Western Europe

on a shoestring

Geert Cole	**Andrea Schulte-Peevers**
Steve Fallon	**David Peevers**
Helen Gillman	**Sean Sheehan**
Mark Honan	**Corinne Simcock**
John King	**Dorinda Talbot**
Clem Lindenmayer	**Bryn Thomas**
Frances Linzee Gordon	**Julia Wilkinson**
Leanne Logan	**David Willett**
John Noble	**Pat Yale**

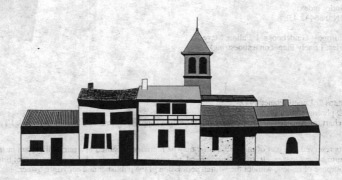

Western Europe

3rd edition

Published by
   Lonely Planet Publications
   Head Office: PO Box 617, Hawthorn, Vic 3122, Australia
   Branches: 155 Filbert St, Suite 251, Oakland, CA 94607, USA
                  10 Barley Mow Passage, Chiswick, London W4 4PH, UK
                  71 bis rue du Cardinal Lemoine, 75005 Paris, France

Printed by
   The Bookmaker Pty Ltd
   Printed in Hong Kong

Photographs by

Austrian National Tourist Office (ANTO)	Vicki Beale (VB)	Bethune Carmichael (BC)
Greg Elms (GE)	Richard Everist (RE)	John Gillman (JG)
Mark Honan (MH)	James Lyon (JL)	John Murray (JM)
Bryn Thomas (BT)		

Front cover photograph by Murray Alcosser, The Image Bank

First Published
   January 1993

This Edition
   January 1997

Although the authors and publisher have tried to make the information as accurate as possible, they accept no responsibility for any loss, injury or inconvenience sustained by any person using this book.

National Library of Australia Cataloguing in Publication Data

Western Europe

   3rd ed.
   Includes index.
   ISBN 0 86442 438 8.

   1. Europe – Guidebooks. I. Fallon, Steve.
   (Series: Lonely Planet on a shoestring).

914

text & maps © Lonely Planet 1997
photos © photographers as indicated 1997
climate chart for Amsterdam compiled from information supplied by Patrick J Tyson, © Patrick J Tyson, 1997

Geert Cole

Geert updated the Benelux chapters with Leanne Logan. Born in Antwerp in Belgium, Geert swapped university and art studies in the 1970s to discover broader horizons and other cultures. Each trip resulted in an extra diary being put on the shelf and another job experience being added to life's list. In more recent times, when not running his stained-glass studio, Geert could be found sailing the Pacific, sorting Aussie sheep, and amongst other challenges, trekking through Alaska and diving tropical reefs. A spark of destiny saw this artist, traveller, writer, cook and landscaper linked to companion, Leanne, with whom he now lives in Australia. In recent years they have worked together on a variety of Lonely Planet guides including *France, New Caledonia, India, Africa, The Middle East* and *Egypt*.

Steve Fallon

Steve worked on the introductory chapters and updated the Ireland chapter. Steve, whose forebears left counties Roscommon and Cork for America at the end of the last century, was born in Boston, Massachusetts, and graduated from Georgetown University in 1975 with a Bachelor of Science in modern languages. The following year he taught English at the University of Silesia near Katowice, Poland. After he had worked for several years for a Gannett newspaper and obtained a master's degree in journalism, his fascination with the 'new' Asia took him to Hong Kong, where he lived and worked for 13 years for a variety of publications and was editor of *Business Traveller* magazine. In 1987, he put journalism on hold when he opened Wanderlust Books, Asia's only travel bookshop. Steve lived in Budapest for 2½ years from where he wrote *Hungary – travel survival kit* and *Slovenia – travel survival kit* before moving to London in 1994.

Helen Gillman

Helen wrote the Italy chapter. She worked as a journalist and editor in Melbourne, Australia, for 12 years, including three years as the editorial manager of 10 suburban newspapers. Trying to manage journalists is not easy, so Helen decided to 'retire' in 1990 and go to live in Italy. She continues to work on a freelance basis as an editor and writer, and has co-authored and is currently updating Lonely Planet's *Italy – travel survival kit*. She now lives in Rome with her husband, Stefano Cavedoni and their three-year-old daughter, Virginia.

Frances Linzee Gordon

Frances worked on the France chapter with Dorinda Talbot. She grew up in Scotland but later went to London University, where she read Latin. Overcome by her usefulness to society, she decided modern languages might be more the thing, and went and worked in Spain, Germany and Belgium for a number of years. After returning to London, she worked for a travel trade publisher's, and read French and European Studies with the University of Lille at the French Institute. She now works – even more usefully – as a freelance travel writer and photographer. She lives in London with her zebra finch, George.

Mark Honan

Mark wrote the Austria, Liechtenstein and Switzerland chapters. After a university degree in philosophy opened up a glittering career as an office clerk, Mark decided 'the meaning of life' lay elsewhere and set off on a two-year trip around the world. As a freelance travel writer, he then went camper vanning around Europe to write a series of articles for a London magazine. When the magazine went bust, Mark joined a travel agency, from where he was rescued by Lonely Planet. Mark wrote the *Vienna city guide* and coordinated, and wrote part of, *Central America on a shoestring*. He also wrote *Switzerandl* and *Austria* and is currently updating the *Solomon Islands*.

Clem Lindenmayer

Clem updated the southern half of the Germany chapter. Clem has worked as a dishwasher, telex operator, translator and assembler of exhibition stands. With a keen interest in languages and mountain sports, he remains a proud undergraduate despite years of scattered studies. Clem researched and authored Lonely Planet's *Trekking in the Patagonian Andes* and *Walking in Switzerland*, and has previously worked on *China – travel survival kit*.

Leanne Logan

Leanne wrote the Benelux chapters. Bitten by the travel bug before even reaching her teens, Leanne has long been lured by travel. From Brisbane, Australia, she explored her homeland while reporting for several newspapers and Australian Associated Press and then set off for Asia and the Middle East. In London, as deputy editor of a travel magazine, her wander lust was temporarily fed but never sated. Eventually she bought a one-way ticket to Africa.

Leanne joined Lonely Planet in 1991 and, while conducting research into Belgium's 350-odd beers, she met a local connoisseur, Geert Cole. Together they have worked on many travel guides, including *France, New Caledonia, India, Africa* and, most recently, the *Middle East* and *Egypt*.

John Noble

John updated the Spain and Andorra chapters. He comes from the Ribble Valley in northern England. After studies at Cambridge University, a spell in mainstream journalism carried him to London's Fleet Street. Increasing interruptions for foreign travel eventually led to him updating Lonely Planet's *Sri Lanka* guide, since when he has been mixed up in numerous Lonely Planet titles, from *Mexico* and *Indonesia* to *Russia, Ukraine & Belarus* and *Central Asia* – supported on many expeditions by his wife and co-author Susan Forsyth and, in recent years, their children Isabella and Jack.

Andrea Schulte-Peevers & David Peevers

Andrea and David updated the northern half of the Germany chapter and are still together after six years of marriage and thousands of miles on German roads. Collectively, they have guided rivers, edited magazines, translated for governments, flown airplanes and fallen in love with Germany. From their base in Los Angeles, they write and photograph their way around the world on assignment for educational and publishing clients in the USA and Germany. Having used Lonely Planet guidebooks in their own travels, they got curious about how it was done. Now, many grey hairs later, they know.

Sean Sheehan

Sean updated part of the Britain chapter. Despite what his name suggests, Sean was born and brought up in London. After teaching for a number of years he took an escape route to South-East Asia where he lived and worked for six years. During that time, alongside acquiring a thirst for travel, he wrote a travel guide to Malaysia and Singapore, edited Shakespeare, ran a computer column for a British publication and worked for a Japanese magazine. He now lives in London.

Corinne Simcock

Corinne helped to update the Greece chapter. Born in London, she spent the first 10 years of her career as a sound engineer in the music industry. In 1988, sick of spending 18 hours a day in a basement listening to people who can't play make mistakes, she chucked it all in to become a journalist, writing for national newspapers and magazines about everything from travel and crime to business and personal finance. She has travelled through more than 30 countries and her passion in life is deserts.

Dorinda Talbot

Dorinda helped to update the France chapter. Born in Melbourne, she began travelling at the age of 18 months – to visit her grandparents in blighty – and has since taken in a fair slice of the world, including Papua New Guinea, South East Asia, the USA, Britain and Continental Europe. Dorinda studied journalism at Deakin University in Geelong before working as a reporter in Alice Springs and sub-editor in Melbourne and London. Still based in London, she now works as a freelance journalist and aspiring travel writer. Dorinda also helped to update LP's *Canada – travel survival kit*.

Bryn Thomas

Bryn worked on the Britain chapter with Pat Yale and Sean Sheehan. Born in Zimbabwe, where he grew up on a farm, Bryn contracted an incurable case of wanderlust during camping holidays by the Indian Ocean in Mozambique. An anthropology degree at Durham University in England earned him the job of polishing leaves of pot plants in London. He has also worked as a ski-lift operator in Colorado, encyclopaedia seller in South Dakota and English teacher in Cairo, Singapore and Tokyo. Travel on four continents has included a 2500-km Andean cycling trip and eight visits to India. Bryn's first guide, the *Trans-Siberian Handbook*, was shortlisted for the Thomas Cook Guidebook of the Year award. He is co-author of LP's guides to *Britain* and *India* and has contributed to the forthcoming LP guide, *Walking in Britain*.

Julia Wilkinson & John King

Julia first set off on her own at the age of four, when she grabbed a backpack and headed down the road in a moment of furious independence. Some 20 years later, en route to Australia, she discovered Asia. With Hong Kong as her base, she has worked as a freelance travel writer and photographer for the past 15 years, writing about the remoter parts of Asia for publications worldwide. The author or contributor to guidebooks on Thailand and Hong Kong, she wrote a guidebook to Portugal some years ago and also updated the Portugal chapter for the last edition of *Western Europe*. When she really wants to get away from it all, she takes to the sky, flying hot-air balloons.

John grew up in the USA, destined for the academic life, but in a rash moment in 1984 he took off for China, teaching English and travelling for a year. In Tibet he met Julia and in Hong Kong they laid plans for future 'joint ventures'. Since then John has squeezed out a living as a travel writer. John is also author of LP's *Karakoram Highway*, and co-author of *Czech & Slovak Republics, Prague, Pakistan, Russia, Ukraine & Belarus* and *Central Asia*.

Julia and John now split their time at 'home' between south-west England and remoter parts of Hong Kong. Life and work have been considerably altered by the arrival of their son Kit, who complicated and enlivened the Portugal research on his first trip out of Hong Kong.

David Willett

David updated the Greece chapter with Corinne Simcock. David is a freelance journalist based near Bellingen on the north coast of New South Wales, Australia. He grew up in Hampshire, England, and wound up in Australia after stints on newspapers in Iran (1975-78) and Bahrain. He spent two years as a sub-editor on the Melbourne *Sun* newspaper before trading a steady job for a warmer climate. Between jobs, David has travelled extensively in Europe, the Middle East and Asia. He has previously worked on LP's guides to *Greece* and *North Africa*, as well as contributing to the books on *Indonesia* and *Australia*.

Pat Yale

Pat helped update the Britain chapter. She spent several years selling holidays before throwing up sensible careerdom to mix teaching with extensive travel in Europe, Asia, Africa, and Central and South America. A full-time writer now, Pat has also worked on the Lonely Planet guides to *Ireland, Dublin, Turkey* and *Britain*. She has lived in London, Cambridge and Cirencester but presently resides with her cat in Bristol.

From the Authors

Steve Fallon *Go raibh maith agat* to Bill Morrison and Catherine McKewitt of Bord Fáilte in Dublin for their assistance and to Clare D'Arcy of Cork, Joan Pyne of Derry, and Mr & Mrs Sexton of Galway for their warmth and hopitality. A *póg* for Roseanne & Michael Rayle of Dingle for Joycean updates and sustenance along the way, and one again for Michael Rothschild, whose soul might just be part Irish.

Helen Gillman Special thanks to my sister Nicole and to Stefano for their invaluable assistance. Thanks also to the various tourism offices in Italy for their help, in particular to Aldo Cianci (Naples EPT), Cecilia and Giovanni (Pisa APT's station branch), Mimmo Ziino (AAST delle Isole Eolie), Signora Albani (Syracuse AAT), Giuseppe (Agrigento AAST), Dottoressa Benci (Siena APT) and Pierluigi and Fulvia (Enjoy Rome).

Frances Linzee Gordon With thanks for endless patience shown at tourist boards across France, and particularly to: Vanina Plotard (Lyon), Sophie Leloup (Normandy), Mélanie Sylvester (Calvi) and Sandra Oliel (French Alps). Thanks also to M Lavêcque for a wonderful day touring his château; to Xavier, to Stéphane and his beautiful island of Corsica, and to M Jacques Tartarin of Crédit Agricole

for miracle-working at a dark hour. Finally to all those little, old men across France who helped me always so gallantly back onto the right route. I dedicate my infinitesimal contribution to this book to my father.

Mark Honan Thanks to Marion and Ingrid at ANTO and Heidi and Evelyn at Switzerland Tourism, who always dealt with my obscure enquiries with patience and diligence. Many thanks to my Switzerland and Austria-based friends for support and information during research trips: Sue, Jim, Imre, Beata, Beat, Irmgard, Ewa and Reinhard.

Clem Lindenmayer General thanks go to the helpful staff at the dozens of tourist offices I visited in southern Germany. Special thanks to Christina Schüler (Stuttgart), Andrea Höchstötter (Nuremberg), Claudia Wachowitz (Frankfurt), Ollie Collins (Maine, USA), Susanna Petrow (Berlin) and a second Swiss kiss goes to Romi, whose on-the-road company was a welcome distraction from the gruelling task of updating.

John Noble Special thanks to Mark Armstrong, Susan Forsyth and Damien Simonis for their generous help on the Spain chapter, and Albert Padrol and Josep Maria Romero for their hospitality and insights into Catalonia and Andorra.

Sean Sheehan I would like to express my thanks to the editor Steve Womersley, Shiva Jahangir-Tafreshi at the London Tourist Board and Bob Barton at the British Travel Authority. A big thankyou also to Danny Gralton in Camden Town and the Furzer family in Chadwell Heath.

Corinne Simcock Thanks to Adrienne Costanzo at LP for bothering to take my details to Australia, and to Mike Elder from *Ourios Travel* in Iraklio and Anna from Dakoutros Travel on Santorini for their spectacular assistance. Among the other friends who helped with fact-finding missions, thanks to Josette and Dimitri at *Pension Andreas* and Jean from *Le Bistrot* on Rhodes, George at *Olga's Pension* in Rethymno, *Rooms for Rent* George in Hania and Vasso and Manolis at *Pension Vasso* on Samos.

Dorinda Talbot Thanks to Mark Baker, Virginie Patheron, Corinne Gripekoven and Dawn Chapman for their unbounded hospitality and support. Also special thanks to Lydia Megert, Claudia Rohrbach, tourist office staff in Paris and across France, fellow travellers and all the staff at the LP Paris office.

Bryn Thomas Thanks to Anna Jacomb-Hood for help with information on Britain's complex rail and bus systems; and also to the staff at TICs around the country.

Andrea Schulte-Peevers & David Peevers Warmest thanks to Andrea's mother, Ingrid Schulte, for her love and hard work. Our deepfelt gratitude to Gunter Winkler, Iris Müller and Iris Hebling (GNTO Frankfurt), Knut Hänschke and Helga Brenner-Khan (NTO New York), Helmut Helas (GNTO Los Angeles) and Dr Wolfgang Rieke for coming through on all fronts. Big thanks also to everyone else who helped us accomplish this project, with special mention to the Mohr family, Dr Peter Rohrsen, John Gottburg and Lonely Planet's own Jane Fitzpatrick and Rob van Driesum.

Leanne Logan & Geert Cole In Belgium,

thanks to Machteld Leducq and Jan Wittouck from the Flanders Tourist Office as well as Madame Gillis (Namur Province). In the Netherlands, thankyou to Ine van der Lof and Gwendola Piek from the Netherlands Board of Tourism as well as the following tourist office staff: Els Wamsteeker (Amsterdam), Marianne van der Zalm (The Hague), Gervaise Frings and Jan Jeronimus (Rotterdam), Anne Marie Beunder (Utrecht), Thea Meinderts (Leeuwarden) and Jan Kappenburg (Groningen). And lastly, special thanks to Roos & Bert Cole for their generous hospitality and for sharing their home and Duvels.

Julia Wilkinson & John King Thanks to Robert Strauss and Deanna Swaney for laying the groundwork for the Portugal chapter, upon which we have depended heavily. Again we are indebted to Pilar Pereira of the London ICEP office for significant logistical support and information gathering. For extraordinary help, both with research and with our two-year-old 'research assistant', we are indebted to Amélia Paulo (Sintra Turismo) and her daughter Andráia. Staff at the municipal tourist offices at Tavira, Évora, Sintra and Coimbra, and at the ICEP offices at Porto and Lisbon, provided assistance well beyond the call of duty. Finally, *obrigado* to Barry Girling for his house and the soft landing it gave us on arrival.

David Willett In Greece, my thanks go to Tolis and Steve (Athens) and to George and Magda (Corfu) for their help and hospitality.

Pat Yale Thanks to the many friends who shared their thoughts on Britain, but most particularly Sharon North, Tony Churchill and Nathan who was doing tourism research before he was old enough to stand!

This Book
Many people have helped to bring about this 3rd edition. In past editions we had the benefit of the following writers on whose sound foundations this edition was laid: Mark Balla, Rob van Driesum, Richard Everist, Rosemary Hall, Daniel Robinson, David Stanley, Robert Strauss, Mark Armstrong, Tony Wheeler, Gary Walsh and Greg Videon.

Western Europe is part of LP's Europe shoestring series, which includes *Eastern Europe, Mediterranean Europe, Central Europe* and *Scandinavian & Baltic Europe.* Lonely Planet also publishes phrasebooks to these regions.

From the Publisher

The editing of this book was co-ordinated by Steve Womersley and Jane Fitzpatrick. The mapping and design were coordinated by Tamsin Wilson and Rachel Black. All four coordinators were ably assisted by a cast of thousands, in particular: Rob van Driesum, Adrienne Costanzo, Mary Neighbour, Jane Hart, Michelle Stamp, Brigitte Barta, Cathy Oliver, Liz Filleul, Katie Cody, Dorothy Natsikas, Tony Fankhauser, Suzi Petkovski, Paul Harding, Tom Smallman, Bethune Carmichael, Anne Mulvaney and Diana Saad. Simon Bracken and David Kemp designed the cover, Paul Clifton designed the colour and back cover maps, Paul Hellander helped with e-mail advice, Vicky Wayland and Sacha Pearson helped with the introductory chapters, and Dan 'the Wonder Boy' Levin saved us from a life without Greek script and many other near disasters.

Thanks

Many thanks to the following travellers who used the last edition and wrote to us with helpful hints, useful advice and interesting anecdotes:

Mark & Maria Anderson, Mr M Barnard, Ian & Claudia Bass, J B Booth, Conrad Benedict, K Bolte, Jon Bowen, M Brighouse, Andrew Bullock, Michelle Burrell, J Burton, A C Sureshbabu, Daria Casinelli, Ben & Thanh Chesry, Kathleen Chesterton, Lisa Crofts, Mr J Cronen, Karen Davies, Raul De Anda, Cate Deans, C Deuscher, Holly Diagle, Mr Diblee, L Dickstein, Rossana Dudziak, Humphrey Evans, Rod Evenden, Craig Garrioch, Susan Gerber, Dean Gould, Mr & Mrs Harrison, C J Hattrick, Lisa Hayes, Geordie Heard, Eirik Helleve, Allen Hendrick, M Hood, Sharon Horwood, Mr J F Houtman, Simon Huang, Alan Jackson, Nadine Jwata, E Kalev, Judith Keegan, Kevin & Kathy Kerns, Warrick King, Ross Klein, Christian Koller, Sonja Kuntze, Stephen Lawton, Steve Lord, D Loucks, George Manetakis, David Manuell, Dr Marc Hasselaar, Bart Maton, Barrie McCormick, Gavin McDonald, Suzanne McNabb, Robert McNeil, Glenn Miller, Elissa Mittman, Philip Mooney, Ian Moseley, P Muller, Debbie Neich, Catherine Nicholson, J Norton, Belinda O'Berry, L & T Orgill, Sue Pavasaris, A & V Pearson, G Peene, Karen Peradon, P Poutaven, Jasmine Read, Sonya Reading, Darrell Rose, Brad & Jodie Sewell, Paul Shapiro, Bill Simpson, John & Wendy Sinton, Simon Skerritt, Greg Slatcher, David Spicer, Nigel Steel, Sarah Stratton, Keith Supko, Lesley & Hugh Sykes, Beatrice Valero, Geert Van de Wiele, J Veragaten, Scott & Jennifer Vinson, Rachel Wernert, Richard Wheeler, Roy Whitehead, Lynda Whitting, Marion Williams, Nancy Wise, Daniel Wolf, Gina Woods, Gordon Woods, Humphrey Yiu, Stefan Zager.

Warning & Request

Things change – prices go up, schedules change, good places go bad and bad places go bankrupt – nothing stays the same. So, if you find things better or worse, recently opened or long since closed, please tell us and help make the next edition even more accurate and useful.

We value all of the feedback we receive from travellers. Julie Young coordinates a small team who read and acknowledge every letter, postcard and email, and ensure that every morsel of information finds its way to the appropriate authors, editors and publishers.

Everyone who writes to us will find their name in the next edition of the appropriate guide and will also receive a free subscription to our quarterly newsletter, *Planet Talk*. The very best contributions will be rewarded with a free Lonely Planet guide.

Excerpts from your correspondence may appear in updates (which we add to the end pages of reprints); new editions of this guide; in our newsletter, *Planet Talk*; or in the Postcards section of our Web site – so please let us know if you don't want your letter published or your name acknowledged.

Contents

Map Legend

BOUNDARIES

.... International Boundary
.... State/Province Boundary
.... Disputed Boundary

ROUTES

.... Freeway
.... Highway
.... Major Road
.... Unsealed Road or Track
.... City Road
.... City Street
.... Train Line, Train Station
.... Underground Railway
.... Tram
.... Walking Track
.... Walking Tour
.... Ferry Route
.... Cable Car or Chairlift

AREA FEATURES

.... Parks
.... Built-Up Area
.... Pedestrian Mall
.... Market
.... Cemetery
.... Non-Christian Cemetery
.... Beach or Desert
.... Key area hatch

HYDROGRAPHIC FEATURES

.... Coastline
.... River, River Flow, Creek
.... Intermittent River or Creek
.... Rapids, Waterfalls
.... Lake, Intermittent Lake
.... Swamp
.... Canal

SYMBOLS

✪ CAPITAL	National Capital		Buddhist Temple, Tomb
◉ Capital	Regional Capital		Bicycle Track, Public Toilets
CITY	Major City	✪ ★	Hospital, Police Station
● City	City		Embassy, Petrol Station
● Town	Town	✈	Airport, Cave
● Village	Village		Swimming Pool, Gardens
■ ▼	Place to Stay, Place to Eat		Shopping Centre, Zoo
	Cafe, Pub or Bar		Winery or Vineyard, Castle
✉ ☎	Post Office, Telephone	← A25	One Way Street, Route Number
❶ ❸	Tourist Information, Bank		Stately Home, Monument
◐ ℗	Transport, Parking	▲ ※	Mountain or Hill, Lookout
ⓜ ⓤ	Metro Station, U-Bahn Station		Lighthouse, Ski Field
🏛 ⌂	Museum, Youth Hostel	)(◎	Pass, Spring
⛺ ⛺	Caravan Park, Camping Ground		Beach, Archaeological Site/Ruins
	Church, Cathedral		Golf Course, Border Crossing
	Mosque, Synagogue		Ancient or City Wall
	Temple (Generic), Classical		Cliff or Escarpment, Tunnel

Note: not all symbols displayed above appear in this book

Introduction

Western Europe is many things to many people. Some marvel at the diversity of culture and language crammed into such a small area, the wealth of the region's museums, theatre and architecture, and the shopping, restaurants and nightlife on offer in the bustling cities. Others are attracted to Western Europe's varied scenery, from sun-drenched beaches and dense forests to snow-capped peaks. Citizens of the Americas and Australasia see Western Europe as the origin of much of their culture and civilisation, while almost all visitors are gladdened by the minimal amount of bureaucracy, the well-developed tourist facilities and the efficient transport that make it possible to explore the region with a minimum of bother.

Western Europe is often looked upon as the hub of the developed world – at least historically. Although other regions may be changing faster nowadays, Western Europe remains an economic powerhouse and a leader in art, literature and music. For the visitor to the region the biggest problem is simply choosing where to go and what to see and do. There are magnificent museums and galleries such as the British Museum in London, the Louvre in Paris and the Pergamon Museum in Berlin. There are architectural treasures such as the Parthenon in Athens, Gaudí's fantastic church in Barcelona and fairy-tale castles in Germany. There are superb natural features, such as the soaring Swiss Alps, the magnificent stretches of rough coastline in western Ireland and the tranquil

islands of Greece. For the energetic, there are walking trails ranging from the high-altitude circuit of Mt Blanc in France to the Cotswolds Way in England, ski runs from Andorra to Zermatt in Switzerland and water sports all along the Atlantic, Baltic and Mediterranean coasts. And there are places where it's simply just fun to be, whether it's after dark in Amsterdam, pub-crawling through Dublin or watching the world go by from a sidewalk café in Paris or Rome.

Western Europe on a shoestring covers this diverse collection of countries with an insight into their history, people and culture as well as practical information to help you make the most of your time and money.

There's information on how to get to Europe and how to get around once you're there. There are extensive details on what to see, when to see it and how much it all costs. The thousands of recommendations about places to stay range from Spanish camping grounds and German hostels to French pensions and Irish B&Bs. Cafés, restaurants and bars are covered in equally exhaustive detail with suggestions ranging from the cheapest of cheap eats to the ideal place for that long-awaited splurge. There are even recommendations on what to buy and where to buy it.

Western Europe is a great place and there's lots out there waiting to be enjoyed. All you have to do is go and this newly updated edition of *Western Europe* will guide you.

Facts for the Visitor

There are those who say that Europe – especially Western Europe – is so well developed you don't have to plan a thing before your trip, since anything can be arranged on the spot. As any experienced traveller knows, the problems you thought about at home often turn out to be irrelevant, or will sort themselves out once you're on the move.

This is fine if you've decided to blow the massive inheritance sitting in your bank account, but if your financial status is somewhat more modest, a bit of prior knowledge and careful planning can make your hard-earned travel budget stretch further than you thought it would. You'll also want to make sure that the things you plan to see and do will be possible at the particular time of year when you'll be travelling.

PLANNING
When to Go

Any time can be the best time to visit Western Europe, depending on what you want to do. Summer lasts roughly from June to September, and offers the most pleasant climate for outdoor pursuits in the northern half of Europe. In the southern half (the Mediterranean coast, the Iberian Peninsula, southern Italy and Greece), where the summers tend to be hotter, you can extend that period by one or even two months either way, when temperatures may also be more agreeable.

Unfortunately, you won't be the only tourist during summer – all of France and Italy, for instance, goes on holiday in August. Prices can be high, accommodation fully booked, and the sights packed. You'll find much better deals – and far fewer crowds – in the shoulder seasons either side of summer; in April and May, for instance, flowers are in bloom and the weather can be surprisingly mild, and indian summers are common in September and October.

On the other hand, if you're keen on winter sports, resorts in the Alps and the Pyrenees begin operating in November and move into full swing after the New Year, closing down when the snows begin to melt in March il.

The Climate & When to Go sections in the individual country chapters explain what to expect and when to expect it, and the Climate Charts appendix in the back of the book will help you compare the weather in different destinations. As a rule, spring and autumn tend to be wetter and windier than summer and winter in Western Europe. The temperate maritime climate along the Atlantic seaboard is relatively wet all year, with moderate extremes in temperature. The Mediterranean coast is hotter and drier, with most rainfall during the mild winter. The continental climate in eastern Germany and the Alps tends to show much stronger extremes between summer and winter.

What Kind of Trip?
Travelling Companions Travelling alone is not a problem in Western Europe; the region is well developed and relatively safe.

If you decide to travel with others, keep in mind that travel can put relationships to the test like few other experiences can. Many a long-term friendship has collapsed under the strains of constant negotiations about where to stay and eat, what to see and where to go next. But many friendships have also become closer than ever before. You won't find out until you try, but make sure you agree on itineraries and routines beforehand and try to remain flexible about everything – even in the heat of an August afternoon in Paris.

If travel is a good way of testing established friendships, it's also a great way of making new ones. Hostels and camping grounds are good places to meet fellow travellers, so even if you're travelling alone you need never be lonely.

The Getting Around chapter has information on organised tours.

Move or Stay? 'If this is Tuesday, it must be Brussels.' Though often ridiculed, the mad dash that crams six countries into a month does have its merits. If you've never visited Europe before, you won't know which areas you'll like, and a quick 'scouting tour' will give an

A	B	C
D	E	F
G	H	I

A: Spain (VB)　　　　B: Portugal (BC)　　　C: Italy (VB)
D: Britain (BT)　　　E: Ireland (JM)　　　F: Austria (MH)
G: Switzerland (MH)　H: Spain (BC)　　　I: Italy (JG)

A	B
C	D	E
F	G

A: France (GE)
C: Britain (RE)
F: Austria (ANTO)

B: Greece (VB)
D: Spain (BC)
G: Portugal (BC)

E: Switzerland (JL)

overview of the options. A rail pass that offers unlimited travel within a set period of time is the best way to do this.

But if you know where you want to go, or find a place you like, the best advice is to stay put for a while, discover some of the lesser known sights, make a few local friends and settle in. It's also cheaper in the long run.

For information on working in Western Europe, see the Work section later in this chapter.

Maps

Good maps are easy to come by once you're in Europe, but you might want to buy a few beforehand. The maps in this book will help you get an idea of where you might want to go and will be a useful first reference when you arrive in a city. Proper road maps are essential if you're driving or cycling.

You can't go wrong with Michelin maps and, because of their soft covers, they fold up easily so you can stick them in your pocket. Some people prefer the meticulously produced Freytag & Berndt, Kümmerly & Frey or Hallwag maps. The British AA maps are also good – as a rule, maps published by European automobile associations are excellent, and they're sometimes free if membership of your local association gives you reciprocal rights. Some of the best city maps are produced by Falk. Tourist offices are often another good source for (usually free) maps.

Online Services

The following web sites offer useful general information about Western Europe, its cities, transport systems, currencies etc.

Lonely Planet
  http://www.lonelyplanet.com. Lonely Planet's own web site is packed with information on Western Europe and other destinations, and is extensively hot-linked to other useful sites.
Tourist Offices
  http://www.mbnet.mb.ca/lucas/travel. Lists tourist offices at home and around the world for most countries.
Rail Information
  http://www.raileurope.com. Train fares and schedules on the most popular routes in Europe, including information on rail and youth passes.
Airline Information
  http://www.travelocity.com. What airlines fly where, when and for how much.

Currency Converters
  http://bin.gnn.com/cgi-bin/gnn/currency & http://pacific.commerce.ubc.ca/xr. Exchange rates of hundreds of currencies worldwide.

See the E-mail section under Post & Communications for some general advice on gaining access to the Internet while on the move in Europe.

What to Bring

Taking along as little as possible is the best policy. It's very easy to find almost anything you need in Western Europe, and since you'll probably buy things as you go, it's better to start with too little rather than too much.

A backpack is still the most popular method of carrying gear as it is convenient, especially for walking. On the down side, a backpack doesn't offer too much protection for your valuables, the straps tend to get caught on things and some airlines may refuse to accept responsibility if the pack is damaged or tampered with.

Travelpacks, a combination backpack/shoulder bag, are very popular. The backpack straps zip away inside the pack when they are not needed, so you almost have the best of both worlds. Some packs have sophisticated shoulder-strap adjustment systems and can be used comfortably even on long hikes. Packs are always much easier to carry than a bag. Backpacks or travelpacks can be made reasonably theft-proof with small padlocks. Another alternative is a large, soft zip-bag with a wide shoulder strap so it can be carried with relative ease if necessary. Forget suitcases unless you're travelling in style.

As for clothing, the climate will have a bearing on what you bring along. Remember that insulation works on the principle of trapped air, so several layers of thin clothing are warmer than a single thick one (and will be easier to dry, too). You'll also be much more flexible if the weather suddenly turns warm on you. Just be prepared for rain at any time of year. Bearing in mind that you can buy virtually anything on the spot, a minimum packing list could include:

• underwear, socks and swimming gear
• a pair of jeans and maybe a pair of shorts or skirt
• a few T-shirts and shirts

- a warm sweater
- a solid pair of walking shoes
- sandals or thongs for showers
- a coat or jacket
- a raincoat, waterproof jacket or umbrella
- a medical kit and sewing kit
- a padlock
- a Swiss Army knife
- soap and towel
- toothpaste, toothbrush and other toiletries

A padlock is useful to lock your bag to a luggage rack in a bus or train; it may also be needed to secure your hostel locker. A Swiss Army knife comes in handy for all sorts of things. Any pocket knife is fine, but make sure it includes such essentials as a bottle opener and strong corkscrew! Soap, toothpaste and toilet paper are readily obtainable almost anywhere, but you'll need your own supply of paper in many public toilets and those at camping grounds. In some countries, using toilets in public areas costs a nominal sum, so have coins handy. Tampons are available at pharmacies and supermarkets in all but the most remote places. Condoms, both locally made and imported, are widely available in Western Europe.

A tent and sleeping bag are vital if you want to save money by camping. Even if you're not camping, a sleeping bag is still very useful. Get one that can be used as a quilt. A sleeping sheet with pillow cover (case) is necessary if you plan to stay in hostels – you may have to hire or purchase one if you don't bring your own. In any case, a sheet that fits into your sleeping bag is easier to wash than the bag itself. Make one yourself out of old sheets (include a built-in pillow cover), or buy one from your hostel association.

Other optional items include a compass, a torch (flashlight), an alarm clock, an adapter plug for electrical appliances (such as a cup or immersion water heater to save on expensive tea and coffee), a universal bath/sink plug (a film canister sometimes works), sunglasses, a few clothes pegs and premoistened towelettes or a large cotton handkerchief that you can soak in fountains and use to cool off while touring cities in the hot summer months. During city sightseeing, a small daypack is better than a shoulder bag at deterring snatch thieves (see Theft in the later Dangers & Annoyances section).

Finally, consider using plastic carry bags or garbage bags inside your backpack to keep things separate but also dry if the pack gets soaked. Airlines do lose luggage from time to time, but you have a much better chance of it not being yours if it is tagged with your name and address *inside* the bag as well as outside; outside tags can always fall off or be removed.

Appearances & Conduct

Although dress standards are fairly informal in northern Europe, your clothes may well have some bearing on how you're treated in southern Europe. By all means dress casually, but keep your clothes clean, and ensure sufficient body cover (trousers or a knee-length dress) if your sightseeing includes churches, monasteries, synagogues or mosques. Apart from the lederhosen (leather shorts with H-shaped braces/suspenders) seen at German cultural events and beer festivals, wearing shorts away from the beach or camping ground is not very common among men in Europe. Some nightclubs and fancy restaurants may refuse entry to people wearing jeans, a tracksuit or sneakers (trainers); men might consider packing a tie as well, just in case.

Most border guards and immigration officials are too professional to judge people entirely by their appearance, but first impressions do count, and you may find life easier if you're well presented.

While nude bathing is usually restricted to certain beaches, topless bathing is very common in many parts of Europe. Nevertheless, women should be wary of taking their tops off as a matter of course. The rule is, if nobody else seems to be doing it, you shouldn't either.

You'll soon notice that Europeans are heavily into shaking hands and even kissing when they greet one another. If you can't handle the kissing, that's fine, but at least get into the habit of shaking hands with virtually everyone you meet. In many parts of Europe, it's also customary to greet the proprietor when entering a shop, café or quiet bar, and to say goodbye when you leave.

The Top 10

There is so much to see in Western Europe that compiling a top 10 is almost impossible. But we asked the authors involved in this book to list their personal highlights. The results are as follows:

1. Paris
2. Rome
3. London
4. Berlin
5. Amsterdam
6. The Alps
7. Venice
8. Scotland & islands
9. Florence & Tuscany
10. Munich

Other nominations included Greek island-hopping, Barcelona, the Algarve, Ireland, Umbria, Provence, Corsica and the Pyrenees.

The Bottom 10

The writers were also asked to list the 10 worst 'attractions' of the region:

1. Spanish coastal resorts
2. Paris
3. Frankfurt Airport
4. Traffic jams in Paris, London and Rome
5. The *Sound of Music* tour in Salzburg
6. France's northern coast
7. Munich *Bierfest*
8. Monte Carlo casino
9. British coastal resorts
10. Bullfights in Spain

Other nominations included the English weather, drunken Scandinavian tourists, rising racism, Madame Tussaud's in London, the Scottish east coast, Milan, Rotterdam and Palma de Mallorca. A visit to any of these places could leave you feeling that you've wasted your time. Note that Paris is almost as good at repelling our authors as attracting them.

VISAS & DOCUMENTS
Passport

Your most important travel document is your passport, which should remain valid until well after you return home. If it's just about to expire, renew it before you go. This may not be easy to do overseas, and some countries insist your passport remain valid for a specified period (usually three months after you visit).

Applying for or renewing a passport can take anything from an hour to several months, so don't leave it till the last minute. Bureaucracy usually grinds faster if you do everything in person rather than relying on the mail or agents, but check first what you need to take with you: photos of a certain size, birth certificate, population register extract, signed statements, exact payment in cash etc.

Australian citizens can apply at a post office or the passport office in their state capital; Britons can pick up application forms from major post offices, and the passport is issued by the regional passport office; Canadians can apply at regional passport offices; New Zealanders can apply at any district office of the Department of Internal Affairs; US citizens must apply in person (but may usually renew by mail) at a US Passport Agency office or at some courthouses and post offices.

Once you start travelling, carry your passport at all times and guard it carefully. (See the following Photocopies section for advice about carrying copies of your passport and other important documents.) Camping grounds and hotels sometimes insist that you hand over your passport for the duration of your stay, which is very inconvenient, but a driving licence or Camping Card International usually solves the problem.

Citizens of many European countries don't always need a valid passport to travel within the region; a national identity card may be sufficient. A citizen of the European Union (EU) travelling to another EU country will generally face the least problems. But if you want to exercise any of these options, check with your travel agent or the embassies of the countries you plan to visit.

Visas

A visa is a stamp in your passport or on a separate piece of paper permitting you to enter the country in question and stay for a specified period of time. Often you can get the visa at the border or at the airport on arrival, but not always – check first with the embassies or consulates of the countries you plan to visit – and seldom on trains. There's a wide variety of visas, including tourist, transit and business ones. Transit visas are usually cheaper than tourist or business visas, but they only allow a very short stay (one or two days) and can be difficult to extend. Most readers of this book, however, will have very little to do with visas. With a valid passport they'll be able to visit most European countries for up to three (sometimes even six) months, provided they have some sort of onward or return ticket and/or 'sufficient means of support' (money).

In line with the Schengen Agreement there are no passport controls at the borders between Germany, France, Spain, Portugal and the Benelux countries (Belgium, the Netherlands and Luxembourg) and an identity card should be sufficient, but it's always safest to carry your passport. The other EU members are not yet (full) members of 'Schengen' and still maintain (low-key) border controls over traffic from other EU countries. Border procedures between EU and non-EU countries can still be fairly thorough. For those who do require visas, it's important to remember that these will have a 'use-by date', and you'll be refused entry after that period has elapsed.

In the past South Africans have had little joy travelling on their passports, but this is changing. Citizens of Hong Kong may need visas to several countries, depending on the endorsements in their British National Overseas (BNO) passports. Australians still need a so-called Schengen visa to visit France or Spain – it may not be checked when entering these countries overland, but major problems can arise if it is requested during your stay or on departure and you can't produce it.

Visa requirements can change, and you should always check with the individual embassies or a reputable travel agent before travelling. It's generally easier to get your visas as you go along, rather than arranging them all beforehand. Carry spare passport photos (you may need one to four every time you apply for a visa). The accompanying table lists visa requirements for some nationalities.

Photocopies

The hassles created by losing your passport can be considerably reduced if you have a record of its number and issue date, or even better, photocopies of the relevant data pages. A photocopy of your birth certificate can also be useful.

Also add the serial numbers of your travellers' cheques (cross them off as you cash them) and photocopies of your credit cards, airline ticket and other travel documents. Keep all this emergency material separate from your passport, cheques and cash, and leave extra copies with someone you can rely on back home. Add some emergency money, say US$50 in cash, to this separate stash as well. If you do lose your passport, notify the police immediately to get a statement, and contact your nearest consulate.

	Aust	Can	Ire	Isr	NZ	Sing	UK	USA
Visa Requirements								
Country of Origin								
Andorra	-	-	-	-	-	-	-	-
Austria	-	-	-	-	-	-	-	-
Belgium	-	-	-	-	-	-	-	-
Britain	-	-	-	-	-	-	N/A	-
France	✓	-	-	-	-	-	-	-
Germany	-	-	-	-	-	-	-	-
Greece	-	-	-	-	-	✦	-	-
Ireland	-	-	N/A	-	-	-	-	-
Italy	-	-	-	-	-	-	-	-
Liechtenstein	-	-	-	-	-	-	-	-
Luxembourg	-	-	-	-	-	-	-	-
Netherlands	-	-	-	-	-	-	-	-
Portugal	-	★	-	-	-	✓	-	-
Spain	✓	-	-	-	-	-	-	-
Switzerland	-	-	-	-	-	-	-	-

✓ Tourist visa required
★ 60-day maximum stay without visa
✛ 30-day maximum stay without visa
✦ 14-day maximum stay without visa

Travel Insurance

You should seriously consider taking out travel insurance. This not only covers you for medical expenses and luggage theft or loss, but also for cancellation or delays in your travel arrangements. (You could fall seriously ill two days before departure, for example.) Cover depends on your insurance and type of airline ticket, so ask both your insurer and your ticket-issuing agency to explain where you stand. Ticket loss is also covered by travel insurance.

Buy travel insurance as early as possible. If you buy it the week before you fly, you may find, for instance, that you're not covered for delays to your flight caused by strikes or other industrial actions that may have been in force before you took out the insurance.

Paying for your airline ticket with a credit card often provides limited travel accident insurance, and you may be able to reclaim the payment if the operator doesn't deliver. In the UK, for instance, institutions issuing credit cards are required by law to reimburse consumers if a company goes into liquidation and the amount in contention is more than UK£100. Ask your credit-card company what it's prepared to cover.

Like passports, travellers' cheques and the like, photocopies of relevant travel insurance paperwork should be kept somewhere safe and details left with a reliable contact person at home. See also Health Insurance under Health, later in this chapter.

International Driving Permit

If you don't hold a European driving licence and plan to drive in the region, obtain an International Driving Permit (IDP) from your local automobile association before you leave – you'll need a passport photo and a valid licence. They are usually inexpensive and valid for one year only. An IDP helps Europeans make sense of your unfamiliar local licence (make sure you take that with you, too) and can make life much simpler, especially when hiring cars and motorcycles.

Also ask your automobile association for a letter of introduction. This entitles you to services offered by affiliated organisations in Europe, usually free of charge (touring maps and information, help with breakdowns, technical and legal advice etc). See the Getting Around chapter for more details on driving with your own vehicle.

Camping Card International

Your local automobile association also issues the Camping Card International, which is basically a camping ground ID. Cards are also available from your local camping federation, and sometimes on the spot at camping grounds. They incorporate third-party insurance for damage you may cause, and many camping grounds offer a small discount if you sign in with one.

Hostelling Card

A hostelling card is useful – if not always mandatory – for those staying at hostels. Some hostels in Western Europe don't require that you be a hostelling association member, but they often charge less if you have a card. Many hostels will issue one on the spot or after a few stays, though this might cost a bit more than getting it in your home country. See Hostels in the later Accommodation section.

Student & Youth Cards

The most useful of these is the International Student Identity Card (ISIC), a plastic ID-style card with your photograph, which provides discounts on many forms of transport (including air travel and local public transport), cheap or free admission to museums and sights, and cheap meals in some student restaurants.

There is a worldwide industry in fake student cards, and many places now stipulate a maximum age for student discounts or, more simply, they've substituted a 'youth discount' for a 'student discount'.

If you're aged under 26 but not a student, you can apply for a GO25 card issued by the Federation of International Youth Travel Organisations (FIYTO), or the Euro<26 card, which go under different names in various countries (UNDER 26 in England and Wales, Young Scot in Scotland, Carte Jeune in France, CJP in the Netherlands etc). Both give much the same discounts and benefits as an ISIC.

All these cards are issued by student unions, hostelling organisations or youth-oriented travel agencies. They do not automatically entitle you to discounts, and some companies and institutions refuse to recognise them altogether, but you won't find out until you flash the card.

Senior Cards

Museums and other sights, public swimming pools and spas and transport companies frequently offer discounts to retired people/old age pensioners/those over 60 (slightly younger for women). Make sure you bring proof of age; that suave *signore* in Italy or that polite Parisian *mademoiselle* is not going to believe you're a day over 39.

European nationals aged over 60 can get a Rail Europe Senior Card. For more information see Cheap Tickets under Train in the Getting Around chapter.

International Health Certificate

You'll need this yellow booklet only if you're coming to the region from certain parts of Asia, Africa and South America, where diseases such as yellow fever are prevalent. See Immunisations in the Health section for more information on jabs.

CUSTOMS

Throughout most of Western Europe, the usual allowances on tobacco (eg 200 cigarettes), alcohol (two litres of wine, one of spirits) and perfume (50 grams) apply to duty-free goods purchased at the airport or on ferries. Do not confuse these with *duty-paid* items (including alcohol and tobacco) bought at normal shops and supermarkets in one EU country and brought into another EU country, where certain goods might be more expensive. Then the allowances are more than generous: 800 cigarettes; 10/90 litres of spirits/wine; unlimited quantities of perfume.

Customs inspections among EU countries have now ceased. At most border crossings and airports elsewhere they are pretty cursory but don't be lulled into a false sense of security. When you least expect it...

MONEY
Costs

The secret to budget travel in Western Europe is cheap accommodation. Europe has a highly developed network of camping grounds and hostels, some of them quite luxurious, and they're great places to meet people.

Other money-saving strategies include preparing your own meals and avoiding alcohol; using a student card (see the previous Visas & Documents section) and buying any of the

various rail and public transport passes (see the Getting Around chapter). Also remember that the more time you spend in any one place, the lower your daily expenses are likely to be as you get to know your way around.

Including transport but not private motorised transport, your daily expenses could work out to around US$30 to US$40 a day if you're operating on a rock-bottom budget. This means camping or staying in hostels, eating economically and using a transport pass.

Travelling on a moderate budget, you should be able to manage on US$60 to US$80 a day. This would allow you to stay at cheap hotels, guesthouses or B&Bs. You could afford meals in economical restaurants and even a few beers! Greece and Portugal would be somewhat cheaper, while Switzerland and the UK would be pricier.

Price Levels

A general warning about all those prices that we list throughout this book: they're likely to change, usually moving upward, but if last season was particularly slow they may remain the same or even come down. Nevertheless, relative price levels should stay fairly constant – if hotel A costs twice as much as hotel B, it's likely to stay that way.

Cash

Nothing beats cash for convenience...or risk. If you lose it, it's gone forever and very few travel insurers will come to your rescue. Those that will, limit the amount to about US$300.

It's still a good idea, though, to bring some local currency in cash, if only to tide you over until you get to an exchange facility or find an automatic teller machine (ATM). The equivalent of, say, US$50 should usually be enough. Some extra cash in an easily exchanged currency (eg US dollars or Deutschmarks) is also a good idea. Remember that banks will always accept paper money, but very rarely coins in foreign currencies.

Travellers' Cheques

The main idea of carrying travellers' cheques rather than cash is the protection they offer from theft, though they are losing their popularity as more travellers – including those on tight budgets – deposit their money in their bank at home and withdraw it as they go along through ATMs.

American Express, Visa and Thomas Cook cheques are widely accepted and have efficient replacement policies. If you're going to remote places, it's worth sticking to American Express since small local banks may not always accept other brands.

Keeping a record of the cheque numbers and those you have used is vital when it comes to replacing lost travellers' cheques. You should keep this separate from the cheques themselves. Cheques are available in various currencies; choose the currency you're likely to need most – say, pounds sterling if you're going to spend a lot of time and money in the UK – or one you can easily 'think' in.

When you change cheques, don't look at just the exchange rate; ask about fees and commissions as well. There may be a per-cheque service fee, a flat transaction fee, or a percentage of the total amount irrespective of the number of cheques. Some banks charge fees to cash cheques and not cash; others do the reverse. But in most European countries these days, the exchange rate for travellers' cheques is slightly better than the exchange rate for cash.

Plastic Cards & ATMs

If you're not familiar with the options, ask your bank to explain the workings and relative merits of credit, credit/debit, debit, charge and cash cards.

A major advantage of credit cards is that they allow you to pay for expensive items (eg airline tickets) without your having to carry great wads of cash around. They also allow you to withdraw cash at selected banks or from the many ATMs that are now linked up internationally in many European countries. However, if an ATM in Europe swallows a card that was issued outside Europe, it can be a major headache. Also, credit cards usually aren't hooked up to ATM networks unless you specifically ask your bank to do this.

Cash cards, which you use at home to withdraw money directly from your bank account or savings account, are rapidly being linked up internationally – ask your bank at home for advice.

Credit and credit/debit cards like Visa and MasterCard are widely accepted. MasterCard (also known as Access in the UK) is linked to Europe's extensive Eurocard system, and Visa (sometimes called Carte Bleue) is particularly strong in France and Spain. However, these cards often have a credit limit that is too low to cover major expenses like long-term car rental or airline tickets and can be difficult to replace if lost abroad.

Charge cards like American Express and Diners Club have offices in the major cities of most countries that will replace a lost card within 24 hours. However, charge cards are not widely accepted off the beaten track.

The best advice is not to put all your eggs in one basket. If you want to rely heavily on bits of plastic, go for two different cards – an American Express or Diners Club, for instance, along with a Visa or MasterCard. Better still is a combination of credit or cash card and travellers' cheques so you have something to fall back on if an ATM swallows your card or the banks in the area are closed.

A word of warning: fraudulent shopkeepers have been known to quickly make several charge-slip imprints with your credit card when you're not looking, and then simply copy your signature from the one that you authorise. Try not to let your card out of sight, and always check your statements upon your return.

International Transfers

Transferring money from your home bank will be easier if you've authorised someone back home to access your account. Also, a transfer to a tiny bank branch in a remote village in Corsica is obviously going to be more difficult than to the bank's head office in Paris. If you have the choice, find a large bank and ask for the international division.

Money sent by telegraphic transfer (which typically costs from US$40) should reach you within a week; by mail, allow at least two weeks.

You can also transfer money by American Express or Thomas Cook; the former charges US$40 for amounts up to US$300 and US$70 for amounts over US$500. Western Union Money Transfers can be collected at associated banks throughout Europe.

Guaranteed Cheques

Guaranteed personal cheques are another way of carrying money or obtaining cash. The most popular of these is the Eurocheque. To get

Eurocheques, you need a European bank account and a cheque-cashing card; depending on the bank, it takes at least two weeks to apply for the cheques.

Some countries have similar systems operating nationally. The most advanced of these is the Dutch 'postgiro' system, with cheques issued to Postbank account holders. The cheques are only valid for purchases within the Netherlands, but allow cash withdrawals at post offices in 40 countries.

Currency Exchange

By the year 2000, the EU should have a single currency called the euro. Until then francs, marks, pesetas and pounds remain in place.

In general, US dollars, Deutschmarks, pounds sterling, and French and Swiss francs are the most easily exchanged currencies in Europe, followed by Italian lire and Dutch guilders, but you may well decide that other currencies suit your purposes better. You lose out through commissions and customer exchange rates every time you change money, so if you only visit Portugal, for example, you may be better off buying escudos straight away if your bank at home can provide them.

All Western European currencies are fully convertible, but you may have trouble exchanging some of the more obscure ones at small banks, while currencies of countries with high inflation face unfavourable exchange rates. Try not to have too many leftover Portuguese escudos, Spanish pesetas, Irish punts, Belgian or Luxembourg francs, or Austrian Schillings. Get rid of Scottish and Northern Irish pounds before leaving those areas; nobody outside the UK will touch them and you'll even have a lot of trouble spending them in England.

Most airports, central railway stations, some big hotels and many border posts have banking facilities outside normal office hours, sometimes on a 24-hour basis. You'll often find automatic exchange machines outside banks or tourist offices that accept the currencies of up to two dozen countries. Post offices in Europe often perform banking tasks, tend to be open longer hours, and outnumber banks in remote places. Be aware, though, that while they always exchange cash, they might balk at handling travellers' cheques.

The best exchange rates are usually at banks. *Bureaux de change* usually (but not always) offer worse rates or charge higher commissions. Hotels are almost always the worst places to change money. American Express and Thomas Cook offices usually do not charge commission for changing their own cheques, but may offer a less favourable exchange rate than banks.

Tipping

In many European countries it's common (and the law in France) for a service charge to be added to restaurant bills, in which case no tipping is necessary. In others, simply rounding up the bill is sufficient. See the individual country chapters for more details.

Taxes & Refunds

A kind of sales tax called value-added tax (VAT) applies to most goods and services throughout Western Europe. In most countries visitors can claim back the VAT on purchases that are being taken out of the country. Those actually residing in one EU country are not entitled to a refund on VAT paid on goods bought in another EU country. The procedure for making the claim is fairly straightforward, though it may vary somewhat from country to country and there are minimum-purchase amounts imposed (see individual country chapters for more information). When making your purchase ask the shop attendant for a VAT refund voucher filled in with the correct amount and the date. This can either be refunded directly at international airports on departure or stamped at ferry ports or border crossings and mailed back for refund.

POST & COMMUNICATIONS

Post

From major European centres, air mail typically takes about five days to North America and a week to Australasian destinations, though mail to/from the UK can be much faster and can be to/from Greece much slower. Postage costs do vary from country to country, and so does post office efficiency – the Italian post office is notoriously unreliable and Lonely Planet manuscripts sent special delivery air mail have taken up to two months to reach Australia.

You can collect mail from poste restante sections at major post offices. Ask people writing to you to print your name clearly and underline your surname. When collecting mail, your passport may be required for identification and you may have to pay a small fee. If an expected letter is not awaiting you, ask to check under your given name: letters commonly get misfiled. Post offices usually hold mail for about a month, but sometimes less (in Germany, for instance, they only hold mail for a fortnight). Unless the sender specifies otherwise, mail will always be sent to the city's main post office or GPO (UK and Ireland).

You can also have mail (but not parcels) sent to you at American Express offices so long as you have an American Express card or are carrying Amex travellers' cheques. When you buy American Express cheques, ask for a booklet listing all its office addresses worldwide.

Telephone

You can ring abroad from almost any phone box in Europe. Public telephones accepting stored-value phonecards, available from post offices, telephone centres, newsstands or retail outlets, are almost the norm now; in some countries, coin-operated phones are almost impossible to find. The card solves the problem of finding the correct coins for calls (or lots of correct coins for international calls), but it can be annoying having to buy a 100FF phonecard when you just want to make a 2FF call.

A new product called the Country Card is available in some areas. With one of these cards (available from post offices or telephone centres), you get a 15% to 20% discount on calls to certain countries, making it even cheaper to use than one of the standard phonecards. Country Cards in the Netherlands, for example, are now available for the USA and Canada (f25), Australia and New Zealand (f50) and South Africa (f50).

Without a phonecard or Country Card, you can ring from a booth inside a post office or telephone centre and settle your bill at the counter. Reverse-charge (collect) calls are often possible, but not always – for a start, you'll have to be able to communicate with the local operator, who might not always speak English. From many countries, however, you can dial direct to your home operator, which solves the problem. See the Telephones appendix in the back of this book for information on international dialling, local phones, costs and country codes.

Fax & Telegraph

You can send telegrams and faxes from most main post offices in Western Europe.

E-mail

Maintaining your Internet connectivity while you are on the road in Europe can be done with a little planning and forethought. All European countries are now connected to the Internet and finding access is becoming easier. You have a few options. You can take your laptop PC and modem and dial your home country service provider, or take out a local account in the region you will be visiting most (there are kits to help you cope with local telephone plugs). For more information have a look at Lonely Planet's site at http://www.lonelyplanet.com.

Internet cafés, where you can buy online time and have a coffee are springing up all over Europe. Check http://www.cyberiacafe.net/cyberia/guide/ccafe.htm for the latest list. Failing that make friends with local students and ask if you can sneak time on a university, or even private machine. Before leaving home, contact your service provider to see if they can offer any specific advice about the countries you intend to visit.

See the earlier Online Services section for useful sites for travellers to Western Europe.

NEWSPAPERS & MAGAZINES

Keeping up with the news in English is obviously no problem in the UK or Ireland. In larger towns in the rest of Europe you can buy the excellent *International Herald Tribune* on the day of publication, as well as the colourful but superficial *USA Today*. The *Guardian*, *Financial Times* and some other UK papers are often available, but usually a day or so late. The lightweight weekly newspaper *The European* can be found everywhere, as can the news magazines *Time*, *Newsweek* and *The Economist*.

RADIO & TV

Close to the Channel, you can pick up British radio stations, particularly BBC's Radio 4. Otherwise, the BBC World Service can be found on medium wave at 648 kHz, on short wave at 6195, 9410, 12095 and 15575 kHz, and on long wave at 198 kHz, the appropriate frequency depending on where you are and the time of day. The Voice of America (VOA) can usually be found on short wave at 15205 kHz. There are also numerous English-language broadcasts (or even BBC World Service and VOA re-broadcasts) on local AM and FM radio stations.

Cable and satellite TV have spread across Europe with much more gusto than radio. Sky TV can be found in many hotels throughout Western Europe, as can CNN and other networks. You can also pick up many cross-border TV stations, including British stations close to the Channel.

VIDEO SYSTEMS

If you want to record or buy video tapes to play back home, you won't get a picture if the image registration systems are different. Europe generally uses PAL (SECAM in France), which is incompatible with the North American and Japanese NTSC system. Australia uses PAL.

PHOTOGRAPHY

Europe and its people are extremely photogenic, but where you'll be travelling and the weather will dictate what film to take or buy locally. In places like Ireland and Britain where the sky is often overcast, photographers should bring high-speed film (eg 200 ASA). For southern Europe (or northern Europe under a blanket of snow and sunny skies) slower film is the answer.

Film and camera equipment is available everywhere in Western Europe, but obviously shops in the larger cities and towns have a wider selection. Avoid buying film at tourist sites in Europe – eg at kiosks below the Eiffel Tower in Paris or the Coliseum in Rome. It may have been stored badly or reached its sell-by date. It certainly will be expensive.

ELECTRICITY
Voltage & Cycle

Most of Europe runs on 220 V, 50 Hz AC. The exceptions are the UK, which has 240 V, and Spain, which usually has 220 V but sometimes still the old 125 V, depending on the network (some houses can have both). Some old buildings and hotels in Italy might also have 125 V. All EU countries should have been standardised at 230 V by now, but like everything

else in the EU, this is taking a bit longer than anticipated.

Check the voltage and cycle (usually 50 Hz) used in your home country. Most appliances that are set up for 220 V will handle 240 V without modifications (and vice versa); the same goes for 110 and 125 V combinations. It's always preferable to adjust your appliance to the exact voltage if you can (some modern battery chargers and radios will do this automatically). Just don't mix 110/125 V with 220/240 V without a transformer (which will be built into an adjustable appliance).

Several countries outside Europe (such as the USA and Canada) have 60 Hz AC, which will affect the speed of electric motors even after the voltage has been adjusted to European values, so CD and tape players (where motor speed is all-important) will be useless. But things like electric razors, hair dryers, irons and radios will be fine.

Plugs & Sockets

The UK and Ireland use a design with three flat pins – two for current and one for earth/grounding. The rest of Europe uses the 'europlug' with two round pins. Many europlugs and some sockets don't have provision for earth, since most local home appliances are double-insulated; when provided, earth usually consists of two contact points along the edge, although Italy, Greece and Switzerland use a third round pin in such a way that the standard two-pin plug still fits the sockets (though not always in Italy).

If your plugs are of a different design, you'll need an adapter. Get one before you leave, since the adapters available in Europe usually go the other way. If you find yourself without one, however, a specialist electrical-supply shop should be able to help.

HEALTH

Europe is generally a healthy place. Your main risks are likely to be sunburn, foot blisters, insect bites, or an upset stomach from overeating and drinking. You might experience mild gut problems in southern Europe if you're not used to copious amounts of olive oil, but you'll get used to it after a while.

If you're reasonably fit, the only things you should organise before departure are a visit to your dentist to get your teeth in order and travel insurance with good medical cover (see the following section). You should also make sure that your normal childhood vaccines (against measles, mumps, rubella, diphtheria, tetanus and polio) are up to date and, depending on where you will be travelling, consider one or more of the immunisations listed below.

Predeparture Preparations

Health Insurance A travel insurance policy to cover theft, personal liability, loss and medical problems is a must. There is a wide variety of policies available and your travel agent will have recommendations. The international student travel policies handled by STA Travel or other student travel organisations are usually good value. Some policies offer lower and higher medical-expense options – go as high as you can afford, especially if you're visiting Switzerland, Germany or any of the Scandinavian countries, where medical costs can be high. Check the small print:

- Some policies specifically exclude 'dangerous activities' such as scuba diving, motorcycling, skiing, mountaineering or even trekking.
- A policy that pays doctors or hospitals directly may be preferable to one where you pay on the spot and claim later. If you have to claim later, make sure you keep all documentation. Some policies ask you to call back (reverse charges) to a centre in your home country where an immediate assessment of your problem is made.
- Check if the policy covers ambulances or helicopter rescue, and an emergency flight home. If you have to stretch out you will need two seats and somebody has to pay for them!

EU citizens are covered for emergency medical treatment in all EU countries on presentation of an E111 form. Enquire about these at your national health service or travel agent well in advance; in some countries post offices have them. Similar reciprocal arrangements exist between the Scandinavian countries. Australian Medicare covers emergency treatment in Finland, Italy, Malta, the Netherlands, Sweden and the UK. You may still have to pay on the spot, but you'll be able to reclaim these expenses at home. However, travel insurance is still advisable because of the flexibility it offers as to where and how you're treated, as well as covering expenses for ambulance and repatriation.

Medical Kit A small, straightforward medical kit is a good thing to carry. A possible list includes:

- Aspirin or Panadol – for pain or fever
- Antihistamine (such as Benadryl) – useful as a decongestant for colds, allergies, to ease the itch from insect bites or stings or to help prevent motion sickness
- Kaolin preparation (eg Pepto-Bismol), Imodium or Lomotil – for possible stomach upsets
- Antiseptic, such as Betadine, and antibiotic powder or similar 'dry' spray – for cuts and grazes
- Calamine lotion – to ease irritation from insect bites or stings
- Bandages and Band-aids – for minor injuries
- Scissors, tweezers and a thermometer (note that mercury thermometers are prohibited by airlines)
- Insect repellent, sunscreen, lip balm and perhaps water-purification tablets

When buying medicines over the counter, especially in southern Europe, check the expiry date and make sure that correct storage conditions have been followed.

Health Preparations If you wear glasses, take a spare pair as well as your prescription. Losing your glasses can be a problem, but you can usually get new spectacles made up quickly, cheaply and competently in Western Europe.

If you need a particular medication, take an adequate supply, as it may not always be available in remote places. The same applies for your oral contraceptive. Take the prescription, or better still, part of the packaging showing the generic rather than the brand name (which may not be locally available), as it will make getting replacements easier.

It's a good idea to have a legible prescription to show that you legally use the medication – it's surprising how often over-the-counter drugs from one place are illegal without a prescription or even banned in another. If you're carrying a syringe for some reason, have a note from your doctor to explain why you're doing so.

A Medic Alert tag is a good idea if your medical condition is not always easily recognisable (heart trouble, diabetes, asthma, allergic reactions to antibiotics etc).

Immunisations Jabs are not really necessary for Europe, but they may be an entry requirement if you're coming from an infected area –

yellow fever is the most likely requirement. If you're going to Europe with stopovers in Asia, Africa or South America, check with your travel agent or with the embassies of the countries you plan to visit.

There are, however, a few routine vaccinations that are recommended whether you're travelling or not, and this Health section assumes that you've had them: polio (usually administered during childhood), tetanus and diphtheria (usually administered together during childhood, with a booster shot every 10 years), and measles. See your physician or nearest health agency about these. You might also consider having an immunoglobulin or hepatitis A (Havrix) vaccine before extensive travels in southern Europe; a tetanus booster; an immunisation against hepatitis B before travelling to Malta; or a rabies (pre-exposure) vaccination.

All vaccinations should be recorded on an International Health Certificate, which is available from your physician or government health department. Don't leave this till the last minute, as the vaccinations may have to be staggered over a period of time.

Basic Rules

Many health problems can be avoided by taking care of yourself. Wash your hands frequently. Clean your teeth. Avoid climatic extremes: keep out of the sun when it's hot, dress warmly when it's cold. Minimise insect bites by covering bare skin when insects are around, or by using insect repellents.

Care in what you eat and drink is also important in the remoter parts of southern Europe; stomach upsets are the most likely travel health problem here, but the majority of these upsets will be relatively minor.

Water Tap water is almost always safe to drink in Europe, but be wary of natural water unless you can be sure that there are no people or cattle upstream; run-off from fertilised fields is also a concern. If you are planning extended hikes where you have to rely on natural water, it may be useful to know about water purification.

The simplest way of purifying water is to boil it thoroughly. Technically this means boiling for 10 minutes, something which

happens very rarely. Remember that at high altitude water boils at a lower temperature, so germs are less likely to be killed.

Simple filtering will not remove all dangerous organisms, so if you cannot boil water it should be treated chemically. Chlorine tablets (Puritabs, Steritabs or other brand names) will kill many but not all pathogens. Iodine is very effective in purifying water and is available in tablet form (such as Potable Aqua), but follow the directions carefully and remember that too much iodine can be harmful.

Food Salads and fruit should be safe throughout Europe. Ice cream is usually OK, but beware of ice cream that has melted and been refrozen. Take great care with fish or shellfish (for instance, cooked mussels that haven't opened properly can be dangerous), and avoid undercooked meat.

If a place looks clean and well run and if the vendor also looks clean and healthy, then the food is probably safe. In general, places that are packed with travellers or locals will be fine. Be careful with food that has been cooked and left to go cold.

Picking mushrooms is a favourite pastime in Europe as autumn approaches, but make sure you don't eat any mushrooms that haven't been positively identified as safe. Many cities and towns set up inspection tables at markets or at entrances to national parks to separate the good from the deadly.

Nutrition If you don't vary your diet, if you're travelling hard and fast and therefore missing meals, or if you simply lose your appetite, you can soon start to lose weight and place your health at risk – just as you would at home.

If you rely on fast food, you'll get plenty of fats and carbohydrates but little else of value. Remember that overcooked food loses much of its nutritional value. If your diet isn't well balanced, it's a good idea to take vitamin and iron pills (women lose a lot of iron through menstruation). Fruit and vegetables are good sources of vitamins.

In hot climates make sure you drink enough liquids – don't rely on feeling thirsty to indicate when you should drink. Not needing to urinate or very dark-yellow (or strong-smelling) urine is a danger sign. Carry a water bottle on long trips. Excessive sweating can lead to loss of salt and therefore muscle cramps. Salt tablets are not a good idea as a preventative, but in places where salt is not used much, adding salt to food can help.

Medical Problems & Treatment

Local pharmacies or neighbourhood medical centres are good places to visit if you have a small medical problem and can explain what the problem is. Hospital casualty wards will help if it's more serious. Major hospitals and emergency numbers are mentioned in the various country chapters of this book and sometimes indicated on the maps. Tourist offices and hotels can put you on to a doctor or dentist, and your embassy or consulate will probably know one who speaks your language.

Sunburn In southern Europe, and anywhere on water, ice, snow or sand, you can get sunburned surprisingly quickly, even through cloud cover. Use a sunscreen and take extra care to cover areas that don't normally see sun, eg your feet. A hat provides added protection, and it may be a good idea to use sunscreen on your nose and lips. Calamine lotion is good for mild sunburn.

Remember that too much sunlight can damage your eyes, whether it's direct or reflected (glare). If your plans include activities on water, ice, snow or sand, then good

---

Vital Signs
The normal body temperature for an adult human being is 37°C (98.6°F); more than 2°C (4°F) higher than that is a 'high' fever. A normal adult pulse rate is 60 to 100 per minute (children 80 to 100, babies 100 to 140). You should know how to take a temperature and a pulse rate. As a general rule, the pulse increases about 20 beats per minute for each 1°C (2°F) rise in body temperature.

The respiration rate is also an indicator of illness. Count the number of breaths per minute: between 12 and 20 is normal for adults and older children (up to 30 for younger children, 40 for babies). People with a high fever or serious respiratory illness (like pneumonia) breathe more quickly than normal. More than 40 shallow breaths a minute could indicate pneumonia. ■

---

sunglasses are doubly important. Make sure they're treated to absorb ultraviolet radiation – if not, they'll do more harm than good by dilating your pupils and making it easier for ultraviolet light to damage the retina.

Prickly Heat Prickly heat is an itchy rash caused by excessive perspiration trapped under the skin. It usually strikes people who have just arrived in a hot climate and whose pores have not yet opened sufficiently to cope with greater sweating. Keeping cool by bathing often, using a mild talcum powder or even resorting to air-conditioning may help until you acclimatise.

Heat Exhaustion Dehydration or salt deficiency can cause heat exhaustion. Take time to acclimatise to high temperatures and make sure you get sufficient liquids (nonalcoholic). Salt deficiency is characterised by fatigue, lethargy, headaches, giddiness and muscle cramps, and in this case salt tablets may help. Vomiting or diarrhoea can deplete your liquid and salt levels.

Anhydrotic heat exhaustion, caused by an inability to sweat, is quite rare. Unlike the other forms of heat exhaustion, it is likely to strike people who have been in a hot climate for some time, rather than recent arrivals.

Heat Stroke This serious, sometimes fatal, condition can occur if the body's heat-regulating mechanism breaks down, and the body temperature rises to dangerous levels. Long, continuous periods of exposure to high temperatures can leave you vulnerable to heat stroke. You should avoid excess alcohol or strenuous activity when you first arrive in a hot climate.

The symptoms are feeling unwell, not sweating very much or at all, and a high body temperature (39°C to 41°C). Where sweating has ceased, the skin becomes flushed and red. Severe, throbbing headaches and lack of coordination will also occur, and the sufferer may be confused or aggressive. Eventually the victim will become delirious or begin to convulse. Hospitalisation is essential, but in the meantime get victims out of the sun, remove their clothing, cover them with a wet sheet or towel and then fan them continually.

Fungal Infections Hot-weather fungal infections are most likely to occur on the scalp, between the toes or fingers (athlete's foot), in the groin (jock itch or crotch rot) and on the body (ringworm). You get ringworm (a fungal infection, not a worm) from infected animals or by walking on damp areas, like shower floors.

To prevent fungal infections, wear loose, comfortable clothes, avoid artificial fibres, wash frequently and dry carefully. Also, wear plastic sandals or thongs in showers you suspect might be less than hygienic. If you do get an infection, wash the infected area daily with a disinfectant or medicated soap and water, and rinse and dry well. Apply an anti-fungal powder like the widely available Tinaderm. Try to expose the infected area to air or sunlight as much as possible and wash all towels and underwear in hot water as well as changing them often.

Hypothermia Too much cold is just as dangerous as too much heat, particularly if it leads to hypothermia. Cold combined with wind and moisture (ie soaking rain) is particularly risky. If you are trekking at high altitudes or in a cool, wet environment, be prepared.

Hypothermia occurs when the body loses heat faster than it can produce it and the core temperature of the body falls. It is surprisingly easy to progress from very cold to dangerously cold through a combination of wind, wet clothing, fatigue and hunger, even if the air temperature is above freezing. It is best to dress in layers – silk, wool and some of the new artificial fibres are all good insulating materials. A hat is important, as a lot of heat is lost through the head. A strong, waterproof outer layer is essential. Carry basic supplies, including food that contains simple sugars to generate heat quickly, and lots of fluid to drink.

Symptoms of hypothermia are exhaustion, numb skin (particularly toes and fingers), shivering, slurred speech, irrational or violent behaviour, lethargy, stumbling, dizzy spells, muscle cramps and violent bursts of energy. Irrationality may take the form of sufferers claiming they are warm and trying to take off their clothes.

To treat hypothermia, first get the person out of the wind and/or rain, remove their clothing if it's wet and replace it with dry, warm clothing. Give them hot, nonalcoholic liquids and some high-kilojoule (high-calorie), easily digestible food. Do not rub victims' skin. Place them near a fire or, if possible, in a warm (not hot) bath. This should be enough for the early stages of hypothermia. The early recognition and treatment of mild hypothermia is the only way to prevent severe hypothermia, which is a critical condition.

Altitude Sickness Acute mountain sickness (AMS) occurs at high altitude and can be fatal. There is no hard-and-fast rule as to how high is too high: AMS can strike at altitudes of 3000 metres, although 3500 to 4500 metres is the usual range. Very few treks or ski runs in the Alps and Pyrenees reach heights of 3000 metres or more, so it's unlikely to be a major concern.

Motion Sickness Eating lightly before and during a trip will reduce the chances of motion sickness. If you are prone to the syndrome, try to find a place that minimises disturbance – near the wing on an aircraft, close to midships on boats, near the centre on buses. Fresh air and a steady reference point like the horizon usually help, whereas reading or cigarette smoke exacerbate the problem. Commercial antimotion-sickness preparations, which can cause drowsiness, have to be taken before the trip commences – when you're feeling sick, it's already too late. Ginger is a natural preventative and is available in capsule form.

Jet Lag Jet lag is experienced when a person travels by air across more than three time zones (each time zone usually represents a one-hour time difference). It occurs because many of the functions of the human body (such as temperature, pulse rate and the emptying of the bladder and bowels) are regulated by internal 24-hour cycles called circadian rhythms. When we travel long distances rapidly, our bodies take time to adjust to the 'new time' of our destination, and we may experience fatigue, disorientation, insomnia, anxiety, impaired concentration and loss of appetite. These effects will usually be gone within three days of arrival, but there are ways of minimising the impact of jet lag:

- Rest for a couple of days prior to departure; try to avoid late nights, too many bon voyage parties, and last-minute dashes for travellers' cheques, visas etc.
- Try to select flight schedules that minimise sleep deprivation; arriving late in the day means you can go to sleep soon after you arrive. For very long flights, try to organise a stopover.
- Avoid excessive eating (which bloats the stomach) and alcohol (which causes dehydration) during the flight. Instead, drink plenty of non-carbonated, non-alcoholic drinks such as fruit juice or mineral water.
- Avoid smoking, as this reduces the amount of oxygen in the aircraft cabin even further and causes greater fatigue.
- Make yourself comfortable by wearing loose-fitting clothes and perhaps bringing an eye mask and ear plugs to help you sleep.

Diarrhoea A change of water, food or climate can all cause the runs; diarrhoea caused by contaminated food or water is more serious. Despite all your precautions, you may still have a bout of mild travellers' diarrhoea, but a few rushed toilet trips with no other symptoms is not indicative of a serious problem.

Moderate diarrhoea, involving a half-dozen loose movements in a day, is more of a nuisance. Dehydration is the main danger with any diarrhoea, particularly for children, so fluid replenishment is the number one treatment. Weak black tea with a little sugar, soda water, or soft drinks allowed to go flat and diluted 50% with water are all good.

With any diarrhoea more severe than this, go straight to the casualty ward of the nearest hospital and have yourself checked. You may need a rehydrating solution to replace minerals and salts. Stick to a bland diet as you recover.

Viral Gastroenteritis This is caused not by bacteria but, as the name suggests, by a virus. It is characterised by stomach cramps, diarrhoea, and sometimes by vomiting and/or a slight fever. All you can do is rest and drink lots of fluids.

Hepatitis B This disease is spread through contact with infected blood, blood products or bodily fluids, for example through sexual contact, unsterilised needles and blood transfusions. Other risk situations include tattooing and ear and body-piercing. The symptoms are fever, chills, headache and fatigue followed by vomiting, abdominal pain, dark urine and jaundiced skin. Hepatitis B can lead to irreparable liver damage, even liver cancer. There is no treatment (except rest, drinking lots of fluids and eating lightly) but an effective prophylactic vaccine is now readily available in most countries.

Rabies Rabies is nonexistent in the UK and Ireland and rare (or under control) in the rest of Western Europe. It is caused by a bite or scratch from an infected animal. Dogs are a noted carrier, but cats, foxes and bats can also be affected. Any bite, scratch or even lick from a warm-blooded, furry animal should be cleaned immediately and thoroughly. Scrub with soap and running water, and then clean with an alcohol solution. If there is any possibility that the animal is infected, particularly if it froths at the mouth and behaves strangely, medical help should be sought immediately. Even if it is not rabid, all bites should be treated seriously as they can become infected or can result in tetanus.

A rabies vaccination is available and should be considered if you are in a high-risk category – eg if you intend to explore caves (bat bites can be dangerous), work with animals, or travel so far off the beaten track that medical help is more than two days away.

Tuberculosis Although TB is widespread in many developing countries and used to be a scourge in Europe, it is not a serious risk to healthy travellers. Young children are more susceptible than adults, and vaccination is a sensible precaution for children aged under 12 travelling in endemic areas. TB is commonly spread by coughing or by unpasteurised dairy products from infected cows. Milk that has been boiled is safe to drink; the souring of milk to make yoghurt or cheese also kills the bacilli.

Sexually Transmitted Diseases Sexual contact with an infected partner spreads what are now commonly called STDs. Abstinence – admittedly an unrealistic expectation – is the only 100% preventative, but the proper use of condoms can also be almost as effective. Gonorrhoea and syphilis are the most common of these diseases: sores, blisters or rashes around the genitals, discharges, or pain when urinating are common symptoms. Symptoms may be less marked or not observed at all in women.

Syphilis symptoms eventually disappear completely, but the disease continues and can cause severe problems in later years. The treatment of gonorrhoea and syphilis is by antibiotics. STD clinics are widespread in Europe. Don't be shy about visiting them if you think you may have contracted something; they are there to help and have seen it all before.

There are numerous other STDs – effective treatment is available for most – but as yet there is no cure for herpes or HIV/AIDS. The latter has become a considerable problem in Europe. HIV, the 'human immunodeficiency virus', may develop into AIDS (acquired immune deficiency syndrome). Apart from abstinence, the most effective preventive is always to practise safe sex using condoms. It is impossible to detect the HIV-positive status of an otherwise healthy-looking person without a blood test.

HIV/AIDS can also be spread through infected blood transfusions or by dirty needles – vaccinations, acupuncture, tattooing and body-piercing can potentially be as dangerous as intravenous drug use if the equipment is not sterile.

Bites & Stings Bee and wasp stings are usually painful rather than dangerous. Calamine lotion will give relief; ice packs will reduce the pain and swelling. There are some spiders with dangerous bites (though rare in Europe), but antivenins are usually available. Scorpion stings are notoriously painful, but the small scorpions occasionally found in southern Europe are not considered fatal. Scorpions often shelter in shoes or clothing – always give your shoes a good shake-out before donning them in the morning, especially when camping.

Mosquitoes can be a nuisance in southern Europe, but can almost drive you insane during the summer months in northern Europe, particularly around lakes and rivers. They also cause sleepless nights in a swampy country like the Netherlands. Fortunately, mosquito-borne diseases like malaria are for the most part unknown in Western Europe. Most people get used to mosquito bites after a few days as their bodies adjust, and the itching and swelling will become less severe. An antihistamine cream may help alleviate the symptoms. For some people, a daily dose of vitamin B will keep mosquitoes at bay.

Midges – small, blood-sucking flies related to mosquitoes – are a major problem in some parts of Europe (eg Scotland and parts of England) during summer.

All lice cause itching and discomfort. They make themselves at home in your hair (head lice), your clothing (body lice) or in your pubic hair (crabs). You catch lice through direct contact with infected people or by sharing combs, clothing and the like. Powder or shampoo treatment will kill the lice, and infected clothing should then be washed in very hot water.

One insect that can bring on more than just an itch in parts of eastern Austria and in Eastern Europe is the forest tick, which burrows under the skin, causing inflammation and even encephalitis. You might consider getting an FSME (meningo-encephalitis) vaccination if you plan to do extensive hiking and camping between May and September.

Snakes tend to keep a very low profile in Western Europe, but to minimise your chances of being bitten, try to wear boots, socks and long trousers when walking through undergrowth or rocky areas where snakes may be present. Tramp heavily and they'll usually slither away before you come near. Don't put your hands into holes and crevices, and be careful when collecting firewood (scorpions also like dead wood).

Snake bites do not cause instantaneous death and antivenins are usually available. Keep the victim calm and still, wrap the bitten limb tightly, as you would for a sprained ankle, and then attach a splint to immobilise it. Then seek medical help, if possible with the dead snake for identification. Don't attempt to catch the snake if there is even a remote possibility of it biting again. Tourniquets and sucking out the poison are now completely discredited.

Women's Health

Some women experience an irregular menstrual cycle when travelling because of the upset in routine. Don't forget to take time zones into account if you're on the pill. Ask your physician about these matters.

Poor diet, lowered resistance through the use of antibiotics for stomach upsets, and even contraceptive pills, can predispose women to vaginal infections when travelling in hot climates. Maintaining good personal hygiene, and wearing skirts or loose-fitting trousers and cotton underwear will help to prevent infections.

Yeast infections (thrush), characterised by a rash, itch and discharge, can be treated with a vinegar or even lemon-juice douche, or with yoghurt. Nystatin suppositories are the usual medical prescription.

Trichomonas is a more serious infection; symptoms are a discharge and a burning sensation when urinating, and if a vinegar-water douche is not effective, medical attention should be sought. Metronidazole (Flagyl) is the prescribed drug. In both cases, male sexual partners must also be treated.

WOMEN TRAVELLERS
For women travellers, common sense is the best guide to dealing with possibly dangerous situations like hitchhiking, walking alone at night etc.

Women are more likely to experience problems in rural Spain and southern Italy, particularly Sicily, but the potential is, sadly, everywhere. Slightly conservative dress can help to avoid unwanted attention, and dark sunglasses help to avoid unwanted eye contact. Marriage is highly respected in southern Europe, and a wedding ring (on the left ring finger) sometimes helps, along with talk about 'my husband'. Hitchhiking alone in these areas is asking for trouble. The *Handbook for Women Travellers* by M & G Moss is recommended reading.

GAY & LESBIAN TRAVELLERS
Gays and lesbians should get in touch with their national organisation. This book lists contact addresses and gay and lesbian venues in the individual country chapters, but your organisation should be able to give you much more information.

The *Spartacus Guide for Gay Men* (Bruno Gmünder, Berlin) is a good international directory of gay entertainment venues in Europe and elsewhere. It's best used in conjunction with listings in local papers. For lesbians, *Places for Women* (Ferrari Publications) is the best international guide.

DISABLED TRAVELLERS
If you have a physical disability, get in touch with your national support organisation (preferably the 'travel officer' if there is one) and ask about the countries you plan to visit. They often have complete libraries devoted to travel, and they can put you in touch with travel agents who specialise in tours for the disabled.

The British-based Royal Association for Disability & Rehabilitation (RADAR) publishes a useful guide titled *Holidays & Travel Abroad: A Guide for Disabled People* (UK£5), which gives a good overview of facilities available to disabled travellers in Europe (published in even-numbered years) and farther afield (in odd-numbered years). Contact RADAR (☎ 0171-250 3222) at 12 City Forum, 250 City Rd, London EC1V 8AF.

SENIOR TRAVELLERS
Senior citizens are entitled to many discounts in Europe on things like public transport, museum admission fees etc, provided they show proof of their age. In some cases they might need a special pass. The minimum qualifying age is generally 60 or 65 for men and slightly younger for women.

In your home country, a lower age may already entitle you to all sorts of interesting travel packages and discounts (on car hire, for instance) through organisations and travel agents that cater for senior travellers. Start hunting at your local senior citizens advice bureau. European residents over 60 are eligible for the Rail Europe Senior Card; see the Getting Around chapter for details.

TRAVEL WITH CHILDREN
Successful travel with young children requires planning and effort. Don't try to overdo things; even for adults, packing too much into the time available can cause problems. And make sure the activities include the kids as well – balance that day at the Louvre with a day at Euro Disney. Include children in the trip planning; if they've helped to work out where you will be going, they will be much more interested when they get there. Lonely Planet's *Travel with Children* by Maureen Wheeler is a good source of information.

In Western Europe most car-rental firms have children's safety seats for hire at a nominal cost, but it is essential that you book them in advance. The same goes for highchairs and cots (cribs); they're standard in most restaurants and hotels, but numbers are limited. The choice of baby food, infant formulas, soy and cow's milk, disposable nappies (diapers) and the like is as great in the supermarkets of most Western European countries as it is at home, but the opening hours may be quite different. Run out of nappies on Saturday afternoon and you're facing a very long and messy weekend.

DANGERS & ANNOYANCES

On the whole, you should experience few problems in Western Europe, so long as you exercise common sense. Whatever you do, don't leave friends and relatives back home worrying about how to get in touch with you in case of emergency. Work out a list of places where they can contact you or, best of all, phone home now and then.

Theft

Theft is definitely a problem in Europe, and it's not just other travellers you have to be wary of. The most important things to guard are your passport, papers, tickets and money – in that order. It's always best to carry these next to your skin or in a sturdy leather pouch on your belt. Train station lockers or luggage storage counters are useful places to store your bags (but *never* valuables) while you get your bearings in a new town. Be very suspicious about people who offer to help you operate your locker. Carry your own padlock for hostel lockers.

You can lessen the risks further by being careful of snatch thieves. Cameras or shoulder bags are great for these people, who sometimes operate from motorcycles or scooters and expertly slash the strap before you have a chance to react. A small daypack is better, but watch your rear. Be very careful at cafés and bars; loop the strap around your leg while seated.

Pickpockets are most active in dense crowds, especially in busy train stations and on public transport during peak hours. A common ploy is for one person to distract you while another zips through your pockets. Beware of gangs of kids (dishevelled-looking or well dressed) waving newspapers and demanding

attention. In the blink of an eye, a wallet or camera can go missing.

Be careful even in hotels; don't leave valuables lying around in your room. Parked cars are prime targets for petty criminals in most cities, and cars with foreign number plates and/or rental agency stickers in particular. Remove the stickers (or cover them with local football club stickers or something similar), leave a local newspaper on the seat and generally try to make it look like a local car. Don't ever leave valuables in the car, and remove all luggage overnight, even if it's in a parking garage. In some places, freeway service centres have become unsafe territory: in the time it takes to drink a cup of coffee or use the toilet, your car can be broken into and cleared out.

Another ploy is for muggers to pull up alongside your car and point to the wheel; when you get out to have a look, you become one more robbery statistic. While driving in cities, beware of snatch thieves when you pull up at the lights – keep doors locked and windows rolled up high. In case of theft or loss, always report the incident to the police and ask for a statement. Otherwise your travel insurance won't pay up.

Drugs

Always treat drugs with a great deal of caution. There is a fair bit of dope available in Western Europe, sometimes quite openly, as in the Netherlands, but that doesn't mean it's legal. Even a little harmless hashish can cause a great deal of trouble.

Don't bother bringing drugs home with you either. With what they may consider 'suspect' stamps in your passport (eg Amsterdam's Schiphol Airport), energetic customs officials could well decide to take a closer look.

ACTIVITIES

Europe offers countless opportunities to indulge in more active pursuits than sightseeing. The varied geography and climate supports the full range of outdoor pursuits: windsurfing, skiing, fishing, trekking, cycling and mountaineering. For more local information, see the individual country chapters.

Windsurfing & Surfing

After swimming and fishing, windsurfing could well be the most popular of the many water sports on offer in Europe. It's easy to rent sailboards in many tourist centres, and courses are usually available for beginners.

Believe it or not, you can also go surfing in Europe. Forget the shallow North Sea and Mediterranean and the calm Baltic. But there can be excellent surf, and an accompanying surfer scene, in south-west England and west Scotland (wetsuit advisable!), along Ireland's west coast, the Atlantic coast of France, in Portugal, and along the north and south-west coasts of Spain.

Skiing

In winter, Europeans flock to the hundreds of resorts in the Alps and Pyrenees for downhill skiing, though cross-country has also become very popular.

Skiing is quite expensive due to the costs of ski lifts, accommodation and the inevitable après-ski drinking sessions. Equipment hire (or even purchase), on the other hand, can be relatively cheap if you follow the tips in this book, and the hassle of bringing your own skis may not be worth it. As a rule, a skiing holiday in Europe will work out twice as expensive as a summer holiday of the same length. Cross-country skiing costs less than downhill since you don't rely as much on ski lifts.

The skiing season generally lasts from early December to late March, though at higher altitudes it may extend an extra month either way. Snow conditions can vary greatly from one year to the next and from region to region, but January and February tend to be the best (and busiest) months.

Ski resorts in the French and Swiss Alps offer great skiing and facilities, but are also the most expensive. Expect high prices, too, in the German Alps, though Germany has cheaper (but far less spectacular) options in the Black Forest and Harz Mountains. Austria is generally slightly cheaper than France or Switzerland (especially in Carinthia). Prices in the Italian Alps are similar to Austria (with some up-market exceptions like Cortina d'Ampezzo), and can work out relatively cheaply with the right package. Cheaper still is the skiing in Slovenia's Julian Alps, across the border from Austria and Italy, which offer some attractive deals.

Possibly the cheapest skiing in Western Europe is to be found in the Pyrenees in Spain

and Andorra, and in the Sierra Nevada range in the south of Spain. Greece and Scotland also boast growing ski industries – good value in Greece, disappointing in Scotland. See the individual country chapters for more information.

Hiking

Keen hikers can spend a lifetime exploring Europe's many exciting trails. Probably the most spectacular are to be found in the Alps and Italian Dolomites, which are crisscrossed with well-marked trails during the summer months; food and accommodation are available along the way. The equally sensational Pyrenees are less developed, which can add to the experience as you often rely on remote mountain villages for rest and sustenance. Hiking areas that are less well known but nothing short of stunning are Corsica and Sardinia.

The Ramblers' Association (☎ 0171-582 6878) is a London charity that promotes long-distance walking in the UK and can help with maps and information. The British-based Ramblers Holidays (☎ 01707-331133) offers hiking-oriented trips in Europe and elsewhere.

Every country in Europe has national parks and other interesting areas that may qualify as a trekker's paradise, depending on your preferences. Guided treks are often available for those who aren't sure about their physical abilities or who simply don't know what to look for. Read the Hiking information in the individual country chapters in this book and take your pick.

Cycling

Along with hiking, cycling is the best way to really get close to the scenery and the people, keeping yourself fit in the process. It's also a good way to get around many cities and towns.

Much of Europe is ideally suited to cycling. In the north-west, the flat terrain ensures that bicycles are a popular form of everyday transport, though rampant headwinds often spoil the fun. In the rest of the continent, hills and mountains can make for heavy going, but this is offset by the dense concentration of things to see. Cycling is a great way to explore many of the Mediterranean islands, though the heat can get to you after a while (make sure you drink enough fluids).

Popular holiday-cycling areas include the Belgian Ardennes, most of Ireland, the upper reaches of the Danube in southern Germany, the coasts of Sardinia and Apulia, anywhere in the Alps (for those fit enough), and the south of France. The French in particular take their cycling very seriously, and the annual Tour de France marathon is followed closely by much of the population.

If you are arriving from outside Europe, you can often bring your own bicycle along on the plane (see Bicycle in the Getting Around chapter). Alternatively, this book lists many places where you can hire one (make sure it has plenty of gears if you plan anything serious), though apart from in Ireland they might take a dim view of rentals lasting more than a week.

See the Getting Around chapter for more information on bicycle touring, and the individual country chapters for rental agencies and tips on places to go to.

Boating

Europe's many lakes, rivers and diverse coast-lines offer a variety of boating options unmatched anywhere in the world. You can canoe in Finland, raft down rapids in Slovenia, charter a yacht in the Aegean, hire a catamaran in the Netherlands, row on a peaceful Alpine lake, join a Danube River cruise from Basel all the way to Budapest (see the Getting Around chapter), rent a sailing boat on the Côte d'Azur, or dream away on a canal boat along Britain's extraordinary canal network – the possibilities are endless. The country chapters have more details.

COURSES

If your interests are more cerebral, you can enrol in courses in Western Europe on anything from language to alternative medicine. Language courses are often available to foreigners through universities or private schools, and are justifiably popular since the best way to learn a language is in the country where it's spoken. But you can also take courses in art, literature, architecture, drama, music, cooking, alternative energy, photography and organic farming, among other subjects.

The individual country chapters in this book give pointers on where to start looking. In general, the best sources of information are the cultural institutes maintained by many Euro-pean countries around the world; failing that, try their national tourist offices or embassies. Student exchange organisations, student travel agencies, and organisations like the YMCA/YWCA and Hostelling International (HI) can also put you on the right track. Ask about special holiday packages that include a course.

WORK

European countries aren't keen on handing out jobs to foreigners with unemployment as high as it is in some areas. Officially, an EU citizen is allowed to work in any other EU country, but the paperwork isn't always straightforward for longer term employment. Other country/nationality combinations require special work permits that can be almost impossible to arrange, especially for temporary work. That doesn't prevent enterprising travellers from topping up their funds occasionally by working in the hotel or restaurant trades or teaching a little English, and they don't always have to do this illegally either.

The UK, for example, issues special 'working holidaymaker' visas to Commonwealth citizens aged between 17 and 27, and Switzerland has a system of work permits allocated by employers. Your national student exchange organisation may be able to arrange temporary work permits to several countries through special programmes. For more details on working as a foreigner, see Work in the Facts for the Visitor sections of the individual country chapters.

If you have a parent or grandparent who was born in an EU country, you may have certain rights you never knew about. Get in touch with that country's embassy and ask about dual citizenship and work permits – if you go for citizenship, also ask about any obligations, such as military service and residency. Ireland is particularly easy-going about granting citizenship to people with an Irish parent or grandparent, and with an Irish passport, the EU is your oyster. Be aware that your home country may not recognise dual citizenship.

If you do find a temporary job, the pay may be less than that offered to local people. The one big exception is teaching English, but these jobs are hard to come by – at least officially. Other typical tourist jobs (picking grapes in France, washing dishes in Alpine resorts) often come with board and lodging, and the pay is little more than pocket money, but you'll have a good time partying with other travellers.

Work Your Way Around the World by Susan Griffith gives good, practical advice on a wide range of issues. Its publisher, Vacation Work, has many other useful titles, including *The Au Pair and Nanny's Guide to Working Abroad* by Susan Griffith & Sharon Legg.

If you play an instrument or have other artistic talents, you could try working the streets. As every Peruvian pipe player (and his fifth cousin) knows, busking is fairly common in major Western European cities like Amsterdam and Paris, but is illegal in some parts of Switzerland and Austria, and illegal but more or less tolerated in Germany and Belgium. Most other countries require municipal permits that can be hard to obtain. Talk to other street artists before you boogie.

Selling goods on the street is generally frowned upon and can be tantamount to vagrancy, apart from at flea markets. It's also a hard way to make money if you're not selling something special. Most countries require permits for this sort of thing. It's fairly common, though officially illegal, in the UK, Germany and Spain.

ACCOMMODATION

The cheapest places to stay in Europe are camping grounds, followed by hostels and accommodation in student dormitories. Cheap hotels are virtually unknown in the northern half of Europe, but guesthouses, pensions, private rooms and B&Bs often offer good value. Self-catering flats and cottages are worth considering with a group, especially if you plan to stay somewhere for a while.

See the Facts for the Visitor sections in the country chapters for an overview of the local accommodation options. During peak holiday periods, accommodation can be hard to find, and unless you're camping, it's advisable to book ahead. Even camping grounds can fill up, especially in or around big cities.

Making Reservations

If you arrive in a country by air, there is often an airport hotel-booking desk, although it rarely covers the lower strata of hotels. Tourist offices often have extensive accommodation lists, and the more helpful ones will go out of their way to find you something suitable. In most countries the fee for this service is very low, and if accommodation is tight, it can save you a lot of running around. This is also an easy way to get around any language problems. Agencies offering private rooms can be good value. Staying with a local family doesn't always mean that you'll lack privacy, but you'll probably have less freedom than in a hotel.

Sometimes people will come up to you on the street offering a private room or a hostel bed. This can be good or bad, there's no hard-and-fast rule – just make sure it's not way out in a dingy suburb somewhere, and that you negotiate a clear price. As always, be careful when someone offers to carry your luggage: they might carry it away altogether.

Camping

Camping is immensely popular in Western Europe (especially among Germans and Dutch) and provides the cheapest accommodation. There's usually a charge per tent or site, per person and per vehicle. National tourist offices should have booklets or brochures listing camping grounds all over their country. See the earlier Visas & Documents section for information on the Camping Card International.

In large cities, most camp sites will be some distance from the centre. For this reason, camping is most popular with people who have their own transport. If you're on foot, the money you save by camping can quickly be outweighed by the money you spend on commuting to/from a town centre. You may also need a tent, sleeping bag and cooking equipment, though not always: many camping grounds hire bungalows or cottages accommodating from two to eight people.

Camping other than on designated camping grounds is difficult because the population density makes it hard to find a suitable spot to pitch a tent away from prying eyes. It is also illegal without permission from the local authorities (the police or local council office) or from the owner of the land (don't be shy about asking – you may be pleasantly surprised by the response).

In some countries, such as Austria, the UK and Germany, free camping is illegal on all but private land, and in Greece it's illegal altogether. This doesn't prevent hikers from occasionally pitching their tent for the night, and they'll usually get away with it if they keep a low profile (don't make a lot of noise and don't build a fire or leave rubbish). At worst, they'll be woken up by the police and asked to move on.

Hostels

Hostels offer the cheapest roof over your head in Europe, and you don't have to be a youngster to use them. Most hostels are part of the national YHA (Youth Hostel Association), which is affiliated with what was formerly called the IYHF (International Youth Hostel Federation) and has now been renamed Hostelling International (HI) in order to attract a wider clientele and move away from the emphasis on 'youth'. The situation remains slightly confused at the moment, however. Some countries, such as the USA and Canada, immediately adopted the new name, but many European countries may take a few years to change their logos. In practice it makes no difference: IYHF and HI are the same thing and the domestic YHA almost always belongs to the parent group.

There are also some privately run hostels, although it's only in Ireland (and less so in England and Wales) that private backpacker hostels have really taken off.

Technically, you're supposed to be a YHA or HI member to use affiliated hostels, but you can often stay by paying an extra charge and this will usually be set against future membership. Stay enough nights as a nonmember and you're automatically a member.

Bavaria in Germany is the only place with an age limit for hostelling members. To join the HI, ask at any hostel or contact your local or national hostelling office. The offices for English-speaking countries appear below. Otherwise, check the individual country chapters for addresses.

Australia
Australian Youth Hostels Association, Level 3, 10 Mallett St, Camperdown, NSW 2050 (☎ 02-9565 1699)
Canada
Hostelling International Canada, 1600 James Naismith Drive, Suite 608, Gloucester, Ontario K1B 5N4 (☎ 613-237 7884)

England & Wales
Youth Hostels Association, Trevelyan House, 8 St Stephen's Hill, St Albans, Herts AL1 2DY (☎ 01727-855215)
Ireland
An Óige, 61 Mountjoy St, Dublin 7 (☎ 01-830 4555)
New Zealand
Youth Hostels Association of New Zealand, PO Box 436, 173 Gloucester St, Christchurch 1 (☎ 03-379 9970)
Northern Ireland
Youth Hostel Association of Northern Ireland, 22-32 Donegall Rd, Belfast BT12 5JN (☎ 01232-324733)
Scotland
Scottish Youth Hostels Association, 7 Glebe Crescent, Stirling FK8 2JA (☎ 01786-451181)
South Africa
Hostel Association of South Africa, 101 Boston House, 46 Strand St, Cape Town 8001 (☎ 021-419 1853)
USA
Hostelling International/American Youth Hostels, 733 15th St NW, Suite 840, Washington DC 20005 (☎ 202-783 6161)

At a hostel, you get a bed for the night, plus use of communal facilities, which often include a kitchen where you can prepare your own meals. You are usually required to have a sleeping sheet – simply using your sleeping bag is not permitted. If you don't have your own approved sleeping sheet, you can usually hire or buy one. Hostels vary widely in character, but the growing number of travellers and the increased competition from other forms of accommodation, particularly private 'backpacker hostels', have prompted many hostels to improve their facilities and cut back on rules and regulations. Increasingly, hostels are open all day, curfews are disappearing and 'wardens' with a sergeant-major mentality are an endangered species. In some places you'll even find hostels with single and double rooms. Everywhere the trend has been towards smaller dormitories with just four to six beds.

There are many hostel guides with listings available, including the HI *Europe* guide, the England & Wales YHA *YHA Accommodation Guide* as well as a couple of cooperatively produced guides to the Irish backpacker hostels. Many hostels accept reservations by phone or fax, but usually not during peak periods; they'll often book the next hostel you're heading to for a small fee. You can also book hostels through national hostel offices. Popular hostels can be heavily booked in

summer and limits may even be placed on how
ma· you can stay.

ommodation

ity towns rent out student accom-
ing holiday periods. This is very
ance (see the France chapter for
and becoming more common in
iversities become more finan-
ble.

tion will sometimes be in
ore commonly in doubles or
ay have cooking facilities.
ollege or university, at student
ices or at local tourist offices.

ses & Hotels

ge of accommodation above
 the UK and Ireland the
e real bargains in this field,
n (a bed) and breakfast in
a some areas every other
h sign out front. In other
co accommodation may
go pension, guesthouse,
Ga , chambre d'hôte and so
on. the majority of B&Bs are simple
affai., there are more expensive ones where
yo'll find en suite bathrooms and other luxuries.

Above this level are hotels, which at the
bottom of the bracket may be no more expensive than B&Bs or guesthouses, while at the
other extreme extend to luxury five-star properties with price tags to match. Although
categorisation depends on the country, the
hotels recommended in this book will generally range from no stars to one or two stars.
You'll often find inexpensive hotels clustered
around the bus and train station areas – always
good places to start hunting.

Check your hotel room and the bathroom
before you agree to take it, and make sure you
know what it's going to cost – discounts are
often available for groups or for longer stays.
Ask about breakfast: sometimes it's included,
but other times it may be obligatory and you'll
have to pay extra for it. If the sheets don't look
clean, ask to have them changed right away.
Check where the fire exits are.

If you think a hotel room is too expensive,
ask if there's anything cheaper. (Often, hotel
owners may have tried to steer you into more
expensive rooms.) In southern Europe in particular, hotel owners may be open to a little
bargaining if times are slack. In France and the
UK it is now common practice for business
hotels (usually more than two stars) to slash
their rates by up to 40% on Friday and Saturday
nights when business is dead. Save your big
hotel splurge for the weekend.

FOOD

Few regions in the world offer such a variety
of cuisines in such a small area. The Facts for
the Visitor sections in the individual country
chapters contain details of local cuisine, and
there are many suggestions on places to eat of
all kinds in the chapters themselves.

Restaurant prices vary enormously. The
cheapest places for a decent meal are often the
self-service restaurants in department stores.
University restaurants are dirt cheap, but the
food tends to be bland and it's not always clear
whether you'll be allowed in if you're not a
local student. Kiosks often sell cheap snacks
that can be as much a part of the national
cuisine as the fancy dishes.

Self-catering – buying your ingredients at a
shop or market and preparing them yourself –
can be a cheap and wholesome way of eating.
Even if you don't cook, a lunch on a park bench
with a fresh stick of bread, some local cheese
and salami and a tomato or two, washed down
with a bottle of local wine, can be one of the
recurring highlights of your trip. It also makes
a nice change from restaurant food.

If you have dietary restrictions – you're a
vegetarian or you keep kosher, for example –
tourist organisations may be able to advise you
or provide lists of suitable restaurants. Some
vegetarian and kosher restaurants are listed in
this book.

In general, vegetarians needn't worry about
going hungry in Western Europe; many restaurants have one or two vegetarian dishes, and
southern European menus in particular tend to
contain many vegetable dishes and salads.
Some restaurants will prepare special dishes
on request (approach them about this in
advance).

Getting There & Away

Step one is to get to Europe and, in these days of severe competition among airlines, there are plenty of opportunities to find cheap tickets to a variety of 'gateway' cities.

Forget shipping, unless by 'shipping' you mean the many ferry services between Europe and North Africa. Only a handful of ships still carry passengers across the Atlantic; they don't sail often and are expensive, even compared with full-fare air tickets. The days of ocean liners as modes of transport are well and truly over, but if you're still keen, see the Sea section at the end of this chapter for more details.

Some travellers still arrive or leave overland – the options being Africa, the Middle East and Asia, and what used to be the Soviet Union. The Trans-Siberian and Mongolian express trains could well begin to carry more people to and from Europe as Russia opens up to tourism. See the Land section later in this chapter for more information.

AIR

Remember always to reconfirm your onward or return bookings by the specified time – at least 72 hours before departure on international flights. Otherwise there's a real risk that you'll turn up at the airport only to find that you've missed your flight because it was rescheduled, or that you've been reclassified as a 'no show' and 'bumped' (see the Air Travel Glossary in this chapter).

Buying Tickets

Your plane ticket will probably be the single most expensive item in your travel budget, and it's worth taking some time to research the current state of the market. Start early: some of the cheapest tickets have to be bought well in advance, and some popular flights sell out early. Have a talk to recent travellers, look at the ads in newspapers and magazines, and watch for special offers.

Cheap tickets are available in two distinct categories: official and unofficial. Official ones have a variety of names including advance purchase tickets, advance purchase excursion (Apex) fares, super-Apex and simply budget fares.

Unofficial tickets are simply discounted tickets that the airlines release through selected travel agents (usually not sold by the airline offices themselves). Airlines can, however, supply information on routes and timetables and make bookings; their low-season, student and senior citizens' fares can be competitive. Also, normal, full-fare airline tickets sometimes include one or more side trips in Europe free of charge, which can make them good value.

Return (round-trip) tickets usually work out cheaper than two one-way fares – often *much* cheaper. Be aware that immigration officials often ask for return or onward tickets, and that if you can't show either, you'll have to provide proof of 'sufficient means of support', which means you have to show a lot of money or, in some cases, valid credit cards.

Round-the-world (RTW) tickets are often real bargains, and can work out to be no more expensive or even cheaper than an ordinary return ticket. The official airline RTW tickets are usually put together by a combination of two or more airlines, and permit you to fly anywhere you want on their route systems so long as you don't backtrack. Other restrictions are that you (usually) must book the first sector in advance and cancellation penalties then apply. There may be restrictions on how many stops (or km/miles) you are permitted, and usually the tickets are valid for 90 days up to a year. Prices start at about UK£1000/US$1500/A$1800, depending on the season and length of validity. An alternative type of RTW ticket is one put together by a travel agent using a combination of discounted tickets. These can be much cheaper than the official ones, but usually carry a lot of restrictions.

Generally, you can find discounted tickets at prices as low as, or lower than, advance purchase or budget tickets. Phone around the travel agencies for bargains. You may discover that those impossibly cheap flights are 'fully booked, but we have another one that costs a bit more...' Or that the flight is on an airline notorious for its poor safety standards and leaves you in the world's least favourite airport in mid-journey for 14 hours – where you're confined to the transit lounge because you don't have a visa. Or the agent claims to have the last two seats available for that country for the whole of August, which will be held for you for a maximum of two hours as long as you come in and pay cash. Don't panic – keep ringing around.

If you are travelling from the USA or South-East Asia, or you are trying to get out of Europe from the UK, you will probably find that the cheapest flights are being advertised by obscure agencies whose names probably haven't even reached the telephone directory. Many such firms are honest and solvent, but there are a few rogues who will take your money and disappear – only to reopen elsewhere a month or two later under a new name.

If you feel suspicious about a firm, don't give them all the money at once – leave a deposit of 20% or so and pay the balance when you get the ticket. If they insist on cash in advance, go somewhere else or be prepared to take a very big risk. And once you have the ticket, ring the airline to confirm that you are actually booked onto the flight.

You may decide to pay more than the rock-bottom fare by opting for the safety of a better-known travel agent. Firms such as STA Travel, which has offices worldwide, Council Travel in the USA and elsewhere or Travel CUTS in Canada offer good prices to most destinations, and won't disappear overnight leaving you clutching a receipt for a nonexistent ticket.

Use the fares quoted in this book as a guide only. They are approximate and based on the rates advertised by travel agents at the time of research. Most are likely to have changed by the time you read this.

Travellers with Special Needs

If you have special needs of any sort – you're vegetarian or require a special diet, you're travelling in a wheelchair, taking the baby, terrified of flying, whatever – let the airline people know as soon as possible so that they can make the necessary arrangements. Remind them when you reconfirm your booking (at least 72 hours before departure) and again when you check in at the airport. It may also be worth ringing around the airlines before you make your booking to find out how they can handle your particular needs.

Children aged under two travel for 10% of the full fare (or free on some airlines) as long as they don't occupy a seat. They don't get a baggage allowance in this case. 'Skycots', baby food and nappies (diapers) should be provided by the airline if requested in advance. Children aged between two and 12 can usually occupy a seat for half to two-thirds of the full fare. They do get a standard baggage allowance.

The USA

The North Atlantic is the world's busiest long-haul air corridor, and the flight options are bewildering. The *New York Times*, *LA Times*, *Chicago Tribune*, *San Francisco Chronicle* and the *Boston Globe* all publish weekly travel sections in which you'll find any number of travel agents' ads. Council Travel and STA Travel have offices in major cities nationwide. You should be able to fly New York-London return for around US$370 in the low season, US$600 in the high season. Tack on another US$80 or so from the West Coast

One-way fares can work out to about half of this on a stand-by basis. Airhitch (☎ 212-864 2000) specialises in this sort of thing and can get you to Europe one way for US$169/$269/$229 from the East Coast/West Coast/elsewhere in the USA.

An interesting alternative to the boring New York-London flight is offered by Icelandair (☎ 800-223 5500), which has competitive year-round fares to Luxembourg with a stop-over in Iceland's capital, Reykjavík – a great way of spending a few days in an unusual country that's otherwise hard to get to.

Another option is a courier flight, where you accompany a parcel or freight to be picked up at the other end. A New York-London return courier flight can be had for about US$300/$400 low/high season or even less. You can also fly one way. The drawbacks are that your stay in Europe may be limited to one or two weeks on a return ticket, that your luggage is usually restricted to hand baggage (the parcel or freight you carry comes out of your luggage allowance) and that you may have to be a

Air Travel Glossary

Apex Tickets Apex ('advance purchase excursion') fares are usually between 30% and 40% cheaper than full economy ones, but there are restrictions. You must purchase the ticket at least 21 days (sometimes more) in advance, be away for a minimum period (normally 14 days) and return within a maximum period (90 or 180 days). Stopovers are not allowed, and if you have to change your travel dates or routing, there will be extra charges. These tickets are not fully refundable; if you cancel your trip, the refund is often considerably less than what you paid for the ticket. Take out travel insurance to cover yourself in case you have to call off your trip unexpectedly (eg due to illness).

Baggage Allowance This will be written on your ticket; you are usually allowed one item weighing 20 kg to go in the hold, plus one item of hand luggage. Many airlines flying transatlantic routes allow for two pieces of luggage with relatively generous limits on their dimensions and weight.

Bucket Shops At certain times of the year and/or on certain routes, many airlines fly with empty seats. This isn't profitable (or good PR) and it's often more cost-effective for them to fly full, even if that means having to sell a certain number of drastically discounted tickets. They do this by off-loading them onto bucket shops (or consolidators), travel agents who specialise in such discounted fares. The agents, in turn, sell them to the public at reduced prices. These tickets are often the cheapest you'll find, but you usually can't purchase them directly from the airlines, restrictions abound and long-haul journeys can be extremely time-consuming, with several stops along the way. Availability varies widely, so you'll not only have to be flexible in your travel plans, you'll also have to be quick off the mark as soon as an advertisement appears in the press.

Bucket-shop agents advertise in newspapers and magazines, and there's a lot of competition – especially in places like Amsterdam, London and Hong Kong, three places that are crawling with them. It's always a good idea to telephone first to ascertain availability before rushing to some out-of-the-way shop. Naturally, they'll advertise the cheapest available tickets, but by the time you get there, these may be sold out (or were nonexistent in the first place), and you may be looking at something slightly more expensive.

Bumping Just because you have a confirmed seat doesn't mean you're going to get on the plane (see Overbooking).

Cancellation Penalties If you have to cancel or change an Apex or other discounted ticket, there may be heavy penalties involved; travel insurance can sometimes be taken out against these penalties. Some airlines now impose penalties on regular tickets as well, particularly against 'no show' passengers.

Check In Airlines ask you to check in a certain time ahead of the flight departure (usually two hours on international flights but longer on particularly security-conscious ones like El Al, the Israeli carrier). If you fail to check in on time and the flight is overbooked, the airline can cancel your reservation and give your seat to somebody else.

Confirmation Having a ticket written out with the flight and date on it doesn't mean you have a seat until the agent has confirmed with the airline that your status is 'OK' and has written or stamped that on your ticket. Prior to this confirmation, your status is 'on request'.

Courier Fares Businesses often send their urgent documents or freight through courier companies. These companies hire people to accompany the package through customs and, in return, offer cheap tickets that used to be phenomenal bargains but nowadays are just like decent discounted fares. In effect, what the courier companies do is ship their goods as your luggage on regular commercial flights; you are usually only allowed carry-on luggage. This is a legitimate operation – all freight is completely legal. There are two drawbacks, however: the short turnaround time of the ticket (usually not longer than a month) and the limitation on your baggage allowance.

Discounted Tickets There are two types of discounted fares: officially discounted (such as Apex) ones and unofficially discounted tickets (see Bucket Shops). The latter can save you more than money – you may be able to pay Apex prices without the associated advance-purchase and other requirements. The lowest prices often impose drawbacks, such as flying with unpopular airlines, inconvenient schedules, or unpleasant routings and connections.

Economy Class Economy-class tickets are usually not the cheapest way to go, but they do give you maximum flexibility and they are valid for 12 months. If you don't use them, most are fully refundable, as are unused sectors of a multiple ticket.

Full Fares Airlines traditionally offer first class (coded F), business class (coded J) and economy class (coded Y) tickets. These days there are so many promotional and discounted fares available that the only passengers paying full fare are on expense accounts or at the gate and in a hurry.

Lost Tickets If you lose your ticket, an airline will usually treat it like a travellers' cheque and, after inquiries, issue you with a replacement. Legally, however, an airline is entitled to treat it like cash, so a loss could be permanent. Consider them as valuables.

MCO An MCO (Miscellaneous Charges Order) is a voucher for a given amount, usually issued by an airline as a refund or against a lost ticket. It can be used to pay for a flight with any IATA (International Air Transport Association) airline. MCOs, which are more flexible than a regular ticket, may satisfy the irritating onward ticket requirement, but some countries are now reluctant to accept them.

No Shows No shows are passengers who fail to turn up for their flight for whatever reason. Full-fare no shows are sometimes entitled to travel on a later flight. The rest are penalised (see Cancellation Penalties), but it all depends on the circumstances and availability of space.

Open-Jaw Tickets These are return tickets that allow you to fly to one place but return from another, and travel between the two 'jaws' by any means of transport at your own expense. If available, this can save you backtracking to your arrival point.
Overbooking Airlines hate empty seats, and since every flight has some no shows, they often book more passengers than there are seats available. Usually the excess passengers balance those who fail to show up, but occasionally somebody gets bumped – usually the last passenger(s) to check in.

Promotional Fares These are officially discounted fares, such as Apex ones, which are available from travel agents or direct from the airline.

Reconfirmation If you break your journey, you must contact the airline at least 72 hours prior to departure of the ongoing flight to 'reconfirm' that you intend to fly. If you don't do this, the airline is entitled to delete your name from the passenger list.
Restrictions Discounted tickets often have various constraints placed on them, such as advance purchase, limitations on the minimum and maximum period you must be away, restrictions on breaking the journey or changing the booking or routing etc.
Round-the-World Tickets These tickets have become very popular in the last decade and basically there are two types: airline RTW tickets and agent (or 'tailor-made') RTW tickets. An airline RTW ticket is issued by two or more airlines that have joined together and allows you to fly around the world in *one continuous direction* on their combined routes. Other restrictions are that you (usually) must book the first sector in advance and cancellation penalties then apply. There may be restrictions on how many stopovers you are permitted. RTW tickets are usually valid for from 90 days up to a year.

The other type of RTW ticket is a combination of cheap fares strung together by an experienced travel agent. These may be much cheaper than airline RTW tickets, but the choice of routes will be limited.

Stand-by This is a discounted ticket where you only fly if there is a seat free at the last moment. Stand-by fares are usually only available directly at the airport, but may sometimes also be handled by an airline's city office. To give yourself the best possible chance of getting on the flight you want, get there early and have your name placed on the waiting list immediately. It's first come, first served.
Student Discounts Some airlines offer student-card holders 15% to 25% off on certain fares. The same often applies to anyone under the age of 26. These discounts are generally only available on normal economy-class fares; you wouldn't get one, for instance, on an Apex or an RTW ticket, since these are already discounted. Take a calculator and do the sums; discounted tickets – both the official and bucket-shop ones – are often better value than student fares.

Tickets Out An entry requirement for many countries is that you have an onward (ie out of the country) ticket. If you're not sure of your travel plans, the easiest solution is to buy the cheapest onward ticket to a neighbouring country or a ticket from a reliable airline that can be refunded later if you do not use it.
Transferred Tickets Airline tickets cannot be transferred from one person to another. Travellers sometimes try to sell the return half of their ticket, but officials can ask you to prove that you are the person named on the ticket. This may not be checked on domestic flights, but on international flights, tickets are usually compared with passports. Remember that if you are flying on a transferred ticket and something goes wrong with the flight (hijack, crash), there will be no record of your presence on board.
Travel Periods Some officially discounted fares – Apex fares in particular – vary with the seasons. There is often a low (off-peak) season and a high (peak) season. Sometimes there's an intermediate (or shoulder) season as well. At peak times, when everyone wants to fly, both officially and unofficially discounted fares will be higher and discounted tickets may not be available. Usually the fare depends on your outward flight – if you depart in the high season and return in the low season, you still pay the high-season fare. ■

resident and apply for an interview before they'll take you on.

Find out more about courier flights from Discount Travel International in New York (☎ 212-362 3636; fax 212-362 3236). Call two or three months in advance and at the start of the calendar month when rosters are being written.

The *Travel Unlimited* newsletter, PO Box 1058, Allston, Massachusetts 02134, USA, publishes details of the cheapest airfares and courier possibilities for destinations all over the world from the USA and other countries, including the UK. The newsletter is a treasure trove of information. A single monthly issue costs US$5 and a year's subscription US$25 (US$35 abroad).

Canada

Travel CUTS has offices in all major Canadian cities. Scan the budget travel agents' ads in the *Toronto Globe & Mail*, *Toronto Star* and *Vancouver Province*.

See the previous the USA section for general information on courier flights. For those originating in Canada, contact FB on Board Courier Services (☎ 905-612 8095 in Toronto, ☎ 604-278 1266 in Vancouver). A courier return flight to London will cost from about C$350 from Toronto or Montreal, C$570 from Vancouver, depending on the season. Airhitch (see the USA section) has stand-by fares to/from Toronto, Montreal and Vancouver.

Australia

STA Travel and Flight Centres International are major dealers in cheap airfares. Check the travel agents' ads in the Yellow Pages and ring around.

The Saturday travel sections of the *Sydney Morning Herald* and Melbourne's *The Age* newspapers have many ads offering cheap fares to Europe, but don't be surprised if they happen to be 'sold out' when you contact the agents: they're usually low-season fares on obscure airlines with conditions attached. With Australia's large and well-organised ethnic populations, it pays to check special deals in the ethnic press – Olympic Airways sometimes has good deals to Athens, for example.

Discounted return fares on mainstream airlines through a reputable agent like STA Travel cost between A$1500 (low season) and A$2500

(high season). Flights to/from Perth are a couple of hundred dollars cheaper. Another option for travellers wanting to go to Britain between November and February is to hook up with a charter flight returning to Britain. These low-season, one-way fares do have restrictions, but may work out to be considerably cheaper. Ask your travel agent for details.

New Zealand

As in Australia, STA Travel and Flight Centres International are popular travel agencies. Not surprisingly, the cheapest fares to Europe are routed through the USA, and a RTW ticket can be cheaper than an advance purchase return ticket.

Africa

Nairobi is probably the best place in Africa to buy tickets to Europe, thanks to the strong competition between its many bucket shops. Several West African countries such as Burkina Faso and The Gambia offer cheap charter flights to France, and charter fares from Morocco can be incredibly cheap if you're lucky enough to find a seat.

From South Africa, Air Namibia has particularly cheap return youth fares to London from as low as R2819. The big carriers' return fares range from R2900 to R3815. These fares are expected to rise shortly following the devaluation of the rand. Students' Travel (☎ 011-716 3945) in Johannesburg, and the Africa Travel Centre (☎ 021-235 555) in Cape Town are worth trying for cheap tickets.

Asia

Hong Kong is still the discount plane-ticket capital of Asia, and its bucket shops offer some great bargains. But be careful: not all are reliable. Ask the advice of other travellers before buying tickets. Many of the cheapest fares from South-East Asia to Europe are offered by Eastern European carriers (eg LOT or Aeroflot). STA Travel has branches in Hong Kong, Tokyo, Singapore, Bangkok and Kuala Lumpur.

To/from India, the cheapest flights tend to be with Eastern European carriers or certain Middle Eastern airlines like Syrian Arab Airlines. Bombay is India's air transport hub, with many transit options to/from South-East Asia, but tickets are slightly cheaper in Delhi.

From the UK

If you're looking for a cheap way out of Europe, London is Europe's major centre for discounted fares. The Trailfinders head office in London is an amazing place complete with travel library, bookshop, visa service and immunisation centre. STA Travel also has branches in the UK. Campus Travel is helpful and has many interesting deals. See the London Information section in the Britain chapter for addresses and phone numbers of these and other discount travel agencies. Also ask them about courier flights.

The listings magazine *Time Out*, the weekend papers and the *Evening Standard* carry ads for cheap fares. Also look out for the free magazines and newspapers widely available in London, especially *TNT* and *Southern Cross* – you can often pick them up outside main train and tube stations.

Make sure the agent is a member of some sort of traveller-protection scheme, such as that offered by the Association of British Travel Agents (ABTA). If you have paid for your flight to an ABTA-registered agent who then goes out of business, ABTA will guarantee a refund or an alternative. Unregistered bucket shops are riskier but usually cheaper.

From Continental Europe

Though London is the travel discount capital of Europe, there are several other cities in the region where you'll find a wide range of good deals, particularly Amsterdam and Athens. See the country chapters for details.

Many travel agents in Europe have ties with STA Travel, where cheap tickets can be purchased and STA tickets can often be altered free of charge the first time around. Outlets in important transport hubs include: CTS Voyages (☎ 01-43 25 00 76), 20 Rue des Carmes, 75005 Paris; SRID Reisen (☎ 069-70 30 35), Bockenheimer Landstrasse 133, 60325 Frankfurt; and International Student & Youth Travel Service (☎ 01-322 1267), Nikis 11, 10557 Athens.

LAND
Train

Morocco and most of Turkey lie outside Europe, but the rail systems of both countries are still covered by Inter-Rail (though only the 26+ version is valid in Turkey). The price of a cheap return train ticket from London to Morocco compares favourably with equivalent bus fares.

To/from central and eastern Asia, a train can work out at about the same price as flying, depending on how much time and money you spend along the way, and it can be a lot more fun. There are three routes to/from Moscow across Siberia: the Trans-Siberian to/from Vladivostok, and the Trans-Mongolian and Trans-Manchurian, both to/from Beijing. There's a fourth route south from Moscow and across Kazakstan, following part of the old Silk Road to Beijing. Prices can vary enormously, depending on where you buy the ticket and what is included – the prices quoted here are a rough indication only.

The Trans-Siberian takes just under seven days from Moscow via Khabarovsk to Vladivostok, from where there is a boat to Niigata in Japan from May to October. Otherwise you can fly to Niigata as well as to Seattle and Anchorage, Alaska, in the USA. The complete journey from Moscow to Niigata costs from about US$600 per person for a 2nd-class sleeper in a four-berth cabin.

The Trans-Mongolian passes through Mongolia to Beijing and takes about 5½ days. A 2nd-class sleeper in a four-berth compartment would cost around US$265 if purchased in Moscow or Beijing. If you want to stop off along the way or spend some time in Moscow, you'll need 'visa support' – a letter from a travel agent confirming that they're making your travel/accommodation bookings required in Russia or Mongolia. Locally based companies that do all-inclusive packages (with visa support) include the Travellers Guest House (☎ 095-971 4059; fax 280 9786) in Moscow; and Monkey Business (☎ 2723 1376; fax 2723 6653) in Hong Kong, with an information centre in Beijing. There are a number of other budget operators.

The Trans-Manchurian passes through Manchuria to Beijing and takes 6½ days, costing about US$225.

A trans-Central Asia route runs from Moscow to Almaty in Kazakstan, crosses the border on the new line to Ürümqi (northwestern China), and follows part of the old Silk Road to Beijing. At present you can't buy through tickets. Moscow to Ürümqi in 2nd class costs about US$160 and takes five or more days, depending on connections.

There are countless travel options between Moscow and the rest of Europe. Most people will opt for the train, usually to/from Berlin, Helsinki, Munich, Budapest or Vienna. The *Trans-Siberian Handbook* (Trailblazer) by Bryn Thomas is a comprehensive guide to the route, and Lonely Planet's *Russia, Ukraine & Belarus* has a separate chapter on trans-Siberian travel.

Overland Trails

Asia In the early 1980s, the overland trail to/from Asia lost much of its popularity as the Islamic regime in Iran made life difficult for most independent travellers, and the war in Afghanistan closed that country off to all but the foolhardy. Now that Iran seems to be rediscovering the merits of tourism, the Asia route has begun to pick up again, though unsettled conditions in Afghanistan, southern Pakistan and north-west India could prevent the trickle of travellers turning into a flood for the time being.

A new overland route through what used to be the Soviet Union could become important over the next decade. At this stage the options are more or less confined to the Trans-Siberian/Trans-Mongolian railway lines to/from Moscow (see the previous Train section), but other modes of transport are likely to become available beyond the Urals as the newly independent states open up to travellers.

Africa Discounting the complicated Middle East route, going to/from Africa involves a Mediterranean ferry crossing (see the Sea section later on). Due to political problems in Africa (eg war between Morocco and the Polisario in the west, civil wars in Algeria and Sudan), the most feasible Africa overland routes of the past have all but closed down.

Travelling by private transport beyond Europe requires plenty of paperwork and other preparations. A detailed description is beyond the scope of this book, but the following Getting Around chapter tells you what's required within Europe.

SEA
Mediterranean Ferries

There are many ferries across the Mediterranean between Africa and Europe. The ferry you take will depend on your travels in Africa, but options include: Spain-Morocco, Italy-Tunisia and France-Algeria/Morocco/Tunisia. There are also ferries between Greece and Israel. Ferries are often filled to capacity in summer, especially to/from Tunisia, so book well in advance if you're taking a vehicle across. See the relevant country chapters.

Passenger Ships & Freighters

Regular, long-distance passenger ships disappeared with the advent of cheap air travel and were replaced by a small number of luxury cruise ships. Cunard's *Queen Elizabeth 2* sails between New York and Southampton 20 times a year; the trip takes six nights each way and costs around UK£1500 for the return trip, though there are also one-way and 'fly one-way' deals. Your travel agent will have more details. The standard reference for passenger ships is the *OAG Cruise & Ferry Guide* published by the UK-based Reed Travel Group (☎ 01582-600111), Church St, Dunstable, Bedfordshire LU5 4HB.

A more adventurous (though not necessarily cheaper) alternative is as a paying passenger on a freighter. Freighters are far more numerous than cruise ships and there are many more routes from which to choose. With a bit of homework, you'll be able to sail between Europe and just about anywhere else in the world, with stopovers at exotic ports that you may never have heard of. The previously mentioned *OAG Cruise & Ferry Guide* is the most comprehensive source of information though *Travel by Cruise Ship* (Cadogan, London) is also a good source.

Passenger freighters typically carry six to 12 passengers (more than 12 would require a doctor on board) and, though less luxurious than dedicated cruise ships, give you a real taste of life at sea. Schedules tend to be flexible and costs vary, but seem to hover around US$100 a day; vehicles can often be included for an additional fee.

DEPARTURE TAXES

Some countries charge you a small fee for the privilege of leaving from their airports. Some also charge port fees when departing by ship. Such fees are usually included in the price of your ticket, but it pays to check this when purchasing it. If not, you'll have to have the fee ready when leaving. Details of departure taxes are given at the end of the Getting There & Away sections of individual country chapters.

WARNING

This chapter is particularly vulnerable to change – prices for international travel are volatile, routes are introduced and cancelled, schedules change, special deals come and go, and rules and visa requirements are amended. Airlines seem to take a perverse pleasure in making price structures and regulations as complicated as possible; you should check directly with the airline or travel agent to make sure you understand how a fare (and ticket you may buy) works. In addition, the travel industry is highly competitive and there are many schemes and bonuses. The upshot of this is that you should get opinions, quotes and advice from as many airlines and travel agents as possible before you part with your hard-earned cash. The details given in this chapter should be regarded as pointers and are not a substitute for careful, up-to-date research.

Getting Around

AIR

From 1997, as part of the EU's 'open skies' policy, national airlines will no longer have to include a domestic airport in their routings and can fly directly from one EU city to another. Pundits forecast increased competition and lower prices, but there are problems. Additional take-off slots at oversubscribed airports are hard to come by, and inefficient state-run carriers are still being propped up by EU subsidies (notably Air France and the Spanish flag-carrier Iberia). But look out for the new breed of small airlines, such as the UK-based EasyJet, which sell budget tickets directly to the customer.

Refer to the Air Travel Glossary in the previous Getting There & Away chapter for information on types of air tickets. London is a good centre for picking up cheap, restricted-validity tickets through bucket shops. Amsterdam and Athens are other good places for bucket-shop tickets in Europe. For more information, see the individual country chapters.

For longer journeys, you can sometimes find airfares that beat surface-travel alternatives in terms of cost. A restricted return (valid for one month only) from London to Munich, for example, is available through discount travel agents for about UK£100 to UK£140; a two-month return by rail between the same cities costs UK£195.

However, air travel is best viewed as a means to get you to the starting point of your itinerary rather than as your main means of travel, since it lacks the flexibility of ground transport. Also, if you start taking flights for relatively short hops it gets extremely expensive, particularly as special deals are not as common on domestic flights as they are on international ones.

So-called open-jaw returns, by which you can travel into one city and exit from another, are worth considering, though they sometimes work out more expensive than simple returns. In the UK, Trailfinders (☎ 0171-938 3232) and STA Travel (☎ 0171-581 4132) can give you tailor-made versions of these tickets. Your chosen cities don't necessarily have to be in the same country. Lufthansa has Young Europe Special (YES) flights, which allow travel around Europe by air at UK£59 or UK£69 per flight (minimum four flights, maximum 10). Britain is the starting point, and the offer is open to students under 31 years of age and anybody under 26. Alitalia's Europa Pass is a similar deal.

If you are travelling alone, courier flights are a possibility. You get cheap passage in return for accompanying a package or documents through customs and delivering it to a representative at the destination airport. EU integration and electronic communications means there's increasingly less call for couriers, but you might find something. British Airways, for example, offers courier flights through the Travel Shop (☎ 0181-564 7009). Sample return fares from London are UK£80 to Barcelona and the same to Lisbon.

Getting between airports and city centres is rarely a problem in Europe thanks to ever improving underground/subway networks and good bus services, though it can be rather time-consuming in cities like London and Paris.

BUS

International Buses

International bus travel tends to take second place to going by train. The bus has the edge in terms of cost, sometimes quite substantially, but is generally slower and less comfortable. Eurolines (☎ 0990-143219), 52 Grosvenor Gardens, London SW1W 0AU, is the main international bus company. See the Getting Around section in the Britain chapter for more details.

Eurolines' European representatives include:

Eurolines Nederland (☎ 020-627 51 51), Rokin 10, 1012 KR Amsterdam
Eurolines Belgium (☎ 02-217 00 25), Place de Brouckère 50, 1000 Brussels
Eurolines France (☎ 01-49 72 51 51), Gare Routière Internationale, 28 Ave du Général de Gaulle, 75020 Paris

Deutsche Touring (☎ 089-545 8700), Arnulfstrasse 3, Im Stamberger, 80335 Munich

Eurolines Italy (☎ 06-44 23 39 28), Ciconvallazione Nonentana 574, Lato Stazione Tiburtina, Rome

Eurolines Austria (☎ 0222-712 0453), Autobusbahnhof Wien-Mitte, Landstrasser Hauptstrasse 1/b, 1030 Vienna.

These may also be able to advise you on other bus companies and deals.

Eurolines has 10 circular explorer routes, always starting and ending in London. The popular London-Amsterdam-Paris route costs UK£71 (no youth reductions) while London-Dublin-Galway-Cork-London is UK£63 and London-Budapest-Prague-London is UK£112. Eurolines now also offers passes, but they're neither as extensive nor as flexible as rail passes. They cover 18 European cities as far apart as London, Barcelona, Rome, Budapest and Copenhagen, and cost UK£229 for 30 days (UK£199 for students and senior citizens) or UK£279 for 60 days (UK£249). The passes are cheaper off-season.

On ordinary return trips, youth (under 26) fares are around 10% less than the adult full fare, eg a London-Munich return ticket costs UK£94 for adults or UK£84 for youths. Explorer or return tickets are valid for six months. One of Eurolines' three daily London-Paris buses goes on Le Shuttle via Channel Tunnel.

Eurobus started up in 1995. In addition to hop-on, hop-off buses equipped with WC and video, the company offers services such as on-board guides and mail-forwarding. Buses complete a figure-of-eight loop of Europe every two days, taking in Amsterdam, Brussels, Paris, Zürich, Prague, Vienna, Budapest and major cities in Germany and Italy; there's also a Spanish link reaching as far as Valencia and Madrid and one into Italy to Florence and Rome. Unlimited travel costs are: US$360/ $460 for two/three months for students and those under 26; US$499/$599 for those 26 years of age and over. Tickets are available in many countries worldwide (eg from STA Travel in the UK), though you need to make your own way to a city on the loop to start off. Eurobus also has a Great Britain Pass.

See the individual country chapters for more information about long-distance buses.

National Buses

Domestic buses provide a viable alternative to the rail network in most countries. Again, compared to trains they are usually slightly cheaper and somewhat slower. Buses tend to be best for shorter hops such as getting around cities and reaching remote villages. They are often the only option in mountainous regions where rail tracks don't exist. Advance reservations are rarely necessary. On many city buses you usually buy your ticket in advance from a kiosk or machine and cancel it on entering.

See the individual country chapters and city sections for more details on local buses.

TRAIN

Trains are a popular way of getting around: they are comfortable, frequent, and generally on time. In some countries, such as Italy, Spain and Portugal, fares are heavily subsidised; in others, European rail passes make travel more affordable. Supplements and reservation costs are not covered by passes, and pass holders must always carry their passport for identification purposes.

If you plan to travel extensively by train, it might be worth getting hold of the *Thomas Cook European Timetable*, which gives a complete listing of train schedules and indicates where supplements apply or where reservations are necessary. It is updated monthly and is available from Thomas Cook outlets in the UK and Australia, in the USA from Forsyth Travel Library (☎ 800-367 7984), 9154 West 57th St, PO Box 2975, Shawnee Mission, Kansas 66201-1375. If you are planning to do a lot of train travel in one or a handful of countries – Benelux, say – it might be worthwhile getting hold of the national timetable(s) published by the state railroad(s).

Paris, Amsterdam, Munich, Milan and Vienna are all important hubs for international rail connections. See the relevant city sections for details and budget-ticket agents. Note that European trains sometimes split en route in order to service two destinations, so even if you know you're on the right train, make sure you're in the correct carriage too.

Express Trains

Fast trains or those that make few stops are identified by the symbols EC (EuroCity) or IC (InterCity). The French TGV, Spanish AVE and German ICE trains are even faster. Supplements can apply on fast trains, and it is a good idea (sometimes obligatory) to make seat reservations at peak times and on certain lines.

Overnight Trains
Overnight trains will usually offer a choice of couchette or sleeper if you don't fancy sleeping in your seat with somebody else's head on your shoulder. Again, reservations are advisable as sleeping options are allocated on a first-come, first-served basis. Couchettes are bunks numbering four in 1st class or six in 2nd class per compartment and are comfortable enough, if lacking a bit in privacy. A bunk costs a fixed price of around US$25 for most international trains, irrespective of the length of the journey.

Sleepers are the most comfortable option, offering beds for one or two passengers in 1st class, and two or three passengers in 2nd class. Charges vary depending upon the journey, but they are significantly more expensive than couchettes. Most long-distance trains have a dining or buffet (café) car or an attendant who wheels a snack trolley through carriages. Prices tend to be steep.

Security
Stories occasionally surface about train passengers being gassed or drugged and then robbed, though bag-snatching is more of a worry. Sensible security measures include not letting your bags out of your sight (especially when stopping at stations), chaining them to the luggage rack, and locking compartment doors overnight.

Rail Passes
Shop around, as pass prices can vary between different outlets. Once purchased, take care of your pass, as it cannot be replaced or refunded if lost or stolen. European passes get reductions on Eurostar through the Channel Tunnel and ferries on certain routes (eg between France and Ireland).

Channel Tunnel
The Channel Tunnel, which opened in November 1994, links England and France by rail. At 50 km it's the longest undersea tunnel in the world and a remarkable engineering feat. There are two ways of using the tunnel: the Eurostar passenger train and Le Shuttle for cars, motorcycles, buses and freight vehicles and their passengers.

Eurostar The Eurostar train link enables passengers to take a direct train from London's Waterloo Railway Station to Paris' Gare du Nord (three hours) or Brussels Midi/Zuid (3¼ hours). These times will come down once high-speed rail has been laid on the British side, but that's not expected until 2002. From about 6.30 am to 8 pm there's a train every one or two hours in each direction between London and Paris, and London and Brussels. There are easy onward connections from London to Scotland and Wales, and from Brussels to Germany and the Netherlands. Tickets are widely available – from some 3000 travel agencies and at major train stations – and include a seat reservation on a particular train. For information and credit-card bookings, call ☎ 0345-881 881 in the UK, ☎ 01233-617 575 from abroad. Passengers can transport bicycles on Eurostar.

Le Shuttle Le Shuttle, the vehicle-carrying service, runs only between the two tunnel terminals, Folkestone and Calais (actually just west of Calais at Coquelles). The crossing takes 35 minutes, but actual travel time with loading and unloading is closer to an hour. Shuttle trains run 24 hours a day, departing every 15 minutes in each direction at peak times and at least every 1¼ hours during the quietest periods of the night. Shuttles are designed to carry up to 180 cars (or 120 cars and 12 coaches). Bicycles, motorcycles, cars, camper vans, caravans and trailers can all be carried, though the maximum vehicle length is 6.5 metres. Ferries normally have a limit of five passengers per car, but with Le Shuttle you can transport up to eight, if you can cram them all in (hitchers, take note!). Facilities are minimal and travellers stay in or with their vehicle. Prices vary according to the time of year, and may also fluctuate as the tunnel and the ferry companies compete for market share. You can pre-pay or pay on arrival (by cash or credit card at a toll booth), but you can't reserve a place on a particular shuttle. For further information or credit-card bookings, call the customer service centre on ☎ 0990-353 535. Passport and immigration controls for the UK and France in either direction are passed before boarding Le Shuttle.■

Eurail These passes can only be bought by residents of non-European countries, and are supposed to be purchased before arriving in Europe. However, Eurail passes can be purchased within Europe, so long as your passport proves you've been there for less than six months, but the outlets where you can do this are limited, and the passes will be more expensive than getting them outside Europe. The Rail Shop (☎ 0990-300003), 179 Piccadilly, London W1V 0BA, is one such outlet. If you've lived in Europe for more than six months, you are eligible for an Inter-Rail pass, which is a better buy.

Eurail passes are valid for unlimited travel on national railways and some private lines in Austria, Belgium, Denmark, Finland, France (including Monaco), Germany, Greece, Hungary, Ireland, Italy, Luxembourg, the Netherlands, Norway, Portugal, Spain, Sweden and Switzerland (including Liechtenstein). The UK is not covered.

Eurail is also valid on some ferries between Ireland and France, between Italy and Greece, and from Sweden to Finland, Denmark or Germany. Reductions are given on some other ferry routes and on steamer services in various countries.

Eurail passes offer reasonable value to people aged under 26. A Youthpass is valid for unlimited 2nd-class travel for 15 days (US$418), one month (US$598) or two months (US$798). The Youth Flexipass, also for 2nd class, is valid for freely chosen days within a two-month period: 10 days for US$438 or 15 days for US$588. Overnight journeys commencing after 7 pm count as the following day's travel. The traveller must fill out (in ink) the relevant box in the calendar before starting a day's travel; not validating the pass in this way earns a fine of US$50. Tampering with the pass (eg using an erasable pen and later rubbing out earlier days) costs the perpetrator the full fare plus US$100.

For those aged over 26, a Flexipass (available in 1st class only) costs US$616 or US$812 for 10 or 15 freely chosen days in two months. The standard Eurail pass has five versions, costing from US$522 for 15 days unlimited travel up to US$1468 for three months. Two or more people travelling together (minimum three people between April and September) can get good discounts on a Saverpass, which

works like the standard Eurail pass. Eurail passes for children are also available.

Europass Also for non-Europeans, the Europass gives between five and 15 freely chosen days unlimited travel within a two-month period. Youth (aged under 26) and adult (solo, or two sharing) versions are available, and purchasing requirements and sales outlets are as for Eurail passes. They are a little cheaper than Eurail passes as they cover fewer countries. You can choose to travel in between three and five countries out of France, Germany, Italy, Spain and Switzerland. For a small additional charge each or all of Austria, Belgium (including Luxembourg and the Netherlands), Greece (including ferries from Italy) and Portugal can be added on. Chosen countries must be adjacent.

Inter-Rail Inter-Rail passes are available to European residents of six-months standing (passport identification is required). Terms and conditions vary slightly from country to country, but in the country of origin there is only a discount of around 50% on normal fares.

Travellers over 26 can get the Inter-Rail 26+, valid for unlimited rail travel in Austria, Bulgaria, Croatia, Czech Republic, Denmark, Finland, Germany, Greece, Hungary, Luxembourg, Netherlands, Norway, Poland, Romania, Ireland, Slovakia, Slovenia, Sweden, Turkey and Yugoslavia. The pass also gives free travel on shipping routes from the Italian port of Brindisi to Patras in Greece, as well as 30% to 50% discounts on various other ferry routes (more than covered by Eurail) and certain river and lake services. A 15-day pass costs UK£215 and one month costs UK£275.

The Inter-Rail pass for those under 26 has been split into zones. Zone A is Ireland; B is Sweden, Norway and Finland; C is Denmark, Germany, Switzerland and Austria; D is the Czech Republic, Slovakia, Poland, Hungary, Bulgaria, Romania and Croatia; E is France, Belgium, Netherlands and Luxembourg; F is Spain, Portugal and Morocco; G is Italy, Greece, Turkey and Slovenia. The price for any one zone is UK£185 for 15 days. Multi-zone passes are better value and are valid for one month: two zones is UK£220, three zones is UK£245, and all zones is UK£275.

Euro Domino There is a Euro Domino pass (called a Freedom pass in Britain) for each of the countries covered in the zonal Inter-Rail pass, except for Croatia and Romania. Adults (travelling 1st or 2nd class) and youths under 26 can choose from three, five, or 10 days validity within one month. Examples of adult/youth prices for 10 days in 2nd class are UK£109/£79 for the Netherlands and UK£209/£159 for Germany.

National Rail Passes If you intend to travel extensively within one country, check which national rail passes are available. These can sometimes save you a lot of money; details can be found in the Getting Around sections in the individual country chapters. You need to plan ahead if you intend to take this option, as some passes can only be purchased prior to arrival in the country concerned.

Cheap Tickets

European rail passes are only worth buying if you plan to do a reasonable amount of inter-country travelling within a short space of time. Some people tend to overdo it and spend every night they can on the train, ending up too tired to enjoy sightseeing the next day.

When weighing up options, consider the cost of other cheap ticket deals. Travellers aged under 26 can pick up Billet International de Jeunesse (BIJ) tickets which cut fares by up to about 30%. Unfortunately, you can't always bank on a substantial reduction. London to Zürich return is UK£142 instead of UK£189, London to Munich return is UK£184 rather than UK£198. Various agents issue BIJ tickets in Europe, eg Campus Travel (☎ 0171-730 8832), 52 Grosvenor Gardens, London SW1 0AG, which also sells Eurotrain tickets for people aged under 26. Eurotrain options include circular Explorer tickets, allowing a different route for the return trip: London to Madrid, for instance, takes in Barcelona, Paris and numerous other cities. The fare for this 'Spanish Explorer' ticket is UK£195, valid for two months. British Rail International (☎ 0171-834 2345) and Wasteels (☎ 0171-834 7066), both in London's Victoria Railway Station, sell BIJ tickets and other rail products.

For a small fee, European residents aged over 60 can get a Rail Europe Senior Card as an add-on to their national rail senior pass. It entitles the holder to reduced European fares. The percentage saving varies according to the route: London-Munich return is UK£164, London-Zürich return is UK£121 against the standard fares of UK£198 and UK£189 respectively.

TAXI

Taxis in Europe are metered and rates are high. There might also be supplements (depending on the country) for things like luggage, the time of day, the location from which you were picked up, and extra passengers. Good bus, rail and underground/subway railway networks make the taking of taxis all but unnecessary, but if you need one in a hurry they can usually be found idling near train stations or outside big hotels. Lower fares make taxis more viable in some countries (eg Spain, Greece and Portugal).

CAR & MOTORCYCLE

Travelling with your own vehicle is the best way to get to remote places and it gives you the most flexibility. Unfortunately, the independence you enjoy does tend to isolate you from the local people. Also, cars are usually inconvenient in city centres, where it is generally worth ditching your vehicle and relying on public transport. Various car-carrying trains can help you avoid long, tiring drives.

A useful general reference on motoring in Europe is Eric Bredesen's *Moto Europa*. It's updated annually, and contains information on rental, purchase, documents, tax and road rules. It can be ordered from US and Canadian bookshops (US$24.95) or directly from Seren Publishing (☎ 800-EUROPA-8 or 319-583 1068 from abroad) at PO Box 1212, Dubuque, Iowa 52004 (add US$3 for shipping).

Paperwork & Preparations

Proof of ownership of a private vehicle should always be carried (Vehicle Registration Document for British-registered cars) when touring Europe. An EU driving licence is acceptable for driving throughout Europe. However, old-style green UK licences are no good for Spain and should be backed up by an Italian translation in Italy and a German translation in Austria. If you have any other type of licence it is advisable or necessary to obtain an International Driving

Permit (IDP) from your motoring organisation (see Visas & Documents in the earlier Facts for the Visitor chapter). An IDP is recommended for Turkey even if you have a European licence.

Third-party motor insurance is a minimum requirement in Europe. Most UK motor insurance policies automatically provide this for EU countries and some others. Get your insurer to issue a Green Card (which may cost extra), an internationally recognised proof of insurance, and check that it lists all the countries you intend to visit. You'll need this in the event of an accident outside the country where the vehicle is insured. Also ask your insurer for a European Accident Statement form, which can simplify things if worse comes to worst. Never sign statements you can't read or understand – insist on a translation and sign that only if it's acceptable.

If you want to insure a vehicle you've just purchased (see the following Purchase section) and have a good insurance record, you might be eligible for considerable discounts if you can show a letter to this effect from your insurance company back home.

Taking out a European motoring assistance policy is a good investment, such as the AA Five Star Service or the RAC Eurocover Motoring Assistance. Expect to pay about UK£46 for 14 days cover with a small discount for association members. Both of these include a bail bond for Spain, which is also recommended. Ask your motoring organisation for a Letter of Introduction, which entitles you to free services offered by affiliated organisations around Europe (see Documents in the earlier Facts for the Visitor chapter).

Every vehicle travelling across an international border should display a sticker showing its country of registration (see the International Country Abbreviations appendix). A warning triangle, to be used in the event of breakdown, is compulsory almost everywhere. Recommended accessories are a first-aid kit (compulsory in Austria, Slovenia, Croatia, Yugoslavia and Greece), a spare bulb kit, and a fire extinguisher (compulsory in Greece and Turkey). Contact the RAC (☎ 0800-550055) or the AA (☎ 0990-500600) in the UK for more information.

Road Rules

With the exception of Britain and Ireland, driving is on the right. Vehicles brought over from either of these countries should have their headlights adjusted to avoid blinding oncoming traffic at night (a simple solution on older headlight lenses is to cover up the triangular section of the lens with tape). Priority is usually given to traffic approaching from the right in countries that drive on the right-hand side.

The RAC publishes an annual *European Motoring Guide*, which gives the visiting motorist an excellent summary of regulations in each country, including parking rules. Motoring organisations in other countries have similar publications.

Take care with speed limits, as they vary from country to country. You may be surprised at the apparent disregard of traffic regulations in some places (particularly in Italy and Greece), but as a visitor it is always best to be cautious. Many driving infringements are subject to an on-the-spot fine in all countries except Britain and Ireland. Always ask for a receipt.

European drink-driving laws are particularly strict. The blood-alcohol concentration (BAC) limit when driving is between 0.05% and 0.08%, but in certain areas – Gibraltar, some Eastern European countries, Scandinavia – it can be *zero* per cent. See the introductory Getting Around sections in the country chapters for more details on traffic laws.

Roads

Conditions and types of roads vary across Europe, but it is possible to make some generalisations. The fastest routes are four or six-lane dual carriageways/highways, ie two or three lanes either side (motorway, *Autobahn*, *autoroute*, *autostrada* etc). These tend to skirt cities and plough though the countryside in straight lines, often avoiding the most scenic bits. Some of these roads incur tolls, often quite hefty (eg in Italy, France and Spain), or have an annual charge for visitors (Switzerland and Austria), but there will always be an alternative route you can take. Motorways and other primary routes are almost always in good condition.

Road surfaces on minor routes are not so reliable in some countries (eg Portugal, Greece and Ireland) although normally they will be more than adequate. These roads are narrower and progress is generally much slower. To compensate, you can expect much better scenery and plenty of interesting villages along the way.

Rental

The big international firms – Hertz, Avis, Budget Car, Eurodollar, and Europe's largest rental agency, Europcar – will give you reliable service and a good standard of vehicle. Usually you will have the option of returning the car to a different outlet at the end of the rental period.

Unfortunately, if you walk into an office and ask for a car on the spot, you will pay over the odds, even allowing for special weekend deals. If you want to rent a car and haven't prebooked, look for national or local firms, which can often undercut the big companies by up to 40%. Nevertheless, you need to be wary of dodgy deals where they take your money and point you towards some clapped-out wreck, or where the rental agreement is bad news if you have an accident or the car is stolen – a cause for concern if you can't even read what you sign.

Prebooked and prepaid rates are always cheaper, and there are fly-drive combinations and other programmes that are worth looking into. Holiday Autos (☎ 909-949 1737), 1425 W Foothill Blvd, Upland, California 91786, has good rates for Europe, for which you need to prebook; it has offices in the UK (☎ 0990-300400; this has a lowest price guarantee) and many European countries. Ask in advance if you can drive a rented car across borders; it's OK to hire a Holiday Autos car in Germany (where hire prices are low) and use it to tour neighbouring countries, for example.

No matter where you rent, make sure you understand what is included in the price (unlimited or paid km, tax, injury insurance, collision damage waiver etc) and what your liabilities are. Always take the collision damage waiver, though you can probably skip the injury insurance if you and your passengers have decent travel insurance.

The minimum rental age is usually 21 or even 23, and you'll probably need a credit card. Note that prices at airport rental offices are usually higher than at branches in the city centre.

Motorcycle and moped rental is common in some countries, such as Italy, Spain, Greece and the south of France, but it is all too common to see inexperienced riders leap on bikes and very quickly fall off them again.

Purchase

The purchase of vehicles in some European countries is illegal for nonresidents of that country. Britain is probably the best place to buy: second-hand prices are good and, whether buying privately or from a dealer, the absence of language difficulties will help you establish exactly what you are getting and what guarantees you can expect in the event of a breakdown. See the Britain Getting Around section for information on purchase paperwork and European insurance.

Bear in mind that you will be getting a car with the steering wheel on the right in Britain. If you want left-hand drive and can afford to buy new, prices are reasonable in the Netherlands and Greece (without tax), in France and Germany (with tax), and in Belgium and Luxembourg (regardless of tax). Paperwork can be tricky wherever you buy, and many countries have compulsory roadworthiness checks on older vehicles.

Leasing

Leasing a vehicle has none of the hassles of purchasing and can work out considerably cheaper than hiring over longer periods. The Renault Eurodrive Scheme provides new cars for non-EU residents for a period of between 17 days and six months. Under this scheme, a Renault Clio 1.2 for 30 days, for example, would cost FF4688 (US$938), including insurance and roadside assistance. Peugeot's European Self-Drive programme is slightly more expensive.

Camper Van

A popular way to tour Europe is for three or four people to band together to buy or rent a camper van. London is the usual embarkation point. Look at the advertisements in London's free magazine *TNT* if you wish to form or join a group. *TNT* is also a good source for purchasing a van, as is the *Loot* newspaper and the Van Market in Market Rd, London N7 (near the Caledonian Rd tube station), where private vendors congregate on a daily basis. Some second-hand dealers offer a 'buy-back' scheme for when you return from the Continent, but buying and re-selling privately should be more advantageous if you have the time.

Camper vans usually feature a fixed high-top or elevating roof and two to five bunk beds.

Apart from the essential camping gas cooker, professional conversions may include a sink, fridge and built-in cupboards. You will need to spend from at least UK£1500 (US$2325) for something reliable enough to get you around Europe for any length of time. An eternal favourite for budget travellers is the VW Kombi; they aren't made anymore but the old ones seem to go on forever, and getting spare parts isn't a problem. Once on the road you should be able to keep budgets lower than backpackers using trains, but don't forget to set some money aside for emergency repairs.

The main advantage of going by camper van is flexibility: with transport, eating and sleeping requirements all taken care of in one unit, you are tied to nobody's timetable but your own.

A disadvantage of camper vans is that you are in a confined space for much of the time. (Four adults in a small van can soon get on each other's nerves, particularly if the group has been formed at short notice.) Another disadvantage is that they're not very manoeuvrable around town, and you'll often have to leave your gear unattended inside (many people bolt extra locks onto the van). They're also expensive to buy in spring and hard to sell in autumn. As an alternative, consider a car and tent.

Motorcycle Touring

Europe is made for motorcycle touring, with good-quality winding roads, stunning scenery, and an active motorcycling scene. Just make sure your wet-weather gear is up to scratch.

The wearing of crash helmets for rider and passenger is compulsory everywhere in Western Europe. Austria, Belgium, France, Germany, Luxembourg, Portugal and Spain also require that motorcyclists use headlights during the day; in other countries it is recommended.

On ferries, motorcyclists rarely have to book ahead as they can generally be squeezed in. Take note of local custom about parking motorcycles on pavements (sidewalks). Though this is illegal in some countries, the police usually turn a blind eye so long as the vehicle doesn't obstruct pedestrians. Don't try this in Britain, however.

Anyone considering a motorcycle tour from Britain might benefit from joining the International Motorcyclists Tour Club (UK£19 per annum plus UK£3 joining fee). It organises European (and worldwide) cycling jaunts, and members regularly meet to swap information. Contact James Clegg (☎ 01489-664868), Membership Secretary, 238 Nettham Rd, Netherton, Huddersfield, HD4 7HL.

Fuel

Fuel prices can vary enormously from country to country; refuelling in Luxembourg or Andorra will save about 30% compared to prices in neighbouring countries. The Netherlands, France and Italy have Europe's most expensive petrol; Gibraltar and Andorra are by far the cheapest in Western Europe. Britain, Spain and Switzerland are also reasonably cheap. Motoring organisations such as the RAC can supply more details.

Unleaded petrol is widely available throughout Europe and is usually slightly cheaper than super (premium grade, the only 'leaded' choice in some countries). Diesel is usually significantly cheaper, though the difference is only marginal in Britain, Ireland and Switzerland.

BICYCLE

A tour of Europe by bike may seem a daunting prospect, but one organisation that can help in the UK is the Cyclists' Touring Club (CTC; ☎ 01483-417 217), Cotterell House, 69 Meadrow, Godalming, Surrey GU7 3HS. It can supply information to members on cycling conditions in Europe as well as detailed routes, itineraries, maps and cheap specialised insurance. Membership costs UK£25 per annum, UK£12.50 for students and people under 18, or UK£16.50 for senior citizens.

Europe by Bike, by Karen & Terry Whitehall, a paperback available in the USA and selected outlets in the UK, is a little out of date but has good descriptions of 18 cycling tours of up to 19 days duration.

A primary consideration on a cycling tour is to travel light, but you should take a few tools and spare parts, including a puncture repair kit and an extra inner tube. Panniers are essential to balance your possessions on either side of the bike frame. A bike helmet is also a very good idea. Take a good lock and always use it when you leave your bike unattended.

Seasoned cyclists can average 80 km a day, but there's no point in overdoing it. The slower you travel, the more local people you are likely to meet. If you get tired of pedalling or simply want to skip a boring transport section, you can put your feet up on the train. On slower trains, bikes can usually be transported as luggage, subject to a small supplementary fee. Fast trains can rarely accommodate bikes: they need to be sent as registered luggage and may end up on a different train from the one you take. British Rail is not part of the European luggage registration scheme, but Eurostar is: it charges UK£20 to send a bike as registered luggage on its routes.

The European Bike Express is a coach service where cyclists can travel with their bicycles. It runs in the summer from north-east England to France and Spain, with pick-up/drop-off points en route. The return fare is UK£149 (£139 for CTC members); phone ☎ 01642-251 440 in the UK for details.

For more information on cycling, see Activities in the earlier Facts for the Visitor chapter and in the individual country chapters.

Rental

It is easy to hire bikes throughout most of Western Europe on an hourly, half-day, daily or weekly basis. Many train stations have bike-rental counters, some of which are open 24 hours a day. See the country chapters for more details. Often it is possible to return the machine at a different outlet (as in Ireland) so you don't have to retrace your route.

Purchase

For major cycling tours, it's best to have a bike you're familiar with, so consider bringing your own (see following section) rather than buying on arrival. There are plenty of places to buy in Europe (shops sell new and second-hand bicycles or you can check local papers for private vendors) but you'll need a specialist bicycle shop for a machine capable of withstanding European touring. CTC can provide a leaflet on purchasing. Cycling is very popular in the Netherlands and Germany, and they are good places to pick up a well-equipped touring bicycle. European prices are quite high (certainly higher than in North America), but non-Europeans should be able to claim back VAT on the purchase.

Bringing Your Own

If you want to bring your own bicycle to Europe, you should be able to take it along with you on the plane relatively easily. You can either take it apart and pack everything in a bike bag or box, or simply wheel it to the check-in desk, where it should be treated as a piece of luggage. You may have to remove the pedals and turn the handlebars sideways so that it takes up less space in the aircraft's hold; check all this with the airline well in advance, preferably before you pay for your ticket. If your bicycle and other luggage exceed your weight allowance, ask about alternatives or you may suddenly find yourself being charged a fortune for excess baggage.

HITCHING

Hitching is never entirely safe in any country in the world, and we don't recommend it. Travellers who decide to hitch should understand that they are taking a small but potentially serious risk. People who do choose to hitch will be safer if they travel in pairs and let someone know where they plan to go.

Hitching can be the most rewarding and frustrating way of getting around. Rewarding, because you get to meet and interact with local people and are forced into unplanned detours that may yield unexpected highlights off the beaten track. Frustrating, because you may get stuck on the side of the road to nowhere with nowhere (or nowhere cheap) to stay.

That said, hitchers can end up making good time, but obviously your plans need to be flexible in case a trick of the light makes you appear invisible to passing motorists. A man and woman travelling together is probably the best combination. Two or more men must expect some delays; two women together will make good time and should be relatively safe. A woman hitching on her own is taking a big risk, particularly in parts of southern Europe.

Don't try to hitch from city centres: take public transport to suburban exit routes. Hitching is usually illegal on motorways (freeways) – stand on the slip roads, or approach drivers at petrol stations and truck stops. Look presentable and cheerful and make a cardboard sign indicating your intended destination in the local language. Never hitch where drivers can't stop in good time or without causing an obstruction. At dusk, give up and think about finding somewhere to stay. If your itinerary includes a ferry crossing (for instance, across the Channel), it might be worth trying to score a ride before the ferry rather than after, since vehicle tickets sometimes include a number of passengers free of charge. This also applies to Le Shuttle via the Channel Tunnel.

It is sometimes possible to arrange a lift in advance: scan student notice boards in colleges, or contact car-sharing agencies. Such agencies are particularly popular in France (Allostop Provoya, Auto-Partage) and Germany (Mitfahrzentralen). See the relevant country chapters.

BOAT
Ferry
Several different ferry companies compete on all the main ferry routes. The resulting service is comprehensive but complicated. The same ferry company can have a host of different prices for the same route, depending upon the time of day or year, the validity of the ticket, or the length of your vehicle. Vehicle tickets include the driver and often up to five passengers free of charge. It is worth planning (and booking) ahead where possible as there may be special reductions on off-peak crossings and advance purchase tickets. On English Channel routes, apart from one-day or short-term excursion returns, there is little price advantage in buying a return ticket as against two singles.

Stena Line is the largest ferry company in the world and serves British, Irish and Scandinavian routes (but from England to/from Norway, contact Color Line). P&O European Ferries and Brittany Ferries sail direct between England and northern Spain, taking 24 to 35 hours. The shortest cross-Channel routes (Dover to Calais, or Folkestone to Boulogne) are also the busiest, though there is now great competition from the Channel Tunnel. Italy (Brindisi or Bari) to Greece (Corfu, Igoumenitsa and Patras) is also a popular route. Greek islands are connected to the mainland and each other by a spider's web of routings; the excellent *Thomas Cook Guide to Greek Island Hopping* gives comprehensive listings of ferry times and routes, as well as information on sightseeing.

Rail-pass holders are entitled to discounts or free travel on some lines (see the earlier Train section), and most ferry companies give discounts to disabled drivers. Food on ferries is often expensive (and lousy), so it is worth bringing your own when possible. It is also worth knowing that if you take your vehicle on board, you are usually denied access to it during the voyage.

Steamer
Europe's main lakes and rivers are served by steamers, and not surprisingly, schedules are more extensive in the summer months. Railpass holders are entitled to some discounts (see the earlier Train section). Extended boat trips should be considered as relaxing and scenic excursions; viewed merely as a functional means of transport, they can be very expensive.

It is possible to take a cruise up the Rhine from the Netherlands as far as Switzerland, but you'll need a boatload of cash. The main operator along the Rhine is the Cologne-based Köln-Düsseldorfer (KD) Line (☎ 0221-208 8288). Boats also sail from Basel in Switzerland to Budapest in Hungary, making use of the recently opened Main-Danube Canal. Contact Triton Reisen (☎ 061-271 9430) in Basel.

ORGANISED TOURS
Tailor-made tours abound; see your travel agent or look in the small ads in newspaper travel pages. Specialists in Britain include Ramblers Holidays (☎ 01707-331133) for walkers and Arctic Experience Discover the World (☎ 016977-48361) for wilderness and wildlife holidays.

Young revellers can party on Europe-wide bus tours. An outfit called Tracks offers budget coach/camping tours for under US$40 per day, plus food fund. It has a London office (☎ 0171-937 3028) and is represented in Australia and New Zealand by Adventure World; in North America, call ☎ 800-233 6046. Contiki (☎ 0181-290 6422) and Top Deck (☎ 0171-370 4555) offer camping or hotel-based bus tours, also for the 18 to 35 age group. The latter's 12-day 'Taste of Europe' tour costs UK£299 plus food fund. Both have offices or representatives in North America, Australasia and South Africa.

For people aged over 50, Saga Holidays (☎ 0800-300500), Saga Building, Middelburg Square, Folkestone, Kent CT20 1AZ, offers holidays ranging from cheap coach tours to luxury cruises (and has cheap travel insurance). Saga also operates in the USA as Saga International Holidays (☎ 617-262 2262) 222 Berkeley St, Boston, Massachusetts 02116, and in Australia as Saga Holidays Australasia (☎ 02-9957 5660), Level One, 110 Pacific Highway, North Sydney, NSW 2060.

National tourist offices in most countries offer organised trips to points of interest. These may range from one-hour city tours to several-day circular excursions. They often work out more expensive than going it alone, but are sometimes worth it if you are pressed for time. A short city tour will give you a quick overview of the place and can be a good way to begin your visit.

Andorra

The princedom of Andorra, covering just 468 sq km, is nestled between France and Spain in the midst of the Pyrenees. Though it *is* tiny, this political anomaly is at the heart of some of the most dramatic scenery in Europe.

Once a real backwater, Andorra has developed since the 1950s as a skiing centre and duty-free shopping haven, bringing not only wealth and foreign workers but also some unsightly development around the capital, Andorra la Vella. Until 1993, the country was a 'co-princedom' with its sovereignty invested in two 'princes': the Catholic bishop of the Spanish town of La Seu d'Urgell and the French president (who inherited the job from France's pre-Revolutionary kings). This arrangement dated back some seven centuries. Now Andorra has a constitution which puts full control in the hands of its people. The elected parliament, the Consell General (General Council), has 28 members, four from each parish. Andorra is not a member of the European Union (EU).

Andorrans form only about a quarter of Andorra's total population (65,000) and are outnumbered by Spaniards. The official language is Catalan, which is related to both Spanish and French. Most people speak a couple of these languages, sometimes all three.

Facts for the Visitor

VISAS & EMBASSIES
You do not need a visa to visit Andorra, but you must carry your passport or national identity card. Andorra does not have any diplomatic missions abroad, but Spain and France have embassies in Andorra la Vella.

MONEY
Andorra, which has no currency of its own, uses both the French franc and the Spanish peseta. Except in Pas de la Casa on the French border, prices are usually given in pesetas. It's best to use pesetas: the exchange rate for francs in shops and restaurants is seldom in your favour. See the France and Spain chapters for exchange rates.

```
1FF      =  24.50 ptas
100 ptas =  4.08FF
```

Andorra's very low tax regime has made it a famous duty-free bazar for electronic goods, cameras, alcohol, etc. Today prices for these things no longer justify a special trip, but if you're prepared to shop around, you can find some cameras or electronic goods about 20% or 30% cheaper than in France or Spain. There are limits on what you can take out of Andorra duty-free – tourist offices have details.

POST & COMMUNICATIONS
Post
Andorra has no postal system of its own; France and Spain each operate separate systems with their own Andorran stamps.

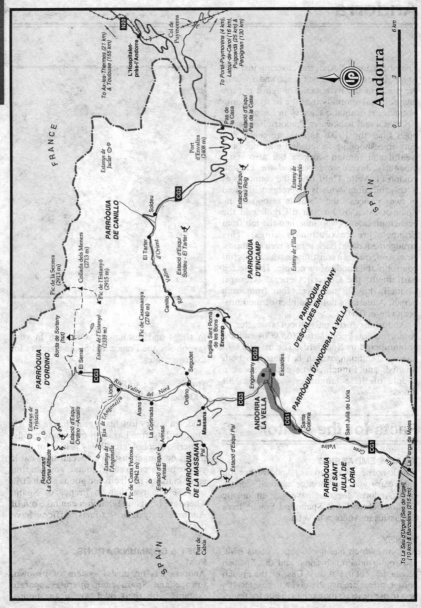

Andorra

Andorran stamps of both types are valid only for mail posted in Andorra and are needed only for international mail – letters within the country are free and do not need stamps. Regular French and Spanish stamps cannot be used in Andorra.

Postal rates are the same as those of the issuing country, with the French tariffs slightly cheaper. You are better off routing all international mail (except letters to Spain) through the French postal system. Poste restante mail to Andorra la Vella goes to the French post office there.

Telephone
Andorra's country code is ☎ 376. To call Andorra from any other country, dial the international access code, then ☎ 376, then the six-digit local number. To call other countries from Andorra, dial ☎ 00, then the country code, area code and local number.

Public telephones take pesetas (francs in Pas de la Casa) or an Andorran *teletarja*, which works like telephone cards in most European countries. Teletarges (plural) worth 500 and 900 ptas are sold at post offices, tourist offices and some shops. Andorra does *not* have reverse-charge (collect) calling facilities.

TIME & ELECTRICITY
Andorra is one hour ahead of GMT/UTC in winter and two hours ahead from the last Sunday in March to the last Sunday in September. Electric current is either 220V or 125V, both at 50 Hz.

MEDICAL & EMERGENCY SERVICES
Medical care has to be paid for. For emergency medical help, call ☎ 116; for an ambulance ☎ 118; for the police ☎ 110.

BUSINESS HOURS
Shops in Andorra la Vella are open daily from 9.30 am to 1 pm and 3.30 to 8 pm, except (in most cases) Sunday afternoon.

ACTIVITIES
Above the main valleys where most people live is plenty of high, attractive, lake-dotted mountain country, good for skiing in winter and walking in summer. Some peaks remain snow-capped until July or even later. Tourist offices give out a useful English-language booklet,

Sport Activities, describing numerous walking and mountain-bike routes. In summer, mountain bikes can be rented at several places for around 2500 ptas a day.

Hiking
There are some beautiful hiking areas in the north and north-west of Andorra (see the Parròquia d'Ordino section for more information). Several long-distance walking routes, including the Spanish GR11 and the mainly French Haute Randonnée Pyrenéenne, which both traverse the Pyrenees from the Mediterranean to the Atlantic, cross the country. The best season for hiking is June to September, when temperatures climb well into the 20s in the day, though they drop to around 10°C at night. June can be wet.

A 1:25,000-scale *mapa topogràfic* of the country costs 1200 ptas in bookshops and tourist offices. Maps at 1:10,000 (10 cm = 1 km) are also available. Hikers can sleep for free in more than two dozen *refugi* (mountain huts).

Skiing
Andorra has the best inexpensive skiing and snowboarding in the Pyrenees. The season lasts from December to April (snow cover permitting). For information on the five downhill ski areas (*estaciós d'esquí*), ask at one of the capital's tourist offices or contact Ski Andorra (☎ 864389). The largest and best resorts are Soldeu-El Tarter and Pas de la Casa/Grau Roig, but the others – Ordino-Arcalís, Arinsal and Pal – are a bit cheaper. Ski passes cost 2500 to 3700 ptas a day, depending on the location and season; ski-gear rental is around 1500 ptas a day.

ACCOMMODATION
There are no youth hostels, but plenty of camping grounds, hotels and cheaper *pensiós*, *residències*, etc. Prices in many places are the same year-round, though some go up in August and/or at Christmas, Easter and the height of the ski season.

The 26 mountain refuges have bunks and fireplaces, and all except one are free. Nearly all have drinking water. Tourist offices have more info, and maps indicating their locations.

Getting There & Away

The only way into Andorra is by road. If you're coming from France, you won't soon forget Port d'Envalira (2408 metres), the highest pass in the Pyrenees. The municipal tourist office in Andorra la Vella has bus timetables and knows ticket office hours.

From France, by public transport you need to approach by train and then get a bus for the final leg. The nearest station is L'Hospitalet-près-l'Andorre, two hours from Toulouse by four daily trains (102 FF). The two daily buses between L'Hospitalet and Plaça Guillemó in Andorra la Vella (1½ to 2¼ hours, 925 ptas) connect with trains.

From Barcelona, Alsina Graells runs five buses daily to and from Andorra la Vella's Estació d'Autobusos on Carrer Bonaventura Riberaygua (four hours, 2500 ptas). Other services to/from the Estació d'Autobusos include: Tarragona daily (four hours, 1260 ptas); Zaragoza and Madrid Estación Sur (8½ hours, 4300 ptas), three per week; Burgos, Valladolid and Tuy, two per week. There are up to eight buses daily between La Seu d'Urgell and Plaça Guillemó in Andorra la Vella (30 minutes, 315 ptas).

The nearest Spanish train station to Andorra is Puigcerdà. The first two trains from Barcelona's Estació Sants (6.15 and 9.18 am) get you to Puigcerdà in time to reach Andorra la Vella (with a change of bus at La Seu d'Urgell) the same day – a trip of about 6½ hours in total for about 2000 ptas.

Getting Around

BUS

Cooperativa Interurbana (☎ 820412) runs eight bus lines along the three main highways from Andorra la Vella. Autobus Parroquial de La Massana i d'Ordino operates a few services from La Massana. The municipal tourist office in Andorra la Vella has timetables. Destinations from Andorra la Vella include Ordino (125 ptas), daily every 20 or 30 minutes from 7.30 am to 8.30 pm; Arinsal (175 ptas) three times daily; Soldeu (325 ptas) hourly from 9

am to 8 pm; Pas de la Casa (560 ptas) at 9 am. Buses to all these places leave from the Plaça Príncep Benlloch stop in Andorra la Vella.

CAR & MOTORCYCLE

With all the twists and turns, it's almost impossible to reach the inter-hamlet speed limit of 90 km/h. The biggest problems are Andorra la Vella's traffic jams and the ever-vigilant parking officers. If you don't buy a coupon (available from machines everywhere) and place it on the dashboard, you will be fined for sure.

Petrol in Andorra is about 15% cheaper than in Spain and 25% cheaper than in France.

Andorra la Vella

Andorra la Vella (Vella is pronounced 'VEY-yah'; population 22,000) is in the Riu Valira valley at an elevation of just over 1000 metres. The town is given over almost entirely to retailing of electronic and luxury goods. With its mountains, constant din of jack-hammers and 'mall' architecture, travellers familiar with Asia may be reminded of Hong Kong. The only differences seem to be the snow-capped peaks and lack of noodle shops!

Orientation

Andorra la Vella is strung out along the main drag, called Avinguda Meritxell in the east and Avinguda Príncep Benlloch in the west. The tiny historic quarter (Barri Antic) lies south-west of Plaça Príncep Benlloch. The town merges with the once-separate villages of Escaldes and Engordany to the east and Santa Coloma to the south-west.

Information

Tourist Offices The helpful municipal tourist office (Oficina d'Informació i Turisme; ☎ 827117), on Plaça de la Rotonda, has maps, all sorts of brochures, stamps and telephone cards. It's open daily from 9 am to 1 pm and 3.30 to 8 pm (on Sunday to 7 pm). In July and August it foregoes the afternoon break.

The national tourist office (Sindicat d'Iniciativa Oficina de Turisme; ☎ 820214) is on Carrer Doctor Vilanova just down from

Plaça Rebés; it's open Monday to Saturday from 10 am (9 am from July to September) to 1 pm and 3 to 7 pm, and on Sunday mornings.

Money Banks are open weekdays from 9 am to 1 pm and 3 to 5 pm and on Saturday to noon. There are banks every 100 metres or so along Avinguda Meritxell and Avinguda Príncep Benlloch in the town centre, most with ATMs. American Express is represented by Viatges Relax (☎ 822044) at Carrer Roc dels Escolls 12. It doesn't change money but can replace American Express cards and travellers' cheques, and sell travellers' cheques against card-holders' personal cheques.

Post & Communications The main French post office (La Poste) is at Carrer Pere d'Urg 1. It is open Monday to Friday from 8.30 am to 2.30 pm (to 7 pm in July and August), Saturday from 9 am to noon. Payment is in French francs only.

The main Spanish post office (Correus i Telègrafs) is nearby at Carrer Joan Maragall 10. It's open Monday to Friday from 8.30 am to 2.30 pm, and Saturday from 9.30 am to 1 pm, and only accepts pesetas.

You can make international telephone calls from street pay phones.

Medical Services The main hospital is the modern Hospital Nostra Senyora de Meritxell (☎ 868000) at Avinguda Fiter i Rossell 1-13, about 1.5 km east of Plaça Guillemó.

Things to See & Do

Casa de la Vall Built in 1580 as a private home, Casa de la Vall (☎ 829129), on Carrer de la Vall in the Barri Antic, has been the seat of Andorra's parliament and its forerunners for almost three centuries. Downstairs is the Sala de la Justicia, the only courtroom in the whole country. Free guided tours (sometimes in English) are given about once an hour on weekdays from 9 am to 1 pm and 3 to 7 pm: you should book a week ahead to ensure a place, but individuals can sometimes join a group at the last minute.

Caldea Caldea (☎ 865777) in Escaldes is an enormous spa complex of pools, hot tubs and saunas fed by thermal springs, all enclosed in

what looks like a futuristic cathedral. Three-hour tickets (2000 ptas) are available from the tourist offices. Caldea is just east of Avinguda Fiter i Rossell, the continuation of Avinguda Doctor Mitjavila, a two-km walk from Plaça Guillemó.

Places to Stay

Camping About 1.5 km south-west of Plaça Guillemó on Avinguda de Salou, *Camping Valira* (☎ 822384) charges 500 ptas per person and the same for a tent and for a car. It's open all year, and has a heated covered swimming pool.

Hotels – Plaça Guillemó & Barri Antic At Carrer La Llacuna 21, just off Plaça Guillemó, *Residència Benazet* (☎ 820698) has large, serviceable rooms with washbasin and bidet at 1300 ptas per person. *Hotel Les Arcades* (☎ 821355) at Plaça Guillemó 5 has singles/doubles with shower and toilet from 2000/3000 to 3000/5400 ptas depending on the season.

In the Barri Antic, the nondescript rooms at *Pensió La Rosa* (☎ 821810) at Antic Carrer Major 18, not far from the Casa de la Vall, are 1700/3000 ptas. Quiet *Hostal Calones* (☎ 821312), Antic Carrer Major 8, has better rooms with big bathrooms for 2800/3700 ptas. *Habitacions Baró* (☎ 821484) at Carrer del Puial 21 – up the steps opposite Avinguda Príncep Benlloch 53 – has rooms for 1300/2600 ptas, or 1800/3600 ptas with bath.

Hotel Pyrénées (☎ 860006; fax 820265), at Avinguda Príncep Benlloch 20, has a tennis court, swimming pool, and all mod cons and is priced accordingly at 5300/8700 ptas including breakfast.

Hotels – further east At Avinguda Meritxell 44, *Hotel Costa* (☎ 821439) has basic but clean rooms for 1300/2600 ptas. Bathrooms are shared. *Hotel Residència Albert* (☎ 820156) at Avinguda Doctor Mitjavila 16 has rooms for 1500/3000 ptas, or doubles with shower for 3500 ptas.

Places to Eat

The *Hotel Les Arcades* restaurant, Plaça Guillemó 5, has a decent three-course Spanish set meal for 800 ptas. *El Timbaler del Bruch*

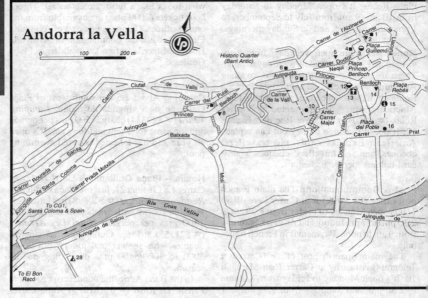

Andorra la Vella

0   100   200 m

Historic Quarter
(Barri Antic)

PLACES TO STAY
1   Residència Benazet
4   Hotel Les Arcades
6   Hotel Pyrénées
7   Habitacions Baró
9   Pensió La Rosa
11 Hostal Calones
19 Hotel Costa
22 Hotel Residència Albert
28 Camping Valira

PLACES TO EAT
2   El Timbaler del Bruch
5   Pizzeria Primavera

8   Tex-Mex Café
14 Pans & Company
21 Pizzeria La Mossegada
23 Pans & Company

OTHER
3   Plaça Guillemó Bus
    Stop
10 Casa de la Vall
12 Plaça Príncep Benlloch
    Bus Stop
13 Església de Sant
    Esteve
15 National Tourist Office

16 Public Lift to Plaça del
    Poble
17 Viatges Relax/Ameri-
    can Express
18 Pyrénées Department
    Store
20 Municipal Tourist Office
24 Spanish Post Office
25 French Post Office
26 Police Station
27 Estació d'Autobusos

on the same square does good, generous torrades (open toasted sandwiches) from 375 ptas. *Pizzeria Primavera* nearby at Carrer Doctor Nequi 4 has pizzas and pasta for 500 to 750 ptas, and a set meal for 900 ptas. It is closed on Wednesday. *Pans & Company* at Plaça Rebés 2 and Avinguda Meritxell 91 is good for hot and cold baguettes with a range of fillings (300 to 400 ptas).

Pizzeria La Mossegada, closed Wednesday, overlooks the Riu Valira at Avinguda Doctor Mitjavila 3. Pizzas cost between 750 and 875 ptas. Fancy Mexican in Andorra? The *Tex-Mex Café* at Avinguda Príncep Benlloch 49 has tacos with chilli (850 ptas) and Mexican spareribs (1200 ptas).

The best place for real Catalan cooking is the up-market *El Bon Racó* (☎ 822085) at

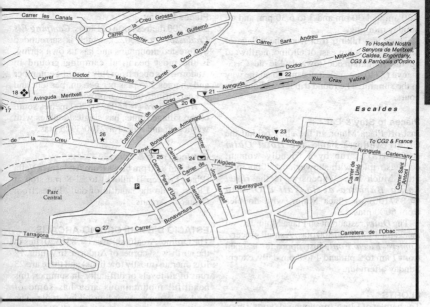

Avinguda de Salou 86 in Santa Coloma, about a km west of Camping Valira. Meat – especially xai (lamb) – roasted in an open hearth is the speciality (1200 ptas). The big supermarket on the 2nd floor of the Pyrénées department store at Avinguda Meritxell 21 is open Monday to Saturday from 9.30 am to 8 pm and on Sunday to 7 pm.

Getting There & Away
See the Getting There & Away and Getting Around sections at the start of this chapter for international and domestic transport options to/from Andorra la Vella.

Parròquia d'Ordino

The mountainous parish of Ordino, north of Andorra la Vella, is arguably the country's most beautiful region, with slate and fieldstone farmhouses, gushing streams and picturesque

stone bridges. Virtually everything of interest is along the 35-km highway CG3.

ORDINO
Ordino (population 1000; 1300 metres) is much larger than other villages in the area, but remains peaceful and Andorran in character, with most buildings still in stone.

Orientation & Information
The tourist office (☎ 836963), on highway CG3, is open Monday to Saturday from 9 am to 1 pm and 3 to 7 pm, and on Sunday morning. There are several banks and two post offices.

Things to See & Do
The **Museu d'Areny i Plandolit** (☎ 836908), just off Plaça Major, is a 17th-century house of typically rugged Andorran design that once belonged to one of the princedom's most illustrious families. The library and dining room are particularly fine. Half-hour guided visits cost 200 ptas; it's open Tuesday to Saturday from

ANDORRA

9.30 am to 1.30 pm and 3 to 6.30 pm, and on Sunday morning.

There is a **hiking trail** from the village of Segudet, half a km east of Ordino, northward up the mountainside towards Pic de Casamanya (2740 metres). It doesn't go all the way to the summit. The round trip takes about four hours.

Places to Stay & Eat
Just off Plaça Major, in the alley behind the Crèdit Andorrà bank, the *Hotel Quim* (☎ 835013) is run by a friendly woman; doubles/triples with shower cost 3000/3500 ptas. Much more expensive is the *Hotel Santa Bàrbara de la Vall d'Ordino* (☎ 837100) on Plaça Major, with doubles from 6000 ptas.

The *Quim* restaurant on Plaça Major has set meals for 1350 and 1500 ptas. A small grocery, *Comerç Fleca Font*, just opposite, is open from 7 am to 2 pm and 4 to 8 pm daily, except Sunday afternoon.

LLORTS
The hamlet of Llorts (pronounced 'yorts'; population 100; 1413 metres), six km north of Ordino, has traditional architecture set amid tobacco fields and near-pristine mountains. This is one of the most unadulterated spots in the whole country.

Things to See & Do
Llorts is a good area for **hiking** trails. One leads west from the village up the Riu de l'Angonella valley to a group of lakes, Estanys de l'Angonella, at about 2300 metres. Count on about three hours to get there.

From slightly north of the village of El Serrat (population 60; 1600 metres), which is three km up the valley from Llorts, a secondary road leads four km east to the Borda de Sorteny mountain shelter.

From there, trails go on to Estany de l'Estanyó (2339 metres) and to peaks such as Pic de la Serrera (2913 metres) and Pic de l'Estanyó (2915 metres), Andorra's fourth and second highest.

The partly Romanesque **Església de Sant Martí** in La Cortinada, 2.5 km south of Llorts, has 12th-century frescos in remarkably good condition.

Places to Stay
Some 200 metres north of Llorts, *Camping Els Pradassos* (☎ 850022), which is surrounded by forested mountains and has its own spring, is the most beautiful camping ground in Andorra. It's open from July to mid-September and charges 275 ptas per person, per tent and per car. Bring your own provisions.

Hotel Vilaró (☎ 850225), 200 metres south of the village limits, has singles/doubles with washbasin and bidet for 2100/3925 ptas.

Getting There & Away
The 1 and 8.30 pm buses from Andorra la Vella (Plaça Príncep Benlloch) to El Serrat stop at Llorts, as do the handful of daily buses from Ordino to Arcalís.

ESTACIÓ D'ESQUÍ ORDINO-ARCALÍS
The Ordino-Arcalís ski area (☎ 836320) lies in the north-west corner of Andorra. In winter, 12 lifts operate (mostly tow lines) and there are 23 runs of all levels of difficulty. In summer, this beautiful mountainous area has some of Andorra's most rewarding hiking trails. The nearest accommodation is in El Serrat or Llorts.

Restaurant La Coma Altitude, at 2200 metres near the third car park, is a useful landmark. It is open from December to early May and, except on Monday, from the end of June to early September. The long Telecadira La Coma chairlift rises opposite.

Things to Do
The souvenir kiosk opposite the foot of Telecadira La Coma rents out mountain bikes for 3100 ptas a day between late June and mid-September (daily, except Monday in June and July, from 10 am to 6 pm). The trail behind Restaurant La Coma Altitude leads eastward across the hill then north over the ridge to a group of beautiful lakes, Estanys de Tristaina. You can also start walking from the top of Telecadira La Coma (2700 metres), which operates daily from late June to early September from 10 am to 6 pm.

Getting There & Away
There are a few buses (150 ptas) daily from Ordino, through Llorts and El Serrat.

Austria

Austria (Österreich) is situated at the cross-roads of Europe. In the heady days of the Habsburgs, its empire encompassed both east and west. This foot-in-both-doors status has served Austria well, enabling it to bring its strong trading links with the East into the European Union, the capitalist club of the West.

The country thrives on tourism, and is one of the most popular destinations in Europe. Its rich cultural heritage, historic cities, winter sports and stunning scenery are a hard combination to beat. Its capital, Vienna, is one of the world's great cities; Salzburg is a living, baroque museum; and Innsbruck is dramatically situated in a perfect panorama of peaks. And everywhere you go, the country moves to the rhythm of its unrivalled musical tradition.

Facts about the Country

HISTORY

In its early years, the land that became Austria was invaded by a succession of tribes and armies using the Danube Valley as a conduit – the Celts, Romans, Vandals, Visigoths, Huns, Avars and Slavs all came and went. Charlemagne established a territory in the Danube Valley known as the Ostmark in 803, and the area became Christianised and predominantly Germanic. The Ostmark was undermined by invading Magyars but re-established by Otto I in 955. In 962, Pope John XII crowned Otto as Holy Roman Emperor of the German princes.

A period of growth and prosperity followed under the reign of the Babenbergs, and the territory acquired the status of a duchy in 1156. Influence in what is now Lower Austria expanded and the duchy of Styria came under central control in 1192. The last Babenberg died in battle in 1246 without an heir. The future of the duchy was uncertain until, in 1278, it fell into the hands of the Habsburgs, who ruled Austria until WWI.

The Habsburg Dynasty

Austrian territory gradually expanded under the rule of the Habsburgs. Carinthia (Kärnten) and Carniola were annexed in 1335, followed by Tirol in 1363. However, the Habsburgs preferred to extend their territory without force. Much of Vorarlberg, for example, was purchased from bankrupt lords and significant gains were achieved by politically motivated marriages. Intermarriage was extremely effective, although it did have a genetic side-effect: a distended lower jaw became an increasingly visible family trait, albeit discreetly ignored in official portraits.

In 1477, Maximilian gained control of Burgundy and the Netherlands by marriage to Maria of Burgundy. His eldest son, Philip, was married to the infanta of Spain in 1496. In 1516, Philip's son became Charles I of Spain (a title which granted control of vast overseas territories). Three years later, he also became Charles V of the Holy Roman Empire.

These acquisitions were too diverse for one person to rule effectively, so Charles handed over the Austrian territories to his younger brother Ferdinand in 1521. Ferdinand, the first

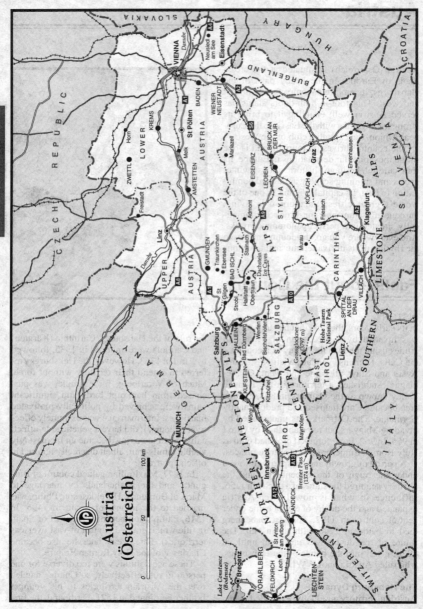

Austria
(Österreich)

Habsburg to live in Vienna, also came to rule Hungary and Bohemia after the death of his brother-in-law, King Lewis II in 1526. In 1556, Charles abdicated as emperor and Ferdinand I was crowned in his place. Charles' remaining territory was inherited by his son, Philip II, splitting the Habsburg dynasty into two distinct lines – the Spanish and Austrian.

In 1571, when the emperor granted religious freedom, the vast majority of Austrians turned to Protestantism. In 1576, the new emperor, Rudolf II, embraced the Counter-Reformation and much of the country reverted to Catholicism – not always without coercion. The attempt to impose Catholicism on Protestant areas of Europe led to the Thirty Years' War, which started in 1618 and devastated much of central Europe. Peace was finally achieved in 1648 with the Treaty of Westphalia, which signalled the end of the push for a Catholic empire over Europe. Austria was preoccupied for much of the rest of the century with halting the advance of the Turks into Europe.

In 1740, Maria Theresa ascended the throne, despite the fact that as a woman she was ineligible to do so. A war followed to ensure that she stayed there. Her rule lasted 40 years, and is generally acknowledged as the era in which Austria developed as a modern state. She centralised control, established a civil service, reformed the army and the economy, and introduced a public education system.

Progress was halted when Napoleon defeated Austria at Austerlitz in 1805 and forced the abolition of the title of Holy Roman Emperor. European conflict dragged on until the settlement at the Congress of Vienna in 1814-15, which was dominated by the Austrian foreign minister, Klemens von Metternich. Austria was left with control of the German Confederation but suffered internal upheaval during the 1848 revolutions and eventual defeat in the 1866 Austro-Prussian War.

Defeat led to the formation of the dual monarchy of Austria-Hungary in 1867 under emperor Franz Josef, and exclusion from the new German empire unified by Bismarck. The dual monarchy established a common defence, foreign and economic policy, but retained two separate parliaments.

Another period of prosperity followed and Vienna, in particular, flourished. The situation changed in 1914 when the emperor's nephew, Archduke Franz Ferdinand, was assassinated in Sarajevo on 28 June. A month later, Austria-Hungary declared war on Serbia and WWI began.

Post Habsburgs

Franz Josef died in 1916. His successor abdicated at the conclusion of the war in 1918 and the Republic of Austria was created on 12 November. In 1919 the new, shrunken state was forced to recognise the independent states of Czechoslovakia, Poland, Hungary and Yugoslavia which, along with Romania and Bulgaria, had previously been largely under the control of the Habsburgs. The loss of so much land caused severe economic difficulties and political and social unrest.

More problems were created by the rise of Germany's Nazis, who tried to start a civil war in Austria and succeeded in killing Chancellor Dolfuss. Hitler manipulated the new chancellor to increase the power of the National Socialists in Austria, and was so successful that German troops met little resistance when they invaded Austria in 1938 and incorporated it into the German Reich. A national referendum in April of that year supported the Anschluss (annexation).

Austria was bombed heavily in WWII, and in 1945 the victorious Allies restored Austria to its 1937 frontiers. Allied troops from the USA, UK, Soviet Union and France remained in the country and divided it into four zones. Vienna, in the Soviet zone, was also divided into four zones. Fortunately there was free movement between zones, which allowed Vienna to escape the fate that eventually befell Berlin. The ratification of the Austrian State Treaty and the withdrawal of the occupying powers was not completed until 1955, when Austria proclaimed its neutrality and agreed not to confederate with Germany.

Since WWII, Austria has worked hard to overcome economic difficulties. It established a free-trade treaty with the European Union (EU; then known as the EC) in 1972, and full membership was applied for in July 1989. Terms of membership were agreed early in 1994, and the Austrian people endorsed Austria's entry in a referendum on 12 June 1994; a resounding 66.4% were in favour. Austria became part of the union on 1 January 1995.

AUSTRIA

AUSTRIA

GEOGRAPHY & ECOLOGY

Austria occupies an area of 83,855 sq km, extending for 560 km from west to east, and 280 km from north to south. Two-thirds of the country is mountainous, with three chains running west to east. The Northern Limestone Alps reach nearly 3000 metres. They are separated from the High or Central Alps, which form the highest peaks in Austria, by the valley of the River Inn. Many of the ridges in the Central Alps are topped by glaciers and most of the peaks are above 3000 metres, making north-south travel difficult. The Grossglockner is the highest peak at 3797 metres. The Southern Limestone Alps form a natural barrier along the border with Italy.

The most fertile land is in the Danube Valley. Cultivation is intensive and 90% of Austria's food is home-grown. North of Linz is an area of forested hills; the only other relatively flat area is south-east of Graz.

Austria is highly environmentally conscious. Recycling is enforced by law, and flora and fauna are protected in Hohe Tauern, Europe's largest national park.

GOVERNMENT & POLITICS

The head of state is the president, who is chosen by the electorate for a six-year term. Austria's international image suffered following the election in 1986 of President Kurt Waldheim, who, it was revealed, served in a German Wehrmacht unit that was implicated in WWII war crimes. In 1992 Waldheim was succeeded by Thomas Klestil, who, like Waldheim, was a candidate of the right-wing Austrian People's Party (ÖVP).

The country is divided into nine federal provinces (Bundesländer), each of which has its own head of government (Landeshauptmann) and provincial assembly (Landtag). Each provincial assembly has a degree of autonomy over local issues and elects representatives to the Federal Council (Bundesrat), the upper house of the national legislative body. The lower house, the National Council (Nationalrat), is elected every four years by voters over the age of 18.

The chancellor, appointed by the president, is the head of the federal government and the most influential political figure. Franz Vranitzky has been chancellor since 1986.

The 1970s saw the dominance of the Social-ist Party, now called the Social Democrats (SPÖ). In the 1990 election, the SPÖ formed a ruling coalition with the ÖVP. This coalition retained power in the October 1994 general election.

ECONOMY

Austria is poor in natural resources. Deposits of oil and natural gas are supplemented by hydroelectric power and imported coal. Agriculture and forestry employ 5% of the population. The economy is bolstered by a large contingent of foreign labour, particularly from Eastern Europe. Austria generally has a trade deficit in visible earnings, which is offset by income from tourism. The main exports are machinery, metallurgical products and textiles. The country's wide-ranging welfare services include free education and medicine (for locals), good pensions and a generous housing policy. A continuing privatisation programme has bitten into Austria's large nationalised sector. In mid-1996, unemployment was under 4% and inflation under 2%.

POPULATION & PEOPLE

Austria has a population of 7.9 million; Vienna has the highest city population with 1.54 million people, followed by Graz (243,000), Linz (203,000), Salzburg (144,000), and Innsbruck (118,000). On average, there are 94 inhabitants per sq km. Native Austrians are mostly of Germanic origin.

ARTS

Austria is renowned for its musical heritage. Composers throughout Europe were drawn to Austria in the 18th and 19th centuries by the willingness of the Habsburgs to patronise music. The various forms of classical music – symphony, concerto, sonata, opera and operetta – were developed and explored in Austria by the most eminent exponents of the day. The waltz originated in Vienna in the 19th century and was perfected as a musical genre by Johann Strauss senior and junior. The musical tradition continued in the 20th century with the innovative work of Arnold Schönberg. Today, Austrian orchestras have a worldwide reputation, and important annual musical festivals are held in Vienna, Salzburg and Graz.

Architecture is another important part of Austria's cultural heritage. The Gothic style was popular in the 14th, 15th and 16th centuries. The next major stylistic influence was baroque. Learning from the Italian model, Fischer von Erlach developed a national style called Austrian baroque; examples in Vienna are the National Library and the Church of St Charles.

CULTURE

Traditional costumes are still worn in rural areas of Tirol, but you're more likely to see local costumes during celebrations and processions. Typical dress for men is shorts with wide braces, and jackets without collars or lapels. The best known form of dress for women is the Dirndl: pleated skirt, apron, and white, pleated corsage with full sleeves.

Many festivals act out ancient traditions, such as welcoming the spring with painted masks and the ringing of bells. The departure of herders and cattle to high alpine pastures in early summer and their return in autumn are the cause of much jollity in village life.

It is customary to greet people, even shop assistants, with the salute *Grüss Gott*. Austrians tend to dress up when going to the opera or theatre; jeans and trainers may be tolerated, but they won't be appreciated.

RELIGION

Roman Catholicism is embraced by 80% of the population; most of the remainder are Protestants, who are concentrated in Burgenland and Carinthia, or non-denominational. Religion plays an important part in the lives of many Austrians. It is not unusual to see small, roadside shrines decorated with fresh flowers.

LANGUAGE

Austrians speak German, although in the eastern province of Burgenland about 25,000 people speak Croatian, and in the southern province of Carinthia about 20,000 people speak Slovene.

English is widely understood in the main cities and tourist resorts. In smaller towns, hotel and railway staff usually know some English, but don't bank on it.

Knowledge of some German phrases would be an asset and would be appreciated by locals. See the Language Guide at the back of the book for pronunciation guidelines and useful words and phrases.

Facts for the Visitor

PLANNING

Climate & When to Go

Average rainfall is 71 cm per year. Maximum temperatures in Vienna are: January 1°C, April 15°C, July 25°C and October 14°C. Minimum temperatures are lower by about 10°C (summer) to 4°C (winter). Salzburg and Innsbruck match the maximum temperature of Vienna, but average minimum temperatures are a couple of degrees lower. Some people find the *Föhn*, a hot, dry wind which sweeps down from the mountains, rather uncomfortable. Summer sightseeing and winter sports make Austria a year-round destination, but the high season is in July and August and (in ski resorts) Christmas to late February.

What to Bring

Pack warm clothing for nights at high altitude. Sheets are usually included in hostel prices; occasionally you can save the 'sheet charge' if you have your own.

Books & Maps

Lonely Planet has published *Austria – a travel survival kit* and *Vienna city guide*. *Off the Beaten Track 'Austria'* (various authors) concentrates on less well-known regions. The Insight Guides to Austria and Vienna are good for background information. *The Xenophobe's Guide to the Austrians* by Louis James is informative and amusing. Graham Greene's famous spy story, *The Third Man*, and John Irving's *Setting Free the Bears* are both set in Austria.

Freytag & Berndt of Vienna publishes good maps in varying scales. Its 1:100,000 series and 1:50,000 blue series are popular with hikers. Extremely detailed maps are produced by the Austrian Alpine Club.

Online Services

On the Internet, the Austrian National Tourist Office is at: http://austria-info.at/

SUGGESTED ITINERARIES

Depending on the length of your stay, you might want to see and do the following things:

Two days
Vienna – see the central sights and visit the Opera and a few *Heurigen* (wine taverns).
One week
Spend four days in Vienna, two days in Salzburg and one day visiting the Salzkammergut lakes.
Two weeks
Spend five days in Vienna, three days in Salzburg (with a day trip to the Werfen ice caves and fortress), two days at the Salzkammergut lakes, two days in Innsbruck and two days at a ski resort.
One month
Visit the same places as the two-week scenario at a more leisurely pace, and add a tour of the south, taking in Graz, Klagenfurt and Lienz.
Two months
Visit all the places mentioned in this chapter.

HIGHLIGHTS

Vienna is the Habsburgs' legacy to the world, offering awe-inspiring public buildings, art treasures culled from the old empire, and music, music and more music – don't miss a trip to the opera. Salzburg is another shrine to music, and its baroque skyline is a breathtaking sight. A cruise on the not-quite-blue Danube is a must. Visits to the distinctive, provincial capitals of Innsbruck and Graz will be rewarded with interesting sights. Away from the cities, there are endless mountain views and hikes to enjoy. For skiing and glitz, head for Kitzbühel or Lech; for a less elitist ambience, try St Anton.

TOURIST OFFICES
Local Tourist Offices

Local tourist offices (called *Kurverein* or *Verkehrsamt*) are efficient and helpful, and can be found in all towns and villages of touristic interest. At least one of the staff will speak English. Most offices have a room-finding service, often without commission. Maps are always available and usually free. Each region has a provincial tourist board.

Tourist Offices Abroad

Austrian National Tourist Office (ANTO) branches abroad include:

Australia
1st floor, 36 Carrington St, Sydney, NSW 2000 (☎ 02-9299 3621; fax 9299 3808)

Canada
2 Bloor St East, suite 3330, Toronto, Ont M4W 1A8 (☎ 416-967 3381; fax 967 4101)
UK
30 St George St, London W1R OAL (☎ 0171-629 0461; fax 730 4568)
USA
500 Fifth Ave, suite 2009-2022, New York, NY 10108-1142 (☎ 212-944 6880)

There are also tourist offices in Los Angeles, Milan, Munich, Paris, Rome and Zürich. New Zealanders can get information from the Austrian consulate in Wellington (see the Austrian Embassies section).

VISAS & EMBASSIES

Visas are not required for EU, US, Canadian, Australian or New Zealand citizens. Visitors may stay a maximum of three months (six months for Japanese). There are no time limits for EU and Swiss nationals, but they should register with the police before taking up residency. Some Third World and Arab nationals require a visa.

Austrian Embassies Abroad

Australia
12 Talbot St, Forrest, Canberra, ACT 2603 (☎ 06-295 1376; fax 239 6751)
Canada
445 Wilbrod St, Ottawa, Ont KIN 6M7 (☎ 613-789 1444; fax 789 3431)
New Zealand
Austrian Consulate, 22-4 Garrett St, Wellington (☎ 04-801 9709; fax 385 4642) – does not issue visas or passports; contact the Australian office for these services
UK
18 Belgrave Mews West, London SW1 8HU (☎ 0171-235 3731; fax 235 8025)
USA
3524 International Court NW, Washington, DC 20008 (☎ 202-895 6700; fax 895 6750)

Foreign Embassies in Austria

The following is a list of foreign consulates and embassies in Vienna. Note that there are also foreign consulates in Salzburg and Innsbruck; see those sections for details.

Australia
4 Mattiellistrasse 2-4 (☎ 0222-512 85 80)
Canada
1 Laurenzerberg 2 (☎ 0222-531 38 3000)
Czech Republic
14 Penzingerstrasse 11-13 (☎ 0222-894 37 41)

Germany
   3 Metternichgasse 3 (☎ 0222-711 540)
Hungary
   1 Bankgasse 4-6 (☎ 0222-533 26 31)
Italy
   3 Rennweg 3 (☎ 0222-712 51 210)
New Zealand
   Consulate is at 19 Springsiedelgasse 28 (☎ 0222-318 85 05). The embassy (☎ 0228-22 80 70) is in Bonn, Germany
Slovakia
   19 Armbrustergasse 24 (☎ 0222-318 90 55)
Switzerland
   3 Prinz Eugen Strasse 7 (☎ 0222-795 050)
UK
   3 Jauresgasse 12 (☎ 0222-713 15 75)
USA
   9 Boltzmanngasse 16 (☎ 0222-313 39)

CUSTOMS

People aged 17 or over can bring 200 cigarettes (or 50 cigars or 250 grams of tobacco), two litres of wine and one litre of spirits. There's no set limit on these goods for personal use if bought duty-paid in another EU country.

MONEY
Currency

The Austrian Schilling (AS, or *ÖS* in German) is divided into 100 Groschen. There are coins to the value of one, five, 10, 25, 50, 100 and 500 Schillings, and for two, five, 10 and 50 Groschen. Banknotes come in denominations of AS20, AS50, AS100, AS500, AS1000 and AS5000. Visa and MasterCard credit cards are more widely accepted than American Express and Diners Club, though some places accept no cards at all.

Exchange rates and commission charges can vary between banks, so it pays to shop around. Changing cash attracts a negligible commission, but the exchange rate is usually between 1% and 4% lower than that offered for travellers' cheques. American Express offices have good rates and the lowest commission charges – AS15 to AS30 for cash and AS25 to AS40 for travellers' cheques; no commission applies on Amex's own travellers' cheques. The post office charges nothing for cash and AS80 for cheques. Train stations charge about AS20 for cash and AS64 minimum for cheques. Banks typically charge AS30 and AS95. Avoid changing a lot of low-value cheques because commission costs will be higher. Perhaps the most efficient way to manage your money in Austria is to get cash advances with a Visa card, Eurocard or MasterCard; there are numerous Bankomat machines offering this service, even in small villages.

A telegraphic transfer of funds is easily arranged, but the receiving bank will charge a small fee. There's no charge at the Austrian end to receive an American Express Moneygram.

Exchange Rates

Australia	A$1	=	AS8.14
Canada	C$1	=	AS7.57
Germany	DM1	=	AS7.02
France	1FF	=	AS2.07
Japan	¥100	=	AS9.60
New Zealand	NZ$1	=	AS7.24
South Africa	Sfr1	=	AS8.60
United Kingdom	UK£1	=	AS16.17
United States	US$1	=	AS10.38

Costs

Expenses are a little above average for Western Europe, and prices are highest in big cities and ski resorts. Budget travellers can get by on AS300 to AS350 a day, after rail-card costs; double this if you want to avoid self-catering or staying in hostels. Prices are fixed, so bargaining for goods is not generally an option.

Tipping

It is customary to tip an extra 5% to 10% in restaurants (pay the server direct, don't leave it on the table); taxi drivers will expect tips of 10%.

Consumer Taxes

Ice cream and hot and cold drinks are expensive because they're subject to a refreshment tax on top of the inevitable value-added tax (*Mehrwertsteuer; MWST*). Prices are always displayed inclusive of all taxes.

For purchases over AS1000, non-EU residents can reclaim the MWST, either upon leaving Austria or afterwards. First ensure the shop has the relevant forms, as they must be filled out at the time of purchase. Present the documentation to customs on departure for checking and stamping. The airports at Vienna, Salzburg, Innsbruck, Linz and Graz have counters for instant refunds, as do some land crossings, or you can reclaim by post.

AUSTRIA

POST & COMMUNICATIONS

Post office hours vary: typical hours are Monday to Friday from 8 am to noon and 2 to 6 pm (money exchange to 5 pm), and Saturday from 8 to 11 am, but a few main post offices in big cities are open 24 hours. Stamps are also available in tobacco (*Tabak*) shops.

Postcards and letters within Austria cost AS5.50 and AS6 respectively. To other countries in Europe, they cost AS6 and AS7; elsewhere the cost is AS7 and AS10. Sending by airmail (*Flugpost*) outside Europe incurs a surcharge.

Poste restante is *Postlagernde Briefe* in German. Mail can be sent care of any post office and is held for a month (address it to 'Postamt', followed by the postcode); a passport must be shown to collect mail. American Express will also hold mail for 30 days for customers who have its card or cheques.

Telephone calls are expensive, although just AS1 will get you connected. Calls are around 33% cheaper on weekends and between 6 pm and 8 am on weekdays. International direct dialling is nearly always possible, otherwise dial ☎ 09 for the operator.

Post offices invariably have telephones. Be wary of using telephones in hotels, because they can cost several times as much as public pay phones. You can save money and avoid messing around with change by buying a phonecard (*Telefon-Wertkarte*). For AS48 you get AS50 worth of calls, and for AS95 and AS190 you gain AS5 and AS10 worth of free calls respectively. To send a fax via the post office costs AS12 plus the call charge.

Note: The Austrian telephone system is being upgraded; many numbers have already changed, others may change in the near future. When dialling Viennese numbers from outside Austria, dial ☎ 1 instead of the normal ☎ 0222 code.

NEWSPAPERS

English-language newspapers are widely available for AS25 to AS35.

RADIO & TV

Blue Danube Radio is a news and music station, mostly in English, with news on the half-hour. Find it round about 100 FM (103.8 FM in Vienna). Austria has only two national TV channels, but many hotels have multi-language cable TV.

PHOTOGRAPHY & VIDEO

Niedermeyer and Foto Nettig are the cheapest stores for buying film; a 36 exposure roll costs AS50 for Kodak Gold 100 and AS129 for Kodachrome 64. Note that slide film usually *excludes* mounting, and sometimes processing too. Austria uses the PAL video system.

TIME

Austrian time is GMT/UTC plus one hour. If it's noon in Vienna it's 4 am in San Francisco, 7 am in New York and Toronto, 10 pm in Sydney and midnight in Auckland. Clocks go forward one hour on the last Saturday in March, and back an hour on the last Saturday in September.

ELECTRICITY

The current used is 220 V, 50 Hz, and the socket used is the round two-pin variety.

WEIGHTS & MEASURES

The metric system is used. Like other Continental Europeans, Austrians indicate decimals with commas and thousands with points.

LAUNDRY

Look out for a *Wäscherei* for self-service or service washes. The minimum charge is around AS100 to wash and dry a load. Many hostels have cheaper laundry facilities.

TOILETS

There's no shortage of public toilets, though cubicles may have a charge of up to AS5.

HEALTH

No inoculations are required for entry, but consider getting an encephalitis immunisation (against tick bites) if you intend doing lots of hiking in forests. There is a charge for hospital treatment and doctor consultations, so private medical insurance is advised. EU nationals can get free emergency treatment; enquire before leaving home about documentation required. Chemist shops (*Apotheken*) operate an out-of-hours service in rotation.

WOMEN TRAVELLERS

Women should experience no special problems. Physical violations and verbal harassment are less common than in many other countries.

Vienna has a Rape Crisis Hotline: ☎ 0222-408 70 66.

GAY & LESBIAN TRAVELLERS
Public attitudes to homosexuality are less tolerant than in most other European countries, except perhaps in Vienna. A good information centre in Vienna is Rosa Lila (☎ 0222-586 8150), 6 Linke Wienziele 102. The age of consent for gay men is 18; for everyone else it's 14.

DISABLED TRAVELLERS
Many sights and venues have wheelchair ramps. Local tourist offices usually have good information for the disabled; the Vienna office, for example, has a free 90-page booklet in English. Car drivers have free, unlimited parking in blue zones with the international disabled sticker.

DANGERS & ANNOYANCES
Dial ☎ 133 for the police, ☎ 144 for an ambulance, or ☎ 122 in the event of a fire. Take care in the mountains: helicopter rescue is expensive unless you are covered by insurance (that's assuming they find you in the first place). Austrian train stations are a habitual haunt of drunks and dropouts, who can be annoying and occasionally intimidating.

BUSINESS HOURS
Shops are open Monday to Friday from 8 am to 6.30 pm, and from 8 am to 1 pm on Saturday (until 5 pm on the first Saturday in the month). They generally close for up to two hours at noon, except in big cities, and sometimes on Wednesday afternoon too. Banking hours can vary but are commonly Monday to Friday from 9 am to 12.30 pm and 1.30 to 3 pm, with late closing on Thursday.

PUBLIC HOLIDAYS & SPECIAL EVENTS
Public holidays are 1 and 6 January, Easter Monday, 1 May, Ascension Day, Whit Monday, Corpus Christi, 15 August, 26 October, 1 November, and 8, 25 and 26 December.

Numerous events take place at a local level throughout the year, so it's worth checking with the tourist office. ANTO compiles an updated list of annual and one-off events. Vienna and Salzburg have almost continuous music festivals (see their Special Events

heading). Linz has the Bruckner Festival in September.

There are trade fairs in Vienna, Innsbruck and Graz in September. Religious holidays provide an opportunity to stage colourful processions. Look out for *Fasching* (Shrovetide carnival) week in early February, maypoles on 1 May, midsummer night's celebrations on 21 June, the autumn cattle roundup at the end of October, much flag-waving on national day on 26 October and St Nicholas Day parades on 5 and 6 December.

ACTIVITIES
Skiing
Austria has world-renowned skiing areas, particularly in Vorarlberg and Tirol. There's also skiing in Salzburg province, Upper Austria and Carinthia, where prices can be lower. Equipment can always be hired at resorts.

Ski coupons for ski lifts can sometimes be bought, but usually there are general passes available for complete or partial days. For one day, count on spending AS250 to AS450 for a ski pass, AS290 for downhill rental and AS160 for cross-country rental; rates drop for multiple days. The skiing season starts in December and lasts well into April at higher altitude resorts. Year-round skiing is possible at the Stubai Glacier near Innsbruck.

Hiking & Mountaineering
Walking and climbing are popular with visitors and Austrians alike. Mountain paths are marked with direction indicators, and most tourist offices have maps of hiking routes. There are 10 long-distance, national hiking routes, and three European routes pass through Austria. Options include the northern alpine route from Lake Constance to Vienna, via Dachstein, or the central route from Feldkirch to Hainburger Pforte, via Hohe Tauern.

Mountaineering should not be undertaken without proper equipment and some previous experience. Tirol province has many mountain guides and mountaineering schools; these are listed in the *Mountains* booklet from the tourist office. The Austrian Alpine Club (Österreichischer Alpenverein, ÖAV; ☎ 0512-58 78 28), Wilhelm-Greil-Strasse 15, A-6010 Innsbruck, has touring programmes, and also maintains alpine huts. These are situated between 900 and 2700 metres in hill-walking regions; they're inexpensive and often have meals or cooking facilities. Members of the club take priority but anyone can stay.

Spa Resorts

There are spa resorts throughout the country. They are identifiable by the prefix *Bad* (Bath); eg Bad Ischl. Long, leisurely walks and much wallowing in hot springs are typical ingredients of these salubrious locations.

WORK

EU nationals can work in Austria without a work permit. Everyone else must obtain in advance a work permit and (except for seasonal work) a residency permit. In ski resorts, where there are often vacancies for jobs with unsociable hours, employers may be prepared to bend the rules. Otherwise, you may be able to find casual work in return for free board and lodging and pocket money. Likely opportunities are in snow clearing, chalet cleaning, restaurants and ski-equipment shops.

ACCOMMODATION

Reservations are recommended in July and August and at the peak times of Christmas and Easter. Reservations are binding on either side and compensation may be claimed if you do not take a reserved room or if a reserved room is unavailable.

A cheap and widely available option is to take a room in a private house (AS150 to AS250 per person). Look out for *Zimmer frei* (room(s) available) signs. See Hiking & Mountaineering for information on alpine huts. Tourist offices can supply listings of all types of accommodation, and often make reservations. Accommodation sometimes costs more for a single night's stay. Prices are lower out of season. Assume breakfast is *included* in places listed in this chapter, unless otherwise stated.

In many resorts (rarely in towns) a guest card is issued to people who stay overnight (a three nights' minimum sometimes applies). They offer useful discounts and are well worth having. Check with the tourist office if you're not offered one at your resort accommodation. Guest cards are funded by a resort tax of around AS10 to AS20 per night, paid to the accommodation. Prices quoted in accommodation lists generally include this tax.

Camping

There are over 400 camping grounds, but most close in the winter. They charge around AS35 to AS65 per person, plus about the same again for a tent and a car. Free camping in camper vans is OK (in tents it's illegal), except in urban and protected rural areas, as long as you don't set up camping equipment outside the van. The Austrian Camping Club (Österreichischer Camping Club; ☎ 0222-711 99 1272), is at Schubertring 1-3, A-1010 Vienna.

Hostels

In Austria there is an excellent network of HI-affiliated hostels (*Jugendherbergen*).

Membership cards are always required, except in a few private hostels. Nonmembers pay a surcharge of AS40 per night for a guest card; after six nights, the guest card counts as a full membership card. Most hostels will accept reservations by telephone, and 20 Austrian hostels are part of the worldwide computer reservations system. Hostel prices are around AS110 to AS170. Austria has two hostel associations but either can give information on hostels. Contact the Österreichischer Jugendherbergswerk (☎ 0222-533 18 33), 1 Helfersdorferstrasse 4, Vienna.

Hotels & Pensions

With very few exceptions, rooms are clean and adequately appointed. Expect to pay from AS280/500 for a single/double. In low-budget accommodation, a room with a private shower may mean a room with a shower cubicle rather than a proper *en suite* bathroom. Prices in major cities are significantly higher than in rural areas, particularly in Vienna. A small country inn (*Gasthaus*) or a guesthouse (*Pension*) tends to be more intimate than a hotel. Self-catering chalets or apartments are common in ski resorts.

FOOD

The main meal is taken at midday. Most restaurants have a set meal or menu of the day (*Tagesteller* or *Tagesmenu*) which gives the best value for money. The cheapest deal around is in university restaurants (*mensas*); these are only mentioned in the text if they are open to all. Wine taverns are fairly cheap places to eat, and some food shops have tables for customers to eat on the premises. A McDonald's awaits in every town, but more authentically Austrian sausage stands (*Würstel Stand*) are also common.

Soups are good, often with dumplings (*Knödel*) and pasta added. *Wiener Schnitzel* is a veal or pork cutlet coated in breadcrumbs. Chicken *Huhn* is also popular. Paprika is used to flavour several dishes including *Gulasch* (beef stew). Look out for regional dishes such as *Tiroler Bauernschmaus*, a selection of meats served with sauerkraut, potatoes and dumplings. Austrians eat a lot of meat; vegetarians will have a fairly tough time finding suitable or varied dishes.

Famous desserts include the *Strudel* (baked dough filled with a variety of fruits) and *Salzburger Nockerl* (an egg, flour and sugar pudding); pancakes are also popular.

Hofer is the cheapest of the supermarket chains.

DRINKS
Nonalcoholic Drinks
Tea and coffee are expensive, but bottled water isn't and tap water is fine to drink anyway. Coffee houses are an established part of Austrian life, particularly in Vienna. Strong Turkish coffee is popular. Linger over a cup (from AS20) and read the free newspapers.

Alcohol
Eastern Austria specialises in producing white wines. Heuriger wine is the year's new vintage. It's avidly consumed, even (in autumn) when still semi-fermented (called *Sturm*). Austria is famous for its lager beer; some well-known brands include Gösser, Schwechater, Stiegl and Zipfer. Also try *Weizenbier* (wheat beer). Beer is usually served by the half-litre or third of a litre; in eastern Austria, these are respectively called a *Krügerl* and a *Seidel*.

ENTERTAINMENT
Late opening is common in the cities, and in Vienna you can party all night long. It isn't hard to find bars or taverns featuring traditional or rock music.

In cinemas (cheaper on Monday) some films are dubbed, but look for *OF* meaning *Original Fassung* (original-language production) or *OmU* meaning *Original mit Untertiteln* (original language with subtitles).

The main season for opera, theatre and concerts is September to June. Cheap, standing-room tickets are often available shortly before performances begin and they represent excellent value.

Gamblers can indulge at a dozen casinos around the country, including in Vienna, Graz, Linz and Salzburg. Admission is free. To gamble, you will pay AS260 for an initial AS300-worth of chips. Smart dress is required; opening hours are typically 3 pm to midnight or later.

THINGS TO BUY
Local crafts such as textiles, pottery, painted glassware, woodcarving and wrought-iron work make popular souvenirs.

Getting There & Away

AIR
The airports at Vienna, Linz, Graz, Salzburg, Innsbruck and Klagenfurt all receive international flights. Vienna is the busiest airport, with several daily, nonstop flights to major transport hubs such as Amsterdam, Berlin, Frankfurt, London, Paris and Zürich.

LAND
Bus
Buses depart London's Victoria Station three times a week (daily in summer), arriving in Vienna 23 hours later (UK£115 return). See the Vienna Getting There & Away section for services to Eastern Europe.

Train
Austria has excellent rail connections to all important destinations. Vienna is the main hub (see its Getting There & Away section for details). Salzburg has at least hourly trains to Munich (AS280) with onward connections north. Express services to Italy go via Innsbruck or Villach; trains to Slovenia are routed through Graz.

Reserving train seats in 2nd class within Austria (either on national IC or international EC trains) costs AS30; in 1st class, IC costs AS30, and EC AS50. Supplements sometimes apply on international trains.

Car & Motorcycle

There are numerous entry points from the Czech Republic, Germany, Hungary, Italy, Slovakia, Slovenia, and Switzerland. Main border crossings are open 24 hours a day.

RIVER

Steamers and hydrofoils operate along the Danube in the summer. See the Vienna and Danube Valley sections for details.

LEAVING AUSTRIA

There is no departure tax to pay at the airport, as all taxes are automatically included in the ticket price.

Getting Around

AIR

Vienna has several flights a day to Graz, Klagenfurt and Innsbruck, and at least two a day to Salzburg and Linz. The main national carrier is Austrian Airlines; its subsidiary, Tyrolean Airlines, has nonstop flights between most domestic airports. Schedules change half-yearly.

BUS

Buses are yellow or orange, respectively run by the post office or Austrian Railways. Either way, they're called 'Bundesbus', which is the term used throughout this chapter. Some rail routes are duplicated by buses, but buses generally operate in the more inaccessible mountainous regions. Buses are clean, efficient and on time. Advance reservations are possible, but sometimes you can only buy tickets from the drivers. Fares work out at around AS140 per 100 km. For Bundesbus information, a national local-rate number is ☎ 0660-51 88.

TRAIN

Trains are efficient and frequent. The state network covers the whole country, and is supplemented by a few private lines. Eurail and Inter-Rail passes are valid on the former; enquire before embarking on the latter. Many stations have information centres where the staff speak English. Tickets can be purchased on the train, but they cost AS30 extra. In this chapter, fares quoted are for 2nd class.

Trains are expensive (eg AS156 for 100 km, AS276 for 200 km) but the cost can be reduced by special passes. The *Bundes-Netzkarte*, a one-month pass valid on all state railways, rack railways and Wolfgangsee ferries, costs AS4300. The *Österreich Puzzle* is not particularly puzzling – it divides the country into four zones – north, south, east and west. You can buy a pass for each zone for AS1090 (under 26-year-olds AS660) giving you four days unlimited travel in a 10-day period. Areas overlap, so you can cover the whole country without needing to buy the east zone. The Kilometerbank pass allows up to six people to travel on journeys over 51 km; the cost is AS2400 for 2000 km, AS3540 for 3000 km, and AS5850 for 5000 km.

The German words *Bahnhof* (train station) and *Hauptbahnhof* (main train station) have been used in this chapter. Ordinary single/return tickets (over 71 km) are valid for four days/two months, and you can break your journey as many times as you like, but tell the conductor first. 'Spar' return tickets (journeys under 50 km) are cheaper than two singles. Reduced fares are sometimes available for those aged under 26: wave your passport and ask. In the larger towns, train information can be obtained by dialling ☎ 1717.

CAR & MOTORCYCLE

Austrians drive on the right. Roads are generally good, but sufficient respect should be given to difficult mountain routes. There are toll charges for some tunnels through the mountains. The tourist office has details of a few roads and passes which are closed in winter.

Give priority to vehicles coming from the right. On mountain roads, Bundesbuses always have priority, otherwise priority lies with uphill traffic. Drive in low gear on steep downhill stretches. The penalty for drink-driving (over 0.08% BAC) is a hefty on-the-spot fine and confiscation of your driving licence. Speed limits are 50 km/h in towns, 130 km/h on motorways and 100 km/h on other roads. Snow chains are highly recommended in winter. Many city streets have restricted parking (called blue zones); parking is free and unrestricted outside the specified times, which normally correspond to shopping hours. Parking is unrestricted on unmarked streets.

Cars can be transported by train: Vienna is linked by a daily motorail service to Feldkirch, Innsbruck, Salzburg and Villach. Motorcycles must have their headlights on during the day. The Austrian Automobile Club (Österreichischer Automobil, Motorrad und Touring Club, ÖAMTC; ☎ 0222-71 19 90) is at Schubertring 1-3, A-1010 Vienna. Dial ☎ 120 for emergency assistance.

Rental

Hertz, Avis, Budget and Europcar all have offices in main cities. Budget (☎ 07242-777 74) and Europcar (☎ 0222-799 61 76) have the best unlimited-km rates: from AS708 per day. Budget's weekend rates (noon Friday to 9 am Monday) are lower: from AS948. Local rental agencies often have cheaper rates; the local tourist office will be able to supply details.

BICYCLE

Bicycles can be hired from most train stations. The rate is AS100 per day, or AS50 with a train ticket valid for that day or for after 3 pm the previous day. There's a surcharge of AS40 to return bikes to a different station. Cycling is popular even though minor roads can be steep and have sharp bends. You can take your bike on slow trains (AS30 for a day ticket); fast trains will accept bikes only as registered luggage (AS80).

HITCHING

Hitching is patchy, but not too bad. Trucks are often the best bet, and can be enticed to stop at border posts, truck stops or truck parking stops (signposted as *Autohof*). Always display a sign showing your destination. It is illegal for minors under 16 to hitch in Burgenland, Upper Austria, Styria and Vorarlberg. Austria has only one *Mitfahrzentrale* hitching agency – see the Vienna section for details.

BOAT

Services along the Danube are slow, expensive, scenic excursions rather than functional transport. Nevertheless, a boat ride is definitely worth it if you like lounging on deck and having the scenery come to you rather than the other way round. The larger Salzkammergut lakes have ferry services.

LOCAL TRANSPORT

Buses, trams and underground railways are efficient and reliable. Most towns have an integrated system and offer excellent-value daily or 24-hour tickets (AS26 to AS50), which are available in advance from Tabak shops. Even single tickets can sometimes only be purchased in advance. On-the-spot fines apply to people caught travelling without tickets, though some locals are prepared to take the risk.

Taxis are metered, although all but unnecessary given the good public transport. If you need one, look around train stations and large hotels.

For a rundown on mountain transport, see the introductory Getting Around section in the Switzerland chapter.

ORGANISED TOURS

These vary from two-hour walks in city centres to all-inclusive packages at ski resorts. Enquire at tourist offices.

Vienna

The character of modern Vienna (Wien) owes much to its colourful political and cultural past. It proffers impressive architecture, world-renowned museums and an enviable musical tradition alongside characteristic Viennese institutions such as coffee houses and wine taverns. Vienna is not as staid as some would make out. You can party all night if you want to. The city that gave the waltz to the world has also pursued radical socialist policies through most of this century.

The Habsburgs settled in Vienna in 1278 and made it the capital of the Austrian empire. The city flourished under their strong leadership, despite being dragged into various European conflicts and withstanding attacks by the Turks in 1529 and 1683. Vienna's 'golden years' as the cultural centre of Europe were the 18th and 19th centuries. Musically, there was only one place to be during this period. Strauss, Mozart, Beethoven, Brahms and Schubert are only a few of the great composers who made Vienna their home. Anybody with an interest in the arts will love this city.

AUSTRIA

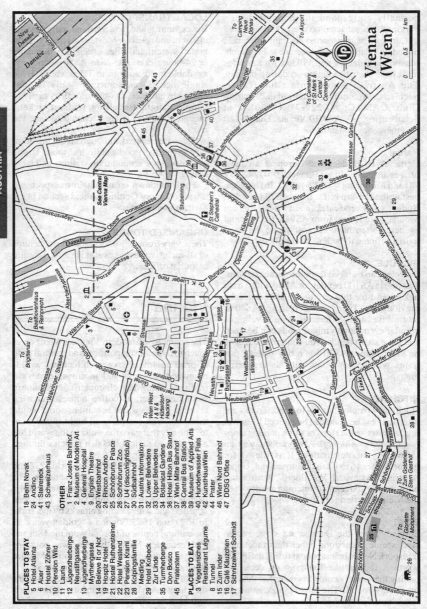

Vienna (Wien)

0   0.5   1 km

To Airport

To Camping Neue Donau

To Cemetery of St Mark & Central Cemetery

New Danube

Danube

Danube Canal

See Central Vienna Map

To Beethovenhaus & Heiligenstadt

To Brigittenau

St Stephen's Cathedral

To Wien West I & II & Hütteldorf Hacking

To Schloss Schönbrunner strasse

To Zum Goldenen Stern Gasthof

To Gloriette Monument

PLACES TO STAY
5 Hotel Atlanta
6 Auer
7 Hostel Zöhrer
10 Pension Wild
11 Lauria
12 Jugendherberge Neustiftgasse
13 Jugendherberge Myrthengasse
14 Believe It or Not
19 Hospiz Hotel
21 Hostel Ruthensteiner
22 Hotel Westend
26 Pension Kraml
28 Kolpingsfamilie Meidling
29 Hotel Kolbeck
31 Zur Linde
35 Turmherberge Don Bosco
45 Praterstern

PLACES TO EAT
3 Vegetarisches Restaurant Legume
8 Tunnel
15 Zum Inder
16 Café Käuzchen
17 Schnitzelwirt Schmidt

18 Beim Novak
24 Andino
41 Steirereck
43 Schweizerhaus

OTHER
1 Franz Josefs Bahnhof
2 Museum of Modern Art
4 General Hospital
9 English Theatre
20 Westbahnhof
23 Rincon Andino
25 Schönbrunn Palace
27 U4 (disco/nightclub)
30 Schönbrunn Zoo
32 Südbahnhof
33 Austria Information
34 Lower Belvedere
37 Upper Belvedere
36 Botanical Gardens
38 Hotel Hilton Bus Stand
38 Wien Mitte Bahnhof
38 Central Bus Station
40 Museum of Applied Arts
42 Hundertwasser Flats
44 KunstHausWien
46 Prater
46 Wien Nord Bahnhof
47 DDSG Office

Orientation

Many of the historic sights are in the old city, which is encircled by the Danube Canal (to the north-east) and a broad boulevard known as the Ring. The Ring changes its name along its sections, eg Opern Ring, Kärntner Ring etc. St Stephen's Cathedral is in the heart of the city and is the principal landmark. Most attractions in the centre are within walking distance of each other.

Take care when reading addresses. The number of a building within a street *follows* the street name. Any number *before* the street name denotes the district, of which there are 23. District 1 (the Innere Stadt) is the central region, mostly within the Ring. Generally speaking, the higher the district number, the further it is from the city centre. The middle two digits of postcodes always refer to the district, hence places with a postcode 1010 are in the first district, and 1230 means district 23.

The main train stations are Franz Josefs Bahnhof to the north, Westbahnhof to the west and Südbahnhof to the south; transferring between them is easy. The majority of hotels and pensions are to the west of the centre, roughly within a triangle bounded by Franz Josefs Bahnhof, Westbahnhof and Karlsplatz. The vicinity of the university, around Universitätsstrasse and Währinger Strasse, just north of Dr K Lueger Ring, is a good area for cheaper restaurants.

Information

Tourist Offices The main tourist office (☎ 513 88 92) is at 1 Kärntner Strasse 38. It is small and hectic, but there is extensive free literature on hand. The city map is excellent, as is the *Youth Scene* booklet, which despite the chummy style contains lots of hard information for young and old. The office is open daily from 9 am to 7 pm. There is a tourist office in the arrival hall of the airport, open daily from 8.30 am to 9 pm.

Information and room reservations are available in Westbahnhof, open daily from 6.15 am to 11 pm; Südbahnhof, open daily from 6.30 am to 10 pm (9 pm in winter); and the DDSG Blue Danube boat-landing stage, Reichsbrücke, open April to mid-October from 8 am to 5 pm (7 am to 9 pm May to September). Tourist offices at major road approaches to the city are sited for the convenience of car drivers. In the west, the office is at the A1 autobahn exit Wien-Auhof, open daily from 8 am to 10 pm (Easter to October), from 9 am to 7 pm (November) and from 10 am to 6 pm (December to Easter). The southern office is at the A2 exit Zentrum, Triesterstrasse, open daily from 9 am to 7 pm (Easter to June, and October) and 8 am to 10 pm (July to September). The office in the north-east is at Floridsdorfer Brücke/Donauinsel, open May to September from 9 am to 7 pm. All of these offices have a room-finding service, which is subject to around AS40 commission. Telephone and postal enquiries are best addressed to the Vienna Tourist Board (☎ 211 140; fax 216 84 92), Obere Augartenstrasse 40, A-1025 Wien. Tourist offices and hotels sell the Vienna Card (AS180), providing admission discounts and a free 72-hour travel pass.

The Austrian Information Office (☎ 587 20 00), 4 Margaretenstrasse 1, is open Monday to Friday from 10 am to 5 pm (6 pm Thursday). The Lower Austria Information Centre (☎ 533 31 14), 1 Heidenschuss 2, is open Monday to Friday from 8.30 am to 5.30 pm. Jugend-Info Wien (☎ 526 46 37), a youth information centre at 1 Dr Karl Renner Ring, Bellaria Passage, can get tickets for varied events at reduced rates for those aged between 14 and 26. It is open Monday to Friday from noon to 7 pm, and Saturday and school holidays from 10 am to 7 pm.

Money Banks are open Monday to Friday from 8 am to 3 pm, with late opening on Thursday until 5.30 pm; smaller branches close from 12.30 to 1.30 pm. Numerous Bankomat machines allow cash advances with Visa, Eurocard and MasterCard. Train stations have extended hours for exchanging money.

Post & Communications The main post office is at 1 Fleischmarkt 19. There are also post offices open 24 hours daily at Süd-bahnhof, Westbahnhof and Franz Josefs Bahnhof.

The telephone code for Vienna is ☎ 0222, or ☎1 if you're ringing from outside the country.

Travel Agencies American Express (☎ 515 40), 1 Kärntner Strasse 21-23, is open Monday to Friday from 9 am to 5.30 pm, and Saturday from 9.30 am to noon. The Österreichisches Komitee für Internationalen Studienaustausch (ÖKISTA: ☎ 401 480), 9 Garnisongasse 7, is a specialist in student and budget fares. It's open Monday to Friday from 9.30 am to 5.30 pm. There are other offices at 9 Türkenstrasse 4-6 and 4 Karlsgasse 3 (☎ 505 01 28).

Bookshops The British Bookshop (☎ 512 19 45), 1 Weihburggasse 24-6, has the most English-language titles; Shakespeare & Co Booksellers (☎ 535 50 53), 1 Sterngasse 2, also has second-hand books from around AS30. Freytag & Berndt (☎ 533 20 94), 1 Kohlmarkt 9, stocks a vast selection of maps. Reiseladen (☎ 513 75 77), 1 Dominikanerbastei 4, is a travel agent and bookshop with many Lonely Planet guides.

Medical & Emergency Services Dial ☎ 144 for an ambulance, ☎ 141 for medical emergencies and ☎ 133 for the police. For out-of-hours dental treatment call ☎ 512 20 78. The general hospital (☎ 404 00) is at 9 Währinger Gürtel 18-20.

Things to See
Walking is the best way to see the centre. Architectural riches confront you at nearly every corner, testimony to the power and wealth of the Habsburg dynasty. Ostentatious public buildings and statues line both sides of the Ring. Those that stand out include the neo-Gothic **Rathaus** (city hall), the Greek Revival-style Parliament (in particular the Athena statue), the 19th-century National Theatre and the baroque St Charles' Church. Carefully tended gardens and parks break up the brickwork.

Walking Tour From the tourist office, walk north up the pedestrian-only Kärntner Strasse, a walkway of plush shops, trees, café tables and street entertainers. It leads directly to Stephansplatz and the prime landmark of **St Stephen's Cathedral** (Stephansdom).

The latticework spire of this 13th-century Gothic masterpiece rises high above the city. Interior walls and pillars are decorated with fine statues; the stone pulpit is particularly striking. Take the lift up the north tower (AS40) or the stairs up the higher south tower (AS25) for an impressive view.

The internal organs of the Habsburgs reside in the catacombs (open daily, AS40). One of the privileges of being a Habsburg was to be dismembered and dispersed after death: their hearts are in the Augustinian Church, 1 Augustinerstrasse 3; the rest of their bits are in the Imperial Burial Vaults in the Church of the Capuchin Friars, 1 Neuer Markt.

From Stephansplatz, turn west down Graben, which is dominated by the knobbly outline of the Plague Column. Turn left into Kohlmarkt, which leads to the St Michael's Gateway of the **Hofburg** (Imperial Palace).

The Hofburg has been periodically enlarged since the 13th century, resulting in the current mixture of architectural styles. The Spanish Riding School office is to the left within the entrance (see the Entertainment section). Opposite are the **Imperial Apartments**, which cost AS70 to visit (students aged under 25 AS50). The apartments in Schönbrunn (see the following section) are more impressive. Walk south into the large courtyard, and take a left into the small Swiss Courtyard. Here you'll find the Royal Chapel, and the **Imperial Treasury** (Schatzkammer), which contains treasures and relics spanning 1000 years, including the crown jewels. Allow up to one hour to get round (entry AS60, students under 30 AS30; closed Tuesday).

Schönbrunn Palace The palace can be reached by U-Bahn No 4. Daily guided tours (in English) take in 40 of its 1440 rooms and cost AS140 (daily, open year round). Self-guided tours of 20 rooms are AS80. The interior is suitably majestic, with frescoed ceilings, crystal chandeliers and gilded ornaments. The pinnacle of finery is reached in the Great Gallery. Mozart played his first royal concert in the Mirror Room at the ripe age of six in the presence of Maria Theresa and her family. Extensive formal gardens are enlivened by several fountains. You can enjoy excellent views from the **Gloriette monument** on the hill (entry AS20, open May to October only). The attractive zoo (Tiergarten) is also worth a look (entry AS80).

Belvedere Palace This baroque palace is within walking distance of the Ring and has good views of the city. It contains the Austrian

Gallery, located in the two main buildings which flank the spacious gardens. Lower (Untere) Belvedere (entrance Rennweg 6A) contains some interesting baroque pieces, but the more important art collection is in Upper (Obere) Belvedere, and includes instantly recognisable works by Gustav Klimt, Egon Schiele and other Austrian artists from the 19th and 20th centuries (entrance Prinz Eugen Strasse 27). It is open Tuesday to Sunday from 10 am to 5 pm, entry for both is AS60, (students AS30).

Museum of Fine Arts This must-see museum, known as the Kunsthistorisches Museum, houses a huge collection of 16th and 17th-century paintings, ornaments and glassware, and Greek, Roman and Egyptian antiquities.

The huge extent of the Habsburg empire led to many important works of art being funnelled back to Vienna. Rubens was appointed to the service of a Habsburg governor in Brussels, so it's not surprising that the Kunsthistorisches has one of the world's best collections of his works. There is also an unrivalled collection of paintings by Peter Brueghel the Elder. Look out for Vermeer's *Allegory of Painting*, Cellini's stunning saltcellar, and the unbelievably lavish clocks from the 16th and 17th centuries. The composite paintings by Archimboldo in room No 29 predate modern surrealism by nearly 400 years.

The museum is open Tuesday to Sunday from 10 am to 6 pm, with the picture gallery closing at 9 pm on Thursday. Entry is AS45 (students AS30). Guided tours in English at 3 pm cost AS30 extra.

Secession Building This Art-Nouveau 'temple of art', built at 1 Friedrichstrasse 12 in 1898, bears a golden dome that looks like an enormous Ferrero Rocher chocolate wrapper (or a 'golden cabbage', according to some Viennese). The 1902 exhibition here featured the famous 34-metre-long *Beethoven Frieze* by Klimt, which has been restored and can be seen in the basement. The rest of the building is primarily devoted to contemporary art. 'Sometimes people just walk past the art, they think they're in empty rooms', the lady at the desk told me. You have been warned! It's open Tuesday to Friday from 10 am to 6 pm, and

Saturday and Sunday to 4 pm; entry costs AS60 (students AS30).

KunstHausWien This gallery at 3 Untere Weissgerberstrasse 13 looks like something out of a toyshop. It was designed by Friedensreich Hundertwasser to house his own works of art. It features coloured ceramics, uneven floors, irregular corners and grass on the roof. His vivid paintings are equally distinctive and there are some interesting models of other building projects. It is open daily from 10 am to 7 pm and costs AS80 to get in (students AS40), or AS120 (students AS80) including temporary exhibitions. Monday is half-price. When you're in the area, walk down the road to see a block of residential flats built by Hundertwasser on the corner of Löwengasse and Kegelgasse. It is now one of Vienna's most prestigious addresses.

Other Museums The **Museum of Natural History**, at 1 Maria Theresien Platz, is the architectural mirror image of the Fine Arts Museum. It holds temporary exhibitions and houses a collection of minerals, meteorites and an assortment of animal remains in jars. The museum is open daily except Tuesday; entry costs AS40 (students AS20). If you're going to Salzburg, the equivalent museum there is superior.

You can certainly overdose on art in Vienna. The **Albertina** may be closed until 1999 (except for a room of facsimiles; AS10), but other important collections are dotted around the city, notably in the **Museum of Modern Art**, 9 Fürstengasse 1, the **Museum of Applied Arts**, 1 Stubenring 5 and the **Academy of Fine Arts**, 1 Schillerplatz 3. The former homes of the great composers are also open to the public; some of these are municipal museums, which are free on Friday morning.

Cemeteries Beethoven, Schubert, Brahms and Schönberg have memorial tombs in the **Central Cemetery** at 11 Simmeringer Hauptstrasse 232-244. Mozart also has a monument here, but he was actually buried in an unmarked grave in the **Cemetery of St Mark**, 3 Leberstrasse 6-8 – nobody quite knows where. It was only many years after the true location had been forgotten that grave diggers

AUSTRIA

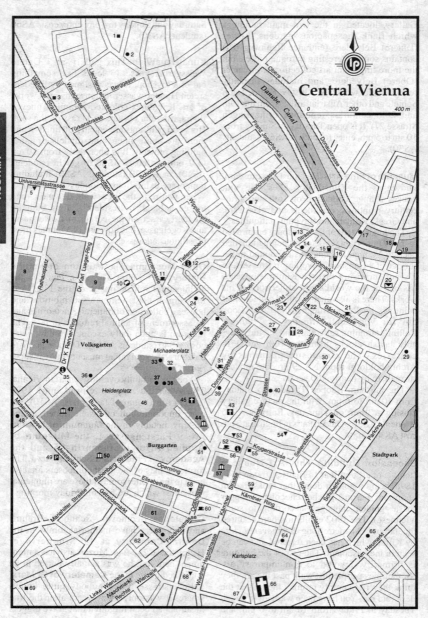

Central Vienna

0   200   400 m

PLACES TO STAY		4	Reisebuchladen	36	Volksgarten
1	Pension Falstaff		(Bookshop & Tourguide)	37	Royal Chapel
3	Hotel Am Schottenpoint	6	University	38	Imperial Treasury
7	Schweizer Pension	8	City Hall (Rathaus)	39	Dorotheum
	Solderer	9	National Theatre	40	American Express
25	Pension Nossek		(Burgtheater)	41	US Consulate
55	Pension Am Operneck	10	Hungarian Embassy	42	British Bookshop
62	Hotel-Pension	11	Café Central	43	Imperia Buria Vaultsè
	Schneider	12	Lower Austria	44	Albertina
69	Kolping-Gästehaus		Information Office	45	Augustinia Church
		14	Shakespeare & Co	46	Hofburg
PLACES TO EAT			Booksellers	47	Natural History
5	University Mensa	15	Roter Engel		Museum
13	China Restaurant	16	Krah Krah	48	Volkstheater
	Turandot	17	Marienbrücke	49	Parking Garage
22	Pizza Bizi	18	Schwedenbrücke	50	Museum of Fine Arts
23	Wrenkh	19	DDSG Canal Tour		(Kunsthistorisches
27	DO & CO Restaurant		Landing Stage		Museum)
30	La Creperie	20	Main Post Office	51	State Ticket Office
53	Rosenberger Markt	21	Alt Wien	52	Hotel Sacher Café
54	Music Academy Mensa	24	Esterházykeller	56	Main Tourist Office
58	Restaurant Smutny	26	Freytag & Berndt	57	State Opera
59	Restaurant Marché	28	St Stephen's Cathedral		(Staatsoper)
	Movenpick		(Stephansdom)	60	Café Museum
68	Technical University	29	Reiseladen	61	Academy of Fine Arts
	Mensa	31	Café Bräunerhof	63	Secession Building
		32	Spanish Riding School	64	Musikverein
OTHER		33	Imperial Apartments	65	Konzerthaus
2	International Theatre	34	Parliament	66	St Charles' Church
		35	Jugend-Info Wien	67	ÖKISTA

cobbled together a poignant memorial from a broken pillar and a discarded stone angel.

Naschmarkt The Naschmarkt is along 6 Linke Wienzeile, and is open Monday to Saturday from 8 am to 6 pm. It consists mainly of fruit, vegetable and meat stalls, but there are a few stalls selling clothing and curios as well. There is also an atmospheric flea market on Saturday, which is well worth a visit. Snack bars provide cheap, hot food.

Activities

Prater This large amusement park is dominated by the giant Ferris Wheel, built in 1897, which featured prominently in *The Third Man*. Rides in the park cost AS10 to AS45, but it is also a great place to just have a wander. As you walk, you're liable to bump into one of the colourful metal sculptures depicting humans caught up in strange hallucinogenic happenings. The park adjoins a complex of sports grounds and a large forested area ideal for rambling.

Wienerwald To the west of the city, the rolling hills and marked trails of the Vienna Woods are perfect for walkers; a brochure (*Wandern in der Stadt*) shows trails and how to get there and is available from the information office in the city hall (open Monday to Friday from 8 am to 6 pm). The Lower Austria Information office has a free map of routes further from the city.

Watersports In the north-east of the city, the Old Danube and the New Danube provide opportunities for swimming, sailing, boating and windsurfing. There are stretches with free swimming access, or bathing complexes like **Gänsehäufel** (open May to September) have swimming pools and charge AS50 for a full day, including a locker (AS40 after noon).

Special Events

The cycle of musical events is unceasing. Mozart features heavily, but all varieties of music get a look-in. The Vienna International Festival (from mid-May to mid-June) has a wide-ranging programme of the arts. Contact Wiener Festwochen (☎ 589 22 22), Lehárgasse

11, A-1060 Vienna, for details. Vienna's Summer of Music runs from mid-July to mid-September. In advance, contact Klangboden (☎ 4000 8410), Laudongasse 29, A-1080 Vienna. Tickets are available from early May at the box office, 1 Friedrich Schmidt Platz 1, open daily from 10 am to 6 pm. Reduced student tickets go on sale 10 minutes before the performance. At the end of June, look out for free rock, jazz and folk concerts in the Donauinselfest.

Vienna's traditional Christmas market takes place in front of the city hall between mid-November and 24 December. Other seasonal events include New Year concerts and gala balls (January and February), the Vienna Spring Marathon (March/April), Vienna trade fairs (March and September), a flower parade in the Prater (June) and the Schubert Festival (November). The tourist office does not sell tickets, but has full details.

Organised Tours

Several companies offer tours of the city and surrounding areas, including walking and cycling tours. An interesting tour is the Third Man Tour, which visits spots featured in the famous film, including the underground sewer. Reisebuchladen (☎ 317 33 84), a travel bookshop, gives an interesting tour of 'alternative' Vienna. DDSG Blue Danube conducts tours of the Danube Canal, which depart from Schwedenbrücke in the Ring; the tourist office has details. See also under Boat in the following Getting There & Away section.

Places to Stay – bottom end

Vienna can be a nightmare for backpackers. Prices are high and the budget places are often full, especially in the summer. Reserve ahead or at least use the telephone before you trek around everywhere. Tourist offices have lists of private rooms, as well as the useful *Camping* pamphlet which details hostels and camping grounds.

Private accommodation agencies can often find cheaper accommodation than the tourist office, though commission charges are higher. ÖKISTA (☎ 401 48), 9 Türkenstrasse 8, charges AS50 to find rooms for a minimum three nights. For longer stays, it charges a AS500 fee to find a room in a family house (from AS170 per night). The Mitwohnzentrale

(☎ 402 60 61), 8 Laudongasse 7, charges 24% of the rent to find good-value private rooms or apartments.

Camping Vienna has several camping grounds in the outer suburbs. *Wien West II* (☎ 914 23 14), is open all year except February. It costs AS62 per person and AS35 per tent, rising to AS68 and AS40 in July and August. In August, it opens a cheaper annex, *Wien West I*, at 14 Hüttelbergstrasse 40. To get there, take U4 or S45 to Hütteldorf, then bus No 152. *Camping Neue Donau* (☎ 220 93 10), 22 Am Kleehäufel, is open from the end of April to mid-September and costs AS60 per person and AS56 for a tent. Take the U1 to Kaisermühlen, then the No 91A bus.

Hostels No hostels invade the imperial elegance of the Ring. The nearest are two linked HI *Jugendherbergen*, at 7 Myrthengasse 7 (☎ 523 63 16) and round the corner at 7 Neustiftgasse 85 (☎ 523 74 62). Both are well run and have new facilities and knowledgeable staff. Enjoy the good showers, lockers and personal bedside light (sheer luxury!). Beds are AS155, lunch or dinner AS60 and laundry AS50 per load. Double rooms (bunk beds) are AS370. Curfew is at 1 am. You can check in for either hostel any time during the day at Myrthengasse; the Neustiftgasse hostel closes from 11.15 am (10.15 am Sunday) to 3.45 pm. Telephone reservations are accepted and strongly advised.

Believe it or Not (☎ 526 46 58), Apartment 14, 7 Myrthengasse 10, is a small private hostel. There's no clue on the main door that it's anything other than a private house. It has a friendly atmosphere, but one room has triple-level bunks and can get hot in summer. There's no breakfast; use the kitchen facilities instead. Beds are AS160 in summer or AS110 during winter, and you get your own key for 24-hour access.

Hostel Zöhrer (☎ 406 07 30), 8 Skodagasse 26, is a private hostel close to the Ring. Four to six-bed dorms are AS170 and doubles (bunk beds) are AS460 with private shower. There's a kitchen, courtyard and own-key entry; reception is open from 7.30 am to 10 pm. *Turmherberge Don Bosco* (☎ 713 14 94), 3 Lechnerstrasse 12, south-east of the Ring, is unrenovated but has a kitchen and the cheapest beds in town – AS70 without breakfast. Sheets are AS25. Reception is closed between noon and 5 pm, the hostel is closed from December to February.

Near Westbahnhof, *Hostel Ruthensteiner* (☎ 893 42 02), 15 Robert Hamerling Gasse 24, is open 24 hours. Ten-bed dorms are AS139 (own sheets needed). Basic singles/doubles (sheets supplied) are AS239/450. Breakfast costs AS25, but there's a kitchen and also a shady, rear courtyard. Non-HI members pay AS40 extra. *Kolpingsfamilie Meidling* (☎ 813 54 87), 12 Bendlgasse 10-12, is near the U6 stop, Niederhofstrasse, south of Westbahnhof. Beds are AS100 to AS145 in different-sized dorms. Non-HI members pay AS20 extra and don't get the guest stamp. Breakfast costs AS45 and sheets are AS65. Curfew is around 11 pm, though reception is open 24 hours.

There are two large HI hostels out in the suburbs. *Brigittenau* (☎ 332 82 940), 20 Friedrich Engels Platz 24 (take tram N north), has a 1 am curfew, though reception is open 24 hours. Huge dorms are AS120, alternatively two to four-bed rooms are AS155 per person. At 13 Schlossberggasse 8 (take the U4 west), *Hütteldorf-Hacking* (☎ 877 02 63), has 271 beds and charges AS149. Reception and the doors are open from 7 am to midnight.

Lauria (see Hotels & Pensions) has dorm beds.

Student Rooms These are available to tourists from 1 July to 30 September while students are on holiday. The cheapest is *Porzellaneum* (☎ 317 72 82), 9 Porzellangasse 30, which has singles/doubles for AS175 per person, without breakfast. Other *Studentenheime* to try, in ascending price order, are: (☎ 34 92 64), 19 Peter Jordan Strasse 29; (☎ 34 76 31) 19 Gymnasiumstrasse 85; (☎ 979 25 38), 14 Linzer Strasse 429; 8 Pfeilgasse 4-6 (☎ 408 34 45); and (☎ 514 84 48), 1 Johannesgasse 8.

Hotels & Pensions *Lauria* (☎ 52 22 555), Kaiserstrasse 77, in a residential building, has friendly staff, own-key entry, kitchen facilities (no breakfast), and thoughtful, homy touches. Hostel beds cost AS160, doubles AS530 (AS480 with bunks), triples AS700, quads AS850; fully-equipped apartments are also

available, but there may be a two-day minimum stay.

Hospiz Hotel (☎ 523 13 04), 7 Kenyongasse 15, is run by the YMCA (CVJM) but anyone can stay here. Simple singles/doubles are AS330/640 with shower or AS350/660 without. There are triples and quads (from AS900/1060), or it's AS180 for an extra mattress in the room. Reception is open from 8 am to 10 pm. There's no lift and lots of stairs.

Kolping-Gästehaus (☎ 587 56 31), 6 Gumpendorfer Strasse 39, has singles without shower for AS260, and doubles with shower for AS820, but it's a newish building with an institutional aura (long-term students stay here). *Auer* (☎ 406 21 21), 9 Lazarettgasse 3, is small and pleasant and feels more Viennese. Singles/doubles start from AS320/490 using hall shower, or doubles with a shower cubicle in the room are AS550.

Pension Wild (☎ 406 51 74), 8 Langegasse 10, is quieter than the name suggests and very close to the Ring. Singles/doubles start from AS450/590 and there are some triples/quads from AS960/1020. There are hall showers and kitchen facilities. The reception is staffed until 9 pm – ring the bell after that.

Hotel Westend (☎ 597 67 29), at 6 Fügergasse 3, close to Westbahnhof, has reasonable singles/doubles for AS330/590 in a nice building. Reception is open 24 hours. *Pension Kraml* (☎ 587 85 88) is nearby at 6 Brauergasse 5. It's small and friendly, and has singles/doubles for AS280/590 and large doubles with a private shower from AS780.

Pension Falstaff (☎ 317 91 27), 9 Müllnergasse 5, has singles/doubles for AS360/600 (AS30 charge to use the hall shower) or AS480/720 with private shower. Prices are around AS100 lower in winter. Fittings are ageing but adequate, and it's convenient for tram D to the Ring and Nussdorf. *Praterstern* (☎ 214 01 23), 2 Mayergasse 6, east of the Ring, has singles/doubles for AS250/465. It's another place that encourages guests to stay dirty, charging AS50 to use the hall shower (for stays of under five nights). Rooms with private shower/WC are AS385/615. Breakfast is AS40.

The small *Zum Goldenen Stern Gasthof* (☎ 804 13 82), 12 Breitenfurter Strasse 94, has singles/doubles without breakfast for AS220/400 using a hall shower. Telephone ahead for weekend arrivals. It is 10 minutes walk south-west of Hetzendorf (S Bahn No 1 or 2). *Hotel Kolbeck Zur Linde* (☎ 604 17 73), 10 Laxenburger Strasse 19, is a 10-minute walk from Südbahnhof. Singles/doubles using hall shower are AS400/700; those with private shower/WC and TV are AS600/1020. Reception is open 24 hours.

Inside the Ring, you inevitably pay more for the convenience of a central location. *Schweizer Pension Solderer* (☎ 533 81 56), 1 Heinrichsgasse 2, has singles/doubles for AS700/980 with private shower/WC or AS430/700 without. Doubles with shower only are AS860. *Pension Nossek* (☎ 533 70 41), 1 Graben 17, has good value, clean, comfortable singles from AS480 to AS770 and doubles from AS950 to AS1500. Rooms are priced according to their size, view and private facilities. *Pension Am Operneck* (☎ 512 93 10), 1 Kärntner Strasse 47, opposite the tourist office, has singles/doubles for AS620/900 with private shower and WC. Reserve well in advance.

Places to Stay – middle

The *Hotel Atlanta* (☎ 42 12 30), 9 Währinger Strasse 33, is located in a typically grand Viennese building. It's a good four-star hotel, with spacious, well furnished rooms and elegant touches. Singles/doubles/triples with shower/WC and TV are AS980/1450/AS1750, reducing to AS800/950/1200 from November to March.

Also good is *Hotel Am Schottenpoint* (☎ 310 87 87), Währinger Strasse 22. The entrance is through a small gallery decorated with murals and a stucco ceiling, but the rest of the hotel hasn't got quite the same style. Singles/doubles are AS900/1400, reducing to AS890/1250 in the low season.

Hotel-Pension Schneider (☎ 58 83 80), Getreidemarkt 5, is close to the Theater an der Wien, and the theatrical connection is obvious when you enter the lobby and see the signed photos of the actors and opera stars who have stayed here. Singles are AS980 to AS1350, doubles are AS1640, and the excellent self-contained two-person apartments are AS2100; prices are lower during winter.

Places to Eat

Supermarkets are shut Saturday afternoon and Sunday, but you can stock up on groceries during these times at the stations, though prices are higher. Westbahnhof has a large shop which is open daily from 6 am to 10.50 pm in the main hall; in Franz Josefs Bahnhof there's one open daily from 6 am (8 am on Sunday) to 10 pm; Südbahnhof has a few tiny kiosks. Würstel stands are scattered around the city and provide a quick snack of sausage and bread for around AS30.

Vienna's best known dish, the Wiener Schnitzel, is available everywhere; Goulash is also common. Vienna is well known for its excellent pastries and desserts, which are best avoided if your money belt is emptier than your stomach.

Budget Restaurants The best deal is in student cafeterias (mensas), which anyone can visit; *Youth Scene* has a full listing. They're usually only open for weekday lunches between 11 am and 2 pm. Meals are AS34 to AS60, with AS4 reduction for students. The *University mensa*, 9 Universitätsstrasse 7, has an adjoining café with full meals open weekdays from 8 am to 7 pm. The *Technical University mensa*, 4 Resselgasse 7-9, is also convenient. The *Music Academy Mensa*, 1 Johannesgasse 8, is the only one inside the Ring.

Tunnel (☎ 405 34 65), 8 Floriangasse 39, is another student haunt. The food is satisfying and easy on the pocket; breakfast costs AS29, vegetarian lunch specials AS45, spaghetti from AS38, big pizzas from AS60 and salads from AS20. Bottled beer costs from AS25 for half a litre. There is a cellar bar which has live music nightly from 9 pm; entry costs from AS30, though on Monday there's generally free jazz. Tunnel is open daily from 9 am to 2 am.

Rosenberger Markt Restaurant is at 1 Maysedergasse 2. Its downstairs buffet offers a fine array of meats, drinks and desserts, but if you really want to save Schillings, concentrate on the salad or vegetable buffet (from AS29). Don't be ashamed to pile a Stephansdom-like spire of food on your plate; everyone else does. It's open daily from 11 am to 11 pm. *Restaurant Marché Movenpick*, Ringstrassen Galerien, Kärntner Ring 5-7, is similar, with small plates from AS25. Another good feature (after 4 pm) is the pizza for AS57, where you can help yourself to a variety of toppings.

Chinese Restaurants are numerous, and many offer weekday lunches from around AS60. *China Restaurant Turandot*, 1 Vorlaufstrasse 2, is no exception, and also has an all-you-can-eat weekday lunch buffet for AS79. Indian Restaurants are rare, but try *Zum Inder*, 7 Burggasse 64, for weekday lunches from AS50.

Pizza Bizi, 1 Rotenturmstrasse 4, is a convenient self-service place with hot food daily from 11 am to 11 pm. Pasta with a choice of sauces is AS65, pizzas are AS60 to AS75.

Schnitzelwirt Schmidt (☎ 523 37 71), 7 Neubaugasse 52, is the best place for schnitzels (from AS60, plus garnishes). Service is sloppy but portions are ridiculously large. It's closed Sunday.

Wrenkh (☎ 533 15 26), 1 Bauernmarkt 10, is a fairly up-market specialist vegetarian restaurant. Meticulously prepared dishes are AS75 to AS190 and it's open Monday to Saturday from 11.30 am to 2.30 pm and 6 pm to midnight.

Vegetarisches Restaurant Légume (☎ 407 82 87), Währinger Strasse 57, has a three-course daily menu for AS102, and dishes like cheese schnitzel for AS79. It's open lunchtimes Sunday to Friday, and adjoins a health food shop.

For a complete contrast, head down to *Schweizerhaus* in the Prater, 2 Strasse des Ersten Mai 116. It's famous for its roasted pork hocks (Hintere Schweinsstelze). A meal consists of a massive chunk of meat on the bone (AS85 for 500 grams; the smallest are around 700 grams), with mustard and grated horseradish (AS15). Chomping your way through vast slabs of pig smacks of medieval banqueting, but it's very tasty when washed down with draught Czech Budweiser. Schweizerhaus is open daily from 10 am to 11 pm (March to October only) and has many outside tables.

Restaurant Smutny (☎ 587 13 56), 1 Elisabethstrasse 8, serves typical Viennese food in a typical Viennese environment. Dishes are filling and reasonably priced (from around AS85). It's open daily from 10 am to midnight.

Mid-Range & Expensive Restaurants *La Creperie* (☎ 512 56 87), 1 Grünangergasse 10, has different rooms with varied and creative décor. Meat and fish dishes are above AS110. Savoury crêpes (AS58 to AS112) are tasty, if not overly large. The attentive *Beim Novak* (☎ 523 32 44), 7 Richtergasse 12, has Austrian food above AS100. A house speciality is *Überbackene Fledermaus* (gratinated bat) for AS160. The 'bat wings' are actually cuts of beef. It's closed on weekends and holidays.

DO & CO (☎ 535 39 69 18), 1 Stephansplatz 12, is in the modern Haas Haus by Stephansdom. It has good food to match the view, and specialises in fish and Thai dishes around the AS220 mark. It's open daily from noon to 3 pm and 6 pm to midnight. There's an adjoining café open in the afternoons.

The classy *Steirereck* (☎ 713 31 68), 8 Rasumofskygasse 2, is one of the best restaurants in Austria. Different rooms have a different ambience, but it's pretty formal throughout. Tempting main courses all top AS300, but you get to choose from lobster, rabbit, pigeon and venison. It's open Monday to Friday; book at least a week in advance.

Coffee Houses The coffee house is an integral part of Viennese life. The tradition supposedly began after retreating Turkish invaders left behind their supplies of coffee beans in the 17th century. Today, Vienna has hundreds (some say thousands) of coffee houses. They're great places for observing the locals in repose and recovering after a hard day's sightseeing. Small coffees cost at least AS20 and the custom is to take your time. Most places have lots of newspapers to read (including expensive British titles), which make a coffee an excellent investment.

Coffee houses basically fall into two types, though the distinction is rather blurred nowadays. A *Kaffeehaus*, traditionally preferred by men, offers games such as chess and billiards and serves wine, beer, spirits and light meals. The *Café Konditorei* attracts more women and typically has a salon look, with rococo mouldings and painted glass. A wide variety of cakes and pastries is usually on offer.

Café Museum, 1 Friedrichstrasse 6, is open daily from 7 am to 11 pm and has chess, many newspapers and outside tables. *Café Bräunerhof*, 1 Stallburggasse 2, offers free classical music on weekends and holidays from 3 to 6 pm, and British newspapers. It's open weekdays to 7.30 pm (8.30 pm in winter) and weekends to 6 pm. *Alt Wien*, 1 Bäckerstrasse 9, is a rather dark coffee house by day and a good drinking hall by night. It's open daily from 10 am to 2 am and is well known for its goulash (AS80 large, AS55 small).

Café Central, 1 Herrengasse 14, has a fine ceiling and pillars, and piano music from 4 to 7 pm. Trotsky came here to play chess. Opening hours are Monday to Saturday from 8 am to 10 pm.

The *Hotel Sacher Café*, 1 Philharmonikerstrasse 4, behind the State Opera, is a picture of opulence, complete with chandeliers, battalions of waiters and rich, red walls and carpets. It's famous for its chocolate apricot cake, Sachertorte (AS50 a slice; coffee from AS32).

Heurigen *Heurigen* are wine taverns that only sell 'new' wine produced on the premises, a concession granted by Joseph II. They can be identified by a green wreath or branch hanging over the door. Outside tables are common and you can bring your own food or make a selection from inexpensive hot and cold buffet counters.

Heurigen usually have a relaxed atmosphere, which gets more and more lively as the customers and mugs of wine get drunk. Many feature traditional live music; these can be a bit touristy but great fun nonetheless. Native Viennese tend to prefer a music-free environment. Opening times are approximately 4 to 11 pm, and wine costs around AS26 a Viertel (1/4 litre).

Heurigen are concentrated in the winegrowing suburbs to the north, south and west of the city. Taverns are so close together that it is best to pick a region and just explore.

The Heurigen areas of Nussdorf and Heiligenstadt are near each other at the terminus of tram D. In 1817, Beethoven lived in the *Beethovenhaus*, at 19 Pfarrplatz 3, Heiligenstadt. Down the road (bus No 38A from Heiligenstadt or tram 38 from the Ring) is Grinzing, a large, lively area favoured by tour groups (count the buses lined up outside in the evening). There are several good Heurigen in a row where Cobenzlgasse and Sandgasse meet. *Reinprecht* at Cobenzl-gasse 22 has mobile musicians and a real sing-along environment.

Stammersdorf (tram No 31) and Strebersdorf (tram No 32) are cheaper, quieter regions. *Esterházykeller*, 1 Haarhof 1, off Naglergasse, in the city centre, has cheap wine (from AS22 a Viertel), meals and snacks; it's open daily from 11 am (4 pm Sunday) to 10 pm.

Entertainment

The tourist office has copies of *Vienna Scene* and produces a monthly listing of events. Weekly magazines with extensive listings include *City* (AS8) and *Falter* (AS28).

Cheap standing-room (*Stehplatz*) tickets for the *Staatsoper*, *Volksoper*, *Burgtheater* and *Akademietheater* go on sale about an hour before the start of the performance. You'll need to start queuing around three hours before the start to get tickets for major productions; less popular works require only minimal queuing. Don't join the student queue by mistake: all remaining seats are sold to students aged under 27, 30 minutes before the performance at the same price as the cheapest seats (home university ID necessary, not ISIC card). The state ticket office, Bundestheaterverkassen (☎ 514 44 2959) at 1 Goethegasse 1 does not charge a commission.

Cinema & Theatre Check local papers for listings. All cinema seats are AS60 on Monday. There are performances in English at the *English Theatre* (☎ 402 12 60), 8 Josefsgasse 12, and the *International Theatre* (☎ 319 62 72), 9 Porzellangasse 8.

Classical Music Classical music is so much a part of Vienna that you really should make an effort to sample some. In fact, it's difficult to avoid because so many of the buskers playing along Kärntner Strasse and Graben are classical musicians.

Check with the tourist office for free events around town. There are sometimes free concerts at the Rathaus.

Productions in the *Staatsoper* (state opera) are lavish affairs. Advance tickets for performances are expensive at AS150 to AS800. AS30 standing-room ticket holders get a good position at the back of the stalls; AS20 ticket holders are closer to the roof than the stage. The Viennese take their opera very seriously and dress up accordingly. Wander around the foyer and the refreshment rooms in the interval to fully appreciate the gold and crystal interior. There are no performances in July and August. The Vienna Philharmonic Orchestra performs in the *Musikverein*.

Vienna Boy's Choir The Wiener Sängerknaben sings Mass every Sunday (except during July and August) at 9.15 am in the Royal Chapel in the Hofburg. Tickets are expensive, but standing room is free. Queue by 8.30 am to find a place inside the open doors, but you can get a flavour of what's going on from the TV in the foyer. Also interesting is the scrum afterwards when everybody struggles to photograph and be photographed with the serenely patient choirboys. The choir also regularly sings a mixed programme of music in the *Konzerthaus*.

Spanish Riding School The famous Lipizzaner stallions strut their stuff in the Spanish Riding School behind the Hofburg. Performances are sold out months in advance, so write to the Spanische Reitschule, Michaelerplatz 1, A-1010 Wien or ask in the office about cancellations (cancelled tickets are sold two hours before performances). Deal directly with the school to avoid the hefty 22% commission charged by travel agents.

You need to be pretty keen on horses to be happy about paying AS240 to AS800 for seats or AS190 for standing room, although a few of the tricks, such as seeing a stallion bounding along on only its hind legs like a demented kangaroo, do tend to stick in the mind. Tickets to watch them train can be bought the same day (AS100). Training is from 10 am to noon, Tuesday to Friday and some Saturdays, from mid-February to the end of October – except in July and August when the stallions go on their summer holidays. Queues are very long early in the day, but if you try around 11 am you can usually get in fairly quickly.

Nightclubs & Bars Vienna has no shortage of good spots for a night out. The best-known area is around Ruprechtsplatz, Seitenstettengasse and Rabensteig in the Ring, dubbed the 'Bermuda Triangle' because drinkers can disappear into the numerous pubs and clubs and apparently be lost to the outside world. Most places are lively and inexpensive; some have live music, which is sometimes free. *Krah Krah*, 1 Rabensteig 8, has 50 different brands of beer (from AS37 a half-litre bottle) and is open daily from 11 am until late. *Roter Engel* is opposite at 1 Rabensteig 5. It has live music nightly (cover charge between AS40 and AS70) and is open until 4 am (2 am on Sunday).

Volksgarten (☎ 533 05 18), 1 Burgring 1, is three linked venues: a café with DJs and a garden, a disco with theme evenings, and a more formal 'Walzer Dancing' place. Late-night bars are by no means limited to the first district. *Café Käuzchen*, 7 Garde Gasse 8, has interesting décor, including part of an old VW Kombi bursting out of one wall. It's open daily from 8 am until 2 or 4 am and is good for late-night conversation (and food). *Andino* (☎ 587 61 25), 6 Münzwardeingasse 2, is a Latin American bar with live rock, soul or funk three times a week upstairs (entry averages AS100). It has lively murals, food, and is open daily from 11 am to 2 am.

One of the best-known discos in Vienna is *U4* (☎ 815 83 18), 12 Schönbrunner Strasse 222, open daily from 11 pm to 4 or 5 am. Drink prices are reasonable (small beers from AS38). Each night has a different theme. Sunday (1960s and 1970s music, cover charge AS50) is a popular night; Thursday is gay night.

Things to Buy
Local specialities include porcelain, ceramics, handmade dolls, wrought-iron work and leather goods. Selling works of art is big business; check the art auctions at the state-owned *Dorotheum* (☎ 515 600), 1 Dorotheergasse 17. Lots can be inspected in advance with their opening prices marked. Some prices include VAT, which can be claimed back (see Consumer Taxes in the Facts for the Visitor section).

Getting There & Away
Air Regular scheduled flights link Vienna to Linz, Salzburg, Innsbruck, Klagenfurt and Graz. There are daily nonstop flights to all major European destinations. Austrian Airlines (☎ 505 57 57) has a city office at 1 Kärntner Ring 18.

Bus Austrobus (☎ 53 41 10) has buses to Prague leaving from 1 Rathausplatz 5 at 7 am daily except Sunday, and at 3 pm daily except Saturday (AS315; five hours). Blaguss Reisen (☎ 501 80) operates daily buses to Budapest at 7 am from the central bus station at Wien Mitte (AS310; 3½ hours). A new, small-scale operation runs a minibus to/from Budapest for AS165; phone the day before on ☎ 0036-1-140 85 85.

Train Train schedules are subject to change, and not all destinations are exclusively serviced by one station, so check with train information centres in stations or call ☎ 1717.

Westbahnhof has trains to western and northern Europe and western Austria. Approximately hourly services head to Salzburg, some continue to Munich and terminate in Paris. To Zürich, there are two day trains (AS1106) and one night train (AS830, including fold-down seat). A direct train goes to Bucharest; to Athens, change at Budapest. Seven trains a day go to Budapest (AS338; three to four hours).

Südbahnhof has trains to Italy (two to Rome, two to Venice and Florence), Slovakia, the Czech Republic, Hungary (once daily to Budapest) and Poland. Trains depart every two hours to Graz. Four trains a day go to Bratislava (AS94), and four go to Prague (AS412; five hours), some continuing to Berlin.

Franz Josefs Bahnhof and Wien-Mitte Bahnhof handle local trains only.

Car & Motorcycle The Gürtel is an outer ring road which joins up with the A22 on the north bank of the Danube and the A23 south-east of town. All the main road routes intersect with this system, including the A1 from Linz and Salzburg, and the A2 from Graz.

Hitching Mitfahrzentrale Josefstadt (☎ 408 22 10), 8 Daungasse 1A, links hitchhikers and drivers. It's open daily from 10 to 5 pm (6 pm Thursday and Friday, 2 pm Saturday and Sunday). Telephone to check availability before going to the office. There are usually many cars going into Germany. Examples of fares are: Salzburg AS210, Innsbruck AS270, Paris AS790 and Munich AS310.

Boat DDSG Blue Danube (☎ 727 500), Handelskai 265, by the Reichsbrücke bridge, operates boats along the Danube. Fast hydrofoils travel eastwards to Bratislava and Budapest. There's one daily departure to Bratislava (AS210/AS330 one way/return; one hour) from mid-April to mid-October. There is one daily departure to Budapest (AS750/AS1100 one way/return; four hours 40 minutes) from 1 April to 31 October, and two daily from mid-July to early September.

A series of boats ply the Danube from Vienna to Passau, on the German border. See the Danube Valley section for operators.

Getting Around

To/From the Airport Wien Schwechat Airport (☎ 7007) is 19 km from the city centre. There are buses every 20 or 30 minutes from 6 am to at least midnight between the airport and the Hotel Hilton. Hourly buses also run from Westbahnhof and Südbahnhof (AS70). It's cheaper to take the S-Bahn (S7 line, two an hour) from Wien Mitte. The fare is AS34, or AS17 additional to a city pass. A taxi should cost under AS400.

Public Transport Vienna has a comprehensive and unified public transport network. Flat-fare tickets are valid for trains, trams, buses, the underground (U-Bahn) and the rapid transport system (S-Bahn). Routes are outlined in the free tourist office map; for a more detailed listing, buy a map from a Vienna Transit window (AS15). Single tickets cost AS20 from ticket machines, or AS17 each in multiples of four or five from Transit windows or Tabak shops (these must be validated before use). You may change lines on the same trip. Children under six always travel free; those under 15 go free on Sunday, public holidays and during Vienna school holidays (photo ID necessary).

Daily passes (Stunden-Netzkarte) are a better deal at AS50 (valid 24 hours from first use) or AS130 (valid 72 hours). Validate the ticket in the machine at the beginning of your first journey. An eight-day, multiple-user pass (Acht-TageStreifenkarte) costs AS265. The validity depends upon the number of people travelling on the same card – one person valid eight days, two people valid four days, and so on. Validate the ticket once per day per person. Weekly tickets, valid Monday to Sunday, cost AS142. Ticket inspections are not very frequent, but fare dodgers who are caught pay an on-the-spot fine of AS500, plus the fare. Austrian and European rail passes are valid on the S-Bahn only. Public transport finishes around midnight, but there's also an excellent night bus service, with 22 lines. They run every 30 minutes nightly, around the Ring and to the suburbs, and tickets are AS25 (day tickets/passes not valid).

Taxi Taxis are metered for city journeys: AS26 or AS27 flag fall, plus AS23 per 143 or 167 metres – the higher rate is on Sunday and at night. There is a AS16 surcharge for phoning a radio taxi.

Car & Motorcycle Parking is a problem in the city centre and the Viennese are impatient drivers. The tourist office encourages visitors to use public transport for sightseeing and it might be worth heeding their advice. Blue parking zones allow a maximum stop of 1½ hours on weekdays from 9 am to 7 pm. Parking vouchers (AS6 per 30 minutes) for these times can be purchased in Tabak shops. Parking garages are expensive; the cheapest in the centre is at Messeplatz (AS245 for 24 hours).

Bicycle Bikes can be hired daily from the main train stations. Pick up the tourist office's leaflet, *See Vienna by Bike*.

Fiacres The ponies and traps lined up at St Stephen's are strictly for the well-heeled tourist. Commanding prices of AS500 for a 20-minute trot, these ponies must be among Vienna's richest inhabitants.

AROUND VIENNA
Eisenstadt
The provincial capital of Burgenland lies 50 km south of Vienna. From the train station, walk nearly one km along Bahnstrasse to reach Hauptstrasse, a central pedestrian-only street. Turn right to get to the tourist office (☎ 673 90) at Schubertplatz 1. The office is in the plush Hotel Burgenland, on the far side, and is open daily from 9 am to noon and 2 to 5 pm (no lunch break in summer; closed weekends in winter).

The provincial tourist office (☎ 633 84 16) is the other way down Hauptstrasse in the Esterházy Palace. It's open daily from 9 am to 5 pm (weekdays only from October to May). The post office and Bundesbus ticket office are near the cathedral at Domplatz.

The telephone code for Eisenstadt is ☎ 02682.

Things to See & Do Joseph Haydn lived and worked in Eisenstadt for 31 years and, although he died in Vienna, his remains were transferred here to the **Bergkirche**, where they now reside in a white, marble tomb. Haydn's skull was stolen from a temporary grave shortly after he died in 1809, and was reunited with his body only in 1954. The church itself is remarkable for the Kalvarienburg, a unique display of life-sized figures depicting the stations of the cross in a series of suitably austere, dungeon-like rooms. It's open between 1 April and 31 October, daily from 9 am to noon and 2 to 5 pm; entry is AS25 (students AS10) and includes the mausoleum.

The baroque **Esterházy Palace** features the frescoed Haydn Hall, and a new exhibition on the Esterházy family. Opening hours are the same as for the provincial tourist office. Entry costs AS50, (students AS30) and includes a 40-minute guided tour (sometimes in English, or ask for the English notes). There's a large, relaxing park behind the palace.

Places to Stay & Eat The nearest HI *Jugendherberge* (☎ 02167-22 52), Herbergsgasse 1, Neusiedl, is 30 minutes away by train, on the shores of Lake Neusiedl. It's open from 1 March to 31 November.

Excluding rooms in private houses, *Gasthof Kutsenits Ludwig* (☎ 635 11), Mattersburger Strasse 30, has the cheapest singles/doubles (AS250/400). It's 1.5 km south of Eisenstadt centre.

For lunch, think Chinese: *Asia*, Hauptstrasse 32, and *Mandarin*, Wiener Strasse 2, both have excellent three-course menus from AS49 and AS55 respectively (both open daily). *Gasthof Zum Haydnhaus*, Joseph Haydngasse 24, has regional and Austrian dishes for AS60 to AS150 (open daily). There's a *Billa* supermarket near the cathedral.

Getting There & Away Trains depart from Vienna Südbahnhof every two hours from 6.20 am (AS68; 1½ hours – change in Neusiedl). On weekdays, it's quicker to take the direct train from Wien Meidling (65 minutes). Buses take about 1¼ hours, and depart from Wien Mitte (AS85). Wiener Neustadt is on the Vienna-Graz train route: buses from there take 30 minutes.

The Danube Valley

AUSTRIA

The strategic importance of the Danube (Donau) Valley as a corridor between the East and Western Europe meant that control of the area was hotly contested. As a result, there are hundreds of castles and fortified abbeys in the region. The Wachau section of the Danube, between Krems and Melk, is considered to be the river's most scenic stretch, with wine-growing villages, forested slopes, vineyards and imposing fortresses at nearly every bend.

Several companies run boats along the Danube. The operator with the most extensive services along the Wachau is DDSG Blue Danube (see the Vienna boat section). A short return tour costs AS90 or the full trip from Melk to Krems (takes 1¾ hours) or Krems to Melk (three hours) costs AS170. Boats sail daily in each direction from late March to late October, and there's also a weekend service from Dürnstein to Vienna. DDSG carries bicycles free of charge.

Brandner (☎ 07433-25 900) has similar prices for Wachau tours. Donauschiffahrt Ardagger (☎ 07479-64 640), connects Linz to Krems, three times a week in summer. Schiffahrt Wurm + Köck runs a regular service between Linz and the German town of Passau; its offices are at Untere Donaulände 1 in Linz (☎ 0732-78 36 07) and Höllgasse 26 in Passau (☎ 0851-92 92 92). The fare is AS228 and it takes at least six hours.

The route by road is also scenic. Highway 3 links Vienna and Linz and stays close to the north bank of the Danube for much of the way. There is a cycle track along the south bank from Vienna to Krems, and along both sides of the river from Krems to Linz.

St Pölten is the state capital of Lower Austria, but refer to the provincial information office mentioned in the Vienna section for region-wide information. If you stay in the Wachau, be sure to get the Wachau guest card – one useful benefit is a day's free bike rental in Melk (apply to the Melk tourist office).

KREMS
The historic town of Krems reclines on the north bank of the Danube, surrounded by terraced vineyards.

Orientation & Information
The main post office (Postamt 3500) is to the left of the train station on Brandströmstrasse 4. Walk 300 metres north for the main pedestrian street, Landstrasse. Two km west of Krems is the suburb of Stein. The tourist office (☎ 82 6 76) is halfway between the two, at Undstrasse 6, in the Kloster Und. It is open Monday to Friday from 8 am to 6 pm. Between Easter and 31 October it is also open weekends from 10 am to noon and 1 to 6 pm.

The telephone code for Krems is ☎ 02732.

Things to See & Do
There's little to do in Krems except relax and enjoy the peaceful ambience. Take your time and wander round the cobbled streets, adjoining courtyards and ancient city walls. The most interesting streets are Landstrasse in Krems and Steiner Landstrasse in Stein. There are several churches worth a look, including the **St Veit**, high on the hill, and the **Dominican Church**, which contains a collection of religious and modern art and wine-making artefacts. There's wine tasting in the Kloster Und (AS130). The street plan from the tourist office details points of interest.

Places to Stay & Eat
Camping Donau (☎ 84 4 55), Wiedengasse 7, near the boat station, is open from mid-April to 31 October and costs AS50 per person, from AS30 for a tent and AS40 for a car.

The HI *Jugendherberge* (☎ 83 4 52), Ringstrasse 77, has excellent facilities for cyclists, including a garage and on-site repair service. Beds in four or six-bed dorms are AS180 (AS160 if three nights or more), and it's open April to September.

Many hotels have a surcharge for a single-night stay. The cheapest singles/doubles (AS350/520 with shower/WC and TV) are at *Aigner* (☎ 84 5 58), Weinzierl 53. In Stein, *Frühstückspension Einzinger* (☎ 82 3 16) at Steiner Landstrasse 82 offers similar doubles for AS550, and singles without the private WC for AS320.

Hotel Restaurant Alte Poste (☎ 82 2 76), Obere Landstrasse 32, is in a historic 500-year-old house. It has good singles/doubles for AS 300/580, or AS470/740 with private shower, and an enchanting rear courtyard. It's a good place to eat too, with dishes from AS90 and local wine from AS30 per quarter litre.

To conserve Schillings, construct a meal in one of several supermarkets (eg the *Spar* at Obere Landstrasse 15). *Schwarze Kuchl*, Untere Landstrasse 8, has basic cheap food (closes 7 pm weekdays, 1 pm Saturday), and there are takeaway places nearby. Ask the tourist office for the opening schedules of the local Heurigen (wine taverns).

Getting There & Away

The boat station (*Schiffsstation*) is a 20-minute walk from the train station towards Stein on Donaulände. Three or four buses a day to Melk (AS64; 65 minutes) leave from outside the train station. Trains to Vienna (AS119; one hour) arrive at Franz Josefs Bahnhof.

DÜRNSTEIN

East of Krems, under 30 minutes away by boat, lies Dürnstein. Ascend to the ruins of Kuenringer Castle for a sweeping view of the river. This castle is where King Richard the Lionheart of England was imprisoned in 1192. In the village, visit the parish church, a baroque structure that has been meticulously restored.

MELK

Lying in the lee of its imposing monastery/fortress, Melk is an essential stop on the Wachau stretch.

Orientation & Information

The train station is 300 metres from the town centre. Walk straight ahead for 50 metres down Bahnhofstrasse to get to the post office (Postamt 3390), where money exchange is available to 5 pm on weekdays and 10 am on Saturday. Turn right for the HI hostel or carry straight on, taking the Bahngasse path, for the central Rathausplatz. Turn right for the tourist office (☎ 23 07 32) on Babenberger-strasse 1, which is open weekdays from 9 am to noon and 2 to 6 pm, and weekends from 10 am to 2 pm; winter hours are shorter. In July and August, hours are daily from 9 am to 7 pm.

The telephone code for Melk is ☎ 02752.

Things to See & Do

The **Benedictine Abbey** dominates the town from the hill and offers excellent views. Guided tours (up to two a day in English) explain its historical importance and are well worth taking.

The huge monastery church is baroque gone mad, with endless prancing angels and gold twirls – but it's very impressive nonetheless. The fine library and the mirror room both have an extra tier painted on the ceiling to give the illusion of greater height. The ceilings are slightly curved to aid the effect.

It is open from the Saturday before Palm Sunday to All Saints' Day from 9 am to 5 pm, except between May and September when it closes at 6 pm. Entry costs AS50 (students aged up to 27 years AS25), and the guided tour is AS15 extra. During winter, the monastery may only be visited by guided tour (☎ 23 12 for information).

There are other interesting buildings around town. Try following the walking route outlined in the tourist office pamphlet. **Schallaburg Castle**, five km south of Melk (AS30 by bus), is a 16th-century Renaissance palace which has marvellous terracotta arches and hosts various exhibitions. It's open from May to October and costs AS60 (students AS20). A combination ticket, which includes Melk monastery, costs AS95.

Places to Stay & Eat

Camping Melk is on the west bank of the canal which joins the Danube. It's open from April to October and charges AS35 per person, AS35 per tent and AS25 for a car. Reception is in the restaurant *Melker Fährhaus* (☎ 32 91), Kolomaniau 3, which is open Wednesday to Sunday (daily in summer) from 8 am to midnight. When it's closed, just camp and pay later. The restaurant has decent lunchtime fare from AS75.

AUSTRIA

The HI *Jugendherberge* (☎ 26 81), Abt Karl Strasse 42, has good showers and four-bed dorms. Beds are AS141 (AS110 for those aged under 19), or AS167 (AS135) for single night stays. The reception and main doors are closed from 10 am to 5 pm, but during the day you can reserve a bed and leave your bags behind the door to the left of the entrance. The hostel is closed from mid-October to mid-March.

The renovated *Gasthof Goldenen Hirschen* (☎ 22 57), Rathausplatz 13, in the centre of town, offers singles/doubles with private shower from AS320/560. The restaurant is open daily and has dishes from AS75. *Gasthof Goldener Stern* (☎ 22 14), Sterngasse 17, offers slightly cheaper rooms.

There is a *Spar* supermarket at Rathausplatz 9. *Gasthof Baumgartner*, Bahnhofstrasse 12, is by the train station. This basic place serves a good Wiener schnitzel, chips and salad for AS75, and beer is just AS26 a Krügerl (open daily).

Getting There & Away

Boats leave from the canal by Pionierstrasse, 400 metres to the rear of the monastery. Bicycle hire is available in the train station and at the boat station. Trains to Vienna Westbahnhof (AS118; one to two hours) travel via St Pölten.

LINZ

Despite the heavy industry based in Linz, the provincial capital of Upper Austria retains a picturesque old-town centre. It's just a pity about the belching smokestacks on the outskirts that smudge your view of the Alps.

Orientation & Information

Most of the town is on the south bank of the Danube. The tourist office (☎ 7070 1777), Hauptplatz, is on the main square and has a free room-finding service and an interesting walking tour pamphlet. It is open daily to 7 pm (6 pm from late October to 30 April). To get there from the train station, walk right, then turn left at the far side of the park and continue along Landstrasse for 10 minutes; alternatively, catch tram No 3.

There's also an information office in the station, and 24-hour bike rental. The large post office, opposite the station and to the left, is open 24 hours.

American Express (☎ 66 90 13) is at Bürgerstrasse 14. The provincial tourist office (☎ 97 30 24), which has information on Salzkammergut, is at Kapuzinerstrasse 3. Opening hours are Monday to Thursday from 9 am to 12.30 pm and 2 to 6 pm, and Friday from 9 am to 12.30 pm.

The telephone code for Linz is ☎ 0732.

Things to See & Do

The large, baroque **Hauptplatz** has the Pillar of the Holy Trinity at its centre. The pillar was sculpted in Salzburg marble in 1723. From Hauptplatz, turn into Hofgasse and climb the hill to **Linz Castle**. The castle has been periodically rebuilt since 799 AD and provides a good view of the many church spires in the centre. It also houses the **Schlossmuseum**, open daily except Monday (entry AS50; temporary exhibitions cost extra).

The neo-Gothic **New Cathedral**, built in 1855, features exceptional stained-glass windows, including one depicting the history of the town. Walk, or take the special tram (AS40), up **Pöstlingberg**, on the north bank. It's recognisable by the twin-spired church at the summit of the hill. There is a great view from the top, and a children's grotto railway. The **Neue Galerie** at Blütenstrasse 15 is also on the north bank. It exhibits modern German and Austrian art. Entry costs from AS40 (students AS20), depending on exhibitions. It's open daily except Sunday. The *Posthof* (☎ 77 05 48), Posthofstrasse 43, is a centre for contemporary music, dance and theatre.

Places to Stay

The nearest *camping ground* (☎ 30 53 14) is out of town at Wiener Bundesstrasse 937, Pichlinger See.

There are three HI hostels in Linz. The *Jugendgästehaus* (☎ 66 44 34), Stanglhofweg 3, near the Linz Stadium, has singles/doubles for AS303/406, and four-bed rooms for AS153 per person. The *Jugendherberge* (☎ 78 27 20), Kapuzinerstrasse 14, is nearer the centre. It has beds, without breakfast, for AS100 to AS140, depending on whether you're under/over 19 or need sheets. It's the smallest hostel, with a kitchen and no curfew. Phone ahead if arriving after 6 pm.

The *Landesjugendherberge* (☎ 23 70 78), at Blütenstrasse 23, on the north bank, has two to five-bed rooms. Per person charges are AS130 (AS105 if under 19), plus AS25 in winter and AS20 for breakfast. You should be able to check in at all of them during the day, except at Kapuzinerstrasse on weekends and Friday, when you'll have to wait until 5 pm.

Goldenes Dachl (☎ 67 54 80), Hafnerstrasse 27, one block away from the New Cathedral, provides singles/doubles for AS260/460, without breakfast. Doubles with private shower are AS480. *Wienerwald* (☎ 77 78 81), Freinbergstrasse 18, is next to the western terminus of bus No 26, 1.5 km from the town centre. It has a restaurant and good rooms from AS270/470. *Goldener Anker* (☎ 77 10 88) at Hofgasse 5, off Hauptplatz, has rooms from AS315/620. Breakfast is AS80 per person.

Places to Eat

There are plenty of cheap Würstel stands around the park on Landstrasse, and a *Mondo* supermarket at the south-eastern corner of the park in Blumauerplatz. One of the cheapest places to sit down and eat is *Goldenes Kreuz*, Pfarrplatz 11, behind the parish church. It has varied Austrian food from AS65 (closed Sunday evening and Saturday).

Mangolds, Hauptplatz 3, is a self-service vegetarian restaurant, open daily except Sunday from 11 am to 8 pm. *Klosterhof*, at the junction of Bischofstrasse and Landestrasse, occupies many rooms in a 17th-century building. It's open daily from 8 am to midnight, and has midday meals from AS75 and evening dishes between AS90 and AS190.

On the corner of Waltherstrasse and Klammstrasse, are *El Mexicano*, which serves inexpensive Mexican and Italian food, and *China-Restaurant Taiwan*; both are open daily. *Café Ex-Blatt*, along Waltherstrasse, is more of a young drinking joint (beer for AS36 a half-litre), though it also has pizza for AS76. It's open daily to at least 1 am.

Getting There & Around

Linz is on the main rail and road route between Vienna and Salzburg. Buy city transport tickets before boarding: AS18 per journey or AS35 for a day card.

The South

The two principal states in the south, Styria (Steiermark) and Carinthia (Kärnten), are often neglected by visitors, yet they offer mountains, lakes, varied cities and interesting influences from the neighbouring countries of Italy, Slovenia and Hungary.

GRAZ

Graz is the capital of Styria, a province characterised by mountains and dense forests. In former times, Graz was an important bulwark against invading Turks; today, it is fast becoming an essential stop on the tourist trail.

Orientation

Graz is dominated by the Schlossberg, the castle hill which rises over the medieval town centre. The river Mur cuts a north-south path west of the hill, dividing the old centre from the main train station. Tram Nos 3 and 6 run from the station to Hauptplatz in the centre. A number of streets radiate from the square, including Sporgasse, an important shopping street, and Herrengasse, the main pedestrian thoroughfare. Jakominiplatz is a major transport hub.

Information

There is a tourist information office (☎ 91 68 37) in the main train station on platform 1. It's open Monday to Saturday from 9 am to 1 pm and 2 to 6 pm, and Sunday and holidays from 10 am to 3 pm. The station also has bike rental, a money exchange office and a Bankomat (for credit card cash advances).

The main tourist office (☎ 80 75 11), Herrengasse 16, shares the same hours as the station office. The main post office is at Neutorgasse 46 (Hauptpostamt 8010), and is open 24 hours daily for some services (including telephones).

The telephone code for Graz is ☎ 0316.

Things to See & Do

The tourist office organises daily guided walks of the city in summer (AS75), and on Saturday in winter. Paths wind up the **Schlossberg** from all sides. The climb up takes less than 30 minutes and repays the effort with excellent

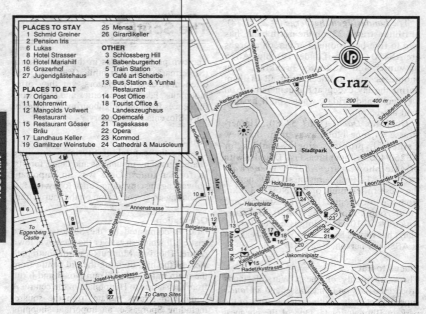

PLACES TO STAY
1 Schmid Greiner
2 Pension Iris
6 Lukas
8 Hotel Strasser
10 Hotel Mariahilf
16 Grazerhof
27 Jugendgästehaus

PLACES TO EAT
7 Origano
11 Mohrenwirt
12 Mangolds Vollwert
   Restaurant
15 Restaurant Gösser
   Bräu
17 Landhaus Keller
19 Gamlitzer Weinstube

25 Mensa
26 Girardikeller

OTHER
3 Schlossberg Hill
4 Babenburgerhof
5 Train Station
9 Café art Scherbe
13 Bus Station & Yunhai
   Restaurant
14 Post Office
18 Tourist Office &
   Landeszeughaus
20 Operncafé
21 Tageskasse
22 Opera
23 Kommod
24 Cathedral & Mausoleum

views. At the top is an open-air theatre, a small military museum and the bell tower which dates from 1588. Unusually, the larger hand on the clock face shows the hours. The townsfolk paid the French not to destroy it during the Napoleonic Wars.

The nearby **Stadtpark** (City Park) is a relaxing place to sit or wander. The **cathedral**, which is on the corner of Hofgasse and Bürgergasse, is worth a look. The impressive baroque **Mausoleum** next door is the resting place of Ferdinand II and several other Habsburgs. It is open Monday to Saturday from 11 am to noon and (May to September only) from 2 to 3 pm. Admission costs AS15.

Visit the **Landeszeughaus** (Armoury), Herrengasse 16, which houses an incredible array of gleaming armour and weapons, enough to equip about 30,000 soldiers. Most of it dates from the 17th century, when the original Armoury was built. Some of the armour is beautifully engraved; other exhibits are crude and intimidating. The view from the 4th floor to the Landhaus courtyard and the

Schlossberg is perfect. The Armoury is open between 1 April and 31 October, Monday to Friday from 9 am to 5 pm, and on Saturday and Sunday to 1 pm. Entry costs AS25; students free (students get free entry to several other museums in town).

A good activity for those with kids is the **Schlossberg Cave Railway**. It's the longest grotto railway in Europe, and winds its way for two km around scenes from fairy tales. It's open daily and admission prices are on a sliding scale: AS30 for one (adults or children), AS55 for two, AS75 for three etc. The entrance is on Schlossbergplatz. **Eggenberg Castle**, Eggenbergen Allee 90, is four km west of the centre (take tram No 1). The interior of this sumptuous 17th-century residence can be visited by guided tour; it also has three museums and extensive parklands. Entry to the state rooms, the *Prunkräume*, is AS25 (students free); they're open between 31 March and 31 October from 10 am to 1 pm and 2 to 5 pm daily. The park is open daily all year and costs AS2 to enter.

Places to Stay

Waldcamping Riederhof (☎ 28 43 80), Riederhof Mantscha 1, costs AS204 for two people or AS162 for one. There's no direct public transport and it's open year round. *Camping Central* (☎ 28 18 31), Martin-hofstrasse 3, is open from 1 April to 31 October, and costs AS230 for a two-person site, including swimming pool entry. Take bus No 32 from Jakominiplatz. Both camping grounds are about six km south-west of the city centre.

The HI *Jugendgästehaus* (☎ 91 48 76), at Idlhofgasse 74, has computer terminals, extensive lawns and parking. Seven-bed dorms are AS135, renovated four-bed dorms with private shower/WC are AS170, and singles/doubles with shower/WC are AS320/440. Sheets if required are AS20. Reception is open all day, except on Sunday from 9 am to 5 pm, but even then the doors stay open. Phone ahead in winter, as it may close for a couple of months. Laundry costs from AS40 to wash and dry.

Five minutes from the station is *Hotel Strasser* (☎ 91 39 77), Eggenberger Gürtel 11. It has functional but pleasant singles/doubles for AS440/660 with private shower, or AS340/560 without. Around the back of the station, *Lukas* (☎ 58 25 90) at Waagner Biro Strasse 8 offers a similar standard without breakfast for AS300/510 with shower, or AS250/440 without. The sleazy reputation of this place no longer applies.

Schmid Greiner (☎ 68 14 82), Graben-strasse 64, north of Schlossberg, is cosy and old-fashioned, but the traffic outside can be noisy. Singles/doubles are AS370/480, using the hall shower. The only place in the old centre is *Grazerhof* (☎ 82 98 24) on Stubenberggasse 10. Smallish, innocuous rooms are AS460/740, or AS650/980 with private shower. The hotel borders two pedestrian streets, but the receptionist can tell you where to park.

The three-star *Hotel Mariahilf* (☎ 91 31 630), Mariahilfer Strasse 9, has singles/doubles with private shower from AS700/1200. The rooms are very large, but the furnishing is variable – grand in some, mixed-and-mismatched in others, with ancient rugs that should have been chucked out with the Third Reich. Three-star comfort is generally a better deal in pensions. *Pension Iris* (☎ 32 20 81), Bergmanngasse 10, has comfort-able rooms with shower and WC for AS600/800 (closed July). Double-glazing eliminates traffic noise.

Places to Eat

The Forum shopping centre opposite the train station has a supermarket and a cheap *Origano* self-service restaurant. Also look out for cheap weekday lunches in Chinese restaurants, such as at *Yunhai*, Andreas Hofer Platz 3. But the best deal is at the *University mensa*, downstairs at Schubertstrasse 2-4. Main meals (including a vegetarian choice) cost AS35 to AS60, with discounts for students. Food is served Monday to Friday from 11 am to 2 pm. The café on the ground floor is open Monday to Friday from 8 am to 4 pm, and has breakfasts for AS35. Explore the university vicinity for other restaurants and bars.

Girardikeller, Leonhardstrasse 28, is a cellar bar (free live music every Sunday in winter) with cheap food – the Monday to Thursday special is just AS45 or AS50. Huge pizzas with seven toppings are AS60. It's open daily from 5 pm (6 pm on weekends) till 2 am. Vegetarian heaven is *Mangolds Vollwert Restaurant*, a self-service place on Griesgasse 11. Salad is AS14 per 100 grams and daily dishes are AS60 to AS90. It's open from 11 am to 8 pm (4 pm on Saturday).

Mohrenwirt, Mariahilfer Strasse 16, is a typical small Gasthof with snacks and meals from AS20 to AS85. Ask the server about daily specials as they're not written down (open Saturday to Wednesday). A little more expensive but also with authentic Styrian cooking is *Gamlitzer Weinstube*, Mehlplatz 4; try the tasty Steinerpfandl (AS80). *Restaurant Gösser Bräu*, Neutorgasse 48, is a large place which has many different rooms and outside tables. Food is AS60 to AS200, and there's a wide selection of local Gösser beer from AS30. Opening hours are Sunday to Friday from 9 am to midnight.

For a splurge, head to the 16th-century *Landhaus Keller* (☎ 83 02 76), Schmiedgasse 9. Floral displays, coats of arms, medieval-style murals, and soft background music contribute to the historic ambience. Most dishes, including interesting Styrian specialities, exceed AS175. It's open Monday to Saturday from 11.30 am to midnight.

AUSTRIA

AUSTRIA

Entertainment

Graz has several traditional coffee houses, including *Operncafé*, Opernring 22, which is open daily from 8 am (9 am Sunday) to midnight. In the centre of town, many bars and clubs are around Mehlplatz and Prokopigasse.

Kommod, Burggasse 15, is a bright and busy bar, often packed with students, which serves inexpensive pizza and pasta; it's open daily from 5 pm to 2 am. *Café art Scherbe*, Stockergasse 2, off Lendl Platz, is a more relaxed bar, with paintings, plants and sofas (open daily from 5 pm). *Babenburgerhof*, Babenburgerstrasse 39, is a friendly bar with free live jazz on Tuesday, Wednesday and Thursday.

Graz is an important cultural centre and hosts musical events throughout the year. The Tageskasse (☎ 8000), Kaiser Josef Platz 10, sells tickets without commission for the Schauspielhaus (theatre) and Opernhaus (opera), and also dispenses information. Students aged under 27 pay half price. An hour before performances, students can buy leftover tickets for AS60 at the door, and anybody can buy standing room tickets for AS25 to AS35.

Getting There & Away

Direct IC trains to Vienna's Südbahnhof depart every two hours (AS296; two hours 40 minutes). Trains depart every two hours to Salzburg (AS396), either direct or changing at Bischofshofen. A daily direct train departs for Zagreb (AS202; 3½ hours) at 6.58 pm. The quickest service to Budapest leaves at 6.20 am (AS562, 3¾ hours; change at Bruck), though later trains also have onward connections. Trains to Klagenfurt go via Leoben. The bus station is at Andreas Hofer Platz. The A2 autobahn from Vienna to Klagenfurt passes a few kilometres south of the city.

Getting Around

Public transport tickets cost AS20 each or AS140 for a block of 10 tickets. These cover the Schlossbergbahn (castle-hill railway) that runs from Sackstrasse up the castle hill. The Touristenkarte costs AS40 and is valid for 24 hours, including rides on the Schlossbergbahn. The weekly pass is AS82. Blue parking zones allow a three hour stop (AS8 for 30 minutes) during specified times.

AROUND GRAZ

The stud farm of the famous Lipizzaner stallions who perform in Vienna is about 40 km west of Graz at **Piber**. The farm can be visited from Easter to the end of October (AS100, students AS30). Get more details from the Graz tourist office or the Köflach tourist office (☎ 03144-25 19 70), which is three km from the farm. Köflach can be reached by train or bus from Graz. The return train fare is AS156, but buy instead the Graz four-zone 24-hour ticket for AS124. One stop nearer Graz on the train line is **Bärnbach**, where there's a remarkable parish church created by Hundertwasser and other artists.

KLAGENFURT

The capital of Carinthia since 1518, Klagenfurt may not be prominent as a tourist destination but it is not without its attractions.

Orientation & Information

Neuer Platz, the heart of the city, is one km north of the main train station. To get there from the station, walk straight ahead down Bahnhofstrasse and take a left at Paradieser Gasse. The tourist office (☎ 53 72 23) is in the Rathaus on Neuer Platz. Opening hours are weekdays from 8 am to 8 pm, weekends and holidays from 10 am to 5 pm; from 1 October to 30 April, hours are reduced to Monday to Friday from 8 am to 6 pm. The staff find rooms (no commission), and rent bikes at a low rate of AS40 for three hours or AS80 for the day. The Hauptbahnhof also rents bikes, and is open 24 hours a day. The main post office is on Dr Hermann Gasse (Postamt 9010), one block to the west of Neuer Platz.

The telephone code for Klagenfurt is ☎ 0463.

Things to See & Do

The **Neuer Platz** (New Square) is dominated by the Dragon Fountain, the emblem of the city. The statue of Maria Theresa dates from 1873. **Alter Platz** (Old Square) is the oldest part of the city, and an interesting area to explore. The walls of the Hall of Arms (Wappensaal) in the 16th-century **Landhaus** are covered in paintings of 655 coats of arms. The ceiling has a gallery painted on it, giving the illusion that it is vaulted; stand in the centre of the room for the best effect. The Landhaus is open between 1 April and 31 September, weekdays only (AS10, students AS5).

Lake Wörth (Wörther See), four km west of the city centre, is one of the warmer lakes in the region thanks to subterranean thermal springs. It is ideal for water sports. STW (☎ 21 155), St Veiter Strasse 31, runs steamers on the lake from early May to late September. A one-day circular tour costs AS170 (AS150 in advance), or AS380 (AS330 in advance).

You can swim or go boating in summer at the lakeside **Strandbad**, near the boat station; there is also tennis and crazy golf close by. The adjoining **Europa Park** has various attractions, including a reptile zoo and a planetarium. The most touristy offering is **Minimundus**, which displays 150 models of famous international buildings on a 1:25 scale; it is open daily from late April to early October and costs AS85 (children AS25).

Klagenfurt is ringed by castles and stately homes. The tourist office has a free map detailing tour routes – ideal if you have your own transport. It also has a *Radwandern* cycling map listing sights and distances. The longest tour is 34 km.

Places to Stay

Camping Strandbad (☎ 21 1 69) is in a good location by the lake in Europa Park. It costs up to AS92 per person and AS20 to AS100 for a site.

HI *Jugendgästehaus Kolping* (☎ 56 9 65), Enzenbergstrasse 26, is a 10-minute walk from Neuer Platz and costs from AS150 per person, but it's only open in July and August. HI *Jugendherberge Klagenfurt* (☎ 23 00 20), Neckheimgasse 6, near Europa Park, has four-bed dorms with own shower/WC for AS175. Single/double occupancy costs AS275/450, and dinner is AS80. Reception shuts from 9 am to 5 pm, though you can leave your bags during the day.

Lehrerhausverein (☎ 51 38 40), Bäckergasse 17, is a central private home with eight beds for AS212 per person. *Klepp* (☎ 32 2 78), Platzgasse 4, has beds without breakfast for AS250/450. *Hotel Liebetegger* (☎ 56 9 35), Völkermarkter Strasse 8, charges AS400/750 with shower/WC or AS220/350 without; breakfast is AS50. For style by the lake, go to *Hotel Wörther See* (☎ 21 1 58), Villacher Strasse 338. It has well-presented rooms, some

with balcony, all with cable TV and bath or shower. Singles/doubles start at AS490/790.

Places to Eat

The university *mensa*, Universitätsstrasse 90, by Europa Park, is open to all for cut-price meals, Monday to Friday from 11 am to 2.30 pm. Eating cheaply in the centre isn't too hard either. There are several *Imbiss* (snack) stands dotted around, especially in the Benediktinerplatz market. The *KGM* supermarket on Bahnhofstrasse has a self-service *Oregano* restaurant, with two-course menus from AS55. *Stefanitsch*, Lidmanskygasse, is a combination deli and stand-up snack bar which has weekday lunches under AS60. On the same street, at No 19, is *Zur Chinesischen Mauer*, offering weekday Chinese lunches for AS65. *Gasthaus Pirker*, on the corner of Adlergasse and Lidmanskygasse, has a good selection of Austrian fare from AS70 to AS180. It's open Monday to Friday from 8 am to midnight.

Getting There & Around

The airport has five flights a day to Vienna and two a day to Zürich and Frankfurt; get there by bus No 40, 41 or 42 from the train station or the town centre, and transfer to bus No 45 or 46 at Annabichl. Trains to Graz depart every one to two hours (AS316; three hours). Trains to west Austria, Italy and Germany go via Villach, which is 40 minutes away by train.

City buses cost AS20 for one journey (including changes) or AS40 for a 24-hour pass. They're available from the driver, but are cheaper in advance from the ticket office on Heiligen Geist Platz. For the Europa Park vicinity, take bus No 10, 11, 12, 20, 21, or 22 from Heiligen Geist Platz.

Salzburg

The city that delivered Mozart to the world has much to recommend it, despite the fact that in more recent years the nearby hills have been alive to *The Sound of Music*. The influence of Mozart is everywhere. There is Mozartplatz, the Mozarteum, Mozart's Birthplace and Mozart's Residence. He even has chocolate bars and liqueurs named after him.

AUSTRIA

But even Mozart must take second place to the powerful bishop-princes who shaped the skyline and the destiny of the city after 798 AD.

Orientation

The centre of the city is split by the River Salzach. The old part of town (mostly pedestrian-only) is on the left (south) bank, with the unmistakable Hohensalzburg Fortress dominant on the hill above. Most of the attractions are on this side of the river. The new town and the centre of business activity is on the right (north) bank, along with most of the cheaper hotels.

Information

Tourist Offices The central office (☎ 84 75 68) is at Mozartplatz 5. It's open daily between Easter and October from 9 am to 7 pm or later (up to 9 pm in July and August), and from 9 am to 6 pm Monday to Saturday between November and Easter. The provincial information section (☎ 84 32 64) in the same building is open Monday to Saturday from 9 am to 6 pm.

Information offices open throughout the year are also in the Hauptbahnhof (☎ 87 17 12) on platform 2A; in the airport (☎ 85 12 11); at Mitte (☎ 43 22 28), Münchner Bundesstrasse 1; and in the south (☎ 62 09 66) at Park & Ride Parkplatz, Alpensiedlung Süd, Alpenstrasse. The office in the north (☎ 66 32 20) at Autobahnstation Kasern, is open from 1 April to 31 October. Tourist offices and hotels sell the Salzburg Card. This provides free museum entry and free public transport, and gives various reductions. The price is AS180/260/350 for 24/48/72 hours.

Foreign Consulates The British Consulate (☎ 84 81 33) is right in the centre of the old town at Alter Markt 4. The US Consulate (☎ 84 87 76) is at Herbert von Karajan Platz 1. The German Consulate (☎ 84 15 910) is near the Mönchsberg lift at Bürgerspitalplatz 1-II. The Swiss Consulate (☎ 62 25 30), Alpenstrasse 85, and Italian Consulate (☎ 62 52 33), Alpenstrasse 102-II, are both south of the old town. Foreign embassies are located in Vienna; see the Facts for the Visitor section.

Money Banks are open Monday to Friday from 8 am to noon and from 2 to 4.30 pm. Currency exchange at the Hauptbahnhof counters is available daily 24 hours. At the airport, money can be exchanged on any day of the week between 8 am and 8 pm.

Post & Communications The post office at the train station (Bahnhofspostamt 5020) is open 24 hours daily (including for money exchange), with poste restante only from 7 am to 10 pm. In the town centre, the main post office (Hauptpostamt 5010), at Residenzplatz 9, is open Monday to Friday from 7 am to 7 pm, and Saturday from 8 to 10 am.

The telephone code for Salzburg is ☎ 0662.

Travel Agencies American Express (☎ 80 80) is next to the tourist office at Mozartplatz 5. It is open Monday to Friday from 9 am to 5.30 pm, and Saturday to noon. ÖKISTA (☎ 88 32 52) at Wolf Dietrich Strasse 31 is open Monday to Friday from 9.30 am to 5.30 pm. Young Austria (☎ 62 57 580), at Alpenstrasse 108A, is open Monday to Friday from 9 am to 6 pm, and Saturday to noon.

Medical Services The Landeskrankenhaus hospital, St Johanns-Spital (☎ 44 820), is at Müllner Hauptstrasse 48, just north of the Mönchsberg; ☎ 141 for an ambulance.

Things to See & Do

Walking Tour The old town is a baroque masterpiece set amid the Kapuzinerberg and Mönchsberg mountains, both of which have a good network of footpaths. Take time to wander around the many plazas, courtyards, fountains and churches.

Start at the vast **cathedral** (Dom) on Domplatz, which has three bronze doors symbolising faith, hope and charity. Head west along Franziskanergasse, and turn left into a courtyard for **St Peter's Abbey**, dating from 847 AD. The interesting graveyard contains the catacombs, and 20-minute guided tours are conducted every hour in summer, less frequently in low season (AS12; students AS8). The western end of Franziskanergasse opens out into Max Reinhardt Platz, where you'll see the back of Fisher von Erlach's **Collegiate Church** on Universitätsplatz. This is considered an outstanding example of baroque,

AUSTRIA

PLACES TO STAY
1 Jugendherberge Haunspergstrasse
6 Elizabeth Pension
7 Sandwirt
9 International Youth Hotel
18 Jugendherberge Glockengasse
19 Amadeus
21 Junger Fuchs
22 Goldene Krone
23 Institut St Sebastian
29 Naturfreundehaus
31 Blaue Gans
38 Zur Goldenen Ente
48 Hinterbrühl
49 Jugendgästehaus

PLACES TO EAT
8 Café-Bistro Tabasco
10 Restaurant Wegscheidstuben
13 Fred's Vegy
15 Fred's Vegy
16 Hotel Restaurant Hofwirt
25 Mozarteum Mensa
30 Sternbräu
36 Mensa
40 K+K Restaurant am Waagplatz
45 Weisses Kreuz
46 St Paul's Stuben

OTHER
2 Avis & Hertz
3 Bundesbus Station
4 Railway Station Post Office
5 Hauptbahnhof
11 ÖKISTA (Travel Agency)
12 Augustiner Bräustübl
14 Mirabell Castle & Gardens
17 Hofer Supermarket
20 St Sebastian Church
24 Schnaitl Musik Pub
26 Mozart's Residence
27 Museum of Natural History
28 Mönchsberg Lift
32 Festival Halls
33 Collegiate Church
34 Mozart's Birthplace
35 Café Tomaselli
37 Residenz Gallery & State Rooms
39 Bar & Disco Area
41 Main Tourist Office & American Express
42 Cathedral
43 Main Post Office
44 St Peter's Abbey & Catacombs
47 Stieglkeller
50 Hohensalzburg Fortress

Salzburg

OLD TOWN

although the cherubs and clouds above the altar are a bit ridiculous.

Hohensalzburg Fortress In many ways this is the high point of a visit to Salzburg. It's a 15-minute walk up the hill to the castle, or you can take the Festungbahn (AS22 up, AS32 return) from Festungsgasse 4. Admission is AS35 (students AS20). Note the many turnip reliefs – this was the symbol of Archbishop Leonhard von Keutschach who greatly extended the fortress. It's worth paying for the guided tour (AS30; students AS25) which allows entrance to the torture chambers, state rooms, the tower and two museums. The view from the castle over the city is stupendous. Look also at the view on the south side: the isolated house in the middle of the big field once belonged to the archbishop's grounds-keeper, though tour guides will tell you it was the home of the shunned official executioner.

Museums The outstanding **Museum of Natural History** (Haus der Natur) is at Museumsplatz 5. You could spend hours wandering round its diverse and well-presented exhibits. In addition to the usual flora, fauna and mineral displays, it has good hands-on exhibits on physics and astronomy, plus bizarre oddities such as the stomach-churning display of deformed human embryos. There are also many tropical fish and an excellent reptile house with lizards, snakes and alligators. It even has an inexpensive terrace café with a lunch menu. The museum is open daily from 9 am to 5 pm, and admission costs AS55 (students AS30).

The other museums don't take too long to get round. In the **Residenz**, Residenzplatz 1, you can visit the baroque state rooms of the archbishop's palace (by guided tour only) and the gallery which houses some good 16th and 17th-century Dutch and Flemish paintings. A combined ticket costs AS80. The **Rupertinium**, Wiener Philharmoniker Gasse 9, has 20th-century works of art and temporary exhibitions. Entry costs AS40 (students AS20).

Mozart's Birthplace (Geburtshaus), at Getreidegasse 9, and **Residence** (Wohnhaus), at Makartplatz 8, are popular but overrated. Entry costs AS65/AS55 respectively, or AS100 (students AS75) for a combined ticket. They both contain musical instruments, sheet music and other memorabilia of the great man. The birthplace also houses the Mozart Sound and Film Museum (free).

Mirabell Palace The castle was built by the worldly prince-archbishop Wolf Dietrich for his mistress in 1606. Its attractive gardens featured in *The Sound of Music*, and they're a great place to spend some time. 'Musical Spring' concerts (among others) are held in the palace. Take a look inside at the marble staircase, which is adorned with baroque sculptures.

Mausoleum of Wolf Dietrich Located in the graveyard of the 16th-century St Sebastian Church on Linzer Gasse, this restored mausoleum has some interesting epitaphs. In a wonderful piece of arrogance, the archbishop commands the faithful to 'piously commemorate the founder of this chapel' (ie himself) and 'his close relations', or expect 'God Almighty to be an avenging judge'. Mozart's father and widow are buried in the graveyard.

Organised Tours
One-hour walking tours of the old city leave from the main tourist office (AS80). Other tours of the city and environs mostly leave from Mirabellplatz, including *The Sound of Music* tour.

The film was a flop in Austria, but this is the most popular tour with English-speaking visitors. Tours last three to four hours, cost around AS330, take in major city sights featured in the movie and include a visit to Salzkammergut. If you go with a group with the right mix of tongue-in-cheek enthusiasm, it can be brilliant fun. It is hard to forget memories of loutish youths skipping in the summer house, chanting 'I am 16 going on 17', or manic Julie Andrews impersonators flouncing in the fields, screeching 'the hills are alive' in voices to wake the dead. On the other hand, if you go with a serious, earnest group, it can be quite dull. See the Jugendgästehaus under Places to Stay for the cheapest tour.

Special Events
The Salzburg International Festival takes place from late July to the end of August, and includes music ranging from Mozart (of

course!) to contemporary. Several events take place per day in different locations. Prices vary from AS50 to a mere AS4200, with reductions for those aged under 26. Most things sell out months in advance. Write for information as early as September to: Kartenbüro der Salzburger Festspiele, Postfach 140, A-5010 Salzburg. Try checking closer to the event for cancellations. Some venues sell standing-room tickets a day or 45 minutes before performances (AS50 to AS200). Enquire at the ticket office (☎ 84 45 01), Hofstallgasse 1. Opening hours during the festival are 10 am to noon and 3 to 5 pm daily. Other important music festivals are at Easter and Whit Sunday.

Places to Stay – bottom end

Accommodation is at a premium during festivals. Ask for the tourist office's list of private rooms (from AS250) and apartments, and the *Hotelplan* map which lists hotels, pensions, six hostels and six camping grounds.

Camping *Camping Kasern* (☎ 50 576), Carl Zuckmayer Strasse 4, just north of the A1 Nord exit, costs AS55 per adult and AS30 each for a car and tent. *Camping Gnigl* (☎ 64 14 44), Parscher Strasse 4, east of Kapuzinerberg, costs marginally less (open mid-May to mid-September).

Hostels If you're travelling to party, head for the sociable *International Youth Hotel* (☎ 87 96 49), Paracelsusstrasse 9. There's a bar with loud music and cheap beer (AS25 for 0.5 litre), and discounts offered on town sights. The staff are almost exclusively young, native English-speakers. Not surprisingly, it is very popular; phone reservations are accepted no earlier than one or two days before. Beds per person are AS130 (eight-bed dorm), AS150 (four-bed dorm, own key) and AS180 (double room, own key). There's a 1 am curfew and it's open all day. Showers cost AS10, lockers AS10 and sheets (if required) AS20. Breakfasts cost AS30 to AS55, dinners AS60 to AS75. The hotel also organises outings and shows *The Sound of Music* daily.

The HI *Jugendherberge* (☎ 87 62 41) at Glockengasse 8 is a bit old, and has a tendency to be overrun by noisy school groups, but it's the cheapest HI hostel in town. Beds in large

dorms are AS130 (AS120 after the first night); dinner is AS70. Curfew is at midnight, and the doors are locked from 9 am to 3.30 pm. The hostel is open from 1 April to 30 September, and is conveniently central.

The HI *Jugendherberge* (☎ 87 50 30), Haunspergstrasse 27, near the train station, is only open in July and August, and costs AS140. *Institut St Sebastian* (☎ 87 13 86), Linzer Gasse 41, has a roof terrace and kitchens, and dorms for AS160 plus AS30 for sheets. Singles/doubles are great value at AS330/630 with shower/WC or AS250/400 without. Reception is closed from noon to 5 pm.

The *Naturfreundehaus* (☎ 84 17 29), Mönchsberg 19, is clearly visible high on the hill between the fortress and the casino. Take the footpath up from near Max Reinhardt Platz, or the Mönchsberg lift (AS16 up, AS27 return) from A Neumayr Platz. It offers dorm beds for AS110 (showers AS10) and marvellous views. It's open all day, but with a 1 am curfew. The café provides breakfast from AS30 and hot meals from AS68 to AS110. It's open from about mid-May to 1 October, but it depends on the weather (phone ahead).

The HI *Jugendgästehaus* (☎ 84 26 700), Josef Preis Allee 18, is large, modern and busy, and probably the most comfortable hostel. Eight-bed dorms are AS150, four-bed rooms are AS200 and two-bed rooms are AS250; all prices are per person and with a AS10 surcharge for the first night's stay. Telephone reservations are accepted, or turn up at 11 am to be sure of a bed – reception is only open in small shifts during the rest of the day. It has good showers, free lockers, a bar, and bike rental for AS90 per day. Daily *Sound of Music* tours are the cheapest in town at AS280 for anybody who shows up at 8.45 am or 1.30 pm. The film is also shown daily.

If everywhere is full in town, try two HI hostels in the south: at Aignerstrasse 34, Aigen (☎ 62 32 48), and at Eduard Heinrich Strasse 2 (☎ 62 59 76); beds in both are AS140.

Hotels & Pensions *Sandwirt* (☎ 87 43 51), Lastenstrasse 6A, is near the rail tracks. Singles/doubles are AS280/440 using hall shower; triples/quads are AS630/720 with private shower/WC. The rooms are clean and reasonably large. *Elizabeth Pension* (☎ 87 16

AUSTRIA

64) is on Vogelweiderstrasse 52. The rooms are smaller and the street is fairly noisy but the pension is close to the Breitenfelderstrasse stop of bus No 15, which heads for the town centre every 15 minutes. Singles/doubles are from AS300/440 using hall shower, or AS350/520 with shower cubicle in the room. Singles are not available in summer.

Junger Fuchs (☎ 87 54 96), Linzer Gasse 54, has singles/doubles/triples for AS260/400/500, without breakfast. The rooms are better than the cramped corridors would suggest and it's in a convenient location. More expensive, but merited by its position in the old town, is *Hinterbrühl* (☎ 84 67 98), Schanzlgasse 12. Singles/doubles are AS420/520 using hall shower, and breakfast is AS50. Reception, in the restaurant downstairs, is open daily from 8 am to midnight.

Places to Stay – middle
Goldene Krone (☎ 87 23 00), Linzer Gasse 48, has singles/doubles with private shower/WC for AS570/970; some of the rooms have church-like groined ceilings which add a bit of character. *Amadeus* (☎ 87 14 01) is down the road and opposite, at No 43-45. Prices are from AS680/1100 for singles/doubles with private shower/WC and TV.

All the rooms in *Zur Goldenen Ente* (☎ 84 56 22), Goldgasse 10, have private bath/shower and TV but prices vary depending upon size and situation – starting at AS720/980 per single/double. The atmospheric restaurant (closed weekends) offers quality meals such as duck from AS128. Also in the old town is *Blaue Gans* (☎ 84 13 17), Getreidegasse 43. It has similarly varied prices, starting at AS500/950 with private shower/WC or AS450/750 without.

Places to Eat – bottom end
There's a fruit and vegetable market at Mirabellplatz on Thursday mornings. On Universitätsplatz and Kapitelplatz there are market stalls and fast-food stands. There's a *Hofer* supermarket at Schallmooser Hauptstrasse 5.

Between sightseeing, nip into *Eduscho*, Getreidegasse 34, for a small, strong cup of coffee for just AS7; you'll have to stand.

The best budget deals are in the university mensas. Lunches are served from 11.30 am to

2 pm on weekdays, and cost from AS35 for ISIC-card holders and AS48 for others. The *Mozarteum Mensa* is between the Aicher Passage and Mirabellgarten. There are several *mensas* on the left bank, including one at Sigmund Haffner Gasse 11.

One of the few vegetarian places in town is *Fred's Vegy*, Schwarzstrasse 33. It's a shop and snack bar with a salad buffet from AS35, and a lunch menu for AS78, including soup. It is open Monday to Friday from 10.30 am to 6 pm. Another branch is at Wolf Dietrich Strasse 17; this one is open till 9 pm on Friday. *Restaurant Wegscheidstuben* (☎ 87 46 18), Lasserstrasse 1, has a three-course menu for AS118, available lunchtime and evening. It offers traditional Austrian cooking, which is popular with locals, and it's open Tuesday to Saturday from 10 am to midnight and on Sunday from lunchtime.

It's almost as if they're trying to keep *St Paul's Stuben*, Herrengasse 16, a secret from the tourists. It's the yellow house, completely anonymous from the outside but for the 1st-floor terrace tables. Pasta and tasty pizzas (from AS72) are served upstairs until late. Long tables make it easy to meet the students who drink there. It's open daily from 6 pm to 1 am.

Sternbräu, set in a courtyard between Getreidegasse 36 and Griegasse 23, is a bit touristy, but it has a nice garden and many different rooms. It serves good Austrian food and fish specials from AS80 to AS210. Opening hours are 9 am to midnight daily. The adjoining courtyard has a self-service buffet place and a pizzeria.

Blaue Gans (see Places to Stay) has a good restaurant with Austrian and Mexican specialities from AS80, affordable set meals, and live music on Thursday. Its Mexican tavern (open from 8 pm; closed Tuesday and Wednesday) is more atmospheric, and has varied live music on Friday and Saturday. *Weisses Kreuz* (☎ 84 56 41), Bierjodlgasse 6, has Austrian food above AS100, but a better choice is its Balkan specialities. Djuvec (rice, succulent pork and paprika) for just AS70 is excellent. It's a small place, so reservations are advised in summer (closed Tuesday except in summer).

Places to Eat – middle
Hotel Restaurant Hofwirt (☎ 87 21 720), Schallmooser Hauptstrasse 1, is really a

mid-price place, with meals above AS110 (English menus). But take advantage of the weekday two-course lunches for AS75. *Café-Bistro Tabasco*, Rainerstrasse 25, offers a tempting array of international and Austrian dishes (AS90 to AS240). The salad buffet is AS62 per bowl. This comfortable, family-oriented place is open daily to midnight.

K+K Restaurant am Waagplatz (☎ 84 21 56), Waagplatz 2, has cheapish food in the casual ground floor Stüberl, or at outside tables. Upstairs, the restaurant is more formal and restrained, with quality Austrian fare for around AS170 to AS260 (open daily).

Entertainment

The atmospheric *Augustiner Bräustübl*, Augustinergasse 4-6, proves that monks can make beer as well as anybody. The quaffing clerics have been supplying the lubrication for this huge beer hall for years. Beer is served in litre (AS52) or half-litre (AS26) mugs. Buy meat, bread and salad ingredients in the deli shops (some are pricey) in the foyer. Eat inside or in the large, shady beer garden. It's open daily from 3 pm (2.30 pm weekends) to 11 pm.

Stieglkeller, Festungsgasse 10, is another beer hall. It's rather touristy, as indicated by the live *Sound of Music* show (AS360) in the summer, but there is a good garden overlooking the town. Food in the restaurant costs between AS90 and AS170. Opening hours are 10 am to 10 pm daily. The *Schnaitl Musik Pub*, at Bergstrasse 5, has pool, videos and a young and vaguely alternative local clientele. Most Fridays (rarely in summer) there's live rock or indie music; cover charge is nil to AS100. The pub is open daily in the summer from 7.30 pm to 1 am, and in the winter from 6.30 pm to midnight. The liveliest area for bars and discos is either side of the Radisson Hotel on Rudolfskai. Try also the vicinity of the Mönchsberg lift.

Coffee houses are a well-established tradition in Salzburg. *Café Tomaselli* and *Café Konditorei Fürst* face each other in an ideal central position overlooking Alter Markt. Both have newspapers, lots of cakes and outside tables.

Things to Buy

Not many people leave without sampling some Mozart confectionery. Chocolate-coated com-binations of nougat and marzipan cost around AS6 per piece, available individually or in souvenir presentation packs. Getreidegasse is the main shopping street.

Getting There & Away

Air The airport (☎ 85 800) has regular scheduled flights to Brussels, Frankfurt, London, Paris and Zürich. Austrian Airlines (☎ 87 55 440) shares an office with Swissair at Schrannengasse 5, and British Airways (☎ 84 21 08) has one at Griesgasse 29.

Bus Bundesbuses depart from outside the Hauptbahnhof. A timetable is displayed in the ticket office, or ☎ 167 for information. There are at least four departures a day to Kitzbühel (AS118; 2¼ hours), changing at Lofer. Buses to Lienz run only from July to September (AS217, change at Franz Josefs Höhe). Numerous buses leave for the Salzkammergut region between 6.30 am and 8 pm – destinations include Bad Ischl (AS95), Mondsee (AS57), St Gilgen (AS57) and St Wolfgang (AS86).

Train Fast trains leave for Vienna via Linz every hour. The express service to Klagenfurt goes via Villach. The quickest way to Innsbruck is by the 'corridor' train through Germany via Kufstein (no passport required, no disembarkation possible in Germany). Trains depart at least every two hours and the fare is AS336. There are trains every 30 to 60 minutes to Munich (AS280; about two hours), some of which continue to Karlsruhe via Stuttgart.

Car & Motorcycle Three autobahns converge on Salzburg and form a loop round the city: the A1 from Linz, Vienna and the east, the A8/E52 from Munich and the west, and the A10/E55 from Villach and the south. Heading south to Carinthia on the A10, there are two tunnels through the mountains; the combined toll is AS190 (AS120 in winter).

Getting Around

To/From the Airport Salzburg airport is four km west of the city centre. Bus No 77 goes there from the Hauptbahnhof.

Public Transport Single bus tickets cost AS19 from the bus driver, but it's cheaper to buy in advance from Tabak shops: a book of five tickets costs AS75. The 24-hour pass valid for all city buses (including those to/from Hellbrunn) is excellent value at AS32. Prices are 50% less for children aged six to 15 years; those aged under six travel free.

Car & Motorcycle Driving in the city centre is hardly worth the effort. Parking places are limited and much of the old town is pedestrian access only. The largest car park near the centre is the Altstadt Garage under the Mönchsberg. Attended car parks cost around AS25 per hour. On streets with automatic ticket machines (blue zones), a three-hour maximum applies (AS42, or AS7 for 30 minutes) during specified times.

Other Transport Taxis cost AS30, plus AS10 per km inside the city or AS20 per km outside the city. To book a radio taxi, call ☎ 87 44 00. Bike rental in the Hauptbahnhof is open 24 hours; bikes for rent in Residenzplatz are more expensive. Rates for a pony-and-trap (fiacre) for up to four passengers are AS380 for 25 minutes and AS740 for 50 minutes.

AROUND SALZBURG
Hellbrunn
Eight km south of Salzburg's old-town centre is the popular **Hellbrunn Palace**, built in the 17th century by bishop Marcus Sitticus, Wolf Dietrich's nephew. The main attraction is the ingenious trick fountains and water-powered figures installed by the bishop and activated today by the tour guides. Expect to get wet! This section of the gardens is open daily from April to October, with the last tour at 4.30 pm (later in summer). Tickets cost AS60 (students AS30). You can also visit the baroque palace (AS20) and the small Folklore Museum on the hill (AS20). There is no charge to stroll round the attractive palace gardens, which are open from February to November (until 9 pm in summer).

The **Hellbrunn Zoo** is as naturalistic and as open-plan as possible: the more docile animals are barely confined. It is open every day from 8.30 am to 5.30 pm (4 pm from October to March). Admission costs AS70 (students AS50).

Getting There & Away City bus No 55 runs to the palace every half-hour from Salzburg's Hauptbahnhof, via Rudolfskai in the old town.

Hallein
Hallein is primarily visited for the **salt mine** at Bad Dürrnberg, on the hill above the town. Much of Salzburg's past prosperity was dependent upon salt mines, and this one is the closest and easiest to visit from the city. The mine stopped production in 1989 to concentrate on guided tours. Some people rave about the experience, others find the one-hour tour disappointing and overpriced (AS170; students AS150). Careering down the wooden slides in the caves is fun, and you get to take a short boat trip on the salt lake, but there's little else to see. It is open daily from 9 am to 5 pm (11 am to 3 pm in winter). Overalls are supplied for the tour.

The tourist office in Hallein (☎ 06245-85 3 94), Unterer Markt 1, is open Monday to Friday from 9 am to 4.30 pm. There's also a summer kiosk at the Stadtsbrücke bridge, open daily from 4 to 9 pm.

Getting There & Away Hallein is an easy half-hour from Salzburg by bus or train (AS34). There are several ways to reach Bad Dürrnberg. The easiest option is to take the cable car, which is a signposted 10-minute walk from the train station. The AS240 (students AS210) return fare includes entry to the mines. A cheaper option is the 15-minute bus ride (AS19) from outside the station; departures are synchronised with train arrivals. You could also hike to the mine, but it's a steep 40-minute climb: at the church with the bare concrete tower, turn left along Ferchl Strasse, and follow the sign pointing to the right after the yellow Volksschule building.

Werfen
Werfen is a rewarding day trip from Salzburg. The **Hohenwerfen Fortress** stands on the hill above the village. Originally built in 1077, the present building dates from the 16th century and can be visited daily from April to early November. Entry costs AS100 (students AS90) and includes an exhibition, a guided tour of the interior and a dramatic falconry show, where birds of prey swoop low over the heads of the

crowd. The walk up from the village takes 20 minutes.

The **Eisriesenwelt Höhle** in the mountains are the largest accessible ice caves in the world. The ice formations inside are vast, elaborate and beautiful, yet completely naturally formed. The 70-minute tour (in German) costs AS80, and the caves are open from 1 May to early October. Some elderly visitors find the going too arduous. Take warm clothes because it can get cold inside.

Both attractions can be fitted into the same day if you start early (visit the caves first, and be at the castle by 3 pm for the falconry show). The tourist office (☎ 06468-388) in the village main street is open Monday to Friday 9 am to 5 pm; in July and August it's open till 7 pm on weekdays and on weekends from 5 to 7 pm.

Getting There & Away Werfen (and Hallein) can be reached from Salzburg by Highway 10. By train (AS78) it takes 50 minutes. The village is a five-minute walk from Werfen station. Getting to the caves is more complicated, though it yields fantastic views. A minibus service (AS65 return) from the station operates along the steep, six-km road to the car park, which is as far as cars can go. A 15-minute walk brings you to the cable car (AS110 return) from which it is a further 15-minute walk to the caves. Allow four hours return from the station, or three hours from the car park (peak-season queues may add an hour). The whole route can be hiked, but it's a hard four-hour ascent, rising 1100 metres above the village.

Salzkammergut

Salzkammergut, named after its salt mines, is a holiday region of mountains and lakes to the east of Salzburg. It's an area where you can simply relax and take in the scenery, or get involved in the numerous sports and activities on offer.

The main season is summer, when hiking and water sports are the preferred pursuits. In winter, some hiking paths stay open but downhill and cross-country skiing are far more popular.

A winter ski pass is available for the Salzkammergut-Tennengau region, which includes 140 cable cars and ski lifts in 21 ski resorts. It costs AS1420 for five days. Six, seven and 10-day passes are also available.

Orientation
The largest lake is Attersee to the north. West of Attersee is Mondsee, a picturesque warm water lake which is a favoured swimming spot. The village of Mondsee has an attractive church which was used in the wedding scenes of *The Sound of Music*. To the east of Attersee is Traunsee and its three main resorts: Gmunden, Traunkirchen and Ebensee. Gmunden is famous for twin castles linked by a causeway on the lake, and the manufacturing of ceramics. South of Traunsee is Bad Ischl, the geographical centre of Salzkammergut. Most of the lakes south of Bad Ischl are much smaller, the largest being Hallstätter See. West of Bad Ischl is the Wolfgangsee.

Information
The Salzburg provincial tourist office has information on the area, including bus and train schedules and a list of camping grounds. Most of Salzkammergut is in Upper Austria, so the Linz provincial tourist office is another good source of information. Styria stretches up to claim the area around Bad Aussee – the relevant brochures are dispensed by the Graz tourist offices. Alternatively, write to the Tourismusregion Salzkammergut, Wirerstrasse 10, A-4820 Bad Ischl.

The area is dotted with hostels and affordable hotels, but often the best deal is a room in a private home or farmhouse, despite the prevalence of single-night surcharges. Tourist offices can supply lists of private rooms, and will sometimes make free hotel bookings. Most resorts have a holiday/guest card (*Gästekarte*) which offers a variety of discounts. Make sure you ask for a card if it is not offered spontaneously. It must be stamped at the place where you're staying (even camping grounds) to be valid.

Getting Around
The main rail routes pass either side of Salzkammergut, but the area can be crossed by regional trains on a north-south route. You can get on this route from Attnang Puchheim on the

Salzburg-Linz line. The track from here connects Gmunden, Traunkirchen, Ebensee, Bad Ischl, Hallstatt and Obertraun. At small unstaffed stations, marked 'Hu' on timetables, you'll need to buy your ticket on the train (surcharge not applicable). After Obertraun, the railway continues east via Bad Aussee before connecting with the main Bischofshofen-Graz line at Stainach Irdning. Attersee can also be reached from the Salzburg-Linz line prior to the Attnang Puchheim stop.

Regular bus services connect all towns and villages in the area. Timetables are displayed at stops, and tickets can be bought from the driver. Enquire locally if the regional train and bus pass has been re-introduced. See the Salzburg Getting There & Away section for more bus information.

Passenger boats ply the waters of the Attersee, Traunsee, Mondsee, Hallstätter See and Wolfgangsee.

To reach Salzkammergut from Salzburg by car or motorcycle, take the A1 or Highway 158.

BAD ISCHL

This spa town's reputation snowballed after Princess Sophie took a treatment to cure her infertility in 1828. Within two years she had given birth to Franz Josef (the penultimate

Habsburg emperor), and two other sons followed.

Orientation & Information

The centre of town is compactly contained within a bend of the River Traun.

The tourist office or *Kurdirektion* (☎ 235 200) is close to the train station (straight ahead and bear left) at Bahnhofstrasse 6. It is open Monday to Friday from 8 am to 6 pm, Saturday 9 am to 4 pm and Sunday 9 am to 11.30 am. The post office (Postamt 4820) is nearby on Bahnhofstrasse. There are money changing facilities at both the post office and the train station. The station also rents bikes between 5 am and 8.10 pm daily.

The telephone code for Bad Ischl is ☎ 06132.

Things to See & Do

Salzkammergut became popular in the mid-19th century when Emperor Franz Josef I began spending his summers in Bad Ischl in the **Kaiservilla**. Not only did he sign the declaration of war here that started WWI, he also had a habit of getting up every day at 3.30 am for his bath. The villa was his hunting lodge and contains an obscene number of hunting trophies. It can be visited only by guided tour, which is given in German, but there are written English translations. The tour takes 40 minutes, costs AS88, and includes entry to the Kaiserpark grounds (which costs AS35 on its own). The small **Photomuseum** in the park nearby has some interesting old photographs and cameras (entry AS15; students AS10).

Free 'spa concerts' take place usually twice a day (except Tuesday) during summer; the tourist office has a list of venues and times. An operetta festival takes place in July and August; for advance details and reservations, call ☎ 238 39.

Bad Ischl has downhill skiing from **Mt Katrin** (a winter day-pass costs AS214) and a variety of cross-country skiing routes. In summer, the Mt Katrin cable car costs AS159 return (AS139 with the guest card). There's a **salt mine** to the south of town; tours cost AS135 and are conducted daily from early May to late September.

The tourist office has information on health treatments available in the resort.

Places to Stay & Eat

The HI *Jugendgästehaus* (☎ 265 77) is at Am Rechensteg 5, in the town centre behind Kreuzplatz. Dorms are AS130 and dinner is AS65. It's closed from 9 am to 5 pm. *Frau Unterreiter* (English not spoken), at Stiegengasse 1 (☎ 267 83), has four singles and two doubles for around AS160 per person, using a hall shower. There are TVs in most rooms.

B&B pensions also offer good value. *Stadlmann Josefa* (☎ 231 04), west of town at Masteliergasse 21, has rooms from AS180 per person, some with private shower. *Haus an der Traun* (☎ 234 72) is just to the right of the station, at Bahnhofstrasse 11. It has rooms at AS320 per person with radio, TV and balcony, or AS370 including a private shower/WC.

The *China Restaurant Happy Dragon*, by the Schröpferplatz bridge, overlooks the river. It has lunch menus from AS64, and is open daily. *Pizzeria Don Camillo*, Wiesingerstrasse 5, has good-value pizza and spaghetti dishes from AS55. It's also open daily. *Blauen Enzian*, Wirerstrasse 2, is back from the main street. This informal place offers a varied menu (AS80 to AS170 per dish) covering pasta, salads, and regional and national food (closed Sunday in the low season).

There's a central supermarket, *Julius Meinl*, on Pfarrgasse.

Getting There & Away

Bundesbuses leave from outside the station. There are hourly buses to Salzburg (AS95) between 5.05 am and 8.10 pm, via St Gilgen. To St Wolfgang (AS38), you have to change at Strobl at weekends (the bus will be waiting, and the same ticket is valid). Buses run to Hallstatt every one to two hours (AS48; 50 minutes). Three buses a day go to both Mondsee and Obertraun.

Trains depart hourly. It costs AS34 to Hallstatt but, unlike the bus, you must add the cost of the boat (see the Hallstatt Getting There & Away section). The fare to Salzburg by train is AS180, via Attnang Puchheim.

HALLSTATT

Hallstatt has a history stretching back 4500 years. In 50 AD, the Romans were attracted by the rich salt deposits. Today, the village is prized mainly for its picturesque location.

Orientation & Information

Seestrasse is the main street. Turn left from the ferry to reach the tourist office (☎ 8208), Seestrasse 169. It is open Monday to Friday from 9 am to 5 pm and weekends from 10 am to 2 pm; from September to June it is closed at weekends and for one hour at noon. The post office (Postamt 4830) is around the corner, and changes money.

The telephone code for Hallstatt is ☎ 06134.

Things to See & Do

Hallstatt is set in idyllic, picture-postcard scenery between the mountains and the lake. It is invaded by crowds of day-trippers; fortunately they only stay a few hours and then the village returns to its natural calm.

Above the village are the **saltworks**, open April to October, daily from 9.30 am. During the shoulder seasons the last tour is at 3 pm; in summer it's at 4.30 pm. Admission costs AS135 (AS120 with guest card). The cable car to the top costs AS100 return (AS85 with guest card), but there are two scenic hiking trails you can take instead. Near the mine, 2000 flat graves were discovered dating from 1000 to 500 BC. Don't miss the macabre **Bone House** (Beinhaus) near the village parish church; it contains rows of decorated skulls (AS10). Around the lake at Obertraun are the **Dachstein Giant Ice Caves**, open May to mid-October. Entry costs AS81 (AS76 with guest card), or AS120 (AS105) in combination with the nearby Mammoth cave. A cable car provides easy access.

Places to Stay & Eat

Some private rooms in the village are only available during the busiest months of July and August; others require a minimum three-night stay. The tourist office can provide details.

Campingplatz Höll (☎ 8329), Lahnstrasse 7, costs AS55 per person, AS40 per tent and AS30 per car. It's open from 1 May to 30 September.

The HI *Jugendherberge* (☎ 8212), Salzbergstrasse 50, is open from around 1 May to 30 September, depending on the weather. Beds cost AS100 and, if required, breakfast and sheets cost another AS25 each. Daytime check-in is sometimes possible, and getting a key avoids the 10 pm curfew. *TVN Naturfreunde Herberge* (☎ 8318), Kirchen-

weg 36, is just below the road tunnel, by the waterfall. It has dorm beds for AS110, plus AS40 each for sheets and breakfast (if required). Dorms vary in size in both places – some are cramped. TVN is part of and is run by the *Zur Mühle Gasthaus*, which has pizza and pasta from AS65, and Austrian dishes from AS70. It's closed on Wednesday, when there's also no TVN check-in.

Go to *Bräu Gasthof* (☎ 8221), Seestrasse 120, if you want typical Austrian food in an old-fashioned atmosphere. Lunchtime specials start from AS105, other dishes from AS85. It's open daily, but only from 1 May to 31 October. Double rooms with private WC and shower are available all year for AS900. *Gasthof Hallberg* (☎ 8286), Seestrasse 113, has pizzas and Austrian food for AS85 to AS160. It also has a few rooms for AS400 per person with private WC and shower.

Getting There & Away

There are around six buses a day to/from Obertraun and Bad Ischl, but none after 6 pm. Get off the 'Lahn' Bundesbus by the stream at the southern end of the road tunnel for the hostel; get off at the 'Parkterrasse' stop for the centre and the tourist office. The train station is across the lake. The boat service from there to the village (AS20) coincides with train arrivals (at least nine a day from Bad Ischl; total trip 45 minutes). Parking in the village is free if you have a guest card (car access is restricted in the summer without one).

WOLFGANGSEE

This lake can become crowded in summer because of its proximity to Salzburg, but its scenery and lakeside villages make it well worth a visit.

Orientation & Information

The lake is dominated by the Schafberg (1783 metres) on the northern shore. Next to it is the resort of St Wolfgang. The tourist office (☎ 06138-2239) is on the main street near the bus stop, open Monday to Friday and (in July and August) Saturday. St Gilgen, on the western shore, provides easy access to Salzburg, which is 29 km away. Its tourist office (☎ 06227-2348), Mozartplatz 1, in the Rathaus, is open Monday to Friday, or daily in July and August.

Things to See & Do

The major sight in St Wolfgang is the **Pilgrimage Church**, built in the 14th and 15th centuries. This incredible church is virtually a gallery of religious art. The best piece is the winged high altar made by Michael Pacher between 1471 and 1481, which has astonishing detail on the carved figures and Gothic designs. The church wardens used to be so protective that the wings were kept closed except for important festivals. Now they are always open, except for eight weeks before and during Easter. The double altar by Thomas Schwanthaler is also excellent. The church is open daily from 7.30 am to 6 pm. The **White Horse Inn** in the village centre was the setting for a famous operetta.

Ascend the **Schafberg** for good hikes and views. The Schafberg cog-wheel railway runs from early May to mid-October approximately every hour during the day and reaches 1734 metres. The cost is AS140 up and AS250 return; holders of Eurail or Bundes-Netzkarte passes ride free, and an Inter-Rail pass secures a 50% reduction.

St Gilgen has good views of the lake and some swimming spots, but little else of interest – unless you want to see the birthplace of Mozart's mother. In winter, there's downhill and cross-country skiing. You can get information from the St Gilgen tourist office or the director of the ski school, Josef Resch (☎ 06227-2275), Liam 136, St Gilgen.

Places to Stay & Eat

Camping Appesbach (☎ 06138-2206), Au 99, is on the lakefront, one km from St Wolfgang in the direction of Strobl. It's open from Easter to 30 September and costs AS69 per person, from AS50 for a tent and AS30 for a car.

St Gilgen has a modern HI *Jugendherberge* (☎ 06227-2365), at Mondseestrasse 7. Prices are from AS115 to AS270 per person, in anything from singles to 10-bed dorms, with or without WC and lake view but always with shower. Check-in is from noon to 5 pm.

Both St Wolfgang and St Gilgen have a good selection of pensions (from AS180 per person) and private rooms (from AS150 per person). Lists are available from the respective tourist offices. Convenient pensions to try are *Gästehaus Raudaschl* (☎ 06138-2329), at Pilgerstrasse 4, opposite the St Wolfgang tourist office, which has singles/doubles from AS280/380; and *Gasthof Rosam* (☎ 06227-2591), Frontfestgasse 2, two minutes from the St Gilgen boat station, which charges from AS320/500. Rosam has decent, hearty meals from about AS80. It's open daily from 8 am to 9 pm (Easter to 31 October only).

There are lots of places to eat in the centre of St Wolfgang, ranging from cheap snack joints to quaint touristy restaurants. *Gasthof Rudolfshöhe* is in the north-east of the village, up the small hill near the tunnel. It has an excellent menu offering a range of Hungarian, Austrian, Indian and vegetarian food from AS65. Look out for its special evenings, eg barbecues on Monday in summer.

Buy picnic materials at the *supermarket* 100 metres from the Schafberg cog-wheel railway ticket office, towards the village centre.

Getting There & Away

An hourly ferry service operates from Strobl to St Gilgen, stopping at various points en route. Services are more frequent during the high season from mid-June to mid-September. The journey from St Wolfgang to St Gilgen takes 40 minutes (AS52), and boats sail approximately hourly from 8.22 am to 6 pm (8.30 pm in the high season). In the reverse direction, the first departure from St Gilgen is at 9.14 am. The operating season and rail card validity are the same as for the Schafberg cog-wheel railway.

Buses from St Wolfgang to St Gilgen and Salzburg go via Strobl, on the east side of the lake. St Gilgen is 50 minutes from Salzburg by bus, with hourly departures until 7.05 pm. The fare is AS570.

Tirol

The province of Tirol (sometimes spelled Tyrol) has some of the best mountain scenery in Austria. It's an ideal playground for skiers, hikers, mountaineers and anglers, and the tourist offices release plenty of glossy material to promote these pursuits. The province is divided into two parts: East Tirol has been isolated from the main part of the state ever since prosperous South Tirol was ceded to Italy at the end of WWI.

Train and bus journeys within Tirol are cheaper using VVT tickets, which can only be bought within Tirol (from train stations etc). These tickets can be combined with city passes. The system is quite complicated; for information you can contact the VVT Büro (☎ 0512-36 59 20), Eduard Bodem Gasse, Innsbruck.

INNSBRUCK

Innsbruck has been an important trading post since the 12th century, thanks in part to the Brenner Pass, the gateway to the south. It wasn't long before the city found favour with the Habsburgs, particularly Emperor Maximilian and Maria Theresa, who built many of the important buildings that still survive in the well-preserved, old town centre. More recently, the capital of Tirol has become an important winter sports centre, and staged the Winter Olympics in 1964 and 1976.

Orientation

Innsbruck is in the valley of the River Inn, scenically squeezed between the northern chain of the Alps and the Tuxer mountain range to the south. Extensive mountain transport facilities surround the city and provide ample hiking and skiing opportunities. The centre of town is very compact, with the main train station (Hauptbahnhof) only a 10-minute walk from the pedestrian-only, old town centre (Altstadt). The main street in the Altstadt is Herzog Friedrich Strasse.

Information

Tourist Offices The main tourist office (☎ 53 56), Burggraben 3, sells ski passes and public transport tickets, books hotel rooms (AS40 commission), and gives out free maps. Ask here about 'Club Innsbruck'. Membership is free and provides various discounts; it also allows you to go on free, guided mountain hikes from June to September. Office opening hours are from 8 am to 7 pm Monday to Saturday, 9 am to 6 pm on Sunday.

There are hotel reservation centres in the Hauptbahnhof (open daily from 9 am to 9 pm; 8 am to 10 pm in summer) and at motorway exits near the city. The youth waiting room (*Jugendwarteraum*) in the Hauptbahnhof also offers useful information; it's closed mid-July to mid-August.

The Tirol Information office (☎ 72 72), Maria Theresien Strasse 55, is open Monday to Friday from 8 am to 6 pm.

Foreign Consulates The British Consulate (☎ 58 83 20) is at Matthias Schmid Strasse 12/I, and the German Consulate (☎ 59 6 65) is at Adamgasse 5. Foreign embassies are in Vienna; see the Facts for the Visitor section earlier in this chapter.

Money The train station has exchange facilities (compare rates and commission between the ticket counters and the office) and a Bankomat. The tourist office also exchanges money.

Post & Communications The main post office is at Maximilianstrasse 2 (Hauptpostamt 6010), and is open daily 24 hours. The train station post office, Brunecker Strasse 1-3, is open Monday to Saturday from 6.30 am to 9 pm.

The telephone code for Innsbruck is ☎ 0512.

Travel Agencies American Express (☎ 58 24 91), Brixnerstrasse 3, is open Monday to Friday from 9 am to 5.30 pm and Saturday to noon. ÖKISTA (☎ 58 89 97), Wilhelm Greil Strasse 17, is open Monday to Friday from 9.30 am to 5.30 pm.

Medical Services The University Clinic (☎ 50 40), also called the Landeskrankenhaus, is at Anichstrasse 35.

Things to See & Do

Consider buying the three-day museum pass for AS150 (students AS90), which entitles you to enter 11 museums from May through to September.

Walking Tour For an overview of the city, climb the 14th-century **City Tower** (Stadtturm) in Herzog Friedrich Strasse. It's open daily between 1 March and 31 October from 10 am to 5 pm, except in July and August when it closes at 6 pm. Entry costs AS20 (students and children AS10). Across the square is the famous **Golden Roof** (Goldenes Dachl); it comprises 2657 gilded copper tiles dating from the 16th century. Emperor Maximilian used to observe street performers from the balcony.

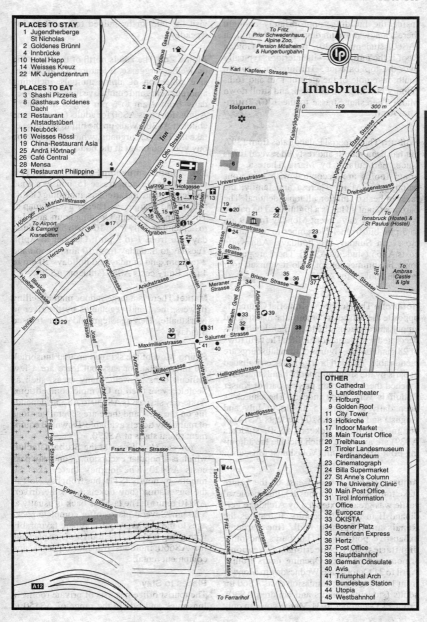

PLACES TO STAY
1 Jugendherberge St Nicholas
2 Goldenes Brünnl
4 Innbrücke
10 Hotel Happ
14 Weisses Kreuz
22 MK Jugendzentrum

PLACES TO EAT
3 Shashi Pizzeria
8 Gasthaus Goldenes Dachl
12 Restaurant Altstadtstüberl
15 Neuböck
16 Weisses Rössl
19 China-Restaurant Asia
25 Andrä Hörtnagl
26 Café Central
28 Mensa
42 Restaurant Philippine

OTHER
5 Cathedral
6 Landestheater
7 Hofburg
9 Golden Roof
11 City Tower
13 Hofkirche
17 Indoor Market
18 Main Tourist Office
20 Treibhaus
21 Tiroler Landesmuseum Ferdinandeum
23 Cinematograph
24 Billa Supermarket
27 St Anne's Column
29 The University Clinic
30 Main Post Office
31 Tirol Information Office
32 Europcar
33 ÖKISTA
34 Bosner Platz
35 American Express
36 Hertz
37 Post Office
38 Hauptbahnhof
39 German Consulate
40 Avis
41 Triumphal Arch
43 Bundesbus Station
44 Utopia
45 Westbahnhof

Innsbruck

AUSTRIA

Inside the building, appropriately enough, there's a new museum devoted to Maximilian (AS60, students AS30). Behind the Golden Roof is the **cathedral** – its interior is typically over-the-top baroque. Turning back to the south, take note of the elegant 15th and 16th-century buildings on all sides, and stroll down Maria Theresien Strasse to the 1767 **Triumphal Arch**.

Hofburg The Imperial Palace dates from 1397, but has been rebuilt and restyled several times since, particularly by Maria Theresa. The grand rooms are decorated with numerous paintings of Maria Theresa and family; the faces of her 16 children all look identical. The baroque Giant's Hall is a highlight. The palace is open every day except Monday from 9 am to 5 pm, but from 1 November to 30 April it closes on Sunday and holidays. Admission costs AS55 (students AS35). There are guided tours in summer, or for a do-it-yourself tour buy the booklet for AS25.

Hofkirche The Hofkirche (Imperial Church) is opposite the palace. It contains the massive but empty sarcophagus of Maximilian I, which is decorated with scenes of his life. The twin rows of 28 giant bronze figures of the Habsburgs are memorable. The dull bronze has been polished in parts by the sheer number of hands that have touched them; a certain private part of Kaiser Rudolf is very shiny indeed! The church is open daily to 5 pm (5.30 pm in July and August) and it costs AS20 (students AS14) to get in. Combined tickets (AS50; students AS39) are available which include the adjoining **Folk Art Museum** (Volkskunst Museum).

Ambras Castle Located east of the centre (take tram No 3 or 6, or bus K), this medieval castle was greatly extended by Archduke Ferdinand II in the 16th century. It features the Renaissance Spanish Hall, fine gardens, exhaustive portraits of Habsburgs and other dignitaries, and collections of weapons, armour and oddities. Opening hours from 1 April to 31 October are Wednesday to Monday from 10 am to 5 pm; admission costs AS60 for adults (students, seniors and children AS30). From 27 December to 31 March you can only

visit the interior by guided tour at 2 pm on weekdays.

Alpine Zoo The zoo is north of the River Inn on Weiherburggasse. It features a comprehensive collection of alpine animals, including amorous bears and combative ibexes. It is open daily from 9 am to 6 pm (5 pm in winter). Admission costs AS60 for adults (students and children AS30). Walk up the hill to get there or take the Hungerburgbahn, which is free if you buy your zoo ticket at the bottom.

Tiroler Landesmuseum Ferdinandeum This museum, at Museumstrasse 15, houses a good collection of art and artefacts, including Gothic statues and altarpieces. There's a relief map of Tirol in the basement. Opening hours are May to September daily from 10 am to 5 pm (Thursday also from 7 to 9 pm); October to April, Tuesday to Saturday from 10 am to noon and 2 to 5 pm, and Sunday and holidays 10 am to 1 pm. Entry costs AS50 (students AS30).

Market There is a large indoor market selling flowers, meat and vegetables by the river in Markthalle, Herzog Siegmund Ufer (closed Sunday).

Skiing Most of the ski runs around Innsbruck are intermediate or easy but there are a few difficult ones as well. Many areas, such as Seefeld, were used in Olympic competitions. A one-day ski pass is AS250 to AS350, depending on the area, and there are several versions of multi-day tickets available. Downhill equipment rental starts at AS270.

You can ski all year at the **Stubai Glacier**, which is a popular excursion. A one-day pass costs AS420. The journey there takes 80 minutes by hourly 'STB' bus from bay No 1 in the bus station (buy tickets from the driver; AS110 return). The last bus back is usually at 5.30 pm. Several places offer complete packages to the glacier, which compare favourably with going it alone. The tourist office package for AS660 includes transport, passes and equipment rental.

Places to Stay
The tourist office has lists of private rooms in Innsbruck and Igls in the range of AS150 to

AS250 per person. Igls is south of town; get there by tram No 6 or bus J.

Camping *Camping Innsbruck Kranebitten* (☎ 28 41 80), Kranebitter Allee 214, is west of the town centre and open from April to October. Prices are AS61 per person, AS35 for a tent and AS35 for a car. There is a restaurant on site.

Hostels A convenient hostel for the centre is *Jugendherberge St Nicholas* (☎ 28 65 15), Innstrasse 95. Reception is also here for the *Glockenhaus* pension, up the hill at Weiherburggasse 3, which has more secluded singles/doubles for AS300/380 with private shower but no breakfast. The hostel is HI-affiliated but it seems more like an independent backpacker place. There's a cellar bar which can be noisy, and a not very friendly pay-up-or-get-out wake-up call. Dorm beds are AS115 for the first night and AS100 for additional nights, including sheets but not breakfast. Shower tokens are AS10 and reception is open from 8 to 10 am and 5 to 8 pm. Get a key for late nights out. The attached restaurant is open to all and is a good place for socialising. The food is so-so; spaghetti bolognaise (AS69) and Wiener schnitzel (AS85).

Two HI hostels down Reichenauerstrasse are accessible by bus No O from Museumstrasse. *Innsbruck* (☎ 34 61 79), at No 147, costs AS135 the first night, AS105 thereafter (AS6 less if you're aged under 18). Curfew is at 11 pm, and the place is closed from 10 am to 5 pm. It has a kitchen, and slow washing machines (AS45). *St Paulus* hostel (☎ 34 42 91), at No 72, has large dorms for AS100 and sheets for AS20. Breakfast costs AS30, although kitchen facilities are available. Curfew is at 10 pm (but you can get a key) and the doors are locked from 10 am to 5 pm. The hostel is only open from mid-June to mid-August.

Two other hostels to try in the summer are: *MK Jugendzentrum* (☎ 57 13 11), centrally situated at Sillgasse 8A, which has beds for AS150 (open from July to mid-September); and *Fritz Prior Schwedenhaus* (☎ 58 58 14), at Rennweg 17B, where beds cost AS120, breakfast is AS45 and sheets are AS20 (open July and August).

Hotels & Pensions *Ferrarihof* (☎ 58 09 68), Brennerstrasse 8, is south of town, just off the main road. Singles/doubles are AS260/520 with either private or hall shower. Reception is in the bar downstairs, open from 8 am to midnight. There is plenty of parking space. *Pension Möslheim* (☎ 26 71 34), Oberkoflerweg 8, to the north in Mühlau, has singles/doubles for AS220/440, using hall showers. Reception is next door at No 4; telephone ahead as it's often full with long-term students.

Goldenes Brünnl (☎ 28 35 19), St Nikolaus Gasse 1, is on the other side of the river from the old town. It's basic but good value: singles/doubles with hall showers are AS240/460. Reception is in the restaurant, and is open to midnight (closed Tuesday). *Innbrücke* (☎ 28 19 34), Innstrasse 1, is nearby. Rooms are AS350/650 with shower/WC or AS290/480 without.

The pick of the hotels in the Altstadt is *Weisses Kreuz* (☎ 59 479), Herzog Friedrich Strasse 31, which has singles/doubles for AS430/800, or AS710/1100 with private shower/WC. The 'superior' doubles for AS1180 are worth the extra cost. This 500-year-old inn played host to Mozart when he was 13, and all the rooms are spacious, well presented and comfortable. Prices drop slightly in winter. If it's full, try the *Hotel Happ* (☎ 58 29 80) across the street at No 14. It's almost as atmospheric, and rooms with shower/WC and TV are AS700/1200. Pre-book for a Sunday arrival as the reception is closed on that day.

Places to Eat
There are various Würstel stands and Imbiss shops for fast, cheap snacks around the city, and two supermarkets are close together on Museumstrasse. *Andrä Hörtnagl*, Maria Theresien Strasse 5, is the self-service restaurant of the supermarket around the corner on Burggasse. Snacks and meals are inexpensive and the salad buffet is AS26/49 for a small/large bowl. It's open weekdays to 5 pm and Saturday to 1 pm. Another inexpensive option is the deli shops which offer hot and cold food. *Neuböck*, Herzog Friedrich Strasse 30, is one such place (open daily), and has a sit-down section.

The *University mensa*, Herzog Siegmund Ufer 15, on the 1st floor, serves good lunches between 11 am and 2 pm from Monday to Friday. For AS45 to AS65 you can get a main dish, soup and salad. The mensa closes for the Christmas and Easter holidays.

Restaurant Philippine (☎ 589 157), Müllerstrasse 9, is a specialist vegetarian restaurant, decked out in light colours. It has a wide selection of main dishes in the range of AS85 to AS185, and a fine salad buffet for AS52/94 for a small/big plate. It is open Monday to Saturday from 10 am to midnight (the kitchen closes at 10 pm).

Café Central, Gilmstrasse 5, is a typical Austrian coffee house. It has English newspapers, daily menus (with soup) from around AS90, and piano music on Sunday from 8 to 10 pm. It opens daily from 8 am to 11 pm. The **China-Restaurant Asia** is nearby at Angerzellgasse 10. It offers excellent three-course weekday lunch specials: you get a *lot* of food for AS69. **Shashi Pizzeria**, Innstrasse 81, has very big pizzas from AS60, and Indian dishes. On Friday and Saturday there's also a good Indian buffet where you can eat as much as you want for AS100 (open daily).

Most places in the Altstadt are a little pricey, and generally serve a combination of Tirolean, Austrian and international food. **Gasthaus Goldenes Dachl**, Hofgasse 1, provides a civilised environment for tasting Tirolean specialities such as Bauerngröstl, a pork, bacon, potato and egg concoction served with salad (AS118). It is open daily from 7.30 am to midnight. **Weisses Rössl** (☎ 58 30 57), Kiebachgasse 8, is good for regional food for around AS90 to AS190 (daily menus and 'senior' meals are cheaper). It's closed on Sunday and holidays. For more up-market eating, **Restaurant Altstadtstüberl** (☎ 58 23 47), Riesengasse 13, is one of the best places to try typical Tirolean food. Main dishes are in the range of AS120 to AS240; it's closed on Sunday and holidays.

Entertainment

Ask the tourist office about 'Tirolean evenings' (AS200 for brass bands, folk dancing, yodelling and one drink) and summer classical concerts. The **Landestheater** has year-round performances ranging from opera and ballet to drama and comedy. Get information and tickets (commission charged) from the tourist office.

Utopia (☎ 58 85 87), Tschamlerstrasse 3, stages theatre, art, parties and live music in the cellar downstairs, around five nights a week; entry costs AS60 to AS200 (AS20 less for students). There's also a café, open Monday to Saturday from 5.30 pm to midnight.

Treibhaus (☎ 58 68 74), Angerzellgasse 8, has live music most nights (in a circus-style tent in summer). Entry costs AS150 to AS200, though free jazz enlivens Sunday lunchtimes. There's also a play area for kids, and pizzas are great value (from AS50/70 for small/large). It's open daily to 1 am.

Cinematograph (☎ 57 85 00), Museumstrasse 31, shows independent films in their original language. Tickets are AS70. Cinemas around town are cheaper on Monday, when all seats are AS60.

Getting There & Away

Air Tyrolean Airlines, the small airport's main carrier, flies daily to Amsterdam, Frankfurt, Paris, Vienna and Zürich.

Bus Bundesbuses leave from by the Hauptbahnhof. The bus ticket office is near the youth waiting room in the smaller of the station's two halls.

Train Fast trains depart every two hours for Bregenz and Salzburg. Regular express trains head north to Munich (via Kufstein) and south to Verona. Connections are hourly to Kitzbühel (AS122). Three daily trains (four on Saturday) go to Lienz, passing through Italy. The 7.10 am and 5.04 pm trains (AS136) are Austrian 'corridor' trains, and you can disembark in Italy. The 12.48 pm train is an international train; it costs AS200, and if you're travelling on an Austrian rail pass you must pay for the Italian section (AS72). For train information, call ☎ 1717.

Car & Motorcycle The A12 and the parallel Highway 171 are the main roads to the west and east. Highway 177, to the west of Innsbruck, heads north to Germany and Munich. The A13 motorway is a toll road (AS130) southwards through the Brenner Pass to Italy; it includes the impressive Europabrücke (Europe Bridge) several km south of the city.

Toll-free Highway 182 follows the same route, passing under the bridge.

Getting Around
To/From the Airport The airport is four km to the west of the centre. To get there, take bus F, which leaves every 20 minutes from Maria Theresien Strasse (AS21).

Tickets bought on buses and trams cost AS21. In advance, you can buy a block of four for AS54, or a day pass for AS30. These are not valid for the Hungerburgbahn. A seven-day pass costs AS105 and is valid from Monday to Sunday.

It's hardly worth using private transport in the compact city centre. Most central streets are blue zones with maximum parking of 1½ hours; the charge is AS5/10/20 for 30/60/90 minutes (tickets from pavement dispensers). Parking garages (eg under the Altstadt) are around AS200 per day.

Taxis cost AS52 for the first 1.3 km, then AS18 per km. Bike rental in the Hauptbahnhof is open 24 hours daily.

KITZBÜHEL
Kitzbühel is a fashionable and prosperous winter resort, offering excellent skiing and a variety of other sports. It also boasts some of the glossiest tourist brochures in the country.

Orientation & Information
The main train station is one km from the town centre. To reach the centre, turn left from Bahnhofstrasse into Josef Pirchl Strasse. Take the right fork (no entry for cars), which is still Josef Pirchl Strasse, and continue past the post office (Postamt 6370). The tourist office (☎ 215 50), Hinterstadt 18, is in the centre, open every day (except Sunday in the low season). Ask about the summer guest card, which offers various discounts.

The telephone code for Kitzbühel is ☎ 05356.

Activities
In winter, there is good intermediate **skiing** on Kitzbüheler Horn to the north and Hahnenkamm to the south. A one-day general ski pass costs AS390; a day's equipment rental is around AS190 for downhill or AS115 for cross-country skiing. The professional Hahnenkamm downhill ski race takes place in January.

Dozens of summer **hiking** trails surround the town and provide a good opportunity to take in the scenery; a free map from the tourist office shows routes. Get a head start to the heights with the three-day cable-car pass for AS320. There is an alpine flower garden with free admission on the slopes of the Kitzbüheler Horn.

Places to Stay & Eat
A single-night surcharge (AS20 to AS40) usually applies, but try to negotiate. Many private rooms and apartments are available and there is a year-round *camping ground* (☎ 2806) near Schwarzsee lake. Prices are higher at Christmas and in February, July and August – peaking in the winter high season, which are the prices quoted here.

The three-star *Hotel Kaiser* (☎ 4708), Bahnhofstrasse 2, has unbeatable rates specially for backpackers, only AS250/400 with shower or AS200/300 without (closed mid-April to mid-May). *Pension Schmidinger* (☎ 3134), at Ehrenbachgasse 13, has rooms for AS300 per person with shower, or AS240 without. The owner, Barbara, gives a discount to students with this book. *Pension Neuhaus* (☎ 2200), Franz Reisch Strasse 23, is also near the centre of the resort. It has singles/doubles from AS330/600. Unusually, discounts are offered to motorcyclists. Both pensions are usually open in the off season.

On Bichlstrasse there's a *Spar* supermarket and *Prima*, a cheap self-service restaurant (open every day in season). *Huberbräu Stüberl*, Vorderstadt 18, offers good Austrian food and an AS85 menu. After the kitchens close at 9.30 pm it stays busy with drinkers enjoying the low beer prices. It's open daily until midnight. *Adria* is near the post office. It serves Italian food from AS65, and is open daily all year. Next door is *La Cantina*, where Mexican food costs from AS75 (closed Monday).

Gasthof Eggerwirt (☎ 24 55), Untere Gänsbachgasse 12, down the steps from the three churches, provides quality regional cuisine for AS100 to AS250. It also has mid-priced rooms.

Getting There & Away
There are approximately hourly train departures from Kitzbühel to Innsbruck (AS122; 1¼ hours) and Salzburg (AS228; 2½ hours).

Slower trains stop at Kitzbühel-Hahnenkamm, which is closer to the centre than the main Kitzbühel stop.

Getting to Lienz is awkward by train: two changes are required and it takes over four hours. The bus is much easier. It leaves from outside the main train station daily at 5 pm (AS128; tickets from the driver), with extra buses at weekends. Heading south to Lienz, you pass through some marvellous scenery. Highway 108 (the Felber Tauern Tunnel) and Highway 107 (the Grossglockner mountain road, closed in winter) both have toll sections.

KUFSTEIN
Tourists are drawn to Kufstein, near the German border, by its lakes and the 13th-century castle.

Orientation & Information
The tourist office (☎ 62207) at Münchner Strasse 2 is opposite the train station. It's open Monday to Friday from 8.30 am to 12.30 pm and 2 to 5 pm, and Saturday from 9 am to noon. Hours are extended during the peak summer period. It makes room reservations without charge. The main square, Stadtplatz, is on the other side of the River Inn.

The telephone code for Kufstein is ☎ 05372.

Things to See & Do
The **fortress** dominates the town from a central hill. There is a lift to the fortress (AS25 return), but the 15-minute walk up is not demanding. The **Heimat Museum** in the castle has a bit of everything but can only be visited by a guided tour (in English, if there is sufficient demand), which lasts around 1¼ hours. Entry costs AS34 (students AS27), and there are five tours a day. It's open Tuesday to Sunday from late April to October, except in July and August when it's open daily (and tours are more frequent).

The **lakes** around Kufstein are an ideal destination for cyclists; you can rent bikes in the train station. Buses visit some of the lakes; they leave from outside the Bahnhof.

Places to Stay & Eat
If you decide to stay overnight, ask for the guest card. There is a *camping ground* by the river (☎ 636 89), Salurner Strasse 36, which

charges AS51 per person, and AS30 each for a tent and a car. *Gasthof Zellerhof* (☎ 62415), Schluiferstrasse 20, behind the station, has rooms from AS290 (restaurant closed Tuesday). There are several places to eat and a supermarket on Stadtplatz.

Getting There & Away
Kufstein is on the main Innsbruck-Salzburg 'corridor' train route. To reach Kitzbühel (AS72; takes an hour), change at Wörgl; the easiest road route is also via Wörgl.

LIENZ
The capital of East Tirol combines winter sports and summer hiking with a relaxed, small-town ambience. The jagged Dolomite mountain range crowds the southern skyline.

Orientation & Information
The town centre is within the junction of the rivers Isel and Drau. The pivotal Hauptplatz is by the train station, beyond the post office (Postamt 9900, money exchange available). The tourist office (☎ 65265) is at Europaplatz 1, open Monday to Friday from 8 am to noon and 2 to 6 pm, and Saturday from 9 am to noon. It also opens on Sunday in the summer and winter high seasons. Staff will make room reservations free of charge, or you can use the hotel board (free telephone) outside.

The telephone code for Lienz is ☎ 04852.

Things to See & Do
Bruck Castle overlooks the town and contains folklore displays and the work of local, turn-of-the-century artist Albin Egger. Between Palm Sunday and 31 October, it is open Tuesday to Sunday from 10 am to 5 pm, except between mid-June and mid-September when it is open daily from 10 am to 6 pm. Admission costs AS50 (students AS25). Most of the downhill skiing takes place on the **Zettersfeld** peak north of town (mostly medium to easy runs), and there are several cross-country trails in the valley. **Hochstein** is another skiing area. A one-day ski pass for both peaks is AS290. In summer, hiking is good in the mountains. The cable cars are closed during the off-season (April, May, October and November).

Places to Stay
Camping Falken (☎ 64022), Eichholz 7, is

AUSTRIA

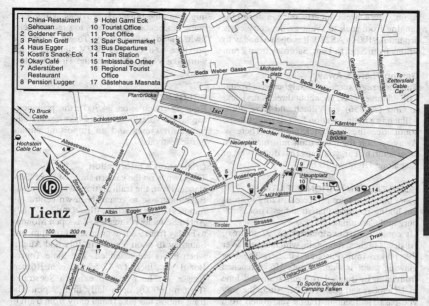

1 China-Restaurant Sehcuan	9 Hotel Garni Eck
2 Goldener Fisch	10 Tourist Office
3 Pension Gretl	11 Post Office
4 Haus Egger	12 Spar Supermarket
5 Kostli's Snack-Eck	13 Bus Departures
6 Okay Café	14 Train Station
7 Adlerstüberl Restaurant	15 Imbisstube Ortner
8 Pension Lugger	16 Regional Tourist Office
	17 Gästehaus Masnata

south of the town, and closed from November to mid-December. Private rooms in and around the town start at AS130 per person. They are excellent value and a single night's stay is often possible. This is the case at *Egger* (☎ 72098), Alleestrasse 33, which costs AS170 per person. *Pension Lugger* (☎ 62104), Andrä Kranz Gasse 7, is plain but it's right in the town centre. Doubles are AS500 with private shower, but without breakfast. There's only one single for AS250.

Gästehaus Masnata (☎ 65536), Drahtzuggasse 4, has good doubles and three-person apartments for around AS540. *Pension Gretl* (☎ 62106), Schweizergasse 32, has courtyard parking and is closed in the off-season. There are big singles/doubles with own shower/WC for AS280/480, and one apartment.

The atmospheric, spacious *Hotel Garni Eck* (☎ 64785) on Hauptplatz has been run by the same family for 500 years. It has large rooms with high ceilings, shower/WC, sofa and comfy chairs, for just AS400 to AS500 per person.

Places to Eat

Imbissstube Ortner, Albin Egger Strasse 5, has the best spit-roasted chicken in Austria, sprinkled with spices. That's all it does in the off-season. The smell of the chickens sizzling on the spit outside is enough to make vegetarians join Meat Eaters Anonymous. It's open daily from 11 am to 9 pm; a half chicken (Hendl) with a roll is just AS32. *Kostli's Snack-Eck*, Kreuzgasse 4, offers cheap snacks, pizzas and schnitzels (open till 8 pm; closed Sunday). *China-Restaurant Sehcuan*, Beda Weber Gasse 13, has weekday lunches for AS55.

There are lots of places to try regional dishes, such as *Adlerstüberl Restaurant*, Andrä Kranz Gasse 5. Most meals are above AS100, though daily specials are cheaper. *Goldener Fisch*, at Kärntner Strasse 9, is also good; meals start at AS70. Both places are open daily.

Entertainment

The *Okay Café* in the Creativ Centre off Zwergergasse is a dark and smoky meeting place for local, young people. In the back room, there are concerts once a fortnight ranging from rock to avant-garde; entry costs around AS100 to AS220. It is open Monday to Friday from 5 pm to 1 am, Saturday from 7 pm.

Getting There & Away
There are regular trains to Salzburg via Spittal Millstättersee (AS296; about three hours), and to Graz (AS456) via Villach and Klagenfurt. Villach is a main junction for rail routes to the south. See the Innsbruck Getting There & Away section for more train information. To head south by car, you must first divert west or east along Highway 100.

HOHE TAUERN NATIONAL PARK
Flora and fauna are protected in this 1786 sq km hiking paradise that straddles Tirol, Salzburg and Carinthia.

It contains **Grossglockner** (3797 metres), Austria's highest mountain, which towers over the 10-km long Pasterze Glacier. The best viewing point is Franz Josefs Höhe, reached from Lienz by Bundesbus; it runs from mid-June to 1 October and costs AS124. Along the way you pass Heiligenblut (buses year-round from Lienz), where there's a HI *Jugendherberge* (☎ 04824-22 59) at Hof 36. It is closed from September to Christmas. By car, you can reach Franz Josefs Höhe from May to November, but the daily toll for using the route (Highway 107, the Grossglockner Hochalpenstrasse) is AS280 for cars and AS230 for motorcycles. An eight-day pass is AS460 and AS310 respectively. There are places to stay overnight. Cyclists and hikers pay nothing to enter the park.

Further west, the Felbertauernstrasse also goes north-south through the park. For the tunnel section, there's a toll of AS190 for cars (AS110 in winter) and AS100 for motorcycles. At the northern end of the park, turn west along Highway 165 to reach the **Krimml Falls**. These triple-level falls make a great spectacle. It takes 1½ hours to walk to the top, where there's an equally good view looking back down the valley.

Vorarlberg

The small state of Vorarlberg encompasses the plains of Lake Constance (Bodensee) and mighty alpine ranges. It provides skiing, dramatic landscapes and access to Liechtenstein, Switzerland and Germany. To get around the province you can buy VVV tickets, which work like VVT tickets (see the Tirol introduction).

BREGENZ
Bregenz (population 24,700), the provincial capital of Vorarlberg, offers lake excursions, mountain views and an important annual music festival.

Orientation & Information
The town is on the eastern shore of Lake Constance. From the train station, walk left along Bahnhofstrasse to reach the town centre (10 minutes). The tourist office (☎ 43 39 10), Anton Schneider Strasse 4A, is open Monday to Friday from 9 am to noon and 1 to 5 pm, and Saturday to noon, except in July and August when hours are extended. The State Tourist Board Vorarlberg (☎ 42 52 50) is at Römerstrasse 7. The post office is on Seestrasse (Postamt 6900), open daily until 9 pm. The train station has bike rental daily from 6 am to 9.40 pm; Bundesbuses leave from outside.

The telephone code for Bregenz is ☎ 05574.

Things to See & Do
The old town merits a stroll. Its centrepiece and the town emblem is the bulbous, baroque **St Martin's Tower**, built in 1599. Follow the walking route described in the tourist office leaflet.

The **Pfänder** mountain offers an impressive panorama over the lake and beyond. A cable car to the top operates daily from 9 am to 6 pm (7 pm in summer). Fares are: up AS77, down AS55 and return AS110.

The **Bregenz Festival** takes place from late July to late August. Operas and classical works are performed from a vast floating stage on the edge of the lake. Contact the Kartenbüro (☎ 49 20 223), Postfach 311, A-6900, about nine months prior to the festival, for tickets and information.

Places to Stay & Eat
Seecamping (☎ 71 8 95/6), Bodangasse 7, is a lakeside site three km west of the station. It's open from mid-May to mid-September, and

prices are AS55 each per person, tent and car, plus AS16 tax.

The HI *Jugendherberge* (☎ 42 8 67), Belruptstrasse 16A, is open from April to September. Yes, it is those two sheds that look like army barracks. Beds are AS121, plus AS24 or AS12 for sheets. It's closed from 9 am to 5 pm, though there's a place to leave your bags during the day.

Private rooms (from AS200 per person) and apartments (from AS500) are good value; enquire at the tourist office, which also has a room-booking service (AS30). A surcharge normally applies for a single night's stay.

Hotel Krone (☎ 42 1 17), Leutbühl 3, is ideally central, and open all year. Large doubles cost from AS700 with shower/WC or AS500 without; there are no singles. *Pension Paar* (☎ 42 3 05), Am Steinenbach 10, is a two-star place near the boat landing stage. Rooms (hall showers) are AS380/680 and it's closed from November to April.

Restaurant Charly (☎ 45 9 59), Anton Schneider Strasse 19, serves good pizza and pasta from AS65 (closed Thursday). It gets busy, so you may need to reserve a table. For Austrian food, try *Gasthaus Maurachbund*, Maurachgasse 11, which has main dishes from AS90 to AS195 (closed Thursday), or the similarly priced but more atmospheric *Alte Weinstube Zur Ilge*, Maurachgasse 6 (open daily).

There's a *Familia* supermarket with a cheap self-service restaurant downstairs in the GWL shopping centre on Römerstrasse.

Getting There & Away

Trains to Munich (AS379) go via Lindau; trains to Constance go via the Swiss shore of the lake. There are also regular departures to St Gallen (AS106) and Zürich. Trains to Innsbruck (AS276; 2¾ hours) depart every one to two hours. Feldkirch is on the same rail route (AS54).

Boat services operate from late May to late October, with a reduced schedule from late March. For information, call ☎ 428 68. Bregenz to Constance by boat (via Lindau) takes about 3½ hours and there are up to six departures per day. Enquire about special boat passes. Eurail and Inter-Rail passes give 50% off fares.

FELDKIRCH

Feldkirch, the gateway to Liechtenstein, was granted its town charter in 1218, and retains some medieval buildings.

Orientation & Information

The tourist office (☎ 734 67), Herrengasse 12, is open Monday to Friday from 8 am to noon and 2 to 6 pm, and Saturday from 9 am to noon. It reserves rooms free of charge.

The telephone code for Feldkirch is ☎ 05522.

Things to See & Do

There are good views from the 12th-century **Schattenburg Castle**, which houses a museum (AS25, students AS10; closed Monday and winter). There's a free **animal park** *(Wildpark)*, with 200 species, one km from the centre. Feldkirch hosts the important **Schubertiade** summer music festival; call ☎ 380 01 well in advance.

Ski slopes are at Laterns, 15 minutes away by car. Alternatively, take the ski bus (calling at the town, the station and the hostel) which is free if you buy that day's ski pass (AS290) from the driver.

Places to Stay & Eat

The HI *Jugendherberge* (☎ 731 81), Reichsstrasse 111, is 1.5 km north of the train station in an historic building. It has been completely modernised inside and has good facilities. Beds are AS140 and dinners are AS65. From 9.30 am to 5 pm reception is closed and the doors are locked; curfew is at 10 pm. The hostel shuts from 1 November to early January and at Easter.

Gasthof Löwen (☎ 728 68), Egelseestrasse, is one km west of the centre, and has rooms from AS380/600 with shower and AS330/500 without (restaurant closed Monday).

For cheap eating in town, go to *Löwen City*, Neustadt 17, which has self-service meals from AS55. It's open Monday to Friday from 9 am to 6 pm and Saturday from 9 am to 2 pm. There's a *Familia* supermarket next door.

Getting There & Away

Two buses an hour (one at weekends) depart for Liechtenstein from in front of the train station. To reach Liechtenstein's capital, Vaduz (AS30; 40 minutes away), change buses in

Schaans. Trains to Buchs on the Swiss border pass through Schaans, but only a few stop there. Buchs has connections to major destinations in Switzerland, including Zürich and Chur.

ARLBERG REGION

The Arlberg region, shared by Vorarlberg and neighbouring Tirol, comprises a number of resorts and is considered to have some of the best skiing in Austria. Summer is less busy, and many of the bars are closed then.

St Anton is the largest resort, enjoying an easy-going atmosphere and vigorous nightlife. There's always a large contingent of Australasian skiers. It has good, medium-to-advanced runs, as well as nursery slopes on Gampen and Kapall. Get information from the tourist office (☎ 05446-226 90), A-6580 St Anton, Tirol.

Lech, a more up-market resort, is a favourite with royalty and film stars. Runs are predominantly medium to advanced. For details, contact the tourist office (☎ 05583-21610), A-6764 Lech, Vorarlberg.

A ski pass valid for 88 ski lifts in Lech, Zürs, Stuben, St Anton and St Christoph costs AS460 for one day and AS2330 for one week (reductions for children and senior citizens). Rental starts at AS190 for skis and poles, and AS100 for boots.

Places to Stay & Eat

Accommodation is mainly in small B&B places – there are nearly 200 in St Anton alone. Tourist office brochures have full listings, or try the accommodation boards with free telephones outside the tourist offices. Bottom-end prices start at around AS350 per person in winter high season, reducing by about 30% to 50% in low season and summer. Try *Enzian* (☎ 05446-2403) in St Anton's main street, or the cheaper *Schuler* (☎ 05446-3108) in nearby St Jakob. There are good pizzas at *Pomodoro*, otherwise try the takeaway stands which are scattered around town. There are several supermarkets; *Spar* has hot lunches (before noon). Good après-ski bars include *Krazy Kanguruh*, on the slopes, and *Piccadilly*, in the village.

Despite its sophisticated profile, Lech has a *Jugendherberge* (☎ 05583-2419), Stubenbach 244, two km from the main resort. It is closed in May, June, and mid-September to mid-December.

Getting There & Away

St Anton is on the main railway route from Bregenz to Innsbruck, under 1½ hours from either place. St Anton is close to the eastern entrance of the Arlberg Tunnel, the toll road connecting Vorarlberg and Tirol. The tunnel toll is AS150 for cars and minibuses. You can avoid the toll by taking the B197, but no vehicles with trailers are allowed on this winding road. There are at least three buses a day to Lech (AS36; 40 minutes) from St Anton.

Belgium

Think of Belgium (België in Flemish, Belgique in French) and it's 'Bruges, beer and chocolate' that generally spring to mind. While certainly exceptional, they are hardly the whole. Yet surprisingly little else is commonly known about this much-embattled country which spawned Western Europe's first great towns, and whose early artists are credited with inventing the oil painting.

Perhaps it's a lack of fervent nationalism – the result of many dominant cultures integrating here over the centuries – which has kept Belgium's spotlight dim on the European stage. Rarely boastful, the country has in fact plenty to fascinate the visitor – from historically rich art towns to the serenity of the hilly Ardennes, and everywhere wonderful bars and cafés where Belgians feel at home.

Facts about the Country

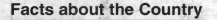

HISTORY

Belgium's position between France, Germany and, across the North Sea, England has long made it one of Europe's main battlegrounds. Prosperous throughout the 13th and 14th centuries, the Flemish towns of Ypres, Bruges and Ghent were the first major cities, booming on the manufacturing and trading of cloth. Their craftspeople established powerful guilds (organisations to stringently control arts and crafts) whose elaborate guildhalls you'll see in many cities. Alas the Flemish weavers were ruined by competition from England and, due largely to Bruges' refusal to handle the foreign cloth as well as the silting of its river, the towns faded. Trade moved east to Antwerp which soon became the greatest port in Europe.

When Protestantism swept Europe in the 16th century, the Low Countries (present-day Belgium, the Netherlands and Luxembourg, often referred to as the Benelux) embraced it, much to the chagrin of their ruler, the fanatically Catholic Philip II of Spain. He sent the cruel Inquisition to enforce Catholicism, thus inflaming the smouldering religious tensions. The eruption came with the Iconoclastic Fury, in which Protestants ran riot, ransacking the churches. Philip retaliated with a force of 10,000 soldiers, and thousands were imprisoned or executed before war broke out in 1568. The Revolt of the Netherlands lasted 80 years, and in the end roughly laid the present-day borders – Holland and its allied provinces victoriously expelling the Spaniards while Belgium and Luxembourg stayed under their rule.

For the next 200 years, Belgium remained a battlefield for successive foreign powers. After the Spaniards, the Austrians came and in turn the French. Napoleon's defeat at the Battle of Waterloo near Brussels led, in 1814, to the creation of the United Kingdom of the Netherlands, incorporating Belgium and Luxembourg into the Netherlands. But the Catholic Belgians revolted, winning independence from the Netherlands in 1830 and forming their own kingdom.

The ensuing years saw the start of Flemish nationalism, with tension growing between the

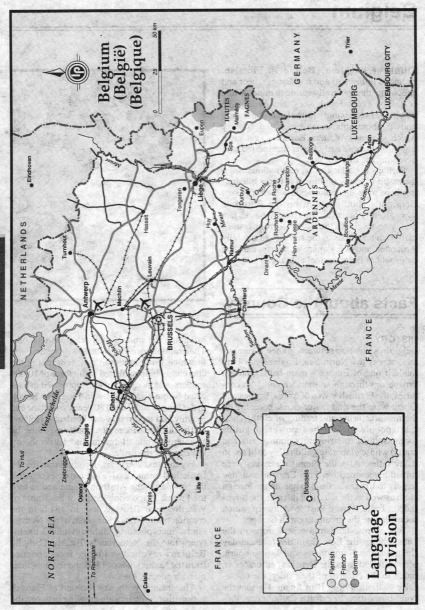

Belgium (België) (Belgique)

0 25 50 km

GERMANY

LUXEMBOURG

LUXEMBOURG CITY

Trier

NETHERLANDS

Eindhoven

HAUTES FAGNES

Eupen
Malmédy
Spa

Bastogne

Arlon

Meuse

Tongeren

Liège

Durbuy
La Roche
Champlon
Ourthe

Marcourt
Marteuange
Semois

ARDENNES

Hasselt

Huy

Namur

Rochefort
Han-sur-Lesse
Lesse

Bouillon

Turnhout

Louvain

Meuse

Dinant

Mechlin

Antwerp

Schelde

BRUSSELS

Charleroi

Meuse

FRANCE

Sambre

Mons

Ghent

Courtrai

Tournai

Schelde

Lille

Lys

Bruges

Ypres

FRANCE

Westerschelde

To Hull

Zeebrugge

Ostend

Calais

To Ramsgate

NORTH SEA

BELGIUM

Language Division

Brussels

Flemish
French
German

Flemish (Dutch) and French speakers which would eventually lead to a language partition dividing the country (see the following Population & People section). The question of whether Belgium can survive as a sovereign state is still moot.

In 1885 the then king, Leopold II, personally acquired the Congo (now Zaïre) in Africa. He was later scandalised over the continuing slave trade there. In the early 1900s the country was made a Belgian colony; much-disputed independence was granted in 1960.

Despite Belgium's neutral policy, the Germans invaded in 1914. Used as a bloody battleground throughout WWI, the town of Ypres was wiped off the map. In WWII the whole country was taken over within three weeks of the surprise attack in May 1940. Controversy over the questionably early capitulation by the then king, Leopold III, led to his abdication in 1950 in favour of his son, King Baudouin, whose popular reign ended with his death (at age 62) from a heart attack in 1993. Childless, Baudouin was succeeded by his brother, the present King Albert II.

Postwar Belgium was characterised by an economic boom, later accentuated by Brussels' appointment as the headquarters of the European Union (EU) and the North Atlantic Treaty Organisation (NATO).

GEOGRAPHY

Occupying just 30,000 sq km, Belgium is one of Europe's smallest nations, sandwiched between the Netherlands, Germany, Luxembourg and France. The north is flat, the south dominated by the hilly, forested Ardennes, and the 65-km North Sea coastline monopolised by resorts, save for a few patches of windswept dunes.

GOVERNMENT & POLITICS

A constitutional parliamentary monarchy is led by King Albert II. Up until 1980 the government was centralised, but the long-standing division between the two language communities led to the national government being partially regionalised. In 1993 it was taken a step further with the creation of three regional governments representing the Flemish and French-speaking communities and the Brussels region. The political scene has long been dominated by the (Catholic) Christian Demo-

crats, Socialists and Liberals, though support for the Green parties and the ultra-right-wing Vlaams Blok (Flemish Block) is increasing.

In recent years, political scandals such as the Agusta affair, in which bribes of US$1.7 million were allegedly paid to the Socialists to sweeten the sale of Italian helicopters, have left Belgium with the nickname of the 'Italy of the north'. Despite such scandals, the existing four-party coalition led by prime minister, Jean-Luc Dehaene, emerged virtually unscathed from general elections in 1995.

ECONOMY

Over the centuries, Belgium's economic prosperity has swung from one language community to the other, starting with Flanders' medieval textile wealth which was later supplanted by Wallonia's mining and steel industries. The latter's decline means Flanders is again the country's industrial backbone. The economy is struggling with a public debt of 130% of GDP (more than double that permitted for countries wishing to join the European monetary union) and high unemployment. The main industries are chemicals, car manufacturing, textiles and iron and steel. Agriculture (cereals), horticulture and stock breeding are also important.

POPULATION & PEOPLE

While spread over nine provinces, Belgium's population is basically split in two: the Flemish and the Walloons. Language is the dividing factor, made official in 1962 when an invisible line – or Linguistic Divide as it's called – was drawn across the country, cutting it almost equally in half. To the north lies Flanders, whose Flemish speakers make up 60% of Belgium's population of 10 million. To the south is Wallonia with the 40%, French-speaking Walloons. To further complicate matters, Brussels is officially bilingual but predominantly French speaking, and lies within the Flemish region but is governed separately from both. There's also a tiny German-speaking enclave in the far east.

The language issue stems from discrimination against the Flemish when the Belgian constitution was drawn up – French was official, Flemish banned – and over the years has caused many political and social conflicts.

BELGIUM

ARTS

The arts first flourished in Belgium as early as the 15th century, starting with the realist paintings of the Flemish Primitives, whose leading figure, Jan van Eyck, is said to have invented oil painting. The mid-16th century gave way to Pieter Brueghel with his often grotesque depictions of peasant life. Pieter Paul Rubens dominated the start of the 17th century, spending much of his early career in Italy where he was heavily influenced by baroque painting. Returning to his native Antwerp, he set up a highly productive studio of painters and turned out sensational religious allegories such as his famous *Descent from the Cross*. Two other Antwerp natives who achieved considerable success at this time were Anthony van Dyck and Jacob Jordaens.

At the turn of this century, the sinuous architecture of Art Nouveau started in Brussels led by Henri van de Velde and Victor Horta. Horta was famed for his interiors which displayed few straight lines – ceilings simply became curved continuations of walls. Stained glass and wrought iron were much used to accentuate this whiplash of lines.

Very little local literature has been translated into English. One book you may want to get hold of is *The Sorrow of Belgium* by Bruges-born author, Hugo Claus, which describes wartime Belgium through the eyes of a Flemish adolescent.

Comic strips are a Belgian forte and, while there are many local favourites, Hergé, the creator of the quiffed Tintin, is the best internationally known cartoonist.

CULTURE

With their history of foreign domination, Belgians are used to visitors and their different habits, and there are few social taboos that travellers are likely to break. It is customary to greet shopkeepers and café/pub owners when entering their premises.

RELIGION

Long a Catholic stronghold, Belgium has experienced a decrease in church attendances but religious traditions continue, influencing many aspects of daily life, including politics and education.

LANGUAGE

See the History and Population & People sections for information on the language issue. For a rundown of the Flemish (Dutch) and Walloon (French) languages, see the Language Guide at the back of the book. English is widely, if somewhat haltingly, spoken, although less frequently in Wallonia and the Ardennes.

For travellers, the Linguistic Divide will cause few problems. The most confusing part will be on the road, when the sign you're following to Bergen (as it's known in Flemish) disappears and the town of Mons (the French name) appears. A list of alternative place names is included at the back of this book.

Facts for the Visitor

PLANNING

Climate & When to Go

The country generally has a mild, maritime climate. July and August are the warmest months. They are also the wettest, although precipitation is pretty evenly over the year. The Ardennes are often a few degrees colder than the rest of the country, with snow from November to March.

SUGGESTED ITINERARIES

Depending on the length of your stay, you might want to see and do the following:

Two days
Spend one day each in Brussels and Bruges.
One week
Spend two days each in Brussels and the Ardennes, and one day each in Antwerp, Bruges and Ypres.
Two weeks
Spend three days in Brussels and surrounds, two days each in Antwerp and the Ardennes, two days in Bruges and Ypres, two days in Ostend and other coastal resorts, and one day each in Ghent, Namur and Liège.
One month
This should give you plenty of time to explore the above-mentioned places and to discover a few new places of your own.

HIGHLIGHTS

The following are some of Belgium's highlights:

Museums & Sights
   Horta Museum, Brussels; Begijnhof, Bruges; Rubens' House; Antwerp
Pubs
   Falstaff in Brussels, 't Brugs Beertje in Bruges, De Ware Jacob in Antwerp
Beers
   Duvel, Westmalle Tripel, Timmermans Gueuze
Hiking
   La Roche or Haute Fagnes areas of the Ardennes

TOURIST OFFICES
The head office of the Flemish and Walloon tourist authorities is at Rue du Marché aux Herbes 63, B-1000 Brussels (☎ 504 03 90). Much of the tourist literature they supply is free.

Tourist Offices Abroad
UK
   Belgian Tourist Office, 29 Princes St, London W1R 7RG (☎ 0171-629 3977)
USA
   Belgian Tourist Office, 780 Third Ave, Suite 1501, New York, NY 10017 (☎ 212-758 8130)

VISAS & EMBASSIES
Visitors from many countries need only a valid passport for three-month visits. Regulations are basically the same as for entering the Netherlands (for more details, see the Facts for the Visitor section in that chapter).

Belgian Embassies Abroad
Australia
   19 Arkana St, Yarralumla, Canberra, ACT 2600 (☎ 06-273 2501/2502)
Canada
   80 Elgin St, 4th floor, Ottawa, Ont K1P 1B7 (☎ 613-236 7267/7269)
New Zealand
   1-3 Willeston St, Wellington (☎ 04-472 9558)
UK
   103 Eaton Square, London SW1 W9AB (☎ 0171-235 5422)
USA
   3330 Garfield St, NW Washington DC 20008 (☎ 202-333 6900)

Foreign Embassies in Belgium
All the following embassies are in Brussels (telephone code ☎ 02):

Australia
   Rue Guimard 6, B-1040 (☎ 231 05 00)
Canada
   Ave de Tervueren 2, B-1040 (☎ 741 06 11)
France
   Rue Ducale 65, B-1000 (☎ 548 87 11)

Germany
   Ave de Tervueren 190, B-1150 (☎ 774 19 11)
Japan
   Ave des Arts 58, B-1000 (☎ 513 23 40)
Luxembourg
   Rue Noyer 211, B-1040 (☎ 733 99 77)
Netherlands
   Ave Herrmann-Debroux 48 B-1160 (☎ 679 17 11)
New Zealand
   Blvd du Régent 47, B-1000 (☎ 512 10 40)
UK
   Rue Arlon 85, B-1040 (☎ 287 62 11)
USA
   Blvd du Régent 27, B-1000 (☎ 508 21 11)

CUSTOMS
Duty-free allowances for travellers entering Belgium are the same as the Netherlands (see the Customs section in that chapter and in the Facts for the Visitor chapter for details).

MONEY
Banks are the best place to change money, charging between f120 and f150 commission on travellers' cheques. Out of hours there are exchange bureaus which mostly have lower rates and higher fees. All the major credit cards are widely accepted.

Currency
The money unit is the Belgian franc, written as f or Bf. Coins come in f1, f5, f20 and f50, notes in f100, f200, f500, f1000, f2000 and f10,000. Belgian francs are equal to Luxembourg francs and are widely used there, but the reverse does not apply.

Exchange Rates
Australia	A$1	=	f23.91
Canada	C$1	=	f22.22
France	1FF	=	f6.08
Germany	DM1	=	f20.61
Japan	¥100	=	f28.20
Netherlands	Nethf1	=	f18.31
New Zealand	NZ$1	=	f21.27
United Kingdom	UK£1	=	f47.50
United States	US$1	=	f30.49

Costs
Travelling modestly – hostels and cheap restaurants – you can get by on about f850 a day. Tipping is not obligatory, and because of the country's size, getting around is not a major outlay. Bargaining is not customary.

BELGIUM

Consumer Taxes

Value-added tax, or VAT (BTW in Flemish, TVA in French), is calculated at 6% (food, hotels, camping) and either 17% or the more common 21% for everything else. To get a rebate, you must get your purchase invoice stamped by customs as you leave. You then send it back to the shop and they'll forward the refund. Alternatively, buy from a 'Tax Free for Tourists' shop (see the Money section in the Netherlands chapter for details).

POST & COMMUNICATIONS

Post offices are generally open weekdays from 9 am to 5 pm and in cities on Saturday mornings. Letters (under 20g) cost f16 within Europe, or f34 elsewhere. They average a week to nine days to reach places outside Europe, two to three days inside. Poste restante attracts a f14 fee.

Local phone calls cost f10 for about three minutes. Call boxes take f5 and f20 coins, or f200, f500 and f1000 Belgacom phonecards available from post offices and newsagents. Econophone cards (used in normal public phones but valid for international calls only) are sold from various agents such as Thomas Cook offices. These phonecards are better value than Belgacom phonecards, and range from f350 to f3150. International calls can be made from public boxes, the post office or telephone centres. Rates from hotels, including hostels, are exorbitant – ask before you dial.

Faxes can be sent from telephone offices and cost f125/175/350 for the first page to the UK/USA/Australia, and f75/125/200 for consecutive pages.

NEWSPAPERS & MAGAZINES

The English-language *Bulletin* magazine (f85) comes out Thursdays and has national news and a good entertainment guide. American and English newspapers and magazines are widely available.

RADIO & TV

The BBC's World Service is on 648 kHz medium wave. The main Belgian TV channels are TV1 and VTM (in Flanders) and RTBF (in Wallonia). Most homes have cable TV and can access about 30 stations including the BBC and CNN.

PHOTOGRAPHY & VIDEO

A Kodak 100 ASA (36-exposure) slide film costs f250, while developing averages f19 per photo plus f140 for film processing. A normal/Hi8 8mm video cassette (90 minutes) costs about f300/500.

TIME

Belgium runs on Central European Time. Noon is 11 am in London, 6 am in New York, 3 am in San Francisco, 6 am in Toronto, 9 pm in Sydney and 11 pm in Auckland. Daylight-saving time comes into effect at 2 am on the last Sunday in March, when clocks are moved an hour forward; they're moved an hour back again at 2 am on the last Sunday in October. The 24-hour clock is commonly used.

ELECTRICITY

The current used is 220V, 50 Hz, and the socket used is the two-pin variety.

WEIGHTS & MEASURES

The metric system is in force. Like other Continental Europeans, Belgians indicate decimals with commas and thousands with points. In Flemish shops, 250g is called a *half pond* and 500g a *pond*.

LAUNDRY

Self-service laundries (*wassalon*, *laverie*) on average charge f120 for a five-kg wash and f10 per dryer cycle. Take plenty of f5 and f20 coins.

TOILETS

Public toilets tend to be few and far between which is why most people avail themselves of the toilets in pubs and cafés. However, such places often have only one tiny toilet squeezed into a nook next to an unshielded urinal. A f10 fee is commonly charged in public toilets or toilets in popular cafés.

HEALTH

There are reciprocal health arrangements only with EU and other European countries. For others, it's wise to have travel insurance. For treating minor ailments, head to an *apotheek* (chemist); tourist offices and hotels will be able to assist in finding a *ziekenhuis* (hospital) with an English-speaking doctor.

WOMEN TRAVELLERS

Women should encounter few problems travelling around Belgium. However, in the event of rape or attack, contact SOS Viol (☎ 02-512 90 20) or Help Line (☎ 02-648 40 14).

GAY & LESBIAN TRAVELLERS

Attitudes to homosexuality are slowly becoming less conservative. The age of consent is 16.

The biggest gay/lesbian organisation is FWH (☎ 09-223 69 29), Vlaanderenstraat 22, 9000 Ghent, which recently established an information/help hotline called Holebifoon (☎ 09-238 26 26), open nightly (except Sunday) from 6 to 10 pm.

Artemys (☎ 02-512 03 47), Galerie Bortier, Rue St Jean, 1000 Brussels, is a women's bookshop and lesbian information centre.

DISABLED TRAVELLERS

Belgium is not terribly user-friendly for travellers with a mobility problem. Some government buildings, museums, hotels and restaurants have lifts and/or ramps, but not the majority. Wheelchair users will be up against rough, uneven pavements, and will need to give a days' notice when travelling by train.

For more information, contact Mobility International (☎ 03-236 51 19) at Drink 13, 2140 Antwerp or the Belgian Red Cross (☎ 02-645 46 26; fax 02-343 89 90), Rue Joseph Stallaert 1 bte 8, 1060 Brussels.

SENIOR TRAVELLERS

Travellers over 60 years can buy a Golden Railpass which gives six one-way train trips in one year. It costs f1190/1850 in 2nd/1st class. There are no standard museum discounts.

On the whole, getting around should pose few major problems although, at some train stations, platforms are lowset making it difficult to climb into carriages.

DANGERS & ANNOYANCES

The only danger you're likely to encounter is a big night on the Belgium beers. The national emergency numbers are police ☎ 101 and fire/ambulance ☎ 100.

BUSINESS HOURS

Shops are open weekdays from 8.30 or 9 am to 6 pm – often closing for lunch – with similar hours on Saturdays. Banks are open weekdays from 9 am to noon or 1 pm, and 2 to 4 or 5 pm, and Saturday mornings; in large cities, they often don't close for lunch.

PUBLIC HOLIDAYS & SPECIAL EVENTS

Public holidays are: New Year's Day, Easter Monday, Labour Day (1 May), Ascension Day, Whit Monday, National Day (21 July), Assumption (15 August), All Saints' Day (1 November), Armistice Day (11 November) and Christmas Day.

The religious festival of Carnival is celebrated throughout Belgium. There's a swarm of local and national, artistic or religious festivals – pick up the tourist office's free brochure.

ACTIVITIES

The Ardennes is Belgium's outdoor playground. Here you can ski in winter and, in summer, kayak or go hiking or mountain biking (using a *vélo tout terrain* or *VTT*) along a good network of forest tracks. The Institut Géographique National publishes detailed regional maps (scale 1:25,000) which are sold in many tourist offices or travel bookshops.

WORK

For non-EU nationals it's officially illegal, but it may be possible to pick up work in hostels and in resorts along the coast.

ACCOMMODATION

Hostels and camping grounds are plentiful, low-budget hotels scarce, and in summer everything's heavily booked. The national tourist office will book accommodation for free and has camping and hotel leaflets, and booklets on B&Bs *(chambres d'hôtes* in French) and rural houses available for weekly rental *(gîtes ruraux)*.

There are two official hostel groups. Les Auberges de Jeunesse (☎ 02-215 31 00) at Rue Van Oost 52, 1030 Brussels runs hostels in Wallonia; its Flemish counterpart is the Vlaamse Jeugdherbergcentrale (☎ 03-232 72 18) at Van Stralenstraat 40, 2060 Antwerp. Rates range from f365 to f395 per night in a dorm, including breakfast. Some of the hostels also have more expensive single and double rooms. In cities, you'll also find private hostels. At most of the hostels you'll pay f100 extra for sheets.

Camping rates vary widely, but on average

you'll be looking at f60 per adult, tent and vehicle in a basic ground. The cheapest hotels charge about f1000/1400 for singles/doubles in a room without facilities but with breakfast; B&Bs average the same.

FOOD

Belgian cuisine is highly regarded throughout Europe – some say it's second only to the French while in others' eyes it's equal. Combining French style with German portions, you'll rarely have reason to complain. Meat and seafood are abundantly consumed and then of course there are *frites – chips or fries* – which the Belgians swear they invented and which, judging by availability, is a claim few would contest.

Snacks

The popularity of frites cannot be understated. Every village has at least one *friture* where frites are served up in a paper cone or dish, smothered until almost unrecognisable with large blobs of thick mayonnaise and eaten with a small wooden fork in a mostly futile attempt to keep your fingers clean.

On the sweet side, waffles *(wafels* or *gaufres)* are eaten piping hot from market stalls. Then there are filled chocolates *(pralines)* whose fame rivals Belgian beer. One of the most exclusive is Godiva, where you'll pay for the white gloves they wear to hand-pick each piece, or there's the poor person's delicious equivalent, the elephant-emblazoned Côte d'Or.

Main Dishes

Meat, poultry and hearty vegetable soups are high on menus, but it's *mosselen* (mussels) cooked in white wine and served with a mountain of frites that's known as the national dish. Grown mainly in the Delta region in the Netherlands, the rule of thumb for mussels is: eat them during the months which include an 'r', and don't touch the ones that haven't opened properly when cooked.

Eating out is rarely cheap: pizzas start at f160, while a *dagschotel* or *plat du jour* (dish of the day) in a cheap bar or café costs f250 to f280.

DRINKS

Beer rules...and deservedly so. The quality is excellent and the variety incomparable –

somewhere upwards of 350 types, from standard lagers to specialist brews. The most noted are the traditionally abbey-brewed *Trappist* beers, dark in colour, grainy in taste and dangerous in quantity (from 6% to 10% alcohol by volume). Then there's *lambic*, a spontaneously fermented beer which comes sweet or sour depending on what was added during fermentation: *gueuze* is the sour alternative, and *kriek* (with cherries) or *framboise* (with raspberries) two of the sweet varieties. Prices match quality, with a 250-ml lager costing f35 to f50, and a 330-ml Trappist f70 to f120, depending on the café.

ENTERTAINMENT

Nightlife almost uniformly centres around the ubiquitous bars and cafés. Cinemas in Flanders usually screen films in their original language with Flemish subtitles, while those in Wallonia tend to dub them into French. Screenings are sometimes cheaper on Mondays.

THINGS TO BUY

Chocolate, lace and beer are the specialities, but the first two don't come cheap. Five individual Godiva pralines will set you back f100, a lace handkerchief anywhere from f150 to f700.

Getting There & Away

AIR

Belgium has two international airports. The main one is Zaventem, 14 km north-east of Brussels and the hub for international flights. The other airport, Deurne, is close to Antwerp and has less frequent flights to Amsterdam, London, Liverpool and Dublin only. Depending on when you leave, flights to London can be cheaper from Deurne. The national airline, Sabena, sometimes has good deals to West African destinations.

LAND
Bus

Eurolines and Hoverspeed Citysprint operate international bus services to and from Belgium. Tickets can be bought for Eurolines in its offices in Antwerp, Brussels or Liège.

Alternatively, many travel agencies sell tickets for both companies. Reduced fares for people aged under 26 are offered by both lines.

Eurolines/Europabus has regular buses to many Western, Eastern, Mediterranean and central European destinations as well as Scandinavia and North Africa. Depending on the destination and the time of year, its buses stop in Antwerp, Bruges, Brussels, Ghent, Liège, Mons, Charleroi and Namur. Hoverspeed runs only between London, Belgium and the Netherlands, with routes via Antwerp and Brussels.

Some Eurolines and all Hoverspeed buses go via Calais in France – intending travellers should check whether a French visa is needed. For more detailed information on these services, see the Getting There & Away section in the relevant city.

Train

Belgium Railways – symbolised by a 'B' surrounded by an eye-shaped oval – has frequent international services. Eurail, Inter-Rail, Europass and Flexipass tickets are valid throughout the country. Brussels is the central international hub, with lines in all directions. Large train stations have information offices, usually open until about 9 pm, or you can ask at the ticket windows. Travellers under 26 years can get a 'youth fare' discount on international tickets (the discount varies depending on the destination) – for other special fares, see the following Getting Around section.

Brussels has three main train stations. Most international services pass through two of them – Gare du Nord and Gare du Midi – but some trains (such as to Amsterdam, Cologne and London) also stop at Gare Centrale. The Eurostar and Thalys fast trains stop only at Gare du Midi.

Examples of one-way, 2nd-class, adult fares and journey times with ordinary trains from Brussels to some destinations on the main neighbouring routes are as follows: Trains going north pass Antwerp en route to Amsterdam (f1080, three hours, hourly trains). Southwards, the line goes via Mons (Bergen in Flemish) to Paris' Gare du Nord (f1290, three hours, six per day). Heading south-east, trains run via Namur to Luxembourg City (f760, 2¾ hours, hourly), while east, the line passes Liège to Cologne (f1400, four hours, hourly).

To London (f2200, eight hours), ordinary trains connect with ferries or jetfoils in Ostend; there are at least seven services per day. With the quicker jetfoil, there's a f200 supplement.

Eurostar trains operate through the Channel Tunnel with at least seven services per day in each direction between Brussels and London (3¼ hours). Standard 2nd-class fares are f3680/1400 for adults/children but there are also cheaper Apex fares (these must be reserved and paid 14 days in advance) and discounts for holders of Eurail, Europass and Benelux Tourrail passes. For more information about Eurostar call ☎ 02-203 36 40.

The brand-new Thalys fast trains connect Brussels with Amsterdam (f1140, 2¾ hours, via Antwerp) and Paris (f1750, two hours, via Mons). However, as these trains are still using old tracks through Belgium and the Netherlands, there is as yet little difference in journey time between Brussels and Amsterdam. Thalys trains also run to Liège and will eventually continue to Cologne in Germany. In general, prices are reduced on weekends and those under 26 years get a 40% discount.

SEA

Two companies operate car/passenger ferries to Britain from either Ostend or Zeebrugge. Tickets can be bought from most travel agencies. For details on train/ferry or jetfoil services, see the preceding Train section.

North Sea Ferries sails overnight from Zeebrugge to Hull (14 hours) and charges f3210/3670 for a car in the low/high season and f1950/2480 for adult passengers.

Oostende Lines/Sally Ferries has services between Ostend and Ramsgate with either the ferry (four hours, six per day) or the jetfoil (1¾ hours, three to five per day). One-way fares for cars plus one adult range from f2650 to f6250, depending on the season. Passengers are charged f800, with an extra f200 to f300 surcharge if you take the jetfoil.

For quicker Channel crossings, you can go from Calais in France – for details, see the France chapter in this book.

LEAVING BELGIUM

Airline passengers departing from Brussels pay a f520 departure tax, f260 from Antwerp. There's no departure tax when leaving by sea.

BELGIUM

Getting Around

BUS

Buses are used to connect towns and villages in more remote areas, particularly throughout the Ardennes. Local tourist offices will generally have details, or contact the bus information office in Namur (see the Ardennes section).

TRAIN

Belgium's transport system is dominated by its efficient rail network. The fastest services are the InterCity (IC) trains, backed up by InterRegional (IR) and local trains. Depending on the line, there will be an IC and an IR train every half-hour or hour. Most train stations have either luggage lockers (f60/100 for small/large lockers for 24 hours) or luggage rooms, which are generally open from 5 am until midnight and charge f60 per article.

Tickets & Passes

On weekends, return tickets within Belgium are reduced by 40% for the first passenger, 60% for the rest of the group (to a maximum of six people). On trips to the Netherlands or Luxembourg, the discount is 25% and 50% respectively. Discount excursion tickets, known as B-Excursions, to places such as the coast or Ardennes are also available.

Several rail passes are available. The Benelux Tourrail, which gives five days travel in one month in Belgium, the Netherlands and Luxembourg, costs f6320/4220 1st/2nd class for adults and f3160 (2nd class only) for those aged under 26. This pass can no longer be bought in the Netherlands, but passes bought in either Belgium or Luxembourg are valid for all three countries.

The Belgian Tourrail pass gives five days travel in one month within Belgium for f2995/1995 for 1st/2nd class. A Fixed Price Reduction Card gives up to 50% off all train tickets for a month and costs f570. The Go Pass, which costs f1360, entitles those under 26 years of age to 10 one-way journeys anywhere in Belgium and is valid for six months.

CAR & MOTORCYCLE

Drive on the right and give way to the right! The speed limit in towns is 50 km/h, outside,

90 km/h and on motorways, 120 km/h. The permissible blood alcohol concentration level is 0.05%. Fuel prices per litre are f38 for super, f33 for lead-free and f24 for diesel. More motoring information can be obtained from the Touring Club de Belgique (☎ 02-233 22 11) Rue de la Loi 44, 1040 Brussels.

BICYCLE

Bicycles are popular in the flat north. Many roads have separate cycle lanes, and bikes can be hired from some train stations for f325 per day (plus a f1500 deposit). They must be returned to the same station. Bikes can be taken on trains (only from stations in cities and major towns) for f200.

HITCHING

It's illegal on motorways but there are plenty of secondary roads. In the Ardennes, hitching is a good way to get around. TaxiStop agencies (see Travel Agencies in the Brussels Information section) match drivers with travellers on the road for a reasonable fee.

BOAT

Although fluvial tourism is not as developed here as, say, in France, it is possible to hire a boat to cruise along Belgium's many rivers and canals. Contact Reko (☎ 053-78 40 27) at Heilig Hartlaan 30, 9300 Aalst for details.

LOCAL TRANSPORT

Buses and trams (and small metro systems in Brussels and Antwerp) are efficient and reliable. Single tickets cost f50 but often you can buy a multistrip ticket – 10 strips for f250, for example – which works out cheaper or a one-day card for about f105 (in Flanders, one-day cards are valid for use on the same day in Antwerp, Ghent, Bruges and 10 other towns but not in Brussels). Services generally run until about 11 pm or midnight. You'll find public-transport ticket/information kiosks near most train stations.

Taxis are metered and expensive. You'll find them outside train stations.

ORGANISED TOURS

From Brussels, it's possible to take bus day trips to Ghent, Bruges and Antwerp, or even to the Ardennes and Luxembourg City, Amsterdam, Paris or Cologne. The main operator is

De Boeck (for details see Organised Tours in the Brussels section).

Brussels

Not a capital that sets out to seduce, Brussels (Bruxelles in French, Brussel in Flemish) is an unpretentious mix of grand edifices and modern skyscrapers. Its character largely follows that of the nation it governs: modest, confident, but rarely striving to overtly impress. Having grown from a 6th-century, marshy village on the banks of the River Senne (filled in long ago for sanitary reasons), this bilingual city is now headquarters of the EU and NATO, and home to Europe's most impressive central square.

Orientation

The city reverberates around the Grand Place, its imposing 15th-century market square, which sits dead centre in the Petit Ring, a pentagon of boulevards enclosing central Brussels and within which are many of the sights. But there's also plenty to see outside the Ring, where you'll also find much of the budget accommodation, often about 20 minutes walk from the Grand Place but accessible by tram, bus or metro.

There are three main train stations: Gare du Nord in the north, Gare du Midi in the south, and Gare Centrale about five minutes walk from the Grand Place. (Brussels' streets and stations are written in French and Flemish – we have used the French versions here.)

Information

Tourist Offices There are two offices: one for Brussels, the other for national information. The Tourist Information Brussels (TIB) (☎ 513 89 40), in the town hall on the Grand Place, has city guff and is open every day from 9 am to 6 pm (from October to December it's open Sundays from 10 am to 2 pm, from 1 January to 28 February it's closed Sundays). The national office (☎ 504 03 90), nearby on Rue du Marché aux Herbes 63, is open June to September daily from 9 am to 7 pm. The rest of the year it's open Monday to Saturday from 9 am to 6 pm and Sunday from 1 to 5 pm.

Money Outside banking hours, there are exchange bureaus at the airport, at Gare Centrale and Gare du Nord (both open until 8 pm) and at Gare du Midi (until 9.30 pm). The GWK exchange bureau at Rue du Marché aux Herbes 88 is open daily from 9 am to 9 pm and has good rates. Thomas Cook (☎ 513 28 45) is at Grand Place 4 and American Express (☎ 676 27 27) is at Place Louise 2.

Post & Communications The main post office is in the Centre Monnaie (1st floor) near Place de Brouckère on Blvd Anspach, open weekdays from 8.30 am to 6 pm and Saturday 9 am to 3 pm (poste restante can be collected only on weekdays). The telephone office at Blvd l'Impératrice 17 is open from 8.30 am to 8 pm, Monday to Saturday.

Brussels' telephone code is ☎ 02.

Travel Agencies Some of the more useful agencies include:

Acotra student travel agency – Rue de la Madeleine 51 (☎ 512 70 78)
AirStop/TaxiStop – organises 40 to 60% off seats on charter flights to southern Europe and paid rides in cars going to other European cities – Rue du Fossé aux Loups 28 (☎ 223 22 60 for AirStop, ☎ 223 23 10 for TaxiStop)
Connections Travel Shop – Rue du Midi 19 (☎ 512 50 60)

Bookshops W H Smith (☎ 219 27 08), Blvd Adolphe Max 71, has English-language novels, travel guides and maps.

Laundry The self-service Ipsomat at Place Hauwaert near CHAB hostel is open daily from 7 am to 9 pm. Close to Bruegel hostel, the Salon Lavoir de la Chapelle on Rue Haute is open weekdays from 8 am to 6 pm.

Medical & Emergency Services For medical emergencies (24 hours), dial ☎ 648 80 00 or ☎ 479 18 18, and for dental problems, dial ☎ 426 10 26.

Help Line (☎ 648 40 14) is a Brussels-based, 24-hour English-speaking crisis line and information service.

Things to See & Do

Walking Tour The **Grand Place** is the obvious start for exploring within the Petit Ring.

BELGIUM

BELGIUM

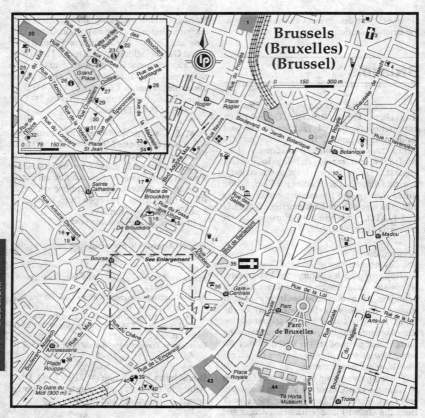

Brussels
(Bruxelles)
(Brussel)

PLACES TO STAY		OTHER		24	National Tourist Office
2	Hôtel Albert	1	Gare du Nord	25	Connections Travel
8	Sleep Well Hostel	3	Saint Maria Church	26	Tourist Information
9	CHAB Hostel	5	De Ultieme Hallucinatie		Brussels (TIB)
10	Jacques Brel Hostel	6	W H Smith Bookshop	28	Sabena Office
11	Hôtel Sabina	7	City 2 Shopping Centre	29	Blues Corner
12	Hôtel la Tasse d'Argent	13	Belgian Comic Strip	31	Goupil le Fol
38	Hôtel Windsor		Centre	32	Manneken Pis
40	Bruegel Hostel	14	À la Mort Subite	33	Acotra Travel
		15	Air Stop/Taxi Stop	34	Artemys Bookshop
PLACES TO EAT		16	Post Office	35	St Michel Cathedral
4	Metin	17	Eurolines/Europabus	36	Telephone Office
18	La Femme du		Office	37	Gare Centrale (Train
	Boulanger	19	L'Archiduc		Station)
27	't Kelderke	20	Bourse	39	Laundry
30	Pitta & Frites Places	21	Falstaff	43	Ancient & Modern Art
41	L'Orféo	22	Galeries St Hubert		Museums
42	La Fleur d'Orange	23	GWK Exchange Bureau	44	Royal Palace

Formerly the Grand Place was home to the craft guilds, whose rich guildhouses line the square, topped by golden figures which glisten by day, and which are fanfared with a sound-and-light show by night (from April to September – check with the TIB for times).

Off the Grand Place to the south on Rue Charles Buls is one of the first glimpses of the city's once-famous Art-Nouveau cult: an 1899 gilded plaque dedicated to the city from its appreciative artists. It's beside a reclining 14th-century hero whose gleaming arm passers-by rub for good luck. A couple of blocks further is **Manneken Pis**, the famous statue of a small boy weeing on the corner of Rue du Chêne and Rue de l'Étuve.

One block north-east of the Grand Place is the **Galeries St Hubert**, Europe's oldest glass-covered shopping arcade and, further north, the **Belgian Comic Strip Centre** (see the following section). Alternatively, head east up the hill past Gare Centrale to Rue Royale and the refinement of the upper town, where near the **Royal Palace** you'll find the modern and ancient art museums.

Museums One of the most central museums – and perhaps for Belgium the most appropriate to start with – is the **Brewery Museum** in the Maison des Brasseurs at Grand Place 10. It's not much more than a collection of everything associated with the consumption of beer but it's a good way to see inside one of the guildhouses. Admission is f100 (including a drink) and it's open daily from 10 am to 5 pm.

Also on the Grand Place, in the Maison du Roi, is the **City of Brussels Museum**, which gives a historical rundown on the city and exhibits every piece of clothing ever worn by Manneken Pis. It's open weekdays (except Friday) from 10 am to 12.30 pm and from 1.30 to 5 pm (until 4 pm from 1 October to 31 March), and weekends from 10 am to 1 pm; entry costs f80.

The **Ancient Art Museum**, Rue de la Régence 3, has works by Flemish Primitives, Brueghel and Rubens. It's open Tuesday to Sunday from 10 am to noon and 1 to 5 pm. For contemporary Belgian works, head to the **Modern Art** section at Place Royale 1, open Tuesday to Sunday from 10 am to 1 pm and 2 to 5 pm. Admission to both is free.

Tintin fans must not miss the **Comic Strip Centre** in an Art-Nouveau building designed by Horta at Rue des Sables 20. It's open Tuesday to Sunday from 10 am to 6 pm; admission is f180.

There are several museums to draw you out of the Petit Ring. The **Horta Museum**, Rue Américaine 25 in St Gilles, was Horta's house and is a superb introduction to his turn-of-the-century architectural movement – open daily except Monday from 2 to 5.30 pm, admission is f100/200 on weekdays/weekends (tram: No 92).

To the east, **Cinquantenaire** is a large museum conglomerate – art, history, military and motor vehicles together in a huge park (metro: Merode).

A few minutes walk from Gare du Midi is the **Gueuze Museum** at Rue Gheude 56 in Anderlecht – a working brewery still using traditional methods, and where you can sample the real thing. It's open weekdays from 8.30 am to 4.30 pm and on Saturday from 10 am to 6 pm (until 1 pm on Saturday from June to mid-October); entry is f90 and includes a guided tour.

Other Attractions The space-age leftover from the 1958 World Fair, **Atomium**, at Blvd du Centenaire in the suburb of Laeken, has virtually become a symbol of the city. It's open from 1 April to 31 August daily from 9 am to 8 pm (the rest of the year from 10 am to 6 pm) and costs f180 (tram: No 81 to Heysel). The **Mini Europe** theme park, next door to the Atomium, shows Europe in miniature. The biggest **market** is Sunday morning's food and general goods market around Gare du Midi.

Organised Tours
Three-hour bus tours of Brussels are run by De Boeck (☎ 513 77 44) at Rue de la Colline 8 (just off the Grand Place).

From 1 June to 15 September, Chatterbus (☎ 673 18 35), Rue des Thuyas, has three-hour walking/minibus tours led by Brusselians; phone for details.

For specialised tours – Horta and Art Nouveau, or Brussels in the Art-Deco era, for example – contact Arau (☎ 219 33 45) at Blvd Adolphe Max 55.

Special Events

The most prestigious annual event is Ommegang, a 16th century-style procession staged within the illuminated Grand Place in early July. Just as popular is the biennial flower carpet that colours the square in August every second year (even numbers).

Places to Stay

There's no shortage of hotels for f2500 and upwards, but the budget class is a different story.

Camping The closest ground to the city centre is *Espace International* (☎ 644 16 81), Chausée de Wavre 205, just outside the Petit Ring to the south-east. It's expensive – f250 per person plus f200 for a tent; cars are not allowed. To get there, take bus No 95 or 96 from Gare Centrale to Place de Luxembourg and walk 500 metres.

Paul Rosmant (☎ 782 10 09), at Warandeberg 52 in Wezembeek-Oppem to the east, charges f200 for an adult and a tent, and is open from April to September; take the metro to Crainhem and then bus No 30 to Église Saint Pierre.

Heading south, *Beersel* (☎ 331 05 61) at Steenweg op Ukkel 75, charges f50/30 for a person/tent and is open all year.

Hostels The newly expanded *Bruegel* (☎ 511 04 36) at Rue du St Esprit 2, is an official hostel with singles/doubles for f660/1100 and dorms for f395 per person. Equally as central is *Sleep Well* (☎ 218 50 50) at Rue du Damier 23. This place has been around for years but it recently opened a brand-new complex and must now rate as Belgium's most modern hostel. Rooms go for f640/1020/1260, and there are six-bed dorms for f380 per person.

The other official hostel, *Jacques Brel* (☎ 218 01 87) at Rue de la Sablonnière 30, is 15 minutes from the centre, impersonal but with parking. It charges the same as Bruegel. Just north is *CHAB* (☎ 217 01 58) at Rue Traversière 8, popular with backpackers, with rooms for f620/1020/1260 and beds in a sleep-in for f300. It has a pleasant garden and bar.

B&Bs Bed & Brussels (☎ 646 07 37) at Rue Victor Greyson 58, 1050 Brussels, can organise accommodation in B&Bs. Prices start at f790/1250 for a single/double room.

Hotels The best budget option is *Les Bluets* (☎ 534 39 83) at Rue Berckmans 124 (metro: Porte de Hal, then a three-block walk east). This attractive house in a quiet backstreet has a lavish assortment of furniture, stained-glass windows, and much, much more. Single rooms range from f900 to f2000, doubles from f1250 to f2450. Smoking is not allowed.

Sabina (☎ 218 26 37), at Rue du Nord 78 (metro: Madou), is popular with weekend travellers and weekday Eurocrats. Rooms, all with shower, start at f1700 and there's street parking. Two blocks south, *Hôtel la Tasse d'Argent* (☎ 218 83 75), Rue du Congrès 48, has decent rooms from f1450/1750; breakfast is f150 extra.

Further north, the friendly *Hôtel Albert* (☎ 217 93 91) at Rue Royale Sainte-Marie 27 has rooms from f1400/1800 including private parking. Heading towards Gare du Midi, the little *Hôtel Windsor* (☎ 511 20 14) at Place Rouppe 13 offers somewhat overpriced rooms from f1970/2375, and there's parking on the square in front.

Places to Eat

expensive but very nice

City Centre Brussels' dining heart is Rue des Bouchers ('Butcher's Street'), near the Grand Place. Here you'll find lobster, crab, mussels and fish awaiting conspicuous consumption in one terrace restaurant after another.

At Grand Place 15 is *'t Kelderke* (☎ 513 73 44), a 16th-century cellar where you can get a variety of Belgian specialities; main courses cost about f440. *La Femme du Boulanger* (☎ 502 40 26) at Rue Antoine Dansaert 18 serves a lunch-time salad buffet for f395. *La Fleur d'Orange* (☎ 511 24 37) at Rue de Rollebeek 21 is a pricey Moroccan restaurant in a quaint street lined with restaurants. Around the corner, *L'Orféo* on Rue Haute 18 has huge stuffed pitta breads from f150.

If you're just after frites or a pitta bread, take your pick of the swarm of places along Rue Marché aux Fromages near the Grand Place.

For self-caterers, there's a *GB* supermarket in the basement of the City 2 shopping centre which is open Monday to Saturday until 8 pm.

Outside the City Centre For authentic moussaka and retsina, try one of the Greek restaurants on Rue d'Argonne near Gare du Midi – *Le Cheval de Troie* (☎ 538 30 95) at No 32 is very good. Equally delicious Turkish fare can be had at one of the cheap *pide* (Turkish pizza) saloons in St Josse to the north; *Metin* (☎ 217 68 63) at Chaussée de Haecht 94 is by far the best. For vegetarian food, *Le Paradoxe* (☎ 649 89 81) at Chaussée d'Ixelles 329 has a plat du jour for f350.

Entertainment
The *Bulletin's* 'What's On' guide lists the live-music and cinema scenes. Otherwise there are enough bars and cafés to keep you on a long pub crawl.

Falstaff, by the stock exchange at Rue Henri Maus 17, is an Art-Nouveau showpiece, trendy with the fashionable young and eccentric old. Alternatively, the auspiciously named *De Ultieme Hallucinatie* at Rue Royale 316 has more subtle Art-Nouveau tones and occasional live music. Those into Art Deco and live jazz should head to the (expensive) *L'Archiduc* at Rue Antoine Dansaert 6. *À la Mort Subite* (literally, 'instant death') at Rue Mont-aux-Herbes-Potagères 7 has one of the many brews named after it. If you're after specialist beers try *Toone,* a puppet theatre/tavern off Petite rue des Bouchers, or for loud live rock, the *Blues Corner* off the Grand Place at Rue des Chapeliers 12. One street away at Rue de la Violette 22 there's ample French ambience at *Goupil le Fol* (Crazy Folk).

On Rue Borgval, *Sappho* and *Le Féminin* are two weekends-only, lesbian bars. *Le Garage* at Rue Duquesnoy 16 is a loud, weekend gay and lesbian nightclub.

Getting There & Away
Air Airline offices in Brussels include the following:

British Airways
    Zaventem Airport (☎ 725 30 00)
KLM
    Ave Marnix 28 (☎ 507 70 70)
Sabena
    Rue du Marché aux Herbes 110 (☎ 723 89 40)

Bus Eurolines/Europabus has three offices in Brussels. The main office (☎ 302 07 07) is on the west side of Gare du Nord. Another office (☎ 217 00 25) is at Place de Brouckère 50 and the third office (☎ 538 20 49) at Ave Fonsny 9 near Gare du Midi. Eurolines buses for cities throughout Europe and Scandinavia leave from Gare du Nord only. Europabus buses leave from King Baudouin stadium at Heysel. To London (f1850) there's an overnight bus (8½ hours) arriving at London's Victoria Station about 6 am, as well as a daytime service (seven hours). Both services go via Ghent and Calais in France (check whether you need a French visa). Other destinations include Amsterdam (f700, four hours), Cologne (f700, four hours), Luxembourg (f600, 2¾ hours) and Paris (f900, four hours).

Hoverspeed (☎ 537 10 47) Citysprint buses to London (f1850, 7½ hours) pick up at Alsa Voyages at Place de la Constitution 12 near Gare du Midi. They go via Calais in France (check if you need a French visa). It has one bus a day, arriving at Victoria Station at 3 pm. During summer, an additional bus leaves Brussels at midnight.

Train The train information office (☎ 224 60 10) at Gare Centrale is open every day from 6.30 am to 9.45 pm.

For prices and journey times from Brussels to other Belgian cities and towns, check the Getting There & Away section in those places. For international services, see the Getting There & Away section at the beginning of this chapter.

Hitching North to Antwerp or Amsterdam, get tram No 52 or 92 to Heysel for the A12 motorway; east towards Liège or Cologne, take tram No 90 to metro Diamant for the E40; south-east to Namur and Luxembourg, get the metro (line 1) to Station Delta for the E411; south to Mons and Paris, get tram No 52 to Rue de Stalle and follow it to the E19; west to Ghent, Bruges or London, get bus No 85 to one stop before the terminus, and then follow the E40 signs.

Getting Around
Brussels' transport network consists of buses, trams and a metro. Transport maps are handed out from the tourist offices or metro information kiosks.

To/From the Airport The national airport, Zaventem, lies 14 km to the north-east and is connected to all three central stations by three trains per hour (f85, 20 minutes). Taxis generally charge about f1200.

Bus, Tram & Underground Single rides cost f50, five/10-journey cards f230/320 and a one-day card f125. Valid on all transport, tickets can be bought from the metro stations or bus drivers, the one-day card also from the TIB. Public transport runs until about midnight.

Taxi There are plenty of ranks, or phone ATR (☎ 647 22 22) or Taxis Orange (☎ 511 22 33).

Car Car rental (including insurance, VAT and unlimited km) starts at about f3200 a day or f11,400 a week, with local operators such as Alamo offering some of the cheapest rates. Rental firms include the following:

Alamo
    Zaventem Airport (☎ 753 20 60)
Avis
    Rue Américaine 145 (☎ 537 12 80)
Budget
    Ave Louise 327 (☎ 646 51 30)
Europcar
    Ave Louise 235 (☎ 640 94 00)
Hertz
    Blvd Lemonnier 8 (☎ 513 28 86)

AROUND BRUSSELS

A huge stone lion and nearly a million visitors a year look out over the plains where Napoleon was defeated and European history changed course at the Battle of **Waterloo**, south of Brussels. There's a visitors' centre (☎ 385 19 12) at Route du Lion 252 – take bus W from Place Rouppe. Those interested in the British version of events should head to the **Wellington Museum** at Chaussée de Bruxelles 147, five km away – bus W also passes here.

The **Central African Museum** at Tervuren, 20 km to the east, is old and in parts musty but it has an impressive range of Zaïrian artefacts. Admission is f80; take the metro to Montgomery, then tram No 44.

About 25 km east of Brussels, **Louvain** (Leuven in Flemish) is a lively student town and home to Belgium's oldest university (dating from 1425). The town's main sight is the 15th-century town hall, a flamboyant struc-

ture with terraced turrets and wrought stonework. From Brussels, there are two trains an hour (f135, 30 minutes).

Antwerp

Second in size to the capital and often more likeable, Antwerp (Antwerpen in Flemish, Anvers in French) is perhaps Belgium's most underrated tourist city. It's compact and heavily beautified by many baroque edifices, and was once home to 17th-century artist Pieter Paul Rubens.

With a prime spot on the Scheldt River, Antwerp came to the fore as Western Europe's greatest economic centre in the early 16th century. But the times of prosperity were relatively short-lived. When the city's Protestants smashed up a cathedral in 1566 as part of the Iconoclastic Fury, the Spanish ruler Philip II sent troops to take control. Ten years later the unpaid garrison mutinied, ransacking the city and in three nights massacring 8000 people in the Spanish Fury. The final blow came in 1648 when the Dutch closed the Scheldt to all non-Dutch ships, blocking Antwerp's vital link to the sea. It wasn't until Napoleon arrived and the French rebuilt the docks that Antwerp got back on its feet.

Today it's brimming with a self-confidence that is rarely extolled outside its boundaries. As a world port, its air is international but at times seedy, while from behind the discreet façades of the Jewish quarter runs the world's largest diamond industry.

Orientation

Antwerp is bordered by the Scheldt and the 'Ring', a highway built on a 16th-century moat which encircled the city. Most of the sights are concentrated between the impressive Centraal Station (CS) and the old centre – a 15-minute walk away, based around the Grote Markt.

Information

Tourist Office At Grote Markt 15, the tourist office (☎ 232 01 03) is open Monday to Saturday from 9 am to 5.45 pm, and Sunday 9 am to 4.45 pm.

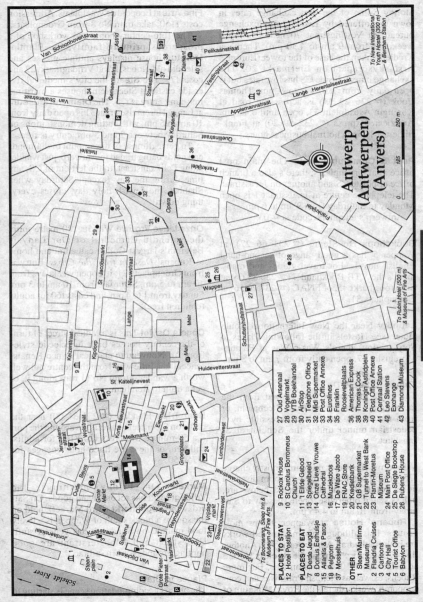

Antwerp (Antwerpen) (Anvers)

Scheldt River

To New International
Youth Hostel (300 m)
& Berchem Station

To Rubin Hotel (500 m)
& Museum of Fine Arts

To Boomerang, Sleep Inn &
Museum of Fine Arts

0   125   250 m

BELGIUM

PLACES TO STAY
12 Hotel Postiljon

PLACES TO EAT
7   Derde Jeugd
8   Domus Eethuisje
15 Atlantis & Paros
16 Pelgrom
37 Mosselhuis

OTHER
1   Steen/Maritime
    Museum
2   Flandria Cruises
3   Cartoons
4   City Hall
5   Tourist Office
6   Babylon
9   Rockox House
10 St Carolus Borromeus
    Church
11 't Elfde Gebod
13 Spiegelbeeld
14 Onze Lieve Vrouwe
    Cathedral
16 Muziekdoos
17 De Ware Jacob
19 FNAC Store
20 Kredietbank
21 GB Supermarket
22 Tunnel to West Bank
23 Plantin-Moretus
    Museum
24 Main Post Office
25 De Slegte Bookshop
26 Rubens' House
27 Oud Arsenaal
28 Vogelmarkt
29 VTB Boekhandel
30 AirStop
31 Telephone Office
32 Midi Supermarket
33 Post Office Annexe
34 Eurolines
35 Franklin
36 Rooseveltplaats
38 American Express
39 Thomas Cook
40 Koningin Astridplein
41 Post Office Annexe
42 Centraal Station
43 Leo Stevens
    Exchange
43 Diamond Museum

Money Some of the best exchange rates in town are offered by Leo Stevens exchange bureau on Vestingstraat 70 near CS (open weekdays from 9 am to 4.30 pm). There's a Kredietbank in the base of the tower (Europe's first skyscraper) on Eiermarkt 20. The exchange bureau inside CS has low rates but is open daily from 7.30 am to 9 pm. Thomas Cook (☎ 226 29 53) is across the road at Koningin Astridplein 33, open until 8.45 pm. American Express (☎ 232 59 20) at Frankrijklei 21 is open normal business hours.

Post & Communications The main post office is at Groenplaats; there's also a branch office opposite CS and another on Jezusstraat. The telephone centre at Jezusstraat 1 is open Monday to Saturday from 9 am to 6 pm.

Antwerp's telephone code is ☎ 03.

Bookshops De Slegte (☎ 231 66 27), at Wapper 5, has a good range of second-hand English novels. For travel guides and maps, there's the VTB Boekhandel (☎ 220 33 66) at St Jakobsmarkt 45, or FNAC (☎ 231 20 56) at Groenplaats 31.

Laundry Near the New International Youth Hotel (see Hostels in the following Places to Stay section) there's Was-o-Was at Plantin-Moretuslei 77, open daily from 7 am to 8 pm.

Things to See & Do
The city's skyline is best viewed from the raised quays leading off from Steenplein, or from the river's west bank, accessible by a pedestrian tunnel under the Scheldt at St Jansvliet.

Museums The major museums mostly charge f75, or you can buy a three-museum discount ticket for f150. All those listed below are, unless stated otherwise, open Tuesday to Saturday from 10 am to 4.45 pm.

Rubens' House at Wapper 9 tops most visitors' lists although his most noted works are in the cathedral. Admission is f75. Another fine 17th-century home is the **Rockox House** at Keizerstraat 10, admission free. For more Rubens, as well as Flemish Primitives and contemporary works, there's the **Royal Museum of**

Fine Arts at Leopold de Waelplaats. Admission costs f150; take tram No 8 from Groenplaats.

The 16th-century home and workshop of a prosperous printing family, the **Plantin-Moretus** house displays antique presses and splendid old globes. It's at Vrijdagmarkt 22 and costs f75. The **Steen**, the city's medieval riverside castle at Steenplein, houses a maritime museum; entry is f75. The **Diamond Museum** at Lange Herentalsestraat 31 is open daily from 10 am to 5 pm, with cutting demonstrations on Saturday between 2 and 5 pm; entry is free.

To get a glimpse of the amount of diamonds and golds being traded in Antwerp, just wander along Pelikaanstraat, to the left out of CS, any time during the day (except Saturday when Shabbat, the Jewish holy day, closes everything down).

Onze Lieve Vrouwe With its 120-metre spire, the splendid Cathedral of Our Lady is Belgium's largest Gothic cathedral and home to Rubens' *Descent from the Cross*. Entry is from Groenplaats 21; it's open weekdays from 10 am to 5 pm, Saturday from 10 am to 3 pm, Sunday from 1 to 4 pm, and costs f60 for adults (children free).

Cogels Osylei This is a radical street of turn-of-the-century houses built in eclectic styles from Art Nouveau to classical or neo-Renaissance. It's a little way from the centre but well worth a wander – tram No 11 runs along it, or get a train to Berchem.

Boat Trips Flandria (☎ 231 31 00) near the castle on Steenplein has cruises around the port – a 50-minute trip costs f240/160 for adults/children, or there are three-hour voyages for f375/250.

Markets On Friday mornings, the **Vrijdagmarkt** has second-hand goods. On Saturday the **Vogelmarkt** (Bird Market), held on the square a block south of Wapper, is a lively food market; on Sunday it has general stuff. Hoogstraat and Kloosterstraat are good hunting grounds for bric-a-brac.

Places to Stay
The budget accommodation scene is starting to

improve, and there are now a few cheap, and relatively central hotels and B&Bs.

Camping There are two camp grounds, both open from April to September and charging f65 for each adult or child, plus f35 for a tent, caravan or a car. *De Molen* (☎ 219 60 90) is on the west bank of the Scheldt at St Annastrand (bus No 81 or 82). *Vogelzang* (☎ 238 57 17) is at Vogelzanglaan near the Bouwcentrum (tram No 2 direction 'Hoboken').

Hostels The cheapest option is the modern, official *hostel* (☎ 238 02 73) at Eric Sasselaan 2, about 10 minutes by tram No 2 (direction 'Hoboken') or bus No 27 (direction 'zuid', ie south) from CS – get off at Bouwcentrum and follow the signs. Open all year, it costs f365, and there are parking and laundry facilities.

The closest private hostel-cum-hotel to CS is the friendly *New International Youth Hotel* (☎ 230 05 22) at Provinciestraat 256. It's 10 minutes walk through the Jewish neigh bourhood – turn left out of the station, follow Pelikaanstraat to the Plantin-Moretuslei inter-section, go left through the tunnel and it's the third street on the right. There are rooms/quads for f920/1320/2320 or dorms (eight beds) for f430.

Near the Royal Museum of Fine Arts, the laid-back *Boomerang* (☎ 238 47 82) at Volkstraat 58 has dorms for f380 – get bus No 23 (direction 'Zuid') from CS. Four blocks south, the *Sleep Inn* (☎ 237 37 48) at Bolivarplaats 1 has rooms for f500/1000, and laundry facilities; take bus No 1 (direction 'Zuid').

Hotels The sage budget choice is *Rubenshof* (☎ 237 07 89) at Amerikalei 115. It has clean rooms, all with communal showers, for f900/1350/1850, or rooms with private facili-ties for f1050/1850. To get there, take bus No 1 from Koningin Astridplein next to CS, or tram No 12 or 24 (direction 'Zuid'), which can be picked up at Franklin Rooseltplaats.

Similarly priced is the lovely *B&B* (☎ 238 39 88) at Edward Pécherstraat 37 near the Museum for Fine Arts. There are four rooms – all fur-nished with antique bits and pieces – and several communal bathrooms; bus No 23 (direction 'Zuid') stops one block away on Kasteelstraat. Catch it in Koningin Astridplein next to CS.

Wonderfully sited on a quiet pedestrian lane smack in the centre is *Hotel Postiljon* (☎ 231 75 75), Blauwmoezelstraat 6. The rooms are tastefully furnished but very small. Rooms with communal facilities start at f1000/2000; breakfast is f200 extra.

The *Hotel Granducale* (☎ 239 37 24) at St Vincentiusstraat 3, about two km south of the centre, has comfortable rooms with communal facilities starting at f1350/1900; rooms with private shower go from f1700/2300. Tram No 8 from Groenplaats stops close by.

Places to Eat

Antwerp's old centre is well endowed with cafés and restaurants but most will cripple your budget. *Pelgrom* (☎ 231 93 35), Pelgrimstraat 15, is a cavernous, candle-lit cellar which, before you descend, offers sweeping views of the cathedral.

The *Domus Eethuisje* (☎ 225 15 06) at Wolstraat 11, is a laid-back place specialising in pasta dishes from f240. Round the corner at Korte Koepoortstraat 61 is the *Derde Jeugd* (☎ 233 28 46), one of the cheapest and most unpretentious diners in the centre of town, with meals from f200.

Nearby on Korte Nieuwstraat there are two good budget choices: *Paros* (☎ 226 26 18) at No 8 is a great-value Greek taverna, closed Tuesday, and full every other night; next door is the vegetarian *Atlantis* (☎ 234 05 17), to its regulars as legendary as its namesake (also closed Tuesday).

Pitta-bread places reign in the streets in front of CS, where you'll also find the *Mosselhuis* (☎ 231 00 28), one of Antwerp's oldest mussel restaurants, at Statiestraat 32.

Self-caterers will find an expensive *Midi* supermarket at Jezusstraat 22, and a *GB* super-market in the basement of the shopping centre next to the Groenplaats.

Entertainment

Antwerp's nightlife consists of its 2500 bars and cafés, most of which serve the sweet local liqueur, Elixir d'Anvers. Terraces line the cobbled streets around the cathedral, one of the most popular (and expensive) being the angel-adorned *'t Elfde Gebod* (the 11th Com-mandment) at Torfbrug 10. *Cartoons* at Kaasstraat 6 is located under a cinema of the same name which screens alternative films.

The *Oud Arsenaal* at M Pijpelinckxstraat, near the Vogelmarkt, is a popular local haunt (the beers are amongst the cheapest in town), as is the brown café-style *De Ware Jacob* on Vlasmarkt. Nearby, *De Vagant* at Reyndersstraat 21 serves more than 150 *genevers* (Belgian gins). The *Spiegelbeeld* on Grote Pieter Potstraat is one of the city's original art/kitsch pubs. In winter, warm your toes by an open fire at the *Babylon*, a rock and blues stronghold on Jeruzalemstraat.

The *Muziekdoos* at Lange Nieuwstraat 7 often has live bands or a succession of buskers on its free podium.

Alternatively, the streets off De Keyserlei near CS blaze with clubs and discos, while the riverside quarter north of Grote Markt is home to a red-light district. North of CS a few gay bars dot Van Schoonhovenstraat off Koningin Astridplein.

Getting There & Away

Air Antwerp airport (also known as Deurne airport) is five km south-east of the centre, connected by bus No 16 from CS. Sabena has an office in Antwerp (☎ 231 68 25) at Appelmansstraat 12 near CS, or at the airport (☎ 239 19 76). AirStop (☎ 226 39 22) at St Jakobsmarkt 86 can arrange cheap charter flights. For details on flights from Antwerp, see the Getting There & Away section at the beginning of this chapter.

Bus Eurolines (☎ 233 86 62) has an office at Van Stralenstraat 8, with buses from here to Amsterdam (f700, 3½ hours), Cologne (f700, four hours) and Paris (f1000, 5½ hours). There's an overnight bus to London (f1850, nine hours) and, during summer, a daytime bus (7½ hours) which goes via Bruges and Calais in France (check if you need a French visa).

Hoverspeed has no office in Antwerp, but tickets can be bought from American Express (see Money in the previous Information section) and other travel agents. The daytime Citysprint bus to London (f1850, seven hours) leaves from Stationsplein at Berchem Station. It goes via Calais in France.

Train Depending on their destination, international trains stop at either CS and/or Berchem Station to the south-east (from where there are regular train connections to CS). Trains to Paris (f1530, 3½ hours, 12 per day) leave from Berchem only. To Amsterdam (f920, 2¼ hours, hourly) and London (f2230, seven per day), they pass through both stations. London trains go via Ostend where they connect with a ferry or jetfoil. The total journey takes eight hours with the ferry, or 6½ hours with the jetfoil. The Thalys fast train connects with Amsterdam (f990, two hours) and Paris (f1900, 2¼ hours) via Brussels.

National connections include IC trains to Bruges (f380, 70 minutes), Brussels (f195, 35 minutes) and Ghent (f240, 45 minutes).

The CS train information office (☎ 204 20 40) is open Monday to Saturday from 6 am to 9.30 pm and Sunday from 7 am to 5.30 pm.

Getting Around

There's a good network of buses, trams and a tiny two-line metro – pick up the f50 public transport map from metro kiosks at Diamant (in front of CS) or Groenplaats (near Grote Markt). The main bus hubs are Koningin Astridplein next to CS and Franklin Rooseveltplaats two blocks west. Single tickets (valid for one hour) cost f40, 10-strip cards f250, or a 24-hour unlimited card f105.

Bruges 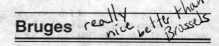 really nice better than Brussels

Known as the 'perfect' tourist attraction, Bruges (Brugge in Flemish) is one of Europe's best-preserved medieval cities and, hardly surprising, Belgium's most visited town. Its richly ornate 13th-century centre was suspended in time five centuries ago (and has remained that way because of strict building regulations) due largely to the silting of the Zwin River. At that time, Bruges was a prosperous cloth manufacturing town and the centre of Flemish Primitive art. When the river silted, Bruges died, its wealthy merchants abandoning it for Antwerp, leaving unoccupied homes and deserted canals.

That air has long gone. Today, particularly in summer, this 'living museum' is smothered with people. Go out of season or stay around late on summer evenings, when the carillon chimes seep through the cobbled streets and

**Bruges
(Brugge)**

0   150   300 m

BELGIUM

PLACES TO STAY		19	De Hobbit	15	Holy Blood Basilica
1	B&B	25	't Koffiehuisje	16	Town Hall
3	Hotel Cordoeanier			17	Bike Rental
21	Speelmanshuys Hotel		**OTHER**	18	Canal Cruises
23	Bruno's Passage Hostel	5	De Versteende Nacht	20	't Brugs Beertje
24	Imperial Pension	6	BBL Bank	22	L'Obcé dé
26	Salvators Hotel	7	Post Office	27	Brangwyn Museum
31	Hotel Lybeer	8	Telephone Office	28	Groeninge Museum
33	Rembrandt-Rubens	9	Nopri Supermarket	29	Gruuthuse Museum
	Hotel	10	Wasteels Reizen	30	Church of Our Lady
		11	Chagall	32	Memling Museum
PLACES TO EAT		12	Tourist Office	34	Begijnhof
2	In den Wittenkop	13	Belfry		
4	Lotus	14	GWK Exchange Bureau		

local boys (illegally) cast their fishing rods into willow-lined canals, and Bruges will show its age-old beauty.

Orientation
Neatly encased by an oval-shaped canal, Bruges is an amblers' ultimate dream, its sights sprinkled within leisurely walking distance of its compact centre. There are two central squares, the Markt and the Burg. Many local buses stop at the former, while the more impressive latter is home to the tourist office. The train station is 20 minutes walk south of the Markt – buses shuttle regularly between the two.

Information
Tourist Office The main tourist office (☎ 44 86 86) at Burg 11 is open summer (1 April to 30 September) weekdays from 9.30 am to 6.30 pm and weekends from 10 am to noon and 2 to 6.30 pm. In winter it's open weekdays from 9.30 am to 5 pm and Saturday 9.30 am to 1 pm and 2 to 5.30 pm. In the foyer there's a handful of luggage lockers. The branch office at the train station is open Monday to Saturday from 10.30 am to 6.30 pm.

Money There's a BBL Bank on the Markt and a GWK exchange bureau on Wollestraat. The exchange bureau at the tourist office is open weekdays from 9.15 am to 6.30 pm and weekends from 10 am to 6.30 pm. Alternatively, you can change cash, with lower rates, at the train station ticket counters from 5.45 am to 10.45 pm.

Post & Communications The post office is at Markt 5. The telephone office at Meestraat, two blocks east of the Burg, is open weekdays from 9 or 10 am to 6 pm and on Saturday from 9 am to 2 pm.

Bruges' telephone code is ☎ 050.

Laundry Next door to Snuffel Travellers Inn (see Hostels in the following Places to Stay section), is a wassalon open daily from 7 am to 10 pm.

Things to See & Do
There are many sights but also a wealth of things to do, from climbing the belfry to cruising the canals.

Walking Tour The **Markt** and neighbouring **Burg** are the dual medieval cores. From the Markt rises the 83-metre-high **belfry** with its 47-bell carillon, while the Burg, connected by a lace-lined alley next to the post office, is home to Belgium's oldest **city hall** as well as the **Basilica of the Holy Blood** where a few coagulated drops of Christ's blood are said to be stored.

From the Burg, go through the tunnelled Blinde Ezelstraat (Blind Donkey St) to the **fish market** and Huidenvettersplein, where canal boats leave. It's the start of the Dijver, along which you'll find the **Groeninge Museum**. The Dijver also leads past the **Brangwyn** and **Gruuthuse** museums – the former housing artwork including lace, the latter a 15th-century lord's mansion. Nearby, the **Church of Our Lady** is home to Michelangelo's *Madonna and Child* – his only sculpture to leave Italy during his lifetime – while across from the church on Mariastraat is the **Memling Museum**, housing works by Hans Memling, one of the early Flemish Primitives. Further down Mariastraat, signs lead to the **Begijnhof**.

Museums There's a f400 discount ticket available if you're visiting the Groeninge, Memling, Gruuthuse and Brangwyn museums. The **Groeninge Museum** at Dijver 12 houses Flemish art, from early Primitives through to contemporary. It's open every day in summer from 9.30 am to 5 pm. In winter it's open from 9.30 am to 12.30 pm and from 2 to 5 pm but closed Tuesday. Admission costs f200/100 for adults/students.

See Walking Tour above for details of other museums.

Belfry The view from the top of the 366 steps is rosy at sunset. It's open daily in summer from 9.30 am to 5 pm, in winter from 9.30 am to 12.30 pm and 1.30 to 5 pm, and costs f100/50 for adults/children.

Begijnhof Once home to unmarried women and widows, this serene 13th-century grassy square, enclosed by modest, whitewashed houses, is today inhabited by Benedictine nuns. It's about 10 minutes walk south of the Markt.

Organised Tours

Bruges by boat, bike, bus, foot or horse-drawn carriage – name it and you can tour by it. The tourist office has copious details. Alternatively, Quasimodo's (☎ 37 04 70) day tours will take you either to Ypres and around the battlefields of Flanders or on a 'Triple Treat' tour to indulge in waffles, beers and chocolate – prices start at f1300 (or f1000 for students and backpackers) and include a picnic lunch.

Places to Stay

Bruges' attractiveness has resulted in a mass of accommodation – all oppressively booked in summer.

Camping East at St Kruis, *Memling* (☎ 35 58 45) at Veltemweg 109 is open all year and charges f100/120 per person/tent. Get bus No 11 from the station. The slightly more expensive (and noisier) *St Michiel* (☎ 38 08 19), Tillegemstraat 55, is reached by bus No 7.

Hostels There are three unofficial hostels, all with lively, traveller-filled beds, less than 10 minutes walk from the Markt. *Passage Budget Hotel* (☎ 34 02 32) at Dweersstraat 26-28 is run by a friendly couple and has modern, clean dorms as well as a new hotel section next door. A bed in a dorm/four-bed room costs f310/375 per person, or there are comfortable doubles for f1200/1500 without/ with private bathroom. An extensive range of meals (including vegetarian fare) is served in the atmospheric bar. Bus No 16 from the train station stops nearby.

Snuffel Travellers Inn (☎ 33 31 33) at Ezelstraat 49 has dorms ranging from f285 to f325, and doubles for f900. There's a kitchen for travellers to use, but no restaurant. To get there from the Markt, head up St Jakobsstraat; from the train station take bus No 3 or 13. *Bauhaus International Youth Hotel* (☎ 34 10 93) at Langestraat 135 is big and bustling with a wide range of meals (including vegetarian options) until midnight. It charges from f300 to f320 for dorms and f550/950 for rooms with communal bathrooms – get bus No 6 from the train station or follow Hoogstraat from the Burg.

The official *hostel* (☎ 35 26 79), Baron Ruzettelaan 143, has dorms/four-bed rooms for f365/470, and a car park. It's closed between 10 am and 1 pm. Get bus No 2 from the station to the 'Wantestraat' stop.

Hotels Most of the cheaper hotels are away from the centre but rarely more than a 15-minute walk. The cosy *'t Keizershof* (☎ 33 87 28), at Oostmeers 126 opposite the train station, has rooms from f925/1300, and a car park. Next door, *Breugelhof* (☎ 34 34 28) has rooms for f1200/1400, and triples/quads for f2100/2900. The *Rembrandt-Rubens Hotel* (☎ 33 64 39), on the horse-and-carriage route at Walplein 38, has an old-world atmosphere and charges from f1000/1500, including parking; it's closed from 1 October to 1 April.

On the restaurant-lined Vrijdagmarkt, *'t Speelmanshuys* (☎ 33 95 52) at No 3 has rooms from f950/1550. *The Imperial Pension* (☎ 33 90 14) on Dweersstraat 28 costs f950/1400. Nearby, the *Hotel Lybeer* (☎ 33 43 55) at Korte Vuldersstraat 31 has decent rooms from f900/1550. The stained-glass entry to *Salvators* (☎ 33 19 21) at St Salvatorskerkhof 17 hides comfortable singles at f1100, doubles for f1750. Very central but on a quiet backstreet is *Hotel Cordoeanier* (☎ 33 90 51) at Cordoeanierstraat 16, which has rooms from f1800/2100/f2750. More intimate is Mrs Nyssen's little *B&B* (☎ 34 31 71) at Moerstraat 50, where rooms cost f900/1400.

Places to Eat

Mainly geared for big budgets, Bruges has a sprinkling of reasonable restaurants, backed up by the hostels (see the previous section) which offer traveller-sized meals. *De Hobbit* (☎ 33 55 20), on Kemelstraat, has charcoal-grilled spare ribs for f300. On Simon Stevinplein, *'t Koffiehuisje* (☎ 33 79 50) serves mussels in white wine for slightly less (f525) than its Markt counterparts.

Toermalijn (☎ 34 01 94) wholefood restaurant in the Alfa Dante Hotel at Coupure 29, 10 minutes walk from the Burg, has a mouth-watering (but pricey) vegetarian menu (closed Sunday night, and Monday and Tuesday). For cheaper, more central vegetarian fare, head for the pleasant little *Lotus* (☎ 33 10 78) at Wapenmakersstraat 5. It's open Monday to Saturday for lunch only (11.45 am to 1.45 pm) and has a good f250 dagschotel.

Popular and affordable, with a smooth jazz atmosphere, is the two-tiered bistro *In den Wittenkop* (☎ 33 20 59) at St Jakobstraat 14 (closed Sunday). A variety of mains start from f300. Self-caterers will find a *Battard* supermarket at Langestraat 55 and a *Nopri* supermarket on Geldmuntstraat, open Monday to Saturday from 9 am to 6 pm.

Entertainment
Besides the lively hostel bars, *De Versteende Nacht* at Langestraat 11 is a jazz café open nightly, except Monday, from 7 pm. Further along at No 121, the spacious *Cactus Café* draws a hip crowd.

In the centre, there's a throng of noisy bars on the Eiermarkt. For a little beer house with more than 300 types of brews, go no further than *'t Brugs Beertje* at Kemelstraat 5 (closed Wednesday). *Chagall* at St Amandsstraat 40 is a laid-back pub, and *L'Obcédé* on 't Zand is a lively nightclub with occasional bands.

Getting There & Away
Bus From April to October, the daytime Eurolines and Hoverspeed buses from Antwerp to London stop at Bruges (at the train station). They go via Calais in France (check if you need a visa) and take six hours. Tickets (f1850) can be bought from Wasteels Reizen (☎ 33 65 31) at Geldmuntstraat 30a.

Train The station information office (☎ 28 32 83) is open weekdays from 7 am to 7 pm and weekends from 9.30 am to 5.30 pm. There are IC trains to Antwerp (f380, 70 minutes), Brussels (f360, one hour), Courtrai (f195, 40 minutes, from where there are hourly connections to Ypres), Ghent (f165, 20 minutes) and Ostend (f105, 15 minutes).

Getting Around
There's a small network of buses, most leaving from the Markt, and many pass by the train station. The boards outside the tourist office list the routes and timetables, or you can ring ☎ 059-56 53 53.

Bicycle The train station shop (☎ 38 58 71), open daily from 7 am to 8.30 pm, charges f325 for a bike for the day. Better value is Eric Popelier (☎ 34 32 62), Hallestraat 14, which charges f70/150/250 for an hour/half-day/day, or Bauhaus (see the previous Hostels section) which has city/mountain bikes for f250/300 per day.

AROUND BRUGES
The famous, poppy-filled **battlefields of Flanders** draw many people south for a day or longer (see the Ypres section). In the opposite direction, the former fishing village of **Damme** is just five km away, connected by the Napoleon Canal, and popular as a lunchtime destination for day-trippers. A paddle wheeler plies between the two towns (30 minutes one way), leaving from Noorweegse Kaai 31, a good 45-minute walk from the Markt (or take bus No 4 or, in summer, the special bus from outside the post office). A one-way voyage costs f170/130 for adults/children, and f210/150 return.

Ypres

The stories have long been told about the WWI battlefields of Flanders. There were the tall red poppies which rose over the flat, flat fields; the soldiers who disappeared forever in the quagmire of battle; and the little town of Ypres (Ieper in Flemish) which was wiped off the map.

Sitting in the country's south-west corner, Ypres and its surrounding land were the last bastion of Belgian territory unoccupied by the Germans in WWI. As such, the region was a barrier to a German advance towards the French coastal ports around Calais. More than 300,000 Allied soldiers were killed here during four years of fighting that left the medieval town flattened. Convincingly rebuilt, its outlying farmlands are today dotted with cemeteries, and in early summer, the poppies still grow.

Orientation & Information
The town's hub is the Grote Markt. It's about five minutes walk from the train station – head straight up Stationsstraat and, at the end, turn left into Tempelstraat and then right into Boterstraat. Three blocks on, at the beginning

of the Markt, rises the Renaissance-style town hall.

Inside this building is the tourist office (☎ 20 07 24) at Grote Markt 34, which is open Monday to Saturday between 1 April and 30 September from 9 am to 5.30 pm and Sunday from 9.30 am; the rest of the year, it's open Monday to Friday from 9 am to 5 pm, Saturday until 4.30 pm and Sunday from 11 am to 4 pm.

Ypres' telephone code is ☎ 057.

Things to See
Ypres ranked alongside Bruges and Ghent as an important cloth town in medieval times, and its postwar reconstruction holds true to its former prosperity. On the 1st floor of the town hall, the **Ypres Salient '14-'18 Museum** details the wartime destruction of the town; it's open daily (except Monday) from Easter to 15 November from 9.30 am to noon and 1.30 to 5.30 pm (entry f50).

Around the town, in outlying fields and hamlets, are 150 British cemeteries and row upon row of white crosses. The tourist office sells a car/bike map (f20) known as the *'14-'18 Route* which winds for 70 km around the north-eastern battlefields past many of these cemeteries. But within the town itself stands perhaps the saddest reminder: the **Menin Gate**, inscribed with the names of 55,000 British and Commonwealth troops who were lost in the quagmire of the trenches and who have no graves. A bugler sounds the last post here every evening at 8 pm. It's about 300 metres from the tourist office – up Meensestraat to the right of the courthouse.

Places to Stay & Eat
For camping, there's the *Jeugdstadion* (☎ 21 72 82) at Leopold III laan 16, about 900 metres south-east of the town centre, or *YPRA* (☎ 44 46 31) at Pingelarestraat 2 in Kemmel, 10 km south.

The closest private hostel is *De Iep* (☎ 20 88 11) at Poperingseweg 34, about two km west of town. Otherwise, heading towards the coast, the official *De Sceure Hostel* (☎ 40 09 01) is at Veurnestraat 4 in Vleteren, 15 km away.

One of the most affordable central hotels, *Gasthof 't Zweerd* (☎ 20 04 75) at Grote Markt 2 next to the courthouse, has good-value singles/doubles from f1000/1375. Also on the Grote Markt is *Old Tom* at No 8 and *Hotel Sultan* at No 33.

Restaurants line the Grote Markt. *Pita Pyramide* (☎ 20 65 72) at Tempelstraat 7, halfway to the train station, has excellent stuffed pitta breads for f140 and cheap beers. *Ter Posterie* (☎ 20 05 80), Rijselstraat 57, opposite the post office, has a quiet garden terrace and meals and snacks. The *Shamrock*, Boterstraat 15, has a small selection of vegetarian meals for about f250.

Getting There & Away
Bus Regional buses leave to the left out of the train station. To Kemmel, take bus No 743 which runs until 5.25 pm on weekdays, and until 6.20 pm on weekends. To Vleteren, take the 'Veurne' bus (No 773) and get off halfway.

Train The station information office is open weekdays from 5.30 am to 8.30 pm and weekends from 6.30 am to 9.30 pm. There are hourly trains to Courtrai (f135, 30 minutes) and direct to Ghent (f295, one hour); for Bruges, Antwerp and Brussels, you have to change in Courtrai.

Getting Around
Bicycles can be rented from the luggage room at the station.

Ghent

Medieval Europe's largest city outside Paris is Ghent (known as Gent in Flemish, Gand in French). Its glory lives in its industrious and rebellious past. Sitting on the junction of the Leie and Scheldt rivers, by the mid-14th century it had become Europe's largest cloth producer, importing wool from England and employing thousands of people. The townsfolk were well known for their armed battles for civil liberties and against the heavy taxes imposed on them. Today home to many students, it's grey and somewhat begrimed, not picturesque like Bruges, but ultimately more realistic.

Orientation
Unlike many Belgian cities, Ghent does not have one central square. Instead, the medieval core is a row of large open squares connected by three imposing edifices: St Nicholas'

Church, the belfry and St Baaf's Cathedral, their line of towers long the trademark of Ghent's skyline. The Korenmarkt is the westernmost square, technically known as the town centre and a 25-minute walk from the main train station, St Pietersstation, but regularly connected by tram Nos 1, 10 and 11. Halfway between the two is the university quarter, based along St Pietersnieuwstraat.

Information

Tourist Office Housed in the city hall crypt on Botermarkt, the tourist office (☎ 266 52325) is open daily from 9.30 am to 6.30 pm from April to early November, and 9.30 am to 4.30 pm the rest of the year.

Money Europabank has a branch at St Pietersstation, open daily from 7.30 am to 1 pm and 2 to 6.30 pm, but commissions here are high. Better is the GWK office at Mageleinstraat 36 in the centre. It's open Monday to Saturday from 9 am to 6 pm and Sunday from 10 am to 4 pm.

Post & Communications The post office is at Korenmarkt 16. International calls can be made from the office at Keizer Karelstraat 1.
Ghent's telephone code is ☎ 09.

Laundry There's a big, modern laundrette at Oudburg 25, open daily from 7 am to 10 pm.

Things to See & Do

Ghent's attractions are largely medieval, its most noted sight being the Van Eyck brothers' *Adoration of the Mystic Lamb* (see St Baaf's Cathedral).

Museums About 10 minutes walk north-east of the station and well worth an hour is the **Museum voor Schone Kunsten** (Museum of Fine Arts) at Nicolaas de Liemaeckereplein 3 (take bus No 9 from the train station). It's home to Flemish Primitives and a couple of typically nightmarish works by Hieronymus Bosch, with a separate contemporary section. Both sections are open Tuesday to Sunday 9.30 am to 5 pm and admission to each costs f80/40.

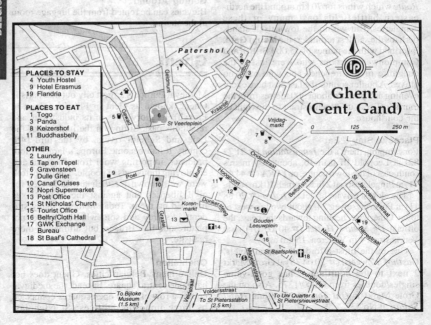

PLACES TO STAY
4 Youth Hostel
9 Hotel Erasmus
19 Flandria

PLACES TO EAT
1 Togo
3 Panda
8 Keizershof
11 Buddhasbelly

OTHER
2 Laundry
5 Tap en Tepel
6 Gravensteen
7 Dulle Griet
10 Canal Cruises
12 Nopri Supermarket
13 Post Office
14 St Nicholas' Church
15 Tourist Office
16 Belfry/Cloth Hall
17 GWK Exchange Bureau
18 St Baaf's Cathedral

Ghent
(Gent, Gand)

Patershol

St Veerleplein

Vrijdagmarkt

Korenmarkt

Gouden Leeuwplein

St Baafsplein

To Bijloke Museum (1.5 km)

Voldersstraat

To St Pietersstation (2.5 km)

To Uni Quarter & St Pietersnieuwstraat

BELGIUM

The **Bijloke Museum** at Godshuizenlaan 2 houses antiquities in a stunning 13th-century abbey. Hours and prices are the same as for the above museums. It's a 10-minute walk from the station or take one of the Korenmarkt-bound trams and get off at the Ijzerlaan intersection.

Belfry & Cloth Hall Rising from the old Cloth Hall, the 14th-century belfry in Gouden Leeuwplein affords spectacular views of the city and can be reached either by a lift or stairs. It's open daily from mid-April to mid-November from 10 am to 12.30 pm and 2 to 5.30 pm; entry costs f100/80 with/without a guide.

St Baaf's Cathedral Unimpressive from the outside, it's Hubert and Jan van Eyck's 15th-century *Adoration of the Mystic Lamb* – a lavish representation of medieval religious thinking and one of the earliest known oil paintings – that draws the crowds. The cathedral is open daily from 8.30 am to 6 pm. The crypt with the Mystic Lamb is open in summer Monday to Saturday from 9.30 am to noon and 2 to 6 pm and Sunday from 1 to 6 pm (in winter it's open daily from 10.30 am to noon and 2.30 to 4 pm, and Sunday from 2 to 5 pm). Entry to the cathedral is free but it costs f60 to see the Mystic Lamb.

Gravensteen With moat, turrets and arrow slits, the fearsome 12th-century Count's Castle is the quintessential castle, built to protect the townsfolk as well as intimidate them into law-abiding submission. It's at St Veerleplein north of the Korenmarkt, open every day from 9 am to 6 pm (5 pm in winter) and costs f80 for adults (free for those aged under 12).

Organised Tours
City canal cruises – 45 minutes, f150/75 for adults/children – depart from the Graslei and Korenlei, west of Korenmarkt.

Places to Stay
Ghent's dearth of budget accommodation has been eased by the relatively recent opening of a modern hostel.

Camping West of the city, *Camping Blaarmeersen* (☎ 221 53 99) at Zuiderlaan 12 is open from 1 March to mid-October and charges f110/55 per adult/child, plus f120/60 per tent/car. Take bus No 38 from the centre or the station.

Hostel Ghent's *hostel* (☎ 233 70 50) occupies a renovated old warehouse at St Widostraat 11. A bunk in a six-bed room, all with private facilities, costs f365, or there are double rooms for slightly more. There's no curfew. From the train station, take tram No 1, 10 or 11 to St Veerleplein.

Colleges From mid-July to late September, single rooms in the university colleges can be rented for a minimum of three nights for f1350. To book, contact Home Vermeylen (☎ 264 71 00) at Stalhof 6, 9000 Ghent.

Hotels The only cheap option is *Flandria* (☎ 223 06 26), near the centre at Barrestraat 3, which charges f1300/1400 for decent singles/doubles including breakfast. Otherwise, to the left out of the train station's rear entrance, *Adoma* (☎ 222 65 50), at Sint Denijslaan 19, has doubles for f1950; breakfast is f180 extra and the hotel is closed for several weeks in summer.

If you can afford a bit more, the best option is *Hotel Erasmus* (☎ 225 75 91) at Poel 25. This renovated, 16th-century house has 12 rooms, some with stained-glass windows and oak beam ceilings. Prices start at f2500/3500; breakfast is f350.

Places to Eat
The student ghetto, about 10 minutes walk south-east of the Korenmarkt, is the best area for well-priced meals. Here on St Pietersnieuwstraat and its continuation, Overpoortstraat, you'll find plenty of cheap cafés and bars including the popular pizzeria *La Rustica* (☎ 233 07 08) at St Pietersnieuwstraat 154. There is also a vegetarian lunchtime café, *De Paddestoel* (☎ 225 13 30), at Guinardstraat 9, a block west of La Rustica. Otherwise, the best-value eateries are the two *mensas* (student cafeterias): the *Octopus* at Overpoortstraat 49 is open weekdays for lunch, while the *mensa* on St Pietersnieuwstraat 45 is open weekdays from noon to 2.30 pm and 6 to 9 pm.

In the centre, *Buddhasbelly* (☎ 225 17 32) on Hoogpoort 30 is open until 9 pm and has good eat-in or takeaway vegetarian fare. At Oudburg 38, the *Panda* (☎ 225 07 86) has biologically sound, three-course vegetarian specialities for f525, or main courses only for f320.

In a thicket of cobbled lanes west of here is the restored Patershol quarter. The choice of restaurants here is ample, but the old-world ambience means prices are high. *Togo* at Vrouwebroersstraat 21 is recommended.

To the south-east, across the bridge on the Vrijdagmarkt (once the city's forum for public meetings and executions), *Keizershof* (☎ 223 44 46) tavern at No 47 has snacks and a dagschotel for f280.

Self-caterers have a *Nopri* supermarket at Hoogpoort 42, open Monday to Saturday from 9 am to 6 pm, and *Gimsel*, a health-food shop on Prinses Clementinalaan to the right out of the train station.

Entertainment
As always, there are plenty of atmospheric bars in which to while away the evenings. The student quarter has a lively selection – the *Pole Pole* (Swahili for 'Slowly Slowly') at St Pietersnieuwstraat 158 has an African ambience and is open nightly from 8 pm to 2 am. Behind the Gravensteen, the *Tap en Tepel* at Gewad 7 is dark by day and lit up like a shrine at night, while on Vrijdagmarkt, the *Dulle Griet* specialises in Trappist beers.

Getting There & Away
Bus Eurolines buses leave from in front of St Pietersstation. Tickets can be bought from the Kris Kras travel shop (☎ 221 08 05) at Prinses Clementinalaan 205 immediately to the right out of the station. There are at least twice-daily buses to London (f1850) – the overnight bus takes eight hours; the daytime bus (via Calais in France – check whether you need a French visa) takes seven hours. Other services include to Cologne (f700, 4¾ hours) and Amsterdam (f700, 5¼ hours).

Train The station information office (☎ 222 44 44) is open daily from 6 am to 9.30 pm. There are IC trains to Antwerp (f240, 45 minutes), Bruges (f165, 20 minutes), Brussels (f230, 45 minutes) and direct to Ypres (f295, one hour).

Getting Around
The public transport information kiosks at the station and on the Korenmarkt sell tickets and tram/bus maps.

Liège

Compared with other cities in Belgium, it's hard to rave about Liège (Luik in Flemish). Sprawled along the Meuse River in the eastern part of Wallonia, this noisy city is seemingly forever shrouded in an atmosphere of grey. Its two main drawing cards are its many museums and its position as the northern gateway to the forested Ardennes (see the following section).

Orientation
The 'central' district is strewn along the western bank of the Meuse River, which splits in two here creating the island of Outremeuse. The main train station, Gare Guillemins, is two km south of Place St Lambert, the city's nominal heart.

Information
The main Office du Tourisme (☎ 221 92 21), Féronstrée 92, is open weekdays from 9 am to 5 or 6 pm and weekends from 10 am to 4 pm (to 2 pm on Sunday).

For regional information head to the Fédération du Tourisme de la Province de Liège (☎ 222 42 10) at Blvd de la Sauvenière 77, open weekdays from 8.30 am to 5 pm and Saturday from 9 am to 1 pm.

At Gare Guillemins there's a small bureau dispensing both city and provincial information. It's open Monday to Saturday from 9 am to noon and 1 to 5.30 pm (on Sunday 10 am to 4 pm).

There's an exchange office at the station open from 6 am to 6 pm. When it's closed, you can change money at the international ticket windows but the rates are lousy. Alternatively, there's a BBL Bank one block up Rue des Guillemins from the train station. A block further is a Hypernet laundry.

Liège's telephone code is ☎ 04.

Things to See & Do
Above the city sits the **citadelle**, a half-hour walk up the Montagne de Bueren stairs (they

lead up from Hors Château), and on Sunday mornings there's **La Batte**, a street market which stretches along 1.5 km of riverfront quays.

Museums If you plan on visiting a few of Liège's many museums, consider the 'Passeport TEC – Musées' which gives entry to most museums as well as free travel on bus No 4 (which connects the museums). It costs f250, is valid for two days and is available from the museums or the tourist office.

Depending on your taste, the highlights are probably the **Musée d'Art Religieux et d'Art Mosan** (Museum of Religious Art and Art from the Meuse Valley) at Rue Mère Dieu, open Tuesday to Saturday from 1 to 6 pm and Sunday from 11 am to 4 pm, and the nearby **Musée de la Vie Wallonne** (Walloon Life Museum) at Cour des Mineurs, which is open Tuesday to Saturday from 10 am to 5 pm and Sunday until 4 pm.

Life as it was for some in the 18th century is depicted in the **Musée d'Ansembourg**, a

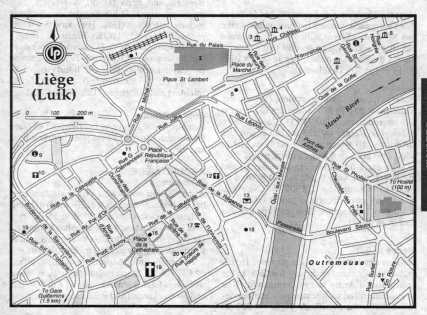

Liège (Luik)

PLACES TO STAY		2	Palais des Princes Évêques	9	Provincial Tourist Information Office
14	Hôtel Simenon	3	Musée de la Vie Wallonne	10	St Jean Church
15	Hôtel le Berger	4	Musée d'Art Religieux et d'Art Mosan	11	Théâtre Royale
		5	Hôtel de Ville (City Hall)	12	St Denis Church
PLACES TO EAT		6	Musée de l'Art Wallon	13	Post Office
20	La Feuille de Vigne	7	Tourist Office	16	Delhaize Supermarket
21	La Pergola	8	Musée d'Ansembourg	17	Telephone Office
				18	University
OTHER				19	Cathédrale Saint Paul
1	Gare du Palais				

rich, Regency-styled mansion at Féronstrée 114, open Tuesday to Sunday from 1 to 6 pm. Wallonian art from the 16th century to the present is housed in the **Musée de l'Art Wallon** at Féronstrée 86, open Tuesday to Saturday from 1 to 6 pm and Sunday from 11 to 4.30 pm.

Places to Stay
Camping The closest ground is *Camping an der Hill* (☎ 087-74 46 17) at Hütte 46 in Esneux, about 20 km to the south, and open all year.

Hostels There's a new *hostel* (☎ 344 56 89) at Rue Georges Simenon 2 in Outremeuse – take bus No 4 from Gare Guillemins. In Tongeren (see the Around Liège section that follows), there's the pleasant hostel, *Begijnhof* (☎ 012-39 13 70) at Sint Ursulastraat 1.

Hotels Opposite the train station, *Pension des Nations* (☎ 252 44 34) at Rue des Guillemins 139 has rooms from f700/1200. Closer to town is *Hôtel le Berger* (☎ 223 00 80) at Rue des Urbanistes 10 which has rooms from f1000/1400. Bus No 1 or 4 stops a block away.

With extra francs head to Outremeuse and the *Hôtel Simenon* (☎ 342 86 90) at Blvd de l'Est 16. Occupying a 1908 Art-Nouveau house, the gaily decorated rooms reflect the writings of local author, Georges Simenon, and cost from f2000.

Places to Eat
Pension des Nations (see the previous Hotels section) has a menu of the day for f295. In the centre, Rue d'Amay and its continuation Rue St Paul are filled with restaurants and brasseries. Nearby, *La Feuille de Vigne* (☎ 222 20 10) at Rue Soeurs de Hasque 12 is a vegetarian restaurant open weekdays from noon to 3 pm, and from 7 to 10 pm on Wednesday, Friday and Saturday.

For more serene surroundings, cross the river to Outremeuse where there's an old cobbled street, En Roture, lined with little restaurants. *La Pergola* (☎ 342 57 08), an Italian place at No 46, is one of the reasonable options.

For self-caterers there's a *Delhaize* supermarket on Place de la Cathédrale, open Monday to Saturday from 9 am to 6.30 pm.

Getting There & Away
Bus Eurolines (☎ 252 69 49) has an office at Rue des Guillemins 77, from where a nightly bus departs to London (f1850, 10 hours) and less frequent buses leave to a pick of European destinations.

Train The principal hub is Gare Guillemins, two km from Place St Lambert but connected by bus No 1 or 4. The train information office (☎ 229 26 10) is open every day from 6 am to 10 pm.

The Thalys fast train connects Liège with Brussels and Paris (f1950, 3¼ hours, two trains per day). Other regular connections include to Brussels (f380, 1¼ hours, two trains per hour), Maastricht (f250, 30 minutes, hourly trains), Cologne (f670, 1½ hours, 11 per day) and Luxembourg City (f740, 2½ hours, seven per day). Locally there are hourly trains to Namur (f230, 50 minutes), Spa (f135, 50 minutes) and Tongeren (f120, 30 minutes).

Getting Around
Inner-city buses leave to the right out of Gare Guillemins. Bus No 1 or 4 plies between here and the centre.

AROUND LIÈGE
Tongeren
About 20 km north-west of Liège, Tongeren has the honour (together with Tournai) of being Belgium's oldest town. Settled in 15 BC as a base for Roman troops, the town has an important collection of Gallo-Roman remains, and is surrounded by Roman and medieval walls.

For more information, the tourist office (☎ 012-39 02 55), Stadhuisplein 9, is open weekdays from 8 am to noon and 1 to 4.30 pm and on weekends from 9.30 am to 5 pm.

Spa
Spa was for centuries the luxurious retreat for royalty and the wealthy who came to drink, bathe and cure themselves in the mineral-rich waters which bubble forth here. But like Vichy, its French thermal counterpart, Spa had its day in the 18th and 19th centuries, only to appear now as a rather run-down reminder of what was.

The town is about 35 km south-east of Liège, connected by regular trains (see the Liège Getting There & Away section). The local Office du Tourisme (☎ 087-77 17 00) is at Place Royale 41, open daily from 9 am to 12.30 pm and 2 to 6 pm (from 10 am on weekends).

Hautes Fagnes Park

Bordering the Eifel hills in Germany, the Hautes Fagnes park is a region of swampy heath and woods. Within the park is the Centre Nature de Botrange (☎ 080-44 57 81) which sits on the highest point in Belgium – 694 metres – and is where many Belgians come to walk, cycle, study nature, and in winter, to ski. About 50 km east of Liège, it takes about 1¼ hours to get to the centre with public transport from Liège – take the train to Verviers and then the bus marked 'Rocherath'.

The Ardennes

Home to deep river valleys and high forests, Belgium's south-east corner is often overlooked by travellers hopping between the old art towns and the capital. But here, in the provinces of Namur, Liège and Luxembourg, you'll find tranquil villages nestled into the grooves of the Meuse, Lesse and Ourthe valleys or sitting atop the verdant hills. Historically, this is where the Battle of the Bulge once raged.

The town of Namur is the best base for exploration – well positioned on the railway line to Luxembourg and with rail and bus connections to some of the more inaccessible spots. However, if you don't have transport, getting around once you're 'inaccessible' can take time.

NAMUR

Just 50 km south-east of Brussels, Namur (Namen in Flemish) is a picturesque town, towered over by its 15th-century citadel.

The tourist office (☎ 22 28 59) is on Ave de la Gare, 200 metres to the left out of the station. It's open daily from 9 am to noon and 1 to 5 pm, later in summer.

Namur's telephone code is ☎ 081.

Things to See & Do

Perched dramatically above the town, the **citadel** is easily reached either by a 15-minute cable-car ride (adults/children f190/150

return) starting at Rue Notre Dame, or by car along the Route Merveilleuse. Open from April to 1 October, admission to the citadel costs f195/110 for adults/children.

There are several museums, including the **Félicien Rops** at Rue Fumal 12, which has works by the 19th-century Namur-born artist who fondly illustrated debauched and erotic lifestyles; it's open daily from 10 am to 5 pm (but closed Monday except in July and August) and costs f100/50 for adults/children.

Places to Stay & Eat

If you're camping, try **Camping des 4 Fils Aymon** (☎ 58 02 94) on Chaussée de Liège about eight km east – get bus No 8 from the station. There's a riverfront **hostel** (☎ 22 36 88) at Ave F Rops 8, 30 minutes' walk from the train station, or jump on bus No 3 or 4. **Queen Victoria Hôtel** (☎ 22 29 71) on Ave de la Gare 11 (to the left of the train station) has rooms from f1250/1800. Just up at No 22, **Taverne de Rome** (☎ 23 04 24) has wonderful stained-glass windows, doubles from f1250 (breakfast is f140 extra) and cheap meals.

Rapido Pat (☎ 22 18 46) at Rue du Pont 4 has sterile decor but the pasta dishes (from f170) are reasonable. The glass-roofed **Grand Café les Galleries** at 27 Rue de Collège is great for a (pricey) snack or drink. A cheaper alternative is **Café le Collège** next door.

Getting There & Away

Namur's train information office (☎ 25 22 21) is open until 9.30 pm – after that ask at the ticket windows. There are two trains an hour to Brussels (f230, one hour) plus hourly trains to Luxembourg City (f710, 1¾ hours) and Liège (f230, 50 minutes). For information on regional trains see the Getting There & Away section in each of the following towns.

Europabus buses en route to regions in France, Italy, Austria, Croatia and Spain stop at Place St Nicolas. Local and regional buses are operated by TEC (☎ 72 08 40) which has an information bus (open until 7 pm) outside the train station. Regional buses leave from the bus station near the C&A department store (to the left out of the train station).

DINANT

This heavy, distinctive town, 28 km south of Namur, is one of the Ardennes' real touristy hot spots. Its bulbous cathedral competes for attention with the cliff-front citadel, while below, a hive of boat operators compete for the Meuse River day-trippers or the Lesse Valley kayakers. The tourist office (☎ 082-22 28 70), Rue Grande 37, is open on weekdays from 9 am to 5 pm (until 8 pm in summer) and from 10 am on weekends.

Dinant's telephone code is ☎ 082.

Things to See & Do

The **citadel** is open all year and accessible by cable car – a combined ticket costs f180/140 for adults/children.

For **kayaking**, several companies have trips leaving in the morning upriver from Houyet, ending in Anseremme next to Dinant several hours later. Try Kayaks Ansiaux (☎ 22 23 25) at 15 Rue du Vélodrome in Anseremme.

More sedate are the **boat cruises** down the Meuse. Companies include Bayard (☎ 22 30 42) at Quai de Meuse 1, which has a range of voyages including a 45-minute trip to Anseremme (f160/120 for adults/children) and a nine-hour haul to Givet over the French border and back (f520/400). Mountain bikes can be hired from Adnet (☎ 22 32 43) at Rue St Roch 17.

Places to Stay

Hotels are not cheap here and there's no hostel to turn to. Two of the most affordable are *Hôtel le Plateau* (☎ 22 28 34) at Plateau de la Citadelle 13 and *Taverne le Derby* (☎ 22 41 96) at Rue de la Station 23, which both have rooms from f950/1250.

Getting There & Away

There are hourly trains from Namur to Dinant (f120, 30 minutes). Bus Nos 433 and 34 (one every two hours) also connect the two.

HAN-SUR-LESSE & ROCHEFORT

The millennium-old underground **limestone grottoes** are the drawing card of these two villages, which sit just eight km apart on the Lesse and Lomme rivers respectively. The Han caves are touristy and situated a little way out of town – a tram takes you to the entrance and a boat brings you back. Open from mid-March to mid-November from 9.30 am to 5 pm, they cost f315/220 for adults/ children. Rochefort's grottoes are of equal

magnitude but the presentation is more low-key. Open from April to mid-November, hour-long tours start at 10 am and cost f190/135 for adults/children.

There are tourist offices in both towns: in Han (☎ 37 75 76) at Place Lannoy, and in Rochefort (☎ 21 25 37) at Rue de Behogne 5.

The telephone code for Han-Sur-Lesse and Rochefort is ☎ 084.

Places to Stay

In Han, *Camping de la Lesse* (☎ 37 72 90), on Rue du Grand Hy a few hundred metres from the tourist office, is open all year. The *Gîte d'Étape* hostel (☎ 37 74 41) at Rue du Gîte d'Étape 10, one block behind the tourist office, charges f350 and is open all year. Alternatively, there's *Hôtel le Central* (☎ 37 72 61) at Rue des Grottes 20 which has singles/doubles with bathroom for f1250/1500.

In Rochefort, *Le Vieux Moulin* (☎ 21 46 04) at Rue de Hableau 25 is a hostel-type place with half-pension deals (bed plus breakfast and one meal) for f670. Just up the road is *Camping Communal* (☎ 21 19 00), open from Easter to 31 October. Otherwise, *Hôtel la Fayette* (☎ 21 42 73) at Rue Jacquet 87 has rooms from f1020/1220.

Getting There & Away

To get to either of these towns, take the Namur-Luxembourg train to Jemelle and from there, the hourly bus No 29.

LA ROCHE-EN-ARDENNE

Hugging a bend in the Ourthe River, La Roche is hidden in a deep valley and surrounded by verdant hills which are much enjoyed by hikers. The tourist office (☎ 41 13 42) is at Place du Marché 15.

The telephone code is ☎ 084.

Places to Stay

Camping Floréal (☎ 21 94 67) at Route d'Houffalize 14 is open all year. The nearest *hostel* (☎ 45 52 94) is at Rue de la Gendarmerie 4 at Champlon, 13 km south. Near the heart of town, *Hôtel de Liège* (☎ 41 11 64) at Rue de la Gare 16 has singles/doubles from f900/1000; similarly priced is *Hôtel le Moderne* (☎ 41 11 24) at Rue Châmont 26.

Getting There & Away
From Namur, take the Luxembourg-bound train to Marloie then bus No 15 (every two hours) to La Roche (35 minutes).

BASTOGNE
North of Arlon, close to the Luxembourg border, it was here that thousands of soldiers and civilians died during the Battle of the Bulge in the winter of 1944-45. A huge, star-shaped American memorial, on the hill two km out of town, is next to the Bastogne Historical Centre, open daily from 1 March to mid-November. The tourist office (☎ 21 27 11) is at Place McAuliffe.

The telephone code for Bastogne is ☎ 061.

Places to Stay
Camping de Renval (☎ 21 29 85), about one km from the tourist office on Rue du Marché, is open all year. The nearest hostel is at Champlon (see the previous La Roche section). As for hotels, there are two of them on Rue du Marché near the tourist office: *Hôtel Lebrun* (☎ 21 54 21) at No 8 has singles/doubles from f900/1300, and *Hôtel du Sud* (☎ 21 11 14) at No 39 has rooms starting at f1050/1640.

Getting There & Away
From Namur, take the Luxembourg train to the rail junction of Libramont, from where there are buses every two hours to Bastogne's defunct train station (35 minutes).

BELGIUM

Britain

At one stage of its history this small island ruled half the world's population and had a major impact on many of the rest. For those whose countries once lay in the shadow of its great empire a visit may almost be a cliché, but it's also essential – a peculiar mixture of homecoming and confrontation.

To the surprise of many, Britain remains one of the most beautiful islands in the world. All the words, paintings and pictures that have been produced are not just romantic, patriotic exaggerations.

In terms of area, Britain is small, but the more you explore the bigger it seems to become. Visitors from the New World are often fooled by this magical expansion and try to do too much too quickly. JB Priestley observed of England, 'She is just pretending to be small'. Covering it all in one trip is impossible – and that's before you start thinking of Scotland and Wales.

The United Kingdom comprises Britain (England, Wales and Scotland) and Northern Ireland. Its full name is the United Kingdom of Great Britain and Northern Ireland. This chapter confines itself to the island of Britain, the largest of the British Isles, and Scotland's outlying islands – the Hebrides in the west and Orkney and Shetland in the north-east. For reasons of geographical and practical coherence, Northern Ireland is dealt with alongside the Irish Republic in the Ireland chapter.

Sometimes in summer it can feel as if the whole world has come to Britain. Don't spend all your time in the big, tourist-ridden towns; rather, pick a small area and spend at least a week or so wandering around the country lanes and villages.

Facts about the Region

HISTORY
Celts & Romans
England had long been settled by small bands of hunters when, around 4000 BC, a new group of immigrants arrived from Europe. The new arrivals used stone tools, and they were the first to leave enduring marks on the island. They farmed the chalk hills radiating from Salisbury Plain, and began the construction of stone tombs and, around 3000 BC, the great ceremonial complexes at Avebury and Stonehenge.

The next great influx of people were the Celts, a people from central Europe who had mastered the smelting of bronze, and later of iron. They brought two forms of the Celtic language: the Gaelic, which is still spoken in parts of Ireland and Scotland, and the Brythonic, which was spoken in England and is still spoken in parts of Wales.

In 43 AD, the Romans arrived in force and, despite fierce resistance, established themselves in England. The mountains of Wales and Scotland remained Celtic strongholds, but England was a part of the Roman Empire for 350 years. Paved roads radiated from London to important regional centres – Ermine St ran north to Lincoln, York and Hadrian's Wall, and Watling St ran north-west to Chester. Christianity arrived in the 3rd century.

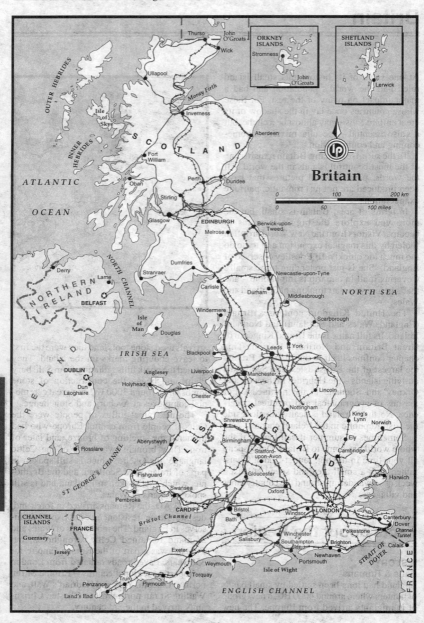

BRITAIN

Britain

Orkney Islands
- Stromness
- John O'Groats

Shetland Islands
- Lerwick

0   100   200 km
0   50   100 miles

Thurso
John O'Groats
Wick
Ullapool
Moray Firth
Inverness
Aberdeen

SCOTLAND

Outer Hebrides
Isle of Skye
Inner Hebrides

ATLANTIC OCEAN

Fort William
Oban
Perth
Dundee
Stirling
Glasgow
EDINBURGH
Melrose
Berwick-upon-Tweed

Derry
Larne
BELFAST
NORTHERN IRELAND

NORTH CHANNEL

Dumfries
Stranraer
Carlisle
Newcastle-upon-Tyne
Durham
Middlesbrough
NORTH SEA
Scarborough

Windermere

IRISH SEA

Isle of Man
Douglas

DUBLIN
Dun Laoghaire

IRELAND

Blackpool
Leeds   York
Anglesey
Liverpool
Manchester
Holyhead
Chester
Lincoln

ENGLAND

Nottingham
King's Lynn   Norwich
Shrewsbury
Ely
Cambridge

Rosslare

ST GEORGE'S CHANNEL

Aberystwyth
Birmingham
Stratford-upon-Avon

WALES

Fishguard
Gloucester
Oxford
Harwich

Pembroke
Swansea
CARDIFF
Bristol
Bath
Windsor
LONDON
Canterbury/Dover
Channel Tunnel

Bristol Channel
Salisbury
Winchester
Southampton
Brighton
Folkestone
Calais

CHANNEL ISLANDS
FRANCE
Guernsey
Jersey

Exeter
Weymouth
Torquay
Newhaven
Portsmouth
Isle of Wight
STRAIT OF DOVER

FRANCE

Penzance
Truro
Plymouth
Land's End

ENGLISH CHANNEL

English

By the 4th century the empire was in retreat, and in 410 the last Roman troops withdrew. The British were left to the tender mercies of the heathen Angles, Jutes and Saxons – Teutonic tribes originating from north of the Rhine. During the 5th century they advanced across what had been Roman England and by the 7th century they had come to think of themselves collectively as English. The Celts, particularly in Ireland, kept Latin and Roman Christian culture alive.

Vikings & Normans

The English were ill-prepared to meet the challenge posed by the next wave of invaders. The Norwegian Vikings conquered northern Scotland, Cumbria and Lancashire, and the Danes conquered eastern England, making York their capital. Eastern England (north of the Romans' Watling St) was called the Danelaw. They were finally stopped by Alfred the Great, and he and his successors created a tenuously unified country. Danish raids continued, however, and in 1016 the crown was taken by Canute the Great, who was also King of Norway and Denmark.

After a brief period of Danish rule, St Edward the Confessor was made king. He had been brought up in Normandy – a Viking duchy in France – alongside his cousin Duke William, the future Conqueror. Edward's death left two contenders for the crown: Harold Godwin, his English brother-in-law, and William, his Norman cousin. In 1066 William landed with 12,000 men and defeated Harold at the Battle of Hastings.

The conquest of England by the Normans was completed rapidly: English aristocrats were replaced by French-speaking Normans, dominating castles were built and the feudal system was imposed.

Middle Ages

In the 12th century, after a disastrous civil war fought over the succession to the crown, Henry II, the Count of Anjou, was made king. He had inherited more than half of modern France and clearly surpassed the King of France in the extent of his power.

The struggle to retain this empire was a dominant concern of the Plantagenet and Lancastrian kings – leading to the Hundred Years' War, and finally to English defeat. In order to finance these adventures, the Plantagenet kings conceded a considerable amount of power to Parliament, which jealously protected its traditional right to control taxation.

Further disputes over the royal succession allowed Parliament to consolidate its power. The Wars of the Roses, a dynastic struggle between the houses of York and Lancaster, lasted for 30 years. The final victor in 1485 was Henry VII, the first Tudor king.

Tudors & Stuarts

Under Henry VIII, the long struggle of the English kings against the power of the pope came to a head. Parliament made Henry the head of the Church of England and the Bible was translated into English. In 1536 the monasteries were dissolved – a largely popular move because the wealthy and often corrupt religious orders were widely resented.

The 16th century was a golden age. Greek learning was rediscovered, the European powers explored the world, trade boomed, Shakespeare wrote his plays, and Francis Bacon laid the foundations for modern science.

An age of religious intolerance was beginning, however, and after Elizabeth I the relationship between Parliament and the autocratic Stuart kings deteriorated. In 1642 the conflict became a civil war.

Catholics, traditionalist members of the Church of England and the old gentry supported Charles I, whose power base was the north and west. The Protestant Puritans and the commons, based in London and the towns of the south-east, supported Parliament.

Parliament found a brilliant leader in Oliver Cromwell; the royalists were defeated and in 1649 Charles I was executed. Cromwell assumed dictatorial powers, but he also laid the foundation for the British Empire by modernising the army and navy. Two years after his death in 1658, a reconstituted Parliament recalled Charles II from exile.

The Restoration was a period of expansion: colonies stretched down the American coast and the East India Company established its headquarters in Bombay.

Empire & Industry

In the 18th century, the Hanoverian kings increasingly relied on Parliament to govern the

BRITAIN

kingdom, and Sir Robert Walpole became the first prime minister in all but name.

By 1770 France had ceded all of Canada and surrendered all but two of its trading stations in India, while Captain Cook claimed Australia for Britain in 1778. The empire's first major reverse came when the American colonies won their independence in 1783.

Also in the 1780s, there were the first developments that would lead to the Industrial Revolution – and Britain was its crucible. Canals, trains, coal, water and steam power transformed the means of production and transport, and the rapidly growing towns of the Midlands became the first industrial cities.

By the time Queen Victoria took the throne in 1837, Britain was the greatest power in the world. Its fleets dominated the seas linking an enormous empire, and its factories dominated world trade.

Under prime ministers Disraeli and Gladstone, the worst excesses of the Industrial Revolution were addressed, education became universal and the right to vote was extended to most men (women did not get equal voting rights until 1928).

The 20th Century

Victoria died at the very beginning of the new century and the old order was shattered by the Great War (WWI). By the war's end in 1918 a million British men had died and 15% of the country's accumulated capital had been spent.

The euphoria of victory didn't last long. In the late 1920s the world economy slumped, ushering in more than a decade of misery and political upheaval. The Labour Party first came to power in 1924, but lasted less than a year.

On 1 September 1939, Hitler provoked a new war by invading Poland. By mid-1940, most of Europe was either ruled by or under the direct influence of the Nazis, Stalin had negotiated a peace, the USA was neutral, and Britain, under the extraordinary leadership of Winston Churchill, was virtually isolated. Between July and October 1940 the Royal Air Force fought and won the Battle of Britain and Hitler's invasion plans were blocked (43,000 Britons died in the bombing raids of 1940-41).

The postwar years have been challenging. The last of the empire has gained independence (India in 1947, Malaya in 1957, Kenya in 1963), many traditional industries have collapsed and the nation has had to accept a new role as a partner in the EU. Britain is still a wealthy and influential country, but it's no longer a superpower and no longer able to maintain that it is anything more than an island, just off the mainland of Europe.

GEOGRAPHY & ECOLOGY

Britain has an area of 240,000 sq km, about the same size as New Zealand or half the size of France. It is less than 600 miles from south to north and under 300 miles at its widest point.

There are no great mountains in terms of height, but this does not prevent a number of ranges from being spectacular. The mountains of Snowdonia in north-west Wales, the Cumbrian mountains in north-west England, and the Glenkens in south-west Scotland all reach around 1000 metres. The Grampians form the mountainous barrier between the Scottish Lowlands and Highlands, and include Ben Nevis, at 1343 metres the highest mountain on the island.

The seas surrounding the British Isles are shallow, and relatively warm because of the influence of the warm North Atlantic Current, also known as the Gulf Stream. This creates a temperate, changeable, maritime climate with few extremes of temperature and few cloudless, sunny days!

With almost 57 million people living on a relatively small island there is, not surprisingly, a number of ecological issues confronting the country; the mad cow disease scare which erupted in 1996 is only the most dramatic example. There are a number of environmental groups in Britain. For more information try Greenpeace (☎ 0171-354 5100), Cannonbury Villas, London N1 2PN.

GOVERNMENT & POLITICS

The United Kingdom does not have a written constitution, but operates under a mixture of Parliamentary statutes, common law (a body of legal principles based on precedents that go back to Anglo-Saxon customs) and convention.

The monarch is the head of state, but real power has been whittled away to the point where the current Queen is a figurehead who acts almost entirely on the advice of 'her' ministers and Parliament.

Parliament has three separate elements – the

Queen, the House of Commons and the House of Lords. In practice, the supreme body is the House of Commons, which is directly elected every five years. Voting is not compulsory, and candidates are elected if they win a simple majority in their constituencies. There are 650 constituencies (seats) – 523 for England, 38 for Wales, 72 for Scotland and 17 for Northern Ireland.

The House of Lords consists of the Lords Spiritual (26 senior bishops of the Church of England) and the Lords Temporal (all hereditary and life peers) and the Lords of Appeal (or 'law lords'). None are elected by the general population. If the Lords refuses to pass a bill, but it is passed twice by the Commons, it is sent to the Queen for her automatic assent.

The Queen appoints the leader of the majority party in the House of Commons as prime minister; all other ministers are appointed on the recommendation of the prime minister, most from the House of Commons. Ministers are responsible for government departments. The senior 20 or so ministers make up the Cabinet, which, although answerable to Parliament, meets confidentially and in effect manages the government and its policies.

For the last 150 years a predominantly two-party system has operated. Since 1945 either the Conservative Party or the Labour Party has held power, the Conservatives drawing their support from suburbia and the countryside, and Labour from urban industrialised areas.

Put crudely, the Conservatives are right-wing, free-enterprise supporters, and Labour is left-wing in the social-democratic tradition. In recent years, however, the Labour Party has shed most of its socialist credo, and the Conservatives have softened their hard-right approach. In the 1992 elections, John Major led the Conservatives to their fourth consecutive victory but all the polls point to a long-awaited Labour victory in the next election which must be held before May 1997. If the polls are correct Tony Blair will be the new prime minister.

ECONOMY
Up to the 18th century the economy was based on agriculture and the manufacture of woollen cloth. In the late 18th century the empire and the Industrial Revolution allowed Britain to become the first industrialised trading nation,

and the population of south Wales, the Midlands, Yorkshire and the Scottish Lowlands expanded rapidly. Conditions for workers were appalling, but 19th-century Britain dominated world trade.

In the 20th century, a considerable proportion of industry was nationalised (railways, services, coal mines, steel, shipbuilding, even the motor industry), a process that was reversed under Margaret Thatcher.

Today the economy is based primarily on free enterprise, and although manufacturing continues to play an important role (particularly in the Midlands), service industries like banking and finance have grown rapidly (particularly in London and the south-east). A great deal of the traditional mining, engineering and cotton industries (especially in the Midlands and north) have disappeared.

The last 20 years have seen a battle against unemployment and inflation. In late 1996 the economy seemed to be emerging from a long recession, and although unemployment was still high (around 10%) inflation was low (around 2.5%).

POPULATION & PEOPLE
Britain has a population of almost 57 million, an average 236 inhabitants per sq km, making the island one of the most crowded on the planet. The majority are concentrated in and around London, and in the Midlands around Birmingham, Manchester, Liverpool, Sheffield and Nottingham.

The big cities are multicultural, and since the war there has been significant immigration from many ex-colonies, especially the West Indies, Bangladesh, Pakistan and India. Outside London and the big Midlands cities, however, the population is overwhelmingly white (although even small towns have Chinese and Indian restaurants).

ARTS
The greatest artistic contributions of the British have been in theatre, literature and architecture. Although there are notable individual exceptions, there is not an equivalent tradition of great painters, sculptors or composers.

Literature
Anyone who has studied 'English' literature will find that to some extent the landscapes and

BRITAIN

164 Britain – Facts about the Region

people they have read about can still be found. Travelling in the footsteps of the great English, Scottish and Welsh writers, and their characters, can be one of the highlights of visiting Britain. There is a phenomenal wealth of books that capture a moment in time, a landscape, or a group of people. This guide only gives a few suggestions as to where to start.

In the beginning was Chaucer with his *Canterbury Tales*. This book may be responsible for more boring lectures than any other, but in its natural environment it comes to life, giving a vivid insight into medieval society, in particular into the lives of pilgrims on their way to Canterbury. Neville Coghill has written a good modern translation.

The next great figure to blight schoolchildren's lives was Shakespeare. Despite this, many will be tempted to follow in his footsteps – to Stratford-upon-Avon where he lived and the site of the Globe Theatre in London where he played.

The most vivid insight into 17th-century life, particularly in London, is courtesy of *Samuel Pepys' Diary*. In particular, he gives the most complete account of the plague and the Great Fire of London.

The popular English novel, as we know it, did not really appear until the 18th century with the upsurge of the literate middle class. If you plan to spend time in the Midlands, read Elizabeth Gaskell's *Mary Barton*, which paints a sympathetic picture of the plight of the workers during the Industrial Revolution. This was also the milieu about which Charles Dickens wrote most powerfully. *Hard Times* is set in fictional Coketown and paints a brutal picture of the capitalists who prospered in it.

Jane Austen wrote about a very different social class – a prosperous, provincial middle class. The intrigues and passions boiling away under the stilted constraints of 'propriety' are beautifully portrayed in *Emma* and *Pride & Prejudice*.

If you visit the Lake District, you will find constant references to William Wordsworth, the romantic poet who lived there for the first half of the 19th century. Modern readers may find him difficult, but at his best he has an exhilarating appreciation for the natural world.

More than most writers, Thomas Hardy depended heavily on a sense of place and on the relationship between place and people. This makes his best work an evocative picture of Wessex, the region of England centred on Dorchester (Dorset) where he lived. *Tess of the D'Urbervilles* is one of his greatest novels.

Moving into the 20th century, DH Lawrence chronicled life in coal-mining towns in the brilliant *Sons & Lovers*. Joseph Conrad's *The Secret Agent* explores a murky world of espionage in London.

Written in the 1930s in the middle of the Depression, George Orwell's *Down & Out in Paris & London* describes Orwell's destitute existence as a temporary vagrant. Shoestringers in the 1990s may find they can identify with him. About the same time, Graham Greene wrote of the seamy side of Brighton in *Brighton Rock*.

One of the funniest and most vicious portrayals of late 20th-century Britain is by Martin Amis in *London Fields*, but there are many other interesting perspectives. Hanef Kureishi writes of growing up in England's Pakistani community in *The Buddha of Suburbia*; Caryl Phillips writes of the Caribbean immigrants' experience in *The Final Passage*; Irvine Welsh in *Trainspotting* explores the world of heroin addiction, and Jonathan Coe satirises Thatcher's legacy in *what a carve up*.

There are also some more straightforward modern travelogues, the most recent being Bill Bryson's highly entertaining and perceptive *Notes from a Small Island*. *The Kingdom by the Sea* by Paul Theroux and Jonathan Raban's *Coasting* were both written in 1982 and so are now a little dated, but they're nonetheless very readable.

Architecture

Perhaps the most distinctive architectural phenomenon is the huge number of extraordinary country houses that litter the landscape. The aristocrats of the 18th and 19th centuries knew quality when they saw it, and they surrounded themselves with treasures in the most beautiful houses and gardens of Europe. Waited on hand and foot, the elite of a mighty empire, they believed with certainty they were at the absolute pinnacle of civilisation.

Fortunately, although their successors have often inherited the arrogance intact, inheritance taxes have forced many to open their houses and priceless art collections to the public. Britain is a treasure house of master-pieces from every age and continent.

Today, British publishers churn out 80,000 books a year, and the range and quality of theatre, music, dance and art is outstanding by any measure, but modern architecture has almost totally failed. The heritage is incom-parable but, with a few notable exceptions, the 20th century has failed to add anything more inspiring than motorways, high-rise housing estates and tawdry suburban devel-opment.

CULTURE

It is difficult to generalise about the British, but there is no doubt they are a creative, energetic and aggressive people whose impact on the world has been entirely disproportionate to their numbers. They are a diverse bunch, as one would expect given the variety of peoples who have made this island their home – from the original inhabitants, to the Celts, Romans, Angles, Jutes, Saxons, Vikings, Normans, Huguenots and Jews, to the relatively recent Asian, African and Middle Eastern arrivals.

Many people have strong preconceptions about British characteristics but, if you do, you would be wise to abandon them. The most common is of reserve, anal-retentive polite-ness and conservatism. Remember, however, that this is one of the most crowded islands on the planet and some of these characteristics have developed as a defensive veneer in response to dealing with a constant crush of people. Remember also that although regional and class differences have shrunk, accents and behaviour still vary widely depending on where you are and with which class you are mingling.

Terms like 'stiff-upper-lip', 'cold' and 'inhibited' might be used to describe elements of the middle and upper classes, but in general they do not apply to the working classes, the northern English, the Welsh or the Scots. Visit a nightclub in one of the big cities, a football match, a historic steam train run by volunteers, a good local pub, or a country B&B and other terms might spring to mind: uninhibited, exhi-bitionist, passionate, aggressive, obsessive, humorous, sentimental and hospitable.

No country in the world has more obsessive hobbyists – they very often teeter on the edge of complete madness – train *and* bus spotters,

twitchers (or bird-watchers), sports supporters, fashion victims, royalists, model-makers and collectors of every description, preserva-tionists and historical societies, ramblers, pet owners, gardeners...

Britain is a country of sceptical individual-ists who deeply resent any intrusion on their privacy or freedom, so it is not surprising that their flirtation with socialism was brief. Change happens slowly, and only after pro-ceeding through endless consultations, committees, departments and layers of govern-ment. As a result, most things (including the cities) have developed organically and chaoti-cally. This is a country where the streets are not straight and the trains do not run on time.

There are some cynics who proclaim that Britain is in a state of terminal decline, but there is no doubt the major cities are still cul-tural powerhouses. You can only wonder what will appear next – perhaps a new tribe on the cutting edge of popular culture (like mods, hippies, new romantics, punks and goths), or perhaps a political or economic movement (like industrialisation, imperialist capitalism, Parliamentary democracy, socialism and Thatcherism).

RELIGION

The Church of England, a Christian church that became independent from Rome in the 16th century, is the largest, wealthiest and most influential in the land. Along with the Church of Scotland, it is an 'established' church, meaning it is officially the national church, and it has a close relationship with the state; the Queen appoints archbishops and bishops on the advice of the prime minister.

Attendances at Sunday services average only 1.2 million, but the majority of English would still consider themselves members. The C of E has traditionally been aligned with the ruling classes, but over recent years has been critical of the Conservative government's social policies. In 1994, after many years of debate, the first women were ordained as priests.

The Church of Scotland, although in a similar position as a national church, is quite different from the C of E – it is not subject to any outside authority, and is much more a child of the Reformation. Other significant Protes-tant churches, or 'free' churches with no connection to the state, include Methodist, Baptist and United Reformed churches and the Salvation Army. Women have been priests in all these churches for some years.

Roman Catholics have at times since the 16th century been terribly persecuted; one modern legacy is the intractable problem of Northern Ireland. They did not gain political rights until 1829 or a formal structure until 1850, but today about one in 10 Britons considers themselves Catholic.

Recent estimates suggest there are now over one million Muslims, and there are also significant numbers of Sikhs and Hindus.

LANGUAGE

English as it is spoken in Britain is sometimes incomprehensible to overseas visitors – even to those who assume they have spoken it all their lives. It's OK to ask someone to repeat what they have said, but try not to laugh.

Facts for the Visitor

PLANNING
Climate & When to Go

Anyone who spends an extended period in Britain will soon sympathise with the locals' conversational obsession with the weather. Although in relative terms the climate is mild (London can go through winter without snowfall) and the rainfall not spectacular (912 mm, or 35 inches), grey skies can make for an utterly depressing atmosphere. Settled periods of sunny weather are rare.

Even in midsummer you can go for days without seeing the sun, and showers (or worse) should be expected. To enjoy England you have to convince yourself that you *like* the rain – after all, that's what makes it so incredibly green! The average July temperature in London is 17.6°C (64°F), and the average January temperature is 4°C (39°F).

July and August are the busiest months, and should be avoided if possible. The crowds in London and popular towns like Oxford, Bath and York have to be seen to be believed. You are just as likely to get good weather in spring and autumn, so May/June and September/October are the best times to visit, although

October is getting too late for the Scottish Highlands.

Books & Maps

There are countless guidebooks covering every nook and cranny in the British Isles. When you arrive, one of your first stops should be at a good book/map shop – see the London Bookshops section.

Guidebooks For greater detail there's Lonely Planet's *Britain: – a travel survival kit*. For in-depth information on history, art and architecture, the *Blue Guide* series is excellent. There are separate guides to *England* (£14.99), *Scotland* (£16.99), and *Wales* (£12.99). They have a wealth of scholarly information on all the important sites.

If you're going to spend more than a few days in London, it's definitely worth buying the outstanding *Time Out London Guide* (£9.99). It manages to be densely packed with detail (sights, shops, clubs, pubs, opening hours, prices, etc) and yet still covers the off-beat corners of London that really make the city.

Numerous books list B&Bs, restaurants, hotels, country houses, camping and caravan parks, self-catering cottages etc. The objectivity of most of these books is questionable as the places they cover have to pay for the privilege of being included; however, they can still be useful. Those published by the tourist authorities are reliable (although not comprehensive) and are widely available in information centres; most are around £5.

Hikers should check out the new Lonely Planet title, *Walking in Britain*. Individual long-distance trails are all covered by the *Countryside Commission National Trail Guide* series published by Aurum Press. Each book in the extensive series is £9.99. For shorter day walks the *Bartholomew Map & Guide* series (£5.99) is recommended. They are spiral-bound books with good maps and descriptions; most walks they describe take around two to three hours.

Maps The best introductory map to Britain is published by the British Tourist Authority (BTA), and is widely available.

Drivers will find there is a range of excellent road atlases. If you plan to go off the beaten

BRITAIN

track you will need one that shows at least three miles to the inch. The spiral-bound *Ordnance Survey Motoring Atlas of Great Britain* (£8.99) is recommended.

The Ordnance Survey also caters to walkers, with a wide variety of maps at different scales. Its Landranger maps at 1:50,000 or about 1¼ inches to the mile are ideal.

Online Services

Britain is second only to the USA in its number of web sites, and there are many that are of interest to cyber travellers. Many sites offer general information. The Lonely Planet site (http://www.lonely planet.com.au) offers a speedy link to numerous sites for travellers. Also comprehensive is the Virtual Traveller (http://www.wings.buffalo.edu/world), which seeks to provide a one-stop link to all travel web sites. The UK Directory (http://www.ukdirectory.com/travel) specialises in British sights.

What to Bring

Since anything you think of can be bought in London (including Vegemite), pack light and pick up extras as you go along.

SUGGESTED ITINERARIES

Depending on the length of your stay, you might want to see and do the following things:

Two days
   Visit London.
One week
   Visit London, Oxford, the Cotswolds, Bath and Wells.
Two weeks
   Visit London, Salisbury, Avebury, Bath, Wells, Oxford, York and Edinburgh.
One month
   Visit London, Cambridge, York, Edinburgh, Inverness, Isle of Skye, Fort William, Oban, Glasgow, the Lake District, Snowdonia (North Wales), Shrewsbury, the Cotswolds, Wells, Bath, Avebury and Oxford, before returning to London.
Two months
   As for one month, but stay in one or two places for a week, and do a week-long walk.

HIGHLIGHTS

Of Britain's many attractions, the most outstanding are listed here:

Islands
   Orkney, Skye, Lewis and Harris (Scotland)

Coastline
   Beachy Head (East Sussex), Land's End to St Ives (Cornwall), Tintagel (Cornwall), Ilfracombe to Lynton/Lynmouth (Devon), St David's to Cardigan (Wales), Scarborough to Saltburn (North Yorkshire), the Scottish coastline (particularly the west coast)
Museums & Galleries
   British Museum, Victoria & Albert Museum, National Gallery, Tate Gallery (London); Castle Museum (York); HMS *Victory* (Portsmouth); Ironbridge Gorge (near Shrewsbury); Burrell Collection (Glasgow)
Historic Towns
   Wells, Salisbury, Winchester, Durham, Oxford, Cambridge, York, Edinburgh, St David's, Whitby, St Andrews
Houses
   Hampton Court Palace (London), Castle Howard (North Yorkshire), Knole House (Kent), Blenheim Palace (Oxfordshire)
Castles
   Dover, Windsor, Edinburgh, Conwy, Leeds (near Canterbury), Alnwick, Tower of London
Cathedrals
   Wells, Salisbury, Winchester, Canterbury, York, Durham
Regions
   Exmoor National Park, Cotswolds, Brecon Beacons National Park, Pembrokeshire National Park, North York Moors National Park, Lake District National Park, Hadrian's Wall, Scottish Highlands and especially the west coast
Other Highlights
   Avebury prehistoric complex

TOURIST OFFICES

The British Tourist Authority (BTA) has a remarkably extensive collection of information, quite a lot of it free and relevant to shoestringers. Make sure you contact BTA before you leave home, because some of the material and discounts are only available outside Britain. Overseas, it represents the English, Scottish and Welsh tourist boards.

Tourist Information Centres (TICs) can be found in even small towns. They can give invaluable advice on accommodation and cheap ways of seeing the area, often including excellent guided walking tours.

Tourist Offices Abroad

The addresses of some overseas offices are as follows:

Australia
   8th floor, University Centre, 210 Clarence St, Sydney, NSW 2000 (☎ 02-9267 4555; fax 02-9267 4442; e-mail 100247.243@compuserve.com)

BRITAIN

Canada
  suite 450, 111 Avenue Rd, Toronto, Ont M5R 3J8
  (☎ 416-925 6326; fax 416-961 2175)
New Zealand
  3rd floor, Dilworth Building, corner Queen and
  Customs Sts, Auckland 1 (☎ 09-303 1446; fax 09-377
  6965)
South Africa
  Lancaster Gate, Hyde Park Lane, Hyde Lane, Hyde
  Park, Sandton 2196 (☎ 011-325 0343; fax 011-325
  0344)
USA – Chicago
  625 North Michigan Ave, suite 1510, Chicago, IL
  60611 (personal callers only – no phone calls)
USA – New York
  551 5th Ave, 7th floor, New York, NY 10176-0799
  (☎ 1-800-462 2748, ☎ 212-986 2200; fax 212-286
  1188; E-mail 74443.1520@compuserve.com)

There are more than 40 BTA offices worldwide. Addresses are listed on their web site
(http://www.bta.org.uk).

USEFUL ORGANISATIONS

Membership of the Youth Hostels Association
(YHA) is a must (£9.30 over-18, £3.20 under-
18). There are around 320 hostels in Britain
and members are also eligible for an impressive list of discounts. See this book's
introductory Facts for the Visitor chapter for
information on the various ISIC and FIYTO
cards.

Membership of English Heritage and the
National Trust is worth considering, especially
if you are going to be in the country for an
extended period and are interested in historical
buildings. Both are non-profit organisations
dedicated to the preservation of the environment, and both care for hundreds of spectacular
sites.

Australasian Clubs
  The London Walkabout Club/Tracks (☎ 0171-937
  3028), at 70 North End Rd W14, Deckers London
  Club (☎ 0171-244 8641), at 135 Earl's Court Rd SW5
  9RH and Drifters (☎ 0171-402 9171), at 22A Craven
  Terrace W2, all offer back-up services like mail
  holding, local information, social events and cheap
  tours. They're mainly aimed at Aussies and Kiwis,
  but any nationality is welcome – membership is
  around £15. The clubs are all associated with tour
  companies and their hope is that you will use them if
  and when you book tours.
English Heritage (EH)
  Most EH properties charge nonmembers around £2
  to enter. Adult membership is £20 and gives free entry
  to all EH properties, half-price entry to Historic Scotland and Cadw (Wales) properties, and an excellent

guidebook and map that together sell for £5. You can
join at most major sites.
Great British Heritage Pass
  The pass gives you access to National Trust and
  English Heritage and some of the fiercely expensive
  private properties. It ain't cheap, but it can easily pay
  for itself: seven days is £25, 15 days is £36, one month
  is £50. It's available overseas or at the British Travel
  Centre in London.
National Trust (NT)
  Most NT properties cost nonmembers from £1 to £5
  to enter. Adult membership is £26, and for those under
  23 it's £12. It gives free entry to all NT properties in
  England and Wales and there are reciprocal arrangements with the National Trust organisations in Scotland, Australia, New Zealand and Canada, most of
  which are cheaper to join. Membership includes an
  excellent guidebook; and you can join at most major
  sites.

VISAS & EMBASSIES
Visas
Visa regulations are always subject to change,
so it's essential to check with your local
embassy, high commission or consulate before
leaving home.

Currently, you don't need a visa if you are a
citizen of Australia, Canada, New Zealand,
South Africa or the USA. Tourists are generally
permitted to stay for up to six months, but are
prohibited from working. If you are a citizen
of the EU you may live and work in Britain free
of immigration control – you do not need a visa
to enter the country.

The immigration authorities have always
been tough, and this is unlikely to change;
dress neatly and carry some evidence that you
have sufficient funds to support yourself. A
credit card and/or an onward ticket will help.
People have been refused entry because they
happened to be carrying documents (perhaps
work references) that suggest they intended to
work.

Work Permits
EU nationals don't need a work permit, but all
other nationalities must have one to work
legally. If the *main* purpose of your visit is to
work, you basically have to be sponsored by a
British company.

However, if you are a citizen of a Commonwealth country, and aged between 17 and 26
inclusive, you may apply for a Working
Holiday Entry Certificate that allows you to
spend up to two years in the UK, and to take
work that is 'incidental to a holiday'. You are

not allowed to engage in business, pursue a career or provide services as a professional sportsperson or entertainer.

You must apply to your nearest UK mission overseas, prior to your arrival. It is not possible to switch from being a visitor to a working holiday-maker, nor is it possible to claim back any time spent out of the UK during the two-year period. When you apply, you must satisfy the authorities that you have the means to pay for a return or onward journey, and will be able to maintain yourself without recourse to public funds.

If you are a Commonwealth citizen and have a parent born in the UK you may be eligible for a Certificate of Entitlement to the Right of Abode, which means you can live and work in Britain free of immigration control.

If you are a Commonwealth citizen and have a grandparent born in the UK, or if the grandparent was born before 31 March 1922 in what is now the Republic of Ireland, you may qualify for a UK Ancestry-Employment Certificate, which means you can work full time for up to four years in the UK.

Visiting students from the USA can get a work permit allowing them to work for six months; you have to be at least 18 years old and a full-time student at a college or university. The permit costs US$200 and is available through the Council on International Educational Exchange (☎ 212-822 2600; http://www.ciee.org), 205 East 42nd St, New York, NY 10017. Contact the council for current details and fees.

If you have queries once you are in the UK, contact the Home Office, Immigration & Nationality Department (☎ 0181-686 0688), Lunar House, Wellesley Rd, Croydon CR9 2BY (East Croydon BR).

UK Embassies Abroad

UK embassies in Western Europe are listed in the relevant country chapters in this book. Other UK embassies abroad include:

Australia – British High Commission
    Commonwealth Ave, Yarralumla, Canberra, ACT 2600 (☎ 06-270 6666)
Canada – British High Commission
    80 Elgin St, Ottawa K1P 5K7 (☎ 613-237 1530)
Japan – British Embassy
    1 Ichiban-cho, Chiyoda-ku, Tokyo (☎ 03-3265 5511)

New Zealand – British High Commission
    44 Hill St, Wellington 1 (☎ 04-472 6049)
South Africa – British High Commission
    255 Hill St, Pretoria (☎ 012-433 3121)
USA – British Embassy
    3100 Massachusetts Ave NW, Washington DC 20008 (☎ 202-462 1340)

Foreign Embassies in the UK

Countries with diplomatic representation in the UK include the following:

Australian High Commission
    Australia House, The Strand, London WC2B 4LA; tube: Temple (☎ 0171-379 4334)
Canadian High Commission
    Macdonald House, 1 Grosvenor Square, London W1X 0AD; tube: Bond St (☎ 0171-258 6600)
French Consulate General
    6A Cromwell Place, London SW7 7JT; tube: South Kensington (☎ 0171-838 2000)
German Embassy
    23 Belgrave Square, London SW1X 8PZ; tube: Hyde Park Corner (☎ 0171-235 5033)
Japanese Embassy
    46 Grosvenor St, London W1X 0BA; tube: Bond St (☎ 0171-493 6030)
New Zealand High Commission
    New Zealand House, Haymarket, London SW1Y 4TQ; tube: Piccadilly Circus (☎ 0171-930 8422)
Spanish Embassy
    20 Draycott Place, London SW3; tube: Sloane Square (☎ 0171-589 8989)
US Embassy
    24 Grosvenor Square, London W1A 1AE; tube: Bond St (☎ 0171-499 9000)

DOCUMENTS

No special documents are required. Your normal driving licence is legal for 12 months from the date you last entered the country; you then apply for a British licence at a post office.

See the introductory Facts for the Visitor chapter for information on international student identity and discount cards.

CUSTOMS

Entering Britain you'll be faced with three colour-coded customs' channels. If you have nothing to declare go through the green channel; if you may have something to declare go through blue if you're coming from an EU country, or red if from outside the EU.

For imported goods there's a two-tier system: the first for goods bought duty free, the second for goods bought in an EU country where tax and duty have been paid.

BRITAIN

The second tier is relevant because a number of products (eg alcohol and tobacco) are much cheaper on the Continent. Under single market rules, however, as long as tax and duty have been paid somewhere in the EU there is no prohibition on importing them within the EU, so long as the goods are for individual consumption. Consequently, a thriving business has developed with Britons making day trips to France to load their cars up with cheap beer, wine and cigarettes – the savings can more than pay for the trip.

Duty Free

If you purchase from a duty-free shop, you can import 200 cigarettes or 250 grams of tobacco, two litres of still wine plus one litre of spirits or another two litres of wine (sparkling or otherwise), 60 cc of perfume, 250 cc of toilet water, and other duty-free goods (eg cider and beer) to the value of £136 (£75 within the EU).

Tax & Duty Paid

If you buy from a normal retail outlet, customs uses the following guidelines to distinguish personal imports from those on a commercial scale: 800 cigarettes or one kg of tobacco, 10 litres of spirits, 20 litres of fortified wine, 90 litres of wine (not more than 60 sparkling) and 110 litres of beer!

MONEY
Currency

The currency is the pound sterling (£). There are 100 pence (p) in a pound. One and 2p coins are copper; 5p, 10p, 20p and 50p coins are silver; and the bulky £1 coin is gold (coloured). The word pence is rarely used in common language; like its written counterpart it is abbreviated and pronounced 'pee'.

Notes (bills) come in £5, £10, £20 and £50 denominations and vary in colour and size. You may also come across notes issued by several Scottish banks, including a £1 note; they are legal tender on both sides of the border, though shopkeepers in England and Wales may be reluctant to accept them – in which case ask a bank to swap them for you.

Exchange Rates

Australia	A$1	=	£0.50
Canada	C$1	=	£0.47
France	1FF	=	£0.13
Germany	DM1	=	£0.43
Japan	¥100	=	£0.59
New Zealand	NZ$1	=	£0.45
United States	US$1	=	£0.64

Costs

Britain is extremely expensive and London is horrendous. While you are in London you will need to budget for around £20 a day just for bare survival. Any sightseeing, restaurant meals or nightlife will be on top of that. There's not much point visiting if you can't participate in some of the city's life, so if possible add another £15. Costs will obviously be even higher if you choose to stay in a central hotel and eat restaurant meals.

Once you start moving around the country, particularly if you have a transport pass of some description, or you're walking or hitching, the costs can drop. Fresh food is roughly the same price as in Australia and the US. However, without including long-distance transport, and assuming you stay in hostels, you'll still need £15 to £20 per day.

If you hire a car or use a transport pass, stay in B&Bs, eat one sit-down meal a day, and don't stint on entry fees, you'll need £30 to £40 per day (still not including long-distance transport costs). If you are travelling by car you will probably average a further £6 per day on petrol and parking; if you travel by some sort of pass you will probably need to average a couple of pounds a day on local transport or for hiring a bike.

Bureaux de Change & Banks

Be careful using *bureaux de change*; they may offer good exchange rates, but they frequently levy outrageous commissions and fees. Make sure you establish the rate, the percentage commission and any fees in advance.

The bureaus at international airports are exceptions to the rule. They charge less than most high-street banks (ie major or city-centre banks) and cash sterling travellers' cheques for free.

Bank hours vary, but you'll be safe if you visit between 9.30 am and 3.30 pm, Monday to Friday. Some banks are open on Saturday, generally from 9.30 am till noon. Once again, the total cost of foreign exchange can vary quite widely; in particular, watch for the minimum charge.

It's difficult to open a bank account, although if you're planning to work, it may be essential. Building societies tend to be more welcoming and often have better interest rates. You'll need a (semi) permanent address, and you'll smooth the way considerably if you have a reference or introductory letter from your bank manager at home, *plus* bank statements for the previous year. Owning credit/charge cards also helps.

Personal cheques are still widely used in Britain, but they are validated and guaranteed by something that looks similar to a credit card. Look for a bank or building society current account that pays interest, gives you a cheque book and guarantee card, and has access to automatic teller machines (cashpoints).

Cheques & Cards

Travellers' cheques are rarely accepted outside banks or used for everyday transactions (as they are in the US, for example) so you need to cash them in advance.

Your cheques should ideally be in pounds. Use American Express or Thomas Cook – they are widely recognised, well represented and don't charge for cashing their own cheques. Thomas Cook has an office in every decent-sized town, and American Express has representation in most cities.

Visa, MasterCard, Access, American Express and Diners Club cards are widely used, although most B&Bs require cash. MasterCard is operated by the same organisation that issues Access and Eurocards and can be used wherever you see one or other of those signs. You can get cash advances by using your Visa card at the Midland Bank and Barclays, or by using MasterCard at National Westminster (NatWest), Lloyds and Barclays. If your bank has an agreement with an international money system such as Cirrus, Maestro or Plus, you may be able to withdraw money direct from your home account using ATMs in Britain.

If you plan to stay for an extended period, and have a permanent address, it's usually straightforward to change the billing address for your card.

Tipping & Bargaining

Taxi drivers and waiters all expect 10% tips. Some restaurants automatically include a service charge (tip) of 10% to 15% on the bill, but this should be clearly advertised. If the service was satisfactory you must pay, or explain the reasons for your dissatisfaction to the manager. You do not add a further tip.

Some restaurants have been known to quietly include the service charge in the total cost shown on a credit card voucher, but still leave a blank for a further tip/gratuity. This is a scam – if you want to tip don't tip more than once.

In general, prices are fixed. Bargaining is only really expected if you're buying second-hand gear, but you could try your Delhi delivery in the markets. Always check whether there are discounts for students, young/old people or hostel members.

Value-Added Tax (VAT) & Refunds

VAT is a 17.5% sales tax levied on virtually all goods and services, but not on food and books. Restaurant menu prices must by law include VAT.

In some cases it's possible to claim a refund of VAT paid on goods – a considerable saving. If you have spent fewer than 365 days out of the two years prior to making the purchase living in Britain, and if you are leaving the EU within three months of making the purchase, you are eligible.

Not all shops participate in a VAT refund scheme, and different shops will have different minimum-purchase conditions, which are normally around £40. On request, participating shops will give you a special form/invoice; they will need to see your passport. This form must be presented with the goods and receipts to customs when you depart (VAT-free goods cannot be posted or shipped home). After customs has certified the form, it should be returned to the shop which will give you a refund less an administration fee.

There are a number of companies that offer a centralised refunding service to shops. Participating shops carry a sign in their window. You can avoid bank charges usually encountered when cashing pound travellers' cheques by using a credit card for purchases and requesting that your VAT refund is credited to your card account. In some cases, cash refunds are now available at the major airports.

BRITAIN

POST & COMMUNICATIONS
Post
Post-office hours can vary, but most are open from 9 am to 5 pm, Monday to Friday, and 9 am to noon on Saturday. First-class mail is quicker and more expensive (26p per letter) than 2nd-class mail (20p).

Air-mail letters to EU countries are 26p, to non-EU European countries 31p, to the Americas and Australasia 43p (up to 10 grams) and 63p (up to 20 grams).

If you don't have a permanent address, mail can be sent to poste restante in the town or city where you are staying. American Express Travel offices will also hold mail free for card-holders.

An air-mail letter to the USA or Canada will generally take less than a week; to Australia or New Zealand, around a week.

Telephone
Since British Telecom (BT) was privatised a number of companies have started competing for its business. However, most public phone booths are still operated by BT.

The famous red phone booth survives in conservation areas. More usually you'll see glass cubicles of two types: one takes money, while the other uses prepaid, plastic debit cards and, increasingly, credit cards.

All phones come with reasonably clear instructions. If you're likely to make some calls (especially international) and don't want to be caught out, make sure you buy a BT phonecard. They're widely available from all sorts of retailers, including post offices and newsagents.

Most BT services are expensive; make your directory assistance calls from a public telephone – they're free that way.

Note in this chapter, telephone codes have been included in the telephone number for the local TIC only, or in cases where no TIC is listed the telephone code will be given with the first local phone number, rather than for every single number in a section.

Local & National Calls Dial ☎ 100 for a BT operator. Local calls are charged by time, and national calls (including Scotland, Wales and Northern Ireland) are charged by time and distance. Standard rates are from 8 am to 6 pm, Monday to Friday; the cheap rate is from 6 pm to 8 am, Monday to Friday; and the weekend rate is from midnight Friday to midnight

Sunday. The latter two rates offer substantial savings.

International Calls Dial ☎ 155 for the international operator. Direct dialling is cheaper, but some shoestringers have been known to prefer operator-connected reverse-charges (collect) calls.

To get an international line (for international direct dialling) dial ☎ 00, then the country code, area code (drop the first zero if there is one) and number.

It's usually cheaper to phone overseas between 8 pm and 8 am Monday to Friday and on weekends; for Australia and New Zealand, however, it's cheapest from 2.30 to 7.30 pm and from midnight to 7 am every day.

Fax & E-mail
Most hotels now have faxes. Some shops also offer fax services, advertised by a sign in the window. To collect your e-mail visit one of the growing number of cybercafés and pubs.

NEWSPAPERS & MAGAZINES
There are few countries in the world where you can wake up to such a range of newspapers. The quality daily papers are the *Independent*, the *Guardian*, the *Telegraph* and the *Times*. At the other extreme the outrageous tabloids like the *Sun*, and on Sundays the *News of the World*, continue to plumb new depths. Curiously, media magnate Rupert Murdoch owns both the *Times* and the *Sun*. There's an equally diverse range of magazines.

RADIO & TV
There are four regular TV channels – mainstream BBC1 and ITV, BBC2 and Channel 4 which are rather more serious – plus Murdoch's satellite Sky TV and numerous cable channels. Radio also has a mix of BBC and commercial stations. Try BBC Radio Four for news and drama, Virgin or Capital Radio (London) for pop/rock, Kiss FM for soul, and Classic FM for classical music.

PHOTOGRAPHY & VIDEO
Print film is widely available, but slide film can be harder to find except in specialist photographic retailers (Boots, the high-street chemist chain, often stocks it). Dull, overcast conditions are common, so high-speed films

(ISO 200 or ISO 400, around £5 for 36 exposures) are useful.

Most videos sold in Britain are for VHS format, incompatible with Betamax as used in the USA.

TIME

Wherever you are in the world, the time on your watch is measured in relation to the time in London's Greenwich – Greenwich Mean Time (GMT) – although strictly speaking, GMT is used only in air and sea navigation, and is otherwise referred to as Universal Time Coordinated (UTC).

Daylight-saving time confuses the issue, but to give you an idea, New York is five hours behind GMT, San Francisco is eight hours behind, and Sydney is 10 hours ahead of GMT. Phone the international operator on ☎ 155 to find out the exact difference.

ELECTRICITY

The standard voltage throughout the country is 240 V, 50 Hz. Plugs have three pins.

WEIGHTS & MEASURES

In theory Britain has made the switch to metric weights and measures, although non-metric equivalents are likely to be used by much of the population for some time to come. Distances continue to be given in miles and yards – except on some of the Scottish islands where hostel distances are indicated in kilometres!

Note in this chapter uses miles to indicate distance, but most other measurements (including distances under one mile) are in metric form. For conversion tables, see the back pages of this book.

LAUNDRY

You'll find a laundrette on every high street. The average cost for a single load is £1.20 for washing, and between 60p and £1 for drying.

TOILETS

Public toilets are well signposted. There may be a charge of 10p to 20p for their use.

HEALTH

Aside from the threats posed by the nightlife and widely available liquids, herbs and chemical substances, there are no major health hazards. International Certificates of Vaccination are not required.

Reciprocal arrangements with the UK allow Australians, New Zealanders, EU citizens and a number of other nationalities to receive free emergency medical treatment and subsidised (but still quite costly) dental care through the beleaguered National Health Service – you can use hospital emergency departments, GPs and dentists (check any Yellow Pages phone book). All other holiday-makers have to pay. Make sure you're insured.

Chemists can give advice for minor ailments. Phone ☎ 100 (free call) for a telephone operator who can give you the address of a local doctor or hospital. In an emergency phone ☎ 999 (free call) for an ambulance.

WOMEN TRAVELLERS

Women will find Britain a reasonably enlightened country. Lone travellers should have no problems, although common-sense caution should be observed in big cities, especially when walking alone at night. Hitchhiking, while possible, is extremely risky. Some pubs still retain a heavy masculine atmosphere but increasingly they are becoming family-friendly places.

The London Rape Crisis Centre (☎ 0171-837 1600) is run by women and gives confidential advice and support to women who have been sexually assaulted.

GAY & LESBIAN TRAVELLERS

London, Manchester and Brighton are Britain's main gay and lesbian centres. You'll also find gay and lesbian information centres in most other cities and large towns. Check the listings in *Gay Times*, available from newsagents. Note that the age of consent is 16 for lesbians and heterosexuals but 18 for gays.

DISABLED TRAVELLERS

The Royal Association for Disability and Rehabilitation (RADAR) publishes a useful guide: *Holidays and Travel Abroad: A Guide for Disabled People*, which gives a good overview of facilities available. Contact RADAR (☎ 0171-250 3222) at 12 City Forum, 250 City Rd, London EC1V 8AF.

SENIOR TRAVELLERS

All senior citizens (over 60s) are entitled to

BRITAIN

discounts on public transport, museum admission fees etc, provided they show proof of their age. Sometimes a pass must be purchased to qualify for discounts. Rail companies offer a Senior Citizens' Railcard (£16 for one year) giving a 30% reduction on fares. Bus companies have similar cards.

DANGERS & ANNOYANCES

Britain is remarkably safe considering its size and the disparities in wealth. However, city crime is certainly not unknown, so caution, especially at night, is necessary. Pickpockets and bag snatchers operate in crowded public places.

When travelling by tube at night in London, choose a carriage with other people and avoid some of the deserted tube stations in the suburbs; a bus can be a better choice.

Drugs of every description are widely available, especially in the clubs where Ecstasy is at the heart of the rave scene – to the extent that a number of clubs don't even bother to sell alcohol, just lots of Lucozade! Nonetheless, all the usual dangers associated with black-market drugs apply. Cannabis is still illegal, although for possession of small quantities a small fine (but still a criminal conviction) is usual.

Hotel/hostel touts descend on backpackers at underground stations like Earl's Court, Liverpool St and Victoria. Treat their claims with scepticism and don't accept an offer of a free lift (you could end up miles away). Be careful of unauthorised taxi drivers approaching you at these same stations; play safe and stick with the regulated black cabs.

The big cities, particularly London, have many beggars; if you must give don't wave a full wallet around, carry some change in a separate pocket. It is preferable, however, to donate to a recognised charity. Shelter (☎ 0171-253 0202), 88 Old St EC1, is a voluntary organisation that helps the homeless; or consider buying the *Big Issue*, an interesting weekly newspaper available from street vendors who benefit directly from sales.

Britain is not without racial problems, particularly in some of the deprived suburbs of big cities, but in general tolerance prevails. Few visitors have problems associated with their skin colour, although non-whites may well feel conspicuous in country villages.

The British don't understand that a good shower (at least once daily) is one of life's essentials. Particularly in B&Bs and private houses you may be faced with a bath or, if you're lucky, with a highly complicated contraption that produces a thin trickle of scalding hot or freezing cold water. Get the homeowner to explain exactly how it works if you want a half-decent shower.

BUSINESS HOURS

Offices are open from 9 am to 5 pm, Monday to Friday. Shops may be open for longer hours, and all shops are open on Saturday from 9 am to 5 pm. Except in rural areas some shops also open on Sundays, from 10 am to 4 pm. In country towns, particularly in Scotland and Wales, there may be an early closing day for shops – usually Tuesday or Wednesday afternoon. Late-night shopping is usually Thursday or Friday.

PUBLIC HOLIDAYS & SPECIAL EVENTS

Most banks, businesses and a number of museums and other places of interest are closed on public holidays: New Year's Day; 2 January (bank holiday in Scotland); Good Friday; Easter Monday (not in Scotland); May Day Bank Holiday (first Monday in May); Spring Bank Holiday (last Monday in May); Summer Bank Holiday (first Monday in August in Scotland, last Monday in August outside Scotland); Christmas Day; and Boxing Day.

There are countless, diverse special events held around the country all year. Even small villages have weekly markets, and many still enact traditional customs and ceremonies, some of which are believed to date back thousands of years.

New Year
    Hogmanay – huge street parties in Edinburgh
Last week in March
    Edinburgh Folk Festival
    Oxford/Cambridge University Boat Race – traditional rowing race; River Thames, Putney to Mortlake, London
First Saturday in April
    Grand National – famous horse-racing meeting; Aintree, Liverpool
Early May
    FA Cup Final – deciding match in premier football tournament; Wembley, London

Glasgow Mayfest – high-quality arts festival; runs for three weeks

Late May

Bath International Festival – arts festival; runs for two weeks

Last week in May

Chelsea Flower Show – premier flower show; Royal Hospital, London

First week in June

Beating Retreat – military bands and marching; Whitehall, London

Derby Week – horse racing and people watching; Epsom, Surrey

Mid-June

Trooping the Colour – the Queen's birthday parade with spectacular pageantry; Whitehall, London

Royal Ascot – more horses and hats; Ascot, Berkshire

Appleby Horse Fair traditional Gypsy fair; Appleby, Cumbria

Late June

Lawn Tennis Championships – runs for two weeks; Wimbledon, London

Henley Royal Regatta – premier rowing and social event; Henley-on-Thames, Oxfordshire

Glastonbury Festival – enormous, open-air music festival and hippy happening; Pilton, Somerset

Late July

Cowes Week – yachting extravaganza; Isle of Wight

Early August

Edinburgh Military Tattoo – pageantry and military displays; runs for three weeks

Mid-August

Edinburgh International & Fringe festivals – premier international arts festivals; run for three weeks

Late August (August Bank Holiday)

Notting Hill Carnival – enormous Caribbean carnival; London

Reading Festival – three days of outdoor rock & roll; Reading, Berkshire

Early September

Royal Braemar Gathering (Highland Games) – kilts and cabers; Braemar, Grampian region

5 November

Guy Fawkes Day – in memory of an unsuccessful Catholic coup, bonfires and fireworks around the country

ACTIVITIES
Hiking

Shoestringers are inevitably going to do plenty of walking, but this is also the best way to see Britain. With the exception of Scotland, you are rarely going to be far away from civilisation, so it's easy to put together walks that connect with public transport and take you from hostel to hostel, village to village. A tent and cooking equipment will not be necessary. Some warm and waterproof clothing, sturdy footwear and a map and compass are all you will need.

The countryside is crisscrossed by a network of countless rights of way, or public footpaths, most of them crossing private land. They have existed for centuries and are marked on the excellent Ordnance Survey maps.

Every small town and village is surrounded by walks; look for local guidebooks in TICs, newsagents and bookshops. Consider spending a week based in one spot and doing a series of circular walks in the surrounding countryside.

For long-distance walks, the best areas include the Cotswolds, the Exmoor National Park, the North York Moors National Park, the Yorkshire Dales National Park, the Lake District, the Pembrokeshire Coast National Park, and the Scottish islands. There are many superb long-distance walks in Scotland but, day walks aside, these tend to require more preparation.

The national parks were set up to protect the finest landscapes, but much of the land remains privately owned. It's almost always necessary to get permission from a landowner before pitching a tent.

Several national long-distance trails have been developed (a number of them traverse the national parks) to offer walkers access to the best countryside. They have been created by linking existing public footpaths and often follow routes that have carried travellers for thousands of years.

There are 15 national long-distance trails in England and Wales, and three in Scotland, created and administered by the relevant countryside commissions (which, along with Aurum Press, publish excellent guides). A number of these are mentioned in this chapter. There are also a growing number of regional routes created by county councils, some of which are well organised and excellent. Finally, there are unofficial long-distance routes, often devised by individuals or groups like the Ramblers' Association (see below). Bear in mind that some walks, particularly along the coast and in the Yorkshire Dales and Lake District, can be very crowded on weekends and in July/August.

The British countryside looks deceptively gentle. Especially in the hills or on the open moors, however, the weather can close in and turn nasty very quickly at any time of the year. It is vital if you're walking in upland areas to carry good maps and a compass (and know how to use them), plus, of course, warm and waterproof clothing.

The Ordnance Survey publishes a wide variety of maps. For walkers, its Landranger maps at 1:50,000 or about 1¼ inches to the mile are recommended. If you're focusing on one small area, the 1:25,000 maps give you a huge amount of detail.

Those intent on a serious walking holiday should contact the Ramblers' Association (☎ 0171-582 6878), 1 Wandsworth Rd, London SW8 2XX; the group's *Yearbook* (£4.99) is widely available and itemises the information available for each walk, the appropriate maps, and nearby accommodation (hostels, B&Bs and bunkhouses).

Guidebooks cover every possible walk. For a general introduction look for Lonely Planet's *Walking in Britain*.

Boating

Even shoestringers should consider the possibility of hiring a canal boat and cruising part of the extraordinary 2000-mile network of canals that has survived the railway era.

Especially if you go outside the high season, prices are quite reasonable, ranging, for example, from about £300 per week in April to £600 in August for a boat that sleeps four. Try Alvechurch Boat Centres (☎ 0121-445 2909) or Hoseason's Holidays (☎ 01502-501501).

The Inland Waterways Association (☎ 0171-586 2556), 114 Regent's Park Rd, London NW1 8UQ, publishes an annual *Directory* (£2.75) and can provide mail-order maps and guides.

Cycling

The scenery changes swiftly, you're never far away from food and accommodation, and there is a great network of backroads and lanes that are comparatively traffic-free. It's also cheap, and you see more from a bike than from any other form of transport.

Most airlines allow you to carry a bicycle as part of your baggage allowance, but if this isn't possible there are numerous places where you can hire them. Prices vary, but you should be able to get a three-speed bike for around £20 per week, or a mountain bike for £60. Book ahead if you want a bike in July or August. Hiring is easiest if you have a credit card; a signed slip is used in lieu of a large deposit (ranging from £20 to £100). You will also need ID (a passport will do). Most touring bikes are set up to take panniers, but few shops actually hire them so you'll either have to buy them or bring them with you.

Bicycles can be taken on most rail services, but the regulations are complex and inconsistent so it is essential to check in advance. In some cases it is also necessary to make a reservation, and although you can do so up to a few minutes before the train leaves there's usually very limited space so you could miss out. The major coach operators (National Express, Citylink, etc) don't carry bikes, but most local bus lines do.

The Cyclists' Touring Club (☎ 01483-417217), Cotterell House, 69 Meadrow, Godalming, Surrey GU7 3HS, is a national cycling association that can provide a great deal of helpful information for visiting cyclists, including detailed information on a range of routes. Call or write for a list of its publications. The *CTS Route Guide to Cycling Britain & Ireland* by Christa Gausden & Nick Crane is widely available.

WORK

See the Visas section earlier in this chapter for details on how to go about it legally. The economic downturn has made it difficult to find jobs; however, if you're prepared to do almost anything and to work long hours for lousy pay, you'll almost certainly find something. It's difficult to find a job that pays sufficiently well to be able to save money; although you should be able to break even, you are almost certainly better off saving in your country of origin.

Traditionally, unskilled visitors have worked in bars and restaurants and as nannies. Both jobs may provide live-in accommodation, but the hours are long, the work is exhausting and the pay is lousy. If you live in, you'll be lucky to get £110 per week; if you have to find your own accommodation, you'll be lucky to get £150.

In good economic times, accountants, nurses, medical personnel, computer programmers, lawyers, teachers and clerical workers (with computer experience) quickly find well-paid work. Over the last few years jobs have been scarce, although the situation may be improving. Even so, you'll probably need some money to tide you over while you search. Don't forget copies of your qualifications, references and a CV. Teachers should contact London borough councils (they administer separate education departments). Medics should approach hospital trusts directly.

TNT Magazine is a good starting point for jobs and agencies aimed at travellers. For au pair and nanny work buy the quaintly titled *The Lady*. Also check the *Evening Standard*, national newspapers and the government-operated Jobcentres. Jobcentres are scattered around London; they're listed under the Manpower Services Commission in the telephone book, and have a branch at 195 Wardour St, off Oxford St. Whatever your skills, it's worth registering with several temporary agencies.

ACCOMMODATION

This will almost certainly be your single largest expense. Even camping – the cheapest option – can be expensive at official sites. For shoestringers, there are really only three options: hostels, B&Bs and some hotels. With the exception of London, there are few independent backpackers' hostels, although the number is growing, particularly in Scotland and some of the popular hiking regions.

Camping

Free camping is rarely possible, except in Scotland. Camping grounds vary widely in quality but most have reasonable facilities, although they're usually ugly and inaccessible unless you have a car or bike. For an extensive listing, buy *Camping & Caravanning in Britain* published by the Automobile Association (£7.99); local TICs also have lists.

The tourist boards rate caravan and camping grounds with one to five ticks; the more ticks, the higher the standard. Don't forget the probably unfavourable weather.

YHA Hostels

Youth Hostel Association (YHA) membership gives you access to a huge network of hostels throughout England, Wales, Scotland and Ireland.

There are separate, local associations for England/Wales, Scotland, Northern Ireland and Ireland, and each publishes individual accommodation guides. If you're travelling extensively it's *absolutely essential* to get hold of these. Most importantly, they include the (often complicated) days and hours during which the hostels are open, as well as information on price, facilities and how to reach each place.

Accommodation guides and membership (£3.20 for under 18s, £9.30 for adults) is available at the YHA Adventure Shop at 14 Southampton St, London WC2 (tube: Covent Garden).

All hostels have facilities for self-catering and some have cheap meals. Advance booking is advisable, especially on weekends, bank holidays and at any time over the summer months. Booking policies vary: most hostels accept phone bookings and payment with Visa or Access (MasterCard) cards; some will accept same-day bookings, although they will usually only hold a bed until 6 pm; some work on a first come, first served basis.

The advantages of hostels are position (especially for walkers), price (although the difference between a cheap B&B and an expensive hostel is shrinking – for people travelling alone this may be the only way to avoid having to pay for two beds!) and the opportunity to meet other travellers. The disadvantages are that some are still run on dictatorial lines (although they are improving), you are usually locked out between 10 am and 5 pm, the front door is locked at 11 pm, you usually sleep in bunks in a single-sex dormitory, and many are closed during winter.

Overnight prices are in two tiers: under 18, with prices from £3.75 to £8.20, but mostly around £5.50; and adult, with prices from £5.50 to £19.75, but mostly around £7.45. When hostel prices are 'average' they are not shown in this chapter. Bear in mind that when you add £2.80 for breakfast, you can get very close to cheap B&B prices. Bed linen is free at hostels in England and Wales but costs 60p in Scotland.

Independent Hostels

The growing network of independent hostels offers the opportunity to escape curfews and lockouts for a price of around £8.50 to £9.50 per night in a basic bunkroom. Like youth hostels these are great places to meet other travellers, and they tend to be in town centres rather than out in the sticks. *The Independent Hostel Guide* (£3.95) covers England, Scotland, Wales and the whole of Ireland, but new

BRITAIN

places are opening fast so it's always worth asking at the TIC.

Universities

Many British universities offer their student accommodation to visitors during the term or semester holidays. Most of the rooms are comfortable and functional single bedrooms (single supplements are not charged). Increasingly, however, there are *en suite* rooms, twin and family units, self-contained flats and shared houses.

University catering is usually reasonable these days and can range from bars, self-service cafés and takeaways to restaurants. Full board, half board, bed and breakfast and self-catering options are available.

The main student holidays are, in most cases, taken from late June to late September, although the increasing number of universities operating on a semester system have rooms early in June. Bed and breakfast will normally cost from £18 to £25 per person.

For more information contact the British Universities Accommodation Consortium (BUAC), Box No 967, University Park, Nottingham NG7 2RD (☎ 0115-950 4571; fax 0115-942 2505).

B&Bs, Guesthouses & Pubs

B&Bs are a great British institution and the cheapest private accommodation you can find. At the bottom end (£12 to £16 per person) you get a bedroom in a normal house, a shared bathroom and an enormous cooked breakfast (juice, cereal, bacon, eggs, sausage, baked beans and toast). Small B&Bs may only have one room to let, and you can really feel like a guest of the family – they may not even have a sign.

More up-market B&Bs have *en suite* bathrooms and TVs in each room. There are three types of room – twin rooms come with two single beds, singles with one, and doubles with one double bed. Single rooms are in short supply, however, and many B&B owners would rather not let a room at all than let a single person have it for less than the price of both beds.

Guesthouses, which are often just large converted houses with half a dozen rooms, are an extension of the idea. They range from £12 to £50 a night, depending on the quality of the food and accommodation. In general, they tend to be less personal than B&Bs, and more like small budget hotels (which is what they are really). Local pubs and inns also often have cheap rooms; they can be good fun since they place you at the hub of the community.

All these options are promoted and organised by local TICs, which can provide you with a free list of nearby possibilities.

Booking The TICs can usually make both local and national bookings. These services are particularly handy for big cities and over weekends and during the summer high season. Don't be embarrassed to ask for the cheapest available option.

Local bookings for accommodation within the next two nights usually cost £1 (£5 in the case of London). In addition you often pay a 10% deposit which is subtracted from the nightly price. Most TICs also participate in the Book-a-Bed-Ahead (BABA) scheme which allows you to book accommodation for the next two nights anywhere in Britain. Most charge a fee of about £2.75 and take a 10% deposit.

Classification & Grading The national tourist boards operate a classification and grading system; participating hotels, guesthouses and B&Bs have a plaque at the front door. If you want to be reasonably confident that your accommodation reaches basic standards of safety and cleanliness, the first classification is 'Listed', denoting clean and comfortable accommodation. Better places are indicated by one to five crowns – the more crowns, the more facilities and, generally, the more expensive the room. One crown means each room will have a washbasin and there is a public phone. Two crowns means washbasins, public phone, bedside lights and a TV in a lounge or in bedrooms. Three crowns means at least one-third of the rooms have *en suite* bathrooms and that hot evening meals are available. And so on.

In addition to the classifications there are gradings which are perhaps more significant. 'Approved', 'commended' and 'highly commended' gradings reflect a subjective judgment of quality.

Although this sounds useful, in practice there's a wide range within each classification and some of the best B&Bs don't participate at all. A high-quality 'listed' B&B can be 20 times nicer than a low-quality 'three crown' B&B, and it may or may not be graded. In practice, actually seeing the place, even from the outside, will give you a better idea of what to expect. Don't be afraid to ask to have a look at your room before you sign up.

Bear in mind that some accommodation providers prefer not to pay the TIC to promote them, so there are always more places available than appear in the lists. Unlisted places are often as good as those that are listed, but in big towns it's wise to stick with registered places since some B&Bs now earn their living from accommodating homeless people...not necessarily the atmosphere you'd expect for a holiday.

Rental

There has been a huge increase in the number of houses and cottages available for short-term rent. These can easily fall within the budget of couples or groups on a shoestringer budget. Staying in one place – preferably an attractive village – gives you an unmatched opportunity to get a real feel for a region and a community. Cottages for four can be as little as £100 per week; some even let for three days.

It's often possible to book through TICs, but there are also a number of excellent agencies who can supply you with glossy brochures to help the decision-making process. Outside weekends and July/August, it's not essential to book a long way ahead. Most organisations have agents in North America and Australasia. Among them, Country Holidays (☎ 01282-445095), Spring Mill, Earby, Colne, Lancashire BB8 6RN, has been highly recommended. English Country Cottages (☎ 01328-864041), Grove Farm Barns, Fakenham, Norfolk NR21 9NB, is one of the largest agencies.

The tourist boards rate self-catering accommodation with one to five keys; the more keys, the more facilities. One key indicates a property is clean and comfortable, has adequate heating, lighting and seating, a TV, cooker, fridge and crockery and cutlery.

FOOD

Although the quality of British food is now steadily rising, the legacy of decades of unhealthy eating is a high incidence of obesity and heart disease. The native cuisine's most consistent success has been with the potato, but although baked and mashed potatoes are consistently good, there's only a 50% success rate with chips/fries.

Fortunately, things are improving fast, especially in the south. Vegetarianism has taken off in a big way, and in the main towns and cities a cosmopolitan range of cuisines is available. Particularly if you like pizza, pasta and curry, these days you should be able to get a reasonable meal for under £10 pretty well anywhere. Chain restaurants like Pierre Victoire and Café Rouge have also brought 'French' cuisine to most tourist-frequented high streets, again for moderate prices.

Vegetarians should buy a copy of *The Vegetarian Travel Guide*, published annually by the UK Vegetarian Society and covering hundreds of places to eat and stay. Most restaurants have at least a token vegetarian dish, although, as anywhere, vegans will find the going tough. Indian restaurants offer welcome salvation.

Takeaways, Cafés & Pubs

Britain has a full complement of takeaway chains, from McDonald's, Burger King and Pizza Hut to the home-grown and aptly named Wimpy.

On every high street, especially in the bigger towns, you will find a café, usually referred to as a 'caff' or greasy spoon. Although they often look pretty seedy, they're usually warm, friendly very English places and invariably serve cheap breakfasts (eggs, bacon and baked beans) and English tea (strong, sweet and milky). They also have plain but filling lunches, usually a roast with three veg, or bangers (sausages) and mash (mashed potato).

A step up from there come pub meals about which it's difficult to generalise. At the cheap end they don't vary significantly from cafés, at the expensive end they're closer to restaurants. Chilli con carne or lasagne is often the cheapest offering on the cooked menu. A filling 'ploughman's lunch' of bread, cheese and pickle rarely costs more than £3.

Self-Catering

The cheapest way to eat in Britain is to cook for yourself. Hopefully, however, you won't be forced to the extremes of an Australian shoestringer who was arrested and jailed for

BRITAIN

attempting to cook a Canada goose in Hyde Park. Even if you don't have great culinary skills it is possible to buy very good-quality pre-cooked meals from the supermarkets (Marks & Spencer may be best but they're also pretty pricey).

DRINKS

English pubs generally serve an impressive range of beers – lagers, bitters, ales and stouts. The drink most people from the New World know as beer is actually lager, and much to the distress of local connoisseurs, lagers (including Foster's and Budweiser) now take a huge proportion of the market. Fortunately, the traditional English bitter has made something of a comeback, thanks to the Campaign for Real Ale (CAMRA) organisation. Look for their endorsement sticker on pub windows.

If you've been raised on lager, a traditional bitter or ale is something of a shock – a warm, flat and expensive shock. Ale is similar to bitter – it's more a regional difference in name than anything else. The best ales and bitters are actually hand-pumped from the cask, because they are not carbonated and under pressure. Stout is a dark, rich, foamy drink; Guinness is the most famous brand.

Don't think of any of these drinks as beers, but as something completely new; if you do, you'll discover subtle flavours that a cold and chemical lager cannot match.

Beers are usually served in pints (from £1.50 to £2), but you can also ask for a 'half' (a half-pint). The stronger brews are usually 'specials' or 'extras'. Beware – potency can vary from around 2 to 8%.

Pubs are allowed to open daily for any 12 hours a day they choose. Most maintain the traditional 11 am to 11 pm hours; the bell for last drinks rings out at about 10.45 pm.

Good wines are widely available and very reasonably priced (except in pubs). Check out the supermarkets; an ordinary but drinkable *vin de pays* will cost less than £3.

Takeaway alcoholic drinks are sold from 'off-licence' shops, not from pubs. Every neighbourhood has one. The best off-licence chain is Oddbins, which has branches throughout the country.

Opening hours for off-licences vary, but although some stay open to 8 or 9 pm, Monday to Saturday, many have ordinary shop hours. They all close between 3 and 7 pm on Sunday.

Unfortunately, most restaurants are licensed and their alcoholic drinks, particularly good wines, are always expensive. There are very few BYO restaurants (where you can Bring Your Own bottles for free), although there are a small number in London. Most places charge an extortionate amount of money for 'corkage' – opening your own bottle for you.

ENTERTAINMENT

For many Brits, the local (pub) is still the main focus for a good night out. For the visitor, the country offers some of the world's best drama, dance and music. A visit to a London theatre is almost obligatory. TICs have lists of nightclubs and discos.

SPECTATOR SPORT

The British are responsible for either inventing or codifying many of the world's most popular spectator sports: tennis, football (soccer), rugby and golf. To this list add billiards and snooker, lawn bowls, boxing, darts, hockey, squash and table tennis.

The country also hosts premier events for a number of sports, Wimbledon (tennis) and the FA Cup Final (football) among them. See Public Holidays & Special Events earlier in this section.

THINGS TO BUY

Napoleon once described the British dismissively as a nation of shopkeepers; today, as chains take over the high streets, it would be truer to say they are a nation of shoppers. Shopping is the most popular recreational activity in the country.

Multinational capitalism being what it is, there are very few things you can buy that are unique to Britain. On the other hand, if you can't find it for sale in London it probably doesn't exist.

London has some of the greatest department stores in the world (Harrods, Fortnum & Mason, Liberty, Harvey Nichols, Marks & Spencer), some of the best bookshops (Waterstones, Dillons, Foyles), some of the best fashion (Camden Market, Kensington Market, Covent Garden, Oxford St, Kings Rd), some of the best record shops (HMV, Virgin, Tower) and specialised shops of every description.

Although shop assistants are often rude and few things are cheap, books and clothing can be good value – and you really don't know you need something until you see it...

Check *TNT Magazine* for the names of shipping companies when you realise you've hopelessly exceeded your baggage limit. Choose an established company; don't just go with the cheapest quote if you want to see your stuff again.

Getting There & Away

London is one of the most important transport hubs in the world. As a result there is an enormous number of travel agents, some of dubious reliability. All the main 'student' travel services have offices in London; they understand shoestringers and are competitive and reliable. You don't have to be a student to use their services. See the London section for details.

As always, buses are the cheapest and most exhausting method of transport, although discount rail tickets are competitive, and budget flights (especially last-minute offers) can be very good value. Shop around. A small saving on the fare may not adequately compensate you for an agonising two days on a bus that leaves you completely exhausted for another two days. When making an assessment don't forget the hidden expenses: getting to and from airports, airport departure taxes and food and drink consumed en route.

See the introductory Getting There & Away chapter at the beginning of this book for information on long-haul flights from Australia, Canada, New Zealand and the USA; the Getting Around chapter for details on Eurail, Inter-Rail, BIJ (*Billet International de Jeunesse* – international youth) tickets, and other European travel passes; and the Ireland chapter for details of transport to and from Ireland.

See the Land section (following) for information on combined rail/ferry or coach/ferry tickets and the Channel Tunnel. Of course, it is also possible to get to and from the ferry ports under your own steam and just pay for the ferry itself.

AIR

There are international air links with London, Manchester, Newcastle, Edinburgh and Glasgow, but shoestringers will find cheap flights all wind up in one of the four main London airports: Heathrow is the largest, followed by Gatwick, Stansted and Luton.

London is an excellent centre for cheap tickets; the best resource, however, is *TNT Magazine*, but Sunday papers also carry travel ads. If you are prepared to shop around and don't mind flying at short notice, you can pick up some interesting bargains.

Excellent discount charter flights are often available to full-time students aged under 30 and all young travellers aged under 26 (you need an ISIC or youth card), and are available through the large student travel agencies. See Information under the London section.

Typical low-season one-way/return flights from London bucket shops include Amsterdam £69/74, Athens £85/129, Frankfurt £65/104, Istanbul £99/119, Madrid £75/89, Paris £50/69 and Rome £77/128. Official scheduled flights with carriers like British Airways can cost a great deal more.

LAND

For the first time since the ice ages, Britain has a land link (albeit a rail-only tunnel) with Europe. Even without using the tunnel, however, you can still get to Europe by bus or train – it's just that there's a short ferry/hovercraft ride thrown in as part of the deal. The ferries/hovercraft all carry cars and motorbikes.

Channel Tunnel

Two services operate through the tunnel: Eurotunnel operates a rail shuttle service (Le Shuttle) for motorbikes, cars, buses and freight vehicles, using specially designed railway carriages, between terminals at Folkestone in the UK and Calais (Coquelles) in France; and the railway companies of Britain, France and Belgium operate a high-speed passenger service, known as Eurostar, between London, Paris and Brussels.

Le Shuttle Trains run 24 hours a day, departing every hour in each direction between 7 am and 11 pm and every two hours between 11 pm and 7 am.

BRITAIN

Eurotunnel terminals are clearly signposted and connected to motorway networks. British and French Customs and Immigration formalities are carried out before you drive on to Le Shuttle.

Eurotunnel claims the total time from motorway to motorway, including loading and unloading, is one hour; the shuttle itself takes 35 minutes. This sounds impressive, but the total time if you travel by hovercraft is already under two hours, and ferries only take 2½ hours.

Price is obviously an important factor; a car and up to five passengers costs £126. You can buy prepaid tickets (☎ 0990-353535) or simply pay by cash or credit card at a toll booth. The shuttle operates on the basis of first come, first served; reservations for particular services are not possible.

Eurostar Eurostar (☎ 0345-881881) runs a service between London and Paris (up to 15 a day), and London and Brussels (up to eight a day). There are now direct Eurostar services from Glasgow and Manchester to both Paris and Brussels, and from Birmingham to Paris. There are easy onward connections from London to Wales and from Brussels to Germany and the Netherlands. A new overnight service offers evening departures from UK stations to give morning arrivals on the continent.

In England, trains arrive at and depart from the international terminal at Waterloo station. Some trains stop at the Ashford international station in Kent, and at Frethun (near Calais) or Lille. Immigration formalities are completed on the train, but British Customs are at Waterloo.

The London to Paris journey takes three hours, Brussels takes another 15 minutes. Get tickets from travel agents and major train stations. The normal single/return fare to Paris is £77/155 but various special offers may reduce this to as little as £49 return.

Bus

Eurolines (☎ 01582-404511), a division of National Express (the largest UK bus line), has an enormous network of European destinations, including Ireland and Eastern Europe.

You can book through any National Express office, including Victoria Coach Station in London (which is where Eurolines' buses depart and arrive), and at many travel agents. Eurolines also has agents all around Europe, including Paris (☎ 01-49 72 51 51), Amsterdam (☎ 020-627 51 51), Frankfurt (☎ 069-790 32 40), Madrid (☎ 91-530 7600), Rome (☎ 06-884 08 40), Budapest (☎ 1-117 2562) and Istanbul (☎ 1-547 7022).

The following single/return prices and journey times are representative: Amsterdam £36/49 (12 hours), Athens £126/218 (56 hours), Frankfurt £52/88 (18½ hours), Madrid £76/137 (27 hours), Paris £36/49 (10 hours) and Rome £85/129 (36 hours).

Eurolines also has some good-value explorer tickets that are valid for up to six months and allow travel between a number of major cities. For example, you can visit Amsterdam, Barcelona, Rome and Paris and then return to London for £227.

Train

Trains that connect with European ferries leave from London's Victoria or Liverpool St stations. The prices given here are for adults; youth tickets and passes are considerably lower.

For those bound for France, there are a number of different options, depending on whether you cross the Channel on a hovercraft or ferry, or from Dover, Harwich or Newhaven. The cheapest option to Paris is 2nd class via Newhaven and the Sealink ferry; singles/returns are £39/65 and the journey takes nine hours. If you travel via Dover and Hoverspeed the fares change to £45/59, but the journey time drops to six hours.

Direct trains to Rome and Madrid travel via Dover and Sealink. Singles/returns to Madrid are £125/212 (34 hours); to Rome they're £108/176 (23 hours).

For Holland, Belgium and Germany you cross the Channel from Harwich. Singles/returns to Amsterdam are £55/69 (13 hours); to Berlin they're £122/174 (19½ hours).

Travellers aged under 26 can pick up BIJ tickets which cut fares by up to 50%. Unfortunately, you can't always bank on a substantial reduction. The £120 return from London to Zürich represents a £17 saving on the normal fare; in contrast, London to Munich return saves £39 on the full fare of £203.

Various agents issue BIJ tickets in London,

including Campus Travel (☎ 0171-730 3402), 52 Grosvenor Gardens, London SW1 0AG (tube: Victoria), which sells Eurotrain (BIJ) tickets. Eurotrain options include circular Explorer tickets, allowing a different route for the return trip: London to Madrid, for instance, takes in Barcelona, Paris and numerous other cities. The fare for this Spanish Explorer ticket is £175, valid for two months. International Rail (☎ 0171-834 2345) and Wasteels (☎ 0171-834 7066), Platform 2, Victoria Station, London SW1, also sell BIJ tickets. For an extensive trip around Europe, however, the Eurail or Inter-Rail tickets are still better value.

SEA
There are a bewildering array of alternatives between Britain and mainland Europe. It is impossible to list all the services because of space limitations. See the Ireland chapter for details on links between Britain and Ireland.

Prices vary widely depending on the time of year that you travel, and return tickets often cost much less than two single one-way fares. There are very cheap day-return tickets available (like £8 Dover-Calais), but they are strictly policed; a backpack would definitely give the game away. Unless otherwise noted, the prices quoted for cars do not include passengers.

France
On a clear day, one can actually see across the Channel. A true shoestringer would obviously swim – only seven hours and 40 minutes if you can match the record. Those who are prepared to compromise their shoestring principles have a number of options.

Dover & Folkestone The shortest ferry link to Europe is from Dover and Folkestone to Calais and Boulogne.

Dover is the most convenient port for those who plan onward travel (in England) by bus or train. P&O (☎ 0990-980980), Hoverspeed (☎ 01304-240241) and Stena Line (☎ 0990-707070) all operate between Dover and Calais every one to two hours. It is worth checking prices for all three.

Stena Line charges one-way adult/student passengers £28/26; cars and drivers, depending on the date and time, from £54 to £136

including the driver only up to £70 to £156 for up to four passengers; motorcycles and riders from £42 to £68. These fares are for their fast 45-minute catamaran service; the 90-minute ferry costs a few pounds less.

Prices for P&O and Hoverspeed are generally similar to those of Stena Line – special offers can make a big difference, however. The hovercraft operated by Hoverspeed only take 35 minutes to cross the Channel rather than the 90 minutes taken by ferries.

Ramsgate Another short, cheap hop worth investigating is the Sally Line (☎ 01843-595522) route to Dunkerque. There are five sailings a day that take 2½ hours; a single costs £22 and a car costs from £71 to £106.

Portsmouth P&O (☎ 0990-980555) operates three or four ferries a day to/from Cherbourg and Le Havre. The day ferries take five to six hours and the night ferries take from seven to eight hours. A single is from £18 to £28 and a car costs from £63 to £148. Brittany Ferries (☎ 0990-360360) has at least one sailing a day to/from Caen and St Malo. Portsmouth-Caen takes six hours and costs the same as the P&O routes. The Portsmouth route, unlike the St Malo route which costs a little more, only runs from mid-November to mid-March. Brittany also has a ferry from Plymouth to Roscoff.

Spain
Plymouth Brittany Ferries (☎ 0990-360360) operates at least one ferry a week to Santander, which is on the north coast of Spain. The journey time is 24 hours; a single is from £46 to £76 and a vehicle costs from £146 to £254. Brittany also operates a service between Santander and Portsmouth that takes 30 hours. P&O (☎ 0990-980555) operates a service between Portsmouth and Bilbao at similar rates.

Scandinavia
Until one looks at the ferry possibilities, it's easy to forget how close Scandinavia and Britain are to each other.

Aberdeen & Shetland One of the most interesting possibilities is the summer-only link

BRITAIN

between Shetland, Norway, the Faroe Islands, Iceland and Denmark. The agent is P&O (☎ 01224-572615), but the operator is the Smyril Line.

P&O has daily sailings from Aberdeen to Lerwick (Shetland) from Monday to Friday (£52 for a reclining seat). Every Saturday between June and August there is a sailing from Lerwick to Bergen in Norway (£55 for a reclining seat). Alternatively, every Friday between June and 25 August, there is a sailing from Aberdeen via Shetland to Bergen. A reclining seat is £90 and fares allow for a stopover in Shetland.

Every Sunday all year round, as well as Thursday between 14 June and 18 August, there is a sailing from Aberdeen to the Faroe Islands.

The Smyril Line operates from June to 31 August. The sailing order is Denmark (Saturday), the Faroes (Monday), Norway (Tuesday), the Faroes (Wednesday), Iceland (Thursday), the Faroes (Friday), Denmark (Saturday), and so on. Depending on the season, one-way couchette fares from Shetland to Norway are £55, and one-way student/adult fares to the Faroes are £43/61, to Denmark £84/120 and to Iceland £132/189.

Newcastle The Norwegian Color Line (☎ 0191-296 1313) operates ferries all year to Stavanger and Bergen in Norway. They depart on Saturday and Tuesday from January to May and September to December, and on Saturday, Monday and Wednesday from mid-May to early-September. They're overnight trips, and the high-season fare for a reclining chair is £93; a car and four people costs £300. Bicycles are free.

During summer, Scandinavian Seaways (☎ 0990-333000) operates ferries to Gothenburg (Sweden), departing on Friday from early-June to mid-August; it's an overnight journey taking around 24 hours. A single in a two-berth couchette costs from £132 to £156; a car costs £54 or £64.

Harwich Harwich is the major port linking southern England and Scandinavia. Scandinavian Seaways (☎ 0990-333000) has ferries to Esbjerg (Denmark) and Gothenburg (Sweden). In summer, ferries leave every two days; the

trip to Esbjerg takes 20 hours, and to Gothenburg it's 24 hours. To Esbjerg, a single in a four-berth couchette costs from £72 to £124; a car costs from £42 to £64. To Gothenburg, a single in a four-berth couchette costs from £90 to £156; a car costs from £42 to £64.

Belgium, the Netherlands & Germany
There are two direct links with Germany; many people prefer to drive to/from the Dutch ferry ports.

Harwich Scandinavian Seaways (☎ 0990-333000) has ferries to Hamburg (Germany) every two days; the trip takes 21 hours. A single in a four-berth couchette is from £62 to £100; a car costs from £42 to £64 extra.

Stena Line (☎ 0990-707070) has two ferries a day to the Hook of Holland, the Netherlands; the day ferry takes 7½ hours and the night ferry takes 9½ hours. A single is £36 and a car plus passengers costs from £88 to £156.

Note that the P&O service from Felixstowe to Zeebrugge now carries freight only – no passengers.

Newcastle Scandinavian Seaways (☎ 0990-333000) has a twice-weekly ferry to Hamburg from late-March to October, taking 20 hours. A single in a four-berth couchette is from £72 to £110 and a car is from £42 to £64 extra.

Ramsgate Sally Line (☎ 01843-595522) has six ferries and a number of jet foils to Ostend every day. The ferry takes four hours and the jet foil (passengers only) takes 95 minutes. A single on the ferry costs £22, on the jet foil £26.50. A car plus passengers costs from £50 to £170.

LEAVING BRITAIN
People taking flights from Britain need to pay an Air Passenger Duty: those flying to countries in the EU will pay £5; those flying beyond it, £10. At present, there is no departure tax if you depart by sea or tunnel.

See Money in the Facts for the Visitor section of this chapter for details on how to reclaim VAT when you depart.

Getting Around

Although public transport is generally of a high standard, most shoestringers are going to want to get to the national parks and small villages where transport is worst. If time is limited, a car becomes a serious temptation, although with a mix of local buses, the occasional taxi, plenty of time, walking and occasionally hiring a bike, you can get almost anywhere.

Buses are nearly always the cheapest way to get around. Unfortunately, they're also the slowest (sometimes by a considerable margin) and on main routes they are confined to major roads, which screen you from the small towns and landscapes that make travel worthwhile in the first place. With discount passes and tickets (especially Apex), trains can be competitive; they're quicker and often take you through beautiful countryside that is still relatively unspoilt by the 20th century.

Ticket types and prices vary considerably. For example, a standard single (one-way) rail ticket from London to Edinburgh is £61, but a SuperApex return ticket is £34! A standard single bus ticket from London to Edinburgh is £20.50, but with a small company you might find a return ticket for £20.

See the Rail and Coach/Bus fares tables in this section to get a full picture of the way the different tickets stack up. If you know how far you are travelling (even if your planned journey is not specifically covered) you can get a *rough* idea of costs by working from the mileage columns.

The BTA distributes an excellent brochure, *Getting About Britain for the Independent Traveller*, which gives details of bus, train, plane and ferry transport around Britain and into mainland Europe.

See the Scotland and Wales introductory Getting Around sections for information on deals that relate specifically to those countries.

AIR

Most regional centres and islands are linked to London. However, unless you're going to the outer reaches of Britain, in particular northern Scotland, planes (including the time it takes to get to and from airports) are only marginally quicker than trains. Prices are generally higher than 1st-class rail, but see the Scotland Getting There & Away section for details of new no-frills flights from London to Scotland (from £29).

BUS

Road transport in Britain is almost entirely privately owned and run. National Express (☎ 0990-808080) runs the largest national network – it completely dominates the market and is a sister company to Eurolines – but there are often smaller competitors on the main routes.

In Britain, long-distance express buses are usually referred to as coaches, and in many towns there are separate terminals for coaches and local buses. Over short distances, coaches are more expensive (though quicker) than buses.

A number of counties operate telephone enquiry lines which try to explain the fast-changing and often chaotic situation with timetables; wherever possible, these numbers have been given. Before commencing a journey off the main routes it is wise to phone for the latest information.

Unless otherwise stated, prices quoted in this chapter are for economy single (one-way) tickets; see the Rail and Coach/Bus fares tables in this section.

Passes & Discounts

The National Express Discount Coach Card allows 30% off standard adult fares. It is available to full-time students, and those aged from 16 to 25 and 60 or over. The cards are available from all National Express agents. They cost £7 and require a passport photo – ISIC cards are accepted as proof of student status and passports for date of birth.

The National Express BritExpress Card gives a 30% discount for any journey taken in a nominated 30-day period. It costs £12 and is available to all overseas visitors on presentation of a passport. The card can be bought overseas, at Heathrow or Gatwick, or at the National Express/Eurolines office (☎ 0990-143219), 52 Grosvenor Gardens, London (tube: Victoria).

National Express Tourist Trail Passes are available to UK and overseas citizens. They provide unlimited travel on all services for three days travel within three consecutive days

BRITAIN

Coach/Bus Fares from London

The sample fares below are for single/return travel from London on the National Express coach (bus) system. To qualify for the discount fares you must have a Discount Coach Card (£8 – see Bus in this section for details). The discount is applicable on nonadvance-purchase fares only.

If you're not eligible for a Discount Coach Card you'll need to buy your ticket at least seven days in advance and avoid travelling on a Friday (or Saturday in July and August) to avoid paying the full fares.

Fares below have been rounded up to the next pound.

| | | | Nonadvance Purchase | | | | 7-Day Advance | |
| | | | Not Fri✦ (Economy) | | Fri (Standard) | | Not Fri✦ | Fri |
miles	to	hours	Adult sgl/rtn(£)	Discount sgl/rtn(£)	Adult sgl/rtn(£)	Discount sgl/rtn(£)	Adult rtn(£)	Adult rtn(£)
23	Windsor✳	1	(serviced by other operators – see text)					
51	Brighton✳	1¾	7/10	5/7	7/10	5/7	7/10	5/7
54	Cambridge	2	7/9	5/7	7/9	5/7	7/9	5/7
56	Canterbury	2	10/11	7/8	12/13	8/9	10	12
57	Oxford✳	1¾	3/6	3/5	3/6	3/5	3/6	3/6
71	Dover	2½	11/12	8/8	14/14	10/10	11	13
83	Salisbury	2¾	13/14	9/10	16/17	11/12	13	15
92	Stratford	2¾	13/14	9/10	16	11/12	12	15
106	Bath✳	3	17/19	12/13	21/22	15/16	17	20
110	Birmingham	2½	14/15	10/10	16/17	11/12	13	16
115	Bristol✳	2¼	18/19	13/14	22/23	16/17	17	21
131	Lincoln	4¾	22/23	16/17	26/28	16/17	21	25
150	Shrewsbury	4½	17/18	12/13	20/21	14/15	16	19
155	Cardiff	3¼	20/22	14/16	25/26	18/19	20	23
172	Exeter✳	3¾	23/25	17/18	28/30	20/21	22	27
184	Manchester	4	21	15	21	15	18	18
188	York✳	4	26	18	26	18	20	20
193	Liverpool	4¼	21	15	21	15	18	18
211	Aberystwyth	7¼	20/22	14/16	25/26	18/19	20	23
215	Scarborough	5¾	30	21	37	26	24	24
255	Durham	4¾	26	18	26	18	20	20
259	Windermere	7	30/33	22/23	37/39	26/28	30	35
280	Penzance	6	33/35	23/25	40/42	28/30	32	38
290	St Ives	7	33/35	23/25	40/42	28/30	32	38
299	Carlisle	5½	21/26	20/24	21/26	20/24	26	26
350	Galashiels	8	33/35	23/25	39/42	28/30	31	31
375	Edinburgh✳	8	21/26	20/24	21/26	20/24	26	26
397	Glasgow✳	7	21/26	20/24	21/26	20/24	26	26
434	Dundee	8¼	36/43	26/30	36/43	26/30	34	34
450	Perth	8¼	36/43	26/30	36/43	26/30	34	34
489	Oban	12	46/54	32/38	46/54	32/38	41	41
503	Aberdeen	10½	41/49	29/34	41/49	29/34	40	40
536	Inverness	12	41/49	29/34	41/49	29/34	40	40
590	Ullapool	14	48/60	34/42	48/60	34/42	51	51
652	Thurso	15½	40/50	33/45	40/50	33/45	50	50

✦ Not on Friday or Saturday in July and August.

✳ Other companies also operate this route and are often cheaper. See main text for more information. National Express may have some special EarlyBird fares but they are usually only applicable for the journey into London.

Rail Fares from London

Rail travel is faster than coach travel but usually more expensive. The sample fares below are for 2nd-class single/return travel from London.

A Eurail pass cannot be used in Britain. If you're studying full-time in the UK, or are under 25, or are over 60, or are disabled, or have children, you can purchase a railcard which allows a discount (usually 34%) on all standard class fares except Apex and SuperApex.

If you don't have a BritRail pass and are not eligible for a railcard you can still save money by buying your ticket in advance, though these tickets are usually available only on journeys of more than 150 miles. Cheap tickets include Apex which must be bought seven days in advance, SuperApex (14 days in advance) and SuperAdvance (see note below). Even cheaper promotional fares are sometimes available.

Fares below have been rounded up to the next pound. Where two routes are available between London and the station below, the fare for the cheaper route has been listed.

			Nonadvance Purchase					7/14-Day Advance	
			Peak	*Saver (Off Peak✷)*		*SuperSaver (Not Fri✦)*		*Apex/SuperApex*	
miles	*to*	*hours*	*Adult sgl/rtn(£)*	*Adult sgl/rtn(£)*	*Railcard sgl/rtn(£)*	*Adult sgl/rtn(£)*	*Railcard sgl/rtn(£)*	*Adult sgl/rtn(£)*	*Adult sgl/rtn(£)*
23	Windsor	½	6/6	5/5	3/3	–	–	–	–
51	Brighton	¾	13/15	12/13	8/8	(Awaybreak £17)		(Stayaway £20)	
54	Cambridge	1	15/16	12/14	8/9	(Awaybreak £17)		–	–
56	Canterbury	1½	15/15	13/14	9/10	–	–	–	–
57	Oxford	¾	15/28	13/14	8/9	(Awaybreak £17)		–	–
71	Dover	1¼	19/20	17/18	11/12	(Awaybreak £20)		–	–
83	Salisbury	1¼	21/21	19/19	13/13	(Awaybreak £24)		(Stayaway £28)	
92	Stratford	2¼	15/29	15/21	10/14	(Cheap day return £18)		–	–
106	Bath	1¼	18/22	18/19	12/12	18/22	12/15	15/15	–
110	Birmingham	1½	17/34	16/23	–	17/20	–	14/14	–
115	Bristol	1½	18/22	18/32	12/22	18/19	12/12	16/17	–
131	Lincoln	1¾	33/66	33/39	22/26	31/32	20/21	–	–
150	Shrewsbury	2½	38/69	36/37	24/24	29/29	19/19	18/18	–
155	Cardiff	2	28/37	28/37	18/24	28/28	18/19	23/23	–
172	Exeter	2	39/40	34/35	22/23	34/35	22/23	24/25	–
184	Manchester	2½	53/96	44/45	29/29	34/35	22/23	26/26	19/19
188	York	2	51/102	51/56	34/37	45/46	30/30	34/35	–
193	Liverpool	2½	51/93	44/45	29/29	34/35	22/23	26/26	19/19
211	Aberystwyth	5¼	50/91	45/46	29/30	36/37	24/25	25/25	–
215	Scarborough	2¾	53/106	53/61	35/40	50/51	33/34	40/41	–
255	Durham	2¾	64/128	64/70	42/46	56/57	37/38	38/39	28/28
259	Windermere	3¾	62/112	56/57	37/38	46/47	30/31	33/34	–
280	Penzance	5	50/99	50/55	33/36	46/47	30/31	30/31	–
290	St Ives	5½	50/99	50/56	33/37	47/48	31/32	31/32	–
299	Carlisle	3½	64/118	62/63	41/42	50/51	33/34	37/38	29/29
350	Galashiels	6	69/129	69/71	46/47	58/59	38/39	–	–
375	Edinburgh	4	68/72	68/72	45/48	61/62	40/41	45/46	33/34
397	Glasgow	5	68/72	68/72	45/48	61/62	40/41	45/46	33/34
434	Dundee	5¾	68/76	68/76	45/50	62/63	41/42	52/53	–
450	Perth	6	68/76	68/76	45/50	62/63	41/42	52/53	–
489	Oban	9½	79/90	79/90	52/60	75/76	50/50	59/60	–
503	Aberdeen	6½	76/83	76/83	50/55	70/71	47/47	57/58	–
536	Inverness	8¼	76/83	76/83	50/55	70/71	47/47	57/58	–
590	Ullapool		(No rail service – bus from Inverness)						–
652	Thurso	13	84/96	84/96	55/63	83/84	55/55	70/71	–

✷ You may travel back on a peak-time train, but not on your outward journey.

✦ Not on Friday or Saturday in July and August, but you can travel on these days for this price if you buy a SuperAdvance ticket. This must be bought before 2 pm on the day before (ie Thursday for Friday travel).

(£49/39 for an adult/discount card-holder), any five days travel within 10 consecutive days (£79/65), any eight days travel within 16 consecutive days (£119/95) and any 15 days travel within 30 consecutive days (£179/145). The passes can be bought overseas, or at any National Express agent in the UK.

Slowcoach

Slowcoach (☎ 01249-891959) is an excellent bus service designed especially for those staying in hostels, but useful for all budget travellers. Buses run on a regular circuit between London, Windsor, Bath, Stratford-upon-Avon, Manchester, the Lake District, Edinburgh, York, Nottingham, Cambridge and London, calling at hostels. You can get on and off the bus where you like, and an £89 ticket is valid for the whole circuit (no time limit). Tickets are available from branches of Campus Travel; look in the Yellow Pages for the nearest branch.

See Scotland's introductory Getting Around section for information on two similar operations.

Postbus

Many small places can only be reached by postbuses – minibuses that follow postal delivery routes (which are circuitous through many of the most beautiful areas of England, Wales and Scotland). For the free *Postbus Guide to England & Wales* contact Postbus Services (☎ 0171-490 2888), Post Office HQ, 130 Old St, London EC1V 9PQ; for the Scottish version contact Postbus Services (☎ 01463-256723), Royal Mail, 7 Strothers Lane, Inverness IV1 1AA.

TRAIN

Despite the cutbacks of the last decade, and the privatisation programme which is now in full swing, Britain still has an impressive rail service – if you're using it as a tourist rather than a commuter, that is. There are several particularly recommended trips on beautiful lines through sparsely populated country, the most famous being in Wales and Scotland.

Unfortunately, Eurail passes are not recognised in Britain. There are local equivalents, but they aren't recognised in Europe.

Rail Privatisation

British Rail is no more. The former company's three main operating regions – Network South East (covering the entire south-east of England), Regional Railways (the rest of England and Wales) and ScotRail (Scotland) – have been split into 25 train operating companies (TOCs). A separate company, Railtrack, owns the tracks and stations. The government hopes to complete the sell-off by 1997 but, so far, only half of the TOCs have been sold. This transport section is therefore likely to change considerably – visitors must get up-to-date information.

A condition of the privatisation process is that main rail cards will still be issued, and travellers must be able to buy a ticket to any destination from any train station. When privatisation is complete, passengers will only be able to travel on services provided by the company who issued their ticket and each company will be free to set whatever fare they choose. Currently, companies using the same route must charge the same fares but if they use a different route they can charge what they like. Thus, between some stations, passengers can buy a cheaper ticket for a more roundabout journey or pay more for a direct route.

The main routes are served by excellent InterCity trains that travel at speeds of up to 140 mph and whisk you from London to Edinburgh in just over four hours.

If you're planning a long journey (over 150 miles) and do not have one of the passes listed below, the cheapest tickets must be bought two weeks in advance. Phone the general enquiry line (☎ 0345-484950) for timetables, fares and the numbers to ring for credit-card bookings. For shorter journeys, it's not really necessary to purchase tickets or make seat reservations in advance. Just buy them at the station before you go.

Unless otherwise stated the prices quoted in this chapter are for adult single tickets; see the Rail and Coach/Bus fares tables in this section.

BritRail Passes

BritRail passes are the most interesting possibility for visitors, but they are *not available in Britain* and must be bought in your country of origin. Contact the BTA in your country for details.

A BritRail pass, which allows unlimited travel, can be bought for four, eight, 15, 22 or 31 days. An eight-day pass for an adult/youth is (in US$ or other local currency) $235/189, a 15-day pass is $365/289, a 22-day pass is $465/369 and a 31-day pass is $545/435. The four-day pass costs the equivalent of $165/135, but is not available in North America.

An even more useful deal is the Flexipass, which allows four days unlimited travel in a month ($199/160), eight days in one month ($280/225), 15 days in one month for adults ($425) and 15 days in two months for young people ($340).

It's possible to combine a Flexipass with a single or return Eurostar trip to Paris or Brussels. A return four/eight-day pass costs $363/445; only adult fares are available and the ticket cannot be bought in Europe.

BritRail/Drive

BritRail/Drive combines a Flexipass (see previous section) with the use of a Hertz rental car for side trips. The car-rental price is competitive; the following prices assume you use a small car.

The package is available in the following combinations: a three-day Flexipass plus three days car hire in one month ($265) and a six-day Flexipass with seven days car hire in one month ($490). Contact the BTA in your country for details.

Rail Rovers

The domestic version of the passes are BritRail Rovers: a seven-day All Line Rover is £220/145, and 14 days is £360/238. There are also regional Rovers and some Flexi Rovers to Wales, north and mid-Wales, the North Country, the north-west coast and Peaks, the south-west, and Scotland. Details have been given in the appropriate sections.

Railcards

Various railcards, available from major stations, give a third off most tickets and are valid for a year.

The Young Person's Railcard (£16) is for people aged from 16 to 25, or for those studying full time. You'll need two passport photos and proof of age (birth certificate or passport) or student status. There are also railcards for seniors (over 60s), disabled people and families.

If you're planning to do a lot of rail travel in the south of England, a Network card may be worth considering. This is valid for the region previously known as Network South East – London and the entire south-east of England, from Dover to Weymouth, Cambridge to Oxford. It costs £14, or £10 for holders of the Young Person's Railcard. Discounts apply to up to four adults travelling together providing one of the card-holders is a member of the party. Children pay a flat fare of £1. Travel is permitted only after 10 am Monday to Friday and at any time on the weekend. A couple of journeys can pay for the card.

Tickets

If the various train passes are complicated enough, try making sense of the different tickets:

Single ticket – Valid for a single one-way journey at any time on the day specified; expensive

Day Return ticket – Valid for a return journey at any time on the day specified; relatively expensive

Cheap Day Return ticket – Valid for a return journey on the day specified on the ticket, but there may be time restrictions and it is usually only available for short journeys; often about the same price as a single

Apex – A very cheap return fare, rivalling National Express prices; for distances of more than 150 miles; you must book at least seven days in advance, but seats are limited so book early

SuperApex – A very cheap return fare for journeys to and from north-east England or Scotland; you must book at least 14 days in advance, but seats are limited and not available on all trains so book early

SuperSaver – A cheap return ticket with up to 50% savings; not available in south-eastern England; cannot be used on Friday, Saturday in July and August, nor in London before 9.30 am or between 4 and 6 pm

SuperAdvance – For travel on Friday, and also Saturday in July and August; similarly priced to the Super-Saver, but must be bought before noon on the day before travel, or earlier

Saver – Higher priced than the SuperSaver, but can be used any day and there are fewer time restrictions

AwayBreak ticket – For off-peak travel in the old Network South East region (south-eastern England). Valid for four nights (five days) for journeys over 30 miles or 40 miles from London

StayAway ticket – As above but valid for one month

CAR & MOTORCYCLE

There are five grades of road. Motorways are dual or triple carriageway and deliver you quickly from one end of the country to the other. In general, they are not a particularly

BRITAIN

pleasant experience. You miss the most interesting countryside, and the driving can be very aggressive. Avoid them whenever possible, and be very careful if you use them in foggy or wet conditions when their usually good safety record plummets. Unfortunately, the primary routes (main A roads) are often very similar.

Minor A roads are single carriageway and are likely to be clogged with slow-moving trucks, but life on the road starts to look up once you join the B roads and minor roads. Fenced by hedgerows, these wind through the countryside from village to village. You can't travel fast, but you won't want to.

Americans and Australians will find petrol expensive (around 57p per litre, or £2.16 for a US gallon), but distances aren't great.

Road Rules

Anyone using the roads should get hold of the *Highway Code* (99p), which is often available in TICs. If you're bringing a car from Europe make sure you're adequately insured.

Briefly, vehicles drive on the left-hand side of the road; front seat belts are compulsory and belts must be worn if they are fitted in the back; the speed limit is 30 mph in built-up areas, 60 mph on single carriageways and 70 mph on dual carriageways and motorways; you give way to your right at roundabouts (that is, traffic already on the roundabout has the right of way); and motorcyclists must wear helmets.

A yellow line painted along the edge of the road indicates there are parking restrictions. The only way to establish the exact restrictions is to find the nearby sign that spells them out. A single line means no parking for at least an eight-hour period between 7 am and 7 pm, five days a week; a double line means no parking for at least an eight-hour period between 7 am and 7 pm more than five days a week; and a broken line means there are some restrictions.

Rental

Rates are expensive in the UK; often you will be best off making arrangements in your home country for some sort of package deal. See this book's introductory Getting Around chapter for more details. The big international rental companies charge from around £150 for a small car (Ford Fiesta, Peugeot 106).

Holiday Autos (☎ 0990-300400) operates through a number of rental companies and can generally offer excellent deals. A week's all-inclusive hire starts at £129 for a Fiat Panda. For other cheap operators check the ads in *TNT Magazine*. TICs have lists of local car-hire companies.

If you're travelling as a couple or a group, a camper van is worth considering. Sunseeker Rentals (☎ 0181-960 5747) has four-berth and two-berth vans for £200 to £300 per week.

Purchase

In Britain all cars require a Ministry of Transport (MOT) safety certificate (the certificate itself is usually referred to simply as an MOT) valid for one year and issued by licensed garages; full third party insurance – shop around but expect to pay at least £300; registration – a standard form signed by the buyer and seller, with a section to be sent to the Ministry of Transport; and tax (£140 for one year, £77 for six months) – from main post offices on presentation of a valid MOT certificate, insurance and registration documents.

You are strongly recommended to buy a vehicle with valid MOT and tax. MOT and tax remain with the car through a change of ownership; third-party insurance goes with the driver rather than the car, so you will still have to arrange this (and beware of letting others drive the car). For further information about registering, licensing, insuring and testing your vehicle, contact a post office or Vehicle Registration Office for leaflet V100.

See the introductory Getting Around and Facts for the Visitor chapters at the beginning of this book for general information on private transport and the paperwork involved.

BICYCLE

See the Activities section earlier in this chapter.

HITCHING

If you're not worried about the safety implications, hitching is reasonably easy, except around the big cities and built-up areas, where you'll need to use public transport. It's against the law to hitch on motorways or the immediate slip roads; make a sign and use approach roads, nearby roundabouts, or the service stations.

BOAT

See the appropriate sections later in this chapter for ferry information and the Activities section earlier in this chapter for canal boating.

LOCAL TRANSPORT

See the London Getting Around section for information on the famous London taxis and their minicab competitors. Outside London, you could expect to pay around £1 per mile, which means they are definitely worth considering to get to an out-of-the-way hostel or sight, or the beginning of a walk. If there are three or four people to share the cost, a taxi over a short distance will often be competitive with the cost of a local bus.

ORGANISED TOURS

Since travel is so easy to organise in Britain, there is very little need to consider a tour. Still, if your time is limited and you prefer to travel in a group there are some interesting possibilities; the BTA has information. Top Deck (☎ 0171-370 4555), 131 Earl's Court Rd, London SW5, Drifters (☎ 0171-262 1292), 10 Norfolk Place London W2, and Tracks (☎ 01303-814949), 8 Evesgate Park Barn, Smeeth, Ashford, Kent TN25 6SX, have trips pitched at a young crowd.

London

Once the capital of the greatest empire the world has ever known, London is still the largest city in Europe. It is embedded in the culture, the vocabulary and the dreams of every English speaker. At times it will be more grand, evocative, beautiful and stimulating than you could have imagined; at others it will be colder, greyer, dirtier and more expensive than you believed possible.

It is a cosmopolitan mixture of the Third World and First World, of chauffeurs and beggars, of the establishment and the avant-garde. There are seven to 12 million inhabitants, depending on the count, and 20 million visitors a year. As you will soon discover, an amazing number of visitors are extremely wealthy. Fortunately for the shoestringer, however, the majority aren't. It

will soon become clear what side of this divide you are on, and you will also discover a London that caters to those who work long hours for lousy wages.

For the shoestring traveller, London is a challenge. Money has a way of mysteriously evaporating every time you move. If you have limited funds it's necessary to plan, book ahead and prioritise. There's little point putting up with the crowds, the underground and the pollution if you can't budget to take advantage of at least some of the theatre, exhibitions, shops, pubs and clubs, cafés and restaurants. A peg or two above desperation, you can find reasonable value. And some of the very best is free, or very cheap.

History

Although a Celtic community had already established itself around a ford across the River Thames, it was the Romans who first developed the sq mile now known as the City of London. They built a bridge and an impressive city wall, and made the city an important port and the hub of their road system.

The Romans left, but trade went on. Few traces of London dating from the Dark Ages can now be found, but London survived the incursions of the Saxons and Vikings. Fifty years before the Normans arrived, Edward the Confessor built his abbey and palace at Westminster.

William the Conqueror found a city that was, without doubt, the richest and largest in the kingdom. He raised the White Tower (part of the Tower of London) and confirmed the city's independence and right to self-government.

During the reign of Elizabeth I the capital began to expand rapidly. Unfortunately, medieval, Tudor and Jacobean London was virtually destroyed by the Great Fire of 1666. The fire gave Christopher Wren the opportunity to build his famous churches, but did nothing to halt or discipline the city's growth.

By 1720 there were 750,000 people, and London, as the seat of Parliament and focal point for a growing empire, was becoming ever richer and more important. Georgian architects replaced the last of medieval London with their imposing symmetrical architecture and residential squares.

The population exploded in the 19th century, creating a vast expanse of Victorian

BRITAIN

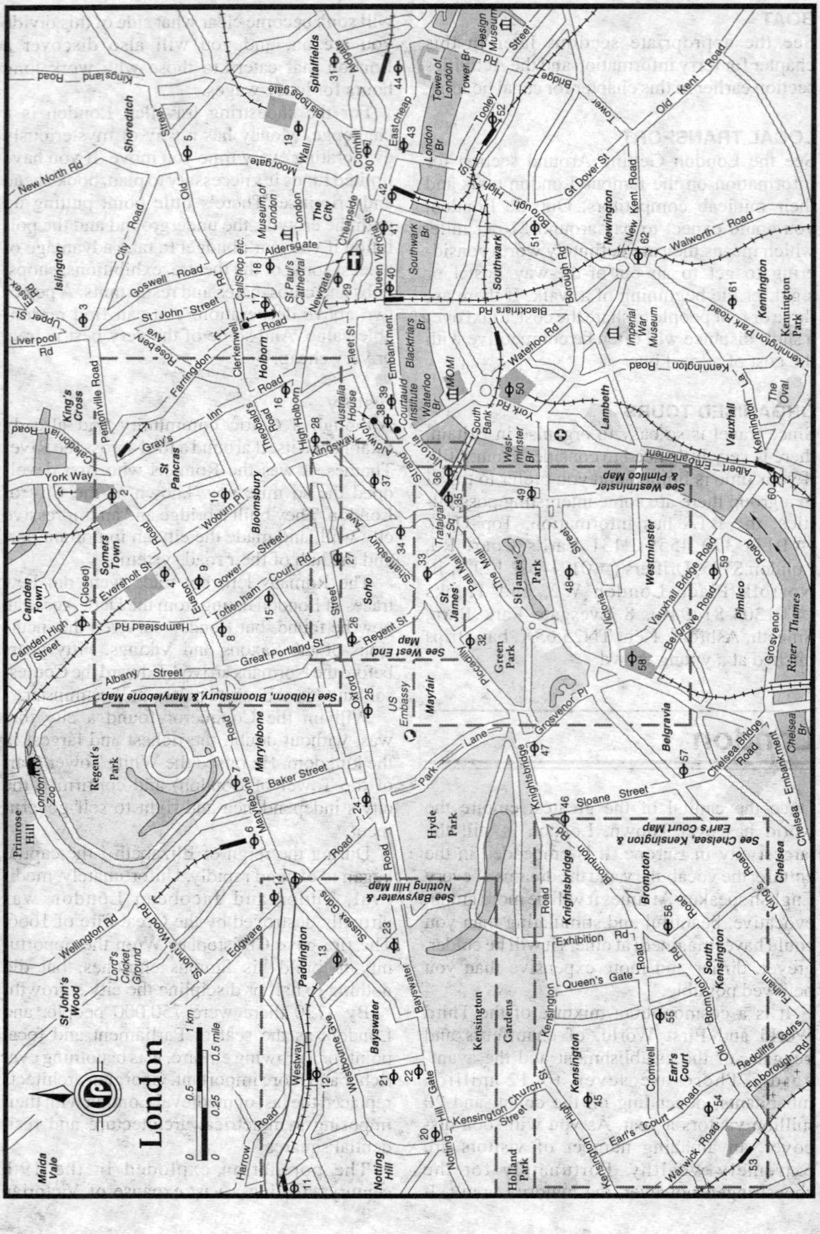

London

1 km
0.5 mile
0.5
0.25
0

BRITAIN

Map labels: Kingsland Road, Shoreditch, Spitalfields, Tower of London, Tower Br, Design Museum, Old Kent Road, New North Rd, Wall, Cornhill, Moorgate, Museum of London, The City, Cheapside, London Br, Tooley St, Bridge, Gt Dover St, Newington, New Kent Road, Walworth Road, Islington, City Road, Goswell Road, Aldersgate, Call/Shop etc, St Paul's Cathedral, Newgate, Queen Victoria St, Southwark, Southwark Br, Borough Rd, Kennington Park Road, Kennington Park, Upper St, Essex Rd, Liverpool Rd, St John Street, Clerkenwell Road, Holborn, Fleet St, Embankment, Blackfriars, Blackfriars Bridge Rd, Blackfriars Rd, Waterloo Rd, Imperial War Museum, Kennington Road, The Oval, King's Cross, Pentonville Road, Gray's Inn, Rosebery Ave, High Holborn, Kingsway, Australia House, Courtauld Institute, Waterloo, MOMI, South Bank, York Rd, Lambeth, Vauxhall, Kennington, Caledonian Road, Gray's Inn, St Pancras, Bloomsbury, Woburn Pl, High Holborn, Strand, Aldwych, Victoria Embankment, Westminster Br, See Westminster & Pimlico Map, Albert Embankment, York Way, Somers Town, Euston Road, Euston, Gower St, Tottenham Court Rd, Soho, Kingsway, Trafalgar Sq, The Mall, St James's Park, Grosvenor Rd, River Thames, Pimlico, Camden Town (Closed), Camden High Street, Eversholt St, Hampstead Rd, Great Portland St, Regent St, See West End Map, St James's Park, Green Park, Victoria St, Victoria, Belgrave Road, Vauxhall Bridge Road, Chelsea Bridge, Albany Street, Marylebone Road, Oxford St, US Embassy, Mayfair, Park Lane, Grosvenor Pl, Belgravia, Chelsea Embankment, Chelsea Br, Regent's Park, London Zoo, Baker Street, Hyde Park, Knightsbridge, Sloane Street, Chelsea, Chelsea Bridge Road, See Holborn, Bloomsbury & Marylebone Map, Primrose Hill, St John's Wood, Lord's Cricket Ground, Wellington Rd, St John's Wood Rd, Edgware Road, Marylebone Road, See Bayswater & Notting Hill Map, Sussex Gdns, Paddington, Bayswater, Knightsbridge, Brompton Road, Exhibition Rd, South Kensington, Old Brompton Road, Fulham Rd, See Chelsea, Kensington & Earl's Court Map, Maida Vale, Westway, Westbourne Gve, Bayswater, Kensington Gardens, Queen's Gate, Kensington Road, Cromwell Road, Earl's Court, Redcliffe Gdns, Finborough Rd, Harrow Road, Notting Hill, Kensington Church St, Kensington High Street, Holland Park, Earl's Court Rd, Warwick Rd, Primrose Hill

Lonely Planet logo

TUBE STATIONS	15	Goodge St	13	Paddington (BR)
(in alphabetical order)	32	Green Park	33	Piccadilly Circus
31 Aldgate			59	Pimlico
38 Aldwych	28	Holborn		
3 Angel	47	Hyde Park Corner	22	Queensway
7 Baker St	61	Kennington	12	Royal Oak
30 Bank	45	Kensington High St	10	Russell Square
18 Barbican	2	King's Cross (BR)		
21 Bayswater	46	Knightsbridge	57	Sloane Square
40 Blackfriars			56	South Kensington
25 Bond St	23	Lancaster Gate	48	St James' Park
51 Borough	34	Leicester Square	29	St Paul's
	19	Liverpool St (BR)		
42 Cannon St (BR)	52	London Bridge (BR)	39	Temple
16 Chancery Lane			27	Tottenham Court Rd
35 Charing Cross (BR)	41	Mansion House	44	Tower Hill (BR)
37 Covent Garden	24	Marble Arch		
	6	Marylebone (BR)	60	Vauxhall (BR)
54 Earl's Court	43	Monument	58	Victoria (BR)
14 Edgware Rd	1	Mornington Crescent		
62 Elephant & Castle (BR)		(Closed for Rebuilding)	8	Warren St
36 Embankment			50	Waterloo (BR)
4 Euston (BR)	20	Notting Hill Gate	11	Westbourne Park
9 Euston Square			49	Westminster
	5	Old St		
17 Farringdon	53	Olympia (BR)		
	26	Oxford Circus		
55 Gloucester Rd				

suburbs. As a result of the Industrial Revolution and rapidly expanding commerce, the population jumped from 2.7 million in 1851 to 6.6 million in 1901.

Georgian and Victorian London was devastated by the Luftwaffe in WWII – huge swathes of the centre and the East End were totally flattened. After the war, ugly housing and low-cost developments were thrown up on the bomb sites. The docks never recovered – shipping moved to Tilbury, and the Docklands declined to the point of dereliction, until rediscovery by developers in the 1980s.

Riding on a wave of Thatcherite confidence and deregulation, London boomed in the 1980s. The new wave of property developers proved to be only marginally more discriminating than the Luftwaffe, and their buildings are only slightly better than the eyesores of the 1950s. There are ambitious plans to rebuild parts of the South Bank, with proceeds from the National Lottery, and Greenwich will undergo a facelift now that it has been chosen as Britain's official site for ushering in the third millennium.

Orientation

London's main geographical feature is the Thames, a tidal river that enabled an easily defended port to be established far from the dangers of the Channel. Flowing around wide bends from west to east, it divides the city into northern and southern halves.

London sprawls over an enormous area. Fortunately, the underground rail system – the 'tube' – makes most of it easily accessible, and the ubiquitous (though geographically misleading) underground map is easy to use. Any train heading from left to right on the map is designated as eastbound, any train heading from top to bottom is southbound. Each line has its own colour.

Most important sights, theatres, restaurants and even some cheap places to stay lie within a reasonably compact rectangle formed by the underground railway's Circle line, just to the north of the river. All the international airports lie some distance from the city centre but transport is easy. See the Getting Around section later for details on airport transport.

Although London's relatively few skyscrapers stick out like sore thumbs, they are

BRITAIN

not easily accessible to shoestringers. The best and most central lookout to help you orient yourself is, surprisingly, over 300 years old: the Golden Gallery at St Paul's Cathedral.

London blankets mostly imperceptible hills, but there are also good views from Hampstead Heath (north of Regent's Park) and Greenwich Park (pronounced 'Grenitch', downriver, east of central London).

Maps A decent map is vital. First, get a single-sheet map so you can see all of central London at a glance; the BTA produces a good one. Even if you only plan to stay for a night or two, buy a copy of the *London A-Z* street directory (black & white £2.75, colour £3.95) as soon as possible. A compass is also handy, as it is easy to be totally disoriented when you emerge from a tube station.

Terminology 'London' is an imprecise term used loosely to describe over 2000 sq km of Greater London enclosed by the M25 ring road, although it is now difficult to see outlying towns like Luton, Reading and Guildford (each around 30 miles from the city centre) as anything more than suburbs.

London is not administered as a single unit, but divided into widely differing boroughs governed by local governments with significant autonomy.

Boroughs are further subdivided into districts (or suburbs, or precincts if you prefer), which to a large degree tally with the first group of letters and numbers of the postal code. The letters correspond to compass directions from the centre of London, which according to the post office must lie somewhere not too far from St Paul's Cathedral: EC means East Central, WC means West Central, W means West, NW means North West, and so on. The numbering system after the letters is less helpful: 1 is the centre of the zone, further numbers relate to the alphabetical order of the postal-district names, which are not always in common use.

Districts and postal codes are often given on street signs, which is obviously vital when names are duplicated (there are 47 Station Rds), or cross through a number of districts. To further confuse visitors, many streets change

name – Holland Park Ave becomes Notting Hill Gate, which becomes Bayswater Rd, which becomes Oxford St... Sometimes they duck and weave like the country lanes they once were. Street numbering can also bewilder: on big streets the numbers on opposite sides can be way out of kilter (315 might be opposite 520) or, for variation, they can go up one side and down the other.

To add to the confusion, some London suburbs – well within the M25 – do not give London as a part of their addresses, and do not use London postal codes. Instead they're considered part of a county.

The City & the East The City refers to the area that was once the old walled city, before the inexorable colonisation of the surrounding towns and villages had begun. Although it lies in the south-eastern corner of the Circle line, it is regarded as the centre – ground zero. As you may have guessed, the West End (much more the tourist's centre) lies to the west.

The City is still one of the most important financial centres in the world. Full of bankers during the working week, it is deserted outside working hours. The same is not true of its most famous sights: the Tower of London, St Paul's Cathedral and the market at Petticoat Lane.

To the east, beyond the Circle line, is the East End, once the exclusive habitat of the cockney, now a cultural melting pot. This incorporates districts like Smithfield, Hackney, Shoreditch and Bethnal Green. There are some lively corners, and cheap rents, but in general it is blighted by traffic and council estates. Much of the East End was flattened during WWII and it shows.

Further east again lie the Docklands. Once part of the busiest port in the world, hundreds of hectares of prime real estate fell into disuse after WWII, graphically mirroring the decline of the empire. In the early 1980s, a light railway (an interesting excursion from Tower Gateway) was built and developers were unleashed.

Across the river (accessible by foot tunnel) is beautiful Greenwich, home to the merchant clipper *Cutty Sark*, superb Wren architecture, open space and the prime meridian.

West West of the City, but before the West End proper, is Holborn and Bloomsbury. Holborn (pronounced 'Hoeburn') is Britain's sedate legal heartland, the home of Rumpole and common law. Bloomsbury is still synonymous with the literary and publishing worlds. There are dozens of specialist shops, and it still has the incomparable British Museum, stuffed to the seams with loot from every age and every corner of the globe.

The West End proper lies west of Tottenham Court Rd and Covent Garden, which is trendy and tourist-ridden but fun, and south of Oxford St, an endless succession of department stores packed with vicious, bargain-hunting shoppers. It includes such icons as Trafalgar Square, the restaurants and clubs of today's not-so-seedy Soho, the famous West End cinemas and theatres around Piccadilly Circus and Leicester Square, and the elegant shops of Regent and Bond Sts – and not to forget Mayfair, the most valuable property on the Monopoly board.

St James' and Westminster are south-west, SW1 to be precise. Would this sq mile be a nuclear target? Well, in no particular order, it includes Whitehall, No 10 Downing St, the Houses of Parliament, Westminster Abbey and Buckingham Palace.

To the south of Victoria station lies Pimlico. It's not a particularly attractive district, but it's central and has a good supply of cheapish, decentish hotels.

Kensington, Earl's Court, South Kensington and Chelsea are in the south-west corner formed by the Circle line.

Earl's Court, once infamous as 'Kangaroo Valley' and home to countless expatriate Australians, now has a strong Middle Eastern influence. It's pretty tacky, and seems to get tackier by the year, but there are still some cheap hotels, a number of backpackers' hostels and a couple of Australian pubs, plus cheap restaurants and travel agents. It is not a bad place to start your visit.

South Kensington is more chic and trendy, and there is a clutch of interesting museums (the Victoria & Albert, Science, Natural History and Geological). Chelsea has abandoned the bohemian for comfort, and Kings Rd has bid farewell to the punks, but it is still an interesting centre for young fashion.

North Accessible from Notting Hill Gate, but more easily reached from Ladbroke Grove, Notting Hill is a lively, interesting district, with a large West Indian population. It gets trendier by the day, but the Portobello Rd market is still good value and there are pubs, a new crop of wine bars and interesting shops.

North of Kensington Gardens and Hyde Park, Bayswater and Paddington are pretty much tourist ghettos, but there are plenty of hostels, cheap and mid-range hotels, good pubs and interesting restaurants (particularly along Queensway and Westbourne Grove).

From west to east, the band of suburbs to the north of the Central line include Kilburn, Hampstead, Camden Town, Kentish Town, Highgate and Highbury. Kilburn is London's Irish capital and bedsit land; it's not a bad place to live. Hampstead, with its great views, is fashionable, quiet and civilised; Camden Town, although well advanced on the road to gentrification, still has some ordinary people and a gaggle of trendy but very enjoyable weekend markets.

South Cross the Thames from Central London and you could be excused for thinking you've arrived in a different country. This is working-class London and it seems a long way from the elegant, antiseptic streets of Westminster. By contrast, much of South London is very poor and very dirty, but very alive.

For the short-term visitor there may be few pressing reasons to visit, although there are middle-class beachheads like the South Bank Centre (a venue for interesting exhibitions and concerts), Kew, with its superb gardens, and Wimbledon, with its tennis.

If you stay for any length of time, however, there's a fair chance you will end up living in suburbs like Clapham, Brixton and Camberwell, or even further out.

Brixton was notorious for racial problems in the early 1980s, but it is definitely no Harlem, even though unemployment is estimated at 18% and the crumbling buildings and piles of rubbish may look the part. You'll enjoy its tatty market and arcades whatever your skin colour. Most of the district is as safe as anywhere else, but don't wander too far off the main streets. The 'front line' – an area around Railton Rd – is best left to the locals.

BRITAIN

Information

There's no shortage of information; the problem is wading through it to find the nuggets relevant to shoestringers. For details of London Regional Transport's information services see the London Getting Around section later. For details of BritRail's information services see the London Getting There & Away section later.

Time Out magazine (issued every Tuesday, £1.60) is a mind-bogglingly complete listing of everything happening and is recommended for every visitor. From the same company, the *Time Out London Guide* (paperback, £9.99) is an excellent, practical guide for those planning to spend more than a week or so in London. They also publish the *Time Out Guide to Eating & Drinking in London* (magazine format, £7.50), which lists over 1700 restaurants and bars, although only some are cheap.

If you baulk at paying, there are free magazines available from pavement bins, especially in Earl's Court, Notting Hill and Bayswater: *TNT Magazine*, *Southern Cross*, *Traveller Magazine* and *SA Times*. They include Australian, New Zealand and South African news and sports results, but they're really invaluable for the information they contain for the budget traveller, with entertainment listings, excellent travel sections and useful classifieds covering jobs, cheap tickets, shipping services and accommodation. *TNT Magazine* is the glossiest and most comprehensive; phone ☎ 0171-373 3377 for the nearest distribution point.

Loot (£1.30) is a daily paper made up entirely of classified ads that are placed free by sellers. You can find everything from second-hand wrestling magazines to kitchen sinks and cars, as well as an extensive selection of flats and house-share ads.

Tourist Offices London is a major European travel centre, so aside from information on London there are also offices that deal specifically with England, Scotland, Wales, Ireland and most European countries.

British Travel Centre
   12 Regent St, Piccadilly Circus SW1Y 4PQ. Two minutes walk from Piccadilly Circus, this is a chaotic and comprehensive information and booking service under one roof: tours; *bureau de change*; theatre tickets; train, air and car travel; accommodation; map and guidebook shop; and the Wales and Ireland tourist boards. It's very busy and open every day: Monday to Friday from 9 am to 6.30 pm, Saturday and Sunday from 10 am to 4.30 pm. For general enquiries telephone ☎ 0181-846 9000.

London Tourist Information Centres
   There are centres in the four Heathrow terminals, and at Gatwick, Luton and Stansted airports, Harrods and the Tower of London. The main centre on the Victoria station forecourt has a number of services including accommodation bookings, information and a book and map shop. They're open every day and can be extremely busy. There is also a TIC at the Arrivals Hall in Waterloo International Terminal. Written enquiries to 26 Grosvenor Gardens SW1W 0DU (☎ 0171-730 3488).
   It is possible to make same-day accommodation bookings at the TICs at Victoria station and Heathrow, although they charge £5 for a hotel or B&B booking and £1.50 for hostels.
   Alternatively, at Victoria station, there are a couple of private-hotel reservation centres (one on the main concourse, one outside near the steps to the underground) that charge £3 for a booking. Backpackers can seek out the Accommodation Express, a free service for backpackers to be found outside the station on Buckingham Palace Rd. They have a courtesy bus to the Chelsea Hotel (see the Private Hostels section under Places To Stay) and other hostels.

Money Whenever possible, avoid using *bureaux de change* to change your money. For more info, see the Facts for the Visitor chapter at the beginning of this book.

There are 24-hour bureaus in Heathrow Terminals 1, 3 and 4. Terminal 2's bureau is open daily from 6 am to 11 pm. Thomas Cook has branches at Terminals 1, 3 and 4. There are 24-hour bureaus in Gatwick's South and North Terminals and one at Stansted. The airport bureaus are actually good value; they don't charge commission on sterling travellers' cheques, and on other currencies it's 1.5% with a £3 minimum.

At Victoria train station near the tourist office, Thomas Cook has a bureau that's open daily from 6 am to 11 pm.

The main American Express office (☎ 0171-930 4411), 6 Haymarket (tube: Piccadilly), is open for currency exchange Monday to Friday from 9 am to 5.30 pm, Saturday from 9 am to 6 pm, and Sunday from 10 am to 5 pm. Other services are available on weekdays from 9 am to 5 pm and Saturday from 9 am to noon.

The main Thomas Cook office (☎ 0171-499 4000), 45 Berkeley St (tube: Green Park), is open from 9 am (10 am on Thursday) to 5.30 pm Monday to Friday, from 9 am to 4 pm on Saturday. There are many branches scattered around the centre of London.

Post & Communications Unless otherwise specified, poste restante mail is sent to London Chief Office (☎ 0171-239 5047), King Edward Building, King Edward St EC1 (tube: St Paul's). It's open from 9 am to 6.30 pm, Monday to Friday. It's more convenient to have your mail sent to Poste Restante, Trafalgar Square Branch Office, London WC2N 4DL. The physical address is 24-28 William IV St (tube: Charing Cross). Mail will be held for four weeks; ID is required.

To get a telephone operator phone ☎ 100; for telephone directory enquiries phone ☎ 192; and for international calls phone ☎ 153. For the international operator (for reverse charges) phone ☎ 155.

CallShop etc has lower charges than British Telecom (BT) for international calls, and faxes may also be sent or received. It has shops at 181a Earls Court Rd (tube: Earl's Court) and 88 Farringdon Rd (tube: Farringdon).

Net surfers can connect at the Cyberia Café (☎ 0171-209 0982), with branches at 39 Whitfield St W1 (tube: Goodge St) and New Broadway W5 (tube: Ealing Broadway). They are open Monday to Friday 11 am to 10 pm, Saturday 9 am to 10 pm, and on Sunday from 11 am to 9 pm.

London telephone numbers have two codes (☎ 0171 or ☎ 0181) before a seven-digit number.

Travel Agencies London has always been a centre for cheap travel. Refer to the Sunday papers (especially the *Sunday Times*), *TNT Magazine* and *Time Out* for listings of cheap flights, but watch out for sharks.

The long-standing and reliable firms include:

Campus Travel
    174 Kensington High St W8; tube: High St Kensington (☎ 0171-938 2188)
Council Travel
    28A Poland St, London W1; tube: Oxford Circus – the USA's largest student/budget travel agency (☎ 0171-437 7767)

STA Travel
    86 Old Brompton Rd SW7; tube: South Kensington – the largest worldwide student/budget agency (☎ 0171-361 6262)
Trailfinders
    194 Kensington High St W8; tube: High St Kensington – a complete travel service, including a bookshop, information centre, visa service and immunisation centre (☎ 0171-938 3939)

Bookshops All the major chains are good, but Waterstones and Dillons have particularly strong travel sections. There are a number of specialist travel bookshops and several shops that are tourist attractions in their own right:

Books for Cooks
    4 Blenheim Crescent W11; tube: Ladbroke Grove – the best collection of cook books in the world (☎ 0171-221 1992)
Daunt Books
    83 Marylebone High St W1; tube: Baker St – a wide selection of travel guides in a beautiful old shop (☎ 0171-224 2295)
Dillons the Bookstore
    82 Gower St WC1E; tube: Euston Square – an enormous bookshop with particularly strong academic sections (☎ 0171-636 1577)
Foyles
    119 Charing Cross Rd WC2; tube: Leicester Square – the biggest, most disorganised bookshop in the world (☎ 0171-437 5660)
Stanfords
    12 Long Acre WC2; tube: Covent Garden – has the largest and best selection of maps and guides in the world (☎ 0171-836 1321)
Travel Bookshop
    13 Blenheim Crescent W11 – across the road from Books for Cooks, has all the new guides, plus a selection of out-of-print and antiquarian gems (☎ 0171-229 5260)

Cultural Centres These are all worth checking out: they'll provide information, often with free entertainment, and, of course, a civilised way of escaping the weather.

Barbican Centre
    Silk St EC2; tube: Barbican (☎ 0171-638 8891, or for recorded information phone ☎ 01771-628 2295).
Institute for Contemporary Arts (ICA)
    Nash House, The Mall SW1; tube: Piccadilly Circus (☎ 0171-930 3647). An interesting, innovative complex including a small bookshop, an art gallery, cinema, bar, café and theatre. There is invariably something worthwhile to see, the bar and restaurant are good value, and there's a young and relaxed crowd. A day pass is £1.50, £1 with any ticket purchase.

BRITAIN

Riverside Studios complex

Crisp Rd W6; tube: Hammersmith (☎ 0181-741 2255). Originally a TV studio, it is now an innovative centre with an excellent gallery, a café and restaurant, a bar, two performance spaces (often showing dance or theatre), an art gallery and a bookshop.

South Bank Centre

Belvedere Rd, Waterloo SE1; tube: Embankment (☎ 0171-928 3002). London's centre for classical music, South Bank includes the Royal Festival Hall, Queen Elizabeth Hall, Purcell Room, Hayward Gallery, the National Film Theatre, the National Theatre, the excellent but expensive Museum of the Moving Image, and a range of restaurants and cafés. There are free foyer events every day from 12.30 to 2 pm.

Laundry There are countless laundries and there should be one within walking distance of your accommodation. Try Forco at 60 Parkway in Camden Town; Bendix at 395 Kings Rd in Chelsea; Notting Hill Launderette at 12 Notting Hill Gate.

Medical Services Reciprocal arrangements within the EU and with Australia and New Zealand mean that citizens of these countries do not pay for emergency medical treatment. Non EU residents would however have to pay if admitted to a hospital ward. Regardless of nationality, anyone should receive free emergency treatment if it's a simple matter like bandaging a cut.

Hospitals with 24-hour emergency departments include:

Guy's Hospital

St Thomas St, SE1; tube: London Bridge (☎ 0171-955 5000)

St Bartholomew's Hospital (Barts)

West Smithfield, EC1; tube: Farringdon Rd (☎ 0171-601 8888)

St Thomas' Hospital

Lambeth Palace Rd, SE1; tube: Waterloo (☎ 0171-928 9292)

University College Hospital

Gower St, W1; tube: Euston Sq (☎ 0171-387 9300)

Emergency dental treatment is also available at Guy's Hospital.

Visas & Immunisation A number of companies have visa and medical (immunisation) services; a few advertise in *TNT Magazine*. Charges can differ widely. Trailfinders (☎ 0171-938 3999), 194 Kensington High St W8, has both a visa service and an immunisation centre. The International Medical Centre (☎ 0171-486 3063) has two branches, including one at the Top Deck (Deckers) headquarters, 131 Earl's Court Rd SW5. Top Deck also hosts the Rapid Visa Service (☎ 0171-373 3026). Nomad (☎ 0171-889 7014), 3 Turnpike Lane N8, sells travel equipment and medical kits, and gives immunisations (Saturday only).

Medical & Emergency Services Dial ☎ 999 for fire, police or ambulance. The local police station can advise you of the nearest late-night pharmacy.

Dangers & Annoyances London is not an especially dangerous city and there are no areas that need to be avoided, but travellers should take all reasonable precautions against thieves who may operate on the streets in tourist locations. Women should be careful about travelling alone after pub closing hours, particularly in areas off the main tourist tracks.

Left Luggage See the London Getting Around section later in this chapter for left-luggage facilities at Heathrow and Gatwick airports. The main train stations also have left-luggage facilities.

Things to See & Do
Walking Tour The centre of London can easily be explored on foot. The following tour could be covered in a day, but it does not allow you the chance to explore any of the individual sights in detail; it will, however, give you an introduction to the West End and Westminster.

Start at **St Paul's Cathedral**, Christopher Wren's masterpiece that was completed in 1710. Entry to the cathedral and crypt costs £3.60, or £6 if you wish to see the galleries (which give you access to one of the best views of London). Unless you're feeling very energetic, catch a tube from St Paul's tube station to Covent Garden (west on the Central line to Holborn, then west on the Piccadilly line).

Covent Garden's piazza, once London's fruit and vegetable market, has been restored as a bustling tourist attraction. It's one of the very few places in London where pedestrians rule, and you can watch the buskers for a few coins and the tourists for free.

Return to the tube station and turn left into Long Acre (look for Stanfords bookshop on your left) and continue across Charing Cross Rd to **Leicester Square** with its cinemas and franchise food. Note the Leicester Square Theatre Ticket Booth, which sells half-price tickets on the day of performance.

Continue along Coventry St, past the Trocadero and Madame Tussaud's Rock Circus, until you get to **Piccadilly Circus**, with Tower Records, the best music shop in London. Shaftesbury Ave enters the circus on the north-eastern corner, with a collection of cheap kebab/pizza counters. This street lined with theatres runs back into Soho, with its myriad restaurants. Regent St curves out of the north-western corner.

Continue west along Piccadilly to the Royal Academy of Arts and St James' Church (with its excellent cheap restaurant). Detour into the extraordinary **Burlington Arcade**, just after the academy; beware the uniformed beadles (private 'police') who, amongst other things, are supposed to stop you whistling.

Return to Piccadilly and continue until you get to St James' St on your left. This takes you down to **St James' Palace**, the royal home from 1660 to 1837 until it was judged insufficiently impressive. Skirt around its eastern side and you come to the Mall.

Trafalgar Square is to the east, **Buckingham Palace** to the west. From 3 April to 3 August the changing of the guard happens daily at 11.30 am; from August to April it is at 11.30 am on alternate days. The best place to be is by the gates of Buckingham House, but the crowds are awesome. Cross back into St James' Park, the most beautiful in London, and follow the lake to its eastern end. Turn right onto Horse Guards Rd. This takes you past the **Cabinet War Rooms** (£4), which give an extraordinary insight into the dark days of WWII.

Continue along Horse Guards Rd and then turn left onto Great George St, which takes you through to beautiful Westminster Abbey, the Houses of Parliament and Westminster Bridge. **Westminster Abbey** is so rich in history you need half a day to do it justice. The coronation chair, where all but two monarchs since 1066 have been crowned, is behind the altar, and many greats – from Darwin to Chaucer – have been buried here. An admission fee (£4) is charged for the royal chapels; alternatively, there are guided tours for £7. The best way to soak in the atmosphere is to attend evensong, which takes place at 5 pm on Monday, Tuesday, Thursday and Friday, and 3 pm on Saturday and Sunday.

The **Houses of Parliament** and the clock tower (actually its bell), **Big Ben**, were built in the 19th century in mock medieval style. The best way to get into the building is to attend the Commons or Lords visitors' galleries during a Parliamentary debate. Phone ☎ 0171-219 4272 to find out if anything is happening.

Walking away from Westminster Bridge, turn right into Parliament St, which becomes Whitehall. On your left, Downing St has an ordinary-looking house at **No 10** that offers temporary accommodation to prime ministers. Further along on the right is the Inigo Jones-designed **Banqueting House**, outside which Charles I was beheaded. Continue past the **Horse Guards**, where you can see a changing of the guard (less crowded than Buck House) at 11 am Monday to Saturday, 10 am on Sunday.

Finally, you reach **Trafalgar Square** and Nelson's Column. The National Gallery and National Portrait Gallery are on the northern side.

River Tour If walking doesn't seem like a good idea, consider catching a boat from Westminster Pier (beside Westminster Bridge) down the river to Greenwich (every half-hour from 10 am, single/return £4.40/5.40). You pass the site of Shakespeare's Globe Theatre, stop at the Tower of London, and continue under Tower Bridge and past many famous docks.

Greenwich can absorb the best part of a day. Start with the *Cutty Sark* (£3.25), the only surviving tea and wool clipper and arguably one of the most beautiful ships ever built. Wander around the Greenwich market, then visit the **Queen's House**, a Palladian masterpiece designed in 1616 by Inigo Jones. If you're interested in boats and naval history, continue to the **National Maritime Museum** (£5.50 each for the museum, house and observatory). The **Royal Naval College**, beside the river, was designed by Wren; open daily from 2.30 to 4.45 pm; free.

BRITAIN

West End

0   125   250 m
0   125   250 yards

To Australia
House &
the City

River Thames

Victoria
Embankment
Gardens

Victoria Embankment

Northumberland Ave

Charing Cross

To Buckingham
Palace & Victoria

Pall Mall East

Cockspur Street

Trafalgar Square

Charing Cross Road

Leicester Square

Piccadilly Circus

Haymarket

Regent Street

Waterloo Place

ST JAMES'

Shaftesbury Avenue

Cambridge Circus

SOHO

Oxford Circus

Oxford Street

Wardour Street

Dean Street

Frith Street

Greek Street

Old Compton Street

Brewer Street

Berwick Street

Wardour Street

Marshall Street

Carnaby Street

Kingly Street

Regent Street

Savile Row

Old Bond Street

New Bond Street

Conduit Street

Dover Street

Burlington Arcade

Sackville Street

Piccadilly

Duke of York St

St James's Sq

Jermyn Street

Charles II Street

King St

Charing Cross Road

Shaftesbury Avenue

Gerrard Street

New Oxford Street

High Holborn

To Bloomsbury

St Giles High Street

Neal Street

Endell Street

Shelton Street

Long Acre

Drury Lane

Bow Street

Russell Street

Tavistock Street

Exeter Street

Southampton St

Maiden Lane

Bedford Street

Garrick Street

King Street

St Martins Lane

Strand

John Adam Street

Villiers Street

Craven Street

Savoy

William IV Street

Irving Street

St Martin's Place

To Marble Arch

To Regent St

Mortimer St

Great Portland St

Great Titchfield St

Mortimer Street

Wells St

Poland Street

Lexington Street

Brewer Street

Great Pulteney St

Beak Street

Golden Square

Air St

Sherwood St

Gt Windmill St

Rupert Street

Coventry St

Whitcomb St

Panton St

Oxendon St

See Westminster &
Pimlico Map

Restricted access, 7am–7pm, Monday to Friday

PLACES TO STAY			
4	Oxford St Youth Hostel		

PLACES TO EAT			
5	Pizza Express		
6	Nusa Dua		
10	Mildred's		
13	Living Room		
15	Pollo		
16	Café Pasta		
17	Neal's Yard Bakery & Tea Room		
18	Food for Thought		
19	Diana's Diner		
21	La Perla		
24	Bunjies		
29	Hamine		
30	Melati		
31	New Piccadilly		
34	The Criterion		
35	Wong Kei		
36	Poons		
40	The Wren at St James		

46	Café in the Crypt

OTHER	
1	Oxford Circus Tube Station
2	100 Club
3	Council Travel
7	Tottenham Court Rd Tube Station
8	Astoria
9	Velvet Underground
11	Borderline
12	Foyle's Bookshop
14	Marquee
20	Hamleys
22	Berwick St Market
23	Ronnie Scott's
25	Covent Garden Tube Station
26	Stanfords Bookshop
27	Covent Garden
28	YHA Headquarters Adventure Shop

32	Piccadilly Circus Tube Station
33	Rock Circus
37	Leicester Square Tube Station
38	Museum of Mankind
39	Royal Academy of Arts
41	British Travel Centre
42	American Express
43	National Gallery
44	National Portrait Gallery
45	Trafalgar Square Post Office
47	New Zealand House
48	Scottish Tourist Board
49	Canada House
50	Charing Cross Tube Station
51	South Africa House
52	Charing Cross Train & Tube Station
53	Embankment Tube Station

Climb the hill behind the museum to the **Old Royal Observatory**. A brass strip in the observatory courtyard marks the prime meridian that divides the world into eastern and western hemispheres. There are great views over the Docklands – with the massive Canary Wharf development just over the river – and back to London.

Walk back down the hill and through the Greenwich foot tunnel (near the *Cutty Sark)* to Island Gardens. From this side of the river there is a superb view of the Naval College and the Queen's House – a classic arrangement of buildings. The Docklands Light Railway whisks above ground from Island Gardens back to Tower Gateway, and there are good views of the new Docklands developments. Unfortunately, it only runs on weekdays (buses run on weekends); Zone 1 & 2 travelcards are valid.

If you are still raring to go, you could dash in to the **Tower of London**. The Tower dates from 1078, when William the Conqueror began to construct the White Tower. The castle was turned into an enormous concentric fortress by Henry III; it has been a fortress, royal residence and prison. It now houses the crown jewels and royal armoury, and there are inevitably big crowds (visit during the week); entry is £8.30/6.25. Or, on Sunday, visit Petticoat Lane market, a short walk north up the Minories.

Museums The greatest of them all is the British Museum with its unparalleled Egyptian, Mesopotamian, Greek and Roman collections. London's main museum precinct, however, is in Kensington, just north of the South Kensington tube station; the brilliant Victoria & Albert Museum (decorative arts) and the rejuvenated Science, Natural History and Geological museums (animated dinosaurs and interactive displays) are all highly recommended.

The **British Museum**, Great Russell St WC1 (tube: Tottenham Court Rd), has the world's greatest collection of antiquities; open from 10 am to 5 pm Monday to Saturday, 2.30 to 6 pm on Sunday; free.

The **Victoria & Albert Museum**, Cromwell Rd SW7 (tube: South Kensington), has the world's greatest collection of decorative arts, including clothes; open from 10 am to 5.50 pm Tuesday to Sunday, noon to 5.50 pm on Monday; £4.50 donation requested. The V&A has the best café in the Kensington museums.

The **Museum of London**, 150 London Wall EC2 (tube: St Paul's), displays the history of London, from the Romans on; open 10 am to 6 pm Tuesday to Saturday, noon to 6 pm on Sunday; £3.50.

The **Imperial War Museum**, Lambeth Rd SE1 (tube: Lambeth North), has an extraordinary collection and some amazing re-creations

BRITAIN

(the 'Blitz Experience' is recommended); open from 10 am to 6 pm daily; £4.10.

The **Museum of the Moving Image (MOMI)**, South Bank Centre SE1 (tube: Embankment, then cross the foot and rail bridge over the Thames), deals with the history of film and TV with interactive displays; open daily from 10 am to 6 pm; £5.95.

The **Museum of Mankind**, 6 Burlington Gardens W1 (tube: Piccadilly Circus), presents a series of fascinating exhibitions that illustrate non-Western societies and cultures. The collections come from the Americas, Africa, parts of Asia and Europe, and the Pacific; open from 10 am to 5 pm Monday to Saturday, and from 2.30 to 6 pm on Sunday; free.

Galleries A visit to the National and Tate galleries is a must, but there are also likely to be interesting exhibitions at the Hayward Gallery (South Bank Centre), the ICA (see Cultural Centres), Riverside Studios and the Royal Academy of Arts – among many others. Check *Time Out* for current shows.

The **National Gallery**, Trafalgar Square (tube: Charing Cross), covers all leading European schools from the 13th to 20th centuries; open from 10 am to 6 pm Monday to Saturday, 2 to 6 pm on Sunday; free.

The **Courtauld Institute Galleries**, Somerset House, the Strand (tube: Temple), has an excellent collection of postimpressionists (Cézanne, Gauguin, Van Gogh); open from 10 am to 6 pm Monday to Saturday, 2 to 6 pm on Sunday; £3.

The **Tate Gallery**, Millbank SW11 (tube: Pimlico), features the history of British art, especially Turner, and international modern art; open from 10 am to 5.50 pm Monday to Saturday, 2 to 5.50 pm on Sunday; free.

Markets The markets are where you see London life at its best; they're bustling, interesting and full of character(s).

Berwick St (tube: Piccadilly) in Soho is one of the last strongholds of real life in the West End. The stall holders are as theatrical as you can find, and the fruit and vegetables are among the best and cheapest in London (stock up for a picnic). There are also some good record shops.

Camden (tube: Camden Town) attracts huge crowds all weekend. It's trendy, but a lot of fun. The Electric Ballroom on High St sells second-hand clothes from 9 am on Sunday, but all you need to do is start at Camden Lock and follow your nose.

Petticoat Lane, Middlesex St (tube: Aldgate), is open from 9 am to 2 pm on Sunday. It's the home of the cockney, and has a wide selection of clothing (particularly leather) and odds and ends.

Brick Lane (tube: Aldgate East), open from 5 am to 2 pm on Sunday, is cheap, chaotic and very East End. It's now dominated by Bengalis, but there are still some fresh bagels to be found (at the northern end, away from Whitechapel).

Portobello Rd (tube: Ladbroke Grove) has fruit and vegetables from 8 am to 5 pm Monday to Saturday except Thursday afternoon, and general goods from 8 am to 3 pm on Friday and from 8 am to 5 pm on Saturday. There are reasonable second-hand stalls at the Westway end, and expensive antiques at the Notting Hill end.

Brixton (tube: Brixton) is open from 9 am to 5.30 pm Monday to Saturday except Wednesday afternoon. Barrows are piled high with fruit and vegetables, and there are lively arcades that *must* be explored – the Caribbean comes to London.

Other Sights A number of London's major sights have been covered in the Walking Tour and River Tour sections. All visitors, but especially shoestringers, should make the most of London's glorious parks. A long walk starting at St James' and continuing through Green, Hyde, Kensington and Holland parks will banish any urban blues.

Hyde Park is central London's largest park. Row a boat on the Serpentine, listen to a military band (on summer Sundays) or heckle the soapbox orators on Sundays at Speakers' Corner (Marble Arch corner).

Harrods, Knightsbridge SW1 (tube: Knightsbridge), is a shop, but not just any shop. Wander through the double-storey Egyptian room on the ground floor that stocks Egyptian merchandise of every kind.

Hamleys, 188 Regent St (tube: Oxford Circus), is the biggest toy shop in the world, for children aged three months to 90 years.

Hampton Court Palace is the grandest Tudor house in the country. Built by Cardinal Wolsey in 1514 and 'adopted' by Henry VIII, it is a beautiful mixture of architectural styles – from Henry's splendid Great Hall to the State Apartments built for King William III and Queen Mary II by Wren. The superb palace grounds, near the Thames, include deer and a 300-year-old maze. It's open every day from 9.30 am to 6 pm (4.30 pm in winter) and admission is £7.50; the grounds are free. There are trains every half-hour from Waterloo (£3.90 return, Zone 6), or you can catch a ferry from Westminster Pier. Ferries sail from April to October at 10.30 and 11.15 am, and noon; they take 3½ hours and cost £7.

Kew Gardens (tube: Kew Gardens, Zone 3), the Royal Botanic Gardens, are a beautiful, restful escape from the real world. Entry costs £5. As an alternative to the tube, ferries sail from Westminster Pier every 30 minutes from 10.15 am to 2.30 pm (April to October). They take 1½ hours and cost £5. While you're out here, cross Kew Bridge and walk to the right along the (left) bank of the Thames, where there are a number of pleasant riverside pubs.

Tourist Traps If you feel jaded and uninspired by history and culture, perhaps you need to spend money and see the human zoo at Madame Tussaud's and the Rock Circus.

London Zoo (☎ 0171-722 3333) in Regent's Park has had a struggle to survive and is now trying to concentrate on conservation issues. The cages are still pretty small and admission is expensive: £7.

Madame Tussaud's (☎ 0171-935 6861), Marylebone Rd (tube: Baker St), is permanently crowded, proving that people do want to see wax versions of the people they see on TV every day. Why? Admission is £8.75. It opens at 9 am, but the queues are horrendous, so get there at 8.30 am.

Rock Circus (☎ 0171-734 8025), London Pavilion, Piccadilly Circus, is a high-tech rock'n'roll version of Tussaud's. The robots are remarkable, and it is, after all, as close as you will ever get to John Lennon or Madonna. Admission is £7.50.

Organised Tours
A number of companies offer tours around the main sights in double-decker buses. They're all expensive and are really only worth considering if you've either got plenty of money or you're only going to be in London for a day or two.

The Original London Sightseeing Tour (☎ 0171-222 1234) has a 1½-hour tour departing from Victoria St near Victoria station (as well as a number of other stops). They have a system where you can buy a ticket from Piccadilly and Oxford Circus TICs for £8; other TICs charge £9 and on the bus you pay £10. London Plus has a more extensive route and you can hop on and off the buses at a number of major attractions. Tickets are the same prices.

Places to Stay
Whichever way you cut it, accommodation in London is ridiculously expensive. In spite of the shoestring take-it-as-it-comes ethos, it is worth booking a night or two's accommodation, especially in July and August. The official TICs at the airports and at Victoria station can arrange last-minute bookings, but they charge £5 for a booking. In summer, the Victoria office has enormous queues, but there are also cheaper, less busy, private operators who charge as much as £5. Outside the station on Buckingham Palace Rd towards the coach station, Accommodation Express (☎ 0171-233 8139) has free bookings and a courtesy bus for a number of private hostels.

Hostel dorm accommodation will cost from £10 to £19.75. You can expect to pay £25/30 for very basic singles/doubles without bathroom, £25/35 with bathroom. There are, of course, some superb hotels in London, but they are *very* expensive. If you have enough money for one or two splurges wait until you get into the countryside, where you will get much better value.

The TICs also have a useful booklet on budget accommodation – get it from the BTA before you leave home.

Camping *Tent City* (☎ 0181-743 5708), Old Oak Common Lane W3 (tube: East Acton, Central line), is the cheapest option in London, short of sleeping rough. There are dormitory-style tents with beds for £5.50. It's open from June through August and you are advised to book. It also has tent sites but doesn't take

BRITAIN

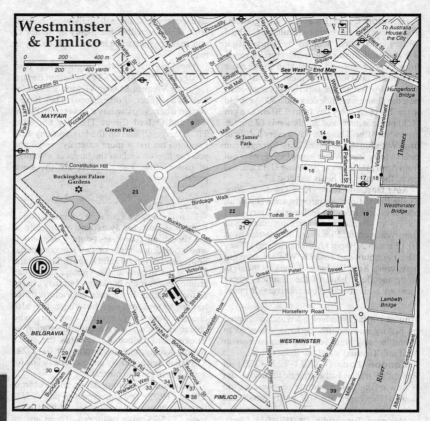

Westminster & Pimlico

0   200   400 m
0   200   400 yards

MAYFAIR

Green Park

Curzon St

Berkeley St

Burlington Arc

Piccadilly

Jermyn Street

St James's Street

Pall Mall

St James' Square

Regent St

Haymarket

Waterloo Pl

Trafalgar Square

Strand

Villers St

To Australia House & the City

See West End Map

Whitehall

Horse Guards Rd

Downing St

Parliament St

Hungerford Bridge

Thames

Embankment

Victoria

Park Lane

Piccadilly

Constitution Hill

Buckingham Palace Gardens

Grosvenor Place

The Mall

St James' Park

Birdcage Walk

Buckingham Gate

Victoria

Tothill St

Parliament Square

Westminster Bridge

Westminster

Great Peter Street

Millbank

Lambeth Bridge

Horseferry Road

WESTMINSTER

Eccleston St

BELGRAVIA

Wilton Rd

Vauxhall Bridge Road

Francis Street

Rochester Row

Regency Street

John Islip Street

Millbank

River

Embankment

Albert

Elizabeth St

Buckingham Palace Road

Belgrave Rd

Warwick Way

Tachbrook

PIMLICO

caravans or camper vans. They also have a place in Millfield Rd E5 where a pitch for a tent or caravan or van is £5.

Lee Valley Park, Picketts Lock Sport & Leisure Centre (☎ 0181-345 6666), Picketts Lock Lane, Edmonton N9, has 200 pitches for tents or caravans. It's open all year and the nightly charge is £4.75 per person, plus £2.20 for electricity.

YHA Hostels There are presently seven YHA hostels in London, but they are crowded during summer. Sometimes they can't even accept advance bookings. If they have room, they all

take advance bookings by phone (if you pay by Visa or MasterCard). They do hold some beds for those who wander in on the day, but wander in early, and be prepared to queue. They all offer 24-hour access. Adults will have to pay £12.25 to £19.75, juniors £8.50 to £16.55.

You can join the association at the YHA London headquarters (☎ 0171-836 8541), 14 Southampton St WC2 (tube: Covent Garden), where there's also a bookshop, excellent outdoor equipment and a branch of Campus Travel. Telephone here also to find out about a new 150-bed hostel that should be opening soon in Euston Rd. It will be called *St Pancras International*.

PLACES TO STAY		4	Charing Cross Train &	17	Westminster Tube
31	Brindle House Hotel		Tube Station		Station
32	Belgrave House Hotel	5	Embankment Tube	18	Westminster Pier
33	Hamilton House		Station	19	House of Parliament
34	Victoria Hotel	6	Thomas Cook	20	Westminster Abbey
38	Luna & Simone Hotels	7	Green Park Tube	21	St James' Park Tube
			Station		Station
PLACES TO EAT		8	Hyde Park Corner	22	Home Office
29	The Well		Tube Station	23	Buckingham Palace
35	Manners	9	St James' Palace	24	London Student Travel
36	Mekong	10	ICA (Institute for	25	American Express
37	O Sole Mio & Grumbles		Contemporary Arts)	26	Westminster Cathedral
		11	Admiralty Arch	27	Victoria Train & Tube
OTHER		12	Horse Guards		Station
1	Piccadilly Circus Tube	13	Banqueting House	28	Accommodation
	Station	14	No 10 Downing St		Express
2	Post Office	15	Cenotaph War	30	Victoria Coach Station
3	Charing Cross Tube		Memorial	39	Tate Gallery
	Station	16	Cabinet War Rooms		

Rotherhithe (☎ 0171-232 2114), Island Yard, Salter Rd SE16 (tube: Rotherhithe), is an impressive, purpose-built hostel. Unfortunately, it's a bit far out, and the area is not great; transport is fair. On the other hand, the hostel is good; rooms are mainly six-bed, although there are some fours and a few doubles; all have *en suite* bathrooms. There's a cheap restaurant as well as kitchen facilities. Rates for seniors/juniors are £19.75/16.55.

Carter Lane (☎ 0171-236 4965), 36 Carter Lane EC4 (tube: St Paul's), is virtually next door to St Paul's Cathedral in an intelligently restored old building, which was the cathedral choir's school. The position and the hostel are excellent, although this end of town does get pretty quiet outside working hours. Rooms are mainly four, three or two beds. There's a cafeteria and kitchen. Rates are £19.75/16.55.

Earl's Court (☎ 0171-373 7083), 38 Bolton Gardens SW5 (tube: Earl's Court), is an old townhouse in a tacky, though lively, part of town; it is not the best equipped of the hostels, however. Rooms are mainly 10-bed dorms. There's a cafeteria. Rates are £17.70/15.55.

Hampstead Heath (☎ 0171-081-458 9054), 4 Wellgarth Rd NW11 (tube: Golders Green), is in a beautiful setting with a well-kept garden, although it is a bit isolated. The dorms are comfortable, and each room has a basin with hot and cold water. There's a rather average cafeteria. Rates are £14.40/12.30.

Highgate Village (☎ 0181-340 1831), 84 Highgate West Hill N6 (tube: Archway), is in an attractive Georgian house close to Hampstead Heath; once again it is a bit isolated. There are kitchen facilities, but no evening meals. It's the cheapest YHA option in London with rates at £12.25/8.50.

Holland House (☎ 0171-937 0748), Holland Walk, Kensington W8 (tube: High St Kensington), has a great location in the middle of Holland Park and is close to everything. It's large, very busy, and rather institutional, but the position really can't be beaten. There's a cafeteria. Rates are £17.70/15.55.

Oxford St (☎ 0171-734 1618), 14-18 Noel St W1 (tube: Oxford Circus), is the most basic of the London hostels, but it is right in the centre of town. There's a large kitchen, but no meals. Rates are £17.30/14.10.

University Colleges University halls of residence are let to nonstudents during the holidays, usually from June to September. They're a bit more expensive than the HI/YHA hostels, but you usually get a single room (there are a small number of doubles) with shared facilities, plus breakfast. Bookings are coordinated by the British Universities Accommodation Consortium (BUAC; ☎ 0115-950 4571), Box 653, University Park, Nottingham NG7 2RD, although you can also contact the colleges direct.

BRITAIN

The London School of Economics (Room B508, LSE, Houghton Street, WC2A 2AE) has a number of its halls available at Easter and summer. *Carr Saunders Hall* (☎ 0171-323 9712), 18-24 Fitzroy St W1 (tube: Great Portland St), is not the greatest part of town, but it's central enough; open Easter and summer holiday; singles/doubles with full breakfast are £17.50/30 over Easter, £22/42 in the summer. Self-catering flats of different sizes are also available on a weekly basis in the summer only, ranging from £238 for a two person flat to £539 for five persons. *High Holborn* (☎ 0171-379 5589), 178 High Holborn WC1 (tube: Holborn), is centrally located and has self-catering singles/doubles for £25/43, with continental breakfast, in the summer only. *Passfield Hall* (☎ 0171-387 3584), Endsleigh Place WC1 (tube: Euston), consists of 10 late-Georgian houses in the heart of Bloomsbury. A bed and full breakfast is £17.50/30 at Easter, £19/35 in the summer. Similar rates apply at *Rosebery Avenue Hall* (☎ 0171-278 3251), 90 Rosebery Ave EC1 (tube: Angel).

Imperial College of Science & Technology (☎ 0171-589 5111), 15 Prince's Gardens SW7 (tube: South Kensington), is in a brilliant position near the Kensington museums; it's open Easter and summer; B&B costs £25/40.

Regent College (☎ 0171-487 7483), Inner Circle, Regent's Park NW1 (tube: Baker St), is a converted Regency manor right in the middle of beautiful Regent's Park, convenient to Camden and central London; it's open May to September; singles/doubles cost £25/36.

John Adams Hall (☎ 0171-387 4086), 15-23 Endsleigh St WC1 (tube: Euston), is central and facilities include a swimming pool; it's open Easter and summer; B&B is £19 per night for more than seven nights, £21.40 for less.

King's Campus Vacation Bureau (☎ 0171-351 6011), 552 Kings Rd SW10 0UA, administers bookings for a number of central King's College residence halls. Rates range from £14 to £23 per person, include access to excellent facilities, and most include a continental breakfast.

Finsbury Residences (☎ 0171-477 8811), Bastwick St EC1 (tube: Old Street), comprises two modern halls belonging to City University. A bed and continental breakfast is £19.50 per person, £97.50 a week; rooms are available over Christmas, Easter and the summer and evening meals are also available.

University of Westminster (☎ 0171-911 5000), 35 Marylebone Rd NW1 (tube: Marylebone), has singles and doubles for £15.70 per person under 26, £21.50 over 26, and £3 for an optional continental breakfast.

Private Hostels There are a number of hotels/hostels that operate on the simple principle that if you squash six people in a room and charge them £10 each you make more profit than if you have a couple at £20 per person. They are not suitable for fastidious, antisocial claustrophobics.

In terms of facilities offered, most of the hostels don't vary much. Most have three or four small bunk beds jammed into a room, a small kitchen and some kind of lounge room. Some have budget restaurants and a few even have a bar. They are cheaper and much more relaxed than the official YHA hostels, but the standards are more hit and miss. Problems with theft are relatively unusual, but be careful with your possessions and deposit your valuables in the office safe. Some hostels have an irresponsible attitude to fire safety – check that the fire escapes are accessible.

Apart from noise levels, safety, and cleanliness, the most important variable is the atmosphere. This can change by the week, as to a certain extent it is dependent on the people who happen to be staying. If you're not happy with your first pick, try somewhere new.

The largest number of private hostels are in Earl's Court (SW5), which consequently has the biggest backpacker scene, but there are also some in Paddington and Bayswater (W2), Notting Hill and Holland Park (W11), Bloomsbury (WC1) and Pimlico (SW1). With the possible exception of Notting Hill and Bloomsbury, all these areas are pretty seedy. Notting Hill and Bayswater are both central and close to Hyde Park; Notting Hill, in particular, is a great part of London.

Private Hostels – Notting Hill The *Palace Hotel* (☎ 0171-221 5628), 31 Palace Court W2 (tube: Notting Hill Gate), has dorm beds for £10. It has a pleasant and convenient location and isn't quite as run-down and manic as some of the others.

The *London Independent Hostel* (☎ 0171-229 4238), 41 Holland Park W11 (tube:

Holland Park), is on an elegant street and is well positioned. It's also good value (all things being relative) with dorms for £8, quads for £9, triples for £10 and doubles for £11 per person.

The *Centre Français* (☎ 0171-221 8134), 61 Chepstow Place W2 (tube: Notting Hill Gate), is like a cross between a YHA hostel and a college residence. It's immaculately maintained, comfortable in an institutional sort of way, and only about half the clientele is French. A bed in a bright and cheery dorm of eight beds is £11.70, and in a three or four-bed dorm it's £15. The singles/doubles (£22.50/36) are spartan, but they do include washbasins and desks.

Private Hostels – Earl's Court The *Curzon House Hotel* (☎ 0171-581 2116), 58 Courtfield Gardens SW5 (tube: Gloucester Rd), is one of the best private hostels – much loved by *Let's Go* researchers, but don't hold that against it. There's a relaxed and friendly atmosphere. Dorms are £13 per person, and singles/doubles with facilities are £23/36.

The *Chelsea Hotel* (☎ 0171-244 6892), 33 Earl's Court Square SW5 (tube: Earl's Court), is a classic hostel. There's a restaurant with meals for £3, and hundreds of cheery backpackers wandering around. They have some good-value singles and doubles as well as dorms. A dorm bed is £10, a twin is £27 and a single is £16.

Regency Court Hotel (☎ 0171-244 6615), 14 Penywern Rd SW5 (tube: Earl's Court), is in need of renovation and some travellers have a low opinion of the place. Dorms are £10; doubles £20; triples £40 and quads £50. A better bet is *Windsor House* (☎ 0171-373 9087) next door at 12 Penywern Rd. A dorm bed is £10, a single £28, a double £38 and triples £48, all including a breakfast.

The *Court Hotels* (tube: Earl's Court), at 194-196 Earl's Court Rd SW5 (☎ 0171-373 0027) and 17-19 Kempsford Gardens (☎ 0171-373 2174), are both under Australasian management and have well-equipped kitchens and TV in most rooms. A dorm bed is £11, singles/doubles are £21/24, and weekly rates are available.

Private Hostels – Paddington & Bayswater The *Palace Court Hotel* (☎ 0171-727 4412 or ☎ 0171-221 9228), 64 Prince's Square W2 (tube: Bayswater), is in a good position, and has clean rooms and a good atmosphere. The bar is open until late for guests, and there's a budget restaurant. Arrive early if you can. You'll pay £9 for a quad, and £12 for a twin. Prices drop outside summer. Ring for details of the hotel's free minibus from Victoria.

The *Quest Hotel* (☎ 0171-229 7782), 45 Queensborough Terrace W2 (tube: Bayswater), is just around the corner from all the action on Queensway and a minute from Hyde Park. It has a friendly atmosphere and a pool table, but it's pretty crowded. There are kitchen facilities; dorms cost £11.50 and £12.50 and a limited number of beds are available on a weekly basis for about £2 less a night.

Next door, the *Royal Hotel* (☎ 0171-229 7225), 43 Queensborough Terrace W2 (tube: Bayswater), is much like many other hostels, but they do make an effort not to overcrowd the rooms. As a result, many people stay for quite long periods of time. A very basic double is £9 per person, and quads are £8 per person.

Private Hostels – Bloomsbury The *Museum Inn* (☎ 0171-580 5360), 27 Montague St WC1 (tube: Holborn), has an excellent position opposite the British Museum. There's a party atmosphere and the management is friendly. Quite a few rooms have colour TVs, there are decent kitchen facilities, and a basic breakfast is included in the price: £17 per person in the one double, £15 in a four-bed dorm and £13 in a nine-bed dorm.

The *International Students House* (☎ 0171-631 8300), 229 Great Portland St W1 (tube: Great Portland St), is really in a different class, more like a university residential college. For a start you can get singles or doubles; they're ordinary, but clean. There are excellent facilities and a friendly atmosphere – you don't have to be a student, and it's open all year. B&B ranges from £23.40 for a single to £14 for a quad. Book in advance.

Private Hostels – Pimlico The *Victoria Hotel* (☎ 0171-834 3077), 71 Belgrave Rd SW1 (tube: Victoria), is a 15-minute walk from Victoria station. It has been criticised for being overcrowded and poorly maintained but it may be worth considering if you arrive in London

BRITAIN

late at night, or have to leave early in the morning. Reception is open 24 hours. It's cheerful and basic, and beds are around £14.

Hotels & B&Bs Bloomsbury (WC1), Bayswater (W2), Paddington (W2), Pimlico (SW1) and Earl's Court (SW5) are the centres for budget hotels. Each area has advantages and disadvantages, but the prices remain pretty consistent. If you want an attached bathroom you will be lucky to find anything for less than £25, even in winter.

Outside the high season, prices are nearly always negotiable; don't be afraid to ask for the 'best' price and for a discount if you are either staying more than a couple of nights or don't want a cooked breakfast. In July, August and September prices can jump by 25%, and it is definitely worth phoning ahead. Many of the cheapies don't take credit cards.

B&Bs in Londoners' private houses can be good value; double-room prices range from £14 to £30 per person per night. At £14 you would be quite a distance out and share a bathroom, at £16 a little closer, at £18 you should be in a central location like Bloomsbury, and from £25 to £30 in a central area with a private bathroom.

Bookings (minimum three days) can be made free in advance through London Homestead Services (☎ 0181-949 4455, 24 hours), Coombe Wood Rd, Kingston-upon-Thames, Surrey KT2 7. Bed & Breakfast (GB) (☎ 01491-578803), PO Box 66, Henley-on-Thames RG9 1XS specialises in central London. Or contact the BTA or local TICs.

Hotels & B&Bs – Notting Hill The *Holland Park Hotel* (☎ 0171-792 0216), 6 Ladbroke Terrace W11 (tube: Notting Hill Gate), has a great position on a quiet street near Holland Park and the hubbub of Notting Hill. The rooms are very pleasant and it's particularly good value, with singles/doubles without bathroom for £40/54, and with bathroom for £54/72.

At the beginning of Portobello Rd, the *Gate Hotel* (☎ 0171-221 2403), 6 Portobello Rd W11 (tube: Notting Hill Gate), has classic frilly English décor in an old townhouse. Rooms are well equipped and they all have bathrooms. Singles/doubles are £38/70.

It's stretching the definition to put the *Hillgate Hotel* (☎ 0171-221 3433), 6 Pembridge Gardens W2 (tube: Notting Hill Gate), in a shoestring guide, but it is a proper hotel, with a great position. Singles/doubles are £50/60.

Hotels & B&Bs – Earl's Court has been a hang-out for refugees from the far-flung corners of the empire for a long time. At one stage it was infamous as Kangaroo Valley, but now Australians are less conspicuous than Africans, Arabs and Indians. Most people seem to be in transit, and it shows in the grubby, unloved streets. It's relatively convenient, although not quite as convenient as the other districts in this guide – it's not really within walking distance of many places you will want to be, so you're heavily dependent on the tube.

The *Philbeach Hotel* (☎ 0171-373 1244), 30 Philbeach Gardens SW5 (tube: Earl's Court), is a pleasant, well-decorated hotel, popular with a gay and lesbian clientele. There's a decent restaurant and bar and a nice garden. Singles with/without bathroom are £50/45; doubles are £65/55.

The *York House Hotel* (☎ 0171-373 7519), 27 Philbeach Gardens SW5, just down the street from the Philbeach (tube: Earl's Court), is relatively cheap, but you get what you pay for. The rooms are basic, although some have showers. Singles/doubles without bath are £26/42; doubles/triples with bath are £58/68.

London Tourist Hotel (☎ 0171-370 4356), 15 Penywern Rd SW5 (tube: Earl's Court), is a pleasant mid-range hotel. Singles/doubles with bathroom are £39/54.

The *Shellbourne Hotel* (☎ 0171-373 5161), 1 Lexham Gardens W8 (tube: Gloucester Rd), is tatty but clean, and the rooms are well equipped for their price – TVs, showers, direct-dial telephones – and you get a full breakfast. Singles/doubles/triples are £26/37/60.

The *Merlyn Court Hotel* (☎ 0171-370 1640), 2 Barkston Gardens SW5 (tube: Earl's Court), is an unpretentious place with a nice atmosphere. The rooms are clean, small and reasonable value if you are sharing. Singles with/without bathroom are £45/30, doubles are £55/45 and triples and quads with/without bathrooms are £70/65.

The *St Simeon* (☎ 0171-373 0505), 38 Harrington Gardens SW7 (tube: Gloucester Rd), is within walking distance of the South Kensington museums. There are dorms as well as singles and doubles; prices are around £14 per person but seem to be negotiable.

The **Boka Hotel** (☎ 0171-370 1388), 33 Eardley Crescent SW5 (tube: Earl's Court), is a relaxed place where guests have the use of a kitchen. Most rooms don't have bathrooms. Singles/doubles start at £22/35 and there's also a dorm from £12.

Hotels & B&Bs – Paddington This area is even seedier than Earl's Court, and, although there are lots of cheap hotels (or is it because there are lots of cheap hotels?), single women in particular will probably feel more comfortable elsewhere. It is convenient, however, and there are some decent places at decent prices.

Right in the centre of the action, the **Norfolk Court & St David's Hotel** (☎ 0171-723 4963), 16 Norfolk Square W2 (tube: Paddington), is a friendly place with the usual out-of-control décor. It's clean, though, and comfortable. Basic singles/doubles have basins and colour TVs and cost £28/40. With showers and toilets prices jump to £45 for a double.

Sussex Gardens is lined with small hotels, but, unfortunately, it's also a major traffic route. Most places aren't inspiring, but there are some gems among the dross. **Balmoral House** (☎ 0171-723 7445), 156 Sussex Gardens W2 (tube: Paddington), is an immaculate and very comfortable place with singles with/without bathroom for £40/30, and doubles with facilities for £52. All rooms have TVs and a full English breakfast is served.

The **Europa House** (☎ 0171-723 7343), 151 Sussex Gardens W2 (tube: Paddington), is clean, quiet and well equipped. All rooms have bathrooms, TVs and telephones. Singles/doubles cost £45/60.

The **Glynne Court Hotel** (☎ 0171-262 4344), 41 Great Cumberland Place W1 (tube: Marble Arch), is not in the main hotel zone at all. In fact, it has a great position behind Marble Arch. All rooms have TVs and telephones. Singles/doubles are £42/60, but you only get a continental breakfast.

Hotels & B&Bs – Bayswater This is extremely convenient and some parts feel as if they are under constant invasion. Some of the streets immediately to the west of Queensway, which has an excellent selection of restaurants, are depressingly run-down.

The **Oxford Hotel** (☎ 0171-402 6860), 13 Craven Terrace (tube: Lancaster Gate), is reasonable value. Singles/doubles with TV are £65 and this goes down to £48 if rented for eight days.

Sass House (☎ 0171-262 2325), 11 Craven Terrace (tube: Lancaster Gate), is fairly basic and threadbare and there are only doubles at £46, including continental breakfast.

One of the best options in Bayswater is the **Garden Court Hotel** (☎ 0171-229 2553), at 30 Kensington Gardens Square W2 (tube: Bayswater). It's a well-run, well-maintained family hotel, with well-equipped rooms. They all have telephones and TVs, and the breakfasts are good. Singles/doubles without bathrooms are £32/48; with bathrooms they're £45/65.

Hotels & B&Bs – Bloomsbury Bloomsbury is very convenient, especially for the West End. It's a peculiar mix made up of London University, the British Museum, beautiful squares, Georgian architecture, traffic, office workers, students and tourists. In general, it is a little more expensive than the other areas, but the hotels also tend to be a little better. It's definitely worth considering.

Tucked away to the north of Russell Square, around Cartwright Gardens, there is a group of the most comfortable, attractive and best value hotels in London, and they're still within easy walking distance of the West End. They're on a crescent around a leafy garden, and although they aren't the cheapest places in London, they are worth it if you have the money to spend.

Jenkin's Hotel (☎ 0171-387 2067), 45 Cartwright Gardens WC1 (tube: Russell Square), has attractive, comfortable rooms, with style. All have basins, TVs, telephones and fridges, and prices include English breakfasts. Singles/doubles are £39/52; doubles with private facilities are £62. Guests can even use the tennis courts in the gardens across the road.

The **Crescent Hotel** (☎ 0171-387 1515), 49 Cartwright Gardens WC1 (tube: Russell Square), is a bigger place, but it is still a family-owned operation of a high standard, with basically the same prices as Jenkin's. The **Euro**

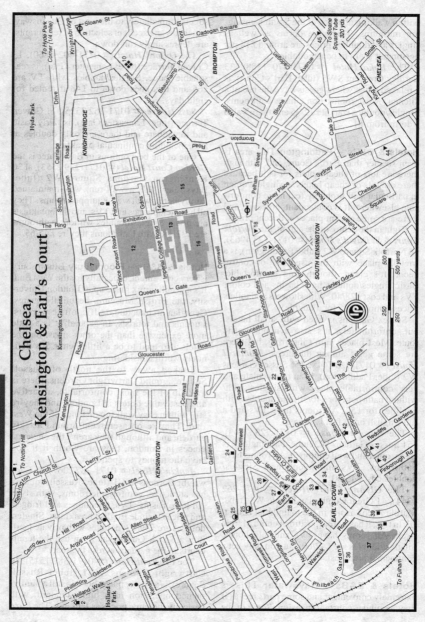

BRITAIN

Chelsea, Kensington & Earl's Court

To Hyde Park
Corner (1/4 mile)

Hyde Park

To Sloane
Square Tube
320 yds

BROMPTON

Cadogan Square

CHELSEA

KNIGHTSBRIDGE

Kensington Gardens

The Ring

SOUTH KENSINGTON

KENSINGTON

The Boltons

To Notting Hill

EARL'S COURT

Holland Park

To Fulham

500 m
500 yards

250
250

0
0

PLACES TO STAY		PLACES TO EAT			10	Harrods
1	Vicarage Private Hotel	14	Ognisko Polskie		11	Brompton Oratory
2	Holland House Youth	18	Spago		12	Imperial College of
	Hostel	19	La Bouchée & STA			Science &
8	Imperial College of		Travel			Technology
	Science & Technology	26	China Kitchen		13	Science Museum
	Residence	29	Benjys		15	Victoria & Albert
22	St Simeon	40	Troubadour			Museum
23	Curzon House Hotel	41	La Papardella		16	Natural History
24	Shelbourne Hotel	44	Chelsea Farmers'			Museum
28	Court Hotels		Market		17	South Kensington Tube
31	Merlyn Court Hotel	45	Chelsea Kitchen			Station
33	Windsor House &				20	STA Travel
	Regency Court Hotel	OTHER			21	Gloucester Rd Tube
34	London Tourist Hotel	3	Commonwealth			Station
35	Chelsea Hotel		Institute		25	Airbus, Route A1,
36	Philbeach Hotel	4	Trailfinders & Campus			Stop 6
38	Boka Hotel		Travel		27	Top Deck Travel
39	Court Hotels	5	YHA Shop		30	CallShop etc.
42	Earl's Court Youth	6	High St Kensington		32	Earl's Court Tube
	Hostel		Tube Station			Station
43	Swiss House Hotel	7	Royal Albert Hall		37	Earl's Court Exhibition
		9	Knightsbridge Tube			Centre
			Station			

and *George* hotels, in the same street, are also good and cost around the same price.

There's a row of places along Gower St, and they all seem to be pretty fair value. Not all of them have double glazing on the front windows, which is essential if you are sensitive to traffic noise. Otherwise, insist on one of the back rooms overlooking the garden, which happen to be the nicest anyway.

The *Arran House Hotel* (☎ 0171-636 2186), 77 Gower St WC1 (tube: Goodge St), is a friendly, welcoming place with a great garden. Singles range from £31 to £41 (with shower and toilet), doubles from £46 to £61, and there are also triples and quads. The hotel has soundproofing on its front rooms, and all have colour TV and telephones. There are also laundry facilities.

The *Hotel Cavendish* (☎ 0171-636 9079), at No 75, and the *Jesmond Hotel* (☎ 0171-636 3199), at No 63, are both fairly basic, but are clean and entirely adequate. They have singles/doubles for £28/42. You share bathrooms, although all rooms have basins, and you get a full English breakfast.

The *Repton Hotel* (☎ 0171-436 4922), 31 Bedford Place WC1 (tube: Russell Square), is pretty good value considering its position – Bedford Place is not nearly as busy as Gower St. There are TVs and telephones in all rooms;

singles/doubles are £48/60. They also have one dorm with six beds at £14 per person.

If all you want is a room, and you don't mind noise and primitive facilities, you'll be happy with the *Royal Hotel* (☎ 0171-636 8401), Woburn Place WC1 (tube: Russell Square). There certainly aren't many cheaper options, and it is clean enough. Singles/doubles are £18/36.

Hotels & B&Bs – Chelsea & Kensington

These are trendy and expensive districts, but they are convenient, especially for museums and shopping, and they don't feel like tourist ghettoes.

The *Magnolia Hotel* (☎ 0171-352 0187), 104 Oakley St SW3 (tube: South Kensington), has a good position, and is remarkably good value. The only drawback is it's a bit of a hike to the nearest tube station. The rooms are pleasant, but if possible get one at the back away from traffic noise. There's colour TV in all rooms, but only some have *en suite* bathrooms. Singles with/without bathroom are £43/33, doubles are £48/43 and triples are £60.

The *Swiss House Hotel* (☎ 0171-373 2769), 171 Old Brompton Rd, is a clean, good-value hotel, on the edge of Earl's Court. Singles/doubles without shower and toilet are £36/53 rising to £68 for doubles only with facilities, which is a bit steep since they only give you a continental breakfast. It is a nice place, however, and you do get a TV and a direct-dial phone.

The **Vicarage Private Hotel** (☎ 0171-229 4030), 10 Vicarage Gate W8 (tube: High St Kensington), is in a good location close to Hyde Park between Notting Hill and Kensington. It's a pleasant, well-kept place with good showers. Singles/doubles are £36/58. This place is recommended in a number of guidebooks so you have to book ahead.

Hotels & B&Bs – Pimlico This is not the most attractive part of London to stay, but you are very close to the action, even if there's not much happening immediately around you. For an area that sees a large transient population, the quality of the hotels is reasonably good. In general, the cheap hotels (around £30 per person) are better value than their counterparts in Earl's Court.

If only all London's budget hotels were like the **Luna & Simone** hotels (☎ 0171-834 5897), 47 Belgrave Rd SW1 (tube: Victoria). They're central, spotlessly clean and comfortable. They don't have offensive décor. Doubles without bathrooms are from £38, and with bathrooms they're £54. Facilities vary from room to room, but a full English breakfast is included. There are storage facilities if you want to leave some bags behind while you go travelling.

The **Belgrave House Hotel** (☎ 0171-828 1563), 32 Belgrave Rd SW1 (tube: Victoria), is another pleasant hotel that doesn't have a doss-house atmosphere. Singles/doubles are £30/40 and include breakfast.

The **Brindle House Hotel** (☎ 0171-828 0057), 1 Warwick Place North SW1 (tube: Victoria), is in an old building off the main thoroughfares. Although the décor is a mess, the rooms are much more pleasant than the foyer suggests – they're light and clean. Singles are £30 (with shared facilities); doubles are £45/40 (with/without facilities).

A step up in quality and price, **Hamilton House** (☎ 0171-821 7113), 60 Warwick Way SW1 (tube: Victoria), has singles/doubles with private bathrooms, TV and telephones for £56/68. The doubles are worth considering.

Rental Prices for rental accommodation are high and standards are low. At the bottom end of the market there are bedsits – a single furnished room, usually with a shared bathroom and kitchen, although some have basic cooking facilities. Expect to pay £50 to £100 per week. The next step up is a studio, which normally has a separate bathroom and kitchen for between £75 and £120. One-bedroom flats average between £90 and £135. Shared houses and flats are the best value, with a bedroom for between £40 and £60 plus bills. Most landlords demand a security deposit (normally one month's rent) plus a month's rent in advance.

Rooms and flats are advertised at the *New Zealand News* UK office in the Royal Opera Arcade behind New Zealand House, in *TNT Magazine*, *Time Out*, the *Evening Standard* and *Loot*. If you decide to use an agency, check that it doesn't charge fees to tenants; Jenny Jones (☎ 0171-493 4381) and Derek Collins (☎ 0171-930 2773) are free agencies.

Places to Eat
It's difficult to eat out in London at a reasonable price, although the situation is gradually improving. In general, eating out is the province of those with money; you'll be lucky to get a decent meal and a glass of wine for less than £10 per head, except in pubs where the food is usually very average. If you do want to keep your costs down, resist the temptation of alcohol, which is always ridiculously expensive.

Indian restaurants are consistently good value; unfortunately, they often tone down their spices for the English palate. There are an increasing number of pasta places, which can be good, especially if they're run by Italians (a lot aren't). It's very difficult to find good-quality English cuisine at a reasonable price.

There's a surprising lack of good guides to London restaurants – the best is the *Time Out Guide to Eating & Drinking in London* (£7.50), but it doesn't have much for shoestringers and it's difficult to wade through. Harden's *Good Cheap Eats* (£4.95) is an annual guide to budget establishments.

There are a number of hunting grounds in the West End: around Covent Garden, especially north-east between Endell St and St Martin's Lane; around Soho, especially north-west of the intersection of Charing Cross Rd and Shaftesbury Ave (including Old Compton and Frith Sts); north of Leicester Square on Lisle and Gerrard Sts (for Chinese). If you're looking for a peaceful oasis, make for Neal's Yard in Covent Garden, a flower-bedecked courtyard surrounded by cheap vegetarian eateries.

Camden Town (NW1) has a cosmopolitan range of restaurants and cafés that can become very crowded on the weekend. For a good selection, start at Mornington Crescent and wander north-west along Camden High St and its continuation Chalk Farm Rd.

The hotel zone around Bayswater (W2) is well served by moderately priced restaurants along Queensway and Westbourne Grove. There are some interesting possibilities around Notting Hill – a couple of places at the southern end of Pembridge Rd and on Hillgate St across Notting Hill Gate, and around Blenheim Crescent and its intersection with Portobello Rd.

Earl's Court (SW5) is full of uninspiring budget eateries – along Earl's Court Rd and the streets opposite the tube station (Hogarth Rd for one), and around the intersection of Earl's Court Rd and Old Brompton Rd. Go somewhere else.

There are a number of places to look for Indian food. Brick Lane (E1) in the East End has a number of cheap, but good, Bangladeshi restaurants; Stoke Newington Church St (N16) has a row of interesting restaurants, a number of which are Indian; and for South Indian menus, which are particularly good for vegetarians, there are some excellent places on Drummond St (NW1).

The main centre for Chinese food is still around Gerrard St, Soho, which has been given the obligatory Chinatown visual effects.

Covent Garden *Café Pasta* (☎ 0171-379 0198), 184 Shaftesbury Ave (tube: Covent Garden), produces simple but good food at reasonable prices. It's a pleasant little restaurant, not part of an enormous chain. Pastas range from £4 to £6 and are generous in size. A glass of house wine is £2.15.

Diana's Diner (☎ 0171-240 0272), 39 Endell St (tube: Covent Garden), is very basic, but it's also very cheap. The food is not inspiring, but it's OK. Spaghetti costs from £3.50 and you'll find a range of grills and roasts around £4.50.

Food for Thought (☎ 0171-836 0239), 31 Neal St WC2 (tube: Covent Garden), is a small and reliable vegetarian place. The menu features dishes like spinach and mushroom South Indian bake for £2.90, stir-fried vegetables for £2.70. It's nonsmoking, but you can bring your own bottle.

Neal's Yard is a peaceful escape from the West End bustle. There are a number of good-value and healthy takeaway places all grouped around a flower-bedecked courtyard. *Neal's Yard Bakery & Tea Room* (☎ 0171-836 5199), 6 Neal's Yard (tube: Covent Garden), is the star performer, however. It has limited, but very good, wholefood vegetarian offerings for around £3. Unfortunately, they're only open until 4.30 pm. Neal's Yard is signposted from Neal St and is off Short's Gardens.

Café in the Crypt (☎ 0171-839 4342), St Martin-in-the-Fields Church, on Trafalgar Square (tube: Charing Cross), is in an atmospheric crypt under the church. The food is good and there are plenty of offerings for vegetarians, but it can be a bit noisy and hectic. Most mains are from £5 to £6. Dinner is served daily from 5 to 7.30 pm.

Cheap fuel is available from a number of pizza counters on the north-eastern corner of Leicester Square. Check the current offers, but you should be able to get a slice of pizza and some salad for £2.

Soho *Poons* (☎ 0171-437 4549), 27 Lisle St WC2 (tube: Leicester Square), is where the up-market Poons empire started. It's tiny, with classic laminated tables and fluorescent lights, but it has exceptional food at very good prices. It specialises in superb wind-dried meats. The dried duck is heavenly, and the steamed chicken is equally sensational. If you're hungry, start with soup and order perhaps two dishes and rice – you'll pay around £9 per person. Be prepared to queue at busy times, and to be hustled out the door pretty quickly.

Wong Kei (☎ 0171-437 6833), 41 Wardour St W1 (tube: Leicester Square), is famous for the rudeness of its waiters. Some find this adds to the experience, but even if you don't you might be tempted by the food, which is cheap and good Cantonese. A set menu starts at £5 (minimum two persons).

BRITAIN

BRITAIN

Holborn, Bloomsbury & Marylebone

To Islington

Rosebery Avenue

CLERKENWELL

Farringdon Road

Clerkenwell Road

HOLBORN

Road

To the City

Lane

Chancery

Gray's Inn

Holborn

Gray's Inn Road

Lincoln's Inn Fields

Red Lion St

Theobald's Road

Lincoln's Inn

High

St

Kingsway

Procter St

Row

Pentonville Road

King's Cross Road

Swinton St

Acton St

Gray's Inn Road

Cromer St

ST PANCRAS

Judd Street

Coram's Fields

Guilford Street

Great Ormond Street

Southampton Row

See West End Map

Holborn

New Oxford Street

High

Pancras Rd

Euston Road

Place

Tavistock

Woburn Place

Russell Square

Bloomsbury

BLOOMSBURY

Montague Street

Bedford Square

Great Russell Street

New Oxford Street

SOHO

St Giles High St

Oxford Street

Everholt Street

Gower

Bloomsbury Street

Charlotte St

Rathbone St

Woburn Place

University College Hospital

Torrington Place

Gower Street

Tottenham Court Road

Court Road

Newman St

Eastcastle St

To Camden Town

Drummond St

Hampstead Road

Warren Street

Euston Street

Whitfield Street

Fitzroy Square

Cleveland Street

Mortimer Street

Great Portland Street

MARYLEBONE

Regent Street

REGENT'S PARK

Stanhope St

Albany Street

Park Square

Outer — Circle

Regent's Park

Marylebone Road

To Madam Tussaud's

Portland Place

Weymouth St

Wigmore Street

To Bayswater

Scale: 0 — 200 — 400 m / 0 — 200 — 400 yards

PLACES TO STAY		PLACES TO EAT		7	Warren St Tube Station
5	International Students House	4	Ravi Shankar	8	Euston Square Tube Station
9	John Adams Hall	13	North Sea Fish Restaurant	14	London University
10	Passfield Hall	22	The Greenhouse	16	Telecom Tower
11	Jenkin's Hotel	25	Mille Pini	17	Dillons the Bookstore
12	Crescent Hotel	28	Wagamama	21	Russell Square Tube Station
15	Carr Saunders Hall			23	Goodge St Tube Station
18	Arran House Hotel	**OTHER**		27	British Museum
19	Hotel Cavendish	1	King's Cross Train & Tube Station	29	YMCA
20	Royal Hotel	2	St Pancras Train Station	30	Tottenham Court Rd Tube Station
24	Repton Hotel	3	Euston Train & Tube Station	32	Holborn Tube Station
26	Museum Inn	6	Great Portland St Tube Station	33	Chancery Lane Tube Station
31	High Holborn Residence				

Nusa Dua (☎ 0171-437 3559), 11 Dean St W1 (tube: Tottenham Court Rd), is a rather garish Indonesian restaurant, but the prices are fair. Most main courses are around £5. The tofu and tempeh are excellent and there are plenty of vegetarian offerings.

Pizza Express (☎ 0171-437 9595), 10 Dean St W1 (tube: Tottenham Court Rd), might not sound very appealing, but it is in fact part of a chain which serves unusually good pizzas. At street level you get cheap, tasty pizzas from £3.40 to £7 and a glass of wine for £2.10; downstairs you get to eat accompanied by excellent jazz (admission downstairs is between £8 and £20).

La Perla (☎ 0171-437 2060), 28 Brewer St W1 (tube: Piccadilly Circus), is a classic Italian restaurant, with good service and good-quality food. A main-course pasta will cost £5.10, but if the budget allows, try something like the fritto misto di mare (including sole, calamari, whitebait and scampi) for £7.80.

Hamine (☎ 0171-439 0785), 84 Brewer St W1 (tube: Piccadilly Circus), is a spartan Japanese noodle restaurant. The food is very good, with dishes around £8.

Pollo (☎ 0171-734 5917), 20 Old Compton St W1 (tube: Leicester Square), attracts an art-student crowd with numerous pastas for around £3. It can be very busy.

Stepping into the *New Piccadilly* (☎ 0171-437 8530), 8 Denman St (tube: Piccadilly Circus), is like stepping into a time warp – nothing, except the prices, has changed since it first opened in the 1950s. Even the prices

haven't changed as much as you would expect: pastas and pizzas are around £3.50, and chicken and steaks weigh in at around £4.50.

Melati (☎ 0171-437 2745), 21 Great Windmill St W1 (tube: Piccadilly Circus), is a highly acclaimed Indonesian/Malaysian/Singaporean restaurant with excellent food and a good range of options for vegetarians. Various noodle and rice dishes are around £5. You'll probably spend around £12.

Mildred's (☎ 0171-494 1634), 58 Greek St W1 (tube: Tottenham Court Rd), is only small, so you may need to share a table. The chaos is worth it, however, because the vegetarian food is both good and well priced. Expect to pay around £4.50 for a main meal with delicious fresh flavours, and £2.10 for a glass of wine.

The *Living Room*, Bateman St between Frith and Greek Sts W1 (tube: Tottenham Court Rd), is a unique oasis and although it is favoured by the young and the hip of Soho it's not intimidating. It's basically a coffee shop, serving meat and vegetable sandwiches (£4), but there are comfortable sofas at the back.

Bunjies (☎ 0171-240 1796), 27 Litchfield St WC2 (tube: Leicester Square), is a folk club tucked away off Charing Cross Rd where you can also get cheap and reasonable vegetarian food. Main dishes are around £4.

St James' The *Wren at St James'* (☎ 0171-437 9419), 35 Jermyn St SW3 (tube: Piccadilly Circus), is the perfect escape from the West End, but it is only open during the day. It adjoins St James' Church (which often has free

BRITAIN

lunchtime concerts) and in summer it spills out into the shady churchyard. There are plenty of vegetarian dishes for around £3.50, and excellent home-made cakes.

Right on Piccadilly Circus, the *Criterion* (☎ 0171-930 0488) has a spectacular interior and quite an atmosphere, so you won't feel comfortable if you look like a scuzzball. The menu offers fashionable Mediterranean-style food like sautéed goats cheese and roasted peppers, but there are also some British classics like fish and chips. Main courses cost from £10.50 to £15.

Bloomsbury & Holborn *Wagamama* (☎ 0171-323 9223), 4 Streatham St WC1, off Coptic St (tube: Tottenham Court Rd), is a deservedly successful Japanese restaurant. It's spartan with shared long tables, but the food is generous, delicious and cheap. Dishes cost around £5.

The *Greenhouse* (☎ 0171-637 8038), 16 Chenies St WC1 (tube: Goodge St), is part of the Drill Hall complex. It's busy, so expect to share a table. The reason it's busy is the excellent vegetarian food, with main courses for £3.95.

The *North Sea Fish Restaurant* (☎ 0171-387 5892), 7 Leigh St WC1 (tube: Russell Square), sets out to cook fresh fish and potatoes well. A limited ambition, but one that British fish-and-chip shops rarely achieve; the North Sea does. The fish (deep-fried or grilled) and a huge serving of chips will set you back from £6 to £7.

Mille Pini (☎ 0171-242 2434), 33 Boswell St WC1 (tube: Holborn), is a true Italian restaurant with reasonable prices. You'll waddle out, but you'll only spend about £10 if you have two courses and coffee.

Bayswater There are literally dozens of places on Queensway and Westbourne Grove – from cheap takeaways to good-quality restaurants. Surprisingly, there are even some decent restaurants on the 2nd floor of Whiteley's shopping centre – although they are not particularly cheap.

The cheapest pit-stop on Queensway is *Quick*, near the intersection with Moscow Rd, which has fish and chips with salad for £3.50 and pizza with salad for £1.

For something a little more interesting, you could try the *Rasa Sayang* (☎ 0171-229 8417), 38 Queensway W2 (tube: Queensway), which is part of a small but reliable chain – there's another branch in Frith St, Soho. The speciality is Malaysian/Singaporean food, with good-sized portions and plenty of dishes under £5. From noon to 6 pm they have an all-you-can-eat buffet for £4.95.

For something even more interesting, try *The Mandola* (☎ 0171-229 4734), 139 Westbourne Grove W2 (tube: Bayswater), which offers vegetarian Sudanese dishes like tamiya, a kind of falafel, for £3.50 and meat dishes for £6. The portions are small so it would be better value if a couple were sharing dishes.

Khan's (☎ 0171-727 5420), 13 Westbourne Grove W2 (tube: Bayswater), is one of the largest and best Indian restaurants – it's authentic, the décor is smart and it's good value, with vegetarian dishes and a selection of meat curries for around £4.

Nachos (☎ 0171-792 0954), 147 Notting Hill Gate W11 (tube: Notting Hill Gate), is a large and popular Mexican joint with better-than-average food at decent prices.

Notting Hill & Ladbroke Grove *Costa's Grill* (☎ 0171-229 3794), 14 Hillgate St W8 (tube: Notting Hill Gate), is a reliable Greek place with dips at £1.50 and mains like souvlaki for £4.50.

Modhubon (☎ 0171-243 1778), 29 Pembridge Rd W11 (tube: Notting Hill Gate), has been recommended for its inexpensive Indian food. Main dishes are under £5 and a set lunch is £3.90.

Topo D'Oro (☎ 0171-727 5813), Farmer St W8 (tube: Notting Hill Gate), offers tasty Italian cuisine in a dimly lit and intimate restaurant. Pasta dishes are around £5, or you could try the petto di pollo con gorgonzola e avocado (£6.80).

Across the road, *Geales* (☎ 0171-727 7969), 2 Farmer St W8 (tube: Notting Hill Gate), is a very popular fish restaurant in the old-fashioned English style. The fish is priced according to weight and season, and is always fresh. Fish and chips average out at about £7 a person, which is a lot more than you'd pay in a fish shop, but worth it. It's closed on Sunday.

The *Ark* (☎ 0171-229 4024), 122 Palace Gardens Terrace W8 (tube: Notting Hill Gate), is an old survivor, with a relaxed and pleasant atmosphere. The food is French – good quality, simple and reasonably priced. Most mains are from £5 to £7. Booking is recommended.

Pimlico *Manners* (☎ 0171-0171-828 2471), 1 Denbigh St SW1 (tube: Victoria), offers a decent range of dishes at a very good price: starters are £2, and a three-course £8 set dinner is £5 between 5.30 and 8 pm. Lunch is £5. Closed Sunday.

O Sole Mio (☎ 0171-976 6887), 39 Churton St SW1 (tube: Victoria), is a standard, decent-value Italian restaurant with pizzas and pastas under £6. Next door, *Grumbles* is a pleasant wine bar with, amongst other things, vegetable risotto for £5.95, kebabs for £6.25 and entre-cote steak for £9.95.

Mekong (☎ 0171-834 6896), 46 Churton St SW1 (tube: Victoria), is reputed to be one of the best Vietnamese restaurants in London. It's a bit beyond a shoestring budget, but it does have a set meal for £12 (minimum two persons), and house wine is reasonable at £1.70.

If you have to wait around Victoria station, head to the *Well* across Ecclestone Place – it's a clean, peaceful oasis with cheap food.

Chelsea The *Chelsea Kitchen* (☎ 0171-589 1330), 98 King's Rd SW3 (tube: Sloane Square), has some of the cheapest food in London – and it ain't half bad. The surroundings are pretty spartan, however. Minestrone is 70p, spaghetti is £2 and apple crumble is 80p.

If the weather is decent make for the *Chelsea Farmers' Market* on Sydney St. There are a number of small stalls that spill out onto a pleasant outdoor area. Among them, the *Sydney St Café* has burgers and steak sandwiches for around £6. The *Il Cappuccino* has coffee for £1.

South Kensington *Spago* (☎ 0171-225 2407), 6 Glendower Place SW7 (tube: South Kensington), is the best value restaurant in the vicinity, which can be reflected in the queues. The reason? A good range of pastas and pizzas from £4.

La Bouchée (☎ 0171-589 1929), 56 Old Brompton Rd SW7 (tube: South Kensington),

is a small but atmospheric bistro with good-quality food, including some excellent-value set menus for £5.95 and £9.95 before 8 pm. It can get much more expensive ordering from the menu (starters around £4, mains around £9), and you pay for all extras, including bread. Booking is recommended.

Ognisko Polskie (☎ 0171-589 4635), 55 Prince's Gate, Exhibition Rd SW7 (tube: South Kensington), is based in the Polish Hearth Club. It's a bit intimidating and you should make an effort to look presentable, but non-Poles are welcome. The food is very good value (a bit meaty for many), with a three-course set menu from £7.50. In summer you can dine on a terrace overlooking the Royal College gardens.

Earl's Court *La Papardella* (☎ 0171-373 7777), 253 Old Brompton Rd SW5 (tube: Earl's Court), is a busy pizzeria opening onto the pavement. The pizzas are good, but cost from £6 to £7.

The *Troubadour*, 265 Old Brompton Rd (tube: Earl's Court), has an illustrious history as a coffee shop and folk venue. Amongst others it has hosted Dylan, Donovan and Lennon. These days it still occasionally has bands, and it also has good-value food. Service is slow, but the wait is worthwhile; order at the counter. Vegetable soup is £1.85; pasta is £4.

Benjys, 157 Earl's Court Rd SW5 (tube: Earl's Court), is an institution. It's really nothing more than a fairly traditional café, but it's always busy and the food, although nothing to write home about, is cheap and filling. Serious breakfasts with as much tea or coffee as you can drink are around £3.50. There are grills for around £4.

China Kitchen (☎ 0171-370 2533), 36A Kenway Rd SW5 (tube: Earl's Court), is a pleasant Chinese restaurant, a step up from the laminated décor one expects. Main dishes around £5.

Camden A quiet place is the *El Parador* (☎ 0171-834 8746), 245 Eversholt St (tube: Camden Town). There's a good vegetarian selection including quesos for £3.50, with meat and fish dishes just a little more expensive.

Ruby in the Dust (☎ 0171-485 2744), 102 Camden High St (tube: Camden Town), is an

BRITAIN

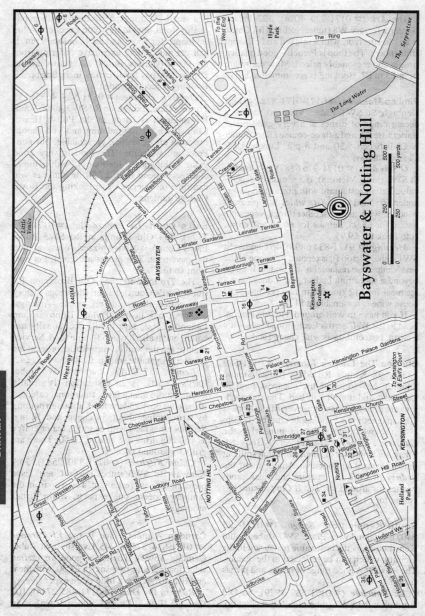

Bayswater & Notting Hill

PLACES TO STAY		PLACES TO EAT		5	Porchester Baths
7	Norfolk Court & St David's Hotel	14	Rasa Sayang	6	Edgware Rd Tube Station
8	Balmoral House	17	Quick	10	Paddington Train & Tube Station
9	Europa House	19	Khan's		
12	Oxford Hotel & Sass House	20	The Mandola	11	Lancaster Gate Tube Station
13	Quest Hotel	26	Modhubon	15	Queensway Tube Station
21	Garden Court Hotel	30	The Ark		
22	Palace Court Hotel	31	Topo D'Oro and Geales	16	Bayswater Tube Station
23	Centre Français	32	Costa's Grill	18	Whiteley's Shopping Centre
24	Gate Hotel	33	Nachos		
25	Palace Hotel	**OTHER**		28	Notting Hill Tube Station
27	Hillgate Hotel	1	Westbourne Park Train Tube Station		
34	Holland Park Hotel			29	Airbus, Route A2, Stop 14
36	London Independent Hostel	2	Portobello Rd Market		
		3	Books for Cooks	35	Holland Park Tube Station
		4	Royal Oak Tube Station		

atmospheric bar/café – it's worth a trek across town. There isn't a huge menu, but it's interesting: Mexican snacks, soup for £2.85 and mains like mussels and noodles for £5.45.

The Raj (☎ 0171-388 6663), 19 Camden High St (tube: Camden Town) is a small Indian place with all-you-can-eat lunch and dinner buffets for £3.50 and £3.75 respectively.

Belgo Noord (☎ 0171-267 0718), 72 Chalk Farm Rd NW1 (tube: Chalk Farm), is a beautifully designed Belgian fish restaurant/bar. Waiters wear monks' habits and, despite the place's trendiness and popularity, the food is really good value. If unsure, go for the set menu: a starter, a beer, a bowl of mussels and chips for £12. There are three sittings, but it is still necessary to book in advance.

Hampstead *Coffee Cup* (☎ 0171-435 7565), 74 Hampstead High St NW3 (tube: Hampstead), is a popular café with a wide-ranging menu from bacon and eggs to pasta. There's something for every taste and every time of day. Good value.

The *Everyman Café* (☎ 0171-431 2123), Holly Bush Vale NW3 (tube: Hampstead), is attached to the cinema of the same name. If you're looking for a quiet place to eat in Hampstead with reasonable food, this is a good choice. The three-course set menu is £7.

East End *Ravi Shankar* (☎ 0171-833 5849), 422 St John St EC1 (tube: Angel), is a small but inexpensive restaurant favoured by vege-

tarians – the all-you-can-eat lunchtime buffets for £4.50 are extremely popular. It has another branch at 133 Drummond St NW1 (tube: Warren St).

There are a number of cheap Bangladeshi restaurants on Brick Lane, including *Aladin* (☎ 0171-247 8210) at 132 and *Nazrul* at 130 (tube: Aldgate East). Both are unlicensed, but you should eat for around £7. Many people believe this is the best subcontinental food in London.

The *Kosher Luncheon Club* (☎ 0171-247 0039), 13 Greatorex St E1 (tube: Aldgate East), is open from noon to 3 pm from Monday to Friday and on Sunday. It's ideally placed if you've worked up an appetite at the Brick Lane or Petticoat Lane markets. The décor is plain, but the food is good quality and authentic. You could eat for less than a fiver.

Beigel Bake (☎ 0171-729 0616), 159 Brick Lane E1 (tube: Whitechapel), is at the Bethnal Green Rd end of Brick Lane – and open 24 hours. You won't find bagels better, fresher or cheaper.

Entertainment
The essential tool is *Time Out* (£1.60), which is published every Tuesday and covers a week of events. The only danger is that there is so much happening you'll be paralysed with indecision.

The biggest problem is transport. The last underground trains leave between 11.30 pm and 12.30 am, so you either have to figure out

BRITAIN

the night buses or pay for a minicab. The second-biggest problem is that most pubs close at 11 pm. That's not a misprint. Fortunately, there are clubs where you can continue partying, although you'll have to pay to enter (£5 to £10), and the drinks are always expensive.

Late-night venues often choose to have a 'club' licence, which means you have to be a member to enter. In practice, they usually include the membership fee as part of the admission price. Many venues have clubs that only operate one night a week, and have a particular angle – whether it be the style of music they play or the kind of people they attract.

Venues can change with bewildering speed – and they sometimes use the membership requirement to exclude people they don't think will fit in. In some places you'll be excluded if you wear jeans, runners and a T-shirt, in others you'll be excluded if you don't. It's not a bad idea to phone in advance to get an idea of cost and membership policy.

Music Venues The major venues for live contemporary music include the *Brixton Academy* (☎ 0171-924 9999), 211 Stockwell Rd SW9 (tube: Brixton); the *Astoria* (☎ 0171-434 0403), 157 Charing Cross Rd WC2 (tube: Tottenham Court Rd); the *Hammersmith Odeon* (☎ 0171-416 6080), Queen Caroline St W6 (tube: Hammersmith); and the *Wembley Arena* (☎ 0181-900 1234), Empire Way, Middlesex (tube: Wembley Park).

Smaller places with a more 'club-like' atmosphere that are worth checking for interesting bands include the *Borderline* (☎ 0171-734 2095), Orange Yard, off Manette St WC2 (tube: Tottenham Court Rd); the *100 Club* (☎ 0171-636 0933), 100 Oxford St W1 (tube: Tottenham Court Rd); the *Forum* (☎ 0171-284 2200), 9-17 Highgate Rd NW5 (tube: Kentish Town); and the *Marquee* (☎ 0171-437 6603), 105 Charing Cross Rd WC2 (tube: Leicester Square). Ring ahead to find what kind of band you'll get.

Venues that are usually reliable for club nights and recorded music include: the *Camden Palace* (☎ 0171-387 0428), 1 Camden Rd NW1 (tube: Camden Town); the *Fridge* (☎ 0171-326 5100), Town Hall Parade SW2 (tube: Brixton); *Velvet Underground* (☎ 0171-734 4687), 143 Charing Cross Rd WC2 (tube: Tottenham Court Rd); and the *Electric Ballroom* (☎ 0171-485 9006), 184 Camden High St NW1 (tube: Camden Town).

If you're a jazz fan, keep your eye on *Ronnie Scott's* (☎ 0171-439 0747), 47 Frith St W1 (tube: Leicester Square); and the *Jazz Café* (☎ 0171-916 6000), 5 Parkway NW1 (tube: Camden Town).

Theatre & Cinema London theatre and music are extraordinarily diverse, high quality (at their best) and extremely reasonably priced by world standards. Even if you don't normally go to the theatre, you really should have a look at the reviews and organise yourself cheap tickets for one or two of the best productions. The *National Theatre* (which is three theatres in one: the Olivier, the Lyttleton and the Cottesloe) puts on consistently good performances, often with some of the best young actors and directors around.

The Leicester Square Theatre Ticket Booth (tube: Leicester Square), on the southern side of Leicester Square, sells half-price tickets (plus £2 commission) on the day of performance. It opens from noon Tuesday to Saturday for matinee tickets only and from 1 to 6.30 pm, Monday to Saturday, for evening tickets only. The queues can be awesome.

A number of theatres and concert halls have stand-by tickets 90 minutes before performances. A ticket to the Royal Shakespeare Company ranges from £5 for students to £20 for the best seats. If you're prepared to watch from the highest seats in the house, you can see the opera at Covent Garden from £2.50. The National Theatre on the South Bank sells cheap back-row tickets for each of its theatres from 10 am on the day of performance – get there an hour early to get near the front of the queue – with a maximum of two tickets to each customer. All these offers are advertised in *Time Out*.

The *Prince Charles Cinema* (☎ 0171-437 8181), Leicester Place WC2 (tube: Leicester Square), is the cheapest in London, with tickets for new-release films from only £1.99. It screens a number of films each day so check the programme carefully.

Spectator Sport
Tickets for league football matches start at £11 and some of the big teams worth watching are

Arsenal (☎ 0171-354 5404), Tottenham Hotspur (☎ 0181-365 5050) and West Ham (☎ 0181-548 2700). International fixtures at Wembley Stadium (☎ 0181-902 8833) will cost more.

Rugby internationals at Twickenham (☎ 0181-892 8161) cost £28 or £33. At the ground there is also a Museum of Rugby (£2.50), which can include a tour of the stadium (£4, including the museum), but advance booking is necessary (☎ 0181-892 2000).

Crystal Palace (☎ 0181-778 0131) is the venue for important athletics events and tickets start at £10. Expect to pay a lot more to watch tennis at Wimbledon (☎ 0181-946 2244).

Getting There & Away

As London is the major gateway to Britain, Getting There & Away information has been given in the introductory transport sections of this chapter. Look up your proposed British destination for prices and possibilities to and from London.

Air See the following Getting Around section for details on transport to and from the airports.

Bus Bus travellers will arrive at Victoria coach station, Buckingham Palace Rd, about 10 minutes walk south of Victoria station.

Train There are eight major train stations in London, and all are connected by tube. For those of you with a combined rail/ferry ticket, if your train goes via south-east England (to and from France, Belgium, Spain or Italy), Victoria is your station; to and from Harwich (for Germany, the Netherlands and Scandinavia), Liverpool St is your station; and to and from Newcastle (for Scandinavia), King's Cross is your station. The international terminal at Waterloo is for all services that use the Channel Tunnel.

For national rail enquiries, fares and timetables phone ☎ 0345-484950.

Getting Around

To/From the Airports Transport to and from London's four airports is as follows:

Heathrow The airport is accessible by bus and underground, but the underground is the cheapest, most reliable method (between 5 am and 11 pm). The station for Terminals 1, 2 and 3 is directly linked to the terminus buildings; there is a separate station for Terminal 4. Check which terminal your flight uses when you reconfirm. The adult single fare is £3.20, or you can use an All Zone travelcard which is £3.90. The journey time from central London is about 50 minutes – allow an hour.

The Airbus (☎ 0171-222 1234) services are also useful. There are two routes: the A1, which runs along Cromwell Rd to Victoria, and the A2, which runs along Notting Hill Gate and Bayswater Rd to Russell Square. Buses run every half-hour and cost £5. A minicab to and from central London will cost from around £15; a metered black cab around £30.

Baggage Hold has left-luggage facilities in Terminal 1 (☎ 0181-745 5301) and Terminal 4 (☎ 0181-745 7460) from 6 am to 11 pm. The charge is £2 per item up to 12 hours and £3 per item up to 24 hours. Excess Baggage (☎ 0181-759 3344) offers a similar service in Terminals 2 and 3. Both companies also have a baggage forwarding service.

Gatwick The Gatwick Express train runs nonstop between the main terminal and Victoria railway station from 4.30 am to 11 pm. Singles are £8.90 and the journey time is half an hour. The regular service takes just a little longer, runs day and all night, and costs £7.50. Gatwick has north and south terminals linked by a monorail; check which terminal your flight uses when you reconfirm. British Airways customers can check in at Victoria. A minicab to central London will cost around £35; a metered black cab around £70.

Excess Baggage PLC (☎ 01293-569 9900), in both the North and South terminals, has left-baggage facilities available daily from 6 am to 10 pm. The charge is £2 per item up to 12 hours and £3 per item up to 24 hours. It also has a baggage forwarding service.

Stansted There is a direct train link to Liverpool St, which takes 45 minutes and costs £10.10. You can change at Tottenham Hale for the West End and other Victoria line stations, including Victoria. There are trains every half-hour.

Luton Catch the airport-to-station Luton Flyer bus outside the arrivals hall for a 15-minute trip to the train station, then take the train for King's Cross or St Pancras (another 45 minutes); the all-in price is £9.90. There are regular services approximately every 20 minutes, starting early and finishing late.

Bus & Underground London Regional Transport is responsible for the buses and the tube. It has a number of information centres where you can get free maps, tickets and information on night buses. Amongst others, there are centres in each Heathrow terminal, and at Victoria, Piccadilly and King's Cross stations; or phone ☎ 0171-222 1234.

Buses are much more interesting and pleasant to use than the tube, although they can be frustratingly slow. There are four types of tickets: one-journey bus tickets sold on the bus (minimum 50p), daily and weekly bus passes, single or return tube tickets (sold at stations, sometimes from vending machines, minimum £1.10), and travelcards.

Travelcards are the easiest and cheapest option, and they can be used on all forms of transport (Network SouthEast trains in London, buses and tubes) after 9.30 am. London is divided into concentric rings, or zones, and the travelcard you need will depend on how many zones you cross. Most visitors will find that a Zone 1 & 2 card will be sufficient (£3.70). Weekly travelcards are also available; they require an ID card with a passport photo (Zone 1 & 2 costs £14.80). If you plan to start moving before 9.30 am you can buy a Zone 1 & 2 LT Card (London Transport Card) for £4.90.

Times of the last tube trains tend to vary from 11.30 pm to 12.30 am, depending on the station and the line. A reasonably comprehensive network of night buses runs from or through Trafalgar Square – get to the square and ask. London Regional Transport publishes a free timetable, *Buses for Night Owls*, which lists them all. One-day travelcards cannot be used on night buses, but weekly travelcards can.

Train Most lines interchange with the tube. Travelcards can be used. See the Getting Around section at the start of this chapter.

Taxi The classic London black cabs (☎ 0171-253 5000 or ☎ 0171-272 0272) are excellent, but not cheap. A cab is available for hire when the yellow sign is lit. Fares are metered and a 10% tip is expected. They can carry five people.

Minicabs are cheap, freelance competitors to the black cabs; anyone with a car can work, but they can only be hired by phone. Some have a very limited idea of how to get around efficiently (and safely). They don't have meters, so it is essential to get a quote before you start. They can carry four people. Women are advised to use black cabs.

Small minicab companies are based in particular areas – ask a local for the name of a reputable company – or phone one of the large 24-hour operations (☎ 0171-272 2612, ☎ 0171-602 1234, ☎ 0181-340 2450 or ☎ 0181-567 1111).

Car & Motorcycle If you're blessed/cursed with private transport, avoid peak hours (7.30 to 9 am, 4.30 to 7 pm), and plan ahead if you will need to park in the centre. Cars parked illegally will be clamped, which is as agonising as it sounds. A clamp is locked on a wheel and in order to have it removed you have to travel across town, pay an enormous fine, then wait most of the day for someone to come and release you. Phone National Car Parks (☎ 0171-499 7050) for car-park addresses; rates vary. You're best to forget this option and stick with public transport – you don't need the aggro.

Bicycle At Bikepark 14 1/2 Stukeley St WC2, the minimum rental charge is £4 for four hours, £10 for the first day, £5 the second day and £3 for subsequent days; helmets, racks, lights and panniers are £1.50 a day (☎ 0171-430 0083).

Boat There are quite a range of services on the river. See the Greenwich, Kew Gardens and Hampton Court Palace sections under Things to See & Do earlier for two popular trips. The main starting points are at Westminster Bridge and Charing Cross. For information on downriver trips (towards Greenwich) phone ☎ 0171-515 1415; for information on upriver trips (towards Kew) phone ☎ 0171-930 4721.

AROUND LONDON

Because of the speed of the train system, a surprisingly large region can be visited on day trips – all of England south-east of an arc drawn through Bournemouth to Bath, Stratford-upon-Avon, Leicester and Norwich.

Windsor & Eton

Home for British royalty for over 900 years, **Windsor Castle** is one of the greatest surviving medieval castles. It was built in stages between 1165 and the 16th century on chalk bluffs overlooking the Thames.

The strategic value of Windsor has long since disappeared, but its symbolic importance has never waned. The current royal family made this connection clear when George V, the current queen's grandfather, changed the family name from the rather too Germanic Saxe-Coburg-Gotha to Windsor.

Inside the castle, St George's Chapel is a masterpiece of Perpendicular Gothic architecture. There is also a collection of royal treasures and the State Apartments. The castle is open daily from 10 am, but it can be closed at short notice such as when members of the royal family are in residence; for opening arrangements, phone ☎ 01753-831118. In summer, the changing of the guard takes place from Monday to Saturday, weather permitting, at 11 am. Entry to the castle is £8.50, except on Sunday when it drops to £6.50 because the chapel does not open until 2 pm.

A short walk along Thames St and across the river and you come to yet another enduring symbol of Britain's class system, **Eton College**, a famous public (meaning private) school that has educated no fewer than 18 prime ministers. It is open to visitors from 2 to 4.30 pm during term, and from 10.30 am during Easter and summer holidays (admission £2.20). A number of buildings date from the mid-15th century, when the school was founded by Henry VI.

Easily accessible from London, Windsor crawls with tourists. If at all possible, avoid weekends. The *Youth Hostel* (☎ 01753-861710) is a mile from the central train station, and open from February through mid-December. There are numerous trains direct from London's Waterloo to the Windsor Riverside station and via Slough from London's Paddington to the central Windsor & Eton station.

The return trip costs £5.40. If you're on your way to Bath or Oxford, pick up the main west-bound trains five minutes away in Slough.

Hatfield House

Six miles from St Albans, north of London, Hatfield House (☎ 01707-262823) is the most celebrated Jacobean (meaning built in the reign of James I) house – a graceful red-brick and stone mansion full of treasures. It's open Tuesday to Saturday from noon to 4.15 pm, and Sunday from 1 pm; admission is £5.20. The entrance is just opposite Hatfield train station. There are numerous trains from King's Cross.

South-East England

At times, the counties of Kent, Surrey, East and West Sussex and Hampshire seem like a rural extension of London. Fast, regular trains make it possible for thousands of commuters to work in the city but, equally, make it possible to see much of this region on day trips. For this very reason, you'd do best to avoid most of the popular sights on weekends.

While many of the towns and villages are virtual dormitories for London workers, it is still a region exceptionally rich in beauty and history. This has always been Britain's frontline, a mere 22 miles from the French coast, and names like Hastings, Dover and Portsmouth inevitably evoke images of invasion and war.

A controversial new invasion began in 1994 when the Channel Tunnel finally opened, drawing Britain into an even closer European orbit. Those bold enough to travel underwater from France will pop up near Folkestone. Those brave enough to use the ferries also find this coastline is their landfall, as it was for the Romans and Normans, amongst many others.

From a visitor's point of view, this region's convenience to London is both its strength and weakness. On the one hand, parts are very beautiful, very English and very convenient. There are few regions more densely packed with sights. On the other hand, crowds of English tourists can be difficult to evade and there are wide swathes of suburban development.

BRITAIN

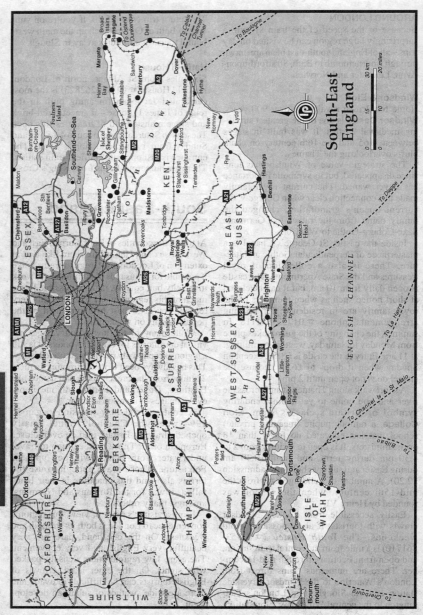

South-East
England

Whatever images you have of England, you can find them in this region: picturesque villages and towns with welcoming old pubs (Chilham, Sandwich, Rye, Arundel, Lewes and Winchester, amongst many others), spectacular coastline (the famous white cliffs of Dover and Beachy Head), impressive castles (Dover, Leeds and Bodiam), great houses (Knole, Penshurst and Petworth), gardens (Sissinghurst, Hever, Scotney Castle, Great Dixter, Chilham), great cathedrals at Canterbury and Winchester and, finally, the kitsch and vibrant seaside resort of Brighton.

Kent is often justly called the 'Garden of England' but many other parts of the region also have an atmosphere of gentle, cultivated prettiness. There are a number of popular walks, including the South Downs Way. Again, because of their accessibility, sections can easily be undertaken as day trips from London. Eastbourne to Brighton along the South Downs Way is a good three-day walk.

Orientation & Information

The main roads and railway lines radiate from London like spokes in a wheel, linking the south-coast ports and resorts with the capital. Chalk country runs through the region along two hilly east-west ridges, or 'downs'.

The North Downs curve from Guildford towards Rochester, then to Dover where they become the famous white cliffs. The South Downs run from north of Portsmouth to end spectacularly at Beachy Head near Eastbourne. Lying between the two is the Weald, once an enormous stretch of forest, now orchards and market gardens.

There are HI/YHA hostels in Canterbury, Dover, Hastings, Brighton, Arundel, Portsmouth, Winchester and Southampton, and several on the Isle of Wight.

Getting Around

Bus Fast, regular buses follow the spokes out from London, but it is very difficult to travel east-west by bus without resorting to the slow, local buses. For information on all public-transport options in Kent, ring ☎ 0800-696996; for West Sussex, ring ☎ 01243-777556; for East Sussex, ring ☎ 01273-474747; and for Hampshire, ring ☎ 01962-868944. Virtually all services in Kent, Sussex and Hampshire accept Explorer tickets, which

give unlimited travel and cost £5/3.50 for adults/children. These can be bought from the bus drivers or from bus stations, and are nearly always the best value option if you are travelling reasonably extensively.

Train It is possible to do an interesting rail loop from London via Canterbury East, Dover, Ashford, Rye, Hastings, Battle (via Hastings), Brighton, Littlehampton, Arundel, Portsmouth, Southampton and Winchester. If you are considering this kind of extensive rail travel, a Network SouthEast Card (see the introductory Getting Around section at the beginning of this chapter) is essential. Network SouthEast has a 24-hour enquiry service (☎ 0171-928 5100).

CANTERBURY

Canterbury's greatest treasure is its magnificent cathedral, the successor to the church St Augustine built after he began converting the English to Christianity in 597. In 1170 Archbishop Thomas á Becket was murdered in the cathedral by four of Henry II's knights as a result of a dispute over the church's independence. An enormous cult grew up around the martyred Becket and Canterbury became the centre of one of the most important medieval pilgrimages in Europe, which was immortalised by Geoffrey Chaucer in the *Canterbury Tales*.

The Archbishop of Canterbury is the Primate of All England, the head of the Church of England and the worldwide Anglican Communion – he plays an important symbolic and leadership role, but exercises little direct authority.

The cathedral is the Archbishop of Canterbury's 'seat', and is therefore considered the most important Anglican cathedral. Although it is not the most beautiful, it is certainly one of the most evocative – the ghosts of saints, soldiers and pilgrims seem to crowd around. Not even crowds of French school children can shatter the atmosphere (although if possible go late in the day to avoid school groups).

Canterbury was severely damaged during the WWII Blitz, and parts, especially to the south of the cathedral, have been rebuilt insensitively. However, there's still plenty to see and the bustling town centre has a good atmosphere.

BRITAIN

The place crawls with tourists, but that simply means all is well with the world – they've been coming for a very long time.

Orientation & Information

The centre of Canterbury is enclosed by a medieval city wall and a modern ring road. The centre is easy to get around on foot, and virtually impossible to get around by car; park by the wall. There are two train stations, both a short walk from the centre. The bus station is just within the city walls at the eastern end of High St.

The TIC (☎ 01227-766567), 34 St Margaret's St, is open daily from 9.30 am to 5.30 pm. It has a *bureau de change* and free booking service for local B&Bs.

Canterbury Cathedral

The present cathedral (☎ 762862) was built in two stages between 1070 and 1184, and 1391 and 1505. The cathedral complex, including the beautiful cloisters, can easily absorb half a day. It is a massive rabbit warren of a building, with treasures tucked away in corners and a trove of associated stories, so a tour is recommended. Admission is £2/1.

There are one-hour guided tours at 10.30 am, noon and 2 and 4 pm for £2.80, or if the crowd looks daunting, you can take a Walkman tour for £2.50 (30 minutes). An excellent guidebook is available for 95p. On weekdays and Saturday the cathedral is open from 9 am to 7 pm from Easter to September, and from 9 am to 5 pm from October to Easter; choral evensong is at 5.30 pm, and 3.15 pm on Saturday. On Sunday it is open from 12.30 to 2.30 pm, and 4.30 to 5.30 pm; choral evensong is at 3.15 pm.

Places to Stay

The *Youth Hostel* (☎ 462911), 54 New Dover Rd, is a half-mile or so from the eastern train station. Continue out St George's St (the continuation of High St) which eventually becomes New Dover Rd. The hostel is in an old Victorian villa and is closed from late December to the end of January; the nightly charge is £9.10.

Most Canterbury accommodation is quite expensive, particularly in July and August. In some cases, prices almost double; ring ahead to avoid nasty surprises and/or use the TIC. *Kingsbridge Villa* (☎ 766415), 15 Best Lane,

in the centre of town just off High St, is a comfortable B&B with colour TVs in rooms; some rooms have their own bathrooms. Prices start from £18/30 for singles/doubles.

Nearby, *Tudor House* (☎ 765650), 6 Best Lane, is also good. It's a bit smaller and, in addition to the usual facilities, it has canoes and boats for guests to hire. Singles/doubles are from £17/28.

Castle Court Guest House (☎ 463441), 8 Castle St, is a pretty straightforward B&B, but it's clean and decent. There is a mixture of singles, doubles and twins for around £16 per person.

You can stay in the heart of the city, right by the cathedral, at the *Cathedral Gate Hotel* (☎ 462800), 36 Burgate, which has comfortable singles/doubles from £21/40, but rising to almost double in high season.

There are quite a number of places on St Dunstan's St (near the West Gate) and on London Rd (its continuation).

Four miles away, the *Thruxted Oast* (☎ 730080), Mystole, Chartham, is an excellent B&B in converted oast houses (where hops were dried). The buildings have loads of character. Rates are £75 for luxurious twin accommodation.

Places to Eat

There's a good range of reasonably priced eating places in Canterbury. If you want to do some window-menu shopping start in St Margaret's St and then walk down High St to West Gate. There are a couple of interesting places outside the gate.

Il Vaticano (☎ 765333), 35 St Margaret's St, has excellent Italian food, in particular a wide range of pastas from £4.25 to £7.95.

The *Three Tuns Hotel*, at the end of St Margaret's St, stands on the site of a Roman theatre, and itself dates from the 16th century. It serves good-value pub meals from around £4.

Fungus Mungus (☎ 781922), 34 St Peter's St, has vegetarian dishes around £5 but may be closing down, so don't expect it to be there.

Café des Amis (☎ 464390) just beyond the West Gate actually serves authentic Mexican cuisine – which is very different from the usual repetitive combinations of beans, cheese and chilli. There's a cheerful atmosphere and the prices are reasonable. Starters are from £3 to £4; for main courses try mole poblano – roast loin of pork in a sauce made of chillies, spices, nuts, seeds and tomato with rice and salad for £6.95.

There are lots of more interesting possibilities. Bookings are recommended, especially on Friday and Saturday nights.

Entertainment
Get hold of a copy of *What & Where When* – a free guide to what's on in Canterbury, available from the TIC. There are quite a few lively pubs, thanks in no small part to the student population. Two on St Radigunds St worth checking out are *Simple Simon's*, which has a beer garden and usually features some sort of folk music in the evenings, and the *Miller's Arms*, which is a classic student hang-out.

Getting There & Away
Canterbury makes a good base for exploring Kent and the High Weald. See the Rail and Coach/Bus fares tables in this chapter's introductory Getting Around section.

Bus Stagecoach East Kent (☎ 581333) has a good network around the region. There are numerous buses to and from London and Dover. There's an interesting service to Hastings across an attractive part of Kent (No 400/404, £4.10) via Chilham, Ashford and Tenterden. There are four buses a day from Monday to Saturday, but none on Sunday, although there is a link from Ashford to Hastings.

National Express has regular buses linking Dover, Folkestone, Hythe, Ashford and Canterbury.

Train There are two train stations: Canterbury East (for the YHA hostel) is accessible from London's Victoria station, and Canterbury West is accessible from London's Charing Cross and Waterloo stations. (£13 day return). There are regular trains between Canterbury East and Dover Priory (45 minutes, £3.70).

BROADSTAIRS
Broadstairs is a small, traditional seaside resort that may be of interest to shoestringers because it has a helpful *Youth Hostel* (☎ 01843-604121), 3 Osborne Rd, convenient for those using the cheap Sally Line ferry between

Ramsgate and Dunkerque. You can make ferry bookings at the hostel.

There are frequent East Kent buses (Nos 34 and 36) to and from Ramsgate and there's sometimes a courtesy bus provided by Sally Line. There are regular buses to Canterbury (No 81). There are also regular trains to and from London's Victoria station via Canterbury West.

SANDWICH
Sandwich is literally a backwater – once a thriving Cinque Port (a port that provided ships for the monarch in return for special favours), it has been deserted by the sea and pretty much forgotten by the world. As a result, the town is a remarkable medieval time capsule that has not been substantially altered since the 16th century. Even more remarkably, the town has avoided being turned into Ye Cute Olde Englishe Village.

The TIC (☎ 01304-613565), on the New St side of the Guildhall, is open 11 am to 3 pm daily from May through to September. The range of places to stay is quite limited, so you may be forced to make a day trip from Canterbury, Ramsgate or Dover. East Kent Buses has regular services linking these three places, and the town is on the railway line between Margate and Dover Priory.

DOVER
Dover has two things going for it: it has the world's busiest passenger harbour and a spectacular castle. It's the only Cinque Port that hasn't yet sunk, although it will come under increasing pressure from the Channel Tunnel. The foreshore of Dover is basically an unattractive (though well-signposted) vehicle ramp for the ferries, and the rest of town is not much more attractive.

Orientation & Information
Dover is dominated by the looming profile of the castle to the east. The town itself runs back from the sea along a valley formed by the unimpressive River Dour.

Ferry departures are from the Eastern Docks (accessible by bus) below the castle, but the Hoverport is below the Western Heights. Dover Priory train station is a short walk to the west of the town centre and the ferry companies run

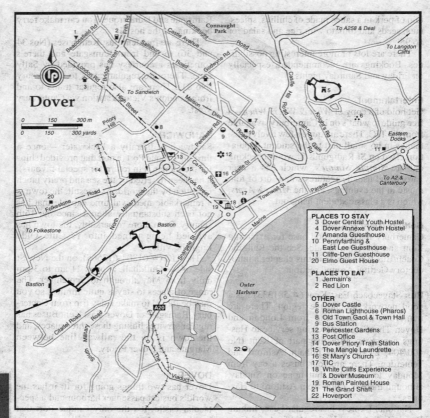

Dover

PLACES TO STAY
3 Dover Central Youth Hostel
4 Dover Annexe Youth Hostel
7 Amanda Guesthouse
10 Pennyfarthing &
   East Lee Guesthouse
11 Cliffe-Den Guesthouse
20 Elmo Guest House

PLACES TO EAT
1 Jermain's
2 Red Lion

OTHER
5 Dover Castle
6 Roman Lighthouse (Pharos)
8 Old Town Gaol & Town Hall
9 Bus Station
12 Pencester Gardens
13 Post Office
14 Dover Priory Train Station
15 The Mangle Laundrette
16 St Mary's Church
17 TIC
18 White Cliffs Experience
   & Dover Museum
19 Roman Painted House
21 The Grand Shaft
22 Hoverport

complimentary buses from Dover Priory. The bus station is in the centre of town.

The TIC (☎ 01304-205108) is on Townwall St near the seafront, and is open from 9 am to 6 pm. It has an accommodation and ferry-booking service.

Things to See

Dover's main attraction, **Dover Castle** (☎ 201628), is a well-preserved medieval fortress with a beautiful location and spectacular views. To add to its fascination, within the fortifications there are the remains of a Roman lighthouse, or **Pharos**, built in 50 AD, as well as a restored Saxon church. The excellent tour

of **Hellfire Corner** covers the castle's history during WWII, and takes you through the tunnels which burrow through the chalk beneath the castle.

The castle is open daily from 10 am to 6 pm April to September; from 10 am to 4 pm between October and March. Entry is £6/4.50, including Hellfire Corner.

Places to Stay & Eat

There are two YHA hostels, both of which can fill up very quickly in summer; one or other may close during winter. Finding any accommodation at all can be tough in high summer, so making a booking is advisable.

The main hostel, ***Dover Central Youth Hostel*** (☎ 201314), 306 London Rd, has been recently renovated. Charges are £9.10 per night. The ***Dover Annexe*** (☎ 206045), 14 Godwyne Rd, is also comfortable, although a bit cramped.

B&Bs are mainly strung out along Folkestone Rd (the A20), but there is another batch on Castle St and Maison Dieu Rd in town. The ***Elmo Guest House*** (☎ 206236), 120 Folkestone Rd, is reasonable value with a per person rate from £12 to £19.

Tucked under the castle, near the Eastern Docks (ideal if you have an early ferry), the ***Cliffe-Den*** (☎ 202418), 63 East Cliff, Marine Parade, is quiet and pleasant with a per-person rate from £14 to £18. Two places on Maison Dieu are worth considering: ***Pennyfarthing*** (☎ 205563) at No 109 and ***East Lee Guesthouse*** (☎ 210176) at No 108. Rooms start at £17 per person, and ***Amanda Guesthouse*** (☎ 201711), on nearby Harold St, is similarly priced.

There are a number of restaurants along Cannon St, but you will probably do best with a pub meal. The ***Red Lion***, just off Frith Rd, has excellent, filling meals for around £4.50, and is convenient to both YHA hostels. ***Jermain's*** serves roast beef for £3.30.

Getting There & Away

See the introductory Getting There & Away section at the beginning of this chapter for details on ferries, hovercraft and so on to Continental Europe. Also see the Rail and Coach/Bus fares tables in this chapter's introductory Getting Around section.

Bus National Express has numerous buses between Dover and London, and most stop at Canterbury. Stagecoach East Kent (☎ 240024) has an office on Pencester Rd. Canterbury is the bus hub for the region; there is no direct link, for instance, between Dover and Brighton, which makes a bus loop around the coast complicated. There is one bus per day from Canterbury to Brighton.

Train There are over 40 trains a day from London's Victoria and Charing Cross stations to Dover Priory.

There's an enjoyable hourly service that runs across the rich Romney Marsh farmlands from Ashford to Rye and Hastings. Ashford to Hastings takes 45 minutes and costs £6.50. There are hourly trains from Hastings to Battle (15 minutes, £2.20). Hastings to Brighton is another hour and costs £8.

Getting Around

Fortunately, the ferry companies run complimentary buses between the docks and train stations – they're a long walk apart, especially if you've got some heavy bags. There are infrequent town buses, or you could try Central Taxis (☎ 240441).

SISSINGHURST

Sissinghurst Gardens (☎ 01580-715330), off the A262 between the village of Sissinghurst and Cranbrook, is an enchanted place, the creation of the Kentish novelist and poet Vita Sackville-West. She developed a superb garden around the (now restored) ruins of an Elizabethan mansion. Anyone who has ever doubted the rich seductiveness of the English landscape has not been to Sissinghurst in spring or summer.

The gardens are managed by the National Trust. They're open 2 April to 15 October from 1 to 6.30 pm from Tuesday to Friday, and 10 am to 5.30 pm on Saturday and Sunday. The ticket office opens at noon from Tuesday to Friday. Admission is £5. The garden is very popular and if you have no option but to visit on a weekend, arrive early.

The nearest station is Staplehurst on the line between Tonbridge and Ashford. Maidstone & District's Maidstone to Hastings service (bus Nos 4 and 5) passes the station and Sissinghurst.

HEVER

Idyllic Hever Castle (☎ 01732-865224), near Edenbridge a few miles west of Tonbridge, was the childhood home of Anne Boleyn, mistress to Henry VIII and then his tragic queen. Restored by the Astor family, it also has magnificent gardens. It's open daily from 1 March to late November from noon to 6 pm; admission is £6. The nearest train station is Hever, a mile from the castle itself (£5.60 from London's Victoria station).

BRITAIN

KNOLE HOUSE

In a country that is full of extraordinary country houses, Knole (☎ 01732-450608) is outstanding. It seems as if *nothing* substantial has changed since early in the 17th century. Vita Sackville-West, the creator of Sissinghurst, was born here and her friend Virginia Woolf based the novel *Orlando* on the history of the house and family.

Now a National Trust property, it is open from April through to October on Wednesday, Friday, Saturday and Sunday 11 am to 5 pm, and on Thursday from 2 to 5 pm; admission is £4.50.

Knole is 1½ miles to the south of Sevenoaks, which is on the rail line from London's Charing Cross to Tonbridge.

LEEDS CASTLE

Near Maidstone in Kent, Leeds Castle (☎ 01622-765400) is justly famous as one of the world's most beautiful castles. It stands on two small islands in a lake, and was transformed by Henry VIII from a fortress into a palace surrounded by a superb park. Unfortunately, at weekends it is overrun by families and the atmosphere is more hysterical than historical.

It's open daily from March to October from 10 am to 5 pm, and from November to February from 10 am to 3 pm; admission is £7. National Express has one bus a day direct from Victoria coach station (leaving at 10 am); it must be prebooked and the combined cost of admission and travel is £15. The nearest train station is Bearsted on the Kent Coast Line to Ashford. British Rail has a combined admission/travel ticket for £15.90.

BRIGHTON

Brighton is Britain's number one seaside town – a fascinating mixture of seediness and sophistication. Just an hour away from London by train, Brighton is the perfect choice for day-trippers looking for a drop of froth and ozone.

In fact, jaded Londoners have been travelling to Brighton ever since the 1750s, when a shrewd doctor suggested that bathing in, and drinking, the local sea water was good for them. Although the town has spent £36 million on a sewage scheme, it's not recommended that you do either.

Brighton has some of the best nightlife outside London, including the largest gay club on the south coast, a vibrant student population, excellent shopping, a thriving arts scene and countless restaurants, pubs and cafés.

Orientation & Information

Brighton station is a 15-minute walk north of the beach. When you leave the station, go straight down the hill along Queen's Rd. The interesting part of Brighton lies to the left. When you reach the major intersection at the clock tower, turn left into North St, which will take you down towards the Royal Pavilion. To find the TIC, turn right at East St and follow the signs to Bartholomew Square. To get to the briny and the unmistakable Palace Pier, continue down North St and turn right into North Steine (it's a road and it's pronounced 'steen').

The bus station is tucked away in a small square sandwiched between the beach and Palace Pier (south) and the main traffic roundabout (north) formed by the Old Steine. There's an information/booking office on Old Steine.

The TIC (☎ 01273-333755), 10 Bartholomew Square, has public-transport maps and should also have copies of Brighton's listings magazine, the *Punter* (70p). If not, pick up a copy from any good newsagent.

Brighton hosts the largest arts festival outside Edinburgh for three weeks every May; though mostly mainstream, there are fringe events too.

Things to See

The **Royal Pavilion** (☎ 603005) is an extraordinary fantasy: an Indian palace on the outside, a Chinese brothel on the inside. It was built between 1815 and 1822 for George IV (then Prince Regent). George is said to have cried when he first saw the Music Room, which confirms that he was a very strange man indeed. The whole edifice is over the top in every respect and is not to be missed. It's open June through September every day from 10 am to 6 pm, and October through May to 5 pm; admission is £3.75.

The **Brighton Museum & Art Gallery** houses a quickie collection of Art-Deco and Art-Nouveau furniture, archaeological finds, surrealist paintings, and costumes. The most famous exhibit is Salvador Dali's lip-shaped sofa, but it's often away on loan. Entry is free, and it's open every day except Wednesday from 10 am to 5 pm, and from 2 to 5 pm on Sunday.

Nearby, the **Palace Pier** is the very image of Brighton, with its Palace of Fun. In this case, fun is taken to mean takeaway food and 1000 machines, all of which have flashing lights, and all of which take your money. This is *the* place to stick your head on a cardboard cutout of Prince Charles or Princess Diana...

Just south of North St (and north of the TIC) you'll find **The Lanes**, a maze of narrow alleyways crammed with antique, jewellery and fashionable clothes shops. Some of the best restaurants and bars are around here too. But for trendier, cheaper shops, good cafés and a slightly less touristy feel, explore **North Laine**, a series of streets north of North St, including Bond, Gardner, Kensington and Sydney Sts. Check out the flea market on Upper Gardner St on Saturday mornings.

Places to Stay

Brighton now has two independent hostels, which provide a more relaxed alternative to the YHA hostel. *Baggies Backpackers* (☎ 733740), 33 Oriental Place, is a spacious place with wonderful décor and truly excellent showers. Beds are £8 per night and there are three double rooms for £20. It's close to the seafront and plenty of cheap restaurants, but quite a trek from the station. Call for a free local pick-up, or turn right off Queen's Rd into Western Rd, then left into Little Preston St, right at Sillwood St and left into Oriental Place.

Brighton Backpackers Hostel (☎ 777717), 75-6 Middle St, is a little more central – turn left off West St (which is the continuation of Queen's Rd) into Duke St, then right into Middle St. Beds are £9 per night and doubles from £25 per room. There's a new annex 50 metres away on the seafront.

There's no shortage of hotels, guesthouses and B&Bs. Though you're unlikely to find much for under £15, it's worth scouting around. The main cluster of cheap B&Bs is to the east of the Palace Pier. Cross the Old Steine roundabout and walk up St James' St. There are several streets with B&Bs, particularly Madeira Place and Charlotte St.

Pebbles (☎ 684898), 8 Madeira Place, has comfortable singles/doubles for £18/30. The

Dorset Guest House (☎ 694646), at 17 Dorset Gardens, is recommended and has singles/doubles at £11 per person.

Brighton's hotels are further west, with many overlooking the sea. The *Dove Hotel* (☎ 779222), 18 Regency Square, is close to restaurant-filled Preston St and the ghost of the West Pier. All bedrooms have attached bathrooms and cost from £22 per person.

Places to Eat

Brighton is jam-packed with good-value eating places. Wander around The Lanes or head down to Preston St, which runs back from the seafront near West Pier, and you'll turn up all sorts of interesting, affordable possibilities. If you can't eat well for less than £7, buy a hot dog at the pier, or throw yourself off the end.

The *Queen Adelaide Tea Rooms* on the top floor of the Royal Pavilion is a very pleasant spot to rest and recuperate. A pot of tea is 80p, sandwiches are around £1.60, and salads and simple meals like ploughman's lunch are around £3.

Food for Friends (☎ 736236), 41 Market St, is Brighton's most enduring vegetarian haunt – it's always busy, so avoid peak times to be sure of a seat. Main meals are around £5 and there are takeaways and snacks as well. There are also branches at 17 Prince Albert St (☎ 202310) and 12 Sydney St (☎ 57163).

The *Dorset Street Bar* (☎ 605423), 28 North Rd, is a friendly pub in the heart of the buzzy North Laine area. You can order snacks, or larger meat or fish dishes for around £5. It has a good selection of wines and bottled beers and excellent coffee.

Entertainment

Brighton is literally jumping with pubs, bars and clubs, but, as always, fashion is fickle – check the *Punter* and bar and café walls for places of the moment.

Getting There & Away

Transport to and from Brighton is fast and frequent. See the Rail and Coach/Bus fares tables in this chapter's introductory Getting Around section.

Bus National Express has numerous buses from London. Its coast link west to Cornwall is basically a one-a-day service. It leaves

Brighton at 8.20 am. You would get off at Portsmouth 1¾ hours later and £6.75 poorer.

Train There are over 40 fast trains a day from London's Victoria, Kings Cross and London Bridge stations (one hour). There are plenty of trains between Brighton and Portsmouth (1½ hours, £10.30). There are also frequent services to Eastbourne, Hastings, Canterbury and Dover. Phone ☎ 206755 for information.

PORTSMOUTH

For much of British history, Portsmouth has been the home of the Royal Navy and it is littered with reminders that this was, for hundreds of years, a force that shaped the world.

After 437 years underwater, Henry VIII's favourite ship, the *Mary Rose*, and its time-capsule contents can now be seen. And you can walk the decks of the magnificent 1765 HMS *Victory*, Lord Nelson's flagship and shrine. Portsmouth is still a busy naval base and the sleek, grey killing machines of the 20th century are also very much in evidence.

Unfortunately, Portsmouth is not a particularly attractive city, largely due to WWII bombing, so there is no persuasive reason to stay overnight. Consider staying on the Isle of Wight, which is quick and easy to reach.

Orientation & Information

The train and bus stations, the harbour and the ferry terminal for the Isle of Wight are conveniently grouped together a stone's throw from the Naval Heritage Area. When you leave the station, or your bus, you'll immediately see HMS *Warrior*. If you walk around the quay towards the vessel you'll see the TIC and the Victory Gate, the entrance to the heritage area which houses the old ships and the Royal Navy Museum. The TIC (☎ 01705-826722) is on the Hard, or quay.

Things to See

At various times the navy has shown a fairly flexible attitude to fund-raising techniques, so at the end of a day in Portsmouth you should not be surprised to find you have been separated from many gold coins. Seeing the sights is expensive.

Portsmouth's centrepiece is the **Naval Heritage Area**. Entry is £5.15 for one ship, or £10

for all three. Entry to any of the ships includes entry to the museum.

Exploring HMS *Victory*, and walking in the footsteps of Lord Nelson and his multicultural crew of ruffians and gentlemen, is about as close as you can get to time travel – an extraordinary experience. The *Mary Rose* is also fascinating. The museum, however, is really for naval buffs, and HMS *Warrior* does not have the same magic as the *Victory*.

Tours of the harbour leave from beside the station and from Southsea. They cost £2.50 and give you an opportunity to see the modern navy at work. There's also Old Portsmouth and, across the harbour, Gosport Town and the **Submarine Museum** with a tour through a large submarine and the chance to look at Britain's first underwater vessel.

Places to Stay & Eat

There are a handful of places across from the Hard but most B&Bs and restaurants are in the adjacent resort of Southsea. Old Portsmouth, between the Hard and Southsea, has a couple of slightly higher-priced B&Bs. The TIC makes free bookings. The *Youth Hostel* (☎ 375661), Old Wymering Lane, Cosham, is about three miles from the main sights. It opens on a restricted basis most of the year; only between July and August is it open every day. Far more convenient is the friendly *Southsea Lodge* (☎ 832495) at 4 Florence Rd in Southsea, an independent hostel charging £8 a night.

Getting There & Away

Bus National Express has a daily service between Brighton and Portsmouth (£6.75). There are numerous buses to London, some via Heathrow airport (2½ hours, £12.50). One bus a day heads west as far as Penzance in Cornwall (11 hours, £31).

Train There are over 40 trains a day from London's Victoria and Waterloo stations (1½ hours, £16.80). There are plenty of trains between Brighton and Portsmouth (1½ hours, £10.30), and there are trains about every hour to Winchester (£6.10).

Ferry Passenger ferries to Ryde on the Isle of Wight operate from beside the train station, connecting with trains and buses. They take just 15 minutes and cost £5.80 for a day return, and £6.80 for a standard return. Contact Wightlink Ferries (☎ 827744), which also operates the car ferries to Fishbourne. There are also hovercrafts from Southsea to Ryde – a 10-minute trip for £7.70 return.

P&O (☎ 827677) has several ferries a day to Cherbourg and Le Havre in France; see the introductory Getting There & Away section at the beginning of this chapter.

WINCHESTER

Winchester is a small, beautiful cathedral city surrounded by rolling chalk downland, crystal-clear streams and water meadows. If any one place lies at the centre of English history and embodies the romantic vision of the English heartland, it is Winchester. Despite this it seems to have escaped inundation by tourists – certainly by comparison to nearby Salisbury and to theme parks like Bath and Oxford.

An Iron-Age hill fort overlooks the city. The Romans built a city on the present-day site; part of their defensive wall can still be seen incorporated into a later medieval defence. King Alfred the Great and many of his successors, including Canute and the Danish kings, made Winchester their capital, and William the Conqueror came to the city to claim the crown of England. Much of the present-day city, however, dates from the 18th century, by which time Winchester was merely a prosperous market centre, bypassed by history.

There are lots of good walks in the surrounding countryside. Winchester can be covered in a day trip from London, but it can also be a base for exploring the south coast (ie Portsmouth or the National Motor Museum at Beaulieu) or the country further west towards Salisbury.

Orientation & Information

The city centre is compact and easily negotiated on foot, and it has a good system of signposts. The train station is a 10-minute walk to the west of the city centre, and the bus and coach station is right in the centre directly opposite the Guildhall and TIC.

The TIC (☎ 01962-840500), the Guildhall, Broadway, is open daily (shorter hours on Sunday) from June to September. It produces the excellent *Winchester City Guide* (£1), which includes information on sights and

places to stay and eat. Regular guided walking tours (£2) operate from April to October.

Things to See

One of the most beautiful cathedrals in the country is **Winchester Cathedral**. If you go on the tours (run by enthusiastic local volunteers), spend some time in the Triforium, explore the cathedral close (the grounds and associated buildings) and go to a service (evensong at 5.30 pm most nights or 3.30 pm on Sundays is highly recommended) – you'll need a whole afternoon. A £2.50 donation is requested.

The present cathedral is a mixture of Norman, Early English and Perpendicular styles. The north and south transepts (the arms of the cross) are a magnificent example of pure Norman architecture, and the south transept houses a fascinating display of medieval sculpture and the famous 12th-century, illuminated Winchester Bible.

Nearby is **Winchester College**, founded in 1382 and the model for the great public (meaning private) schools of England. The chapel and cloisters are open to visitors from 10 am to 1 pm and 2 to 5 pm daily, except Sunday mornings. Guided tours operate several times daily and cost £2.50.

From the college there's a beautiful one-mile walk to the **Hospital of St Cross**, which was founded in 1136. It's open Monday to Saturday from 9.30 am to 12.30 pm and from 2 to 5 pm (shorter hours in winter); admission is £2.

In town, it's also worth visiting the **Great Hall**, begun by William the Conqueror and the site of many dramatic moments in English history, including the trial of Sir Walter Raleigh in 1603. It houses **King Arthur's Round Table**, now known to be a fake at 'only' 600 years of age.

Places to Stay & Eat

The **Youth Hostel** (☎ 853723), City Mill, 1 Water Lane, is in part of a beautiful 18th-century restored water mill; the other part is used by the National Trust. It's close to the centre of the city; walk down High St, which becomes the Broadway, cross the River Itchen (where you'll see the National Trust section) and take the first left into Water Lane.

There are also camping facilities a 10-minute walk north from the centre of town. The

BRITAIN

River Park Leisure Centre (☎ 869525), Gordon Rd, North Walls, is open from June to September and has tent sites for around £8.

There are plenty of B&Bs (the TIC charges £2 for bookings) but most only have one or two rooms and are in the £15 to £18 bracket. *Mrs B Sullivan* (☎ 862027), 29 Stockbridge Rd, near the train station, has singles/doubles from £15/28. *Mrs R Wright* (☎ 855067), 56 St Cross Rd, charges from £18/34. There are other B&Bs in St Cross Rd and the parallel Christchurch Rd.

Jewry St has several restaurant possibilities, including *Muswell's* (☎ 842414) at No 9. The ever-reliable *Pizza Express* (☎ 841845), at 1 Bridge St, near the old mill at the end of the Broadway, serves excellent pizzas at £4 to £6. The *Wykeham Arms* at 75 Kingsgate St, on the eastern side of the college, is a good example of the perfect British pub and has a cheaper bar menu as well as a more expensive restaurant.

Getting There & Away

Bus There are regular National Express buses to London via Heathrow (two hours, £9). Stagecoach/Hampshire Bus (☎ 852352) has a good network of local buses linking Salisbury, Southampton, Portsmouth and Brighton. Its Explorer ticket (£4.25) is also good on most Wilts & Dorset buses, which serve the region further to the west. In summer there are buses to the National Motor Museum at Beaulieu.

Train There are fast links with London's Waterloo, the south coast and the Midlands. The trip to London takes 1½ hours and costs £15.10. The regular services to Salisbury involve a change of train at Basingstoke or Southampton.

CHANNEL ISLANDS

Across the Channel from Dorset and just off the coast of France lie the small islands of Jersey, Guernsey, Alderney, Sark and Herm. As well as being a tax haven, the Channel Islands are a popular summer holiday resort for the British. Although there are pleasant beaches, good walks and cycle rides on some islands, and there's the famous conservation zoo (☎ 01534-864666) started by Gerald Durrell on Jersey, compared to mainland Britain or the Scottish islands there's really not a lot to see

and do. Jersey is the biggest and busiest of the islands, Alderney the most peaceful. There are no youth hostels but there are several campsites and B&Bs from £13 per person. For more information contact Jersey Tourism (☎ 01534-500777) and, for all the other islands, Guernsey Tourism (☎ 01481-723552).

Getting There & Away

There are daily flights to Jersey and Guernsey from nine UK airports on several airlines including British Airways (☎ 0345-222111). Return airfares range from around £70 up to £200.

Flights to Alderney are on Aurigny Air Services (☎ 01481-822866) from Southampton. Aurigny also operates inter-island flights.

Condor (☎ 01534-601000) runs twice-daily ferries between Weymouth (in 1997 from Poole) in Dorset and Jersey (3½ hours, from £65 return) via Guernsey. They also have a slower overnight ferry from Britain to Guernsey and Jersey; return fares start at £50. Ferry links to France are run by Emeraude (☎ 01481-711414) with services between Guernsey or Jersey and St Malo in Brittany; and also to Granville, Carteret and Diélette in Normandy.

South-West England

The counties of Wiltshire, Dorset, Somerset, Devon and Cornwall include some of the most beautiful countryside and spectacular coastline in Britain. They are also littered with the evidence of successive cultures and kingdoms that have been swept away by one invader after another.

The region can be divided between Devon and Cornwall out on a limb in the far west, and Dorset, Wiltshire and Somerset in the east, which are more readily accessible.

In the east, the story of English civilisation is signposted by some of its greatest monuments: the Stone Age left Stonehenge and spellbinding Avebury; the Iron Age Britons left Maiden Castle just outside Dorchester; between them, the Romans and the Georgians created Bath; the legendary King Arthur is said to be buried at Glastonbury; the Middle Ages left the great cathedrals at Exeter, Salisbury and Wells; and the landed gentry left great houses like Montacute and Wilton.

The east is densely packed with things to see, and the countryside, though varied, is a classic English patchwork of hedgerows, thatched cottages, stone churches, great estates and emerald-green fields.

Parts of Somerset and Wiltshire, particularly Bath and Salisbury, are major tourist attractions, but they are still, unquestionably, worth visiting. Dorset and North Devon are counties where you can happily wander without too many plans and without stumbling over too many people.

Devon and particularly Cornwall were once Britain's 'wild west', and smuggling was rife. Until the 18th century there were still Cornish speakers in Cornwall. The 'English Riviera' is almost too popular for its own good. It's wise to steer clear of the coastal towns in July and August, not least because the narrow streets are choked with traffic.

The weather is milder in the south-west all year round and there are beaches with golden sand and surfable surf. And then there are the exquisite villages tucked into unexpected valleys or overlooking beautiful harbours, and lanes squeezed between high hedges...

Some people find Cornwall disappointing, however. You'll certainly feel cheated if you think because you have reached the extreme south-western tip of the island you'll find untouched, undiscovered hideaways. Land's End – a veritable icon – has been reduced to a commercially minded tourist trap and inland, much of the peninsula has been devastated by generations of tin and china-clay mining. However, many of the coastal villages retain their charm, especially if you visit out of season.

The South West Coast Path, a long-distance walking route, follows the coastline round the peninsula for 613 miles from Poole, near Bournemouth in Dorset, to Minehead in Somerset, giving spectacular access to the best and most untouched sections. Walkers can also head to the Dartmoor and Exmoor national parks.

Orientation & Information

The chalk downs centred on Salisbury Plain run across Wiltshire and down through the centre of Dorset to the coast. In the west,

Exmoor and Dartmoor dominate the landscape. The railways converge on Exeter, the most important city in the west, then run round the coast, skirting the granite *tors* (outcrops) of Dartmoor to Truro, the uninspiring administrative centre of Cornwall, and Penzance. Bristol and Salisbury are also important crossroads.

Amongst others, there are several YHA hostels in Dartmoor and Exmoor national parks, and at Salisbury, Bath, Bristol, Winchester, Exeter, Plymouth, Penzance, Land's End, Tintagel and Ilfracombe.

Activities

Hiking The south-west has plenty of beautiful countryside, but walks in Dartmoor and Exmoor national parks, and round the coastline, are the best known. The barren, open wilderness of Dartmoor can be an acquired taste, but Exmoor covers some of the most beautiful countryside in England, and the coastal stretch from Ilfracombe to Minehead is particularly spectacular. See the separate sections on Dartmoor and Exmoor for more information.

The South West Coast Path is not a wilderness walk – villages (with food, beer and accommodation) are generally within easy reach. It's the longest national trail and follows a truly magnificent coastline. Completing a section of the path should be considered by any keen walker; if possible avoid busy summer weekends.

The official Countryside Commission/ Aurum Press guides cover Exmouth to Poole, Falmouth to Exmouth, Padstow to Falmouth and Minehead to Padstow, and cost £10.99 each. The South West Way Association (☎ 01803-873061) publishes a single-volume guide and accommodation list for the whole route (no maps) for £3.99.

Another famous walk, the Ridgeway, starts near Avebury and runs north-east for 85 miles to Ivinghoe Beacon near Aylesbury. Much of it follows ancient roads over the high open ridge of the chalk downs, before descending to the Thames Valley and climbing into the Chilterns. The western section (to Streatley) can be used by mountain bikes, horses, farm vehicles and recreational 4WDs. For peace and quiet, walk during the week.

The best guide is *The Ridgeway* by Neil Curtis (Countryside Commission/Aurum

BRITAIN

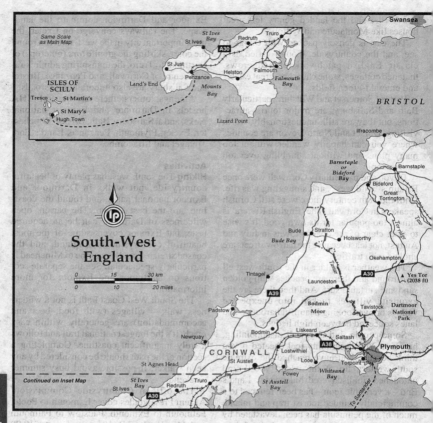

Same Scale
as Main Map

ISLES OF
SCILLY

Tresco
St Martin's
St Mary's
Hugh Town

Land's End

St Ives
Bay
St Ives
Penzance
St Just
Helston
Mounts
Bay
Redruth
Truro
A30
Falmouth
Falmouth
Bay
Lizard Point

Swansea

BRISTOL

Ilfracombe

Barnstaple
or
Bideford
Bay
Barnstaple
Bideford
Great
Torrington

Bude
Bude Bay
Stratton
Holsworthy
Okehampton
Yes Tor
2038 ft

South-West
England

0   15   30 km
0   10   20 miles

Tintagel
Launceston
A39
A30
Bodmin
Moor
Tavistock
Dartmoor
National
Park

Padstow

Newquay

St Agnes Head

Bodmin
Liskeard
A38
Saltash
Plymouth
CORNWALL
St Austell
Lostwithiel
Looe
Torpoint
Fowey
St Austell
Bay
Whitsand
Bay
To Santander

Continued on Inset Map

St Ives
Bay
St Ives
Redruth
Truro
A30

BRITAIN

Press, £9.99). A range of useful publications, including an excellent *Information and Accommodation Guide* (£1.50 plus 40p for UK postage), is available from the Ridgeway Officer (☎ 01865-810224), Countryside Service, Department of Leisure & Arts, Holton, Oxford OX33 1QQ. Cyclists should get a copy of *The Mountain Biker's Guide to the Ridgeway* by Andy Bull & Frank Barrett (Newspaper Publishing, £5.99).

Surfing The capital of British surfing is Newquay on the west Cornish coast, and it's complete with surf shops, bleached hair, Kombis and neon-coloured clothes (for

anyone suffering withdrawal symptoms). The surfable coast runs from Porthleven (near Helston) in Cornwall, west around Land's End and north to Ilfracombe. The most famous reef breaks are at Porthleven, Lynmouth and Milbrook; though good, they are inconsistent.

Cycling Bikes can be hired in most major regional centres, and the infrequent bus connections make cycling more than usually sensible. There's no shortage of hills, but the mild weather and quiet back roads make this excellent cycling country.

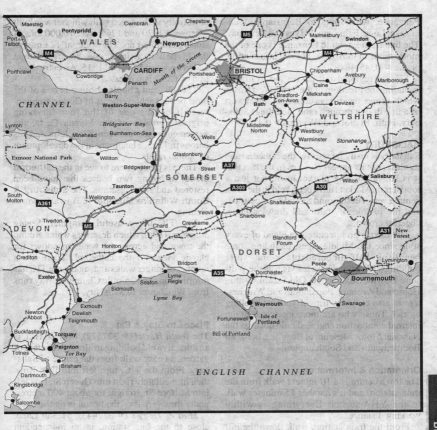

Getting Around

Bus National Express buses provide reasonable connections between the main towns, particularly in the east, but the further west you go the more dire the situation becomes. Transport around Dartmoor and Exmoor is very difficult in summer, and nigh on impossible at any other time. This is territory that favours those with their own transport.

Phone numbers for regional timetables include Bristol and Bath ☎ 0117-955 5111, Somerset ☎ 01823-255696, Wiltshire ☎ 0345-090899, Dorset ☎ 01305-224535, Devon ☎ 01392-382800 and Cornwall ☎ 01872-322142.

The Key West bus pass gives unlimited travel in South Devon and Cornwall for three/seven days for £12/20. There are also a number of one-day Explorer passes for around £4.50; it's always worth asking about them. For example, the Wiltshire Day Rover (£4.75) gives unlimited travel in Wiltshire (Salisbury, Avebury, Bradford-on-Avon etc), but also includes Bath.

Train Train services in the east are reasonably comprehensive, linking Bristol, Bath, Salisbury, Weymouth and Exeter. Beyond Exeter a single line follows the south coast as far as

Penzance, with spurs to Barnstaple, Gunnislake, Looe, Falmouth, St Ives and Newquay. The line from Exeter to Penzance is one of the most beautiful in Britain. For rail information, phone ☎ 0345-484950.

Several regional rail passes are available, including the Freedom of the SouthWest Rover which allows seven days unlimited travel west of a line drawn through (and including) Salisbury, Bath, Bristol and Weymouth (£47).

SALISBURY

Salisbury is justly famous for the cathedral and its close, but its appeal also lies in the fact that it is still a bustling market town, not just a tourist trap. Markets have been held in the town centre every Tuesday and Saturday since 1361, and the jumble of stalls still draws a large, cheerful crowd.

The town's architecture is a blend of every style since the Middle Ages, including some beautiful, half-timbered black-and-white buildings. It's a good base for visiting the Wiltshire Downs, Stonehenge, Old Sarum, Wilton House and Avebury. Portsmouth and Winchester are also easy day trips if you're travelling by rail. Those who are more interested in the internal combustion engine should not miss the National Motor Museum at Beaulieu, between Bournemouth and Southampton.

Orientation & Information

The town centre is a 10-minute walk from the train station, and it's another 15 minutes walk to the YHA hostel. Everything is within walking distance.

From the train station, walk down the hill and turn right at the T-junction into Fisherton St. This leads directly into town (which is well signposted). The bus station is just north of the centre of town; just two minutes down Endless St and you'll be in the thick of things.

The helpful TIC (☎ 01722-334956), Fish Row, is behind the impressive 18th-century Guildhall, which stands on the south-eastern corner of Market Square.

Things to See & Do

Beautiful **St Mary's Cathedral** is built in a uniform style known as Early English (or Early Pointed). This period is characterised by the first pointed arches and flying buttresses, and has a rather austere feel. The cathedral owes its

uniformity to the speed with which it was built – between 1220 and 1266, over 70,000 tons of stone were piled up. The spire, at 123 metres the highest in Britain, was an afterthought added between 1285 and 1315. An entry donation of £2.50 is requested.

The adjacent **chapter house** is one of the most perfect achievements of Gothic architecture. It houses one of the four surviving original versions of the Magna Carta, the agreement made between King John and his barons in 1215, a landmark in the development of human rights.

There is plenty more to see in the **cathedral close**, including two houses that have been restored and two museums. The **Salisbury & South Wiltshire Museum** (£3) is also worth visiting.

The TIC has a useful pamphlet, *Seeing Salisbury* (80p), which describes walks around the town and across the water meadows for classic views of the cathedral. There are a number of longer walks and, again, the TIC has information. The 26-mile Clarendon Way runs from Winchester to Salisbury.

Places to Stay & Eat

The *Youth Hostel* (☎ 327572), Milford Hill, is an attractive old building in almost a hectare of garden, an easy walk from the centre of Salisbury. From the TIC, turn left into Fish Row, then immediately right into Queen St, first left into Milford St, straight for about 400 metres, under the overpass – the hostel is on the left.

Matt & Tiggy's (☎ 327443), 51 Salt Lane, close to the bus station, is an independent hostel-like guesthouse with dorm rooms, but without a curfew. It's a pleasant old house and very welcoming. A bed costs £8.50, breakfast another £2.

Popular cafés include *Michael Snell's* and *Mr Christopher's*, near St Thomas' Church. Fisherton St, running from the centre to the train station, has Chinese, Thai, Indian and other restaurants. Try the Turkish *Charcoal Grill* (☎ 322134) at No 18. Continue under the railway bridge to *Pinocchio's* (☎ 413069) at No 139 for Italian food.

Pub food can be found at the old *Pheasant Inn* (☎ 327069) on the corner of Salt Lane and Rollestone St or at the popular *Coach & Horses* (☎ 336254) on Winchester St.

Entertainment

There is often interesting live entertainment in the *Salisbury Arts Centre* (☎ 321744), Bedwin St, including high-quality contemporary music and performances. Get a programme from the TIC.

Getting There & Away

See the Rail and Coach/Bus fares tables in this chapter's introductory Getting Around section.

Bus National Express has one bus a day via Salisbury from Portsmouth to Bath and Bristol. It's more expensive than the local bus lines, with the Portsmouth to Salisbury and Salisbury to Bath sectors both costing around £6. Badgerline/Wiltshire buses also run the regular X4 to Bath (two hours, £3) via Wilton and Bradford-on-Avon.

Three buses a day run from London via Heathrow to Salisbury (three hours).

There are three unlimited travel tickets available in Wiltshire – the Wiltshire Day Rover (£4.85), the Wilts & Dorset Explorer (£4.25) and the Badgerline Day Rambler (£4.60). Wiltshire Bus Lines (☎ 0345-090899) or Wilts & Dorset (☎ 336855) can tell you more. There are daily buses to and from Avebury, Stonehenge and Old Sarum. If you're going through to Bristol or Bath, or plan to spend time exploring Somerset (Wells, Glastonbury) or Gloucestershire (Cotswolds), get the Badgerline Day Rambler, which is also good for the X4 to Bath.

Train Salisbury is linked by rail to Portsmouth (numerous, 1¼ hours), Bath (numerous, two hours, £9) and Exeter (eight per day, two hours). There are numerous daily trains from London's Waterloo station (1½ hours) – see the Rail and Coach/Bus fares tables in this chapter's introductory Getting Around section.

Getting Around

Local buses are reasonably well organised and link Salisbury with Stonehenge, Old Sarum and Wilton House; phone ☎ 336855 for details. Bikes can be hired from the Hayball Cycle Shop (☎ 411378) on Winchester St at £7.50 per day.

AROUND SALISBURY
Stonehenge

Stonehenge is the most famous prehistoric site in Europe – a ring of enormous stones (some of which were brought from Wales), built in stages beginning 5000 years ago. Reactions vary; some find that the car park, gift shop and crowds of tourists swamp the monument, which is actually quite small. Avebury, 18 miles to the north, is much more impressive in scale and recommended for those who would like to commune with the ley lines in relative peace.

Stonehenge is two miles west of Amesbury at the junction of the A303 and A344/A360, and nine miles from Salisbury (the nearest station); entry is £3. Some feel that it is unnecessary to pay the entry fee, because you can get a good view from the road and even if you do enter you are kept at some distance from the stones. There are seven buses a day from Salisbury, costing £2.70 one way and £4.25 return. First departure is 11 am, and in summer there's an additional departure at 10 am. Consider a Wilts & Dorset Explorer ticket for £4.25. Phone ☎ 01722-336855 for details.

AVEBURY

Avebury (between Calne and Marlborough, just off the A4) stands at the hub of a prehistoric complex of ceremonial sites, ancient avenues and burial chambers dating from 3500 BC. In scale the remains are more impressive than Stonehenge, and if you visit outside summer weekends it's quite possible to escape the crowds. The impact made by the Neolithic people on the environment is so dramatic you can almost feel them breathing down your neck.

In addition to an enormous stone circle, there's Silbury Hill (the largest constructed mound in Europe), West Kennet Long Barrow (a burial chamber) and a pretty village with an ancient church. The Avebury Museum (£1.50) helps explain (as far as this is possible, which is not far) the complex and is a good place to start your exploration.

Avebury TIC (☎ 01672-539425) can help with accommodation. The *Old Vicarage* (☎ 539362) does B&B for £20 per person, or there's *The Red Lion* (☎ 539266) with doubles for £37. The very popular *Stones Restaurant* has great food served cafeteria style.

Avebury can be easily reached by frequent buses from Salisbury (Wiltshire Bus No 5 or 6) or Swindon. To travel to and from Bath you'll have to change buses at Devizes; check connections with the county enquiry line (☎ 0345-090899).

DORSET

The greater part of Dorset is designated as an area of outstanding natural beauty but, with the exceptions of Poole and Weymouth, it avoids inundation by tourists.

The coast varies from sandy beaches to shingle banks and towering cliffs. Lyme Regis is a particularly attractive spot, made famous as the setting for John Fowles' book *The French Lieutenant's Woman*, and the subsequent film.

For those who've read Thomas Hardy, however, Dorset is inextricably linked with his novels. You can visit his birthplace at Higher Bockhampton, or Dorchester (Casterbridge), the unspoilt market town where he lived. Maiden Castle, the largest Iron Age fort in England, is two miles south-west of Dorchester.

Orientation & Information

Dorchester makes a good base for exploring the best of Dorset, but on the coast colourful Weymouth or quieter Bridport are good alternatives. One of the reasons for Dorset's backwater status is that no major transport routes cross it. A rail loop runs west from Southampton to Dorchester, then north to Yeovil, and the main westbound InterCity trains stop at Axminster (East Devon).

There are good TICs in all the main towns.

Places to Stay

There is no YHA hostel in Dorchester or Weymouth but there are hostels in Swanage, Lulworth Cove, Litton Cheney and Bridport, all convenient for walkers on the Dorset Coast Path. Dorchester has some B&Bs but Weymouth is positively packed with them. In Lyme Regis try the *Cliff Cottage* (☎ 01297-443334) in Cobb Rd which has rooms with bath for £17 and without for £15.50.

Getting There & Away

Trains to Dorchester from London depart about every hour; they take about three hours, cost £28.70 and continue to Weymouth. Dorchester to Weymouth takes just 10 to 15 minutes by train and costs £2.10. Trains continue west to Bath and Bristol from Dorchester.

There are also buses on these routes but, although cheaper, they tend to be much slower. The buses from London take four hours! Axminster is also a reasonable transport hub.

Getting Around

There are regular buses between Dorchester and Weymouth, Salisbury, Bournemouth and Bridport. Buses also operate regularly between Bridport and Axminster, while the hourly buses between Lyme Regis and Axminster cost £1.45. Contact Southern National (☎ 01305-783645) or Wilts & Dorset (☎ 01202-673555) for more information.

EXETER

Exeter is the largest city in the West Country, with a population of 102,000. It was devastated during WWII and as a result first impressions are not particularly inspiring; if you get over these, you'll find a livable university city with a thriving nightlife. It's a good starting point for Dartmoor and Cornwall.

The cathedral is one of the most attractive in England, with two massive Norman towers surviving from the 11th century. From 50 AD, when the city was established by the Romans, until the 19th century, Exeter was an important port, and the waterfront (including a large boat museum) is gradually being restored.

There are a number of highly recommended free tours, which cover both cathedral and town.

Orientation & Information

There are two train stations, but most InterCity trains use St David's, which is a 20-minute walk west of the city centre and Central station. From St David's, cross the station forecourt and Bonhay Rd, then climb some steps to St David's Hill and then turn right up the hill for the centre. You'll pass a batch of reasonably priced B&Bs on your right; keep going for ¾ mile, then turn left up High St. The centre of the city is well signposted.

The TIC (☎ 01392-265700) in the Civic Centre, Paris St, is just across the road from the bus station, a short walk north-east of the cathedral; it's not open on Sunday.

Places to Stay & Eat

The *Youth Hostel* (☎ 873329), 47 Countess Wear Rd, is two miles south-east of the city towards Topsham. It's open from early January through November. From High St, catch minibus K or T (10 minutes) and ask for the Countess Wear post office.

The best value accommodation in central Exeter is the university's *St Luke's Hall* (☎ 211500) – just £12.50 per person, including breakfast. The catch is that it's available only in March, April, July, August and September (college vacations).

There are several reasonable B&Bs on St David's Hill. The *Highbury* (☎ 434737), 89 St David's Hill, is good value with singles/doubles for £13.50/25. There's another batch on Blackall Rd (near the prison). *Rhona's Guest House* (☎ 77791), 15 Blackall Rd, has doubles for £24.

There are a number of busy wine bars on medieval Gandy St, which is signposted off High St. The *Ship Inn*, down the alley between the cathedral and the High St, was where Drake used to drink. *Herbies*, on North St, is an excellent vegetarian restaurant. Carnivores should be satisfied by the steaks at *Mad Meg's* (☎ 221225), on Fore St. Students get a 20% discount on Monday nights and special prices (from £3.95 for main courses) on Wednesdays.

Getting There & Away

See the Rail and Coach/Bus fares tables in this chapter's introductory Getting Around section.

Bus Half a dozen buses run between London, Heathrow airport and Exeter daily (four hours). The daily south-coast service between Brighton and Penzance (via Portsmouth, Weymouth, Dorchester, Bridport, Exeter and Plymouth) departs Exeter for Brighton at 12.40 pm (eight hours, £23 if you don't travel on a Friday). Dorchester to Exeter takes two hours and costs £8.75. Buses for Penzance leave Exeter at 11.15 am and 4.35 pm (five hours, £16). Phone ☎ 0990-808080 for National Express information, ☎ 01392-427711 for Stagecoach bus information.

Train Exeter is at the hub of lines running from Bristol (numerous, 1½ hours), Salisbury (hourly, two hours) and Penzance (12 per day,

three hours). There are hourly trains from London's Waterloo and Paddington stations (three hours). The train to and from London is much quicker than the bus.

The 39-mile branch line to Barnstaple is promoted as the Tarka Line and gives good views of traditional Devon countryside with its characteristic, deep-sunken lanes. Barnstaple is a useful starting point for North Devon. There are 11 trains a day from Monday to Friday, nine on Saturday and four on Sunday.

For rail information, phone ☎ 0345-484950.

PLYMOUTH

Plymouth's renown as a maritime centre was established long before Sir Francis Drake's famous game of bowls on Plymouth Hoe in 1588. Devastated by WWII bombing raids, much of the city is modern but the Barbican (the old quarter by the harbour where the Pilgrim Fathers set sail for the New World in 1620) has been preserved.

Orientation & Information

The TIC (☎ 01752-264849), Island House, the Barbican, is open daily. North of here are the bus station (½ mile) and train station (one mile). To the west is Plymouth Hoe, a grassy park with wide views over the sea.

Places to Stay

The *Youth Hostel* (☎ 562189), Bemont Places, Stoke, is 1½ miles from the centre. It's open daily from March through October; phone for other opening hours. B&Bs cluster round the north-western corner of the Hoe and are generally good value, from £13. *Plymouth Backpackers International Hostel* (☎ 225158) at 172 Citadel Rd, The Hoe, has 48 beds for £7.50 a night.

Getting There & Away

Devon General has frequent buses to and from Exeter (1¼ hours, £4.05). National Express has direct connections to numerous cities, including London (4½ hours, £27.50) and Bristol (2½ hours, £18). Trains are faster – London (3½ hours) and Penzance (1½ hours) – but more expensive.

DARTMOOR NATIONAL PARK

Although the park is only about 25 miles from north to south and east to west, it encloses some of the wildest, bleakest country in England – a suitable terrain for the Hound of the Baskervilles (one of Sherlock Holmes' most famous opponents).

The park covers a granite plateau punctuated by distinctive tors, which can look uncannily like ruined castles, and cut by deep valleys known as *coombs*. The high moorland is covered by windswept gorse and heather (there are no trees, apart from some limited plantations), and is grazed by sheep and semi-wild Dartmoor ponies.

Habitation is sparse. There are several small market towns surrounding the tableland, but the only village of any size on the moor is Princetown, which is not a particularly attractive place.

The countryside in the south-east is more conventionally beautiful, with wooded valleys and thatched villages. There are no specific tourist sights of note on Dartmoor. This is hiking country par excellence.

Orientation & Information

Dartmoor is accessible from Exeter and Plymouth, and rare buses run from these regional centres to the surrounding market towns. There are only two roads across the moor and they meet near Princetown.

The National Park Authority (NPA) has eight information centres in and around the park, but it is also possible to get information in the TICs at Exeter and Plymouth before you set off. The new High Moorland Visitor Centre (☎ 01822-890414) in Princetown is open all year. The Ministry of Defence (☎ 01392-70164) has a large training area and three live firing ranges in the north-western section.

Places to Stay

Most of Dartmoor is privately owned, but the owners of unenclosed moorland don't usually object to backpackers who keep to a simple code: don't camp on moorland enclosed by walls or within sight of roads or houses; don't stay on one site for more than two nights; and leave the site as you found it.

There are YHA hostels bang in the middle near Postbridge and at Steps Bridge, near Dunsford between Moretonhampstead and Exeter, as well as at Exeter, Plymouth and Dartington.

The *Bellever Youth Hostel* (☎ 01822-880227), Postbridge, is very popular. It closes from November to mid-March and on Sunday, except in July and August. The *Steps Bridge Youth Hostel* (☎ 01647-252435) is closed from October through March. The *Plume of Feathers Inn Bunkhouse* (☎ 01822-890240) in Princetown has 42 beds for £5.50 a head, but warns that three months advance booking may be needed for summer weekends. Beds cost the same at *Dartmoor Expedition Centre* (☎ 01364-621249) in Widecombe-in-the-Moor. Phone ☎ 01722-337494 for information on the camping barn network which offers basic beds in unheated 'stone tents' from £2.75 a night.

The larger towns on the edge of the park (like Buckfastleigh, Moretonhampstead, Okehampton and Tavistock) all have plentiful supplies of B&Bs in the £13 to £16 bracket.

Getting There & Away

Exeter or Plymouth are the best starting points for the park, but Exeter has the better transport connections to the rest of England. Public transport in and around the park is lousy, so consider hiring a bike (about £6 a day) from Flash Gordon (☎ 01392-213141) in Exeter or Action Sports (☎ 01752-662901) in Plymouth.

From Exeter, DevonBus 359 follows a circular route through Steps Bridge, Moretonhampstead and Chagford (Monday to Saturday). The most important bus that actually crosses Dartmoor is DevonBus 82, the Transmoor Link (☎ 01752-382800), running between Exeter and Plymouth via Moretonhampstead and Princetown. Unfortunately, it only runs daily from late May to late September, and even then there are only three buses each way.

A one-day Rover ticket (£3.50) allows you to get on and off as often as you like. Alternatively, you can catch the Transmoor Link in one direction and catch the hourly buses between Plymouth and Exeter (along the A38) in the other direction but it'll cost you more.

Outside summer, life becomes considerably more difficult, with infrequent services and changing schedules. The best idea is to work out roughly what you want to do, then contact the Devon County Public Transport Help Line (☎ 01392-382800).

BRITAIN

SOUTH CORNWALL COAST
Truro
You may need to use Cornwall's uninspiring regional centre as a transport hub. For bus information, ring Western National (☎ 01209-719988).

Penzance
At the end of the line from London, Penzance is a busy little town that has not yet completely sold its soul to tourists. You may want to stay here if you're just about to start or finish the section of the Coast Path around Land's End to and from St Ives. This dramatic 25-mile section can be broken at the YHA hostel at St Just (near Land's End), and there are many cheap farm B&Bs along the way.

The TIC (☎ 01736-62207) is just outside the train station.

Places to Stay The *Youth Hostel* (☎ 62666), Castle Horneck, Alverton, is an 18th-century mansion on the outskirts of town. Walk west through town on the Land's End road (Market Jew St) until you get to a thatched cottage opposite the Pirate Inn, turn right and cross the A30 bypass road until you get to the signposted lane.

Getting There & Away There are four buses a day from Penzance to Bristol via Truro and Plymouth; one direct bus a day to Exeter (five hours); and five buses a day from London and Heathrow (7½ hours).

The train is definitely the civilised way to get to Penzance – a very enjoyable, though expensive, trip. There are five trains a day from London's Paddington station (five hours, £30 if you buy your ticket a week in advance). There are frequent trains from Penzance to St Ives between 7 am and 8 pm (20 minutes, £2.50).

Land's End
The coastal scenery on either side of Land's End is some of the finest in Britain, although the development at Land's End itself is the pits. However, the *Youth Hostel* (☎ 01736-788437) at St Just, eight miles from Penzance, is highly recommended. It's closed from January to mid-February. You can also stay at the independent *Whitesand's Lodge* (☎ 871776) backpackers hostel in Sennen village; dorm beds cost £8. Even cheaper is *Kelynack Bunk-barn* (☎ 787633), one mile south of St Just; a bunk bed costs £5 but with only 10 beds advance booking is wise.

The coastal hills between St Just and St Ives, with their dry stone walling, form one of the oldest, most fascinating agricultural landscapes in Britain, still following an Iron Age pattern. There are numerous prehistoric remains and the abandoned engine houses of old tin and copper mines.

WEST CORNWALL COAST
St Ives
Artists have long been attracted to St Ives, and in 1993 a branch of London's Tate Gallery was opened here. This is an exceptionally beautiful little town, but steer clear in July and August. The omnipresent sea, the harbour, the beaches, the narrow alleyways, steep slopes and hidden corners are captivating. It's easily accessible by train from Penzance and London via St Erth. There are numerous B&Bs in the £13 to £16 bracket.

The TIC (☎ 01736-796297), the Guildhall, Street-an-Pol, a short walk from the train station, is open all year. There are several surf shops on the Wharf (the street edging the harbour) where it is possible to rent boards. Windansea (☎ 796560) on Fore St has seven-foot surfboards for £5, wetsuits, and mountain bikes at £10 per day.

The main road into St Ives from Penzance, above Carbis Bay, is lined with B&Bs, but the closer you are to the town centre the better. Climb the steep streets immediately behind the harbour (towards Porthmeor Beach) and you'll find several blocks of B&Bs. There are a number of cheap restaurants around the harbour and in Fore St behind.

Newquay
This is a brash and tacky tourist centre – a schizophrenic cross between a 1970s surf town and a traditional English beach resort. There are numerous sandy beaches, several of them right in town (including Fistral Beach for board riders).

The TIC (☎ 01637-871345) is near the bus station in the centre of town. There are several surf shops on Fore St and they all hire fibreglass boards and wetsuits, each for £5 to

£6 per day. Compare prices; they're competitive.

Newquay has several independent hostels geared up for surfers. *Newquay Cornwall Backpackers* (☎ 874668), in an excellent central position overlooking Towan Beach in Beachfield Ave, has dorm beds for £6.50 per night, or £39 per week. There are no curfews, and it's open all day. *Fistral Backpackers* (☎ 873146), 18 Headland Rd, is a clean, new place close to Fistral Beach where the world surfing championships take place each July. Dorm beds cost £5 each.

There are four trains a day between Par, on the main London to Penzance line, and Newquay, and numerous buses to Truro.

Tintagel

Even the summer crowds and the grossly commercialised village can't destroy the surf-battered grandeur of Tintagel Head. According to legend the scanty ruins mark the birthplace of King Arthur, hence the plethora of King Arthur tea shops etc. Entry costs £2.20. It's also worth visiting the picturesque 14th-century **Old Post Office**; admission £2. The *Tintagel Youth Hostel* (☎ 01840-770334), at Dunderhole Point, is open April through September. Alternatively *Boscastle Youth Hostel* (☎ 250287) has a lovely situation overlooking the harbour. It's open daily from mid-May through September; phone for other opening hours.

For information on the irregular bus services phone ☎ 322000.

NORTH DEVON

North Devon is one of the most beautiful regions in England, with a spectacular, largely unspoilt coastline and the superb Exmoor National Park, which protects the best of it.

Barnstaple

Barnstaple is a large town and transport hub: a good starting point for North Devon. There are some handsome old buildings, but there's no reason to stay, and there's no YHA hostel. Contact the TIC (☎ 01271-388583) for B&Bs.

Barnstaple is at the western end of the Tarka Line from Exeter and connects with a number of bus services around the coast. Filer's (☎ 863819) bus No.301 service runs along the A39 south of Bideford, where you can connect

with a Red Bus (☎ 45444) to Bude. Red Bus service No 310 runs direct to Lynton (1½ hours, £2.15, five buses a day, with the last bus at 5.30 pm), but the most interesting option is the excellent No 300 scenic service (summer only) that crosses Exmoor from Barnstaple, through Lynton to Minehead (£4.50 for a one-day Explorer Pass).

Mountain bikes are available from Tarka Trail (☎ 24202) in the train station for £8 per day.

Exmoor National Park

Exmoor is a small national park (265 sq miles) enclosing a wide variety of beautiful landscapes. In the north and along the coast the scenery is particularly breathtaking, with dramatic humpbacked headlands giving superb views across the Bristol Channel.

A high plateau rises steeply behind the coast, but is cut by steep, fast-flowing streams. The bare, high hills of heather and grass run parallel to the coast. On the southern side the two main rivers, the Exe and Barle, wind their way south along the wooded coombs. Pony herds descended from ancient hill stock still roam the commons, as do England's last herds of wild red deer.

There are a number of particularly attractive villages: Lynton/Lynmouth, twin villages joined by a water-operated railway; Porlock at the edge of the moor in a beautiful valley; Dunster, which is dominated by a castle, a survivor from the Middle Ages; and Selworthy, a National Trust village with many classic thatched cottages.

Arguably the best and easiest section of the South West Coast Path is between Minehead and Padstow (sometimes known as the Somerset & North Devon Coast Path).

Orientation & Information Exmoor is accessible from Barnstaple (train from Exeter) and Taunton (bus/train from Bristol or London, bus from Wells).

The NPA has five information centres in and around the park, but it's also possible to get information in the TICs at Barnstaple, Ilfracombe, Lynton and Minehead. The NPA centres at Dunster (☎ 01643-821835) and Lynmouth (☎ 01598-752509) are open from the end of March to November. The main visitor centre (☎ 01398-323841), Fore St, Dulverton (between Bampton and Minehead), is open all year.

The *Exmoor Visitor* is a free newspaper listing useful addresses, numerous guided walks run by the NPA, accommodation and general information.

Places to Stay In addition to the YHA hostel at Ilfracombe, there are hostels at Minehead (☎ 01643-702595), near Lynton (☎ 01598-53237) and Exford (☎ 01643-831288) in the centre of the park. All these hostels close over winter (Lynton only in January) and are only open daily in July and August.

The main swarm of B&Bs can be found around Lynton/Lynmouth, but they are scattered throughout the park. They aren't cheap: you're probably looking at £16. Contact the Lynton TIC (☎ 01598-752225) for specific suggestions.

Getting There & Away From Exeter catch the Tarka Line to Barnstaple, from where buses run to Ilfracombe, Lynton and Minehead. See the Exeter and Barnstaple sections for more details.

Alternatively, there are hourly buses from Taunton (one hour, £3.10) to Minehead. Contact Southern National (☎ 01823-272033) for details; the last bus leaves at 7.55 pm. Taunton can be reached from Bristol (Bristol to Plymouth line), Wells and Glastonbury (Badgerline bus No 163), or London (London to Penzance line). A timetable covering local public transport is available from TICs or you can phone Devon County Council's bus enquiry line (☎ 01392-382800).

BATH

For more than 2000 years, Bath's fortune has been linked to its hot springs and tourism. The Romans developed a complex of baths and a temple to Sulis-Minerva. Today, however, Bath's Georgian architecture is almost as important an attraction.

Throughout the 18th century, Bath was the most fashionable and elegant haunt of English society. Aristocrats flocked here to gossip, gamble and flirt. Fortunately, they had the good sense and fortune to employ a number of brilliant architects who designed the Palladian terrace housing (characterised by simplicity and symmetry) that dominates the city.

Like Florence, Italy, Bath is an architectural jewel. As in Florence, there is a much-photographed, shop-lined bridge, and like Florence, in high summer the town can seem little more than an exotic shopping mall for wealthy tourists. However, when sunlight brightens the honey-coloured stone, and buskers and strollers fill the streets and line the river, no one could deny Bath's exceptional beauty.

Orientation & Information

Bath sprawls more than you'd expect and some suburbs are a long way out (as you'll discover if you stay at the hostel). Fortunately, the centre is compact and easy to get around, although the tangle of streets, arcades and squares can be confusing. The train and bus stations are both south of the TIC, by the river.

From mid-June to mid-September, the TIC (☎ 01225-462831), Abbey Chambers, Abbey Churchyard, is open until 7 pm Monday to Saturday and until 6 pm on Sunday. For the rest of the year it closes at 5 pm (4 pm on Sunday). Advance booking of accommodation is essential over Easter, during the Bath International Festival, over summer weekends and throughout July and August.

Things to See & Do

Bath was designed for wandering around – you need at least a full day. Don't miss the **covered market** next to the Guildhall, or the maze of passageways just north of the Abbey Churchyard. Free walking tours (recommended) leave from the Abbey Churchyard at 10.30 am (except Saturday).

Try to see a play at Bath's sumptuous Theatre Royal (☎ 448844), which often features shows on their pre-London run. The Bath International Festival is held from the last week of May through the first week of June.

Bath's flea market (antiques and clothes) is a popular place for bargain hunters. It's held on Saturday and Sunday mornings on Walcot St, near the YMCA.

Walking Tour A convenient starting point for a walking tour is **Bath Abbey** (donation £1.50). Built between 1499 and 1616, it's more glass than stone.

BRITAIN

BRITAIN

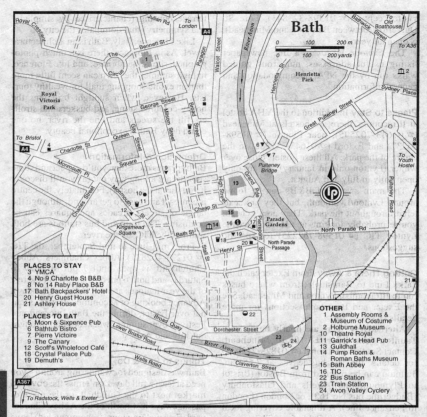

Bath

0   100   200 m
0   100   200 yards

To
Old
Boathouse

To A36

Henrietta
Park

Sydney Place

To
Youth
Hostel

Pulteney Road

North Parade Rd

Parade
Gardens

North Parade
Passage

21

Royal Crescent

To
London A4

Bennett St

The
Circus

1

Paragon

Walcot Street

River Avon

Bathwick Street

Royal
Victoria
Park

George Street

Broad Street

Milsom Street

Henrietta St

3

Great Pulteney Street

To Bristol
A4

4

Charlotte St

Queen
Square

Monmouth Pl

Gay Street

5

6

7

Pulteney
Bridge

Monmouth St

Charles Street

10

11

12

Kingsmead
Square

Cheap St.

15

High Street

13

Grand Pde

9

14

16

19

17

Bath St

Stall St

Henry St

20

Pierrepont Street

Broad Quay

Lower Bristol Road

Dorchester Street

Wells Road

22

Claverton Street

River Avon

23

24

To Radstock, Wells & Exeter

A367

A4

PLACES TO STAY
3 YMCA
4 No 9 Charlotte St B&B
8 No 14 Raby Place B&B
17 Bath Backpackers' Hotel
20 Henry Guest House
21 Ashley House

PLACES TO EAT
5 Moon & Sixpence Pub
6 Bathtub Bistro
7 Pierre Victoire
9 The Canary
12 Scoff's Wholefood Café
18 Crystal Palace Pub
19 Demuth's

OTHER
1 Assembly Rooms &
   Museum of Costume
2 Holburne Museum
10 Theatre Royal
11 Garrick's Head Pub
13 Guildhall
14 Pump Room &
   Roman Baths Museum
15 Bath Abbey
16 TIC
22 Bus Station
23 Train Station
24 Avon Valley Cyclery

On the southern side of the Abbey Churchyard (an open square), the **Pump Room** houses
an opulent restaurant that exemplifies the
elegant style that once drew the aristocrats.

Nearby, the **Roman Baths Museum** is a
series of excavated passages and chambers
beneath street level, taking in the sulphurous
mineral springs (still flowing after all these
years), the ancient central-heating system and
the bath itself, which retains its Roman paving
and lead base. This is Bath's top attraction
(open year round from 9 am to 6 pm daily (5
pm in winter and on Sunday) and entry is
£5.60, or £7.50 including the Museum of
Costume in the Assembly Rooms, a 20-minute

walk up the hill. It can get hopelessly overcrowded in summer.

From the Roman Baths, walk north until you
come to the main shopping drag, Milsom St,
and finally the **Assembly Rooms** and the
Museum of Costume, which contains an
enormous collection of clothing from 1590 to
the present day.

Turn left on Bennet St and walk west to the
Circus, an architectural masterpiece by John
Wood the Elder, designed so that a true cres-
cent faces each of its three approaches.
Continue to **Royal Crescent**, designed by
John Wood the Younger and even more highly
regarded than his father's effort. No 1 has been

superbly restored to its 1770 glory, down to the minutest detail (entry is £3.50/2.50 for adults/students, and worth it).

From Royal Crescent, wander back to the Abbey, then keep going east until you find yourself overlooking the formal **Parade Gardens** with their famous view up the Avon to **Pulteney Bridge**, built by Robert Adam and lined with tiny shops. Continue along Great Pulteney St from the bridge and you will reach Sydney Place. Jane Austen lived at No 4 with her parents.

Places to Stay

Hostels The new *Bath Backpackers Hotel* (☎ 446787) in Pierrepont St is just five minutes walk from the bus and train stations, with dorm beds for £9.50. The *YMCA International House* (☎ 460471) offers the best budget accommodation. Centrally located, it takes men and women and there's no curfew, but it's heavily booked. Approaching from the south along Walcot St, look out for an archway and steps on the left about 150 metres past the post office. Singles/doubles with continental breakfast are £12.50/23, and dorms are £10.

The *Youth Hostel* (☎ 465674) is out towards the University of Bath, a good 25-minute walk, or you can catch Badgerline bus No 18 (75p return) from the bus station. There are compensatory views and the building is magnificent. It's open daily year round.

B&Bs Bath's B&Bs are expensive. In the summer most charge at least £18/32 for a single/double. The main areas are along Newbridge Rd to the west, Wells Rd to the south and around Pulteney Rd in the east.

Considering its central location, *Henry Guest House* (☎ 424052), 6 Henry St, is a bargain at £16 per person. *No 9 Charlotte St* (☎ 424193) is also dead central, and good value at £30 for a double room.

There are numerous B&Bs on and around Pulteney Rd. *Ashley House* (☎ 425027), 8 Pulteney Gardens, has eight rooms, some with attached shower, from £20 to £25 per person. *No 14 Raby Place* (☎ 465120), off Bathwick Hill just after you turn off Pulteney Rd, is a non-smoking establishment charging £18 to £21 per person. Continue along Bathwick Hill over the canal to *No 14 Dunsford Place* (☎ 464134), a two-room B&B that charges from £15 a head.

In an idyllic location beside the River Avon, the *Old Boathouse* (☎ 466407), Forester Rd, is an Edwardian boating station within walking distance of the centre. Comfortable rooms with attached bathrooms are from £20 per person.

Places to Eat

Scoff's Wholefood Café, on Kingsmead Square, has excellent filled rolls and light lunches (tandoori burgers, spinach pancakes, etc) with up to 30% off if you don't eat in. There are several fast-food places in this area.

The *Moon & Sixpence* (☎ 460962), 6 Broad St, is a pleasant pub which offers two-course all-you-can-eat lunches for £5. Pubs will probably be your best bet for evening meals, too. The *Crystal Palace* (☎ 423944), Abbey Green (south of Abbey Churchyard), has a beer garden, traditional ale and meals like lasagne and salad for £4.55.

The excellent Edinburgh chain *Pierre Victoire* (☎ 334334) has a branch at 16 Argyle St, serving French food that's very good value. The three-course set lunch (£4.90) is popular. Nearby at 2 Grove St, *Bathtub Bistro* (☎ 460593) is recommended and also good value. It serves interesting dishes like black bean moussaka (£5.50). *Demuth's* (☎ 446059) in North Parade Passage is a very popular vegetarian restaurant where delicacies like pesto toast cost £4.25.

The *Canary* (☎ 424846), 3 Queen St, is in one of Bath's most attractive streets. It has an interesting menu with a range of main dishes for around £5.50 – honey spiced chicken, for example. Cream teas are £3.50 at the Canary but the real place for such indulgences is the *Pump Room*. Here one sips one's tea and heaps one's scones with jam and cream while one is being serenaded by the Pump Room Trio. It's not cheap at £5.10, but it's very much part of the Bath experience.

Getting There & Around

See the Rail and Coach/Bus fares tables in this chapter's introductory Getting Around section.

Bus There are National Express (☎ 0990-808080) buses every two hours from London (three hours), but Turners (☎ 0117-955 5333) currently sells the cheapest tickets – just £6.50/12.50 for a single/return. Bakers Dolphin

BRITAIN

(☎ 0117-961 4000) charges £8.50/13.95 for a single/return.

There's one bus a day between Bristol and Portsmouth via Bath and Salisbury – see the Salisbury section for details. There's also a link with Oxford (two hours, £9.50) and Stratford-upon-Avon via Bristol (2½ hours, £14).

Some excellent map/timetables are available from the bus station (☎ 464446). The Badgerline Day Rambler (£4.60) gives you access to a good network of buses in Bristol, Somerset (Wells, Glastonbury), Gloucestershire (Gloucester via Bristol) and Wiltshire (Lacock, Bradford-on-Avon, Salisbury).

See the Salisbury section for information on the Wiltshire Day Rover, if you're planning to spend the bulk of a day in Wiltshire en route to Salisbury.

Train There are numerous trains from London's Paddington station (1½ hours). There are also plenty of trains through to Bristol for onward travel to Cardiff, Exeter or the North. There are hourly trains between Portsmouth and Bristol via Salisbury and Bath. A single ticket from Bath to Salisbury is £8.70.

Bicycle The Bristol & Bath Cycle Walkway is an excellent footpath and cycleway that follows the route of the disused railway. Bikes are available from Avon Valley Cyclery (☎ 461880), from £9 per day. They're just behind the train station.

AROUND BATH
Lacock
Three miles south of Chippenham, Lacock is a classic, dreamy Cotswolds village with the further attraction of an abbey dating back to the 13th century (open April through October, daily except Tuesday, 1 to 5.30 pm; £4.20) and a museum of photography. Badgerline bus No 234/7 (Chippenham to Trowbridge) serves Lacock.

Bradford-on-Avon
Eight miles east of Bath, this beautiful, small town has somehow managed to avoid becoming a tourist trap. Its narrow streets tumble down a steep bluff overlooking the Avon. There are good bus connections with Bath, and hourly trains (15 minutes), so the town could easily be used as a base. There's a reasonable

range of B&Bs from £13 up. Contact the TIC (☎ 01225-865797) for more information.

WELLS
Wells is a small cathedral city that has kept much of its medieval character; many claim that the cathedral is England's most beautiful, and it is certainly one of the best surviving examples of a full cathedral complex.

Wells is 21 miles south-west of Bath on the edge of the Mendip Hills. The TIC (☎ 01749-672552) is in the town hall on the picturesque Market Place. City Cycles (☎ 675096), 80 High St, has bikes for hire from £7.50 per day, and there are lots of possible routes.

Things to See
The **cathedral** was built in stages from 1180 to 1508 and incorporates several styles. The most famous features are the extraordinary west façade, an immense sculpture gallery with over 300 surviving figures; the interior scissor arches, a brilliant solution to the problem posed by the subsidence of the central tower; the delicate chapter house; and the ancient mechanical clock in the north transept. Try and join one of the free tours.

Beyond the cathedral is the moated **Bishop's Palace**, with its beautiful gardens (open Tuesday, Thursday and Sunday summer afternoons only; daily in August; £2.50), Market Place (markets Wednesday and Saturday) and the 14th-century Vicars' Close.

Places to Stay & Eat
The nearest YHA hostel is at Street near Glastonbury (see the following section), but there are plenty of B&Bs with prices around £13.

The B&B at *9 Chamberlain St* (☎ 672270) is very central and charges £17 per person. Opposite St Cuthbert's church is *19 St Cuthbert St* (☎ 673166) with rooms at £14 per person. The *Old Poor House* (☎ 675052) is a comfortable 14th-century cottage just outside the cathedral precincts, with singles from £16.50.

The *City Arms* (☎ 673916), 69 High St, used to be the city jail but now serves good pub grub with main dishes from around £5. Near the bus station the *Good Earth Restaurant* produces excellent home-made pizzas and puddings; a three-course lunch is £4.69.

Getting There & Away

Badgerline operates hourly buses from Bath and Bristol (1¼ hours, £2.35). No 376 from Bristol continues through Wells to Glastonbury and Street. No 163 runs from Wells to Taunton (for Exmoor) via Glastonbury and Street.

GLASTONBURY

Legend and history combine at Glastonbury to produce an irresistible attraction for romantics and nuts of every description. It's a small market town with the ruins of a 14th-century abbey, and a nearby tor with superb views.

According to various legends, Jesus travelled here with Joseph of Arimathea and the chalice from the Last Supper, it is the burial place of King Arthur and Queen Guinevere, and the tor is either the Isle of Avalon or a gateway to the underworld. Whatever you choose to believe, a climb to the top of the tor is well worthwhile. Turn right at the top of High St (the far end from the TIC) into Chilkwell St and then left into Dod Lane; there's a footpath to the tor from the end of the lane.

The TIC (☎ 01458-832954) can supply maps and accommodation information; there are plenty of B&Bs for around £15. The nearest hostel is *Street Youth Hostel* (☎ 442961), four miles south. It's open April through October except Tuesday, and every day in July and August.

The Glastonbury Festival, a three-day festival of theatre, music, circus, mime, natural healing etc, is a massive affair with over 1000 acts. It takes place at Pilton, eight miles from Glastonbury; admission is by advance ticket only (around £60 for the whole festival). Phone ☎ 01839-668899 for details.

There are Badgerline buses from Bristol to Wells, Glastonbury and Street (for the YHA hostel, alight at Marshalls Elm, then it's a 500-metre walk). Glastonbury is only six miles from Wells, so walking or hitching is feasible. Bus No 163 from Wells continues to Taunton, from where there are buses to Minehead (for Exmoor).

BRISTOL

Bristol is a large city, and if you approach through the unlovely southern suburbs, you might wonder what the hell you're getting into. The centre, however, has atmospheric old streets and canals, some magnificent architecture, docks and warehouses that are being rescued from ruin, and a plethora of bars, pubs and restaurants.

Although the city definitely has an eye to the tourists, it has not become ossified in the way of some of the more famous nearby towns and, as a result, some people may prefer it. There's lots to see and do and the city has an interesting history that stretches back 1000 years. Bristol is most famous as a port, although it is six miles from the Severn estuary, and it grew rich on the 17th-century trade with the North American colonies and the West Indies (rum, slaves, sugar and tobacco).

It continues to prosper today (although it has had to switch some commodities) and it is an important transport hub, with connections north to the Cotswolds and the Midland cities, west to southern Wales, south-west to Devon and Cornwall, and east to Bath (which would be an easy day trip).

Orientation & Information

The city centre is to the north of the Floating Harbour – a system of locks, canals and docks fed by the tidal River Avon. The central area is compact and easy to get around on foot.

The main train station is Bristol Temple Meads, about one mile to the south-east of the centre, although some trains use Bristol Parkway five miles to the north, which is accessible from the centre by bus and train. There are also some suburban train stations. The bus and coach station is to the north of the city centre.

Open daily, the TIC (☎ 0117-926 0767) is now impressively located in St Nicholas Church, St Nicholas St, with the magnificent 18th-century altarpiece by William Hogarth still in place. The comprehensive *Visitors Guide* (£1.50) is worth buying, and there is also a good (free) public transport map.

Things to See

The first thing on a visitor's agenda should be a wander around the twisting streets of the old city centre, followed by a ferry trip on the Floating Harbour (see Getting Around later in this section).

From the TIC, start by exploring **St Nicholas Market**, then continue westwards to medieval **St John's Church** and across busy

Rupert St to the **Christmas Steps**. Walk south to College Green, flanked by the impressive council offices and **Bristol Cathedral**.

Up the hill (Park St) there are numerous restaurants, the university and, 1½ miles beyond, the suburb of Clifton, which is dominated by fine Georgian architecture. The spectacular **Clifton Suspension Bridge**, designed by Brunel to cross the equally spectacular Avon Gorge, is also here.

Back in the centre, you could visit the **Arnolfini Centre**, an important contemporary arts complex, or the **Watershed**, on opposite sides of St Augustine's Reach. Then walk down King St, with its old buildings, now used as restaurants and clubs, and the **Llandoger Trow**, a 17th-century pub reputed to be the Admiral Benbow in Robert Louis Stevenson's *Treasure Island*.

There are numerous other important sights: the beautiful **Church of St Mary Redcliffe**; the **Maritime Heritage Centre** (free) with Brunel's **SS Great Britain** (£3.70), the first ocean-going iron ship with a screw propeller; and the **Industrial Museum** (£1).

Places to Stay

The *Youth Hostel* (☎ 922 1659), 14 Narrow Quay St, is an excellent place to stay. It occupies a converted warehouse five minutes from the centre of town. The dorms are small, mostly four-bed (£10.90), and most have shower rooms attached. There's also a good, cheap café.

Very well situated and good value, *St Michael's Hill Guest House* (☎ 973 0037), 145 St Michael's Hill, has singles/doubles from £13/19 without breakfast, or £15/22 with. Most of the other cheap B&Bs tend to be a fair distance from the centre, although there is a good town bus service. There are a number on Bath Rd (the A4) and Wells Rd (the A37).

Clifton, 1½ miles from the centre, is a very attractive suburb but most of the B&Bs here cost £20 to £25 per person. On Oakfield Rd (off Whiteladies Rd), the *Oakfield Hotel* (☎ 973 5556) has singles/doubles for £26/37. In Tyndalls Park Rd the *Alandale* (☎ 973 5407) charges from £30/45 a single/double.

Places to Eat

Bristol is well endowed with restaurants, and most are reasonably priced.

If you're dining on a very short shoestring, a couple of basic cafés on the corner of College Green (opposite the Watershed) can provide sustenance. Much nicer are the cafés in the *Watershed* and *Arnolfini* art centres on either side of the Floating Harbour where you should be able to get something to eat for under £5.

There are a number of restaurants along Park St, which becomes Queen's Rd and Whiteladies Rd (a 20-minute walk from the centre). At 75 Park St the *Boston Tea Party* (☎ 929 8601) is an excellent place for a sandwich. *Rosinantes* (☎ 973 4482), 85 Whiteladies Rd, is a lively tapas bar with good choices for vegetarians. *Johnny Yen's Wok Diner* (☎ 973 0730), 113 Whiteladies Rd, is an entertaining Japanese-Malaysian-Thai-Chinese DIY diner. You pay £4.95 for a three-course lunch which mixes the four vital characteristics of oriental cuisine (form, aroma, colour and flavour). At 119 Whiteladies Rd, a branch of *Pierre Victoire* (☎ 973 0716) serves good, cheap French food – £4.90 for a three-course lunch.

Across the road from the TIC there's *Las Iguanas* (☎ 927 6233), 10 St Nicholas St, with Mexican and South American dishes; a three-course lunch costs £4.95. Park St has several possible places for pizza but best, if not necessarily cheapest, is *Pizza Express* (☎ 926 0300) at 31 Berkeley Square, near the University.

Entertainment

There's plenty going on at night, ranging from high culture to low. Get a copy of *Venue* (£1.70) from newsagents; it's a similar listings mag to London's *Time Out* with details on theatre, music, the works, for both Bath and Bristol.

There are several options on King St, ranging from the *Old Duke* (pub jazz) to the *New Vic* (theatre). On St Nicholas St, there's often live music at *Las Iguanas* (see Places to Eat above) and at *St Nicholas House* at the weekends.

The legendary *Bierkeller* (☎ 926 8514), All Saints St, which has played host to luminaries like the Stone Roses and the Stranglers, is a good bet. Depending on the night of the week and who's playing entry costs from £1 to £12.

Getting There & Away

See the Rail and Coach/Bus fares tables in this chapter's introductory Getting Around section.

Bus Bristol has excellent bus connections. There are hourly National Express (☎ 0990-808080) buses to London via Heathrow airport (2½ hours), but Turners (☎ 955 5333) currently sells the cheapest tickets – just £4.95/9.50 for a single/return. Also check prices from Bakers Dolphin (☎ 961 4000).

National Express has frequent buses to Cardiff (1¼ hours, £6). There are a couple of buses a day to Barnstaple (2¾ hours, £14) and regular buses to Exeter (1¾ hours, £9.50), Oxford (2½ hours, £12.50) and Stratford-upon-Avon (2½ hours, £13).

Badgerline has numerous services a day to and from Bath. There are also services to Salisbury and north to Gloucester. A Day Rambler ticket is £4.60. For city-wide information, phone ☎ 955 5111.

Train Bristol is an important rail hub, with regular connections to London's Paddington station (1½ hours). Most trains (except those to the south) use both Temple Meads and Parkway stations. Bath is only 20 minutes, so it is an easy day trip (£4.30 for a day return). There are frequent links to Cardiff (45 minutes, £6.10), Exeter (one hour, £13.90), Fishguard (3½ hours, £19.40), Oxford (1½ hours, £18) and Birmingham (1½ hours, £12). Phone ☎ 0345-484950 for timetable information.

Getting Around

The nicest way to get around is on the ferry which, from April to September, plies the Floating Harbour. There are a number of stops including at Bristol Bridge, the Industrial Museum, the SS *Great Britain* and Hotwells. The ferry (☎ 927 3416) runs every 40 minutes; a single fare is 80p, and a round trip £1.80.

There's a taxi rank in the city centre opposite the Hippodrome Theatre but it's not a good idea to hang around here late at night. To call a cab free, ring 1A Premier Cabs on ☎ 0800-716777.

There's a good local bus system – phone ☎ 955 5111 for details. The suspension bridge is quite a walk from the centre of town – catch bus No 8 or 9 (Nos 508 and 509 at weekends) from bus stop 'Cu' on Colston Ave, or from Temple Meads station.

Southern Midlands

Sometimes known as the Heart of England, this patchwork of small counties contains some of the country's best and worst aspects. The worst can be found in a wide corridor either side of the M1 motorway. Hertfordshire, Bedfordshire and Buckinghamshire are a graveyard for modern town planning, exemplified by Milton Keynes, which was founded in 1967.

London's uninspiring suburban sprawl continues to advance into the Chilterns, and Birmingham and Coventry – never famous for their beauty – have struggled to survive the bombing of WWII and the industrial decline of the 1970s and 1980s.

To the west, however, it's a different story. Oxford is not without modern urban problems, but it's still a very beautiful city. The southwest sections of the Chilterns remain largely unspoilt and are accessible to walkers of the Ridgeway.

The Cotswolds, more than any other region, embody the popular image of English countryside. The prettiness can be forced, and the villages are certainly not strangers to mass tourism, but there are also moments when you will be transfixed by the beauty of the landscape. The combination of golden stone, flower-draped cottages, church spires, towering chestnuts and oaks, rolling hills and green, stone-walled fields can be too extraordinarily picturesque to seem quite real.

West again, you reach the Bristol Channel and the wide Severn Valley, a natural border to the county of Hereford & Worcester and the region known as the Welsh Marches. Hereford & Worcester has rich agricultural countryside with orchards and market gardens. The Wye Valley is a famous beauty spot, popularised by the first romantic poets in the 18th century. Approaching England from the Welsh plateau, there are wonderful views.

Some of England's most popular tourist sites are in the southern Midlands, amongst them Blenheim Palace, Hatfield House, Windsor Castle, Warwick Castle, Stratford-upon-Avon and Oxford.

Orientation & Information

The Midlands is a vague term at best; dividing

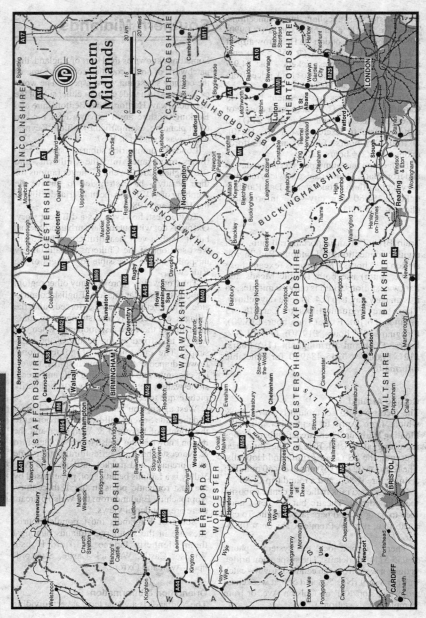

it between north and south is thoroughly arbitrary. However, the region is cut by two ranges of hills and two major rivers. From east to west, you first meet the chalk ridge of the Chilterns which runs north-east from Salisbury Plain to Hertfordshire, then come the Thames Valley, the limestone Cotswolds which run north from Bath, and finally the Severn Valley.

Major northbound transport arteries (including the M1 and M40) cross the region, so it's highly likely you'll pass through it at some stage. There are YHA hostels at Windsor, Oxford, Stow-on-the-Wold, Stratford-upon-Avon and Birmingham, amongst others.

Activities

Hiking The best hiking is in the Chilterns and the Cotswolds, although there are a number of other interesting paths in the region.

The Cotswolds Way, with easy accessibility to accommodation, is the best way to discover the Cotswolds. The path follows the western escarpment overlooking the Bristol Channel for 100 miles from Chipping Campden to Bath, but it is quite feasible to tackle a smaller section. Bath is obviously easily accessible, but you'll have to contact the Gloucestershire enquiry line (☎ 01452-425543) for information about the infrequent buses that run between Chipping Campden and Stratford or Moreton-in-Marsh.

Contact the Ramblers' Association (☎ 0171-582 6878), 1 Wandsworth Rd, London SW8 2XX, for copies of the *Cotswold Way Handbook*, which includes accommodation and transport information (£1.50 plus 70p UK p&p). *The Cotswold Way – a complete walker's guide* by Mark Richards is available in some local bookshops.

The Ridgeway starts near Avebury and runs north-east for 85 miles to Ivinghoe Beacon near Aylesbury. See Activities under the South-West England section earlier for more information.

OXFORD

It's impossible to pick up any tourist literature about Oxford without reading about its dreaming spires. Like all great clichés it's strikingly apt. Looking across the meadows or rooftops to Oxford's golden spires is certainly an experience to inspire purple prose.

These days, however, Oxford battles against a flood of tourists and some typical Midlands social problems. It is not just a university city, but the home of Morris cars, later British Leyland and now the Rover Group, and it has expanded rapidly this century. This has created a city with a congested centre (housing the most important university buildings and shops) surrounded by sprawling industrial suburbs.

Oxford University is the oldest university in Britain, but no-one can find an exact starting date. It evolved during the 11th century as an informal centre for scholars and students.

The colleges began to appear from the mid-13th century onwards. There are now about 14,500 undergraduates and 36 colleges.

Orientation

The city centre is surrounded by rivers and streams on the eastern, southern and western sides, and can easily be covered on foot. Carfax Tower at the intersection of Queen St and Cornmarket St/St Aldate's is a useful central marker. The tower is all that remains of St Martin's Church. There's a fine view from the top, which is good for orienting yourself. It's open daily, March through October; admission is £1.20.

The train station is to the west of the city, with frequent buses to Carfax Tower. Alternatively, turn left off the station concourse into Park End St and it's a 15-minute walk.

The bus station is nearer the centre, on Gloucester Green (there's no green).

Information

A visit to the hectic TIC (☎ 01865-726871), Gloucester Green, is essential. It's open Monday to Saturday from 9.30 am to 5 pm, and Sundays during summer 10 am to 3.30 pm. A hefty £2.75 charge (plus 10% deposit) is made for local B&B bookings.

You need more information than this guide can give if you're going to do the place justice. The *Welcome to Oxford* brochure (£1) has a walking tour with college opening times. The TIC has daily two-hour walking tours of the colleges (at 10.30 and 11 am, and 1 and 2 pm; £4/2.50). Oxford Classic (☎ 01235-819393) is the cheapest bus-tour operator and for £6 (£4 for students under 21) you can use its service all day.

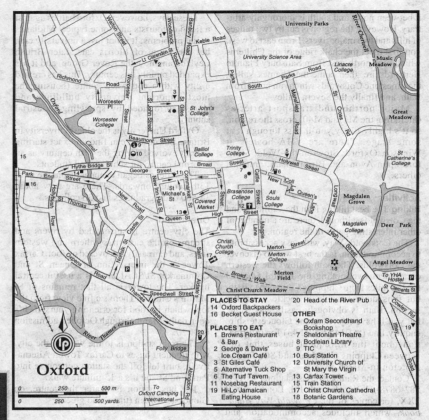

PLACES TO STAY
14 Oxford Backpackers
16 Becket Guest House

PLACES TO EAT
1 Browns Restaurant & Bar
2 George & Davis' Ice Cream Café
3 St Giles Café
5 Alternative Tuck Shop
6 The Turf Tavern
11 Nosebag Restaurant
19 Hi-Lo Jamaican Eating House
20 Head of the River Pub

OTHER
4 Oxfam Secondhand Bookshop
7 Sheldonian Theatre
8 Bodleian Library
9 TIC
10 Bus Station
12 University Church of St Mary the Virgin
13 Carfax Tower
15 Train Station
17 Christ Church Cathedral
18 Botanic Gardens

Oxford

0   250   500 m
0   250   500 yards

Things to See & Do

Colleges You need more than a day to 'do' Oxford, but, at a minimum, make sure you visit the following colleges: Christ Church (with Oxford Cathedral), Merton and Magdalen (pronounced 'maudlen'). The colleges remain open throughout the year (unlike Cambridge) but their hours vary; many are closed in the morning. Some never admit visitors.

Starting at the Carfax Tower, cross Cornmarket St and walk down the hill, along St Aldate's, to Christ Church, perhaps the most famous college in Oxford. The main entrance is beneath Tom Tower, which was built by

Wren in 1680, but the usual visitors' entrance is further down the hill via the wrought-iron gates of the War Memorial Gardens and the Broad Walk facing out over Christ Church Meadow. There's a £3 admission charge. The college chapel is the smallest cathedral in England, but it is a beautiful example of late Norman (1140-80) architecture.

Return to the Broad Walk, follow the stone wall, then turn left up Merton Grove, through wrought-iron gates, then right into Merton St. **Merton College** was founded in 1264 and its buildings are amongst the oldest in Oxford. The present buildings mostly date from the 15th to the 17th centuries. The entrance to the

14th-century Mob Quad, with its medieval library, is on your right.

Turn left into Merton St, then take the first right into Magpie Lane, which will take you through to High St with its fascinating mix of architectural styles. Turn right down the hill until you come to **Magdalen** just before the river on your left. Magdalen is one of the richest Oxford colleges and has the most extensive and beautiful grounds, with a deer park, river walk, three quadrangles and superb lawns. This was C S Lewis' college and the setting for the film, *Shadowlands*.

Walk back up High St until you come to the **University Church of St Mary the Virgin** on your right (there's a good view from the tower), turn right up Cattle St to the distinctive, circular **Radcliffe Camera**, a reading room for the Bodleian Library. Continue up Cattle St passing the **Bridge of Sighs** on your right, then turn left into Broad St. On your left you pass Wren's **Sheldonian Theatre**, and on your right **Trinity** and **Balliol** colleges. Turn left at Cornmarket St and you'll be back where you started.

Punts Punts and boats can be hired at Follybridge and Magdalen Bridge (£8 per hour, £25 deposit). There is no better way of letting the atmosphere of Oxford seep in. The seepage can be dramatic: punting is not as easy as it looks. Go left for peace and quiet, and right for views back to the colleges across the Botanic Gardens and Christ Church Meadow. Punts are available from Easter to September.

Places to Stay
The most convenient hostel is *Oxford Backpackers* (☎ 721761) at 9A Hythe Bridge Rd, less than five minutes walk from the train station. Beds in dorms cost £9 each. The *Youth Hostel* (☎ 62997), 32 Jack Straw's Lane, is not centrally located despite which it gets booked up very quickly in summer. Bus Nos 13, 14 and 14A run from outside the St Aldate's post office to the hostel.

Oxford Camping International (☎ 246551), 426 Abingdon Rd, is conveniently located by the Park & Ride car park roughly three miles south of the centre. Charges are £2.50 for a tent, £2.50 for a car and £1.50 per person.

B&Bs are expensive and suburban, the two main areas being Abingdon Rd and Cowley/ Iffley Rds – both on regular bus routes. You're looking at £18 per person, rising to over £20 in peak season.

The *Brenal Guest House* (☎ 721561), 307 Iffley Rd, charges from £18 to £20 per person. The *Athena Guest House* (☎ 243124), 253 Cowley Rd, is within walking distance of shops and restaurants and has singles/doubles for £18/36. A bit further out, the *Earlmont* (☎ 240236) at No 322 is a large and comfortable B&B with rooms for £36/48.

The *Sportsview Guest House* (☎ 244268), 106 Abingdon Rd, is a two-star guesthouse for non-smokers, with rooms from £18/30. *Becket Guest House* (☎ 724675), 5 Becket St, is convenient to the train station, with doubles from £36.

Places to Eat
There's quite a range of places to eat, but most of them aren't cheap. Generally, pubs will be your best bet. There's excellent pub grub at the *Turf Tavern*, Bath Place, a recommended watering hole hidden away down an alley. The *Head of the River*, ideally situated by Folly Bridge, is very popular.

Self-caterers should visit the *covered market*, on the northern side of High St near Carfax Tower, for fruit and vegetables. The *Alternative Tuck Shop*, Holywell St, is the place to go for filled rolls and sandwiches at lunchtime, but the queues of students can be long.

The *Nosebag Restaurant* (☎ 721033) has main dishes for around £4.50 and a good range of vegetarian choices. *George & Davis' Ice Cream Café*, Little Clarendon St, serves light meals as well as delicious home-made ice cream. It's open until midnight.

A popular place for snacky meals is *St Giles Café* in St Giles where fry-ups cost around £3.75. *Browns Restaurant & Bar* (☎ 511995), 5 Woodstock Rd, is a popular, stylish brasserie. Main dishes here are around £7.50.

There are several interesting places to eat in the Cowley Rd student area. The *Hi-Lo Jamaican Eating House* (☎ 725984), 70 Cowley Rd, is an unusual restaurant with old-fashioned furniture and good music. Large portions of healthy food (including vegetarian dishes) are around £7.

Getting There & Away

See the Rail and Coach/Bus fares tables in this chapter's introductory Getting Around section.

Bus Oxford is easily and quickly reached from London, and there are a number of competitive bus lines on the route. The Oxford Tube (☎ 772250) starts at London's Victoria Coach Station but also stops at Marble Arch, Notting Hill Gate and Shepherd's Bush; a 24-hour return from Victoria is £6.50. The journey takes around 1½ hours and the service operates 24 hours a day.

National Express (☎ 0990-808080) has numerous buses to London and Heathrow airport. There are two or three services a day to and from Bath (two hours) and Bristol (2¼ hours), and two services to and from Gloucester (1½ hours) and Cheltenham (one hour). From Bristol there are connections to Wales, Devon and Cornwall. Buses to Shrewsbury, north Wales, York and Durham go via Birmingham.

Oxford Citylink (☎ 711312) is the third major operator, with frequent departures to London, Heathrow, Gatwick, Birmingham and Stratford. Stagecoach (☎ 20077) runs six buses a day to Cambridge.

Train There are very frequent trains from London's Paddington station (1½ hours, £15.10 single). Network SouthEast cards apply.

There are regular trains north to Coventry and Birmingham, and north-west to Worcester and Hereford (for Moreton-in-Marsh, Gloucester and Cheltenham in the Cotswolds). Birmingham is the main hub for transport further north.

To connect with trains to the south-west you have to change at Didcot Parkway (15 minutes). There are plenty of connections to Bath; with a bit of luck the whole trip won't take longer than 1½ hours. Change at Swindon for another line running into the Cotswolds (Kemble, Stroud and Gloucester). For train enquiries, phone ☎ 0345-484950.

Getting Around

Local buses and minibuses leave from the streets around Carfax Tower. For information on Thames Transit services phone ☎ 772250.

There are a number of places where you can hire bicycles: Pennyfarthing (☎ 249368), 5 George St, not far from the bus station, has three-speeds at £5 per day or £9 per week, and mountain bikes for £10/25.

Boat trips and punts are available at Folly Bridge and at Magdalen Bridge. Salter Bros (☎ 243421) offers several interesting boat trips from Folly Bridge between May and September; a return trip to Abingdon costs £8.85.

BLENHEIM PALACE

Blenheim Palace (☎ 01993-811325), one of the largest palaces in Europe, was a gift to John Churchill from Queen Anne and Parliament as a reward for his role in defeating Louis XIV. Curiously, the palace was the birthplace of Winston Churchill, who perhaps more than any other individual was responsible for checking Hitler.

Designed and built by Vanbrugh and Hawksmoor between 1704 and 1722 with gardens by Capability Brown, Blenheim is an enormous baroque fantasy, and is definitely worth visiting. The house is open from mid-March through October, and costs adults £7.30 or £5.30 with a student card; the park is open every day, all year.

Blenheim is just south of the village of Woodstock. Catch a Thames Transit Minibus No 20/A/B/C from Gloucester Green in Oxford (30 minutes, £2.40 return) to the palace's entrance.

STRATFORD-UPON-AVON

Stratford is an ordinary Midlands market town that happened to be William Shakespeare's home. Due to shrewd management of the cult of Bill, it's one of England's busiest tourist attractions. If you're a fan you can visit a number of buildings associated with his life, including Shakespeare's Birthplace, New Place, Nash's House, Hall's Croft, Anne Hathaway's Cottage and Mary Arden's House. A passport ticket to all the Shakespearian properties costs £9.

As it's just beyond the northern edge of the Cotswolds, Stratford can be a handy stopover on your way to and from the North. The Royal Shakespeare Company has three theatres here, in addition to its London venues, and there is nearly always something on. Warwick, with its wonderful castle, is just to the north.

Information
The TIC (☎ 01789-293127), Bridgefoot, has plenty of information about the numerous B&Bs. Seeing a production by the Royal Shakespeare Company (☎ 205301) is definitely worthwhile. Tickets are often available on the day of performance, but get in early; the box office opens at 9 am. Stand-by tickets are available to students immediately before performances (£10.50 or £14.50) and there are almost always standing room tickets (£4.50 or £5).

Places to Stay & Eat
The *Youth Hostel* (☎ 297093), Hemmingford House, Alveston, is 1½ miles out of town. From the train station walk into town along Alcester Rd, which becomes Greenhill, Wood, Bridge and Bridgefoot (with the TIC). Cross Clopton Bridge and follow the B4086. You can take bus No 18 from Wood St near the TIC.

Prices for B&Bs can lurch skywards in summer but there are plenty of places at around £17 on Evesham Place, Grove Rd and Broad Walk, just west of the centre. Try the cheerful *Grosvenor Villa* (☎ 266192) at No 9, the good-value *Clomendy* (☎ 266957) at No 157 or the *Dylan* (☎ 204819; where Bob has never stayed) at No 10. Alcester Rd, by the train station, also has a number of places although they are a bit further from the centre.

Sheep St has a fine selection of dining possibilities or try *Fatty Arbuckle's* (☎ 267069) at 9 Chapel St for its reasonably priced and *very* comprehensive menu.

Getting There & Away
Bus National Express (☎ 0990-808080) buses link Birmingham, Stratford, Warwick, Oxford, Heathrow and London.

Phone ☎ 01788-535555 for local bus information. The X20 operates regularly to Birmingham (one hour, £2.60), the X16 to Warwick (15 minutes, £1.75) and Coventry (1¼ hours, £2.20) and the X50 to Oxford (1½ hours, £3.50).

Train Direct services to and from London's Paddington station cost £14.50. There are trains to Warwick (£2.10) and Birmingham (£3.10 after 9 am). For further information phone ☎ 0345-484950.

BIRMINGHAM
Birmingham is the most southerly of the great Midlands industrial cities and the second-largest city in Britain, with over one million inhabitants. There's plenty of vitality but it's not beautiful, there are no essential sights and it's not particularly accessible to the short-term visitor. It is, however, a major transport hub.

The TIC (☎ 0121-693 6300) on Victoria Square is open every day. Try a balti restaurant for the Midlands' own version of Indian cooking.

COTSWOLDS
The Cotswolds are a range of limestone hills rising gently from the Thames and its tributaries in the east but forming a steep escarpment overlooking the Bristol Channel in the west. The hills are characterised by honey-coloured stone villages and a gently rolling landscape. The villages were built on the wealth of the medieval wool trade.

Many of the villages are extremely popular with tourists; it's difficult to escape commercialism unless you have your own transport or are walking. The best advice is to take your time and wander off the beaten track in search of your own ideal Cotswold village.

Orientation & Information
The hills run north from Bath for 100 miles to Chipping Campden. The most attractive countryside is bounded in the west by the M5 and Chipping Sodbury, and in the east by Stow-on-the-Wold, Burford, Bibury, Cirencester and Chippenham.

There are train stations at Cheltenham, Kemble (serving Cirencester), Moreton-in-Marsh (serving Stow-on-the-Wold) and Stroud.

Bath, Cheltenham, Stratford-upon-Avon and Oxford are the best starting points for the Cotswolds. Cirencester calls itself the region's capital.

The TICs in surrounding towns all stock information on the Cotswolds, but the TICs dealing specifically with the region are at Market Place, Cirencester (☎ 01285-654180), and The Square, Stow-on-the-Wold (☎ 01451-831082).

Stow-on-the-Wold
Stow, as it is known, is one of the most impressive (and visited) towns in the Cotswolds. It's a

BRITAIN

terrific base if you don't have a vehicle, because several particularly beautiful villages (Longborough, Broadwell, Upper and Lower Slaughter) are within a day's walk or cycle ride.

The **Youth Hostel** (☎ 01451-830497) is in a 16th-century building and is open Monday to Saturday from March through October and also on Sunday in July and August.

Stow can be reached by bus from Moreton-in-Marsh, which is on the main Cotswolds line between Worcester and Oxford. Regular buses (75p) leave from the town hall, a five-minute walk from the station, and take between 10 and 30 minutes to get to Stow. Contact Pulhams' Coaches (☎ 820369) for a timetable.

Cheltenham

Cheltenham is a large, but still elegant, spa town easily accessible by bus and train. The TIC (☎ 01242-522878) is helpful. Cheltenham is on the main Bristol to Birmingham train line, and can be easily reached by train from South Wales, Bath and south-west England, and Oxford (changing at Didcot and Swindon).

Places to Stay

The Cotswolds area is not particularly well served by YHA hostels, but there are countless B&Bs. There are hostels at Slimbridge and Wantage (the Ridgeway), but the most central and most interesting are at Stow-on-the-Wold (see the earlier Stow-on-the-Wold section) and Duntisbourne Abbots (which, unfortunately, has no public transport). In Gloucester there's an independent hostel at *23 Alvin St* (☎ 01452-418152). Beds are £7.50 but there are only six of them.

Getting Around

As you may have gathered, it's difficult to use public transport around the Cotswolds. If you're trying anything ambitious, contact the Gloucestershire enquiry line (☎ 01452-425543). Bikes can be hired in Bath, Oxford (see appropriate sections) and Cheltenham. Crabtrees (☎ 01242-515291), 50 Winchcombe St, Cheltenham, rents mountain bikes at £8/35 a day/week (£50 deposit required).

Eastern England

With the exception of the city of Cambridge, most of the eastern counties – Essex, Suffolk, Norfolk and Cambridgeshire – have been overlooked by tourists. East Anglia, as the region is often known, has always been distinct, historically separated from the rest of England by the fens and the Essex forests.

The fens were strange marshlands that stretched from Cambridge north to the Wash and beyond into Lincolnshire. They were home to people who led an isolated existence amongst a maze of waterways – fishing, hunting and farming scraps of arable land. In the 17th century, however, Dutch engineers were brought in to drain the fens, and the flat open plains with their rich, black soil were created. The region is the setting for Graham Swift's novel *Waterland*.

To the east of the fens, Norfolk and Suffolk have gentle, unspectacular scenery that can still be very beautiful. John Constable and Thomas Gainsborough painted in the area known as Dedham Vale, the valley of the River Stour. Villages like East Bergholt (Constable's birthplace), Thaxted and Cavendish are quintessentially English with their beautiful churches and thatched cottages.

The distinctive architectural character of the region has been determined by the lack of suitable building stone. Stone was occasionally imported for important buildings, but for humble churches and houses three local materials were used: flint, clay bricks and oak. The most unusual of the three, flint, can be chipped into usable shapes, but a single stone is rarely larger than a fist. Often the flint is used in combination with dressed stone or bricks to form decorative patterns.

More than any other part of England, East Anglia has close links with northern Europe. In the 6th and 7th centuries it was overrun by the Norsemen. From the late Middle Ages, Suffolk and Norfolk grew rich by trading wool and cloth with the Flemish; this wealth built scores of churches and helped subsidise the development of Cambridge. The windmills, the long straight drainage canals and even sometimes the architecture (especially in King's Lynn) call the Low Countries to mind,

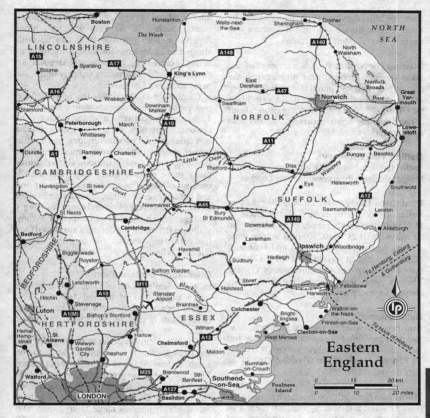

Eastern
England

Orientation & Information

East Anglia lies to the west of the main north-bound transport arteries. Its southern boundary is the Thames estuary, and its western boundary (now marked by the M1 and A1) was formed by that huge expanse of almost impenetrable marshland – the fens. Norwich is the most important city. Harwich is the main port for ferries to Germany, Holland and Denmark.

There are YHA hostels at Cambridge, Colchester, Ely, King's Lynn and Norwich, among others. The East Anglia Tourist Board (☎ 01473-822922) can provide further information.

Activities

Hiking The 94-mile Peddars Way & Norfolk Coast Path runs across the middle of Norfolk from Knettishall Heath until it reaches the beautiful north Norfolk coast at Holme-next-the-Sea. It follows this coastline through a number of attractive, untouched villages, like Wells-next-the-Sea, to Cromer. The Peddars Way Association (☎ 01603-503207), 7 Lowther St, Norwich NR4 6QN, publishes a guide and accommodation list for £2.35 (including UK p&p).

Cycling This is ideal cycling country. Where

there are hills, they're gentle. Bicycles can be hired in Cambridge, and the TIC there can suggest several interesting routes.

Boating The Norfolk Broads, a series of inland lakes (ancient flooded peat diggings) to the east of Norwich, are popular with boat people of every description. Contact Blake's Holidays (☎ 01603-782911) for information about hiring narrow boats, cruisers, yachts and houseboats.

Getting There & Away
Train Harwich, Norwich, King's Lynn and Cambridge are all easily accessible from London.

Boat Stena Line (☎ 01255-243333) runs two ferries a day from Harwich to the Hook of Holland (the Netherlands); Scandinavian Seaways (☎ 01255-240240) runs at least three a week to Esbjerg (Denmark) and Hamburg (Germany), and at least two a week to Gothenburg (Sweden). See the introductory Getting There & Away section at the beginning of this chapter for more details.

Getting Around
Bus Bus transport around the region is slow and disorganised. For regional timetables and information phone Cambridgeshire (☎ 01223-317740), Norfolk (☎ 01603-613613) or Suffolk (☎ 01473-265676).

Train From Norwich you can catch trains to the Norfolk coast and Sheringham, but there's an unfortunate gap between Sheringham and King's Lynn (bus or hitch?) which prevents a rail loop back to Cambridge. It may be worth considering Anglia Plus passes which offer three days travel out of seven for £16, one day for £7.

CAMBRIDGE
Cambridge can hardly be spoken of without reference to Oxford – so much so that the term Oxbridge is used to cover them both. The two cities are not just ancient and beautiful university towns; they embody preconceptions and prejudices that are almost mythical in dimension.

An Oxbridge graduate is popularly characterised as male, private-school educated, intelligent and upper class, but the value judgments attached to the term will very often depend on who is using it. It can be both abusive and admiring: for some it means academic excellence, for others it denotes an elitist club whose members unfairly dominate many aspects of British life.

Cambridge University is the newer of the two, probably beginning some time early in the 13th century, perhaps a century later than Oxford. There is a fierce rivalry between the two cities and the two universities, and a futile debate over which is best and most beautiful. If you have the time, visit both. Oxford draws many more tourists than Cambridge. Partly because of this, if you only have time for one and the colleges are open, choose Cambridge. Its trump card is the choir and chapel of King's College, which should not be missed by any visitor to Britain. If the colleges are closed (see the following section for opening dates), choose Oxford.

Orientation & Information
Fifty-four miles north of London, Cambridge has a population of around 100,000. The central area, which lies in a wide bend of the River Cam, is easy to get around on foot or bike.

The bus station is in the centre of town, but the train station is a 20-minute walk to the south. Sidney St is the main shopping street. The most important group of colleges (including King's) and the Backs (the meadows adjoining the Cam) are to the west of Sidney St, which changes its name many times. The bus station is on Drummer St; Sidney St is 50 metres to the west.

The TIC (☎ 01223-322640), Wheeler St, is open Monday to Saturday all year, and also on Sunday (10.30 am to 3.30 pm) from Easter to September. It organises walking tours at 2 pm every day, all year, with more during summer. Group sizes are limited, so buy your ticket in advance (£5.75 including St John's or King's colleges).

The university has three eight-week terms: Michaelmas (October to December), Lent (mid-January to mid-March) and Easter (mid-April to mid-June). Exams are held from mid-May to mid-June. There's general mayhem for the 168 hours following exams – the so-called May Week. Most colleges are

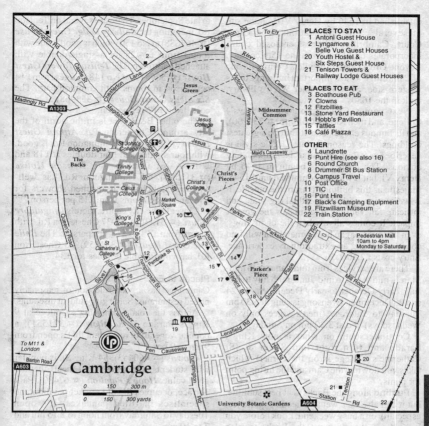

PLACES TO STAY
1 Antoni Guest House
2 Lyngamore &
  Belle Vue Guest Houses
20 Youth Hostel &
  Six Steps Guest House
21 Tenison Towers &
  Railway Lodge Guest Houses

PLACES TO EAT
3 Boathouse Pub
7 Clowns
12 Fitzbillies
13 Stone Yard Restaurant
14 Hobb's Pavilion
15 Tatties
18 Café Piazza

OTHER
4 Laundrette
5 Punt Hire (see also 16)
6 Round Church
8 Drummer St Bus Station
9 Campus Travel
10 Post Office
11 TIC
16 Punt Hire
17 Black's Camping Equipment
19 Fitzwilliam Museum
22 Train Station

Pedestrian Mall
10am to 4pm
Monday to Saturday

Cambridge

0   150   300 m
0   150   300 yards

University Botanic Gardens

closed to visitors for the Easter term, and all are closed for exams. Precise details of opening hours vary from college to college and year to year, so contact the TIC for up-to-date information.

There's a laundrette at 12 Victoria Ave, just north of the bridge and near Chesterton Rd.

Things to See & Do

Cambridge is an architectural treasure house. If you are seriously interested you will need considerably more information than this guide can give, and more than a day.

Starting at Magdalene Bridge walk south down Bridge St until you reach the unmistakable **Round Church**, one of only four surviving medieval round churches, dating from the 12th century. Turn right down St John's St (immediately across the road) which is named in honour of **St John's College** (on the right). The gatehouse dates from 1510 and on the other side there are three beautiful courts, the second and third dating from the 17th century. From the third court, the picturesque **Bridge of Sighs** (not open to the public) crosses the river.

Next door, **Trinity College** is one of the largest and most attractive colleges. It was established in 1546 by Henry VIII on the site of several earlier foundations. The Great Court, Cambridge's largest enclosed court, incorporates buildings from the 15th century. Beyond Great Court is Nevile's Court with one of Cambridge's most important buildings on its western side: Sir Christopher Wren's library, built in the 1680s.

Next comes Caius (pronounced 'keys') College, and then **King's College** (☎ 331100), and its famous chapel, one of Europe's greatest buildings. The reason its late Gothic style is described as Perpendicular is immediately obvious. The chapel was begun in 1446 by Henry VI, but it was not completed until 1545. Majestic as this building is from the outside, it is its interior, with its breathtaking scale and intricate fan vaulting, that makes the greater impact. It comes alive when the choir sings; even the most pagan heavy-metal fan will find choral evensong an extraordinary experience. Entry costs £2.50/1.50.

There are services from mid-January to mid-March, mid-April to mid-June, mid-July to late July, early October to early December, and 24 and 25 December. Evensong is sung at 5.30 pm Tuesday to Saturday (men's voices only on Wednesdays) and at 3.30 pm on Sunday.

Continue south on what is now King's Parade and turn right into Silver St (St Catherine's College is on the corner) which takes you down to the Cam and the hiring point for punts.

Punting along the Backs is at best sublime, but it can also be a wet and hectic experience, especially on a busy weekend. Look before you leap. If you do wimp out, the Backs are also perfect for a walk or a picnic – cross the bridge and walk along the river to the right. Scudamore's rents punts (for up to six people) at £8 per hour, but requires a £30 to £50 deposit. Punting the three miles up the river to the idyllic village of Grantchester makes a great day out.

Places to Stay

The *Youth Hostel* (☎ 354601), 97 Tenison Rd, has small dormitories and a restaurant. Near the train station, it's very popular – book ahead. For B&B, seniors/juniors are charged £12.80/9.60.

There are numerous B&Bs at all times, even more during university vacation from late June

to late September. There are several on Tenison Rd, including the *Railway Lodge Guest House* (☎ 467688) at No 150 which is good value with rooms from £24/28 for a single/double with attached bathroom. The *Tenison Towers Guest House* (☎ 566511) at No 148 charges from £14 per person in rooms with common bath. The *Six Steps Guest House* (☎ 353968) at No 93 costs from £17 per person.

The other B&B area is in the north of the city around Chesterton Rd. *Antoni Guest House* (☎ 357444), 4 Huntingdon Rd, is good, with four singles and four doubles at £18 and £30. A bit further out, *Benson House* (☎ 311594), 24 Huntingdon Rd, has well-equipped doubles with attached showers for £36, and basic rooms from £15 per person.

Closer to the city centre, there's *Lyngamore House* (☎ 312369), 35-37 Chesterton Rd, with rooms from £14 to £18 per person. The *Belle Vue Guest House* (☎ 351859), 33 Chesterton Rd, has comfortable doubles for £34.

Places to Eat

Cambridge has a good selection of reasonably priced restaurants. Some give student discounts.

Across the road from King's College at 9 King's Parade is *Rainbow* (☎ 321551), a popular vegetarian restaurant that's open from 9 am to 9 pm.

Clowns (☎ 460453), 54 King St, is popular with students, and serves light meals that are good value. *Hobb's Pavilion* (☎ 67480), Park Terrace, occupies the old cricket pavilion and specialises in filled pancakes. It's open Tuesday to Saturday from noon to 2.15 pm and 7 to 10 pm.

There are quite a number of reasonably priced restaurants on Regent St. Now revamped, and with a liquor license, *Tatties* (☎ 358478), at No 26, has long been a budget favourite. Open 10 am to 10 pm daily, it specialises not only in baked potatoes stuffed with a variety of tempting fillings (from £1.75 to £4.95) but also in breakfasts, filled baguettes, salads and cakes.

During the day, the *Stone Yard Restaurant*, next door to St Andrew's Baptist Centre, serves very cheap cafeteria-style food. *Café Piazza* (☎ 356666), 83 Regent St, has pizzas from £3.95, with a resident DJ some nights.

Fitzbillies (☎ 352500), 52 Trumpington St, is a brilliant bakery/restaurant. The Chelsea buns are an outrageous experience, and so is the chocolate cake beloved by generations of students, but there are many other temptations in addition to the usual sandwiches and pies – stock up before you go punting.

The *Boathouse*, 14 Chesterton Rd, is a good riverside pub.

Getting There & Away

Cambridge can easily be visited as a day trip from London (although it is worth staying at least a night) or en route to the North. See the Rail and Coach/Bus fares tables in this chapter's introductory Getting Around section. It's well served by trains, but not so well by buses.

Bus For more detailed bus information phone ☎ 317740. National Express (☎ 0990-808080) has hourly buses to London (two hours). There are four buses a day to and from Bristol (two stop at Bath). Unfortunately, links to the North aren't very straightforward. To get to Lincoln or York you'll have to change at Peterborough or Nottingham respectively. King's Lynn is also only accessible via Peterborough.

Cambridge Coach Services (☎ 236333) runs the Inter-Varsity Link via Stansted airport to Oxford (three hours, six per day, £7/10 for a single/return). It also runs buses to Heathrow (£13) and Gatwick (£15) airports.

Train There are trains every half-hour from London's King's Cross and Liverpool St stations (one hour). Network SouthEast cards are valid. If you catch the train at King's Cross you travel via Hatfield (see Hatfield House in the Around London section) and Stevenage. There are also regular train connections to Bury St Edmunds, Ely (£2.70) and King's Lynn (£8.50). There are connections at Peterborough with the main northbound trains to Lincoln, York and Edinburgh. If you want to head west to Oxford or Bath, you'll have to return to London first. For more information, phone ☎ 311999.

Getting Around

Cambus (☎ 423554) runs numerous buses around town from Drummer St, including bus No 1 from the train station to the town centre. It's easy enough to get around Cambridge on foot, but if you're staying out of the centre, or plan to wander into the fens (fine flat country for the lazy cyclist), a bicycle can be hired from Geoff's Bike Hire (☎ 365629), 65 Devonshire Rd, near the youth hostel.

ELY

Ely is a small city set on a low hill that was once an island deep in the watery world of the fens. It is dominated by the overwhelming bulk of Ely Cathedral, a superb example of the Norman Romanesque style, built between 1081 and 1200. Phone the TIC (☎ 01353-662062) for places to stay.

There are regular trains from Cambridge (20 minutes, £2.70).

NORFOLK
Norwich

This ancient capital was for many years larger than London, its prosperity based on trade with the Low Countries. Norwich's medieval centre has been retained along with its castle, cathedral and no fewer than 33 churches. There are numerous B&Bs – contact the TIC (☎ 01603-666071), the Guildhall, Gaol Hill, for details. The *Youth Hostel* (☎ 627647) is at 112 Turner Rd. There are direct rail and bus links with Cambridge and London.

King's Lynn

King's Lynn is an interesting old port with some notable buildings, some of which were distinctly influenced by the trading links with Holland. Contact the TIC (☎ 01553-763044), Saturday Market Place (but may move soon to the Custom House), for further information. The *Youth Hostel* (☎ 772461), College Lane, is fully open from 1 July to 31 August and haphazardly outside that time. There are regular trains from Cambridge (one hour, £8.50).

SUFFOLK
Harwich & Felixstowe

These are typically ugly shipping terminals; Harwich is used by passenger ferries, Felixstowe currently for freight only. Contact the TIC (☎ 01255-506139) if you need a B&B.

There are numerous trains from Harwich (International Port) to London (Liverpool St station); on some services you will have to change trains at Manningtree or Colchester.

BRITAIN

Alternatively, you could go north to Norwich, or change for Bury St Edmunds and Cambridge at Ipswich. See the introductory Getting There & Away section at the beginning of this chapter for details on the ferries.

Northern Midlands

The northern Midlands are often dismissed as England's industrial back yard. The dense network of motorways you see on maps gives forewarning of both the level of development and the continuing economic importance of the region, despite the decline of some traditional industries. On the other hand, there are still some beautiful corners, and the larger cities are important cultural centres with a legacy of brilliant Victorian architecture.

In a very real sense this is England's working-class heartland. There is a wide gap between these northern cities and those south of Birmingham. Since the Industrial Revolution created them, life for their inhabitants has often been an uncompromising struggle. The horrific excesses of 19th-century capitalism gave birth to a bitter and protracted class struggle that continues today.

Orientation & Information

The main industrial corridor runs from Merseyside (Liverpool) to the River Humber. All the major cities – Liverpool, Manchester, Leeds, Doncaster, Sheffield, Nottingham, Derby and Leicester – sprawl into the countryside, burying it under motorways, grim suburbs, power lines, factories and mines.

There are, nonetheless, some important exceptions: Lincoln, one of the great cathedral cities; walled Chester, a starting point for north Wales; and attractive Shrewsbury. On the eastern and western extremes in Shropshire and Lincolnshire (especially the Wolds) there is beautiful, little-visited countryside. In the centre there's the Peak District National Park, and in the north some of the dramatic Yorkshire Dales.

There are HI/YHA hostels in Ludlow, Shrewsbury, Chester, Haworth and Lincoln, and many closely spaced hostels in the Peak District National Park (most a day's walk apart).

Getting Around

Bus transport around the region is fairly efficient, and particularly good in the Peak District.

There's also a good network of railway lines; you'll rarely need to resort to buses other than for financial reasons. See Shrewsbury for details on an interesting rail loop around northern Wales.

SHREWSBURY

Shrewsbury is the attractive regional capital for Shropshire, and is famous for its black-and-white, half-timbered buildings. It's a good base for Ironbridge, Stokesay Castle and Wales. Two famous small railways into Wales terminate here and it's possible to do a fascinating circuit of north Wales – see Trains under the Getting There & Away section later.

Orientation & Information

The station lies across the narrow land bridge formed by the loop of the Severn, a five-minute walk north of the centre of town. The bus station is central and the whole town is well signposted.

There's an efficient TIC (☎ 01743-350761), The Square, with theatre-booking facilities (including for the Royal Shakespeare Company at Stratford).

Things to See & Do

There are no vitally important sights, and, because of this, Shrewsbury has been saved from inundation by tourists. Strategically sited within a loop of the River Severn, there are **medieval streets** (including Butcher's Row and Fish St), **Quarry Park** (with a famous flower show in August) and river walks.

The city provides the setting for the *Brother Cadfael Chronicles*. In case you've never heard of him, Brother Cadfael is a fictional medieval sleuth, the subject of the books by Ellis Peters. Across the street from the abbey, the **Shrewsbury Quest** (☎ 243324) plays on this theme with clues to find amongst the displays of 12th-century monastery life.

There are daily walking tours of the town (£2/1) at 2.30 pm from May to October.

Places to Stay & Eat

The *Youth Hostel* (☎ 360179), Abbey Foregate, is one mile from the train and bus stations, 10 minutes after crossing English Bridge. Walk down High St, cross the bridge and veer right when Abbey Foregate splits in two around the abbey. There are numerous cheap B&Bs in this area. *Prynce's Villa Guest House* (☎ 356217), 15 Monkmoor Rd, has B&B accommodation from £13 per person.

The *Lucroft Hotel* (☎ 362421), Castlegates, on the way into town from the train station, is clean, comfortable and central. Rooms are £18/34 for singles/doubles.

There's a branch of *Pierre Victoire* (☎ 344744) at 15 St Mary's St, offering set lunches for £4.90 and more expensive dinners. The *Good Life Wholefood Restaurant* (☎ 350455), Barracks Passage, 73C Wyle Cop, does light lunches and teas that are good value. It's open 9.30 am to 4.30 pm, Monday to Saturday.

Getting There & Away

See the Rail and Coach/Bus fares tables in this chapter's introductory Getting Around section.

Bus National Express (☎ 0990-808080) has three buses a day to and from London (five hours) via Telford and Birmingham. Change at Birmingham for Oxford and Stratford-upon-Avon.

For information on transport in Shropshire, contact the county help line (☎ 0345-056785). Williamsons (☎ 01473-231010) runs an interesting service, the X96 Wrekin Rambler, between Birmingham and Shrewsbury via Ironbridge. There are daily departures in both directions. Midland Red West (☎ 01905-763888) has regular buses to and from Ludlow (service No 435).

Train Two fascinating small railways terminate at Shrewsbury, in addition to plenty of main-line connections. It's possible to do a brilliant, highly recommended rail loop from Shrewsbury around north Wales. Timetabling is a challenge – phone ☎ 01743-364041 for information. The journey is possible in a day as long as you don't miss any of the connections, but it's much better to allow at least a couple of days as there are plenty of interesting

places to visit along the way. The North & Mid-Wales Flexi Rover ticket is the most economical way of covering this route. It costs £23/15.20 and allows travel on three days out of seven.

From Shrewsbury you head due west across Wales to Dovey Junction (1¾ hours), where you connect with the famous Cambrian Coast Line, which hugs the beautiful coast on its way north to Porthmadog (1½ hours).

At Porthmadog you can pick up the Ffestiniog Railway, a superb restored narrow-gauge steam train that winds up into Snowdonia National Park to the slate-mining town of Blaenau Ffestiniog (1¼ hours). From Blaenau another small railway carves its way through the mountains and down the beautiful, tourist-infested Conwy Valley to Llandudno (1¼ hours) and Conwy. From there it's a short trip to Chester.

Another famous line, promoted as the Heart of Wales Line, runs south-west to Swansea (four hours), connecting with the main line from Cardiff to Fishguard (six hours, £22.70).

There are numerous trains to and from London's Euston station (three hours), and regular links to Chester (one hour, £5.50). There are also regular trains from Cardiff to Manchester via Bristol, Ludlow and Shrewsbury.

AROUND SHREWSBURY
Ironbridge Gorge

The World Heritage Site at Ironbridge, on the southern edge of Telford, is a monument to the Industrial Revolution. It was the wonder of its age, developing iron smelting on a scale never seen before – easy transport on the Severn and rich deposits of iron and coal in the gorge itself made it all possible.

The **Ironbridge Gorge Museum** (☎ 01952-433522) is open daily and comprises seven main museums and several smaller sites strung along the gorge. There's Blists Hill Open Air Museum, which recreates an entire community, including shops, houses, forges and pub; the Coalport China Museum with more than you ever wanted to know about porcelain; the beautiful first iron bridge; the Museum of Iron; and the Museum of the River and Visitor Centre (the best starting point). A passport ticket allowing entrance to all the museums is £8.95/5.30 for adults/students.

BRITAIN

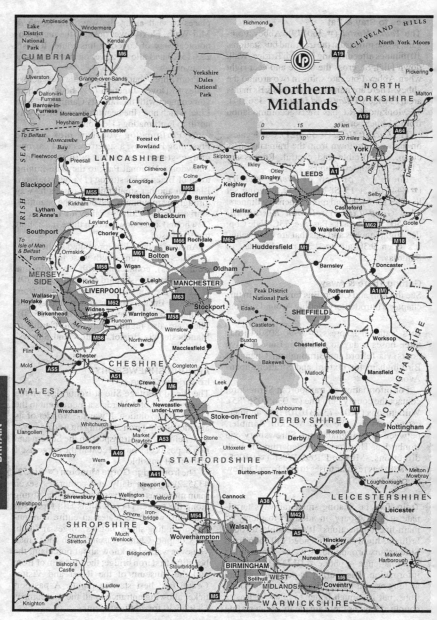

Northern
Midlands

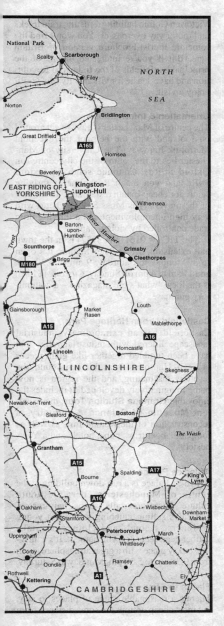

The excellent *Youth Hostel* (☎ 01952-433281) is fully open from February through November. From the bridge, follow Wellington Rd towards the power station; turn right after ¾ mile on the A4169 to Wellington.

Trains and buses run regularly to Telford from Shrewsbury (see Getting There & Away under Shrewsbury earlier), and some go on to the Gorge. Otherwise, there are regular buses from Telford's town centre. You'll need a car or a bike to get around the sites – it's three miles from Blists Hill to the Museum of Iron.

CHESTER

Despite steady streams of tourists Chester remains a beautiful town, ringed by an unbroken, red sandstone city wall which is the best in Britain and dates back to the Romans. Many of the city's 'medieval' looking buildings are actually only Victorian! Chester has excellent transport connections, especially to and from north Wales.

The two-mile walk along the top of the wall is the best way to see the town – allow a couple of hours to include detours down to the river and a visit to the cathedral.

Orientation & Information

Built in a bow formed by the River Dee, the walled centre is now surrounded by suburbs. The train station is a 15-minute walk from the city centre: go up City Rd, then turn right into Foregate at the large roundabout. From the bus station, turn left into Northgate St.

The TIC (☎ 01244-318356) is in the town hall opposite the cathedral. There's a second information centre just outside Newgate opposite the Roman amphitheatre, and another at the train station. There are excellent guided walks around the city every day at 10.45 am.

Places to Stay & Eat

The *Youth Hostel* (☎ 680056), 40 Hough Green, is over a mile from the centre and on the opposite side from the train station. Leave by Grosvenor Rd past the castle on your left, cross the river and turn right at the roundabout.

There are numerous good-value B&Bs along Hoole Rd, the road into the city from the M53/M56. The *Glen-Garth Guest House* (☎ 310260) at No 59 is typical. The *Aplas Guest House* (☎ 312401), 106 Brook St, is very comfortable and only a five-minute walk

BRITAIN

from the train station. Rooms are from £15/27 for a single/double. B&Bs can also be found inside the city walls.

Chester's pubs have good, basic food at reasonable prices. Try *Scruffy Murphy's* and *Pied Bull* on Northgate or *Scandals* on Music Hall Pass by the cathedral. *Francs* (☎ 317952) at 14 Cuppin St turns out reasonably priced traditional French food. *Alexander's Jazz Theatre* (☎ 340005) at Rufus Court by Northgate is a wine, coffee and tapas bar with great music.

Getting There & Away

Bus National Express (☎ 0990-808080) has numerous connections with Chester, including Birmingham (two hours) and on to London (five hours), Manchester (one hour), Glasgow (six hours), Liverpool (one hour) and Llandudno (1¾ hours). There's a late night bus to Holyhead (two hours) for the Irish ferry. For many destinations to the south or east it will be necessary to change at Birmingham; to the north, change at Manchester.

For information on the well-organised local bus services ring the Cheshire Bus Line (☎ 602666). Local buses leave from Market Square behind the town hall.

Train Any bus from the station goes into the centre. There are numerous trains to Shrewsbury (one hour); Manchester (one hour) and Liverpool; Holyhead (2¼ hours, £11), via the north Wales coast, for Ireland; and London's Euston station (three hours). Phone ☎ 0151-709 9696 for details.

MANCHESTER

Probably best known around the world for its football team (Manchester United), the city that produced Oasis, Take That and Simply Red is a grim monument to the industrial history of Britain. In the 19th century, Friedrich Engels (the co-author of the *Communist Manifesto)* used the city to illustrate the evils of capitalism, and after decades of painful decline it would again make a fascinating study.

Following its successful bid as the venue for the Commonwealth Games in 2002, the city will, no doubt, be given a makeover. As yet, the streets are dominated by empty warehouses and factories, the fantastical grandeur of Victorian Gothic buildings, rusting train tracks and motorway overpasses. You won't find the romantic tourist-brochure version of Britain here. But if you're interested in one of the principal battlefields of the Industrial Revolution and have a taste for vibrant city life, you'll enjoy a visit.

Orientation & Information

The centre of Manchester is easy to get around on foot and with the help of the excellent Metrolink tramway. The University of Manchester lies to the south of the city centre (on Oxford St/Rd). Continue south on Oxford St/Rd and you reach Rusholme, a thriving centre for cheap Indian restaurants. To the east of the university is Moss Side, a ghetto with very high unemployment and a thriving drug trade controlled by violent gangs.

The TIC (☎ 0161-234 3157) is in the town hall extension, off St Peter Square. It's open from Monday to Saturday, 9 am to 5.30 pm, and 11 am to 4 pm on Sunday. *City Life* (£1.40) is the local 'what's on' magazine – a compulsory purchase.

Castlefield Urban Heritage Park

Castlefield has an extraordinary industrial landscape littered with industrial relics that have been tumbled together like giant pieces of Lego. Unpromising as this may sound, the result is fascinating, and the region is now being imaginatively developed. It includes the enjoyable **Granada Studios Tour**, the excellent **Museum of Science & Industry**, a reconstruction of the Roman fort, as well as footpaths, boat trips, pubs, hotels and a YHA hostel.

Affleck's Palace

Affleck's Palace is a run-down building at the centre of Manchester's energetic youth culture. There are stalls, shops, hairdressers and cafés selling clubbing gear from young designers, second-hand clothes, crystals, leather gear, records – you name it. It's a thriving, buzzy place with a great atmosphere, open from 9.30 am to 5.30 pm, Monday to Saturday.

Places to Stay

There's a reasonable range of places to stay, but most cheap options are some distance from the city centre. The TIC's free booking service is recommended.

The stunning new *Youth Hostel* (☎ 839 9960) is across the road from the Museum of Science & Industry in the Castlefield area, and has comfortable four-bedded rooms for £11.60/8.20 per person. From late June to late September, the University of Manchester lets students' rooms to visitors from around £9 per person. Contact *Montgomery House* (☎ 226 3434), *Loxford Tower* (☎ 247 1334) and *Woolaton Hall* (☎ 224 7244).

The *Commercial Hotel* (☎ 834 3504), 125 Liverpool Rd, Castlefield, is a smartly renovated traditional pub close to the museum. Singles/doubles are £20/34.

Didsbury is an attractive suburb to the south of the university. There are some good local pubs and the bus links into the city are frequent. There's quite a strip of hotels in converted Victorian houses along Wilmslow and, particularly, Palatine Rds.

The *Crescent Gate Hotel* (☎ 224 0672), Park Crescent, has a particularly good location within walking distance of the Indian restaurants in Rusholme and is well served by numerous buses into the city centre. Most of the comfortable rooms have bathrooms; singles/doubles are £35/48.

Places to Eat
The most distinctive restaurant zones are Chinatown in the city centre and Rusholme in the south. Chinatown is bounded by Charlotte, Portland, Oxford and Mosley Sts, and it has a number of restaurants – not all Chinese, and most not particularly cheap. Rusholme is to the south of the university on Wilmslow Rd, the extension of Oxford St/Rd, and has numerous popular, cheap and very good Indian/Pakistani places.

Café bars have taken off in a big way in Manchester. The first, *Dry 201* (☎ 236 5920), 28 Oldham St, and *Manto* (☎ 236 2667), 46 Canal St are both still among the best. If you're shopping in Affleck's Palace, there are several good cafés there.

Homesick Vietnamese, Thais and Australians should check out the *Hong Pat Restaurant* (☎ 228 2485), 78 Portland St, Manchester's only Vietnamese restaurant, with set menus from £20 for two.

Entertainment
Manchester comes into its own at night, offering a remarkable range of high-quality entertainment. One of the best venues for live music is *Band on the Wall* (☎ 832 6625), Swan St, which has an eclectic variety of acts from jazz, blues and folk to pop. The *Hacienda* (☎ 236 5051), Whitworth St West, once the undisputed centre of Manchester's nightlife, survives and still has the occasional live band.

Canal St is the centre of Manchester's enormous gay nightlife scene – there are over 20 bars and clubs in the so-called 'Gay Village'.

Getting There & Away
Manchester is about 200 miles from London, 215 from Glasgow, 65 from York and 35 from Liverpool. See the Rail and Coach/Bus fares tables in this chapter's introductory Getting Around section.

Bus There are numerous coach links with the rest of the country. National Express (☎ 0990-808080) serves 1000 destinations! Chorlton St station is in the centre of the city.

Train Piccadilly is the main station for trains to and from the rest of the country, although Victoria serves Halifax and Bradford. The two stations are linked by Metrolink. For information phone ☎ 832 8353.

Getting Around
For general enquiries about local transport, including night buses, phone ☎ 228 7811 (open daily, 8 am to 8 pm).

Bus Buses from the city centre to West Didsbury cost around £1; to the university it's 70p.

Metrolink Metrolink is a new system of light-rail vehicles (trams) that operate on a combination of disused rail tracks and tracks laid along the city-centre's streets. In the centre there are frequent links between Victoria and Piccadilly train stations and G-Mex (for Castlefield). Buy tickets from the machines on the platforms.

LIVERPOOL
Liverpool was one of the world's greatest ports – exporting the cotton fabrics and manufactured

goods produced further inland, as well as millions of immigrants.

Since WWII it has suffered a cruel decline. In 1931 the population peaked at 855,000, today it is only 510,000. The city's combination of grandeur and decay, of decrepit streets, boarded-up windows and imperious buildings creates some of the most striking sights in Britain.

There aren't many large cities of note in the UK; Liverpool, however, is one that is definitely worth visiting. The Albert Docks, the Western Approaches Museum, the looming cathedrals, the brilliant architecture and the city streets themselves give vivid testimony to the city's rugged history and the perverse exhilaration of its present-day decline.

Orientation
Liverpool stretches north-south along the Mersey estuary for more than 13 miles. The main visitor attraction is Albert Dock (which is well signposted) to the south of the city centre. The centre, including the two cathedrals to the east, is quite compact – about 1½ by one mile.

Lime St, the main train station, is just to the east of the city centre. The National Express coach station is on the corner of Norton and Islington Sts in the north of the city. The bus station is in the centre on Paradise St.

Information
The main TIC (☎ 0151-709 3631) is in Clayton Square Shopping Centre. It's open from Monday to Saturday 9.30 am to 5.30 pm. There's also a branch at Albert Dock (☎ 708 8854) which is open daily from 10 am to 5.30 pm. Both have accommodation-booking services.

A little caution is justified in Liverpool. Although the main hazard is likely to be over-friendly drunks, one should avoid dark side streets.

Albert Dock
In the 1980s the derelict Albert Dock was restored and it has become a deservedly popular tourist attraction. There are a number of outstanding modern museums (the **Merseyside Maritime Museum**, the **Museum of Liverpool Life** and the **Tate Gallery Liverpool**), shops and restaurants, a branch of the

TIC and several tacky tourist attractions (the **Beatles Story** is disappointing).

Western Approaches Museum
The Combined Headquarters of the Western Approaches (☎ 227 2008), the secret command centre for the Battle of the Atlantic, was buried under yards of concrete beneath an undistinguished building behind the town hall in Rumford Square. At the end of the war the bunker was abandoned, with virtually everything left intact. It's open daily except Friday and Sunday.

Beatles Tour
There are numerous sites around Liverpool associated with the Beatles, all of whom grew up here. Both TICs sell tickets to the Magical Mystery Tour, a 2¼-hour bus trip taking in homes, schools, venues, Penny Lane, Strawberry Fields and many other landmarks. It departs daily from inside the Albert Dock TIC at 2.20 pm and from the Merseyside Welcome Centre at 2.30 pm. Tickets are £7.95.

A re-creation of the original Cavern Club (☎ 236 9091) in Mathew St still attracts a big crowd. Phone for opening times.

Places to Stay
There's no official YHA hostel in Liverpool, but there are several other options. The *YMCA* (☎ 709 9516), 56 Mount Pleasant, offers a passable alternative for men and women, though it's definitely spartan. Singles/doubles are £12.50/22.60, including a full English breakfast. There's a good *YWCA* (☎ 709 7791) at 1 Rodney St (off Mount Pleasant) for women only. Rooms are £11/20.

The *Embassie Youth Hostel* (☎ 707 1089), 1 Falkner Square, to the west of the Anglican Cathedral, but still within walking distance of the centre, has dorm beds from £9.50, and facilities including a laundry.

The *University of Liverpool* (☎ 794 6440) has single rooms at Mulberry Court, Oxford St, near the Metropolitan Cathedral, and self-catering apartments from March to April and July to September from £13.

The weekend rate at the *Britannia Adelphi Hotel* (☎ 709 7200), Ranelagh Place, makes Liverpool's top hotel a worthwhile splurge. When it was completed in 1912 it was considered one of the most luxurious hotels in the world. Singles/doubles are £30/60 at weekends, £49/87 during the week. Breakfast (£8.95) is extra.

There are a number of well-positioned hotels on Mount Pleasant, between the city centre and the Metropolitan Cathedral. The *Feathers Hotel* (☎ 709 9655), 119 Mount Pleasant, is a particularly good mid-range hotel. There are 80 rooms with a variety of facilities. Singles/doubles start at £25/35.

Places to Eat
There are lots of places to eat down Bold St in the city centre. At the eastern end of this street is *Café Tabac* (☎ 709 3735), No 124, a relaxed wine bar that attracts a young crowd.

Everyman Bistro (☎ 708 9545), 5 Hope St, underneath the famous Everyman Theatre is highly recommended. It's a cafeteria-style set-up, but the food is cheap and good (main dishes under £4.50). The *refectory* at the Anglican Cathedral serves excellent lunches that are great value.

Entertainment
On a long summer evening, it's hard to imagine a more perfect programme than starting with a pint in the Philharmonic Hotel (on the corner of Hope and Hardman Sts), eating and seeing a show at the Everyman, wandering into town to listen to some music, and finally collapsing, in comfort, at the Adelphi.

The *Everyman Theatre* (☎ 709 4776) is one of the best repertory theatres in the country. If possible, get hold of the free *In Touch* or *L: Scene* (£1), both monthly entertainment guides. Wander around Mathew St and south-west to Bold, Seel and Slater Sts and you'll stumble over an amazing array of clubs and pubs catering to every style you can imagine.

Getting There & Away
There are National Express (☎ 0990-808080) services linking Liverpool to most major towns.

Numerous InterCity services run to Lime St station (☎ 709 9696). See the Rail and Coach/Bus fares tables in this chapter's introductory Getting Around section.

Getting Around
Public transport in the region is coordinated by Merseytravel (☎ 236 7676), which has a branch in the TIC at Clayton Square. There are various zone tickets, such as the £3.10 ticket for bus, train and ferry (except cruises). These are also sold at post offices.

Bus There are a number of bus companies. Smart Bus No 1 runs from Albert Dock through the city centre to the university, and vice versa, every 20 minutes.

Ferry The ferry across the Mersey (85p), started 800 years ago by Benedictine monks but made famous by Gerry & the Pacemakers, still offers one of the best views of Liverpool. Boats depart from Pier Head ferry terminal, to the north of Albert Dock and next to the Liver Building, going to Woodside and Seacombe. Special one-hour commentary cruises run all year round, departing every hour from 10 am to 3 pm on weekdays and until 6 pm on weekends (£3.10/2.15). Phone ☎ 630 1030 for more information.

ISLE OF MAN
Equidistant from Liverpool, Dublin and Belfast in the Irish Sea, the number one industry on this island is tax avoidance. The capital, Douglas, is a run-down relic of Victorian tourism, but the island also has beautiful countryside and a proud heritage as the site of the world's oldest continuous parliament. The annual TT races (May-June) draw 45,000 motorcycle fans.

Phone the Douglas TIC (☎ 01624-686766) for B&Bs. The Isle of Man Steam Packet Company (☎ 661661) has several sailings a week to Douglas from Liverpool (four hours, from £25 single), daily departures from Heysham (near Lancaster), and connections to Belfast and Dublin (see the Ireland chapter).

PEAK DISTRICT
Squeezed between the industrial Midlands to the south, Manchester to the west and Sheffield to the east, the Peak District seems an unlikely site for one of England's most beautiful regions. Even the name is misleading – being derived from the tribes who once lived here, not from the existence of any significant peaks (there are none!). Nonetheless, the 542-sq-mile Peak District National Park is a delight, particularly for walkers and cyclists.

The Peak District divides into the green fields and steep-sided dales of the southern White Peak and the bleak, gloomy moors of the northern Dark Peak. Buxton, to the west, and Matlock, to the east, are good bases for exploring the park or you can stay right in the centre at Bakewell or Castleton. In May and June the ancient custom of 'well dressing' can be seen at many villages. There are also prehistoric sites, limestone caves, the tragic plague village of Eyam and the fine stately homes of Chatsworth and Haddon Hall.

Castleton and nearby Edale are popular villages on the border between the White and Dark peaks. From Edale, the Pennine Way starts its 250-mile meander northwards. From Castleton, the 25-mile Limestone Way is a superb day walk covering the length of the White Peak to Matlock. In addition, a number of disused railway lines in the White Peak have been redeveloped as walking and cycling routes, with strategically situated bicycle-rental outlets at old station sites.

There are information centres at Edale (☎ 01433-670207), Castleton (☎ 01433-620679), and Bakewell (☎ 01629-813227). The Peak District is packed with B&Bs, YHA hostels and a collection of camping barns (☎ 01433-620373), together with plenty of convivial pubs and good restaurants. Visitors to Bakewell should make sure to sample Bakewell pudding – not tart.

The regular Transpeak bus service cuts right across the Peak District from Nottingham and Derby to Manchester via Matlock, Bakewell and Buxton.

LINCOLN

Since it's not on a direct tourist route, many people bypass Lincoln, missing a magnificent 900-year-old cathedral (the third largest in Britain) and an interesting city with a compact medieval centre of narrow, winding streets. The suburbs are unattractive and depressed; however, perhaps because Lincoln escapes the hordes of visitors that places like York attract, the people are particularly friendly.

The TIC (☎ 01522-529828), 9 Castle Hill, has information on cheap B&Bs; the *Youth Hostel* (☎ 522076), 77 South Park, is an excellent hostel.

Lincoln is 132 miles from London, with direct bus and rail services.

Northern England

Northern England is quite different from the rest of the country, although it is misleading to think of it as a single entity. The three major sections are Yorkshire to the south; Durham and Northumberland in the north-east; and Cumbria in the north-west. The latter two areas border on Scotland.

As a rule, the countryside is more rugged than in the south and it is as if the history reflects this, because every inch has been fought over. The central conflict has been the long struggle between north and south, with the battle lines shifting over the centuries. The Romans were the first to attempt to delineate a border with Hadrian's Wall, but the struggle continued into the 18th century.

The Danes made York their capital and ruled the Danelaw – all of England north and east of a line between Chester and London. Later, their Norman cousins left a legacy of spectacular fortresses and the marvellous Durham Cathedral. The region prospered on the medieval wool trade, which sponsored the great cathedral at York, and enormous monastic communities, the remains of which can be seen at Rievaulx and Fountains abbeys.

The countryside is a grand backdrop to this human drama, with four of England's best national parks and some spectacular coastline. The Lake District and the Yorkshire Dales are the best known and arguably most beautiful of the parks, but the North York Moors have a great variety of landscapes and a superb coastline. All three parks can be very crowded in summer, but it is easier to escape the masses in the North York Moors National Park.

Orientation & Information

The dominating geological feature is the Pennine Hills, which form a north-south spine dividing the region into eastern and western halves and provide the source for numerous major rivers.

The major transport routes – both rail and road – basically run either side of the hills from York (which is east of Manchester), to Newcastle (which is east of Carlisle) and Edinburgh (which is east of Glasgow). East-west transport, except between these paired cities, is slow.

There are YHA hostels at York and Newcastle and, even more importantly, dozens scattered about the national parks. Book ahead in summer.

Activities

Hiking There are more great hikes in this region than any other in England. The most famous is the Pennine Way, which stretches 250 miles from Edale in the Peak District to Kelso in Scotland. Unfortunately, its popularity means that long sections turn into unpleasant bogs.

An alternative like the Cleveland Way in the North York Moors National Park (see that section) is likely to be quieter and drier underfoot. The Cumbria Way, from Ulverston to Carlisle, and the Dales Way, from Ilkley to Windermere, are among many other interesting possibilities.

Getting There & Around

Bus Bus transport around the region can be difficult, particularly around the national parks. For timetables and information covering Cumbria phone ☎ 01228-812812; for County Durham phone ☎ 0191-383 3337; and for Northumberland phone ☎ 0191-232 4211. For North Yorkshire transport phone ☎ 01609-780780, and for the Newcastle area phone ☎ 0191-232 5325. Phone numbers for individual operators are given in the following sections. For onward travel into the Scottish Borders phone ☎ 01289-307461.

There are a number of one-day Explorer tickets; always ask if one might be appropriate. The Explorer North East is particularly interesting, covering a vast area north of York to the Scottish Borders and west to Carlisle and Hawes (in the Yorkshire Dales).

The major operator in the scheme is Northumbria (☎ 0191-232 4211) – they'll help plan an itinerary. Unlimited travel by bus and metro for one day is £4.75, and there are also numerous admission discounts for holders of Explorer tickets. You can purchase the tickets on the buses.

Train In addition to the main-line routes running north to Edinburgh and Glasgow there are several useful branch lines, a number of which centre on Carlisle.

There are numerous special-price Rover tickets, for single-day travel and longer periods, so ask if one might be appropriate. For example, the North Country Flexi Rover allows unlimited travel throughout the North (not including Northumberland) for any four days out of eight for £49.

Boat The Norwegian Color Line (☎ 0191-296 1313) operates two ferries a week to Stavanger and Bergen (Norway). During summer, Scandinavian Seaways (☎ 0990-333000) operates a weekly ferry from Newcastle to Gothenburg (Sweden). See the introductory Getting There & Away section at the beginning of this chapter for details.

YORK

For nearly 2000 years York has been the capital of the North. It existed before the Romans, but entered the world stage under their rule. In 306 AD, Constantine the Great, the first Christian emperor and founder of Constantinople (now Istanbul), was proclaimed emperor here, probably on the site of the cathedral.

In Saxon times York became an important centre for Christianity and learning – the first church on the site of the current cathedral was built in 627. Danish invaders captured the city in 867, transforming it into an important trading centre and port – the River Ouse providing the link with the sea – and the capital of the Danelaw.

York continued to prosper as a political and trading centre after William the Conqueror's initial 'pacification'. In the 15th and 16th centuries, however, it declined economically. Although it remained the social and cultural capital of the North, it was the arrival of the railway in 1839 that gave York a new lease of commercial life, allowing the expansion of Rowntree's and Terry's confectionery factories and the development of tourism.

The city walls were built during the 13th century and are among the most impressive surviving medieval fortifications in Europe. They enclose a thriving, fascinating centre with medieval streets, Georgian town houses, riverside pubs, McDonald's and Marks & Spencer. The crowning glory is the Minster, the

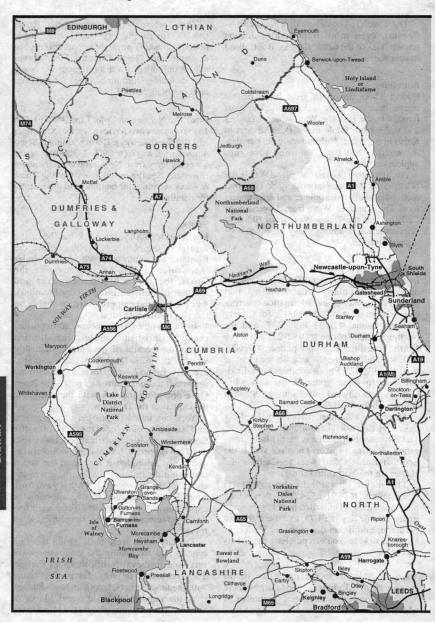

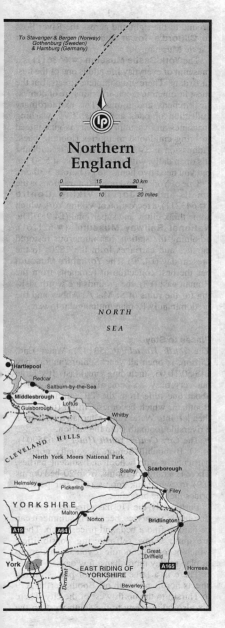

Northern England

To Stavanger & Bergen (Norway)
Gothenburg (Sweden)
& Hamburg (Germany)

0   15   30 km
0   10   20 miles

NORTH
SEA

Hartlepool
Redcar
Saltburn-by-the-Sea
Middlesbrough
Guisborough   Loftus
                          Whitby

CLEVELAND HILLS

North York Moors National Park

Helmsley   Pickering   Scalby   Scarborough
                                              Filey

YORKSHIRE
          Malton
          Norton   Bridlington

A19   A64

York   Great
        EAST RIDING OF   Driffield   A165
        YORKSHIRE   Hornsea
          Derwent
                        Beverley

largest Gothic cathedral in England. York attracts millions of visitors, and the crowds can get you down, especially in July and August. But it's too old, too impressive, too real and too convinced of its own importance to be totally overwhelmed by mere tourists.

Orientation
York is not the easiest city to find your way around – signposting leaves something to be desired and the streets are a medieval tangle. Bear in mind that *gate* means street, and *bar* means gate.

There are five major landmarks: the 2½-mile wall that encloses the city centre; the Minster at the northern corner; Clifford's Tower, a 13th-century castle and mound at the southern end; the River Ouse that cuts the centre in two (the most important part being the north-eastern two-thirds); and the enormous train station just outside the western corner.

The main bus terminal is on Rougier St (off Station Rd, inside the city walls on the western side of Lendal Bridge), but some local buses leave from the train station.

Information
There are small TICs at the train and bus stations (handy for an introductory map), but the main centre is across the river near Bootham Bar (☎ 01904-621756), De Grey Rooms, Exhibition Square. The main TIC is open Monday to Saturday from 9 am to 5 pm (to 7pm during August), and on Sunday from 9.30 am to 2 pm.

Things to See
There's a lot to see in York, and this guide just scratches the surface with an introductory ramble. Before you start, buy a York Visitor Card from the TIC; it costs £1 and gives significant discounts at the major sights.

It is also worth considering taking the innovative and excellent Yorspeed Walkman Guided Tour – also available from the TIC. For £4 you can hire a Walkman (if required) and an informative tape with atmospheric sound effects, enabling you to wander around at your own speed with a private guide in your pocket.

If you want to walk, start at the main TIC, Exhibition Square. Climb the city wall at **Bootham Bar** (on the site of a Roman gate)

BRITAIN

and walk north-east along the wall to Monk Bar, from where there are beautiful views of the Minster.

York Minster took over 250 years to complete (from 1220 to 1480), so it incorporates a number of architectural styles. From the wall you can see the nave, which was built in the Decorated style between 1291 and 1350; the central or lantern tower in the Perpendicular style, which was the last addition (there are brilliant views from the top); the north transept (Early English, 1241-60) and, extending from it, the octagonal chapter house, a Decorated masterpiece (1260-1300); and the choir (the eastern end), also in the Decorated style. The cathedral is most famous for its extensive medieval stained glass, particularly the enormous Great Eastern Window (1405-08) which depicts the beginning and end of the world.

By the 1960s the cathedral was in danger of collapse. If you go down to the foundations you can see how it was saved, as well as traces of earlier buildings on the site going back as far as the Roman garrison. There are worthwhile free guided tours. Evensong is at 5 pm Monday to Friday, and at 4 pm on Saturday and Sunday (said, not sung, on Wednesday).

Monk Bar is the best preserved medieval gate, with a working portcullis. Leave the walls here, walk along Goodramgate and take the first right into Ogleforth, then left into Chapter House St. The **Treasurer's House** (open April through October; £3), on the right, has been restored by the National Trust. Turn left again into College St (back towards Goodramgate) and pass a 15th-century, timber-framed building, **St William's College**, with a good restaurant.

Turn right into Goodramgate again, passing the ancient Lady Row houses. Cross diagonally over King's Square and you'll reach the much-photographed **Shambles**, a medieval butcher's street. Walk down the Shambles, then turn left and immediately right into Fossgate for the **Merchant Adventurers' Hall** (£1.80), which was built in the 14th century by a guild of merchants who controlled the cloth export trade.

Continue down Walmgate (the continuation of Fossgate) to **Walmgate Bar**, the only city gate in England with an intact barbican – an extended gateway designed to make life very difficult for uninvited guests. Follow the wall

around to the right and across the River Foss to **Clifford's Tower** and the brilliant York Castle Museum.

The **York Castle Museum** (☎ 653611) is a museum of everyday life and is one of the best in Britain. There are complete streets, but the most fascinating reconstructions are of domestic kitchens and rooms. The extraordinary collection of odds and ends, TVs, washing machines and vacuum cleaners is guaranteed to bring childhood memories flooding back. Admission is £4.20/2.90 for adults/students; it's open daily, with last admission at 5.30 pm but you need two hours, so go before 3.30 pm.

One of York's most popular attractions is the smells-and-all **Jorvik Viking Centre** (☎ 643211), a recreation of Viking York which some think glitzy and superficial (£4.95). The **National Railway Museum** (☎ 621261), adjoining the station, has numerous restored engines and carriages from the 1820s to the present day (£4.20). The **Yorkshire Museum** has the best collection of remnants from the Roman past (£3); the grounds are worth visiting for the ruins of St Mary's Abbey and the predominantly Roman multangular tower.

Places to Stay

The *Youth Hostel* (☎ 653147), Water End, Clifton, is open all year. Seniors/juniors pay £13.50/10.05, including breakfast. It's large but very busy, so book ahead. The hostel is about one mile from the TIC: turn left into Bootham, which becomes Clifton (the A19), then left into Water End. Alternatively, there's a riverside footpath from the station.

The *City Centre Youth Hotel* (☎ 625904), at 11 Bishophill Senior, is equally popular, particularly with school and student parties. There is a range of rooms, from 20-bed dorms (£9) to twin bunk rooms (£12 per person); prices include breakfast.

Fortunately, the TIC has a free accommodation-booking service, because in summer it can be hard to find a bed, and prices jump. There are quite a few self-catering possibilities, which become economic if you are in a group or plan to stay more than a few days.

There is a large number of places on the streets north and south off Bootham (the A19 to Thirsk) to the north-west of the city. There are also quite a few to the south-west on the

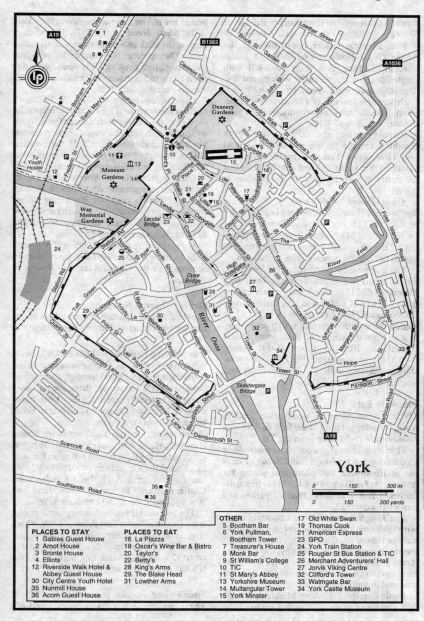

York

0   150   300 m
0   150   300 yards

PLACES TO STAY
1 Gabies Guest House
2 Arnot House
3 Bronte House
4 Elliots
12 Riverside Walk Hotel &
   Abbey Guest House
30 City Centre Youth Hostel
35 Nunmill House
36 Acorn Guest House

PLACES TO EAT
16 La Piazza
18 Oscar's Wine Bar & Bistro
20 Taylor's
22 Betty's
28 King's Arms
29 The Blake Head
31 Lowther Arms

OTHER
5 Bootham Bar
6 York Pullman,
   Bootham Tower
7 Treasurer's House
8 Monk Bar
9 St William's College
10 TIC
11 St Mary's Abbey
13 Yorkshire Museum
14 Multangular Tower
15 York Minster
17 Old White Swan
19 Thomas Cook
21 American Express
23 GPO
24 York Train Station
25 Rougier St Bus Station & TIC
26 Merchant Adventurers' Hall
27 Jorvik Viking Centre
32 Clifford's Tower
33 Walmgate Bar
34 York Castle Museum

streets between Bishopthorpe Rd (over Skeldergate Bridge) and the A1036 to Leeds.

With a central position beside the river, the *Abbey Guest House* (☎ 627782), 14 Earlsborough Terrace, is a standard B&B with singles/doubles from £15/30 with colour TV. The *Riverside Walk Hotel* (☎ 620769), at 9 Earlsborough Terrace, is a comfortable place; rooms mostly have bathrooms, and singles/doubles are from £24/44.

Running along the railway line, both Bootham Terrace (to the south of Bootham) and Grosvenor Terrace (to the north of Bootham) are virtually lined with B&Bs. Most are pretty standard issue, but the position is good.

Arnot House (☎ 641966), 17 Grosvenor Terrace, has shared facilities but is good value at £13 to £16 per person. *Bronte House* (☎ 621066), 22 Grosvenor Terrace, is a pleasant hotel with *en suite* rooms ranging from £10 to £20 per person depending on the season.

There are some nice places on Sycamore Terrace, off Bootham Terrace, including *Elliots* (☎ 623333) with good *en suite* rooms from £22 to £27 per person. On Bishopthorpe Rd, *Nunmill House* (☎ 634047), at No 85, is a good place with rooms from £16 per person. Just in from the corner of Bishopgate St and Southlands Rd, the *Acorn Guest House* (☎ 620081), 1 Southlands Rd, is a decent two-star guesthouse with TV in all rooms and singles/doubles from £16.50/33.

Places to Eat

There's no shortage of good-value food in York; for pubs get hold of the free *Yorkshire & Humberside Pub Guide* from the TIC.

There are several decent restaurants along Goodramgate from Monk Bar. *Caesar's Pizzeria & Ristorante* has pasta and pizzas for around £5. *La Piazza* (☎ 642641) is in a half-timbered hall and does standard pizzas and pasta for around £5.

. The *King's Arms* on King's Staith is a pub with tables overlooking the river on the southeastern side of the Ouse Bridge (the middle of the three main bridges). Nearby, the *Lowther Arms* on the corner of King's Staith and Cumberland has cheap bar meals and a reasonable-value restaurant.

Further up the hill, along Micklegate, there is a variety of places, including some of the best in town. The most acclaimed café in York is the *Blake Head* (☎ 623767), 104 Micklegate, at the back of a book store with the same name. The emphasis is on simple, but imaginative, vegetarian cooking. It is open every day from 10 am to 5 pm; soup and a roll costs £2.25, a main-course salad £4.25.

Back in the centre of town, *St William's College Restaurant* is a great spot to relax after exploring the cathedral. It's open from 10 am to 5 pm. Lunch includes various casseroles and vegetarian dishes under £3. If the weather allows, there are few more pleasant spots in the city than the beautiful cobbled courtyard.

Oscar's Wine Bar & Bistro, Little Stonegate, is an atmospheric spot with an outdoor area and a wide range of interesting dishes (including vegetarian). Most main meals – for example, smoked haddock pasta or chicken tikka masala – are around £5.

For teas you're spoilt for choice. Try *Betty's* in St Helen's Square, *Taylor's*, upstairs at 46 Stonegate or the *Grand Assembly Rooms* in Blake St.

Getting There & Away

See the Rail and Coach/Bus fares tables in this chapter's introductory Getting Around section.

Bus National Express (☎ 0990-808080) buses leave from Rougier St. One bus a day runs from Birmingham (4½ hours) through to Scarborough via York. Curiously, there are no buses direct to Durham. There are at least three buses a day to London (4½ hours) and one to Edinburgh (six hours).

For information on local buses (to Castle Howard, Helmsley, Scarborough, Whitby, etc), contact the information office on Rougier St. Yorkshire Coastliner (☎ 01653-692556) has a useful service that links Leeds, York, Castle Howard, Pickering, Goathland and Whitby; check the £7.50 Freedom ticket.

The best deal if you're heading north or east is the Explorer North East ticket (£4.50), which is valid on most bus services and gives unlimited travel for one day. United Auto (☎ 01325-465252) has a bus north to Ripon (£2.85) where you can link into the network.

Train For information phone ☎ 0345-484950. There are numerous trains from London's

King's Cross station (two hours) and on to Edinburgh (2¾ hours).

North-south trains also connect with Peterborough (1¼ hours, £20.50) for Cambridge and East Anglia (three hours, £26.50). There are good connections with south-west England, via Bristol (4½ hours, £37), Cheltenham, Birmingham and Sheffield. There is also a service from Oxford (4½ hours, £26.50), via Birmingham.

Local trains to Scarborough take 45 minutes and cost £7.60. For Whitby it's necessary to change at Middlesbrough. Trains to and from the west and north-west go via Leeds.

Getting Around

You can hire a bike for £9.50 a day from Bob Trotter by Monk Bar (☎ 622868), but you need your own helmet.

If you are energetic you could do an interesting loop out to Castle Howard (15½ miles), Helmsley and Rievaulx Abbey (12½ miles) and Thirsk (another 12½ miles), where you could catch a train back to York. There's also a Trans-Pennine Trail cycle path section from Bishopthorpe in York to Selby (15 miles) along the old railway line; call ☎ 01757-703263 for a free visitors' pack.

AROUND YORK
Castle Howard

There are few buildings in the world that are so perfect their visual impact is almost a physical blow – Castle Howard (☎ 01653-648333), of *Brideshead Revisited* fame, is one. The house has a picturesque setting in the rolling Howardian Hills and is surrounded by 400 hectares of superb terraces and landscaped grounds dotted with monumental follies.

Castle Howard is 15 miles north of York off the A64. It's open mid-March through October from 10 am (grounds) and 11 am (house) to 4.30 pm. Entry to the house and garden is £6.50/3.50.

The castle can be reached by several tours and occasional buses from York. Check with the York TIC for up-to-date schedules. Tours cost around £5. Yorkshire Coastliner bus Nos 840 and 842, running between York and Whitby, stop at the castle.

NORTH YORK MOORS NATIONAL PARK

Only rivalled by Exmoor in the south and the

Lake District, the North York Moors are less crowded than the Lake District and more expansive than Exmoor. The coast is superb, with high cliffs and long, sandy beaches backing onto unspoilt countryside. From the ridge-top roads and open moors there are wonderful views, and the dales shelter abbeys, castles and small stone villages.

One hundred mile Cleveland Way, the long-distance path, curves around the edge of the park along the western hills from Helmsley to Saltburn-by-the-Sea, then down the coast to Scarborough. For further information, see *The Cleveland Way* by Ian Sampson (Countryside Commission/Aurum Press, £9.99). A leaflet with information on accommodation is available from TICs. The North Yorkshire Moors Railway, a privately owned steam train, runs up the beautiful wooded Newtondale from Pickering to Grosmont (with train connections to Whitby and Middlesbrough).

Orientation & Information

The western boundary of the park is a steep escarpment formed by the Hambleton and Cleveland Hills; the moors run east-west and stretch along the coast between Scarborough and Staithes. Rainwater escapes from the moors down deep, parallel dales – to the Rye and Derwent rivers in the south and the Esk in the north. After the open space of the moors, the dales form a gentler, greener landscape, sometimes wooded, and often with a beautiful stone village or two.

The coastline is as impressive as any in Britain, and considerably less spoilt than most; Scarborough and Whitby are both popular resorts, but Whitby in particular retains its charm.

There's a useful, tabloid visitors' guide (50p), which is widely available in surrounding towns. There are visitors' centres at Helmsley (☎ 01439-770173) and Danby (☎ 01287-660654), but they are open daily only from April to October (weekends from November to March). The TICs in Whitby, Pickering and Scarborough are open year round.

Getting Around

The excellent free brochure *Moors Connections* is available from TICs and is a must for public-transport users. Transport on the A roads is quite good, but beyond them you'll have to find your own way.

The North York Moors Railway (NYMR; ☎ 01751-472508) cuts through the park from Pickering to Grosmont, which is on the Esk Valley Line (no Sunday service) between Whitby and Middlesbrough. It operates from late March to early November (one hour, £6.90), but there are only three trains a day at either end of the season. There are pleasant walks from most of the stations along the line; brochures are available from NYMR shops.

Bicycles are hired by Footloose (☎ 01439-770886) in Helmsley; mountain bikes are £10 per day and 10-speeds £5 per day.

Helmsley

Helmsley is a perfect base for walking a short stretch of the Cumberland Way. There's a picturesque ruined castle on the edge of town, and Rievaulx Abbey, Duncombe Park and Nunnington Hall are all within easy walking distance.

Helmsley itself is an attractive market town (Friday market) with excellent short walks in the beautiful surrounding countryside. There's a hostel and a number of B&Bs with prices around £14; a group of them on Ashdale Rd. The TIC (☎ 01439-770173) offers a booking service. The *Youth Hostel* (☎ 770433) is open from February through November, but only between 15 July and the end of September on a daily basis. There are several camping grounds in the area, the nearest being the one at Harome (☎ 770416) two miles to the southeast of town.

Everything is grouped around the marketplace; it's worth checking out the elegant little shops off Borogate, including the Footloose Walking & Outdoor Shop (☎ 770886), where you can hire bikes; see the preceding Getting Around section'.

There are two Stephenson's buses (☎ 01347-838990) a day between York and Helmsley (No 57, 1¼ hours). Scarborough & District (☎ 01723-375463) has six buses a day, Monday to Saturday, and three on Sunday, between Helmsley and Scarborough via Pickering (No 128, 2¼ hours).

Rievaulx Abbey A 3½-mile uphill walk from Helmsley along the Cleveland Way, the remains of this 13th-century abbey are arguably the most beautiful monastic ruins in England. They are open daily from 10 am; admission is £2.50/1.90.

Pickering

Pickering is a terminus for the NYMR – see the preceding Getting Around section. The TIC (☎ 01751-473791) will be able to suggest one of the numerous B&Bs. The nearest *Youth Hostel* (☎ 460376) is at Lockton, about four miles north. It's another good walking base, and is open from April to 28 September, except Sunday.

Pickering can be reached from Leeds, York or Whitby on Yorkshire Coastliner (☎ 01653-692556) or from Helmsley or Scarborough on Scarborough & District (☎ 01723-375463).

Scarborough

Scarborough is a traditional seaside resort with a spectacular location. It's jam-packed with arcades, boarding houses and B&Bs. The coastline to the north, especially around Robin Hood's Bay, is beautiful. With its ruined castle looming over the harbour, Scarborough must once have been very beautiful itself.

If you do need to stay, contact the TIC (☎ 01723-373333). There's a *Youth Hostel* (☎ 361176) in Burniston Rd which is open most nights, except some Sundays and Mondays.

Scarborough is a good transport hub, connected by rail with York and Kingston-upon-Hull. There are reasonably frequent buses west along the A170 to Pickering and Helmsley; contact Scarborough & District (☎ 375463). Tees & District (☎ 01947-602146) has regular buses to Whitby via Robin Hood's Bay.

Whitby

Somehow Whitby transcends the coaches and fish-and-chip shops – the imposing ruins of the abbey loom over red-brick houses that spill down a headland to a beautiful harbour. Captain James Cook was apprenticed to a Whitby shipowner in 1746, and HMS *Endeavour* was built here, originally to carry coal.

The *Youth Hostel* (☎ 01947-602878) is beside the abbey and has fantastic views. Alternatively, the well-designed *Harbour Grange Hostel* (☎ 600817), Spital Bridge, on the eastern side of the harbour, is open all year. There are plenty of B&Bs and a helpful TIC (☎ 602674). The *Magpie Café* on the harbour has a reputation as the best place for fish and chips in England!

Consider attempting the 5½-mile cliff-top walk to Robin Hood's Bay, but don't plan on staying there as accommodation is limited and always pre-booked; the last Tees & District bus returns to Whitby around 4 pm. There are also some beautiful fishing villages to the north.

There are buses from Scarborough and York, or you can catch the Esk Valley train from Middlesbrough (four per day, Monday to Saturday, 1½ hours), which connects with the NYMR at Grosmont.

DURHAM
Durham is the most dramatic cathedral city in Britain; the massive Norman cathedral stands on a high, wooded promontory above a bend in the River Wear. Other cathedrals are more refined, but none has more impact. This extraordinary structure was built to survive to the end of time, with utter confidence in the enduring qualities of faith and stone.

Durham is also home to the third-oldest university in England (founded in 1832); the banks of the river and the old town are worth exploring.

Orientation & Information
The marketplace (and TIC), castle and cathedral are all on the teardrop-shaped peninsula surrounded by the River Wear. The train station is above and to the north-west of the cathedral on the other side of the river. The bus station is also on the western side. The TIC (☎ 0191-384 3720), Market Place, is just a short walk to the north of the castle and cathedral.

Things to See & Do
The World Heritage-listed **cathedral** is the most complete Norman cathedral, with characteristic round arches, enormous columns and zigzagged chevron ornament. The vast interior is like a cave that is only partly artificial. Don't miss the beautiful Galilee Chapel at the western end. There are tours in July and August, Monday to Friday at 10 am. Evensong is at 5.15 pm weekdays and at 3.30 pm on Sunday.

The **castle** dates from 1093 and served as the home for Durham's prince-bishops. These bishops had powers and responsibilities more normally associated with a warrior king than a priest, but this was wild frontier country. It is now a residential college for the university, and it is possible to stay there during summer holidays (see the following Places to Stay & Eat section). There are guided tours (£1.75/1.20) although their schedule is erratic, especially during summer weekends when the castle is booked out for weddings.

There are superb views back to the cathedral and castle from the outer bank of the river; walk around the bend between Elvet and Framwelgate bridges, or hire a boat at Elvet Bridge.

Places to Stay & Eat
Several colleges rent their rooms during the university vacations (particularly July to September); enquire at the TIC. The most exciting possibility is *University College* in the old Durham Castle (☎ 374 3863), which has B&B at £18.50 per person.

The TIC makes local bookings free, which is useful since convenient B&Bs are not particularly numerous; the situation is particularly grim during graduation week in late June. There are a number of B&Bs for around £15 per person on Gilesgate – leave the market square from its northern end, over the freeway onto Claypath, which becomes Gilesgate – *Mrs Koltai* (☎ 386 2026) is at No 10, *Mr Nimmins* (☎ 384 6485) is at No 14, Mrs Miles' *Pink House* is at No 16 (☎ 386 7039) and *Mrs Elliott* (☎ 384 1671) is at No 169.

Most of the eating possibilities are around the market square. Near the old Elvet Bridge, *Pizzaland* and *Bella Pasta*, which offers the usual good-value Italian fare, have great views, set among trees overlooking the river.

Getting There & Away
See the Rail and Coach/Bus fares tables in this chapter's introductory Getting Around section.

Bus There are five National Express (☎ 0990-808080) buses a day to London (4½ hours), one to Edinburgh (4½ hours), two to Birmingham (5¾ hours), and numerous buses to/from Newcastle (half an hour).

BRITAIN

Train There are numerous trains to York (one hour), a good number of which head on to London (three hours) via Peterborough (for Cambridge). Frequent trains from London continue through to Edinburgh (three hours). For further details, phone ☎ 0345-484950.

NORTHUMBERLAND

Taking its name from the Anglo-Saxon kingdom of Northumbria (north of the River Humber), Northumberland is one of the wildest and least spoilt of England's counties. There are probably more castles and battlefield sites here than anywhere else in England, testifying to the long and bloody struggle with the Scots.

The Romans were the first to attempt to draw a line separating north from south: Hadrian's Wall, which stretches for 73 miles from Newcastle to Bowness-on-Solway near Carlisle, was the northern frontier of the empire for almost 300 years. It was abandoned around 410 AD, but enough of the structure remains to bring the past dramatically alive.

After the arrival of the Normans, large numbers of castles and fortified houses (or *peles*) were built. Most have now lapsed into peaceful ruin, but others, like Bamburgh and Alnwick, were converted into great houses which can be visited today.

The Northumberland National Park lies north of Hadrian's Wall, incorporating the sparsely populated Cheviot Hills. The walks can be challenging, and cross some of the loneliest parts of England. The most interesting part of Hadrian's Wall is also included – see the Hadrian's Wall section later. There are information centres open from Good Friday to the end of October at Rothbury (☎ 01669-620887) and Once Brewed (☎ 01434-344396). There is another at Housesteads (☎ 01434-344525) on Hadrian's Wall. All of the centres handle accommodation bookings.

Newcastle-upon-Tyne

Newcastle is the largest city in the north-east. It grew famous as a coal-exporting port and in the 19th century it became an important industrial centre, before falling into serious decline after WWII. Newcastle has retained some 19th-century grandeur, but it has had a grim struggle to survive.

There are no major sights, although both **St Nicholas Cathedral** and **Castle Garth** are

worth visiting. Shopaholics might be tempted by the Metro Centre – the largest shopping centre in Europe – with 350 shops, 50 places to eat (mostly fast food), fairground rides... Needless to say, old Grainger Market in the centre, is much more interesting.

Orientation & Information The city centre is easy to get around on foot, and the metro (for the hostel and B&Bs) is cheap and pleasant to use. The central train station is just to the south of the city centre and the coach station is just to the east.

There's a convenient and helpful TIC at the train station, but the main office is in the Central Library, Prince's Square (☎ 0191-261 0691); both have a free map, guide and accommodation list. The train-station TIC is open Monday to Saturday from 10 am to 5 pm from October to May, and Monday to Friday to 8 pm, Saturday to 6 pm and Sunday to 5 pm from June to September.

Places to Stay & Eat The *Youth Hostel* (☎ 281 2570), 107 Jesmond Rd, is open from February to November (not Monday or Tuesday in February and November). Catch the metro to Jesmond station (40p), turn left from the station, cross Osborne Rd and continue for five minutes. Call in advance, as it can be busy.

There are quite a number of B&Bs within easy walking distance of Jesmond station, mostly along Jesmond and Osborne Rds. *Herron's Hotel* (☎ 281 4191), 40 Jesmond Rd, is in a Georgian building with a private car park, and has singles/twins from £22/36.

On Osborne Rd, consider the *Gresham Hotel* (☎ 281 4341), at No 92, a medium-sized, comfortable hotel with singles/doubles from £22.50/32.50, although at that price in Newcastle you still get shared bathrooms. The *Minerva Hotel* (☎ 281 0190), at No 105, is a small place with decent prices: rooms are £18/31.

For interesting restaurants and nightlife walk south down Grey St (lined with beautiful Georgian and Victorian offices), which becomes Dean St and takes you down to the River Tyne and Quayside. On Grey St itself, *Don Vito's* (☎ 232 8923) is extraordinarily good value with pizzas and pastas from £2.

Café Procope (☎ 232 3848) has vegetarian dishes from £6. There are a number of interesting pubs at the bottom of the hill. *Flynns Waterfront Bar* right on Quayside has a beer garden and cheap food and drink. Also check out the *Pumphouse*, *Bob Trollop* and *Redhouse*; the latter two have pub meals from about £3.

The *Cooperage* (☎ 232 8286), 32 The Close, Quayside, is a popular dance club with a wide-ranging clientele. Not far away at 57 Melbourne St, the *Riverside* (☎ 261 4386) is a popular live-music venue.

Getting There & Away Newcastle is a transport hub, so there are many options. See the Rail and Coach/Bus fares tables in this chapter's introductory Getting Around section.

Bus There are numerous National Express (☎ 0990-808080) connections with virtually every major city in the country.

For local buses around the north-east, don't forget the excellent-value Explorer North East ticket, valid on most services (£4.75). A travel line (☎ 232 5325) has details on services to Berwick-upon-Tweed and along Hadrian's Wall (see the appropriate sections).

Train Newcastle (☎ 0345-484950) is on the main London to Edinburgh line, so there are numerous trains to Edinburgh (1¾ hours), London (four hours) and York (1¼ hours). Berwick-upon-Tweed and Alnmouth (for Alnwick) are further north on this line. There is also an interesting, scenic line known as the Tyne Valley Line west to Carlisle, roughly every two hours (1½ hours).

Boat There are regular ferry links to Stavanger and Bergen (Norway) and in summer to Gothenburg (Sweden). See the introductory Getting There & Away section in this chapter for details.

Getting Around There's an excellent metro with fares from 40p. The service also links up with Newcastle airport. For advice and information use the travel line (☎ 232 5325). Bus No 327 links the ferry (at Tyne Commission Quay), the central train station and Jesmond Rd (for the hostel and B&Bs). The fare is

£2.50, and it leaves the station 2½ and 1½ hours before ferry departure times.

Berwick-upon-Tweed

Between the 12th and 15th centuries, Berwick changed hands between the Scots and the English 14 times. This merry-go-round ceased after the construction of massive ramparts that still enclose the town centre. It is beautifully sited at the mouth of the River Tweed. The TIC (☎ 01289-330733) should help you find a B&B for around £15; there's no YHA hostel.

There are two superb castles between Newcastle and Berwick: **Alnwick Castle** (☎ 01665-510777) is particularly fascinating (inside and out), while **Bamburgh Castle** (☎ 016684-208) is a dramatic looking pile, but not so interesting inside.

Getting There & Away Berwick is on the main London to Edinburgh line, so it is easy to get to by train. Northumbria (☎ 0191-232 4211) has several bus services linking Newcastle and Berwick. From Monday to Saturday, Service No 505 has four buses a day to and from Newcastle via Bamburgh and Alnwick.

Berwick is a good starting point if you wish to explore the Scottish Borders. There are buses on to Edinburgh around the coast via Dunbar and west to Coldstream, Kelso and Galashiels; the TIC will be able to advise.

Hadrian's Wall

Hadrian's Wall stretches 73 miles from Newcastle-upon-Tyne past Carlisle to Bowness-on-Solway. It follows a naturally defensible line and peaks at the bleak and windy Winshields Crags. The most spectacular section is between Hexham and Brampton. It's possible to walk the entire length (allow at least five days), but the first section through Newcastle is pretty uninteresting (the TICs in Newcastle and Carlisle have information). There are many fascinating Roman sites, often set in beautiful countryside.

Chesters Fort & Museum (☎ 01434-681379) is in a pleasant valley by the River Tyne (£2.50). There's an interesting museum, a superb military bath house and the remains of a massive bridge.

Housesteads Fort (☎ 344363) is the most dramatic of the ruins. The very well-preserved foundations include a famous latrine and are perched on a ridge overlooking the Northumbrian countryside (£2.50).

Vindolanda Fort & Museum (☎ 344277), 2½ miles to the south, is an extensively excavated fort and civil settlement with a museum that has some unusual artefacts, including shoes and evocative letters (£3).

Birdoswald Roman Fort (☎ 016972-602) overlooks a picturesque valley, and is less inundated with visitors than some of the other sites (£1.95).

Places to Stay Corbridge, Hexham, Haltwhistle and Brampton are attractive small towns with plentiful B&Bs, although Carlisle is also a good base for exploring the wall. Starting in the east, the *Acomb Youth Hostel* (☎ 602864) is about 2½ miles north of Hexham and two miles south of the wall. Hexham can be reached by bus or train.

Once Brewed Youth Hostel (☎ 344360) is central for both Housesteads Fort (three miles) and Vindolanda (one mile). The Northumbria bus No 685 (from Hexham or Haltwhistle stations) will drop you at Henshaw, two miles south; bus Nos 682 and 890 will drop you at the front door. The nearest train station is at Bardon Mill 2½ miles to the south-east.

Greenhead Youth Hostel (☎ 016977-47401) is three miles west of Haltwhistle station, but is also served by the trusty bus No 685.

Getting There & Away West of Hexham the wall parallels the A69, between Carlisle and Newcastle. The hourly Northumbria bus No 685 (☎ 01228-812812) runs along the A69, two to three miles south of the main sites. The Newcastle to Carlisle railway line (☎ 0345-484950) has stations at Hexham, Haydon Bridge, Bardon Mill, Haltwhistle and Brampton, but all trains do not stop at all stations.

From mid-July to early September a daily Hadrian's Wall Tourist Bus No 890 (☎ 01434-605225) runs between Hexham and Haltwhistle stations along the B6318 calling at the main sites. Earlier and later in the season a Monday to Friday service (bus No 682) operates along a similar route (☎ 01228-812812). Rover tickets on all the bus services cost £4.50.

During the summer there are guided coach tours from Carlisle to Birdoswald; contact Carlisle's TIC (☎ 01228-512444) for details.

CARLISLE

For 1600 years, Carlisle defended the north of England, or south of Scotland, depending on who was winning. In 1745 Bonnie Prince Charlie proclaimed his father king at the market cross.

The city's character was diminished by industrialisation in the 19th century; however, it's still an interesting place and its strategic location can be exploited by visitors to Northumberland, Dumfries & Galloway and the Borders (the beautiful Scottish border counties), and the Lake District. It is also the hub for five excellent railway journeys.

Orientation & Information

The train station is to the south of the city centre, a five-minute walk to Greenmarket (the market square) and the TIC. The bus station is on Lowther St, just one block east of the square. Both the TIC and visitors' centre in the old town hall (☎ 01228-512444) offer free accommodation booking for Cumbria.

Things to See

The 11th-century **Carlisle Castle** is to the north of the cathedral, overlooking the River Eden (£2). **Tullie House Museum** (☎ 34781) is one of the best in Britain, drawing on the fascinating history of the region and presenting it imaginatively (£3.50).

Places to Stay

The existing *Youth Hostel* (☎ 23934) is for sale, although a new one may replace it – ring ahead. Fortunately, there are plenty of comfortable and accessible B&Bs in the £13 to £15 bracket.

There are plenty of reasonable options on Warwick Rd. From the station, cross Butchergate, walk around the crescent and then take Warwick Rd on your right. *Cornerways Guest House* (☎ 21733), No 107, is large and convenient, with B&B for £13 per person. *East View Guesthouse* (☎ 22112), No 110, charges £18. The *Calreena Guest House* (☎ 25020), No 123, charges from £13.

Getting There & Away

See the Rail and Coach/Bus fares tables in this chapter's introductory Getting Around section.

Bus There are numerous National Express (☎ 0990-808080) connections. There are four buses to and from London (5½ hours) and many to Glasgow (two hours). One service a day comes through from Cambridge (eight hours), Bristol (eight hours) and York (five hours).

There is a Rail Link coach service that runs to Galashiels in the Scottish Borders – see the South-Eastern Scotland section later.

Train Carlisle is the terminus for five famous scenic railways – phone ☎ 0345-484950 for information. There are 15 trains a day to Carlisle from London's Euston station (3½ hours). Most of the following lines have Day Ranger tickets that allow you unlimited travel – ask for details.

Leeds-Settle-Carlisle Line (LSC)
  This very famous line cuts south-east across the Yorkshire Dales through beautiful countryside and is one of the great engineering achievements of the Victorian railway age – the Ribblehead Viaduct is 32 metres high. Several stations are good starting points for walks in the Yorkshire Dales National Park. There are trains every two hours from Monday to Saturday and three on Sunday from April through October (three hours, £15.50 for a day return).
Lake District Line
  This line branches off the main north-south line between Preston and Carlisle at Oxenholme, just outside Kendal, for Windermere. The landscape on the main line is beautiful, but you're whisked through pretty quickly. The Windermere branch is only about 10 miles long, but it takes nearly half an hour. There are plenty of trains seven days a week.
Tyne Valley Line
  This line follows Hadrian's Wall to and from Newcastle. There are sme fine views, and it is useful for visitors to the wall; see the Newcastle-upon-Tyne and Hadrian's Wall sections.
Cumbrian Coast Line
  This line follows the coast in a great arc around to Lancaster, with views over the Irish Sea and back to the Lake District. There are five trains a day Monday to Saturday and two on Sunday from Carlisle to Barrow (2½ hours), where you change for a train to Lancaster on the main line (one hour). Ulverston, on the line just past Barrow, is the starting point for the Cumbria Way, which traverses the lakes to Carlisle. There are bus connections with Windermere from Barrow-in-Furness.

Glasgow to Carlisle Line
  This is the main route north to Glasgow, and it gives you a taste of the grand scale of Scottish landscapes. Most trains make few stops (1½ hours).

LAKE DISTRICT

I wandered lonely as a cloud
That floats on high o'er dales and hills
When all at once I saw a crowd...
                from *Daffodils* by William Wordsworth

The Lake District is the most beautiful corner of England: a combination of green dales, so perfect they could almost be parks, rocky mountains that seem to heave themselves into the sky, and lakes that multiply the scenery with their reflections. The Cumbrian Mountains are not particularly high – none reach 1000 metres – but they're much more dramatic than their height would suggest.

This is Wordsworth country, and his houses at Grasmere (Dove Cottage, ☎ 015394-35544) and Rydal (☎ 015394-33002, between Ambleside and Grasmere) are literary shrines.

Unfortunately, there are over 10 million visitors a year, and they ain't all daffodils. The crowds are so intense it is questionable whether it is worth visiting on any weekend between May and October, or any time at all from mid-July to the end of August. It is particularly bizarre and horrible to be stuck in a traffic jam in such idyllic surroundings. It is also common. A good time to visit is weekdays in May and June, followed by September and October.

Orientation

The two main bases for the Lake District are Keswick in the north (particularly for walkers) and Bowness/Windermere in the south (two contiguous tourist traps). Coniston, Ambleside, Grasmere and Cockermouth are less hectic alternatives. All these towns have hostels, numerous B&Bs and places to eat.

Ullswater, Grasmere, Windermere, Coniston Water and Derwent Water are often considered to be the most beautiful lakes, but they also teem with boats. Wastwater, Crummock Water and Buttermere are equally spectacular and less crowded.

In general, the mob stays on the A roads, and the crowds are much thinner west of a line drawn from Keswick to Coniston.

BRITAIN

Information

A frightening quantity of guidebooks and brochures on this region are available from TICs.

Start at the Windermere or Keswick TICs (both have free booking services). The Windermere TIC (☎ 015394-46499), Victoria St, is excellent; it's near the train station at the northern end of town. Keswick TIC (☎ 017687-72645), Market Square, is also helpful.

If you are staying more than a day or so, buy a copy of *The Good Guide to the Lakes* by Hunter Davies (paperback, £4.95), an idiosyncratic guide covering the area's background, practicalities, walks and where to stay and eat.

The classic walking guides are the seven volumes of Alfred Wainwright's *Pictorial Guide to the Lakeland Fells*. Each is a work of art – handwritten and hand drawn – and they are still useful despite their age.

There are numerous walking/climbing shops in the region, particularly in Ambleside and Keswick; they are good sources of local information. The Climber's Shop (☎ 015394-32297), Compston Rd, Ambleside, and George Fisher (☎ 017687-72484), Lake Rd, Keswick, are both excellent shops that hire equipment.

There are over 30 YHA hostels in the region, many of which can be linked by foot. Look for *Inter Hostel Walks in the Lake District* (£1.50).

Getting There & Away

See the Rail and Coach/Bus fares tables in this chapter's introductory Getting Around section.

There are two National Express (☎ 0990-808080) buses a day from Manchester via Preston (three hours) and on to Keswick. There's also a service from London via Birmingham (seven hours) and on to Keswick, and a train service from Manchester airport to Windermere (two hours).

There's a free paper, *Explorer*, available from TICs, which gives bus and boat timetable details for Cumbria and the lakes. Cumberland (☎ 01946-63222) has a number of important services. One of the best is bus No 555 which links Lancaster with Carlisle, via Kendal, Windermere, Ambleside, Grasmere and Keswick. No 518 runs between Windermere and Barrow-in-Furness, via Ulverston on the Cumbrian Coast Line. No 505/506, the Coniston Rambler, runs from Bowness Pier to Coniston via the Steamboat Museum, Brockhole, Ambleside and Hawkshead.

Cumberland also has open-topped double-deckers (W1/W2) which run a frequent service: Ambleside, Waterhead, Brockhole, Troutbeck Bridge, Windermere station, Windermere, Bowness and Bowness Pier.

Cumberland's X9 service runs between York and Keswick via Harrogate (Yorkshire Dales), Skipton, Kendal and Ambleside on Wednesday, Friday and Saturday. Connections can be made at Skipton for Leeds. Ask about Day Ranger and Explorer tickets.

Windermere is at the end of a spur line off the main line between London's Euston station and Glasgow. Windermere trains leave the main line at Oxenholme.

Getting Around

Walking or cycling are the two best ways to get around, but bear in mind that conditions can be treacherous, and the going can be very, very steep. Mountain bikes can be hired from Ashtons (☎ 015349-47779), 12 Main Rd, Windermere for £12 per day , or from Lakeland Leisure (☎ 015394-44786) on Lake Rd in Bowness.

There are numerous boat trips and a number of steam railways; the TICs have countless brochures covering the alternatives in detail.

Bowness & Windermere

Thanks to the railway, the Bowness/Windermere conglomerate is the largest tourist town in the Lake District. At times it feels like a seaside resort. The town is quite strung out, with Windermere (including the train station and the TIC) a 30-minute uphill walk from Bowness on the lakeside.

The *Youth Hostel* (☎ 015394-43543) is a two-mile walk from the station. Book in advance. There are a million B&Bs in Windermere at about £15 a night, and a stack of restaurants in both towns.

If you can't face a fight for cardboard-flavoured pizza, buy a fresh roll or pastries from one of the bakeries in both centres and row out for a picnic on the lake. Boat hire is about £3 per person per hour. Alternatively, escape for the evening to Troutbeck, which is a classic Lakeland village a steep three miles away; the bar meals at either the *Mortal Man* (☎ 015394-33193) or the *Queen's Head*

(☎ 015394-32174) are around £6 and highly recommended.

Keswick

Keswick is an important walking centre, but although the town centre lacks the green charm of Windermere, the lake is beautiful. The *Youth Hostel* (☎ 017687-72484) is open most of the year, a short walk down Station Rd from the TIC (☎ 017687-72645).

See the Bowness/Windermere Getting There & Away section for information on buses. Keswick can also be reached from Penrith station (only one service on Sunday) with Wright's No 888 service. This service continues eastwards to Langwathby on the LSC Line, to Hexham and Corbridge on Hadrian's Wall, and finally to Newcastle. There are plenty of buses linking Windermere, Ambleside and Keswick.

Coniston

This is still very definitely a tourist town, but decidedly less busy than Keswick or Bowness/Windermere. The TIC (☎ 015394-41533) is open in the summer only.

There are two excellent YHA hostels near the town. *Holly How Youth Hostel* (☎ 41323) is just north of Coniston on the Ambleside Rd. It's open between 19 January and 24 November, except some weekends. The other hostel, *Coppermines* (☎ 41261), is one mile along the minor road between the Black Bull Hotel and the Co-op – a good walking base.

Cumberland's 505/506 Coniston Rambler service runs from Bowness Pier to Ambleside, Hawkshead and Coniston.

YORKSHIRE DALES

Austere stone villages with simple and functional architecture; streams and rivers cutting through the rolling hills; empty moors and endless stone walls snaking over the slopes – this is the region that was made famous by James Herriot and the TV series *All Creatures Great & Small*.

The landscape of the Dales is completely different from that of the Lake District. The high tops of the limestone hills are exposed moorland, and the sheltered dales between them range from Swaledale, which is narrow and sinuous, Wensleydale and Wharfedale,

which are broad and open, to Littondale and Ribblesdale, which are more rugged.

The Yorkshire Dales are very beautiful, but unfortunately, in summer, like the Lake District, they are extremely crowded. Avoid weekends and the peak summer period, or try to get off the beaten track. The Pennine Way runs through the area, and can be unbelievably busy, while other footpaths are often deserted.

Orientation & Information

The Dales can be broken into northern and southern halves. In the north, the two main dales run parallel and east-west. Swaledale, the northernmost, is particularly beautiful. If you have private transport, the B6270 from Kirkby Stephen to Richmond is highly recommended.

In the southern half, the north-to-south extent of Ribblesdale is the route taken by the LSC Line (see Trains under Carlisle's Getting There & Away section for more information). Wharfedale is parallel to the east.

Skipton is the most important transport hub for the region, while Richmond is a beautiful town which is handy for the North. For visitors without transport, the best bet will be those places accessible on the LSC Line: Kirkby Stephen, Dent and Settle all have nearby YHA hostels.

The main National Park Centre (☎ 01756-752774) is at Grassington, six miles north of Skipton; open daily from November to April. It publishes the useful *Visitor* newspaper.

Getting Around

With the exception of the LSC Line, public transport is grim. Bus users need a copy of the *Dales Connections* timetable available from TICs. Cycling is an excellent way to get around; there are some steep climbs, but most of the time the roads follow the bottom of the Dales.

Kirkby Stephen

Kirkby Stephen is a small, little-visited market town on the LSC Line. The TIC (☎ 017683-71199) has complicated opening hours during winter. The *Youth Hostel* (☎ 71793) is in a converted chapel in the centre of town, just south of Market Square.

Skipton

Skipton is a major centre for the Dales, but there's little to hold you once you've raided the

TIC (☎ 01756-792809) and stormed the castle. The nearest hostel is actually closer to Grassington, which is one of the prettiest and most popular Dales villages.

Apart from being on the LSC Line, there is a National Express (☎ 0990-808080) bus direct from London. During summer, Cumberland (☎ 01946-63222) has a service between York and Ambleside (Lake District) via Skipton on Monday, Wednesday, Friday and Saturday. Bikes are available from Cycle Sports (☎ 794386), Water St, at £12 a day.

Grassington

Grassington is home to a National Park Centre and is a good base for walks in Wharfedale. The *Youth Hostel* (☎ 01756-752400) is just south of Grassington and can be reached by the Skipton to Grassington bus.

From Skipton station, Keighley & District buses (☎ 01535-603284) depart irregularly Monday to Saturday. There's a Sunday service from April to September. Bikes are available from The Hardware Shop (☎ 752592) from £12 a day.

Scotland

No visitor to Britain should miss the opportunity to visit Scotland. Despite its official union with England in 1707, it has managed to maintain an independent national identity that extends considerably further than the occasional kilt and bagpipes. There are similarities and close links, but there are also considerable differences.

With few exceptions the entire country is beautiful; the Highlands, however, are exceptional. You could hardly call it a secret, but for a region that has some of the world's most dramatic and unspoilt scenery, it is curiously underrated. Surprisingly few English realise what an extraordinary neighbour they have.

Scottish urban culture is also quite different. Edinburgh is one of the most beautiful cities in the world; Glasgow is vigorously reinventing itself after the collapse of its traditional industries; St Andrews is Scotland's small version of Cambridge; and prosperous Aberdeen

surveys the North Sea with a proprietorial interest.

FACTS ABOUT THE COUNTRY
History

Celts It is believed that the earliest settlement of Scotland was undertaken by hunters and fishers 6000 years ago. They were followed by the Celtic Picts, whose loose tribal organisation survived to the 18th century in the clan structure of the Highlands. They never bowed to the Romans, who retreated and built Hadrian's Wall, defining the North as a separate entity for the first time.

A new Celtic tribe, the Gaels (or Scots), arrived from northern Ireland (Scotia) in the 6th century. They finally united with the Picts in the 9th century in response to the threat posed by the Scandinavians who dominated the northern islands and west coast. By the time the Normans arrived, most of Scotland was loosely united under the Canmore dynasty.

Normans The Normans never conquered Scotland, although they wielded a major influence over several weak kings, and the Lowlands (with the most important arable land) were controlled by French-speaking aristocrats imported from northern England. The Highland clans remained staunchly Gaelic, the Islands remained closely linked to Norway, and neither paid much attention to central authority.

Despite almost continuous border warfare, it was not until a dispute over the Canmore succession that Edward I attempted the conquest of Scotland. Beginning in 1296, a series of battles finally ended in 1328 with Robert the Bruce the recognised king of an independent country. Robert, who was more Norman than Scottish in his ancestry, cemented an alliance with France that was to complicate the political map for 400 years.

Stuarts In 1371 the kingship passed to the Fitzalan family. The Fitzalans had served William the Conqueror and his descendants as High Stewards, and Stuart became the name of the dynasty.

In 1503 James IV married the 12-year-old daughter of Henry VII of England, the first of the Tudor monarchs, linking the two families.

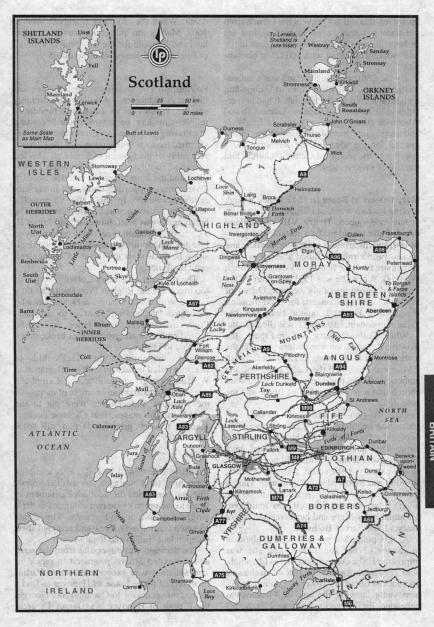

SHETLAND ISLANDS

Unst
Yell
Mainland
Lerwick

Same Scale as Main Map

Scotland

0 — 25 — 50 km
0 — 15 — 30 miles

To Lerwick,
Shetland Is
(see inset)

Westray
Sanday
Stronsay
Mainland
Stromness
Kirkwall
ORKNEY ISLANDS
South Ronaldsay
John O'Groats

Butt of Lewis
Durness
Scrabster
Thurso
Tongue
Melvich
Wick
A9
Helmsdale
Brora
WESTERN ISLES
Stornoway
Lewis
Lochinver
Loch Shin
Lairg
Bonar Bridge
Dornoch Firth
OUTER HEBRIDES
Tarbert
Ullapool
Invergordon
North Uist
Gairloch
Loch Maree
Dingwall
Moray Firth
Cullen
Fraserburgh
Lochmaddy
Uig
Benbecula
Portree
Skye
Inverness
MORAY
Elgin
A96
Huntly
A98
Peterhead
South Uist
Loch Ness
Kyle of Lochalsh
Grantown-on-Spey
To Bergen & Faroe Islands
Lochboisdale
Aviemore
ABERDEEN SHIRE
Aberdeen
Barra
A87
Kingussie
Newtonmore
Braemar
A93
Rhum
INNER HEBRIDES
Mallaig
Loch Lochy
Coll
Fort William
Glencoe
A82
GRAMPIAN MOUNTAINS
Nith
Esk
Tiree
Aberfeldy
Pitlochry
ANGUS
Montrose
A94
Mull
Oban
A85
Loch Awe
PERTHSHIRE
Loch Tay
Dunkeld
Blairgowrie
Dundee
Arbroath
Crieff
Perth
St Andrews
Inveraray
A83
Loch Lomond
Callander
Kinross
M90
FIFE
NORTH SEA
Colonsay
STIRLING
Stirling
Kirkcaldy
Firth of Forth
ATLANTIC OCEAN
ARGYLL
Dunoon
Greenock
Falkirk
M9
M8
EDINBURGH
Dunbar
Jura
Bute
GLASGOW
Berwick-upon-Tweed
Islay
Motherwell
LOTHIAN
Duns
Ardrossan
Kilmarnock
Lanark
A72
Galashiels
Kelso
Coldstream
Arran
M74
A7
Campbeltown
Firth of Clyde
Ayr
AYRSHIRE
BORDERS
Jedburgh
A83
Girvan
A77
A74
A68
Dumfries
DUMFRIES & GALLOWAY
ENGLAND
NORTHERN IRELAND
Larne
Stranraer
A75
Kirkcudbright
Luce Bay
Solway Firth
Carlisle
M6

North Minch
Little Minch
Sound of Jura
North Channel

BRITAIN

However, this did not prevent the French from persuading James to go to war against his in-laws; he was killed at the disastrous battle of Flodden Hill along with 10,000 of his subjects.

By the 16th century, Scotland was a nationalistic society, with close links to Europe and a visceral hatred for the English. It had universities at St Andrews, Glasgow, Edinburgh and Aberdeen (there were only two in England) and a lively intellectual climate that was fertile ground for the ideas of the Reformation, a critique of the medieval Catholic church, and the rise of Protestantism.

Mary Queen of Scots In 1542 James V died, leaving his two-week-old daughter Mary to be proclaimed queen. Henry VIII of England decided she would make a suitable daughter-in-law, and his armies ravaged the Borders and sacked Edinburgh in a failed attempt to force agreement from the Scots (they called it Rough Wooing). When she was 15, Mary married the French dauphin and duly became Queen of France as well as Scotland; for good measure she claimed England, on the basis that her Protestant cousin, Elizabeth I, was illegitimate.

While Catholic Mary was in France, the Scottish Reformation was underway under the leadership of John Knox. In 1560 the Scottish Parliament abolished the Latin mass and the authority of the pope, creating a Protestant church that was independent of Rome and the monarchy.

Eighteen-year-old Mary, one of the most acclaimed beauties of her time, returned to Scotland on the death of her husband. In Edinburgh she married Henry Darnley and gave birth to a son. Domestic bliss did not last, and, in a scarcely believable train of events, Darnley was involved in the murder of Mary's Italian secretary Rizzio (rumoured to be her lover). Then Darnley himself was murdered, presumably by Mary and her lover and future husband, the Earl of Bothwell.

At this point, Mary was forced to abdicate in favour of her son James, and she was imprisoned. She escaped and fled to Elizabeth, who, recognising a security risk when she saw one, locked her in the Tower of London. Nineteen years later, at the age of 44, she was beheaded for allegedly plotting Elizabeth's death. When the childless Elizabeth died in 1603, Mary's son united the crowns of Scotland and England for the first time as James I of England and James VI of Scotland.

Revolution The Stuarts have become romantic figures, but their royal skills were extremely suspect. When Charles I began to meddle in religious matters, he provoked the Scots into organising a National Covenant that reaffirmed the total independence of the General Assembly of the Church of Scotland. This led to armed conflict. Civil war between Parliament and the king followed, with the Scottish Covenanters supporting Cromwell in his successful revolution. In 1660, after Cromwell's death, the Stuart monarchy was restored. The honeymoon was brief, however, and James II, a Catholic, appeared to set out determinedly to lose his kingdom. Amongst other poor decisions, he made worshipping as a Covenanter a capital offence.

The prospect of another Catholic king was too much for the English Protestants, so they invited William of Orange, a Dutchman who was James' nephew and married to his oldest Protestant daughter, to take power. In 1689 he landed with a small army; James broke down and fled to France.

When the chief of the MacDonalds of Glencoe failed to take an oath of allegiance to William by a given deadline, the Campbells were ordered to make an example of them – 40 men, women and children were put to the sword, and the massacre at Glencoe became Jacobite (Stuart) propaganda that still resonates today.

Union with England In 1707, after complex bargaining (and buying a few critical votes), England persuaded the Scottish Parliament to agree to the union of the two countries under a single parliament and crown. The Scots received trading privileges and retained their independent church and legal system.

The decision was unpopular from the start, and the exiled Stuarts promised to repeal it. The situation was exacerbated when Parliament turned to the house of Hanover to find a Protestant successor to Queen Anne. George, the Elector of Hanover, was James I's great grandson, but he was German and spoke no English.

Scotland was the centre for Jacobitism (Stuart support) and there were two major rebellions – in 1715, and 1745 when Bonnie Prince Charlie failed to extend his support beyond the wild, Catholic Highland clans. The Jacobite cause was finally buried at the Battle of Culloden, and the English set out to destroy the clans, prohibiting Highland dress, weapons and military service.

The Scottish Enlightenment The old Scotland was already fast disappearing by the mid-18th century. There was considerable economic growth and the beginning of industrialisation. Eighteenth-century Scotland was a sceptical, well-educated society and, among other figures, it produced David Hume the philosopher, Adam Smith the economist and Robert Burns the poet.

The great Highland Clearances began when the lairds (landowning aristocrats) sought to improve their estates. Sheep were considered more profitable than crofters (subsistence peasants), so the people had to go. They went to the burgeoning slums of the new industrial cities – especially Glasgow and Dundee – and to the four corners of the British Empire.

Modern Scotland By the end of the 19th century the population was concentrated in the grim industrial towns and cities of the Lowlands. Working-class disillusionment led to the development of fierce left-wing politics. After WWI Scotland's ship, steel, coal, cotton and jute industries began to fail, and, though there was a recovery during WWII, since the 1960s they have been in terminal decline.

In the 1970s the economy received a tremendous boost when oil was found in the North Sea – Scottish oil, as many will tell you. Despite the bonanza, Thatcherism failed to impress the Scots. Of the 72 Scottish seats in the House of Commons only nine are held by the ruling Conservative Party.

Today, with the creation of the Scottish National Party (SNP), nationalism is still very much a live issue. The most radical are dreaming of a Scottish Parliament within the framework of the EU.

Geography & Ecology

Scotland can be divided into three areas: the south, or southern uplands, with ranges of hills bordering England; the central Lowlands, a triangular slice from Edinburgh and Dundee in the east to Glasgow in the west, containing the majority of the population; and the Highlands and Islands in the north.

The Lowlands is an imprecise, unprepossessing term that is often used to describe everything south of a line from Aberdeen to Loch Lomond. It suggests that mountains and spectacular scenery will only be found in the north which is incorrect. Just one example: Scotland's highest village is actually Wanlockhead in Dumfries in the south-west.

Edinburgh is the capital and financial centre, Glasgow the industrial centre, and Aberdeen and Dundee are the two largest regional centres.

Some two-thirds of Scotland is mountain and moorland. Once it was almost entirely covered by the Caledonian Forest, most of which has now been chopped down. In parts of the country no new trees have been able to grow since the red deer population started to increase 300 years ago, a worrying ecological problem.

Population

Scotland has a population of just over five million, around 9% of the total population of Britain.

Language

Gaelic is now only spoken by some 66,000 people, mainly in the Islands and north-west of Scotland. Aye, but the Scottish accent can make English almost impenetrable to the Sassenach (the English or Lowland Scots) and other foreigners, and there are numerous Gaelic and Scots words that linger in everyday speech. Ye ken? Some common terms you might encounter include:

aye	yes/always
bairn	child
bap	bread roll
ben	mountain
brae	hill
burn	creek
ceilidh (pronounced 'kaylee')	informal evening entertainment & dance

croft	small farm
firth	estuary
glen	valley
haar	fog off the North Sea
Hogmanay	New Year's Eve
ken	know
kirk	church
Munro	mountain of 3000 feet (914 metres) or higher
wynd	lane

FACTS FOR THE VISITOR

Planning

Climate & When to Go The climate varies widely. The west and east coasts have relatively mild climates, but the Highlands can have extreme weather at any time. Aside from the ski resorts, many facilities (including B&Bs and TICs) are closed between the end of September and the end of March.

The east coast tends to be cool and dry; rainfall averages around 650 mm, and winter temperatures rarely drop below 0°C, although winds off the North Sea can rattle your teeth. The west coast is milder and wetter, with over 1500 mm of rain and average summer highs of 19°C.

May and June are generally the driest months, but expect rain at any time. The best time to visit is between May and September – April and October are acceptable weather risks, although many things are closed in October. The Highlands are pretty much off limits during winter, but Edinburgh and Glasgow are still worth visiting. Edinburgh is very crowded during the festival which is held in the last two-thirds of August; if possible, book ahead if you plan to visit during this time. The same is true of Hogmanay.

The further north you go in Scotland in summer, the longer the days become; the midsummer sun sets at 10.30 pm in the Shetland Islands, but even in Edinburgh there are seemingly endless evenings.

Tourist Offices

Outside of Britain, contact the British Tourist Authority (BTA) for information (see Tourist Offices in the Facts for the Visitor section at the start of this chapter). The Scottish Tourist Board (☎ 0171-930 8661) has an information centre at 19 Cockspur St, London SW1 5BL, just off Trafalgar Square. It can suggest routes, provide detailed information and make all kinds of reservations. There is a special help line for visitors to the Highlands and Islands, with booking facilities – phone ☎ 01253-290431.

Most towns in Scotland have TICs that are open weekdays from 9 am to 5 pm, often extending to weekends during the summer. In small places, particularly in the Highlands, TICs only open from Easter to September.

Useful Organisations

The Scottish Youth Hostels Association (SYHA) markets an Explore Scotland ticket that includes a seven-day Citylink Bus Pass, six overnight accommodation vouchers, a bus timetable, a Scotpass Discount Card, free YHA membership and an SYHA handbook, and a Historic Scotland Pass – for £130. The savings are worthwhile, especially if you're not a student. The association also offers a Scottish Wayfarer ticket, a similar package but including travel by rail and ferry – eight days for £170, 15 days for £270. Contact the SYHA headquarters (☎ 01786-451181) at 7 Glebe Crescent, Stirling FK8 2JA.

Visas & Embassies

No visas are required if you arrive from England, Wales or Northern Ireland. If you arrive from the Republic of Ireland or any other country, normal British regulations apply (see the introductory Facts for the Visitor section in this chapter). There are numerous diplomatic missions in Edinburgh.

Customs

If you arrive from the Republic of Ireland or any other country, normal British regulations apply (see the introductory Facts for the Visitor section at the beginning of this chapter).

Money

The same currency is valid on both sides of the border; however, the Clydesdale Bank, the Royal Bank of Scotland and the Bank of Scotland have retained the right to issue their own currency. All these banks print pound notes. You may have difficulty trying to change one of these notes in a *bureau de change* in Greece, but they don't usually present a problem in Britain.

If you have an Access/MasterCard, you can use the cash machines belonging to the Royal Bank of Scotland and Clydesdale Bank; if you have a Visa card you can use the Bank of Scotland, Royal Bank of Scotland, Clydesdale Bank and Trustee Savings Bank (TSB); if you have an American Express card you can use the Bank of Scotland.

Because accommodation for backpackers is more readily available in Scotland than in England, you'll be able to keep sleeping costs right down. Edinburgh is more expensive than most other mainland towns but prices also rise quite steeply in remote parts of the Highlands and in the Islands where supplies depend on ferries.

Dangers & Annoyances

Edinburgh and Glasgow are big cities with the usual problems, so normal caution is required.

Hikers in the Highlands should be properly equipped and cautious: the weather can become vicious at any time of the year. After rain peaty soil can become boggy; always wear stout shoes and carry a change of clothing.

The most infuriating and painful problem facing visitors to the west coast and Highlands, however, is midges. These are tiny blood-sucking flies, related to mosquitoes and under certain conditions they can be prolific. They are at their worst in the evenings or in cloudy or shady conditions; their season lasts from late May to mid-September, peaking from mid-June to mid-August.

There are several possible defences: cover up, particularly in the evening; wear light-coloured clothing (midges are attracted to dark colours); and, most importantly, buy a reliable insect repellent which includes either DEET or DMP.

Business Hours

Minimum banking hours are weekdays from 9.30 am to 3.30 pm; a few banks close between 12.30 and 1.30 pm, but the tendency is to longer hours. Post offices and shops are open from 9 am to 5.30 pm on weekdays; post offices close at 1 pm on Saturday and shops in small towns sometimes have an early closing day mid-week.

Public Holidays & Special Events

In Scotland, bank holidays apply only to banks and some other commercial offices, although in England they are general public holidays. Christmas and New Year's Day are usually taken by everybody, and Scottish towns normally have a Spring and Autumn holiday. Dates vary.

In 1997, Scottish banks will be closed on 1 and 2 January, 28 March, 5 and 26 May, 4 August and 25 and 26 December.

The Edinburgh Festival, one of the world's largest arts festivals, runs from mid-August to early September each year.

Activities

Hiking There are four long-distance hiking routes in Scotland: the Southern Upland Way (see the Stranraer section), the West Highland Way (see the Glasgow section), the Fife Coastal Walk and the Speyside Way. Beyond this, there is a network of thousands of miles of paths and tracks. Scotland has a long tradition of relatively free access to open country. Numerous guidebooks are available.

The southern Highlands are popular (but this does not mean crowded), particularly the Cairngorms west of Aberdeen and the Grampians east of Oban and Fort William. The walking and climbing is spectacular, but Scottish mountains can be killers. Caution is required – the climate over 1000 metres is equivalent to that north of the Arctic Circle. Bad weather is normal so you must be properly equipped to deal with cold and wet conditions and if necessary to stay put until the weather improves; thick mist can descend suddenly at any time so it's essential to be able to use a map and compass. It is also important to notify someone reliable of your plans.

Skiing Scotland has a flourishing skiing industry. The ski season runs between December and April. Although there is nothing to rival the European Alps, there are several resorts of international standard within a day's drive of London. There are several resorts in the Cairngorms (near Braemar and Aviemore) and around Ben Nevis (Scotland's highest mountain, near Fort William). The Scottish Tourist Board can provide details.

Surfing The north coast of Scotland offers some of the best and coldest surfing in Britain.

Accommodation

Budget travellers are spoilt for choice in Scotland because the Scottish Youth Hostels Association (SYHA) hostels and normal B&Bs are now supplemented by a growing number of independent hostels and bunkhouses, most with prices around £8. Look out for *Independent Hostel Guide – budget accommodation* (20p) which lists 50 hostels in Scotland and is available from some TICs. Alternatively send a stamped, addressed envelope to Independent Backpackers Hostels of Scotland (☎ 01478-640254), Croft Bunkhouse, 7 Portnalong, Isle of Skye IV47 8SL.

The SYHA is a separate organisation and it produces its own handbook (£1.50), which gives details on around 80 hostels it operates, including transport links. Its hostels are generally cheaper and often better than its English counterparts. In big cities costs are £10.45/9 for seniors/juniors; the rest range from £4.10/3.40 to £7.80/6.40.

B&Bs and small hotels are also cheaper than their English counterparts; you are unlikely to have to pay more than £15 per person. The TICs have local booking services (usually £1) and a Book-a-Bed Ahead scheme (£2.75). A 10% deposit is also required for most bookings. The service is worth using in July and August, but is not necessary outside this peak time, unless you plan to arrive in a town after business hours (when the local TIC will be closed). If you arrive without accommodation in the evening it may still be worth going to the TIC, since most leave a list in the window showing the B&Bs that had rooms free when it closed.

You can camp free on all public land (unless it is specifically protected). Commercial camping grounds are geared to caravans and vary widely in quality. A tent site will cost around £6. If you plan to use a tent regularly, invest in *Scotland: camping & caravan parks* (£3.99), available from most TICs.

Food

Scotland's culinary reputation is as dismal as England's, and the fact that the Scots have the highest rate of heart attacks in Europe gives fair warning. In small villages and hotels the alternatives will usually be bleak, although village bakeries are generally excellent.

There are a surprising number of restaurants that cater to vegetarians; look for *The Vegetarian Guide to the Scottish Highlands & Islands* (£2.85), which lists B&Bs, hotels and restaurants.

GETTING THERE & AWAY
Air

There are direct services from many European cities to Edinburgh, Glasgow, Dundee, Aberdeen and Inverness, and from North America to Glasgow and Edinburgh. New York to Glasgow is around US$590 (£391). You can also connect with numerous flights to Scotland from London (including to Inverness).

Coming from overseas it often works out cheaper to buy a cheap fare to London and then take a train or an internal flight to Scotland. London to Glasgow or Edinburgh is around £95, but price wars have been known to break out on these routings. Flying from Luton, north of London, Easyjet (☎ 01582-445566) has seats from £29 to £49 one way, booked on a first-come, first-served basis.

Land

Bus Long-distance buses (coaches) are usually the cheapest method of getting to Scotland. The main operator is Scottish Citylink (☎ 0990-505050), part of the nationwide National Express group, with numerous regular services from London and other departure points in England (see the Glasgow Getting There & Away section).

Advance-purchase return tickets from London (Victoria) to Edinburgh or Glasgow start at around £25 return – a saving of about 30% on a ticket bought on the day of travel. Tickets from London (King's Cross) are sometimes cheaper (perhaps £18 return). The cheap tickets sell out quickly so booking in advance is recommended. See the introductory Getting Around section at the beginning of this chapter for more information.

Train InterCity services (☎ 0345-550033) can take you from London's King's Cross to Edinburgh in as little as four hours or to Glasgow in five hours (see the Getting There & Away sections for those cities).

The cheapest adult return ticket between London and Edinburgh or Glasgow is the SuperApex which costs only £34. Numerous restrictions apply to these tickets which must be purchased 14 days in advance and are particularly difficult to get hold of in summer. Apex tickets (£46 return) must be bought seven days in advance and are more readily available. See the introductory Getting Around section at the beginning of this chapter for more information.

Car & Motorcycle The main roads are busy and quick. Edinburgh is 373 miles from London and Glasgow is 392. Allow eight hours.

Hitching If you're not worried about the safety aspects, it's easy enough to hitch to Scotland along the A68 to Edinburgh or the A74 to Glasgow. The coastal routes are slow.

Sea

Scotland has ferry links to Larne, near Belfast in Northern Ireland, from Cairnryan (P&O, ☎ 01574-274321) and Stranraer (Stena Line, ☎ 0990-455455), both south-west of Glasgow. For details, see the Ireland chapter.

From June to late August P&O also operates one ferry a week between Bergen (Norway), Lerwick (Shetland Islands) and Aberdeen. Bergen to Lerwick, leaving at 2 am on Sunday morning, costs from £55. There's also a twice weekly Stradfaraskip Landsins ferry between the Faroe Islands and Aberdeen (leaving Aberdeen on Thursday and Sunday), with the cheapest tickets ranging from £60 to £105.

To make a fascinating northern sea route you could link these two ferries with the Smyril Line's Denmark-Norway-Iceland-Faroes service, also summer only. The sailing order is Denmark (Saturday), the Faroes (Monday), Norway (Tuesday), the Faroes (Wednesday), Iceland (Thursday), the Faroes (Friday), Denmark (Saturday), and so on. During the high season the one-way couchette fare from Norway to the Faroes is £61. P&O (☎ 01224-572615) is the agent for Smyril Line and Stradfaraskip Lansins and can book this complete route.

GETTING AROUND

If you're not a student, it's worth considering ScotRail's Freedom of Scotland Travelpass. The pass gives unlimited travel on ScotRail

trains and most Caledonian MacBrayne (CalMac) ferries to the west-coast islands; 33% discount on P&O's Scrabster to Orkney ferry; 20% discount on P&O services from Aberdeen to Shetland, Aberdeen to Orkney and Orkney to Shetland; 20% discount on Stena Line services to Northern Ireland; 33% on postbuses and most of the important regional bus lines; and discounts on entry fees to some attractions.

A Travelpass for eight days consecutive travel costs £99; for eight days out of 15 costs £110; and 15 days consecutive travel costs £139. Students get equivalent discounts anyway and could get the much cheaper rail Rover ticket (see the Train information below). For more information contact ScotRail (☎ 0345-484950), which administers the scheme. Tickets are available from the Scottish Travel Centres at London's Victoria and King's Cross stations, and from the ScotRail stations in Glasgow and Edinburgh.

Unfortunately, Scottish Citylink, the major coach operator, no longer participates, but it does have a tourist pass and discount cards of its own (see the following Bus section).

Another possibility is Haggis Backpackers, which runs a jump-on, jump-off circuit from hostel to hostel around the Highlands (see the following Bus section).

Air

British Airways Express (☎ 0345-222111) connects the main towns, the Western Isles, Orkney and Shetland.

Bus

Privatisation, takeovers and buyouts have reduced Scotland's internal bus network to one major player, Scottish Citylink (☎ 0990-505050), which is part of the nationwide National Express group, and numerous smaller regional companies. These companies come and go with astonishing rapidity.

During summer, Haggis Backpackers (☎ 0131-557 9393), at 11 Blackfriars St, Edinburgh, operates an almost daily service on a circuit between the hostels in Edinburgh, Perth, Pitlochry, Aviemore, Inverness, Loch Ness, Isle of Skye, Fort William, Glencoe, Oban, Inverary, Loch Lomond and Glasgow, finishing up back in Edinburgh. You can hop on and off the minibus wherever and whenever you like, and you can book your stages up to 24 hours before departure. There's no compulsion to stay in hostels either. Fares start at a bargain £65.

Go Blue Banana (☎ 0131-220 6868), Suite 8, North Bridge House, 28 North Bridge, Edinburgh, also runs a jump-on, jump-off service on the same circuit for the same price (£65). It also offers two excellent-value three-day tours, leaving from Edinburgh but based in Inverness and on the Isle of Skye. The transport cost is £65 and the tour covers a good cross-section of sights.

Otherwise, since no single bus company provides anything like full coverage of Scotland, you're likely to be using the services of a number of different operators. Scottish Citylink, for example, does not currently run buses to St Andrews.

The National Express Tourist Trail Pass (see Getting Around at the beginning of this chapter) can be used on all Scottish Citylink services. Citylink also honours all European under-26 cards, including the Young Scot card which costs £7 and provides discounts all over Scotland and Europe. If they don't have one of these cards, full-time students and people aged under 26 can buy the ironically titled Smart Card (more bureaucratic insanity and you can't even blame the government). This is equivalent to the National Express Discount Coach Card and can be purchased when you're buying your ticket. On presentation of proof of age or student status (an NUS or ISIC card), a passport photo and a £7 fee, you get the Smart Card to add to your collection. All this entitles you to a 30% discount, so the chances are you'll be ahead after buying your first ticket.

Regional enquiry telephone numbers have been given throughout the text; you are advised to use them. There are a large number of Royal Mail postbuses, which can be particularly useful for walkers. For information and timetables contact Royal Mail Communications (☎ 0131-228 7407), 102 West Port, Edinburgh EH3 9HS.

Scottish Citylink buses don't carry bicycles, but most of the local buses will.

Train

Scotland has some fantastic train lines; however, they are limited and expensive, so it is quite likely you'll have to turn to alternatives

at some point. The West Highland Line through Fort William to Mallaig and the routes from Stirling to Inverness, Inverness to Thurso and Inverness to Kyle of Lochalsh are considered to be among the best in the world.

The BritRail pass, which includes travel in Scotland, must be bought outside Britain. ScotRail's Freedom of Scotland Travelpass (see the previous Getting Around section) and its regional Rover tickets can be bought in Britain, including from most train stations in Scotland. Regional Rover tickets cover the North Highlands (£39 for four out of eight consecutive days), West Highlands (£39 for four out of eight consecutive days) and the central area (Festival Cities, £24 for three out of seven consecutive days). The ScotRail Rover covers all the ScotRail network and costs £60 for four out of eight consecutive days, £88 for eight consecutive days or £115 for 12 out of 15 consecutive days.

Reservations for bicycles (£3) are compulsory on many services.

Hitching

Hitching is reasonably good in Scotland, although the north-west is difficult, simply because there is so little traffic. You could easily be stuck for a day or two – and public transport won't necessarily rescue you. Also in the north and west, the Sunday Sabbath is still widely observed, so the traffic virtually dries up.

Boat

Caledonian MacBrayne (CalMac; ☎ 0990-650000) is the most important ferry operator on the west coast, with services from Ullapool to the Outer Hebrides, from Mallaig to Skye and on to the Outer Hebrides. Its main west-coast port, however, is Oban, with ferries to virtually all the west-coast islands except Harris and Lewis.

As an example, a single passenger fare from Oban to Lochboisdale, South Uist (Hebrides) is £15.95. Island Hopscotch tickets are usually the best deal, with ferry combinations over 23 set routes. CalMac also has Rover tickets offering unlimited travel for eight and 15 days (£36/51).

P&O Scottish Ferries (☎ 01224-589111) has ferries from Aberdeen and Scrabster to Orkney and from Aberdeen to Shetland. From

June through August, the cheapest one-way tickets to Stromness (Orkney) cost £14 from Scrabster and £38 from Aberdeen. Between Aberdeen and Shetland fares start at £52. There's a 10% student discount.

EDINBURGH

Edinburgh is one of the greatest European cities. It has an incomparable location, studded with volcanic hills and situated on the edge of an enormous estuary, and superb architecture, from extraordinary 16th-century tenements to monumental Georgian and Victorian master-pieces. Sixteen thousand of the city's buildings are listed as architecturally or historically important.

The royal capital since the 11th century, all the great dramas of Scottish history played at least one act in Edinburgh. Even after the union of 1707 it remained the centre for government administration (now the Scottish Office), the separate Scottish legal system and the Presbyterian Church of Scotland.

In some ways, however, it is the least Scottish of Scotland's cities – partly because of the impact of tourism, partly because of its closeness to England and the links between the two countries' upper classes, and partly because of its multicultural population.

History

Edinburgh Castle dominates the city from its rocky crag. This natural defensive position was probably the feature that first attracted settlers; it has been fortified since at least 600 and there are even older traces of habitation.

The old, walled city grew on the east-west ridge (the Royal Mile, which runs from Holyrood Palace to the castle) and south of the castle around Grassmarket. This restricted, defensible zone became a medieval Manhattan, forcing its densely packed inhabitants to build multistoreyed tenements. Even so, the city was sacked by the English seven times.

In the second half of the 18th century a new city was created across the ravine to the north of the old city. Before it was drained, this valley was a lake – it is now a superb park, cut but not spoilt by the railway line.

The population was expanding, defence declined in importance, and the thinkers and architects of the Scottish Enlightenment planned to distance themselves from Edinburgh's Jacobite past. Built on a grid, the new city's brilliance is owed to the way that it opens onto the castle, the old city and the Firth of Forth, and to the genius of architects like Robert Adams whose gracious, disciplined buildings line the streets.

The population exploded in the 19th century – Edinburgh quadrupled in size to 400,000, not much less than it is today – and the tenements of the old city were taken over by refugees from the Irish famines. A new ring of crescents and circuses was built to the south of the new town, and then grey Victorian terraces sprung up. In the 20th century the slums were emptied into new housing estates even further out, and these now have massive social problems.

Orientation

The most important orientation point is Arthur's Seat, the 800-foot-high rocky peak that lies to the south-west of the city. The old and new towns are separated by the valley park (and Waverley station), and the castle dominates them both.

Princes St, the main shopping street, runs along the northern side of the valley. Buildings are restricted to its northern side, which has the usual selection of high-street shops. Princes St runs west from Calton Hill, which is crowned by several monuments – an incomplete war memorial modelled on the Parthenon, and a tower honouring Nelson. The Royal Mile (made up of Lawnmarket, High St and Canongate) is the parallel equivalent in the old town.

Information

Edinburgh and Glasgow's answer to *Time Out* is the *List* (£1.80), a fortnightly guide to films, theatre, cabaret, music – the works. It's essential if you're staying for a couple of days.

Tourist Offices The frantically busy main TIC (☎ 0131-557 1700) is at Waverley Market, 3 Princes St EH2 2QP. There's also a branch at Edinburgh airport (☎ 338-2167). It has information about all of Scotland, and sells a very useful guide to the city (25p). It also has an accommodation service, but charges £3, so you should consider using its excellent free accommodation brochure, or the free booking service (for bookings worth less than £20) in the train station operated by Thomas Cook (open daily).

BRITAIN

BRITAIN

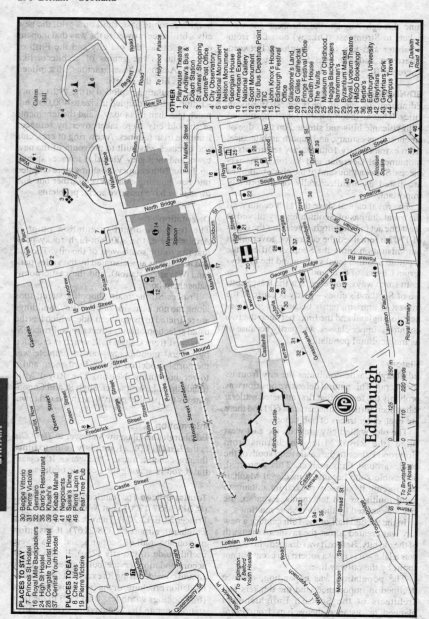

Edinburgh

To Holyrood Palace

To Dalkeith Road & A4

To Leith Walk

To Eglinton & Belford Youth Hostels

To Braidfield Youth Hostel

Edinburgh Castle

Waverley Station

0   125   250 m
0   110   220 yards

The TIC is open daily all year, except Sunday from October to April. In summer it stays open to 8 pm.

Money There's a *bureau de change* at the tourist office, with long opening hours, including 10 am to 6 pm on Sunday from May to September. American Express (☎ 225 7881) has an office at 139 Princes St, open business hours from Monday to Friday, and from 9 am to noon on Saturday.

Emergency Dial ☎ 999 for police, fire or medical emergencies (free call).

Things to See
The best place to start any tour of Edinburgh is **Edinburgh Castle**, which has excellent views overlooking the city.

The castle is still the headquarters for the army's Scottish Division, and is a complex of buildings that has been altered many times by war and the demands of the military. The smallest and oldest building is **St Margaret's Chapel**, built in the 12th century. The castle was the seat of Scottish kings, and the royal apartments include the tiny room where Mary Queen of Scots gave birth to the boy who became King James VI of Scotland and James I of England. It's open seven days a week from 9.30 am to at least 5 pm; admission is £5.50.

The castle is at the western end of the Royal Mile, which runs all the way down to Holyrood Palace. The streetscape is an extraordinarily complete survival from the 16th and 17th centuries, and an exploration of the closes and wynds that run into it evokes the crowded and vital city of that time.

On the left, **Gladstone's Land** and **Lady Stair's House** are restored townhouses that give fascinating insights into urban life of the past. Gladstone's Land was completed in 1620 and has been skilfully restored; it's open from April to October, and costs £2.60. Lady Stair's House contains relics and portraits of Robert Burns, Sir Walter Scott and Robert Louis Stevenson.

Turn right onto the George IV Bridge, which crosses Cowgate (an ancient narrow street). Grassmarket, below and to the right, has a number of pubs and restaurants. Continue until you reach the angled intersection with Candlemaker Row and **Greyfriars Kirk** with its

beautiful old churchyard, where the National Covenant was signed; there are views from here across the roofs to the castle.

Return to the Royal Mile and turn right past the much-restored 15th-century **St Giles Cathedral**. At the rear of the cathedral is **Parliament House**, now the seat of the supreme law courts of Scotland. Immediately to the east of St Giles stands the **Mercat Cross**, which was where public proclamations were made.

Continue down the Royal Mile over North/South Bridge until you come to the **Museum of Childhood** on your right and **John Knox's House** on your left. The Museum of Childhood has a fascinating collection of toys (free entry). John Knox was the fiery leader of the Scottish Reformation (open Monday to Saturday; £1.75).

Holyrood Palace is at the eastern end of the Royal Mile, a Stuart palace mostly dating from a reconstruction by Charles II in 1671. Holyrood is the official Scottish residence of the current royal family, so it can be closed at any time (usually in late May and late June) and, anyway, it's not particularly interesting inside. It's open daily from April to late October except when the Queen is in residence; admission is £5.

From the palace, turn right and climb Abbey Hill (under the railway overpass). Turn left into Regent Rd which takes you back to Princes St. On your right you pass **Calton Hill**, which is worth climbing for its superb views across to the castle.

Continue along Princes St until you get to the extravagant 200-foot spire of the **Sir Walter Scott Monument**. Turn right and walk up the slight hill to **St Andrew Square**, which is home to numerous financial institutions, including the Bank of Scotland. Turn left down George St, the main street of the new town, which is lined with many fine buildings.

If you're a little thirsty at this stage, turn left and then right into Rose St, which is famous for its large number of pubs. Then continue west until you come out onto Charlotte Square – the northern side is Robert Adam's masterpiece. No 7 is the **Georgian House**, which has been furnished by the National Trust to bring it back to its full 18th-century glory. It's open daily from April to October (Sunday from 2 to 4.30 pm only); admission is £3.60.

BRITAIN

Special Events

Born in 1947, the Edinburgh International Festival has established itself as one of the largest, most important arts festivals in the world – the world's premier companies play to packed audiences.

The Fringe Festival has grown up alongside, presenting the would-be stars of the future. It now claims to be the largest event of its kind in the world, with over 500 amateur and professional groups presenting every possible kind of avant-garde performance. Just to make sure that every B&B for 40 miles around is full, the Edinburgh Military Tattoo is held at the same time.

The International and Fringe festivals run from mid-August to early September; normally the Tattoo finishes four or five days earlier than the festivals, so the last week is less hectic. If you want to attend the International Festival, it is necessary to book; the programme is published in April and is available from the Edinburgh Festival Office (☎ 225 5756), 21 Market St EH1 1BW. The Fringe Festival is less formal, and many performances will have empty seats the day before. Programmes are available from the Fringe Office (☎ 226 5257), 180 High St EH1 1QS. For bookings for the Military Tattoo, contact the Tattoo Office (☎ 225 1188), 33-34 Market St EH1 1QS.

Book accommodation as far in advance as possible. Contact the Edinburgh & Lothian Tourist Board (☎ 557 9655), 3 Princes St EH2 2QP, or for a reservation in a university college, Reservations Office (☎ 667 1971), Pollock Halls, 18 Holyrood Park Rd EH16 5AY.

In recent years the street parties for Hogmanay (New Year) have got bigger and bigger. Edinburgh has now overtaken London as *the* place to see in the New Year and you'll need to book well ahead if you want to be part of the fun.

Places to Stay

Edinburgh has numerous accommodation options, but the city can fill up very quickly at Easter and between mid-May and mid-September, particularly in August. Single rooms are always in short supply. Book in advance if possible, or use the accommodation services operated by the TIC, or Thomas Cook.

Camping The *Mortonhall Caravan Park* (☎ 664 1533), Frogston Rd, East Edinburgh, is 15 minutes from the centre. Sites are from £7.75; it's open from March through to October.

Hostels & Colleges The most popular hostel accommodation is the friendly, central, independent *High St Hostel* (☎ 557 3984), 8 Blackfriars St. From Princes St, turn right onto North Bridge and walk up the hill until you get to the Royal Mile (High St at this point), turn left and Blackfriars is the second on the right. It's £8.90 per night. Not far away at 105 Royal Mile is the new *Royal Mile Backpackers* (☎ 557 6120) with beds for £9.50.

The *Princes St Hostel* (☎ 556 6894), 5 West Register St, has an equally good location just behind Princes St and close to the bus station, although you do have to negotiate 77 exhausting steps. It charges £8.50 in a dorm or £22 in a double.

The fourth independent option, the *Belford Youth Hostel* (☎ 225 6209), 6 Douglas Gardens, is in a converted church and, although some people have complained of noise, it's a well-run, cheerful place. The nightly rate is £8.50, and it has a couple of doubles for £27.50.

There are also three good official SYHA hostels: Eglington is closed in December, Bruntsfield in January, and Central is open from July to early September; all have 2 am curfews and the senior rates are £10.40, £7.80 and £8.80 respectively.

Eglington Youth Hostel (☎ 337 1120), 18 Eglington Crescent, is about one mile west of the city near the Haymarket train station. Walk down Princes St and continue along Shandwick Place, which becomes West Maitland St; veer right at the Haymarket along Haymarket Terrace, then turn right into Coates Gardens which runs into Eglington Crescent.

Bruntsfield Youth Hostel (☎ 447 2994), 7 Bruntsfield Crescent, is a bit more difficult to get to; it has an attractive location overlooking Bruntsfield Links about 2½ miles from Waverley station. Catch bus No 11 or 16 from the garden side of Princes St and alight at Forbes Rd just after the gardens on the left.

Central Youth Hostel (☎ 229 8660), Robertson Lane, Cowgate, has a great position in a college residence with single bedrooms; advance bookings are required.

During university vacations the *Pollock Halls of Residence* (☎ 667 0662), 18 Holyrood Park Rd, has modern (often noisy) single rooms from £23.50 per person, including breakfast. *Cowgate Tourist Hostel* (☎ 226 2153), 112 Cowgate, has singles and doubles with self-catering facilities from £9.80 per person.

B&Bs The best budget bet will be one of the numerous private houses; get the TIC's free accommodation guide and make some phone calls. Outside festival time you should have no trouble getting something for around £13, although most are scattered around the suburbs and will be a bus ride to the centre.

Guesthouses are generally two or three pounds more expensive, and to get a private bathroom you'll have to pay around £20. The main concentrations are around Minto St (a southern continuation of North Bridge), Newington; Pilrig St, Pilrig; and Leamington Terrace, Bruntsfield.

The *Ardenlee Guest House* (☎ 556 2838), 9 Eyre Place, is reasonably central, north of the new town and one mile from the centre; singles/doubles are from £16 (£2 more for a private bathroom). *Blairhaven Guest House* (☎ 556 3025) at 5 Eyre Place has B&B from £15.

Pilrig St, left off Leith Walk (veer left at the eastern end of Princes St), is a happy hunting ground for guesthouses. *Balmoral Guest House* (☎ 554 1857), at No 32, has easy access to the city and singles/doubles from £17 to £19. The *Barrosa* (☎ 554 3700), at No 21, has some similarly priced rooms with bathrooms. At No 94, *Balquhidder Guest House* (☎ 554 3377) is a very pleasant two-crown place with rooms with bathrooms from £17 to £24.

There are numerous guesthouses around the suburb of Newington, which is south of the city centre and university on either side of the continuation of North/South Bridge, which continues to change its name about every 400 metres. This is the main traffic artery from the south and carries traffic from the A7 and A68 (both routes are signposted); there are plenty of buses to the centre.

The *Salisbury Guest House* (☎ 667 1264),

45 Salisbury Rd, is 10 minutes from the centre by bus, and is quiet and very comfortable. Rates, including private bathrooms, are from £22 to £26 per person. *Casa Buzzo* (☎ 667 8998), 8 Kilmaurs Rd, has two doubles at £13 per person.

Using the same bus stop as for the Bruntsfield Youth Hostel you can get to the *Lugton's Guest House* (☎ 229 7033), 29 Leamington Terrace, which has singles/doubles from £20 to £28 per person. Virtually next door, the *Menzies Guest House* (☎ 229 4629) is similar.

Places to Eat

For cheap eats, the best areas are around Grassmarket just north of the castle, and near the university around Nicolson St, the extension of North/South Bridge.

Those staying at Bruntsfield will find the quirky and popular *Parrots* (☎ 229 3252) at 5 Viewforth, which runs off Bruntsfield Place. It has an interesting, good-value menu with offerings like baltis for £5.95 or mushroom and nut fettucine for £3.45.

Those staying in the West End, will find a batch of interesting Indian restaurants at the Haymarket end of Dalry Rd, including *The New Star of Bengal* (☎ 346 0204), which does a two-course lunch for £3.95.

There are some lively pubs and reasonable restaurants on the northern side of Grassmarket, catering to a young crowd. *Gennaro* (☎ 226 3706) at No 64 has standard Italian fare, with pizzas and pastas from £5 to £8. Nearby, *Mamma's* (☎ 225 6464) at No 30 is an informal and extremely popular pizzeria where you can get a full meal for under £8.

The most interesting possibility is *Pierre Victoire* (☎ 226 2442), 38 Grassmarket, which has a relaxed style and an interesting contemporary menu emphasising fresh ingredients. Main meals are from £6 to £8. Pierre is credited with bringing a culinary revolution to Edinburgh with his reasonably priced, interesting food and he has been extraordinarily successful.

There are now Pierre Victoire branches at 8 Union St and 10 Victoria St and several offspring: *Chez Jules* (☎ 225 7983), 61 Frederick St – a French bistro which is even cheaper; *Pierre Lapin* (☎ 668 4332), 113 Buccleuch St – a vegetarian restaurant which serves four courses for £9.60; and, finally, *Beppe Vittorio* (☎ 226 7267), 7 Victoria St – Italian, of course, with main courses for around £5.

The university students' budget favourites are between Nicolson St and Bristo Place at the end of the George IV Bridge. *Kebab Mahal* (☎ 667 5214), 7 Nicolson Square, is a legendary source of cheap sustenance with kebabs from £3.50.

Vegetarians should also look for *Susie's Diner* (☎ 667 8729), 51 West Nicolson St, which has good, inexpensive and healthy food; chunky soup and a main course will set you back around £5. *Negociants* (☎ 225 6313), 45 Lothian St, is a hip, but nonetheless comfortable, café and music venue. The food is good value with main courses from £5 to £6 – and the music downstairs is often free.

The *Kalpna* (☎ 667 9890), 2 St Patrick's Square, is a highly acclaimed Gujarati (Indian) restaurant that is not only very good, but also very reasonable. Thalis are from £7 and most main courses are under £5. One of the cheapest and most eccentric possibilities in town is *Khushi's* (☎ 556 8996), 16 Drummond St, which serves a set lunch for £5.45 in simple café surroundings. Bring your own wine, or duck next door for a pint of beer.

Entertainment

There are several rowdy pubs on the northern side of Grassmarket, often with live music. Turn up Cowgate from Grassmarket and you reach a batch of good pubs (several with live music), including the relaxed *Bannerman's*. The *Pear Tree* on West Nicolson St has a large outdoor courtyard – pleasant on sunny afternoons and warm evenings.

There are some interesting music/club venues in old vaults under the George IV and South bridges. *Bertie's*, at the end of Merchant St off Candlemaker Row, has good live music, and the *Vaults*, 15 Niddry St under South Bridge, has a café as well as a variety of club nights. Under the Tron Tavern, *The Ceilidh House* is home to the Edinburgh Folk Club; most nights there are informal jamming sessions.

Getting There & Away

See Scotland and Britain's introductory Getting Around sections.

Bus Buses from London are very competitive and you may be able to get cheap promotional tickets. See Getting There & Away under the Glasgow section; prices are the same and the journey takes half an hour less.

There are numerous links with cities in England, including a service from Newcastle (2¾ hours) and one from York (5½ hours). As you might expect, Citylink has buses to virtually every major town in Scotland. Most of the west-coast towns are reached via Glasgow. There are numerous buses to Glasgow, with off-peak singles/returns for £4.50/6.50, and also to St Andrews, Aberdeen and Inverness.

The bus station is in the new town and is a little difficult to find, just off the south-eastern corner of St Andrew Square to the north of Princes St.

Train There are 20 trains a day from London's King's Cross station (☎ 0171-278 2477); apart from SuperApex fares which must be booked two weeks in advance and can't be changed they're expensive, but they're also much quicker and more comfortable than a bus.

ScotRail (☎ 0345-484950) has two northern lines from Edinburgh: one cuts across the Grampians to Inverness (3½ hours) and on to Thurso, and the other follows the coast around to Aberdeen (three hours) and on to Inverness.

There are numerous trains to Glasgow (50 minutes, £6.70).

Getting Around

To/From the Airport There are regular bus links with Waverley station; they take 35 minutes and cost £3.20. A taxi would cost around £12.

Bus Bus services are frequent and cheap, but the two main competitors do not issue interchangeable tickets. You can buy tickets when you board buses, but on Lothian Regional Transport buses (with the maroon livery) you have to have the exact change. For short trips in the city, fares are 40p to 55p. After midnight there are special night buses. The TIC has a map that shows the most important services, or during the week you can contact Traveline (☎ 225 3858), 24 St Giles St – an information service near St Giles Cathedral.

Bicycle David's Bicycle Store (☎ 229 8528), 39 Argyle Place, hires out bikes for £8 a day (mountain bikes £12 a day); prices are less for longer rentals. He also has used bikes from £30 and will buy them back from people staying for fewer than six months, the price depending on the state they come back in.

GLASGOW

Glasgow, with a population of nearly 700,000, is one of Britain's largest and most interesting cities. It doesn't have the beauty of Edinburgh, although it does have a legacy of interesting Victorian architecture and some distinguished suburbs of terraced squares and crescents. What makes it appealing is its vibrancy and energy. 'Glasgow's Alive', say the billboards in the city, and it's true.

Although influenced by thousands of Irish immigrants, this is the most Scottish of cities – quite different from Edinburgh and completely different from anything south of the border. There's a unique blend of friendliness, urban chaos, black humour and energy. There are some excellent art galleries and museums (all free), numerous cheap restaurants, countless pubs and bars and a lively arts scene. If the English cities were too bland for your taste, Glasgow should be the antidote.

History

Glasgow grew up around the cathedral founded by St Mungo in the 6th century. In 1451 the University of Glasgow was founded – the fourth-oldest university in Britain. Unfortunately, with the exception of the cathedral, virtually nothing of the medieval city remains. It was swept away by the energetic people of a new age – the age of capitalism, the Industrial Revolution, and the empire.

In the 19th century, Glasgow – transformed by cotton, steel, coal, shipbuilding and trade – justifiably called itself the second city of the empire. Grand Victorian public buildings were built, but the working class lived in ghastly slums.

In the 20th century, Glasgow's port and its engineering industries went into terminal decline. By the early 1970s Glasgow looked doomed, but it has fought back by developing service industries. The spooky emptiness of the River Clyde – once one of the greatest shipbuilding ports in the world – and the city's soulless housing estates are outweighed by a renewed confidence in the city.

Orientation

The city centre is built on a grid system on the northern side of the River Clyde. The two train stations (Central and Queen St), the bus station (Buchanan St) and the TIC are all within a couple of blocks of George Square, the main city square.

Running along a ridge in the northern part of the city, Sauchiehall St has a pedestrian mall with numerous high-street shops at its eastern end, and pubs and restaurants to the west. The university and the SYHA hostel are north-west of the city centre around Kelvingrove Park. Motorways bore through the suburbs and the M8 sweeps round the western and northern edges of the centre. The airport is 10 miles to the west.

Information

The *List* (£1.80), available from newsagents, is Glasgow and Edinburgh's comprehensive and invaluable fortnightly entertainment guide.

Glasgow's telephone code is ☎ 0141.

Tourist Offices The main TIC (☎ 204 4400), George Square, has a free accommodation-booking service and a *bureau de change*. It's open all year from 9 am to 6 pm Monday to Saturday, and from 10 am to 6 pm on Sunday from May to September. In July and August it stays open until 7 pm during the week. There's also a branch at Glasgow airport.

Make sure you pick up a copy of the *Visitors Transport Guide Map* (free) which gives all the local transport options on a useful map. Travel information is also available from the Strathclyde Transport Travel Centre (☎ 226 4826), St Enoch Square. It's open from Monday to Saturday.

Money Full American Express services are available at 115 Hope St (☎ 221 4366); it's open during commercial hours from Monday to Friday, and until noon on Saturday.

Emergency Dial ☎ 999 on any phone (free call).

Glasgow

0   250   500 m

0   220   440 yards

Many Streets One-way only

Ⓤ Underground Station

PLACES TO STAY
1 Glasgow Backpackers
2 Glasgow Youth Hostel
4 McLay's Guest House
5 Baird Hall
6 Berkeley Globetrotters

PLACES TO EAT
7 Ristoro Ciao Italia
8 Loon Fung
9 Centre for
   Contemporary Arts
11 The Willow Tearoom

12 Delifrance

OTHER
3 Tenement House
10 Glasgow School of Art
13 Buchanan St
    Bus Station
14 Queen St Train Station
15 City Chambers
16 Post Office
17 TIC
18 Central Train Station
19 Travel Centre

Things to See

A good starting point for exploring the city is **George Square**. It's surrounded by imposing Victorian architecture, including the post office, the Bank of Scotland and, along its eastern side, the City Chambers. The chambers were built in the 1880s at the high point of the city's wealth; their interior is even more extravagant than their exterior. There are free tours from the main entrance, Monday to Friday at 10.30 am and 2.30 pm.

The current **Glasgow Cathedral** is a direct descendant of St Mungo's simple church. It was begun in 1238 and is regarded as a perfect example of pre-Reformation Gothic architec-

ture. The lower church is reached by a stairway, and its forest of pillars creates a powerful atmosphere around St Mungo's tomb, the focus of a famous medieval pilgrimage that was believed to be as meritorious as a visit to Rome.

Beside the cathedral, the **St Mungo Museum of Religious Life & Art** (☎ 553 2557), opened in 1993, is well worth visiting. In the main gallery, Dali's *Christ of St John of the Cross* hangs beside statues of the Buddha and Hindu deities. Outside, there's Britain's only Zen garden. The museum is open daily until 5 pm; entry is free.

The **Burrell Collection** (☎ 649 7151) was

amassed by a wealthy local before it was given to the city and housed in a superb museum in the Pollok Country Park, three miles south of the city. It's an idiosyncratic collection, including Chinese porcelain, medieval furniture and paintings by Renoir and Cézanne. It is not so big as to be overwhelming, and the stamp of the individual collector seems to create a weird coherence.

It's open from 10 am to 5 pm Monday to Saturday, and from 11 am on Sunday. Catch a train to Pollokshaws West from Central station (one service every half-hour; the second station on the light-blue line to the south) and then walk for 10 minutes through the pleasant park – bring a picnic lunch if the weather allows.

There are a number of superb Art-Nouveau buildings designed by the Scottish architect and designer Charles Rennie Mackintosh. In particular, check out the **Glasgow School of Art** (☎ 353 4526), 167 Renfrew St, which has guided tours Monday to Saturday mornings (£3.50/2), and the **Willow Tearoom** (☎ 332 0521), 217 Sauchiehall St.

For an extraordinary time-capsule experience, visit the small apartment in the **Tenement House** (☎ 333 0183), 145 Buccleuch St. It gives a vivid insight into middle-class life at the turn of the century, and is open daily from 2 to 5 pm from April to October (£2.60).

Special Events

Not to be outdone by Edinburgh, Glasgow has developed two major festivals of its own. Mayfest, in the first three weeks of May, has a strong mix of Scottish and international performers, and there is an excellent international jazz festival early in July.

Places to Stay

Finding somewhere decent in July and August can be difficult – for a B&B, get into town reasonably early and use the TIC's free booking service. Unfortunately, Glasgow's B&Bs are expensive by Scottish standards – you may have to pay up to £16.

Camping *Craigendmuir Caravan Park* (☎ 779 4159), Campsie View, Stepps (six miles north-east of Glasgow), is the nearest,

but it's still a 15-minute walk from Stepps station. It takes vans and tents for £5.50 (two people).

Hostels & Colleges The excellent *Youth Hostel* (☎ 332 3004), is at 7 Park Terrace. The building was once a hotel, so there are mainly four-bed rooms, many with *en suite* facilities, as well as a small number of doubles. In summer, it is advisable to make a booking. It's open all day and the nightly charge is £10.45/9. From Central station take bus No 44 or 59 and ask for the first stop on Woodlands Rd.

Berkeley Globetrotters (☎ 221 7880), 63 Berkeley St, has beds from £8 (£6.50 if you have your own bedding) in dorms, £9.50 in twin rooms. Phone ahead for bookings. Berkeley St is a western continuation of Bath St (one block south of Sauchiehall St). The hostel's just past the Mitchell Library.

Near the SYHA hostel, the *Glasgow Backpackers Hostel* (☎ 332 5412), Kelvin Lodge, 8 Park Circus, is one of the university's halls of residence, and so is only open from July through September. Beds are from £8.90. This is an Independent Backpackers Hostel, and very popular.

The *University of Glasgow* (☎ 330 5385) has a range of B&B accommodation at £20.50/36, and self-catering at £11 from mid-March to mid-April, and July, August and September.

The *University of Strathclyde* (☎ 553 4148) also opens its halls of residence to tourists during the vacation period; charges are from £8.50. If you don't mind staying further out of town, its cheapest B&B accommodation is at Jordanhill Campus, 76 Southbrae Drive. Comfortable singles/doubles are £18/28, and bus No 44 from Central station goes to the college gates. The university's impressive Art-Deco Baird Hall offers some B&B accommodation year round for £22/36. It's in a great location at 460 Sauchiehall St.

B&Bs *McLay's Guest House* (☎ 332 4796) is labyrinthine, but brilliantly located at 264 Renfrew St, which is behind Sauchiehall St. Considering the location, you can't quibble at £17.50 for a single room without bathroom, or

£19.50 with. There are doubles for £33, or £37 with bath.

There's a batch of reasonable-value B&Bs to the east of the Necropolis. *Brown's Guest House* (☎ 554 6797), 2 Onslow Drive, has singles/doubles from £15/26. *Craigpark Guest House* (☎ 554 4160), 33 Circus Drive, charges from £16/28.

Places to Eat
Glasgow has an excellent range of moderately priced restaurants. Wander along Sauchiehall St or around the city centre and you're certain to find the ethnic cuisine of your choice. The set lunches offered by many restaurants are usually very good value at £3 to £5. *Delifrance*, on Sauchiehall St, does excellent filled baguettes for £1.70.

Those staying in the vicinity of Kelvingrove Park will find a scattering of restaurants along Gibson St and on and around Great Western Rd. The *Bay Tree* (☎ 334 5898), 403 Great Western Rd, is a vegetarian café with an imaginative menu (eg Peruvian potato bake with tofu) that's good value. Carnivores should seek out the *Back Alley* (☎ 334 7165), 8 Ruthven Lane (off Byres Rd), for excellent burgers and a wide range of sauces and toppings.

There are a number of interesting choices on Sauchiehall St. The *Centre for Contemporary Arts* (☎ 332 7521), at No 346, is an interesting visual and performing-arts venue – it also has a pleasant café with sandwiches, salads and a range of main courses. Main dishes from £4 to £6. Check out the centre's gallery and theatre programme.

Ristoro Ciao Italia (☎ 332 4565), 441 Sauchiehall St, is an efficient Italian restaurant with pasta from around £5 and delicious home-baked bread. *Loon Fung* (☎ 332 1240), 417 Sauchiehall St, is one of the best Chinese places in town. A set lunch costs £5.95. There are also a number of Indian restaurants at the western end of Sauchiehall St but, relatively speaking, they're expensive.

The *Willow Tearoom* (☎ 332 0521), above a jewellery shop at 217 Sauchiehall St, was designed as a tearoom by Charles Rennie Mackintosh in 1903. Last orders are at 4.15 pm, and for lunch and tea the queues can be long. Avoid them by arriving when it opens at 9 am (11 am on Sunday) and splash out on a superior breakfast of smoked salmon, scrambled eggs and toast (£3.25).

Entertainment
Some of the best nightlife in Scotland is to be found in the pubs and clubs of Glasgow. See the *List* for the latest information.

There's a good range of rowdy bars and nightclubs at the western end of Sauchiehall St, and around the intersection of Bath and Renfield Sts.

Getting There & Away
See the introductory Getting Around sections for Scotland and Britain.

Air Glasgow airport (☎ 887 1111) handles domestic and international flights.

Bus Buses from London are very competitive. The London Liner (☎ 332 2283) is currently the best deal at £16/18 for a single/return, and the journey takes 7¾ hours. The service is very popular so you'll need to book. Tickets are available from any branch of the travel agent A T Mays, and buses leave London from Transpak, 71 Pancras Rd (near King's Cross station).

Silver Choice (☎ 333 1400) costs £20/24 and leaves from Victoria coach station in London. National Express (☎ 0990-808080) also leaves from here and costs £20.50/25.50. The best option is to catch the 8.30 am bus, so that you arrive in good time to organise accommodation. There are direct links with Heathrow and Gatwick airports.

There are numerous links with other English cities. National Express services include: three buses per day from Birmingham (5¼ hours); one from Cambridge (nine hours); numerous from Carlisle (two hours); one from Newcastle (four hours); and one from York (6½ hours).

National Express/Scottish Citylink has buses to most major towns in Scotland. Most of the east-coast towns are reached via Edinburgh. There are numerous buses to Edinburgh with singles/returns from £4.50/6.50 (off peak), Stirling (one hour), Inverness (4¼ hours), three to Oban (2¾ hours), Aberdeen (four hours), Fort William (three hours) and Skye (5¼ hours). There's a summer service for

Stranraer, connecting with the ferry to Larne in Northern Ireland (five hours).

Fife Scottish/Stagecoach Express (☎ 01592-261461) operates buses to St Andrews (2¼ hours, £5, hourly) and Dundee (2½ hours, £5, hourly) via Glenrothes.

Midland Bluebird (☎ 01324-613777) runs hourly buses to Milngavie (30 minutes), the start of the West Highland Way.

Train As a general rule, Central station serves southern Scotland, England and Wales, and Queen St serves the north and east. There are frequent buses between the two (40p). There are 20 trains a day from London's Euston station (☎ 0345-484950); they're not cheap, but they are much quicker (4¾ hours) and more comfortable than the bus.

ScotRail (☎ 0345-484950) has one major line north to Oban and Fort William (see those Getting There & Away sections) and direct links to Dundee, Aberdeen and Inverness. There are numerous trains to Edinburgh (50 minutes, £6.70).

Getting Around
The Roundabout Glasgow ticket (£3.20/1.60) covers all public transport in the city for a day; the Roundabout Glasgow Plus ticket (£5.80/2.90) also includes the Discovering Glasgow hop-on hop-off tourist buses that run along the main sightseeing routes.

To/From the Airport There are buses every 20 minutes from the airport to Buchanan St bus station; they take 20 minutes and cost £2.20. A taxi would cost about £12.

Bus Bus services are frequent and cheap. You can buy tickets when you board buses, but on some you have to have the exact change. For short trips in the city, fares are around 50p. After midnight there are special night buses.

Train There's an extensive suburban network; tickets should be bought before travel if the station is staffed, or from the conductor if it isn't.

There's also an underground line that serves 15 stations in the centre, west and south of the city (60p). An Underground Heritage Trail Pass (£2) gives unlimited travel on the system for a day.

SOUTH-WESTERN SCOTLAND
The tourist board bills this region as Scotland's surprising south-west, and it is surprising if you expect magnificent mountain and coastal scenery to be confined to the Highlands. What really is surprising is that you can escape the crowds that flock to the better known Western Highlands.

Ayrshire to the immediate south-west of Glasgow is the least spectacular part of the region, though it was the home of Scotland's national poet, Robert Burns. Dumfries & Galloway covers the southern half of this western elbow, and this is where the coast and mountains really do approach the grandeur of the north. Warmed by the Gulf Stream, this is also the mildest corner of Scotland, and there are a number of famous gardens. There are many notable historic and prehistoric attractions linked by the Solway Coast Heritage Trail (information from TICs). Sweetheart Abbey, spectacular Caerlaverock Castle and fascinating Whithorn Priory are just three of many. Kirkcudbright is a beautiful town, and would make a good base.

This is excellent cycling and walking country, and it is crossed by the coast-to-coast Southern Upland Way (see the Stranraer section) and a number of cycle trails (the TICs have brochures).

Orientation & Information
Southern Scotland is divided from east to west by the southern uplands. The western coast from Glasgow to Girvan is quite busy, but south from there, the crowds evaporate. Stranraer is the ferry port to Larne in Northern Ireland; it's the shortest link from Britain to Ireland, taking less than 2½ hours. The area's only YHA hostels are at Ayr, Newton Stewart (Minnigaff), Kendoon and Wanlockhead.

Getting There & Around
Bus National Express (☎ 0990-808080) has coaches from London and Birmingham (via Manchester and Carlisle), and Glasgow/Edinburgh to Stranraer. These coaches service the main towns and villages along the A75 (including Ayr, Dumfries and Newton Stewart).

Stagecoach Western (☎ 01387-253496) provides a variety of local bus services.

Train See Getting There & Away under the Carlisle section for info on the Carlisle to Glasgow rail link, and the Glasgow section for the Glasgow to Stranraer link.

Boat Frequent car and passenger ferries operate between Stranraer and Larne in Northern Ireland (Stena Line, ☎ 01776-702262) and between Cairnryan, which is close to Stranraer, and Larne (P&O, ☎ 01581-200276). The fastest option is the SeaCat (☎ 0345-523523) between Stranraer and Belfast. See the Northern Ireland section of the Ireland chapter for details.

Isle of Arran
Often described as 'Scotland in Miniature' because of its varied scenery, Arran is an hour's ferry ride from Ardrossan, conveniently accessible from Glasgow.

With 10 peaks over 600 metres, this is excellent walking country. A coastal road right around the island provides a good cycle route, except at weekends at the height of the season when traffic can be bad. Avoid Brodick, the main town – although the castle (☎ 01770-302202) is worth visiting – and head for the peaceful village of **Lochranza**, 14 miles to the north. The *Youth Hostel* (☎ 01770-830631) at Lochranza is a great place to stay.

The TIC (☎ 01770-302140), by the pier in Brodick, has details of other accommodation on the island.

Stranraer & Cairnryan
Stranraer is rather more pleasant than the average ferry port, but there is really no pressing reason to stay. Make for the south coast, or Glasgow. The train station is right on the docks beside the ferry terminal. Cairnryan is a couple of miles away on the other side of the bay (basically only an option if you have transport). The TIC (☎ 01776-702595) is in town and can provide the usual information on the region and accommodation.

The **Southern Upland Way** starts at Portpatrick near Stranraer and runs for 212 miles to Cockburnspath near Berwick-upon-Tweed on the east coast. It offers varied walking country, but includes some very long and demanding stretches – those tackling the whole route should be experienced. The TIC stocks guides and maps covering the trail.

London to Stranraer by rail is nine hours.

Kirkcudbright
Kirkcudbright, with its dignified streets of 17th and 18th-century merchants' houses and its lively harbour, is the ideal base if you wish to explore the beautiful southern coast. There's no SYHA hostel but the TIC (☎ 01557-330494) by the harbour can provide all the necessary information about local B&Bs.

SOUTH-EASTERN SCOTLAND
There is a tendency to think that the real Scotland doesn't start until you are north of Perth, but the castles, forests and glens of the Borders have a romance of their own. The region survived centuries of war and plunder and was romantically portrayed by Robert Burns and Sir Walter Scott.

Few people pause in their rush to get to Edinburgh, but if you do stop, you'll find the lovely valley of the Tweed, rolling hills, castles, ruined abbeys and sheltered towns. The cycling and walking opportunities are excellent. Two possibilities among many include the challenging coast-to-coast Southern Upland Way (see the Stranraer & Cairnryan section for details) and the Tweed Cycleway, a signposted route between Biggar (on the A702 west of Peebles) to Berwick-upon-Tweed.

Orientation & Information
The Borders region lies between the Cheviot Hills along the English border, and the Pentland, Moorfoot and Lammermuir hills, which form the border with Lothian, and overlook the Firth of Forth. The most interesting country surrounds the River Tweed and its tributaries.

Getting There & Around
Bus There's a good network of local buses. For those coming from the south-west, there is a Rail Link coach service that runs between Carlisle in north-west Cumbria and Galashiels; there are six services a day from Monday to Saturday, and three on Sunday (£14). Lowland (☎ 01896-753337) has numerous buses between Galashiels, Melrose and Edinburgh.

Regular Lowland buses also run between Berwick-upon-Tweed and Galashiels via Melrose. Another useful and frequent Lowland service links Jedburgh, Melrose and Galashiels.

To get to and from Edinburgh there are at least four Lowland services a day direct to and from Jedburgh, and, as previously noted, numerous buses to and from Galashiels. Lowland's Waverley Wanderer ticket allows a day's unlimited travel around the Borders, and includes Edinburgh (£9.50).

National Express has one bus a day (No 383) between Chester and Edinburgh via Manchester, Leeds, Newcastle, Jedburgh and Melrose.

Train The main lines from Carlisle and Newcastle/Berwick skirt the region. Buses are the only option.

Bicycle Neither Jedburgh nor Melrose have bicycle hire; however, Scottish Border Trails (☎ 01721-722934) will deliver bikes in the region.

Jedburgh
The most complete of the ruined Border abbeys is **Jedburgh Abbey**. After a famous ride to visit her lover, the Earl of Bothwell, at Hermitage Castle, Mary Queen of Scots was nursed back to health in a Jedburgh house (now a museum) that bears her name. The TIC (☎ 01835-863435) stays open all year.

Hermitage Castle, off the B6399 from Hawick, is only accessible if you have transport, but it's well worth a detour; its forbidding architecture bears testimony to the Borders' brutal history.

Melrose
Melrose is an attractive small town four miles east of Galashiels, and is a popular base for exploring the Borders. This is the only Borders town with a convenient *Youth Hostel* (☎ 01896-822521). Open all year, it overlooks the ruined abbey.

Sir Walter Scott's house, **Abbotsford** (☎ 752043), is on the banks of the Tweed, a short walk from the intersection of the B6360 and the A6091 between Galashiels and Melrose. It's a beautiful spot, and the house has an extraordinary collection of historical relics.

Thirlestane Castle (☎ 01578-722430), 10 miles north, just off the A68, is one of Scotland's most fascinating castles. The original keep was built in the 13th century, but was refashioned and added to in the 16th century – with fairy-tale turrets and towers. It has complicated opening times; phone ahead.

STIRLING
Twenty-six miles north of Glasgow, and occupying the most strategically important location in Scotland, Stirling has witnessed many of the struggles of the Scots against the English. Like Edinburgh, the town is dominated by its castle (☎ 01786-450000) perched dramatically on a rock. Mary Queen of Scots was crowned here and it was a favourite royal residence. Open daily, it's one of the most interesting castles in the country.

The cobbled streets of the attractive old town surround the castle. The *Youth Hostel* (☎ 473442), St John St, is centrally located and an excellent place to stay. The TIC (☎ 475019), 41 Dumbarton Rd, is open all year. For local transport in the area, phone ☎ 442707.

ST ANDREWS
St Andrews is a beautiful, unusual seaside town – a concoction of medieval ruins, obsessive golfers, windy coastal scenery, tourist glitz and a schizophrenic university, with wealthy English undergraduates rubbing shoulders with Scottish theology students.

Although St Andrews was once the ecclesiastical capital of Scotland, both its cathedral and castle are now in ruins. For most people, the town is the home of golf. It's the headquarters of the game's governing body, the Royal & Ancient Golf Club, and home of the world's most famous golf course, the Old Course, which was laid out in the 16th century.

Orientation & Information
The most important parts of old St Andrews, lying to the east of the bus station, are easily explored on foot. The TIC (☎ 01334-472021), 70 Market St, is open all year. Pick up a copy of *Getting Around Fife*, a free guide to public transport.

To play the Old Course (which is a public course, not owned by the exclusive Royal & Ancient Golf Club), you must book months in advance or present a handicap certificate or letter of introduction to the St Andrews Links Management Committee (☎ 475757), and enter a ballot before 2 pm the day before you wish to play. Green fees are a mere £60; the course is closed on Sunday.

Places to Stay
There's no SYHA hostel here. The cheapest accommodation in the area is eight miles outside the town at the *Bunkhouse* (☎ 310768), in West Pitkierie, near Anstruther. The nightly charge is £6, and it's so popular you must phone ahead.

Back in St Andrews, the central B&Bs and hotels that line Murray Park and Murray Place are expensive, charging around £20 per person.

There are two B&Bs on Nelson St that are excellent value at about £13 per person. *Maria Haston* (☎ 473227) is at No 8, and *Mrs Lusk* (☎ 472575) at No 2. To reach Nelson St from the bus station, walk south along City Rd, into Alexandra Place and then into Bridge St. Nelson St is on the right, after about half a mile.

Places to Eat
Brambles, 5 College St, is a good place for lunch. There are excellent vegetarian choices. *Ziggy's* (☎ 473686), 6 Murray Place, is popular with students, and has burgers from £3.60 and also has a good range of vegetarian dishes. *Ogston's* (☎ 473473), 114 South St, is a bar and bistro that's good value.

If you're on a very tight budget, *PM*, on the corner of Market St and Union St, often has half-price baked potatoes. Finally, don't leave town without sampling one of the 52 varieties of ice cream from *B Jannetta*, 31 South St.

Getting There & Away
See the Rail and Coach/Bus fares tables in this chapter's introductory Getting Around section.

Fife Scottish (☎ 474238) has four buses a day from St Andrew's Square, Edinburgh, to St Andrews (two hours; £4.50, or £3 for students) and on to Dundee (45 minutes; £1.75).

The nearest station to St Andrews is eight miles away at Leuchars (one hour from Edinburgh) on the Edinburgh, Dundee, Aberdeen, Inverness coastal line. There are No 94 or 95 buses every half-hour to St Andrews.

EASTERN HIGHLANDS
A great elbow of land juts into the North Sea between Perth and the Firth of Tay in the south and Inverness and Moray Firth in the north. The Cairngorm Mountains are as bleak and demanding as any of the Scottish mountains, and the coastline, especially from Stonehaven to Buckie, is excellent. The valley of the Dee – the Royal Dee thanks to the Queen's residence at Balmoral – has sublime scenery.

Orientation & Information
The Grampian Mountains march from Oban in a great arc to the north-east, becoming the Cairngorm Mountains in this eastern region. Aberdeen is the main ferry port for Shetland, and Inverness is the centre for the northern Highlands. The division between the eastern and western Highlands reflects the transport realities – there are few coast-to-coast links between Perth and Inverness.

Getting Around
The main bus and train routes from Edinburgh to Inverness run directly north through Perth, or around the coast to Aberdeen and then north-west and inland back to Inverness.

Bus Citylink (☎ 0990-505050) links the main towns. Edinburgh to Inverness via Perth takes four hours (£11.20); to Aberdeen, changing at Dundee, takes 3¾ hours (£11.70). There are also regular buses from both cities to Glasgow for much the same price. Aberdeen to Inverness takes three hours for £8.60 and passes through Elgin.

For local buses in Perthshire and Angus, contact the Transport Unit, Dundee (☎ 01382-303714). For information on the Aberdeenshire region, phone Aberdeen (☎ 01224-664581).

Train The train journey from Perth to Inverness is one of the most spectacular in Scotland, with a beautiful climb through the Cairngorms from Dunkeld to Aviemore. There are 10 trains daily from Monday to Saturday, and five on Sunday (2¼ hours). There are many trains from Edinburgh and Glasgow to Aberdeen (2½ hours from Edinburgh) and from Aberdeen to Inverness (2¼ hours).

Perthshire & Cairngorms

On the direct route from Edinburgh to Inverness, Perth, once the capital of Scotland, is an attractive town ringed by castles. Both Dunkeld and Pitlochry to the north are appealing, but touristy, villages. The *Youth Hostel* at Aviemore (☎ 01479-810345) is open from 22 December to 15 November. Aviemore is a very touristy town, best used just as a walking base. Frequent buses and trains service this route.

Grampian Country – Coast

Following the coastal route to Aberdeen and Inverness you quickly reach Dundee, one of Scotland's largest cities. Despite its excellent location it has suffered from (often corrupt) modern development and the loss of its jute and shipbuilding industries. It's worth pausing to visit Captain Scott's Antarctic ship, *Discovery*, moored here by the Discovery Point Visitor Centre.

The Grampian range meets the sea at Stonehaven, with its spectacular Dunnottar Castle. Continuing around the coast from Aberdeen there are long stretches of sand, and, on the north coast, some magical fishing villages like Pennan, where the film *Local Hero* was shot.

Old and new hippies should check out the Findhorn Foundation (☎ 01309-673655), Forres IV36 0RD, just east of Inverness. The foundation is an international spiritual community, founded in 1962. There are about 150 members and many more sympathetic souls who have moved into the vicinity. The community is dedicated to creating 'a deeper sense of the sacred in everyday life, and to dealing with work, relationships and our environment in new and more fulfilling ways'. In many ways it's very impressive, although it can become a bit outlandish. A recent course was entitled 'Devas, Fairies and Angels – a practical approach'. There are week-long residential programmes from £230, including food and accommodation.

The community is not particularly attractive itself – it started life in the Findhorn Bay Caravan Park and still occupies one end of the site. Far more attractive are the nearby fishing village of Findhorn (one mile) and the town of Forres (2½ miles). It's possible to stay in the *caravan park* (☎ 01309-690203) where camping costs from £3.50.

Buses and trains follow the coast to Aberdeen, then the train cuts back directly to Inverness (via Forres). Bus transport around the north-east coast is reasonable.

Grampian Country – Inland

The region between Braemar and Huntly and east to the coast is castle country, and includes the Queen's residence at Balmoral. There are more fanciful examples of Scottish baronial architecture, with its turret-capped towers, than anywhere else in the country. The TICs have information on a Castle Trail, but you really need private transport. Balmoral Castle is open Monday to Saturday from May to July, and attracts large numbers of visitors; it can be reached by the Aberdeen to Braemar bus (see later in this section).

Braemar is an attractive, small town surrounded by mountains. There's a good regional TIC (☎ 013397-41600), open all year, and the town makes a fine walking base. There are a number of B&Bs, the *Youth Hostel* (☎ 41659) and the *Braemar Bunkhouse* (☎ 41242). The bunkhouse has dorm accommodation from £8. On the first Saturday in September the town is invaded by 20,000 people for the Royal Braemar Gathering (Highland Games); bookings are essential.

It's a beautiful drive between Perth and Braemar. Check whether the summer bus service known as the Bluebird Heather Hopper (☎ 01738-629339) has been reinstated on this route. From Aberdeen to Braemar there are several buses a day operated by Bluebird Buses (☎ 01224-212266), which travel along the beautiful valley of the River Dee.

The direct inland route from Aberdeen to Inverness, serviced by bus and train, cuts across rolling agricultural country that, thanks to a mild climate, produces everything from grain to flower bulbs. The grain is turned into a magical liquid known as malt whisky. Aficionados might be tempted by the Malt Whisky Trail (information from TICs) which gives you an inside look and complimentary tastings at a number of famous distilleries (including Cardhu, Glenfiddich and Glenlivet).

Aberdeen

Aberdeen is an extraordinary symphony in grey. Almost everything is built of granite. In the sun, especially after a shower of rain, the stone turns silver and shines like a fairy tale, but with low grey clouds and rain scudding in off the North Sea it can all be a bit much.

Aberdeen was a prosperous North Sea trading and fishing port centuries before oil was considered a valuable commodity. Now it services one of the largest oilfields in the world. Start with 200,000 Scots, add multinational oil workers and a large student population – the result: a thriving nightlife.

Orientation & Information Aberdeen is built on a ridge that runs east-west to the north of the train and bus stations (next to each other off Guild St) and the ferry quay. Open year round, the TIC (☎ 01224-632727) is in St Nicholas House, Broad St.

Places to Stay The *Youth Hostel* (☎ 646988), 8 Queen's Rd, is 1½ miles from the train station. It's open all year except January. Walk east along Union St and take the right fork along Albyn Place until you reach a roundabout; Queen's Rd continues on the eastern side.

There are batches of B&Bs, which centre on Bon Accord St and Springbank Terrace (both close to the centre) and Great Western Rd (the A93, a 20-minute walk); they're more expensive than is usually the case in Scotland. *Crynoch Guest House* (☎ 582743), 164 Bon Accord St, has singles/doubles for £18/30. Around the corner at 63 Springbank Terrace, *Nicoll's Guest House* (☎ 572867) is a friendly place with rooms at around £20/30. There are plenty of other alternatives.

Places to Eat The *Lemon Tree* (☎ 621610), West North St, is an excellent café attached to the theatre of the same name. It's open daily from 10 am to 5 pm; there's great coffee, cakes and lunches that are good value.

Despite its wimpy name, *Owlies Brasserie* (☎ 649267), in Littlejohn St, is highly recommended and very popular. French-run, it produces tasty food with unusual flavours and it has the best range of vegetarian food in Aberdeen. Main dishes start at £4.

There's a branch of the reliable chain *Littlejohn's* (☎ 635666) on School Hill. For a classier ambience and delicious patisserie, try the *Wild Boar* (☎ 625357), 19 Belmont St.

The *Prince of Wales*, 7 St Nicholas Lane, is a good, traditional pub. There are many others

up and down Union St and Belmont St, some with live music.

Getting There & Away For transport around the region, see the preceding Getting Around section under Eastern Highlands. Also see the Rail and Coach/Bus fares tables in this chapter's introductory Getting Around section.

Bus & Train Scottish Citylink (☎ 0990-505050) has daily buses from London, but it's a tedious 12-hour trip. There are numerous trains from London's King's Cross station taking an acceptable seven hours, although they are more expensive. Bluebird Buses (☎ 212266) is the major local bus operator, with reasonable coverage of the Aberdeenshire region.

Ferry P&O (☎ 572615) has daily sailings from Monday to Friday leaving in the evening for Lerwick (Shetland). The trip takes approximately 14 hours. A reclining seat will cost £46/52 in the low/high season, one way. In summer there are departures on Tuesday and Saturday to Stromness (Orkney); 10 hours, £35/38. The passenger terminal is a short walk east of the train and bus stations.

WESTERN HIGHLANDS

This is the Highlands of the tour bus, but there are also some unspoilt peninsulas and serious mountains where you can be very isolated. The scenery is unquestionably dramatic – Ben Nevis is Britain's highest mountain (1343 metres); brooding Glencoe still seems haunted by the massacre of the MacDonalds; the Cowal and Kintyre peninsulas have a magic of their own; and Loch Lomond may be a tourist cliché but is still very beautiful.

This area provides challenges for the most experienced and well-equipped mountaineers, rock climbers and walkers, but there are also moderate walks that are quite safe if you are properly equipped and take the normal precautions. The West Highland Way runs 95 miles between Fort William and Glasgow.

Orientation & Information

Fort William is a major tourist centre, easily reached by bus and train and a good base for the mountains. Oban is the most important ferry port for boats to the Inner Hebrides (Mull, Coll, Tiree, Colonsay, Jura and Islay) and the Outer Hebridean islands of South Uist and Barra. There's a reasonable scattering of SYHA hostels, including those at Glencoe, Oban and Crianlarich. There are also independent bunkhouses at Glencoe, Onich and Corpach.

Getting There & Around
Although the road network is comprehensive, travel around this region is still difficult – many of the roads are single-track switchbacks with sparse traffic.

Bus Out of Glasgow, Scottish Citylink (☎ 0990-505050) and its subsidiary Skye-Ways (☎ 01599-534328), are the main operators, with daily connections to Oban (three hours, £9.50), Fort William (three hours, £9.50) and Inverness (from 3½ hours, £10.30). Highland Country Buses (☎ 01397-702373) also runs buses along these routes for similar prices.

Train The spectacular West Highland Line runs north to Fort William and Mallaig, with a spur to Oban from Crianlarich. There are four trains a day to Oban (three hours) from Monday to Saturday, and one or two on Sunday. There are the same number of Glasgow to Fort William trains (3¾ hours). The West Highland Rover ticket (£39) gives unlimited travel for four days in an eight-day period.

Fort William
Fort William has lost any charm it may once have had to modern development. It's an excellent base for the mountains but don't plan on hanging around.

The town meanders along the edge of Loch Linnhe for a number of miles. The rather bleak centre and its small selection of shops, takeaways and pubs is easy to get around on foot unless you're staying at a very far-flung B&B. The TIC (☎ 01397-703781) is in the centre of town in Cameron Square, and is open all year. Bicycles are available from Off-Beat Bikes (☎ 704008), 117 High St.

Fort William Backpackers' Guest House (☎ 700711), Alma Rd, is a short walk from the station. It costs £8.50 per night and is very popular. Three miles from Fort William, up magical Glen Nevis, there's the *Glen Nevis Youth Hostel* (☎ 702336) and, across the river, *Ben Nevis Bunkhouse* (☎ 702240), Achintee Farm (£6).

There are several other independent hostels in the area – the TIC has details. In beautiful Glencoe, 16 miles from Fort William, there's the *Leacantuim Farm Bunkhouse* (☎ 01855-811256) and, close by, the popular *Glencoe Youth Hostel* (☎ 01855-811219). Particularly favoured by mountain-climbing types, the Glencoe hostel is a 1½-mile walk from the main road, which is the Fort William to Glasgow bus route.

Getting There & Away See the preceding Western Highlands Getting Around section, and the Rail and Coach/Bus fares tables in this chapter's introductory Getting Around section.

Fort William is at the northern end of the West Highland Way which runs to Glasgow. This is an excellent walk through some of Scotland's finest scenery. Parts of the Way can be tackled, or the whole 95 miles could easily be walked in a week. If you do plan to walk the whole route, it's best to start in Glasgow and walk north. The best map/guide is Harveys Walker's Route *West Highland Way* (£5.95), which also gives tourist information. The TICs have a free brochure listing accommodation.

Oban
Oban can be inundated by visitors, but as the most important ferry port on the west coast it manages to hold its own. Although quite a large town by Highland standards, you can easily get around it on foot. There isn't a great deal to see or do, but it's on a beautiful bay, the harbour is interesting and there are some lovely coastal and hill walks in the vicinity.

The bus, train and ferry terminals are all grouped conveniently together by the side of the harbour. The TIC (☎ 01631-563122) on Argyll Square, one block behind the harbour, is open all year and until 9 pm in summer. The *Oban Backpackers Lodge* (☎ 562107), Breadalbane St, charges £8.50. There are numerous B&Bs in this area. The *Youth Hostel* (☎ 562025) is on the Esplanade to the north of town, on the other side of the bay to the terminals.

Getting There & Away See the introductory Getting Around sections for Scotland at the start of this chapter. Numerous CalMac (☎ 562285) boats link Oban with the Inner and Outer Hebrides (Lochboisdale). There are six ferries a day to Craignure (Mull); the trip takes 40 minutes and costs £3.05.

NORTHERN HIGHLANDS & ISLANDS

Forget the castles (although there are some romantic ruins), and forget the towns and villages (more often than not they are plain and utilitarian). The Highlands and Islands are all about mountains, sea, heather, moors, lakes – and wide, empty, exhilarating space. This is one of Europe's last great wildernesses, and it's more beautiful than you can imagine.

The east coast is dramatic, but it's the north and west, where the mountains and sea collide, that exhaust superlatives. Orkney and Shetland are bleak and beautiful, and the Outer Hebrides are the last stronghold of Gaelic culture and the old crofting ways.

Orientation & Information

For more information on the Hebrides, contact the Western Isles Tourist Board (☎ 01851-703088), 26 Cromwell St, Stornoway, Isle of Lewis HS1 2DD.

Getting There & Around

This is a remote and scarcely populated region, so you need to be well organised or have plenty of time if you are relying on public transport. All transport services are drastically reduced after September so double-check timetables in the off season. Car rentals are available in Inverness, Oban and Stornoway, and if you can get a group together, this can be a worthwhile option.

Air British Airways Express (☎ 0345-222111) has daily flights to Benbecula, Stornoway and Inverness, and from Inverness to the Outer Hebrides. They have daily scheduled flights from Glasgow to the beach airport at Barra, to Benbecula and to Stornoway on the Outer Hebrides, and also fly regularly from Glasgow to Inverness and from Edinburgh to Wick.

Bus Wick, Thurso, Ullapool and Kyle of Lochalsh can all be reached by regular buses from Inverness, or from Edinburgh and Glasgow; contact Scottish Citylink (☎ 0990-505050) and Highland Country Buses (☎ 01463-233371) in Inverness. The major problem is in the far north-west where there is no straightforward link around the coast between Thurso and Ullapool.

Train The Highland lines are all justly famous. There are two routes from Inverness: up the east coast to Thurso, and west to Kyle of Lochalsh (see the Inverness section for details). There's also a regular train from Glasgow to Oban, Fort William and Mallaig (for Skye and the Inner Hebrides). Contact ScotRail on ☎ 0345-484950 for more information.

Ferry CalMac (☎ 01475-650100) sails car and passenger ferries to all the major islands. The ferries can be expensive, especially if you're taking a vehicle. Check out Island Rover tickets for unlimited travel between islands for eight or 15 days and Island Hopscotch tickets that offer various route combinations at reduced rates. Inter-island ferry timetables depend on tides and weather so check departures with TICs.

Inverness

Inverness is the capital of the Highlands, and the hub for Highlands transport. It's a pleasant place to while away a few days although it lacks major attractions. In summer it crawls with visitors. Fortunately, most are intrepid monster hunters and their next stops will be Loch Ness and Fort William.

Orientation & Information The River Ness flows through the town from the loch to Moray Firth. The bus and train stations, the TIC and the hostels are all on the eastern side of the river within 10 minutes walk of each other. The TIC (☎ 01463-234353) is on Bridge St in the corner of the museum building. In summer it's open from 9 am daily.

Places to Stay & Eat In peak season it's best to start looking for accommodation early;

better still, book a bed ahead. The Inverness TIC charges a hefty £2 for local bookings.

The three hostels are clustered together, just 10 minutes from the train or bus station and just past the castle. The *Inverness Student Hotel* (☎ 236556), 8 Culduthel Rd, is in the same family as the High St Hostel in Edinburgh – you can make phone bookings from there. It's a friendly, homy place with a great view, and costs £8.50. Across the road, the *Youth Hostel* (☎ 231771), 1 Old Edinburgh Rd, is very busy at Easter and in July and August. A little further down the hill *Bazpackers Backpackers Hotel* (☎ 717663) is clean and new and charges £8.50 a head.

Within easy walking distance of town (on the eastern side) there's *Crownleigh Guest House* (☎ 220316), 6 Midmills Rd, and *Leinster Lodge Guest House* (☎ 233311), 27 Southside Rd.

Heathfield Guest House (☎ 230547), 2 Kenneth St, is immaculate. These places all cost around £15 to £18 per person. Old Edinburgh Rd and Kenneth St have plenty of B&Bs; cheaper places can be found along Argyle St, and more expensive, if very inviting ones along the river.

Near the hostels, the *Castle Restaurant* (☎ 230925), 41 Castle St, is cheap and cheerful. *Littlejohn's* (☎ 713005) at 28/30 Church St is bright and noisy with a very descriptive menu. The *River Café and Restaurant* near the footbridge over the river is a pleasant place for a snack.

Getting There & Away Many people take tours from Inverness to Loch Ness, and there's a wide variety costing from £5 to £10. See the introductory Getting Around sections for Scotland and Britain.

Bus Scottish Citylink (☎ 0990-505050) has bus connections with a number of major centres in England, including London via Perth and Glasgow. There are numerous buses to and from Glasgow (3½ hours, £10.30) and Edinburgh via Perth (four hours, £11.20).

There are two buses a day for Ullapool (1½ hours, £6.30), connecting with the CalMac ferry to Stornoway on Lewis (not on Sunday). The 3½-hour ferry trip costs £11.05.

Highland Country Buses (☎ 233371) oper-ates two buses a day (one on Sunday) travelling from Inverness to Kyle of Lochalsh and on to Portree on Skye. The total journey takes three hours and costs £8. From Portree there are buses to Uig, whence there are ferries to Tarbert on Harris and Lochmaddy on North Uist (both destinations cost £7.35).

There are three Citylink buses a day for Thurso and Scrabster (3¾ hours, £8.10), connecting with ferries to Orkney. From late April to early September the Orkney Bus (☎ 01955-611353) operates a daily bus from Inverness to John O'Groats, connecting straight through to Kirkwall. It costs £12 to John O'Groats, £22 to Orkney or £35 for a return permitting a stop-over in John O'Groats.

It's possible to head up to the north-west through Lairg. Inverness Traction (☎ 239292) has a Monday to Saturday service (Sunday as well in summer). The service goes through to Durness in summer, and there is also a Monday to Saturday postbus (☎ 256228) covering the Lairg-Tongue-Durness route. The Inverness bus station number is ☎ 233371.

Train The two onward train journeys from Inverness are both famous; the line to Kyle of Lochalsh, however, is one of the greatest scenic journeys in Britain. There are three trains a day on both routes (none on Sunday). The trip to Kyle of Lochalsh (2½ hours, £13.50) leaves you within walking distance of the pier for buses across the new Skye Bridge. The trip to Thurso (3¾ hours, £11.50) connects with the ferry to Orkney. From Inverness to and from Glasgow or Edinburgh costs £26.50.

Car & Bicycle The TIC has a list of the numerous car and bicycle-rental operators; book ahead in summer. The big car agencies all have branches (and charge around £36 per day), or you could try Sharp's Reliable Wrecks (☎ 236694), 1st floor, Highland Rail House, Station Square. Sharp's also rents bicycles, as do Thornton Cycles (☎ 222810) at 23 Castle St, Clive Rowland Mountain Sports (☎ 238746) at 9/11 Bridge St and Pedalway Mountain Bike Hire (☎ 233456) at 7 Lovat Rd.

East Coast
The coast really starts to get interesting when you leave behind the industrial development at

Invergordon. Great, heather-covered hills heave themselves out of the wild North Sea, with towns like Dornoch and Helmsdale moored precariously at its edge.

There are SYHA hostels at *Carbisdale Castle* (☎ 01549-421232) and *Helmsdale* (☎ 01431-821577). Book early for Helmsdale in midsummer. Don't miss Wick's wonderful heritage museum (summer only) but otherwise keep going to John O'Groats and beyond.

John O'Groats By Scottish standards, the coast at the island's north-eastern tip is understated, and John O'Groats is nothing more than a second-rate tourist trap – but there is something magical about the view across the water to Orkney. There's a *Youth Hostel* (☎ 01955-611424) at Canisbay just beyond John O'Groats, open April through October. There are regular buses Monday to Saturday from Wick (£2.25) and Thurso (£2.20), but none on Sunday. Passenger ferries shuttle across from John O'Groats to Orkney and offer a free connection from the Thurso train station.

Thurso & Scrabster Thurso is a largish, bleak town overlooking the north Atlantic. It's the end of the line, both for the east-coast railway and the big bus lines. Surprisingly, the nearby coast has arguably the best and most regular surf in Britain. On the eastern side of town, directly in front of Lord Caithness' castle, there's a right-hand reef break. There's another shallow reef break five miles west at Brimms Ness.

The TIC (☎ 01847-892371), Riverside, is open Easter to October, every day in midsummer. In July and August the *Thurso Youth Club* (☎ 892964), Old Mill, Millbank, has dorm accommodation for £8 with breakfast. There are plenty of B&Bs around town. The *Fountain Restaurant* (☎ 896351) at 2 Sinclair St serves Chinese, Indian and European food.

The Bike & Camping Shop (☎ 896124), The Arcade, 34 High St, has mountain bikes for £6.50 a day.

Scrabster, from where car ferries run to Orkney, is a two-mile walk or a 70p bus ride from Thurso.

Orkney Islands
Just six miles off the north coast of Scotland, this magical group of islands is known for its dramatic coastal scenery (which ranges from 300-metre cliffs to white, sandy beaches) and abundant marine-bird life, and for a plethora of prehistoric sites, including an entire 4500-year-old village at Skara Brae. If you're anywhere in the area around mid-June, don't miss the St Magnus Arts Festival.

Twenty of these 70 islands are inhabited. Kirkwall, with 6000 inhabitants, is the main town, and Stromness the major port; both are on the largest island, which is known as Mainland. The land is treeless, but lush and level rather than rugged. The climate, warmed by the Gulf Stream, is surprisingly moderate, with April and May being the driest months. Contact the TIC (☎ 01856-872856), 6 Broad St, Kirkwall KW15 1NX for more information.

Places to Stay There's a good selection of cheap B&Bs, six SYHA hostels and four independent hostels.

In Stromness, the *Youth Hostel* (☎ 850589) is a 10-minute walk from the ferry. Also in Stromness, *Brown's Hostel* (☎ 850661) is popular, and charges £7.50. On beautiful Papa Westray, the most northerly island, the excellent *Papa Westray Hostel* (☎ 01857-644267), Orkney KW17 2BU, is open all year.

Getting There & Away There are car ferries from Scrabster, near Thurso, to Stromness operated by P&O (☎ 850655). There's at least one departure a day all year, with single fares around £14. P&O also sails from Aberdeen (see that section).

John O'Groats Ferry (☎ 01955-611353) has a passenger ferry from John O'Groats to Burwick on South Ronaldsay from May to September. A one-way ticket is £13, but the company also offers an excellent special deal: a return fare of £20 as long as you leave John O'Groats in the afternoon, and Orkney in the morning. A free bus meets the afternoon train from Inverness, and a bus for Kirkwall (20 miles away) meets the ferry in Burwick.

Shetland Islands
Sixty miles north of Orkney, the Shetland Islands remained under Norse rule until 1469, when they were given to Scotland as part of a Danish princess' dowry. Even today, these remote, windswept and treeless islands are

almost as much a part of Scandinavia as of Britain – the nearest mainland town is Bergen, Norway.

Much bleaker than Orkney, Shetland is famous for its varied bird life, its rugged coastline and a 4000-year-old archaeological heritage. There are 15 inhabited islands and a population of 23,000. Lerwick is the largest town on Mainland Shetland, which is used as a base for the North Sea oilfields. Oil has brought a certain amount of prosperity to the islands. There are well-equipped leisure centres in many villages, and the wide roads seem like motorways after Orkney's tiny, winding lanes.

Small ferries connect a handful of the smaller islands. Contact the TIC (☎ 01595-693434), Lerwick ZE1 0LU, for information on B&Bs and camping *böds* (barns). The *Youth Hostel* (☎ 692114) is open from April to October.

Getting There & Away Lerwick can be reached by P&O ferries from Aberdeen (see the Aberdeen Getting There & Away section), or from Orkney – leaving Stromness on Tuesday morning and Sunday evening (eight hours, £35/70 for a single/return). British Airways Express (☎ 0345-222111) operates low-flying ATPs (with great views of the islands) daily between Orkney and Shetland, from £55 return if you spend Saturday night away. See Scotland's introductory Getting There & Away section for ferry links to Scandinavia.

North Coast
The coast from Dounreay, with its nuclear power station, around to Ullapool is mindblowing. Everything is on a massive scale: vast emptiness, enormous lochs and snowcapped mountains. The unreliable weather and terrible public transport are the only drawbacks. There are two *SYHA hostels*: one at Tongue (☎ 01847-611301), with a spectacular lochside location, and another at Durness (☎ 01971-511244).

Transport in the north-west is very patchy. Thurso by bus or train is no problem, but from there your troubles start. Monday to Saturday there are Thurso to Bettyhill (east of Tongue) services, but they travel no further along the

coast. Your only hope is the school buses, which only operate during school time and take passengers only if the driver is willing.

The alternative is to come up to the coast from Inverness via the town of Lairg. There are trains and Inverness Traction buses to Lairg, but neither have services on Sunday. In summer Inverness Traction continues to Durness. The post office operates postbus services (☎ 01463-256228) from Monday to Saturday, covering Lairg-Tongue-Durness and Lairg to Lochinver, and around the coast between Elphin and Scourie, Drumbeg and Lochinver and Shieldaig-Applecross-Kishorn. These services all leave gaps between towns. There are regular bus services between Inverness and Ullapool. Renting cars or hitching are the other options.

West Coast
Ullapool is the most northerly town of any significance and the jumping-off point for the Isle of Lewis. There's more brilliant coast round to Gairloch, along the incomparable Loch Maree and down to the Kyle of Lochalsh and Skye. From here on you are well and truly back in the land of the tour bus; civilisation (or whatever it is you find in Fort William) is a shock.

Ullapool The small fishing village of Ullapool attracts the crowds because it is easily accessible along beautiful Loch Broom from Inverness. Everything is strung along the harbour, including the *Youth Hostel* (☎ 01854-612254), but the TIC (☎ 612135) is in Argyle St, one block inland. The hostel is open from mid-March through October; book ahead in Easter and summer. There are a great many B&Bs. Try the *Ceilidh Place* (☎ 612103) for food and entertainment.

See the Inverness Getting There & Away section for the ferry to Stornoway on the Isle of Lewis, and bus connections.

Kyle of Lochalsh Kyle, as it is known, is a small village that overlooks the lovely island of Skye across the narrow Loch Alsh. There's a TIC (☎ 01599-534276) in the car park, but the nearest hostels are just across the loch on Skye. The *Seagreen Café* (☎ 534388) on Plockton Rd has good wholefood dishes.

BRITAIN

The new, and controversial, Skye Bridge charges £4.30 one way for a car, rising to £5.20 in summer.

Kyle can be reached by bus and train from Inverness (see that section), and by direct Scottish Citylink buses from Glasgow (five hours, £13.80), which continue across to Kyleakin and on to Uig (6½ hours, £16) for ferries to Tarbert on Harris and Lochmaddy on North Uist.

Skye

Skye is a large, rugged island, 50 miles north to south and east to west. The island is ringed by beautiful coastline and is dominated by the Cuillins, immensely popular for the sport of 'Munro bagging' – climbing the Scottish mountains which top 3000 feet (914 metres). Tourism is a mainstay of the island economy, so until you get off the main roads, don't expect to escape from the hordes. Contact the Portree TIC (☎ 01478-612137) for more information. Bicycles can be hired from Bikes of Skye (☎ 01599-534795) in Kyleakin, Island Cycles (☎ 01478-613121) in Portree and Fairwinds Cycle Hire (☎ 01471-822270) in Broadford.

Places to Stay & Eat There are more than a dozen SYHA and independent hostels on the island and numerous B&Bs. The SYHA hostels most relevant to ferry users are at *Kyleakin* (☎ 01599-534585) for Kyle of Lochalsh, which is open all year; *Uig* (☎ 01470-542211) for the Western Isles, which is open from Easter to October; and *Armadale* (☎ 01471-844260) for Mallaig, which is also open from Easter to October.

The pick of the independent pack is *Skye Backpackers* (☎ 01599-534510), Kyleakin, a short walk from the Skye Bridge. There's a friendly atmosphere, beds at £8.50 and even some double rooms.

There's also the nearby *Fossil Bothy* (☎ 01471-822644), Lower Breakish, and on the west coast there's *Croft Bunkhouse* (☎ 01478-640254).

Portree is the main centre on the island and the *Ben Tianavaig Vegetarian Bistro* (☎ 01478-612152) at 5 Bosville Terrace has excellent food.

Getting There & Away There are still two ferries from the mainland to Skye. CalMac (☎ 01475-650100) operates between Mallaig and Armadale (30 minutes, £2.30). The Mallaig to Armadale ferry does not operate in the winter and it's wise to book. There's also a private Glenelg to Kylerhea service from April through September (not always on Sunday) which also takes 10 minutes and costs 50p.

From Uig on Skye, CalMac has daily services to Lochmaddy on North Uist and (excluding Sunday) to Tarbert on Harris; both destinations take 1¾ hours and cost £7.35.

The beautiful West Highland railway line runs south from Mallaig to Fort William, Oban and Glasgow (five hours all the way). There are three trains a day from Monday to Saturday, and just one on Sunday. In July one train each day is steam operated between Fort William and Mallaig (£6.80).

Outer Hebrides

The Outer Hebrides are bleak, remote and treeless. The climate is fierce – the islands are completely exposed to the gales that sweep in from the Atlantic, and it rains on more than 250 days of the year. Some people find the landscape mournful, but others find that the stark beauty and isolated world of the crofters create a unique and strangely captivating atmosphere.

The islands are much bigger than might be imagined (stretching in a 120-mile arc); those that do fall under the islands' spell will need plenty of time to explore. Don't forget that the Sabbath is strictly observed – nothing moves on a Sunday and it can be hard finding anything to eat. Tarbert (Harris) and Lochmaddy (North Uist) are reasonably pleasant villages, but the real attraction lies in the landscape.

See the Skye and Kyle of Lochalsh sections for details of CalMac ferries to Tarbert and Lochmaddy, and the Oban section for ferries to Lochboisdale. All the TICs are open for late ferry arrivals in summer but close between September and May.

Lewis & Harris Lewis (Stornoway, by ferry from Ullapool) and Harris (Tarbert, by ferry from Uig on Skye) are in fact just one island with a border of high hills between them. Lewis has low, rolling hills and miles of untouched moorland and freshwater lochs; Harris is rugged, with stony mountains bordered by meadows and sweeping, sandy beaches.

Stornoway is the largest town, with a population of 8000; it's not particularly attractive, but does have a reasonable range of facilities, including a TIC (☎ 01851-703088) and several banks. It's also possible to rent cars, but they can't be taken off the islands: contact Arnol Motors (☎ 71548) or Mackinnon Self-Drive (☎ 702984).

Book a B&B by ringing around, or stay at the *Stornoway Hostel* (☎ 703628) at £8 a night. There's also a *hostel*, open all year, at Garenin, 18 miles from Stornoway (buses twice daily). There's at least one bus a day between Tarbert and Stornoway (except Sunday). Alex Dan hires bikes; he can be contacted through the TIC.

Tarbert has a bank, a TIC (☎ 01859-502011, open Easter to October only) and a few shops. The nearest hostel is almost seven miles south at *Stockinish* (☎ 530373); there's one bus a day from Tarbert. There is also a hostel at *Rhenigidale*, 10 miles north of Tarbert; a bus can take you to the end of the road at Maraig, but it's a two-hour walk from there; alternatively, walk the whole way – it's a great hike.

North & South Uist North Uist (Lochmaddy, by ferry from Uig on Skye, or Tarbert or Leverburgh on Harris), Benbecula (by air from Inverness and Glasgow) and South Uist (Lochboisdale, by ferry from Oban) are actually joined by bridge and causeway. These are low, flat, green islands half-drowned by sinuous lochs and open to the sea and sky.

Barra (Castlebay, by ferry from Lochboisdale and, for passengers only, Ludag on South Uist) lies at the southern tip of the island chain and is famous for its wild flowers and glorious white, sandy beaches.

Lochmaddy has a bank, hotel and TIC (☎ 01876-500321). There's a *Youth Hostel* (☎ 500368) open mid-May through September, and you can also stay at the *North Uist Outdoor Centre* (☎ 500438), open all year. Mr Morrison hires bikes and can be contacted through the TIC.

There's one postbus a day between Lochmaddy and Lochboisdale, which also has

a bank and TIC (☎ 01878-700286). The only hostel is at *Howmore* (no phone), 15 miles north on the west coast; it's open all year and there's a bus from Lochboisdale.

Castlebay on Barra has a TIC (☎ 01871-810336) and 20-odd B&Bs, but no hostel.

Wales

Wales has had the misfortune to be so close to England that it could not be allowed its independence, and yet to be far enough away to be conveniently forgotten. It sometimes feels rather like England's unloved back yard – a suitable place for mines, pine plantations and nuclear power stations. Even the most enduring of its symbols – the grim mining towns and powerful castles – represent exploitation and colonialism.

It is almost miraculous that anything Welsh should have survived the onslaught of its dominating neighbour. However, Welsh culture has proved to be remarkably enduring and the language stubbornly refuses to die.

Huge swathes of the countryside have been vandalised by mining, grossly insensitive forestry operations and power lines, but magnificent corners remain. Miles of coastline have been ruined by shoddy bungalows and ugly caravan parks, but some of it is still breathtakingly beautiful.

Wales' appeal lies in its countryside. In general, the towns and cities are not particularly inspiring. The best way to appreciate the Great Welsh Outdoors is by walking, bicycling, canal boating or hitching, or by some other form of private transport. Simply catching buses or trains from one regional hub to another is not recommended. Instead, base yourself in a small town or farm B&B, and explore the surrounding countryside for a few days. Hay-on-Wye, Brecon, St David's, Dolgellau, Llanberis and Betws-y-Coed are possibilities that come to mind.

Much of the most beautiful countryside is now protected by the Pembrokeshire Coast National Park, the Brecon Beacons National Park and the Snowdonia National Park, but the Gower and Lyn peninsulas are also outstanding.

Wales also has an unsurpassed legacy of

BRITAIN

Wales

LP

To Dublin &
Dun Laoghaire
(Ireland)

Holyhead
Bay

Amlwch

Isle of Anglesey

LIVERPOOL

Birkenhead

Widnes

ANGLESEY

Holyhead

Holy
Island

A5

Menai
Bridge

Llangefni

Conwy
Bay

Llandudno

Colwyn Bay

Rhyl

Mersey

M56

0   10   20 km
0   6   12 miles

Caernarfon
Bay

Bangor

Caernarfon

Llanberis

A487

Conwy

Llanfairfechan

Abergele

A55

Holywell

Flint

ABERCONWY
& COLWYN

Denbigh

Chester

CHESHIRE

Llanrwst

DENBIGHSHIRE

Mold

A55

▲ Snowdon
(3560 ft)

Betws-y-Coed

Ruthin

Wrexham

WREXHAM

LLYN

Criccieth

Porthmadog

Blaenau-
Ffestiniog

Ffestiniog

A5

Llangollen

Whitchurch

PENINSULA

Pwllheli

Bala

Snowdonia
National Park

Oswestry

Ellesmere

IRISH

SEA

CAERNARFONSHIRE
& MERIONETHSHIRE

SHROPSHIRE

Llanfyllin

A49

Pembrokeshire
Coast NP

Fishguard

St David's

PEMBROKE-
SHIRE

Haverfordwest

Milford
Haven

To Rosslare

Pembroke

Pembrokeshire
Coast NP

Same Scale as Main Map

Barmouth

Dolgellau

CARDIGAN
BAY

Tywyn

Machynlleth

A458

Welshpool

Shrewsbury

M

O

U

N

T

A

I

N

S

A487

Newtown

Church
Stretton

Aberystwyth

A44

Llanidloes

POWYS

Bishop's
Castle

Ludlow

Knighton

A49

Aberaeron

CARDIGANSHIRE

New Quay

Tregaron

Wye

Llandrindod
Wells

A44

Kington

Leominster

HEREFORD &
WORCESTER

Cardigan

Lampeter

C

A

M

B

R

I

A

N

Llanwrtyd
Wells

Builth
Wells

Hay-on-
Wye

Hereford

Fishguard

Newcastle
Emlyn

Teifi

Llandovery

Brecon

E

N

G

L

A

N

D

Pembrokeshire
Coast
National Park

CARMARTHENSHIRE

Llandeilo

A40

Brecon Beacons
National Park

PEMBROKE-
SHIRE

GOWER PENINSULA

Carmarthen

Llandeilo

Abergavenny

Monmouth

A40

Haverfordwest

A40

Narberth

Ammanford

Ebbw Vale

MONMOUTH-
SHIRE

See
Inset

Kidwelly

Tywi

Blaenafon

Usk

To
Rosslare
(Ireland)

A487

To Cork (Ireland)

Pembroke

Tenby

Llanelli

M4

NEATH &
PORT
TALBOT

Neath

Merthyr
Tydfil

Mountain Ash

Pontypool

Pontypridd

Cwmbran

Caerphilly

Chepstow

A449

M4

Pembrokeshire
Coast
National Park

Carmarthen
Bay

Swansea

SWANSEA

Port
Talbot

Maesteg

A470

Newport

M5

BRISTOL CHANNEL

Porthcawl

Bridgend

Cowbridge

CARDIFF

VALE OF
GLAMORGAN

Penarth

Mouth of the Severn

Barry

Weston-Super-Mare

BRITAIN

magnificent medieval castles. All of the following are within a mile of a train station: Caerphilly, north of Cardiff; Kidwelly, north of Llanelli; Harlech, south of Porthmadog; Caernarfon, in the north-west; and Conwy, near Llandudno in the north.

FACTS ABOUT THE COUNTRY
History
The Celts arrived from their European homeland sometime after 500 BC. Little is known about them, although it is to their Celtic forebears that the modern Welsh attribute national characteristics like eloquence, warmth and imagination.

The Romans invaded in 43 AD, and for the next 400 years kept close control over the Welsh tribes from their garrison towns at Chester and Caerlon. From the 5th century to the 11th, the Welsh were under almost constant pressure from the Anglo-Saxon invaders of England. In the 8th century, a Mercian king, Offa, constructed a dyke marking the boundary between the Welsh and the Mercians. Offa's Dyke can still be seen today – in fact you can walk its length.

The Celtic princes failed to unite Wales, and local wars were frequent. However, in 927, faced with the destructive onslaught of the Vikings, the Welsh kings recognised Athelstan, the Anglo-Saxon king of England, as their overlord in exchange for an alliance against the Vikings.

By the time the Normans arrived in England, the Welsh had returned to their warring, independent ways. To secure his new kingdom, William I set up powerful feudal barons along the Welsh borders. The Lords Marcher, as they were known, developed virtually unfettered wealth and power and began to advance on the lowlands of south and mid-Wales.

Edward I, the great warrior king, finally conquered Wales in a bloody campaign. In 1302 the title of Prince of Wales was given to the monarch's eldest son, a tradition that continues today. To maintain his authority, Edward built the great castles of Rhuddlan, Conwy, Beaumaris, Caernarfon and Harlech.

The last doomed Welsh revolt began in 1400 under Owain Glyndwr and was crushed by Henry IV. In 1536 and 1543, the Acts of Union made Wales, for all intents and purposes, another region of England.

From the turn of the 18th century, Wales, with its plentiful coal and iron, became the most important source of Britain's pig iron. By the end of the 19th century, almost a third of the world's coal exports came from Wales, and an enormous network of mining villages, with their unique culture of Methodism, rugby and male-voice choirs, had developed.

The 20th century, especially the 1960s, 1970s and 1980s, saw the coal industry and the associated steel industry collapse. Large-scale unemployment persists as Wales attempts to move to more high-tech and service industries. Tourism is now a major industry accounting for almost 10% of all jobs in the principality.

Geography
Wales has two major mountain systems: the Black Mountains and Brecon Beacons in the south, and the more dramatic mountains of Snowdonia in the north-west. The population is concentrated in the south-east along the coast between Cardiff and Swansea and the old mining valleys that run north into the Brecon Beacons. Wales is approximately 170 miles long and 60 miles wide. Cardiff is the capital.

Population
Wales has a population of 2.9 million – around 5% of the total population of Britain.

Language
Welsh is now only spoken by some 500,000 people, mainly in the north, although a major effort is being made to reverse its slide into extinction. Although almost everyone speaks English, there is Welsh TV and radio, and most signs are now bilingual.

At first sight, Welsh looks impossibly difficult to get your tongue around. Once you know that 'dd' is pronounced 'th', 'w' can also be a vowel pronounced 'oo', 'f' is 'v' and 'ff' is 'f', and you've had a native speaker teach you how to pronounce 'll' (roughly 'cl'), you'll be able to ask the way to Llanfairpwllgwyngllgogerychwyrndrobwllllantysiliogogogoch (a village in Anglesey reputed to have Britain's longest place name – no joke) and be understood. Try the following (pronunciation in brackets):

Bore da (bora-da) Good morning
Shw'mae (shoo-my) Hello

BRITAIN

Peint o gwrw (paint-o-guru)	Pint of beer
Diolch yn fawr (diolkh in far)	Thank you
Da boch (da bokh)	Goodbye

FACTS FOR THE VISITOR

Planning

Climate & When to Go The climate is unpredictable: the closeness of the mountains to the coast creates conditions that can vary widely over a short distance. May/June and September/October are the best months to visit. July/August can be very wet, and very crowded.

Tourist Offices

Outside of Britain, contact the BTA for information (see Tourist Offices in the Facts for the Visitor section at the start of this chapter). The Wales Tourist Board (☎ 01222-499909) has its headquarters at Brunel House, 2 Fitzalan Rd, Cardiff CF2 1UY, and also operates a branch at the British Travel Centre (☎ 0171-409 0969), 12 Regent St, Piccadilly Circus, London SW1Y 4PQ.

Most major towns in Wales have TICs that are open weekdays from 9 am to 5 pm, sometimes extending to weekends during the summer. In small places, TICs only open from Easter to September.

Visas & Customs

No visas are required if you arrive from England. If you arrive from the Republic of Ireland or any other country, normal British regulations apply (see the introductory Facts for the Visitor section at the beginning of this chapter).

Money

The same currency is used on both sides of the border. Wales is less expensive than England. As a general rule, accommodation and food are around 15% cheaper.

Business Hours & Public Holidays

Business hours and holidays are the same as in England. In the countryside, shops often close early on Wednesday.

Activities

Hiking Wales has numerous popular walks; the most challenging are in the rocky Snowdonia National Park (around Llanberis and Betws-y-Coed) and the grassy Brecon Beacons National Park (around Brecon). There are seven long-distance walks, the most famous being the Pembrokeshire Coast Path and Offa's Dyke Path.

Most of the 186-mile Pembrokeshire Coast Path is in the Pembrokeshire Coast National Park, an area rich in coastal scenery and historical associations. From Amroth to Cardigan, there are wide, sandy beaches; rocky, windswept cliffs; and picturesque villages. Accommodation is widely available and it is easy to undertake shorter sections. The walk can be crowded on summer weekends. *The Pembrokeshire Coast Path* by Brian John (Aurum Press, £9.99) has maps and detailed information. The National Park people publish an accommodation guide; phone ☎ 01437-764636 for further info.

Offa's Dyke Path follows the English/Welsh border for 168 miles from Chepstow on the River Severn, through the beautiful Wye Valley and Shropshire Hills and ending on the north Wales coast at Prestatyn. There are two guides (*Chepstow to Knighton* and *Knighton to Prestatyn*) by Ernie & Kathy McKay & Mark Richards (Aurum Press, £9.99 each). The *Offa's Dyke Path Accommodation & Transport* guide is available from the Ramblers' Association (☎ 0171-582 6878) for £1.50 plus 70p UK p&p.

Surfing The south-west coast of Wales has a number of surf spots. From east to west, try Porthcawl, Oxwich Bay, Rhossili, Manorbier, Freshwater West and Whitesands.

Accommodation

The YHA (England & Wales) publishes a single accommodation guide, available from YHA Adventure Shops and from many hostels.

There are reasonably priced B&Bs everywhere you look. The TICs have local booking services (free) and a Book-a-Bed-Ahead scheme allowing you to book 24 hours in advance. This is worth using in July and August, but is not necessary outside this peak time, unless you are going to arrive at your destination late.

Always check with landowners before pitching a tent; this includes the national parks, which are all privately owned. Commercial camping grounds are geared to caravans and vary widely in quality. A tent site will cost around £5. If you plan to use a tent regularly, invest in the AA's *Camping & Caravanning in Britain* (£7.99).

GETTING THERE & AWAY
Land
Bus Long-distance buses (coaches) are the cheapest method of getting to Wales. National Express (☎ 0990-808080) has routes from London and Bristol along the south coast through Cardiff to Pembroke (for ferries to Ireland), from Birmingham through Shrewsbury to Aberystwyth and from Chester and the Midlands along the north coast to Holyhead (for ferries to Ireland).

London to Cardiff should cost around £20 (£4.50 more if you travel on a Friday). As in England, return tickets usually cost only a fraction more than singles. London to Pembroke takes six hours and costs £25.

Train InterCity services can take you from London's Paddington station (☎ 0171-262 6767) to Cardiff in as little as 1¾ hours, or to Fishguard (for the Ireland ferry) in four hours. A SuperSaver return ticket from Cardiff to London will cost £28 – about the same price as a single. Fast InterCity trains also link south Wales with Birmingham, York and Newcastle.

There are also trains from London's Euston station (☎ 0171-387 7070) to north Wales and Holyhead via Birmingham, Chester and Llandudno. There are about five trains a day from Euston to Holyhead; they take 4½ hours and a SuperSaver ticket costs £43.

Car & Motorcycle Motorways bring you into Wales quickly and easily. The three-mile long Second Severn Crossing, Britain's longest bridge, opened in June 1996 downstream from the old Severn Bridge. The M4 travels west from London, across either bridge (both £3.80 toll, westbound traffic only) and deep into south Wales. The A55 coastal expressway whisks traffic along the north coast. London to Cardiff is 155 miles and takes about three hours.

Sea
There are ferry links with Ireland from four towns in Wales: Holyhead, in the north-west,

to Dublin (Irish Ferries) and Dun Laoghaire, near Dublin (Stena Line); Pembroke, in the south-west, to Rosslare in south-east Ireland (Irish Ferries); Fishguard, in the south-west, to Rosslare (Stena Line); and, from March to early January, from Swansea to Cork (Swansea Cork Ferries). See the Ireland chapter for details.

GETTING AROUND
Distances in Wales are small, but, with the exception of links around the coast, public-transport users have to fall back on infrequent and complicated bus timetables.

Bus
The major operators serving Wales are Crosville Cymru (☎ 01492-596969), for the north and west, and South Wales Transport (☎ 01792-580580). There are Rover tickets available that can be very good value. For example, the Crosville Day Rover, covering all points north and west of Shrewsbury, costs £5.70 a day.

Crosville has two particularly useful daily Traws Cambria services, but there's only one bus a day each way. The 701 (west coast) link runs between Cardiff, Swansea, Carmarthen, Aberystwyth, Porthmadog, Caernarfon and Bangor. Cardiff to Aberystwyth (four hours) costs £9.70; Aberystwyth to Porthmadog (two hours) costs £7.30. Service No 702 runs north from Cardiff along the border with England, via Brecon to Chester.

Bus Gwynedd (☎ 01286-679535) is a council-sponsored network of buses operating in the north-western corner of Wales – from Llandudno to Machynlleth, including all of Snowdonia. Those using a British Rail North & Mid-Wales Rover ticket (see the following section) can travel free on these buses as well. Bus Gwynedd public-transport guides are available at TICs.

Train
Wales has some fantastic train lines – mainline services (☎ 01222-228000) and narrow-gauge survivors. Apart from the main lines along the north and south coasts to the Irish ferry ports, there are some interesting lines that converge on Shrewsbury (see Getting There & Away in the Shrewsbury section). The lines along the

BRITAIN

west coast, and down the Conwy Valley, are exceptional.

There are several Rover tickets: the North & Mid-Wales Regional Rover gives seven days travel north of Aberystwyth and Shrewsbury – plus Bus Gwynedd services (which means virtually all north-western buses) and the Blaenau Ffestiniog Railway – for £36/23.75; the Flexi Rover ticket for the same area allows travel on three days out of seven for £23/15.20; the Freedom of Wales Rover gives seven days travel for £54/35.65. Again, see also the Getting There & Away information in the Shrewsbury section.

SOUTH WALES

The valleys of the Usk and Wye, with their castles and Tintern Abbey, are beautiful, but can be packed with day-trippers. The south coast from Newport to Swansea is heavily industrialised, and the valleys running north into the Black Mountains and the Brecon Beacons National Park are still struggling to come to grips with the loss of the coal-mining industry.

Even so, the little villages that form a continuous chain along the valleys have their own stark beauty and the people are very friendly. The traditional market town of Abergavenny is also worth a look. The Big Pit (☎ 01495-790311), near Blaenafon, gives you a chance to experience life underground, and guided tours by former miners (£5.50/3.50) are highly recommended.

The Black Mountains and Brecon Beacons have majestic, open scenery and their northern flanks overlook some of the most beautiful country in Wales.

Cardiff

The Welsh are proudly defensive of their capital, which has rapidly been transformed from a dull provincial backwater into a prosperous university city with an increasingly lively arts scene.

Cardiff Castle is worth seeing for its outrageous interior refurbishment. Revamped by the Victorians, it's more Hollywood than medieval. Nearby, the **National Museum of Wales** packs in everything Welsh but also includes one of the finest collections of impressionist art in Britain. The **Welsh Folk Museum**, at St Fagan's, five miles from the centre, is a popular open-air attraction with reconstructed buildings and craft demonstrations.

If you are planning to explore south Wales, it's worth stocking up on maps and information from the excellent TIC (☎ 01222-227281), open daily, at the central train station.

The *Youth Hostel* (☎ 462303), 2 Wedal Rd, Roath Park, is about two miles from the city centre. It operates seven days a week from March to October, opens at 5 pm and costs £9.10. See the preceding Getting There & Away information for details on transport to and from London.

Swansea

Swansea is the second-largest town (it would be stretching the definition to call it a city), and the gateway to the Gower Peninsula and its superb coastal scenery (crowded in summer). Dylan Thomas grew up in Swansea and later called it an 'ugly, lovely town'. The town's position is certainly lovely, but there's no pressing reason to stay.

For more information, contact the TIC (☎ 01792-468321), then move on west to the Gower. The *Youth Hostel* (☎ 390706) is a converted lifeboat house, superbly situated right on the beach. Bus No 18/A/C covers the 16 miles from Swansea.

Brecon Beacons National Park

The Brecon Beacons National Park covers 522 sq miles of high bare hills, surrounded on the northern flanks by a number of attractive market towns; Llandovery, Brecon, Crickhowell, Talgarth and Hay-on-Wye make good bases. The railhead is at Abergavenny. A 77-mile cycleway/footpath, the Taff Trail, connects Cardiff with Brecon.

There are three mountain ridges in the park: the popular Brecon Beacons in the centre, the Black Mountains in the east and the confusingly named Black Mountain in the west.

The National Park Mountain Centre (☎ 01874-623366) is in open countryside near Libanus, five miles south-west of Brecon. Other information offices are in Brecon (☎ 623156), at the Cattle Market Car Park, and in Llandovery (☎ 01550-20693), 8 Broad St. Both make B&B bookings. The Monmouthshire & Brecon Canal, which runs south-east from Brecon, is popular both with hikers (especially the 33 miles between Brecon and Pontypool) and canal boaters, and cuts through beautiful country.

Brecon Brecon is an attractive, historic market town, with a cathedral dating from the 13th century. The market is on Tuesday and Friday. There's a highly acclaimed jazz festival in August. The TIC (☎ 01874-622485) can organise B&Bs. The *Youth Hostel* (☎ 01874-86270) is three miles from town; ask directions from the TIC.

Brecon has no train station, but there are regular bus links. Silverline (☎ 623900) has daily links to Swansea and Cardiff; Stagecoach Red & White (☎ 01633-266336) has regular buses to Hereford via Hay-on-Wye.

Hay-on-Wye At the north-eastern tip of the Black Mountains, Hay-on-Wye is an eccentric market village that is now known as the world centre for second-hand books – there are 27 shops and two million books, everything from first editions costing £1000 to books by the yard (literally).

Contact the TIC (☎ 01497-820144) for info on the excellent restaurants and B&Bs in the neighbourhood. The *Youth Hostel* (☎ 01873-890650) is eight miles south of Hay on the road to Abergavenny. The walk here from Hay follows part of Offa's Dyke and is highly recommended.

SOUTH-WESTERN WALES

The coastline north-east of St David's to Cardigan is particularly beautiful, and, as it is protected by the national park, it remains unspoilt. The Pembrokeshire Coast Path begins at Amroth, north of Tenby, on the western side of Carmarthen Bay and continues to St Dogmaels to the west of Cardigan.

Carmarthen Bay is often referred to as Dylan Thomas Country; Dylan's boathouse at Laugharne (☎ 01994-427420), where he wrote *Under Milk Wood*, has been preserved exactly as he left it, and it is a moving memorial (£2/1). Llanstephan has a beautiful Norman castle overlooking sandy beaches. On west-facing beaches, there can be good surf; the Newgale filling station (☎ 01437-721398), Newgale, hires the necessary equipment and has daily surf reports.

Irish Ferries (☎ 01646-684161) leave Pembroke Dock for Rosslare in Ireland; ferries

connect with buses from Cardiff and destinations east. Stena Line (☎ 0990-707070) has ferries to Rosslare from Fishguard; these connect with buses and trains. See the Ireland chapter for more details.

Pembroke Dock is a classically unpleasant ferry port and the surrounding region is not particularly inspiring either, although nearby Pembroke Castle, the home of the Tudors and birthplace of Henry VII, is magnificent. Fishguard is surprisingly pleasant.

Pembrokeshire Coast National Park

The national park protects a narrow band of magnificent coastline, broken only by the denser development around Pembroke and Milford Haven. The only significant inland portion is the Preseli Hills to the south-east of Fishguard. There are National Park Information Centres and TICs at Tenby (☎ 01834-842402), St David's (☎ 01437-720392) and Fishguard (☎ 01348-873484), amongst others. Get a copy of their free paper, *Coast to Coast*, which has detailed local information. Apart from hostels, there are loads of B&Bs from around £13.

There's quite good public transport in the area (except on a Sunday). Contact the Public Transport Unit (☎ 01437-769832) for information. Around Pembroke the main operator is Silcox (☎ 01646-683143), with buses from Pembroke and Pembroke Dock to Tenby; Richards Bros (☎ 01239-613756) is the main operator from St David's to Cardigan.

St David's The linchpin for the south-west is beautiful St David's, one of Europe's smallest cities. There's a web of interesting streets, and, concealed in the Vale of Roses, beautiful **St David's Cathedral**. There is something particularly magical about this isolated, secretive 12th-century building. Unfortunately, it's not an undiscovered secret.

Contact the TIC (☎ 01437-720392) for more information. There are regular Richards Bros (☎ 01239-613756) buses to and from Fishguard (four a day from Monday to Saturday, but none on Sunday). There's an interesting section of the coast path between St David's and Fishguard.

There are four handy *youth hostels*: near St David's (☎ 720345), open from March to

October except Thursday (daily in July and August); near Newgale and Solva (☎ 720959); at Trevine (☎ 01348-831414), 11 miles from St David's; and at Pwll Deri (☎ 01348-891233), eight miles from Trevine and just over 4½ miles from Fishguard.

Fishguard Fishguard stands out like a jewel amongst the depressing ranks of ugly ferry ports. It is on a beautiful bay, and the old part of town – Lower Fishguard – was the location for the 1971 film version of *Under Milk Wood*, which starred Richard Burton and Elizabeth Taylor. The train station and harbour (for Stena Line ferries to Rosslare) are at Goodwick, a 20-minute walk from the town proper.

The TIC (☎ 01348-873484) is open seven days a week from Easter to October. In Goodwick, the *Beach House* (☎ 872085), above the railway line and overlooking the bay five-minutes walk from the ferry, is remarkably welcoming given the constant flow of visitors – B&B is £13. By rail, Fishguard to London is £40 for a SuperSaver single.

MID-WALES
Most visitors to Wales head either for the easily accessible south or the scenically more dramatic north, leaving the quiet valleys of mid-Wales to the Welsh.

This is unspoilt walking country: farming land interspersed with bare rolling hills and small lakes. The 120-mile Glyndwr's Way visits sites associated with the Welsh hero between Knighton (on Offa's Dyke Path) and Welshpool via Machynlleth. Sixteen leaflets are available from TICs in the area and are invaluable – route-finding is difficult in places.

Machynlleth is an attractive market town that is a good base for exploring mid-Wales. The **Centre for Alternative Technology** (☎ 01654-702400) is an interesting working community that can be visited. The TIC (☎ 01654-702401), Owain Glyndwr Centre, is open year round.

Aberystwyth, the only place of any size on the west coast, is a remarkably pleasant university town, which has good transport connections. Steam trains run through the Vale of Rheidol to Devil's Bridge, with spectacular views of the waterfall. The *Youth Hostel* (☎ 01970-890693) is 1½ miles from the

bridge. Contact the TIC (☎ 01970-612125) for B&Bs and more information.

NORTH WALES
North Wales is dominated by the Snowdonia Mountains, which loom over the beautiful coastline. Unfortunately, this is the holiday playground for much of the Midlands, so the coast is marred by tacky holiday villages and the serried ranks of caravan parks.

Heading east from Chester, the country is flat, industrialised and uninteresting until you reach Llandudno. Llandudno is virtually contiguous with Conwy – either spot would make a good base. From Llandudno and Conwy you can catch buses or trains to Betws-y-Coed or Llanberis, the main centres for exploring the Snowdonia National Park. From Betws-y-Coed there's a train to the bleak but strangely beautiful mining town of Blaenau Ffestiniog. One of Wales' most spectacular steam railways runs from Blaenau to the bustling coastal market town of Porthmadog. From Porthmadog you can loop back to Shrewsbury, via Harlech with its castle.

The remote Lyn Peninsula in the west escapes the crowds to a large extent; start from Caernarfon, with its magnificent castle, or Pwllheli. Near Porthmadog is whimsical Portmeirion, a holiday village built in the Italianate style – it's very attractive, but crowded in summer. Holyhead is one of the main Irish ferry ports.

Bus Gwynedd (☎ 01286-679535) has a Red Rover day ticket (£4.20) that covers most of the region.

Llandudno
Llandudno seethes with tourists, which in this instance seems entirely fitting. It was developed as a Victorian holiday town and it has retained its beautiful architecture and 19th-century atmosphere. There's a wonderful pier and promenade – and donkeys on the beach.

Llandudno is on its own peninsula between two sweeping beaches, and is dominated by the spectacular limestone headland – the Great Orme – with the mountains of Snowdonia as a backdrop. The Great Orme, with its tramway, chair lift, superb views and Bronze-Age mine, is quite fascinating.

There are hundreds of guesthouses, however, it can be difficult to find somewhere in the peak July/August season. Contact the TIC (☎ 01492-876413) for more information.

Getting There & Away There are numerous trains and buses between Llandudno and Chester, and between Llandudno and Holyhead.

Buses and trains run between Llandudno Junction, Betws-y-Coed (for the Snowdonia National Park) and Blaenau Ffestiniog (for the brilliant narrow-gauge railway to Porthmadog). There are six trains a day from Monday to Saturday and the journey takes a bit over an hour. A Flexi Rover ticket (£23/15.20) gives three days travel over one week. See the Shrewsbury Getting There & Away section for information on the complete Llandudno, Blaenau, Porthmadog, Dovey Junction, Shrewsbury loop.

Bus Gwynedd (No 5) has frequent services between Llandudno, Bangor and Caernarfon; there are plenty of buses from Bangor to Holyhead for the ferry.

Conwy

Conwy has been revitalised since the through traffic on the busy A55 was consigned to a tunnel which burrows under the estuary of the River Conwy and the town. It is now a picturesque and interesting little town, dominated by superb **Conwy Castle** (£3/2), one of the grandest of Edward I's castles and a medieval masterpiece.

The TIC (☎ 01492-592248) is in the Conwy Castle Visitor Centre. Five miles west of Llandudno, Conwy is linked to Llandudno by several buses an hour and a few trains. There are, however, numerous trains from Llandudno to Llandudno Junction, a 15-minute walk from Conwy.

Snowdonia National Park

Although the Snowdonia Mountains are fairly compact, they loom over the coast and are definitely spectacular. The most popular region is in the north around Mt Snowdon, at 1085 metres the highest peak in Britain south of the Scottish Highlands. Hikers must be prepared to deal with hostile conditions at any time of the year.

There are National Park Information Centres at Betws-y-Coed (☎ 01690- 710665), Blaenau Ffestiniog (☎ 01766-830360) and Harlech (☎ 01766-780658), amongst others; they all have a wealth of information, and all make B&B bookings.

Betws-y-Coed Betus (as it is known and pronounced) is a tourist village in the middle of the Snowdonia National Park. Despite bus loads of tourists it just can't help being beautiful. There's nothing to do except go for walks and take afternoon tea, which in this case is enough.

The TIC (☎ 01690-710426) is useful, but the National Park Information Centre is excellent. Both are near the train station. There are plenty of B&Bs, and the two hostels are both about five miles away. *Capel Curig Youth Hostel* (☎ 720225) is to the west on the A5; *Ledr Valley Youth Hostel* (☎ 750202), Pont-y-Pant, is on the A470. There are numerous other hostels in the Snowdon area.

Snowdon Sherpa Buses, which is part of Bus Gwynedd, runs from Llandudno to Conwy, Betws-y-Coed, Capel Curig and Pen-y-Pas (for the hostels), and then on to Llanberis and Caernarfon. There are regular services daily from mid-May to late September. A Rover ticket (£4.20) can be bought on the bus.

Llanberis This tourist town lies at the foot of Mt Snowdon and is packed with walkers and climbers. If you're neither, for a mere £13.50 you can take the Snowdon Mountain Railway (☎ 01286-870223) for the ride to the top and back. The TIC (☎ 01286-870765) is in the High St.

The best hostel in the area is *Youth Hostel* (☎ 870428), six miles up the valley in a spectacular site at the start of one of the paths up Snowdon. Back in Llanberis there are numerous B&Bs. *Pete's Eats* (☎ 870358) is a warm café where hikers swap information over large portions of healthy food. In the evenings climbers hang out in the *Heights* (☎ 871179), a hotel with a pub that even has its own climbing wall.

Llangollen
In the north-east, eight miles from the border with England, Llangollen is famous for its **International Musical Eisteddfod**. This six-day music and dance festival, held in July, attracts folk groups from around the world. Phone ☎ 01978-860236 for details.

For the rest of the year the town makes an excellent base for outdoor activities – walks to ruined **Valle Crucis Abbey** and the Horseshoe Pass, horse-drawn canal-boat trips, and canoeing on the River Dee. **Plas Newydd** was the 'stately cottage' of the eccentric Ladies of Llangollen, fascinating as much for their unorthodox (for those days – 1780-1831) lifestyle as for the building's striking black-and-white decoration.

The ***Llangollen Youth Hostel & Activity Centre*** (☎ 860330) is 1½ miles from the centre. Contact the TIC (☎ 860828) for B&Bs. There are frequent buses from Wrexham, but public transport to Snowdonia is limited.

Holyhead
Holyhead is a grey and daunting ferry port. Both Irish Ferries (☎ 01407-760222) and Stena Line (☎ 0990-707070) run ferries to Ireland. Irish Ferries runs direct to Dublin, Stena Line goes to Dun Laoghaire, just outside Dublin.

The TIC (☎ 01407-762622) is in the new ferry terminal. Nearby there's a batch of B&Bs that are used to dealing with late ferry arrivals. The ***Min-y-Don*** (☎ 762718) is pleasant, with rooms for £14 per person. The TIC has a 24-hour information terminal in the train station. There are hourly trains east to Llandudno, Chester, Birmingham and London.

France

France's most salient characteristic is its exceptional diversity. The largest country in Western Europe, France stretches from the rolling hills of the north to the seemingly endless beaches of the south; from the wild coastline of Brittany to the icy crags of the Alps, with cliff-lined canyons, dense forest and vineyards in between. France's towns and cities also hold many charms. Whether strolling along grand boulevards, sitting at a café terrace or picnicking in the beautiful public parks, it's easy to sense the famous *joie de vivre* of the country. Outstanding museums and galleries are also a nationwide phenomenon. This chapter will help you decide where to go and what to see.

Over the centuries, France has received more immigrants than any other country in Europe. From the ancient Celtic Gauls and Romans to the more recent arrivals from France's former colonies in Indochina and Africa, these peoples have introduced new elements of culture, cuisine and art, all of which have contributed to create France's unique and diverse civilisation.

At one time, France was on the western edge of Europe. Today, as Europe moves towards unification of one sort or another, it is at the crossroads: between England and Italy, Belgium and Spain, North Africa and Scandinavia. Of course, this is exactly how the French have always regarded their country – at the very centre of things.

Facts about the Country

HISTORY
Prehistory

Human presence in France is known to date from the middle Palaeolithic period, about 90,000 to 40,000 years ago. Around 25,000 BC the Stone Age Cro-Magnon people appeared on the scene and left their mark in the form of cave paintings and engravings. The most visible evidence of France's Neolithic age are the menhirs and dolmens dating from 4000 to 2500 BC. With the dawning of the Bronze Age, and the demand for copper and tin for bronze, trade began to develop between France and the rest of Europe around 2000 BC.

Ancient & Medieval History

The Celtic Gauls moved into what is now France between 1500 and 500 BC. By about 600 BC, they had established trading links with the Greeks, whose colonies on the Mediterranean coast included Massilia (Marseille). After several centuries of conflict between Rome and the Gauls, Julius Caesar's legions took control of the territory around 52 BC, when a revolt led by the Gallic chief Vercingétorix was crushed. Christianity was introduced to Roman Gaul early in the 2nd century AD.

France remained under Roman rule until the 5th century, when the Franks (thus 'France') and other Germanic groups overran the country. These peoples adopted important parts of Gallo-Roman civilisation – including Christianity – and their eventual assimilation resulted in a fusion of Germanic, Roman and Celtic cultures.

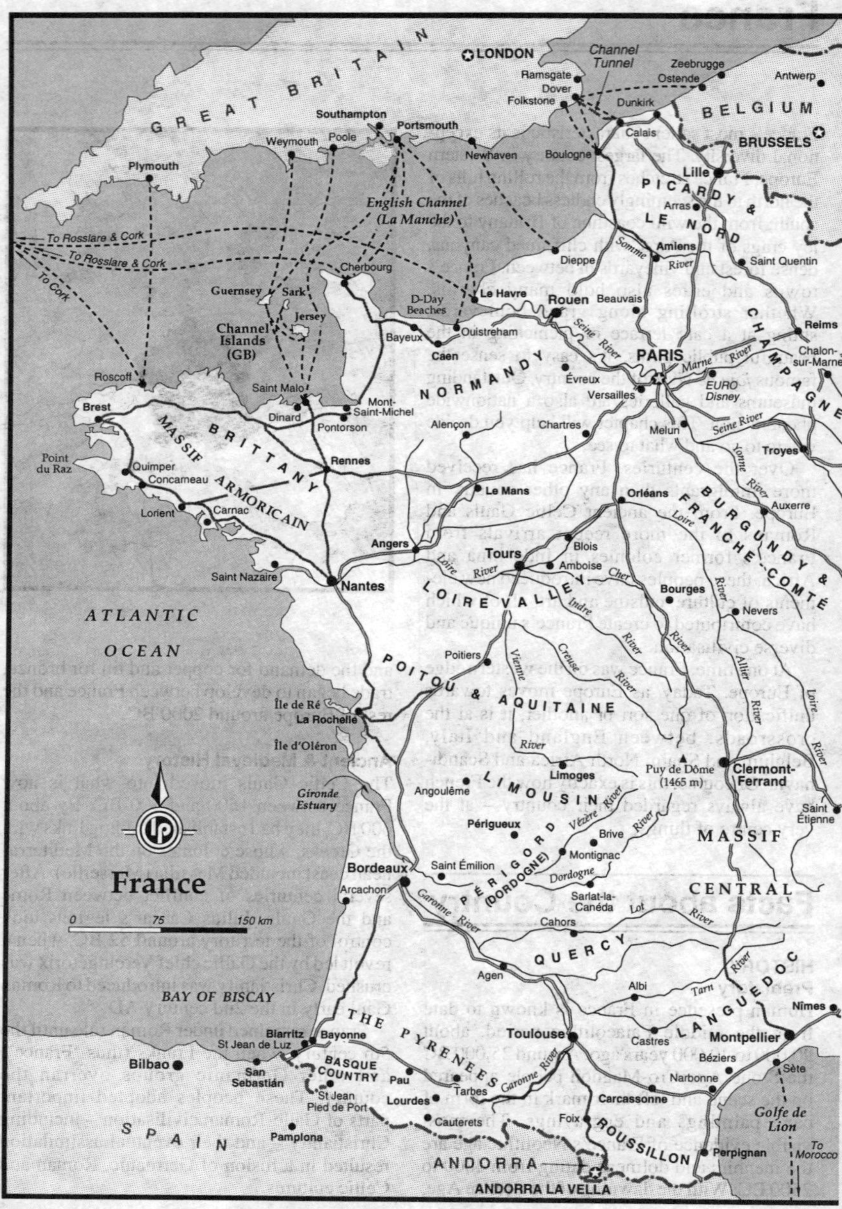
France
0
75
150 km
GREAT BRITAIN
LONDON
Channel Tunnel
Ramsgate
Dover
Folkstone
Zeebrugge
Ostende
Antwerp
Dunkirk
BELGIUM
BRUSSELS
Calais
Boulogne
Lille
Arras
Southampton
Portsmouth
Weymouth
Poole
Newhaven
Plymouth
English Channel
(La Manche)
To Rosslare & Cork
To Rosslare & Cork
To Cork
PICARDY & LE NORD
Amiens
Somme River
Saint Quentin
Dieppe
Cherbourg
Guernsey
Sark
Jersey
Channel Islands
(GB)
D-Day Beaches
Le Havre
Rouen
Beauvais
CHAMPAGNE
Reims
Ouistreham
Bayeux
Caen
Seine River
PARIS
Marne River
Chalon-sur-Marne
Roscoff
NORMANDY
Évreux
Versailles
EURO Disney
Saint Malo
Mont-Saint-Michel
Brest
Dinard
Pontorson
Alençon
Chartres
Melun
Seine River
Troyes
MASSIF ARMORICAIN
BRITTANY
Rennes
Point du Raz
Quimper
Concarneau
Le Mans
Yonne River
Orléans
Auxerre
Lorient
Carnac
BURGUNDY & FRANCHE-COMTÉ
Loire
Angers
Blois
Tours
Amboise
Loire River
Cher
Saint Nazaire
Nantes
LOIRE VALLEY
Indre
Bourges
Nevers
River
River
ATLANTIC
OCEAN
Poitiers
Vienne
Creuse
River
River
POITOU & AQUITAINE
Allier River
Loire River
Île de Ré
La Rochelle
Île d'Oléron
River
Puy de Dôme
(1465 m)
Limoges
Clermont-Ferrand
Gironde Estuary
Angoulême
LIMOUSIN
Vézère River
River
Saint Étienne
Périgueux
Brive
MASSIF
PÉRIGORD
(DORDOGNE)
Montignac
Bordeaux
Saint Émilion
CENTRAL
Dordogne
Arcachon
Sarlat-la-Canéda
Lot
River
Garonne River
Cahors
QUERCY
LANGUEDOC
River
Agen
Albi
Tarn
BAY OF BISCAY
Nîmes
THE PYRENEES
Biarritz
Bayonne
St Jean de Luz
Toulouse
Castres
Montpellier
Bilbao
San Sebastián
BASQUE COUNTRY
Pau
Tarbes
Garonne River
Béziers
Sète
Narbonne
St Jean Pied de Port
Lourdes
Carcassonne
Golfe de Lion
Cauterets
Foix
SPAIN
Pamplona
ROUSSILLON
Perpignan
To Morocco
ANDORRA
ANDORRA LA VELLA

Two Frankish dynasties, the Merovingians and the Carolingians, ruled from the 5th to the 10th century. The Frankish tradition by which the king was succeeded by all of his sons led to power struggles and the eventual disintegration of the kingdom into a collection of small, feudal states. In 732, Charles Martel defeated the Moors at Poitiers, thus ensuring that France would not follow Spain and come under Muslim rule.

Charles Martel's grandson, Charlemagne, significantly extended the power and boundaries of the kingdom and was crowned Holy Roman Emperor (Emperor of the West) in 800. But during the 9th century, the Scandinavian Vikings (also known as the Normans, ie Northmen) began raiding France's western coast. They eventually settled in the lower Seine Valley and formed the Duchy of Normandy in the early 10th century.

The Capetian dynasty was founded in 987, when the nobles elected Hugh Capet as their king. At the time, the king's domains were quite modest, consisting mostly of small pieces of land around Paris and Orléans.

Under William the Conqueror, Duke of Normandy, Norman forces occupied England in 1066, making Normandy – and later, Plantagenet-ruled England – a formidable rival of the kingdom of France. A further third of France came under the control of the English Crown in 1154, when Eleanor of Aquitaine married Henry of Anjou (later King Henry II of England). The subsequent battle between France and England for control of Aquitaine and the vast English territories in France lasted for three centuries.

The struggle between the Capetians and the English king Edward III (a member of the Plantagenet family) over the powerful French throne set off the Hundred Years' War, which was fought on and off from 1337 to 1453. The Black Death ravaged the country in 1348, killing about a third of the population, but the plague only briefly interrupted the fighting.

In 1415, French forces were defeated at Agincourt; in 1420, the English took control of Paris, and two years later King Henry IV of England became king of France. Just when it seemed that the Plantagenets had pulled off a dynastic union of England and France, a 17-year-old peasant girl known to history as Jeanne d'Arc (Joan of Arc) surfaced in 1429

FRANCE

and rallied the French troops at Orléans. She was captured, convicted of heresy by a court of French ecclesiastics and burned at the stake two years later, but her efforts helped to turn the war in favour of the French. With the exception of Calais, the English were expelled from French territory in 1453.

The Renaissance

The ideals and aesthetics of the Italian Renaissance arrived in France towards the end of the 15th century, introduced in part by the French aristocracy returning from military campaigns in Italy. The influence was most evident during the reign of François I, and the chateaux of Fontainebleau, near Paris, and Chenonceau in the Loire are good examples of Renaissance architectural style.

The Reformation

By the 1530s the position of the Protestant Reformation sweeping Europe had been strengthened in France by the ideas of the Frenchman John Calvin, an exile in Geneva. The Edict of January (1562), which afforded the Protestants certain rights, was violently opposed by ultra-Catholic nobles, whose fidelity to their religion was mixed with a desire to strengthen their power base in the provinces.

The Wars of Religion (1562-98) involved three groups: the Huguenots (French Protestants); the Catholic League, led by the House of Guise; and the Catholic monarchy. The fighting severely weakened the position of the king and brought the French state close to disintegration. The most outrageous massacre took place in Paris in 1572, when some 3000 Huguenots who had come to Paris to celebrate the wedding of Henry of Navarre were slaughtered in the Saint Bartholomew's Day Massacre (24 August).

Henry of Navarre, a Huguenot who had embraced Catholicism, eventually became King Henry IV. In 1598, he promulgated the Edict of Nantes, which guaranteed the Huguenots freedom of conscience and many civil and political rights. It was revoked by Louis XIV less than 100 years later.

Louis XIV & the Ancien Régime

Le Roi Soleil (the Sun King) ascended the throne in 1643 at the age of five and ruled until 1715. Throughout his long reign, he sought to extend the power of the French monarchy – bolstered by claims of divine right – both at home and abroad. He involved France in a long series of costly wars that gained it territory but nearly bankrupted the treasury. Louis XIV was not known for his parsimony domestically either, and poured huge sums of money into building his extravagant palace at Versailles.

His successor, Louis XV (ruled 1715-74), was followed by the incompetent – and later universally despised – Louis XVI. As the 18th century progressed, new economic and social circumstances rendered the old order (ancien régime) dangerously at odds with the needs of the country. The regime was further weakened by the anti-Establishment and anticlerical ideas of the Enlightenment, whose leading lights included Voltaire, Rousseau and Montesquieu. But entrenched vested interests, a cumbersome power structure and royal lassitude delayed reform until it was too late.

The Seven Years' War (1756-63), fought by France and Austria against Britain and Prussia, was one of a series of ruinous wars pursued by Louis XV, culminating in the loss of France's flourishing colonies in Canada, the West Indies and India to the English. It was in part to avenge these losses that Louis XVI sided with the colonists in the American War of Independence. But the Seven Years' War cost a fortune and, even more disastrous for the monarchy, it helped to disseminate in France the radical democratic ideas which the American Revolution had thrust onto the world stage.

The French Revolution

By the late 1780s, Louis XVI and his queen, Marie-Antoinette, had managed to alienate virtually every segment of society – from enlightened groups to conservatives. When the king tried to neutralise the power of the more reform-minded delegates at a meeting of the Estates General in 1789, the urban masses took to the streets and, on 14 July, a Parisian mob stormed the Bastille prison – the ultimate symbol of the despotism of the ancien régime.

At first, the Revolution was in the hands of relative moderates. France was declared a constitutional monarchy and various reforms were made, including the adoption of the Declaration of the Rights of Man. But as the masses armed themselves against the external threat to the Revolution posed by Austria, Prussia and the many exiled French nobles, patriotism and nationalism melded with revolutionary fervour, thereby popularising and radicalising the Revolution. It was not long before the moderate, republican Girondists (Girondins in French) lost power to the radical Jacobins, led by Robespierre, Danton and Marat who established the First Republic in 1792, after Louis XVI proved unreliable as a constitutional monarch. In January 1793, Louis was guillotined in what is now Place de la Concorde in Paris. In March, the Jacobins set up the notorious Committee of Public Safety. This body had virtually dictatorial control over the country during the Reign of Terror (September 1793 to July 1794), which saw religious freedoms revoked and churches desecrated.

By autumn, the Reign of Terror was in full swing, and by the middle of 1794 some 17,000 people in every part of the country had been beheaded. In the end, the Revolution turned on its own, and many of its leaders, including Robespierre, followed their victims to the guillotine.

Napoleon

In the resulting chaos, the leaders of the French military began disregarding instructions from the increasingly corrupt and tyrannical Directory (the executive power in Paris), pursuing instead their own ambitions on the battlefield. One dashing young general by the name of Napoleon Bonaparte was particularly successful in the Italian campaign of the war against Austria, and his victories soon turned him into an independent political force. In 1799, when it appeared that the Jacobins were again on the ascendancy in the legislature, Napoleon overthrew the discredited Directory and assumed power himself.

At first, Napoleon took the title of First Consul. In 1802, a referendum declared him 'consul for life' and his birthday became a national holiday. By 1804, when he had himself crowned Emperor of the French by Pope Pius VII at Notre Dame Cathedral in Paris, the scope and nature of Napoleon's ambitions were obvious to all. But to consolidate and legitimise his authority, Napoleon needed more victories on the battlefield. So began a seemingly endless series of wars in which France came to control most of Europe.

But in 1812, in an attempt to do away with his last major rival on the continent, Tsar Alexander I, Napoleon invaded Russia. Although his Grande Armée (Grand Army) captured Moscow, it was wiped out shortly after by the brutal Russian winter. Prussia and Napoleon's other enemies quickly recovered from their earlier defeats, and less than two years after the fiasco in Russia, the Allied armies entered Paris. Napoleon abdicated and left France for his tiny Mediterranean island-kingdom of Elba.

At the Congress of Vienna (1814-15), the Allies restored the House of Bourbon to the French throne, installing Louis XVI's brother as Louis XVIII (Louis XVII, Louis XVI's son, had died in exile in 1795). But in March 1815, Napoleon escaped from Elba, landed in southern France and gathered a large army as he marched northward towards Paris. His 'Hundred Days' back in power ended when his forces were defeated by the English at Waterloo in Belgium. Napoleon was exiled to the remote South Atlantic island of Saint Helena, where he died in 1821.

Although reactionary in some ways – slavery was re-established in the colonies, for instance – Napoleon instituted a number of important reforms, including a reorganisation of the judicial system and the promulgation of a new legal code, the Code Civil (or Napoleonic Code), which forms the basis of the French legal system (and many others in Europe) to this day. More importantly, he preserved the essence of the changes wrought by the Revolution. Napoleon is therefore remembered by the French as a great hero.

The 19th Century

The 19th century was a chaotic one for France. Louis XVIII's reign (1815-24) was dominated by the struggle between extreme monarchists, who wanted a return to the ancien régime, and those who saw the changes wrought by the Revolution as irreversible. Charles X (ruled 1824-30) handled the struggle between reactionaries and liberals with great ineptitude and was overthrown in the July Revolution of 1830. Louis-Philippe (ruled 1830-48), an ostensibly constitutional monarch of upper bourgeois sympathies and tastes, was then chosen by parliament to head what became known as the July Monarchy.

Louis-Philippe was in turn overthrown in the February Revolution of 1848, in whose wake the Second Republic was established. In presidential elections held that year, Napoleon's undistinguished nephew Louis-Napoleon Bonaparte was overwhelmingly elected. A legislative deadlock led Louis-Napoleon to lead a coup d'état in 1851, after which he was proclaimed Napoleon III, Emperor of the French.

The second empire lasted from 1852 until 1870. During this period, France enjoyed significant economic growth. But as his uncle had done, Napoleon III embroiled France in a number of conflicts, including the disastrous Crimean War (1853-56). It was the Prussians, however, who ended the second empire. In 1870, the Prussian prime minister Bismarck goaded Napoleon III into declaring war on Prussia. Within months the thoroughly unprepared French army had been defeated and the emperor taken prisoner.

When news of the debacle reached the French capital, the Parisian masses took to the streets and demanded that a republic be declared. The Third Republic began as a provisional government of national defence – the Prussians were, at the time, advancing on Paris. But in the Assemblée Nationale (National Assembly) elections of February 1871 (required by the armistice which had been signed after a four-month siege of Paris by the Prussians), the republicans, who had called on the nation to continue resistance, lost to the monarchists, who had campaigned on a peace platform.

As expected, the monarchist-controlled National Assembly ratified the Treaty of Frankfurt (1871). However, when ordinary Parisians heard of its harsh terms – a five billion franc war indemnity and surrender of the provinces of Alsace and Lorraine – they revolted against the government. The Communards, as the supporters of the Paris Commune were known, took over the city but were slowly pushed back in bloody fighting in which several thousand rebels were killed. A further 20,000 or so Communards, mostly from the working class, were summarily executed.

The greatest moral and political crisis of the Third Republic was the infamous Dreyfus Affair, which began in 1894 when a Jewish army officer named Captain Alfred Dreyfus

was framed as a German spy, court-martialled and sentenced to life imprisonment. Despite bitter opposition from the army command, right-wing politicians and many Catholic groups, the case was eventually reopened and Dreyfus vindicated. The affair greatly discredited both the army and the Church. The result was more rigorous civilian control of the military and, in 1905, the legal separation of church and state.

WWI

Central to France's entry into WWI was the desire to regain Alsace and Lorraine, lost to Germany in 1871. This was achieved but at immense human cost: of the eight million French men who were called to arms, 1.3 million were killed and almost one million crippled. The war was officially ended by the Treaty of Versailles in 1919, whose severe terms (Germany was to pay US\$33 billion in reparations) were heavily influenced by the uncompromising French prime minister Georges Clemenceau.

WWII

During the 1930s the French, like the British, did their best to appease Hitler, but two days after the 1939 German invasion of Poland, the two countries reluctantly declared war on Germany. By June of the following year, France had capitulated. The British expeditionary force sent to help the French barely managed to avoid capture by retreating to Dunkirk and crossing the English Channel in small boats. The hugely expensive Maginot Line, a supposedly impregnable wall of fortifications along the Franco-German border, had proved useless: the German armoured divisions had simply outflanked it by going through Belgium.

The Germans divided France into a zone under direct German occupation (in the north and along the west coast) and a puppet state based in the spa town of Vichy, which was led by the ageing WWI hero, General Philippe Pétain. Both Pétain's collaborationist government (whose leaders and supporters assumed that the Nazis were Europe's new masters and had to be accommodated) and French police forces in German-occupied areas were very helpful to the Nazis in rounding up French

Jews and other targeted groups for deportation to concentration camps.

After the capitulation, General Charles de Gaulle, France's undersecretary of war, fled to London and set up a French government-in-exile. He also established the Forces Françaises Libres (Free French Forces), a military force dedicated to continuing the fight against Germany. The underground movement known as the Résistance, which included no more than perhaps 5% of the population (the other 95% either collaborated or did nothing), engaged in such activities as railway sabotage, collecting intelligence for the Allies, helping Allied airmen who had been shot down, and publishing anti-German leaflets.

The liberation of France began with the US, British and Canadian landings in Normandy on D-Day (6 June 1944). On 15 August, Allied forces also landed in southern France. After a brief insurrection by the Résistance, Paris was liberated on 25 August by an Allied force spearheaded somewhat superficially by Free French units.

The Fourth Republic

De Gaulle soon returned to Paris and set up a provisional government, but in January 1946 he resigned as its president, miscalculating that such a move would create a popular outcry for his return. A few months later, a new constitution was approved by referendum. The Fourth Republic was a period of unstable coalition cabinets that followed one another with bewildering speed (on average one every six months). It was characterised by slow economic recovery helped by massive US aid (the Marshall Plan), an unsuccessful war to reassert French colonial control of Indochina and an uprising by Arab nationalists in Algeria, whose population included over one million French settlers.

The Fifth Republic

The Fourth Republic came to an end in 1958, when extreme right-wingers, furious at what they saw as defeatism in dealing with the uprising in Algeria, began conspiring to overthrow the government. De Gaulle was brought back to power to prevent a military coup and even civil war. He soon drafted a new constitution that gave considerable powers to the president at the expense of the National Assembly.

The Fifth Republic (which continues to this day) was rocked in 1961 by an attempted coup staged in Algiers by a group of right-wing military officers. When it failed, the Organisation de l'Armée Secrète (OAS; a group of French settlers and sympathisers opposed to Algerian independence) turned to terrorism, trying several times to assassinate De Gaulle. In 1962, de Gaulle negotiated an end to the war in Algeria. Some 750,000 *pieds noirs* ('black feet' – as Algerian-born French people are known in France) flooded into France. In the meantime, almost all of the other French colonies and protectorates in Africa had demanded and achieved independence. Shrewdly, the French government began a programme of economic and military aid to its former colonies in order to bolster France's waning international importance.

The crisis of May 1968 took the government, and much of the country, by total surprise. A seemingly insignificant incident, in which police broke up yet another protest by university students, sparked a violent reaction on the streets of Paris: students occupied the Sorbonne, barricades were erected in the Latin Quarter and unrest spread to other universities. Workers then joined in the protests. About nine million people participated in a general strike, virtually paralysing the country. But just when the country seemed on the brink of revolution, de Gaulle defused the crisis by successfully appealing to people's fear of anarchy. With stability restored, the government made a number of important changes, including a reform of the higher education system.

In 1969, de Gaulle was succeeded as president by the Gaullist leader Georges Pompidou, who was in turn succeeded by Valéry Giscard d'Estaing in 1974. François Mitterrand, a Socialist, was elected president in 1981 and re-elected for a second seven-year term in 1988. In the 1986 parliamentary elections, the right-wing opposition led by Jacques Chirac received a majority in the National Assembly. For the next two years, Mitterrand was forced to work with a prime minister and cabinet from the opposition, an unprecedented arrangement which became known as *cohabitation*.

Cohabitation was again the order of the day after the 1993 parliamentary elections, in

FRANCE

which a centre-right coalition took 480 of 577 seats in the National Assembly and Édouard Balladur of Chirac's party was named prime minister.

The closely contested presidential election of May 1995 resulted in Chirac winning the mandate with 52% of the vote, and naming Alain Juppé as prime minister. More surprising was the considerable success of the extreme-right Front National (FN) led by Jean-Marie Le Pen. In the presidential elections, this party took 15% of votes in the first round, and in the municipal elections of June that year won some 1249 seats, notably in southern France.

Chirac has earned credit for decisive words and actions in matters relating to the EU and the war in former Yugoslavia. His decision however to resume nuclear testing on the Polynesian island of Moruroa was met with outrage both in France and abroad. On the home front, Chirac's moves to restrict welfare payments led to the largest protests and strikes since 1968. In January 1996, François Mitterrand died.

GEOGRAPHY & ECOLOGY

France covers an area of 551,000 sq km and is the largest country in Europe after Russia and Ukraine. It is shaped like a hexagon bordered by either mountains or water except for the relatively flat, north-east frontier which abuts Germany, Luxembourg and Belgium.

France has a rich variety of flora and fauna, including some 113 species of mammals (more than any other country in Europe). Unfortunately, intensive agriculture, the draining of wetlands, the encroachment of industry and the expansion of the tourism infrastructure are amongst the problems threatening some species. The proportion of protected land is relatively low in France, but animal reintroduction programmes, such as storks bred in Alsace, have met with some success. France is home to nearly two million hunters. The 1979 Directive de Bruxelles, introduced to protect wild birds and their habitats, was signed by the French government but has yet to become part of French law.

France's nuclear energy industry continues to thrive and about three-quarters of the country's electricity is produced in this way. Since 1960, France has also maintained an independent arsenal of nuclear weapons. In 1992, the French government finally agreed to suspend nuclear testing on the Polynesian island of Moruroa and a nearby atoll, and this decision was reaffirmed in 1994. In 1995, however, Jacques Chirac decided to conduct one last round of tests before supporting a worldwide test ban treaty. The tests were concluded in January 1996, but France has yet to commit itself to the test ban.

GOVERNMENT & POLITICS

Despite a long tradition of highly centralised government, the country remains linguistically and culturally heterogeneous, and in some areas there's less than complete acceptance of control by Paris. There are even groups in the Basque Country, Brittany and Corsica demanding complete independence from France.

France has had 11 constitutions since 1789. The present one, which was instituted by de Gaulle in 1958, established what is known as the Fifth Republic (see the previous History section). It gives considerable power to the president of the republic.

The 577 members of the National Assembly are directly elected in single-member constituencies for five-year terms. The 321 members of the rather powerless Sénat, who serve for nine years, are indirectly elected. The president of France is elected directly for a seven-year term. The voting age is 18 and women were given the franchise in 1944.

Executive power is shared by the president and the Council of Ministers, whose members, including the prime minister, are appointed by the president but are responsible to parliament. The president, who resides in the Palais de l'Élysée in Paris, makes all major policy decisions.

France is one of the five permanent members of the UN Security Council. It withdrew from NATO's joint military command in 1966.

Local Administration

Before the Revolution, the country consisted of about two dozen regions. Their names are still widely used, but for administrative purposes the country has been divided into units called *départements* since 1790. At present, there are 96 departments in metropolitan

France and another five overseas. The government in Paris is represented in each department by a *préfet* (prefect). A department's main town, where the departmental government and the prefect are based, is known as a *préfecture*.

ECONOMY

The recession hit France especially hard in the early 1990s. Unemployment, which has plagued the country for years, has risen to near crisis proportions with over 3.3 million workers (12.2% of the workforce) jobless in the first half of 1995. The situation among young people is so bleak that since 1994 the government has been offering bonuses and tax exemptions to employers for hiring anyone under 25 years of age who has never held a steady job.

The government has long played a significant interventionist *(dirigiste)* role in managing and running the French economy, which during the 1950s was one of the most tariff-protected and government-subsidised in Europe. Under direct government control is the world-famous Renault car works and most of the major banks. Although privatisation has been embraced in some sectors and will probably accelerate under Chirac, the lack of competition in other areas can mean poor service.

Union activity is strongest in the public sector where strike action is often a daily occurrence. But only about 15% of the French workforce is unionised – amongst the lowest rates in the EU – despite the fact that France is one of the most industrialised nations in the world, with around 40% of the workforce employed in the industrial sector. France is also the largest agricultural producer and exporter in the EU. Nearly one in 10 workers is engaged in agricultural production, which helps to account for the attention given by the government to French farmers during their periodic protests against cheaper imports.

POPULATION & PEOPLE

France has a population of 58 million, more than 20% of whom live in the Paris greater metropolitan area. The number of French people living in rural and mountain areas has been declining since the 1950s. For much of the last two centuries, France has had a considerably lower rate of population growth than its neighbours.

On the other hand, during the last 150 years France has received more immigrants than any other European country (4.3 million between 1850 and 1945), including significant numbers of political refugees. During the late 1950s and early 1960s, as the French colonial empire collapsed, more than one million French settlers returned to metropolitan France from Algeria, Morocco, Tunisia and Indochina.

In recent years, there has been a racist backlash against France's nonwhite immigrant communities, especially Muslims from North Africa. The extreme-right FN party has fanned these racist sentiments in a bid to win more votes. In 1993, the French government tightened its immigration laws, making it harder for immigrants to get French citizenship.

ARTS
Architecture

A religious revival in the 11th century led to the construction of a large number of Romanesque churches, so called because their architects adopted many elements (eg vaulting) from Gallo-Roman buildings still standing at the time. Romanesque buildings typically have round arches, heavy walls that let in very little light and a lack of ornamentation bordering on the austere.

The Gothic style originated in the mid-12th century in northern France, whose great wealth enabled it to attract the finest architects, engineers and artisans. Gothic structures are characterised by ribbed vaults, pointed arches and stained-glass windows, with the emphasis on space, verticality and light. The invention of the flying buttress (a structural support which conducts the thrust of the building down through a series of arches to the ground) meant that greater height and width were now possible. This new technology subsequently spread to the rest of Europe. By the 15th century, decorative extravagance led to the Flamboyant Gothic style, so named because its wavy stone carving was said to resemble flames.

Painting

An extraordinary flowering of artistic talent took place in France during the late 19th and early 20th centuries. The impressionists, who dealt with colour as a property of light (rather than of objects) and endeavoured to capture the ever-changing aspects of reflected light, included Édouard Manet, Claude Monet, Edgar Degas, Camille Pissarro and Pierre-Auguste Renoir. They were followed by a diverse but equally creative group of artists known as the postimpressionists, among whose ranks were Paul Cézanne, Paul Gauguin and Georges Seurat. A little later, the Fauves (literally, 'wild beasts'), the most famous of whom was Henri Matisse, became known for their radical use of vibrant colour. In the years before WWI Pablo Picasso, who was living in Paris, and Georges Braque pioneered cubism, a school of art which concentrated on the analysis of form through abstract and geometric representation.

Music

When French music comes to mind, most people hear accordions and *chansonniers* (cabaret singers) like Édith Piaf. But they're only part of a much larger and more complex picture. At many points in history France has been at the centre of musical culture in Europe.

In the 17th and 18th centuries, French baroque music greatly influenced European musical output. Composers such as François Couperin (1668 -1733), noted for his harpsicord studies, and Jean Phillipe Rameau (1683-1764), a key figure in the development of modern harmony, were two major contributors. The opulence of the baroque era is reflected also in the art and architecture of the time.

France's two greatest classical composers of the 19th century were the Romantic Hector Berlioz, the founder of modern orchestration, and César Franck. Berlioz's operas and symphonies and Franck's organ compositions sparked a musical renaissance in France that would produce such greats as Gabriel Fauré and the impressionists Claude Debase and Maurice Ravel.

Jazz hit Paris in the 1920s and has remained popular ever since. France's contribution to the world of jazz includes the violinist Stéfane Grappelli and, in the 1950s, Claude Luter and his Dixieland Band.

Popular music has come a long way since the *yéyé* (imitative rock) of the 1960s sung by Johnny Halliday – though you might not think

so listening to middle-of-the-roaders Vanessa Paradis and Patrick Bruel. Watch out for rappers MC Solaar, Reg'lyss and I Am from Marseille. Evergreen balladeers/folk singers include Francis Cabrel and Julien Clerc. Some people like the new age space music of Jean-Michel Jarre; others say his name fits his sound.

France's claim to fame over the past decade has been *sono mondial* (world music) – from Algerian *raï* (Cheb Khaled, Zahouania) and Senegalese *mbalax* (Youssou N'Dour) to West Indian *zouk* (Kassav, Zouk Machine). La Mano Negra and Négresses Vertes are two bands that combine many of these styles – often with outstanding results.

Literature

To get a feel for France and its literature of the 19th century, you might pick up a translation of any novel by Victor Hugo (*Les Misérables* or *The Hunchback of Notre Dame*), Stendahl (*The Red and the Black*), Honoré de Balzac (*Old Goriot*), Émile Zola (*Germinal*) or Gustave Flaubert (*A Sentimental Education*).

After WWII, existentialism, a significant literary movement, emerged. Based upon the philosophy that people are self-creating beings, it placed total moral responsibility upon individuals to give meaning to their existence. The most prominent figures of the movement – Jean-Paul Sartre (*Being & Nothingness*), Simone de Beauvoir, and Albert Camus (*The Plague*) – stressed the importance of the writer's political commitment. De Beauvoir, author of the ground-breaking study *The Second Sex*, has had a profound influence on feminist thinking.

In the late 1950s, some younger novelists began to experiment with the novel in an attempt to show different aspects of reality. Critics began to speak of the *nouveau roman* (new novel), referring to the works of Alain Robbe-Grillet, Nathalie Sarraute, Michel Butor and Claude Simon among others. Although these writers did not form a school, they all rejected the traditional novel with its conventions of plot, linear narrative and identifiable characters. Other authors who enjoy a wide following are: Marguerite Duras, Françoise Sagan, Patrick Modiano, Pascal Quignard and Denis Tillinac.

Cinema

Film has always been taken very seriously as an art form in France, and as such has attracted artists, intellectuals and theorists. Some of the most innovative and influential film-makers of the 1920s and 1930s were Jean Vigo, Marcel Pagnol and Jean Renoir.

After WWII, a new generation of directors burst onto the scene with experimental films that abandoned such constraints as temporal continuity and traditional narrative. Known as the *nouvelle vague* (new wave), this genre includes many disparate directors such as Jean-Luc Godard, François Truffaut, Claude Chabrol, Alain Resnais, Agnès Varda and Eric Rohmer, whose main tenet was that a film should be the conception of the film-maker – not the product of a studio or a producer.

Despite the onslaught of American films in Europe, France is still producing commercially viable (albeit subsidised) films. Contemporary directors of note include Bertrand Blier *(Trop belle pour toi)*, Jean-Jacques Beineix *(Betty Blue)* and Jacques Rivette *(Jeanne la Pucelle)*. The French film industry's main annual event is the Cannes Film Festival held in May, when the coveted Palme d'Or is awarded to French and foreign films.

CULTURE

Some visitors to France conclude that it would be a lovely country if it weren't for the French. As in other countries, however, the more tourists a particular town or neighbourhood attracts, the less patience the locals tend to have for them. The following tips might prove useful when interacting with the French:

Never address a waiter or bartender as *garçon* (boy); *s'il vous plaît* is the way it's done nowadays. Avoid discussing money, keep off the manicured French lawns *(Pelouse Interdite)*, and resist handling produce in markets; trust the shopkeeper to choose for you.

Perhaps the easiest way to improve the quality of your relations with the French is always to address people as *Monsieur/ Madame/Mademoiselle*. Monsieur means 'sir' and can be used with any male person who isn't a child. Madame is used where 'Mrs' would apply in English; Mademoiselle is equivalent to 'Miss' and is used when addressing unmarried women. When in doubt, use 'Madame'.

Finally, when you go out for the evening, it's a good idea to follow the local custom of being relatively well dressed, particularly in a restaurant. If invited to someone's home or a party, always bring some sort of gift, such as good wine.

RELIGION

Some 80% of French people say they are Catholic, but although most have been baptised very few attend church – especially among the middle classes. The French Catholic church is generally progressive and ecumenically minded.

Protestants, who were severely persecuted during much of the 16th and 17th centuries, now number about one million. They are concentrated in Alsace, the Jura, the south-eastern part of the Massif Central and along the Atlantic coast.

France now has at least four million Muslims, making Islam the second-largest religion in the country. The vast majority are immigrants (or their offspring) who came from North Africa during the 1950s and 1960s.

There has been a Jewish community in France almost continuously since the Roman period. About 75,000 Jews resident in France were killed during the Holocaust. The country's Jewish community now numbers some 600,000.

LANGUAGE

Around 122 million people worldwide speak French as their first language; it is an official language in Belgium, Switzerland, Luxembourg, Canada and over two dozen other countries, most of them former French colonies in Africa. It is also spoken in the Val d'Aosta region of north-western Italy. Various forms of creole are used in Haiti, French Guiana and parts of Louisiana. France has a special government ministry (Ministère de la Francophonie) to deal with the country's relations with the French-speaking world.

The French tend to take it for granted that all human beings should speak French; it was the international language of culture and diplomacy until WWI. Your best bet is always to approach people politely in French, even if the only words you know are *'Pardon, Monsieur/Madame/Mademoiselle, parlez-vous anglais?'* ('Excuse me Sir/Madam/Miss, do you speak English?').

See the Language Guide at the back of the book for pronunciation guidelines and useful words and phrases.

Facts for the Visitor

PLANNING

Climate & When to Go

Weather-wise, France is at its best in spring, though winter-like relapses are not unknown in April and the beach resorts only begin to pick up in mid-May. Autumn is pleasant, too, but later on (late October) it gets a bit cool for sunbathing. Winter is great for snow sports in the Alps and Pyrenees, but Christmas, New Year and the February/March school holidays create surges in domestic and foreign tourism that can make it very difficult to find accommodation. On the other hand, Paris always has all sorts of cultural activities during its rather wet winter.

In summer, the weather is warm and even hot, especially in the south, which is one reason why the beaches, resorts and camping grounds are packed to the gills. Also, millions of French people take their annual month-long holiday (congé) in August. Resort hotel rooms and camp sites are in extremely short supply, while in the half-deserted cities – only partly refilled by the zillions of foreign tourists – many shops, restaurants, cinemas, cultural institutions and even hotels simply shut down. If at all possible, avoid travelling in France during August.

Books

There are many excellent histories of France in English. Among the best is Fernand Braudel's two-volume The Identity of France (History & Environment and People & Production). Citizens, a very readable work by Simon Schama, looks at the first few years of the French Revolution. France Today by John Ardagh provides excellent insights into the way French society has evolved since WWII.

Paul Rambali's French Blues is a series of uncompromising yet sympathetic snapshots of modern France, while Paris Notebooks by veteran journalist Mavis Gallant reviews the years 1968 to 1985. Patrick Howarth's When the Riviera Was Ours traces the lives of expatriates who frequented the Mediterranean coast during the two centuries up to WWII. A Year in Provence by Peter Mayle is an irresistible account of country life in southern France. Toujours Provence is its witty sequel.

France has long attracted expatriate writers from the UK, North America and Australasia, many of whom spent at least part of their stay writing in the country. A Moveable Feast by Ernest Hemingway portrays Bohemian life in 1920s Paris. Henry Miller also wrote some pretty dramatic stuff set in the French capital of the 1930s, including Tropic of Cancer and Tropic of Capricorn. Gertrude Stein's The Autobiography of Alice B Toklas is an entertaining account of Paris' literary and artistic circles from WWI to the mid-1930s, featuring such figures as Picasso, Matisse and Apollinaire.

Travel Guides Lonely Planet's France – a travel survival kit by Steve Fallon & Daniel Robinson is a comprehensive guide to France and includes chapters on Andorra and Monaco.

Michelin's hardcover Guide Rouge (red guide) to France, published annually, has more than 1200 pages of maps and practical travel information (hotels, restaurants, garages for car repairs, etc) for every corner of the country, but it's best known for rating France's greatest restaurants with one, two or three stars. Michelin's green guides, covering France in 24 regional volumes (10 of which are available in English), are full of generally interesting historical information, though the prose can hardly be called lively. The green guide to all of France, with brief entries on the most touristed sights, is also available in English.

Maps

For driving, the best road map is Michelin's Motoring Atlas France, which covers the whole country in 1:200,000 scale (1 cm = 2 km). If you'll only be in one or several regions of France, you might prefer to use Michelin's yellow-jacketed 1:200,000 scale sheet maps.

Éditions Didier & Richard's series of 1:50,000 scale trail maps are adequate for most hiking and cycling excursions. The Institut Géographique National (IGN) publishes maps of France in both 1:50,000 and 1:25,000 scale. Topoguides are little booklets for hikers that include trail maps and information (in French) on trail conditions, flora, fauna, villages en route etc.

Abbreviations commonly used on city maps include: *R* for *rue* (street); *Boul* or *Bd* for boulevard; *Av* for avenue; *Q* for *quai* (quay); *C* or *Cr* for *cours* (avenue); *Pl* for *place* (square); *Pte* for *porte* (gate); *Imp* for *impasse* (dead-end street); and *St* and *Ste* for saint (masculine and feminine, respectively). The street numbers 14bis (14 twice) or 92ter (92 thrice) are the equivalent of 14A or 92B.

What to Bring

English-language books, including used ones, cost about 50% more in France than in the UK (double North American prices), so voracious readers might want to bring along a supply. A pocketknife (penknife) and eating utensils are invaluable for picnicking. Bikini tops are not used much in France; you might leave them at home! And, of course, bring as much money as you can afford – France can be an expensive (and a very tempting) place to visit.

SUGGESTED ITINERARIES

Depending on the length of your stay, you might want to consider the following options:

Two days
    Paris – the most beautiful city in the world.
One week
    Paris plus a nearby area, such as the Loire Valley, Champagne, Alsace or Normandy.
Two weeks
    As above, plus one area in the west or south, such as Brittany, the Alps or Provence.
One month
    As above, but spending more time in each place and visiting more of the west or south – Brittany, say, or the Côte d'Azur.
Two months
    In summer, hiking in the Pyrenees or Alps; hanging out at one of the beach areas on the English Channel, Atlantic coast or the Mediterranean; spending some time in more remote areas (eg the Basque Country or Corsica).

HIGHLIGHTS
Beaches

The Côte d'Azur – the French Riviera – has some of the best known beaches in the world, but you'll also find lovely beaches further west on the Mediterranean coast as well as on Corsica, along the Atlantic coast (eg at Biarritz) and even along the English Channel (eg Dinard).

Museums

Every city and town in France has at least one museum, but a good number of the country's most exceptional ones are in Paris. In addition to the rather overwhelming Louvre, Parisian museums not to be missed include the Musée d'Orsay (late 19th and early 20th-century art), the Pompidou Centre (modern and contemporary art), the Musée Rodin, and the Musée National du Moyen Age (Museum of the Middle Ages) at the Hôtel de Cluny. Other cities known for their museums include Nice, Bordeaux, Strasbourg and Lyon.

Chateaux

The royal palace at Versailles is the largest and most grandiose of the hundreds of chateaux located all over the country. Many of the most impressive ones, including Chambord, Cheverny, Chenonceau and Azay-le-Rideau, are in the Loire Valley around Blois and Tours.

Cathedrals

The cathedrals at Chartres, Strasbourg and Rouen are among the most beautiful in France.

TOURIST OFFICES
Local Tourist Offices

Virtually every French city, town and one-chateau village has some sort of tourist office. See Information under each town or city for details.

Tourist Offices Abroad

French Government Tourist Offices are located in the following countries and can provide brochures and tourist information.

Australia
    BNP Building, 12 Castlereagh St, Sydney, NSW 2000 (☎ 02-9231 5244; fax 02-9221 8682)
Canada
    30 Saint Patrick St, suite 700, Toronto, Ontario M5T 3A3 (☎ 416-593 4723; fax 416-979 7587)
UK
    178 Piccadilly, London W1V OAL (☎ 0891-244 123; fax 0171-493 6594)
USA
    444 Madison Ave, New York, NY 10020-2452 (☎ 212-838-7800; fax 212-838-7855)

FRANCE

VISAS & EMBASSIES

Citizens of the USA, Canada, most European countries and a handful of other nations can enter France for up to three months without a visa. Australians, however, must have visas to visit France, even as tourists. The usual length of a tourist visa is three months.

If you plan to stay in France for over three months to study or work, apply to the French consulate nearest where you live for the appropriate sort of long-stay visa. If you're not an EU citizen, it is extremely difficult to get a work visa; one of the few exceptions is the provision that people with student visas can apply for permission to work part-time. For any sort of long-stay visa, begin the paperwork several months before you leave home. By law, everyone in France, including tourists, must carry identification with them. For visitors, this means a passport. A national identity card is sufficient for EU citizens.

Visa Extensions

Tourist visas *cannot* be extended. If you qualify for an automatic three-month stay upon arrival, you'll get another three months if you exit and then re-enter France. The fewer French entry stamps you have in your passport, the easier this is likely to be.

French Embassies Abroad

Australia
    6 Perth Ave, Yarralumla, ACT 2600 (☎ 06-270 5111)
Canada
    42 Sussex Drive, Ottawa, Ontario K1M 2 C9
    (☎ 613-789 1795)
Germany
    Kappellenweg 1A, 5300 Bonn 2 (☎ 228-35 18 32)
Italy
    consulate: Via Giulia 251, 00186 Rome
    (☎ 06-68 80 64 37)
New Zealand
    Robert Jones House, 1-3 Willeston St (PO Box 1695),
    Wellington (☎ 04-472 0200)
Spain
    consulate: Calle Marques de la Enseñada 10, 28004
    Madrid (☎ 91-319 7188)
UK
    consulate: 6A Cromwell Place, London SW7
    (☎ 0171-838 2051; 0891-887733 for general information on visa requirements)
USA
    4101 Reservoir Rd, NW Washington, DC, 20007-2185 (☎ 202-944 6195)

Foreign Embassies in Paris

Australia
    4 Rue Jean Rey, 15e; metro Bir Hakeim
    (☎ 01 40 59 33 00)
Canada
    35 Ave Montaigne, 8e; metro Alma Marceau or
    Franklin D Roosevelt (☎ 01 44 43 29 00)
New Zealand
    7ter Rue Léonard de Vinci, 16e; metro Victor Hugo
    (☎ 01 45 00 24 11)
Spain
    consulate: 165 Blvd Malesherbes, 17e; metro
    Wagram (01 47 66 03 32)
UK
    Embassy: 35 Rue du Faubourg Saint Honoré, 8e;
    metro Concorde (☎ 01 42 66 91 42)
    consulate: 16 Rue d'Anjou, 8e; metro Concorde
    (☎ 01 42 66 38 10)
USA
    2 Ave Gabriel, 8e; metro Concorde
    (☎ 01 43 12 22 22)

MONEY

Generally you'll get a better exchange rate for travellers' cheques than for cash. The most useful travellers' cheques are those issued by American Express in US dollars or French francs, which can be exchanged at many post offices.

Do not bring travellers' cheques in Australian dollars as they are hard to change, especially outside Paris. US$100 dollar bills are also difficult to change because there are so many counterfeits around; many Banque de France branches refuse them.

Visa (Carte Bleue in France) is more widely accepted than MasterCard (Eurocard). Visa card-holders with a 'PIN' number can get cash advances from banks and automatic teller machines nationwide – even in remote Corsican towns. American Express cards are not very useful except to get cash at American Express offices in big cities or to pay for things in up-market shops and restaurants. To have money sent from abroad, have it wired to either Citicorp's Paris office (see Money in the Paris section) or to a specific branch of a French or foreign bank. You can also have money easily sent via American Express.

Currency

One French franc (FF) equals 100 centimes. French coins come in denominations of five, 10 and 20 centimes and half, one, two, five, 10 and 20FF (the last two are two-tone). Banknotes are issued in denominations of 20, 50,

100, 200 and 500FF. The higher the denomination, the larger the bill. It can be difficult to get change for a 500FF bill.

Exchange Rates

Australia	A$1	=	3.93FF
Canada	C$1	=	3.66FF
Germany	DM1	=	3.39FF
Japan	¥100	=	4.64FF
New Zealand	NZ$1	=	3.50FF
Spain	100 ptas	=	3.99FF
United Kingdom	UK£1	=	7.81FF
United States	US$1	=	5.02FF

Banque de France, France's central bank, offers the best exchange rates, especially for travellers' cheques, and it does not charge any commission (except 1% for travellers' cheques in French francs). There are Banque de France bureaus in the prefectures of each department.

Many post offices make exchange transactions at a very good rate. They accept banknotes in a variety of currencies as well as American Express travellers' cheques, but *only* if the cheques are in US dollars or French francs.

In large cities, *bureaux de change* (currency exchange offices) are faster, easier, have longer opening hours and often give better rates than the banks, but are not beyond milking clueless tourists. As always, your best bet is to compare the rates offered by various banks, which charge at least 20 to 30FF per transaction, and exchange bureaus, which are not allowed to charge commission.

If your American Express travellers' cheques or credit card are lost or stolen, call ☎ 08 00 90 86 00, American Express' 24-hour toll-free number in France. For lost or stolen Visa cards, call ☎ 01 42 77 11 90.

Costs

If you stay in hostels (or, if there are two or more of you, the cheapest hotels) and buy provisions from grocery stores rather than eating at restaurants, it is possible to tour France on as little as US$35 a day per person (US$45 in Paris). Eating out, lots of travel or treating yourself to France's many little luxuries can increase this figure dramatically. A student card can significantly reduce the price of getting into museums and other sights,

cinemas etc. Always check to see if you qualify for the *tarif réduit* (reduced price), as the rules vary tremendously.

Tipping

It is not necessary to leave a tip (*pourboire*) in restaurants, hotels etc; under French law, the bill must already include a 15% service charge. Some people leave a few francs on the table for the waiter, but this is not expected (especially for drinks). At truly posh restaurants, however, a more generous gratuity will be anticipated. For a taxi ride, the usual tip is about 2 or 3FF no matter what the fare.

Consumer Taxes

France's VAT (value-added tax, ie sales tax) is known in French as TVA (*taxe sur la valeur ajoutée*). The TVA is 20.6% on the purchase price of most goods (and for noncommercial vehicle rental). Prices that include TVA are often marked TTC (*toutes taxes comprises*), which means 'all taxes included'.

It is possible (though rather complicated) to get a reimbursement for TVA if you meet several conditions: 1) You are not an EU national and are over 15 years of age; 2) you have stayed in France less than six months; 3) you are buying more than 2000FF worth of goods at a single shop (not including foodstuffs); and 4) the establishment offers duty-free sales (*vente en détaxe*).

To claim a TVA, you fill out the proper export sales invoice (*bordereau de vente*) at the time you make your purchase. This is then stamped at your port of exit, thereby proving that you have taken the goods out of the country. The shop then reimburses you – by mail or bank transfer within 30 days – for the TVA you've paid.

POST & COMMUNICATIONS

Post

Postal Rates Postal services in France are fast, reliable and expensive. Postcards and letters up to 20g cost 3FF within the EU, 4.40FF to the USA and Canada and 5.20FF to Australasia. Aerograms cost 5.10FF to all destinations. All overseas packages are now sent by air only, which is very expensive.

Receiving Mail All mail to France *must* include the area's five-digit postcode, which begins with the two-digit number of the department. In Paris, all postcodes begin with 750 and end with the arrondissement number, eg 75004 for the 4th arrondissement, 75013 for the 13th. The local postcode appears in each destination in this book under Information or Post.

Since poste restante mail is held alphabetically by family name, it is important that you follow the French practice of having your last name written in capital letters. Poste restante mail not sent to a particular branch post office ends up at the town's main post office *(recette principale)*. In Paris, this means it goes to the central post office (☎ 01 40 28 20 00) at 48-52 Rue du Louvre (1er; metro Sentier or Les Halles). See Post in the Paris section for details. There is a 2.80FF charge for every poste restante claimed.

It is also possible to receive mail care of American Express offices, although if you do not have an American Express card or travellers' cheques there is a 5FF charge each time you check to see if you have received any mail.

Telephone

Once saddled with one of the worst telephone systems in Western Europe, over the last two decades France has leapfrogged into the era of high-tech telecommunications. Today, you can dial direct to almost anywhere in the world from any phone in France. The Minitel system, which gives online access to computer data bases, allows you to look up phone numbers throughout France and to make air, rail and concert reservations as well as access a wide range of data bases and services. Minitel is available in most major post offices.

Public Telephones Most public phones in France now require phonecards *(télécartes)*, which are sold at post offices, tobacconists' shops *(tabacs)*, Paris metro ticket counters and supermarket check-out counters. Cards worth 50/120 units cost 40.60/97.50FF. Each unit is good for one three-minute local call. Rates for calls abroad vary according to the time of day, so you will need to ask the French operator (see International Dialling below). To make a call with a phonecard, pick up the receiver, insert

the card and dial when the LCD screen reads 'Numérotez'.

All telephone cabins can take incoming calls, so if you want someone to call you back, give them the new 10-digit number (see Domestic Dialling below) written after the words *'ici le'* on the information sheet next to the phone.

Domestic Dialling In October 1996, the old system of dialling ☎ 16 to the provinces and ☎ 1 to Paris was abolished. France is now divided into five telephone zones and all telephone numbers, no matter what number you are calling or where you are calling from, are 10-digit rather than eight-digit.

Paris and Île de France numbers now begin with ☎ 01. The other codes are: ☎ 02 for areas in the north-west; ☎ 03 for the north-east; ☎ 04 for the south-east; and ☎ 05 for the south-west.

Toll-free numbers *(numéros verts)* now begin with ☎ 0800 instead of ☎ 05. Two-digit emergency numbers have not changed. For directory assistance *(service des renseignements)*, dial ☎ 12.

International Dialling To call France from abroad, first dial the international access code, then ☎ 33 (France's country code), but omit the 0 at the beginning of the new 10-digit number (see Domestic Dialling above).

Direct-dial calls to almost anywhere in the world can be placed using a phonecard. Just dial ☎ 00, wait for the second tone, and then add the country code, area code and local number. If the country code is not on the information sheet posted in phone cabins, consult a phone book or dial ☎ 12 (directory assistance).

To make a reverse-charge call *(en PCV)* or person-to-person *(avec préavis)* from France to other countries, dial ☎ 00 (the international operator), wait for the second tone and then dial ☎ 33 plus the country code of the place you're calling. If you're using a public phone, you must insert a phonecard (or, in the case of coin telephones, deposit 1FF) first.

For directory enquiries outside France, dial ☎ 00, and when the second tone sounds, dial ☎ 33, then ☎ 12, and finally the country code. For information on home-country direct calls, see the Telephones Appendix in the back of this book.

Fax & Telegram

Virtually all French post offices can send and receive domestic and international faxes (*télécopies* or *téléfaxes*), telexes and telegrams. It costs around 20FF to send a one-page fax within France, 45FF to the USA and 60FF to Australia.

NEWSPAPERS & MAGAZINES

The excellent *International Herald Tribune*, published six times a week and distributed around the globe, is edited in Paris. It is sold at many news kiosks throughout France for 10FF. Other English-language papers you can find include two British papers with European editions, the *Guardian* and the *Financial Times*; *The European*; and the colourful *USA Today*. *Newsweek*, *Time* and the *Economist* are also widely available.

RADIO & TV

The BBC World Service can be picked up on 195 kHz AM and 6195 kHz, 9410 kHz, 9760 kHz and 12095 kHz short wave. In northern France, BBC for Europe is on 648 kHz AM. Up-market hotels often offer cable TV access to CNN, BBC TV and other networks. Canal+ (pronounced 'ka-NAHL pluce'), a French subscription TV station available in many mid-range hotels, sometimes screens non-dubbed English movies.

PHOTOGRAPHY & VIDEO

Be prepared to have your camera and film forced through the ostensibly film-safe x-ray machines at airports and when entering sensitive public buildings such as any Palais de Justice (Law Courts) or Banque de France branch. The most you can do is ask that they hand-check your film, if not your whole camera.

Unlike the rest of Western Europe and Australia, which use PAL (phase alternation line), French TV broadcasts are in SECAM (*système électronique couleur avec mémoire*). North America and Japan use a third incompatible system, NTSC (National Television Systems Committee). French videotapes cannot be played on video cassette recorders or TVs that are not equipped with SECAM.

TIME

France is one hour ahead of GMT/UTC in winter and two hours ahead in summer. The 24-hour clock is widely used in France – even informally. Thus 14.30 (or 14h30) is 2.30 pm, 00.15 (00h15) is 12.15 am and so on.

ELECTRICITY

The electric current in France is 220V, 50 Hz. Plugs have two round pins.

WEIGHTS & MEASURES

France uses the metric system, which was invented by the French Academy of Sciences and adopted by the French government in 1795. For a chart of metric equivalents, see the inside back cover of this guide.

LAUNDRY

To find a self-service laundrette (*laverie libre service*), ask at the front desk of your hotel or hostel. Be prepared to pay about 22FF per load and around 2FF for six minutes of drying and a cup of washing powder (*lessive*). Bring lots of coins; few laundrettes have change machines.

TOILETS

Public toilets, signposted as *toilettes* or *wc*, are few and far between, though small towns often have them near the town hall (*mairie*). In Paris, you're more likely to come upon one of the tan, self-disinfecting toilet pods. Get your change ready: many public toilets cost 2FF or even 2.50FF. In the absence of public amenities, you can try ducking into a fast-food outlet or department store. Except in the most tourist-filled areas, café owners are usually amenable to your using their toilets provided you ask politely (and with just a hint of urgency).

HEALTH
Public Health System

France has an extensive public health care system. Anyone who is sick can receive treatment in the emergency room (*service des urgences*) of any public hospital. Such treatment costs much less in France than in many other countries, especially the USA. Hospitals usually ask that foreigners settle their account right after receiving treatment.

Condoms

Many pharmacies have 24-hour automatic condom (*préservatif*) dispensers near the door.

Some brasseries and discothèques also have condom-vending machines.

WOMEN TRAVELLERS

In general, women need not walk around in fear of passers-by – women are rarely physically attacked on the street. However, you are more likely to be left alone if you have about you a purposeful air that implies that you know exactly where you're going – even if you haven't a clue!

If you are subject to catcalls or are hassled in any way while walking down the street, the best strategy is usually to carry on and ignore the macho lowlife who is disrupting your holiday. Making a cutting retort is ineffective in English and risky in French if your slang isn't extremely proficient.

France's national rape crisis hotline, which is run by a women's organisation called Viols Femmes Informations, can be reached toll-free by dialling ☎ 0800 05 95 95. It is staffed by volunteers Monday to Friday from 10 am to 6 pm.

GAY & LESBIAN TRAVELLERS

Most of France's major gay organisations are based in Paris. Centre Gai et Lesbien (CGL; ☎ 01 43 57 21 47), 3 Rue Keller (11e; metro Ledru Rollin) 500 metres east of Place de la Bastille, serves as a headquarters for lots of organisations that hold a variety of meetings and activities each week. The bar, library etc are open Monday to Saturday from 2 to 8 pm; the Sunday activities (2 to 7 pm) are mainly for people who are HIV positive.

Archives Lesbiennes (☎ 01 43 56 11 49) holds meetings on the ground floor of the Maison des Femmes (☎ 01 43 48 24 91) at 8 Cité Prost (11e; metro Charonne) every Friday from 7 to 10 pm. Écoute Gaie runs a hotline (☎ 01 44 93 01 02) for gays and lesbians that's staffed on weekdays from 6 to 10 pm.

Gay male-oriented publications include *Illico*, published at the beginning of each month, with articles (in French) and lots of ads for places that cater to gays, and the monthly *Double Face*, which has fewer articles and more information on nightlife. For lesbians, the monthly national magazine *Lesbia* gives a rundown of what's happening around the country.

DISABLED TRAVELLERS

France is not particularly well equipped for disabled people *(handicapés)*: kerb ramps are few and far between, older public facilities and bottom-end hotels often lack lifts, and the Paris metro, most of it built decades ago, is hopeless. But physically disabled people who would like to travel in France can overcome these problems. For instance, most hotels with two or more stars are equipped with lifts, and Michelin's *Guide Rouge* indicates hotels with lifts and facilities for disabled people.

Hostels in Paris that cater to disabled travellers include the Foyer International d'Accueil de Paris Jean Monnet and the Centre International de Séjour de Paris Kellermann (see Hostels & Foyers under Places to Stay in the Paris section).

The Comité National Français de Liaison pour la Réadaptation des Handicapés (☎ 01 53 80 66 66), at 236 Rue de Tolbiac (13e; metro Glacière) in Paris, can provide information on accommodation, sports and leisure pursuits, transport and access to tourist sites throughout France. The Association des Paralysés de France (☎ 01 40 78 69 00), at 17 Blvd Auguste Blanqui (13e; metro Porte d'Italie), may be able to help with specific enquiries and can supply the addresses of branches across France.

SENIOR TRAVELLERS

People aged over 60 are eligible for a reduction of up to 50% on 1st and 2nd-class train travel with a Carte Vermeil Plein Temps. It costs 270FF and is valid in 21 European countries for one year (see Train in the Getting Around section). Entry to most museums and monuments in France is half price for people over 60 – always check the tariff rules to see if you are eligible for a reduction. Senior citizens are usually offered a reduction on cinema tickets during the week. Some hostels, particularly in Paris, only offer accommodation to 'young' people; again, check the rules if you're thinking of hostelling.

DANGERS & ANNOYANCES

The biggest crime problem for tourists in France is theft – especially of and from cars. Never, *ever* leave anything in a parked motor vehicle or you'll learn the hard way. Pickpockets are a problem, and women are a common target because of their handbags. Be especially careful at airports and on crowded public transport in cities.

France's laws regarding even small quantities of drugs are very strict. Thanks to the Napoleonic Code, the police have the right to search anyone they want at any time, whether or not there is probable cause, and they have been known to stop and search charter buses coming from Amsterdam.

If stopped by the police for any reason, your best course of action is to be polite and to remain calm. It is a very bad idea to be overly assertive, and being rude or disrespectful is asking for serious trouble. Emergency telephone numbers in use all over France include:

Ambulance (SAMU)	☎ 15
Fire Brigade	☎ 18
Police	☎ 17

The rise in support for the extreme right-wing National Front in recent years reflects the growing racial intolerance in France, particularly against Muslim North Africans and, to a lesser extent, blacks from sub-Saharan Africa and France's former territories in the Caribbean. In many parts of France, especially in the south (eg Provence and the Côte d'Azur), entertainment places such as bars and discos are, for all intents and purposes, segregated: owners and their ferocious-looking bouncers make it quite clear who is 'invited' to use their public facilities and who is not.

BUSINESS HOURS

Most museums are closed on either Monday or Tuesday and on public holidays (jours fériés), though during the summer some stay open seven days a week. Most small businesses are open from 9 or 10 am to 6.30 or 7 pm daily except Sunday and perhaps Monday, with a break between noon and 2 pm or 1 and 3 pm. In the south, midday closures are more like siestas and may continue until 3.30 or even 4 pm.

Many food shops are open daily except Sunday afternoon and Monday. As a result, Sunday morning may be your last chance to stock up on provisions until Tuesday. Most restaurants are open only for lunch (noon to 2 or 3 pm) and dinner (6.30 to about 10 or 11 pm); outside Paris, very few serve meals throughout the day. All are closed at least one full day per week and sometimes a lunchtime as well. In August, lots of establishments simply close so that their owners and employees alike can take their annual month-long holiday. With most museums and other sights closed at midday and lunch menus cheaper than dinner ones, it pays to take your main meal at lunch and picnic at night.

Banque de France branches throughout France are open Monday to Friday from around 8.45 am to 12.15 pm and 1.30 to 3.30 pm. The opening hours of other banks vary. The main post office in towns and cities, and all branches in Paris, are open weekdays from 8 am to 6.30 or 7 pm and on Saturday to noon. Branches outside Paris are generally open from 8.30 am to noon and 1.30 or 2 to 5.30 or 6.30 pm weekdays and on Saturday morning.

PUBLIC HOLIDAYS & SPECIAL EVENTS

National public holidays in France include New Year's Day, Easter Sunday & Monday, May Day (1 May), 1945 Victory Day (8 May), Ascension Thursday (40th day after Easter), Pentecost Sunday and Whit Monday (seventh Sunday and Monday after Easter), Bastille Day (14 July), Assumption Day (15 August), All Saints' Day (1 November), 1918 Armistice Day (11 November) and Christmas Day.

Most French cities have at least one major cultural festival each year. For details about what's on and when (dates change from year to year), contact the main tourist office in Paris or a French Government Tourist Office abroad.

ACTIVITIES
Skiing

The French Alps have some of the finest skiing in Europe. Smaller, low-altitude stations are much cheaper than their classier, high-altitude cousins. There are quite a few low-altitude ski stations in the Pyrenees.

Surfing

The best surfing in France (and some of the best in all of Europe) is on the Atlantic coast around Biarritz.

Hiking

France has thousands of km of hiking trails in every region of the country and through every kind of terrain. These include sentiers de *grande randonnée*, long-distance hiking paths whose alphanumeric names begin with the letters GR and are sometimes hundreds of km long (as in Corsica).

Canoeing

The Fédération Française de Canoë-Kayak (☎ 01 45 11 08 50) at 87 Quai de la Marne, 94340 Joinville-le-Pont, can supply information on canoeing and kayaking clubs around the country. The sports are very popular in the Périgord (Dordogne) area. See Getting Around for information about houseboats and canal boats.

COURSES

For details on language and cooking courses, see Courses in the Paris section. For water sports courses see Courses in Bayonne.

Information on studying in France is available from French consulates and French Government Tourist Offices abroad. In Paris, the Centre Régional des Œuvres Universitaires et Scolaires (CROUS; ☎ 01 40 51 37 10), 39 Ave Georges Bernanos (5e; metro Port Royal), provides information on matters of interest to students.

WORK

Getting a *carte de séjour* (temporary residence permit), which in most cases lets you work in France, is almost automatic for EU citizens; contact the Préfecture de Police in Paris or, in the provinces, the *mairie* (town hall) or nearest prefecture. For anyone else, it is almost impossible, though the government does seem to tolerate undocumented workers helping out with some agricultural work, especially the apple and grape harvests in autumn. It's hard work and you are usually put up in barracks, but it's paid.

Working as an au pair – a kind of mother's helper – is very common in France, especially in Paris. Single young people – particularly women – receive board, lodging and a bit of money (500FF per week is the going rate) in exchange for taking care of the kids and doing light housework. Knowing at least a bit of French may be a prerequisite. Even US and other non-EU citizens can become au pairs, but they must be studying something (eg a recognised language course) and have to apply

for an au pair's visa three months *before* leaving home.

For information on au pair placement, contact a French consulate or the Paris tourist office. Most private agencies charge the au pair 600 to 800FF and collect an additional fee from the family. Some agencies check the family and the living conditions they are offering; others are less thorough. In any case, be assertive in dealing with the agency to make sure you get what you want.

ACCOMMODATION

More and more cities and towns in France are instituting a *taxe de séjour*, which is a tax on each night you stay in a hotel and sometimes even hostels or camping grounds. In Paris, the tax ranges from 1 to 7FF per person per night but is usually included in the quoted price.

Camping

France has thousands of seasonal and year-round camping grounds, many of which are situated near streams, rivers, lakes or the ocean. Facilities and amenities, which are reflected in the number of stars the site has been awarded, determine the price. At the less fancy places, two people with a small tent should expect to pay 25 to 55FF a night. Another option in some rural areas is farm camping (*camping à la ferme*). Tourist offices will have details.

Camping grounds near cities and towns covered in this guide are detailed under Places to Stay for each city or town. For information on other camping grounds, enquire at a tourist office or consult the *Guide Officiel Camping/Caravaning* or Michelin's *Camping/Caravaning France*. Both are updated annually.

Campers who arrive at a camping ground without a vehicle can usually get a spot, even late in the day, but not in July and especially not in August, when most are packed with families on their annual holiday.

If you'll be doing overnight backpacking, remember that in national and regional parks camping is permitted only in proper camping grounds. Camping elsewhere, eg in a road or trailside meadow (*camping sauvage*), is tolerated to varying degrees (but not at all in Corsica); you probably won't have any problems with the police if you're not on private land, have only a small tent, are discreet, stay only one night and are at least 1500 metres from a camping ground.

Refuges & Gîtes d'Étape

Refuges (mountain huts or shelters) are basic dorm rooms operated by national park authorities, the Club Alpin Français and other private organisations along trails in uninhabited mountainous areas frequented by hikers and mountain climbers. They are marked on hiking and climbing maps. Some are open all year, others only during the warm months.

In general, refuges are equipped with mattresses and blankets but not sheets, which you have to bring yourself. Charges average 50 to 70FF per night per person. Meals, prepared by the *gardien* (attendant), are sometimes available. Most refuges are equipped with a telephone, so it's a good idea to call ahead and make a reservation. For details on refuges, contact a tourist office near where you'll be hiking.

Gîtes d'étape, which are usually better equipped and more comfortable than refuges (some even have showers), are found in less remote areas, often in villages. They also cost around 50 to 70FF per person. *Les Gîtes d'Étape* published annually by Fivedit covers the whole of France and should be available in bookshops or at newsstands.

Hostels

In the provinces, hostels (*auberges de jeunesse*) generally charge from 45FF (for out-of-the-way places with basic facilities) to 70FF for a bunk in a single-sex dorm room. A few of the more comfortable places that aren't officially auberges de jeunesse charge from 70 to 90FF, usually including breakfast. In Paris, expect to pay 95 to 120FF a night, including breakfast. In the cities, especially Paris, you will also find *foyers*, student dorms used by travellers in summer. Information on hostels and foyers is available from tourist offices. Most of France's hostels belong to one of three Paris-based organisations:

Fédération Unie des Auberges de Jeunesse (FUAJ)
    27 Rue Pajol, 18e; metro La Chapelle (☎ 01 44 89 87 27; fax 01 44 89 87 10). FUAJ has 190 hostels in France and is the only group affiliated with Hostelling International (HI).

Ligue Française pour les Auberges de la Jeunesse (LFAJ)
    38 Blvd Raspail, 7e; metro Sèvres Babylone (☎ 01 45 48 69 84; fax 01 45 44 57 47)
Union des Centres de Rencontres Internationales de France (UCRIF)
    27 Rue de Turbigo, 2e; metro Étienne Marcel (☎ 01 40 26 57 64; fax 01 40 26 58 20)

Cheap Hotels

Staying in an inexpensive hotel often costs less than a hostel when two or more people share a room.

Unless otherwise indicated, prices quoted in this chapter refer to rooms in unrated or one-star hotels equipped with a washbasin (and usually a bidet, too) but without a toilet or shower. Most doubles, which generally cost the same or only marginally more than singles, have only one bed. Doubles with two beds usually cost a little more. Taking a shower (*douche*) in the hall bathroom can be free or cost between 10 and 25FF.

Reservations If you'll be arriving after noon (or after 10 am during peak tourism periods), it is a good idea to call ahead and make reservations; it will probably save you a lot of time and hassle in the long run.

For advance reservations, most hotels require that you send them a deposit by post. But if you call on the day you'll be coming and sound credible, many hotels will hold a room for you until a set hour (rarely later than 6 or 7 pm). At small hotels, reception is usually closed on Sunday morning or afternoon. Local tourist offices will also make reservations for you, usually for a small fee.

FOOD

A fully fledged traditional French dinner – usually begun about 8.30 pm – has quite a few distinct courses: an apéritif or cocktail; a first course (*entrée*); the main course (*plat principal*); salad (*salade*); cheese (*fromage*); dessert (*dessert*); fruit (*fruit*); coffee (*café*); and a *digestif*.

France has lots of restaurants where several hundred francs gets you excellent French cuisine, but inexpensive French restaurants are in short supply. Fortunately, delicious and surprisingly cheap ethnic cuisine is available from the many restaurants specialising in dishes from France's former colonies in Africa, Indochina, India, the Caribbean and the South

Pacific. One of the most delicious of the North African dishes is *couscous*, steamed semolina eaten with vegetables and some sort of meat: lamb shish kebab, *merguez* (North African sausage), *mechoui* (lamb on the bone) or chicken.

Restaurants & Brasseries
There are two principal differences between restaurants and brasseries: restaurants usually specialise in a particular cuisine while brasseries – which look very much like cafés – serve quicker meals of more standard fare (eg steak and chips/French fries, omelettes etc). Restaurants are usually open only for lunch and dinner; brasseries, on the other hand, serve meals (or at least something solid) throughout the day.

Most restaurants offer at least one fixed-price, multicourse meal known in French as a *menu*, *menu à prix fixe* or *menu du jour*. In general, menus cost much less than ordering each dish separately (*à la carte*), but some may be only available at lunch. When you order the menu, you usually get to choose a first course, a main meat or fish dish and a cheese or dessert course. A *formule* usually allows you to choose two of the three courses. Drinks (*boissons*) cost extra unless the menu says *boisson comprise* (drink included), which usually means a quarter litre of wine.

Cafés
Sitting in a café to read, write or talk with friends is an integral part of everyday life in France. People use cafés as a way to keep in touch with their neighbourhood and friends, and to generally participate in the social life of their town or city.

A café located on a grand boulevard (such as Blvd du Montparnasse or the Champs Élysées in Paris) will charge considerably more than a place that fronts a side street. Once inside, progressively more expensive tariffs apply at the counter (*comptoir*), in the café itself (*salle*) and outside on the *terrasse*. The price of drinks goes up at night, usually after 8 pm, but the price of a cup of coffee (or anything else) earns you the right to sit for as long as you like.

Self-Catering
France is justly renowned for its extraordinary

chefs and restaurants, but one of the country's premier culinary delights – especially for vegetarians, who will find France's restaurants obsessed with meat and seafood – is to stock up on fresh breads, cheeses, fruit, vegetables, prepared dishes etc and have a picnic. Although prices are likely to be much higher than you're used to, you will find that the food is of excellent quality.

While supermarkets (*supermarchés*) and slightly more expensive grocery shops (*épiceries*) are more and more popular with working people in cities, many people still buy their food from small neighbourhood shops, each with its own speciality. The whole setup is geared towards people buying fresh food each day, so it's completely acceptable to purchase very small quantities – a few slices (*tranches*) of sliced meat or a few hundred grams of salad.

Fresh *baguettes* and other breads are baked and sold at a *boulangerie*. They may also sell sandwiches, quiches and small (very ordinary) pizzas. Mouthwatering pastries are available from a *pâtisserie*. For chocolate and sweets, look for a *confiserie*. (These three shops are often combined.) For a selection of superb cheeses, such as *chèvre* (goat's-milk cheese) and a half-round of perfectly ripe Camembert, go to a *fromagerie* (also called a *crémerie*). Fruit and vegetables are sold by a *marchand de legumes et de fruits*. Wine is sold by a *marchand de vin*.

A general butcher is a *boucherie*, but for specialised poultry you have to go to a *marchand de volaille*, and a *boucherie chevaline* will sell you horsemeat, still popular in France all these years after the war. Fish is available from a *poissonnerie*. A *charcuterie* is a delicatessen offering pricey but delicious sliced meats, seafood salads, pâtés and ready-to-eat main dishes. Most supermarkets have a charcuterie counter. The word *traiteur* (caterer) means the establishment sells ready-to-eat takeaway dishes.

In most towns and cities, most foods are available one or more days a week at open-air markets (*marchés découverts*) or their covered equivalents (*marchés couverts* or *halles*).

DRINKS
Nonalcoholic Drinks
There is no medical reason to buy expensive

bottled water; the tap water in France is perfectly safe. Make sure you ask for *une carafe d'eau* (a jug of water) or *de l'eau du robinet* (tap water) or you may get costly mineral water (*eau de source*).

A small cup of espresso is called *un café*, *un café noir* or *un express*. You can also ask for a large (*grand*) version. *Un café crème* is espresso with steamed cream. *Un café au lait* is espresso served in a large cup with lots of steamed milk. Decaffeinated coffee is *un café décaféiné* or simply *un déca*.

Other hot drinks that are popular include: tea (*thé*), but if you want milk you ask for '*un peu de lait frais*'; herbal tea (*tisane*); and usually excellent hot chocolate (*chocolat chaud*).

Alcohol

The French almost always take their meals with wine – red (*rouge*), white (*blanc*) or *rosé*, chosen to complement what's being eaten. The least expensive wines cost less per litre than soft drinks. Wines that meet stringent regulations governing where, how and under what conditions the grapes are grown, fermented and bottled, bear the abbreviation AOC (*Appellation d'Origine Controlée*, which means 'mark of controlled place of origin'). The cheapest wines have no AOC certification and are known as *vins ordinaires* or *vins de table* (table wines). They sell for as little as 5FF a litre in wine-producing areas and closer to 10 or 12FF a litre in supermarkets, but spending an extra 5 or 10FF per bottle can make all the difference.

Alcoholic drinks other than wine include apéritifs, such as kir (dry white wine sweetened with *cassis* – blackcurrant liqueur), *kir royale* (champagne with cassis), and *pastis* (anise-flavoured alcohol drunk with ice and water); and *digestifs* such as brandy or Calvados (apple brandy). Beer is usually either from Alsace or imported. A *demi* (about 250 ml) is cheaper on draught (*à la pression*) than from a bottle.

ENTERTAINMENT

If you don't fancy seeing your favourite actors lip-synching in French, look in the film listings and on the theatre marquee for the letters 'VO' (*version originale*) or 'VOST' (*version originale sous-titrée*), which mean the film retains its original foreign soundtrack but has been

given French subtitles. If there's no VO or if you see 'VF' (*version française*), the film has been dubbed.

THINGS TO BUY

France is renowned for its luxury goods, including *haute couture* fashion, expensive accessories (eg Hermès scarves), perfume and such alcoholic beverages as champagne and brandy. Purchases of over 2000FF by people who live outside the EU are eligible for a rebate of the value added tax (TVA) on most goods. See Consumer Taxes under Money earlier in this section.

Getting There & Away

AIR

Air France and scores of other airlines link Paris with every part of the globe. Other French cities with direct international air links include Nice, Lyon and Marseille. For details on agencies selling discount international tickets in Paris, see Travel Agencies in the Paris section. For information on Paris' two international airports, Orly and Roissy-Charles de Gaulle, see Getting There & Away in the Paris section. Information on how to get from the airports into Paris (and vice versa) is given under Getting Around in the Paris section.

Britain

Return flights between Paris' Charles de Gaulle airport and London start at 611FF (British Midland) to Heathrow and 618FF (British Airways and Air UK) to Gatwick and Stanstead. You must stay over a Saturday night. In Paris contact Nouvelles Frontières (☎ 01 46 34 55 30) at 66 Blvd Saint Michel (6e; metro Luxembourg). SOS Charters (☎ 01 49 59 09 09; recorded message) has information on round-trip packages. On Minitel, key in 3615 SOS Charters.

Elsewhere in Europe

One-way discount charter fares available for flights from Paris start at 580FF to Rome; 920FF to Athens; 730FF to Dublin; 940FF to Istanbul; and 710FF to Madrid. Contact a travel agent or call SOS Charters for more information.

LAND
Britain

The highly civilised Eurostar – the passenger train service through the Channel Tunnel – began operating between Paris' Gare du Nord and London's Waterloo Station in late 1994. The journey takes about three hours (20 minutes through the tunnel) and will be shortened when Britain completes its portion of high-speed track at the end of the decade. The full one-way/return fare between Paris and London is 645/1290FF, but if you travel during the week and spend more than three nights away you can get a return fare for as little as 490FF.

Le Shuttle, which also began operating in 1994, whisks buses and cars (and their passengers) on single and double-deck wagons from near Folkstone to Coquelles just west of Calais in 35 minutes. Actual travel time from *autoroute* (the A26 to/from Paris) to motorway (the M20 to/from London) is closer to an hour, though. One-way fares start at 590FF. Shuttles run round the clock, and no bookings are required.

The Eurostar and Le Shuttle office in Paris (☎ 01 44 51 06 02) is in the Maison de la Grande Bretagne at 19 Rue des Mathurins (9e; metro Havre Caumartin), north-west of Place de l'Opéra. Information is also available on Minitel 3615 SNCF/Le Shuttle.

Elsewhere in Europe

Bus For bus services between France and other parts of Europe, see Getting There & Away in the Paris section.

Train Paris, France's main rail hub, is linked with every part of Europe. Depending on where you're coming from, you may have to transit through Paris to get to the provinces. For details on Paris' six train stations, each of which handles traffic to/from different parts of France and Europe, see Train under Getting There & Away in the Paris section.

BIJ (Billet International Jeunes) tickets, which are available to people under 26, cost about 20% or 25% less than regular tickets on international 2nd-class train travel started during off-peak periods. See Discounts under Train in the following Getting Around section for details. BIJ tickets are not sold at train station ticket windows; you have to go to an office of Transalpino, Frantour Tourisme or Voyages Wasteels. There's usually one in the vicinity of a major train station.

SEA
Britain & the Channel Islands

The hovercraft *(aéroglisseur)* takes 30 minutes to cross the Channel. Hoverspeed (☎ 01 40 25 22 00 in France, 01304-24 0241 in Dover) runs both giant catamarans (SeaCats) and hovercraft from Calais to Dover (Douvres), Boulogne to Dover and Boulogne to Folkstone. Passage costs from 200FF one way, up to 400FF for a five-day return. A small car with four passengers costs at least 525FF return on a SeaCat. Bus-boat combos from Victoria Coach Station in London to 165 Ave de Clichy (17e; RER C Porte de Clichy) take about eight hours and start at 270FF one way. Train-boat combos are sold at train stations. Hoverspeed's Paris office is at 165 Ave de Clichy (17e; RER C Porte de Clichy).

Sealink (☎ 01 44 94 40 40 in Paris, 03 21 34 55 00 in Calais and 01304-20 4204 in Dover), in Paris' Maison de la Grande Bretagne at 19 Rue des Mathurins (9e; metro Havre Caumartin), runs car ferries from Calais to Dover (1½ hours). One-way fares for passengers and cyclists start at 180FF. Cars cost from 400 to 1180FF one way.

Stena Line (☎ 01 53 43 40 00), 38 Ave de l'Opéra (2e; metro Opéra), operates car ferries (from 180FF one way, four hours) and catamarans (from 220FF, two hours) from Dieppe to Newhaven; and ferries from Cherbourg to Southampton (180 to 390FF one way, six/eight hours during the day/night).

P&O European Ferries (☎ 01 44 51 00 51 in Paris, 01304-22 3000 in Dover), in the same building as Sealink in Paris, runs car ferries from Calais to Dover (1¼ hours), Le Havre to Portsmouth (5¾ hours) and Cherbourg to Portsmouth (3¾ hours). If you're going to far northern France, you might consider the company's Dover-Ostende (Belgium) route.

For information on ferries from Saint Malo to Weymouth, Poole, Portsmouth, Jersey, Guernsey (Guernesey) and Sark (Sercq), see Ferry under Getting There & Away in the Saint Malo (Brittany) section.

Ireland

Irish Ferries (☎ 01 42 66 90 90) links Le Havre and Cherbourg with Cork and Rosslare. The trip takes about 20 hours. There are only two or three ferries a week from October to March but daily runs the rest of the year. Passengers pay from 530FF one way, depending on when they travel, and students get a small discount. The cheapest couchette is an extra 38FF. Irish Ferries' Paris office is at 32 Rue du 4 Septembre (2e; metro Opéra). Eurail passes are valid on some of these ferry services.

Italy

For information on ferry services between Italy and Corsica, see Getting There & Away in the Corsica section. You can purchase tickets from many French travel agents.

North Africa

The Société Nationale Maritime Corse Méditerranée (SNCM) and its Algerian counterpart, Algérie Ferries, operate ferry services from Marseille to the Algerian ports of Algiers (Alger), Annaba, Bejaia, Skikda and Oran. Passage to the first four cities (from 950FF one way) takes 18 to 24 hours – and slightly more to Oran (from 1050FF one way). SNCM also has services from Marseille to Tunis in Tunisia (from 915FF) and Porto Torres in Sardinia. For details, see Ferry under Getting There & Away in the Marseille section.

The Compagnie Marocaine de Navigation (☎ 04 91 56 32 00 in Marseille) runs ferries from Sète (near Montpellier) to the Moroccan cities of Tangier (Tanger) and Nador. The trip takes about 36 hours.

Getting Around

AIR

Air France Europe (Air Inter until the end of 1996; ☎ 01 45 46 90 00 in Paris) handles domestic passenger flights. Flying within France is quite expensive, but people under 25 (and students under 27) can get discounts of 50% and more on certain Air Inter flights. The most heavily discounted flights may be cheaper than long-distance rail travel. Details are available from travel agents.

BUS

Because the French train network is state-owned and the government prefers to operate a monopoly, the country has only a limited intercity bus service. Buses are widely used, however, for short-distance intra-departmental routes, especially in rural areas with relatively few train lines (eg Brittany and Normandy).

Costs

In some areas (eg along the Côte d'Azur), you may have the choice of going by either bus or train. For longer trips, buses tend to be much slower but slightly cheaper than trains. On short runs they are slower and usually more expensive.

TRAIN

France's excellent rail network, operated by the Société Nationale des Chemins de Fer (SNCF), reaches almost every part of the country. Places not served by train are linked with major railheads by SNCF buses. France's most important train lines fan out from Paris like the spokes of a wheel, making rail travel between certain provincial towns and cities infrequent and rather slow. In some cases, you have to transit through Paris, which may require transferring from one of Paris' six train stations to another (see Train under Getting There & Away in the Paris section for details).

The pride and joy of the SNCF is the world-famous TGV (train à grande vitesse), which means 'high-speed train'. There are three TGV lines: the TGV Sud-Est, which links Paris' Gare de Lyon with Lyon, Valence and – via non-TGV tracks – the south-east; the TGV Atlantique, which runs from Paris' Gare Montparnasse to the Loire Valley, Bordeaux and the south-west; and the TGV Nord Europe, which goes from Paris' Gare du Nord to Calais and London. Although it usually travels at 300 km/h, the TGV Atlantique has, in test runs, reached over 515 km/h, the world speed record for trains. Going by TGV costs the same as travelling on regular trains except that you must pay a reservation fee (see Costs & Reservations below) of 18 to 99FF, depending on when you travel.

Most larger SNCF stations have a left-luggage office (consigne manuelle) which charges 30FF per bag (35FF for a bicycle) for 24 hours.

Information

Most train stations have both ticket windows (*guichets*) and an information and reservation office or desk. SNCF now has a nationwide telephone number (☎ 08 36 35 35 35 in French, ☎ 08 36 35 35 39 in English) for all rail enquiries and reservations.

Formalities

Before boarding the train on each leg of your journey, you must validate your ticket *and* your reservation card by time-stamping them in one of the *composteurs*, postbox-like orange machines that are located somewhere between the ticket windows and the tracks. Eurail passes and France Railpasses *must* be time-stamped before you begin your first journey to initiate the period of validity.

Costs & Reservations

Train fares consist of two parts: the cost of passage, which is calculated according to the number of km you'll be travelling, and a reservation fee. The reservation fee is optional unless you travel by TGV or want a couchette or special reclining seat. In addition, on especially popular trains (eg on holiday weekends) you may have to make advance reservations in order to get a seat. Eurail-pass holders should bear in mind that they must pay any applicable reservation fees. Since some overnight trains are equipped only with couchettes – eg most of the overnight trains on the Paris-Nice run – there's no way Eurail-pass holders can avoid the reservation fee except by taking a day train with a supply of unreserved seats.

Discounts

For the purpose of granting discounts, SNCF now divides train travel into two periods: blue (*bleue*), when the largest discounts are available, and white (*blanche*), when there are far fewer bargains. To be eligible for the discount, your journey must begin during a period of the appropriate colour. For a chart of blue and white periods, ask for a *Calendrier Voyageurs* at any SNCF information counter.

Discounts for Non-EU Citizens The France Vacances Pass (called the France Railpass in North America) allows unlimited travel by rail in France for three to nine days over the course of a month. The pass can be purchased in

France (from Gare du Nord, Gare de Lyon, Gare Saint Lazare and the two airports in Paris, and the main train stations in Nice and Marseille only) but will be more expensive than buying it before you leave home. A three-day pass bought in France costs 1169FF. In the USA, the three-day 2nd-class version costs US$145; each additional day is US$30. The pass is available through travel agents anywhere outside Europe and from a limited number of places within Europe. In North America, Rail Europe (☎ 800-438 7245) has all the information.

Discounts Available in France The Carrissimo card, valid for travel within France *only*, grants the holder (who must be 12 to 25 years old) and up to four travelling companions (who must also be aged 12 to 25) a 50% discount for journeys begun during blue periods and a 20% discount for travel begun during white periods. A Carrissimo card costs 190FF for four trips or 295FF for eight trips and is available from SNCF information offices.

For travel within France, students aged 12 to 25 can purchase BSE (Billet Scolaire et Étudiants) tickets, which cost 20% to 25% less than regular one-way or return fares. Like BIJ tickets (see Train in the Getting There & Away section), they cannot be purchased from SNCF – you have to go to a Wasteels, Transalpino or Frantour Tourisme office.

No matter what age you are, the Billet Séjour excursion fare gives you a 25% reduction for round-trip travel within France if you meet three conditions: the total length of your trip is at least 1000 km; you'll be spending at least part of a Sunday at your destination; and you begin travel in both directions during blue periods. It is available at ticket counters or the station's information and reservation office. With a Carte Couple – which is available free to any two people who are living together and can prove it – one of the two people who appear on the card pays full fare and the other gets 50% off on travel undertaken together provided it's begun during blue periods.

People aged 60 or over can get a Carte Vermeil Plein Temps, which entitles the bearer to a 50% reduction for 1st or 2nd-class travel begun during blue periods and 20% during white periods. It costs 270FF, is valid for one year in 21 European countries and is available from the information offices of major European train stations. A four-journey version valid for France only, the Carte Vermeil Quatre Temps, costs 135FF.

The Carte Kiwi is useful for people travelling with a child under 16. With the Carte Kiwi 4 x 4 (285FF), the child (who is the cardholder) and up to four companions of any age or relation get 50% off four trips for a year. The Carte Kiwi Tutti (444FF) allows unlimited travel under the same conditions for a year.

Anyone can take advantage of *les prix Joker* (Joker prices). Buy your ticket eight days in advance and you'll get a 30% discount. More than a month before earns you 60% off. But discounts are not available on all lines.

TAXI
France's cities and larger towns all have 24-hour taxi service. French taxis are always equipped with meters; prices range from 3.23FF per km in Paris to as high as 10FF in Corsica. Tariffs are quite a bit higher after 7 pm and on Sunday and public holidays. There are often surcharges (5FF or so) for each piece of heavy luggage or if you are picked up or dropped off at a train station or airport. Passengers always sit in the back seat.

CAR & MOTORCYCLE
There's nothing like exploring the back roads of the Loire Valley or the Alps on your own, free of train and bus schedules. Unfortunately, travelling around France by car or motorcycle is expensive: petrol is costly and tolls can reach hundreds of francs a day if you're going cross-country in a hurry. Three or four people travelling together, however, may find that renting a car is cheaper than taking the train. Throughout France, you must use a meter to park. Buy a ticket from the machine you'll see on every block and display it *inside* the car on the dashboard.

Road Rules
To drive in France, you must carry a passport or EU national identity card, a valid driver's licence, proof of insurance and car-ownership papers.

Unless otherwise posted, speed limits are 130 km/h (110 km/h in the rain) on the *auto-routes* (dual carriageways/expressways whose

alphanumeric names begin with A); 110/90 km/h on the *routes nationales* (highways whose names begin with N); and 90 km/h on the *routes départementales* (rural highways whose names start with D). The moment you pass a sign indicating that you've entered the boundaries of a town, village or hamlet, the speed limit automatically drops to 50 km/h (or less as posted) and stays there until you pass an identical sign with a red bar across it.

The maximum permissible blood-alcohol level in France is 0.07%.

Expenses
Petrol prices in France can vary by half a franc or more per litre depending on the station – it pays to shop around. Regular leaded petrol (*essence*) with an octane rating of 97, usually sold as *super*, costs about 5.90FF a litre. Unleaded (*sans plomb*) petrol with an octane rating of 98 costs around 5.80FF a litre. Diesel fuel (*gasoil* or *gazole*) is about 4.20FF a litre. Fuel is most expensive at the rest stops along the autoroutes.

Tolls are another major expense: expect to pay around 40FF per 100 km.

Rental
Renting a car in France is expensive, especially if you do it through one of the international car-hire companies. In the Getting Around sections for many cities, the Car & Motorcycle entry supplies details on the cheapest places to rent cars.

If you get into a minor accident, fill out a Constat Aimable d'Accident Automobile (joint car accident report) – there should be one in the glove compartment – with the other driver. You both sign and each of you gets a copy. If you were not at fault, make sure all the facts reflecting this are included on the form which, unless your French is really fluent, should be filled out with the assistance of someone who can translate all the French automobile terms.

Purchase-Repurchase Plans
If you'll be needing a car in France for a minimum of 23 days and a maximum of 180, it is *much* cheaper to 'purchase' one from the manufacturer and then 'sell' it back than it is to rent one. In reality, you only pay for the number of days you use the vehicle, but the

purchase-repurchase *(achat-rachat)* aspect of the paperwork, none of which is your responsibility, lets you save France's whopping 20.6% VAT on noncommercial car rentals.

Both Renault and Citroën have excellent-value purchase-repurchase plans – contact the dealer in your country. It can be up to 35% cheaper arranging your purchase-repurchase car abroad, where various discounts are available, than in France. You usually have to book and pay about a month before you pick up the car.

Useful Organisations

For further information on driving in France contact the Automobile Club de France (☎ 01 43 12 43 12; fax 01 43 12 43 43) at 8 Place de la Concorde (8e; metro Concorde) or its Paris affiliate, the Automobile Club de l'Île de France (☎ 01 40 55 43 00; fax 01 43 80 90 51) at 14 Ave de la Grande Armée (17e; metro Argentine).

BICYCLE

Most large towns have at least one cycling shop that hires out bikes by the hour, day or week. You can still get low-tech one and three-speeds or 10-speeds *(vélos à 10 vitesses)*, but in some areas such antiquated contrivances are going the way of the penny-farthing. A growing number of shops only have mountain bikes *(vélos tout-terrain* or VTTs), which generally cost 70 to 120FF a day. Most places, especially those renting expensive mountain bikes, require a substantial deposit (though a passport will often suffice).

HITCHING

Hitching in France is more difficult than almost anywhere else in Europe. (See the Hitching section in the introductory Getting Around chapter for general information.) Getting out of big cities like Paris, Lyon and Marseille or travelling around the Côte d'Azur by thumb is well nigh impossible. Remote rural areas are your best bet, but few cars are likely to be going further than the next large town. Women should not hitch alone.

It is an excellent idea to hold up a sign with your destination followed by the letters *s.v.p.* (for *s'il vous plaît* – 'please'). Some people have reported good luck hitching with truck drivers from truck stops. It is illegal to hitch on autoroutes and other major expressways, but you can stand near the entrance ramps.

In Paris, Allostop-Provoya (☎ 01 53 20 42 42; metro Cadet) at 8 Rue Rochambeau (9e) can put you in touch with a driver who is going your way. If you are not a member (250FF for up to eight journeys over two years), there is a per-trip fee of between 30FF (for distances under 200 km) and 70FF (for distances over 500 km). In addition, you have to pay the driver 0.20FF per km for expenses.

BOAT

Travelling through some of France's 7500 km of navigable waterways on a houseboat or canal boat is a unique and relaxing way to see the country. For a brochure listing boat-rental companies around France, contact the Paris-based Syndicat National des Loueurs de Bateaux de Plaisance (☎ 01 44 37 04 00) at Port de Javel Haut (15e; metro Javel).

ORGANISED TOURS

Though independent travel is usually far more rewarding then being led from coach to sight and back to coach, some areas in France are difficult to visit on your own unless you have wheels. Tour options are mentioned under Organised Tours in sections where they are relevant (eg Loire Valley, the D-Day Beaches in Normandy, the Vézère Valley in Périgord). A number of Paris-based companies have tours of various lengths into the hinterland (Champagne, Burgundy, the Loire Valley, Normandy) including Cityrama Gray Line (☎ 01 44 55 61 00; metro Palais Royal) at 4 Place des Pyramides (1er). The tourist office in Paris has a complete list.

Paris

By now, Paris (population 2.15 million; metropolitan area 10.6 million) has almost exhausted the superlatives that can reasonably be applied to a city. Notre Dame and the Eiffel Tower – at sunrise, at sunset, at night – have been described ad nauseam as have the Seine and the subtle (and not-so-subtle) differences between the Left and Right banks. But what writers have been unable to capture is the grandness and even the magic of strolling along the city's broad avenues – a legacy of the 19th century – which lead from impressive public buildings and exceptional museums to parks, gardens and esplanades. Paris is enchanting at any time, in every season. You too may find yourself humming that old Cole Porter favourite as you walk the streets: 'I love Paris in the springtime, I love Paris in the fall...'

Orientation

In central Paris (which the French call Intra-Muros – 'within the walls'), the Rive Droite (Right Bank) is north of the Seine, while the Rive Gauche (Left Bank) is south of the river. For administrative purposes, Paris is divided into 20 *arrondissements* (districts), which spiral out clockwise from the centre of the city. Paris addresses always include the arrondissement number. In this section, these numbers are listed in parentheses immediately after the street address, using the usual French notation. For example, *1er* stands for *premier* (1st), *4e* for *quatrième* (4th) and 19e for *dix-neuvième* (19th). When an address includes the full five-digit postal code, the last two digits indicate the arrondissement: 75001 for the 1st, 75014 for the 14th etc.

As there is nearly always a metro station within 500 metres, you can whiz around under the traffic and pop up wherever you choose. To help you find your way, we've included the station nearest each hotel, museum etc, immediately after the telephone or arrondissement number.

Maps The best map of Paris is Michelin's 1:10,000 scale *Paris Plan*. It comes both in booklet *(Paris Plan 11)* and sheet form *(Paris Plan 10)* and is available in bookshops, stationery stores and kiosks around the city.

Information

Tourist Offices Paris' main tourist office (☎ 01 49 52 53 54; fax 01 49 52 53 00; metro Charles de Gaulle-Étoile) is 100 metres east of the Arc de Triomphe at 127 Ave des Champs Élysées (8e). It is open every day of the year except 1 May from 9 am to 8 pm. This is the best source of information on the city's museums, concerts, expositions, theatre performances and the like. Information on other parts of France is also available. For a small fee and a deposit, the office can find you a place to stay in Paris for that night or in the provinces up to eight days in advance.

There are tourist office annexes open Monday to Saturday from 8 am to 8 pm (9 pm in summer) in all of Paris' train stations except Gare Saint Lazare. From May to September, the tourist office annexe (☎ 01 45 51 22 15) at the Eiffel Tower (7e) is open from 11 am to 6 pm.

Both international airports have Aéroports de Paris (ADP) tourist information desks. The one at Orly is in the Orly-Sud terminal on the ground floor opposite Gate H; it is open daily from 6 am to 11.45 pm. At Roissy-Charles de Gaulle, there's a tourist information bureau (☎ 01 48 62 27 29) on the arrival level of Aérogare 1 and one in each of the three terminals of Aérogare 2.

For recorded information on cultural and other events taking place in Paris, call ☎ 01 49 52 53 56 (English) or ☎ 01 49 52 53 55 (French) any time. Many French regions and departments such as Périgord, Pyrénées and Hautes-Alpes have tourist outlets (Maisons du Tourisme) in Paris. Ask at the main tourist office for a list.

Money All of Paris' six major train stations have exchange bureaus open seven days a week until at least 8 pm (7 pm at Gare Montparnasse), but the rates are not very good. The exchange offices at Orly (Orly-Sud terminal) and Roissy-Charles de Gaulle (both Aérogares) are open until 10 or 11 pm. Unless you want to get about 10% less than a fair rate, avoid the big exchange-bureau chains like Chequepoint and ExactChange.

Banque de France By far the best rate in town is offered by Banque de France, France's central bank, whose headquarters (☎ 01 42 92 22 27; metro Palais Royal-Musée du Louvre) is three blocks north of the Louvre at 31 Rue Croix des Petits Champs (1er). The exchange service is open Monday to Friday from 9.30 am to 12.30 pm and 1.30 to 4 pm. The Banque de France branch (☎ 01 44 61 15 30; metro Bastille) at 5 Place de la Bastille (4e), which is opposite the new Opéra-Bastille, is open weekdays from 9 am to noon and 1.30 to 3.30 pm.

FRANCE

FRANCE

To Grande Arche de la Défense
(Tête Défense)

La Défense

Seine River

Pont de Neuilly

Avenue Charles de Gaulle

Les Sablons

Route du M Gandhi

47

48

Blvd Bineau

49

Rue A France

Rue V Hugo

Boulevard

51

50

Cimetière de Montmartre

17ᵉ

Blvd Pereire

Avenue de Wagram

Rue d'Amsterdam

Parc de Monceau

Gare St Lazare

See Central Paris map

Boulevard Haussmann

Arc de Triomphe

8ᵉ

Avenue Foch

46

Avenue des Champs Elysées

Place de la Concorde

To Camping du Bois de Boulogne

45

Blvd Périphérique

Lac Inférieur

Bois de Boulogne

44

43

Avenue Victor Hugo

Avenue Kléber

Avenue d'Iéna

16ᵉ

Eiffel Tower

7ᵉ

Hôtel des Invalides

LEFT BANK

Blvd Raspail

To Camping du Bois de Boulogne (1 km)

42

41

To Autoroute A13,
Versailles (12 km),
Chartres (via N10, 80 km),
Rouen (128 km),
Bayeux (257 km) &
Normandy

Quai André Citroën

Seine River

Rue de la Convention

15ᵉ

Avenue de Versailles

Avenue Félix Faure

Lecourbe

Vaugirard

Gare Montparnasse

Blvd du Montparnasse

Cimetière du Montparnasse

31

Rue

Rue

Avenue du Maine

Avenue Edouard Vaillant

40

Avenue P Grenier

39

38

Rue des Morillons

37

14ᵉ

Place Denfert Rochereau

Blvd

Lefebvre

36

Blvd Brune

35

34

Rue d'Alésia

Périphérique

33

32

Périphérique

To Charles de Gaulle Airport (21 km), Autoroute A1, Calais (289 km), Brussels & Antwerp

Blvd Ney

Blvd Ornano

18e

Rue de la Chapelle

Ave de Flandre

Canal de l'Ourcq

Parc de la Villette

19e

Blvd Barbès

Sacré Cœur Basilica

Blvd de Clichy

See Montmartre map

Gare du Nord

Avenue Jean Jaurès

Parc des Buttes Chaumont

Belleville

Rue de

9e

Gare de l'Est

Rue La Fayette

Blvd de Magenta

10e

Opéra-Garnier

2e

Blvd Jules Ferry

20e

Place de la République

RIGHT BANK

1er

Blvd Sébastopol

See Marais & Île St Louis map

3e

Blvd de Ménilmontant

11e

Cimetière du Père Lachaise

Louvre

Rue de Rivoli

4e

Notre Dame

Rue de la Roquette

Rue de Lappe

Germain

6e

Place de la Bastille

Rue du Faubourg St Antoine

Blvd de Charonne

16

To Château de Vincennes (1.5 km) & Jardin Tropical (4.4 km)

Blvd St Michel

Rue St Jacques

5e

Panthéon

See the Latin Quarter & Île de la Cité map

Diderot

Gare de Lyon

Rue de Bercy

Avenue Daumesnil

Place de la Nation

Cours de Vincennes

12e

Blvd Soult

17

18

19

To Château de Vincennes (1.6 km), Park Floral (2.4 km) & Jardin Tropical (4 km)

Gare d'Austerlitz

Blvd de l'Hôpital

Seine River

Quai de Bercy

Quai de la Gare

20

21

Zoo

Blvd Arago

30

Blvd Saint Jacques

28

Place d'Italie

Glacière

29

Blvd Vincent Auriol

Avenue d'Italie

13e

Boulevard Poniatowski

22

Bois de Vincennes

Rue de Tolbiac

To Orly Airport, Autoroutes A6, A10 & A11, Chartres, Brittany, Blois, Tours, Bordeaux, Dijon, Lyon, Alps, Marseille & Nice

23

Jourdan

Blvd Kellermann

Blvd Masséna

27

26

25

24

To Reims (136 km), Strasbourg (482 km), Alsace, Lorraine, Luxembourg & Stuttgart

Autoroute A4

To Autoroutes A1 & A3

9

10

Paris

0   0.5   1 km

- - - arrondissement boundaries

FRANCE

PLACES TO STAY		6	Porte de Pantin	32	Porte d'Orléans
14	Hôtel Sainte Marguerite	7	Porte du Pré St Gervais	33	Porte de Châtillon
15	Maison Internationale	8	Porte des Lilas	34	Porte de Vanves
	des Jeunes	9	Gare Routière	35	Porte Brancion
19	CISP Ravel		Internationale	36	Porte de la Plaine
26	CISP Kellermann		(International Bus	37	Lost Property Office
28	Maison des Clubs		Terminal)	38	Porte de Sèvres
	UNESCO	10	Porte de Bagnolet	39	Paris Heliport
29	FIAP Jean Monnet	12	Le Balajo Discothèque	40	Porte de St Cloud
		16	Porte de Montreuil	41	Porte Molitor
PLACES TO EAT		17	Porte de Vincennes	42	Porte d'Auteuil
11	Ethnic Restaurants	18	Porte de St Mandé	43	Porte de Passy
13	Hamilton's Fish & Chips	20	Musée des Arts	44	Porte de la Muette
31	La Cagouille		d'Afrique et	45	Paris Cycles
	Restaurant		d'Océanie	46	Porte Dauphine
		21	Porte Dorée	47	Paris Cycles
OTHER		22	Porte de Charenton	48	Porte Maillot
1	Porte de Saint Ouen	23	Porte de Bercy	49	Porte de Champerret
2	Porte de Clignancourt	24	Porte d'Ivry	50	Porte d'Asnières
3	Porte de la Chapelle	25	Porte d'Italie	51	Porte de Clichy
4	Porte d'Aubervilliers	27	Porte de Gentilly		
5	Porte de la Villette	30	Catacombs		

American Express Paris' landmark American Express office (☎ 01 47 77 77 07; metro Auber or Opéra) at 11 Rue Scribe (9e) faces the west side of Opéra-Garnier. Exchange services, cash advances, refunds and poste restante are available Monday to Saturday from 9 am to 6.30 pm (5.30 pm on Saturday). Since you can get slightly better exchange rates elsewhere and the office is usually jammed, try to avoid it.

Citibank Money wired from abroad by or to Citibank usually arrives at its head office (☎ 01 49 06 10 10; metro Grande Arche de la Défense) in the suburb of La Défense, which is west of the Arc de Triomphe. The address is 19 Le Parvis, and it is open Monday to Friday from 10 am to 5.30 pm.

Notre Dame (4e & 5e) Le Change de Paris (☎ 01 43 54 76 55; metro Saint Michel) at 2 Place Saint Michel (6e) has some of the best rates in all of Paris. It is open daily from 10 am to 7 pm. There is another exchange bureau (☎ 01 46 34 70 46; metro Saint Michel) with good rates one block south of Place Saint Michel at 1 Rue Hautefeuille (6e). This place is open daily from 9 am (11 am on Sunday) to 8 pm (11 pm from May to October).

Panthéon (5e) The Banque Nationale de Paris (☎ 01 43 29 45 50; metro Luxembourg) at 7 Rue Soufflot exchanges foreign currency Monday to Friday from 9 am to noon and 1 to 5 pm.

Champs Élysées (8e) Thanks to fierce competition, the Champs Élysées is an excellent place to change money. The bureau de change (☎ 01 42 25 38 14; metro Franklin D Roosevelt) at 25 Ave des Champs Élysées is open every day of the year from 9 am to 8 pm.

Montmartre (18e) There's a bureau de change (☎ 01 42 52 67 19; metro Abbesses) at 6 Rue Yvonne Le Tac, two blocks east of Place des Abbesses. It is open Monday to Saturday from 10 am (10.30 am on Saturday) to 6.30 pm.

Post & Communications Paris' main post office (☎ 01 40 28 20 00; metro Sentier or Les Halles) at 48-52 Rue du Louvre (1er) offers all the usual services every day round the clock. Foreign exchange is only available on weekdays from 8 am to 7 pm and Saturday from 8 am to noon. All poste restante mail not specifically addressed to a particular branch post office ends up here.

At the post office (☎ 01 44 13 66 00; metro

George V) at 71 Ave des Champs Élysées (8e), you can place telephone calls with phonecards, pick up poste restante mail and send letters, telegrams and faxes Monday to Saturday from 8 am to 10 pm and on Sunday and public holidays from 10 am to noon and 2 to 8 pm. See Orientation for an explanation of Paris postcodes.

Travel Agencies Nouvelles Frontières (☎ 01 46 34 55 30; metro Luxembourg) at 66 Blvd Saint Michel (6e) specialises in discount long-distance airfares and is open Monday to Saturday from 9 am to 7 pm. Another agent, Selectour Voyages (☎ 01 43 29 64 00; metro Saint Michel) at 29 Rue de la Huchette (5e), is open weekdays from 9 am to 7 pm and on Saturday from 10 am to 6.30 pm. Council Travel (☎ 01 44 55 55 65; metro Pyramides) has its main Paris office at 22 Rue des Pyramides (1er). It is open Monday to Friday from 9.30 am to 6.30 pm and on Saturday from 10 am to 5.30 pm.

Bookshops Paris' famous English-language bookshop Shakespeare & Company (☎ 01 43 26 96 50; metro Saint Michel) is at 37 Rue de la Bûcherie (5e), which is across the Seine from Notre Dame Cathedral. The shop has an unpredictable collection of new and used books in English, but even the second-hand stuff doesn't come cheap. There's a library/reading room on the 1st floor. Shakespeare & Company is generally open daily from noon to midnight.

The largest English-language bookshop in the city, WH Smith (☎ 01 44 77 88 99; metro Concorde) at 248 Rue de Rivoli (1er), is a block east of Place de la Concorde. It's open Monday to Saturday from 9.30 am to 7 pm and on Sunday from 1 to 6 pm. At 29 Rue de la Parcheminerie (5e), the mellow, Canadian-run Abbey Bookshop (☎ 01 46 33 16 24; metro Cluny-La Sorbonne) has an eclectic, though somewhat limited, selection of titles. It's open daily from 10 am to 7 pm (10 pm Wednesday to Saturday in the summer).

Lonely Planet books and other travel guides are available from Ulysse (☎ 01 43 25 17 35; metro Pont Marie) at 26 Ave St Louis en L'Île (4e); from FNAC Librairie Internationale (☎ 01 44 41 31 50; metro Cluny-La Sorbonne)

at 71 Blvd Saint Germain (5e); and from L'Astrolabe Rive Gauche (☎ 01 46 33 80 06; metro Cluny-La Sorbonne) at 14 Rue Serpente (6e).

Cultural & Religious Centres The British Council (☎ 01 49 55 73 00; metro Invalides) at 9-11 Rue de Constantine (7e) has a lending library (230FF a year for membership) and a free reference library. The bulletin board outside the entrance has information on the many cultural activities sponsored by the council.

The newly restored Canadian Cultural Centre (☎ 01 44 43 21 31; metro Invalides) at 5 Rue de Constantine has an art gallery, a reference library and an extensive multimedia section which, among other things, offers access to the Internet. The centre is open Monday to Friday from 9 am to 7 pm.

The American Church (☎ 01 47 05 07 99; metro Invalides) at 65 Quai d'Orsay (7e) is a place of worship and something of a community centre for English speakers, and its announcement board is an excellent source of information on all sorts of subjects, including job openings and apartments for rent. Reception is staffed daily from 9 am to 10 pm (7.30 pm on Sunday).

Laundry The laundrettes *(laveries)* mentioned here are near many of the hotels and hostels listed under Places to Stay. Near the BVJ hostels, the Laverie Libre Service (metro: Louvre Rivoli) at 7 Rue Jean-Jacques Rousseau (1er) is open daily from 7.30 am to 10 pm. In the Marais, the Laverie Libre Service (metro: Saint Paul) at 25 Rue des Rosiers (3e) is open daily from 7.30 am to 10 pm.

Thanks to the Latin Quarter's student population, laundrettes are plentiful in this part of Paris. Three blocks south-west of the Panthéon, the laundrette (metro: Luxembourg) at 216 Rue Saint Jacques (5e), near the Hôtel de Médicis, is open from 7 am to 10.30 pm. Just south of the Arènes de Lutèce, the Lavomatique (metro: Monge) at 63 Rue Monge (5e) is open daily from 6.30 am to 10 pm.

Near Gare de l'Est, the Lav' Club (metro: Gare de l'Est) at 55 Blvd de Magenta (10e) stays open daily until 10 pm. In Montmartre, the Laverie Libre Service (metro: Blanche) at

4 Rue Burq (18e) is open daily from 7.30 am to 10 pm.

Lost & Found Paris' Bureau des Objets Trouvés (Lost & Found Office; ☎ 01 45 31 14 80), run by the Préfecture de Police, is at 36 Rue des Morillons (15e; metro Convention). The only lost objects that do not make their way here are those found in SNCF train stations. Since telephone enquiries are impossible, you have to go in person and fill out forms to see if what you've lost has been located. The office is open weekdays from 8.30 am to 5 pm (8 pm on Tuesday and Thursday).

Medical Services Paris has about 50 Assistance Publique hospitals. An easy one to find is the Hôtel Dieu hospital (☎ 01 42 34 82 34; metro Cité), on the northern side of Place du Parvis Notre Dame (4e), the square in front of the cathedral. The emergency room (*service des urgences*) is open 24 hours a day.

Dangers & Annoyances For its size, Paris is a safe city, but you should always use common sense; for instance, avoid the large Bois de Boulogne and Bois de Vincennes forested parks after nightfall. Although it's fine to use the metro until it stops running at about 12.45 am, some stations may be best avoided late at night, especially if alone. These include Châtelet (1er) and its many seemingly endless tunnels to the Les Halles and Châtelet-Les Halles stops; Château Rouge in Montmartre (18e); Gare du Nord (10e); Strasbourg-Saint Denis (2e & 10e); Réaumur-Sébastopol (2e); and Montparnasse-Bienvenüe (6e and 15e).

Museum Hours & Discounts Paris has more than 100 museums of all sizes and types; a comprehensive list is available from the tourist office for 10FF. Government-run museums (*musées nationaux*) in Paris and the Île de France (eg the Louvre, the Musée Picasso) are open daily except Tuesday. The only exceptions are the Musée d'Orsay, Musée Rodin and Versailles, which are closed Monday. Entry to most of the national museums is free for people 17 or younger and half-price for those aged 18 to 25 or over 60. Paris' municipal museums (Musées de la Ville de Paris; ☎ 01 42 76 65 68)

are open daily except Monday and are free on Sunday.

The Carte Musées et Monuments (☎ 01 44 78 45 81) museum pass gets you into some 75 museums and monuments in Paris and the surrounding region without having to queue for a ticket. The card costs 70/140/200FF for one/three/five consecutive days and is on sale at the museums and monuments it covers, at some metro ticket windows and at the tourist office.

Things to See – Left Bank

Île de la Cité (1er & 4e) Paris was founded sometime during the 3rd century BC, when members of a tribe known as the Parisii set up a few huts on Île de la Cité. By the Middle Ages, the city had grown to encompass both banks of the Seine, but Île de la Cité remained the centre of royal and ecclesiastical power.

Notre Dame Paris' cathedral (☎ 01 42 34 56 10; metro Cité or Saint Michel) is one of the most magnificent achievements of Gothic architecture. Its construction was begun in 1163 and completed around 1345. Exceptional features include the three spectacular rose windows, especially the one over the west façade, and the window on the north side of the transept, which has remained virtually unchanged since the 13th century. One of the best views of Notre Dame is from the lovely little park behind the cathedral, where you can see the mass of ornate flying buttresses that encircle the chancel and hold up its walls and roof. (While there, have a look at the haunting **Mémorial des Martyrs de la Déportation** in memory of the more than 200,000 people deported by the Nazis and French fascists during WWII.)

Notre Dame is open daily from 8 am to 7 pm (but is closed on Saturday from 12.30 to 2 pm). There is no entrance fee. Free concerts are held every Sunday at 5.30 pm. The **Trésor** (Treasury) at the back of the cathedral, which contains precious liturgical objects, is open Monday to Saturday from 9.30 to 11.45 am and 12.30 to 5.30 pm (2 to 5.30 pm on Saturday); admission is 15FF (10FF for students). The top of the west façade, from where you can view many of the cathedral's most ferocious-looking gargoyles and a good deal of Paris, can be reached via 387 steps. It is open daily from 9.30 am to 6.30 pm during summer; until 5 pm in winter. The entrance is at the base of the north tower. Entry is 28FF (18FF reduced rate).

The **Crypte Archéologique** (☎ 01 43 29 83 51) under the square in front of the cathedral displays Gallo-Roman and later remains found on the site. Entrance costs 28FF (18FF reduced rate).

Sainte Chapelle The gem-like upper chapel of Sainte Chapelle (☎ 01 43 54 30 09; metro Cité), illuminated by a veritable curtain of 13th-century stained glass, is inside the **Palais de Justice** (Law Courts) at 4 Blvd du Palais (1er). Consecrated in 1248, Sainte Chapelle was built in only 33 months to house a crown of thorns (supposedly worn by the crucified Christ) and other relics purchased by King Louis IX (later Saint Louis) earlier in the 13th century. From October to March, it is open daily from 10 am to 5 pm; the rest of the year, from 9.30 am to 6.30 pm. Tickets cost 32FF (21FF reduced rate). A ticket valid for both Sainte Chapelle and the nearby Conciergerie costs 45FF. The high-security visitors' entrance to the Palais de Justice is opposite 7 Blvd du Palais (1er).

Conciergerie The Conciergerie (☎ 01 43 54 30 06; metro Cité) was a luxurious royal palace when it was built in the 14th century – the **Salle des Gens d'Armes** (Cavalrymen's Room) is the oldest medieval hall in Europe – but was later transformed into a prison and continued as such until 1914. During the Reign of Terror (1793-94), the Conciergerie was used to incarcerate 'enemies' of the Revolution before they were brought before the tribunal, which met next door in what is now the Palais de Justice. Among the almost 2800 prisoners held here before being bundled off to the guillotine were Queen Marie-Antoinette and the Revolutionary radicals Danton and Robespierre. The Conciergerie is open daily from 10 am to 5 pm (9.30 am to 6.30 pm from April to September). Guided visits in French leave every half-hour. The entrance is at 1 Quai de l'Horloge (1er) and tickets cost 28FF (18FF reduced rate).

Île Saint Louis (4e) Île Saint Louis, the smaller of Paris' two islands, is just east of Île de la Cité. The 17th-century houses of grey stone and the small-town shops that line the streets and quays impart an almost provincial feel, making this quarter a great place for a quiet stroll. If circumnavigating the island makes you hungry, you might want to join the line in front of Berthillon at 31 Rue Saint Louis en l'Île (4e; metro Pont Marie), which is reputed to have Paris' best ice cream. On foot, the shortest route between Notre Dame and the Marais passes through Île Saint Louis.

Latin Quarter (5e & 6e) This area is known as the Quartier Latin because, up till the Revolution, all communication between students and their professors took place here in Latin. The 5e has become increasingly touristy but still has a large population of students and academics affiliated with the University of Paris and other institutions. Shop-lined **Blvd Saint Michel**, known as the 'Boul Mich', runs along the border of the 5e and the 6e.

Panthéon (5e) The Latin Quarter landmark now known as the Panthéon (☎ 01 43 54 34 51; metro Luxembourg or Cardinal Lemoine), which is at the eastern end of Rue Soufflot, was commissioned as an abbey church in the mid-18th century. In 1791, the Constituent Assembly converted it into a mausoleum for the 'great men of the era of French liberty'. Permanent residents include Victor Hugo, Émile Zola, Voltaire and Jean-Jacques Rousseau. The Panthéon's ornate marble interior is gloomy in the extreme, but you get a great view of the city from around the colonnaded dome (261 steps). From October to March, the Panthéon is open daily from 10 am to 5.30 pm (9.30 am to 6.30 pm the rest of the year when there are guided visits). Entrance costs 32FF (21FF reduced rate).

Sorbonne (5e) Paris' most famous university was founded in 1253 as a college for 16 poor theology students. After serving for centuries as France's major theological centre, it was closed in 1792 by the Revolutionary government but reopened under Napoleon. Today, the Sorbonne's main campus complex (bounded by Rue Victor Cousin, Rue Saint Jacques, Rue des Écoles and Rue Cujas) and other buildings nearby house several of the 13 autonomous

Central Paris

FRANCE

RIGHT BANK

LEFT BANK

Jardin des Tuileries

Palais du Louvre

Place de la Concorde

Place Vendôme

Jardin du Luxembourg

Île de la Cité

Jardin des Plantes

Champ de Mars

Seine River

arrondissement boundaries

1 km / 0.5 / 0

To Gare du Nord (800 m)
To Montmartre (1 km)
To La Défense Skyscraper District (3.7 km)
To La Place d'Italie Centre Rocheareau (650 m)

See Marais & Île St Louis Map
See the Latin Quarter & Île de la Cité Map

Blvd Jules Ferry
Blvd de la République
Place de la République
Blvd de Magenta
Blvd de Strasbourg
Rue St Denis
Rue du Faubourg du Temple
Rue de Turbigo
Rue de Beaubourg
Blvd Sébastopol
Rue Réaumur
Rue Montmartre
Rue Montorgueil
Rue La Fayette
Blvd Haussmann
Blvd des Italiens
Rue de Richelieu
Rue Croix des Petits Champs
Pont Neuf
Quai Saint Bernard
Quai de la Tournelle
Blvd de l'Hôpital
Rue Geoffroy St Hilaire
Rue Monge
Rue des Écoles
Panthéon
Rue Saint Jacques
Blvd St Germain
Blvd St Michel
Blvd Saint Michel
Rue d'Assas
Blvd du Montparnasse
Blvd Raspail
Rue de Sèvres
Rue de Babylone
St Placide
Rue de Vaugirard
Rue du Bac
Rue de Rennes
Blvd des Invalides
Blvd de la Tour Maubourg
Ave de la Motte Picquet
Ave Duquesne
Ave de Suffren
Ave Bosquet
Ave Rapp
Ave de la Bourdonnais
Ave de Grenelle
Blvd de Grenelle
Rue du Commerce
Rue de Vaugirard
Rue de Lourmel
Rue des Entrepreneurs
Rue Cambronne
Champ de Mars / Tour Eiffel
Pont d'Iéna
Ave d'Iéna
Place d'Iéna
Trocadéro
Place du Trocadéro
Avenue Kléber
Ave Victor Hugo
Ave Foch
Ave de la Grande Armée
Place Charles de Gaulle
Ave de Friedland
Ave Marceau
Ave Georges V
Ave des Champs Élysées
Ave Montaigne
Ave F D Roosevelt
Ave W Churchill
Ave du Président Wilson
Blvd Malesherbes
Rue du Faubourg St Honoré
Rue St Honoré
Rue de Rivoli
Rue du Louvre
Rue des Halles
Châtelet–Les Halles
Place de la Madeleine
Ave de l'Opéra
Blvd des Capucines
Quai de l'Université
Rue de l'Université
Esplanade des Invalides
Quai d'Orsay
Esplanade des Invalides
Notre Dame

1er 2e 3e 4e 5e 6e 7e 8e 9e 10e 11e 12e 13e 15e 16e 17e

PLACES TO STAY		8	Au Printemps	36	Bateaux Mouches
28	Auberge de Jeunesse		(Department Store)		(Boat Tours)
	Jules Ferry	9	Galeries Lafayette	37	Cinémathèque
31	Centre International		(Department Store)	38	Palais de Chaillot
	BVJ Paris-Louvre &	10	Galeries Lafayette	39	Jardins du Trocadéro
	Laundrette	11	Eurostar & Ferry Offices	40	American Church
50	Three Ducks Hostel &	12	American Express	41	Aérogare des Invalides
	Bicycle Tours/Rental	13	Opéra-Garnier		(Buses to Orly)
51	Aloha Hostel	16	Canadian Embassy	42	Palais Bourbon
		17	Grand Palais		(National Assembly
PLACES TO EAT		18	Musée du Petit Palais		Building)
14	Chartier Restaurant	19	US Embassy	43	British Council
15	Le Drouot Restaurant	20	WH Smith Bookshop	44	Musée d'Orsay
33	Léon de Bruxelles &	21	Food Shops	45	Eiffel Tower
	Batifol	22	Council Travel	46	Hôtel des Invalides
56	Le Caméléon	23	Musée de l'Orangerie	47	Église du Dôme
	Restaurant	24	Banque de France	48	Musée Rodin
57	CROUS Restaurant	25	Main Post Office	49	École Militaire
	Universitaire (6e)	26	Rue Saint Denis Sex	52	FNAC Store & Ticket
58	CROUS Restaurant		District		Outlet
	Universitaire Bullier	27	Cinémathèque	53	Montparnasse Tower
		29	Louvre Museum	54	Gare Montparnasse
OTHER		30	Change du Louvre	55	Cimetière du
1	Gare Saint Lazare		(Currency		Montparnasse
2	Gare de l'Est		Exchange)	59	Institut du Monde Arabe
3	Arc de Triomphe	32	Église Saint Eustache	60	Paris Mosque &
4	Main Tourist Office	34	Forum des Halles		Hammam
5	Post Office		(Shopping Mall &	61	Museum of Natural
6	Bureau de Change		Park)		History
7	La Madeleine Church	35	Musée Guimet	62	Gare d'Austerlitz

universities created when the University of Paris was reorganised in 1968. **Place de la Sorbonne** links Blvd Saint Michel with **Église de la Sorbonne**, the university's domed 17th-century church.

Jardin du Luxembourg (6e) When the weather is warm, Parisians flock to the Luxembourg Gardens (metro: Luxembourg) in their thousands to sit and read, write, relax, talk and sunbathe while their children sail little boats in the fountains. The gardens' main entrance is across the street from 65 Blvd Saint Michel. The **Palais du Luxembourg**, fronting Rue de Vaugirard at the northern end of the Jardin du Luxembourg, was built for Maria de' Medici (Marie de Médicis in French), queen of France from 1600 to 1610. It now houses the Sénat, the upper house of the French parliament.

Musée du Moyen Age (5e) The Museum of the Middle Ages (☎ 01 43 25 62 00; metro Cluny-La Sorbonne) houses one of France's finest collections of medieval art. Its prized

possession is a series of six late 15th-century tapestries from the southern Netherlands known as *La Dame à la Licorne* (the Lady & the Unicorn). The museum is housed in two structures: the frigidarium (cold room) and other remains of Gallo-Roman baths from around the year 200 AD, and the late 15th-century residence of the abbots of Cluny. The museum's entrance is at 6 Place Paul Painlevé, and is open from 9.15 am to 5.45 pm daily except Tuesday. Entry is 27FF (18FF reduced rate). On Sunday, everyone pays 18FF.

Paris Mosque (5e) Paris' central mosque (☎ 01 45 35 97 33; metro Monge) at Place du Puits de l'Ermite was built between 1922 and 1926 in an ornate Moorish style. There are tours from 10 am to noon and 2 to 6 pm daily except Friday. The mosque complex includes a small souk (marketplace), a salon de thé, an excellent couscous restaurant and a public bath *(hammam)*. The hammam (☎ 01 43 31 18 14) is open from 10 am to 9 pm on Monday, Wednesday, Thursday, Friday and Saturday for

FRANCE

women and from 2 to 9 pm on Tuesday and 10 am to 9 pm on Sunday for men. It costs 85FF. The entrance is at 39 Rue Geoffroy Saint Hilaire.

The mosque is opposite the western end of the **Jardin des Plantes** (Botanical Gardens), which includes a small **zoo** (☎ 01 40 79 37 94) as well as the recently renovated **Muséum d'Histoire Naturelle** (☎ 01 40 79 30 00; metro Monge). It is open weekdays except Tuesday from 10 am to 6 pm (until 10 pm on Thursday). Entrance is 40FF (30FF reduced rate).

Institut du Monde Arabe (5e) Established by 20 Arab countries to showcase Arab and Islamic culture and to promote cultural contacts, this institute (☎ 01 40 51 38 38; metro Jussieu) at 1 Rue des Fossés Saint Bernard occupies one of the most graceful and highly praised modern buildings in Paris. The 7th-floor **museum** (buy your tickets on the ground floor) of 9th to 19th-century Muslim art and artisanship is open daily except Monday from 10 am to 6 pm and costs 25FF (20FF reduced rate).

Catacombs (14e) In 1785, it was decided that the hygiene problems posed by Paris' overflowing cemeteries could be solved by exhuming the bones and storing them in the tunnels of three disused quarries. One such ossuary is the Catacombes (☎ 01 43 22 47 63; metro Denfert Rochereau), in which the bones and skulls of millions of Parisians from centuries past are neatly stacked along the walls. During WWII, these tunnels were used by the Résistance as headquarters. The route through the Catacombs begins from the small green building at 1 Place Denfert Rochereau. The site is open Tuesday to Friday from 2 to 4 pm and on weekends from 9 to 11 am and 2 to 4 pm. Tickets cost 27FF (15FF reduced rate).

Musée d'Orsay (7e) The Musée d'Orsay (☎ 01 40 49 48 14; metro Musée d'Orsay), along the Seine at 1 Rue de Bellechasse, exhibits paintings, sculptures, *objets d'art* and other works of art produced between 1848 and 1914, including the fruits of the impressionist, post-impressionist and Art-Nouveau movements. It thus fills the chronological gap between the Louvre and the Musée d'Art Moderne at the Centre Pompidou. The Musée d'Orsay is spectacularly housed in a former train station built in 1900 and re-inaugurated in its present form in 1986. It is open daily, except Monday, from 10 am (9 am on Sunday) to 6 pm (9.45 pm on Thursday). Entrance costs 35FF (24FF reduced rate).

Musée Rodin (7e) The Musée Auguste Rodin (☎ 01 44 18 61 10; metro Varenne) at 77 Rue Varenne is one of the most pleasant museums in Paris. Rodin's extraordinarily vital bronze and marble sculptures (look for *The Kiss*, *Cathedral* and, of course, *The Thinker*) are on display both inside the 18th-century Hôtel Biron and in the delightful garden out the back. The Musée Rodin is open from 9.30 am to 5.45 pm (4.45 pm during winter) daily except Monday. Entrance costs 27FF (18FF reduced rate). On Sunday, everyone gets in for 18FF.

Invalides (7e) The **Hôtel des Invalides** (metro Invalides for the Esplanade, metro Varenne or Latour Maubourg for the main building) was built in the 1670s by Louis XIV to provide housing for 4000 disabled veterans *(invalides)*. On 14 July 1789, the Paris mob forced its way into the building and, after fierce fighting, took 28,000 rifles before heading for the Bastille prison.

The **Église du Dôme**, whose dome sparkles again after a 1989 regilding, was built between 1677 and 1735 and is considered one of the finest religious edifices erected under Louis XIV. The church was initially a mausoleum for military leaders in 1800, and in 1861 received the remains of Napoleon, encased in six concentric coffins.

The buildings on either side of the **Cour d'Honneur** (Main Courtyard) house the **Musée de l'Armée** (☎ 01 44 42 37 72), a huge military museum. The Musée de l'Armée and the light and airy **Tombeau de Napoléon 1er** (Napoleon's Tomb) are open daily from 10 am to 5 pm (6 pm in summer). Entrance costs 34FF (24FF reduced rate).

Eiffel Tower (7e) The Tour Eiffel (☎ 01 44 11 23 11; metro Champ de Mars-Tour Eiffel) faced massive opposition from Paris' artistic and literary elite when it was built for the 1889 Exposition Universelle (World's Fair), held to commemorate the Revolution. It was almost torn down in 1909 but was spared for practical reasons – it proved an ideal platform for new-fangled transmitting antennae. The Eiffel Tower is 318 metres high, including the television antenna at the very tip. This figure can vary by as much as 15 cm as the tower's 7000 tonnes of steel, held together by 2.5 million rivets, expand in warm weather and contract when it's cold.

You can choose to visit any of the three levels open to the public. The lift (west and north pillars) costs 20FF for the 1st platform (57 metres above ground), 40FF for the 2nd (115 metres) and 56FF for the 3rd (276 metres). Walking up the stairs (south pillar) to the 1st or 2nd platforms costs 12FF. The tower is open every day from 9.30 am to 11 pm (9 am to midnight in summer). You can walk up from 9 am to 6.30 pm (11 pm or midnight from early July to mid-September).

Champ de Mars (7e) The Champ de Mars, the grassy park around the Eiffel Tower, was originally a parade ground for the **École Militaire** (France's military academy), the huge, 18th-century building at the south-eastern end of the lawns.

Things to See – Right Bank
Jardins du Trocadéro (16e) The Jardins du Trocadéro (metro: Trocadéro), whose fountain and nearby statue garden are grandly illuminated at night, are across the Pont d'Iéna from the Eiffel Tower. The colonnaded Paris and Passy wings of the **Palais de Chaillot**, built in 1937, house a number of museums, including the Musée de la Marine (☎ 01 45 53 31 70), the Musée du Cinéma (☎ 01 45 53 21 86) and the Musée des Monuments Français (☎ 01 44 05 39 10), all of which are closed on Tuesday. The view from the terrace between the two wings is one of the most impressive in Paris.

Musée Guimet (16e) The Guimet museum (☎ 01 47 23 61 65; metro Iéna) at 6 Place d'Iéna, about midway between the Eiffel Tower and the Arc de Triomphe, displays a fabulous collection of antiquities and works of art from throughout Asia. Large sections of the museum, however, will be closed for renova-

tion until 1999. It is open daily except Tuesday from 9.45 am to 6 pm. Entrance costs 27FF (18FF reduced rate and on Sunday for all).

Louvre (1er) The Louvre Museum (☎ 01 40 20 53 17, 01 40 20 51 51; metro Palais Royal-Musée du Louvre), constructed around 1200 as a fortress and rebuilt in the mid-16th century as a royal palace, became a public museum in 1793. The paintings, sculptures and artefacts on display have been assembled by French governments over the past five centuries and include works of art and artisanship from all over Europe as well as important collections of Assyrian, Egyptian, Etruscan, Greek, Coptic, Roman and Islamic art. The Louvre's most famous work is undoubtedly Leonardo da Vinci's *Mona Lisa*. Since it takes several serious visits to get anything more than the briefest glimpse of the offerings, your best bet – after seeking out a few things you really want to see (eg masterpieces such as the Winged Victory of Samothrace and Venus de Milo) – is to choose a period or section of the museum and pretend the rest is somewhere across town.

The Louvre's entrance is covered by a glass pyramid designed by American architect IM Pei. Commissioned by François Mitterrand and completed in 1990, the design generated bitter opposition but is now generally acknowledged as a brilliant success.

The Louvre is open daily except Tuesday from 9 am to 6 pm (until 9.45 pm on Monday and Wednesday). Ticket sales end 30 minutes before closing time. The entry fee is 45FF (26FF reduced rate), but on Sunday and every day after 3 pm everyone pays just 26FF. Entry is free for all on the first Sunday of every month.

Free brochures with rudimentary maps of the museum are available at the information desk in Hall Napoléon, where you can also get details on guided tours. Cassette tours in six languages can be rented for 28FF on the mezzanine level. Detailed explanations in a variety of languages, printed on heavy plastic-coated pages, are stored on racks in each display room.

Place Vendôme (1er) The arcaded buildings around Place Vendôme (metro: Tuileries) and the square itself were designed in the 17th century to display a giant statue of Louis XIV that was later destroyed during the Revolution. The present 44-metre column in the middle of Place Vendôme consists of a stone core wrapped in a spiral of bronze made from 1250 cannons captured by Napoleon at the Battle of Austerlitz (1805). The shops around the square are among the most fashionable – and expensive – in Paris.

Musée de l'Orangerie (1er) The Musée de l'Orangerie (☎ 01 42 97 48 16; metro Concorde), which is in the south-east corner of Place de la Concorde, displays important impressionist works, including a series of Monet's spectacular *Nymphéas* (Water Lilies) and paintings by Cézanne, Matisse, Modigliani, Picasso and Renoir. It is open daily except Tuesday from 9.45 am to 5 pm. The entry fee is 27FF (18FF reduced rate and on Sunday for all).

Place de la Concorde (8e) This vast, cobbled square, set between the Jardin des Tuileries and the eastern end of the Champs Élysées, was laid out between 1755 and 1775. Louis XVI was guillotined here in 1793 – as were another 1343 people over the next two years including his wife, Marie-Antoinette, and Robespierre. The 3300-year-old Egyptian **obelisk** in the middle of the square was given to France in 1829 by the ruler of Egypt, Mohammed Ali.

La Madeleine (8e) The church of Saint Mary Magdalene (☎ 01 44 51 69 00; metro Madeleine) is 350 metres north of Place de la Concorde along Rue Royale. Built in the style of a Greek temple, it was consecrated in 1842 after almost a century of design changes and construction delays. The front porch affords a superb view of the square and, across the river, the 18th-century **Palais Bourbon**, whose façade dates from the early 19th century. It is now the home of the National Assembly.

Fauchon (☎ 01 47 42 60 11; metro Madeleine) at 26 Place de la Madeleine, Paris' most famous gourmet food shop, is open daily except Sunday from 9.40 am to 7 pm.

Champs Élysées (8e) The two-km-long Ave des Champs Élysées links Place de la Concorde with the Arc de Triomphe. Once popular

with the aristocracy as a stage on which to parade their wealth, it has, in recent decades, been partly taken over by fast-food restaurants and overpriced cafés. The nicest bit is the park with the Petit Palais and the Grand Palais between Place de la Concorde and Rond Point des Champs Élysées.

Musée du Petit Palais (8e) The Petit Palais (☎ 01 42 65 12 73; metro Champs Élysées-Clemenceau), built for the 1900 Exposition Universelle, is on Ave Winston Churchill, which runs between Ave des Champs Élysées and the Seine. Its museum specialises in medieval and Renaissance porcelain, clocks, tapestries, drawings and 19th-century French painting and sculpture. It is open from 10 am to 5.40 pm daily except Monday. The entry fee is 27FF (14.50FF reduced tariff). Temporary exhibitions usually cost 35FF extra (25FF if you qualify for the reduction).

The **Grand Palais** (☎ 01 44 13 17 17), which is across Ave Winston Churchill from the Petit Palais on Square Jean Perrin, was also built for the 1900 World's Fair. It is now used for temporary exhibitions.

Arc de Triomphe (8e) The Arc de Triomphe (☎ 01 43 80 31 31; metro Charles de Gaulle-Étoile), Paris' second most famous landmark, is a couple of km north-west of Place de la Concorde in the middle of Place Charles de Gaulle. Also called Place de l'Étoile, this is the world's largest traffic roundabout and the meeting point of 12 avenues. The Arc de Triomphe was commissioned in 1806 by Napoleon to commemorate his imperial victories but remained unfinished when he started losing battles and then entire wars. It was finally completed in the 1830s. An Unknown Soldier from WWI is buried under the arch, his fate and that of countless others like him commemorated by a memorial flame that is lit with ceremony each evening.

The platform atop the arch (lift up, steps down) is open from 9.30 am to 6 pm (10 pm on Friday) daily except on public holidays. Winter hours are 10 am to 5.30 pm. It costs 31FF (20FF reduced rate), and there's a small **museum** with a short videotape. The only sane way to get to the base of the arch is via the underground passageways from its perimeter; trying to cross the traffic on foot is suicidal.

From the Arc de Triomphe, the **Voie Triomphale** (Triumphal Way) stretches another 4.5 km north-west along Ave de la Grande Armée and beyond to the new skyscraper district of **La Défense**. Its best known landmark, the **Grande Arche** (Grand Arch), is a hollow cube (112 metres to a side) completed in 1989.

Centre Georges Pompidou (4e) This centre (☎ 01 44 78 12 33; metro Rambuteau or Châtelet-Les Halles), also known as the Centre Beaubourg, is dedicated to displaying and promoting modern and contemporary art. Thanks in part to its outstanding temporary exhibitions, it is by far the most frequented sight in Paris and the tens of thousands of daily visitors have forced a major renovation of the building. **Place Igor Stravinsky** and its crazy fountains south of the centre and the large square to the west attract street artists, mimes, musicians, jugglers and 'artisans' who will write your name on a grain of rice.

The design of the Centre Pompidou has not ceased drawing wide-eyed gazes and critical comment since it was built between 1972 and 1977. In order to keep the exhibition halls as spacious and uncluttered as possible, the architects put the building's 'insides' on the outside.

The Centre Pompidou consists of six floors and several sections. The **Musée National d'Art Moderne**, which displays the national collection of modern and contemporary art on the 4th floor, is open daily except Tuesday from noon (10 am on weekends and public holidays) to 10 pm. Entrance costs 35FF (24FF reduced rate), but everyone gets in for free on Sunday from 10 am to 2 pm. The free **Bibliothèque Publique d'Information**, with the same opening hours, is a huge, nonlending library equipped with the latest high-tech information retrieval systems. The entrance is on the 2nd floor.

If you'll be visiting several parts of the complex in the same day, the one-day pass (Forfait Journalier), which costs 70FF (45FF if you're 13 to 25), is a good deal, especially if you take a guided tour. Tours in English, which last 1½ hours, leave at 2.30 and 3.30 pm daily except Tuesday from the main information desk (accueil général).

Les Halles (1er) Paris' central food market, Les Halles, occupied this site from the 12th century until 1969, when it was moved out to the suburb of Rungis. A huge underground shopping mall (Forum des Halles) was built in its place and has proved highly popular with Parisian shoppers. Just north of the grassy area on top of Les Halles is one of Paris' most attractive churches, the mostly 16th-century **Église Saint Eustache**, noted for its wonderful pipe organ.

Hôtel de Ville (4e) Paris' city hall (☎ 01 42 76 40 40; metro Hôtel de Ville) at Place de l'Hôtel de Ville was burned down during the Paris Commune of 1871 and rebuilt in the neo-Renaissance style between 1874 and 1882. There are guided tours in French every Monday at 10.30 am, and the small **museum** has imaginative exhibits on Paris. The visitors' entrance is at 29 Rue de Rivoli.

Marais Area (4e) The Marais, the part of the 4e east of the Centre Pompidou and north of Île Saint Louis, was a marsh (marais) until the 13th century, when it was converted to agricultural use. During the 17th century this was the most fashionable part of the city, and the nobility erected luxurious but discreet mansions known as hôtels particuliers. When the aristocracy moved to trendier pastures, the Marais was taken over by ordinary Parisians. By the time renovation was begun in the 1960s, the Marais had become a poor but lively Jewish neighbourhood centred around **Rue des Rosiers**. In the 1980s the area underwent serious gentrification and is today one of the trendiest neighbourhoods to live and shop in. It is also something of a gay quarter.

Place des Vosges (4e) In 1605, King Henri IV decided to turn the Marais into Paris' most fashionable district. The result of this initiative, completed in 1612, was the Place Royale – now Place des Vosges (metro: Chemin Vert) – a square ensemble of 36 symmetrical houses with ground-floor arcades, steep slate roofs and large dormer windows north of Rue Saint Antoine. Duels were once fought in the elegant park in the middle. Today, the arcades around Place des Vosges are occupied by up-market art galleries, antique shops and salons de thé.

The **Maison de Victor Hugo** (☎ 01 42 72 10 16), where the author lived from 1832 to 1848, is open daily except Monday from 10 am to 5.40 pm. The entry fee is 17.50FF (9FF reduced rate).

Musée Picasso (3e) The Picasso Museum (☎ 01 42 71 25 21; metro Saint Sébastien-Froissart), housed in the mid-17th century Hôtel Salé, is a few hundred metres north-east of the Marais at 5 Rue de Thorigny. Paintings, sculptures, ceramic works, engravings and drawings donated to the French government by the heirs of Pablo Picasso (1881-1973) to avoid huge inheritance taxes are on display, as is Picasso's personal art collection (Braque, Cézanne, Matisse, Rousseau etc). The museum is open daily except Tuesday from 9.30 am to 6 pm (5.30 pm in the winter). The entry fee is 27FF (18FF reduced rate).

Bastille (4e, 11e & 12e) The Bastille is the most famous nonexistent monument in Paris; the notorious prison was demolished shortly after the mob stormed it on 14 July 1789 and freed all seven prisoners. Today, the site where it stood is known as Place de la Bastille; the 52-metre **Colonne de Juillet** in the centre was erected in 1830. The new (and rather drab) **Opéra-Bastille** (☎ 01 40 01 19 71; metro Bastille) at 2-6 Place de la Bastille (12e) is another grandiose project initiated by President François Mitterrand.

Opéra-Garnier (9e) Paris' better known opera house (☎ 01 40 01 25 14; metro Opéra) at Place de l'Opéra was designed in 1860 by Charles Garnier to display the splendour of Napoleon III's France and is one of the most impressive monuments erected during the second empire. The extravagant **entrance hall**, with its grand staircase, is decorated with multicoloured marble and a gigantic chandelier. The **ceiling** of the auditorium was painted by Marc Chagall in 1964. Opéra-Garnier is open to visitors from 10 am to 5 pm daily except Sunday. Entrance is 30FF (18FF reduced rate). Opéra-Garnier is used for concerts and ballets; opera performances now take place at Opéra-Bastille.

Montmartre (18e) During the 19th century – and especially after 1871, when the Commu-

nard uprising began here – Montmartre's Bohemian lifestyle attracted artists and writers, whose presence turned the area into Paris' most vibrant centre of artistic and literary creativity. In English-speaking countries, Montmartre's mystique of unconventionality has been magnified by the notoriety of the **Moulin Rouge** (☎ 01 46 06 00 19; metro Blanche) at 82 Blvd de Clichy, a nightclub founded in 1889 and known for its twice-nightly *revue* (at 10 pm and midnight) of nearly naked chorus girls. Today it is an area of mimes, buskers, tacky souvenir shops and commercial artists.

Basilique du Sacré Cœur Perched at the very top of Butte de Montmartre, the Basilica of the Sacred Heart (metro: Lamarck Caulaincourt) was built to fulfil a vow taken by many Parisian Catholics after the disastrous Franco-Prussian War of 1870-71. On warm evenings, groups of young people gather on the steps below the church to contemplate the view, play guitars and sing. Although the basilica's domes are a well-loved part of the Parisian skyline, the architecture of the rest of the building, which is typical of the style of the late 19th century, is not very graceful.

The basilica is open daily from 6.45 am to 11 pm. The entrance to the **dome** and the **crypt**, which costs 15FF (8FF for students), is on the west side of the basilica. Both are open daily from 9 am to 6 pm; they say you can see for 30 km on a clear day from the dome. The recently rebuilt funicular up the hill's southern slope costs one metro/bus ticket each way. It runs from 6 am to 12.45 am.

The **Musée d'Art Naïf** (Museum of Naive Art) in Halle Saint Pierre (☎ 01 42 58 72 89; metro Anvers), south-west of the basilica at 2 Rue Ronsard, is worth a visit (40FF; 30FF for students).

Place du Tertre Just west of **Église Saint Pierre**, the only building left from the great abbey of Montmartre, Place du Tertre is filled with cafés, restaurants, portrait artists and tourists and is always animated. But the real attractions of the area, apart from the view, are the quiet, twisting streets and shaded parks. Look for the two **windmills** west on Rue Lepic and the last **vineyard** extant in Paris on the corner of Rue des Saules and Rue Saint Vincent.

Pigalle (9e & 18e) Pigalle, only a few blocks south-west of the tranquil, residential areas of Montmartre, is one of Paris' major sex districts. Although the area along Blvd de Clichy between the Pigalle and Blanche metro stops is lined with sex shops and striptease parlours, the area has plenty of legitimate nightspots too, including La Locomotive discothèque (see Entertainment later in the Paris section) and several all-night cafés.

Cimetière du Père Lachaise (20e) Père Lachaise Cemetery (☎ 01 43 70 70 33; metro Père Lachaise), final resting place of such notables as Chopin, Proust, Oscar Wilde, Édith Piaf and Sarah Bernhardt, may be the most visited cemetery in the world. The best known tomb (and the one most visitors come to see) is that of 1960s rock star Jim Morrison, lead singer for the Doors, who died in 1971. It is in Division 6. Maps indicating the graves' locations are posted around the cemetery.

The cemetery is open daily from 8.30 am to 5 pm (7.30 am to 6 pm from mid-March to early November). On Sundays and public holidays, it opens at 9.30 am. The cemetery has five entrances; the main one is opposite 23 Blvd de Ménilmontant. Admission is free.

Bois de Vincennes (12e) This large English-style park, the 9.29-sq-km Bois de Vincennes, is in the far south-eastern corner of the city. Highlights include the **Parc Floral** (Floral Garden; metro Château de Vincennes) on Route de la Pyramide; the Parc Zoologique de Paris (Paris Zoo; ☎ 01 44 75 20 10) at 53 Ave de Saint Maurice (metro: Porte Dorée); and, at the park's eastern edge, the **Jardin Tropical** (Tropical Garden; RER stop Nogent-sur-Marne) on Ave de la Belle Gabrielle.

Château de Vincennes (12e) The Château de Vincennes (☎ 01 43 28 15 48; metro Château de Vincennes), at the northern edge of the Bois de Vincennes, is a bona fide 14th-century royal chateau complete with massive fortifications and a moat. You can walk around the grounds for free, but to see the Gothic **Chapelle Royale**, built between the 14th and 16th centuries, and the 14th-century **donjon** (keep), with its small historical museum, you must take a guided tour (26FF; 17FF reduced rate). Daily opening hours are from 10 am to 5 pm (6 pm in summer). The main entrance, which is opposite 18 Ave de Paris in the inner suburb of Vincennes, is right next to the Château de Vincennes metro stop.

Musée des Arts d'Afrique et d'Océanie (12e) This museum (☎ 01 44 74 84 80; metro Porte Dorée) at 293 Ave Daumesnil specialises in art from Africa and the South Pacific. It is open weekdays except Tuesday from 10 am to noon and 1.30 to 5.30 pm (12.30 to 6 pm on weekends). The entry fee is 27FF (18FF reduced rate).

Bois de Boulogne (16e) The 8.65-sq-km Bois de Boulogne, located on the western edge of the city, is endowed with meandering trails, gardens, forested areas, cycling paths and *belle époque*-style cafés. Rowing boats can be rented at the **Lac Inférieur** (metro: Ave Henri Martin), the largest of the park's lakes.

Paris Cycles (☎ 01 47 47 76 50) rents city and mountain bicycles at two locations: on Route du Mahatma Gandhi (metro: Les Sablons), opposite the Porte des Sablons entrance to the Jardin d'Acclimatation amusement park; and near the Pavillon Royal (metro: Ave Foch) at the northern end of the Lac Inférieur. Charges are 30FF an hour or 80FF a day. From mid-April to mid-October, bicycles are available daily from 10 am to sundown. During the rest of the year, you can rent them on Wednesday, Saturday and Sunday only.

Courses
Language Courses The Alliance Française (☎ 01 45 44 38 28; metro Saint Placide) at 101 Blvd Raspail (6e) has month-long French courses beginning the first week of each month. The registration office is open Monday to Friday from 9 am to 6 pm. French courses with the same schedule offered by the Accord Language School (☎ 01 42 36 24 95; metro Rambuteau or Les Halles) at 72 Rue Rambuteau (1er) get high marks from students. A one-month course (10 hours a week) costs 1900FF.

Cooking Courses Several cooking schools offer courses of various lengths including the famed École Ritz Escoffier (☎ 01 42 60 38 30; metro Concorde) at 38 Rue Cambon (1er) and École Le Cordon Bleu (☎ 01 48 56 06 06; metro Vaugirard) at 8 Rue Léon Delhomme (15e). A one-day hands-on course at the latter is 1250FF and from 4590FF for a week.

Organised Tours

Bus The cheapest way to see Paris on wheels between mid-April and late September is to hop aboard RATP's Balabus (☎ 01 43 46 14 14) which follows a 50-minute route from the Gare de Lyon to the Grande Arche de la Défense and back, passing many of the city's most famous sights. Buses leave every 10 to 20 minutes from 12.30 to 8 pm; the fare is one to three bus/metro tickets, depending on how far you go. ParisBus (☎ 01 42 30 55 50) offers a longer (2¼ hours) tour with English and French commentary year-round on red double-decker buses. There are nine stops (including the Eiffel Tower and Notre Dame) and you can get on and off as you wish. Tickets, available on the bus, are 125FF (half-price for children under 12).

Bicycle Mountain Bike Trip (☎ 01 48 42 57 87; metro Commerce), based in the Three Ducks Hostel at 6 Place Étienne Pernet (15e, metro Commerce), runs popular six-hour mountain bike tours of Paris in English for 135FF. Phone to reserve a place between 8 am and 9 pm the day before. Here you can also rent a mountain bike for 90FF a day.

Boat In summer, the Batobus river shuttle (☎ 01 44 11 33 44) stops at half a dozen places along the Seine, including Notre Dame and the Musée d'Orsay. The boats come by every 35 minutes and cost 12FF per journey or 60FF for the whole day. The Bateaux Mouches company (☎ 01 40 76 99 99; metro Alma Marceau), which is based on the north bank of the Seine just east of Pont de l'Alma (8e), runs the biggest tour boats on the Seine. The cost for a one-hour cruise with commentary is 40FF (no student discount). Vedettes du Pont Neuf (☎ 01 46 33 98 38; metro Pont Neuf), whose home port is on the western tip of Île de la Cité (1er) near the newly cleaned Pont Neuf, oper-

ates one-hour boat circuits day and night for 45FF.

Places to Stay

Accommodation Services Accueil des Jeunes en France (AJF) can always find anyone accommodation in a hostel, hotel or private home, even in summer. It works like this: you come in on the day you need a place to stay and pay AJF for the accommodation, plus a 10FF fee, and they give you a voucher to take to the establishment. The earlier in the day you come the better, as the convenient and cheap places always go first. Prices start at 120FF per person. AJF's main office (☎ 01 42 77 87 80; metro Rambuteau) is at 119 Rue Saint Martin (4e), just west of the Centre Pompidou's main entrance. It is open Monday to Saturday from 10 am to 6.45 pm. Be prepared for long queues during the summer. The AJF annexe (☎ 01 42 85 86 19; metro Gare du Nord) at the Gare du Nord train station (10e) is open daily from June to mid-September.

The main Paris tourist office (☎ 01 49 52 53 54) can also find you accommodation in Paris for the evening of the day you visit its office. There is an 8FF charge for a spot at a hostel and a 20FF charge for reservations at a one-star hotel. For information on the tourist office and its annexes, see Tourist Offices under Information at the start of the Paris section.

Camping The only camping ground actually within the Paris city limits, *Camping du Bois de Boulogne* (☎ 01 45 24 30 00) on Allée du Bord de l'Eau (16e), is along the Seine at the far western edge of the Bois de Boulogne. In summer, two people with a tent pay around 65FF or 80FF with a car. From April to September, privately operated shuttle buses from the Porte Maillot metro stop (16e & 17e) run daily from 8.30 am to 1 pm and 5 pm to sometime between 11 pm and 1 am. During July and August, the shuttles run every half-hour from 8.30 am to 1 am. Throughout the year, you can take either bus No 244 from Porte Maillot or bus No 144 from the Pont de Neuilly metro stop from 6 am to about 9 pm.

Hostels & Foyers Many hostels allow guests to stay for only three nights, especially in summer. Places that have age limits (eg up to

30) tend not to enforce them very rigorously. Only official hostels require that guests present Hostelling International cards. Curfews at Paris hostels tend to be 1 or 2 am though some are earlier. Few hostels accept reservations by telephone; those that do are noted in the text.

Louvre Area (1er) The *Centre International BVJ Paris-Louvre* (☎ 01 42 36 88 18; metro Louvre-Rivoli) at 20 Rue Jean-Jacques Rousseau is only a few blocks north-east of the Louvre. Beds in single-sex rooms cost 120FF, including breakfast. There is a second BVJ hostel, the *Centre International BVJ Paris-Les Halles* (☎ 01 40 26 92 45), around the corner at 5 Rue du Pélican.

Marais (4e) The Maison Internationale de la Jeunesse et des Étudiants, better known as MIJE, runs three hostels (☎ 01 42 74 23 45 for all) in attractively renovated 17th and 18th-century residences in the Marais. A bed in a single-sex dorm with shower costs 120FF, including breakfast. The nicest of the three, *MIJE Fourcy* is at 6 Rue de Fourcy (metro: Saint Paul), 100 metres south of Rue de Rivoli. *MIJE Fauconnier* is two blocks away at 11 Rue du Fauconnier (metro: Pont Marie). *MIJE Maubisson* is at 12 Rue des Barres (metro: Hôtel de Ville). Individuals can make reservations for all three hostels, up to seven days in advance, by calling in at MIJE Fourcy.

Panthéon Area (5e) The clean and friendly *Y&H Hostel* (☎ 01 45 35 09 53; metro Monge) is at 80 Rue Mouffetard, a hopping, happening street known for its restaurants and pubs. A bed in a cramped room with a sink costs 97FF plus 15FF for sheets. Reservations can be made only if you leave a deposit for the first night. Reception is open from 8 to 11 am and 5 pm to 2 am.

11e Arrondissement The *Auberge de Jeunesse Jules Ferry* (☎ 01 43 57 55 60; metro République) is at 8 Blvd Jules Ferry. This hostel is a bit institutional but the atmosphere is fairly relaxed and – an added bonus – it doesn't accept large groups. A bed costs 110FF, including breakfast.

The friendly *Hôtel Sainte Marguerite* (☎ 01 47 00 62 00; metro Ledru Rollin) at 10 Rue Trousseau, 700 metres east of Place de la Bastille, is run like an HI hostel and attracts a young, international crowd. Beds in rooms for two, three or four people cost 91FF per person, including breakfast.

The *Maison Internationale des Jeunes* (☎ 01 43 71 99 21; metro Faidherbe Chaligny) at 4 Rue Titon is about a km east of Place de la Bastille. A bed in a spartan dorm room for two, three, five or eight people costs 110FF, including breakfast. If you don't have your own sheets, there's a 15FF rental charge. Telephone reservations are accepted only for the day you call.

12e Arrondissement The *Centre International de Séjour de Paris (CISP) Ravel* (☎ 01 44 75 60 00; metro Porte de Vincennes) is on the south-eastern edge of the city at 4-6 Ave Maurice Ravel. A bed in a 12-person dormitory is 105FF. Rooms for two to five people cost 118FF per person, and singles are 135FF. All prices include breakfast (provided you stay more than one night) and student card-holders get a 10% discount. Reservations are accepted from individuals no more than 24 hours in advance.

13e & 14e Arrondissements The *Foyer International d'Accueil de Paris (FIAP) Jean Monnet* (☎ 01 45 89 89 15; metro Glacière) is at 30 Rue Cabanis (14e), a few blocks south-east of Place Denfert Rochereau. A bed costs 126/151FF (including breakfast) in modern rooms for eight/four people. Singles/doubles cost 260/170FF per person. Rooms specially outfitted for disabled people (handicapés) are available.

The *Centre International de Séjour de Paris (CISP) Kellermann* (☎ 01 44 16 37 38; metro Porte d'Italie) is at 17 Blvd Kellermann (13e). A bed in an attractive dorm for eight costs 109FF, and staying in a double or quad will cost 134FF per person. Singles are 151FF (181FF with toilet and shower). All prices include sheets and breakfast. This place also has facilities for disabled people on the 1st floor. Telephone reservations are accepted if you call the same day you arrive.

The rather institutional *Maison des Clubs UNESCO* (☎ 01 43 36 00 63; metro Glacière) is at 43 Rue de la Glacière (13e), midway

FRANCE

Quai du Louvre

1er

To the
Louvre (300 m)

2

Seine River

Châtelet

Place du
Châtelet

Ave Victoria

3

Rue de Rivoli

To Centre
Pompidou (200 m)

Hôtel
de Ville

10

Quai de l'Horloge

Quai de Conti

To the Musée
d'Orsay (900 m)

Pont Neuf

5

Place
Dauphine

Île de
la Cité

7

8

Cité

10

Place de
l'Hôtel
de Ville

4

Rue de Seine

Rue de
Nesle

Rue Dauphine

6

9

Blvd du Palais

12

13

Rue d'Arcole

Rue Mazarine

11

Place
St Michel

14

Rue de la Cité

St Michel

Place du
Parvis
Notre Dame

22

Rue du
Cloître Notre Dame

15

St André des Arts

18

19

Rue de la Huchette

28

23

Pont St
Louis

16

Rue de
l'Ancienne
Comédie

Place
St André
des Arts

Rue Git
le Cœur

25

26

Rue Hautefeuille

29

20

21

Rue St Séverin

27

30

31

Square
R Viviani

24

To the
Marais
(200 m)

Mabillon

Rue Serpente

Rue de la Harpe

32

33

34

Rue Dante

35

Odéon

17

Blvd Saint Germain

Cluny-La
Sorbonne

36

37

38

39

Maubert
Mutualité

40

Place
Maubert

41

Blvd Saint Germain

Rue Saint Sulpice

Rue de l'Odéon

Rue de Tournon

Rue Racine

Monsieur le Prince

Rue du Sommerard

Rue des Écoles

Rue de la Montagne Sainte Geneviève

Rue des Bernardins

Lemoine

Rue de Vaugirard

42

6e

Blvd Saint Michel

Place
de la
Sorbonne

43

44

Rue Saint Jacques

Rue des Carmes

45

5e

Rue Monge

Cardinal
Lemoine

Jardin
du
Luxembourg

Rue Cousin

47

Rue Soufflot

Cujas

Place
du
Panthéon

49

50

51

Rue

Descartes

Place de la
Contrescarpe

60

61

Luxembourg

46

48

Rue Gay Lussac

52

53

54

55

56

Rue St Jacques

Rue de l'Estrapade

59

Rue Rollin

Rue Lacépède

62

Rue Auguste
Comte

57

58

Rue d'Ulm

Rue Lhomond

Place
Monge

64

Monge

65

The Latin Quarter
& Île de la Cité

63

Rue Erasme

Rue du Pot de Fer

66

To Boulevard
Montparnasse
(200 m) & Place
Denfert
Rochereau
(900 m)

0   150   300 m

--- arrondissement boundaries

FRANCE

PLACES TO STAY		OTHER		29	Église Saint Séverin
5	Hôtel Henri IV	1	Samaritaine	30	Shakespeare & Co
6	Hôtel de Nesle		(Department Store)		Bookshop
16	Hôtel Petit Trianon	2	Vedettes du Pont Neuf	32	Abbey Bookshop
19	Hôtel Saint Michel		(Boat Tours)	37	Musée du Moyen Age
31	Hôtel Esmerelda	3	Noctambus (All-Night		(Thermes du Cluny)
34	Hôtel du Centre, Le		Bus) Stops	38	Musée du Moyen Age
	Cloître Pub & Polly	4	Hôtel de Ville (City Hall)		Entrance
	Maggoo Pub	7	Palais de Justice &	39	Eurolines Bus Office
52	Hôtel de Médicis		Conciergerie	40	Food Shops
58	Hôtel Gay Lussac	8	Conciergerie Entrance	41	Fromagerie (Cheese
61	Hôtel des Arènes	9	Sainte Chapelle		Shop)
63	Grand Hôtel du Progrès	10	Flower Market	42	Palais du Luxembourg
66	Y & H Hostel	11	Préfecture de Police		(French Senate
		12	Préfecture Entrance		Building)
PLACES TO EAT		13	Hôtel Dieu (Hospital)	43	Sorbonne (University
27	Restaurants ('Bacteria	14	Hospital Entrance		of Paris)
	Alley')	15	Food Shops	44	Église de la Sorbonne
28	L'Année du Dragon	17	Carrefour de l'Odéon	45	Le Violon Dingue Pub
	Chinese Restaurant	18	Le Change de Paris	47	Post Office
33	McDonald's	20	Selectour Voyages	48	Banque Nationale de
35	Au Coin des Gourmets		(Travel Agent)		Paris
	Indochinese	21	Caveau de la Huchette	49	Panthéon
	Restaurant		Jazz Club	50	Panthéon Entrance
36	Pâtisserie Viennoise	22	Notre Dame Tower	51	Église Saint Étienne du
46	McDonald's		Entrance		Mont
54	Tashi Delek Tibetan	23	Notre Dame Cathedral	53	Food Shops
	Restaurant	24	WWII Deportation	55	Laundrette
56	Aleka Restaurant		Memorial	57	Nouvelles Frontières
59	La Rose de Mouffetard	25	Bureau de Change		(Travel Agency)
64	Restaurants	26	L'Astrolabe Rive	60	Arènes de Lutèce
65	Crêpe Stand		Gauche Travel	62	Laundrette
			Bookshop		

between Place Denfert Rochereau and Place d'Italie. A bed in a large, unsurprising room for three or four people is 120FF; singles/doubles cost 160/140FF per person.

15e Arrondissement The friendly, helpful *Three Ducks Hostel* (☎ 01 48 42 04 05; metro Commerce), a favourite with young backpackers, is at 6 Place Étienne Pernet. A bunk bed costs 97FF, and if you don't have your own sheets, there is a one-time charge of 15FF. Telephone reservations are accepted. For information on their mountain bike tours, see Bicycle under Organised Tours earlier in this section. The *Aloha Hostel* (☎ 01 42 73 03 03; metro Volontaires), run by the same people, is at 1 Rue Borromée about a km west of Gare Montparnasse. Beds cost 107FF and sheets, if you don't have your own, cost 15FF.

Hotels A rash of renovations, redecorations and other improvements has turned many of

Paris' best budget hotels into quaint and spotless two-star places where the sheets are changed daily and the minibar is full. But there are still bargains to be had.

Marais (4e) One of the best deals in town is the friendly *Hôtel Rivoli* (☎ 01 42 72 08 41; metro Hôtel de Ville) at 44 Rue de Rivoli. Room rates range from 110FF (for singles without shower) to 230FF (for doubles with bath and toilet). The front door is locked at 2 am. The *Grand Hôtel du Loiret* (☎ 01 48 87 77 00; metro Hôtel de Ville) is two buildings away at 8 Rue des Mauvais Garçons. Singles/doubles start at 140/160FF. Rooms with shower and toilet start at 250FF.

The *Hôtel Moderne* (☎ 01 48 87 97 05; metro Saint Paul) at 3 Rue Caron has basic singles/doubles for 130/160FF, 190FF with shower and 220FF with shower and toilet. The *Hôtel Pratic* (☎ 01 48 87 80 47; metro Saint Paul) is just around the corner at 9 Rue

FRANCE

d'Ormesson. Singles/doubles cost 150/230FF with washbasin; double rooms cost 275FF with shower, 340FF with bath and toilet.

One of the most attractive medium-priced hotels in the area is the *Hôtel de Nice* (☎ 01 42 78 55 29; fax 01 42 78 36 07; metro Hôtel de Ville), a comfortable oasis at 42bis Rue de Rivoli. Doubles/triples/quads with shower and toilet are 400/500/600FF and many of the rooms have balconies. The completely overhauled *Grand Hôtel Mahler* (☎ 01 42 72 60 92; fax 01 42 72 25 37; metro Saint Paul) is at 5 Rue Mahler. Singles/doubles with everything start at 470/570FF (add 100FF in summer).

Notre Dame Area (5e) The run-down *Hôtel du Centre* (☎ 01 43 26 13 07; metro Saint Michel) at 5 Rue Saint Jacques has very basic singles/doubles starting at 100/150FF. Doubles with shower cost from 180FF. Hall showers are 20FF. Reservations are not accepted, but reception is open 24 hours a day.

Because of its location at 4 Rue Saint Julien le Pauvre directly across the Seine from Notre Dame, the *Hôtel Esmerelda* (☎ 01 43 54 19 20; metro Saint Michel) is everybody's favourite. Its three simple singles (160FF) are almost always booked up months in advance – other singles/doubles (with shower and toilet) start at 320FF.

Panthéon Area (5e) The *Hôtel de Médicis* (☎ 01 43 54 14 66; metro Luxembourg) at 214 Rue Saint Jacques is exactly what a dilapidated Latin Quarter dive for impoverished travellers should be like. Very basic singles start at 75FF, but the cheapest rooms are usually occupied. Basic doubles/triples are 150/240FF and hall showers are 10FF.

A much better deal is the *Grand Hôtel du Progrès* (☎ 01 43 54 53 18; metro Luxembourg) at 50 Rue Gay Lussac. Singles with washbasin start at 150FF and there are larger rooms with fine views of the Panthéon for 240FF. Hall showers are free. There are also large old-fashioned singles/doubles with shower and toilet for 310/330FF. A cut above, the *Hôtel Gay Lussac* (☎ 01 43 54 23 96; metro Luxembourg) at No 29 on the same street has small singles/doubles with washbasin for 200/260FF; doubles/quads with shower and toilet are 360/500FF.

A quiet, up-market hotel with views from the back of a 2nd-century Roman amphitheatre (Arènes de Lutèce) is the *Hôtel des Arènes* (☎ 01 43 25 09 26; fax 01 43 25 79 56; metro Monge) at 51 Rue Monge. Singles/doubles/triples with shower and toilet are 595/662/900FF.

Saint Germain des Prés (6e) The wonderfully eccentric *Hôtel de Nesle* (☎ 01 43 54 62 41; metro Odéon or Mabillon) at 7 Rue de Nesle, with its frescoed rooms and cool garden out the back, is a favourite with students and young people from all over the world. Singles cost 195FF, and a bed in a double is 220FF. Doubles with shower and toilet are 350FF. The only way to get a place here is to book in person in the morning. The nearby *Hôtel Petit Trianon* (☎ 01 43 54 94 64; metro Odéon) at 2 Rue de l'Ancienne Comédie also attracts lots of young travellers. Singles start at 170FF. Doubles with shower are 320FF.

The well-positioned *Hôtel Henri IV* (☎ 01 43 54 44 53; metro Pont Neuf) is at 25 Place Dauphine (1er), a quiet square at the western end of Île de la Cité near Pont Neuf. Perfectly adequate singles without toilet or shower are 140FF, doubles are 195 to 270FF, and hall showers are 15FF. This place is usually booked up months in advance.

The *Hôtel Saint Michel* (☎ 01 43 26 98 70; metro Saint Michel) is a block west of Place Saint Michel and a block south of the Seine at 17 Rue Gît le Cœur. Singles/doubles are 215/240FF, with shower 310/335FF. All prices include breakfast.

Montmartre (18e) The metro station Abbesses is convenient for all the following hotels. The *Idéal Hôtel* (☎ 01 46 06 63 63) at 3 Rue des Trois Frères has simple but acceptable singles/doubles starting at 125/170FF. A hall shower is 20FF; rooms with showers are 250FF. The *Hôtel Bonséjour* (☎ 01 42 54 22 53), a block north of Rue des Abbesses at 11 Rue Burq, has basic but pleasant singles from 110 to 130FF and doubles for 170FF; showers are 10FF.

The *Hôtel Audran* (☎ 01 42 58 79 59) is on the other side of Rue des Abbesses at 7 Rue Audran. Singles/doubles start at 100/140FF with showers costing 10FF. A cut above is the renovated **Hôtel des Arts** (☎ 01 46 06 30 52; fax 01 46 06 10 83) at 5 Rue Tholozé. This two-star place has singles/doubles with shower and toilet starting at 340/460FF.

Places to Eat

Restaurants Except for those in touristy areas (Notre Dame, Louvre, Champs Élysées), most of the city's thousands of restaurants are pretty good value for money – at least by Parisian standards. Intense competition tends to rid the city quickly of places with bad food or prices that are out of line. Still, you can be unlucky. Study the posted menus carefully and check to see how busy the place is before entering.

Forum des Halles One of a chain of seven restaurants, **Léon de Bruxelles** (☎ 01 42 36 18 50; metro Les Halles) at 120 Rue Rambuteau (1er) is dedicated to only one thing: moules et frites (mussels and chips/French fries). Meal-size bowls of the bivalves start at 60FF. This place is open nonstop from 11.45 am to midnight (1 am on Friday and Saturday nights). A favourite with young Parisian branchés (trendies), **Batifol** (☎ 01 42 36 85 50; metro Les Halles or Étienne Marcel) at 14 Rue Mondétour (1er) excels at making pot au feu (beef and vegetables cooked in a clay pot) for 60FF. It's open daily from noon to midnight.

Opéra Area (2e & 9e) On the 1st floor at 103 Rue de Richelieu (2e), 500 metres east of Opéra-Garnier, is **Le Drouot** (☎ 01 42 96 68 23; metro Richelieu Drouot), whose décor and ambience haven't changed much since the late 1930s. A three-course traditional French meal with wine costs only 80FF. Le Drouot is open daily for lunch and dinner. **Chartier** (☎ 01 47 70 86 29; metro Rue Montmartre) at 7 Rue du Faubourg Montmartre (9e), under the same management, is famous for its ornate, late 19th-century dining room. Prices, fare and hours are similar to those at Le Drouot, but it closes a little earlier (9.30 pm).

Marais (4e) The heart of the old Jewish neighbourhood, Rue des Rosiers (metro: Saint Paul), has quite a few kosher (cacher) and kosher-style restaurants but most of them are European-orientated. If you're after kosher

couscous and kebabs, check out the restaurants along Blvd de Belleville (11e and 20e; metro Belleville or Couronnes).

Société Rosiers Alimentation (☎ 01 48 87 63 60), at 34 Rue des Rosiers, is one of several places along Rue des Rosiers selling Israeli takeaway food and Middle Eastern snacks such as shwarma and felafel. Paris' best known Jewish restaurant, founded in 1920, is **Restaurant Jo Goldenberg** (☎ 01 48 87 20 16) at 7 Rue des Rosiers. The food (main dishes about 70FF) is Jewish but not kosher. Jo Goldenberg is open from 8.30 am until about midnight daily except on Yom Kippur.

Le P'tit Gavroche (☎ 01 48 87 74 26; metro Hôtel de Ville), at 15 Rue Sainte Croix de la Bretonnerie, is a favourite with crowds of raucous working-class regulars. It is open daily except Sunday for lunch and dinner to midnight. The menu, available until about 10 pm or whenever the food runs out, costs around 48FF.

For vegetarian food, a good bet is **Aquarius** (☎ 01 48 87 48 71; metro Rambuteau) at 54 Rue Sainte Croix de la Bretonnerie, which has a calming, airy atmosphere. It is open Monday to Saturday from noon to 10 pm but the plat du jour is available only at lunch and dinner times. There's a two-course menu for 56FF.

Bastille (4e, 11e & 12e) Lots of ethnic restaurants line Rue de la Roquette and Rue de Lappe (11e), which intersects Rue de la Roquette 200 metres north-east of Place de la Bastille. Among the pizza joints and Chinese, North African and Japanese places, you'll find Paris' only fish and chips shop, **Hamilton's** (☎ 01 48 06 77 92; metro Bastille or Ledru Rollin) at 51 Rue de Lappe, which gets good reviews from homesick English expats. It is open Monday to Friday from noon to 2.30 pm and 6 pm to midnight and on Saturday from 1 pm to 1 am.

Notre Dame Area (4e, 5e & 6e) The Greek, North African and Middle Eastern restaurants in the area bounded by Rue Saint Jacques, Blvd Saint Germain, Blvd Saint Michel and the Seine attract mainly foreign tourists, unaware that some people refer to Rue de la Huchette and its nearby streets as 'bacteria alley' because of the frequency of food poisoning at

Montmartre

arrondissement
boundaries

0   100   200 m

18e

9e

10e

5e

Boulevard de Magenta

To Gare du Nord (300 m)

Barbès
Rochechouart

Boulevard Barbès

Rue de Clignancourt

Marcadet
Poissonniers

Château
Rouge

Rue Poulet

Rue Marcadet

Rue Ramey

Rue Ramey

Rue Custine

Rue Muller

Rue Lamarck

Rue Lamarck

Rue Lamarck

Rue de la
Bonne

Rue Seveste

Rue de Steinkerque

Place du Parvis
du Sacré Cœur

Square
Willette

Anvers

Rue d'Orsel

Rue Mont Cenis

Rue du Mont Cenis

Rue Saint Vincent

Cimetière
St Vincent

Rue de l'Abreuvoir

Rue Cortot

Rue Norvins

Place du
Tertre

Rue Gabrielle

Rue des Trois Frères

Place des
Abbesses

Abbesses

Rue Yvonne le Tac

Rue des Martyrs

Boulevard de Rochechouart

Rue de
Rochechouart

Lamarck
Caulaincourt

Place
Constantin
Pecqueur

Rue Caulaincourt

Ave Junot

Rue Tholozé

Rue Lepic

Rue Durantin

Rue des
Abbesses

Rue des
Abbesses

Rue Lepic

Rue Germain Pilon

Rue Houdon

Place
Emile
Goudeau

Rue Véron

Rue Lepic

Rue J de Maistre

Rue Caulaincourt

Cimetière
de
Montmartre

Rue J de Maistre

To Gare Saint
Lazare (1 km)

Rue Blanche

Place
Blanche

Boulevard de Clichy

Place
Pigalle

Pigalle

Boulevard de Clichy

Blanche

6
5
4
3
2
1
7
8
9
10
11
12
13
14
15
16
18
19
20
21
22

PLACES TO STAY
7   Hôtel des Arts
8   Hôtel Bonséjour
11 Hôtel Audran
21 Idéal Hôtel

PLACES TO EAT
10 Le Mono African Restaurant
19 Refuge des Fondus Restaurant
22 Le Delta Brasserie

OTHER
1   Vineyard
2   Moulin de la Galette (Windmill)
3   Moulin Radet (Windmill)
4   Église Saint Pierre
5   Crypt & Dome Entrance
6   Sacré Cœur Basilica
9   Laundrette
12 Food Shops
13 Funicular Railway
14 Museum of Naive Art
15 La Locomotive Discothèque
16 Moulin Rouge Nightclub
17 Pigalle Sex & Entertainment District
18 Post Office
20 Bureau de Change

restaurants there. But the takeaway kebab and shwarma sandwiches (20FF) aren't bad.

L'Année du Dragon (☎ 01 46 34 23 46; metro Saint Michel) at 10 Rue Saint Séverin (5e), which serves Chinese and Vietnamese food, has menus for as little as 36FF. It is open daily for lunch and dinner.

Sandwich shops sell baguette halves with various delicious fillings for around 18FF, and, of course, there's always *McDonald's* (metro: Cluny-La Sorbonne) on the corner of Blvd Saint Germain and Rue de la Harpe (5e) open to midnight.

East of Rue Saint Jacques, *Au Coin des Gourmets* (☎ 01 43 26 12 92; metro Maubert Mutualité) at 5 Rue Dante (5e) serves decent Indochinese food. It is open for lunch and dinner every day but Tuesday. The lunch menu is 68FF; main dishes are 40 to 55FF.

For a delightful selection of scrumptious central European pastries and tourtes (quiche-like pies), drop by *Pâtisserie Viennoise* (☎ 01 43 26 60 48; metro Cluny-La Sorbonne or Saint Michel) at 8 Rue de l'École de Médicine (6e), which is on the other side of Blvd Saint Michel from the Musée du Moyen Age. It is open

weekdays from 9 am to 7.15 pm but is closed from mid-July to the end of August.

Panthéon (5e) The area around Rue Mouffetard is filled with dozens of places to eat and is especially popular with students. Some of the best discount crêpes in Paris are sold from a little stall across the street from 68 Rue Mouffetard between 11 am and 2 am. They start at 11FF. *La Rose de Mouffetard* (☎ 01 43 26 66 43; metro Monge) at 6 Rue Mouffetard serves some of the cheapest sit-down food in town, including generous portions of tasty couscous starting at only 25FF. This place is open daily from 11 am to midnight.

For Tibetan food, a good choice is the friendly *Tashi Delek* (☎ 01 43 26 55 55; metro Luxembourg) – that's 'bon jour' in Tibetan – at 4 Rue des Fossés Saint Jacques. Tashi Delek is open for lunch and dinner from Monday night to Saturday. Lunch/dinner menus start at 40/105FF. If someone else is treating, try *Aleka* (☎ 01 44 07 02 75) at 187 Rue Saint Jacques for some of the freshest Greek-style hors d'oeuvres (from 25FF) and grilled salmon and tuna (79FF) in Paris. Aleka is open weekdays for lunch and every night to 2 am for dinner.

Montparnasse (6e & 14e) Two somewhat pricey places but real 'finds' in this area are *Le Caméléon* (☎ 01 43 20 63 43; metro Vavin) at 6 Rue de Chevreuse (6e), which has never-to-be-forgotten lobster ravioli on its menu, and *La Cagouille* (☎ 01 43 22 09 01; metro Gaîté) at 10-12 Place Brancusi (14e), which faces 23 Rue de l'Ouest. Fish and shellfish are the latter's speciality. Bookings at both are essential.

Montmartre (9e & 18e) There are dozens of cafés and restaurants around Place du Tertre but they tend to be touristy and overpriced. An old Montmartre favourite is *Refuge des Fondus* (☎ 01 42 55 22 65) at 17 Rue des Trois Frères (18e), whose speciality is fondues. For 87FF, you get wine and a good quantity of either cheese fondue Savoyarde or meat fondue Bourguignonne (minimum of two). It's open daily from 7 pm to 2 am and is very popular, so book. *Le Mono* (☎ 01 46 06 99 20) at 40 Rue Véron (18e) serves West African

FRANCE

dishes (Togolese to be exact) priced from 25 to 70FF. It's open every night except Wednesday. Get off at metro station Abbesses for the above restaurants.

Le Delta Brasserie (☎ 01 42 85 74 15; metro Barbès Rochechouart) at 17 Blvd Rochechouart (9e) caters to shoppers perusing the clothing and fabric stalls in the area and has plats du jour for 55FF.

University Restaurants The Centre Régional des Œuvres Universitaires et Scolaires, or CROUS (☎ 01 40 51 37 10), runs 15 student cafeterias (restaurants universitaires) in the city. Tickets (on sale at meal times) cost 21.10FF for students and 26.40FF for others. Some of the restaurants also have à la carte brasseries. In general, CROUS restaurants have rather confusing opening times that change according to rotational agreements among the restaurants and school holiday schedules (eg most are closed on weekends and during July and August).

Restaurant Universitaire Bullier (metro: Port Royal) is on the 2nd floor of the Centre Jean Sarrailh at 39 Rue Bernanos (5e). Lunch and dinner are served Monday to Friday and, during some months, on weekends as well. The ticket window, which is up one flight of stairs, is open from 11.30 am to 2 pm and 6.15 to 8 pm. One of the nicest CROUS restaurants in town is on the 7th floor of the Faculté de Droit et des Sciences Économiques (Faculty of Law & Economics; metro Vavin), which is south of the Jardin du Luxembourg at 92 Rue d'Assas (6e). It's open weekdays from 11.30 am to 3 pm. The ticket window is on the 6th floor.

Self-Catering Buying your own food is one of the best ways to keep down the cost of visiting Paris. Supermarkets are always cheaper than small grocery shops.

Food Markets The freshest and best-quality fruits, vegetables, cheeses and meats at the lowest prices in town are on offer at Paris' neighbourhood food markets. The city's dozen or so covered markets are open from 8 am to sometime between 12.30 and 1.30 pm and from 3.30 or 4 to 7.30 pm daily except Sunday afternoon and Monday. The open-air markets – about 60 scattered around town – are set up two or three mornings a week in squares and streets like Rue Mouffetard (5e) and Rue Daguerre (14e) and are open from 7 am to 1 pm.

Notre Dame Area (4e & 5e) On Île Saint Louis, there are boulangeries, fromageries and fruit and vegetable shops on Rue Saint Louis en l'Île and Rue des Deux Ponts (4e; metro Pont Marie). There is a cluster of food shops in the vicinity of Place Maubert (5e; metro Maubert-Mutualité), which is 300 metres south of Notre Dame, and on Rue Lagrange. On Tuesday, Thursday and Saturday from 7 am to 1 pm, Place Maubert is transformed into an outdoor produce market. There's an excellent fromagerie (metro: Maubert-Mutualité) at 47 Blvd Saint Germain (5e).

Saint Germain des Prés (6e) The largest cluster of food shops in the neighbourhood is one block north of Blvd Saint Germain around the intersection of Rue de Buci and Rue de Seine. There are also food shops along Rue Dauphine and the two streets that link it with Blvd Saint Germain, Rue de l'Ancienne Comédie and Rue de Buci.

Panthéon Area (5e) There are several food shops (metro: Luxembourg) along Rue Saint Jacques between Nos 172 and 218 (the area just south of Rue Soufflot).

Marais (4e) Fresh breads and Jewish-style central European pastries are available at the two *Finkelsztajn* bakeries (metro: Saint Paul) at 27 Rue des Rosiers and 24 Rue des Écouffes. There are quite a few food shops on Rue de Rivoli and Rue Saint Antoine around the Saint Paul metro stop.

Louvre Area (1er) You'll find a number of food shops one block north of where the western part of the Louvre meets the eastern end of Jardin des Tuileries.

Montmartre (18e) Most of the food shops in this area are along Rue des Abbesses, which is about 500 metres south-west of Sacré Cœur, and Rue Lepic.

Entertainment

Information in French on cultural events, music concerts, theatre performances, films, museum exhibitions, festivals, circuses etc is listed in two publications that come out each Wednesday: *Pariscope* (3FF), which includes an eight-page English section, and *L'Officiel des Spectacles* (2FF). They are available at most news kiosks.

Tickets Reservations and ticketing for all sorts of cultural events are handled by the ticket outlets in the FNAC stores at 136 Rue de Rennes (6e; ☎ 01 49 54 30 00; metro Saint Placide) and at the 3rd underground level of the Forum des Halles shopping mall (☎ 01 40 41 40 00; metro Châtelet-Les Halles) at 1-7 Rue Pierre Lescot (1er).

Cinemas The fashionable cinemas on Blvd du Montparnasse (6e & 14e; metro Montparnasse Bienvenüe) show both dubbed (VF) and original (VO) feature films. There's another cluster of cinemas at Carrefour de l'Odéon (6e; metro Odéon) and lots more movie theatres along the Ave des Champs Élysées (8e; metro George V) and Blvd Saint Germain (6e; metro Saint Germain des Prés).

The *Cinémathèque Française* (☎ 01 47 04 24 24) almost always leaves its foreign offerings non-dubbed. Several screenings take place almost every day at two locations: in the far eastern tip of the Palais de Chaillot on Ave Albert de Mun (16e; metro Trocadéro or Iéna) and at 18 Rue du Faubourg du Temple (11e; metro République). Tickets cost 30FF.

Parisian movie-going is rather pricey. Expect to pay around 45FF for a ticket. Students and people under 18 and over 60 usually get discounts of about 25% except on weekend nights. On Monday and/or Wednesday most cinemas give everyone discounts.

Pubs At 19 Rue Saint Jacques (5e), *Le Cloître* (☎ 01 43 25 19 92; metro Saint Michel) is an unpretentious, relaxed place with mellow background music which seems to please the young Parisians who congregate there. It is open daily from 3 pm to 2 am. Informal, friendly *Polly Maggoo* (☎ 01 46 33 33 64; metro Saint Michel), up the street at 11 Rue Saint Jacques, was founded in 1967 and still

plays music from that era. It is open daily from 3 pm to the wee hours.

Another favourite with Anglo-Saxons is a rather loud American-style bar named *Le Violon Dingue* (☎ 01 43 25 79 93; metro Maubert-Mutualité), which is at 46 Rue de la Montagne Sainte Geneviève (5e). It is open daily from 7.30 pm to 2 am; live bands start at 10 pm on Thursday, Friday and Saturday. *Café Oz* (☎ 01 43 54 30 48; metro Luxembourg), at 18 Rue Saint Jacques, is a casual, friendly Australian pub with Fosters on tap. It is open daily from 11 am to 1.30 am.

Discothèques The discothèques – not really 'discos' as we know them but any place where there's music and dancing – favoured by the Parisian 'in' crowd change frequently, and many are officially private, which means that the gorilla-like bouncers can refuse entry to whomever they don't like the look of. Single men, for example, may not be admitted simply because they're alone and male. Women, on the other hand, get in free on some nights. Expect to pay at least 50FF on weekdays and 100FF on weekends.

Le Balajo (☎ 01 47 00 07 87; metro Bastille), a mainstay of the Parisian dance-hall scene since the time of Édith Piaf, is at 9 Rue de Lappe (11e), two blocks north-east of Place de la Bastille. It offers accordion music on Friday, Saturday and Sunday afternoons from 3 to 7 pm and dancing on Thursday, Friday and Saturday nights from 11.30 pm to 5 am. On Saturday and Sunday admission costs 40/50FF. At night admission is 100FF and includes one drink.

La Locomotive (☎ 01 42 57 37 37; metro Blanche) at 90 Blvd de Clichy (18e), which is in Pigalle next to the Moulin Rouge nightclub, occupies three floors, each offering a different ambience and kind of music. It is open from 11 pm until 6 am nightly except Monday. Entrance costs 65FF on weekdays and 100FF on Friday and Saturday nights, including one drink.

Jazz For the latest on jazz happenings in town, check the listings (see the beginning of this section). *Caveau de la Huchette* (☎ 01 43 26 65 05; metro Saint Michel) at 5 Rue de la Huchette (5e) is an old favourite with live jazz.

FRANCE

Marais & Île Saint Louis

To Gare de l'Est (1.7 km)

2e

Blvd de Sébastopol

Rue St Martin

Rue Beaubourg

Rambuteau

Place Georges Pompidou

Rue Rambuteau

Rue des Archives

Temple

3e

Rue des Fils

To Forum des Halles (350 m)

Rue du Temple

Rue des Archives

Rue Vieille du Temple

Rue de la Perle

Rue de Thorigny

5

11

Place Igor Stravinsky

3

To the Louvre (1 km)

Rue du Renard

Rue des Francs Bourgeois

Rue du Parc Royal

Rue de Turenne

11e

Hôtel de Ville

4

Rue St Gilles

Chemin Vert

Bréguet Sabin

Place de l'Hôtel de Ville

15

Marais

6   7

Rue des Rosiers

Rue des Écouffes

R de Béarn

Boulevard Beaumarchais

Boulevard Richard Lenoir

14   16

8

R Traséé

Rue de Rivoli

Rue F Miron

R des Barres

17

R de Lobau

13

R Mahler

10

Rue de Séviqué

Place des Vosges

18

R Geoffroy l'Asnier

19

Saint Paul

11

12

Rue de Birague

22

23

Île de la Cité

Pont Louis Philippe

Metro Pont Marie

20

Rue Charlemagne

Rue Saint Antoine

Bastille

24

Place de la Bastille

25

4e

R du Fauconnier

Rue St Paul

Bastille

26

29

Pont St Louis

Rue St Louis

Seine River

Pont Marie

27

30

Île Saint Louis

Rue des Deux Ponts

31

32

33

en l'île

Boulevard Henri IV

Boulevard Bourdon

Boulevard de la Bastille

28

12e

5e

To Place Maubert (200 m) & the Latin Quarter

Pont de la Tournelle

Pont de Sully

Sully Morland

0   150   300 m

arrondissement boundaries

It is open every night from 9.30 pm to 2.30 am (Sunday to Thursday nights), 3.30 am (Friday night) or 4 am (Saturday and holiday nights). From Sunday to Thursday, entry costs 60FF (55FF for students) and 70FF on Friday and Saturday.

Concerts & Opera Paris has all sorts of orchestra, organ and chamber music concerts. Some are even free, such as the organ concerts held at Notre Dame every Sunday at 5.30 pm. *Opéra-Bastille* (☎ 01 44 73 13 99; metro Bastille) at 2-6 Place de la Bastille (12e) has been Paris' main opera house since its opening in 1989. The old – some would say real – opera house, *Opéra-Garnier* (☎ 01 44 73 13 99; metro Opéra) at Place de l'Opéra (9e) now stages concerts and ballets. The cheapest regular tickets, which get you a seat with an obstructed view high above the stage, cost as little as 20 to 30FF. Subject to availability, people under 25 and over 65 may be able to purchase decent seats 15 minutes before the curtain rises for the 100FF tarif spécial.

Things to Buy

Fashion For fashionable clothing and accessories, some of the fanciest shops in Paris are along Ave Montaigne (8e), Rue Saint Honoré (1er & 8e), Place Vendôme (1er) and Rue du Faubourg Saint Honoré (8e). Rue Bonaparte (6e) offers a good choice of mid-range boutiques.

Department Stores Right behind Opéra-Garnier are two of Paris' largest department stores. Au Printemps (☎ 01 42 82 50 00; metro Havre Caumartin) is at 64 Blvd Haussmann (9e) and Galeries Lafayette (☎ 01 42 82 36 40; metro Auber or Chaussée), at 40 Blvd Haussmann (9e), is housed in two adjacent buildings linked by a pedestrian bridge. The third of Paris' 'big three', Samaritaine (☎ 01 40 41 20 20; metro Pont Neuf), consists of four buildings between Pont Neuf and Rue de Rivoli. There is an amazing 360° view of the city from the 10th-floor terrace of Building 2 at 19 Rue de la Monnaie. Take the lift to the 9th floor and walk up the narrow staircase. All three stores are open Monday to Saturday from 9.30 am to 7 pm (10 pm on Thursday).

Getting There & Away

Air Paris has two major international airports. Aéroport d'Orly is 14 km south of central Paris. For flight and other information, call ☎ 01 49 75 15 15. Aéroport Charles de Gaulle (☎ 01 48 62 22 80), also known as Roissy-Charles de Gaulle because it is in the Paris suburb of Roissy, is 23 km north-east of central Paris. Telephone numbers for information at Paris' airline offices are:

Airline Office	Telephone
Air France	☎ 01 44 08 22 22
Air Inte	☎ 01 45 46 90 00
American Airline	☎ 01 42 89 05 22
British Airways	☎ 01 47 78 14 14
Continental Airline	☎ 01 42 99 09 09
Delta Air Lines	☎ 01 47 68 92 92
Northwest Airlines	☎ 01 42 66 90 00
Qantas Airways	☎ 01 44 55 52 00
Singapore Airlines	☎ 01 45 53 90 90
Thai Airways	☎ 01 44 20 70 80
Tower Air	☎ 01 44 51 56 56
TWA	☎ 01 49 19 20 00
United Airlines	☎ 01 48 97 82 82

Bus Eurolines runs buses from Paris to cities all over Europe. The company's terminal, Gare Routière Internationale (☎ 01 49 72 51 51; metro Gallieni), is at Porte de Bagnolet (20e) on the eastern edge of Paris. Its ticket office in town (☎ 01 43 54 11 99; metro Cluny-La Sorbonne) at 55 Rue Saint Jacques (5e) is open Tuesday to Friday from 9.30 am to 1 pm and 2.30 to 7 pm and on Monday and Saturday to 6 pm.

Cities served include Amsterdam (250FF one way, eight hours), London (290FF, nine hours), Madrid (590FF, 17 hours) and Rome (590FF, 26 hours). People under 26 and over 60 get a discount of about 10%. Because the French government prefers to avoid competition with the state-owned rail system and regulated domestic airlines, there is no domestic, intercity bus service to or from Paris.

Train Paris has six major train stations (*gares*), each handling traffic to different parts of France and Europe. For information in English call ☎ 08 36 35 35 39; the switchboards are staffed from 7 am to 10 pm. All the stations have exchange bureaus, and there is a tourist office annexe at each one except Gare Saint Lazare. The metro station attached to each

FRANCE

train station bears the same name as the gare. Paris' major train stations are:

Gare d'Austerlitz (13e) Quai d'Austerlitz (metro: Gare d'Austerlitz) – trains to the Loire Valley, Spain and Portugal and non-TGV trains to south-western France (Bordeaux, the Basque Country)

Gare de l'Est (10e) Place du 11 Novembre 1918 (metro: Gare de l'Est) – trains to parts of France east of Paris (Champagne, Alsace, Lorraine), Luxembourg, parts of Switzerland (Basel, Lucerne, Zürich), southern Germany (Frankfurt, Munich) and Austria

Gare de Lyon (12e) Place Louis Armand (metro: Gare de Lyon) – regular and TGV Sud-Est trains to points south-east of Paris, including Dijon, Lyon, Provence, Côte d'Azur, Alps, parts of Switzerland, Italy and Greece

Gare Montparnasse (15e) Blvd de Vaugirard (metro: Montparnasse Bienvenuë) – trains to Brittany and places on the way (Chartres, Angers, Nantes); and the TGV Atlantique, which serves Tours, Bordeaux and other places in south-western France

Gare du Nord (10e) Rue de Dunkerque (metro: Gare du Nord) – trains to northern France (Lille, Calais), the UK via the Channel Tunnel (TGV Nord), Belgium, Netherlands, northern Germany, Scandinavia, Moscow etc

Gare Saint Lazare (8e) Rue Saint Lazare (metro: Saint Lazare) – trains to Normandy and, via the Channel ports, ferries to England. The SNCF information office (☎ 01 53 42 00 00), which is 50 metres behind *voie* 2 (track 2), can also help tourists with matters not concerning train travel.

Getting Around

RATP, Paris' public transit system, is one of the most efficient in the world and one of the biggest urban transport bargains (see Metro/Bus Tickets). Free metro/RER/bus maps are available at the ticket windows of most stations and at tourist offices. For information on metros and RER commuter trains and buses, call ☎ 08 36 68 77 14 between 6 am and 9 pm.

To/From Orly Airport Orly Rail is the quickest way to get to the Left Bank and the 16e. Take the free shuttle bus to the Pont de Rungis-Aéroport d'Orly RER (commuter rail) station, which is on the C2 line, and get on a train (30FF) heading into the city. Another fast way into town is to hop on the Orlyval shuttle train (52FF); it stops near Orly-Sud's Porte F and links Orly with the Antony RER station, which is on line B4. Orlybus (30FF or six bus/metro tickets), takes you to the Denfert-Rochereau metro station (14e).

Air France buses charge 40FF to take you to Ave du Maine at the Gare Montparnasse (15e) or the Aérogare des Invalides, which is next to Esplanade des Invalides (7e). RATP bus No 183 (four tickets) goes to Porte de Choisy (13e) but is very slow. All the services between Orly airport and Paris run every 15 minutes or so (less frequently late at night) from early in the morning (sometime between 5.30 and 6.30 am) to 11 or 11.30 pm.

Taking a taxi from Orly airport can work out cheaper per person if there are four people to share it.

To/From Charles de Gaulle (CDG) Airport
The fastest way to get to/from the city is by Roissy Rail. Free shuttle buses take you from the airport terminals to the Roissy-Charles de Gaulle RER (commuter rail) station. You can buy tickets to CDG (45FF) at RER stations. If you get on at an ordinary metro station you can buy a ticket when you change to the RER or pay at the other end or on the train (with a fine) if you get caught.

Air France buses will take you to Porte Maillot (16e & 17e; metro Porte Maillot) or the corner of Ave Carnot near the Arc de Triomphe (17e) for 55FF. Its buses to Blvd de Vaugirard at the Gare Montparnasse (15e) cost 65FF. Roissybus (RATP bus No 352) goes to the American Express office (9e) near Place de l'Opéra and costs 35FF. RATP bus No 350 goes to Gare du Nord (10e) and Gare de l'Est (10e). Until 9.15 pm (heading into the city) and 8.20 am (towards the airport), RATP bus No 351 goes to Ave du Trône (11e & 12e), on the eastern side of Place de la Nation. Both RATP buses require six tickets.

Unless otherwise indicated, the buses and trains from CDG to Paris run from sometime between 5 and 6.30 am until 11 or 11.30 pm.

Bus Paris' extensive bus network tends to get overlooked by visitors, in part because the metro is so quick, efficient and easy to use. Bus routes are indicated on the free RATP maps No 1, *Petit Plan de Paris*, and No 3, *Grand Plan Île de France*.

Short trips cost one bus/metro/RER ticket (see Underground/Bus Tickets below), while longer rides require two. Travellers without tickets can purchase them from the driver.

Whatever kind of ticket (coupon) you have, you must cancel it in the little machine next to the driver. The fines are hefty if you're caught without a ticket or without a cancelled ticket. If you have a Carte Orange, Formule 1 or Paris Visite pass (see the following Metro & RER section), just flash it at the driver – do not cancel your ticket.

After the metro shuts down at around 12.45 am, the Noctambus network, whose symbol is a black owl silhouetted against a yellow moon, links the Châtelet-Hôtel de Ville area (4e) with lots of places on the Right Bank (lines A to H) and a few on the Left Bank (lines J and R). Noctambuses begin their runs from the even-numbered side of Ave Victoria (4e), which is between the Hôtel de Ville and Place du Châtelet, every hour on the half-hour from 1.30 to 5.30 am. A ride requires three tickets (four tickets if your journey involves a transfer).

Metro & RER Paris' underground rail network consists of two separate but linked systems: the Métropolitain, known as the metro, which has 13 lines and over 300 stations, many marked by Hector Guimard's famous noodle-like Art-Nouveau entrances with the red 'eyes', and the suburban commuter rail network, the RER which, along with certain SNCF lines, is divided into eight concentric zones. The term 'metro' is used in this chapter to refer to the Métropolitain and any part of the RER system within Paris. The whole system has been designed so that no point in Paris is more than 500 metres from a metro stop; in fact, some places in the city centre are within a few hundred metres of up to three stations.

You may be able to reduce the number of transfers you'll have to make by going to a station a bit further on from your destination. For metro stations to avoid late at night, see Dangers & Annoyances earlier in the Paris section.

How it Works Each metro train is known by the name of its terminus; trains on the same line have different names depending on which direction they are travelling in. On lines that split into several branches and thus have more than one end-of-the-line station, the final destination of each train is indicated on the front, sides and interior of the train cars. In the sta-

tions, white-on-blue sortie signs indicate exits and black-on-orange correspondance signs show how to get to connecting trains. The last metro train sets out on its final run at 12.30 am. Plan ahead so as not to miss your connection. The metro starts up again at 5.30 am.

Metro/Bus Tickets The same green 2nd-class tickets are valid on the metro, the bus and, for travel within the Paris city limits, the RER's 2nd-class carriages. They cost 7.50FF if bought separately and 44FF for a booklet (carnet) of 10. For children aged four to nine a carnet costs 22FF. One ticket lets you travel between any two metro stations, including stations outside of the Paris city limits, no matter how many transfers are required. You can also use it on the RER commuter rail system for travel within Paris (within zone 1).

For travel on the RER to destinations outside the city, purchase a special ticket before you board the train or you won't be able to get out of the station and could be fined. Always keep your ticket until you reach your destination and exit the station; if you're caught without a ticket, or with an invalid one, you'll be fined. A weekly and monthly bus/metro/RER pass, known as the Carte Orange, is available for travel in two to eight urban and suburban zones; you must present a photograph of yourself to buy one. The weekly ticket (coupon hebdomadaire), which costs 67FF for travel in zones 1 and 2 (covering all of Paris proper plus a few RER stops in the inner suburbs), is valid from Monday to Sunday. The validity of the monthly (mensuel) ticket (230FF for zones 1 and 2) begins on the first day of each calendar month. You must write your name on the Carte Orange and the number of your Carte Orange on your weekly/monthly ticket.

Formule 1 and Paris Visite passes, designed to facilitate bus, metro and RER travel for tourists, are on sale in many metro stations, the train stations and international airports. The Formule 1 card (and its coupon) allows unlimited travel for one day in two to four zones. The version valid for zones 1 and 2 costs 30FF. The four-zone version (60FF) lets you go all the way out to Versailles and both airports (but not on Orlyval). Paris Visite passes are valid for three consecutive days of travel in three to five zones. The 1 to 3-zone version costs 105/165FF (three/five days). Obviously a Paris Visite pass is much dearer than a weekly two-zone Carte Orange ticket.

Taxi Paris' 15,000 taxis have a reputation for paying little heed to riders' convenience. Another common complaint is that it can be difficult to find a taxi late at night (after 11 pm) or in the rain. The flag fall is 12FF; within the city, it costs 3.23FF per km between 7 am and 7 pm Monday to Saturday. On nights, Sunday and holidays, it's 5.10FF per km. Animals, a fourth passenger and heavy luggage cost extra. Tips are not obligatory, but no matter what the fare is, usual tips range from 2FF to a maximum of 5FF.

The easiest way to find a taxi is to walk to the nearest taxi stand (*tête de station*), of which there are 500 scattered around the city and marked on any of the Michelin 1:10,000 maps. Radio-dispatched taxis include Taxis Bleus (☎ 01 49 36 10 10), G7 Taxis (☎ 01 47 39 47 39), Alpha Taxis (☎ 01 45 85 85 85), Taxis-Radio Étoile (☎ 01 42 70 41 41) and Artaxi (☎ 01 42 41 50 50). If you order a taxi by phone, the meter is switched on as soon as the driver gets word of your call – wherever that may be (but usually not too far away).

Car & Motorcycle Driving in Paris is nerve-racking but not impossible. Most side streets are one way (*sens unique*) and, without a good map, trying to get around town by car will make you feel like a rat in a maze. In general, the best way to get across the city is via one of the major boulevards, except during rush hour. If you're caught in rush hour, all you can do is find a parking space and take the metro. You must feed Paris meters every two hours. The fastest way to get all the way across Paris is usually the Blvd Périphérique, the ring road (beltway) around the city.

Rent A Car (☎ 01 43 45 15 15), has offices at 79 Rue de Bercy (12e; metro Bercy) and 84 Ave de Versailles (16e; metro Mirabeau), and has Fiat Pandas with unlimited km for 298FF a day, including insurance. The weekly rate is 1398FF. The Rue de Bercy office is open Monday to Thursday from 8 am to 6.30 pm, Friday from 8 am to 7 pm and on Saturday from 9 am to 6 pm. Avis (☎ 01 46 10 60 60) has

offices at all six train stations, both airports and several other locations in the Paris area. Europcar (☎ 01 30 43 82 82) has bureaus at both airports and almost 20 other locations. Hertz (☎ 01 47 88 51 51) also has offices at the airports and at many other places around Paris.

For information on purchase/repurchase plans, see the Getting Around section at the start of this chapter.

Bicycle With its heavy traffic and impatient drivers Paris has never been a cyclist's paradise. But things are improving. In early 1996 the city unveiled a plan to establish a 50-km network of bicycle lanes across Paris. By early 1997, there will be lanes stretching from Porte de Pantin in the north to Porte de Vanves in the south, and east to west from the Bois de Vincennes to the Bois de Boulogne. Centrally, the lanes run along Rue de Rivoli and the Blvd Saint Germain. The tourist office should have detailed maps.

Maison du Velo (☎ 01 42 81 24 72), at Rue Fénélan (10e; metro Gare du Nord), has bicycles available for 150FF per day, 260FF per weekend and 575FF per week.

Cyclic (☎ 01 43 25 63 67), at 19 Rue Mange (5e; metro Cardinal Lemoine), rents bikes by the hour (20FF), day (100FF) and week (300FF).

See the sections on Bois de Boulogne (under Things to See) and Bicycle (under Organised Tours) for more information.

Around Paris

The region surrounding Paris is known as the Île de France (Island of France) because of its position between four rivers: the Aube, Marne, Oise and Seine. It was from this relatively small area that, starting around 1100 AD, the kingdom of France began to expand. Today, the region's proximity to Paris and a number of remarkable sights make it an especially popular day-trip destination for people staying in Paris.

EURODISNEY
It took US$4 billion to turn beet fields 32 km east of Paris into the much hyped EuroDisney

theme park (☎ 01 64 74 30 00), which opened in April 1992 amid much moaning from France's intellectuals. Though far from turning a profit, the park is pulling in European crowds by the hundreds of thousands.

From June to September EuroDisney is open daily from 9 am to 8 pm (11 pm on Saturday and Sunday), the rest of the year it's open daily from 10 am to 6 pm (8 pm on Sunday). All-day entry costs 195FF for everyone over age 12 (150FF for children aged three to 11). Three-day passes are 505/390FF.

To get there, take RER line A4 to the terminus (Marne-la-Vallée Chessy), but check the destination boards to ensure your train goes all the way to the end. Trains, which take 35 minutes from the Nation stop on Place de la Nation (12e), run every 10 or 15 minutes or so. Sometimes, usually during the off-peak season, RER/EuroDisney offer cheap promotional fares. There are also shuttle buses from Orly and Roissy-Charles de Gaulle airports (80FF one way).

VERSAILLES

Site of France's grandest and most famous chateau, Versailles (population 92,000) served as the country's political capital and the seat of the royal court from 1682 until 1789, when Revolutionary mobs massacred the palace guard and dragged Louis XVI and Marie-Antoinette off to Paris, where they were later guillotined. After the Franco-Prussian War of 1870-71, the victorious Prussians proclaimed the establishment of the German empire from the chateau's Galerie des Glaces (Hall of Mirrors). In 1919 the Treaty of Versailles was signed in the same room, officially ending WWI and imposing harsh conditions on a defeated Germany, Austria and Hungary.

Because Versailles is on most travellers' 'must-see' lists, the chateau can be jammed with tourists, especially on weekends, in summer and most especially on summer Sundays. The best way to avoid the lines is to arrive early in the morning.

Information

The tourist office (☎ 01 39 50 36 22) is at 7 Rue des Réservoirs, just north of the chateau. From November to April, it is open Monday to Saturday from 9 am to 12.30 pm and 2 to 6.15 pm (on Saturday to 5 pm). During the rest of the year, it is open daily from 9 am to 7 pm.

Château de Versailles

The enormous Château de Versailles (☎ 01 30 84 74 00) was built in the mid-17th century during the reign of Louis XIV (the Sun King). Among the advantages of Versailles was its distance from the political intrigues of Paris; out here, it was much easier for the king to contain and keep an eye on his scheming nobles. The plan worked brilliantly, all the more so because court life turned the nobles into sycophantic courtiers who expended most of their energy vying for royal favour à la *Les Liaisons Dangereuses*.

The chateau essentially consists of four parts: the main palace building, which is a classical structure with innumerable wings, sumptuous bedchambers and grand halls; the vast 17th-century gardens, laid out in the formal French style; and two out-palaces, the late 17th-century Grand Trianon and the mid-18th century Petit Trianon.

Opening Hours & Tickets The main building is open daily except Monday and public holidays from 9 am to 5.30 pm (6.30 pm from May to September). Entrance to the **Grands Appartements** (State Apartments), which include the 73-metre-long **Galerie des Glaces** (Hall of Mirrors) and the **Appartement de la Reine** (Queen's Suite), costs 45FF (35FF reduced rate). Everyone pays 35FF on Sunday. Tickets are on sale at Entrée A (Entrance A), which is off to the right from the equestrian statue of Louis XIV as you approach the building. You won't be able to visit other parts of the main palace unless you take one of the guided tours (see Guided Tours below). Entrée H has facilities for the disabled, including a lift.

The **Grand Trianon**, which costs 25FF (15FF reduced rate), is open daily except Monday. From October to April, opening hours are 10 am to 12.30 pm and 2 to 5.30 pm (10 am to 5.30 pm on weekends). During the rest of the year, hours are 10 am to 6.30 pm. The **Petit Trianon**, open the same hours as the Grand Trianon, costs 15FF (10FF reduced rate).

The gardens are open every day of the week from 7 am to nightfall. Entry is free except on Sundays from May to early October when the baroque fountains 'perform'. The **Grandes Eaux** show takes place from 3.30 to 5 pm and costs 25FF.

At the time of writing, Versailles was in the process of being privatised; you may want to call the chateau or tourist office to check whether hours and prices have changed drastically.

Guided Tours Eight different guided tours are available in English. A one-hour tour costs 25FF in addition to the regular entry fee. To buy tickets and make advance reservations (☎ 01 30 84 76 18), go to entrées C or D. Cassette-guided tours in six different languages are also available at entrées A and C for 25FF.

Other Attractions
The city of Versailles is filled with beautiful buildings from the 17th and 18th centuries. The tourist office has a brochure of historic walks (*promenades historiques*) pinpointing more than two dozen of these structures. They include: the **Jeu de Paume** (check the opening hours with the tourist office) on Rue du Jeu de Paume, where the representatives of the Third Estate constituted themselves as a National Assembly in June 1789; the **Musée Lambinet** (☎ 01 39 50 30 32) at 54 Blvd de la Reine (open Tuesday to Sunday from 2 to 6 pm); and the mid-18th century **Cathédrale Saint Louis** at Place Saint Louis, renowned for its enormous pipe organ.

Getting There & Away
Bus Bus No 171 takes you from the Pont de Sèvres metro stop in Paris all the way to Place d'Armes, right in front of the chateau.

Train Versailles, 23 km south-west of central Paris, has three train stations: Versailles-Rive Gauche, Versailles-Chantiers and Versailles-Rive Droite. Each is served by one of the three rail services that link Versailles with Paris.

RER line C5 takes you from Paris' Gare d'Austerlitz and various other RER stations on the Left Bank (including Saint Michel and Champ de Mars-Tour Eiffel) to Versailles-Rive Gauche, which is 700 metres south-east of the chateau on Ave Général de Gaulle. Check the electronic destination lists on the platform to

make sure you take a train that goes all the way there.

SNCF trains go from Paris' Gare Montparnasse to Versailles-Chantiers, which is 1.3 km south-east of the chateau just off Ave de Sceaux. SNCF trains also run from Paris' Gare Saint Lazare to Versailles-Rive Droite, 1.2 km north-east of the chateau. Many of the trains from Gare Montparnasse to Versailles continue on to Chartres. Eurail-pass holders can travel free on the SNCF trains but not on those operated by the RER.

CHARTRES
The indescribably beautiful 13th-century cathedral of Chartres (population 43,000) rises abruptly from the corn fields 88 km south-west of Paris. Crowned by two soaring spires – one Gothic, the other Romanesque – it dominates the attractive medieval town clustered around its base. The present cathedral has been attracting pilgrims for eight centuries, but the city has been a site of pilgrimage for over two millennia: the Gallic Druids may have had a sanctuary here, and the Romans apparently built a temple dedicated to the Dea Mater (mother goddess).

Orientation
The medieval sections of Chartres are situated along the Eure River and the hillside to the west. The cathedral, which is visible from almost everywhere, is about 500 metres east of the train station.

Information
Tourist Office The tourist office (☎ 02 37 21 50 00) is one block south-west of the cathedral's main entrance at Place de la Cathédrale. It is open Monday to Friday from 9.30 am to 6, 6.30 or 6.45 pm, depending on the season. Saturday hours are 9.30 am to 5 pm (6 pm from March to October). From May to September, the office is also open on Sunday from 10.30 am to 12.30 pm and 2.30 to 5.30 pm; during the rest of the year it is open on Sunday morning only. Hotel reservations cost 10FF (plus a 50FF deposit).

Money & Post Banks are usually open Tuesday to Saturday, including the Banque de France (☎ 02 37 91 59 03) at 32 Rue du Docteur Maunoury about a km south of the train station. The main post office is at Place des Épars. Chartres' postcode is 28000.

Things to See & Do

Cathédrale Notre Dame Chartres' cathedral (☎ 02 37 21 56 33) was built in the first quarter of the 13th century and, unlike so many of its contemporaries, it has not been significantly modified since then. Built to replace an earlier structure devastated by fire in 1194, the construction of this early Gothic masterpiece took only 25 years, which is why the cathedral has a high degree of architectural unity. It was almost torn down during the Reign of Terror and managed to survive WWII bombing raids unscathed.

The cathedral is open daily from 7 am to 7 pm (7.30 pm from April to September). From April to November (and sometimes in winter), Englishman Malcolm Miller gives fascinating tours (30FF) of what he calls 'this book of stained glass and sculpture' at noon and 2.45 pm every day except Sunday.

The 105-metre **Clocher Vieux** (old bell tower), the tallest Romanesque steeple still standing, is to the right as you face the Romanesque **Portail Royal** (the main entrance). The **Clocher Neuf** (new bell tower) has a Gothic spire dating from 1513 and can be visited daily, except Sunday morning, from 9.30 or 10 to 11.30 am and 2 to 4 or 4.30 pm (October to March) or 5.30 pm (April to September). The fee is 14FF (10FF reduced rate).

Inside, the cathedral's most exceptional feature is its extraordinary **stained-glass windows**, most of which are 13th-century originals and are slowly being cleaned at great expense. The three exceptional windows over the main entrance date from around 1150. The strange **labyrinth** on the nave floor in dark and light stone was used by medieval pilgrims while praying. The **trésor** (treasury) displays a piece of cloth given to the cathedral in 876 said to have been worn by the Virgin Mary. It is open every afternoon from Tuesday to Saturday and in the morning as well from April to October.

The early 11th-century Romanesque **crypt**, the largest in France, can be visited by a half-hour guided tour in French for 11FF. Tours depart from the cathedral's gift shop, La Crypte, which is outside the south entrance at 18 Rue du Cloître Notre Dame, every day at 11 am, 2.15, 3.30 and 4.30 pm. From mid-June to

mid-September there's an additional tour at 5.15 pm.

Centre International du Vitrail The International Centre of Stained Glass Art (☎ 02 37 21 65 72), partly housed in a 13th-century underground storehouse north of the cathedral at 5 Rue du Cardinal Pie, has exhibits on stained-glass production, restoration, history and symbolism; it's not a bad idea to stop by here before visiting the cathedral if you read French. The centre is open Monday to Friday from 9.30 am to 12.30 pm and 1.30 to 6 pm and on weekends and holidays from 10 am to 12.30 pm and 2.30 to 6 pm. The entry fee is 15FF (12FF reduced rate).

Musée des Beaux-Arts The fine arts museum (☎ 02 37 36 41 39), which is behind (north of) the cathedral at 29 Cloître Notre Dame, is housed in the 17th and 18th-century **Palais Épiscopal** (Bishop's Palace). Its collections include paintings from the 16th to 19th centuries, wooden sculptures from the Middle Ages, a number of 17th and 18th-century harpsichords and some tapestries. The museum is open daily, except Tuesday, from 10 am to noon and 2 to 5 pm (10 am to 6 pm from April to October). Entrance is 10FF (5FF reduced rate).

Old City During the Middle Ages, the city of Chartres grew and developed along the banks of the Eure River. Among the many buildings remaining from that period are private residences, stone bridges, tanneries, wash houses and a number of churches. Streets with buildings of interest include **Rue de la Tannerie**, which runs along the Eure, and **Rue des Écuyers**, which is midway between the cathedral and the river. **Église Saint Pierre** at Place Saint Pierre has a massive bell tower dating from around 1000 and some fine (and often overlooked) medieval stained-glass windows.

Walking Tour Self-guided cassette-tape tours of the old city can be rented at the tourist office for 35/40FF for one or two people (plus 100FF deposit).

Places to Stay

Camping About 2.5 km south-east of the train station on Rue de Launay is *Les Bords de* *l'Eure* camping ground (☎ 02 37 28 79 43), which is open from April to early September. Two adults with a tent and car pay 47FF. To get there from the train station take bus No 8 to the Vignes stop.

Hostel The pleasant and calm *Auberge de Jeunesse* (☎ 02 37 34 27 64) at 23 Ave Neigre is about 1.5 km east of the train station via the ring road (Blvd Charles Péguy and Blvd Jean Jaurès). By bus, take line No 3 from the train station and get off at the Rouliers stop. Reception is open daily from 8 to 10 am and from 3 to 10 pm (11 pm in summer). A bed costs 65FF, including breakfast. The hostel may be closed between December and January.

Hotels The cheapest hotel in town is the *Hôtel Le Goût Royal* (☎ 02 37 36 57 45) at 17 Rue Nicole, which is 200 metres south-west of the train station. Very basic doubles with communal showers and toilets cost 120FF. The *Hôtel de l'Ouest* (☎ 02 37 21 43 27), a two-star place opposite the train station at 3 Place Pierre Sémard, has clean, carpeted doubles/triples for 120/170FF (with washbasin and bidet), 140/240FF (with shower) and 210/260FF (with shower and toilet).

A lovely two-star choice is *Hôtel de la Poste* (☎ 02 37 21 04 27; fax 02 37 36 42 17), north-west of Place des Épars at 3 Rue du Général Koening, with singles/doubles from 215FF with shower (265/290FF with shower and toilet). Triples/quads with shower cost 360/430FF.

Places to Eat

Café Serpente (☎ 02 37 21 68 81), a brasserie and salon de thé across from the south porch of the cathedral at 2 Rue du Cloître Notre Dame, has main dishes for 72 to 98FF and large salads for 40 to 68FF. It is open daily from 10 am to 1 pm. *Le Petit Bistro* (☎ 02 37 21 09 23), three blocks south of the cathedral at 12 Place Billard, is a casual wine bar/bistro with generous charcuterie (42FF) and cheese platters (25FF). It is open daily from 9 am to 10 pm. The *Monoprix* supermarket at 21 Rue Noël Ballay north-east of Place des Épars is open daily from 9 am to 7.30 pm.

Getting There & Around

Train The train station (☎ 08 36 35 35 39) is at Place Pierre Sémard. The trip from Paris' Gare Montparnasse (69FF one way) takes 50 to 70 minutes. The last train back to Paris leaves Chartres just after 9 pm on weekdays and an hour or so later on weekends. There is also direct rail service to/from Nantes, Quimper, Rennes and Versailles.

Taxi For a taxi in Chartres, call ☎ 02 37 36 00 00.

Alsace

Alsace, the easternmost part of northern France, is nestled between the Vosges Mountains and, about 30 km to the east, the Rhine River, marking the Franco-German border. The area owes its unique language, architecture, cuisine and atmosphere to both sides of this river.

Most of Alsace became part of France in 1648, although Strasbourg, the region's largest city, retained its independence until 1681. But more than two centuries of French rule did little to dampen 19th and early 20th-century German enthusiasm for a foothold on the west bank of the southern Rhine, and Alsace was twice annexed by Germany: from the Franco-Prussian War (1871) until the end of WWI and again between 1939 and 1944.

Language

The Alsatian language, a Germanic dialect similar to that spoken in nearby parts of Germany and Switzerland, is still used by many Alsatians, especially older people in rural areas. Alsatian is known for its singsong intonations, which also characterise the way some Alsatians speak French.

STRASBOURG

The cosmopolitan city of Strasbourg (population 256,000), just a couple of km west of the Rhine, is Alsace's great metropolis and its intellectual and cultural capital. Towering above the restaurants, pubs and *bars à musique* of the lively old city is the cathedral, a medieval marvel in pink sandstone near which is clustered one of the finest ensembles of museums in France. Strasbourg's distinctive architecture, including the centuries-old half-timbered houses, and its exemplary orderliness impart an unmistakably Alsatian ambience.

When it was founded in 1949, the Council of Europe (Conseil de l'Europe) decided to base itself in Strasbourg. The organisation's huge headquarters, the Palais de l'Europe, is used for one week each month (except in summer) by the European Parliament, the legislative branch of the EU.

Orientation

The train station is 350 metres west of the old city, which is an island delimited by the Ill River to the south and the Fossé du Faux Rempart to the north. The main public square in the old city is Place Kléber, which is 400 metres north-west of the cathedral. The quaint Petite France area is in the old city's south-west corner.

Information

Tourist Office The main tourist office (☎ 03 88 52 28 28) at 17 Place de la Cathédrale is open from 9 am to 6 pm, and from May to September daily from 8.30 am to 7 pm.

There's a tourist office annexe (☎ 03 88 32 51 49) in the underground complex beneath the Place de la Gare in front of the train station. It's open weekdays from 9 am to 12.30 pm and 1.45 to 6 pm. From April to June it's also open on the weekend, and from June to September hours are 8.30 am to 7 pm daily. This is a good place to pick up bus tickets. The office also sells the Strasbourg Pass (50FF, valid for three days) which includes free/reduced admission to museums.

Money The Banque de France is at 9 Place Broglie. The Banque CIAL bureau in the train station is open weekdays from 9 am to 1 pm and 2 to 7.30 pm and weekends from 9 am to 8 pm. The commission is 15FF on weekdays and 26FF on weekends. There's a 24-hour exchange machine outside the Sogenal bank at Place Gutenberg; American Express (☎ 03 88 75 78 75) at 31 Place Kléber is open weekdays from 8.45 am to noon and 1.30 to 6 pm.

Post The main post office (☎ 03 88 52 31 00), opposite 8 Ave de la Marseillaise, is open weekdays from 8 am to 7 pm and on Saturday till noon. The branch post office to the left of the train station keeps the same hours. Both offer currency exchange. The postcode of central Strasbourg is 67000.

Things to See & Do

Walking Tour Strasbourg is a great place for an aimless stroll. The bustling **Vieille Ville** is filled with pedestrian malls, up-market shopping streets and lively public squares. There are river views from the quays and paths along the Ill River and the Fossé du Faux Rempart, and in **La Petite France**, half-timbered houses line the narrow streets and canals. The city's parks – **Parc de l'Orangerie** and **Place de la République** particularly – provide a welcome respite from the traffic and bustle. Guided tours of the town (38FF) are organised by the tourist office every Saturday from April to December and from Tuesday to Saturday in July and August.

Cathédrale Strasbourg's impossibly lacy Gothic cathedral was begun in 1176 after an earlier cathedral had burnt down. The west façade was completed in 1284, but the spire (its southern companion was never built) was not in place until 1439. Following the Reformation and a long period of bitter struggle, the cathedral came under Protestant control and was not returned to the Catholic Church until 1681. Many of the statues decorating the cathedral are copies – the originals can be seen in the Musée de l'Œuvre Notre-Dame (see the Museums section).

The cathedral is open from 7 to 11.30 am and 12.40 to 7 pm daily except during masses. The 30-metre-high Gothic and Renaissance contraption just inside the south entrance is the **horloge astronomique**, a 16th-century clock (the mechanism dates from 1842) that strikes every day at precisely 12.30 pm. There is a 5FF charge to see the carved wooden figures do their thing.

The 66-metre-high platform above the façade (from which the tower and its spire soar another 76 metres) can be visited daily – if you don't mind the 330 steps to the top. It's open from 9 am (8.30 am in July and August) to 4.30 pm (November to February), 5.30 pm (March and October), 6.30 pm (April to June and September) or 7 pm

PLACES TO STAY
2 CIARUS (Hostel)
19 Hôtel de Bruxelles
21 Hôtel Le Colmar
24 Hôtel Weber
36 Hôtel Michelet
43 Hôtel de la Cruche d'Or
44 Hôtel Patricia
49 Hôtel de l'Ill

PLACES TO EAT
18 Restaurant Le Cappadoce
22 Pâtisserie
28 Au Crocodile
33 Aldo Pizzeria
42 Winstub Zuem Strissel
45 Au Pont Saint Martin Restaurant
51 Le Bouchon & Festival Bar Américain
53 La Michaudière
54 Adan Vegetarian Restaurant

OTHER
1 Synagogue de la Paix
3 Law Courts
4 Palais du Rhin
5 Préfecture
6 Bibliothèque Nationale et Universitaire
7 US Consulate
8 Église Saint Paul
9 Main Post Office
10 Théâtre National
11 Banque de France
12 Église Saint Pierre-le-Jeune (Prostestant)
13 Post Office Branch
14 Train Station
15 Tourist Office Annexe
16 Europcar Car Rental
17 Voyages Wasteels (Travel Agency)
20 Budget Car Rental
23 Coop Supermarket
25 L'Académie de la Bière

26 Église Saint Pierre-le-Vieux (Catholic)
27 Cinéma Club
28 Cinéma Star
29 Printemps (Department Store)
30 American Express
31 Nouvelles Galefies-Magmod (Department Store)
34 Main Tourist Office
35 24-Hour Exchange Machine (Sogenal Bank)
37 Cathédrale Notre Dame
38 Bar des Aviateurs
39 Château des Rohan, Musée Archéologique, Musée des Arts Décoratifs & Musée des Beaux-Arts
40 Musée d'Art Moderne & Post Office Branch
41 Musée de l'Œuvre Notre-Dame
46 Église Saint Thomas
47 Musée Alsacien
48 Bierstub Le Trou
50 Café des Anges (Live Music Bar)
53 Bus Station

To Auberge de Jeunesse
René Cassin (1.2 km),
Camping de la Montagne Verte
(1.8 km) & Airport (12 km)

FRANCE

Boulevard Clemenceau

Contades Park

Rue Oberlin

Avenue de la Paix

1

Rue Finkmatt

2

Avenue des Vosges

Rue du Maréchal Foch

Rue du Général Gouraud

3

4

5

Place de la République

6

Quai Jacques Sturm

Quai d'Alsace

Fossé du Faux Rempart

7

Quai Schoepflin

Rue de la Fonderie

10

Avenue de la Liberté

To Parc de l'Orangerie & Palais de l'Europe (1 km)

8

Quai Koch

9

Ave de la Marseillaise

Pont d'Auvergne

R de la Nuée Bleue

11

Place Broglie

Rue Brûlée

Quai Lezay Marnésia

Quai du Maire

Place de l'Université

University

Rue de la Mésange

Grande Île

32

Rue des Juifs

Rue du Dôme

33

R Faubn

du

Place Saint Etienne

Ill River

Quai des Pêcheurs

Boulevard de la Victoire

Place Gutenberg

Rue des Hallebardes

Rue des Frères

38

Rue des Sœurs

To Pont de l'Europe (3 km) & Kehl, Germany

34

37

Rue St Guillaume

35

R Mercière

Place de la Cathédrale

40

41

R de la Râpe

39

Place du Château

Rue de l'Académie

R de la Division Leclerc

R des Serruriers

36

Rue du Vieux Marché aux Poissons

42

Place de la Grande Boucherie

Quai des Bateliers

Rue des Bateliers

49

Rue de Zurich

50

Rue des Poules

44

Rue

43

48

Rue des Couples

Place de Zurich

51

Quai Saint Nicolas

47

Rue des Orphelins

Rue du Saint Gothard

52

Rue de Zurich

Thomas

Rue d'Austerlitz

Place d'Austerlitz

53

Rue des de la 1ère Armée

Bouchers

Place de l'Hôpital

54

R. Sédillot

Strasbourg

0   100   200 m

To Place de l'Étoile (for Buses to Kehl, Germany; 200m) & Pont de l'Europe (4 km)

FRANCE

(July and August). The entrance (☎ 03 88 32 59 00) is at the base of the tower that was never built. Tickets cost 13FF (10FF for students).

Église Saint Thomas This church on Rue Martin Luther was built in the late 12th century and turned into a Lutheran church in 1529. It's best known for the mausoleum of Marshal Maurice of Saxony, a masterpiece of 18th-century French sculpture erected on the order of Louis XV. The church is open from 10 am to noon and 2 to 5 pm (6 pm from April to November).

Museums Strasbourg's most important museums are in the immediate vicinity of the cathedral. All are closed on Tuesday except the Musée de l'Œuvre Notre-Dame which is closed on Monday. Hours are 10 am to noon and 1.30 to 6 pm (10 am to 5 pm on Sunday). Each museum charges 15FF (8FF for students under 25, free for those under 18). For information on all these museums, call ☎ 03 88 52 50 00.

The **Musée de l'Œuvre Notre-Dame**, housed in a group of 14th- and 15th-century buildings at 3 Place du Château, is Strasbourg's single most outstanding museum. It displays one of France's finest collections of Romanesque, Gothic and Renaissance sculpture, including many of the cathedral's original statues, brought here for preservation. Don't overlook the beautiful and celebrated statue *Synagoga*. The booklet for sale at the ticket desk (28FF) provides a useful though rather pricey introduction to items on display.

The **Château des Rohan** or Palais Rohan, at 2 Place du Château, was built between 1732 and 1742 as a residence for the city's princely bishops. It now houses three museums; entry for each is 15FF though a combined ticket for all three costs 30FF (students 16FF). Information sheets in English are available. The large **Musée Archéologique** in the basement covers the period from prehistory to 800 AD. The **Musée des Arts Décoratifs**, which takes up the ground floor, includes clocks, ceramics and a series of episcopal state rooms decorated in the 18th-century style. The **Musée des Beaux-Arts**, which displays paintings from the 14th to the 19th century, is on the 1st floor. The **Musée d'Art Moderne**, at 5 Place du Château (2nd floor), specialises in painting and sculpture from the late 19th-century impressionists to the present. There are plans to enlarge and relocate it by the end of 1997.

The **Musée Alsacien** at 23 Quai Saint Nicolas, housed in three 16th and 17th-century houses, affords a glimpse into Alsatian life over the centuries.

Places to Stay
During the one week each month from September to June when the European Parliament is in session, many of the city's hotel rooms are reserved up to a year in advance. The tourist office will tell you the parliament's schedule.

Place de la Gare and nearby Rue du Maire Kuss are lined with two and three-star hotels.

Camping The municipal *Camping de la Montagne Verte* (☎ 03 88 30 25 46) at 2 Rue Robert Forrer is open from March to October. It costs 23FF for a tent and car and 18FF per person. There are also facilities for the disabled. The *Auberge de Jeunesse René Cassin* (see the next section) has a place to pitch tents at the back. The charge, including breakfast, is 41FF per person. Bus Nos 3 and 23 link the city centre (Rue du Vieux Marché aux Vins) and the train station (Rue Sainte Marguerite) with the camping ground and the auberge. Get off at the Auberge de la Jeunesse stop.

Hostels The modern *Centre International d'Accueil et de Rencontre Unioniste de Strasbourg* (CIARUS; ☎ 03 88 32 12 12), a 200-bed Protestant-run hostel at 7 Rue Finkmatt, is about a km north-east of the train station. Per-person tariffs, including breakfast, range from 86FF in a room with eight beds to 177FF in a single. CIARUS also has facilities for the disabled. To get there from the train station, take bus No 10 and get off at the Place de Pierre stop.

The 286-bed *Auberge de Jeunesse René Cassin* (☎ 03 88 30 26 46) is two km south-west of the train station at 9 Rue de l'Auberge de Jeunesse. A bed costs 68FF (in a room for four to six people), 97FF (in a double) or 147FF (in a single), including breakfast. See the earlier Camping section for bus transport.

Hotels Strasbourg's cheapest hotels are to be found near the train station but the old city also offers several good options.

Train Station Area The *Hôtel Le Colmar* (☎ 03 88 32 16 89) at 1 Rue du Maire Kuss (1st floor) is a bit sterile, but it's convenient and clean. Singles/doubles start at 130/150FF, or 190/200FF with shower. Hall showers are 15FF. The *Hôtel Weber* (☎ 03 88 32 36 47) at 22 Blvd de Nancy is on the grim side, but it's cheap, and convenient if you arrive by train. Singles or doubles cost 110 to 150FF and 205/240FF with shower. Triples or quads with shower and toilet are 290FF. Hall showers are 12FF.

The two-star *Hôtel de Bruxelles* (☎ 03 88 32 45 31) at 13 Rue Kuhn has clean and fairly large singles/doubles from 145FF, or 215/250FF with shower, toilet and TV; triples/quads are 280/350FF.

Old City The small, family-run *Hôtel Michelet* (☎ 03 88 32 47 38) is at 48 Rue du Vieux Marché aux Poissons. Singles/doubles cost 125/135FF, or 170/200FF with shower and 190/220FF with shower and toilet. An extra bed costs 30FF. Breakfast in your room costs 15FF. The *Hôtel Patricia* (☎ 03 88 32 14 60) at 1a Rue du Puits, a few blocks further west, has very ordinary singles/doubles for 135/160FF and doubles with shower and toilet for 210FF. Hall showers at both these hotels are 12FF.

The pleasant two-star *Hôtel de l'Ill* (☎ 03 88 36 20 01), across the river from the cathedral at 8 Rue des Bateliers, has comfortable singles/doubles for 190/230FF with shower, and more spacious rooms with TV for 275/298FF. Hall showers are free. Breakfast is 29 to 38FF.

More expensive is the two-star *Hôtel de la Cruche d'Or* (☎ 03 88 32 11 23) at 6 Rue des Tonneliers, south-west of the cathedral. Singles/doubles cost 160/280FF with shower, toilet and TV. Breakfast is 35FF.

Places to Eat

Local specialities can be sampled at two uniquely Alsatian kinds of eating establishments. Winstub ('VEEN-shtub') serve both wine and typically hearty Alsatian fare such as choucroute (sauerkraut) and baeckeoffe (pork, beef and lamb marinated in wine for one to two days before being cooked with vegetables in a baeckeoffe, or baker's oven). Some places serve baeckeoffe only on certain days (eg Friday).

Bierstubs ('BEER-shtub') primarily serve beer – the selection may include dozens, scores, even hundreds! Although they do have food (such as tarte flambée, a pastry base with cream, onion and bacon), they don't usually serve multicourse meals (see also Entertainment).

Restaurants In La Petite France, *Au Pont Saint Martin* (☎ 03 88 32 45 13) at 15 Rue des Moulins specialises in Alsatian dishes, including choucroute (68FF) and baeckeoffe (86FF). Vegetarians can order the fricassée de champignons (46FF). The restaurant is open daily except Sunday afternoon and Monday.

The hugely popular *Aldo Pizzeria* (☎ 03 88 36 00 49) at 3 Rue du Faisan has design-it-yourself pizzas for 44FF, huge salads for 42FF and pasta dishes from 44FF. It's open daily. *Le Bouchon* (☎ 03 88 37 32 40) at 6 Rue Sainte Catherine offers Lyonnais specialities at reasonable prices. A chanteuse (singer) performs most evenings. It's open Monday to Saturday from 7 pm to 4 am; meals are served until 2 am.

The area of La Krutenau, south-east of the centre, has quite a few up-market restaurants, including *La Michaudière* (☎ 03 88 24 28 12) at 52 Rue de Zurich; it's closed on Sunday and Monday evening.

Near the train station, *Restaurant Le Cappadoce* (☎ 03 88 32 88 95) at 15 Rue Kuhn serves excellent, freshly prepared Turkish food in an informal dining room. Main dishes are 35 to 85FF, salads 15 to 25FF. It's open Monday to Saturday till 1 am.

For all-out indulgence, head for the three-Michelin-star *Au Crocodile* (☎ 03 88 32 13 02) at 10 Rue de l'Outre, east of Place Kléber. On offer are dishes such as truffle-flavoured pig's trotters and ears, and foie gras set in Gewürztraminer jelly. The four-course menus start at a mere 295/395FF for lunch/dinner. Au Crocodile is closed on Sunday and Monday and during the last three weeks of July.

Winstubs The *Winstub Zuem Strissel* (☎ 03 88 32 14 73), close to the the cathedral at 5 Place de la Grande Boucherie, has a typical winstub ambience – wooden floors, benches and panelling and colourful stained-glass windows. A quarter-litre of wine costs 17 to 27FF and menus start at 60FF. Strissel is open Tuesday to Saturday from 10 am to 11 pm.

Self-Catering There is an excellent selection of picnic food at the *Suma* supermarket. It's on the 3rd floor of the Nouvelles Galeries-Magmod store at 34 Rue du 22 Novembre, just off Place Kléber, and is open every day except Sunday.

Entertainment

Live Music The mellow *Café des Anges* (☎ 03 88 37 12 67) at 5 Rue Sainte Catherine is a music bar that puts on live jazz or blues concerts almost every night at around 9 pm. Tickets cost around 50FF (40FF for students), though entry to the bœufs (jam sessions) on Monday is free. Beers are 9FF (17FF after 10 pm). The café is open Monday to Saturday from 5 pm until late and on Saturday from 3 pm to 1 am or later.

Bars The *Festival Bar Américain* (☎ 03 88 36 31 28), a fashionable American-style bar at 4 Rue Sainte Catherine, is open daily from 8 pm to 4 am (from 9 pm during October to March). The lively *Bar des Aviateurs* (☎ 03 88 36 52 69) at 12 Rue des Sœurs, whose poster-covered walls and long wooden counter impart a 1940s sort of atmosphere, is open from 6 pm to 4 am (closed Sunday evening).

Bierstubs Housed in a vaulted brick cellar at 5 Rue des Couples, *Le Trou* (☎ 03 88 36 91 04) serves over 100 kinds of beer and is open daily from 8 pm to 4 am. Prices for a demi (33 ml) on tap start at 15FF. At *L'Académie de la Bière* (☎ 03 88 32 61 08), 17 Rue Adolphe Seyboth, you can sit at rough-hewn wooden tables and sip one of 80 beers (from 12FF). It's open from 8 pm (7.30 pm Wednesday and Friday, 10 am on Saturday, 11 am Sunday) to 4 am.

Brewery Tours Free guided tours of the city's brasseries are conducted on weekday mornings and afternoons – ask at the tourist office for details.

Getting There & Away

Bus Strasbourg's municipal bus No 21 goes from Place de l'Étoile (take a tram from the train station) to Kehl across the Rhine in Germany.

Train For information on trains call (☎ 08 36 35 35 39). At the train station, there is always at least one ticket counter open every day from 6 am to midnight. Strasbourg is well connected by rail with Basel (Bâle; 100FF), Colmar (56FF, 30 minutes, a dozen a day), Munich (368FF) and Paris (263FF, four to 4½ hours, at least 10 a day). There are also trains to Amsterdam (463FF), Chamonix (332FF) and Nice (460FF). Certain trains at the weekend to/from Paris require payment of a 30FF supplement.

BIJ discounted tickets are available for those under 26 from Wasteels (☎ 03 88 32 40 82) at 13 Place de la Gare, which is open Monday to Saturday from 9 am to 7 pm (6 pm on Saturday).

Car Near the train station, Budget (☎ 03 88 52 87 52) at 14 Rue Déserte rents small cars at 395FF a day with 300 km included, and 525FF (with 700 km) for a two-day weekend. The office is open Monday to Saturday from 8 am to noon and 2 to 7 pm. Cheaper cars can be found at Europcar (☎ 03 88 22 18 00) at 16 Place de la Gare. Prices are 375FF a day (200 km) and 398/459FF for a two/three-day weekend with 400/600 km. Opening hours are Monday to Saturday from 8 am to noon and 2 to 7 pm (3 pm on Saturday).

Free parking can be found along Quai du Woerthel in La Petite France.

Getting Around

Bus and tram tickets (7FF) or a Multipass (29/56FF) good for five/10 trips are available from the tourist office and the CTS office in the train station. Tourpasses (22FF) are valid for 24 hours of travel from the moment you time-stamp them. Buses from Strasbourg's city centre run until about 11.30 pm.

Strasbourg's new 12.6-km-long tram line stops at various places in the city centre, including the train station, Place de l'Homme de Fer, Place Kléber and Place de l'Étoile. Tickets can be bought from the machines at each stop.

There are taxi ranks at the train station and

Place de la République. To order a cab, call ☎ 03 88 36 13 13.

COLMAR

Colmar (population 64,000), an easy day trip from Strasbourg, is famous for the typically Alsatian architecture of its older neighbourhoods and the unparalleled *Issenheim Altarpiece* in the Musée d'Unterlinden.

Orientation

Ave de la République stretches from one block in front of the train station to the Musée d'Unterlinden; the streets of the old city are to the south-east. Petite Venise, a neighbourhood of old, half-timbered buildings, runs along the Lauch River at the southern edge of the old city.

Information

Tourist Office The efficient tourist office (☎ 03 89 20 68 92) is opposite the museum at 4 Rue d'Unterlinden. It's open Monday to Saturday from 9 am to 6 pm (7 pm in July and August), and Sunday from 10 am to 2 pm.

Money & Post The Banque de France is at 46 Ave de la République. The main post office (☎ 03 89 41 19 19) at 36 Ave de la République also has exchange services. Colmar's postcode is 68000.

Things to See

Musée d'Unterlinden This museum (☎ 03 89 20 15 50) houses the famous *Issenheim Altarpiece (Retable d'Issenheim)*, acclaimed as one of the most dramatic and moving works of art ever created. The gilded wooden figures of this reredos (ornamental screen) were carved by Nicolas of Hagenau in the late 15th century; the wooden wings – which originally closed over each other to form a three-layered panel painting – are the work of Matthias Grünewald, and were painted between 1512 and 1516.

The museum's other displays include an Alsatian wine cellar, 15th and 16th-century armour and weapons, pewterware and Strasbourg faïence.

From November to March, the museum is open from 9 am to noon and 2 to 5 pm (closed Tuesday); from April to October, it's open

daily from 9 am to 6 pm. Tickets cost 30FF (20FF for students under 30).

Musée Bartholdi This museum (☎ 03 89 41 90 60) at 30 Rue des Marchands – once the home of Frédéric Auguste Bartholdi (1834-1904), creator of the *Statue of Liberty* – displays some of the sculptor's work and personal memorabilia. The museum is open from 10 am to noon and 2 to 6 pm (closed Tuesday and in January and February). Entry is 20FF (10FF for students).

Église des Dominicains This desanctified church at Place des Dominicains is known for its 14th and 15th-century stained glass and the celebrated triptych, *La Vierge au Buisson de Roses* (The Virgin & the Rosebush), painted by Martin Schongauer in 1473. It's open from 10 am to 6 pm daily from mid-March to November only. Entry is 8FF (5FF for students under 30).

Old City The medieval streets of the old city, including **Rue des Marchands** and much of **Petite Venise**, are lined with half-timbered buildings. **Maison Pfister**, opposite 36 Rue des Marchands, was built in 1537 and is remarkable for its exterior decoration (frescos, medallions and a carved wooden balcony). The **Maison des Têtes** at 19 Rue des Têtes is known for its façade covered with all manner of carved stone heads and faces; it was built in 1609.

Places to Stay

Camping The *Camping de l'Ill* (☎ 03 89 41 15 94) is four km from the train station in Horbourg-Wihr. It's open from February to November, but tent camping is only possible from May to mid-September. It costs 16FF for a tent and car plus 14FF per person. Take bus No 1 from the train station.

Hostels The *Maison des Jeunes et de la Culture* (MJC; ☎ 03 89 41 26 87) is five minutes walk south of the train station at 17 Rue Camille Schlumberger. A bed costs 40FF, and curfew is at 11 pm. The *Auberge de Jeunesse Mittelharth* (☎ 03 89 80 57 39) at 2 Rue Pasteur is just over two km north of the station. You can take bus No 4 from here or

FRANCE

from the Unterlinden stop and get off at the Pont Rouge stop. Reception is open before 10 am or after 5 pm. A bed costs 64FF and singles are 89FF, including breakfast. Curfew is at midnight.

Hotels The one-star *Hôtel La Chaumière* (☎ 03 89 41 08 99) at 74 Ave de la République is Colmar's cheapest hotel with simple rooms for 150FF. Singles/doubles with shower, toilet and TV are 220/240FF. The two-star *Hôtel Rhin et Danube* (☎ 03 89 41 31 44) at 26 Ave de la République has old-fashioned and rather dark doubles for 250FF or 320FF with shower. A triple/quad with bath is 390/400FF.

The *Hôtel Primo* (☎ 03 89 24 22 24) at 5 Rue des Ancêtres is two blocks from the Musée d'Unterlinden. The rooms, which are accessible by lift, are modern in a tacky sort of way and cost 139/199FF or 219/279FF with shower. All rooms have TV and hall showers are free.

Places to Eat
Reasonably priced restaurants are not Colmar's forte, but one good bet is *La Maison Rouge* (☎ 03 89 23 53 22) at 9 Rue des Écoles, which specialises in Alsatian cuisine, including ham on the bone cooked on a spit (57FF). The four-course menu costs 78FF. The restaurant is open daily except Sunday evening and Wednesday. The inexpensive *Flunch cafeteria* (☎ 03 89 23 56 56) at 8 Ave de la République is open daily from 11 am to 9.30 pm.

There is a *Monoprix* supermarket (closed Sunday) across the square from the Musée d'Unterlinden. *Fromagerie Saint Nicolas* at 18 Rue Saint Nicolas sells fine, traditionally made cheeses. It's closed all day Sunday and Monday morning.

Getting There & Around
The train trip to/from Strasbourg takes about 30 minutes and costs 56FF each way.

All nine of Colmar's bus lines – which operate Monday to Saturday until 7.30 or 8 pm – serve the Unterlinden (Point Central) stop next to the tourist office and the Musée d'Unterlinden. To get to the museum from the train station, take bus No 1, 2, 3, 4 or 5. On Sunday, lines A and B operate about once an hour between 1 and 6.30 or 7 pm.

ROUTE DU VIN
The Route du Vin winds its way some 120 km south of Strasbourg to Thann, south of Colmar. This area is famous not only for its excellent Alsatian wines but also for its picturesque villages of half-timbered houses set amid vine-covered hills and overlooked by hilltop castles. The tourist office in Colmar has brochures on the wine route and information about tours.

Riquewihr and Ribeauvillé are perhaps the most attractive villages – and the most visited. Less touristy places include Mittelbergheim, Eguisheim and Turkheim, all of which can be seen on a day trip from Colmar. If you have your own transport, you might visit the imposing chateau of Haut-Koenigsbourg, rebuilt early this century by Emperor William II. The wine route is also where you're most likely to see some of Alsace's few remaining storks.

Normandy

The one-time duchy of Normandy (Normandie) derives its name from the Norsemen (or Vikings) who took control of the area in the early 10th century.

Often compared with the countryside of southern England, Normandy is the land of the *bocage*, farmland subdivided by hedges and trees. Set among this lush, pastoral landscape are Normandy's cities and towns. Rouen, the region's capital, is especially rich in medieval architecture, including a spectacular cathedral. Bayeux is home to the 11th-century Bayeux Tapestry and is only about 12 km from the D-Day landing beaches. In Normandy's southwestern corner is one of France's greatest attractions: the island abbey of Mont-St-Michel. Because of its proximity to Paris, the Normandy coastline is lined with beach resorts, including the fashionable twin towns of Deauville and Trouville. Rural Normandy is famed for its cheeses and other dairy products, apples and cider brandy (Calvados).

Ferries link southern England with four ports in Normandy: Dieppe, Le Havre,

Cherbourg and Ouistreham, north-east of Caen.

Getting Around

Given rural Normandy's beauty and its limited public transport, renting a car will add more to your visit here than almost anywhere else in France.

ROUEN

The city of Rouen (population 105,000), for centuries the furthest point downriver where you could cross the Seine by bridge, is known for its many spires and church towers. The old city is graced with over 800 half-timbered houses, a renowned Gothic cathedral and a number of excellent museums. The city can be visited on an overnight or even a day trip from Paris.

Orientation

The train station (Gare Rouen-Rive Droite) is at the northern end of Rue Jeanne d'Arc, the major thoroughfare running south to the Seine. The old city is centred around Rue du Gros Horloge between the Place du Vieux Marché and the cathedral.

Information

Tourist Office The tourist office (☎ 02 32 08 32 40) is in an early 16th-century building at 25 Place de la Cathédrale. It's open Monday to Saturday from 9 am to 6.30 pm and Sunday from 10 am to 1 pm. From May to September, opening hours are Monday to Saturday from 9 am to 7 pm and on Sunday and holidays from 9.30 am to noon and 2.30 to 6 pm. In summer, guided tours of the city (30FF) depart from the tourist office daily at 10 am and 3 pm. The Carte des Musées de Rouen (60FF) is also available here and allows entry to five of the city's museums.

Money & Post The Banque de France is at 32 Rue Jean Lecanuet. Albuquerque Bureau de Change near the cathedral at 9 Rue des Bonnetiers offers good rates. It is open from 10 am to 7 pm daily except Sunday.

Rouen's main post office (☎ 02 35 08 73 73), which also has exchange services, is at 45bis Rue Jeanne d'Arc. Rouen's postcode is 76000.

Things to See

Old City Rouen's old city suffered enormous damage during WWII but has since been painstakingly restored. The main street, **Rue du Gros Horloge**, runs from the cathedral to **Place du Vieux Marché**, where 19-year-old Joan of Arc was burned at the stake for heresy in 1431. The striking **Église Jeanne d'Arc** marking the site was completed in 1979; you'll learn more about her life from its stained-glass windows than at the tacky **Musée Jeanne d'Arc** across the square at No 33.

The pedestrians-only Rue du Gros Horloge is spanned by an early 16th-century gatehouse holding aloft the **Gros Horloge**, a large medieval clock with only one hand. The late 14th-century belfry above it was under renovation at the time of going to press and could not be visited.

The incredibly ornate **Palais de Justice** (law courts) was left a shell at the end of WWII, but has since been restored to its early 16th-century Gothic glory. The courtyard, entered through a gate on Rue aux Juifs, is well worth a look for its spires, gargoyles and statuary. Under the courtyard is the **Monument Juif**, a stone building used by Rouen's Jewish community in the early 12th century.

Cathédrale Notre Dame Rouen's cathedral, which was the subject of a series of paintings by the impressionist painter Claude Monet, is considered a masterpiece of French Gothic architecture. Built between 1201 and 1514, it suffered extensive damage during the war and has been undergoing restoration and cleaning for decades. The Romanesque **crypt** was part of a cathedral completed in 1062 and destroyed by fire in 1200. There are several guided visits (15FF) a day to the crypt, ambulatory (containing Richard the Lion-Heart's tomb) and **Chapel of the Virgin** between July and August but only on weekends the rest of the year. The cathedral is open Monday to Saturday from 8 am to 7 pm (6 pm on Sunday).

Museums The **Musée Le Secq des Tournelles** (☎ 02 35 71 28 40) is dedicated to the blacksmith's craft and displays some 12,000 locks, keys, scissors, tongs and other wrought-iron utensils made between the 3rd and 19th centuries. Located on Rue Jacques Villon

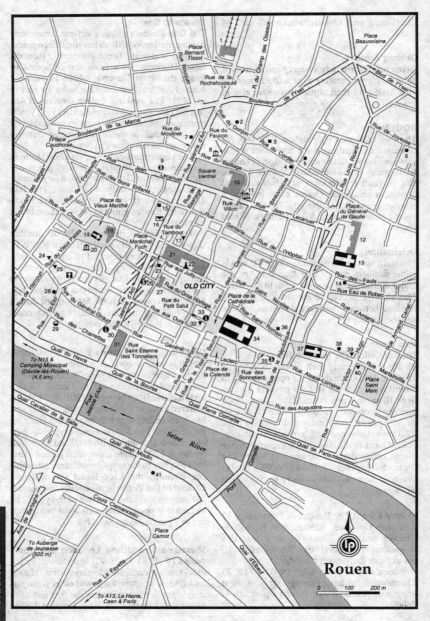

Rouen

0   100   200 m

FRANCE

PLACES TO STAY		OTHER		22	Palais de Justice
3	Hôtel Normandya	1	Gare Rouen-Rive		Courtyard &
5	Hôtel Sphinx		Droite (Train Station)		Monument Juif
6	Hostellerie du Vieux	2	La Tour Jeanne d'Arc	26	Banks
	Logis	4	Laundrette	27	Gros Horloge (Medi-
7	Hôtel du Square	8	Musée de la Céramique		eval Clock)
14	Hôtel Saint Ouen	9	Banque de France	28	Rouen Cycles
15	Hôtel des Flandres	10	Musée des Beaux-Arts	29	Bus Station
23	Hôtel Le Palais	11	Musée Le Secq des	30	Métrobus (Local Bus
36	Hôtel de la Cathédrale		Tournelles		Information)
		12	Hôtel de Ville	31	Théâtre des Arts
PLACES TO EAT		13	Église Saint Ouen	33	Tourist Office
17	Pascaline	16	Main Post Office	34	Cathédrale Notre Dame
24	Chez Pépé	18	Covered Food Market	35	Albuquerque Bureau
25	La Galetteria	19	Église Jeanne d'Arc		de Change
32	Natural	20	Musée Jeanne d'Arc	37	Église Saint Maclou
39	Kim Ngoc	21	Palais de Justice	38	Aître Saint Maclou
40	Chez Zaza			41	Prefecture

(opposite 27 Rue Jean Lecanuet), it is open from 10 am to 1 pm and 2 to 6 pm daily except Tuesday. The entry fee is 13FF (9FF for students).

The **Musée de la Céramique** (☎ 02 35 07 31 74), whose speciality is 16th to 19th-century Rouen ceramics, is north of Square Verdrel up some stairs at 1 Rue du Faucon. Opening hours and ticket prices are the same as at the Musée Le Secq des Tournelles. The recently renovated **Musée des Beaux-Arts** (☎ 02 35 71 28 40) facing the square at 26bis Rue Jean Lecanuet features some major paintings from the 16th to 20th centuries, including some of Monet's cathedral series. The museum is open from 10 am to 6 pm and entry is 20FF (13FF for students).

Aître Saint Maclou Behind the Gothic **Église Saint Maclou** at 186 Rue Martainville is the *aître*, or ossuary, a rare surviving example of a medieval burial ground for plague victims. The curious ensemble of 16th-century buildings that surround the courtyard is decorated with macabre carvings of skulls, crossbones, grave-diggers' tools and hourglasses. It's open every day from 8 am to 6 pm, and entry is free.

La Tour Jeanne d'Arc This tower (☎ 02 35 98 16 21) in Rue du Donjon south of the train station is the only one left of the eight that once ringed the chateau built by Philippe Auguste in the early 13th century. Joan of Arc was imprisoned here before her execution. The

tower and its two exhibition rooms are open from 10 am to noon and 2 to 5.30 pm daily except Tuesday. Entrance is 10FF (free for students).

Places to Stay
Camping The *Camping Municipal* (☎ 02 35 74 07 59) in the suburb of Déville-lès-Rouen is five km north-west of the train station on Rue Jules Ferry. From the Théâtre des Arts on Rue Jeanne d'Arc or the nearby bus station, take bus No 2 and get off at the mairie (town hall) of Déville-lès-Rouen. Two people with a tent are charged 51FF, or 58FF with a car. It is open from March to December.

Hostel Rouen's *Auberge de Jeunesse* (☎ 02 35 72 06 45) is at 118 Blvd de l'Europe, three km south of the train station. The new metro runs there: take the train in the direction of Hôtel de Ville and get off at the Europe station. A bed in a dorm costs 56FF, including breakfast, shower and sheets (100FF deposit required).

Hotels – north of the centre The spotless and friendly *Hôtel Normandya* (☎ 02 35 71 46 15), at 32 Rue du Cordier, is on a quiet street 300 metres south-east of the train station. Singles (some with shower) are 90 to 140FF, doubles are 10FF more; an additional bed costs 40FF and a hall shower is 15FF. The quiet *Hôtel du Square* (☎ 02 35 71 56 07) at 9 Rue du Moulinet, a few hundred metres south of the station, has singles/doubles without shower for 110 to 130FF, and with shower for 150 to 180FF. There are no hall showers.

The *Hôtel Sphinx* (☎ 02 35 71 35 86) at 130 Rue Beauvoisine is a cosy, friendly place with some timbered rooms. Doubles range from 90 to 100FF; an additional bed is 60FF. Showers cost 10FF.

The very French *Hostellerie du Vieux Logis* (☎ 02 35 71 55 30) at 5 Rue de Joyeuse, almost a km to the east of the train station, has a relaxed and pleasantly frayed atmosphere with a lovely little garden out the back. Singles/doubles start at 120FF, two-bed triples cost 150FF. Showers are free.

Hotels – city centre The attractive *Hôtel Saint Ouen* (☎ 02 35 71 46 44) is opposite the garden of Église Saint Ouen at 43 Rue des Faulx. Simple singles/doubles cost from 115/125FF and 130/140FF with shower. Hall showers are 16FF. The *Hôtel des Flandres* (☎ 02 35 71 56 88) at 5 Rue des Bons Enfants has doubles for 120/145FF without/with shower. The *Hôtel Le Palais* (☎ 02 35 71 41 40), between the Palais de Justice and the Gros Horloge at 12 Rue du Tambour, has singles and doubles without/with shower for 130/150FF.

If you're feeling flush, the *Hôtel de la Cathédrale* (☎ 02 35 71 57 95) sits in the shadow of Rouen's cathedral in a 17th-century house at 12 Rue Saint Romain. Rooms are from 300 to 415FF. Ask for a room looking onto the courtyard.

Places to Eat
Near Place du Vieux Marché *La Galetteria* (☎ 02 35 88 98 98), opposite 17 Rue du Vieux Palais, has savoury-filled galettes and crêpes for 12 to 43FF. It is open daily except Saturday at midday and Sunday.

Chez Pépé (☎ 02 35 07 44 94) at 19 Rue du Vieux Palais is a pizzeria open from noon to 2 pm and 7 to 11.30 pm daily except Monday at lunchtime and Sunday. *Natural* (☎ 02 35 98 15 74), near the tourist office at 3 Rue du Petit Salut, is a lunchtime vegetarian café with good salads and health-food menus for 39 and 61FF.

Near Église Saint Maclou, *Chez Zaza* (☎ 02 35 71 33 57) at 85 Rue Martainville specialises in couscous (from 45FF) and is open daily. *Kim Ngoc* (☎ 02 35 98 76 33), nearby at No 168, is

one of Rouen's many Vietnamese restaurants with menus for 65 and 80FF. It is open every day but Monday.

For a splurge, the old-time bistro *Pascaline* (☎ 02 35 89 67 44) at 5 Rue de la Poterne has two/three-course menus for 77/97FF. It's open until 11.30 pm every day.

Dairy products, fish and fresh produce are on sale from 7 am to 12.30 pm daily except Monday at the covered market at Place du Vieux Marché.

Getting There & Away
Bus Buses to Dieppe and Le Havre are slower and more expensive than the train. The bus station (☎ 02 35 52 92 29) is on 25 Rue des Charrettes near the Théâtre des Arts.

Train There are 24 trains a day to and from Paris' Gare Saint Lazare (70 minutes). The last leaves at about 9 pm for Paris and 10 pm for Rouen. The information office at Rouen's train station (☎ 08 36 35 35 39) is open Monday to Saturday from 7.15 am to 7 pm.

Getting Around
Bus & Metro TCAR operates Rouen's local bus network as well as its metro line. The metro links the train station with the Théâtre des Arts before crossing the Seine into the southern suburbs, and runs between 5.30 am and 11 pm daily. Bus tickets cost 7.50FF, a carnet of 10 is 56FF, and the Carte Découverte, good for one/two/three days unlimited travel, costs 20/30/40FF. They can be purchased at the Métrobus counters in the train station, in front of the Théâtre des Arts and in the Place du Général de Gaulle near the Hôtel de Ville.

Bicycle Rouen Cycles (☎ 02 35 71 34 30) at 45 Rue Saint Éloi rents mountain bikes and 10-speeds for 120FF a day (320FF a week). The shop is open Tuesday to Saturday from 9 am to noon and 2 to 7.30 pm.

BAYEUX
Bayeux (population 15,000) is celebrated for two trans-Channel invasions: the conquest of England by the Normans under William the Conqueror in 1066 (an event chronicled in the Bayeux Tapestry) and the Allied D-Day landings of 6 June 1944, which launched the

liberation of Nazi-occupied France. Bayeux was the first town in France to be freed.

Bayeux is an attractive – though fairly touristy – town with several excellent museums. It also serves as a base for visits to the D-Day beaches (see that section for details).

Orientation & Information

The cathedral, the major landmark in the centre of Bayeux and visible throughout the town, is one km north-west of the train station. The tourist office (☎ 02 31 92 16 26) is at Pont Saint Jean just off the northern end of Rue Larcher. It is open Monday to Saturday from 9 am to noon and 2 to 6 pm. During July and August, it opens on Sunday from 10 am to 12.30 pm and 3 to 6.30 pm.

Money & Post

Banks are open Tuesday to Saturday from 8.30 am to noon and from about 2 to 5 pm. There is a Société Générale at 26 Rue Saint Malo and a Caisse d'Épargne at No 59 of the same street. The main post office (☎ 02 31 92 01 00), at 29 Rue Larcher opposite the Hôtel de Ville, also has exchange operations. Bayeux's postcode is 14400.

Things to See

A multipass ticket *(billet jumelé)* valid for all four museums listed here, and available at each, costs 65FF (30FF for students).

Bayeux Tapestry The world-famous Bayeux Tapestry – actually a 70-metre-long strip of coarse linen decorated with woollen embroidery – was commissioned by Odo, bishop of Bayeux and half-brother to William the Conqueror (Guillaume le Conquérant), sometime between the Norman invasion of England in 1066 and 1082, when Odo was disgraced for raising troops without William's consent. The tapestry, which was probably made in England for the consecration of the cathedral in Bayeux in 1077, recounts the dramatic story of the Norman invasion and the events that led up to it – from the Norman perspective. The story is told in 58 panels presented like a modern comic strip, with action-packed scenes following each other in quick succession. The events are accompanied by a written commentary in dog Latin. The scenes themselves are filled with depictions of 11th-century Norman and Saxon dress, food, cooking, weapons and tools. Halley's Comet, which passed through our part of the solar system in 1066, also makes an appearance.

The tapestry is housed in the **Musée de la Tapisserie de Bayeux** (☎ 02 31 92 05 48), on Rue de Nesmond. It is open daily from 9.30 am (8 am in July and August) to 12.30 pm and 2 to 6 or 6.30 pm. From May to mid-September, the museum is open all day until 7 pm. Entry is 35FF (14FF for students). There is an excellent taped commentary available (5FF) and a 14-minute video (screened in English eight times a day).

Cathédrale Notre Dame Most of Bayeux's spectacular cathedral, an exceptional example of Norman-Gothic architecture, dates from the 13th century, though the crypt, the arches of the nave and the lower portions of the towers on either side of the main entrance, are Romanesque from the late 11th century. Look out for the 15th-century frescos of angels playing musical instruments in the south transept. The cathedral is open daily from 9 am (8 am in July and August) to 12.30 pm and 2 to 6.30 or 7 pm.

Musée Diocésain d'Art Religieux The Diocesan Museum of Religious Art (☎ 02 31 92 14 21), full of liturgical objects and clerical garb, is just south of the cathedral at 6 Rue Lambert Leforestier. It is open daily from 10 am to 12.30 pm and 2 to 6 pm (7 pm from July to September). The 15FF entry fee (6FF for students), also gets you in to the **Conservatoire de la Dentelle** (☎ 02 31 92 73 80) in the same building. It's dedicated to the preservation of traditional Norman lace-making techniques.

Musée Baron Gérard This pleasant museum (☎ 02 31 92 14 21), next to the cathedral at Place de la Liberté, specialises in local porcelain, lace and 15th to 19th-century European paintings. Out front there is a huge plane tree known as the Arbre de la Liberté which, like many such 'Freedom Trees', was planted in the years after the French Revolution (1797). It is one of only nine left in all of France. The museum is open daily from 10 am to noon and from 2 to 6 pm (9 am to 7 pm from June to mid-September). The entry fee is 20FF (10FF for students).

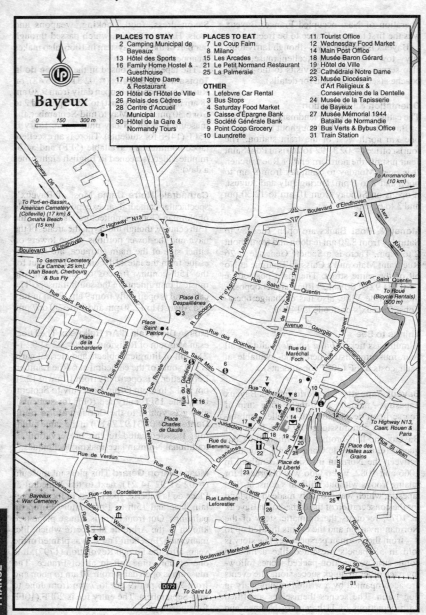

Bayeux

0   150   300 m

PLACES TO STAY
2 Camping Municipal de Bayeux
13 Hôtel des Sports
16 Family Home Hostel & Guesthouse
17 Hôtel Notre Dame & Restaurant
20 Hôtel de l'Hôtel de Ville
26 Relais des Cèdres
28 Centre d'Accueil Municipal
30 Hôtel de la Gare & Normandy Tours

PLACES TO EAT
7 Le Coup Faim
8 Milano
15 Les Arcades
21 Le Petit Normand Restaurant
25 La Palmeraie

OTHER
1 Lefebvre Car Rental
3 Bus Stops
4 Saturday Food Market
5 Caisse d'Épargne Bank
6 Société Générale Bank
9 Point Coop Grocery
10 Laundrette
11 Tourist Office
12 Wednesday Food Market
14 Main Post Office
18 Musée Baron Gérard
19 Hôtel de Ville
22 Cathédrale Notre Dame
23 Musée Diocésain d'Art Religieux & Conservatoire de la Dentelle
24 Musée de la Tapisserie de Bayeux
27 Musée Mémorial 1944 Bataille de Normandie
29 Bus Verts & Bybus Office
31 Train Station

To Arromanches (10 km)

Boulevard d'Eindhoven

Aure River

To Port-en-Bessin, American Cemetery (Colleville) (17 km) & Omaha Beach (15 km)

Highway N13

To Port-en-Bessin & Eindhoven

Boulevard d'Eindhoven

To German Cemetery (La Cambe, 25 km), Utah Beach, Cherbourg & Bus Fly

Rue du Docteur Michel

Rue Saint Patrice

Rue Montfiquet

Rue d'Aprigny

R Louvière

Rue Saint Quentin

To Roué (Bicycle Rentals) (500 m)

Place G Despaillières

R Cabourg

Place Saint Patrice

Rue de la Vallée des Prés

Rue des Bouchers

Avenue Georges Clemenceau

Rue Saint Laurent

Place de la Lombarderie

Rue des Bilettes

Rue Saint Malo

Rue Royale

Rue du Général de Dais

Rue du Maréchal Foch

Avenue Conseil

Place Charles de Gaulle

Rue Saint Martin

Rue des Cuisiniers

Rue Larcher

Rue de la Juridiction

Rue des Terres

Rue du Bienvenu

R Chanoines

Rue de la Poterie

Place de la Liberté

To Highway N13, Caen, Rouen & Paris

Place des Halles aux Grains

Rue St Jean

Rue de Verdun

Boulevard Fabien Ware

Bayeux War Cemetery

Rue des Cordeliers

Rue Lambert Leforestier

Rue Tardif

Rue de Nesmond

Rue aux Coqs

Rue de Crémel

27

28

Rue des Marettes

Rue de Saint Loup

Boulevard Sadi Carnot

Boulevard Maréchal Leclerc

29 30

31

D572

To Saint Lô

Musée Mémorial 1944 Bataille de Normandie
Bayeux's huge war museum (☎ 02 31 92 93 41) on Blvd Fabien Ware displays a rather haphazard collection of photos, uniforms, weapons, newspaper clippings and life-like scenes associated with D-Day and the Battle of Normandy. It is open daily from 10 am to 12.30 pm and from 2 to 6 pm (9.30 am to 6.30 pm from May to mid-September). Entry costs 30FF (12FF for students). There's an excellent 30-minute film compiled from archive newsreels which is screened in English three to five times a day.

The **Bayeux War Cemetery**, a British cemetery on Blvd Fabien Ware a few hundred metres west of the museum, is the largest of the 18 Commonwealth military cemeteries in Normandy. It contains the tombs of 4868 soldiers from 11 countries, including the graves of 466 Germans. Many of the headstones are inscribed with poignant epitaphs.

Places to Stay
Camping The *Camping Municipal de Bayeux* (☎ 02 31 92 08 43) is two km north of the town centre, just south of Blvd d'Eindhoven. It's open from mid-March to mid-November. A tent site costs from 7.40FF and adults pay 13.60FF each.

Bus Nos 5 and 6 from the train station will take you there.

Hostels The *Family Home* hostel and guesthouse (☎ 02 31 92 15 22) in three old buildings at 39 Rue du Général de Dais is an excellent place to meet other travellers. A bed in a dorm room costs 100FF (90FF if you've got a HI card), including breakfast. Singles with showers are 160FF. Multicourse French dinners, prepared by the indefatigable Mme Lefebvre, cost 65FF, including wine. Vegetarian dishes are available on request or you can cook for yourself.

The efficient *Centre d'Accueil Municipal* hostel (☎ 02 31 92 08 19) is housed in a large, modern building at 21 Rue des Marettes, one km south-west of the cathedral. Sterile but comfortable singles are good value at 89FF, including breakfast. A HI card is not necessary.

Hotels The old but well-maintained *Hôtel de la Gare* (☎ 02 31 92 10 70) at 26 Place de la Gare opposite the train station has singles/doubles from 85/100FF. Two-bed triples/quads are 160FF and showers are free.

The *Hôtel de l'Hôtel de Ville* (☎ 02 31 92 30 08), in the centre of town at 31 Rue Larcher, has large, quiet singles/doubles for 150FF. An extra bed is 50FF, and showers are free. Telephone reservations are not accepted. A few hundred metres north at 19 Rue Saint Martin, the *Hôtel des Sports* (☎ 02 31 92 28 53) has decent singles/doubles (most with shower or free use of those along the hall) starting at 160/200FF.

The *Relais des Cèdres* (☎ 02 31 21 98 07), somewhat fussily done out in 'French country' style, is in an old mansion at 1 Blvd Sadi Carnot. Doubles cost 150 to 220FF, or 270FF with shower. Hall showers are free.

If you can afford something more upmarket, you might try *Hôtel Notre Dame* (☎ 02 31 92 87 24) at 44 Rue des Cuisiniers, a two-star (though not officially) place opposite the western façade of the cathedral. Doubles are 240 to 250FF with shower or bath, but they have half a dozen cheaper rooms for 150FF. Hall showers cost 20FF.

Places to Eat
Le Petit Normand (☎ 02 31 22 88 66) at 35 Rue Larcher specialises in traditional Norman food prepared with apple cider, and is popular with English tourists. Simple fixed-price menus start at 58FF. The restaurant is open every day except Sunday evening (daily in July and August). *Les Arcades* (☎ 02 31 92 72 79), at 10 Rue Laitière close to Hôtel des Sports, is popular with the locals and has excellent four-course menus from 68FF. It's open every day and serves dinner until 11 pm.

For couscous (from 55FF), try *La Palmeraie* (☎ 02 31 92 72 08) near the Bayeux Tapestry Museum at 62-64 Rue de Nesmond. It's open for lunch and dinner every day except Monday and midday on Saturday. *Milano* (☎ 02 31 92 15 10) at 18 Rue Saint Martin serves very good pizza. It's open every day except Sunday and daily from June to October.

The food at the *Hôtel Notre Dame* restaurant (☎ 02 31 92 87 24) is Norman at its best; count on 55FF for a lunch menu and 88FF per person at dinner. It is open every day except Sunday midday and Monday (daily from June to August).

There are lots of takeaway places and food shops along or near Rue Saint Martin and Rue Saint Jean, including *Le Coup Faim* at 42 Rue Saint Martin and the *Point Coop* grocery at 25 Rue du Maréchal Foch, open Tuesday to Saturday from 8.30 am to 12.15 pm and 2.30 to 7.15 pm and on Sunday from 9 am to noon. There are open-air markets in Rue Saint Jean on Wednesday morning and in Place Saint Patrice on Saturday morning.

Getting There & Away
The train station (☎ 02 31 92 80 50) is open daily from about 6 am to 9.30 or 10 pm. Trains serve Paris' Gare Saint Lazare (via Caen), Cherbourg, Rennes and points beyond.

Getting Around
The local bus line, Bybus, schedules buses to meet train arrivals. Bus Nos 1 and 3 go to the centre and end up at Place Saint Patrice. See the D-Day Beaches section for information on car rental and transport to places in the vicinity of Bayeux.

Taxis can be ordered 24 hours a day by calling ☎ 02 31 92 92 40.

D-DAY BEACHES
The D-Day landings, codenamed 'Operation Overlord', were the largest military operation in history. Early on the morning of 6 June 1944, swarms of landing craft – part of a flotilla of almost 7000 boats – hit the beaches, and tens of thousands of soldiers from the USA, UK, Canada and elsewhere began pouring onto French soil. Most of the 135,000 Allied troops stormed ashore along 80 km of beach north of Bayeux codenamed (from west to east) Utah and Omaha (in the American sector) and Gold, Juno and Sword (in the British and Canadian ones). The landings on D-Day – Jour J in French – were followed by the start of the 76-day battle of Normandy that would lead to the liberation of Europe from Nazi occupation.

Things to See
Arromanches In order to unload the vast quantities of cargo necessary for the invasion, the Allies established two prefabricated ports codenamed **Mulberry Harbour**. The remains of one of them, Port Winston, can still be seen at Arromanches, a seaside town 10 km northeast of Bayeux. The harbour consisted of 146 massive cement caissons towed over from England and sunk to form a semicircular breakwater in which floating bridge spans were moored. In the three months after D-Day, 2½ million men, four million tonnes of equipment and 500,000 vehicles were unloaded there. At low tide you can walk out to many of the caissons. The best view of Port Winston is from the hill east of town topped with a statue of the Virgin Mary.

The well-regarded **Musée du Débarquement** (Landing Museum; ☎ 02 31 22 34 31) explains the logistics and importance of Port Winston and makes a good first stop before visiting the beaches. It is open daily from 9.30 am (10 am on Sunday) to 5 pm (until 6 pm in April). From May to September, it's open from 9 am to 7 pm. The museum is closed for most of January. Entrance is 32FF (17FF for students). The last guided tour (in French, with a written text in English) leaves 45 minutes before closing time. Forget about the diorama/slide show, but don't miss the film showing archival news footage. Both are screened in English, last about 10 minutes and run throughout the day.

Omaha Beach The most brutal fighting of 6 June was fought 20 km west of Arromanches along Omaha Beach, which had to be abandoned in storms two weeks later. A memorial marks the site of the first US military cemetery on French soil, where soldiers killed right on the beach were first buried. Today, Omaha Beach is lined with holiday cottages and is popular with swimmers and sunbathers. Little evidence of the war remains except the bunkers and munitions sites of a German fortified point to the west (look for the tall obelisk on the hill).

American Military Cemetery The remains of the Americans who lost their lives during the Battle of Normandy were either sent back to the USA or buried in the American Military Cemetery (☎ 02 31 51 62 00) at Colleville-sur-Mer above Omaha Beach. The cemetery contains the graves of 9386 American soldiers and a memorial to 1557 others whose bodies were never found. The huge, immaculately tended expanse of white crosses and Stars of David, set on a hill overlooking Omaha Beach, testifies to the extent of the killing which took

Normandy & Brittany

ENGLISH CHANNEL

ATLANTIC OCEAN

place around here in 1944; there's a large colonnade memorial, a reflecting pond and a chapel for silent meditation. The cemetery is open from 8 am to 5 pm (6 pm from mid-April to September). From Bayeux, it can be reached by Bus Verts' line No 70, but service is infrequent.

Pointe du Hoc Ranger Memorial At 7.10 am on 6 June, 225 US Army Rangers scaled the 30-metre rocky cliffs at Pointe du Hoc, where the Germans had positioned a battery of mammoth artillery guns. The guns, as it turns out, had been transferred elsewhere, but the American commandos captured the gun emplacements (the two huge circular cement structures) and the German command post (next to the two flagpoles) and then fought off German counterattacks for two days. By the time they were relieved on 8 June, 81 of the Rangers had been killed and 58 wounded. The ground is still pockmarked with three-metre bomb craters. Visitors can walk among and inside the German fortifications, but they are warned not to dig: there may still be mines and explosive materials below the surface. In the German command post, you can still see where the wooden ceilings were charred by American flame-throwers. Pointe du Hoc is 12 km west of the American Military Cemetery.

Commonwealth Military Cemeteries By tradition, soldiers from the Commonwealth killed in the war were buried close to where they fell. As a result, the 18 Commonwealth military cemeteries in Normandy follow the line of advance of British and Canadian troops. The Canadian cemetery at Bény-sur-Mer is a few km south of Juno Beach and 18 km east of Bayeux. See the Bayeux section for information on the mostly British Bayeux War Cemetery. The cemeteries are permanently open.

German Military Cemetery Some 21,000 German soldiers are buried in the military cemetery near La Cambe, a village 25 km west of Bayeux. Hundreds of German dead were also buried in the Commonwealth cemeteries, including the Bayeux War Cemetery.

Organised Tours
Given the limitations posed by other forms of transport, a bus tour is an excellent way to see the D-Day beaches. Normandy Tours (☎ 02 31 92 10 70), based at Hôtel de la Gare in Bayeux, has tours stopping at Juno Beach, Arromanches, Omaha Beach, the American Military Cemetery and Pointe du Hoc for 100FF a person. Times and itineraries are flexible.

Bus Fly (☎ 02 31 22 00 08) has an office on the D13 in Les Sablons (Vaucelles) west of Bayeux, but reservations are most easily made through the Family Home hostel (☎ 02 31 92 15 22) in Bayeux. An afternoon tour to major D-Day sites costs 150FF (130FF for students with a hostel card), including museum entry fees.

Getting There & Away
Bus Bus No 70 run by Bus Verts (☎ 02 31 92 02 92 in Bayeux), goes westward to the American cemetery at Colleville-sur-Mer and Omaha Beach and on to Pointe du Hoc and the town of Grandcamp-Maisy. Bus No 74 serves Arromanches, Gold and Juno beaches and Courseulles. During July and August only, Bus No 75 goes to Caen via Arromanches, Gold, Juno and Sword beaches and the port of Ouistreham. The Bus Verts office, across the parking lot from the train station, is open weekdays from 9 am to noon and 2 to 6 pm. Timetables are also posted in the train station and at Place Saint Patrice.

Car & Motorcycle For three or more people, renting a car can actually be cheaper than a tour. Lefebvre Car Rental (☎ 02 31 92 05 96) on Blvd d'Eindhoven (at the Esso petrol station) charges 320FF per day with 100 km free (about the distance of a circuit to the beaches along coastal route No 514) and 600FF for two days with 300 km free. The excess (deductible) is 2000FF. The office is open every day from 7 am to 9 pm.

Bicycle The Family Home hostel has one-speeds for 60FF a day (plus 200FF deposit). Roué (☎ 02 31 92 27 75) on Blvd Winston Churchill rents mountain bikes for 80FF a day or 350FF a week, but you have to leave a deposit of 1500FF. It's open every day from 8.30 am to noon and 2 to 7 pm.

MONT-SAINT-MICHEL

It is difficult not to be impressed with your first sighting of Mont-Saint-Michel. Covering the summit is the massive abbey, a soaring ensemble of buildings in a hotchpotch of architectural styles. Topping the abbey – 80 metres above the sea – is a slender spire, at the tip of which is a gilded copper statue of Michael the Archangel slaying a dragon. Around the base are the ancient ramparts and a jumble of buildings that house the 120 people who still live there.

Mont-Saint-Michel's fame derives equally from the bay's extraordinary tides. Depending on the orbits of the moon and, to a lesser extent, of the sun, the difference in the level of the sea between low tide and high tides can reach 12 metres. At low tide, the Mont looks out onto bare sand stretching many km off into the distance. At high tide – only about six hours later – this huge expanse of tideland will be under water (though the Mont and its causeway are completely surrounded by the sea only during the highest of tides, which occur at seasonal equinoxes).

History

According to Celtic mythology, Mont-Saint-Michel was one of the sea tombs to which the souls of the dead were conveyed. In 708 AD, Saint Michel appeared to Aubert, Bishop of Avranches, and told him to build a devotional chapel at the top of the Mont. In 966, Richard I, Duke of Normandy, transferred Mont-Saint-Michel to the Benedictines, who turned it into an important centre of learning. The monastery was at its most influential in the 12th and 13th centuries, and pilgrims journeyed from miles around to honour the cult of St Michel. In the 13th century, the Mont became something of an ecclesiastical fortress, with a military garrison at the disposal of the abbot and the king.

In the early 15th century, during the Hundred Years' War, the English blockaded and besieged Mont-Saint-Michel three times. But the fortified abbey withstood these assaults; it was the only place in all of western and northern France not to fall into English hands. After the French Revolution, Mont-Saint-Michel was turned into a prison. In 1966 the abbey was symbolically returned to the Benedictines as part of the celebrations marking its millennium.

Orientation

There is only one opening in the ramparts, Porte de l'Avancée, immediately to the west as you walk down the causeway. The single street (Grande Rue), for pedestrians only, is lined with restaurants, a few hotels, souvenir shops and entrances to some rather tacky exhibits in the crypts below. **Pontorson**, the nearest town, is nine km south and the base for most travellers. Route D976 from Mont-Saint-Michel runs right into Pontorson's main thoroughfare, Rue du Couësnon.

Information

Tourist Office The tourist office (☎ 02 33 60 14 30) is up the stairs to the left as you enter Porte de l'Avancée. It is open every day except Sunday from 9 am to noon and 2 to 5.45 pm (6.30 pm from Easter to September). In July and August hours are from 9 am to 7 pm daily. If you are interested in what the tide will be doing during your visit, look for the *horaire des marées* posted outside. In July and August – when up to 9000 people a day visit – children under eight can be left at the day nursery (*garderie*) near the abbey church.

The friendly staff at Pontorson's tourist office (☎ 02 33 60 20 65) in the Place de l'Église (just west of the Place de l'Hôtel de Ville) are on duty from 9.30 am to 12.30 pm and from 2.30 to 5 pm (to 7.30 pm from mid-June to mid-September).

Money & Post There are several places to change money in Mont-Saint-Michel, but the best rate is at the CIC bank at 98 Rue du Couësnon in Pontorson. It's open Tuesday to Friday from 8.30 am to 12.15 pm and 1.45 to 5.45 pm (4.50 pm on Saturday).

The Pontorson post office (☎ 02 33 60 01 66) is on the east side of the Place de l'Hôtel de Ville.

Things to See & Do

Walking Tour When the tide is out, you can walk all the way around Mont-Saint-Michel, a distance of about one km. Straying too far from the Mont is extremely inadvisable: you might get stuck in quicksand – from which Norman soldiers are depicted being rescued in one scene of the Bayeux Tapestry. For information on guided tours, call the Maison de la Baie (☎ 02 33 70 86 46).

Abbaye du Mont-Saint-Michel The Mont's major attraction is the renowned abbey (☎ 02 33 89 80 00), at the top of the Grande Rue, up the stairway. It's open daily from 9.30 am to 4.30 pm. From mid-May to September, it's open from 9 am to 5.30 pm, and there are also night-time visits of the abbey (60FF) every evening except Sunday (May to August from 10 pm to 1 am, and September from 9 pm to midnight). Visitors explore at their own pace the illuminated and music-filled rooms.

During the day, it's worth taking the guided tour included in the ticket price (36FF or 23FF for students under 25). One-hour tours in English depart three to eight times a day.

In the 11th century, the Romanesque **Église Abbatiale** (Abbey Church) was built on the rocky tip of the mountain cone over its 10th-century predecessor, now the underground chapel of **Notre Dame de Sous Terre**. When the Romanesque choir collapsed in 1421, a Flamboyant Gothic choir replaced it in the 15th century, held up from below by crypts with vast supporting columns. The church is famous for this mixture of architectural styles.

In the early 13th century, **La Merveille** (literally, the 'wonder' or 'marvel') monastery was built on three levels and added to the church's north side. Considered a Gothic masterpiece, it was completed in only 16 years. The famous **cloître** (cloister) is an ambulatory surrounded by a double row of delicately carved arches resting on slender marble pillars, and is a good example of the Anglo-Norman style. The early 13th-century **réfectoire** (dining hall) is illuminated by a wall of recessed windows, a remarkable arrangement given that the sheer drop-off precluded the use of flying buttresses. The High Gothic **salle des hôtes** (guest hall), which dates from 1213, has two giant fireplaces.

Places to Stay
Camping The *Camping du Mont-Saint-Michel* (☎ 02 33 60 09 33) is on the road to Pontorson (D976), two km from the Mont. It's open from mid-February to mid-November and charges 15FF per person, 11FF for a tent

and 13FF for a car. Bungalows with shower and toilet are also available for 210 to 230FF for two people. There are several other camping grounds a couple of km further towards Pontorson.

Hostel *Centre Duguesclin* (☎ 02 33 60 18 65) in Pontorson operates as a hostel from Easter to mid-September. A bed in a three-bunk room costs 43FF a night, but you must bring your own sheets. There are kitchen facilities on the ground floor. The hostel is closed from noon to 5 pm, but there is no curfew. The hostel is about one km west of the train station on Rue du Général Patton, which runs parallel to the Couësnon River north of Rue du Couësnon. The hostel is on the left side in an old three-storey stone building opposite No 26.

Hotels Mont-Saint-Michel has about 15 hotels but almost all are at least two-star and expensive. Don't forget that you'll have to drag your luggage up here too, as vehicles must be left in the parking lot below. *La Mère Poulard* (☎ 02 33 60 14 01), the first hotel on the left as you walk up the Grande Rue, has twins with shower from 250FF.

Your best bet is to stay in Pontorson. Across Place de la Gare from the train station, there are a couple of cheap hotels. The *Hôtel de l'Arrivée* (☎ 02 33 60 01 57) at 14 Rue du Docteur Tizon has doubles for 87/150FF without/with shower. Triples/quads are 160/200FF and from 200FF with shower. Hall showers are 15FF. The *Hôtel Le Rénové* (☎ 02 33 60 00 21), nearby at 2 Rue de Rennes, has doubles for 140/180FF without/with shower. Triples or quads cost 250FF.

The *Hôtel La Tour de Brette* (☎ 02 33 60 10 69) at 8 Rue du Couësnon is an excellent deal. Its singles and doubles – all with shower and TV – are 165FF to 220FF. The tourist office can arrange private accommodation or farm stays from 150 to 200FF per double, including breakfast.

Places to Eat
The tourist restaurants around the base of the Mont have lovely views but they aren't bargains; menus start at about 90FF.

In Pontorson, *La Squadra* (☎ 02 33 68 31 17) at 102 Rue Couësnon has decent pizza (from 37FF), salads and pasta and is open daily. For crêpes and savoury galettes (15FF), try *La Crêperie du Couësnon* (☎ 02 33 60 16 67) at 21 Rue du Couësnon. *La Tour de Brette* (☎ 02 33 60 10 69), across from the river at 8 Rue du Couësnon, has very good menus from 57FF.

The supermarket nearest the Mont is next to the Camping du Mont-Saint-Michel on the D976. It's open daily except Sunday from 9 am to 1 pm and 2.30 to 7 pm from mid-February to October and from 7.30 am to 10 pm in July and August.

Getting There & Away

Bus Bus No 15 run by STN (☎ 02 33 58 03 07 in Avranches) goes from Pontorson train station to Mont-Saint-Michel. There are nine buses a day in July and August (six on weekends and holidays) and three or four during the rest of the year. Most of the buses connect with trains to/from Paris, Rennes and Caen.

For information on bus transport to/from Saint Malo, 43 km to the west, see Getting There & Away in the Saint Malo section. The Pontorson office of Courriers Bretons buses (☎ 02 33 60 11 43; ☎ 02 99 56 79 09 in Saint Malo) is 50 metres west of the train station at 2 Rue du Docteur Tizon. It is open weekdays from 9.30 to 11.30 am and 5.45 to 7 pm.

Train There are trains to the Pontorson train station (☎ 02 33 60 00 35) from Caen (via Folligny) and Rennes (via Dol). From Paris, take the train to Caen (from Gare Saint Lazare), Rennes (from Gare Montparnasse) or direct to Pontorson via Folligny (Gare Montparnasse).

Bicycle Bikes can be rented at the train station (55FF per day plus 1000FF deposit) and from E Videloup (☎ 02 33 60 11 40) at 1bis Rue du Couësnon, which charges 35FF/70FF per day for one-speeds/mountain bikes. E Videloup is open from 8.30 am to 12.30 pm and 2 to 7 pm from Monday afternoon to Saturday.

Brittany

Brittany (Bretagne in French, Breizh in Breton), the westernmost region of France, is famous for its rugged countryside and wild coastline. The area is also known for its many colourful religious celebrations *(pardons)*. Traditional costumes, including extraordinarily tall headdresses of lace worn by the women, can still be seen at some of these and other local festivals, including night-time dance meets called *fest-noz*.

Breton customs are most in evidence in Cornouaille, the area at the south-western tip of the Breton peninsula, whose largest city is Quimper. Saint Malo is a popular tourist destination and seaside resort on Brittany's north coast.

Breton Identity

The people of Brittany, driven from their homes in what is now Great Britain by the Anglo-Saxon invasions, migrated across the English Channel in the 5th and 6th centuries, bringing with them their Celtic language and traditions. For centuries a rich and powerful duchy, Brittany became part of France in 1532. To this day, many Bretons have not abandoned the hope that their region will one day regain its independence or at least a greater degree of autonomy.

Language

The indigenous language of Brittany is Breton, a Celtic language related to Welsh and, more distantly, to Irish and Scottish Gaelic. Breton – which, to the untrained ear, sounds like Gaelic with a French accent – can sometimes still be heard in western Brittany and especially in Cornouaille, where perhaps a third of the population understands it. However, only a tiny fraction of the people speak Breton at home.

Getting Around

Brittany's lack of convenient, intercity public transport and the appeal of exploring out-of-the-way destinations make renting a car or motorcycle worth considering. Brittany – especially Cornouaille – is an excellent area for cycling, and bike-rental places are never hard to find.

QUIMPER

Situated at the confluence *(kemper* in Breton) of two rivers, the Odet and the Steïr, Quimper (which is pronounced 'cam-PAIR'; population 62,000) has managed to preserve its Breton architecture and atmosphere and is considered by many to be the cultural and artistic capital of Brittany. Some even refer to the city as the 'soul of Brittany'.

The Festival de Cornouaille, a showcase for traditional Breton music, costumes and culture, is held here every year between the third and fourth Sundays in July.

Orientation
The old city, largely pedestrianised, is to the west and north-west of the cathedral. The train and bus stations are just under a km east of the old city. Mont Frugy overlooks the city centre from the south bank of the Odet River.

Information
Tourist Office The tourist office (☎ 02 98 53 04 05) at Place de la Résistance is open Monday to Saturday from 9 am to noon and 1.30 to 6 or 7 pm. In July and August, the hours are from 8.30 am to 8 pm. From May to mid-September, the office is also open on Sunday from 9.30 am to 12.30 pm.

Money & Post The Banque de France is 150 metres from the train station at 29 Ave de la Gare, and is open Tuesday to Saturday from 8.45 am to noon and 1.30 to 3.30 pm. Crédit Agricole at 10 Rue René Madec is open Monday to Saturday and keeps similar hours but closes at 5.30 pm (4 pm on Monday and Saturday). The main post office (☎ 02 98 64 28 28) is at 37 Blvd Amiral de Kerguélen. Quimper's postcode is 29000.

Things to See
Walking Tour Strolling the quays that flank both banks of the Odet River is a fine way to get a feel for the city. The old city is known for its centuries-old houses, which are especially in evidence on **Rue Kéréon** and around **Place au Beurre**. To climb 72-metre-high **Mont Frugy**, which offers great views of the city, follow the switchback path **Promenade du Mont Frugy** next to the tourist office.

Cathédrale Saint Corentin Built between 1239 and 1515 (with spires added in the 1850s), Quimper's cathedral incorporates many Breton elements, including – on the west façade between the spires – an equestrian statue of King Gradlon, the city's mythical 5th-century founder. The early 15th-century nave is out of line with the choir, built two centuries earlier. The cathedral's patron saint is Saint Corentin, the city's first bishop who, according to legend, ate half a fish each morning and threw the rest back in the river. The next day the miraculous fish would reappear whole and offer itself once again to the saint. The loaf of bread you'll see in the south transept in front of a relic of Blessed Jean Discalcéat (1279-1349) was left by one of the faithful asking for a blessing. The really poor – not you – are entitled to it. Mass in Breton is said on the first Sunday of every month. In July and August, there are guided tours of the cathedral every day at 3 pm; in May and June tours are every other day at 2 pm.

Museums The **Musée Départemental Breton** (☎ 02 98 95 21 60), next to the cathedral in the former bishop's palace on Place Saint Corentin, houses exhibits on the history, furniture, costumes, crafts and archaeology of the area. It opens from 9 am to noon and 2 to 5 pm daily except Sunday morning and Monday. From June to September it's open daily from 9 am to 6 pm. Entry is 20FF (10FF for students) but rises to 25/12FF in summer. The **Musée des Beaux-Arts** (☎ 02 98 95 45 20), in the Hôtel de Ville at 40 Place Saint Corentin, has a wide collection of European paintings from the 16th to early 20th centuries. It is open from 10 am to noon and 2 to 6 pm every day except Tuesday, and in July and August daily from 10 am to 7 pm. The entry fee is 25FF (15FF for students).

Faïencerie Tour
Faïenceries HB Henriot (☎ 02 98 90 09 36) has been turning out the famous Quimper (or Kemper) porcelain since 1690. It has tours of the factory, which is on Rue Haute south-west of the cathedral, on weekdays from 9 to 11.15 am and 1.30 to 4 pm on weekdays (3 pm on Friday). The cost is 15FF (12FF for students).

Places to Stay
It is extremely difficult to find accommodation in Quimper during the Festival de Cornouaille. The tourist office can make bookings for you for 2FF in Quimper, and 10FF elsewhere in

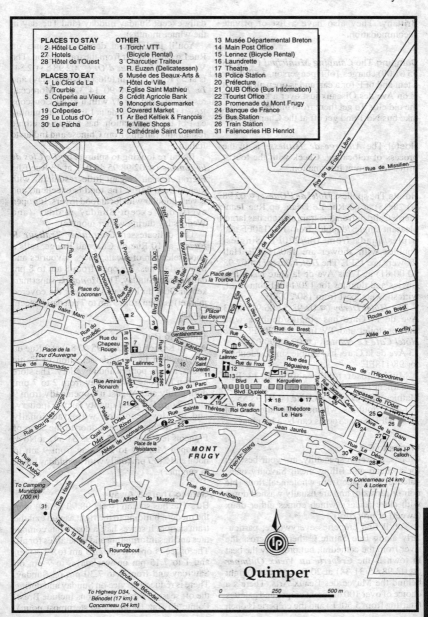

PLACES TO STAY
2 Hôtel Le Celtic
27 Hotels
28 Hôtel de l'Ouest

PLACES TO EAT
4 Le Clos de La Tourbie
5 Crêperie au Vieux Quimper
19 Crêperies
29 Le Lotus d'Or
30 Le Pacha

OTHER
1 Torch' VTT (Bicycle Rental)
3 Charcutier Traiteur R. Euzen (Delicatessen)
6 Musée des Beaux-Arts & Hôtel de Ville
7 Église Saint Mathieu
8 Crédit Agricole Bank
9 Monoprix Supermarket
10 Covered Market
11 Ar Bed Keltiek & François le Villec Shops
12 Cathédrale Saint Corentin

13 Musée Départemental Breton
14 Main Post Office
15 Lennez (Bicycle Rental)
16 Laundrette
17 Theatre
18 Police Station
20 Préfecture
21 QUB Office (Bus Information)
22 Tourist Office
23 Promenade du Mont Frugy
24 Banque de France
25 Bus Station
26 Train Station
31 Faïenceries HB Henriot

Quimper

0   250   500 m

To Camping Municipal (700 m)

To Highway D34, Bénodet (17 km) & Concarneau (24 km)

To Concarneau (24 km) & Lorient

MONT FRUGY

FRANCE

Brittany. They also have a list of private accommodation.

Camping The *Camping Municipal* (☎ 02 98 55 61 09) charges 16FF per person, 3.50FF for a tent and 6FF for a car, and is open all year. It is on Ave des Oiseaux just over a km west of the old city. To get there from the train station, take bus No 1 and get off at the Chaptal stop.

Hostel The *Auberge de Jeunesse* is in the process of relocating. Check with the tourist office for current information.

Hotels The spotless *Hôtel de l'Ouest* (☎ 02 98 90 28 35) at 63 Rue Le Déan, up Rue Jean-Pierre Calloch from the train station, has large, pleasant singles/doubles from 100/150FF and triples/quads from 180/220FF. Singles/doubles with shower are 180/190FF. Hall showers are 15FF. The *Hôtel Pascal* (☎ 02 98 90 00 81) at 17bis Ave de la Gare has a few singles and doubles for 120/140FF, but most, with showers, cost from 180/200FF.

The *Hôtel Derby* (☎ 02 98 52 06 91) at 13 Ave de la Gare has singles/doubles with shower, toilet and TV from 150/200FF. The *Hôtel Café Le Nantaïs* (☎ 02 98 90 07 84) at 23 Ave de la Gare, has simple singles/doubles for 98/118FF.

Much closer to the action at 13 Rue Douarnenez (100 metres north of Église Saint Mathieu), the *Hôtel Le Celtic* (☎ 02 98 55 59 35) has doubles without/with shower for 120/160FF. Some rooms can be a bit noisy.

Places to Eat
Crêpes, a Breton speciality, are your best bet for a cheap and filling meal. Savoury ones, galettes, are made from wholemeal flour (blé noir or sarrazin) and are usually washed down with cidre (cider), which comes either doux (sweet) or brut (dry).

You'll find crêperies everywhere, particularly along Rue Sainte Catherine, across the river from the cathedral, but probably the best in town is the *Crêperie au Vieux Quimper* (☎ 02 98 95 31 34) at 20 Rue Verdelet, right behind the Mu"ee des Beaux Arts. There's a choice of over 100 different crêpes and galettes (starting from 5.50FF) and the crêperie is open daily except Sunday midday (and Tuesday in the winter months).

You'll find several decent restaurants on Rue Le Déan not far from the train station. The Vietnamese *Le Lotus d'Or* (☎ 02 98 53 02 54) is at 53 Rue Le Déan (closed Wednesday) and *Le Pacha* (☎ 02 98 90 14 32), a Moroccan restaurant, is at No 37 with a killer Couscous Royal for 99FF. Ave de la Libération, running east of the train station, has a strip of ethnic restaurants ranging from Chinese and Indian to Italian.

If you're looking to splurge, try *Le Clos de la Tourbie* (☎ 02 98 95 45 03), at 43 Rue Elie Fréron. It's an elegant little restaurant with menus from 74FF. The food is excellent, and is very popular with local food lovers. It's open every day except Sunday midday (and Wednesday during winter months).

The delicatessen *Charcutier Traiteur R Euzen*, at 10 Rue du Chapeau Rouge, sells a good selection of meats, patés, savouries and prepared dishes. It's open from 8 am to 8 pm daily except Sunday. The *Monoprix* supermarket on Quai du Port au Vin (near the covered market) is open from 9 am to 7 pm daily except Sunday.

Things to Buy
Ar Bed Keltiek (☎ 02 98 95 42 82) at 2 Rue du Roi Gradlon has a wide selection of Celtic books, music, pottery and jewellery. The store is open Monday to Saturday from 2 to 7 pm; during July and August it's open daily from 9 am to 7 pm. For good-quality faïence (pottery) and textiles decorated with traditionally inspired designs, go next door to the shop of François le Villec (☎ 02 98 95 31 54) at No 4. It's open Monday to Saturday from 9 am to noon and 2 to 7 pm (daily with no midday break in summer).

Getting There & Away
Bus The bus station (☎ 02 98 90 88 89) is in the modern building to the right as you exit the train station. It serves half a dozen bus companies and has information and timetables for all. The office is open from 7.15 am to 12.30 pm and 1 to 7.15 pm on weekdays, to 7 pm on Saturday and from 5 to 7.30 pm on Sunday. There is reduced service on Sunday and during the off season. Bus destinations include Brest, Pointe du Raz (France's westernmost point),

Roscoff (from where there are ferries to Plymouth, England), Concarneau and Quimperlé. For information on SNCF buses to Douarnenez, Camaret-sur-Mer, Concarneau and Quiberon, enquire at the train station.

Train The train station (☎ 08 36 35 35 39) is east of the city centre on Ave de la Gare. The information counters are open daily from 8.30 am to 6.30 pm (8 am to 7 pm in July and August). A one-way ticket on the TGV to Paris' Gare Montparnasse costs 357FF (4½ hours). You can also reach Saint Malo by train via Rennes. The station has luggage lockers (30FF).

Getting Around
Bus QUB (☎ 02 98 95 26 27), which runs the local buses, is opposite the tourist office at 2 Quai de l'Odet. It's open weekdays from 8 am to 12.15 pm and 1.30 to 6.30 pm and on Saturday from 9 am to noon and 2 to 6 pm. Tickets are 6FF each or 45FF for a carnet of 10. Buses stop running around 7 pm and do not operate on Sunday. To reach the old city from the stations, take any bus from No 1 to No 7.

Taxi Radio taxis can be reached on ☎ 02 98 90 21 21.

Bicycle Possible cycling destinations from Quimper include Bénodet, Concarneau and even Pointe du Raz in Cornouaille. Torch' VTT (☎ 02 98 53 84 41) at 58 Rue de la Providence rents mountain bikes for 90/50FF a day/half day (70/45FF from October to April). The shop, which is open from 9.30 am to 7 pm daily except Sunday, is a good source of information on cycling routes. Bikes are a little bit cheaper at Lennez (☎ 02 98 90 14 81) just west of the train station at 13 Rue Aristide Briand. Lennez also rent *cyclos* and scooters for 150FF and 200FF a day.

CONCARNEAU
Concarneau (Konk-Kerne in Breton; population 19,000), 24 km south-east of Quimper, is France's third most important trawler port. Much of the tuna brought ashore here is caught in the Indian Ocean and off the coast of Africa; you'll see handbills announcing the size of the incoming fleet's catch all around town. Concarneau is slightly scruffy and at the same time a bit touristy, but it's refreshingly unpretentious and is near several decent beaches.

Orientation & Information
Concarneau curls around the busy fishing port, the Port de Pêche, with the two main quays running north-south along the harbour. The tourist office (☎ 02 98 97 01 44) is on Quai d'Aiguillon, 150 metres north of the main (west) gate to the Ville Close. It is open Monday to Saturday from 9 am to noon and from 2 to 6 pm. From mid-May to June, it keeps Sunday hours from 9 am to 12.30 pm, and in July and August, it's open daily from 9 am to 8 pm.

Money & Post The Société Générale at 10 Rue du Général Morvan, half a block west of the tourist office, is open weekdays from 8.10 am to noon and from 1.35 to 5.10 pm. Caisse d'Épargne on Rue Charles Linement, which runs parallel two streets south, keeps similar hours but is open on Saturday (until 4 pm) and closed Monday. The main post office, which has an exchange service, is at 14 Quai Carnot. Concarneau's postcode is 29900.

Things to See & Do
The **Ville Close** (walled city), built on a small island measuring 350 metres by 100 metres and fortified between the 14th and 17th centuries, is reached from Place Jean Jaurès by a footbridge. As you enter, note the sundial warning us all that 'Time passes like a shadow'. Ville Close is packed with shops and restaurants, and there are nice views of the town, the port and the bay from the **ramparts**, which are open throughout the year for strolling. From mid-June to mid-September, however, there is a charge of 5FF, and opening times are from 10 am to 7.30 pm daily. The ticket office is up the stairs to the left just inside the main gate.

The **Musée de la Pêche** (☎ 02 98 97 10 20), on Rue Vauban just beyond the gate, has four aquariums and interesting exhibits on everything you could possibly want to know about fish and the fishing industry over the centuries. It's open daily from 9.30 am to 12.30 pm and 2 to 6 pm (9.30 am to 7 pm from mid-June to mid-September). The entry fee is 30/20FF for adults/under 18s.

The **Château de Keriolet** (02 98 97 36 50) about three km north of town is an extravagant neo-Gothic building with a colourful history. Five rooms are open to the public from June to September from 10.30 am to 6.30 pm. Entry is 25FF and includes a guided tour lasting an hour. To get there, take the bus to Beuzec-Conq which departs about every 10 minutes from the bus terminal at Place Jean Jaurès.

Plage des Sables Blancs (White Sands Beach) is 1.5 km north-west of the tourist office on Baie de la Forêt; **Plage du Cabellou** is several km south of town. Both beaches can be reached by taking bus No 2.

From April to September, three companies offer excursions to **Îles Glénan**, nine little islands about 20 km south of Concarneau with sailing and scuba-diving schools, an 18th-century fort, a bird sanctuary and a few houses. Fares are around 100FF. See Vedettes Glenn (☎ 02 98 97 10 31) at 17 Ave du Docteur Nicolas or call Vedettes de L'Odet (☎ 02 98 57 00 58) or Vedette Taxi (☎ 02 98 97 25 25).

Places to Stay
Camping Concarneau's half a dozen camping grounds include *Camping du Moulin d'Aurore* (☎ 02 98 50 53 08), 600 metres south-east of the Ville Close at 49 Rue de Trégunc. It's open from April to September and costs 18.50FF per person and 16.50FF for a tent and car. To get there take bus No 1 or 2 (to stop: Le Rouz) or the little ferry from Ville Close to Place Duquesne and walk south along Rue Mauduit Duplessis.

Hostel The *Auberge de Jeunesse* (☎ 02 98 97 03 47) is right on the water at Quai de la Croix, next to the Marinarium. To get there from the tourist office, walk south to the end of Quai Peneroff and turn right. A bed is 45FF, breakfast is 18FF. Reception is open from 9 am to noon and 6 to 8 pm.

Hotels The cheapest hotel in town is the *Hôtel Renaissance* (☎ 02 98 97 04 23) at the northern end of town at 56 Ave de la Gare. Rooms start at 130/185FF without/with shower. Opposite the tourist office, *Hôtel Le Jockey* (☎ 02 98 97 31 52) at Ave Pierre Guéguin has singles/

doubles with shower from 230FF. Just south at 9 Place Jean Jaurès, the *Hôtel Les Voyageurs* (☎ 02 98 97 08 06) has doubles without/with shower for 165/190FF. Hall showers are free.

If you can afford a bit more, *Hôtel des Halles* (☎ 02 98 97 11 41) around the corner from Hotel Les Voyageurs on Place de l'Hôtel de Ville charges from 260FF for a double with shower and TV. *Hôtel Modern* (☎ 02 98 97 03 36) is north of the port at 5 Rue du Lin, a quiet back street. It has singles/doubles with shower from 260FF (190FF without) and use of a private garage (40FF).

Places to Eat
Designed like the interior of an old fishing boat, *L'Écume* (☎ 02 98 97 33 27) at 3 Place Saint Guénolé in the Ville Close has excellent wholemeal crêpes and draught cider served in pewter cups. Back on the mainland, *Le Men Fall* (☎ 02 98 50 80 80), down narrow Rue Fresnel from Quai de la Croix, has good pizzas and pasta and is open daily to 11 pm except Monday and Sunday at midday. *Le Chalut* (☎ 02 98 97 02 12) at 20 Quai Carnot has a 50FF menu which is popular with local people.

The covered market on Place Jean Jaurès is open to 1 pm daily except Sunday. There's a large *Super U* supermarket on Quai Carnot next to the post office.

Getting There & Away
The bus station is in the parking lot next to the tourist office. Caoudal (☎ 02 98 56 96 72) runs nine buses a day (three on Sunday) between Quimper and Quimperlé (via Concarneau and Pont Aven). The trip from Quimper to Concarneau costs 23FF and takes 30 minutes.

Getting Around
Bus Concarneau's three bus lines run by Busco operate between 7.20 am and 6.30 pm daily except Sunday. All of them stop at the bus terminal next to the tourist office and tickets are 5FF (44FF for a 10-ticket carnet). For information, consult the Busco office (☎ 02 98 60 53 76) in the covered market on Ave de Docteur Nicolas. It's open from 9.30 am to noon and from 2 to 5 pm on weekdays.

Taxi For taxis in Concarneau call ☎ 02 98 97 24 18.

Boat A small passenger ferry links the Ville Close and Place Duquesne on Concarneau's eastern shore year-round. From mid-June to August, sailings are between 7 am and 8.30 pm. Off season, they start an hour later, take a lunch break and finish at 6.20 pm (7.20 pm at the weekend). One way is 3FF (20FF for 10 tickets).

SAINT MALO

The Channel port of Saint Malo (population 48,000) is one of the most popular tourist destinations in Brittany – and with good reason. Situated at the mouth of the Rance River, it is famed for its walled city and nearby beaches. The Saint Malo area has some of the highest tidal variations in the world – depending on the lunar and solar cycles, the high-water mark is often 13 metres or more above the low-water mark.

Saint Malo is an excellent base from which to explore the Côte d'Émeraude, the northern 'Emerald Coast' of Brittany between Pointe du Grouin and Le Val André. Mont-Saint-Michel (see Normandy, earlier) can be visited easily as a day trip from Saint Malo.

Saint Malo reached the height of its importance during the 17th and 18th centuries, when it was one of France's most active ports for both merchant ships and privateers, whose favourite targets were, of course, the English.

Orientation

Saint Malo consists of the resort towns of Saint Servan, Saint Malo, Paramé and Rothéneuf. The old city, signposted as Intra-Muros ('within the walls') and also known as the Ville Close, is connected to Paramé by the Sillon Isthmus. Esplanade Saint Vincent, where the tourist office and bus station are located, is a giant parking lot just outside Porte Saint Vincent, one of the old city gates. The train station is 1.2 km east of Esplanade Saint Vincent.

Information

Tourist Office Saint Malo's tourist office (☎ 02 99 56 64 48) is just outside the old city on Esplanade Saint Vincent. It's open Monday to Saturday from 9 am to noon and 2 to 6.30 pm. From April to September, it's also open on Sunday from 10 am to noon and 2 to 5.30 pm. In July and August, it's open Monday to Satur-day from 8.30 am to 8 pm and on Sunday from 10 am to 6.30 pm.

Money There are half a dozen banks near the train station, along Blvd de la République and at Place de Rocabey. All are open on weekdays and keep about the same hours: 8.30 am to noon and 1.30 to 4.30 pm. In the old city, the Banque de France is at 7 Rue d'Asfeld.

Post The main post office (☎ 02 99 20 51 78) is near Place de Rocabey at 1 Blvd de la Tour d'Auvergne. Currency exchange services are available. In the old city, there's a branch at 4 Place des Frères Lamennais. Saint Malo's postcode is 35400.

Things to See & Do

Old City During the fighting of August 1944, which drove the Germans from Saint Malo, 80% of the old city was destroyed. After the war, the principal historical monuments were faithfully reconstructed but the rest of the area was rebuilt in the style of the 17th and 18th centuries. **Cathédrale Saint Vincent**, begun in the 11th century, is noted for its medieval stained-glass windows. The striking modern altar in bronze reveals a Celtic influence.

The **ramparts**, built over the course of many centuries, survived the war and are largely original. They afford superb views in all directions: the freight port, the interior of the old city and the English Channel. There is free access to the **ramparts walk** at Porte de Dinan, the Grande Porte, Porte Saint Vincent and elsewhere. The remains of the 17th-century **Fort National**, for many years a prison, are just beyond the northern stretch.

The **Musée de la Ville** (☎ 02 99 40 71 57), in the Château de Saint Malo at Porte Saint Vincent, deals with the history of the city and the Pays Malouin (the area around Saint Malo). It is open daily from 10 am to noon and 2 to 6 pm (closed on Monday in winter). Entry is 25FF (12.50FF for students).

The **aquarium** (☎ 02 99 40 91 86), with over 100 tanks, is built into the walls of the old city, next to Place Vauban. It's open daily from 9.30 am to noon and 2.30 to 6 pm (to 11 pm with no midday break from July to mid-August). Entry is 30FF (22FF for students). (A giant new aquarium, **Le Grand Aquarium**

Saint Malo

ENGLISH CHANNEL
(LA MANCHE)

0 — 250 — 500 m

Sillon Isthmus

Chaussée du Sillon

Quai Duguay Trouin

Grande Plage

Rue de l'Industrie

Boulevard Théodore Botrel

Blvd de la Tour d'Auvergne

Place de Rocabey

Boulevard de la République

R Ernest Renan

Avenue Jean Jaurès

To Auberge
de Jeunesse (1 km),
Plage de Rochebonne (1.2 km),
Paramé & Rothéneuf,

Avenue Pasteur

R du Calvaire

Rue Sainte Barbe

Place Vauban

Intra-Muros

To Île
du Grand Bé

*Place des
Frères
Lamennais*

*Rue
du Boyer*

*Plage de Bon
Secours*

*Rue de
Dinan*

Rue de Toulouse

Rue Brousais

Quai Saint Louis

Quai Saint Vincent

Esplanade Saint Vincent

Bassin Duguay Trouin

Avenue Louis Martin

Place de la Grande

Boulevard des Talards

*Bassin
Jacques
Cartier*

Rue Albhonse Thébaut

**Saint
Malo**

To Le Grand
Aquarium (1.5 km),
Barrage de la
Rance (5 km) &
Dinard (10 km)

Rue Hochelaga

Chaussée des Corsaires

*Bassin
Vauban*

Jetty

*Bassin
Bouvet*

Quai de Trichet

Rue Georges Clémenceau

*Pleasure Craft
Port*

Plage des Bas Sablons

R Dauphine

Rue des Bas

Rue Pré Bréal

**Saint
Servan**

Rue de la Cité

*Place
Saint
Pierre*

*Rue du
Dick*

Quai Solidor

*Port
Solidor*

Corniche d'Aleth

*Rance
Estuary*

*Esplanade Commandant
Yves Menguy*

PLACES TO STAY

3	Hôtel Le Neptune
8	Hôtel de l'Avenir
15	Hôtel Port Malo
23	Hôtel Le Victoria
27	Hôtel Aux Vieilles Pierres
35	Hôtel de l'Europe & Hôtel de la Petite Vitesse
41	Camping Municipal Cité d'Aleth

PLACES TO EAT

2	Chez Jean-Pierre
16	Le Maclou
18	Tourist Restaurants
20	Le Chasse Marée
31	Crêperie Gaby
39	Crêperie du Val de Rance

OTHER

1	Fort National
4	Cycles Diazo
5	Intermarché Supermarket
6	Main Post Office
7	Laundrette
9	Église de Rocabey
10	Aquarium
11	Musée de Cire
12	Château de Saint Malo
13	Musée de la Ville
14	Porte Saint Vincent
19	Tourist Office & Bus Station
21	Post Office Annexe
22	Cathédrale Saint Vincent
24	Grande Porte
25	Porte des Bés
26	Porte Sainte Pierre
28	Rue de l'Orme (Food Shops)
29	Banque de France
30	Porte de Dinan
32	Émeraude Lines & Ferries to Dinard
33	Esplanade de la Bourse
34	Banks
36	Train Station
37	Gare Maritime de la Bourse (Ferry Terminal)
38	Gare Maritime du Naye (Car Ferry Terminal)
40	Fort de la Cité
42	Musée International du Long Cours Cap-Hornier & Tour de Solidor

FRANCE

(☎ 02 99 21 19 02) is scheduled to open in June 1996 on Ave Général Patton, about a km to the south of St Malo's centre. It will spread over 4000 sq metres, with exotic fish, turtles, crocodiles and sharks displayed in 40 aquariums (including a circular one offering a 360-degree panoramic view). Entry is expected to cost 50FF (students, 44FF). Bus No 5 from the railway station should run past there, but check with the tourist office first.

Île du Grand Bé You can reach the Île du Grand Bé, where the 18th-century writer Chateaubriand is buried, on foot at low tide via the Porte des Bés and the nearby old city gates. Be warned: when the tide comes in (and it comes in fast), the causeway remains impassable for about six hours.

Saint Servan Saint Servan's fortress, **Fort de la Cité**, was built in the mid-18th century and served as a German base during WWII. The German pillboxes of thick steel flanking the fortress walls were heavily scarred by Allied shells in August 1944. The interior of the fort is now used by camper vans.

The **Musée International du Long Cours Cap-Hornier** (☎ 02 99 40 71 58), housed in the 14th-century **Tour de Solidor** on Esplanade Menguy, displays nautical instruments, ship models and other exhibits relating to the sailors who sailed around Cape Horn between the early 17th and early 20th centuries. There is a great view from the top of the tower. The museum is open from 10 am to noon and 2 to 6 pm daily (closed Monday from October to April). Tickets cost 25FF (12.50FF for students).

Beaches Just outside the old city walls to the west is **Plage de Bon Secours**. Saint Servan's **Plage des Bas Sablons** is popular with older sunbathers. The **Grande Plage**, which stretches north-eastward from the Sillon Isthmus, is spiked with tree trunks that act as breakers. **Plage de Rochebonne** is a km or so to the north-east.

Places to Stay

Camping The *Camping Municipal Cité d'Aleth* (☎ 02 99 81 60 91) is at the northern tip of Saint Servan next to Fort de la Cité. It's

open all year and charges 18.50FF per person and 26FF for a tent and car. In summer, take bus No 1. During the rest of the year, your best bet is to take bus No 6 and walk.

Hostel The *Auberge de Jeunesse* (☎ 02 99 40 29 80) is at 37 Ave du Père Umbricht in Paramé, a bit under two km north-east of the train station. A bed in a four or six-person room costs from 64 to 67FF, doubles are from 74 to 81FF per person, and singles with shower and toilet are 108FF, all including breakfast. From the train station, take bus No 5.

Hotels It can be difficult finding a hotel room in Saint Malo during July and August. Among the cheaper places, the noisy and charmless hotels near the train station are the first to fill up. If you're looking for a bargain, the hotels around Place de Rocabey are probably your best bet, though there are also a few good deals in the old city.

Place de Rocabey The small *Hôtel de l'Avenir* (☎ 02 99 56 13 33) at 31 Blvd de la Tour d'Auvergne has singles and doubles for 120FF (150FF with shower). Hall showers cost 15FF. Close to the Grande Plage, *Hôtel Le Neptune* (☎ 02 99 56 82 15) is an older, family-run place at 21 Rue de l'Industrie. Adequate doubles with free hall showers cost from 120FF. Doubles with shower and toilet cost 170FF.

Train Station Area The *Hôtel de l'Europe* (☎ 02 99 56 13 42) is at 44 Blvd de la République, across the roundabout from the train station. Modern, nondescript doubles start at 140FF (175FF from mid-April to August). Shower-equipped rooms without/ with toilet are 170/180FF (220/250FF from mid-April to August). There are no hall showers. Like other places in this area, it's somewhat noisy. The *Hôtel de la Petite Vitesse* (☎ 02 99 56 01 93), next door at No 42, has good-sized but noisy doubles from 160FF (180FF with shower) and two-bed quads from 270FF. Hall showers are 20FF.

Old City The friendly, family-run *Hôtel Aux Vieilles Pierres* (☎ 02 99 56 46 80) is in a quiet part of the old city at 4 Rue des Lauriers.

Singles/doubles start at 135FF (160FF with shower); hall showers are free. The *Hôtel Le Victoria* (☎ 02 99 56 34 01) is more in the thick of things at 4 Rue des Orbettes. It has doubles from 150FF (185FF with shower). Hall showers are free.

The *Hôtel Port Malo* (☎ 02 99 20 52 99), 150 metres from Porte Saint Vincent at 15 Rue Sainte Barbe, has singles/doubles with shower and toilet for 180/240FF (200/260FF from May to September). The *Hôtel Brochet* (☎ 02 99 56 30 00), due south at 1 Rue Corne de Cerf, has singles/doubles (accessible by lift) with shower and TV for 180/200FF (230/290FF in summer).

Places to Eat

The old city has lots of tourist restaurants, crêperies and pizzerias in the area between Porte Saint Vincent, the cathedral and the Grande Porte, but if you're after better food, and better value, avoid this area completely.

The *Auberge Aux Vieilles Pierres* (☎ 02 99 56 46 80), below the Hotel in 4 Rue des Lauriers, has excellent menus from 85FF. The building was one of the very few in Saint Malo to survive the war. It is open daily (except Monday midday) until 11 pm. Popular with the locals is *Le Chasse Marée* (☎ 02 99 40 85 10) at 4 Rue du Grout Saint-Georges, off Place des Frères Lamennais. Menus start at 87FF, and it's open daily (except Monday in winter). For crêpes and galettes, try *Crêperie Gaby* at 2 Rue de Dinan, which has become a bit of an institution; the indefatigable Mme Gaby has been turning out her delicious crêpes for over 30 years. Crêpes start at 8.50FF, galettes at 7.50FF.

Chez Jean-Pierre (☎ 02 99 40 40 48), popular for pizza and pasta (from 44FF), has an enviable location across from the Grande Plage at 60 Chaussée du Sillon. It's open daily.

For takeaway sandwiches available until 1 am daily, head for *Le Maclou* (☎ 02 99 56 50 41) at 22 Rue Sainte Barbe. Near Plage des Bas Sablons in Saint Servan, *Crêperie du Val de Rance* (☎ 02 99 81 64 68) at 11 Rue Dauphine serves Breton-style crêpes and galettes all day. Order a bottle of Val de Rance cider and drink it, as they do here, from a teacup.

In the old city, you'll find a number of food shops along Rue de l'Orme, including the excellent cheese shop *Bordier* at No 9 (closed Sunday and Monday), a fruit and vegetable shop (closed Sunday) at No 8 and two boulangeries. A large *Intermarché* supermarket is two blocks from Place de Rocabey on Blvd Théodore Botrel.

Getting There & Away

Bus The bus station, from which several bus companies operate, is at Esplanade Saint Vincent, next door to the tourist office. Many of the buses departing from here also stop at the train station.

Les Courriers Bretons (☎ 02 99 56 79 09) has regular services to destinations such as Cancale (20.50FF), Fougères (48FF, Monday to Saturday only) and Mont-Saint-Michel (50FF, one hour). The daily bus to Mont-Saint-Michel leaves at 11.10 am and returns around 6.30 pm. During July and August, there are five return trips a day. The Courriers Bretons office is open Monday to Friday from 8.30 am to 12.15 pm and 2.15 to 6 pm and Saturday morning (all day in summer).

Tourisme Verney (☎ 02 99 40 82 67), with identical opening hours, has buses to Cancale (19.50FF), Dinan (33FF), Dinard (18.50FF) and Rennes (54FF).

Voyages Pansart (☎ 02 99 40 85 96), whose office is open Monday to Saturday (daily in July and August), offers various excursions. All-day tours to Mont-Saint-Michel (110FF; 99FF for students) operate daily from June to mid-September and three times a week in April and May.

Train The train station (☎ 02 99 40 70 20) is one km east of the old city along Ave Louis Martin. The information counters are open daily from 9 am to 12.30 pm and 2 to 7 pm. There is direct service to Paris' Gare Montparnasse (248FF, 4½ hours) in summer only. During the rest of the year, you have to change trains at Rennes. There are also services to Dinan (44FF) and Quimper (210FF).

Ferry Ferries link Saint Malo with the Channel Islands, Weymouth, Portsmouth and Poole in England and Cork in Ireland. There are two ferry terminals: hydrofoils, catamarans and the like depart from Gare Maritime de la Bourse; car ferries leave from Gare Maritime du Naye. Both are south of the walled city. Shuttles to

Dinard (see the Dinard section for details) depart from just outside the old city's Porte de Dinan.

From Gare Maritime de la Bourse, Condor (☎ 02 99 20 03 00) has hydrofoil services to Jersey (275FF one-day excursion) and Guernsey (315FF) from mid-April to October and up to mid-September to Sark and Alderney (560FF three-day excursion). Condor's service to Weymouth (579FF one way, seven hours) operates daily from late April to October.

Émeraude Lines (☎ 02 99 40 48 40) has ferries to Jersey, Guernsey and Sark. Service is most regular between late March and mid-November. Car ferries to Jersey run all year long, except in January.

Between mid-March and mid-December, Brittany Ferries (☎ 02 99 40 64 41) has boats to Portsmouth once or twice a day (except Sunday during some months) leaving from the Gare Maritime du Naye. One-way fares are 210 to 240FF and 910 to 1210FF for a car. In winter, ferries sail twice a week. There are also services to Poole (four times weekly) from late May to September, and to Portsmouth, Plymouth and Cork.

Getting Around

Bus Saint Malo Bus has seven lines, but line No 1 runs only in summer. Tickets cost 7FF and can be used as transfers for one hour after they're time-stamped; a carnet of 10 costs 49FF and a one-day pass, 20FF. In summer, Saint Malo Bus tickets are also valid on Courriers Bretons buses for travel within Saint Malo. Buses run until about 7.15 pm, but in summer certain lines keep running until about midnight. The company's information office at Esplanade Saint Vincent (☎ 02 99 56 06 06) is open from 8.30 to noon and 2 to 6.15 or 6.30 pm daily except Saturday afternoon and Sunday (daily except Sunday in summer).

Esplanade Saint Vincent, where the tourist office and bus station are, is linked with the train station by bus Nos 1, 2, 3 and 4.

Taxi Taxis can be ordered on ☎ 02 99 81 30 30.

Bicycle Cycles Diazo (☎ 02 99 40 31 63) at 47 Quai Duguay Trouin is open Monday to Friday from 9 am to noon and 2 to 6 pm. Three-speeds cost 50FF and mountain bikes are 80FF a day.

DINARD

While Saint Malo's old city and beaches are oriented towards middle-class families, Dinard (population 10,000) attracts a well-heeled clientele – especially from the UK – who have been coming here since the town first became popular with the English upper classes in the mid-19th century. Indeed, Dinard has the feel of a turn-of-the-century English beach resort, especially in summer, with its candy-cane bathing tents, beachside carnival rides and spiked-roof *belle époque* mansions perched above the waters.

Staying in Dinard can be a bit hard on the budget, but since the town is just across the Rance Estuary from Saint Malo, a day trip by bus or boat is an easy option.

Orientation

Plage de l'Écluse (also called Grande Plage), down the hill from the tourist office, runs along the northern edge of town between Pointe du Moulinet and Pointe de la Malouine. To get there from the Embarcadère (the pier where boats from Saint Malo dock), climb the stairs and walk 200 metres along Rue Georges Clemenceau. Place de Newquay (formerly Place de la Gare) is one km south-west of the tourist office.

Information

The tourist office (☎ 02 99 46 94 12) is in a round, colonnaded building at 2 Blvd Féart. It is open Monday to Saturday from 9 am to noon and 2 to 6 pm (from 9.30 am to 7.30 pm with no midday break in July and August and including Sunday).

There are a number of banks on Rue Levavasseur east of Blvd Féart and a Caisse d'Épargne at Place Rochaid close to the post office, open weekdays from 8.45 am to 12.15 pm and 1.45 to 5.30 pm (4 pm on Saturday). The main post office (☎ 02 99 16 34 00) is just south of Ave Édouard VII at Place Rochaid. Dinard's postcode is 35800.

Things to See & Do

Musée du Site Balnéaire The town's only real museum (☎ 02 99 46 81 05), at 12 Rue des Français Libres, focuses on the history of the area and, in particular, Dinard's development as a seaside resort. The Villa Eugénie was built in 1868 for the wife of Napoleon III who – alas

– never got to stay here. It's open April to October from 10 am to noon and 2 to 6 pm (on Saturday and Sunday, only in the afternoon) and costs 16FF (10FF for students).

Walks Beautiful seaside trails extend along the coast in both directions from Dinard. The tourist office sells a topoguide (5FF) with maps and information in French on five coastal trails entitled *Sentiers du Littoral du Canton du Dinard*.

Dinard's famous **Promenade du Clair de Lune** (Moonlight Promenade) runs along the Baie du Prieuré, which is south-west of the Embarcadère at the Place du Général de Gaulle. Perhaps the town's most attractive walk is the one which links the Promenade du Clair de Lune with **Plage de l'Écluse** via the rocky coast of **Pointe du Moulinet**, from where Saint Malo's old city can be seen across the water. This trail continues westward along the coast, passing **Plage de Saint Énogat** en route to Saint Briac, some 14 km away. Bikes are not allowed. There's a sound-and-light show on the Promenade du Clair de Lune from mid-June to mid-September.

If you are in the mood for a bit of a hike, you can take the bus or ferry over from Saint Malo and walk the 12 km back via the Barrage de la Rance (see below).

Swimming Wide, sandy **Plage de l'Écluse** is surrounded by fashionable hotels, a casino and changing cubicles. Next to the beach is the **Piscine Olympique** (☎ 02 99 46 22 77), an Olympic-sized swimming pool filled with heated sea water. It's open mornings, afternoons or evenings (except in December) depending on the day and costs 12FF/10FF for adults/students on weekdays and 24FF/15FF on weekends, holidays and during July and August. **Plage du Prieuré**, one km to the south along Blvd Féart, isn't as smart but it's less crowded. **Plage de Saint Énogat** is a km west of Plage de l'Écluse on the other side of Pointe de la Malouine.

Windsurfing The Wishbone Club (☎ 02 99 88 15 20) next to the swimming pool on the Plage de l'Écluse offers windsurfing instruction for 150FF per hour and rents boards. Depending on the make, they're 80 and 100FF an hour

(190 and 240FF for half a day). Wishbone operates every day from 9 am to 7 pm from March to October, and on weekends only during the rest of the year.

Barrage de la Rance If you're driving or walking along the D168 between Saint Malo and Dinard, you'll pass over the Rance Tidal Power Station (☎ 02 99 16 37 00), a hydroelectric dam across the estuary of the Rance River that uses Saint Malo's extraordinarily high tides to generate 3% of the electricity consumed in Brittany. The 750-metre-long dam, built between 1961 and 1966, has 24 generators that are turned at high tide by sea water flowing into the estuary and at low tide by water draining into the sea. Near the lock on the Dinard side is a small, subterranean visitors' centre open daily from 8.30 am to 8 pm. It has a film in English on how the power station works.

Places to Stay

Hostel The *Auberge de Jeunesse Ker Charles* (☎ 02 99 46 40 02) at 8 Blvd l'Hôtelier (about 600 metres west of the tourist office) is open all year. A bed costs 80FF including breakfast; evening meals are 40FF.

Hotels A number of relatively inexpensive hotels can be found around Place de Newquay. The friendly *Hôtel de la Gare* (☎ 02 99 46 10 84) at 28 Rue de la Corbinais has doubles without shower for 120 to 170FF. The reception is inside the ground-floor restaurant. The newly refurbished *Hôtel L'Étoile de Mer* (☎ 02 99 46 11 19) at 52 Rue de la Gare has singles/doubles with shower from 150/190FF.

The *Hôtel du Parc* (☎ 02 99 46 11 39), a bit closer to the centre of town at 20 Ave Édouard VII, has rooms starting at 145FF for one or two people. Doubles with shower and toilet are 270FF.

If you can afford a little more, *Hôtel du Prieuré* (☎ 02 99 46 13 74) is a lovely little place overlooking the beach and the town at 1 Place du Général de Gaulle. Singles/doubles with shower are 260/270FF.

Places to Eat

There are plenty of places around the tourist office that sell crêpes and the like. *L'Épicurien* at the Hôtel de la Gare (☎ 02 99 46 10 84) is a family-style restaurant with a good-value lunch menu for 45FF which includes a choice from the salad bar.

Le Grill de la Croisette (☎ 02 99 16 00 01), a few steps west of the tourist office at 2 Place de la Republique, specialises in meat grilled over an open fire and has a good three-course meal available for 59FF. The restaurant is open until around midnight daily except Tuesday.

The *Shopi* supermarket north of the Place de Newquay at 45 Rue Gardiner is open from 8.30 am to 12.30 pm and 2.30 to 7.30 pm Monday to Saturday and on Sunday morning.

Getting There & Around

Bus TIV buses (☎ 02 99 40 83 33, 02 99 82 26 26 in Saint Malo) leave Esplanade Saint Vincent in Saint Malo and pick up passengers at the train station before continuing on via the Barrage de la Rance to Dinard. The buses run almost once an hour until about 6 pm (to Saint Malo) and 7 pm (to Dinard).

Taxi You can order a taxi on ☎ 02 99 46 88 80.

Boat From April to September, the Bus de Mer ferry run by Émeraude Lines links Saint Malo with Dinard. The trip costs 20/30FF one way/return and takes 10 minutes. In Saint Malo, the dock (☎ 02 99 40 48 40) is just outside the Porte de Dinan; the Dinard dock (☎ 02 96 46 10 45) is at 27 Ave George V. There are eight to 17 trips a day from 9.30 am to around 6 pm, and until 11 pm in July and August.

Loire Valley

From the 15th to 18th centuries, the Loire Valley (Vallée de la Loire) was the playground of kings, princes, dukes and nobles who expended family fortunes and the wealth of the nation to turn it into a vast neighbourhood of lavish chateaux. Today, the region is a favourite destination of tourists seeking architectural testimony to the glories of the Middle Ages and the Renaissance.

The earliest chateaux in the Loire Valley were medieval fortresses (*châteaux forts*), some constructed hastily in the 9th century as a defence against the marauding Vikings. These structures were built on high ground and, from the 11th century, when stone came into wide use, were often outfitted with fortified keeps, massive walls topped with battlements, loopholes (arrow slits) and moats spanned by drawbridges.

As the threat of invasion diminished – and the cannon (in use by the mid-15th century) rendered castles almost useless for defence – the architecture of new chateaux (and the new wings added to older ones) began to reflect a different set of priorities, including aesthetics and comfort. Under the influence of the Italian Renaissance, with its many innovations introduced to France at the end of the 15th century, the defensive structures so prominent in the early chateaux metamorphosed into whimsical, decorative features such as can be seen at Azay-le-Rideau, Chambord and Chenonceau. Instead of being built on isolated hilltops, the Renaissance chateaux were placed near a body of water or in a valley and proportioned to harmonise with their surroundings. Most chateaux from the 17th and 18th centuries are grand country houses built in the neoclassical style and set amid formal gardens.

BLOIS

The medieval town of Blois (population 50,000), whose name is pronounced 'blwah', was a major centre of court intrigue between the 15th and 17th centuries, and during the 16th century served as something of a second capital of France. A number of dramatic events, involving some of the most important kings and other personages of French history (Louis XII, François I and Henri III among them), took place inside the city's outstanding attraction, the Château de Blois. The old city, seriously damaged by German attacks in 1940, retains its steep, twisting medieval streets. Several of the most rewarding chateaux in the Loire Valley, including Chambord and Cheverny, are within a 20-km radius of the city.

Orientation

Blois, lying on the north bank of the Loire River, is quite a compact town and almost everything is within walking distance of the train station. The old city is both south and east of the Château de Blois, which towers over Place Victor Hugo.

Information

Tourist Office The local tourist office (☎ 02 54 74 06 49) at 3 Ave Jean Laigret is housed in an early 16th-century pavilion which used to stand in the middle of the chateau's gardens. From October to April, it's open Monday to Saturday from 9 am to noon and 2 to 6 pm, and on Sunday from 10.30 am to 12.30 pm and 2 to 5 pm. From May to September it's open daily from 9 am to 7 pm.

Money & Post The Banque de France (☎ 02 54 55 44 00), one block east of the train station at 4 Ave Jean Laigret, is open Tuesday to Saturday from 8.45 am to 12.15 pm and 1.45 to 3.45 pm. Crédit Agricole (☎ 02 54 74 30 68) at 6 Place Louis XII is open Tuesday to Saturday from 8.45 am to 5.30 pm (4.30 pm on Saturday) but charges a 40FF commission for changing money. The post office (☎ 02 54 78 08 01), which also has a currency exchange service, is north of Place Victor Hugo at 2 Rue Gallois. The postcode for Blois is 41000.

Things to See

Château de Blois This chateau (☎ 02 54 74 16 06) is not the most impressive in the Loire Valley, but it has a compellingly bloody history and an extraordinary mixture of architectural styles. The chateau's four distinct sections are: early Gothic (13th century), Flamboyant Gothic (the reign of Louis XII around 1500), early Renaissance (from the reign of François I, about 1520) and classical (towards the end of the reign of Louis XIII, around 1630). In the Louis XII section, look out for the porcupines (his symbol) carved into the stonework. The Italianate François I wing, which includes the famous **spiral staircase**, is decorated with repetitions of François I's insignia, a capital 'F' and the salamander.

The chateau also houses a small **archaeological museum** (closed until 1998 for refurbishment) and the **Musée des Beaux-Arts**. The chateau is open daily from 9 am to noon and 2 to 5 pm from October to mid-March. During the rest of the year, opening hours are from 9 am to 6 pm (until 7.30 pm during July and August). The entry fee is 33FF

(17FF if you are under 25 or over 60). There is a sound-and-light show at the chateau during some evenings in May and every night from June to September. Prices are 60FF. For show times, check with the tourist office.

The entry ticket for the chateau also gets you into the museums of religious art and natural history in the 15th-century **Les Jacobins convent** across from 15 Rue Anne de Bretagne. Both are open every day from 2 to 6 pm except Sunday and Monday.

A new museum, the **Maison de la Magie** (House of Magic; ☎ 02 54 55 26 26) is due to open towards the end of 1997 across the square from the chateau at 1 Place du Château. It will exhibit a collection of clocks and other objects invented by the 19th-century scientist/magician Robert Houdin (after whom the great Houdini named himself), and will stage magic shows in the theatre.

Old City Much of the area has been turned into a pedestrian mall and there are informative explanatory signs (in brown) tacked up around the old city in English. The tourist office has a good brochure suggesting walking tours (*itinéraires*), and guided tours (in French) leave every day from the chateau at 6 pm in July and August, and on Saturdays at 3 pm during May, June, September and October. Prices are 42FF (26FF for students).

Cathédrale Saint Louis is named after Louis XIV, who assisted in rebuilding it after a devastating hurricane in 1678. The crypt dates from the 10th century. There's a great view of both banks of the Loire River from the **Terrasse de l'Évêché** (terrace of the bishop's palace), directly behind the cathedral. The 15th-century **Maison des Acrobates** at 3 Place Saint Louis, with its carved faces of acrobats, is one of the few medieval houses in Blois not destroyed during WWII.

Places to Stay

Camping The *Camping Municipal de la Boire* (☎ 02 54 74 22 78), open from March to November, is 2.5 km east of the train station on the south bank of the Loire. It is on Blvd René Gentil near the heliport and Pont Charles de Gaulle, a highway bridge over the river. Two people with a tent are charged 34FF, 40FF with a car. There's no bus service from town.

Blois

PLACES TO STAY
4 Hôtel Saint Jacques
5 Hôtel Le Savoie
11 Hôtel du Bellay
12 Hôtel L'Étoile d'Or
13 Hôtel Le Lys

PLACES TO EAT
21 La Salamandre
22 La Mesa
28 Au Bouchon Lyonnais
30 Restaurant Le Maïdi
31 Banquettes Rouges

OTHER
1 Bus Station
2 Taxi Booth
3 Train Station
6 Banque de France
7 Avis Car Rental
8 Tourist Office
9 Église Saint Vincent
10 Post Office
14 Palais de Justice
15 Bus Stops
16 Prefecture Building
17 Palais de la Culture et de Congrès
18 Maison des Acrobates
19 Cathédrale Saint Louis
20 Hôtel de Ville
23 Laundrette
24 Sports Motos Cycles
25 Maison de la Magie
26 Point Bus Office
27 Château de Blois
29 Crédit Agricole
32 Église Saint Nicolas
33 Les Jacobins

Old City

Quartier Saint Nicolas

Loire River

FRANCE

Hostel The *Auberge de Jeunesse* (☎ 02 54 78 27 21), open during the same period as the camp site, is 4.5 km south-west of the train station at 18 Rue de l'Hôtel Pasquier in the village of Les Grouëts. Call before heading out there as it's often full. Beds in a dorm are 40FF and breakfast (optional) is 18FF. The hostel is closed from 10 am to 6 pm. To get there, take bus No 4, which runs until 7 or 7.30 pm, from Place de Valin-de-la-Vaissière.

Hotels Near the train station, your best bet is the friendly *Hôtel Saint Jacques* (☎ 02 54 78 04 15) at 7 Rue Ducoux. Basic doubles start at 125FF; with shower, toilet and TV they're 176FF. Just opposite at No 6-8, the family-run *Hôtel Le Savoie* (☎ 02 54 74 32 21) has well-kept singles/doubles with shower, toilet and TV for 210/230FF.

A couple of hundred metres north-west of the old city, the *Hôtel du Bellay* (☎ 02 54 78 23 62) at 12 Rue des Minimes has doubles for 135FF; hall showers are free. Doubles with shower are 160FF, or 185FF with shower, toilet and cable TV. The hotel is closed during February. Nearby, the *Hôtel L'Étoile d'Or* (☎ 02 54 78 46 93) at 7 Rue du Bourg Neuf has doubles from 120FF (240FF with shower and toilet). Hall showers cost 12FF. Another good medium-priced deal in this area is the *Hôtel Le Lys* (☎ 02 54 74 66 08) at 3 Rue des Cordeliers, where singles/doubles with shower are 200FF.

Places to Eat

Le Maïdi (☎ 02 54 74 38 58), a North African restaurant in the old city at 42 Rue Saint Lubin, serves excellent couscous from 55FF, and menus from 65FF. It's open till 10 or 11 pm daily except Thursday. *La Mesa* (☎ 02 54 78 70 70) is a pleasant place at 11 Rue Vauvert, up tiny Rue du Grenier à Sel from 44 Rue Foulerie. It serves good pizzas (from 35FF) and salads, and you can eat al fresco in the courtyard.

For something a bit more up-market, try the local favourite *Au Bouchon Lyonnais* (☎ 02 54 74 12 87) at 25 Rue des Violettes (above Rue Saint Lubin). Menus are 110 and 165FF. The restaurant is open daily except Monday. Another good bet is *Banquettes Rouges* (☎ 02 54 78 74 92), an old-fashioned bistro at 16 Rues des Trois Marchands with a menu at 120FF. By

far the best value in town is the restaurant *La Salamandre* (☎ 02 54 74 09 18) at 34 Rue Foulerie. Good four-course menus including an aperitif are 72 and 98FF. It is open every day except Saturday and Sunday midday.

In the old city, there's a food market along Rue Anne de Bretagne, off Place Louis XII, on Tuesday, Thursday and Saturday until 1 pm.

Getting There & Away

The train station (☎ 08 36 35 35 39) is at the western end of Ave Jean Laigret on Place de la Gare. The information office is open from 9 am to 6.30 pm daily except Sunday. Service between Blois and Paris' Gare d'Austerlitz takes about 1½ hours by direct train (119FF) but less than an hour via Orléans. Tours (50FF) is 30 minutes away and Bordeaux (228FF) is four hours by direct train (less if you change to a TGV at Saint Pierre des Corps near Tours).

Getting Around

Bus Buses within Blois proper – run by TUB – operate from Monday to Saturday until 7.30 pm (to 11 pm on Saturday). On Sundays, service is greatly reduced. All lines except TUB No 4 stop at the train station. Tickets cost 5.80FF or 39.50FF for a carnet of 10. For information, consult the Point Bus office (☎ 02 54 78 15 66) at 2 Place Victor Hugo beneath the chateau (closed Sunday).

Taxi Taxis (☎ 02 54 78 07 65) can be hired for trips into the Loire Valley (see Getting There & Away in the Blois Area Chateaux section).

Car & Bicycle See Getting There & Away in the Blois Area Chateaux section for rental information.

BLOIS AREA CHATEAUX

The Blois area is endowed with some of the finest chateaux in the Loire Valley, including the spectacular Château de Chambord, the magnificently furnished Château de Cheverny, the beautifully situated Château de Chaumont (also accessible from Tours) and the modest but more personal Beauregard. The town of Amboise (see the Tours Area Chateaux section) can also be reached from Blois. Don't try to visit too many though; you'll soon find yourself 'chateau-saturated'.

Organised Tours

Without your own wheels, the best way to see more than one chateau in one day is with an organised tour. The regional TLC bus company (same office as Point Bus; ☎ 02 54 78 15 66) in Blois offers two Circuits Châteaux itineraries (prices do not include admission fees): Chambord and Cheverny (65FF return, 50FF for students) and Chaumont and Chenonceau (110/90FF for students). Both operate daily from mid-June to mid-September and on weekends between late May and mid-June.

Getting There & Away

Bus TLC runs limited bus services to destinations in the vicinity of Blois. All times quoted here are approximate and should be verified with the company first. Buses depart from Place Victor Hugo (in front of the Point Bus office) and from the bus station to the left of the train station as you exit.

Taxi If there are a few of you, you might consider visiting one or several chateaux by taxi (☎ 02 54 78 07 65 in Blois), which can be boarded at the taxi booth just outside the train station. Sample fares on weekdays/Sundays are: Chaumont 250/350FF; Cheverny 240/340FF; Chambord 260/365. For 950/1340FF you can (somehow) manage Chaumont, Cheverny, Chambord, Amboise and Chenonceau in one day.

Car Avis (☎ 02 54 74 48 15) at 6 Rue Jean Moulin is open Monday to Saturday from 8 am to noon and 2 to 7 pm.

Bicycle The countryside around Blois, with its quiet country back roads, is perfect for cycling. Unfortunately, Chambord, Cheverny and Chaumont are each about 20 km from Blois. An excursion to all, which are 20 km apart, is a 60-km proposition – quite a bit for one day if you're not in shape. A 1:200,000 scale Michelin road map or a 1:50,000 scale IGN is indispensable to find your way around the rural back roads.

Sports Motos Cycles (☎ 02 54 78 02 64) at 6 Rue Henry Drussy rents 10-speeds at 35FF a day. It is open Tuesday to Saturday from 9 am to noon and 2 to 6.30 pm.

Château de Chambord

The Château de Chambord (☎ 02 54 20 40 18), begun in 1519 by François I (1515-47), is the largest and most visited chateau in the Loire Valley. Its Renaissance architecture and decoration, grafted onto a feudal ground plan, may have been inspired by Leonardo da Vinci who, at the invitation of the king, lived in Amboise (45 km south-west of here) from 1516 until his death three years later.

Chambord is the creation of François I, whose emblems – a royal monogram of the letter F and a salamander of a particularly fierce disposition – adorn many parts of the building. Though forced by liquidity problems to leave his two sons unransomed in Spain and to help himself to both the treasuries of his churches and his subjects' silver, the king kept 1800 workers and artisans at work on Chambord for 15 years. At one point he even demanded that the Loire River be rerouted so that it would pass by Chambord; eventually, a smaller river, the Cosson, was diverted instead (you can still see a bridge spanning dry land on the road from Blois). Molière first staged two of his most famous plays at Chambord to audiences that included Louis XIV.

The chateau's famed **double-helix staircase**, attributed by some to Leonardo, consists of two spiral staircases that wind around the same central axis but never meet. The rich ornamentation is in the style of the early French Renaissance. Of the chateau's 440 rooms, only about 10 are open to the public. Watch out for the **tapestries** in the lovely chapel, the **Count de Chambord bedroom** (a late 19th-century pretender to the throne) and the fine collection of **Dresden tiles** on the 1st floor.

The royal court used to assemble on the Italianate **rooftop terrace** to watch military exercises, tournaments and the hounds and hunters returning from a day of stalking deer. As you stand on the terrace (once described as resembling an overcrowded chessboard), you will see all around you the towers, cupolas, domes, chimneys, dormers and slate roofs with geometric shapes that create the chateau's imposing skyline.

Tickets to the chateau are on sale daily from 9.30 am to 5.15 pm (October to March), to 6.15 pm (April to June and in September) and to 7.15 pm (July and August). The entry fee is

36FF (22FF for those under 24). A brochure in English (3FF) is available, but there are good (multilingual) explanatory signs posted in the major rooms. There are also tours of the chateau in English; these last about an hour and the price is included in the entry fee. During July and August, a nursery is available for children over two years. A sound-and-light show (50FF or 40FF for students) takes place nightly at 10.30 pm between mid-June and mid-September and on weekends from mid-April to mid-June and mid-September to mid-October.

The Centre d'Information Touristique (☎ 02 54 20 34 86) is at Place Saint Michel, the parking lot surrounded by tourist shops. It's open from mid-March to September daily from 10 am to 6 pm.

Getting There & Away Chambord is 16 km east of Blois and 18 km north-east of Cheverny. During the school year, TLC line No 2 averages three daily return trips from Blois to Chambord (18.40FF one way). The first bus out to Chambord leaves Blois at 12.10 pm Monday to Saturday and at 1.45 pm on Sundays. The last bus back to Blois leaves Chambord at 6.45 pm every day except Friday (6.03 pm) and Sunday (5.15 pm). There is very limited service in July and August.

Getting Around Bicycles are available from the Centre d'Information Touristique for 25FF an hour, 40FF for two hours and 80FF a day.

Château de Cheverny

The Château de Cheverny (☎ 02 54 79 96 29), the most magnificently furnished of the Loire Valley chateaux and still privately owned, was completed in 1634. After entering the building through its finely-proportioned neoclassical façade, visitors are treated to some 17 sumptuous rooms outfitted with the finest of period appointments: canopied beds, tapestries (note the *Abduction of Helen* in the **Salle d'Armes**, the former armoury), paintings, mantelpieces, parquet floors, painted ceilings and walls covered with embossed Córdoba leather. The pamphlet provided is extremely useful. Don't miss the three dozen panels illustrating the story of *Don Quixote* in the 1st-floor dining room.

On exiting the chateau, you can visit the **Salle des Trophées** – exhibiting the antlers of almost 2000 stags – and the kennels where a pack of some 80 hounds are still kept.

Cheverny is open daily from 9.15 or 9.30 am to noon and 2.15 to 5 pm (November to February), to 5.30 pm (October and March), to 6 pm (the last half of September) or 6.30 pm (April and May). From June to mid-September, the chateau stays open every day from 9.15 am to 6.45 pm. The entry fee is 32FF (21FF for students).

Getting There & Away Cheverny is 15 km south-east of Blois. TLC bus No 4 from Blois to Romorantin stops at Cheverny. Buses leave Blois Monday to Saturday at 6.50 am and 12.20 pm, Sundays at 11.10 am. Heading back to Blois, the last buses depart before 7 pm from Monday to Saturday (6.30 pm during July and August) and at 8.25 pm on Sunday and holidays.

By car from Blois, follow route D765 south to Cour-Cheverny. From Chambord, take the D112 south to Bracieux and then head west on route D102.

Château de Beauregard

Beauregard (☎ 02 54 70 46 64), the closest chateau to Blois, is relatively modest in size and a bit scruffy on the outside, which somehow adds to its charm. Built in the early 16th century as a hunting lodge for François I and enlarged 100 years later, it is set in the middle of a large park which is now being converted (with EU assistance) to what will be one of the largest gardens (70 hectares) in Europe. The count and countess who own the place still live in one wing, which is why only five rooms are open to the public.

Beauregard's most famous feature is the **Galerie des Portraits** on the 1st floor, featuring 327 portraits of 'who was who' in France from the 14th to 17th centuries. The floor is very unusual also, covered with 17th-century Dutch tiles.

From April to September, Beauregard is open daily from 9.30 am to noon and 2 to 6.30 pm; there is no closure at midday during July and August. During the rest of the year (except from mid-January to mid-February, when it's closed), the chateau is open from 9.30 am to noon and 2 to 5 pm daily except Wednesday. Entry is 35FF (25FF for students under 25 and people over 60).

Getting There & Away The Château de Beauregard, only six km south of Blois, makes a good destination for a short bike ride. There is road access to the chateau from both the D765 (the Blois-Cheverny road) and the D956 (turn left at the village of Cellettes).

TLC bus No 5 heading towards the town of Saint Aignan stops at the village of Cellettes, one km south-west of the chateau, on Wednesday, Friday and Saturday. The first leaves at noon. Unfortunately, there is no afternoon bus back except the one operated by Transports Boutet (☎ 02 54 34 43 95), which passes through Cellettes at about 6.30 pm from Monday to Saturday and at about 6 pm on Sunday (except during August).

Château de Chaumont

The Château de Chaumont (☎ 02 54 20 98 03), set on a bluff overlooking the Loire, looks as much like a feudal castle as any chateau in the area. Built in the late 15th century, it served as a 'booby prize' for Diane de Poitier when her lover, Henry II, died in 1559, and hosted Benjamin Franklin several times when he served as ambassador to France after the American Revolution. The luxurious **stables** (*écuries*) are Chaumont's most famous feature, but the **Salle du Conseil** (Council Chamber) on the 1st floor with its majolica-tile floor and tapestries and **Catherine de' Medici's bedroom** overlooking the chapel are remarkable.

Tickets are on sale daily from 10 am to 4.30 pm (9.30 am to 6 pm from mid-March to mid-October); the chateau stays open for half an hour after sales end. The entry fee is 28FF (18FF for people under 24). The park around the chateau, with its many cedar trees, is open daily from 9 am to 5 pm (7 pm from April to September).

Wine Tasting There are many wine cellars in the area offering tastings; consult the tourist office (☎ 02 54 20 91 73) just below the chateau on Rue du Maréchal Leclerc as times vary. From around Easter to September, for example, there is free tasting in the small building 50 metres up Rue du Village Neuf from the beginning of the path up to the chateau.

Getting There & Away The Château de Chaumont is 21 km south-west of Blois and 15 km north-east of Amboise in the village of Chaumont-sur-Loire. The path leading up to the park and the chateau begins at the intersection of Rue du Village Neuf and Rue Maréchal Leclerc (route D751). By rail, you can take a local train on the Orléans-Tours line and get off at Onzain (16FF), which is a two-km walk across the river from the chateau.

TOURS

While Blois remains essentially medieval in layout and small-townish in atmosphere, Tours (population 136,000) has the cosmopolitan and bourgeois air of a real French provincial city. Tours was devastated by German bombardment and an accompanying fire in June 1940; much of it has been rebuilt since WWII. It is said that the French spoken in Tours is the purest in all of France.

Orientation

Tours' focal point is Place Jean Jaurès, where the city's major thoroughfares (Rue Nationale, Blvd Heurteloup, Ave de Grammont and Blvd Béranger) join up. The train station is 300 metres to the east along Blvd Heurteloup. The old city, centred around Place Plumereau, is about 400 metres west of Rue Nationale.

Information

Tourist Office The tourist office (☎ 02 47 70 37 37) is at 78-82 Rue Bernard Palissy opposite the new Centre International de Congrès (International Convention Centre). From June to September, the office is open Monday to Saturday from 8.30 am to 7 pm and on Sunday from 10 am to 12.30 pm and 3 to 6 pm. The rest of the year it opens daily from 9 am to 12.30 pm and 1.30 to 6 pm and on Sunday from 10 am to 1 pm.

Money & Post Most banks in Tours are closed on Monday. The Crédit Agricole (☎ 02 47 20 84 85), just east of the train station at 10 Rue Édouard Vaillant, is open Tuesday to Saturday from 9 am to 12.30 pm and 1.30 to 5.15 pm (4.15 pm on Friday). Banque de France, at 2

FRANCE

Rue Chanoineau, has similar opening hours but closes at 3.30 pm.

The main post office (☎ 02 47 60 34 20) is 200 metres west of Place Jean Jaurès on 1 Blvd Béranger. It also offers currency exchange. Tours' postcode is 37000.

Things to See

Walking Tour Tours is a great city for strolling. Areas worth exploring include the **old city** around Place Plumereau, which is surrounded by half-timbered houses, **Rue du Grand Marché** and **Rue Colbert**. Also of interest is the neighbourhood around the Musée des Beaux-Arts, which includes **Cathédrale Saint Gatien**, built between 1220 and 1547 and renowned for its spectacular 13th and 15th-century stained glass. It is open from 8.30 am to noon and 2 to 7.30 pm (8 pm in July and August). Tours of the cathedral's Renaissance **cloître** (cloister) can be visited with a guide (14FF) daily except Sunday morning from 10 am to noon and 2 to 5 pm (9 am to noon and 2 to 6 pm from April to September).

Museums The tourist office offers a 'Carte multi-visite' for 50FF allowing entry to seven museums in Tours.

The **Musée Archéologique de Touraine** (☎ 02 47 66 22 32) is at 25 Rue du Commerce in the Hôtel Goüin, a splendid Renaissance residence built around 1510 for a wealthy merchant. Its Italian-style façade, all that was left after the 1940 conflagration, is worth seeing even if the eclectic assemblage of pottery, scientific instruments, art etc inside doesn't interest you. The museum is open from 10 am to 12.30 pm and 2 to 5.30 or 6.30 pm; in July and August, it's open until 7 pm. Entry is 18FF (15FF for students).

The **Musée du Compagnonnage** (☎ 02 47 61 07 93) overlooking the courtyard of **Église Saint Julien** at 8 Rue Nationale, is a celebration of the skill of the French artisan; exhibits include examples of woodcarving, metalwork and even cake-icing. It's open every day except Tuesday from 9 am to noon and 2 to 5 or 6 pm, and from 9 am to 6.30 pm (mid-June to mid-September). Tickets cost 21FF (12FF for students). The **Musée des Vins de Touraine** (Museum of Touraine Wines; ☎ 02 47 61 07 93), a few metres away at No 16, is in the 13th-century wine cellars of Église Saint Julien. Hours are the same as those of the Musée du Campagnonnage, and so is the level of interest: neither are must-sees. Entry costs 12FF (6FF for students).

The **Musée des Beaux-Arts** (☎ 02 47 05 68 73) at 18 Place François Sicard has a good collection of works from the 14th to 20th centuries but is especially proud of two 15th-century altar paintings by the Italian painter Andrea Mantegna, brought from Italy by Napoleon. The museum is open every day except Tuesday from 9 am to 12.45 pm and 2 to 6 pm. Entry costs 30FF (15FF for students).

Places to Stay

Camping The *Camping Édouard Péron* (☎ 02 47 54 11 11) at Place Édouard Péron, about 2.5 km north-east of the train station on the north bank of the Loire, is open from June to mid-September. To get there, take bus No 7 towards Sainte Radegonde Ermitage. The per-person charge is 14FF and a tent site is 10 to 18FF.

Hostels At 16 Rue Bernard Palissy, 400 metres north of the train station, *Le Foyer* (☎ 02 47 60 51 51) has singles/doubles for 80/160FF. Reception is open weekdays from 9 am to 7 pm (to 2.30 pm on Saturday).

The *Auberge de Jeunesse* (☎ 02 47 25 14 45) is five km south of the train station in Parc de Grand Mont. A bed with/without breakfast costs 63/45FF a night, and sheets/sleeping bag are an extra 17FF. Rooms are locked from 10 am to 5 pm. To get there, take bus No 1 or 6 from Place Jean Jaurès (Auberge de Jeunesse stop). Between about 9.30 pm and midnight, take the Bleu de Nuit line N1 (southbound) and get off at the Monge stop.

Hotels Most of the cheapest hotels – those close to the train station – are pretty basic. The ones near the river are slightly more expensive but are also good value.

Train Station Area The cheapest hotel in town is the *Tours Hôtel* (☎ 02 47 05 59 35), directly to the east of the train station at 10 Rue Édouard Vaillant. Basic singles/doubles start at 70/75FF, and a two-bed quad is 120FF. Showers cost 10FF. On the other side of the station, the

PLACES TO STAY

6 Hôtel Colbert
7 Hôtel Voltaire
13 Hôtel Berthelot
14 Hôtel Regina
24 Le Foyer
33 Hôtel Olympia
35 Hôtel de l'Europe
37 Tours Hôtel
42 Hôtel Thé au Rhum & Restaurant
43 Hôtel Français
45 Hôtel Comté
50 Hôtel Vendôme

PLACES TO EAT

4 Restaurant Les Tuffeaux
5 Au Lapin qui Fume
12 Le Yang Tse Restaurant
16 Restaurants & Food Shops
17 Nuit de Saïgon
36 Surya Indian Restaurant
46 Le Centenaire
48 Le Point du Jour

OTHER

1 Municipal Library
2 Monument des Américains
3 Château de Tours
8 Église Saint Julien
9 Musée du Compagnonnage
10 Musée des Vins de Touraine
11 Musée Archéologique de Touraine (Hôtel Goüin)
15 Théâtre
18 Laundrette
19 Cathédrale Saint Gatien
20 Musée des Beaux-Arts
21 Flower Garden
22 Chapelle Saint Michel
23 Laundrette
25 Prefecture Building
26 Basilique Saint Martin
27 Les Halles (Covered Food Market)
28 Banque de France
29 Main Post Office
30 Palais de Justice
31 Hôtel de Ville
32 Centre International de Congrès
34 Tourist Office, Eurolines & Europcar
38 Crédit Agricole
39 Gare Routière (Bus Terminal)
40 Atac Supermarket
41 Fil Bleu Office (Local Bus Information)
44 Train Station & Amster Cycles
47 Église Saint Étienne
49 Boulangerie-Pâtisserie Dardeau

Tours

To Amboise (23 km)
To Camping Édouard Péron (2 km) & Vouvray (10 km)
Loire River
Pont de Fil (Pedestrian Bridge)
Pont Wilson
Place Anatole France
Rue Albert Thomas
Rue Lavoisier
Place de la Cathédrale
Rue des Ursulines
Rue Jules Simon
Boulevard Heurteloup
Rue Édouard Vaillant
Rue Bernard Palissy
Rue François Sicard
Jardin de la Préfecture
Place du Général Leclerc
Rue Blaise Pascal
Place des Aumônes
To ADA Car Rental, Cher River (1.5 km) & Auberge de Jeunesse (4.5 km)
Quai d'Orléans
Rue des Jacobins
Rue du Cygne
Place François Sicard
Rue Buffon
Rue Victor Laloux
Rue Michelet
Rue Auguste Comté
Rue de Bordeaux
Rue Gilles
Rue Chalmel
Avenue de Grammont
Rue des Minimes
Rue Colbert
Rue Voltaire
Rue de la Scellerie
Rue Émile Zola
Rue Berthelot
Rue Nationale
Place Jean Jaurès
Rue Victor Hugo
Rue des Halles
Rue Marceau
Rue Georges Sand
Rue d'Entraigues
Rue Roger Salengro
Jardin des Prébendes d'Oé
Place de la Résistance
Rue des Déportés
Rue du Commerce
Rue Marceau
Rue de Jérusalem
Rue de Constantine
Rue Néricault Destouches
Rue de la Grandière
Boulevard Béranger
Rue Jehan Fouquet
Rue de Clocheville
Rue Rabelais
Rue Chanoineau
Old City
Rue des Tanneurs
Rue de la Paix
Rue Briçonneau
Rue du Grand Marché
Rue Bretonneau
Rue Dr Bretonneau
Rue de la Grosse Tour
Place Gaston Paihou
Rue de la Victoire
Place de la Victoire
Rue des Halles
Rue Plumereau

0   100   200 m

FRANCE

Hôtel Français (☎ 02 47 05 59 12) at 11 Rue de Nantes has simple singles/doubles for 120FF, or 150/180FF with shower. Hall showers cost 10FF. Neither of these places accepts telephone reservations. A couple of metres north of the tourist office, the friendly *Hôtel Olympia* (☎ 02 47 05 10 17) at 74 Rue Bernard Palissy has singles/doubles from 95FF, or 135FF with shower. Shower-equipped rooms for up to four people are 200FF.

The *Hôtel Thé Au Rhum* (☎ 02 47 05 06 99) at 4-6 Place des Aumônes has clean singles/doubles/triples from 90/110/140FF. Hall showers are free. Reception is closed on Sundays and holidays. Another good choice is *Hôtel Comté* (☎ 02 47 05 53 16) at 51 Rue Auguste Comte. Basic singles/doubles/triples start at 74/97/130FF.

An excellent choice a bit further from the station to the south-west is *Hôtel Vendôme* (☎ 02 47 64 33 54) at 24 Rue Roger Salengro. This cheerful place, run by a very friendly couple, has simple but decent singles/doubles starting at 105/110FF. A triple with shower is 210FF. Hall showers cost 15FF. If you can afford a bit more, the *Hôtel de l'Europe* (☎ 02 47 05 42 07) at 12 Place du Maréchal Leclerc has high ceilings and carpeted hallways that give it a sort of belle époque ambience. Rooms with shower and toilet are 250/300FF a single/double; triples cost from 320 to 350FF.

River Area The *Hôtel Voltaire* (☎ 02 47 05 77 51) is 900 metres north of the train station at 13 Rue Voltaire. Comfortable but rather noisy singles/doubles start at 100FF, or 130FF with shower. Hall showers are 15FF. A two-bed triple with shower costs 170FF. The *Hôtel Regina* (☎ 02 47 05 25 36) is due south at 2 Rue Pimbert. Well-maintained singles/doubles start at 105/120FF, or 135/165FF with shower. Hall showers cost 15FF. The *Hôtel Berthelot* (☎ 02 47 05 71 95), a block west at 8 Rue Berthelot, has clean, basic doubles for 105/125FF without/with shower. Two-bed triples with shower cost 175FF.

A cut above in this area is the *Hôtel Colbert* (☎ 02 47 66 61 56) at 78 Rue Colbert, with large singles/doubles with shower, toilet and TV for 225/260FF.

Places to Eat
In the old city, Place Plumereau and Rue du Commerce are filled with bars, cafés, crêperies, pâtisseries and restaurants.

Near Place Plumereau at 83bis Rue du Commerce is *Le Yang Tse* (☎ 02 47 61 47 59), a Chinese/Vietnamese restaurant which has main dishes from 30 to 35FF. It's open daily till around midnight.

There are plenty of places to splurge along or just off Rue Colbert, including *Restaurant Les Tuffeaux* (☎ 02 47 47 19 89) at 19-21 Rue Lavoisier which is open until 9.30 pm daily except Sunday and Monday at midday. The innovative cuisine gastronomique is made with lots of fresh local products. Menus are 110 to 200FF, and reservations are a good idea on weekends. Another good place – more relaxed and much cheaper with menus from 65FF – is *Au Lapin qui Fume* (☎ 02 47 66 95 49) at 90 Rue Colbert. It's open for lunch and dinner every day except Tuesday evening and Sunday.

Near the train station, *Le Centenaire* (☎ 02 47 61 86 93) at 39 Rue Blaise Pascal prides itself on its home-made, classic French cuisine. It's open daily except Monday evening and all day Sunday, and has menus for 52 and 59FF. *Thé Au Rhum* (☎ 02 47 05 06 99), on the ground floor of the hotel, has crêpes (10 to 35FF), meat dishes (30 to 45FF) and menus (45 to 70FF).

Surya (☎ 02 47 64 34 04), at 65 Rue Colbert, is a North Indian restaurant open every day but Monday lunch.

Les Halles covered market, 500 metres west of Rue Nationale at Place Gaston Pailhou, is open daily until 7 pm and Sunday until 1 pm. The *Atac* supermarket in front of the train station at 5 Place du Maréchal Leclerc is open weekdays to 8 pm (Sunday to 12.30 pm). For a good selection of freshly baked bread and exquisite cakes and tarts, try the *Boulangerie-Pâtisserie Dardeau* (☎ 02 47 64 35 18) on 29 Ave de Grammont. It's open from 7 am to 1 pm and from 4 to 7.30 pm. The strawberry tarts are to die for.

Getting There & Away
Bus The long-haul international carrier Eurolines (☎ 02 47 66 45 56) has a ticket office next to the tourist office at 76 Rue Bernard Palissy. It's open Monday to Saturday from 9 am to noon and 1.30 to 6.30 pm. La Compagnie

d'Autocars de Touraine (CAT; ☎ 02 47 37 81 81) handles services within the department of Indre-et-Loire. Schedules are posted at the bus terminal, which is in front of the train station at Place du Maréchal Leclerc. The information office is open from 7 am to 12.15 pm and 2 to 6.30 pm Monday to Friday and on Saturday from 8 am to 12.15 pm and 2 to 5.30 pm. See each Getting There & Away section under Tours Area Chateaux for details.

Train The train station (☎ 08 36 35 35 39) is off Blvd Heurteloup at Place du Maréchal Leclerc. The information office is open Monday to Saturday from 8.30 am to 6.30 pm. Paris' Gare Montparnasse is about an hour away by TGV (196 to 251FF). There is also service to Paris' Gare d'Austerlitz, Bordeaux (218FF, 2½ hours) and Nantes (134FF, two hours). Some of the chateaux around Tours can be reached by train or SNCF bus, both of which accept Eurail passes. See the Getting There & Away section under Tours Area Chateaux for details.

Car Europcar (☎ 02 47 64 47 76), next to the tourist office at 76 Blvd Bernard Palissy, is open from 8 am to noon and 2 to 6.30 pm Monday to Saturday.

Getting Around
Bus Fil Bleu is the bus network serving Tours and its suburbs. Almost all lines stop near Place Jean Jaurès. Three Bleu de Nuit lines operate about every hour from around 9.15 pm to just after midnight. Tickets (6.50FF) are valid for one hour after being time-stamped; a carnet of five/10 tickets is 29/56FF. A day pass costs 23FF.

Fil Bleu has an information office (☎ 02 47 66 70 70) in the Jean Jaurès centre, at 5bis Rue de la Dolve, 50 metres west of Place Jean Jaurès. It's open daily except Sunday from 7.30 am to 7 pm (9 am to 6.30 pm on Saturday).

Taxi Call Taxi Radio (☎ 02 47 20 30 40) to order a cab 24 hours a day.

Bicycle See the Getting There & Away section under Tours Area Chateaux for information on renting a bike.

TOURS AREA CHATEAUX
Tours makes a good base for visits to some of the Loire chateaux, including Chenonceau (which you can also visit on a tour from Blois), Azay-le-Rideau, Amboise (also accessible from Blois) and Chaumont (listed under Blois Area Châteaux). If you have a Eurail pass, more chateaux can be reached from Tours than from any other railhead in the region.

Organised Tours
Three companies offer English-language tours of the chateaux. Reservations can be made at the Tours tourist office or you can phone the company directly. Prices quoted here do not include entrance fees – a major expense if you go alone – but you will benefit from group prices on arrival with a tour.

Touraine Évasion (☎ 02 47 60 30 00), which uses minibuses, charges from 75 to 170FF for half-day and from 215 to 245FF for full-day tours. Half-day tours with Acco-Dispo (☎ 02 47 57 67 13) are from 100 to 130FF, and from 180 to 200FF for full days. Services Touristiques de Touraine (☎ 02 47 58 32 06), based at the train station, has bus tours from 158 to 176FF for a half-day and 245 to 260FF for a full day.

Getting There & Away
Bus CAT (☎ 02 47 37 81 81) runs a limited bus service to the area around Tours every day except Sunday. If you work fast, you can see two chateaux – Chenonceau and Amboise – by public transport on the same day. Take the bus from Quai 7 at the bus station in Tours to Chenonceaux (the town has an 'x' at the end) at 10 am, arriving at 11.14 am, and have a quick look at the chateau. The bus to Amboise leaves at 12.40 pm and returns to Tours at 5.25 pm. The total price is 65.90FF.

All times quoted are approximate, so verify them before making plans.

Train Some of the chateaux (including Azay-le-Rideau, Chenonceau and Chaumont) can be reached from Tours by train or SNCF bus. In summer, certain trains allow you to take a bicycle along free of charge, which makes it possible to cycle either there or back. For up-to-date schedules, ask for the brochure *Les Châteaux de la Loire en Train* at the Tours train station.

Bicycle From May to September, Amster Cycles (☎ 02 47 61 22 23) has a rental point inside the train station. For an 18-speed/ tandem the price is 65/140FF per day (cheaper for longer periods). They can also lend you maps.

Château de Chenonceau

With its stylised (rather than defensive) moat, drawbridge, towers and turrets straddling the Cher River, 16th-century Chenonceau (☎ 02 47 23 90 07) is everything you imagine a fairy-tale castle to be. The chateau's interior, however, filled with period furniture, tourists, paintings, tourists, tapestries and more tourists, is of only moderate interest.

One of the series of remarkable women who created Chenonceau, Diane de Poitiers, mistress of King Henri II, planted the garden to the left (east) as you approach the chateau down the avenue of plane trees. After Henri's death in 1559, she was forced to give up her beloved Chenonceau by the vengeful Catherine de' Medici, Henri's wife. Catherine then applied her own formidable energies to the chateau and, among other works, laid out the garden to the west. (Diane's is prettier.)

The 60-metre-long **Galerie**, spanning the Cher River, was built by Catherine de' Medici and was converted into a hospital during WWI. Between 1940 and 1942, the demarcation line between Vichy-ruled France and the German-occupied zone ran down the middle of the Cher. For many people trying to escape to Vichy, this room served as a crossing point. Two other must-see rooms are Catherine's lovely little **library** on the ground floor with the oldest original ceiling (1521) in the castle and the **bedroom** where Louise de Lorraine lived out her final days after the assassination of her husband, Henri III, in 1589. Macabre illustrations of bones, skulls, shovels and teardrops adorn the walls.

Chenonceau is open all year from 9 am to 4.30 pm from mid-November to January, until 5 to 6.30 pm for the rest of the year (check with the tourist office for exact times). From mid-March to mid-September it's open until 7 pm. The entry fee is 40FF (25FF for students). You'll be given an easy-to-follow tour brochure in English as you enter.

Getting There & Away The Château de Chenonceau is 34 km east of Tours, 10 km south-east of Amboise and 40 km south-west of Blois. A couple of trains a day go from Tours to the town of Chenonceaux (33FF one way), 500 metres from the chateau. There are two CAT buses a day from Monday to Saturday, one departing at 10 am, the other at 2.15 pm; both take about an hour. The one-way/return fare is 36.60/65.90FF.

Château d'Azay-le-Rideau

Azay-le-Rideau (☎ 02 47 45 42 04), built on an island in the Indre River and surrounded by a quiet pool and lovely park, is one of the most harmonious and elegant of the Loire chateaux. It is adorned with stylised fortifications and turrets intended both as decoration and to indicate the owners' rank. But only seven rooms are open to the public, and their contents are disappointing (apart from a few 16th-century Flemish tapestries). The self-guiding brochure is a bit sketchy.

The chateau can be visited daily from October to March from 9 am to noon and 2 to 5.30 pm. From April to June and in September it's open from 9.30 am to 6 pm. During July and August, the hours are from 9 am to 7 pm. Tickets cost 32FF (21FF under 25). There's a sound-and-light show nightly from May to September at 10 or 10.30 pm (60FF).

Getting There & Away Azay-le-Rideau is 26 km south-west of Tours. SNCF has a year-round service two or three times a day from Tours to Azay (the station is 2.5 km from the chateau) by either train or bus for 27FF one way. The train is faster, but the bus goes direct to the chateau. The last train/bus back to Tours leaves Azay at about 6 pm (just after 8 pm on Sunday).

Amboise

The picturesque hillside town of Amboise (population 11,400), an easy day trip from Tours, is known for its chateau which reached the pinnacle of its importance around the turn of the 16th century.

Tourist Office The tourist office (Accueil d'Amboise; ☎ 02 47 57 09 28), along the river opposite 7 Quai Général de Gaulle, is open

Monday to Saturday from 9 am to 12.30 pm and from 2 or 3 pm to 6 or 6.30 pm, depending on the season. Between mid-June and mid-September there's no midday break and the office stays open to 8.30 pm. It also keeps Sunday hours from 10 am to noon and 4 to 7 pm. 'Passport tickets' which allow entry to Amboise's five museums are available for 80FF.

Château d'Amboise The rocky outcrop overlooking the town has been fortified since Gallo-Roman times, but the Château d'Amboise (☎ 02 47 57 00 98), which now lies atop it, began to take form in the 11th and 12th centuries. King Charles VIII, who grew up here, began work to enlarge it in 1492 after a visit to Italy, the artistic creativity and luxurious lifestyle of which had deeply impressed him. François I lived here during the first few years of his reign, a wild period marked by balls, masquerade parties and tournaments.

The chateau's ramparts and open gallery afford a panoramic view of the town, the Loire Valley and – on a clear day – Tours. The most notable features of the chateau are the **Tour des Chevaliers**, with a vaulted spiral ramp once used to ride horses in and out of the castle, and the Flamboyant Gothic **Chapelle Saint Hubert**, with a curious spire decorated with antlers. The remains of Leonardo da Vinci (1452-1519), who lived in Amboise for the last three years of his life, are supposedly under the chapel's northern transept. Exit the chateau via the souvenir shop: the side door leads to the 15th-century **Tour Hurtault**, whose interior consists of a circular ramp decorated with sculptured faces, animals and angels.

The entrance to the chateau is on Rue François Ier, a block east of Quai Général de Gaulle. It's open daily from 9 am to noon and 2 to 5 or 6.30 pm, depending on the season. During July and August, the hours are 9 am to 6.30 pm without a break. The entry fee is 34FF (24FF for students under 26). Tours are in French only, but you are given a fact sheet in the language of your choice.

Le Clos Lucé Leonardo da Vinci came to Amboise at the invitation of François I in 1516. Until his death at the age of 67 three years later, Leonardo lived and worked in Le Clos Lucé

(☎ 02 47 57 62 88), a 15th-century brick manor house 500 metres south-east of the chateau on Rue Victor Hugo. The building now contains restored rooms and scale models of some 40 of Leonardo's inventions – including a proto-automobile, armoured tank, parachute and hydraulic turbine. It's a fascinating place with a lovely garden, watchtower and recorded Renaissance music – infinitely more evocative of the age than the chateau. Le Clos Lucé is open daily from 9 am to 7 pm (closed in January). The entry fee is 37FF (28FF for students). Rue Victor Hugo to Clos Lucé passes several troglodyte dwellings – caves in the limestone hillside in which local people still live (with all the mod cons and a mortgage, of course).

Wine Tasting If you are driving, you can't see for all the *caves* (wine cellars) and wine-tasting places on route No 751, which runs parallel to the Loire (south side) from Chaumont. Closer to town the Caveau de Dégustation (wine-tasting cellar run by local growers; ☎ 02 47 57 23 69), in the base of the south side of the chateau, is open from April to September daily from 10 am to 7 pm.

Getting There & Away Amboise is 23 km east of Tours and 35 km west of Blois. Several trains a day between those two cities stop right across the river from Amboise (27FF one way from Tours). The last train back to Tours departs around 8.30 pm. From Tours, you can also take the CAT bus from Quai No 7 (23.50/42.30FF one way/return).

South-Western France

The south-western part of France includes a number of diverse regions, ranging from the Bordeaux wine-growing area near the beach-lined Atlantic seaboard to the Basque Country and the Pyrenees mountains in the south. There is convenient rail transport from this region to Paris, Spain and the Côte d'Azur.

LA ROCHELLE
La Rochelle (population 78,000) is a lively city midway down France's Atlantic coast and is

popular with middle-class French families and students on holiday. A university opened there in 1995, further boosting the student population. The nearby Île de Ré is surrounded by tens of km of fine-sand beaches. The quais of La Rochelle are lined with pleasant cafés and bars.

La Rochelle was one of France's most important seaports between the 14th and 17th centuries, and it was here that Protestantism first took root in France, incurring the wrath of Catholic authorities during the Wars of Religion in the latter half of the 16th century. In 1628 this Huguenot stronghold surrendered to Louis XIII's forces after all but 5000 of its 28,000 residents had starved to death during a 15-month siege orchestrated by Cardinal Richelieu, the principal minister to Louis XIII. There was a German submarine base here during WWII; Allied attacks on it devastated La Rochelle.

Orientation

The old city is at the northern end of Quai Valin, which runs more or less north-south along the Vieux Port (old port). Quai Valin is linked to the train station – 500 metres southeast – by Ave du Général de Gaulle. To get to Place du Marché, with a covered market and lots of restaurants, walk 250 metres north along Rue des Merciers from the old city's Hôtel de Ville. Rue du Palais, with its arcades and 18th-century merchants' homes, is the main shopping street.

Information

The tourist office (☎ 05 46 41 14 68) is in Le Gabut, the area due west of where Quai Valin and Ave du Général de Gaulle meet. It is open Monday to Saturday from 9 am to 12.30 pm and 2 to 6 pm. From June to September, opening hours are Monday to Saturday from 9 am to 7 pm (8 pm in July and August) and Sunday from 11 am to 5 pm.

The Banque de France is at 22 Rue Réaumur. The main post office (☎ 05 46 30 41 35) is to the north-east on Place de l'Hôtel de Ville. La Rochelle's postcode is 17000.

Things to See & Do

Old City To protect the harbour at night and defend it in times of war, a chain used to be stretched between the two 14th-century stone towers at the harbour entrance. Visitors can climb to the top of the 36-metre **Tour Saint Nicolas** (☎ 05 46 41 74 13) daily except Tuesday between 9.30 am and 12.30 pm and from 2 to 6.30 pm for 22FF (10FF for students). It's open every day to 7 pm in July and August with no midday break. **Tour de la Chaîne** (☎ 05 46 50 52 36), which houses a rather corny exhibition called 'La Rochelle in the Middle Ages', costs 20FF (12FF for students). West along the old city wall is **Tour de la Lanterne** (☎ 05 46 41 56 04), which was used for a long time as a prison. It now houses a museum with essentially the same hours and entry fees as the other two towers. The English-language graffiti you'll see on the walls was written by English privateers held here during the 18th century.

Parts of the **Tour de la Grosse Horloge** (☎ 05 46 51 51 51), the imposing clock tower on Quai Duperré, were built in the 13th century but most of it dates from the 18th century. From July to mid-September, the archaeological museum (15FF) inside is open from 10 am to 7 pm. There's an excellent view of the city from the roof.

The **Hôtel de Ville** (☎ 05 46 41 14 68) at Place de l'Hôtel de Ville in the old city was begun in the late 15th century and still houses the municipal government. Guided tours of the interior (16FF, 10FF for students) take place on Saturday and Sunday at 3 pm and daily from June to September.

Île de Ré & Beaches The Île de Ré, a 30-km-long island whose eastern tip is nine km west of La Rochelle's centre, is reached by a three-km toll bridge. In summer, the island's many beaches are a favourite destination for families with young children. The island is accessible from Quai Valin and the train station by Autoplus bus No 1, which goes to Sablanceaux (the narrow bit of the island nearest La Rochelle). The entire island is served by Rébus (☎ 05 46 09 20 15 in Saint Martin de Ré) from Place de Verdun and the train station. Eight buses a day go to both Saint Martin de Ré (23FF one way) and La Flotte (17FF). If you decide to drive, be prepared for the 110FF bridge toll from June to September (60FF at other times).

Another excellent beach about 10 km south of La Rochelle is **Châtelaillon**. It is accessible by Autoplus bus No 16.

Places to Stay

During July and August, most places in La Rochelle are full by noon and prices are higher than during the rest of the year.

Camping In summer, many camping grounds open up in the La Rochelle area, especially on the Île de Ré. The closest is *Camping du Soleil* (☎ 05 46 44 42 53) on Ave des Minimes in Les Minimes, a beachside suburb of La Rochelle about 1.5 km south of the city centre. It's open from mid-May to mid-September and is often full. Two people with a tent are charged about 45FF. From Quai Valin or the train station, take bus No 10.

Hostel The *Auberge de Jeunesse* (☎ 05 46 44 43 11) is half a km south of Camping du Soleil on Ave des Minimes. Beds are 72FF and singles/doubles are from 107FF including breakfast. There's a bus service (No 10; get off at the Lycée Hôtelier stop) until about 7.15 pm.

Hotels The *Hôtel Henri IV* (☎ 05 46 41 25 79), near the Vieux Port at 31 Rue des Gentilshommes, has doubles from 150FF but for 50FF more you get a room with shower, toilet and TV. Just south, the *Hôtel de Bordeaux* (☎ 05 46 41 31 22) at 43-45 Rue Saint Nicolas has pleasant singles/doubles for 145FF (185FF from May to September). For something a little more up-market, try *Hôtel de l'Arrivée et des Voyageurs* (☎ 05 46 41 40 68), some 50 metres south at 5 Rue de la Fabrique. Its comfortable doubles/quads with shower, toilet and TV are 275/440FF (cheaper off season). Breakfast is 30FF.

A number of cheap hotels can be found in the vicinity of Place du Marché, 250 metres north of the old city. The renovated *Hôtel Printania* (☎ 05 46 41 22 86) at 9 Rue du Brave Rondeau has singles/doubles from 150FF and triples/quads with shower for 195FF. Hall showers cost 10FF. Breakfast is 28FF. The *Hôtel de la Paix* (☎ 05 46 41 33 44), housed in an 18th-century building at 14 Rue Gargoulleau, has a few doubles for 150FF (170FF with shower, 180FF with shower and toilet). There are also triples and quads with shower for 230 to 310FF. Hall showers are free.

One of the nicest hotels in La Rochelle and convenient to the Place du Marché is the *Hôtel François Ier* (☎ 05 46 41 28 46) at tranquil 13-15 Rue Bazoges. It has doubles with all the mod cons for 278 to 475FF (cheaper in winter). Several French kings stayed in this building in the 15th and 16th centuries.

Places to Eat

There's always room at the *Brasserie Spaten* (☎ 05 46 41 42 88), a large seafood place at 15 Quai Valin with a 79FF menu. It's open daily from noon to midnight. A pizzeria in the immediate area can be recommended: the friendly *Papageno* (☎ 05 46 41 05 34) at 46 Rue Saint Nicolas. Homesick Yanks may want to try *Molly's Lone Star* (☎ 05 46 41 57 05) at 16 Rue de la Chaîne with buffalo wings, chilli, real cheeseburgers and brownies. It's open seven days a week from noon to 1 am.

Two areas chock-a-block with restaurants are the streets around the Place du Marché and Rue Saint Jean du Pérot, which is west of the Vieux Port. Choose the former for ethnic eateries – Moroccan, Chinese, Vietnamese – and food shops. On Rue Saint Jean du Pérot, three French restaurants worthy of a splurge are *La Marmite* (☎ 05 46 41 17 03) at No 14 with seafood menus from 185FF (closed Wednesday); the more reasonably priced *L'Assiette Saint Jean* (☎ 05 46 41 75 75) at No 18 with a 95FF seafood menu; and *Bistro l'Entr'acte* (☎ 05 46 50 62 60) at No 22 with an astonishing three-course meal for 145FF (closed Sunday).

Coop, a small grocery store near the Hôtel de Bordeaux on Rue Sardinerie, is open daily from 9 am to 1 pm and from 4 to 9 pm. For the sweetest North African pastries this side of the Mediterranean, try *El Souk* at 3 Rue de la Ferté which is open to 7.30 pm Tuesday to Saturday. It also has an excellent choice of olives and nuts.

Getting There & Away

Bus Océcars (☎ 05 46 00 21 01) and Citram (☎ 05 46 99 01 36 in Rochefort), which handle destinations in the department of Charente-Maritime, have buses which stop at Place de Verdun.

Train La Rochelle's train station (☎ 08 36 35 35 39) is at the southern end of Ave du Général de Gaulle. The information office is open

Monday to Saturday from 9 am to 6.45 pm. Destinations served by direct trains include: Bordeaux (131FF, two hours); Nantes (123FF, two hours); Marseille (404FF, nine hours); and Toulouse (243FF, 4½ hours). From Paris (320FF), you can take a TGV from Gare Montparnasse (three hours) or a non-TGV from Gare d'Austerlitz (five hours), which usually requires a change at Poitiers.

Getting Around

Bus Local buses run by Autoplus (☎ 05 46 34 02 22) all stop at the central station (gare centrale) on Place de Verdun. Most of the 10 lines run until sometime between 7.15 and 8 pm. A single ticket is 8FF; one-day and three-day passes are available for 24FF (including bicycle hire) and 58FF. The information office at the bus station is open Monday to Friday from 9 am to noon and 2 to 6 pm and on Saturday morning.

Car A small fleet of bright yellow electric cars and scooters are available for rent from the Autoplus bus company at Place de Verdun. The cars are good for 50 km and cost 100FF per day; scooters need to be recharged after 35 km and cost 70/40FF per day/half-day. Both require a 2500FF deposit.

Bicycle The Autoplus bus company runs an unusual bicycle rental called Les Vélos Autoplus opposite 11 Quai Valin from May to September. An adult's or child's yellow bike (lock included) is free for the first two hours; after that the charge is 6FF per hour and 60FF overnight (the one-day bus pass also covers bicycle rental). The bike depot is open every day from 9 am to 12.30 pm and 1.30 to 7 pm. The tourist office has a good biking map brochure called *Guide des Itinéraires Cyclables*.

Boat Autoplus' Bus de Mer links the Vieux Port with the beach at Les Minimes. From April to September boats leave from the pier just north of Tour de la Chaîne every hour from 10 am to 8 pm (10FF one way). In July and August departures are increased to two per hour to 11.30 pm. During the rest of the year Bus de Mer runs only at weekends.

BORDEAUX

Bordeaux (population 260,000) is known for its neoclassical architecture, wide avenues, colossal statues and well-tended public squares and parks. The city's ethnic diversity (there are three universities here with 60,000 students, many from developing countries), excellent museums and untouristed atmosphere make it much more than just a convenient stop between Paris and Spain.

Bordeaux was founded by the Romans in the 3rd century BC. From 1154 to 1453, it prospered under the rule of the English, whose fondness for the region's red wines (known as claret across the Channel) gave impetus to the local wine industry. The marketing and export of Bordeaux wine remains the single most important economic activity.

Orientation

Cours de la Marne stretches from the train station to Place de la Victoire, which is linked to Place de la Comédie by the pedestrians-only Rue Sainte Catherine. The city centre lies between Place Gambetta and the Garonne River. Cours de l'Intendance is the city's main shopping street. Rue de la Porte Dijeaux is also a pedestrian mall.

Information

Tourist Office The very efficient main tourist office (☎ 05 56 00 66 00) at 12 Cours du 30 Juillet is open daily from 9 am to 6 pm (to 8 pm from June to September). Its free maps and brochures are first-class, and there are daily city and 'theme' tours on foot from 40FF (30FF for students). The tourist office annexe at the train station (☎ 05 56 91 64 70) is open daily from 9 am (10 am on off-season Sundays) to 7 pm, and there is an airport branch (☎ 05 56 34 50 50).

For information about the Gironde department, contact the Maison du Tourisme de la Gironde (☎ 05 56 52 61 40) at 21 Cours de l'Intendance Monday to Saturday from 9 am to 7 pm.

Foreign Consulates Bordeaux has some 40 consulates, including the UK's at 353 Blvd du Président Wilson (☎ 05 56 42 34 13). The US consulate, however, has recently closed.

Money & Post Banque de France is around the corner from the tourist office at 13 Rue Esprit des Lois. American Express (☎ 05 56 52 40 52) at 14 Cours de l'Intendance is open Monday to Friday from 8.45 am to noon and 1.30 to 6 pm. The rate at the Thomas Cook bureau (☎ 05 56 91 58 80) in the train station is lower than that of the banks, but its services are available Monday to Saturday from 9 am to 6.50 pm and on Sunday from 10 am to 5.50 pm. It's open daily until 9 pm in summer.

The main post office (☎ 05 56 48 87 48) is west of the city centre at 52 Rue Georges Bonnac. Central Bordeaux's postcode is 33000.

Laundry The laundrette at 6 Rue de Fondaudège, near Place de Tourny, is open seven days a week from 7 am to 8.30 pm. At 10 Rue La Faurie de Monbadon, near the Hôtel Balzac, there's a laundrette open daily from 7 am to 9 pm. The laundrette on Rue La Boetie, around the corner from the Hôtel Boulan, is also open daily from 7 am to 9 pm.

Things to See
The most prominent feature of the **Esplanade des Quinconces**, laid out in 1820, is a towering fountain-monument to the Girondists, a group of moderate, bourgeois legislative deputies during the French Revolution, 22 of whom were executed in 1793 for alleged counter-revolutionary activities. The **Jardin Public**, an 18th-century 'English park', is along Cours de Verdun. It includes Bordeaux's **botanical garden** and **Musée d'Histoire Naturelle** (Natural History Museum).

The much-praised, neoclassical **Grand Théâtre** at Place de la Comédie was built in the 1770s. Lovely **Place de la Bourse**, flanked by the old Hôtel de la Douane (customs house) and the Bourse du Commerce (stock exchange), was built between 1731 and 1755. The riverside area nearby is run-down and fairly lifeless.

Porte Dijeaux, which dates from 1748 and is one of the few city gates still standing, leads to **Place Gambetta**, a beautiful garden by a pond. Today it is an island of calm in the midst of the urban hustle and bustle, but during the Reign of Terror, a guillotine was used here to sever the heads of 300 people.

Cathédrale Saint André in the Place Pey-Berland was where the future King Louis VII married Eleanor of Aquitaine in 1137. The cathedral's 15th-century belfry, **Tour Pey-Berland**, stands behind the choir, whose chapels are nestled among the flying buttresses. The cathedral is open Monday to Saturday from 8 am to noon and 2 to 7 pm (on Sunday from 8 am to noon and 3 to 6 pm).

Bordeaux' Moorish **synagogue** (☎ 05 56 91 79 39), inaugurated in 1882, is just west of Rue Sainte Catherine on Rue du Grand Rabbin Joseph Cohen. During WWII, the interior was ripped apart by the Nazis, who turned the complex into a prison. Visits are possible Monday to Thursday from 3 to 5 pm from the rabbi's office at 213 Rue Sainte Catherine.

Museums Most museums in Bordeaux charge adults 18FF (9FF for students), but almost all are free on Wednesday. The outstanding **Musée d'Aquitaine** (☎ 05 56 01 51 00) at 20 Cours Pasteur illustrates the history and ethnography of the Bordeaux area from prehistory to the 19th century and the exhibits are exceptionally well designed. The museum is open daily except Monday from 10 am to 6 pm.

At 20 Cours d'Albert, the **Musée des Beaux-Arts** (☎ 05 56 10 16 93) occupies two wings of the 18th-century Hôtel de Ville, between which is an attractive public garden called Jardin de la Mairie. The museum houses a large collection of paintings, including 17th-century Flemish, Dutch and Italian works and a major painting by Delacroix. It's open from 10 am to 5 or 6 pm daily except Tuesday.

At 39 Rue Bouffard, the **Musée des Arts Décoratifs** (☎ 05 56 00 72 50) specialises in porcelain, silverware, glassware, furniture and so on. It is open daily except Tuesday from 2 to 6 pm. Temporary exhibits stay open from 10 am to 6 pm.

The excellent **Musée d'Art Contemporain** (☎ 05 56 44 16 35) at 7 Rue Ferrère hosts temporary exhibits by contemporary artists on three floors. It is open from noon to 7 pm (to 10 pm on Wednesday) daily except Monday. Entry is 30FF (20FF for students), but is free if you arrive between noon and 2 pm. The museum is housed in the Entrepôts Lainé, built in 1824 as a warehouse for the exotic products of France's colonies: coffee, cocoa, peanuts, vanilla etc.

FRANCE

Bordeaux

Map labels

Jardin Botanique
Jardin Public
Duplessy
Rue Foy
Rue Ferrère
Cours du Maréchal Foch
Cours de Verdun
Rue de Fondaudège
Rue Turenne
Rue Lafaurie de Monbadon
Rue du Palais Gallien
Rue Huguerie
Cours Georges Clemenceau
Place de Tourny
Cours de Tournon
Allées de Chartres
Esplanade des Quinconces
Allées de Tourny
Rue JJ Rousseau
Place des Grands Hommes
Rue Montesquieu
Voltaire
Cours du 30 Juillet
Cours de l'Intendance
Rue Judaïque
Place Gambetta
Rue Saint Sernin
Rue du Château d'Eau
To Airport (10 km)
Rue de la Porte Dijeaux
Rue de la Grasse
Rue Bouffard
R des Remparts
Rue Vital Carles
Rue La Boëtie
Rue Boulan
Rue Montbazon
Place Pey-Berland
Rue des Trois Conils
Place du Colonel Raynal
Cours d'Albret
Cours du Maréchal Joffre
Rue du Hâ
Rue de Cursol
Rue de Belfort
Rue Mouneyra
Rue Lalande
Rue Jean Burguet
Cours Pasteur
Rue Paul Louis Lande
Cours de la Libération
Cours Aristide Briand
Rue Esprit des Lois
Place de la Comédie
Cours du Chapeau Rouge
Galerie Bordelaise
Rue Saint Rémi
Place de la Bourse
Rue Sainte Catherine
Rue Margaux
Rue du Cancéra
Place du Parlement
Place Saint Pierre
Rue du Pas Saint Georges
Cours d'Alsace et Lorraine
Cours Victor Hugo
Rue Sainte Catherine
Rue des Ayres
Rue Saint James
Rue Saint François
Rue du Mirail
Rue Leyteire
Rue des Augustins
R Grassi
Place de la Victoire
Cours de la Marne
Quai Louis XVIII
Place Jean Jaurès
Garonne River
Quai Richelieu
To Pont de Pierre
Rue des Faures
Rue des Menuts
Rue Borderet

Gare Saint Jean Area (inset)
To Place de la Victoire (700m)
Cours de la Marne
Cours Barbey
Rue Malbec
Rue Eugène Leroy
Rue Charles Domercq
Rue Vidal
Rue de Tauzia
Place de Casablanca
Rue Furtado

0   100   200 m

To / direction notes
To Airport (10 km)
To Pont de Pierre
To Camping Les Gravières (10 km)
To Camping Beausoleil (10 km via Cours de l'Argonne)
To Auberge de Jeunesse (800 m) & Gare Saint Jean (1,4 km - See Inset)

0   150   300 m

FRANCE

PLACES TO STAY		OTHER		33	
5	Hôtel Touring & Hôtel Studio	1	Musée d'Histoire Naturelle	35	Brad...
6	Hôtel de Sèze	2	Musée d'Art Contemporain	36	Musée de... Décoratifs
14	Hôtel Le Provence			37	Musée des Beaux...
16	Hôtel Balzac & Laundrette	3	CITRAM Bus Station	38	Jardin de la Mairie
		4	Laundrette	39	Hôtel de Ville
19	Hôtel Blayais	7	Monument des	40	Cathédrale Saint André
28	Hôtel Bristol		Girondins	41	Tour Pey-Berland
29	Hôtel de Lyon	8	Bordeaux Magnum	42	Musée d'Aquitaine
34	Hôtel Boulan		(Wine Shop)	43	Porte de la Grosse Cloche
49	Maison des Etudiantes	9	Banks & Cash Machines		
55	Auberge de Jeunesse			44	Porte des Salinières
56	Hôtel Les Deux Mondes & Hôtel La Terasse	10	Maison du Vin de Bordeaux	45	Église Saint Michel
		11	Tourist Office	46	Tour Saint Michel
		13	Banque de France	48	Hôpital Saint André
PLACES TO EAT		17	Église Notre Dame	50	Synagogue
12	Les Quatre Sœurs Bistro	18	Maison du Tourisme de la Gironde	51	Champion Supermarket
				53	Porte d'Aquitaine
15	Le Mechoui	20	Grand Théâtre	54	Marché des Capucins
23	La Galluchat	21	Bourse du Commerce		(Wholesale Food
24	Chez Edouard	22	Hôtel de la Douane		Market)
26	Pizza Paï		(Customs)	57	Thomas Cook
30	Cân Tho Restaurant	25	American Express	58	SNCF Information
47	The Blarney Stone	27	Porte Dijeaux (Gate)		Office
52	La Dakaroise	31	Laundrette	59	Bus Stops
		32	Main Post Office	60	Train Station (Gare Saint Jean)

Places to Stay

Camping *Camping Beausoleil* (☎ 05 56 89 17 66; open all year) charges 59FF for two people with their own tent (84FF with a car). It is about 10 km south-west of the city centre at 371 Cours du Général de Gaulle (route N10) in Gradignan. To get there, take bus G from Place de la Victoire towards Gradignan Beausoleil and get off at the terminus.

Camping Les Gravières (☎ 05 56 87 00 36; open all year) charges 28FF for a tent and 19FF per person; there's no extra charge for a car. It's 10 km south-east of central Bordeaux at Place de Courréjean in Villenave d'Ornon. Take bus B from Place de la Victoire towards Courréjean and get off at the terminus.

Hostels The *Maison des Étudiantes* (☎ 05 56 96 48 30) at 50 Rue Ligier, a dormitory during the academic year, offers accommodation from July to September. A bed costs 55FF with a student card (75FF without), including sheets and use of the showers and kitchen. To get there from the train station, take bus No 7 or 8 to the Bourse du Travail stop and walk 400 metres west on Cours de la Libération.

The charmless *Auberge de Jeunesse* (☎ 05 56 91 59 51) at 22 Cours Barbey is 650 metres west of the train station. A spot in a utilitarian, eight-bed room is only 40FF but the 1st floor (women's section) and the 2nd floor (men's section) are reached by separate staircases! There's an 11 pm curfew, but have a word with the manager in advance if you'll be staying out late. The hostel accepts telephone reservations and reception is open daily from 8 to 9.30 am and 6 to 11 pm.

Hotels Hotels in the area around the train station are convenient for rail passengers, but the neighbourhood is rather seedy. In terms of both price and value, you're much better off staying around the tourist office, Place de Tourny or Place Gambetta.

Tourist Office Area The old-fashioned *Hôtel Blayais* (☎ 05 56 48 17 87), east of the baroque Église Notre Dame at 17 Rue Mautrec, has fairly large singles/doubles for 110FF (with washbasin and bidet) and 150FF (with shower). Hall showers are free.

Place de Tourny The best inexpensive choice here is the two-star *Hôtel Touring* (☎ 05 56 81 56 73) at 16 Rue Huguerie, which has gigantic, spotless singles/doubles for 120/140FF (with washbasin and bidet), 180/200FF (with shower and TV) and 200/220FF (with shower, toilet and TV). The *Hôtel Studio* (☎ 05 56 48 00 14), nearby at No 26, has basic singles from 98FF, doubles from 120FF and triples from 180FF. All have shower, toilet and TV with cable.

The best choice in a higher price range in this area is *Hôtel de Sèze* (☎ 05 56 52 65 54) at 7 Rue de Sèze with comfortable singles/doubles from 250/380FF. South-west of Place de Tourny the *Hôtel Le Provence* (☎ 05 56 52 00 05), at 2 Rue Castéja, has basic singles/doubles from 110/130FF.

Place Gambetta There are several excellent deals in the area between Place Gambetta and the Musée des Beaux-Arts. The quiet *Hôtel Boulan* (☎ 05 56 52 23 62) at 28 Rue Boulan has pleasant singles/doubles with high ceilings for 100/110FF (120/130FF with shower). Hall showers cost 15FF.

The friendly *Hôtel de Lyon* (☎ 05 56 81 34 38, at 31 Rue des Remparts has singles/doubles with shower, toilet and TV for 120/135FF. Try not to get one of the cramped rooms on the 3rd floor though.

The excellent *Hôtel Bristol* (☎ 05 56 81 85 01) at 2 Rue Bouffard has pleasant singles/doubles with four-metre-high ceilings, a bathroom, toilet and TV for 210/300FF.

Train Station Area The popular *Hôtel La Terrasse* (☎ 05 56 91 42 87) at 20 Rue Saint Vincent de Paul has clean singles/doubles from 70/120FF. Doubles with shower cost 150FF. Hall showers are 20FF. The *Hôtel Les Deux Mondes* (☎ 05 56 91 63 09), nearby at No 10, is a decent place with lots of foreign guests during the summer. Rates are 110/165FF for singles/doubles with shower.

Places to Eat

The plats du jour at *Les Quatre Sœurs* (☎ 05 56 48 16 00), a bistro next to the tourist office at 6 Cours de 30 Juillet, are tasty and reliable. A two-course menu is 65FF. *Pizza Paï* (☎ 05 56 81 35 80) at 26 Cours de l'Intendance has that most un-French of things: an all-you-can-

eat salad bar (40FF). Generous pizza menus start at 50FF. It's open every day from 11 am to 10 pm. Looking out onto the attractive square and fountain at Place du Parlement, *Chez Edourd* (☎ 05 56 81 48 87) has traditional French lunch menus from 58FF. Nearby, at 29 Rue du Parlement St Pierre, *Le Galluchat* (☎ 05 56 44 86 67) has excellent lunch menus from 45FF. It's open every day except Tuesday for lunch and dinner.

Bordeaux is a multicultural city and its restaurants reflect that. Around Place de La Victoire, *La Dakaroise* (☎ 05 56 92 77 32) at 9 Rue Gratiolet specialises in West African dishes like yassa poisson (fish cooked with lime) and maffé (beef in a peanut sauce) from around 65FF. It's open daily from 7 to 11.30 pm. A few minutes walk to the north-west at 144 Cours Victor Hugo is the *Blarney Stone* (☎ 05 56 31 87 20), an Irish bar and restaurant with pub food from 25FF. It's open Monday to Saturday from 11.30 am to 2 am and on Sunday from 6.30 pm to 2 am. There's live music on Monday evenings.

Rue du Palais Gallien is loaded with Chinese, Vietnamese and North African restaurants. *Le Mechoui* (☎ 05 56 44 58 81) at No 20 has decent couscous from 65FF. The *Cân Tho* (☎ 05 56 81 40 38), south of Place Gambetta at 16 Rue Villeneuve, has good Chinese and Vietnamese dishes from 30FF. It's open seven days a week.

If price is no object, eat at *La Chanterelle* (☎ 05 56 81 75 43), one of the best restaurants in Bordeaux with menus starting at 95FF (65FF at lunch). It's at 3 Rue Martignac (heading east, Rue Martignac is left off Cours de l'Intendance, just after Place de la Comédie) and is open for lunch and dinner every day except Monday night and all day Sunday.

The modern, mirrored *Marché des Grands Hommes* at Place des Grands Hommes, 100 metres north of Cours de l'Intendance, has stalls in the basement selling fruit, vegetables, cheese, bread, pastry and sandwiches. It's open Monday to Saturday from 7 am to 7.30 pm. *Champion* supermarket at 190 Rue Sainte Catherine is open from 8.30 am to 8 pm daily except Sunday.

Things to Buy

Bordeaux wine in all price ranges is on sale at three speciality shops near the main tourist office: Vinothèque de Bordeaux at 8 Cours du 30 Juillet, L'Intendant at 2 Allées de Tourny and Bordeaux Magnum at 3 Rue Gobineau.

Getting There & Away

Bus Buses to places all over the Gironde and nearby departments leave from the CITRAM bus station (☎ 05 56 43 68 43) at the western end of Allée de Chartres, north-east of Place de Tourny. The information office is open Monday to Friday from 9 am to noon and 2 to 6 pm (5 pm on Friday). Destinations include Soulac (on the coast near the mouth of the Gironde River) and Cap Ferret (south-west of Bordeaux near the Bassin d'Arcachon, a bay on the coast west of Bordeaux). There's also year-round service to the medieval vineyard town of Saint Émilion. See the Bordeaux Vineyard Visits section for fares and frequencies.

Train Bordeaux's train station, Gare Saint Jean (☎ 08 36 35 35 39), is about three km south-east of the city centre at the end of Cours de la Marne. It is one of France's major rail transit points – there are trains from here to almost everywhere. The station's information office is open Monday to Saturday from 9 am to 7 pm. If you take the TGV Atlantique, Bordeaux is only about three hours from Paris' Gare Montparnasse (non-TGV trains use the Gare d'Austerlitz).

Getting Around

Bus Single tickets on Bordeaux's urban bus network, CGFTE (☎ 05 57 57 88 88), cost 7.50FF (52FF for 10) and are valid for one hour after being time-stamped. Bus information bureaus (*espaces rouges*) on Place Gambetta and at the southern end of the train station (open every day to 7.30 pm) have user-friendly route maps. Carte Bordeaux Découverte allows unlimited bus travel for one day (22FF) or three days (52FF).

Bus Nos 7 and 8 link the train station with the city centre. Place de la Comédie is the correct stop for the tourist office; the Place Gambetta stop is also good for Place de Tourny.

Taxi To order a cab in central Bordeaux, ring ☎ 05 56 48 03 25 or ☎ 05 56 91 47 05.

BORDEAUX VINEYARD VISITS

The Bordeaux wine-producing region is subdivided into 53 production areas (*appellations*), whose climate and soil impart distinctive characteristics upon the wine produced there. These are grouped into six families (*familles*). The majority of the region's diverse wines (reds, rosés, sweet and dry whites, sparkling wines) have earned the right to include the abbreviation AOC on their labels, indicating that the contents have been grown, fermented and aged according to strict regulations. The region's production averages 660 million bottles of wine a year.

The areas to the east, north-east and south-east of Bordeaux have many thousands of chateaux, which indicates properties where grapes are raised, fermented and matured, and some of the names may be familiar: Graves, Sauternes, Pommarol, Saint Émilion. The smaller chateaux often accept walk-in visitors year-round except in August, but many of the larger and better known ones (eg Château Mouton-Rothschild) accept visitors only by appointment. Each vineyard has different rules about tasting – at some it's free, others make you pay, and others do not serve wine at all. As you drive around, look for signs that say *dégustation* (wine tasting), *en vente directe* (direct sales) or *vin à emporter* (wine to take away/to go).

Information

Opposite Bordeaux's main tourist office at 3 Cours du 30 Juillet, the Maison du Vin de Bordeaux (☎ 05 56 00 22 66) has lots of information on visiting vineyards. First decide which growing area you would like to visit (use the maison's colour-coded map of *appellations*); the staff will give you the address of the local *maison du vin* (a sort of tourist office for wine-growing areas), which has details on which chateaux are open and when.

The Maison du Vin de Bordeaux is open weekdays from 8.30 am to 5.30 or 6 pm. From mid-June to mid-October it is also open on Saturday from 9 am to 12.30 pm and 1.30 to 7 pm. There is free wine tasting here at 10.30 and 11.30 am and at 2.30 and 4.30 pm.

Organised Tours

Bus tours organised by the tourist office to various chateaux in the Bordeaux area are a solution to transport difficulties. Afternoon excursions, which take place throughout the year on Wednesday and Saturday (daily from mid-June to mid-September) and last from 1.30 to 6.30 pm, cost 150FF (130FF for students). Commentary is in French and English.

Saint Émilion

One easily accessible wine-producing area to visit on your own is Saint Émilion, a medieval gem of a village 42 km east of Bordeaux and famous for its full-bodied, deeply coloured reds. The local tourist office (☎ 05 57 24 72 03) is open daily at Place du Clocher. From Bordeaux, Saint Émilion is accessible by train with at least one return trip every day (8 or 9 am, returning at 6.30 pm, 42FF one way). CITRAM buses go there and back about five times a day (there may be a transfer at Libourne). The one-way fare is 37FF. If you're driving take route D89 east to D670.

Virtually every shop in Saint Émilion sells wine (which you can also sample) but stick with the professionals. Maison du Vin (☎ 05 57 55 50 55) around the corner from the tourist office on Place Pierre Meyrat has an enormous selection and one-hour introductory wine-tasting courses (100FF) in summer. The English proprietor at Maison des Vins du Libournais (☎ 05 57 24 65 60) on Rue Guadet, with a more eclectic selection, is particularly knowledgeable and helpful.

If you get hungry in Saint Émilion, *L'Envers du Décor* (☎ 05 57 74 48 31) next to the tourist office on Rue Clocher has excellent plats du jour for around 65FF and vintage wine by the glass from 20 to 35FF. For something more romantic, try the excellent *Le Tertre* (☎ 05 57 74 46 33) on Rue du Tertre de La Tente. Macaroons – soft cookies made from almond flour, egg whites and sugar – are a speciality of Saint Émilion. Fabrique de Macarons Matthieu Mouliérac just up from Le Tertre has the best.

BAYONNE

Bayonne (population 41,000) is the most important city in the French part of the Basque Country (Euzkadi in Basque, Pays Basque in French), a region straddling the French-Spanish border with its own unique language, culture, history and identity. Unlike the up-market beach resort of Biarritz a short bus ride

away, Bayonne retains much of its Basqueness: the riverside buildings with their green, red and white shutters are typical of the region and you'll hear almost as much Euskara (Basque language) as French. Most of the graffiti you'll see around town – like *Amnistia!* in bold letters on the massive Château Neuf – is the work of nationalist groups seeking an independent Basque state.

Bayonne's most important festival is the annual Fête de Bayonne, which begins on the first Wednesday in August. The festival includes a 'running of the bulls' like the one in Pamplona except that here they have cows rather than bulls and usually it's the people – dressed in white with red scarves around their necks – who chase the cows rather than the other way around. The festival also includes Basque music, bullfighting, a float parade and rugby matches (a favourite sport in south-west France).

Orientation

The Adour and Nive rivers split Bayonne into three parts: Saint Esprit, the area north of the Adour, where the train station is located; Grand Bayonne, the oldest part of the city, on the west bank of the Nive; and very Basque Petit Bayonne to the east. The suburban area of Anglet is sandwiched between Bayonne and the beach resort of Biarritz, eight km to the west.

Information

Tourist Office The tourist office (☎ 05 59 46 01 46) is on Place des Basques just north-west of Grand Bayonne. It's open Monday to Friday from 9 am to 6.30 pm and on Saturday from 10 am to 6 pm. In July and August, it's open daily from 9 am to 7 pm and from 10 am to 1 pm on Sunday. Its brochure *Programme des Fêtes en Pays Basque* is useful for cultural and sporting events. The freebie *Découverte et Activités en Pays Basque* is indispensable for organising hiking, biking, climbing, diving etc.

The tourist office for the Basque Country, the Agence de Tourisme du Pays Basque (☎ 05 59 46 46 64), is a km north of Place des Basques at 1 Rue Donzac.

Money & Post Banks in Bayonne are open from Monday to Friday; those in Anglet open

Tuesday to Saturday. The Banque de France is at 18 Rue Albert 1er, and there are more banks in Grand Bayonne near the Hôtel de Ville, along Rue Thiers and on Rue du 49ème Régiment d'Infanterie behind the post office.

The post office (☎ 05 59 59 32 00), which has exchange operations, is at 11 Rue Jules Labat. Bayonne's postcode is 64100.

Things to See & Do

Cathédrale Sainte Marie This Gothic cathedral is on Rue de la Monnaie at the southern end of the Rue du Port Neuf pedestrian mall in the heart of the oldest part of town. Construction of the cathedral was begun in the 13th century, when Bayonne was ruled by the English, and completed after the area came under French control in 1451. These political changes are reflected in the ornamentation on the vaulted ceiling of the nave, which includes both the English arms, three leopards, and that most French of emblems, the *fleur-de-lis*. Some of the stained glass dates from the Renaissance but many of the statues that once graced the church's very crumbly exterior were smashed during the Revolution.

Sainte Marie is open daily from 7 am to 12.30 pm and 2.30 to 7.30 pm. The **cloître**, the beautiful 13th-century cloister south of the cathedral on Place Louis Pasteur, is open every day except Saturday from 9.30 am to 12.30 pm and 2 to 5 pm (to 6 pm from April to October). Entry is 14FF (10FF reduced).

Musée Bonnat This museum (☎ 05 59 59 08 52) at 5 Rue Jacques Laffitte in Petit Bayonne has a diverse collection of works, including a whole room of paintings by Peter Paul Rubens (1577-1640). It is open from 10 am to noon and 2.30 to 6.30 pm (8.30 pm on Friday) daily except Tuesday. From mid-September to mid-June, opening hours on Friday are 3 to 8.30 pm only. The entry fee is 20FF (10FF for students).

Izarra Tasting Izarra, a local liqueur supposedly distilled from '100 flowers of the Pyrenees', is produced at the **Distillerie de la Côte Basque** (☎ 05 59 55 07 48) at 9 Quai Amiral Bergeret in Saint Esprit. Half-hour free tours of the plant and the little museum with a tasting at the end take place on weekdays from

9 to 11.30 am and 2 to 4.30 pm (to 6 pm from mid-July to August).

Sports Courses

The Auberge de Jeunesse d'Anglet (see Places to Stay) offers very popular one-week courses *(stages)* in surfing, body-boarding *(morey boogie)*, scuba diving and horse riding throughout the year. The courses, which are in French (though the instructors usually speak a little English), last from Sunday evening to Saturday afternoon and cost between 2150 and 2800FF, including accommodation, meals and equipment.

Places to Stay

Accommodation is most difficult to find from mid-July to mid-August, especially during the five-day Fête de Bayonne in August.

Camping There are several camping grounds in Anglet. The one-star *Camping du Fontaine Laborde* (☎ 05 59 03 48 16), open June to September, is on Allée Fontaine Laborde not far from the hostel. It often fills up in July and August. To get there, follow the instructions for taking the bus to the auberge de jeunesse (see Hostel below) but get off at Fontaine Laborde two stops later. You can also take bus No 2 from Bayonne's train station and get off at Place Leclerc.

You might also try *Camping de Parme* (☎ 05 59 23 03 00), open all year, which is on Route l'Aviation in Anglet. It costs 29FF to pitch a tent and 29FF per adult. Take bus line No 6 and ask for Camping de Parme.

Hostel The *auberge de jeunesse* (☎ 05 59 63 86 49) nearest Bayonne is at 19 Route des Vignes in Anglet. It is open all year and charges 69FF for a bed, including breakfast. To get there from the Bayonne train station, take bus No 4 heading for Biarritz and get off at the Auberge de Jeunesse stop. From the Biarritz train station, it's bus No 2 (direction Bayonne) to the Hôtel de Ville stop where you change to bus No 4.

Hotels There are a number of hotels right around the train station in Saint Esprit. The *Hôtel Paris Madrid* (☎ 05 59 55 13 98) is to the left (east) as you exit the station. The cheapest singles cost 90FF. Big, pleasant singles and

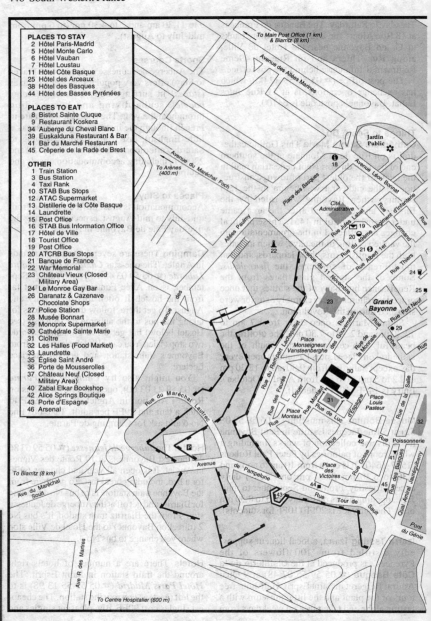

PLACES TO STAY
2   Hôtel Paris-Madrid
5   Hôtel Monte Carlo
6   Hôtel Vauban
7   Hôtel Loustau
11 Hôtel Côte Basque
25 Hôtel des Arceaux
38 Hôtel des Basques
44 Hôtel des Basses Pyrénées

PLACES TO EAT
8   Bistrot Sainte Cluque
9   Restaurant Koskera
34 Auberge du Cheval Blanc
39 Euskalduna Restaurant & Bar
41 Bar du Marché Restaurant
45 Crêperie de la Rade de Brest

OTHER
1   Train Station
3   Bus Station
4   Taxi Rank
10 STAB Bus Stops
12 ATAC Supermarket
13 Distillerie de la Côte Basque
14 Laundrette
15 Post Office
16 STAB Bus Information Office
17 Hôtel de Ville
18 Tourist Office
19 Post Office
20 ATCRB Bus Stops
21 Banque de France
22 War Memorial
23 Château Vieux (Closed
     Military Area)
24 Le Monroe Gay Bar
26 Daranatz & Cazenave
     Chocolate Shops
27 Police Station
28 Musée Bonnart
29 Monoprix Supermarket
30 Cathédrale Sainte Marie
31 Cloître
32 Les Halles (Food Market)
33 Laundrette
35 Église Saint André
36 Porte de Mousserolles
37 Château Neuf (Closed
     Military Area)
40 Zabal Elkar Bookshop
42 Alice Springs Boutique
43 Porte d'Espagne
46 Arsenal

Citadelle

Rue Sainte

Quai de Lesseps

Ursule

6

Place de
la Gare

1

2

3

Rue Maubec

4

5

R Neuve

R du

Graouillats

Rue des Hayes

Rue Chemin

11

10

9

8

7

*Saint
Esprit*

Place de la
République

Adour River

Pont Saint Esprit

Square
Gambetta

Rue Sainte Catherine

Avenue Maréchal Leclerc

Place
Charles
de Gaulle

16

17

Place de
la Liberté

Bernède

Quai Amiral Lesseps

Esplanade
de Réduit

Place de
Réduit

12

Boulevard

14

13

Quai Amiral Bergeret

Rue de l'Esté

15

Alsace-Lorraine

Rue Denis
Etcheverry

26

Rue Lormand

Victor Hugo

Pont Mayou

Quai Amiral Dubourdieu

Alfées Boufflers

Lafitte

27

28

Rue Jacques

*Petit
Bayonne*

Square
Léo
Pouzac

Rue Frédéric Bastiat

Ravignan

Avenue du Capitaine Resplandy

Quai des Corsaires

Rue Marsan

Rue

Bourgneuf

Rue Marengo

34

Nive River

33

Quai Galuperie

Rue Pontrique

Rue du Trinquet

Rue des Tonneliers

Rue des Lisses

35

36

Pont Pannecau

Rue Pannecau

39

38

40

Place
Paul Bert

37

Quai Augustin Chao

Rue des Cordeliers

Rue Pelletier

Place de
l'Arsenal
& Marché
de Brocante

46

Bayonne

0   50   100 m

doubles without/with shower cost 120/145FF. Doubles with shower and toilet are 165FF. The *Hôtel Monte Carlo* (☎ 05 59 55 02 68) opposite the train station at 1 Rue Sainte Ursule has singles/doubles from 100FF (120FF with shower). Hall showers are free.

The *Hôtel Vauban* (☎ 05 59 55 11 31) at 13 Rue Sainte Ursule has singles/doubles from 195FF. All rooms have shower, toilet and TV. The *Hôtel Côte Basque* (☎ 05 59 55 10 21), opposite the station at Place de la Gare, has large singles/doubles with shower, toilet and TV for 295/320FF.

Saint Esprit's nicest hotel is the *Hôtel Loustau* (☎ 05 59 55 16 74; fax 05 59 55 69 36) facing the Adour River on Quai de Lesseps (the actual address is 1 Place de la République) in an 18th-century building. Doubles/triples with shower are 285/350FF.

In the centre of Grand Bayonne, the *Hôtel des Arceaux* (☎ 05 59 59 15 53) at 26 Rue du Port Neuf has doubles from 125FF (210FF with shower, toilet and TV). The two-star *Hôtel des Basses Pyrénées* (☎ 05 59 59 00 29; fax 05 59 59 42 02), close to the Porte d'Espagne on Place des Victoires, has doubles/triples/quads with shower and toilet for 280/340/380FF. There are a few simple rooms with washbasin from 150FF.

The least expensive hotel in the colourful Petit Bayonne quarter is the *Hôtel des Basques* (☎ 05 59 59 08 02), which is next to 3 Rue des Lisses at Place Paul Bert. Large, nondescript singles or doubles start at 100FF (one bed) and 150FF (two beds); one-bed singles with shower are 135FF. Hall showers cost 10FF.

Places to Eat

Bayonne is an excellent place to sample Basque cuisine. The *Euskalduna Restaurant & Bar* (☎ 05 59 59 28 02), near the Hôtel des Basques at 61 Rue Pannecau, has a menu for 100FF and main dishes for 70 to 90FF. It's open Monday to Saturday for lunch only (the bar stays open until 9 pm). *Restaurant Koskera* (☎ 05 59 55 20 79), south of the train station at 3 Rue Hugues, has plats du jour for 35FF and menus from 59FF. It's open Monday to Saturday (and Sunday in the summer) for lunch only (for dinner to 10.30 pm from mid-June to September). An excellent choice is the *Bistrot Sainte Cluque* (☎ 05 59 55 82 43) at 9 Rue Hugues. Its speciality is paella (55FF) and

there are menus from 50FF. It's open Tuesday to Saturday from 11 am to 1 am.

In Grand Bayonne, a good bet is the very pleasant *Bar du Marché* (☎ 05 59 59 22 26) at 39 Rue des Basques. It is open Monday to Saturday for lunch and dinner. menus with a choice of local dishes start at 39FF. For a selection of crêpes, stop by the *Crêperie de la Rade de Brest* at 7 Rue des Basques. It's open Tuesday to Saturday from noon to 2 pm and 7 to 10 pm (11 pm on Friday and Saturday).

If your budget can support it, some of the most creative dishes in town can be had at the elegant French *Auberge du Cheval Blanc* (☎ 05 59 59 01 33) at 68 Rue Bourgneuf in Petit Bayonne. It's open Tuesday to Sunday for lunch and dinner (daily from July to September). Menus start at 105FF.

The central market *Les Halles* is in a new building on the west quay (Quai Amiral Jauréguiberry) of the Nive River and is open every morning except Sunday. The *Monoprix* supermarket at 8 Rue Orbe is open Monday to Saturday from 8 or 8.30 am to 7 pm. In Saint Esprit, the *ATAC* supermarket on Blvd d'Alsace-Lorraine is open Monday to Saturday from 8.30 am to 12.30 pm and from 2.45 to 7.15 pm (no midday closure on Saturday).

Spectator Sport

Bullfights *Corrida*, Spanish-style bullfighting in which the bull is killed, has its devotees all over the south of France, including Bayonne. Tournaments are held about half a dozen times each summer. Advance reservations are usually necessary – information is available at the tourist office.

Pelote *Pelote Basque* or *pelota* is the name given to several games native to the Basque Country which are played with a *chistera* (a curved leather and wicker racquet strapped to the wrist) and a *pelote* (a hard ball with a rubber centre). The best known variety of pelota in the Basque Country is *cesta punta*, the world's fastest ball game, played in a covered court with three walls. For information on matches, which take place in Bayonne, Biarritz, Saint Jean de Luz and elsewhere year-round, enquire at one of the area's tourist offices. See the Biarritz section for information on cesta punta lessons.

Things to Buy

Bayonne is famous throughout France for its ham and chocolate. Buy the former at Au Jambon de Bayonne Brouchican (☎ 05 59 59 27 18) at 20 Quai Augustin Chao in Petit Bayonne; the latter at the very traditional *chocolaterie* Cazenave (☎ 05 59 59 03 16) at 19 Rue Port Neuf.

Zabal Elkar (☎ 05 59 25 43 90) at 52 Rue Pannecau has a large selection of cassettes and CDs of Basque music. It also carries lots of books on Basque history and culture and hiking in the Basque Country as well as maps. The shop is open from 9.15 am to 12.30 pm and 2.30 to 7.30 pm daily except Monday morning and all day Sunday.

Homesick Aussies should check out Alice Springs (☎ 05 59 59 13 72), a *boutique australienne* at 25 Rue Poissonnerie open weekdays from 10 am to 7 pm.

Getting There & Away

Bus The tiny bus station (☎ 05 59 55 17 59) is in front of the train station at Place de la Gare. The information office is open weekdays from 8.45 am to 12.15 pm and 2 to 5.30 pm. RDTL serves destinations in Les Landes, the department to the north, including Dax, Léon and Vieux Boucau. To get to the beaches along the coast north of Bayonne such as Mimizan and Moliets, take the bus heading for Vieux Boucau (37FF, 1¼ hours).

Buses run by ATCRB (☎ 05 59 26 06 99 in Saint Jean de Luz) serve Saint Jean de Luz (20FF), Hendaye (40.50FF) and San Sebastián (Spain). They leave from the bus stop at 9 Rue du 49ème Régiment d'Infanterie.

Train The train station (☎ 08 36 35 35 39) is in Saint Esprit at Place de la Gare. The information office is open Monday to Saturday from 9 am to noon and 2 to 6.30 pm (daily from 9 am to 7.30 pm in July and August). TGVs to/from Paris (406FF) take 4½ hours and go to Gare Montparnasse. Other Paris-bound trains take about eight hours and stop at Gare d'Austerlitz. There are also trains to Bordeaux (141FF, two hours), Lourdes (102FF), Pau (79FF, one hour), Saint Jean de Luz (24FF) and Saint Jean Pied de Port (45FF).

For travel to Spain, change trains at Irún. Night trains to the Italian border town of Ventimiglia go via Lourdes, Marseille and the Côte d'Azur.

Getting Around

Bus The bus network serving the BAB metropolitan area – Bayonne, Anglet and Biarritz – is called STAB. Single tickets cost 7FF (31/62FF for a carnet of five/10) and remain valid for an hour after they are time-stamped.

In Bayonne, STAB has an information office (☎ 05 59 59 04 61) in the Hôtel de Ville. It is open Monday to Saturday from 8 am to noon and 1.30 to 6 pm. Line No 1 links Bayonne's train station with the centre of Biarritz (Hôtel de Ville stop). Line No 2 starts at Bayonne's train station and passes through the centre of Biarritz before continuing on to the Biarritz-La Négresse train station. Bus No 4 links the train station in Bayonne and the centre of Biarritz via the Anglet coast and its beaches. No 9 is a scenic – if slow – way to get from Bayonne to Biarritz.

Taxi To order a taxi, call ☎ 05 59 59 48 48. There's a large rank in front of the train station.

BIARRITZ

The classy coastal town of Biarritz (population 30,000 but four times that in summer), which is eight km west of Bayonne, got its start as a resort in the mid-19th century when Emperor Napoleon III and his Spanish-born wife, Eugénie, began coming here. In later decades, Biarritz became popular with wealthy Britons and was visited by Queen Victoria and King Edward VII, both of whom have streets named in their honour. These days, Biarritz is known for its fine beaches and some of the best surfing in Europe.

Biarritz can be a real budget-buster. Consider making it a day trip from Bayonne or the HI hostel in Anglet.

Information

Tourist Office The tourist office (☎ 05 59 24 20 24) is one block east of Ave Édouard VII at 1 Square d'Ixelles. It's open daily from 9 am to 6.45 pm. From June to September it's open from 8 am to 8 pm when there is also an annexe at the train station open from 8.30 am to 7.30 pm.

Money & Post Change Plus (☎ 05 59 24 82 47) at 9 Rue Mazagram, west off Place Bellevue, offers pretty good rates and is open Monday to Friday from 9.30 am to 12.30 pm and 2 to 7 pm. From June to September it's open Monday to Saturday from 8 am to 8 pm and on Sunday from 10 am to 1 pm and 4 to 7 pm.

The main post office is between Place Clemenceau and Ave Jaulerry on Rue de la Poste. Biarritz' postcode is 64200.

Things to See & Do

The **Grande Plage**, lined in season with striped bathing tents, stretches from the Casino Bellevue to the grand old Hôtel du Palais, built in the mid-19th century as a villa for Napoleon III and Empress Eugénie. North of the Hôtel du Palais is **Plage Miramar**, bounded to the north by **Pointe Saint Martin** and the **Phare de Biarritz** (lighthouse), erected in 1834. There are four km of beaches north of Pointe Saint Martin in Anglet.

Heading southward from the Grande Plage, you can walk along the coast past the old fishing port and around the mauve cliffs of **Rocher de la Vierge**, a stone island topped with a white statue of the Virgin Mary and reached by a footbridge. There's a small beach just south of Rocher de la Vierge at the **Port Vieux**. The long **Plage de la Côte des Basques** begins a few hundred metres further down the coast.

The **Musée de la Mer** (☎ 05 59 24 02 59), Biarritz' sea museum, is on the esplanade near the Rocher de la Vierge footbridge. It has a 24-tank aquarium, exhibits on commercial fishing, and seal and shark pools. The museum is open daily from 9.30 am to 12.30 pm and 2 to 6 pm (to 7 pm with no midday closure from July to September and to midnight from mid-July to mid-August). Entry is 45FF (40FF reduced rate).

Introductory one-hour **cesta punta lessons** (100FF per person) are available at the Biarritz Athletic Club (☎ 05 59 23 91 09) in the Parc des Sports d'Aguilera south of the town centre.

Places to Stay

Most hotels raise their rates substantially in summer, sometimes by almost 100%.

The friendly *Hôtel Berthouet* (☎ 05 59 24 63 36), near the market at 29 Rue Gambetta, has clean singles/doubles with hardwood floors and outdated furniture for 90/130FF with washbasin and 150/210FF with shower. Hall showers are 20FF. The *Hôtel La Marine* (☎ 05 59 24 34 09) at 1 Rue des Goélands, off Rue Mazagram west from Place Bellevue, is a popular place with young travellers. Singles/doubles with shower are 130/150FF. Doubles with shower and toilet are 180FF.

One of the most attractive – and quiet – hotels in Biarritz is the *Hôtel Etche-Gorria* (☎ 05 59 24 00 74) at 21 Ave du Maréchal Foch. Situated in an old villa with a terrace and charming garden, it has doubles with washbasin and bidet from 200FF and with shower and toilet from 280FF.

Places to Eat

An excellent place for lunch is the central *O Frango* (☎ 05 59 24 20 12) at 11 Ave du Maréchal Foch with Portuguese and Spanish specialities starting at 45FF. Try the morue (salt cod) in garlic and olive oil or the tortilla española. Around the corner at 6 Rue Jean Bart, *Le Dahu* (☎ 05 59 22 01 02) serves traditional French cuisine daily except Monday in a rustic setting. Menus start at 85FF.

Pizzeria Les Princes (☎ 05 59 24 21 78) at 13 Rue Gambetta has pizzas for 45 to 55FF and pasta from 45FF. It's open for lunch and dinner (to 11.30 pm) daily except Wednesday and at lunch on Thursday. *Bar Jean* (☎ 05 59 24 80 38), right by the market at 5 Rue des Halles, serves super fresh tapas from 5FF.

Les Halles, the large food market south along Rue Gambetta, is open seven days a week from 5 am to 1.30 pm.

Getting There & Away

Bus For information on STAB buses to/from Bayonne and Anglet, see Getting Around in the Bayonne section. The STAB information office in Biarritz (☎ 05 59 24 26 53) is across Square d'Ixelles from the tourist office. It's open Monday to Saturday from 8 am to noon and 1 to 6 pm.

Train The Biarritz-La Négresse train station (☎ 08 36 35 35 39) is three km south of the centre at the southern end of Ave du Président John F Kennedy (the continuation of Ave du Maréchal Foch). SNCF has a downtown office

(☎ 05 59 24 00 94) at 1 Rue Étienne Ardoin at the corner of Ave du Maréchal Foch. It is open Monday to Friday from 9 am to noon and 2 to 6 pm.

Getting Around
Taxi To summon a taxi, call ☎ 05 59 23 18 18 or 05 59 63 17 17.

Motorcycle & Bicycle Two-wheeled conveyances of all sorts can be rented from Sobilo (☎ 05 59 24 94 47) at 24 Rue Peyroloubilh, which is south of Place Clemenceau where Rue Gambetta becomes Ave Beaurivage. Mountain bikes cost 70FF a day; scooters/motorcycles are 240/360FF.

AROUND BAYONNE
Saint Jean de Luz
The seaside town of Saint Jean de Luz (Donibane Lohitzun in Basque; population 13,000), 23 km south-west of Bayonne and 15 km from Biarritz, is an attractive beach resort with a colourful history of whaling and piracy. It's still an active fishing port and is celebrated for its fine Basque linen.

The richly decorated (and almost windowless) **Église Saint Jean Baptiste**, a mid-17th century church built in the traditional Basque style on Rue Gambetta, was the scene in 1660 of the marriage of King Louis XIV to the Spanish princess Marie-Thérèse, only an infant at the time. Don't miss the exceptional 17th-century **altar screen** with gilded wooden statues.

The tourist office (☎ 05 59 26 03 16) is south of the Église Saint Jean Baptiste on Place du Maréchal Foch and is open Monday to Sunday from 9 am to 12.30 pm and 2 (3 pm on Sunday) to 7 pm (to 8 pm without interruption in July and August).

If you want to spend the night (Saint Jean de Luz is an easy day trip from Bayonne or Biarritz), one of the nicest – if not cheapest – places is the two-star *Hôtel Ohartzia* (☎ 05 59 26 00 06), a few steps from the ocean at 28 Rue Garat. Doubles with shower and TV start at 280FF (higher in summer).

For a meal, *Tarterie-Saladerie Muscade* (☎ 05 59 26 96 73) nearby at 20 Rue Garat specialises in savoury tartes (30 to 45FF) and mixed salads (38 to 75FF). The speciality at *La Vieille Auberge* (☎ 05 59 26 19 61) at 22 Rue Tourasse, the street running parallel to the west, is ttoro (Basque fish soup). menus start at 75FF.

Frequent trains and buses link Saint Jean de Luz with Bayonne and Biarritz (see Getting There & Away and Getting Around in the Bayonne section). Buses leave from Place du Maréchal Foch. The train station is 200 metres south.

Saint Jean Pied de Port
The walled Pyrenean town of Saint Jean Pied de Port (Donibane Garazi in Basque; population 1800), 54 km south-east of Bayonne, was once the last stop in France for pilgrims on their way south to the Spanish city of Santiago de Compostela, the most important Christian pilgrimage site after Jerusalem and Rome in the Middle Ages. Today the town, which is in a hilly rural area, retains much of its Basque character. The views from the 17th-century **Citadelle** are picture-postcard perfect.

The tourist office (☎ 05 59 37 03 57), at 14 Place Charles de Gaulle just north of the Nive River, has a set of five maps for hiking in the area. The office is open Monday to Saturday from 9 am to noon and 2 to 7 pm (to 6 pm on Saturday). It opens on Sunday from mid-June to mid-September.

The cheapest place to stay in town is the *Hôtel des Remparts* (☎ 05 59 37 13 79) south of the Nive at 16 Place Fouquet. Singles/doubles with shower are 180/205FF. For more comfort, head north from the tourist office to the *Hôtel Itzalpea* (☎ 05 59 37 03 66) at 5 Place du Trinquet which has doubles with shower and toilet from 220FF. It also has a restaurant with hearty regional cuisine and menus from around 65FF. For a real splurge, try the *Restaurant des Pyrénées* (☎ 05 59 37 01 01), which boasts two Michelin stars. Menus are from 220 to 500FF.

Half the reason for coming to Saint Jean Pied de Port is the scenic train trip (three to six a day) from Bayonne, which takes about an hour. The cost from Bayonne is 45FF one way.

LOURDES
Lourdes (population 16,300) was just a sleepy market town on the edge of the snowcapped Pyrenees in 1858 when Bernadette Soubirous, a 14-year-old peasant girl, saw the Virgin Mary in a series of 18 visions that took place in a

FRANCE

grotto near the town. The girl's account was eventually investigated by the Vatican, which confirmed them as bona fide apparitions. Bernadette, who lived out her short life as a nun and died in 1879, was canonised as Saint Bernadette in 1933.

These events set Lourdes on the path to becoming one of the world's most important pilgrimage sites. Some five million pilgrims from all over the world converge on Lourdes annually, including many sick people seeking cures. But accompanying the fervent, almost medieval piety of the pilgrims is an astounding display of commercial exuberance that can seem unspeakably tacky. Wall thermometers, snowballs and plastic statues of the Virgin are easy to mock; just remember that people have spent their life savings to come here and for many of the Catholic faithful Lourdes is as sacred a place as Mecca, the Ganges, or the Wailing Wall in Jerusalem.

Orientation

Lourdes' two main east-west streets are Rue de la Grotte and, 300 metres north, Blvd de la Grotte. Both lead to the Sanctuaires Notre Dame de Lourdes, but Blvd de la Grotte takes you to the main entrance at Pont Saint Michel. The principal north-south thoroughfare, known as Chaussée Maransin when it passes over Blvd de la Grotte, connects Ave de la Gare and the train station with Place Peyramale.

Information

Tourist Office The new horseshoe-shaped glass-and-steel tourist office (☎ 05 62 42 77 40) at Place Peyramale is open Monday to Saturday from 9 am to noon and 2 to 6 pm (7 pm from Easter to mid-October when it's also open on Sunday). From May to September, there is no midday closure. The office sells a pass called Visa Passeport Touristique (139FF; 69.50FF for children under 12) allowing entry to seven museums in Lourdes.

Money & Post The Caisse d'Épargne at 17 Place du Marcadal is open weekdays from 8.45 am to noon and from 1.15 to 5 pm. There are several other banks nearby. The main post office (☎ 05 62 42 72 00), east of the tourist office at 1 Rue de Langelle, has a foreign exchange service. Lourdes' postcode is 65100.

Things to See

The huge religious complex that has grown around the cave where Bernadette saw the Virgin, **Sanctuaires Notre Dame de Lourdes**, is west of the city centre across the small Gave de Pau River. The grounds can be entered 24 hours a day via the Entrée des Lacets, which is on Place Monseigneur Laurence at the end of Rue de La Grotte. The Pont Saint Michel entrance is open from 5 am to midnight.

The more noteworthy sites in the complex include the **Grotte de Massabielle**, where Bernadette had her visions and which today is hung with the crutches of cured cripples, the nearby **pools** in which 400,000 people seeking to be healed immerse themselves each year and the **Basilique du Rosaire** (Basilica of the Rosary), which was built at the end of the 19th century in an overwrought pseudo-Byzantine style. Proper dress is required within the complex (don't wear short shorts, skirts or sleeveless shirts) and smoking is prohibited.

From the Sunday before Easter to at least mid-October, there are solemn **torch-lit processions** nightly at 8.45 pm from the Grotte de Massabielle. The **Procession Eucaristique** (Blessed Sacrament Procession), in which groups of pilgrims carrying banners march along the esplanade, takes place daily during the same period at 4.30 pm.

Other attractions in Lourdes include the **Musée Grévin** wax museum (☎ 05 62 94 33 74) at 87 Rue de la Grotte, where you can see life-size dioramas of important events in the lives of both Jesus Christ and Bernadette Soubirous, and the **Musée de Lourdes** (☎ 05 62 94 28 00), with similar exhibits a few steps south in the Parking de l'Égalité. The museums are open from 9 to 11.40 am and 1.30 to 6.30 pm (from 8.30 to 10 pm in July and August). Admission to the Musée Grévin is 33FF (17FF reduced rate), and 30FF (15FF reduced rate) to the Musée de Lourdes.

Sites directly related to the life of Saint Bernadette include: her birthplace, the **Moulin de Boly** (Boly Mill), down the alley next to 55 Blvd de la Grotte (12 Rue Bernadette Soubirous); the **Cachot**, the former prison where the impoverished Soubirous family was forced to move in 1857, at 15 Rue des Petits Fossés; and **Bernadette's school** in the Centre Hospitalier Général west of the train station on Chaussée

Maransin. Visits to all three are free and self-guided.

Between April and mid-October, the same two films about Saint Bernadette play at the **Cinéma Pax** (☎ 05 62 94 52 01), which is down the small street opposite 64 Rue de la Grotte. The eyrie-like medieval **Château Fort**, with the majority of its present buildings dating from the 17th or 18th centuries, houses the **Musée Pyrénéen** (☎ 05 62 94 02 04). The entrances to the chateau (opposite 42 Rue du Fort and off Rue du Bourg) are open daily (except Tuesday from mid-October to March) from 9 am to noon and 2 to 6 pm. Entry is 26FF.

Places to Stay
Lourdes has over 350 hotels, more than any city in France except Paris; even in winter, when many places close, it is no problem finding a relatively cheap room.

Camping The camping ground nearest the centre of town is *Camping de la Poste* (☎ 05 62 94 40 35) at 26 Rue de Langelle, a few blocks east of the main post office. It's open from late April to mid-October and charges 42FF for two people plus a tent. It also has doubles/quads with washbasin and bidet for 120/160FF in a nearby building.

Hotels The family-run *Hôtel de l'Annonciation* (☎ 05 62 94 22 78) at 23 Blvd de la Grotte has ordinary singles/doubles/quads with shower and toilet from 160/170/330FF. It's open from April to the end of October. The tidy *Hôtel Saint Sylve* (☎ 05 62 94 63 48) to the south at 9 Rue de la Fontaine has large singles/doubles with washbasin for 70/120FF. With shower, they're 90/140FF and with shower and toilet 100/150FF. Half-board, which includes room, breakfast and dinner, costs 120FF per person. The Saint Sylve is open all year.

A much more stylish place (and priced accordingly) is the fin de siècle *Hôtel de la Grotte* (☎ 05 62 94 58 87; fax 05 62 94 20 50) at 66 Rue de la Grotte, with balconies and a pretty garden. Singles/doubles with all the mod cons start at 320/340FF (higher in summer).

Places to Eat
Most hotels offer pilgrims half or full-board plans; some even require guests to stay on those terms. It usually works out cheaper than eating elsewhere, but the food is seldom very inspiring. Restaurants close early in this pious town; even *McDonald's* at 7 Place du Marcadal is slammed shut at 10 pm.

The friendly *Restaurant Les Tilleuls* (☎ 05 62 94 01 63) at 75 Rue de la Grotte has one of the cheapest menus around – 55FF for four courses. The *Restaurant Croix du Périgord* (☎ 05 62 94 26 65) at 13-15 Rue Basse just west of the tourist office serves up steak frites and a salad at lunch for only 38FF. *Restaurant La Rose des Sables* (☎ 05 62 42 06 82) across from the tourist office at 8 Rue des Quatre Frères Soulas specialises in couscous (from 66FF) and is open for lunch and dinner every day except Tuesday.

Les Halles, the covered market on Place du Champ Commun south of the tourist office, is open Monday to Saturday from 7 am to 2 pm. There's a *Prisunic* supermarket across the road on Rue Laffitte open Monday to Saturday from 8.30 am to 7.30 pm.

Getting There & Away
Bus The bus station (☎ 05 62 94 31 15), down Rue Anselme Lacadé from the covered market, has TER services to regional towns and cities including Pau (34.50FF, 1¼ hours). SNCF buses to the Pyrenean towns of Cauterets (36FF, one hour) and Luz Saint Sauveur (36FF, 1¼ hours) leave from the train station parking lot.

Train The train station (☎ 08 36 35 35 39) is one km east of the Sanctuaires on Ave de la Gare. Trains connect Lourdes with many cities including Bayonne (107FF, two hours), Bordeaux (169FF, 2½ hours) and Marseille (304FF, six hours). To Paris (395FF) there are three non-TGV trains to Gare d'Austerlitz and several TGVs to Gare Montparnasse. Local buses link the train station with the Grotte de Massabielle from April to mid-October.

AROUND LOURDES
The resort town of **Cauterets** (population 1200), 30 km south of Lourdes and accessible from there by SNCF bus, makes an excellent base for exploring the Parc National des

FRANCE

Pyrénées, which stretches for about 100 km along the Franco-Spanish border.

Cauterets (935 metres) is in a valley surrounded by mountains of up to 2800 metres, which offer some of the best skiing in the Pyrenees (at **Circuit du Lys** and **Pont d'Espagne**). The École de Ski Français (☎ 05 62 92 58 16) at Place Georges Clemenceau gives group and individual lessons. Other activities include taking the waters in the **Thermes César** (☎ 05 62 92 51 60) at 3 Place de la Victoire or hiking in the park. For information and maps, contact the Maison du Parc National des Pyrénées (☎ 05 62 92 52 56) at Place de la Gare.

The helpful tourist office (☎ 05 62 92 50 27) at Place du Maréchal Foch can book hotel rooms, but the cheapest places in town are the *Hôtel du Béarn* (☎ 05 62 92 53 54), around the corner at 4 Ave du Général Leclerc, and the friendly *Hôtel Le Grum* (☎ 05 62 92 53 01) at 4 Rue de l'Église. Both have simple rooms from 95FF; doubles with shower and toilet are around 190FF.

Périgord (Dordogne)

Although the name Périgord dates from pre-Roman times, the region is better known in English-speaking countries as the Dordogne, referring both to the department that covers most of the area and one of Périgord's seven rivers.

Périgord was one of the cradles of human civilisation. A number of local caves, including the world-famous Lascaux, are adorned with extraordinary prehistoric paintings, and there have been major finds here of the remains of Neanderthal and Cro-Magnon people. Périgord is also justly renowned for its cuisine, which makes ample use of those very French products, black *truffes* (truffles – subterranean fungi with a very distinct aroma and taste) and *foie gras*, the fatty liver of force-fed geese served on its own or used in preparing the finest *pâté*.

PÉRIGUEUX
Built over 2000 years ago around a curve in the gentle Isle River, Périgueux (population 36,000) rests these days on its two laurels: its proximity to the prehistoric sites of the Vézère Valley to the south-east and its status as the capital of one of France's true gourmet regions.

Orientation
The town is composed of three sections. The main one is the medieval and Renaissance old city (Puy Saint Front), which was built on a hill and whose pedestrians-only streets sweep down from Blvd Michel Montaigne to the Isle River. To the south-west is the older Gallo-Roman quarter (La Cité), whose centre is a ruined 2nd-century amphitheatre. The train station area and its cheap hotels are about one km north-west of the old city.

Information
The tourist office (☎ 05 53 53 10 63) is at 26 Place Francheville next to the 15th-century Tour Mataguerre. It's open Monday to Saturday from 9 am to noon and 2 to 6 pm; from mid-June to mid-September, the hours are 9 am to 7 pm, and 10 am to 5 pm on Sunday. For regional information, contact the Comité Départementale du Tourisme de la Dordogne (☎ 05 53 35 50 24) at 25 Rue du Président Wilson. It's open Monday to Friday from 9.30 am to noon and 2 to 5.30 pm and on Saturday from 9.30 am to noon (to 2 pm in summer).

The Banque de France is on Place Franklin Roosevelt. Other banks line Blvd Montaigne. The main post office (☎ 05 53 53 60 82) is 150 metres south-east at Rue du 4 Septembre. Périgueux's postcode is 24000.

Things to See & Do
The most appealing part of Périgueux is the **Puy Saint Front** quarter around the cathedral, which has a marked circuit you can follow with a walking map provided by the tourist office. When viewed at sunset, the five-dome **Cathédrale Saint Front** looks like something transported from Istanbul. Originally Romanesque, the massive church (the largest in south-western France) was almost totally rebuilt in a mock-Byzantine style in the mid-19th century. The interior (open from 8 am to 12.30 pm and 2.30 to 7.30 pm) is devoid of distinctive characteristics while the 12th-century cloister displays an odd mixture of styles.

The **Musée du Périgord** (☎ 05 53 53 16 42), north of the cathedral at 22 Cours Tourny, is France's second-most important prehistoric museum after the one at Les Eyzies de Tayac (see that section). It is open daily except Tuesday from 10 am to noon and 2 to 5 pm (6 pm in summer). Admission for adults/students is 12/6FF and free for those under 18.

The regional tourist office organises hiking, bicycling, horse riding and canoe excursions from April to October. Two days on the Vézère River costs 520FF per person, including equipment, board and tent accommodation. A weekend of guided mountain biking in the Dordogne Valley costs 750FF.

Organised Tours
Taxi Flanchec (☎ 05 53 53 70 47) offers regional circuits, including a trip to Les Eyzies de Tayac and Lascaux II (see Montignac in the Vézère Valley section) from 240FF. There must be a minimum of three people, and bookings will need to be made by telephone two days in advance.

Places to Stay
Camping The *Barnabé Plage* camp site (☎ 05 53 53 41 45) is about 2.5 km east of the train station along the Isle River. Open all year, it charges 15FF per adult and 14.50/9.50FF for a tent/car. To get there take bus No D from Place Michel Montaigne to the Rue des Bains stop.

Hostel The small *Foyer Des Jeunes Travailleurs* (☎ 05 53 53 52 05) south of the Puy Saint Front quarter is open all year and charges 65FF a night, including breakfast. Reception is open weekdays from 4 to 8 pm and weekends from noon to 1 pm and 7 to 8 pm. Bus No G from Place Montaigne goes to the nearby Lakanal stop.

Hotels One of the cheapest places near the train station is the *Hôtel des Voyageurs* (☎ 05 53 53 17 44) at 26 Rue Denis Papin, with basic singles/doubles for 74/80FF (hall showers are free) and 100FF for a double with shower. The *Hôtel du Midi et Terminus* (☎ 05 53 53 41 06), on the same street at No 18-20, is a huge, amiable place with basic singles from 125FF and doubles with shower from 155FF. Quads with two beds plus shower go for 185FF.

Near the old city, *Le Lion d'Or* (☎ 05 53 53 49 03) at 17 Cours Fenelon is on a busy road and locks the front door at 11 pm, but the large singles/doubles start at only 140FF (160FF with shower). A much more pleasant option is the two-star *Hôtel de l'Univers* (☎ 05 53 53 34 79) at 18 Cours Michel Montaigne. It has three small attic doubles without shower (hall showers are free) for 150FF and rooms with shower from 250FF.

Places to Eat
A few places, such as the homely *Vieux Pavé* (☎ 05 53 08 53 97) at 4 Rue de la Sagesse, have three-course formule rapide menus (quick-order meals) from 68FF. Inexpensive salads and vegetarian snacks can be found at *Le Tonic* (☎ 05 53 53 51 94), a café in a health club/gym at 4 Rue Gambetta. *Le Grange* (☎ 05 53 53 74 88) on Place Saint Silain is a popular pizzeria with tables set out in a pleasant, shady square. Daily specials start at 36FF. *Sorrentino* (☎ 05 53 53 20 45) at 1 Rue Chanzy near the amphitheatre is another pizzeria and pasta place.

The *Monoprix* on Place Bugeaud has a huge grocery section upstairs and is open Monday to Saturday from 8.30 am to 8 pm.

Getting There & Away
Bus The bus station (☎ 05 53 08 91 06) is on Place Francheville south-west of the city tourist office. CFTA runs three buses a day to Bergerac (42.20FF) and Sarlat (43.20FF), and there's a bus to Montignac weekdays at 6 pm (31.50FF, one hour).

Train Périgueux's train station (☎ 08 36 35 35 39) is on Rue Denis Papin, about one km north-west of the city tourist office. It's connected to Place Montaigne by bus Nos A and C. There are connections from here to Bordeaux (97FF, 1¼ hours), Limoges (78FF, one hour) and Toulouse (170FF, four hours). Short-haul destinations include Bergerac (74FF, 1½ hours), Sarlat (73FF, 1½ hours) and Les Eyzies de Tayac (39FF, 40 minutes).

Getting Around
Péribus' main hub is Place Montaigne; for information go to the Péribus kiosk (☎ 05 53 53 30 37) there. Single tickets are 7FF; a 10-ticket carnet costs 45FF.

VÉZÈRE VALLEY

Périgord's most important prehistoric caves are in the Vézère Valley south-east of Périgueux. Stretching from Le Bugue, near where the Vézère and Dordogne rivers meet, north to Montignac, the valley's centre is the village of Les Eyzies de Tayac, 45 km from Périgueux. Another 22 km south-east is Sarlat-la-Canéda, a lovely Renaissance town and the most pleasant base from which to explore the valley with a car. Montignac is the town closest to the Lascaux II cave. Those not under their own steam might consider a day tour (see Organised Tours in the Périgueux and Sarlat sections). Bus and train connections are very limited in the valley.

Les Eyzies de Tayac

As one of the world's major prehistoric centres, this tiny village (population 800) at the confluence of the Vézère and Beune rivers attracts a great many tourists. Most come to see some of the oldest art works in the world at the **Musée National de la Préhistoire** (☎ 05 53 06 97 03) or visit the **Musée de l'Abri Pataud** (☎ 05 53 06 92 46), an impressive Cro-Magnon rock shelter towering above the town. From mid-November to March, the museum is open daily except Tuesday from 9.30 am to noon and 2 to 5 pm (6 pm the rest of the year with no midday closure in July and August). Entry is 20FF (13FF for students and free for those under 18). The rock shelter is open daily except Monday and all of January from 10 am to noon and 2 to 5.30 pm (10 am to 7 pm in July and August). Entry is 25FF (12FF for students).

Two caves, **Grotte de Font de Gaume** and **Grotte des Combarelles**, are one and three km respectively north-east of Les Eyzies de Tayac on Route D47 (Route de Sarlat). Combarelles has thousands of animal engravings dating back some 15,000 years, but the narrow passages of Font de Gaume (with Lascaux and, in Spain, Altamira, one of only three Palaeolithic polychrome caves in the world) are covered with lifelike paintings of bison, reindeer, woolly rhinoceros and wolves in red, brown, white and black. Each cave costs 32/21FF for adults/students and both are open from 9 or 10 am to noon and 2 to 5 or 6 pm (Combarelles closes on Wednesday, Font de Gaume on Tuesday). Because the number of visitors allowed in each day is limited, you must book ahead on site or by phone (☎ 05 53 06 90 80).

Les Eyzies de Tayac's tourist office (☎ 05 53 06 97 05) is in the centre of the village at Place de la Mairie and is open weekdays (and weekends from April to October) from 9 am to noon and from 2 to 6 pm. The **Restaurant Chateaubriant** (☎ 05 53 06 91 74), a few steps to the north along the village's single road, is a good place to sample local specialities like cou d'oie farci (stuffed goose neck) or confit de canard (duck joints cooked very slowly in their own fat). There's an excellent-value lunch menu for 60FF. Train service to/from Périgueux and Sarlat exists but is infrequent.

Montignac

Montignac (population 2900), picturesquely situated on the Vézère River, is near Lascaux Cave and the facsimile Lascaux II. The tourist office (☎ 05 53 51 82 60) is on Place Bertran de Born and can help with bicycle rentals.

Lascaux Cave About 2.5 km south of Montignac off route D704 is the Lascaux Cave, discovered by four teenage boys in 1940 and sometimes called 'the Sistine Chapel of prehistoric art'. The cave was closed to visitors in 1960 when it was discovered that carbon dioxide and condensation from human breath were creating green fungus and even tiny stalactites on the 17,000-year-old paintings. Today the cave is kept at a constant 12°C (98% humidity), and visitors are allowed in at a rate of five a day, three times a week. The waiting list for visits is more than two years long.

But everyone can visit **Lascaux II** (☎ 05 53 51 95 03), a very exact paint and cement replica of the most important section of the original. The reproductions of the bison, horses and reindeer are so clear and alive that the paintings in the real caves may be disappointing! Only 2300 people can enter Lascaux II daily. Tours take 40 people and in the high season leave every 10 or 15 minutes.

Lascaux II is open Tuesday to Sunday (closed January) from 10 am to noon and 2 to 5.30 pm. In July and August, when tickets *must* be purchased from the Montignac tourist office, Lascaux II is open daily from 9.30 am to 7 pm. There are guided visits in English every hour.

Tickets, which cost 50FF (no discounts), also allow entry into **Le Thot** (☎ 05 53 50 70 44), a prehistoric theme park with a museum, mock-ups of Palaeolithic huts and living examples of some of the animals as seen in the cave paintings. It's all very *Flintstones*. Le Thot is just off lovely route D706 about four km south of Lascaux II and has the same opening hours.

Sarlat-la-Canéda

Despite centuries of war and conflagration, this beautiful Renaissance town (population 10,650) north of the Dordogne River has managed to retain most of its 16th and 17th-century limestone buildings.

Orientation & Information Modern Sarlat stretches for 2.5 km from the town hospital in the north to the train station in the south. The main drag linking the two is known as Rue de la République where it slices the heart-shaped old town almost in half. Three lovely squares – Place du Marché aux Oies, Place de la Liberté and Place du Peyrou – are in the restored eastern half.

The tourist office (☎ 05 53 59 27 67) is in the beautiful Hôtel de Maleville on Place de la Liberté. It's open Monday to Saturday from 9 am to noon and 2 to 6 pm. From June to September, it's also open on Sunday from 10 am to noon and 2 to 6 pm.

Things to See & Do The **Cathédrale Saint Sacerdos** on Place du Peyrou was originally part of a 9th-century Benedictine abbey but has been extended and rebuilt in a mixture of styles over the centuries. To the east is the **Jardin des Pénitents**, Sarlat's medieval cemetery, and the beehive-shaped **Lanterne des Morts** (Light of the Dead), a 12th-century tower dedicated to Saint Bernard. There's a colourful **Saturday market** on Place de la Liberté chock-full with truffles, mushrooms, geese and parts thereof.

Organised Tours HEP! Excursions (☎ 05 53 28 10 04) runs various tours to regional destinations, including the southern Vézère Valley (180FF, excluding entry to sights).

Places to Stay The closest camping ground to Sarlat is the expensive *Les Périères* (☎ 05 53 59 05 84), about 800 metres to the north-east

along route D47 towards Sainte Nathalène. It charges 104FF for two people including tent and is open from April to September. From the train station take the minibus to the La Bouquerie stop.

Hostel Sarlat's *Auberge de Jeunesse* (☎ 05 53 59 47 59) at 77 Ave de Selves is open from mid-March to late November. Charges are 40FF a night or 25FF for those who want to pitch their tent in the tiny backyard. It's just over two km from the train station, but the minibus stops close by at Le Cimetière on Rue du 26 Juin 1944.

Hotels One of the cheapest places in this relatively expensive town is the *Hôtel de la Mairie* (☎ 05 53 59 05 71) near the tourist office at 13 Place de la Liberté. Pleasant singles/doubles start at 170FF. Hall showers are free. The renovated *Hôtel les Récollets* (☎ 05 53 59 00 49), west of Rue de la République at 4 Rue Jean-Jacques Rousseau, has attractive rooms with washbasin and bidet for 190FF, with toilet and shower for 240FF.

Rooms with shower, toilet and TV at the large, chateau-like *Hôtel La Couleuvrine* (☎ 05 53 59 27 80; fax 05 53 31 26 83) start at 200FF though there is one small room for 160FF.

Places to Eat Two reasonably priced places facing each other on steep, narrow Côte de Toulouse west of Rue de la République are the *Pizzeria Romane* (☎ 05 53 59 23 88) at No 3 with pasta and pizza (from 35FF) and *La Petite Taverne* (☎ 05 53 28 35 52), opposite at No 2, with a 60FF Périgord menu.

For more salubrious surrounds, head for the *Auberge de Mirandol* (☎ 05 53 29 53 89) in a lovely Renaissance house at 7 Rue des Conseils just north of the Place du Marché aux Oies. An excellent-value menu costs 85FF.

Getting There & Away CFTA buses to Périgueux via Montignac (22.50FF, 25 minutes) leave from Place de la Petite Rigaudie north of the old town. The CFTA information office (☎ 05 53 59 01 48) is at 31 Rue de Cahors halfway between the old town and the train station.

Sarlat's tiny train station (☎ 08 36 35 35 39) is just over a km south of town at the end of

Ave de la Gare. Trains go to Périgueux (73FF, 1½ hours), Les Eyzies de Tayac (50FF, 40 minutes), Bordeaux (two via Saint Émilion: 117FF, 2½ hours) and Toulouse via Souillac (120FF, three hours).

Getting Around Sarlat's two bus routes (Nos A and B), serviced by minibus, run the length of the modern town and point north and south. To reach the old town from the train station, take bus No B and get off at the Jules Ferry stop.

Peugeot Cycles (☎ 05 53 28 51 87), north of the train station at 36 Ave Thiers, rents bicycles for 50FF a day and organises excursions in the countryside.

Burgundy & the Rhône Region

The Duchy of Burgundy (Bourgogne), situated on the great trade route between the Mediterranean and northern Europe, was wealthier and more powerful than the kingdom of France during the 14th and 15th centuries. These days, the region and its capital, Dijon, are known for their superb wines, great gastronomy and a rich architectural heritage.

By far the most important urban centre in the Rhône region, which lies south of Burgundy, is Lyon, France's second-largest city in area. Lyon's centuries of commercial and industrial prosperity, made possible by the mighty Rhône River and its tributary the Saône, have created an appealing city with superb museums, an attractive centre, shopping to rival that of Paris and a flourishing cultural life.

DIJON

Dijon (population 150,000), the prosperous capital of the dukes of Burgundy for almost 500 years, is one of France's most appealing provincial cities, its centre graced by elegant residences built during the Middle Ages and the Renaissance. Despite its long history, Dijon has a distinctly youthful air, in part because of the major university situated there. The city is a good starting point for visits to the nearby vineyards of the Côte d'Or, arguably the greatest wine-growing region in the world.

Orientation

Dijon's main thoroughfare runs eastward from the train station to Église Saint Michel. Ave Maréchal Foch links the train station with the tourist office. Rue de la Liberté, the principal shopping street, runs between Porte Guillaume (a triumphal arch erected in 1788) and the Palais des Ducs. The social centre of Dijon is Place François Rude, a popular hang-out in good weather.

Information

Tourist Office The tourist office (☎ 03 80 43 42 12), 300 metres east of the train station at Place Darcy, is open daily from mid-October to April from 9 am to 1 pm and 2 to 7 pm. During the rest of the year, hours are 9 am to 9 pm. The tourist office annexe (☎ 03 80 44 11 44) at 34 Rue des Forges, opposite the north side of the Palais des Ducs, is open from 9 am to noon and 1 to 6 pm.

Money & Post The Banque de France is at 2 Place de la Banque (just north of the covered market). There are quite a few banks along Rue de la Liberté. The main post office (☎ 03 80 50 62 14) is at Place Grangier. Exchange services are available. Dijon's postcode is 21000.

Things to See

The classical appearance of the **Palais des Ducs et des États de Bourgogne** (Palace of the Dukes & States-General of Burgundy) is the result of 17th and 18th-century remodelling. The mid-15th century **Tour Philippe le Bon**, in the palace's central building, offers a great view of the city. Between April and mid-November the tower is open daily from 9 am to noon and 1.45 to 5.30 pm. For the rest of the year, it's open on weekends only from 9 to 11 am and 1.30 to 3.30 pm, and on Wednesday from 1.30 to 3.30 pm. Across the courtyard are the vaulted **Cuisines Ducales** (Ducal Kitchens) built in 1445, a fine example of Gothic civic architecture. The front of the palace looks out onto the semicircular **Place de la Libération**, a gracious, arcaded public square laid out in 1686.

Some of the finest of Dijon's many medieval and Renaissance hôtels particuliers are along

Rue Verrerie and **Rue des Forges**, Dijon's main street until the 18th century. The splendid Flamboyant Gothic courtyard of the **Hôtel Chambellan** (1490) at 34 Rue des Forges, now home to a branch of the tourist office, is worth at least a peek. There's some remarkable vaulting at the top of the spiral staircase. **Rue de la Chouette**, where there are more old residences, runs along the north side of Église Notre Dame. It is named after the small stone owl (*chouette*) carved into the corner of one of the church's chapels, which people stroke for good luck and happiness.

Churches The Burgundian-Gothic **Cathédrale Saint Bénigne**, built in the late 13th century over what may be the tomb of St Benignus (who by tradition is believed to have brought Christianity to Burgundy in the 2nd century), is open daily from 8.45 am to 7 pm. Many of the great figures of Burgundy's history are buried here. The multicoloured tile roof is typically Burgundian.

The **Église Saint Michel**, begun in 1499, is a flamboyant Gothic church with an impressive Renaissance façade added in 1661. The unusual **Église Notre Dame** was built in the Burgundian-Gothic style during the first half of the 13th century. The three tiers of the extraordinary façade are decorated with dozens of false gargoyles (they aren't there to throw rainwater clear of the building). The **Horloge à Jacquemart** (mechanical clock) on the right tower dates from the late 14th century.

Museums The Carte d'Accès aux Musées is a combo ticket that gets you into seven major museums. It costs 20FF (10FF for students and people over 60). The Clé de la Ville-Dijon is similar but is valid for three days and includes a guided visit of the town. You can purchase both at museum ticket counters or at the tourist office. All museums are closed on Tuesday except the Musée Magnin, which is closed on Monday.

The **Musée des Beaux-Arts** (☎ 03 80 74 52 70), one of the most renowned fine arts museums in the provinces, is in the east wing of the Palais des Ducs. It's worth a visit just for the magnificent **Salle des Gardes** (Room of the Guards), rebuilt after a fire in 1502, which houses the extraordinary 15th-century Flamboyant Gothic sepulchres of two of the first Valois dukes of Burgundy. The museum is open from 10 am to 6 pm. Entry is 18FF (9FF for students and free for those under 18 and for everyone on Sunday).

Next to the cathedral at 5 Rue du Docteur Maret is the **Musée Archéologique** (☎ 03 80 30 88 54), containing a number of very rare Celtic and Gallo-Roman artefacts. It's open from 9 am to noon and 2 to 6 pm. From June to September hours are 9.30 am to 6 pm. Entry costs 12FF (6FF for students and free for teachers with ID and everyone on Sundays).

The **Musée Magnin** (☎ 03 80 67 11 10) is just off Place de la Libération at 4 Rue des Bons Enfants. This pleasant, mid-17th century residence contains a collection of 2000 assorted works of art assembled by Jeanne Magnin and her brother Maurice around the turn of the century. It's open from 10 am to noon and 2 to 6 pm (closed Monday). From June to September, it does not close at midday. Admission is 15FF (10FF for students, and free for art, art history and archaeology students and teachers with ID).

Places to Stay

Camping The *Camping du Lac* (☎ 03 80 43 54 72) at 3 Blvd Chanoine Kir is 1.2 km west of the train station, behind the psychiatric hospital. It's open from April to mid-November and charges 14/12/8FF per person/tent/car. From the train station, take bus No 12 and get off at the Hôpital des Chartreux stop.

Hostels The *Centre de Rencontres Internationales et de Séjour de Dijon* (CRISD; ☎ 03 80 71 32 12), Dijon's large, institutional hostel, is 2.5 km north-east of the town centre at 1 Blvd Champollion. A bed in a dorm costs 64FF, a single room 150FF, including breakfast. The hostel is closed from 10 am to 5 pm, but if you stay for a few days and pay in advance you can still get in during these hours. There's no curfew but you will need a hostelling card or an international student card. There are facilities for the disabled. To get to CRISD, take bus No 5 (towards Épirey) from Place Grangier. From 8.30 pm to midnight, Line A buses run hourly from the station or the centre.

Central Dijon

0   50   100 m

Many streets are one way
or pedestrian only

**To Chartreuse
de Champmol
(1 km), Camping
du Lac (1.2 km)
& Paris (313 km)**

Avenue Victor Hugo

Rue Guillaume Tell

Rue des Fleurs

Rue Jacques Cellerier

Rue Devosge

Place
St Bernard

Rue Audra

Avenue de la 1ère Armée

Rue Devosge

Boulevard de Brosses

Temple

Rue du Château

Rue

Rue des Godrans

Rue des Perrières

Jardin
Darcy

Avenue Maréchal Foch

Place
Darcy

5

3   4

Rue de la Poste

9

Place
Grangier

10

R Musette

Place
François
Rude

6

Boulevard de Sévigné

Rue Dr Chaussier

7

Rue du Docteur Maret

8

Place
de la Liberté

Rue Mariotte

32

31   30   29

33

Place
Saint
Bénigne

Rue Michelet

Rue du Chapeau Rouge

Rue Bossuet

Avenue Albert Premier

Jardin de
l'Arquebuse
(Botanical
Gardens)

Rue de l'Arquebuse

Rue Jehan de Marville

Rue du Faubourg Raines

Ouche River

Quai Nicolas Rolin

Rampart

Misericorde

Rue Danton

28

Rue Piron

Place
Bossuet

34

35

36

Rue Berbisey

Rue Monge

Place
Émile Zola

Rue Berbisey

Rue Sainte Anne

38

37

Rue Cordorcet

Rue de la Mandention

Rue de l'Hôpital

Rue de Tivoli

Rue du Transvaal

Blvd du
Castel

**To ADA Car
Rental (1 km),
Chenôve (4 km)
& Lyon
via A31**

Avenue Jean Jaurès

FRANCE

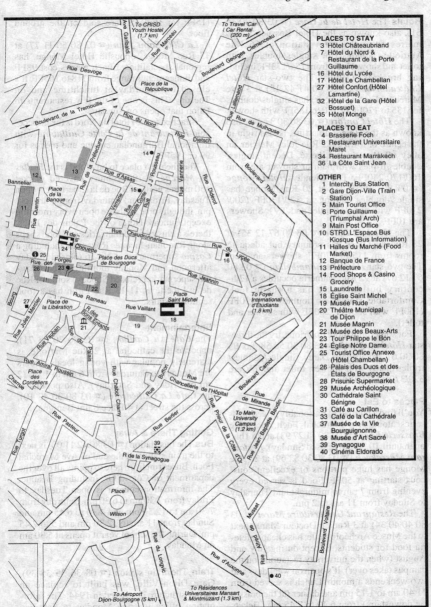

To CRISD
Youth Hostel
(1.7 km)

To Travel 'Car
l Car Rental
(200 m)

PLACES TO STAY
3 Hôtel Châteaubriand
7 Hôtel du Nord &
Restaurant de la Porte
Guillaume
16 Hôtel du Lycée
17 Hôtel Le Chambellan
27 Hôtel Confort (Hôtel
Lamartine)
32 Hôtel de la Gare (Hôtel
Bossuet)
35 Hôtel Monge

PLACES TO EAT
4 Brasserie Foch
8 Restaurant Universitaire
Maret
34 Restaurant Marrakech
36 La Côte Saint Jean

OTHER
1 Intercity Bus Station
2 Gare Dijon-Ville (Train
Station)
5 Main Tourist Office
6 Porte Guillaume
(Triumphal Arch)
9 Main Post Office
10 STRD L'Espace Bus
Kiosque (Bus Information)
11 Halles du Marché (Food
Market)
12 Banque de France
13 Préfecture
14 Food Shops & Casino
Grocery
15 Laundrette
18 Église Saint Michel
19 Musée Rude
20 Théâtre Municipal
de Dijon
21 Musée Magnin
22 Musée des Beaux-Arts
23 Tour Philippe le Bon
24 Église Notre Dame
25 Tourist Office Annexe
(Hôtel Chambellan)
26 Palais des Ducs et des
États de Bourgogne
28 Prisunic Supermarket
29 Musée Archéologique
30 Cathédrale Saint
Bénigne
31 Café au Carillon
33 Café de la Cathédrale
37 Musée de la Vie
Bourguignonne
38 Musée d'Art Sacré
39 Synagogue
40 Cinéma Eldorado

To Foyer
International
d'Etudiants
(1.8 km)

To Main
University Campus
(1.2 km)

To Résidences
Universitaires Mansart
& Montmuzard (1.3 km)

To Aéroport
Dijon-Bourgogne (5 km)

FRANCE

Hotels The *Hôtel de la Gare* (☎ 03 80 30 46 61), also known as the Hôtel Bossuet, is 300 metres from the train station at 16 Rue Mariotte. Nondescript singles/doubles with toilet and shower start from 154/173FF, including breakfast (19FF). The two-star *Hôtel Châteaubriand* (☎ 03 80 41 42 18) at 3 Ave Maréchal Foch (1st floor) has singles/doubles for 135 to 170FF or 140 to 185FF with shower.

The *Hôtel Confort* (☎ 03 80 30 37 47), also known as the Hôtel Lamartine, is also right in the centre of town at 12 Rue Jules Mercier, an alley off Rue de la Liberté. Decent singles/doubles/triples with bath or shower are from 160/170/240FF. The friendly *Hôtel Monge* (☎ 03 80 30 55 41) at 20 Rue Monge has singles/doubles starting at 120/130FF (200/210FF with shower, toilet and TV). Showers are 10FF.

The *Hôtel du Lycée* (☎ 03 80 67 12 35) at 28 Rue du Lycée has ordinary but adequate rooms from 115 to 170FF; showers are free. The two-star *Hôtel Le Chambellan* (☎ 03 80 67 12 67) at 92 Rue Vannerie occupies a 17th-century building and has a rustic feel. Comfortable singles or doubles are 110FF (160FF with shower, 200FF with shower and toilet).

For something more luxurious, try the three-star *Hôtel du Nord* (☎ 03 80 30 58 58; fax 03 80 30 61 26) at Place Darcy. Singles/doubles/triples/quads with shower, toilet and TV are 320/370/455/470FF.

Places to Eat

You'll find a number of reasonably priced brasseries along Ave Maréchal Foch, including *Brasserie Foch* (☎ 03 80 41 27 93) at No 1bis, open until 10.30 pm (closed Sunday). *Restaurant Marrakech* (☎ 03 80 30 82 69) at 20 Rue Monge has huge portions of excellent couscous starting at 50FF. Food is served every evening from 7 pm to midnight and Thursday to Sunday from 11 am to 2 pm.

The *Restaurant Universitaire Maret* (☎ 03 80 40 40 34) at 3 Rue du Docteur Maret, next to the Musée Archéologique, has cheap cafeteria food for students. Except during July and August (when the university restaurant on the campus takes over), it's open on weekdays and two weekends a month. Lunch is served from 11.40 am to 1.15 pm and dinner (at the brasserie downstairs) from 6.40 to 7.45 pm. Tickets (15FF for students) are sold on the ground floor.

La Côte Saint Jean (☎ 03 80 50 11 77) at 13 Rue Monge, opposite Hôtel Monge, has regional specialities. Lunch menus cost 98FF and dinner menus range from 118 to 165FF. It's closed on Saturday at lunchtime and on Tuesday. This is one of the few restaurants in Dijon that opens on Sunday.

Attached to the Hotel du Nord is the impeccable *Restaurant de la Porte Guillaume* with traditional Burgundian cuisine and menus for 99 or 195FF.

The cheapest place to buy food is the *Halles du Marché*, a 19th-century covered market 150 metres north of Rue de la Liberté. It is open Tuesday, Friday and Saturday from 6 am to 1 pm, though some stalls are open every morning except Sunday. North of the Palais des Ducs, there's a cluster of boulangeries and food shops along Rue Jean-Jacques Rousseau, including a *Casino* supermarket at No 16 (closed Sunday afternoon and Monday morning). The *Prisunic* supermarket (closed Sunday) south of Rue de la Liberté at 11-13 Rue Piron has a food section upstairs.

Entertainment

The *Café Au Carillon* (☎ 03 80 30 63 71), opposite the cathedral at 2 Rue Mariotte, is extremely popular with young locals. Hours are Monday to Saturday from 6 am to 1 am (2 am on Friday and Saturday). Also popular is the *Café La Cathédrale* (☎ 03 80 30 42 10), across the street at 4 Place Saint Bénigne.

Getting There & Away

Bus The bus station (☎ 03 80 42 11 00) is next to the train station at the end of Ave Maréchal Foch. Buses run from here to points all over the department of Côte d'Or, including Beaune. The information counter is open Tuesday to Friday from 7.30 am to 6.30 pm, Saturday from 7.30 am to 12.30 pm and 4.30 to 6.45 pm and Sunday from 11 am to 12.30 pm and 5 to 7.45 pm. During the school year it opens at 5.30 am on Monday.

Train The train station (☎ 08 36 35 35 39), Gare Dijon-Ville, was built to replace an earlier structure destroyed in 1944. The information office is open Monday to Saturday from 9 am to 7 pm (6 pm on Saturday). At least one ticket counter is always open every day from 7 am to 10 pm. Going to/from Paris' Gare de Lyon by TGV (215 to 274FF) takes about 1¾ hours. Prices vary according to the day of travel; Friday and Saturday are generally the most expensive. There are non-TGV trains to Lyon (132 to 145FF, two hours) and Nice (from 372FF, eight hours).

Getting Around

Dijon's extensive urban bus network is run by STRD (☎ 03 80 30 60 90). Single trips cost 5.20FF; various bus passes are available, including a day ticket (15.14FF) and a 12-trip ticket (40FF). Eight different bus lines stop along Rue de la Liberté and six more stop at Place Grangier. Most STRD buses run Monday to Saturday from 6 am to 8 pm, and on Sunday from 1 to 8 pm. Six lines (A, B, C D, E and F) run from 8 pm to 12.15 am. STRD's L'Espace Bus Kiosque (information office) in the middle of Place Grangier is open Monday to Friday from 7.15 am to 7.15 pm, and Saturday from 8.30 am to 12.15 pm and 2.15 to 7.15 pm.

VINEYARDS AROUND DIJON

Burgundy's finest vineyards come from the vine-covered Côte d'Or, the eastern slopes of the limestone, flint and clay escarpment running for about 60 km south of Dijon. The northern section is known as the Côte de Nuits and the southern section as the Côte de Beaune. The tourist offices in Dijon, Beaune and nearby towns can provide details on wine cellars (caves) that offer tours and wine tasting (dégustation).

For detailed information on the region's wines, vineyards, wine cellars and merchants, get a copy of the booklet *Guide des Caves* (25FF), available at the tourist office in Beaune. The tourist office can also book you onto an organised tour of vineyards in a minibus. The trips last two hours, include a guide, and some wine tasting. There are three Safari Tours a day, and prices start at 170FF per person.

North of Beaune are the picturesque wine-making villages of Nuits Saint Georges, Vosne-Romanée, Clos de Vougeot and Gevrey-Chambertin, which are known for their fine reds and offer excellent wine-tasting opportu-

nities. You can also visit the **Clos de Vougeot chateau**, which was founded by Cistercian monks in the 12th century and owned by them until the Revolution. The chateau (☎ 03 80 62 89 09) is open daily from 9 to 11.30 am and 2 to 5.30 pm (from 9 am to 6.30 pm with no midday break from April to September). Entrance is 16FF (students 8FF) and includes a 45-minute guided tour (departing every half-hour in summer) but no tasting.

Gevrey-Chambertin chateau, where the staunchly monarchist and octogenarian Madame Masson gives you a charming tour (in English) of her home and cellar, is also worth visiting. Entry costs 20FF and includes one tasting.

Beaune

The attractive town of Beaune (population 22,000), a major wine-making centre about 40 km south of Dijon, makes an excellent day trip. Its most famous historical site is the Hôtel-Dieu, France's most opulent medieval charity hospital. The tourist office (☎ 03 80 26 21 30) is at Rue de l'Hôtel-Dieu, opposite the entrance to the Hôtel-Dieu.

The **Hôtel-Dieu**, founded in 1443 by Nicolas Rolin, is built in Flemish-Burgundian Gothic style and features a distinctive multicoloured tile roof. Of particular interest are the hospice's **Hall of the Poor** and the **Apothecary**, with a vast array of china and glass jars full of herbal potions. Don't miss the extraordinary polyptych of *The Last Judgment*, a medieval masterpiece by Roger van der Weyden. You'll find it in the darkened room off the hall. The Hôtel-Dieu is open from late March to late November from 9 am to 6.30 pm; the rest of the year, hours are 9 to 11.30 am and 2 to 5.30 pm. Entry is 29FF (22FF for students). Make sure you pick up the informative brochure (in English) at the ticket counter.

For wine tasting in Beaune, you can visit the **Marché aux Vins** at Rue Nicolas Rolin, where you can sample 15 wines for 50FF. It is closed from mid-December to 26 January. **Patriarche Père et Fils** at 7 Rue du Collège has the largest wine cellars in Burgundy, containing several million bottles. You can taste 13 wines for 40FF. It is open daily from 9 to 11.30 am and 2 to 5.30 pm.

FRANCE

Places to Eat As one of France's prime gastronomic centres, Beaune is a great place to indulge your taste buds. The town has an abundant selection of restaurants, including the *Restaurant Bernard Morillon* (☎ 03 80 24 12 06) at 31 Rue Maufoux, with one Michelin star and with menus from 180FF. *Les Jardins du Rempart* (☎ 03 80 24 79 41) at 10 Rue de l'Hôtel-Dieu offers impeccable food and service; menus range from 130 (170 at weekends) to 280FF. The restaurant is closed on Sunday evening and Monday. Another good (and more informal) choice is *La Grilladine* (☎ 03 80 22 22 36), just up the road from Bernard Morillon at 17 Rue Maufoux. Menus cost from 72 to 199FF.

The city also has a fantastic collection of food shops – if you want to prepare a gourmet picnic, this is the place to do it. The boulangerie-pâtisserie *Aux 3 Épis*, at 31 Rue d'Alsace, and the boucherie *J Rossignol* close by at 19 Rue Faubourg Madeleine have a great selection of edibles.

Getting There & Away You can get from Dijon to Beaune by train (36.80FF, about 30 minutes) or bus (36.40FF, one hour). Trains also stop at various villages along the way, including Gevrey-Chambertin, Vougeot and Nuits Saint Georges but services are limited in winter. Transco bus No 44 is a good bet if you want to stop along the way as there are vineyards at virtually every stop. Service is greatly reduced on Sunday.

LYON

The grand city of Lyon, with a population of 423,000, is part of a prosperous urban area of 1.26 million people, making it the second-largest conurbation in France. Founded by the Romans over 2000 years ago, it has spent the last 500 years as a commercial, industrial and banking powerhouse. Lyon is endowed with outstanding museums, a dynamic cultural life, an important university, up-market shops, lively pedestrian malls and excellent cuisine – it is, after all, one of France's gastronomic capitals, even for people on a budget.

Lyon, founded in 43 BC as the Roman military colony of Lugdunum, served as the capital of the Roman territories known as the Three Gauls under Augustus. The 16th century marked the beginning of the city's extraordinary prosperity. Banks were established, great commercial fairs were held, and trade flourished. Printing arrived before the end of the 15th century; within 50 years Lyon was home to several hundred printers. The city became Europe's silk-weaving capital in the mid-1700s. The famous *traboules*, a network of covered passageways in Croix Rousse and Vieux Lyon, originally built to facilitate the transport of silk during inclement weather, proved very useful to the Résistance during WWII. In 1944, the retreating Germans blew up all but one of the city's two dozen bridges.

Orientation

Lyon's city centre is on the Presqu'île, a long, thin peninsula bounded by the Rhône and Saône rivers. The elevated area north of Place des Terreaux is known as Croix Rousse. Place Bellecour is one km south of Place des Terreaux and one km north of Place Carnot, which is next to one of Lyon's train stations, Gare de Perrache. The city's other train station, Gare de la Part-Dieu, is two km east of the Presqu'île in a huge, modern commercial district known as La Part-Dieu. Vieux Lyon (the old city) is on the west bank of the Saône River between the city centre and Fourvière hill.

Information

Tourist Offices The main tourist office (☎ 04 78 42 25 75) is in the south-east corner of Place Bellecour. It is open Monday to Friday from 9 am to 6 pm and Saturday until 5 pm. From mid-June to mid-September, hours are 9 am to 7 pm (6 pm on Saturday). The same building houses an SNCF information and reservations desk, open Monday to Saturday from 9 am to 6 pm (5 pm on Saturday).

The tourist office annexe at Gare de Perrache (in the pedestrian flyover that links the train station with the upper level of the Centre d'Échange) is open Monday to Friday from 9 am to 6 pm and to 5 pm on Saturday; in summer, weekday hours are 9 am to 6 pm and to 7 pm on Saturday.

In Vieux Lyon, the tourist office annexe (☎ 04 78 42 25 75) on Ave Adolphe Max, right next to the lower funicular station, is open Monday to Friday from 9 am to 6 pm, on Saturday until 5 pm, and on Sunday from 10 am to 5 pm. Summer hours are 10.30 am to 7.30

pm Monday to Saturday and 10 am to 6 pm on Sunday.

Money The Banque de France is at 14 Rue de la République on Place de la Bourse. There is a Caisse d'Épargne de Lyon (open Tuesday to Friday and on Saturday mornings) at 2 Place Ampère, and there are other banks on Rue Victor Hugo just north of Place Ampère. Near Place des Terreaux, there are a number of banks on Rue de la République and Rue du Bât d'Argent.

American Express (☎ 04 78 37 40 69), near Place de la République at 6 Rue Childebert, is open weekdays from 9 am to noon and 2 to 6 pm and, from May to September, on Saturday morning also. At Gare de la Part-Dieu, Thomas Cook (☎ 04 72 33 48 55) is open daily from October to April from 8 am (10.30 am on Sunday) to 7 pm. During the rest of the year it's open daily from 8 am to 8 pm. The Thomas Cook office (☎ 04 78 38 38 84) at Gare de Perrache keeps roughly the same hours, but shuts at midday from 12.15 to 1.25 pm.

Post The main post office (☎ 04 72 40 60 50) at 10 Place Antonin Poncet has foreign currency services. The branch office at 3 Rue du Président Édouard Herriot, near Place des Terreaux, can also change money. There is another office at 8 Place Ampère.

Lyon's postcodes consist of the digits 6900 followed by the number of the arrondissement (one to nine).

Bookshops The Eton English Bookshop (☎ 04 78 92 92 36) at 1 Rue du Plat has lots of new paperbacks as well as some Lonely Planet titles. Students get a 5% discount.

Things to See
The tourist office has details of guided tours of Lyon on foot, by boat and by bus. You can also buy a Clé de la Ville ticket for 90FF which includes an audio-guided tour, and entrance to the six principal museums.

Vieux Lyon The old city, whose narrow streets are lined with over 300 meticulously restored medieval and Renaissance houses, lies at the base of Fourvière hill. The area underwent urban renewal two decades ago and has since become a trendy place in which to live and socialise. Many of the most interesting old buildings are along Rue du Bœuf, Rue Juiverie, Rue des Trois Maries and Rue Saint Jean. Traboules that can be explored include those at 68 Rue Saint Jean and 1 Rue du Bœuf; a comprehensive list is available at the tourist office.

Begun in the late 12th century, the mainly Romanesque **Cathédrale Saint Jean** has a Flamboyant Gothic façade and portals decorated with stone medallions from the early 14th century. Don't miss the 14th-century astronomical clock in the north transept. The cathedral can be visited daily from 8 am to noon and 2 to 7.30 pm (5 pm on weekends and holidays).

The **Musée Gadagne** (☎ 04 78 42 03 61) at 12 Rue de Gadagne (or Place du Petit Collège) has two sections: the Musée de la Marionette, featuring puppets of all sorts, including *guignol* (a French 'Punch-and-Judy'), created by the museum's founder, Laurent Mourguet (1769-1844), which has become one of the city's symbols; and the Musée Historique, which illustrates the history of Lyon. Both are open daily except Tuesday from 10.45 am to 6 pm (8.30 pm on Friday). The entry fee is 20FF (10FF for students). Puppet performances are held, amongst other places, at the Guignol de Lyon Theatre (☎ 04 78 28 92 57) at 2 Rue Louis Carrand north of Place du Change.

Fourvière Two millenniums ago, the Romans built the city of Lugdunum on the slopes of Fourvière. Today, the hill – topped by the Tour Métallique, a sort of stunted Eiffel Tower erected in 1893 and now used as a TV transmitter – offers spectacular views of Lyon and its two rivers.

Several paths lead up the slope, but the easiest way to get to the top is to take the funicular railway (metro: Vieux Lyon) from Place Édouard Commette in Vieux Lyon. The Fourvière line, with an upper terminus right behind the basilica, operates daily until 6 pm. You can use a bus/metro ticket or you can purchase a special return ticket for 12FF, which is valid all day for one trip up and one trip down.

The exceptional **Musée Gallo-Romain** (☎ 04 78 25 94 68) at 17 Rue Cléberg is well

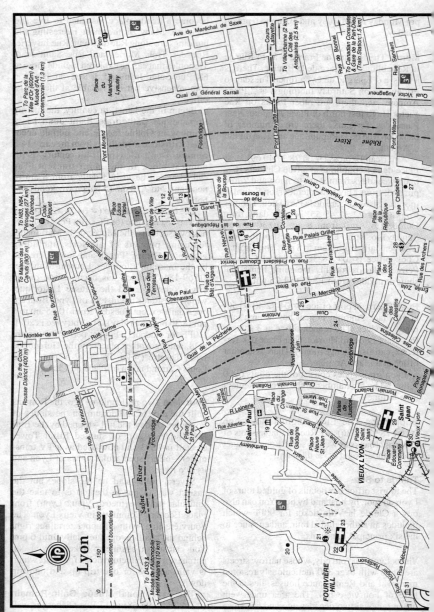

Lyon

0   150   300 m

arrondissement boundaries

FRANCE

To Parc de la
Tête d'Or (600m) &
Musée d'Art
Contemporain (1.3 km)

Ave du Maréchal de Saxe

To Villeurbanne (2 km)
& Cité de la
Antiquaires (2.5 km)

To Canadian Consulate (4 km),
& Gare de la Part-Dieu
(Train Station) (1.5 km)

Place du
Maréchal
Lyautey

Quai du Général Sarrail

Quai Victor Augagneur

Foch

Cours
Lafayette

Rue de Bonnel

Rue Servient

3e

6e

Pont Morand

Footbridge

Footbridge

Pont Lafayette

Rhône River

Pont Wilson

To N83, N84,
Pérouges (27 km)
& La Dombes

To Maison des
Canuts (900 m)

1er

Place
Louis
Pradel

Hôtel de Ville

Place de
la Bourse

Rue du Président Carnot

Rue Childebert

27

Croix
Paquet

Rue Romarin

Rue de la République

Rue Neuve

Rue Grenette

Rue Cordeliers

Rue Palais Grillet

Rue Ferrandière

Place
de la
République

Place
des
Jacobins

Rue de la République

28

R du Garet

Sec

Place
des
Terreaux

Rue Paul
Chenavard

Rue du Bât d'Argent

Rue du Président Édouard Herriot

Rue de Brest

Rue Mercière

Rue des Archers

Emile Zola

R des Capucins

Rue Ste-Catherine

Rue d'Algérie

St Antoine

Quai

Place
des
Célestins

Quai des Célestins

Montée de la Grande Côte

Rue Terme

Rue de la Martinière

Quai de la Pêcherie

Pont Alphonse Juin

Footbridge

Pont
Bonaparte

To the Croix
Rousse District (400 m)

Montée de la

Rue Burdeau

Rue de l'Annonciade

O Octavio May

Quai Romain Rolland

Quai Romain Rolland

Saône River

Footbridge

Rue Carriès

Place
St Paul

R Lainerie

R Juiverie

Barthélemy

Rue de Gadagne

Place
du
Change

Rue St-Jean

Rue des Trois Maries

Saint Jean

Place
Neuve
St-Jean

Palais
de
Justice

Saint Jean

Vieux Lyon

Place
Édouard
Commette

VIEUX LYON

Saint Paul

To D433 &
Musée de l'Automobile
Henri Malartre (10 km)

FOURVIÈRE
HILL

Montée

Roger Radisson

Rue Cléberg

31

21

22

23

20

19

24

25

26

29

30

5e

1

2

3

4

5

6

7

8

9

10

11

12

13

14

15

16

17

18

PLACES TO STAY

4 Hôtel Le Terme
43 Hôtel Vaubecour
48 Hôtel d'Ainay
49 Hôtel Vichy
51 Hôtel Le Beaujolais
52 Hôtel Dubost
53 Hôtels, Restaurants & Food Shops

PLACES TO EAT

3 Chouettel Un Tonneaul
6 Le Canut
11 Chez Georges
12 Le Garet
13 Alyssaar
25 Le Saint-Joseph
58 Brasserie Georges Lyon

OTHER

1 Amphithéâtre des Trois Gauls (Roman Amphitheatre)
2 Les Halles de la Martinière (Food Market)
5 Albion Public House
7 Musée des Beaux-Arts
8 Post Office Branch
9 Hôtel de Ville
10 Opéra
14 Banks
15 Cinéma Ambiance
16 Banque de France
17 Musée de l'Imprimerie
18 Église Saint Nizier
19 Musée Gadagne
20 Tour Métallique
21 Tourist Office Branch
22 Fourvière Funicular Station
23 Basilique Notre Dame de Fourvière
24 Outdoor Food Market
26 Prisunic Supermarket
27 UK Consulate
28 American Express
29 Cathédrale Saint Jean
30 Saint Jean Tourist Office Annexe
31 Musée Gallo-Romain
32 Roman Theatres
33 Minimes Funicular Stop
34 Express Market & Boulangerie
35 Laundrette
36 Eton English Bookshop
37 Louis XIV Statue
38 Main Tourist Office & SNCF Desk
39 Main Post Office
40 Laundrette
41 Fromagerie Victor Hugo
42 Food Shops
44 Post Office Branch
45 Caisse d'Épargne
46 Musée des Arts Décoratifs
47 Musée Historique des Tissus
50 Commissariat de Police
54 Centre d'Échange & Bus Terminal
55 Tourist Office Annexe
56 Airport Bus (Satobus)
57 Gare de Perrache

To Institut Lumière (2.3 km), Hôpital Édouard Herriot (3 km) & Grande Mosque (4 km)

Cours de la Liberté

Cours Gambetta

LYON RIVE GAUCHE

Quai Victor Augagneur

Rhône River

Pont de la Guillotière

Pont de l'Université

Quai du Docteur Gailleton

To University

PRESQU'ÎLE

Rue des Marronniers

Rue Antonin Poncet

Bellecour

Place Bellecour

Rue Colonel Chambonnet

Rue de la Barre

Rue

Rue Charité

la

Rue Sala

Hélène

Rue des Remparts d'Ainay

Rue Franklin

Rue

de

Condé

Rue A. Fochier

Rue Victor Hugo

Rue Sainte-Hélène

Rue Duhamel

Rue

Rue Jarente

Ampère

Place Ampère

Rue Henri IV

Rue d'Enghien

Rue de Condé

Place Carnot

Saône River

Quai Tilsitt

Rue du Plat

Fulchiron

Footbridge

Saint Georges

Quai Sainte Georges

Rue Sainte Georges

Rue du Doyenné

To Saint-Just Funicular Station

To Saint Just

To Place Jean Macé, Locasport Bike Rental (800m), Centre International de Séjour (3.8 km), Auberge de Jeunesse (4.5 km), A43, Airport (25 km) & Grenoble

Perrache

Cours de Verdun Perrache

Rue de Verdun

Rue du Bélier

Ave Berthelot

Pont Gallieni

To A7 & Marseille

To Camping International de la Porte de Lyon (10 km), Beaujolais (40 km) & Paris

FRANCE

worth seeing even if you don't consider yourself a fan of Roman history. Among the museum's extraordinary artefacts, almost all of which were found in the Rhône Valley area, are the remains of a four-wheeled vehicle from around 700 BC, several sumptuous mosaics and lots of Latin inscriptions, including the bronze text of a speech made by the Lyon-born Roman emperor Claudius in 48 AD. The two rebuilt Roman theatres next to the museum are still used for concerts in June. The museum is open from 9.30 am to noon and 2 to 6 pm (closed Monday, Tuesday and bank holidays). Admission is 20FF (10FF for students).

Like Sacré Cœur in Paris, the **Basilique de Notre Dame de Fourvière**, completed in 1896, was built by subscription to fulfil a vow taken by local Catholics during the disastrous Franco-Prussian War (1870-71). If overwrought marble and mosaics are not your cup of tea, the panoramic view from the nearby terrace still merits a visit. From November to March, the basilica is open from 6 am to noon and 2 to 6 pm; otherwise, hours are 6 am to 7 pm.

Presqu'île In the middle of the **Place des Terreaux** there is a monumental 19th-century fountain by Bartholdi, sculptor of the Statue of Liberty. The four horses represent the four major French rivers galloping seaward. Fronting the square is the **Hôtel de Ville**, built in 1655 but given its present façade in 1702. To the south, there are up-market shops along and around **Rue de la République**, known for its 19th-century buildings; it's a pedestrian mall, as is Rue Victor Hugo, which runs southward from 17th-century **Place Bellecour**, one of the largest public squares in Europe.

The Lyonnais are especially proud of their **Musée Historique des Tissus** (History of Textiles Museum; ☎ 04 78 37 15 05) at 34 Rue de la Charité. Its collection includes extraordinary Lyonnais silks and fabrics from around the world. The museum is open from 10 am to 5.30 pm (closed Monday and holidays). Entry is 26FF (13FF for students under 25), but is free on Wednesdays. The ticket also gets you into the **Musée des Arts Décoratifs**, nearby at No 30, which closes between noon and 2 pm.

The history of printing, a technology that had firmly established itself in Lyon in the 1480s (less than 40 years after its invention) is illustrated by the **Musée de l'Imprimerie** (☎ 04 78 37 65 98) at 13 Rue de la Poulaillerie. Among the exhibits are some of the first books ever printed, including a page of a Gutenberg Bible (1450s) and several incunabula (books printed before 1500). The museum is open from 9.30 am to noon and 2 to 6 pm (all day Friday) but is closed Monday and Tuesday. The entry fee is 20FF (10FF for students).

Lyon's outstanding fine arts museum, the **Musée des Beaux-Arts** (☎ 04 72 10 17 40), whose 90 rooms house sculptures and paintings from every period of European art, is at 20 Place des Terreaux. It's open from 10.30 am to 6 pm (closed Monday and Tuesday). The entry fee is 20FF (10FF for students aged 18 to 25).

Set up by the Guild of Silk Workers (called *canuts* in French), the **Maison des Canuts** (☎ 04 78 28 62 04) at 10-12 Rue d'Ivry (300 metres north of the Croix Rousse metro stop) traces the history of Lyon's silk-weaving industry. Weavers are usually on hand to demonstrate the art of operating traditional silk looms. It is open weekdays from 8.30 am to noon and 2 to 6.30 pm and Saturday from 9 am to noon and 2 to 6 pm. Opening times may vary in August. Tickets cost 10FF (5FF for students under 26).

Other Attractions At the time of writing, the **Musée d'Art Contemporain** (☎ 04 72 69 17 17) was being relocated to the Cité Internationale, Quai Charles-de-Gaulle, and was due to open in June 1996. It specialises in work produced after 1960, but check with the tourist office for all details.

The **Institut Lumière** (☎ 04 78 78 18 95) at 25 Rue du Premier-Film (8e) has a permanent exhibition (25FF entry) on the work of the motion-picture pioneers Auguste and Louis Lumière. The institute is open daily except Monday from 2 to 7 pm, and tickets cost 27FF (22FF concession). Films (non-dubbed also) are shown daily at 6, 8 and 10 pm. In summer, open-air films are screened for free in the square.

Places to Stay
Camping The *Camping International de la Porte de Lyon* (☎ 04 78 35 64 55), about 10 km north of Lyon in Dardilly, is open year-

round. This attractive and well-equipped camping ground (with facilities for the disabled) charges 32FF to park and pitch a tent and 17FF per person. It closes at 9 pm in winter and midnight in summer. Bus No 19 (towards Ecully-Dardilly) from the Hôtel de Ville metro station stops right in front of it. To get there by car, take the A6 towards Paris.

Hostels The *Auberge de Jeunesse* (☎ 04 78 76 39 23) is about five km south-east of Gare de Perrache at 51 Rue Roger Salengro in Vénissieux. Beds cost 48FF, breakfast 18FF and sheets 16FF. Reception is open from 7.30 am to noon and from 5 pm to 12.30 am; curfew is also at 12.30 am. To get there from the Presqu'île, take bus No 35 from Place Bellecour (Georges Lévy stop); from Gare de Perrache take bus No 53 (Etats-Unis-Viviani stop), and from Gare de la Part-Dieu take bus No 36 (Viviani-Joliot-Curie stop).

The *Centre International de Séjour* (☎ 04 78 01 23 45, 04 78 76 14 22) is about four km south-east of Gare de Perrache at 46 Rue du Commandant Pégoud, behind 101 Blvd des États-Unis. Guests staying more than one night must buy a membership card, which costs 14FF and is valid for a year. Weekday rates range from 83FF (for a bed in a quad with shower and breakfast) to 130FF (for a single with sheets and breakfast). Weekend rates are 78/123FF. From the train stations, take the same buses as for the Auberge de Jeunesse.

Hotels The neighbourhood around Place Carnot, just north of Gare de Perrache, is a bit on the seedy side, but the hotels here are convenient if you're travelling by train. The cheapest place in town is the very basic and unwelcoming *Hôtel Le Beaujolais* (☎ 04 78 37 39 15) at 22 Rue d'Enghien. Singles/doubles cost between 130 and 142FF; rooms with shower cost 161/162FF. Hall showers are 17FF. The two-star *Hôtel Dubost* (☎ 04 78 42 00 46) is at 19 Place Carnot, to the left as you come out of the train station. There are two singles for 215FF. Singles/doubles/triples with shower, toilet and TV are from 245/257/340FF.

In the area north of the train station, the old-fashioned *Hôtel Vaubecour* (☎ 04 78 37 44 91) at 28 Rue Vaubecour has singles from 105 to 120FF and doubles from 140 to 200FF.

Hall showers cost 15FF. The friendly, family-run *Hôtel d'Ainay* (☎ 04 78 42 43 42) at 14 Rue des Remparts d'Ainay (2nd floor), just off Place Ampère, has simply furnished singles/doubles for 155/165FF or 198/208FF with shower, and 215/225FF with shower, toilet and TV. Quads with shower are 416FF. Hall showers are 15FF and breakfast is 24FF.

One of the most affordable places in town is the family-run *Hôtel Vichy* (☎ 04 78 37 42 58) at 60bis Rue de la Charité (1st floor). Basic rooms range from 103 to 138FF or 148 to 175FF with shower. Hall showers are 20FF. The *Hôtel Le Terme* (☎ 04 78 28 30 45) at 7 Rue Sainte Catherine (1er) is in a lively area a few blocks north-west of the Hôtel de Ville. It has simply furnished singles or doubles from 150FF and more comfortable rooms for around 220FF.

Places to Eat

There are two *bouchons* – small, friendly, unpretentious restaurants that serve traditional Lyonnais cuisine – near Place des Terreaux. One is *Chez Georges* (☎ 04 78 28 30 46) at 8 Rue du Garet. The other is the cosy *Le Garet* (☎ 04 78 28 16 94) at 7 Rue du Garet, which is popular with locals. Both are open Monday to Friday. *Alyssaar* (☎ 04 78 29 57 66), a Syrian restaurant specialising in dishes from Aleppo (49 to 68FF), is at 29 Rue du Bât d'Argent. It's open Monday to Saturday until midnight.

Chouette! Un Tonneau! (☎ 04 78 27 42 42) at 17 Rue d'Algérie serves decent French food daily until midnight. *Le Canut* (☎ 04 78 28 19 59; closed Sunday) at 4 Place des Terreaux is a small, friendly place offering good Lyonnais cuisine as well as more innovative dishes. Dinner menus range from 68 to 127FF. Restaurants abound on the pedestrianised Rue Mercière (2e). A good choice is *Le Saint Joseph* (☎ 04 78 37 37 25) at No 46, which is open daily. There are also lots of places to eat, including several hamburger joints, along the Rue Victor Hugo pedestrian mall.

For a splurge, you might try *Brasserie Georges Lyon* (☎ 04 72 56 54 54) at 30 Cours de Verdun Perrache by the train station. It has been serving food in its vast Art Deco dining room since 1836 and has become a bit of an institution. Good-value menus are from 82FF (71FF for lunch).

The Presqu'île has lots of food shops along

FRANCE

Rue Vaubecour, including several boulangeries. *Fromagerie Victor Hugo* is a particularly good cheese shop at 26 Rue Sainte Hélène. The *Prisunic* (with an upstairs supermarket section) at 31 Rue de la République is open Monday to Saturday from 8.30 am to 7.30 pm.

In the old city, there are a number of food shops on Rue du Doyenné, including a Tunisian boulangerie and an *Express Market* grocery, both at No 11. The outdoor food market along the Saône River (Quai Saint Antoine and Quai des Célestins) on the Presqu'île is open from 7 am to 12.30 pm (closed Monday).

Entertainment

Ask at the tourist office for the free bimonthly publication *Lyon. Spectacles Evènements*. It gives the latest on Lyon's lively cultural life, which includes theatre, opera, dance, classical music, jazz, variety shows, sporting events and films.

The *Albion Public House* (☎ 04 78 28 33 00) at 12 Rue Sainte Catherine is one of the city's most popular hang-outs at night. Live music, such as blues, jazz and R&B, is played on weekends after 9.30 pm. It is open Monday to Saturday from 5 pm to 2 am (3 am on Friday and Saturday) and Sunday from 6 pm to 1 am.

Getting There & Away

Air Aéroport Lyon-Satolas (☎ 04 72 22 72 21) is 25 km east of the city.

Bus Intercity buses (of which there are relatively few) depart from the bus terminal under the Centre d'Échange (the building next to Gare de Perrache). Timetables and other information are available from the information office of Lyon's mass transit authority, TCL (☎ 04 78 71 70 00 for intercity bus information), which is on the lower level of the Centre d'Échange. Tickets for travel on buses run by private companies are sold by the driver.

Train Lyon has two train stations: Gare de Perrache and Gare de la Part-Dieu. There are lots of exceptions, but in general trains which begin or end their runs in Lyon use Perrache, whereas trains passing through the city stop at Part-Dieu. As you would expect, trains to/from Paris (292 to 390FF) use the capital's Gare de Lyon. Some trains, including all the Lyon-Paris TGVs, stop at both stations. For travel between the stations, you can go by metro (change at Charpennes), but if there happens to be an SNCF train going from one station to the other you can take it without buying an additional ticket. Fares from Lyon include Marseille (201 to 221FF), Nice (293 to 313FF) and Bordeaux (323 to 343FF). Prices vary according to the day on which you travel, and are more expensive on weekends.

The complex that includes Gare de Perrache (☎ 08 36 35 35 39) consists of two main buildings: the Centre d'Échange, the inside of which serves as a bus terminal and metro station; and, southward over the pedestrian bridge, the SNCF station itself. In the latter, the information office on the lower level is open Monday to Saturday from 9 am to 6.30 pm.

Gare de la Part-Dieu (same phone number as Perrache) is two km east of Place de la République. The information office (same opening hours as Perrache) is to the right as you go out from the Sortie Vivier-Merle exit.

Getting Around

To/From the Airport The Navette (shuttle) buses to Aéroport Lyon-Satolas run daily from 5 am to 9 pm departing every 20 minutes. They cost 47FF and take about 40 minutes from Gare de Perrache (near the taxi stand), and 30 minutes from Gare de la Part-Dieu. From the airport, there are buses to the city between 5 am and 11 pm.

Bus & Metro The metro's four lines (A, B, C and D) start operating at 5 am; the last trains begin their final run at about midnight. Tickets, which cost 7.80FF if bought individually, are valid for one-way travel on buses, trolleybuses, the funicular and the metro for an hour after time-stamping. A carnet of 10 tickets is 66.50FF (55FF for students under 26). On the metro, tickets have to be validated before you enter the platform.

Shuttle buses (Navette Presqu'île) run between Saint Paul, Place des Terreaux, Place Bellecour, Gare de Perrache and Cours Charlemagne; tickets valid only for these buses cost 6FF each (55FF for a carnet of 10).

TCL (☎ 04 78 71 70 00) has information offices on the lower level of the Centre d'Échange; at 43 Rue de la République; underground at Place Bellecour at the entrance to line A; at Vieux Lyon next to the entrance to the line D metro; and at 19 Blvd Marius Vivier-Merle (near Gare de la Part-Dieu).

Taxi Taxi Lyonnais (☎ 04 78 26 81 81) operates 24 hours a day.

Bicycle Except in winter, mountain bikes can be rented for 100/350FF a day/week from Locasport (☎ 04 78 61 11 01), which is at 62 Rue Colombier, a block east of Place Jean Macé (east of Gare de Perrache). The shop is open Tuesday to Saturday from 9 am to noon and 2 to 7 pm.

The French Alps

The French Alps, where fertile valleys meet soaring peaks topped with craggy, snowbound summits, are without doubt one of the most awe-inspiring mountainscapes in the world. In summer, visitors can take advantage of hundreds of km of magnificent hiking trails and engage in all sorts of warm-weather sporting activities. In winter, the area's profusion of fine ski resorts attracts enthusiasts from around the world.

If you're going to ski, expect to pay at least 250FF a day (including equipment hire, lifts and transport) at low-altitude stations, which usually operate from December to March. The larger, high-altitude stations cost 350 to 450FF a day. The cheapest time to go skiing is in January, between the school holiday periods. Tourist offices have up-to-the-minute information on ski conditions, hotel availability and prices.

GRENOBLE

Grenoble (population 155,000) is the undisputed intellectual and economic capital of the French Alps. Set in a broad valley surrounded by the Alps on all sides, this spotlessly clean city has a Swiss feel to it.

Orientation

The old city is centred around Place Grenette, with its many cafés, and Place Notre Dame.

Both are about a km east of the train and bus stations.

Information

Tourist Offices The Maison du Tourisme at 14 Rue de la République houses the tourist office (☎ 04 76 42 41 41), an SNCF train information counter and a desk for information on the local bus network (TAG). The tourist office is open Monday to Saturday from 9 am to 12.30 pm and 1.30 to 6 pm (7 pm in summer) and Sunday from 10 am to noon. The TAG and SNCF counters are open Monday to Friday from 8.30 am to 6.30 pm and on Saturday from 9 am to 6 pm. The Maison du Tourisme is served by both tram lines.

Money & Post There are several banks along Blvd Édouard Rey, including the Lyonnaise de Banque at No 11 and the Banque de France on the corner of Blvd Édouard Rey and Ave Félix Viallet (open weekdays from 8.45 am to 12.15 pm and 1.30 to 3.30 pm). There's also a 24-hour exchange machine outside the tourist office that accepts foreign banknotes and credit cards. The branch post office next door to the tourist office is open on weekdays from 8 am to 6.30 pm (6 pm on Monday) and Saturday to noon. Grenoble's postcode is 38000.

Things to See

Built in the 16th century (and expanded in the 19th) to control the approaches to the city, **Fort de la Bastille** sits on the north side of the Isère River, 263 metres above the old city. The fort affords superb views of Grenoble and the surrounding mountain ranges, including Mont Blanc on clear days. A sign near the disused Mont Jalla chair lift (300 metres beyond the arch next to the toilets) indicates the hiking trails that pass by here. To reach the fort you can take the *téléphérique* (cable car) de Grenoble Bastille (☎ 04 76 44 33 65) from Quai Stéphane Jay, which costs 21/33FF one way/return (12/17FF for students).

Housed in a 17th-century convent, the **Musée Dauphinois** (☎ 04 76 85 19 00) at 30 Rue Maurice Gignoux (at the foot of the hill on which Fort de la Bastille sits) has displays on the history of the old Dauphiné region. It's open from 9 am to noon and 2 to 6 pm (closed

French Alps & Jura

To Chaumont (95 km)
To Belfort (98 km)
To Dijon (43 km)
Besançon
DOUBS
SWITZERLAND
Dole
Doubs River
Arc-et-Senans
A36
N57
Morteau
Neuchâtel
N5
To Chalon-sur-Saône (55 km)
N83
Pontarlier
Lac de Neuchâtel
Frasne
Lac St Point
Malbuisson
Métabief
JURA
Mont d'Or (1463 m)
Mouthe
Vallorbe
Lons-le-Saunier
N78
N5
Lac de Joux
Lausanne
To Bern
0   20   40 km
Lac de Vouglans
Les Rousses
N1
Lake Geneva (Lac Léman)
Saint Claude
Gex
Évian-les-Bains
Yvoire
Thonon-les-Bains
Sion
To Bourg-en-Bresse (46 km) & Lyon (108 km)
Lajoux
Lelex
N5
Châtel
HAUTE-SAVOIE
La Chapelle d'Abondance
Rhône River
Geneva
Annemasse
Avoriaz
Nantua
A40
Les Gets
Morzine
Martigny
Bellegarde
N201
Cluses
Col des Montets
To Lyon (70 km)
AIN
N508
N205
Chamonix
Argentière
Le Grand Bornand
Annecy
Megève
Saint Gervais
Mont Blanc Tunnel
La Clusaz
Mont Blanc (4807 m)
Courmayeur
A41
Duingt
N212
Aosta
Lac Bourget
Le Semnoz
Col du Petit Saint Bernard
Aix-les-Bains
Le Châtelard
Albertville
Bourg Saint Maurice
Seez
To Lyon (45 km)
Chambéry
Tarentaise Valley
Les Arcs
La Plagne
N90
Val d'Isère
Col de l'Iséran
A43
Moûtiers
Tignes
A48
N75
Méribel
Brides-les-Bains
SAVOIE
N6
Sainte Pierre de Chartreuse
ISÈRE
Courchevel
Bonneval
N6
Les Menuires
Parc National de la Vanoise
Bessans
Col de Porte
Le Sappey
Val Thorens
Lanslebourg
To Valence (42 km)
St Nizier
DAUPHINÉ
Maurienne Valley
Modane
Col du Mont Cénis
To Turin, Italy (33 km)
A49
Autrans
Grenoble
Alpe d'Huez
Col du Lautaret
La Grave
Susa
Lans-en-Vercors
Bourg d'Oisans
Col du Galibier
Fréjus Tunnel
Villard de Lans
Les Deux Alpes
N91
Le Monêtier-les-Bains
Chantemerle
Parc Régional du Vercors
Venosc
Villeneuve-la-Salle
Briançon
Col du Montgenèvre
To Sisteron (40 km)
N85
La Bérarde
Parc National des Écrins
Barre des Écrins (4102 m)
Col d'Izoard
Parc Régional du Queyras
Drac River
Romanche River
Isère River
Rhône River

Tuesday). Tickets cost 15FF (10FF for students and people over 60).

Grenoble's fine arts museum, the **Musée de Grenoble** (☎ 04 76 63 44 44) at 5 Place de Lavalette, is known for its fine collection of painting and sculpture, including a well-regarded modern section that features pieces by Matisse, Picasso and Chagall. The museum is open daily except Tuesday from 11 am to 7 pm (10 pm on Wednesday). Admission costs 25FF (15FF for students).

The **Musée de la Résistance et de la Déportation** (☎ 04 76 42 38 53) at 14 Rue Hébert examines the region's role in the Résistance, and the deportation of Jews from Grenoble to Nazi concentration camps. It's open daily except Tuesday from 9 am till noon and 2 to 6 pm. Tickets cost 20FF (15FF for students).

At the time of writing, both **Cathédrale Notre Dame** and the adjoining **Bishop's Palace** on Place Notre Dame were getting complete face-lifts. They will contain three new museums towards the end of 1996. Check with the tourist office for current details.

Activities

Skiing Downhill skiing *(ski de piste)* and cross-country skiing *(ski de fond)* are possible at a number of inexpensive, low-altitude ski stations which are day trips from Grenoble. These include Col de Porte and Le Sappey (both north of the city) and Saint Nizier du Moucherotte, Lans-en-Vercors, Villard-de-Lans and Méaudre (west of the city).

Summer skiing, which is relatively expensive, is possible during June and July (and even into August) at several high-altitude ski stations east of Grenoble. These include the Alpe d'Huez (tourist office ☎ 04 76 80 35 41), which offers skiing (during July) on glaciers at elevations of 2530 to 3350 metres, and Les Deux Alpes (see Around Grenoble).

Hiking A number of beautiful trails can be picked up in Grenoble or nearby (eg from Fort de la Bastille). The northern part of the Parc Naturel Régional du Vercors (☎ 04 76 95 15 99 for the administrative headquarters) is just west of town.

The place in Grenoble to go for hiking information is CIMES and La Maison de la Randonnée (☎ 04 76 42 45 90) at 7 Rue Vol-

taire. They have a large selection of hiking maps (57 to 79FF), topoguides, day-hike guides and information on places where you can stay overnight (gîtes d'étape and refuges) when hiking. They can also suggest itineraries. The office is open Monday to Saturday from 9 am to noon and 2 to 6 pm.

Places to Stay

Camping The *Camping Les Trois Pucelles* (☎ 04 76 96 45 73; open all year) is at 58 Rue des Allobroges, one block west of the Drac River, in Grenoble's western suburb of Seyssins. To get there from the train station, take the tram towards Fontaine and get off at the Maisonnat stop. Then take bus No 51 to Mas des Îles and walk east on Rue du Dauphiné. A place to camp and park costs 25/50FF for one/two people.

Hostel The *Auberge de Jeunesse* (☎ 04 76 09 33 52) is at 10 Ave du Grésivaudan in Échirolles, 5.5 km south of the train station. To get there from Cours Jean Jaurès, take bus No 8 (direction Pont de Claix, which runs until about 9 pm) and get off at the Quinzaine stop – look for the Casino supermarket. Reception is open from 7.30 am to 11 pm. Charges are 67FF per person, including breakfast, but you must have a hostelling card.

Hotels Near the train station, the *Hôtel Alizé* (☎ 04 76 43 12 91) at 1 Place de la Gare has ultramodern and somewhat sterile singles/doubles from 120/200FF.

Quite a few cheap hotels are within a few blocks of Place Condorcet, a bit under a km south-east of the train station. The *Hôtel des Doges* (☎ 04 76 46 13 19) at 29 Cours Jean Jaurès has singles/doubles from 100/120FF. Rooms with shower or bath, toilet and TV are 160/170FF. Hall showers are 15FF.

The *Hôtel Victoria* (☎ 04 76 46 06 36), a quiet, well-maintained place at 17 Rue Thiers, has comfortable singles/doubles with shower for 165FF. All rooms have TV. The *Hôtel Beau Soleil* (☎ 04 76 46 29 40) at 9 Rue des Bons Enfants has simple singles/doubles from 130/140FF, and from 155/170FF with shower and TV. There is a 16FF charge for showers.

Hôtel du Moucherotte (☎ 04 76 54 61 40) at 1 Rue Auguste Gaché has huge, well-kept

Boulevard Maréchal Leclerc

Rue Sainte Ursule

Rue des Minimes

Rue des Cloîtres

Rue Servan

Rue des Dauphins

Rue Cornille Gifford

Rue Dominique Villars

Rue Hubert Dubedout

Rue E. Faure

Rue Doudart

To University District & Foyer Les Écrins (2 km)

Hôtel de Ville

Parc Paul Mistral

Boulevard Jean Pain

Pl de Lavalette

Place Notre Dame

Rue Chenoise

Rue Bayard

Rue Auguste Gâché

Rue de la Paix

Rue Voltaire

Jardin des Plantes

Rue Haxo

Préfecture

Place de Verdun

Rue de Strasbourg

Rue Maréchal Lyautey

Blvd Maréchal Lyautey

To Village Olympique (2.5 km)

Quai Mounier

Pont de la Citadelle

Pont Saint Laurent

Quai Perrière

Isère River

Quai Jongkind

Quai Créqui

Place de la Cymaise

Rue Renauldon

Rue Barnave

Place Sainte Claire

La Fayette

Rue Raoul Blanchard

Rue de la République

Rue Casimir Perrier

Rue Lesdiguières

Rue de Liberté

R Vicat

Rue de la Poste

Montée de Chalemont

To Fort de la Bastille

Rue Maurice Gignoux

Isère River

Quai de France

Pont Marius Gontard

Place Saint André

Place Aux Herbes

Place de Gordes

Rue Hector Berlioz

Jardin de Ville

Place de Philippe-ville

Rue Montorge

R St François

R Félix Poulat

Rue Montorge

Belgrade

Rue de Bonne

Boulevard Agutte Sembat

Cours La Fontaine

Rue Lakanal

Rue Albert Dubayet

Place Championnet

Place Marval

Jardin des Dauphins

Place Aristide Briand

Pont de la Porte de France

Quai Créqui

Boulevard Édouard Rey

Rue Docteur Mazet

Boulevard

Rue Vialet

Avenue Félix Viallet

Rue Jay

Rue Billerey

Place Victor Hugo

Rue Béranger

Gambetta

Rue des Bergers

Place Condorcet

Rue Turenne

Rue Génissieu

Cours Berriat

Place Thiers

Rue des Arts

To Auberge de Jeunesse (5 km)

Quai de l'Isère

Rue de l'Isère

Rue Bernard

Rue Claude

Rue Casimir Brenier

Rue d'Arsonval

Avenue Alsace-Lorraine

Rue Rochereau

Rue Colonel Denfert

Rue Gabriel Péri

Cours Jean Jaurès

Rue Colbert

Rue Joseph Rey

Avenue de Vizille

Rue Nicolas Chorier

Quai Jean Macé

Rue Émile Gueymard

Place de la Gare

Rue Crépu

To Camping Les Trois Pucelles (3.5 km)

Rue Michelet

Place Saint Bruno

Grenoble

0   100   200 m

FRANCE

PLACES TO STAY		27	Lotus d'Or	16	Lyonnaise de Banque
4	Foyer de l'Étudiante (Summer Hostel)		**OTHER**	17	Église Saint Louis
14	Hôtel Alizé	1	Musée Dauphinois	18	Prisunic Supermarket
23	Hôtel du Moucherotte	2	Musée de Grenoble	19	Post Office
28	Hôtel de la Poste	3	Police Headquaters	20	Tourist Office, TAG
29	Hôtel des Doges	5	Cathédrale Notre		Bureau &
30	Hôtel Victoria		Dame &		SNCF Counter
31	Hôtel Beau Soleil		Bishop's Palace	21	Laundrette
		9	Téléphérique to Fort de	22	Les Halles Sainte
PLACES TO EAT			la Bastille		Claire
6	Le Tonneau de Diogène	11	Bus Station		Market
7	Le Tunis Restaurant	12	Train Station	25	CIMES & Maison de la
8	Namastay Indian	13	Post Office &		Randonnée
	Restaurant		Gare Europole Tram	26	Musée de la Résistance
10	University Restaurant		Station	32	Main Post Office
24	La Panse Restaurant	15	Banque de France		

rooms and a central location. Singles/doubles without shower are from 130/168FF, and hall showers cost 25FF. Singles/doubles/triples/quads with showers start at 140/194/218/256FF.

The pleasant and friendly *Hôtel de la Poste* (☎ 04 76 46 67 25) at 25 Rue de la Poste has singles from 100 to 120FF, doubles and triples for 160 to 190FF and quads for 200FF. Showers are free. Overall, this is an excellent deal.

Places to Eat
For reasonable French food at good prices, try *Le Tonneau de Diogène* (☎ 04 76 42 38 40) at 6 Place Notre Dame, which attracts a young, lively crowd. It's open daily from 8.30 am to 1 am. The 38FF three-course 'student' menu (lunchtime only) is excellent value. *La Panse* (☎ 04 76 54 09 54) at 7 Rue de la Paix offers traditional French cuisine at lunch and dinner every day but is closed Sunday. The 71FF lunch menu is especially good value; dinner menus are 98 and 148FF.

The popular *Lotus d'Or* (☎ 04 76 51 20 10) at 6 Rue Vicat offers Vietnamese specialities to have there or take away; the plat du jour costs 30FF. It's open from 10 am to 7 pm (closed on Sunday). You can get vegetarian and non-vegetarian main dishes for 39 to 59FF at the *Namastay Indian Restaurant* (☎ 04 76 54 29 89) at 2 Rue Renauldon. It's open from Monday evening to Saturday for lunch and dinner. *Le Tunis Restaurant* (☎ 04 76 42 47 13) at 5 Rue Chenoise, open daily for lunch and dinner, has good Tunisian couscous from 38FF.

Les Halles Sainte Claire food market, near the tourist office, is open daily except Tuesday from 6.45 am to 12.30 pm. The *Prisunic* (closed Sunday) at 22 Rue Lafayette, a block west of the tourist office, has a supermarket in the basement.

Getting There & Away
Bus The bus station (Gare Routière) is next to the train station at Place de la Gare. VFD (☎ 04 76 47 77 77), which is open daily from 6.45 am to 7 pm, has services to Geneva (140FF), Nice (287FF), Annecy (90FF), Chamonix (149FF), and many places in the Isère region, including a number of ski stations. Unicar (☎ 04 76 87 90 31) handles tickets to Aéroport Lyon-Satolas (the international airport for Lyon and the Alps, 130FF), Marseille (145FF), Gap (53FF), Valence (49FF) etc. Unicar is open Monday to Saturday from 6.30 am to 7 pm and Sunday from 7 am to 7 pm.

Train The train station (☎ 04 76 47 50 50) is served by both tram lines (get off at the Gare Europole stop). The information office is open daily from 8.30 am to 7 pm and at least one ticket counter will remain open from 5.15 am to 11 pm. By TGV, the trip to Paris' Gare de Lyon (from 342 to 430FF) takes about 3½ hours. There is also service to Lyon (93FF), Nice (285FF) and Chamonix (160FF).

Getting Around
Bus & Tram The buses and trams (line Nos A and B) take the same tickets (7.50FF, or 51FF

for a carnet of 10), which are sold by bus (but not tram) drivers and by ticket machines at tram stops. They are valid for same-direction transfers within one hour of time-stamping. Most buses stop running sometime between 6.30 and 9 pm, while the trams run until 11.30 pm or midnight. TAG (☎ 04 76 20 66 66), the local bus company, has an information desk inside the tourist office building and an office to the left as you exit the train station (open Monday to Friday from 7.15 am to 6.30 pm).

Taxi Radio taxis can be ordered by calling ☎ 04 76 54 42 54.

AROUND GRENOBLE
Les Deux Alpes
Les Deux Alpes (1650 metres) is the largest summer skiing area in Europe (mid-June to early September) and is also a popular winter resort. There are 196 km of marked ski runs and 64 ski lifts.

Information The tourist office (☎ 04 76 79 22 00) in the Maison des Deux Alpes on Place des Deux Alpes is open from 8 am to 7 pm daily, except in spring, when it's open from 8.30 am to 12.30 pm and 2 to 6.30 pm. There's a reservation centre here (☎ 04 76 79 75 10) which can help with accommodation.

In winter, equipment hire (skis, stocks/poles and boots) costs from about 60/300FF per day/seven days. Ski passes, available at the tourist office, start at 78FF for a one-day beginners' blue pass. The all-lifts red pass costs 170/965FF per day/seven days. In summer, a full/half-day ski pass costs 200/150FF. For ski lessons, contact the École de ski Français (☎ 04 76 79 21 21) which charges from 120FF for a 2½-hour group lesson.

Places to Stay The *Auberge de Jeunesse Les Brûleurs de Loups* (☎ 04 76 79 22 80) in the heart of the ski station at Ave de Muzelle is open from mid-June to early September and from late October to April. Dorm beds cost 66FF, including breakfast; sheets are 21FF. Reception is closed between 2 and 5 pm. The hostel sells ski passes, runs both winter and summer skiing courses (with a 10% discount for students) and organises various activities in summer.

Le Bel Alpe (☎ 04 76 80 52 11) at Place de Venosc, opposite the tourist office, has simple singles/doubles for 150/240FF (160/250FF in summer). Singles/doubles with shower, toilet and TV cost from 200/270FF (230/300FF in summer). The hotel is closed in May.

Getting There & Away Les Deux Alpes is 77 km south-east of Grenoble. VFD (☎ 04 76 47 77 77) runs buses from Grenoble (99FF, 1¾ hours) and Briançon.

CHAMONIX
The town of Chamonix (population 10,000; 1037 metres) sits in a valley surrounded by the most spectacular scenery in the French Alps. The area is almost Himalayan in its awesomeness: deeply crevassed glaciers many km long ooze down the valley in the gullies between the icy spikes and needles around Mont Blanc, which soars 3.8 vertical km above the valley floor. In late spring and summer, the glaciers and high-altitude snow serve as a glistening white backdrop for meadows and hillsides rich in flowering plants, bushes and trees.

There are some 330 km of hiking trails in the Chamonix area. In winter, Chamonix and its environs offer superb skiing, with dozens of ski lifts and over 200 km of downhill and cross-country ski runs.

Orientation
The mountain range to the east of the Chamonix Valley, the Aiguilles de Chamonix, includes the mind-boggling mass of Mont Blanc (4807 metres), the highest mountain in the Alps. The almost glacierless Aiguilles Rouges range – its highest peak is Le Brévent (2525 metres) – runs along the western side of the valley.

Information
Tourist Office The tourist office (☎ 04 50 53 00 24) at Place du Triangle de l'Amitié (opposite Place de l'Église) is open daily from 8 or 8.30 am to 12.30 pm and 2 to 7 pm. In July and August, it is open from 8.30 am to 7.30 pm. Useful brochures on ski-lift hours and costs, refuges, camping grounds and parapente schools are available. In winter it sells a range of ski passes, including two-day/seven-day passes, valid for bus transport and all the ski lifts in the valley (except Lognan-Les Grands

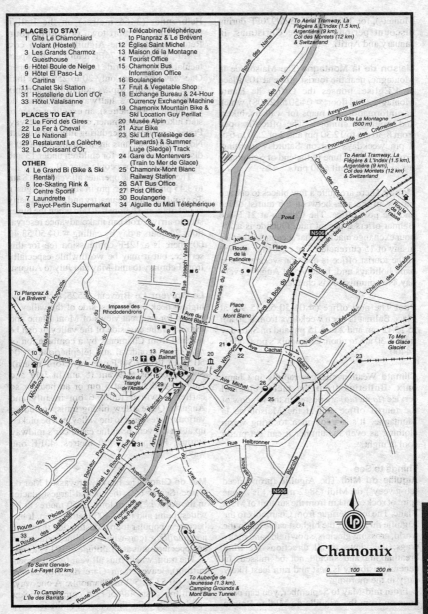

PLACES TO STAY
1 Gîte Le Chamoniard Volant (Hostel)
3 Les Grands Charmoz Guesthouse
6 Hôtel Boule de Neige
9 Hôtel El Paso-La Cantina
11 Chalet Ski Station
31 Hostellerie du Lion d'Or
33 Hôtel Valaisanne

PLACES TO EAT
2 Le Fond des Gires
22 Le Fer à Cheval
28 Le National
29 Restaurant Le Calèche
32 Le Croissant d'Or

OTHER
4 Le Grand Bi (Bike & Ski Rental)
5 Ice-Skating Rink & Centre Sportif
7 Laundrette
8 Payot-Pertin Supermarket
10 Télécabine/Téléphérique to Planpraz & Le Brévent
12 Église Saint Michel
13 Maison de la Montagne
14 Tourist Office
15 Chamonix Bus Information Office
16 Boulangerie
17 Fruit & Vegetable Shop
18 Exchange Bureau & 24-Hour Currency Exchange Machine
19 Chamonix Mountain Bike & Ski Location Guy Perillat
20 Musée Alpin
21 Azur Bike
23 Ski Lift (Télésiège des Planards) & Summer Luge (Sledge) Track
24 Gare du Montenvers (Train to Mer de Glace)
25 Chamonix-Mont Blanc Railway Station
26 SAT Bus Office
27 Post Office
30 Boulangerie
34 Aiguille du Midi Téléphérique

Chamonix

FRANCE

Montets), for 350/1050FF (325/920FF during discount periods – before Christmas, in January and April).

Maison de la Montagne The Maison de la Montagne, near the tourist office at 109 Place de l'Église, houses the Office de Haute Montagne (2nd floor; ☎ 04 50 53 22 08), which has information and maps for walkers, hikers and mountain climbers. The office is open from 8.30 am to 12.30 pm and 2 or 2.30 to 6 or 7 pm weekdays and on Saturday morning. From the end of June to the end of September it's open daily until 6.30 pm.

Money There are quite a few places to change money in the area between the tourist office and the post office. The Change at 21 Place Balmat offers a decent rate. Outside is a 24-hour exchange machine that accepts banknotes in any of 15 currencies. The exchange service at the tourist office is open on weekends and bank holidays and, in July and August, every day. No commission is charged.

Post The post office (☎ 04 50 53 15 90) at Place Balmat is open weekdays from 8.30 am to 12.15 pm and 2 to 6.15 pm and on Saturday from 8.30 am to noon. Chamonix's postcode is 74400.

Climate Weather changes rapidly in Chamonix. Bulletins from the meteorological service (la météo) are posted in the window of the tourist office and at the Maison de la Montagne. It's a good idea to bring warm clothing as even in summer it can get pretty cool at night.

Things to See
Aiguille du Midi The Aiguille (pronounced 'eh-gweey') du Midi (3842 metres) is a lone spire of rock eight km from the summit of Mont Blanc. The téléphérique from Chamonix to the Aiguille du Midi is the highest cable car in the world, crossing glaciers, snowfields and rocky crags; the views in all directions are truly breathtaking and should not be missed. In general, visibility is best and rain least likely early in the morning.

From mid-May to September, you can continue on from the Aiguille du Midi to **Pointe**

Helbronner (3466 metres) on the Italian border and the resort town of **Courmayeur**. Return tickets to the Aiguille du Midi cost 174FF; it's an extra 76FF return for the spectacular transglacial ride to Pointe Helbronner. One-way prices are only 20 to 25% less than those for a return trip. A ride from Chamonix to the cable car's halfway point, Plan de l'Aiguille (2308 metres), an excellent place to start hikes during summer, costs 55FF one way. Prices are 10FF higher during July and August. No student discounts are available but a 50% discount is available for children under 13 and a 20% discount for people over 60.

The téléphérique operates all year from 8 am to 3.45 pm (6 am to 5 pm in July and August). To avoid the long queues, try and arrive as early as possible, and before 9.30 am when the buses start to arrive. You can make advance reservations 24 hours a day by calling ☎ 04 50 53 40 00; there is a 12FF commission fee for this service, but it may be worthwhile especially from February to mid-May and July to August.

Le Brévent Le Brévent (2525 metres), the highest peak on the west side of the valley, is known for its great views of Mont Blanc and the rest of the east side of the valley. It can be reached from Chamonix by a combination of télécabine (gondola) and téléphérique (☎ 04 50 53 13 18) for 54FF one way (76FF return). Service begins at 9 am (8 am in July and August) and stops at 5 pm or an hour or so earlier in winter (until 6 pm in July and August). Quite a few hiking trails, including various routes back to the valley, can be picked up at Le Brévent or at the cable car's midway station, Planpraz (1999 metres; 43FF one way).

Mer de Glace The heavily crevassed Mer de Glace (Sea of Ice), the second-largest glacier in the Alps, is 14 km long, 1950 metres at its widest point and up to 400 metres deep. It has become a popular tourist destination thanks to a crémaillère (cog-wheel rail line) which has an upper terminus at an altitude of 1913 metres.

The train, which runs all year (weather permitting), leaves from Gare du Montenvers (☎ 04 50 53 12 54) in Chamonix. A one-way/return trip costs 48/65FF. A combined ticket valid for the train, the gondola to the ice cave

(Grotte de la Mer de Glace; 13FF return) and entry to the cave (14FF) costs 86FF. There are often long queues for the train during July and August. The ride takes 20 minutes each way.

The Mer de Glace can also be reached on foot from Plan de l'Aiguille (take the Grand Balcon Nord – see Activities below) and Chamonix. The uphill trail, which takes about two or 2½ hours, begins near the summer bob sleigh track. Traversing the glacier, with its many crevasses, is dangerous without a guide and proper equipment.

Musée Alpin This museum (☎ 04 50 53 25 93) at 89 Ave Michel Croz in Chamonix displays artefacts, lithographs and photos illustrating the history of mountain climbing and other Alpine sports. From June to September, it's open daily from 2 to 7 pm; between Christmas and Easter, hours are 3 to 7 pm. It's closed the rest of the year. The entry fee is 15FF (8FF for those under 16).

Activities

Hiking In late spring and summer (mid-June to October), the Chamonix area has some of the most spectacular hiking trails anywhere in the Alps. In June and July there is enough light to hike until at least 9 pm.

The *Carte des Sentiers de Montagne en Été* (summer mountain trails map; 25FF) is adequate for straightforward day hikes. It includes lots of trails and the locations of refuges. The best map of the area is the 1:25,000 scale IGN map (No 3630OT) entitled *Chamonix-Massif du Mont Blanc* (54FF).

The fairly flat **Grand Balcon Sud** trail along the Aiguilles Rouges (western) side of the valley, which remains at about 2000 metres, offers great views of Mont Blanc and the glaciers along the eastern side of the valley. If you prefer to avoid a km of hard uphill walking, take either the Planpraz lift (43FF one way) or La Flégère lift (40FF one way).

From Plan de l'Aiguille (55FF one way), the midway point on the Aiguille du Midi cable car, the **Grand Balcon Nord** takes you to the Mer de Glace, from where you can hike down to Chamonix. There are a number of other trails from Plan de l'Aiguille.

There are also trails to **Lac Blanc** (2350 metres), a turquoise lake surrounded by moun-

tains, from either the top of Les Praz-L'Index cable car (55FF one way) or La Flégère (40FF one way), the line's midway transfer point.

Cycling Many of the trails around the valley are perfect for mountain biking (although the well-known Petit Balcon Sud is no longer open to cyclists during July and August). See Getting Around in this section for information on bike rentals.

Skiing The Chamonix area has 160 km of marked ski runs, 42 km of cross-country trails and 64 ski lifts of all sorts. These include *téléskis* (tow lines), *télésièges* (chair lifts), télécabines and téléphériques.

Many sports shops around Chamonix rent skiing equipment. Count on paying around 39/220FF a day/week for regular skis or boots. Ski Location Guy Perillat (☎ 04 50 53 54 76) at 138 Rue des Moulins is open daily and also rents out snowboards (99/148FF a day without/with boots or 590/690FF a week). Cross-country skis are available from Le Grand Bi (☎ 04 50 53 14 16) at 240 Ave du Bois du Bouchet.

Parapente Parapente is the sport of floating down from somewhere high – the top of a cable car line, for instance – suspended from a wing-shaped, steerable parachute that allows you to catch updraughts and fly around for quite a while. An initiation flight *(baptême de l'air)* with an instructor costs 500FF. A five-day beginners' course *(stage d'initiation)* costs around 3000FF. For information, contact the tourist office.

Places to Stay

Camping Open from May to September, *L'Île des Barrats* (☎ 04 50 53 51 44) is near the base of the Aiguille du Midi cable car. The three-star *Camping Les Deux Glaciers* (☎ 04 50 53 15 84) on the Route des Tissières in Les Bossons, three km south of Chamonix, is open all year except from mid-November to mid-December. Two people with a car and tent pay 64FF. To get there, take the train to Les Bossons or Chamonix Bus to the Tremplin-le-Mont stop. There are a number of camping grounds a couple of km south of Chamonix in the village of Les Pélerins (near the turn-off to the Mont

FRANCE

Blanc Tunnel to Italy), including *Camping Les Arolles* (☎ 04 50 53 14 30; open from late June to September) at 281 Chemin du Cry.

Refuges Most mountain refuges, which have dorm beds from 35 to 150FF a night, are accessible to hikers, though a few can be reached only by climbers. They are generally open from mid-June to mid-September. Half-board (demi-pension) costs from 145 to 290FF.

The easier-to-reach refuges include one at Plan de l'Aiguille (☎ 04 50 53 55 60) at 2308 metres, the intermediate stop on the Aiguille du Midi cable car, and another at La Flégère (☎ 04 50 53 06 13) at 877 metres, the midway station on the Les Praz-L'Index cable car. It is advisable to call ahead to reserve a place, especially in July and August. For information on other refuges, contact the Maison de la Montagne (☎ 04 50 53 22 08).

Hostels The *Chalet Ski Station* (☎ 04 50 53 20 25) is a gîte d'étape at 6 Route des Moussoux in Chamonix (next to the Planpraz/Le Brévent télécabine station). Beds cost 60FF a night, there's a 15FF charge for sheets, and showers are 5FF. Guests receive a discount on the Brévent cable car. This place is closed from 10 May to 20 June and from 20 September to 20 December. The semi-rustic *Gîte Le Chamoniard Volant* (☎ 04 50 53 14 09) is on the north-eastern outskirts of town at 45 Route de la Frasse. A bunk in a cramped, functional room of four, six or eight beds costs 65FF; sheets are 20FF, and an evening meal is available for 65FF. Showers and use of the kitchen are free. Reception is open from 10 am to 10 pm. The nearest bus stop is La Frasse.

The *Auberge de Jeunesse* (☎ 04 50 53 14 52) is a couple of km south-west of Chamonix at 127 Montée Jacques Balmat in Les Pélerins. By bus, take the Chamonix-Les Houches line and get off at the Pélerins École stop. Beds in rooms of four or six cost 74FF; doubles are 89/94FF per person without/with shower. The HI hostel is closed from October to November.

Hotels At 468 Chemin des Cristalliers next to the railway tracks, *Les Grands Charmoz Guesthouse* (☎ 04 50 53 45 57) is run by a friendly, easy-going American couple. Doubles cost 184FF, including use of the

shower and sheets (but not towels); dorm beds are 72FF. Guests also have use of the kitchen. This place is closed in November and sometimes also in October. *Hôtel El Paso-La Cantina* (☎ 04 50 53 64 20) at 37 Impasse des Rhododendrons has comfortable rooms from 182/224FF in the low/high season, and from 252/284FF with shower and toilet. Quads are 340/428FF in the low/high season. Some rooms can be a bit noisy as there's a lively bar downstairs.

The *Hôtel Valaisanne* (☎ 04 50 53 17 98) is a small, family-owned place at 454 Ave Ravanel Le Rouge, about a km south of the centre of town. Doubles cost 160FF (256FF with bath and toilet). At the *Hostellerie du Lion d'Or* (☎ 04 50 53 15 09) at 255 Rue du Docteur Paccard, singles/doubles start at 175/220FF; showers are free.

Places to Eat

Le Fer à Cheval restaurant (☎ 04 50 53 13 22) at 118 Rue Whymper is reputed to have the best fondue Savoyarde (cheese fondue) in town. Prices range from 71 to 120FF. During summer and the skiing seasons, it's a good idea to reserve a day in advance. This place is closed on Tuesday during the off season and for the month of June.

Le Fonds des Gires (☎ 04 50 55 85 76), a self-service restaurant on the north side of town at 350 Route du Bois du Bouchet, is a favourite with people staying at the nearby gîtes. It's open for lunch all year (except January) every day and for dinner until 9 pm in July and August.

Countless restaurants offering pizza, fondue etc can be found in the centre of town. One of these is *Le National* (☎ 04 50 53 02 23) on 3 Rue du Docteur Paccard, a friendly place offering huge portions of local specialities. Menus go for 89 and 145FF. *La Cantina*, the Tex-Mex restaurant attached to Hôtel El Paso-La Cantina, has copious main dishes from 55 to 110FF.

The *Payot-Pertin* supermarket at 117 Rue Joseph Vallot is open Monday to Saturday and Sunday morning.

Getting There & Away

Bus Chamonix's bus station is next to the train station. SAT Autocar (☎ 04 50 53 01 15) has buses to Annecy (89FF), Courmayeur in Italy

(50FF, 40 minutes), Geneva (188FF, two hours), Grenoble (152FF) and Turin (140FF, three hours).

Train The narrow-gauge train line from Saint Gervais-Le Fayet (20 km west of Chamonix) to Martigny, Switzerland (42 km north of Chamonix), stops at 11 towns in the Chamonix Valley. There are nine to 12 return trips a day. You have to change trains at Châtelard or Vallorcine on the Swiss border. Le Fayet serves as a railhead for long-haul trains to destinations all over France.

Chamonix-Mont Blanc train station (☎ 04 50 53 00 44) is in the middle of Chamonix. The information office is open Monday to Saturday from 9 am to noon and 2 to 6.30 pm. From June to September and December to April, it's open on Sunday as well. Major destinations include Paris' Gare de Lyon (400 to 480FF, six to seven hours, five trains a day plus one night train), Lyon (179FF, four to 4½ hours, four trains a day) and Geneva (95FF, two to 2½ hours via Saint Gervais).

Getting Around

Bus Bus transport in the valley is handled by Chamonix Bus, whose stops are marked by black-on-yellow roadside signs. From mid-December to early April, there are 21 lines to all the ski lifts in the area; from April to early May there are 12 lines; and during the rest of the year, there are only two, both of which leave from Place de l'Église and pass by the Chamonix Sud stop. Chamonix Bus summer lines do not run after about 7 pm (6 or 6.30 pm in June and September).

The Chamonix Bus information office (☎ 04 50 53 05 55) at Place de l'Église (opposite the tourist office) is open daily in winter from 8 am to 7 pm. The rest of the year, hours are 8 am to noon and 2 to 6.30 pm (7.45 am to 7 pm from June to August).

Taxi There is a taxi stand (☎ 04 50 53 13 94) outside the train station.

Bicycle Chamonix Mountain Bike (☎ 04 50 53 54 76) at 138 Rue des Moulins, run by an Aussie and an Englishman, is open daily from 9 am to 7 pm. Their hire charges are 50FF for two hours and 95FF a day. Azur Bike (☎ 04 50

53 50 14) at 79 Rue Whymper rents bikes for 140FF a day. It's open daily from 9 am to 7 pm during the biking season. Between April and October, Le Grand Bi (☎ 04 50 53 14 16) at 240 Ave du Bois du Bouchet has 10-speeds for 70FF a day and mountain bikes for 100FF. It is open Monday to Saturday from 9 am to noon and 2 to 7 pm.

ANNECY

Annecy (population 51,000; 448 metres), situated at the northern tip of the incredibly blue Lac d'Annecy, is the perfect place to spend a relaxing holiday. Visitors in a sedentary mood can sit along the lake and feed the swans or mosey around the geranium-lined canals of the old city. Museums and other sights are limited, but for the athletically inclined, the town is an excellent base for water sports, hiking and biking. In winter, there is bus transport to low-altitude ski stations nearby.

Orientation

The train and bus stations are 500 metres northwest of the old city, which is centred around the canalised Thiou River. The modern town centre is between the main post office and the Centre Bonlieu complex, home to the tourist office. The lake town of Annecy-le-Vieux is just east of Annecy.

A 1:25,000 scale map of the Lac d'Annecy area is on sale at the tourist office for 55FF.

Information

The tourist office (☎ 04 50 45 00 33), at 1 Rue Jean Jaurès in the Centre Bonlieu north of Place de la Libérations, is open Monday to Saturday from 9 am to noon and 1.45 to 6.30 pm and on Sunday from 3 to 6 pm. In July and August it does not close at midday and opens on Sunday from 9 am to noon and 1.45 to 6.30 pm.

There are several banks in the vicinity of the main post office. The Banque de Savoie opposite the tourist office at 2 Rue du Pâquier is open Monday to Friday from 9 am to 12.25 pm and 1.30 to 5.30 pm. There is a 24-hour currency exchange machine outside the Crédit Lyonnais in the Centre Bonlieu. In the old city, the Change at 20 Rue Perrière is generally open Tuesday to Saturday (daily from June to September). It's closed in January and February.

FRANCE

Annecy

Lake Annecy

Île des Cygnes

0   50   100 m

To Plage de l'Impérial (700m),
Plage d'Annecy-le-Vieux &
Camping Grounds in
Annecy-le-Vieux (1.2 km)

To Base Nautique des Marquisats
(300m), Plage des Marquisats
(500m) & Sévrier (5 km)

To Camping Municipal Le
Belvédère (800m), Auberge
de Jeunesse (500m) &
Forêt du Crêt du Maure

To Basilique
de la Visitation

To Hôtel
Plaisance

To Hôtel
Plaisance

Champ
de Mars

Place de la
Libération

Jardins
de
l'Europe

Place de
l'Hôtel
de Ville

Place du
Château

Place de la
Gare

Canal du Vassé

Canal du Thiou

Quai Jules Philippe

Quai Napoléon III

Quai de la Tournette

Quai des Marquisats

Quai de la Corniche

Quai Perrière

Quai de l'Isle

Quai de l'Évêché

Rue de la Providence

Avenue de Trésum

Boulevard de la Visitation

Avenue de la Visitation

Rue des Marquisats

Faubourg des
Annonciades

Avenue des Balmettes

Faubourg
de Lesse

Avenue du Crêt du Maure

Avenue de la
Corniche

Chemin de la Tour

Rue Perrière

Porte
Perrière

Place aux
Bois

Porte du
Sépulcre

Porte du
Sépulcre

Rue Royale

Rue de la Poste

Rue de la République

Rue Carnot

Rue Vaugelas

Rue Sommeiller

Rue du Pâquier

Rue Notre Dame

Rue Filaterie

Rue J-J Rousseau

Rue de l'Isle

Rue Grenette

Rue de l'Annexion

Rue E Chappuis

Rue Président Favre

Rue Jean Jaurès

Rue Guillaume
Fichet

Rue Louis Revon

Rue de la Paix

Avenue d'Aléry

Avenue de Chambéry

Rue des Glières

Rue de la Gare

Rue de l'Industrie

Avenue de Chevennes

Avenue Bertholet

Avenue Bovard

Rue Louis Chaumontet

Ave de l'Industrie

Rue Royale

Rue du Lac

Rue du Pont Morens

Rue de la Tour

Rue Perrière

Rue Claire

Côte

Rue Nemours

Rue de l'Île

Rue du Château

St S.F.F.

PLACES TO STAY
1   Hôtel Les Terrasses
12 Central Hôtel
23 Hôtel de Savoie
27 Auberge du Lyonnais
29 Hôtel du Château

PLACES TO EAT
17 Pomme de Pain
24 Le Ramoneur Savoyard
32 Salle des Gardes
34 Le Pichet

OTHER
2   Bus Station & Voyages
    Crolard Office
3   Train Station
4   Lyonnaise de Banque
6   Centre Bonlieu
    Tourist Office &
    SIBRA Office
7   24-Hour Currency
    Exchange Machine
8   Boat Rental
9   Boulangerie
10 Banque de Savoie
11 Banque Populaire
    Savoisienne de Crédit
13 Main Post Office
14 Boulangerie
    Pâtisserie Royale
15 Église Notre Dame
    de Liesse
16 Prisunic Supermarket
18 Église Saint Maurice
19 Hôtel de Ville
20 Boat Rental
21 Boat Rental
22 Église Saint François
25 Food Shop
26 Cathédrale Saint Pierre
28 Morning Food Market
30 Château d'Annecy
31 Musée d'Histoire d'Annecy
33 Boulangerie
35 Pedal Boat Rental
36 Police Station
37 Hospital
38 Stade Nautique des
    Marquisats
39 Sports Évasion (Bicycle
    & Ski Rental)

The main post office (☎ 04 50 33 67 00) is at 4 Rue des Glières. Foreign exchange services are available. Annecy's postcode is 74000.

Things to See & Do
Walking Tour Just walking around, taking in the water, flowers, grass and quaint buildings, is the essence of a visit to Annecy.

Just east of the old city, behind the Hôtel de Ville, are the flowery **Jardins de l'Europe**, shaded by giant redwoods from California. There's a pleasant stroll from the Jardins de l'Europe along Quai de Bayreuth and Quai de la Tournette to the Base Nautique des Marquisats and beyond. Another fine promenade begins at the **Champ de Mars**, across the Canal du Vassé from the redwoods, and goes eastward around the lake towards **Annecy-le-Vieux**.

Old City The Vieille Ville, an area of narrow streets on either side of the Canal du Thiou, retains much of its 17th-century appearance despite recent 'quaintification'. On the island in the middle, the Palais de l'Isle (a former prison) houses the **Musée d'Histoire d'Annecy et de la Haute-Savoie** (☎ 04 50 33 87 31), which is open daily except Tuesday from 10 am to noon and 2 to 6 pm (daily from July to September). Entry costs 20FF (5FF for students).

Château d'Annecy The **Musée d'Annecy** (☎ 04 50 33 87 31), housed in the 13th to 16th-century chateau overlooking the town, puts on innovative temporary exhibitions and has a permanent collection of local craftwork and miscellaneous objects relating to the region's natural history. It keeps the same hour as Musée d'Histoire d'Annecy et de la Haute-Savoie. Entry is 30FF (10FF for students). The climb up to the chateau is worth it just for the view.

Activities
Beaches A km east of the Champ de Mars there is a free beach, **Plage d'Annecy-le-Vieux**. Slightly closer to town, next to the casino, is the **Plage de l'Impérial** (open from May to September), which costs 21FF (14FF for those under 13 or over 60) and is equipped with changing rooms, sporting facilities and

other amenities. Perhaps Annecy's most pleasant stretch of lawn-lined swimming beach is the free **Plage des Marquisats**, one km south of the old city along Rue des Marquisats.

Hiking The Forêt du Crêt du Maure, the forested area south of the old city, has lots of trails. There are nicer hiking areas, though, in and around two nature reserves: **Bout du Lac** (20 km from Annecy at the southern tip of the lake) and **Roc de Chère** (10 km from town on the east coast of the lake). Both can be reached by Voyages Crolard buses (see Getting There & Away).

Cycling There is a bike path along the western side of the lake. It starts 1.5 km south of Annecy (off Rue des Marquisats) and goes all the way to the lakeside town of Duingt, about 14 km to the south.

Bicycles can be rented from Sports Évasion (☎ 04 50 51 21 81) at 30 Rue des Marquisats, which is open Monday to Saturday from 9 am to noon and 2 to 7 pm (9 am to 7 pm in July and August). Mountain bikes cost 90/70FF a day/half-day.

Boating From late March to late October, pedal boats (60/70FF an hour for two/four people) and small boats with outboard motors can be hired (210FF an hour for four or five people, 250FF for up to seven) along the shore near the Jardins de l'Europe and the Champ de Mars. Boats are available daily (unless it's raining) from 9 am until sometime between 6 pm (in March) and 9 pm (in July and August). Various clubs at the Base Nautique des Marquisats, 800 metres south of the old city, rent kayaks, canoes, sailboats, sailboards, rowing hulls and diving equipment.

Swimming Pools The Stade Nautique des Marquisats (☎ 04 50 45 39 18) at 29 Rue des Marquisats has four swimming pools (including one for children) and acres of lawn. The complex is open from May to early September. Entry is 19FF.

The covered pool (☎ 04 50 57 56 02) at 90 Chemin des Fins, on the corner of Blvd du Fier, is open year-round except from 29 June to 29 August. The entry fee is 19FF (15FF for those under 18). The pool is served by bus Nos 2 and

3. There is an ice-skating rink (*patinoire*) in the same complex, open until mid-June. Entry and skate rental is 32FF (28FF for students).

Parapente Col de la Forclaz, the huge ridge overlooking Lac d'Annecy from the east, is a perfect spot from which to descend by parapente (see the Chamonix section for an explanation of this sport). For details on parapente and hang-gliding (*delta-plane*) schools, contact the tourist office in Annecy.

Winter Sports Not much snow falls in Annecy itself, but there's cross-country and downhill skiing at **Le Semnoz** (☎ 04 50 01 25 98 for information), about 15 km from town, and at **La Clusaz** (☎ 04 50 32 65 00) and **Le Grand Bornand** (☎ 04 50 02 78 00), both of which are 32 km east of Annecy. Count on paying 120 to 140FF a day for lift tickets. All three can be reached by Voyages Crolard buses.

In Annecy, skis can be rented from Sports Évasion (see Cycling earlier), which is also open on Sunday during the skiing season.

Places to Stay

Camping The *Camping Municipal Le Belvédère* (☎ 04 50 45 48 30) is 2.5 km south of the train station in the Forêt du Crêt du Maure. To get there, turn off Rue des Marquisats onto Ave de Trésum, take the first left and follow Blvd de la Corniche. From mid-June to early September you can take bus No 91 (Ligne des Vacances) from the train station. Charges are 23FF for a tent site and 25FF per person.

There are several other camping grounds near the lake in Annecy-le-Vieux. *Le Pré d'Avril* (☎ 04 50 23 64 46; open from Easter to 20 September) at 56 Rue du Pré d'Avril, charges 25FF for a place to camp and park and 20FF per person (70FF for two people with a tent and car in summer).

Hostels The *Auberge de Jeunesse* (☎ 04 50 45 33 19) is on Route du Semnoz, close to the camping ground. From mid-June to early September, bus No 91 goes there. Beds cost 67FF with a hostelling card, 86FF without, including breakfast. Sheets are an extra 17FF. You can check in between 8 am and noon and from 2 to 10 pm.

Hotels The *Hôtel Plaisance* (☎ 04 50 57 30 42) at 17 Rue de Narvik has simple but bright singles/doubles from 120/135FF and triples for 235FF. Rooms with shower are 180FF. Hall showers are 11FF and breakfast is 25FF. Free parking is available. The pleasant *Hôtel Les Terrasses* (☎ 04 50 57 08 98) at 15 Rue Louis Chaumontet, 300 metres north of the train station, has singles/doubles from 120/150FF (170/200FF in the high season). Rooms with shower and toilet are 160/190FF (210/240FF). From June to September, guests must pay half-board (255/440FF for singles/doubles without shower, 295/480FF with). It is closed in December and January.

One of the cheapest places close to the old city is the *Central Hôtel* (☎ 04 50 45 05 37) at 6bis Rue Royale (enter through the courtyard). Basic rooms start at 200FF and go up to 220FF with bath and toilet. Triples/quads are around 210/230FF. In the heart of the old city, the *Auberge du Lyonnais* (☎ 04 50 51 26 10) at 9 Rue de la République (on the corner of Quai de l'Évêché) occupies an idyllic setting just next to the canal. Comfortable singles/doubles are from 160/200FF, from 170/200FF with shower and toilet. All rooms have TV. This place does not take reservations and has only a few rooms, so come by before 9 am.

Places to Eat

In the old city, there are a number of cheap, hole-in-the-wall sandwich shops along Rue Perrière and Rue de l'Isle, including a couple of good crêperies. Further north, *Pomme de Pain* at 2 Rue Joseph Blanc has decent sandwiches for 16 to 26FF. It is open daily from 11 am to 7 pm (8 pm or later in summer).

The popular *Le Ramoneur Savoyard* (☎ 04 50 51 99 99) at 7 Rue de Grenette has reasonably priced regional dishes, with menus from 69 to 175FF. It's open daily for lunch and dinner. *Le Pichet* (☎ 04 50 45 32 41) at 13 Rue Perrière has three-course menus from 61 to 110FF. The rather touristy *Salle des Gardes* (☎ 04 50 51 52 00) at Quai des Vieilles Prisons, facing the old prison, has Savoyard specialities, such as fondue and tartiflette (a filling concoction of oven-baked potatoes, reblochon cheese, and other ingredients such as onions and bacon). Menus start at 89FF (55FF for lunch). It is closed on Monday and Tuesday at midday during the low season.

In the old city, there is a food market along Rue Sainte Claire on Sunday, Tuesday and Friday from 6 am to 12.30 pm. Fancy vegetables, fruit, cheese and wine (at fancy prices) are on sale at the food shop *Mme de Warens* at 7 Rue Jean-Jacques Rousseau.

Getting There & Away
Bus The bus station, Gare Routière Sud, is on Rue de l'Industrie next to the train station. Voyages Crolard's office (☎ 04 50 45 08 12) there is open Monday to Saturday from 6.15 am to 12.10 pm and 1.30 to 7.30 pm. The company has regular services to Roc de Chère on the eastern shore of Lac d'Annecy and Bout du Lac at the far southern tip, as well as to places east of Annecy, including La Clusaz and Le Grand Bornand ski stations and the towns of Albertville and Chamonix. Autocars Frossard (☎ 04 50 45 73 90), open from 7.45 am to 12.30 pm and 1.45 to 7 pm (closed Sunday and holidays), sells tickets to Geneva, Grenoble, Nice and elsewhere.

Autocars Francony (☎ 04 50 45 02 43) has buses to Chamonix. The office at the bus station is open weekdays from 7.15 to 11 am and 2.15 to 6.15 pm.

Train The train station (☎ 08 36 35 35 39) is a modernistic structure at Place de la Gare. The information office, which is on the lower level, is open daily from 8.35 am (9 am on Sunday) to 7.15 pm. There is also at least one ticket office open from 4.45 am to 11.45 pm. There are frequent trains, not all of them direct, to Paris' Gare de Lyon (335 to 423FF, 3¾ hours), Nice (347FF via Lyon, 328FF via Grenoble, eight to nine hours, faster with a change of train), Lyon (110FF, two hours), Chamonix (102FF, 2½ to three hours) and Aix-les-Bains (37FF, 30 to 45 minutes).

Getting Around
Bus The local bus company SIBRA (☎ 04 50 51 72 72) has an information bureau (☎ 04 50 51 70 33) across the covered courtyard from the tourist office. It's open Monday to Saturday from 8.45 am to 7 pm. Tickets cost 7FF each or 37.50FF for a carnet of eight. Students and those aged five to 20 pay 27FF for a carnet of 10. Annecy's buses run Monday to Saturday from 6 am to 8 pm. On Sundays, 20-seat

minibuses (identified by letters rather than numbers) provide limited service. Ligne des Vacances bus No 91 runs only from mid-June to early September.

Taxi Taxis based at the bus station can be ordered by calling ☎ 04 50 45 05 67.

Provence

Provence stretches along both sides of the Rhône River from just north of the town of Orange down to the Mediterranean and along France's southern coast from the Camargue salt marshes in the west to Marseille and beyond in the east. The spectacular Gorges d'Ardèche, created by the often torrential Ardèche River, are west of the Rhône, and to the east are the region's famous upland areas: 1909-metre Mt Ventoux, the Vaucluse Plateau, the Lubéron Range and the chain of hills known as the Alpilles. East of Marseille is the Côte d'Azur and its hinterland, which, though part of Provence, is treated as a separate region in this guide.

Provence was settled by the Ligurians, the Celts and the Greeks, but it was after its conquest by Julius Caesar in the mid-1st century BC that the region really began to flourish. Many exceptionally well-preserved amphitheatres, aqueducts (particularly Pont du Gard) and other buildings from the Roman period can still be seen in Arles, Nîmes and Orange. During the 14th century, the Catholic Church, then led by a series of French-born popes, moved its headquarters from feud-ridden Rome to Avignon, thus beginning the most resplendent period in that city's history.

Language
A thousand years ago, *oïl* and *oc* were the words for 'yes' in the Romance languages of what is now northern and southern France respectively. As Paris-based influence and control spread, so did the Langue d'Oïl, and thus the Langue d'Oc (the language of Provence) was gradually supplanted. The Provençal language is not spoken much these days, but it has left the world a rich literary legacy – the Langue d'Oc was used by the medieval troubadours,

whose melodies and poems were motivated by the ideal of courtly love.

Climate

Provence's weather is bright and sunny for much of the year, and the extraordinary light has attracted a number of painters, including Van Gogh, Cézanne and Picasso. The cold, dry winds of the mistral, which gain surprising fury as they careen down the Rhône Valley, can turn a fine spring day into a bone-chilling wintry one with little warning.

MARSEILLE

The cosmopolitan and much maligned port of Marseille, France's second-largest city with a population of 800,000 and third-most populous urban area (population 1.23 million), is not in the least bit prettified or quaintified for the benefit of tourists. Its urban geography and atmosphere are a function of the diversity of its inhabitants, the majority of whom are immigrants (or their descendants) from the Mediterranean basin, West Africa and Indochina. Although Marseille is notorious for organised crime and racial tensions (the extreme right polls about 17% here), the city has more to reward the visitor who likes exploring on foot than almost any other city in France.

Orientation

The city's main street, La Canebière, stretches eastward from the Vieux Port. The train station is north of La Canebière at the top of Blvd d'Athènes. The city centre is around Rue Paradis, which becomes more fashionable as you move south.

Information

Tourist Office The tourist office (☎ 04 91 13 89 00), next to the Vieux Port at 4 La Canebière, is open Monday to Saturday from 9 am to 7.15 pm and on Sunday from 10 am to 5 pm. From June to September, opening hours are 8.30 am to 8 pm daily. The tourist office annexe (☎ 04 91 50 59 18) at the train station (on the right as you exit the station's main doors) is open weekdays from 10 am to 1 pm and 1.30 to 6 pm (9 am to 7 pm from June to September).

Foreign Consulates There is a UK consulate (☎ 04 91 53 43 32) at 24 Ave du Prado (near Place Castellane and the Castellane metro stop). The US consulate (☎ 04 91 54 92 00) is across from the préfecture building at 12 Blvd Paul Peytral.

Money The Banque de France is at Place Estrangin Pastré, a block west of the préfecture. There are a number of banks on La Canebière near the tourist office. Change de la Bourse at 3 Place du Général de Gaulle will exchange dozens of currencies.

American Express (☎ 04 91 13 71 26) at 39 La Canebière is open weekdays from 8 am to 6 pm and on Saturday from 8.30 am to noon and 2 to 4.30 pm. The Comptoir de Change Méditerranéen at the train station will exchange foreign currencies daily.

Post The main post office (☎ 04 91 1 47 00) is at 1 Place de l'Hôtel des Postes. E ange services are available. The postcode fo 1ar-seille consists of the digits 130 plu he arrondissement number (01 to 16). The s covered by the Marseille map in this book a in 13001 except the area south of Rue Grignan, which is in 13006, and the area south of the Vieux Port, which is 13007.

Laundry The Laverie des Allées at 17 Allées Léon Gambetta is close to many of the hotels mentioned under Places to Stay and is open seven days a week from 9 am to 8 pm.

Dangers & Annoyances Despite its fearsome reputation for underground crime, Marseille is probably no more dangerous than other French cities. As elsewhere, street crime such as bag-snatching and pickpocketing is best avoided by keeping your wits about you and your valu-ables hard to get at. Guard your luggage very carefully, especially at the train station, and *never* leave anything inside a parked vehicle. One Lonely Planet researcher did just that – and lost all his clothes!

At night, it is best to avoid the Belsunce area, the poor, immigrant neighbourhood south-west of the train station bounded by La Canebière, Cours Belsunce/Rue d'Aix, Rue Bernard du Bois and Blvd d'Athènes.

Things to See & Do
Walking Tour Marseille grew up around the

Vieux Port, where Greeks from Asia Minor established a settlement around 600 BC. The quarter north of Quai du Port (around the Hôtel de Ville) was blown up by the Germans in 1943 and rebuilt after the war. The lively **Place Thiars** pedestrian zone, with its many late-night restaurants and cafés, is south of the Quai de Rive Neuve. To get from one side of the harbour entrance to the other, you can walk through the Saint Laurent Tunnel, which surfaces in front of the cathedral (near Fort Saint Jean) and, on the south side, just east of Fort Saint Nicolas. Also worth a stroll is the more fashionable **6e arrondissement**, especially the area between La Canebière and the préfecture building, and the Rue Saint Ferréol pedestrian mall.

Corniche Président John F Kennedy runs along the coast from 200 metres west of the **Jardin du Pharo**, a park with good harbour views, to the Plages Gaston Defferre, 4.5 km to the south. Along its entire length, the corniche is served by bus No 83, which goes to the Quai des Belges (the old port) and the Rond-Point du Prado metro stop.

If you like great panoramic views or over-wrought mid-19th century architecture, consider a walk up to the **Basilique Notre Dame de la Garde**, which is one km south of the Vieux Port on a hilltop (154 metres) – the highest point in the city. The basilica and the crypt are open from 7.30 am to 5.30 pm (7 am to 7.30 pm in summer). Bus No 60 will get you back to the Vieux Port.

Museums Except where noted, the museums listed here are open daily from 10 am to 5 pm (11 am to 6 pm from June to September). All of them admit students and teachers for half the regular price.

The **Centre de la Vieille Charité** (☎ 04 91 56 28 38), which used to be a charity centre and is housed in a hospice built between 1671 and 1745, has superb permanent exhibits on ancient Egypt and Greece and all sorts of temporary exhibitions. It is in the mostly North African Panier quarter (north of the Vieux Port) at 2 Rue de la Charité. Adult entry fees are 10FF for the Museum of Mediterranean Archaeology, 10FF for the Museum of African Art and 20FF for special exhibitions.

The **Musée du Vieux Marseille** (☎ 04 91 55 10 19), behind the Hôtel de Ville in a 16th-century mansion at 2 Rue de la Prison, displays antique household items from Provence, playing cards (for which Marseille has been known since the 17th century) and the equipment to make them, and photos of the city under German occupation – among other things. Admission costs 10FF (5FF for students). The museum was closed for restoration at the time of writing, but was due to reopen in late 1996.

The **Musée Cantini** (☎ 04 91 54 77 75), off Rue Paradis at 19 Rue Grignan, has changing exhibitions of modern and contemporary art. From October to May the museum is open from 10 am to 5 pm (11 am to 6 pm from June to September); it's closed on Monday. Entry is 15FF.

Roman history buffs might want to visit the **Musée d'Histoire de Marseille** (☎ 04 91 90 42 22) on the ground floor of the Centre Bourse shopping mall (just north of La Canebière). Its exhibits include the freeze-dried remains of a merchant ship that plied the waters of the Mediterranean in the late 2nd century AD. It is open Monday to Saturday from noon to 7 pm. Entry is 10FF. The remains of Roman buildings, uncovered by accident during construction of the shopping mall, can be seen nearby in the **Jardin des Vestiges**, which lies between the Centre Bourse and Rue Henri Barbusse and can be entered via the museum.

Château d'If Château d'If (☎ 04 91 59 02 30), the 16th-century island fortress-turned-prison made infamous by Alexandre Dumas' *The Count of Monte Cristo*, can be visited daily from 9 am until 7 pm (or whenever the last boat of the day departs). The entry fee is 22FF for all. Boats (45FF return, 20 minutes each way) leave from near the GACM office (☎ 04 91 55 50 09) on Quai des Belges (old port) and go on to the nearby **Îles du Frioul** (45FF return, or 70FF for both the chateau and islands).

Beaches The city's most attractive beach, the **Plages Gaston Defferre** (commonly known as the Plage du Prado), is four km south of the city centre. To get there, take bus No 19, 72 or 83 from the Rond-Point du Prado metro stop or bus No 83 from the Quai des Belges. You

MEDITERRANEAN

SEA

Bassin de la Grande Joliette

● 1

Place de
la Joliette

2 ■

🚇 Joliette

Rue Fauchier

Rue

Rue de la Joliette

● 3
● ●

Rue de Mazenod

Quai de la Joliette

Avenue Robert Schuman

Boulevard
des
Dames

Rue de la République

Malaval

Jules
Guesde

● 4

Rue de l'Évêché

● 9
● 10
† 1

11 ■

Place
Sadi-
Carnot

Colbert

Rue

13 ●

2ᵉ

Panier
Quarter

● 12

Rue H Barbusse

Avant-Port

de la

Joliette

Quai de la Tourette

Ave. Vaudoyer

Rue St-Laurent

Esplanade de la Tourette

Pl des
Moulins

Rue Caisserie

Grand' Rue

30 🏛

29 Loge

Rue de la

Vieux Port -
Hôtel de Ville 🚇

Quai du Port

31

Tunnel St Laurent

Vieux Port

🟊
Jardin
du
Pharo

32

Quai de Rive   Neuve

Place
Thiars

33

Boulevard Charles   Livon

Rue   Sainte   Catherine

Rue Neuve Sainte Dame

Rue   Sainte

Rue Fort N. Dame

Rue Grignan

Avenue Pasteur

Avenue de la Corse

Boulevard de la Corderie

Jardin
Pierre Puget 🟊

Cours Pierre Puget

Corniche Président
John F Kennedy

Ave. de la Corse

Rue Cap

Dessemond

Rue Vauvenargues

Boulevard André Aune

Boulevard Notre Dame

To Plages Gaston
Deferre (4 km)

d'Endoume

Boulevard

Teisseire

Boulevard

Rue Jules Moulet

Rue

Rue du Fort

7ᵉ

Boulevard Marius Thomas

Sanctuaire

50 🚉

🅛🅟

Marseille

0   200   400 m

- - - - arrondissement boundaries

PLACES TO STAY
2   Hôtel Breton
17 Hôtel de Bourgogne
18 Hôtel Gambetta
19 Hôtel Ozea & Hôtel
    Pied-à-Terre
21 Hôtel de Nice
22 Hôtel Sphinx
23 Cheap Hotels
49 Hôtel Béarn

PLACES TO EAT
12 Auberge 'In' Vegetarian
    Restaurant
25 Takeaway Restaurants
37 La Caucase & Le Resto
    Provençal
38 Ethnic Restaurants
40 Restaurant Antillais
    Madiana
41 Le Quinze

OTHER
1   Passenger Ferry Terminal
3   SNCM Ferries Office
4   Algérie Ferries
5   Bus Station
6   Taxi Stand
7   Post Office
8   Gare Saint Charles
9   Nouvelle Cathédrale
10 Ancienne Cathédrale de
    la Major
11 Centre de la Vielle
    Charité
13 Main Post Office
14 Jardin des Vestiges
    (Roman Ruins)
15 Musée d'Histoire de
    Marseille
16 Laundrette
20 New Can-Can Disco
24 Marché des Capucins
    (Food Market)
26 American Express
27 Espace Infos RTM (Bus &
    Metro Information)
28 Nouvelles Galeries
    Supermarket
29 Hôtel de Ville
30 Musée du Vieux Marseille
31 Fort Saint Jean
32 Bas Fort Saint Nicolas
33 Fort d'Entrecasteaux & Fort
    Saint Nicolas
34 Tourist Office
35 Opera
36 Change de la Bourse
39 La Maison Hantée
42 Musée Cantini
43 Law Courts
44 Préfecture de Police
45 Préfecture
46 US Consulate
47 Banque de France
48 Fruit & Vegetable Morning
    Market
50 Basilique Notre Dame de
    la Garde

FRANCE

can walk there along the Corniche Président John F Kennedy. For more information about beaches and the great range of water activities, ask for the *Marseille by the Sea* brochure at the tourist office.

Places to Stay

Camping All of Marseille's municipal camping grounds are presently closed. Contact the tourist office to find out if any have reopened. Travellers with tents can camp at the Auberge de Jeunesse de Bonneveine.

Hostels The *Auberge de Jeunesse de Bonne-veine* (☎ 04 91 73 21 81) is at 47 Ave Joseph Vidal, about 4.5 km south of the Vieux Port. To get there, take bus No 44 from the Rond-Point du Prado metro stop and get off at Place Louis Bonnefon. A bed in a room for six is 66FF (72FF in summer), including breakfast. Sheets cost 16FF. Valuables should be kept in the 24-hour lockers, which cost 25FF.

There's another hostel, the *Auberge de Jeunesse de Bois Luzy* (☎ 04 91 49 06 18), 4.5 km east of the city centre at 76 Ave de Bois Luzy (in the Montolivet neighbourhood). To get there, take bus No 6 from near the Canebière-Réformés metro stop to the Marius-Richard stop. Beds are 43FF and breakfast is 18FF. The hostel is closed between 10 am and 5 pm.

Hotels Marseille has some of France's cheapest hotels; you can still find rooms for 50FF a night but most are filthy dives in unsafe areas which rent out rooms by the hour. All of the places listed by name in this section are reputable and relatively clean.

Ferry Terminal Area The *Hôtel Breton* (☎ 04 91 90 00 81), a stone's throw away from the ferry terminal at 52 Rue Mazenod, has clean, well-kept singles/doubles with shower, telephone and TV for 110/170FF.

Train Station Area The *Hôtel de Bourgogne* (☎ 04 91 62 19 49) at 31 Allées Léon Gambetta has singles/doubles from 80/140FF and triples for 180FF; showers are 10FF. Singles/doubles with shower are 150/160FF. If requested, they can add an extra bed. The *Hôtel Gambetta* (☎ 04 91 62 07 88), nearby at No 49, has singles without shower for 95FF and singles/doubles with shower from 130/160FF. Doubles with shower and toilet start at 215FF. Hall showers are 15FF.

There are several other one and two-star hotels nearby and a cluster of small, extremely cheap hotels of less-than-pristine reputation along Rue des Petites Maries.

South of La Canebière The *Hôtel Ozea* (☎ 04 91 47 91 84) is at 12 Rue Barbaroux, across Square Léon Blum from the eastern end of Allées Léon Gambetta. This place, which welcomes new guests 24 hours a day (if you arrive late at night just ring the bell), has clean, old-fashioned doubles without/with shower for 120/150FF. There are no hall showers. Nearby, the *Hôtel Pied-à-Terre* (☎ 04 91 92 00 95) at No 18 has singles/doubles without/with shower for 120/150FF.

There are lots of rock-bottom hotels along Rue Sénac de Meilhan and around Place du Lycée and a number of one-star hotels along Rue des Feuillants. The *Hôtel Sphinx* (☎ 04 91 48 70 59), at 16 Rue Sénac, has simple but well-kept singles/doubles from 68/116FF or 120/160FF with shower. Triples with shower are 200FF. Hall showers are 17FF. Another possibility is the *Hôtel de Nice* (☎ 04 91 48 73 07) on the same street at No 11. Doubles without/with rather dismal showers are 100/120FF; hall showers cost 20FF. Guests can register 24 hours a day.

Préfecture Area The *Hôtel Béarn* (☎ 04 91 37 75 83), at 63 Rue Sylvabelle, has comfortable singles/doubles with shower for 120FF and singles/doubles with shower, toilet and TV for 170FF.

Places to Eat

There are lots of cheap takeaway places selling pizza and Middle Eastern sandwiches of various sorts on Rue des Feuillants, which intersects La Canebière just east of Cours Saint Louis. Cours Belsunce is lined with inexpensive food kiosks.

Restaurants along and near the pedestrianised Cours Julien, a few blocks south of La Canebière, offer an incredible variety of cuisines: Antillean, Pakistani, Thai, Lebanese, Tunisian, Italian and more. *La Caucase* (☎ 04

91 48 36 30) at No 62 specialises in Armenian dishes. It's open for dinner seven nights a week from about 6 pm and has menus for 85 and 145FF. If you'd rather have something French, try *Le Resto Provençal* (☎ 04 91 48 85 12) at No 64. There are pleasant outdoor tables and a good-value three-course lunch menu for 100FF. It's closed Sunday and Monday.

Le Quinze (☎ 04 91 92 00 52), at 15 Rue des Trois Rois, a small street running parallel to Cours Julien, offers Provençal menus from 89FF. Nearby, the West Indian restaurant *Antillais Madiana* (☎ 04 91 94 25 55) on Rue des Trois Mages has menus from 65FF.

Countless sandwich shops, cafés and restaurants line the pedestrian streets around Place Thiars, which is on the south side of the Vieux Port. Though many offer bouillabaisse, the rich fish stew for which Marseille is famous, it is difficult to find the real thing. Recommended for the real thing, however, is *La Maronaise* (☎ 04 91 73 25 21) at 'Les Gourdes' on Route de la Maronaise west of the city, on the way to Plages Gaston Defferre. Avoid the touristy restaurants on the Quai de Rive Neuve.

The *Auberge 'In'* (☎ 04 91 90 51 59) is a vegetarian restaurant a few hundred metres north of the Vieux Port at 25 Rue du Chevalier Roze. Giant salads cost 45 to 50FF. Meals are served at lunch and dinner daily except on Sunday. The attached food shop and salon de thé are open from 8 am to 11 pm.

There is an up-market supermarket, open Monday to Saturday, in the Nouvelles Galeries department store a block north of La Canebière in the Centre Bourse shopping mall complex. The most convenient entrance is at 28 Rue de Bir Hakeim. At the *Marché des Capucins*, one block south of La Canebière on Rue Longue des Capucins, you can buy fruit and vegetables Monday to Saturday from 7 am to 7 pm.

Getting There & Away
Air The Aéroport de Marseille-Provence (☎ 04 42 14 14 14) is 28 km north-west of the city.

Bus The bus station (☎ 04 91 08 16 40) at Place Victor Hugo, 150 metres to the right as you exit the train station, offers service to Aix-en-Provence, Arles, Avignon, Cannes, Carpentras, Nice (direct and via the coast), Nice airport, Orange and Salon. The buses, which are slower than the train, cost more or less the same unless you're a student under 26 (30% discount). The information counter and the left-luggage office are open Monday to Saturday from 7.45 am to 6.30 pm and on Sunday from 9 am to noon and 2 to 6 pm. Tickets are sold on the bus.

Train Marseille's passenger train station, Gare Saint Charles (☎ 08 36 35 35 39), is served by both metro lines. Trains from here go everywhere, including Paris' Gare de Lyon (409FF, five to eight hours), Bordeaux (339FF, five to six hours), Toulouse (232FF, three to four hours) and Nice (143FF, 1½ to two hours). The information office, one floor under the platforms, is open Monday to Saturday from 9 am to 8 pm. There's an SNCF office (☎ 04 91 54 42 61) at 17 Rue Grignon, off Rue St Ferréol a couple of blocks north of the préfecture. It's open weekdays from 9 am to 5 pm.

Ferry The Société Nationale Maritime Corse-Méditerranée (SNCM; ☎ 04 91 56 30 10) at 61 Blvd des Dames offers ferry service from the gare maritime (at the foot of Blvd des Dames) to Corsica (Corse), Sardinia (Sardaigne), Tunisia and Algeria. Discounts of up to 30%, some limited to the off season (October to April) or applicable only if you're a student or under 25 (or both), are available. The SNCM office is open weekdays from 8 am to 6 pm and on Saturday from 8.30 am to noon and 2 to 6 pm.

Getting Around
To/From the Airport TRPA buses from Gare Saint Charles go to the Marseille-Provence airport every 20 minutes from 5.30 am to 9.50 pm. From the airport, they go to the train station from 6.20 am to 10.20 pm. The trip takes about 25 minutes and costs 42FF.

Bus & Underground Marseille has two easy-to-follow metro lines (look for the white-on-brown signs bearing an angular letter 'M') and an extensive bus network.

Numbered buses run until 9 pm; lines identified with letters, known as the *autobus de nuit*, run from 9 pm to 12.30 am. Tickets (8FF) are valid for travel on both the bus and the metro for 70 minutes from when they've been time-stamped. When you buy a carnet of six tickets (available in metro stations for 42FF) you get two coupons (talons or souches) with the same serial number as your tickets; to use a ticket as a transfer you must show one of the coupons.

For more information, visit the Espace Infos RTM (☎ 04 91 91 92 10) at 6-8 Rue des Fabres, which is open weekdays from 8.30 am to 6 pm.

Taxi Marseille Taxi (☎ 04 91 02 20 20) and Allô Taxis (☎ 04 91 49 59 99) will dispatch taxis 24 hours a day.

AIX-EN-PROVENCE

One of the most appealing cities in Provence, Aix (population 159,000) is very lively, perhaps because of the high number of students, which make up over 20% of the population. One of the city's most prominent citizens was the postimpressionist painter Cézanne. Aix's main festival is the Festival International d'Art Lyrique, which is held in July. The city is also renowned for its *calissons*, almond-paste confectionery made with candied melon.

The mostly pedestrianised old city is a great place to explore, with its maze of tiny streets full of ethnic restaurants, specialist food shops and tempting designer shops. Apart from this, there are lots of mossy fountains, elegant 17th and 18th-century hôtels particuliers and popular outdoor cafés which give the city a relaxed, friendly atmosphere.

Aix also has several interesting museums, the finest of which is the **Musée Granet** (☎ 04 42 38 14 70) at Place Saint Jean de Malte. The collection includes Italian, Dutch and French paintings from the 16th to 19th centuries as well as some of Cézanne's lesser known paintings. Admission is 18FF (10FF for students). The **Musée des Tapisseries** (☎ 04 42 23 09 91), in the former bishop's palace at 28 Place des Martyrs de la Résistance, is worth visiting for its tapestries and sumptuous costumes. Entry is 15FF (9FF for students); during special exhibitions the fee goes up to 18FF (10FF concession). Both museums are closed on Tuesday.

Atelier Paul Cézanne (☎ 04 42 21 06 53), at 9 Ave Paul Cézanne, was the painter's last studio and has been left as it was when he died in 1906. It's open daily except Tuesday and entry is 16FF (10FF for students).

The tourist office (☎ 04 42 16 11 61) is on Place Général de Gaulle. Numerous cafés, brasseries and restaurants can be found in the heart of the city on Place des Cardeurs and Place de l'Hôtel de Ville. One of these is the *Brasserie de la Mairie* which has good, inexpensive salads. *Les Tournesols* (☎ 04 42 27 93 78) at 1 Rue Cardinale, close to Rue d'Italie, offers delectable, seasonal food at very reasonable prices. A colourful morning fruit and vegetable market is held on Place Richelme.

Frequent trains run between Marseille and Aix (32FF, 30 minutes).

AVIGNON

Avignon (population 100,000) acquired its ramparts and its reputation as a city of art and culture during the 14th century, when Pope Clement V and his court, fleeing political turmoil in Rome, established themselves here. From 1309 to 1377 huge sums of money were invested in building and decorating the popes' palace and other important church edifices. Even after the pontifical court returned to Rome amid bitter charges that Avignon had become a den of criminals and brothel-goers, Avignon, which remained under Vatican rule until the Revolution, continued to serve as an important cultural centre.

Today, Avignon maintains its tradition as a patron of the arts, most notably through its annual performing arts festival. The city's other attractions include a bustling (if slightly touristy) walled town and a number of interesting museums, including several across the Rhône in Villeneuve-lès-Avignon. Avignon is a good base for day trips to other parts of Provence.

The world-famous Festival d'Avignon, held every year during the last three weeks of July, attracts many hundreds of performers (actors, dancers, musicians etc) who put on some 300 performances of all sorts each day.

Orientation

The walled city's main avenue runs northward from the train station to Place de l'Horloge; it's called Cours Jean Jaurès south of the tourist office and Rue de la République north of it. Place de l'Horloge is 200 metres south of Place du Palais, which is next to the Palais des Papes.

The island that runs down the middle of the Rhône between Avignon and Villeneuve-lès-Avignon is known as Île de la Barthelasse.

Information

Tourist Office The tourist office (☎ 04 90 82 65 11) is 300 metres north of the train station at 41 Cours Jean Jaurès. The free guide *Avignon en Poche* has all the information you're likely to need while in Avignon. The office is open Monday to Saturday from 9 am to 1 pm and 2 to 6 pm (5 pm on Saturday). During the festival, hours are 10 am to 7 pm (5 pm on weekends and holidays). From October to March the tourist office annexe at the Pont Saint Bénézet (Pont d'Avignon) is open from 9 am to 1 pm and 2 to 5 pm (closed Monday); from April to September it's open daily from 9 am to 6.30 pm.

Money & Post There's a Banque de France at the northern end of Place de l'Horloge. The main post office (☎ 04 90 86 78 00) is on Cours Président Kennedy, which is through Porte de la République from the train station. It has currency exchange services. Avignon's postcode is 84000.

Laundry Laverie La Fontaine at 64 Place des Corps Saint, just around the corner from Rue Agricol Perdiguier, is open Monday to Saturday from 7 am to 8 pm.

Things to See

Avignon's most interesting areas are within the walled city *(intra-muros)*. The ramparts were restored during the 19th century but the original moats were not re-excavated, leaving the crenellated fortifications looking rather less imposing than they once probably did.

Palais des Papes Avignon's leading tourist attraction is the fortified Palace of the Popes (☎ 04 90 27 50 73/4) at Place du Palais, built during the 14th century. Six centuries ago, the seemingly endless halls, chapels, corridors and staircases were sumptuously decorated with tapestries, paintings etc but these days, except for a few damaged frescos, they are nearly empty. As a result, the palace is of interest more as a result of the dramatic events that took place here than for the inherent beauty of its stone halls.

The palace is open daily from 9 am to 12.45 pm and 2 to 6 pm. From April to October, hours are 9 am to 7 or 8 pm. When the palace closes at midday, morning ticket sales end at noon; in the evening, the ticket window closes 45 to 60 minutes before the palace does. Entry to the palace's interior is 34FF (26FF for students and people over 60). One-hour guided tours (43FF, or 38FF concession) are available in English from April to November *only*, usually at 10 am and 3.30 pm (10 am and 3 pm in July and August). Special exhibitions, especially during summer, may raise the entry fee by 10FF or so.

Around Place du Palais At the far northern end of Place du Palais, the **Musée du Petit Palais** (☎ 04 90 86 44 58) houses an outstanding collection of 13th to 16th-century Italian religious paintings. It's open from 9.30 am to noon and 2 to 6 pm (closed Tuesday); from July to August hours are 10 am to 6 pm. Tickets cost 20FF (10FF concession) but entry is free on Sunday from October to March. Just up the hill is **Rocher des Doms**, a delightful bluff-top park that offers great views of the Rhône, Pont Saint Bénézet, Villeneuve-lès-Avignon, the Alpilles, and so on.

Pont Saint Bénézet (☎ 04 90 85 60 16) was built in the 12th century to link Avignon with Villeneuve-lès-Avignon. The 900-metre-long structure was repaired and rebuilt several times, but four of its 22 spans were washed away once and for all in the mid-1600s. Yes, this is the Pont d'Avignon mentioned in the French nursery rhyme. If you want to stand *on* the bridge, you can do so – for 15FF (7FF concession) Tuesday to Sunday from 9 am to 1 pm and 2 to 5 pm (from April to September, daily from 9 am to 6.30 pm).

Synagogue The synagogue (☎ 04 90 85 21 24), at 2 Place Jérusalem, was established on this site in 1221. A 13th-century oven used to bake unleavened bread for Passover is still in place, but the rest of the present dome-topped, neoclassical structure dates from the 19th century. You can visit the synagogue Monday to Friday from 10 am to noon and 3 to 5 pm.

FRANCE

To Lyon

To Orange
& Lyon

Route de Lyon

Rhône River

Route de Lyon

• 10
• 11
Imp. Moure

Montfavet

To Airport;
Aix-en-Provence
& Marseille

Boulevard Limbert

Boulevard du Quai Saint Lazare

• 8

Avenue Pierre

Rue Louis Pasteur

Rue des Infirmiers

Rue Carreterie

Place des
Carmes

Rue Palapharnerie

Rue Campane

Rue Paul Saïn

Rue Philonarde

Rue Thiers

Rue Guillaume

Rue Saint Christophe

Rue des Teinturiers

• 38

Boulevard Saint Michel

37 •

To Centre Hospitalier
(2.5 km) & Arles

Rocher des
Doms

R Bertrand

Rue Carnot

Place
Pie
21
23
24

Rue Bonneterie

Rue du Roi-René

Place des
Corps Saints

Rue des
Fourbisseurs

Rue St. Michel

• 49
Avenue
Mondar

Boulevard de la Ligne

Banasterie

7 •

12

6

Place du
Palais

5

13
14

Place de
l'Horloge

Place
Jérusalem

Rue Rouge

Rue Racine

26

Place
St. Didier

Rue Henri Fabre

36
39
7

Rue Agricol Perdiguier

40
41

48

50 •
52
51

R de la
Balance

Place
Campana

Place des Grottes

Rue de la République

19
20
25

Rue St. Agricol

32

35

31

Square
Agricol
Perdiguier

Cours Jean Jaurès

42

Rue Bouquerie

33

43

46

Pont
Saint
Bénézet

11

Place
Crillon

18
16 17
15

Rue Joseph Vernet

Rue St. Charles

29

34

Rue
Joseph
30

Vernet

Rue Saint Charles

Boulevard Saint Roch

47

28

Rue Victor Hugo

Rue Annanelle

Rue du Rempart de l'Oulle

Boulevard de l'Oulle

Boulevard du Rhône

Allées des Oulles

Boulevard Raspail

Cours Président Kennedy

Rue Veloùterie

44

Ave Eisenhower

To Saint Bénézet (300m)

To Villeneuve-lès-
Avignon (500m);
Tour Philippe Le Bel
(1.2 km) & Fort Saint
André (2.1 km)

Chemin des Berges

• 1

2

Île de la
Barthelasse

• 3

Pont Edouard Daladier

Rhône River

Boulevard de Saint Dominique

Rue Paul
Mérindol

45

To Hameau Champfleury (250m)

Pont de l'Europe

0   150   300 m

Avignon

LP

Museums Housed in an 18th century mansion, and only partially reopened after extensive renovation, the **Musée Calvet** (☎ 04 90 86 33 84) at 65 Rue Joseph Vernet has a collection of Egyptian, Greek and Roman artefacts as well as paintings from the 16th to 20th centuries. Admission is free. The **Musée Lapidaire** (☎ 04 90 85 75 38) at 27 Rue de la République houses the city's archaeological collection. It's open from 10 am to noon and 2 to 6 pm (closed Tuesday). Entry is 10FF (free for students).

At 17 Rue Victor Hugo, the **Musée Louis Vouland** (☎ 04 90 86 03 79) exhibits a fine collection of faïence (ceramics) and some superb pieces of 18th-century French furniture. It's open Tuesday to Saturday from 2 to 6 pm (also 10 am to noon from June to September). Entry costs 20FF (10FF for students and people over 65).

Villeneuve-lès-Avignon Avignon's picturesque sister city also has a few interesting sights. The **Chartreuse du Val de Bénédiction** (☎ 04 90 15 24 24) at 60 Rue de la République, a Carthusian charterhouse founded in the 14th century, is open daily from 9.30 am to 5.30 pm (9 am to 6.30 pm from April to September), but the ticket office closes half an hour earlier. Entry is 27FF (18FF for those

under 25 or over 60). You can also buy a 50FF combined ticket which allows you to visit all of the town's major sights.

The **Musée Pierre de Luxembourg** (☎ 04 90 27 49 66) on Rue de la République near Place Jean Jaurès has a fine collection of religious paintings, many of them from the 15th to the 17th centuries. The museum is open from 10 am to noon and 2 to 5.30 pm (closed Tuesday); from April to September hours are 10 am to 12.30 pm and 3 to 7 pm. Admission is 20FF (12FF concession).

The **Tour Philippe le Bel** (☎ 04 90 27 49 68), a defensive tower built in the 14th century at what was then the western end of Pont Saint Bénézet, has great views of Avignon's walled city, the river and the surrounding countryside. Another place to visit for a wonderfully Provençal panorama is the 14th-century **Fort Saint André**, which is open daily from 10 am to noon and 2 to 5 pm (October to March) and 9.30 am to 12.30 pm and 2 to 7 pm (April to June and September). In July and August it's open from 9 am to 7 pm. Entry is 21FF (14FF for students and those over 60).

From Avignon, Villeneuve can be reached by bus No 10, which you can catch in front of the main post office. Unless you want to take the grand tour of the Avignon suburb of Les

Angles, take a bus marked 'Villeneuve puis (then) Les Angles' (rather than 'Les Angles puis Villeneuve').

Places to Stay

Camping The attractive, shaded *Camping Bagatelle* (☎ 04 90 85 78 45; open all year) is on Île de la Barthelasse, slightly north of Pont Édouard Daladier. Charges are 20FF per adult, 8.50FF to pitch a tent and 8.50FF to park a car. To get there take bus No 10 from the main post office and get off at La Barthelasse stop.

Hostels The 210-bed *Auberge Bagatelle* (☎ 04 90 86 30 39) and its many amenities are part of a large, park-like area on Île de la Barthelasse that includes Camping Bagatelle. A bed costs 58FF; doubles with twin beds cost 137FF. Rooms are locked from 1 to 5 pm, but there's no curfew. See the previous Camping section for bus directions.

The friendly *Avignon Squash Club* (☎ 04 90 85 27 78) at 32 Blvd Limbert also serves as a hostel. A bunk in a converted squash court costs only 54FF (74FF in summer). Breakfast is 16FF; sheets cost 16FF also. Travellers can check in Monday to Saturday from 10 am to 10 pm; from May to October reception is open daily from 9 to 11 am and 5 to 11 pm (10 to 11 am and 6 to 7 pm on Sunday). The hostel is closed in winter. There is a bus from the main post office (get off at the Thiers stop).

Hotels During the festival, it is nearly impossible to find accommodation in Avignon unless you've booked months in advance.

Walled City The very proper *Hôtel du Parc* (☎ 04 90 82 71 55) at 18 Rue Agricol Perdiguier, only 300 metres from the train station, has singles without/with shower for 120/145FF and doubles without/with shower for 140/155FF. Rooms with shower and toilet are 190FF and a quad with shower is 245FF. Hall showers are 10FF. Across the street at No 17 is the *Hôtel Splendid* (☎ 04 90 86 14 46). Small well-kept rooms – most have showers – start at 140FF (160FF in summer). Doubles with all the amenities cost from 160FF (200FF in summer). Prices are cheaper if you stay a week or more. The friendly *Hôtel Innova* (☎ 04 90 82 54 10) at 100 Rue Joseph Vernet has doubles without/with run-down showers for 130/160FF; doubles with shower and toilet cost 200 to 250FF. Hall showers are free.

The *Hôtel Mignon* (☎ 04 90 82 17 30; fax 04 90 85 78 46), three blocks west of Place de l'Horloge at 12 Rue Joseph Vernet, has beautifully decorated rooms with shower for 185 to 210FF and doubles/triples with shower, toilet and TV for 250/300FF. To get there by bus, take No 10 from in front of the main post office and get off at the Porte de l'Oulle.

Outside the Walls The family-run *Hôtel Monclar* (☎ 04 90 86 20 14) is across the tracks from the train station at 13 Ave Monclar. Eminently serviceable singles/doubles cost 100/160FF, 184FF with shower and 215FF with shower and toilet. Triples/quads with shower and toilet are 245/265FF. Parking is available at 20FF a day. The pleasant *Hôtel Saint Roch* (☎ 04 90 82 18 63) at 9 Rue Paul Mérindol has large, airy singles or doubles with bath, toilet and TV for 200 to 250FF and triples/quads for 280/375FF. Several rooms look out onto the lovely garden at the back. Prices in winter are about 10% cheaper. Breakfast is 30FF.

Places to Eat

The *Brasserie Le Palais* (☎ 04 90 82 53 42) at 36 Cours Jean Jaurès has lunch menus starting at 56FF and dinner menus for 76 and 92FF. Meals are served every day of the year from 11.30 am to 3 pm and 6.45 pm to midnight; during the festival, hours are 11.30 am to 1 am. There are several cheap places along Rue de la République, including the excellent sandwich shop *Sur Le Pouce* at No 26.

Restaurant Song-Long (☎ 04 90 86 35 00) at 1 Rue Carnot (next to Place Carnot) offers a wide variety of Vietnamese dishes, including vegetarian soups, salads, first courses and main dishes. menus start at 45FF (lunch) and 55 or 78FF (dinner to 11 pm). There are quite a few restaurants on Rue Galante (a small street running south off Rue Rouge, near Place de l'Horloge), including Chinese and Vietnamese places and a very popular tapas bar.

If you're in the mood to splurge on French cuisine, you might try *Le Petit Bedon* (☎ 04 90 82 33 98) at 70 Rue Joseph Vernet, whose specialities include frogs' legs and escargots.

Menus (there's no à la carte service) cost 100FF (lunch only) and 150FF. The restaurant is closed on Sunday. The attractive *Café des Artistes* (☎ 04 90 82 63 16), at 21 Place Crillon by the Porte de l'Oulle, serves very good French fare at reasonable prices. Excellent lunch menus start at 55FF. It's open Monday to Saturday (daily during the festival) from noon to 2 pm and 8 to 11 pm.

On the other side of town, a good choice is *Woolloomooloo* (☎ 04 90 85 28 44) at 16bis Rue des Teinturiers. This informal, lively restaurant is open Tuesday to Saturday from noon to 2 pm and 7.30 pm to 1 am. Lunchtime menus are 48 to 58FF and vegetarian and Antillean dishes are on offer.

Near Place de l'Horloge, there's a *Casino* grocery at 22 Rue Saint Agricol (closed on Sunday). Avignon's fanciest food shops are along Rue Joseph Vernet and Rue Saint Agricol.

Entertainment

The Australian-run *Koala Bar* (☎ 04 90 86 80 87), a popular hang-out for English speakers, is at 2 Place des Corps Saints. A small beer on tap costs from 10FF, but the price drops to 6FF during happy hour (9 to 10 pm on Wednesday, Friday and Saturday).

The only movie theatre in town with non-dubbed movies is *Cinéma Utopia* (☎ 04 90 82 65 36) at 4 Rue Escaliers Ste Anne, just north of the Palais des Papes (there's also one screen in the centre of town at 5 Rue Figuière). The cinema also functions as a mini-cultural centre and jazz club. Tickets cost 30FF (24FF each if you buy a carnet of 10).

The *Opéra d'Avignon* (☎ 04 90 82 42 42) at Place de l'Horloge stages operas, operettas, theatre, symphonic concerts, chamber music and ballet from October to June. Performance prices in the fourth gallery/orchestra range from 30/120FF to 120/360FF, depending on what's playing. The ticket office is open Monday to Saturday from 11 am to 6 pm except during August.

Getting There & Away

Bus The bus station (☎ 04 90 82 07 35) is down the ramp to the right as you exit the train station. The information windows are open Monday to Friday from 8 am to noon and 2 to 6 pm (5 pm on Friday). Tickets are sold on the buses, which are run by 19 different companies.

Places you can get to by bus include Aix-en-Provence (11 a day), Arles (four direct a day), Carpentras (about 15 a day), Nice (one a day), Nîmes (five a day), Orange (17 a day) and Marseille (five a day). Service on Sundays and during winter is less frequent. A schedule is posted in the waiting room.

Train The train station (☎ 08 36 35 35 39) is across Blvd Saint Roch from Porte de la République. The information office is open from 9 am to 6.15 pm (closed on Sunday and holidays). There are frequent trains to Arles (33FF, 25 minutes, 18 a day), Nice (180FF, four hours), Nîmes (44FF, 30 minutes, 16 a day) and Paris (400FF).

Car & Motorcycle Europcar Interent (☎ 04 90 14 40 80), at 2a Ave Monclar, rents cars for 415FF a day (with 200 free km) and 775FF for the weekend (with 600 free km), including tax and insurance. It's open Monday to Saturday.

Getting Around

TCRA municipal buses operate from 7 am to about 7.40 pm. On Sunday, buses are less frequent and most lines run only between 8 am and 6 pm. TCRA has offices in the walled city at Porte de la République (☎ 04 90 82 68 19) and at Place Pie (☎ 04 90 85 44 93; closed on Sunday). Tickets cost 6.50FF.

AROUND AVIGNON

The Provençal cities of Arles and Nîmes, famed for their well-preserved Roman antiquities, are only a short train or bus ride from Avignon. See Getting There & Away under Avignon for transport details.

Arles

Arles (population 52,000), set on the northern edge of the Camargue alluvial plain, began its ascent to prosperity and political importance in 49 BC when Caesar (to whom the city had given its support) captured and despoiled Marseille, which had backed the Roman general Pompey. It soon became a major trading centre, the sort of place that, by the late 1st century, needed a 20,000-seat amphitheatre and a 12,000-seat theatre. Now known as the

Arènes and the **Théâtre Antique** respectively, the two structures are still used to stage bull-fights and cultural events.

Arles is also known for its **Cathédrale Saint Trophime** and **Cloître Saint Trophime**; significant parts of both date from the 12th century and are in the Romanesque style. It is probably best known as the place where Van Gogh painted some of his most famous works, including *The Sunflowers*. The tourist office (☎ 04 90 18 41 20) is on Esplanade des Lices.

Nîmes
The city of Nîmes (population 130,000) has some of the best preserved Roman structures in all of Europe. The **Arènes** (amphitheatre), which, unlike its counterpart at Arles, retains its upper storey, dates from around 100 AD and could once seat 24,000 spectators. Entry is 30FF (22FF for students). The rectangular **Maison Carrée**, a Greek-style temple measuring 26 by 15 metres, dates from the late 1st century BC and is largely intact.

The most important festival in Nîmes is La Feria at the end of March, with bullfights and concerts in the Arènes and parades and music in the streets. The helpful tourist office (☎ 04 66 67 29 11) is at 6 Rue Auguste. There is an annexe (☎ 04 66 84 18 13) at the train station.

Pont du Gard
Built by the Roman general Agrippa around 19 BC, the mighty Pont du Gard is not to be missed. This aqueduct, which spans the Gard River, is 275 metres long and 49 metres high. Apart from admiring the Romans' handiwork from a distance, you can also walk inside the aqueduct, where the water once flowed. There are buses to the Pont du Gard from Avignon, but there are more services from Nîmes.

Côte d'Azur

The Côte d'Azur, also known as the French Riviera, stretches along France's Mediterranean coast from Toulon to Menton and the Italian border. Many of the towns along the coast – Saint Tropez, Cannes, Antibes, Nice, Monaco – have become world-famous thanks to the recreational activities of the rich, idle and tanned. The reality

is rather less glamorous, but the Côte d'Azur still has a great deal to attract visitors: sun, 40 km of beaches, all sorts of cultural activities and, sometimes, even a bit of glitter.

Unless you'll be camping or hostelling, your best bet is to stay in Nice, which has a generous supply of cheap hotels, and take day trips to other places in the area. The Côte d'Azur includes many seafront and hillside towns, such as Toulon, Saint Tropez, the Massif de l'Esterel, Grasse (renowned for its perfume production), Vence, Saint Paul de Vence and Roquebrune-Cap Martin. Make sure you don't miss Villefranche-sur-Mer and Èze; though close to Nice they offer a completely different view of the Riviera.

Trains run between Ventimiglia (just across the border in Italy) and Saint Raphaël – via Menton, Monaco, Nice, Antibes, Cannes and the many smaller towns – from early morning until late at night. See Getting There & Away in the Nice section for details.

Radio
The English-language Riviera Radio, based in Monte Carlo, can be heard on 106.3 MHz FM (in Monaco) and 106.5 MHz FM (along the rest of the Côte d'Azur). It broadcasts BBC World Service news every hour.

Dangers & Annoyances
Theft from backpacks, pockets, cars and even laundrettes is a serious problem along the Côte d'Azur. To avoid unpleasantness, keep a sharp eye on your bags, especially at train and bus stations, and use the lockers at train and bus stations if you'll be sleeping outside (say, on the beach). Again, *never* leave anything in a parked vehicle.

Getting Around
The Côte d'Azur is notorious for its traffic jams, so if you'll be driving along the coast, especially in summer, be prepared for slow going. Around Saint Tropez, for instance, it can sometimes take hours to move just a few km, which is why some of the truly wealthy have taken to reaching their seaside properties by helicopter.

NICE
Known as the capital of the Riviera, the fashionable yet relaxed city of Nice (population

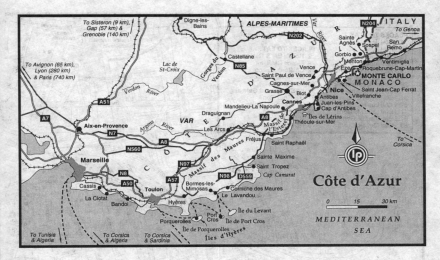

346,000) makes a great base from which to explore the entire Côte d'Azur. The city, which did not become part of France until 1860, has plenty of relatively cheap accommodation and is only a short train or bus ride away from the rest of the Riviera. Nice's beach may be nothing to write home about, but the city is blessed with a fine collection of museums.

Orientation

Ave Jean Médecin runs from near the train station to Place Masséna. The Promenade des Anglais follows the curved beachfront from the city centre all the way to the airport, six km to the west. Vieux Nice is the area delineated by the Quai des États-Unis, Blvd Jean Jaurès and the 92-metre hill known as Le Château. The neighbourhood of Cimiez, home to several very good museums, is north of the town centre.

Information

Tourist Office From July to September, the main tourist office (☎ 04 93 87 07 07) at the train station is open daily from 8 am to 8 pm (until 7 pm the rest of the year). The tourist office annexe (☎ 04 93 87 60 60) at 5 Promenade des Anglais is open Monday to Saturday from 8 am to 6 pm.

Money There's a Banque de France at 14 Ave Félix Faure. There are numerous places where you can change money along Ave Jean Médecin near Place Masséna. The Banque Populaire de la Côte d'Azur at 17 Ave Jean Médecin has a 24-hour currency exchange machine. The Office Provençal Change at 17 Ave Thiers (to the right as you exit the train station) offers less-than-optimal rates but is open every day of the year from 7 am to midnight.

American Express (☎ 04 93 16 53 53) at 11 Promenade des Anglais is open Monday to Saturday from 9 am to 8 pm and on Sunday from 10 am to 6 pm.

Post The main post office (☎ 04 93 82 65 00), which will exchange foreign currency, is at 23 Ave Thiers, one block to the right as you exit the train station. There are branch post offices at 4 Ave Georges Clemenceau, on the corner of Rue de Russie, and in the old city at 2 Rue Louis Gassin. Nice's postcode is 06000 north of Ave Jean Jaurès (including the train station area) and 06

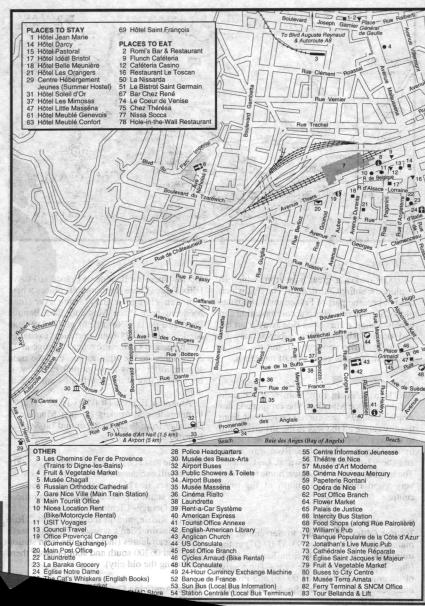

PLACES TO STAY
1 Hôtel Jean Marie
14 Hôtel Darcy
15 Hôtel Pastoral
17 Hôtel Idéal Bristol
18 Hôtel Belle Meunière
21 Hôtel Les Orangers
29 Centre Hébergement
   Jeunes (Summer Hostel)
31 Hôtel Soleil d'Or
37 Hôtel Les Mimosas
47 Hôtel Little Masséna
61 Hôtel Meublé Genevois
63 Hôtel Meublé Confort

69 Hôtel Saint François

PLACES TO EAT
2 Romi's Bar & Restaurant
9 Flunch Cafétéria
12 Cafétéria Casino
16 Restaurant Le Toscan
50 La Nissarda
51 Le Bistrot Saint Germain
67 Bar Chez René
74 Le Coeur de Venise
75 Chez Thérésa
77 Nissa Socca
78 Hole-in-the-Wall Restaurant

OTHER
3 Les Chemins de Fer de Provence
   (Trains to Digne-les-Bains)
4 Fruit & Vegetable Market
5 Musée Chagall
6 Russian Orthodox Cathedral
7 Gare Nice Ville (Main Train Station)
8 Main Tourist Office
10 Nicea Location Rent
   (Bike/Motorcycle Rental)
11 USIT Voyages
13 Council Travel
19 Office Provençal Change
   (Currency Exchange)
20 Main Post Office
22 Laundrette
23 La Baraka Grocery
24 Église Notre Dame
25 The Cat's Whiskers (English Books)

28 Police Headquarters
30 Musée des Beaux-Arts
32 Airport Buses
33 Public Showers & Toilets
34 Airport Buses
35 Musée Masséna
36 Cinéma Rialto
38 Laundrette
39 Rent-a-Car Système
40 American Express
41 Tourist Office Annexe
42 English-American Library
43 Anglican Church
44 US Consulate
45 Post Office Branch
46 Cycles Arnaud (Bike Rental)
48 UK Consulate
49 24-Hour Currency Exchange Machine
52 Banque de France
53 Sun Bus (Local Bus Information)
54 Station Centrale (Local Bus Terminus)

55 Centre Information Jeunesse
56 Théâtre de Nice
57 Musée d'Art Moderne
58 Cinéma Nouveau Mercury
59 Papeterie Rontani
60 Opéra de Nice
62 Post Office Branch
64 Flower Market
65 Palais de Justice
66 Intercity Bus Station
68 Food Shops (along Rue Pairolière)
70 William's Pub
71 Banque Populaire de la Côte d'Azur
72 Jonathan's Live Music Pub
73 Cathédrale Sainte Réparate
79 Église Saint Jacques le Majeur
80 Buses to City Centre
81 Musée Terra Amata
82 Ferry Terminal & SNCM Office
83 Tour Bellanda & Lift

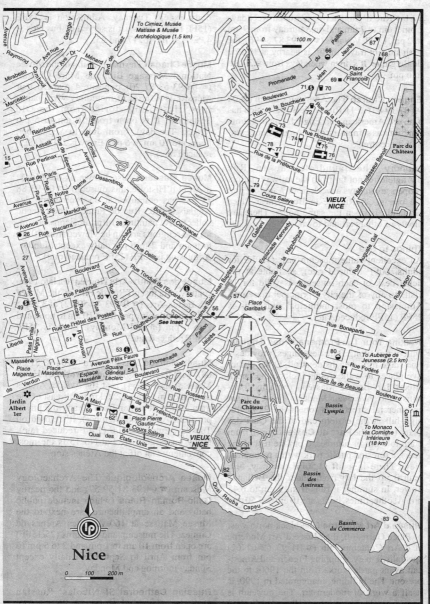

Nice

0   100   200 m

37 bis Rue d'Angleterre. It's open weekdays from 9 am to 7 pm and on Saturday from 9 am to 2 pm. USIT Voyages (☎ 04 93 87 34 96), the Irish student travel outfit, is nearby at 10 Rue de Belgique. It's open weekdays from 9.30 am to 6 pm.

English Church The Anglican Church (☎ 04 93 87 19 83) at 11 Rue de la Buffa, which has a mixed American and English congregation, functions as something of an Anglophone community centre.

Laundry The laundrette at 16 Rue d'Angleterre, not far from the railway station, is open seven days a week from 7 am to 9 pm; the one at 39 Rue de la Buffa, near Place Grimaldi, is open the same hours. There are plenty of others around town.

Things to See
An excellent-value museum pass (120FF for adults, 60FF reduced rate), available at the ticket desk of each museum, is valid for 15 visits to any of the city's principal museums. Admission to most municipal museums is 25FF (15FF reduced rate).

Walking Tour The **Promenade des Anglais**, which runs along Baie des Anges, provides a fine stage for a beachside stroll. Other attractive places to walk around include the Jardin Albert 1er, Espace Masséna (with its fountains) and Ave Jean Médecin (Nice's main commercial street). On top of the 92-metre-high hill at the eastern end of the Quai des États-Unis is the **Parc du Château** (open from 8 am to 7 pm in summer, 6 pm the rest of the year), a forested public park with a panoramic view. There is a lift (3.50FF one way, 5FF return) up the hill from under the Bellanda Tower. In summer it runs from 9 am to 6.45 pm. At other times, hours are 10 am to 5.50 pm.

Musée d'Art Moderne One block north-west of Place Garibaldi, the Musée d'Art Moderne et d'Art Contemporain (☎ 04 93 62 61 62) specialises in eye-popping French and American avant-garde works from the 1960s to the present. The building, inaugurated in 1990, is itself a work of modern art. The museum is open from 11 am to 6 pm (10 pm on Friday)

daily except Tuesday. Admission is 25FF (15FF for students). It is served by bus Nos 3, 4, 5, 7, 9, 10, 16, 17 and 25.

Musée Chagall The main exhibit of the Musée National Message Biblique Marc Chagall (☎ 04 93 53 87 20), opposite 4 Ave Docteur Ménard, is a series of incredibly vivid paintings illustrating stories from the Old Testament. It is open from 10 am to 5 pm (closed Tuesday). From July to September, hours are 10 am to 6 pm. Entry is 28FF (18FF reduced rate).

Musée Masséna Also known as the Musée d'Art et d'Histoire, this museum (☎ 04 93 88 11 34) has entrances at 35 Promenade des Anglais and 65 Rue de France. The eclectic collection of paintings, furniture, icons, ceramics and religious art can be viewed from 10 am to noon and 2 to 6 pm daily except Monday. Admission is 25FF (15FF reduced rate).

Musée des Beaux-Arts Housed in a late 19th-century villa just off Rue de France, the Musée des Beaux-Arts (☎ 04 93 44 50 72) at 33 Ave des Baumettes is open from 10 am to noon and 2 to 6 pm (closed Monday). Entry is 25FF (15FF reduced rate).

Musée Matisse This museum (☎ 04 93 81 08 08), with its fine collection of works by Henri Matisse (1869-1954), is at 164 Ave des Arènes de Cimiez in Cimiez, 2.5 km north-east of the train station. It's open from 10 am to 5 pm (6 pm from April to September). It's closed on Tuesday. Entry is 25FF (15FF reduced rate). Many buses go there but No 15 is the most convenient. Get off at the Arènes stop.

Musée Archéologique The Archaeology Museum (☎ 04 93 81 59 57) and the nearby **Gallo-Roman Ruins** (which include public baths and an amphitheatre) are next to the Musée Matisse at 160 Ave des Arènes de Cimiez. The museum and the ruins (25/15FF) are open from 10 am to 1 pm and 2 to 5 pm (6 pm from April to September) daily except Sunday morning and Monday.

Russian Cathedral St Nicolas' Russian Orthodox Cathedral (☎ 04 93 96 88 02), crowned by six onion-shaped domes, was built between 1903 and 1912 in the style of the early 17th century. Step inside and you'll be transported to Imperial Russia, a world of Cyrillic script and gilded icons. The cathedral, opposite 17 Blvd Tzaréwitch, is open from 9 or 9.30 am to noon and 2.30 to 5 pm (5.30 pm in spring and autumn, and 6 pm in summer). The entry fee is 12FF (10FF for students). Shorts or short skirts and sleeveless shirts are forbidden.

Activities

Nice's **beach** is covered with smooth little rocks. Between mid-April and mid-October, the sections of beach open to the public without charge alternate with private beaches (60 to 70FF a day) offering all sorts of amenities (mattresses, showers, changing rooms, parasols, a reduced chance of theft etc). Along the beach you can hire catamaran paddle boats, sailboards and jet skis (300FF for 30 minutes), and go parasailing (200FF for 10 minutes) and water-skiing (100 to 130FF for 10 minutes). There are indoor showers (12FF) and toilets (2FF) open to the public opposite 50 Promenade des Anglais.

Places to Stay

In summer, lots of young people sleep on the beach. Theoretically this is illegal, but the Nice police usually look the other way.

Hostels The *Auberge de Jeunesse* (☎ 04 93 89 23 64) is five km east of the train station on Route Forestière du Mont Alban. Beds cost 64FF, including breakfast, and sheets are 15FF. There is a midnight curfew (1 am in summer). It's often full so call ahead. Take bus No 14 from the Station Centrale (the local bus terminal) on Square Général Leclerc, which is linked to the train station by bus Nos 15 and 17.

The *Relais International de la Jeunesse* (☎ 04 93 81 27 63; open all year) at 26 Ave Scuderi is four km north of the city centre in the wealthy neighbourhood of Cimiez. Take bus No 15 to get out there and get off at the Scuderi stop; it's a five-minute walk along Ave Scuderi. A dorm bed costs 70FF (including breakfast and showers) for the first night and 60FF for subsequent nights. The maximum stay in summer is three nights, but you can stay

longer if you take half-board, which costs 120FF. This place is closed between 10 am and 5 pm and there is an 11 pm curfew. You can't make reservations, so call ahead to find out if there's room.

From mid-June to 10 September the *Centre Hébergement Jeunes* (☎ 04 93 86 28 75) serves as a hostel. It's at 31 Rue Louis de Coppet, half a block from 173 Rue de France. A bed in a six-bed room costs only 50FF. There is a midnight curfew. Bags must be stored in the luggage room during the day, which costs 10FF a day.

Hotels There are quite a few cheap hotels near the train station and lots of places in a slightly higher price bracket along Rue d'Angleterre, Rue d'Alsace-Lorraine, Rue de Suisse, Rue de Russie and Rue Durante, also near the station. There are plenty more to the east of the station, clustered around Rue Assalit and Rue Pertinax. In summer the inexpensive places fill up by late morning – come by or call ahead by 10 am.

Train Station Area The *Hôtel Belle Meunière* (☎ 04 93 88 66 15) at 21 Ave Durante, a clean, friendly place that attracts lots of young people, is an excellent bet. Dorm beds are 75 to 80FF. Large doubles/triples with high ceilings, some with century-old décor, or kitchenettes, start at 160/240FF (265/321FF with shower and toilet). All prices include breakfast. There's room to park out the front. This place is closed in December and January. Down the block at No 10bis, the *Hôtel Les Orangers* (☎ 04 93 87 51 41) has renovated but plain rooms with shower, hotplate and fridge. It costs 80FF for a dorm bed and from 90FF for a single. Doubles are 180 to 200FF and triples/quads are 270/340FF.

The *Hôtel Darcy* (☎ 04 93 88 67 06) at 28 Rue d'Angleterre has singles/doubles for 130/160FF (165/190FF with shower and toilet), breakfast included. From May to September, prices are increased by 10 to 30FF. The friendly *Hôtel Idéal Bristol* (☎ 04 93 88 60 72) at 22 Rue Paganini has cheaply furnished doubles, some with fridge, from 145FF (180FF with shower and toilet). Rooms with shower and toilet for four/five people are 340/425FF. There's no charge for showers and there's a rooftop terrace.

FRANCE

The **Hôtel Pastoral** (☎ 04 93 85 17 22) is just off Ave Jean Médecin at 27 Rue Assalit. Large, simple singles/doubles with fridge start at 105/120FF; showers cost 10FF. Doubles with shower and toilet are 170FF. Reception is open daily from 8 am to 3 pm and 6 to 10 pm.

Vieux Nice The **Hôtel Saint François** (☎ 04 93 85 88 69) at 3 Rue Saint François has small singles with small windows from 85FF, doubles with one/two beds for 127/164FF and triples from 216FF. Showers cost 15FF.

The **Hôtel Meublé Genevois** (☎ 04 93 85 00 58), in an unmarked building at 11 Rue Alexandre Mari (3rd floor), has 1950s-style singles/doubles with kitchenette from 120FF (with washbasin and bidet) and 180FF (with shower and toilet). Large studios with shower and toilet cost from 200FF for two people. Reception is open from 9.30 to 11 am and 3 to 6 pm. The **Hôtel Meublé Confort** (☎ 04 93 85 00 58), which is run by the same people and has similar prices, is down the block in an unmarked building at No 17 (4th floor). Both are near the Station Centrale – to get there take bus No 15 (or any of several other lines) from the train station.

Elsewhere in Town The **Hôtel Little Masséna** (☎ 04 93 87 72 34) is right in the centre of things at 22 Rue Masséna. Reception, which stays open until 7 pm, is on the 5th floor and, yes, there's a lift. Small studios for one or two people with hotplate, fridge and TV range from 130 to 220FF; showers are free. The relaxed, family-style **Hôtel Les Mimosas** (☎ 04 93 88 05 59) is at 26 Rue de la Buffa (2nd floor), a block north of the Musée Masséna. Depending on the season, good-sized, utilitarian rooms cost 100 to 130FF for one person and 120 to 180FF for two. Showers are free. You can check in here 24 hours a day.

The quiet **Hôtel Soleil d'Or** (☎ 04 93 96 55 94) is 1.3 km south-west of the train station at 16 Ave des Orangers. Simple singles with high ceilings cost 100FF, doubles start at 150FF, and an extra bed costs 50FF. Doubles with shower and toilet are 210FF. Hall showers cost 10FF.

The **Hôtel Jean Marie** (☎ 04 93 84 87 23) is 600 metres north of the train station at 15-17 Rue André Theuriet. The less-than-convenient location means that there may be rooms here

when other places are full. Dim but serviceable rooms (doubles only) start at 120/145FF without/with shower. There are no hall showers, but you can take a shower (11FF) in the annexe. Buses from Ave Jean Médecin include Nos 1, 2 and 22. Also in the northern part of town, **Madame Gregori Maurin** (☎ 04 93 52 84 15) has four rooms in a large house at 2 Rue Gare du Sud. A room for two costs 150FF including breakfast, lunch or dinner. Heading west from Place Général de Gaulle, Rue Gare du Sud is the first street on the left.

Places to Eat

Cheap places near the train station include the **Flunch Caféteria** (☎ 04 93 88 41 35), which is to the left as you exit the station building and is open daily from 11 am to 9.30 pm (10 pm in summer) and, across the street at 7 Ave Thiers, the **Caféteria Casino** (☎ 04 93 82 44 44), which is open from 8 am to 10 pm.

In the same vicinity, **Restaurant Le Toscan** (☎ 04 93 88 40 54; closed Sunday), a family-run Italian place at 1 Rue de Belgique, offers large portions of home-made ravioli. The menus (from 62FF) let you choose from a wide selection of dishes. There are lots of Vietnamese and Chinese restaurants on Rue Paganini, Rue d'Italie and Rue d'Alsace-Lorraine.

North of the railway station, **Romi's Bar & Restaurant** (☎ 04 93 51 83 71) at 7 Place Général de Gaulle offers a variety of wonderfully fresh plats du jour from 50FF. It's open for lunch and dinner daily except Tuesday. A huge traditional vegetable, fruit, flower and fish market is held nearby, along Ave Malaussena, every morning except Monday.

La Nissarda (☎ 04 93 85 26 29; closed Sunday) at 17 Rue Gubernatis has specialities of both Nice and Normandy. The menus are reasonably priced at 60, 78, 98 and 138FF. This place serves dinner to 9 pm. Nearby, **Le Bistrot Saint Germain** (☎ 04 93 13 45 12; closed Sunday) at 9 Rue Chauvain brings a touch of Paris to Nice, its walls decorated with photos of famous Parisian scenes. It offers fresh, seasonal food at affordable prices: you can choose from three plats du jour (59FF) or the menu (129FF).

In the old city, a perennial favourite with locals is **Nissa Socca** (☎ 04 93 80 18 35) at 5 Rue Sainte Reparate. Niçois specialities include socca, whose main ingredients are chickpea flour and olive oil. Pasta dishes are 36 to 40FF. Nissa Socca is closed all day Sunday, at midday on Monday, and all of January. Nearby streets, such as Rue de l'Abbaye, are lined with restaurants. For socca (10FF), Niçois-style sandwiches (12 to 17FF), pizza (6 to 10FF per piece) and other takeaway dishes, try *Bar Chez René* at 2 Rue Miralheti.

The *Prisunic* supermarket opposite 33 Ave Jean Médecin is open Monday to Saturday. A few blocks south-east of the train station, *La Baraka* grocery at 10 Rue de Suisse is open daily from 5 pm to 2 am. In Vieux Nice, there are a number of food shops along Rue Pairolière.

Entertainment
William's Pub-Biererie (☎ 04 93 85 84 66), opposite the intercity bus station at 4 Rue Centrale, has live rock music every night starting at around 10 pm (9 pm on Sunday). The pub itself is open Monday to Saturday from 9 pm to 6 am. There's pool, darts and chess in the basement. *Jonathan's Live Music Restaurant* (☎ 04 93 62 57 62), another bar à musique at 1 Rue de la Loge, near Rue Centrale, has live music (country, boogie-woogie, Irish folk etc) every night except Monday. *Hole-in-the-Wall Restaurant* (☎ 04 93 80 40 16) at 3 Rue de l'Abbaye offers both food and live music. Open from 8 pm to 1 am nightly except Monday, it has main dishes for 35 to 79FF and the famous salade niçoise for 38FF. Bottled beer is 22 to 40FF.

Getting There & Away
Air Nice's airport, Aéroport International Nice-Côte d'Azur (☎ 04 93 21 30 30), is six km west of the centre of town.

Bus Lines operated by some two dozen bus companies stop at the bus station, which is opposite 10 Blvd Jean Jaurès. The information counter (☎ 04 93 85 61 81) is open Monday to Saturday from 8 am to 6.30 pm. There is slow but frequent service every day until about 7.30 pm to Cannes (30FF one way, 1½ hours), Antibes (24.50FF one way, 1¼ hours), Monaco (18FF return, 45 minutes), Menton (24FF return, 1¼ hours) and Grasse (36FF one way, 1¼ hours).

Train The train station's information office (☎ 08 36 35 35 39) is open Monday to Saturday from 8 to 6.30 pm and Sunday from 8 to 11.30 am and 2 to 5.30 pm. There is fast, frequent service (up to 40 trains a day in each direction) to points all along the coast, including Monaco (18FF, 20 minutes), Antibes (21FF, 24 minutes) and Cannes (30FF, 35 minutes). From June to September there are trains every 20 minutes between 5 am and 11 or 11.30 pm. The rest of the year trains run at least once an hour except between 2 and 4 pm and after 8.30 pm. One of the two overnight trains to Paris (Gare de Lyon) is a sleeper (564FF). Second-class tickets cost 214FF to Rome and 362FF to Barcelona.

Ferry The fastest and least expensive ferries from mainland France to Corsica depart from Nice (see Getting There & Away in the Corsica section). The SNCM office (☎ 04 93 13 66 99) at the ferry port on Quai du Commerce is open from 8 am to noon and 2 to 5.45 pm daily except Saturday afternoon and Sunday. From mid-June to September, weekday hours are 6 am to 8 pm and Saturday hours are 6 am to noon. SNCM tickets can be purchased at many travel agencies. To get to the ferry port from Ave Jean Médecin, take bus No 1 or 2 and get off at the Port stop.

Getting Around
To/From the Airport From the bus station or the Promenade des Anglais, take the bus with the aeroplane logo (22FF). Buses run daily every 20 minutes (30 minutes on Sunday) from 5.50 am to 8.15 pm. From the train station or Rue de France, take bus No 23 (8FF). From the airport, buses run from 6.05 am to 10.45 pm (11.45 pm on Friday).

Bus Tickets cost 8FF for a single ride or 68FF for a carnet of 10. Bus No 12 links the train station with the beach. To go from the train station to Vieux Nice and the bus station, take bus No 15 or 17. Bus information and one, five and seven-day passes are available from the Centre d'Information (☎ 04 93 16 52 10) at 10 Ave Félix Faure (next to the Station Centrale, the main terminal for municipal buses).

Taxi Call ☎ 04 93 80 70 70 to order a taxi.

Car & Motorcycle Rent-a-Car Système (☎ 04 93 87 87 37) at 25 Promenade des Anglais rents Fiat Pandas for 298FF a day, including insurance and unlimited km. The excess is 1000FF. For 199FF a day, the excess is an outrageous 8000FF. The office is open Monday to Saturday from 8.30 am to 12.30 pm and 2 to 7 pm and Sunday from 9 am to noon.

Mopeds (from 150FF), scooters (from 325FF) and motorcycles can be rented from Nicea Location Rent (☎ 04 93 82 42 71) at 9 Ave Thiers, which is open Monday to Saturday from 9 am to 6 pm.

Bicycle Bicycles (120FF a day) can be rented from Nicea Location Rent (see Car & Motorcycle above). Cycles Arnaud (☎ 04 93 87 88 55) at 4 Place Grimaldi has mountain bikes for 100FF a day or 180FF for the weekend. It's open Monday to Friday from 9 am to noon and 2 to 7 pm.

ANTIBES

Across the Baie des Anges from Nice, Antibes has beautiful, sandy beaches, 16th-century ramparts that run along the sea, an attractive pleasure-boat harbour (Port Vauban) and an old city with narrow, winding streets and flower-bedecked houses. The tourist office (☎ 04 92 90 53 00) is at 11 Place de Gaulle.

The Château Grimaldi, set on a spectacular site overlooking the sea, now serves as the **Musée Picasso** (☎ 04 93 34 91 91). This outstanding museum at Place Mariejol is open from 10 am to noon and 2 to 6 pm (3 to 7 pm from July to September). It's closed on Tuesday and in November; entry is 20FF (10FF for students).

For accommodation, there is a *Relais International de la Jeunesse* (☎ 04 93 61 34 40; open all year) at 60 Blvd de la Garoupe at Cap d'Antibes. Dorm beds are 70FF a night. *La Belle Époque* (☎ 04 93 34 53 00) at 10 Ave du 24 Août, close to the bus station, has well-kept singles/doubles with shower for 173/196FF (223/246FF, including breakfast, from May to September). Doubles with shower and toilet are 236FF (286FF in the high season). From July to August you have to take half-board: 303/406FF for singles/doubles. For more luxurious accommodation try the *Relais du Postillon* (☎ 04 93 34 20 77) at 8 Rue Cham-

pionnet, across the park from the post office, or the *Auberge Provençale* (☎ 04 93 34 13 24) at 61 Place Nationale.

In the old city, Rue James Close has the greatest concentration of restaurants and food shops, but these establishments are fairly touristy. Further away, at 3 Rue Frédéric Isnard near the town hall, the friendly *Le Brulot* (☎ 04 93 34 17 76) has lunch menus for 58FF. There are more restaurants nearby and on Place Nationale. A food market is held on Tuesday to Saturday mornings (daily from June to August) on Place Masséna, next to the Hôtel de Ville.

The bus station (☎ 04 93 34 37 60) is at Place Guynemer, just off Rue de la République. The train station is on Ave Robert Soleau; call ☎ 08 36 35 35 39 for information. There are frequent trains from Nice and Cannes.

CANNES

The harbour, the bay, Le Suquet hill, the beachside promenade, the beaches and the people sunning themselves provide more than enough natural beauty to make at least a day trip to Cannes (population 68,000) worth the effort. It's also fun watching the rich drop their money with such fashionable nonchalance.

Cannes is famous for its many festivals and cultural activities, the most renowned of which is the International Film Festival, which runs for two weeks in mid-May. People come to Cannes all year long, but the tourist season runs from May to October. During the off season, however, local people are more inclined to be friendly, prices are lower and there are no crowds to contend with.

Orientation

Rue Jean Jaurès, which runs in front of the train station, is four or five blocks north of the huge Palais des Festivals et des Congrès, to the west of which is the old port. Place Bernard Cornut Gentille (formerly Place de l'Hôtel de Ville), where the bus station is located, is on the north-western corner of the Vieux Port. Cannes' most famous promenade, the magnificent, hotel-lined Blvd de la Croisette, begins at the Palais des Festivals and continues eastward around the Baie de Cannes to Pointe de la Croisette.

Cannes

PLACES TO STAY
1 Pension Les Glycines
10 Hôtel de Bourgogne
13 Hôtel Atlantis
19 Hôtel Chantéclair

PLACES TO EAT
9 Au Bec Fin
17 Restaurant Le Croco
20 Restaurants
21 Aux Bons Enfants

OTHER
2 Morning Food Market
3 Location Deux Roues
  (Bicycle & Scooter Rental)
4 Laundrette
5 Bus Station (to Grasse,
  Vallauris & Valbonne)
6 Tourist Office Annexe
7 Train Station
11 Office Provençal Change
12 Monoprix Supermarket
14 Champion Supermarket
15 Zanzi Bar
16 Food Shops
18 Marché Forville
22 Cristal Bar
23 Bus Station (To Nice)
24 Musée de la Castre
25 Cannes Info Jeunesse
26 CMC Ticket Office
   (Ferries to the
   Îles de Lérins)
27 Cannes English Bookshop
28 Post Office
29 American Express
30 Main Tourist Office
31 Palais des Festivals
   et des Congrès
32 Banque de France
33 Plages de la Croisette
   (Private Beaches)

FRANCE

Information
Tourist Office The main tourist office (☎ 04 93 39 24 53) is on the ground floor of the Palais des Festivals. It's open Monday to Saturday from 9 am to 6.30 pm and, during festivals and conventions, on Sunday as well. In July and August, the office is open daily to 8 pm. The tourist office annexe (☎ 04 93 99 19 77) at the train station is open from 9 am to 1 pm and 2 to 6 pm. In July and August, it opens half an hour earlier and closes half an hour later. To get there, go left as you exit the terminal building and then walk up the stairs next to Frantour Tourisme.

Money & Post There are banks along Rue d'Antibes (two blocks towards the beach from Rue Jean Jaurès) and on Rue Buttura (across Blvd de la Croisette from the main tourist office). American Express (☎ 04 93 99 05 45) at 8 Rue des Belges, two blocks north-east of the Palais des Festivals, is open Monday to Friday from 9 am to 6 pm and on Saturday from 9 am to 1 pm.

There's a post office (☎ 04 93 39 14 11) at 22 Rue Bivouac Napoléon, two blocks inland from the Palais des Festivals, that exchanges foreign currency. Cannes' postcode is 06400.

Things to See & Do
Walking Tour Not surprisingly, the best places to walk are not far from the water. Some of the largest yachts you've ever seen are likely to be sitting in the **Vieux Port**, which was once a fishing port but is now given over to pleasure craft. The streets around the old port are particularly pleasant on a summer's night after dark, when the many cafés and restaurants – overflowing with well-heeled patrons – light up the whole area with coloured neon.

The hill just west of the old port, **Le Suquet**, affords magnificent views of Cannes, especially in the late afternoon and on clear nights. Musée de la Castre (see the following entry) is at the summit. The pine and palm-shaded walkway along **Blvd de la Croisette** is probably the classiest promenade on the whole Riviera.

Musée de la Castre This museum (☎ 04 93 38 55 26), housed in a chateau atop Le Suquet, has a diverse collection of Mediterranean and Middle Eastern antiquities as well as objects of ethnographic interest from all over the world. The museum, which costs 10FF (free for students), is open from 10 am to noon and 2 to 5 pm (closed Tuesday). From April to June and in September, afternoon hours are 2 to 6 pm; during July and August, they're 3 to 7 pm.

Beaches Each of the fancy hotels that line Blvd de la Croisette has its own private section of the beach. Unfortunately, this arrangement leaves only a small strip of sand near the Palais des Festivals for the bathing pleasure of the masses. Free public beaches, the **Plages du Midi** and **Plages de la Bocca**, stretch for several km westward from the old port along Blvd Jean Hibert and Blvd du Midi.

Islands The eucalyptus and pine-covered **Île Sainte Marguerite**, where the Man in the Iron Mask (made famous in the novel by Alexandre Dumas) was held captive during the late 17th century, lies just over a km from the mainland. The island, which measures 3.2 by 0.95 km, is crisscrossed and circumnavigated by many trails and paths. The smaller **Île Saint Honorat** was once the site of a renowned and powerful monastery founded in the 5th century.

The Compagnie Maritime Cannoise (☎ 04 93 38 66 33) and the Compagnie Esterel Chanteclair (☎ 04 93 39 11 82) run ferries to Île Saint Honorat (50FF return, 20 minutes) and Île Sainte Marguerite (45FF return, 20 minutes). Both islands (known as the Îles de Lérins) can be visited for 70FF. The ticket office, at the old port across Jetée Albert Édouard from the Palais des Festivals, is open daily from 7.30 am to 12.15 pm and 2 to 4.15 pm. From early May to August, it's open from 8.30 am to 6 pm and later for special outings.

Places to Stay
Hotel prices in Cannes fluctuate wildly according to seasonal demand. Tariffs can be up to 50% higher in July and August – when you'll be lucky to find a room at any price – than in winter. During the film festival, all the hotels are booked up to a year in advance.

Hostels Cannes' *Auberge de Jeunesse* (☎ 04 93 99 26 79), in a small villa at 35 Ave de Vallauris about 400 metres north-east of the train station, has beds in dorm rooms for four to six people for about 80FF, though you must have an HI card (available for 75/104FF for those under/over 26). Sheets cost 10FF. Each of the three floors has a kitchen, and there's a laundry room. Reception is open from 8 am to 10.30 pm daily; curfew is at midnight (1 am at weekends). The hostel is open all year.

An alternative to the official hostel is a very pleasant private one called *Le Chalit* (☎ 04 93 99 22 11) at 27 Ave du Maréchal Galliéni about five minutes walk north-west of the station. It charges 80FF for a bed in rooms for four to eight people. Sheets are 15FF extra. There are two kitchens. Le Chalit is open year-round and there is no curfew, but you must leave a deposit to get a key.

Hotels Cannes should have more places like the *Hôtel Chanteclair* (☎ 04 93 39 68 88) at 12 Rue Forville. This well-maintained and friendly hotel, a favourite with backpackers, has singles/doubles from 140/180FF (mid-October to mid-April) and rooms with shower and toilet for 260FF (during the film festival and from mid-July to mid-August). Triples/quads with shower are 240/280FF (300/400FF in the high season). Hall showers are free. The *Hôtel National* (☎ 04 93 39 91 92) at 8 Rue Maréchal Joffre has doubles starting at 160FF (190FF in the high season). Rooms with shower are 190FF (250FF high season) or 220FF (300FF) with shower and toilet.

The large *Hôtel Atlantis* (☎ 04 93 39 18 72) is half a block south of the train station at 4 Rue du 24 Août. Despite its two-star rating, it has singles/doubles with washbasin, bidet and TV from only 145/160FF in the low season. Rooms with shower cost 200/230FF or 230/250FF with shower and toilet. Prices are hiked up by about 50FF during the festival and in July and August. The *Hôtel de Bourgogne* (☎ 04 93 38 36 73) at 13 Rue du 24 Août has singles/doubles for 160/180FF in the off season and 170/220FF in summer. Showers are free. Singles or doubles with shower, toilet and TV are 200FF (220 to 250FF in summer).

Places to Eat

There are a few small, cheap restaurants around the Marché Forville (a block north of Place Bernard Cornut Gentille) and many little

(but not necessarily cheap) restaurants along Rue Saint Antoine, which runs north-west from Place Bernard Cornut Gentille.

Near the train station, *Au Bec Fin* (☎ 04 93 38 35 86) at 12 Rue du 24 Août is often filled with regulars. You can choose from two excellent plats du jour for 50 to 55FF. This place is open for lunch and dinner, but is closed on Saturday evening and Sunday. Another good choice is the popular *Aux Bons Enfants* at 80 Rue Meynadier. It offers regional dishes in a convivial atmosphere; menus are 59FF (lunch only) and 90FF. It's open for lunch and dinner on weekdays and for lunch on Saturday (in June and July it's also open on Saturday evening). There are several other small restaurants at this end of Rue Meynadier.

One of the cheapest restaurants in Cannes is *Restaurant Le Croco* (☎ 04 93 68 60 55), on Rue Louis Blanc, just south of Ave des Anciens Combatants. Pizzas, grilled meat and fish and shish kebabs are the main items on the menu. Plats du jour start at 40FF and menus are 59FF (lunch) and 89FF.

There's a *Monoprix* supermarket (closed Sunday) on the corner of Rue Buttura and Rue Vénizélos, half a block towards the beach from the train station. A morning food market is held on Place Gambetta from Tuesday to Sunday (daily in summer). There are quite a few food shops along Rue Meynadier, a pedestrian mall two blocks inland from the old port. One block north of Place Bernard Cornut Gentille along Rue du Docteur Gazagnaire is the *Marché Forville*, a fruit and vegetable market that's open every Tuesday to Saturday morning (daily in summer).

Getting There & Away

Bus Buses to Nice (30FF one way, 1½ hours), Nice's airport (70FF one way, 45 minutes), Antibes (12.50FF, 25 minutes) and other destinations, most of them operated by Rapides Côte d'Azur, leave from Place Bernard Cornut Gentille. Buses to Nice's airport leave every hour on the hour from 8 am to 7 pm; the last bus is at 9.15 pm. The bus information office (☎ 04 93 39 11 39) is open Monday to Saturday from 8 am to noon and 2 to 6 pm and Sunday to 2 pm.

Buses to Grasse (line No 600), Vallauris, Valbonne and elsewhere depart from the bus station, which is to the left as you exit the train station. The information counter (☎ 04 93 39 31 37) is open from 9 am to noon and 2 to 6.30 pm (closed Wednesday, Sunday and holidays).

Train The train station (☎ 08 36 35 35 39) is five blocks inland from the Palais des Festivals on Rue Jean Jaurès. The information office (on the 1st floor over the left-luggage office) is open Monday to Saturday from 8.30 am to 6 pm. Opening hours are 8.30 am to 7 pm from mid-July to mid-September. Trains to Antibes cost 13FF and take 10 minutes; to Fréjus-Saint Raphaël, the fare is 32FF (30 minutes).

Getting Around
Bus Bus Azur serves Cannes and destinations up to 11 km from town. Its office (☎ 04 93 39 18 71) at Place Bernard Cornut Gentille, in the same building as Rapides Côte d'Azur, is open Monday to Saturday from 7 am to 7 pm. Tickets cost 7FF and a carnet of 10 is 49FF.

Taxi Call ☎ 04 92 99 27 27 to order a taxi.

MENTON
Menton (population 30,000), reputed to be the warmest spot on the Côte d'Azur, is next to the Italian frontier. Set in the Baie du Garavan and the Baie du Soleil, it is encircled by mountains which protect it from the mistral. It's very pleasant to wander around the narrow, winding streets of the old city and up to the cemetery, from where there are scenic views of the bay and surrounding hills.

Menton is renowned for its production of lemons and holds a two-week Fête du Citron that begins every year sometime between mid-February and early March. During the Fête Médiévale de la Saint Jean (held on the third weekend in June) people don medieval garb for a historic parade complete with troubadours. Menton is a good base from which to explore the nearby historic villages of Sospel, Gorbio and Sainte Agnès, as well as the Parc National du Mercantour.

Orientation
The Promenade du Soleil runs more or less east-west along the beach; the railway tracks run more or less east-west about 400 metres inland. Ave Boyer and Ave de Verdun (on either side of the wide centre strip) run perpendicular

to both. The Vieille Ville is on and around the hill at the eastern end of the Promenade du Soleil. The port is east of the old city. Ave Édouard VII links the train station with the beach. Ave Boyer, where the tourist office is, is 200 metres west of the station along Ave de la Gare.

Information
The helpful tourist office (☎ 04 93 57 57 00) is in the Palais de l'Europe at 8 Ave Boyer. It's open Monday to Saturday from 8.30 am to 6 pm and, during winter festivals, on Sunday from 10 am to 12.30 pm. From mid-June to mid-September it's open from 8.30 am to 7.30 pm every day except Sunday, when hours are 8.30 am to 12.30 pm. There are lots of banks on Ave Carnot and Ave Félix Faure.

Things to See & Do
The **beach** along the Promenade du Soleil is public and, like Nice's, is carpeted with smooth pebbles. The better, private beaches lie east of the old city in the pleasure port area, the main one being **Plage des Sablettes**.

Église Saint Michel, the grandest baroque church in this part of France, sits perched in the centre of the **Vieille Ville**, with its many narrow and winding passageways. The church is open from 10 am to noon and 3 to 6 pm except Saturday mornings. The ornate interior is Italian in inspiration. Further up the hill is the cypress-shaded **Cimetière du Vieux Château**, which is open from 7 am to 6 pm (8 pm from May to September). Graves of English, Irish, North Americans, New Zealanders and other foreigners who died here during the 19th century can be seen in the cemetery's southwest corner (along the road called Montée du Souvenir). The view is worth the climb.

The **Musée Jean Cocteau** (☎ 04 93 57 72 30) is near the old city on Quai de Monléon and features the artist's drawings, tapestries and ceramics. It is open from 10 am to noon and 2 to 6 pm (closed Tuesday); afternoon hours are 3 to 7 pm from mid-June to mid-September. Entry is free. More of Cocteau's distinctive work can be seen in the Hôtel de Ville's Salle des Mariages (☎ 04 93 57 87 87) at Place Ardoïno, which is still used for wedding ceremonies. It is open Monday to Friday from 8.30 am to 12.30 pm and 1.30 to 5 pm. Entry is 5FF.

Places to Stay

Camping The *Camping Saint Michel* (☎ 04 93 35 81 23; open from April to 30 September), just off Route des Ciappes de Castellar, is best reached by walking eastward from the bus and train stations along Chemin des Terres Chaudes, which runs along the north side of the train tracks (turn left at the end). Tariffs are 16FF per person, 16FF for a small tent and 17FF for a car.

Camping Fleur de Mai (☎ 04 93 57 22 36; open from Easter to mid-October) at 67 Val de Gorbio is two km west of the train station. Two people with a car and a small tent pay 90FF. The simplest way to get there is to walk westward on the street one block inland from the Promenade du Soleil, and then turn right onto Ave Florette, which becomes Route de Gorbio. Both camping grounds have a two-star rating.

Hostel The *Auberge de Jeunesse* (☎ 04 93 35 93 14) on Plateau Saint Michel (the hill northeast of the train station) is next to Camping Saint Michel. Bed and breakfast is 64FF and sheets are 12FF. Daytime closure is from 10 am to 5 pm, and there is a midnight curfew. The hostel is closed in December and January. Between 7 am and 7 pm (8 pm in summer), you can get to the hostel from the train station by a privately run minibus that operates something like a shared taxi. From the bus station it only runs twice in the morning and twice in the afternoon. You can also take bus No 6 – get off at the Saint Michel stop.

Hotels Opposite the train station at Place de la Gare, *Hôtel Le Terminus* (☎ 04 93 35 77 00) has a few basic singles or doubles for 150FF; rooms with shower and toilet are 210FF. Showers are free. Reception is closed after noon on Saturday and after 5 pm on Sunday. The hotel may be closed for one week in mid-November. The friendly *Hôtel de Belgique* (☎ 04 93 35 72 66) at 1 Ave de la Gare has singles/doubles from 140/187FF or doubles with shower and toilet for 260FF. All rooms have TV. The *Hôtel Le Parisien* (☎ 04 93 35 54 08) at 27 Ave Cernuschi is just west of the train station and only 100 metres from the beach. Singles/doubles start at 160/200FF or 220/250FF with shower and toilet; all rooms have TV and air-con. Parking is free.

Places to Eat

Au Pistou (☎ 04 93 57 45 89) at 2 Rue du Fossan, behind the Nouvelles Galeries department store, has local specialities. The *Marché Municipal*, also known as Les Halles, is in the old city on Quai de Monléon. Food of all sorts is on sale daily from 5 am to 1 pm. Just across the border in Vintimille (Ventimiglia) is a huge market selling everything from food to imitation designer clothes every Friday until 5 pm.

Getting There & Away

Bus The bus station (☎ 04 93 35 93 60) is next to 12 Promenade Maréchal Leclerc, the northern continuation of Ave Boyer. The information office is open Monday to Friday from 9 am to noon and 2 to 6 pm and from 8 am to noon on Saturday.

Train The information desk at the train station, which is at Place de la Gare, is open daily. The ticket offices offer the same services daily from 5 am to 7.30 pm. Call ☎ 08 36 35 35 39 for more information.

Monaco

The Principality of Monaco, which has been under the rule of the Grimaldi family for most of the period since 1297, is a sovereign state whose territory, surrounded by France, covers only 1.95 sq km. It has been ruled since 1949 by Prince Rainier III (born in 1923), whose sweeping constitutional powers make him far more than a figurehead. The citizens of Monaco (Monégasques), of whom there are only 5070 (out of a total population of 30,000), pay no taxes. The official language is French, although efforts are being made to revive the country's traditional dialect. The official religion is Catholicism. There are no border formalities upon entering Monaco and a visit here makes a perfect day trip from Nice.

Orientation

Monaco consists of four principal areas: Monaco Ville, a 60-metre-high outcrop of rock 800 metres long (also known as the old city or the Rocher de Monaco), south of the Port of Monaco; Monte Carlo, famed for its casino and

Monaco

0   100   200 m

N7

Beausoleil

FRANCE

To Menton

To Nice

To Menton

To Menton

Place des Moulins

To Larvotto, Cinéma d'Eté & Monte Carlo Sporting Club

Boulevard de Verdun

Avenue Méridienne Foch

Avenue du Carnier

Blvd de la République

Avenue de Grande Bretagne

Avenue Princesse Grace

Boulevard du Larvotto

Avenue des Moulins

Blvd du Général Leclerc

Escalier du Riviéra

Rue Ste Cée

Boulevard Princesse Charlotte

Boulevard des Spélugues

Avenue de la Madone

Monte Carlo

Avenue de la Costa

Avenue Henri Dunant

Square Beaumarchais

Place du Casino

Avenue Princesse Alice

Avenue de Monte Carlo

Rue Pasteur

Boulevard de Suisse

Avenue de la Costa

Avenue d'Ostende

Avenue du Quai des États-Unis

Avenue Président JF Kennedy

Boulevard Louis II

MEDITERRANEAN SEA

Ave Paul Doumer

Ave Paul Doumer

Rue J Jaures

Rue Grimaldi

Rainier III

Rue Princesse Antoinette

Boulevard Albert 1er

Quai Albert 1er

Quai Albert 1er

Quai Antoine 1er

Quai de la Quarantaine

Avenue de la Porte Neuve

Port de Monaco

Place Saint Dévote

Route de la Moyenne Corniche

Jardin Exotique

Ave Hector Otto

Avenue Hector Otto

Boulevard de Belgique

Rue Plati

Avenue Crovetto Frères

Rue Plati

Boulevard Rainier III

Boulevard Charles III

Avenue du Hérédiaire Albert

Boulevard du Prince

Rue Suffren Reymond

Rue Princesse Caroline

R Princesse Caroline

Rue de Millo

Ave de la Turbie

Ave des Pins

Rue Pierre

Place d'Armes

La Condamine

Rue des Remparts

Rue des Remparts

Rue Saint Martin

Avenue Saint Martin

Monaco Ville

Place de la Visitation

Place du Palais

Avenue des Pins

Port de Fontvieille

Quai des Sanbarbani

Quai des

Avenue des Papalins

Fontvieille

To Cap d'Ail, France (200 m) & Nice (16 km)

FRANCE

PLACES TO STAY		4	Public Lift Entrance	22	Public Lift to Parking
6	Hôtel Cosmopolite (Beausoleil)	5	Public Lift		Pêcheurs
		7	Laundrette	23	Musée
29	Hôtel Cosmopolite (La Condamine) & Hôtel de France	8	American Express		Océanographique
		9	Codec Top Supermaket	24	Cathedral
		11	Tourist Office	25	Musée des Souvenirs
30	Youth Hostel	12	Casino of Monte Carlo		Napoléoniens
		14	Main Post Office	26	Palais du Prince
PLACES TO EAT		15	CAM Office (Local Bus Company)	27	Rampe Major (Path to Palais du Prince)
10	Le Bistroquet	16	Public Lift Entrance	28	Food Market
13	Café de Paris	17	Public Lift Entrance	31	Train Station
19	Stars 'n' Bars	18	Monaco Market Super- market	32	Post Office
OTHER		20	Fort Antoine	33	Musée d'Anthropologie Préhistorique
1	Plages du Larvotto	21	Post Office	34	Public Lift
2	Public Lift Entrance				
3	Musée National				

its Grand Prix motor race in late May, north of the port; La Condamine, the flat area around the port; and Fontvieille, an industrial area south-west of Monaco Ville and the port of Fontvieille. The French town of Beausoleil is just north of Monte Carlo.

Information

Tourist Office The Office National de Tourisme (☎ 04 92 16 61 16) is at 2a Blvd des Moulins, across the public gardens from the casino. It is open Monday to Saturday from 9 am to 7 pm, and Sunday from 10 am to noon. From mid-June to mid-September, several tourist office kiosks are set up around the principality, including one at the train station, next to the Jardin Exotique and on the Quai des États-Unis, which runs along the north side of the port.

Money The currency of Monaco is the French franc. Both French and Monégasque coins are in circulation, but the latter are not widely accepted outside the principality.

In Monte Carlo, you'll find lots of banks in the vicinity of the casino (along Ave Princesse Alice, for instance). In La Condamine, try Blvd Albert 1er. American Express (☎ 04 93 25 74 45), near the tourist office at 35 Blvd Princesse Charlotte, is open weekdays from 9 am to noon and 2 to 6 pm, and on Saturday to noon.

Post & Communications Monégasque stamps, one of the principality's few symbols of independence, are valid only within Monaco. Postal rates are the same as in France. The main post office (☎ 04 93 25 11 11) is in Monte Carlo at 1 Ave Henri Dunant (inside the Palais de la Scala). It does not exchange foreign currency. Other post offices are at Place de la Mairie in Monaco Ville, near the Musée Océanographique, and near the train station (look for the sign of the Hôtel Termi-nus). Monaco's postcode is 98000.

Monaco's public telephones accept either Monégasque or French phonecards. The country telephone code for Monaco is ☎ 377.

Things to See & Do

Palais du Prince The changing of the guard takes place outside the Palais du Prince de Monaco (☎ 04 93 25 18 31) every day at pre-cisely 11.55 am. From June to September about 15 rooms in the palace are open to the public every day from 9.30 am to 6.30 pm (10 am to 5 pm in October). Entry is 30FF (15FF for children and students). Guided visits (35 minutes) in English leave every 15 or 20 minutes.

Musée des Souvenirs Napoléoniens In the south wing of the Palais du Prince, this museum (☎ 04 93 25 18 31) displays some of Napoleon's personal effects (handkerchiefs, a sock etc) and a fascinating collection of princely bric-a-brac (medals, coins, swords, uniforms). The museum is open daily except Monday and is closed in November. Tickets, which costs 20FF (10FF for children), are sold from 10.30 am to 12.30 pm and 2 to 5 pm. From

FRANCE

June to September they're on sale from 9.30 am to 6.30 pm.

Musée Océanographique If you're going to go to one aquarium on your whole trip, the world-renowned Oceanographic Museum (☎ 04 93 15 36 00), with its 90 sea-water aquariums, should be it. This is also one of the few aquariums in the world to have living coral. Upstairs are all sorts of exhibits on ocean exploration. The museum, which is on Ave Saint Martin in Monaco Ville, is open daily from 9 or 9.30 am to 7 pm (8 pm from June to August); from November to February hours are 10 am to 6 pm. The entry fee – brace yourself – is 60FF (30FF for students).

Walk around the Rock The touristy streets and alleys facing the palace are surrounded by beautiful, shaded gardens offering great views of the entire principality (as well as a good bit of France and some of Italy).

Jardin Exotique The steep slopes of the wonderful Jardin Exotique (☎ 04 93 30 33 65), which is at one end of the No 2 bus line, are home to some 7000 varieties of cacti and succulents from all over the world. The spectacular view is worth at least half the admission fee of 36FF (18FF for students), which also gets you into the **Musée d'Anthropologie Préhistorique** and includes a half-hour guided visit to the **Grottes de l'Observatoire**, caves located 279 steps down the hillside. The garden is open daily from 9 am to 6 or 7 pm depending on the season.

Casino The drama of watching people risk their money in Monte Carlo's incredibly ornate casino (☎ 04 92 16 21 21), built between 1878 and 1910, makes visiting the gaming rooms almost worth the stiff entry fees: 50FF for the Salon Ordinaire (which has French roulette and trente-quarante) and 100FF for the Salons Privés (baccarat, blackjack, craps, American roulette etc). You must be at least 21 to enter. Shorts are forbidden in the Salon Ordinaire; men must wear a tie and jacket after 9 pm in the Salons Privés. Income from gambling accounts for 4.95% of Monaco's total state revenues.

Places to Stay

There are no cheap places to stay in Monaco, and less expensive accommodation is scarce and often full. Over 75% of Monaco's hotel rooms are classified as 'four-star deluxe'.

Hostels The *Centre de la Jeunesse Princesse Stéphanie* (☎ 04 93 50 83 20), Monaco's HI hostel, is at 24 Ave Prince Pierre, 120 metres up the hill from the train station. You must be aged between 16 and 31 to stay here. The cost is 70FF per person, including breakfast and sheets. Stays are usually limited to one night during summer. Beds are given out each morning on a first-come-first-served basis; numbered tickets are distributed from 7.30 or 8 am. Registration begins at 10.30 am but rooms only become free after 11.30 am.

The *Relais International de la Jeunesse* (☎ 04 93 78 18 58) on the waterfront at Ave R Grammaglia in Cap d'Ail is another good option, as it is very close to the train station, which is the stop just before Monaco. This place, which is open from April to October, is run by the same people as the Relais International in Nice. See Places to Stay in the Nice section for information on prices, curfew and daytime closure.

Hotels The *Hôtel Cosmopolite* (☎ 04 93 30 16 95) at 4 Rue de la Turbie in La Condamine still has some of the cheapest rooms in the principality. Basic singles/doubles cost 186/200FF or 272/310FF with shower.

The other, unrelated *Hôtel Cosmopolite* (☎ 04 93 78 36 00), at 19 Blvd du Général Leclerc in Beausoleil and up the hill from the casino, offers better value if you want all the amenities. Very comfortable singles/doubles with shower, toilet and TV cost 250/280FF. The all-you-can-eat breakfast buffet is 30FF. The even-numbered side of the street is in Monaco and is called Blvd de France. The nearest bus stop is Crémaillère, served by bus Nos 2 and 4. The *Hôtel de France* (☎ 04 93 30 24 64) at 6 Rue de la Turbie has similar singles/doubles/triples with shower, toilet and TV for 295/360/450FF.

Places to Eat

There are a few cheap restaurants in La Condamine along Rue de la Turbie. Lots of touristy restaurants of more or less the same quality can be found in the streets leading off from Place du Palais.

Le Bistroquet (☎ 04 93 50 65 03) at 11 Galerie Charles III on Ave des Spélugues in Monte Carlo is fairly up-market but has good-value plats du jour for 55FF. It's open from noon to 6 am (7 am on weekends) and is closed on Wednesday during the off season. A local favourite is *Tea for Two* (☎ 04 93 50 10 10) at 11 Blvd Albert 1er in La Condamine. The *Café de Paris* (☎ 04 92 16 23 00) at Place du Casino is a great place to sit but a beer and a sandwich will cost you around 72FF!

The *Codec Top* supermarket opposite 33 Blvd Princesse Charlotte, a block from the main tourist office, is open daily except Sunday. It has an in-house bakery. In La Condamine, there's a covered food market every morning in the new building at Place d'Armes.

Getting There & Away

Bus There is no single bus station in Monaco; intercity buses leave from various points around the city.

Train The train station, which is part of the French national railway network, is on Ave Prince Pierre. See Getting There & Away in the Nice section for more information. The station's information office is open daily from 9.15 am to noon and 2.30 to 4.20 pm; in summer it closes at 6 pm. You can exchange foreign currency here, but the rates are not very good.

Getting Around

Bus Monaco's urban bus system has six lines. You're most likely to use line No 2, which links Monaco Ville with Monte Carlo and then loops back to the Jardin Exotique. Rides cost 8.50FF and eight-ride magnetic cards are on sale from bus drivers for 30FF. The bus system operates daily until 8.45 or 9 pm; bus maps are available at the tourist office. CAM, the bus company (☎ 04 93 50 62 41 for information), has offices at 3 Ave Président John F Kennedy, on the north side of the port.

Taxi Taxis can be ordered by calling ☎ 04 93 15 01 01 or 04 93 50 56 28.

Lift Twelve large public lifts *(ascenceurs publics)* operate up and down the hillside. Most of them operate from 6 am to 10 pm.

Corsica

Corsica (Corse in French) is the most mountainous and geographically diverse of all the islands of the Mediterranean. Though measuring only 8720 sq km, in many ways Corsica resembles a miniature continent, with 1000 km of coastline, soaring granite mountains that stay snowcapped until July, a huge national park (the Parc Naturel Régional de Corse), flatland marshes (along the east coast), an uninhabited desert (the Désert des Agriates) in the north-west and a 'continental divide' running down the middle of the island. Much of the island is covered with the typically Corsican form of vegetation called *maquis*, with its low, dense shrubs providing many of the spices used in Corsican cooking. During WWII, the French Résistance became known as Le Maquis because the movement was so active in Corsica.

Corsica was ruled by Genoa from the 13th century until the Corsicans *(u populu corsu)*, led by the extraordinary Pasquale (Pascal in French) Paoli, declared the island independent in 1755. But its independence was short-lived. France took over Corsica in 1769 and has ruled it ever since – except for a period in 1794-96, when it was under English domination, and during the German and Italian occupation of 1940-43.

Despite having spent only 14 years as a self-governed country, the people of Corsica (who now number about a quarter of a million) have retained a fiercely independent streak. Though few support the Front de Libération National de la Corse (FLNC) and other violent separatist organisations, whose initials and slogans are spray-painted on walls and road signs all over the island, they remain very proud of their language, culture and traditions.

The symbol of a black head wearing a bandanna that you see everywhere in Corsica is the Tête de Maure (Moor's Head), the island's emblem, which dates back to the time of the Crusades. The Corsicans, like the Irish, have a

FRANCE

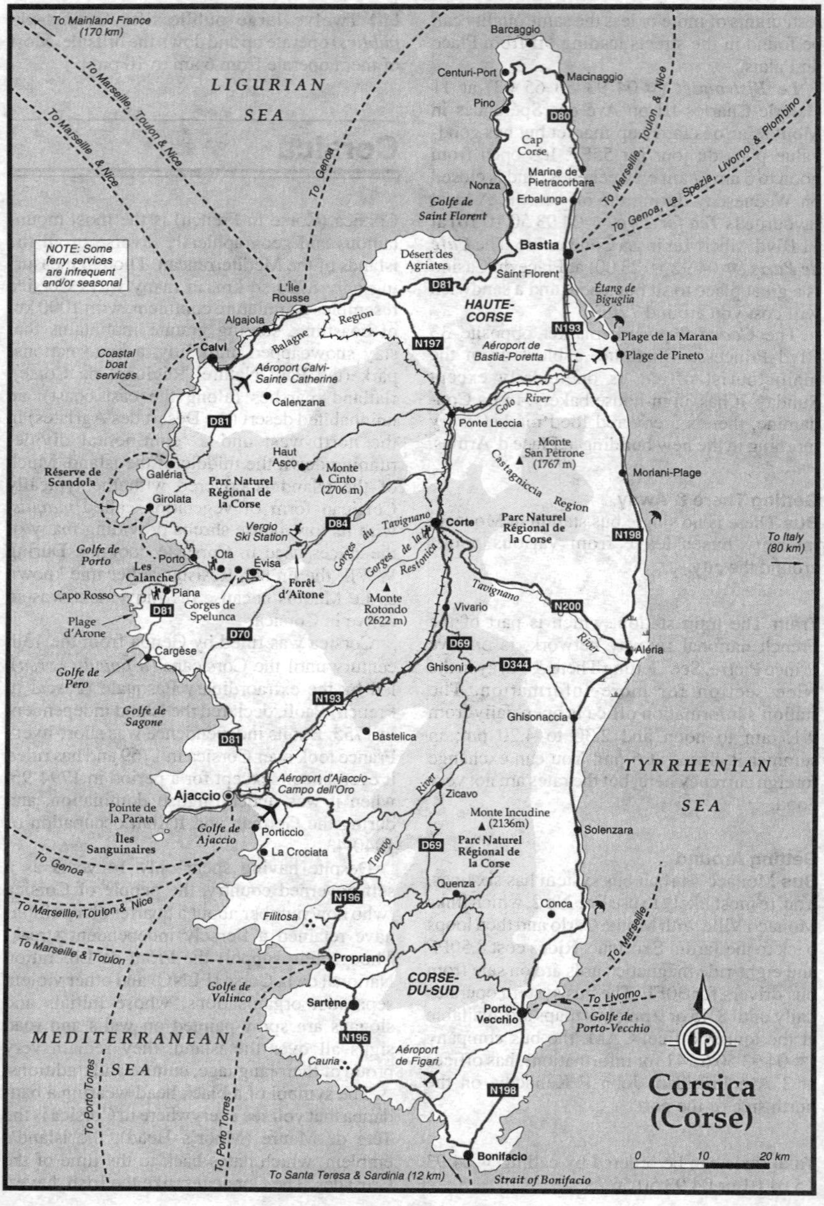
To Mainland France
(170 km)
To Marseille, Toulon & Nice
To Marseille & Nice
LIGURIAN
SEA
To Genoa
NOTE: Some
ferry services
are infrequent
and/or seasonal
Barcaggio
Centuri-Port
Macinaggio
Pino
D80
Cap
Corse
Marine de
Pietracorbara
Nonza
Erbalunga
Golfe de
Saint Florent
To Marseille, Toulon & Nice
To Genoa, La Spezia, Livorno & Plombino
Bastia
Désert des
Agriates
Saint Florent
D81
L'Île
Rousse
HAUTE-
CORSE
Étang de
Biguglia
Algajola
Region
Balagne
N193
N197
Calvi
Coastal
boat
services
Aéroport Calvi-
Sainte Catherine
Aéroport de
Bastia-Poretta
Plage de la Marana
Plage de Pineto
Calenzana
Golo
River
D81
Ponte Leccia
Monte
San Petrone
(1767 m)
Haut
Asco
Castagniccia
Monte
Cinto
(2706 m)
Moriani-Plage
Réserve de
Scandola
Galéria
Parc Naturel
Régional de
la Corse
Girolata
Region
Vergio
Ski Station
D84
Gorges du Tavignano
Corte
Parc Naturel
Régional de
la Corse
N198
To Italy
(80 km)
Golfe de
Porto
Porto
Ota
Évisa
Gorges de la Restonica
Les
Calanche
Forêt
d'Aïtone
Capo Rosso
Piana
Tavignano
Monte
Rotondo
(2622 m)
D81
Gorges de
Spelunca
Plage
d'Arone
D70
Vivario
N200
D69
River
Aléria
Cargèse
Ghisoni
D344
Golfe de
Pero
N193
Golfe de
Sagone
Ghisonaccia
Bastelica
D81
TYRRHENIAN
SEA
Aéroport d'Ajaccio-
Campo dell'Oro
River
Ajaccio
Zicavo
Pointe de
la Parata
Monte Incudine
(2136m)
Golfe de
Ajaccio
Porticcio
Solenzara
Îles
Sanguinaires
D69
Parc Naturel
Régional de
la Corse
La Crociata
Taravo
To Genoa
Quenza
N196
To Marseille, Toulon & Nice
Conca
Filitosa
To Marseille
To Marseille & Toulon
Propriano
CORSE-
DU-SUD
Golfe de
Valinco
Sartène
To Livorno
Porto-
Vecchio
Golfe de
Porto-Vecchio
MEDITERRANEAN
N196
SEA
Aéroport
de Figari
Cauria
To Porto Torres
To Porto Torres
N198
Corsica
(Corse)
Bonifacio
0
10
20 km
To Santa Teresa & Sardinia (12 km)
Strait of Bonifacio

long tradition of emigration. Many of the settlers in France's colonies were Corsican émigrés, and many young people still leave the island in search of better opportunities.

Language

The Corsican language (Corsu), which has been almost exclusively oral until recently, is more closely related to Italian than French. It constitutes an important component of Corsican identity and there is a movement afoot to ensure its survival (notably at the university of Corte). Street signs are now often bilingual or exclusively in Corsican.

Climate & When to Go

The best time of year to visit Corsica is in May and June. Outside these months, there are fewer visitors but a reduced tourist infrastructure (many hotels etc operate only seasonally). Avoid July and August when the island' is overrun with mainly Italian and German holiday-makers.

Dangers & Annoyances

When Corsica makes the newspapers around the world, it's usually because separatist militants have engaged in some act of violence, such as bombing a public building, robbing a bank or blowing up a vacant holiday villa. But such attacks, which in 1994 included over 400 bombings and some 40 murders, are *not* targeted at tourists and there is no reason for visitors to fear for their safety.

Activities

Corsica's superb hiking trails include three *mare à mare* (sea-to-sea) trails that cross the island from east to west. The legendary GR20, also known as Li Monti (literally, 'between the mountains'), stretches over 160 km from Conca (20 km north of Porto-Vecchio) to Calenzana (10 km south-east of Calvi), and is passable from mid-June to October.

Some 600 km of trails are covered in the invaluable *Walks in Corsica*, published by Robertson McCarta, London. The book is currently out of print in Corsica itself, but you can get it in the UK for £9.95. If you read French, the Parc Naturel Régional de la Corse (☎ 04 95 21 56 54), based in Ajaccio, has useful fact sheets and a couple of guide books including

A Travers la Montagne Corse for 89FF. These are all available by mail order.

Accommodation

Camping Almost all of Corsica's many camping grounds close during the colder half of the year and some are open only from June to September. Charges are quite a bit higher than on the mainland – a rate of 28FF per person (minus tent) is usual. Camping outside recognised camping areas *(camping sauvage)* is strictly prohibited, partly because of the risk of fires.

Gîtes If you're staying put for a while and there are several of you, *gîtes ruraux* (country cottages) can be a good deal, ranging from 1000 to 3000FF a week from October to May but increasing considerably from June to September. Some are also rented out for weekends, and by the night in a bed and breakfast arrangement (from 200FF for a double room). In Ajaccio, contact Relais des Gîtes Ruraux (☎ 04 95 51 72 82; fax 04 95 51 72 89) at 1 Rue Général Fiorella, which provides information on available cottages.

Hotels Corsica's bottom-end hotel rooms are much more expensive than mainland counterparts and virtually nothing is available for less than 180FF. Many hotels in all price ranges raise their tariffs considerably in July and August (in some cases by over 200%!). But unless you make reservations months in advance (or arrive early in the morning and get lucky) you probably won't have the opportunity to pay them anyway. On the other hand, wintertime visitors will find that outside of Bastia and Ajaccio, most hotels shut down completely between November and Easter.

Getting There & Away

Visitors pay an arrival *and* departure tax of 30FF; this will probably have been calculated into your ferry or airfare.

Air Corsica's four main airports are at Ajaccio, Bastia, Calvi and Figari (near Bonifacio). Flights from Nice cost 464FF, but people under 25 or over 60 may qualify for a fare of 330FF. The regular one-way fare from Paris starts at 954FF, but charters and certain discounted

FRANCE

(and very restricted) fares cost about 675FF one way, which is much cheaper than going by train and ferry.

Ferry During the summer – especially from mid-July to early September, reservations for vehicles and couchettes (berths) must be made well in advance (several months for the most popular routes).

To/From France Car and passenger ferry services between the French mainland (Nice, Marseille and Toulon) and Corsica (Ajaccio, Bastia, Calvi, L'Î Rousse, Propriano and Porto-Vecchio) are handled by the Société National Maritime Corse-Méditerranée, or SNCM (☎ 04 91 56 30 10 in Marseille).

For a one-way passage, individuals pay 304 to 340FF to/from Nice and 292 to 308FF to/from either Marseille or Toulon. Daytime crossings take from about three to 8½ hours, depending on where you get on and off. For overnight trips (departing at 8 pm and arriving at 7.30 or 8 am), the cheapest couchette costs an additional 80FF; the charge per person in a very comfortable cabin is 174FF. For people under 25, the basic passenger fare is from 177 to 249FF one way on all sailings to/from Nice. There are currently no youth fares available to/from Marseille and Toulon.

To/From Italy Corsica Ferries (☎ 04 95 32 95 95 in Bastia) has year-round car ferry services between Bastia and Genoa, La Spezia and Livorno (four to six hours or overnight). From mid-May to mid-September, the company also runs ferries between Genoa and Calvi. Depending on which route you take and when you travel, individuals pay 150 to 190FF. Bringing a car over costs from an additional 235 to 650FF (depending on the season).

From late March to October, Mobylines (☎ 04 95 31 46 29 in Bastia) also links Bastia with Genoa and Livorno. Between early July and early September, their car ferries also sail to/from Piombino. Depending on when you travel, the one-way passenger fare between Genoa and Bastia is 180 to 220FF. The smallest car costs 236 to 650FF.

SNCM has very infrequent sailings between Propriano or Ajaccio and Porto-Torres, in Sardinia, between April and September (147FF per person). For information on ferries from Sardinia to Bonifacio, see Getting There & Away in the Bonifacio section.

Getting Around

Bus Bus transport around the island is slow, infrequent (one to four runs a day), relatively expensive (105FF from Ajaccio to Bastia) and handled by an enormously complicated network of independent companies. Outside July and August, only a handful of intercity buses operate on Sunday and public holidays. Student discounts are available on some routes.

Train Chemins de Fer de la Corse, Corsica's metre-gauge, single-track train system has more in common with the Kalka-Simla line through the Himalayan foothills of northern India than it does with the TGV. The two and four-car trains make their way unhurriedly through the stunning mountain scenery, stopping at tiny rural stations and, when necessary, for sheep and cows. The two-line network links Ajaccio, Corte, Bastia, Ponte Leccia and Calvi on 232 km of track and is definitely the most interesting (and comfortable) way to tour the island.

Corsica's train system does *not* accept Eurail passes or give any discounts except to holders of Inter-Rail passes, who get 50% off. Tariffs are 118FF to go from Ajaccio to Bastia, 63FF to Corte and 89FF to travel from Bastia to Calvi. Transporting a bicycle is 63FF. Leaving luggage and bikes at the stations' ticket offices costs a flat 19FF.

Car There's no doubt that a car is the most convenient way to get around Corsica. It's also the most stressful. Many of the roads are spectacular but narrow and serpentine (particularly D81 between Calvi and Porto and N196 from Ajaccio to Bonifacio). Count on averaging 50 km/h. A good road map is indispensable. Car-rental agencies in Corsica are listed under Getting There & Away in the Ajaccio and Bastia sections.

AJACCIO

The port city of Ajaccio (Aiacciu in Corsican; population 58,000), birthplace of Napoleon Bonaparte in 1769, is a great place to begin a visit to Corsica. This pastel-shaded, Mediterranean town is a fine place for strolling, but spending some time here can also be educational: Ajaccio's several museums and many statues dedicated to Bonaparte (who, local people will neglect to mention, never came back to visit after becoming emperor) speak volumes, not about Napoleon himself, but about how the people of his native town prefer to think of him.

Orientation
Ajaccio's main street is Cours Napoléon, which stretches from Place du Général de Gaulle northward to the train station and beyond. The old city is south of Place Foch.

Information
Tourist Office The tourist office (☎ 04 95 21 40 87) at 1 Place Foch is open Monday to Friday from 8.30 am to 6 pm and on Saturday from 9 am to noon. Between mid-June and mid-September, it is open daily from 8.30 am to 8 pm. At the airport, the information desk (☎ 04 95 21 03 64) is open daily from 6 am to 10.30 pm.

Money & Post The Banque de France is at 8 Rue Sergent Casalonga. The main post office (☎ 04 95 21 13 60), which has an exchange service, is at 5 Cours Napoléon. Ajaccio's postcode is 20000.

Hiking Information The Maison d'Information (☎ 04 95 51 79 10) at 2 Rue Sergent Casalonga has lots of information on the Parc Naturel Régional de Corse and the island's many hiking trails. It's open Monday to Friday from 9 am to noon and 2 to 6 pm.

Things to See & Do
Museums The house where Napoleon was born and raised, the **Maison Bonaparte** (☎ 04 95 21 43 89) on Rue Saint Charles in the old city, was sacked by Corsican nationalists in 1793 but rebuilt (with a grant from the government in Paris) later in the decade. It is open from 9 am (10 am from October to April) to noon and 2 to 6 pm (5 pm from October to April) daily except Sunday afternoon and Monday morning. The entry fee of 17FF (11FF for those 18 to 25 and over 60) includes a guided tour in French.

The sombre **Salon Napoléonien** (☎ 04 95 21 90 15), which exhibits memorabilia of the emperor on the 1st floor of the Hôtel de Ville at Place Foch, is open Monday to Friday from 9 am to noon and 2 to 6 pm. The fee is 5FF but visitors must be properly dressed. The **Musée A Bandera** (☎ 04 95 51 07 34) at 1 Rue Général Lévie deals with Corsican military history and costs 20FF (10FF for students) to visit. It's open Monday to Friday from 9 am to noon and from 2 to 6 pm.

The **Musée Fesch** (☎ 04 95 21 48 17) at 50 Rue du Cardinal Fesch has a fine collection of Italian primitive-art paintings (14th to 19th centuries) and yet another collection of Napoleonia in the basement. It is open from 9.30 am to 12.15 pm and 2.15 to 6 pm (3 to 7 pm from May to September) daily except Sunday and Monday. During July and August it's also open on Friday night from 9 pm to midnight. Entry costs 25FF (15FF for students aged 18 to 25 and people over 60). There is a separate fee of 10FF (5FF for students) to get into the Renaissance **Chapelle Impériale**, the Bonaparte family sepulchre built in 1857.

Cathédrale Ajaccio's Venetian Renaissance cathedral is in the **old city** on the corner of Rue Forcioli Conti and Rue Saint Charles. Built in the late 1500s, it contains Napoleon's marble baptismal font, which is to the right of the entrance, and the painting *Vierge au Sacré Cœur* (Virgin of the Sacred Heart) by Eugène Delacroix (1798-1863), which is to the left.

Pointe de la Parata This wild, black granite promontory is 12 km west of the city on Route des Sanguinaires (route D111). It's famed for its sunsets, which can be watched from the base of a crenellated, early 17th-century Genoan watchtower. Bus No 5 links Ajaccio with the Pointe.

The **Îles Sanguinaires**, a group of small islands visible offshore, can be visited on two to three-hour boat excursions between April and November which cost 100FF (120FF during July and August). Boats leave from the quayside opposite Place Foch.

Beaches Ajaccio's beaches are nothing special. Plage de Ricanto, popularly known as

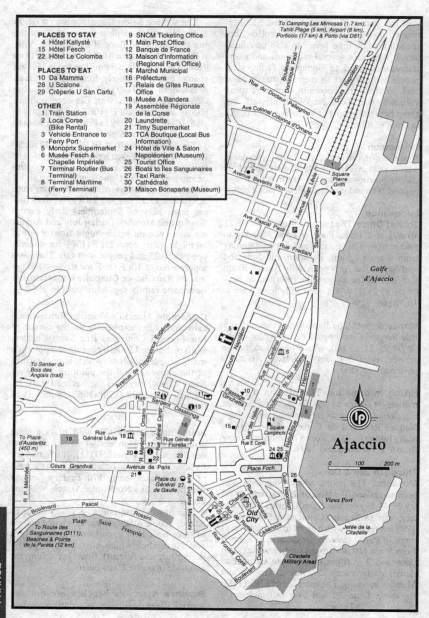

PLACES TO STAY
4 Hôtel Kallysté
15 Hôtel Fesch
22 Hôtel Le Colomba

PLACES TO EAT
10 Da Mamma
28 U Scalone
29 Crêperie U San Carlu

OTHER
1 Train Station
2 Loca Corse (Bike Rental)
3 Vehicle Entrance to Ferry Port
4 Monoprix Supermarket
6 Musée Fesch & Chapelle Impériale
7 Terminal Routier (Bus Terminal)
8 Terminal Maritime (Ferry Terminal)

9 SNCM Ticketing Office
11 Main Post Office
12 Banque de France
13 Maison d'Information (Regional Park Office)
14 Marché Municipal
16 Préfecture
17 Relais de Gîtes Ruraux Office
18 Musée A Bandera
19 Assemblée Régionale de la Corse
20 Laundrette
21 Timy Supermarket
23 TCA Boutique (Local Bus Information)
24 Hôtel de Ville & Salon Napoléonien (Museum)
25 Tourist Office
26 Boats to Iles Sanguinaires
27 Taxi Rank
30 Cathédrale
31 Maison Bonaparte (Museum)

To Camping Les Mimosas (1.7 km),
Tahiti Plage (5 km), Airport (8 km),
Porticcio (17 km) & Porto (via D81)

Boulevard Dominique Paoli

Cours Napoléon

Rue du Docteur Pellegrino

Ave Colonel Colonna d'Ornano

Avenue Beverini Vico

Avenue Jean Lévie

Square Pierre Griffi

Ave Pascal Paoli

Rue Frediani

Sampiero

Boulevard

Golfe d'Ajaccio

Cours Napoléon

Rue du Cardinal Fesch

Rue du Roi Jérôme

Quai l'Herminier

To Sentier du Bois des Anglais (trail)

Avenue de l'Impératrice Eugénie

Rue Serpent Casalonga

Passage Guincheta

Boulevard

Rue des Halles

Square Campinchi

Quai de la République

Rue Général Campi

Rue Maréchal

Rue Général Fiorella

Rue E Conti

To Place d'Austerlitz (450 m)

Rue Général Lévie

Ajaccio

0   100   200 m

Cours Grandval

Avenue de Paris

Place du Général de Gaulle

Rue du Charles

Rue Bonaparte

Vieux Port

R P Mérimée

Boulevard   Pascal

Plage   Saint   François

Rossini

Rue St Charles

Rue St de Rome

Old City

Rue Eugène Macchini

Rue Forcioli Conti

Danielle

Rue Casanova

Boulevard

Jetée de la Citadelle

To Route des Sanguinaires (D111),
Beaches & Pointe de la Parata (12 km)

Citadelle (Military Area)

Tahiti Plage, is about five km east of town on the way to the airport and can be reached on bus No 1. The more attractive and smaller, segmented beaches between Ajaccio and Pointe de la Parata (Ariane, Neptune, Palm Beach and Marinella) are served by bus No 5.

Places to Stay

Camping The *Camping Les Mimosas* (☎ 04 95 20 99 85; open April to October) is about three km north of the centre on Route d'Alata. To get there, take bus No 4 to the roundabout at the western end of Cours Jean Nicoli and walk up Route d'Alata for about one km. A tent site and a place to park cost 11FF each; adults pay 28FF each.

Hotels The best deal in town is the central *Hôtel Le Colomba* (☎ 04 95 21 12 66) on the 3rd floor at 8 Ave de Paris opposite Place du Général de Gaulle. It's run by a feisty Italian woman who offers clean, pleasant doubles without/with shower for 180/250FF and triples for 250FF. The friendly *Hôtel Kallysté* (☎ 04 95 51 34 45) at 51 Cours Napoléon has serviceable singles/doubles with shower and air-con off a large central stairway for 200/235FF (15 to 25% more from May to mid-November). Studios with kitchenettes for one/two people range from 235/260FF to 280/335FF, depending on the season.

The two-star *Hôtel Fesch* (☎ 04 95 21 50 52; fax 04 95 21 83 36) at 7 Rue du Cardinal Fesch has singles/doubles with satellite TV for 280/305FF (350/395FF from June to September). An extra bed costs 100FF (150FF during summer).

Places to Eat

U Scalone (☎ 04 95 21 50 05) at 2 Rue Roi de Rome caters to a well-heeled crowd (mains are 60 to 150FF) but it's a relaxing, comfortable place for a splurge.

The restaurant *Da Mamma* (☎ 04 95 21 39 44) is a charming, tucked-away place reached through a little tunnel off Rue du Cardinal Fesch. It has a small, outdoor terrace and serves menus from 60 to 145FF. For a taste of the local cuisine, the four-course menu Corse at 135FF is good value. It's open daily except Sunday and Monday lunchtime.

Crêperie U San Carlu (☎ 04 95 21 30 21)

at 16 Rue Saint Charles has crêpes of all descriptions for 15 to 50FF. It's open April to September from 11 am to 9.30 or 10 pm.

There's a big *Timy* supermarket opposite 4 Cours Grandval which is open Monday to Saturday from 9 am to 12.30 pm and 3.15 to 7.30 pm. The *Monoprix* supermarket opposite 40 Cours Napoléon is open Monday to Saturday from 8.30 am to 7.15 pm.

Getting There & Away

Air Aéroport d'Ajaccio-Campo dell'Oro is eight km east of the city along Cours Napoléon and its continuation. Bus No 1 links Place du Général de Gaulle and Cours Napoléon with the airport (20FF).

Bus The Terminal Routier (Ajaccio's bus terminal) is on Quai l'Herminier next to (and connected with) the Terminal Maritime (ferry terminal). About a dozen companies have daily services (except on Sunday and public holidays) to Bastia (105FF), Bonifacio (115FF), Calvi via Ponte Leccia (120FF), Corte (60FF), Porto (65FF), Sartène (70FF), Propriano and many other destinations.

The bus station's information booth (☎ 04 95 21 28 01), which can provide schedules for all routes, is open Monday to Saturday from 7 am to 6.30 or 7 pm. Eurocorse (☎ 04 95 21 06 30), which handles many of the long-distance lines, keeps its kiosk open Monday to Saturday from 7 to 11.30 am and from 2 to 6.30 pm (no break in July and August).

Train Trains to Corte, Bastia, Calvi and intermediate destinations are boarded at the train station (☎ 04 95 23 11 03) on Square Pierre Griffi. See Train under Getting Around at the start of the Corsica section for more information.

Car & Motorcycle About a dozen car-rental companies have bureaus at the airport, but the least expensive is Aloha (☎ 04 95 20 52 00). For a Fiat Panda, the charge is 975FF for three days, including insurance and unlimited km.

Loca Corse (☎ 04 95 20 71 20) at 10 Ave Beverini Vico rents 50/80 cc scooters for 200/250FF a day and 125 cc motorbikes for 350FF. It's open April to September from 9 am to noon and 2 to 6.30 pm.

FRANCE

Ferry The Terminal Maritime is on Quai l'Herminier next to the bus station. SNCM's ticketing office (☎ 04 95 29 66 99), across the street at 3 Quai l'Herminier, is open Monday to Friday from 8 to 11.45 am and 2 to 6 pm and on Saturday morning. For evening ferries, the SNCM bureau in the ferry terminal opens two or three hours before the scheduled departure time.

Getting Around

Bus Local bus maps and timetables can be picked up at the TCA Boutique (☎ 04 95 51 43 23) at 2 Ave de Paris from 8 am to noon and 3 to 6 pm Monday to Saturday. Local bus tickets cost 7.50FF (58FF for a carnet of 10).

Taxi There's a taxi rank on the east side of Place du Général de Gaulle or you can order one from Radio Taxis (☎ 04 95 51 15 67).

Bicycle Mountain bikes are available for 80/440FF a day/week from Loca Corse (see Car & Motorcycle earlier).

BASTIA

Bustling Bastia (population 38,000), Corsica's most important business and commercial centre, has rather an Italian feel to it. It was the seat of the Genoese governors of Corsica from the 15th century, when the *bastiglia* (fortress) from which the city derives its name was built. Though it's a pleasant enough place, there's not all that much to see or do here, and most travellers simply pass through. Bastia does, however, make a good base for exploring **Cap Corse**, the wild, 40-km-long peninsula to the north.

Orientation

The focal point of the town centre is 300-metre-long Place Saint Nicolas. Bastia's main thoroughfares are the east-west Ave Maréchal Sébastiani, which links the ferry terminal with the train station, and the north-south Blvd Paoli, a fashionable shopping street one block west of Place Saint Nicolas.

Information

The tourist office (☎ 04 95 31 00 89) at the northern edge of Place Saint Nicolas is open daily from 8 am to 6 pm (from 7 am to 10 pm

during July and August when there's also tourist information available in the ferry terminal building). It has information on companies offering day trips to Cap Corse.

Banque de France is at 2bis Cours Henri Pierangeli, half a block south of Place Saint Nicolas. The main post office is on the even-numbered side of Ave Maréchal Sébastiani, a block west of Place Saint Nicolas. Exchange services are available. Bastia's postcode is 20200.

Things to See & Do

Place Saint Nicolas, a palm and plane tree-lined esplanade as long as three football pitches, was laid out in the late 19th century. The narrow streets and alleyways of **Terra Vecchia**, which is centred around Place de l'Hôtel de Ville, lie just south. The **Oratoire de l'Immaculée Conception**, opposite 3 Rue Napoléon, was decorated in rich baroque style in the early 18th century.

The picturesque, horseshoe-shaped **Vieux Port** is between Terra Vecchia and the **Citadelle**; you can reach the latter by climbing the stairs through the **Jardin Romieu**, the hillside park on the south side of the port. Inside the Citadelle, built by the Genoese in the 15th and 16th centuries, stands the mustard-coloured **Palais des Gouverneurs** (Governors' Palace). It houses a rather dull anthropology museum, but the views from the gardens behind the submarine conning tower (which served active and heroic duty during WWII) are worth the climb. **Église Sainte Marie**, whose entrance is on Rue de l'Evêché, was rebuilt in 1604 on the site of a much earlier church. Much more interesting is the **Église Saint Croix** down the alley to the right (south) of Sainte Marie. It's older (1543), the gilded coffered ceiling is Renaissance and the chapel to the right of the main altar contains a miraculous black statue of the crucified Christ found by two fishermen in the early 15th century.

Bastia's best beach is **Plage de la Marana**, about 12 km south at the southern edge of the Étang de Biguglia lagoon, a favourite nesting area for waterfowl. In summer it can be reached by bus No 8 from Rue du Nouveau Port.

Places to Stay

Camping In Miomo, about five km north of

Bastia, you'll find **Camping Casanova** (☎ 04 95 33 91 42), which is open from early May to October and charges 12FF for a tent and 22FF per person. To get there, take the bus towards Erbalunga from the terminal on Rue du Nouveau Port.

Hotels One of the most convenient hotels in Bastia is the **Hôtel de l'Univers** (☎ 04 95 31 03 38) at 3 Ave Maréchal Sébastiani. Singles/doubles/triples cost 130/170/200FF with washbasin and bidet and 200/300/350FF with shower and toilet. The hotel sometimes closes during the winter months, so check first. The one-star **Hôtel Le Riviera** (☎ 04 95 31 07 16) is 100 metres north of Place Saint Nicolas at 1bis Rue du Nouveau Port. Fairly large singles/doubles with washbasin and bidet cost 150/180FF. Singles/doubles with shower, toilet and TV are 200/250FF (250/300FF during July and August).

If your budget can handle it, the very central, up-market **Hôtel Napoléon** (☎ 04 95 31 60 30; fax 04 95 31 77 83) at 43 Blvd Paoli is good value between October and May with fully equipped doubles at 290FF. Unfortunately the price jumps to 450FF in summer.

Places to Eat
There are plenty of restaurants around the Vieux Port, especially on the north side. Try **A Scaletta** (☎ 04 95 32 28 70) at 4 Rue Saint Jean and ask for a table on the tiny balcony overlooking the port. Scaletta's excellent-value menus include omelette with white brocciu cheese and mint (75FF) and fresh stuffed sardines (85FF). About 200 metres west in a square near the start of Rue Laurent Casanova, the **Chiangmai** (☎ 04 95 32 73 61) has reasonable, Vietnam-influenced Thai food.

The **Timy** supermarket at 2 Rue Campanelle (one block north of Ave Maréchal Sébastiani) is open Monday to Saturday from 8.30 am to 12.30 pm and 3.30 to 7.30 pm. The mammoth **Hyper Toga** supermarket north of the town centre on Rue de l'Impératrice Eugénie is open Monday to Saturday from 9 am to 8 pm.

Getting There & Away
Air France's fifth-busiest airport, Aéroport de Bastia-Poretta (☎ 04 95 54 54 54), is 20 km south of the town. Municipal buses to the

airport (42FF) depart from the roundabout in front of the préfecture building (opposite the train station) about an hour before each flight's departure (nine to 10 times a day). A timetable is available at the tourist office.

Bus Rapides Bleus, whose buses serve Porto-Vecchio and Bonifacio (110FF), has a ticket office (☎ 04 95 31 03 79) at 1 Ave Maréchal Sébastiani from where the buses depart. Twice-daily buses run by Eurocorse (☎ 04 95 31 03 79) to Corte (55FF) and Ajaccio (105FF) also leave from here. The bus to Calvi (80FF), run by Autocars Beaux Voyages (☎ 04 95 65 15 02), leaves from the stop a short way up the block. Short-haul buses serving the Bastia area stop at the terminal along Rue du Nouveau Port, which is opposite the north-west corner of Place Saint Nicolas.

Train The train station (☎ 04 95 32 60 06) is across the roundabout at the northern end of Ave Maréchal Sébastiani. See Getting Around at the start of the Corsica section for information on the train system. Fares from Bastia are 118FF to Ajaccio, 89FF to Calvi and 55FF to Corte.

Car The cheapest place in Bastia to rent a car is ADA (☎ 04 95 31 48 95) next to the Renault office at 35 Rue César Campinchi, the street two blocks west of Place Saint Nicolas. It is open Monday to Saturday from 8 am to noon and 2 to 7 pm. Small cars (eg the Peugeot 106) cost 560FF for a weekend and 1790FF for a week, including unlimited km and insurance.

Ferry The ferry terminal is at the quayside end of Ave Maréchal Sébastiani. SNCM's office (☎ 04 95 54 66 88) is across the roundabout; it handles ferries to mainland France and is open from 8 to 11.30 am and 2 to 5.30 pm daily except Sunday, and Saturday afternoon in the winter, unless a boat has just arrived or departed. The SNCM counter in the ferry terminal itself is open two hours before each sailing (three hours on Sunday).

If you're headed for Italy, Mobylines' office (☎ 04 95 31 46 29) is 200 metres north of Place Saint Nicolas at 4 Rue du Commandant Luce de Casabianca. It is open Monday to Saturday

FRANCE

from 8.30 am to noon and 2 to 6 pm. There is also a bureau (☎ 04 95 31 46 29) in the ferry terminal which is open daily from 9 to 11.30 am and 2 to 5.30 pm. Corsica Ferries' office (☎ 04 95 32 95 95) is 250 metres north of the ferry terminal at 5 Rue Chanoine Leschi next to the Mobil petrol station. It's open daily except Sunday from 8.30 am to noon and from 2 to 6 pm, and on Saturday from 8.30 am to noon. See Ferry under Getting There & Away at the start of the Corsica section for more information.

CALVI

Calvi (population 5000), where Nelson lost his eye, serves both as a military town and rather down-market holiday resort. The citadel, garrisoned by a crack regiment of the French Foreign Legion, sits atop a promontory at the western end of a beautiful half-moon shaped bay.

Orientation

The Citadelle – also known as the Haute Ville (upper town) – is north-east of the port. Blvd Wilson, the major thoroughfare in the Basse Ville (lower town), is set up the hill from Quai Landry and the marina.

Information

The tourist office (☎ 04 95 65 16 67) is on the marina just behind the train station. It's open Monday to Saturday from 9 am to noon and 2 to 6 pm (from mid-June to mid-September, it's open every day from 8.30 am to 7.30 pm). Guided visits of Calvi are available in English between mid-April and October for 45FF.

The Crédit Lyonnais opposite 10 Blvd Wilson is open weekdays from 8.20 am to 12.20 pm and from 1.50 to 4.40 pm. The main post office (☎ 04 95 65 00 40) is about 100 metres to the south on the same street. Calvi's postcode is 20260.

Things to See & Do

The **Citadelle**, set atop an 80-metre-high granite promontory and enclosed by ramparts built by the Genoese, affords great views of the surrounding area. **Église Saint Jean Baptiste** was built in the 13th century and rebuilt in 1570; inside is yet another miraculous ebony icon of Christ. West of the church, a marble plaque marks the site of the house where,

according to local tradition, Christopher Columbus was born. The imposing **palace of the Genoan governors**, built in the 13th century and enlarged in the mid-16th century, is above the entrance to the citadel. Now known as Caserne Sampiero, it serves as a barracks and mess hall for officers of the French Foreign Legion.

Beaches Calvi's four-km-long beach begins just east of the marina and stretches around the Golfe de Calvi. There are a number of other nice beaches, including one at **Algajola**, west of town. The port and resort town of L'Île Rousse (Red Island) east of Calvi is also endowed with a long, sandy beach with some of the cleanest water in the Mediterranean.

Between late April and October, many of the beaches between Calvi and L'Île can be reached by shuttle train (see Getting There & Away for details).

Places to Stay

Camping & Studios The *Camping Les Castors* (☎ 04 95 65 13 30), open from April to mid-October, is 800 metres south-east of the centre of town on Route de Pietra Maggiore. Campers pay 29FF per adult, 15FF for a camp site and 10FF for parking. Small studios for two people with shower, toilet and kitchenette cost 1040FF a week in the low season and between 2150 and 2450FF in summer.

Hostel The friendly, 133-bed *BVJ Corsotel* hostel (☎ 04 95 65 14 15), open from late March to October, is on Ave de la République, 70 metres to the left as you exit the train station. Beds in rooms for two to eight people cost 120FF per person, including breakfast, and 175/230FF for half/full board. No reservations are accepted from guests staying less than a week. A hostel card is not necessary.

Hotels The *Hôtel du Centre* (☎ 04 95 65 02 01), in an airy old building at 14 Rue Alsace-Lorraine (parallel to and one block down the hill from Blvd Wilson), is open from early June to mid-October. Basic doubles without/with shower are 180/200FF and rise to 250/280FF in the middle of summer. *Hôtel Le Belvédère* (☎ 04 95 65 01 25) at Place Christophe Colomb is open all year. Small, cheaply appointed doubles/triples/quads with shower and toilet start at 180/200/250FF (300/400/450FF during the summer).

The three-star **Grand Hôtel** (☎ 04 95 65 09 74; fax 04 95 65 25 18) at 3 Blvd Wilson charges 328FF for a double with shower and 358FF with shower and toilet (380 and 550FF in July and August).

Places to Eat

Calvi's attractive marina is lined with restaurants and cafés, and there are several budget places on Rue Clemenceau, which runs parallel to Blvd Wilson. One of the cheapest, **Astalla Crêperie-Snack** (☎ 04 95 65 06 29) at No 11, has crêpes and omelettes. **Au Poussin Bleu** (☎ 04 95 65 01 58) at 8 Blvd Wilson is good for sandwiches in the 17 to 22FF range.

The pleasant open-air restaurant at the **Grand Hôtel** (☎ 04 95 65 09 74) has pizza, pasta and one of the better three-course menus in town for a reasonable 80FF. Try the mixed deep-fried seafood.

There are a couple of supermarkets south of the town centre on Ave Christophe Colomb: **Timy** (next to the Mobil petrol station) and the massive **Super U**.

Getting There & Away

Air Aéroport Calvi-Sainte Catherine is seven km south-east of Calvi. There is no bus service from Calvi to the airport; taxis (☎ 04 95 65 03 10) cost between 70 and 90FF (depending on the time of day) to the centre of town.

Bus From Monday to Saturday, Autocars Beaux Voyages (☎ 04 95 65 15 02) runs a daily bus to Bastia (80FF) which leaves from Place de la Porteuse d'Eau opposite the post office. During summer, one bus a day goes to Calenzana (30FF) and another to Porto (100FF) from Place du Monument every day but Sunday.

Train Calvi's train station is between the marina and Ave de la République. Fares to Ajaccio are 137FF, Corte 75FF and Bastia 89FF.

From mid-April to mid-October, one-car shuttle trains (navettes) of Tramways de la Balagne make 19 stops between Calvi and L'Île Rousse. The line is divided into three sectors, and it costs one ticket (9FF or 44FF for a carnet of six) for each sector you travel in. Getting to and from L'Île Rousse takes all six tickets. The navettes run on Sundays and holidays only in summer.

Ferry SNCM ferries (☎ 04 95 65 20 09) sail to Calvi from Nice, Marseille and Toulon, but during winter they can be very infrequent. Between mid-May and mid-September, Corsica Ferries links Calvi with Genoa. See Ferry under Getting There & Away at the start of the Corsica section for more information.

PORTO

The pleasant seaside town of Porto, nestled among huge outcrops of red granite and renowned for its sunsets, is an excellent base for exploring some of Corsica's natural wonders. **Les Calanche** (Les Calanques de Piana in French), a truly spectacular mountain landscape of red-and-orange granite forms resembling humans, animals, fortresses etc, towers above the azure waters of the Mediterranean slightly south of Porto along route D81. The **Gorges de Spelunca**, Corsica's most famous river gorges, stretch almost from the town of Ota, five km east of Porto, to the town of Evisa, 22 km away.

Orientation & Information

The marina is about 1.5 km down the hill from Porto's pharmacy – the local landmark – and the nearby Timy supermarket, both of which are on the D81. The area, known as Vaïta, is spread out along the road linking the D81 to the marina. The Porto River just south of the marina is linked by an arched pedestrian bridge to a fragrant eucalyptus grove and a small, pebble beach.

The tourist office (☎ 04 95 26 10 55) is built into the wall that separates the marina's upper and lower parking lots and is open from 9.30 am to noon and 2 to 6 pm Monday to Saturday (no break in July and August). Just around the corner is a Parc Naturel Régional de Corse office, open in summer only. Porto's postcode is 20150.

Things to See & Do

A short trail leads to the 16th-century **Genoese tower** on the outcrop above the town. It is open from April to September between 11 am and 7 pm (10FF).

From April to mid-October, the Compagnie des Promenades en Mer (☎ 04 95 26 15 16), whose bureau is across the parking lot from the tourist office, has two **boat excursions** a day (170FF) to Girolata (passing by the Scandola Nature Reserve), and occasionally to Les Calanche in the evenings. There are also glass-bottom boat excursions during July and August for 180FF. Keep a look out for dolphins following the boat as you leave and return to the port. Patrick & Toussaint (☎ 04 95 26 12 31), close to the bridge leading to the pebble beach, rents **motorboats** for up to seven people between April and October. Prices start at 400/600FF for a half/full day, not including petrol.

Places to Stay
Camping The *Camping Sole e Vista* (☎ 04 95 26 15 71), open from April to early November, is behind the Timy supermarket near the pharmacy. Charges are 10FF each for a tent and for a parking place and 30FF per person.

Hostels There are two hostels in the nearby village of Ota. *Gîte d'Étape Chez Félix* (☎ 04 95 26 12 92) and *Gîte d'Étape des Chasseurs* (☎ 04 95 26 11 37) are both open all year and charge 60/50FF respectively for a bed in a dormitory room. Chez Félix has doubles and triples for 200FF and a room for five for 320FF.

Hotels There are plenty of hotels in Vaïta and at the marina. One of the best deals, with great views of the marina, is the *Hôtel Le Golfe* (☎ 04 95 26 13 33), which charges 220FF for shower-equipped doubles with toilet (add 10FF in summer). *Hôtel Monte Rosso* (☎ 04 95 26 11 50) nearby has doubles with shower and toilet for 240FF (300FF in July and August). If you're not staying, at least have a cup of coffee at its lovely terrace café.

Places to Eat
Most of Porto's hotels double as restaurants. For a splurge and some seafood try the restaurant *Le Soleil Couchant* (☎ 04 95 26 10 12) on the marina. It has good-value menus from 85FF, pizzas from 38FF, and is open from April to mid-October. The grocery *Super Viva* near

the Porto River, just before the bridge to the beach, is open from April to September.

Getting There & Away
Between July and mid-September, two buses a day run daily (except on Sunday) between Porto and Ajaccio (65FF) operated by SAIB (☎ 04 95 26 13 70 in Porto; ☎ 04 95 22 41 99 in Ajaccio). From mid-May to mid-October, one bus a day goes to/from Calvi (100FF). Several buses a day link the village of Ota to both Ajaccio and Porto.

CORTE
When Pasquale Paoli led Corsica to independence in 1755, one of his first acts was to make Corte (Corti in Corsican; population 6000), a fortified town at the geographical centre of the island, the country's capital. To this day, the town remains a potent symbol of Corsican independence. In 1765, Paoli founded a national university there, but it was closed when his short-lived republic was taken over by France in 1769. The Università di Corsica Pasquale Paoli was reopened in 1981 and now has about 3000 students, making Corte the island's liveliest and least touristy town.

Information
The tourist office (☎ 04 95 46 24 20) is at the far end of the long building on your right as you pass through the Citadelle's main gate; look for the entrance with a '1' above it. It is open Monday to Friday from 9 am to noon and 1.30 to 5 pm. In summer, the office moves to the building on the left as you walk through the citadel gate.

There are several banks and automatic tellers on Cours Paoli, the main street which runs north-south through the town. The main post office is just off the northern end on Ave du Baron Mariani. Corte's postcode is 20250.

Things to See & Do
The **Citadelle**, built in the early 15th century and largely reconstructed during the 18th and 19th centuries, is perched on top of a hill, with the steep and twisted alleyways and streets of the **Ville Haute** and the Tavignanu and Restonica river valleys below. The Citadelle's **Belvédère** can be visited any time; the 15th-century **Nid d'Aigle** (eagle's nest) lookout 100

metres above is open from May to October (10FF).

The Citadelle houses the **Font Régional d'Art Contemporain** (☎ 04 95 46 22 18), which puts on temporary exhibitions of contemporary art. An ambitious anthropological museum, the **Musée de la Corse**, is being built with EU funding and is scheduled to open in June 1997.

The **Palazzu Naziunale** (National Palace; ☎ 04 95 61 02 62), down the hill from the Citadelle on Place Gaffori, was the governmental seat of the short-lived Corsican republic. It contains temporary exhibitions.

Università di Corsica Pasquale Paoli, Corsica's only university, is east of the town centre on Ave Jean Nicoli, on the way to the train station.

The **Gorges de la Restonica**, a deep valley cut through the mountains by the Restonica River, is a favourite with hikers. The river passes Corte, but some of the choicer trails begin about 16 km south-west of town at the Bergeries Grotelle sheepfolds. The trails are indicated on the free town map available at the tourist office.

Places to Stay

Camping The *Camping Alivetu* (☎ 04 95 46 11 09; open from Easter to mid-October), is in Faubourg Saint Antoine just south of Pont Restonica, the second bridge on Allée du Neuf Septembre crossing the Restonica River. It costs 13FF per tent and per car and 28FF per person.

Hostel The quiet and very rural *Gîte d'Étape U Tavignanu* (☎ 04 95 46 16 85), which is open all year, charges 60FF per person (or 160FF with half-board). To get there from Pont Tavignanu (the first bridge on Allée du Neuf Septembre over the Tavignanu River), walk westward along Chemin de Baliri and follow the signs (almost a km).

Hotels The 135-room *Hôtel HR* (☎ 04 95 45 11 11), housed in a complex of converted apartment blocks at 6 Allée du Neuf Septembre, is 300 metres to the left (south-west) as you exit the train station. Utilitarian singles/doubles/triples with a washbasin and bidet cost 135/145/170FF; doubles with shower and toilet are

195FF. Prices are slightly higher from August to mid-September.

The *Hôtel de la Poste* (☎ 04 95 46 01 37) is a few blocks north of the centre of town at 2 Place du Duc de Padoue. Simply furnished doubles with tiny shower cost 165 to 190FF, depending on how big it is and whether you want a window. They're 230FF with shower and toilet. The friendly *Hôtel Colonna* (☎ 04 95 46 01 09), in the centre just north of the main square (Place Paoli), has 18 rooms at 3 Ave Xavier Luciani and in an annexe opposite at No 4. Decent, renovated doubles are 180 to 250FF, and triples are 300FF.

Places to Eat

Le Bip's (☎ 04 95 46 06 26), down the steps and behind 14 Cours Paoli, is a cellar restaurant specialising in Corsican cuisine. The daily menu costs 75FF and is good value. Le Bip's is closed on Saturday, except in summer. *U Muntagnone* (☎ 04 95 61 09 77) has a pleasant terrace on 3 Place Paoli and is popular with the locals for its good-value fare. Pizzas start at 32FF, menus at 59FF and there's a special student deal for 54FF. It's open every day from mid-January to mid-November. The *Hôtel HR* (see above) also does student menus (49FF with a student card) at its brasserie. *Les Delices du Palais* pâtisserie diagonally opposite Le Bip's on Cours Paoli has a great selection of pastries.

Supermarkets in Corte include the *Eurospar* next to the Hôtel Colonna on Ave Xavier Luciani and the much larger *Casino*, a few steps west of the Hôtel HR. Both are open Monday to Saturday from 8.30 am to noon and 3 to 7 or 7.30 pm. Eurospar is also open on Sunday morning.

Getting There & Away

Corte is on Eurocorse's twice-daily (except Sunday) service in each direction between Bastia (50FF) and Ajaccio (60FF). The stop is in front of the Hôtel Colonna (3 Ave Xavier Luciani).

The train station (☎ 04 95 46 00 97) is about a km south-east of the town centre along Ave Jean Nicoli. Trains link Corte with Ajaccio (63FF, two hours), Bastia (55FF, 1½ hours) and Calvi (75FF, almost three hours).

SARTÈNE

The town of Sartène (Sartè in Corsican; population 3500), whose unofficial slogan is 'the most Corsican of Corsica's towns', is a delightful place to spend a morning or afternoon. Local people chatting in Corsican gather in **Place de la Libération**, the town's main square, where you'll find **Église Sainte Marie** – which contains a huge and very heavy wooden cross carried by a penitent every year on the eve of Good Friday – and the **Hôtel de Ville**, once the Genoan governor's palace. The **Musée de la Préhistoire Corse** (☎ 04 95 77 01 09) is up the hill. It's open Monday to Friday from 10 am to noon and 2 to 4 or 5 pm depending on the season. The tourist office (☎ 04 95 77 15 40) at 6 Rue Médecin-Capitaine Louis Bénédetti is open from 9 am to noon and, in summer, after lunch to 5 or 6 pm.

Places to Stay & Eat

The only hotel in Sartène is the two-star *Hôtel Les Roches* (☎ 04 95 77 07 61), just off the northern end of Ave Jean Jaurès. Singles/doubles/triples are 220/250/340FF, rising to 250/295/405FF from April to September.

A popular restaurant in Sartène is *La Chaumière* (☎ 04 95 77 07 13) at 39 Rue Médecin-Capitaine Louis Bénédetti, a couple of hundred metres south of the tourist office. Its evening menu is 90FF.

Getting There & Away

Given Sartène's dearth of reasonably priced hotels, your best bet is to stop off here on your way from Ajaccio to Bonifacio or to make it a day trip from the capital. Buses operated by Eurocorse between Ajaccio (70FF) and Bonifacio (55FF, two a day Monday to Saturday) stop at the Ollandini travel agency (☎ 04 95 77 18 41) on Cours Gabriel Péri.

BONIFACIO

The famed **Citadelle** of Bonifacio (Bunifaziu in Corsican; population 2700) and its medieval streets sit 70 metres above the translucent, turquoise waters of the Mediterranean, atop a long, narrow and eminently defensible promontory sometimes called 'Corsica's Gibraltar'. On all sides, limestone cliffs sculpted by the wind and the waves – topped in places with precariously perched apartment houses – drop almost vertically to the sea. The north side of the promontory looks out on 1.6-km-long Bonifacio Sound, at the eastern end of which is Bonifacio's **marina**. The southern ramparts of the citadel afford views of the coast of Sardinia, 12 km away.

Bonifacio was long associated with the Republic of Genoa. The local language – unintelligible to the rest of Corsicans – is a Genoan dialect and many of the traditions (including cooking methods) are Genoa-based.

Information

The tourist office (☎ 04 95 73 11 88) is in the old town at Place de l'Europe – go in through the ground-floor entrance on the eastern side of the Hôtel de Ville. It's open Monday to Friday from 8.30 am to 12.30 pm and 1.30 to 5.15 pm. From mid-June to mid-September, the hours are 9 am to 1 pm and 3 to 7 pm Monday to Saturday. There's also an annexe at the marina in summer.

In the port area, there's a Société Générale at 7 Rue Saint Erasme and a bureau de change with longer hours just opposite. The main post office (☎ 04 95 73 01 55) is in the old town, up the hill south of the tourist office, in Place Corega. Bonifacio's postcode is 20169.

Things to See

Walking around the old town and looking down the dramatic cliffs to the sea is a delight; the best views are to be had from **Place du Marché** and from the walk west towards and around the cemetery. Don't miss **Porte de Gênes**, which is reached by a tiny 16th-century drawbridge, or the Romanesque **Église Sainte Marie Majeure**, the oldest building in Bonifacio. **Rue des Deux Empereurs** (Street of the Two Emperors) is so-called because both Charles V and Napoleon himself slept there; look for the plaques at Nos 4 and 7. The **Foreign Legion Monument** east of the tourist office was brought back from Algeria in 1963 when that country won its independence.

Places to Stay

The olive-shaded *Camping Araguina* (☎ 04 95 73 02 96), open from mid-March to October, is 400 metres north of the marina on Ave Sylvère Bohn. Two people with a tent are charged 65FF (71FF during July and August) and 11FF to park.

Your best bet for budget hotel accommodation is the *Hôtel des Étrangers* (☎ 04 95 73 01 09), on Ave Sylvère Bohn 100 metres up the hill from the camping ground. It's open from April to October. Plain doubles with shower and toilet cost 180FF; from June to September, prices are 40 to 90FF higher.

In the citadel, the two-star *Hôtel Le Royal* (☎ 04 95 73 00 51) at 8 Rue Fred Scamaroni has doubles for 290FF (from 450 to 600FF from July to September).

Places to Eat
U Castille (☎ 04 95 73 04 99) on Rue Simon Varsi is a charming, family-run place converted from an old mill. Decent pizzas cost from 30FF, menus from 95FF. *Les Terrasses d'Aragon* (☎ 04 95 73 51 07) is just up the road at Place de la Poste. It has pizzas/menus from 39/70FF. It's a great place also for a cup of coffee (6FF); the terrace has good views over the cliffs. There's a supermarket at 15 Rue Oloria which is open from 8 am to noon and 3 to 6.30 pm.

For a real treat, visit *Boulangerie-Pâtisserie Faby* at 4 Rue Saint Jean Baptiste. It specialises in Corsican-Genoan treats like fougazi – big, flat biscuits flavoured with anis – and lemon canistrelli. It's open daily from 7.30 am to 12.30 pm and 3.30 to 7 pm (no midday closure from June to October).

Getting There & Away
Bus From Monday to Saturday, Rapides Bleus (☎ 04 95 70 10 36 in Porto-Vecchio) has up to two buses a day to Porto-Vecchio and daily buses to Bastia (110FF). Eurocorse (☎ 04 95 21 06 30 in Ajaccio; ☎ 04 95 70 13 83 in Porto-Vecchio) runs buses the 137 km to Ajaccio (115FF) via Sartène twice a day. All buses leave from the parking lot across the street from the eastern end of the marina.

Ferry Saremar (☎ 04 95 73 00 96) offers year-round car ferry service every day from Bonifacio's ferry port to Santa Teresa in Sardinia. One-way pedestrian passage costs 48 to 60FF depending on the season plus the 30FF departure tax (see Getting There & Away at the start of the Corsica section). If you want to get a vehicle across (from 124 to 234FF), make sure you have reservations at least a week in advance. Fares charged by their competition, Moby Lines (☎ 04 95 73 00 29), which has more frequent sailings, are a couple of francs more. The tax is the same.

Germany

Perhaps no other country in Western Europe has such a fascinating past, as well as history in the making, as Germany. Its reunification in 1990 was the beginning of yet another riveting chapter. Much of this history is easily explored by visitors today, in a country of sheer beauty where outdoor activity is a way of life. There is a huge variety of museums, architecture from most periods and a heavy emphasis on cultural activity. Infrastructure is extremely well organised, there is plenty of accommodation and the beer, food and wine are excellent.

Though it's now one country, the cultural, social and economic differences of the formerly separate Germanys will take many years to disappear altogether. Nevertheless the integration of the two is well advanced, and first-time visitors to Germany may not notice many big differences between them.

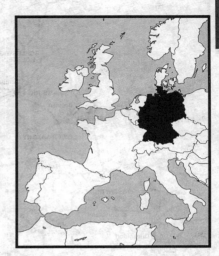

Facts about the Country

HISTORY

Events in Germany have often dominated the history of Europe. For many centuries, however, Germany was a patchwork of semi-independent principalities and city-states, preoccupied with internal quarrels and at the mercy of foreign conquerors. In the 18th and 19th centuries, these squabbling territories gradually came under the control of Prussia, a state created by the rulers of Brandenburg. Germany only became a nation-state in 1871 and, despite the momentous events that have occurred since then, many Germans still retain a strong sense of regional identity.

Ancient & Medieval History

Germany west of the Rhine and south of the Main was part of the Roman Empire, but Roman legions never managed to subdue the proud warrior tribes beyond. As the Roman Empire crumbled, these tribes spread out over much of Europe, establishing small kingdoms. The Frankish conqueror Charle-magne, from his court in Aachen, forged a huge empire that covered most of Christian Western Europe, but it broke up after his death in 814 AD.

The eastern branch of Charlemagne's empire developed in 962 AD into the Holy Roman Empire, organised under Otto I (Otto the Great). It included much of present-day Germany, Austria, Switzerland and Benelux. The term 'Holy Roman' was coined in an effort to assume some of the authority of the defunct Roman Empire.

The house of Habsburg, ruling from Vienna, took control of the empire in the 13th century. By this stage the empire had already begun to contract, and eventually it was little more than a conglomerate of German-speaking states run by local rulers who paid mere lip service to the Habsburg emperor. A semblance of unity in northern Germany was maintained by the Hanseatic League, a federation of German and Baltic city-states with Lübeck as its centre. The League began to form in the mid-12th century and dissolved in 1669.

Germany
(Deutschland)

The Reformation

Things would never be the same in Europe after Martin Luther, a scholar from the monastery in Erfurt, nailed his '95 Theses' to the church door in Wittenberg in 1517. Luther opposed a Church racket involving the selling of so-called 'indulgences', which absolved sinners from temporal punishment. In 1521 he was condemned by the Church and went into hiding in Wartburg castle in Eisenach. There he translated the Bible from the original Greek version into an everyday form of German. This Bible was printed on the presses developed by Gutenberg in Mainz and was then read by the masses.

Luther's efforts at reforming the Church gained widespread support from merchants, wealthy townsfolk and, crucially, several ambitious German princes. This protest against the established Church began the Protestant movement and the Reformation. The Peace of Augsburg in 1555 declared that the religion of a state would be determined by its ruler.

Meanwhile the established Church, which some people began to refer to as the 'Roman' Catholic Church, began a campaign known as the Counter-Reformation to stem the spread of Protestantism.

Thirty Years' War

The tensions between Protestant and Catholic states across Europe led to the catastrophic Thirty Years' War (1618-48). Germany became the battlefield for the great powers of Europe, losing over a third of its population and many of its towns and cities. It took the country centuries to recover.

The Peace of Westphalia in 1648 established the rights of both faiths in Germany but also sealed the country's political division. The German-speaking states remained a patchwork of independent principalities within the loose framework of the Holy Roman Empire, but were weakened further by the loss of important territories to other countries.

Prussia Unites Germany

In the 18th century, the Kingdom of Prussia, with its capital in Berlin, became one of Europe's strongest powers. Thanks to the organisational talents of Friedrich Wilhelm I (the Soldier King) and his son Friedrich II (Frederick the Great), it expanded eastwards at the expense of Poland, Lithuania and Russia.

In the early 19th century, the fragmented German states proved easy pickings for Napoleon. The Austrian emperor, Francis II, relinquished his crown as Holy Roman Emperor in 1806 following his defeat at Austerlitz. But the French never quite managed to subdue Prussia, which became the centre of German resistance. After Napoleon's disastrous foray into Russia, Prussia led the war that put an end to Napoleon's German aspirations in a decisive battle at Leipzig in 1813.

In 1815 the Congress of Vienna again redrew the map of Europe. The Holy Roman Empire was replaced with a German Confederation of 35 states; it had a parliament in Frankfurt and was led by the Austrian chancellor Klemens von Metternich. The Confederation was shaken by liberal revolutions in Europe in 1830 and 1848, but the Austrian monarchy continued to dominate a divided Germany.

The well-oiled Prussian civil and military machine eventually smashed this arrangement. In 1866, Otto von Bismarck (the Iron Chancellor) took Prussia to war against Austria, and rapidly annexed northern Germany. Another successful war in 1870-71 saw Prussia defeat France and seize from its neighbour the provinces of Alsace and Lorraine. The Catholic, anti-Prussian states in southern Germany were forced to negotiate with Bismarck, who had achieved his dream of German unity. The Prussian king, Wilhelm I, became *Kaiser* (German emperor).

WWI & the Rise of Hitler

Wilhelm II dismissed Bismarck in 1890, but Germany's rapid growth overtaxed the Kaiser's political talents, and led to mounting tensions with England, Russia and France. When war broke out in 1914 Germany's only ally was a weakened Austria-Hungary.

Gruelling trench warfare on two fronts sapped the nation's resources and by late 1918 Germany was forced to sue for peace. The Kaiser abdicated and escaped to Holland. Anger on the home front, which had been mounting during the fighting and deprivation, exploded when the troops returned home. A full-scale socialist uprising, based in Berlin and led by the Spartacus League, was put down and its leaders, Karl Liebknecht and Rosa Luxemburg, were murdered. A new republic, which became known as the Weimar Republic, was proclaimed.

The Treaty of Versailles in 1919 chopped huge areas off Germany and imposed heavy reparation payments. These proved virtually impossible to meet, and when France and Belgium occupied the Rhineland to ensure continued payments, the subsequent hyperinflation and miserable economic conditions provided fertile ground for political extremists. One of these was Adolf Hitler.

Led by Adolf Hitler, an Austrian drifter and German army veteran, the National (or Nazi) Socialist German Workers' Party staged an abortive coup in Munich in 1923. This landed Hitler in prison for nine months, during which time he wrote *Mein Kampf*.

From 1929 the worldwide economic depression hit Germany particularly hard, leading to massive unemployment, strikes and demonstrations. The Communist Party under Ernst Thälmann gained strength, but wealthy industrialists began to support the Nazis and police turned a blind eye to Nazi street thugs.

The Nazis increased their strength in general elections and in 1933 replaced the Social Democrats as the largest party in the Reichstag. Hitler was appointed chancellor and a year later assumed absolute control as *Führer* (leader) of what he called the Third Reich (the 'third empire', the previous two being the Holy Roman Empire and Wilhelm I's German Empire).

WWII & the Division of Germany

From 1935 Germany began to rearm and build its way out of depression with strategic public works such as the autobahns. Hitler reoccupied the Rhineland in 1936, and in 1938 annexed Austria and parts of Czechoslovakia. Finally, in September 1939, after signing a pact that allowed both Stalin and himself a free hand in the east of Europe, Hitler attacked Poland, which led to war with Britain and France.

Germany quickly invaded large parts of Europe, but after 1943 began to suffer increasingly heavy losses. Massive bombing reduced Germany's centres to rubble and the country lost 10% of its population. Germany accepted unconditional surrender in May 1945, soon after Hitler's suicide. Chief among the horrors of WWII was the extermination of millions of Jews, Gypsies, Communists and others in history's first 'assembly-line' genocide. Camps were designed specifically to rid Europe of people considered undesirable according to racist Nazi doctrine.

At conferences in Yalta and Potsdam, the Allies redrew the borders of Germany, making it a quarter smaller than it had already become after the Treaty of Versailles 26 years earlier. Some 6.5 million ethnic Germans migrated or were expelled to Germany from their homes in eastern Europe, where they had lived for centuries. Germany was divided into four occupation zones and Berlin was occupied jointly by the four victorious powers.

In the Soviet zone, the communist Socialist Unity Party (SED) won the 1946 elections and began a rapid nationalisation of industry. In June 1948 the Soviet Union stopped all land traffic between Germany's western zones and Berlin. This forced the Western allies to mount a military operation known as the Berlin Airlift, which brought food and other supplies to West Berlin by plane until the Soviets lifted the blockade in May 1949.

In September 1949 the Federal Republic of Germany (FRG) was created out of the three western zones; in response the German Democratic Republic (GDR) was founded in the Soviet zone the following month, with (East) Berlin as its capital.

From Division to Unity

As the West's bulwark against Communism, the FRG received massive injections of US capital in the postwar years, and experienced rapid economic development under the leadership of Konrad Adenauer. At the same time the GDR had to pay US$10 billion in war reparations to the Soviet Union and rebuild itself from scratch.

A better life in the West increasingly attracted skilled workers away from the miserable economic conditions in the East. As these were people the GDR could ill afford to lose, in 1961 it built a wall around West Berlin and sealed its border with the FRG. As the Cold War intensified, TV and radio stations in both Germanys beamed programmes heavy with propaganda to the other side.

Coinciding with a change to the more flexible leadership of Erich Honecker in the East, the *Ostpolitik* of FRG chancellor Willy Brandt allowed an easier political relationship between the two Germanys. In 1971 the four occupying powers – the Soviet Union, the USA, the UK and France – formally accepted the division of Berlin. Many Western countries, but not West Germany itself, then officially recognised the GDR.

Honecker's policies produced higher living standards in the GDR, yet East Germany barely managed to achieve a level of prosperity half that of the FRG. After Mikhail Gorbachev came to power in the Soviet Union in March 1985, the East German Communists gradually lost Soviet backing. In May 1989 Hungary relaxed its border controls, allowing East Germans to escape to the West. Mass demonstrations demanding reforms similar to those in other Eastern European countries began in Leipzig and soon spread to other cities in the GDR. The East German government countered by prohibiting travel to Hungary, and would-be defectors began taking refuge in the FRG's embassy in Prague.

Gorbachev urged the East German Politburo to introduce reforms, but Honecker resisted. Forced to resign, Honecker was replaced by his security chief, Egon Krenz, who also proved unable to rescue the regime despite introducing some minor reforms. The demonstrations continued, attracting hundreds of thousands of people. Then suddenly on 9 November 1989, to everyone's surprise, Politburo member Gunter Schabowski announced – mistakenly as it turned out – the opening of all GDR borders with West Germany, including the Berlin Wall. That same night thousands of people streamed into the West past stunned border guards. Millions more followed in the next few days, and dismantling of the Wall began soon thereafter. On 13 November the East German parliament elected the reformist Hans Modrow as prime minster.

Opposition within the GDR had long been led by peace and human-rights activists who nevertheless had liberal-socialist sympathies. But the popular mood quickly shifted away from favouring reform to complete reunification with the West. Offering a fast-track unification plan with generous one-for-one exchange rates for the otherwise inconvertible East German currency, on 18 March 1990 FRG chancellor Helmut Kohl's Christian Demo-cratic Union (CDU) easily won the first East German elections. The Communists – but also the citizen-based opposition groups who had been so instrumental in their downfall – were completely marginalised.

Leading economists had warned that attempts to rapidly integrate the two Germanys' fundamentally different economies would cause the collapse of many less efficient East German industries. But the GDR's new CDU prime minister, Lothar de Mazière, pushed monetary union forward to 1 July 1990 and Kohl reassured West Germans that reunification would not lead to tax rises.

In September 1990 the two Germanys and the wartime Allies signed the Two-Plus-Four Treaty, ending the postwar system of occupation zones. Germany recognised its eastern borders, officially accepting the loss of territories annexed by Poland and the Soviet Union after 1945. On 3 October 1990, the German Democratic Republic was incorporated into the Federal Republic of Germany. In the ensuing national euphoria Kohl's CDU-led coalition soundly defeated the Social Democrat opposition in the all-German elections of 2 December 1990.

The 'Land in the Middle'

The social and economic costs of absorbing East Germany were grossly underestimated – even by many pessimists. East and West Germans, who began to refer to each other as *Wessis* and *Ossis* (westies and easties), discovered that their differences were greater than they had previously liked to believe.

Many uncompetitive and highly polluting East German industries had to be shut down, causing the loss of millions of jobs. The government countered with enormous public spending, bringing about a short-lived 'unification boom'. Revelations that respected figures cooperated with the Stasi, the GDR's secret police, deepened public distrust of eastern Germany's 'new' democrats. Hundreds of former SED office holders and senior judges were charged with human-rights violations allegedly committed during the GDR years. Erich Honecker escaped manslaughter charges due to his declining health and died in exile in Chile in May 1994.

Despite continuing problems, eastern Germany's longer-term future looks promising.

The region is receiving state-of-the-art technology that many parts of western Germany will have to wait years for. Nevertheless, while social and economic conditions have improved markedly, they continue to lag behind the West. With unemployment running as high as 35% in some eastern towns, there's widespread restlessness and impatience among the citizenry.

Dislocation in the east and a general economic downturn throughout Germany have been exploited by neo-Nazi organisations. Although their support is too weak to win them more than a handful of parliamentary seats, attacks on immigrants and asylum-seekers by right-wing elements have occurred repeatedly. Having regained its historical role as the 'land in the middle', Germany now finds itself torn between an inward-looking reunification process and support for further European integration.

GEOGRAPHY & ECOLOGY

Germany covers 356,866 sq km and can be divided from north to south into several geographical regions.

The Northern Lowlands are a broad expanse of flat, low-lying land that sweeps across the northern third of the country from the Netherlands into Poland. The landscape is characterised by moist heaths interspersed with pastures and farmland.

The complex Central Uplands region divides northern Germany from the south. Extending from the deep schisms of the Rhineland massifs to the Harz Mountains and the Bavarian Forest, these low mountain ranges are Germany's heartland. The Rhine and Main rivers, important waterways for inland shipping, cut through the south-west of this region. With large deposits of coal and favourable transport conditions, this was one of the first regions in Germany to undergo industrialisation.

The Alpine Foothills take in the Swabian and Bavarian highlands, from the Black Forest to Munich, and are largely drained by the Danube River. The landscape is typified by rolling subalpine plateaux and rounded, heavily forested mountain ranges with occasional peaks that rise above 1400 metres.

Germany's Alps lie entirely within Bavaria and stretch from the large, glacially formed Lake Constance in the west to Berchtesgaden in Germany's south-eastern corner. Though lower than the mountains to their south, many summits are well above 2000 metres, rising dramatically from the Alpine Foothills to the 2966-metre Zugspitze, Germany's highest mountain.

Germans are fiercely protective of their natural surroundings, and environmental science is one area where they excel. German households and businesses enthusiastically participate in waste recycling programmes. In 1994 a newly created article of German basic law made it the duty of the government to protect the nation's natural resources. Perhaps this new law was a reaction to some stark figures: in a land where people cherish the outdoors, about two thirds of all trees are damaged to some extent. This sad fact led to a recent attempt to pass a law limiting speeds on the autobahns: it failed. The Germans may love their forests, but they adore their cars.

GOVERNMENT & POLITICS

Germany has one of the most decentralised governmental structures in Europe, with a federal system based on regional states. With reunification, eastern Germany's six original (pre-1952) states of Berlin, Brandenburg, Mecklenburg-Vorpommern (Mecklenburg-Western Pomerania), Sachsen (Saxony), Sachsen-Anhalt (Saxony-Anhalt) and Thüringen (Thuringia) were re-established. In the context of the Federal Republic of Germany they are called *Bundesländer* (federal states). The Bundesländer in western Germany are Schleswig-Holstein, Hamburg, Niedersachsen (Lower Saxony), Bremen, Nordrhein-Westfalen (North Rhine-Westphalia), Hessen (Hesse), Rheinland-Pfalz (Rhineland-Palatinate), Saarland, Baden-Württemberg and Bayern (Bavaria). Germans commonly refer to the eastern states as the *neue Bundesländer* (new states) and to the western states as the *alte Bundesländer* (old states).

The Bundesländer have a large degree of autonomy in internal affairs and exert influence on the central government through the *Bundesrat* (upper house). The *Bundestag* (lower house) is elected by direct universal suffrage with proportional representation, although a party must have at least 5% of the vote to gain a seat. The federal government has alternated between the Christian Democrats (CDU, or CSU in Bavaria) and the Social Democrats (SPD), with the balance of power generally held by a small but influential liberal party, the Free Democrats (FDP). In October 1994 Kohl's ruling CDU-led coalition again won the national elections, though with a greatly reduced working majority in the Bundestag. The SPD continued to dominate the Bundesrat.

In June 1991 the Bundestag voted to transfer the capital from Bonn to Berlin (although some administrative functions are to remain in Bonn). The move to Berlin is scheduled to be completed by the year 2000.

ECONOMY
The Marshall Plan helped to produce West Germany's *Wirtschaftswunder* (economic miracle), which in the 1950s and '60s turned the FRG into the world's third-largest economy. The trade unions and industrial corporations developed a unique economic contract by which the workers refrained from strikes in return for higher wages and better conditions. Important industries include electrical manufacturing, precision and optical instruments, chemicals and vehicle manufacturing.

East Germany's recovery was even more remarkable given the wartime destruction, postwar looting by the USSR, loss of skilled labour, and isolation from Western markets. Although some of its own economic data may now be seriously questioned, the GDR was by any measure an important industrial nation, with major metallurgical, electrical, chemical and engineering industries.

At the time of unification, West Germany's per-capita income was almost three times that of the GDR. The post-unification years of 1991 and 1992 saw a worsening of this situation, as eastern Germany's export markets in the socialist Comecon trading bloc collapsed and its industries proved unable to compete in Western markets. Industrial production in the east fell by 65%. Five years after reunification, Germany's unemployment level hit a post-war record of 10.8% in January 1996.

Under the Treuhandanstalt (Trust Agency) almost all state-owned enterprises of the former GDR were privatised, many with binding pledges for new investments. Rather than turning a profit, however, this massive sell-off left liabilities of around DM300 billion.

Annual investments of around DM150 billion have been necessary to pay for welfare and badly needed infrastructure in the east. With public debt running at DM2 trillion (and climbing), major tax rises coupled with cutbacks in social welfare have been necessary to ease the government's enormous budget deficits. Industries in eastern Germany continue to struggle with low productivity levels. In cash terms, east Germans buy 30 times more goods from the west than they sell to them.

On the other hand, the per-capita level of company investment – one of the more telling long-term economic indicators – is now higher in the east than in west Germany. Taxpayer-funded spending has been pumped into everything from new roads, building construction and renovation, and ultramodern communications systems to education and the conversion of brown coal to cleaner natural gas. Despite continuing high unemployment, economic growth in eastern Germany during the last three years has averaged 9%, as many new industries have been rebuilt.

It will be at least a decade before the eastern German economy catches up to its western counterpart. Before WWII, northern Germany was the richest part of the country, but after the war the focus of technological excellence fell increasingly on the southern states of Bavaria and Baden-Württemberg, where many big names of German industry – Mercedes, BMW, Siemens – are based. A similar shift may well occur towards the east, but it may come too late to benefit many members of the present generation.

POPULATION & PEOPLE
There are 65 million people in western Germany and 16 million in eastern Germany, making the unified country the most populous in Europe apart from Russia. Germany's main native minority is the tiny group of Slavonic Sorbs, in the far east of the country (Saxony and Brandenburg). In political and economic terms, Germany is Europe's most decentralised nation, but considerable variation in population density exists. The Ruhr district in the northern Rhineland has

Germany's densest concentration of people and industry, while Mecklenburg-Western Pomerania in the north-eastern corner is relatively sparsely settled. A third of the population lives in 84 cities each with over 100,000 people, while 54.5% of the people live in smaller towns, cities and villages.

Nearly seven million foreigners also live in Germany. Most hail from Turkey, Italy, Greece and the former Yugoslavia and arrived as 'guest workers' in the FRG from the early 1960s onward to work in lower-paid jobs. By now, many of them and their descendants are thoroughly integrated into German society. Though entitled to apply for German citizenship, a majority choose not to do so because German law requires them to renounce their former citizenship on becoming Germans. Eastern Germany has fewer resident foreigners, though some of the roughly 200,000 workers who arrived in the GDR during the 1980s from 'fellow socialist' countries remain. In effect, Germany has become a nation of immigration, thus compensating for the extremely low birth rate among the established German population. (The number of Germans living in the country's eastern states has now dropped to levels last recorded in 1906!)

ARTS

Germany's meticulously creative population has made major contributions to European culture. Indeed Germans take their *Kultur* so seriously that visitors sometimes wonder how on earth they ever manage to actually enjoy it. The answer lies, perhaps, in a German musician's proverb: True bliss is absolute concentration.

Architecture, Painting & Literature

The scope of German art is such that it could be the focus of an entire visit. The arts first blossomed during the Romanesque period (800-1200), of which examples can be found at the Germanisches Nationalmuseum in Nuremberg, Trier Cathedral and the churches of Cologne.

The Gothic style (1200-1500) is best viewed at Freiburg's Münster cathedral, Meissen Cathedral and the Marienkirche in Lübeck. Artists from the Cologne school of painters and sculptor Peter Vischer and his sons produced famous Gothic paintings and sculpture. The

Renaissance came late to Germany but flourished once it took hold. The draughtsman Albrecht Dürer of Nuremberg (1471-1528) was one of the world's finest portraitists, as was the prolific Lucas Cranach the Elder (1472-1553) who worked in Wittenberg for over 45 years.

The baroque period brought great sculpture, including works by Andreas Schlüter in Berlin. Balthasar Neumann's superb Residenz in Würzburg and the magnificent cathedral in Passau are foremost examples of baroque architecture.

The Enlightenment During the 18th century, the Saxon court at Weimar attracted some of the major cultural figures of Europe. Among them was Johann Wolfgang von Goethe (1749-1832), the poet, dramatist, painter, scientist, philosopher and perhaps the last European to achieve the Renaissance ideal of excellence in many fields. His greatest work, the drama *Faust*, is a masterful epic of all that went before him, as the archetypal human strives for meaning and knowledge.

Goethe's close friend, Friedrich Schiller (1759-1805), was a poet, dramatist and novelist. His most famous work is the dramatic cycle *Wallenstein*, based on the life of a treacherous Thirty Years' War general who plotted to make himself arbiter of the empire. Schiller's other great play, *William Tell*, dealt with the right of the oppressed to rise against tyranny. Large museums dedicated to both Schiller and Goethe exist in Weimar today.

The 19th & Early 20th Centuries Berlin too produced remarkable individuals, such as Alexander von Humboldt (1769-1859), an advanced thinker in environmentalism through his studies of the relationship of plants and animals to their physical surroundings. His contemporary, the philosopher Georg Wilhelm Friedrich Hegel (1770-1831), created an all-embracing classical philosophy that is still influential today. The neoclassical period in Germany was led by Karl Friedrich Schinkel and the Munich neoclassical school. The romantic period is best exemplified by the paintings of Caspar David Friedrich.

Art Nouveau also made great contributions to German architecture, as exemplified by

Alfred Messel's Wertheim department store in Berlin. Next came expressionism, with great names like Paul Klee and the Russian-born painter Vasili Kandinsky. In 1919, Walter Gropius founded the Bauhaus movement in an attempt to meld the theoretical concerns of architecture with the practical problems faced by artists and craftspeople. With the arrival of the Nazis, Gropius accepted a chair at Harvard.

In the 1920s, Berlin was the theatrical capital of Germany, and its most famous practitioner was the Marxist poet and playwright Bertolt Brecht (1898-1956). Brecht introduced Marxist concepts into his plays, and his work was distinguished by the simplicity of its moral parables, its language and its sharp characterisation. Brecht revolutionised the theatre by detaching the audience from what was happening on stage, enabling them to observe the content without being distracted by the form. In 1933 Brecht fled the Nazis and lived in various countries, eventually accepting the directorship of the Berliner Ensemble in East Berlin, where his work has been performed ever since.

WWII & Beyond During the Third Reich, the arts were devoted mainly to propaganda, with grandiose projects and realist art extolling the virtues of Germanhood. Max Ernst, resident in France and the USA, was a prominent exponent of dada and surrealism who developed the technique of collage.

Postwar literature in both Germanys was influenced by the Gruppe 47, a loose grouping whose members took a deliberately political stance. It included writers such as Günter Grass, whose modern classic, *Die Blechtrommel* ('The Tin Drum'), is about a young boy who stops growing in order to survive WWII. Christa Wolf, an East German novelist and Gruppe 47 writer, won high esteem in both Germanys. Her 1963 story *Der geteilte Himmel* ('Divided Heaven') tells of a young woman whose fiancé abandons her for life in the West.

Since the late 1980s, Patrick Süskind has been one of Germany's more popular young writers. Süskind's first novel, *Das Parfum* ('The Perfume'), published in 1985, is the extraordinary tale of a psychotic 18th-century perfume-maker with an obsessive genius.

Music
Few countries can claim the impressive musical heritage of Germany. A partial list of household names includes Johann Sebastian Bach, Georg Friedrich Händel, Ludwig van Beethoven, Richard Wagner, Richard Strauss, Felix Mendelssohn-Bartholdy, Robert Schumann, Johannes Brahms and Gustav Mahler.

The two greatest baroque composers were born in Saxony in the same year. Johann Sebastian Bach (1685-1750) was born at Eisenach into a prominent family of musicians. During his tenures as court organist at Weimar and city musical director at Leipzig, Bach produced some 200 cantatas, plus masses, oratorios, passions and other elaborate music for the Lutheran service, and sonatas, concertos, preludes and fugues for secular use.

Georg Friedrich Händel (1685-1759) left his native Halle for Hamburg at 18. He composed numerous operas and oratorios, including his masterpiece *Messiah* (1742). The birthplaces of both Händel and Bach are now large museums.

In the 19th century, the musical traditions of Saxony continued unabated with the songwriter Robert Schumann (1810-56) born at Zwickau. In 1843 Schumann opened a music school at Leipzig in collaboration with composer Felix Mendelssohn-Bartholdy (1809-47), director of Leipzig's famous Gewandhaus Orchestra.

These musical traditions continue to thrive: the Dresden Opera and Leipzig Orchestra are known around the world, and musical performances are hosted almost daily in every major theatre in the country.

The Studio for Electronic Music in Cologne is a centre for cutting-edge developments in this field. Contemporary music is also popular: jazz, folk, rock & roll, new wave, techno and much more can be found in every large city – the emphasis is often on beat and volume rather than melody. Traditional German oompah music is still popular with some locals and tourists.

CULTURE
Once viewed as overly disciplined, humourless and domineering, today's Germans are generally more relaxed, personable and interested in enjoying life. Reunification has strengthened this trend, which is spreading

eastwards. English-speaking travellers readily identify with Germans and normally find it easy to strike up conversations with them.

Despite their penchant for continual improvement and modernisation, tradition remains dear to the German heart. Hunters still wear green, master chimney sweeps get around in pitch-black suits and top hats, Bavarian women don the *Dirndl* (skirt and blouse), while menfolk occasionally sport the typical Bavarian *Lederhosen* (leather shorts), a *Loden* (short jacket) and felt hat.

There are few real taboos left in modern Germany and Germans are generally not prudish. Millions regularly visit nude beaches (identifiable by the abbreviation FKK), and even public figures may sometimes express themselves in earthy Germanic terms.

Formal manners are still important, though less so than a decade or two ago. Except with close friends, most Germans still use *Herr* and *Frau* in daily discussion. (In fact, the transition from the formal *Sie* to the informal *du* is often celebrated.) Similarly, professional titles are often used instead of surnames (eg *Herr Professor* or *Frau Doktor*). Germans usually shake hands when greeting or leaving. Hugging and cheek kissing is standard between males and females who know one another.

The holocaust and WWII, while by no means taboo topics, should be discussed with tact and understanding in Germany. In western Germany these themes have been dealt with openly for decades, but Germans sometimes feel their country's postwar role as a model for peace continues to be under-emphasised against its relatively short period under the Nazis. Germans understandably take great offence at the presumption that fascist ideas are somehow part of – or even compatible with – their national culture.

RELIGION

Most Germans belong to a church, and there are almost equal numbers of Catholics and Protestants: roughly speaking, Catholics predominate in the south, Protestants in the north and east. A majority of citizens pay contributions to their church, which the government collects along with their taxes, but in practice few Germans regularly attend church services.

Despite their bitter historical rivalry, conflict between Catholics and Protestants in Germany is a nonissue these days, but conflict *within* the two faiths is great. Catholics are concerned with old and new problems, such as abortion. Protestants are struggling with the church's involvement in political issues, like the environment.

In eastern Germany, the Protestant Church, which claims support among the overwhelming majority of the population there, played a major role in the overthrow of German Communism by providing a gathering place for antigovernment protesters. Despite the fall of Communism, however, active church membership remains even lower than in western Germany.

In 1933 some 530,000 Jews lived in Germany. Today Germany's Jewish citizens number around 50,000, with the largest communities being those in Berlin, Frankfurt and Munich. Their population is growing, though, with the recent influx of Russian Jews. There are also more than 1.7 million Muslims, most of them Turks.

LANGUAGE

It might come as a surprise to know that German is a close relative of English. English, German and Dutch are all known as West Germanic languages. This means that you know lots of German words already – *Arm, Finger, Gold* – and you'll be able to figure out many others, such as *Mutter* (mother), *trinken* (drink), *gut* (good). A primary reason why English and German have grown apart is that when the Normans invaded England in 1066 they brought in many non-Germanic words. For this reason, English has many synonyms, usually with the more basic word being German, and the more literary or specialised one coming from French; for instance, 'start' and 'green' as opposed to 'commence' and 'verdant'.

German is spoken throughout Germany and Austria and in much of Switzerland. It is also useful in Eastern Europe, especially with older people. Although you will hear different regional dialects, the official language, *Hochdeutsch*, is universally understood. In some tourist centres, English is so widely spoken that you may not have a chance to use German, even if you want to! However, as soon as you try to meet ordinary people or move out of the big cities, especially in eastern Germany, the situation is rather different. Your efforts to speak the local language will be appreciated and will make your trip much more enjoyable and fulfilling.

Words that you'll often encounter on maps and throughout this chapter include: *Altstadt* (old city), *Bahnhof* (train station), *Brücke* (bridge), *Hauptbahnhof* (main train station), *Markt* (market, often the central square in old towns), *Platz* (square), *Rathaus* (town hall) and *Strasse* (street). German nouns are always written with a capital letter.

See the Language Guide at the back of the book for pronunciation guidelines and useful words and phrases.

Facts for the Visitor

PLANNING
Climate & When to Go
The German climate can be variable, so it's best to be prepared for all types of weather throughout the year. That said, the most reliable weather is from May to October. This, of course, coincides with the standard tourist season (except for skiing). The shoulder periods can bring fewer tourists and surprisingly pleasant weather.

Eastern Germany lies in a transition zone between the temperate maritime climate of Western Europe and the rougher continental climate of Eastern Europe – continental and Atlantic air masses meet here. The mean annual temperature in Berlin is 11°C, the average range of temperatures varying from -1°C in January to 18°C in July. The average annual precipitation is 585 mm and there is no special rainy season. The camping season is from May to September.

Books & Maps
The German literary tradition is strong and there are many works that provide excellent background to the German experience. Mark Twain's *A Tramp Abroad* is recommended for his comical observations of German life. For a more modern analysis of the German character and the issues facing post-unification Germany, pick up the Penguin paperback *Germany and the Germans* by John Ardagh.

The green *Michelin Guide* to Germany is strong on culture, but weak on practical travel details. A good collection of motoring itineraries is presented in *German Country Inns & Castles*, written by Karen Brown and published by Harrap, but it only concentrates on up-market accommodation.

Locally produced maps of Germany are among the best in the world. Most tourist offices have free city maps. The automobile clubs ADAC and AvD produce excellent road maps. More detailed maps can be obtained at most bookshops. The best city maps are made by Falkplan with a patented folding system.

Online Services
For up-to-date information on Germany via the internet, try the web site maintained by the German Information Centre at http://www.germany-info.org.

Most of the information is in English and it also lists hyperlinks to other German information sites. The site offers travel information and homepages for various German cities.

Another German web site is at http://www.langlab.uta.edu.

What to Bring
If you forget to bring it, you can buy it in Germany.

Standard dress can be casual, but should be fairly conservative. Jeans are generally accepted throughout the country. A layering system is best, as weather can change drastically from region to region and from day to night.

SUGGESTED ITINERARIES
Depending on the length of your stay, you might want to see and do the following things:

Two days
  Depending on where you enter the country, try to spend at least two days in either Berlin or Munich.
One week
  Divide your time between Berlin and Munich, and throw in a visit to Dresden or Bamberg.
Two weeks
  Berlin (including Potsdam), Dresden, Munich, Bamberg and Lübeck.
One month
  Berlin (including Potsdam), Dresden, Meissen, the Harz Mountains, the Moselle River, Munich, the Alps, Lake Constance and Bamberg or Lübeck.

Two months
  As for one month, plus Weimar, Regensburg, Passau, the Romantic Road, the Rhine valley, Cologne, and the North Frisian Islands.

HIGHLIGHTS
Museums & Galleries
Germany is a museum-lover's dream. Munich features the huge Deutsches Museum, and Frankfurt's Museumsufer (Museum Bank) has enough museums for any addict. The Dahlem Museum in Berlin and the Neue Meister Gallery in Dresden are among the chief art museums, while treasures of another sort are at Dresden's Grünes Gewölbe.

Castles
Germany has castles of all periods and styles. If you're into castles, make sure to hit Heidelberg, Neuschwanstein, Burg Rheinfels on the River Rhine, Burg Eltz on the Moselle, the medieval Königstein and Wartburg castles, Renaissance Wittenberg Castle, baroque Schloss Moritzburg and romantic Wernigerode Castle.

Historic Towns
Time stands still in much of Germany, and some of the best towns in which to find this flavour are Rothenburg ob der Tauber, Goslar and Regensburg. Meissen and Quedlinburg have a fairy-tale air, Weimar has a special place in German culture, and Bamberg and Lübeck are two of Europe's true gems. The old parts of many large cities also impart this historic feel.

Places to Stay & Restaurants
Some sleeping highlights include the hostels along the Rhine and Moselle rivers, in Rothenburg and in Nuremberg, and summer camping at 'the Tent' in Munich. The Hotel zum Ritter is in a 16th-century building on the main square in picturesque Heidelberg.

The restaurants along Frankfurt's Berger Strasse offer a cosmopolitan setting, and in Düsseldorf's lively city centre you can eat and drink on the pedestrian streets. Leipzig wouldn't be the same without its Auerbachs Keller. Zur Letzten Instanz, Schwarzes Café and Café Voltaire are Berlin eateries you'll enjoy.

TOURIST OFFICES
Tourism in Germany runs like the train system: very efficiently. Small and large tourist offices are incredibly helpful and well informed. Don't hesitate to make use of their services.

Local Tourist Offices
The German National Tourist Office (Deutsche Zentrale für Tourismus, DZT) is headquartered at Beethovenstrasse 69, 60325 Frankfurt/Main (☎ 069-7 57 20; fax 75 19 03). For local information, the office to head for in cities and towns in eastern and western Germany alike is the *Verkehrsamt* (tourist office) or *Kurverwaltung* (resort administration).

Tourist Offices Abroad
DZT representatives abroad include:

Australia & New Zealand
  German National Tourist Office, 464 Kent St, Sydney, NSW 2000 (☎ 02-9267 8148; fax 02-9267 9035)
Canada
  German National Tourist Office, 175 Bloor St East, North Tower, 6th Floor, Toronto, Ont M4W 3R8 (☎ 416-968 1570)
South Africa
  German National Tourist Office, c/o Lufthansa German Airlines, 22 Girton Rd, Parktown, Johannesburg 2000 (☎ 011-643 1615)
UK
  German National Tourist Office, Nightingale House, 65 Curzon St, London W1Y 8PE (☎ 0171-495 0081)
USA
  German National Tourist Office, 52nd floor, 122 East 42nd St, Chanin Building, 52nd Floor, New York, NY 10168-0072 (☎ 212-661 72 00)
  German National Tourist Office, 11766 Wilshire Blvd, suite 750, Los Angeles, CA 90025 (☎ 310-575 97 99)

There are also offices in Amsterdam, Brussels, Chicago, Copenhagen, Helsinki, Hong Kong, Madrid, Milan, Moscow, Oslo, Paris, São Paulo, Stockholm, Tel Aviv, Tokyo, Vienna and Zürich.

VISAS & EMBASSIES
Americans, Australians, Britons, Canadians, New Zealanders and Japanese require only a valid passport (no visa) to enter Germany. Citizens of the EU and some other Western European countries can enter on an official identity card. Unless you're a citizen of a Third

World country you can probably stay up to three months.

German Embassies Abroad

Australia
119 Empire Circuit, Yarralumla, ACT 2600 (☎ 06-270 1911)

Canada
1 Waverley St, Ottawa, Ont K2P 0T7 (☎ 613-232 1101)

New Zealand
90-92 Hobson St, Wellington (☎ 04-473 6063)

South Africa
180 Blackwood St, Arcadia, Pretoria 0083 (☎ 012-344 3854)

UK
23 Belgrave Square, London SW1 (☎ 0171-824 13 00)

USA
4645 Reservoir Rd, NW Washington, DC 20007-1998 (☎ 202-298 4000)

Foreign Embassies in Germany

The transferral of the German capital from Bonn to Berlin will begin in earnest from 1998, but until the foreign ministry moves to Berlin the main diplomatic missions of other countries will remain in Bonn (see Berlin later in this chapter for details). Embassies in Bonn (telephone code ☎ 0228) include:

Australia
Godesberger Allee 105-107, 53175 Bonn (☎ 8 10 30)

Austria
Johanniterstrasse 2, 53113 Bonn (☎ 53 00 60)

Canada
Godesberger Allee 119, 53113 Bonn (☎ 812 3410)

France
An der Marienkapelle 3, 53179 Bonn (☎ 955 60 00)

New Zealand
Bundeskanzlerplatz 2-10, 53113 Bonn (☎ 22 80 70)

Switzerland
Gotenstrasse 156, 53175 Bonn (☎ 81 00 80)

UK
Friedrich-Ebert-Allee 77, 53113 Bonn (☎ 23 40 61)

USA
Deichmanns Aue 29, 53179 Bonn (☎ 33 91)

CUSTOMS

Most items needed for personal use during a visit are duty-free. When entering Germany from another EU country, visitors can bring 800 cigarettes, 200 cigars, or one kilogram of tobacco; 10 litres of spirits (more than 22% alcohol by volume), 20 litres of fortified wine or aperitif; 90 litres of wine or 110 litres of beer.

All other goods for personal use are free. From non-EU countries, duty-free allowances are 200 cigarettes, 50 cigars, or 250 grams of tobacco; one litre of strong liquor or two litres of less than 22% alcohol by volume; two litres of wine; 50 grams of perfume and 0.25 litres of toilet water; and other products to a value of DM115. Petrol reserves up to 10 litres are duty-free.

When entering from a non-European country, visitors can bring 400 cigarettes, 100 cigars, or 500 grams of tobacco; liquor, perfume and import restrictions are the same as for non-EU neighbours.

Tobacco products and alcohol may only be brought in by people aged 17 and over. There are no currency import restrictions.

MONEY

The German Mark, or Deutschmark (DM), consists of 100 pfennig (Pf). Germans refer to it as the Mark or D-Mark (pronounced 'day-mark'). The easiest places to change cash in Germany are banks or foreign exchange counters at airports and train stations, particularly those of the Deutsche Verkehrs Bank (DVB). Main banks in larger cities generally have automatic money-changing machines for after-hours use, but they don't give very good rates. Post offices often have money-changing facilities as well, and rates for cash – but not for travellers' cheques – tend to be better than at banks.

Travellers' cheques are widely used and accepted, especially if issued in Deutschmark denominations. If that's the case, you'll usually get the full amount, though bank branches at borders often charge a small commission, and post offices charge a flat DM6-per-cheque fee for any cheques outside the postal financial system. A commission of up to DM10 (ask first!) is charged every time you change foreign currency into DM.

The most widely accepted travellers' cheques are American Express, Thomas Cook and Barclays. American Express charges no commission on its own cheques, but the exchange rates aren't great if the cheques have to be converted into DM. Eurocheques are widely accepted (up to DM400 per cheque). DVB banks charge a commission of DM4 for cash payments on Eurocheques.

Credit cards are not always accepted outside major cities, but are handy for emergencies.

GERMANY

Hotels and restaurants often accept MasterCard, Visa and American Express. German banks prefer Eurocard, which is linked with Access and MasterCard, and in small towns you may have difficulty drawing cash with cards other than these three. Typically, over-the-counter cash advances against cards at major banks cost a flat DM10 per withdrawal, so it's better if you have automatic teller linkage (check fees and availability of services with your bank before you leave home). DVB offers the most convenient cash-for-card services and has offices at main train stations, but charges 1% commission or a minimum of DM7.50 (DM3 for small amounts) to change travellers' cheques.

Having money sent to Germany is fairly straightforward. American Express is a good bet, and transfers to large commercial banks are also easy, although you may have to open an account. For emergencies, DVB (Western Union) and Thomas Cook (MoneyGram) offer ready and fast international cash transfers through agent banks, but the commissions are costly.

Currency

Coinage includes one, two, five, 10, and 50 Pf, as well as DM1, DM2, and DM5. There are banknotes of DM5, 10, 20, 50, 100, 200, 500 and 1000. Beware of confusing the old DM5 and new DM20 banknotes, which are the same colour and have similar designs, although the DM20 note is larger, and watch out for counterfeit banknotes made on colour photocopy machines!

Exchange Rates

Australia	A$1	=	DM1.19
Austria	AS1	=	DM0.14
Canada	C$1	=	DM1.12
Denmark	Dkr1	=	DM0.26
France	1FF	=	DM0.29
Japan	¥100	=	DM1.38
Netherlands	Nethf1	=	DM0.89
New Zealand	NZ$1	=	DM0.98
Switzerland	Sfr	=	DM1.21
United Kingdom	UK£1	=	DM2.36
United States	US$1	=	DM1.52

Costs

With the monetary restructuring caused by reunification now easing, inflation has fallen

and the Deutschmark is relatively stable against most other European currencies. Prices have almost reached western levels in the cities of eastern Germany, but food and accommodation are generally quite affordable by Western European standards.

Tipping

Tipping is not widespread in Germany. In restaurants, service *(Bedienung)* is usually included but it is normal to round the bill up a bit if you're satisfied with the service. Do this as you pay, rather than leave money on the table. Taxi drivers, too, expect a slight tip. A tip of 10% is considered generous and is gratefully received.

Bargaining

Bargaining rarely occurs in Germany, but when paying cash for large purchases of more than, say, DM100, you could try asking for *Skonto*, which is a 3% discount. This doesn't apply to services like hotel and restaurant bills, however.

Consumer Taxes

Most German goods and services include a value-added tax (VAT, or *Mehrwertsteuer)* of 15%. Non-EU residents leaving the EU can have this tax refunded for goods (not services) bought, which is definitely worth it for large purchases.

Check that the shop where you're buying has the necessary Tax Refund Cheque forms which, together with the bills, must be stamped by German customs as you're leaving the country. You're not allowed to use the items purchased until you're out of Germany. Bus drivers and train conductors aren't likely to want to wait at the border while you're getting your paperwork stamped, so if you're travelling this way, ask the shop (or the tourist office) for the nearest customs authority that can do this beforehand. If you're flying out, have the paperwork stamped at the airport before you check in. Note that you will have to show the goods. The stamped forms, together with the bills, must be returned to the shop where the goods were bought. The shop will mail the refund, minus costs, to your home address.

Some 17,000 shops, including Germany's biggest department stores, are affiliated with the Tax Cheque Refund Service; they can be identified by a special label on their window – this makes the procedure a lot easier. The shop will issue you a cheque for the amount of value-added tax to be refunded, which you can have stamped and cash in when leaving the country (or the EU, if you are moving on to another EU country). You can obtain literature at affiliated shops, some tourist offices, major hotels, airports and harbours.

POST & COMMUNICATIONS

Post
Post offices are generally open from 8 am to 6 pm Monday to Friday and main offices to noon on Saturday. Many train station post offices stay open later.

Postal Rates Postcard rates are DM1 within Europe, DM2 to North America and Australasia; a 20-gram letter to anywhere in Europe costs DM1, a 50-gram letter DM2. Aerograms cost DM2, a 20-gram letter (by air to North America and Australasia) DM3. A 500-gram parcel to destinations outside Europe costs DM12 (surface) and DM24 (by air).

Receiving Mail Mail can be sent poste restante (*Postlagernde Briefe*) to the main post office in your city (no fee for collection). German post offices will only hold mail for two weeks, so plan your drops carefully.

You can also have your mail sent c/o American Express in any large city (address it with 'Client's Mail'). American Express holds mail for 30 days but won't accept registered mail or parcels. This service is free if you have an American Express card or travellers' cheques.

Telephone
Most pay phones in Germany accept only phonecards. These cards (available at post offices, news kiosks and some banks) can be used throughout the country. When using coins or the DM3, DM6 and DM12 phonecards, call units cost DM0.20, but with the DM50 card it's only DM0.19 per unit. Rates vary somewhat depending on when you ring. Within Germany, daytime call units last from around four minutes (local calls under 20 km), and decrease progressively to a minimum of 11.5 seconds per unit (calls over 200 km).

To ring abroad from Germany, dial ☎ 00 followed by the country code, area code and number. To EU countries and Germany's neighbours, daytime call units last 7.2 seconds, to the rest of Europe 5.3 seconds, to the USA and Canada five seconds, and to Australia, NZ, Hong Kong and Singapore 2.6 seconds.

Both domestic and international rates may drop significantly, however, once Germany opens up the monopolised telecommunications market to private competition from early 1998.

A reverse-charge call or *R-Gespräch* from Germany is only possible to a limited number of countries. For calls through the German operator, dial ☎ 0010. To reach the operator direct in the USA and Canada dial ☎ 0130 followed by 00 10 (AT&T), 00 12 (MCI), 00 13 (Sprint) or 00 14 (Canada). To Australia, dial ☎ 0130-80 06 61 for the Optus operator and ☎ 0130-80 00 61 for Telecom.

For international information call ☎ 0 01 18 (costs five telephone units); for local information, call ☎ 0 11 88 (three units).

Fax & Telegram
The best places to send faxes and telegrams from are main post offices. Faxes (sending or receiving) are expensive; some shops and businesses offer fax services a little more cheaply. Telegrams can be sent through the post office, from many hotels, or by calling ☎ 11 31.

NEWSPAPERS & MAGAZINES
Germany's cities can provide an overload of information, but away from major train stations and airports it's often difficult to obtain reading material of any kind in English.

The most widely read newspapers in Germany are *Die Welt*, *Bild*, *Frankfurter Allgemeine*, Munich's *Süddeutsche Zeitung*, and the green-leaning *Die Tageszeitung (Taz)*. Germany's most popular magazines are *Der Spiegel*, *Die Zeit* and *Stern*. The *International Herald Tribune*, *The European* and the *Economist* are available in most major cities, as are the international editions of *Time* and *Newsweek*.

RADIO & TV
Germany's two main TV channels are ARD and ZDF, while a third, *Drittes Programm*, features regional programming. The BBC World Service (on varying AM and FM wavelengths depending on which part of the country

GERMANY

you happen to be in) and National Public Radio (available via Astra 1B satellite or channel 22) have radio programmes in English.

PHOTOGRAPHY & VIDEO

Germany is a photographer's dream, whether in the Alps or the picturesque old towns. German film and photography equipment is among the best in the world and gear of all makes and types is readily available. For a roll of 36-exposure standard film (Kodak Gold or Agfa) expect to pay around DM7. Developing (if not included) will cost about DM6. Many 24-hour processing outlets also handle slides. The Porst chain offers specials with developing.

Camcorder users will pay around DM12 for a 60-minute Video 8 tape, or DM7 for a 30-minute VSC tape.

TIME

Germany is on Central European Time (GMT/UTC plus one hour), the same time zone as Madrid and Warsaw. Daylight-saving time comes into effect at the end of March, when clocks are turned one hour forward. At the end of September they're turned an hour back again. Times are usually indicated with the 24-hour clock, eg 6.30 pm is 18.30.

ELECTRICITY

Electricity is 220V, 50 Hz. European standard two-pronged plugs are used.

WEIGHTS & MEASURES

Germany uses the metric system. Like other Continental Europeans, Germans indicate decimals with commas and thousands with points. Cheese and other food items are often sold per *Pfund*, which means 500 grams.

LAUNDRY

You'll find a coin-operated laundry (*Münzwäscherei*) in most cities. Average costs are DM7 for the wash, plus DM1 per 15 minutes for drying. Some camping grounds and a few hostels also have them. Your best bet is to ask your hotel, hostel or camping ground manager. If you're staying in a private room, chances are your host will take care of your washing for a reasonable fee. Most major hotels provide laundering services for fairly steep fees.

TOILETS

Finding a public lavatory when you need one is not usually a problem in Germany, but you may have to pay anything from 20 to 80 Pf for the convenience. All train stations have toilets, and at those in main stations you can even shower for around DM3.50. The standard of hygiene is usually very high, although occasionally toilets can be surprisingly grotty – even in places where you'd least expect it, such as Nuremberg train station. Public toilets also exist in larger parks, pedestrian malls and inner-city shopping areas, where ultra-modern self-cleaning pay toilets (with wide automatic doorways that allow easy wheelchair access) are increasingly being installed.

HEALTH

Germany is a clean and healthy nation, with no particular health concerns. No vaccinations are required to visit Germany, except if you're coming from certain Third World areas. Tap water is safe to drink everywhere.

Most major hotels have doctors available. In an emergency, look in the telephone book under *Ärztlicher Notdienst* (Emergency Doctor Service). Emergency health care is free for EU citizens with an E111 form, but otherwise, any form of treatment can be very expensive, so make sure you have travel insurance.

WOMEN TRAVELLERS

Women should not encounter particular difficulties while travelling in Germany. The Lübeck-based organisation Frauen gegen Gewalt (☎ 0451-70 46 40), Marlesgrube 9, can offer advice if you are a victim of harassment or violence. Frauenhaus München (☎ 3 54 83 11, 24-hour service ☎ 35 48 30) in Munich also offers advice, and Frauennotruf (☎ 76 37 37) at Güllstrasse 3 in Munich can counsel victims of assault.

The women's movement is very active in Germany. Most larger cities have women-only cafés, ride and accommodation-sharing services, or cultural organisations exclusively for women such as the Frauenkulturhaus (☎ 4 70 52 12), at Richard-Strauss-Strasse 21 in Munich, or the Frankfurt Frauenkulturhaus (☎ 70 10 17) at Industriehof 7-9.

GAY & LESBIAN TRAVELLERS

Germans are generally fairly tolerant of homosexuality, but gays (who call themselves *Schwule*) and lesbians (or *Lesben*) still don't enjoy quite the same social acceptance as in certain other northern European countries. Most progressive are the largest cities, particularly Berlin and Frankfurt, where the sight of homosexual couples holding hands is not uncommon, although kissing in public is rather less common. Larger cities have many gay and lesbian bars as well as other meeting places for homosexuals, such as the Lesbisch-Schwules Kulturhaus (☎ 069-297 72 96), at Klingerstrasse 6, a gay and lesbian cultural centre in Frankfurt.

DISABLED TRAVELLERS

Germany caters well to the needs of disabled travellers, with access ramps for wheelchairs and/or lifts where necessary in public buildings, including toilets (see special heading above), train stations, museums, theatres and cinemas. All InterCity Express (ICE), InterCity/EuroCity (IC/EC), and InterRegio (IR) trains, suburban (S-Bahn) and underground (U-Bahn) trains and ferry services have easy wheelchair access, but stepped entrances to trams and buses remain obstacles.

DANGERS & ANNOYANCES

Theft and other crimes against travellers are relatively rare. In the event of problems, the police are helpful and efficient. In most areas, the emergency number for the police is ☎ 110.

Be careful in crowded train stations, where pickpockets are often active. Don't allow anyone to help you put your luggage into a coin locker. Once they've closed the locker, they might switch keys and later come back to pick up your things. Begging for small change is becoming prevalent in crowded city centres.

Africans, Asians and southern Europeans may encounter racial prejudice, especially in eastern Germany where they have been singled out as convenient scapegoats for economic hardship, though the animosity is directed against immigrants, not tourists. People in eastern Germany are becoming used to foreigners, though a few may still feel a bit awkward in your presence.

BUSINESS HOURS

Shop opening hours in Germany have recently been extended to allow trading from 6 am until 8 pm on weekdays, until 4 pm on Saturday, and for a maximum of three hours on Sunday. Larger stores – particularly supermarkets – are expected to take full advantage of this.

Banking hours are generally from 8.30 am to 1 pm and from 2.30 to 4 pm Monday to Friday (many stay open later on Thursday). Government offices close for the weekend at 1 or 3 pm on Friday. Museums are generally closed on Monday; opening hours vary greatly, although many art museums are open later one evening per week.

Restaurants tend to open from 10 am to midnight, with varying closing days. Many of the cheap restaurants are closed on Saturday afternoon and Sunday. All shops and banks are closed on public holidays (see below).

PUBLIC HOLIDAYS & SPECIAL EVENTS

Germany has many holidays, some of which vary from state to state. Public holidays include New Year's Day; Good Friday to Easter Monday; 1 May (Labour Day); Whit Monday, Ascension Day, Pentecost, Corpus Christi (10 days after Pentecost); 3 October (Day of German Unity); 1 November (All Saints' Day); 18 November (Day of Prayer and Repentance); and usually Christmas Eve to the day after Christmas.

There are many festivals, fairs and cultural events throughout the year. Famous and worthwhile ones include:

January
   The carnival season (Shrovetide, known as *Fasching* in Bavaria) begins, with many carnival events in large cities, most notably Cologne, Munich, Düsseldorf and Mainz; the partying peaks just before Ash Wednesday.
February
   International Toy Fair in Nuremberg, International Film Festival in Berlin
March
   Frankfurt Music Fair; Frankfurt Jazz Fair; Thuringian Bach Festival; many spring fairs throughout Germany; Sommergewinn Festival in Eisenach
April
   Stuttgart Jazz Festival; Munich Ballet Days; Mannheim May Fair; Walpurgis Festivals – the night before May Day in Harz Mountains
May
   International Mime Festival in Stuttgart; Red Wine Festival in Rüdesheim; Dresden International Dixie-

land Jazz Festival; Dresden Music Festival (last week of May into first week of June)

June

Moselle Wine Week in Cochem; Händel Festival in Halle; sailing regatta in Kiel; Munich Film Festival; International Theatre Festival in Freiburg

July

Folk festivals throughout Germany; Munich Opera Festival; Richard Wagner Festival in Bayreuth; German-American Folk Festival in Berlin; Kulmbach Beer Festival; International Music Seminar in Weimar

August

Heidelberg Castle Festival; wine festivals throughout the Rhineland area

September-October

Munich's Oktoberfest, the world's biggest beer festival; Berlin Festival of Music & Drama

October

Frankfurt Book Fair; Bremen Freimarkt; Gewandhaus Festival in Leipzig; Berlin Jazzfest

November

St Martin's Festival throughout Rhineland and Bavaria

December

Many Christmas fairs throughout Germany, most famously in Munich, Nuremberg, Berlin, Essen and Heidelberg

ACTIVITIES

The Germans are active outdoors people, which means there are plenty of facilities for like-minded visitors.

Cycling

Cycling is a favoured recreation. You'll often find marked cycling routes, and eastern Germany has much to offer cyclists in the way of lightly travelled back roads and a well-developed hostel network, especially in the flat, less populated north. Offshore islands like Amrum and Rügen are ready-made for pedal-powered travellers.

For details on Deutsche Bahn's Fahrrad am Bahnhof network and more tips, see Cycling in the following Getting Around section. Always have a good lock for your bike.

Hiking & Mountaineering

Walking trails crisscross the German landscape, with more than 100,000 km of marked trails throughout the country. Popular areas for hiking are the Black Forest, Harz Mountains, the Bavarian Forest, the so-called Saxon Switzerland area and the Thuringian Forest. The Bavarian Alps offer the most inspiring scenery, however, and are the centre of mountaineering

in Germany, with some 50 mountain huts available to climbers and walkers.

The Verband Deutscher Gebirgs-und Wandervereine (Federation of German Hiking Clubs), at Reichsstrasse 4, 66111 Saarbrücken, and the Deutscher Alpenverein (German Alpine Club, ☎ 089-14 00 30) at Von-Kahr-Strasse 2-4, 80997 Munich, are the best sources of information on walking and mountaineering in Germany.

Steam Train Excursions & Joy Flights

Railway enthusiasts will be excited by the wide range of special excursions by old steam trains organised by the Deutsche Bahn. For more information, ask for the free booklet Nostalgiezüge at any large train station in Germany.

For an experience with a difference, consider the special Lufthansa flights available from 40 airports in and around German cities. Flown by slow, angular 1930s Junkers JU-52/3 transport planes, these flights, though expensive, give breathtaking views of German cities in a 30-minute circuit. One way to cut the DM260 cost is to head to eastern Germany, where flights are only 20 minutes long and cost DM175. To book in advance, write or send a fax to Lufthansa Traditionsflug GmbH (fax 040-50 70 50 61), Box 630300, 22313 Hamburg. In Germany, call ☎ 040-50 70 17 17.

Skiing

The Bavarian Alps are the most extensive area for downhill and cross-country skiing, and Garmisch-Partenkirchen is the most popular Alpine resort. Those who wish to avoid the glitz, glamour and prices there may want to try the Black Forest or the Harz Mountains. The skiing season generally runs from early December to late March. In the shoulder season, discounted ski package weeks are advertised by Weisse Wochen signs in tourist offices, hotels and ski resorts.

All winter resorts have rental facilities. The lowest daily rate for a set of downhill gear is DM20, and daily ski-lift passes start at around DM30.

WORK

With unemployment running at historically high levels, Germany is not what you'd call a prime job-hunting area. Citizens of the EU may work in Germany; otherwise no temporary work permits are available. Street artists and hawkers are widespread in the cities, though you should ask the municipal authority about permits.

To get an idea of the sorts of jobs available, check the *Stellenmarkt* (Employment Market) ads in the classified sections of big-city newspapers. Sometimes advertisers for unskilled labour are mainly interested in finding cheap workers and are not concerned whether or not you're legally authorised to work in Germany. Jobs are offered under the heading *Biete*, while people looking for work advertise themselves under *Suche*.

Two organisations that organise *unpaid* cooperative work and study camps (many of which are conducted in English) are the Christlicher Friedensdienst (☎ 069-45 90 72), Rendeler Strasse 9-11, 60385 Frankfurt/Main, and the Studienkreis für Tourismus (☎ 081-77 17 83), at Kapellenweg 3, 82541 Ammerland.

ACCOMMODATION

Accommodation in Germany is generally well organised, though since privatisation eastern Germany has been a little short on budget beds; private rooms are one option in these emergencies. If you're after a hotel or private room, head straight for the tourist office and use the room-finding service *(Zimmervermittlung)*, which normally costs DM3 to DM5. Staff will usually go out of their way to find something in your price range, although telephone bookings are not always available. The German Tourist Board associate ADZ Room Reservation Service (☎ 069-75 10 56), Corneliusstrasse 34, 60325 Frankfurt/Main is a national booking agency.

Accommodation usually includes breakfast. Look for signs saying 'Zimmer frei' (rooms available) or 'Fremdenzimmer' (tourist rooms) in house or shop windows of many towns. In official resorts and spas, displayed prices usually include *Kurtaxe* (resort tax) levies, but you should check (see the following Hostels section).

Camping

With over 2000 organised camping grounds, tenting makes an excellent overnighting alternative. If you want to make camping your main form of accommodation, however, you'll probably need your own transport, since sites tend to be far from city centres.

Most camping grounds are open from April to September, but several hundred stay open throughout the year. The range of facilities varies greatly, from the primitive to the over-equipped and serviced. In eastern Germany camping grounds often rent out small bungalows. For camping on private property, permission from the landowner is required.

The best overall source of information is the Deutscher Camping Club, Mandlstrasse 28, 80802 Munich. Local tourist information sources can help too.

Hostels

The Deutsches Jugendherbergswerk or DJH (☎ 05231-7 40 10; fax 05231- 74 01 49, or write to: Hauptverband, Postfach 1455 32704 Detmold), coordinates all affiliated Hostelling International (HI) hostels in Germany.

With more than 600 of them conveniently located throughout the country, Germany's youth hostel network is arguably the best and most extensive in the world – which is to be expected of the country that pioneered the concept. Almost all hostels in Germany are open all year. Guests must be members of a Hostelling International-affiliated organisation, but it's possible to join the DJH when checking in for an annual fee of DM19/32 juniors/seniors.

The charge for a dorm bed in a DJH hostel varies from about DM18 to DM30. Camping at a hostel (where permitted) is usually half-price. If you don't have a hostel-approved sleeping sheet, it usually costs from DM5 to DM7 to hire one (some hostels insist you hire one anyway). Breakfast is always included in the overnight price. Lunch or an evening meal cost between DM5 and DM9.

Theoretically, visitors aged under 27 get preference, but in practice prior booking or arrival determines who gets rooms, not age. In Bavaria, though, the strict maximum age for anyone except group leaders or parents accompanying a child is 27. Check-in hours vary, but you must usually be out by 9 am. You don't need to do chores at the hostels and there are few rules.

The DJH's *Jugendgästehäuser* (youth guesthouses) offer some better facilities, freer hours and sometimes good single rooms from DM35.

Pensions & Guesthouses

Pensions offer the basics of hotel comfort without asking hotel prices. Many of these are private houses with several rooms to rent, a bit out of the centre of town. Some proprietors are a little sensitive about who they take in and others are nervous about telephone bookings – you may have to give a time of arrival and stick to it (many well-meaning visitors have lost rooms by turning up late).

Cheap Hotels

Budget hotel rooms can be a bit hard to come by in Germany during the summer months, although there is usually not much seasonal price variation. The cheapest hotels only have rooms with shared toilets (and showers) in the corridor.

Expensive Hotels

Expensive hotels in Germany provide few advantages for their up-market prices. The best time to splurge on them is during weekends or lulls in trade-fair activity, when you can sometimes take advantage of a package deal or special discounts.

Longer-Term Rentals

Renting an apartment for a week or more is a popular form of holiday accommodation in Germany. Look in newspaper classifieds for *Ferienwohnungen* or *Ferien-Apartments*, or – particularly if you want shared accommodation somewhere in an urban centre – contact the local *Mitwohnzentrale* (accommodation-finding service). Rates vary widely, but are invariably lower than hotels and decrease dramatically with the length of stay.

FOOD

Germans are hearty eaters, but this is truly a meat-and-potatoes kind of country, though vegetarian and health-conscious restaurants are beginning to sprout. Restaurants always display their menus outside with prices, but watch for daily specials chalked onto blackboards. Beware of early closing hours, and of the *Ruhetag* (rest day) at some establishments. Tipping is not necessary, although you might round up the bill as you're paying. Lunch is the main meal of the day; getting a main meal in the evening is never a problem, but you may find that the dish or menu of the day only applies to lunch.

A *Gaststätte* is somewhat less formal than a *Restaurant*, while a *Weinkeller* or *Bierkeller* would be fine for a lighter meal. Many town halls have an atmospheric restaurant, or *Ratskeller*, in the basement, serving traditional German dishes at reasonable prices.

A good German breakfast usually includes rolls, butter, jam, cheese, several sliced meats, a hard-boiled egg, and coffee or tea. Germans at home might eat their heaviest meal at noon and then have lighter evening fare (*Abendbrot* or *Abendessen*, consisting of cheeses and bread).

Cafés & Bars

Much of the German daily and social life revolves around these institutions, which are often hard to separate as both coffee and alcohol are usually served. They're great places to meet locals without spending too much money. A wonderful German invention is the quick-and-cheap *Stehcafé*, a 'stand-up' café where you can go to indulge in that sinful European habit of coffee and cakes – without spending too much time and money doing so.

Snacks

If you're on a low budget, you can get a feed at stand-up food stalls *(Schnellimbiss* or simply *Imbiss)* in all the towns. The food is usually quite reasonable and filling, ranging from döner kebabs to traditional German sausages with beer.

Main Dishes

Sausage *(Wurst)*, in its hundreds of forms, is by far the most popular main dish. Regional favourites include *Bratwurst* (spiced sausage), *Weisswurst* (veal sausage) and *Blutwurst* (blood sausage). In Berlin, *Eisbein* (pickled pork knuckles) is the dish of choice. Other popular choices include *Rippenspeer* (spare ribs), *Rotwurst* (black pudding), *Rostbrätl* (grilled meat) and many forms of *Schnitzel* (breaded pork or veal cutlet).

Potatoes feature prominently in German meals, either fried *(Bratkartoffeln)*, mashed *(Kartoffelpüree)*, grated and then fried (the Swiss *Rösti*), or as French fries *(Pommes*

Frites); a Thuringian speciality is Klösse, a ball of mashed and raw potato which is then cooked to produce something like a dumpling. In Baden-Württemberg, potatoes are often replaced by Spätzle – wide, flattened noodles.

Italian, Chinese and other ethnic cuisines are available as mid-price options.

Desserts
Germans are keen on rich desserts. A popular choice is the Schwarzwälder Kirschtorte (Black Forest cherry cake), which is one worthwhile tourist trap. Desserts and pastries are also often enjoyed during another German tradition, the 4 pm coffee break.

Fruit
Except, perhaps, for bananas, Germans are modest fruit eaters. However, groceries and markets generally have a broad, if expensive, selection of fruits, which are often air-freighted from as far away as California, South Africa and New Zealand.

Self-Catering
It's very easy and relatively cheap to put together picnic meals in any town. Simply head for the local market or supermarket and stock up on breads, sandwich meats, cheeses, wine and beer. Chains such as Penny-Markt and Norma can be good places to start, though they may lack a wide range.

DRINKS
Buying beverages can get very expensive. Be very careful at restaurants and, if you like lots of liquids, make a point of buying your drinks in supermarkets.

Nonalcoholic Drinks
The most popular choices are mineral water and soft drinks. Nonalcoholic beers are very good and have become quite popular. Löwenbräu makes an especially tasty nonalcoholic beer that is frequently served on tap.

Alcohol
Beer is the national beverage and it's one cultural phenomenon that must be adequately explored. The beer is excellent and still relatively cheap. Each region and brewery has its own distinctive taste and body.

Beer-drinking in Germany has its own vocabulary. Vollbier is 4% alcohol by volume, Export is 5% and Bockbier is 6%. Helles Bier is light, while dunkles Bier is dark. Export is similar to, but much better than, typical international brews, while the Pils is more bitter. Alt is darker and more full-bodied. A speciality is Weizenbier, which is made with wheat instead of barley malt and served in a tall, half-litre glass with a slice of lemon.

Eastern Germany's best beers hail from Saxony, especially Radeberger Pils from near Dresden and Wernesgrüner from the Erzgebirge on the Czech border. Berliner Weisse, or 'Berlin white', is a foaming, low-alcohol wheat beer mixed with red or green fruit syrup. The breweries of Cologne produce their own specialities, and in Bamberg Schlenkerla Rauchbier is smoked to a dark-red colour.

German wines are exported around the world, and for good reason. German wines are typically white, light and relatively sweet. As with beer, the cheaper wines are almost as cheap as bottled water or soft drinks, and quite good. Germans usually ask for a Schoppen of whatever – a solid wine glass holding 200 or 250 ml. A Weinschorle or Spritzer is white wine mixed with mineral water. Wines don't have to be drunk with meals. The Rhine and Moselle valleys are the classic wine-growing regions, but Franconian labels are also popular. The Ebbelwei of Hesse is a strong apple wine with an earthy flavour.

ENTERTAINMENT
The German heritage is associated with high culture, and the standard of theatre performances, concerts and operas is among the best in Europe. Berlin is unrivalled when it comes to concerts and theatre, Dresden is famed for its opera, and Hamburg is (by now) synonymous with Cats.

Cinemas
Films are widely appreciated in Germany, but foreign films are usually dubbed into German. English-language subtitled options (usually identifiable by the letter-code 'OF') are mostly limited to large cities like Berlin, Munich, Hamburg and Frankfurt.

Nightclubs
Because of the German preference for pubs offering beer and conversation, nightclubs are

not especially popular outside large cities. Many of these clubs are in international hotels, patronised by foreigners with money to burn. There are, however, exceptions, and any young local or tourist office can point you in the right direction.

SPECTATOR SPORT

Soccer is the sport of choice for the masses who like to watch rather than participate; almost every city or town has at least one team and stadium. The international success of German players has greatly boosted the popularity of tennis. Motor racing attracts huge and enthusiastic crowds, reflecting both the Germans' special relationship with the automobile and the driving expertise of Michael Schumacher. Winter sports have always held a special place in the German heart.

THINGS TO BUY

Products made in Germany are rarely cheap, but the higher prices are generally compensated for by much better quality. Worthwhile industrial goods include optical lenses, fine crystal glassware (particularly from the Bavarian Forest), fine porcelain (particularly from Meissen) and therapeutic footwear, such as the sandles and shoes made by Birkenstock, or orthopaedic inlays by Scholl. Art reproductions, books and posters are sold in some museums and specialty shops. Germany's fine regional wines give you a real taste of the country to take back home. More predictable souvenirs include colourful heraldic emblems, cuckoo clocks from the Black Forest, Bavarian wooden carvings and traditional Bavarian clothing.

Getting There & Away

AIR

The main arrival/departure points in Germany are Frankfurt, Munich, Düsseldorf and Berlin – Frankfurt is Europe's busiest airport after Heathrow. Flights are generally priced competitively among all major airlines, but Lufthansa offers the most flexibility. The German charter company LTU makes regular

scheduled international flights, but these fill up quickly.

Flights to Frankfurt are usually cheaper than to other German cities. Regular flights from Western Europe to Germany tend to be more expensive than the train or bus, but not always: discount air tickets from London can be less than £100 return. Lufthansa alone has about 40 flights a day from the UK to Germany. It also flies from North America, Australia and New Zealand. Munich's new airport handles most main Lufthansa flights to and from southern Germany. Lufthansa's central reservation and flight information number is ☎ 01803-80 38 03 and can be dialled from anywhere in Germany at 24 Pf per minute.

It might be worth looking into the various fly/drive or flight/accommodation packages put together by travel agents or the airlines. Lufthansa often has special deals, particularly from the USA, and if you plan to hire a car, prices can be very attractive.

Lufthansa also has regular connections with the Baltic States, Belarus, Ukraine and cities in Russia, including Moscow and St Petersburg. It flies to Prague from Düsseldorf, Hamburg and Frankfurt and to Budapest and Warsaw from Berlin; there are many discount options.

LAND
Bus

If you're already in Europe, it's generally cheaper to get to/from Germany by bus than it is by train or plane. Some of the coaches are quite luxurious, with toilet, air-con and snack bar. Advance reservations may be necessary, and any German travel agency should be able to tell you where to place them. Return fares are noticeably cheaper than two one-way fares.

Eurolines has a youth fare for those aged under 26 that saves around 10%. The company operates daily services between London and Frankfurt which cost DM120/182 (adult one way/return), and four services a week (Thursday, Friday, Saturday and Monday) between London and Munich (DM140/216). Frankfurt-Paris tickets cost DM92/163. Other Eurolines services include Frankfurt-Warsaw (DM95/155), Nuremberg-Prague (DM55/90), Munich-Paris (DM125/209) and Munich-Budapest (DM110/165). Eurolines is represented in

Germany by Deutsche Touring (☎ 069-7 90 30 or 7 90 32 51), Am Römerhof 17, 60486 Frankfurt/Main, though travel agents should be able to help you with tickets. For frequent travellers, there's a Eurolines Pass, offering unlimited travel for either 30 days (DM515) or 60 days (DM620), but you must buy it in person from the company's offices at Frankfurt Hauptbahnhof.

Train

Train is a good way to get to Germany if you're already in Western Europe and it's a lot more comfortable (if quite a bit more expensive) than the bus. But it is worth noting that, although the daytime services are frequent, rapid, and comfortable, overnight international trains are increasingly being made up of sleeping cars only, and the few seats are usually 2nd class. Generally speaking, though, travelling in 2nd class on German trains is perfectly acceptable and comfortable, and considerably cheaper than 1st.

Berlin-Warsaw services via Poznan run several times a day (to and from Berlin Hauptbahnhof or Berlin-Lichtenberg); at least once daily these connect to Paris (the *Nord-Express* runs each evening through Berlin-Zoo). There are also daily trains to Moscow and St Petersburg, both via Warsaw from Berlin-Lichtenberg.

Berlin-Prague trains leave several times daily to and from Berlin-Lichtenberg (a few of these originate in or continue to Hamburg) and they run via Dresden. Some continue to Vienna or Bratislava and Budapest, and at least one train daily connects to and from Bucharest. There are also a few direct services to Prague from Dresden, Munich and Nuremberg. Direct Salzburg-Munich trains leave almost every half-hour, and most connect hourly to and from Vienna or with services to and from Zagreb and Budapest. Several direct trains run daily between Munich and Innsbruck (via Kufstein), and there are also connections available via Garmisch-Partenkirchen. You can also get trains to Bregenz in western Austria, from where you can connect for Switzerland. There are direct trains from Frankfurt to Basel and Konstanz and fast links between Stuttgart and Zürich (and further into Italy).

Eurail passes are not valid to Prague, but you can buy a 'Eurodomino' extension that lets you travel in the Czech Republic. A three-day ticket costs DM80 for adults and DM59 for those under 26; a five-day ticket is DM115/86 and a 10-day ticket costs DM191/143. It's best to buy these tickets at the Eurail Aid offices at train stations in nine German cities, including Berlin, Frankfurt and Hamburg. Details are in the information brochures issued with your ticket.

Train passes are also valid on some suburban trains (S-Bahns), such as Munich-Augsburg, Berlin and the system encompassing Cologne, Düsseldorf and Bonn. Beware: you cannot use other local transport, including underground trains (U-Bahns) in this way.

Car & Motorcycle

Germany is served by an excellent highway system. If you're coming from the UK, the quickest option (apart from the Channel Tunnel) is to take the car ferry or Hovercraft from Dover, Folkestone or Ramsgate to Boulogne or Calais in France. You can be in Germany three hours after the ferry docks.

In the south, the main gateways are Munich, Freiburg and Passau, although the mountain autobahn Felbertauernstrasse gives superb Alpine views as it takes you through Kufstein into Austria at Kitzbühel (and on to Trieste or Venice if you wish).

Heading for Poland during main holidays, you might find border delays, particularly during Easter at the main crossing of Frankfurt an der Oder.

You must be third-party insured to enter Germany with a car or motorcycle.

Hitching & Ride Services

Hitchhikers should not have too many problems getting to and from Germany via the main highways. Aside from hitchhiking, the cheapest way to get to Germany from elsewhere in Europe is as a paying passenger in a private car. Leaving Germany, or travelling within the country, such rides are arranged by *Mitfahrzentrale* agencies in many German cities. You pay a reservation fee to the agency and a share of petrol and costs to the driver. The local tourist office will be able to direct you to several such agencies, or you can check under 'Mitfahrzentrale' in the Yellow Pages phone book. Most of those mentioned in this chapter belong either to the large Arbeitsgemeinschaft

GERMANY

Deutscher Mitfahrzentralen (ADM – ☎ 1 94 40 in most cities), where you pay DM45 from Hamburg to Amsterdam (DM90 to Paris), or the computer-equipped Citynetz Mitfahr-Service (☎ 1 94 44), which has booking fees up to DM33, and inclusive prices from Frankfurt to Paris of DM60 (to Basel DM38).

SEA

If you're heading to/from the UK or Scandinavia, the port options are Hamburg, Cuxhaven, Lübeck and Kiel. The Hamburg-Harwich run carries a growing volume of passengers, and a Newcastle-Hamburg ferry sails every four days from April to October. The Puttgarden-Rødbyhavn ferry is popular with those heading to Copenhagen (see the Hamburg Getting There & Away section for details). In eastern Germany, there are five ferries in each direction daily all year between Trelleborg (Sweden) and Sassnitz Hafen near Stralsund (see the Rügen Island section).

There is a daily service between Kiel and Gothenburg (Sweden). A ferry between Travemünde (near Lübeck) and Trelleborg (Sweden) runs four times daily. Ferries also run several times a week between the Danish island of Bornholm and Sassnitz Hafen. Carferry service is also good from Gedser (Denmark) to Rostock. Travemünde-Helsinki 24-hour high-speed runs are available in summer. Baltic Line sails from Kiel (on Saturday only) to St Petersburg (with connections to Riga). See the Rostock, Warnemünde, Kiel, Stralsund and Rügen Island Getting There & Away sections for more details.

LEAVING GERMANY

There is an airport departure tax of DM6 to DM8 per person leaving Germany. This cost is included in ticket prices. There is no departure tax if you depart by sea or land.

Getting Around

AIR

There are lots of flights within the country, but costs can be prohibitive compared to the train. Lufthansa, together with its charter subsidiary,

LTU, has the most frequent air services within Germany. Foreign airlines also offer services between major cities. There are several small airlines that offer services between regional cities, as well as to and from the North Frisian Islands.

BUS

As with the train system, the bus network in Germany is excellent and comprehensive. For trips of any distance, however, the train is faster and generally as cheap. Buses are better geared towards regional travel in areas where the terrain makes train travel more difficult.

Europabus, the motorcoach system of Europe's railways, operates within Germany as Deutsche Touring GmbH, a subsidiary of the German Federal Railways (Deutsche Bahn, DB). Europabus services include the Romantic and Castle roads buses in southern Germany, as well as organised bus tours of Germany lasting a week or more. See the Frankfurt and Romantic Road sections for details, or contact the Deutsche Touring GmbH main booking office (☎ 069-790 30), Römerhof 17, 60486 Frankfurt/Main.

TRAIN

Operated almost entirely by the Deutsche Bahn (DB), the German train system is arguably the best in Europe.

DB's InterCity Express (ICE) trains offer ultrarapid services and special fares apply. Travelling at speeds of over 250 km/h, ICE trains now dominate some long distance routes between large cities, such as Frankfurt-Berlin (DM266/178 1st/2nd class) and Hamburg-Munich (DM359/239 1st/2nd class). ICE trains also run other major city-to-city routes such as Cologne-Nuremberg, but these routes are still mainly serviced by rather less rapid InterCity (IC) and international EuroCity (EC) trains or the long distance InterRegio (IR) express trains. For all IC trains a supplementary charge applies (DM6, or DM8 if purchased from the conductor); holders of Eurail, Inter-Rail and German rail passes do not pay supplements on ICE or IC trains. There are also slower D and E trains, which generally run regional and night services.

At many train stations passengers are required to buy tickets from vending machines for distances under 100 km – it's generally more convenient anyway. If you're travelling further than anywhere indicated on the machine, press button X for the maximum fare and contact the conductor on board. Holders of the BahnCard (see below) should press the '½' or 'Kind' (child) button for a half-price ticket. Tickets can usually be bought from the conductor for a surcharge of DM5 (or DM10 for ICE trains), but an increasing number of (generally slower, regional) services operate without a conductor. For these trains passengers are required to buy a ticket *before* boarding, so ask if in any doubt. Anyone caught without a valid ticket receives a fine of DM60.

All larger train stations in Germany have coin-operated 24-hour left-luggage lockers (DM2/4 for small/large lockers). *Gepäckaufbewahrung* (left-luggage) counters are sometimes more convenient and charge similar rates. Luggage can be sent door to door by *Kuriergepäck* to any address within Western Europe for DM28.

Tickets & Reservations

For ticket and timetable information (available in English) you can call ☎ 1 94 19 from anywhere in Germany for the cost of a local call.

The per-km price for train travel in western Germany is roughly 26 Pf/39 Pf for 2nd/1st class. Fares in the eastern states are still around 10% lower, but are gradually being adjusted up to those in the west.

Single tickets of over 100 km are valid up to four days, and there's normally no problem breaking your journey (though you should advise the conductor). Return tickets cost exactly double, but if the combined distance is more than 100 km they're valid for one month (two months for international return tickets). Train tickets and passes are also valid on the S-Bahn except in Berlin.

On holidays and in the busy summer season, reservations are recommended for longer journeys or sleeping compartments. Seat reservation costs a flat DM3, regardless of the number of people. Most night trains are equipped with 1st-class and 2nd-class sleeping compartments (four or six people per compartment), which must be booked at least one day beforehand; otherwise turn up on the platform and ask the conductor. The surcharge for the simplest 2nd-class D-train sleeping bunk is DM8 (or DM26 with sheets and other services); more expensive sleeping car tickets are available for three or two-bed compartments, and also one-bed compartments in 1st class.

German Rail Passes

German Rail Passes are a relatively inexpensive way of getting around and allow you to avoid the often long ticket queues. The standard German Rail Pass is available to anyone not resident in Germany, and entitles you to unlimited 1st or 2nd-class travel for five, 10 or 15 days within a one-month period. The 1st-class German Rail Pass costs US$260, US$410 and US$530 respectively, or for the 2nd-class version US$178, US$286 and US$386. A similar setup is the German Rail Youth Pass, limited to 2nd-class travel by those aged between 12 and 25, which costs US$138, US$188 and US$238 respectively. The German Rail Twin Pass for couples costs US$267, US$429 and US$579 respectively (2nd class). These passes can be obtained in the UK, Australia or the USA, and at all major train stations in Germany itself (passport required). They are valid on all trains, DB buses, and some river services operated by the Köln-Düsseldorfer Line. Of course, Inter-Rail and Eurail passes are also good within Germany.

Ticket Discounts

Apart from youth, student and senior discounts on some tickets, there are various permanent and temporary reduced-rate ticket offers available.

If you intend travelling entirely within Germany for longer than one month, the BahnCard may be a cheaper option. The Bahncard is available for half price (DM110) to all 'juniors' over 17 and under 23 years of age, as well as to students under 27. People aged 17 or less pay only DM50 for the Bahncard. The 1st-class/2nd-class BahnCard costs DM220/440 (DM110/220 for juniors, people over 60 years, students and cardholders' spouses) and is valid for one year; it allows you to buy train tickets (including IC and ICE, but *not* S-Bahn or U-Bahn trains) and many regional bus tickets for half-price.

The Sparpreis, a return ticket between any two stations in Germany, costs DM199, and accompanying passengers pay only DM99. It remains valid for 30 days, but you may not

GERMANY

complete the return trip within a *single* Monday-to-Friday period.

If arriving very late is not a problem, the Guten-Abend-Ticket is good value. It's valid for unlimited train travel from 7 pm until 2 am, and costs DM59/99 in 2nd/1st class (or DM69/109 in 2nd/1st class with ICE option); there's a flat DM15 surcharge on weekends. Another great deal is the Schönes-Wochenende-Ticket for just DM35. It's valid from 12 am Saturday until 2 am Monday - that's a whole weekend - and allows up to five people to travel together on slower local trains but *not* ICE, IC, IR, or SE trains anywhere in Germany; in most cities it even gives free travel on public transport, but check first.

CAR & MOTORCYCLE

German roads are excellent, and motorised transport can be a great way to tour the country. Prices for fuel vary from DM1.50 to DM1.65 per litre for unleaded super, and DM1.60 to DM1.75 per litre for leaded super. Avoid buying fuel at more expensive autobahn filling stations.

The autobahn system of motorways runs throughout Germany. Road signs (and most motoring maps) indicate national autobahn routes in blue with an 'A' number, while international routes have green signs with an 'E' number. Though very efficient, the autobahns are often busy, and literally present life in the fast lane. Tourists often have trouble coping with the very high speeds and the dangers involved in overtaking – don't overestimate the time it takes for a car in the rearview mirror to close in at 180 km/h. Secondary roads are easier on the nerves, much more scenic, and still present a fairly fast way of getting from A to B.

Cars are less practical in the centre of most cities because one-way streets and extensive pedestrian zones are common. Vending machines in the streets of many innercity areas sell parking vouchers which must be displayed clearly behind the windscreen, but it's usually more convenient to leave your car at a central *Parkhaus* (car park) and proceed on foot. Most cities have automated car parks with signs indicating available space; rates are roughly DM20 per day or DM2.50 per hour.

To find passengers willing to pay their share of the petrol (gasoline) costs, drivers should contact the local *Mitfahrzentrale* (see Hitching & Ride Services in Getting There & Away section).

Germany's main motoring organisation is the Allgemeiner Deutscher Automobil Club (ADAC, ☎ 089-7 67 60 or fax 089-76 76 28 01), whose main office is at Am Westpark 8, 81373 Munich; it also has offices in all major cities. Call the ADAC road patrol if your car breaks down.

Road Rules

Road rules are easy to understand and standard international signs are in use. The usual speed limits are 50 km/h in built-up areas (in effect as soon as you see the yellow nameboard of the town) and 100 km/h on the open road. The speed on autobahns is unlimited, though there's an advisory speed of 130 km/h; exceptions are clearly signposted. The highest permissible blood-alcohol level for drivers is 0.08%. Obey the road rules carefully: the German police are very efficient and issue heavy on-the-spot fines; speed and red-light cameras are in widespread use, and notices are sent to the car's registration address wherever that may be.

Rental

Germany's four main rental companies are Avis, Europcar, Hertz and Sixt, but there are numerous smaller local rental companies. Three days car rental (of an Opel Corsa or a Ford Fiesta) can cost as little DM99. To hire you must usually be at least 21 years of age.

Fly/drive packages can give excellent value for money; Lufthansa offers deals from around US$25 per day if you book for longer than three weeks. Otherwise, shopping around upon arrival is preferable to making prior bookings.

Purchase

Due to the costs and paperwork hassles involved, buying a car in Germany tends to be an unwise option. Experienced car dealers from Eastern Europe pick over the bargains, so it's a lot easier purchasing (and reselling) a vehicle in other Western European countries.

Within Germany, Berlin is one of the best places to shop around for used cars if you know what to look for. Don't buy any vehicle without checking first that it has a current TÜV certificate of roadworthiness. The Berlin newspaper

Zweite Hand has a separate car edition with thousands of listings each week. Opel Corsas with more than a few years on the clock can sometimes be snapped up for as little as DM3000.

BICYCLE

Radwandern (bicycle touring) is very popular in Germany. In urban areas the pavement (sidewalk) is often divided into separate sections for pedestrians and cyclists – be warned that these divisions are taken very seriously. Even outside towns and cities there are often also separate cycling routes so you don't have to use the roads and highways. Favoured routes include the Rhine, Moselle and Danube rivers and the Lake Constance area. Of course, cycling is strictly *verboten* on the autobahns. Hostel-to-hostel biking is an easy way to go, and route guides are often sold at local DJH hostels. There are well-equipped cycling shops in almost every town, and a fairly active market for used touring bikes.

Simple three-gear bicycles can be hired from train stations for DM12/56 per day/week, and more robust mountain bikes from DM15/90; holders of rail passes or valid train tickets get a small discount. See DB's *Fahrrad am Bahnhof* brochures for lists of stations offering this service. If you plan to spend longer than several weeks in the saddle, buying a second-hand bike works out cheaper than renting a bike or bringing your own; good reconditioned models cost from DM300 to DM400.

A separate ticket must be purchased whenever you carry your bike on a train. These cost DM5.60 (DM5 in eastern Germany) for distances under 100 km, DM9.40 for distances over 100 km, and DM16 to destinations outside Germany.

Germany's main cyclists' organisation is the Allgemeiner Deutscher Fahrrad Club (ADFC, ☎ 08955 35 75), Landwehrstrasse 16, 80336 Munich. See also Activities in the earlier Facts for the Visitor section.

HITCHING

Trampen (hitching) is considered an acceptable way of getting around in Germany and average waits are short. Don't waste time hitching in urban areas: take public transport to the main exit routes. It's illegal to hitchhike on autobahns or their entry/exit roads, but service stations can be very good places to pick up a ride. Prepare a sign clearly showing your intended destination in German (eg 'München', not 'Munich'). You can save yourself a lot of trouble by arranging a lift through a *Mitfahrzentrale* (see Hitching & Ride Services in the earlier Getting There & Away section).

BOAT

Boats are most likely to be used for basic transport when travelling to or between the Frisian Islands, though tours along the Rhine and Moselle rivers are also popular. In summer there are frequent services on Lake Constance, but, except for the Constance to Meersburg and the Friedrichshafen to Romanshorn car ferries, these boats are really more tourist craft than a transport option. From April to October, excursion boats ply the lakes and rivers of eastern Germany and are an excellent, inexpensive way of seeing the country. Paddlewheel steamers operating out of Dresden are a fine way to tour the Elbe. Cruises are popular between Berlin and Potsdam (see Activities in the Berlin section).

LOCAL TRANSPORT

Local transport is excellent within big cities and small towns, and generally based on buses, trams, S-Bahn (suburban train system) and/or U-Bahn (underground train system). Most public transport systems integrate buses, trams and trains; fares are determined by the zones or the time travelled, or sometimes both. Multi-ticket strips or day passes are generally available and offer far better value than single-ride tickets. See the individual Getting Around entries in this chapter for details.

Bus & Tram

Cities and towns operate their own local bus, trolleybus and/or tram services. In most places you must have a ticket before embarking, and stamp it once aboard (or pay a fine of around DM60 if caught without a validated ticket). Tickets are sold mainly from vending machines at train stations and tram or bus stops. Bus drivers usually sell single-trip tickets as a service to forgetful passengers, but these are more expensive than tickets bought in advance.

GERMANY

Train

Most large cities have a system of suburban train lines called the S-Bahn. Trains on these lines cover a wider area than buses or trams, but tend to be less frequent. S-Bahn lines are often linked to the national rail network, and sometimes interconnect urban centres; rail cards or tickets are generally valid on these services (except in Berlin).

Underground

The larger cities, such as Berlin, Munich and Frankfurt, have an underground metro system known as the U-Bahn. Although fast and efficient, U-Bahns don't let you see where you're going, which can be quite disorienting.

Taxi

Taxis are expensive and, given the excellent public transport system, not recommended unless you're in a screaming hurry. (They can actually be slower if you're going to or from the airport.) For fast service, look up 'TaxiRuf' in the local telephone directory to find the nearest taxi rank. Taxis are metered and cost up to DM2.40 per km and DM4 flag fall; in some places higher night tariffs apply.

ORGANISED TOURS

Local tourist offices offer various tour options, from short city sightseeing trips to multiday adventure, spa-bath and wine-tasting packages. Apart from city tours, other good sources for organised tours in and around Germany are Europabus and Deutsche Bahn.

There are many other international and national tour operators with specific options. Your travel agent should have some details, and it's also worth contacting the German National Tourist Office in your home country. Many airlines also offer tour packages with their tickets.

Berlin

Berlin, the largest city in Germany, has more to offer visitors than almost any city in Europe. Divided by a 162-km wall until mid-1990, East and West Berlin remain separate and will continue to be so until the sentiments and associations of the past are put aside. Even though the German government is scheduled to return to Berlin, it will be years before the wounds of the Cold War are fully healed.

The centre of 19th-century Prussian military and industrial might, this great city finally reached maturity in the 1920s, only to be bombed into rubble in WWII. Today, despite having lost a large part of its prewar population, Berlin's gross domestic product equals that of countries such as Ireland and Greece.

History

The first recorded settlement at present-day Berlin was a place named Cölln (1237) around the Spree River south of Museumsinsel ('museum island'), although Spandau, the junction of the Spree and the ponded Havel River, is considered to be older. Medieval Berlin developed on the bank of the Spree around the Nikolaikirche and spread north-east towards today's Alexanderplatz. In 1432, Berlin and Cölln, which were linked by the Mühlendamm, merged.

In the 1440s, Elector Friedrich II of Brandenburg established the rule of the Hohenzollern dynasty, which was to last until Kaiser Wilhelm II's escape from Potsdam in 1918. Berlin's importance increased in 1470 when the elector moved his residence here from Brandenburg and built a palace near the present Marx-Engels-Platz.

During the Thirty Years' War Berlin's population was decimated, but the city was reborn stronger than before under the so-called Great Elector Friedrich Wilhelm in the mid-17th century. His vision was the basis of Prussian power, and he sponsored Huguenot refugees seeking princely tolerance.

The Great Elector's son, Friedrich I, the first Prussian king, made the fast-growing Berlin his capital, and his daughter-in-law Sophie Charlotte encouraged the development of the arts and sciences and presided over a lively and intellectual court. Friedrich II sought greatness through building and was known for his political and military savvy. All this led to the city being nicknamed *Spreeathen* ('Athens-on-Spree').

The Enlightenment arrived with some authority in the persons of Gotthold Ephraim Lessing and the thinker and publisher Friedrich

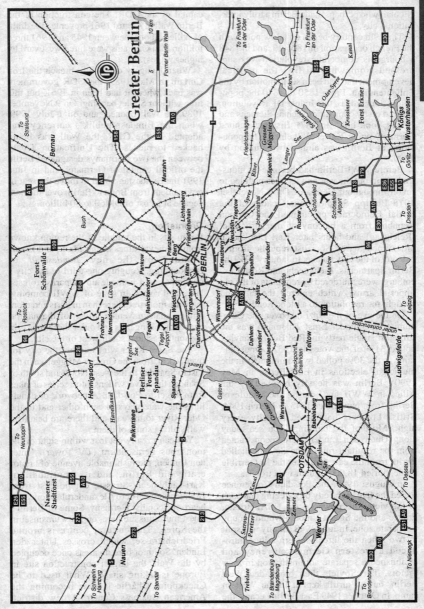

Greater Berlin

0   5   10 km

– – – Former Berlin Wall

Nicolai, who perhaps made Berlin a truly international city.

The 19th century began on a low note, with the French occupation of 1806-13, and in 1848 a bourgeois democratic revolution was suppressed, somewhat stifling the political development that had been set in motion by the Enlightenment. From 1850 to 1870 the population doubled as the Industrial Revolution, spurred on by companies such as Siemens and Borsig, took hold. In 1871 Bismarck united Germany under Kaiser Wilhelm I. The population of Berlin was almost two million by 1900.

Before WWI Berlin had become an industrial giant, but the war and its aftermath led to revolt throughout Germany. On 9 November 1918 Philipp Scheidemann, leader of the Social Democrats, proclaimed the German Republic from a balcony of the parliament (Reichstag) and hours later Karl Liebknecht proclaimed a free Socialist republic from a balcony of the City Palace. In January 1919 the Berlin Spartacists, Liebknecht and Rosa Luxemburg, were murdered by remnants of the old imperial army, which entered the city and brought the revolution to a bloody end.

On the eve of the Nazi takeover, the Communist Party under Ernst Thälmann was the strongest single party in 'Red Berlin', having polled 31% of the votes in 1932 (almost the same as the 30% polled by Communists in the municipal elections in East Berlin in May 1990). Berlin was heavily bombed by the Allies in WWII and, during the 'Battle of Berlin' from November 1943 to March 1944, British bombers hammered the city every night. Most of the buildings you see today along Unter den Linden were reconstructed from the resultant ruins. The Soviets shelled Berlin from the east, and after the last terrible battle, buried 18,000 of their own troops.

In August 1945, the Potsdam Conference sealed the fate of the city by agreeing that each of the victorious powers – the USA, Britain, France and the Soviet Union – would occupy a separate zone. In June 1948 the city was split in two when the three Western Allies introduced a western German currency and established a separate administration in their sectors. The Soviets then blockaded West Berlin, but an airlift kept it in the Western camp. In October 1949 East Berlin became the capital of the GDR. The construction of the Berlin Wall in August 1961 prevented the drain of skilled labour (between 1945 and 1961 three million East Germans were lured westward by higher wages).

When Hungary decided to breach the Iron Curtain in May 1989, the GDR government was back where it had been in 1961, but this time without Soviet backing. On 9 November 1989 the Wall opened, and on 1 July 1990, when the Bundesrepublik's currency was adopted in the GDR, the Wall was being hacked to pieces. The Unification Treaty between the two Germanys designated Berlin the official capital of Germany, and in June 1991 the Bundestag voted to move the seat of government from Bonn to Berlin over the next decade at a cost of DM60 to 80 billion.

Orientation

Berlin sits in the middle of the region known from medieval times as the Mark, and is surrounded by the new *Bundesland* of Brandenburg. Roughly one-third of the city's municipal area is made up of parks, forests, lakes and rivers. In spite of WWII bombing, there are more trees here than in Paris and more bridges than in Venice. Much of the natural beauty of rolling hills and quiet shorelines is in the south-east and south-west of the city.

The Spree River winds across the city for over 30 km, from the Grosser Müggelsee in the east to Spandau in the west. North and south of Spandau the Havel widens into a series of lakes from Tegel to Potsdam. A network of canals links the waterways to each other and to the Oder River to the east and there are beautiful walks along some of them.

You can't really get lost within sight of the monstrous Fernsehturm (TV Tower). Unter den Linden, the fashionable avenue of aristocratic old Berlin, and its continuation, Karl-Liebknecht-Strasse, extend east from Brandenburger Tor to Alexanderplatz, once the heart of Socialist Germany. Some of Berlin's finest museums are here, on Museumsinsel in the Spree. The cultural centre is around Friedrichstrasse, which crosses Unter den Linden. South of here, in areas once occupied by the Wall, the largest construction site in Europe is taking shape. What used to be Checkpoint Charlie is now becoming the American Business Center. A new district, which will be dominated by futuristic high-rises built by international corporations, is being erected all around Potsdamer Platz. Still, some sections of the Wall will be left for public view.

The ruin and modern annexes of Kaiser-Wilhelm-Gedächtnis-Kirche, the shattered memorial church on Breitscheidplatz a block away from Zoologischer Garten station, form a most visible landmark. The tourist office and hundreds of shops are in Europa-Center at the end of the square farthest from the station. The Kurfürstendamm (known colloquially as the 'Ku'damm') runs 3.5 km south-west from Breitscheidplatz. To the north-east, between Breitscheidplatz and the Brandenburger Tor, is Tiergarten, a district named after the vast city park which was once a royal hunting domain. The area adjacent to the park, along the Spree, has been chosen for the new national government complex, to be completed between 2000 and 2005.

While in central Berlin, keep in mind that the street numbers usually run sequentially up one side of the street and down the other (important exceptions are Martin-Luther-Strasse in Schöneberg and Unter den Linden), although number guides appear on most corner street signs. Be aware, too, that a continuous street may change names several times, and that on some streets (Pariser Strasse, Knesebeckstrasse) numbering sequences continue after interruptions caused by squares or plazas. The names of some streets and other landmarks have been changed for political reasons and more will follow.

Information

Tourist Offices The main office of Berlin Touristen-Information is at Budapester Strasse 45 in Europa-Center, and is open Monday to Saturday from 8 am to 10 pm, Sunday from 9 am to 9 pm. This office also handles hotel room reservations. Other offices are in the southern wing of the Brandenburger Tor (open 10.30 am to 7 pm daily) and in the main hall of Lufthansa Airport Center in Tegel Airport (open 5.15 am to 10 pm daily). For information over the phone, call ☎ 25 00 25.

The tourist office sells the new Berlin Welcome Card (DM29) which entitles you to unlimited transport for 48 hours after purchase and 72 hours of discounted admission to major museums, shows, attractions, sightseeing tours, and boat cruises in both Berlin and Potsdam. It is also available at hotels and public transport ticket offices. A 24-hour version costs DM16.

Foreign Consulates The following consulates are in Berlin:

Australia
  Uhlandstrasse 181-183 in Kempinski Plaza (☎ 8 80 08 80), open weekdays 9 am to noon and 2 to 4 pm. New Zealand has no representation in Berlin as yet, and the Australians will only help those they call 'stressed New Zealanders' (lost or stolen passport, money, luggage etc).
Bulgaria
  Mauerstrasse 11 (☎ 2 01 09 22). Visas are issued between 2 and 4 pm on Thursday.
Canada
  Friedrichstrasse 95, on the 23rd floor of the International Trade Centre (☎ 2 61 11 61 or 20 96 30 01), open weekdays from 8.30 am to 12.30 pm and 1.30 pm to 5 pm.
France
  Kurfürstendamm 211 on the corner of Uhlandstrasse (☎ 88 59 02 43). The office issues visas Monday to Thursday 9 am to noon and 2 to 3.30 pm and on Friday mornings. Visas (required for Australians) cost DM18 for up to five days and DM60 for over five days. You are asked to show identification as you enter.
Hungary
  Unter den Linden 76 (☎ 2 29 16 66), open weekdays 9 am to noon. Visas (required by Australians and New Zealanders) cost DM60.
Poland
  Unter den Linden 74 (☎ 2 20 24 51), open weekdays 9 am to 1 pm. Single-entry tourist visas, required by Canadians, Australians and New Zealanders, cost DM66.
Russia
  Reichensteiner Weg 34-36 (☎ 8 32 70 04). The consular section is open from 9 am to 1 pm Monday, Wednesday and Friday, and from 2 to 5 pm Tuesday and Thursday. If you are booking tours to Russia, travel agencies will often take care of applications. A few private agencies will handle these quicker than Intourist, though generally at a higher price.
UK
  Unter den Linden 32-34 (☎ 20 18 40), open weekdays from 9 am to noon and 2 to 4 pm.
USA
  Clayallee 170 (U-Bahn: Oskar-Helene-Heim); ☎ 8 32 40 87 or 8 32 92 33 for consular services, open weekdays from 8.30 am to noon.

Money Main post offices exchange travellers' cheques at the exorbitant rate of DM6 per cheque. American Express (☎ 8 82 75 75), at

GERMANY

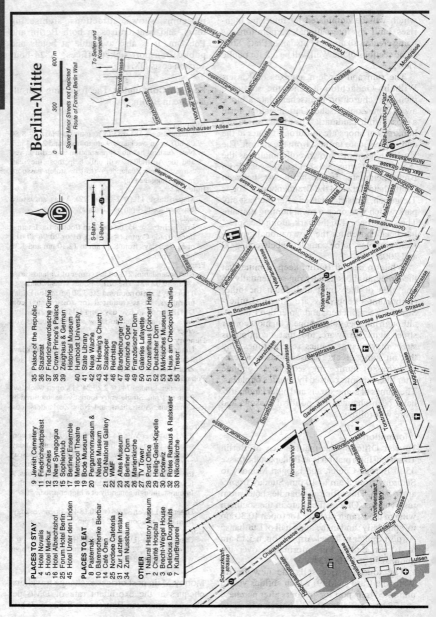

Berlin-Mitte

S-Bahn
U-Bahn

Some Minor Streets not Depicted
Route of Former Berlin Wall

0   300   600 m

To Seifen und Kosmetik

PLACES TO STAY
4 Hotel Novalis
5 Hotel Merkur
16 Hotel Albrechtshof
45 Forum Hotel Berlin
Hotel Unter den Linden

PLACES TO EAT
8 Pastemak
10 Bärenschenke Bierbar
14 Café Oren
25 Nordsee Cafeteria
31 Zur Letzten Instanz
34 Zum Nussbaum

OTHER
1 Natural History Museum
2 Charité Hospital
3 Brecht-Weigel House
6 Delicious Doughnuts
7 KulturBrauerei

9 Jewish Cemetery
11 Friedrichstadtpalast
12 Tacheles
13 New Synagogue
15 Sophienklub
17 Berliner Ensemble
18 Metropol Theatre
19 Bode Museum
20 Pergamonmuseum & Neues Museum
21 Old National Gallery
22 WMF
23 Altes Museum
24 Berliner Dom
26 Marienkirche
27 TV Tower
28 Post Office
29 Heilig-Geist-Kapelle
30 Podewiz
32 Rotes Rathaus & Ratskeller
33 Nikolaikirche

35 Palace of the Republic
36 Staatsrat
37 Friedrichswerdesche Kirche
38 Crown Prince's Palace
39 Zeughaus & German Historical Museum
40 Humboldt University
41 State Library
42 Neue Wache
43 St Hedwig's Church
44 Staatsoper
46 Reichstag
47 Brandenburger Tor
48 Komische Oper
49 Französischer Dom
50 Galeries Lafayette
51 Konzerthaus (Concert Hall)
52 Deutscher Dom
53 Märkisches Museum
54 Haus am Checkpoint Charlie
55 Tresor

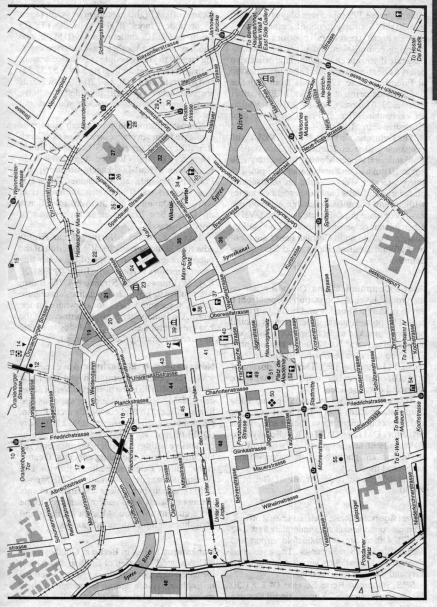

Uhlandstrasse 173 (open weekdays from 9 am
to 5.30 pm, Saturday to noon), cashes American Express travellers' cheques without
charging commission, but gives a very ordinary rate if you are converting. This office also
offers a client-mail service. Other branches are
at Friedrichstrasse 172 across from Galeries
Lafayette department store, and at Bayreuther
Strasse 23. Thomas Cook (☎ 2 01 72 20) has
an exchange office at Friedrichstrasse near
Kochstrasse in Mitte.

The Deutsche Verkehrs-Bank (DVB) has an
exchange office at Hardenbergplatz outside
Zoo station. It is open Monday to Saturday 7.30
am to 10 pm and on Sunday 8 am to 7 pm. The
Europa-Center Wechselstube on Breitscheidplatz buys and sells banknotes of all countries
without any commission charge and you can
easily compare the daily rate with the DVB or
other exchange services around Zoo station.
Branches of the main German banks are plentiful around Breitscheidplatz and Kurfürstendamm.

Post & Communications The post office on
the ground level of Zoo station is open from 6
am to midnight (Sunday and holidays from 8
am). The poste restante is here; letters should
be clearly marked as 'Hauptpostlagernd', and
addressed to you at 10612 Berlin 120, Bahnhof
Zoo. You can also send a fax (phone charges
plus DM4 handling fee). There are dozens of
post offices all over Berlin, but most have more
restricted opening hours.

You can make international phone calls
from just about any post office but it's cheaper
and more convenient to use phonecards, which
cost either DM12 or DM50. This allows you to
make calls of any length to anywhere in the
world from any phone booth that accepts these
cards (and most do).

The telephone code for all of Berlin is
☎ 030.

Travel Agencies Reise Welt has several offices,
the most convenient at Alexanderplatz 5 (☎ 2 42
73 52). Others are at Schönefeld airport and
Bahnhofstrasse 18 in Köpenick. These are good
places to buy train tickets very cheaply or make
ferry and package reservations.

SRS Studenten Reise Service (☎ 2 83 30
94), at Marienstrasse 25 near Friedrichstrasse

station, offers flights at student or youth (aged
25 or under) fares. It also sells the FIYTO
youth and ISIC student cards (DM15; one
photo required). Another travel service catering largely to young people is Atlas Reisewelt,
with offices at Mandrellaplatz 5 (☎ 6 57 57 72)
and Münzstrasse 14 (☎ 2 47 70 42). ISIC cards
are issued here as well, provided you have
proper and recognisable student and personal
ID.

Tourist information on Eastern Europe is
available from several sources: Cedok (Czech
Republic) at Leipziger Strasse 60; Ibusz
(Hungary), centrally located at ground level in
Haus Ungarn (Karl-Liebknecht-Strasse 9); and
Polorbis (Poland), at Warschauer Strasse 5.
The Russian travel specialist Intourist is at
Kurfürstendamm 63 and the Aeroflot office is
on Unter den Linden near the corner of
Friedrichstrasse.

Travel agencies offering cheap flights
advertise in the *Reisen* classified section of the
popular magazine *Zitty*. One of the better discount operators is Alternativ Tours (☎ 8 81 20
89), Wilmersdorfer Strasse 94 (U-Bahn:
Adenauerplatz), which specialises in unpub-
lished, discounted fares to anywhere in the
world. On Budapester Strasse north-east of the
zoo are several agencies specialising in exotic
locations, including the Middle East.

Newspapers & Magazines An excellent
source of general information and the latest
news about Berlin is the bi-lingual *Berlin Magazine* (DM3.50), available at newsstands and
tourist offices. To find out what's on in Berlin,
check out *Berlin Programm* (DM2.80), *Zitty*
(DM3.60) or *Tip* (DM4). All offer comprehensive listings (though in German only) of
all current events, including concerts, theatre,
clubs, gallery exhibits, readings, movies, etc.
An English-language alternative is *Metropolis*
(DM3) which has a less extensive events
listing but offers good general guidance to the
city's current hot spots. Most newsstands and
bookshops carry all these magazines.

Bookshops Books in Berlin at Goethestrasse
69 has a good selection of English and American literature. For paperbacks (mostly fiction)
in English, try the Marga Schoeller Bücher-
stube, Knesebeckstrasse 33-34 or the British

Bookshop at Mauerstrasse 83-84 in Mitte. Kiepert, at the corner of Knesebeckstrasse and Hardenbergstrasse, has many departments, from guidebooks to foreign-language dictionaries. Herder Buchhandlung on Tauentzienstrasse 13, across from the Gedächtniskirche, has guidebooks and maps (some discounted) covering Berlin and its cultural background (ground and second floors). Europa Presse Center at ground level in Europa-Center has the whole range of international papers and magazines. Berliner Universitätsbuchhandlung at Spandauer Strasse 2 has a huge selection of everything from glossy art books, German travel guidebooks and maps, to cultural and historical material about Berlin and surrounds.

Laundry The Schnell und Sauber Waschcenter chain has laundrettes (open from 6 am to 11 pm) at Uhlandstrasse 53; on the corner of Hohenstaufenstrasse and Martin-Luther-Strasse; at Hauptstrasse 127 in Schöneberg; and on Mehringdamm, at the U-Bahn station exit, in Kreuzberg. To wash and dry a load costs about DM10.

Medical & Emergency Services For 24-hour medical aid, dial ☎ 31 00 31. The general emergency number for a doctor (*Notarzt*) or fire brigade *(Feuerwehr)* throughout Berlin is ☎ 112. If you need a pharmacy after hours, dial ☎ 0 11 41.

Charité hospital on Luisenstrasse near Hannoversche Strasse (U-Bahn: Oranienburger Tor) has an emergency department. As you come from the station, look for an unmarked driveway (probably with a couple of ambulances parked on the right), just beyond the walk-over between the hospital buildings. This Humboldt University-operated facility is open 24 hours. It is central and just as good as anything in Berlin. If you can't get to this facility, you should call the emergency number or go to the nearest hospital. For information on where to find an emergency dentist *(Zahnarzt)*, dial ☎ 0 11 41 or 89 00 43 33.

Call ☎ 110 for police emergencies only. Otherwise, there are police stations all over the city, including City-Wache at Joachimsthaler Strasse 15 near Zoo station. In eastern Berlin, there's a station at Hans-Beimler-Strasse 27-

37. For mishaps on trains, your first recourse should be the *Bahnpolizei*, located at ground level inside Zoo station. The main police centre and lost-and-found office (☎ 69 95) is at Platz der Luftbrücke 6 beside Tempelhof airport. If you've lost something on public transport, contact the Berlin public transport office, or BVG (☎ 7 51 80 21), at Lorenzweg 5 in Tempelhof.

Dangers & Annoyances By all accounts, Berlin is among the safest and most tolerant of European cities. Walking alone at night on city streets shouldn't be considered a threat for anyone, bearing in mind the caveat that there is always safety in numbers in any urban environment. You may want to avoid the area along the Spree south of the Hauptbahnhof, which has become the haunt of occasionally violent punks, urban drifters and druggies.

Things to See & Do
Around Alexanderplatz Soaring above Berlin is the recently restored 365-metre **TV Tower** or Fernsehturm (1969), open daily from 10 to 1 am. If it's a clear day and the queue isn't too long, it's worth paying the DM7 (discount DM3) to go up the tower or have a drink at the 207-metre level Telecafé, which revolves twice an hour. The complex also houses nine radio and two TV stations.

On the opposite side of the elevated train station from the tower is **Alexanderplatz** (or, affectionately, 'Alex'), the square named after Tsar Alexander I who visited Berlin in 1805. The area was redesigned several times in the late 1920s but nothing was ever actually built because of the Depression. It was bombed in WWII and completely reconstructed in the 1960s. The **World Time Clock** (1969) is nearby in case you want to check the time before making a telephone call home.

Museum Island West of the TV tower, on an island between two arms of the Spree River, is the GDR's **Palace of the Republic** (1976), which occupies the site of the damaged baroque City Palace that was demolished in 1950. During the Communist era, the People's Chamber (Volkskammer) used to meet in this showpiece which faces Marx-Engels-Platz. In 1990 it was discovered that asbestos had been used in the construction, so this 'palace' too is expected to go, although nobody is volunteering to pay for the planned reconstruction of the original palace.

On the southern side near the Spree bank is the former **Staatsrat** (Council of State) building (1964), with a portal from the old city palace incorporated in the façade. The modern white building just across the canal on the eastern side of Marx-Engels-Platz used to house the GDR foreign ministry and is intended to house that of united Germany in the future.

North of Marx-Engels-Platz looms the great neo-Renaissance **Berliner Dom** (1904), the former court church of the Hohenzollern family. The imposing edifice beside it is Karl Friedrich Schinkel's 1829 neoclassical **Altes Museum** with its famed rotunda area featuring statues of the Greek divinities. It's currently used for special exhibitions only. The **Neues Museum** behind is being reconstructed, but you can visit the adjacent **Alte Nationalgalerie**, with art from the 18th and 19th centuries, including sculpture by Johan Gottfried Schadow and Christian Daniel Rauch. Besides the Renoirs, Monets, Manets, Cézannes and Constables, you can take in the brooding and Romantic death images of Arnold Böcklin, the Prussian military scenes of Adolph Menzel and, in the 'Berlin' rooms, the works of Max Liebermann, Max Beckmann, Max Slevogt and Lovis Corinth. There's a similar collection in the **Martin-Gropius-Bau** on Stresemannstrasse 110 in Kreuzberg.

The **Pergamon Museum** is a feast of classical Greek, Babylonian, Roman, Islamic and Oriental antiquity. The world-renowned Ishtar Gate from Babylon (580 BC), the reconstructed Pergamon Altar from Asia Minor (160 BC) and the Market Gate from Greek Miletus (Asia Minor, 2nd century AD) are among the beautiful artefacts hauled from the Middle East. The **Bode Museum** houses collections of sculpture, paintings, coins and Egyptian art, though not all sections are open every day.

Admission to all these museums is DM4, discount is DM2, and Sunday is free. All are closed on Monday.

Nikolaiviertel The rebuilt 13th-century **Nikolaikirche** stands amid the interesting Nikolaiviertel quarter, conceived and executed

under the GDR's Berlin restoration programme. Inside is a fascinating museum (admission DM3, discount DM1; closed Monday) that exhibits relics of early Berlin, Cölln, the Mark and the remains of the church's original interiors. Another medieval church, **Marienkirche** (admission free; open Monday to Thursday from 10 am to noon and 1 to 5 pm, Saturday noon to 5 pm, Sunday 1 to 4 pm), is on Karl-Liebknecht-Strasse. It stands near the monumental red **Rotes Rathaus** (known as such for its appearance, not its politics), a neo-Renaissance structure from 1860, which has been proudly restored and is once again the centre of Berlin's municipal government. Across Grunerstrasse, the medieval remains of the **Heilig-Geist-Kapelle** mark the spot of the former Spandauer Tor and the earliest town wall. Nearby on Klosterstrasse (U-Bahn: Klosterstrasse) is the bombed-out shell of the **Franciscan Abbey** (admission free, closed Monday and Saturday).

Märkisches Ufer Several interesting sights can be covered from the Märkisches Museum U-Bahn station. The collections of the **Märkisches Museum** (admission DM3; discount DM1, open Wednesday to Sunday from 10 am to 6 pm) cover the early history of Berlin. Permanent exhibits include a quite magnificent scale model of Berlin around 1750 and another that brings back the atmosphere of long-gone theatres and the colourful cabaret, stage and magic shows of Berlin's 1920s and 1930s. The brown bears housed in a pit in the park behind the main museum are the official mascots of the city and are fed daily at 12.30 pm.

Unter den Linden A stroll west of Museumsinsel along Unter den Linden takes in the greatest surviving monuments of the former Prussian capital. The **German Historical Museum** in the former Armoury (or Zeughaus, 1706, by Andreas Schlüter) contains an extensive and fascinating collection of objects, maps and photos (free; closed Wednesday). Be sure to see the baroque building's interior courtyard with Schlüter's famous 22 masks of dying warriors. Opposite the museum is the beautiful colonnaded **Crown Prince's Palace** (Kronprinzenpalais,

1732). Next to the museum is Schinkel's **Neue Wache** (1818), a memorial to the victims of fascism and despotism which harbours Käthe Kollwitz's sculpture *Mother and Dead Son* (open daily). **Humboldt University** (1753), the next building to the west, was originally a palace of the brother of King Friedrich II of Prussia. It was converted to a university in 1810. Beside this is the massive **State Library** (1914). An equestrian **statue of Friedrich II** stands in the middle of the avenue in front of the university.

Across the street from the university, beside the **Old Library** (1780) with its curving baroque façade, is Wenzeslaus von Knobelsdorff's **State Opera** (Deutsche Staatsoper, 1743). Behind this site is the Catholic **St Hedwig's Church** (1773), which was modelled on the Pantheon in Rome.

Just south of here lies Gendarmenmarkt, a quiet square framed by a trio of magnificent buildings. The **Deutscher Dom** at the south end of the square is being remodelled to house an excellent exhibit on German history from 1800 to the present – previously shown at the Reichstag – by 1997. The **Französischer Dom** contains the **Hugenottenmuseum** (DM2, discount DM1) which covers the Huguenot contribution to Berlin life. For a great view, climb the tower (weekdays from 10 am to 4 pm, free). The statuesque **Concert Hall** completes the picture. The **Berlin Museum** further to the south is scheduled to reopen in 1998.

Around Oranienburger Tor North of Unter den Linden is the **Brecht-Weigel Memorial House** at Chausseestrasse 125 (U-Bahn: Zinnowitzer Strasse or Oranienburger Tor), where the socialist playwright Bertolt Brecht and his wife Helene Weigel lived from 1953 until his death in 1956. It's open Tuesday to Friday 10 am to noon, on Thursday also from 5 to 7 pm, and on Saturday from 9.30 am to noon and 12.30 to 2 pm. Admission is DM4, discount DM2. Go into the rear courtyard and up the stairs to the right. Behind is **Dorotheenstadt Cemetery** with tombs of the illustrious, such as the architect Schinkel, the philosopher Georg Friedrich Hegel, the poet Johannes Becher, and Brecht. There are two adjacent cemeteries here: you want the one

closer to Brecht's house. The **Natural History Museum** (1810) nearby at Invalidenstrasse 43 (admission DM3, discount DM1.50; closed Monday) has a good collection of dinosaur and mineral exhibits.

Also of interest is the nearby **New Synagogue** on Oranienburger Strasse 28 (admission free, closed Saturday). Built in the Moorish-Byzantine style in 1866, it was destroyed during the pogroms in 1938 and recently reopened as 'centrum judaicum', with a permanent exhibit on the history of the synagogue.

Tiergarten Unter den Linden ends at the **Brandenburger Tor**, or Brandenburg Gate (1791, by Karl Gotthard Langhans), a symbol of Berlin and once the boundary between East and West (S-Bahn: Unter den Linden). It is crowned by the winged Goddess of Victory and a four-horse quadriga by Schadow. At the open-air stalls around the gate you can buy GDR and Soviet military souvenirs and ever-smaller painted pieces of the Wall. Compare prices before buying, and bargain. And mind the traffic – Pariser Platz is now full of tour buses and vehicles of all sorts and is dangerous to cross or photograph in.

Beside the Spree River, just north of the Brandenburger Tor, is the **Reichstag** (1894), the German parliament until it was burned down on the night of 27 February 1933. At midnight on 2 October 1990 the reunification of Germany was enacted here. After the artist Christo wrapped the edifice in fabric in 1995, construction began that, by 1998, will turn the building once again into the seat of the German Federal Parliament. Between the Reichstag and the river is a small memorial to some of the 191 people who died trying to cross the Wall.

Just west of the Reichstag, along the Spree River, is the **Haus der Kulturen der Welt** (House of World Cultures, 1957), nicknamed the 'pregnant oyster' for its shape. The arched roof collapsed in 1980 but has since been rebuilt. The photo and art exhibits (often with Third World themes) are worth a look (closed Monday). The soft seats here will provide some welcome rest and you can board excursion boats behind the building during the summer months.

Tiergarten,
Schöneberg
& Kreuzberg

0   0.5   1 km

Route of Former Berlin Wall

S-Bahn

U-Bahn   U

The huge city park, **Tiergarten**, stretches west from the Brandenburger Tor towards Zoo station. It became a park in the 18th century and from 1833 to 1838 was landscaped with streams and lakes. Strasse des 17 Juni (named for the 1953 workers' uprising), which leads west from the Brandenburger Tor through the park, was known as the East-West Axis during the Nazi era, Hitler's showplace entrance to Berlin. On the north side of this street, just west of the gate, is a **Soviet War Memorial** flanked by the first Russian tanks to enter the city in 1945.

Further to the west, in the middle of Strasse des 17 Juni, is the **Victory Column** (Siegessäule, 1873), which commemorates 19th-century Prussian military adventures. It is crowned by a gilded statue of the Roman victory goddess, Victoria, which is visible from much of Tiergarten. A spiral staircase

leads to the top and affords a worthwhile view (DM1.50). Just north-east is **Schloss Belle-vue** (1785), built for Prince Ferdinand, brother of Friedrich II ('the Great'), and now an official residence of the President of Germany.

Potsdamer Platz One of Berlin's biggest tourist attractions is the monumental construction site around Potsdamer Platz. Over the next decade or so, an entire city is being built on the space once occupied by the Wall, including corporate headquarters, hypermodern train stations and futuristic-looking shopping and apartment complexes. The so-called **Infobox** on Leipziger Platz 21, a gleaming red container on stilts, houses a free multi-media exhibit that explains this gigantic project (daily 9 am to 7 pm). From an outside walkway you have a view of the dusty spectacle created by a phalanx of cranes, sledge-hammers and bulldozers.

West of the construction site is the angular **Berliner Philharmonie** (1963, by Hans Scharoun), a strikingly modern concert hall. The **Musical Instruments Museum**, Tiergartenstrasse 1 beside the Philharmonie (admission DM4, discount DM2; closed Monday), has a rich collection that is beautifully displayed. The red-brick **Mattäikirche** (1846) stands just south from here in the centre of Berlin's *Kulturforum*, and beyond it is the **New National Gallery** at Potsdamer Strasse 50 (admission DM8, discount DM4, Sunday and holidays free; closed Monday), with a collection of 19th and 20th-century paintings that includes works by Picasso and Klee. This sleek gallery, built in 1968, is a creation of the architect Mies van der Rohe. The **State Library** (1976) across the street contains reading, periodical and exhibition rooms (closed Sunday).

The **Museum for Design** at Klingelhöferstrasse 14 near the Landwehrkanal is dedicated to the artists of the Bauhaus school (1919-33), who laid the basis for much contemporary architecture. The collection includes works by Kandinsky, Klee and Oskar Schlemmer and is housed in a building designed by the school's founder, Walter Gropius. Admission is DM4, discount DM2, Monday free; closed on Tuesday.

Around Checkpoint Charlie On Stresemannstrasse 110 in Kreuzberg is the site of the former SS/Gestapo headquarters where the **Topographie des Terrors** exhibition (admission free; open until 6 pm daily) documents Nazi crimes, especially the 'Jewish solution'. A booklet in English costs DM1. Nearby, on the corner of Wilhelmstrasse and Vossstrasse is the site of **Hitler's bunker**. The Chancellery built here by Albert Speer in 1938 was demolished after the war, and the bunker below it (where Hitler shot himself on 30 April 1945) was completely effaced in the late 1980s when the Communists built the apartment complex that occupies the site.

Almost nothing remains at the site of the famous **Checkpoint Charlie**, where the American Business Center is now being built. If you want to see where it once stood, get off at Kochstrasse and walk north on Friedrichstrasse. Because of the construction, the remains of the Wall that occupied the site have been moved a three-minute walk away to the corner of Zimmerstrasse and Charlottenstrasse. The structure at Friedrichstrasse 207-208 was, until 1990, the headquarters of all Western intelligence organisations in Berlin, and from here photos were taken of everyone crossing the border. The history of the Wall is commemorated nearby in the **Haus am Checkpoint Charlie**, a private museum of escape memorabilia and photos (admission DM7.50, discount DM4.50). Such is the attraction of the Wall that it's crawling with visitors daily from 9 am to 10 pm.

The longest surviving stretch of the **Berlin Wall** is just across the bridge from the Schlesisches Tor terminus of the U1, about which the film *Linie 1* was made. As the Wall was being demolished in mid-1990, this 300-metre section was turned over to artists who created the **East Side Gallery**, a permanent open-air art gallery along the side facing Mühlenstrasse (the side facing the river is sprayed with graffiti), now threatened with demolition. Be careful when you visit this area (see Dangers & Annoyances).

Kurfürstendamm The stark ruins of the **Kaiser-Wilhelm-Gedächtnis-Kirche** (1895) in Breitscheidplatz, engulfed in the roaring commercialism all round, marks the heart of west Berlin. The British bombing of 22 November 1943 left only the broken west

tower standing. The foyer (Gedenkhalle) below the tower may be visited from Monday to Saturday, 10 am to 5 pm. The modern church (1961) and its overwhelmingly blue stained glass is open to visitors from 9 am to 7 pm daily, except during services.

Adjacent to Bahnhof Zoo station, on the corner of Kantstrasse and Joachimsthaler is the new **Erotik-Museum**, which displays erotic sculptures, drawings and objects from around the world (open daily 9 am to midnight, admission DM10, discount DM8). You have to be 18 or over to get in.

On the other side of Gedächtniskirche rises the **Europa-Center** (1965), a shopping and restaurant complex that's still bustling when other shops are closed. North-east of Europa-Center on Budapester Strasse is the elephant gate of Germany's oldest **Zoo & Aquarium** (over 150 years old). It contains some 1400 species and is open daily 9 am to 5 pm, the aquarium till 6 pm. Admission for the zoo is DM10, children DM5; for the aquarium it's DM9/4.50; and a combined ticket is DM15/7.50.

Charlottenburg Built as a summer residence for Queen Sophie Charlotte, **Schloss Charlottenburg** (1699) is an exquisite baroque palace on Spandauer Damm three km northwest of Zoo station (U-Bahn: Sophie-Charlotten-Platz). The palace was bombed in 1943 but has been completely rebuilt. Before the entrance is an equestrian statue of the Great Elector (1620-1688), Sophie Charlotte's father-in-law. Along the Spree River behind the palace are extensive French and English gardens (free admission).

In the central building below the dome are the former royal living quarters. The winter chambers of Friedrich II, upstairs in the new wing (1746) to the east, may be visited individually, or on an DM8 general admission ticket that takes in the **Schinkel Pavilion**, the neoclassical **Mausoleum** and the rococo **Belvedere pavilion**. Huge crowds are often waiting for the guided tour of Charlottenburg Palace and it may be difficult to get a ticket. This is especially true on weekends and holidays in summer. If you can't get into the main palace, content yourself with the façades and gardens.

In addition to the splendour of the royal private quarters, three museums are worth visiting. The **Romantic Gallery** of the National Gallery (closed Monday) is housed downstairs in the new wing and contains works by such artists as Caspar David Friedrich and Carl Blechen. The **Museum of Prehistory** occupies the west wing of the palace, and across the street at the beginning of Schlossstrasse is the **Egyptian Museum**, whose highlight is the 14th-century BC bust of Queen Nefertiti, an incredible sight to behold. Both museums are closed on Friday. Entry to the museums and the gallery is DM4, discount DM2, but a combined ticket to all three is DM8, discount DM4. Admission is free on Sunday.

Zehlendorf A complex of museums that perhaps is worth all the others combined is the **Dahlem Museums** in south-west Berlin (U-Bahn: Dahlem-Dorf). The **Gemäldegallerie** houses the better part of the Prussian art collections amassed by Friedrich the Great, evacuated from Museumsinsel during WWII and never returned to east Berlin (DM4, discount DM2, Sunday free; closed Monday). The fantastic museum full of old master paintings as well as sculpture, ethnographical exhibits and Indian, Oriental and Islamic art will knock you over. Other museums in the complex house sculpture, metal and gold work, ceramics, woodcuts, and more. Arrive early in the morning and plan to spend the day. A couple of blocks away is the **Botanical Garden**, Königin-Luise-Strasse 6-8, with over 18,000 plant species on display (open daily; admission DM4.40, discount DM2.20).

Cruises

Central Berlin may be crowded with roads, office buildings and apartments, but the southeast and south-west sections of the city are surprisingly green with forests, rivers and lakes. From April to October, tourist boats cruise the waterways, calling at picturesque villages, parks and castles. Food and drink are sold on board but they're quite expensive, so take along something to nibble or sip.

Shipping company Bruno Winkler (☎ 3 91 70 70) offers sightseeing cruises on the Spree River or the Landwehr Canal from March to the end of October. The main landing stage is at Schlossbrücke, Charlottenburger Ufer, next to Charlottenburg Palace. Three-hour tours leave twice daily and cost DM18. You can also hop aboard at the Friedrichstrasse landing at the Reichstagsufer, which cuts down the travelling time to two hours and the cost to DM15. Spreefahrt (☎ 3 94 49 54) has one-hour cruises through historical Berlin for DM10 and two-hour trips for DM15.

Stern und Kreisschiffahrt (☎ 5 36 36 00) operates many different cruises, except in winter. A 3½-hour cruise from Jannowitzbrücke in Mitte through Tiergarten to Schlossbrücke and back costs DM22 and is offered several times daily from late April to October. A one-hour spin around Museum Island will set you back DM12.50, and a four-hour voyage from Treptow in the east along the Spree and down the Havel to the castle of Cecilienhof in Potsdam is DM18 return (DM12 one way). Other cruises cover the Havel lakes from Wannsee and various canals.

Places to Stay – bottom end

Things are tight east of Tiergarten, as hotels close, are demolished, or renovated into the exclusive class. This has diverted the attention of budget travellers to the west until the accommodation scene settles down. The tourist office has an excellent booklet with a fairly comprehensive listing of hotel and pension options.

Camping Camping facilities in Berlin are not good. There are several camping grounds charging DM8.50 per person plus from DM5.50 to DM8.50 per tent, but they're far from the city centre, crowded with caravans and often full. They cater almost exclusively to permanent residents who live in their caravans all year, and although you may be admitted if you're polite and persistent, they aren't really set up to receive casual tourists.

The only camping ground convenient to public transport is *Campingplatz Kohlhasenbrück* (☎ 8 05 17 37), Neue Kreisstrasse 36, in a peaceful location overlooking the Griebnitzsee in the far south-west corner of Berlin. Bus No 118 from Wannsee S-Bahn station runs directly there. If the gate is locked when you arrive, just hang around until someone with a key arrives, and then ask for the manager at the

GERMANY

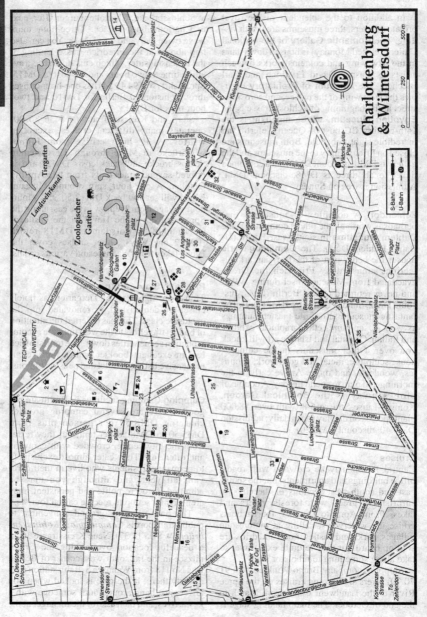

Charlottenburg
& Wilmersdorf

S-Bahn
U-Bahn

To Deutsche Oper &
Schloss Charlottenburg

PLACES TO STAY		35	Jugendgästehaus	9	Erotik Museum
1	Hotel-Pension Brinn		Central	10	Filmzentrum Zoo-Palast
2	Jugendgästehaus am	**PLACES TO EAT**		11	Kaiser-Wilhelm-
	Zoo	7	Dicke Wirtin		Gedächtnis-Kirche
5	Pension Knesebeck	20	Café Bleibtreu	12	Europa-Center
6	Hotel-Pension Bialas	21	Zillemarkt	13	Zoo & Aquarium
16	Hotel-Pension Majesty	24	Schwarzes Café	14	Museum for Design
18	Hotel-Pension Modena	25	Piccola Taormina	15	Kurbel Cinema
22	Hotel Crystal & Hotel-	26	Café Kranzler	17	Salsa
	Pension Cortina	27	Pizzeria Amigo	19	Big Eden
23	Pension Peters			28	Ku'damm Eck
30	Steigenberger Hotel	**OTHER**			Shopping Arcade
31	Pension Fischer &	3	School of Art Concert	29	Wertheim Department
	Hotel-Pension		Hall		Store
	Nürnberger Eck	4	Post Office	32	KaDeWe Department
33	Hotel-Pension Pariser	8	Theater des Westens		Store
	Eck		& Quasimodo		
34	Pension Elton				

Stay @ Circus Hostel

caravan near the gate. It is open from 1 April to 30 September.

If Kohlhasenbrück is full, two km to the east along the Teltowkanal is *Campingplatz Drei-linden* (☎ 8 05 12 01), at Albrechts-Teerofen (open from 1 March to 31 October, bus No 118 from Wannsee).

Hostels The three DJH hostels in Berlin fill up fast on weekends and throughout summer. Until early July, the hostels are often fully booked by noisy school groups. None of the hostels offer cooking facilities but breakfast is included in the overnight charge, and lunch and dinner are available. The hostels stay open all day throughout the year.

The only hostel within walking distance of the city centre is the impersonal 364-bed *Jugendgästehaus Berlin* (☎ 2 62 30 24), which costs DM31 for juniors, DM40 for seniors. It's at Kluckstrasse 3 in Schöneberg near Landwehrkanal (U-Bahn: Kurfürsten-strasse, bus No 129).

The most pleasant location surely belongs to the modern 264-bed *Jugendgästehaus am Wannsee* (☎ 8 03 20 34) at Badeweg 1 (not the nearby Wannseebad-Weg), on lake Grosser Wannsee south-west of the city. The hostel is at most an eight-minute walk from Nikolassee S-Bahn station and direct trains to Zoo station. Walk west out of the station over the foot-bridge, turn left at Kronprinzessinnenweg, and the hostel is soon in sight on the right. The cost is DM31 for juniors, DM40 for seniors, and the key deposit is DM20.

Jugendherberge Ernst Reuter (☎ 4 04 16 10), Hermsdorfer Damm 48, is in the far north-west of Berlin. Take the U6 to Tegel, then bus No 125 right to the door. The 110 beds are DM25 for juniors, DM32 for seniors.

It is a good idea to book DJH hostels in writing with the Deutsches Jugendher-bergswerk (☎ 2 64 95 20), Tempelhofer Ufer 32, 10963 Berlin, several weeks in advance. State precisely which nights you'll be in Berlin and enclose an international postal reply coupon so they can send back confirmation. You must give an address where the confirma-tion can be sent to. Otherwise you could just try calling a hostel to ask if they'll reserve a place.

Guesthouses Handiest of the private hostels is *Jugendgästehaus am Zoo* (☎ 3 12 94 10), Hardenbergstrasse 9a, three blocks from Zoo station, which charges DM47 for doubles, DM85 for triples and DM35 per person for dormitory beds, breakfast not included. It's limited to people aged under 27, but the loca-tion is great if you get in. The giant *Jugendgästehaus Central* (☎ 8 73 01 88) at Nikolsburger Strasse 2 offers bed and break-fast at DM36 in double and multi-bed rooms; the DM7 sheet charge applies to the first two nights only. It helps if you are gregarious – there are more than 450 beds! Take the U1 to Hohenzollernplatz or the U9 to Güntzelstrasse.

Studentenwohnheim Hubertusallee (☎ 8 91 97 18) at Delbrückstrasse 24 offers dis-counts to students with a recognised card

GERMANY

(singles/doubles/triples DM45/70/90), otherwise you pay DM80/110/126; all prices include breakfast. This establishment operates only from March to October. The *Studentenhotel Berlin* (☎ 7 84 67 20), Meininger Strasse 10 (U-Bahn: Rathaus Schöneberg), operates like a youth hostel but you don't need a card. Bed and breakfast is DM41 per person in a double, DM37 per person in a quad. It's often full.

In July and August you can sleep in a big tent at the *Internationales Jugendcamp* (☎ 7 91 30 40) in north-west Berlin. From the U-Bahn at Alt-Tegel take bus No 222 (towards Lübars) four stops to the corner of Ziekowstrasse and Waldmannsluster Damm. The tents are behind the *Jugendgästehaus Tegel* (☎ 4 33 30 46), a huge, red-brick building opposite the bus stop. Beds in large communal tents are DM10 per person (blankets and foam mattresses provided) and check-in is after 5 pm (no curfew). Officially this place is only for those aged 14 to 27, but they don't turn away foreigners who are a little older. The maximum stay is three nights and there are no reservations. Self-catering facilities are available. Beds in the guesthouse's four-bed rooms go for DM36 each, including breakfast.

Private Rooms The Berlin Tourist Information office no longer books private rooms, but you can try the private agency *Ariba* (☎ 3 27 54 38), which charges from DM45 per person but no booking fee.

An excellent way to find inexpensive private rooms is through the various Mitwohnzentrale agencies. Most of these have singles from DM35, doubles from DM60 and apartments from DM80 a day and there is usually no minimum stay. Monthly rates for rooms range from DM350 to DM550 and apartments start at DM500. Depending on the length of your stay, it may work out cheaper to pay the monthly rent, even if you don't stay the whole time.

Mitwohnzentrale Ku'damm-Eck (☎ 1 94 45), on the 2nd floor of the Ku'damm Eck shopping arcade at Kurfürstendamm 227, has apartments with one to four beds. The office is open from 9 am to 7 pm weekdays and 11 am to 3 pm Saturday. *Erste Mitwohnzentrale* in Charlottenburg (☎ 3 24 30 31), Sybelstrasse 53 (U-Bahn: Adenauerplatz), is open weekdays from 9 am to 8 pm and Saturday from 10 am to 6 pm. *Mitwohnagentur 2 Domizil* (☎ 7 86 20 03), on the 3rd floor at Mehringdamm 72 in Kreuzberg, is open Monday to Friday 10 am to 7 pm and Saturday 11 am to 4 pm.

Places to Stay – middle
Mid-priced pensions and hotels garni do exist in Berlin but most are small, plain and uncommercial, so expect no luxury. Rooms begin at around DM50/90 singles/doubles with shared facilities. Some places charge extra for showers, though others offer a shower in the room. Breakfast can cost extra. Many are upstairs from shop fronts and some signs are hard to find; often you must ring to enter. There are a few big places, but many have 20 beds or less.

Charlottenburg There are many places near Zoo station and north of Ku'damm. The excellent *Pension Knesebeck* (☎ 3 12 72 55), Knesebeckstrasse 86, just off Savignyplatz, has singles/doubles at DM75/120 (triples available, breakfast included). The *Hotel-Pension Bialas* (☎ 3 12 50 25) at Carmerstrasse 16 is about the biggest, with rooms starting at DM72/100. *Pension Peters* (☎ 3 12 22 78), upstairs at Kantstrasse 146, is one of the smallest, but good value, with rooms starting at DM70/100, including breakfast buffet. *Hotel-Pension Brinn* (☎ 3 12 16 05) at Schillerstrasse 10, also small and friendly, has good but bathless rooms at DM100/130 in attractive surroundings, and relaxed buffet breakfasts.

Hotel-Pension Cortina (☎ 3 13 90 59) at Kantstrasse 140 has plenty of rooms, starting at DM60/90. *Hotel Crystal* (☎ 3 12 90 47) at Kantstrasse 144 is large and reasonably priced from DM70/90. The *Hotel Charlottenburger Hof* (☎ 32 90 70), Stuttgarter Platz 14, is large and convenient, opposite Charlottenburg S-Bahn station (singles/doubles from DM70/80). A good breakfast is downstairs at Café Voltaire (from DM6 to DM8).

Among the best offers around Ku'damm is *Hotel-Pension Modena* (☎ 8 85 70 10) at Wielandstrasse 26, starting at DM65/110 and ranging up to DM120/160 with all facilities.

Hotel-Pension Majesty (☎ 3 23 20 61), Mommsenstrasse 55, is one of the least expensive at DM50/75. South of Breitscheidplatz are *Hotel-Pension Nürnberger Eck* (☎ 2 18 53 71), Nürnberger Strasse 24a, with rates at DM80/130, and *Pension Fischer* (☎ 2 18 68 08) in the same building from DM60/80, breakfast DM10 extra.

South of Ku'damm, you'll find *Hotel-Pension Pariser Eck* (☎ 8 81 21 45), Pariser Strasse 19 (singles/doubles from DM50/90, three to five-bed rooms available), and *Pension Elton* (☎ 8 83 61 55), Pariser Strasse 9 (from DM100/130).

Kreuzberg You'll find lots of inexpensive accommodation in this lively quarter. Try *Pension Kreuzberg* (☎ 2 51 13 62), Grossbeeren-strasse 64, which has singles/doubles for DM70/90 and multi-bed rooms for DM40 per person. *Hotel Transit* (☎ 7 85 50 51), Hagelberger Strasse 53-54 (U-Bahn: Mehringdamm), a youth hotel crowded with travellers, offers rooms from DM80/99 single/double and multi-bed rooms with shower at DM42 per person, big breakfast included. The Transit tends to fill up with school groups from March to May and in September and October, but in other months it should have beds available. *Hostel Die Fabrik* (☎ 6 11 71 16), Schlesische Strasse 18, has singles for DM58, doubles for DM85 and multi-bed rooms at DM28 per person. The downstairs café serves breakfast (extra charge). The budget option on the edge of Schöneberg is the large *Hotel Sachsenhof* (☎ 2 16 20 74) at Motzstrasse 7, which has depressing rooms but a good breakfast buffet (DM10) and starts at an affordable DM57/99.

Mitte The family-operated *Hotel Merkur* (☎ 2 82 95 23), at Torstrasse 156, ranges from DM75/110 for a single/double to DM110/160 with bath and breakfast. It's a little overpriced for what you get, but it has a few moderate family rooms. The small *Hotel Novalis* (☎ 2 82 40 08), Novalisstrasse 5 off Torstrasse, is fairly central and starts at DM125/165 a single/double with all facilities.

Spandau A budget pension north-west of the centre out in Spandau, and handy to Altstadt Spandau U-Bahn station, is *Hotel Hamburger Hof* (☎ 3 33 46 02) at Kinkelstrasse 6, where singles/doubles start at DM50/80.

Places to Stay – top end
The 324-room *Hotel Unter den Linden* (☎ 23 81 10), near Friedrichstrasse train station, charges from DM160/195 a single/double and over DM350 for suites, and gives you a spot at No 14 on one of the world's famous avenues, though the hotel is not beautiful to look at. The monstrous *Forum Hotel Berlin* (☎ 2 38 90) with its 941 rooms dominates Alexanderplatz. Prices start at DM195/245 (breakfast buffet DM21). The smaller, renovated and well located *Hotel Albrechtshof* (☎ 30 88 60), Albrechtstrasse 8, starts at DM195/245 for a single/double with all facilities (S-Bahn: Friedrichstrasse).

Riehmers Hofgarten (☎ 7 86 60 59), Yorckstrasse 83 in Kreuzberg (U-Bahn: Mehringdamm) is one up-market hotel that deserves special attention. Rooms (25 in all) cost DM180/220 singles/doubles, including a big breakfast. Bus No 119 from Ku'damm passes the door. This elegant, eclectic edifice erected in 1892 will delight romantics, and it's a fun area in which to stay. For a real splurge, you can't get more central than the *Steigenberger* (☎ 2 12 70) on Los-Angeles-Platz 1. This pleasant 397-room hotel offers all amenities and is one minute away from Ku'damm and Gedächtniskirche. Rates start at DM290/340 and the lavish breakfast buffet is an extra DM29 per person.

Long-Term Rentals If you'd like to spend some time in Berlin, look for people willing to sublet their apartment. Many Berliners take off for extended holidays and are only too happy to have the bills paid while they're gone. The Mitwohnzentrale agencies handle many long-term rentals, and six months or more is usually no problem if the price suits you. Check the *Wohnungen* classified section in *Zitty* or *Zweite Hand*. The Mitwohnzentrale agencies (see the earlier Private Rooms section) charge up to 20% of the monthly rental rate. If you're staying for under a month, you may end up sharing a flat with others, a good way to meet people. Australians and New Zealanders who advertise for rooms often get quicker responses by putting their nationality first in the ad ('Australian seeks room...').

Places to Eat

There's a restaurant of every cuisine under the sun in Berlin – in fact, there are so many *Spezialitäten* that you will soon regard native fare as the real speciality. Yet among this variety, the best food is generally available at (by local standards) reasonable prices. A cooked lunch or dinner at an unpretentious restaurant will cost less than DM15 if you order carefully.

Restaurants *Pizzeria Amigo*, Joachimstaler Strasse 39-40 near Zoo station (open daily from 11 to 1 am), serves a wicked plate of spaghetti napoli or a pizza margherita for only DM6. It's self-service but the food is good and there's a fine place to sit down. *Piccola Taormina* on Uhlandstrasse 29 in Charlottenburg is a noisy blue-walled labyrinth serving fast, good-value pizzas (from the DM2 variety up to a quite filling DM16) and it is possible to escape for DM10 (including coffee). Locals like the style, and the smell wafting along the nearby Ku'damm can be irresistible. The *Noodle Company* at Yorckstrasse 83 in Kreuzberg offers international noodle dishes of good value in tasteful surroundings. *Pasternak*, on Knaackstrasse 24 in Prenzlauer Berg, revives Russian nostalgia with updated versions of traditional Russian dishes (main dishes around DM14).

German One of the easiest places to experience a typical German meal is the *Ratskeller* (daily from 11 am to 1 am) below Berlin Rathaus just south of the TV tower (S/U-Bahn: Alexanderplatz). Prices are reasonable but the service tends to be slow. *Dicke Wirtin*, Carmerstrasse 9 off Savignyplatz, is an earthier *Kneipe* (pub) offering goulash soup and beer. In Kreuzberg, there's *Gasthaus Herz* on Marheinekeplatz 15, with an extensive menu of stick-to-the-ribs fare. The *Bärenschenke Bierbar*, Friedrichstrasse 124 (U-Bahn: Oranienburger Tor), is an unpretentious local pub serving local specialities from 10 am to 11 pm (closed Monday). Typical are the Schlachteplatte mit Blut und Leberwurst (a mixed meat plate typical of Berlin) and the Wildsuppe (venison soup). There's a long bar where you can chat with Berliners as you swill your beer.

Vegetarian The Krishna snack bar *Higher Taste* at Kurfürstendamm 157 is an excellent speciality restaurant and very reasonably priced but is, like most of its type, closed on Sunday. Always open and a good café and restaurant for any purpose is *Café Voltaire* on Stuttgarter Platz opposite the Charlottenburg S-Bahn station. The speciality is fresh food prepared while you wait, which is not hard to do as this restaurant attracts an interesting crowd from across the spectrum of Berlin cultural life. The vegie menu is quite respectable and tasty. A bit more expensive, with average main courses around DM18, is the trendy *Café Ören* on Oranienburger Strasse 28, where most dishes are not just meatless but also Kosher.

Cafés In the Berlin café culture, the distinctions between pub, restaurant and bar become blurred; you can roll into most places at most times and order most things. *Café Kranzler* (open daily till midnight), on Kurfürstendamm 18 near Zoo station, is one of Berlin's oldest coffee houses and a traditional *Konditorei*. It's popular with grandmas and tourists and has a nice terrace for people-watching. Berlin's most elegant literary café is *Café Einstein*, a Viennese-style coffee house on Kurfürstenstrasse 58 (U-Bahn: Kurfürstenstrasse). It's open daily from 10 to 2 am. This is a good place to go with friends if you want to talk.

A good late-evening place is *Café Arkade*, Französische Strasse 25 near Platz der Akademie (U-Bahn: Französische Strasse), which stays open until midnight. Here you can get excellent Viennese coffee, ice cream or drinks in a pleasant, relaxed atmosphere.

Breakfast Cafés These are a Berlin institution catering to the city's late risers. You can get a filling brunch of yoghurt, eggs, meat, cheese, bread, butter and jam for around DM12 (coffee extra). Some of the breakfasts are huge, so consider sharing one between two people. Many restaurants serve these 'breakfasts' until a rather civilised hour and so they also make a good lunch.

On Bleibtreustrasse (S-Bahn: Savignyplatz), you'll find two establishments typical of the genre. At No 45 there's *Café Bleibtreu*, which serves breakfast from 9.30 am to 2 pm and at No 48 is the old-timey *Zillemarkt*, where you can indulge until 4 pm. Another longtime favourite, though a bit pricey, is *Schwarzes Café*, Kantstrasse 148 near Zoo station. It serves breakfast any time and is open around the clock from 9 pm Tuesday to 1.30 am Monday. This is one place to get off the street if you happen to roll into Berlin in the middle of the night. Also in Charlottenburg try *Café Voltaire* (see the preceding Vegetarian section). *Sidney*, in Schöneberg, right on Winterfeldplatz square, gives you front-row seats to watch the trendy crowds, with breakfast served till 5 pm.

Fast Food One of the best places for felafel and shawarma is *Habibi* on Goltzstrasse 24 in Schöneberg. It's open till 3 am and is especially popular with night-time crowds. A little more expensive is the *Nordsee* cafeteria on the corner of Spandauer Strasse and Karl-Liebknecht-Strasse, which specialises in freezer-package fare that is nonetheless filling and locally popular.

Substantial snacks are available at the many *Schnellimbiss* stands around the city. In addition to German stand-bys like *Rostbratwurst* and *Currywurst*, most Imbiss stands also have döner kebab (usually DM4, though a mini-dösner here and there costs about DM2.50) and mini-pizzas are often advertised for DM2. Many Schnellimbiss also offer smallish barbecued half-chickens (about DM5).

For big cups of coffee for DM1.50, visit the stand-up cafés in many *Eduscho* and *Tchibo* coffee retailers around Berlin. Because these stores are bound by regular shopping hours, this deal isn't offered on evenings or weekends.

Cafeterias On weekdays, you can enjoy a hot subsidised meal (DM5 to DM10) in a government cafeteria where you clear your own table. The *Kantine* in Rathaus Charlottenburg, Otto-Suhr-Allee 100 close to Schloss Charlottenburg (U-Bahn: Richard-Wagner-Platz) is in the basement inside the building (not the expensive Ratskeller outside). What's available is usually written on a blackboard at the far end of the counter.

The *Rathaus Casino* cafeteria on the 10th floor of Rathaus Kreuzberg, Yorckstrasse 4-11 (U-Bahn: Mehringdamm), is open weekdays from 7.30 am to 3 pm and offers cheap lunch specials, vegetarian dishes and great views. Everyone is welcome.

Almost any Arbeitsamt (employment office) will have a cheap *Kantine*. A good one is in Arbeitsamt IV at Charlottenstrasse 90 (U-Bahn: Kochstrasse); it's open weekdays from 9 am to 1 pm. Just walk straight in and take the lift on the left up to the 5th floor.

If you have a valid student card there's the *mensa* of the Technical University, Hardenbergstrasse 34 three blocks from Zoo station (open weekdays from 8 am to 5 pm), where you can fill up a tray for DM10.

Self-Catering To prepare your own food, start your shopping at the discount *Aldi* or *Penny Markt* chains, which have outlets throughout Berlin, or the less common *Tip* stores. You sometimes have to wait in long checkout queues and the variety of goods can occasionally be scant, but you will pay considerably less for the basic food items available. Handy travelling food such as powdered fruit drinks and soups, dried and fresh fruit, bread, cheese, packaged salads, sandwich meats and chocolate bars are among the worthwhile items. They are also the cheapest places to buy beer and table wines.

Aldi is upstairs on Joachimstaler Strasse opposite Zoo station, at Uhlandstrasse 42 and on the corner of Kantstrasse and Kaiser-Friedrich-Strasse in Charlottenburg. Tip and Penny Markt are side-by-side near the corner of Hohenzollernstrasse and Martin-Luther-Strasse. *Plus* is another discounter – probably with more outlets and a slightly bigger range of goods – often competing with the others on price.

Vegetarians could try the *Einhorn* buffets on Wittenbergplatz and on Mommsenstrasse near Bleibtreustrasse. For good-quality fruit and vegetables, though, consider the various street markets outside the city centre (see the following Things to Buy section).

Entertainment
Opera & Musicals Most of the best theatres are conveniently clustered in Berlin-Mitte and Charlottenburg. All performances are listed in

GERMANY

the various events magazines (see the earlier Newspapers & Magazines section). Many theatres are dark on Monday and from mid-July to late August.

Good seats are usually obtainable on the evening of a performance because unclaimed tickets are sold an hour before the show. Some theatres (such as the Metropol) give students and pensioners a 50% discount on unsold tickets 30 minutes or one hour before curtain. The best way to get in is simply to start making the rounds of the box offices at about 6 pm. If there's a big crowd waiting at one theatre, hurry on to the next. You're allowed to move to unoccupied, better seats just as the curtain is going up. Berlin's not stuffy, so you can attend theatre and cultural events dressed as you please.

The *Staatsoper*, Unter den Linden 5 in Mitte, hosts lavish productions with international stars. The box office (☎ 20 25 45 55) is open weekdays from 10 am to 6 pm and weekends from 2 to 6 pm; tickets cost from DM6 to DM190. Nearby, at Behrenstrasse 55-57 at the corner of Glinkastrasse (S-Bahn: Unter den Linden) is the *Komische Oper*. The box office (☎ 20 26 03 60) at Unter den Linden 41 is open Monday to Saturday from 11 am to 7 pm, Sunday from 1 pm until 90 minutes before curtain; tickets cost DM10 to DM80.

In Charlottenburg, at Bismarckstrasse 35, you'll find the *Deutsche Oper* from 1961 (U-Bahn: Deutsche Oper), a glass and steel behemoth. Its box office (☎ 3 41 02 49) opens Monday to Saturday from 11 am to 7 pm, Sunday from 10 am to 2 pm; tickets range from DM15 to DM135.

Musicals and operettas are presented at the *Metropol-Theater* at Friedrichstrasse 101 in Mitte, directly in front of Friedrichstrasse station. It's not as famous as the operas, so tickets are easier to obtain – highly recommended! The box office (☎ 20 24 61 17) opens Monday to Saturday from 10 am to 6 pm; tickets are DM10 to DM70. (Don't confuse this Metropol theatre with the Metropol disco in Schöneberg.)

Seats at Charlottenburg's *Theater des Westens*, Kantstrasse 12 near Zoo station, cost DM20 to DM76 most days, Friday and Saturday DM23 to DM84. The box office across the street is open Tuesday to Saturday from noon to 6 pm, Sunday from 2 to 4 pm. Though this

beautiful old theatre (1896) has style and often features excellent musicals, it's hard to see much from the cheap seats.

Back in Mitte, *Friedrichstadtpalast*, Friedrichstrasse 107, offers vaudeville musical revues, but it's often sold out. The box office (☎ 23 26 24 74) is open Monday 1 to 6 pm, Tuesday to Saturday 1 to 7 pm and Sunday 2 to 7 pm; tickets cost from DM17 to DM87. Tickets are also hot at the *Wintergarten*, Potsdamer Strasse 96, which features a 1920s-style variety show updated for the 1990s. You can get in for DM50 to DM92. There's no box office, but you can make reservations by calling ☎ 2 62 70 70.

Theatre & Concerts Even if you speak little or no German, the *Berliner Ensemble*, Bertolt Brecht's original theatre near Friedrichstrasse station is worth attending for its architecture and the musical interludes as well as the brilliance of the classic Brecht plays. *The Threepenny Opera*, Brecht's first great popular success, premiered here in 1928. The box office (☎ 2 82 31 60) opens Monday to Saturday from 11 am to 6 pm, Sunday 3 to 8 pm; tickets cost from DM10 to DM55.

Try to hear at least one concert at the *Philharmonie*, Matthäikirchstrasse 1 (U-Bahn: Kurfürstenstrasse, then bus No 148). All seats are excellent, so just take the cheapest. Another treat is a concert at the *Konzerthaus* (Concert Hall) in Mitte, formerly the Schauspielhaus Berlin.

Cinemas Movies are quite expensive in Berlin; tickets on Saturday night can cost as much as DM17. It's cheaper on Tuesday or Wednesday and before 5 pm, when tickets are DM8 to DM11. The *Filmzentrum Zoo-Palast*, Hardenbergstrasse 29a near Zoo station, contains nine cinemas (the Berlin Film Festival is held here). There are many other movie houses along Kurfürstendamm, but foreign films are dubbed into German. (If the film is being shown in the original language with German subtitles it will say 'O.m.U.' on the advertisement. If it's in English the ad will be marked 'engl. OF'.)

The *Kurbel Cinema* (☎ 8 83 53 25), Giesebrechtstrasse 4 off Kurfürstendamm (U-Bahn: Adenauerplatz), usually has at least one film in English (seats DM12). See movies in the original English at the *Odeon Cinema* (☎ 7 81 56 67), Hauptstrasse 116 (U-Bahn: Innsbrucker Platz, or S-Bahn: Schöneberg). There are three shows daily.

Culture Centres Much of Berlin's nightlife is concentrated in three main neighbourhoods: along Oranienstrasse in Kreuzberg, around Käthe-Kollwitz-Square in Prenzlauer Berg (locals say Prenz'lberg) north-east of Alexanderplatz, and along Oranienburger Strasse in Berlin-Mitte. Much of the action takes place in cultural centres which offer a rainbow of entertainment – concerts, discos, readings, theatre, among them – all under one roof. What's on varies, so it is best to ring ahead, check the events listings in the city magazines, or drop by and check the programmes usually posted at the door. The price of admission depends on the event.

Podewil (☎ 24 74 96), at Klosterstrasse 68-70 in Mitte (U-Bahn: Klosterstrasse), offers a mixed bag of film, theatre and live music as well as a café, all in a historic building from 1704. The café is open Monday to Friday 11 am to 7 pm and for all performances.

An adventure playground for adults is *Tacheles* (☎ 2 82 61 85, U-Bahn: Oranienburger Tor), which is housed in a dilapidated, graffiti-covered building on Oranienburger Strasse 54-56 near the New Synagogue. Its scrappy look belies an active cultural programme that includes dance, jazz concerts, a café, cabaret, readings, workshops and a steady stream of characters.

Another multi-media culture club, though a bit more tame, is the *UFA-Fabrik* on Victoriastrasse 13 in Tempelhof (U-Bahn: Ullsteinstrasse). It is housed in the former UFA film studios. The hot spot in Prenzlauer Berg is the *KulturBrauerei* on Knaackstrasse 97, on the corner of Dimitroffstrasse, where artists from around the world work in a space of 8000 square metres.

Discos & Nightclubs Berlin has a reputation for its nightlife, and nothing happens until 10 pm. Just as in every metropolis, the nightclub scene changes quickly and it's hard to keep up. Before heading out, call ahead to make sure the club's still there.

You'll always find lots of discos around Ku'damm, such as *Big Eden* at Kurfürstendamm 202 (open daily from 7 pm). Other than Friday and Saturday nights there's no cover charge, but they make up for it with the price of the drinks. If you'd rather dance with Berliners it's *Far Out* (☎ 32 00 07 23), Kurfürstendamm 156 (U-Bahn: Adenauerplatz). The entrance to this Bhagwan disco is beneath the bowling alley around the side of the building (open from 10 pm except Monday). Admission varies.

Several nightclubs have perfected the fine art of the rave, and techno music has become quintessentially Berlin, as evidenced by the Love Parade held in summer every year. Among the pioneering clubs is the giant *E-Werk* (☎ 6 18 10 07), a former electricity plant on Wilhelmstrasse 43, now charged by about 2000 ravers every Friday and Saturday from midnight till morning (DM15 to DM30). *Tresor* (☎ 6 09 37 02), on Leipziger Strasse 128a in Mitte, is a techno haven inside the actual money vault of a former department store. It opens at 10 pm but things don't get humming until way past midnight (DM10 to DM15).

Among the latest entries on the scene is *WMF* (☎ 2 82 79 01), Burgstrasse 22, in Mitte. It's big but cosy, with plump sofas and two elegant dance floors playing underground dance music. One of the best-known places in Berlin is *Delicious Doughnuts* (☎ 61 68 85 00), a café-bar-club at Rosenthaler Strasse 9 near Humboldt University and therefore popular with students (DM8).

Pubs Many pubs offer live music and food. A cover charge of up to DM20 may be asked if there's live music, although some places only charge admission on Friday and Saturday nights. The *Sophienklub*, Sophienstrasse 6 off Rosenthaler Strasse (S-Bahn: Weinmeisterstrasse), has jazz nightly from 9 pm, with a special programme on Tuesday and Saturday nights. *Quasimodo*, Kantstrasse 12a near Zoo station (open from 9 pm, music from 10 pm), is a jazz cellar with live jazz, blues or rock every night. There are cover charges for 'name' acts.

Salsa, Wielandstrasse 13, features Latin American and Caribbean music. It opens at 8 pm, has live music from 10.30 pm and offers free admission Sunday to Thursday (as well as happy hours from 8 to 10 pm). In Schöneberg, you'll find a couple of cocktail bars that tend to be packed nightly. *Mr Hu*, on Goltzstrasse 39 (U-Bahn: Eisenacher Strasse) has an exotic feel while the *Zoulou Bar* on Hauptstrasse 3 (U-Bahn: Kleistpark) is trendy and intimate.

Counterculture pub-cafés with an earthy atmosphere are *Seifen und Kosmetik*, at Schliemannstrasse 21 in Prenzlauer Berg (S-Bahn: Prenzlauer Allee), and *Café Anfall*, at Gneisenaustrasse 64 in Kreuzberg (S-Bahn: Südstern). Anfall opens only in the evening and has wild décor and good, but loud, music, while Seifen und Kosmetik can offer you a laid-back afternoon.

Berliner Kneipen Typical Berlin pubs have their own tradition of hospitality – good food (sometimes small courses or daily soups only), good beer, good humour and *Schlagfertigkeit* (repartee). You can find this atmosphere in a few backstreet, unassuming places (the tendency to add modern music is inevitable), where a handful of fine establishments maintain a living and evolving tradition. Part of the charm of the following three venues is that each, in its own way, claims to be the oldest Berlin inn.

Stories abound about the historic *Zur letzten Instanz* ('The Last Resort') at Waisenstrasse 14 (U-Bahn: Klosterstrasse). The pub claims traditions dating back to the 1600s and for good measure is next to a stretch of medieval town wall. The place got its present name 150 years ago when a newly divorced couple (we are told) came in from the nearby courthouse with their witnesses, but by the time they were ready to leave they'd decided to remarry the next day, at which one of those present exclaimed, 'This is the court of last resort!' A course of wholesome local fare, beer and coffee here costs less than DM25.

E&M Leydicke, Mansteinstrasse 4 on the corner of Goebenstrasse (S/U-Bahn: Yorckstrasse), is one of Berlin's oldest surviving pubs (founded in 1877) and bottles its own liqueurs on the premises. It is open odd hours, for lunch and then from early evening until late, but is primarily a drinking place.

The inn *Zum Nussbaum*, associated in the past with the artist Heinrich Zille and the humorist Otto Nagel, has been re-established as part of the Nikolaiviertel (beside the church on the corner of Propststrasse near the Mühlendamm). You can enjoy the good, reasonably priced fare while examining some of Zille's sketches on the walls.

Things to Buy

Shopping in Berlin is surprisingly difficult because there is no central shopping district or street, though Tauentzienstrasse, running south-east of Gedächtniskirche, perhaps comes closest. Here you'll find KaDeWe (Kaufhaus des Westens, U-Bahn: Wittenbergplatz), an amazing, six-storey, turn-of-the-century department store selling just about everything. Wertheim, Kurfürstendamm 232, Berlin's second-largest department store, is less pretentious and less expensive. New among department stores is a transplant of the French chain Galeries Lafayette on Friedrichstrasse (U-Bahn: Stadtmitte) which has an interesting interior. Europa-Center next to Gedächtniskirche stays open late and has a large supermarket, newsstands, boutiques and restaurants.

Shops selling discount cameras can be found along Augsburger Strasse near Ku'damm. Meissner Porzellan, Unter den Linden 39, sells the famous Meissen porcelain – fun to look at but, with prices starting at DM100, an expensive buy. For funky, second-hand attire, try Made in Berlin, Potsdamer Strasse 106 (U-Bahn: Kurfürstenstrasse).

Berlin has several street markets hawking a hotchpotch of produce, clothing, toiletries, books and other wares. The one at Rathaus Schöneberg, where John F Kennedy once said, 'Ich bin ein Berliner', is hard to beat for its range and quality (Tuesday and Friday to 1 pm). A visit to the market on Winterfeldplatz square in trendy Schöneberg (Wednesday and Saturday to 1 pm) should be rounded out with crowd-watching during a lavish breakfast in one of the surrounding cafés.

There's an outdoor flea market (*Trödelmarkt*) every Saturday and Sunday on Strasse des 17 Juni at Tiergarten S-Bahn station. Don't buy any GDR paraphernalia here, as you can get it much cheaper from the stands around Brandenburger Tor (but try to make sure it's authentic) or from the market at Am Kupfergraben near the Pergamon Museum. On Sunday, you can rummage through bric-a-brac at the market on Arkonaplatz in Prenzlauer Berg until 4 pm.

Second-hand cars are lined up on Stuttgarter Platz in Charlottenburg (just west of the S-Bahn station) on most days of the week. Prices start at about DM1500, but most of the respectable-looking Golfs and Corsas are in the DM3000 to DM5000 range. Varied information appears in the windows and, although some offer service histories, it seems very much a case of *caveat emptor*. Perhaps it is better to ring around using the auto edition of *Zweite Hand* if you want a wide choice of marque or a particular car or features.

You can buy solid second-hand bicycles from about DM120 through the listings in *Zweite Hand*, although used touring models start at about DM230. Mehring Hof Fahrrad Laden (☎ 6 91 60 27), at Gneisenaustrasse 2a in Kreuzberg, is a handy showroom for good second-hand makes, and solid, three-gear models cost from about DM280. Fahrrad Station (see Bicycle Rental in the following Getting Around section) sells fully tested used machines from DM400.

For outdoor gear and camping equipment, investigate the range at Der Aussteiger, Schliemannstrasse 46 in Prenzlauer Berg, and compare with the big Alles für Tramper specialist store at Bundesallee 88 in west Berlin.

Getting There & Away

Air Most Eastern European and Third World carriers use Berlin-Schönefeld airport, next to Flughafen Berlin-Schönefeld station just outside the southern city limits. The S9 runs via Zoo station and Alexanderplatz every 20 minutes between 4 am and midnight (or take the U7 to Rudow and bus No 171, also every 20 minutes). The more occasional S45 links Schönefeld and Tempelhof airports.

Berlin-Tegel, Berlin's main commercial airport six km north-west of Zoo station, receives most flights from Western Europe (bus No 109 from the Inter-Continental Hotel on Kurfürstendamm via Zoo station, or express bus X9 from Kurfürstenstrasse/Lützowplatz). These buses operate every 15 minutes from 5 am to midnight. There's a baggage storage office (open from 5.30 am to 10 pm), a tourist information counter and a bank in the main hall of the airport.

Tempelhof airport receives mostly domestic flights (U6 to Platz der Luftbrücke or bus No 119 from Kurfürstendamm via Kreuzberg).

Bus The Funkturm bus station (U-Bahn: Kaiserdamm) is open from 5.30 am to 10 pm. Witzleben S-Bahn station is within walking distance. Bayern Express-Berlinien bus (☎ 8 60 09 60) has buses to Amsterdam, Hanover, Munich, Nuremberg, Würzburg and Rothenburg ob der Tauber as well as a DM110 fare to Frankfurt/Main (9 hours, students to age 26 DM76). Tickets are available from most travel agencies in Berlin. Sperling GmbH (☎ 33 10 31) has services to Bremen, Goslar, Hamburg, Kiel, Lübeck and other cities in northern Germany.

Train Train services in Berlin can be confusing because the extensive construction around town affects several stations. Trains scheduled to leave from or arrive at one station may be spontaneously rerouted to another, so it's best to check in advance. You may also find that services arriving at one station link with services leaving from another. To connect, take the U-Bahn or S-Bahn (DM2.50 or DM3.90, depending on the distance), but allow ample time for this transfer because unexpected delays on these trains are frequent.

Conventional train tickets to and from Berlin are valid for all train stations in the city S-Bahn, which means that on arrival you may use the S-Bahn network (but not the U-Bahn) to connect or to proceed to your destination. Conversely, you can use the S-Bahn to go to the station from where your train leaves for another city, if you have a booked ticket.

Berlin Hauptbahnhof in Friedrichhain handles trains going south to Munich and east to Leipzig and Warsaw; there's also one daily train to Malmö in Sweden. This station has more of the large DM3 lockers than Zoo, as well as a DM4 per day left-luggage office (open from 6.15 am to 10.30 pm daily) and an exchange office (weekdays 7 am to 10 pm, Saturday to 6 pm, Sunday 8 am to 4 pm).

Berlin Lichtenberg handles trains to Stralsund, Rostock and other cities in Mecklenburg-Pomerania, as well as services to

GERMANY

Dresden, Erfurt, Halle, Magdeburg, Moscow, Prague and other destinations in Eastern Europe. The reservation office is open on weekdays from 6 am to 8 pm, on weekends from 8 am to 6 pm. The left-luggage room is always open (DM2 per piece per day) and there are coin lockers.

Bahnhof Zoo, on Hardenbergplatz, is the main station for long-distance trains to cities in the West, including Hanover, Frankfurt and Cologne, as well as Paris, Amsterdam and Brussels. There's also frequent service to Hamburg and a direct train to Sylt. Coin lockers cost DM2 or DM3 depending on the size, and the left-luggage station charges DM4 per item per day. There's a large remodelled reservation and information office with quick service (open 5.15 am to 11 pm) and – outside on Hardenbergplatz – is a local transit office where you can get information and tickets.

Bahnhof Friedrichstrasse and Alexanderplatz station can be good places to dump your gear as big lockers cost only DM2 (though many will be out of order at any time).

Hitching You can hitch to Dresden, Hanover, Leipzig, Munich, Nuremberg and beyond from Checkpoint Dreilinden at Wannsee (S-Bahn: Wannsee, then walk less than a km up Potsdamer Chaussee and follow the signs to Raststätte Dreilinden). There's always a bunch of hitchhikers here, but everyone gets a ride eventually. Bring a sign showing your destination, and consider waiting until you find a car going right where you want to go.

There are several Mitfahrzentrale agencies, which charge a fixed amount payable to the driver plus commission ranging from DM7 for short distances to DM20 for trips abroad.

Generally, a ride to Magdeburg goes for DM16, Frankfurt is DM48, Budapest DM90 and Paris is DM84; all prices include commission.

One central agency is Mitfahrerzentrale im Bahnhof Zoo (☎ 1 94 40), on Vinetastrasse platform of the U2 line. It is open weekdays from 9 am to 8 pm and weekends from 10 am to 6 pm. Also open daily are Mitfahrerzentrale im U-Bahnhof Alexanderplatz (☎ 2 41 58 20) as you cross from the U2 to the U8, and Citynetz Mitfahr-Service (☎ 1 94 44), which has offices on the 2nd-floor of Ku'damm-Eck

shopping arcade at Kurfürstendamm 227, at Sybelstrasse 53 and three other locations. The people answering the phone in these offices usually speak good English.

If you arrange a ride a few days in advance, be sure to call the driver the night before and again on departure morning to make sure he/she is still going.

Getting Around
Berlin is probably easier to drive around than many other big cities, but you will still run into roadworks in the eastern parts for some time yet. You can park immediately west of the zoo for DM20 for the day; the going rate is about DM2 per hour. Underground parking at similar rates is on Augsburger Strasse not far from Breitscheidplatz. The ring roads get you easily around the urban perimeter. Above-ground parking is easier to find in eastern areas and is generally cheaper. Better yet, use the efficient public transport network – or a bicycle.

To/From the Airports Berlin's three airports can be reached by train and/or bus. See the previous Getting There & Away section for routes and times.

Public Transport Usually, the Berliner Verkehrs-Betriebe (BVG) operate an efficient suburban train (S-Bahn), metro (U-Bahn), ferry and bus system which reaches every corner of Berlin and the surrounding area. At the moment, however, the extensive construction around town causes frequent delays and schedule changes.

Trams exist only in east Berlin. The BVG ferry from Kladow to Wannsee operates hourly all year (except when there's ice or fog), with regular tickets, passes and transfers accepted. The S-Bahn differs from the U-Bahn in that more than one line uses the same track. Destination indicators on the platforms tell you where the next train is going. Route maps are posted in all stations and carriages or you can pick one up from the information kiosks.

The system is easy to use, but you have to pay attention. The next station (including an *Übergang*, or place to change) is announced in most trains and even displayed at the end of carriages on some new trains. It's best, though, to know the name of the station before the one you need.

Most stations now have orange ticket machines with English instructions and usually accept DM5 coins or notes up to DM50, although you can often buy a ticket from a ticket window at the station entrance. A single DM2.50 *(Kurzstrecke)* ticket will take you three stops (with one change, if necessary) on a train or half a dozen stops on a bus; if in doubt, ask. The DM3.90 ticket allows unlimited transfers on all forms of public transport for two hours; in train stations validate the ticket as your train arrives to ensure full value.

A *Sammelkarte* with four trip blocks of two hours each works out cheaply at DM13, and a 24-hour ticket costs DM16. If two of you (and up to three children) are travelling together, a 24-hour group card at DM20 is the best value. The DM40 weekly pass is a good buy if you are travelling a lot. Monthly passes cost DM93.

Bus drivers sell single tickets and 24-hour tickets, but other multiple, weekly or monthly tickets must be purchased in advance. Most passes are available from the orange machines in mass transit stations or from the BVG information kiosk (open daily from 10 am to 6 pm) in front of Zoo station.

You validate your own ticket in a red machine *(Entwerter)* at the platform entrances to S-Bahn and U-Bahn stations or at bus stops. If you're caught by an inspector without a valid ticket, there's a DM60 fine (random checks have been stepped up and no excuses are accepted). Cultural cringe is such that less than 1.5% of passengers ride illegally.

You can take a bicycle in specially marked cars on the S-Bahn or U-Bahn for a DM2.50 fare or for free if you hold a monthly ticket. You're not allowed, however, to take a bike on U-Bahn trains weekdays from 2 to 5.30 pm.

The double-decker buses offer great views from the upstairs front seats. Among the most popular routes is bus No 119 from Grunewald to Kreuzberg via Ku'damm. An even better option is bus No 100, which passes all major sights on its way from Bahnhof Zoo to Prenzlauer Berg, providing you with a great overview and cheap orientation to Berlin.

The S-Bahn and U-Bahn lines close down between 1 and 4 am, but buses run every 30 minutes all night from Zoo station to key points such as Rathaus Spandau, Alt-Tegel, Hermannplatz, Rathaus Steglitz etc. Regular fares apply.

Taxi There are taxi stands beside all main train stations. The basic flag fall tariff is DM4.80, then it's DM2.20 for the first km, DM1.80 for each additional km. Night and weekend fares are higher by DM0.20. If you need to travel quickly over a short distance, you can use the DM5 flat rate which entitles you to ride for five minutes or 2 km, whichever comes first. This deal only applies if you flag down a moving taxi and ask for the DM5 rate before getting into the car. You can call a taxi at ☎ 96 44, 69 02 and 21 02 02, though for faster response try the 'Taxi-Ruf' listings for your area in the telephone directory (for instance ☎ 8 81 52 20 for the Ku'damm-Uhlandstrasse area).

Car & Motorcycle Rental All the large car-rental chains are represented in Berlin, and their standard rates for the cheapest car begin at around DM99 daily or DM449 weekly, including tax and unlimited km. Some arrangements also include collision insurance which can save you up to DM40 a day. There are also special weekend tariffs for rental from Friday at noon to Monday 9 am, starting at DM99. Rental cars are often fully booked in Berlin, so advance reservations are advisable, and you'll probably get a better rate by booking from abroad. Weekends are usually the best times to rent.

Hertz (☎ 2 61 10 53), Budapester Strasse 39 across from the Zoo, has Opel Corsas or equivalent for DM99 a day on weekdays, including theft and collision insurance; ask for the 'city-hit' rate. On weekends, the same money will let you keep the car from Friday through to Monday, but insurance is extra. Weekly rentals are perhaps the best deal, starting at an all-inclusive DM449.

Avis next door offers pretty much the same deals. There's also a Budget/Sixt Rent-a-Car (☎ 2 61 13 57) at Budapester Strasse 18 and a Europcar at Kurfürstendamm 178 (☎ 8 81 80 93). You must be at least 21 years old to rent and practically all credit cards are accepted by these companies. For small companies offering discount car rentals, check the 'PKW – Vermietung' section of the classified newspaper *Zweite Hand*.

For motorcycle rentals try Classic Rent (☎ 6 14 73 43) at Skalitzer Strasse 127 in Kreuzberg near Schlesisches Tor. Weekly rental rates vary from DM570 to DM980 and there is a deposit of DM1500 on cash rentals. The first 250 km are free. Another prospect is S7 Motorradvermietung (☎ 7 71 73 69) at Breite Strasse 22 in Steglitz. Rates start at around DM500 per week for 650cc models, with a DM350 deposit.

Bicycle Rental Bicycles can be rented at Fahrrad Station (☎ 285 99 895), Rosenthaler Strasse 40/41 in the Hackeschen Höfen in Mitte. Another office is nearby at Gipsstrasse 7 and at Möckernstrasse 92 in Kreuzberg, where it's called Berlin by Bike. This company offers carefully inspected and maintained machines from DM17 per 24 hours for city use, DM80 per week. You might also try Fahrradvermietung Berlin am Europa-Center (☎ 2 61 20 94) on the 15th floor of the Europa-Center.

Brandenburg

The state of Brandenburg surrounds the city-state of Berlin, and plans to merge these two political entities were dashed in a May 1996 referendum. Brandenburg is a flat region of lakes, marshes and rivers, and canals connecting the Oder and Elbe rivers (utilising the Havel and Spree rivers, which meet at Spandau west of Berlin). The Spreewald, a marshy area near Cottbus, was inhabited by the Slavonic Sorbs until WWII. The electors of Brandenburg acquired the eastern Baltic duchy of Prussia in 1618, merging the two states into a powerful union called the Kingdom of Prussia. This kingdom eventually brought all of Germany under its control, leading to the establishment of the German Empire in 1871.

POTSDAM
Potsdam, on the Havel River just beyond the south-west tip of Berlin, became important in the 17th century as the residence of the Elector of Brandenburg. Later, with the creation of the Kingdom of Prussia, Potsdam became a royal seat and garrison town, and in the mid-18th century Friedrich the Great built many of the marvellous palaces in Sanssouci Park, where visitors flock today.

In April 1945, British bombers devastated the historic centre of Potsdam, but fortunately most of the palaces escaped undamaged (only the City Palace was badly hit). To make a point of their victory over German militarism, the Allies chose the city for the Potsdam Conference of August 1945, which set the stage for the division of Berlin and Germany into four occupation zones.

Orientation & Information
Potsdam Stadt train station is just south-east of the town centre across the Havel River. The next stop after Potsdam Stadt is Potsdam West, which is closer to Sanssouci Park; most trains also stop at Bahnhof Wildpark (closer still, but check in advance). The city centre and Sanssouci Palace are both reached from Hauptbahnhof by tram or bus (buy your ticket in advance at a kiosk or machine). You can walk from Schloss Cecilienhof to Glienicker Brücke (and bus No 116 to Wannsee) in about 10 minutes.

Potsdam-Information (☎ 29 11 00 or 27 55 80), at Friedrich-Ebert-Strasse 5 beside Alter Markt, sells a variety of maps and brochures but can be crowded. Its opening hours vary with the season: in summer it is open from 9 am to 8 pm weekdays, 10 am to 6 pm on Saturday, and 10 am to 4 pm on Sunday. From November to March its hours are weekdays from 10 am to 6 pm, weekends from 10 am to 2 pm. A smaller branch is at Brandenburger Strasse 18. In both places you can buy the joint Berlin-Potsdam WelcomeCard (see Information in the Berlin section) which entitles you to 48 hours of unlimited transportation and free or discounted admission to many attractions in both cities for 72 hours (DM29). Sanssouci-Information (☎ 9 69 42 02) is near the historical windmill adjacent to Schloss Sanssouci.

Potsdam's telephone code is ☎ 0331.

Things to See
Sanssouci Park This large park is open from dawn till dusk with no admission charge. Begin with Knobelsdorff's **Schloss Sanssouci** (1747), a famous rococo palace with glorious interiors (closed Monday). You have to take the

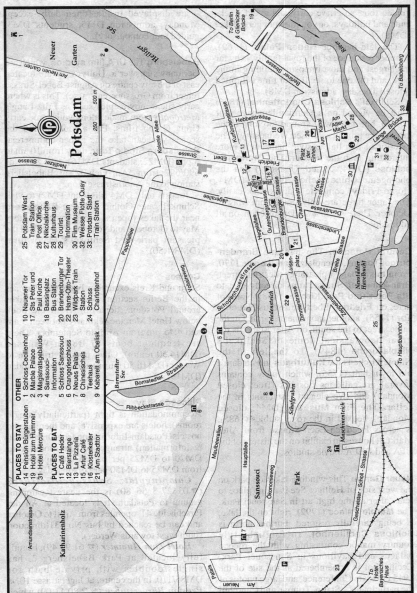

Potsdam

PLACES TO STAY
14 Pension Bürgerstuben
19 Hotel zum Hummer
31 Hotel Mercure

PLACES TO EAT
11 Café Heider
12 Bierstange
13 La Pizzeria
15 Artur Café
16 Klosterkeller
21 Am Stadttor

OTHER
1 Schloss Cecilienhof
2 Marble Palace
3 Magistratsgebäude
4 Sanssouci-
  Information
5 Schloss Sanssouci
6 Orangerieschloss
7 Neues Palais
8 Chinesisches
  Teehaus
9 Kabarett am Obelisk

10 Nauener Tor
17 Sts Peter und
  Paul Kirche
18 Bassinplatz
  Bus Station
20 Brandenburger Tor
22 Hans-Otto-Theater
23 Wildpark Train
  Station
24 Schloss
  Charlottenhof

25 Potsdam West
  Train Station
26 Post Office
27 Nikolaikirche
28 Kulturhaus
29 Tourist
  Information
30 Film Museum
32 Weisse Flotte Quay
33 Potsdam Stadt
  Train Station

guided tour, so arrive early and avoid weekends and holidays, or you may not get a ticket (DM8).

The late-baroque **Neues Palais** (1769), summer residence of the royal family, is by far the largest and most imposing building in the park, and the one to see if your time is limited (closed Tuesday, admission DM8).

Schinkel's **Schloss Charlottenhof** (1826) must be visited on a German-language tour (DM6), but don't wait around too long if the crowds are immense (closed Wednesday). The exterior of this Italian-style mansion is more interesting than the interior. The **Orangerieschloss** (DM4, closed Thursday) and the photogenic **Chinesisches Teehaus** (DM4, closed Friday) complete a day's walk easily. The latter three are only open from May to October. There's a 50% student discount on all admissions.

Central Potsdam The baroque **Brandenburger Tor** on Luisenplatz bears the date 1770. From this square a pleasant pedestrian street, Brandenburger Strasse, runs directly east to **Sts Peter und Paul Kirche** (1868). North of here, on Friedrich-Ebert-Strasse, is **Nauener Tor** (1755), another monumental arch. On the same street to the south, on Alter Markt, is the great neoclassical dome of Schinkel's **Nikolaikirche** (1849). To the left of the Nikolaikirche is the **Kulturhaus** in Potsdam's old town hall (1755), which today contains several art galleries upstairs (free; closed Monday) and two elegant restaurants in the cellar. The **Film Museum** (DM4; closed Monday), housed in the royal stables (1685), is across Friedrich-Ebert-Strasse from Alter Markt. It houses an exhibit on the history of the UFA and DEFA movie studios.

Neuer Garten This winding lakeside park on the west side of Heiliger See is a fine place to relax after all the high art in Sanssouci Park. The **Marble Palace** (1792), right on the lake, is being carefully restored. Further north is **Schloss Cecilienhof**, an English-style country manor contrasting with the rococo palaces and pavilions in Sanssouci Park. Cecilienhof is remembered as the site of the 1945 Potsdam Conference, and large photos of the participants – Stalin, Truman and Churchill

– are displayed inside (open daily except Monday, admission DM5, students DM3, guided tour compulsory).

Babelsberg The **UFA film studios**, which are Germany's answer to Hollywood, are located east of the city centre on August-Bebel-Strasse (enter from Grossbeerenstrasse). This is where early silent movie epics such as Fritz Lang's *Metropolis* were made, along with some early Greta Garbo films. For a look behind the scenes you can take the rather commercial **Babelsberg Studio Tour**, daily from 10 am to 6 pm (DM22, students DM16); take bus Nos 690/692 from 'Am Gehölz' at Babelsberg station to the Ahornstrasse stop.

It costs only DM4 (discount DM2) to visit Schinkel's neo-Gothic **Schloss Babelsberg** near the lakes (open all year, tour obligatory May to October), and you can also stroll in the pleasant park past Schinkel's **Flatowturm** (DM3/1.50).

Cruises

Stern und Kreis excursion boats (see Cruises in the Berlin section) operate on the lakes around Potsdam, departing from the dock below Hotel Mercure regularly between 9 am and 4.45 pm from April to September. There are frequent boats to Berlin-Wannsee (DM14.50 return). Other popular trips are to Werder (DM16.50 return) and Berlin-Spandau (DM19.50).

Places to Stay

Accommodation is tight (particularly single rooms), hotels are expensive, and there are no hostels. Potsdam-Information (see Orientation & Information) arranges private rooms from DM20 to DM25 per person and apartments from DM25 to DM50 per person a day.

Campingplatz Sanssouci/Gaisberg (☎ 03327-5 56 80) is the nearest camping ground to Potsdam. It is located at An der Pirschheide 41, operates from April to October and can be reached by bus No 631(direction south-west towards Werder).

Hotel Zum Hummer (☎ 61 95 49), beautifully located at Park Babelsberg 2, has singles/doubles with private bath for DM85/110. In the centre, at Jägerstrasse 10, is *Pension Bürgerstuben* (☎ 2 80 11 09) which also has a restaurant. Rooms go for DM90/170. *Hotel Bayerisches Haus* (☎ 96 37 90) at Im Wildpark 1 is a bit on the pricey side, with singles starting at DM115, doubles at DM195. Rooms at the three-star *Hotel Schloss Cecilienhof* (☎ 3 70 50) in Neuer Garten are even higher at DM165/280 and up, but you get to sleep in one of Potsdam's most famous buildings. If you don't mind the price, have a travel agent book your room well in advance.

Places to Eat

The *Klosterkeller*, Friedrich-Ebert-Strasse 94 on the corner of Gutenbergstrasse, harbours a restaurant, wine bar, beer garden and night bar. The restaurant serves traditional regional dishes at moderate prices. *La Pizzeria*, Gutenbergstrasse 90, is popular with locals for its well-priced pizzas and pastas. *Am Stadttor*, by the gate at the western end of Brandenburger Strasse, has good lunch specials and offers a pleasant view.

Young people congregate at *Café Artur*, Dortustrasse 16, where you can get small dishes for under DM10. The airy décor of the new two-floor *Bierstange* at Friedrich-Ebert-Strasse 88 matches the contemporary menu that includes generous fish dishes at DM13. *Café Heider*, another lively meeting place, is just up the street at No 28, adjacent to Nauener Tor.

Entertainment

The Besucherservice (☎ 2 80 06 93), in Theaterhaus on Alter Markt (open Monday to Friday 9 am to 4 pm, Saturday 9 am to noon), has tickets for performances at the *Hans-Otto-Theater*, Zimmerstrasse 10, and the *Schlosstheater* in the Neues Palais. On some Wednesdays at 7.30 pm from July to mid-September, there are organ concerts at various churches in Potsdam (ask Potsdam-Information for locations). The *Potsdamer Kabarett am Obelisk* (☎ 29 10 69), Schopenhauerstrasse 27, presents satirical programmes (in German) with contemporary themes.

Getting There & Away

Bus Bassinplatz bus station is accessible from Berlin on bus No 638 from Rathaus Spandau (hourly from 5 am to 9 pm). If you're headed for Schloss Cecilienhof, take bus No 116 from

Berlin-Wannsee to Glienicker Brücke in Potsdam and walk from there.

Train Hourly S-Bahn trains run from Berlin-Wannsee to Potsdam Stadt, near the centre of town. There is no direct service to Berlin-Schönefeld airport, but you can take the S3 and S7 from Potsdam Stadt to Westkreuz in western Berlin and change for the S45. All Berlin transit passes are valid for the trip to Potsdam by either S-Bahn or BVG transit bus, and for local trams and buses around Potsdam.

Many trains between Hanover and Berlin-Zoo also stop at Potsdam Stadt. For Schwerin, take a train from Potsdam Hauptbahnhof to Stendal or leave from Potsdam Stadt and change in Magdeburg. Train connections from Potsdam Stadt south to Leipzig are poor and most require a change in Magdeburg also. Going to Dresden means changing trains at Berlin-Lichtenberg.

Getting Around

Potsdam is part of Berlin's S-Bahn network and has its own buses; these converge on Lange Brücke near Potsdam Stadt train station. Comparable in price (DM3.50 per trip) are the summer excursion buses around Sanssouci to Neues Palais, through the town centre to the park, or to Babelsberg. Most run direct from outside Potsdam Stadt station. For a taxi dial ☎ 81 04 04.

Saxony

The Free State of Saxony (Sachsen) is the most densely populated and industrialised region in eastern Germany. Germanic Saxon tribes originally occupied large parts of north-western Germany, but in the 10th century they expanded south-eastward into the territory of the pagan Slavs.

The medieval history of the various Saxon duchies and dynasties is complex, but in the 13th century the Duke of Saxony at Wittenberg obtained the right to participate in the election of Holy Roman emperors. Involvement in Poland weakened Saxony in the 18th century, and ill-fated alliances, first with Napoleon and

GERMANY

then with Austria, led to the ascendancy of Prussia over Saxony in the 19th century.

In the south, Saxony is separated from Czech Bohemia by the Erzgebirge, eastern Germany's highest mountain range. The Elbe River cuts north-west from the Czech border through a picturesque area known as the 'Saxon Switzerland' towards the capital, Dresden. Leipzig, a great educational and commercial centre on the Weisse Elster River, rivals Dresden in historic associations. Quaint little towns like Bautzen, Görlitz and Meissen punctuate this colourful, accessible corner of Germany.

DRESDEN
In the 18th century the Saxon capital Dresden was famous throughout Europe as 'the Florence of the north'. During the reigns of Augustus the Strong (ruled 1694-1733) and his son Augustus III (ruled 1733-63), Italian artists, musicians, actors and master craftsmen, particularly from Venice, flocked to the Dresden court. The Italian painter Canaletto depicted the rich architecture of the time in many paintings which now hang in Dresden's Alte Meister Gallery alongside countless masterpieces purchased for Augustus III with income from the silver mines of Saxony.

In February 1945 much of Dresden was devastated by Anglo-American fire-bombing raids. At least 35,000 people died in this atrocity, which happened at a time when the city was jammed with refugees and the war was almost over. In the postwar years quite a number of Dresden's great baroque buildings have been restored, but the city's former architectural masterpiece, the Frauenkirche, is still in the early stages of a laborious and enormously expensive reconstruction.

The Elbe River cuts a curving course between the low, rolling hills, and in spite of modern rebuilding in concrete and steel, this city invariably holds visitors' affection. With its numerous museums and many fine baroque palaces, a stay of three nights is the minimum required to fully appreciate Dresden.

Orientation
Dresden has two important train stations: the main station, or Dresden Hauptbahnhof, on the southern side of town, and Dresden-Neustadt north of the river. Most trains stop at both, but

the Hauptbahnhof is more convenient unless you're staying in Neustadt.

At present most of Dresden's priceless art treasures are housed in two large buildings, the Albertinum and the Zwinger, which are at opposite sides of the Dresden's largely restored Altstadt. From Dresden Hauptbahnhof, the pedestrian mall of Prager Strasse leads north into this old centre. Major redevelopment is planned for the area around the Hauptbahnhof and Prager Stasse, including a dozen new high-rise buildings as well as pedestrian and traffic underpasses.

Information
Dresden-Information (☎ 49 19 20) is at Prager Strasse 10, on the eastern side of the pedestrian street leading away from the Hauptbahnhof. It's open weekdays from 10 am to 6 pm, and Saturday 9.30 am to 5 pm (closed Sunday). Dresden-Information's Neustädter Markt office (☎ 5 35 39), in the underpass below the Goldener Reiter statue in Neustadt, is open from Monday to Friday between 10 am to 6 pm. Ask about the 48-hour Dresden-Card (DM19) which gives free entry to six museums, concessions on city tours and river boats as well as free use of public transport.

The Deutsche Verkehrs Bank has a branch in the main train station (open daily), and American Express is at Münzgasse 4 near the Frauenkirche. There is a useful post office on Prager Strasse near the tourist office.

Dresden's telephone code is ☎ 0351.

Things to See & Do
Altstadt A 10-minute walk north along Prager Strasse from the Dresden train station brings you into the Altmarkt area, the historic hub of Dresden. On the right you'll see the rebuilt **Kreuzkirche** (1792), famous for its boys' choir, and behind it the 1912 **Neues Rathaus** (New Town Hall).

Cross the wide Wilsdruffer Strasse to the **City Historical Museum** (entry DM3, closed Monday) in a building erected in 1776. Northwest up Landhausstrasse is Neumarkt and the site of the ruined **Frauenkirche** (Church of Our Lady) built in 1738. Until 1945 it was Germany's greatest Protestant church, and is now in the early stages of a painstaking reconstruction expected to last almost two decades. To view the progress, you can take a one-hour guided tour (several daily in German only) of the Frauenkirche site; it's free, but donations are warmly accepted.

Leading north-west from Neumarkt is Augustusstrasse with the 102-metre-long *Procession of Princes* mural depicted on the outer wall of the old royal stables. Here you'll also find the interesting **Museum of Transport** (DM4, closed Monday). Augustusstrasse leads directly to Schlossplatz and the baroque Catholic **Hofkirche** (1755), whose crypt contains the heart of Augustus the Strong. Just south of the church is the Renaissance **Royal Palace**, which is being reconstructed as a museum. The restoration work is well advanced, and the tower and a palace exhibit are now open to the public (DM3, closed Monday).

On the western side of the Hofkirche is Theaterplatz, with Dresden's glorious opera house, the neo-Renaissance **Semperoper**. The first opera house on the site opened in 1841 but burned down in 1869. Rebuilt in 1878, it was again destroyed in 1945 and only reopened in 1985 after the Communists invested millions in the restorations. The Dresden opera has a tradition going back 350 years, and many works by Richard Strauss, Carl Maria von Weber and Richard Wagner premiered here.

The baroque **Zwinger** (1728) occupies the southern side of Theaterplatz and houses five museums. The most important are the **Old Masters Gallery** (entry DM7, closed Monday), which features numerous old masters, including Raphael's *Sistine Madonna*, and the **Historisches Museum** (DM3, closed Monday), which has a superb collection of ceremonial weapons. There are also the **Mathematics Salon** with old instruments and timepieces (DM3, closed Thursday), the **Museum für Tierkunde** (DM2, closed Monday), with natural history exhibits, and the **Porcelain Collection** (DM3, closed Thursday), all housed in opposite corners of the complex with separate entrances. The grey porcelain bells of the clock on the courtyard's eastern gate chime on the hour.

To reach the **Albertinum**, on Brühlsche Garten just off Terrassenufer, stroll east along the terrace overlooking the river. Here you'll find the **New Masters Gallery**, with renowned 19th and 20th-century paintings, and the **Grünes Gewölbe** (Green Vault), one of the world's finest collections of jewel-studded precious objects; both are closed Thursday and admission is DM7 (students DM3.50). Eventually the Grünes Gewölbe will be relocated to its original site in the Royal Palace. In a park to the south of the Albertinum is the unique **Hygiene Museum** (DM5, closed Monday), Lignerplatz 1, which will appeal to anyone with a healthy interest in the human body.

Neustadt Neustadt is an old part of Dresden largely untouched by the wartime bombings. After unification Neustadt became the centre of the city's alternative scene, but as entire street blocks are renovated it's gradually losing its hard-core Bohemian feel.

The **Goldener Reiter** statue (1736) of Augustus the Strong stands at the northern end of the Augustusbrücke (bridge), leading to Hauptstrasse, a pleasant pedestrian mall with the **Museum of Early Romanticism** (DM3, closed Monday and Tuesday) at No 13. On Albertplatz at its northern end there's an evocative marble monument to the poet Schiller. Other museums in the vicinity of the Goldener Reiter include the **Museum für Volkskunst** (Museum of Folk Art, DM2, closed Monday) at Grosse Meissner Strasse 1, and the **Japanisches Palais** (1737), Palaisplatz, with Dresden's famous Ethnological Museum (closed Friday).

Special Events
Dresden's International Dixieland Festival takes place every year in the first half of May.

Places to Stay
Camping There are two camping grounds near Dresden. The closest is *Camping Mockritz* (☎ 4 71 82 26, open March to December), five km south of the city. (Take the frequent No 76 'Mockritz' bus from behind the Dresden train station.) It has bungalows, but like the camping ground itself they're often full in summer.

A more appealing, if more distant, choice is the spacious *Camping Mittelteich Moritzburg* (☎ 035207-4 23; open April to mid-October) on a lake called Mittelteich, a 10-minute walk beyond Schloss Moritzburg (see the following Around Dresden section).

Hostels Best and most central is the large *Jugendgästehaus Dresden* (☎ 49 26 20), a

Dresden

0   0.5   1 km

Minor streets not depicted
Some streets pedestrian-only

PLACES TO STAY
3   Pension Edith
4   Hotel Stadt Rendsburg
8   Hotel Rothenburger Hof
10 Hotel Martha Hospiz
28 Hotel Taschenbergpalais
34 Jugendgästehaus
40 Hotel Königstein
44 Youth Hostel

PLACES TO EAT
1   Café Europa
2   Café 100
5   Café Scheune
6   Planwirtschaft
9   Raskolnikoff
16 Topinambur
31 aha
33 Walterrasse Restaurant
35 Gaststätte Zur Keule
36 Zum Goldenen Ring

OTHER
7   Dresden-Neustadt
    Train Station
11 Museum of
    Early Romanticism
12 ADM-Mitfahrzentrale
13 Japanisches Palais
14 Dresden-Information
    & Goldener Reiter
15 Museum of Folk Art
17 Semperoper
18 Hofkirche
19 Museum of Transport
20 Dock for Steamer Boats
21 Frauenkirche
22 Albertinum
23 Bärenzwinger
24 Jazzclub Tonne
25 Royal Palace
26 Zwinger
27 Staatsschauspiel
29 Kulturpalast
30 City Historical Museum
32 Kreuzkirche
37 Neues Rathaus
38 Hygiene Museum
39 Post Office
41 Dresden-Information
42 Main Train Station
43 Zoo

former Communist party training centre 15 minutes walk north-west of the main station at Maternistrasse 22. Beds cost DM30.50/35.50 junior/senior in basic twin or triple rooms, or DM35.50/40.50 junior/senior in better twins with private shower and WC. The *youth hostel* (☎ 4 71 06 67), at Hübnerstrasse 11, is 10 minutes walk south of the main train station and offers dorm beds for DM21.50/26 junior/ senior. On the outskirts of Dresden are two other youth hostels, the *Jugendherberge Radebeul* (☎ 8 30 52 07), Weintraubenstrasse 12, in Radebeul, and the *Jugendherberge Ober-loschwitz* (☎ 3 66 72) at Sierksstrasse 33, which both charge DM21/25 for seniors/juniors.

Private Rooms Dresden-Information, Prager Strasse 10, finds private rooms priced from around DM35 per person (plus a fee of DM5 per person).

Hotels & Pensions Average hotel rates in Dresden are among the highest in Germany, with few genuine budget places near the centre.

South of the Elbe New on the scene is *Artis Suites* (☎ 5 20 03), one km west of the centre at Berliner Strasse 25, which offers basic singles/doubles from DM60/90 (without breakfast). The *Hotel Cosel* (471 94 95), August-Bebel-Strasse 46, is two km south-east of the centre and charges DM65/100 for similar rooms.

Along Prager Strasse are the *Hotel Bastei* (☎ 4 85 63 88), the *Hotel Königstein* (☎ 4 85 64 42) and the *Hotel Lilienstein* (☎ 4 85 64 89), three large hotels belonging to the Ibis group. Their rates are as similar as their 1960s-style architecture, with rooms from DM135/220. Dresden's most central and ritzi-est place is the *Hotel Taschenbergpalais* (☎ 4 12 20), at Taschenberg 3 opposite the Zwinger. It's a complete reconstruction of the early 18th-century mansion that stood here until 1945, and offers luxurious suites starting from DM395/ 455 a single/double.

North of the Elbe Over in Neustadt, *Hotel Stadt Rendsburg* (☎ 8 04 15 51), built in 1884, is at Kamenzer Strasse 1, and offers basic singles/doubles with shared bath for DM65/95

including breakfast. The *Pension Edith* (☎ 57 90 58), in a quiet backstreet at Priesnitzstrasse 63, has doubles with private shower for DM100; it only has a few rooms, so you'd better book well ahead. *Hotel Martha Hospiz* (☎ 5 67 60), at Nieritzstrasse 11 close to Neu-stadt train station, has a few simple single rooms for DM85, but most other rooms are singles/doubles with private toilet and shower costing DM140/230. The *Rothenburger Hof* (☎ 801 17 17), Rothenburger Strasse 15-17, has single/double rooms with shared bath for DM95/145.

East of the Centre A reasonable option in the suburb of Blasewitz, several km from the centre, is the *Waldparkhotel* (☎ 3 44 41), at Prellerstrasse 16, with basic singles/doubles from DM70/100. The nearby *Pension Andreas* (☎ 33 77 76), Mendelssohnallee 40-42, whose rooms all have private facilities, charges DM90/140 per single/double.

Places to Eat
Interesting restaurants are scattered pretty thinly around the Dresden Altstadt. A pleasant but unexciting place is *Walterrasse Restau-rant*, on Wallstrasse overlooking Antonsplatz, which serves drinks and meals to tables on its spacious 1st-floor terrace. Also reasonable is the *Zum Goldenen Ring* at Altmarkt 18 oppo-site the Kreuzkirche, with main courses around DM13. The *Gaststätte Zur Keule* (☎ 4 95 15 44), below a cabaret at Sternplatz 1, is a lively beer hall that offers good, solid meals.

Dresden's down-to-earth folk eat at *Topinambur*, Schützengasse 18 (next to the environment centre), where menu favourites include wholemeal noodles with gorgonzola sauce (DM11.50) and tofu schnitzels with baked vegies (DM14.50). Catering to slightly more up-market organic-vegetarian tastes is *aha*, just off Altmarkt at Kreuzstrasse 7. Both places are open daily.

North of the river the food scene is much less tame. Worth a brief re-mention is the *Rothenburger Hof* (see Places to Stay), whose restaurant has alternating evening menus for around DM12.50 (closed Monday). For some-thing special, dine at the *Restaurant Kügelgenhaus* (☎ 5 27 91, open daily), at Hauptstrasse 13, below the Museum of Early

Romanticism in Neustadt. It has a good range of local Saxon dishes, and there's a beer cellar below the restaurant.

Neustadt's selection of late-night restaurant-bars include the *Planwirtschaft*, in a beer cellar at Luisenstrasse 20 (head through the small courtyard), the *Café 100*, another cellar pub at the corner of Alaunstrasse and Bischofsweg, and the *Café Scheune*, Alaunstrasse 36, whose tasty five-course Indian menu is amazingly good value at just DM35 for two people. The Bohemian *Raskolnikoff* at Böhmische Strasse 34, has cheap Russian dishes like borscht (beetroot soup) and wareniki (dough baked with potatoes and mushrooms). *Café Europa* at Königsbrücker Strasse 68 in Neustadt is a convenient place to drop in for a meal or a drink; it only closes for one hour every day (from 5 to 6 am, to get rid of long-staying guests).

Entertainment
Dresden is synonymous with opera, and performances at the *Semperoper*, opposite the Zwinger, are brilliant. Dresden's two other great theatres are the *Staatsschauspiel*, also near the Zwinger, and the *Staatsoperette*, at Pirnaer Landstrasse 131, in Leuben in the far east of the city. Tickets for all three theatres can be bought at the Besucherdienst office on Sofienstrasse (at the side of the palace opposite the Semperoper), from Dresden-Information, or an hour before each performance at either theatre's box office. Tickets for the Semperoper cost from DM30, but they're usually booked-out well in advance. Many theatres close for holidays from mid-July to the end of August.

A variety of musical events are presented in the *Kulturpalast* (☎ 4 86 63 06), which changes its programmes daily. The *Bärenzwinger* (☎ 4 95 14 09) is a cheap students' bar in an old cellar at Brühlscher Garten in front of the Albertinum. It has pantomime, cabaret or live music most nights. The *Jazzclub Tonne* (☎ 4 95 13 54) at Tzschirnerplatz 3 has live jazz five nights per week (entry DM12 to 20).

Getting There & Away
Dresden is just over two hours south of Berlin-Lichtenberg by fast train. The Leipzig-Riesa-Dresden service (120 km, 1½ hours) operates

hourly. The double-decker S-Bahn trains run half-hourly to Meissen (40 minutes). There are also direct trains to Frankfurt/Main (six hours), Munich (7½ hours), Vienna (8½ hours), Prague (2¾ hours), Budapest (via Prague, 10½ hours), Warsaw (via Görlitz and Kraków, 11 hours) and Wroclaw (Breslau in German, four hours).

There's an ADM-Mitfahrzentrale (☎ 1 94 40) at Königstrasse 10; some destinations and prices (including fees) are: Berlin DM20.50, Hamburg DM46.50, Prague DM15 and Munich DM46.

Getting Around
Dresden's bus and tram-based transport network is surprisingly cheap. Fares are charged for the time travelled – there are no zones. Seven-ride strip tickets cost DM7.50; stamp once for 10 minutes travel (but no more than four stops), or twice for 60 minutes travel. Day/weekly tickets cost DM7/18.

AROUND DRESDEN
Pillnitz Palace
From 1765 to 1918, Pillnitz Palace, on the Elbe about 10 km directly south-east of Dresden, was the summer residence of the kings and queens of Saxony. The most romantic way to get there is on one of Dresden's old steamers. Otherwise, take tram No 14 from Wilsdruffer Strasse or tram No 9 from in front of the Dresden train station east to the end of the line, then walk a few blocks down to the riverside and cross the Elbe on the small ferry, which operates throughout the year. The museum at Pillnitz (open from May to mid-October) closes at 5.30 pm, but the gardens (which stay open till 8 pm) and the palace exterior with its Oriental motifs are far more interesting than anything inside, so don't worry if you arrive too late to get in.

Schloss Moritzburg
This palace rises impressively from its lake 14 km north-west of Dresden. Erected as a hunting lodge for the duke of Saxony in 1546, the Moritzburg was completely remodelled in baroque style in 1730, and it has an impressive interior. Entry costs DM6 (students DM4), and it's open Tuesday to Sunday from 10 am to 5.30 pm (until 3.30 in winter). Behind the palace are

lovely parklands ideal for strolling. There are buses to Moritzburg from Dresden Hauptbahnhof.

Elbe River Excursions

From May to November the Sächsische Dampfschifffahrts GmbH (☎ 0351-86 60 90) – which prides itself on having the world's oldest fleet of paddle-wheel steamers – has frequent services upriver from Dresden via Pirna and Bad Schandau to Schmilka. Here the Elbe River has cut a deep valley through the sandstone, producing abrupt pinnacles and other striking rock formations. Local trains return to Dresden from Schmilka-Hirschmühle opposite Schmilka about every half-hour until late in the evening, with stops all along the river. On weekends, boats also run downriver as far as Meissen.

MEISSEN

Meissen, just 27 km north-west of Dresden, is a perfectly preserved old German town and the centre of a rich wine-growing region. Its medieval quarter, Albrechtsburg, crowns a ridge high above the Elbe River, and contains the former ducal palace and Meissen Cathedral, a magnificent Gothic structure. Augustus the Strong of Saxony created Europe's first porcelain factory here in 1710.

Orientation & Information

Meissen straddles the Elbe, with the old town on the western bank and the train station on the eastern bank. The train/pedestrian bridge behind the station is the quickest way across, and presents you with a picture-postcard view of the river and the Altstadt. From the bridge, continue up Obergasse then bear right through Hahnemannsplatz and Rossplatz to Markt, the town's central square. A new road bridge is being built one km downriver; from 1998 it will replace the vehicle-choked Elbbrücke and divert traffic away from the historic heart.

The helpful Meissen-Information (☎ 45 44 70), just off Markt at An der Frauenkirche 3 in an old brewery, charges a service fee of DM5 per person for finding private-room accommodation. In summer the office is open Monday to Friday from 10 am to 6 pm, as well as Saturday and Sunday from 10 am to 3 pm; the shorter winter opening hours are from 9 am to 5 pm on weekdays only.

Meissen's telephone code is ☎ 03521.

Things to See & Do

On Markt are the **town hall** (1472) and the 15th-century **Frauenkirche** (open 10 am to 4 pm daily from May to October). The church's tower (1549) has a porcelain carillon, which chimes every quarter-hour. It's well worth climbing the tower (DM2) for fine views of Meissen's Altstadt; pick up the key in the church or from the adjacent *Pfarrbüro* (parish office).

Various steeply stepped lanes lead up to the **Albrechtsburg**, whose towering medieval **cathedral** (open daily; DM3.50 or DM2.50 for students), with its altarpiece by Lucas Cranach the Elder, is visible from afar. Beside the cathedral is the remarkable 15th-century Albrechtsburg **palace** (open daily but closed all January; DM6, students DM3). Constructed with an ingenious system of internal arches, it is the first palace-style castle ever built in Germany.

Meissen has long been famous for its chinaware, with its easily distinguishable blue crossed-swords insignia. The Albrechtsburg palace was originally the manufacturing site, but the **porcelain factory** is now at Talstrasse 9, one km south-west of town. There are often long queues for the workshop demonstrations (DM7, students DM5), but you can view the fascinating porcelain collection in the museum upstairs at your leisure (another DM7, students DM5). Even if you're not interested in buying, it's still worth having a look at the factory's porcelain shop downstairs.

Places to Stay

Budget accommodation is fairly scarce, but Meissen-Information can often find private rooms from around DM30 per person (plus a service fee of DM5 each).

Camping Rehbocktal (☎ 45 26 80) is in a beautiful forest at Scharfenberg on the banks of the Elbe, three km south-east of Meissen. Charges are DM3 per car, DM4 per tent plus DM6 per person, and its four-person bungalows are good value at DM17.50 per person for the first night, DM12.50 thereafter; take bus No 404 from the station. The non-DJH *Jugendgästehaus* (☎ 45 30 65) which is at

Wilsdruffer-strasse 28, about 20 minutes walk south of Markt, offers beds in small dorms for DM18.

The *Pension Burkhardt* (☎ 45 81 98), at Neugasse 29 in a renovated building about halfway between Rossmarkt and the porcelain factory, offers fair value for money. It has attractive rooms all with toilet, shower, phone and TV from DM60/90 a single/double. The *Pension Schweizerhaus* (☎ 45 71 62), off Talstrasse at Rauhentalstrasse 1, has seven double rooms, all with private shower and toilet, from DM90. A similar deal is offered by the *Haus Hartlich* (☎ 45 25 01), on the southern edge of town at Goldgrund 15.

Places to Eat

Meissen's cheapest surprise is the *Meissner Hof*, Lorenzgasse 7 (closed weekends). Here, a bowl of vegetable stew costs DM3, a steaming serving of soljanka (Sorbian sour soup) with bread is DM2.80, and half-litre mugs of frothy ale go down the hatch for just DM3 – definitely lower than average prices! The *Kellermeister*, a simple pub at Neugasse 10, has daily set meals from DM7.40.

On the way up to the Albrechtsburg is the *Gaststätte Winkelkrug*, Schlossberg 13 (closed Monday and Tuesday). It's in a quaint old building with many cosy corners, and you can eat from as little as DM8. The *Rabener Keller*, in an old arched wine cellar below at Elbstrasse 4, offers local specialities from around DM15.

The *Weinschänke Vincenz Richter*, An der Frauenkirche 12 (closed Sunday and Monday), is rather expensive but it's in an old woodenbeam house whose interior looks more like a museum – check the torture chamber – and it has plenty of atmosphere. The food menu is short but the wine list is pages long. A better place to sample Meissen's fine fermentations is the *Probierstube* (☎ 73 55 33), 10 minutes walk north-east of the train station at Bennoweg 9. It's run by the local winegrowers' cooperative and dishes up hearty food to complement the excellent wines.

Getting There & Away

Meissen is most directly accessible by the half-hourly S-Bahn trains from Dresden (DM4.80, 40 minutes) or Dresden-Neustadt train stations, but a more interesting way to get there is by steamer (between May and September).

LEIPZIG

Since the discovery of rich silver mines in the nearby Erzgebirge (the 'Ore Mountains') in the 16th century, Leipzig has enjoyed almost continual prosperity. Today Leipzig is a major business and transport centre, and the second-largest city in eastern Germany. It has a strong cultural tradition and still offers much for book and music lovers (Bach's time here is celebrated by a museum and an active choir).

Since medieval times Leipzig has hosted annual trade fairs, and during the Communist era these provided an important exchange window between East and West. After unification, the city spent a huge sum of money on a new ultra-modern fairground in order to re-establish its position as one of Europe's great 'fair cities'. Never as heavily bombed as nearby Dresden, in recent years central Leipzig has undergone a restoration and construction boom that has brought new life to its many fine old buildings.

Orientation

With its 26 platforms, the impressive Leipzig train station (1915) is the largest terminal station in Europe. This massive structure is undergoing total renovation, including the construction of a large underground shopping and services complex. Until this is completed in late 1997, rail passengers may experience some inconvenience.

To reach the city centre, head through the underpass below Willy-Brandt-Platz and continue south for five minutes; the central Markt square is just a couple of blocks south-west. Ring roads surround the old city centre, more or less where the former city walls once stood. The wide Augustusplatz, three blocks east of Markt, is ex-socialist Leipzig, with the space-age lines of the university (1975) and Gewandhaus concert hall (1983) juxtaposed against the functional opera house (1960). The main post office is also here.

Leipzig's dazzling new trade fairgrounds (or Neue Messe) are five km north of the Hauptbahnhof (take tram No 16).

Information

Leipzig-Information (☎ 10 42 65, open Monday to Friday from 9 am to 7 pm, and at weekends from 9.30 am to 2 pm) is at Sachsenplatz 1, between the main train station and the

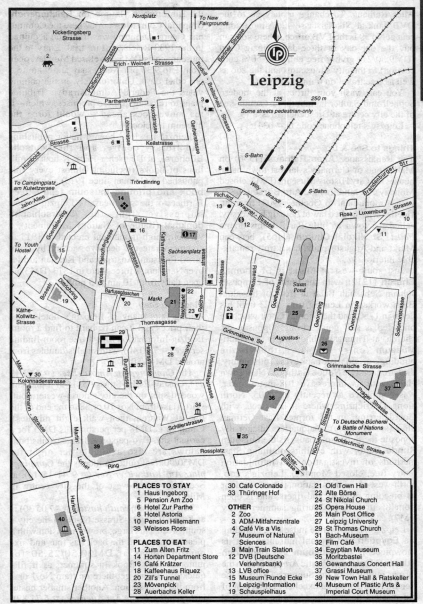

Leipzig

0   125   250 m

Some streets pedestrian-only

PLACES TO STAY
1 Haus Ingeborg
5 Pension Am Zoo
6 Hotel Zur Parthe
8 Hotel Astoria
10 Pension Hillemann
38 Weisses Ross

PLACES TO EAT
11 Zum Alten Fritz
14 Horten Department Store
16 Café Krätzer
18 Kaffeehaus Riquez
20 Zill's Tunnel
28 Mövenpick
28 Auerbachs Keller

30 Café Colonade
33 Thüringer Hof

OTHER
2 Zoo
3 ADM-Mitfahrzentrale
4 Café Vis a Vis
7 Museum of Natural
   Sciences
9 Main Train Station
12 DVB (Deutsche
   Verkehrsbank)
13 LVB office
15 Museum Runde Ecke
17 Leipzig-Information
19 Schauspielhaus

21 Old Town Hall
22 Alte Börse
24 St Nikolai Church
25 Opera House
26 Main Post Office
27 Leipzig University
29 St Thomas Church
31 Bach-Museum
32 Film Café
34 Egyptian Museum
35 Moritzbastei
36 Gewandhaus Concert Hall
37 Grassi Museum
39 New Town Hall & Ratskeller
40 Museum of Plastic Arts &
   Imperial Court Museum

GERMANY

Altes Rathaus. To change money go to the DVB bank at Nikolaistasse 42. Almost adjacent at No 59 is the LVB office, where you can buy the one-day or three-day Leipzig Card (DM9.50/21) giving free entry (or 50% concession) to the city's museums and the zoo as well as free travel on trams and buses.

You can wash your dirties at the modern Schnell-und-Sauber laundrette just south-east of the city centre at Dresdener Strasse 19.

Leipzig's telephone code is ☎ 0341.

Things to See & Do
The Renaissance **Altes Rathaus** (1556) on Markt, one of Germany's largest town halls, houses the City History Museum (DM3, closed Monday). Behind it is the **Alte Börse** (1687), with a monument to Goethe (1903) in front. Goethe, who studied law at Leipzig University, called the town a 'little Paris' in his drama *Faust*. **St Nikolai Church** (1165), between Markt and Augustusplatz, has a truly remarkable interior.

Just south-west of Markt is **St Thomas Church** (1212), with the tomb of composer Johann Sebastian Bach in front of the altar. Bach worked in Leipzig from 1723 until his death in 1750, and the Thomas Choir which he once led is still going strong. Opposite the church, at Thomaskirchhof 16, is the **Bach-Museum** (entry DM4). Although the building's origins date back to the 16th century, the baroque-style **Neues Rathaus** (New Town Hall), with its impressive 108-metre tower, was completed as recently as 1905. North along Dittrichring where it intersects with Goerdelerring, in the former East German Stasi (secret police) headquarters (diagonally opposite the Schauspielhaus), is the **Museum Runde Ecke**, with exhibits outlining Stasi methods of investigation and intimidation (entry free, closed Monday). Leipzig's **zoo**, north-west of the train station, is renowned for its breeding of lions and tigers, and is open from 8 am to 7 pm during summer (entry DM7).

Leipzig has many fine museums, including the **Egyptian** and **Grassi** museums, but its showpiece is the **Museum der bildenden Künste** (Museum of Plastic Arts) housed in the former buildings of the Supreme Court of the Reich (1888), with an excellent collection of old masters downstairs. Upstairs you'll find

the **Historische Räume im Reichsgericht** (Imperial Court Museum), where the Communist Georgi Dimitrov was tried and acquitted in the 1933 Reichstag Fire trial. Entry to the museum costs DM5; it's closed Monday, open from 1 to 9.30 pm Wednesday and 9 am to 5 pm other days. Unfortunately, in the coming years the Federal Administrative Tribunal plans to relocate to these premises, which – if the move goes ahead – would force the museum to relocate

Leipzig has long been a major publishing and library centre, and the **Deutsche Bücherei**, at Deutscher Platz 1, houses millions of books (including almost every title published in German since 1913) as well as a **book and printing museum** (entry free). Further to the south-east is Leipzig's most impressive sight, the **Völkerschlacht-denkmal** (Battle of Nations Monument), a 91-metre high monument erected in 1913 to commemorate the decisive victory by combined Prussian, Austrian and Russian armies over Napoleon's forces here in 1813 (DM3.50, open daily from 10 am to 5 pm).

Places to Stay
During fairs many of Leipzig's hotels raise their prices and it can be hard to find a room. Leipzig-Information runs a free room-finding service (☎ 7 10 40), with singles/doubles from around DM45/80.

The *Campingplatz Am Auensee* (☎ 4 61 19 77), Gustav-Esche-Strasse 5, is in a pleasant wooded spot on the city's north-western outskirts (take tram Nos 10 or 28 to the end of the line at Wahren, then walk eight minutes). Camping is DM8 per person plus DM5 for a car/tent site. Two-person A-frame cabins/bungalows are also available per night for DM50/90. Not quite so nice is the *Campingplatz Am Kulkwitzer See* (☎ 9 41 15 14), at Seestrasse south-west of the city centre in Miltitz.

Leipzig's main *youth hostel* (☎ 47 05 30) is at Käthe-Kollwitz-Strasse 62-66 in the city's south-west. This large, prewar mansion with a pleasant garden at the back has four and six-person dorms at DM20.50/25.50 for juniors/seniors. Book in summer, as it fills quickly; you can get there on tram No 1 or 2 from the train station. Another smaller hostel is *Jugendherberge Am Auensee* (☎ 5 71 89), at Gustav-Esche-Strasse 4 on the lake near the previously mentioned camping ground, which charges DM20/24 for juniors/seniors.

The best value in rooms in Leipzig is offered by the small *Pension Hillemann* (☎ 9 60 27 43), at Rosa-Luxemburg-Strasse 2, less than five minutes walk east of the main train station. Here clean and cosy singles/doubles cost just DM40/80 (excluding breakfast). Surrounded by idle GDR-era factories in Plagwitz (tram No 2 or bus No 52 evenings and weekends) is *Elster Pension* (☎ 4 79 80 39), at Giesser-strasse 15, which charges DM44/86 per single/double with semi-private shower and toilet.

Other reasonable options include the newly renovated *Weisses Ross* (☎ 9 60 59 51), Rossstrasse 20, which offers rooms for DM65/110 with shower or DM55/90 without, and the *Pension Prima* (☎ 6 88 34 81) at Dresdener Strasse 82, with simple rooms for DM55/95 (without breakfast). It's two km east of the centre, but easily reached from Willy-Brandt-Platz by tram No 4, 6 or 20.

North-west of the station is the *Pension Am Zoo* (☎ 9 60 24 32), Pfaffendorfer Strasse 23, which charges DM60 for simple singles, and DM90/130 for single/double rooms with private shower. Not far away are *Haus Inge-borg* (☎ 9 60 31 43), Nordstrasse 58, and the *Hotel Zur Parthe* (☎ 9 80 43 26), Löhrstrasse 15, which both offer basic rooms with shared bath for DM70/110.

The Art Deco *Hotel Astoria* (☎ 1 28 30), conveniently situated at Willy-Brandt-Platz 2 (opposite the station's western hall), offers perhaps the best value in the upper-market range, with singles/doubles from DM155/208.

Places to Eat

Always good for a filling feed is the cafeteria on the 5th floor of the *Horten* department store on Trondlinring, where a meal costs around DM10. *Zum Alten Fritz* (closed weekends), a simple tavern at Chopinstrasse 6, offers good-sized meals from around DM15. The *Café Colonade*, on the corner of Max-Beckmann-Strasse and Kolonnadenstrasse, serves sound dishes for less than DM15; there's a small beer garden out the back. *Mövenpick*, Am Naschmarkt 1-3, offers outstanding value with a nightly buffet where you can help yourself to imaginative salads, casseroles and desserts for DM19.50 per person.

Founded in 1525, *Auerbachs Keller* (☎ 2 16 10 40), just south of the Altes Rathaus in the Mädler-Passage, is one of Germany's classic restaurants. Goethe's *Faust* includes a scene at Auerbachs Keller, in which Mephistopheles and Faust carouse with students before they leave riding on a barrel. Other Leipzig eating houses with long culinary traditions are the *Thüringer Hof* (☎ 9 94 49 99), Burgstrasse 19, which was Luther's favourite pub, and *Zill's Tunnel* at Barfussgässchen 9. Both are open daily and serve up Saxon specialities from around DM18. At the *Ratskeller* (☎ 1 23 62 02) in the Neues Rathaus, try the cream goulash with red cabbage and dumplings for DM12.90.

The *Kaffeehaus Riquez*, a somewhat up-market café in a superb Art Nouveau building (identifiable by the two enormous bronze ele-phant heads above the entrance), stands on the corner of Reichsstrasse and Schuhmach-ergässchen. Other good cafés are the *Bachstübl* and the *Café Concerto* on Thomaskirchhof next door to the Bach-Museum, and the *Krätzer*, a cheap stand-up café and bakery on Hainstrasse.

Entertainment

Live theatre and music are major features in Leipzig's cultural offerings. With a tradition dating back to 1743, the *Gewandhaus* concert hall on Augustusplatz has Europe's longest established orchestra – one of its conductors was the composer Mendelssohn. Leipzig's modern *Opernhaus* is just across the square. The *Schauspielhaus* is a few blocks west of Markt, at Bosestrasse 1.

Moritzbastei, at Universitätsstrasse 9 in a spacious cellar below the old city walls, has live bands or disco most nights. *Film Café*, Burgstrasse 9, is a café-pub popular among young Leipzigers. *Café Vis a Vis*, just north of the station at Rudolf-Breitscheid-Strasse 33, draws a largely gay clientele (open 24 hours).

Getting There & Away

Leipzig's huge main train station has depar-tures and arrivals to and from all important German cities as well as other European cities.

The local ADM-Mitfahrzentrale (☎ 1 94 40) is at Rudolf-Breitscheid-Strasse 39; fare prices (including booking fee) include: Berlin DM19, Munich DM43, and Frankfurt DM40.

GERMANY

Getting Around

Trams are the main form of public transport in Leipzig, with the most important lines running via Willy-Brandt-Platz in front of the main train station. The S-Bahn circles the city's outer suburbs. Fares are time-based (ie *not* zone-based), with DM1.40 (15-minute) and DM2 (60-minute) adult tickets available. A 24-hour ticket (if stamped on Saturday it's valid all-day Sunday) costs DM7, while strip-tickets valid for four journeys cost DM5 for 15-minute rides, or DM7.50 for 60-minute rides.

GÖRLITZ

Situated 100 km east of Dresden on the Neisse River, Görlitz emerged from WWII with its beautiful old town virtually undamaged. Today its Renaissance and baroque architecture is better preserved than that of any city its size in Saxony, and Görlitz is receiving special federal funding to restore the entire Altstadt. Of particular interest are the **town hall** (1537), the **Peterskirche** (1497), the 16th-century **Dreifaltigkeitskirche** on Obermarkt and the **Lange Läuben**, a row of opulent town houses built by medieval cloth merchants.

The tourist office (☎ 4 75 70) is at Obermarkt 29.

Görlitz' telephone code is ☎ 03581.

Places to Stay & Eat

The *DJH hostel* (☎ 40 65 10), south of the station at Goethestrasse 17, charges juniors/seniors DM21/25. The central *Gästehaus Lisakowski* (☎ 40 05 39), Landeskronstrasse 23, offers simple singles/ doubles for DM60/90. The *Restaurant Destille* (☎ 40 53 02), beside a medieval tower at Nikolaistrasse 6, serves local cuisine and has a few doubles with shower and toilet for DM130.

Getting There & Away

Over a dozen daily trains run in either direction between Görlitz and Dresden (1 hour 40 minutes). Görlitz is also an important border-crossing point, and daily Frankfurt-Warsaw and Berlin-Kraków trains make a stop here before crossing into Poland (via the historic Neisseviadukt bridge, completed in 1847).

Thuringia

The state of Thuringia (Thüringen) occupies a basin cutting into the heart of Germany between the Harz Mountains and the hilly Thuringian Forest. The Germanic Thuringians were conquered by the Franks in 531 and converted to Christianity by St Boniface in the 8th century. The duke of Saxony seized the area in 908 and for the next 1000 years the region belonged to one German principality or another. Only in 1920 was Thuringia reconstituted as a state with something approaching its original borders. Under the Communists it was again split into separate districts, but since 1990 it has been a single unit once again.

ERFURT

This trading and university centre, founded as a bishop's residence by St Boniface in 742, is the capital of Thuringia. Erfurt was only slightly damaged during WWII, and due to the numerous burgher town houses, churches and monasteries that grace its surprisingly well-preserved medieval quarter, the city has been listed by UNESCO as a place of world cultural heritage.

Orientation & Information

As you come out of the train station, turn left, then right and walk straight up Bahnhofstrasse. In a few minutes you'll reach Anger, a large square in the heart of the city. Continue straight ahead and follow the tram tracks along Schlösserstrasse past the town hall till you come to Domplatz, Erfurt's most impressive sight.

Erfurt has two tourist offices. Erfurt-Information (☎ 5 62 62 67), at Bahnhofstrasse 37, halfway between the station and Anger, is open Monday to Friday from 10 am to 6 pm, and Saturday to 1 pm. The main tourist office (☎ 5 62 34 36) is at Krämerbrücke 3; its opening hours are Monday to Friday 10 am to 6 pm, Saturday to 4 pm, and Sunday to 1 pm. A one-day card for entry to all of the city's museums is available and offers good value at only DM5.

The main post office is on Anger.

There is a convenient laundrette (SB-Waschsalon) at Bahnhofstrasse 22, below the rail bridge.

Erfurt's telephone code is ☎ 0361.

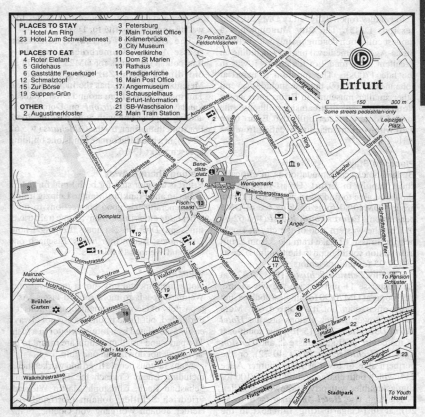

PLACES TO STAY
1 Hotel Am Ring
23 Hotel Zum Schwalbennest

PLACES TO EAT
4 Roter Elefant
5 Gildehaus
6 Gaststätte Feuerkugel
12 Schmalztopf
15 Zur Börse
19 Suppen-Grün

OTHER
2 Augustinerkloster
3 Petersburg
7 Main Tourist Office
8 Krämerbrücke
9 City Museum
10 Severikirche
11 Dom St Marien
13 Rathaus
14 Predigerkirche
16 Main Post Office
17 Angermuseum
18 Schauspielhaus
20 Erfurt-Information
21 SB-Waschsalon
22 Main Train Station

Erfurt

0   150   300 m
Some streets pedestrian-only

Things to See & Do

The numerous interesting backstreets and laneways in Erfurt's surprisingly large Altstadt make this a nice place to explore on foot. Begin by visiting the **Angermuseum** (DM4, closed Monday), Anger 18, then take Schlösserstrasse north-west to Fischmarkt, the medieval city centre. Historical buildings such as the **town hall** (1873), the **Haus Zum Breiten Herd** (1584) and the **Haus Zum Roten Ochsen** (1562) surround this square.

The 13th-century Gothic **Dom St Marien** and **Severikirche** stand together on a hillock in the centre of town dominating the central square of Domplatz. The wooden stools (1350)

and stained glass (1410) in the choir, and figures on the portals, make the cathedral one of the richest medieval churches in Germany. From here you can walk north-west up the stairway to **Petersburg**, the former site of a medieval church and abbey later converted by the Prussians into a fortress.

From Fischmarkt, the eastbound street beside the town hall leads to the medieval restored **Krämerbrücke** (1325), which is lined on each side with timber-framed shops. This is the only such bridge north of the Alps. Further north, on the same side of the River Gera, is Augustinerkloster, a late-medieval monastery that was home to Martin Luther early in the

GERMANY

16th century (open daily; entry DM4.50, concessions DM3). The **City Museum** has a modest collection dealing mainly with Erfurt's Stone-Age and medieval history (including an excellent scale model of the city as it was in the late 1700s). The museum is based at Johannesstrasse 169, but also includes several other smaller museums in Erfurt such as the **Neue Mühle**, an old streamside millhouse (the last of some 60 water mills that Erfurt once had) with working machinery dating from the early 1880s.

Places to Stay

Budget hotel accommodation is in critically short supply in Erfurt. Erfurt-Information should be able to find you a private room from around DM40/80 (plus booking fee of DM5 per person). Erfurt's *youth hostel* (☎ 5 62 67 05), on the western side of the city at Hochheimer Strasse 12 (take tram No 5 from Erfurt train station southbound to the terminus), costs DM21/25 for juniors/seniors.

The tiny *Pension Schuster* (☎ 3 50 42), at Rubenstrasse 11 just outside the city centre, has rooms at DM70/90 for singles/doubles, but more often than not it's booked out. More reliable lower-budget options are the *Hotel Garni Daberstedt* (☎ 3 15 16), just south-east of the centre at Buddestrasse 2, and *Pension Zum Feldschlösschen* (☎ 71 40 72), on the northern side of town at Magdeburger Allee 214, which both charge around DM70/100 for singles/doubles with private shower and toilet.

The high-rise *Hotel Am Ring* (☎ 6 46 55 20), at Juri-Gagarin-Ring 148 next to the Museum für Thüringer Volkskunde offers two-bed apartments with shared toilet and shower from DM79/119 single/double. Behind the station, at Spielbergtor 20, is the *Zum Schwalbennest* (☎ 3 48 10), where rooms with all mod cons start at DM95/120.

Places to Eat

If you feel like something other than the 'Thuringian specialities' offered at most of Erfurt's restaurants, the *Suppen-Grün*, a soup bar at Regierungsstrasse 70, has wholesome organic-vegetarian broths from DM5.40 a bowl; it's open until 7 pm every day except Sunday. The *Roter Elefant* (closed Sunday) is a trendy café-restaurant on the corner of Turnierstrasse and Allerheiligenstrasse that serves good coffee and interesting dishes like walnut and fetta soufflé for DM11.50.

The *Gaststätte Feuerkugel*, Michaelisstrasse 4 (near Krämerbrücke), has daily four-course set menus for DM23 served in an old dining room. *Zur Börse*, a pub at Meienbergstrasse 19, has the inevitable local Thuringian dishes from around DM15 (closed Sunday). The *Schmalztopf* on Domplatz is another popular pub with quite passable food. For something finer, try the *Gildehaus* (☎ 5 62 32 73), in a beautiful ornate sandstone building at Fischmarkt 13-16.

Getting There & Away

Erfurt is a major stop for both Frankfurt/Main to Berlin and Frankfurt/Main to Leipzig trains, and generally has good connections to most other large cities in Germany. Some train travel times are: Dresden 2¾ hours, Leipzig 1 hour 20 minutes, Berlin four hours, Eisenach one hour and Weimar 15 minutes.

WEIMAR

Not a monumental city, nor a medieval one, Weimar appeals to more refined tastes. As a repository of German humanistic traditions it's unrivalled, but these traditions are not always easily assimilated by a foreign visitor in a rush. The parks and small museums are meant to be savoured, not downed in one gulp.

Many famous people lived and worked here, including Lucas Cranach the Elder, Johann Sebastian Bach, Christoph Martin Wieland, Friedrich Schiller, Johann Gottfried von Herder, Johann Wolfgang von Goethe, Franz Liszt, Friedrich Nietzsche, Walter Gropius, Lyonel Feininger, Vasili Kandinsky, Gerhard Marcks and Paul Klee. The Bauhaus movement, which laid the foundations of modern architecture, functioned in the city from 1919 to 1925. Today Weimar is a centre for architecture and music studies.

Weimar is best known abroad as the place where the German republican constitution was drafted after WWI (hence, the 1919-33 Weimar Republic), though you won't find much evidence of it here. The horrors of Buchenwald concentration camp (see the Around Weimar section) are well remembered, however.

Because of its historical significance to all Germans, Weimar has received particularly large handouts for the restoration of its many fine buildings. Weimar has been declared European Cultural City for 1999, and a range of (generously funded) cultural activities are planned for the years leading up to the major festivities.

Orientation & Information

The centre of town is just west of the Ilm River and a 20-minute walk south of the train station. Buses run fairly frequently between the station and Goetheplatz, from where it's a short walk east along small streets to Herderplatz or Markt.

The Tourist-Information Weimar (☎ 2 40 00), at Markt 10, is open weekdays from 9 am to 6 pm, Saturdays from 9 am to 4 pm, and Sundays from 10 am to 4 pm. Regular guided city tours in English start here every Friday and Saturday at 2 pm (DM8). Available here is the three-day Weimar Card (DM25), a combined ticket giving free entry to most of Weimar's museums and travel on city buses (plus various other benefits).

Most of Weimar's museums and many cultural activities are managed by a trust foundation, the Stiftung Weimarer Klassik, (☎ 54 51 02), which has a visitor's information office just off Markt at Frauentorstrasse 4. It sells a wide range of relevant literature (mostly in German).

Weimar's telephone code is ☎ 03643.

Things to See & Do

City Centre A good place to begin your visit is on Herderplatz. The Herderkirche (1500), in the centre of the square, has an altarpiece (1555) by Lucas Cranach the Elder, who died before he could finish it. His son, Lucas Cranach the Younger, completed the work and included a portrait of his father (to the right of the crucifix, between John the Baptist and Martin Luther).

A block east of Herderplatz towards the Ilm River is Weimar's main art museum, the Schlossmuseum (DM4, closed Monday) on Burgplatz. This large collection, with masterpieces by Cranach, Dürer and others, occupies three floors of this castle, which was formerly the residence of the Elector of the Duchy of Saxony-Weimar. A new museum of contemporary and modern art, the Neues Museum Weimar, is currently being constructed at Rathenauplatz, north of the centre. It is

expected to open at the end of 1998, and will house the Paul Maenz collection.

Platz der Demokratie, with the renowned music school founded in 1872 by Franz Liszt, is up the street running south from the castle. This square spills over into Markt, where you'll find the neo-Gothic town hall (1841), and the Cranachhaus, in which Lucas Cranach the Elder spent his last two years and died (in 1553). West of Markt via some narrow lanes is Theaterplatz, with statues (1857) of Goethe and Schiller, and the German National Theatre, where the constituent assembly drafted the constitution of the German Republic in 1919. Opposite the theatre on this same square are the new Bauhaus Museum (entry DM4, closed Monday) and the Wittumspalais (DM6, closed Monday), a museum dedicated to the poet Christoph Martin Wieland (1733-1813), who first translated Shakespeare's works into German.

Houses & Tombs From Theaterplatz, the elegant Schillerstrasse curves around to the Schillerhaus at No 12 with the modern Schiller Museum immediately behind it (entry DM4, closed Monday). Schiller lived in Weimar from 1799 to 1805.

Goethe, his contemporary, spent the years 1775 to 1832 here. The Goethehaus (DM6, closed Monday), a block ahead and then to the right, is where the immortal work *Faust* was written. To the right are the personal quarters where Goethe resided, and upstairs an exhibition on his life and times. The museum will be closed for renovations until late 1998.

The Goethe-Schiller Archive at Hans-Wahl-Strasse has more information but it is only open (weekdays) to serious researchers.

The Liszthaus (entry DM4, closed Monday) is south on Marienstrasse by the edge of Park an der Ilm. Liszt resided in Weimar during 1848 and from 1869 to 1886, and here he wrote his *Hungarian Rhapsody* and *Faust Symphony*. In the yellow complex across the road from the Lisztshaus, Walter Gropius laid the groundwork for all modern architecture. The buildings themselves were erected by the famous architect Henry van de Velde between 1904 and 1911 and now house the Academy of Architecture.

The tombs of Goethe and Schiller lie side by

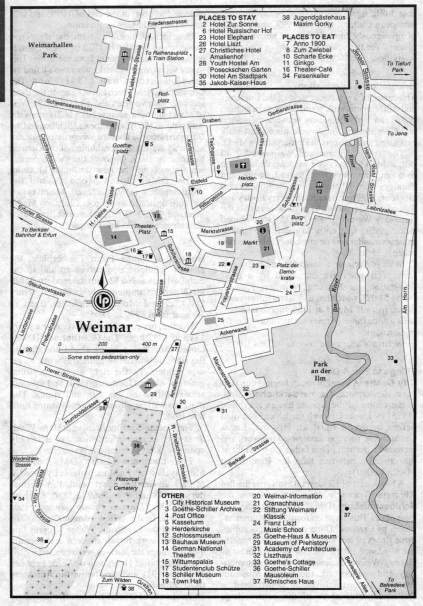

PLACES TO STAY
2   Hotel Zur Sonne
6   Hotel Russischer Hof
23 Hotel Elephant
26 Hotel Liszt
27 Christliches Hotel
    Amalienhof
28 Youth Hostel Am
    Poseckschen Garten
30 Hotel Am Stadtpark
35 Jakob-Kaiser-Haus

38 Jugendgästehaus
    Maxim Gorky
PLACES TO EAT
7   Anno 1900
8   Zum Zwiebel
10 Scharfe Ecke
11 Ginkgo
16 Theater-Café
34 Felsenkeller

Weimar

0   200   400 m

Some streets pedestrian-only

OTHER
1   City Historical Museum
3   Goethe-Schiller Archive
4   Post Office
5   Kasseturm
9   Herderkirche
12 Schlossmuseum
13 Bauhaus Museum
14 German National
    Theatre
15 Wittumspalais
17 Studentenclub Schütze
18 Schiller Museum
19 Town Hall

20 Weimar-Information
21 Cranachhaus
22 Stiftung Weimarer
    Klassik
24 Franz Liszt
    Music School
25 Goethe-Haus & Museum
29 Museum of Prehistory
31 Academy of Architecture
32 Liszthaus
33 Goethe's Cottage
36 Goethe-Schiller
    Mausoleum
37 Römisches Haus

side in a neoclassical crypt in the **Historischer Friedhof** (Historical Cemetery), two blocks west of the Liszthaus.

Parks & Palaces Weimar boasts three large parks, each replete with monuments, museums and attractions. Most accessible is **Park an der Ilm** which runs right along the eastern side of Weimar and contains **Goethe's cottage** (entry DM4, closed Tuesdays). Goethe himself landscaped the park.

Several km further south is the **Belvedere Park**, with its baroque castle housing the **Rokokomuseum** and the **orangery coach museum** (DM4 combined, both open from April to October, closed Monday). The surrounding park is beautiful and spacious, and could absorb hours of your time. In summer you can take the hourly No 12 bus from Goetheplatz straight to Belvedere.

Tiefurt Park, a few km east of the train station, is similar but smaller (palace closed Monday, and also Tuesday from November to February, DM6). Duchess Anna Amalia organised famous intellectual 'round-table gatherings' here in the late 18th century. Get here on bus No 3, which leaves hourly from Goetheplatz.

Places to Stay

Budget accommodation can get tight just about any time in Weimar. During the week its often busy (and noisy) with school excursion groups and business travellers, while at weekends and on public holidays the city is a popular tourist destination. For a flat fee of DM5 Weimar-Information arranges private rooms (from DM25 to DM40 per person).

Camping The closest camping ground is the **Campingplatz Oettern** (☎ 036453-2 64, open from May to November) at Oettern in the scenic Ilm Valley, seven km south-east of Weimar. Charges are DM4.50 per person, DM2 per vehicle, plus DM5 for a site.

Hostels At last count Weimar had four DJH hostels. The **Jugendherberge Germania** (☎ 20 20 76), at Carl-August-Allee 13 in the street running south (downhill) from the station, charges DM20/24 for juniors/seniors. Most central, though least comfortable, is the hostel **Am Poseckschen Garten** (☎ 6 40 21) at Humboldtstrasse 17 near the Historischer Friedhof, which charges DM19/23 for seniors/juniors. Two better options are **Jugendgästehaus Maxim Gorki** (☎ 34 71), on the southern uphill side of town at Zum Wilden Graben 12 (take bus No 8 from the station), and the **Jugendgästehaus Am Ettersberg** (☎ 34 71), at Ettersberg-Siedling (bus No 6 from the main train station to Obelisk), which both offer beds for DM22/26 senior/junior.

Pensions The tiny **Pension Savina I** (☎ 51 33 52), at Rembrandtweg 13, charges DM58/102 per single/double with private bath and shower. Its near namesake, the **Savina II** (☎ 51 33 52), near to the station at Meyerstrasse 60, has rooms (with attached kitchen) from DM50/90. **Pension Am Kirschberg** (☎ 6 19 68), Am Kirschberg 27, and **Zum Alten Zausel** (☎ 50 16 63), in Carl-Von-Ossietzky-Strasse, both offer doubles and twins for around DM90. West of the centre, but still conveniently close to town is the **Am Berkaer Bahnhof** (☎ 20 20 10), Peter-Cornelius-Strasse 7, with singles/doubles for DM65/95 and triples costing DM160.

Hotels Prices given here include private shower/toilet and breakfast.

The best deal in the centre of Weimar is **Hotel Zur Sonne** (☎ 8 62 90), on the little square of Rollplatz, which has quiet singles/ doubles for DM70/110. The historic **Hotel Russischer Hof** (☎ 77 40), at Goetheplatz 2, has been doing business since 1805, and has singles/doubles starting at DM125/ 180. Not far from the Goethemuseum is the **Christliches Hotel Amalienhof** (☎ 54 90), at Amalienstrasse 2, with singles/doubles from DM125/ 185. Weimar's charming old classic, the **Hotel Elephant** (☎ 6 14 10), which is right in the heart of town at Markt 19, charges from DM170/230.

On the southern side of town are several reasonable medium-range options. At Lisztstrasse 1-3 is the **Hotel Liszt** (☎ 5 40 80), with rooms from DM95/140. **Hotel Am Stadtpark** (☎ 2 48 30), Amalienstrasse 19, only has twin and double rooms on offer for DM165. A bit further out is the **Jakob-Kaiser-Haus** (☎ 2 46 30), an Art Nouveau style suburban villa at Wilhelm-Külz-Strasse 22 (take bus No 6 from the train station). It charges DM90/135 single/double, but rooms are often unavailable as seminars are held here.

Places to Eat

Despite its slightly posh ambience, the *Anno 1900* (☎ 50 13 37), in a restored turn-of-the-century winter garden at Geleitstrasse 12a, offers quite good value. On the menu are almost a dozen vegetarian dishes. Nearby, at Eisfeld 2, you'll find the *Scharfe Ecke* (☎ 24 30; closed Wednesdays), with home-cooked cuisine from DM16.50 and a wide range of beers. Just along the way at Teichgasse 6 is *Zum Zwiebel*, a nice place to come with friends for a late meal and a drink.

The *Ginkgo* (whose name alludes to Goethe's fascination for these east-Asian trees), is upstairs at Grüner Markt 4. It's open daily and serves excellent Chinese food at very reasonable prices. The *Zum Weissen Schwan*, next to the Goethemuseum on Frauenplan, is a classic Weimar eating house whose patrons included Goethe, Schiller and Liszt. (This place is, unfortunately, also haunted by other ghosts from by-gone days; at the time of research it was closed due to a legal dispute over payments for renovations done during the GDR!)

Another Weimar institution is the *Felsenkeller* at Humboldtstrasse 37, run by the local Felsenbräu brewery. The atmosphere is great, the beer is cheap, the food is good and well priced – no wonder it's often full.

Hard to pass is the *Theater-Café* at Theaterplatz 1a, which serves to outside tables bordering the quiet pedestrian square. The *Café Sperling* at Schillerstrasse 18 prepares excellent breakfasts, including numerous coffee variations.

Entertainment

The *German National Theatre* on Theaterplatz is the main stage of Weimar's cultural activities. Goethe's theatrical works are regularly performed here along with many other productions. Tickets to the German National Theatre and other events can be bought at the tourist office.

The *Kasseturm*, a beer cellar in the round tower on Goetheplatz, has live music, disco or cabaret most nights. The *Studentenclub*

Schütze just off Theaterplatz at Schützengasse 2 is a lively student bar that serves cheap drinks.

Getting There & Away

Very few IC or EC trains stop at Weimar, so for longer trips changing in Erfurt (just 22 km and 15 minutes away) may be quicker. There are direct InterRegio and D trains between Weimar and Berlin-Lichtenberg (3½ hours), Frankfurt/Main (four hours and 20 minutes), Dresden (three hours), Halle/Leipzig (one hour) and Eisenach (one hour 20 minutes).

AROUND WEIMAR

Buchenwald

The Buchenwald museum and memorial are on Ettersberg Hill, seven km north-west of Weimar. You first pass the memorial with mass graves of some of WWII's 56,500 victims from 18 nations, including German antifascists, Jews, and Soviet and Polish prisoners of war. The concentration camp and museum are one km beyond the memorial. Many prominent German Communists and Social Democrats, Ernst Thälmann and Rudolf Breitscheid among them, were murdered here. On 11 April 1945, as US troops approached, the prisoners rebelled at 3.15 pm (the clock tower above the entrance still shows that time), overcame the SS guards and liberated themselves.

After the war the Soviet victors turned the tables by establishing Special Camp No 2, in which thousands of (alleged) anti-Communists and former Nazis were worked to death.

The main Buchenwald museum and concentration camp are open every day except Monday from 9.45 am to 5.15 pm (8.45 am to 4.15 pm in winter). A new museum dealing with the post-1945 oppression at Buchenwald has recently been opened. Bus No 6 runs via Goetheplatz and Weimar train station to Buchenwald roughly every 40 minutes.

EISENACH

The birthplace of Johann Sebastian Bach, Eisenach is a small picturesque city on the edge of the Thuringian Forest. From the nearby Wartburg castle, the landgraves (German counts) ruled medieval Thuringia. Richard Wagner based his opera *Tannhäuser* on a minstrel's contest which took place in the castle in 1206-07. Martin Luther went into hiding here under the assumed name of Junker Jörg after being excommunicated and put under the ban of the empire by the pope.

Orientation & Information

Markt, Eisenach's central square, can be reached on foot from the train station by following Bahnhofstrasse to Karlsplatz, then continuing west via the shopping mall of Karlstrasse. Except for the Wartburg, which is two km south-west of town, most sights are close to Markt.

The friendly and well-organised Eisenach-Information (π 67 02 60) is also on Markt at No 2; it's open Monday from 10 am to 6 pm, Tuesday to Friday from 9 am to 6 pm, and Saturday from 9 am to 2 pm.

Eisenach's telephone code is π 03691.

Things to See & Do

The superb old **Wartburg** castle, on a forested hill overlooking Eisenach, is world famous. Martin Luther translated the New Testament from Greek into German while in hiding here during 1521 and 1522, thus making an enormous contribution to the development of the written German language. You can only visit the castle's interior with a guided tour (most tours are in German), which includes the museum, Luther's study room and the amazing Romanesque great hall. Tours run every 15 minutes from 8.30 am to 4.30 pm (9 am to 3.30 pm in winter) and cost DM11 (students DM6); arrive early to avoid the crowds. Guided tours in English are only possible by prior reservation (at least five days beforehand) through Wartburg-Information (π 7 70 73) at Am Schlossberg 2. A free English-language leaflet set out in the sequence of the tour is available.

To get to the Wartburg on foot from the station, follow Bahnhofstrasse west under the arch, cross the square and continue west on Karlstrasse to Markt. Two blocks west of Markt you'll find a steep signposted lane called Schlossberg which leads two km south-west through forest to the castle. Between 1 May and 31 August there's also a shuttle bus running up to the castle; it leaves from the terminal in front of the train station roughly every $1\frac{1}{2}$ hours (DM2.50 return).

At Markt 24 is the **Thuringian Museum** in the former Town Palace (1751), which has a collection of ceramics and paintings. (The long-planned renovation of this building has been delayed for years, and it seems unlikely that the museum will open soon; a tiny part of the collection is on display in the foyer, however.) The interior of the **Georgenkirche** (rebuilt in 1676) on Markt has three balconies which run all the way around, plus a glorious organ and pulpit. Four members of the Bach family served as organists here between 1665 and 1797.

Up the hill from the Georgenkirche is the late-Gothic **Lutherhaus** (open daily; DM5 or DM2 for students), the reformer's home from 1498 to 1501. It contains original manually inscribed and illustrated works, as well as early printed editions of Luther's Bible translations. The **Bachhaus** (open daily; admission DM5, or DM4 for students), on Frauenplan, is where the composer was born in 1685.

The first country-wide proletarian political movement, the Social Democratic Workers' Party, was founded in Eisenach by August Bebel and Wilhelm Liebknecht in 1869. The **Gedenkstätte Parteitag 1869** (closed Wednesday and on weekends), nearby at Marienstrasse 57, has an interesting exhibit on the 19th-century workers' movements in Germany.

Places to Stay

The nearest camping ground is the *Campingplatz Altenberger See* (π 21 56 37), at Neubau 24, seven km south of town in Wilhelmsthal. Charges are DM5 for a site plus DM5 per person. There are two hostels in Eisenach: the 65-bed *Jugendherberge Erich Honstein* (π 73 20 12), at Bornstrasse 7, which charges DM18/22 for juniors/seniors, and the 102-bed *Jugendherberge Arthur Becker* (π 20 36 13), Mariental 24 in the valley below the Wartburg (DM20/24). For the latter, take bus No 3 from the station to the 'Liliengrund' stop.

Eisenach-Information has a free room-finding service (from DM30/50 single/double). Otherwise, the cheapest accommodation in central Eisenach is at *Gasthof Storchenturm* (π 21 52 50), Georgenstrasse 43, which has double rooms with shower and toilet from DM70. In Eisenach's southern suburbs is the small *Pension Christine Kilian* (π 21 11 22), Kapellenstrasse 8, which has rooms from DM40/80.

Pension Kesselring (☎ 73 20 49), just 10 minutes walk up from Bachplatz at Hainweg 32, offers nicer rooms for DM60/90. The *Hotel Villa Karoline* (☎ 73 28 84), in an early Art Nouveau building at Mariental 26 (next door to the hostel), charges DM55/95 for simpler rooms or DM110/140 for rooms with private bath and toilet.

Places to Eat

The *Altdeutsche Bierstube* (closed Monday), Alexanderstrasse 8, is an unpretentious worker's pub that dishes up simple meals for as little as DM5.90. Not quite as down-market is the *Gaststätte Wartburghof* at Frauenberg 6, though its meat-and-potato variations are mainly under DM10.

One of Eisenach's favourite Altstadt eating houses is the *Alt Eisenach*, at Karlstrasse 51. This restaurant specialises in pan-fried meat dishes (from DM12), although it also does interesting vegetarian food. In an old monastery wine cellar opposite the Georgenkirche is the *Brunnenkeller* (☎ 9 81 26), Markt 10, whose menu includes hearty Thuringian dishes like beef roulade with red cabbage and dumplings for DM14. 50. It's open daily for lunch, and evenings until 1 am.

Getting There & Away

Eisenach has good train connections to Erfurt (56 km); through-trains running between Frankfurt/Main and Berlin-Lichtenberg also stop here.

Saxony-Anhalt

The State of Saxony-Anhalt (Sachsen-Anhalt) comprises the former East German districts of Magdeburg and Halle. Originally part of the duchy of Saxony, medieval Anhalt was split into smaller units by the sons of various princes. In 1863 Leopold IV of Anhalt-Dessau united the three existing duchies, and in 1871 his realm was made a state of the German Reich.

The mighty Elbe River flows north-west across Saxony-Anhalt, past Lutherstadt Wittenberg and Magdeburg on its way to the North Sea at Hamburg. On the Saale River south of Magdeburg is Halle.

The Harz Mountains fill the south-west corner of Saxony-Anhalt and spread across into Lower Saxony to Goslar (see the Harz Mountains map in the Lower Saxony section). Quaint historical towns like Quedlinburg and Wernigerode hug the gentle, wooded slopes.

WERNIGERODE

Wernigerode is flanked by the foothills of the Harz Mountains. A romantic ducal castle rises above the old town, which contains some 1000 half-timbered houses from five centuries in various states of repair. In summer this is a busy tourist centre attracting large throngs of German holiday-makers. It is also the northern terminus of the steam-powered, narrow-gauge Harzquerbahn, which has chugged the 60 km south to Nordhausen for almost a century. The line to the summit of the Brocken, the highest mountain (1142m) in northern Germany, also leaves from here.

Orientation & Information

The bus and train stations are adjacent on the north side of town. From Bahnhofsplatz, Rudolf-Breitscheid-Strasse leads south-east to Breite Strasse, which runs south-west to Markt, the old town centre. The tourist office (☎ 4 42 95) is at Nicolaiplatz 1, just off Breite Strasse near Markt. The roads of Burgberg, Nussallee and Schlosschaussee all lead towards the fairy-tale castle on the hill at Agnesberg, to the south-east.

Wernigerode's telephone code is ☎ 03943.

Things to See

Wander along the streets of the old town centre and admire the medieval houses. The **Rathaus** (1277) on Markt, with its pair of pointed black-slate towers, is a focal point. A block behind, the **Harz Museum** at Klint 10 features local and natural history (closed Sunday).

From Marktstrasse or Breite Strasse, you can join one of the two 'Bimmelbahn' wagon rides (DM3 one way) up to the neo-Gothic **castle**, though it's not a long climb. First built in the 12th century, the castle has been renovated and enlarged over the centuries and got its current fairy-tale façade from Count Otto of Stolberg-Wernigerode in the last century. The castle's museum (entry DM7, discount DM6;

open daily; closed Monday in winter) has a nice chapel and Great Hall. For an extra DM2 you can climb the main tower, but the views of Wernigerode from the castle terrace are free and just as good.

Activities
There are plenty of short walks and day hikes nearby, foremost to the castle or to the inn Zur Harburg on the hill south of town. The more serious might tackle the 30-km route (marked by blue crosses) from Mühlental south-east of the town centre to Elbingerode, Königshütte with its 18th-century wooden church, and the remains of medieval Trageburg castle at Trautenstein. Popular too is the 11-km route (marked by red dots) past the rocks at Ottofelsen and the waterfall and inn at Steinerne Renne, south-west of Wernigerode.

You can also take the steam train to the station at Drei-Annen-Hohne, the departure point for several loop trails around Hochharz National Park. The tourist office will make suggestions and you'll need a good topographic sheet for some of them. The *Auto + Wanderkarte: Harz* (DM9.80) is worth inspecting.

The Harzquerbahn train line runs south from the main station to Nordhausen (60 km, three hours) four times daily all year. Tickets (DM28 return) are available at the station. Rail passes are not valid. The other steam-train ride is up Brocken on the Brockenbahn, a train that connects with services from Wernigerode (2¾ hours; DM40 return). There are direct trains connecting Nordhausen with Halle, Erfurt and Kassel. If you are a steam nut or just particularly taken by the mountains, the three-day steam-train pass at DM60, including connections (and the Selketalbahn, which runs from Gernrode), is fine value, as is the one-week pass at DM100.

Places to Stay
The City of Wernigerode runs three *Youth Guesthouses* (☎ 3 20 61) where beds cost DM14.50 for adults, DM11 for those under 18 (breakfast not included). All are located somewhat outside of town. The tourist office arranges private rooms from DM30, free and by telephone if you wish, and Harz-Tourist-Service (☎ 2 32 34), at Burgberg 9b, handles bookings in the area.

Hotel zur Tanne (☎ 3 25 54), Breite Strasse 59, charges DM40/60 for bathless singles/doubles. The *Hotel Schlossblick* (☎ 3 20 04), Burgstrasse 58, has rooms with all facilities from DM55/75. *Pension Schweizer Hof* (☎ 3 20 98) at Salzbergstrasse 13 should be the first choice for those keen on hiking, with route information and rooms from DM65/100. If you want to splurge, try the very traditional *Hotel Weisser Hirsch* (☎ 3 24 34), Marktplatz 5, with rooms from DM115/180.

Places to Eat
The *Gaststätte zur Sonne* has plain décor but serves 16 varieties of Schnitzel at DM14.50 each and also has daily specials under DM10. More atmospheric is the woodsy *Nonnenhof* where regional specialities range from DM11 to DM20. Younger locals meet at the *Filmkneipe Capitol*, a modern restaurant with a movie-theme décor and standard dishes from DM8. For true budget eats and take-away, visit *Kochlöffel* on the corner of Burgstrasse and Breite Strasse; burgers are DM4.50.

Getting There & Away
For details on train and bus services from Wernigerode to Bad Harzburg in the western Harz, see the Getting Around section under Western Harz Mountains in Lower Saxony. In Bad Harzburg you can connect with trains to Hanover and Göttingen. There are also trains from Wernigerode to Halberstadt (30 minutes), where you can connect for Quedlinburg, Magdeburg or Berlin.

QUEDLINBURG
Unspoiled Quedlinburg just celebrated 1000 years of existence and is a popular destination, especially since becoming a UNESCO World Heritage Site in 1992. Almost all buildings in the centre are half-timbered, street after cobbled street of them, and they are slowly being restored. One of the drawbacks is the current shortage of hotels, but it is worth visiting Quedlinburg before it becomes one of Germany's busiest tourist centres.

Orientation & Information
The centre of the old town is a 10-minute walk from the train station down Bahnhofstrasse. Quedlinburg-Information (☎ 77 30 10) is at Markt 2. From May to October it is open

GERMANY

Monday to Friday 9 am to 8 pm, on weekends 9 am to 6 pm. Hours are reduced during the rest of the year.

Quedlinburg's telephone code is ☎ 03946.

Things to See

The Renaissance **Rathaus** (1615) on Markt has its own Roland statue. Nearby, the **Ständerbau** (closed Thursday, DM3, discount DM2) in Wordgasse 3 ranks among Germany's oldest half-timbered houses and contains a museum on the history of half-timbered construction. However, the real focal point for visitors is the hill just south-west – the old castle district, known as **Schlossberg**. The area features the Romanesque **Church of St Servatii** (1129), or 'Dom' (closed Monday, DM5, discount DM3), with a 10th-century crypt. The Dom treasure contains priceless reliquaries and early Bibles. In 1938 SS meetings were held in the Dom – a 'Germanic solemn shrine'. The adjacent **Schlossmuseum** (closed Monday, DM5, discount DM3) in the 16th-century castle has a good historical collection. The view of Quedlinburg from the castle is one of the most evocative in Germany.

Activities

To get in some hiking, take a bus or train 10 km south-west to Thale, at the mouth of the lovely Bode Valley in the Harz Mountains. Here you'll find a cable car (closed November) to the Hexentanzplatz, site of a raucous celebration during *Walpurgisnacht* every 30 April. A trail leads up the valley and there are several caves. Outdoor stage performances are held in the amphitheatre nearby.

Places to Stay

Quedlinburg-Information has good private rooms from about DM30, but it is a good idea to ring ahead and book. *Pension Am Dippeplatz* (☎ 42 00) in Breite Strasse 16 has rooms with private shower/WC for DM60/80 singles/doubles. Excellent value is the new and friendly *Hotel Zum Augustinern* (☎ 70 12 34) in Reichenstrasse 35a where rooms with all facilities (shower/WC, TV, phone) go for DM60/90. The *Motel Quedlinburg* (☎ 28 55), Wipertistrasse 9, has singles/doubles from DM90/120.

Places to Eat

A wooden décor gives the *Prinz Heinrich* restaurant-bar in Pölle 29 a cosy ambience. Most dishes here cost between DM10 and DM15. At the *Alsatian* restaurant down the street at Steinweg 9, you'll get French specialities at reasonable prices. The speciality at *Lüdde-Bräu* brewery in Blasiistrasse 14 is a sweetish low-alcohol beer, accompanied by hearty German meals, many under DM10.

Getting There & Away

There are regular trains to Quedlinburg from Berlin via Magdeburg. Coming from Halle, you must change at the isolated siding of Wegeleben; the link operates several times daily. Connections to Halberstadt (25 minutes away) are by local trains, and from there you can ride to Wernigerode or Magdeburg.

MAGDEBURG

Magdeburg, on the Elbe River, lies at a strategic crossing of transport routes from Thuringia to the Baltic and Western Europe to Berlin. It was severely damaged by wartime bombing and much of it was rebuilt in steel and concrete. But the city centre also has generous boulevards lined with lovely refurbished 19th century buildings, a Gothic cathedral and a few Romanesque churches. Budget accommodation is tight, so Magdeburg is perhaps best visited on a long day trip from Berlin. The city is the capital of Saxony-Anhalt.

Orientation & Information

From the broad square in front of the train station, Ernst-Reuter-Allee leads east to a bridge over the Elbe, with Alter Markt a block back on the left. Magdeburg-Information (☎ 5 40 49 01) is at Alter Markt 12.

The telephone code for Magdeburg is ☎ 0391.

Things to See

The centre of the old town is Alter Markt, with a copy of the bronze **Magdeburg Rider** figure (1240) of King Otto the Great facing the **Rathaus** (1698). Behind the Rathaus are the ruins of 15th-century **Johanniskirche**, undergoing restoration after long being a memorial to the catastrophic bombing. To the north are arrayed the **Wallonerkirche**, the Gothic **Magdalenenkapelle** and **Petrikirche**.

South of the bridge is Magdeburg's oldest building, the 12th-century Romanesque convent **Unser Lieben Frauen**, now a museum (closed Monday; DM2, although you can enter the cloister and church for free). It also serves as a concert hall for the music of Georg Phillipp Telemann, who was born in Magdeburg, and other composers. Further south is the soaring Gothic **cathedral** (open daily 10 am to 4 pm), with the tomb of Otto I and art from eight centuries. The quarter behind the Dom, along Hegelstrasse and Hasselbachplatz, has nicely restored villas from the last century and a healthy amount of restaurants and pubs. The **Kulturhistorisches Museum** (DM2, closed Monday) is on Otto-von-Guericke-Strasse at the corner of Danzstrasse. The original 'Rider' statue is kept here.

Places to Stay

There are no camping grounds or hostels nearby, but you can get good private rooms from about DM40 through Magdeburg-Information for a DM5 fee. Several hotels with reasonable prices are also close to the town centre. Among them is the *Bildungshotel* (☎ 22 34 30) at Lorenzweg 56 which charges DM70/90 for singles/doubles. Near the university, on W-Rathenau-Strasse 6, you'll find the *Uni-Hotel* (☎ 55 11 44) with rooms for DM105/130. The *Hotel Stadtfeld* (☎ 73 80 60) is at Maxim-Gorki-Strasse 57. Rooms here with half board go for DM130/160. Rooms at all these hotels have shower, toilet, phone and TV.

Getting There & Away

Trains to/from Berlin-Zoo take about 70 minutes direct or almost two hours via Potsdam. Magdeburg is on the main route from Rostock and Schwerin to Leipzig or Erfurt. There are hourly direct trains from Leipzig to Magdeburg.

HALLE

The former state capital and largest city in Saxony-Anhalt, Halle is as untouristy as you might expect of a city that was the centre of the GDR chemical industry. Most buildings are still in various states of disrepair, but there are a few churches and museums in the old town that warrant a brief visit. Halle is also a univer-

sity town and a centre of modest cultural activities.

Orientation

To walk to the city centre from the main train station, head through the underpass and down the long pedestrian Leipziger Strasse past the 15th-century Leipziger Turm to Markt, Halle's central square.

Information

Halle-Information (☎ 2 02 33 40) is in the unmistakable elevated gallery built around the Roter Turm in the middle of Markt. It's open weekdays from 9 am to 6 pm (from 10 am Wednesday), Saturday from 9 am to 1 pm, and on Sunday (April to October only) from 10 am to 2 pm.

Halle's telephone code is ☎ 0345.

Things to See

Halle-Information runs guided city tours (DM8.50, discount DM5, times vary), but the town is easily explored independently on foot. Start at Markt with its statue (1859) of the great composer Georg Friedrich Händel, who was born in Halle in 1685. The four tall towers of **Marktkirche** (1529) loom above the square. It's worth going inside to see the exquisitely decorated Gothic interior. Also on Markt is the **Roter Turm** (1506), a tower that is now an art gallery. Just south, at Grosse Märker Strasse 10, is the **City Historical Museum** (open daily).

The **Händelhaus** (open daily), at Grosse Nikolai Strasse 5, was the composer's birthplace and now houses a major collection of musical instruments. Händel left Halle in 1703 and, after stays in Hamburg, Italy and Hanover, spent the years from 1712 to 1759 in London, where he achieved great fame. Nearby, on Friedemann Bachplatz, is the 15th-century **Moritzburg castle** (DM5, discount DM3, closed Monday), a former residence of the archbishops of Magdeburg that now contains a museum of 19th and 20th century art, including some pretty impressive German expressionist works.

Places to Stay

The closest camping ground is the municipal *Campingplatz* (☎ 34 00 85) at Pfarrstrasse near the Saale River on the northern edge of

GERMANY

town; it's open from early May until late September. The 72-bed *Youth Hostel* (☎ 2 02 47 16) at August-Bebel-Strasse 48a in the town centre charges DM23/28.50 for juniors/seniors (including breakfast).

For private rooms (from DM30 per person plus a DM5 service fee), contact Halle-Information at ☎ 2 02 83 71. Otherwise, it's lean pickings for budget accommodation. The small *Cafehaus Sasse Hotel* (☎ 2 02 30 88), at Geiststrasse 22 near the Thalia Theater, has rooms with shower/WC at DM95/135, while *Pension Am Markt* charges DM95/125. If you like modern digs, check out the brand new *Steigenberger Esprix Hotel* (☎ 6 93 10), the 'budget' version of the chain, where rooms cost DM120/150. The *Congresshotel Rotes Ross* (☎ 3 72 71), Leipziger Strasse 76 between the train station and the centre of town, has a few rooms for DM90/130, but those with private bath cost a steep DM150/180.

Places to Eat

For a bit of atmosphere, try the *Zum Schad*, a brewery-restaurant at Reilstrasse 10, with a menu heavy on hearty meat dishes. You can get smaller portions (around DM10) of most meals. *Strieses Biertunnel*, around the corner from the Neues Theater on Schulstrasse, serves food until midnight and has many beers on tap. Also historic – and popular with students – is *Gasthof zum Mohr*, right on the Saale River across from Giebichstein Castle. Another favourite haunt is the lively *Café Nöö* at Grosse Klaussstrasse 11, near the old cathedral.

Getting There & Away

Just 40 km apart, Leipzig and Halle are linked by hourly *Stadtexpress* shuttle trains. Halle is also on the route of fast trains from Rostock and Magdeburg to Leipzig or Erfurt, and also from Berlin-Lichtenberg to Erfurt and Frankfurt. If you're coming from Dresden, you may have to change at Leipzig. Between Lutherstadt Wittenberg and Halle, you may have to take a local train (68 km, one hour).

NAUMBURG

Naumburg is one of those pretty little medieval towns for which Germany is famous. It is strategically located between Halle/Leipzig and Weimar and has frequent train services to these centres. The scenic Unstrut Valley lies to

the north-west, and there are several hostels and camping grounds in the area. All of this makes Naumburg well worth including in a German itinerary.

Orientation & Information

The main train station (Naumburg/Saale) is 1.5 km north-west of the old town. You can walk into town along Rossbacher Strasse, visiting Naumburg's famous cathedral on the way. Alternatively, bus Nos 1 and 2 run frequently from the main train station to Markt, Naumburg's central square.

Naumburg-Information (☎ 20 16 14 or 1 94 33) at Markt 6 is open from 9 am to 6 pm weekdays, 10 am to 4 pm on Saturday, and 10 am to 2 pm on Sunday.

Naumburg's telephone code is ☎ 03445.

Things to See

Naumburg's picturesque **Town Hall** (1528) and Gothic **Stadtkirche St Wenzel**, built between 1218 and 1523, rise above Markt. In the ancient western quarter of the town stands the magnificent late Romanesque/early Gothic **Cathedral of Sts Peter & Paul**, with many unique features, including the famous 13th-century statues of Uta and Ekkehard in the west choir. The cloister, crypt, sculptures and four tall towers of this great medieval complex are unique. The boringly delivered but informative German-language tour is included in the admission price (DM5, discount DM3), but you can also walk around on your own. Fans of Friedrich Nietzsche will want to make a pilgrimage to the **Nietzsche Haus** at Weingarten 18, which houses a permanent exhibition on his days in Naumburg.

Places to Stay

Naumburg is one place in the east where you can find affordable accommodation. For a private room see Naumburg-Information; expect to pay around DM30 per person (plus a DM2 service fee) for somewhere central.

Camping Blütengrund (☎ 20 27 11), 1.5 km north-east of Naumburg at the confluence of the Saale and Unstrut rivers, charges DM5 per person and DM2 for a tent site; there are also bungalows with private facilities from DM30 per night.

Naumburg's large and well-equipped *Youth Hostel* (☎ 70 34 22), Am Tennisplatz 9, two km south of the town centre, has double rooms at DM26/30 juniors/seniors. Multi-bed rooms go for DM21/27.

Gasthaus St Othmar (☎ 20 12 13) is a recently restored historic hotel with rooms from DM40/80. *Gasthaus Zum Alten Krug* (☎ 20 04 06), at Lindenring 44 halfway between the cathedral and Markt, has lovely furniture, a great atmosphere and rooms for DM80/110. Almost next door at No 40 is the *Caféhaus-Pension Kattler* (☎ 20 28 23), which has nice rooms with private bath and TV for DM60/120.

Five km south-west of Naumburg, in Bad Kösen, the *Jugendherberge Bad Kösen* (☎ 034463-2 75 97), at Bergstrasse 3, has beds for DM14/18.

Getting There & Away
There are fast trains to Naumburg from Halle (one hour), Leipzig (one hour), Jena (45 minutes) and Weimar (45 minutes). A local line runs to Artern via Laucha and Freyburg. Frankfurt/Main-Leipzig and Berlin-Munich IC trains stop in Naumburg.

FREYBURG
Eight km north-west of Naumburg and easily accessible by train or bus, Freyburg lies in the lovely Unstrut Valley. The large medieval **Neuenburg castle**, now undergoing major restoration, stands on the wooded hilltop directly above the town (admission DM5). The adjacent tower (DM2) offers a splendid view. Both are closed on Monday. Freyburg's vineyards are the northernmost in Europe, and there are wine festivals from May to October, including eastern Germany's largest wine festival, held on the second weekend in September.

LUTHERSTADT WITTENBERG
Wittenberg is most famous as the place where Martin Luther did most of his work, but the Renaissance painter Lucas Cranach the Elder also lived here for 43 years. Wittenberg was a famous university town and the seat of the Elector of Saxony until 1547. It was here that Luther launched the Reformation in 1517, an act of the greatest cultural importance to all of Europe. A relaxed city, Wittenberg can be seen in a day from a Berlin base, but is well worth a longer look.

Orientation & Information
There are two train stations. You'll probably arrive at Hauptbahnhof Lutherstadt Wittenberg, the stop for all of the fast trains to/from Berlin, Leipzig, Magdeburg and Halle. Bahnhof Wittenberg-Elbtor is a minor stop for local trains. From the main station, the city centre is a 15-minute walk between the two train lines and then under the tracks and into Collegienstrasse. Wittenberg-Information (☎ 40 22 39) is at Collegienstrasse 29. It's open weekdays from 9 am to 6 pm, Saturday 10 am to 2 pm, and Sunday 11 am to 3 pm.

Wittenberg's telephone code is ☎ 03491.

Things to See
The **Lutherhaus** is a Reformation museum inside Lutherhalle, a former monastery at Collegienstrasse 54 (DM6, discount DM3; closed Monday). It contains an original room furnished by Luther in 1535. Luther stayed here in 1508 when he came to teach at Wittenberg University and made the building his home for the rest of his life after returning in 1511. The home of his friend and supporter, the humanist Philipp Melanchthon, nearby at Collegienstrasse 60, is also a museum (scheduled for renovation from summer 1996 to early 1997).

The large altarpiece in the **Stadtkirche St Marien** was created jointly by Lucas Cranach the Elder and his son in 1547. It shows Luther, Melanchthon and other Reformation figures, as well as Cranach the Elder himself, in Biblical contexts. In June 1525 Luther married ex-nun Katharina von Bora in this church, where he also preached. Note the baptismal font and marble tombstones. The **Luthereiche**, the site where Luther burnt the papers threatening his excommunication, is at the corner of Lutherstrasse and Am Bahnhof.

Imposing monuments to Luther and Melanchthon stand in front of the impressive **Old Town Hall** (1535) on Markt. On one corner of Markt is the **House of Lucas Cranach the Elder**, Schlossstrasse 1, with a picturesque courtyard you may enter.

At the west end of town is **Wittenberg Castle** (1499) with its huge, rebuilt church (DM2) onto whose door Luther allegedly nailed his *95 Theses* on 31 October 1517. His tombstone lies below the pulpit, and Melanchthon's is opposite.

Places to Stay

The nearest camping ground is *Bergwitz* (☎ 034921-2 82 28), in the village of Kemberg, some 11 km south of town on Lake Bergwitz. You can get private rooms through Wittenberg-Information from about DM40 per person (plus a DM3 fee). The Regional Tourist Office (☎ 40 26 10) at Mittelstrasse 33 also books accommodation in and around the city.

The 104-bed *Youth Hostel* (☎ 40 32 55) is housed upstairs in Wittenberg Castle (DM19/25 juniors/seniors, sheets DM6.50). *Gasthaus Central* (☎ 41 15 72) at Mittelstrasse 20 has bathless singles for DM57.50 and doubles with shower/WC for DM92. Up the street at No 7 is *Pension An der Stadtkirche* which charges DM60/80. The 34-room *Hotel Goldener Adler* (☎ 41 01 47), Markt 7, starts at DM70/80 for singles/doubles without bath.

Getting There & Away

Wittenberg is on the main train line to Leipzig and Halle, 90 minutes south of Berlin-Lichtenberg. All the Berlin trains stop at Schönefeld airport. For train tickets and times, go to the train station or to Reise Welt at Markt 12.

Mecklenburg-Western Pomerania

The state of Mecklenburg-Western Pomerania (Mecklenburg-Vorpommern) is a low-lying, postglacial region of lakes, meadows, forests and the beaches of the Baltic Sea (German: Ostsee), stretching across northern Germany from Schleswig-Holstein to Poland. Most of the state is historic Mecklenburg; only the island of Rügen and the area from Stralsund to the Polish border traditionally belong to Western Pomerania, or Vorpommern.

In 1160 the Duke of Saxony, Heinrich (Henry the Lion), conquered the region under the guise of introducing Christianity and made the local Polish princes his vassals. Germanisation gradually reduced the Slavonic element, and in 1348 the dukes of Mecklenburg became princes of the Holy Roman Empire. Sweden became involved in the area during the Thirty Years' War (1618-48). In

1867 the whole region joined the North German Confederation and, in 1871, the German Reich.

Some of the offshore islands, like Poel and Hiddensee, are still undiscovered paradises, while others, including Rügen, are becoming increasingly popular with tourists. Just keep in mind the very short swimming season (July and August only). Spring and autumn can be cold.

SCHWERIN

Almost surrounded by lakes, Schwerin is one of the most picturesque towns in eastern Germany and its popularity as a tourist attraction is rising. The town gets its name from a Slavonic castle known as Zaurin ('animal pasture') on the site of the present Schloss. This former seat of the Grand Duchy of Mecklenburg – now the capital of Mecklenburg-Western Pomerania – is an interesting mix of 16th and 17th-century half-timbered town houses (many of which are being painstakingly renovated) and 19th-century architecture. It's also small enough to explore on foot.

Orientation & Information

Down the hill to the east of the train station is Pfaffenteich, the lake where you will find the crenellated arsenal. South of the lake is the town centre, focused on Markt. Further south, around Alter Garten on the Schweriner See, are the monumental Marstall (the former royal stables), the Schloss (ducal castle), and the museums, parks and tour boats that will keep you entertained. Schwerin-Information (☎ 56 09 31) is at Am Markt 11.

Schwerin's telephone code is ☎ 0385.

Things to See

Above Markt rises the tall 14th-century Gothic **cathedral** (open daily); you can climb the 19th-century church tower (DM1) for the view. The cathedral is a superb example of north German red-brick architecture; another is the **Paulskirche** south of the train station, which is currently undergoing restoration.

South-east of Alter Garten over the causeway is Schwerin's neo-Gothic **Schloss** (closed Monday), on an island connected to the **Schlossgarten** by a further causeway. Admission to the superb interior costs DM6, discount DM3. On the city side of Alter Garten is the **Staatliches Museum** (closed Monday, entry

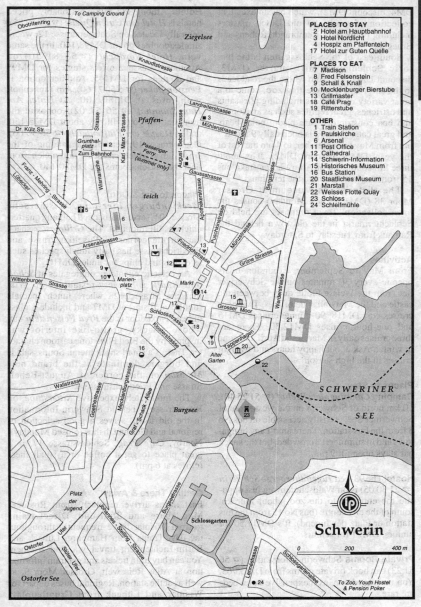

PLACES TO STAY
2 Hotel am Hauptbahnhof
3 Hotel Nordlicht
4 Hospiz am Pfaffenteich
17 Hotel zur Guten Quelle

PLACES TO EAT
7 Madison
8 Fred Felsenstein
9 Schall & Knall
10 Mecklenburger Bierstube
13 Grillmaster
18 Café Prag
19 Rittterstube

OTHER
1 Train Station
5 Paulskirche
6 Arsenal
11 Post Office
12 Cathedral
14 Schwerin-Information
15 Historisches Museum
16 Bus Station
20 Staatliches Museum
21 Marstall
22 Weisse Flotte Quay
23 Schloss
24 Schleifmühle

Ziegelsee

Obotritenring

To Camping Ground

Knaudtstrasse

Pfaffen-teich

Passenger Ferry (summer only)

Landreiterstrasse

Mühlenstrasse

Grunthal-platz

Zum Bahnhof

Dr. Külz Str.

Franz - Mehring - Strasse

Lübecker Strasse

Wismarsche Strasse

Karl - Marx - Strasse

Strasse

August - Bebel - Strasse

Gaussstrasse

Apothekerstrasse

Puschkinstrasse

Münzstrasse

Grüne Strasse

Schelfstrasse

Bergstrasse

Werderstrasse

Arsenalstrasse

Friedrichstrasse

Marienplatz

Wittenburger Strasse

Markt

Grosser Moor

Schlossstrasse

Klosterstrasse

Pappenhagen

Alter Garten

Wallstrasse

Goethestrasse

Mecklenburgstrasse

Graf - Schack - Allee

Burgsee

SCHWERINER

SEE

Platz der Jugend

Johannes - Stelling - Strasse

Lennéstrasse

Schlossgartenallee

Burgseestrasse

Schlossgarten

Ostorfer Uter

Slüter Ufer

Ostorfer See

To Zoo, Youth Hostel & Pension Poker

Schwerin

0   200   400 m

DM4, discount DM2), which has an excellent collection of works by old Dutch masters including Frans Hals, Rembrandt, Rubens and Brueghel.

South-east of the Schlossgarten is the historic **Schleifmühle** mill quarter (DM3, discount DM1.50), from where the road leads to the surprisingly interesting **zoo**, home to a great variety of denizens including pheasants and ostriches, great reptiles such as anacondas and boa constrictors, rare bison, polar bears and great cats. The zoo is open daily 9 am to 7 pm from May to September, to 4 pm the rest of the year (DM5, discount DM2). It is about three km south-east of Alter Garten (take bus 15 from the bus station to the terminus).

The **Historisches Museum** at Grosser Moor 38 (DM1; closed Monday) houses the town collection. Town **markets** are held on Schlachtermarkt in the old town behind the Rathaus from Tuesday to Saturday.

Activities

From May to September, excursion boats operate every 30 minutes on the Schweriner See from the Weisse Flotte quay between the castle and the Marstall state offices. Two-hour cruises cost DM18, 90-minute cruises DM15 and one-hour cruises DM12.50. There are three cruises daily in March and April, but none in winter. Ask about happy hours and twilight cruises in the high season.

Places to Stay

Camping *Campingplatz Seehof* (☎ 51 25 40), 10 km north of Schwerin on the west shore of Schweriner See, is easily accessible on bus No 8 from the bus station. There aren't any bungalows and in summer it's crowded, but the snack bar stays open till 9 pm.

Hostel The 93-bed *Jugendherberge Schwerin* (☎ 21 30 05) is on Waldschulenweg just opposite the entrance to the zoo, about four km south of the city centre (bus No 15 from the bus station or Platz der Jugend). It's DM17.50 for juniors, DM21 for seniors.

Private Rooms Schwerin-Information (☎ 56 51 23) can book private rooms from DM35/65. You may need one, as inexpensive hotel beds are rare.

Hotels Among the more reasonably priced hotels is *Hotel Zur Guten Quelle* (☎ 56 59 85), centrally located on Schusterstrasse 12, where singles/doubles go for DM98/140. In the same vein, *Hotel Nordlicht* (☎ 55 81 50) on Apothekerstrasse 2 offers singles for DM97 and doubles for DM145. Another option is *Pension Poker* (☎ 5 50 71 60), Am Tannenhof, with rates at DM80/100. At *Hotel Am Hauptbahnhof* (☎ 56 57 02), opposite the train station, you will pay about DM75/150, and at *Hospiz am Pfaffenteich* (☎ 56 56 06), Gaussstrasse 19, near the far landing of the small ferry which crosses Pfaffenteich from near the station, rooms are DM80/140.

Places to Eat & Drink

Mecklenburger Bierstube, Wismarsche Strasse 104, serves barbecued half and quarter-chickens till midnight. The *Grillmaster* snack bar on the corner of Puschkinstrasse and Friedrichstrasse has daily lunch specials such as cutlets and chips for under DM10.

An eclectic clientele congregates at *Schall und Knall*, a brewery-restaurant on Wismarsche Strasse 128 where lunch specials (until 5 pm) start at DM7 and include a glass of beer. Next door is the *Fred Felsenstein* bar, whose whacky, grotto-like interior was inspired by the Fred Flintstone cartoon character. There's a small snack menu. Soups, salads and burgers dominate at the brand new *Madison* on the corner of August-Bebel-Strasse and Friedrichstrasse.

The moderately expensive *Ritterstube*, on Ritterstrasse 3 behind Schwerin-Information in the old town, serves a good selection of regional and German dishes (closed Monday). Nearby, *Café Prag*, Schlossstrasse 17, is a great place to get a coffee or a small meal (closes at 6 pm).

Getting There & Away

Fast trains arrive regularly from Rostock, Magdeburg and Stralsund. Direct trains to/from Wismar leave frequently throughout the day. Trains from Hamburg, Lübeck and Berlin-Lichtenberg travel via Bad Kleinen. You can buy train tickets and get train information at Atlas Reisewelt, Grosser Moor 9, as well as at the station. Regional buses depart for Wismar and Lübeck from Grunthalplatz outside the train station; tickets are available from the bus driver.

WISMAR

Wismar, about halfway between Rostock and Lübeck, became a Hanseatic trading town in the 13th century. For centuries Wismar belonged to Sweden, and traces of Scandinavian rule can still be seen (and heard). It's less hectic than Rostock or Stralsund and a pretty little town worth seeing for itself. It's also the gateway to Poel Island.

Information

Wismar-Information (☎ 28 29 58) at Am Markt 11 (open daily 9 am to 6 pm) has maps, brochures, stickers etc.

Wismar's telephone code is ☎ 03841.

Things to See

Like many other German cities, Wismar was a target for Anglo-American bombers just a few weeks before the end of WWII. Of the three great red-brick churches that once rose above the rooftops, only **St Nikolai** is intact. The massive red shell of **St Georgenkirche** is being restored for future use as a concert hall and exhibit space. In 1945, a freezing populace was sadly driven to burn what was left of a beautiful wooden statue of St George and the dragon. Cars now park where the 13th-century **St Marienkirche** once stood, although the great brick steeple (1339), now partly restored, still towers above.

Apart from this, it's hard to believe that Wismar's gabled houses were seriously bombed. In a corner of Markt are the graceful old **Waterworks** (1602) and the **Rathaus** (1819). The town's historical museum (closed Monday) is in the Renaissance **Schnabbelhaus** at Schweinsbrücke 8 near St Nikolai. It has many interesting exhibits on Wismar's past as a maritime Hanseatic power and a Swedish garrison town. Busy town **markets** are held on Tuesday, Thursday and Saturday on Markt. On Saturday, a lively fish market takes place at Alter Hafen.

Activities

From May to September, Clermont Reederei operates hour-long harbour cruises five times daily (DM10) from Alter Hafen. By arrange-ment, boats also go to Poel Island, a summer bathing resort popular among Germans.

Places to Stay

Wismar-Information arranges private singles and doubles from DM30 per person (DM5 booking fee). The nearest hostel is *Youth Hostel Beckerwitz* (☎ 0384-2 83 62) at Haus Nr. 21 in Beckerwitz. Take bus No 240, direction Boltenhagen, from the train station. The nearest *camping ground* is at Am Strand 19c in Zierow (☎ 03841-64 23 77) and can be reached with bus No 320.

Gothia-Hotel (☎ 73 41 56), Sella-Hasse-Strasse 11, is a good deal at DM75 for singles and from DM45 per person for apartments. Also affordable is *Hotel Lippold* (☎ 28 35 77), Poeler Strasse 138, which has doubles only at DM60 to DM80.

The historic *Hotel Altes Brauhaus* (☎ 21 14 16), Lübschestrasse 37, has rooms from DM85/140 singles/doubles. At the elegant *Hotel Alter Speicher* (☎ 21 47 61), Bohrstrasse 12, rates start at DM110/160.

Places to Eat

Wismar's 'restaurant row' is along the car-free Am Lohberg near the fishing harbour. The string of atmospheric restaurants and bars includes *Brauhaus*, the town's first brewery. *Zum Weinberg* is a wine restaurant in the Renaissance house at Hinter dem Rathaus 3. Possibly the best situated restaurant is the historic and exclusive *Alter Schwede*, Am Markt 18. The local *Grillmaster* budget grill bar is at Lübsche Strasse 49; it's fast and filling for DM8 or less.

Getting There & Away

Trains run to/from Rostock every couple of hours and regularly to/from Schwerin. Trains to/from Berlin-Lichtenberg, Lübeck and Hamburg travel via Bad Kleinen. There are daily buses to/from Lübeck – and from there on to Kiel, Rendsburg and Hamburg – from beside the train station. There is also frequent bus service to Schwerin and to Poel Island. There are no lockers at the train station.

ROSTOCK

Rostock, the largest city in lightly populated north-eastern Germany, is a major Baltic port and shipbuilder. The giant shipyards on the estuary of the Warnow River were built from scratch after 1957. In the 14th and 15th centuries, Rostock was an important Hanseatic city trading with Riga, Bergen and Bruges. Rostock University, founded in 1419, was the first in northern Europe. The city centre along Kröpeliner Strasse retains the flavour of this period and much is being redeveloped, including the remains of the old city walls, medieval churches and the local transit system. It's a popular tourist centre, and the beach resort of Warnemünde is only 12 km north.

Orientation & Information

Rostock-Information (☎ 1 94 33 or 49 79 90) is at Schnickmannstrasse 13-14, about two km from the train station. Take tram Nos 11 or 12 outside the station and get off at the Lange Strasse stop. Rostock's main post office is adjacent to the Rathaus.

Rostock's telephone code is ☎ 0381.

Things to See

Rostock's greatest sight is the 13th-century **St-Marien-Kirche**, which survived WWII unscathed. This great medieval brick edifice contains a functioning astronomical clock (1472), a Gothic bronze baptismal font (1290), a Renaissance pulpit (1574) and a baroque organ (1770) – all artistic treasures. Ascend the 207 steps of the 50-metre-high church tower for the view.

Kröpeliner Strasse, a broad pedestrian mall lined with 15th and 16th-century burgher houses, runs west from the **Rathaus** on Neuer Markt to the 14th-century **Kröpeliner Tor** (closed Monday) near a stretch of old city wall. Halfway along, off the south-west corner of Universitätsplatz, is the **Kloster 'Zum Heiligen Kreuz' Museum** (closed Monday) in an old convent (1270). Ask at the museum about visiting the recently restored convent church.

Rostock also has a good **Maritime Museum** (DM4; closed Monday) on the corner of Richard-Wagner-Strasse and August-Bebel-Strasse, near the **Steintor**.

Places to Stay

The 85-berth **Jugendgästeschiff 'Traditionsschiff'** (☎ 71 62 24) is in a converted freighter on the harbour at Schmarl-Dorf, between Rostock and Warnemünde (S-Bahn to Lütten

Klein station, then walk east past the apartment blocks for 25 or 30 minutes, turn left at the three-way intersection and past the small lighthouse and the two car parks to the far gangway marked for the museum). It's a good deal at DM26/32 for juniors/seniors because the rooms and setting are very pleasant and it's run more like a pension. But you are a long way from anything else, so shop first if you arrive late in the afternoon or evening.

Rostock-Information can book private singles/doubles from around DM30/60 for a DM5 fee. If you arrive after hours, you can call ☎ 1 94 14 for a recorded message (in German only) about all vacant rooms in the city.

Small but central and worth trying is **City-Pension** (☎ 4 59 08 29) at Krönkenhagen 3, with singles/doubles with private facilities from DM85/150. **Landhaus Immenbarg** (☎ 77 69 30), Gross Kleiner Weg 19, has rooms for DM108/158. More expensive but central is the new **Ramada Hotel** (☎ 4 97 00) at Universitätsplatz in a pedestrian-only zone. Rooms here go for DM155/190. Pricey but nice is the nine-storey Radisson SAS Hotel, Lange Strasse 40, at DM175/210.

Places to Eat

For a quick snack of fruits, fish, pizza and the like, go to **Gallerie Rostocker Hof** at Universitätsplatz, beneath the Ramada Hotel. For a late lunch, it's hard to beat the **Rostocker Ratskeller** in the Rathaus building on Neuer Markt, where everything is half-price between 3 and 5 pm on weekdays. The local stand-by is **Jimmy's Hamburger** at Kröpeliner Strasse 71, on the corner of Breite Strasse at Universitätsplatz (good burgers, big coffees for DM2.30). There's a new **Burger King** across the street. **Kartoffelhaus No. 1**, Am Strande 3a, serves delicious potato-based dishes at reasonable prices in a city harbour setting. The **Gastmahl des Meeres** opposite the Maritime Museum on August-Bebel-Strasse specialises in seafood and is expensive.

Getting There & Away

There are direct trains to Rostock from Berlin-Lichtenberg and trains run to Stralsund, Wismar and Schwerin several times daily. Atlas Reisewelt at Lange Strasse in front of the Radisson sells train tickets, as does the main station's ticket office.

Several ferry companies offer crossings to Trelleborg (Sweden) and Gedser (Denmark) from Rostock Seaport. Among them, TT-Line ferries depart Rostock for Trelleborg five times daily. The crossing takes three hours and costs DM46-50 one way (depending on the season). Bicycles are DM10 extra and cars are DM120 (DM210 in high season). Hansa/DFO charges from DM120 to DM180 to take your car (and up to four passengers), depending on the season and day of the week. Motorbikes are DM25 to 35.

DFO Vogelfluglinie also has frequent ferries all year to Gedser (DM8 one way, DM10 from June to mid-September). Cars cost DM80 (in summer DM100, Friday to Sunday).

Getting Around

The double-deck S-Bahn has 1st (50% dearer) and 2nd class – be careful which one you get into and check exactly from which platform the next service will depart. The Rostock transit area, which includes Warnemünde, is divided into zones and you pay DM2 for one zone, DM2.80 for two or more zones, single journeys. Day cards are DM7.50, and the discounted after-9 am day card is excellent value at DM3.80 (one zone) and DM5 (two or more zones). Local tickets are available at machines at nearly all tram stops and S-Bahn stations.

WARNEMÜNDE

Warnemünde, at the mouth of the Warnow River on the Baltic Sea just north of Rostock, is among eastern Germany's most popular beach resorts. S-Bahn trains (see the Getting Around section above) connect Warnemünde to Rostock every 15 minutes on weekdays, every 30 minutes in the evenings, and hourly from midnight to dawn, so the town can easily be used as a base for day trips to Rostock, Wismar, Stralsund and even Schwerin. It's a good choice if you want to enjoy the comforts of city life while staying in what is essentially a small fishing village on the beach.

Information

Warnemünde Tourist-Information (☎ 5 11 42) is on the corner of Wachtler Strasse and Heinrich-Heine-Strasse. It's open weekdays from 10 am to 5 pm and in summer also on Saturday morning. Outside the office, you'll find an information board with push-button screen and a coin telephone.

For currency exchange, DVB Bank, Am Bahnhof in the station area, is open Monday to Friday from 8.30 am to 6 pm, Saturday 9 am to noon. Otherwise, you can exchange on the ferry if you are crossing to Scandinavia.

Warnemünde has the same telephone code as Rostock: ☎ 0381.

Things to See

The old harbour, **Alter Strom,** is a picturesque inlet lined with quaint fishermen's cottages. One of these has been converted into a **Heimatmuseum** (open Wednesday to Sunday, 11 am to 6 pm; DM3), on Alexandrinenstrasse just south of Kirchenstrasse, the church and the main square. Lining the inlet on the west side are tempting restaurants, while boats moored at the quay below sell fish and rolls, offer cruises (DM9-15 all year, weather permitting), or present themselves as restaurants (some manage all three). The result is a pleasant atmosphere that can be experienced at little or no cost.

The crowded **promenade** to the north, on the sea, is where tourists congregate. Warnemünde's broad, sandy beach stretches west from the **lighthouse** (1898), and is chock-a-block with bathers on a hot summer's day.

Places to Stay

For private rooms, turn to Warnemünde Tourist-Information or *Warnemünde Zimmervermittlung* (☎ 5 91 76) at Am Bahnhof 1 just outside the train station. Otherwise, look for the 'Zimmer frei' signs in the windows along Parkstrasse.

Apart from private rooms, reasonably priced accommodation is basically non-existent. You might try *Pension Katy* (☎ 54 39 40), Kurhausstrasse 9, which has doubles with private bath for DM55 to DM75. *Hotel am Alten Strom* (☎ 5 25 81), Am Strom 60, has rooms starting at DM45/70 (shared facilities), ranging up to DM100/160. *Hotel Stolteraa* (☎ 5 43 20), Strandweg 17, offers doubles at DM130 to DM220.

Places to Eat

Eating in Warnemünde can be very expensive. You may find reasonably priced daily specials

GERMANY

in the cafés along Alter Strom or just pick up a fish snack sold straight from the boats. *Café zur Traube* at Alexandrinenstrasse 72 is cosy but pricey. You can find better prices at *Zur Gemütlichkeit* on Mühlenstrasse 25, where many dishes go for around DM12. Also affordable are the daily fish specials at *Kettenkasten*, Am Strom 71.

Getting There & Away
It's easy to get to Warnemünde station on the double-decker S-Bahn from Rostock station (DM2.80; see Getting Around in the Rostock section).

STRALSUND
Stralsund, an enjoyable city on the Baltic Sea north of Berlin, is nearly surrounded by lakes and the sea, which once contributed to its defence. Stralsund was a Hanseatic city in the Middle Ages and later formed part of the Duchy of Pommern-Wolgast. From 1648 to 1815 it was under Swedish control. Today it's an attractive historic town with fine museums and buildings, pleasant walks and a restful, uncluttered waterfront. The island of Rügen is just across the Strelasund, and in summer the ferry to Hiddensee Island leaves from here.

Orientation & Information
The old town and port are connected by causeways to their surrounds; the main train station is across the Tribseer Damm causeway, west of the old town. Neuer Markt is the south-western hub and the bus station is a few blocks south past the Marienkirche. Stralsund-Information (☎ 2 46 90) is at Ossenreyerstrasse 1, near the northern focus of the old town at Alter Markt. Ask about the tourist pass (DM19, discount DM9 in summer; DM15/9 in winter) that will admit you to the main attractions and summer organ concerts. The post office is on Neuer Markt, opposite the Marienkirche.

Stralsund's telephone code is ☎ 03831.

Things to See
On Alter Markt is the medieval **Rathaus**, where you can stroll through the vaulted and pillared structures and around to the impressive **Nikolaikirche**. Long-term restoration of the church's magnificent painted medieval interior is continuing, but parts of it are open on weekdays except Monday from 10 am to 4

pm, Saturday to noon and Sunday from 11 am to noon. The 14th-century **Marienkirche** on Neuer Markt is a massive red-brick edifice typical of north German Gothic architecture. You can climb the 350 or so steps of the tower (on a daunting network of steep ladders) for a sweeping view of Stralsund from 10 am and 3 pm on the hour and half-hour (DM2).

On Mönchstrasse are two excellent museums. Stralsund's highlight is the **Meeresmuseum**, an oceanic complex and aquarium in a 13th-century convent church (open 10 am to 5 pm daily from May to October, closed Monday in winter; DM7, discount DM3.50). There's a large natural-history section and much information on the fishing industry. Some aquariums in the basement contain tropical fish and coral, others display creatures of the Baltic and North seas. The **Kulturhistorisches Museum** (DM4, discount DM1.50, closed Monday) has a large collection housed in the cloister of an old convent (and an annexe for local history at Böttcherstrasse 23 near the battered Jakobikirche – one ticket admits you to both). Maritime and naval history is covered at the **Marinemuseum** (closed Monday, DM3, discount DM1) on the island of Dänholm, off the B96 towards Rügen.

Many fine buildings have been restored on the showpiece **Mühlenstrasse** near Alter Markt. The old harbour is close by and you'll want to stroll along the sea wall, then west along the waterfront park for a great view of Stralsund's skyline.

Activities
From May to September, Weisse Flotte ferries depart from the old harbour for Neuendorf on Hiddensee Island (DM13/22 one way/return). If you want to take a bicycle on this boat (DM10), check first. Large baggage costs DM1 per piece. There are also short crossings to Altefähr (DM3) and one-hour harbour cruises daily at 2.30 pm (DM6). You can book at ☎ 26 81 16 or buy tickets from the kiosk at the quay.

There are organ recitals on the 1659 instrument in Marienkirche and in the Gothic splendour of Nikolaikirche, alternating on Wednesday in summer at 8 pm; the bill is occasionally filled by chamber music. Performances at Marienkirche cost DM8, discount DM5; at Nikolaikirche it's DM7, discount DM4.

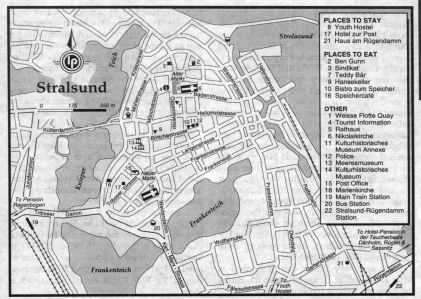

PLACES TO STAY
8 Youth Hostel
17 Hotel zur Post
21 Haus am Rügendamm

PLACES TO EAT
2 Ben Gunn
3 Sindikat
7 Teddy Bär
9 Hansekeller
10 Bistro zum Speicher
16 Speichercafé

OTHER
1 Weisse Flotte Quay
4 Tourist Information
5 Rathaus
6 Nikolaikirche
11 Kulturhistorisches Museum Annexe
12 Police
13 Meeresmuseum
14 Kulturhistorisches Museum
15 Post Office
18 Marienkirche
19 Main Train Station
20 Bus Station
22 Stralsund-Rügendamm Station

Places to Stay

As no camping ground is handy you should plan to camp on Rügen Island (see the following Rügen section). Stralsund's excellent 180-bed *Youth Hostel* (☎ 29 21 60) is in the 17th-century waterworks at Am Kütertor 1 (bus Nos 4, 5 or 50 or 15 minutes walk from the main train station). It's DM18 for juniors, DM22 for seniors and is closed in January. Another *Youth Hostel* (☎ 27 03 58) is at Strandstrasse 21 off the Greifswald road in nearby Devin (20 minutes by bus Nos 3 or 60 from the main train station, closed in December and January).

Stralsund-Information handles reservations for private rooms, pensions and hotels. A budget option, especially handy to Stralsund-Rügendamm station, is *Haus am Rügendamm* (☎ 29 50 51), at Reiferbahn 29 in a former housing development. The hostel-class bathrooms are shared, but singles/doubles go for DM60/90. Enter from the Strelasund side. The *Hotel-Pension in der Taucherbasis* (☎ 29 70 90) is at Haus 93 on Dänholm Island, about four km from the town centre, and offers quiet rooms from DM60/90. Another candidate is *Pension Regenbogen* (☎ 49 76 74) at Richtenberger Chaussee 2a, which costs from DM70/90, less during off season. For a worthwhile splurge, try *Hotel Zur Post* (☎ 20 05 00), at Tribseer Strasse 22 near Marienkirche, where rooms start at DM145/210.

Places to Eat & Drink

For budget eating, go directly to the tiny *Bistro zum Speicher* on the corner of Böttcherstrasse and Filterstrasse, where main dishes come in under DM10. *Teddy Bär* is a snack bar and café on the corner of Ossenreyerstrasse and Badenstrasse near the Rathaus. The pub *Ben Gunn* at Fährstrasse 27 behind Alter Markt is a popular youth hangout, as is the nearby *Sindikat* on Knieperstrasse at the corner of Schillstrasse, and the new *Speichercafé* at Katharinenberg 34. The *Hansekeller* at Mönchstrasse 48 serves hearty regional dishes at moderate prices in the earthy atmosphere of a vaulted cellar.

Getting There & Away

Express trains run to/from Rostock (one hour, about 15 daily) and Berlin-Lichtenberg (three hours, 15 daily). Connections to Hamburg and Leipzig are less frequent but regular. International trains between Berlin and Stockholm or Oslo use the car ferry connecting Sassnitz Hafen on Rügen Island with Trelleborg and Malmö (Sweden). Some trains to/from Sassnitz Hafen don't stop at Stralsund's main train station but instead call at Stralsund-Rügendamm south-east of the city (some stop at both). Boarding for Sweden, use the cars labelled for Sassnitz Hafen and Malmö, as the train will split up at Sassnitz. Two or three daily connections to Stockholm (changing at Malmö) are available, some from Stralsund-Rügendamm only (see also Rügen Island, and the Getting There & Away section at the beginning of this chapter). There are about 20 daily trains to Sassnitz (one hour) from Stralsund or Stralsund-Rügendamm, and at least 10 daily run to/from Binz on Rügen Island.

Train and ferry tickets can be booked at Atlas Reisewelt at Heilgeiststrasse 85. Buses run between Bergen (on Rügen) and Sassnitz several times daily, departing from the bus station by Frankenteich south of the city centre.

HIDDENSEE ISLAND

Hiddensee is a narrow island about 17 km long off Rügen's west coast, north of Stralsund. No cars are allowed on Hiddensee. Hotels are few and concentrate in the town of Vitte. At *Godewind* (☎ 038300-2 35) at Süderende 53 prices start at DM50 per person for bathless rooms. Singles/doubles at *Pension Lachmöwe* (☎ 038300-2 53) on Wallweg 5 go for DM80/140 (includes shower/WC) during high season. There are no camping grounds or hostels.

Ferries from Schaprode on Rügen's west coast run frequently across to Hiddensee (DM10/17.50 one way/return to Neuendorf, DM12/20.50 to Kloster and Vitte, DM10 for bicycles). In summer there are also ferries from Stralsund (see Activities in the Stralsund section).

RÜGEN ISLAND

Germany's largest island, Rügen is just northeast of Stralsund and connected by a causeway. The island's highest point is Königsstuhl (117

metres), reached by car or by bus from Sassnitz. The **chalk cliffs** which tower above the sea are the main attraction. Much of Rügen and its surrounding waters are either national park or protected nature reserves. The **Bodden** inlet area is a bird refuge and therefore popular with bird-watchers. Several maps are available, but Nordland's *Rügen mit Hiddensee* 1:75,000 sheet (about DM9 at most shops and tourist offices) is adequate for walking or cycling.

The main resort area is around Binz, Sellin and Göhren, on a peninsula on Rügen's east side. A lovely hike from Binz to Sellin skirts the cliffs above the sea through beech and pine forest and offers great coastal views. Another destination is **Jagdschloss Granitz** (1834), also surrounded by lush forest.

Rügen Information (☎ 038303-14 70) is at August-Bebel-Strasse 12 in Sellin (information only, no room reservations). In Sassnitz, the tourist office (☎ 038392-3 20 37) at Seestrasse 1 handles enquiries and also books hotel and private rooms, as does Binz Information (038393-27 82) at Schillerstrasse 15 in Binz.

Places to Stay

Rügen has 18 camping grounds, the largest concentration of them at Göhren. Rügen Information publishes a booklet with details and prices, available at all tourist offices.

The newly renovated *Youth Hostel* (☎ 038393-3 25 97) at Strandpromenade 35 in Binz was scheduled to reopen in mid-1996. The huge 360-bed *Youth Hostel Prora* (☎ 038393-32 844) is at Prora-Ost, near the road to Sassnitz (bus from Binz, DM18/22 juniors/seniors). The small *Hotel-Pension Granitz* (☎ 038393-26 78) at Bahnhofstrasse 2 in Binz has rooms for DM70/160 singles/doubles, less in low season. At *Vier Jahreszeiten* (☎ 038393-5 00), also in Binz at Zeppelinstrasse 8, rooms start at DM120/170. In Sassnitz, the recently renovated four-star *Rügenhotel*, at Seestrasse 1 near the ferry harbour, offers doubles with all amenities for DM160.

Getting There & Away

Local trains run almost hourly between 8 am and 9 pm from Stralsund to Sassnitz or Binz (one hour). Both services pass Lietzow, 13 km before Sassnitz, where you may have to change trains. An historic and fun narrow-gauge train chugs from Putbus to Göhren via Binz.

DFO HansaFerry runs five ferries daily from Sassnitz to Trelleborg (Sweden) and return. The crossing takes four hours and costs DM20/40 one way/return (DM30/60 from June to mid-September). If you want to take a car, you pay DM175/350 in summer; motorcycles are DM70/140. Prices include passengers and are slightly lower in winter. Cabins are available on night crossings. For bookings, call ☎ 038392/6 41 80 or visit a travel agent. There is also a ticket kiosk at Trelleborger Strasse on the street corner between Sassnitz train station and the harbour.

If you are taking the train to the Sweden ferry, find out whether it ends at Sassnitz main station or goes right to the quayside at Sassnitz Hafen (in the case of a split train you need to be in the appropriately labelled carriage). It's about a 10-minute walk downhill from the station to the harbour and about 20 minutes going uphill in the other direction. Generally, local trains from Stralsund end at the main station, while through services to/from Malmö connect with the ferry.

DFO HansaFerry also has four services daily (June to mid-September) between Neu-Mukran near Sassnitz and Rønne on Bornholm (Denmark) for DM30/60. There are two daily crossings in winter (DM20/40).

See the previous Hiddensee Island section regarding transport from Rügen to Hiddensee.

Bavaria

For many visitors to Germany, Bavaria (Bayern) is a microcosm of the whole country. Here you will find fulfilled the German stereotypes of *Lederhosen*, beer halls, oompah bands and romantic castles. Yet the Bavarians themselves are proudly independent and pursue a separate course from the rest of Germany in a number of ways, not least in the refusal of its youth hostels to accept any guests over the age of 26.

Bavaria was ruled for centuries as a duchy under the line founded by Otto I of Wittelsbach, and eventually graduated to the status of a kingdom in 1806. The region suffered amid numerous power struggles between Prussia and Austria and was finally brought into the German Empire in 1871 by Bismarck. The last king of Bavaria was Ludwig II (1845-86), who earned the epithet the 'mad monarch' due to his obsession for building fantastic fairy-tale castles at enormous expense. He was found drowned in Lake Starnberg in suspicious circumstances, and left no heirs.

Bavaria draws visitors all year. If you only have time for one part of Germany after Berlin, this is it. Munich, the capital, is the heart and soul of the area. The Bavarian Alps, Nuremberg and the medieval towns on the Romantic Road are other important attractions. Try getting off the beaten track in a place like the Bavarian Forest for a glimpse of Germany away from the tour buses.

MUNICH
Munich (München) is the Bavarian mother lode. But this beer-belching, sausage-eating city can be as cosmopolitan as anywhere in Europe. Munich residents have figured out how to enjoy life and are perfectly happy to show outsiders – as a visit to the Hofbräuhaus (or some other beer hall) will confirm. There's much more to Munich, however, than beer halls. Decide on one of the many fine museums and take a leisurely look.

Munich has been the capital of Bavaria since 1503, but really achieved eminence under the guiding hand of Ludwig I in the 19th century. It has seen many turbulent times, but this century has been particularly rough. WWI practically starved the city, and WWII brought bombing and more than 200,000 deaths.

Orientation
The main train station (Hauptbahnhof) is less than one km west of the centre of town. Although there's an extensive metro and S-Bahn system, old-town Munich is enjoyable for walking. Head east along Bayerstrasse, through Karlsplatz, and then along Neuhauser Strasse and Kaufingerstrasse to Marienplatz, the hub of Munich.

North of Marienplatz are the Residenz (the former royal palace), Schwabing (the famous student section) and the parklands of Englischer Garten. East of Marienplatz is the Platzl quarter for beer houses and restaurants, as well as Maximilianstrasse, a fashionable street that's fun for strolling and window-shopping.

Information

The main tourist office (☎ 23 33 02 56) is at Hauptbahnhof, beside the south entrance near platform No 11. Its hours are 8 am to 10 pm from Monday to Saturday and 11 am to 7 pm on Sunday. Despite the efficiency of the staff, you can expect to stand in line during summer. The room-finding service costs DM5 and you must book in person (or in writing, to: D-80313, München).

There's also a more central tourist office at Sendlinger Strasse 1 near Rindermarkt (go upstairs to Room 213), open Monday to Thursday from 8.30 am to 4 pm, to 2 pm on Friday. The Munich airport tourist office (☎ 97 59 28 15) is open from Monday to Saturday, 8.30 am to 10 pm, and from 1 to 9 pm on Sunday and holidays.

EurAide (☎ 59 38 89), near platform 11 at the train station, is another excellent source of information in English. The office gives information on train travel, and its room-finding service (DM6 per booking) is at least as skilful as the tourist office. It's open daily from May to the end of October, from 7.30 am to 6 pm (to 4 pm only during May), but closes for lunch.

Yet another useful office is the Jugendinformationszentrum (51 41 06 60) at the corner of Paul-Heyse-Strasse and Landwehrstrasse. Open from noon to 6 pm Monday to Friday (until 8 pm on Thursday), it has a wide range of printed information for young visitors to Germany.

The excellent *Young People's Guide to Munich* is available for DM1 from all of these tourist offices.

Foreign Consulates Among the many consulates in the city are the British Consulate (☎ 21 10 90) at Bürkleinstrasse 10, the US Consulate (☎ 2 88 80) at Königinstrasse 5, and the Canadian Consulate (☎ 22 26 61) at Tal 29. The Czech Consulate (☎ 95 01 24) is at Siedlerstrasse 2 in Unterföhring (open 8.30 to 11 am only).

Money The DVB bank has two offices at Hauptbahnhof. Otherwise there are Deutsche Bank and Stadtsparkasse branches on Marienplatz. Post offices offer good rates for cash, but charge DM6 per travellers' cheque. You'll find American Express at Promenadeplatz 6 and Thomas Cook at Kaiserstrasse 45.

Post & Communications Munich's central post office and telephone exchange is directly opposite the station at Bahnhofplatz 1, and is open daily from 7 am to 10 pm (from 8 am on weekends and holidays). The poste restante address is Postlagernd, 80074 München 32. The post office in the station closes at 7 pm Monday to Friday, and at 2 pm on Saturday (closed Sunday).

Munich's telephone code is ☎ 089.

Travel Agencies ABR Reisebüro (☎ 1 20 40) in the main station building handles train-ticket sales (including under-26 discount TwenTickets). Studiosus Reisen (☎ 2 35 05 20) at Oberanger 6 organises educational trips within Germany and abroad.

Bookshops Munich is one of the best German cities for getting hold of English-language reading matter. In the university quarter you'll find the Anglia English Bookshop (☎ 28 36 42) at Schellingstrasse 3, which has a formidable range of paperbacks. Just down the street in the courtyard at No 21a is Words' Worth Books. The best travel and cultural book range is at the multilevel Hugendubel branch opposite the Rathaus at Marienplatz.

Laundry Conveniently close to the main train station, and open from 6 am to 10 pm daily, is Prinz Münz-Waschsalon at Paul-Heyse-Strasse 21. Loads cost DM7, drying DM1 for 15 minutes, and the last wash must be in by 8 pm.

Medical & Emergency Services Medical help is available at the Kassenärztlicher Notfalldienst on ☎ 55 77 55; for ambulances dial ☎ 1 92 22. The police are at Hauptbahnhof on the Arnulfstrasse side, and their emergency number is ☎ 110.

Dangers & Annoyances Crime and staggering drunks leaving the beer halls are major problems in Munich. Watch valuables carefully around touristy areas and the seedy streets south of Hauptbahnhof. A common trick is to steal your gear if you strip off in the Englischer Garten.

Things to See & Do
The pivotal **Marienplatz** contains the towering neo-Gothic **Altes Rathaus** (old town hall) and the incessantly photographed **Glockenspiel** (carillon), which does its number at 11 am, noon and 5 pm (only at 11 am from 1 November to 30 April). Many other attractions are within easy walking distance.

Walking Tour Start at Marienplatz. Two important churches are on this square: **Peterskirche** and, behind the Altes Rathaus, the **Heiliggeistkirche**. Head west along the shopping street Kaufingerstrasse to the late Gothic **Frauenkirche** (Church of Our Lady), the landmark church of Munich; the monotonous red brick is very Bavarian in its simplicity. Continue west on Kaufingerstrasse to **Michaelskirche**, Germany's grandest Renaissance church.

Further west is the **Richard Strauss fountain** and then the medieval **Karlstor** (an old city gate). Double back towards Marienplatz and turn right onto Eisenmannstrasse, which becomes Kreuzstrasse, and Herzog-Wilhelm-Strasse. The two streets converge at the medieval gate of Sendlinger Tor. Go down the left side of the shopping street Sendlinger Strasse to the **Asamkirche**, a remarkable church designed by the Asam brothers. It shows a rare unity of style, with scarcely a single unembellished surface.

Continue along Sendlinger Strasse and turn right on Hermann-Sack-Strasse to reach the **Stadtmuseum** (admission DM5; closed Monday) on St-Jakobs-Platz, where the outstanding exhibits cover beer brewing, fashion, musical instruments, photography and puppets. Walk around the left side of the museum and turn left onto Sebastiansplatz and Prälat-Zistl-Strasse. The **Viktualienmarkt** (food market), one of Europe's great markets, is nearby.

Residenz This huge palace housed Bavarian rulers from 1385 to 1918, and features more than 500 years of architectural history. Apart from the palace itself, the **Residenz Museum** (entry DM5) has an extraordinary array of 100

rooms containing the Wittelsbach house's belongings, while the **Schatzkammer** (entry DM5) exhibits a ridiculous quantity of jewels, crowns and ornate gold. The Residenz is open Tuesday to Sunday from 10 am to 4.30 pm.

If this doesn't satisfy your passion for palaces, visit **Schloss Nymphenburg** (general admission DM6, or just castle and gallery DM4) north-west of the city centre. This was the royal family's equally impressive summer home. The surrounding park is worth a long, royal stroll.

Deutsches Museum The world's largest science and technology museum, this is like a combination of Disneyland and the Smithsonian Institute all under one huge roof. You can explore anything from the depths of coal mines to the stars, but it's definitely too large to see everything so pursue specific interests. A major extension is planned, though it already covers some 55,000 sq metres, requiring over 13 km of walking to see all exhibits. The museum's hours are 9 am to 5 pm daily (closed on important holidays) and admission is DM10 for adults and DM4 for students and children (free for those aged under six). A visit to the planetarium costs DM3 extra. To get to the museum, take the S-Bahn to Isartor, U1 or U2 to Fraunhoferstrasse, or tram No 18 to Deutsches Museum.

Alte Pinakothek A veritable treasure house of European masters between the 14th and 18th centuries, including Dürer's Christ-like *Self Portrait* and his *Four Apostles*, Rogier van der Weyden's *Adoration of the Magi* and Botticelli's *Pietà*, the Alte Pinakothek is due to reopen in early 1997 after a thorough renovation. Immediately adjacent, at Barer Strasse 29, is the **Neue Pinakothek**, which contains mainly 19th-century painting and sculpture (DM6, students DM3.50). The museum is free on Sunday and holidays, and closed on Monday.

Other Museums On Königsplatz there are two museums worth a look. The **Glyptothek** and the **Staatliche Antikensammlungen** feature one of Germany's best antiquities collections (mostly Greek and Roman stuff). To visit either museum costs DM6 (students DM3.50), to

PLACES TO STAY

13	4 you münchen
30	Jugendhotel Marienherberge
31	Pension Schiller
33	Hotel Arosa
39	Hotel-Pension am Markt
46	CVJM-YMCA Jugendgästehaus
47	Pension Marie Luise
48	Hotel Gebhardt
53	Hotel Blauer Bock

PLACES TO EAT

6	News Bar
19	Haxenbauer
20	Hofbräuhaus
21	Alois Dallmayr
22	Münchner Suppenküche
23	Nürnberger Bratwurst Glöckl am Dom
29	Mathäser Bierstadt
32	Augustiner Bierhalle
42	Altes Hackerhaus
43	Prinz Myschkin
45	Café Ziegler
44	Bella Roma
40	Löwenbräu Stadt Kempten
49	Café Höflinger

OTHER

1	Citynetz Mitfahr-Service
2	Chinesischer Turm
3	University
4	Neue Pinakothek
5	Words' Worth Books
7	Anglia English Bookshop
8	Alte Pinakothek
9	Glyptothek
10	Staatliche Antikensammlungen
11	Staatsgalerie Moderner Kunst
12	ADM-Mitfahrzentrale
14	Main Train Station (Hauptbahnhof)
15	Tourist Information
16	Post Office
17	Residenz
18	Nationaltheater
24	Frauenkirche
25	Museum of Hunting & Fishing
26	Michaelskirche
27	Richard Strauss Fountain
28	Karlstor
34	Sport Schuster
35	Altes Rathaus
36	Peterskirche
37	Heiliggeistkirche
41	Tourist Information
38	Viktualienmarkt
50	Sendlinger Tor
51	Asamkirche
52	Stadtmuseum
54	Deutsches Museum

visit both costs DM10 (DM6). Try to go on a Sunday when they're free; both are closed on Monday.

Also interesting is the **Staatsgalerie Moderner Kunst** at Prinzregentenstrasse 1. This gallery displays some of the great German and international contributions to modern art, including wild paintings by Munch, Picasso and Magritte, as well as funky sculpture and some pop art (admission DM5, students DM3; closed Monday).

North of the city is the somewhat self-congratulatory **BMW Museum** (DM5.50, open daily), at Peutelring 130. Unfortunately, guided public tours of the adjoining BMW motor works are currently unavailable. Take the U2 to Scheidplatz and then the U3, or take the U3 direct from Marienplatz to Olympia-zentrum.

Englischer Garten One of the largest city parks in Europe, this is a great place for strolling, especially along the Schwabinger Bach. In balmy summer weather, nude sunbathing is the rule rather than the exception. It's not unusual for hundreds of naked people to be in the park on a normal business day, with their coats, ties and dresses stacked primly on the grass.

Olympiaturm If you like heights, go up the lift of the 290-metre tower Olympiaturm in the Olympia Park complex (DM5; open until midnight).

Dachau Don't miss this. Dachau was the very first Nazi concentration camp, built by Heinrich Himmler in March 1933. It 'processed' more than 200,000 prisoners, though it's not known exactly how many died. In 1933 Munich had 10,000 Jews. Only 200 survived the war. An English-language documentary is shown at 11.30 am and 3.30 pm. A visit includes camp relics, a memorial, and a very sobering museum. It's open from 9 am to 5 pm every day except Monday, and admission is free. Take the S2 to Dachau and then bus No 722, which departs from Dachau station (you need a two-zone ticket to cover the journey).

Activities
Munich makes a perfect base for outdoor activities. The Deutscher Alpenverein (German Alpine Club, ☎ 14 00 30) is west of the centre at Von-Kahr-Strasse 2-4; the club can give information on walking and climbing in the mountains.

The Sport Schuster outdoor goods store at Rosenstrasse 1-5 has five floors of everything imaginable for the adventurer, from simple camping gear to expedition wear, plus an excellent bookshop. It has a travel service on the 1st floor, offering organised outdoor trips.

Special Events
Try to get to Munich for the Oktoberfest, one of the continent's biggest and best parties, running from the last Saturday in September to the first Sunday in October. Reserve accommodation well ahead. The Oktoberfest takes place at the Theresienwiese grounds south-west of the main station. No entrance fee is charged, but most of the fun costs something. There are carnival rides, food stands and, best of all, lots of beer tents.

Places to Stay
No-one older than 26 (unless travelling with children aged under 18) can stay in Bavarian youth hostels. This puts extra pressure on budget hotels and pensions, of which there are precious few in Munich. Reserve ahead if possible and arrive early in the day.

Camping The most centrally located camping ground is *Campingplatz Thalkirchen* (☎ 7 23 17 07), south-west of the city centre at Zentralländstrasse 49, close to the hostel on Miesingstrasse. Closed from November to mid-March, it can be incredibly crowded in summer, but there always seems to be room for one more tent. Take the U3 to Thalkirchen and bus No 57 to the last stop, 'Thalkirchen' (about 20 minutes from the city centre).

A bit further from the city centre are *Waldcamping Obermenzing* (☎ 8 11 22 35) and *Langwieder See* (☎ 8 64 15 66); the latter has a great location but can only be reached by car on the autobahn towards Stuttgart. It is open from early April to the end of October.

Youth Hostels All of Munich's youth hostels (DJH-affiliated) are open only to those aged 26 and under.

The most central is the *Jugendherberge München* (☎ 13 11 56), north-west of the city centre at Wendl-Dietrich-Strasse 20 (U1: Rotkreuzplatz). It's one of the largest in Germany and is relatively loud and busy. Beds cost from DM22.50. Still decently close, and a better deal, is the more modern *Jugendgästehaus München* (☎ 7 23 65 50/60), south-west of the city centre in the suburb of Thalkirchen, at Miesingstrasse 4. Take the U3 to Thalkirchen, and then follow the signs. Per-person costs are DM26 in dorms, DM28 in triples and quads, DM30 in doubles, and DM34 in singles. Both hostels have a 1 am curfew.

Jugendherberge Burg Schwaneck (☎ 7 93 06 43) at Burgweg 4-6 is in a great old castle in the southern suburbs, 10 minutes walk from the Pullach station on S-Bahn No 7. Dorm beds cost from DM19.50.

Munich's summer budget favourite is the *Jugendlager am Kapuziner Hölzl* (☎ 1 41 43 00) on In den Kirschen, north of Schloss Nymphenburg. Nicknamed 'The tent', this mass camp is only open from late June to early September. There's no night curfew, but the usual 26-year age limit applies (with priority given to people under 23). Take the U1 to Rotkreuzplatz and change to tram No 12 for the Botanischer Garten. The cheapest 'beds' – a thermal mattress and blanket in the big tent – cost DM13 with breakfast; showers are available.

Other Hostels Munich has quite a few non-DJH hostels or hotels that offer cheaper dormitory accommodation as well as simple rooms.

Newest on the inner-Munich budget scene is the ecologically inspired *4 you münchen* (☎ 5 52 16 60), at Hirtenstrasse 18. The downstairs 'hostel' section – where, unfortunately, the under-27 rule also applies – has dorm beds from just DM18, as well as very nice singles/doubles from DM48/64; the wholemeal-organic breakfast costs an extra DM6. Guests over 26 can stay in the 'hotel' section upstairs for DM89/110 a single/double (including breakfast).

At the *CVJM-YMCA Jugendgästehaus* (☎ 5 52 14 10) at Landwehrstrasse 13, an overnight stay in three/two/single-bed rooms cost

DM38/41/48 (or DM53 for a larger single), but prices are 15% higher for guests over 26. The *Kolpinghaus St Theresia* (☎ 12 60 50) at Hane-bergestrasse 8, a 10-minute walk north of Rotkreuzplatz (U-Bahn), has beds for DM37/ 47/53 in triple/double/single rooms.

Women aged under 26 can try the *Jugendhotel Marienherberge* (☎ 55 58 05) at Goethestrasse 9, where beds start at DM25 and singles/doubles cost only DM35/60. *Haus International* (☎ 12 00 60) at Elisabethstrasse 87 has more than 500 beds in all; prices range from DM40 in five-person dorms to DM83/ 140 for excellent singles/doubles with mod cons.

Hotels Prices in Munich are higher than in most other parts of Germany. Accommodation services (see Information) can help, but even if you insist on the lowest price range, it's unlikely they'll find anything under DM55/90 for a single/double.

There are plenty of fairly cheap, if seedy, places near the station. The best option is *Hotel Gebhardt* (☎ 53 94 46) on the corner of Goethestrasse and Landwehrstrasse, with singles/doubles starting at DM60/85 (or DM85/110 with private bath). Other acceptable options are *Pension Schiller* (☎ 59 24 35) at Schillerstrasse 11, with rooms for DM50/85 (without breakfast), and the cramped *Pension Marie-Luise* (☎ 55 42 30) upstairs at Landwehrstrasse 35, which offers rooms from DM50/80. Phone for vacancies at the 11 am check-out time.

An ideal compromise of location, price and cleanliness is *Pension Haydn* (☎ 53 11 19) at Haydnstrasse 9, near the Goetheplatz U-Bahn station and within walking distance of the main station. Rooms without bath start at DM50/80. If they're full, head around Kaiser-Ludwig-Platz to *Pension Schubert* (☎ 53 50 87), which is upstairs at Schubertstrasse 1. Rooms without bath are DM50/85, while a fully equipped double isn't bad for DM95.

Another value-for-money deal is the *Hotel-Pension am Markt* (☎ 22 50 14) at Heiliggeiststrasse 6, just off the Viktualienmarkt. Rooms start at DM60/102. Clean, comfortable, central and reasonably spacious rooms can be found at *Hotel Blauer Bock* (☎ 23 17 80), Sebastiansplatz 9. Rooms with private shower

GERMANY

and toilet start at DM105/145, or DM75/110 with communal facilities. A buffet breakfast is included and garage parking is available. Of a similar standard and price is *Hotel Arosa* (☎ 26 70 87), Hotterstrasse 2.

The best mid-price deal is the *Hotel Petri* (☎ 58 10 99) at Aindorferstrasse 82. Rooms have distinctive old wooden furniture and a TV, and there's also a garden and a small indoor swimming pool. Singles/doubles with private shower and WC start at DM110/170.

Places to Eat

Eating cheaply in Munich is much like anywhere else in Germany. Go where the locals go – mostly to the less touristy beer halls and restaurants, or one of the many markets.

At *Viktualienmarkt*, just south of Marienplatz, you can put together a picnic feast of breads, cheeses and salad vegetables to take to Englischer Garten for DM10 or less per person. Make sure you figure out the price before buying, and don't be afraid to move on to another stall. More prosperous picnickers might prefer the legendary *Alois Dallmayr* at Dienerstrasse 14, one of the world's greatest (and priciest) delicatessens, with an amazing range of exotic foods imported from every end of the earth. The upstairs restaurant (☎ 21 35 100) is expensive, but if you can afford it, you can expect the best.

Student-card holders can fill up for around DM4 in any of the university *mensas*, at Leopoldstrasse 13, at Arcisstrasse 17, and at Helene-Mayer-Ring 9. Cheap eating is also available in various department stores in the centre, and the *Münchner Suppenküche* at Schäfflerstrasse 7 has meaty and vegetarian soups from DM3.50. You don't have to be staying at the hotel to eat at the *CVJM Jugendrestaurant* at Landwehrstrasse 13; it's open until 11 pm on weekdays and Saturday.

The beer halls like the *Hofbräuhaus* are not particularly appetising or cheap for eating, unless you're just munching on a pretzel or a few sausages. Instead, head to one of the local Bavarian beer restaurants, where the company is just as lively, the beer just as cold, and the food generally far superior.

On the Viktualienmarkt, seek out *Löwenbräu Stadt Kempten* at No 4 (closed Sunday). There, you'll get a half-litre of Löwenbräu for DM4.90 and the daily set menus start at around DM13.

The speciality of *Nürnberger Bratwurst Glöckl am Dom*, in the shadow of the Frauenkirche at Frauenplatz 9, is the small Nuremberg-style sausages, served with sauerkraut (DM12). *Haxenbauer* (☎ 29 16 21 00), at Sparkassenstrasse 8, is a mid-range inner-Munich establishment offering hearty four-course menus for DM50 per person.

Vegetarianism stubbornly survives in this sausage-oriented city. For imaginative vegetarian cuisine at acceptable prices, nothing beats *Prinz Myschkin* (☎ 26 55 96) at Hackenstrasse 2. It offers gourmet vegetarian cooking blending East Asian, Indian and Italian influences, with rotating daily menus and main courses for as little as DM16. A culinary contrast just a bone's throw away is *Altes Hackerhaus* (☎ 2 60 50 26), Sendlinger Strasse 14. This old Munich inn dishes up big, beefy Bavarian fare at mid-range prices.

Italian food is a good deal in Munich and one of the better-value restaurants is *Bella Roma* in the Asam-Hof, a small courtyard just off Sendlinger Strasse.

Cafés Centrally situated cafés cater largely to tourists and therefore tend to be rather expensive. Two cheap and central stand-up cafés that serve excellent home-made sweet and savoury pastries are *Höflinger*, at the corner of Sendlinger-Tor-Platz and Sonnenstrasse, and *Ziegler*, at Bornstrasse 11. *Stadtcafé* at the Stadtmuseum is a popular haunt for Munich's intellectual types. Of the many lively student hang-outs in Schwabing are the *Vorstadt Café*, Türkenstrasse 83, and the *News Bar* at the corner of Amalienstrasse and Schellingstrasse; both are open daily at least until 1 am.

A women-only teahouse, the *Frauenteestube* (☎ 77 40 91), is at Dreimühlenstrasse 1, on the corner of Isartalstrasse south of the city centre (closed Wednesday and Saturday).

Entertainment

Munich is one of the cultural capitals of Germany. The *Nationaltheater* on Max-Joseph-Platz is the home of the Bavarian State Opera and the site of many cultural events (particularly during the opera festival in July). You can buy tickets at Maximilianstrasse 11 between 10 am and 6 pm Monday to Friday (to 1 pm Saturday) or dial ☎ 21 85 19 20.

Munich is also a hot scene for jazz, and the place to go is *Jazzclub Unterfahrt* (☎ 4 48 27 94) at Kirchenstrasse 96, near the Ostbahnhof station. It has live music from 9 pm (except Monday), and jam sessions open to everyone on Sunday nights.

Two larger cinemas that show films in English daily are *Museum-Lichtspiele* (☎ 48 24 03) at Lilienstrasse 2 and *Cinema* (☎ 55 52 55) at Nymphenburger Strasse 31.

For other events and locations, pick up the *Monatsprogramm* for DM2.50 at any news-stand or tourist office.

Beer Halls & Beer Gardens Beer drinking is an integral part of Munich's entertainment scene. Germans drink an average of 250 litres of the amber liquid each per year, while Munich residents average some 350 litres!

Several breweries run their own beer halls, so try at least one large, frothy, litre mug (called a *Mass*) of beer before heading off to another hall. Most famous is the enormous *Hof-bräuhaus*, Am Platzl 9, where Hitler publicly announced his programme at a meeting on 20 February 1920. There's a live band playing Bavarian folk music every night, and the place is generally packed with tipsy tourists. The *Augustiner Bierhalle*, at Neuhauser Strasse 27, has a less raucous atmosphere than the Hofbräuhaus (not to mention decent food), yet it's a more authentic example of an old-style Munich beer hall. Also much less touristy is the *Mathäser Bierstadt* at Zweigstrasse 5, which is run by the Löwenbräu brewery and is Munich's main blue-collar beer hall.

On a summer day there's nothing better than sitting and sipping amongst the greenery at one of Munich's beer gardens. In the Englischer Garten is the classic *Chinesischer Turm* beer garden, although the nearby *Hirschau beer garden* on the banks of the Kleinhesseloher See is less crowded. The *Augustiner Keller's* large and leafy beer garden, at Arnulfstrasse 52, also has that laid-back atmosphere ideal for recreational drinking.

Things to Buy
Bavarian dress is one of the world's most distinctive traditional styles of clothing. *Loden-Frey*, a specialist department store at Maffeistrasse 5-7, stocks an incredible range

of Bavarian wear, but expect to pay at least DM400 for a good leather jacket or a women's *Dirndl* dress.

Also look out for optical goods (Leica cameras and binoculars), handicrafts and beer steins (best bought from breweries or beer halls). The *Christkindlmarkt* (Christmas Market) on Marienplatz in December is large and well stocked but often expensive. The *Auer Dult*, a huge flea market on Mariahilfplatz, has great buys and takes place during the last weeks of April, July and October.

Getting There & Away
Air Munich is second in importance only to Frankfurt for international and national connections. Flights will take you to all major destinations including London, Paris, Rome, Athens, New York and Sydney. Main German cities are serviced by at least half a dozen flights daily. The main carrier is Lufthansa (☎ 54 55 99), Lenbachplatz 1. For general flight information, call ☎ 97 52 13 13.

Bus Munich is linked to the Romantic Road by the Europabus Munich-Frankfurt service (see Getting Around in the following Romantic Road section). Enquire at Deutsche Touring GmbH (☎ 59 18 24) near platform 26 of the main train station. This is also the agent for Eurolines' bus services to Budapest (10 hours, DM110/165 one way/return), and other central European destinations. For some fare comparisons see the introductory Getting There & Away section at the beginning of this chapter.

Train Train services to/from Munich are excellent. There are rapid connections at least every two hours to all major cities in Germany, as well as frequent services to other European cities such as Vienna (five hours), Prague (6½ hours) and Zürich (4¼ hours). High-speed ICE services from Munich include Berlin-Zoo (seven hours, DM246), Frankfurt (3½ hours, DM130) and Hamburg (six hours, DM239). Prague extension passes to your rail pass (see the introductory Getting There & Away section of this chapter) are sold at the rail-pass counters (Nos 19 and 20) at the main station.

GERMANY

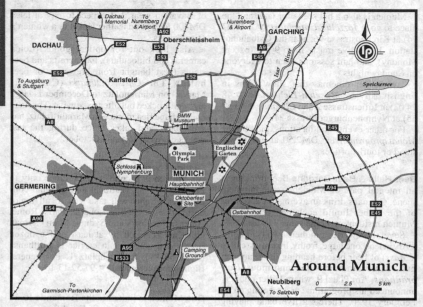

Around Munich

DACHAU

Dachau Memorial

To Nuremberg & Airport

To Nuremberg & Airport

GARCHING

A92

Oberschleissheim

E52

E52

E53

A9

E45

Isar River

Speichersee

Karlsfeld

E52

To Augsburg & Stuttgart

E52

A8

BMW Museum

E45

E52

Olympia Park

Englischer Garten

Schloss Nymphenburg

MUNICH

Hauptbahnhof

GERMERING

Oktoberfest Site

A94

Ostbahnhof

E52

E45

A96

E54

A95

Camping Ground

E533

A8

Neubiberg

0   2.5   5 km

To Garmisch-Partenkirchen

E54

To Salzburg

Car & Motorcycle Munich has autobahns radiating outwards on all sides. Take the A9 to Nuremberg, the A92 to Passau, the A8 to Salzburg, the A95 to Garmisch-Partenkirchen and the A8 to Ulm or Stuttgart. The main rental companies have counters together on the second level of the Hauptbahnhof. For arranged rides, the ADM-Mitfahrzentrale (☎ 1 94 40) is near Hauptbahnhof at Lämmerstrasse 4 and open daily to 8 pm. ADM charges (including booking fees) are: to Berlin DM52, Frankfurt DM40, and Prague DM39. The Citynetz Mitfahr-Service (☎ 1 94 44) at Amalienstrasse 87 is slightly cheaper.

Getting Around

Even in the summer throngs, the central pedestrian zone leading from the main station to Marienplatz makes for very pleasant walking.

To/From the Airport Munich's new Flughafen Franz Josef Strauss is connected by S-Bahn to Hauptbahnhof (via the S8, DM13.20 with a single ticket). The service takes 40 minutes and runs every 20 minutes from 4 am until around 1 am. The airport bus also runs at 20-minute intervals from Arnulfstrasse near the main train station (DM15, 45 minutes) between 6.50 am and 8.50 pm. Forget taxis (at least DM80!).

Bus & Train Getting around is easy on Munich's excellent public transport network (MVV). The system is zone-based, and most places of interest to tourists (except Dachau and the airport) are within the 'blue' inner-city zone *(Innenraum)*. MVV tickets are valid for the S-Bahn, U-Bahn, trams and buses, but must be validated before use. The U-Bahn ends around 12.30 am on weekdays and 1.30 am on weekends, but there are some later buses. Rail passes are valid on S-Bahn trains. Bicycle transport is free, but forbidden on weekdays during the morning and evening rush hour.

Short rides (over four stops with no more than two U-Bahn or S-Bahn stops) cost DM1.70, and longer trips cost DM3.30; children pay a maximum of DM3 per trip. It's cheaper to buy a strip-card of 10 tickets

(Mehrfahrtenkarte) for DM13, and stamp one strip per adult on short rides, two strips for longer rides. Day passes for the inner zone cost DM8/12 single-person/partner (covers two adults and up to three kids), and three-day inner-zone passes are DM20/30 single-person/partner.

Taxi Taxis are expensive (more than DM5 flag fall, plus DM2.20 per km) and not much more convenient than public transport. For a radio-dispatched taxi dial ☎ 2 16 10.

Car & Motorcycle It's not worth driving in the city centre – many streets are pedestrian only. The tourist office map shows city parking places.

Bicycle Pedal power is popular in Munich. Radius Radverleih (☎ 59 61 13), conveniently located at the end of platform 31 of Hauptbahnhof, rents out two-wheelers for DM20/80 per day/week. For cheaper rental, however, go to A-Z Fahräder (☎ 22 32 72) at Zweibrückenstrasse 8, which charges just DM10 per day. Mike's Bike Tours (6 51 42 75) runs 3½-hour guided city cycling tours in English every day leaving from Marienplatz at 11.30 am or 4 pm (DM28).

AUGSBURG

Originally established by the Romans, Augsburg later became a centre of Luther's Reformation. Today it's a medium-sized provincial city with an ambience and vitality matched by few other places in Germany. For some it will be a day trip from Munich, for others an ideal base or a gateway to the Romantic Road. Its tourist offices are at Bahnhofstrasse 7 (☎ 50 20 70), open to 6 pm Monday to Friday, and at Rathausplatz (☎ 50 20 724), which is open weekdays until 5 pm and on Saturday until 1 pm.

Augsburg's telephone code is ☎ 0821.

Things to See & Do

The onion-shaped towers of the modest **St Maria Stern Kloster** in Elias-Holl-Platz started a fashion which spread throughout southern Germany after these cloisters were constructed in the 16th century. More impressive are those on the **Rathaus** (open to 6 pm daily), the adjacent **Perlachturm** and the soaring tower of **St Ulrich und Afra Basilika** (on Ulrichsplatz near the south edge of the old town). The **Dom Mariae Heimsuchung** on Hoher Weg north of Rathausplatz is more conventionally styled, although one of Martin Luther's more unconventional anti-papal documents was posted here after he was run out of town in 1518.

From later ages is the family home of the dramatist Bertolt Brecht on the stream at Am Rain 7, now the **Bert-Brecht-Gedänkstätte**, a museum dedicated to Brecht and the work of young artists (DM3; closed Monday and from 1 to 2 pm). The **Maximilianmuseum** at Philippine-Welser-Strasse 24 (DM4; open Wednesday to Sunday) contains Augsburg's art treasures.

Places to Stay & Eat

Campers can turn to *Campingplatz Augusta* (☎ 70 75 75) near the airport, half a km from the Augsburg Ost autobahn interchange northeast of the city (there are a few family rooms). Juniors can get a bed for DM18 at Augsburg's central *DJH hostel* (☎ 3 39 09) at Beim Pfaffenkeller 3.

Perhaps the best value in Augsburg is the *Hotel von den Rappen* (☎ 41 20 66), Aussere Uferstrasse 3, where modern bathless singles/doubles go for DM50/80. Behind the train station at Thelottstrasse 2 is the *Lenzhalde* (☎ 52 07 45), with simple rooms from DM42/78.

For ethnic eaters, the *Ristorante Dragone* at Wintergasse 3 has standard Italian food, while *Die Pyramide*, Johannesgasse 2, serves quite classy Egyptian dishes, including vegetarian main courses from DM9 up to DM21 for fish cooked in the 'Suez Canal style'. The old *Gaststätte am Roten Tor* (☎ 15 63 67, closed Monday), just inside the southern city gate, is recommended for mid-range cuisine.

Getting There & Away

Augsburg is just off the autobahns north-west of Munich. Trains between Munich and Augsburg are frequent (30 minutes, DM15.40 one way). Connections to/from Regensburg take two hours, either via Munich (DM51) or Ingolstadt (DM36). There are also main-line links to Stuttgart and Nuremberg.

GERMANY

ROMANTIC ROAD

Originally conceived as a way of promoting tourism in western Bavaria, the Romantic Road (Romantische Strasse) links a series of picturesque Bavarian towns and cities. The trip has become one of the most popular in Germany, but despite its touristiness it's well worth falling for the sales pitch and taking time to explore this delightful route.

Orientation & Information

The Romantic Road runs north-south through western Bavaria, from Würzburg to Füssen near the Austrian border, passing through Rothenburg ob der Tauber, Dinkelsbühl and Augsburg. The best places for information about the Romantic Road are the tourist offices in Rothenburg (☎ 09861-4 04 92), at Markt 1, and in Dinkelsbühl (☎ 09581-9 02 40), at Marktplatz 1. Füssen's tourist office (☎ 08362-70 77) is at Kaiser-Maximilian-Platz 1 (closed for lunch, Saturday afternoon and Sunday).

Things to See & Do

Rothenburg ob der Tauber Rothenburg is the main tourist attraction along the route. Granted the status of a 'free imperial city' in 1274, it's full of cobbled lanes and picturesque old houses and enclosed by towered walls, all of which are worth exploring. Crowded in summer, its museums open for short afternoon hours from November to March.

The **Rathaus** on Markt was commenced in Gothic style in the 14th century but completed in Renaissance style. The tower gives a majestic view over the town and the Tauber valley. According to legend, the town was saved during the Thirty Years' War when the mayor won a challenge by the Imperial general Tilly and downed more than three litres of wine at a gulp. The **Meistertrunk** scene is re-enacted by the clock figures on the tourist office building (eight times daily in summer), and in costumed ceremonies in the Rathaus hall during the Whitsun celebrations (mid to late May). A very entertaining walking tour of the old town is conducted every evening except Sunday by the town crier, dressed in his traditional costume (DM6, meet at Markt at 7.55 pm).

The fascinating and extensive **Mittelalterliches Kriminalmuseum** at Burggasse 3 south of Markt displays brutal instruments of torture and punishment used in centuries past (DM5, students DM4). The **Puppen und Spielzeugmuseum** of dolls and toys at Hofbronnengasse 13 is the largest private collection in Germany (DM5, students DM3.50). The **Reichsstadt Museum** in the former convent (DM4) features the superb Rothenburger Passion in 12 panels (Martinus Schwarz, 1494) and the Judaika room, with a collection of gravestones with Hebrew inscriptions.

Dinkelsbühl Another walled town of cobbled streets, south of Rothenburg, Dinkelsbühl celebrates the **Kinderzeche** ('children's festival') in mid-July, commemorating a legend from the Thirty Years' War that the children of the town successfully begged the invading Swedish troops to leave Dinkelsbühl unharmed. The festivities include a pageant, re-enactments, lots of music and other entertainment. It is a pleasant walk of about an hour around the town's **walls** and its almost 30 towers.

Nördlingen The town of Nördlingen is encircled by original 14th-century walls – you can climb the tower of the **St Georg Kirche** for a bird's-eye view. The town is within the basin of the Ries, a huge crater created by a meteor more than 15 million years ago. It's one of the largest in existence (25 km in diameter) and was used by US astronauts to train for the exploration of the moon. The **Rieskrater Museum** gives details.

Füssen After passing through the 1000-year-old **Donauwörth**, at the confluence of the Danube and Wörnitz rivers, and **Schongau**, a lovely medieval town in the Alpine foothills, the road continues on to Fussen, just short of the Austrian border. Füssen has a monastery, castle and splendid baroque architecture, but it is primarily visited for the two castles in nearby Schwangau associated with King Ludwig II. The castles provide a fascinating glimpse into the king's state of mind. **Hohenschwangau** is where Ludwig lived as a child, but more interesting is the adjacent **Neuschwanstein**, his own creation. Although it was unfinished at the time of his death in 1886, there is plenty of evidence of Ludwig's twin obsessions: swans and Wagnerian operas. The fantastic pastiche of architectural styles inspired Walt Disney's

Fantasyland castle. There's a great view of Neuschwanstein from the Marienbrücke (bridge) over a waterfall and gorge just above the castle, from where you can hike the Tegelberg for even better vistas.

Take the bus from Füssen train station (DM4.40 return), share a taxi (DM14) or walk the five km. Both castles are open daily from 9 am to 5.30 pm (from 10 am to 4 pm between 1 November and 31 March), and entry is only by guided tour (DM10, students DM7). Go early to avoid the crowds.

Places to Stay
Considering the number of tourists, accommodation along the Romantic Road can be surprisingly good value. Tourist offices in most towns are very efficient at finding accommodation in almost any price range. All the DJH hostels listed below only accept people aged under 27.

Rothenburg ob der Tauber Camping options are a km or two north of the town walls at Detwang, west of the road on the river. There are signs to *Campingplatz Tauber-Idyll* (☎ 09861-31 77) and the larger *Tauber-Romantik* (☎ 61 91). Both are open from Easter to late October.

Rothenburg's *youth hostel* (☎ 9 41 60), housed in two enormous renovated old buildings at Mühlacker 1, has beds for DM20. The tourist office can find singles/doubles from around DM35/50 (plus a fee of DM2). *Pension Eberlein* (☎ 46 72), behind the train station at Winterbachstrasse 4, offers excellent value, with basic singles/doubles from DM36/54. Inside the old town are the *Pension Raidel* (☎ 31 15), at Wenggasse 3, which is only slightly more expensive, and the *Gasthof Butz* (☎ 22 01) at Kapellenplatz 4, where singles/doubles with bath cost from DM48/90.

Dinkelsbühl The *DCC-Campingplatz Romantische Strasse* (☎ 09851-78 17) is open all year. Dinkelsbühl's *youth hostel* (☎ 95 09), at Koppengasse 10, charges DM17.50. The small *Pension Lutz* (☎ 94 54), Schäfergässlein 4, offers singles/doubles for DM35/70 and the *Fränkischer Hof* (☎ 5 79 00) has similar rooms from DM41/76. The ornate façade of the *Deutsches Haus* (☎ 60 59), Weinmarkt 3, is

one of the town's attractions, yet singles/doubles start at just DM80/120.

Nördlingen The *youth hostel* (☎ 09081-8 41 09) is at Kaiserwiese 1 and charges DM17.50. By the church at Hallgasse 15 is *Gasthof Walfisch* (☎ 31 07), with singles/doubles for DM30/60. The *Drei Mohren* (☎ 31 13), Reimlinger Strasse 18, has rooms from DM35/70 (and a more than passable restaurant).

Füssen The *youth hostel* (☎ 77 54), Mariahilferstrasse 5, is by the train tracks, 10 minutes west of the station. Dorm beds cost DM19, curfew is at 10 pm and the hostel is closed from mid-November to Christmas. The central *Hotel Alpenhof* (☎ 32 32), at Theresienstrasse 8, has attractive singles/doubles from DM40/75. The tourist office has lists of private rooms from DM25 per person. In Füssen there's a resort tax of DM3 per person per night.

Places to Eat
It pays to picnic or eat takeaway, as most restaurants cater to the hordes of tourists.

Rothenburg ob der Tauber Two cheap options in Hafengasse with sit-down and takeaway food are *Albig's Schnell Imbiss* at No 2, where Turkish kebabs cost from DM6, and *Albig's Quick Restaurant*, immediately opposite at No 3, with German schnitzels from DM8. At *Gasthof zum Ochsen* at Galgengasse 26 you can fill up on local Franconian fare from DM12 (closed Thursday). The *Bräustüble*, Alter Stadtgraben 2, has daily set menus for around DM14.

Füssen *Infooday* at Ritterstrasse 6 (open weekdays until 6.30 pm and Saturday until 1 pm) has excellent and cheap buffet food (including salads, pastas and desserts) to take away or eat in-house. The old *Franziskaner Stüberl* (☎ 08362-3 71 24), at the corner of Ritterstrasse and Kemptener Strasse, specialises in fleshy delicacies like roast trotters served with beer sauce and rye-bread (DM10.80), for which Bavaria is renowned.

Getting There & Away
Though Frankfurt is the most popular starting

point for the Romantic Road, Munich is a better choice if you decide to take the bus (the stop is directly north of Hauptbahnhof). To start at the southern end, take the hourly train link from Munich to Füssen (DM34, 2½ hours, some services change at Buchloe). Rothenburg is linked by train to Würzburg and Munich via Steinach, and Nördlingen to Augsburg via Donauwörth (DM18.40).

There are half a dozen daily bus connections between Füssen and Garmisch-Partenkirchen (DM14.80, all via Neuschwanstein and most via Schloss Linderhof), as well as several connections between Füssen and Oberstdorf (via the Tirolean town of Reutte and/or Pfronten). Europabus runs a daily 'Castle Road' coach service in each direction between Heidelberg and Rothenburg (DM47/94 single/return, 4¼ hours). The OVF has a daily morning bus (No 8805) from Nuremberg train station to Rothenburg, which returns in late afternoon. Berlinien buses (☎ 030-3 30 00 10) running between Zürich and Berlin pass through Rothenburg (seven hours from Berlin, DM96 one way).

Getting Around
It is possible to do this route using train connections, local buses or by car (just follow the brown 'Romantische Strasse' signs), but most travellers prefer to take the Europabus. From the beginning of April until the end of October Europabus runs one coach daily in each direction between Frankfurt and Munich (12 hours), and another in either direction between Dinkelsbühl and Füssen (4½ hours). The bus makes short stops in some towns, but it's silly to do the whole trip in one go, since there's no charge for breaking the journey and continuing on the next day (you can reserve a seat for the next day before you disembark). The full fare from Frankfurt to Füssen is DM126/252 single/return (change buses in Dinkelsbühl, Nördlingen, Augsburg or Munich). Eurail and German Rail passes are valid and Inter-Rail gets 50% discount, Europass 30%, students under 27 10%, and passengers over 60 get 50% off. Tickets are available for short segments of the trip, and reservations are only necessary on peak-season weekends. For information and reservations, contact Deutsche Touring GmbH (☎ 069-7 90 30; fax 7 90 32 19) at Am Römerhof 17, 60486 Frankfurt/Main.

With its gentle gradients and ever-changing scenery, the Romantic Road makes an ideal bike trip. Bikes can be rented from most large train stations, and Radl-Tour (☎ 08191-4 71 77 or 09341-53 95) offers nine-day cycling packages along the entire route from Würzburg to Füssen for DM848, which covers accommodation, bike rental and daily luggage transport.

WÜRZBURG
Surrounded by forests and vineyards, the charming city of Würzburg straddles the upper River Main. Although not very famous outside Germany, Würzburg is a centre of art, beautiful architecture and of delicate wines.

Information
There are tourist offices outside the main train station on Röntgenring (☎ 3 74 36), in the Rathaus, and at the congress centre on Pleichtorstrasse. The main station office is open until 8 pm Monday to Saturday, but all are closed on Sunday.

Würzburg's telephone code is ☎ 0931.

Things to See & Do
Spread along Balthasar-Neumann-Promenade, the magnificence of the **Residenz**, a baroque masterpiece by Neumann, took a generation to build, and is well worth the DM5 admission (students DM3.50). The two-hour **guided city tour** in English (daily except Sunday at 11 am; DM12) includes the Residenz. The open **Hofgarten** and **Rosenbach Park** behind are favourite spots. The **Dom St Kilian** interiors and the adjacent **Neumünster** in the old town continue the baroque themes of the Residenz.

The fortress **Marienberg**, across the river on the hill, is reached by crossing the 15th-century stone **Alte Mainbrücke** from the city. The fortress encloses the **Fürstenbau Museum** (featuring the episcopal apartments; entry DM4) and the regional **Mainfränkisches Museum** (DM3.50). Both museums (combined card DM6) are closed on Monday.

More practical is Neumann's fortified **Alter Kranen**, which serviced a dock on the river bank south of Friedensbrücke. Today it is the **Haus des Frankenweins**, where you can wander in and inspect, sample and buy Franconia's finest wines (for around DM2 per glass). You can view riverside vineyards on a river cruise to the **Veitshöchheim castle** (entry DM3); in summer boats depart hourly from Alter Kranen (about 40 minutes; DM13 return).

Würzburg's most important son is Wilhelm Conrad Röntgen, discoverer of the X-ray. The **Röntgen Gedächtnisstätte** at Röntgenring 8 is a tribute to his work and is open, free, from Monday to Friday.

Places to Stay & Eat
The nearest camping ground is *Kanu-Club* (☎ 7 25 36) on the west bank of the River Main at Mergentheimer Strasse 13b (take tram No 5 from the train station). The hostel *Jugendgästehaus Würzburg* (☎ 4 25 90), on Burkarder Strasse below the fortress, charges DM27 for beds (juniors only; tram No 3 or 5 from the train station).

The *Gasthof Goldener Hahn* (☎ 5 19 41), Marktgasse 7, offers perhaps the best value for a central location, with no-frills singles/doubles from DM40/70, while *Hotel Dortmunder Hof* (☎ 5 61 63) at Innerer Graben 22 has comparable rooms from DM50/100. *Hotel Meesenburg* (☎ 5 33 04) at Pleichtorstrasse 8 has various rooms, from simple singles (DM55) to fully equipped doubles (DM120), while *Hotel Barbarossa* (☎ 5 59 53) at Theaterstrasse 2 charges similar rates.

The *City Café*, at Eichhornstrasse 21, serves just about everything that's easy to prepare, tastes good and doesn't cost (much) more than DM10, like salads, soups, pastas, pancakes, toasted sandwiches, baked camembert, fried sausages, vegetable dishes – get the idea? One of Würzburg's most popular eating and drinking addresses is *Bürgerspital* (☎ 1 38 61) at Theaterstrasse 19 (closed Tuesday). Originally a medieval hospice, it offers a broad selection of Franconian wines (including its own vintages), and serves tasty house specialities from DM15.

Getting There & Away
Würzburg lies 80 minutes by train from Frankfurt and one hour from Nuremberg, and Frankfurt-Nuremberg and Hanover-Munich trains stop here several times daily. It is also handily placed if you want to join Europabus Romantic Road tours (from Rothenburg by bus 2½ hours/DM26, or by train, via Steinach, about one hour/DM15.40). The main bus station is next to the train station off Rönt-

genring. Berlinien Bus (☎ 030-3 30 00 10) runs daily from Berlin (six hours for DM87 one way, DM95 return).

BAMBERG
Tucked off the main routes in northern Bavaria, Bamberg is practically a byword for magnificence; an unwalled, untouched monument to the Holy Roman Emperor Heinrich II (who conceived it), to its prince-bishops and clergy and to its patriciate and townsfolk. Walk, behold, drink the unique beers, but experience Bamberg for at least a day. It is recognised as perhaps the most beautiful city in Germany, and one of the finest in Europe.

The tourist office (☎ 87 11 54) is at Geyersworthstrasse 3 on the island in the River Regnitz (closed Sunday).

Bamberg's telephone code is ☎ 0951.

Things to See & Do
Bamberg's appeal rests in its sheer number of fine buildings, their jumble of styles and the ambience this helps create. Most attractions are spread either side of the River Regnitz, but the colourful **Altes Rathaus** (old town hall) is actually on or it, built on twin bridges. The princely and ecclesiastical district is centred on Domplatz, where the Romanesque and Gothic **cathedral**, housing the statue of the chivalric king-knight, the *Bamberger Reiter*, is the biggest attraction. The **Diözesan Museum** in the cloister (DM3; closed Monday) represents one aspect of the city's past; the adjacent courtyard, the **Alte Hofhaltung** (partly Renaissance in style), contains the secular **Historisches Museum** (DM4, students free; closed Monday). The episcopal **Neue Residenz**, not as large as Würzburg's, is stately and superb within (DM4, students DM3; closed Monday) and the **Rosengarten** behind offers one of the city's fine views. Another view is from the tower of the castle **Altenburg** a few km away (take bus No 10 from Promenadestrasse and finish with a walk to the hilltop).

Above Domplatz is the former Benedictine monastery of St Michael, at the top of Michaelsberg. The **Kirche St Michael** is a must-see for its baroque art and the herbal compendium painted on its ceiling. The garden terraces grant another marvellous overview of the city's splendours. There is also the **Fränkisches Brauereimuseum** (entry DM3), which shows how the monks brewed their robust *Benediktiner Dunkel* beer.

Places to Stay

Camping options are limited to *Campingplatz Insel* (☎ 5 63 20), at Bug on the west bank of the Regnitz a few km south of the city, but the camping ground is large and pleasant (DM11 per site plus DM6.50 per adult). The youth hostel *Jugendherberge Wolfsschlucht* (☎ 5 60 02) at Oberer Leinritt 70 (DM18, juniors only) is on the same bank but closer to town; turn south off Münchener Ring towards the clinic complex, then east at Bamberger Strasse, then north along the river.

Near the train station are *Gasthof Zum Goldenen Anker* (☎ 6 65 05), at Obere Königsstrasse 21, with simple singles for DM40 and doubles with shower/WC for DM80, while *Café-Gästehaus Graupner* (☎ 98 04 00), Lange Strasse 5, has singles/doubles with shower from DM60/90, without for DM50/80. *Hotel Garni Hospiz* (☎ 98 12 60), Promenadestrasse 3, is highly recommended at DM60/88 with all facilities (budget singles are only DM45). *Hotel Alt-Bamberg* (☎ 2 52 66), in a quiet location at Habergasse 11, is great value at DM68/115 with all facilities.

Places to Eat

The 17th-century *Wirtshaus zum Schlenkerla*, at Dominikanerstrasse 6, offers Frankonian specialities from DM12, along with its own house-brewed *Rauchbier*, a dark-red ale with a smooth, smoky flavour (just DM3.10 per half-litre mug). Another of Bamberg's lovely old half-timbered breweries is *Klosterbräu* (☎ 5 77 22), Obere Mühlbrücke 3, which also offers excellent beers to complement its solid standard specialities (between DM12 and DM18). *Dom Terrassen*, Untere Kaulberg 36, presents quite tasty pastas, salads and other vegetable-based dishes all for around DM10; sit outside on the scenic terrace looking across to the town cathedral.

Getting There & Away

The most regular train connections to Bamberg are from Nuremberg (30 minutes) or Würzburg (1¼ hours), though several through services run daily to Leipzig and there are daily trains from Munich and Berlin. The autobahn con-

nection to Nuremberg is direct, but buses from anywhere else are few.

NUREMBERG

Nuremberg (Nürnberg) is the capital of the Franconia (Franken) region of northern Bavaria. Though the flood of tourists to this historical town never seems to cease, it's still worth the trip. The people of the city completely rebuilt Nuremberg after Allied bombs reduced it to rubble on the night of 2 January 1945. That includes the castle and the three old churches in the Altstadt, which were painstakingly rebuilt using the original stone.

Orientation & Information

The train station is just outside the city walls of the old town; the main artery, the mostly pedestrian Königsstrasse, takes you through the old town and its main squares. There are tourist offices at the train station's main hall (☎ 2 33 60, open Monday to Saturday from 9 am to 5 pm), and at Hauptmarkt (☎ 2 33 61 35, open until 6 pm). The main post office is at Bahnhofplatz 1 by the station. There's a very central laundrette on Obstmarkt.

The telephone code for Nuremberg is ☎ 0911.

Things to See & Do

The modern **Germanisches National-museum** on Kornmarkt is the most important general museum of German culture. It shows works by German painters and sculptors, an archaeological collection, arms and armour, musical and scientific instruments and toys. It's open Tuesday to Sunday from 10 am to 5 pm (to 9 pm Wednesday) and entry costs DM6.

The scenic **Altstadt** (old town) is easily covered on foot. The **Handwerkerhof**, a recreation of the crafts quarter of old Nuremberg, is walled in opposite the main train station and opens from March to December. It's about as quaint as they can possibly make it, but the goods are overpriced. On Lorenzer Platz is the **St Lorenzkirche**, noted for the 15th-century tabernacle which climbs a pillar like a vine, all the way up to the vaulted ceiling.

To the north is the bustling **Hauptmarkt**. This is the site of the most famous *Christkindlmarkt* in Germany, lasting from the Friday before Advent to Christmas Eve. The church here is the ornate **Pfarrkirche Unsere**

Nuremberg (Nürnberg)

Liebe Frau; the figures around the clock go walkabout at noon. Near the Rathaus is **St Sebalduskirche**, Nuremberg's oldest church (13th century), with the shrine of St Sebaldus.

It's a hard climb up Burgstrasse to the **Kaiserburg** castle area, but this location offers one of the best views of the city. You can visit the palace complex, chapel, well and tower on a DM5 ticket (students DM3.50). The walls spread west to the tunnel-gate of **Tiergärtnertor**, where you can stroll behind the castle into the garden zone.

Near Tiergärtnertor is the **Albrecht-Dürer-Haus**, where Dürer, Germany's Renaissance draughtsman, lived from 1509 to 1528. This house made it through WWII and features a large number of Dürer artefacts (entry DM4). At Karlstrasse 13-15, the **Spielzeugmuseum** (DM5) displays toys from throughout the ages.

Much less charming was Nuremberg's role during the Third Reich. Despite – or because of – their very low popularity in Nuremberg, the Nazis chose this city as their propaganda centre and for mass rallies, which were held at **Luitpoldhain**, a (never completed) sports complex of megalomaniac proportions. After the war, the Allies deliberately chose Nuremberg as the site for the trials of Nazi war criminals. A chilling documentary film, *Fascination and Force*, can be seen in the museum at the rear of the Zeppelin stand (on the Zeppelin field) at Luitpoldhain; the museum is open from 10 am to 6 pm, Tuesday to Sunday, May to October (entry free). Get there by S-Bahn or U-Bahn to Dutzendteich, or take tram No 9.

Places to Stay
Campingplatz im Volkspark Dutzendteich (☎ 81 11 22), Hans-Kalb-Strasse 56, is near the lakes in the Volkspark, south-east of the city centre (the U-Bahn No 1 from the main station takes you to Messezentrum, which is fairly close). It costs DM8 per person plus DM10 per site, and is open from early in May to the end of September.

The excellent *Jugendgästehaus* (☎ 24 13 52) is in the historical Kaiserstallung next to the castle. Dorm beds including sheets cost DM27 (juniors only). The cheapest option for those aged over 27 is the *Jugend-Hotel Nürnberg* (☎ 5 21 60 92) at Rathsbergstrasse 300, north of the city (take the U2 to Herrnhütte, then bus No 21 north four stops). Dorm beds start at DM26, and there are singles/doubles from DM39/64; prices exclude breakfast. The *Jugend + Economy Hotel* (☎ 9 26 20), south-west of the city centre at Gostenhofer Hauptstrasse 47, has good facilities. Doubles start at DM117, singles DM69.

The most reasonable pension in the city centre is *Altstadt* (☎ 22 61 02), Hintere Ledergasse 4, with bathless singles/doubles from DM50/90. Near the station is *Gasthof Schwänlein* (☎ 22 51 62), Hintere Sterngasse 11, which has basic singles/doubles from DM45/80. The quiet and central *Pfälzer Hof* (☎ 22 14 11), at Am Gräslein 10 (near the Germanisches Nationalmuseum), has rooms from DM50/80. *Haus Vosteen* (☎ 53 33 25), just north-east of the old city at Lindenaststrasse 12, charges from DM38/80 a single/double.

Places to Eat
At *Alte Küch'n*, Albrecht-Dürer-Strasse 3, the house speciality is 'Backers', a kind of savoury cake baked from grated potato and served with apple or bacon sauce accompanied by sauerkraut (from DM8.50). A classic Nuremberg restaurant is the *Heilig Geist Spital* (☎ 22 17 61), Spitalgasse 16, whose large dining hall spans the river. There's an extensive wine list and Franconian specialities from DM17.

Try Nuremberg's famous sausages at *Bratwursthäusle*, Rathausplatz 1 (closed Sunday), or *Pizza Sombrero*, at Schlotfegergasse 2 (closed Sunday), which offers Italian-Mexican arrangements from as little as DM12.50 per main course.

A tip for money-conscious diners is *Sabberlodd*, at Wiesentalstrasse 21 just northwest of the old town in the backstreets of St Johannis (tram No 6). It offers generous plates of ravioli and mixed salads for around DM10, along with inexpensive house wines and draught beers. A popular student bar is *Café Treibhaus*, Karl-Grillenberger-Strasse, with filling baguettes from DM7. The crowded *Irish Castle Pub*, Schlehengasse 31, has typical pub food and Guinness on tap (DM6.20 a pint); there's live music most nights.

Getting There & Away
Trains run approximately hourly to/from Frankfurt ($2\frac{1}{2}$ hours) and Stuttgart (just over two hours). There are connections several times daily to Berlin ($6\frac{1}{2}$ hours). Hourly trains run to/from Munich ($1\frac{1}{2}$ hours), and several daily trains travel to Vienna and to Prague (six hours). Eurolines buses also run daily between Nuremberg and Prague ($5\frac{1}{2}$ hours, DM63). Several autobahns converge on Nuremberg, but only the north-south A73 joins the B4 ring road.

Getting Around
In the mainly pedestrian-only city centre, walking is usually best. Tickets on the bus, tram and U-Bahn system cost DM2.50/3.30 per short/long ride in the central zone, and 24-hour passes are DM7.20. A strip of 10 short-ride tickets costs DM12.50.

REGENSBURG
Located on the Danube River, Regensburg has relics of all periods, yet lacks the packaged feel of some other German cities. Its Roman, medieval and later beauties escaped the fate of carpet bombing. Here, as nowhere else in Germany, you enter the misty ages between the Roman and the Carolingian.

The tourist office (☎ 5 07 21 41) is in the Altes Rathaus and is open daily. Ask about the

DM10 *Verbundkarte* giving free entry to four of the city's main museums.

Regensburg's telephone code is ☎ 0941.

Things to See & Do

Dominating the skyline are the twin spires of the cathedral **Dom St Peter**, which also has striking stained glass. The **Diözesanmuseum** houses an interesting collection of religious art. It's at Domplatz 2 in the painted medieval church of St Ulrich (open from April to October, except Monday). Admission costs DM3, or DM5 when combined with a visit to the cathedral's **treasury**. The patrician **tower-houses** in the city's centre are arresting.

The fascinating castle **Schloss Thurn und Taxis** is near the train station, and is divided into three separate sections: the castle proper (Schloss), the monastery (Kreuzgang) and the royal stables (Marstall). A combined ticket for all three costs DM17 (students DM12); for tours in English call ☎ 5 04 81 33. Nearby is **St Emmeram Basilika**, a baroque masterpiece of the Asam brothers containing untouched Carolingian and episcopal graves and relics (entry free).

The **Altes Rathaus** (old town hall) was progressively extended from medieval to baroque times and remained the seat of the Reichstag for almost 150 years (tours in English at 3.15 pm Monday to Saturday; DM5). The astronomer and mathematician Johannes Kepler lived and died in the house at Keplerstrasse 5, which is now the **Kepler-Gedächtnishaus** (DM4; closed Monday).

The **Roman wall**, with its **Porta Praetoria** arch, follows Unter den Schwibbögen onto Dr-Martin-Luther-Strasse and is the most tangible reminder of the ancient Castra Regina, whence the name 'Regensburg' comes. Ask at the tourist office for guides to the town's other attractions.

Places to Stay & Eat

Camp at the *Campingplatz* (☎ 2 68 39), Am Weinweg 40 (adults DM8.80 plus DM11.60 site fee). The *youth hostel* (☎ 5 74 02), Wöhrdstrasse 60, costs DM20 (juniors only; closed all of December). Both *Gaststätte Roter Hahn* (☎ 59 50 90), Rote-Hahnen-Gasse 10, and *Hotel Peterhof* (☎ 57 5 14), at Fröhliche-Türken-Strasse 12, have simple rooms for around DM60/95 a single/double. The

Diözesanzentrum Obermünster (☎ 56 81 249) charges DM50/95 for singles/doubles; ring ahead if you can't arrive before 5 pm.

The *Hinterhaus*, in a roofed-over lane at Rote-Hahnen-Gasse 2, serves vegetarian and meat dishes from DM10. Just across the river at Müllerstrasse 1 is the *Alte Linde* (☎ 8 80 80, closed Wednesday), which serves fairly routine but well-prepared food to its large and leafy beer garden in view of the cathedral. The *Dampfnudelküche*, in a medieval tower at Am Watmarkt 4, serves steamed doughnuts with custard (DM7.80), a local speciality of Regensburg; it's closed after 6 pm, and all day Sunday and Monday.

Getting There & Away

Main-line trains run from Frankfurt through Regensburg on their way to Passau and Vienna (nine daily) and several Munich-Leipzig and Munich-Dresden services also pass through. Sample ticket prices are: Munich DM35 (1½ hours), Nuremberg DM37 (one hour), Passau DM42 (one hour). The A3 autobahn runs north-west to Nuremberg and south-east to Passau, while the A93 runs south to Munich and north towards Dresden.

PASSAU

As it exits Germany for Austria, the Danube River flows through the lovely baroque town of Passau, where it is joined by the rivers Inn and Ilz. Passau is not only at a confluence of inland waterways, but also forms the hub of long-distance cycling routes, some eight of which converge here.

There are two useful tourist offices: at Rathausplatz 3 (☎ 3 51 07, open weekdays and summer weekends), and the tourist centre for Passau and Upper Bavaria (95 59 80) at Bahnhofstasse 27 (opposite the train station), which is especially useful for bicycle and boat travellers along the Danube.

Passau's telephone code is ☎ 0851.

Things to See & Do

The Italian-baroque essence has not doused the medieval feel and you can wander through the narrow lanes, tunnels and archways of the old town and monastic district to Ortspitze, where the rivers meet. The 13th-century **Veste Oberhaus** (closed Monday and all February; DM6) contains the **Cultural History Museum**;

there's a great view over the city from the castle tower (DM1). The impressive baroque cathedral **Dom St Stephan** houses the world's largest church organ (17,388 pipes), and also has a **treasury** and **museum**. The half-hour concerts held in the cathedral daily at noon (DM4) are acoustically stunning. The glockenspiel in the colourful **Rathaus** chimes several times daily and wall markings show historical flood levels. In Kastell Boiotro, across the Inn footbridge from the city centre, is the **Römermuseum** (DM2), which covers Passau's original settlement by the Romans (closed Monday).

Places to Stay & Eat

There's camping at *Zeltplatz an der Ilz* (☎ 4 14 57), Halser Strasse 34, with a DM9 fee per adult and no tent price (over the Ilz River bridge with bus No 1, 2 or 3; no campervans allowed). It's a wheezy climb up to the castle which contains the *youth hostel* (☎ 4 13 51). The hostel only accepts juniors (DM18), but travellers of all ages may well prefer the more central *Rotel Inn* (☎ 9 51 60; open from early May to late October). Situated right beside the Danube at Donaugelände (just two minutes walk from the train station), the Rotel Inn offers small yet clean rooms for an amazing DM25/50 per single/double with hall shower/toilet. Breakfast is not included, but only costs an extra DM8 in the cafeteria.

The *Hotel Wienerwald* (☎ 3 30 69), Grosse Klingergasse 17, has basic singles/doubles from DM50/80 (but there's no hall shower and the kitchen is noisy until very late), while the *Gasthof Blauer Bock* (☎ 3 46 37) on Fritz-Schäffer-Promenade has quieter rooms from DM49/98.

Café Nyhavn, Theresienstrasse 31, has light-style Danish food including yoghurt salads. *Peschl-Terrasse* (☎ 24 89) at Rosstränke 4, an old-style pub/brewery with a spacious dining terrace overlooking the Danube, offers hearty fare of generous servings. The *Weisses Kreuz*, in a back alley at Milchgasse 15, is popular with local students and serves big plates of cheesy wholemeal spätzle for DM14 and half-litre glasses of local ale for DM3.80; it's open daily to 1 am.

Getting There & Away

Regional buses to/from Zwiesel (DM16),

Grafenau and Bayerisch Eisenstein stop at the train station concourse outside the main post office. Buses to/from Plattling use the stop on the lower level. Trains run direct to/from Munich (DM50), Regensburg (DM31) and Nuremberg (you change at Plattling for the Bavarian Forest), Linz (DM24) and Vienna.

From April to October Wurm + Köck (☎ 92 92 92), Höllgasse 26, has a twice-daily boat service down the Danube to Linz in Austria (five hours, DM32 or AS228). Another line, DDSG (☎ 3 30 35), Im Ort 14a, runs boats downstream as far as Vienna (DM152 or AS1075).

BAVARIAN ALPS

While not quite as high as their sister summits further south in Austria, the Bavarian Alps (Bayerische Alpen) rise so abruptly from the rolling hills of southern Bavaria that their appearance seems all the more dramatic.

Orientation

Stretching westwards from Germany's remote south-eastern corner to the Allgäu region near Lake Constance, the Bavarian Alps take in most of the mountainous country fringing the southern border with Austria. The year-round resort of Garmisch-Partenkirchen is Munich's favourite getaway spot, though nearby Mittenwald is a less hectic alternative. Other suitable bases from which to explore the Bavarian Alps are Berchtesgaden, the Tegernsee area, Füssen (see the Romantic Road section) and Oberstdorf.

Information

The Berchtesgaden tourist office (☎ 08652-96 70), just across the river from the train station at Königsseer Strasse 2, is open in summer from 8 am to 6 pm Monday to Friday, 8 am to 5 pm Saturday, and 9 am to 3 pm Sunday and public holidays. At other times of the year it is open Monday to Friday from 8 am to 5 pm, and Saturday from 9 am to noon.

In Garmisch-Partenkirchen, the tourist office (☎ 08821-18 06), on Richard Strauss Platz, is open Monday to Saturday from 8 am to 6 pm, and Sunday and holidays from 10 am to noon. In nearby Mittenwald, the tourist office (☎ 08823-3 39 81) is at Dammkarstrasse 3. It's open weekdays from 8 am to noon then from 1 to 5 pm.

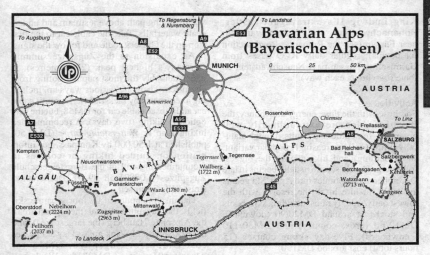

Bavarian Alps (Bayerische Alpen)

Over in the western part of the Bavarian Alps, the car-free resort of Oberstdorf has a tourist office (☎ 08322-70 00) at Marktplatz 7. It's open weekdays from 8.30 am to noon then from 2 to 6 pm. There's also a convenient room-finding service near the train station.

Things to See & Do

Berchtesgaden Berchtesgaden is perhaps the most romantically scenic place in the Bavarian Alps. A tour of the **Salzbergwerk** (☎ 08652-6 00 20) is a must. Visitors change into protective miners' gear before descending into the depths of the salt mine for a 1½-hour tour. It's open daily from 8.30 am to 5 pm between 1 May and 15 October, and from 12.30 to 3.30 pm Monday to Saturday during the rest of the year. Admission is DM17 for adults and DM8.50 for children.

At **Kehlstein**, at 1834 metres atop the sheer-sided mountain of **Obersalzberg** that overlooks Berchtesgaden, is Hitler's former mountain retreat (open from late May to early October). Better known as the **Eagle's Nest**, this is one of the most scenic spots in Germany. Here Hitler established his holiday house (which he called 'Berghof'), complete with a maze-like bunker complex built into the Alpine rock. Kehlstein is reached from

Berchtesgaden by RVO bus to Hintereck, then by special bus to the Kehlstein car park, from where a lift goes 120 metres up to the summit; a combined return ticket from Berchtesgaden costs DM26.50. On foot it's a 30-minute brisk climb from the Kehlstein car park to the summit.

The Berchtesgaden area's other great attraction is the **Königssee**, a beautiful Alpine lake five km to the south. There are frequent boat tours (DM21; 1½ hours) in all seasons across the lake to the quaint chapel at St Bartholomä. In summer, boats continue to the far end of the lake.

Garmisch-Partenkirchen The huge **ski stadium** on the slopes right outside town has two ski jumps and a slalom course; it hosted more than 100,000 people for the Winter Olympics of 1936. Take a peek at the chapel of **St Anton**, at the edge of Partenkirchen, and then walk along **Philosophenweg** for great Alpine views.

Around Garmisch-Partenkirchen About 20 km west of Garmisch by road is **Schloss Linderhof** (open daily 8.30 am to 5.30 pm; DM6.50; bus fare DM11 return). Garmisch can also serve as a base for excursions to crazy

King Ludwig II's extravagant castles, **Hohenschwangau** and **Neuschwanstein** near Füssen (see the Romantic Road section for details); regular daily RVO buses from Garmisch to Füssen pass Neuschwanstein en route (two hours each way).

Activities

For those with the time, energy and money, the Bavarian Alps are extraordinarily well organised for outdoor pursuits, though naturally skiing (or its increasingly popular variant, snowboarding) and hiking have the biggest following. The ski season usually begins in late December and continues into April. Ski gear is available for hire in all the resorts, with the lowest daily/weekly rates including skis, boots and stocks at around DM20/90 (downhill), DM12/60 (cross-country) and DM30/110 (snowboard). Five-day skiing courses (15 hours total) cost around DM190.

The hiking season goes from late May right through to November, but the higher trails may be icy or snowed over before mid-June or after October. Large lakes are another feature of the landscape and are ideal for water sports. Canoeing, rafting, mountain biking and paragliding are popular summer activities.

Berchtesgaden The wilds of Berchtesgaden National Park unquestionably offer some of the best hiking in Germany. A good introduction to the area is a two-km path up from St Bartholomä beside the Königssee to the Watzmann-Ostwand, a massive 2000-metre-high rock face which has claimed the lives of scores of mountaineers attempting to climb it. Another popular hike goes from the southern end of the Königssee to the Obersee.

Berchtesgaden's main ski-field is the Jenner area at Königssee. Daily/weekly ski-lift passes cost DM37/179. The Erste Skischule Mittenwald (☎ 08652-85 48), Mathias-Klotz-Strasse 5, rents skiing and snowboarding equipment at good rates. The Outdoor Club (☎ 50 01), Ludwig-Ganghofer-Strasse 20½, organises a vast range of activities and courses, from hiking and mountaineering to paragliding and rafting.

Garmisch-Partenkirchen A great short hike from Garmisch is to the Partnachklamm gorge

via a winding path above a stream and underneath waterfalls. Take the cable car to the first stop on the Graseck route and follow the signs.

An excursion to the Zugspitze summit, Germany's highest peak (2963 metres), is understandably the most popular outing from Garmisch. There are various ways up, including a return trip by rack-railway, summit cable car and Eibsee cable car for DM58, but the best option is hiking (two days). A recommended hiking map is *Wettersteingebirge* (DM7.50) published at 1:50,000 by Kompass. For information on guided hiking or courses in mountaineering call at the Bergsteigerschule Zugspitze (☎ 08821-58 99 9), Dreitorspitzstrasse 13, Garmisch.

Garmisch is bounded by four separate ski-fields: the Zugspitze plateau (the highest area), the Alpspitze/Hausberg (the largest area), and the Eckbauer and Wank areas. Day ski passes cost DM58 for Zugspitze, DM46 for Alpspitze/Hausberg, DM33 for Wank and DM28 for Eckbauer. The Happy Ski Card covers all four areas, but it's available for a minimum of three days (DM136). Cross-country ski trails run along the main valleys, including a long section from Garmisch to Mittenwald.

For ski hire, Flori Wörndle (☎ 08821-5 83 00) has the cheapest rates and convenient outlets at the Alpspitze and Zugspitze lifts. For skiing information and instruction (downhill) you can contact the Skischule Garmisch-Partenkirchen (☎ 08821-49 31), Am Hausberg 8, or (cross-country) the Skilanglaufschule (☎ 08821-15 16), Olympia-Skistadion. Sport Total (☎ 08821-14 25), at Marienplatz 18, also runs skiing courses and organises numerous outdoor activities like paragliding, mountain biking, rafting and ballooning, as well as renting a wide range of gear.

Mittenwald Popular local hikes with cable-car access go to the Alpspitze (2628 metres), the Wank (1780 metres), Mt Karwendel (2384 metres) and the Wettersteinspitze (2297 metres). The Karwendel skifield has the longest run (seven km) in Germany. Combined day ski passes covering the Karwendel and nearby Kranzberg skifields cost DM38. For ski hire and instruction, contact the Vereinigte Skischule (☎ 08823-80 80), Bahnhofstrasse 6.

Oberstdorf Like Garmisch, Oberstdorf is surrounded by towering peaks and offers superb hiking. For an exhilarating day walk, ride the Nebelhorn cable car to the upper station then hike down via the Gaisalpseen, two lovely Alpine lakes.

In-the-know skiers value Oberstdorf for its friendliness, lower prices and generally uncrowded pistes. The village is surrounded by several major skifields: the Nebelhorn, Fellhorn/Kanzelwand and Söllereck. Combined daily/weekly ski passes that include all three areas (plus the adjoining Kleinwalsertal lifts on the Austrian side) cost DM55/272. For ski hire and tuition, try the Neue Skischule (☎ 08322-27 37), which has convenient outlets at the valley stations of the Nebelhorn and Söllereck lifts.

The Oberstdorf Eislaufzentrum, behind the Nebelhorn cable-car station, is the biggest ice-skating complex in Germany, with three separate rinks.

Places to Stay
Most of the resorts have plenty of reasonably priced guesthouses and private rooms, though it's still a good idea to ring ahead and book accommodation. Tourist offices near the local train stations can help you find a room; otherwise look out for *Zimmer frei* signs. During the busy winter and summer seasons, some places levy a surcharge (usually at least DM5 per person) for stays of less than two or three days. In most resorts a local tax (or *Kurtaxe*, usually an extra DM3) is levied for each night a guest stays.

Berchtesgaden Of the five camping grounds in the Berchtesgaden area (telephone code ☎ 08652), the nicest are up at Königssee: *Grafenlehen* (☎ 41 40) and *Mühleiten* (☎ 45 84). The *youth hostel* (☎ 21 90) is at Gebirgsjägerstrasse 52 and charges DM20.50 (including tourist tax and breakfast) for a bed. From the train station, take bus No 3 to Strub, then continue a few minutes on foot. The hostel is closed from the start of November to late December.

The *Hotel Watzmann* (☎ 20 55) is at Franziskanerplatz 2, just opposite the chiming church in the old town. Simple singles/doubles cost just DM33/66 (DM39/78 in summer). The hotel closes in November and December. Only

15 minutes walk up from the station but with great views over valley is the *Pension Haus am Berg* (☎ 50 59), Am Brandholz 9, which charges DM78 for doubles with bath and toilet.

Garmisch-Partenkirchen The camping ground nearest to Garmisch (telephone code ☎ 08821), *Zugspitze* (☎ 31 80), is along highway B24. Take the blue-and-white bus outside the train station in the direction of the Eibsee. Sites cost DM8, plus DM9 per person and DM5 per vehicle.

The *youth hostel* (☎ 29 80) is at Jochstrasse 10, in the suburb of Burgrain. Beds cost DM21 (including tourist tax) and there's an 11.30 pm curfew; it's closed from November until Christmas. From the train station take bus No 3, 4 or 5 to the Burgrain stop.

Five minutes walk from the station is the quiet *Hotel Schell* (☎ 9 57 50), Partnachauenstrasse 3 (*not* Partnachstrasse), with singles/doubles from DM45/90. In the town centre, *Haus Weiss* (☎ 46 82), Klammstrasse 6, *Gasthaus Pfeuffer* (☎ 22 38), Kreuzstrasse 9, and the nearby *Haus Trenkler* (☎ 34 39) at Kreuzstrasse 20 all offer simple but pleasant rooms for around DM35/70.

Mittenwald The camping ground closest to Mittenwald (telephone area code ☎ 08823) is *Am Isarhorn* (☎ 52 16), two km north of town off the B2 highway. The local *youth hostel* (☎ 17 01) is in Buckelwiesen, four km outside Mittenwald. It charges DM18 per night and closes from early November until late December.

Two good budget places in the middle of town are *Hotel Alpenrose* (☎ 50 55), Obermarkt 1, with singles/doubles for DM45/85, and *Gasthaus Bergfrühling* (☎ 80 89), at Dammkarstrasse 12, which has basic but bright rooms from DM30/60.

Oberstdorf The local *camping ground* (☎ 08322-65 25) is at Rubinger Strasse 16, two km north of the station beside the train line. The *youth hostel* (☎ 22 25) at Kornau 8, on the outskirts of town near the Söllereck chairlift, charges DM20 per night; take the Kleinwalsertal bus to the Reute stop.

Geiger Hans (☎ 36 74), at Frohmarkt 5, has small rooms from DM35 per person. The *Zum*

Paulanerbräu (☎ 23 43), at Kirchstrasse 1 right in the heart of the old town, charges DM45/84 for simple rooms (or DM60/114 with private shower). Also central is *Gasthaus Binz* (☎ 44 55), in a quaint wooden inn at Bachstrasse 14, with simple rooms for DM40 per person.

Places to Eat
Berchtesgaden *Hotel Watzmann* (see Places to Stay) deserves another mention for the well-priced dishes served to outside tables. The *Hubertus Stuben* next door to the Hotel Vier Jahreszeiten on Maximilianstrasse offers vegetarian as well as hearty meat dishes from around DM18. *Gasthaus Bier-Adam*, Marktplatz 22, has a good range of traditional fare to suit all budgets, and the nearby *Gasthaus Neuhaus* at Marktplatz 1 has a beer garden.

Garmisch-Partenkirchen For bottom-priced greasy food go to the *Cafeteria Sirch*, behind Marienplatz at Griesstrasse 1. Here a schnitzel or half a grilled chicken costs DM7.20 and a half-litre glass of Löwenbräu is just DM3.30; it closes at 8 pm. Directly opposite is the *Gasthaus zur Schranne*, an old tavern with three-course evening menus from just DM12.80. The *Hofbräustüberl* (☎ 08821-7 17 16), on the corner of Chamonixstrasse and Olympia-strasse, has home-made Hungarian specialities like *hajducki cevap* (grilled meat pieces on a skewer with paprika, DM18). One of the best restaurants in town is *Isi's Goldener Engel* (☎ 08821-56 67 7; closed Wednesday), at Bankgasse 5, complete with outside frescos and stags' heads. The menu varies widely, from the game platter with deer loin and roast boar for two at DM80 to more modest dishes like *Leberknödel* (liver dumplings) with sauerkraut for DM14.50.

Mittenwald *Gasthof Alpenrose* (☎ 50 55), in an ornate 18th century building at Obermarkt 1, offers affordable old-style eating – there's nothing on the menu over DM18 – and live Bavarian music almost every night. *Gasthof Stern*, at Fritz-Brösl-Platz 2 (closed Thursday), also has local dishes at reasonable prices.

Oberstdorf The large *Zum Paulanerbräu* (see also Places to Stay) has a wide range of belly-filling selections priced from around DM12. The restaurant is closed on Tuesday. *Zum wilde Männle*, at Oststrasse 15, is a bit classier, and the extra you pay is worth it.

Getting There & Away
Berchtesgaden For the quickest train connections to Berchtesgaden it's usually best to take a Munich-Salzburg train and change at Freilassing. It's a 2½-hour train trip from Munich (DM46), but less than an hour from Salzburg, although from Salzburg it's more convenient to take a bus or even a tour. Berchtesgaden is south of the Munich-Salzburg A8 autobahn.

Garmisch-Partenkirchen Garmisch is serviced from Munich by hourly trains (1½ hours; DM26). A special return train fare from Munich or Augsburg for DM68 (DM84 on weekends) includes the trip up the Zugspitze (or a day ski pass). The A95 from Munich is the direct road route. Trains from Garmisch to Innsbruck pass through Mittenwald.

Oberstdorf The direct 'Alpenland' InterRegio train runs daily in either direction between Hamburg and Oberstdorf (via Hanover, Würzburg and Augsburg), and there are several daily bus connections to Füssen (via Reutte in Austria and/or Pfronten).

Getting Around
While the public transport network is very good, the mountain geography means there are few direct routes between main centres; sometimes a short cut via Austria works out quicker (such as between Garmisch and Füssen or Oberstdorf). Road rather than rail routes are often more practical. For those with private transport, the German Alpine Road (Deutsche Alpenstrasse) is a more scenic way to go – though obviously much slower than the autobahns and highways that fan out across southern Bavaria.

Regional (RVO) passes giving free travel (with certain route restrictions) on the upper-Bavarian bus network between Füssen and Salzburg are excellent value; the day pass is DM13/6.50 for adults/children and a pass giving five free days travel within one month costs DM40/20.

BAVARIAN FOREST

The largest continuous mountain forest in all of Europe, the Bavarian Forest (Bayerischer Wald) is a lovely landscape of rolling wooded hills intersected by tiny little-disturbed valleys. Being mostly visited by other Germans, the locals here speak little English. Go out of your way to do some hiking in this surprisingly wild and rugged region.

Orientation & Information

The ranges of the Bavarian Forest stretch north-west to south-east along the German-Czech border, and its wild frontier nature is still the region's chief attribute. Situated at its heart is the town of Zwiesel, which makes an ideal base for exploring the Bavarian Forest. Zwiesel's helpful tourist office (☎ 09922-96 23) is in the town hall at Stadtplatz 27, about one km from the station. It has lots of free brochures, maps and helpful hints for exploring the area.

The tourist office (☎ 08552-9 62 30) in Grafenau is at Rathausgasse 1. The best information about wildlife areas and trails is available from the Dr-Hans-Eisenmann-Haus (☎ 08558-13 00) in Neuschönau.

Things to See & Do

Zwiesel's **Waldmuseum** (Forest Museum) deals with forestry and the wood industry (open daily), and the **Glasmuseum** covers local glass-making. Lindberg's **Bauernhaus-museum** features traditional Bavarian Forest houses, Regen has the **Landwirtschaftsmuseum** (Agricultural Museum), and there's the **Handwerks-museum** (Handicrafts Museum) at Deggendorf.

The Bavarian Forest is known for its unusual alcoholic beverages. The **Dampfbier-brauerei** (☎ 09922-14 09) at Regener Strasse 9-11 in Zwiesel has a brewery tour at 10 am every Wednesday (DM13), which includes generous samplings of its peppery local ales. The **Bayerwald-Bärwurzerei** (☎ 09922-15 15), two km out of Zwiesel at Frauenauer Strasse 80-82, produces some 26 Bavarian liqueurs that you can sample and purchase. The production of superior-quality glass is another important local industry. You can buy wares and watch glass being blown in many places, such as the Glasbläserei Schmid (☎ 09922-94 62), A.M. Daimingerstrasse 24 in Zwiesel.

Hiking & Skiing South of Zwiesel is the 130-sq-km Bavarian Forest National Park, a paradise for the outdoors enthusiast. There are several superb long-distance hiking routes, with mountain huts along the way. The most famous is the 180-km Nördliche Haupt-wanderlinie or E6 trail, a 10-day trek from Furth im Wald to Dreisessel. The Südliche Hauptwanderlinie or E8 is its shorter sibling at 105 km, while the 50-km trek from Kötzting to Bayerisch Eisenstein near the Czech border is the quickest way to experience the Bavarian Forest. A recommended walking map is the 1:50,000 *Mittlerer Bayerischer Wald* published by Fritsch (DM11.80).

Downhill skiing in the Bavarian Forest is relatively low-key, with the best resorts in the north around peaks such as Geisskopf (1097 metres), Grosser Arber (1456 metres), Pröller and Hoher Bogen (1079 metres). More exciting and popular here is cross-country skiing, with numerous routes through the ranges.

Places to Stay

Zwiesel's camping ground is **AZUR Camping** (☎ 09922-18 47), one km from the train station, near public pools and sports facilities. The local **youth hostel** (☎ 09922-10 61) is at Hinden-burgstrasse 26, where beds are DM18. Other dormitory accommodation in the region includes the Frauenau **youth hostel** (☎ 09926-543), Hauptstrasse 29 (DM15.50), and the **Wald-häuser** (☎ 08553-6000), at Herbergsweg 2 in Neuschönau (DM20). All these hostels close for at least a month in early winter, and only accept guests under 27 years of age.

Zwiesel is full of budget pensions and apartments; prices include resort tax. Excellent value is the **Pension Haus Inge**, (☎ 09922-10 94), Buschweg 34, which stands at the edge of the forest and has comfortable rooms with private shower and toilet from just DM36/61 for a single/double. The **Naturkost Pension Waldeck** (☎ 09922-32 72) at Ahornweg 2, a non-smokers' pension featuring organic vegetarian cooking, costs from DM49 to DM58 per person for half board. Two quiet places in the hills at nearby Rabenstein are the **Pension Fernblick** (☎ 09922-94 09), Brücklhöhe 48, and the smaller **Berghaus Rabenstein** (☎ 09922-12 45), Grosses Feld 8, which both charge around DM35 per person.

Grafenau's central **Gasthof Schraml** (☎ 08552-12 29), at Stadtplatz 14, has basic rooms for DM26 per person (excluding breakfast).

Nearby at Stadtplatz 8 is *Gasthof Keller-mann* (☎ 08552-12 13), with better rooms for DM35/65 a single/double.

Places to Eat
In Zwiesel, *Bistro Flair*, Dr-Schott-Strasse 16, has schnitzels from just DM7.80. Another good tip in Zwiesel is the *Musikantenkeller*, a live-music pub at Stadtplatz 42, where a pork cutlet served with chips and salad costs DM11.50; wash it down with a half-litre glass of local draught beer for DM3.80. The *Zwieseler Hof Hotel-Restaurant*, Regener Strasse 5, has a comfortable ambience despite the plastic plants. The extensive menu (DM12 to 25) includes fish, lamb and Bavarian dishes.

Two good restaurants in Grafenau are the *Gasthof Jägerwirt*, Hauptstrasse 18, and *Zum Kellermann*, at Stadtplatz 8.

Getting There & Away
From Munich, Regensburg or Passau, Zwiesel is reached by rail via Plattling; most trains continue to Bayerisch Eisenstein on the Czech border, with connections to Prague. The direct buses between Zwiesel and Passau work out cheaper than a change of trains at Plattling, and run several times daily (DM13, 2⅓ hours). Two scenic small-gauge railways from Zwiesel go to Grafenau (DM4.60 one way) and to Bodenmais (DM3.10).

Baden-Württemberg

Baden-Württemberg is one of Germany's main tourist regions. With recreational centres such as the Black Forest (Schwarzwald), Lake Constance (Bodensee), medieval towns such as Heidelberg and the health spa of Baden-Baden it's also one of the most varied parts of Germany.

The prosperous modern state of Baden-Württemberg was created in 1951 out of three smaller regions: Baden, Württemberg and Hohenzollern. Baden was first unified and made a grand duchy by Napoleon, who was also responsible for making Württemberg a kingdom in 1806. Both areas, in conjunction with Bavaria and 16 other states, formed the Confederation of the Rhine under French protection, part of Napoleon's plan to undermine the might of Prussia. Baden and Württemberg sided with Austria against Prussia in 1866, but were ultimately drafted into the German Empire in 1871.

STUTTGART

Stuttgart enjoys the status of being Baden-Württemberg's state capital and the hub of its industries. Lacking historical monuments, Stuttgart nevertheless attracts visitors with its impressive museums and air of relaxed prosperity. At the forefront of Germany's economic recovery from the ravages of WWII, Stuttgart started life somewhat less auspiciously, as a stud farm.

Orientation & Information

The main train station (Hauptbahnhof) is immediately to the north of the central pedestrian shopping street, Königstrasse. As part of an enormous inner-city redevelopment project, Stuttgart's Hauptbahnhof is being remodelled from the present terminal station into an underground station that will allow through-trains. The tourist office (☎ 2 22 82 40), Königstrasse 1a, is diagonally opposite the Hauptbahnhof. It's open Monday to Friday from 9.30 am to 8.30 pm, Saturday to 6 pm and Sunday from 11 am to 6 pm (1 to 6 pm between 1 November and 30 April). Room reservations can be made here for no fee.

The main post office is at Lautenschlagerstrasse 17, but there's a more convenient branch at Hauptbahnhof. The most central laundrette is Waschsalon, at Hohenheimer Strasse 33.

Stuttgart's telephone code is ☎ 0711.

Things to See & Do

Stretching south-west from the Neckar River to the city centre is the **Schlossgarten**, an extensive strip of parkland divided into three sections (Unterer, Mittlerer and Oberer), complete with swan ponds, street entertainers and modern sculptures. At their northern edge the gardens take in the **Wilhelma** zoo and botanical gardens (entry DM8, students DM4; open daily). At their southern end they encompass the sprawling baroque **Neues Schloss** (New Castle, now government offices) and the Renaissance **Altes Schloss** (Old Castle), housing the Württembergisches Landesmuseum (DM5/3, closed Monday). Adjoining the park, at Konrad-Adenauer-Strasse 30, you'll find the **Staatsgalerie** (closed Monday, DM5/3) housing Stuttgart's best art collection. The new section concentrates on modern art and has a good selection of works by Picasso; the old section has works from the Middle Ages to the 19th century.

Motor Museums The motor car was first developed by Gottlieb Daimler and Carl Benz at the end of the 19th century. The impressive **Mercedes-Benz Museum** (☎ 1 72 25 78) in Sindelfingen, a high-tech satellite city of Stuttgart, tells the story of their partnership and achievements via recorded commentary and numerous gleaming vehicles. It's open Tuesday to Sunday from 9 am to 5 pm (free; take S-Bahn No 1 to Gottlieb-Daimler-Stadion), and is larger and more fun than the equivalent **Porsche Museum** at Porschestrasse 42 (open daily, entry free); take S-Bahn line S6 to Neuwirkshaus.

Better than either museum is a **factory tour** where you can view the whole production process from unassembled components to completed cars. Porsche does a free daily tour in English at 10 am. It's often possible to join at short notice (☎ 8 27 53 84), but it's best to book at least six weeks ahead. Write to Porsche Besucherservice, Frau Schlegl, Postfach 400640, D-70435 Stuttgart. Mercedes-Benz also runs free tours of its Sindelfingen plant at

GERMANY

Stuttgart

0   200   400 m

Some streets pedestrian-only

S-Bahn ━━━ Ⓤ

U-Bahn ━━━ Ⓤ

To Wilhelma Zoo
& Nuremberg

Mittlerer
Schloss-
garten

Oberer
Schloss-
garten

Akademie-
garten

Stadtgarten

Keplerstrasse

Schellingstrasse

Bolzstrasse

Schloss-
platz

Planie

Schiller-
platz

Karls-
platz

Dorotheenstr

Charlotten-
platz

Stadtmitte

Rotebühlplatz

Markt-
platz

Marktstr

To Karlsruhe

To Pension
Schaich

Eberhardstrasse

Torstr

8.50 am and 2.05 pm weekdays (kids under 14 years are not allowed), but it's strongly advisable to call beforehand (☎ 07031-90 75 27) to check details.

Places to Stay

Camping & Hostels You can camp at *Campingplatz Stuttgart* (☎ 55 66 96), by the river at Mercedesstrasse 40, just 500 metres from the Bad Cannstatt S-Bahn station. The DJH-*youth hostel* (☎ 24 15 83), Haussmannstrasse 27, is a signposted 15-minute walk east of Hauptbahnhof. Beds cost DM20.80/25 for juniors/seniors, and the curfew is from midnight. The non-DJH *Jugendgästehaus* (☎ 24

11 32), south-east of the centre at Richard-Wagner-Strasse 2, charges DM35/60 for singles/doubles. (Take the U-Bahn line No 15 Heumaden tram seven stops from the train station.)

Hotels & Pensions You'll need to book for the plain but central *Pension Märklin* (☎ 29 13 15), Friedrichstrasse 39, which charges DM50/90 for singles/doubles (without breakfast). The Greek-run *Hotel Dieter* (☎ 23 51 61), Brennerstrasse 40, has spartan rooms for 50/90 (but try bargaining). Rooms at the *Gasthof Alte Mira* (☎ 29 51 32), Büchsenstrasse 24, start at DM60/100 or DM75/130.

PLACES TO STAY

5 Pension Märkiln
9 Youth Hostel
13 Museumstube
14 Gasthof Alte Mira
15 Holl's Arche
18 Wirt Am Berg
23 Hotel Dieter

PLACES TO EAT

4 University Mensa
10 Urbanstuben
12 Stuttgarter Kellerschenke
16 Markthalle
19 iden
20 Ali's Brasserie
21 Pica Pao
22 Weinstube Stetter

OTHER

1 Main Train Station
2 Bus Station
3 Tourist Office
6 Main Post Office
7 Staatstheater
8 Staatsgalerie
11 Neues Schloss
17 Altes Schloss
24 Waschsalon

Just around the corner at Hospitalstrasse 9 is the smaller *Museumstube* (☎ 29 68 10), with simple rooms from DM55/82.

The best value in the city centre is offered by *Holl's Arche* (☎ 24 57 59), an old tavern just off Marktplatz at Bärenstrasse 2. Here, singles/doubles with private shower and toilet cost only DM70/110.

The *Pension Schaich* (☎ 60 26 79), at Paulinenstrasse 16, has large and sunny rooms (soundproofed to combat the noisy overpass outside) for DM65/100, or DM75/110 with shower cubicle in the room. The *Wirt am Berg* (☎ 262 20 08), in a quiet backstreet at Gaisburgstrasse 12a, has simple rooms for DM70/110.

Places to Eat

The *Markthalle*, a superb Art Nouveau-style market gallery on Dorotheenstrasse, is the perfect place to pick up delicatessen goodies for your picnic in the nearby parks; it's open weekdays from 7 am to 6 pm and to 2 pm on Saturday. For a really cheap lunch though, try the university *mensa*, at Holzgartenstrasse 11. The upstairs dining hall is officially reserved

for students (although student IDs are not regularly checked), and has set menus for around DM4. The ground-floor cafeteria and the small *Mensa Stüble* in the basement, where meals only cost around DM7, are open to non-universitarians.

Otherwise, join the shoppers and office workers at the *iden*, Eberhardtstrasse 1, a spacious vegetarian cafeteria-type restaurant with a healthy spread of whole-food selections from salads to sweets. It's open weekdays until 8 pm (or 9 pm on Thursday) and Saturday until 4 pm.

Stuttgart is a good place to sample the (Swabian) flavours of central Baden-Wüttemberg. The *Weinstube Stetter* (☎ 24 01 63), at Rosenstrasse 32, has simple Swabian specialities like Linsen und Spätzle (lentils with noodles) or Maultaschen (meat and spinach inside pasta envelopes) for under DM8. There's also a great assortment of regional wines at the earthiest prices. It's open weekdays until 11 pm, and Saturday until 4 pm.

The *Stuttgarter Kellerschenke* (☎ 29 44 45) is downstairs in the unpretentious trade union hall at Theodor-Heuss-Strasse 2a, and offers daily three-course Swabian menus from DM12.50. It's open Monday to Friday from 10 am to midnight. The cosy *Urbanstuben*, on the corner of Urbanstrasse and Eugenstrasse, has predominantly vegetarian dishes from around DM20 and some excellent local wines.

Ali's Brasserie, at Eberhardtstrasse 49, is popular with young Stuttgarters, and serves more than passable Turkish cuisine. More adventurous is *Pica Pao*, Pfarrstrasse 7, which features Latin American-inspired combinations like maize pancakes (DM12.50) and cauliflower with avocado cream (DM14.50) along with the more predictable tortillas.

Entertainment

The Stuttgart area has dozens of theatres and live music venues. The *Staatstheater* (☎ 22 17 95), in the Oberer Schlossgarten near to Konrad-Adenauer-Strasse, holds regular orchestral, ballet and opera performances. The *Theaterhaus* (☎ 40 20 70) at Ulmer Strasse 241, east of the centre in Wangen (take U-Bahn line 4 or 9 and get off at the Im Degen stop) stages anything from serious theatre to jazz concerts and cabaret. The *Laboratorium* (☎ 3 41 14 66), east of the centre at Wagenburgstrasse 147 (take bus No 42 from Schlossplatz), has live bands most nights. See the tourist office for ticket reservations.

Getting There & Away
Stuttgart's international airport, south of the city, is accessible by S-Bahn (lines 2 and 3; the trip from the Hauptbahnhof takes about 30 minutes). There are frequent departures for all major German and many international cities, including ICE and IC trains, to Frankfurt (1⅓ hours), Berlin (six hours) and Munich (2¼ hours). Eurolines runs international buses to numerous cities in Europe from the bus station next to the Hauptbahnhof. The A8 from Munich to Karlsruhe passes Stuttgart, as does the A81 from Würzburg south to Lake Constance. There is an ADM-Mitfahrzentrale (☎ 6 36 80 36) at Lerchenstrasse 65.

Getting Around
On Stuttgart's public transport network single fares are DM1.80/2.70 for short/long trips within the central zone. A four-ride strip ticket costs DM9.80, but a three-day central-zone ticket is better value at DM10.

AROUND STUTTGART
Tübingen
This gentle, picturesque university town, just 35 km south of Stuttgart, is a place to wander winding laneways and enjoy views of half-timbered houses and old stone walls. On **Marktplatz**, the centre of town, is the **Rathaus** with its ornate baroque façade and astronomical clock. The nearby late-Gothic **Stiftkirche** houses tombs of the Württemberg dukes and has excellent medieval stained-glass windows. From the heights of the Renaissance **Schloss Hohentübingen** (now part of the university) there are fine views over the steep, red-tiled rooftops of the old town. The tourist office (☎ 9 13 60) is on the way into town by the main bridge, Neckarbrücke.

The telephone code is ☎ 07071.

Places to Stay & Eat There is a convenient *camping ground* (☎ 4 31 45) at Rappenberghalde 61. The *DJH hostel* (☎ 2 30 02) can be found at Gartenstrasse 22/2. The *Hotel Am Schloss* (☎ 9 29 40) at Burgsteig 18 has a few simple singles/ doubles from DM50/100 – very reasonable considering the central location. The *Markthalle Kelter* on the corner of Kel-

ternstrasse and Schmiedtorstrasse is a food hall with various cheap takeaway stalls and restaurants. The *Collegium* on the corner of Collegiumsgasse and Lange Gasse has good-sized main dishes from DM13.

Getting There & Away Tübingen can easily be visited as a day excursion from Stuttgart, from where there are direct trains every two hours (DM34.60 return).

Schwäbisch Hall
The site of ancient saltworks dating back to pre-Germanic times, today Schwäbisch Hall is a household name throughout Germany – not so much because of the town's quaint medieval streetscapes but for the highly successful Schwäbisch Hall insurance and banking company that still maintains strong links with its tiny home base.

The tourist office (☎ 75 13 75) is on **Marktplatz**, where you'll also find **Pfarrkirche St Michael**, begun in 1156, and the town hall (1735). The 15th-century **Keckenburg**, on the eastern side of town by the river, serves as the city museum.

Schwäbisch Hall's telephone code is ☎ 0791.

Places to Stay & Eat The nearby *Campingplatz Steinbacher See* (☎ 29 84; open April to mid-October) charges DM7 per person plus DM9 per site. The local *DJH hostel* (☎ 4 10 50) at Langenfelder Weg 5 charges juniors/seniors DM19.50/ 24.50. The *Krone* (☎ 60 22), next to Pfarrkirche St Michael at Klosterstrasse 1, offers singles/ doubles priced from DM70/100 with shower and toilet, and from DM55/85 without. The *Gasthof Hirsch* (☎ 23 22), at Sulzdorfer Strasse 14 near the Hessental train station, has simple rooms from DM40/75. A good place to eat is *Zum Grünen Baum* at Gelbinger Gasse 33, which serves main courses priced from around DM10 (closed Sunday).

Getting There & Away Depending on available connections, there are two ways of reaching Schwäbisch Hall by train from Stuttgart: the quickest option is usually direct to the Schwäbisch Hall-Hessental station, then by public bus into town. The other alternative is to change trains in Heilbronn and continue to the main Schwäbisch Hall station, from where it's a 10-minute walk to Marktplatz.

HEIDELBERG

Although Heidelberg was all but destroyed by invading French troops in 1693, its magnificent castle and medieval town are irresistible drawing cards for most travellers in Germany. Mark Twain began his European travels here and recounted his comical observations in *A Tramp Abroad*. Britain's JMW Turner loved Heidelberg and it inspired him to produce some of his greatest landscape paintings.

With a sizeable student population (attending the oldest university in the country), Heidelberg is surprisingly lively for a city of only 140,000. But be warned: this place is chock-a-block with tourists during the high season (July and August), so try to avoid coming here then.

Orientation

Arriving in Heidelberg can be something of an anticlimax. Expectations of a quaint old town clash with the modern and less interesting western side of the city near the train station. To find out what this city is really all about continue down Kurfürsten-Anlage to Bismarckplatz, where the romantic old Heidelberg begins to reveal itself.

The Hauptstrasse is the pedestrian way leading eastwards through the heart of the old city from Bismarckplatz via Markplatz to Karlstor. The two-km walk past old buildings, shops, bars and restaurants makes a nice introduction.

Information

The main tourist office (☎ 2 13 41), outside the train station, is open from 9 am to 7 pm Monday to Saturday throughout the year, plus Sunday from 10 am to 6 pm between mid March and mid November. It charges a DM4 room-finding fee. There are smaller tourist offices at the funicular train station near the castle and on Neckarmünzplatz.

The main post office is just to the right as you leave the train station. You can exchange foreign currency at the Deutsche Verkehrsbank at the station and the money-changers in town. You can drop off your dirties at Waschsalon Wojtala (closed Sunday), a fast and economical laundry service at Kettengasse 17.

Heidelberg's telephone code is ☎ 06221.

Things to See & Do

Heidelberg's large **castle** is one of Germany's finest examples of Gothic-Renaissance castles and the city's chief attraction. The building's half-ruined state actually adds to its romantic appeal. Seen from anywhere in the Altstadt, the striking red-sandstone castle (open daily) dominates the hillside. Entry costs DM2 (students DM1), but it costs nothing to wander the grounds and garden terraces; there's also a rather dull guided tour of the interior (DM4, students DM2). Make sure you see the **Grosses Fass** (Great Vat), an enormous 18th-century keg capable of holding 221,726 litres (DM1, students DM0.50, or part of the guided tour).

The German Pharmaceutical Museum, **Deutsches Apothekenmuseum**, which is also located in the castle, does a good job of recalling earlier times (DM3, students DM1.50). You can take the funicular railway to the castle from lower Kornmarkt station (DM2.50), otherwise you can enjoy an invigorating 10-minute walk up steep stone-laid lanes. The funicular continues up to the **Königstuhl**, where there's a TV and lookout tower; the return fare from Kornmarkt with a stop at the castle is DM7.

Dominating Universitätsplatz are the 18th-century **Alte Universität** (Old University) and the **Neue Universität** (New University). Head south down Grabengasse to the **University Library** and then down Plöck to Akadamiestrasse and the old **Institute of Natural Sciences**. Robert Bunsen, inventor of the Bunsen burner, taught here for more than 40 years. The **Studentenkarzer** (students' jail) is on Augustinergasse (entry DM1.50, students DM1, closed Sunday and Monday). From 1778 to 1914 this jail was used for uproarious students. Many 'convicts' passed their time by carving inscriptions and drawing on the walls. Sentences (usually two to 10 days) were earned for heinous crimes such as drinking, singing and womanising. The **Marstall** is the former arsenal, now a student refectory. The **Palatinate Museum** on Haupstrasse contains regional artefacts and works, plus the jawbone of 600,000-year-old Heidelberg Man (DM5, students DM3; closed Monday).

A stroll along the **Philosophenweg**, north of the Neckar River, gives a welcome respite from Heidelberg's tourist hordes. Leading

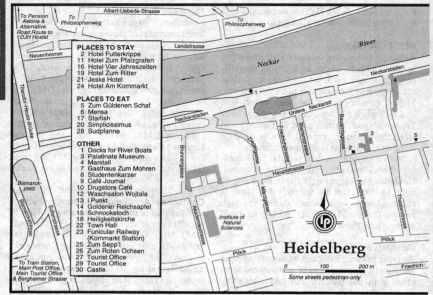

PLACES TO STAY
2   Hotel Futterkrippe
11 Hotel Zum Pfalzgrafen
16 Hotel Vier Jahreszeiten
19 Hotel Zum Ritter
21 Jeske Hotel
24 Hotel Am Kornmarkt

PLACES TO EAT
5   Zum Güldenen Schaf
6   Mensa
17 Starfish
20 Simplicissimus
28 Sudpfanne

OTHER
1   Docks for River Boats
3   Palatinate Museum
4   Marstall
7   Gasthaus Zum Mohren
8   Studentenkarzer
9   Café Journal
10 Drugstore Café
12 Waschsalon Wojtala
13 i Punkt
14 Goldener Reichsapfel
15 Schnookeloch
18 Heiligkeitskirche
22 Town Hall
23 Funicular Railway (Kornmarkt Station)
25 Zum Sepp'l
26 Zum Roten Ochsen
27 Tourist Office
29 Tourist Office
30 Castle

Heidelberg

0   100   200 m

Some streets pedestrian-only

through steep vineyards and orchards, the path offers those great views of the Altstadt and the castle that were such an inspiration to the German philosopher Hegel. There are also many other hiking possibilities in the surrounding hills.

Places to Stay

You don't get very good value for your Deutschmarks here, and in the high season finding any accommodation can be difficult. Arrive early in the day or book ahead.

Camping *Camping Neckartal* (☎ 06223-21 11) is about eight km east of the city by the river, and costs DM7.50 per person and DM8 per site. Take bus No 35 from Bismarckplatz and get off at the Neckargemünd post office (one stop after the Neckargemünd train station). It's open from Easter to 1 November. The more expensive *Camping Haide* (☎ 80 25 06) is across the river and back towards town about one km.

Hostels The local *DJH hostel* (☎ 41 20 66) is across the river from the train station at Tiergartenstrasse 5. The rates are DM20/25 for juniors/seniors (including breakfast). To get there from the station or Bismarckplatz, take bus No 33 (towards Ziegelhausen). The veteran *Jeske Hotel* (☎ 2 37 33) is ideally situated at Mittelbadgasse 2. Frau Jeske offers beds in simple rooms for just DM24 without breakfast.

Hotels & Pensions With a few notable exceptions, the cheapies are well outside the old part of town. Many places have seasonally variable rates.

The *Kohler* (☎ 97 00 97), east of the station at Goethestrasse 2 and within walking distance, has singles/doubles from DM64/82. The tiny *Astoria* (☎ 40 29 29), Rahmengasse 30, is in a quiet residential street north of the river just across Theodor-Heuss-Brücke, and has rooms for DM65/110. At the *Hotel Elite* (☎ 2 57 34), Bunsenstrasse 15, all rooms come with private shower; it charges DM75/95. More central is the *Hotel Futterkrippe* (☎ 9 00 00),

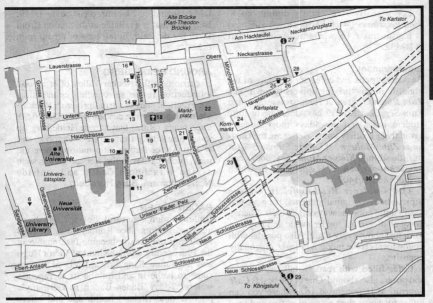

Hauptstrasse 93, which offers rooms with mod cons from DM85/130.

Near the Alte Brücke (Karl-Theodor-Brücke) is the *Hotel Vier Jahreszeiten* (☎ 2 41 64), Haspelgasse 2, with rooms varying from DM75/110 (low season) to DM75/120 (high season). It's claimed that Goethe himself once creased the sheets here. Another lower-budget hotel in Heidelberg's old town is *Hotel Am Kornmarkt* (☎ 2 43 25), Kornmarkt 7, whose rates are DM120/165 for rooms with shower and toilet or DM80/115 without. Similar is the *Hotel Zum Pfalzgrafen* (☎ 2 04 89), Kettengasse 21, where fully equipped rooms cost from DM95/150 single/double.

The superbly ornate 16th-century *Hotel Zum Ritter* (☎ 2 42 72), at Hauptstrasse 178 on Marktplatz, was one of the few buildings in Heidelberg to survive the French invasion of 1693. Standard rooms start at DM95/130, or from DM135/245 with private shower and toilet.

Places to Eat

You might expect a student town to have plenty of cheap eating, but unfortunately, free-spending tourists outweigh frugal scholars. If you can bluff your way into the *mensa*, a meal will only cost about DM4. For takeaways and picnics, seek out fast-food places and delicatessens along Hauptstrasse, though for cheaper sit-down food, Bergheimer Strasse, west of Bismarckplatz, is a better bet. There are also many student pubs (see Entertainment) with main courses priced from around DM14, though they tend to attract customers for the lively atmosphere rather than their culinary offerings.

Heidelberg's current favourite is the *Starfish* (☎ 1 25 87), at Steingasse 16a, which has quality 'natural food' like vegetarian Balinese curry with basmati rice for DM15.50; it's small, so it fills up quickly. The *Zum Güldenen Schaf*, a large old tavern at Hauptstrasse 115, has an extensive menu, with vegetarian fare from DM13 and local specialities priced from around DM20. The *Sudpfanne*, at Hauptstrasse 223, has similar cuisine.

For a really fine night's dining, go to *Simplicissimus* (☎ 18 33 36; closed Tuesday) at Ingrimstrasse 16, where main courses start at DM32.

Entertainment

Backstreet pubs and cafés are a feature of the nightlife in this thriving university town. The *Zum Roten Ochsen* at Hauptstrasse 217, and *Zum Sepp'l* at No 213 next door, are historic student pubs, but nowadays most students avoid these touristy joints. Better are the *Gasthaus Zum Mohren*, at Untere Strasse 5-7 (or its little sibling, *Kleiner Mohr*, next door), and the *Schnookeloch* at Haspelgasse 8, which first opened in 1407.

The *Goldener Reichsapfel* in Untere Strasse is one original students' hangout that hasn't quite gone the way of the others. There's noisy chatter, even louder music and nowhere to sit just about every night. Also popular with young locals is the modern *i Punkt*, diagonally opposite.

Cafés filled with readers, talkers, thinkers and posers also abound. One of the best is *Café Journal* at Hauptstrasse 162, where you can linger for hours over a cup of coffee and read the English-language magazines. Serious chess players (and other quiet guests) gather at the small *Drugstore Café*, at Kettergasse 10.

Getting There & Away

Heidelberg is on the Castle Road route from Mannheim to Nuremberg. From mid May until the end of September the Europabus has a daily coach service, with one bus in either direction between Heidelberg and Rothenburg ob der Tauber (4¼ hours, DM47/94 one way/return). Enquire at Deutsche Touring GmbH (☎ 069-7 90 30), Am Römerhof 17, Frankfurt/Main. There are frequent train connections to/from Frankfurt (one hour), Stuttgart (45 minutes), Baden-Baden (one hour), Munich (three hours) and Nuremberg (3½ hours). The north-south A5 links Heidelberg with Frankfurt and Karlsruhe. You can arrange a lift through the local Citynetz Mitfahr-Service (☎ 1 94 44) at Bergheimer Strasse 125.

Getting Around

Bismarckplatz is the main transport hub. The bus and tram system in and around Heidelberg is extensive and efficient. Single tickets are DM3.10 and a 24-hour pass costs DM9. Bicycle rental is available at the station (from DM9 per day with Eurail pass or recent train ticket).

AROUND HEIDELBERG

Excursions to the Neckar Valley offer a good introduction to the surrounding countryside. An excellent start is a trip upriver to **Neckarsteinach** and its four castles. Boats (DM16.50, three hours return) leave from Heidelberg up to six times daily from April to October; call ☎ 2 01 81 for further information. There are many more castles in the Neckar Valley, such as the **Hirschhorn Castle** and, outside Neckarzimmern, **Burg Hornberg**.

BADEN-BADEN

Baden-Baden's natural hot springs have attracted visitors since Roman times, but this small city only really became fashionable in the 19th century when the likes of Victor Hugo and the future King Edward VII of Britain came to bathe in and imbibe its therapeutic waters. Today Baden-Baden is Germany's premier (and ritziest) health spa and offers many other salubrious activities in a friendly and relaxed atmosphere.

Orientation

The train station is at Oos, which is four km north-west of town. The No 1 bus runs frequently between Oos and Leopoldsplatz, the heart of Baden-Baden. Almost everything is within walking distance of this square. Sophienstrasse leads east to the more historic part of town. North of Sophienstrasse are the baths, the Stiftskirche and the Neues Schloss (New Castle). Across the river to the west you'll find the Trinkhalle (pump room) and, past Goetheplatz, the Kurhaus, which houses the Spielhalle (casino).

Information

The tourist office (or Kurverwaltung, ☎ 27 52 00), Augustaplatz 8, is set in elegant park surroundings, with staff eager to promote the spa facilities. Opening hours are Monday to Saturday from 9 am to 8 pm (7 pm in winter), and Sunday and holidays from 10 am. There is a spa Kurtaxe (visitors' tax) of DM4 (central zone) or DM1.50, entitling you to a Kurkarte

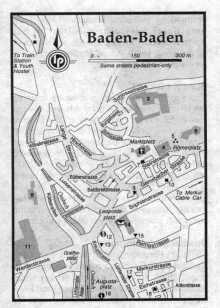

Baden-Baden

0   150   300 m
Some streets pedestrian-only

To Train
Station
& Youth
Hostel

1	Hotel Schweizer Hof
2	Neues Schloss
3	Stiftskirche
4	Friedrichsbad
5	Römische Badruinen
6	Caracalla-Therme
7	Hotel Am Markt
8	Trinkhalle
9	Manzur
10	Hotel Römerhof
11	Kurhaus/Casino
12	Deutsche Bank
13	Namaskaar Restaurant
14	Post Office
15	Zum Nest
16	Tourist Office
17	Café Löhr
18	Hotel & Gästehaus Löhr

from your hotel which brings various discounts. The tax doesn't apply to the hostel.

Baden-Baden's telephone code is ☎ 07221.

Things to See & Do
The ancient **Römische Badruinen** (Roman Bath Ruins) on Römerplatz are worth a quick look, but for a real taste of Baden-Baden head for the **Trinkhalle** at Kaiserallee 3. Here, in an ornate setting, the springs of Baden-Baden dispense curative drinking water (free with Kurkarte, open daily). Next door is the **Kurhaus**, from the 1820s, which houses the opulent **casino** (guided tours daily every 20 minutes between 9.45 and 11.45 am; DM4).

The **Merkur Cable Car** takes you up to the 660-metre summit (DM7 return), from where there are fine views and numerous 'terrain treatment' trails, each with a specific gradient designed to therapeutically exercise your muscles. (Take bus No 5 from Leopoldplatz.) A good hiking/driving tour is to the wine-growing area of **Rebland**, six km to the west.

Spas On either side of Römerplatz are the two places where you can take to the waters: the **Friedrichsbad** (☎ 27 59 20) at Römerplatz 1, and the **Caracalla-Therme** (☎ 27 59 40) at Römerplatz 11. A visit to one (or both) is an experience not to be missed.

The 19th-century Friedrichsbad is ornately Roman in style and offers two special bathing options: the Roman-Irish programme (DM36), or the Roman-Irish Plus (DM48); there's a 10% reduction with Kurkarte or for Hostelling International members. Your two-odd hours of humid bliss consist of a timed series of hot and cold showers, saunas, steam rooms and baths that leave you feeling scrubbed, lubed and loose as a goose. The highlight of the Plus programme is the all-too-short soap-and-brush massage. At the end of the session they wrap you in a blanket for a half-hour's rest.

No clothing is allowed inside, and several of the bathing sections are mixed on most days, so leave your modesty at the reception desk. The Friedrichsbad is open Monday to Saturday from 9 am to 10 pm. Mixed bathing is all day on Wednesday and Saturday, from 12 pm on Sunday, and from 4 pm on Tuesday and Friday.

The Caracalla-Therme, opened in 1985, has more than 1700 sq metres of outdoor and indoor pools, hot and cold-water caves ('grottoes') and whirlpools, showers and saunas. You're free to try any of these, but here you must wear a bathing costume (not available for hire). Two-hour, three-hour and four-hour visits cost DM18/24/32. It's open

GERMANY

daily from 8 am to 10 pm, but the latest admission is two hours before closing time.

Places to Stay

The closest camping ground is the **Campingplatz Adam** (☎ 07223-2 31 94), at Bühl-Oberbruch, about 12 km outside town (take bus No 3 from the train station). Baden-Baden's **DJH hostel** (☎ 5 22 23) is at Hardbergstrasse 34, two km from the town centre, and costs DM20/25 for juniors/seniors. (Take bus No 1 to Grosse-Dollenstrasse.)

The tourist office may be able to find you a cheaper pension or a private room (there's no charge for this service). Otherwise, the **Hotel-Löhr** (☎ 2 62 04) and the **Gästehaus Löhr** (☎ 3 13 70) are a bargain by Baden-Baden's standards. Located in neighbouring buildings just off Augustaplatz at Adlerstrasse 2 and Stahlbadstrasse, the two are jointly managed. The reception is in the Café Löhr at Lichtentaler Strasse 19. Rooms cost from DM40/75 a single/double, or DM60/120 with private shower.

The **Zum Nest** (see Places to Eat) offers a few singles/doubles for DM52/88. Another good place is the **Schweizer Hof** (☎ 3 04 60) at Lange Strasse 73, where basic rooms start at DM50/100.

The **Hotel Am Markt** (☎ 2 27 47), Marktplatz 17, up by the Stiftskirche, charges DM52/95 for simple rooms and DM90/140 with private facilities. Classier, but still affordable, is the **Hotel Römerhof** (☎ 2 34 15) at Sophienstrasse 25, where bright clean rooms with private shower and toilet cost DM75/150.

Places to Eat

The **Café Löhr** (see Places to Stay) has simple set menus for DM9. For something just as cheap but tastier, go for the **Manzur**, Gernsbacherstrasse 18, which has oriental dishes from D8.50. Another Eastern tip is the Indian **Namaskaar** (☎ 2 46 81; closed Tuesday) at Kreuzstrasse 1, with imaginative meat, fish and vegetarian meals from DM15 per main course. Locals favour the **Zum Nest** (☎ 2 30 76; closed Tuesday), Rettigstrasse 1, which serves up Baden specialities from as little as DM14.

Getting There & Away

Baden-Baden is on the main north-south corridor. Trains leave every hour to most important destinations, including Frankfurt/Main, Freiburg/Basel, Heidelberg (direct or via Karlsruhe) and Stuttgart. The town is also close to the north-south A5 autobahn. Access the westward A8 at Karlsruhe.

BLACK FOREST

There are lots of tourists and hikers roaming the Black Forest (Schwarzwald), but it's not hard to get away from the busy areas. Home of the cuckoo clock, the moniker 'Black Forest' comes from the dark canopy of evergreens. The fictional Hansel and Gretel encountered their wicked witch in these parts, but 20th-century hazards are rather more ominous. While superficially it seems as lush as ever, experts will tell you the Black Forest is being steadily destroyed by acid rain, air pollution and insect plagues. Enjoy it while you can.

Orientation & Information

The Black Forest lies east of the Rhine between Karlsruhe and Basel. It's roughly triangular in shape, about 160 km long and 50 km wide. Baden-Baden, Freudenstadt, Triberg and Freiburg act as convenient information posts for Black Forest excursions. Even smaller towns in the area generally have tourist offices.

Freudenstadt's tourist office (☎ 07441-86 40) is at Am Promenadeplatz 1. In Triberg, you'll find the tourist office (☎ 07722-95 32 30) at Luisenstrasse 10, and in Furtwangen (☎ 07723-93 91 11) at Marktplatz 4.

Things to See & Do

Though enjoying the natural countryside will be the main focus, there's still much history and culture to explore in the region.

Halfway between Baden-Baden and Freudenstadt along the Schwarzwald-Hochstrasse, the first major tourist sight is the **Mummelsee** south of the Hornisgrinde peak. It's a small, deep lake steeped in folklore. (Legend has it that an evil sea king inhabits the depths.) If you want to escape the busloads, hike down the hill to the peaceful and inappropriately named **Wildsee**.

Further south, the friendly town of **Freudenstadt** is mainly used as a base for excursions into the countryside. Be sure to visit the central marketplace, which is the largest in Germany and great for photos.

The area between Freudenstadt and Freiburg

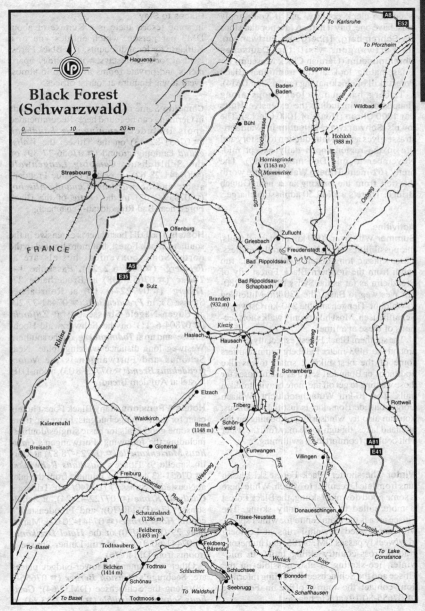

Black Forest
(Schwarzwald)

0   10   20 km

GERMANY

is cuckoo-clock country, and if you simply must have one, buy it here. A few popular stops are **Schramberg, Triberg** and **Furtwangen**. In Furtwangen, visit the **Deutsches Uhrenmuseum** (German Clock Museum) for a fascinating look at the traditional Black Forest skill of clockmaking (admission DM4).

Triberg has many clock shops along Hauptstrasse, including the extensive **Haus der 1000 Uhren** (House of 1000 Clocks). The town's **Schwarzwald-Museum** in Wallfahrtstrasse gives a vivid introduction to history and life in the region (open daily except mid-November to mid-December; DM5). The pretty 162-metre **Triberg Waterfalls** are worth the trek from the parking area near Gutach Bridge. There's a DM2.50 admission charge.

Activities

Summer With over 7000 km of marked trails, the possibilities are, almost literally, endless. Three classic long-distance hiking trails run south from the northern Black Forest city of Pforzheim as far as the Swiss Rhine: the 280-km Westweg to Basel, the 230-km Mittelweg to Waldhut-Tiengen and the 240-km Ostweg to Schaffhausen. Most hikers only walk short sections of these at a time.

The southern Black Forest, especially the area around the 1493-metre Feldberg summit, offers some of the best hiking; small towns like Todtmoos or Bonndorf serve as useful bases for those wanting to get off the more heavily trodden trails. The 10-km **Wutachschlucht** (Wutach Gorge) outside Bonndorf is justifiably famous. You can also try windsurfing or boating on the highland lakes, though some may find the water a bit cool for (comfortable) swimming.

Winter The shorter Black Forest ski season runs from late December to March. While there is some good downhill skiing, the Black Forest is more suited to cross-country skiing. The Titisee area is the main centre for winter sports, with uncrowded downhill runs at Feldberg (day/weekly passes DM36/185) and numerous graded cross-country skiing trails. In midwinter, ice-skating is also possible on the Titisee and the Schluchsee. For skiing information, contact the tourist office in Feldberg (☎ 07655-80 19) at Kirchgasse 1.

Places to Stay

In some resorts there is a Kurtaxe of about DM3 per person, which entitles you to a Kurkarte for local discounts. The Black Forest is ideal for longer stays, with holiday apartments and private rooms available in almost every town. Enquire at tourist offices.

Camping Some of the best camping grounds in Germany can be found here. Recommended spots include: *Campingplatz Sandbank* (☎ 07651-82 43) on the Titisee; the *Wolfsgrund* camping ground (☎ 07656-77 39) on the Schluchsee; *Camping Langenwald* (☎ 07441-28 62), three km outside Freudenstadt; and *Schwarzwald-Camping-Alisehof* (☎ 07839-2 03) in the centre of the Black Forest near Bad Rippoldsau-Schapbach.

Hostels The DJH hostel net is extensive in the southern Black Forest, but more limited in the north. Some convenient hostels are at *Feldberg* (☎ 07676-2 21), Passhöhe 14; *Titisee* (☎ 07652-238) at Bruderhalde 27; *Triberg* (☎ 07722-41 10) at Rohrbacher Strasse 35; in *Freudenstadt* (☎ 07441-77 20) at Eugen-Nägele-Strasse 69; at *Zuflucht* (☎ 07804-6 11) on the Schwarzwald-Hochstrasse; and up at *Todtnauberg*, on the southern Westweg long-distance walking route. Near Schönau and Furtwangen is the *Naturfreudehaus Brend* (☎ 07723-8 03), a non-DJH hostel at Auf dem Brend.

Hotels & Pensions Many Black Forest hotels cater for higher-range budgets; however, there are some good deals for basic singles/doubles, including the following: Furtwangen's *Gasthaus Marienkapelle* (☎ 07723-78 87) at Martinskapelle 9; Titisee's *Gasthaus Rehwinkel* (☎ 07651-83 41), a few minutes from the lake at Neustädter Strasse 7 (DM40/ 80); Triberg's *Gasthaus Krone* (☎ 07722-45 24), at Schulstrasse 37, (DM40/70); and Freudenstadt's central *Hotel Krone* (☎ 07441-20 07), Marktplatz 29 (DM35/70) or the *Hotel Dreikönig* (☎ 07441-60 16) at Martin-Luther-Strasse 3 (rooms from DM40/76).

Other recommended lower-budget places are: Seebrugg's *Pension Berger* (☎ 07656-2 38) along the Schluchsee (DM32/64); *Gasthaus Schwarzwaldstüble* (☎ 07722-33 24), at

Obervogt, Huber-Strasse 25a (DM38 per person); the *Gasthof Württemberger Hof* (☎ 07422-44 89) at Oberdorfer Strasse 34 in Schramberg (DM40/80) and Schönwald's *Hotel-Pension Schätzle* (☎ 07722-41 06) at Ludwig-Uhland-Strasse 6 (DM34/68).

Places to Eat

Black Forest specialities include Schwarzwälderschinken (ham) and the much imitated cherry cake. But restaurants are often expensive, so picnic whenever possible.

In ultratouristy Titisee, try the *Hirschstüble* (☎ 07651-84 86), near the church at Im Winkel 3. It has healthy-sized main courses for around DM15 (and double rooms from DM80). Further north in Triberg, the *Restaurant Krone* (at Gasthaus Krone), Schulstrasse 37, has basic German dishes from DM15 (and cheap rooms as well – see Places to Stay). The *Sonneck*, at Schwarzbachweg 5 in Feldberg-Altglasshütten, offers better standard Black Forest specialities for reasonable prices. Schramberg's *Restaurant-Café Haas*, Berneckstrasse 2, has local specialities at budget prices.

Good value in Freudenstadt is the *Poseidon*, below the Hotel Dreikönig (see Places to Stay), with Greek dishes priced from DM13. Also worthwhile is *Gasthof Kaiser*, Schulstrasse 9, just off the main square.

Getting There & Away

The north-south train route allows easy access to the region. Trains run very frequently between Karlsruhe and Basel, calling at Baden-Baden and Freiburg en route. There are also direct train connections to some of the hub towns from Strasbourg, Stuttgart and Constance. Road access is good too, with the A5 skirting the western side of the forest and the A81 the eastern side.

Getting Around

The rail network is surprisingly extensive for such a mountainous area. The most useful lines link Baden-Baden, Freudenstadt and Freiburg. One of the prettiest stretches runs between Freiburg and Titisee (DM9).

Where rail fails to go, the bus system usually leads the way, but travel times can be slow in this rugged terrain. If you plan to spend several days in the southern Black Forest, consider the seven-day Südbaden Bus-Pass for DM35 (DM50 for two people) which is valid for the entire SBG network between Constance and Freiburg, and from Sulz right down to the Swiss border. Similar bus passes are available in other areas. Cycling is a good way to get about, despite the hills. Bikes can be hired at larger train stations.

Drivers enjoy flexibility in an area that rewards it. The main tourist road, the Schwarzwald-Hochstrasse (B500), runs from Baden-Baden to Freudenstadt and Triberg to Waldshut. Other thematic roads to explore are the Schwarzwald-Bäderstrasse (spa town route), Schwarzwald-Panoramastrasse (which affords good views) and Badische Weinstrasse (wine route).

FREIBURG

The gateway to the southern Black Forest, Freiburg (full name: Freiburg im Breisgau) has a relaxed atmosphere accentuated by the city's large and thriving university community. Ruled for centuries by the Austrian Habsburgs, Freiburg has retained many traditional features, although major reconstruction was necessary following severe bombing damage during WWII. The monumental 13th-century cathedral is the city's key landmark.

Orientation

The city centre is a convenient 10 minutes walk from the train station. Walk east along Eisenbahnstrasse to the tourist office, then continue through the bustling pedestrian zone to Münsterplatz, dominated by the red stone cathedral. All the sights are within walking distance of here.

Information

The tourist office (☎ 368 90 90), Rotteckring 14, is open Monday to Saturday from 9 am to 9.30 pm, and Sunday and holidays from 10 am to 2 pm (from 1 October to 31 May it closes at 6 pm on weekdays, 2 pm on Saturday and noon on Sunday and public holidays). Pick up the excellent official guide in English (DM5). The office has a free room-finding service. Ask here about daily guided tours of the city in English (DM8).

The main post office, Eisenbahnstrasse 58-62, is open from 8.30 am to 6.30 pm on weekdays, to 2 pm on Saturday. Like the

GERMANY

Freiburg

PLACES TO STAY
11   Hotel Löwen
20   Hotel Markgräfler Hof

PLACES TO EAT
12   Engler's Weinkrügle
14   Papala Pub
16   UC Uni-Café
17   Mensa
18   Salatstuben
23   Hausbrauerei Feierling
24   Enoteca Restaurant

OTHER
1   Main Train Station
2   Volksbank Freiburg
3   Main Post Office
4   Museum of Prehistory
5   Café Fleck
     Waschsalon
6   Tourist Office
7   Universitätskirche
8   Old University
9   Münster
10   Kaufhaus
13   Jazzhaus
19   University
19   Martinstor
21   Museum of Modern Art
22   Augustiner Museum
25   Zum Roten Bären
26   Schwabentor

0   100   200 m
Some streets pedestrian-only

Volksbank Freiburg opposite the station, it's a convenient place to change money and cheques. The central Café Fleck Waschsalon, on the corner of Gutenbergstrasse and Predigerstrasse, is a laundrette (open daily until 1 am) with an adjoining café (open until 6 pm weekdays, or 4 pm on Saturday).

Freiburg's telephone code is ☎ 0761.

Things to See

The major sightseeing goal is the **Münster** cathedral, a classic example of both high and late-Gothic architecture looming over Münsterplatz, Freiburg's active market square. Of particular interest are the stone and wood carvings, the stained-glass windows and the west porch. Ascend the tower to the stunning pierced spire (DM2) for great views of Freiburg and, on a clear day, the Kaiserstuhl and the Vosges. South of the Münster stands the picturesque **Kaufhaus**, the 16th-century merchants' hall.

Be sure to notice the pavement mosaics on the pedestrian laneways, but take care to sidestep the old drainage system, the **Bächle** (tiny, permanently flowing canals which run through many of the streets and laneways of the Freiburg Altstadt). In former times the townsfolk used the water from the Büchle to clean their beasts and combat fire. From the cathedral, wander south to the beautiful city gate, the **Schwabentor**, and peer into **Zum Roten Bären**, reputedly the oldest inn in Germany. The **University quarter** is north-west of the Martinstor (one of the old city gates) and is usually bustling with students. Along Bertoldstrasse, check the **Universitätskirche** (University Church) and then walk round the back to the picturesque Rathausplatz.

Freiburg's main museum is the **Augustiner Museum** (entry DM4, free on Sunday) on Augustinerplatz. The **Museum of Prehistory** (DM3.50/1.50) is in Columbipark, on the corner of Eisenbahnstrasse and Rotteckring. Most of the city's other museums, including the **Museum of Modern Art**, at Marienstrasse 10, are free and closed on Monday.

Activities

Wine Tasting Freiburg is a great place to buy and taste the local wines of the Baden region. The best times for this are late June for the five days of *Weintagen* (Wine Days), or mid-August for the nine days of *Weinkost* (Wine Fare).

Schauinsland The popular trip by gondola lift (cable car) to the 1286-metre Schauinsland peak is a quick way to reach the Black Forest highlands. Numerous easy and well-marked trails make the Schauinsland area ideal for day walks. From Freiburg take tram No 4 south to Günterstal and then the shuttle bus to Talstation. The five-hour hike from Schauinsland to the Untermünstertal offers some of the best views with the fewest people; return to Freiburg via the train to Staufen and then take the bus.

Cable-car tickets cost DM11/18 single/return (DM8/14 for students and rail-pass holders).

Places to Stay

The most convenient camping ground is *Camping Hirzberg* (☎ 3 50 54, open all year) at Kartäuserstrasse 99. Take tram No 1 to Messeplatz (direction: Littenweiler), and then go under the road and across the stream.

Freiburg's *DJH hostel* (☎ 6 76 56), on the eastern edge of the city at Kartäuserstrasse 151, is often full with groups of German students, so phone ahead. Take tram No 1 to

Römerhof (direction: Littenweiler) and follow the signs down Fritz-Geiges-Strasse. A bed costs DM20/25 for juniors/seniors. Reception is open all day and there is an 11.30 pm curfew.

Finding an affordable room anywhere near the centre of town can be difficult – even Freiburg's students get frustrated. The tourist office may be able to find a private room for you, but don't count on it.

The least expensive place in central Freiburg is *Pension Schemmer* (☎ 27 20), behind the train station at Eschholzstrasse 63, where singles/doubles cost DM55/85, or DM90 for a double with a shower. The historic *Hotel Zum Schützen* (☎ 7 20 21), at Schützenallee 12 on the way to the youth hostel, is also a reasonable compromise for centrality and good value, with doubles from DM80. A bit further out is the 16-bed *Hotel Dionysos* (☎ 2 93 53), at Hirschstrasse 2, which has simple but nice rooms for DM45/80. (Take tram No 4 from near the train station south to Klosterplatz.)

If you're willing to pay more to stay in the Altstadt, a good choice is *Hotel Löwen* (☎ 3 31 61), Herrenstrasse 47, which has simple singles/doubles for DM60/90 or DM120/150 with toilet and shower. Though mainly oriented to the wealthier guests who dine in its celebrated restaurant, the *Markgräfler Hof* (☎ 3 25 40), Gerberau 22, also has a few simpler rooms for DM65/110; more luxurious rooms with shower, toilet and TV cost from DM95/130.

The *Zum Löwen*, at Breisgauer Strasse 62 in Freiburg's north-western suburbs (take tram No 1 to Padua-Allee in the direction of Landwasser), has singles/doubles from DM45/80. Down the road are two middle-range places: the *Hirschengarten-Hotel* (☎ 8 03 03) at Breisgauer Strasse 51, which has rooms with private shower and cable TV starting at DM85/130, and *Hotel Bierhäusle* (☎ 8 83 00), which offers similar rooms at slightly higher rates.

Places to Eat

Being a university town, Freiburg virtually guarantees cheap eats. Take advantage of this while you can, as Black Forest food is more expensive. The university-subsidised *mensas* at Rempartstrasse 18 and Hebelstrasse 9a have salad buffets and other filling fodder. You may be asked to show a student ID when buying meal tickets, but it's worth a try.

The **Papala Pub**, at Moltkestrasse 30, is a typical Freiburg student hang-out with a slightly nostalgic 1970s feel (complete with sweet-smelling smokey atmosphere). You can fill up here on spaghetti, pizza or pancakes from as little as DM5, or risk the 'surprise menu' that includes several (undisclosed) courses for DM22.

There are other good student joints around the university. The popular **UC Uni-Café**, on the corner of Universitätsstrasse and Niemanstrasse, serves drinks, snacks and build-your-own breakfasts. Nearby is the **Salatstuben**, Löwenstrasse 1, with a wide choice of wholesome salads for DM2.09 per 100 grams. It's open to 8 pm on weekdays and 4 pm on Saturday. Another lively place is **Brasil** at Wannerstrasse 21 (open daily to 1 am), whose kitchen chef takes a spicy Afro-Latin American approach to cooking; try the mosqueca de piexe for DM15.50.

For affordable Badener food and wine, seek out **Engler's Weinkrügle**, at Konviktstrasse 12, which has three-course meals from around DM20 (closed Monday). The trendy **Hausbrauerei Feierling** (☎ 2 66 78), in a renovated old brewery at Gerberau 46, has imaginative dishes such as meat loaf with curry sauce and salad (DM10.50). Nearby is the **Enoteca Restaurant** (☎ 389 91 30, closed Sunday), at Gerberau 21, which offers finer dining for around DM25 per main course, plus an array of delicate wines.

Entertainment

The **Jazzhaus** (☎ 3 49 73) at Schnewlinstrasse 1 is one of Germany's hottest music venues, with live jazz every night (admission generally costs no more than DM20) and appearances by internationally acclaimed artists. For a detailed programme, pick up a free copy of the monthly *Jazzhaus Journal* from the tourist office, university or cafés around town.

Getting There & Away

Freiburg lies directly on the north-south train corridor, and is therefore highly accessible. Trains frequently depart for Basel, Baden-Baden, Freudenstadt and Donaueschingen. The main A5 autobahn linking Frankfurt and Basel also passes Freiburg. This is an easy

hitching route, but for more certainty call the Citynetz Mitfahr-Service (☎ 1 94 44) at Belfortstrasse 55.

Getting Around

On the efficient local bus-and-tram network single rides cost DM3. The 24-hour Freiburger Stadtkarte allows unlimited travel with up to four children and two adults (DM9) or one adult (DM6.50), so it's more than paid for itself after just three rides.

DANUBE RIVER

The Danube (Donau), one of Europe's great rivers, rises in the Black Forest. In Austria, Hungary and Romania it is a mighty, almost intimidating, waterway, but in Germany it's narrower and more tranquil, making it ideal for hiking, biking and motoring tours.

Orientation & Information

The Danube flows from west to east through central Europe, finally finding an outlet in the Black Sea. In a nominal sense, Donaueschingen is the source of the river proper, though the Black Forest town of Furtwangen, on the Breg River, has a superior claim to being the true source of its waters – a rivalry that stimulates tourism to both places.

Donaueschingen has a tourist office (☎ 0771-85 72 21) at Karlstrasse 58 that is open weekdays, and also Saturday morning in summer. The Danube leads north-east through the large regional centres of Ulm and Regensburg. Ulm's tourist office (☎ 0731-161 28 30) is in an incongruous new building on Münsterplatz, and is open Monday to Friday from 9 am to 6 pm and on Saturday until 12.30 pm. The river then sweeps south-east and leaves Germany at Passau (see the Regensburg and Passau entries in the Bavaria section).

Things to See & Do

Donaueschingen To mark the source of the Danube, the town has the **Donauquelle** (Danube Source) monument in the park of the Fürstenberg Schloss. A sign at this arbitrarily positioned pool points out that it's 2840 km to the Black Sea. However, the two tributaries that meet one km down the path, the Brigach and the Breg, actually rise further from the Black Sea. Both these rivers are worth exploring.

Ulm *The* reason for coming to Ulm is to see the huge **Münster**, famous for its 161-metre-high steeple – the tallest anywhere in the world. Though the first stone was laid in 1377, it took just over 500 years for the entire structure to be completed. Only by climbing to the top (DM3) via the 768 spiralling steps do you fully appreciate the tower's astonishing height. The nearby **town hall**, adorned with frescos and an interesting astronomical clock, also demands inspection. Stroll past the **Schwörhaus** (Oath House) into the charming **Fischerviertel** – the old city's artisan quarter built along canals running into the Danube – then head downstream beside the river, with the old **Stadtmauer** (city walls) on your left.

Cycling The river's course can be followed by car, boat or on foot, but perhaps the most enjoyable way is by bicycle. The Donauradweg bike track runs the entire length of the German Danube, from Donaueschingen to Passau and beyond into Austria. Bikes can be hired at train stations in Ulm, Regensburg and Passau and returned to any of the others. It's also possible to send your pack ahead on the train. Donaueschingen's Southern Cross Independent Hostel (see Places to Stay & Eat) also rents out bikes.

Places to Stay & Eat
Donaueschingen The excellent *Southern Cross Independent Hostel* (☎ 0771-1 29 11), Josefstrasse 13, is run by an ex-traveller who knows what backpackers want most: cheap, convenient and friendly accommodation. The hostel has a kitchen, a bar and several dorms with beds for DM20; breakfast is DM6.50 extra. The owner, Martin, also runs Southern Cross Travel on the premises, offering cheap worldwide flights. The *Hotel Ochsen* (☎ 0771-8 09 90), at Käferstrasse 18, has a few simple singles for DM45 and better singles/doubles with amenities from DM75/105.

The *SB Restaurant*, at Käferstrasse 18, is a good option for cheap meals on weekdays until 5 pm, and the adjoining *Restaurant Ochsen* (☎ 0771-80 99 22) offers local specialities from around DM15.

Ulm The *DJH hostel* (☎ 0731-38 44 55) at Grimmelfinger Weg 45 charges juniors/seniors DM20/24 with breakfast. From the train station, take the S-Bahn line No 1 to Ehinger Tor, then bus No 4 to Schulzentrum, from where it's five minutes walk. Across the river in Neu-Ulm the *Rose* (☎ 0731-7 78 03), at Kasernstrasse 42a, has singles/doubles for DM40/80. In the centre are the *Münster-Hotel*, Münsterplatz 14, and the *Spanische Weinstube* (☎ 0731-6 32 97), right beside the Münster at Rabengasse 2; both have rooms from around DM50/90. The latter place also has a good restaurant downstairs. In the Fischerviertel, the *Allgäuer Hof* at Fischergasse 12 has basic dishes for around DM15, while the more up-market *Zunfthaus* at Fischergasse 31 offers local Swabian specialities.

Getting There & Away
Donaueschingen is on the Constance-Freiburg train route; Ulm is on the main Stuttgart-Munich train line. The Danube is shadowed by a series of roads, most notably the B311 (Tuttlingen to Ulm), the B16 (Ulm to Regensburg) and the B8 (Regensburg to Passau). North-south autobahns intersect at various points.

LAKE CONSTANCE
Lake Constance (Bodensee) is a perfect cure for travellers stranded in landlocked southern Germany. Often jokingly called the 'Swabian Ocean', this giant bulge in the sinewy course of the Rhine offers a choice of water sports, relaxation or cultural pursuits. The lake's southern side belongs to Switzerland and Austria, whose snow-capped mountaintops provide a perfect backdrop when viewed from the northern (German) shore.

The town of Constance (Konstanz) achieved historical significance in 1414 when the Council of Constance convened to try to heal huge rifts in the Church. The consequent burning at the stake of the religious reformer, Jan Hus, as a heretic, and the scattering of his ashes over the lake, failed to block the impetus of the Reformation.

Orientation & Information
The German side of Lake Constance features three often-crowded tourist centres in Constance, Meersburg and the island of Lindau.

GERMANY

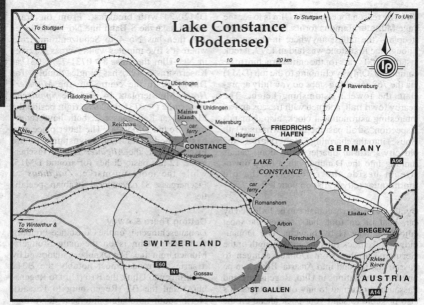

It's essentially a summer area, too often foggy or at best hazy in winter.

In the west, Constance straddles the Swiss border, a good fortune that spared it from Allied bombing in WWII. The tourist office (☎ 07531-13 30 30) is at Bahnhofplatz 13 (150 metres right from the station exit). In summer it's open weekdays between 9 am and 6.30 pm, and Saturday to 1 pm.

Meersburg lies across the lake from Constance and is an ideal base for exploring the long northern shore. The helpful tourist office (☎ 07532-43 11 11) is in the city museum building at Kirchstrasse 4; its summer opening times are Monday to Friday from 9 am to noon and 2 to 5.30 pm, and Saturday from 10 am to 2 pm. Nearby Friedrichshafen, the largest and most 'central' city on the lake's northern shore, has its own tourist office (☎ 07541-3 00 10) near the train station at Bahnhofsplatz 2.

Most of the German part of Lake Constance lies within Baden-Württemberg, but Lindau in the east is just inside Bavaria, near the Austrian border. The tourist office (☎ 08382-26 00 30),

directly opposite the station, is open weekdays and Saturday from 9 am to 1 pm in summer.

Things to See & Do
The lake itself adds special atmosphere to the many historic towns around its periphery, which can be explored by boat, bicycle and on foot.

Constance The city's most visible feature is the Gothic spire of the **cathedral**, added only in 1856 to a church that was started in 1052, which gives excellent views over the old town. Visit the bohemian **Rheingasse** quarter or relax in the parklands of the **Stadtgarten**. If you have time, head across to **Mainau Island** with its baroque castle established by the royal house of Sweden (admission DM16); it's set amongst palmy gardens which include a butterfly house.

Meersburg Meersburg is the prettiest town on the lake, with terraced streets and vineyard-patterned hills. The **Marktplatz** offers great vistas and leads to **Steigstrasse**, lined with lovely half-timbered houses. The fascinating 11th-century **Altes Schloss** (Old Castle) is the oldest structurally intact castle in Germany (open daily; DM8, students DM6). The baroque **Neues Schloss** (New Castle) houses the town's art collection (open daily from April to October; DM4, students DM3).

Lindau Connected by bridges with the nearby lakeshore, key sights of this lovely historic island town are the muralled **Altes Rathaus** (Old Town Hall) on Reichsplatz, the **city theatre** on Barfüsserplatz and the harbour's **Seepromenade** with its Bavarian Lion monument and lighthouse.

Elsewhere There is a wide choice of excursions around the lake. Count Zeppelin was born in Constance, but first built his cigar-shaped balloons over in Friedrichshafen, an endeavour commemorated in that town's superb new **Zeppelin Museum** (admission DM8; closed Monday). Überlingen features the astonishing **Cathedral of St Nicholas**, which boasts a dozen side altars and a wooden four-storey central altar dating from the 17th century. Another impressive baroque church can be found at Birnau.

Activities
Water Sports In season, the lake offers plenty of possibilities. In Constance, five public beaches are open from May to September, including the Strandbad Horn with nude bathing. See 3 UP (☎ 07531-2 31 17), Münzgasse 10, Constance, for equipment and courses.

Meersburg is perhaps a better base for watery pursuits, and some of the best windsurfers hang out here. Windsurfing Keetmann (☎ 07532-53 30) at Uferpromenade 37 hires out sailboards (DM28 per hour with wetsuit) and also runs courses. Meersburg's Bodensee-Yachtschule (☎ 07532-55 11) offers sailing courses and the Tauchschule Barakuda-Club (☎ 07532-92 77) at Von-Lassberg-Strass 1 runs very professional courses in scuba diving for beginners and more advanced divers. Call Motorboot-Charter (☎ 07532-3 64) for sailing boat and motorboat rental.

Lindau's water isn't as crowded as the land; Windsurf-Schule Kreitmeir (☎ 08382-2 33 30) at Strandbad Eichwald has a windsurfing school and equipment rental. For boat rental contact Grahneis (☎ 08382-55 14).

Cycling A 270-km international bike track circumnavigates Lake Constance through Germany, Austria and Switzerland, tracing the often steep shoreline beside vineyards and pebble beaches. The route is well signposted, but Regio Cart's 1:50,000 cycling/hiking map, *Rund um den Bodensee* (DM9.80), is useful.

All the larger train stations rent out standard 12-gear bicycles from around DM13 per day, and most lakeside towns also have private bike rentals. Velotours (☎ 07531-9 82 80), at Mainsaustrasse 34 in Constance, rents out better quality two-wheelers (daily/weekly DM20/100), and organises cycling tours.

Special Events
In the low season, the pre-Lent Fasnacht celebrations can be lively, helped along by Constance's large student population.

Places to Stay
The lake's popularity among German tourists pushes up accommodation prices; fortunately excellent hostel and camping facilities exist around the lake. See tourist offices for apartments and private rooms.

Camping Though there are many others along the shore, recommended camping grounds include: *Campingplatz Mainau* (☎ 07531-4 43 21) opposite Mainau Island near Constance; *Camping Hagnau* (☎ 07545-64 13), four km east of Meersburg (one of three camping grounds side by side); *Camping Seefelden* (☎ 07556-54 54) at Uhldingen, seven km west of Meersburg; and *Campingplatz Lindau-Zech* (☎ 08382-7 22 36), three km south-east of Lindau (open 1 April to 15 October).

Hostels The *DJH hostel* (☎ 07531-3 22 60) at Zur Allmannshohe 18 in Constance is open from March to October and costs DM19/24 for juniors/seniors; take bus No 1 or 4 from the station. The *DJH hostel* (☎ 07551-42 04), Alte Nussdorfer Strasse 26 in Überlingen, 15 km west of Meersburg, costs DM20/25. Lindau's newly rebuilt *DJH hostel* (☎ 08382-58 13 at Herbergsweg 11 charges DM25 (juniors only). The Friedrichshafen *DJH hostel* (☎ 07541-7 24 04) is at Lindauer Strasse 3 (DM19/23).

Hotels In central Constance is the *Hotel Barbarossa* (☎ 07531-2 20 21), at Obermarkt 8-12, which has simple singles/doubles from DM50/80 or DM55/98 with private shower. Also in the old town is the *Pension Gretel* (☎ 07531-2 32 83), Zollernstrasse 6, with simple rooms from DM45/85.

In Meersburg, the *Hotel Zum Lieben Augustin* (☎ 07532-65 11), at Unterstadtstrasse 35, offers excellent value with attractive singles/doubles for DM40/80. Not far out of town, the *Gasthaus zum Letzten Heller* (☎ 07532-61 49), Daisendorfer Strasse 41, has basic singles from DM38 and doubles with shower/WC for DM92.

In Lindau, the best budget deals on the island are the *Gästehaus Limmer* (☎ 08382-58 77), at In der Grub 16, and the nearby *Gästehaus Lädine* (☎ 08382-53 26), In der Grub 25, which both have basic rooms from around DM40/70 single/double.

Places to Eat
You'll pay extra to eat anywhere overlooking the water, and the food rarely matches the prices.

In Constance, check the *Seekuh*, a student-type bar on the corner of Zollernstrasse and Konzilstrasse, which dishes up great food and company; salads, pasta and pizza are priced from around DM10. It's open every evening at least until 1 am, and has live music on most summer Saturdays. The *Cleopatra* at Bahnhofstrasse 8 has take-away and sit-down Egyptian food including felafels for DM5 and daily menus from DM6.50.

In Meersburg, the *Gasthof zum Bären*, at Marktplatz 11, has hearty main courses from DM14. The *Alemannen-Torkel* (☎ 07532-10 67; open daily) is in an old wine cellar at Steigstrasse 16-18, and specialises in wines from the Lake Constance region as well as local dishes (from DM24).

In Lindau the *Früchtehaus Hannes*, In der Grub 36, has an array of fine delicatessen food including fruit, vegetables, meats, fish, pastas as well as a selection of ready-mixed salads;

there's a wine cellar/bistro at the rear. Although touristy, the *Goldenes Lamm* (☎ 08382-57 32) on Paradiesplatz nevertheless offers respectable dishes from DM12.

Getting There & Away
Constance has train connections every one to two hours to Zürich, Donaueschingen and Stuttgart. Meersburg is most easily reached by bus from Friedrichshafen (DM5), or by the car ferry from Constance (every 15 minutes all year; DM2.20, plus DM1.50 per bicycle, motorcycles DM3 and cars DM7). The car ferry between Friedrichshafen and Romanshorn (Switzerland) runs at least hourly in each direction (adults DM8.40). Lindau can be reached by train from Zürich (several daily), Bregenz (hourly, 15 minutes) and Munich (hourly, 2½ hours).

Getting Around
Although trains link Lindau, Friedrichshafen and Constance, buses provide the easiest land connections. By car, the B31 hugs the northern shore of Lake Constance, but it can get rather busy. By far the most enjoyable way to get around is on the ferries (☎ 07541-20 13 89), which, from Easter to late October, call in several times a day at all the larger towns along both sides of the lake; there are concessions for holders of rail passes. The seven-day Bodensee-Pass costs DM57 and gives two free days travel plus five days at half-price on all boats, buses, trains and mountain cableways on and around Lake Constance (including its Austrian and Swiss shores).

Rhineland-Palatinate

Rhineland-Palatinate (Rheinland-Pfalz) has a rugged topography characterised by thinly populated mountain ranges and forests cut by deep river valleys. Created after WWII from parts of the former Rhineland and Rhenish Palatinate regions, its turbulent history saw the area settled by the Romans and later hotly contested by the French and a variety of German states. The state capital is Mainz.

This land of wine and great natural beauty is still a secret spot for many travellers willing

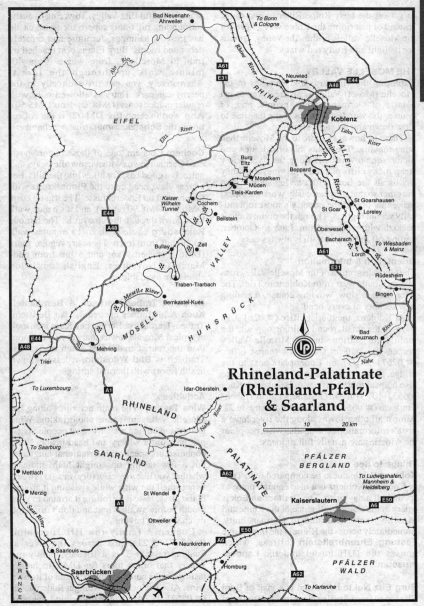

Rhineland-Palatinate
(Rheinland-Pfalz)
& Saarland

0   10   20 km

Map labels:
- Bad Neuenahr-Ahrweiler
- To Bonn & Cologne
- Ahr River
- A61
- E31
- Rhine River
- Neuwied
- A48
- E44
- RHINE
- EIFEL
- Eltz River
- Koblenz
- Lahn River
- RHINE VALLEY
- Burg Eltz
- Moselkern
- Müden
- Treis-Karden
- Boppard
- Kaiser Wilhelm Tunnel
- Cochem
- Beilstein
- St Goarshausen
- St Goar
- Loreley
- E44
- A48
- Oberwesel
- Bacharach
- Bullay
- Zell
- MOSELLE VALLEY
- Lorch
- To Wiesbaden & Mainz
- A61
- E31
- Rüdesheim
- Traben-Trarbach
- Bingen
- Moselle River
- Bernkastel-Kues
- HUNSRÜCK
- Piesport
- Bad Kreuznach
- Nahe River
- A48
- E44
- Mehring
- MOSELLE
- Trier
- To Luxembourg
- A1
- RHINELAND
- Idar-Oberstein
- Nahe River
- PFÄLZER BERGLAND
- To Saarburg
- SAARLAND
- Mettlach
- Merzig
- St Wendel
- A62
- PALATINATE
- To Ludwigshafen, Mannheim & Heidelberg
- Kaiserslautern
- A6
- E50
- A1
- Ottweiler
- Saar River
- Saarlouis
- Neunkirchen
- A6
- E50
- Homburg
- PFÄLZER WALD
- Saarbrücken
- FRANCE
- A62
- To Karlsruhe

GERMANY

to get off the busy Rhine River tourist route. Instead of just riding the Rhine wave, head for the Moselle Valley, or the Ahr Valley, famous for its light and fruity red wines.

THE MOSELLE VALLEY
Exploring the vineyards and wineries of the Moselle (Mosel) Valley is an ideal way to get a taste of German culture, people, and, of course, the wonderful wines. Take the time to slow down and do some sipping.

There is, however, more to the Moselle than wine-making. The many historical sites and picturesque towns built along the river below steep rocky cliffs planted with vineyards (they say locals are born with one leg shorter than the other so that they can easily work the vines) make this one of the country's most romantically scenic regions. Though the entire route is packed with visitors from June to October, getting off the beaten path is always easy.

Orientation & Information
The German section of the Moselle Valley runs 195 km south-west from Koblenz to Trier. The river takes a slow, winding course, revealing new scenery at every bend.

At Koblenz, the tourist office (☎ 0261-3 13 04) is in the small, round building opposite the main train station. In the Moselle Valley proper, the staff in Cochem's tourist office (☎ 02671-39 71), on Endertplatz next to the bridge, are especially keen to please. There are also helpful tourist offices in Bernkastel-Kues (06531-40 23) at Am Gestade 5, and in Traben-Trarbach (☎ 06541-8 39 80) at Bahnstrasse 22. Almost all other towns along the river have a visitor information centre; otherwise, people at the wineries are usually full of ideas.

Things to See
Koblenz While not to be compared with Trier or Cochem, Koblenz is a nice enough place to spend half a day or so. The **Deutsches Eck** is a park at the sharp confluence of the Rhine and Moselle rivers dedicated to German unity. Immediately across the Rhine is the impressive **Festung Ehrenbreitstein** fortress, which houses the DJH hostel and the **Landesmuseum**.

Burg Eltz Not to be missed is a visit to Burg Eltz (open from April to November) at the head of the beautiful Eltz Valley. Towering over the surrounding hills, this superb medieval castle has frescos, paintings, furniture and ornately decorated rooms. Burg Eltz is best reached by train to Moselkern, from where it's a 40-minute walk up through the forest. Alternatively, you can drive directly to the nearby car park. Entry is allowed only with regular guided tours (DM8, students DM5.50). Also worth seeing (for DM4/2) is the collection in the **Schatzkammer** (treasure chamber).

Cochem Cochem, one of those picture-postcard German towns with narrow alleyways and gates, is a good base for hikes into the hills. For a great view, head up to the **Pinnerkreuz** with the chairlift on Endertstrasse. The trip up costs DM6.90 (DM8.90 return), and it's a nice walk back down through the vineyards. The famous **Reichsburg** castle is about 15 minutes walk up the hill from town. There are regular tours (DM6) between 9 am and 5 pm from mid-March to November; English translation sheets are available.

Beilstein, Traben-Trarbach & Bernkastel-Kues A bit further upstream, visit Beilstein, Traben-Trarbach or Bernkastel-Kues for a look at typical Moselle towns that survive on more than the tourist trade. Just south of Traben-Trarbach is **Bad Wildstein**, a lesser known health resort with thermal springs.

Activities
Wine Tasting The main activities along the Moselle Valley are eating and drinking. Wine tasting and buying are why most people visit – just pick out a winery and head inside. Wine connoisseurs speak an international language, but a few tasting tips might help: indicate whether you like a *trocken* (dry) or *süss* (sweet) wine; smell the wine while swishing it around in the glass; taste it by rolling it around in your mouth before swallowing; and don't drink too much without buying.

Cochem's family-run HH Hieronimi (☎ 02671-2 21), just across the river at Stadionstrasse 1-3, is a friendly, family-run winery that offers tours for DM8, including tastings and a complimentary bottle of its own wine. Also in Cochem is Weingut Rademacher (☎ 02671-41 64), diagonally behind the train station at Pinnerstrasse 10, whose tours of the winery and cellar (an old WWII bunker) cost DM8.50/11.50 with four/six wine tastings.

In Bernkastel-Kues, the private Weingut Dr Willkomm (☎ 06531-80 54), Gestade 1, is in a lovely old arched cellar; the winery also distils its own brandy. The Moselland Winzergenossenschaft (☎ 06531-5 70), at In der Bornwiese, is the local winegrowers' cooperative; there are guided tours in English every Thursday morning.

Hiking The Moselle Valley is especially scenic walking country, but plan on some steep climbs if you venture away from the river. The views are worth the sore muscles. The Moselle region is covered by a series of three 1:50,000 hiking maps that cost DM8.80 per sheet.

Places to Stay

There are camping grounds, hostels and rooms with classic views all along the Moselle Valley. If possible, stay at a winery – many winemakers have their own small pensions. Then, after a long tasting session, you shouldn't have to worry about finding your way home. As usual, the local tourist offices operate well-organised room-finding services.

Koblenz The *Rhein Mosel* camping ground (☎ 0261-80 24 89; open April to mid-October) is on Schartwiesenweg, at the confluence of the Moselle and Rhine rivers opposite the Deutsches Eck. The daytime passenger ferry across the Moselle puts the camping ground within five minutes walk of town.

Koblenz has a wonderful *DJH hostel* (☎ 0261-7 37 37) in the old Ehrenbreitstein fortress (DM21/26 for juniors/seniors), but it's advisable to book ahead in summer. From the main train station take bus No 7, 8, 9 or 10; there's also a chairlift (DM7/10 up/return, concessions for youth hostel card-holders) from Ehrenbreitstein station by the river. If you want to stay somewhere more central, the *Hotel Weinand* (☎ 3 24 92), Weissernonnengasse 4-6, has clean no-frills singles/doubles priced from DM32/64.

Cochem For lovely riverside camping, go to the *Campingplatz Am Freiheitszentrum* (☎ 02671-44 09; open from 10 days before

Easter to the end of October) in Stadionstrasse, downstream of the northern bridge. Also on the eastern bank near the bridge is Cochem's *DJH hostel* (☎ 02671-86 33), at Klottener Strasse 9. A good budget place is *Pension Dapper* (☎ 02671-74 71), at Moselstrasse 24 near the train station, which has basic doubles from DM54 (or from DM62 with private shower and toilet). On summer weekends and during the local wine harvest (mid-September to mid-October), you can forget about finding any bargain accommodation anywhere.

Bernkastel-Kues The *Campingplatz Kueser Werth* (☎ 06531-82 00) has pleasant tent sites by the river, and there's a nice *DJH hostel* (☎ 06531-23 95) at Jugendherbergsstrasse 1. The small *Haus Waldkönig* (☎ 06531-63 69), at Brünigstrasse 35 in Kues, offers singles/doubles with shower and toilet for only DM35/70.

Traben-Trarbach For campers, there's the *Rissbach* (☎ 06541-31 11; open April to mid-October) at Rissbacher Strasse 170. The *DJH hostel* (☎ 06541-92 78), at Hirtenpfad, has beds in small dorms for DM24/30 for juniors/seniors. The small and central *Pension Germania* (☎ 06541-93 98), at Kirchstrasse 101, offers simple singles/doubles from just DM30/60.

Bullay The *Bären-Camp* (☎ 06542-90 00 97), Am Moselufer 1, is tailored to riverside tents. Bullay's *Hotel Mosella/Gästehaus Brück* (☎ 06542-25 77), at Zehnthausstrasse 8, offers simple singles/doubles from DM38/76.

Places to Eat

Good wine often means good food and this is true all along the Moselle, with dozens of inexpensive family places to choose from. The Moselle is also an ideal place for picnics – enjoying the peaceful river and countryside with good local food and wine.

Koblenz The lively *Domino*, at Altenhof 3, offers pancakes (from DM6.80), as well as large salads and plates of home-made noodles for under DM10; it's closed Tuesday. The *Alt Coblenz* (☎ 0261-16 06 56) at Am Plan serves main courses from DM18 to tables on the square.

Cochem A good sit-down fast-food choice is *Kochlöffel*, opposite the town hall at Am Markt 10, where a schnitzel with salad and fries only costs DM7.50. A few paces uphill at Oberbachstrasse 4 is the *Zum Christophorus*, a restaurant that serves a broad range of dishes ranging from fish (from DM19), pizzas (from 9.50) and vegetarian/diabetic meals (from DM14).

Getting There & Away
It's most practical to begin your Moselle Valley trip from either Trier or Koblenz. If you have private transport and are coming from the north, however, you might head up the Ahr Valley and cut through the scenic High Eifel mountain area.

Getting Around
The Moselle Valley can be explored on foot or by bike, car, boat or other public transport.

Bus The only scheduled bus service along the Moselle is between Trier and Bullay, about three-fifths of the way towards Koblenz. (In this section the train line is too far from the river for convenience.) The private Moselbahn (☎ 0651-2 10 76) runs seven daily buses in each direction (DM16.60, three hours each way). It's a highly scenic route, following the river's winding course and passing through numerous quaint villages along the way. Buses leave from outside the train stations in Trier and Bullay.

Train The trains running along the Moselle are frequent and run even to the smallest towns, but often they won't let you enjoy much of the beautiful scenery. The private Moselweinbahn line goes from Bullay to Traben-Trarbach.

Car & Motorcycle Driving along the Moselle is ideal, though drivers will risk cramped necks (not to mention nervous passengers) from looking up at the majestic slopes. One possibility is to rent a car in either Koblenz or Trier and drop it off at the other end.

Hitchhiking is good, especially during summer, when the roads are crowded with friendly drivers. Just make sure that whoever picks you up hasn't spent too much time at one of the wineries.

Bicycle The Moselle is a popular area among cyclists, and for much of the river's course there's a separate 'Moselroute' bike track. The ADFC map *Radtourenkarte Mosel-Saarland* (DM12.80) indicates optimum routes and is also useful for hiking. Touren-Rad (☎ 0261-9 11 60 16), at Hohenzollernstrasse 127, near the main train station in Koblenz, rents quality mountain and touring bicycles from DM10/18 per day. Bikes can be returned in Trier or Bingen (on the Rhine, across the river from Rüdesheim). Larger train stations also have rental bikes; you can send luggage ahead on the train and drop off bikes at other stations.

Boat A great way to explore the Moselle is by boat. While much of the river's charm comes from its constantly winding course, this does make water travel particularly slow. To get from Koblenz to Trier using scheduled ferry services takes three days.

Between early May and mid-October, ferries of the Köln-Düsseldorfer (KD) Line (☎ 0221-20 88 318) sail daily from Koblenz to Cochem (DM35 one way). From Cochem, the Gebrüder Kolb Line (☎ 02673-15 15) runs boats upriver as far as Trier (DM68 one way) between April and early November. Various smaller ferry companies also operate on the Moselle.

Eurail and Germanrail passes are valid for all normal KD Line services and – something to consider when planning your itinerary – travel on your birthday is free. There are numerous other possible excursions, ranging from short return cruises to multiday wine-tasting packages.

TRIER
Trier is touted as Germany's oldest town. Although settlement of the site dates back to 400 BC, Trier itself was founded in 15 BC as Augusta Treverorum, the capital of Gaul, and was second in importance only to Rome in the Western Roman Empire. You'll find more Roman ruins here than anywhere else north of the Alps. There's a university too, and Trier can get pretty lively.

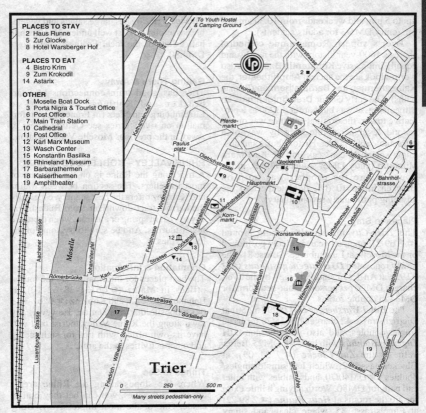

PLACES TO STAY
 2 Haus Runne
 5 Zur Glocke
 8 Hotel Warsberger Hof

PLACES TO EAT
 4 Bistro Krim
 9 Zum Krokodil
14 Astarix

OTHER
 1 Moselle Boat Dock
 3 Porta Nigra & Tourist Office
 6 Post Office
 7 Main Train Station
10 Cathedral
11 Post Office
12 Karl Marx Museum
13 Wasch Center
15 Konstantin Basilika
16 Rhineland Museum
17 Barbarathermen
18 Kaiserthermen
19 Amphitheater

Trier

0   250   500 m

Many streets pedestrian-only

Orientation & Information

From the main train station head west along Bahnhofstrasse and Theodor-Heuss-Allee to the Porta Nigra, where you'll find Trier's tourist office (☎ 97 80 80). It has a free and efficient room-finding service. Ask here about daily guided city walking tours in English (DM9), and the Trier-Card (DM17), a combined ticket to the city's main sights and museums. From Porta Nigra, walk along Simeonstrasse's pedestrian zone to Hauptmarkt, the pivotal centre of the old city. Most of the sights are within this area of roughly one sq km.

There's a convenient and cheap laundrette, the Wasch Center, at Brückenstrasse 19-21.

Trier's telephone code is ☎ 0651.

Things to See

The town's chief landmark is the **Porta Nigra**, the imposing city gate on the northern edge of the town centre, which dates back to the 2nd century AD (entry DM4, or DM2 for students). The **Rheinisches Landesmuseum** (Rhineland Museum), Weimarer Allee 1, is one of Germany's finest museums, with works of art dating from Palaeolithic, Roman and modern times; it's open Tuesday to Friday from 9.30

GERMANY

am to 5 pm, and weekends from 10.30 am to 5 pm (entry DM5/3 for adults/students).

Trier's superb Romanesque **cathedral** shares a 1600-year history with the nearby and equally impressive **Konstantin Basilika**. Also worth a look are the ancient **Amphitheater**, the **Kaiserthermen** and **Barbarathermen** (Roman baths). The early Gothic **Dreikönigenhaus** on Simeonstrasse was built around 1230 as a protective tower: the original entrance was on the second level accessible only by way of a retractable rope ladder. History buffs and nostalgic socialists can seek out the **Karl Marx Museum** (entry DM3, students DM2), in the house where the prophet was born on Brückenstrasse 10 (but don't expect to see anything particularly revolutionary).

Places to Stay

The *Trier-City* municipal camping ground (☎ 8 69 21; open all year) is nicely positioned on the Moselle at Luxemburger Strasse 81. The newly renovated *DJH Jugendgästehaus* (☎ 2 92 92), at An der Jugendherberge 4 by the river, charges DM26 per person in four-bed dorms or DM34 in double rooms.

The *Hotel Warsberger Hof* (☎ 97 52 50) at Dietrichstrasse 42 charges DM35/70 for basic singles/doubles, and also runs the non-DJH *Jugendgästehaus* with beds for DM25. Better value is the *Zur Glocke* (☎ 7 31 09), at Glockenstasse 12, which has simple singles/doubles for DM40/70, and doubles with toilet and bath for DM80. Worth paying a little extra for are the rooms at *Haus Runne* (☎ 2 89 22) at Engelstrasse 35, where clean and sunny rooms with private toilet and shower cost just DM45/85. The restaurant is known for its excellent Franco-Germanic cooking.

Places to Eat

Trier is a great place to sample Franco-German cooking. A typical example is *Zum Krokodil*, a historic old inn on Nikolaus-Koch-Platz, which has half a dozen daily set menus for between DM15 and DM27. *Bistro Krim* (☎ 7 39 43), an innovative eatery at Glockenstrasse 7, serves tasty combinations like baked fetta (DM12.50) and Argentinian meat salad (DM16.50) as well as three-course 'Mediterranean' set menus including coffee for DM27.50. A favourite student hang-out is *Astarix*, down an arcade at Karl-Marx-Strasse

11. Meaty rice dishes, large salads and vegetable casseroles all cost well under DM10, while half a litre of the local Erdinger brew costs DM4.80.

Getting There & Away

Trier has good train connections to Saarbrücken and Koblenz, as well as to Luxembourg and Metz (in France). For information on river ferries see Getting There & Away in the previous Moselle Valley section.

RHINE VALLEY – KOBLENZ TO MAINZ

A trip along the Rhine is on the itinerary of most travellers. The section between Mainz and Koblenz offers the best scenery, especially the narrow tract downriver from Rüdesheim. Try to visit in spring or autumn, when there are fewer tourists. And be sure to try some of the local wines.

Orientation & Information

The best places for information are the tourist offices in Mainz (☎ 06131-28 62 10), at Bahnhofstrasse 15, and Koblenz (☎ 0261-3 13 04), opposite the train station. However, any town along the Rhine Valley tourist trail will have its own office, with tips for sightseeing and other activities in the area.

Things to See

Where the slopes along the Rhine aren't covered with vines, you can bet they built a castle. One of the most impressive is **Burg Rheinfels** in St Goar. Across the river, just south of St Goarshausen, is the Rhine's most famous sight: the **Lorelei Cliff**. Legend has it that a maiden sang sailors to their deaths against its base. It's worth the trek to the top of the Lorelei for the view, but try to get up there early in the morning before the hordes ascend.

Rüdesheim Although it's rolling drunk on tourism, this town is well worth a visit. To get some perspective of the area and the wines you'll be sampling, take the **Weinlehrpfad** walking route (from above Drosselgasse) which leads through vineyard slopes to the **Brömserburg**, an old riverside castle that houses an interesting wine museum (adults DM5, students DM3).

Mainz Half an hour's ride by train from Frankfurt, Mainz has an attractive old town. Of particular interest are the massive **St Martins cathedral** and the **Stephanskirche**, with stained-glass windows by Marc Chagall. Mainz's museums include the **Gutenberg Museum**, which contains the first printed Bible, and the **Roman Ship Museum**, which houses an ancient Rhine galley built by the Romans.

Activities
Wine Tasting As with the Moselle Valley, the Koblenz-to-Mainz section of the Rhine Valley is great for wine tasting. Along with Rüdesheim, the best towns for a true Rhine-wine experience are Oberwesel and Bacharach, respectively 40 km and 45 km south of Koblenz. For wine tasting in other towns, ask for recommendations at the tourist offices or just follow your nose.

Hiking Though the trails here may be a bit more crowded with day-trippers than those along the Moselle, hiking along the Rhine is also excellent. The slopes and trails around Bacharach are justly famous and offer a great way to work off Rhine wine and cooking.

Places to Stay
Camping Camping facilities line the Rhine, but amenities and views vary greatly. Good possibilities include: Oberwesel's *Schönburg* (☎ 06744-2 45), open April to October and right beside the river; Bacharach's *Sonnenstrand* (☎ 06743-17 52), open from April to mid-November and offering riverside camping just 500 metres south of the centre; and St Goarshausen's *Auf der Loreley* (☎ 06771-4 30), right on the legendary rock and open Easter to October.

Hostels There are *DJH hostels* in Oberwesel (☎ 06744-9 33 30), at Auf dem Schönberg; St Goar (☎ 06741-3 38), at Bismarckweg 17; St Goarshausen (☎ 06771-2619), Auf der Loreley (like the nearby camping ground, it's right on top of the Lorelei); Bacharach (☎ 06743-12 66), a legendary facility housed in the Burg Stahleck castle; and Rüdesheim (☎ 06722-27 11), at Am Kreuzburg. In Mainz, the DJH-*Jugendgästehaus* (☎ 06131-8 53 32) is at Otto-Brunfels-Schneise 4.

Hotels & Pensions In St Goar, the *Hotel Germania* (☎ 06741-16 10), at Heerstrasse 47 near the ferry dock, offers simple singles/doubles from DM35/70. In Bacharach, the *Gasthaus Zur Alten Mühle* (☎ 06743-14 43), below the castle at Blücherstrasse 105, has rooms with toilet and shower for DM35/64. Best value in Rüdesheim is the *Haus Felzen* (☎ 06722-24 30), Schmidtstrasse 23, with simple singles for DM35 and doubles with shower and toilet for DM80. Apart from its excellent youth hostel, Mainz has no (recommendable) budget accommodation.

For accommodation in Koblenz, see Places to Stay in the previous Moselle Valley section.

Places to Eat
Whether you put together a modest picnic by the river or dine in one of the numerous local restaurants, this is the place to savour fine Rhine wine and food.

St Goarhausen's *Zum Goldenen Löwen*, by the water at Heerstrasse 1, serves game and other specialities priced from DM22 (also have a look at the historic flood-level markings on the outside wall). In Rüdesheim, *Drosselmüller's Bierstube* at Oberstrasse 26 (near the chair-lift station) offers simple three-course meals priced from DM15. Avoid eating anywhere in Rüdesheim's appropriately named Drosselgasse (Strangle Lane), an oversold row of touristy shops and restaurants. In Mainz, the *Altstadtcafé* at Schönbornstrasse 9a is a popular student hang-out.

Getting There & Away
Koblenz or Mainz are the best starting points. The Rhine Valley is also easily accessible from Frankfurt on a long day trip, but that won't do justice to the region.

Getting Around
Each mode of transport has its own advantages and all are equally enjoyable. Try combining several of them by going on foot one day, cycling the next, and then taking a boat for a view from the river.

Boat The Köln-Düsseldorfer (KD) Line (☎ 0221-20 88 318) earns its bread and butter on the Rhine, with many slow and fast boats daily between Koblenz and Mainz. The most scenic stretch is between Koblenz and

Rüdesheim; the journey downstream (Rüdesheim-Koblenz) takes about 3¾ hours (DM52.40) and about 5½ hours upstream (DM41 – KD Line says it's cheaper because it's more popular). See Getting Around in the previous Moselle Valley section for information about concessions. Depending on demand, boats stop at riverside towns along the way.

Train Important train lines run on both banks of the Rhine. Providing you can get across the river easily, this increases the number of possible train connections.

Car Touring the Rhine Valley by car is also ideal. The route between Koblenz and Mainz is short enough for a car to be rented and returned to either city. There are no bridge crossings between Koblenz and Rüdesheim, but there are frequent ferries.

Saarland

In the late 19th century, Saarland's coal mines and steel mills fuelled the burgeoning German economy. Since WWII, however, the steady economic decline of coal and steel has made Saarland the poorest region in western Germany. Though distinctly German since the early Middle Ages, Saarland was ruled by France for several periods during its turbulent history. Reoccupied by the French after WWII, it only joined the Federal Republic of Germany in 1957, after the population rejected French efforts to turn it into an independent state.

SAARBRÜCKEN
Saarbrücken, capital of Saarland, has an interesting mixed French and German feel. Though lacking major tourist sights, this city of 200,000 is a matter-of-fact place where people go about their daily business and where tourists are treated as individuals. It's also an easy base for day trips to some of the beautiful little towns nearby, such as Ottweiler, Saarburg and St Wendel.

Orientation & Information
The main train station is in the north-western corner of the old town, which stretches out on

both sides of the Saar River. Tourist-Information (☎ 3 51 97) is just to the left of the main exit at the train station. Its opening hours are from 9 am to 6 pm Monday to Friday, and to 4 pm Saturday. The main tourist office (☎ 3 69 01), at Grossherzog-Friedrich-Strasse 1, just past the town hall, is open Monday to Friday from 8 am to 6 pm.

There are post offices at the main train station and in the city centre at Dudweilerstrasse 17. You'll find a convenient laundrette, the Wasch-Haus, opposite the Ludwigskirche at Eisenbahnstrasse 8.

Saarbrücken's telephone code is ☎ 0681.

Things to See & Do
Start your visit by strolling along the lanes around lively **St Johanner Markt** in the central pedestrian zone. A flea market is held here every second Saturday from April to November. Not far away beside the Saar River are the **Saarländische Staatstheater**, a neoclassical structure built by the Nazis, and the **Saarland-Museum** (entry DM3; closed Monday), the city's main art gallery.

Cross the 1549 **Alte Brücke** (Old Bridge) to **Schloss Saarbrücken**, the former palace on Schlossplatz designed by King Wilhelm Friedrich's court architect, Friedrich Joachim Stengel, in the 18th century. There are several museums (all closed Monday) in the **Alte Rathaus** (old town hall) on Schlossplatz: the small **Museum of Regional History** (entry free), the **Prehistoric Museum** (DM5) and the more interesting **Abenteuer Museum** (Adventure Museum). The latter is a hotchpotch of weird souvenirs and photos collected since 1950 by solo adventurer extraordinaire, Heinz Rox-Schulz, but unfortunately, the opening hours are rather limited.

The nearby **Ludwigsplatz** is a fine example of baroque architecture. The square, also Stengel's work, is dominated by the **Ludwigskirche**, an odd combination of a Lutheran church in a baroque setting. The church also keeps ridiculously inconvenient opening hours, so you may just have to peer through the glass doorway.

Places to Stay
The camping ground *Am Spicherer Berg* (☎ 5 17 80; open April to October), at Am Spicherer Berg, is out on the French border, south of the

city; take bus No 42 to the ZF Gewerbegebiet or the Mercedes tower. The excellent *DJH hostel* (☎ 3 30 40) is at Meerwiesertalweg 31, a half-hour walk north-east of the train station; otherwise take bus No 49 or 69 to Prinzen-weiher. Beds cost DM26/29 for juniors/seniors in four-person dorms, or DM31/35 in two-person rooms.

Unfortunately, Saarbrücken has very few private rooms, and the many French day and weekend trippers keep hotel prices high. The cheapest option in the centre is *Hotel Schlosskrug* (☎ 3 54 48), Schmollerstrasse 14, on the edge of the lively area around Nauwieserplatz. Single/double rooms cost from DM50/100. The *Gästehaus Weller* (☎ 37 19 03), at Neugrabenweg 8 near the DJH hostel, has basic rooms from DM49/69, and rooms with toilet, shower and TV for DM69/98.

Places to Eat

At Saarbrücken's eateries, your taste buds get to visit France while enjoying hearty German servings.

The *Gasthaus Zum Stiefel* (☎ 93 54 50, closed Sunday), in an old brewery at Am Stiefel 2 (a laneway off St Johanner Markt), has an up-market restaurant at the front specialising in fine meat and fish dishes, with main courses from DM25. The pub out the back (enter from Froschgasse) has house beers on tap and serves rather less expensive food. Also try some of the other bistros and fast-food places along Froschgasse.

You'll find most of the cheaper restaurants and student pubs along the streets running off Nauwieserplatz. Perhaps the most popular hang-out is *Uff de Nauwies* on the corner of Nauwieserstrasse and Nassauerstrasse, with salads and pizzas from DM6.50 and beer on tap. The *Café Kostbar* is in an attractive back-street courtyard at Nauwieserstrasse 19; it has several different set menus each day (for between DM9 and DM11), and there's a special breakfast buffet on Sunday.

As its German name implies, the creative *Auflauf* (☎ 3 11 68, open daily), at Johannis-strasse 17, specialises in oven-baked build-your-own soufflés from DM10.50 (small) to DM13.50 (large). Across the river, near Schlossplatz, is *Tomate 2* (☎ 5 78 46), at Schlossstrasse 2. Its Italo-Alsatian cuisine

changes daily, but risotto, fish soup and pasta are staple options.

Getting There & Away

There are hourly trains to the connecting cities of Mannheim, Koblenz, Mainz and Karlsruhe, and two direct trains to Paris each day. The international E50 autobahn connecting Mannheim with Metz in France passes close by Saarbrücken. The ADM-Mitfahrzentrale (☎ 1 94 40), at Grossherzog-Friedrich-Strasse 59, can organise your ride to Frankfurt (DM21), Paris (DM39), Hamburg (DM58) or any other major city.

Hesse

The Hessians, a Frankish tribe, were among the first people to convert to Lutheranism in the early 16th century. Apart from a brief period of unity in that same century under Philip the Magnanimous, Hesse (Hessen) remained a motley collection of principalities and, later, of Prussian administrative districts until it was proclaimed a state in 1945. Its main cities are Frankfurt, Kassel and the capital, Wiesbaden.

As well as being a transportation hub, the city of Frankfurt can also be used as a base to explore some of the smaller towns in Hesse – those that remind you that you're still in Germany. The beautiful Taunus and Spessart regions offer quiet village life and hours of scenic walks.

FRANKFURT/MAIN

They call it 'Bankfurt' and 'Mainhattan' and much more. It's on the Main (pronounced 'mine') River, and is generally referred to as Frankfurt-am-Main, or Frankfurt/Main, since there's another large city called Frankfurt (Frankfurt/Oder) near the Polish border.

Frankfurt/Main is the financial and geo-graphical centre of western Germany, as well as the host of important trade fairs, including the world's largest book, consumer-goods and musical-instrument fairs. Frankfurt's 650,000 inhabitants produce a disproportionately large part of Germany's wealth, and a big part of the city's taxes are devoted to the arts; here you'll find the richest collection of museums in the country.

Frankfurt is Germany's most important transport hub – for air, train and road connections – so you'll probably end up here at some point. Don't be surprised if you find this cosmopolitan melting-pot more interesting than you had expected.

Orientation

The airport is about 15 minutes by train southwest of the city centre. The Hauptbahnhof (main train station) is on the western side of the city, but within walking distance of the old city centre.

One way to walk into the old city from Hauptbahnhof is east along Taunusstrasse. This leads you to Goetheplatz and then to a large square called An der Hauptwache. The area between the former lockup, the Hauptwache, and the Römerberg, in the tiny vestige of Frankfurt's original old city, is the centre of Frankfurt. The Main River runs just south of the Altstadt, with several bridges leading to one of the city's livelier areas, Sachsenhausen. Its north-eastern corner, behind the DJH hostel (see Places to Stay) is known as Alt Sachsenhausen and is full of quaint old houses and narrow alleyways.

Information

Tourist Offices Frankfurt's most convenient tourist office (☎ 21 23 88 49/51) is at Hauptbahnhof, at the head of platform No 23. It's open weekdays from 8 am to 9 pm, weekends and holidays from 9 am to 6 pm. The staff are efficient at finding rooms, but there's a service fee of DM5 plus a DM10 deposit on the room.

People with particular needs or those staying longer in Frankfurt should contact Tourismus + Congress (☎ 21 23 03 98), at Kaiserstrasse 56. This office handles hotel reservation (free of charge) and is open Monday to Friday until 4 pm.

In the centre of the city, the Römer tourist office (☎ 21 23 87 08/09) at Römerberg 27 (in the north-western corner of the square) is open daily (including weekends) from 9 am to 6 pm.

The friendly head office of the German National Tourist Office (☎ 75 72 0), north of Hauptbahnhof at Beethovenstrasse 69, is a good place to visit if you're still planning your trip to Germany, with brochures of all areas of the country.

Ask about the two-day Frankfurt Card, which costs DM13 and gives 50% reductions on admission to all of the city's important museums, the zoo and the Palmengarten, as well as free travel on public transport.

Money The Hauptbahnhof has a branch of the Deutsche Verkehrs Bank or DVB (☎ 2 64 82 01), near the southern exit at the head of platform No 1, which is open daily from 6.30 am to 10.30 pm; otherwise, use the money-exchange machine at the head of platform No 15. There are several banks at the airport, most of them open till about 10 pm, and exchange and automatic teller machines are dotted around the various arrival and departure halls.

American Express and Thomas Cook are opposite each other on Kaiserstrasse at Nos 10 and 11 respectively.

Post & Communications The main post office (☎ 90 90 10) is near Hauptwache at Zeil 108-110. It's open weekdays from 9 am to 6 pm, and to 1 pm Saturday; limited after-hours services are offered until 7 pm weekdays (8 pm Thursday) and until 4 pm Saturday. The post office above the tourist office in Hauptbahnhof is open from 6 am to 10 pm Monday to Friday, and 8 am to 9 pm on weekends and public holidays; the one at the airport (in the waiting lounge of departure hall B) is open 24 hours a day.

Frankfurt's telephone code is ☎ 069.

Bookshops You can stock up on magazines and newspapers at the Internationale Presse shop in the train station, at the head of platform No 15. Sussmann's Presse & Buch, on Hauptwache behind the Katharinenkirche, has a fair selection of English-language material.

Laundry The Wasch-Center chain has useful laundrettes in Frankfurt: at Wallstrasse 8 in Sachsenhausen, and at Sandweg 41 just north-east of the city centre. They're open daily from 6 am to 10 pm and 11 pm respectively, and charge DM6 per wash, DM1 for (optional) use of the spinner, and DM1 (per 15 minutes) for the tumble drier.

Medical Services The Uni-Clinic (☎ 6 30 11), at Theodor Stern Kai 7 in Sachsenhausen, is open 24 hours a day. For medical queries, contact the doctor service on ☎ 1 92 92. The service is open 24-hours a day.

Dangers & Annoyances The area around Hauptbahnhof acts as a base for Frankfurt's sex and illegal drugs trades. Frequent police patrols of the station itself and the surrounding Bahnhofsviertel keep things under control, but it's nevertheless advisable to use 'big city' common sense.

Things to See & Do

Eighty per cent of the old city was wiped off the map by two Allied bombing raids in March 1944, and postwar reconstruction was subject to the demands of the new age. Rebuilding efforts were more thoughtful, however, in the **Römerberg**, the old central square of Frankfurt, west of the cathedral, where restored 14th and 15th-century buildings provide a glimpse of the beautiful city this once was. The old town hall, or **Römer**, is in the north-west corner of Römerberg and consists of three 15th-century houses topped with Frankfurt's trademark stepped gables.

East of Römerberg, behind the Historical Garden (remains of Roman and Carolingian foundations), is the newly restored **cathedral**, the coronation site of Holy Roman emperors from 1562 to 1792. It's dominated by the elegant 15th-century Gothic **tower** (completed in the 1860s) – one of the few structures left standing after the 1944 raids. The small **Wahlkapelle** (Voting Chapel) on the cathedral's southern side is where the seven electors of the Holy Roman Empire chose the emperor from 1356 onwards; the adjoining **choir** has beautiful wooden stalls.

Anyone with an interest in German literature should visit the **Goethe-Haus**, Grosser Hirschgraben 23-25. Johann Wolfgang von Goethe, arguably the last person to master all fields of human knowledge, was born in this house in 1749. This newly renovated museum and library is open Monday to Saturday from 9 am to 6 pm, Sunday and public holidays from 10 am to 1 pm (shorter hours in winter); entry costs DM4 (students DM3).

A bit further afield, the botanical **Palmengarten** (entry DM7, students DM3, or DM5 with a valid RMV ticket) and the creative

Frankfurt Zoo (DM11, students DM5) are perfect reliefs from the cosmopolitan chaos.

There's a great **flea market** along Museumsufer every Saturday between 8 am and 2 pm.

Museums Frankfurt has more top-ranking museums than any other German city; entry to most museums is free on Wednesday.

The **Museum für Moderne Kunst** (Museum of Modern Art), north of the cathedral at Domstrasse 10, features work by Joseph Beuys, Claes Oldenburg and many others; admission is DM7 (students DM3.50).

A string of other museums lines the southern bank of the Main River along the so-called **Museumsufer** (Museum Row). Pick of the crop is the **Städel Museum** at Schaumainkai 63, with a world-class collection of works by artists from the Renaissance to the 20th century, including Botticelli, Dürer, Van Eyck, Rubens, Rembrandt, Vermeer, Cézanne and Renoir, among many other greats. It costs DM8 (DM4 for students, free on Sunday and public holidays). Other interesting possibilities along the way include the **Deutsches Architekturmuseum** (German Architecture Museum), the **Deutsches Filmmuseum** and the **Bundespostmuseum** (Postal Museum).

Places to Stay

Camping The most recommended camping ground is *Heddernheim* (☎ 57 03 32; open all year) at An der Sandelmühle 35, in the Heddernheim district north-west of the city centre. It charges DM10 for a site and DM9 per person, and is a 15-minute ride on the U1, U2 or U3 from the Hauptwache U-Bahn station (one zone) – get off at the Heddernheim stop.

Hostels The *Haus der Jugend* (☎ 61 90 58; fax 61 82 57), on the south side of the Main River at Deutschherrnufer 12 (postcode for postal bookings: 60594 Frankfurt/Main), is within walking distance of the city centre and Sachsenhausen. It's big, bustling and fun. Rates (including breakfast) for beds in large dorms are DM23/28 for juniors/seniors, in four-person rooms DM33. Evening meals of several courses cost DM8.70. From Hauptbahnhof, take bus No 46 to Frankensteiner Platz; or from Hauptbahhof take S-Bahn lines

GERMANY

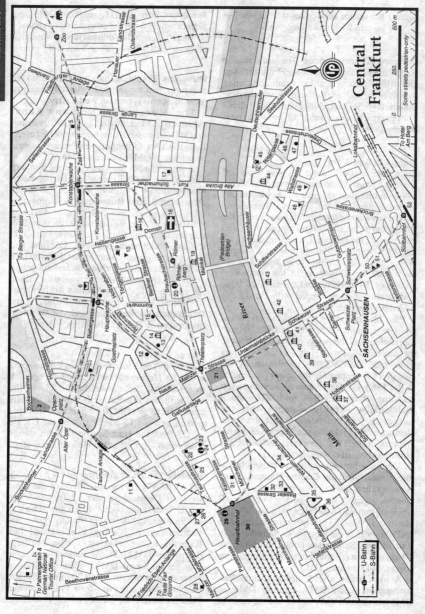

Central
Frankfurt

Some streets pedestrian-only

0   250   500 m

PLACES TO STAY			
1	Hotel-Pension Gölz & Pension Sattler	46	Lorsbacher Tal
		48	Café Satz
5	Hotel Zeil	49	Tagtraum
11	Hotel Atlas	50	Zum Gemalten Haus
17	Hotel-Pension Station	51	Wagner Adolf
22	Pension Schneider		
26	Hotel Carlton		**OTHER**
27	Hotel Adler	2	Alte Oper (Old Opera House)
28	Hotel Glockshuber		
31	Hotel Münchner Hof	3	Sinkkasten
32	Hotel Wiesbaden	4	Zoo
33	Hotel Teheran	6	Main Post Office
36	Pension Wal	7	Jazzkeller
45	Haus der Jugend (Youth Hostel)	8	Sussman's Presse & Buch
		12	American Express
	PLACES TO EAT	13	Thomas Cook
9	Café Mozart	14	Goethe-Haus
10	Kleinmarkthalle	15	Jazz-Kneipe
25	Royal Bombay Palace	16	Museum of Modern Art
34	Ginger Brasserie	18	Cathedral
		19	Historical Museum

20	Tourist Office		
21	Frankfurt Oper		
23	English Theater		
24	Tourismus + Congress		
29	Römer Tourist Office		
30	Main Train Station (Hauptbahnhof)		
35	ADM-Mitfahrzentrale		
37	Liebighaus (Museum of Ancient Sculpture)		
38	Städel Museum		
39	Postal Museum		
40	German Architecture Museum		
41	German Film Museum		
42	Museum of Ethology		
43	Museum of Applied Arts		
44	Icon Museum		
47	Wasch Center		
52	Southern Train Station (Südbahnhof)		

No 2, 3, 4, 5, or 6 to Lokalbahnhof. Check-in begins at 1 pm and it can get very crowded.

Hotels & Pensions In this city, 'cheap' can mean paying over DM100 for a spartan double room. During the many busy trade fairs even that price may turn out to be unrealistic, since most hotels and pensions jack up their prices – in some cases close to double the standard rate.

Predictably, most of Frankfurt's lower-budget accommodation is in the rather sleazy Bahnhofsviertel area surrounding the main train station. A typical though not unpleasant example is the *Hotel Teheran* (☎ 23 30 23) at Baseler Strasse 14, which has basic singles/doubles for DM60/80 and triples with shower and WC for DM150; the mark-up during fairs is only around 10%. The *Hotel Münchner Hof* (☎ 23 00 66) at Münchener Strasse 46 also has cheap singles/doubles from DM70/90 with hall shower. Almost opposite at No 43 is *Pension Schneider* (☎ 25 10 71), which has nicer rooms from DM70/130.

The *Hotel Adler* (☎ 23 34 55), on the 4th floor at Niddastrasse 65 just north of Hauptbahnhof (access via an arcade from Düsseldorfer Strasse), has passable rooms for DM70/105 (DM105/195 during fairs). A bit more up-market is *Hotel Carlton* (☎ 23 20 93), just around the corner at Karlstrasse 11, where rooms with television, telephone, shower and

WC cost DM100/180 (DM120/250 during trade fairs).

The most cheerful budget hotels in Bahnhofsviertel, however, are the *Wiesbaden* (☎ 23 23 47) at Baseler Strasse 52 (right of the station exit), and the *Glockshuber* (☎ 74 26 28), Mainzer Landstrasse 120, which both offer clean and bright rooms from around DM75/120.

Away from the sleaze but still within a convenient distance of the Hauptbahnhof is the modern *Hotel Atlas* (☎ 72 39 46), at Zimmerweg 1, with simple singles/doubles from DM65/90 (DM80/130 during fairs). A similar place closer to the centre is *Hotel-Pension Station* (☎ 28 78 77), at Hinter der Schönen Aussicht 16. Even more central is *Hotel Zeil* (☎ 28 36 38), at Zeil 12, where rooms with private toilet and shower cost DM80/120 (DM120/190 during fairs).

Sachsenhausen has disappointingly few budget places to stay, but the *Hotel Am Berg* (☎ 611 20 21), a lovely old sandstone building at Grethenweg 23 in the quiet backstreets a few minutes walk from Südbahnhof, charges DM60/115 (DM85/140 during fairs) for simple rooms without breakfast; it's clean, pleasant and friendly.

Quite a number of budget pensions lie tucked away in Frankfurt's inner northern suburbs. Close to the quieter Palmengarten area, along Beethovenstrasse at No 44 and No 46 respectively, are *Hotel-Pension Gölz* (☎ 74 67 35) and *Pension Sattler* (☎ 74 60 91). Their rooms start at around DM65/100, but at those prices they're almost continuously full. The *Pension Backer*, (☎ 74 79 92) at Mendelsohnstrasse 92 in Westend, offers rooms from DM50/80.

The friendly and clean *Pension Adria* (☎ 59 45 33), at Neuhausstrasse 21 in Nordend, has pleasant rooms overlooking garden lawns from DM65/110 (without breakfast). The *Hotel Uebe* (☎ 59 12 09), at Grünebrugweg 3 near the Botanical Gardens in Westend-Nord, offers simple singles for DM75 and doubles with private shower for DM105. In the interesting Bornheim district north-east of town is the *Pension Zur Rose* (☎ 45 17 62) at Berger Strasse 283. Basic rooms go for DM60/100 or DM120/140 with shower and bath.

Places to Eat

In Bahnhofsviertel, the eating options are decidedly 'ethnic', with predominantly Southern European, Middle Eastern and Asian eating houses. At the *Restaurant India House*, at Kaiserstrasse 54 (almost next door to the English Theater), a dahl and rice serving costs just DM8.90. For more convincing curry-and-coriander creations head for the nearby *Royal Bombay Palace* (☎ 2 33 93) at Taunusstrasse 17, which offers set four-course menus (vegetarian or meat) for DM30 per person. The pan-Asian *Ginger Brasserie* (☎ 23 17 71) at Windmühlstrasse 14 has everything Eastern on the menu – from Sichuan to sushi, Tandoori to Thai – with most main courses between DM18 and DM23.

Known to locals as Fressgasse (Munch-Alley), the Kalbächer Gasse and Grosse Bockenheimer Strasse area, between Opernplatz and Rathenauplatz, has many cheap restaurants and fast-food places with outdoor tables. For snacks and picnic supplies go to the *Kleinmarkthalle* off Hasengasse. It's an active little city market with displays of fruit, vegetables, meats, fish and hot food. The nearby *Café Mozart* at Töngesgasse 23 is popular for its cakes and coffee.

A Frankfurt eating and drinking tradition are the *apple-wine taverns*, which serve Ebbelwoi (Frankfurt dialect for Apfelwein), an alcoholic apple cider, along with local specialities like Handkäse mit Musik (literally, 'hand-cheese with music'). This is a round cheese first soaked in oil and vinegar with onions, then garnished with a 'green sauce' of yoghurt, mayonnaise, sour cream and herbs, before being served with potatoes and meat or eggs – Goethe's favourite food. The best Ebbelwoi taverns are in Alt Sachsenhausen – the area directly behind the DJH hostel – which is filled with eateries and pubs. Classics include the *Lorsbacher Tal*, Grosse Rittergasse 49, the *Wagner Adolf* at Schweizer Strasse 71, and *Zum Gemalten Haus*, a lively place full of paintings of old Frankfurt, nearby at Schweizer Strasse 67.

Sachsenhausen's *Tagtraum* (☎ 61 87 57; open daily) at Affentorplatz 20, features inspired salads as well as daily specials (consult the blackboard) that average DM15 per main course. Only a block away at Schifferstrasse 36 is the airy *Café Satz*, with vegetarian couscous (DM10.50) and chilli con carne (DM8.50) on offer. At the *Kebabhouse*, a cheap Turkish restaurant on the corner of Paradiesgasse and Kleine Rittergasse, a döner kebab with salad and tzatziki costs just DM6.

In the cosmopolitan Bornheim area north of the zoo, *Café Gegenwart* (☎ 4 97 05 44), at Berger Strasse 6, is a stylish bar/restaurant serving traditional German dishes from DM13; if the weather cooperates you can sit outside. The more way-out *Café Provisorisch* next door does particularly good breakfasts.

Over to the west in Bohemian Bockenheim, *Stattcafé* at Grempstrasse 21 offers vegetarian and meatier fare from around DM13. Near the university on the corner of Gräfstrasse and Bockenheimer Warte is the *Depot Café*, a popular student hang-out that serves great breakfasts. Another restaurant offering sound servings at student prices is *Pielok* (☎ 77 64 68), Jordanstrasse 3.

The Nordend area, east of Bockenheim, also attracts students and trendoids. For fare with flair, try *Grössenwahn* (☎ 59 93 56), Lenaustrasse 97, a lively pub where you can eat for under DM20.

Entertainment

Frankfurt is a true *Weltstadt* – an 'international city' – with an exhaustive amount of evening entertainment. Ballet, opera and theatre are strong points of Frankfurt's entertainment scene. For information and bookings, ring the

Oper Frankfurt on ☎ 21 23 60 61 (Untermain-anlage 11), or the Hertie concert and theatre-booking service on ☎ 29 48 48 (Zeil 90).

Frankfurt's jazz scene is second to none, and the top acts perform at the *Jazzkeller* (☎ 28 85 37), Kleine Bockenheimer Strasse 18a, and the *Jazz-Kneipe* (☎ 28 71 73) at Berliner Strasse 70. Leading reggae and rock bands can be seen (and heard) at *Sinkkasten* (☎ 28 03 85), just north of the city centre at Brönnerstrasse 5. A popular venue in Bornheim is *Mousonturm* (☎ 40 58 95 20), Waldschmidtstrasse 4, a converted soap factory that offers dance performances and politically oriented cabaret.

The *Turm-Palast* (☎ 28 17 87), at Am Eschenheimer Turm, is a large cinema that screens films in original English-language versions. The *English Theater* (☎ 24 23 16 20), at Kaiserstrasse 52, stages English-language plays and musicals, with performances every evening except Monday.

A popular gay bar is *Zum Schwejk* at Schäffergasse 20 (just off Zeil), while *Harvey's* (☎ 49 73 03), a restaurant on Friedberger Platz, is a favoured meeting place for Frankfurt's gay and lesbian yuppie types.

Things to Buy
There are no particular things you should buy in Frankfurt, though the shopping is excellent and it's an ideal place to satisfy any souvenir requirements before boarding the plane or train home. Frankfurt's main shopping street is Zeil, particularly the section between the Hauptwache and the Konstablerwache. It's reputed to do more business than any other shopping district in Europe, but is generally expensive. More interesting areas for shopping are Sachsenhausen's Schweizer Strasse and in Berger Strasse north-east of the city centre, where there are shops stocking all sorts of weird and wonderful stuff.

Getting There & Away
Air Flughafen Frankfurt/Main is Germany's largest airport, with the highest freight and second-highest passenger turnover in Europe. This high-tech town has two terminals linked by an elevated railway ('Sky Line'). Departure and arrival halls A, B and C are in the old Terminal 1, the western half of which handles Lufthansa flights; halls D and E are in the new

Terminal 2. Bus connections are currently on level 1 of Terminal 1, train connections are on level 0 (ground floor), and the S-Bahn is on level -1. A new airport railway station expected to open in 1999 will accommodate higher-speed InterCity trains.

The airport information number is ☎ 69 03 05 11.

Bus Long-distance buses leave from the southern side of Hauptbahnhof, where there's a Europabus office (☎ 23 07 35/6). It caters for most European destinations, but the most interesting possibility is the Romantic Road bus (see the Bavaria section). The Europabus head office is Deutsche Touring GmbH (☎ 7 90 30), Römerhof 17, 60486 Frankfurt.

Train The main train station handles more departures and arrivals than any other station in Germany (almost 1500 trains a day, with more than a quarter of a million travellers), so finding a train to or from almost anywhere is not a problem. The information office for train connections, tickets etc is at the head of platform No 9. For train information, call ☎ 1 94 19.

Car & Motorcycle Frankfurt features the famed Frankfurter Kreuz, the biggest autobahn intersection in the country. All main car rental companies have offices in the main hall of the Hauptbahnhof.

The ADM-Mitfahrzentrale (☎ 1 94 40) is on Baselerplatz, three minutes walk south of the train station. It's open Monday to Friday from 8 am to 6.30 pm, and Saturday till 2 pm. A sample of fares (including fees) is: Berlin DM54, Hamburg DM51 and Munich DM40. The Citynetz Mitfahr-Service (☎ 1 94 44), at Homburger Strasse 36, has slightly cheaper rates.

Getting Around
To/From the Airport The S-Bahn's S8 line runs at least every 15 minutes between the airport and Frankfurt Hauptbahnhof (takes 11 minutes), then continues via Hauptwache and Konstablerwache to Ostbahnhof; a standard fare of DM5.70 applies to/from all these stations. Bus No 61 runs to/from the Südbahnhof in Sachsenhausen. Taxis charge about DM40

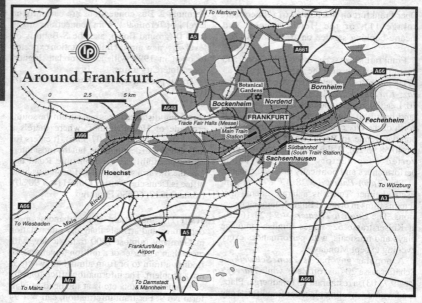

Around Frankfurt

for the trip into town but are slower than the train.

Public Transport Frankfurt's excellent transport network (RMV) integrates all bus, tram, S-Bahn and U-Bahn lines. The RMV has automatic ticket machines at every station and virtually every tram and bus stop (press the left-hand button for explanations in English). A zonal system applies – the core zone (press the *Preisstufe 3* button) covers the large central area of Frankfurt, but to get to or from the airport you'll need a two-zone (*Preisstufe 4*) ticket. Short trips (up to two km irrespective of zones) cost DM2.60, while a longer single trip costs DM3.30/5.70 for one/two zones. If you plan to do much city travelling, buy a 24-hour central-zone ticket for DM8.80 (DM5.30 for students) or a seven-day ticket for DM28.50 (students DM21.50); these tickets are also valid for the airport.

Car & Motorcycle Traffic flows smoothly in Frankfurt, but the extensive system of one-way

streets makes it extremely frustrating to get to where you want to go. You're better off parking your vehicle in one of the many (expensive) car parks and proceeding on foot.

Taxi Taxis are slow compared with public transport and quite expensive at DM3.80 flag fall plus a minimum of DM2.15 per km. There are taxi ranks throughout the city, or you can ring ☎ 23 00 01/33, ☎ 25 00 01 or ☎ 54 50 11 to book a cab.

MARBURG
Situated 90 km north of Frankfurt, Marburg is known for its charming Altstadt with the splendid **Elizabethkirche** and **Philipps-Universität**, Europe's first Protestant university (founded in 1527). Wander up to the museum in the **castle**, from where there are nice views of the old town.

Places to Stay & Eat
Marburg's *DJH hostel* (☎ 06421-2 34 61) is at Jahnstrasse 1, about 10 minutes walk upstream

along the river from Rudolfsplatz in the Altstadt. Rates for juniors/seniors are DM24/29. For other budget accommodation drop in at the tourist office (☎ 06421-20 12 62), directly right as you exit the train station; it has a free room-finding service. At the *Café Local*, Steinweg 1, you can fill up on student food priced from DM8.

North Rhine-Westphalia

North Rhine-Westphalia (Nordrhein-Westfalen) was formed in 1946 from a hotchpotch of principalities and bishoprics, most of which had belonged to Prussia since the early 19th century. A quarter of Germany's population lives here. The Rhine-Ruhr industrial area is the country's economic powerhouse and one of the most densely populated conurbations in the world. Though the area is dominated by bleak industrial cities connected by a maze of train lines and autobahns, some of the cities are steeped in history and their attractions warrant an extensive visit.

COLOGNE
Because of its location at a major crossroads of European trade routes, Cologne (Köln) was an important city even in Roman times. It was then known as Colonia Agrippinensis, the capital of the province of Germania, and had no fewer than 300,000 inhabitants. In later years it remained one of northern Europe's main cities (the largest in Germany until the 19th century), and it is still the centre of the German Roman Catholic church. Though almost completely destroyed in WWII, it was quickly rebuilt and many of its old churches and monuments have been meticulously restored.

It's worth making an effort to visit this city, if only for the famous cathedral, though there's much more to see.

Orientation
Situated on the Rhine River, the skyline of Cologne is dominated by the cathedral. The pedestrianised Hohe Strasse runs straight through the middle of the old town from north to south and is Cologne's main shopping street. The main train station is just north of the cathedral, within walking distance of almost everything. The main bus station is just behind the train station, on Breslauer Platz.

If you arrive by private transport, head for one of the many underground car parks in the city centre; a neat system of electronic signs indicates exactly how many parking spaces are left and where they are.

Information
Tourist Office The tourist office (☎ 2 21 33 45) is conveniently located opposite the cathedral's main entrance, at Unter Fettenhennen 19. In summer it's open Monday to Saturday from 8 am to 10.30 pm, Sunday and public holidays from 9 am; from November to April, opening hours are from 8 am to 9 pm Monday to Saturday and 9.30 am to 7 pm Sunday and public holidays. Browse through the chained guide booklets before deciding which one to buy. *Monatvorschau*, the monthly what's-on booklet, is a good investment at DM2. The room-finding service, at DM5, is a bargain when the city is busy with trade fairs, but you cannot book by telephone.

Money The bank at the train station is open from 7 am to 9 pm, seven days a week. American Express is at Burgmauer 14 and the Thomas Cook office is at Burgmauer 4, near the tourist office.

Post & Communications The main post office is just opposite the train station on An den Dominikanern. It's open weekdays from 7 am to 8 pm, Saturday 8 am to 6 pm and Sunday from 11 am to 6 pm.

Cologne's telephone code is ☎ 0221.

Bookshops Ludwig im Bahnhof, inside the main station, has newspapers and magazines from all over the world. For travel guides in English, try Kösel to the right of the cathedral. The Women's Cultural Centre at Moltkestrasse 66 has a bookshop with a great selection of feminist publications. It's open during regular shopping hours.

Laundry Öko-Express Waschsalon (Monday to Saturday 6 am to 11 pm) is on Weyerstrasse near Barbarossaplatz. Washing costs DM6 per load, 10 minutes of drying is DM1.

GERMANY

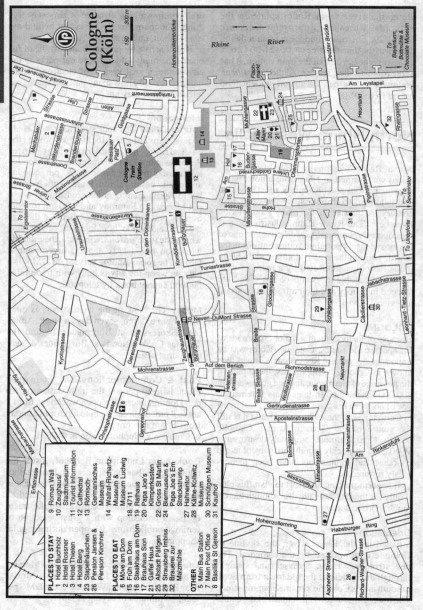

Cologne (Köln)

Rhine River

0   150   300 m

PLACES TO STAY
1 Hotel Buchholz
2 Hotel Rossner
3 Hotel Thielen
4 Hotel Berg
23 Stapelhäuschen
26 Pension Jansen &
   Pension Kirchner

PLACES TO EAT
6 Möve am Dom
15 Früh am Dom
16 Steakhaus am Dom
17 Brauhaus Sion
21 Gaffel Haus
25 Altstadt Päffgen
29 Strausberg Imbiss
32 Brauerei zur
   Malzmühle

OTHER
5 Main Post Office
8 Basilika St Gereon
9 Roman Wall
10 Zeughaus/
   Stadtmuseum
11 Tourist Information
12 Cathedral
13 Römisch-
   Germanisches
   Museum
14 Wallraf-Richartz-
   Museum &
   Museum Ludwig
18 4711
19 Rathaus
20 Papa Joe's
   Klimperkasten
22 Gross St Martin
24 Biermuseum &
   Papa Joe's Em
   Streckstrump
27 Hahnentor
28 Käthe-Kollwitz
   Museum
30 Schnütgen Museum
31 Kaufhof

Medical & Emergency Services The police are on ☎ 110; for fire and ambulance, ring ☎ 112. An on-call doctor can be contacted on ☎ 1 92 92.

Things to See
Cologne has one of the most extensive old town centres in the country, and the cathedral (Dom) is its heart, soul, and tourist draw. Combined with the excellent museums next door, plan to spend at least one full day inside and around the Dom.

Dom Head first to the south side of the Dom for an overall view. The structure's sheer size, with spires rising to a height of 157 metres, is overwhelming. Building began in 1248 in the French Gothic style. The huge project was stopped in 1560 but was started again in 1842, in the style originally planned, as a symbol of Prussia's drive for unification. It was finally finished in 1880. Strangely, it survived WWII's heavy night bombing intact, and acquires a gilt appearance when photographed.

The Dom is open daily from 7 am to 7 pm. Invest DM1 in the informative *Cologne Cathedral* booklet sold at the tourist office. When you reach the transept, you'll be overwhelmed by the sheer size and magnificence of it all. The five **stained-glass windows** along the north aisle depict the lives of the Virgin and St Peter. Behind the high altar, see the **Magi's Shrine** (circa 1150-1210), believed to contain the remains of the Three Wise Men, which was brought to Cologne from Milan in the 12th century. On the south side, in a chapel off the ambulatory, is the 15th-century **Adoration of the Magi altarpiece**. Guided tours in English are held Sunday to Friday at 2 pm, Saturday at 10.30 am and cost DM6, students DM4; meet inside the main portal. Tours in German are more frequent and cost DM4.

For a fitness fix, pay DM3 (students DM1.50; open to 5 pm, to 3.30 pm only from October to April) to climb 509 steps up the Dom's south tower to the base of the stupendous steeple, which towered over all of Europe until the Eiffel Tower was erected. Look at the 24-tonne **Peter Bell**, the largest working bell in the world, on your way up. At the end of your climb, the view from the vantage point, 98.25 metres up, is absolutely stunning: with clear weather you can see

all the way to the Siebengebirge mountains beyond Bonn. The cathedral **treasury**, just inside the north entrance, is pretty average. It is open April to October from 9 am to 5 pm Monday to Saturday (to 4 pm in winter), 1 to 4 pm Sunday; DM3. Cologne's archbishops are interred in the crypt.

Outside, on the cathedral forecourt, artists work on giant chalk reproductions of famous portraits in summer.

Other Churches Many other churches are worth a look, particularly Romanesque ones that have been restored since WWII bombing. The most handsome from the outside is **Gross St Martin**, while the best interior has to be that of **Basilika St Gereon** on Christophstrasse, with its incredible four-storey decagon (open 9 am to noon and 1 to 6 pm Monday to Saturday, Sunday 1.30 to 6 pm; enter from Gereonkloster). A DM2 churches guide is available at the tourist office.

Museums The **Römisch-Germanisches Museum**, next to the cathedral at Roncalliplatz 4, displays artefacts on all aspects of the Roman settlement and, on the 2nd floor, from the Rhine Valley. The highlights are the giant Poblicius grave monument and the *Dionysos mosaic*, around which the museum was built. Entry is DM5 and the museum is open daily (except Monday) to 4 pm.

The **Wallraf-Richartz-Museum & Museum Ludwig** at Bischofsgartenstrasse 1 (DM10, open daily except Monday to 6 pm) is one of the country's finest art galleries, making brilliant use of natural light. The 1st floor is devoted to the Cologne Masters of the 14th to 16th centuries, known for their distinctive use of colour. Further along, look for familiar names like Rubens, Rembrandt and Munch. On the 2nd floor, the contemporary art collection provides a wonderful contrast. Catch some prime Kirchner, Kandinsky and Max Ernst, as well as pop-art works by Rauschenberg and Andy Warhol. The building also houses a unique photography collection from the former Agfa Museum in Leverkusen.

At Cäcilienstrasse 29, the former church of St Cecilia houses the **Schnütgen Museum**, an overwhelming display of church riches, including many religious artefacts and early ivory carvings (DM5; open to 4 pm daily

GERMANY

except Monday). At the **Diözesanmuseum** on Roncalliplatz, admission is free to see the religious treasures (closed Thursday).

One museum is actually in a bank branch: the **Käthe Kollwitz Museum** at Neumarkt 18-24 (DM5; open to 8 pm Thursday, closed Monday). On display are some of the sculptures and stunning black-and-white graphics of the great socialist artist. The **Zeughaus** on Zeughausstrasse, restored as the **Stadtmuseum** (DM5; closed Monday), has a scale model showing old Cologne and a fine arms and armour collection.

In the **Chocolate Museum**, on the river in the Rheinauhafen near the Altstadt (open weekdays 10 am to 6 pm, weekends 11 am to 7 pm; DM10), you will learn everything about the history of making chocolate in a hands-on way – not just for those with a sweet tooth.

All museums offer a 50% discount for children, students and seniors.

Activities

Guided Tours The summer daily city tour in English lasts two hours and departs from the tourist office at 10 and 11 am and at 2 and 3 pm (from November to March at 11 am and 2 pm). The cost is a rather steep DM23.

The 'Cologne Bonbon', a tourist package costing DM26 and available at main hotels, is good value if you want to take a city tour and visit several museums. You can make day trips to nearby cities with KD River Cruises (see Getting There & Away later in this section). A trip down the Rhine to Bonn is DM17, to Koblenz DM57 one way.

Historical Walks You can give yourself a free tour of ancient and medieval Cologne by walking around its restored monuments with a free city-sights map from the tourist office. Starting from the cathedral's main door, you will see the remains of the arch of a Roman gate from the ancient north wall. If you walk west along Komödienstrasse over Tunisstrasse, you reach the Zeughaus museum, the Burgmauer side of which was built along the line of the **Roman wall**. On the pavement at the west end is a plaque tracing the Roman wall line on a modern street plan, which you can pencil on your map (other plaques appear around the city near Roman sites). Continue

west until you find a complete section of the north wall, which leads to a corner tower standing among buildings on the street corner at St-Apern-Strasse. Walk south one block and you come to another tower ruin near Helenenstrasse.

On the south wall of the Römisch-Germanisches Museum are the remains of the **Roman harbour street** that led to the Rhine bank and two **Roman wells**. You can also take a lift down and walk through the **Roman sewer** and see the remains of the palace of the Praetorium under the medieval town hall (entry on Kleine Budengasse; closed Monday). The **Rathaus** itself is open from 7.30 am weekdays (to noon only on Friday); the façades, foyer and tower have been restored.

The city's medieval towers and gates complement its Romanesque churches. The Bayenturm on the Rhine bank at the east end of Severinswall is completely rebuilt, but along the street to the west the vine-bedecked Bottmühle and the mighty main south gate of Severinstor have more of the original basalt and tuff stones. To the north-west along Sachsenring is the vaulted Ulrepforte towergate and a section of wall with two more towers. North of the city centre is the gate of Eigelsteintor on Eigelstein, suspended from which is a boat from the MS *Schiff Cöln*, which sank off Heligoland in 1914. The main west gate, Hahnentor, is at Rudolfplatz.

Special Events

Try to visit Cologne during the wild and crazy period of the Cologne Carnival (Karneval), rivalled only by Munich's Oktoberfest. People dress in creative costumes, clown suits, as popular personalities, and whatever else their alcohol-numbed brains may invent. The streets explode with activity on the Thursday before the seventh Sunday before Easter. On Friday and Saturday evening the streets pep up, Sunday is like Thursday and on Monday *(Rosenmontag)* there are formal and informal parades, and much spontaneous singing and celebrating.

Places to Stay

Cheap accommodation in Cologne is not plentiful, but there are some good pensions around the city, and you should be able to get private rooms unless there's a trade fair. Reasonably central hotel rooms are available for about DM60/90 a single/double.

Camping The most (though not very) convenient camping grounds are the municipal *Campingplatz der Stadt Köln* (☎ 83 19 66; open from May to at least the end of September) on Weidenweg in Poll, five km south-east of the city centre; and *Campingplatz Waldbad* (☎ 60 33 15), on Peter-Baum-Weg in Dünnwald, about 10 km from the city centre but open all year.

Hostels Cologne has two DJH hostels. The first, *Jugendherberge Köln-Deutz* (☎ 81 47 11), is at Siegesstrasse 5a in Deutz, a 15-minute walk east from Hauptbahnhof over the Hohenzollernbrücke or three minutes from Bahnhof Köln-Deutz. The cost for juniors/seniors is DM27/32.50, but the hostel is crowded and not really very pleasant. The *Jugendgästehaus Köln-Riehl* (☎ 76 70 81) is north of the city in Riehl, by the river at An der Schanz 14. It's much more enjoyable and the cost is a flat DM30.50. Take the U5 or U16 to Boltensternstrasse.

Hotels Hotels in Cologne are expensive and prices increase by at least 20% when fairs are on. The cheapest rooms are usually taken, so count on paying DM10 to DM15 above the prices quoted here. If you have private transport, enquire about parking – a night in a car park will set you back DM25 or more (and not all of them operate 24 hours). The tourist office room-finding service can help you with hotel rooms in the lower price range.

Excellent budget bets are the two pensions at Richard-Wagner-Strasse 18, *Pension Jansen* (☎ 25 18 75), with a few singles from DM35 to DM70 and doubles from DM80 to DM120, and *Pension Kirchner* (☎ 25 29 77), with similar singles and doubles starting at DM45/80. *Das Kleine Stapelhäuschen* (☎ 2 57 78 62), at Fischmarkt 1-3 in the middle of the Altstadt, has pleasant singles/doubles from DM48/120, but you'd be lucky to get in at those prices. Further south, you can try the church-operated *Gästehaus St Georg* (☎ 9 37 02 00) at Rolandstrasse 61, where rooms without private shower cost DM58/96, with DM80/140.

In the area north of the train and bus stations, try *Hotel Rossner* (☎ 12 27 03), Jakordenstrasse 19, with rooms from DM55/ 80. *Hotel Berg* (☎ 12 11 24), Brandenburger Strasse 6, has rooms from DM52/90. *Hotel Brandenburger Hof* (☎ 12 28 89) at Brandenburger Strasse 2 and *Hotel Thielen* (☎ 12 33 33) at No 1 have rooms from DM55/75 but fill up quickly. All the cheap rooms have toilet and shower facilities out in the corridor. *Hotel Buchholz* (☎ 12 18 24) at Kunibertsgasse 5 has a few singles from DM55, doubles from DM130.

Places to Eat & Drink

Italian restaurants are generally Cologne's best value, as long as you stick to pizza and pasta, and most pubs serve decent meals for well under DM20. Cologne's beer halls serve cheap and filling (though often bland) meals to go with their home brew (see Beer Halls for details).

Brauhaus Sion at Unter Taschenmacher 9 is a big beer hall, packed most nights and for good reason: you'll eat your fill for well under DM20, including a couple of beers. *Brauerei zur Malzmühle*, at Heumarkt 6 off Am Malzbüchel south of the Deutzer Brücke feeder roads, is smaller but similar. Slightly more up-market and much more of a cosy pub, *Altstadt Päffgen* at Heumarkt 62 (the north or Salzgasse end) serves meals for about DM20. Another *Päffgen* is at Friesenstrasse 64-66, and *Gaffel Haus*, Alter Markt 20-22, is similar.

A bustling stand-up snack bar is *Strausberg* at Schildergasse 92 where you can get good, hot, fast food for DM10 or less. For good DM7 breakfasts (or wurst-and-salad lunches) near the train station, squeeze into *Möve am Dom* at Marzellenstrasse 11. *Kaufhof*, towards the south end of Hohe Strasse, has a self-service restaurant on the 3rd floor with low-budget breakfasts. *Steakhaus am Dom* at Am Hof 48 (closed Tuesday) has splurge main courses from DM18, but salads are included.

To put together a picnic, visit a *market*; the biggest is on Tuesday and Friday at Aposteln-Kloster Strasse near Neumarkt. For hot DM15 vegetarian dishes and Indian curries, seek out *Bombay Palace* on the corner of Am Weidenbach and Am Pantaleonsberg (closed on Monday).

Entertainment

Evenings and weekends in the Altstadt are like miniature carnivals, with bustling crowds and lots to do. The beverage of choice is beer, and there are plenty of places to enjoy it.

For excellent jazz, head for either *Papa Joe's Klimperkasten* at Alter Markt 50, or *Papa Joe's Em Streckstrump* at Buttermarkt 37. The first is large and lively, with a wonderful old pianola, whereas the second is more intimate.

The gay scene centres on the Belgisches Viertel around Bismarckstrasse, west of Altstadt just beyond Kaiser-Wilhelm-Ring.

Cologne's usual venue for rock concerts is *E-Werk*, a converted power station at Schanzenstrasse 28-36 in Mülheim. It turns into a huge techno disco on Friday and Saturday nights (information at ☎ 96 27 90).

For theatre programme information, ring ☎ 1 15 17; for concerts, exhibitions, special events, trade fairs etc, call ☎ 1 15 16. *Monatvorschau* (see Information) has full events listings, and Köln Ticket (☎ 28 01), at Roncalliplatz next to the Römisch-Germanisches Museum, has tickets and information (open Saturday to 2 pm).

Beer Halls Much as in Munich, beer reigns supreme in Cologne. There are more than 20 local breweries, all producing a variety called *Kölsch*, relatively light and slightly bitter. The breweries run their own beer halls and serve their wares in skinny glasses holding a mere 200 ml, but you'll soon agree it's a very satisfying way to drink the stuff. See Places to Eat & Drink or try *Früh am Dom* at Am Hof 12-14. For more of a choice in beers, the *Biermuseum* at Buttermarkt 39 (beside Papa Joe's) serves 39 varieties. Another favourite among connoisseurs is *Küppers Brauerei* at Alteburger Strasse 157 in Bayenthal south of the city (U-Bahn: Bayenthalgürtel). It has an interesting museum (open from 11 am to 4 pm Saturday only).

Things to Buy

A good Cologne souvenir might be a small bottle of *eau de Cologne*, which is still produced in its namesake city. The most famous brand is called 4711, after the house number where it was invented. There's still a perfumery and gift shop by that name at the corner of Glockengasse and Schwertnergasse. Try to catch the Glockenspiel, with characters from Prussian lore parading above the store, hourly from 9 am to 9 pm.

Getting There & Away

Air Cologne/Bonn airport has many connections within Europe and to the rest of the world. For flight information, ring ☎ 02203-40 40 01/2. The Lufthansa office (☎ 92 54 990), together with a general travel agency, is at Am Hof 30.

Bus Deutsche Touring's Eurolines buses have overnight one-way tickets to Paris for DM75 (return DM133) and the journey lasts seven hours. The office is at the train station at the Breslauer Platz exit.

Train S-Bahn as well as main-line trains service Bonn (DM8.20) and Düsseldorf (DM11.60). Most trips to/from Aachen (hourly; DM18.40) take about one hour (via Düren is more direct). Other direct links are to Hanover (about three hours minimum), Dresden (three times daily, 8½ hours), Leipzig (six times daily, 6½ hours), Berlin (nine times daily, 7½ hours) and Frankfurt (regular trains, 2¼ hours).

Car & Motorcycle The city is on a main north-south autobahn route and is thus easy for drivers and hitchhikers. The ADM Mitfahrzentrale (☎ 1 94 40) is at Triererstrasse 47 near Barbarossaplatz, and Citynetz Mitfahr-Service (☎ 1 94 44) is at Saarstrasse 22.

Boat An enjoyable way to travel to/from Cologne is by boat. KD River Cruises (for information ☎ 2 08 83 18), which has its headquarters in the city at Frankenwerft 15, has services all along the Rhine.

Getting Around

To/From the Airport Bus No 170 runs between Cologne/Bonn airport and the main bus station every 15 minutes (DM8.20 for the 20-minute trip).

Public Transport Cologne offers a convenient and extensive mix of buses, trams and local trains – trams go underground in the inner city, and trains handle destinations up to 50 km around Cologne. Ticketing and tariff structures are complicated. The best ticket option is the one-day pass for DM10.50 if you're staying near the city (one or two zones), DM15.50 for most of the Cologne area (three zones), and DM22 including Bonn (eight zones), all valid for up to five persons travelling together. Single city trips cost DM2 and 90-minute two-zone tickets are DM3.20.

Taxi Taxis cost DM3.20 flag fall plus DM2.15 per km (DM0.20 more at night); add another DM1 if you order by phone (☎ 28 82). There are taxi ranks on the city's larger squares.

DÜSSELDORF

More than 80% of Düsseldorf's Altstadt was destroyed in WWII, but it was reconstructed to become one of the most elegant and wealthy cities in all of Germany. Though not particularly strong in historical sights, this capital of North Rhine-Westphalia is an important centre for fashion and commerce and a charming example of big-city living along the Rhine River.

Information

The main tourist office (☎ 17 20 20) is opposite the main exit of the train station towards the north end of Konrad-Adenauer-Platz. It's open 8.30 am to 6 pm weekdays, 9 am to 12.30 pm on Saturday. The main post office, open daily, is right across the street. The bank in the train station's main hall is open to 9 pm daily.

Düsseldorf's telephone code is ☎ 0211.

Things to See & Do

The tourist office runs a two-hour bus/walking city tour for DM25 daily at 11 am and 2.30 pm, April to October; in winter only at 11 am plus at 2.30 pm on Saturday.

To catch a glimpse of Düsseldorf's elegant lifestyle, head for the famed Königsallee, or 'Kö', with its stylish (and pricey) boutiques and arcades. Stroll north along the Kö to the **Hofgarten**, a large park in the city centre.

The city has several interesting museums, particularly art museums. These include the **Kunstmuseum Düsseldorf** at Ehrenhof north of the Oberkasseler Brücke (DM5, discount DM2.50; closed Monday), with a comprehensive European collection, and the

incorporated **Glasmuseum Hentrich**. The **Kunstsammlung Nordrhein-Westfalen** at Grabbeplatz No 5 (DM12, discount DM8, closed Monday) has a huge modern art collection. Across the street, the **Kunsthalle** features changing exhibits (prices vary, closed Monday).

The **Goethe-Museum Düsseldorf** in Schloss Jägerhof, Jacobistrasse 2, pays tribute to the life and work of one of Europe's great men of letters. The large collection includes books, first drafts, letters, medals and much more (DM4, discount DM 2; closed Monday and Saturday morning). German-literature buffs will also want to visit the **Heinrich-Heine-Institut** at Bilker Strasse 12-14, which documents the Düsseldorfer's career (DM4, discount DM2; closed Monday and Saturday morning), or his house at Bolkerstrasse 53, now a literary pub.

On Marktplatz, the restored **Rathaus** town hall looks out onto the **statue of Prince Elector Johann Wilhelm**, known in local speech as 'Jan Wellem'. He lies buried in the ornate early-baroque **St Andreas Kirche** at the corner of Kay-und-Lore-Lorentz-Platz and Andreasstrasse, now in the care of a Dominican monastery. Another church worth visiting is the 13th-century **St Lambertus Basilika** on Stiftsplatz. Nearby, the reconstructed **Schlossturm** of the long-destroyed Residenz stands on Burgplatz as a forlorn reminder of the Palatine elector's glory. In summer, the town's youth congregate on the steps below the tower. From here the just completed pedestrian-only **Rheinuferpromenade** invites strolling along the river.

For a terrific bird's-eye view of the city, head up to the viewing platform of the **Rheinturm** (DM5). **Schloss Benrath**, a late-baroque pleasure palace with park, makes for a lovely excursion. Take tram No 701 from Jan-Wellem-Platz.

Places to Stay

There are two camping grounds close to the city. *Campingplatz Nord Unterbacher See* (☎ 8 99 20 38; open 1 April to 30 September) is at Kleiner Torfbruch in Düsseldorf-Unterbach (S-Bahn No 7 to Düsseldorf-Eller, then bus No 735 to Kleiner Torfbruch). A second camping ground on the southern lake shore does not accept tourists. *Camping*

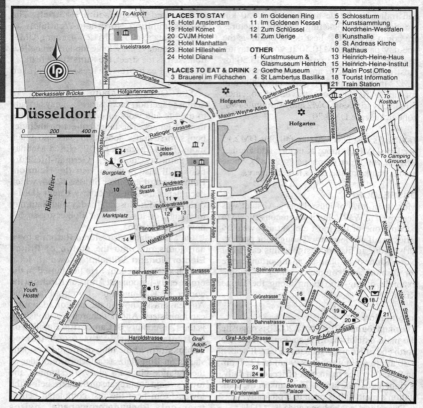

Düsseldorf

PLACES TO STAY
16 Hotel Amsterdam
19 Hotel Komet
20 CVJM Hotel
22 Hotel Manhattan
23 Hotel Hillesheim
24 Hotel Diana

PLACES TO EAT & DRINK
3 Brauerei im Füchschen

6 Im Goldenen Ring
11 Im Goldenen Kessel
12 Zum Schlüssel
14 Zum Uerige

OTHER
1 Kunstmuseum &
   Glasmuseum Hentrich
2 Goethe Museum
4 St Lambertus Basilika

5 Schlossturm
7 Kunstsammlung
   Nordrhein-Westfalen
8 Kunsthalle
9 St Andreas Kirche
10 Rathaus
13 Heinrich-Heine-Haus
15 Heinrich-Heine-Institut
17 Main Post Office
18 Tourist Information
21 Train Station

Oberlörick (☎ 59 14 01; open mid-April to mid-September) is at Lutticherstrasse beside the Rhine in Düsseldorf-Lörick (U-Bahn Nos 70, 76, 74 or 77 to Belsenplatz, and then bus Nos 828 or 838). The trek to the Altstadt is very inconvenient from either camping ground.

The *Jugendgästehaus* (☎ 55 73 10) is located at Düsseldorfer Strasse 1 in posh Oberkassel across the Rhine from the Altstadt. DM32.50 buys bed and breakfast in 3-6 person rooms. A few singles (DM39.50) and doubles (DM36.50 per person) are available. Take U-Bahn Nos 70, 74, 75, 76, or 77 from the main train station to Luegplatz. From there it's a short walk.

Rooms at *Hotel Manhattan* (☎ 37 02 44) at Graf-Adolf-Strasse 39 start at DM50/90. *Hotel Komet* (☎ 17 87 90) at Bismarckstrasse 93 has rooms from DM50/85.

The YMCA's *CVJM-Hotel* (☎ 17 28 50) is at Graf-Adolf-Strasse 102; basic singles/doubles start at DM65/111. Another option is *Hotel Amsterdam* (☎ 8 40 58) at Stresemannstrasse 20, which has rooms with private shower from DM70/130. On Jahnstrasse, *Hotel Diana* (☎ 37 50 71) at No 31 and *Hotel Hillesheim* (☎ 37 19 40) at No 19 have rooms with private bath from DM70/90, without from around DM55/80.

Keep in mind that Düsseldorf frequently

hosts trade shows, and prices are usually higher then. However, many of the comfortable business hotels offer steep discounts on weekends and when no fair is in town. The tourism office can tell you whether such bargains are offered during your stay.

Places to Eat

One of the best places for a hearty German meal with atmosphere to boot is *Brauerei im Füchschen*, one of four pub/restaurants on Ratinger Strasse popular with students. *Zum Schlüssel* on Bolkerstrasse, mentioned in Entertainment below for its beer, also has great food; there are daily specials for DM11 to DM15. Also on Bolkerstrasse, at No 44, is *Im Goldenen Kessel*, serving similar food to Zum Schlüssel. Another street worth taking a look down is Liefergasse, which is lined with drinking and eating places.

Popular with locals too is the *Im Goldenen Ring* on Burgplatz 21-22 where many hearty main dishes go for under DM20. Vegetarians, or those craving a little variety, have to head away from the city centre to Ratingen (S-Bahn Nos 701 or 711), home to the very popular, if somewhat pricey, *Kostbar* on Lintorferstrasse 14.

Entertainment

Besides walking and museum-hopping, one of the best things to do in Düsseldorf is (surprise!) drink beer. There are lots of bars (for drinking and eating) in the Altstadt, affectionately referred to as the 'longest bar in the world'. On evenings and weekends, the best places overflow onto the pedestrian-only streets. Favoured streets include Bolkerstrasse, Kurze Strasse, Andreasstrasse and the surrounding side streets.

The beverage of choice is Alt beer, a dark and semisweet brew typical of Düsseldorf. Try Gatzweilers Alt in *Zum Schlüssel* at Bolkerstrasse 43-47, and check the sign that says that schnapps is bad for 'your health and our business'. Even more local in colour is the spartan *Zum Uerige* on Berger Strasse, the only place where you can buy Uerige Alt beer. It charges DM2.40 per quarter-litre glass, and the beer flows so quickly that the waiters just carry around trays and give you a glass when you're ready.

Getting There & Away

Düsseldorf's Lohausen airport (S-Bahn trains run every 20 minutes between the airport and main train station) is busy with many national and international flights. It's one of the most unpleasant and ill-run airports in Europe and it can only be hoped that the April 1996 fire there, which claimed numerous victims, will cause this situation to change. Düsseldorf is part of a dense S-Bahn network in the Rhine-Ruhr region and regular services run to Cologne and Aachen as well; rail passes are valid on these lines. Regular main-line trains also run to/from Frankfurt and most other major German cities.

Getting Around

As Düsseldorf is very spread out, it's easiest to get around by public transport. However, the extensive network of U-Bahn and S-Bahn trains, trams and buses can be confusing. It is divided into zones, and prices vary depending on how many zones you travel through. Single tickets start at DM1.90 for one zone and go up to DM11.40 for multiple zones. Better value are four-trip tickets which sell for DM5.40 to DM33.60. For unlimited travel within one day, get a TagesTicket, which is good for up to five persons travelling together and costs from DM9.50 to DM25.50. First-class carriages on local trains cost an extra DM2.40 per person. It is best to buy tickets from the orange machines at stops, though bus drivers sell them also. All tickets must be validated before boarding.

BONN

This friendly, relaxed city of 310,000 on the Rhine south of Cologne became West Germany's temporary capital in 1949. Since reunification, it threatens to sink into obscurity once more as the all-German parliament and government ministries shift back to Berlin.

Settled in Roman times, Bonn celebrated its 2000th anniversary in 1989. In the 18th century, it was the seat of the electors of Cologne, and some of their baroque architecture survived the ravages of WWII and the postwar demand for modern government buildings. Organise a day trip out here and to nearby Bad Godesberg, the spa town that forms one city with Bonn and houses most of its diplomats. Classical music buffs can pay homage to Bonn's most famous son, Ludwig van Beethoven.

Information

The tourist office (☎ 77 34 66) is in an arcade called Cassius Bastei at Münsterstrasse 20. Look carefully, because it's not well signposted. It's open from 9 am to 6.30 pm Monday to Friday, to 5 pm on Saturday, and 10 am to 2 pm on Sunday. The office operates a DM3 room-finding service (DM5 for rooms over DM100). The DM12 BonnCard (DM24 for families) entitles you to unlimited travel after 9 am and admission to most main museums for a day.

The bank in the train station operates weekdays from 9 am to 1 pm and 1.30 to 6 pm, Saturday from 8 am to noon and 12.30 to 3 pm. The main post office is on Münsterplatz.

The telephone code for Bonn and Bad Godesberg is ☎ 0228.

Foreign Embassies As long as the German foreign ministry remains in Bonn, most of the foreign embassies will remain too. See the Facts for the Visitor section at the beginning of this chapter for a list.

Things to See & Do

A combined walking/bus city tour (April to October, Monday to Saturday at 2 pm, Sunday at 10.30 am; November to March, Saturday at 2 pm) costs DM18. Themed walking tours cost around DM10.

The recently renovated **Beethoven-Haus** at Bonngasse 20 is open Monday to Saturday from 10 am to 5 pm (to 4 pm in winter), Sunday 11 am to 4 pm (closed in winter); DM8, discount DM4. The composer was born here in 1770 and the house contains much memorabilia concerning his life and music, including his last piano, specially made with an amplified sounding board to accommodate his deafness. The ear trumpets will make you wonder what kind of music he could have created with good hearing. The Beethoven Festival is held every two to three years (the next will be in September 1997) and his music is performed at the **Beethovenhalle** on Fritz-Schroeder-Ufer by the Rhine and occasionally in the concert hall next to his house.

The **Frauenmuseum** at Im Krausfeld 10 promotes and exhibits art created by women in an environment that combines history, mythology and contemporary artistic expressions. Concerts, readings, lectures and theatre performances by women artists also take place. Admission is DM6 (students DM3); opening hours are Tuesday to Saturday 2 to 5 pm, Sunday 11 am to 5 pm. Take tram No 61 to Rosenthal.

Sts Cassius and Florentius, two martyred Roman officers who became the patron saints of Bonn, are honoured in the **Münsterbasilika** on Münsterplatz. It's one of the best examples of the unique Rhenish style of architecture in the transition from Romanesque to Gothic. The interior is mainly baroque.

The **Bundeshaus** complex, south-east of the city centre at Göresstrasse 15, incorporates the new steel and glass Plenary Hall, the meeting place for Germany's Lower House (Bundestag) since 1992. It stands right next to the Bauhaus structure where the country's first parliament convened in 1949. Free guided tours (in German) provide insights into the German political system.

The **Haus der Geschichte der Bundesrepublik Deutschland**, Adenauerallee 250, covers the history of Germany from 1945 (open 9 am to 7 pm, closed Monday, free entry; U-Bahn: Heussallee). It is part of the **Museumsmeile**, a row of four museums that also includes the Museum Alexander Koenig, a natural history museum; the Kunstmuseum with its collection of 20th-century art; and changing exhibitions at the Kunst-und-Ausstellungshalle der Bundesrepublik Deutschland.

Places to Stay

The *Jugendgästehaus Venusberg* (☎ 28 99 70), Haager Weg 42, is inconvenient, large and loud, but beautifully located in the woods on Venusberg south of the city. A bunk costs DM30.50 including breakfast, and meals are available. Take bus No 621.

For the ultimate in German hostel elegance, head for the 90-bed *Jugendgästehaus Bad Godesberg* (☎ 31 75 16) in Bad Godesberg at Horionstrasse 60. It costs DM32.50 including breakfast. Take bus No 615 from this pretty town's train station to the 'Jugendgästehaus' stop. At both hostels, couples may be able to grab one of the rooms reserved for group leaders.

Bonn's hotels are not as pricey as you'd expect – DM65/95 should get you a single/double within easy walking distance of the city centre. Right in the city centre, just off Markt on Kasernenstrasse, are *Hotel Bergmann*

(☎ 63 38 91) at No 13 with rooms for DM55/90 and *Deutsches Haus* (☎ 63 37 77) at No 19-21 where rates start at DM65/100. Or try *Hotel Kurfürstenhof* (☎ 98 50 50) on Baum-schulallee 20 near the train station, where rooms (including private bath and good break-fast) start from DM63/98. Hotel prices in Bad Godesberg are even lower.

Places to Eat

Many traditional pubs in Bonn serve decent food at decent prices. *Zum Gequetschen* at Sternstrasse 78, on the corner of Kasernen-strasse, is a cosy, Cologne-style beer establishment with main courses under DM20. Next to Beethovenhaus, at Bonngasse 30, is the historic *Im Stiefel*, with a hearty lunch menu between DM10 and DM15. Snack bars aren't hard to find, and there's a colourful *food market* on Markt in front of the Rathaus from 8 am to 6.30 pm Monday to Friday, to 2 pm Saturday. In summer, you can also grab a sand-wich and join the throngs of students lounging in the Hofgarten near the university.

Getting There & Away

Bonn makes for a pleasant day trip from Cologne or Düsseldorf, and it can even be seen by just jumping off the train for a few hours on your way through. There are some 70 trains a day to/from Cologne in the north and Koblenz in the south. KD River Cruises (☎ 63 21 34 for the Bonn office at Brassertufer) also runs its Rhine cruises through Bonn.

Getting Around

Many of Bonn's sights are an easy walk from the station. The Bonn transit system is linked with Cologne's and a one-way train ride between the two cities costs only DM8.20 (see the Cologne Getting Around section for passes covering both). A day pass for Bonn only costs DM10.50 (valid for up to five people travelling together). There's a public transit information office in the basement of the station, open Monday to Friday 7 am to 7.30 pm, Saturday 8 am to 4 pm.

AACHEN

Aachen was already known in Roman times for its thermal springs. The great Frankish con-queror Charlemagne was so impressed by their revitalising qualities that he settled here and made it the capital of his kingdom in 794 AD. Ever since, Aachen has held special signifi-cance among the icons of German nationhood. It is now an industrial and commercial city of 260,000 and home to the country's largest tech-nical university.

Orientation

Aachen's compact old centre is contained within two ring roads that roughly follow the old city walls. The inner ring road, or Graben-ring, has different names, most ending in 'graben', and encloses the old city proper. The main train station is south-east of the town centre, just beyond the outer ring road called Alleenring.

Information

The helpful tourist office (☎ 1 80 29 60/1) is at Atrium Elisenbrunnen, just inside the Graben-ring east of the cathedral. The bank across from the tourist office at Friedrich-Wilhelm-Platz 1-4 has exchange facilities. It is open Monday to Wednesday 8.30 am to 4.30 pm, Thursday to 5.30 pm, Friday to 4 pm. The main post office is at Kapuzinergraben 19. The bus station is at the north-eastern edge of the Grabenring on the corner of Kurhausstrasse and Peterstrasse.

Aachen's telephone code is ☎ 0241.

Things to See & Do

Cathedral Aachen's drawing card is its cathe-dral (Dom, Kaiserdom or Münster), open daily from 7 am to 7 pm. Though not very grand, the cathedral's historical significance and interior serenity make a visit almost obligatory – it's on UNESCO's world cultural heritage list. No fewer than 30 Holy Roman emperors were crowned here from 936 to 1531.

The heart of the cathedral is formed by a Byzantine-inspired **octagon**, built on Roman foundations, which was the largest vaulted structure north of the Alps when consecrated as Charlemagne's court chapel in 805. He lies buried here, and it became a site of pilgrimage after his death, not least for its religious relics. The Gothic **choir** was added in 1414; its massive stained-glass windows are impressive even though some date from after WWII. The octagon received its **folded dome** after the city fire of 1656 destroyed the original tent roof.

GERMANY

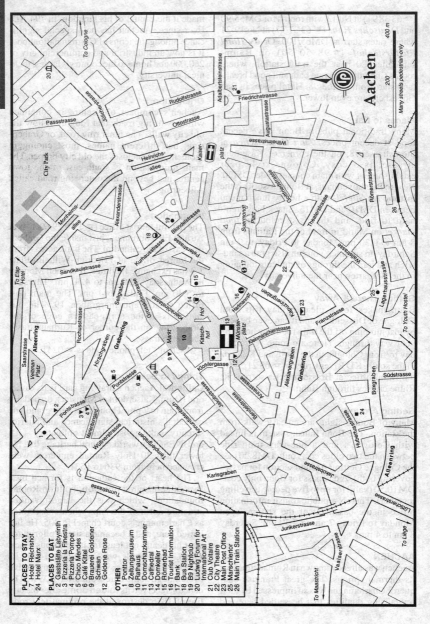

Aachen

Many streets pedestrian-only

0   200   400 m

To Cologne

To Etap Hotel

To Maastricht

To Liège

To Youth Hostel

Passstrasse

Jülicherstrasse

Rudolfstrasse

Ottostrasse

Adalbertsteinstrasse

Friedrichstrasse

Augustastrasse

Wilhelmstrasse

Heinrichs-
allee

Kaiser-
platz

Römerstrasse

Theaterstrasse

Suermondt
Platz

City Park

Monheims-
allee

Alexanderstrasse

Blondelstrasse

Peterstrasse

Kurhausstrasse

Sandkaulstrasse

Seilgraben

Grabenring

Hirschgraben

Rochusstrasse

Saarstrasse

Alleenring

Veltman
Platz

Pontstrasse

Pontstrasse

Wüllnerstrasse

Marienbongard

Annuntiatenbach

Templegraben

Turmstrasse

Karlsgraben

Markt

Katsch-
hof

Kleinkölnstrasse

Grossköln-

Münster-
platz

Klostergasse

Hartmannstr

Hühnermarkt

Annastrasse

Kleinmarschierstrasse

Jakobstrasse

Pontdriesch

Kapuzinergraben

Franzstrasse

Lagerhausstrasse

Südstrasse

Alexianergraben

Grabenring

Boxgraben

Hubertusstrasse

Bendelstrasse

Kockerellstrasse

Karlsgraben

Junkerstrasse

Lütticherstrasse

Vaalserstrasse

Wallstrasse

Gottfriedstrasse

PLACES TO STAY
7   Hotel Reichshof
24 Hotel Marx

PLACES TO EAT
2   Gaststätte Labyrinth
3   Pizzeria la Finestra
4   Pizzeria Pompei
5   Chico Mendes
6   Café Kittel
9   Brauerei Goldener
    Schwan
12 Goldene Rose

OTHER
1   Pontor
8   Zeitungsmuseum
10 Rathaus
11 Domschatzkammer
13 Cathedral
14 Römerbad
15 Tourist Information
16 Bank
17 Bus Station
18 Bank
19 B9 Nightclub
20 Ludwig Forum for
    International Art
21 Club Voltaire
22 City Theatre
23 Main Post Office
25 Marschiertor
26 Main Train Station

The **western tower** dates from the 19th century.

Worth noting is the huge brass **chandelier**, which was added to the octagon by Emperor Friedrich Barbarossa in 1165; the **high altar** with its 11th-century gold-plated Pala d'Oro frontal depicting scenes of the Passion; and the gilded copper ambo, or **pulpit**, donated by Henry II. Unless you join a German-language tour (DM3), you'll only catch a glimpse of Charlemagne's white-marble **throne** on the upper gallery of the octagon, where the nobles sat.

The entrance to the **Domschatzkammer** (cathedral treasury), with one of the richest collections of religious art north of the Alps, is on nearby Klostergasse (open Monday 10 am to 1 pm, Tuesday to Sunday 10 am to 6.30 pm, Thursday to 9 pm; DM5, discount DM3, includes pamphlet).

Other Sights North of the cathedral, the 14th-century **Rathaus** overlooks Markt, a lively gathering place in summer, with its fountain statue of Charlemagne. The eastern tower of the Rathaus, the Granusturm, was once part of Charlemagne's palace. The Rathaus is open daily from 10 am to 1 pm and 2 to 5 pm, and admission is DM3, discount DM1.50. History buffs will be thrilled to stand in the grand Empire Hall upstairs, where Holy Roman emperors enjoyed their coronation feasts.

There are several museums worth visiting, most notably the **Ludwig Forum for International Art** in a former umbrella factory on Jülicherstrasse 97-109; it has works by Warhol, Lichtenstein, Baselitz and others (closed Monday, open Tuesday and Thursday 10 am to 5 pm, Wednesday and Friday to 8 pm; Saturday and Sunday 11 am to 5 pm, admission DM6). The international newspaper collection at the **Zeitungsmuseum**, Pontstrasse 13, has 150,000 titles with many first, last and special editions. It's open Tuesday to Saturday from 9.30 am to 1 pm and 2.30 to 5 pm, on Saturday only to 1 pm. Admission is free.

Thermal Baths The Römerbad at Buchkremerstrasse 1 will let you drift off on cloud nine for DM11 (discount DM6). They're open weekdays from 7 am to 7 pm, to 9 pm Wednesday, and to 1 pm Saturday and Sunday.

Places to Stay
The nearest camping ground to Aachen is *Hoeve de Gastmolen* (☎ 44-5 46 57 55) in the Dutch town of Vaals, about six km outside of town at Lemierserberg 23. Take bus Nos 15 or 65 and get off at the 'Heuvel' stop.

The *Colynshof* hostel (☎ 7 11 01), Maria-Theresia-Allee 280, is four km south-west of the train station on a hill overlooking the city. Catch bus No 2 to the 'Ronheide' stop, or bus No 12 to the closer 'Colynshof' stop at the foot of the hill. It costs DM22/26.50 for juniors/ seniors, including breakfast; other meals are available.

The tourist office has private rooms from DM30/50 single/double (fee DM3), but ask for something within walking distance of the city centre. It's best to call the reservation service ahead of time on ☎ 1 80 29 50/1. Don't be disappointed if the cheapest rooms are taken, even on a Monday in the low season.

The *Etap Hotel* outside the city centre at Strangenhäuschen (☎ 91 19 29) has rooms for DM60/70. Take bus No 51 to the 'Strangenhäuschen' stop. *Hotel Marx* (☎ 3 75 41), Hubertusstrasse 33-35, has singles/ doubles from DM60/100 and an inner courtyard where you can park your car (a bonus in Aachen). At the very central *Hotel Reichshof* (☎ 2 38 68) at Seilgraben 2, rooms with all facilities start at DM80/130.

Places to Eat & Drink
Being a university town, Aachen is full of lively cafés, restaurants and pubs, especially along Pontstrasse, referred to by locals as 'Quartier Latin'. *Café Kittel*, at No 39, is a popular student hang-out with a lively garden out the back. It serves reasonably priced small meals, including vegetarian dishes. The café *Chico Mendes* in the Katakomben Studentenzentrum, at Nos 74-76, is excellent value and also serves breakfast.

For authentic Italian food and a matching ambience, head for *Pizzeria la Finestra*, at No 123, where you can get large pizzas from DM8.50. You'll find similar prices at *Pizzeria Pompei* at No 117. *Gaststätte Labyrinth*, at Nos 156-158, is a rambling beer-hall-type place that lives up to its name. Good, filling meals range from DM8 to DM15, and the menu also lists several vegetarian dishes.

Brauerei Goldener Schwan, Markt 37, is a great old pub with most dishes under DM15 and pizzas for around DM10. *Goldene Rose*, facing the west side of the cathedral at Fischmarkt 1, is busy and boisterous with more than a touch of style, and slightly above-average prices. *Domkeller*, around the other side of the cathedral at Hof 1, has been a student pub since the 1950s and features live music on weekends. The atmosphere is great, but they serve no food.

On Katschhof, the square between the cathedral and the Rathaus, there's a food-and-flower *market* on Tuesday and Thursday from 8 am to 1 pm.

Entertainment
There are several discotheques in Aachen, mainly frequented by the young and very young. Among them is *B9* at Blondelstrasse 9. The more mature crowd heads for *Club Voltaire*, Friedrichstrasse 9, which really starts swinging to funk and other black music from midnight. The *City Theatre* (☎ 4 78 42 44 for bookings) on Theaterplatz has concerts and opera most nights; the tourist office can tell you what's on.

Getting There & Away
Aachen is well served by road and rail. There are fast trains almost every hour to Cologne (43 minutes; DM18.40) and Liège (40 minutes; DM14.80). There's also a frequent bus service to Maastricht (55 minutes; DM8.75).

Getting Around
Aachen's points of interest are clustered around the city centre, which is small enough to be covered easily on foot. Those arriving with private transport can dump their cars in one of the many car parks. City bus tickets bought from the driver cost DM1.20, DM2.50 or DM3, depending on the distance. A batch of five tickets bought in advance (at the train station, machines, or the bus station) costs DM10 or DM12.50, again depending on the distance.

Bremen

The federal state of Bremen covers only the 404 sq km comprising the two cities of Bremen (the state capital) and Bremerhaven. In medi-eval times Bremen was for a time Europe's northernmost archbishopric. The city was ruled by the Church until it joined the Hanse-atic League in the 14th century. Controlled by the French from 1810 to 1813, Bremen went on to join the German Confederation in 1815. In 1871 the city was made a state of the German Empire. In 1949 Bremen was officially declared a state of the Federal Republic of Germany.

BREMEN
Bremen is, after Hamburg, the most important harbour in Germany, even though the open sea lies 113 km to the north. Its Hanseatic past and congenial Altstadt area around Am Markt and Domsheide make it an enjoyable place to explore on foot.

Orientation & Information
The heart of the city is Am Markt, but the soul is the port which provides about 40% of local employment. The tourist office (☎ 30 80 00) is directly in front of the main train station. The staff are helpful and can provide an excellent brochure in English. There is also a booth at the New Town Hall opposite the smaller of the main Altstadt churches, Unser Lieben Frauen Kirche. The main hubs for trams and buses are in front of the Hauptbahnhof and Domsheide. The main post office is also on Domsheide.

If you get lost in the Altstadt streets, look down – often there are stencilled arrows on the foot-paths directing you to other sights. But don't walk with your head down, or you are likely to be knocked over by the local cyclists who seem to claim the pedestrian areas (and just about any other ground) by proprietary right.

Bremen's telephone code is ☎ 0421.

Things to See & Do
Around Am Markt take a look at the splendid and ornate **Rathaus**, the cathedral **St Petri-Dom** which has a tower lookout (DM1; open in summer only) and museum (DM2; both closed Saturday afternoon and Sunday until 2 pm), and the large statue of **Roland**, Bremen's sentimental protector, erected in 1404.

Walk down **Böttcherstrasse**, a re-creation of a medieval alley, complete with tall brick houses, shops, galleries, museums and restaurants. The **Paula-Becker-Modersohn-Haus**, at No 8, has works by its namesake contemporary painter,

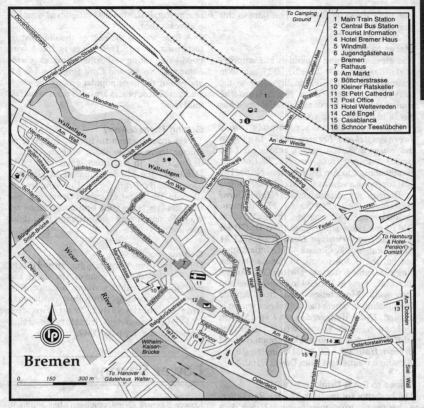

1 Main Train Station
2 Central Bus Station
3 Tourist Information
4 Hotel Bremer Haus
5 Windmill
6 Jugendgästehaus Bremen
7 Rathaus
8 Am Markt
9 Böttcherstrasse
10 Kleiner Ratskeller
11 St Petri Cathedral
12 Post Office
13 Hotel Weltevreden
14 Café Engel
15 Casablanca
16 Schnoor Teestübchen

Bremen

0   150   300 m

and varied exhibits of the **Bernhard Hoetger Collection**; Hoetger's striking sculpture graces much of the Böttcherstrasse. The **Roselius-Haus** is at No 6, with medieval objects. There is a DM8 entry charge to the museums (students DM4). The **Glockenspiel**, in summer hourly from noon to 6 pm (in winter at noon, 3 and 6 pm) plays an extended tune from between rooftops and an adjacent panel swivels to reveal reliefs of fearless seadogs (the best known here being Columbus).

The nearby **Schnoorviertel** area features fishing cottages that are now a tourist attraction, with shops, cafés and tiny lanes.

An excellent walk encircling the Altstadt is along the **Wallanlagen**, parks stretching along the old city walls and moat. They're a peaceful break from the city. On a summer Saturday, look for the **flea market** which might stretch a km or more along the north-east bank of the Weser, from beyond Bürgermeister-Smidt-Brücke to the bridge at Balgebrückstrasse and the lawns to the south-east.

Along with Bremerhaven, 59 km downstream, Bremen has a large port system. The 75-minute **port tour** is excellent and costs DM13 per person (discount DM9).

One great reference around which to frame a Bremen trip is the **Fairy-Tale Road** from Bremen to Hanau, the birthplace of the Brothers Grimm

GERMANY

(see the Fairy-Tale Road section later in this chapter).

Places to Stay

The closest camping ground is at *Camping-platz Bremen* (☎ 21 20 02) at Am Stadtwaldsee 1. It's reasonably close to the university – take tram No 5 from the Hauptbahnhof to Kuhlenkampfallee, then bus No 28 to the camping ground.

The city's hostel accommodation is *Jugendgästehaus Bremen* (☎ 17 13 69), on the Weser at Kalkstrasse 6, across from the Beck's brewery (take bus No 26 from the Hauptbahnhof to Am Brill, or tram No 6). The cost for juniors/seniors is DM26/30.50. Hotels in Bremen are expensive, but *Hotel Garni Gästehaus Walter* (☎ 55 80 27), Buntentorsteinweg 86-88, charges from DM40 to DM70 for a few singles and from DM70 for doubles. *Hotel-Pension Domizil* (☎ 3 47 81 47) at Graf-Moltke-Strasse 42 is a little further out but the dozen rooms all have a shower; singles/doubles start at DM68/110. To get there, take bus No 30 or 34 to Holler Allee and then walk. Most buses leave from outside Hauptbahnhof, where the central bus station is located. *Hotel Weltevreden* (☎ 7 80 15), Am Dobben 62, has rooms without bath for DM60/100. A good up-market option is *Hotel Bremer Haus* (☎ 3 29 40), Löningstrasse 16-20, where rooms cost from DM125/160.

Places to Eat & Drink

The best spot for meals is *Kleiner Ratskeller*, a charming, narrow guesthouse at Hinter dem Schütting 11 (near the head of Böttcherstrasse). Hearty meals usually cost between DM10 and DM14. This place is open from 10 am to midnight. If you would like to sample another popular Bremen beer, the *Schüttinger Brauerei* and pub is next door.

For a good splurge in the Schnoorviertel, head for *Beck's in'n Schnoor*, at Schnoor 34-36. They offer large meals in a pleasant atmosphere from DM15; it costs up to DM39.50 for fish specialities and platters. Just off Schnoor, at Wüstestätte 1, there's a little vegetarian restaurant and teahouse, *Schnoor Teestübchen* (meals DM10 to DM17), which is easiest to find from the riverside, through the narrow lane with the theatre on the left. On Am Markt is the large *Nordsee* seafood chain. The

nearby *Ratskeller* has 600 varieties of wine but no Beck's beer.

A little way to the east of the old town is Ostertorsteinweg. This street is lined with good-value eating and drinking places. *Casablanca*, at No 59, and *Café Engel*, at No 31, are two of the most popular among the city's students. These places are open from breakfast until late.

Getting There & Away

To get from Bremen to Berlin, you have to change trains in Hamburg or Hanover. For destinations in the north-east, change in Hamburg; for Munich, change in Hanover (occasionally Brunswick). For Amsterdam (three to 3½ hours), change in Osnabrück. For Brussels (six hours), the best connections are via Cologne. Direct Frankfurt trains take about five hours.

Getting Around

Directly in front of the train station and tourist office, follow the tram route to Am Markt, and everything is within walking distance. The tram system is simple to follow on the map from the tourist office. Short trips cost DM1.50, a four-trip transferable ticket DM9.60 and a day pass DM7.

Lower Saxony

Lower Saxony (Niedersachsen) has much to offer, and it's a quick train ride or autobahn drive from the tourist centres down south. The scenic Harz Mountains, the old student town of Göttingen, and the picturesque towns along the Fairy-Tale Road are the most popular tourist attractions. British occupation forces created the federal state of Lower Saxony in 1946, when they amalgamated the states of Braunschweig (Brunswick), Schaumburg-Lippe and Oldenburg with the Prussian province of Hanover.

HANOVER

Hanover (Hannover), the capital of Lower Saxony, has close links with the English-speaking world. In 1714, the eldest son of Electress Sophie of Hannover – a granddaughter of James

I of England and VI of Scotland – ascended the British throne as King George I. This English/German union lasted through several generations until 1837. Savaged by heavy bombing in 1943, Hanover was rebuilt into a prosperous city known throughout Europe for its trade fairs. It will host the next World EXPO in the year 2000.

Information

The tourist office (☎ 30 14 20) in Hanover is at Ernst-August-Platz 2 next to the main post office near the main train station. It's open until 6 pm Monday to Friday and 2 pm on Saturday. There is also an information counter in the Rathaus. HannoverCard, which entitles you to unlimited public transportation and discounted admission to museums and other attractions, costs DM14 for a day, DM23 for three days and is valid after 9 am each day.

Hanover's telephone code is ☎ 0511.

Things to See & Do

One way to pick out most city sights on foot is to follow the red line with its numbered attractions, with the help of the *Red Thread Guide* from the tourist office. The chief attractions are the glorious parks of **Herrenhäuser Gärten**, especially the baroque **Grosser Garten** and the **Berggarten** (DM4; open until 8 pm on summer evenings), and their museums (take tram Nos 4 or 5). The **Fürstenhaus** (entry DM5, students DM3) shows what treasures remain from the Guelph palaces, and the **Wilhelm-Busch-Museum** of caricature and satirical art (DM4; closed Monday) contains the work of that artist and others.

The **Sprengel Museum** (DM6; open to 10 pm on Tuesday, closed Monday) exhibits contemporary works, the highlights being Picasso and Max Beckmann, while the **Kestner-Museum** (DM3, Wednesday free; closed Monday) has antiquities, including a bust of the pharaoh Akhenaten. The **Niedersächsisches Landesmuseum** is being renovated and is scheduled to open in 1998. Admission to all museums is half price for students.

At Am Markt in the old town, the 14th-century **Marktkirche**, apart from its truncated tower, is characteristic of the northern red-brick Gothic style; the original stained-glass windows are particularly beautiful. The **Altes Rathaus** across

the marketplace was built in various sections over a century. Around **Burgstrasse** some of the half-timbered town houses remain, as well as the **Ballhof**, originally built for badminton-type games of the 17th century but today offering theatrical plays.

In the domed **Neues Rathaus** off Friedrichswall you can see four city models that show what has been lost and gained in the march of time (entry free). On Breite Strasse the ruin of the **Aegidienkirche**, smashed in 1943, is an eloquent memorial; the peace bell inside is a gift from one of Hanover's sistercities – Hiroshima.

Places to Stay

Hanover's *hostel* (☎ 1 31 76 74) is three km out of town at Ferdinand-Wilhelm-Fricke-Weg 1 (U3 or U7 from Hauptbahnhof to Fischerhof, then cross the river on the Lodemannbrücke bridge and turn right). The price for juniors/seniors is DM21/25 with breakfast.

The city centre has some affordable hotel options, such as *Hospiz am Bahnhof* (☎ 32 42 97), in sight of the main station at Joachimstrasse 2, with basic singles/doubles from DM55/106 and access to a shower (DM3). Similar but bigger is *Hotel am Thielenplatz* (☎ 32 76 91 93), at Thielenplatz, with some rooms starting at DM78/140. *Hotel Flora* (☎ 34 23 34), at Heinrichstrasse 36, has rooms with shared bathroom from DM50/95 (with private bathroom up to DM85/140).

Places to Eat

Restaurant Gilde-Hof, Joachimstrasse 6 near Hauptbahnhof, has big servings of typical German food from DM10. If you've had your fill of this fare, try the slightly more expensive Turkish restaurant *Kreuzklappe*, on the corner of Kreuzstrasse and Kreuzkirchhof. Vegetarians ought to try *Hiller* on Blumenstrasse 3. For fast, fresh and inexpensive fish, there's a *Nordsee* outlet in Karmarschstrasse.

Getting There & Away

Hanover is a major intersection of train lines. Trains to/from Hamburg (1½ hours), Munich (4½ hours, overnight 6½), Frankfurt (2¼ hours) and Berlin (3½ to four hours) leave virtually every hour from 5 or 6 am.

If you are driving, Hanover is well positioned, with autobahns to the same four cities.

There are also good autobahn connections to Bremen, Cologne, Amsterdam and Brussels.

Getting Around

The city centre is best covered on foot, but from either end of Bahnhofstrasse the tram and U-Bahn networks are the handiest ways to reach beyond. Single journeys cost DM3.10, day passes DM9, and blocks of six tickets are DM14.50. The tourist brochure *Travel Tips for Visitors* is packed with information on how to get around town and to most attractions.

FAIRY-TALE ROAD

The Fairy-Tale Road (Märchenstrasse), so called because of the number of legends and fairy tales which sprang from this region, is definitely worth a day or two. The route begins at Bremen, passes near Hanover and then goes further south to Göttingen, Kassel and Hanau. The stretch from Hanover to Göttingen is the most historical section of the route. Among the most interesting towns here are Hamelin (Hameln) of Pied Piper fame, Bodenwerder where the great adventurer Baron von Münchhausen made his home, and the surprising town of Bad Karlshafen.

Information

Every town, village and hamlet along the Fairy-Tale Road has an information office of sorts. The office in Hamelin (☎ 20 26 18) is most helpful. It is at Deister Allee 3, just outside the old town (there is also a counter in the Hochzeitshaus from April to October). In Bodenwerder, you will find the tourist office (☎ 4 05 42) at Brückenstrasse 7. In Bad Karlshafen, it is in the Kurverwaltung (☎ 99 99 24) by the 'harbour'. The office in Hamelin has a colourful map of the entire route.

The telephone codes for Hamelin, Bodenwerder and Bad Karlshafen are ☎ 05151, ☎ 05533 and ☎ 05672 respectively.

Things to See

Hamelin Among the most interesting sights is the **Rattenfängerhaus** ('Rat Catcher's House') on Osterstrasse, the old town's main street, built at the beginning of the 17th century. On the Bungelosenstrasse side is an inscription that tells how, in 1284, 130 children of Hamelin were led past this site and out of town by a piper wearing multicoloured clothes,

never to be seen again. Also have a look at the Rattenfänger **Glockenspiel** at the Weser Renaissance **Hochzeitshaus** at the Markt end of Osterstrasse (daily at 1.05, 3.35 and 5.35 pm). More of the story is at the museum in the ornate **Leisthaus** (DM2; closed Monday). For the other beauties of Hamelin – the restored 16th to 18th-century half-timbered houses with inscribed dedications – stroll through the south-eastern quarter of the old town, around Alte Marktstrasse and Grossehofstrasse or Kupferschmiedestrasse.

Bodenwerder The **Rathaus** is said to be the house in which the legendary Baron von Münchhausen was born. The baron's fame was due to his telling of outrageous tales, the most famous of which was how he rode through the air on a cannonball. This very cannonball is in a room dedicated to the baron in the Rathaus. Also interesting is the statue of the baron riding half a horse, in the garden outside the Rathaus. This was, of course, another of his stories.

There is a pleasant **walking track** along the Weser River in both directions from Bodenwerder.

Bad Karlshafen This place is totally unexpected. After passing through towns like Hamelin and Bodenwerder, the last thing you expect is this whitewashed, meticulously planned, baroque village. Originally the city was planned with an impressive harbour and a canal connecting the Weser River with the Rhine in the hope of diverting trade away from Hanover and Münden in the north. The plans were laid by a local earl with help from Huguenot refugees. The earl's death in 1730 prevented completion of the project, but even today his incomplete masterpiece and the influence of the Huguenots is too beautiful to miss.

Places to Stay & Eat

In Hamelin the camping ground *Fährhaus an der Weser* is on Uferstrasse (☎ 6 11 67), across the Weser River from the old town and 10 minutes walk north. The *DJH hostel* (☎ 34 25) is at Fischbeckerstrasse 33 (bus No 2 from the train station to Wehler Weg). In Bodenwerder, the *DJH hostel* (☎ 26 85) is on Richard-Schirrmann-Weg, above the valley on the eastern edge of town. In Bad Karlshafen, the hostel *Hermann Wenning* (☎ 3 38) is at Winnefelderstrasse 7, a few minutes walk from the train station near the river.

For a hotel in Hamelin, try *Hotel zur Börse* (☎ 70 80), Osterstrasse 41a, which has singles/doubles for DM74/139. The friendly and central *Hotel Altstadtwiege* (☎ 2 78 54), Neue Marktstrasse 10, has rooms from DM55/90. In Bodenwerder, the *Hotel Deutsches Haus* (☎ 39 25), Münchhausen-platz 4, has rooms from DM85/130.

For a gastronomic treat in Hamelin, try *Gaststätte Rattenfängerhaus* in the Rat Catcher's House, where you can lash out or order a DM10.50 daily special.

Getting Around
The easiest way to follow the Fairy-Tale Road is by car. The ADAC map of the Weserbergland covers the area in detail. There are several local trains a day from Hanover to Hamelin and back (40 minutes). From Hamelin's train station about a dozen buses a day (Nos 2612 to 2614, 40 minutes) travel to/from Bodenwerder. There are also buses between Bodenwerder and Höxter, and Höxter-Kassel buses pass through Bad Karlshafen.

GÖTTINGEN
This leafy university town is an ideal stopover on your way north or south; it's on the direct train line between Munich and Hamburg. Though small, Göttingen is a lively town, mostly because of its large student population. A legion of notables, including Otto von Bismarck and the Brothers Grimm, studied and worked here. The university has produced a number of Nobel Prize winners and it's also the site of the prestigious Max Planck Institute, named after the German physicist and a leader in scientific research.

Information
The main tourist office is in the old Rathaus on Markt 9 (☎ 5 40 00). It is open weekdays from 9 am to 1 pm and 2 to 6 pm, weekends from 10 am to 4 pm (closed on Sunday and after 1 pm on Saturday in winter). There's a smaller tourist office just outside the main entrance to the train station (☎ 5 60 00, same hours), and a large post office is just to the left (north).

Göttingen's telephone code is ☎ 0551.

Things to See
The German-language walking tour leaves daily at 2.30 pm (DM5, students DM3) from the Altes Rathaus, but the pedestrian-only old town is easily explored on your own. At Markt, don't miss the **Great Hall** in the Rathaus where colourful frescos cover every inch of wallspace. Just outside, students mill about the **Gänseliesel** fountain, the town's symbol. The bronze beauty has a reputation as 'the most kissed girl in the world' because every student who obtains a doctor's degree must plant a kiss on her cold lips.

The 15th-century **Junkernschänke** on the corner of Jüdenstrasse and Barfüsserstrasse, with its colourful carved facade, is perhaps the most stunning of the town's half-timbered buildings. Walking on top of the old **town wall** along Bürgerstrasse, you come upon the **Bismarckhäuschen**, a modest building where the Iron Chancellor lived in 1833 during his wild student days (open Tuesday 10 am to 1 pm, Thursday and Saturday 3 to 5 pm, admission free).

Places to Stay
Camping am Hohen Hagen (☎ 05502-21 47), about 15 km out of town in Dransfeld, is reached by bus No 120. The *Jugendherberge Göttingen* (☎ 5 76 22) is less than friendly and a bit hard to reach at Habichtsweg 2. From the train station main entrance, head through the tunnel under Berliner Strasse, take the first right to Groner-Tor-Strasse and take bus No 6 from across the street to the 'Jugendherberge' stop. Beds cost DM21/26 juniors/seniors.

For pensions try *Hotel garni zum Schwan* (☎ 4 48 63) at Weender Landstrasse 23, which costs DM46/73 for a bathless single/double, DM56/87 with bath. For a place with character, check out *Hotel Garni Gräfin Holtzendorff* (☎ 6 39 87), where you can room with a real countess from DM48/70. *Hotel Kasseler Hof* (☎ 7 20 81), at Rosdorfer Weg 26 near the edge of the old town, has rooms from DM52/115.

Places to Eat & Drink
Because it's a student centre, eating and drinking in Göttingen is fairly cheap and lively. Students get decent food from 9 am to 9 pm at the large *Zentralmensa*, through the arch off

Weender Landstrasse. *Nudelhaus*, on the corner of Jüdenstrasse at Rote Strasse 13, has plenty of reasonably priced noodle dishes. *Zur Alten Brauerei* features Bavarian décor and a hearty menu with many dishes under DM15. The restaurant is in a courtyard behind the half-timbered building at Düstere Strasse 20 (under the gallery walkover and to the right at No 20a).

Among the many cafés and bars that also serve small dishes are the historic *Zum Altdeutschen* at Prinzenstrasse 16 and the *Irish Pub* at Mühlenstrasse 4, both popular with students.s

Entertainment
Göttingen's bars and clubs come to life after 9 pm and often close with breakfast at 8 am, even on weekdays. *Der Nörgelbuff*, in a vaulted cellar at Groner Strasse 23, has live blues and jazz music. The dance club *Blue Note* on Wilhelmsplatz 3 swings with Latin rhythms. *Musa*, an underground cultural centre in a former bread factory at Hagenweg 2, features dance, music, readings and more.

Getting There & Away
Trains constantly pass through on the Munich-Hamburg line. There are a few direct trains daily from Göttingen to Goslar in the Harz Mountains.

GOSLAR
Goslar is a centre for Harz Mountains tourism, but this 1000-year-old city with its beautifully preserved half-timbered buildings has plenty of charm in its own right. In 1992, the town and the nearby Rammelsberg Mine were included on the list of world cultural heritage sites by UNESCO. On a weekday or in the off-season, it is one of the most relaxed and pleasant towns in Germany to visit.

Information
The tourist office (☎ 28 46) is at Markt 7 and can help when the area's accommodation is packed. For information on the Harz Mountains visit the Harzer Verkehrsverband (☎ 3 40 40) at Marktstrasse 45 (inside the Bäckergildehaus, enter on the side). Streets in the old town number up one side, down the other.

Goslar's telephone code is ☎ 05321.

Things to See & Do
The **Marktplatz** has several photogenic houses. The one opposite the Gothic **Rathaus** has a chiming clock depicting four scenes from the history of mining in the area. It struts its stuff at 9 am, noon, 3 pm and 6 pm. The eagle on the **market fountain** is from the 13th century.

While strolling, look at the **Schuhhof**, **Worthstrasse** and **Marktkirchhof** and historic buildings such as the **Bäckergildehaus** and the **Kaiserworth**, an old textile guildhall decorated with the statues of emperors.

The **Kaiserpfalz** is a restored Romanesque 11th-century palace usually jammed with tour bus visitors. Just below is the recently restored **Domvorhalle** which displays the 11th-century 'Kaiserstuhl' throne, used by German emperors. The **Siemenshaus** in Schreiberstrasse 12 is the ancestral home of the industrial family and can be visited on weekday mornings (call ahead, ☎ 2 38 37).

For an excellent overview of the history of Goslar and the geology of the Harz Mountains, visit the **Goslarer Museum** at Königstrasse 1, on the corner of Abzuchtstrasse (DM3.50; closed Monday).

The **Zinnfiguren Museum** (Pewter Statuette Museum), in the courtyard at Münzerstrasse 11, has hundreds of painted figures in various pretty settings (DM3.50). At the **Rammelsberger Bergbaumuseum**, about one km south of the town centre on Rammelsberger Strasse, you can delve into the mining history of the area and descend into the shafts on a variety of tours costing from DM6 to DM12.

Places to Stay
The pretty *Jugendherberge* (☎ 2 22 40) is at Rammelsberger Strasse 25 behind the Kaiserpfalz (bus 'C' to Theresienhof from the train station). It charges DM20/25 for juniors/seniors (including breakfast) and is often full of high school students.

A better option is *Hotel und Campingplatz Sennhütte* (☎ 2 25 02), three km south on Route B241 at Clausthaler Strasse 28. Take bus No 434 from the train station to the 'Sennhütte' stop. The few rooms are clean and simple and start at DM30/60 for singles/doubles (nice views). Many trails lead away from the camping ground and into the mountains, including the one to Hahnenklee.

Goslar has plenty of private rooms from DM28/46 but it's best to make a reservation through the tourist office. Other inexpensive options are *Haus Bielitza* (☎ 2 07 44) at Abzuchtstrasse 11, where rooms are DM30/50 (shower DM3.50), or *Rühland* (☎ 2 51 62) at An der Abzucht 30 with bathless rooms for DM30/60. *Gästehaus Schmitz* offers perhaps the best value: DM50/65 for rooms with shower/WC.

Places to Eat

The latest trend to sweep Goslar restaurants is the DM10 (or less) lunch menu. Among those offering full meals in this price range are *Effesus*, a Turkish restaurant at Breite Strasse 28, and *Tollis* at Sommerwohlenstrasse 5. For traditional German fare, go to *Wolpertinger* at Marstallstrasse 1, a brewery restaurant with whimsical décor where small dishes go for around DM8. Good beer is also served at *Paulaner* at Gemeindehof 3-5, a rustic joint with meat dishes for between DM10 and DM20. Next door is the bistro-style *Paulinchen*. On sunny days, it's the done thing to loll with coffee or ice cream on Marktkirchhof all afternoon. Note that many places are closed Monday.

Getting There & Away

Goslar is regularly connected by train to Göttingen (about 1¼ hours), Hanover, Brunswick and beyond. For information on getting to/from the eastern Harz region, see Getting Around in the following Western Harz Mountains section and the Getting There & Away sections under Quedlinburg and Wernigerode earlier in this chapter.

WESTERN HARZ MOUNTAINS

Known mostly to Germans and Scandinavians, the Harz Mountains (Harzgebirge) don't have the dramatic peaks and valleys of the Alps, but they offer a great four-seasons sports getaway without some of the Alpine tackiness and tourism. The area provides one of the best opportunities in Europe to get off crowded tourist tracks. Silver, lead and copper mines in the area have been largely exhausted, and many can now be visited.

Orientation & Information

Make sure to pick up the booklet *Grüner Faden* ('Green Thread'), available at any tourist office in the Harz and at many hotels (DM5). For weather reports and winter snow information (in English), contact the Harzer Verkehrsverband in Goslar (☎ 3 40 40). Alpenverein and Harzclub offices in many mountain towns are also good places for further information, specific recommendations, itineraries, hiking partners and guided hikes.

Things to See

Hahnenklee is proud of its Norwegian-style **'stave' church**, but most remarkable is Clausthal-Zellerfeld's 17th-century wooden church **Zum Heiligen Geist** at Hindenburgplatz, built to accommodate over 2000 worshippers! Nearby, the technical university's **mineral collection** at Römerstrasse 12a (DM1) is of particular interest to geology buffs.

For a fine view, take the **Bergbahn** car up to the castle ruins above Bad Harzburg (DM4/6 one way/return, less with resort card). The embarkation point is two km uphill from the train station, so you can promenade among German wealth and ambition and check the array of furs and other luxury goods flaunted in this health resort.

Activities

Hiking Despite 400 km of groomed hiking trails in the National Park Harz, its beauty hasn't suffered. Maps and information are abundant. Make sure to get the latest version of the *Auto + Wanderkarte Harz* hiking and driving map (DM9.80). Most hikes are under 10 km and can be completed in half a day.

Goslar has many highly recommended hikes just outside town. Hikes through the wildly romantic Okertal are particularly scenic, as is the area up to and around the Granestausee reservoir (four or five km west of Goslar train station towards the town of Wolfshagen). You can also hike the 15 km to Hahnenklee from Goslar without ever leaving the forest. From Goslar to Bad Harzburg, you can pick up the medieval Kaiserweg route and follow it towards Walkenried, or turn back to Sennhütte via Langes Tal. From Bad Harzburg back to Altenau is a good 20 km stretch. All along the way rustic mountain restaurants

To Magdeburg

Former West/East German Border

Harz Mountains (Harzgebirge)

0   10   20 km

---

tempt you with hearty German specialties. Among them is the scenic *Molkenhaus*, about a 45-minute walk from Bad Harzburg.

Most trails are well marked and maintained, but it doesn't hurt to ask occasionally to make sure you're heading the way you think you are. At any time of year and no matter what the current weather, be prepared for almost anything mother nature can throw at you.

Cycling Pedalling in the Harz Mountains is popular among those seeking a hilly challenge. If the slopes eventually get to you, hop on any of the local buses which will carry your machine for only DM1. A cycle track follows the main road from Bad Harzburg as far as the old border at Eckertal.

Skiing Downhill skiing is below average, due to uninspiring slopes and inconsistent snow conditions. Locals, however, are passionate about cross-country skiing, which is a better overall option. Most tourist offices have an excellent brochure and map, *Skilanglauf im*

Naturschutzgebiet Oberharz. This gives details of about 10 different loops, ranging from three to 15 km, with information on elevation, difficulty and trailheads. One of the more consistent and popular downhill resorts is Hahnenklee, with five runs and three lifts (one is a cable car).

Rental equipment for both sports is easy to find. Downhill skis and boots or cross-country gear start at about DM15 a day.

Spas The six spa towns in the Western Harz Mountains are Bad Grund, Bad Lauterberg, Bad Harzburg, Bad Sachsa, Braunlage and Bad Gandersheim. Other towns, such as Hahnenklee and Altenau, also have spa amenities and they may well be better value. Practically all the spas have public indoor pools with saunas.

Places to Stay
Many of the 30 or so camping grounds are open all year, but that doesn't mean the weather is suitable for camping, just that they cater for

caravans. Hotels and guesthouses can be expensive. For extended stays, ask the tourist office about apartments or holiday homes, which become pretty good deals when staying for a week or more. In the resorts you will pay about DM2.50 Kurtaxe (visitor's tax) per day.

Hahnenklee *Campingplatz am Kreuzeck* (☎ 05325-25 70) is on the road two km north of Hahnenklee (bus from Goslar). The *Jugendherberge* (☎ 22 56) is at Steigerstieg 1 near the 'Bockswiese' bus stop on the road from Goslar (DM20/24 for juniors/seniors). The tourist office (☎ 20 14) at Rathausstrasse 16 can help you find a private room.

Altenau The *Campingplatz Okertalsperre* (☎ 05328-7 02) is on the B498 just north of town. The *Jugendherberge* (☎ 3 61) is at Auf der Rose 11 (juniors/seniors DM21/25, breakfast included). If you would like a private room, the Kurverwaltung (☎ 80 20) can help.

Bad Harzburg The *Campingplatz Wolfenstein*, at Wolfsklippen on Ilsenburger Strasse east of town, is the only site that accepts tents (bus Nos 74 or 77 from the train station). The youth hostel *Braunschweiger Haus* (☎ 05322-45 82) is at Waldstrasse 5 (bus No 73 from the train station) and has beds for DM20/23 juniors/seniors.

Clausthal-Zellerfeld Beds at the *youth hostel* (☎ 05323-8 42 93) at Altenauer Strasse 55 cost DM20/24 for juniors/seniors. The hostel is usually closed one weekend per month from mid-September to mid-June.

Getting Around

Since June 1996, direct train service between the West Harz and East Harz – once divided by the Iron Curtain – has been restored. You can now go directly from Goslar to Bad Harzburg to Wernigerode. Buses are another option. Bus No 77 shuttles several times daily between Bad Harzburg and Wernigerode (just under an hour; DM5). It stops on the far side of Am Bahnhofsplatz at Bad Harzburg train station and next to the main station in Wernigerode (stop No 4).

Bus Nos 408 and 432 run between Goslar and Altenau, while No 408 and 434 connect

Goslar with Clausthal-Zellerfeld (No 434 via Hahnenklee).

Hamburg

The first recorded settlement on the present site of Hamburg was the moated fortress of Hammaburg, built in the first half of the ninth century AD. The city that developed around it became the northernmost archbishopric in Europe, to facilitate the conversion of the northern peoples. The city was burned down many times, but in the 13th century it became the Hanseatic League's gateway to the North Sea and was second in importance and influence only to Lübeck. With the decline of the Hanseatic League in the 16th century, Lübeck faded into insignificance but Hamburg continued to thrive.

Hamburg strode confidently into the 20th century, but WWI stopped all trade, and most of Hamburg's merchant shipping fleet (almost 1500 ships) was forfeited to the Allies as reparation payment. In WWII, over half of Hamburg's residential areas and port facilities were demolished and 55,000 people killed in Allied air raids. Twenty-five years later, however, Hamburg was as good as rebuilt.

Today it is a sprawling port city and a separate state of Germany, with a stylish shopping district, numerous waterways (with more bridges than Venice), and even a beach (in Blankenese, Germany's most exclusive suburb).

Orientation

The main train station, the Hauptbahnhof, is very central, near Aussenalster lake and fairly close to most of the sights. These are south of Aussenalster and north of the Elbe River, which runs all the way from the Czech Republic to Hamburg before flowing into the North Sea. The city centre features the Rathaus and the beautiful Hauptkirche St Michaelis. The port is west of the city centre, facing the Elbe.

Information

The small tourist office in the Hauptbahnhof (☎ 3 00 51 20) at the Kirchenallee exit offers limited brochures and a room-finding service.

GERMANY

It has great hours (7 am to 11 pm daily) and friendly, if overworked, staff. There's also an office at St Pauli harbour, between piers 4 and 5, open daily from 10 am to 7 pm, in winter 9 am to 5.30 pm (S/U-Bahn: St Pauli-Landungsbrücken).

The handy monthly information booklet *Hamburger Vorschau* (DM2.30) has an English version available at these offices and at newsstands. The Hamburg Card offers unlimited public transportation and free or discounted admission to most attractions, museums and cruises. The 'day card' is valid after 6 pm on the day of purchase and during the following day and costs DM12.50 (single) or DM24 (groups, ie up to four adults and three children under 12). The 'multi-day card' is valid on the day of purchase and the following two days (DM24.50 and DM39). The card is available at tourist offices, where you can also ask to see the leaflet that explains the discounts. An even better deal is the Hamburg Jugend Spass card, only available at youth hostels, which gives you even steeper discounts for a mere DM10.50.

Money There is a DVB bank above the Kirchenallee exit of the Hauptbahnhof (open 7.30 am to 10 pm daily), an exchange counter at Altona train station (closed Sunday) and a Deutsche Bank counter at the airport (6.30 am to 8.30 pm daily). There are several exchange centres scattered around the Hauptbahnhof. Most branches of banks are open until 4 pm on weekdays (to 6 pm on Thursday), and outside the city centre many close from 1 to 2.30 pm. American Express is on Ballindamm near Jungfernstieg (open weekdays from 9 am to 5.30 pm, Saturday 10 am to 1 pm).

Post & Communications There's a small post office with a poste restante counter near the Kirchenallee exit of the Hauptbahnhof (open Monday to Friday from 7 am to 9 pm, Saturday from 8 am to 8 pm). The main post office is on the corner of Dammtorstrasse at Stephansplatz (telephone cubicles are downstairs as you enter).

Hamburg's telephone code is ☎ 040.

Newspapers & Magazines For cultural events and lifestyle information, look for the monthly magazines *Szene* (DM5) and *Oxmox* (DM4.30). For classified ads of all sorts, pick up a copy of *Avis*, published on Tuesday (DM3.20) and Friday (DM3.80).

Bookshops Dr Götze Land & Karte, Bleichenbrücke 9 in the Bleichenhof arcade (S-Bahn: Stadthausbrücke), claims to be the biggest specialist map-and-travel bookshop in Europe and has a smattering of guidebooks in English. A second, smaller shop is in the Wandelhalle shopping arcade at the Hauptbahnhof. The branch of Thalia Bücher on Grosse Bleichen 19 has a large section of English-language books and some guidebooks.

Laundry Hamburg has several Waschcenter laundrettes, where a basic wash costs DM6, although to take away a dry load you will part with DM10 total. The most convenient is probably at Wandsbeker Chaussee 159, at the exit of the Ritterstrasse station on the U1. Another is reasonably central at Mühlenkamp 37 (bus No 108 from Rathausplatz).

Medical & Emergency Services For an ambulance, call ☎ 1 12; in other medical emergencies, contact the 24-hour medical clinic (☎ 4 68 47 17) at Eppendorf hospital on Martinistrasse (U-Bahn: Kellinghusenstrasse, or bus No 102). A medical emergency service is available (☎ 22 80 22), as well as a 24-hour first-aid service (☎ 24 82 81) and dental emergency aid (☎ 1 15 00). The police are on ☎ 1 10; there are stations at the corner of Kirchenallee and Bremer Reihe outside the central train station and at Spielbudenplatz 31, on the corner of Davidstrasse.

Dangers & Annoyances Overall, Hamburg is a very safe city with a low crime rate. The area in the vicinity of Hauptbahnhof and Kirchenallee is down-market, has a pale red-light district and a moderate drug scene. The area around the Reeperbahn is not as seedy as you might expect, and locals say it's the safest place on earth because there are so many police around. The area is generally safe for walking and looking, but you may be more comfortable travelling in groups including at least one male.

Things to See & Do

Altstadt Much of Hamburg's old city centre was lost in WWII, but it's still worth a walking tour. The area is laced with wonderful canals (called 'fleets') running from the Alster Lakes to the Elbe.

The Altstadt centres on Rathausmarkt, where the large **Rathaus** and huge clock tower overlook the lively square. This is one of the most interesting city halls in Germany, and the 40-minute tour is worthwhile at DM2. It's in English hourly Monday to Thursday from 10.15 am to 3.15 pm, Friday to Sunday to 1 pm. The building has 647 rooms – six more than Buckingham Palace.

It is a moving experience to visit the remaining tower of the devastated **St Nikolai Church**, now an anti-war memorial, on Ost-West-Strasse nearby. From there, walk a few blocks west to the baroque **Hauptkirche St Michaelis** and take the lift up the tower (DM4, children DM2, enter through portal No 3) for a great view of the city and the port. Inside, the beautiful interiors and the crypt (a donation of DM1 is requested) are open for viewing. The tower is open Monday to Saturday from 9 am to 6 pm, Sunday from 11 am.

Port After exploring the Altstadt, stroll down to one of the busiest ports in the world. It boasts the world's largest carpet warehouse complex, while the Free Port Warehouses stockpile spices from all continents.

The **port cruises** are admittedly touristy, but still worthwhile. There are many options; for details see Organised Tours later in this section.

If you're in the port area early on a Sunday (5 am to 10 am, in winter from 7 am), head for the **fish market** in St Pauli, right on the Elbe. Hamburg's oldest market (since 1703) is popular with locals and tourists alike and everything under the sun is sold here. Cap your morning with a visit to the live jazz session at Fish Auction Hall, Grosse Elbstrasse 9.

Reeperbahn Though the Altstadt and the port are interesting, Hamburg's biggest tourist attraction is probably the Reeperbahn, one of the world's most famous red-light districts. It is 600 metres long and is the heart of the St Pauli entertainment district, which includes shows, bars, cabarets, clubs, theatres and a casino. In recent years, St Pauli has cleaned up its act somewhat and now peep shows and sex shops rub shoulders with popular restaurants and bars.

If you venture into one of the more 'traditional' Reeperbahn haunts, make sure you understand costs before going in; many times these **bars** or other 'events' can turn out to be more expensive than they appear. Ask for the price list if it's not posted by the entrance. Beer and soft drinks are cheapest but many places with shows or other entertainment have a minimum purchase (up to DM40) in addition to the admission fee (DM5 or DM10). On **Grosse Freiheit**, you'll find Tabu, Safari and Colibri, which feature live sex shows that are not for the faint-hearted. **Herbertstrasse** is the infamous street where the prostitutes sit, stand, and lean out the windows offering their wares. It is fenced off at each end by a metal wall with small entry ways. The scene is almost surreal. You must be at least 18 to get in, and women are not allowed.

Other Sights The waxworks museum **Panoptikum** is one of those unusual places that seems to be fun for the entire family. Founded in 1879, it contains more than 100 well-known (at least to Germans) historical, political and show-business celebrities. It's at Spielbudenplatz 3 and is open from 11 am to 9 pm Monday to Friday, Saturday to midnight, and Sunday from 10 am to 9 pm (closed from mid-January to early February). Admission costs DM7 (children DM4).

Hagenbecks Tierpark is the largest privately owned zoo in Europe. There are around 2500 animals representing over 370 species in 54 enclosures. It's in the suburb of Stellingen, a little way north-east of the centre. The easiest way to get there is to take the U2 line towards Niendorf. Entry costs a hefty DM19 for adults and DM14 for kids (the dolphins cost an extra DM6/DM4). The zoo is open from 9 am daily.

Harry's Hamburger Hafen Basar at Bernhard-Nocht-Strasse 65 (the nearest S-Bahn stations are Reeperbahn and St Pauli-Landungsbrücken) is an incredible 'shop': it's the life's work of Harry, a bearded character known to seamen all over the world, who for decades has been buying trinkets and souvenirs

GERMANY

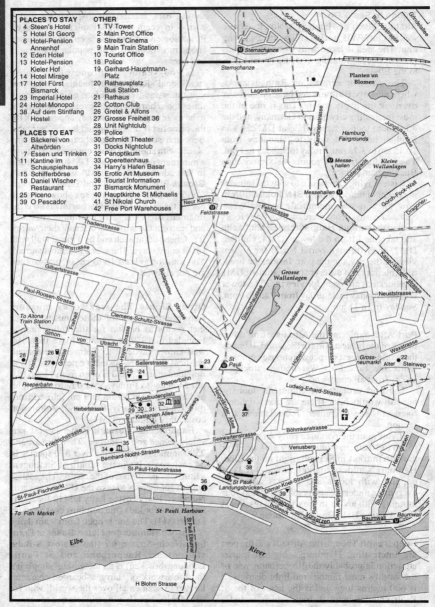

PLACES TO STAY
4 Steen's Hotel
5 Hotel St Georg
6 Hotel-Pension Annenhof
12 Eden Hotel
13 Hotel-Pension Kieler Hof
14 Hotel Mirage
17 Hotel Fürst Bismarck
23 Imperial Hotel
24 Hotel Monopol
38 Auf dem Stintfang Hostel

PLACES TO EAT
3 Bäckerei von Altwörden
7 Essen und Trinken
11 Kantine im Schauspielhaus
15 Schifferbörse
18 Daniel Wischer Restaurant
25 Piceno
39 O Pescador

OTHER
1 TV Tower
2 Main Post Office
8 Streits Cinema
9 Main Train Station
10 Tourist Office
16 Police
19 Gerhard-Hauptmann-Platz
20 Rathausplatz Bus Station
21 Rathaus
22 Cotton Club
26 Gretel & Alfons
27 Grosse Freiheit 36
28 Unit Nightclub
29 Police
30 Schmidt Theater
31 Docks Nightclub
32 Panoptikum
33 Operettenhaus
34 Harry's Hafen Basar
35 Erotic Art Museum
36 Tourist Information
37 Bismarck Monument
40 Hauptkirche St Michaelis
41 St Nikolai Church
42 Free Port Warehouses

Aussenalster

Hamburg

0   250   500 m

To
University
Area

Moorweiden-

Rothenbaumchaussee

strasse

Tesdorpfstrasse

Mittelweg

Warburgstrasse

Alsterufer

Edmund-Siemers-Allee

Dammtor

Alsterglacis

Stephansplatz

Stephans-
platz   Esplanade

2

Stephansplatz

Kennedybrücke

An der Alster

To Pension
Sarah
Petersen

Dammtorwall

Dammtorstrasse

Gänsemarkt

Valentinskamp

Gänse-
markt

3

Colonnaden

Neuer Jungfernstieg

Lombardsbrücke

Ferdinandstor

Holzdamm

Koppel

6

Lange
Reihe

7

8

Jungfernstieg

Binnenalster

ABC Strasse

Jungfernstieg

Ballindamm

Ferdinandstrasse

Glockengiesser-
wall

Ernst-Merck-Strasse

Hachmannplatz

Hauptbahnhof Nord

4

5

11

Ellmenreichstrasse

15

16

12

13

Bremer Reihe

14

Grosse   Bleichen

Poststrasse

Rathausmarkt

Raboisen

Rosenstrasse

Lilienstrasse

9

i   10

Steindamm

Hauptbahnhof Süd

Steindamm

Grosse   Bleichen

Wall

Hermannstrasse

Spitalerstrasse

18

19

Mönckebergstrasse

Mönckebergstrasse

Adenauerallee

Neuer   Wall

Alter Wall

21

20

Gr. Johannisstrasse

Jakobi-
kirchhof

Steinstrasse

Kurt-Schumacher-Allee

Steinstrasse

Stadthausbrücke

Neuer

Rathausmarkt

Rathausstrasse

Speersort

Steinstrasse

Steinstrasse

Stadthausbrücke

Grasbrook

Grosser   Burstah

Domstrasse

Burchardstrasse

Altstädterstrasse

Steinstrasse

Steinwall

Klosterwall

Rödingsmarkt

Rödingsmarkt

41

Ost-West-Strasse

Messburg

Pumpen

Högerdamm

Schaar-Kalen

Katherinenstrasse

Zippelhaus

Alter Wandrahm

Oberbaumbrücke

Bankstrasse

Bei den Mühren

Neuer Wandrahm

Brooktorkai

Kehrwieder

42

Brooktor

Stockmeyerstrasse

Am Sandtorkai

Sandtorhafen

S-Bahn
U-Bahn

710 Germany – Hamburg

from sailors and others. The result is over 2000 sq metres of curiosities such as Zulu drums, stuffed giraffes and even a shrunken head. The admission charge of DM4 is refunded with a minimum purchase of DM10. Next door, at No 69, is the **Erotic Art Museum**, a former brick warehouse containing some 1800 paintings, drawings and sculptures by artists from Delacroix to Picasso (open daily 10 am to midnight, DM15).

Prominent and awesome is the giant and stylised statue of **Otto von Bismarck** (Hugo Lederer, 1906) above Helgoländer Allee in the park past the eastern end of the Reeperbahn. You may share the sentiments of the graffiti artists around the periphery, but they have problems climbing high enough to deface Bismarck himself.

The view from Hamburg's **TV Tower**, Lagerstrasse 2-8, is truly breathtaking by itself (DM6), but for a real scream, you can now also bungee jump off the platform at 130 metres (DM250), Germany's tallest jump. From above you'll see the adjacent sprawling gardens of **Planten un Blomen**, a gorgeous landscaped city park with a large Japanese garden.

Organised Tours

Basic city sightseeing tours in English depart five times daily (11 am to 4 pm) from Kirchenallee next to the Hauptbahnhof (DM26, children DM13) and last 1¾ hours; you can add a harbour cruise for an extra DM12. 'Fleet' (canal) cruises lasting two hours depart from Jungfernstieg three times daily and cost DM23 (children DM14), for which you also get a multi-language guide brochure. The 50-minute Alster Lakes tour departs twice hourly and costs DM14 (children DM7). You can also cover the Alster Lakes in stages with boats leaving hourly; it's DM1.50 for each stop or DM12 for the round trip. There are also canal and special summer cruises.

Port Cruises

The Barkassen launch tours (60 minutes; DM15, half-price for children up to 16) run all year from St Pauli-Landungsbrücken, piers 1 to 9. They depart half-hourly from 9 am to 6 pm from April to October, and hourly from 10.30 am to 3.30 pm from November to March. Tours with English commentary run daily at 11.15 am from March to November

from pier 1 only. A one-hour HADAG steamer grand tour (DM15, children DM7.50) sails from pier No 2 half-hourly from 9.30 am to 6 pm daily (the winter schedule is more limited). Other HADAG tour options are outlined in the leaflet at the pier or by telephone (☎ 3 11 70 70).

Places to Stay

Accommodation can be pricey, although you can find a range of options in *Hamburger Vorschau* (see Information) or the hotel guide available from tourist offices. The tourist office at the Hauptbahnhof charges DM6 per booking. You can also call the Hamburg-Hotline (☎ 300 51 300) daily from 8 am to 8 pm for availability and reservations.

Camping Though inconvenient and catering mainly for caravans, the best camping option is *Campingplatz Buchholz* (☎ 5 40 45 32) at Kieler Strasse 374. From Hauptbahnhof take S-Bahn Nos 2 or 3 to Stellingen or Eidelstedt. It's better to get off the train at Hamburg-Altona station and then take bus No 183 towards Schelsen. It runs straight down Kieler Strasse, where other camping grounds are also located.

Hostels Hamburg's two hostels are large. *Auf dem Stintfang* (☎ 31 34 88) is conveniently located at Albert-Wegener-Weg 5 (U or S-Bahn: St Pauli-Landungsbrücken), and offers a view of the port (juniors DM21.50, seniors DM26.50). The youth guesthouse *Horner Rennbahn* (☎ 6 51 16 71) is less convenient at Rennbahnstrasse 100 (U3: Horner Rennbahn, walk 10 minutes north past the racecourse and leisure centre). It's DM29 for juniors and DM34.50 for seniors. The DM2.50 discount per night for stays of three nights or more only applies if you book, not if you extend your stay. The independent youth hotel *Schanzenstern* (☎ 4 39 84 41) at Bartelsstrasse 12 (U or S-Bahn: Sternschanze) has about 50 beds at DM69/108 for singles/doubles, but it's often full. All prices include breakfast.

Private Rooms Private rooms are hard to come by in Hamburg, and the price is not always a big saving over the more conveniently located budget accommodation around Hauptbahnhof. You could try *Agentur Zimmer*

Frei (☎ 41 20 70 or 41 20 79) at Baumkamp 58, an agency specialising in short-term private accommodation. For longer stays, see Long-Term Rentals below.

Hotels The best budget hotels are along Steindamm, and a few blocks east of the Hauptbahnhof along Bremer Reihe. *Hotel Mirage* (☎ 24 17 62), Steindamm 49, has singles from DM110 and doubles from DM140. Also close to the Hauptbahnhof, *Eden Hotel* (☎ 24 84 80), Ellmenreichstrasse 20, has comfortable rooms, all with TV and telephone. Rooms with shared bathroom cost DM75/120, those with private shower/WC are DM150/220. *Hotel St Georg* (☎ 24 11 41) at Kirchenallee 23 has rooms from DM95/100 and some multi-bed rooms. *Hotel Fürst Bismarck* (☎ 2 80 10 91) at Kirchenallee 49 has rooms from DM85/160. On Holzdamm, try *Steen's Hotel* (☎ 24 46 42) at No 43, which has rooms with shared shower from DM90/130. In the Reeperbahn area there's *Hotel Imperial*, Millerntorplatz 3-5, with rooms from DM95/140, and *Hotel Monopol*, Reeperbahn 48, with singles from DM133 and doubles from DM166. During low season, these rates are sometimes discounted.

Pensions A handful of small pensions are east of Kirchenallee. *Hotel-Pension Kieler Hof* (☎ 24 30 24), at Bremer Reihe No 15, has mostly doubles from DM100 and a few singles from DM60. *Hotel-Pension Annenhof* (☎ 24 34 26) is at Lange Reihe 23, with rooms for DM56/98. *Pension Sarah Petersen* (☎ 24 98 26) at Lange Reihe 50 is a very friendly place (DM65/98), but has only four rooms.

Long-Term Rentals It's best to contact Mitwohnzentrale (☎ 1 94 45) at Schulterblatt 112 (also for short-term private rooms), Mitwohnzentrale Altona (☎ 39 13 73) at Lobuschstrasse 22, or any of the other agencies that you'll find listed in the Yellow Pages under 'Mitwohnvermittlung' or 'Wohnungsund Zimmervermittlung.'

Places to Eat
Hauptbahnhof Hamburg is one of the best spots in Germany for fish, but it doesn't come cheaply. For a splurge and a truly fishy Hamburg experience, head to *Schifferbörse* on Kirchenallee 46 across from the train station exit. Here, you sit amidst original ship furniture and beneath a giant wooden ship dangling from the ceiling. Expect to pay about DM30, including one drink. The food is just as good and the atmosphere almost so at any of the three *Daniel Wischer* locations, with specials costing around DM10 and almost everything else less than DM15. The most convenient is at Spitalerstrasse 12 (250 metres from the Hauptbahnhof). One of the best kept secrets in this part of town is *Kantine im Schauspielhaus*, downstairs in the Deutsches Schauspielhaus on Kirchenallee in front of the Hauptbahnhof. Officially it caters for actors and others working in the theatre, but anyone is welcome. With a new lunch menu every day, and main courses from as little as DM8 on the right day, this place is simply too good to miss.

Gänsemarkt There is a wide variety of establishments around Gänsemarkt and Jungfernstieg near the Binnenalster lake. One lunchtime spot popular with locals is *Essen und Trinken* in the arcade at Gänsemarkt 21, a vaguely buffet-style cooperative setup where you can choose from Greek, Italian, German and other dishes. In general, you should be able to put a meal together (main course and drink) for DM12 or DM15. Close to Dammtorstrasse is *Bäckerei von Altwörden*, a bakery which also supplies shoppers and workers with warm drinks and filling, tasty snacks. It's a great place for breakfast, but a good bet at any time.

Schanzenviertel The lively Schanzenviertel neighbourhood lies west of the TV Tower and north of St Pauli (U-Bahn, S-Bahn: Sternschanze) and is peacefully shared by students and immigrants. Lots of cosy cafés and restaurants string along Schanzenstrasse and Susannenstrasse, including the *Frank and Frei* on the corner of the two, a student hangout with a small menu. On Schulterblatt 36, you'll find *La Sepia*, which serves a terrific paella and lots of fish dishes in a Mediterranean atmosphere, sometimes with live music.

St Pauli/Port Area There's a cluster of Portuguese restaurants, many excellent, along Ditmar-Koel-Strasse and Reimarus-Strasse near St Pauli Landungsbrücken. Where the two meet, the upscale *O Pescador* serves a varied menu of meat and fish dishes; less pricey (around DM15 to DM20) is *Os Amigos* on the corner of Karpfanger-Strasse and Reimarus-Strasse. If you are spending the evening around the Reeperbahn, *Piceno*, Hein-Hoyer-Strasse 8, serves up delicious Italian fare at very reasonable prices. In the evenings it is always full of young people.

Self-Catering Try one of the *Penny Markt* budget groceries. There's one on Baumeister-strasse, one at the corner of Lange Reihe and Schmilinskystrasse to the east of the main station, one near the corner of Königstrasse and Holsten-strasse at the west end of the Reeperbahn, and another at Thielbek 8. A *Plus* outlet is at Alter Steinweg 13 near Grossneumarkt. Good fresh fare is offered at Grossneumarkt on market days (Wednesday and Saturday).

Entertainment
The jazz scene in Hamburg is Germany's best. It's definitely worth catching a show at the *Cotton Club* near Grossneumarkt at Alter Steinweg 10. It opens at 8 pm and shows start at 8.30 pm, Monday to Saturday. On Sunday there's a daytime show from 11 am to 3 pm.

For an English-language fix, head for the plays at the *English Theatre*, Lerchenfeld 14. For kids (their language is more international) there's the personably presented *Theater für Kinder* at Max-Brauer-Allee 76 in Altona (tickets DM19). *Streits* cinema, on Jung-fernstieg near the corner of Grosse Bleichen, shows films in their original version every Sunday at 11 am. Half of Hamburg's expatriate English and American communities seem to show up, so you're advised to come a little early.

Hamburg has an excellent alternative and experimental theatre scene. In particular, *Kampnagelfabrik*, Jarrestrasse 20-24 (bus Nos 172 or 173), is well-respected. *Schmidt Theater*, Spielbudenplatz 27 (S-Bahn: Reeperbahn), is much loved for its wild variety shows and very casual atmosphere.

The Andrew Lloyd Webber musical *Cats* has been showing at the *Operettenhaus*, Spielbudenplatz 1 (S-Bahn: St Pauli), for the past 10 years (tickets from DM70 to DM175). The *Neue Flora Theater*, on the corner of Alsenstrasse and Stresemannstrasse (S-Bahn: Holstenstrasse), hosts *Das Phantom der Oper* (tickets from DM50 to DM200). Tickets and information at ☎ 0180/5 44 44.

For central theatre or concert bookings, go to the Last Minute Theaterkasse (near the travel service counter) on the 2nd floor of the Alsterhaus shopping complex in Poststrasse (open during regular shopping hours).

Not surprisingly, St Pauli is nightclub central. *Unit*, on the corner of Holstenstrasse and Nobistor, is a techno hot spot, while inter-national bands perform at *Docks*, at Spielbudenplatz 19, and *Grosse Freiheit 36* at – surprise, surprise! – Grosse Freiheit 36. At *Gretel & Alfons* next door, you can have a drink in what used to be the Beatles' favourite watering hole.

Getting There & Away
Air Hamburg's international airport is growing in stature as Lufthansa continues to add ser-vices. Apart from links with other German cities, you can fly to/from Brussels, London, Paris, Manchester, Dublin, Oslo, Gothenburg, Stockholm, Helsinki and St Petersburg daily. SAS flies to/from Copenhagen. Airport buses (DM8, return DM12) make the 25-minute trip to the airport from Hauptbahnhof every 20 minutes between 5.40 am and 9.20 pm.

Bus International destinations not served directly by train from Hamburg, such as Amsterdam and London, are served by Eurolines buses. You can buy tickets from the travel agent on the 2nd floor of Hamburg-Altona train station.

A very cheap option for getting to London is Rainbow Tours, which offers a weekend trip to London with accommodation included for DM153. Even if you don't use the return portion of the ticket, you will be hard pushed to find a cheaper one-way fare which includes your first night in London.

Train Hamburg's Hauptbahnhof is one of the busiest in Germany, although it does not handle all the through traffic. There are trains several times per hour to Lübeck, Kiel, Hanover and Bremen, as well as good, direct connections to Berlin and Frankfurt (some stop at the airport; the super-fast ICE trains do not). There is an overnight train to Munich and Vienna and another to Basel which continues to Milan. Hamburg-Altona shares the load, with services north to/from Kiel, Husum and Westerland on Sylt and links with Denmark (Flensburg is the change point for some trains), and south to/from Hanover, though many trains also stop at the Hauptbahnhof. It is important to read the timetables clearly, or you can finish up at the wrong station at the wrong time. Hamburg-Harburg handles some regional services (for instance to/from Cuxhaven, the main port for Heligoland).

Car & Motorcycle The autobahns of the A1 (Bremen-Lübeck) and A7 (Hanover-Kiel) cross south of the Elbe River. Three concentric ring-roads manage linking traffic. The Citynetz Mitfahr-Zentrale (☎ 1 94 44) is at Gotenstrasse 19. The Mitfahrzentrale Altona (☎ 1 94 40) is at Lobuschstrasse 22 on the corner of Am Felde (U or S-Bahn: Altona, west from the square as you leave the station's Elbe exit).

Ferry Hamburg is 20 hours by car ferry from the English port of Harwich. Services run year round, at least twice a week in either direction (except in January); check with Scandinavian Seaways (☎ 3 89 03 71). The Edgar-Engelhard-Kai terminal is at Van-der-Smissen-Strasse, off Grosser Elbe Strasse, about two km west of St Pauli harbour (S-Bahn: Königstrasse, or bus No 183 to/from the city centre). It is open weekdays from 10 am to 5 pm, weekends just before departures (you will have to exchange money before you reach the terminal or on board). The one-way passenger fare to Harwich ranges from DM88 to DM580, depending on the season, the day of the week and cabin amenities. A car costs an extra DM49 to DM121, a motorbike DM41 to DM81, and a bicycle will cost DM19 in the high season and DM5 the rest of the year. Every four days, there's also a ferry to Newcastle.

DFO VogelflugLinie (☎ 0180-5 34 34 41) operates a busy train, car and passenger ferry from Puttgarden to Rødby (the quickest way to Copenhagen), which leaves every half-hour 24 hours a day and takes one hour. If you're travelling by train, the cost of the ferry is included

in your ticket. It costs DM80/160 one way/return (DM100/200 Friday to Sunday) to take a car including up to five people all year. A motorbike including up to two people costs DM40/80, and a bicycle is DM5/10. A single passenger pays DM8 (DM10 from June to September) for a one-way ticket.

Getting Around
Public transport consists of buses, the U-Bahn and the S-Bahn. A day pass for travel after 9 am in most of the Hamburg area is DM7.70 (including the surrounding area, DM12.40) and there are various family passes. Single journeys cost DM2.50 for the city tariff area, DM4 for the city and surrounding area, and DM6.40 within the outer tariff area. Children cost a basic DM1.50. For the Schnellbus or 1st-class S-Bahn the day supplements are DM1.80. A three-day travel-only pass is DM22.30, and weekly cards range from DM20.50 to DM43.50, depending on your status and the distance you want to travel (check the diagrams with the oval-shaped zones marked in yellow). From midnight to dawn the night bus network takes over from the trains, converging on the main city bus station at Rathausmarkt. For the transport options with a Hamburg Card, see the Information section.

A taxi from the Hauptbahnhof to the airport should cost around DM25 (one easy number to use is ☎ 21 12 11). A better airport option is to take the U1 from the main train station to U-Bahn Ohlstedt and from there the No 112 express bus, but it's perhaps easiest to use the shuttle bus (see 'Air' for details). Hamburg's bicycle tracks are extensive and reach almost to the centre of the city.

AROUND HAMBURG
The **Altes Land** area along the southern bank of the Elbe is a welcome relief from the city hustle and bustle. It can be viewed from the city transit network or on one of the cruises to **Lühe**. The area was reclaimed from marshy ground by Dutch experts in the Middle Ages, who then set about growing fruit. The area's jewels are the thatched and panelled **17th-century homes** around Jork (S3: Neugraben, then bus No 257 to Jork), although early in May the **orchards** are a brilliant sight.

The HADAG cruise to Lühe from St Pauli,

lasting about 90 minutes, costs DM20 return and departs four times daily. In good weather there are extra services. You can pay supplements for an on-board feast. Family cards cost up to DM42.

Schleswig-Holstein

Schleswig-Holstein is Germany's northernmost state. Covering an area of 16,696 sq km, it borders Denmark at the lower end of the Jutland Peninsula. Among the many attractions here are the North Frisian Islands and the historical city of Lübeck.

Schleswig and Holstein began the long process of breaking away from Denmark with the help of Sweden in the mid-17th century. Only in 1773 were both finally free of their Danish masters. In 1815, Holstein joined the German Confederation, which resulted in Denmark trying to lure Schleswig back to the motherland.

Ever-increasing tensions finally led to two wars between Germany and Denmark, the first in 1848-50 and the second in 1864. After a short period under combined Prussian and Austrian rule, and yet another war, Austria was forced to accept Schleswig-Holstein's annexation by Bismarck's Prussia in 1866. Under the conditions of the Treaty of Versailles in 1919, North Schleswig was handed over to Denmark. Finally, in 1946, the British military government formed the state of Schleswig-Holstein from the Prussian province of the same name.

LÜBECK

Medieval Lübeck was known as the Queen of the Hanseatic League, as it was the capital of this association of towns which ruled trade on the Baltic Sea from the 12th to the 16th century. You will need a full day or more to explore this beautiful city.

Information

The tourist office in the train station (☎ 7 23 00) is open Monday to Saturday from 10 am to 6 pm. Another office (☎ 1 22 81 09) is in the Kanzleigebäude on Breite Strasse near the Rathaus, open weekdays from 9.30 am to 6 pm, and weekends from 10 am to 2 pm. The central

information office is at Beckergrube 95. Late on Thursday (to 8.30 pm) or on weekends, take booking enquiries to the tourist office in Holstentor-Passage, just inside the arcade at the west end of Holstenstrasse.

Good value is the Lübeck Card which entitles you to unlimited travel and discounts on cruises, museums, cinema, and other attractions. It costs DM9 for 24 hours and DM18 for three days and is available at tourist offices, hotels, youth hostels and museums.

The central post office is on Königstrasse 46, across from the Katarinenkirche.

Lübeck's telephone code is ☎ 0451.

Things to See & Do

Most museums and attractions are free on Friday. One exception is the landmark **Holstentor**, a fortified gate with huge twin towers, which serves as the city's symbol as well as its museum (DM5, discount DM2.50; closed Monday). Another exception is **Buddenbrookhaus**, the family house where Thomas Mann was born and which he made famous in his novel *Buddenbrooks*. The literary works and philosophical rivalry of the brothers Thomas and Heinrich are commemorated here (entry DM6, discount DM3). It is located on Mengstrasse to the north of **Marienkirche** on Markt, which contains a stark reminder of WWII: a bombing raid brought the church bells crashing to the stone floor and the townspeople have left the bell fragments in place, with a small sign saying, 'A protest against war and violence'. Also on Markt is the imposing **Rathaus** which covers two full sides of the square. It can be toured – three times on weekdays – for DM4, discount DM2.

Lübeck's **Marionettentheater** (Puppet Theatre), on the corner of Am Kolk and Kleine Petersgrube, is an absolute must (closed Monday). Usually there is an afternoon performance for children (3 pm) and an evening performance for adults, but times vary. Afternoon seats cost DM7 and evenings DM12 or DM16. It is best to book ahead: the box office is open Monday from 8 am to noon, Tuesday to Friday from 8 am to noon and 1.30 to 4 pm, and weekends in the afternoon only. The **Museum für Figurentheater**, a survey of all types of dolls and puppetry, is just around the corner from the theatre at Kleine Petersgrube

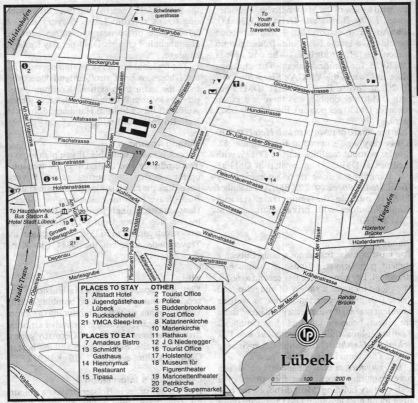

Lübeck

0   100   200 m

PLACES TO STAY
1 Altstadt Hotel
3 Jugendgästehaus
 Lübeck
9 Rucksackhotel
21 YMCA Sleep-Inn

PLACES TO EAT
7 Amadeus Bistro
13 Schmidt's
 Gasthaus
14 Hieronymus
 Restaurant
15 Tipasa

OTHER
2 Tourist Office
4 Police
5 Buddenbrookhaus
6 Post Office
8 Katarinenkirche
10 Marienkirche
11 Rathaus
12 J G Niederegger
16 Tourist Office
17 Holstentor
18 Museum für
 Figurentheater
19 Marionettentheater
20 Petrikirche
22 Co-Op Supermarket

4. It is open daily from 10 am to 6 pm and entry is DM6 (students DM5 and children DM4).

The tower lift at the partly restored **Petrikirche** costs DM3 and affords a superb view over the Altstadt (open 11 am to 4 pm, closed Monday).

Places to Stay

Though a bit of a trek at 18 kilometres, the **camping** is excellent along the Travemünde shoreline to the north. This area, on the mouth of the Trave River, is an international beach resort. The tourist offices have a list of camping grounds.

For budget accommodation, the small

Rucksackhotel (☎ 70 68 92), Kanalstrasse 70, has beds in multi-bed rooms at DM21 to DM26, a few doubles at DM80, and a four-bed room at DM128; there are cooking facilities. It only has 28 beds, so you'd be wise to book ahead.

Lübeck has two DJH hostels. The excellent *Jugendgästehaus Lübeck* (☎ 7 02 03 99), Mengstrasse 33, is well situated in the middle of the old town, 15 minutes walk from the train station (bus Nos 3 or 12 along An der Untertrave to Beckergrube). The cost for juniors/seniors is DM25/30, although there are multi-night discounts and some great singles and doubles costing DM30/35 per person, a few with a view of the Marienkirche. The other hostel, *Folke-Bernadotte-Heim* (☎ 3 34 33), is at Am Gertrudenkirchhof 4, a little outside the old town (same bus routes from the train station, past Burgtorbrücke). The cost here is DM20/25 for juniors/seniors. The cheapest place in town is the YMCA's *Sleep-Inn* (☎ 7 19 20) at Grosse Petersgrube 11 (DM15 per bed, DM40 per double, and there is a group room for DM30 per person). Breakfast is DM5 extra.

In the centre of town, *Altstadt Hotel* (☎ 7 20 83) is very well situated at Fischergrube 52. Singles without facilities start at DM75, with facilities at DM95. Doubles start at DM120. For something a little more up-market, try *Hotel Stadt Lübeck* (☎ 8 38 83), Am Bahnhof 21 just outside the main train station. Singles/doubles with private bath start at DM120/170.

Places to Eat

The most popular restaurant among Lübeck's student population is *Tipasa*, Schlumacherstrasse 14. For atmosphere it is second to none. The menu includes a variety of budget-priced meat, fish and vegetarian dishes as well as excellent pizzas. If you need a good brew, there are several beers on tap, including Guinness. Another place that is always crowded is *Schmidt's Gasthaus*, Dr-Julius-Leber-Strasse 60-62. The menu is similar to Tipasa's.

Hieronymus, at Fleischhauerstrasse 81, is a cosy restaurant spread over four floors of a 15th-century building. Most dishes on the creative menu cost less than DM15 and are quite filling.

Amadeus, Königstrasse 26, is a great bistro with good music. It has a limited menu, but the prices are right. It is also a good place for breakfast (open from 10 am).

Save room for a dessert or a snack of marzipan, which was invented in Lübeck (local legend has it that the town ran out of flour during a long siege and resorted to grinding almonds to make bread). The mecca of marzipan is *JG Niederegger* at Breite Strasse 89, directly opposite the Rathaus.

Getting There & Away

Lübeck is close to Hamburg, with at least one train every hour. The trip takes from 40 minutes to a little over an hour depending on the train. Kiel is nearby, and there are numerous trains to/from Lübeck every day. A left-luggage office near the entrance of the Hauptbahnhof charges DM4 per day for large baggage.

The regional bus services stop opposite the local buses, a brief stroll around the corner from the main train station. Kraftomnibusse services to/from Wismar arrive here, as well as Autokraft buses to/from Hamburg, Schwerin, Kiel, Rostock and Berlin.

Getting Around

Lübeck is easily walkable. If you plan to go to Travemünde, you'll find lots of transport options during the tourist season. Several buses link the city island with the train station. Buses leave from the bus station on adjacent Hansestrasse; a single journey on the island or to one stop beyond costs DM2.80. Lübeck day-travel cards cost DM8 and include the Travemünde area, but the DM4 City-Karte does not.

KIEL

Kiel, the capital of Schleswig-Holstein, was seriously damaged by Allied bombing during WWII, but has since been rebuilt into a vibrant and modern city. Located at the end of a modest firth, it has long been one of Germany's most important Baltic Sea harbours and the host of Olympic sailing events in 1936 and 1972.

Orientation & Information

Kiel's main street is Holstenstrasse, a colourful, pedestrian street a few hundred metres from the sea. It runs from St Nikolai church in the north to the tourist office in the south, although at this end the street is actually an undercover shopping mall. The tourist office at Sophienblatt 30 is reached by an overpass from the Hauptbahnhof – just follow the signs from within the station. At the tourist office you can buy the Kiel Card, which entitles you to unlimited public transportation and discounts for museums and cruises (one-day card DM12, three-day card DM17, seven-day DM27).

Kiel's telephone code is ☎ 0431.

Things to See & Do

Kiel's most famous attraction is the **Kieler Woche** (Kiel Week) in the last full week in June, a festival revolving around a series of yachting regattas attended by over 4000 of the world's sailing elite and half a million spectators. Even if you're not into sailing, the atmosphere is electric – just make sure you book a room in advance if you want to be in on the fun.

To experience Kiel's love for the sea in less energetic fashion, take a ferry ride to the village of **Laboe** at the mouth of the firth. Ferries leave hourly from Bahnhofbrücke pier, no more than five minutes walk from Hauptbahnhof. They take around one hour to reach Laboe, hopping back and forth across the firth along the way. In Laboe, you can visit **U995**, a wartime U-boat on the beach, which is now a technical museum (open daily; DM3). Nearby are the **Naval Memorial** and a **navigation museum** (open daily; DM4.50).

Kiel is also the point at which the shipping canal from the North Sea enters the Baltic Sea. Some 60,000 ships pass through the canal every year, and the **locks** *(Schleusen)*, at Holtenau six km north of the city centre, are well worth a visit. Admission to the viewing platform is DM1; tours of the locks are offered daily at 9 and 11 am and 1 and 3 pm.

The **Schiffahrtsmuseum**, Wallstrasse 65, (closed Monday; admission free), contains an interesting collection of models and other maritime artefacts. Worth seeing, too, is the **Schleswig-Holstein Open Air Museum** in nearby Molfsee (take Autokraftbus No 1680). More than 60 historical houses typical of the region have been relocated here, giving you a thorough introduction to the northern way of life. The museum is open daily from July to September, on weekends from November to March and daily except Monday the rest of the year. Admission is DM7, students DM5.

Places to Stay

Kiel's *Campingplatz Falckenstein* (☎ 39 20 78) is at Palisadenweg 171 in the suburb of Friedrichsort and is open from April to October. The *youth hostel* (☎ 73 14 88) is at Johannesstrasse 1 in the suburb of Gaarden, across the water from the Hauptbahnhof. To get there, take the Laboe ferry from near the train station and get off at the first stop ('Gaarden'), from where it's a 10-minute walk. The other option is to take bus Nos 4 or 54 from Sophienblatt by the tourist office to Kieler

Strasse. The cost for juniors/seniors is DM22/27.

In the budget-hotel range, *Touristhotel Schweriner Hof* (☎ 6 14 16), Königsweg 13, is the most centrally located. It has singles/doubles from DM65/110. *Rabe's Hotel* (☎ 66 30 70) at Ringstrasse 30 is also very central, with rooms from DM70/120.

In Gaarden, not too far from the DJH hostel, is *Hotel Runge* (☎ 73 19 92) at Elisabethstrasse 16. Rooms start at DM55/98 without shower, DM70/98 with. *Hotel Düvelsbek* (☎ 8 10 21), Feldstrasse 111, has well-priced singles with shower/WC from DM66 and doubles from DM100. It's about two km outside the city centre; take bus No 1 from the train station to the 'Esmarch-Strasse' stop.

Places to Eat

There are plenty of eateries with very reasonable prices. Good and typical is the *Friesenhof*, at Fleethörn 9 in the Rathaus building. Daily lunch specials (from 11 am to 3 pm) cost under DM10, and tasty main courses start at DM15. Between 3 and 5pm, all dishes cost half price plus DM2.

The *Klosterbrauerei*, at Alter Markt 9 (at the northern end of Holstenstrasse), is a private brewery with great atmosphere and prices to match. Lunch specials (including some vegetarian dishes) range from DM7.50 to DM8.50. Around the hostel in Gaarden, the best value are the kebab and pizza places within walking distance.

Getting There & Away

Numerous trains run every day between Kiel and Hamburg-Altona or Hamburg Hauptbahnhof. The trip takes from one to 1½ hours. To Lübeck, trains leave just about every hour (sometimes more often). The trip takes about 1¼ hours. Regional buses run to/from Lübeck, Schleswig and Puttgarden.

Langeland-Kiel (☎ 97 41 50) runs two or three ferries a day to Bagenkop on the Danish island of Langeland (not from early January to mid-February). The trip takes 2½ hours and costs DM7/11 one way/return except in July, when it is DM9/17. Bicycles cost DM19/33; cars DM21/29 in low season (including up to four passengers) and DM70 in July (return only, driver included). The ferries leave from Oslokai.

GERMANY

The daily Kiel-Gothenburg ferry (14 hours) leaves from Schwedenkai at 7 pm. From the beginning of November to the beginning of April, the fare is DM66/104 one way/return; from mid-June to the beginning of August it costs DM158/256; the rest of the year it costs DM108/176. Bicycles are carried free. Sleeping berths in four-bed cabins are an additional DM30. For booking and information, call Stena Line on ☎ 90 99.

Color Line ferries (☎ 97 40 90) run direct to/from Kiel and Oslo daily, except on Christmas and New Year's Day. Departures are at 1.30 pm on Tuesday and Thursday, at 4.30 pm on Monday, Wednesday, Friday and Saturday, and at 2.30 pm on Sunday. The trip takes just under 20 hours. Fares start at DM150 one way (around 30% extra in summer) per bed in a two-bed cabin. On all these ferries, occasional student discounts are available.

Getting Around
The bus station is conveniently located on Auguste-Viktoria-Strasse near the Hauptbahnhof. To get to the North-Baltic Sea Canal and the locks, take bus No 4 to Wik; the locks are about five minutes walk from the terminus.

SCHLESWIG
This peaceful town on the Schlei Fjord is worth a day trip if you can fit in all the attractions. It has a restored old centre a short walk south from the bus station on Königstrasse. In the old town is the tourist office (☎ 2 48 78), in the historic building at Plessenstrasse 7. It is closed on weekends, but an interactive computer information display should answer most questions regarding sights and accommodation. The telephone code is ☎ 04621.

Things to See
The Romanesque-Gothic **cathedral** and **Altstadt** are both well worth seeing, but **Schloss Gottorf** and its **Schleswig-Holstein Landesmuseum** collections of cultural history are a bigger attraction (DM7, students DM3). They cover just about everything from prehistoric hunting to 19th-century arts and crafts, and afterwards you can stroll around the castle and its gardens.

The old Viking town of **Hedeby** (Haithabu) lies across the fjord from the town centre and is marked only by the remains of its semicircular wall, on the lagoon of Haddeby Noor. To make it all meaningful, visit the **Viking Museum** (DM4, discount DM2; closed Monday), about a three km walk from the train station, east of B76. A huge Viking longboat has been artfully reconstructed inside. More history, if you can handle it, is in a walk along the old dyke and wall complex of the **Danevirke** (Dannewerk), which runs from the walls of old Hedeby west to Hollingstedt. You can follow its twists for several km on worn trails.

Getting There & Around
The train station is linked by local bus to the town centre and there are trains to/from Kiel daily.

NORTH FRISIAN ISLANDS
The Frisian Islands reward those who make the trek with sand dunes, sea, pure air and – every so often – sunshine. Friesland itself covers an area stretching from the northern Netherlands along the coast up into Denmark. Many inhabitants speak Frisian dialects, very closely related to English but virtually incomprehensible if you hear them spoken. North Friesland (Nordfriesland) is the western coastal area of Schleswig-Holstein up to and into Denmark. The sea area forms the National Park of Wattenmeer, and the shifting dunes, particularly on the islands of Amrum, Föhr and Langeness, are sensitive and cannot be disturbed – paths and boardwalks are provided for strolling. Wild and domesticated animals are protected by stringent regulation. The most popular of the North Frisian Islands is Sylt, a famous resort known for its spa facilities, water sports and fancy restaurants. It can be very crowded in summer; the neighbouring islands of Föhr and Amrum are far more relaxed and less touristy.

Orientation & Information
The information office next to Westerland's train station on Sylt (☎ 99 88) can help with finding accommodation. For other information, try the office of the Bädergemeinschaft Sylt (☎ 82 02 0), near the Westerland Rathaus on Stephanstrasse 6 (open weekdays from 10 am to noon and 2 to 4 pm) or Sylt Tourismus Zentrale, (☎ 60 26) on Keitumer Landstrasse 10b just outside of town in Tinnum (open

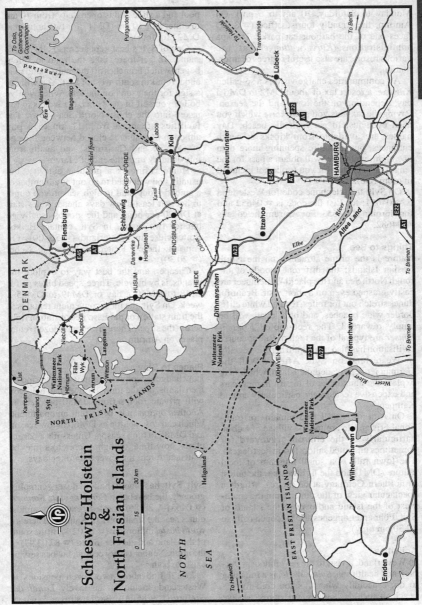

Schleswig-Holstein
&
North Frisian Islands

0   15   30 km

NORTH
SEA

NORTH FRISIAN ISLANDS

EAST FRISIAN ISLANDS

Heligoland

DENMARK

To Oslo,
Gothenburg
& Copenhagen

Langeland

Ærø   Marstal

Bagenkop

Schlei fjord

Laboe

Kiel

Puttgarden

To Heiligenhafen

Travemünde

To Berlin

Lübeck

A1
E22

HAMBURG

Neumünster

E45

A7

Itzehoe

A1
E22

Altes Land

Elbe River

To Bremen

Kampen   List

Westerland   Sylt

Hörnum

Föhr   Wyk
Amrum
Witdün   Langeness

Wattenmeer
National Park

Niebüll

Dagebüll

HUSUM

Danewirke
Hollingstedt

Schleswig

Flensburg

ECKERNFÖRDE

E45   A7

RENDSBURG

Nord-Ostsee Kanal

HEIDE

Dithmarschen

A23

Wattenmeer
National Park

CUXHAVEN

E234
A27

Bremerhaven

To Bremen

Wattenmeer
National Park

Weser River

Wilhelmshaven

Emden

To Harwich

Monday to Saturday, 10 am to 6 pm). On Amrum, the friendly tourist office (☎ 8 91) faces one of the harbour car parks. The spa administrations *(Kurverwaltungen)* at the various resorts are also useful sources of information.

All communities charge visitors a so-called *Kurtaxe*, a resort tax of about DM2 to DM6 a day, depending on the town and the season. Paying the tax gets you a *Kurkarte* which you need even just to get onto the beach. Day passes are available from kiosks at beach entrances, but if you're spending more than one night, your hotel will obtain a pass for the length of your stay for you (price not included in room rate).

On Sylt, the telephone code for Westerland is ☎ 04651; for List the code is ☎ 04652 and for Hörnum ☎ 04653. For Amrum the code is ☎ 04682.

Things to See

Nature is the prime attraction on the North Frisian Islands; the different moods of the rough North Sea and the placid Wattenmeer are easily grasped even on a short visit. Beautiful dunes stretch out for miles, red and white cliffs border wide beaches, and bird lovers will be amply rewarded. The reed-roofed *Friesenhäuser* are typical of the region. But of course civilisation has also taken hold here, especially in Westerland on Sylt. After WWII, the German jet-set invaded the island, which may explain the abundance of luxury homes, cars and expensive restaurants, particularly around Kampen.

On Amrum, you'll find remains of traditional Frisian life around the village of **Nebel**, particularly in the **church graveyard** for sometimes unnamed sailors lost in hostile seas. The town **mill** is a small museum of local culture (DM1) and the **lighthouse**, the tallest in northern Germany at 63 metres, affords a spectacular view of the dunes from the southwest of the island and over to the islands of Sylt, Föhr and Langeness (DM2; open daily to 12.30 pm only).

Activities

In Westerland, a visit to the new indoor waterpark and health spa, *Sylter Welle*, is a fun thing to do, especially when it's too cold for the beach. It includes saunas, solariums, a wave pool and a slide and is open daily from 10 am to either 9 or 10 pm (DM17 for two hours and DM22 for four).

One of Sylt's best kept secrets is the beach sauna. To get there, take the road to Ellenbogen, which branches off the main island road about four km south-west of List. You will see a sign for the sauna on the left. When you've boiled yourself in the sauna, the idea is to run naked into the chilly North Sea – brrr. The facilities are open from 11 am to 5 pm, although the sauna is closed between the end of October and Christmas, and again from mid-January until the end of March.

Horse riding is a popular activity, but usually you will need to go out as a member of a guided group, and in high season you ought to book at least a few days ahead. Rates start at DM20 per hour, and the groups usually go out for two hours. In Sylt, contact Heikos Reiterwiese in Westerland (☎ 56 00). On Amrum, there's Reiterhof Jensen in Nebel (☎ 20 30).

Cheaper, and the best way to explore the islands, is by bicycle. Three-speed bikes go for DM8 to DM10 a day or DM49 to DM55 a week. On Sylt, the most convenient rental is at the train station or the Esso petrol station right across the street. There are about a dozen rental places on Amrum.

Places to Stay

Low budget accommodation is hard to find on the islands, but the tourist offices can help you with private rooms from DM30 per person. Another option may be to rent an apartment, which can cost as little as DM60 in low season and DM85 in high season. Unless it's a particularly slow time, though, proprietors may be reluctant to rent for fewer than three days.

Sylt Sylt has about half a dozen camping grounds, the best being *Campingplatz Kampen* (☎ 04651-4 20 86), located beautifully amidst dunes near the small town of Kampen. There's a *youth hostel* in Hörnum (☎ 88 02 94) in the south of the island and another in List (☎ 87 03 97) in the north. Neither is very central, but bus service exists to both.

You'll find about two dozen pensions in Westerland, including the lovely *Landhaus Nielsen* (☎ 9 86 90), Bastianstrasse 5, where singles/doubles cost DM60/100 in low season and DM 65/110 in high season. *Hotel Garni Diana* (☎ 9 88 60), Elisabethstrasse 19, is decent value at DM85/150 and DM90/160 in low and high seasons respectively. An even better deal is *Haus Wagenknecht* (☎ 2 30 91), Wenningstedter Weg 59, where rooms are DM60/150 in low season and DM65/170 in high season.

Amrum *Campingplatz Amrum* (☎ 04682-22 54) is at the north edge of Wittdün. The *Wittdün hostel* (☎ 20 10), Obere Wandelbahn 9, has plenty of beds but it's best to book ahead, even in the off season. *Haus Südstrand* (☎ 27 08), at Mittelstrasse 30 in Wittdün, has a few singles/doubles for DM58/120 most times of the year.

Places to Eat

Sylt Picnics are a fine option on the islands, but for a splurge try Westerland's *Alte Friesenstube* in the 17th-century building at Gaadt 4. It specialises in northern German and Frisian cooking, with main courses starting at DM30. For good, inexpensive fare, try *Toni's Restaurant*, Norderstrasse 3. It has a variety of main courses at around DM11 and a pleasant garden. *Blum's* on Neue Strasse 4 has some of the freshest fish in town at very reasonable prices. *Kupferkanne*, Stapelhooger Wai in Kampen, is a beautiful stop during a bike tour. Their giant cups of coffee and matching slices of pie are not cheap, but the view of the Wattenmeer is complimentary.

List's harbour sports a number of colourful kiosks. One of them, *Gosch*, which prides itself on being Germany's northernmost fish kiosk, is an institution well known beyond Sylt. The food is delicious, and with prices starting at DM2.50 for fish sandwiches, nobody has to leave hungry.

Amrum Amrum has only a few restaurants and many of them close out of season. But for local fare for lunch or dinner consider *Hotel Ual Öömreng* in Norddorf, or the relaxing teahouse atmosphere of *Burg Haus*, built on an old Viking hill-fort above the eastern beach at Norddorf.

Note that restaurants can be closed by 7 pm in low season.

Getting There & Away

Sylt Sylt is connected with the mainland by a scenic trains-only causeway right through the Wattenmeer. Between 13 and 18 trains a day make the three-hour trek from Hamburg-Altona to Westerland. If you are travelling by car, you must load it onto a train in the town of Niebüll near the Danish border. There are 12 to 15 crossings in both directions every day and no reservations can be made. The cost per car is a shocking DM131 return, but that includes all passengers.

Amrum To get to Amrum and the island of Föhr, you must board a ferry in Dagebüll Hafen. To get there, take the Sylt-bound train from Hamburg-Altona and change in Niebüll. In summer, there are also some through-trains. A day-return from Dagebüll costs DM24, which allows you to visit both islands. If you stay overnight, return tickets cost DM27.40. The trip to Amrum takes around two hours, stopping at Föhr on the way.

There are daily flights between Westerland airport and Hamburg, Munich and Berlin, and several flights weekly from other German cities.

Getting Around

On Sylt, buses run every 20 minutes, with five lines serving every corner of the island. There are seven price zones, costing from DM2 to DM10.50. Some buses have bicycle hangers. On Amrum, a bus runs from the ferry terminal in Wittdün to Norddorf and back every 30 to 60 minutes, depending on the season (day passes are only DM6). The slow, fun inter-island options are the day-return cruises to Föhr (Wyk) and Amrum (Wittdün) from the harbour at Hörnum on Sylt. You pass the shallow banks that attract seals and sea birds on WDR and Adler-Schiffe tour boats for DM32. Bicycles are an extra DM7 or DM8.

HELIGOLAND

Not technically part of the Frisian Islands, Heligoland (Helgoland) lies 70 km out to sea and is a popular day-trip from the islands and a duty-free port. Because of the North Sea's strong currents and unpredictable weather, however, the passage will be most enjoyed by people with iron stomachs. Adler-Schiffe ferries make the excursion from Hörnum on Sylt several times a week (DM42).

It's hard to explain the seasick crowds flocking to Heligoland like lemmings: it's a tiny chunk of red rock sticking up out of the sea. It was used as a submarine base in WWII, and it's still possible to tour the strong bunkers and underground tunnels. The island was heavily bombed and all of the houses are new. Take a walk along Lung Wai ('long way'), filled with duty-free shops, and then up the stairway of 180 steps to Oberland for what view there is. There's also a 'scenic trail' around the island. Neighbouring **Düne** is a tiny island filled with beaches and nudists (there is a ferry service).

Greece

The first travel guide to Greece was written 1800 years ago by the Greek geographer and historian Pausanias, so the tourism industry isn't exactly in its infancy. In the 19th century, wealthy young European aristocrats made it part of their Grand Tour; in this century it has become a mecca for sun and sea worshippers.

The country's enduring attraction is its archaeological sites; those who travel through Greece journey not only through the landscape but also through time, witnessing the legacy of Europe's greatest ages – the Mycenaean, Minoan, classical, Hellenistic and Byzantine.

You cannot wander far in Greece without stumbling across a broken column, a crumbling bastion or a tiny Byzantine church, each perhaps neglected and forgotten but still retaining an aura of former glory.

Greece is much more than beaches and ancient monuments. Its culture is a unique blend of East and West, inherited from the long period of Ottoman rule and apparent in its food, music and traditions. The mountainous countryside is a walker's paradise crisscrossed by age-old donkey tracks leading to stunning vistas.

The magnetism of Greece is also due to less tangible attributes – the dazzling clarity of the light, the floral aromas which permeate the air, the spirit of *place* – for there is hardly a grove, mountain or stream which is not sacred to a deity, and the ghosts of the past still linger.

And then again, many visitors come to Greece simply to get away from it all and relax in one of Europe's friendliest and safest countries.

Facts about the Country

HISTORY
Greece's strategic position at the crossroads of Europe and Asia has resulted in a long and turbulent history.

During the Bronze Age, which lasted from 3000 to 1200 BC in Greece, the advanced Cycladic, Minoan and Mycenaean civi-lisations flourished. The Mycenaeans were eventually swept aside by the Dorians in the 12th century BC. The next 400 years are often referred to as the 'age of darkness' (1200-800 BC), which sounds a bit unfair for a period that saw the arrival of the Iron Age and emergence of geometric pottery. Homer's *Odyssey* and *Iliad* were composed at this time.

By 800 BC, when Homer's works were first written down, Greece was undergoing a cultural and military revival with the evolution of the city-states, the most powerful of which were Athens and Sparta. Greater Greece – Magna Graecia – was created, with south Italy as an important component. The unified Greeks repelled the Persians twice, at Marathon (490 BC) and Salamis (480 BC). The period which followed was an unparalleled time of growth and prosperity, resulting in what is called the classical (or golden) age.

The Golden Age
In this period, the Parthenon was commissioned by Pericles, Sophocles wrote *Oedipus*

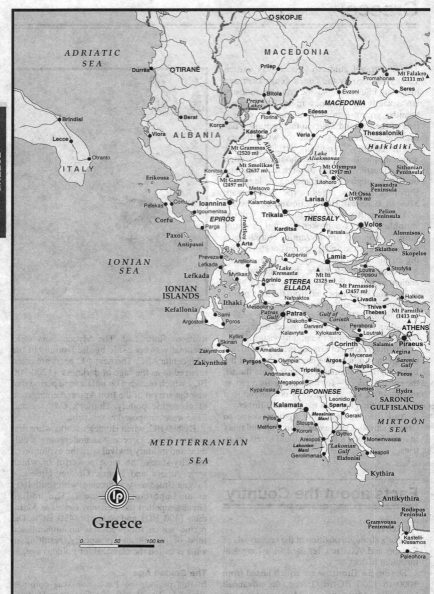

Greece

0   50   100 km

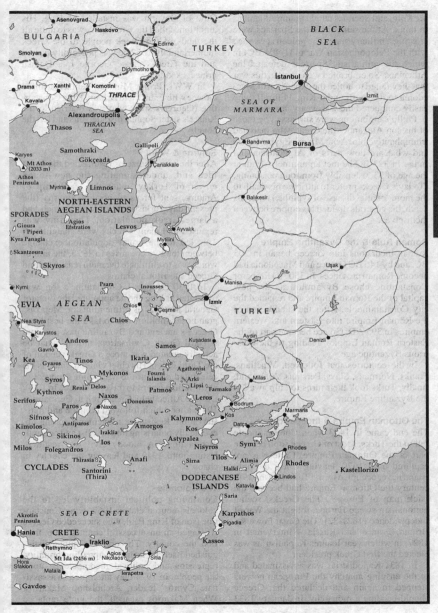

the King, and Socrates taught young Athenians to think. At the same time, the Spartans were creating a military state. The golden age ended with the Peloponnesian War (431-404 BC) in which the militaristic Spartans defeated the Athenians. So embroiled were they in this war that they failed to notice the expansion of Macedonia to the north under King Philip II, who easily conquered the war-weary city-states.

Philip's ambitions were surpassed by those of his son Alexander the Great, who marched triumphantly into Asia Minor, Egypt, Persia and what are now parts of Afghanistan and India. In 323 BC he met an untimely death at the age of 33, ostensibly from food poisoning. (Today's Greeks prefer to attribute his death to the more 'exotic' disease of syphilis.) After his death, his generals divided his empire between themselves.

Roman Rule & the Byzantine Empire

Roman incursions into Greece began in 205 BC, and by 146 BC Greece and Macedonia had become Roman provinces. In 330 AD Emperor Constantine chose Byzantium as the new capital of the Roman Empire and renamed the city Constantinople. After the subdivision of the Roman Empire into Eastern and Western empires in 395 AD, Greece became part of the Eastern Roman Empire, leading to the illustrious Byzantine age.

In the centuries that followed, Venetians, Franks, Normans, Slavs, Persians, Arabs and, finally, Turks took their turns to chip away at the Byzantine Empire.

The Ottoman Empire & Independence

The end came in 1453 when Constantinople fell to the Turks. Most of Greece soon became part of the Ottoman Empire. Crete was not captured until 1670, leaving Corfu the only island never occupied by the Turks. By the 19th century the Ottoman Empire had become the 'sick man of Europe'. The Greeks, seeing nationalism sweep Europe, fought the War of Independence (1821-32). The Great Powers – Britain, France and Russia – intervened in 1827, in which year Ioannis Kapodistrias was elected the first Greek president.

In 1831 Kapodistrias was assassinated and in the ensuing anarchy the European powers stepped in again and declared that Greece should become a monarchy. In January 1833

Otho of Bavaria was installed as king. His ambition, called the Great Idea, was to unite all the lands of the Greek people to the Greek motherland. In 1862 he was peacefully ousted and the Greeks chose George I, a Danish prince, as king.

In WWI, Prime Minister Venizelos allied Greece with France and Britain. King Constantine (George's son), who was married to the Kaiser's sister Sophia, disputed this and left the country.

Smyrna & WWII

After the war, Venizelos resurrected the Great Idea and, underestimating the new-found power of Turkey under the leadership of Atatürk, sent forces to occupy Smyrna (the present-day Turkish port of İzmir) which had a large Greek population. The army was repulsed and many Greeks were slaughtered. This led to the brutal population exchange between the two countries in 1923, the aim of which was to eliminate the main reason behind Greece's territorial claims.

In 1930 George II, Constantine's son, was reinstated as king and he appointed the dictator General Metaxas as prime minister. Metaxas' grandiose ambition was to take the best from Greece's ancient and Byzantine past to create a Third Greek Civilisation, though what he actually created was more a Greek version of the Third Reich. His chief claim to fame is his celebrated *okhi* (no) to Mussolini's request to allow Italian troops to traverse Greece in 1940. Despite Allied help, Greece fell to Germany in 1941, after which followed carnage and mass starvation. Resistance movements sprang up, eventually polarising into royalist and communist factions. A bloody civil war resulted, lasting until 1949 and leaving the country in chaos.

The Colonels

Continuing political instability led to the colonels' coup d'état in 1967. King Constantine (son of King Paul, who succeeded George II) staged an unsuccessful counter coup, then fled the country. The colonels' junta distinguished itself by inflicting appalling brutality, repression and political incompetence upon the people. In 1974 they attempted to assassinate Cyprus' leader, Archbishop Makarios. When Makarios escaped, the junta replaced him with the extremist Nikos Samson, a convicted murderer. The Turks, who comprised 20% of the population, were alarmed at having Samson as leader. Consequently, mainland Turkey sent in troops and occupied North Cyprus, the continued occupation of which is one of the most contentious issues in Greek politics today. The junta, by now in a shambles, had little choice but to hand back power to civilians. In November 1974 a plebiscite voted 69% against restoration of the monarchy, and Greece became a republic. An election brought the right-wing New Democracy (ND) party into power.

The Socialist 1980s

In 1981 Greece entered the EC (European Community, now the EU). Andreas Papandreou's Panhellenic Socialist Movement (PASOK) won the next election, giving Greece its first socialist government. PASOK promised removal of US air bases and withdrawal from NATO, which Greece had joined in 1951.

Six years into government these promises remained unfulfilled, unemployment was high and reforms in education and welfare had been limited. Women's issues had fared better however – the dowry system was abolished, abortion legalised, and civil marriage and divorce were implemented. The crunch for the government came in 1988 when Papandreou's affair with air stewardess Dimitra Liana (whom he subsequently married) was widely publicised and PASOK became embroiled in a financial scandal involving the Bank of Crete.

In July 1989 an unprecedented conservative and communist coalition took over to implement a *katharsis* (campaign of purification) to investigate the scandals. It ruled that Papandreou and four ministers should stand trial for embezzlement, telephone tapping and illegal grain sales. It then stepped down in October 1990, stating that katharsis was completed.

The 1990s

The tough economic reforms that Prime Minister Konstantinos Mitsotakis was forced to introduce to counter a spiralling foreign debt soon made his government deeply unpopular. By late 1992, allegations began to emerge about the same sort government corruption and dirty tricks that had brought Papandreou

unstuck. Mitsotakis himself was accused of having a secret horde of Minoan art. He was forced to call an election in October 1993 after his foreign minister, Antonis Samaras, quit ND to found the Political Spring party.

Greeks again turned to PASOK and the ageing, ailing Papandreou, who had eventually been cleared of all the charges levelled in 1990. He marked his last brief period in power with a conspicuous display of the cronyism that had become his trademark. He appointed his wife as chief of staff, his son Giorgos as deputy foreign minister and his personal physician as minister of health.

He had little option but to continue with the same austerity program begun by Mitsotakis, quickly making his government equally unpopular.

Papandreou was finally forced to hand over the reins in January 1996 after a lengthy spell in hospital. His resignation marked the end of an era. After a tense two-round ballot, party reformist Costas Simitis narrowly defeated Papandreou loyalist Akis Tsochadzopoulos for the PASOK leadership. Simitis, an experienced economist and lawyer, came to power committed to further economic reform in preparation for involvement in the new Europe.

Foreign Policy

Greece's foreign policy is dominated by its extremely sensitive relationship with Turkey, its giant Muslim neighbour to the east. The two uneasy NATO allies have repeatedly come close to blows, most recently after Turkish journalists symbolically replaced the Greek flag on the tiny rocky outcrop of Imia (Kardak to the Turks) in February 1996. Both sides poured warships into the area before being persuaded to calm down.

The break-up of former Yugoslavia and the end of the Stalinist era in Albania have given Greece two new issues to worry about. The attempt by the former Yugoslav republic of Macedonia to become independent Macedonia prompted an emotional outburst from Greece, which argued that the name 'was, is, and always will be' Greek. Greece was able to persuade its EU partners to recognise Macedonia only if it changed its name. That's how the independent acronym of FYROM (Former Yugoslav Republic of Macedonia) came into being.

GREECE

Greece is also at odds with Albania over that country's treatment of its significant Greek-speaking minority.

GEOGRAPHY & ECOLOGY

Greece consists of the southern tip of the Balkan peninsula and about 2000 islands, only 166 of which are inhabited. The land mass is 131,900 sq km and Greek territorial waters cover a further 400,000 sq km.

Most of the country is mountainous. The Pindos Mountains in Epiros are the southern extension of the Dinaric Alps, which run the length of former Yugoslavia. The range continues down through central Greece and the Peloponnese, and re-emerges in the mountains of Crete. Less than a quarter of the country is suitable for agriculture.

The variety of flora is unrivalled in Europe. The wild flowers are spectacular. They continue to thrive because much of the land is too poor for agriculture and has escaped the ravages of modern fertilisers. The best places to see the amazing variety are the mountains of Crete and the southern Peloponnese.

You won't encounter many animals in the wild, mainly due to the macho male habit of blasting to bits anything that moves. The brown bear, Europe's largest mammal, survives in very small numbers in the Pindos Mountains, as does the grey wolf. Lake Mikri Prespa in Macedonia has the richest colony of fish-eating birds in Europe, while the Dadia Forest Reserve in Thrace numbers such majestic birds as the golden eagle and the giant black vulture among its residents.

Looking at the harsh, rocky landscapes of the 20th century, it's hard to believe that in ancient times Greece was a fertile land with extensive forests. The change represents an ecological disaster on a massive scale. The main culprit has been the olive tree. In ancient times, native forest was cleared on a massive scale to make way for a tree whose fruit produced an oil that could be used for everything from lighting to lubrication. Much of the land cleared was hill country that proved unsuitable for the olives. Without the surface roots of the native trees to bind it, the topsoil quickly disappeared. The ubiquitous goat has been another major contributor to ecological devastation.

The news from the Aegean Sea is both good and bad. According to EU findings, it is Europe's least polluted sea – apart from areas immediately surrounding major cities. Like the rest of the Mediterranean, it has been over-fished.

GOVERNMENT & POLITICS

Since 1975, democratic Greece has been a parliamentary republic with a president as head of state. The president and parliament, which has 300 deputies, have joint legislative power. Prime Minister Simitis heads a 41-member cabinet.

Administratively, Greece is divided into regions and island groups. The mainland regions are the Peloponnese, Central Greece (officially called Sterea Ellada), Epiros, Thessaly, Macedonia and Thrace. The island groups are the Sporades, North-Eastern Aegean, Saronic Gulf, Cyclades, Dodecanese, and the Ionian, which is the only group not in the Aegean. The large islands of Evia and Crete do not belong to any group. For administrative purposes each region and group is divided into prefectures (nomoi).

ECONOMY

Traditionally, Greece has been an agricultural country, but the importance of agriculture in the economy is declining. Greece has the second-lowest income per capita in the EU (Portugal's is lowest). Tourism is by far the biggest industry; shipping comes next.

Greece's politicians face a tough battle to meet conditions set down by the EU for the country's proposed entry into Europe's financially integrated elite. Austerity measures forced on previous governments went down like lead balloons, but still tougher measures are required if conditions are to be met. The inflation rate has been brought below 10% for the first time in donkeys' years, but efforts to get the economy moving have been hit hard by the loss of the main overland trade route through the Balkans to Europe. The economy grew by only 1.5% in 1994, well behind the rest of Europe.

POPULATION & PEOPLE

The 1991 census recorded a population of 10,264,146, an increase of 5.4% on the 1981 figure. Women outnumber men by more than 200,000. Greece is now a largely urban society, with 68% of people living in cities. By far the largest is Athens, with more than 3.1 million in the greater Athens area – which includes Piraeus (169,000). Other major cities and their populations are Thessaloniki (740,000), Patras (172,800), Iraklio (127,600), Larisa (113,400) and Volos (106,100). Less than 15% of people live on the islands. The most populous are Crete (537,000), Evia (209,100) and Corfu (105,000).

It is doubtful that any Greek alive today is directly descended from an ancient Greek. Contemporary Greeks are a mixture of all of the invaders who have occupied the country since ancient times. There are a number of distinct ethnic minorities – about 300,000 ethnic Turks in Thrace; about 100,000 Britons (60,000 live in Athens); about 5000 Jews; Vlach and Sarakatsani shepherds in Epiros; Gypsies; and lately, a growing number of Albanians – many in Greece illegally.

ARTS

The arts have been integral to Greek life since ancient times. In summer, Greek dramas are staged in the ancient theatres where they were originally performed.

The visual arts follow the mainstream of modern European art, and traditional folk arts such as embroidery, weaving and tapestry continue.

The bouzouki is the most popular musical instrument, but each region has its own speciality of instruments and sounds. *Rembetika* music, with its themes of poverty and suffering, was banned by the junta, but is now enjoying a revival.

Architecture in the classical, Hellenistic and Roman periods was based on three column orders – simple, clear Doric; slender Ionic, topped with a scroll; and the more ornate Corinthian, surmounted by a flowery burst of elaboration.

The blind bard Homer composed the narrative poems the *Odyssey* and the *Iliad*. These are tales of the Trojan war and the return to Greece of Odysseus, King of Ithaki, linking together the legends sung by bards during the dark age. Plato was the most devoted pupil of Socrates, writing down every dialogue he could recall between Socrates, other philosophers and the youth of Athens. His most widely read work is the *Republic*, which argued that the perfect

State could only be created with philosopher-rulers at the helm.

The Alexandrian, Constantine Cavafy (1863-1933), revolutionised Greek poetry by introducing a personal, conversational style. He is considered the TS Eliot of Greek literary verse. Nikos Kazantzakis, author of *Zorba the Greek* and numerous other novels, plays and poems, is the most famous of 20th-century Greek novelists.

CULTURE

Greece is steeped in traditional customs. Name days (celebrated instead of birthdays), weddings and funerals all have great significance. On someone's name day there is an open house and refreshments are served to well-wishers who stop by with gifts. Weddings are highly festive, with dancing, feasting and drinking sometimes continuing for days.

If you want to bare all, other than on a designated nude beach, remember that Greece is a traditional country, so take care not to offend the locals.

RELIGION

About 97% of Greeks nominally belong to the Greek Orthodox Church. The rest of the population is split between the Roman Catholic, Protestant, Evangelist, Jewish and Muslim faiths. While older Greeks and people in rural areas tend to be deeply religious, most young people are decidedly more interested in the secular.

LANGUAGE

Greeks are naturally delighted if you can speak a little of their language. But many Greeks have lived abroad, usually in Australia or the USA, so even in remote villages there are invariably one or two people who can speak English. If you arrive in such a place and make your presence known, the local linguist will soon be produced.

Greek is the oldest European language, with a 4000-year-old oral tradition and a 3000-year-old written tradition. Its evolution over the four millennia has been characterised by its strength during the golden age of Athens; its spread and use as a lingua franca by Alexander the Great and his successors as far east as India during the Hellenistic period (330 BC to 100 AD); its adaptation instead of Aramaic as the

GREECE

language of the new religion, Christianity; its status as the official language of the Eastern Roman Empire; and its eventual proclamation as the language of the Byzantine Empire (380-1453 AD).

Greek maintained its status and prestige during the Renaissance and was employed as the linguistic perspective for all contemporary sciences and terminologies during the period of the Enlightenment. The Modern Greek (MG) language is a southern Greek dialect now used by most Greek speakers in Greece and abroad. Modern Greek combines ancient vocabulary with Greek regional dialects – namely, Cretan, Cypriot and Macedonian.

See the Language Guide at the back of this book for pronunciation guidelines and useful words and phrases.

Transliteration

Travellers in Greece will frequently encounter confusing, seemingly illogical English transliterations of Greek words. Transliteration is a knotty problem – there are six ways of rendering the vowel sound 'ee' in Greek, and two ways of rendering the 'o' sound and the 'e' sound. This book has merely attempted to be consistent within itself, not to solve this long-standing difficulty.

As a general rule, the Greek letter gamma (γ) appears as a 'g' rather than a 'y'; thus *agios*, not *ayios*. The letter delta (δ) appears as 'd' rather than 'dh', so *domatia*, not dhomatia. The letter phi (φ) can be either 'f' or 'ph'. Here, we have used the general rule that classical names are spelt with a 'ph' and modern names with an 'f' – Phaestos (not Festos), but Folegandros, not Pholegandros. Please bear with us if signs in Greek don't agree with our spelling. It's that sort of language.

Facts for the Visitor

PLANNING
Climate & When to Go

The climate is typically Mediterranean with mild, wet winters followed by hot, dry summers. Spring and autumn are the best times to visit. Winter is pretty much a dead loss, unless you're coming to Greece to take advan-

tage of the cheap skiing. Most of the tourist infrastructure goes into hibernation between late November and early April, particularly on the islands. Hotels and restaurants close up, and buses and ferries operate on drastically reduced schedules.

The cobwebs are dusted off in time for Easter, and conditions are perfect until the end of June. Everything is open, public transport operates normally, but the crowds have yet to arrive. From July until mid-September, it's on for young and old as northern Europe heads for the Mediterranean en masse. If you want to party, this is the time to go. The flip side is that everywhere is packed out, and rooms can be hard to find.

The pace slows down again by mid-September, and conditions are ideal once more until the end of October.

Book & Maps

The 2nd edition of Lonely Planet's *Greece – travel survival kit* has been comprehensively updated, with particular emphasis on some of the less visited areas of central and northern Greece. Lonely Planet's *Trekking in Greece* is recommended for anyone considering any serious walking. Both books are strong on maps.

There are numerous books to choose from if you want to get a feel for the country. *Zorba the Greek* by Nikos Kazantzakis may seem an obvious choice, but read it and you'll understand why it's the most popular of all Greek novels translated into English. *A Traveller's History of Greece* by Timothy Boatswain & Colin Nicholson covers Greek history from Neolithic times to the present day.

Mythology was such an intrinsic part of life in ancient Greece that some knowledge of it will enhance your visit to the country. *The Greek Myths* by Robert Graves is very thorough, if a bit academic. Homer's *Odyssey*, translated by EV Rien, is arguably the best translation of this epic.

The Colossus of Maroussi by Henry Miller is a gripping book. With senses heightened, Miller relates his travels in Greece at the outbreak of WWII with feverish enthusiasm. *Hellas* and *Eleni*, both by Nicholas Gage, are portraits of contemporary Greece that will further whet your appetite for the country.

Detailed, although somewhat outdated ordnance survey maps are available from the

Athens Statistical Service (☎ 01-325 9302), Lykourgou 14; take your passport. Stanfords, 12 Long Acre, London WC2E 9LP, also stocks them. Freytag & Berndt produces 15 maps of Greece which are widely available and cost about US$10 each.

What to Bring

In summer, bring light cotton clothing, a sun hat and sunglasses; bring sunscreen too, as it's expensive in Greece. In spring and autumn, you will need light jumpers (sweaters) and thicker ones for the evenings.

In winter, thick jumpers and a raincoat are essential. You will need to wear sturdy walking shoes for trekking in the country, and comfortable shoes are a better idea than sandals for walking around ancient sites. An alarm clock for catching early-morning ferries, a torch (flashlight) for exploring caves, and a small backpack for day trips will also be useful.

SUGGESTED ITINERARIES

Depending on the length of your stay, you might want to see and do the following things:

Two days
    Spend both days in Athens seeing its museums and
    ancient sites.
One week
    Spend two days in Athens, four days in either Epiros
    or the Peloponnese, or four days visiting the Cycladic
    islands.
Two weeks
    Spend two days in Athens, three days each in Epiros
    and the Peloponnese and four days on the Cycladic
    islands, allowing two days travelling time.
One month
    Spend two days in Athens, four days in Epiros, a week
    in the Peloponnese, six days on the Dodecanese and
    North-Eastern Aegean islands and four days each in
    Crete and the Cyclades.

HIGHLIGHTS
Islands

Many islands are overrun with tourists in summer. For tranquillity, try lesser-known islands such as Kassos, Sikinos, Anafi, Koufonisi, Donoussa, Shinoussa, Iraklia and Kastellorizo. (See the sections on the Cyclades and the Dodecanese islands for more information.) If you enjoy mountain walks, then Naxos, Crete, Samothraki and Samos are all very rewarding. If you prefer the beach, try Paros.

Museums & Archaeological Sites

There are three museums which should not be missed. The National Archaeological Museum in Athens houses Heinrich Schliemann's finds from Mycenae and, temporarily, the Minoan frescos from Akrotiri on Santorini (Thira). The Thessaloniki Museum contains exquisite treasures from the graves of the Macedonian royal family, and the Iraklio Museum houses a vast collection from the Minoan sites of Crete.

Greece has more ancient sites than any other country in Europe. It's worth seeking out some of the lesser lights where you won't have to contend with the crowds that pour through famous sites like the Acropolis, Delphi, Knossos and Olympia.

The Sanctuary of the Great Gods on Samothraki is one of Greece's most evocative sites, and it's off the package-tourist circuit because there's no airport and there are no boats from Piraeus.

Museums and sites are free on Sunday, except for tour groups. They are free all the time for card-carrying students and teachers from EU countries. An International Student Identification Card (ISIC) gets non-EU students a 50% discount.

Historic Towns

Two of Greece's most spectacular medieval cities are in the Peloponnese. The ghostly Byzantine city of Mystras, west of Sparta, clambers up the slopes of Mt Taygetos, its winding paths and stairways leading to deserted palaces and churches. In contrast, Byzantine Monemvassia is still inhabited, but equally dramatic and full of atmosphere.

There are some stunning towns on the islands. Rhodes is the finest surviving example of a fortified medieval town, while Naxos' hora (main village) is a maze of narrow, stepped alleyways of whitewashed Venetian houses, their tiny gardens ablaze with flowers. Pyrgi, on Chios, is visually the most unusual village in Greece – the exterior walls of the houses are all decorated with striking black-and-white geometrical patterns.

TOURIST OFFICES

The Greek National Tourist Organisation (GNTO) is known as EOT in Greece. There is either an EOT office or a local tourist office in almost every town of consequence and on many islands. Most do no more than give out brochures and maps. Popular destinations have tourist police, who can often help in finding accommodation.

Local Tourist Offices

The EOT head office (☎ 01-322 3111) is at Amerikis 2, Athens 10564. This office does not deal directly with the general public. Some of the main tourist offices are:

Athens
  Syntagma/Karageorgi Servias 2 (in the National Bank) (☎ 01-322 2545)
Patras
  Iroön Polytehniou 110 (☎ 061-420 303/304)
Piraeus
  EOT Building, Zea Marina (☎ 01-413 5716)
Thessaloniki
  Plateia Aristotelous 8 (☎ 031-271 888)

Tourist Offices Abroad

Australia
  51 Pitt St, Sydney, NSW 2000 (☎ 02-9241 1663)
Canada
  1300 Bay St, Toronto, Ontario M5R 3K8 (☎ 416-968 2220); 1233 Rue de la Montagne, Suite 101, Montreal, Quebec H3G 1Z2 (☎ 514-871 1535)
France
  3 Ave de l'Opéra, Paris 75001 (☎ 01 42 60 65 75)
Germany
  Neue Mainzerstrasse 22, 6000 Frankfurt (☎ 69-237 735); Pacellistrasse 2, W 8000 Munich 2 (☎ 89-222 035); Abteistrasse 33, 2000 Hamburg 13 (☎ 40-454 498); Wittenplatz 3A,10789 Berlin 30 (☎ 30-217 6262)
Italy
  Via L Bissolati 78-80, Rome 00187 (☎ 06-474 4249); Piazza Diaz 1, 20123 Milan (☎ 02-860 470)
Japan
  Fukuda Building West, 5F 2-11-3 Akasaka, Minato-ku, Tokyo 107 (☎ 03-350 55 911)
UK
  4 Conduit St, London W1R ODJ (☎ 0171-499 9758)
USA
  Olympic Tower, 645 5th Ave, New York, NY 10022 (☎ 212-421 5777); Suite 160, 168 North Michigan Ave, Chicago, Illinois 60601 (☎ 312-782 1091); Suite 2198, 611 West 6th St, Los Angeles, California 92668 (☎ 213-626 6696)

VISAS & EMBASSIES

Nationals of Australia, Canada, EU countries, Israel, New Zealand and the USA are allowed to stay in Greece for up to three months without a visa. For longer stays, apply at a consulate abroad or at least 20 days in advance to the Aliens Bureau (☎ 01-770 5711), Leoforos Alexandros 173, Athens. Elsewhere in Greece apply to the local police authority. Singapore nationals can stay in Greece for 14 days without a visa.

In the past, Greece has refused entry to people whose passport indicates that they have visited Turkish-occupied North Cyprus, though there are reports that this is less of a problem now. To be on the safe side, however, ask the North Cyprus immigration officials to stamp a piece of paper rather than your passport. If you enter North Cyprus from the Greek Republic of Cyprus, no exit stamp is put in your passport.

Greek Embassies Abroad

Greece has diplomatic representation in the following countries:

Australia
  9 Turrana St, Yarralumla, Canberra, ACT 2600 (☎ 062-73 3011)
Canada
  76-80 Maclaren St, Ottawa, Ontario K2P 0K6 (☎ 613-238 6271)
France
  17 Rue Auguste Vacquerie, 75116 Paris (☎ 01 47 23 72 28)
Germany
  Koblenzer Str 103, 5300 Bonn 2 (☎ 228-83010)
Italy
  Via S Mercadante 36, Rome 00198 (☎ 06-854 9630)
Japan
  16-30 Nishi Azabu, 3-chome, Minato-ku, Tokyo 106 (☎ 03-340 0871/0872)
New Zealand
  5-7 Willeston St, Wellington (☎ 04-473 7775)
South Africa
  Reserve Bank Building, St George's Rd, Cape Town (☎ 21-24 8161)
Turkey
  Ziya-ul-Rahman Caddesi 9-11, Gazi Osman Pasa 06700, Ankara (☎ 312-446 5496)
UK
  1A Holland Park, London W11 3TP (☎ 0171-229 3850)
USA
  2221 Massachusetts Ave NW, Washington, DC, 20008 (☎ 202-667 3169)

Foreign Embassies in Greece

The following countries have diplomatic representation in Greece:

Australia
  Dimitriou Soutsou 37, Athens 11521
  (☎ 01-644 7303)
Canada
  Genadiou 4, Athens 11521 (☎ 01-725 4011)
France
  Leoforos Vasilissis Sofias 7, Athens 10671
  (☎ 01-361 1663)
Germany
  Dimitriou 3 & Karaoli, 10675 Kolonaki
  (☎ 01-728 5111)
Italy
  Sekeri 2, Athens 10674 (☎ 01-361 7260)
Japan
  Athens Tower, Leoforos Messogion 2-4, Athens
  11527 (☎ 01-775 8101)
New Zealand (honorary consulate)
  Semitelou 9, Athens 11528 (☎ 01-771 0112)
South Africa
  Kifissias 60, Maroussi, Athens 15125
  (☎ 01-689 5330)
Turkey
  Vasilissis Georgiou B 8, Athens 10674
  (☎ 01-724 5915)
UK
  Ploutarhou 1, Athens 10675 (☎ 01-723 6211)
USA
  Leoforos Vasilissis Sofias 91, Athens 11521
  (☎ 01-721 2951)

CUSTOMS

Duty-free allowances in Greece are the same as for other EU countries. Import regulations for medicines are strict; if you are taking medication, make sure you get a statement from your doctor before you leave home. It is illegal, for example, to take codeine into Greece. The export of antiques is prohibited. You can bring as much foreign currency as you like, but if you want to leave with more than US$1000 in foreign banknotes the money must be declared on entry. It is illegal to bring in more than 100,000 dr, and to leave with more than 20,000 dr.

MONEY

Banks will exchange all major currencies, in either cash or travellers' cheques and also Eurocheques. All post offices have exchange facilities and charge less commission than banks. Most travel agencies also change money, but check the commission charged.

All major credit cards are accepted, but only in larger establishments. If you run out of money, you can get a cash advance on a Visa card at the Greek Commercial Bank and on Access/MasterCard/Eurocard at the National

Bank, or you can find a major bank and ask them to cable your home bank for money (see Money in the Facts for the Visitor chapter at the start of this book).

American Express card-holders can draw cash from Credit Bank automatic teller machines.

Currency

The Greek unit of currency is the drachma (dr). Coins come in denominations of one, two, five, 10, 20, 50 and 100 dr. Banknotes come in 50, 100, 500, 1000, 5000 and 10,000 dr denominations.

Exchange Rates

Australia	A$1	=	185.13 dr
Canada	C$1	=	172.11 dr
France	FF1	=	47.07 dr
Germany	DM1	=	159.60 dr
Italy	L1000	=	154.98 dr
Japan	¥100	=	218.41 dr
New Zealand	NZ$1	=	164.75 dr
United Kingdom	UK£1	=	367.82 dr
United States	US$1	=	236.13 dr

Costs

Greece is no longer dirt cheap. A rock-bottom daily budget would be about 4000 dr, which would mean staying in hostels, self-catering and seldom taking buses or ferries. Allow at least 9000 dr per day if you want your own room and plan to eat out regularly, as well as travelling and seeing the sites. If you want a real holiday – comfortable rooms and restaurants all the way – reckon on close to 15,000 dr per day.

Tipping & Bargaining

In restaurants the service charge is included on the bill, but it is the custom to leave a small tip – just round off the bill. There are plenty of opportunities to practise your bargaining skills. If you want to dive in the deep end, try haggling with the taxi drivers at Athens airport after a long flight! Accommodation is nearly always negotiable outside peak season, especially if you are staying more than one night. Souvenir shops are another place where substantial savings can be made. Prices in other shops are normally clearly marked and non-negotiable.

GREECE

GREECE

Consumer Taxes

The value-added tax (VAT) varies from 15 to 18%. A tax-rebate scheme applies at a restricted number of shops and stores; look for a Tax Free sign in the window. You must fill in a form at the shop and present it with the receipt at the airport on departure. A cheque will (hopefully) be sent to your home address.

POST & COMMUNICATIONS
Post

Postal rates for cards and small air-mail letters (up to 20g) are 120 dr to EU destinations, and 150 dr elsewhere. The service is slow but reliable – five to eight days within Europe and about 10 days to the USA, Australia and New Zealand.

Post offices are usually open from 7.30 am to 2 pm. In major cities they stay open until 8 pm and also open from 7.30 am to 2 pm on Saturday. Do not wrap up a parcel until it has been inspected at the post office.

Mail can be sent poste restante to any main post office and is held for up to one month. Your surname should be underlined and you will need to show your passport when you collect your mail. Parcels are not delivered in Greece – they must be collected from a post office.

Telephone

The phone system is modern and efficient. All public phone boxes use phonecards, sold at OTE telephone offices and *periptera* (kiosks). Three cards are available: 100 units (1300 dr), 500 units (6000 dr) and 1000 units (11,500 dr). A local call costs one unit. The 'i' at the top left hand of the dialling panel on public phones brings up the operating instructions in English. Some periptera have metered phones. On the islands, you can often use the phones at travel agents, but they add a hefty surcharge.

Direct-dial long-distance and international calls can also be made from public phones. Many countries participate in the Home Country Direct scheme, which allows you to access an operator in your home country for reverse-charge calls.

If you're calling Greece from abroad, the country code is ☎ 30. If you're making an international call from Greece, the international access code is ☎ 00.

Fax & Telex

Telegrams can be sent from any OTE office. Larger offices have telex facilities. Main city post offices have fax facilities.

NEWSPAPERS & MAGAZINES

The most widely read Greek newspapers are *Ethnos*, *Ta Nea* and *Apoyevmatini*, all of which are dailies.

Newspapers printed in English include the daily *Athens News* (250 dr) and the weekly *Greek Times* (300 dr). *The Athenian* (600 dr) is a quality monthly magazine with articles on politics and the arts. Foreign newspapers are widely available, although only between April and October in smaller resort areas. The papers reach Athens (Syntagma) at 1 pm on the day of publication on weekdays and 7 pm at weekends. They are not available until the following day in other areas.

RADIO & TV

There are plenty of radio stations to choose from, especially in Athens, but not many broadcast in English. Athens International FM broadcasts the BBC World Service live 24 hours a day, interspersed with occasional Greek programs. If you have a short-wave radio, the best frequencies for the World Service are 618, 941 and 1507 MHz.

The nine TV channels offer nine times as much rubbish as one channel. You'll find the occasional American action drama in English (with Greek subtitles). News junkies can get their fix with CNN and Euronews.

PHOTOGRAPHY

Major brands of film are widely available, but quite expensive outside major towns. In Athens, a 36-exposure role of Kodak Gold ASA 100 costs about 1500 dr. You'll pay at least 500 dr more on the islands.

Never photograph military installations or anything else with a sign forbidding pictures. Greeks usually love having their photos taken, but ask first. Because of the brilliant sunlight in summer, it's a good idea to use a polarising lens filter.

TIME

Greece is two hours ahead of GMT/UTC, and three hours ahead on daylight-saving time, which begins at 12.01 am on the last Sunday in March, when clocks are put forward one hour. Clocks are put back an hour at 12.01 am on the last Sunday in September.

Out of daylight-saving time, at noon in Greece it is also noon in İstanbul, 10 am in London, 11 am in Rome, 2 am in San Francisco, 5 am in New York and Toronto, 8 pm in Sydney and 10 pm in Auckland. These times do not make allowance for daylight saving in the other countries.

WEIGHTS & MEASURES

Greece uses the metric system. Liquids are sold by weight rather than volume – 950g of wine, for example, is equivalent to 1000 ml. Like other Continental Europeans, Greeks indicate decimals with commas and thousands with points.

LAUNDRY

Large towns and some islands have laundrettes. They charge 2000 to 2500 dr to wash and dry a load, whether you do it yourself or leave it to them. Hotels can normally provide you with a wash tub.

ELECTRICITY

The electric current is 220V, 50 Hz, and plugs have two round pins. All hotel rooms have power points, and most camping grounds have power.

TOILETS

You'll find public toilets at all major bus and train stations, but they are seldom very pleasant. You will need to supply your own paper. In town, a café is the best bet, but the owner won't be impressed if you don't buy something.

A warning: Greek plumbing cannot handle toilet paper; always put it in the bin provided.

HEALTH

Tap water is generally safe to drink in Greece. The biggest health risk comes from the sun, so take care against sunburn, heat exhaustion and dehydration. Mosquitoes can be troublesome but coils and repellents are widely available.

Watch out for sea urchins around rocky beaches; if you get some of their needles embedded in your skin, olive oil will help to loosen them. Beware also of jellyfish; although the Mediterranean species are not lethal, their sting can be painful. Greece's only poisonous

snake is the adder, but they are rare. They like to sunbathe on dry-stone walls, so it's worth having a look before climbing one.

Greece's notorious sheepdogs are almost always all bark and no bite, but if you are going to trek in remote areas, you should consider having rabies injections. There is at least one doctor on every island in Greece and larger islands have hospitals or major medical clinics. Pharmacies are widespread – in cities, at least one is rostered to be open 24 hours. All pharmacies have a list of all-night pharmacies on their doors. Remember that codeine is banned in Greece, and ensure that you carry a statement from your doctor if you have prescribed drugs with you.

The number to ring throughout Greece for advice on first aid is ☎ 166. (See the Health section in the Facts for the Visitor chapter at the start of this book for more details on travel health.)

WOMEN TRAVELLERS

Many foreign women travel alone in Greece. Hassles occur, but they tend to be a nuisance rather than threatening. Women travelling alone in rural areas are usually treated with respect. In rural areas it's a good idea to dress conservatively, although it is perfectly OK to wear shorts, short skirts etc in touristy places. If you are pestered, ignore the guy and you'll find that the hint is usually taken.

GAY & LESBIAN TRAVELLERS

Greece is a popular destination amongst gay and lesbian travellers and Mykonos and Lesvos are still the most popular islands. The address of the Greek Gay Liberation Organisation is PO Box 2777, Athens 10022. The monthly magazine *To Kraximo* has information about the local scene.

DISABLED TRAVELLERS

If mobility is a problem, the hard fact is that most hotels, museums and ancient sites are not wheelchair accessible. Lavinia Tours (☎ 031-23 2828), Egnatia 101 (PO Box 11106), Thessaloniki 54110, has information for disabled people coming to Greece.

SENIOR TRAVELLERS

Elderly people are shown great respect in Greece. There are some good deals available

GREECE

for EU nationals. For starters, those over 60 qualify for a 50% discount on train travel plus five free journeys per year. Take your ID card or passport to a Greek Railways (OSE) office and you will be given a Senior Card. The five free journeys may not be taken 10 days before or after Christmas or Easter, or between 1 July and 30 September. Pensioners also get a discount at museums and ancient sites.

DANGERS & ANNOYANCES

Greece has the lowest crime rate in Europe, and crimes are most likely to be committed by other travellers. Drug laws are strict. There's a minimum seven-year sentence for possession of even a small quantity of dope.

BUSINESS HOURS

Banks are open Monday to Thursday from 8.30 am to 2.30 pm, and Friday from 8.30 am to 2 pm. Some city banks also open from 3.30 to 6.30 pm and on Saturday morning. Shops open from 8 am to 1.30 pm and 5.30 to 8.30 pm on Tuesday, Thursday and Friday, and from 8 am to 2.30 pm on Monday, Wednesday and Saturday, but these times are not always strictly adhered to. Periptera (kiosks) are open from early morning to midnight. All banks and shops, and most museums and archaeological sites, close during holidays.

PUBLIC HOLIDAYS & SPECIAL EVENTS

Public holidays are as follows: New Year's Day (1 January); Epiphany (6 January); Lent (first Sunday in March); Greek Independence Day (25 March); Good Friday; Easter Sunday; Spring Festival (1 May); Assumption Day (5 August); Okhi Day (28 October) – Metaxas' refusal to allow Mussolini's troops to cross Greece in WWII – is commemorated with military parades throughout the country; Christmas Day (25 December); and St Stephen's Day (26 December).

Easter is Greece's most important festival, with candle-lit processions, feasting and firework displays. The Orthodox Easter is 50 days after the first Sunday in Lent.

Numerous regional festivals take place throughout the year. If you're in the right place at the right time, you'll certainly be invited to join the revelry.

A number of cultural festivals are also held during the summer months. The most import-

ant is the Athens Festival, when plays, operas, ballet and classical music concerts are staged at the Theatre of Herodes Atticus. The festival is held in conjunction with the Epidaurus Festival, which features ancient Greek dramas at the theatre at Epidaurus. Ioannina, Patras and Thessaloniki also host cultural festivals.

ACTIVITIES
Windsurfing

Sailboards are widely available for hire at about 2000 dr an hour. The top spots for windsurfing are Hrysi Akti on Paros, and Vasiliki on Lefkada – reputedly one of the best places in the world to learn.

Skiing

Greece offers some of the cheapest skiing in Europe. There are 16 resorts dotted around the mainland, most of them in the north. They have all the basic facilities and are a pleasant alternative to the glitzy resorts of northern Europe. What's more, there are no package tours. More information is available from the Hellenic Ski Federation (☎ 01-524 0057), PO Box 8037, Omonia, Athens 10010, or from the EOT.

The largest resort is at Mt Parnassos, near Delphi. There are daily excursions to Mt Parnassos from Athens, organised by the ski department (☎ 01-324 1915) at Klaoudatos, a department store on Athinas. The return fare of 5000 dr includes a lift pass, and an extra 2500 dr gets you all the gear.

Hiking

The mountainous terrain is perfect for trekkers who want to get away from the crowds. Lonely Planet's *Trekking in Greece* is an in-depth guide to Greece's mountain trails. The popular routes are well marked and well maintained, including the E4 and E6 trans-European treks, which both end in Greece. The Hellenic Federation of Mountaineering Clubs (also known as EOS; ☎ 01-323 4555), Karageorgi Servias 7, Athens, has information on conditions.

If you want someone to do the organising for you, Trekking Hellas, Filellinon 7, Athens 10557 (☎ 01-325 0853; fax 01-323 4548) offers a range of treks and other adventure activities throughout the country.

COURSES

If you are serious about learning Greek, an

intensive course at the start of your stay is a good way to go about it. Most of the courses are in Athens. The Athens Centre (☎ 01-701 2268; fax 01-701 8603), Archimidous 48, and the YWCA (XEN in Greek) (☎ 01-362 4291; fax 01-362 2400), Ameriki s 11, both have good reputations.

There are also courses on the islands in summer. The Athens Centre moves to Spetses in June and July, while the Hellenic Culture Centre (☎ & fax 01-647 7465 or 0275-61 482) runs courses on the island of Ikaria from June to October.

More information about courses is available from EOT offices and Greek embassies.

WORK

The unemployment rate is one of the highest in Europe, so Greeks aren't exactly falling over themselves to give jobs to foreigners.

Your best chance of finding work is to do the rounds of the tourist hotels and bars at the beginning of the season. The few jobs available are hotly contested, despite the menial work and dreadful pay. EU nationals don't need a work permit, but everyone else does.

If you are an EU national, an employment agency worth contacting is Working Holidays, Pioneer Tours, Nikis 11, Athens (☎ 01-322 4321). It offers hotel and bar jobs, au pair work, fruit picking, etc.

ACCOMMODATION

There is a range of accommodation in Greece to suit every taste and pocket. All places to stay are subject to strict price controls set by the tourist police. By law, a notice must be displayed in every room, which states the category of the room and the price for each season. If you think you've been ripped off, contact the tourist police.

Many places – especially in rural areas and on the islands – are closed from the end of October until mid-April.

Camping

Greece has almost 350 camping grounds. Prices vary according to facilities, but reckon on about 1000 dr per person and about 750 dr for a small tent. Most sites are open only from April to October. Freelance camping is officially forbidden, but often tolerated in remoter areas.

Hostels

You'll find youth hostels in most major towns and on half a dozen islands. The only place affiliated to Hostelling International (HI) is the superb Athens International Youth Hostel (☎ 01-523 4170). Most hostels are run by the Greek Youth Hostel Organisation (☎ 01-751 9530), Damareos 75, 11633 Athens. There are affiliated hostels in Athens (two), Litohoro (Mt Olympus), Mycenae, Olympia, Patras and Thessaloniki on the mainland; and on the islands of Corfu, Crete, Ios, Naxos, Santorini (Thira) and Tinos. There are six on Crete – at Iraklio, Malia, Myrthios, Plakias, Rethymno and Sitia.

Other hostels belong to the Greek Youth Hostels Association (☎ 01-323 4107), Dragatsaniou 4, 105 59 Athens. It has hostels in Delphi and Nafplio on the mainland, and on the islands of Corfu, Crete (Hersonisos) and Santorini.

Whatever their affiliation, the hostels are mostly very casual places. Their rates vary from 1000 to 1500 dr.

Athens has a number of private hostels catering to budget travellers. Standards vary enormously – from clean, friendly places to veritable fleapits. Most charge from 1500 to 2000 dr for dorm beds.

There are YWCA hostels (XEN in Greek) for women only in Athens and Thessaloniki.

Domatia

Domatia are the Greek equivalent of the British bed and breakfast, minus the breakfast. Once upon a time, domatia consisted of little more than spare rooms that families would rent out in summer to supplement their income. Nowadays many domatia are purpose-built appendages to the family house. Rates start at about 3500/6000 dr for singles/doubles, rising to 5000/8000 dr.

Hotels

Hotels are classified as deluxe, A, B, C, D or E class. The ratings seldom seem to have much bearing on the price, but expect to pay 4000/8000 dr for singles/doubles in D and E class, and about 8000/12,000 dr in a decent C-class place. Some places are classified as pensions and rated differently. Both are allowed to levy a 10% surcharge for stays of less than three nights, but they seldom do. It normally works the other way, and you can bargain if you're staying more than one night. Prices are about 40% cheaper between October and May.

Apartments
Self-contained family apartments are available in some hotels and domatia. There are also a number of purpose-built apartments, particularly on the islands, which are available for either long or short-term rental.

Traditional Settlements
Traditional settlements are old buildings of architectural merit that have been renovated and turned into tourist accommodation. They are terrific places to stay if you can afford 10,000 to 15,000 dr for a double. The EOT has information on the settlements.

Houses & Flats
For long-term rental accommodation in Athens, check the advertisements in the English-language newspapers. (See also Places to Stay in the Athens section.) In rural areas, ask around in tavernas.

Refuges
Greece has 55 mountain refuges, which are listed in the booklet *Greece Mountain Refuges & Ski Centres*, available free of charge at EOT and EOS offices.

FOOD
If Greek food conjures up an uninspiring vision of lukewarm moussaka collapsing into a plate of olive oil, take heart – there's a lot more on offer.

Snacks
Greece has a great range of fast-food options for the inveterate snacker. Foremost among them are the *gyros* and the *souvlaki*. The gyros is a giant skewer laden with slabs of seasoned meat that grills slowly as it rotates, the meat being steadily trimmed from the outside. Souvlaki are small, individual kebabs. Both are served wrapped in pitta bread with salad and lashings of tzatziki (a yoghurt, cucumber and garlic dip). Other snacks are pretzel rings, *spanakopitta* (spinach and cheese pie) and *tyropitta* (cheese pie). Dried fruits and nuts are also very popular.

Starters
Greece is famous for its appetisers, known as *mezedes*, (literally, 'tastes'). Standards include tzatziki, *melitzanosalata* (aubergine dip), taramasalata (fish-roe dip), dolmades (stuffed vine leaves), *fasolia* (beans) and *oktapodi* (octopus). A selection of three or four represents a good meal and can be a good option for vegetarians. Most dishes cost between 400 dr and 800 dr.

Main Dishes
You'll find moussaka (layers of aubergine and mince, topped with cheese sauce and baked) on every menu, alongside a number of other taverna staples. They include *moschari* (oven-baked veal and potatoes), *keftedes* (meatballs), *stifado* (meat stew), *pastitsio* (macaroni with mince meat and béchamel sauce, baked) and *yemista* (either tomatoes or green peppers stuffed with mince meat and rice). Most main courses cost between 1000 dr and 1500 dr.

The most popular fish are *barbouni* (red mullet) and *ksifias* (swordfish), but they don't come cheap. Prices start at about 2000 dr for a serve. *Kalamaria* (fried squid) are readily available and cheap at about 1000 dr for a decent serve.

Fortunately for vegetarians, salad is a mainstay of the Greek diet. The most popular is *horiatiki salata*, normally listed on English menus as Greek or country salad. It's a mixed salad of cucumbers, peppers, onions, olives, tomatoes and feta (white sheep or goat cheese).

Desserts
Turkish in origin, most Greek desserts are variations on pastry soaked in honey. Popular ones include baklava (thin layers of pastry filled with honey and nuts) and *kadaifi* (shredded wheat soaked in honey). Delicious thick yoghurt *(yiaourti)* and rice pudding *(rizogalo)* are also available.

Restaurants
There are several varieties of restaurants. An *estiatoria* is a straightforward restaurant with a printed menu. A taverna is often cheaper and more typically Greek, and you'll probably be invited to peer into the pots. A *psistaria* specialises in charcoal-grilled dishes. *Ouzeria* (ouzo bars) often have such a good range of

mezedes that they can be regarded as eating places.

Kafeneia

Kafeneia are the smoke-filled cafés where men gather to drink coffee, play backgammon and cards and engage in heated political discussion. They are a bastion of male chauvinism that Greek women have yet to break down. Female tourists tend to avoid them too, but those who venture in invariably find they are treated courteously.

Self-Catering

Buying and preparing your own food is easy in Greece as there are well-stocked grocery stores and fruit and vegetable shops everywhere. In addition, villages and each area of a town hold a once or twice-weekly *laiki agora* (street market) where goods are sold. These markets are great fun to stroll around, whether or not you are cooking for yourself.

DRINKS
Nonalcoholic Drinks

The tap water is safe to drink, but many people prefer bottled mineral water. It's cheap and available everywhere, as are soft drinks and packaged juices.

Greeks are great coffee drinkers. Greek coffee (known as Turkish coffee until the words became unspeakable after the 1974 invasion of Cyprus) comes three main ways. Greeks like it thick and sweet *(glyko)*. If you prefer less sugar, ask for *metrio; sketo* means without sugar. Instant coffee is known as Nescafé, which is what it usually is. If you want milk with your coffee, ask for *Nescafé me ghala*.

Alcohol

Greece is traditionally a wine-drinking society. If you're spending a bit of time in the country, it's worth acquiring a taste for retsina (resinated wine). The best (and worst) flows straight from the barrel in the main production areas of Attica and central Greece. Tavernas charge about 700 dr for a litre. Retsina is available by the bottle everywhere. Greece also produces a large range of non-resinated wines from traditional grape varieties.

Amstel is the cheapest of several northern European beers produced locally under

licence. Expect to pay about 180 dr in a supermarket, or 350 dr in a restaurant. The most popular aperitif is the aniseed-flavoured ouzo.

ENTERTAINMENT

The busy nightlife is a major attraction for many travellers. Nowhere is the pace more frenetic than on the islands in high season; Ios and Paros are famous for their raging discos and bars. Discos abound in all resort areas. If you enjoy theatre and classical music, Athens and Thessaloniki are the places to be.

Greeks are great movie-goers. You'll find cinemas everywhere. They show films in the original language (usually English) with Greek subtitles.

SPECTATOR SPORT

Greek men are football mad, both as spectators and participants. If you happen to be eating in a taverna on a night when a big match is being televised, expect indifferent service. Basketball is another boom sport.

THINGS TO BUY

Greece produces a vast array of handicrafts, including woollen rugs, ceramics, leather work, hand-woven woollen shoulder bags, embroidery, copperware and carved-wood products. Beware of tacky imitations in tourist areas.

Getting There & Away

AIR

There are no less than 16 international airports, but most of them handle only summer charter flights to the islands. Athens handles the vast majority of international flights, including all intercontinental flights. Athens has regular scheduled flights to all the European capitals, and Thessaloniki is also well served. Most flights are with the national carrier, Olympic Airways, or the flag carrier of the country concerned.

Europe

Flying is the fastest, easiest and cheapest way of getting to Greece from northern Europe. What's more, the scheduled flights are very competitvely priced these days so it's hardly worth hunting around for charter cheapies.

For example, Olympic Airways, British Airways and Virgin Atlantic all offer 30-day return tickets from London for under UK£220 (midweek departures) in high season, and Olympic and British Airways both offer returns to Thessaloniki for about UK£210.

Charter flights from London to Athens are readily available for UK£99/189 one way/ return in high season, dropping to UK£70/129 in low season. Fares are about UK£109/209 to most island destinations in high season. Similar deals are available from charter operators throughout Europe.

There is one important condition for charter-flight travellers (only) to bear in mind. If you travel to Greece on a return ticket, you will invalidate the return portion if you visit Turkey. If you turn up at the airport for your return flight with a Turkish stamp in your passport, you will be forced to buy another ticket.

Athens is a good place to buy cheap air tickets. Examples of one-way fares include London (25,000 dr), Paris (40,000 dr) and Amsterdam (48,000 dr).

North America
Delta Airlines, Olympic and Trans-World Airlines all have daily flights from New York to Athens. Apex return fares range from US$900 to US$1400. Olympic also has a weekly flight from Boston (same fares), and two flights a week from Toronto via Montreal. Apex fares start at C$1098. You'll get better deals from the discount operators.

Australia
Olympic flies to Athens twice a week from Sydney via Melbourne. Fares range from A$1730 to A$2199.

LAND
Northern Europe
Overland travel between northern Europe and Greece is virtually a thing of the past. Buses and trains can't compete with cheap airfares, and the turmoil in former Yugoslavia has cut the shortest overland route. All bus and train services now go via Italy and take the ferries over to Greece.

Bus Olympic Bus operates the only year-round service between London and Athens, travelling via Brussels, Frankfurt, Munich, Innsbruck, Venice and Brindisi. Buses leave London (☎ 0171-837 9141) on Friday, and Athens (☎ 01-324 4633) on Tuesday. Fares drop as low as UK£50 one way at times. Eurolines operates between London and Athens only during August and September.

Train Unless you have a Eurail pass, travelling to Greece by train is prohibitively expensive. Greece is part of the Eurail network, and passes are valid on ferries operated by Adriatica di Navigazione and Hellenic Mediterranean Lines from Brindisi to Corfu, Igoumenitsa and Patras.

Neighbouring Countries
Bus The Hellenic Railways Organisation (OSE) has two buses a day from Athens to İstanbul (22 hours; 16,600 dr), leaving at 8 am and 7 pm. It also has daily services to Tirana (Albania) and Sofia (Bulgaria). All depart from the Peloponnese train station in Athens.

Train There are daily trains between Athens and İstanbul for 13,250 dr, but the service is incredibly slow, crowded and uncomfortable. Stick to the buses. There is also a daily train from Athens to Sofia (18 hours, 9000 dr).

Car & Motorcycle The crossing points into Turkey are at Kipi and Kastanies; the crossings into the Former Yugoslav Republic of Macedonia (FYROM) are at Evzoni and Niki; and the Bulgarian crossing is at Promahonas. All are open 24 hours a day. The crossing points to Albania are at Kakavia and Krystallopigi.

Hitching If you want to hitchhike to Turkey, look for a through-ride from Alexandroupolis because you cannot hitchhike across the border. If you're heading for Bulgaria, try to get a lift from Thessaloniki through to Sofia, as lifts are difficult to find after Servia.

SEA
Italy
The most popular crossing is from Brindisi to Patras (18 hours), via Corfu (nine hours) and Igoumenitsa (10 hours). There are numerous

services. Deck-class fares start at about 7000 dr one way in low season, 10,000 dr in high season. Eurail pass-holders can travel free with both Adriatica di Navigazione and Hellenic Mediterranean. You still need to make a reservation and pay port taxes – L8000 in Italy, and 1500 dr in Greece.

There are also ferries to Patras from Ancona, Bari, Trieste and Venice, stopping at either Corfu or Igoumenitsa on the way. In summer there are also ferries from Bari and Brindisi to Kefallonia, from Otranto and Ortona to Igoumenitsa and from Ancona to Iraklio on Crete.

Turkey

There are five regular ferry services between the Greek islands and Turkey: Lesvos-Ayvalık, Chios-Çeşme, Samos-Kuşadası, Kos-Bodrum and Rhodes-Marmaris. All are daily services in summer, dropping to weekly in winter. Tickets must be bought a day in advance and you will be asked to hand over your passport. It will be returned on the boat.

Cyprus & Israel

Salamis Lines operates a weekly, year-round service from Piraeus to Lemessos (formerly Limassol) on Cyprus and the Israeli port of Haifa, stopping at Rhodes on the way. Deck-class fares from Haifa are US$105 to Rhodes and US$110 to Piraeus. The fares from Lemessos are US$70 to Rhodes and US$75 to Piraeus. There are two other services in summer, both travelling via Iraklio on Crete.

LEAVING GREECE

An airport tax of 6000 dr for international flights is included in airfares. The tax is to help pay for Athens' new airport. Port taxes are 1500 dr to Italy and 4000 dr to Turkey.

Getting Around

AIR

Most domestic flights are operated by Olympic Airways and its offshoot, Olympic Aviation. They offer a busy schedule in summer with flights from Athens to 22 islands and a range of mainland cities. Sample fares include

Athens-Iraklio for 20,500 dr, Athens-Rhodes for 23,100 dr and Athens-Thessaloniki for 20,700. There are also flights from Thessaloniki to the islands. It is advisable to book at least two weeks in advance, especially in summer. Services to the islands are fairly skeletal in winter. Air Greece provides competition on a few major routes, such as Athens-Iraklio (18,100 dr).

All the above fares include the 3100-dr tax on domestic flights, paid when you buy your ticket.

BUS

Buses are the most popular form of public transport. They are comfortable, they run on time and there are frequent services on all the major routes. Almost every town on the mainland (except in Thrace) has at least one bus a day to Athens. Local companies can get you to all but the remotest villages. Reckon on paying about 1000 dr per hour of journey time. Sample fares from Athens include 7300 dr to Thessaloniki (7½ hours) and 3200 dr to Patras (three hours). Tickets should be bought at least an hour in advance in summer to ensure a seat.

Major islands also have comprehensive local bus networks. In fact, every island with a road has a service of some sort, but they tend to operate at the whim of the driver.

TRAIN

Trains are generally looked on as a poor alternative to bus travel. The main problem is that there are only two main lines: to Thessaloniki and Alexandroupolis in the north and to the Peloponnese. In addition there are a number of branch lines, such as Pyrgos-Olympia and the spectacular Diakofto-Kalavryta mountain railway.

If there are trains going in your direction, they are a good way to travel. Be aware though that there are two distinct levels of service: the painfully slow, dilapidated trains that stop at all stations and the faster, modern intercity trains.

The slow trains represent the cheapest form of transport. It may take five hours to crawl from Athens to Patras, but the 2nd-class fare is only 1580 dr. Intercity trains do the trip in just over three hours for 2580 dr – still cheaper than the bus.

Inter-Rail and Eurail passes are valid in Greece, but you still need to make a reservation. In summer, make reservations at least two days in advance.

CAR & MOTORCYCLE

Car is a great way to explore areas that are off the beaten track. Bear in mind that roads in remote regions are often poorly maintained. You'll need a good road map.

EU nationals need only their normal licence; others need an International Driving Permit. You can bring a vehicle into Greece for four months without a carnet – only a Green Card (international third-party insurance) is required.

Average prices for fuel are 210 dr per litre for super, 195 dr for unleaded and 140 dr for diesel.

Most islands are served by car ferries, but they are expensive. Sample fares for small cars from Piraeus include 15,200 dr to Crete and 18,600 dr to Rhodes. If you are going to take your car island-hopping, do some research first – cars are useless on some of the smaller islands.

Road Rules

Greek motorists are famous for ignoring the road rules, which is probably why the country has the highest road fatality rate in Europe. No casual observer would ever guess that it was compulsory to wear seat belts in the front seats of vehicles, nor that it was compulsory to wear a crash helmet on motorcycles of more than 50 cc – always insist on a helmet when renting a motorcycle.

The speed limit for cars is 120 km/h on toll roads, 90 km/h outside built-up areas and 50 km/h in built-up areas. For motorcycles, the speed limit outside built-up areas is 70 km/h. Speeding fines start at 30,000 dr. Drink-driving laws are strict – a blood alcohol content of 0.05% incurs a penalty and over 0.08% is a criminal offence.

All cars are required to have a first-aid kit, a fire extinguisher and triangular warning sign (in case of a breakdown).

Rental

Car hire is expensive, especially from the multinational hire companies. Their high-season weekly rates with unlimited mileage start at about 105,000 dr for the smallest

models, dropping to 85,000 dr in winter – and that's without tax and extras. You can generally do much better with local companies. Their advertised rates are 25 % lower and they're often willing to bargain.

Mopeds, however, are cheap and available everywhere. Most places charge about 3000 dr per day.

Automobile Association

The Greek automobile club, ELPA, offers reciprocal services to members of other national motoring associations. If your vehicle breaks down, dial ☎ 104.

BICYCLE

People do cycle in Greece, but you'll need strong leg muscles to tackle the mountainous terrain. You can hire bicycles, but they are not nearly as widely available as cars and motorcycles. Prices range from about 1000 to 3000 dr. Bicycles are carried free on most ferries.

HITCHING

The further you are from a city, the easier hitching becomes. Getting out of major cities can be hard work, and Athens is notoriously difficult. In remote areas, people may stop to offer a lift even if you aren't hitching.

BOAT
Ferry

Every island has a ferry service of some sort. They come in all shapes and sizes, from the state-of-the-art 'superferries' that run on the major routes to the ageing open ferries that operate local services to outlying islands.

The hub of the vast ferry network is Piraeus, the main port of Athens. It has ferries to the Cyclades, Crete, the Dodecanese, the Saronic Gulf islands and the North-Eastern Aegean islands. Patras is the main port for ferries to the Ionian islands, while Volos and Agios Konstantinos are the ports for the Sporades.

Some of the smaller islands are virtually inaccessible in winter, when schedules are cut back to a minimum. Services start to pick up in April and are running at full steam from June to September.

Fares are fixed by the government. The small differences in price you may find between ticket agencies are the result of some agencies sacrificing part of their designated

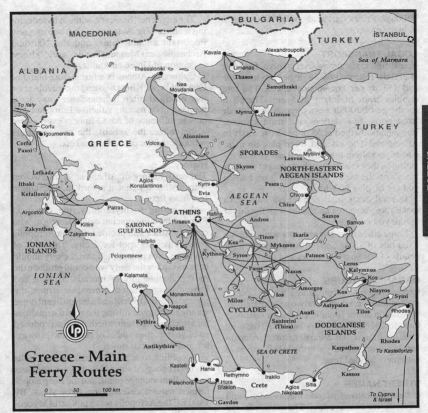

Greece - Main Ferry Routes

0   50   100 km

commission to qualify as a 'discount service'. The discount seldom amounts to more than 50 dr. Tickets can be bought at the last minute from quayside tables set up next to the boats. Prices are the same, contrary to what you will be told by agencies. Unless you specify otherwise, you will automatically be sold deck class, which is the cheapest fare. Sample fares from Piraeus include 3550 dr to Mykonos and 4280 dr to Santorini (Thira).

Hydrofoil

Hydrofoils operate competing services on some of the most popular routes. They cost about twice as much as the ferries, but get you there in half the time.

Yacht

It's hardly a budget option, but *the* way to see the islands is by yacht. There are numerous places to hire boats, both with and without crew. If you want to go it alone, two crew members must have sailing certificates. Prices start at about US$1200 per week for a four-person boat. A skipper will cost an extra US$700 per week.

Individuals can sign up with one of the companies that offer fully catered yachting holidays. Prices start at about US$900 a week in high season.

LOCAL TRANSPORT
You'll find taxis almost everywhere. Flag fall is 200 dr, followed by 58 dr per km in towns and 113 dr per km outside towns. The rate doubles from midnight to 5 am. There's a surcharge of 300 dr from airports and 160 dr from ports, bus stations and train stations. Luggage is charged at 55 dr per item. Taxis in Athens and Thessaloniki often pick up extra passengers along the way (yell out your destination as they cruise by; when you get out, pay what's on the meter, minus what it read when you got in, plus 200 dr).

In rural areas taxis don't have meters, so make sure you agree on a price with the driver before you get in.

Large cities have bus services which charge a flat rate of 75 dr. See the Athens section for details of buses, trolleybuses and the metro.

ORGANISED TOURS
Greece has many companies which operate guided tours, predominantly on the mainland, but also on larger islands. The major operators include CHAT, Key Tours and GO Tours, all based in Athens. It is cheaper to travel independently – tours are only worthwhile if you have extremely limited time.

STREET NAMES
Odos means street, *plateia* means square and *leoforos* means avenue. These words are often omitted on maps and other references, so we have done the same throughout this chapter, except when to do so would cause confusion.

Athens Αθήνα

Ancient Athens ranks alongside Rome and Jerusalem for its glorious past and its influence on Western civilisation, but the modern city is a place few people fall in love with.

However inspiring the Acropolis might be, most visitors have trouble coming to terms with the surrounding urban sprawl, the appalling traffic congestion and the pollution.

The city is not, however, without its redeeming features. The Acropolis is but one of many important ancient sites, and the National Archaeological Museum has the world's finest collection of Greek antiquities.

Culturally, Athens is a fascinating blend of East and West. King Otho and the middle class that emerged after Independence may have been intent on making Athens a European city, but the influence of Asia Minor is everywhere – the coffee, the kebabs, the raucous street vendors and the colourful markets.

History
The early history of Athens is so interwoven with mythology that it's hard to disentangle fact from fiction.

According to mythology, the city was founded by a Phoenician called Cecrops, who came to Attica and decided that the Acropolis was the perfect spot for a city. The gods of Olympus then proclaimed that the city should be named after the deity who could produce the most valuable gift to mortals. Athena and Poseidon contended. Poseidon struck the ground with his trident and a magnificent horse sprang forth, symbolising the warlike qualities for which he was renowned. Athena produced an olive tree, the symbol of peace and prosperity, and won hands down.

According to archaeologists, the Acropolis has been occupied since Neolithic times. It was an excellent vantage point, and the steep slopes formed natural defences on three sides. By 1400 BC the Acropolis was a powerful Mycenaean city.

Its power peaked during the so-called golden age of Athens in the 5th century BC, following the defeat of the Persians at the Battle of Salamis. It fell into decline after its defeat by Sparta in the long-running Peloponnesian War, but rallied again in Roman times when it became a seat of learning. The Roman emperors, particularly Hadrian, graced Athens with many grand buildings.

After the Roman Empire split into east and west, power shifted to Byzantium and the city fell into obscurity. By the end of Ottoman rule, Athens was little more than a dilapidated village (the area now known as Plaka).

Then, in 1834, Athens became the capital of independent Greece. The newly crowned King Otho, freshly arrived from Bavaria, began rebuilding the city along neoclassical lines, featuring large squares and tree-lined boulevards with imposing public buildings. The city grew steadily and enjoyed a brief heyday as the 'Paris of the Mediterranean' in the late 19th and early 20th centuries.

This came to an abrupt end with the forced population exchange between Greece and Turkey that followed the Treaty of Lausanne in 1923. The huge influx of refugees from Asia Minor virtually doubled the population overnight, forcing the hasty erection of the first of the concrete apartment blocks that dominate the city today. The belated advent of Greece's industrial age in the 1950s brought another wave of migration, this time of rural folk looking for jobs. This trend continues.

Orientation

Although Athens is a huge, sprawling city, nearly everything of interest to travellers is located within a small area bounded by Omonia Square (Plateia Omonias) to the north, Monastiraki Square (Plateia Monastirakiou) to the west, Syntagma Square (Plateia Syntagmatos) to the east and the Plaka district to the south. The city's two major landmarks, the Acropolis and Lykavittos Hill, can be seen from just about everywhere in this area.

Syntagma is the heart of modern Athens; it's flanked by luxury hotels, banks and expensive coffee shops and dominated by the old royal palace – home of the Greek parliament since 1935.

Omonia is decidedly sleazy these days. It's more of a transport hub than a square. The major streets of central Athens all meet here. Panepistimiou (El Venizelou) and Stadiou run parallel south-east to Syntagma, while Athinas leads south from Omonia to the market district of Monastiraki. Monastiraki is in turn linked to Syntagma by Ermou – home to some of the city's smartest shops – and Mitropoleos.

Mitropoleos skirts the northern edge of Plaka, the delightful old Turkish quarter which was virtually all that existed when Athens was declared the capital of independent Greece. Its labyrinthine streets are nestled on the north-eastern slope of the Acropolis, and most of the city's ancient sites are close by. It may be touristy, but it's the most attractive and interesting part of Athens and the majority of visitors make it their base.

Streets are clearly signposted in Greek and English. If you do get lost, it's very easy to find help. A glance at a map is often enough to draw an offer of assistance. Anyone you ask will be able to direct you to Syntagma (say SYN-tagma).

Information

Tourist Offices EOT's head office (☎ 322 3111) at Amerikis 2 does not deal with enquiries from the general public. The organisation's public face is a small information window (☎ 322 2545) in the National Bank of Greece building on Syntagma. It's worth asking for their free map of Athens, which has most of the places of interest clearly marked and also shows the trolleybus routes. There's also a notice board with transport information, including ferry departures from Piraeus. This window is open Monday to Friday from 8 am to 6 pm and Saturday from 9 am to 2 pm.

The EOT office (☎ 979 9500) at the East airport terminal is open Monday to Friday from 9 am to 7 pm and Saturday from 10 am to 5 pm.

The tourist police (☎ 902 5992) are open 24 hours a day at Dimitrakopoulou 77, Veïkou. Take trolleybus No 1, 5 or 9 from Syntagma. They also have a 24-hour information service (☎ 171).

Money Most of the major banks have branches around Syntagma, open Monday to Thursday from 8 am to 2 pm and Friday from 8 am to 1.30 pm. The National Bank of Greece and the Credit Bank, on opposite sides of Stadiou at Syntagma, both have 24-hour automatic exchange machines.

American Express (☎ 324 4975), Ermou 2, Syntagma, is open Monday to Friday from 8.30 am to 4 pm, and Saturday from 8.30 am to 1.30 pm. Thomas Cook (☎ 322 0155) has an office at Karageorgi Servias 4, open Monday to Friday from 8.30 am to 8 pm, Saturday from 9 am to 6.30 pm and Sunday from 10 am to 2.30 pm.

In Plaka, Acropole Foreign Exchange, Kydathineon 23, is open from 9 am to midnight every day. The banks at both the East and West airport terminals are open 24 hours a day, although you may have trouble tracking down the staff late at night.

GREECE

GREECE

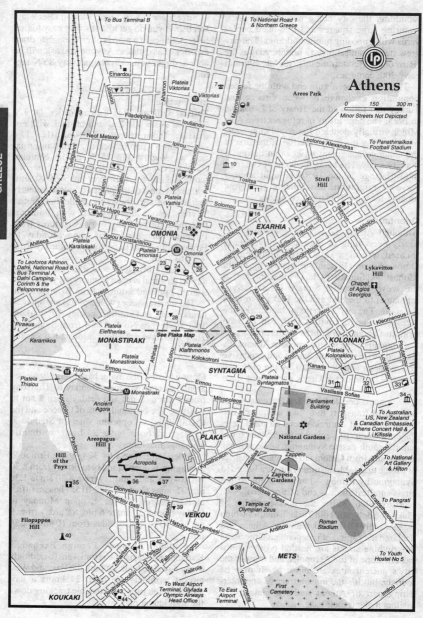

To Bus Terminal B

To National Road 1 & Northern Greece

Athens

0   150   300 m

Minor Streets Not Depicted

1 Einardou

2

3

4

Filadelphias

Neof Metaxa

Ipirou

Plateia Viktorias

7

Viktorias

M

8

9

10

Tositsa

11

Solomou

15

16

EXARHIA

12

13

14

Areos Park

To Panathinaikos Football Stadium

Strefi Hill

5

6

Plateia Vathis

Victor Hugo

20

19

Karolou

Veranzerou

18

OMONIA

Plateia Omonias

M

Omonia

23

24

25

22

26

17

Themistokleous

Emmanuil Benaki

Zosodhou Pigis

Mavrommati

Harilaou Trikoupi

Ippokratous

Solonos

Akadimias

Lykavittou

Asklipiou

Lykavittos Hill

Chapel of Agios Georgios

Kleomenous

KOLONAKI

21

Plateia Karaiskaki

To Leoforos Athinon, Dafni, National Road 8, Bus Terminal A, Dafni Camping, Corinth & the Peloponnese

Pireos

27

28

Plateia Eleftherias

See Plaka Map

MONASTIRAKI

Plateia Monastirakiou

29

30

Plateia Klafthmonos

Kolokotroni

SYNTAGMA

Plateia Syntagmatos

Plateia Kolonakiou

31

32

33

34

Vasilisis Sofias

To Australian, US, New Zealand & Canadian Embassies, Athens Concert Hall & Kifissia

To Piraeus

Keramikos

Plateia Thisiou

M Thision

Ancient Agora

Areopagus Hill

Acropolis

Hill of the Pnyx

35

M Monastiraki

Ermou

Mitropoleos

Nikis

Filellinon

Amalias

Parliament Building

National Gardens

To National Art Gallery & Hilton

36

37

Dionysiou Areopagitou

Rovertou Galli

38

Vasilissis Olgas

Zappeio

Zappeio Gardens

Temple of Olympian Zeus

Roman Stadium

To Pangrati

Filopappos Hill

40

VEIKOU

39

41

42

Veikou

Hatzihristou

Lembesi

Synarou

Kalirois

Ardittou

METS

To Youth Hostel No 5

KOUKAKI

43

44

To West Airport Terminal, Glyfada & Olympic Airways Head Office

To East Airport Terminal

First Cemetery

PLACES TO STAY		OTHER		24	Marinopoulos

PLACES TO STAY
- 1 Hostel Aphrodite
- 11 Museum Hotel
- 19 Athens International Youth Hostel
- 21 Hotel Mystras
- 30 YWCA (XEN) Hostel (women only)
- 41 Art Gallery Pension
- 44 Marble House Pension

PLACES TO EAT
- 2 Taverna Avli
- 5 O Makis Psistaria
- 14 Taverna Barbargiannis
- 17 Ouzeri Refenes
- 27 Fruit & Vegetable Market
- 28 Meat Market Tavernas
- 39 Socrates Prison Taverna
- 43 Gardenia Restaurant

OTHER
- 3 Larisis Train Station
- 4 Peloponnese Train Station
- 6 Rodon Club
- 7 OTE
- 8 Buses to Marathon & Rafina
- 9 Buses to Lavrion and Cape Sounion
- 10 National Archaeological Museum
- 12 Green Door Club
- 13 Supermarket
- 15 Ach Marie Club
- 16 AN Club
- 18 Minion Department Store
- 20 Laundrette
- 22 Buses to Bus Terminal A
- 23 Bus 049 to Piraeus
- 24 Marinopoulos Supermarket
- 25 Buses to Airport
- 26 Main Post Office
- 29 Buses to Dafni
- 31 Benaki Museum
- 32 Goulandris Museum of Cycladic & Ancient Greek Art
- 33 UK Embassy
- 34 Byzantine Museum
- 35 Church of Agios Dimitrios
- 36 Theatre of Herodes Atticus
- 37 Ancient Theatre of Dionysos
- 38 Arch of Hadrian
- 40 Monument of Filopappos
- 42 Hellaspar Supermarket

Post & Communications The main post office is at Eolou 100, Omonia (postcode 10200), which is where poste restante mail will be sent. If you're staying in Plaka, it's best to get mail sent to the Syntagma post office (postcode 10300). Both open weekdays from 7.30 am to 8 pm, Saturday from 7.30 am to 2 pm, and Sunday from 9 am to 1.30 pm.

Parcels over two kg going abroad must be posted from the parcels office at Stadiou 4 (in the arcade). They should not be wrapped until they've been inspected.

The OTE telephone office at 28 Oktovriou-Patission 85 is open 24 hours a day, as is the office at Stadiou 15. The Omonia office, Athinas 50, is open from 7 am to 10 pm every day.

Athens' telephone code is ☎ 01.

Travel Agencies Most of the travel agencies are around Syntagma and Omonia, but only those around Syntagma deal in discount air fares. There are lots of them south of the square on Filellinon, Nikis and Voulis.

The International Student & Youth Travel Service (☎ 01-323 3767), 2nd floor, Nikis 11, is the city's official youth and student travel service. Apart from selling tickets, they also issue student cards.

Bookshops Athens has three good English-language bookshops: Pantelides Books at Amerikis 11, Eleftheroudakis at Nikis 4, and Compendium Bookshop at Nikis 28. Compendium also has a second-hand books section.

Cultural Centres The British Council (☎ 363 3215), Plateia Kolonaki 17, and the Hellenic American Union (☎ 362 9886), Massalias 22, hold frequent concerts, film shows, exhibitions etc. Both have libraries.

Laundry Plaka has a convenient laundry at Angelou Geronta 10, just off Kydathineon near the outdoor restaurants.

Medical & Emergency Services For emergency medical treatment, ring the tourist police (☎ 171) and they'll tell you where the nearest hospital is. Don't wait for an ambulance – get a taxi. Hospitals give free emergency treatment to tourists. For hospitals with outpatient departments on duty, ring ☎ 106. For first-aid advice, ring ☎ 166. You can get free dental treatment at the Evangelismos Hospital, Ipsilandou 45.

GREECE

Dangers & Annoyances Although Athens is one of Europe's safest cities, a warning to solo male travellers about the following practice: a male traveller enters a bar, or is enticed there by a friendly local, and buys a drink; the owner then offers him a second drink. Girls appear, more drinks are provided and the visitor relaxes as he realises that the girls are not prostitutes, just friendly Greeks. The crunch comes when the traveller is eventually presented with an exorbitant bill. Beware of this scam, especially around Syntagma.

Things to See

Walking Tour The following walk starts and finishes at Syntagma Square and takes in most of Plaka's best-known sites. Without detours, it will take about 45 minutes. The route is marked with a dotted line on the Plaka map.

From Syntagma, walk along Mitropoleos and take the first turning left onto Nikis. Continue along here to the junction with Kydathineon, Plaka's main thoroughfare, and turn right. Opposite the church is the **Museum of Greek Folk Art**, which houses an excellent collection of embroidery, weaving and jewellery. It is open Tuesday to Sunday from 10 am to 2 pm; admission is 400 dr. After passing the square with the outdoor tavernas, take the second turning left onto Adrianou. A right turn at end of Adrianou leads to the small square with the **Choregic Monument of Lysicrates**, erected in 334 BC to commemorate victory in a choral festival.

Turn left and then right onto Epimenidou; at the top, turn right onto Thrasilou, which skirts the Acropolis. Where the road forks, veer left into the district of **Anafiotika**. Here the little white cubic houses resemble those of the Cyclades, and olive-oil cans brimming with flowers bedeck the walls of their tiny gardens. The houses were built by the people of Anafi, who were used as cheap labour in the rebuilding of Athens after Independence.

The path winds between the houses and comes to some steps on the right, at the bottom of which is a curving pathway leading downhill to Pratiniou. Turn left onto Pratiniou and veer right after 50 metres onto Tholou. The yellow-ochre Venetian building with brown shutters at No 5 is the old university, now the **Museum of the University**. It is open Monday and Wednesday from 2.30 to 7 pm, and Tues-day, Thursday and Friday from 9.30 am to 2.30 pm. Admission is free.

At the end of Tholou, turn left onto Panos. At the top of the steps on the left is a restored 19th-century mansion which is now the **Paul & Alexandra Kanellopoulos Museum** – closed for repairs at the time of writing. Retracing your steps, go down Panos to the ruins of the **Roman Agora**, then turn left onto Polygnotou and walk to the crossroads. Opposite, Polygnotou continues to the **Ancient Agora**. At the crossroads, turn right and then left onto Poikilis, then immediately right onto Areos. On the right are the remains of the **Library of Hadrian** and next to it is the **Museum of Traditional Greek Ceramics**, open every day, except Tuesday, from 10 am to 2 pm. Admission is 500 dr. The museum is housed in the **Mosque of Tzistarakis**, built in 1759. After Independence it lost its minaret and was used as a prison.

Ahead is Monastiraki Square, named after the small church. To the left is the metro station and the **flea market**. Monastiraki is Athens at its noisiest, most colourful and chaotic; it's teeming with street vendors.

Turn right just beyond the mosque onto Pandrossou, a relic of the old Turkish bazar. At No 89 is Stavros Melissinos, the 'poet sandalmaker' of Athens who names the Beatles, Rudolph Nureyev and Jackie Onassis among his customers. Fame and fortune have not gone to his head – he still makes the best sandals in Athens, costing from 2400 dr per pair.

Pandrossou leads to Plateia Mitropoleos and the **Athens Cathedral**. The cathedral was constructed from the masonry of over 50 razed churches and from the designs of several architects. Next to it stands the much smaller, and far more appealing, old **Church of Agios Eleftherios**. Turn left after the cathedral, and then right onto Mitropoleos and back to Syntagma.

Acropolis Most of the buildings now gracing the Acropolis were commissioned by Pericles during the golden age of Athens in the 5th century BC. The site had been cleared for him by the Persians, who destroyed an earlier temple complex on the eve of the Battle of Salamis.

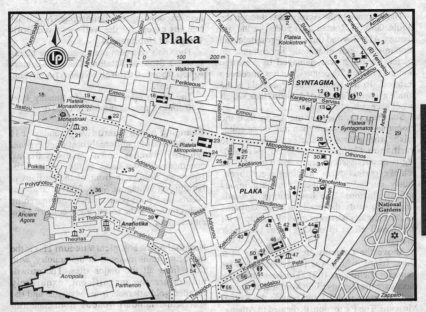

Plaka

PLACES TO STAY
9 Hotel Grande Bretagne
17 Hotel Tempi
27 John's Place
40 Hotel Nefeli
41 Acropolis House
    Pension
42 Kouros Hotel
43 George's Guesthouse
44 Festos Youth &
    Student Guest
    House
50 Student & Travellers'
    Inn

PLACES TO EAT
3 Apotsos Ouzeri
4 Zonar's
7 Brazil Coffee Shop
8 Wendy's
19 Savas & Thanasis
26 Peristeria Taverna
30 Neon Café
39 Eden Vegetarian
    Restaurant
48 Taverna Saita

49 The Cellar
52 Byzantino
53 Plaka Psistaria
54 Ouzeri Kouklis
55 Taverna Damigos

OTHER
1 Pantiledes Books
2 OTE
5 Parcel Post Office
6 Festival Box Office
10 Credit Bank
11 EOT & National Bank
    of Greece
12 Thomas Cook
13 Buses to Airport
14 American Express
15 Eleftheroudakis Books
16 Church of Kapnikarea
18 Flea Market
20 Museum of Traditional
    Greek Ceramics
21 Library of Hadrian
22 Centre of Hellenic
    Tradition
23 Athens Cathedral

24 Church of Agios
    Eleftherios
25 National Welfare
    Organisation
28 Syntagma Post Office
29 Parliament
31 Bus 040 to Piraeus
32 International Student &
    Youth Travel Service
33 Buses to Cape Sounion
34 Compendium Books
35 Tower of the Winds
36 Roman Agora
37 Kanellopoulos Museum
38 Museum of the
    University
45 Trolley Stop for Plaka
46 Church of
    Metamorphosis
47 Museum of Greek Folk
    Art
51 Acropole Foreign
    Exchange
56 Plateia Plakas
57 Laundrette

The entrance to the Acropolis is through the **Beule Gate**, a Roman arch added in the 3rd century AD. Beyond this is the **Propylaia**, the monumental gate that was the entrance in ancient times. It was damaged by Venetian bombing in the 17th century, but has since been restored. To the south of the Propylaia is the small, graceful **Temple of Athena Nike**, which is not accessible to visitors.

Standing supreme over the Acropolis is the monument which more than any other epitomises the glory of ancient Greece: the **Parthenon**. Completed in 438 BC, this building is unsurpassed in grace and harmony. To achieve perfect form, its lines were ingeniously curved to counteract unharmonious optical illusions. The base curves upwards slightly towards the ends, and the columns become slightly narrower towards the top, with the overall effect of making them both look straight.

Above the columns are the remains of a Doric frieze, which was partly destroyed by Venetian shelling in 1687. The best surviving pieces are the famous Elgin Marbles, carted off by Lord Elgin in 1801 and now in the British Museum. The Parthenon, dedicated to Athena, contained an 11-metre-tall gold and ivory statue of the goddess completed in 438 BC by Phidias of Athens; only the statue's foundations exist today).

To the north is the **Erechtheion** with its much-photographed Caryatids, the six maidens who support its southern portico. These are plaster casts – the originals (except for the one taken by Lord Elgin) are in the site's museum. The Erechtheion was dedicated to Athena and Poseidon and supposedly built on the spot where they competed for possession of ancient Athens. The Acropolis Museum has sculptures from the temples.

The site is open Monday to Friday from 8 am to 5.45 pm, and weekends and public holidays from 8.30 am to 2.45 pm. The museum is open on Monday from 11 am to 4 pm, Tuesday to Friday from 8 am to 6.30 pm, and weekends from 8.30 am to 2.30 pm. The combined admission fee is 2000 dr.

Ancient Agora The Agora was the marketplace of ancient Athens and the focal point of civic and social life. Socrates spent much time here expounding his philosophy. Not much remains except for the well-preserved **Doric Temple of Hephaestus**.

The site's museum is housed in the reconstructed **Stoa of Attalos**. The 11th-century **Agiou Apostoli Church** contains fine Byzantine frescos.

The site is open Tuesday to Sunday from 8.30 am to 3 pm; admission is 1200 dr.

Changing of the Guard Every Sunday at 11 am a platoon of traditionally costumed *evzones* (guards) marches down Vasilissis Sofias, accompanied by a band, to the Tomb of the Unknown Soldier in front of the parliament building on Syntagma. Some find the costumes (skirts and pom-pom shoes) and marching style comic, but the ceremony is colourful and entertaining.

National Archaeological Museum This is the most important museum in the country, with finds from all the major sites. The crowd-pullers are the magnificent, exquisitely detailed gold artefacts from Mycenae and the spectacular **Minoan frescos** from Santorini (Thira), which are here until a suitable museum is built on the island. Allow a whole day to see the vast collection. The museum is at 28 Oktovriou-Patission 44, open Monday from 11 am to 7 pm, Tuesday to Friday from 8 am to 7 pm, and on weekends and public holidays from 8.30 am to 3 pm. It closes at 5 pm instead of 7 pm in winter. Admission is 2000 dr.

Benaki Museum This museum, on the corner of Vasilissis Sofias and Koumbari, houses the collection of Antoine Benaki, the son of an Alexandrian cotton magnate named Emmanual Benaki. The collection includes ancient sculpture, Persian, Byzantine and Coptic objects, Chinese ceramics, icons, two El Greco paintings and a superb collection of traditional costumes. The museum was closed for repairs at the time of writing.

Goulandris Museum of Cycladic & Ancient Greek Art This private museum was custom-built to display a fabulous collection of Cycladic art, with an emphasis on the Early Bronze Age. Particularly impressive are the beautiful marble figurines. These simple, elegant forms, mostly of naked women with arms folded under their breasts, inspired 20th-century artists such as Brancusi, Epstein, Modigliani and Picasso. It's at Neofytou Douka 4 and is open Monday, Tuesday, Thursday and Friday from 10 am to 4 pm, and Saturday from 10 am to 3 pm. Admission is 400 dr.

Lykavittos Hill Pine-covered Lykavittos is the highest of the eight hills dotted around Athens. From the summit there are all-embracing views of the city, the Attic basin and the islands of Salamis and Aegina – pollution permitting.

The southern side of the hill is occupied by the posh residential suburb of Kolonaki. The main path to the summit starts at the top of Loukianou, or you can take the funicular railway from the top of Ploutarhou (400 dr).

National Gardens Formerly named the Royal Gardens, these offer a welcome shady retreat from the summer sun, with subtropical trees, peacocks, water fowl, ornamental ponds and a botanical museum.

Courses
The Athens Centre (☎ 701 2268; fax 701 8603), Archimidous 48, has a very good reputation. Its courses cover five levels of proficiency from beginners' to advanced. There are five immersion courses a year for beginners. The YWCA (XEN in Greek) (☎ 362 4291; fax 362 2400), Amerikis 11, has six-week beginners' courses starting in February, May, and October.

Other places in Athens offering courses are the Hellenic American Union (☎ 362 9886), Massalias 22, and the Hellenic Language School, Zalongou 4 (☎ 362 8161; fax 363 9951).

Organised Tours
Key Tours (☎ 923 3166), Kallirois 4; CHAT Tours (☎ 322 3137), Stadiou 4; and GO Tours (☎ 322 5951), Voulis 31-33, are the main operators. You'll see their brochures everywhere, offering identical tours and prices. They include a half-day bus tour (7700 dr), which does no more than point out the major sights.

Special Events
The Athens Festival is the city's most important cultural event, running from mid-June to the end of September, with plays, ballet and classical-music concerts. Performances are held in the Theatre of Herodes Atticus and begin at 9 pm. Information and tickets are available from the Festival Box Office, Stadiou 4.

If this all sounds too staid, the fringe International Jazz Festival runs concurrently. Venues include the theatre on Lykavittos Hill. Both festivals have discounts for students.

Places to Stay
Camping *Dafni Camping* (☎ 581 1562/1563) is a good shady site next to Dafni's famous Byzantine monastery, about 10 km from the city centre on the road to Corinth. Take bus No 880 or 860 from Panepistimiou. There are several camping grounds on the coast road to Cape Sounion.

Hostels There are a few places around town making a pitch for the hostelling market by tagging 'youth hostel' onto their name. There are some dreadful dumps among them.

The only youth hostel worth bothering with is the excellent HI-affiliated *Athens International Youth Hostel* (☎ 523 4170), Victor Hugo 16. Location is the only drawback, otherwise the place is almost too good to be true. The spotless rooms, each with bathroom, sleep two to four people. Rates are 2000 dr per person for HI members, 2500 dr for others.

The *YWCA* (XEN; ☎ 362 4291), Amerikis 11, is an option for women only. It has singles/doubles with shared bathroom for 3500/6000 dr, or 4500/6500 dr with private bathroom. There are laundry facilities and a snack bar. Annual membership is 600 dr.

Hotels Athens is a noisy city and Athenians keep late hours, so an effort has been made to select hotels in quiet areas. Plaka is the most popular place to stay, and it has a good choice of accommodation right across the price spectrum. Rooms fill up quickly in July and August, so it's wise to make a reservation. Some budget hotels let you sleep on the roof in summer. Checkout time in hotels is noon unless otherwise stated.

Plaka The **Student & Travellers' Inn** (☎ 324 4808), right in the heart of Plaka at Kyda thineon 16, is hard to look past. It's a friendly, well-run place with beautiful polished floors and spotless rooms. It has beds in four-person dorms for 2000 dr, while singles/doubles/triples are 4500/6000/7500 dr with shared bathroom. English breakfast is served in the vine-covered courtyard out the back for 1050 dr.

The huge timber spiral staircase at **George's Guesthouse** (☎ 322 6474) speaks of grander times at Nikis 46, but it's a friendly place with dorms for 2000 dr and doubles/triples for 5000/6000 dr with shared bathroom.

The **Festos Youth & Student Guest House** (☎ 323 2455), Filellinon 18, has been a popular place with travellers for a long time despite its noisy situation on one of the busiest streets in Athens. Dorm beds are 2000 dr, but they pack eight into a room. It charges 2500 dr per person in private rooms with shared bathroom.

The rooms at **John's Place** (☎ 322 9719), Patroou 5, are very basic but clean. Singles/doubles with shared bathroom are 4000/6000 dr. Patroou is on the left heading down Mitropoleos from Syntagma.

Slightly more expensive but much better value is the friendly **Hotel Tempi** (☎ 321 3175), near Monastiraki Square on the pedestrian precinct part of Eolou. The rooms at the front have balconies overlooking a little square with a church and a flower market. Rates are 4000/7000 dr with shared bathroom, or 8000 dr for doubles with private bathroom.

Plaka also has some good mid-range accommodation. The **Acropolis House Pension** (☎ 322 2344), Kodrou 6-8, is a beautifully preserved 19th-century house. Singles/doubles with shared bathroom are 7500/9000 dr, or 9100/10,900 dr with private bathroom. All rooms have central heating. Kodrou is the southern (pedestrian) extension of Voulis, leading onto Kydathineon.

Just around the corner from the Acropolis House is the **Hotel Nefeli** (☎ 322 8044/8045), Iperidou 16, a modern place with singles/doubles for 11,000/12,000 dr, including breakfast.

Veïkou & Koukaki There are a few good places to stay in this pleasant residential area just south of the Acropolis. The **Marble House** Pension (☎ 923 4058), Zini 35A, Koukaki, is a quiet, friendly place tucked away on a small cul-de-sac. Rates for the immaculate singles/doubles are 5800/8900 dr with shared bathroom or 6800/9900 dr with private bathroom. Special weekly and monthly rates are available in winter.

The comfortable **Art Gallery Pension** (☎ 923 8376/1933), Erehtheiou 5, Veïkou, is a fine family-run place with singles/doubles for 13,000/15,000 dr with balcony and private bathroom.

Both these places are just a short ride from Syntagma on trolleybus No 1, 5, 9 or 18. Coming from Syntagma, they travel along Veïkou. Get off at the Drakou stop for the Art Gallery Pension, and at Zini for the Marble House. The trolleybuses return to Syntagma along Dimitrakopoulou.

Omonia & Surrounds There are dozens of hotels around Omonia, but most of them are either bordellos masquerading as cheap hotels or uninspiring, overpriced C-class hotels. Only a couple of places are worth a mention.

The **Hostel Aphrodite** (☎ 881 0589), 10 minutes from the train stations, at Einardou 12, is well set up for budget travellers. It is very clean, with dazzling, white walls and good-sized rooms, many with balconies. It has dorm beds for 1500 dr, singles/doubles/triples with shared bathroom for 4000/5000/6000 dr and a few doubles with private bathroom for 6000 dr.

The **Hotel Mystras** (☎ 522 7737), just south of the stations at Kerameon 26, is also geared towards travellers. Singles/doubles/triples are 4000/5000/6000 dr with private bathroom.

The long-established **Museum Hotel** (☎ 380 5611), Bouboulinas 16, is behind the National Archaeological Museum. The rooms are comfortable and reasonably priced at 5000/7000/8400 dr with private bathroom.

Long-Term Accommodation For long-term rentals, look in the classifieds of the English-language newspapers and magazines. Another possibility is to look at the notice board outside Compendium Books, Nikis 28. One-bedroom furnished flats cost from 80,000 dr a month, although less salubrious apartments can be found for 60,000 dr.

GREECE

Places to Eat

Plaka For most people, Plaka is the place to be. It's hard to beat the atmosphere of dining out beneath the floodlit Acropolis.

You do, however, pay for the privilege – particularly at the outdoor restaurants around the square on Kydathineon. The best of this bunch is *Byzantino*, which prices its menu more realistically and is popular with Greek family groups. One of the best deals in the Plaka is the nearby *Plaka Psistaria*, Kydathineon 28, with a range of gyros and souvlakia to eat there or take away.

Ouzeri Kouklis, Tripodon 14, is an old-style ouzeri with an oak-beamed ceiling, marble tables and wicker chairs. It serves only mezedes, which are brought round on a large tray for you to take your pick. They include flaming sausages – ignited at your table – and cuttlefish for 800 dr, as well as the usual dips for 400 dr. The whole selection, enough for four hungry people, costs 6400 dr.

Vegetarian restaurants are thin on the ground in Athens. The *Eden Vegetarian Restaurant*, Lyssiou 12, is one of only three. The Eden has been around for years, substituting soya products for meat in tasty vegetarian versions of moussaka (1250 dr) and other Greek favourites.

With such an emphasis on outdoor eating in summer, it's no great surprise that the three cellar restaurants on Kydathineon are closed from mid-May until October. They are also three of Plaka's cheaper places, charging about 1500 dr for a main dish washed down with half a litre of retsina. The best of them is the *Taverna Saita* at No 21 – near the Museum of Greek Folk Art. The others are *The Cellar* at No 10 and *Damigos* at No 41.

Peristeria Taverna, next to John's Place at Patroou 5, is a good, basic taverna that is open all year.

Monastiraki There are some excellent cheap places to eat around Monastiraki, particularly for gyros and souvlaki fans. *Thanasis* and *Savas*, opposite each other at the bottom end of Mitropoleos, are the places to go.

The best taverna food in this part of town is at the *meat market*, on the right 400 metres along Athinas from Monastiraki Square. The place must resemble a vegetarian's vision of hell, but the food is great and the tavernas are

open 24 hours, except Sunday. They serve traditional meat dishes such as patsas (tripe soup), podarakia (pig-trotter soup) as well as regular dishes like stifado and meatballs. Soups start at 600 dr and main dishes at 1000 dr.

Opposite the meat market is the main *fruit & vegetable market*.

Syntagma The *Neon Café*, opposite the post office, has spaghetti or fettucine with a choice of sauces for 780 dr, moussaka for 1350 dr and roast beef for 1680 dr. It is probably the only eating place in Athens with a no-smoking area.

Apotsos Ouzeri, Panepistimiou 10 (in an arcade opposite Zonar's), is Athens' oldest ouzeri – it opened in 1900. It is a popular lunch-time venue for journalists and politicians. It has a huge choice of mezedes priced from 450 to 2500 dr.

Follow your nose to the *Brazil Coffee Shop* on Vorkourestiou for the best coffee in town.

Veïkou & Koukaki The *Gardenia Restaurant*, Zini 31 at the junction with Dimitrakopoulou, claims to be the cheapest taverna in Athens; it has moussaka for 650 dr and a litre of draught retsina for 450 dr. What's more, the food is good and the service is friendly.

Socrates Prison, Mitseon 20, is not named after the philosopher, but after the owner (also called Socrates) who reckons the restaurant is his prison. It's a stylish place with an imaginative range of mezedes from 450 dr and main dishes from 1250 dr.

Exarhia There are lots of ouzeria and tavernas to choose from in the lively suburb of Exarhia, just east of Omonia. Prices here are tailored to suit the pockets of the district's largely student clientele.

Emmanual Benaki, which leads from Panepistimiou to the base of Strefi Hill, is the place to look. The *Ouzeri Refenes*, at No 51, is a popular place that does a delicious pikilia (mixed plate) of mezedes for 1000 dr. The *Taverna Barbargiannis*, further up the hill on the corner of Emmanual Benaki and Dervenion, is another good place. It does a tasty bean soup for 650 dr as well as a selection of meat dishes for under 1200 dr.

It's quite a long hike to the area from Syntagma. An alternative is to catch bus No 230 from Amalias to Harilau Trikoupi and walk across.

Around the Train Stations Wherever you choose to eat in this area you will find the lack of tourist hype refreshing. The *O Makis Psistaria*, at Psaron 48 opposite the church, is a lively place serving hunks of freshly grilled pork or beef, plus chips, for 1200 dr.

Hidden away at Proussis 21 is one of Athens' real gems, the *Taverna Avli*. Although not a vegetarian restaurant, it has the best vegetarian food in town. It has a fabulous range of mezedes, including spicy Mykonos cheese salad, saganaki of smoked Macedonian cheese or mussels and deep-fried 'sausages' of aubergine and minced walnut. Expect to pay about 2500 dr per person.

Entertainment

Cinema Athenians are avid movie-goers and there are cinemas everywhere. The *Athens News*, *Greek Weekly Times* and *Athenscope* all have listings. Admission is about 1500 dr.

Discos & Bars Discos operate in central Athens only between October and April. In summer, the action moves to the coastal suburbs of Glyfada and Ellinikon.

The highest concentration of music bars is in Exarhia. The *Green Door Music Club*, Kalidromiou 52 at the junction with Emmanual Benaki, is one of the most popular. If you want to hear some good music and have a conversation at the same time, then try the *Passenger Club*, 1st floor, Mavromihali 168. The music is mellow (mostly jazz and R&B), with no hard rock or heavy metal. Cocktails are priced from 1200 dr, spirits are 1000 dr and beer 800 dr.

Popular gay bars include *Granazi Bar*, Lembesi 20, which is south of the Arch of Hadrian, and the *Alexander Club* at Anagnostopoulou 44, Kolonaki. Both attract a mixed clientele. *Iridis* is a lesbian bar on Apostolou Pavlou in the Thision district, west of the Agora.

Rock & Jazz Concerts The *Rodon Club* (☎ 524 7427) at Marni 24 hosts touring international rock bands, while local bands play at the *AN Club* and *Ach Maria Club*, opposite each other on Solomou in Exarhia. Concerts are listed in the *Weekly Greek News*.

Greek Folk Dances The *Dora Stratou Dance Company* performs at its theatre on Filopappos Hill at 10.15 pm every night from mid-May to October, with additional performances at 8.15 pm on Wednesday. Tickets are 1500 dr. Filopappos Hill is west of the Acropolis, off Dionysiou Areopagitou. Bus No 230 from Syntagma will get you there.

Sound-and-Light Show Athens' endeavour at this spectacle is not one of the world's best. There are shows in English every night at 9 pm from the beginning of April until the end of October at the theatre on the Hill of the Pnyx (☎ 322 1459). Tickets are 1500 dr. The Hill of the Pnyx is opposite Filopappos Hill, and the show is timed so that you can cross straight to the folk dancing.

Rembetika Clubs Rembetika is the music of the working classes and has its roots in the sufferings of the refugees from Asia Minor in the 1920s. Songs are accompanied by bouzouki, guitar, violin and accordion. By the 1940s it had also become popular with the bourgeoisie. It was banned during the junta years, but has since experienced a resurgence, especially in Athens.

Rembetika Stoa Athanaton, Sofokleous 19 (in the meat market), is open in the afternoon from 3 to 6 pm as well as in the evenings. *Rembetiki Istoria*, Ippokratous 181, plays host to some top musicians. It's open Thursday to Sunday from 11 pm.

Spectator Sport

Soccer is the most popular sport in Greece. Six of the 18 teams in the Greek first division are from Athens: AEK, Apollon, Ethnikos, Olympiakos, Panathinaïkos and Panionios. The season lasts from September to mid-May. Matches are played on Wednesday and Sunday. Admission is 1200 dr. Fixtures and results are given in the *Weekly Greek News*.

Things to Buy

The National Welfare Organisation shop, on the corner of Apollonos and Ipatias, Plaka, is a good place to go shopping for handicrafts. It has top-quality goods and the money goes to a good cause – the organisation was formed to preserve and promote traditional Greek handicrafts. It has a wide range of knotted carpets, kilims, flokatis, needle-point rugs and embroidered cushion covers as well as a small selection of pottery, copper and wood-work.

The Centre of Hellenic Tradition, Pandrossou 36, Plaka, has a display of traditional and modern handicrafts from each region of Greece. Most of the items are for sale.

Getting There & Away
Air Athens' dilapidated airport, Ellinikon, is nine km south of the city. There are two main terminals: West for all Olympic Airways flights, and East for all other flights. Occasionally, the old military terminal is dusted off for charter flights in peak season.

The Olympic Airways head office (☎ 926 9111) is at Syngrou 96. There was no office on Syntagma at the time of writing, following the closure of the branch at Othonos 6. A new office is due to open on Filellinon in 1997.

Bus Athens has two main intercity bus stations. The EOT gives out comprehensive schedules for both with departure times, journey times and fares.

Terminal A is north-west of Omonia at Kifissou 100 and has departures to the Peloponnese, the Ionian islands and western Greece. To get there, take bus No 051 from the junction of Zinonos and Menandrou, near Omonia. Buses run every 15 minutes from 5 am to midnight.

Terminal B is north of Omonia off Liossion and has departures to central and northern Greece as well as to Evia. To get there, take bus No 024 from outside the main gate of the National Gardens on Amalias. EOT misleadingly gives the terminal's address as Liossion 260, which turns out to be a small workshop. Liossion 260 is where you should get off the bus. Turn right onto Gousiou and you'll see the terminal at the end of the road.

Buses for Attica leave from the Mavromateon terminal at the junction of Leoforos Alexandras and 28 Oktovriou-Patission.

Train Athens has two train stations, located about 200 metres apart on Deligianni, which is about a km north-west of Omonia. Trains to the Peloponnese leave from the Peloponnese station, while trains to the north leave from Larisis station – as do all the international trains.

Trolleybus No 1 stops 100 metres from Larisis station at the junction of Deligianni and Neofiliou Metaxa. Plaka residents can catch the trolleybus from the southern end of the National Gardens on Amalias. Peloponnese station is across the footbridge at the southern end of Larisis Station.

Services to the Peloponnese include 14 trains a day to Corinth (780 dr, or 1430 dr intercity). The Peloponnese line divides at Corinth, with nine trains heading along the north coast to Patras (1580/2580 dr), and five going south. Three of these go to Kalamata (2160 dr) via Tripolis, while two stop at Nafplio (1400 dr).

Services from Larisis station include nine trains a day to Thessaloniki (3500 dr), five of which are intercity services (7150 dr). The 7 am service from Athens is express right through to Alexandroupolis, arriving at 7 pm. There are also trains to Volos and Halkida, Evia.

Tickets can be bought at the stations or at the OSE offices at Filellinon 17, Sina 6 and Karolou 1.

Car & Motorcycle National Rd 1 is the main route north from Athens. It starts at Nea Kifissia. To get there from central Athens, take Vasilissis Sofias from Syntagma and follow the signs. National Rd 8, which begins beyond Dafni, is the road to the Peloponnese. Take Agiou Konstantinou from Omonia.

The northern reaches of Syngrou, just south of the Temple of Olympian Zeus, are packed solid with car-rental firms. Local companies offer much better deals than their international rivals. Motorcycles are available from Motorent (☎ 923 4939), Falirou 5 (parallel to and east of Syngrou), and from Papavassiliou Eleftherios (☎ 325 0677), Asomaton 6, Thision.

Hitching Athens is the most difficult place in Greece to hitchhike from. Your best bet is to ask the truck drivers at the Piraeus cargo wharves. Otherwise, for the Peloponnese, take a bus from Panepistimiou to Dafni, where National Rd 8 begins. For northern Greece, take the metro to Kifissia, then a bus to Nea Kifissia and walk to National Rd 1.

Ferry See the Piraeus section for information on ferries to/from the islands.

Getting Around
To/From the Airport There is a 24-hour express bus service (No 91) between central Athens and both the East and West terminals, also calling at the special charter terminal when in use.

The buses leave Stadiou, near Omonia, every half-hour from 6 am to 9 pm, every 40 minutes from 9 pm until 12.20 am, and then hourly through the night. They stop at Syntagma (outside the Macedonia-Thrace Bank) five minutes later. The trip takes from 30 minutes to an hour, depending on traffic. The fare is 160 dr (200 dr at night), and you pay the driver. There are also express buses between the airport and Plateia Karaïskaki in Piraeus.

A taxi from the airport to Syntagma should cost from 1200 to 2500 dr depending on the time of day.

Bus & Trolleybus You probably won't need to use the normal blue-and-white suburban buses. They run every 15 minutes from 5 am to midnight and charge a flat rate of 75 dr. Route numbers and destinations, but not the actual routes, are listed on the free EOT map.

The map does, however, mark the routes of the yellow trolleybuses, making them easy to use. They also run from 5 am to midnight and cost 75 dr.

There are special green buses that operate 24 hours a day to Piraeus. Bus No 040 leaves from the corner of Syntagma and Filellinon, and No 049 leaves from the Omonia end of Athinas. They run every 20 minutes from 6 am to midnight, and then hourly.

Tickets can be bought from ticket kiosks and periptera. Once on a bus, you must validate your ticket by putting it into a machine; the penalty for failing to do so is 1500 dr.

Metro Central Athens is dotted with construction sites for its new metro line, which is due to open

in 1998. Until then, there is just one metro line, running from Piraeus in the south to Kifissia in the north. The line is divided into three sections: Piraeus-Omonia, Omonia-Perissos and Perissos-Kifissia. The fares are 75 dr for travel within one or two sections, and 100 dr for three sections. Monastirakiou is the closest stop to Plaka.

Taxi Athenian taxis are yellow. Flag fall is 200 dr, with a 160 dr surcharge from ports, train and bus stations and 300 dr from airports. After that the day rate (tariff 1 on the meter) is 58 dr per km. Rates double between midnight and 5 am.

In theory, most trips around the city centre shouldn't cost more than about 400 dr on tariff 1, but Athenian taxi drivers are notorious for pulling every scam in the book. If a taxi driver refuses to use the meter, try another – and make sure it's set on the right tariff.

To hail taxis, stand on the edge of the street and shout your destination as they pass. They will stop if they are going your way even if the cab is already occupied. Take a note of the meter reading when you get in, and pay the difference when you get out – plus 200 dr flag fall.

Radio taxis are useful if you have to get somewhere on time. Operators include Athina (☎ 921 7942), Kosmos (☎ 493 3811), Parthenon (☎ 581 4711), Ermis (☎ 411 5200), Proodos (☎ 643 3400) and Enossi (☎ 644 3345).

Bicycle You'll rarely see anyone riding a bicycle in central Athens, and you'd need to have a death wish to attempt it.

Piraeus & Attica

PIRAEUS Πειραιάς
Piraeus has been the port of Athens since classical times. These days it's little more than an outer suburb of the space-hungry capital, linked by a mish-mash of factories, warehouses and apartment blocks. The streets are every bit as traffic-clogged as Athens, and behind the veneer of banks and shipping offices most of Piraeus is pretty seedy. The only reason to come here is to catch a ferry or hydrofoil.

Orientation & Information

Piraeus consists of a peninsula surrounded by harbours. The most important of them is the Great Harbour. All ferries leave from here, and it has excellent connections to Athens. There are dozens of shipping agents around the harbour, as well as banks and a post office. Zea Marina, on the other side of the peninsula, is the port for hydrofoils to the Saronic Gulf islands (except Aegina). North-east of here is the picturesque Mikrolimano (small harbour). There's a useless EOT office (☎ 413 5716) at Zea Marina.

The telephone code for Piraeus is ☎ 01.

Getting There & Away

Bus There are two 24-hour green bus services between central Athens and Piraeus. Bus No 049 runs from Omonia to the Great Harbour, and bus No 040 runs from Syntagma to the tip of the Piraeus peninsula. This is the service to catch for Zea Marina – get off at the Hotel Savoy on Vasileos Konstantinou. Leave plenty of time – the trip can take over an hour if the traffic is bad.

There are express buses to Athens airport from Plateia Karaïskaki between 5 am and 8.20 pm, and between 6 am and 9.25 pm in the other direction. The fare is 160 dr. Blue bus No 110

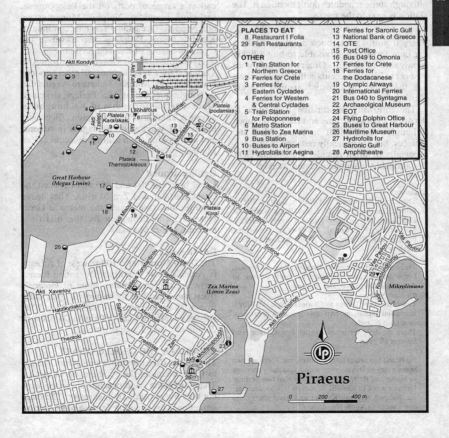

PLACES TO EAT	12	Ferries for Saronic Gulf
8 Restaurant I Folia	13	National Bank of Greece
29 Fish Restaurants	14	OTE
	15	Post Office
OTHER	16	Bus 049 to Omonia
1 Train Station for	17	Ferries for Crete
Northern Greece	18	Ferries for
2 Ferries for Crete		the Dodacanese
3 Ferries for	19	Olympic Airways
Eastern Cyclades	20	International Ferries
4 Ferries for Western	21	Bus 040 to Syntagma
& Central Cyclades	22	Archaeolgical Museum
5 Train Station	23	EOT
for Peloponnese	24	Flying Dolphin Office
6 Metro Station	25	Buses to Great Harbour
7 Buses to Zea Marina	26	Maritime Museum
8 Bus Station	27	Hydrofoils for
10 Buses to Airport		Saronic Gulf
11 Hydrofoils for Aegina	28	Amphitheatre

GREECE

Piraeus

runs from Plateia Karaïskaki to Glyfada and Voula every 15 minutes (75 dr). It stops outside the West terminal.

There are no intercity buses to or from Piraeus.

Metro The metro offers the fastest and most convenient link between the Great Harbour and Athens. The station is close to the ferries, at the northern end of Akti Kalimassioti. There are metro trains every 10 minutes from 5 am to midnight.

Train All services to the Peloponnese from Athens actually start and terminate at Piraeus, although some schedules don't mention it. The station is next to the metro.

Ferry If you want to book a cabin or take a car on a ferry, it is advisable to buy a ticket in advance in Athens. Otherwise, wait until you get to Piraeus; agents selling ferry tickets are thick on the ground around Plateia Karaïskaki.

The following information is a guide to departures between June and mid-September. Schedules are similar in April, May and October, but are radically reduced in winter – especially to small islands. The Athens EOT has a reliable schedule, updated weekly.

Cyclades
There are daily ferries to Kythnos, Serifos, Sifnos, Milos, Kimolos, Syros, Mykonos, Paros, Naxos, Ios and Tinos; two or three ferries a week to Iraklia, Shinoussa, Koufonisi, Donoussa, Amorgos, Folegandros, Sikinos, and Anafi; and one ferry a week to Andros.
Dodecanese
There are daily ferries to Rhodes, Kos, Kalymnos, Leros and Patmos; and two or three a week to Astypalea, Karpathos, and Kassos.
North-East Aegean
There are daily ferries to Chios, Lesvos (Mytilini), Ikaria and Samos; and two or three a week to Limnos.
Saronic Gulf Islands
There are daily ferries to Aegina, Poros, Hydra and Spetses all year.
Crete
No island has better ferry connections. There are two boats a day to Iraklio year-round, and daily services to Hania and Rethymno. There are also two or three ferries a week to Kastelli-Kissamos (via Monemvassia, Neapoli, Gythio, Kythira and Antikythira) and one a week to Agios Nikolaos.

The departure points for the various ferry destinations are shown on the map of Piraeus. Note that there are two departure points for Crete. Check where to find your boat when you buy your ticket. All ferries display a clock face showing their departure time and have their ports of call written in English above their bows. See Boat in this chapter's Getting Around section and the Getting There & Away sections for each island for more information.

Hydrofoil Flying Dolphin hydrofoils operate a busy schedule around the Saronic Gulf between early April and the end of October. There are frequent services to the islands of Aegina, Poros, Hydra and Spetses. They also call at a range of ports on the Peloponnese, including Leonidio, Nafplio, Monemvassia and Neapoli. Occasional services continue to Kythira. Flying Dolphins also travel to the Cycladic islands of Kea and Kythnos.

Hydrofoils to Aegina leave hourly from Akti Tzelepi at the Great Harbour; all other services leave from Zea Marina. Tickets to Aegina can be bought quayside at Akti Tzelepi; tickets to other destinations should be bought in advance. There are Flying Dolphin offices next to the EOT window on Syntagma in Athens, and overlooking the maritime museum at Zea Marina.

Getting Around
Local bus Nos 904 and 905 run between the Great Harbour and Zea Marina. They leave from the bus stop beside the metro at Great Harbour, and drop you by the maritime museum at Zea Marina.

DAFNI Δαφνί
The **Dafni Monastery**, 10 km west of Athens, is Attica's most important Byzantine monument. Its church contains some of Greece's finest mosaics. The monastery is open daily from 8.30 am to 3 pm and entry is 800 dr. Blue Athens bus Nos 860 and 880 run to Dafni every 20 minutes from Panepistimiou.

SOUNION & THE APOLLO COAST
The Apollo Coast stretches south from Athens to Cape Sounion, the southern tip of Attica. There are some good beaches along the way, but they are packed out in summer. The main attraction is the stunning **Temple of Poseidon**

at Cape Sounion, perched on a rocky headland that plunges 65 metres into the sea. The temple is open Monday to Saturday from 9 am to sunset, and from 10 am to sunset on Sunday. Sunset is the best time to be there. Admission is 800 dr.

Getting There & Away
Buses to Cape Sounion (two hours, 1050 dr) leave from the Mavromateon terminal in Athens. Services using the coast road leave hourly on the half-hour and stop on Filellinon 10 minutes later. Services travelling inland via Marcopoulo leave hourly on the hour.

The Peloponnese
Η Πελοπόννησος

The Peloponnese is the southern extremity of the rugged Balkan peninsula. Its strange geography, linked to the rest of Greece only by the narrow Isthmus of Corinth, has long prompted people to declare the Peloponnese to be more an island than part of the mainland. Its name – Peloponnisos in Greek – translates as Island of Pelops, the mythological father of the Mycenaean royal family. It technically became an island after the completion of the Corinth Canal across the isthmus in 1893, and it is now linked to the mainland only by road and rail bridges.

The Peloponnese is an area rich in history. The principal site is Olympia, birthplace of the Olympic Games, but there are many other sites worth seeking out. The ancient sites of Epidaurus, Corinth and Mycenae in the north-east are all within easy striking distance of the pretty Venetian town of Nafplio.

In the south are the magical old Byzantine towns of Monemvassia and Mystras. The rugged Mani peninsula is famous for its spectacular wild flowers in spring, as well as for the bizarre tower settlements that dot its landscape. The beaches south of Kalamata are some of the best in Greece.

NAFPLIO Ναύπλιο
Nafplio is a resort town with some fine Venetian buildings. The municipal tourist office is on 25 Martiou opposite the OTE office and is open from 9 am to 1.30 pm and 4.30 to 9 pm daily. The bus station is on Syngrou, the street which separates the old town from the new.

Nafplio's telephone code is ☎ 0752.

Things to See
Folk Art Museum The museum has a fascinating display of traditional textile-producing techniques as well as beautiful costumes. The museum is in the old town at Ypsilandou 1. It's open Tuesday to Sunday from 9 am to 2.30 pm; admission is 300 dr.

Palamida Fortress There are terrific views of the old town and the surrounding coast from this ruined hill-top fortress. The climb is strenuous – there are almost 1000 steps – so start early and take water with you. The easy way out is to catch a taxi from town for about 1000 dr. The fortress is open daily from 8 am to 7 pm (5 pm in summer); admission is 800 dr.

Places to Stay & Eat
There are *camping grounds* galore along Tolo Beach, nine km east of town. The pleasant *youth hostel* (☎ 27 754) is in the new town at Argonafton 15. Beds cost 1000 dr and an HI card or student ID is required. It takes about 20 minutes to walk there from the bus station. Head east on 25 Martiou and fork left onto Asklipiou at the first traffic lights, then left again onto Argolis at the following traffic lights. Argonafton is the seventh street on the right.

Most of the domatia are in the old town in the streets between Staikopoulou and the Ic Kale fortress. Also in this area is the D-class *Hotel Lito* (☎ 28 093), at the fortress end of Farmakopoulou. The *Hotel King Otto* (☎ 27 585), at the other end of Farmakopoulo, offers a similar deal.

The friendly *Hotel Acropol* (☎ 27 796), near the folk museum at Vasilissis Olgas 9, has clean singles/doubles with bathroom for 5700/8000 dr.

Zorbas and *Taverna Ta Fanaria* are two popular places opposite each other in the centre of the old town on Staikopoulou. Both have main courses priced from around 1000 dr.

Getting There & Away
There are hourly buses to Athens (2½ hours, 2250 dr), as well as services to Argos (for

Peloponnese connections), Mycenae, Epidaurus, Corinth and Tolo.

From May to September, there are hydrofoils to Piraeus every day except Sunday. Buy tickets from Iannopoulos Travel on Plateia Syntagmatos in the old town.

EPIDAURUS Επίδαυρος

The huge well-preserved **Theatre of Epidaurus** is the crowd-puller at this site, but don't miss the more peaceful **Sanctuary of Asclepius** nearby. Epidaurus was regarded as the birthplace of Asclepius, the god of healing, and the sanctuary was once a flourishing spa and healing centre. The setting alone would have been enough to cure many ailments.

The site is open every day from 8 am to 7 pm. Admission is 1000 dr, including the museum – closed on Monday afternoon.

You can enjoy the theatre's astounding acoustics first hand during the **Epidaurus Festival** from mid-June to mid-August.

The expensive *Xenia* is the only hotel in town.

Getting There & Away

There are two buses a day from Athens (2½ hours, 2100 dr), as well as three a day to Nafplio (40 minutes, 495 dr). During the festival, there are excursion buses from Nafplio and Athens.

ANCIENT CORINTH & ACROCORINTH

The sprawling ruins of ancient Corinth lie seven km south-west of the modern city. Corinth (Κόρινθος) was one of ancient Greece's wealthiest and most wanton cities. When Corinthians weren't clinching business deals, they were paying homage to Aphrodite in a temple dedicated to her, which meant they were having a rollicking time with the temple's sacred prostitutes. The only ancient Greek monument remaining here is the imposing **Temple of Apollo**; the others are Roman. Towering over the site is Acrocorinth, the ruins of an ancient citadel built on a massive outcrop of limestone.

Both sites are open daily from 8 am to 7 pm. Admission is 1200 dr for ancient Corinth and 500 dr for Acrocorinth.

Modern Corinth is an unprepossessing town which gives the impression that it has never quite recovered from the devastating earth-

quake of 1928. It is, however, a convenient base from which to visit ancient Corinth.

Corinth's telephone code is ☎ 0741.

Places to Stay & Eat

Buses to ancient Corinth go past **Corinth Beach Camping** (☎ 27 967), about three km west of town, and there are *domatia* near ancient Corinth.

There are a couple of reasonable cheap hotels in Corinth. The **Belle-Vue** (☎ 22 088), facing the harbour at Damaskinou 41, is an old place with clean singles/doubles with shared bathroom for 3500/4500 dr, and doubles with private bath for 6000 dr. The **Hotel Apollon** (☎ 22 587), near the train station at Pirinis 18, has singles/doubles with shower for 4000/5500 dr.

The *Kanita Restaurant*, near the Belle-Vue Hotel, serves generous helpings of traditional fare. Main meals are priced from 800 dr. As the name suggests, the *Restaurant To 24 Hours* never closes. It's on the waterfront south of the port.

Getting There & Away

Corinth has two bus stations. There are buses to Athens (1½ hours, 1350 dr) every 30 minutes from the bus station on Ermou, near the park in the city centre. It is also the departure point for hourly buses to ancient Corinth (20 minutes, 150 dr). Buses to other parts of the Peloponnese leave from the station at the junction of Ethnikis Antistaseos and Aratou.

There are 14 trains a day to Athens, five of them intercity services. There are also trains to Kalamata, Nafplio and Patras.

MYCENAE Μυκήνες

Mycenae was the most powerful influence in Greece for three centuries until about 1200 BC. The rise and fall of Mycenae is shrouded in myth, but the site was settled as early as the sixth millennium BC. Historians are divided as to whether the city's eventual destruction was due to outsiders or internal conflict between the various Mycenaean kingdoms. Described by Homer as 'rich in gold', Mycenae's entrance, the **Lion Gate**, is Europe's oldest monumental sculpture.

Excavations have uncovered the palace complex and royal tombs, shaft graves and extraordinary beehive-shaped tombs. The six shaft graves known as the **First Royal Grave Circle** were uncovered by Heinrich Schliemann in 1873.

The gold treasures he found in these graves, including the so-called **Mask of Agamemnon**, are among the world's greatest archaeological finds. They are now in the National Archaeological Museum in Athens.

The site is open daily from 8 am to 7 pm; admission is 1500 dr.

Getting There & Away

There are buses to Argos and Nafplio.

SPARTA Σπάρτη

The bellicose Spartans sacrificed all the finer things in life to military expertise and left no monuments of any consequence. Ancient Sparta's forlorn ruins lie amidst olive groves at the northern end of town. Modern Sparta is a neat, unspectacular town, but a convenient base from which to visit Mystras.

Orientation & Information

Sparta is laid out on a grid system. The main street, Paleologou, runs north-south through the town. The EOT office (☎ 24 852) is in the town hall on the main square, Plateia Kentriki. It's open Monday to Saturday from 8 am to 2 pm.

Sparta's telephone code is ☎ 0731.

Places to Stay & Eat

Camping Mystra (☎ 22 724), on the Sparta-Mystras road, is open year-round. *Hotel Cecil* (☎ 24 980), at Paleologou 125, has cosy singles/doubles/triples for 4000/6500/8000 dr with shared bath. The *Hotel Maniatis* (☎ 22 665), Paleologou 72, has immaculate singles/doubles with air-con for 9000/11,500 dr.

The *Diethnes Restaurant*, Paleologou 105, does good traditional food and has garden seating in summer.

Getting There & Away

There are frequent buses to Mystras (30 minutes, 175 dr) from Lykourgou, two blocks west of the main square. The main bus terminal is on Vrasidou, off Paleologou. There are eight buses a day to Athens (4½ hours, 3300 dr), three a day to Monemvassia and two to Kalamata.

MYSTRAS Μυστράς

Mystras, seven km from Sparta, was once the shining light of the Byzantine world. Its ruins spill from a spur of Mt Taygetos, crowned by a mighty fortress built by the Franks in 1249. The streets of Mystras are lined with glorious palaces, monasteries and churches, most of them dating from the period between 1271 and 1460, when the town was the effective capital of the Byzantine Empire. The buildings, most of which have been restored, are among the finest examples of Byzantine architecture in Greece and contain many superb frescos.

On no account should you miss the **Church of Perivleptos**, whose walls are decorated with incredibly detailed paintings. Except for the **Pantanassa Convent**, which is occupied by nuns, the buildings are uninhabited.

The site is open every day from 8 am to 7 pm. Admission is 1000 dr, which includes entrance to the museum (closed Monday). You'll need a whole day to do this vast place justice. Take a taxi or hitch a ride to the upper Fortress Gate and work your way down. Take some water.

MONEMVASSIA Μονεμβασία

Monemvassia is no longer an undiscovered paradise, but mass tourism hasn't lessened the impact of one's first encounter with this extraordinary old town – nor the thrill of exploring it.

There's no EOT office but the staff at Malvasia Travel (☎ 61 752), near the bus station, are helpful.

Monemvassia's telephone code is ☎ 0732.

Things to See

Monemvassia occupies a great outcrop of rock that rises dramatically from the sea opposite the village of Gefyra. It was separated from the mainland by an earthquake in 375 AD and access is by a causeway from Gefyra. From the causeway, a road curves around the base of the rock for about a km until it comes to a narrow L-shaped tunnel in the massive fortifying wall. You emerge, blinking, in the **Byzantine town**, hitherto hidden from view.

The cobbled main street is flanked by stairways leading to a complex network of stone houses with tiny walled gardens and courtyards. Steps (signposted) lead to the ruins of the **fortress** built by the Venetians in the 16th century. The views are great, and there is the added bonus of being able to explore the Byzantine **Church of Agia Sophia**, perched precariously on the edge of the cliff.

Places to Stay & Eat

The nearest camping ground is *Camping Paradise* (☎ 61 123), 3.5 km to the north. There is no budget accommodation in Monemvassia, but there are domatia in Gefyra as well as cheap hotels.

The best place is the *Hotel Glyfada* (☎ 61 445, 61 719; fax 61 604), on the beach a short walk from town. It has spacious rooms with private bathroom for 5000/6500 dr. The basic *Hotel Akrogia* (☎ 61 360), opposite the National Bank of Greece, has singles/doubles with shower for 5000/7000 dr, while the *Hotel Aktaion* (☎ 61 234), by the causeway, charges 4000/8000 dr with bathroom.

If your budget permits, treat yourself to a night in one of the beautifully restored traditional settlements in Monemvassia. They include *Malvasia Guest Houses* (☎ 61 113), with singles/doubles for 7500/10,000 dr, and *Byzantino* (☎ 61 254), with doubles for 12,500 dr.

Taverna Nikolas is the place to go for a hearty meal in Gefyra, while *To Kanoni*, on the right of the main street in Monemvassia, has an imaginative menu.

Getting There & Away

Bus There are between two and four buses a day to Athens (six hours, 4900 dr), depending on the season. They travel via Sparta, Tripolis and Corinth. In summer, there is a daily bus to Gythio (1½ hours, 1400 dr).

Ferry In summer, ferries call at Monemvassia twice a week in each direction on the route between Piraeus and Kastelli-Kissamos on Crete, via Gythio, Kythira and Antikythira. Check the schedules at Malvasia Travel.

In July and August, there are at least two hydrofoils a day to Piraeus via the Saronic Gulf islands.

GYTHIO Γύθειο

Gythio, once the port of ancient Sparta, is an attractive fishing town at the head of the Lakonian Gulf. It is the gateway to the rugged Mani peninsula to the south.

The main attraction at Gythio is the picturesque islet of **Marathonisi**, linked to the mainland by a causeway. According to mythology, it is ancient Cranae, where Paris (a prince of Troy) and Helen (the wife of Menelaus of Sparta) consummated the love affair that sparked the Trojan War. An 18th-century tower on the islet has been turned into a **museum** of Mani history.

Gythio's telephone code is ☎ 0731.

Places to Stay & Eat

Gythio's *camping grounds* are dotted along the coast south of town.

There are numerous *domatia* on the waterfront near the main square. The *Saga Pension* (☎ 23 220), between the square and the causeway, has immaculate singles/doubles with bathroom for 5000/6000 dr.

The waterfront tavernas are tourist traps, so make for *Petakos Taverna* in the town's stadium at the northern end of town on the road to Skala. There's also a restaurant at the Saga Pension.

Getting There & Away

Bus There four buses a day to Athens (5½ hours, 3950 dr), and four a day to Kalamata. Two of these services go via the Mani, calling at Areopoli, Itilo, Kardamyli and Stoupa, and two go via Sparta. In summer, there is a daily bus to Monemvassia.

Services to the Inner Mani include three buses a day to the Diros Caves, two to Gerolimenas and one to Vathia – all via Areopoli. All buses heading south can drop you at the camping grounds.

Ferry In summer, there are two ferries a week to Kastelli-Kissamos on Crete via Kythira and Antikythira, and two a week to Piraeus via Monemvassia. For information and ferry tickets, contact Rozakis Travel Agency (☎ 22 207) opposite the port.

THE MANI

The Mani is divided into two regions, the Lakonian (inner) Mani in the south and Messinian (outer) Mani in the north-west below Kalamata.

Lakonian Mani

The Lakonian Mani is wild and remote, its

landscape dotted with the dramatic stone tower houses that are a trademark of the region. They were built as refuges from the clan wars of the 19th century. The best time to visit is in spring, when the barren countryside briefly bursts into life with a spectacular display of wild flowers.

The principal village of the region is **Areopoli**, about 30 km south-west of Gythio. There are a number of fine towers on the narrow, cobbled streets of the old town.

Just south of here are the magnificent **Diros Caves**, where a subterranean river flows. The caves are open 8 am to 6 pm from June to September and 8 am to 4.30 pm from October to May. Admission is 2300 dr and worth it.

Gerolimenas, 20 km further south, is a tranquil fishing village built around a sheltered bay. It's a short walk from Gerolimenas to the almost deserted villages of **Boulari** and **Kato Boulari**. **Vathia**, a village of towers built on a rocky peak, is 11 km south-east of Gero-limenas. Beyond Vathia, the coastline is a series of rocky outcrops sheltering pebbled beaches. At the hamlet of **Porto Kagia**, seven km south of Vathia, a path leads to the light-house at **Cape Matapan**, reckoned by some to be the mythical **Gate of Hades**.

Kotronas is the east coast's largest village, and further south are the villages of **Kokkala** and **Laggia**. The latter, 400 metres above sea level, has magnificent views.

The telephone code for Areopoli and the rest of the Lakonian Mani is ☎ 0733.

Places to Stay & Eat There are no official camp sites in the Lakonian Mani.

Areopoli The cheapest accommodation in Areopoli is at *Perros Bathrellos Rooms* (☎ 51 205) on Kapetan Matapan, the main street of the old town. Singles/doubles are 4000/5000 dr with shared bath.

Tsimova Rooms (☎ 51 301), signposted off Kapetan Matapan, offers beautiful doubles in a renovated tower house for 6000 dr. There's good food at the nameless *taverna* below Perros Bathrellos Rooms.

Gerolimenas & Vathia There are two hotels in Gerolimenas. The *Hotel Akrotenaritis* (☎ 54 254) has singles/doubles for 2500/4500 dr with shared bath, while the more luxurious

Hotel Akroyali (☎ 54 204) has rooms over-looking the beach for 4500/7000 dr with private bath. It also has an excellent restaurant. If you feel like a treat, check out the superb rooms at *Vathia Towers* (☎ 52 222). Doubles are 14,000 dr with breakfast. On the east coast there are domatia at Kotronas and Kokkala.

Getting There & Away There are direct buses to Gythio and Sparta from both Areopoli and Gerolimenas. Getting to Kalamata involves changing buses in Itilo, 11 km north of Areopoli.

Getting Around Areopoli is the focal point of the local bus network. There are three buses a day to Itilo, two a day to the Diros Caves and Gerolimenas, and one a day to Kotronas. There are occasional buses to Vathia.

Hitching in the Mani is fairly easy. An asphalt road skirts the coast, and minor roads lead to isolated churches and villages.

Messinian Mani

The Messinian Mani runs north along the coast from Itilo to Kalamata. The beaches here are some of the best in Greece, set against the dramatic backdrop of the Taygetos mountains.

Itilo, the medieval capital of all the Mani, is split by a ravine that is the traditional dividing line between inner and outer Mani.

The picturesque coastal village of **Karda-myli**, 37 km south of Kalamata, is the starting point for walks up the **Taygetos Gorge**. It takes about 2½ hours to walk to the deserted Monastery of the Saviour. Strong footwear is essential and take plenty of water.

The once small fishing village of **Stoupa**, 10 km south of Kardamyli, has become a popular package destination in summer.

The Messinian Mani's telephone code is ☎ 0721.

Places to Stay There are about half a dozen *camping grounds* along the coast between Kardamyli and Stoupa.

Kardamyli There are numerous domatia, but nowhere cheap. *Olivia Koumounakou* (☎ 73 326), opposite the post office, has immaculate doubles with private bathroom for 7500 dr. *Lela's Taverna & Rooms* (☎ 73 541) occupy a charming stone building overlooking the sea. It has stylish doubles with bathroom for 10,000 dr.

Stoupa Accommodation is monopolised by package operators in summer. Groups of two or more can seek out Thanasis at his small office by the beach. The wacky **Thanasis** rents domatia in a variety of houses. Rates start at 7000 dr for two.

The **Ipocampus Taverna**, between the bus stop and the sea, has good seafood.

Getting There & Away Itilo, Kardamyli and Stoupa are all on the bus route between Kalamata and Gythio. There are two buses a day in each direction. There are also buses between Itilo and Areopoli, the only bus link between inner and outer Mani.

OLYMPIA Ολυμπία
The site of ancient Olympia lies just half a km beyond the modern town, surrounded by the green foothills of Mt Kronion. There is an

excellent tourist office on the main street, open from 8.30 am to 10 pm in summer and until 8.15 pm in winter. It will also change money.

Olympia's telephone code is ☎ 0624.

Things to See
In ancient times, Olympia was a sacred place of temples, priests' dwellings and public buildings, as well as being the venue for the quadrennial Olympic Games. The first Olympics were staged in 776 BC, reaching the peak of their prestige in the 6th century BC. The city-states were bound by a sacred truce to stop fighting for three months and compete.

The site is dominated by the immense, ruined **Temple of Zeus**, to whom the games were dedicated. The site is open Monday to Friday from 8 am to 7 pm, and on weekends from 8.30 am to 3 pm. Admission is 1200 dr. There's also a **museum** north of the archaeological site. It keeps similar hours and admission is also 1200 dr. Allow a whole day to see both.

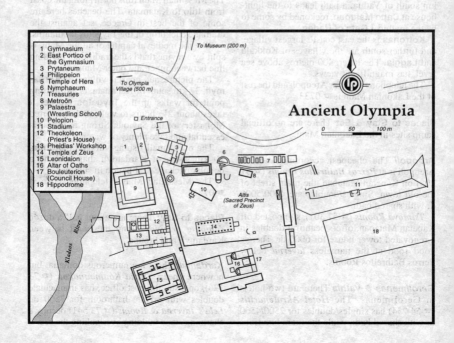

1 Gymnasium
2 East Portico of the Gymnasium
3 Prytaneum
4 Philippeion
5 Temple of Hera
6 Nymphaeum
7 Treasuries
8 Metroön
9 Palaestra (Wrestling School)
10 Pelopion
11 Stadium
12 Theokoleon (Priest's House)
13 Pheidias' Workshop
14 Temple of Zeus
15 Leonidaion
16 Altar of Oaths
17 Bouleuterion (Council House)
18 Hippodrome

To Museum (200 m)
To Olympia Village (500 m)
Entrance

Ancient Olympia

0   50   100 m

Altis (Sacred Precinct of Zeus)

Kladeos River

Places to Stay & Eat
Well signposted and only 250 metres from town is *Camping Diana* (☎ 22 314). It has excellent facilities and a pool.

The *youth hostel* (☎ 22 580), Kondili 18, has dorm beds for 1300 dr. No hostel card is required.

The *Pension Achilleys* (☎ 22 562), Stefanopoulou 4, has singles/doubles with shared bathroom for 3500/5000 dr, while the plant-festooned *Pension Poseidon* (☎ 22 567), at No 9, charges 4000/5000 dr for singles/doubles with shared shower. It also has an outside taverna serving tasty food in summer.

The *Taverna Praxitelous*, behind the tourist office, is a favourite with locals.

Getting There & Away
There four buses a day to Olympia from Athens (5½ hours, 5000 dr), but buses to Athens leave only from the town of Pyrgos, 24 km away. There are hourly buses from Olympia to Pyrgos (330 dr) and five trains a day. Regular buses and trains go from Pyrgos to Patras.

PATRAS Πάτρα
Patras is Greece's third-largest city and the principal port for ferries to Italy and the Ionian islands. It's not particularly exciting and most travellers hang around only long enough for transport connections.

Orientation & Information
The city is easy to negotiate and is laid out on a grid stretching uphill from the port to the old *kastro* (castle). Most services of importance to travellers are to be found along the waterfront, known as Othonos Amalias in the middle of town and Iroön Politehniou to the north. All the various shipping offices are to be found along here. The train station is right in the middle of town on Othonos Amalias, and the bus station is close by. Customs and the EOT office (☎ 42 0303) are clustered together inside the port fence off Iroön Politehniou.

Money The National Bank of Greece on Plateia Trion Symahon has a 24-hour automatic exchange machine. American Express is represented by Albatros Travel at Othonos Amalias 48.

Post & Communications The post office, on the corner of Zaïmi and Mezonos, is open Monday to Friday from 7.30 am to 8 pm and Saturday from 7.30 am to 2 pm. There is also a mobile post office outside customs. The postcode is 26001.

The main OTE office, on the corner of Dimitriou Gounari and Kanakari, is open 24 hours. There are also OTE offices at customs and on Agiou Andreou at Plateia Trion Symahon.

Patras' telephone code is ☎ 061.

Medical & Emergency Services There is a first-aid centre (☎ 27 7386) on the corner of Karolou and Agiou Dionysiou.

The tourist police (☎ 22 0902), opposite the EOT at the port, are open 24 hours.

Things to See & Do
There are great views of Zakynthos and Kefallonia from the Venetian **kastro**, which is reached by the steps at the top of Agiou Nikolaou.

The **Achaïa Clauss Winery**, eight km south-east from Patras, has conducted tours offers free wine sampling between 7 am and 1 pm and 4 and 7 pm (10 am to 4.30 pm in the low season). Take bus No 7 from the corner of Kolokotroni and Kanakari.

Places to Stay & Eat
The nearest camping ground is *Kavouri Camping* (☎ 42 8066), three km east of town. Take bus No 1 from Agios Dionysios church.

The friendly *youth hostel* (☎ 42 7278) was still operating from Iroön Politehniou 68, 1.5 km along the same road, at the time of writing, but it's set to move to a restored neoclassical building at Tofalou 2. Dorm beds are 1500 dr and no card is required.

The best budget hotel is the *Pension Nicos* (☎ 27 6183), at Patreos 3 on the corner of Agiou Andreou. Its cheery singles/doubles cost 3000/4500 dr with shared bath, and doubles with private bath are 6000 dr. The *Hotel Metropolis* (☎ 27 7535), Plateia Trion Symahon, lingers on in faded grandeur; singles/doubles are 5500/9900 dr.

Nicolaros Taverna, Agiou Nikolaou 50, and the nameless *restaurant* at Michalakopoulou 3 both serve good traditional food.

GREECE

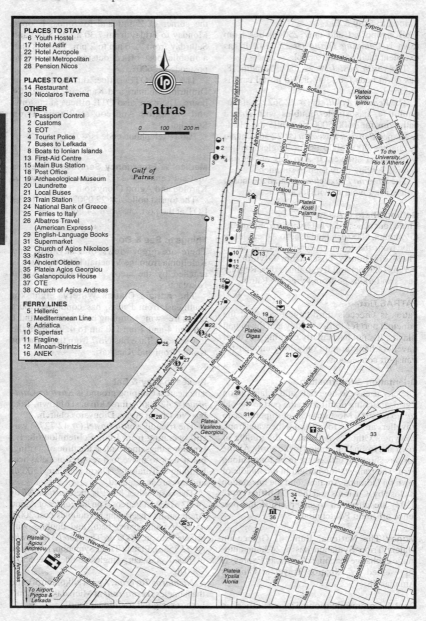

PLACES TO STAY
- 6 Youth Hostel
- 17 Hotel Astir
- 22 Hotel Acropole
- 27 Hotel Metropolitan
- 28 Pension Nicos

PLACES TO EAT
- 14 Restaurant
- 30 Nicolaros Taverna

OTHER
- 1 Passport Control
- 2 Customs
- 3 EOT
- 4 Tourist Police
- 7 Buses to Lefkada
- 8 Boats to Ionian Islands
- 13 First-Aid Centre
- 15 Main Bus Station
- 18 Post Office
- 19 Archaeological Museum
- 20 Laundrette
- 21 Local Buses
- 23 Train Station
- 24 National Bank of Greece
- 25 Ferries to Italy
- 26 Albatros Travel
    (American Express)
- 29 English-Language Books
- 31 Supermarket
- 32 Church of Agios Nikolaos
- 33 Kastro
- 34 Ancient Odeion
- 35 Plateia Agios Georgiou
- 36 Galanopoulos House
- 37 OTE
- 38 Church of Agios Andreas

FERRY LINES
- 5 Hellenic
    Mediterranean Line
- 9 Adriatica
- 10 Superfast
- 11 Fragline
- 12 Minoan-Strintzis
- 16 ANEK

Patras

0   100   200 m

Gulf of Patras

Getting There & Away

Bus Buses to Athens (three hours, 3200 dr) run every 30 minutes, with the last at 9.45 pm. There are also 10 buses a day to Pyrgos (for Olympia) and two a day to Kalamata.

Train There are nine trains a day to Athens. Four are slow trains (five hours, 1580 dr) and five are express intercity trains (3½ hours, 2580 dr). The last intercity train leaves at 6 pm. Trains also run south to Pyrgos and Kalamata.

Ferry There are daily ferries to Kefallonia (2½ hours, 2725 dr), Ithaki (3¾ hours, 2725 dr) and Corfu (10 hours, 4900 dr). Services to Italy are covered in the Getting There & Away section at the start of this chapter. Ticket agents line the waterfront.

DIAKOFTO-KALAVRYTA RAILWAY

This spectacular rack-and-pinion line climbs up the deep gorge of the Vouraikos River from the small coastal town of Diakofto to the mountain resort of **Kalavryta**, 22 km away. It is a thrilling journey, with dramatic scenery all the way. The trains leave Diakofto at 6, 9, 10.50 and 11.50 am, and 1.50 and 4.25 pm, returning at 7.10 and 10.10 am, 12.15, 1.10, 3.05 and 5.35 pm. Kalavryta is 45 minutes east of Patras by bus or train.

Kalavryta has some good hotels, but it can be hard to find a room at weekends and during the ski season. The *Hotel Paradissos* (☎ 22 303) on Kallimani has spotless singles/doubles with bathroom for 4000/7000 dr. To get there, cross the road from the train station and walk up Syngrou, then turn right onto Kallimani at the Hotel Maria. Kalavryta has five buses a day to Patras and two to Athens.

Central Greece

Central Greece has little going for it in terms of attractions – with the notable exception of Delphi and its surroundings.

DELPHI Δελφοί

Like so many of Greece's ancient sites, the setting at Delphi – overlooking the Gulf of Corinth from the slopes of Mt Parnassos – is stunning. The Delphic oracle is thought to have originated in Mycenaean times when the earth goddess Gaea was worshipped here.

By the 6th century BC, Delphi had become the Sanctuary of Apollo and thousands of pilgrims came to consult the oracle, who was always a peasant woman of 50 years or more. She sat at the mouth of a chasm which emitted fumes. These she inhaled, causing her to gasp, writhe and shudder in divine frenzy. The pilgrim, after sacrificing a sheep or goat, would deliver a question, and the priestess' incoherent mumblings were then translated by a priest. Wars were fought, voyages embarked upon, and business transactions undertaken on the strength of these prophecies.

Orientation & Information

The bus station, post office, OTE, National Bank of Greece and tourist office (☎ 82 900) are all on modern Delphi's main street, Vasileon Pavlou. The tourist office, at No 44, is open Monday to Saturday from 8 am to 2 pm. The ancient site is 1.5 km east of modern Delphi.

Delphi's telephone code is ☎ 0265.

Sanctuary of Apollo

The **Sacred Way** leads up from the entrance of the site to the **Temple of Apollo**. It was here that the oracle supposedly sat, although no chasm, let alone vapour, has been detected. The path continues to the theatre and stadium. Opposite this sanctuary is the **Sanctuary of Athena** (free admission) and the much photographed **tholos**, which is a columned rotunda of Pentelic marble. It was built in the 4th century BC and is the most striking of Delphi's monuments, but its purpose and to whom it was dedicated are unknown.

The site is open from Monday to Friday from 7.30 am to 7.15 pm, and on weekends and public holidays from 8.30 am to 2.45 pm. The museum is open similar hours, except on Monday when it's open only from noon until 6.15 pm. Entry to each is 1200 dr.

Places to Stay & Eat

The nearest camping ground to Delphi is *Apollon Camping* (☎ 82 750), 1.5 km west of modern Delphi.

The *youth hostel* (☎ 82 268), Apollonos 29, is one of Greece's best. It has dorm beds for

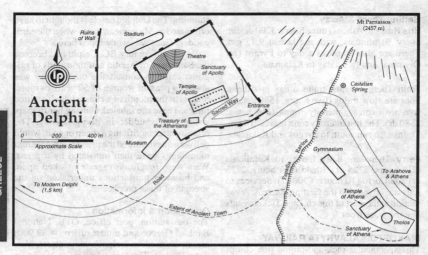

Ancient
Delphi

0   200   400 m
Approximate Scale

1500 dr and doubles for 6000 dr. It's open from March to November.

There are hotels in Delphi to suit every budget. The *Hotel Athina* (☎ 82 239), on the corner of Vasileon Pavlou and Frederikis, has singles/doubles with shared bathroom for 4000/6000 dr, or 5200/7000 dr with private bathroom.

The food is good value at *Taverna Vakhos*, next to the youth hostel.

Getting There & Away
There are five buses a day to Delphi from Athens (three hours, 2600 dr).

Northern Greece

Northern Greece covers the regions of Epiros, Thessaly, Macedonia and Thrace. It includes some areas of outstanding natural beauty, such as the Zagoria region of north-western Epiros.

IGOUMENITSA Ηγουμενίτσα
Igoumenitsa, opposite the island of Corfu, is the main port of north-western Greece. Few people stay any longer than it takes to buy a ticket out. The bus station is on Kyprou. To get

there from the ferries, follow the waterfront (Ethnikis Antistasis) north for 500 metres and turn up El Venizelou. Kyprou is two blocks inland and the bus station is on the left.

Igoumenitsa's telephone code is ☎ 0665.

Places to Stay & Eat
If you get stuck for the night, the *Hotel Lux* (☎ 22 223) has singles/doubles for 2500/4800 dr with shared bathroom, or 4700/5400 dr with private bath. To get there, turn right onto Kyprou from El Venizelou and the hotel is on the left. The nearby *Hotel Egnatias* (☎ 23 648) has better singles/doubles with bathroom for 5500/10,000 dr.

To Astron Restaurant, El Venizelou 9, and *Restaurant Nikolas*, on the corner of 23 Fevrouariou and Gregoris Lambraki, both have main courses priced from 900 dr.

Getting There & Away
Bus Services include nine buses a day to Ioannina (two hours, 1600 dr), and three a day to Athens (8½ hours, 7350 dr).

Ferry In summer, there are daily ferries to the Italian ports of Brindisi and Bari, and occasional boats to Ortona and Otranto. Ticket agents are opposite the port.

There are ferries to Corfu (1½ hours, 850 dr) every hour between 5 am and 10 pm.

IOANNINA Ιωάννινα

Ioannina is the largest town in Epiros, sitting on the western shore of Lake Pamvotis. In Ottoman times, it was one of the most important towns in the country.

Orientation & Information

The main bus terminal is between Sini and Zossimadon. To reach the town centre, find the large pharmacy adjoining the terminal and take the road opposite. Turn right at the Hotel Egnatias, then left onto 28 Oktovriou, which meets Ioannina's main street at Plateia Dimokratias. The street is called Averof on the left and Dodonis on the right.

The helpful EOT office is 100 metres along Dodonis, set back on a small square at Napoleonda Zerva 2. It's open Monday to Friday from 7.30 am to 2.30 pm and from 5.30 to 8.30 pm, and on Saturday from 9 am to 2 pm. Robinsons Travel (☎ 29 402), 8 Merarhias Gramou 10, specialises in treks in the Zagoria region.

Ioannina's telephone code is ☎ 0651.

Things to See

The **old town** juts out into the lake on a small peninsula. Inside the impressive fortifications lies a maze of winding streets flanked by traditional Turkish houses.

The **Nisi** (island) is a serene spot in the middle of the lake, with four monasteries set among the trees. Ferries to the island leave from just north of the old town. They run half-hourly in summer and hourly in winter. The fare is 150 dr.

The **Perama Cave**, four km from Ioannina, has a mind-boggling array of stalactites and stalagmites. It's open from 8 am to 8 pm in summer and 8 am to 6.15 pm in winter; admission is 800 dr.

Places to Stay & Eat

On the lakeside two km north of town is *Camping Limnopoula* (☎ 25 265).

The cheapest hotel is the *Agapi Inn* (☎ 20 541), Tsirigoti 6, near the bus station. Basic doubles cost 4000 dr. Next door is the *Hotel Paris*, which has more comfortable singles/

doubles for 4000/6500 dr. There are domatia on the island.

There are several restaurants outside the entrance to the old town. *To Mantelo Psistaria* is recommended.

Getting There & Away

Air Ioannina has two flights a day to Athens (17,100 dr) and five a week to Thessaloniki (10,800 dr).

Bus Services include 12 buses a day to Athens (7½ hours, 6450 dr), nine to Igoumenitsa, five to Thessaloniki and three to Trikala via Kalambaka. The road from Ioannina to Kalambaka across the Pindos mountains is one of Greece's most spectacular drives.

ZAGORIA & VIKOS GORGE

The Zagoria (Ζαγώρια) region covers a large expanse of the Pindos mountains north of Ioannina. It's a wilderness of raging rivers, crashing waterfalls and deep gorges. Snow-capped mountains rise out of dense forests. The remote villages that dot the hillsides are famous for their impressive grey-slate architecture.

The fairytale village of **Monodendri** is the starting point for treks through the dramatic **Vikos Gorge**, with its awesome sheer limestone walls. It's a strenuous 7½-hour walk from Monodendri to the twin villages of **Megalo Papingo** and **Mikro Papingo**. The trek is very popular and the path is clearly marked. Ioannina's EOT office has information.

Other walks start from **Tsepelovo**, near Monodendri.

The telephone code for the Zagoria villages is ☎ 0653.

Places to Stay & Eat

There are some excellent places to stay, but none come cheap. The options in Monodendri include the lovely, traditional *Monodendri Pension & Restaurant* (☎ 61 233). Doubles are 8100 dr. *Alexis Gouris* (☎ 81 214) has a delightful pension in Tsepelovo with doubles for 7000 dr. Alexis also runs a shop and restaurant and can advise on treks.

Xenonas tou Kouli (☎ 41 138) is one of several options in Megalo Papingo. Rates start at 7000 dr for singles. The owners are official

EOS guides. The only rooms in Mikro Papingo are at *Xenonas O Dias* (☎ 41 257), a beautifully restored mansion with doubles for 9500 dr. It has an excellent restaurant specialising in charcoal grills.

Getting There & Away

Buses to the Zagoria leave from the main bus station in Ioannina. On weekdays, there are buses to Monodendri at 5.30 am and 4.15 pm and to Tsepelovo at 6 am and 3 pm. There are buses to the Papingo villages on Monday, Wednesday and Friday at 5.30 am and 2 pm, and on Sunday at 9 am.

TRIKALA Τρίκαλα

Trikala is a major transport hub, but otherwise has little of interest. Eight buses a day run between Trikala and Athens, (5½ hours, 4750 dr). There are also six buses a day to Thessaloniki, two to Ioannina and hourly buses to Kalambaka (for Meteora).

METEORA Μετέωρα

Meteora is an extraordinary place. The massive, sheer columns of rock that dot the landscape were created by wave action millions of years ago. Perched precariously atop these seemingly inaccessible outcrops are monasteries that date back to the late 14th century.

Meteora is just north of the town of Kalambaka, on the Ioannina-Trikala road. The rocks behind the town are spectacularly floodlit at night. **Kastraki**, two km from Kalambaka, is a charming village of red-tiled houses just west of the monasteries.

The telephone code for the area is ☎ 0432.

Things to See

There were once monasteries on each of the 24 pinnacles, but only five are still occupied. They are Metamorphosis (Grand Meteora, closed on Tuesday), Varlaam (closed Friday), Agios Stefanos (open daily), Agia Triada (open daily), Agios Nikolaos (open daily) and Roussanou (closed Wednesday). All keep similar hours – 9 am to 1 pm and 3 to 5 pm – except Agios Nikolaos, which opens from 9 am to 6 pm. Admission is 600 dr for Grand Meteora, 400 dr for the others.

Meteora is best explored on foot, following the old paths where they exist. Allow a whole

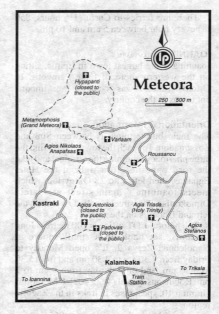

day to visit all of the monasteries and take food and water. Women must wear skirts that reach below their knees, men must wear long trousers, and arms must be covered.

Places to Stay & Eat

Kastraki is the best base for visiting Meteora. *Vrachos Camping* (☎ 22 293), on the edge of the village, is an excellent site. *Zozas Pallas*, on the road to Kalambaka, has luxurious singles/doubles for 4000/8000 dr. The *Hotel France* (☎ 24 186), which is opposite Vrachos Camping, has rooms for 5000/7000 dr and a restaurant. The owner is a good source of information about walks.

In Kalambaka, *Koka Roka Rooms* (☎ 24 554), at the beginning of the path to Agia Triada, is popular travellers' place. Doubles with bath are 6000 dr; the taverna downstairs is good value.

Getting There & Away

Kalambaka is the hub of the transport network. There are frequent buses to Trikala and two a day to Ioannina. Local buses shuttle constantly between Kalambaka and Kastraki; five a day continue to Metamorphosis.

THESSALONIKI Θεσσαλονίκη

Thessaloniki, also known as Salonica, is Greece's second-largest city. It's a bustling, sophisticated place with good restaurants and a busy nightlife. It was once the second city of Byzantium, and there are some magnificent Byzantine churches, as well as a scattering of Roman ruins.

Orientation & Information

Thessaloniki is laid out on a grid system. The main thoroughfares – Tsimiski, Egnatia and Agiou Dimitriou – run parallel to Nikis, on the waterfront. Plateias Eleftherias and Aristotelous, both on Nikis, are the main squares. The city's most famous landmark is the White Tower (no longer white) at the eastern end of Nikis.

The train station is on Monastiriou, the westerly continuation of Egnatia beyond Plateia Dimokratias, and the airport is 16 km to the south-east. The old Turkish quarter is north of Athinas. The EOT office (☎ 271 888), at Plateia Aristotelous 8, is open Monday to Friday from 8 am to 8 pm, and Saturday from 8 am to 2 pm. USIT Travel (☎ 263 814), Ippodromiou 15, sells airline and ferry tickets.

Money The National Bank of Greece and the Commercial Bank have branches on Plateia Dimokratias. American Express (☎ 269 521) has an office at Tsimiski 19.

Post & Communications The main post office is at Tsimiski 45 and is open Monday to Friday from 7.30 am to 8 pm, Saturday from 7.30 am to 2 pm, and Sunday from 9 am to 1.30 pm. The OTE telephone office is at Karolou Dil 27 and is open 24 hours a day.

Thessaloniki's telephone code is ☎ 031.

Laundry Bianca Laundrette, on Antoniadou, charges 1200 dr to wash and dry a load. Antoniadou is just north of the Arch of Galerius, off Gournari.

Medical & Emergency Services There is a first-aid centre (☎ 530 530) at Nav Koun-douriti 6. The tourist police (☎ 548 907) are at Egnatia 10, but the entrance is on Tandalidou. They are open daily from 7.30 am to 11 pm from October to March, and 24 hours a day from April to September.

Things to See

The **archaeological museum**, at the eastern end of Tsimiski, houses a superb collection of treasures from the royal tombs of Philip II. It is open on Monday from 12.30 to 7 pm, Tuesday to Friday from 8 am to 7 pm (5 pm in winter) and on weekends from 8.30 am to 3 pm; admission is 1500 dr. The outstanding **Folkloric & Ethnological Museum of Macedonia**, at Vasilissis Olgas 68, includes traditional household utensils and northern Greek costumes. It's open every day, except Thursday, from 9.30 am to 4 pm; admission is 200 dr.

Places to Stay

The *youth hostel* (☎ 225 946), Alex Svolou 44, has dorm beds for 1800 dr. The doors are locked from 11 am to 7 pm, and there's an 11 pm curfew. An HI card is required and the hostel is closed from December to mid-May.

The best budget hotel in town is the friendly, family-run *Hotel Acropol* (☎ 531 670), on Tandalidou, a quiet side street off Egnatia. It has singles/doubles with shared bath for 5000/7500 dr. The *Hotel Atlantis* (☎ 540 131), Egnatia 14, has doubles with shared bathroom for 4500 dr. The rooms are tiny but clean.

The *Hotel Atlas* (☎ 510 038), Egnatia 40, has good doubles with bath for 8000 dr. The rooms at the front get a lot of traffic noise. Just around the corner from the Atlas is the quiet *Hotel Averof* (☎ 538 498) at Leontos Sofou 24. Pleasant singles/doubles with shared bath are 4500/7500 dr.

Rooms can be hard to find during the international trade fair in September.

Places to Eat

Adventurous eaters should head for *Patsas Ilias*, Egnatia 102, to sample the local speciality, tripe soup. Others may prefer the security of McDonald's, 50 metres away.

A place full of local colour is the lively *O Loutros Fish Taverna*, which occupies an old Turkish hammam near the flower market on Komninon. Excellent fish dishes start from 1000 dr. The place is always packed and there

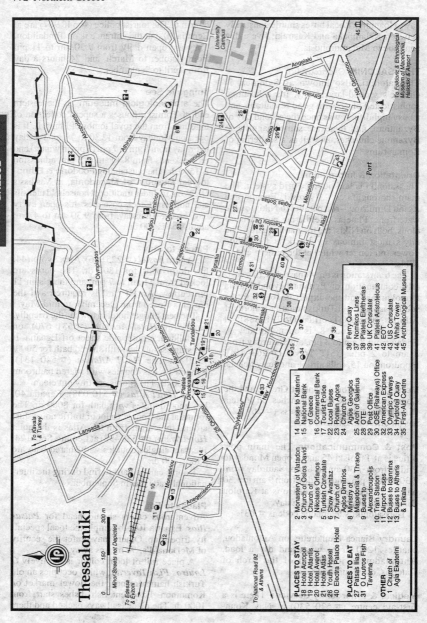

Thessaloniki

0   150   300 m

Minor Streets not Depicted

To Edessa
& Evzoni

To National Road 92
& Athens

To Kávala
& Turkey

PLACES TO STAY
18 Hotel Acropol
19 Hotel Atlantis
20 Hotel Averof
21 Hotel Atlas
26 Youth Hostel
40 Electra Palace Hotel

PLACES TO EAT
27 Patsas Ilias
31 O Loutros Fish
   Taverna

OTHER
1 Church of
  Agia Ekaterini

2 Monastery of Vlatadon
3 Church of Osios David
4 Church of
5 Nikolaos Orfanos
6 Turkish Consulate
7 Show Avantaz
8 Church of
  Agios Dimitrios
9 Ministry of
  Macedonia & Thrace
10 Buses to
   Alexandroupolis
11 Train Station
12 Airport Buses
13 Buses to Ioannina
14 Buses to Athens
   & Trikala

14 Buses to Katerini
15 National Bank
   of Greece
16 Commercial Bank
17 Tourist Police
22 Local Buses
23 Roman Agora
24 Church of
   Agios Georgios
25 Arch of Galerius
28 PTE
29 Pavilion
30 OSE (Railways) Office
32 American Express
33 Olympic Airways
34 Hydrofoil Quay
35 First-Aid Centre

36 Ferry Quay
37 Nomikos Lines
38 Plateia Eleftherias
39 UK Consulate
41 Plateia Aristotelous
42 EOT
43 US Consulate
44 White Tower
45 Archaeological Museum

To Folkloric & Ethnological
Museum of Macedonia,
Halkidiki & Airport

are often spontaneous renderings of rembetika; it's closed at weekends.

Entertainment

Young people frequent the many bars along the waterfront before hitting the clubs. From October to May, the action is in town. You'll find live bouzouki and folk music every night at *Show Avantaz*, opposite the Turkish consulate at Agiou Dimitriou 156. It opens at 11 pm. *Traffic*, east of the university on Tritis Septemvriou, is a popular dance spot. In summer, the city discos close and others open up on the road to the airport.

Getting There & Away

Air The airport is 16 km to the south-east. There are six flights a day to Athens (19,200 dr) and daily flights to Limnos (12,800 dr). Other destinations include Ioannina, Lesvos, Iraklio and Rhodes. Olympic Airways (☎ 230 240) is at Nav Koundouriti 3. See the Getting There & Away section at the start of this chapter for information on international flights.

Bus There are several bus terminals, most of them near the train station. Buses for Athens, Igoumenitsa and Trikala leave from Monastiriou 65 & 67, and buses for Alexandroupolis leave from Plateia Galopourou. Buses for Pella, Florina, Kastoria and Volos leave from Anegeniseos 22, and buses to the Halkidiki peninsula from Karakassi 68 (off the map in the eastern part of town; it's marked on the free EOT map). To reach the Halkidiki terminal, take local bus No 10 to the Botsari stop, near Odos Markou Botsari. The OSE has two buses a day to Athens from the train station, as well as international services to İstanbul, Sofia (Bulgaria) and Korça (Albania).

Train There are eight trains a day to Athens and five to Alexandroupolis. All international trains from Athens stop at Thessaloniki. You can get more information from the OSE office at Aristotelous 18 or from the train station.

Ferry & Hydrofoil There's a Saturday ferry to Lesvos, Limnos and Chios throughout the year. In summer there are two ferries a week to Iraklio (Crete), stopping in the Sporades and the Cyclades on the way. Get your tickets from Nomikos Lines (☎ 524 544) by the port. In summer there are hydrofoils most days to Skiathos, Skopelos and Alonnisos. Tickets can be bought from Egnatias Tours (☎ 22 811), Kambouniou 9.

Getting Around

To/From the Airport There is no bus service from the Olympic Airways office. Take bus No 78 from the train station. A taxi from the airport costs about 1500 dr.

Bus There is a flat fare of 75 dr on city and suburban buses, paid either to a conductor at the rear door or to coin-operated machines on driver-only buses.

HALKIDIKI Χαλκιδική

Halkidiki is the three-pronged peninsula south-east of Thessaloniki. It's the main resort area of northern Greece, with superb sandy beaches right around its 500 km of coastline. **Kassandra**, the south-western prong of the peninsula, has surrendered irrevocably to mass tourism. **Sithonia**, the middle prong, is not as over the top and has some spectacular scenery.

Mt Athos

Halkidiki's third prong is occupied by the all-male Monastic Republic of Mt Athos (also called the Holy Mountain), where monasteries full of priceless treasures stand amid an impressive landscape of gorges, wooded mountains and precipitous rocks.

To acquire a four-day visitor's permit to Mt Athos you must be male and have a letter of recommendation from your embassy or consulate. You take it to either the Ministry of Foreign Affairs, Zalokosta 2, Athens, or the Ministry of Macedonia & Thrace, Plateia Diikitirio, Thessaloniki, between 10 am and 2 pm, Monday to Friday. Thessaloniki's UK consulate (☎ 278 006), which also represents Australian, Canadian and New Zealand citizens, is at El Venizelou 8, and the US consulate (☎ 266 121) is at Nikis 59. For more details, enquire at the EOT office. Armed with your permit, you can explore, on foot, the 20 monasteries and dependent religious communities of Mt Athos. You can stay only one night at each monastery.

MT OLYMPUS Ολυμπος Ορος
Mt Olympus is Greece's highest and mightiest mountain. The ancients chose it as the abode of their gods and assumed it to be the exact centre of the Earth. Olympus has eight peaks, the highest of which is Mytikas (2917 metres). The area is popular with trekkers, most of whom use the village of **Litohoro** as a base. Litohoro is five km inland from the Athens-Thessaloniki highway.

The telephone code is ☎ 0352. The EOS office (☎ 81 944) on Plateia Kentriki has information on the various treks and conditions.

The main route to the top takes two days, overnighting at one of the refuges on the mountain. Good protective clothing is essential, even in summer.

Places to Stay & Eat
Litohoro's *youth hostel* (☎ 82 176) charges 1300 for dorm beds and 500 dr for linen. The manager is a valuable source of information for serious trekkers and also hires out suitable clothing. Luggage can be stored here. The *Olympos Taverna* serves standard fare at reasonable prices.

There are four *refuges* on the mountain at altitudes ranging from 270 metres to 930 metres. They are all open from May to September.

Getting There & Away
There are eight buses a day to Litohoro from Thessaloniki and three from Athens (5½ hours, 6500 dr). There are frequent buses between Litohoro and the coastal village of Katerini.

ALEXANDROUPOLIS Αλεξανδρούπολη
Dusty Alexandroupolis doesn't have much going for it, but if you're going to Turkey or Samothraki, you may end up staying overnight here. There's a tourist office (☎ 24 998) in the town hall on Dimokratias.

Alexandroupolis' telephone code is ☎ 0551.

Places to Stay & Eat
The nearest camping ground, *Camping Alexandroupolis* (☎ 28 735), is on the beach two km west of town. Buses to Makri from Plateia Eleftherias, opposite the port, can drop you there. The *Hotel Lido* (☎ 28 808), one block north of the bus station at Paleologou 15, is a great budget option. Doubles are 2600 dr, or 5200 dr with private bathroom. The *Hotel*

Okeanis (☎ 28 830), almost opposite the Lido, has large, comfortable singles/doubles for 7000/9000 dr.

The *Neraida Restaurant*, on Kyprou, has a range of local specialities priced from 1400 dr. Kyprou starts opposite the pier where ferries leave for Samothraki.

Getting There & Away
There is at least one flight a day to Athens (17,100 dr) from the airport seven km west of town. There are five trains (3440 dr) and five buses (5100 dr) a day to Thessaloniki. There's also a daily train and a daily OSE bus to İstanbul, as well as daily buses to Plovdiv and Sofia in Bulgaria.

In summer there are at least two boats a day to Samothraki (two hours, 2200 dr), dropping to one in winter. There are also hydrofoils to Chios, via Lesvos and Limnos.

Saronic Gulf Islands
Νησιά του Σαρωνικού

The Saronic Gulf islands are the closest island group to Athens. Not surprisingly they are a very popular escape for residents of the congested capital. Accommodation can be hard to find between mid-June and September, and on weekends all year round.

The telephone code is ☎ 0298 for all the islands except Aegina (☎ 0297).

Getting There & Away
Ferries to all four islands, and hydrofoils to Aegina, leave from the Great Harbour in Piraeus. Hydrofoils to the other islands run from Zea Marina in Piraeus.

AEGINA Αίγινα
Aegina is the closest island to Athens and a popular destination for day-trippers. Many make for the lovely **Temple of Aphaia**, a well-preserved Doric temple 12 km east of Aegina town. It is open on weekdays from 8.15 am to 7 pm (5 pm in winter) and on weekends from 8.30 am to 3 pm. Admission is 800 dr. Buses from Aegina town to the small resort of **Agia Marina** can drop you at the site. Agia Marina

has the best beach on the island, which isn't saying much.

Most travellers prefer to stay in Aegina town, where the *Hotel Plaza* (☎ 25 600) has singles/doubles overlooking the sea for 4000/7000 dr.

POROS Πόρος

Poros is a big hit with the Brits, but it's hard to work out why. The beaches are nothing to write home about and there are no sites of significance. The main attraction is pretty Poros town, draped over the Sferia peninsula. Sferia is linked to the rest of the island, known as Kalavria, by a narrow isthmus. Most of the package hotels are here. There are a few domatia in Poros town, signposted off the road to Kalavria.

The island lies little more than a stone's throw from the mainland, opposite the Peloponnesian village of Galatas.

HYDRA Ύδρα

Hydra is the island with the most style and is famous as the haunt of artists and jet-setters. Its gracious stone mansions are stacked up the rocky hillsides that surround the fine natural harbour. The main attraction is peace and quiet. There are no motorised vehicles on the island – apart from a garbage truck and a few construction vehicles.

Accommodation is expensive, but of a high standard. The friendly *Pension Theresia* (☎ 53 983) has quaint rooms around a leafy courtyard for 7000/9000 dr, negotiable on weekdays.

SPETSES Σπέτσες

Pine-covered Spetses is perhaps the most beautiful island in the group. It also has the best beaches, so it's packed with package tourists in summer. The **old harbour** in Spetses town is a delightful place to explore. The travel agents on the waterfront can organise accommodation.

Cyclades Κυκλάδες

The Cyclades, named after the rough circle they form around Delos, are quintessential Greek islands with brilliant white architecture, dazzling light and golden beaches.

Delos, historically the most important island of the group, is uninhabited. The inhabited islands of the archipelago are Mykonos, Syros, Tinos, Andros, Paros, Naxos, Ios, Santorini (Thira), Anafi, Amorgos, Sikinos, Folegandros and the tiny islands of Koufonisi, Shinoussa, Iraklia and Donoussa, which lie east of Naxos. The remaining six – Kea, Kythnos, Serifos, Sifnos, Kimolos and Milos – are referred to as the Western Cyclades.

Some of the Cyclades, like Mykonos, Paros and Santorini, have vigorously embraced the tourist industry, filling their coastlines with discos and bars, and their beaches with sun lounges, umbrellas and water-sports equipment for hire. But others, like Anafi, Sikinos and the tiny islands east of Naxos, are little more than clumps of rock, each with a village, a few secluded coves – and very few tourists.

To give even the briefest rundown on every island is impossible in a single chapter. The following gives information on a cross section of the islands, from those with packed beaches and a raucous nightlife, to those off the tourist circuit, where tranquillity and glimpses of a fast-dying, age-old way of life await the visitor.

History

The Cyclades enjoyed a flourishing Bronze Age civilisation (3000-1100 BC), more or less concurrent with the Minoan civilisation.

By the 5th century BC, the island of Delos had been taken over by Athens, which kept its treasury there.

Between the 4th and 7th centuries AD, the islands, like the rest of Greece, suffered a series of invasions and occupations. During the Middle Ages they were raided by pirates – hence the labyrinthine character of their towns, which was meant to confuse attackers. On some islands the whole population would move into the mountainous interior to escape the pirates, while on others they would brave it out on the coast. This is why on some islands the hora (main town) is on the coast and on others it is inland.

The Cyclades became part of independent Greece in 1827.

Orientation & Information

The islands lie in the central Aegean, south-east of Athens and north of Crete. In July, August and September the Cyclades are prone to the *meltemi*, a ferocious north-easterly wind which sends everything flying and disrupts ferry schedules. Paros, Ios, Milos, Serifos, Sifnos and Syros have either EOT or municipal tourist offices. On other islands, information is available from the tourist police, private travel agents and the regular police.

Getting There & Away

Air Mykonos and Santorini have international airports that receive charter flights from northern Europe. There are daily flights from Athens to Milos, Naxos, Paros, Mykonos and Santorini, and six flights a week between Mykonos and Santorini. Both islands have flights to Crete and Rhodes.

Boat The information on boat services supplied in this section is for April to October; in winter, services are severely curtailed. Most islands are served by daily boats from Piraeus.

A daily excursion boat travels between Mykonos, Paros, Naxos, Ios and Santorini. Hydrofoils and catamarans link Paros, Naxos, Syros, Tinos, Ios, Santorini and Crete in high season. Bear in mind, particularly if you're visiting a remote island, that ferries are prone to delays and cancellations. All the islands are served by car ferry. Hydrofoils do not carry cars.

Getting Around

Most islands have buses that link the port with villages on the island. On many islands caïques (fishing boats) connect the port with popular beaches.

Santorini, Paros, Naxos, Ios, Milos and Mykonos have car-rental firms. Most islands have motorcycle and moped-rental places, and some also have bicycles for rent.

Most islands are crisscrossed by donkey tracks, which are great to walk along.

NAXOS Νάξος

Naxos is the island where Theseus disloyally dumped Ariadne after she helped him to slay the Minotaur (half-bull, half-man) on the island of Crete. She gave him the thread that enabled him to find his way out of the Minotaur's labyrinth once he had killed the monster.

Naxos, the greenest and most beautiful island of the archipelago, is popular but big enough to allow you to escape the hordes.

Orientation & Information

Naxos town, on the west coast, is the island's capital and port. There is no EOT but there's an excellent unofficial tourist office (☎ 24 358) opposite the harbour, run by the inimitable Despina Kitini. Luggage storage is 300 dr, and the office is open daily from 8 am to midnight. The OTE is on the waterfront opposite the National Bank of Greece; for the post office, turn left beyond the OTE and then take the second right.

Naxos' telephone code is ☎ 0285.

Things to See

Naxos Town The winding alleyways of Naxos town, lined with immaculate whitewashed houses, clamber up to the crumbling 13th-century kastro walls. The well-stocked archaeological museum is here, housed in a former school where Nikos Kazantzakis was briefly a pupil. The museum is open Tuesday to Sunday from 8.30 am to 3 pm; admission is 500 dr.

Beaches After the town beach of Agios Georgios, sandy beaches – which become progressively less crowded – continue southwards as far as Pyrgaki Beach.

Apollonas On the north coast, Apollonas has a rocky beach and a pleasant sheltered bay. If you're curious about the *kouros* statues, you can see the largest one, 10.5 metres long, just outside of Apollonas, lying abandoned and unfinished in an ancient marble quarry. There are two more in the Melanes region.

It's worth taking the bus or driving from Naxos town to Apollonas for the scenery. The road winds its way through the Tragaea, gradually ascending through increasingly dramatic mountainscapes. After Apiranthos the road zigzags to Komiaki, the island's highest village. From here the descent begins to the lush valley of Apollonas.

Tragaea This gorgeous region is a vast Arcadian olive grove with Byzantine churches and

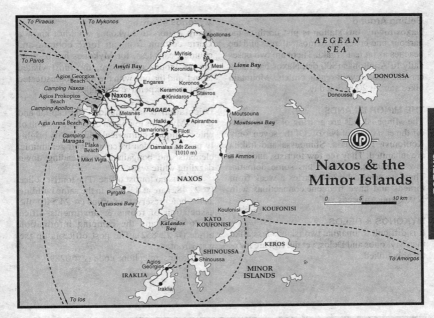

Naxos & the
Minor Islands

0   5   10 km

tranquil villages. **Filoti**, the largest settlement, perches on the slopes of **Mt Zeus** (1004 metres). It takes three hours to climb the trail to the summit.

Filoti is also a good base from which to explore the region on foot. A dirt road leads from the village to the picturesque and isolated hamlets of **Damarionas** and **Damalas**. From Damalas it is a short walk to the village of **Halki**, from where another dirt road leads to the twin hamlets of **Khimaros** and **Tsikalario**.

Another village, **Apiranthos**, has many old houses of uncharacteristically bare stone, and some of the women who live here still weave on looms and wear traditional costumes.

Places to Stay & Eat
Naxos' three camping grounds are *Camping Naxos* (☎ 23 501), one km south of Agios Georgios Beach; *Camping Maragas* (☎ 24 552), Agia Anna Beach; and *Camping Apollon* (☎ 24 117), 700 metres from Agios Prokopios Beach. All are open from May to October.

Hotel Anixis (☎ 22 112) is one of Naxos

town's best budget hotels. Doubles/triples cost 8000/10,000 dr with private bath. Nearby, the unofficial *Dionyssos Hostel* (☎ 22 331) has dorm beds for 1500 dr and doubles/triples for 4000/6000 dr. No card is required. The easiest way to find these establishments is to follow the signs in the old town to the Hotel Panorama. *Pension Sofi* (☎ 25 582), 350 metres from the quay, has spotless doubles/triples for 10,000/12,000 dr.

O Tsitas Restaurant, in Naxos town, up the alleyway by Zas Travel Agency near the harbour, has tasty cheap food. *Maro's*, on the street bearing left after the roundabout 50 metres past the post office, has a wide range of dishes and is superb for breakfasts (omelettes from 400 dr). You will find bakeries, grocery shops and fruit and vegetable shops on Market St.

Getting There & Away
Naxos has daily ferries to Paros and Piraeus (3500 dr) and frequent ferries to the Minor Islands, other Cycladic ports, and to Samos and Chios. For the port police, call ☎ 22 300.

GREECE

GREECE

Getting Around

Naxos town's bus station is just north of the harbour, and buses run to most villages and the beaches as far as Pyrgaki. There are two buses daily to Apollonas (800 dr). Naxos has many car and motorcycle-rental outlets. Mountain bikes start at 2000 dr a day.

THE MINOR ISLANDS

The Minor Islands are a string of tiny islands off the east coast of Naxos. Of the seven, only Koufonisi, Donoussa, Shinoussa and Iraklia are inhabited. They see few tourists, and have few amenities, but each has some domatia. They are served by two ferries a week from Piraeus and have frequent connections with Naxos and Amorgos.

MYKONOS & DELOS

It is difficult to imagine two islands less alike than Mykonos and Delos, yet the two are inextricably linked.

Mykonos Μύκονος

Many visitors to Mykonos wouldn't know a Doric column from an Ionic column and couldn't care less, for Mykonos has become the St Tropez of Greece, the most visited island, and the one with the most sophisticated – and most expensive – nightlife.

Orientation & Information The capital and port is Mykonos town – an elaborate tableau of chic boutiques, chimerical houses with brightly painted wooden balconies, and geraniums, clematis and bougainvillea cascading down dazzling white walls.

There is no tourist office. The tourist police (☎ 22 482) are at the port, in the same building as the hotel reservation office (☎ 24 540), the association of rooms & apartments office (☎ 26 860), and the camping information office (☎ 22 852). The post office is on the waterfront.

Mykonos' telephone code is ☎ 0289.

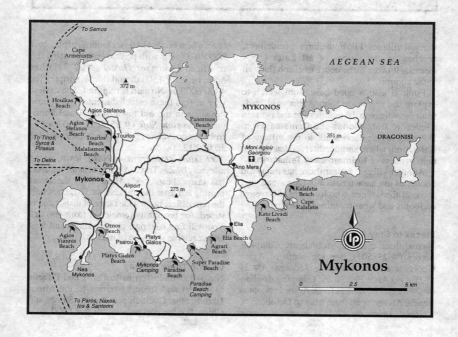

Things to See & Do The **archaeological museum** and **nautical museum** are mediocre, but the **folklore museum** (open Monday to Saturday from 5.30 to 8.30 pm; free entry) is well stocked with local memorabilia. Exhibits include reconstructions of traditional homes, and a somewhat macabre stuffed pelican, the erstwhile Petros, who was run over by a car in 1985. He was hastily supplanted by Petros II, who you will no doubt meet if you loiter around the fish market. The museum is near the Delos quay.

The most popular beaches are the mainly nude **Paradise** and **Super Paradise** (mainly gay), **Agrari** and **Elia**. The less crowded ones are **Panormos**, which is inaccessible by bus or caïque but can be walked to from the inland village of Ano Mera, and **Kato Livadi**, which you can walk to from Elia Beach.

Places to Stay Mykonos has two camping grounds: *Paradise Beach Camping* (☎ 22 937) and *Mykonos Camping* (☎ 24 578). Paradise charges 1500 dr per person and 850 dr per tent.

Rooms fill up quickly in summer, so it's prudent to succumb to the first domatia owner who accosts you.

The delightfully old-world *Apollon* (☎ 22 223) on the waterfront, run by two genteel elderly ladies, has doubles for 15,000 dr with private bath (closed in the low season), and *Angela's Rooms* (☎ 22 967), on Plateia Mavrogenous (usually called Taxi Square), has doubles with bath for 12,000 dr.

Places to Eat The *Sesame Kitchen*, near the nautical museum, serves mostly vegetarian dishes. *Niko's Taverna*, near the Delos quay, is popular, though prices are higher than at waterfront cafés.

Entertainment The *Scandinavian* bar, near Niko's Taverna, and the improbably named *Stavros Irish Pub*, near Taxi Square, have the cheapest drinks. For a more tasteful ambience, make for *Club Verandah* and *Montparnasse* bars in Little Venice, where classical music plays as the sun sets.

Getting There & Away Flights from Mykonos to Athens cost 17,300 dr, to Santorini 13,900

dr, and to both Rhodes and Crete 20,500 dr. The Olympic Airways office (☎ 22 490) is on Plateia Louka.

There are many ferries daily to Mykonos from Piraeus (6500 dr). Mykonos also has hydrofoil and excursion boats to the other major Cycladic islands.

Getting Around The north bus station is near the port, behind the OTE office. It serves Agios Stefanos, Elia, Kalafatis and Ano Mera. The south bus station serves Agios Yiannis, Psarou, Platys Gialos and the airport.

Super Paradise, Agrari and Elia beaches are served by caïque from Mykonos town, but easier access to these and Paradise Beach is by caïque from Platys Gialos.

There are at least six boats daily to Delos, in season, leaving between 8.45 am and 10.45 am. The round-trip is 1600 dr; entrance to the site is 1200 dr.

Most car, motorcycle and bicycle-rental firms are around the south bus station.

Delos Δῆλος
Just south-east of Mykonos, the uninhabited island of Delos is the Cyclades' archaeological jewel. In ancient times, the island was both a religious site and the most important commercial port in the Aegean.

According to mythology, Delos was the birthplace of Apollo – the god of light, poetry, music, healing and prophecy. Delos flourished as a religious and commercial centre from the 3rd millennium BC, reaching its height in the 5th century BC, by which time its oracle was second only to Delphi's. It was sacked by Mithridates, king of the Black Sea region, in 88 BC and 20,000 people were killed.

The site of Delos is basically in three sections. To the north of the harbour is the **Sanctuary of Apollo**, containing temples dedicated to him, and the much photographed **Terrace of the Lions**. These proud beasts were carved in the 4th century BC from marble from Naxos, and their function was to guard the sacred area. The Venetians took a liking to them, and in the 17th century shipped one to Venice, where it can still be seen guarding the arsenal of the city. The **Sacred Lake** (dry since 1926) is where Leto supposedly gave birth to Apollo. The museum is east of this section.

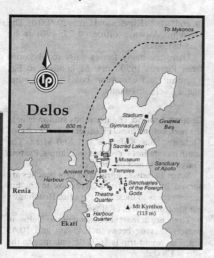

GREECE

South of the harbour is the **Theatre Quarter**, where private houses were built around the **Theatre of Delos**. East of here, towards Mt Kynthos, are the **Sanctuaries of the Foreign Gods**, containing a shrine to the Samothracian Great Gods, the sanctuary of the Syrian Gods, and a sanctuary with temples to Serapis and Isis.

There are boats to Delos from Mykonos. No-one can stay overnight on Delos, and the boat schedule allows you only three hours there. Bring plenty of water and, if you want, some food, because the island's cafeteria is a rip-off.

IOS Ιος

More than any other Greek island, Ios epitomises the Greece of sun, sand, sex and souvlaki. Come here if you want to bake on a beach all day and drink all night. Young people hang out in the village, where the nightlife is. The older set tend to stay in the port.

Ios' telephone code is ☎ 0286.

Places to Stay & Eat

Ios Camping (☎ 91 329) is on the beach next to the port, but the camping grounds at Milopotas beach are preferable. They are *Milopotas Camping* (☎ 91 554), *Stars* (☎ 91 302) and, the best of all, *Far Out Camping* (☎ 91 468).

There is a wonderful view of the bay from *Francesco's* (☎ 91 223), in the village. A dorm bed is 2300 dr, and doubles/triples with private bath are 6000/8000 dr. It's a lively meeting place with a bar and terrace.

The Nest is an excellent eatery, with plenty of dishes at around 800 dr. It's opposite the village's only pharmacy. In season, *Zorba's Restaurant*, *Pithari Taverna* and *Pinocchios* are popular.

Getting There & Away

The island has daily connections with Piraeus (4700 dr) and there are frequent hydrofoils and excursion boats to the major Cycladic islands.

PAROS Πάρος

Physically, Paros is 16 km from Naxos, but metaphysically it hovers somewhere between Ios and Mykonos. It's popular with backpackers who crave style but can't afford Mykonos, yet still attracts some big spenders, as evidenced by its expensive jewellery shops (which are conspicuously absent on Ios). Like Mykonos, it's also popular with gay travellers. Paros is famous for its pure white marble – no less than the *Venus de Milo* herself was created from it.

Paros is an attractive island, although less

dramatically so than Naxos. Its softly contoured and terraced hills culminate in one central mountain, Profitis Ilias. It has some of the finest beaches in the Cyclades.

The small island of Antiparos (Αντίπαρος) lies one km east of Paros. The two were originally joined, but were split by an earthquake many millennia ago.

Orientation & Information
Paros' main town and port is Paroikia, on the west coast. The municipal tourist office is by the port. The OTE is on the south-west waterfront; turn right from the ferry pier. The post office is also on the waterfront, but to the north of the pier.

Paros' telephone code is ☎ 0284.

Things to See & Do
One of the most notable churches in Greece is Paroikia's **Panagia Ekatontapyliani**, which features a beautiful, highly ornate interior.

Petaloudes, 10 km from Paroikia, is better known as the Valley of the Butterflies. In summer, huge swarms of the creatures almost conceal the copious foliage.

The charming village of **Naoussa**, filled with white houses and labyrinthine alleyways, is still a working fishing village, despite an enormous growth in tourism over the last few years.

Paroikia's beaches are disappointing. Take a caïque to a nearby beach or try Naoussa, which has good beaches served by caïque. Most popular are **Kolimvythres**, with bizarre rock formations, **Monastiri**, a mainly nude beach, and **Santa Maria**, which is good for windsurfing.

Paros' longest beach, **Hrysi Akti** (Golden Beach) on the south coast, is reputedly brilliant for windsurfing.

The picturesque villages of **Lefkes**, **Marmara** and **Marpissa** are all worth a visit. The Moni Agiou Antoniou (Monastery of St Anthony), on a hill above Marpissa, offers breathtaking views. From Lefkes, an ancient Byzantine path leads in one hour of easy walking to the village of Prodromos, from where it is a short walk to either Marmara or Marpissa.

Antiparos This small island, less than two km from Paros, has superb beaches, but is becoming too popular for its own good.

One of the chief attractions in Antiparos is the cave, considered one of Europe's most beautiful (open from 10 am to 4 pm daily in summer only). Despite indiscriminate looting of stalagmites and stalactites in times gone by, it still has a profusion of them. Entry is 450 dr.

Places to Stay
Paros has five camping grounds. *Parasporas* (☎ 22 268), *Koula Camping* (☎ 22 081) and *Krios* (☎ 21 705) are near Paroikia, and *Naoussa Camping* (☎ 51 595) and *Surfing Beach* (☎ 51 013) are near Naoussa. Surfing Beach is the largest and has the best facilities.

Antiparos has one camping ground, *Antiparos Camping* (☎ 61 221), on Agios Giannis Theologos Beach.

Rooms Mike (☎ 22 856) is deservedly popular with backpackers. Doubles/triples cost 7000/9000 dr, with a small kitchen and a roof terrace. To get there, walk 50 metres left from the pier and you'll find it next to the Memphis bar. Around the corner, above Taverna Parikia, Mike also has self-contained studios; doubles/triples are 8000/10,000 dr. *Hotel Kypreou* (☎ 21 383) has doubles/triples with private bath for 7000/10,000 dr; turn left from the pier and it's on the first street to the right .

Places to Eat
No matter how late at night you arrive, *To Proto*, 50 metres to the right from the pier, is usually open; it serves bacon and eggs (500 dr), home-made hamburgers (650 dr), gyros and souvlaki (350 dr). *Ouzeri Albadross*, on the south-west waterfront, is cosy and popular; small/big mixed platters cost 900/1800 dr.

Getting There & Away
Flights from Athens cost 17,100 dr. Paros is a major transport hub for ferries. Daily connections with Piraeus take seven hours and cost 3320 dr. There are frequent ferries to Naxos, Ios, Santorini and Mykonos, and less frequent ones to Astypalea, Kalymnos, Kos, Tilos, Symi and Rhodes. There are hourly excursion boats in season to Antiparos. You can contact the port police on ☎ 21 240.

Getting Around
The bus station is 100 metres north of the tourist office. There are frequent buses to Aliki, Naoussa, Lefkes, Piso Livadi and Hrysi Akti. For Petaloudes take the Aliki bus.

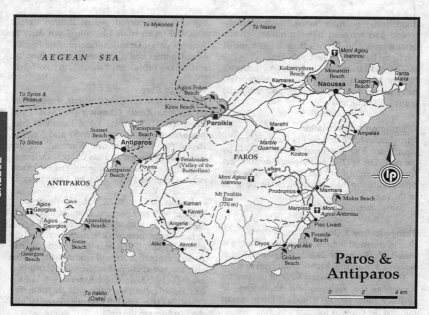

Map: Paros & Antiparos

There are many car and motorcycle-rental places.

FOLEGANDROS & SIKINOS

Of these two sparsely populated islands, Sikinos (Σίκινος) is the less visited – you could be the only visitor during the low season. There are no hotels, but there are some domatia and pensions in the very pretty Hora. The island also has several good beaches.

Folegandros (Φολέγανδρος) has become too popular in recent years and is no longer an island where you can get away from it all. Even so, it is considerably quieter than the major islands in the Cyclades and has a dramatic landscape, with a hora perched precariously on top of a sheer cliff. *Livadi Camping* (☎ 0286-41 204) on Livadi Beach has good facilities. *Hotel Kastro Danassis* (☎ 0286-41 230) has doubles/triples at 12,000/16,000 dr.

Getting There & Away

There are three ferries a week between Sikinos (4650 dr), Folegandros (4030 dr) and Piraeus.

Two go via Kythnos, Serifos, Sifnos, Milos and Kimolos, and one goes via Syros, Paros, Naxos and Santorini.

SANTORINI (THIRA) Σαντορίνη (Θήρα)

Around 1450 BC, the volcanic heart of Santorini exploded and sank, leaving an extraordinary landscape. Today the startling sight of the malevolently steaming core almost encircled by sheer cliffs remains. It's possible that the catastrophe destroyed the Minoan civilisation, but neither this theory nor the claim that the island was part of the lost continent of Atlantis have been proven.

Since ancient times the Atlantis legend has fired the imaginations of writers, scientists and mystics, all of whom depict it as an advanced society destroyed by a volcanic eruption. Egyptian papyruses have been found which tell of a cataclysmic event which destroyed such a civilisation, but they place it further west than the Aegean. Solon, the 6th-century BC Athenian ruler, related that on his visit to Egypt he was told of a continent destroyed 9000 years before his birth. Believers say he merely made a mathematical error and that he meant 900 years, which would correspond with the Santorini eruption. Plato firmly believed in the existence of Atlantis and depicted it as a land of art, flowers and fruit, and the frescos from Akrotiri bear this out.

Orientation & Information

The capital, Fira, perches on top of the caldera on the west coast. The port of Athinios is 12 km away. There is no EOT or tourist police, but, the exceptionally helpful Dakoutros Travel Agency (☎ 22 958) gives advice, sells boat tickets, arranges accommodation and changes currency. It is open from 8 am to 9 pm every day. Facing north, turn right at the Commercial Bank on the main square (Plateia Theotokopoulou).

Santorini's telephone code is ☎ 0286.

Things to See & Do

Fira The commercialism of Fira has not reduced its all-pervasive dramatic aura. The **Megaron**

Gyzi Museum, behind the Catholic monastery, houses local memorabilia, including fascinating photographs of Fira before and immediately after the 1956 earthquake. It's open Monday to Saturday from 10.30 am to 1.30 pm and 5 to 8 pm, and on Sunday from 10.30 am to 4.30 pm. Admission is 400 dr. The **archaeological museum**, opposite the cable-car station, houses finds from ancient Akrotiri and ancient Thira. Opening times are Tuesday to Sunday from 8.30 am to 3 pm, and admission is 800 dr.

Ancient Sites Excavations in 1967 uncovered the remarkably well preserved Minoan settlement of **Akrotiri**. There are remains of two and three-storey buildings, and evidence of a sophisticated drainage system. The site is open Tuesday to Sunday from 8.30 am to 3 pm; admission is 1200 dr.

Less impressive than Akrotiri, the site of **ancient Thira** is still worth a visit for the stunning views. The **Moni Profiti Ilia**, built on the island's highest point, can be reached along a path from ancient Thira.

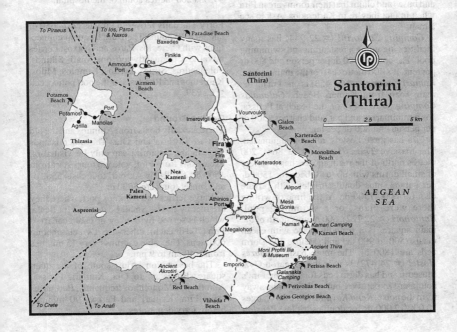

Beaches Santorini's beaches are of black volcanic sand which becomes unbearably hot, making a beach mat essential. Kamari and Perissa get crowded, whereas those near Oia and Monolithos are quieter.

Other Attractions From Imerovigli, just north of Santorini, a 12-km coastal path leads to the picturesque village of **Oia**. On a clear day there are breathtaking views of Folegandros and Sikinos. Oia is built on a steep slope of the caldera, and many of its traditional white Cycladic houses nestle in niches hewn from the volcanic rock.

Of the surrounding islets, only **Thirasia** is inhabited. At Palia Kameni you can bathe in hot springs, and on Nea Kameni you can clamber around on volcanic lava.

Places to Stay
Non-ravers should avoid accommodation near the main square or on the road running east towards Camping Santorini. Beware of aggressive accommodation owners who meet boats and buses and claim that their rooms are in Fira when in fact they're in Karterados. Ask to see a map.

Camping Santorini (☎ 22 944) has many facilities including a restaurant and swimming pool. The cost is 1300 dr per person and 800 dr per tent. It's 400 metres east of the main square. *Kamari Camping* (☎ 31 453) is one km up the main road from Kamari Beach. *Galanakis Camping* (☎ 81 343), on the beach at Perissa, has a minimarket and bar, and charges 1300 dr per person and 800 dr per tent.

Fira has three hostels, all well signposted. The massive *Thira Hostel* (☎ 23 864), 200 metres north of the main square, has a variety of small dorms with up to 10 beds for 1500 dr per person, plus doubles/triples with private bath for 6000/7500 dr. At the time of writing there were plans for a swimming pool. *Kontohori* (☎ 22 722), 500 metres north of the main square, is a friendly place with cheap meals (500 to 900 dr) and satellite TV. Dorm beds are 1800 dr. The more basic *Kamares Hostel* (☎ 24 472) is near the Megaron Gyzi Museum and has dorm beds for 1600 dr. Fira's hotels are expensive, but a short walk away from the noise, *Rena Kavallari Rooms* charges 10,000/12,000 dr for doubles/triples, *Pension*

Horizon charges 11,000/13,000 and *Villa Gianna* – which has a pool – charges 14,000/16,800. All have private bath and balcony. To book, ring Dakoutros Travel (see Orientation and Information).

The same agent has a variety of properties in Oia on its books; most are in traditional houses with heart-stopping views. Prices for a double studio start at 18,000 dr; a house for four costs from 35,000 dr.

Places to Eat
Next to Thira Hostel, the *Bella Thira* looks expensive but isn't – some Italian and Greek dishes are less than 900 dr. *Restaurant Stamna*, towards the main square from Dakoutros, usually has specials for 800 or 900 dr.

There's a supermarket just north of the main square.

Getting There & Away
Air Flights cost 20,200 dr to Athens, 13,900 dr to Mykonos, 13,900 dr to Crete and 20,400 dr to Rhodes. The Olympic Airways office (☎ 22 493) is 200 metres south of the hospital.

Ferry The daily ferries to Piraeus cost 4650 dr and take 10 hours. There are frequent connections with Crete, Ios, Paros and Naxos. Ferries travel less frequently to/from Anafi, Sikinos, Folegandros, Sifnos, Serifos, Kimolos, Milos, Karpathos and Rhodes. For the port police, call ☎ 22 239.

Getting Around
There are daily boats from Athinios and the old port to Thirasia and Oia. The other islands surrounding Santorini can only be visited on excursions from Fira; volcano tours start from 1500 dr. A full-day Akrotiri tour costs 5500 dr and sunset tours are 3500 dr.

Large ferries use Athinios port, where they are met by buses. Small boats use Fira Scala, which is served by donkey or cable car from Fira (700 dr each); otherwise it's a clamber up 600 steps. The cable car runs every 15 minutes from 6.40 am to 9 pm.

The bus station is just south of the main square. Buses go to Oia, Kamari, Perissa, Akrotiri and Monolithos frequently. Port buses leave Fira, Kamari and Perissa 90 minutes before ferry departures.

Car & Motorcycle Fira has many car and motorcycle-rental firms.

ANAFI Ανάφη

Tiny Anafi, lying east of Santorini, is almost entirely overlooked by travellers – the island's amenities are limited and its ferry links with other islands are tenuous. It's a pristine island untainted by concessions to tourism. If you visit, be aware that the island has limited resources. The few tavernas will prevent you from starving but don't expect a wide choice. Take some food along and go easy with the water.

One or two boats a week from Piraeus (4930 dr) call in at Anafi via Paros, Naxos, Ios and Santorini.

Crete Κρήτη

Crete, Greece's largest island, has the dubious distinction of playing host to a quarter of all visitors to Greece. You can escape the hordes by visiting the undeveloped west coast, going into the rugged mountainous interior, or staying in one of the villages of the Lassithi Plateau which, when the tour buses depart, return to rural tranquillity.

Blessed with an auspicious climate and fertile soil, Crete is Greece's cornucopia, producing a wider variety of crops than anywhere else.

As well as water sports, Crete has many opportunities for trekking and climbing. It is also the best place in Greece for buying high-quality, inexpensive leather goods.

History

The island was the birthplace of Minoan culture, Europe's first advanced civilisation, which flourished from 2800 to 1450 BC. The palace of Knossos, discovered at the beginning of this century, gives clues to the advanced nature of Minoan culture. They were literate – their first script resembled Egyptian hieroglyphs, which progressed to a syllable-based script called Linear A (still undeciphered). In the ruins, archaeologists also found clay tablets with Linear B inscriptions, the form of writing used by the Mycenaeans, which suggests that

Mycenaean invaders may have conquered the island, perhaps around 1500 BC.

Later, Crete passed from the warlike Dorians to the Romans, and then to the Genoese, who in turn sold it to the Venetians. Under the Venetians, Crete became a refuge for artists, writers and philosophers who fled Constantinople after it fell to the Turks. Their influence inspired the young Cretan painter Domenikos Theotokopoulos, who moved to Italy and won immortality as El Greco. The Turks finally conquered Crete in 1670. It became a British protectorate in 1898 after a series of insurrections and was united with independent Greece in 1913. There was fierce fighting during WWII when a German airborne invasion defeated Allied forces in the 10-day Battle of Crete. An active resistance movement drew heavy reprisals from the German occupiers.

Orientation & Information

Crete is divided into four prefectures: Hania, Rethymno, Iraklio and Lassithi. All of Crete's large towns are along the north coast, and it is in this area that the package tourist industry is concentrated.

Most of Crete's towns have tourist offices.

Getting There & Away

Air The international airport is at Iraklio, which is Crete's capital city. Hania and Sitia have domestic airports. There are several flights a day from Athens to Iraklio and Hania, and in summer there are two a week to Sitia. From Thessaloniki there are three flights a week to Iraklio and one a week to Hania. There are daily flights to Rhodes from Iraklio and several flights a week in high season to Mykonos and Santorini. In summer, Kassos and Karpathos are served by one flight a week from Sitia.

Ferry Kastelli-Kissamos, Rethymno, Hania, Iraklio, Agios Nikolaos and Sitia have ferry ports. Within Greece, direct ferries travel daily to Piraeus from Iraklio (5450 dr) and Hania (4990 dr), and three times a week from Rethymno (5500 dr), Agios Nikolaos and Sitia. From Monday to Saturday there are daily boats from Iraklio to Santorini.

Regular ferries from Iraklio serve the Cyclades. There are three ferries a week to

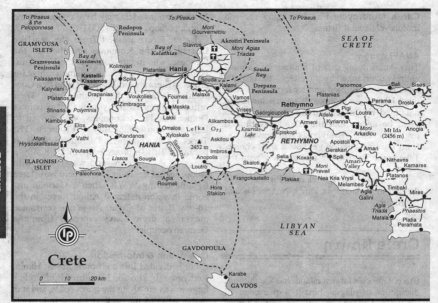

Crete

0   10   20 km

Rhodes (5500 dr) via Karpathos and in season at least two a week from Agios Nikolaos to Rhodes via Sitia, Kassos and Karpathos. Two or three boats a week run between Piraeus and Kastelli-Kissamos via Antikythira, Kythira and the Peloponnese.

In summer, two boats a week go from Iraklio to Cyprus via Rhodes and continue to Israel.

Hydrofoil In summer, four hydrofoils a week link Iraklio with Santorini, Ios, Naxos and Paros.

Getting Around
Frequent buses run between towns on the north coast, and less frequently to the south coast and mountain villages. Parts of the south coast are without roads, so boats are used to connect villages.

IRAKLIO Ηράκλειο
Iraklio, Crete's capital, lacks the charm of Rethymno or Hania, its old buildings having been swamped by modern apartment blocks,

yet it exudes a dynamism from its frenetically paced, neon-lit streets.

Orientation & Information
Iraklio's two main squares are Venizelou and Eleftherias. Dikeosynis and Dedalou run between them, and 25 Avgoustou is the main thoroughfare leading from the waterfront to Venizelou. The EOT (☎ 22 8225), which is open Monday to Friday from 8 am to 2 pm, and Olympic Airways offices (☎ 22 9191) are on Plateia Eleftherias. There is a laundrette and left-luggage storage at Handakos 18 (☎ 28 0858), open from 7.30 am to 9 pm. Lockers cost 400 dr per day.

Money Most of the city's banks are on 25 Avgoustou, but none open in the afternoon or on weekends. The American Express representative is at 25 Avgoustou 23.

Post & Communications The central post office is on Plateia Daskalogiani, and opening hours are Monday to Friday from 7.30 am to 8

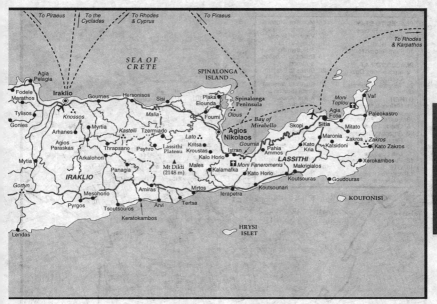

pm. The OTE telephone office is on the west side of Plateia El Greco, and is open 24 hours.

Iraklio's telephone code is ☎ 081.

Medical & Emergency Services The Apollonia Hospital (☎ 22 9713) is on P Nikousiou. The tourist police (☎ 28 3190) is at Dikeosynis 10. It's open from 7 am to 11 pm.

Things to See
Don't leave Iraklio until you've seen the **archaeological museum's** magnificent collection. Opening times are Tuesday to Sunday from 8 am to 6 pm and Monday from 12.30 to 6 pm. Admission is 1500 dr.

You can pay homage to the great writer Nikos Kazantzakis by visiting his grave. To get there, walk south on Evans and turn right onto Plastira.

Places to Stay
Beware of taxi drivers who tell you that the pension of your choice is dirty, dangerous or has a bad reputation. They're paid commissions by the big hotels.

Rent Rooms Hellas (☎ 28 0858), Handakos 24, has a lively atmosphere, with a roof garden and bar. Reception is on the roof. Singles/doubles/triples are 4500/5500/7000 dr, but they can fit up to six beds in some of the rooms for 2000 dr per extra person.

If you don't mind surly service, *Vergina Rooms* (☎ 24 2739), 32 Hortatson, is a turn-of-the-century house with a bit of character. Singles/doubles/triples are 4500/6500/8500 dr.

Hotel Rea (☎ 22 3638), 50 metres away at the junction of Handakos and Kalimeraki, has singles/doubles/triples for 5000/6400/8000 dr with private bath, 4500/5500/7000 dr without.

If you truly can't afford anything else, there is a *hostel* (☎ 28 6281) at Vyronos 5, off 25 Avgoustou. Dorms and roof beds are 1200 dr, but don't even think about the roof beds. There is a midnight curfew.

Places to Eat
The *Ippocampos Ouzeri*, on the waterfront just west of 25 Avgoustou, has a huge range of mezedes on offer from 400 dr. Go early to

PLACES TO STAY
4 Vergina Rooms
6 Hotel Rea
7 YHO Hostel
10 Rent Rooms Hellas

PLACES TO EAT
2 Ippocampos Ouzeri
9 Doukiani
26 Taverna Melandris

OTHER
1 Historical Museum of Crete
3 Venetian Fortress
5 Ourios Travel
8 American Express Representative
11 Laundrette/Left Luggage
12 Planet Bookstore
13 OTE
14 National Bank of Greece
15 Morosini Fountain
16 Buses to Knossos
17 Venetian Loggia
18 Buses to Hania & Rethymno
19 Buses to Knossos & Airport
20 Buses to Eastern Crete (Station A)
21 Buses to Western Crete (Station B)
22 Agios Minos Cathedral
23 Tourist Police
24 EOT
25 Archaeological Museum
27 Post Office
28 Buses to Airport
29 Olympic Airways
30 Appollonia Hospital
31 Grave of Nikos Kazantzakis

Iraklio

get a table. It's closed between 3.30 pm and 7 pm.

Treat yourself to traditional Cretan cuisine – or even just a coffee – at the stylish *Doukiani* at Handakos 30. Mezedes start at 400 dr.

Half-way down the fish market on Karterou is *Taverna Malandris*, a lively restaurant popular with locals, serving main courses for between 900 and 1000 dr.

The bustling, colourful market is on Odos 1866.

Getting There & Away
For air and ferry information, see Getting There & Away at the start of the Crete section.

Iraklio has two main bus stations. Bus station A is 100 metres west of the new harbour, and serves Agios Nikolaos, Ierapetra, Sitia, Malia and the Lassithi Plateau. Bus station B, 50 metres beyond the Hania Gate, serves Phaestos, Matala, Anoghia and Fodele. The Hania/Rethymno terminal is opposite bus station A.

Ourios Travel (☎ 28 2977), in the hi-tech Candia Tower building at Monis Agarathou 20, is particularly helpful.

Getting Around
Bus No 1 goes to/from the airport every 15 minutes between 6 am and 1 am; it stops at

Plateia Eleftherias adjacent to the archaeological museum (120 dr). Local bus No 2 goes to Knossos every 15 minutes from bus station A and also stops on 25 Avgoustou.

Car and motorcycle-rental firms are mostly along 25 Avgoustou.

KNOSSOS Κνωσσός

The most famous of Crete's Minoan sites, Knossos, is eight km south-east of Iraklio. It inspired the myth of the Minotaur.

According to legend, King Minos of Knossos was given a bull to sacrifice to the god Poseidon, but he took such a liking to the bull that he decided to keep it. This enraged Poseidon, who punished the king by causing his wife Pasiphae to fall in love with the animal. The result of this bizarre union was the Minotaur – half-man and half-bull – who lived in a labyrinth beneath the king's palace, feeding on youths and maidens sent as tributes from Athens.

Theseus, an Athenian prince anxious to put an end to these tributes, posed as a sacrificial youth and planned to kill the monster. He fell in love with Ariadne, King Minos' daughter, who gave him a ball of wool to unwind, so that he could find his way out of the labyrinth. Theseus killed the monster and fled with Ariadne, only to later dump her on Naxos.

Classicists have speculated on the origins of the myth; one theory is that it may have been based on a Minoan religious ritual.

In 1900 the ruins of Knossos were uncovered by Arthur Evans, who spent a fortune reconstructing some of the buildings. The site consists of an immense palace, courtyards, public reception rooms, private apartments, baths, storage vaults and stairways. Although archaeologists tend to disparage Evans' reconstruction, the buildings do give the layperson a good idea of what a Minoan palace may have looked like.

Most visitors enter along the Corridor of the Procession Fresco. It is best then to leave the corridor and re-enter from the north, near the Royal Road which brought visitors in ancient times. Entering the Central Court, you will pass the relief Bull Fresco, which depicts a charging bull. The Throne Room is dominated by a simple, beautifully proportioned throne flanked by the Griffin Fresco. The room is thought to have been a shrine, and the throne the seat of a high priestess.

The grand staircase leads to the private apartments and the Hall of the Double Axes, from which a passage leads to the Queen's Megaron, where the exquisite Dolphin Fresco was found. Adjacent is the bathroom with a terracotta bathtub. Also just off the megaron is the water chamber, a masterpiece of archaic plumbing.

Very little is known of Minoan civilisation, which came to an abrupt end around 1450 BC, possibly destroyed by Santorini's volcanic eruption. The delightful frescos depict plants and animals, as well as people participating in sports, ceremonies and festivals, and generally enjoying life, in contrast to the battle scenes found in the art of classical Greece.

A whole day is needed to see the site, and a guidebook is immensely useful – one of the best is *The Palaces of Minoan Crete* by Gerald Cadogan (paperback), which is not always available on Crete. The site is open Monday to Friday from 8 am to 7 pm, and weekends and holidays from 8.30 am to 3 pm; entry is 1000 dr. Try to arrive early, unless you enjoy crowds.

PHAESTOS & OTHER MINOAN SITES

Phaestos (Φαιστός), Crete's second-most important Minoan site, is not as impressive as Knossos but worth a visit for its stunning views of the plain of Mesara. The palace was laid out on the same plan as Knossos, but excavations have not yielded a great many frescos. Opening times are the same as for Knossos and entry is 800 dr.

Crete's other important Minoan sites are **Malia**, 34 km to the east of Iraklio, where there is a palace complex and adjoining town, and **Zakros**, 40 km from Sitia. This was the smallest of the island's palatial complexes. The site is rather remote and overgrown, but the ruins are on a more human scale than at Knossos, Phaestos or Malia.

HANIA Χανιά

Hania, the old capital of Crete, has a harbour with crumbling, softly hued Venetian buildings. It oozes charm; unfortunately it also oozes package tourists.

Orientation & Information

Hania's bus station is on Kydonias, two blocks

south-west of Plateia 1866, the town's main square. Halidon runs from here to the old harbour. The fortress separates the old harbour from the new.

The central post office is at Tzanakaki 3, open from 7.30 am to 8 pm on weekdays, and 7.30 am to 2 pm on Saturday. The OTE telephone office is next door and it operates from 6 am to 11 pm. The EOT office (☎ 92 624) is at Kriari 40, 20 metres from Plateia 1866. It is open Monday to Friday from 8 am to 3 pm. There is a laundrette next to the Fidias Pension on Sarpaki. Hania's port is at Souda, 10 km from town.

Hania's telephone code is ☎ 0821.

Things to See
The **archaeological museum** at Halidon 21 is housed in the former Venetian Church of San Francesco; the Turks converted it into a mosque. Opening hours are Tuesday to Sunday from 8.30 am to 3 pm. Admission is 500 dr.

Places to Stay & Eat
The nearest camping ground is *Camping Hania* (☎ 31 138) which charges 1200 dr per person and 800 dr per tent. Take a Kalamaka bus from Plateia 1866.

If it's character you're after, try *Rooms for Rent George* (☎ 88 715), Zambeliou 30, in a 600-year-old house with antique furniture;

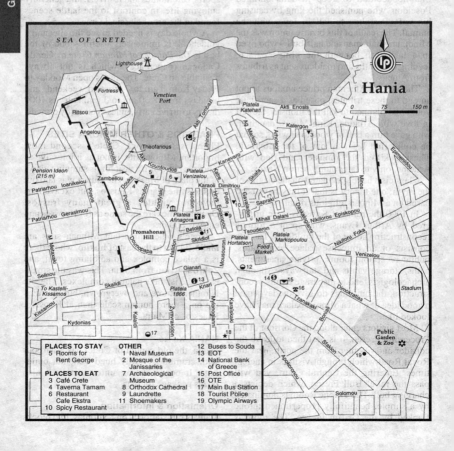

PLACES TO STAY	OTHER	12 Buses to Souda
5 Rooms for	1 Naval Museum	13 EOT
Rent George	2 Mosque of the	14 National Bank
	Janissaries	of Greece
PLACES TO EAT	7 Archaeological	15 Post Office
3 Café Crete	Museum	16 OTE
4 Taverna Tamam	8 Orthodox Cathedral	17 Main Bus Station
6 Restaurant	9 Laundrette	18 Tourist Police
Cafe Ekstra	11 Shoemakers	19 Olympic Airways
10 Spicy Restaurant		

singles/doubles/triples are 3000/5000/6500 dr. Turn left from Halidon onto Zambeliou one block from the waterfront; the pension is on the right.

There are many other pensions and domatia in the old town near the old harbour. The area around the new harbour is easier for parking and has lots of accommodation bargains. The opulent *Pension Ideon* (☎ 70 132) on Patriarhou Ioanikeiou has singles/doubles/triples for 4000/6000/9000 dr.

Come early for a table at *Taverna Tamam*, Zambeliou 51. Meatballs and souvlaki start at 1200 dr. It is open only for dinner. *Restaurant Cafe Ekstra*, at Zambeliou 8, serves Greek and international dishes, with crêpes from 1200 dr. *Spicy Restaurant*, Potie 19, is popular and cheap. The central *food market* is a lively place to go and eat; there are two inexpensive tavernas.

Entertainment
The authentic *Café Crete* at Kalergon 22 has live Cretan music every evening.

Things to Buy
Good-quality, handmade leather goods are available from the market on Skridlof, where shoes cost from 9000 dr.

Getting There & Away
For air and ferry information, see Getting There & Away at the start of the Crete section. Olympic Airways (☎ 57 701) is at Tzanakaki 88.

There are frequent buses to Rethymno and Kastelli-Kissamos, and less frequent ones to Paleohora, Omalos, Hora Sfakion, Lakki and Elafonisi. Buses for Souda (the port) leave frequently from outside the food market.

THE WEST COAST
This is Crete's least developed coastline. At Falassarna, 11 km west of Kastelli-Kissamos, there's a magnificent sandy beach and a few tavernas and domatia. The beach is five km from Platanos, where you get off the bus.

South of Falassarna there are good sandy beaches near the villages of Sfinario and Kambos.

Further south you can wade out to more beaches on Elafonisi islet. Travel agents in Hania and Paleohora run excursions to the area.

SAMARIA GORGE Φαράγγι της Σαμαριάς
It's a wonder the rocks aren't worn away completely as so many people trample through the Samaria Gorge. But it is one of Europe's most spectacular gorges, and worth seeing. You can do it independently by taking a bus to Omalos from Hania, returning by boat to Hora Sfakion, and then returning by bus to Hania. Or you can join one of the daily excursions from Hania.

The first public bus leaves at 6.15 am and excursion buses also leave early so that people get to the top of the gorge before the heat of the day. You need good walking shoes and a hat, as well as water and food. The gorge is 16 km long and takes on average five or six hours to walk. It is closed from autumn to spring because of the danger of flash floods.

LEVKA ORI Λευκά Ορι
Crete's rugged White Mountains are south of Hania. For information on climbing and trekking, contact the EOS (☎ 44 647), Tzanakaki 90, in Hania.

PALEOHORA & THE SOUTH-WEST COAST
Paleohora (Παλαιοχώρα) was discovered by hippies back in the 1960s and from then on its days as a tranquil fishing village were numbered. But it remains a relaxing resort favoured by backpackers.

Further east, along Crete's south-west coast, are the resorts of Sougia, Agia Roumeli, Loutro and Hora Sfakion; of these, Loutro is the most appealing and the least developed.

Paleohora's telephone code is ☎ 0823.

Places to Stay & Eat
One and a half km from town is *Camping Paleohora* (☎ 41 120), which charges 800 dr per person and 400 dr per tent. There are many domatia.

Rooms to Rent Anonymous (☎ 41 509) is a great place for backpackers. It has clean rooms set around a small courtyard; singles/doubles are 3000/4000 dr and there is a communal kitchen.

Oriental Bay Rooms (☎ 41 076), at the northern end of the pebble beach, has comfortable doubles/triples for 6500/8500 dr. The *Lissos Hotel* (☎ 41 266), El Venizelou 12, opposite the bus stop, has singles/doubles for 5000/5500 dr with shared bath, and doubles/triples for 7200/8500 dr with private bath.

Getting There & Away

There is no road linking the coastal resorts, but they are connected by boats from Paleohora in summer. Twice weekly the boat goes to Gavdos Island. Coastal paths lead from Paleohora to Sougia and from Agia Roumeli to Loutro (make sure you take plenty of water, because you'll be walking in full sun). There are five or six buses a day from Paleohora to Hania.

GAVDOS ISLAND Νήσος Γαύδος

The small rocky island of Gavdos, off Crete's southern coast, has some good beaches, a few domatia and tavernas, and as yet, is little visited. Freelance camping is tolerated all over the island.

RETHYMNO Ρέθυμνο

Although similar to Hania in its Venetian and Turkish buildings (not to mention its package tourists), Rethymno is smaller and has a distinct character.

The EOT office (☎ 24 143) is on the beach side of El Venizelou and is open Monday to Friday from 8 am to 2.30 pm. The post office is at Moatsou 21 and the OTE telephone office is at Pavlou Kountouriotou 28. The latter is open from 7 am to 10 pm. There is a laundrette next to the hostel.

SEA OF CRETE

Rethymno

0   150   300 m

PLACES TO STAY
6 Rent Rooms Garden
9 Olga's Pension
10 HI Hostel

PLACES TO EAT
4 Taverna Kyria Maria
5 Gounakis Restaurant & Bar

OTHER
1 Entrance to Fortress
2 Archaeological Museum
3 Rimondi Fountain
7 Historical & Folk Art Museum
8 Nerandjes Mosque
11 The Happy Walker
12 EOT
13 Bus Station
14 OTE
15 Olympic Airways
16 Post Office
17 National Bank of Greece

Fortress

Ferry Quay

Venetian Harbour

Plastira
Makedonias
Melissinou
Mesologiou
Katehaki
Melissinou
Melisinou
Smyrnis
Plateia Iroön Polytehniou
Koroneou
Arabatzoglou
Nikiforou Foka
Vernardou
Paleologou
Soutsou
Arkadiou
National Stadium
Plateia Vardinogianni
Dimakopoulou
Ethnikis Antistaseos
Tombazi
El Venizelou
Alexandrou
Vlastou Sifi
Igoum Gavriil
Igoum Gavriil
Krani
Illakaki
Dimitrakaki
Koumoundourou
Municipal Garden
Moatsou
Hospital
Gerakari
Arkadiou
Kountouriotou
Dimokratias
Plateia Iroön
Kapodistriou

Rethymno's telephone code is ☎ 0831.

Things to See & Do

The imposing **Venetian fortress** is worth a wander around, and the **archaeological museum** opposite the fortress entrance is well stocked but disorganised. The fortress is open daily from 9 am to 7 pm and the museum is open Tuesday to Sunday from 8.30 am to 3 pm. Admission to both is 500 dr. The **historical & folk art museum** at Mesologiou 28 has a well-presented display of Cretan crafts. Its opening hours are Monday to Saturday from 9 am to 1 pm; entry is 400 dr.

The Happy Walker (☎ 52 920), Tombazi 56, has a programme of daily walks in the countryside costing from 6000 dr per person.

Places to Stay

The nearest camping ground is *Elizabeth Camping* (☎ 28 694) on Myssiria beach, three km east of town.

The *youth hostel* (☎ 22 848), Tombazi 41, is a friendly place with a bar; beds are 1000 dr in dorms or on the roof. There is no curfew and a card is not required. *Olga's Pension* (☎ 29 851), in the heart of town at Souliou 57, is spectacularly funky, with a wide choice of rooms spread about in clusters off a network of terraces bursting with greenery. Prices range from basic singles for 4000 dr up to triple rooms with private bath for 9000 dr. **Rent Rooms Garden** (☎ 28 586), Nikiforou Foka 82, is an old Venetian house with many original features and a delightful grape-arboured garden; doubles/triples are 8000/10,000 dr with private bath.

Places to Eat

Taverna Kyria Maria, Diog Mesologiou 20, tucked behind the Rimondi fountain, is a cosy family-run taverna.

Gounakis Restaurant & Bar, Koroneou 6, has live Cretan music every evening and good, reasonably priced food.

Getting There & Away

There are frequent buses to Iraklio and Hania, and less frequent ones to Agia Galini, Arkadi Monastery and Plakias.

For ferries, see Getting There & Away at the start of the Crete section.

AGIOS NIKOLAOS Αγιος Νικόλαος

The manifestations of package tourism gather momentum as they advance eastwards, reaching their ghastly crescendo in Agios Nikolaos, or Ag Nik in package-tourist jargon.

If you don't take the first bus out, you'll find the municipal tourist office (☎ 22 357) next to the bridge between the lake and the harbour; follow the signs from the bus station and pick up a map. The tourist police (☎ 26 900) are at Kontogianni 34.

Ag Nik's telephone code is ☎ 0841.

Places to Stay & Eat

The nearest camping ground is *Gournia Moon Camping* (☎ 0842-93 243), 19 km from Ag Nik and almost opposite the Minoan site of Gournia. Buses to Sitia can drop you off right outside.

In town, the *Sunbeam* hotel (☎ 25 645), Ethnikis Antistaseos 23, is outstanding and certainly the best value for money. Immaculate singles/doubles/triples are 4000/6000/7000 dr with private bath, breakfast included. There is also a bar. Walk up Paleologou and take the fourth left after the lake.

For a balcony over the sea, try the spotless *Pension Mylos* (☎ 23 783), at Sarolidi 24, where doubles/triples cost 8500/10,500 dr with private bath, or 6700/8700 dr without.

The ramshackle *Green House* (☎ 22 025), Modatsou 15, is popular with backpackers; singles/doubles are 3500/4500 dr. Walk up Kapetan Tavla from the bus station and look for the sign.

The waterfront tavernas are expensive – head inland for better value. *Taverna Itanos*, Kyprou 1, is a lively traditional restaurant. The *Taverna Pine Tree*, next to the lake at Paleologou 18, specialises in charcoal-grilled food, such as a plate of king prawns for 1800 dr. *Aouas Taverna*, at Paleologou 44, has traditional décor and a lovely garden.

Things to See & Do

The **archaeological museum**, on Paleologou, is open daily, except Monday, from 8.30 am to 3 pm. Admission is 500 dr. The **folk museum** next to the tourist office is open daily, except Saturday, from 9.30 am to 1 pm. Admission is 250 dr.

GREECE

Getting There & Away

There are frequent buses from Agios Nikolaos to Iraklio, Malia, Ierapetra and Sitia, and two a day to Lassithi.

For boats, see Getting There & Away at the start of the Crete section. To contact the port police, call ☎ 22 312.

Getting Around

Car and motorcycle-rental firms are ubiquitous, but for bicycle rental try Ross Rentals (☎ 23 407), Koundourou 10, which has mountain bikes for 2000/10,500 dr per day/week.

LASSITHI PLATEAU Οροπέδιο Λασιθίου

Sadly, many of the windmills that gave Lassithi its picture-postcard fame have been replaced by electrically operated pumps, although if you're lucky you may still see some white sails unfurled. But windmills or not, the first view of this mountain-fringed plateau, laid out like an immense patchwork quilt, is breathtaking.

Things to See

The **Dikteon Cave**, on the side of Mt Dikti, is not as festooned with stalactites and stalagmites as some of Greece's other caves, but it's still worth a visit. Here, according to mythology, the Titan Rhea hid the newborn Zeus from Cronos, his offspring-gobbling father. It's open Monday to Saturday from 10.30 am to 5 pm; admission is 800 dr.

Places to Stay & Eat

Psychro is the best place to stay: it's near the cave and has the best views. The *Zeus Hotel* (☎ 0844-31 284) has singles/doubles for 5000/7500 dr. The taverna in the main square is good value.

Getting There & Away

From Psychro two or three buses a day go to Iraklio and Agios Nikolaos, and one goes to Malia.

SITIA Σητεία

Back on the north coast the tourist overkill dies down considerably by the time you reach Sitia. Skirting a commanding hotel-lined bay with a long sandy beach (more than can be said of Ag Nik), Sitia is an attractive town.

The post office is on Therissou, off El Venizelou; the OTE telephone office is on Kapetan Sifis, which runs inland from the central square. The tourist office can be contacted on ☎ 24 955.

Sitia's telephone code is ☎ 0843.

Places to Stay & Eat

There are no camp sites near Sitia, but it is possible to camp in the grounds of the *youth hostel* at Therissou 4, on the road to Iraklio. Beds at the hostel are 1300 dr and double rooms are 3000 dr.

The immaculate *Hotel Arhontiko* (☎ 28 172), Kondilaki 16, has singles/doubles/triples for 4000/5000/7000 dr. From the bus station, turn left onto the waterfront and 100 metres along you'll see a small harbour; turn left here and you'll see the sign.

To Kyma, on the waterfront, serves good seafood and grills. There are many grocery shops on Thoyntaladou, one block south of Plateia Agonostos.

Getting There & Away

For air and ferry information, see Getting There & Away at the start of the Crete section. There are at least five buses daily to Ierapetra and eight to Iraklio via Agios Nikolaos. In summer there are two or three buses daily to Vaï and Zakros.

AROUND SITIA

The reconstructed **Toplou Monastery**, 15 km from Sitia, houses some beautifully intricate icons and other fascinating relics.

Vaï Beach, famous for its palm tree forest, gets pretty crowded, but it's a superb beach and well worth a visit.

For Toplou Monastery, get a Vaï bus from Sitia, get off at the fork for the monastery and walk the last three km.

Dodecanese Δωδεκάνησα

More verdant and mountainous than the Cyclades and with comparable beaches, the islands of the Dodecanese offer more than natural beauty, for here more than anywhere else you get a sense of Greece's proximity to

Asia. Ancient temples, massive crusader fortifications, mosques and imposing Italian-built neoclassical buildings stand juxtaposed, vestiges of a turbulent past. Even now, proximity to Turkey makes the islands a contentious issue whenever hostility between the two countries intensifies.

There are 16 inhabited islands in the group; the most visited are Rhodes, Kos, Patmos and Symi.

RHODES Ρόδος

According to mythology, the sun god Helios chose Rhodes as his bride and bestowed light,

warmth and vegetation upon her. The blessing seems to have paid off, for Rhodes produces flowers in profusion and enjoys more sunny days than most Greek islands.

The ancient sites of Lindos and Kamiros are legacies of Rhodes' importance in antiquity.

In 1291 the Knights of St John, having fled Jerusalem under siege, came to Rhodes and established themselves as masters. In 1522 Süleyman I, sultan of the Ottoman Empire, staged a massive attack on the island and took Rhodes city. The island, along with the other Dodecanese, then became part of the Ottoman Empire.

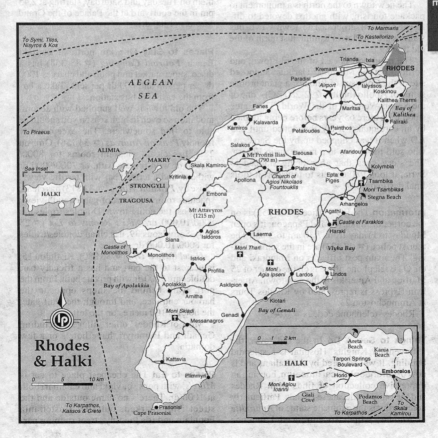

GREECE

In 1912 it was the Italians' turn and in 1944 the Germans took over. The following year Rhodes was liberated by British and Greek commandos. In 1948, Rhodes, along with the other Dodecanese, became part of Greece.

Rhodes City

Rhodes' capital and port is Rhodes city, on the northern tip of the island. Almost everything of interest in the city lies within its walls. The main thoroughfares are Sokratous, Pythagora, Agiou Fanouriou and Ipodamou, with mazes of narrow streets between them. Many parts of the old town are prohibited to cars, but there are car parks around the periphery.

The new town to the north is a monument to package tourism, with ghettos devoted to different national groups. The town's two bus stations are on Plateia Rimini, just north of the old town.

The main port is east of the old town, and north of here is Mandraki Harbour, supposed site of the Colossus of Rhodes, a giant bronze statue of Apollo (built in 292-280 BC) – one of the Seven Wonders of the World. The statue stood for a mere 65 years before being toppled by an earthquake. It lay abandoned until 653 AD when it was chopped up by the Saracens, who sold the pieces to a merchant in Edessa. The story goes that after being shipped to Syria, it took 980 camels to transport it to its final destination.

Information The EOT office (☎ 23 255) is on the corner of Makariou and Papagou; it's open Monday to Friday from 7.30 am to 3 pm. The tourist police (☎ 27 423) are in the same building. The main post office is on Mandraki and the OTE telephone office is on the corner of 25 Martiou and Amerikis in the new town. American Express is represented by Rhodos Tours at Ammochostou 23.

Rhodes' telephone code is ☎ 0241.

Things to See & Do In the old town, the 15th-century Knights' Hospital is a splendid building. It was restored by the Italians and is now the **archaeological museum**, housing an impressive collection of finds from Rhodes and the other Dodecanese islands. Particularly noteworthy is the exquisite statue of *Aphrodite of Rhodes*, which so entranced Lawrence

Durrell that he named his book about the island, *Reflections on a Marine Venus*, after it. Opening times are Tuesday to Sunday from 8.30 am to 3 pm. Admission is 800 dr.

Odos Ippoton – the Avenue of the Knights – is lined with magnificent medieval buildings, the most imposing of which is the **Palace of the Grand Masters**, restored, but never used, as a holiday home for Mussolini. It is open Tuesday to Sunday from 8.30 am to 3 pm. Admission is 1200 dr.

The old town is reputedly the world's finest surviving example of medieval fortification. The 12-metre-thick walls are closed to the public, but you can take a **guided walk** along them on Tuesday and Saturday, starting at 2.45 pm in the courtyard at the Palace of the Grand Masters (1200 dr).

Places to Stay One km north of Faliraki Beach, *Faliraki Camping* (☎ 85 358) has a disco, supermarket and pool, and charges 1000 dr per person and 600 dr per tent. Take a bus from the east-side bus station.

The old town is well supplied with accommodation so even in high season you should be able to find somewhere. The exceptionally friendly *Pension Andreas* (☎ 34 156), Omirou 28D, has clean, pleasant rooms for 8000/10,000 dr with private bath, or 7000/9000 dr without, and a terrace bar with terrific views. Close by, *Pension Minos* (☎ 31 813) has clean, spacious rooms and a roof garden with views of almost the entire town. Doubles/triples are 8000/10,000 dr. *Niki's Rooms to Let* (☎ 25 115), Sofokleous 39, has clean doubles/triples for 8000/10,000 dr.

Hotel Kava d'Oro (☎ 36 980), Kistiniou 15, is nearest to the port and has a friendly bar; doubles are 9000 dr with private bath. From the port, walk behind the shops opposite the harbour entrance, and through the wall gate; the hotel is 100 metres on the left.

Most of Rhodes' other villages, including Genadi and Plimmyri, have hotels or a few domatia.

Places to Eat The cheapest place to eat is *Mike's*, with pork souvlaki and calamari both at 1000 dr. There's no name outside and the street isn't marked, but find Castellania Fountain and it's the tiny street running par-

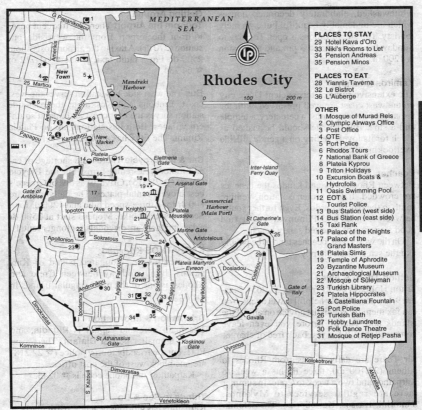

MEDITERRANEAN SEA

Rhodes City

0   100   200 m

GREECE

PLACES TO STAY
29 Hotel Kava d'Oro
33 Niki's Rooms to Let
34 Pension Andreas
35 Pension Minos

PLACES TO EAT
28 Yiannis Taverna
32 Le Bistrot
36 L'Auberge

OTHER
1   Mosque of Murad Reis
2   Olympic Airways Office
3   Post Office
4   OTE
5   Port Police
6   Rhodos Tours
7   National Bank of Greece
8   Plateia Kyprou
9   Triton Holidays
10 Excursion Boats &
    Hydrofoils
11 Oasis Swimming Pool
12 EOT &
    Tourist Police
13 Bus Station (west side)
14 Bus Station (east side)
15 Taxi Rank
16 Palace of the Knights
17 Palace of the
    Grand Masters
18 Plateia Simis
19 Temple of Aphrodite
20 Byzantine Museum
21 Archaeological Museum
22 Mosque of Süleyman
23 Turkish Library
24 Plateia Hippocrates
    & Castelliana Fountain
25 Port Police
26 Turkish Bath
27 Hobby Laundrette
30 Folk Dance Theatre
31 Mosque of Retjep Pasha

allel south of Sokratous. *Yiannis Taverna*, Apellou 41, is also very good value, but if you're sick of Greek food by now, *Le Bistrot*, Omirou 22-24, serves terrific French dishes, with main courses costing around 1500 dr. At the time of writing, the restaurant was planning to split into two, with Le Bistrot offering a variety of Créole appetisers and the French menu being served from *L'Auberge*, Praxitelous 19-21.

South of the old town, *To Steno*, Agion Anargiron 29, near the church, is popular with locals.

Self-caterers will find many food shops in the new market.

Entertainment The *sound-and-light show* at the Palace of the Knights, depicting the Turkish siege, is superior to most such efforts. Check the schedule with the EOT, but there is usually an English performance nightly except on Sunday. Admission is 1000 dr.

Homesick Aussies should make for the *Down Under Bar* at Orfanidi 37, north-west of the old town, where all the staff are Australian.

Lindos Λίνδος
The imposing **Acropolis of Lindos**, Rhodes' most important ancient city, shares a rocky outcrop with a **crusader castle**. Down below it there are labyrinths of winding streets with

whitewashed, elaborately decorated houses which are undeniably beautiful but extremely touristy. The site of Lindos is open Tuesday to Sunday from 8.30 am to 3 pm and admission is 1200 dr.

Kamiros Κάμειρος

The extensive ruins of this ancient Doric city on the west coast are well preserved, with the remains of houses, baths, a cemetery, a temple and a stoa. But the site should be visited as much for its lovely setting on a gentle hillside overlooking the sea.

Beaches

Between Rhodes city and Lindos the beaches are crowded. If you prefer isolation, venture south to the bay of Lardos. Even further south, between Genadi and Plimmyri, you'll find good stretches of deserted sandy beach.

On the west coast, beaches tend to be pebbly and the sea is often choppy.

Getting There & Away

Triton Holidays (☎ 21 690; fax 31 265), Plastira 9, is a particularly helpful travel agent. You can fax them for specialist advice on any of the islands and Turkey before you even leave home and they'll fax you back free of charge.

Air There are daily flights from Rhodes to Athens (23,100 dr), three flights a week to Karpathos and two a week to Crete. In summer there are regular services to Mykonos, Santorini, Kassos, Kastellorizo, Thessaloniki and Kos. The Olympic Airways office (☎ 24 555) is at Ierou Lohou 9.

Ferry There are daily ferries from Rhodes to Piraeus (7000 dr). Some go via Karpathos, Kassos, Crete and the Cyclades, others go via the Dodecanese north of Rhodes. There are two ferries a week to Kastellorizo and daily excursion boats to Symi. The EOT gives out a schedule.

There are regular boats from Rhodes to Marmaris (Turkey) between April and October; one-way tickets cost 16,000 dr by hydrofoil or 10,500 dr by ferry, including the 4000-dr port tax.

In summer there are regular ferries to Israel (from 27,000 dr) via Cyprus (19,000 dr).

Getting Around

To/From the Airport There are frequent buses to/from the airport from the west-side bus station (270 dr). A taxi to the airport costs about 2500 dr. For a radio taxi, phone ☎ 64 712 or ☎ 64 734.

Bus The west-side bus station serves the west coast, Embona and Koskinou; the east-side station serves the east coast and inland southern villages. Both bus stations are on Plateia Rimini. The EOT has a schedule.

Car & Motorcycle There is no shortage of car and motorcycle-rental firms, but the Bicycle Centre (☎ 28 315), Griva 39, is one of Greece's best bicycle-rental places. The daily rates are 800 dr for a three-speed bike and 1200 dr for a Scott mountain bike. Mopeds start at 2500 dr a day and there are discounts for longer rentals.

KARPATHOS Κάρπαθος

The picturesque, elongated island of Karpathos, lying midway between Crete and Rhodes, is one of the most singular islands in the Aegean.

Orientation & Information

The main port and capital is **Pigadia**, and there's a smaller port at **Diafani**. There's no EOT, but the friendly tourist police (☎ 22 218) are one block west of the post office.

Karpathos' telephone code is ☎ 0245.

Things to See & Do

Karpathos has glorious beaches, particularly at Apella and Kira Panagia. The northern village of **Olymbos** is like a living museum and is endlessly fascinating to ethnologists. Young women wear brightly coloured and embroidered skirts, waistcoats and headscarves and goatskin boots. The older women's apparel is more subdued but still distinctive. Interiors of houses are decorated with embroidered cloth and their façades with brightly painted moulded-plaster reliefs. The inhabitants speak a dialect which retains some Doric words, and the houses have wooden locks of the kind described by Homer. A two-hour uphill trail leads from Diafani to Olymbos.

Places to Stay & Eat

In Pigardia the delightfully kitsch *Carlos*

Rooms (☎ 22 477) has doubles and triples for 5000 dr. From the port take the left fork onto Karpathou, turn left two blocks along, turn right two blocks further on again, and turn left at the arts centre. It's 400 metres up the hill on the left. *Konaki Rooms* (☎ 22 908) is sparkling and has doubles/triples for 5000/6000 dr. It's just beyond the arts centre. Accommodation is also available at Diafani, Olymbos and several other villages.

The *Kali Kardia Restaurant* serves superb, fresh fish and inexpensive meat dishes. It's opposite the Hotel Atlantic in Pigadia.

Getting There & Away
Air Karpathos has an international airport that receives charter flights from northern Europe.

There are two flights a week to Athens (24,700 dr), four a week to Kassos (6000 dr), daily flights to Rhodes (12,100 dr), and one a week to Sitia on Crete (11,500 dr).

Ferry There are two ferries a week from Rhodes and from Piraeus (6340 dr) via the Cyclades and Crete. In bad weather, ferries do not stop at Diafani.

KASSOS Κάσσος
On the map, Kassos looks like a bit of Karpathos that has broken away; it's rocky and barren with a couple of sandy beaches, and it's a good choice if you yearn for isolation. Kassos has air connections with Sitia, Karpathos and Rhodes, and has the same ferry connections as Karpathos, but if the weather is bad, the ferries give it a miss.

Hotel Anagennisis (☎ 41 323) is highly recommended; singles/doubles cost 6600/10,750 dr with private bath.

Kassos' telephone code is ☎ 0245.

KOS Κως
Kos is renowned as the birthplace of Hippocrates, father of medicine. Kos town manifests the more ghastly aspects of mass tourism, and the beaches are horrendous, with wall-to-wall sun lounges and beach umbrellas.

Orientation & Information
Kos town, on the north-east coast, is the main town and the port. The municipal tourist office (☎ 26 583) is at Vasileos Georgiou 3, near the hydrofoil pier. It is open Monday to Friday

from 8 am to 2.30 pm. The post office is at El Venizelou 16, one block from the OTE, on the corner of Vironos and Xanthou.

Kos' telephone code is ☎ 0242.

Things to See
Kos Town Before you beat a hasty retreat, check out the ruined **agora** and **odeion**, and also the 13th-century **fortress** and the **museum**, open Tuesday to Sunday from 8.30 am to 3 pm; admission to both the fortress and the museum is 800 dr.

Standing at the entrance to the castle is the **Hippocrates Plane Tree** beneath which, according to the EOT brochure, the great man taught – although plane trees don't usually live for more than 200 years.

Asclepion On a pine-clad hill, four km from Kos town, stand the extensive ruins of the renowned healing centre of Asclepion. The site is open Tuesday to Sunday from 8.30 am to 3 pm; admission is 800 dr.

Around the Island The villages in the **Asfendion** region of the Dikeos Mountains are reasonably tranquil. **Paradise** on the south-east coast is the most appealing beach, but don't expect to have it to yourself.

Places to Stay & Eat
Three km south-east of town is the friendly *Kos Camping* (☎ 23 275). In June, July and August their minibus meets most boats, including the 4 am ferry from Piraeus.

The *Dodekanissos Hotel* (☎ 28 460), Ipsilandou 9, has singles/doubles/triples with private bath for 5200/7700/9200 dr. From the port, with the castle wall to your left, turn right and then left at the sign for the centre. *Hotel Elena* (☎ 22 986), Megalou Alexandrou 5, has doubles with/without private bath for 6500/5500 dr. The street is off Akti Kondourioti in the middle of the waterfront.

Many of Kos' restaurants cater for the package-tourist trade, but one notable exception is the remarkably cheap and good *Olympiada Restaurant* behind the Olympic Airways office. It offers a good range of dishes from 850 dr.

The food market is on Plateia Eleftherias.

GREECE

Getting There & Away

Air Apart from European charter flights, there are daily flights from Kos to Athens (19,800 dr) and two a week to Rhodes (13,200 dr). The Olympic Airways office (☎ 28 330) is at Vasileos Pavlou 22, south of the agora.

Ferry There are frequent ferries from Rhodes which continue on to Piraeus (6330 dr) via Patmos, Leros and Kalymnos. There are less frequent connections to Nisyros, Tilos, Symi, Samos and Crete. Daily excursion boats also go to Nisyros, Kalymnos and Rhodes.

Ferries travel twice daily in summer to Bodrum in Turkey; fares are 10,500 dr one way or 13,000 dr return (including port tax).

Getting Around

Buses for Asclepion leave from opposite the town hall on the harbour; all other buses leave from behind the Olympic Airways office. Motorcycles, mopeds and bicycles are widely available for hire.

NISYROS & TILOS Νίσυρος & Τήλος

Volcanic Nisyros' caldera obligingly bubbles, hisses and spews – you must wear solid shoes as it gets very hot underfoot. Dramatic moonscapes combine with lush vegetation, and after the day-trippers from Kos depart, Nisyros reverts to its peaceful, unspoilt self.

Tilos is less visited than Nisyros and has gentle and enfolding hills offering many opportunities for walking, as well as some of the finest beaches in the Dodecanese.

PATMOS Πάτμος

Starkly scenic Patmos is where St John wrote his book of Revelations. It gets crowded in summer, but manages to remain remarkably tranquil.

Patmos' telephone code is ☎ 0247.

Orientation & Information

The tourist office (☎ 31 666), open Monday to Friday from 9 am to 1.30 pm and from 5 to 8 pm, is behind the post office at Skala, the port. The main town is the hill-top Hora.

Things to See & Do

The **Monastery of the Apocalypse**, on the site where St John wrote the Revelations, is between the port and the Hora. The attraction here is the cave in which the saint lived and dictated his revelations. It's open on Monday, Wednesday, Friday and Saturday from 8 am to 1 pm, on Tuesday and Thursday from 8 am to 1 pm and 4 to 6 pm, and on Sunday from 10 am to noon and 4 to 6 pm. Admission is free.

The Hora's whitewashed houses huddle around the fortified **Monastery of St John**, which houses a vast collection of monastic treasures, including embroidered robes, ornate crosses and chalices, Byzantine jewellery and early manuscripts and icons. It's open the same hours as the Monastery of the Apocalypse. Admission to the monastery is free, but it's 1000 dr to see the treasury.

Patmos' indented coastline provides numerous secluded coves, mostly with pebble beaches.

Places to Stay & Eat

One of Greece's most pleasant camp sites is **Stefanos Flower Camping** (☎ 31 821). It's on the beach, two km north-east of Skala, and charges 1200 dr per person and 400 dr per tent.

Enthusiastic domatia owners will nearly knock you over as you disembark, and there are many rooms for rent in and around the harbour.

The **Pension Akteon** (☎ 31 187) has self-contained studios at 4000/8000/9600 dr for singles/doubles/triples. **Hotel Chris**, **Hotel Maria** and **Hotel Rex**, all close to the harbour and easy to find, are among the cheapest hotels.

O Pantelis Taverna, on the street a block back from the waterfront, and **Taverna Grigoris**, opposite the cafeteria/passenger transit building, are the two most popular eateries. The food market is well signposted from the waterfront.

Getting There & Away

Frequent ferries travel between Patmos and Piraeus (5340 dr), and to Rhodes (4640 dr) via Leros, Kalymnos and Kos. There are also frequent boats to Samos.

Getting Around

Skala, Hora, Grigos and Kambos are connected by buses which depart from beside the ferry port. In summer there are excursion boats from Skala to beaches and also to the island of Lipsi to the east of Patmos.

KASTELLORIZO Καστελλόριζο

Tiny Kastellorizo lies 116 km east of Rhodes, its nearest Greek neighbour, and only 2.5 km from the southern coast of Turkey. Its **Blue Grotto** is spectacular and comparable to its namesake in Capri. The name derives from the blue appearance of the water in the grotto, caused by refracted sunlight. Fishermen will take you to the cave in their boats, and also to some of the surrounding islets, all of which are uninhabited. The island's remoteness is drawing a steady trickle of visitors, but as yet it remains pristine. Three flights (10,600 dr) and two ferries a week operate between Rhodes and Kastellorizo. There are plenty of rooms for rent.

Kastellorizo's telephone code is ☎ 0241.

North-Eastern Aegean Islands

These islands are less visited than the Cyclades and the Dodecanese. There are seven major islands in this group: Chios, Ikaria, Lesvos, Limnos, Samos, Samothraki and Thasos.

Off-shore oil – albeit of a not very high quality – has been found around Thasos, leading to Turkey casting a covetous eye upon the whole group. The Turks claim that as this part of the Aegean lies off their coast, they should have a share of whatever it yields. But on the basis of the 1982 Law of the Sea the Aegean belongs to Greece. Turkey has not ratified this law and is pressing for negotiations. The dispute has necessitated a heavy military presence.

SAMOS Σάμος

Samos was an important centre of Hellenic culture and is reputedly the birthplace of the philosopher and mathematician Pythagoras. Lush and humid, its mountains are skirted by pine, sycamore and oak-forested hills, and its air is permeated with floral scents.

Orientation & Information

Vathy (Samos town) is the main town and port; the smaller port of Pythagorio is on the south-east coast. The municipal tourist office (☎ 28 530) is in Vathy, at 25 Martiou 4, and is open

from 8.30 am to 2.30 pm on weekdays. The post office is on Smyrnis, four blocks from the waterfront. The OTE telephone office is on Plateia Iroön, behind the municipal gardens, and is open from 7.30 am to 3 pm.

Samos' telephone code is ☎ 0273.

Things to See & Do

Very little is left of the **ancient city** of Samos, on which the town of Pythagorio now stands. The Sacred Way, once flanked by 2000 statues, has now metamorphosed into the airport's runway.

The extraordinary **Evpalinos Tunnel** is the site's most impressive surviving relic. It was built in the 6th century BC by Evpalinos who was the chief engineer of the tyrant Polycrates. The one-km-long tunnel was dug by political prisoners and used as an aqueduct to bring water from the springs of Mt Ampelos. Part of it can still be explored. It's two km north of Pythagorio and is open daily, except Monday, from 8.30 am to 3 pm. Entry is 800 dr.

Vathy's **archaeological museum** is outstanding, with an impressive collection of statues, votives and pottery. It is open daily, except Monday, from 8.30 am to 3 pm. Admission is 800 dr.

The villages of **Manolates** and **Vourliotes** on the slopes of Mt Ampelos are excellent walking territory, as there are many marked pathways in the region.

Quiet beaches can be found on the south-west coast in the Marathokampos area.

Places to Stay & Eat

Pythagorio, where you'll disembark if you've come from Patmos, is touristy and expensive.

Vathy – 20 minutes away by bus – is cheaper. The friendly *Pension Vasso* (☎ 23 258) is open all year round and has singles/doubles/triples for 3000/5000/6000 dr with private bath. To get there from the quay, turn right onto the waterfront, left into Stamatiadou and walk up the steps. The owners also have a charming three-bed country cottage for rent, right by the sea in the unspoilt village of Livadaki, on the north coast. It costs 8000/10,000/12,000 dr a day for two/four/six people.

Back in Vathy, *Pension Avli* (☎ 22 939), a former convent girls' school, has doubles for 6500 dr. It's on Kalomiri, close to the port, two blocks back from the waterfront. Nearby,

Hotel Ionia (☎ 28 782) is cheap, with singles/doubles/triples for 2500/3500/4500 dr.

The popular *Taverna Gregory*, near the post office, is one of Greece's most authentic delights, serving good food at reasonable prices. On some nights three locals – the Tris Manolis – sing for their supper.

Getting There & Away

Air Samos has an international airport receiving European charter flights. There are also daily flights to Athens (16,100 dr).

Ferry There are ferries twice a week to Chios and Patmos, and also to Piraeus (4830 dr); some go via Paros and Naxos, others go via Mykonos. Avoid being hustled onto an excursion boat to Patmos. The normal ferry (2500 dr) is a quarter of the price.

There are daily boats to Kuşadası (for Ephesus) in Turkey, costing 11,000 dr one way and 14,000 dr return, including port tax. There are many travel agencies on the waterfront. For the port police, call ☎ 27 318.

Getting Around

To get to Vathy's bus station, turn left onto Lekadi, 250 metres south of Plateia Pythagora. Buses run to all the island's villages.

CHIOS Χίος

'Craggy Chios', as Homer described it, is less visited than Samos and almost as riotously fertile. Chios is famous for its mastic trees, which produce a resin used in chewing gum, and arrack, a liquor distilled from grain.

In 1822 an estimated 25,000 inhabitants of the island were massacred by the Turks.

Orientation & Information

he main town and port is Chios town, which is strident and unattractive; only the old Turkish quarter has any charm. It is, however, a good base from which to explore the island.

The municipal tourist office (☎ 44 389) is on Kanari, the main street running from the waterfront to Plateia Plastira in the town centre. The OTE telephone office is opposite the tourist office. The post office is on Rodokanaki, a block back from the waterfront.

Chios' telephone code is ☎ 0271.

Things to See

The **Philip Argenti Museum**, next to the cathedral in Chios town, contains exquisite embroideries and traditional costumes. It's open daily from 9 am to 1.30 pm except Sunday. Admission is 500 dr.

The **Nea Moni** (New Monastery), 14 km

west of Chios town, houses some of Greece's most important mosaics. They date from the 11th century and are among the finest examples of Byzantine art in Greece. It's open daily from 7 am to 1 pm and 4 to 6 pm; entry is 500 dr.

Pyrgi, 24 km from Chios town and the centre of the mastic-producing region, is one of Greece's most beautiful villages. The façades of its dwellings are decorated with intricate grey and white geometric patterns. **Emboreios**, six km south of Pyrgi, is an attractive, uncrowded black-pebble beach.

Places to Stay
Singles/doubles/triples with private bath and TV are available for 4000/6000/8000 dr at *Anesis Pension* (☎ 44 801). It is just off Aplotaras, the main shopping street, parallel to the waterfront. *Hotel Filoxenia* (☎ 22 813), signposted from the waterfront, has simple singles/doubles for 4800/6500 dr.

Places to Eat
Right opposite the ferry disembarkation point on Neorion is *Ouzeri Theodosiou*, a popular old-style establishment. For the freshest possible fish, try *Iakovos Taverna* on the northern arm of the harbour by the fish terminal.

Getting There & Away
There are daily flights from Chios to Athens (14,600 dr) and twice-weekly flights to Thessaloniki (21,100 dr).

Ferries sail twice a week to Samos (2100 dr) and Piraeus (4800 dr) via Lesvos, and once a week to Thessaloniki via Lesvos and Limnos. There are also four boats a week to the small island of Psara, west of Chios, and in summer daily excursion boats to the even smaller island of Inousses. In summer daily boats travel to Çeşme in Turkey; tickets cost 11,000 dr one way and 14,000 dr return. You can contact the port police on ☎ 44 433.

Getting Around
The bus station is on Plateia Vournakio, just south of Plateia Plastira. Blue buses go to Vrontados, Karyes and Karfas, all near Chios town. Green buses go to Emboreios, Pyrgi and Mesta.

LESVOS (MYTILINI) Λέσβος (Μυτιλήνη)
Lesvos, the third-largest island in the North-Eastern Aegean, has always been a centre of artistic and philosophical achievement and creativity. Sappho, one of the greatest poets of ancient Greece, lived here and today the island is visited by many lesbians paying homage to her. Lesvos was also the birthplace of the composer Terpander and the poet Arion – an influence on both Sophocles and Euripides – and boasted Aristotle and Epicurus among the teachers at its exceptional school of philosophy. It remains to this day a spawning ground for innovative ideas in the arts and politics.

Mytilini
Mytilini, the capital and port of Lesvos, is a large workaday town built around two harbours. All passenger ferries dock at the southern harbour. The tourist police (☎ 22 776) are at the entrance to the quay and the EOT (☎ 42 511) is at James Aristakou 6. The post office is on Vournazon, west of the southern harbour, and the OTE is in the same street.

Mytilini's telephone code is ☎ 0251.

Things to See Mytilini's imposing **castle** was built in early Byzantine times and renovated in the 14th century. It is open daily, except Monday, from 8.30 am to 2.50 pm. The **archaeological museum**, one block north of the quay, is open Tuesday to Sunday from 8.30 am to 3 pm. Admission to both is 500 dr. Don't miss the **Theophilos Museum**, which houses the works of the prolific primitive painter Theophilos; it's open Tuesday to Sunday from 9 am to 1 pm. Entry is 250 dr.

Places to Stay & Eat Domatia owners belong to a cooperative called *Sappho Self-Catering Rooms in Mytilini*. Most of these domatia are in little side streets off Ermou, near the northern harbour. The nearest to the quay is the *Panorea Pension* (☎ 42 650), Komninaki 21, where doubles/triples cost 6800/8500 dr. *Thalia Rooms* (☎ 24 640) has doubles/triples for 7000/8000 dr. *Salina's Garden Rooms* (☎ 42 073), Fokeas 7, has doubles for 7500 dr with private bath.

The *Albatross Ouzeri*, on the corner of Ermou and Adramytiou, is worth a visit just for the experience. It's packed with paraphernalia and looks more like a junk shop than an eating establishment. The *Restaurant Averof*, in the middle of the southern waterfront, is a no-nonsense traditional eatery serving hearty Greek staples. The small, friendly *Ta Stroggylia*, at Komninaki 9, has wine barrels and good food.

Around the Island
Northern Lesvos is best known for its exquisitely preserved traditional town of **Mithymna**. Its neighbouring beach resort of **Petra**, six km south, is affected by low-key package tourism, while the villages surrounding **Mt Lepetymnos** are authentic, picturesque and worth a day or two of exploration.

Western Lesvos is a popular destination for lesbians who come on a kind of pilgrimage in honour of the poet Sappho. The beach resort of **Skala Eresou** is built over ancient Eresos, where she was born in 628 BC.

Southern Lesvos is dominated by 968-metre **Mt Olympus** and the pine forests that decorate its flanks. **Plomari**, a large traditional coastal village, is popular with visitors, and the picturesque village of **Agiasos** is a favourite day-trip destination with some fairly genuine artisan workshops.

Getting There & Away
Air There are three flights a day from Lesvos to Athens (15,800 dr), one a day to Thessaloniki (19,600 dr) and Limnos (12,700 dr) and two a week to Chios (7100 dr). The Olympic Airways office (☎ 28 659) is at Kavetsou 44.

Ferry In summer there are daily boats to Piraeus (12 hours, 5300 dr), some via Chios. There are three a week to Kavala (5100 dr) via Limnos and two a week to Thessaloniki (7000 dr). Ferries to Turkey cost 16,000 dr. From May there are hydrofoils to Limnos, Chios, Samos, Patmos, Kavala and Alexandroupolis. You can contact the port police on ☎ 47 888.

Getting Around
There are two bus stations in Mytilini, both by the harbour. The one for long-distance buses is just beyond the south-western end of Pavlou Kountouriotou. For local villages go to the northernmost section. There are many car and motorcycle-rental firms.

SAMOTHRAKI Σαμοθράκη
Until a decade ago, Samothraki was Greece's best kept secret, visited only by archaeologists and a few adventurers. But inevitably this wild, alluring island has been discovered by holidaymakers. Most people stick to the resorts of Kamariotissa, Therma and Pahia Ammos, leaving the rest of the island untouched.

Orientation & Information
Samothraki's port is Kamariotissa on the north-west coast. The main town, the Hora (also called Samothraki), is five km inland. There is no EOT office or tourist police, but the regular police (☎ 41 203) are in the Hora, near the kastro.

Samothraki's telephone code is ☎ 0551.

Things to See & Do
Sanctuary of the Great Gods This hushed, ancient site at Paleopolis is shrouded in mystery. No-one knows quite what went on here, only that it was a place of initiation into the cult of the Kabeiroi, the gods of fertility. They were believed to help seafarers, and to be initiated into their mysteries was seen as a safeguard against misfortune and in particular against shipwreck. Its winding pathways lead through lush shrubbery to extensive ruins.

The famous Winged Victory of Samothrace, which now has pride of place in the Louvre, was taken from here in the last century. The site's little museum is well laid out, and both the site and the museum are open Tuesday to Sunday from 8.30 am to 3 pm. Admission to each is 500 dr.

Mt Fengari Legend tells that it was from the summit of Mt Fengari (1611 metres) that Poseidon, god of the sea and of earthquakes, watched the progress of the Trojan War. A difficult climb, Mt Fengari should only be tackled by experienced trekkers. Guides can be hired in Therma for about 12,000 dr.

Walks The island is a walker's paradise. The glorious scenery combines the jagged rocks of Mt Fengari's slopes with shady groves of plane trees, bubbling waterfalls, gentle undulating hills and meadows ablaze with wild flowers.

From the kastro ruin in the Hora, a dirt track

leads to Paleopolis. It takes about an hour to get there.

Samothraki's only sandy beach, **Pahia Ammos**, a 700-metre-long stretch of sand sheltered by two rocky headlands, can be reached along a seven-km dirt track from Lakoma.

Places to Stay & Eat

There are several private camping grounds at Therma and free camp sites at Pahia Ammos. There are showers on the beach.

Samothraki's few hotels are expensive. The most pleasant place to stay is the Hora. Its Turkish-era houses are built in amphitheatre fashion on two adjacent mountain slopes and the town is totally authentic. There are no hotels, just rooms in private houses.

Cheap eateries line Kamariotissa's waterfront. The *psistaria* in Hora's main square serves large helpings of barbecued meat. The *nameless taverna* on the left of the nameless street which leads up to the kastro has delicious vegetable stews.

Getting There & Around

See Getting There & Away under Alexandroupolis in the Northern Greece section. There is one boat a week between Kavala and Samothraki. To contact the port police, call ☎ 41 305.

Buses run from Kamariotissa to the Hora, Lakoma, Profitis Ilias, Paleopolis and Therma. In summer, caïques sail between Kamariotissa and Pahia Ammos. There is a motorcycle-rental outlet opposite the harbour.

Sporades Σποράδες

The Sporades group comprises the lush, pine-forested islands of Skiathos, Skopelos and Alonnisos, south of the Halkidiki Peninsula, and far-flung Skyros, off Evia.

Getting There & Away

Air Skiathos receives lots of charter flights from northern Europe. In summer, there are up to three flights a day from Athens to Skiathos (15,300 dr) and daily flights to Skyros (13,900

dr). There's also the odd flight between the two (9100 dr).

Ferry Skiathos, Skopelos and Alonnisos have frequent ferry services to the mainland ports of Volos and Agios Konstantinos, as well as one or two a week to Kymi (Evia), via Skyros.

There's a bewildering array of hydrofoil services buzzing around the islands in summer. They include three services a week connecting Skyros and the other islands.

SKIATHOS Σκίαθος

Skiathos is tagged the Mykonos of the Sporades, which means it's crowded and expensive. If you decide to go, however, the tourist police (☎ 23 172) on Papadiamanti 8, the port's main street, will help you to find accommodation. Ferries dock at Skiathos town.

Skiathos' telephone code is ☎ 0427.

SKOPELOS Σκόπελος

Skopelos is less commercialised than Skiathos, but following hot on its trail. Skopelos town is an attractive place of white houses built on a hillside, with mazes of narrow streets and stairways leading up to the kastro. **Glossa**, the island's other town, lying inland in the north, is similarly appealing with fewer concessions to tourism. There is no tourist office or tourist police. The post office is signposted from the port, as is the OTE, although both are well hidden in the labyrinth of alleyways behind the waterfront.

Skopelos' telephone code is ☎ 0424.

Things to See

Four km from Skopelos town, **Staphylos** is a decent beach that gets very crowded; over a headland is **Velanio**, the island's designated nudist beach.

The two-km stretch of tiny pebbles at **Milia**, 10 km further on, is considered the island's best beach.

Places to Stay & Eat

The lovely traditional *Pension Lina* (☎ 22 637), with oak-beamed ceilings, brass bedsteads, and carpet throughout, has doubles/triples for 10,000/12,000 dr with private bath. The pension is on the waterfront, opposite the taxi stand. *Pension Sotos* (☎ 22 549), also on the waterfront 150 metres from the ferry pier, is another charming alternative. Spacious doubles/triples are 10,000/12,000 dr. There are many rooms to rent in private houses.

H Klimataria restaurant, opposite the ferry pier, has impressive food at reasonable prices.

Getting There & Away
There are frequent ferries to Volos (2820 dr) and Agios Konstantinos (3480 dr). These boats also call at Alonnisos and Skiathos. Many hydrofoil services to Skopelos also call at Loutraki, the port for Glossa.

Getting Around
There are frequent buses from Skopelos town to Glossa, stopping at the beaches on the way.

You can hire cars and motorcycles from Rent-a-Car Bike (☎ 22 986), which is at the southern end of the port, next to the Hotel Lena.

ALONNISOS Αλόννησος
Alonnisos is the least visited of these three islands. In 1963 the island suffered a major earthquake which devastated the inland Hora, and villagers were forced to move to the harbour town of Patitiri.

Alonnisos' telephone code is ☎ 0424.

Things to See & Do
One of the best beaches is **Kokkinokastro** (red castle), so named because the earth around here is red. Other good beaches line the coast. Alonnisos is an ideal island for walking. A winding path starting from just beyond Pension Galini in Patitiri leads within 40 minutes to the Hora. **Gialia Beach**, on the west coast, is a 20-minute walk from the Hora.

Places to Stay & Eat
Outstanding budget accommodation is offered by *Pension Galini* (☎ 65 573). It is well kept and beautifully furnished with lots of pine and has a flower-festooned terrace. Doubles/triples are 8000/9500 dr with private bath, breakfast included. Spacious, well-equipped apartments for five/six people are also available for 13,000/15,000 dr. The pension is on the left, 400 metres up Pelasgon, the main road leading up from the waterfront, to the left of the port. There are also many domatia in Patitiri.

On the waterfront, *To Dixty Taverna* has a larger selection of dishes than most.

Getting There & Away
There are frequent ferries to Volos (3180 dr) and Agios Konstantinos (3850 dr), via Skiathos and Skopelos.

Getting Around
In summer, caïques take passengers to the beaches of Milia, Hrysi Milia and Kokkinokastro.

Ionian Islands
Τα Επτάνησα

The Ionian islands stretch down the west coast of Greece from Corfu in the north to remote Kythira, off the southern tip of the Peloponnese.

Getting There & Away
Air There are lots of charter flights to Corfu from Northern Europe in summer, as well as a few flights to Kefallonia and Zakynthos. Olympic has daily flights from Athens to Corfu, Zakynthos and Kefallonia.

Ferry Most ferries between Italy and Patras call at Corfu. In summer, there are also direct services from Brindisi to Ithaki, Kefallonia, Paxoi and Zakynthos and from Bari to Kefallonia.

For inter-island ferries and ferries to the mainland, see the Getting There & Away sections under the respective islands.

CORFU Κέρκυρα
Corfu is the most important island in the group, with a population of more than 100,000. With its green hills and valleys of graceful cypress trees and olive groves, many visitors rate it Greece's most beautiful island.

Corfu Town
The old town of Corfu, wedged between two fortresses, occupies a peninsula on the island's east coast. The narrow alleyways of high shuttered tenements in mellow ochres and pinks are an immediate reminder of the town's long association with Venice.

Orientation & Information The town's old fortress (Palaio Frourio) stands on an eastern promontory, separated from the town by an

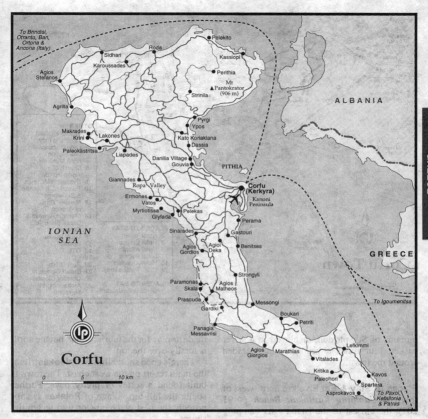

To Brindisi,
Otranto, Bari,
Ortona &
Ancona (Italy)

Agios
Stefanos

Sidhari

Karoussades

Roda

Pelekito

Kassiopi

Perithia

Mt
Pantokrator
(906 m)

Strinila

ALBANIA

Agrilla

Makrades
Krini

Lakones

Paleokastritsa

Liapades

Pyrgi
Ypos

Kato Koriakiana

Dassia

Danilia Village

Gouvia

PITHIA

Giannades

Ropa
Valley

Ermones

Vatos

Myrtiotissa

Glyfada

Pelekas

Corfu
(Kerkyra)

Kanoni
Peninsula

PITHIA

Perama

Sinarades

Gastouri

Agios
Gordios

Agioi
Deka

Benitses

GREECE

IONIAN
SEA

Strongyli

Paramonas

Skala

Agios
Matheos

Prasouda

Gardiki

Messongi

To Igoumenitsa

Boukari

Petriti

Panagia
Messavrisi

Agios
Giorgios

Marathias

Lefkimmi

Vitalades

Kritika
Paleohori

Kavos

Asprokavos

Spartera

To Paxoi,
Kefallonia
& Patras

Corfu

0   5   10 km

GREECE

area of parks and gardens known as the Spianada. The new fortress (Neo Frourio) lies to the north-west. Ferries dock at the new port, just beyond the new fortress. The long-distance bus station in on Avrami, just inland from the port.

The EOT office (☎ 37 520) is on Rizospaston Voulefton, between the OTE and the post office, and the tourist police (☎ 30 265) are at Plateia Neou Frouriou 1. All the major Greek banks are in town, including the National Bank on the corner of Voulgareos and Theotoki. American Express (☎ 30 661) is represented by Greek Skies Tours at Kapodistriou 20A.

Corfu's telephone code is ☎ 0661.

The Corfu General Hospital (☎ 45 811) is on Polithroni Kostanda.

Things to See The **archaeological museum**, Vraili 5, houses a collection of finds from Mycenaean to classical times. The star attraction is the pediment from the Temple of Artemis, decorated with gorgons. Opening times are Tuesday to Saturday from 8.45 am to 3 pm and Sunday from 9.30 am to 2.30 pm; admission is 800 dr.

The **Church of Agios Spiridon**, Corfu's most famous church, has an elaborately decorated interior. Pride of place is given to the

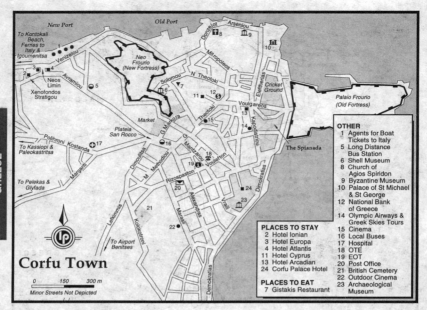

OTHER
1 Agents for Boat Tickets to Italy
5 Long Distance Bus Station
6 Shell Museum
8 Church of Agios Spiridon
9 Byzantine Museum
10 Palace of St Michael & St George
12 National Bank of Greece
14 Olympic Airways & Greek Skies Tours
15 Cinema
16 Local Buses
17 Hospital
18 OTE
19 EOT
20 Post Office
21 British Cemetery
22 Outdoor Cinema
23 Archaeological Museum

PLACES TO STAY
2 Hotel Ionian
3 Hotel Europa
4 Hotel Atlantis
11 Hotel Cyprus
13 Hotel Arcadian
24 Corfu Palace Hotel

PLACES TO EAT
7 Gistakis Restaurant

Corfu Town

0   150   300 m

Minor Streets Not Depicted

remains of St Spiridon, displayed in a silver casket; four times a year they are paraded around the town.

Places to Stay & Eat Five km north-west of town is *Camping Kontokali Beach* (☎ 91 202), the closest of the island's six camping grounds. Take bus No 7 from Plateia San Rocco. Next door is the co-managed *youth hostel* (☎ 91 292) where beds are 1200 dr per person.

There are no decent budget places in town. Most travellers wind up at the *Hotel Europa* (☎ 39 304), mainly because it's right next to the port. It charges 5500/6000 dr for reasonable singles/doubles. A better choice is the *Hotel Cyprus*, between the fortresses at Agiou Paterou 13. Doubles are 5500 dr.

Gistakis Restaurant, Solomou 20, serves excellent Corfiot regional food. Main dishes are priced from 900 dr.

Around the Island
There's hardly anywhere in Corfu that hasn't

made its play for the tourist dollar, but the north is totally over the top.

There's good snorkelling at **Paleokastritsa**, the main resort on the west coast. The town is built round a series of pretty bays. Further south, the hill-top village of **Pelekas** is supposedly the best place on Corfu to watch the sunset.

Many backpackers head straight for the *Pink Palace* (☎ 53 103/104), a huge complex of restaurants, bars and budget rooms that tumbles down a hillside outside the village of **Agios Gordios**. It charges 4500 dr per day for bed, breakfast and dinner. The place is open from April to November, and staff meet the boats.

There's a road from the village of **Strinila** to the top of **Mt Pantokrator** (906 metres), Corfu's highest mountain. You'll find a monastery – and stupendous views over to the mountains of southern Albania.

Getting There & Away
Air Olympic Airways flies to Athens (19,100 dr) three times a day and to Thessaloniki

(19,600 dr) twice a week. The Olympic Airways office (☎ 38 694) is at Kapodistriou 20.

Bus There are daily buses to Athens and Thessaloniki from the Avrami terminal in Corfu town. The fare of 8100 dr to Athens includes the ferry to Igoumenitsa. The trip takes 11 hours.

Ferry There are hourly ferries to Igoumenitsa (1½ hours, 850 dr) and a daily ferry to Paxoi. In summer, there are daily services to Patras (10 hours, 4900 dr) on the international ferries that call at Corfu on their way from Italy. (See Getting There & Away at the start of the Ionian Islands section.)

Getting Around
Buses for villages close to Corfu town leave from Plateia San Rocco. Services to other destinations leave from the bus terminal on Avrami. The EOT gives out a schedule.

ITHAKI Ιθάκη
Ithaki is the fabled home of Odysseus, the hero of Homer's *Odyssey*, who pined for his island during his journeys to far-flung lands. It's a quiet place with some isolated coves. From the main town of Vathy you can walk to the **Arethusa Fountain**, the fabled site of Odysseus' meeting with the swineherd Eumaeus on his return to Ithaki. Take water with you, as the fountain dries up in summer.

Ithaki has daily ferries to the mainland ports of Patras and Astrakos, as well as daily services to Kefallonia and Lefkada.

KEFALLONIA Κεφαλλονιά
Tourism remains relatively low-key on mountainous Kefallonia, the largest island of the Ionian group. Resort hotels are confined to the areas near the capital, the beaches in the south-west, Argostoli and the airport. Public transport is very limited, apart from regular services between Argostoli and the main port of Sami, 25 km away on the east coast. The **Melissani Cave**, signposted off the Argostoli road four km from Sami, is an underground lake lit by a small hole in the cave ceiling. The nearby **Drogarati Cave** has some impressive stalactites.

There are daily ferries from Sami to Patras (2½ hours, 2725 dr), as well as from Argostoli and the south-eastern port of Poros to Kyllini in the Peloponnese. There are also connections to Ithaki, Lefkada and Zakynthos.

ZAKYNTHOS Ζάκυνθος
Zakynthos, or Zante, is a beautiful island surrounded by great beaches – so it's hardly surprising that the place is completely overrun by package groups. Its capital and port, Zakynthos town, is an imposing old Venetian town that has been painstakingly reconstructed after being levelled by an earthquake in 1953.

Some of the best beaches are around **Laganas Bay** in the south, which is where endangered loggerhead turtles come ashore to lay their eggs in August – at the peak of the tourist invasion. Conservation groups are urging people to stay away.

There are regular ferries between Zakynthos and Kyllini in the Peloponnese.

Ireland

This chapter covers both the independent Republic of Ireland and Northern Ireland, which forms part of the United Kingdom.

Ireland is one of the most sparsely populated and least industrialised nations in Western Europe. It's green, relaxed and incredibly friendly, making it a superb holiday destination. But behind those 'smiling Irish eyes' and lively pubs lies one of the longest and most tragic histories in the region.

That long history is easy to trace: from Stone Age passage tombs and ring forts, through medieval monasteries and castles, right up to the stately homes and splendid Georgian architecture of the 18th and 19th centuries. The tragic side is almost as easy to spot; the reminders of Ireland's long and difficult relationship with neighbouring Britain are ubiquitous.

What's in a Name?
When the distinction between Ireland the island and Ireland the nation needs to be made in this chapter, the country is referred to as the Republic of Ireland. Northern Ireland is usually referred to as such. In your travels you may hear the Republic of Ireland referred to as Eire, the Irish Republic, the Republic, southern Ireland or 'the south'. Northern Ireland may be dubbed 'the north' or Ulster. The historical province of Ulster once comprised nine counties. With the partition of Ireland, six of those were ceded to Northern Ireland while the remainder went to the Republic.

Facts about the Country

HISTORY
Ireland Alone
The many Stone Age sites dotted around the island clearly indicate Ireland's long history, and the monastic ruins, round towers and crumbling churches recall the Christian centuries with equal clarity.

Fierce and dashing Celtic warriors and adventurers probably reached Ireland from Continental Europe around 300 BC and were

well ensconced by 100 BC. The Romans never got further west than Wales, but Christianity arrived in Ireland around the 5th century, and the Irish take pleasure in claiming that a raiding party brought St Patrick, the patron saint and national hero, from England as a slave. As the Dark Ages enveloped Europe, Ireland became an outpost of European civilisation – a land of saints, scholars and missionaries, its thriving monasteries producing beautiful illuminated manuscripts, some of which survive to this day.

From the end of the 8th century, the rich monasteries were targets of raids by Vikings until they too began to settle in this green, gentle land. At the height of their power the Vikings ruled Dublin, Waterford and Limerick, but they were eventually defeated by the legendary Celtic hero Brian Ború, the king of Munster, at the battle of Clontarf in 1014.

The British Arrive
In 1169 the Norman conquest of England, by then more than a century old, spread to Ireland when Henry II, fearful of the growing power

IRELAND

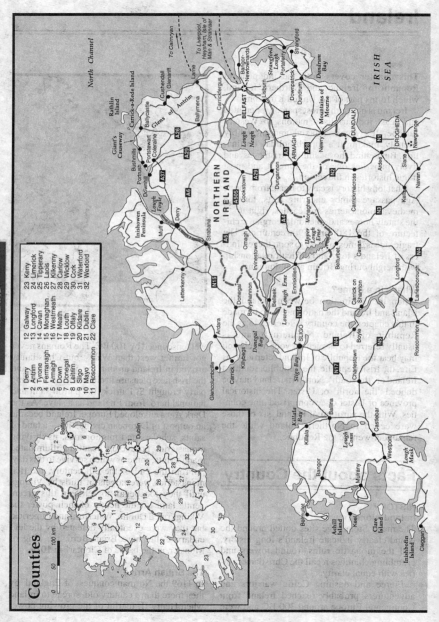

Counties

0   50   100 km

1	Derry	12	Galway	23	Kerry
2	Antrim	13	Longford	24	Limerick
3	Tyrone	14	Cavan	25	Tipperary
4	Fermanagh	15	Monaghan	26	Laois
5	Armagh	16	Westmeath	27	Kilkenny
6	Down	17	Meath	28	Carlow
7	Donegal	18	Louth	29	Wicklow
8	Leitrim	19	Offaly	30	Cork
9	Sligo	20	Kildare	31	Waterford
10	Mayo	21	Dublin	32	Wexford
11	Roscommon	22	Clare		

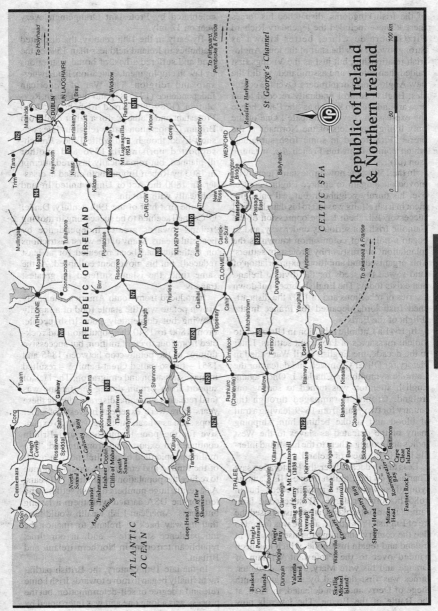

IRELAND

Republic of Ireland & Northern Ireland

0   50   100 km

St George's Channel

CELTIC SEA

ATLANTIC OCEAN

REPUBLIC OF IRELAND

To Holyhead
To Fishguard, Pembroke & France
Rosslare Harbour
To Swansea & France

Malahide
DUBLIN
DUN LAOGHAIRE
Bray
Wicklow
Enniskerry
Powerscourt
Rathdrum
Arklow
Glendalough
Mt Lugnaquilla (924 m)
Gorey
Enniscorthy
WEXFORD
Wellington Bridge
Ballyhack
New Ross
Thomastown
Passage East
Waterford
CARLOW
KILKENNY
Callan
Carrick-on-Suir
CLONMEL
Durrow
Cahir
Dungarvan
Ardmore
Cashel
Mitchelstown
Youghal
Fermoy
Tipperary
Thurles
Roscrea
Birr
Portlaoise
Nenagh
Kilmallock
CORK
Cobh
Mallow
Blarney
Kinsale
Limerick
Rathluirc (Charleville)
Bandon
Clonakilty
Foynes
Tarbert
Killarney
Kenmare
Skibbereen
Baltimore
Cape Clear Island
Fastnet Rock
Mizen Head
Sheep's Head
Bantry
Glengarriff
Beara Peninsula
Kenmare River
Bantry Bay
Roaringwater Bay
Mt Carrantuohill (1038 m)
Killorglin
Glenbeigh
Ring of Kerry
Iveragh Peninsula
Cahirciveen
Waterville
Valentia Island
Skellig Michael Island
Durcan
Dingle
Dingle Bay
Dingle Peninsula
Blasket Islands
TRALEE
Kilrush
Kilkee
Loop Head
Mouth of the Shannon
Shannon
Ennis
Ennistymon
Lisdoonvarna
The Burren
Cliffs of Moher
Doolin
Inisheer
Inishmaan
Inishmór
Aran Islands
North Sound
South Sound
Galway Bay
Spiddal
Rossaveal
Salthill
GALWAY
Kinvarra
Tuam
Cong
Lough Corrib
Clifden
Connemara
ATHLONE
Moate
Clonmacnois
Tullamore
Mullingar
Trim
Tara
Maynooth
Naas
Kildare
Kilcullen
N1
N2
N3
N7
N9
N6
N7
N8
N10
N25
N8
N24
N20
N21
N22

of the Irish kingdoms, dispatched his forces there. (These included the legendary Richard FitzGilbert de Clare, better known as Strongbow.) It was the start of the long Anglo-Irish relationship, but just as the Vikings first raided then settled and assimilated, so did the new Anglo-Norman intruders. Over the centuries, English control gradually receded to an area around Dublin known as 'the Pale', hence the expression 'beyond the pale'. One of the only living reminders of the Normans is the prefix 'Fitz' found in some Irish surnames, which comes from the French *fils*, meaning 'son (of)'.

In the 1500s, the now-Protestant Henry VIII moved once again to enforce English control over his unruly neighbour, but real entanglement in Irish affairs was left to his daughter and successor, Elizabeth I. The oppression of the Catholic Irish got seriously under way, and so began a policy of colonisation known as the 'plantation' by trustworthy Protestant settlers. This organised and ambitious expropriation of land sowed the seeds for the divided Ireland that exists today. The English forces put down a series of rebellions and in 1607 the disheartened Irish lords departed for France in the 'Flight of the Earls'.

In 1641 a Catholic rebellion in Ulster led to violent massacres of Protestant settlers. Later in the decade, the English Civil War ended in victory for Oliver Cromwell and defeat for the Catholic sympathiser Charles I. Once again, English attention was turned to sorting out Ireland. Cromwell rampaged through the country for two years from 1649, leaving a trail of blood and smoke behind him, shipping many of the defeated as slaves to the West Indies and exiling others to the harsh and infertile land in the west of Ireland.

Less than a decade later, the Restoration saw Charles II on the English throne. His Catholic sympathies were kept firmly in check, but in 1685 his brother James II succeeded him. James' more outspoken Catholicism raised the ire of English Protestants, and he was forced to flee the country, intending to raise an army in Ireland and regain his throne, which had been handed over to the Protestant William of Orange and his wife Mary, James' daughter. James was first delayed by the eight-month Siege of Derry and then defeated, in 1690, at the Battle of the Boyne. The latter is now celebrated by Protestant Orangemen every year on 12 July.

By early in the 18th century, the dispirited Catholics in Ireland held less than 15% of the land and suffered a host of brutal restrictions by law in employment, education, land ownership and religion. The War of American Independence (1775-83) and the French Revolution (1789-99) stirred Irish hopes, both Protestant and Catholic, for a fairer deal from Britain. Cooperation across religious lines was short-lived, though, and Wolfe Tone's French-supported uprising in 1796 and another ill-planned, but romantically inspired attempt in 1803 by Robert Emmet both ended in disaster. In 1800 the Act of Union united Ireland politically with Britain.

In the first half of the 19th century, Daniel O'Connell seemed to be succeeding in moving Ireland towards greater independence by peaceful means. Many of the worst restrictions on Catholics had been repealed (or at least reduced), but his movement collapsed. At the same time, the island suffered its greatest tragedy.

Introduced from South America, the easily grown potato was the staple food of a rapidly growing but desperately poor Irish people. From 1800 to 1840 the population had rocketed from four to eight million, but successive failures of the potato crop between 1845 and 1851 – the so-called Great Famine – resulted in mass starvation and emigration. The lack of support from Britain during the famine was (and remains) a national disgrace; during these years there were excellent harvests of other crops such as wheat, but these were too expensive for the poor to purchase and Britain continued to export food from Ireland. Two million people died or quit Ireland as a result of the famine and emigration would continue to reduce the population for another 100 years. As a result, huge numbers of Irish settlers who left for the USA carried with them a lasting bitterness. American-Irish wealth would later find its way back to Ireland to finance the independence struggle – and, in our time, republican terrorism in Northern Ireland and Britain.

In the late 19th century, the British parliament finally began to move towards Irish home rule and a degree of self-determination, but the process was a long one and was interrupted by

WWI and the Ulster question. In the north of the island, the Protestant majority bitterly opposed the move, fearing eventual minority status in a largely Catholic country.

Ireland might still have moved, slowly but peacefully, towards some sort of accommodation were it not for a bungled uprising in 1916. Though it is now celebrated as a glorious bid for freedom, the so-called Easter Rising was, in fact, heavy with rhetoric, light on planning and decidedly lacking in public support. The British response was just as badly conceived. After the insurrection had been put down, a long, drawn-out series of trials and executions – 15 in all – transformed the ringleaders from troublemakers to martyrs and roused international support for Irish independence.

The Road to Independence

In 1919 a guerrilla war broke out, pitting the Irish political movement Sinn Féin ('We Ourselves' or 'Ourselves Alone') and its military wing, the Irish Republican Army (IRA), against the British. The increasingly harsh responses of the notorious Black & Tans further roused anti-British sentiment, and atrocity was met with atrocity until the Anglo-Irish Treaty was signed in 1921, creating the Irish Free State. 'I signed my death warrant,' acknowledged the charismatic IRA leader Michael Collins, for numerous strings were attached to the treaty and the six counties of Northern Ireland were excluded. Ulster had been granted its own parliament in Belfast the year before.

Ireland Since Partition

A bitter civil war followed between those Irish who wanted to accept the agreement as a reasonable compromise and those who continued to seek complete independence for the entire island. The issue at the time was not so much the future of the six Ulster counties, but rather the dominion status of the new state and the need to swear allegiance to the British crown. Within a year, Collins was assassinated.

By 1923 the civil war had ground to a halt, and for nearly 50 years development in the Republic of Ireland was slow and relatively peaceful. The irksome clauses in the treaty, giving Britain a continuing link to Ireland, were one by one jettisoned and the Republic of Ireland left the British Commonwealth in 1949. After WWII, during which the Republic remained neutral, emigration and a declining population finally began to abate.

In the north, however, problems continued to mount. The Protestant majority in Ulster made sure that its rule was absolute by systematically excluding Catholics from power wherever possible, and this 'jobs for the boys' mentality led to the formation of an initially non-sectarian civil-rights movement in 1967. Violent Protestant opposition to the movement eventually required a British army presence in 1969 to keep the sides apart, and soon the long-hibernating IRA reappeared and the struggle for a united Ireland was once more under way.

'The Troubles', as the internecine violence in Ulster has always been called in Ireland, rolled back and forth throughout the 1970s and into the 1980s. The Royal Ulster Constabulary (RUC) was reorganised and retrained, while the IRA split into 'official' and 'provisional' wings from which sprang even more extreme republican organisations like the Irish National Liberation Army (INLA). Protestant loyalist paramilitary organisations arose in opposition, and brutality was met with brutality.

Meanwhile, negotiations toward a possible settlement continued. In 1985 the Anglo-Irish Agreement gave the Dublin government an official consultative role in Northern Irish affairs for the first time. The Downing Street Declaration of December 1993, signed by Britain and the Republic, moved matters forward, with Britain admitting that it had no 'selfish, economic or military interest' in preserving the division of Ireland.

The announcement of a 'permanent cessation of violence' on behalf of the IRA by Sinn Féin leader Gerry Adams in August 1994 offered the almost unimagined prospect of a real end to political violence in Ulster. When Protestant paramilitary forces responded with their own cease-fire in October, the chances of a lasting peace became far greater than at any time in over a generation. Most British troops were withdrawn to barracks and roadblocks were removed.

In 1995 the British and Irish governments published two 'framework documents' intended to act as a basis for discussion on the way forward. The main sticking point for the Republicans was that British Prime Minister

John Major's Conservative government refused to allow all-party talks to start until the IRA first 'decommissioned' their weapons. The IRA argued that no arms could be given up until all British troops had been withdrawn and political prisoners freed.

As history has shown time and again, 18 months of peace in Ireland is a lifetime elsewhere and on a cold Friday evening in February 1996, it was shattered by an IRA bomb in the Docklands area of east London, killing two men, wounding scores more and causing millions of pounds' worth of property damage. The IRA called off its cease-fire and a series of other IRA bombs shook London and Manchester.

With the refusal of the IRA to restore the cease-fire, 'all-party' talks on Ulster's future convened in June 1996 with representatives from Britain, the Republic and Northern Ireland but without the participation of Sinn Féin. At the time of writing, there had been no breakthrough and the success of the negotiations and possibility of genuine peace in this sad and troubled land seemed ever more distant.

GEOGRAPHY & ECOLOGY

Ireland is divided into 32 counties: 26 in the south and six in the north. The island measures 84,421 sq km (about 83% is the Republic) and stretches 486 km north to south and 275 km east to west. The jagged coastline extends for 5631 km. The midlands of Ireland is composed of flat, generally rich farmland or raised bog, huge swaths of brown peat rapidly being depleted for fuel. While the land gets less arable as one approaches the western seaboard, it also becomes more scenic. Cliffs and mountains – Carrantuohill (1038 metres) on the Iveragh Peninsula, County Kerry, is the highest – add grandeur to the seascapes. The Shannon Estuary and Galway Bay form the widest breaches along the western coastline and the River Shannon, the longest in Ireland, flows for 259 km before emptying into the Atlantic west of Limerick.

Ireland's rivers and lakes are well-stocked with fish such as salmon and trout, and the island is home to some three dozen mammal species, including the Irish hare and Irish stoat. The island is home or host to a wide range of locally breeding and migrating birds – some 380 species – with the coastlines especially rich in seabirds. The Office of Public Works (OPW) maintains five national parks and 75 nature reserves in the Republic; the National Trust oversees 26 nature reserves in Northern Ireland. The conservation of Ireland's bogs is a recent phenomenon.

GOVERNMENT & POLITICS

The Republic of Ireland has a parliamentary system of government. The lower house of parliament (Oireachtas) is known as the Dáil and its 166 members are elected by a system of proportional representation; the prime minister is the Taoiseach (pronounced 'teashock'). The 60-strong upper house is called the Seanad (Senate), and it basically rubber-stamps Dáil legislation. The president of Ireland (Uachtarán na hÉireann) is elected for seven years. Though the post lacks political power and is limited to two terms, Mary Robinson's current tenure, which began in 1990, has injected a healthy dose of liberalism into an otherwise highly conservative political structure.

The main political parties in the Republic are Fianna Fáil and Fine Gael, although the Labour Party has managed to capitalise on the growing disenchantment with these two traditional power brokers. Two other parties of note are the Liberal Progressive Democrats, which split from Fianna Fáil in the mid-1980s, and the socialist Democratic Left.

Northern Ireland has been governed from London since its ineffective parliament at Stormont was abolished in 1972. The main Protestant parties are the Ulster Unionists and the controversial Ian Paisley's Democratic Unionists. Catholic parties are the middle-of-the-road Social Democratic & Labour Party, and Sinn Féin, the political wing of the IRA led by Gerry Adams, which has never won more than 12% of the vote in Ulster elections. A total of 17 MPs from Northern Ireland sit in Westminster.

ECONOMY

The Republic of Ireland is still basically an agricultural country although there has been much light-industrial investment since the 1970s. Tourism is an enormously important activity (worth IR£1.4 billion a year), and Ireland now attracts increasing numbers of visitors from all over Western Europe as well as from the traditionally Irish-linked, English-speaking nations. Inflation is relatively low at around 3%, but unemployment accounts for some 14% of the workforce. Ireland joined the European Community (now European Union) in 1973 and has received upwards of US$42 billion in subsidies since then.

Northern Ireland's shipbuilding and other great Industrial Revolution activities have declined dramatically, but new industries have developed and, of course, the region is heavily supported financially by Britain. Almost 37% of the working population is employed in one way or another by the government. Northern Ireland suffers from an unemployment rate of about 13.5%, which is higher than the British average.

POPULATION & PEOPLE

The total population of Ireland is just over five million – 3.571 million in the south and 1.577 million in the north. The remarkable thing about this figure is that it is considerably less than two centuries ago when eight million people made their home here. Deaths during the famine (1845-51) and large-scale emigration for the next 100 years reduced the population by some 35%. It was not until the 1960s that Ireland's population finally began to increase again.

The major cities are metropolitan Dublin with just over one million inhabitants, Belfast with 280,000, Cork with 174,000, Limerick with 75,000 and Galway with 51,000.

ARTS

Music

Traditional Irish music, played on instruments such as the *bodhrán* (a flat, goatskin drum), *uilleann* (or 'elbow') pipes, flute and fiddle, is an aspect of Irish culture that visitors are most likely to encounter. Almost every town and village in Ireland seems to have a pub renowned for its traditional music, and a visit is very worthwhile. Of the Irish music groups, perhaps the best known are the Chieftains, the Dubliners, Clannad, Altan and the wilder Pogues. The Irish are equally keen on country & western and rock music. Among popular Irish singers/musicians who have made it on the international stage are Van Morrison, Enya,

Sinéad O'Connor, Bob Geldof, U2 and the Cranberries.

Literature

The Irish have made a greater impact on literature than they have on most other arts. Important writers include Oscar Wilde, WB Yeats, George Bernard Shaw, Sean O'Casey, James Joyce, Samuel Beckett and, more recently, Roddy Doyle, whose *Paddy Clarke Ha Ha Ha* won the Booker Prize in 1993, and the Ulster-born Séamus Heaney, called 'the greatest poet in English since Yeats', who was awarded the Nobel Prize for Literature in 1995. Earlier Irish Nobel laureates include Shaw (1925), WB Yeats (1938) and Beckett (1969).

Architecture

Ireland is packed with archaeological sites, prehistoric graves, ruined monasteries, crumbling fortresses, abandoned manor houses and many other firm reminders of its long and often dramatic history. You may encounter the following terms on your travels:

cashel – a stone ring fort or *rath*
dolmen – a portal tomb or Stone Age grave consisting of stone 'pillars' supporting a stone roof or capstone
high cross – tall Christian stone cross dating from the 8th to 12th centuries with high-relief figures usually depicting Biblical characters and stories
ogham stone – memorial stone of the 4th to 9th century, marked on its edge with groups of straight lines or notches to represent the Latin alphabet
passage tomb – megalithic mound tomb with a narrow stone passage leading to a burial chamber
ringfort or **rath** – circular fort, originally constructed of earth and timber, later made of stone
round tower – a tall tower or belfry built as a lookout and place of refuge from the Vikings

CULTURE

The Irish are an easy-going, loquacious, fun-loving people. They are used to tourists and there are few social taboos; the old dictum that politics and religion should be avoided at the dinner table would leave most Irish households with nothing to talk about! In the north, people have been wary to discuss the Troubles while in the Republic the subject is more likely to produce resigned indifference, but this is changing. Though Irish people like to talk (and talk), they don't enjoy arguing and generally avoid confrontation. Do not take humorous Irish scepticism or sarcasm too seriously. Irish society is very homogeneous and people have relatively little experience with those of different races and cultures. Most people, especially in the countryside, tend to be socially conservative.

RELIGION

Religion has always played a major role in Irish history. Almost everybody is either Catholic or Protestant, with the south 92% Catholic and the north about 60% Protestant. The Jewish community in Ireland is tiny but long-established.

Though its 'special position' was removed from the Constitution in 1972, the Catholic Church still wields considerable power in the Republic. There is, however, a curious ambivalence towards it, and it is alternately treated with respect and sometimes passionate derision. Attending Mass is often more a social obligation than a spiritual experience. Though condom machines can be found everywhere nowadays, abortion remains illegal. A referendum to allow divorce in the Republic was approved in September 1995 and is now law.

LANGUAGE

Officially the Republic of Ireland is bilingual. English is spoken throughout the island, but there are still parts of western and southern Ireland known as the Gaeltacht where Irish – a Celtic language closely related to Scottish Gaelic and less so to Welsh – is still the native language. It's an attractive but difficult tongue with an orthographical (spelling) system that would have given Charles Berlitz apoplexy ('mh' is pronounced like 'v'; 'bhf' is a 'w'; 'dh' is like 'g'). Most roadsigns in the Republic are bilingual and in the Gaeltacht areas they appear in Irish only; see Appendix I – Alternative Place Names for assistance.

Some useful words in Irish you might come across include:

fáilte	welcome
garda (gardaí pl)	police
fir	men
go raibh maith agat	thank you
an lár	(town) centre
an leithreas	toilet
mná	women
siopa	shop

sláinte	health; cheers!
slán	goodbye

Facts for the Visitor

PLANNING

Climate & When to Go

Ireland has a relatively mild climate with a mean annual temperature of around 10°C. In January and February, average temperatures range from 4° to 7°C. Average maximums in July and August are from 14° to 16°C. May and June are the sunniest months while December is the gloomiest. The sea around Ireland is surprisingly warm for the latitude due to the influence of the Gulf Stream. Snow is relatively scarce – perhaps one or two flurries in winter in high-level areas.

It does tend to rain a lot in Ireland; even the drier parts of Ireland get rain on 150 days in a typical year, and it often rains every day for weeks on end. Annual rainfall is about 1000 mm a year, and there's much local terminology – a 'soft day' is a wet one – and humour about the rain.

The tourist season begins the weekend before St Patrick's Day (17 March) and is in full swing from Easter onward. In July and August the crowds will be the biggest and the prices the highest. In the quieter winter months, however, you may get miserable weather and many tourist facilities could be shut for the season.

Books & Maps

See the earlier Arts section for Ireland's substantial contribution to literature in the English language. Lonely Planet's *Ireland – a travel survival kit* offers a comprehensive guide to the country and its *Dublin City Guide* to the capital.

There are many good-quality maps of Ireland, including the Michelin *Ireland Motoring Map* No 405 (1:400,000) as well as the four-part Ordnance Survey Holiday Map series (1:250,000).

What to Bring

The Irish climate is changeable and even at the height of summer you should be prepared for cold weather and sudden rainfall. A raincoat and/or umbrella is an absolute necessity. Walkers should be particularly well prepared if they are crossing open country. Otherwise, Ireland presents few surprises. Dress is usually casual even in the cities.

SUGGESTED ITINERARIES
Depending on the length of your stay, you might want to see and do the following things:

Two days
Visit Dublin and perhaps a couple of places nearby – Powerscourt and Glendalough to the south, or New-grange, Mellifont and Monasterboice to the north.

One week
Visit Dublin, Newgrange, Mellifont, Monasterboice, the Burren and Kilkenny.

Two weeks
As above, plus the Ring of Kerry (Iveragh Peninsula), Killarney and Cork.

One month
With your own car you could cover all the main attractions around the coast. (This would be more difficult to achieve in the same time by bicycle or on public transport.)

Two months
You'd have time to explore most of Ireland thoroughly. You could do some walking as well.

HIGHLIGHTS
Scenery, Beaches & Coastline
There's a lot of natural beauty in Ireland but among the best is the scenery around the Ring of Kerry and the Dingle Peninsula, the barren stretches of the Burren, the rocky Aran Islands, and the Glens of Antrim in Northern Ireland.

Favourite stretches of coast include the Cliffs of Moher, the Connemara and Donegal coasts, and the Causeway Coast of Northern Ireland. There are some fine beaches (and marginally warmer water) around the south-east coast and some great surfing around the west and north-west coasts.

Museums, Castles & Houses
Trinity College's Old Library with the ancient Book of Kells is a must-see, but Dublin also has the fine National Museum and National Gallery. Belfast has the Ulster Museum and the extensive Ulster Folk Museum just outside the city.

Ireland is littered with castles and forts of various types and in various stages of ruin. The Stone Age forts on the Aran Islands are of particular interest, but there are other ancient ring forts all over Ireland. Castles are equally numerous and prime examples include the ones in Dublin, Kilkenny, Blarney (with its famous stone) and, in Northern Ireland, Carrickfergus.

The Anglo-Irish aristocracy left a selection of fine stately homes, buildings and gardens, many of them now open to the public: Muckross House, Malahide Castle, the beautiful gardens at Powerscourt and, on the Causeway Coast in Ulster, Mussenden Temple.

Religious Sites
The passage tomb at Newgrange is the most impressive relic of pre-Christian Ireland. Early Christian churches, some well over 1000 years old, are scattered throughout Ireland, and ruined monastic sites, many of them with round towers, are also numerous. Glendalough, Mellifont Abbey, Jerpoint Abbey, the Rock of Cashel and the monastic buildings on Skellig Michael, off the coast of Kerry, are all astonishing.

TOURIST OFFICES
Both Bord Fáilte (pronounced 'board fawlchuh' – the proper name for the Irish Tourist Board) and the Northern Ireland Tourist Board (NITB) operate separate tourist offices. Both are usually well organised and helpful though Bord Fáilte will not provide any information on places (such as B&Bs and camping grounds) that it has not approved.

Local Tourist Offices
Dublin and Belfast have Bord Fáilte and NITB offices while the former also has the flashy new Dublin Tourism Centre. Elsewhere in the Republic and Northern Ireland there is some sort of tourist office in almost every town big enough to have half a dozen pubs. Most will find you a place to stay – a useful service in the busy summer months. Weekday hours are usually from 9 am to 6 pm (with a one-hour lunch break) and 9 am to 1 pm on Saturday, but they can be extended in summer. Many of the smaller offices are closed in winter – particularly in the Republic.

Tourist Offices Abroad
Overseas offices of Bord Fáilte include:

IRELAND

Australia
5th floor, 36 Carrington St, Sydney, NSW 2000 (☎ 02-9299 6177; fax 02-9299 6323)
Canada
Suite 1150, 160 Bloor St East, Toronto, Ontario M4W 1B9 (☎ 416-929 2777; fax 416-929 6783)
France
33 Rue de Miromesnil, 75008 Paris (☎ 01-47 42 03 36; fax 1-47 42 01 64)
UK
150 New Bond St, London W1Y OAQ (☎ 0171-493 3201; fax 0171-493 9065)
USA
345 Park Ave, New York, NY 10154 (☎ 212-428 0800; fax 212-371 9052)

Tourist information for Northern Ireland abroad is usually handled by the British Tourist Authority (BTA), though there are a few offices of the NITB in some locations:

Canada
Suite 450, 111 Avenue Rd, Toronto, Ontario M5R 3J8 (☎ 416-925 6368; fax 416-961 2175)
UK
11 Berkeley St, London W1X 5AD (☎ 0171-355 5040; fax 0171-409 0487)
USA
Suite 701, 551 Fifth Ave, New York, NY 10176 (☎ 212-922 0101; fax 212-922 0099)

USEFUL ORGANISATIONS

Many manor houses, monuments and gardens in the Republic are operated by the Office of Public Works (OPW). From the ticket office at any one of these, you can buy a Heritage Card giving you unlimited access to all OPW sites for one year. The card costs IR£15 (senior citizens IR£10, students and children IR£6). In Northern Ireland the National Trust has a similar deal but it's not so useful for most visitors. If, however, you are also visiting Britain you might consider it. One-year membership in the National Trust costs £26 (under 23s £12, family £48).

Office of Public Works (OPW)
51 St Stephen's Green, Dublin 2 (☎ 01-661 3111 ext 2386)
The National Trust
Rowallane, Saintfield, County Down BT24 7LH (☎ 01238-510721)

VISAS & EMBASSIES

Citizens of most Western countries do not require a visa to visit Ireland. UK nationals born in Britain or Northern Ireland do not need

a passport, but it's advisable to carry some form of identification. Irish diplomatic offices overseas include:

Australia
20 Arkana St, Yarralumla, Canberra, ACT 2600 (☎ 06-273 3022)
Canada
130 Albert St, Ottawa, Ontario K1A 0L6 (☎ 613-233 6281)
France
12 Ave Foch, 75116 Paris (☎ 01-45 00 20 87)
Japan
Kowa Building, No 25, 8-7 Sanban-cho, Chiyoda-ku, Tokyo 102 (☎ 3-3263 0695)
UK
17 Grosvenor Place, London SW1X 7HR (☎ 0171-235 2171)
USA
2234 Massachusetts Ave NW, Washington, DC 20008 (☎ 202-462 3939). There are also consulates in Boston, Chicago, New York and San Francisco.

Foreign Embassies in Ireland
Foreign embassies in Dublin include:

Australia
2nd floor, Fitzwilton House, Wilton Terrace, Dublin 2 (☎ 01-676 1517)
Canada
4th floor, Canada House, 65-68 St Stephen's Green, Dublin 2 (☎ 01-478 1988)
France
36 Ailesbury Rd, Dublin 4 (☎ 01-269 4777)
UK
31-33 Merrion Rd, Dublin 4 (☎ 01-269 5211)
USA
42 Elgin Rd, Ballsbridge, Dublin 4 (☎ 01-668 8777)

In Northern Ireland, nationals of most countries other than the USA should contact their embassy in London.

USA
Queens House, 14 Queen St, Belfast (☎ 01232-328239)

CUSTOMS

The usual tobacco, alcohol and perfume allowances apply to duty-free goods purchased at the airport or on the ferry. Do not confuse these with items (including alcohol and tobacco) bought at normal shops in other EU countries, where certain commodities can be considerably cheaper than in Ireland. As long as taxes have been paid somewhere in the EU and the goods are for personal consumption, there are no additional taxes levied in Ireland.

MONEY
Currency

The Irish pound or punt (IR£), like the British pound sterling (£), is divided into 100 pence (p). The best exchange rates are offered by banks, which are usually open on weekdays from 10 am to 3 or 3.30 pm.

In Dublin and some larger towns, most banks stay open until 4 pm (5 pm on Thursday). Exchange bureaus stay open longer, but the rate is worse and the commission higher.

Many post offices have currency-exchange facilities and are open on Saturday morning.

Pounds sterling (see the Britain chapter) are used in Northern Ireland, though several banks also issue their own Northern Irish pound notes, which are equivalent to sterling but not readily accepted in Britain.

Most major currencies and types of travellers' cheques are readily accepted in Ireland. Eurocheques can also be cashed here.

Costs

Ireland is an expensive place – marginally more costly than Britain – but prices vary around the island. Many places to stay, particularly hostels but also hotels and some B&Bs, have low and high-season prices. Entry prices to sites and museums are usually lower for children, students and senior citizens (OAPs).

Exchange Rates

Australia	A$1	=	IR£0.48
Canada	C$1	=	IR£0.45
Germany	DM	=	IR£0.42
France	1FF	=	IR£0.12
Japan	¥100	=	IR£0.57
New Zealand	NZ$1	=	IR£0.43
South Africa	SAfr R1	=	IR£0.14
United Kingdom	UK£1	=	IR£0.96
United States	US$1	=	IR£0.62

Credit & Charge Cards

Major credit cards – particularly Visa and MasterCard (often called Access) – are widely accepted, even at quite a few B&Bs. You can obtain cash advances on your card from a bank and from automatic teller machines (ATMs) in both the north and south.

Tipping

Fancy hotels and restaurants usually add a 10% or 15% service charge onto the bill. Simpler places usually do not add service; if you decide to tip, just round up the bill (or add 10% at most). In any case, in many places in the Republic – even relatively expensive restaurants – you pay the cashier as you leave, not the waiter. Taxi drivers do not have to be tipped, but if you're feeling flush 10% is more than generous.

Taxes & Refunds

Value-added tax (VAT) applies to most goods and services in Ireland. People residing in an EU country are not entitled to a VAT refund. Other visitors can claim back the VAT on purchases that are being taken out of the EU. If you buy something from a so-called Cashback Store (they have signs), you will be given a voucher which can be refunded at most international airports or stamped at ferry ports and mailed back for refund.

POST & COMMUNICATIONS
Post

Post offices (An Post) in the Republic are open on weekdays from 9 am (9.30 am on Tuesday or Wednesday) to 5.30 pm, and on Saturday from 9 am to 1 pm; smaller offices close for lunch.

Postcards cost 28p to EU countries and 38p outside Europe, while aerograms cost 45p. An air-mail letter to the USA or Australia costs 52p.

Post-office hours and postal rates in Northern Ireland are the same as in Britain. Mail can be addressed to poste restante at post offices, but is officially held for only two weeks. Writing 'hold for collection' on the envelope may help.

Telephone

Phonecards are almost essential these days in the Republic, where Telecom Éireann sells Callcards of 10/20/50/100 units for IR£2/ 3.50/ 8/16.

In Northern Ireland, telephone booths (boxes) accepting British Telecom (BT) phonecards are few and far between outside Belfast. International calls can be dialled directly from pay phones.

See the Telephones appendix in the back of this book for information about dialling international calls to or from the Republic or Northern Ireland (ie the UK). The important

IRELAND

difference is that to call Northern Ireland from Ireland, you do not dial ☎ 00-44 as for the rest of the UK. Instead you dial ☎ 08 and then the local Northern Irish area code *without* dropping the initial 0.

Fax, Telegraph & E-mail
Faxes can be sent from post offices or other specialist offices. To send international telegrams, phone ☎ 196 in the Republic or ☎ 190 in Northern Ireland. Dublin's surfeit of cybercafés allows you to send e-mail messages from a half-dozen locations around the city.

NEWSPAPERS
English papers and magazines are readily available, but the main papers in the south are the Dublin-based *Irish Times* and *Irish Independent* and the *Cork Examiner*. In the north you will find the *Belfast Telegraph* and the staunchly Protestant *News Letter* tabloid. British newspapers are readily available as is the *International Herald Tribune* and *USA Today*.

RADIO & TV
Ireland has two state-controlled television channels (RTÉ 1 and Network 2) and three radio stations. Northern Ireland's two TV channels are BBC Northern Ireland and Ulster Television. With the right aerial, Britain's BBC and other stations can now be picked up in most parts of the country. Raidió na Gaeltachta (92.5/96 FM or 540/828/963 MW) is the national Irish-language service. A controversial Irish-language TV station (Teilifís na Gaeilge) was set to begin broadcasting for two hours a day in late 1996.

PHOTOGRAPHY & VIDEO
Ireland and its people are very photogenic, but the sky is often overcast, so photographers should bring high-speed film (eg 200 or 400 ASA). A roll of 24-exposure print film costs around IR£4 and another IR£5 or so to process.

TIME
Ireland is on the same time as Britain and advances the clock by one hour from late March to late October. During the summer months it stays light until very late at night; you could still just about read this page by natural light at 11 pm in August.

ELECTRICITY
Electricity is 220 V, 50 Hz, and plugs are usually of the flat three-pin type, as in Britain.

WEIGHTS & MEASURES
In Ireland progress towards metrication has accelerated though old road markers show distances in miles as do some speed-limit signs. In Northern Ireland – as in Britain – the situation is more confused and miles and km, pints and litres and pounds and kilos are in use. We've used the metric system exclusively in this chapter; there is a conversion table printed on the inside back cover of this book.

LAUNDRY
Most towns will have several laundrettes – usually where an attendant washes, dries and neatly folds your dirty clothes for around IR£4. Hostel laundries are usually good value.

TOILETS
Public toilets in both the Republic (often marked *fir* for men and *mná* for women) and Northern Ireland are often weathered but usually clean, free of charge and stocked with toilet paper/loo rolls. Drunks urinating in the street on a Friday or Saturday night is a common sight in Ireland.

HEALTH
Apart from the dangers posed by the Irish high-cholesterol diet, Ireland presents no serious health problems – sunburn is not a concern, there are no mountains to bring on altitude sickness, and St Patrick banished all reptiles (save the common lizard) from the island way back in the 5th century. The Irish proclivity for tippling can be contagious; watch out for the 'black stuff'.

WOMEN TRAVELLERS
Although women are in some ways second-class citizens in Ireland (the Church's influence), they're also generally treated very respectfully (the Irish mother complex) and, with few exceptions, control the household. In many ways Ireland is one of the safest and least bothersome countries in the world for women. Nevertheless the usual care should be taken.

Rape Crisis Centre
70 Leeson St Lower, Dublin 2 (☎ 01-661 4911; toll-free 1 800 778888)
Women's Centre
30 Donegall St, Belfast (☎ 01232-243363)

GAY & LESBIAN TRAVELLERS

Despite the 1993 decriminalisation of homosexuality for people over the age of 17 in the Republic (1982 in Northern Ireland), gay life is generally not acknowledged or understood. Only Dublin and to a certain extent Belfast and Cork have open gay communities.

National Lesbian & Gay Federation
Hirschfield Centre, 10 Fownes St, Dublin 2 (☎ 01-671 0939)
Northern Ireland Gay Rights Association
Cathedral Buildings, Lower Donegall St, Belfast (☎ 01232-664111)
Gay Switchboard Dublin
(☎ 01-872 1055)
Lesbian Line Dublin
(☎ 01-872 9911)

DISABLED TRAVELLERS

Guesthouses, hotels and sights throughout Ireland are increasingly being adapted for people with disabilities. Bord Fáilte's various accommodation guides indicate which places are wheelchair accessible; the NITB publishes *Accessible Accommodation in Northern Ireland*.

National Rehabilitation Board
Access Department, 25 Clyde Rd, Dublin 4
Disability Action
2 Annadale Ave, Belfast BT7 3UR (☎ 01232-491011)

DANGERS & ANNOYANCES

Ireland is probably safer than most countries in Europe, but the usual precautions should be observed. Drug-related crime is on the increase, and Dublin has its fair share of pickpockets waiting to relieve the unwary of unwatched bags. Be careful with your belongings when you visit pubs and cafés.

If you're travelling by car, do not leave valuables on view inside when the car is parked and try to use covered, guarded garages; Dublin is notorious for car break-ins and petty thieving. Car theft is a big problem in Belfast. Cyclists should always lock their bicycles securely and be cautious about leaving bags on

their bikes, particularly in larger towns or more touristy locations.

The emergency number in both the Republic and Northern Ireland is ☎ 999.

BUSINESS HOURS

Offices are open from 9 am to 5 pm Monday to Friday, shops a little later. On Thursday and/or Friday, shops stay open later. Many are also open on Saturday. In winter tourist attractions are often open shorter hours, fewer days per week or may be shut completely. In Northern Ireland the main thing to remember is that many tourist attractions are closed on Sunday morning, rarely opening until around 2 pm – well after church services (and Sunday lunch) have ended.

PUBLIC HOLIDAYS & SPECIAL EVENTS

Public holidays in Ireland (IR), Northern Ireland (NI) or both are:

New Year's Day.
St Patrick's Day (17 March).
Good Friday.
Easter Monday.
May Holiday (IR) (first Monday in May).
May Bank Holidays (NI) (first and last Mondays in May).
June Bank Holiday (IR) (first Monday in June).
Orangemen's Day (NI) (12 July – Monday if 12th is a Sunday).
August Holiday (IR) (first Monday in August).
August Bank Holiday (NI) (last Monday in August).
October Holiday (IR) (last Monday in October).
Christmas Day.
St Stephen's Day/Boxing Day (26 December).

The All-Ireland hurling and football finals both take place in Dublin in September. There are some great regional cultural events around the country, like the Galway Arts Festival in late July. In Dublin, Leopold Bloom's Joycean journey around the city is marked by various events on Bloomsday (16 June). In Northern Ireland, July is marching month, and every Orangeman in the country hits the streets on the 'glorious 12th'. Other events include the Ould Lammas Fair at Ballycastle in August, and the Belfast Festival at Queen's in November.

ACTIVITIES

Ireland is a great place for outdoor activities, and the tourist boards put out a wide selection

IRELAND

of information sheets covering everything from bird-watching (the Hook area of County Wexford), to surfing (great along the west coast), scuba diving, hang-gliding, trout and salmon fishing, ancestor tracing, horse riding, sailing and canoeing along the way.

Walking is particularly popular although, as usual, you must come prepared for wet weather. There are now well over 20 way-marked trails varying in length from the 26-km Cavan Way to the 900-km Ulster Way.

WORK

With unemployment so high in both the north and south, Ireland is not a good place for casual employment, although there is a certain amount of low-paying seasonal work in the tourist industry, usually in pubs and restaurants.

Citizens of EU countries can work in Ireland without special papers. If you have at least one Irish parent or grandparent, it is easy to obtain Irish citizenship without necessarily renouncing your own, and this opens the door to employment throughout the EU. For information contact an Irish embassy or consulate in your own country.

ACCOMMODATION

Bord Fáilte's comprehensive *Ireland Accommodation Guide*, once published annually, is a thing of the past and has now been split into guides to camping grounds, B&Bs, hotels, etc. These guides, which cost from IR£1.50 to IR£4, do not in any way exhaust the options, however, as Bord Fáilte publications list only 'tourist office approved' places, which is optional. In Northern Ireland all accommodation *must* be inspected and approved by the NITB to operate, and these places are covered in *Where to Stay in Northern Ireland* (£3.99).

Bord Fáilte and NITB offices will book accommodation for a fee of IR£1 or IR£2. All this really involves is phoning a place on their list, but in summer, when it may take numerous calls to find a free room, it can be a pound or two well spent.

Camping

Camping grounds are not as common in Ireland as they are elsewhere in Europe, but there are still plenty of them around. Some hostels also have a space for tents. At commercial camping grounds, costs are typically IR£5 to IR£8 for a tent and two people.

Hostels

If you're travelling on a tight budget, the country's numerous hostels – both official and independent – offer the cheapest accommodation and are also great centres for meeting fellow travellers. In summer they can be heavily booked.

An Óige (meaning 'youth'), the Irish branch of Hostelling International, which is still called the Irish Youth Hostel Association here, has more than 40 hostels scattered round the country, and there are another eight in Northern Ireland administered by the Youth Hostel Association of Northern Ireland (YHANI). These hostels are open to members of HI, members of An Óige/YHANI (annual membership IR£7.50/7.50), or to any overseas visitor for an additional nightly charge of IR£1.25. If you pay the extra charge six times (total IR£7.50), you become a member. To use one of these hostels, you must have or rent a sleeping-bag sheet.

From June to September nightly costs range from IR£5.50 to IR£6.50 except for the more expensive hostels in Dublin, Belfast and a couple of other places. Rates are cheaper in the low season and if you're under 18.

A government-backed enterprise-incentive scheme has seen independent hostels in the Republic pop up like toadstools after rain. They emphasise their easy-going ambience and lack of rules, but not all of them are of a very high standard; some are cold in winter, stuffy in summer and always cramped, with up to 20 people in a room sleeping on flimsy metal bunk beds. Two associations with reliable accommodation include the Independent Holiday Hostels (IHH), a cooperative group with 137 associated hostels in both Northern Ireland and the Republic, and the 'back-to-basics' Independent Hostels Owners in Ireland (IHO) association with 82 members around Ireland.

An Óige
  61 Mountjoy St, Dublin 7 (☎ 01-830 4555; fax 01-830 5808)
Youth Hostel Association of Northern Ireland (YHANI)
  22-32 Donegall Rd, Belfast (☎ 01232-3247333; fax 01232-439699)

Independent Holiday Hostels (IHH)
  57 Gardiner St Lower, Dublin 1 (☎ 01-836 4700; fax 01-836 4710)
Independent Hostels Owners in Ireland (IHO)
  Dooey Hostel, Glencolumbcille, County Donegal (☎ 073-30130; fax 073-30339)

B&Bs

If you're not staying in hostels you will probably end up in a bed & breakfast (B&B), as Irish a form of accommodation as there is. It sometimes seems every other house here is a B&B, and you'll stumble upon them in the most unusual and remote locations. Typical costs are IR£12/16 (without/with *en suite* bathroom) per person a night; you rarely pay less or more than that, although in the big towns there are some more luxurious B&Bs which can cost from IR£25. B&Bs are increasingly adding *en suite* bathrooms so the low end of the scale is disappearing pretty quickly. At some places, single rooms cost several pounds more. Most B&Bs are very small, just two to four rooms, so in summer they can quickly fill up. However, with so many to choose from, there's bound to be someone with a spare room.

Breakfast at an Irish B&B is almost inevitably cereal followed by 'a fry', which means fried eggs, bacon and sausages, plus toast and/or brown bread and butter. A week of B&B breakfasts exceeds every known international guideline for cholesterol intake, but if you decline fried food you're left with toast and cold cereal in most places. It's a shame more B&Bs don't offer alternatives like fruit, yoghurt or the delicious variety of Irish breads and scones, which are widely available.

Other Accommodation

Hotel accommodation in Ireland can range from the local pub to a stately 'heritage house' or even a medieval castle. Another possibility is farmhouse accommodation, which usually means a B&B on a farm. Self-catering accommodation in an apartment or a house is often on a weekly basis and good value if you're staying put for a while.

FOOD

It's frequently said that Irish cooking doesn't match up to the ingredients used and imitates the English variety – ie cook it until it's dead, dead, dead. Fortunately the Irish seem to be doing a better job than the British in overcoming that habit, and you can generally eat quite well in Ireland. Of course, if you want meat or fish cooked to a frazzle with mushy vegetables on the side, there are plenty of places willing to accommodate.

Fast food is well established, from traditional fish and chips to more recent arrivals like burgers, pizzas, kebabs and tacos served at both American and Irish chains. Pubs are often good places to eat, particularly at lunchtime when a bowl of the day's soup and some excellent soda or brown bread can make an economical meal. Seafood, long neglected in Ireland, is often excellent, especially in the west, and there are some good vegetarian restaurants.

DRINKS

In Ireland a drink means a beer – either lager or stout. Stout is usually Guinness, the famous black beer of Dublin, although in Cork it can mean a Murphy's or a Beamish. If you don't develop a taste for stout (and you should at least try one), a wide variety of lagers are available, including Harp or Smithwicks and many locally brewed imports like Budweiser, Foster's or Heineken. Simply asking for a Guinness or a Harp will get you a pint (570 ml, IR£1.85 to IR£2.25 in a pub). If you want a half-pint (285 ml, 95p to IR£1.20), ask for a 'glass' or a 'half'.

In the Republic, pub hours are Monday to Saturday from 10.30 am to 11.30 pm (11 pm from October to May), and Sunday from 12.30 to 2 pm and 4 to 11 pm. In Northern Ireland, the pubs' Monday to Saturday hours are from 11.30 am to 11 pm, Sunday ones from 12.30 to 2 pm and 7 to 10 pm.

ENTERTAINMENT

Listening to traditional music in a pub while nursing a pint of Guinness is the most popular form of entertainment in Ireland. If someone suggests visiting a particular pub for its good 'crack', don't think you've just found the local dope dealer. 'Crack' comes from the Irish *craic* meaning 'a good time' – convivial company, sparkling conversation, scintillating music. Music sessions usually begin at around 9 or 9.30 pm at Irish pubs. Theatre is popular, and a 'medieval banquet' (a sort of Irish theatre-restaurant performance in an old castle) finds its way onto many tourist itineraries.

IRELAND

THINGS TO BUY
Clothing, especially anything woollen and hand-knitted or woven, is the most authentically Irish purchase. The Irish produce some high-quality outdoor gear as they have plenty of experience with wet weather. Jewellery with a Celtic inspiration and fine Waterford crystal and glassware are other popular buys.

Getting There & Away

Students and young people should contact the Union of Students in Ireland Travel (USIT) for information about cheap deals to Ireland from Britain.

Union of Students in Ireland Travel (USIT)
    London Student Travel, 52 Grosvenor Gardens, London SW1W 0AG (☎ 0171-730 3402)
    19 Ashton Quay, Dublin 2 (☎ 01-679 8833)

AIR
Aer Lingus is the Irish national airline with international connections to other countries in Europe and to the USA. Ryanair is the next largest Irish carrier, with routes to Europe and the USA.

Britain
Dublin is linked by a variety of airlines to many cities in Britain, including London's five airports. There are also flights to various regional cities in the Republic of Ireland. The standard one-way economy fare from London to Dublin is around £95, but advance-purchase fares are available offering return tickets for as low as £59. These usually must be booked well in advance as seats are often limited. Ryanair has some of the best deals to Dublin from London's Stansted airport. Virgin Atlantic Airways flies from London City airport to Dublin.

Belfast is also linked with several cities in Britain, including London (Heathrow) by the British Airways Express shuttle service. Costs on the shuttle range from £77 for a saver off-peak one-way or £131 for an advance-purchase return to as high as £113 for a regular one-way with no restrictions. British Midland Airways offers similar fares, and the British Airways Express also has an advance-purchase return

from Luton airport, north of London, to Belfast for £59.

Continental Europe
Dublin is connected with other major centres in Europe; there are also flights to Cork, Shannon and Belfast. From Paris, the standard return fare to Dublin is around 1450FF, to Belfast (via London) 1950FF. One-way/return student flights cost 625/1250FF to/from Dublin and 755/1510FF to/from Belfast.

The USA
Aer Lingus (from New York and other centres) and Delta (from Atlanta) fly direct to Dublin and Shannon. Because competition on flights to London is so much fiercer, it is usually cheaper to fly to London first. During the summer high season, the return fare between New York and Dublin with Aer Lingus is around US$800, though there is an advance-purchase fare for just under US$700 return. In the low season, discount return fares from New York to London will be in the US$500 range, in the high season between US$600 and US$700.

Australia & New Zealand
Advance-purchase excursion fares from Australia or New Zealand to Britain (see the Britain chapter) can have a return flight to Dublin tagged on at no extra cost. Return fares from Australia vary from around A$1600 (low season) to A$2900 (high season), but there are often special deals available.

LAND
Britain
Bus Éireann and National Express operate Eurolines and Supabus services direct from London and other UK centres to Dublin, Belfast and other cities. For details in London contact Eurolines (☎ 0171-730 8235), 52 Grosvenor Gardens, London SW1W 0AU or National Express (☎ 0990-808080), Victoria coach station, Buckingham Palace Rd, London SW1W. Slattery Coaches (☎ 0171-730 3666), 26 Elizabeth St, beside Victoria coach station, is an Irish bus company with routes from a half-dozen British cities to Dublin, Galway, Limerick and other regional centres. London to Dublin by bus takes about 12 hours and costs £20/39 one-way/return during the day in peak season and £32/49 at night. To Belfast it's 13

hours and costs £40/59 (night-time service only).

SEA

There is a great variety of ferry services from Britain and France to Ireland, which use both modern car ferries and high-speed catamarans. Figures quoted here are one-way fares for a single adult foot passenger/a car plus driver and up to four adult passengers. There are often special deals, discounted return fares and other money savers worth investigating. If you can manage to hitch a ride in a less-than-full car leaving Britain or France or returning from Ireland, it will cost the driver nothing extra. He/she may not know that.

Britain

There are services from eight ports in England, Scotland and Wales (plus from Douglas on the Isle of Man) to a half-dozen points in Ireland. Most – but not all – run year round. From south to north, the options are:

Swansea to Cork The 10-hour crossing run by Swansea Cork Ferries (☎ 01792-456116 in Swansea) costs £29/179 in July and August, which drops to £21/99 in the low season.

Fishguard & Pembroke to Rosslare These popular ferry crossings take 3½ hours from Fishguard with Stena Line (☎ 0990-707070 in the UK) or 4¼ hours from Pembroke on Irish Ferries (☎ 0990-171717). They cost up to £29/189 and £30/199 respectively on peak-season weekends, but can drop as low as £20/63 and £20/67 during the low season. The Stena Line high-speed catamaran crossing from Fishguard takes just over 1½ hours and costs £36/209 on peak-season weekends.

Holyhead to Dublin & Dun Laoghaire The Stena Line ferry crossing from Holyhead to Dun Laoghaire takes 3½ hours and costs £30/194 at peak-season weekends, down to £20/99 in the off-season. The Stena Line high-speed catamaran operating on the same route takes 99 minutes and costs from £26/99 (low season) to £32/209 (high season). Irish Ferries makes the Holyhead-Dublin ferry crossing. Peak-season fares are £29/189, dropping to £20/89 in the off-season.

Liverpool & Heysham to Belfast The Norse Irish Ferries (☎ 0151-922 0344 in Merseyside) overnight service is not heavily promoted, but it's easy to get to Liverpool from London. In peak season, the trip costs £53 for foot passengers, £142 for a car and driver and £47 for each additional car passenger; fees include two meals and a berth. There is also the Isle of Man Steam Packet (☎ 01624-661661 in Douglas) from Liverpool and Heysham via Douglas (Isle of Man) to Belfast. A small car costs £75 in the peak season, passengers another £40 each.

Irish Ferry Routes

Stranraer to Belfast Seacat (☎ 0345 523523 in the UK) uses a high-speed catamaran to race across the North Channel in just 1½ hours at a cost of £25/226 at peak times, £22/151 in the off-season. Stena's regular ferry (three hours) on the Stranraer-Belfast run costs £22/120 and £24/165 in the low/high seasons; the 1½-hour Stena catamaran on the same route is £22/130 and £26/180.

Cairnryan to Larne P&O (☎ 01581-200276 in Stranraer) operates the Cairnryan-Larne route. It takes 2¼ hours and costs £36/185 for a five-day return at peak times down to £29/136.

France

You can travel to Cork and Rosslare directly from Roscoff, Cherbourg, Le Havre and Saint Malo in France. Eurail passes are valid for ferry crossings between Ireland and France on Irish Ferries only; Inter-Rail passes give reductions.

Roscoff & Saint Malo to Cork & Rosslare These two services, taking 14 and 18 hours respectively, are operated by Brittany Ferries (☎ 1-44 94 89 00 in Paris). Foot passengers pay from 450 to 670FF one-way; a car plus driver costs 1210 to 1910FF. Irish Ferries (☎ 1-42 66 90 90 in Paris) also makes the Roscoff-Cork and Roscoff-Rosslare runs; pedestrians pay around 500/725FF and a car with up to four adults costs 2290/3290FF in the low/high season.

Cherbourg to Rosslare Cherbourg to Rosslare takes 17½ hours on Irish Ferries. Fares are the same as the Roscoff-Cork run.

Le Havre to Rosslare & Cork Le Havre to Rosslare or Cork takes between 20½ and 22 hours on Irish Ferries. The fares are the same as those from Cherbourg.

LEAVING IRELAND

There is a IR£5 airport departure tax, but this is included in the price of the ticket. There's no departure tax if you leave by ferry.

Getting Around

At a glance, travelling around Ireland looks very simple as the distances are short and there's a dense network of roads and railways. But in Ireland, from A to B is seldom a straight line, and public transport can be expensive (particularly trains), infrequent or both. Plus there are many interesting places that public transport simply does not reach. For these reasons, having your own transport can be a major advantage.

PASSES & DISCOUNTS

Eurail passes are valid for train travel in the Republic of Ireland – but not in Northern Ireland – and entitle you to a reduction on Bus Éireann's three-day Irish Rambler ticket (see the following). They are also valid on some ferries between France and the Republic. Inter-Rail passes offer a 50% reduction on train travel within Ireland and discounts on some ferries to/from France and Britain.

For IR£8.50 students can have a Travelsave Stamp affixed to their ISIC card by any USIT agency. This gives a 50% discount on Iarnród Éireann train services, and 15% on Bus

Éireann and Ulsterbus services for fares over IR£1. There is a great variety of unlimited-travel tickets for buses and trains in both the north and south, but most make sense only if you're planning to travel at the speed of light. Irish Rambler tickets are available from Bus Éireann for bus-only travel within the Republic of Ireland. They cost IR£28 (for travel on three out of eight consecutive days), IR£68 (eight out of 15 days) or IR£98 (15 out of 30 days).

For train-only travel within the Republic, there is the Irish Explorer ticket which costs IR£60 (five out of 15 days), while the Irish Rover ticket entitles you to travel in Northern Ireland as well and costs IR£75 (five days). A bus-and-rail version of the Irish Explorer ticket costs IR£90 (eight days).

Finally, the Emerald Card gives you unlimited travel throughout Ireland on all scheduled train and bus services (including city buses in Dublin and Belfast). The card costs IR£105 (or pounds sterling equivalent) for eight out of 15 days, or IR£180 for 15 out of 30 days. Children under 16 pay half fare on all these passes.

If you're going to be staying in hostels, it's worth considering the Slow Coach (☎ 01-679 2684), 6 South William St, Dublin 2, which is operated in association with An Óige and Independent Holiday Hostels. For IR£89 you can travel by bus around Ireland from hostel to hostel with no time limit on when you complete your trip.

AIR

Ireland is too compact to make flying a necessity, but there are flights between Dublin and Belfast, Cork, Galway and Shannon among other regional centres. You can also fly to the Aran Islands (see that section for details).

BUS

Bus Éireann is the Republic's national bus line, with services all over the south and into the north. Standard one-way fares from Dublin include Belfast IR£9.50, Cork IR£12 and Galway IR£8. These fares are much cheaper than regular rail fares. Return fares are usually only a little more expensive than one-way fares, and special deals (eg same-day returns) are often available.

Ulsterbus is the service in the north. An Ulsterbus Freedom of Northern Ireland ticket gives you unlimited travel on Ulsterbus and

Belfast Citybus services for one day for £9, or seven consecutive days for £28.

TRAIN

Iarnród Éireann, the Republic of Ireland's railway system, operates trains on routes that fan out from Dublin. Distances are short in Ireland, and the longest trip you can make by train from the capital is just over four hours to Tralee. Regular one-way fares from Dublin include Belfast IR£14, Cork IR£32 and Galway IR£24. As with buses, special fares are often available, and a midweek return ticket is often not much more than the single fare. First-class tickets cost from IR£3 to IR£15 more than the standard fare for a single journey; you cannot book a train seat in Ireland. If you're under 26 you can get a Faircard for IR£8.50 which gives you a 50% discount on regular intercity fares. For people over 26, the Weekender card offers one-third off the price of intercity travel between Friday and Tuesday.

Northern Ireland Railways has four routes from Belfast, one of which links up with the Republic's rail system.

CAR & MOTORCYCLE
Road Rules

As in Britain, driving is on the left and you should only overtake (pass) to the right of the vehicle ahead of you. Safety belts must be worn by the driver and front-seat passengers; in the north passengers in the rear must also wear them. Motorcyclists and their passengers must wear helmets; headlights should be dipped. Minor roads may sometimes be potholed and will often be very narrow, but the traffic is rarely heavy except as you go through popular tourist or busy commercial towns.

Speed limits in both north and south appear in km, miles or both and are generally the same as in Britain: 112 km/h (70 mph) on motorways, 96 km/h (60 mph) on other roads and 48 km/h (30 mph) or as signposted in towns. These limits tend to be treated with a certain disregard, but on the quiet, narrow, winding rural roads it's advisable to stick to the limit.

As elsewhere in Europe, parking in car parks or other specified areas in Ireland is regulated by 'pay and display' tickets or disc parking. You buy a disc, available from newsstands, on which you punch out or tick the time you park. Discs usually cost around 30p each and are valid for between one and three hours. In the north, beware of Control Zones in town centres where, for security reasons, cars absolutely must not be left unattended. Double yellow lines by the roadside mean no parking at any time; single yellow lines warn of restrictions, which will be signposted.

The Automobile Association (AA) has offices in Belfast (☎ 01232-328924), Dublin (☎ 01-677 9481) and Cork (☎ 021-276922). The AA breakdown number in the Republic is ☎ 1800-667788; in the north it's ☎ 0800-887766. Also in the north, for members of the Royal Automobile Club (RAC) the breakdown number is ☎ 0800-828282.

Rental

Car rental in Ireland is expensive so you will often be better off booking some package deal from your home country. In high season it's wise to book ahead. In the off-season, some companies simply discount all rates by about 25%, and there are often special deals. Some smaller companies charge an extra daily fee if you go across the border, to the north or south.

People under 21 are not allowed to hire a car; for the majority of rental companies you must be at least 23 and have had a valid driving licence for a minimum of 12 months. Some companies will not rent to those over 70 or 75. Your own local licence is usually sufficient to hire a car for up to three months.

In the Republic typical weekly high-season rental rates with insurance, collision-damage waiver, VAT and unlimited distance are around IR£240 for a small car (Ford Fiesta), IR£270 for a medium-sized car (Toyota Corolla 1.3) and IR£320 for a larger car (Ford Mondeo). In the north, similar cars would cost about 10% less.

The international rental companies Avis, Budget, Hertz, Eurodollar, Thrifty and the major local operators Murray's Europcar and Dan Dooley have offices all over Ireland. There are many local operators with rates from as low as IR£139 a week, including Access (☎ 01-844 4848) and Windsor (toll-free ☎ 1800 515800), both at Dublin airport, and Argus (☎ 01-490 4444) at 59 Terenure Rd East, Dublin 6.

BICYCLE

A large number of visitors explore Ireland by bicycle. Although the distances are relatively short, the most interesting parts of Ireland can be very hilly and the weather is often wet. Despite these drawbacks, it's a great place for bicycle touring, and facilities are good.

You can either bring your bike with you on the ferry or plane or rent one in Ireland. Typical rental costs are IR£7 to IR£10 a day or IR£30 to IR£35 a week. Bags and other equipment can also be rented. Raleigh Rent-a-Bike (☎ 01-626 1333), Raleigh House, Kylemore Rd, Dublin 10, has a dozens of outlets around the country, some of which offer one-way rentals for IR£42 a week. Just plain Rent-a-Bike (☎ 01-872 5399), 58 Gardiner St Lower, Dublin 1, has 15 depots around Ireland and offers one-way rentals for an extra IR£5. In addition, there are also many local independent outlets and most hostels rent bicycles.

Bicycles can be transported on some Bus Éireann and Ulsterbus routes; the charges vary. By train the cost ranges from IR£2 to IR£6 for a one-way journey, depending on the distance.

Numerous tourist-office publications on cycling are available, and there are a number of books and guides on the subject. You might also want to get in touch with the Irish Federation of Cyclists (☎ 01-855 1522), 619 North Circular Rd, Dublin 1.

HITCHING

While we don't recommend hitching – it's never entirely safe in any country – hitching in Ireland is generally easy. The major exceptions are in heavily touristed areas where the competition from other hitchers is stiff and the cars are often full. In the Republic there are usually large numbers of local people on the road who use hitching as an everyday means of travel. Women should travel with someone else (even though many local women appear to hitch alone without problems). If you feel at all doubtful about an offered ride, turn it down.

BOAT

There are many boat services to outlying islands and across rivers and lakes (eg see Bantry and Lough Leane, or the Skellig and Aran Islands). Some of the boat services (eg the Ballyhack-Passage East ferry linking counties Wexford and Waterford) make interesting little short cuts.

LOCAL TRANSPORT

There are comprehensive local bus networks in Dublin, Belfast and some other larger towns. The Dublin Area Rapid Transport (DART) line in Dublin and the service from Belfast to Bangor are the only local railway lines. Taxis in Ireland tend to be expensive, but in Belfast and Derry there are share-taxi services, which operate rather like shuttle buses.

ORGANISED TOURS

Bord Fáilte has details of general tour operators and specialist companies that include angling, walking, cycling, cultural holidays and tours for the disabled. Tír na nÓg Tours (☎ 01-836 4684), 57 Gardiner St Lower, Dublin 1, organises backpacking tours in both the north and south from IR£129 a week. See the Dublin and Belfast sections for information about coach tours in those cities and further afield.

Dublin

Ireland's capital and its largest and most cosmopolitan city, Dublin can shift so rapidly from 'have' to 'have not' that it's virtually impossible to pin down. The elegant and prosperous-looking Georgian squares in the centre can quickly give way to areas where any refinement has long since faded into decay. Dublin has very little contemporary architecture.

Its faults notwithstanding, Dublin is a curious and colourful place, an easy city to like and a fine introduction to Ireland (though not a truly representative one). Travellers returning for the first time in several years will find a somewhat different city – much more modern and European-feeling – with cybercafés and trendy restaurants sitting happily next to smoky pubs and chophouses, and young Dubliners scurrying around in the latest Continental fashions.

Orientation

Dublin is neatly divided by the River Liffey into the more affluent south and the far less prosperous north (where the popular 1991 film *The Commitments* was set). The Viking and medieval city first developed south of the river, spreading north in the early years of the city's Georgian heyday and then moving south again as the northern settlements peaked and declined.

North of the river important streets for visitors are O'Connell St, the major shopping thoroughfare, and Gardiner St, with its many B&Bs and guesthouses. Henry St running west off O'Connell St, is the main shopping street north of the river. Connolly station lies to the east; the main bus station is at the southern end of Gardiner St, which becomes very run-down as it continues north. Immediately south of the river is the atmospheric old Temple Bar district and the expanse of Trinity College. Nassau St, running along the southern edge of the campus, and up-market and pedestrianised Grafton St are the main shopping streets south of the river.

Information

Tourist Offices The new Dublin Tourism Centre (in Ireland 24-hour ☎ 1550-112233; fax 1550-114400; outside Ireland ☎ 605 7777; fax 605 7787) is in desanctified St Andrew's Church in St Andrew St west of Trinity College. In July and August (when it can be a mad house), the centre is open Monday to Saturday from 9 am to 8.30 pm and on Sunday from 11 am to 5.30 pm. At other times of year, the hours from Monday to Saturday are 9 am to 6 pm. There are other city tourist offices at the airport and on the waterfront at Dun Laoghaire. The head office of Bord Fáilte (☎ 676 5871; fax 676 4764) at Baggot St Bridge has an information desk and, although it is less conveniently situated, it is also much less crowded. The office is open weekdays from 9.15 am to 5.15 pm. The Northern Ireland Tourist Board (☎ 679 1977; fax 677 1587) is at 16 Nassau St.

Money There are numerous banks around the centre with exchange facilities. There are also exchange bureaus, which operate longer hours than the banks, but they generally take a bigger commission. American Express has an exchange bureau in the Dublin Tourism Centre; its main office is on College Green across the road from the Bank of Ireland and the Trinity College entrance and Thomas Cook is next door.

Post & Communications The famous GPO – the General Post Office – is on O'Connell St, north of the river. South of the river there's a post office in Anne St South, just off Grafton St, and on St Andrew St.

The telephone code for Dublin is ☎ 01.

Travel Agency The USIT travel office (☎ 679 8833) is at 19 Aston Quay, right by the river and O'Connell Bridge.

Bookshops Directly opposite Trinity College, at 27-29 Nassau St, is Fred Hanna's excellent bookshop, while round the corner, facing each other across Dawson St, Waterstone's at No 7 and Hodges Figgis at No 57 are equally large and well stocked. An Siopa Leabhar – also called the Celtic Bookshop – at 6 Harcourt St, just off St Stephen's Green, has books in Irish. North of the Liffey, Eason, at 40 O'Connell St and near the post office, has a big selection of books and one of the largest ranges of magazines in Ireland.

Medical Services The Eastern Health Board Dublin Area (☎ 671 4711), 138 Thomas St, Dublin 8, has a Choice of Doctor Scheme which can advise you on a suitable doctor from 9 am to 5 pm Monday to Friday. It also provides services for the physically and mentally handicapped.

Other Facilities Most of the hostels offer laundry facilities at lower-than-commercial rates. Otherwise there's the Laundry Shop at 191 Parnell St north of the river near the centre and a laundrette on the corner of Aungier and York Sts opposite Avalon House.

There are left-luggage facilities at the bus station (IR£1.50) and at both Heuston and Connolly railway stations (IR£1, backpacks IR£2 at Connolly).

Things to See & Do

Trinity College & Book of Kells The college, founded in 1592, is right in the centre of Dublin. Its prime attraction is the magnificent Book of Kells, an illuminated manuscript dating from around 800 AD and one of the oldest books in the world. It's on display in the East Pavilion of the Colonnades underneath the college's Old Library. The Book of Kells

IRELAND

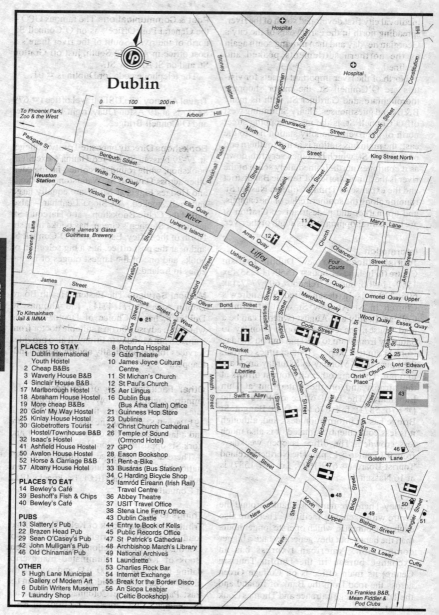

Dublin

0   100   200 m

To Phoenix Park,
Zoo & the West

To Kilmainham
Jail & IMMA

Heuston
Station

Saint James's Gates
Guinness Brewery

Parkgate St

Benburb   Street

Wolfe   Tone   Quay

Victoria   Quay

Ellis Quay

River

Usher's Island

Liffey

Usher's Quay

River

James   Street

Thomas   Street

Bridgefoot   Street

Oliver   Bond   Street

Cornmarket

Swift's Alley

The
Liberties

Dean   Street

New Row

New   Street

Stoney   Batter

Arbour   Hill

North   Brunswick   Street

King   Street

King   Street North

Francis   Street

Meath   Street

Arran   Quay

Inns Quay

Merchants Quay

Cook   Street

High   Street

Christ Church
Place

Nicholas   Street

Patrick   Street

Kevin St Upper

Bride   Street

Kevin St Lower

Grangegorman

Church   Street

Constitution   Hill

Hospital

Hospital

Queen   Street

Smithfield

Bow   Street

Church   Street

Mary's Lane

Chancery   Street

Four
Courts

Ormond Quay Upper

Wood Quay

Essex Quay

Arran   Street

Ormond Quay Upper

St Augustine   St

Bridge   St

Winetavern St

Lord Edward
St

John   Dillon   Street

Nicholas   Street

Werburgh   St

Golden   Lane

Patrick   St

Bride   Street

Aungier   Street

Hospital

11

12

22

21

23

24

25

43

46

47

48

49

50

51

Cuffe

To Frankies B&B,
Mean Fiddler &
Pod Clubs

PLACES TO STAY
1 Dublin International
   Youth Hostel
2 Cheap B&Bs
3 Waverly House B&B
4 Sinclair House B&B
17 Marlborough Hostel
18 Abraham House Hostel
19 More cheap B&Bs
20 Goin' My Way Hostel
25 Kinlay House Hostel
30 Globetrotters Tourist
   Hostel/Townhouse B&B
32 Isaac's Hostel
41 Ashfield House Hostel
48 Avalon House Hostel
52 Horse & Carriage B&B
52 Albany House Hotel

PLACES TO EAT
14 Bewley's Café
39 Beshoff's Fish & Chips
40 Bewley's Café

PUBS
13 Slattery's Pub
22 Brazen Head Pub
29 Sean O'Casey's Pub
42 John Mulligan's Pub
46 Old Chinaman Pub

OTHER
5 Hugh Lane Municipal
   Gallery of Modern Art
6 Dublin Writers Museum
7 Laundry Shop

8 Rotunda Hospital
9 Gate Theatre
10 James Joyce Cultural
   Centre
11 St Michan's Church
12 St Paul's Church
15 Aer Lingus
16 Dublin Bus
   (Bus Átha Cliath) Office
21 Guinness Hop Store
23 Dublinia
24 Christ Church Cathedral
26 Temple of Sound
   (Ormond Hotel)
27 GPO
28 Eason Bookshop
31 Rent-a-Bike
33 Busáras (Bus Station)
34 C Harding Bicycle Shop
35 Iarnród Éireann (Irish Rail)
   Travel Centre
36 Abbey Theatre
37 USIT Travel Office
38 Stena Line Ferry Office
43 Dublin Castle
44 Entry to Book of Kells
45 Public Records Office
47 St Patrick's Cathedral
48 Archbishop March's Library
51 National Archives
51 Laundrette
53 Charlies Rock Bar
54 Internet Exchange
55 Break for the Border Disco
56 An Siopa Leabjar
   (Celtic Bookshop)

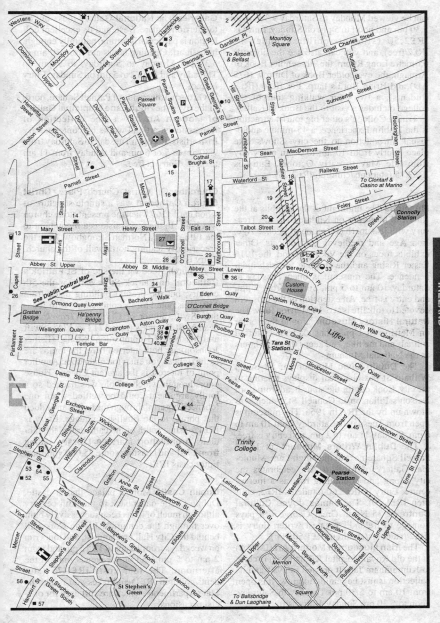

can be viewed Monday to Saturday 9.30 am to 5.30 pm and noon to 5 pm on Sunday. Entry is IR£2.50 (students/children under 12 IR£2/free), and you can also see the library's 65-metre Long Room, the 9th-century Book of Armagh, the even older Book of Durrow (675 AD) and Brian Ború's harp. For IR£4 (IR£3 students), a two-hour walking tour of the college includes a visit to the Book of Kells.

Trinity College's other big tourist attraction is the Dublin Experience, a 45-minute audio-visual introduction to the city. Shows take place hourly from 10 am to 5 pm every day from late May to early October. Entry is IR£2.75 (students/children IR£2.25).

Museums The highlight of the exhibits at the **National Museum** on Kildare St is the Treasury with its superb collection of Bronze Age, Iron Age and medieval gold objects. Other exhibits focus on the Viking period, the 1916 Easter Rising and the struggle for Irish independence. The museum is open Tuesday to Saturday 10 am to 5 pm, Sunday from 2 pm, and entry is free. An extension of the museum devoted to folk life is at 6-10 Merrion Row. The **Natural History Museum**, around the corner on Merrion St Upper, has skeletons, stuffed animals and the like, and keeps the same hours as the National Museum.

The **Dublin Civic Museum** at 58 South William St has historical displays relating to the city. Look out for the stone head from Lord Nelson's Pillar on O'Connell St, which was blown up by the IRA in 1966. The museum is open from Tuesday to Saturday from 10 am to 6 pm, Sunday 11 am to 2 pm, and entry is free.

The **Dublin Writers Museum**, at 18-19 Parnell Square next to the Hugh Lane Municipal Gallery of Modern Art, celebrates the city's long and continuing role as a literary centre. Entry is IR£2.60 (students IR£2, children IR£1.10). The **James Joyce Cultural Centre** at 35 North Great George's St pays homage to Ireland's greatest writer. Entry is IR£2 (students/children IR£1.50/70p).

The **Irish Museum of Modern Art** (IMMA) at the old Royal Hospital Kilmainham is close to Kilmainham Jail. It opened in 1991 and its collection is just beginning to grow. It is open from 10 am to 5.30 pm Tuesday to Saturday, noon to 5.30 pm Sunday. Entry is free.

Galleries The **National Gallery** looks out on to Merrion Square West, and its excellent collection is particularly strong, naturally enough, in Irish art. Opening hours are from 10 am to 5.30 pm Monday to Saturday, to 9 pm on Thursday and from 2 to 5 pm on Sunday. Entry is free.

On the northern side of Parnell Square, north of the river, the **Hugh Lane Municipal Gallery of Modern Art** has a fine collection of Impressionist art and works by contemporary Irish artists. It's open Tuesday to Saturday from 9.30 am to 5 or 6 pm and Sunday from 11 am to 5 pm. Entry is free.

Churches On Christ Church Place, **Christ Church Cathedral** was a simple structure of wood until 1169 when the present stone church was built. In the south aisle is a monument to the 12th-century Norman Strongbow. Note the precariously leaning north wall of the church. Entry is IR£1.

A church stood on the site of **St Patrick's Cathedral** on Patrick St as early as the 5th century, but the present building dates from 1191. It is noted for its connections with Jonathan Swift, author of *Gulliver's Travels* and dean of St Patrick's from 1713 to 1745. Swift and his beloved companion 'Stella' (Esther Johnson) are both interred here; the tombs are to the right as you enter the main door. Another point of interest is the ancient Chapter House door through which a hole was hacked so a lordly argument could be settled when one 'chanced his arm' through the hole – and added that phrase to the English language. Entry is IR£1.20. Just south of the cathedral is the fabulous **Archbishop Marsh's Library**, dating from 1701 and boasting some 25,000 volumes. Entry costs IR£1.

Dublin Castle More a palace than a castle, Dublin Castle dates back to the 13th century although much of it has been successively built over through the centuries. It's on Cork Hill behind the City Hall on Dame St, and tours run on weekdays from 10 am to 12.15 pm and from 2 pm to 5 pm, and on weekends only in the afternoon. The tour costs IR£1.75 (students/children IR£1) and takes you round the State Apartments, which are still used for official occasions.

Other Central Buildings The finest Georgian architecture and colourful doorways can be found around St Stephen's Green and Merrion Square. The Irish parliament meets in **Leinster House** on Kildare St. **Mansion House** on Dawson St is the residence of the Lord Mayor and was the site of the 1919 Declaration of Independence.

The **GPO building** on O'Connell St is an important landmark, both physically and historically. It was the focus for the Easter Rising of 1916 when the building was almost totally destroyed, apart from the façade.

The **Four Courts** building on the north bank of the Liffey dates from 1785. Heavy shelling and a fire during the civil war in 1922 destroyed one of Europe's finest archives as well as genealogical records going back centuries. One of the best views of the River Liffey is from the old pedestrian Liffey Bridge, popularly known as Ha'penny Bridge because that was what it cost to cross it.

Kilmainham Jail Built in 1792, this grey and solid old building played a key role in Ireland's struggle for independence and was the site for the executions after the 1916 Easter Rising. The fateful part it played during the civil war is conspicuously played down in the tour, which follows an excellent audiovisual introduction to the old building. It's in Inchicore Rd, west of Christ Church Cathedral; take bus No 51 or 79 from Aston Quay. Daily hours from May to September are 10 am to 6 pm; the rest of the year it is open from 1 to 4 pm on weekdays and to 6 pm on Sunday. Entry is IR£2 (students/children IR£1).

Guinness Brewery The Guinness Hop Store on Crane St is the historic brewery's old storehouse for hops (a flavouring ingredient in beer-making) where visitors can watch a Guinness audiovisual show and inspect an extensive Guinness museum. It may not be a tour of the brewery, but your entry fee (IR£2/1.50 adults/students) includes a glass of the black stuff. Hours are 10 am to 4 pm Monday to Friday. Take bus No 78A from Aston Quay.

Other Attractions Inside what was once the Synod Hall attached to Christ Church Cathedral, the Medieval Trust has created **Dublinia**,

as bogus a multimedia attempt to recreate history as there ever was. It's shoddy, boring and overpriced (adults/students & children IR£3.95/2.90). Daily opening hours from April to September are from 10 am to 5 pm. In winter it's open from 11 am to 4 pm Monday to Saturday and 10 am to 4.30 pm on Sunday.

The so-so **Dublin Zoo** in the south-eastern corner of Phoenix Park is open 9.30 am to 6 pm Monday to Saturday and from 10.30 am on Sunday. Entry is adults/children IR£5.50/2.90. You can reach it on bus No 10 from O'Connell St.

Not to be missed is the **Casino at Marino** (☎ 833 1618), which is not a casino at all but a pleasure house built for the Earl of Charlemont in the grounds of Marino House in the mid-18th century. By Malahide Rd, north-east of the centre, it's open mid-June to September from 9.30 am to 6.30 pm; at other times of year phone ahead for details of opening hours. Entry (guided tour only) is IR£2 (students & children IR£1). Take bus No 123 from College Green or Dame St.

Organised Tours

Gray Line (☎ 661 9666) has tours around Dublin and further afield, but they're mostly in summer. Different morning and afternoon tours are available; each costs around IR£14, including any admission charges, and lasts just under three hours. Dublin Bus (☎ 873 4222) also has a variety of coach tours including three-hour open-deck ones year round for IR£9 (children IR£4.50). The Heritage Trail bus does a city tour nine times daily (with additional circuits in July and August), and the adults/students/children IR£6/5/3 ticket lets you travel all day, getting on or off at the eight stops.

See the Trinity College section for details of its walking tour. Dublin Footsteps Walking Tours (☎ 496 0641) operates 1½ to two-hour themed walks for IR£4. The tours start from Bewley's Café on Grafton St.

The 2½-hour Jameson Dublin Literary Pub Crawl (☎ 454 0228) operates from Easter to October seven days a week, starting at 7.30 pm from the Duke Pub on Duke St, just off Grafton St. In winter they take place from Thursday to Saturday. There's another tour at noon on Sunday all year round. The walk is great fun and costs IR£6/5 (not including your Guinness consumption!).

IRELAND

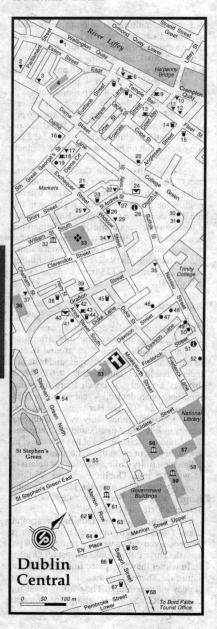

Dublin Central

0   50   100 m

PLACES TO STAY
20 Bloom's Hotel
55 Shelbourne Hotel

PLACES TO EAT
2   Da Pino Pizzeria
3   Les Fréres Jacques
5   La Med
6   Planet Web Cybercafé
9   Chameleon
10 Omar Khayyam
11 Elephant & Castle
12 Gallagher's Boxty House
13 Bad Ass Café
17 Il Gabbiano
18 Bewley's Café
21 Boulevard Café
22 QVII
25 Munchies
27 Trocadero
29 Cornucopia
34 La Taverna
35 Judge Roy Bean's
37 Pasta Fresca
39 Bewley's Oriental Café
42 Eddie Rocket's City Diner
43 Gotham Café
61 Galligan's Restaurant
68 Georgian Fare

PUBS
7   Norseman Pub
8   Temple Bar Pub
14 Auld Dubliner
15 Oliver St John Gogarty Bar & Hostel
23 Old Stand Pub
26 International Bar
38 McDaid's Pub
44 John Kehoe's Pub
45 Davy Byrne's Pub
62 O'Donoghue's Pub
65 Doheny & Nesbitt's Pub
66 Big Jack's Baggot Inn
67 James Toner's Pub

OTHER
1   Kitchen Club (Clarence Hotel)
4   Olympia Theatre
16 The George (Disco)
19 Rí Rá Club (Disco)
24 Post Office (Branch)
28 Dublin Tourism Centre
30 Thomas Cook
31 American Express
32 Dublin Civic Museum
33 Powerscourt Townhouse Shopping Centre
36 Gaiety Theatre
40 Post Office
41 System Club (Disco)
46 Hodges Figgis Bookshop
47 Waterstone's Bookshop
48 Ryanair

continued on next page

continued from previous page

Places to Stay

Camping There's no camping ground convenient to Dublin. The **Shankill Caravan & Camping Park** (☎ 282 0011) is 16 km south of the centre on the Wicklow Rd (N11). A site for two costs IR£6 in summer. The **North Beach Caravan & Camping Park** (☎ 843 7131), which charges IR£7, is 27 km north of the city off the N1.

Hostels – North of the Liffey The An Óige **Dublin International Youth Hostel** (☎ 830 1766) at 61 Mountjoy St is a big, well-equipped hostel in a restored and converted old building. From Dublin airport, bus No 41 (or 41A at the weekend) will drop you off in Dorset St Upper, a few minutes walk from the hostel. The hostel is in the run-down northern area of the city centre; the nightly cost in summer for HI members is IR£9; non-members pay IR£9.50.

The IHH **Goin' My Way Hostel** (☎ 878 8484) is a smaller, older hostel at 15 Talbot St, east of O'Connell St. The nightly cost is IR£7 plus 50p for a shower. Breakfast is included and there are good (and clean) cooking facilities. The IHH **Marlborough Hostel** (☎ 874 7629), 81-82 Marlborough St, has dorms accommodating four to 10 people and the nightly cost is IR£7.50 per person irrespective of the dorm size. Double rooms cost IR£11 per person. Cooking facilities are available.

For convenience you can't beat the big IHH **Isaac's Hostel** (☎ 874 9321), 2-5 Frenchman's Lane, a stone's throw from the bus station or Connolly railway station. In some rooms, traffic noise is the penalty for the convenience of being central. Dorm beds are cheap at IR£6.25 to IR£7 and there are singles/doubles from IR£17.75/29 in the adjoining **Isaac's Hotel**.

Nearby at 46-48 Gardiner St Lower is the much more relaxed and welcoming IHH **Globetrotters Tourist Hostel** (☎ 873 5893), where dorm beds cost IR£10 including continental breakfast. With up to 12 to a dorm there's bound to be some disturbance, but this is a clean, modern place with good security.

At 82-83 Gardiner St Lower is IHH **Abraham House** (☎ 855 0600) where beds in the largest dorms cost IR£7 in low season, IR£8.50 in high.

Hostels – South of the Liffey You won't get any more central than **Ashfield House** (☎ 679 7734), a new and very large place at 19 D'Olier St a few steps south-east of O'Connell Bridge. It has beds in six-berth dorms for IR£7.50 to IR£10.50, in four-bed rooms for IR£11.50 and doubles for IR£27, including breakfast. All rooms have attached bath, there's a large kitchen and laundry, and reception is 24 hours. Another central option is the new **Oliver St John Gogarty Bar Hostel** (☎ 671 1822) at 18-21 Anglesea St, with dorm beds and twins in the high/low seasons for IR£14/10 and IR£36/28.

The less-than-welcoming **Kinlay House** (☎ 679 6644), another IHH member, is beside Christ Church Cathedral at 2-12 Lord Edward St, but some rooms are noisy. Costs are from IR£12 per person for four-bed dorms in summer, from IR£13.50 for the better rooms (some with bathroom) and from IR£18 for a single. Bus Nos 54A, 68A, 78A and 123 stop outside.

The pick of the crop in Dublin has to be the IHH **Avalon House** (☎ 475 0001), in an old building that has been completely renovated at 55 Aungier St, just west of St Stephen's Green. It's very well equipped, and basic accommodation in dorms for up to 12 costs IR£7.50/10.50 in low/high season, including a continental breakfast. In summer, a bed in a four-bed room with attached bathroom costs IR£11.50; in a two-bed it's IR£13.50. To get there take bus No 16, 16A, 19 or 22 right to the door or bus No 11, 13 or 46A to nearby St Stephen's Green.

Morehampton House (☎ 668 8866), further out at 78 Morehampton Rd in Donnybrook, south of the centre. The cheapest beds, at IR£7.95 in summer, are in 10 or eight-bed basement dorms. For eight and four-bed rooms you pay IR£10.95; for twins IR£15. Breakfast is another IR£1, but there are clean, spacious cooking facilities. Bus Nos 10, 46A and 46B pass by.

Next to the ferry port in Dun Laoghaire on Eblana Ave is the IHH *Old School House* (☎ 280 8777), with a variety of room sizes from IR£8 and lots of facilities. Twin rooms cost from IR£11 per person.

B&Bs & Guesthouses If you want something inexpensive and close to the city, Gardiner Sts Upper and Lower are the places to look. It's not the prettiest part of Dublin and can be noisy, but it is cheap.

At the bottom of Gardiner St there is a large collection of places near the bus and train stations, and another group further up near Mountjoy Square. The friendly and newly renovated *Harvey's Guesthouse* (☎ 874 8384) at 11 Gardiner St Upper has singles/doubles from IR£18/32, and *Stella Maris* (☎ 874 0835), next door at No 13, has singles for IR£20 and doubles from IR£34. Hardwicke St is only a short walk west from Gardiner St Upper and has a number of popular B&Bs including *Waverly House* (☎ 874 6132) at No 4 or *Sinclair House* (☎ 855 0792), next door at No 3. Singles/doubles here start at IR£19/28. An excellent, but pricier, choice is the *Townhouse* (☎ 878 8808) at 47-48 Gardiner St Lower, which is connected to the Globetrotters Tourist Hostel and shares a breakfast room with it. Singles/doubles with *en suite* facilities are IR£28/50.

If you're willing to travel further out, you can find a better price/quality combination on the coast south-east of the centre at Dun Laoghaire or to the north-east at Clontarf. The seaside suburbs are easy to reach on the DART local train service. The Ballsbridge embassy district, just south-east of the centre, offers convenience and quality, but you pay for that combination with higher prices. Other suburbs to try are Sandymount and Drumcondra.

There are numerous places along Clontarf Rd, about five km from the centre, including the friendly *Ferryview* (☎ 833 5893) at No 96. Further along there's the slightly more expensive *White House* (☎ 833 3196) at No 125, *San Vista* (☎ 833 9582) at No 237 and *Bayview* (☎ 833 9870) at No 265. These B&Bs typically cost IR£15 to IR£20 for singles, IR£25 to IR£35 for doubles. Bus No 30 from Abbey St will get you there for IR£1.

In Dun Laoghaire, the Rosmeen Gardens area is packed with B&Bs. To get there, walk south along George's St, the main shopping street; Rosmeen Gardens is the first street after Glenageary Rd Lower, directly opposite People's Park. *Mrs Callanan* (☎ 280 6083) is at No 1, *Rathoe* (☎ 280 8070) at No 12 and *Rosmeen House* (☎ 280 7613) at No 13. Prices here are IR£20 to IR£28 for singles, IR£28 to IR£40 for doubles. Dun Laoghaire is easily accessible on the DART or by bus Nos 7, 7A, 8 and 46A from central Dublin.

Ballsbridge and nearby Donnybrook are good areas for better-quality B&Bs such as the *Morehampton Townhouse* (☎ 660 8630) at 46 Morehampton Rd, Donnybrook, with singles/doubles from IR£40/55. *Mrs O'Donoghue* (☎ 668 1105) is a large, convivial place at 41 Northumberland Rd (no sign) and costs from IR£24/44.

Dublin has two gay B&Bs, neither of them highly recommended, but if your pound is pink, they're there and pretty central. The larger of the two, the none-too-salubrious *Horse & Carriage* (☎ 478 3537) at 15 Aungier St adjoins the popular Incognito sauna. Singles/doubles (none with bathroom) start at IR£30/45. *Frankies* (☎ 478 3087) on narrow Camden Place between Camden and Harcourt Sts, has a dozen cramped rooms (only three of them with showers) starting at IR£20/44.

Hotels The distinction between B&Bs/guesthouses and less-expensive hotels is an academic one as far as the traveller is concerned. Facilities and prices can be the same, and often the service is more personal in a guesthouse. Hotel rates can sometimes be negotiated by asking for the commercial rate – 20-30% less than the official (or 'rack') rate.

South-west of St Stephen's in a Georgian townhouse at 84 Harcourt St is *Albany House* (☎ 475 1092; fax 475 1093) with singles/doubles for IR£60/90. Further down at No 60-61 in the erstwhile residence of George Bernard Shaw is the *Harcourt Hotel* (☎ 478

3677; fax 475 2013) with 53 rooms costing from IR£35/60 to IR£56/100. The very central *Bloom's Hotel* (☎ 671 5622; fax 671 5997), on Anglesea St, right behind the Bank of Ireland in the Temple Bar district, has 86 rooms costing IR£90/110 for singles/doubles. Dublin's most exclusive hotel is the celebrated *Shelbourne* (☎ 676 6471; fax 661 6006) at 27 St Stephen's Green. Standard singles/doubles without breakfast start at IR£130/150.

Places to Eat

Restaurants Sandwiched between the south bank of the river and Dame St is Temple Bar, an interesting old area with numerous good eating places, including the very popular *Bad Ass Café*. This cheerful and bright place at 9-11 Crown Alley is just south of the Ha'penny Bridge and offers pretty good pizzas from IR£5 to IR£7. You can also find pizza at the fancier *Da Pino*, 38-40 Parliament St on the corner of Dame St. Side by side on Temple Bar are the popular and bustling *Elephant & Castle* (burgers a speciality) at No 18 and the equally popular *Gallagher's Boxty House* at No 20-21. A boxty is a traditional Irish dish, a potato pancake that tastes like an extremely bland Indian masala dosa when eaten on its own but comes with a variety of stuffings for about IR£7.

If you want something fancier, Dame St and surrounds is a good place to look. *Les Frères Jacques* at No 74 serves authentic Gallic dishes; set lunches/dinners cost IR£13.50/22. Around the corner at 8 South Great George's St, *Il Gabbiano* serves delicious Italian food from 6 pm onwards; two people could dine here for around IR£25. An even better choice is *La Med*, an up-market Italian restaurant at 22 Essex St East with main courses from about IR£10.

At 27 Exchequer St, south of Dame St, there's the popular *Boulevard Café* with a mixed bag of panini, tapas and pasta dishes from around IR£4. On the same street at No 37 is the *Old Stand*, a popular place for pub food from IR£4.25. *Pasta Fresca* is at 3-4 Chatham St just off Grafton St and has authentic pasta dishes from IR£6.50 to IR£8.50.

Head to Mexico at *Judge Roy Bean's* at 45-47 Nassau St on the corner with Grafton St with tacos (IR£7.95) and fajitas (IR£8.95). *Eddie Rocket's City Diner* at 7 Anne St South

is a genuine 1950s-style American diner ready to dish out anything from breakfast to a late-night burger for around IR£5. Next door at No 8 is the trendy and popular *Gotham Café*.

Exotic choices (for Ireland anyway) include: the *Chameleon* in Fownes St just off Wellington Quay, with Indonesian rijstaffel and nasi goreng at IR£9.50; *Omar Khayyam*, a Middle Eastern place at 51 Wellington Quay, with kebabs (IR£9.75), couscous (IR£7.95) and some vegetarian dishes; and the Greek *La Taverna* at 33 Wicklow St, with main courses from IR£7.

Two old stand bys that remain very popular with Dubliners are the *Trocadero*, 3 St Andrew St, which stays open past midnight most nights, and the *QVII*, across the road at No 14-15, with pasta dishes for IR£5.95 to IR£7.95 and main courses for IR£7.25 to IR£12.50.

Cafés *Bewley's Cafés* are a Dublin institution: huge cafeteria-style places offering good-quality food, from breakfasts and lunchtime sandwiches to complete meals. Prices are in the IR£2.80 to IR£4 range. Opening hours vary from branch to branch, but you'll find a Bewley's at 78 Grafton St, 11-12 Westmoreland St, 13 South Great George's St (all south of the river) and at 40 Mary St (north of the river).

Munchies, on the corner of Exchequer St and William St South just west of Grafton St, claims to produce the best sandwiches in Ireland at around IR£2 and the lunch menu is worth a look. A little closer to Grafton St, at 19 Wicklow St, is *Cornucopia*, a popular 'wholefood' café.

There's a so-so but convenient café on the 1st floor of the *Kilkenny Shop* at 6 Nassau St. Also hidden away is *Fitzer's*, the slightly pricier but very popular restaurant in the National Gallery. It's open the same hours as the gallery (on Thursday until 9 pm) and has meals for around IR£5. There is also a Fitzer's at 51 Dawson St. Just off St Stephen's Green at 6 Merrion Row, *Galligan's Restaurant* is a great place for all-day breakfasts and lunch. Further along, *Georgian Fare* at 14 Baggot St Lower is good for basic sandwiches.

Dublin now boasts several cybercafés, with food, drink and non-stop computers, including

IRELAND

Planet Web at 23 Essex St East and *Internet Exchange* in Stephen St Lower.

Fast Food & Cheap Eats *Isaac's*, *Kinlay House*, the *Dublin International Youth Hostel* and especially *Avalon House* (see Hostels under Places to Stay) all have decent cafeteria-style facilities or cafés. For fast food ranging from pizzas to *KFC*, *Burger King*, *McDonald's* and a host of local late-night alternatives like *Abrakebabra*, O'Connell St north of the Liffey is the main hunting ground. *Beshoff's* at 14 Westmoreland St south of the Liffey is reliable for fish and chips (from IR£1.95).

Entertainment
The best single source of information for what's on in Dublin is the biweekly *In Dublin* available from newsstands every Thursday for IR£1.50. Outdoor free entertainment by way of buskers is a Dublin tradition. The best of them work on pedestrianised Grafton St.

Pubs Dublin has some 870 pubs so there's no possibility of being caught without a Guinness should a terrible thirst hit you. The *Old China-man* on the corner of Golden Lane and Ship St is one of the few places where pleasures go up in smoke rather than in a glass.

The *Brazen Head* on Bridge St, just south of the river, opened in 1666 or 1688 (opinions differ but either way it's the oldest pub in Dublin). In the trendy Temple Bar area popular pubs include the *Temple Bar*; the *Norseman* at the corner of Temple Bar and Eustace St; the restored *Oliver St John Gogarty Bar* at 57-58 Fleet St; and the *Auld Dubliner* at 24-25 Temple Bar.

Just off Grafton St, *Davy Byrne's* at 21 Duke St features in *Ulysses* but has been extensively yuppified. On the other side of Grafton St, the *International Bar* at 23 Wicklow St has entertainment almost every night and an excellent Wednesday comedy show at 9 pm upstairs in the Comedy Cellar. *McDaid's*, a Brendan Behan hang-out at 3 Harry St, and *John Kehoe's* with its 'snugs' on Anne St South are other well-frequented drinking holes just off Grafton St.

O'Donoghue's at 15 Merrion Row is one of the most renowned music pubs in Ireland.

Further along Baggot St Lower are a number of good pubs including *James Toner's*, which also has a high reputation for music, *Doheny & Nesbitt's*, with its antique snugs, and the trendy *Big Jack's Baggot Inn*.

At 8 Poolbeg St, between Trinity College and the river, is *John Mulligan's*, reputed to have the best Guinness in Ireland and even more famous after its appearance in the film *My Left Foot*. It's a great place for a pint and very reminiscent of old Dublin.

North of the river, *Slattery's* at 132 Capel St, on the corner of Mary's Lane, and *Sean O'Casey's* at 105 Marlborough St, on the corner of Abbey St Lower, are both busy music pubs where you'll often find traditional Irish music downstairs and loud rock upstairs.

Discos Popular bopping venues include *Break for the Border*, a Mexican-themed place at the Grafton Plaza Hotel on Stephen St Lower, the *Mean Fiddler* at 26 Wexford St and *Charlie's Rock Bar* at 2 Aungier St. Dublin's trendiest clubs (at the moment) are the *Pod* at 35 Harcourt St and *Rí-Rá* at 1 Exchequer St.

Nightly gay venues in Dublin include the multilevel, ever-throbbing *George* at 79 South Great George St and the *Shaft* at 22 Ely Place. Other places, gay or mixed on Sunday night only, include the *Temple of Sound* in the Ormond Hotel on Ormond Quay, the *Kitchen* at the Clarence Hotel, 6-8 Wellington Quay, and the *System* at 21 Anne St South. For more details look out for the monthly *Gay Community News* or *Dublin Guyz* available free at most bars.

Theatre & Concerts Pubs aren't the sole entertainment venues, and Dublin's theatre activity is limited but busy. The famous *Abbey Theatre* (☎ 878 7222) and the smaller *Peacock Theatre* are on Abbey St Lower near the river. The *Gate Theatre* (☎ 874 4045) is on Cavendish Row near Parnell Square, the *Olympia Theatre* (☎ 677 7744) is on Dame St and the *Gaiety Theatre* (☎ 677 1717) on King St South. The *City Arts Centre* (☎ 677 0643) is at 23-25 Moss St.

Concerts take place at the *National Concert Hall* (☎ 671 1888) on Earlsfort Terrace just south of St Stephen's Green. For rock concerts, head for the *Point Depot* (☎ 836 3633) at East

Link Bridge, North Wall Quay, by the river, about one km east of the Custom House.

The *Irish Film Centre* (☎ 677 8079) at 6 Eustace St in the Temple Bar district shows Irish and foreign art films and has a decent café-restaurant.

Things to Buy

If it's made in Ireland you can buy it in Dublin. The wonderful Powerscourt Townhouse Shopping Centre, just west of Grafton St, is housed in a fine old 1774 building. Other good shopping areas are Henry St north of the river and Nassau St south of it. The Kilkenny Shop at 6 Nassau has a decent selection of fine Irish crafts; some people prefer the Blarney Woollen Mills outlet further down at 21-23 Nassau St.

Getting There & Away

Air Dublin is Ireland's major international airport with flights from all over Europe and North America. The Aer Lingus offices (☎ 844 4777 for UK and Ireland enquiries, ☎ 844 4747 for other destinations) are at 13 St Stephen's Green North (on the corner with Dawson St) and at 41 O'Connell St Upper. Ryanair (☎ 677 4422) has an office at 3 Dawson St.

Bus Busáras (☎ 836 6111), Bus Éireann's central bus station, is just north of the Custom House and the Liffey at Store St. Standard one-way fares from Dublin include Cork IR£12 (three daily, 3½ hours), Donegal IR£10 (four daily, 4½ hours), Galway IR£8 (eight daily, 3¾ hours), Rosslare Harbour IR£9 (six daily, three hours), Tralee IR£14 (five daily, six hours) and Waterford IR£6 (seven daily, 2¾ hours). Buses to Belfast in Northern Ireland depart from the Busáras up to seven times a day Monday to Saturday (three times on Sunday) and cost IR£9.50/12 one-way/return.

Train Connolly station (☎ 836 3333), just north of the Liffey and the city centre, is the station for Belfast, Derry, Sligo and other points to the north as well as to Wexford. Heuston station, just south of the Liffey and well west of the centre, is the station for Cork, Galway, Killarney, Limerick, Waterford and most other points to the west, south and southwest. The Iarnród Éireann Travel Centre (☎ 836 6222) is at 35 Abbey St Lower. Regular

one-way fares from Dublin include Belfast IR£15 (six daily, 2¼ hours), Cork IR£32 (up to eight daily, 3¼ hours), Galway IR£24 (four daily, three hours) and Limerick IR£25 (up to 13 daily, 2¼ hours). As with buses, special fares are often available.

Boat Stena Line (☎ 280 8844), 15 Westmoreland St, runs the Dun Laoghaire-Holyhead ferries and catamarans; Irish Ferries (☎ 661 0511) at 2-4 Merrion Row operates the Dublin-Holyhead ferries. See the introductory Getting There & Away section of this chapter for details.

Getting Around

To/From the Airport Dublin airport (☎ 704 4222) is 10 km north of the centre, and there's an express bus service to/from Busáras for IR£2.50 (children IR£1.25). Alternatively, the slower bus Nos 41 and 41A (the latter weekends only), which make a number of useful stops on the way, terminate at Eden Quay and cost IR£1.10. A taxi to the centre should cost about IR£15, plus additional charges for baggage, extra passengers and 'unsocial hours' if travelling at night or on Sunday.

Local Transport Bus Átha Cliath, or the Dublin Bus company, has an information office (☎ 873 4222) at 59 O'Connell St. Buses cost 55p for one to three stages up to a maximum of IR£1.25. Ten-ride tickets are available at a small discount. One-day passes cost IR£3.30 for bus, IR£4.50 for bus and rail. Other passes include a one-week Citizone bus pass for IR£10.50 (students IR£8.50) or a bus-and-rail pass for IR£14.50 plus IR£2 for a photo. Late-night Nitelink buses operate from the College St/Westmoreland St/D'Olier St triangle until 3 am on Friday and Saturday nights.

DART provides quick rail access to the coast as far north as Howth (IR£1.10) and south to Bray (IR£1.30). Pearse station is handy for central Dublin. Taxis in Dublin are expensive, with flag fall at IR£1.80. To order a taxi, ring City Cabs (☎ 872 7272) or All Fives Taxi (☎ 455 7777).

Bicycle The Bike Store (☎ 872 5399) at 58 Gardiner St Lower is a popular place just round the corner from Isaac's Hostel and is the main depot for Rent-a-Bike. The daily/weekly rates are IR£7/30. There are a number of Raleigh Rent-a-Bike agencies including C Harding (☎ 873 2455) at 30 Bachelor's Walk near O'Connell Bridge. All the hostels offer secure areas to park bicycles, but be careful elsewhere; bicycle thefts are rife in Dublin.

NORTH OF DUBLIN

If you head north from Dublin along the coast, you pass through counties Dublin, Meath and Louth before you cross the border into County Down in Northern Ireland. The main areas of interest are the seaside town of Malahide, with its 12th-century castle, and around the town of Drogheda, where you will find sites dating right back to Celtic times, including the finest passage tomb in Europe.

Malahide

Despite the vicissitudes of Irish history, the Talbot family managed to keep **Malahide Castle** (☎ 846 2184) under their control from 1185 to 1973. The castle is packed with furniture and paintings, and Puck, the family ghost, is still in residence. The extensive **Fry Model Railway** in the castle grounds covers 240 sq metres and authentically displays much of Dublin and Ireland's rail and public transport system. The castle is open in summer from Monday to Friday from 10 am to 12.45 pm and 2 to 5 pm, and on Saturday and Sunday from 11.30 am to 6 pm; shorter hours apply the rest of the year. Entry is IR£2.75 (students/children IR£2.15/ 1.40).

To get to Malahide, take bus No 42 from beside Busáras, or from Connolly station a Drogheda train to the Malahide town station, which is only a 10-minute walk from the park. Malahide is 13 km north-east of Dublin.

Boyne Valley & Newgrange

There are numerous historic markers along the Boyne Valley, which are sites of the Battle of the Boyne, the epic struggle between the forces of the Catholic King James and the Protestant King William of Orange. They are really of interest only to students of Irish history, but the fertile and very beautiful valley has other very worthwhile attractions.

The finest Celtic passage tomb in Europe is a huge flattened mound faced with quartz and granite at Newgrange (☎ 041-24488) near the Boyne on the N51, about 10 km west of Drogheda, an attractive little town and a good base. It's believed to date from around 3200 BC, predating the great pyramids of Egypt by some six centuries. The site was extensively restored in the 1970s, and you can walk down the narrow passage to the tomb chamber about a third of the way into the colossal mound. At just before 9 am on the mornings of the winter solstice (December), the rising sun's rays shine directly down the long passage and illuminate the tomb chamber for 17 minutes.

Guided tours of the site run from June to September 9.30 am to 7 pm (between 10 am and 4.30 or 5 pm the rest of the year). Entry is IR£3 (students/children IR£1.25).

Mellifont Abbey & Monasterboice

Mellifont Abbey (☎ 041-26459), about eight km north-west of Drogheda, was Ireland's first Cistercian monastery and in its prime in the 12th century was the most magnificent and important centre of this monastic sect. Entry to the ruins is adults/children IR£1.50/60p, and the grounds are open from 9.30 am to 6.30 in summer. At other times, you can stroll around the grounds for free.

Just off the N1 road, about 10 km north of Drogheda, is Monasterboice with an intriguing little enclosure containing a cemetery, two ancient though unimportant church ruins, one of the finest round towers in Ireland and two of the best high crosses. Monasterboice is open year round and entry is free.

SOUTH OF DUBLIN

Heading south of Dublin, the main place of interest is Dun Laoghaire.

Dun Laoghaire

Dun Laoghaire (pronounced 'dun leary'), only 13 km south of central Dublin, is both a busy harbour with ferry connections to Britain and a popular resort. There is a hostel in Dun Laoghaire, as well as many B&Bs; they're a bit cheaper than in central Dublin, and the fast and frequent rail connections make it easy to stay out here. See the Dublin Places to Stay section for some options.

Dun Laoghaire is very popular for sailing, and the **National Maritime Museum**, housed in an old church, is open May to September from 2 to 5.30 pm from Tuesday to Sunday. Entry is adults/children IR£1.50/75p.

On the southern side of the harbour is the **Martello Tower**, where James Joyce's epic novel, *Ulysses*, opens. It now houses the **James Joyce Museum** (☎ 280 9265). *Ulysses* follows its characters around Dublin during a single day, and many of the places visited on that journey can still be found in the capital; there are several Joycean Dublin guides available with good maps. An annual retracing of the journey takes place on Bloomsday (16 June). The tower is open April to October from Monday to Saturday from 10 am to 5 pm, and on Sunday from 2 to 6 pm. Phone in advance at other times of year. Entry is adults/students/children IR£2/1.60/1.10.

Just below the Martello Tower is the **Forty Foot Pool**. At the close of the first chapter of *Ulysses*, Buck Mulligan heads off to the Forty Foot Pool for a morning swim in the frigid ('scrotum-tightening' in Joyce's words) Irish Sea. A morning wake-up here is still a Dun Laoghaire tradition, winter or summer. The 'wear togs' sign does not apply until 9 am; until then it is mainly patronised by 'Forty Foot gentlemen' and a few brave women. Bus No 7, 7A, 8 or 46A or the DART rail service (IR£1.10, 20 minutes) will take you from Dublin to Dun Laoghaire.

The South-East

COUNTY WICKLOW

Wicklow, bordering County Dublin to the south, has three contenders for the 'best in Ireland': best garden (at Powerscourt), best monastic site (at Glendalough) and best walk (along the Wicklow Way). There are some fine beaches stretching south from Wicklow town to Arklow.

Powerscourt

Near Enniskerry and about 22 km south of Dublin, the 18th-century mansion at Powerscourt Estate (☎ 01-286 7676) was burned to the ground in 1974 shortly after a major renovation had been completed when a bird's nest caught fire in the chimney. One wing survives, but it's the magnificent gardens that attract the crowds. The 20-hectare formal gardens were laid out in the 19th century, with the magnificent natural backdrop of the Great Sugar Loaf Mountain to the east. There are five garden terraces extending for over 500 metres down to Triton Lake.

Opening hours from March to October are 9.30 am to 5.30 pm daily, and entry is adults/students IR£3/2.50. The estate's noted waterfall, open year round, is further south and entry is IR£1.50/1. There's a six-km walking path from the estate to the falls. Bus No 44 runs regularly from Hawkins St in Dublin to Enniskerry.

Glendalough

From its establishment in the late 6th century by St Kevin, Glendalough monastery grew to become one of the most important in Ireland, surviving Viking raids in the 9th and 10th centuries and an English incursion in 1398 before final suppression in the 16th century. The site is entered through the only monastic gateway to survive in Ireland. The ruins include a round tower, cathedral, a fine high cross and the delightful little Church of St Kevin.

Glendalough (pronounced 'glenda-lock') is close enough to Dublin to attract lots of tourists in summer. Entry to the Glendalough Visitor Centre (☎ 45325) is adults/children IR£2/1, but the site is free. The centre has some interesting displays including a model of the monastery in its heyday and a fine audiovisual is shown regularly. The centre is open daily all year round from 9 am to 6.30 pm.

Glendalough's telephone code is ☎ 0404.

The *Glendalough An Óige Hostel* (☎ 45342) is near the site and costs from IR£5 to £7.50 per person. At the village of Laragh, three km west of the monastic site, the IHO *Wicklow Way Hostel* (☎ 45398), beside Lynham's Bar, charges IR£6 for a dorm bed and is open all year. The independent *Old Mill Hostel* (☎ 45156) is housed in farm buildings one km south of Laragh on the road to Rathdrum. The charge is IR£6.50 a night for a bed in dorms or IR£9 in double rooms.

St Kevin's Bus Service (☎ 281 8119) runs daily between St Stephen's Green in Dublin and the site. Departures from Dublin are at 11.30 am, and departures from Glendalough are at 4.15 pm; the one-way/return fare is IR£5/8.

IRELAND

The Wicklow Way

Running for 132 km from County Dublin through County Wicklow to County Carlow, this is the longest established and most popular of Ireland's long-distance walks. The walk is well-documented in leaflets and guidebooks; one of the better ones is *Hill Stroller's Wicklow* (IR£3.50). Much of the trail traverses countryside above 500 metres, so you should be prepared for Ireland's fickle weather.

If you don't feel up to tackling the whole eight to 10-day walk, the three-day section from Enniskerry near Powerscourt to Glendalough is probably the most attractive and has easy transport at each end.

Along with the An Óige hostel in Glendalough and the two independent ones at Laragh (see Glendalough above), An Óige hostels along the route include *Glencree* (☎ 286 4037) and *Knockree* (☎ 286 4036), both at Enniskerry, and *Aghavannagh* (☎ 0402-36366) at Aughrim.

Prices range from IR£4.50 to £6.

WEXFORD

Little remains of Wexford's Viking past, apart from its name (Waesfjord or 'ford of mud flats') and rather narrow streets. Cromwell was in one of his most destructive moods when he included Wexford in his 1649 Irish itinerary, destroying the churches and 'putting to the sword' three-quarters of the town's 2000 inhabitants. Wexford is 21 km north-west of Rosslare, a popular arrival point for visitors by ferry from Wales and France.

Orientation & Information

The quay streets run along the waterfront; North and South Main Sts run parallel a block inland to the south-east.

The tourist office (☎ 23111; fax 41743), open all year, is on the waterfront at Crescent Quay. The main post office is one block west on Anne St. If you need to wash clothes, My Beautiful Laundrette on St Peter's Square, 300 metres south-west of the harbour, is open six days a week. The Book Centre is on South Main St.

The telephone code for Wexford is ☎ 053.

Things to See & Do

Dating from 1300 the huge **West Gate** west of North Main St is the only surviving gate tower to the city, although several stretches of wall remain. The **West Gate Heritage Centre** there has an audiovisual display on the history of Wexford (entry IR£1.50) open from April to December. The ruined condition of nearby **Selskar Abbey** is a result of Cromwell's visit. In 1172 Henry II spent 40 days in the abbey as penance for murdering Thomas à Becket two years before. Bull baiting used to take place at the **Bullring**, on the corner of Cornmarket and North Main St.

About five km north-west of Wexford, right beside the Dublin-Rosslare N11 road at Ferrycarrig, the **Irish National Heritage Park** (☎ 20733) is an outdoor theme park condensing Irish history from the Stone Age to the early Norman period of the 12th century through 14 reconstructions. Entry is adults/children & students IR£3.50/2, and it's open every day from 10 am to 7 pm from mid-March to October.

Places to Stay

The *Ferrybank Camping Park* (☎ 44378), across the River Slaney from the town centre, is open from Easter to October and costs from IR£3 to IR£7 for a tent site. The nearest hostel is the An Óige *Rosslare Harbour Hostel* (☎ 33399; IR£5.50 to 6.50) although there is also the slightly cheaper An Óige *Arthurstown Hostel* (☎ 389411) at Arthurstown, 23 km to the south-west via the R733 and closer to Waterford.

Several B&Bs are convenient to the centre. *Westgate House* (☎ 24428) some 150 metres south of the train station has singles/doubles from IR£17/27. Further south, the *St George* (☎ 43474) on the corner of John and George Sts charges IR£20/34. Almost diagonally opposite on St John's Rd, *Kilderry* (☎ 23848) charges IR£23/32 for rooms with shower and IR£20/28 without. Other places can be found both north and south of town along the N11.

Places to Eat

Parallel to the waterfront, North and South Main Sts have something for most tastes including fish and chips at the *Premier* (104 South Main St), Chinese at *Chan's Restaurant* (90 North Main St) and pub grub at the *Bohemian Girl* (near the Cornmarket at 2-4 North Main St).

Good places at lunchtime include *Joanne's Bakery* at the corner of Cornmarket and North

Main St, the **Wooden Brasserie** with a daily carvery on North Main and Rowe Sts, the **Chapter Coffee Shop** under the Book Centre and **Kelly's Deli** at 80 South Main St. **Green Acres** sells fruit, vegetables and prepared dishes from a 19th-century food hall at 54 North Main St.

Robertino's at 19 South Main St has decent pizzas from IR£4.50. The **Country Kitchen** at White's Hotel on George St can be relied on for a very good meal at lunchtime or dinner.

Entertainment

Many of Wexford's pubs are strung along North and South Main Sts, where you'll find **Tim's Tavern**, the **Commodore** and the **Bohemian Girl**. Just round the corner on Cornmarket is the atmospheric **Thomas Moore Tavern**, where the poet's mother was born, and down on Customs House Quay is the **Wren's Nest**, which often features music. Wexford hosts the country's biggest Opera Festival in late October as well as regular live performances throughout the year at its **Arts Centre** and the **Theatre Royal**.

Getting There & Away

Wexford is connected by train with Dublin (via Wicklow) and Rosslare and Waterford three times daily (twice on Sunday). Bus Éireann services to Rosslare, Dublin, Killarney etc also operate from the train station (☎ 22522) near the waterfront. Buses to Dublin run by the private Ardcavan Coach Company (☎ 22561) stop at Crescent Quay by the tourist office in the morning.

If you're travelling by bike or car between Wexford and Waterford, it's worth taking the short cut via the R733 to Ballyhack, where you cross the river estuary year round by small ferry to the town of Passage East. One-way fares are IR£1 for cyclists and IR£3.50 for cars and passengers.

Getting Around

Dave Allen Cycles (☎ 22516), next to Kelly's Deli at 84-86 South Main St, rents bikes for IR£7/35 per day/week. You can book a taxi in Wexford by ringing ☎ 46666.

WATERFORD

Although Waterford is a busy port and modern commercial centre, it also retains fascinating vestiges of its Viking and Norman past. The legendary Norman Richard FitzGilbert de Clare, Earl of Pembroke and nicknamed Strongbow, took the city in 1170, and in later centuries it was the most powerful centre in Ireland. Today Waterford is famed for its crystal, one of Ireland's better-known exports.

Orientation & Information

Like Wexford, the long quays on the River Suir and the narrow lanes behind them are reminders of the town's Viking origins. The tourist office (☎ 875823; fax 877388), open all year, is at 41 Merchant's Quay. If you need to wash clothes, try Washed Ashore, close by at No 36. It is open daily except Sunday. The main post office is three blocks to the east on Parade Quay. The excellent Book Centre is on Baronstrand St, which runs from the quayside clock tower south to the shopping area.

The telephone code for Waterford is ☎ 051.

Things to See & Do

There are several handsome sections of the old city wall still standing, including **Reginald's Tower**, which dates from 1003. Admission is IR£1/50p for adults/children. Around the corner on Greyfriars St is the **Waterford Heritage Centre** with Viking and medieval displays (entry IR£1/50p).

Next door to the centre is the **French Church**. Founded in 1240, it served as a hospital in the 16th century, which enabled it to survive the suppression of the monasteries. It takes its name from the Huguenot refugees who used it in the 18th century, after which it fell into ruins. Among other important churches in Waterford is the Church of Ireland's **Christ Church Cathedral**, one of the town's many 18th-century buildings constructed by John Roberts.

Self-paced tours of the **Waterford Crystal Factory** (☎ 373311) at Kilbarry, two km west on the Cork Rd, cost adults/students IR£3.50/1.75. You can either buy your ticket at the tourist office or on site.

Guided walking tours of Waterford commence from the Granville Hotel on Merchant's Quay at noon and 2 pm daily from March to October and cost IR£3.

IRELAND

Places to Stay

The *Newtown Cove Caravan & Camping Park* (☎ 381979) is near Tramore, 10 km south of Waterford on the coast. It is open from April to September and charges IR£6 to 11 to pitch a tent.

The place to stay in Waterford is the immaculate *Viking House* (☎ 853827), a smart new IHH hostel on Coffee House Lane, just off Greyfriars St behind the quay. Dorm beds start at IR£8.50 and the price includes breakfast and a personal security locker. Basic singles/twins start at IR£15/26 in summer. An Óige *Arthurstown Hostel* (see Places to Stay under Wexford) is eight km south-east of Waterford across the estuary in County Wexford.

In town you can choose from the usual ample supply of B&Bs. *Beechwood* (☎ 876677) is wonderfully central at 7 Cathedral Square and has singles/doubles for IR£15/26, but there are only three rooms. *Corlea* (☎ 875764) at 2 New St, just off the southern end of Michael St, also has three rooms for IR£14/25.

The *Portree Guesthouse* (☎ 874574) on Mary St, just off Bridge St, has rooms with shower for IR£20/32 and ones without for IR£16/25. *Derrynane House* (☎ 875179) at 19 The Mall charges a punt or two less. For more B&Bs, The Mall and its extension, Parnell St, are good places to look, or try further out along Cork Rd. *Dooley's* (☎ 873531; fax 870262) is at 30 Merchant's Quay and provides the best hotel value. Spacious singles/doubles start at IR£30/57 (IR£41/77 in summer), though packages are available

Places to Eat

Bewley's Café is upstairs in the Broad St Centre on Broad St, the main shopping street. There are various fast-food places along this street and its extension Michael St, including a branch of the popular fast-food chain *Abrakebabra*.

A number of pubs turn out meals. *T & H Doolan* at 32 George's St is particularly good at lunchtimes, and *Egan's* on Baronstrand St serves meals cafeteria style. The *Olde Stand* at 45 Michael St serves bar food downstairs and seafood and steaks upstairs.

At 11 O'Connell St, *Haricot's* is a delightful wholefood restaurant with superb main courses from IR£3.95. It's good for carnivores and vegetarians alike, or for a herbal tea and a slice of apple or banana-walnut cake (IR£1.65) at any time. Haricot's is open Monday to Friday from 9 am to 8 pm, Saturday only to 5.45 pm. More expensive restaurants include *Reginald's* behind Reginald's Tower and the excellent *Dwyer's*, open just for dinner in an old barracks at 8 Mary St. Starters/mains average IR£3/13.

One of the best – and most expensive – Chinese restaurants in Ireland is the *Jade Palace* on The Mall around the corner from Reginald's Tower.

Entertainment

Many Waterford pubs feature music. The venerable *T & H Doolan* at 32 George's St has one wall that could be a contemporary of the 1000-year-old city wall. Equally popular are *Geoff's* and the *Pulpit*, side by side on John St. Diagonally across the road from those two but at 27 Michael St is the *Olde Rogue*. Back towards the river there's *Lord's* just off Broad St in Arundel Lane and *Egan's* on Baronstrand St; the latter has a disco upstairs called *Bourbon Street* at weekends. The *Roxy Theatre Club* on O'Connell St has music and Saturday-night discos.

The *Garter Lane Art Centre*, with branches at 5 and 22 O'Connell St, hosts films and exhibitions and stages plays. Waterford has a Light Opera Festival held in late September.

Getting There & Away

The train and bus stations (☎ 873401) are across the river from the town centre. There are regular train connections to Dublin (IR£11, 2½ hours, four daily), Limerick (IR£10, 2½ hours, one daily), Rosslare (IR£6, 80 minutes, twice daily), Kilkenny and Wexford. There are private as well as Bus Éireann services to Dublin (IR£6), Cork, Limerick, Wexford (IR£7.30) and Rosslare (IR£8.80). Waterford has an airport (☎ 875589) with flights to London's Stansted airport. The USIT office (☎ 872601) is at 36-37 George's St.

Getting Around

Wright's Cycle Depot (☎ 874411) at 19-20 Henrietta St is a Raleigh Rent-a-Bike centre. Taxis can be ordered on ☎ 877777 or ☎ 877775.

CORK

There may be no specific reasons to visit the Irish Republic's second-largest city, but Cork is a surprisingly appealing place where it's easy to lose track of a day or two. Budget accommodation is plentiful, and the crack is right up there with the best in Ireland.

The town dates back to the 7th century and survived Cromwell's visit but it fell to King William in 1690. Cork played a key role in Ireland's independence struggle, with one mayor killed by the Black & Tans in 1920, his successor dying as a result of a hunger strike and much of the town being burned down. Today Cork is noted for its fierce rivalry with Dublin and its citizens' civic pride.

Orientation & Information

The town centre is an island between two channels of the River Lee. Oliver Plunkett St and the curve of St Patrick's St (or Patrick St) are the important central streets. The train station and several hostels are north of the river; MacCurtain St and Glanmire Rd Lower are the main thoroughfares there. The Shandon area, also north of the river, is an interesting older area to wander around.

The less-than-helpful tourist office (☎ 273251; fax 273504), really a big shop, is on Grand Parade south-west of Oliver Plunkett St, where you'll find the main post office. The Quay Co-op Restaurant has a good notice board. Waterstone's bookshop at 69 St Patrick's St runs back as far as Paul St. There's a laundrette at 14 MacCurtain St across from Isaac's Hostel open six days a week, or try the College Laundrette on Western Rd opposite the gates of University College Cork.

The telephone code for Cork is ☎ 021.

Things to See

Around Town Cork's interesting churches include the imposing **St Finbarre's Cathedral** south of the centre. Nearby are the fragmentary remains of 17th-century **Elizabeth Fort**. North of the river there's a fine view from the tower of **St Anne's Church Shandon** (IR£1.50), where you can ring the famous Shandon bells. It's open every day except Sunday from 10 am to 5 pm. Nearby, the **Cork Butter Exchange** now houses the Shandon Craft Centre.

The **Cork Public Museum** is west of the centre in Fitzgerald Park near Cork's An Óige

hostel and is worth a visit. Entry is free, except on Sunday, and it's open Monday to Friday from 11 am to 1 pm and 2.15 to 5 pm (to 6 pm in summer) and Sunday from 3 to 5 pm.

Cork City Gaol, with an interesting history, is open daily from 9.30 am to 6 pm from March to October with shorter hours the rest of the year. Guided tours cost adults/students/children IR£3/2.50/1.50. The gaol is on Sunday's Well Rd, about a half-hour's walk west of the centre.

Blarney Castle Even the most untouristy visitor will probably feel compelled to kiss the **Blarney Stone** at Blarney Castle and get the gift of the gab. It was Queen Elizabeth I who invented the word, due to her exasperation with the ability of one Dermot MacCarthy, Lord Blarney, to talk endlessly without ever getting down to action. Bending over backwards to kiss the hallowed rock requires a head for heights. The castle is eight km north-west of the city and is open daily from 9 am to 6.30 or 7 pm, or sundown depending on the time of year. Entry is adults/students/children IR£3/2/1.

The adjacent **Blarney House**, a 19th-century baronial home, is open from noon until 6 pm Monday to Saturday, June to mid-September. Entry is adults/students/children IR£2.50/ 2/1. A combined ticket costs IR£5/ 3.50/2. About 15 buses a day run from the Cork bus station and cost IR£1.75 one-way or IR£2.60 return. There are also private services from some of the hostels for a little less.

Places to Stay

Hostels The competition among hostels in Cork is fierce. At 48 MacCurtain St, midway between the train station and city centre, the IHH *Isaac's Hostel* (☎ 500011) is a big place in a fine old building. A bed costs IR£6.25 in the large dorms, IR£7.75 in the four to six-bed ones, IR£29 for private doubles or IR£17.75 for a single. It has a good cafeteria, kitchen facilities and bicycle hire (IR£7/30 per day/week), but the dorm rooms are closed every day from 11 am to 5 pm.

Friendly *Kinlay House Shandon* (☎ 508966), also a member of the IHH group, is at Bob & Joan Walk behind St Anne's Church Shandon, just north of the river. It's

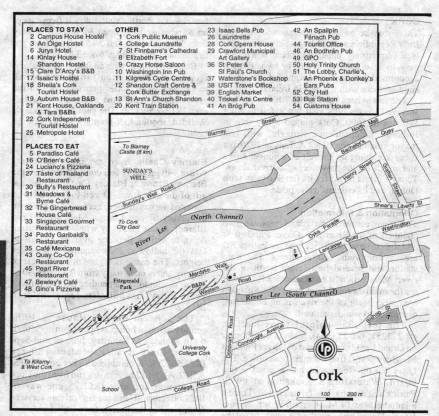

PLACES TO STAY	OTHER	23 Isaac Bells Pub	42 An Spailpín
2 Campus House Hostel	1 Cork Public Museum	26 Laundrette	Fánach Pub
3 An Óige Hostel	4 College Laundrette	28 Cork Opera House	44 Tourist Office
6 Jurys Hotel	7 St Finnbarre's Cathedral	29 Crawford Municipal	46 An Bodhrán Pub
14 Kinlay House	8 Elizabeth Fort	Art Gallery	49 GPO
Shandon Hostel	9 Crazy Horse Saloon	36 St Peter &	50 Holy Trinity Church
15 Clare D'Arcy's B&B	10 Washington Inn Pub	St Paul's Church	51 The Lobby, Charlie's,
17 Isaac's Hostel	11 Kilgrews Cycle Centre	37 Waterstone's Bookshop	An Phoenix & Donkey's
18 Sheila's Cork	12 Shandon Craft Centre &	38 USIT Travel Office	Ears Pubs
Tourist Hostel	Cork Butter Exchange	39 English Market	52 City Hall
19 Auburn House B&B	13 St Ann's Church Shandon	40 Triskel Arts Centre	53 Bus Station
21 Kent House, Oaklands	20 Kent Train Station	41 An Bróg Pub	54 Customs House
& Tara B&Bs			
22 Cork Independent			
Tourist Hostel			
25 Metropole Hotel			
PLACES TO EAT			
5 Paradiso Café			
16 O'Brien's Café			
24 Luciano's Pizzeria			
27 Taste of Thailand			
Restaurant			
30 Bully's Restaurant			
31 Meadows &			
Byrne Café			
32 The Gingerbread			
House Café			
33 Singapore Gourmet			
Restaurant			
34 Paddy Garibaldi's			
Restaurant			
35 Café Mexicana			
43 Quay Co-Op			
Restaurant			
45 Pearl River			
Restaurant			
47 Bewley's Café			
48 Gino's Pizzeria			

almost as convenient to the centre as Isaac's and much quieter. Dorm beds in rooms for four cost IR£7.50, twin rooms are IR£22 and singles are IR£15. All include a continental breakfast.

Beyond Isaac's, towards the train station and back from MacCurtain St on Belgrave Place, Wellington Rd, is the IHH **Sheila's Cork Tourist Hostel** (☎ 505562), which is neat and tidy and very well equipped; there's even a sauna! Dorm beds start at IR£6.50 and private doubles at IR£19. The location is convenient but quiet, and the hostel also rents bicycles for IR£6 a day.

The IHO **Cork Independent Tourist Hostel** (☎ 509089) at 100 Glanmire Rd Lower is just beyond the train station. It's a small, friendly place without the facilities of the larger hostels. The nightly cost is IR£6.

Kellys (☎ 315612), also an IHO member, is south of the river near George's Quay at 25 Summerhill South. It is a newly renovated hostel with beds from IR£6. There's a laundry, sleeping sheets aren't required and there's no afternoon lockout.

On the other side of the centre is the An Óige **Cork Hostel** (☎ 543289) at 1-2 Redclyffe Terrace, Western Rd. It's a big, well-organised

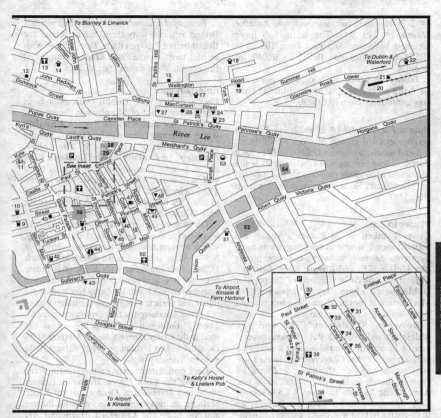

hostel and costs from IR£7 per night, but rooms are shut between 10 am and 2 pm or so. There are bikes for rent. Take bus No 8 from the centre, two km away. *Campus House* (☎ 343531), a stone's throw from the An Óige hostel at 3 Woodland View, Western Rd, is open in summer only. It's a very small hostel but neat and tidy and costs IR£6.

B&Bs Glanmire Rd Lower, a short distance east of the train station towards Dublin, is lined with economical B&Bs, including *Kent House* (☎ 504260) at No 47, *Oaklands* (☎ 500578) at No 51 and *Tara House* (☎ 500294) at No 52.

Singles are IR£15 to IR£17 and doubles IR£28 to IR£30.

More central is *Clare D'Arcy's* (☎ 504658), a very friendly place in a fabulous Georgian mansion at 7 Sydney Place, Wellington Rd, with singles/doubles from IR£22/40 (IR£25/45 with bathroom). About 200 metres to the east at 3 Garfield Place, Wellington Rd, *Auburn House* (☎ 508555) has singles and doubles with/without bathroom for IR£18/15 and IR£32/28.

On the opposite side of town, Western Rd leads towards Killarney and also has plenty of higher-priced B&Bs, including *St Kilda's*

(☎ 273095) and, two doors down, *Antoine House* (☎ 273494). The rooms all have attached bathroom and cost from IR£22 to IR£25 for singles and IR£35 to IR£40 for doubles.

Danny's B&B (☎ 503606), a gay place at 3 St John's Terrace, Upper John St, has singles/doubles from IR£18/30.

Hotels *Jurys Hotel* (☎ 276622; fax 274477) on Western Rd is one of Cork's half-dozen top-end hotels. It charges IR£100 to £119 for a double. More economical (and central) is the old-world *Metropole* (☎ 508122; fax 506450) on MacCurtain St, with singles/doubles from IR£65/90.

Places to Eat

Oliver Plunkett St, St Patrick's St and the pedestrianised streets connecting them have numerous eateries, including fast-food places like *McDonald's* and *Burger King*. *Bewley's Café* at 4 Cook St is a branch of the popular Dublin-based chain. Try *O'Brien's* at 39 MacCurtain St for tea, scones, sandwiches and good, home-made ice cream.

Between St Patrick's St and the pedestrianised area of Paul St are several narrow lanes with good places for a sandwich or full meal. Try the *Gingerbread House Café* on Carey's Lane or *Meadows & Byrne* on French Church St for lunch or coffee or tea. Almost side by side in Carey's Lane there's *Café Mexicana* and *Paddy Garibaldi's*, an Irish-Italian hybrid with pasta, pizzas and hamburgers. There's a branch of the latter in Washington St. The rather expensive *Singapore Gourmet Restaurant* in Carey's Lane serves laksa, noodle dishes (IR£7.50) etc that would be unrecognisable in Asia. *Bully's* at 40 Paul St is a reasonably priced restaurant also good for pizza and pasta.

The *Quay Co-Op Restaurant* upstairs at 24 Sullivan's Quay and *Paradiso Café*, opposite Jurys Hotel on Western Rd, both serve excellent vegetarian meals. Lunch at either place costs IR£4 or £5, with dinner a few pounds more. *Gino's Pizzeria* at 7 Winthrop St off Oliver Plunkett St and *Luciano's* next to the Metropole Hotel on MacCurtain St and open till at least 1 am are two good pizzerias. Gino's also has excellent Italian ice cream.

Taste of Thailand, just across St Patrick's Bridge, offers a tasty three-course dinner for IR£10 before 7.30 pm daily. For Chinese with an Irish twist, try the *Pearl River* upstairs at 20 Princes St. Main dishes start at IR£6.

Entertainment

Cork's rivalry with Dublin even extends to drink. Here a pint of Murphy's is the stout of choice – not Guinness, or even a Beamish, which is cheaper in most pubs. On Union Quay near the corner of Anglesea St, *The Lobby*, *Charlie's*, *An Phoenix* and the *Donkey's Ears* are all side by side, and at least one of them will have some sort of live music most nights. The Lobby at No 1 is arguably the best place in town for traditional music, An Phoenix for rock (Thursday and Sunday nights).

On Oliver Plunkett St *An Bodhrán* at No 42 regularly features music as does *An Bróg*, which attracts a young, alternative crowd, at No 78. More subdued is *An Spailpín Fánach* at 28 South Main St, with traditional music four nights a week. *Isaac Bells*, behind Luciano's on St Patrick's Quay has traditional music and attracts a local crowd. Students hang out at the *Washington Inn* on Washington St. There's traditional Irish dancing across the road at the *Crazy Horse Saloon*. *Loafers* at 26 Douglas St is a lesbian pub that attracts male gays on Tuesday night.

Cork prides itself on its cultural institutions, including the *Cork Opera House* in Emmet Place and *Triskel Arts Centre* just off South Main St, an important venue for films, theatre and the like. The *Crawford Municipal Art Gallery* next to the Opera House is worth a visit and costs nothing. It's open Monday to Saturday from 10 am to 5 pm. The Cork International Jazz Festival takes place in late October and an International Film Festival is held in September.

Getting There & Away

The bus station (☎ 508188) is on the corner of Merchants Quay and Parnell Place east of the centre, while Kent railway station (☎ 506766) is across the river on Glanmire Rd Lower. There are frequent bus and train connections to Dublin and other main centres. One-way bus fares include Dublin IR£12, Limerick IR£9, Killarney IR£8.80, Waterford IR£8 and Wexford IR£12. Trains go to Dublin (IR£33),

Killarney (IR£13.50), Waterford (IR£17), Kilkenny (IR£23) and Galway (IR£30). Beyond the train station, Glanmire Rd Lower is often lined with hitchhikers heading out of town to Cork's big-smoke rival, Dublin.

Cork has an international airport (☎ 313131) six km south, and there are also ferry connections with several ports in Britain and France. Shipping company telephone numbers include Irish Ferries (☎ 504333) and Brittany Ferries (☎ 277801). The USIT office (☎ 270900) is hidden away at 10-11 Market Parade, a narrow arcade off St Patrick St near the Grand Parade junction.

Getting Around

Buses to Cork airport run 15 times a day (four on Sunday) from the bus station. The one-way/return fare is IR£2.50/3.50. You can book a taxi in Cork by ringing ☎ 272222 or ☎ 961961.

A number of the hostels rent bicycles for around IR£7/30 a day/week, or try Kilgrews Cycle Centre (☎ 276255) at 6-7 Kyle St. The cost is the same but you must put down a IR£40 deposit.

KINSALE

If a director were to create a film set of the perfect Irish seaside town, he or she might come up with Kinsale – minus the traffic jams in summer. The tourist office (☎ 774026; fax 774438) is on Pier Rd in the centre of town. There's a small museum in the old courthouse building where the enquiry into the 1915 sinking of the *Lusitania*, which went down off the coast at Cobh to the east, was held. A short distance south-east of the village are the huge ruins of 17th-century **Charles Fort**, a fine example of a star-shaped fort. Entry is adults/children IR£2/1, and it's open from 9 am to 6 pm in summer with slightly shorter hours in spring and autumn.

Buses connect Kinsale with Cork (IR£3.80) half a dozen times a day and stop just south-west of the tourist office. Mylie Murphy (☎ 772703) on Main St rents bicycles.

Kinsale's telephone code is ☎ 021.

Places to Stay & Eat

Kinsale has plenty of B&Bs (ask the tourist office for its *Good Accommodation Guide* pamphlet), an unofficial camping ground close to the waterfront on the edge of town (en route to Summercove and Charles Fort) and the IHH *Dempsey's Hostel* (☎ 772124), a couple of minutes walk from the centre of town on Eastern Rd and costing IR£5 a night plus 50p for showers. Doubles are IR£12.

Not only is Kinsale impossibly cute, it also lays claim to the title of gourmet centre of Ireland (though sheer numbers don't always mean quality). Fortunately, if your credit card can't stretch to a meal at one of the dozen 'Good Food Circle' restaurants, you can still eat well at many more simpler establishments like *Mother Hubbard's Café* at the northern end of Pearse St or *Patsy's Corner Café*, a few steps to the north-west on Market Square. If you want to sample gourmet dining, you would have no trouble spending IR£30 a head at the fancier restaurants, but some of them – like *Max's* on Main St – have less-expensive tourist menus for around IR£12. The *Cottage Loft* about 50 metres north gets consistently good reviews for its seafood. Many restaurants close down from November to March.

CORK TO BANTRY

Travelling west from Kinsale can be tough, as bus services are limited and hitching competition can be fierce. Skibbereen (year-round tourist office ☎ 028-21766; fax 028-21353) does have a bus connection with Cork, and it's very scenic from there down to Baltimore, from where boats run to Cape Clear Island between one and four times a day throughout the year. The IHH *Rolf's Hostel* (☎ 028-20289) in Baltimore is a popular place with dorm beds/doubles costing IR£6/20. There's the An Óige *Cape Clear Hostel* (☎ 028-39144) on Cape Clear Island open from April to October. Dorm beds start at IR£5.

West Cork's three peninsulas – Mizen Head, Sheep's Head and Beara – are scenic alternatives to the better known and much more touristy Iveragh (Ring of Kerry) and Dingle peninsulas in County Kerry. At Allihies village on the wild Beara Peninsula there's the IHH *Village Hostel* (☎ 027-73107), open April to September, and an *An Óige Hostel* (☎ 027-73014). The IHO *Ard na Mara Hostel* (☎ 027-74271) at Eyeries on the north coast is open May to October.

IRELAND

BANTRY

Wedged between hills and the waters of Bantry Bay, this little town's major attraction is colourful old **Bantry House**, superbly situated overlooking the bay. The gardens are beautifully kept, and the house is noted for its French and Flemish tapestries and the eclectic collection of odds and ends assembled by William White, 2nd Earl of Bantry, during his overseas peregrinations between 1820 and 1850. Entry is adults/students/children with family IR£3/1.75/free and it's open from 10 am to 6 pm daily (closed in winter).

In the courtyard of the house (joint tickets will save you IR£2) is a French Armada exhibit (adults/students/children IR£2.50/1.50/1), recounting the sorry saga of France's attempt in 1796 to aid the Irish independence struggle. The exhibit centres around the scuttled French frigate *La Surveillante*, which may one day be raised from Bantry Bay. From the central pier, boats run to nearby **Whiddy Island** (IR£5 return) in season. There's a tourist office (☎ 50229) open from late May to September on New St.

Bantry's telephone code is ☎ 027.

Places to Stay & Eat

The IHH *Bantry Independent Hostel* (☎ 51050), open mid-March to October, is on Bishop Lucey Place just off Glengarriff Rd about 600 metres north-east of the town centre. The nightly cost is IR£6.50 and the two doubles cost IR£16. Much more central and open all year is the IHO *Harbour View Hostel* (☎ 51140) on Marino St near the main square, with dorm beds from IR£7.50 in summer. There are plenty of B&Bs, including a number around the central square, out along the Glengarriff Rd and at the top end of town.

Food possibilities in Bantry include the expensive though highly acclaimed *O'Connor's*, right next to the tourist office, with lunch specials from IR£5, or at the other end of Bridge St, *Ó Síocháin*, which has a standard café-style menu. *Kearney's Kitchen* in Barrack St is a similar place. There are plenty of pubs along New St, including the dumpy but popular *Anchor Tavern & Lounge*.

INLAND
Cahir

Riverside **Cahir Castle** (☎ 052-41011), one of the most complete and best preserved castles in Ireland, has had numerous additions, although its basic structure dates back to the 13th or 14th century. It was besieged and taken in 1559 and surrendered to Cromwell in 1650. Entry is adults/children & students IR£2/1. In summer it's open from 9 am to 7.30 pm and guided tours are available. At other times of the year it opens at 10 am and closes at 4.30 or 6 pm.

Rock of Cashel

One of Ireland's most spectacular medieval sites, the Rock of Cashel (☎ 062-61437) is in the town of Cashel some 18 km north of Cahir. In one complex there's a cathedral, 12th-century Cormac's Chapel, a round tower, the eroded remains of an unusual high cross, the restored Hall of Vicars and several other structures. The complex is open from mid-June to mid-September from 9 am to 7.30 pm, and from 10 am to 4.30 or 6 pm the rest of the year. Entry is adults/children & students IR£2.50/£1. The IHH *Cashel Holiday Hostel* (☎ 062-62330) at 6 John St in Cahel town has dorm rooms for IR£6 and doubles from IR£17.

KILKENNY

Lovely Kilkenny – Ireland's 'medieval capital' – has a long history, some fine reminders of its medieval past and a particularly good collection of music pubs. Kilkenny's glory days came to an end in 1650 when Cromwell ransacked the town.

Orientation & Information

Most places of interest can be found on or close to Parliament St and its continuation (High St), which runs parallel to the River Nore; or along John St, which leads away from it to the north-east. The tourist office (☎ 51500; fax 63955), open all year, is in the old Shee Alms House on Rose Inn St, south-west of the river.

Both the main post office and Book Centre are on High Street. Brett's Laundrette, open six days a week, is on Michael St, just off John St, not far from the bus and train stations. For high-quality Irish goods and souvenirs, visit the Kilkenny Design Centre in an 18th-century coach house and stables opposite the castle on The Parade.

Kilkenny's telephone code is ☎ 056.

Things to See & Do

Kilkenny Castle Stronghold of the powerful Butler family, Kilkenny Castle has a history dating back to 1172 and Strongbow himself, though the present castle is a much more recent structure. The Long Gallery, with its vividly painted ceiling and extensive portrait collection of Butler family members over the centuries, is quite remarkable. In summer the castle is open from 10 am to 7 pm and entry is adults/students & children IR£3/1.25. Hours are shorter for the rest of the year and in winter it closes at lunch and on Monday.

St Canice's Cathedral At the northern end of Parliament St is Irishtown and St Canice's Cathedral, which dates from 1251 and has some interesting tombs and monuments. You can ascend the narrow round tower in the church grounds for under IR£1.

Other Attractions On Parliament St, **Rothe House** is a fine old merchant's house dating from 1594. From April to October it's open from 10.30 am to 5 pm Monday to Saturday, and 3 to 5 pm on Sunday. For the rest of the year the hours are 3 to 5 pm on Saturday and Sunday only. Entry is adults/students/children IR£1.50/1/60p.

The **Smithwick Brewery** (☎ 21014), also on Parliament St, shows a video and has tastings Monday to Friday at 3 pm from June to September. Tickets are available from the tourist office. Kilkenny has many other interesting old buildings including the **Black Abbey** from 1225 (but substantially rebuilt since then) and the **Shee Alms House** (1582) where the tourist office is located. Walking tours of the town leave from there several times a day throughout the year and cost adults/students/children IR£2.50/2/60p.

Places to Stay

The closest camping ground to Kilkenny is **Tree Grove Park** (☎ 21512) about two km south-east of town on the R700. The much larger **Nore Valley Park** (☎ 27229) is at Bennettsbridge, another eight km south on the same road. The nightly cost there is IR£5/8 for a small tent/caravan plus 50p per person.

The friendly IHH **Kilkenny Tourist Hostel** (☎ 63541) at 35 Parliament St, open year round, is very central and has dorm beds for IR£6.50 and private rooms for IR£8 per person a night. There's a kitchen and laundry service. **Ormonde Tourist Hostel** (☎ 52733), on John's Green close to the railway and bus stations, has dorm beds for IR£7 or £8, doubles from IR£18. The closest **An Óige Hostel** (☎ 67674; IR£5.50 in summer) is at Foulksrath Castle in Jenkinstown, 13 km north.

In town there are plenty of B&Bs. You'll find **Mrs Dempsey** (☎ 21954) and **St Mary** (☎ 22091) side by side on James St, very close to the centre; they charge from IR£18/30 for a single/double. Rooms with attached bathroom at Mrs Dempsey cost IR£20/34. On Dean St opposite St Canice's Cathedral is the double-barrelled **Kilmore/Kilkenny** (☎ 64040), where rooms start at IR£18/30 for a single/double. A few doors to the west is **Bregagh** (☎ 22315), with *en suite* rooms from IR£20/34.

Places to Eat

On St Kieran's St and named after Kilkenny's famous witch, **Kyteler's Inn** has a modern interior and does sandwiches and meals in a cellar restaurant called **Alice's**. The **Italian Connection** at 38 Parliament St has good-value pizzas from IR£4.50 and pasta from IR£6.

Across the road from the castle, the restaurant upstairs in the **Kilkenny Design Centre** (open from 9 am to 5 pm daily) is good for lunch. During the summer the restaurant in the **Kilkenny Castle Kitchen** is another good place for lunch or delicious homemade scones. It's open from 10 am to 7 pm.

Michael Dore is a colourful little place at 65 High St, serving meals and snacks at reasonable prices upstairs at its **Nostalgia Café**. **Lautrec's Bistro & Wine Bar** on St Kieran's St serves an eclectic range of dishes including Italian and Mexican from IR£4 and stays open till at least midnight. **Edward Langton's** is a stylish, award-winning pub at 69 John St with affordable lunches but pricey set dinners (from IR£17.50).

Entertainment

The best pub in town for traditional Irish music is **Andrew Ryan's** on Friary St, which runs south-west off High St. The **Flagstone Wine**

IRELAND

Bar at 40 Parliament St has traditional music in summer and a popular weekend disco all year round. *Ó Riada* at 25 Parliament St and the *Pump House* next door are other good music venues.

At the castle end of High St, the stylishly old-fashioned *Caisleán Uí Chuain* is a cosy place for a drink. North of the river on John St there's often music at *Peig's Bar*, and *Edward Langton's* runs a disco for the more mature crowd on Tuesday and Saturday nights. The *Watergate Theatre* on Parliament St hosts musical and theatrical productions throughout the year.

Getting There & Away

Bus Éireann (☎ 64933) operates out of the railway station. There are five buses a day (three on Sunday) to Dublin, three to Cork, up to five to Galway and between one and two to Wexford, Waterford and Rosslare. McDonagh railway station (☎ 22024) is on Dublin Rd, east of the town centre via John St. There are four trains daily each way (five on Monday and Friday, three on Sunday) on the Dublin (IR£10; two hours) to Waterford (IR£5) line.

Getting Around

You can book a taxi in Kilkenny on ☎ 63017 or 27497.

JJ Wall (☎ 21236), 88 Maudlin St, rents bikes for IR£5/25 a day/week. The countryside around Kilkenny is fine cycling territory, and there's a lovely day excursion to Kells, Inistioge, Jerpoint Abbey and Kilfane.

AROUND KILKENNY
Jerpoint Abbey

Dating from the 12th century, Ireland's finest Cistercian monastery (☎ 24623) is in ruins – you'll find it just south of Thomastown, about 20 km south of Kilkenny. The fragments of the monastery's cloister are particularly notable, and there are some fine Irish Romanesque stone carvings on the church walls and tombs. Entry is adults/children & students IR£2/1, and in summer it's open from 9.30 am to 6.30 pm. In the off-season, the hours are shorter, and it's closed on Monday.

The West Coast

KILLARNEY

By the time you reach Killarney you will have seen plenty of touristy Irish towns, but this is Numero Uno, with more than the usual shamrock-'kiss-me-I'm-Irish'-leprechaun trappings. There are, however, lots of easy escapes if you want to explore the delights of Kerry and avoid the excesses.

Information

Killarney's busy but efficient tourist office (☎ 31633; fax 34506), open six days a week year round, is in the town hall on Main St right in the centre of town. There's an American Express office a short distance to the east on East Avenue Rd. The main post office is on New St. There's a laundrette behind the Spar supermarket at the Plunkett St end of College St. The Killarney Bookshop is at 32 Main St.

The telephone code for Killarney is ☎ 064.

Things to See

In Town Most of Killarney's attractions are around the town, not actually in it. **St Mary's Cathedral** (1855) on Cathedral Place is worth a look and the **National Museum of Irish Transport**, set back from East Avenue Rd, has an interesting assortment of old cars, bicycles and other odds and ends. The museum is open from April to October from 10 am to 6 pm daily. Entry is adults/students/children IR£2.50/1.50/1.

Knockreer You can walk to the Knockreer Estate, just beyond the cathedral to the west of town. There's fine scenery around Lough Leane, and the lake's **Innisfallen Island** with its ancient monastery ruins can be reached by a hired rowing boat from behind the restored **Ross Castle** (☎ 35851) dating from the 15th century.

The castle is open daily in summer from 9 am to 6.30 pm; hours are shorter in spring and autumn. Entry to the castle is adults/students & children IR£2.50/1.

Muckross Once you escape the suburbs to the south, you can explore the extensive grounds of Muckross Estate (☎ 31440), six km from

Killarney. Muckross Friary, founded in 1488, had a typically grisly history and was put to the torch in 1652. The tombs of the abbey's founder, some Kerry chieftains and several noted Irish poets are found in the choir.

Muckross House has some lovely period-furnished rooms (don't miss the billiard room) and extensive museum exhibits dealing with traditional crafts. It's open daily in summer from 9 am to 7 pm, and to 5.30 pm in winter. Entry is adults/students & children IR£3.30/

1.50. Prices are the same at nearby **Muckross Traditional Farms**, a museum dedicated to rural life and traditional farming methods, and you'll save a pound or two by buying a joint ticket.

Places to Stay

Camping The *Fossa Caravan & Camping Park* (☎ 31497) is 5.5 km west of town on the road to Killorglin (R562). A tent is IR£3.50 per night for a cyclist or hiker, IR£8.50 for a car

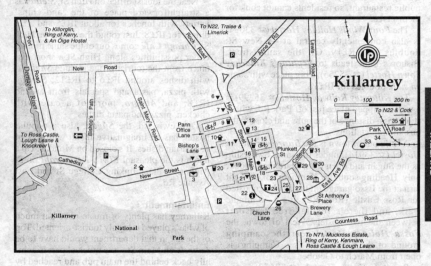

Killarney

PLACES TO STAY
2 Four Winds Holiday Hostel
10 Neptune's Killarney Town Hostel
32 Súgán Hostel & Restaurant
35 Killarney Railway Hostel

PLACES TO EAT
4 Grunt's Restaurant
5 Country Kitchen
6 Buckley's Bakery
7 Scellig Restaurant
11 Sheila's Restaurant
12 Allegro Restaurant
19 Caragh Restaurant
21 Stella's Restaurant
27 Kiwi's Restaurant

PUBS
9 Courtney's Pub
13 O'Connor's Pub
14 Laurels Pub
20 Danny Mann Inn
29 Kiely's Bar
30 Scott's Beer Garden
31 Jug of Punch Bar

OTHER
1 St Mary's Cathedral
3 Post Office
8 O'Sullivan's Bike Hire
15 Bike Hire
16 Old Town Hall
17 Killarney Bookshop
18 O'Neill's Bike Hire
22 Tourist Office
23 Laundrette
24 St Mary's Church
25 American Express
26 Jaunting Cars
28 National Museum of Irish Transport
33 Bus Station
34 Killarney Train Station

and two people. Nearer to town and with similar rates is *Fleming's White Bridge Caravan & Camping Park* (☎ 31590). It's 1.5 km out along the road to Cork (N22).

Hostels Killarney has seven IHH hostels, most of which charge from IR£6 or IR£6.50 for a dorm bed; some have transport waiting to pick you up at the bus or train station. The small and friendly *Súgán Hostel* (☎ 33104) is right in the centre on Lewis Rd, by the junction with College St. At night the kitchen serves as a public restaurant, so residents cannot cook for themselves.

The *Four Winds Holiday Hostel* (☎ 33094) is also conveniently central at 43 New St; doubles are IR£19. Off the same street, Bishop's Lane leads to *Neptune's Killarney Town Hostel* (☎ 35255), a big place with some *en suite* doubles for IR£18.

The *Killarney Railway Hostel* (☎ 35299) is a well-equipped place just off Park Rd, within staggering distance of the pubs and close to the bus and rail stations.

A little out of town is the *Bunrower House Hostel* (☎ 33914), under the same ownership as the Súgán and open from March to October only. Heading south for Kenmare, take a right turn at the Esso garage on the road signposted for Ross Castle (Ross Rd). It's a 20-minute walk, and there's regular free transport between the two hostels. West of town, the *Fossa Holiday Hostel* near the camping ground of the same name (see Camping) is open from March to October.

Peacock Farm Hostel (☎ 33557), open April to September, is in Gortdromakiery near Muckross Estate and charges IR£5/14 for a dorm bed/double. To get there, take a left turn onto the Lough Guitane road just after the jaunting, or horse-drawn, car entrance at Muckross House.

The large An Óige *Killarney Hostel* (☎ 31240) is four km west of the centre at Aghadoe House; it costs IR£6.50 per night in summer. A hostel bus meets trains from Dublin and Cork.

B&Bs Although Killarney has an awesome number of B&Bs, finding a room can be difficult in the high season. As usual, the answer is to throw yourself upon the tourist office and let

them do the looking. Muckross Rd is particularly dense with B&Bs. The current price of an average B&B for a single/double starts at IR£18.50/30.

Places to Eat
Take care when choosing a restaurant; some places have very ordinary menus at rather high prices. For lunchtime sandwiches, try *Grunt's Restaurant* on New St or the *Country Kitchen* three doors down. Another possibility is *Buckley's Bakery* on High Street.

Near the tourist office on High St, *Stella's* is a straightforward place of the 'and chips' variety with lunches for about IR£5 and a set dinner for IR£8. Just round the corner on New St, *Caragh Café* comes out of the same mould. Other possibilities along High St a short distance from the tourist office include *Sheila's*, with dishes around IR£6 to IR£12; *Scellig*, with pizza, pasta and specials from around IR£8; and *Allegro*, more of a café with chicken, pizza and pasta dishes.

On Lewis Rd, the *Súgán*, also a popular hostel, has an imaginative menu with lots of vegetarian dishes. It's closed on Monday. Up a notch is the pleasant *Kiwi's Restaurant* on St Anthony's Place linking College St and East Avenue Rd.

Entertainment
Killarney has plenty of music pubs but much of what's played is highly tourist-oriented. Top of the list in that department would have to be *Laurels* on Main St – the musical part is actually back behind the main pub and reached by the side alley. It's *very* touristy with a nightly show in summer from 9.30 to 11 pm and an entry charge of IR£3.

Pubs where there's a good chance of more-authentic music include the *Danny Mann Inn* in the Eviston House Hotel in New St; *O'Connor's* on High St, which is popular with young people; and *Courtney's*, diagonally opposite on High St. Along College St try *Kiely's Bar* or the *Jug of Punch Bar* in the Arbutus Hotel. *Scott's Beer Garden* between College St and East Avenue Rd also has music most nights in summer.

Getting There & Away
Bus Éireann (☎ 34777) operates from outside the small train station. Bus fares include Cork

IR£8.80, Galway via Limerick IR£13, Kilkenny IR£14 and Limerick IR£9.30. Travelling by train to Cork (IR£9.50) usually involves changing at Mallow, but there is a direct route to Dublin (IR£22) via Limerick Junction. Ring ☎ 31067 for details.

Getting Around
Taxis can be booked on ☎ 31331. Bicycles are the ideal way to explore the Killarney area, as the sights are somewhat scattered. A number of places hire bikes, typically at around IR£6/30 a day/week. They include O'Sullivan's (☎ 31282) in Pawn Office Lane off High St, O'Neill's (☎ 31970) on Plunkett St and the Laurels pub, which has its own bike hire (☎ 32578) in Old Market Lane, alongside the pub.

If you're not on two wheels, Killarney's traditional transport is the jaunting car, complete with a driver known as a 'jarvey'. The pick-up point is on East Avenue Rd just past the tourist office. Prices for four passengers range from IR£12 (Ross Castle) to IR£32 (Muckross Estate and Torc Waterfall).

KENMARE
This pretty little pastel-coloured town is an excellent alternative to Killarney as a base for exploring the Ring of Kerry area. It's somewhat touristy, but not as much or as big as Killarney.

Henry, Main and Shelbourne Sts make a neat triangle defining the town centre. The tourist office (☎ 41233; fax 41688; open April to October) faces the town square on the road to Killarney (the N71) and there's an attached heritage centre (adults/students/children IR£2/1.50/1) open Easter to September. An ancient stone circle is signposted from across the tourist office; it's about a 300-metre walk down Market St.

The excellent Kenmare Bookshop with guides and maps is on Shelbourne St near the southern end of Main St.

The telephone code for Kenmare is ☎ 064.

Places to Stay & Eat
The IHH *Fáilte Hostel* (☎ 41083) at the junction of Henry and Shelbourne Sts charges IR£6.50/18 for a dorm bed/double and is open all year. Seven km south of Kenmare on the N71 road to Glengarriff, the *Bonane Hostel*

(☎ 41098) has beds at IR£6.50, and camping is possible but without use of the kitchen. Naturally, Kenmare has lots of B&Bs, including the excellent *D'Arcy's/Old Bank House* (☎ 41589) at the southern end of Main St, with singles/doubles with *en suite* bathroom costing IR£18/32. The *Wander Inn* on Henry St charges from IR£18/25.

Two of Ireland's most expensive hotels – each boasting a restaurant with a Michelin star – compete for business in Kenmare: the *Park* (☎ 41200; fax 41402) on Shelbourne St and the *Sheen Falls Lodge* (☎ 41600; fax 41386), which is on Glens Rd two km south-east of town next to the old Kenmare cemetery. A double at either will set you back over IR£200.

For a sandwich or coffee, try *Clifford Bakery* or *Micky Ned's* on Henry St. *Foley's Restaurant Pub* on the same street does a good pub lunch. There are lots of restaurants like the *Purple Heather* on Henry St or the more expensive *An Leath Phingin*, an Irish-Italian eatery in an old schoolhouse at 35 Main St. *Giuliano's Pizzeria* is at the southern end of Main St with small/large pizzas from IR£5/8, but for a real treat, go next door to the restaurant at *D'Arcy's Restaurant*, whose owners cooked at the Park Hotel for almost a dozen years. Expect to pay between IR£15 and IR£20.

Entertainment
The best crack and music in town are at *Brennans* on Main St, the *Atlantic Bar* on Market Square and *Ó Donnabháin* on Henry St.

Getting Around
Finnegan's (☎ 41083), opposite the Fáilte Hostel on Shelbourne St, has bikes for hire.

THE RING OF KERRY
The Ring of Kerry, the 179-km circuit of the Iveragh Peninsula, is one of Ireland's premier tourist attractions. Although it can be done in a day by car or bus or in three days by bicycle, the wonderful scenery and quaint villages may detain you for a bit longer.

Getting off the beaten tourist track is also worthwhile. The Ballaghbeama Pass cuts across the peninsula's central highlands with some spectacular views and remarkably little traffic. The shorter Ring of Skellig at the end of the peninsula, with fine views of the Skellig Islands, is also less touristy.

Anticlockwise is the 'correct' way to tackle the ring, but in the high season it's probably worth doing it in the other direction to avoid the mass of tourist buses all following one another from Killarney. You can forgo roads completely by walking the **Kerry Way**, which winds through Macgillycuddy's Reeks and past 1038-metre **Carrantuohill**, the highest mountain in Ireland.

Starting from Killarney and heading for the northern side of the peninsula, the ring's highlights include **Killorglin** during its Puck's Fair on the second weekend in August. **Glenbeigh** offers fine views over Dingle Bay.

The **Skellig Experience Centre** (☎ 064-31633 in Killarney), on Valentia Island just across the bridge from Portmagee, takes you to the two Skellig Islands without actually landing there. For IR£3/2.70/1.50 (adults/students/children) you can visit the centre with its exhibits on the life and times of the monks who lived there from the 7th to the 12th or 13th centuries, the history of the lighthouses on larger Skellig Michael Island and the islands' wildlife. A 15-minute audiovisual show deals with the monastery. For IR£15/13.50/8 you can combine the visit with a daily 2.30 pm boat trip which takes you round the islands. Except for Monday and Friday, the boat also leaves Dingle (IR£20/18/10) at 11.15 am and Cahersiveen (IR£18/16/9) at 12.15 pm.

From Ballinskelligs, Caherdaniel, Portmagee and, on Valentia island, Knightstown, boats run to uninhabited **Skellig Michael** with its superb monastery buildings and bird life. The standard fare is around IR£20 and for most visitors it's more rewarding than the Skellig Experience Centre tour.

Near Caherdaniel to the south-east is fine old **Derrynane House** (☎ 066-75113), the ancestral home of Daniel O'Connell and open to visitors all year round (weekends only in winter; adults/children IR£2/1). A few km further is a turn inland to **Staigue Fort**, with sweeping views down to the coast. The 3rd or 4th-century fort is about three km off the main road, reached by an increasingly narrow country lane that sees some bizarre traffic jams in summer. There are some great beaches and pretty little coves on the stretch from Waterville to the town of **Sneem**.

Places to Stay

Cycling from hostel to hostel around the ring, there's the IHO **Hillside House** (☎ 066-68228) at Glenbeigh; the IHH **Sive Hostel** (☎ 066-72717) at Cahersiveen; the IHO **Ring Lyne** (☎ 066-76103) and **Royal Pier** (☎ 066-76144) hostels as well as the An Óige **Valentia Island Hostel** (☎ 76141) on Valentia Island; the An Óige **Ballinskelligs Hostel** (☎ 066-79229) at Ballinskelligs; the IHH **Waterville Leisure Hostel** (☎ 066-74644) and IHO **Pat's Place** (☎ 066-74383) at Waterville; the IHH **Carrigbeg** (☎ 066-75229) and **Village** (☎ 066-75227) hostels at Caherdaniel; and in Macgillycuddy's Reeks the An Óige **Black Valley Hostel** (☎ 064-34712), which is a good starting point for walking the Kerry Way.

Getting Around

If you're not up to cycling, the Ring of Kerry bus leaves the bus/train station in Killarney in summer at 8.45 am and 1.25 pm (no early bus on Sunday), and stops at Killorglin, Cahersiveen, Waterville, Caherdaniel and Sneem before returning to Killarney. Several travel agents in Killarney, including Deros Tours (☎ 064-31251) opposite the tourist office and O'Connor Autotours (☎ 064-31052) south of town on Ross Rd, offer daily tours of the ring in season for about IR£10.

THE DINGLE PENINSULA

Much less touristy but just as beautiful as the Ring of Kerry, a circuit of the Dingle Peninsula makes a fine alternative to one around the Iveragh Peninsula. This is the Ireland of the British film *Ryan's Daughter* (1970), and it's noted for its extraordinary number of ring forts, high crosses and other reminders of Ireland's ancient history. The western tip of the peninsula is predominantly Irish-speaking.

Ferries run to the bleak **Blasket Islands**, off the tip of the peninsula, from Dunquin, where, between Easter and September, the **Blasket Centre** (☎ 066-56444) focuses on the bygone days of the islanders (IR£2.50/1). The Dingle Peninsula is nearly as mountainous as the Iveragh Peninsula, and, at 951 metres, **Mt Brandon** is the second-highest mountain in Ireland. The snaking Connor Pass, which begins its ascent just outside Dingle, offers spectacular views.

Dingle, the main town on the peninsula, has

a seasonal tourist office (☎ 066-51188) on Main St.

Places to Stay

For accommodation, there's the An Óige *Dún Chaoin Hostel* (☎ 066-56145) at Dunquin; the IHH *Ballintaggart House Hostel & Campsite* (☎ 066-51454) on the Tralee Rd just before Dingle town; the IHH *Seacrest Hostel* (☎ 066-51390) at Kinard West, Lispole, also near Dingle; five hostels in Dingle town including the new *Grapevine Hostel* (☎ 066-51434) with dorm beds from IR£6.50; the IHH *Tigh an Phoist Hostel* (☎ 55109) at Bothar Bui village in Ballydavid; the IHH *Connor Pass Hostel* (☎ 066-39179) at Stradbally; and the IHH *Fuchsia Lodge* (☎ 57150) at Annascaul. There are lots of B&Bs in Dingle town, including *Bolands* (☎ 066-51426) on Upper Main St, with stunning views over Dingle Bay. Basic singles are IR£12, singles/doubles with *en suite* bathroom are IR£18/32.

Places to Eat

For some good lunch spots try *An Café Liteartha* on Dykegate St with a bookshop in the front or *Murphy's Pub* on Strand St along the waterfront) and restaurants noted for their excellent seafood (try *Lord's* on Strand St, the more expensive *Beginish* on Green St or *Doyle's Seafood Bar* at 4 John St).

Entertainment

Among Dingle's many pubs, *O'Flaherty's* near the roundabout and *Dick Mack's* in Green St are a step back in time. *Murphy's* is a raucous, boozy place and *An Droichead* on the corner of Main St and Spa Rd is the best spot for traditional music.

Getting There & Away

A daily bus serves Dingle from Tralee and Killarney.

Getting Around

Bicycles are a fine way to make a circuit of the peninsula, and you can rent them from many of the hostels as well as J J Moriarty (☎ 066-51316) on Main St in Dingle town for IR£7/30 a day/week. There's a Raleigh Rent-a-Bike place on Green St.

LIMERICK

Limerick, an instantly recognisable name, is the Irish Republic's third-largest city. For a long time it was regarded by travellers as one of the dullest cities in the country, but in recent years it has become something of a place of interest in its own right, rather than just a convenient crossroads.

Orientation & Information

The main thoroughfare through town changes names from Patrick St to O'Connell St and then to O'Connell Ave. The helpful tourist office (☎ 317522; 317939), open all year round, is in a modern building at Arthur's Quay near the River Shannon. The main post office is on Lower Cecil St, which links O'Connell and Henry Sts. There are laundrettes on Ellen St (off Patrick St) and Cecil St (off O'Connell St).

The telephone code for Limerick is ☎ 061.

Things to See

In 1691 Limerick was the site of the final Catholic resistance to the Protestant forces of King William. On the other side of the river across Thomand Bridge, the **Treaty Stone** marks the spot where the subsequent treaty was signed; soon afterwards the deceitful English reneged on the agreement, an act that rankles Limerick to this day.

Across the Shannon from the stone is **King John's Castle** dating from 1210 and the 12th-century **St Mary's Cathedral**. The castle's modern centre has displays and audiovisuals focusing on the city and the castle's dramatic history, while underground there are archaeological excavations. The castle is open daily April to October from 9.30 am to 5.30 pm, and entry is adults/students & children IR£3.60/1.95.

The **Limerick City Museum** (free admission) is on St John's Square and is open Tuesday to Saturday from 10 am to 1 pm and 2 to 5 pm.

Places to Stay

The An Óige *Limerick Hostel* (☎ 314672) is at 1 Pery Square, only a short walk south-west across People's Park from the bus and train station. Nearby is the IHO *Finnigan's Holiday Hostel* (☎ 310308) at 6 Pery Square. The large IHH *Limerick Hostel* (☎ 415222) is across the narrow River Abbey at Barrington's Lodge on Georges Quay. All three hostels charge IR£6.50 for a dorm bed in summer.

There are some cheap B&Bs on Davis St, directly opposite the train station. *Alexandra House* (☎ 318472) at 6 Alexandra Terrace, O'Connell Ave, is close to the centre and has singles/doubles from IR£17.50/28. Otherwise the Ennis Rd (N18), running north-west of Limerick, is lined with B&Bs and more expensive accommodation for several km.

Places to Eat

For cheap eats, try the self-service *Sails Restaurant* in the modern Arthur's Quay Centre opposite the tourist office or *Luigi's*, with 15 varieties of burgers, directly opposite the train station on Parnell St.

Decent meals are available from 5.30 pm at *Freddy's Bistro*, tucked away down Theatre Lane which runs between Lower Mallow and Lower Glentworth Sts; it's open every day except Monday and dishes range from various pastas for IR£8 to seafood for IR£12. Upstairs at 103 O'Connell St, *Mustang Sally's* is a bright Tex-Mex joint open all day with mains from about IR£6.

Other higher-priced restaurants include *Moll Darby's* at 8 Georges Quay near the Limerick Hostel with meals from IR£8 to IR£15 and outdoor tables and the grill room at the *Royal George Hotel* along the middle of O'Connell St. Opposite the Royal George is *La Romana*, an Italian place with set dinners for IR£16 (IR£10 before 7 pm).

Entertainment

The music scene in Limerick shifts depending on the evening, but there's often something on at the very popular *Nancy Blake's* at 19 Upper Denmark St. Other good possibilities include the *Locke Bar* at 3 Georges Quay; the *White House* at 52 O'Connell St; and *Costello's Tavern*, opposite the Dominican Church on Dominic St.

Getting There & Away

Bus Éireann services (☎ 313333) operate from the bus and train station, a short walk south of the centre. There are regular bus connections to Dublin (IR£10) via Kildare, Cork (IR£9), Galway (IR£9.30), Killarney (IR£9.30) and other centres. By train from Colbert railway station (☎ 315555) it costs from IR£16 to Dublin and IR£10 to Cork. There's a USIT office at 51-52 O'Connell St.

Getting Around

Buses connect Shannon airport with the bus and train station for IR£3.50. (There are also bus services from Shannon to Dublin IR£10.) Taxis can be reached in Limerick on ☎ 313131 or ☎ 411422. Bicycles are available for hire at Emerald Cycles (☎ 416983), 1 Patrick St, or at the Bike Shop (☎ 315900) on O'Connell Ave.

AROUND LIMERICK

North-west of Limerick on the N18 road to Ennis is **Bunratty Castle & Folk Park** (☎ 361511), another version of an Irish theme park. It's open daily from 9.30 am to 5.30 pm (the park remains open until 7 pm in summer), and entry is IR£4.75 (children IR£2.30). At night, Bunratty Castle features 'medieval banquets' where big tourist crowds enjoy Irish songs, corny jokes and truly dreadful food for about IR£30 a head. Ring ☎ 360788 as far ahead as possible. Near the castle is a pub called **Durty Nelly's**, one of the oldest in Ireland and filled with pipe-smoking tipplers in tweed jackets who look straight out of Central Casting.

THE BURREN

County Clare's greatest attraction is the Burren, a harsh and rocky stretch of country that eventually tips itself into an often rough and stormy Atlantic Ocean. Despite its unwelcoming look, the Burren is an area of great interest, with many ancient dolmens, ring forts, round towers, high crosses and other reminders of Ireland's long and rich history. There's also some stunning scenery, a good collection of hostels and some of Ireland's best music pubs.

The Burren is excellent cycling territory, but there are also some good walks.

For detailed exploration of the Burren get a copy of Tim Robinson's *The Burren* map (IR£3.60 at bookshops and tourist offices). Galway Tours (☎ 091-770066) in Galway organises a daily guided coach tour in summer that takes in the Burren, Aillwee Cave, the Poulnabrone Dolmen and the Cliffs of Moher. The bus leaves every day from Eyre Square at 9.30 am and tickets cost IR£10 each.

Doolin

Doolin, famed for its music pubs, is a convenient base for exploring the Burren and the awesome Cliffs of Moher; it is also a gateway for boats to Inisheer, the easternmost and smallest of the Aran Islands. Doolin is actually the sum of three parts: an upper village spread along the road and called Roadford; the compact cluster of the lower village known as Fisher St; and the harbour area.

Doolin's telephone code is ☎ 065.

Next to Doolin pier, two people can pitch a small tent at *Nagles Doolin Caravan & Camping Park* (☎ 74458) for IR£6. Apart from rather pricey B&Bs – *Cullinan's* (☎ 74183) next to the little River Aille in Roadford has excellent singles/doubles from IR£18/26 – Doolin has four hostels, all of them IHH members: the *Fisher Street Hostel* (☎ 74006) in the lower village (dorm beds/doubles from IR£8/18); *Paddy Moloney's Doolin Hostel* (☎ 74006) across the road (IR£6.75/18); the small *Rainbow Hostel* (☎ 74415) near McGann's pub in Roadford and the only one open all year (IR£6.50/14); and the *Aille River Hostel* (☎ 74260), a converted farmhouse between the upper and lower villages (IR£6.50/15). Both *O'Connor's* in the lower village and *McGann's* in the upper village serve decent pub good; the latter has Irish stew for around IR£5. There's also the *Apple Tree Restaurant* opposite Maloney's and the *Doolin Chipper* next to MacDermott's. If you feel like splashing out, there are several very nice restaurants, including *Bruach na hAille*, in the upper village next door to McGann's.

Two of Doolin's three famed music pubs, *McGann's* and *MacDermott's*, are in the upper village, but *O'Connor's* in the lower village is the best known (though it has become somewhat touristy).

There are direct buses to Doolin from Limerick, Ennis and Galway; the main Bus Éireann stop is outside Paddy Moloney's Doolin Hostel. See the Aran Islands section for information on ferries to and from Inisheer. All the hostels have bikes for around IR£7/35 a day/week plus deposit.

Cliffs of Moher

Eight km south of Doolin are the towering Cliffs of Moher (230 metres). They're one of the most famous natural features in Ireland, so in season the cars and buses are packed in door to door. Near the visitor centre (☎ 065-81171) is **O'Brien's Tower** (entry 75p/50p for adults/children), a picturesque lookout point. Walk south or north and the crowds soon disappear. You can walk all the way from Doolin, and at one point a precipitous path leads right down to the base of the cliffs. This should be tackled in fine weather only.

GALWAY

One of Ireland's fastest-growing and most dynamic cities, Galway has narrow streets, old stone and wooden shopfronts, good restaurants and bustling pubs. The old-fashioned beach resort of Salthill is within easy walking distance, and the Galway area is the main springboard to the fascinating Aran Islands.

Orientation & Information

Galway's tightly packed town centre is spread evenly on both sides of the River Corrib. Just south-west of the river mouth on Galway Bay is the historic – but now totally redeveloped – Claddagh area, while slightly further south-west is Salthill, a popular area for B&Bs.

The main tourist office (☎ 563081; fax 565201) is south-east of Eyre Square on Victoria Place. At the height of the season, it can get very busy and there can be a delay of an hour or more in making accommodation bookings. There's a seasonal tourist office branch (☎ 563081) in Salthill at the junction of Seapoint Promenade and Upper Salthill Rd. The main post office is on Eglington St.

Hawkins House at 14 Churchyard St, opposite St Nicholas Collegiate Church, and Charlie Byrne's in the Cornstore on Middle St are good bookshops. There's also an Eason branch on Shop St. There are laundrettes on Sea Rd, just off Dominick St Upper, and in a courtyard off New Rd on the western side of the river. A more convenient one can be found in the Olde Malte Mall shopping arcade off High St.

The Eyre Square Centre is a big shopping centre right off Eyre Square. Other shopping centres include Bridge Mills, in an old mill building right by the river, and the Cornstore on Middle St.

The telephone code for Galway is ☎ 091.

PLACES TO STAY
1   Corrib Villa Hostel
2   Salmon Weir Hostel
3   Wood Quay Hostel
13 Galway Hostel
17 Kinlay House Hostel
    & USIT Office
20 Celtic Tourist Hostel
45 Quay Street
    House Hostel
51 St Martin's B&B
55 Galway City Hostel
56 Arch View Hostel
60 Westend Hostel

PLACES TO EAT
7   Brannagan's Restaurant
8   Conlon & Sons
    Fish & Chips
23 Food for Thought Café

29 Aideen's Wine Bar
    & Restaurant
31 Brasserie Restaurant
34 Mackens Café
37 Sev'nth Heav'n
40 Fat Freddy's Pizzeria
41 Shama Indian
    Restaurant
43 McDonagh's Restaurant
44 Pasta Mista
47 Hungry Grass
48 Busker Brownes
53 Left Bank Café
54 Le Graal Restaurant
58 Kebab House

OTHER
4   St Nicholas' Cathedral
5   MacSwiggan's Pub
6   Post Office
9   Skeffington Arms Pub

10 Kennedy Park
11 An Púcán Bar
12 Rabbitt's Bar
14 Great Southern Hotel
    & O'Flaherty's Pub
15 Island Ferries Office
16 Train & Bus Station
18 Tourist Office
19 Galway Cycle Hire
21 Celtic Cycles
22 Lynch Castle
24 Nora Barnacle House
    Museum
25 Lynch Memorial
    Window
26 St Nicholas Collegiate
    Church
27 Eason Bookshop
28 Hawkins House
    Bookshop
30 Augustinian Church

32 King's Head Pub
33 Old Malte Mall
    & Laundrette
35 Charlie Byrne's
    Bookshop
36 Mayoralty House
38 Druid Theatre
39 The Quays Bar
42 Spanish Arch &
    Museum
46 Sean O'Nachtain's Pub
49 Lisheen Pub
50 Bridge Mills Shopping
    Centre
52 Laundrette
57 Roísín Dubh Pub
59 Monroe's Tavern
61 Flaherty's Cycles
62 Claddagh Ring Pub
63 Crane's Bar
64 Laundrette

IRELAND

Galway City

0   50   100 m

River Corrib

Waterside St

Eglinton Canal

To N59, University,
Clifden & Westport

Salmon Weir Bridge

St Vincent's Ave

St Francis St

Wood Quay

Eyre Street

To N17
& Sligo

To N6
& Dublin

Nuns
Island

Kings
Gap

Newtown Smith Street

Mary Street

Abbeygate
Street

City Wall

Eyre Square

Forster Street

Station Rd

Victoria Pl

Queen Street

Eyre Square
Centre

City
Wall

River Corrib

Nuns Island Street

Bowling Green

Market Street

Lombard St

St Augustine Street

Middle Street

High Street

Cross Street

Mainguard St

Eyre Square

Williamsgate St
William St

Abbeygate
Street

St Upper

Merchants Road

Dock Rd

The
Comstore

Dock Road

Commercial
Dock

To Aran Islands
Ferry Pier

Mill Street

New Road

Bridge St

Quay Street

Flood Street

Dominick St Lower

Canal

Raven Tce

Wolfe Tone Bridge

Henry St

Eglinton St

To N59

William St West

Sea Rd

Dominick St Upr

Fairhill

To Salthill, Spiddal, Rossaveal & Camping Ground

Galway
Bay

Things to See & Do

Galway is a great place to wander around, and a copy of the *Medieval Galway* walking guide will point out many curiosities. Right in the centre, **St Nicholas Collegiate Church** dates from 1320 and has several interesting tombs. At the end of the south transept is the 'empty frame' which once held an icon of the Virgin Mary. It was taken to Győr in Hungary in the 17th century by an Irish bishop sent packing by Cromwell and is still a pilgrimage site there.

Across the river, **St Nicholas' Cathedral** is a huge and rather ugly structure completed in 1965.

On Shop St, parts of **Lynch Castle**, now a branch of the Allied Irish Bank, date back to the 14th century. Lynch, so the story goes, was a mayor of Galway in the 15th century who was so dedicated to upholding justice that when his own son was condemned for murder he personally acted as hangman, since nobody else was willing to do the job.

The **Lynch Memorial Window** on Market St marks the spot of the sorrowful deed. Across the road in the **Bowling Green** area is the **Nora Barnacle House Museum**, the former home of the wife and life-long inspiration of James Joyce. It's open mid-May to mid-September and costs IR£1.

Little remains of Galway's old city walls apart from the **Spanish Arch** right by the river mouth. The small and unimpressive **Galway City Museum** is in the gateway and opens Monday to Saturday from 10 am to 1 pm and 2.15 pm to 5.15 pm (IR£1/50p adults/children).

Places to Stay

Camping Just west of Galway, *Hunters Silver Strand Caravan Park* (☎ 592452) is on the coast, just beyond Salthill. The *Spiddal Caravan & Camping Park* (☎ 553372) is on the same coastal road (R336), 18 km west of Galway. The *Ballyloughane Caravan & Camping Park* (☎ 755338) is on the Dublin Rd (N6), five km east of Galway. All three charge between IR£6 and IR£7.50 for two people, a car and large tent.

Hostels There are legions of hostels. A new one is the IHO *Galway Hostel* (☎ 566959) in Frenchville Lane adjacent to the bus and train station, with beds for IR£7 plus double rooms (IR£24) and a sauna. The modern 150-room

IHH *Kinlay House* (☎ 565244), opposite the tourist office, is well equipped, and has a variety of rooms from IR£8, including a light breakfast. Around the corner on Queen St the smaller and more personal IHO *Celtic Tourist Hostel* (☎ 566606) has beds from IR£6 and IR£20 doubles.

The IHH *Quay Street House Hostel* (☎ 568644) at 10 Quay St has 97 beds and charges from IR£6.60, doubles IR£23. The IHO *Corrib Villa* (☎ 562892) is at 4 Waterside St, near the Salmon Weir Bridge. It costs from IR£5.50 and there are no doubles. The *Wood Quay Hostel* (☎ 562618) costs IR£6.90 (twins IR£15) and has a decent kitchen but cramped washrooms and rickety bunks. It's just north of the city centre, in St Anne's House at 23-24 Wood Quay. Around the corner in St Vincent's Ave is the *Salmon Weir Hostel* (☎ 561133). Beds cost from IR£6, doubles IR£18.

The *Arch View Hostel* (☎ 586661), with 60 beds from IR£5, is hidden away at the junction of Dominick Sts Upper and Lower, just west of Wolfe Tone Bridge. Close by, on the other side of the canal at 24 Dominick St Lower, is the *Galway City Hostel* (☎ 566367) at IR£6.60. Back on Dominick St Upper at No 20 is the *Westend Hostel* (☎ 583636) with 63 beds from IR£6 and four doubles at IR£20.

In Salthill, the IHH *Grand Holiday Hostel* (☎ 521150) is right on the promenade and has rooms with two or four beds from IR£5.50 a night and doubles from IR£14. The similarly priced IHH *Stella Maris Holiday Hostel* (☎ 521950) is at 151 Upper Salthill.

B&Bs In summer Galway can become very full and you may have to travel to the suburbs. There are not many B&Bs around the city centre, but it's worth trying *St Martin's* (☎ 568286) at 2 Nuns Island Rd, which is delightfully situated right on to the Corrib. Costs are from IR£15 per person.

There are plenty of places less than 10 minutes walk away on the Newcastle Rd, which is west of the river and runs in a north-south direction, becoming the N59 to Clifden. Another good hunting ground is north along Forster St heading toward the Dublin Rd (N6). Salthill and adjacent Renmore have lots of B&Bs which average IR£15 per person. Particularly good places include *Norman Villa*

IRELAND

(☎ 521131) at 86 Lower Salthill for IR£16/26. *Devondell* (☎ 523617) is down a cul-de-sac at 47 Devon Park, Lower Salthill.

Places to Eat

There are lots of restaurants, cafés and pubs around the river end of Quay St. *Hungry Grass* on Cross St Upper has great French-bread sandwiches from IR£1.75 and lots of other possibilities for less than IR£4. A few doors down, *Busker Brownes* is a popular 24-hour eatery with great sandwiches and seafood chowder (IR£2.25). *Food for Thought* is a wholefood lunchtime possibility at Abbeygate St Lower. Nobody does fish and chips better than *Conlon & Sons* on Eglinton St.

There's a *Mackens Café* in the Cornstore on Middle St, while *Sails*, a popular self-service restaurant, is in the Eyre Square Centre. Vegetarians and non-vegetarians alike can head for *Aideen's Wine Bar & Restaurant* tucked away in Buttermilk Walk off Middle St. Pizzas and lots of other delicious dishes are around IR£6.

Sev'nth Heav'n is right beside the Druid Theatre on the corner of Courthouse Lane and Flood St and is an excellent place for pasta (around IR£6) and pizza. *Fat Freddy's* on Quay St has a similar menu (pizzas from IR£3.75) and is equally popular. Other interesting choices include: the Indian restaurant *Shama* on Flood St, with tandoori and Balti specialities from IR£7.50; the *Brasserie* on Middle St, with a great salad bar (IR£2.95); and *Brannagan's* on Abbeygate St Upper, which claims to serve Italian, French, Cajun, Mexican *and* Oriental food. *McDonagh's* on Quay St is excellent for seafood; be sure to try the 'wild' Irish mussels.

The choice isn't so good on the other side of the river, but the *Left Bank Café* on Dominick St Lower is another good sandwich place, or turn the corner to Dominick St Upper for late-night eats at the *Kebab House*. *Le Graal* at 13 Dominick St Lower is a charming choice for lunch or dinner, with mains from IR£5.

Entertainment

The *Galway Edge*, with complete listings of what's on in Galway and surrounds, is available free from the tourist office and other venues around town.

There's lots going on in Galway's pubs. At 17 Cross St is the cosy, 100-year-old *Sean O'Nachtain's*, which has a great atmosphere and sometimes attracts a gay crowd. Back from the river on High St, the *King's Head* has music most nights in summer. *MacSwiggan's* on Daly's Place is big and busy. The upstairs of *The Quays* on Quay St draws a great crowd at weekends and in summer.

There are some glossier pubs around Eyre Square, including the popular *Skeffington Arms* ('the Skeff') and *O'Flaherty's* in the Great Southern Hotel on the square, *An Púcán* just off the square at 11 Forster St (music most nights) and *Rabbitt's Bar* at No 23 of the same street. *Lisheen* at 5 Bridge St is one of the better traditional-music venues on this side of the Corrib.

On the west side of the river the choice spot for traditional music is *Monroe's Tavern* on the corner of Dominick St Upper and Fairhill St. The *Roísín Dubh* opposite on Dominick St Upper is good for alternative music. Round the corner on Sea Rd, the *Claddagh Ring* and *Crane's Bar*, both have music as does *O'Connor's* at Salthill.

Galway parties with a vengeance at such annual events as the Galway Arts Festival in late July or early August. There are regular performances at the small *Druid Theatre* (☎ 568617) on Chapel Lane.

Getting There & Away

Galway airport (☎ 755569) is in Carnmore, 10 km east of the city. The bus station (☎ 562000) is behind the big Great Southern Hotel off Eyre Square in the centre of town, next to Ceannt railway station (☎ 564222). Bus Éireann fares include Doolin IR£8.80, Dublin IR£8, Killarney IR£13, Limerick IR£9 and Sligo IR£10.50. The Dublin services operate up to eight times daily. There are four or more trains to and from Dublin (2¾ hours), Monday to Saturday, fewer on Sunday. Connections with other train routes can be made at Athlone.

There's a USIT travel office (☎ 565177) at the Kinlay House hostel.

Getting Around

There is one bus (IR£2.25) a day to and from the airport and Galway bus station. A taxi to or from the airport costs around IR£10. You can book a taxi in Galway on ☎ 585858 or ☎ 563333. Most of the hostels rent bikes. In the centre, you'll find them around both corners of the tourist office: Galway Cycle Hire (☎ 561600) on Merchants Rd and Celtic Cycles (☎ 566606) on Queen St. On the western side of the river is Flaherty's Cycles (☎ 589230) on Dominick St Upper.

ARAN ISLANDS
The windswept and starkly beautiful Aran Islands have become one of western Ireland's major attractions in recent years. Apart from their natural beauty, the islands have some of the most ancient Christian and pre-Christian remains in Ireland. Inhospitable though the rocky terrain may appear, the islands were settled at a much earlier date than the mainland, since agriculture was easier to pursue here than in the densely forested Ireland of the pre-Christian era.

The Irish passion for stone walls is carried to an absolute fever pitch on the islands, with countless km of stone walls separating off even the tiniest patches of rocky land. The islands are also something of a cultural reserve, and Irish is still widely spoken here.

Orientation & Information
There are three main islands in the group. Most visitors head for long and narrow (14.5 km by a maximum four km) Inishmór (or Inishmore). The land slopes up from the relatively sheltered northern shores of the island and plummets on the southern side into the raging Atlantic. Inishmaan and Inisheer are much smaller and less visited.

Between May and mid-September, a tourist office (☎ 61263) operates on the waterfront at Kilronan, the arrival point and major village of Inishmór. You can change money there. A couple of hundred metres to the north is a small post office and a branch of the Bank of Ireland, which opens a couple of days a week only. Many of the shops (including the Carraig Donn woollen shop next to the tourist office) will change money.

JM Synge's *The Aran Islands* (Oxford University Press) is the classic account of life on the islands and is readily available in paperback. A much less accessible (but more recent) tribute to the islands is mapmaker Tim Robinson's *Stones of Aran* (Penguin). For detailed exploration, pick up a copy of his *The Aran Islands – A Map and Guide*.

Although many visitors make day trips to

the islands, Inishmór alone is worth a couple of days' exploration. The islands can get very crowded at holiday times (St Patrick's Day, Easter) and in July and August, when accommodation is at a premium.

The telephone code for the islands is ☎ 099.

Things to See
Inishmór has four impressive stone forts of uncertain age, though 2000 years is a good guess. Halfway down the island, about eight km west of Kilronan, semi-circular **Dún Aengus**, perched terrifyingly on the edge of the sheer southern cliffs, is the best known of the four. About 1.5 km north is **Dún Eoghanachta**, while halfway back to Kilronan is **Dún Eochla**; both are smaller but perfectly circular ring forts. Directly south of Kilronan and dramatically perched on a promontory is **Dún Dúchathair**.

The ruins of numerous stone churches trace the island's monastic history. The small **Teampall Chiaráin** (St Kieran's Church), with a high cross in the churchyard, is near Kilronan. Beyond Kilmurvey are the ruins of the **Seven Churches**, which consist of a couple of ruined chapels, the restored Teampall Bhreacáin (St Brecan's Church), monastic houses and some fragments of a high cross.

The new **Aran Heritage Centre** at Kilronan introduces the landscape and traditions of the islands. Entry is adults/students/children IR£2/1.50/1 and the centre is open seven days a week from 10 am to 7 pm between April and October.

On the other islands there are more stone walls, ruined churches, ring forts (the magnificent **Dún Chonchúir** on Inishmaan and **Dún Firmina** on Inisheer), *currachs* (the traditional hide-covered boats) and still more music pubs.

Places to Stay
The *Inishmór Camp Site* (☎ 61185) has a fine setting near the beach in Mainistir, almost two km north-west of Kilronan. Facilities are basic and the charge is IR£2 per person. The islands have a number of hostels and the usual collection of B&Bs. In Kilronan, the *Aran Islands Hostel* (☎ 61255) is only a short walk from the pier and has dorm beds for IR£6. It's above Joe Mac's pub but is owned by the people at the Spar Supermarket a few steps north around the

corner so go there first off-season. *St Kevin's Hostel*, between the Aran Islands Hostel and Spar, is usually open only in summer; enquire at the Dormer House B&B opposite.

Dún Aengus Hostel (☎ 61318) is near the beach on the west side of Kilmurvey Bay some seven km from Kilronan. This is a nice country house with 42 beds, two, three or four to a room. The charge is IR£6 a night. The same people own the IHO *Mainistir House Hostel* (☎ 61199), which has beds for IR£7.50 and doubles for IR20; both include a breakfast of porridge and scones. Island Ferries offers special discounts with one or two of the hostels. For example, you can get one night's accommodation at Mainistir House and return fares by bus and ferry from Galway for around IR£20.

The numerous B&Bs include the large *Dormer House* (☎ 61125) right behind Joe Mac's in Kilronan, with rooms for IR£15 per person. About 800 metres from the harbour on the road to Kilmurvey is *An Crugán* (☎ 61150) which costs IR£13.50 per person. Closer to town on the same road is *Claí Bán* (☎ 61111), which charges IR£13, or IR£15 with *en suite* bathroom. Not-so-friendly *Bayview House* (☎ 61260) enjoys an enviable position overlooking the harbour and charges from IR£16 per person.

The smaller islands also have B&Bs, and there's a camping ground and a hostel (the IHH *Brú Radharc na Mara*; ☎ 75024) on Inisheer.

Places to Eat
In Kilronan there are a couple of snack bars – the *Ould Pier* and *An tSean Chéibh* – just up from the tourist office. About the best place for pub food is *Joe Watty's Bar*, a bit further north on the way out of Kilronan. The *Aran Fisherman* has a wide range of pizzas, seafood and vegetarian dishes from around IR£6. *Dún Aengus* to the south-west overlooking Cill Éinne Bay has a set dinner for around IR£12 and serves good grills, steaks, chips and lovely scones and fruitcake.

Mainistir House Hostel serves good buffet dinners at 8 pm that include vegetarian dishes. They cost IR£6 for residents and IR£7 for non-residents.

Entertainment
There's music in most of the Kilronan pubs at night. For traditional Irish music, try *Joe Watty's*, *Joe Mac's* or, west of the village, *Tigh Fitz*. The *American Bar* often has rock music, which draws a younger crowd. Robert O'Flaherty's 1934 film *Man of Aran* is screened regularly at the *Halla Rónáin*, Kilronan's community centre south-west of the tourist office, for IR£3.

Getting There & Away
Air If time is important or seasickness a concern on the rough Atlantic, you can fly to the islands with Aer Árann (☎ 091-593034 in Galway) for IR£35 return (children IR£20). Flights operate to all three islands four times a day and take less than 10 minutes. The mainland departure point is Connemara airport at Minna, near Inverin, 38 km west of Galway. A connecting bus from outside the Galway City or Salthill tourist offices costs IR£4 return. A package including a return flight and one night's B&B accommodation costs IR£47.

Boat There's only one big ferry line making the year-round run to the islands following Island Ferries' purchase of Aran Ferries in March 1996. Island Ferries' services from Rossaveal, 37 km west of Galway, are popular because the crossing is quick and there are frequent sailings. The ferries operate two or three times daily with an adult/student return fare of IR£15/12 for the 45-minute trip. In summer the Island Ferries' service from Rossaveal to Inishmór continues on to the smaller islands of Inishmaan and Inisheer. The Island Ferries office (☎ 091-561767) in Galway is off Victoria Place opposite the tourist office.

Island Ferries also has direct services from Galway between June and September. This is a journey of about 46 km to Inishmór. It takes 90 minutes, costs IR£18 return and operates twice daily in July and August, once a day in June and September. O'Brien Shipping (☎ 091-567676 in Galway) also operates a single daily boat service to all three Aran Islands from June to September, which usually departs from the Galway docks around 10 am.

Doolin Ferries (☎ 065-74455 in Doolin) operates a service from Doolin to Inisheer and Inishmór. It's only eight km to Inisheer, taking about 30 minutes and costing IR£7 one-way or IR£10 return.

Inter-island services run by Island Ferries are not quite so regular (between one and four daily sailings depending on demand), but when they do operate in summer the usual fare is IR£10.

Getting Around
Inisheer and Inishmaan are small enough to explore on foot, but on larger Inishmór mountain bikes are definitely the way to go. Daily rates for bike hire are around IR£5 (IR£3 for groups), but the islands are tough on bikes, so check it over carefully before agreeing to rent it.

Aran Cycle Hire (☎ 61132), just up from the pier, has very good bikes. Costelloes (☎ 61241), opposite the American Bar, has similar bikes for similar prices. You can bring your own bicycle along on the ferries.

There are plenty of small tour buses which offer speedy trips to some of the island's principal sights for around IR£5. Pony traps with a driver are also available for a trip from Kilronan to the west of the island from around IR£20.

CONNEMARA
The north-west corner of County Galway is the wild and barren region known as Connemara. It's a stunning patchwork of bogs, lonely valleys, pale grey mountains and water, water everywhere; some people find it the most beautiful and evocative area of Ireland. Connemara's isolation has allowed Irish to thrive and the language is still widely spoken here; the lack of English signposting can be a little confusing at times.

The telephone code for Connemara is ☎ 095.

Clifden
The unsurprising port town of Clifden is the main centre in Connemara. The seasonal tourist office (☎ 21163) is on Lower Market St; the Clifden Walking Centre (☎ 21379) on Market St organises guided hikes and sells maps.

Accommodation options in Clifden include the IHH *Clifden Town Hostel* (☎ 21076) on Market St, which costs IR£6/16 for a dorm bed/double. Another IHH member, *Leo's*

Hostel (☎ 21429), is nearby, right by the square, and costs a little less. The IHO *Brookside Hostel* (☎ 21812) is down by the river in a quiet location and charges IR£7.

My Tea Shop on Main St next to Barry's Hotel serves wholefood meals and snacks. Opposite is *Fat Freddy's*, a popular spot for pasta and pizza. Three doors west is *D'Arcy's Inn*, where seafood is the emphasis. It has menus in French and German, and meals are under IR£10.

Buses link Clifden with Galway via Oughterard and Maam Cross or via Cong and Leenane. In summer there are three express buses a day to/from Galway and one to Cleggan, 10 km north-west, from where ferries run to Inishbofin Island.

WESTPORT
Tourist pounds didn't help to create the capital of County Mayo's postcard prettiness – it was designed that way. As a result, The Mall, with the River Carrowbeg running right down the middle of it, is as nice a main street as you could find anywhere in Ireland. There's a rather unwelcoming tourist office (☎ 25711; fax 26709) on The Mall open all year round; the main post office is a short distance to the south-east. There's a laundrette on Mill St by the clock tower.

Westport's telephone code is ☎ 098.

Things to See
About three km west of town, on the R335 to Croagh Patrick and Louisburgh, is **Westport House** (☎ 25430), one of the finest stately homes in Ireland. The present house dates from 1730 but, sadly, commercialisation has been taken its toll. Entry to the house is a pricey adults/children IR£6/3, but if you're planning to make a day of it and visit the zoo, take a boat on the lake and picnic in the park, the cost only jumps to IR£6.50/3.25. It's open in July and August from 10.30 am to 6 pm (Sunday from 2 to 6 pm); hours are shorter in spring and autumn.

Westport's other major attraction is **Croagh Patrick**, about seven km west of the town, the hill from where St Patrick performed his snake-expulsion act – Ireland has been serpent-free ever since. Climbing the 765-metre peak is a ritual for thousands of pilgrims on the last Sunday of July.

Places to Stay

Camping is good at the *Club Atlantic Hostel* (see the following). The alternative, the *Parkland Caravan & Camping Park* (☎ 27766) on the Westport House estate, charges an extortionate IR£16 for one night's pitch (IR£10 for hikers and cyclists). There are two IHH hostels: the *Old Mill Hostel* (☎ 27045) in a courtyard off James St, which charges IR£6.50/13 for a dorm bed/double; and the almost luxurious *Club Atlantic Hostel* (☎ 26644), on Altamont St near the railway station, with plenty of facilities and beds/doubles from IR£6.50/17. For B&Bs, try *Altamont House* (☎ 25226), which is a short distance down from the railway station on Altamont St. *En suite* singles/doubles are IR£18/32.

Places to Eat

Bridge St, the main thoroughfare, has a selection of cafés, including *McCormack's* and the simpler *Gavin's*. The *West* is a pub and restaurant with a tourist menu at around IR£7. The *O'Malley Restaurant* has a varied menu of pizza, steak and seafood. Expect to pay around IR£10 for dinner. Almost opposite is the newly renovated *Urchin Restaurant*, with a ploughman's lunch at IR£3 and dinner for under IR£10.

Entertainment

Good music pubs include *Matt Molloy's* on Bridge St, which is owned by one of the Chieftains, or head for the *Three Arches* near the clock tower on High St.

Getting There & Around

There are bus connections to Achill Island, Athlone, Ballina, Belfast, Cork, Galway, Limerick, Shannon, Sligo and Waterford. Buses depart from the Octagon at the end of James St. The railway station (☎ 25253) is on Altamont St south-east of the town centre. There are three daily connections with Dublin (3½ hours) via Roscommon city and Athlone.

Bicycles can be hired from the Club Atlantic Hostel or from Breheny Bike Hire (☎ 25020), which is on Castlebar St east of the tourist office.

ACHILL ISLAND

Joined to the mainland by a bridge, Achill Island combines views, moorland and mountains in one relatively remote location.

The independent *Railway Hostel* (☎ 098-45187) is on the east side of the bridge over Achill Sound, opposite the police station. Beds are IR£5, doubles IR£13, and the hostel is open all year. The excellent IHO *Wild Haven Hostel* (☎ 098-45392) is just across the bridge on the left near the church. The basic rate is IR£6 and two-bed rooms cost IR£2 extra per person. Buses link Achill with Westport and Ballina throughout the year.

The North-West

County Sligo and County Donegal make up the north-west, an area of the 'south' which extends further north than anywhere in the 'north'! The region has scenery the equal of better known regions of Ireland and yet has sufficient distance from Dublin to deter most of the crowds. Perhaps because of this, it's very popular with cyclists.

SLIGO

William Butler Yeats (1865-1939) was educated in Dublin and London, but his poetry is inextricably linked with the county of his mother's family. He returned to Sligo many times, and there are plentiful reminders of his presence in the county town and in the rolling green hills around it.

The tourist office (☎ 61201; fax 60360), open all year round, is on Temple St, just south of the centre. The main post office is on Wine St east of the train/bus station. Pam's Laundrette is in Johnston Court, just off O'Connell St.

The telephone code for Sligo is ☎ 071.

Things to See

The main draw of the **Sligo County Museum** is the Yeats room, chock-a-block with manuscripts, photographs, letters and newspaper cuttings connected with the poet's life and work. The **Sligo Municipal Art Gallery** upstairs has a good selection of paintings by Irish artists like George Russell, Sean Keating and Jack B Yeats, brother of the poet. The museum and gallery are open from 10.30 am to 12.30 pm and 2.30 to 4.30 pm, Tuesday to

Saturday from June to September. In April, May and October it opens in the morning only. Admission is free.

Sligo Abbey was established around 1250 for the Dominicans, but it burned down in the 15th century and was rebuilt. It was put to the torch once more – and for the last time – in 1641, and ruins are all that remain. The site is open mid-June to mid-September, and admission is IR£1.50/60p for adults/students & children.

Sligo's two major attractions are outside town. **Carrowmore**, five km to the south-west, is the site of a megalithic cemetery (☎ 61534) with a varied assortment of over 60 stone rings, passage tombs and other Stone Age remains. It's the largest Stone Age necropolis in Europe. A couple of km north-west of Carrowmore is the hilltop cairn grave of **Knocknarea**. About 1000 years younger than Carrowmore, the huge cairn is said to be the grave of the legendary Maeve, Queen of Connaught in the 1st century AD. Several trails lead to the top of the 328-metre-high grassy hill.

Places to Stay
On Pearse Rd the excellent IHH *Eden Hill Holiday Hostel* (☎ 43204) is about a 10-minute walk south from the centre on Pearse Road. The nightly cost is IR£6.50; doubles are IR£15. Just north of the town centre on Markievicz Rd, the IHH *White House Hostel* (☎ 45160) costs the same for a bed. The independent *Yeats County Hostel* (☎ 46976) is just west of the centre, opposite the bus/train station at 12 Lord Edward St, and costs IR£5.

B&Bs can be found all around town, including a couple on Temple St just along from the tourist office and on Lord Edward St west of the train/bus station. *Renaté Central House* (☎ 62014) at 7 Upper John St is a traditional B&B though overpriced at IR£21/32 for a single/double.

Places to Eat
The *Happy Eater* on O'Connell St is a big place, good for lunch. Also on O'Connell St, *Bistro Bianconi* serves decent Italian dishes for around IR£10, salads and pizzas from IR£6. *Beezies*, a flashy, modern café/bar with food, is down the alleyway around the corner. On the corner of Grattan St and Harmony Hill,

Gullivers is an old-fashioned place with a standard Irish menu ('and chips').

Entertainment
Sligo has the usual number of pubs, some with music on certain nights, including *McLaughlin's* (Tuesday) on Market St, the *Oak Tree* (Thursday) on Cranmore Rd and *Donaghy's* (Sunday) on Lord Edward St. *McGarrigle's* on O'Connell St has a good 'alternative music' bar upstairs. No place in Sligo can beat *Hargadon Bros* on O'Connell St for atmosphere, however. While it doesn't have music, this old place is like a stage set with snugs, nooks, crannies and 19th-century bar fixtures. Don't miss it.

Getting There & Around
Bus Éireann (☎ 60066) has three services a day to/from Dublin (IR£8). The run between Galway (IR£6) and Derry (IR£10) stops in Sligo. Buses operate from below the train station (☎ 69888), which is just to the west of the centre along Lord Edward St. Dublin service by train is via Mullingar. From Mullingar, connections can also be made to Galway and points in County Mayo. Taxis can be booked in Sligo on ☎ 44444 or ☎ 55555. The Eden Hill Hostel and Gary's Cycles (☎ 45418) on Lower Quay St have bikes for hire.

DONEGAL
Donegal Town is not the major centre in County Donegal, but it's a pleasant and popular, laid-back place and well-worth a visit. County Donegal is virtually separated from the rest of the Irish Republic by the westward projection of County Fermanagh in Northern Ireland, and it's worth making your way to or from Donegal via Enniskillen and Lough Erne in the north. The triangular Diamond is the centre of Donegal; a few steps south along the River Eske is the tourist office (☎ 21148; fax 22762), open all year round. The post office is in Tirchonaill St north of the river.

Donegal is principally a jumping-off point for the rest of the county, but the tourist office has *A Signposted Walking Tour of Donegal Town*. Restoration work at **Donegal Castle**, built by Red Hugh O'Donnell in the late 15th century, should be finished by the time you read this. Opening hours are usually 10 am to

IRELAND

6.30 pm mid-June to mid-September and admission is adults/students & children IR£2/1.

Donegal's telephone code is ☎ 073.

Places to Stay

The IHH *Donegal Town Independent Hostel* (☎ 22805) is on Killybegs Rd, about two km from the centre. The nightly cost is IR£5.70, and there are a couple of doubles for IR£13.50. Keep going another four km in the same direction and then turn off to the An Óige *Ball Hill Hostel* (☎ 21174) in Ball Hill. It has an enviable position on Donegal Bay and beds for IR£6.

There are plenty of B&Bs within walking distance of the centre. Waterloo Place, past the castle and down a few steps beside the river, has two: *Riverside House* (☎ 21083) and *Castle View House* (☎ 22100), both of which have doubles from IR£27. On Main St the *Atlantic Guest House* (☎ 21187) has garishly decorated but airy singles/doubles from IR£15/28.

Places to Eat

There are at least half a dozen places to eat within 100 metres or so of the Diamond. *Stella's Salad Bar* at McGroarty's Bar right on the Diamond offers lunches with a healthy twist. The *Atlantic Café* on Main St and the *Errigal Restaurant* further east are inexpensive. The *Midnight Haunt*, also in Main St, has almost unrecognisable Chinese food, with main courses from IR£6.50. The recommended *Belshade Restaurant* on the 1st floor of Magee's store does breakfast for IR£3.95 and lunches with vegetarian possibilities. Numerous music pubs can also be found within a stone's throw of the Diamond, including the *Coach House* at the eastern end of Main St and the *Schooner Inn* just beyond. *Charlie's Star Bar* is a friendly, lively place that has more modern music and attracts a younger crowd.

Getting There & Around

There are Bus Éireann (☎ 21101) connections with Derry, Enniskillen and Belfast in the north; Glencolumbcille, Killybegs, Sligo and Galway to the west; and Limerick and Cork in the south. The bus stop is outside the Abbey Hotel on the Quay south of the Diamond. The

Bike Shop (☎ 22515), across from the castle on Waterloo Place, has bikes for IR£6/30 a day/week.

AROUND COUNTY DONEGAL

County Donegal can match anywhere else in Ireland for soulful beauty, dramatic cliffs and hectare after hectare of peat bog. West of Donegal town is the hill of **Slieve League**, which drops over 300 metres straight into the sea. You can drive to the cliff edge, but after turning off the Glencolumbcille road (R263) at Carrick towards Bunglass Point, try continuing beyond the narrow track signposted Slieve League to the one signposted Bunglass. Walkers can start from Teelin and walk in a day via Bunglass and the thrilling (and very narrow) One Man's Path to Malin Beg, near Glencolumbcille.

The IHO *Hollybush Hostel* (☎ 31118) is in Killybegs, and the IHH *Derrylahan Hostel* (☎ 38079) is between Kilcar and Carrick. Both are open all year and have dorm beds/doubles for IR£5/14.

Continue beyond Carrick to **Glencolumbcille**, where there's a **Folk Village** of 18th and 19th-century buildings with genuine period fittings. There's a IR£1.50 charge (children IR£1) for the hourly tour of the site's buildings and for entry to the museum.

The *Dooey Hostel* (☎ 30130) is about 1.5 km beyond the village and offers everything from camping space and dorm beds (IR£6) to private doubles (IR£13).

Buses from Donegal go via Killybegs to Glencolumbcille, from where you can take the scenic road via the Glengesh Pass to Ardara.

Northern Ireland

More than a quarter-century of internal strife has seriously affected tourism in Northern Ireland and it is far less visited than the Republic. Though this was understandable in the dark days of the late 1960s and early 70s, in actual fact wanton violence was never a serious threat to visitors here. The road signs are British and the accent is not the same as in the south, but otherwise the differences across the border are not as significant as you'd think.

The rewards of a foray to the north are considerable. The Causeway Coast to the north and the Glens of Antrim in the north-east are areas of stunning natural beauty, there are some fascinating early Christian remains around Lough Erne; and Derry has one of the best preserved old city walls in Europe. Nor should the Troubles be ignored – the colourful and very political wall murals in Belfast and Derry, and the military roadblocks are as much a part of Ireland as green fields, haunting music and lively pubs. Travellers should note that for security reasons, there are no left-luggage facilities at train or bus stations anywhere in Northern Ireland.

BELFAST

Without the well-publicised Troubles, Northern Ireland's main city would simply be a big industrial centre – nicely situated on the River Lagan and Belfast Lough, but well past its glory days. If your only view of the city has been through the media, however, it will come as quite a surprise to find that the centre of Belfast is actually quite a bustling and prosperous place. A black-taxi ride through the strictly divided working-class areas of west Belfast will quickly show you the flip side of the coin.

As eye-opening as it all can be, the truth is that there are no compelling reasons to visit Belfast, and many people think it looks and feels just like a large, provincial British city – with all the decay, social problems and uniformity that implies.

Orientation & Information

The city centre is a compact area with the imposing City Hall as the central landmark. Great Victoria St runs south from the centre towards Queen's University, the Botanic Gardens and the Ulster Museum. The giant – and often idle – cranes at the Harland & Wolff shipyards to the east of the city are a visible landmark across the Lagan; the 'unsinkable' *Titanic* was built there. West of the centre, the Westlink Motorway divides the city from 'the wrong side of the tracks'. The (Protestant) Shankill Rd and the (Catholic) Falls Rd run west from there with a virtual no man's land separating them.

The helpful Northern Irish Tourist Board (☎ 246609; fax 312424) is in St Anne's Court at 59 North St and is open Monday to Saturday from 9 am to 5.15 pm (to 7 pm weekdays in summer and noon to 4 pm on Sunday). Bord Fáilte (☎ 327888) is at 53 Castle St. The main post office is on Castle Place, just east of the latter, and there's a branch on Shaftsbury Square. The Youth Hostel Association of Northern Ireland (YHANI) (☎ 315435) has its offices at the Belfast International Youth Hostel at 22 Donegall Rd. Belfast City Hospital (☎ 329241) is on Lisburn Rd south-west of the centre.

Bookshops in Belfast include Waterstone's on Royal Ave, Dillon's on Fountain St, Eason on Ann St and the Queen's University Bookshop opposite the university on University Rd. There's a laundrette in the university area at 160 Lisburn Rd and a Duds 'n Suds at 37 Botanic Ave.

The telephone code for Belfast is ☎ 01232.

Things to See

Around the City The Industrial Revolution transformed Belfast, and that rapid rise to muck-and-brass prosperity is evident to this day. The imposing **City Hall** (1906), crowned with the Union Jack and fronted by a pursed-lipped Queen Victoria, is still the symbol of Belfast.

To the north-east between High St and Queen's Square, the queen's consort, Prince Albert, also makes his Belfast appearance at the slightly leaning **clock tower**.

Other reminders of the city's Victorian past can be found in the narrow alleys known as the Entries off High St and Ann St in the pedestrianised shopping centre, at the wonderful old **Grand Opera House** and in the museum-like **Crown Liquor Saloon**, which still functions as a pub.

Museums & Gardens The **Ulster Museum**, which is in the Botanic Gardens near the university, has excellent exhibits on Irish art, wildlife, dinosaurs, steam and industrial machines, minerals and fossils. Items from the 1588 Spanish Armada wreck of the *Girona* (see Dunluce Castle in the Belfast-Derry Coastal Road section) are a highlight. Entry is free, and the museum is open from 10 am to 5 pm Monday to Friday, from 1 pm Saturday and from 2 pm Sunday. Bus No 69, 70 or 71 will get you there.

IRELAND

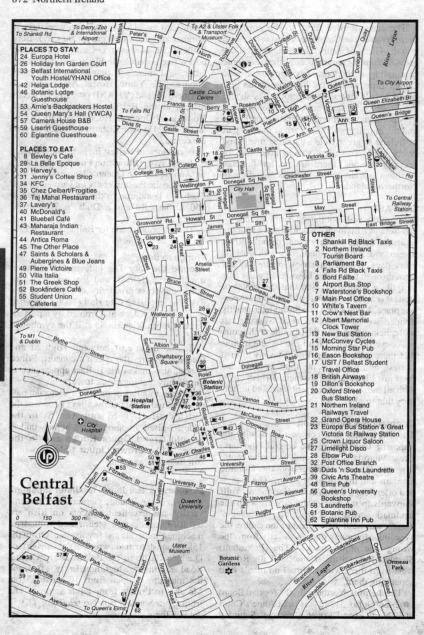

PLACES TO STAY
24 Europa Hotel
26 Holiday Inn Garden Court
33 Belfast International
   Youth Hostel/YHANI Office
42 Helga Lodge
46 Botanic Lodge
   Guesthouse
53 Arnie's Backpackers Hostel
54 Queen Mary's Hall (YWCA)
57 Camera House B&B
59 Liseriri Guesthouse
60 Eglantine Guesthouse

PLACES TO EAT
8 Bewley's Café
29 La Belle Epoque
30 Harvey's
31 Jenny's Coffee Shop
34 KFC
35 Chez Delbart/Frogities
36 Taj Mahal Restaurant
37 Lavery's
40 McDonald's
41 Bluebell Café
43 Maharaja Indian
   Restaurant
44 Antica Roma
45 The Other Place
47 Saints & Scholars &
   Aubergines & Blue Jeans
49 Pierre Victoire
51 Villa Italia
51 The Greek Shop
55 Bookfinders Café
55 Student Union
   Cafeteria

OTHER
1 Shankill Rd Black Taxis
2 Northern Ireland
   Tourist Board
3 Parliament Bar
4 Falls Rd Black Taxis
5 Bord Fáilte
6 Airport Bus Stop
7 Waterstone's Bookshop
9 Main Post Office
10 White's Tavern
11 Crow's Nest Bar
12 Albert Memorial
   Clock Tower
13 New Bus Station
14 McConvey Cycles
15 Morning Star Pub
16 Eason Bookshop
17 USIT / Belfast Student
   Travel Office
18 British Airways
19 Dillon's Bookshop
20 Oxford Street
   Bus Station
21 Northern Ireland
   Railways Travel
22 Grand Opera House
23 Europa Bus Station & Great
   Victoria St Railway Station
25 Crown Liquor Saloon
27 Limelight Disco
28 Elbow Pub
32 Post Office Branch
38 Duds 'n Suds Laundrette
39 Civic Arts Theatre
48 Elms Pub
56 Queen's University
   Bookshop
58 Laundrette
61 Botanic Pub
62 Eglantine Inn Pub

Central Belfast

0   150   300 m

IRELAND

Belfast has a good **zoo** (☎ 776277) on the Antrim Rd on the slopes of Cave Hill. It's open from 10 am to 5 pm in summer (till 3.30 pm at other times) and entry is adults/children £4.40/2.20. Reach here on bus No 2, 3, 8, 9 or 45.

Falls & Shankill Rds The Catholic Falls Rd and the Protestant Shankill Rd in west Belfast have been battle zones for a generation; apart from the odd multicolour wall mural, they're grey, dismal and potentially dangerous places. The best way to visit these sectarian zones if you must is by black taxi – beat-up, recycled London cabs that run a bus-like service to these roads from ranks in the city (see Local Transport under Getting Around).

Ulster Folk & Transport Museum Belfast's biggest tourist attraction (☎ 428428) is 11 km north-east of the centre beside the Bangor road (A2) near Holywood. The fine collection of almost 30 old buildings on a 60-hectare site ranges from city terrace homes to thatched farm cottages and several oddities. A bridge crosses the A2 to the Transport Museum, where you can see a varied collection of Ulster-related transport including a prototype of the vertical take-off and landing (VTOL) aircraft and a gull-wing stainless-steel De Lorean car.

In July and August the museum is open from 10.30 am to 6 pm daily, except Sunday when it opens at noon. During the rest of the year it is open daily but for shorter hours (typically 9.30 am to 4 or 5 pm). Entry to both museums is £3.30/2.20 for adults/children. You can get there on a the Belfast-Bangor Ulsterbus No 1 or on certain Bangor-bound trains that stop at Cultra station by the museum.

Organised Tours
There is a 3½-hour Citybus tour (☎ 458484) for £7/6/4.50 (adults/students/children) taking in all the city sights including Northern Ireland's former parliament, Stormont, the shipyards and Belfast Castle on Cave Hill. It begins at Castle Place at 1.30 pm every Wednesday during the summer months. Citybus' 2½-hour Living History tour, taking in the sites and areas associated with the Troubles and costing the same, leaves Castle Place in summer at 10 am and 2 pm on Tuesday, Thursday and Sunday and at 1 pm on Sunday

only in winter. Ulsterbus also runs evening tours of Belfast during July and August. They leave Castle Place at 7 pm and tickets must be reserved in advance (☎ 265265).

Places to Stay
Camping The only camping option in the Belfast area is at *Jordanstown Lough Shore Park* (☎ 863133), 10 km to the north on Shore Rd (A2) in Newtownabbey. It costs £6.50.

Hostels The cheapest place to stay in Belfast is *Arnie's Backpackers* at 63 Fitzwilliam St (☎ 242867), where a dorm bed costs £7.50. Bus Nos 70 and 71 and Nos 52 and 59 stop at opposite ends of Fitzwilliam St.

The YHANI *Belfast International Youth Hostel* (☎ 315435) is at 22-23 Donegall Rd. Beds cost £9 a head or £10.50/15 in a single/double. Bus Nos 69, 70 and 71 pass nearby, while Nos 89 and 90 stop outside.

From June until the end of September *Queen's Elms* (☎ 381608), run by the university at 78 Malone Rd, offers excellent accommodation for about £7.50 (students) and £12 (non-students). *Queen Mary's Hall* (☎ 240439) is the YWCA at 70 Fitzwilliam St, with dorm rooms for £8 and single and double rooms at £13.50 per person, including breakfast.

B&Bs & Guesthouses The tourist office will make bookings at B&Bs in the Belfast area. Be warned that some levy a 5% surcharge if you opt to use a credit card. There are many B&Bs in the university area, with prices averaging around £19. This area is conveniently close to the centre, safe and secure and well supplied with restaurants and pubs. Botanic Ave, Malone Rd, Wellington Park and Eglantine Ave are other good hunting grounds.

Central places to try include the German-run *Helga Lodge* (☎ 324820) at 7 Cromwell Rd, just off Botanic Ave, which costs £25/45 for singles/doubles with *en suite* bathroom and £20/38 without. This place has more rules than a state penitentiary, and not all rooms are centrally heated. Nearby at 87 Botanic Ave is the more homely *Botanic Lodge* (☎ 327682), where rooms are £18/34. Bus No 83, 85 or 86 will get you to these two places.

The *Eglantine Guesthouse* (☎ 667585) at 21 Eglantine Ave charges from IR£18/34 for singles/doubles. On the same street at No 17 is the friendly *Liserin Guesthouse* (☎ 660769), where rooms start at £19 per person. Another good choice nearby is the Victorian *Camera House* (☎ 660026) at 44 Wellington Park with singles/doubles from £20/40.

Hotels Belfast's hotels tend to be expensive, but the quoted rates can sometimes be negotiated and there are weekend packages. The city's most famous hotel is the *Europa* (☎ 327000; fax 327800); singles/doubles start at £95/130. Across the road and behind the Crown Liquor Saloon at 15 Brunswick St is the recently renamed *Holiday Inn Garden Court* (☎ 333555; fax 232999). Singles/doubles cost £75/85, with prices plummeting to £45/55 at weekends.

Places to Eat

Restaurants The *Greek Shop* at 43 University Rd, open for dinner only, has main dishes like pastitsio and moussaka from £5. The *Villa Italia* (☎ 328356) is a vibrant Italian restaurant and pizzeria at No 37-41 of the same street. There are a number of other bright and cheerful Italian places in the area, including *Harvey's* at 95 Great Victoria St and the more expensive and very stylish *Antica Roma* at 67 Botanic Ave.

Chez Delbart/Frogities is a fairly cheap (around £6) and cheerful French restaurant at 10 Bradbury Place; *Pierre Victoire* at 32 University Rd has set lunches/dinners from £5/9. Still in the university area the *Maharaja* upstairs at 62 Botanic Ave has acceptable Indian food; more authentic is the *Taj Mahal*, a block north on the same street, with main dishes for about £7.

If you can stand the frenetic atmosphere *Aubergines & Blue Jeans* at 1 University St serves all sorts of interesting goodies in a crazy décor; set meals are £5/6/7.50 depending on the number of courses. Next door at No 3 is the up-market *Saints & Scholars*, where excellent meals are available in the £8 to £14 range.

Cafés & Pubs There's a branch of the popular Dublin chain *Bewley's Café* in Rosemary St. Historic *White's Tavern* on Winecellar Entry is good for pub lunches, as is the rough-edged *Morning Star* on Pottinger's Entry with a lunch buffet for £3.95. The *Bookfinders Café*

at 47 University Rd is a good little place at the back of a second-hand bookshop.

Fast Food & Cheap Eats South of Great Victoria St, you'll find such fast-food places as *McDonald's* and *KFC* on Bradbury Place. *Jenny's Coffee Shop* is a pleasant little café/sandwich bar at 81 Dublin Rd. There are a number of bakeries along Botanic Ave, and *Bluebell* is good for a coffee or ice cream. At No 79 of the same street the burgers and chips at *The Other Place* are very popular with students. The *Student Union Cafeteria*, upstairs on University Rd, is so-so for lunchtime cheap eats.

Entertainment

For a complete listing of what's on in Belfast, pick up a copy of the free weekly *That's Entertainment* at one of the tourist offices.

Belfast has several pubs that are as much museums as drinking places. Opposite the Europa Hotel at 42-44 Great Victoria St, is the wonderful old *Crown Liquor Saloon*, built in 1885 and now owned by the National Trust. Other places are the *Morning Star* on Pottinger's Entry or *White's Tavern* dating from 1630 on Winecellar Entry off High St.

The huge lounge bar upstairs at *Lavery's* on Bradbury Place attracts a very young crowd as does the *Elbow* on the corner of Dublin Rd and Ventry St. More comfortable and trendy is the studenty *Elms* at 36 University Rd. Further south and facing each other across Malone Rd are the *Eglantine Inn* and the *Botanic*, known as the Egg and Bott.

Those who want to kick up their heels should head for the *Errigle Inn* at 320 Ormeau Rd, south of the centre, which has great music, or the *Limelight*, south of City Hall at 17 Ormeau Ave. Monday night is gay night at the *Limelight*. Other popular gay hangouts are the *Crow's Nest* on the corner of Skipper and High Sts and the *Parliament Bar* in Dunbar St.

For those with more highbrow tastes, there's often something on at the *Grand Opera House* (☎ 241919) or at the *Civic Arts Theatre* (☎ 324936) on Botanic Ave.

Getting There & Away

The USIT/Belfast Student Travel office (☎ 324073) is at 13B Fountain Centre, College St.

Air Flights from London and some regional airports in Britain arrive at the convenient City Harbour airport (☎ 457745), but everything else goes to Belfast International airport (☎ 018494-422888), 30 km north-west of the city at Aldergrove. British Airways (☎ 0345-222111) and, to a lesser extent, British Midland Airways (☎ 0345-554554) are the main operators. See the introductory Getting There & Away section for more details.

Bus Belfast has two bus stations. Ulsterbus connections to counties Antrim, Down and east Derry operate from the Oxford St bus station, which should have moved to just north of Ann St by the time you read this. Buses to everywhere else in Northern Ireland, the Republic, Belfast International airport and the Larne ferry pier leave from the new Europa bus station in Glengall St, right behind the Europa Hotel. Phone ☎ 320011 for Ulsterbus information or ☎ 333000 for timetable information. There are four Belfast-Dublin services daily which take about three hours and cost £9.50. To Derry (£5.70, 1¾ hours), count on an hourly bus Monday to Saturday (six a day on Sunday).

Train For tickets and information, Northern Ireland Railways Travel (☎ 230671) is at 17 Wellington Place close to the City Hall. Trains to all destinations, including Larne, Derry, Dublin, Newry, Portadown and Bangor, arrive and depart from Belfast Central railway station (☎ 899411) on East Bridge St, which can now be reached by train from the new Great Victoria St railway station (☎ 434424) behind the Europa bus station. Belfast-Dublin trains (£14) run up to six times a day (three on Sunday) and take about two hours. They all stop at Portadown or Dundalk, and some stop at Lisburn and Newry as well. There are a half-dozen daily services to Derry, and local services run to Bangor and Portadown.

Boat See the Getting There & Away section at the beginning of this chapter for more details on the Norse Irish Belfast-Heysham (Liverpool) ferry, the P&O Larne-Cairnryan ferry, the Stena Line Belfast-Stranraer high-speed ferry and the Seacat Belfast-Stranraer catamaran. In Belfast, the dock on Donegall Quay is reasonably close to the centre, and you can

walk, take a taxi or a bus from nearby Great George's St. The Liverpool terminal, used by Norse Irish, is a little further north while the Larne terminal (P&O) is 30 km north-east on the Antrim coast. There are trains from Larne to Belfast Central (50 minutes) and Ulsterbus services to and from Belfast's Europa bus station.

Ferry line phone numbers in Belfast are Norse Irish (☎ 779090) and Seacat (☎ 0345-523523). Stena Line (☎ 01574-273616) and P&O (☎ 01574-274321) have their offices at Larne Harbour.

Getting Around
To/From the Airport Airbus buses link Belfast International airport with the Europa bus station every half-hour for £3.70. There's also a stop in front of Waterstone's on Royal Ave. A taxi costs £18. The Belfast City Harbour airport is only six km north-east of the centre and you can cross the road from the terminal to the Sydenham Halt station, from which trains run to Botanic and Great Victoria St stations.

Local Transport Buses run by Citybus (☎ 246485) cost 73p for a standard fare and 42p for a 'short-distance fare' in the centre, increasing by zones as you travel farther out. A multitrip ticket good for four rides costs £2.30 and daily/weekly passes are £2.10/10. Most local bus services depart from Donegall Square, near the City Hall, where there is a ticket kiosk.

Black taxis operate a shuttle service down the Shankill Rd from North St and down the Falls Rd from Castle St. Fares start at 55p. The flag fall of regular taxis (☎ 233333 or ☎ 323278) is a pricey £2. If you're driving, be fastidious about where you park; automobile theft is a serious problem here. The tourist office has a free leaflet showing all the multi-storey car parks.

McConvey Cycles (☎ 330322) at 10 Pottinger's Entry or south-east of the centre at 467 Ormeau Rd (☎ 491163) rents bicycles for £8/40 a day/week. A deposit of £30 is required.

THE BELFAST-DERRY COASTAL ROAD
It's easy to spend a couple of days between Belfast and Derry, enjoying the magnificent

scenery and historic sites along the coast of counties Antrim and Derry. From late May to late September, you can travel along the coast by the twice-daily Ulsterbus Antrim Coaster service, which runs from Belfast to Coleraine, just beyond Portstewart, and takes four hours. The Bushmills Open Topper makes the one-hour run between the Giant's Causeway and Coleraine – the heart of the Causeway Coast – four times a day in July and August.

Carrickfergus

Only 13 km north-east of Belfast is Carrickfergus with its huge 12th-century Norman castle complete with a museum. The castle is open April to September from 10 am to 6 pm Monday to Saturday and from 2 to 6 pm Sunday; at other times it closes at 4 pm. Entry is £2.70/1.35 for adults/children.

Glens of Antrim

Between Larne and Ballycastle are the nine Glens of Antrim, extremely picturesque stretches of woodland where streams cascade into the sea. The lovely little port of Cushendall has been dubbed the 'Capital of the Glens' while Glenariff, a couple of km to the south, lays claim to the title 'Queen of the Glens'. Between Cushenden and Ballycastle, eschew the main A2 road for the narrower and more picturesque (and roller coaster-like) coastal road (B92) and take the turn-off down to beautiful Murlough Bay.

The YHANI *Cushendall Youth Hostel* (☎ 012667-71344) is about a km north of the village and costs £6.30.

Carrick-a-Rede Island

Open from May to mid-September, but closed any time the wind is too strong, the 20-metre rope bridge connecting Carrick-a-Rede Island to the mainland is a heart-stopper and a half – even in fine weather. The island is the site of a salmon fishery and a nesting ground for gulls and fulmars. The car park costs £2.

Giant's Causeway

Legend tells us that if the giant Finn McCool had finished the job here this would not be merely a 'pier' but a real causeway clear across to Scotland. The bizarre assembly of hexagonal volcanic columns, numbering some 38,000 and formed 55 million years ago, is so artifi-

cial-looking that it's easy to believe it was the work of an Irish Goliath.

Today the Giant's Causeway, a World Heritage Site since 1986, attracts huge crowds of tourists though not everyone has been impressed. On his visit in here early in the last century, the English novelist William Thackery moaned, 'I travelled 150 miles to see *that*?' Today it has a big visitor centre (☎ 012657-31582) complete with an inventive 25-minute audiovisual show. It is open daily from 10 am to 4.30 or 5 pm (to 7 pm in July and August) and costs £1/50p for adults/children.

Two well-established footpaths at different levels start from just outside the visitor centre; for the lazy or infirm minibuses with wheelchair access ply the route every 15 minutes (80p return) from mid-March to the end of October. Entry to the Giant's Causeway itself is free; the car park costs £2. About four buses a day (fewer on Sunday) between Portrush and Ballycastle pass the site.

Dunluce Castle

Abandoned back in 1641, the ruins of 14th-century Dunluce Castle, dramatically sited overlooking the sea between Bushmills and Portrush, still bear a hint of historic power. Some of that came from the Spanish armaments conveniently salvaged from the overloaded Spanish ship *Girona*, wrecked just off the coast in 1588 with the loss of over 1000 crew. Entry to the castle, which has an audiovisual display, is adults/children £1.50/75p and it's open April to September daily from 10 am (11 am on Sunday) to 7 pm; the rest of the year it closes at 4 pm and Sunday hours are from 2 to 4 pm.

Ballycastle, Portrush & Portstewart

Although the Causeway Coast itself is the main attraction, several resort towns along it are not without their charms. On the last Monday and Tuesday in August, Ballycastle hosts the Ould Lammas Fair, dating back to 1606. Just a km east of town along the A2 are the ruins of Bonamargy Friary. Boats run from Ballycastle to **Rathlin Island**, just off the coast, for £5.60 return.

Between Ballycastle and Portrush and a km east of the town of Bushmills is the famous Old Bushmills whiskey distillery, which has held its licence since 1608. Tours, which include a shot of the 'water of life' (*uisce beatha* in Irish, from which the word 'whiskey' comes), operate from 9 am to noon and 1.30 to 3.30 pm Monday to Thursday and on Friday morning. Admission costs £2.50/1 for adults/children.

Portrush and Portstewart are twin resorts only six km apart. Portstewart, the nicer of the two, has a slightly decayed, *fin-de-siècle* feel to it. Portrush is marred by a huge caravan park on its eastern approach.

The IHH *Castle Hostel* (☎ 012657-62337) is at 62 Quay Rd in Ballycastle and costs £6/15 a night for a dorm bed/double. The YHANI *Whitepark Bay Youth Hostel* (☎ 012657-31745) is at 157 Whitepark Rd, Ballintoy, which is 10 km west of Ballycastle, and costs £6.30. The IHO *Causeway Coast Hostel* (☎ 012658-33789) is at 4 Victoria Terrace, Atlantic Circle, in Portstewart and costs £6/7.50 for dorm beds/singles.

Downhill & Mussenden Temple

The eccentric Bishop of Derry was also the Earl of Bristol, and his fine home at Downhill was built in 1722, burned down in 1851, rebuilt in 1870 and abandoned after WWII. The dramatic ruins of the house remain and there are some fine gardens, but the major attraction here is the curious little Mussenden Temple, perched right on the cliff edge and built to house the bishop's library. The circular 'temple', about 20 km west of Portstewart by road, is open April, May, June and September on Saturday and Sunday from noon to 6 pm; in July and August it opens daily.

DERRY

Merely choosing what you call Northern Ireland's second-largest city can be a political statement – it's Derry if you're following signs from Dublin, and Londonderry if you're driving from Belfast. In practice it's better known as Derry whatever your religion. Doire, the original Irish name, means 'oak grove', and the 'London' prefix was add as a reward for the town's central role in the struggle between the Protestant King William III and the Catholic King James II. This was the place where 'No Surrender' entered the Northern Irish lexicon.

In December 1688 the gates of Derry were slammed shut before the forces of King James II, and the great Siege of Derry commenced. For more than eight months the citizens of Derry withstood bombardment, disease and starvation. By the time a relief ship burst through the boom on the River Foyle and broke the siege, a quarter of the city's 30,000 inhabitants had died.

In the 1960s and 70s, Derry was a flashpoint for the Troubles, resentment at the long-running and decisively gerrymandered Protestant-dominated council boiling over in the civil rights march of 1968. Attacks on the Catholic Bogside district in 1969 were a major factor in deploying large numbers of British troops, and 'Bloody Sunday' in Derry in 1972, in which 14 unarmed demonstrators were killed, was the definitive clash between the army and Catholic civilians. Derry is now a much more peaceful place; a 'cease-fire' has been in effect here in all but name for years.

Orientation & Information

The old centre of Derry is the small but delightful walled city on the west bank of the River Foyle; the heart of the walled city is the Diamond. The Catholic Bogside area is below the walls to the north-west while to the south is a Protestant estate known as the Fountain. The Waterside district across the river is mostly Protestant.

The Northern Ireland Tourist Board (☎ 267284) and Bord Fáilte (☎ 369501), both open year round, share an office at 8 Bishop St in the old city. The main post office is on Custom House St just north of the Tower Museum.

The Bookworm, an excellent local bookshop with lots of local and regional titles and maps, is at 16-18 Bishop St. Duds 'n Suds, at 141 Strand Rd, is probably the most glamorous laundrette you'll ever see.

Derry's telephone code is ☎ 01504.

Things to See

The protective iron bars put up by the army have at last been removed from Derry's magnificent **city walls**, allowing you to walk much of the way round. The walls were built between 1613 and 1618, making Derry the last city to be fortified in Ireland. Be sure to visit the striking new **Calgach Centre** near Butcher's Gate on the north-west side, with a 40-minute audiovisual 'journey' relating to the history and culture of the Celts called the Fifth Province. It is open daily from 10 am to 8 pm.

IRELAND

Down to the left as you step out of Butcher's Gate is the famous 'You Are Now Entering Free Derry' mural from the early 1970s. At that time, and until the British army smashed the barricades in July 1972, this was a no-go area for the military. A short distance to the north-east, the **Bloody Sunday Memorial** (1974) honours the 14 people shot dead by British soldiers on Sunday, 30 January 1972. None of the soldiers who fired the 108 bullets or the officers who gave the order to shoot were ever brought to trial.

Just inside Coward's Bastion to the north, O'Doherty's Tower houses the excellent **Tower Museum** which traces the story of Derry from the days of St Columbcille to the present. The museum is open 10 am to 5 pm Monday to Saturday (also on Sunday in July and August from 2 to 5 pm) and costs £3/1.25 for adults/children.

The fine red-brick **Guildhall** was originally built in 1890, reconstructed after a fire in 1908 and bombed by the IRA in 1972. It's just outside the city walls and is noted for its wonderful stained-glass windows. Austere **St Columb's Cathedral** dates from 1628 and stands at the southern end of the walled city.

The **Foyle Valley Railway Centre** in Foyle Rd station by the bridge stands on what was once the junction of four railway lines. Exhibits inside tell the story of the railways, and you can take a 20-minute, four-km train excursion. The centre is open April to September from Tuesday to Saturday from 10 am to 5 pm, Sunday 2 to 6 pm. Admission is free but the excursion costs £2.50/1.25 for adults/children.

Places to Stay

Derry's YHANI hostel is in the restored *Oakgrove Manor* (☎ 372273) at 4-6 Magazine St, inside the city walls near Butcher's Gate and just 150 metres from the bus station. The cheapest dorm beds without breakfast cost £7.60, but there's a variety of rooms ranging up to singles at £17.50 with breakfast. If it's full, the IHH *Muff Independent Hostel* (☎ 077-84188 in Ireland) is just eight km to the north across the border in Muff, County Donegal. The nightly cost is IR£6/16 for a dorm bed/twin room.

Joan Pyne (☎ 269691) offers B&B for £16 a head in a wonderful 19th-century townhouse at 36 Great James St, with comfortable beds,

antique furniture, Oriental rugs and excellent breakfasts. Highly recommended. Farther north, at 15 Northland St, there is *Clarence House* (☎ 265342), charging £16.50 a head, and *Florence House* (☎ 268093) at No 16 with B&B for £15 per person.

Places to Eat

Inside the walled city there is plenty of choice along Shipquay St. *Louis' Restaurant* on the ground floor of the Richmond Shopping Centre serves inexpensive meals throughout the day for around £4. *The Sandwich Company*, at 25 The Diamond, and *Malibu*, beside the tourist office, are also handy lunch stops. More up-market is the *Boston Tea Party* in the Craft Village off Shipquay St.

Thran Maggies, also in the Craft Village, is one of the few places to eat in the walled city after dark. The *City Chinese Restaurant* opposite the Craft Village at 27 Shipquay St has main dishes from as low as £4. Good possibilities outside the walls include: *India House*, at 51 Carlisle Rd heading toward Craigavon Bridge, with curries from £7.50; *La Sosta*, an excellent Italian eatery a few doors up at No 45A; and *Reggies Seafood Restaurant* past Magee University College at 145 Strand Rd.

Entertainment

Derry's liveliest pubs are those along Waterloo St: the *Gweedore*, *Bound for Boston*, *Dungloe* and *Castle Bar*. *Peadar O'Donnell's* is good for traditional music. The *Metro Bar* at 3-4 Bank Place, just inside the walls, is also very popular. Students favour the *Strand Tavern* and *Cole's* on the corner of Rock and Strand Rds north of the centre.

Getting There & Away

Eglinton airport (☎ 810784), about 13 km east of Derry, receives flights from Glasgow and Manchester. The bus station (☎ 262261) is just outside the city walls south-east of the Guildhall. From Monday to Saturday there are five or six daily buses to Belfast (£5.70, 1¾ hours); fewer services operate on Sunday. Other destinations include Omagh, Portstewart, Portrush and, in the Republic, Cork, Sligo, Donegal and Galway. Along with Ulsterbus, Lough Swilly (☎ 262017) has services into Donegal, including Muff (£1.20) and Letterkenny (£4.50). The railway station (☎ 42228) is across the Foyle from the centre, and a free bus connects it with the centre. There are seven trains daily to Belfast (three on Sunday) via Portrush taking about three hours.

There's a USIT travel office (☎ 371888) at 33 Ferryquay St.

Getting Around

As in Belfast, black taxis operate a shuttle service from the centre to the Bogside and outlying suburbs. The stand is on William St. Regular cabs include Auto Cabs (☎ 45100) and Central Taxis (☎ 261911). Bikes can be hired from the Oakgrove Manor hostel.

ENNISKILLEN

Enniskillen, the main town of little County Fermanagh, is a handy centre for activities on Upper and Lower Lough Erne and the antiquities around them. **Enniskillen Castle** (open year round; adults/children and students £2/1) in the centre and the mansions of **Castle Coole** (☎ 322690; £3 per car), three km south-east of Enniskillen, and **Florence Court** (☎ 348249; adults/children £2.60/1.60), eight km south-west of town, are worth a visit.

The town centre is on an island in the River Erne, which connects the upper and lower lakes. The tourist office (☎ 01365-323110; fax 01365-325511), open year round, is on Wellington Rd about 100 metres down the hill from the centre. The main post office is on the East Bridge St section of the main street.

The telephone code for Enniskillen and Lough Erne area is ☎ 01365.

Places to Stay

There is hostel-style accommodation and a camp site at the *Lakeland Canoe Centre* (☎ 324250) on Castle Island, which is reached by free ferry from the Lakeland Forum Leisure Centre southeast of the tourist office. It costs £4 to camp, or £9 in the hostel (£10.50 for B&B).

There are no B&Bs right in the centre of Enniskillen but plenty on the outskirts, particularly along the Sligo Rd (A4) and the A46 up the western shore of Lower Lough Erne. *Carraig Aonrai* (☎ 324889) at 19 Sligo Rd has singles/doubles for £10.50/20, while *Rossole House* (☎ 323462) at No 85 charges £15/30. At the other side of town B&Bs can be found along the B80 road to Tempo. Prices average £16 to 17 per person.

Places to Eat

Johnston's Coffee Lounge on Townhall St, just east of the clock tower in the centre, has good sandwiches. Almost opposite is the *Peppercorn Restaurant*, a pleasant place, serving breakfast and meals for under £5. *Franco's Pizzeria* on Queen Elizabeth Rd on the northern side of town is more adventurous: pizzas and pasta dishes start at around £5 to 6 and there's much more on offer in this very popular restaurant. The main street through town has a number of popular pubs. These include the Victorian-style *William Blake* on Church St, the *Crow's Nest* on High St with good food and music in the evenings, the *Vintage* at 13 Townhall St and the *Bush Bar* at 26 Townhall St.

Getting There & Around

The bus station (☎ 322633) is across from the tourist office on Shore Rd. There are up to 10 Ulsterbus services a day to Belfast via Dungannon (£5.70, two hours) Monday to Saturday, with about eight on Sunday. Buses also run to Derry (3¼ hours) and Cork (11¼ hours) via Omagh (one hour). From Omagh, there are express buses to Dublin. Bicycles can be hired at the Lakeland Canoe Centre for £10 a day or from Erne Tours (☎ 322882) at the Round 'O' Quay at Brook Park west of Enniskillen's centre.

AROUND LOUGH ERNE

There are a number of ancient religious sites on and around Lower Lough Erne, the convoluted stretch of water extending north from Enniskillen (the even more convoluted Upper Lough Erne lies to the south). Between May and September from the Round 'O' Jetty at Brook Park, the MV *Kestrel* waterbus (☎ 322882) operates 1¾-hour tours (£4/2 adults/children) of the lough, including a visit to **Devenish Island**, with its 9th-century church and abbey ruins and one of the best round towers in Ireland.

White Island, close to the eastern shore of the lough, has a line of eight mysterious statues dating from around the 6th century. From April to September, a ferry runs across to White Island from the Castle Archdale marina, 20 km north of Enniskillen on the Kesh road. The return fare is £3 (children £2) and the crossing takes 15 minutes.

Italy

Since the days of the Grand Tour, travellers to Italy have speculated on the 'fatal spell' of the country. This special charm has been attributed to the women, the art, the history, even the air. What is it that makes Italy so seductive? The Italian writer, Luigi Barzini, had this to say on the question:

It made and still makes unwanted people feel wanted, unimportant people feel important and purposeless people believe that the real way to live intelligently is to have no earnest purpose in life.

This land of vibrant, expressive people has given the world pasta and pizza, da Vinci and Michelangelo, Dante and Machiavelli, Catholicism and a vast array of saints and martyrs, Verdi and Pavarotti, Fellini and Sophia Loren, not to mention the Mafia, a remarkable sense of style and *la dolce vita*. In Italy you can visit Roman ruins, study the art of the Renaissance, stay in tiny medieval hill towns, go mountaineering in the Alps and Apennines, feel romantic in Venice, participate in traditional festivals and see more beautiful churches than you imagined could exist in one country. Some people come simply to enjoy the food and wine.

Do your research before coming to Italy, but arrive with an open mind and you will find yourself agreeing with Henry James, who wrote on his arrival in Rome: 'At last, for the first time, I live'.

Facts about the Country

HISTORY

Italy's strategic position in the Mediterranean made it a target for colonisers and invaders over thousands of years. But it also gave the Romans an excellent base from which to expand their empire. Italy's history is thus a patchwork of powerful empires and foreign domination, its people have a diverse ethnic background, and, from the fall of the Roman Empire until the Risorgimento (the Italian unification movement) in 1860, the country was never a unified entity.

The traditional date for the founding of Rome by Romulus is 753 BC, but the country had been inhabited for thousands of years. Palaeolithic Neanderthals lived in Italy during the last Ice Age, more than 20,000 years ago, and by the start of the Bronze Age, around 2000 BC, the peninsula had been settled by several Italic tribes.

The Etruscans

From about 900 BC, or possibly earlier, the Etruscan civilisation developed until these mysterious people, whose origins are still controversial, dominated the area between the Arno and Tiber valleys.

After the foundation of Rome, Etruscan civilisation continued to flourish and Etruscan kings, known as the Tarquins, ruled Rome until 509 BC, when the Roman republic was established. By the end of the 3rd century BC the Romans had overwhelmed the last Etruscan city.

Italy (Italia)

FRANCE
GERMANY
AUSTRIA
HUNGARY

SWITZERLAND
LIECHTENSTEIN

Lake Constance

Livigno
Bolzano
Canazei
Dolomites
Trento

SLOVENIA
TRIESTE

YUGOSLAVIA

0   150   300 km

Sondrio

Grand St Bernard
Courmayeur
Mont Blanc

Milan
VERONA
PADUA
Venice

CROATIA

Turin
Mantua

Ferrara

BOSNIA-
HERCEGOVINA

Genoa
Bologna
Ravenna

Portofino
La Spezia
SAN MARINO

Zadar

To Croatia

Imperia
Pisa
Florence
Urbino

Ancona

Split

LIGURIAN SEA
LIVORNO
Siena
Arezzo

Bastia
Elba
Gubbio
PERUGIA
Assisi

ADRIATIC SEA

Dubrovnik

CORSICA
Orvieto
Spoleto

Tarquinia
Civitavecchia
ROME

Pescara

Promonte del Gargano

To Greece, Turkey & Albania

Fiumicino
Lido di Ostia

BARI

To Greece

Porto Torres
Olbia
Golfo Aranci

TYRRHENIAN SEA

Naples
Vesuvius
Sorrento
Potenza
Alberobello

To Greece

Sassari
Ischia
Salerno
Matera
Brindisi
Lecce

Alghero
Nuoro
Anacapri
Paestum
TARANTO

Bosa
Dorgali
Capri
Amalfi
Velia
Lido di Metaponto
Otranto

Oristano
Arbatax
Gallipoli

SARDINIA
Gennargentu

CAGLIARI

Stromboli

Aeolian Islands
Panarea

MEDITERRANEAN SEA

Alicudi
Salina
Lipari

Filicudi
Vulcano
Milazzo

Palermo
MESSINA
REGGIO DI CALABRIA

Trapani
Cefalù
Mt Etna
Taormina

Agrigento
SICILY
CATANIA

Syracuse

IONIAN SEA

Tunis

MALTA
Valletta

TUNISIA

The Roman Republic

The new Roman republic, after recovering from the invasion of the Gauls in 390 BC, began its expansion into the south of Italy. The Greeks had colonised this area, which they called Magna Grecia, as early as the 8th century BC, and they had established cities such as Syracuse, which rivalled Athens in power.

By about 265 BC Rome had taken the south from Greece, and Sicily was held by Carthage. Rome claimed Sicily following the First Punic War against Hannibal in 241 BC, and although the Romans were defeated by Hannibal at Lake Trasimeno after his legendary crossing of the Alps, Rome defeated and destroyed Carthage in 202 BC. Within another few years they claimed Spain and Greece as colonies and had moved into North Africa.

Expansion & Empire

In the 1st century BC, under Julius Caesar, Rome conquered Gaul and moved into Egypt. After Caesar's assassination by his nephew, Brutus, on the Ides of March in 44 BC, a power struggle began between Mark Antony and Octavius, leading to the deaths of Antony and Cleopatra in Egypt in 31 BC and the establishment of the Roman Empire in 27 BC. Octavius, who had been adopted by Julius Caesar as his son and heir, took the title of Augustus Caesar and became the first emperor. During his rule Roman literature flourished, with great writers including Virgil, Horace and Livy. Augustus was succeeded by Tiberius, Caligula, Claudius and Nero.

The Eastern & Western Empires

By the end of the 3rd century, the empire had grown to such an extent that Emperor Diocletian divided it between east and west for administrative purposes. His reign was also noted for the persecution of Christians. His successor, Constantine, declared religious freedom for Christians and moved the seat of the empire to the eastern capital, Byzantium, which he renamed Constantinople. During the 4th century, Christianity was declared the official state religion and grew in power and influence; at the same time Rome was under constant threat of barbarian invasion.

By the early 5th century, German tribes had entered Rome, and in 476 the Western Roman

Empire ended when the German warrior, Odoacer, deposed the emperor and declared himself ruler of Italy.

While the Eastern Roman Empire continued to exist and even retook part of the country for Byzantium in 553, this was the period of the Dark Ages during which Italy became a battleground of barbarians fighting for control. The south and Sicily were dominated by Muslim Arabs until the Normans invaded in 1036 and established a kingdom there.

With a view to re-establishing the Western Roman Empire, Pope Leo II crowned the Frankish king, Charlemagne, emperor in 800 AD. However, the empire again declined under Charlemagne's successors, culminating in the foundation of the Holy Roman Empire in 962 by the German king Otto I, who also declared himself emperor.

The City-States

The Middle Ages in Italy were marked by the development of powerful city-states in the north, while in the south the Normans were busily imposing a severe feudal system on their subjects. After the mid-12th century, when Frederick Barbarossa was crowned emperor, conflict between Pope Alexander III and the emperor reached the point where Italy again became a battleground as cities became either Guelph (supporters of the pope) or Ghibelline (supporters of the emperor). The factional struggles died gradually, but did not prevent a period of great economic, architectural and artistic development. This was the time of Dante, Petrarch and Boccaccio, Giotto, Cimabue and Pisano. The city-states flourished under the rule of powerful families and the papal states were established, even though the French had moved into the country and installed rival popes based in Avignon.

The Renaissance

It was not until the 15th century and the arrival of the Renaissance that Italy rediscovered its former glory. This period was marked by savage intercity wars, internal feuding and French invasions, but the Renaissance, which began in Florence, spread throughout the country, fostering genius of the likes of Brunelleschi, Donatello, Bramante, Botticelli, da Vinci, Masaccio, Lippi, Raphael and, of course, Michelangelo.

ITALY

By the early 16th century, the Reformation had arrived in Italy, and by 1559 much of the country was under Spanish rule. This lasted until 1713 when, following the War of Spanish Succession, control of Italy passed to the Austrians. The powerful states of the country's north, however, continued to grow in power. It was not until after the invasion by Napoleon in 1796 that a degree of unity was introduced into the country, for the first time since the fall of the Roman Empire. The Congress of Vienna in 1815, which restored power to the nobles and revived the old territorial divisions in Italy, created great discontent among the people and led directly to the Risorgimento, the movement to unite the country under one rule.

The Risorgimento
Under the leadership of Garibaldi, Cavour and Mazzini, the unification movement gained momentum until Garibaldi and his Expedition of One Thousand (also known as the Redshirts) took Sicily and Naples in 1860. The Kingdom of Italy was declared in 1861 and Vittorio Emanuele was proclaimed king. Venice was wrested from Austria in 1866 and Rome from the papacy in 1870. However, the new government had great difficulty achieving national unity. As Cavour noted before his death in 1861: 'To harmonise north and south is harder than fighting with Austria or struggling with Rome'.

Mussolini & WWII
In the years after WWI, Italy was in turmoil and in 1921 the Fascist Party, formed by Benito Mussolini in 1919, won 35 of the 135 seats in parliament. In October 1921, after a period of considerable unrest and strikes, the king asked Mussolini to form a government, and he became prime minister with only 7% representation in parliament.

The Fascists won the 1924 elections, following a campaign marked by violence and intimidation, and by the end of 1925 Mussolini had become head of state, expelled opposition parties from parliament, gained control of the press and trade unions and reduced the voting public by two-thirds. He formed the Rome-Berlin axis with Hitler in 1936 and Italy entered WWII as an ally of Germany in June 1941. After a series of military disasters and an invasion by the Allies in 1943, Mussolini surrendered Italy to the Allies and went into

hiding. He was shot, along with his mistress, Clara Petacci, by partisans in April 1945.

The Italian Republic
In 1946, following a referendum, the constitutional monarchy was abolished and the republic established.

Italy was a founding member of the European Economic Community in 1957 and was seriously disrupted by terrorism in the 1970s following the appearance of the Red Brigades, who kidnapped and assassinated the Christian Democrat prime minister, Aldo Moro, in 1978.

In the decades following WWII, Italy's national government was consistently dominated by the centre-right Christian Democrats, usually in coalition with other parties (excluding the Communists). Italy enjoyed significant economic growth in the 1980s, but the 1990s heralded a new period of crisis for the country, both economically and politically. Against the backdrop of a severe economic crisis, the very foundations of Italian politics were shaken by a national bribery scandal.

The 1990s
The *tangentopoli* (translated as 'kickback cities') scandal broke in Milan in early 1992 when a functionary of the Socialist Party was arrested on charges of accepting bribes in exchange for public works contracts. Investigations eventually implicated thousands of politicians, public officials and businesspeople and left the main parties in tatters, effectively demolishing the centre of the Italian political spectrum.

National elections in March 1994 saw Italy move decisively to the right. A new right-wing coalition known as the Freedom Alliance, whose members include the Neo-Fascist National Alliance, and which is led by billionaire media magnate Silvio Berlusconi, won the elections. Berlusconi, who had entered politics only three months before the elections, was appointed prime minister, but his government fell after only nine months. The latest elections, held in April 1996, resulted in a centre-left coalition, led by economist Romano Prodi, winning the majority of votes. The win by the Olive Tree coalition represented a historic moment in Italian politics: for the first time since the establishment of the republic, the communists will participate in governing the country.

The 1990s have also seen Italy moving more decisively against the Sicilian Mafia, prompted by the 1992 assassinations of two prominent anti-Mafia judges. A major offensive in Sicily, plus the testimonies of several *pentiti* (repentant mafiosi-turned-informers), led to several important arrests – most notably of the Sicilian godfather, Salvatore 'Toto' Riina. The most recent breakthrough in the war against the Mafia came with the arrest in May 1996 of Giovanni Brusca, the man believed to have taken power after Riina's arrest. Brusca was implicated in the murder of anti-Mafia judge, Giovanni Falcone, as well as in the bombings in Florence, Milan and Rome in 1993, which damaged monuments and works of art and killed several people.

GEOGRAPHY & ECOLOGY

Italy's boot-shape makes it one of the most recognisable countries in the world. The country, incorporating the islands of Sicily and Sardinia, is bound by the Adriatic, Ligurian, Tyrrhenian and Ionian seas, which all form part of the Mediterranean Sea. About 75% of the Italian peninsula is mountainous, with the Alps dividing the country from France, Switzerland and Austria, and the Apennines forming a backbone which extends from the Alps into Sicily. There are three active volcanoes: Stromboli (in the Aeolian Islands), Vesuvius (near Naples) and Etna (Sicily). The countryside can be dramatically beautiful, but the long presence of humans on the peninsula has had a significant impact on the environment. Aesthetically the result is not always displeasing – much of the beauty of Tuscany, for instance, lies in the interaction of olive groves with vineyards, fallow fields and stands of cypress and pine.

However, this alteration of the environment, combined with the Italians' passion for hunting *(la caccia)*, has led to many native animals and birds becoming extinct, rare or endangered. Under laws progressively introduced this century, many animals and birds are now protected.

There are numerous national parks in Italy. Among the most important are the Parco Nazionale del Gran Paradiso and the Parco Nazionale dello Stelvio, both in the Alps, and the Parco Nazionale d'Abruzzo.

Pollution caused by industrial and urban waste exists throughout Italy and many beaches are fouled to some extent, particularly on the Ligurian Coast, in the northern Adriatic (where there is an algae problem resulting from industrial pollution), and near major cities such as Rome and Naples. However, it is possible to find a clean beach, particularly in Sardinia. Air pollution is a problem in the industrialised north, as well as in major cities, where car emissions poison the atmosphere with carbon monoxide and lead. Litter-conscious visitors will be astounded by the Italians' habit of dumping rubbish when and where they like.

GOVERNMENT & POLITICS

For administrative purposes Italy is divided into 20 regions, which each have some degree of autonomy. The regions are then divided into provinces and municipalities.

The country is a parliamentary republic, headed by a president who appoints the prime minister. The parliament consists of a senate and chamber of deputies, both of which have equal legislative power. The seat of national government is in Rome. Italy's political situation is in a constant state of flux. Until reforms were introduced in 1994, members of parliament were elected by what was probably the purest system of proportional representation in the world. Two-thirds of both houses are now elected on the basis of who receives the most votes in their district, basically the same as the first-past-the-post system in the UK. The old system generally produced unstable coalition governments – Italy had 53 governments in the 48 years from the declaration of the republic to the introduction of the electoral reforms. But, even under the new system, there has been instability.

ECONOMY

Italy has the fifth-largest economy in the world, after enjoying spectacular growth in the 1980s. However, there has been much debate about the ability of the Italian economy to perform efficiently in the context of a unified Europe – a debate which has intensified following the country's severe economic crisis and political instability of the 1990s. Draconian measures were introduced by the

ITALY

Regions of Italy

0   100   200 km

FRANCE

GERMANY

AUSTRIA

HUNGARY

Lake Constance

LIECHTENSTEIN

SWITZERLAND

Bolzano

SLOVENIA

YUGOSLAVIA

VALLE D'AOSTA

Aosta

TRENTINO-ALTO ADIGE

FRIULI-VENEZIA GIULIA

Trieste

Trento

LOMBARDY

VENETO

CROATIA

BOSNIA-HERCEGOVINA

Turin

Milan

Venice

PIEDMONT

EMILIA-ROMAGNA

FRANCE

Genoa

Bologna

SAN MARINO

LIGURIA

LIGURIAN SEA

Florence

TUSCANY

Ancona

ADRIATIC SEA

THE MARCHES

Perugia

UMBRIA

CORSICA

L'Aquila

LAZIO

ABRUZZO

Rome

MOLISE

Campobasso

Bari

CAMPANIA

APULIA

Naples

Potenza

BASILICATA

TYRRHENIAN SEA

SARDINIA

Cagliari

CALABRIA

Catanzaro

MEDITERRANEAN SEA

Palermo

IONIAN SEA

SICILY

ITALY

TUNISIA

MALTA

government to control public spending and reduce the massive public debt, including partial privatisation of the country's huge public sector.

There remains a significant economic gap between Italy's northern and southern regions, despite years of effort and the expenditure of trillions of lire. The fact remains that Italy's richest regions (Piedmont, Emilia-Romagna and Lombardy) are all northern, and its poorest (Calabria, Campania and Sicily) are all southern. One impact of this gap is that, generally, things don't work as well in the south as they do in the north – notably in hospitals, banks and public services such as the post office.

POPULATION & PEOPLE

The population of Italy is 57.8 million. The country has the lowest birthrate in Europe – a surprising fact considering the Italians' preoccupation with children and family. Foreigners may like to think of Italy as a land of passionate, animated people who gesticulate wildly when speaking, love to eat, drive like maniacs and don't like to work. However, it will take more than a holiday in Italy to understand its vigorous and remarkably diverse inhabitants. Overall the people remain fiercely protective of their regional customs, including their dialects and cuisine.

ARTS
Architecture, Painting & Sculpture

Italy has often been called a living art museum and certainly it is not always necessary to enter a gallery to appreciate the country's artistic wealth – it is all around you as you walk through Rome, or Florence, or Venice, or visit a tiny church in a tiny medieval hill town in Umbria. This visible evidence of the country's history is one of the most fascinating aspects of a visit to Italy. In Rome, for instance, the forum, the Colosseum and the Pantheon are juxtaposed with churches and palaces of the medieval, Renaissance and baroque periods. Near Rome, at Tarquinia, you can visit 2000-year-old Etruscan tombs to see the vibrant funerary artwork of this ancient civilisation.

In the south of Italy and in Sicily, where Greek colonisation preceded Roman domination, there are important Greek archaeological sites such as the temples at Paestum, south of Salerno, and at Agrigento in Sicily. Pompeii and Herculaneum give an idea of how ancient Romans actually lived.

Byzantine mosaics adorn churches throughout Italy, most notably at Ravenna, in the Basilica of San Marco in Venice, and in Monreale cathedral near Palermo. There are also some interesting mosaics in churches in Rome. In Apulia, you can tour the magnificent Romanesque churches, a legacy of the Normans (the region's medieval rulers) and their successors, the Swabians.

The Renaissance The 15th and early 16th centuries in Italy saw one of the most remarkable explosions of artistic and literary achievement in recorded history – the Renaissance. Giotto di Bendone (1267-1337), known simply as Giotto, who revolutionised painting by introducing naturalism into his works, was one of the most important precursors of the Renaissance. Among his most noted works are the frescos of the Scrovegni Chapel in Padua.

Patronised mainly by the Medici family in Florence and the popes in Rome, painters, sculptors, architects and writers flourished and many artists of genius emerged. The High Renaissance (about 1490-1520) was dominated by three men – Leonardo da Vinci (1452-1519), Michelangelo Buonarrotti (1475-1564) and Raphael (1483-1520).

A tour of Renaissance artworks would alone fill an extended trip to Italy. In Florence there is Italy's best known art gallery, the Uffizi. Ten of its rooms trace the development of Florentine and Tuscan painting from the 13th to 16th centuries and works include Botticelli's *Birth of Venus* and *Primavera* (Spring) and Leonardo da Vinci's *Annunciation*. In the Accademia is Michelangelo's *David*, while the Bargello houses Donatello's bronze *David*. At the Vatican in Rome there is Michelangelo's ceiling and *Last Judgment* in the Sistine Chapel and Raphael's frescos in Pope Julius II's private apartment. In St Peter's Basilica is Michelangelo's *Pietà* and his *Moses* is in the church of San Pietro in Vincoli.

Baroque The baroque period (17th century) was characterised by sumptuous, often fantastic architecture and richly decorative painting and sculpture.

ITALY

In Rome there are innumerable works by the great baroque sculptor and architect Gianlorenzo Bernini (1598-1680), including the central fountain in Piazza Navona. Rome's best loved baroque work is the Trevi Fountain. Cities which were literally transformed by baroque architecture include Lecce, Noto and Naples.

Later Styles Neoclassicism in Italy produced the sculptor, Canova (1757-1822). Of Italy's modern artists, Amadeo Modigliani (1884-1920) is perhaps the most famous. The early 20th century also produced an artistic movement known as the Futurists, who rejected the sentimental art of the past and were infatuated by new technology, including modern warfare. Fascism produced its own style of architecture in Italy, characterised by the work of Marcello Piacentini (1881-1960), which includes the *Stadio dei Marmi* at Rome's Olympic Stadium complex.

Music

Few modern Italian singers or musicians have made any impact outside Italy – one exception is Zucchero (Adelmo Fornaciari), who has become well known in the USA and UK as Sugar. Instead, it is in the realms of opera and instrumental music where Italian artists have always triumphed. Antonio Vivaldi (1675-1741) created the concerto in its present form. Verdi, Puccini, Bellini, Donizetti and Rossini, composers from the 19th and early 20th centuries, are all stars of the modern operatic era. Tenor Luciano Pavarotti (1935-) is today's luminary of Italian opera.

Literature

Before Dante wrote his *Divina Commedia* (Divine Comedy) and confirmed vernacular Italian as a serious medium for poetic expression, Latin was the language of writers. Among the greatest writers of ancient Rome were Cicero, Virgil, Ovid and Petronius.

A contemporary of Dante was Petrarch (Francesco Petrarca 1304-74). Giovanni Boccaccio (1313-75), author of the *Decameron*, is considered the first Italian novelist.

Machiavelli's *Il Principe* (The Prince), although a purely political work, has proved the most lasting of the Renaissance works.

Alessandro Manzoni (1785-1873) worked hard to establish a narrative language which was accessible to all Italians in his great historical novel *I Promessi Sposi* (The Betrothed).

The turbulence of political and social life in Italy in the 20th century has produced a wealth of literature. The often virulent poetry of ardent nationalist, Gabriele d'Annunzio, was perhaps not of the highest quality, but his voice was a prestige tool for Mussolini's Fascists.

Italy's richest contribution to modern literature has been in the novel and short story. Cesare Pavese and Carlo Levi both endured internal exile in southern Italy during Fascism. Levi based *Cristo si è Fermato a Eboli* (Christ Stopped at Eboli) on his experiences in exile in Basilicata. The works of Italo Calvino border on the fantastical, thinly veiling his preoccupation with human behaviour in society.

Natalia Ginzburg has produced prose, essays and theatre. Alberto Moravia was a prolific writer who concentrated on describing Rome and its people. The novels of Elsa Morante are characterised by a subtle psychological appraisal of her characters. Umberto Eco shot to fame with his first and best known work, *Il Nome della Rosa* (The Name of the Rose).

Theatre

At a time when French playwrights ruled the stage, the Venetian Carlo Goldoni (1707-1793) attempted to bring Italian theatre back into the limelight with the *commedia dell'arte*, the tradition of improvisational theatre based on a core of set characters including Pulcinella and Arlecchino. Luigi Pirandello (1867-1936) threw into question every preconception of what theatre should be with such classics as *Sei Personaggi in Cerca d'Autore* (Six Characters in Search of an Author). Pirandello won the Nobel Prize in 1934. Modern Italian theatre's most enduring contemporary representative is actor/director Dario Fo.

Cinema

Born in Turin in 1904, the Italian film industry originally made an impression with silent spectaculars. Its most glorious era began as WWII came to a close in Europe, when the Neo-Realists began making their films. One of the earliest examples of this new wave in cinema was Luchino Visconti's *Ossessione* (Obsession). From 1945 to 1947, Roberto Rossellini produced three Neo-Realist master-pieces, including *Roma Città Aperta* (Rome Open City), starring Anna Magnani. Vittorio de Sica produced another classic in 1948, *Ladri di Biciclette* (Bicycle Thieves).

Schooled with the masters of Neo-Realism, Federico Fellini in many senses took the cre-ative baton from them and carried it into the following decades, with films such as *La Dolce Vita*, with Anita Ekberg and Marcello Mastroianni. The career of Michelangelo Antonioni reached a climax with *Blow-up* in 1967. Pier Paolo Pasolini's films included *Accattone* and *Decameron*.

Bernardo Bertolucci had his first interna-tional hit with *Last Tango in Paris*. He made the blockbuster *The Last Emperor* in 1987. Franco Zeffirelli's most recent film was *Jane Eyre*. Other notable directors include the Taviani brothers, Giuseppe Tornatore and Nanni Moretti.

Italy's first international film star was Rudolph Valentino. Among Italy's most suc-cessful actors since WWII are Marcello Mastroianni, Anna Magnani, Gina Lollo-brigida and Sophia Loren.

CULTURE

Religious festivals and soccer are the two great passions of the average Italian, followed closely by eating and the traditional August holidays. The midday meal is a revered tradi-tion which means that all shops, offices and most institutions close for three to four hours in the afternoon.

In August, particularly during the week around the Feast of the Assumption (August 15), known as *ferragosto*, a combination of summer heat and national holidays means that Italians evacuate the cities en masse and head for the hills and beaches. This means that almost *everything* closes down in the big cities during the peak tourist period.

Avoiding Offence

Women should note that light, skimpy clothing which might be acceptable in the north could attract unwanted attention in places such as Sicily and Sardinia. Churches enforce strict dress rules. Anyone wearing shorts (including men) will find it difficult to get into a church anywhere in Italy. Remember that while churches are major tourist attractions in Italy, they are also places of worship, so try to avoid visiting during services.

RELIGION

Some 85% of Italians professed to be Catholic in a census taken in the early 1980s. The remaining 15% included about 500,000 evan-gelical Protestants; the rest professed to have no religion.

LANGUAGE

Although many Italians speak some English (as they study it in school), English is more widely understood in the north, particularly in major centres such as Milan, Florence and Venice, than in the south. Staff at most hotels, *pensioni* and restaurants usually speak a little English, but you will be better received if you at least attempt to communicate in Italian.

Italian is a Romance language which is related to French, Spanish, Portuguese and Romanian. The Romance languages belong to the Indo-European group of languages, which include English. Indeed, as English and Italian share common roots in Latin, you will recog-nise many Italian words.

Modern literary Italian began to be devel-oped in the 13th and 14th centuries, predominantly through the works of Dante, Petrarch and Boccaccio, who wrote chiefly in the Florentine dialect. The language drew on its Latin heritage and the many dialects of Italy to develop into the standard Italian of today. Although many and varied dialects are spoken in everyday conversation, standard Italian is the national language of schools, media and literature, and is understood throughout the country.

There are 58 million speakers of Italian in Italy, half a million in Switzerland (where Italian is one of the four official languages) and 1.5 million speakers in France and former Yugoslavia. As a result of migration, Italian is also widely spoken in the USA, Argentina, Brazil and Australia.

Many older Italians still expect to be addressed by the third person formal, ie *Lei* instead of *tu*. Also, it is not polite to use the greeting *ciao* when addressing strangers, unless they use it first; use *buongiorno* and *arrivederci*.

ITALY

See the Language Section at the back of the book for pronunciation guidelines and useful words and phrases.

Facts for the Visitor

PLANNING
Climate & When to Go
Italy lies in a temperate zone, but the climates of the north and south vary. Summers are uniformly hot, but are often extremely hot and dry in the south. Winters can be severely cold in the north – particularly in the Alps, but also in the Po Valley – whereas they are generally mild in the south and in Sicily and Sardinia. The best time to visit Italy is in the off season, particularly from April to June and September to October, when the weather is good, prices are lower and there are fewer tourists. During July and August (the high season) it is very hot, prices are inflated, the country swarms with tourists, and hotels by the sea and in the mountains are usually booked out. Many hotels and restaurants in seaside areas close down for the winter months.

Books & Maps
For a more comprehensive guide to Italy, pick up a copy of Lonely Planet's *Italy* guide.

For serious research on Italian history, culture and people, try the following books: *The Decline and Fall of the Roman Empire* by Edward Gibbons; *Concise History of Italy* by Vincent Cronin; *Painters of the Renaissance* by Bernard Berenson; and *The Penguin Book of the Renaissance* by J H Plumb.

For lighter reading, you will find many books written by travellers in Italy: *Venice* by James Morris; *Venice Observed* and *The Stones of Florence* by Mary McCarthy; and *A Traveller in Southern Italy* and *A Traveller in Italy* by H V Morton.

Companion Guides (Collins) are excellent and include *Rome* by Georgina Masson, *Venice* by Hugh Honour, *Tuscany* by Archibald Lyall and *Southern Italy* by Peter Gunn.

Luigi Barzini's classic *The Italians* is a must.

For maps of cities, you will generally find those provided by the tourist office adequate.

Excellent road and city maps are published by the Istituto Geografico de Agostini and are available in all major bookshops. If you are driving, invest in the De Agostini *Atlante Stradale Italiano* (L35,000).

What to Bring
A backpack is a definite advantage in Italy, but if you plan to use a suitcase and portable trolley, be warned about the endless flights of stairs at train stations and in many of the smaller medieval towns, as well as the petty thieves who prey on tourists who have no hands free because they are carrying too much luggage. A small pack (with a lock) for use on day trips and for sightseeing is preferable to a handbag or shoulder bag, particularly in the southern cities where motorcycle bandits are very active. A money belt is absolutely essential in Italy, particularly in the south and in Sicily, but also in the major cities, where groups of dishevelled-looking women and children prey on tourists with bulging pockets. While travelling, it is best not to display any valuable jewellery, including rings and expensive watches.

In the more mountainous areas, the weather can change suddenly even in high summer, so remember to bring at least one item of warm clothing. Most importantly, bring a pair of hardy, comfortable, already worn-in walking shoes. In many cities, pavements are uneven and often made of cobblestones.

SUGGESTED ITINERARIES
Depending on the length of your stay, you might want to see and do the following things:

Two days
    Visit Rome to see the Forum, the Colosseum, St Peter's Basilica and the Vatican museums.
One week
    Visit Rome and Florence, with detours to Siena and San Gimignano.
Two weeks
    As above, plus Bologna, Verona, Ravenna and at least three days in Venice.
One month
    As above, but go to Sicily and perhaps Sardinia for one week at least. Explore the north, including Liguria, and the south, including Puglia.

HIGHLIGHTS
Museums & Galleries
The Vatican museums in Rome and the fabulous Uffizi Gallery in Florence are absolutely

not to be missed. The Bargello in Florence, with its excellent sculpture collection, is another must. In Venice visit the Peggy Guggenheim Gallery of Modern Art. The Museo Archeologico Nazionale in Naples houses finds from Pompeii, as well as the spectacular Farnese collection.

Historic Towns
There are so many fascinating and beautiful medieval towns in Italy that it seems a shame to confine your travels to the major cities. In Tuscany visit San Gimignano, Arezzo and Volterra, and in Umbria take a tour of the medieval hill towns, many still surrounded by their walls and crowned with ruined castles. The more interesting towns include Perugia, Assisi, Spoleto, Gubbio and Orvieto. In Liguria walk along the coast to visit the Cinque Terre, five tiny villages linked by a walking track on the Riviera di Levante. One of the most fascinating towns in Italy is Matera in Basilicata. Wandering through its famous *sassi* (stone houses) is an experience not easily forgotten.

Churches
A few highlights include the cathedrals in Florence, Milan, Siena and Orvieto (considered one of the most beautiful in Italy), and one at Monreale, near Palermo, for its beautiful mosaics. The Basilica of San Vitale in Ravenna is notable both for its mosaics and for the design of the church. The Romanesque cathedrals in Apulia are fascinating.

Beaches
Although the water is polluted, the beaches along the Riviera di Levante in Liguria are worth visiting. The beach resorts along the Amalfi Coast are particularly scenic, but again the water is not exactly clean. The cleanest beaches are in Sardinia and there are some lovely spots in Sicily.

Hotels & Restaurants
The following are hotels which are in characteristic locations. The Pensione Bellavista in Florence has two double rooms with views of the Duomo (cathedral) and the Palazzo Vecchio. Just outside Florence, near Fiesole, is Bencistà, a former villa with a terrace overlooking Florence. In Rome the Albergo

Abruzzi is in the same piazza as the Pantheon. In Naples, the best pizzas are at Trianon. In Florence, head for Mario's, a local institution.

General Sights
Italy itself is a virtual museum and in every part of the country you will come across monuments, works of art, views and special places which have the capacity to surprise even the most world-weary traveller. Here are a few of the more special ones: Michelangelo's *Pietà* in St Peter's Basilica, Rome; the Grand Canal in Venice; the Pala d'Oro (gold altarpiece) in the Basilica di San Marco (St Mark's Basilica) in Venice; the view of Tuscany from the top of the town hall tower in San Gimignano; the painted Etruscan tombs at Tarquinia; Giotto's frescos in the Cappella degli Scrovegni in Padua; the Valley of the Temples at Agrigento; and the floor mosaic in Otranto's cathedral.

TOURIST OFFICES
There are three main categories of tourist office in Italy: regional, provincial and local. Their names vary throughout the country, but they all offer basically the same services. Provincial offices are sometimes known as the Ente Provinciale per il Turismo (EPT) or, more commonly, the Azienda di Promozione Turistica (APT). The Azienda Autonoma di Soggiorno e Turismo (AAST) offices usually have information only on the town itself. In most of the very small towns and villages the local tourist office is called a Pro Loco.

The quality of services offered varies dramatically throughout the country and don't be surprised if you encounter lethargic or even hostile staff. You should be able to get a map, a *elenco degli alberghi* (a list of hotels), a *pianta della città* (map of the town) and information on the major sights. Staff speak English in larger towns, but in the more out-of-the-way places you may have to rely on sign language. Tourist offices are generally open from 8.30 am to 12.30 pm and 3 to 7 pm Monday to Friday and on Saturday morning. You can obtain some information on places throughout Italy at the EPT office in Rome, Via Parigi 11, 00185, and at the Rome office of the Italian State Tourist Office, Ente Nazionale Italiano per il Turismo (ENIT), Via Marghera 2.

Tourist Offices Abroad

Information about Italy can be obtained at Italian State Tourist Offices throughout the world, including:

Australia
    Alitalia, Orient Overseas Building, suite 202, 32 Bridge St, Sydney (☎ 02-9247 1308)
Canada
    1, Place Ville Marie, suite 1914, Montreal, Que H3B 3M9 (☎ 514-866 7667)
UK
    1 Princes St, London W1R 8AY (☎ 0171-408 1254)
USA
    630 Fifth Ave, suite 1565, New York, NY 10111 (☎ 212-245 4822)
    124000 Wilshire Blvd, suite 550, Los Angeles, CA 90025 (☎ 310-82 0098)
    401 North Michigan Ave, suite 3030, Chicago, IL 60611 (☎ 312-644 0990)

Sestante CIT, Italy's national travel agency, also has offices throughout the world (known as CIT outside Italy). It can provide extensive information on Italy, as well as book tours and accommodation. It can also make train bookings. Offices include:

Australia
    123 Clarence St, Sydney 2000 (☎ 02-9299 4754)
    suite 10, 6th floor, 422 Collins St, Melbourne 3000 (☎ 03-9670 1322)
Canada
    1450 City Councillors St, suite 750, Montreal, Que H3A 2E6 (☎ 514-954 8608)
    111 Avenue Rd, suite 808, Toronto, Ont M5R 3J8 (☎ 416-927 7712)
UK
    Marco Polo House, 3-5 Lansdown Rd, Croydon, Surrey CR9 1LL (☎ 0181-686 0677)
USA
    242 Madison Ave, suite 207, New York, NY 10173 (☎ 212-697 2497)
    6033 Century Blvd, suite 980, Los Angeles, CA 90045 (☎ 310-338 8615).

USEFUL ORGANISATIONS

The following organisations in Italy might prove useful:

Centro Turistico Studentesco e Giovanile (CTS)
    This agency has offices all over Italy and specialises in discounts for students and young people, but is also useful for travellers of any age looking for cheap flights and sightseeing discounts. It is linked with the International Student Travel Confederation. You can get a student card if you have documents proving that you are a student.

Touring Club Italiano (TCI)
    The head office (☎ 02-852 62 44) is at Corso Italia 10, Milan. It publishes useful trekking guides and maps (in Italian), and has offices throughout Italy.

VISAS & EMBASSIES

Residents of the USA, Australia, Canada and New Zealand do not need to apply for visas before arriving in Italy if they are entering the country as tourists only. While there is an official three-month limit on stays in the country, border authorities no longer stamp the passports of visitors from Western nations. If you are entering the country for any reason other than tourism, you should insist on having your passport stamped. By law, visitors must go to a *questura* (police headquarters) if they plan to stay at the same address for more than one week, to receive a *permesso di soggiorno* – in effect, permission to remain in the country for a nominated period up to the three-month limit. Tourists who are staying in hotels are not required to do this. While it is extremely unlikely that tourists will encounter any problems without a permesso di soggiorno, authorities have the right to put you on the next plane, train or boat out of the country if they find you without one.

It is almost impossible to extend your visa within Italy and visitors of the nationalities just mentioned must theoretically leave the country after three months, even if this means simply crossing a border into France or Switzerland and then re-entering Italy to have their passport restamped.

Foreigners who want to study at a university in Italy must have a student visa. Australians and New Zealanders also require a visa to study at a language school. This can be obtained from the Italian embassy or consulate in your city, but you must have a letter of acceptance from the university or school you will be attending. This type of visa is renewable within Italy, but you will be required to continue studying and provide proof that you have enough money to support yourself during the period of study. It should be noted that the process to obtain a student visa can take some months.

While citizens of EU countries are able to travel and work freely in Italy, it is extremely difficult for other nationalities to obtain a visa to work in the country (see Work in this chapter).

Italian Embassies Abroad
Italian diplomatic missions abroad include:

Australia
   Level 45, The Gateway, 1 Macquarie Place, Sydney
   (☎ 02-9392 7940)
   509 St Kilda Rd, Melbourne (☎ 03-9867 5744)
Canada
   136 Beverley St, Toronto (☎ 416-977 1566)
France
   47 Rue de Varennes, 73343 Paris (☎ 01-44 30 47 00)
New Zealand
   34 Grant Rd, Thorndon, Wellington (☎ 04-735 339)
UK
   14 Three Kings Yard, London (☎ 0171-312 2200)
USA
   690 Park Ave, New York (☎ 212-439 8600)
   2590 Webster St, San Francisco (☎ 415-931 4924)

Foreign Embassies in Italy
The headquarters of most foreign embassies
are in Rome, although there are generally
British and US consulates in other major cities.
The following addresses and phone numbers
are for Rome (the telephone area code is
☎ 06):

Australia
   Via Alessandria 215 (☎ 85 27 21)
Austria
   Via Pergolesi 3 (☎ 855 82 41)
   Consulate, Via Liegi 32 (☎ 855 29 66)
Canada
   Via G B de Rossi 27 (☎ 44 59 81)
   Consulate, Via Zara 30
France
   Palazzo Farnese (☎ 68 60 11)
   visas at Via Giulia 251
Germany
   Via Po 25c (☎ 88 47 41)
   Consulate, Via Francesco Siacci 2c.
Greece
   Via Mercadante 36 (☎ 855 31 00)
   Consulate, Via Stoppani 10 (☎ 807 08 49)
Japan
   Via Sella 60 (☎ 48 79 91)
New Zealand
   Via Zara 28 (☎ 440 29 28)
Spain
   Largo Fontanella Borghese 19 (☎ 687 81 72)
Switzerland
   Via Barnarba Oriani 61 (☎ 808 36 41)
   Consulate, Largo Elvezia 15 (☎ 808 83 71)
UK
   Via XX Settembre 80a (☎ 482 54 41)
USA
   Via Vittorio Veneto 119a-121 (☎ 46 741)

For a complete list of all foreign embassies in
Rome and other major cities throughout Italy,
look in the local telephone book under
Ambasciate or *Consolati*, or ask for a list at the
tourist office.

DOCUMENTS
A passport is the only important document you
will need in Italy if you want to stay as a tourist
for up to three months. It is necessary to
produce your passport when you register in a
hotel or *pensione*. You will find that many
proprietors will want to keep your passport
during your stay. This is not a legal requirement; they only need it long enough to take
down the details. If you want to rent a car or
motorcycle, you will need a valid EU driving
licence, an International Driving Permit, or
your driving permit from your own country.
If you're driving your own car, you'll need
an International Insurance Certificate,
known as a *Carta Verde* (Green Card). Students should carry their student identity card,
or obtain an International Student Identity
Card (ISIC) before leaving home, in order to
take advantage of student discounts while
travelling.

CUSTOMS
People from outside Europe can import,
without paying duty, two still cameras with 10
rolls of film, a movie or TV camera with 10
cartridges of film, a portable record player with
10 records or a tape recorder with 10 tapes, a
CD player, a transistor radio, a pair of binoculars, up to 400 cigarettes, two bottles of wine
and two bottles of liquor.

   Visitors who are residents of a European
country and enter from an EU country can
import a maximum of 300 cigarettes, one
bottle of wine and half a bottle of liquor. There
is no limit on the amount of lire you can import.

MONEY
Anything to do with money and banks is
likely to cause significant frustration and
time-wasting in Italy. Banks are the most
reliable (although not necessarily the fastest)
places to exchange money or to obtain cash
advances on your credit card, although some
will charge up to L8000 commission on
cheques. The dilemma here is that although it
is best to exchange large sums at once to save
on the commission, it is unwise throughout
Italy to carry large amounts of cash. If you buy

ITALY

travellers' cheques in lire, generally there should be no commission charge when cashing them.

There are exchange offices at all major airports and train stations, but it is advisable to obtain a small amount of lire before arriving to avoid problems and queues at the airport and train stations.

Most of the major banks will give cash advances on Visa, but not all will honour MasterCard. The Banca Commerciale Italiana, one of Italy's major banks, *will* give cash advances on MasterCard, as will the Cassa di Risparmio and Credito Italiano. American Express and Thomas Cook have offices throughout the country, and for sheer convenience their travellers' cheques are a good option.

The fastest way to have money sent to you is by 'urgent telex' through the foreign office of a large Italian bank, or through major banks in your own country, to a nominated bank in Italy. It is important to have an exact record of all details associated with the money transfer, particularly the exact address of the Italian bank where the money has been sent. This will always be the head office of the bank in the town to which the money has been sent. Urgent telex transfers will take only a few days, while other means, such as by draft, can take weeks. You will be required to produce identification, usually a passport, in order to collect the money.

Major credit cards, including Visa, MasterCard and American Express, are accepted throughout Italy in shops, restaurants and larger hotels. However, many *trattorias*, *pizzerias*, most *pensioni* and one-star hotels do *not* accept credit cards. You will also find that while most stall holders at large flea markets accept credit cards, they will bargain only if you pay cash.

Currency

Italy's currency is the lira (plural: lire). The smallest note is L1000. Other denominations in notes are L2000, L5000, L10,000, L50,000 and L100,000. Coin denominations are L50, L100, L200 and L500. Remember that like other Continental Europeans, Italians indicate decimals with commas and thousands with points.

Exchange Rates

Australia	A$1	=	L1195
Canada	C$1	=	L1111
France	FF1	=	L304
Germany	DM1	=	L1030
Japan	¥100	=	L1409
New Zealand	NZ$1	=	L1063
United Kingdom	UK£1	=	L2373
United States	US$1	=	L1524

Costs

A *very* prudent traveller could get by on L60,000 per day, but only by staying in youth hostels, eating one meal a day (at the hostel), buying a sandwich or pizza by the slice for lunch and minimising the number of galleries and museums visited, since the entrance fee to most major museums is cripplingly expensive at around L12,000. You save on transport costs by buying tourist or day tickets for city bus and underground services. When travelling by train, by avoiding the fast intercities you can save on the *supplemento rapido*. Italy's railways also offer a few cut-price options for students, young people and tourists for travel within a nominated period (see the Getting Around section in this chapter for more information). Museums and galleries usually give discounts to students, but you will need a valid student card which you can obtain from CTS offices if you have documents proving you are a student. A basic breakdown of costs during an average day could be: accommodation L20,000 to L30,000; breakfast (coffee and croissant) L2000; lunch (sandwich and mineral water) L3000 to L5000; public transport (bus or underground railway in a major town) L5000-L6000; entry fee for one museum L12,000; dinner L15,000.

Tipping & Bargaining

You are not expected to tip on top of restaurant service charges, but it is common practice among Italians to leave a small amount, around 10%. In bars they will leave any small change as a tip, often only L50 or L100.

Bargaining is common throughout Italy in the various flea markets, but not normally in shops. You can try bargaining for the price of a room in a pensione, particularly if you plan to stay for more than a few days.

Consumer Taxes

Whenever you buy an item in Italy you will pay value-added tax, known as IVA. Tourists who are residents of countries outside the EU are able to claim back this tax if the item costs more than a certain amount (L400,000 at the time of writing). The goods must be for personal use, they must be carried with your luggage and you must keep the fiscal receipt. You have to fill in a form at the point of purchase, have the form checked and stamped by Italian customs and then return it by mail within 60 days to the vendor, who will then make the refund, either by cheque or to your credit card. At major airports and border points, there are places where you can get an immediate cash refund.

POST & COMMUNICATIONS

Italy's postal service is notoriously slow and unreliable. Don't expect to receive every letter sent to you, or that every letter you send will reach its destination.

Post

Rates The cost of sending a letter *via aerea* (air mail) depends on weight, but an average letter to Australia will cost L1400, L750 to the UK and around L1100 to the USA. It usually takes 10 days to two weeks for air mail to reach countries outside Europe and approximately one week to reach the UK.

Sending Mail Print the country of destination in block letters and underline it. If you want to mail something urgently, you can ask to send the article *espresso* (express). Registered mail is *raccomandato* and insured mail (for valuable items) is *assicurato*. If you want something to reach its destination quickly, use Express Mail Service (EMS), also known as CAI Post. A parcel weighing one kg will cost approximately L40,000 within Europe, L66,000 to the USA and Canada, and L95,000 to Australia and New Zealand. It will take four to eight days for a letter or parcel to reach Australia and two to four days to reach the USA. Ask at post offices for addresses of EMS outlets. The international courier DHL operates in Italy and offers a low-cost option for packages weighing up to 500 grams.

Francobolli (stamps) are available at authorised tobacconists, but any international mail has to be weighed, so it is best to use the post office.

Fax & Telegraph Public fax services are available at large post offices, otherwise use one of the many private services. Telecom is introducing public fax telephones, although they are still few and far between. Telegrams can be sent from any post office.

Telephone

Rates, particularly for long-distance calls, are among the highest in Europe. Travellers from countries which offer direct dialling services paid for at home country rates (such as AT&T in the USA and Telecom in Australia) should take advantage of them. Local and long distance calls can be made from any public phone, or from a Telecom office in larger towns.

Local calls cost L200 for a few minutes. Most public phones accept only phonecards, however coin-operated phones accept L100, L200 and L500 coins. You can buy L5000, L10,000 and L15,000 phonecards at tobacconists and newsstands, or from vending machines at Telecom offices.

To call Italy from abroad, dial the international access code, ☎ 39 (the country code for Italy), the area code (dropping the initial zero) and the number. Important area codes include: ☎ 06 (Rome), ☎ 02 (Milan), ☎ 055 (Florence), ☎ 081 (Naples), ☎ 070 (Cagliari) and ☎ 091 (Palermo).

To make a reverse-charges (collect) call from a public telephone, dial ☎ 170. For calls to European countries, dial ☎ 15. All operators speak English. Otherwise, you can direct dial an operator in your own country and ask to make your collect call. Numbers for this service include: Australia (☎ 172 10 61), Canada (☎ 172 10 01), New Zealand (☎ 172 10 64), UK (☎ 172 10 44), and USA (through AT&T ☎ 172 10 11).

Receiving Mail

The Italian version of poste restante is fermo posta and is usually reliable. Tell friends and relatives to write your surname in block letters. It often happens that mail is filed under the first letter of your first name, instead of your surname, so ask staff to check under both letters.

ITALY

E-mail

There are Internet cafés in Rome, where you can rent time on a PC and surf the Net or send messages to friends (see under Rome Entertainment).

NEWSPAPERS & MAGAZINES

The major English-language newspapers available in Italy are the *Herald Tribune*, an international newspaper available Monday to Saturday, and the *European* (available Friday). The major English newspapers, including the *Guardian*, *The Times* and the *Telegraph*, are sent from London, so outside major cities such as Rome and Milan, they are generally a few days old. *Time* magazine, *Newsweek* and the *Economist* are available weekly. The French newspaper *Le Monde* is also widely available.

RADIO & TV

At the time of writing, the Telemontecarlo (TMC) station broadcast CNN live from about 3 to 7.30 am. On channel 41, known as Autovox, the American PBS McNeill Lehrer News Hour was broadcast nightly at around 8 pm. Vatican Radio (526 on the AM dial or 93.3 and 105 on FM) broadcasts the news in English at 7 and 8.30 am, 6.15 and 9.50 pm. Pick up a pamphlet at the Vatican tourist office for more information.

PHOTOGRAPHY & VIDEO

A roll of normal Kodak film (36 exposures, 100 ASA) costs around L8000. It costs around L18,000 to have 36 exposures developed and L12,000 for 24 exposures. There are many outlets which provide cheap developing services, but beware of poor quality. A roll of 36 slides costs L10,000, and L7000 for processing. Tapes for video cameras are often available at film processing outlets, otherwise you can buy them at stores selling electrical goods.

TIME

Italy is one hour ahead of GMT/UTC, two hours ahead during summer. Daylight-saving time starts on the last Sunday in March, when clocks are put forward an hour. Clocks are put back an hour on the last Sunday in September. Remember to make allowances for daylight-saving time in your own country. Note that Italy operates on a 24-hour clock.

When it's noon in Rome, it's 11 pm in Auckland, 11 am in London, 6 am in New York, 3 am in San Francisco and 9 pm in Sydney. European cities such as Paris, Munich, Berlin, Vienna and Madrid are on the same time as Italy. Athens, Cairo and Tel Aviv are one hour ahead.

ELECTRICITY

The electric current in Italy is 220V, 50 Hz, but make a point of checking with your hotel management because in some areas, including parts of Rome, 125V is still used. Power points have two or three holes but do not have their own switches, while the plugs have two or three corresponding round pins.

WEIGHTS & MEASURES

Italy uses the metric system. Basic terms for weight include: *un etto* (100 grams) and *un chilo* (one kg). Note that Italians indicate decimals with commas and thousands with points.

LAUNDRY

The best place to wash your clothes is in your hotel room. Most laundries in Italy charge by the kg and do the laundry themselves, which makes it an expensive proposition. In some of the larger towns, particularly where there are universities, you can find laundries with coin-operated machines, but a load will still cost around L8000.

TOILETS

You'll find public toilets in locations such as train stations, service stations on the autostrade, and in department stores. Bars are obliged to have a toilet, but you might need to buy a coffee before they'll permit you to use it. Coin-operated, self-cleaning public toilets are being installed throughout the country, but they are still pretty rare.

HEALTH

Residents of EU countries, including the UK, are covered for emergency medical treatment in Italy on presentation of an E111 form (see the Facts for the Visitor chapter at the start of this book). Australia has a reciprocal arrangement with Italy whereby Australian citizens have access to free emergency medical services. Medicare publishes a brochure with the details. The USA, New Zealand and Canada do not have reciprocal health care arrangements with Italy.

Travellers should seriously consider taking out a travel insurance policy which covers health care, in order to have greater flexibility in deciding where and how you are treated. The quality of public hospital care in Italy can vary dramatically. Basically, the further north you travel, the better the standard of care.

For emergency treatment, go straight to the *pronto soccorso* (casualty section) of a public hospital, where you can also get emergency dental treatment. Your own doctor and dentist may be able to give you some recommendations or referrals before you leave your country. Otherwise, embassies can usually be of assistance.

WOMEN TRAVELLERS

Italy is not a dangerous country for women, but women travelling alone will often find themselves plagued by unwanted attention from men. Most of the attention falls into the nuisance/harassment category and it is best simply to ignore the catcalls, hisses and whistles. However, women on their own should use common sense. Avoid walking alone in dark and deserted streets and look for centrally located hotels which are within easy walking distance of places where you can eat at night.

Women travelling alone should be particularly careful in the south, Sicily, and Sardinia, especially in Naples, Palermo, Brindisi and Bari. Women should also avoid hitchhiking alone.

GAY & LESBIAN TRAVELLERS

Homosexuality is legal in Italy and generally well tolerated in major cities – although overt displays of affection might get a negative response in smaller towns and villages. National gay organisations include Arci Gay (for men; ☎ 051-43 67 00) and ARCI Coordinamento Donne (for women; ☎ 06-325 09 21).

DISABLED TRAVELLERS

Italy has only recently started to become conscious of the particular needs of the disabled. The Italian travel agency CIT can advise on hotels which have special facilities. The UK-based Royal Association for Disability and Rehabilitation (RADAR ☎ 0171-250 3222) publishes a useful guide called *Holidays & Travel Abroad; A Guide for Disabled People*.

TRAVEL WITH CHILDREN

Don't try to pack too much into the time available and make sure activities include the kids. Involve older kids in the planning of the trip and be sure to take time out to let the little ones play – keep an eye out for playgrounds. *Farmacie* (chemists) in Italy sell baby formula and sterilising solutions. Disposable nappies are widely available in supermarkets and chemists. Fresh cow's milk is found in bars bearing the *latteria* sign.

DANGERS & ANNOYANCES

Theft is the main problem for travellers in Italy. Thieves and pickpockets operate in most major cities, particularly in Rome, Florence and Milan. Watch out for groups of dishevelled-looking women and children. They generally work in groups of four or five and carry paper or cardboard which they use to distract your attention while they swarm around and rifle through your pockets and bag. Never underestimate their skill – they are lightning fast and very adept. The best way to avoid being robbed is to wear a money belt. Never carry a purse or wallet in your pockets and hold on tight to your bag. Pickpockets operate in crowded areas, such as markets and on buses. Motorcycle bandits are particularly active in Rome, Naples, Palermo and Syracuse. If you are using a shoulder bag, make sure that you wear the strap across your body and have the bag on the side away from the road.

Never leave valuables in a parked car – in fact, try not to leave anything in the car if you can help it. It is a good idea to park your car in a supervised car park if you are leaving it for any amount of time. Car theft is a major problem in Rome and Naples. Throughout Italy you can call police (☎ 113) or carabinieri (☎ 112) in an emergency.

BUSINESS HOURS

Business hours can vary from city to city, but generally shops and businesses are open Monday to Saturday from 8.30 am to 1 pm and from 5 to 7.30 pm. Banks are generally open Monday to Friday from 8.30 am to 1.30 pm and from 2.30 to 4.30 pm, but hours vary between

ITALY

banks and cities. Public offices are usually open Monday to Saturday from 8 am to 2 pm, although in major cities some open in the afternoon. Large post offices are open Monday to Saturday from 8 am to 6 or 7 pm. Most museums close on Monday, and restaurants and bars are required to close for one day each week. All food outlets close on Sundays and one weekday afternoon, which varies from town to town.

PUBLIC HOLIDAYS & SPECIAL EVENTS

National public holidays include: 6 January (Epiphany); Easter Monday; 25 April (Liberation Day); 1 May (Labour Day); 15 August (ferragosto, or the Feast of the Assumption); 1 November (All Saints' Day); 8 December (the Feast of the Immaculate Conception); 25 December (Christmas Day); and 26 December (the Feast of St Stephen).

Individual towns also have public holidays to celebrate the feasts of their patron saints. Some of these are the Feast of St Mark in Venice on 25 April; the Feast of St John the Baptist on 24 June in Florence, Genoa and Turin; the Feast of St Peter and St Paul in Rome on 29 June; the Feast of St Januarius in Naples on 19 September; and the Feast of St Ambrose in Milan on 7 December.

Annual events in Italy worth keeping in mind include:

Carnevale
During the 10 days before Ash Wednesday, many towns stage carnivals. The one held in Venice is the best known, but there are also others, including at Viareggio in Liguria and Ivrea near Turin, where they hold the only carnival in the world which follows a script.

Holy Week (the week before Easter)
There are important festivals during this week everywhere in Italy, in particular the colourful and sombre traditional festivals of Sicily. In Assisi the rituals of Holy Week attract thousands of pilgrims.

Scoppio del Carro (Explosion of the Cart)
This colourful event held in Florence in Piazza del Duomo on Easter Sunday features the explosion of a cart full of fireworks and dates back to the Crusades. If all goes well, it is seen as a good omen for the city.

Corso dei Ceri
One of the strangest festivals in Italy, this is held in Gubbio (Umbria) on 15 May, and features a race run by men carrying enormous wooden constructions called *ceri*, in honour of the town's patron saint, Sant'Ubaldo.

Il Palio
On 2 July and on 16 August, Siena stages this extraordinary horse race in the town's main piazza.

ACTIVITIES

If the churches, museums, galleries and sightseeing are not sufficient to occupy your time in Italy, there are various options if you want to get off the main tourist routes or have specific interests.

Hiking

It is possible to go on organised treks in Italy, but if you want to go it alone you will find that trails are well marked and there are plenty of refuges, especially in the Alps. The Dolomites in particular provide spectacular walking/trekking opportunities. There are also well-marked trails and refuges in the Alpi Apuane in Tuscany and in parts of the Appennines. In Sardinia the rugged landscape offers some spectacular hikes, particularly in the eastern mountain ranges, such as Gennargentu, and the gorges near Dorgali (see the Sardinia section for more details).

Skiing

The numerous excellent ski resorts in the Alps and the Apennines usually offer good conditions from December to April (see the Alps section).

Cycling

This is a good option if you can't afford a car but want to see the more isolated parts of the country. Classic cycling areas include Tuscany and Umbria. A bicycle would be particularly useful in Sardinia to explore the coast between Alghero and Bosa and the area around Dorgali (see the section on Sardinia).

In the south, try cycling along the coast of Apulia, starting from Lecce and continuing down the coast of Salento Province to the tip of the heel, and then up to Gallipoli.

COURSES

There are numerous private schools which offer Italian language courses, particularly in Rome, Florence and Siena (see under these cities for more details), but the cheapest option is to study at the University for Foreigners in Perugia. The average cost of a course in Florence is around L800,000 a month, whereas in

Perugia it costs L260,000 a month. Schools in Florence and Rome also offer courses in art, sculpture, architecture and cooking.

Italian cultural institutes and embassies in your country will provide information on schools and courses as well as enrolment forms. The university in Perugia and all private schools can arrange accommodation (see under Perugia for further information).

WORK

It is illegal for non-EU citizens to work in Italy without a work permit, but trying to obtain one is extremely difficult. EU citizens are allowed to work in Italy. After finding a job they must go to the questura with a letter promising employment and can then obtain a work permit and permesso di soggiorno for up to two years. For citizens of other countries it is not so simple. You must have a promise of a job which cannot be filled by an Italian or citizens of EU countries, and must apply for the visa in your country of nationality. A type of amnesty in early 1996, when the government gave illegal workers the opportunity to become legitimate, is expected to mean that it will become more difficult to find work which has in the past usually been done by people without permits, such as teaching English in language schools.

Traditionally, the main legal employment for foreigners is to teach English, but even with full qualifications an American, Australian, Canadian or New Zealander will find it difficult to secure a permanent position. Foreign visitors can still find 'black economy' work in bars and restaurants, or as babysitters and housekeepers. Most people get started by placing or responding to advertisements in local publications such as *Wanted in Rome*, or *Secondomano* in Milan. Another option is au pair work. A useful guide is *The Au Pair and Nanny's Guide to Working Abroad* by S Griffith & S Legg. Also see *Work Your Way Around the World* by Susan Griffith.

If you are looking to work legally in Italy for an extended period, you should seek information from the Italian embassy in your country.

ACCOMMODATION

Prices are intended as a guide only. There is generally a fair degree of fluctuation throughout the country, depending on the season.

Prices usually rise by 5% to 10% each year, although sometimes they remain fixed for years, or even drop.

Camping

Facilities throughout Italy are usually reasonable and vary from major complexes with swimming pools, tennis courts and restaurants, to simple camping grounds. Average prices are around L8000 per person and L10,000 or more for a site. Lists of camping grounds in and near major cities are usually available at tourist information offices.

The Touring Club Italiano (TIC) publishes an annual book on all camping sites in Italy, *Campeggi e Villaggi Turistici in Italia* (L22,000), and the Istituto Geografico de Agostini publishes the annual *Guida di Campeggi in Europa* (L20,000), available in major bookshops in Italy. Free camping is forbidden in many of the more beautiful parts of Italy, although the authorities pay less attention in the off season.

Hostels

Hostels in Italy are called *ostelli per la gioventù* and are run by the Associazione Italiana Alberghi per la Gioventù (AIG), which is affiliated with Hostelling International (HI). A HI membership card is not always required, but it is recommended that you have one. Membership cards can be purchased at major hostels, from student and youth travel centre (CTS) offices and from AIG offices throughout Italy. Pick up a list of all hostels in Italy, with details of prices, locations etc, from the AIG office (☎ 06-487 11 52) in Rome, Via Cavour 44.

Many Italian hostels are located in castles and old villas, most have bars and the cost per night often includes breakfast. Many also provide dinner, usually for around L12,000. Prices, including breakfast, range from L15,000 to L23,000. Closing times vary, but are usually from 9 am to 3 or 5 pm and curfews are around midnight. Men and women are often segregated, although some hostels have family accommodation.

Pensioni & Hotels

Establishments are required to notify local tourist boards of prices for the coming year and by law must then adhere to those prices

ITALY

(although they do have two legal opportunities each year to increase charges). If tourists believe they are being overcharged they can make a complaint to the local tourist office. The best advice is to confirm hotel charges before you put your bags down, since many proprietors employ various methods of bill padding. These include charges for showers (usually around L2000), a compulsory breakfast (up to L14,000 in the high season) and compulsory half or full board, although this can often be a good deal in some towns.

The cheapest way to stay in a hotel or pensione is to share a room with two or more people: the cost is usually no more than 15% of the cost of a double room for each additional person. Single rooms are uniformly expensive in Italy (from around L30,000) and quite a number of establishments do not even bother to cater for the single traveller.

There is often no difference between an establishment that calls itself a pensione and one that calls itself an *albergo* (hotel); in fact, some use both titles. *Locande* (similar to pensioni) and *alloggi*, sometimes also known as *affittacamere*, are generally cheaper, but not always. Tourist offices have booklets listing all pensioni and hotels, including prices, and lists of locande and affittacamere.

Rental Accommodation

Finding rental accommodation in the major cities can be difficult and time-consuming and you will often find the cost prohibitive, especially in Rome, Florence, Milan and Venice. For details on rental agencies, refer to the individual city chapters. If you are planning to study in an Italian city, the school or university will help you to find rental accommodation, or a room in the house of a family. In major resort areas, such as the Aeolian Islands and other parts of Sicily, and in the Alps, rental accommodation is reasonably priced and readily available. You can obtain information from local tourist offices, or from specialist travel agencies in your own country.

One organisation which publishes booklets on villas and houses in Tuscany, Umbria, Veneto, Sicily and Rome is Cuendet. Write to Signora N Cuendet, Località Il Cereto/Strove, 53035, Monteriggioni, Siena (☎ 0577-30 10 12; fax 0577-30 11 49) and ask for a catalogue

(US$15). Prices, however, are expensive. CIT offices throughout the world also have lists of villas and apartments for rent in Italy.

Agriturismo

This is basically a farm holiday and is becoming increasingly popular in Italy. Traditionally the idea was that families rented out rooms in their farmhouses. However, the more common type of establishment these days is a restaurant/small hotel. All establishments are working farms and you will usually be able to sample the local produce. Recommended areas where you can try this type of holiday are Tuscany, Umbria and Trentino-Alto Adige. Information is available from local tourist offices.

For detailed information on all facilities in Italy contact Agriturist (☎ 06-6 85 21), Corso Vittorio Emanuele 89, 00186 Rome. It publishes a book listing establishments throughout Italy (L35,000), which is available at their office and in selected bookshops.

Religious Institutions

These institutions offer accommodation in most major cities. The standard is usually good, but prices are no longer low. You can expect to pay about the same as for a one-star hotel, if not more. Information about the various institutions is available at all tourist offices, or you can contact the archdiocese in your city.

Refuges

Before you go hiking in any part of Italy, obtain information about refuges from the local tourist offices. Some refuges have private rooms, but many offer dorm-style accommodation, particularly those which are more isolated. Average prices are L20,000 per person for B&B. A meal costs around the same as at a trattoria. The locations of refuges are marked on good hiking maps and most open only from July to September.

FOOD

Eating is one of life's great pleasures for Italians. Be adventurous and never be intimidated by eccentric waiters or indecipherable menus and you will find yourself agreeing with the locals, who believe that nowhere in the world is the food as good as in Italy and, more specifically, in their own town.

Cooking styles vary notably from region to region and significantly between the north and south. In the north the food is rich and often creamy, and the regional specialities of Emilia-Romagna, including *spaghetti bolognese* (known in Italy as *spaghetti al ragù*), *tortellini*, and *mortadella* are perhaps the best known throughout the world.

In Tuscany and Umbria the locals use a lot of olive oil and herbs, and regional specialities are noted for their simplicity, fine flavour and the use of fresh produce. As you go further south the food becomes hotter and spicier and the *dolci* (cakes and pastries) sweeter and richer. Don't miss the experience of eating a pizza in Naples and don't leave Sicily without trying their *dolce di mandorle* (almond pastries), or the rich and very sweet ricotta cake known as *cassata*.

Vegetarians will have no problems eating in Italy. Though there are very few restaurants devoted to them (and these few tend to be expensive and on the trendy side), vegetable dishes are a staple of the Italian diet. Most eating establishments serve a selection of *contorni* (vegetables prepared in a variety of ways), and the further south you go, the more excellent vegetable dishes you'll find.

Self-Catering

For a light lunch, or a snack, most bars serve *panini* (sandwiches), and there are numerous outlets where you can buy pizza by the slice. Another option is to go to one of the many *alimentari* (grocery stores) and ask them to make a panino with the filling of your choice. At a *pasticceria* you can buy pastries, cakes and biscuits.

If you have access to cooking facilities, you can buy fruit and vegetables at open markets (see the individual towns for information), and salami, cheese and wine at alimentari or *salumerie* (a cross between a grocery store and a delicatessen). Fresh bread is available at a *forno* or *panetteria*.

Restaurants

Eating establishments are divided into several categories. A *tavola calda* (literally hot table) usually offers cheap, pre-prepared meat, pasta and vegetable dishes in a self-service style. A *rosticceria* usually offers cooked meats, but also often has a larger selection of takeaway

food. A pizzeria will of course serve pizza, but usually also a full menu. An *osteria* is likely to be either a wine bar offering a small selection of dishes, or a small trattoria. A trattoria is basically a cheaper version of a *ristorante* (restaurant). The problem is that many of the establishments that are in fact ristoranti call themselves trattorias and vice versa for reasons best known to themselves. It is best to check the menu, which is usually posted by the door, for prices.

Don't panic if you find yourself in a trattoria which has no printed menu, as they are often the ones which offer the best and most authentic food and have menus which change daily according to the availability of fresh produce. Just hope that the waiter will patiently explain the dishes and tell you how much they cost.

Most eating establishments charge a *coperto* (cover charge) of around L1000 to L3000, and a *servizio* (service charge) of 10 to 15%. Restaurants are usually open for lunch from 12.30 to 3 pm, but will rarely take orders after 2 pm. In the evening, opening hours vary from north to south. In the north they eat dinner earlier, usually from 7.30 pm, but in Sicily you will be hard-pressed to find a restaurant open before 8 pm. Note that very few restaurants stay open after 11.30 pm.

Italians rarely eat a sit-down breakfast. Their custom is to drink a cappuccino, usually *tiepido* (lukewarm), and eat a *brioche, cornetto*, or other type of pastry while standing at a bar. Lunch is the main meal of the day, and shops and businesses close for three to four hours each afternoon to accommodate the meal and the siesta which follows.

A full meal will consist of an antipasto, which can vary from *bruschetta*, a type of garlic bread with various toppings, to fried vegetables, or *prosciutto e melone* (ham wrapped around melon). Next comes the *primo piatto*, a pasta dish or risotto, followed by the *secondo piatto* of meat or fish. Italians often then eat an *insalata* (salad) or contorni and round off the meal with dolci and caffè, often at a bar on the way home or back to work.

Numerous restaurants offer tourist menus, at an average price of L18,000 to L24,000. Generally the food is of a reasonable standard, but choices will be limited and you can usually get away with paying less if you want only pasta, salad and wine.

ITALY

After lunch and dinner, head for the nearest *gelateria* to round off the meal with some excellent Italian *gelati* (ice cream), followed by a *digestivo* (liqueur) at a bar.

Remember that as soon as you sit down in Italy, prices go up considerably. A cappuccino at the bar will cost around L1500, but if you sit down, you will pay anything from L2500 to L5000 or more, especially in touristy areas such as Piazza San Marco in Venice (L10,000) and the Spanish Steps in Rome.

DRINKS
Italian wine is justifiably world-famous. Few Italians can live without it, and even fewer abuse it, generally drinking wine only with meals. Going out for a drink is still considered unusual in Italy. Fortunately, wine is reasonably priced so you will rarely pay more than L10,000 for a bottle of drinkable wine and as little as L5000 will still buy OK quality. The styles of wine vary throughout the country, so make a point of sampling the local produce in your travels. Try the famous *chianti* in Tuscany, but also the *vernaccia* of San Gimignano, the *soave* in Verona and the *valpolicella* around Venice. Orvieto's wines are excellent, as are those from Trentino; in Rome try the local *frascati*.

Italians drink wine with lunch and dinner, but prefer to drink beer with pizza, which means that many pizzerias do not serve wine. Beer is known as *birra* and the cheapest local variety is *Peroni*, but a wide range of imported beers are also available, either in bars or at a *birrerria* or pub.

ENTERTAINMENT
Whatever your tastes, there should be some form of entertainment in Italy to keep you amused, from the national obsession, *il calcio* (soccer), to the opera, theatre, classical music concerts, rock concerts and traditional festivals. Major entertainment festivals are also held, such as the Festival of Two Worlds in June/July at Spoleto, Umbria Jazz in Perugia in July, and the Venice Biennale every odd-numbered year. Operas are performed in Verona and Rome throughout summer (for details see the Entertainment sections under both cities) and at various times of the year throughout the country, notably at the opera houses in Milan and Rome.

The main theatre season is during winter, and classical music concerts are generally performed throughout the year. Nightclubs, indoor bars and discotheques are more popular during winter and many close down for the summer months. For up-to-date information on entertainment in each city, buy the local newspaper. Tourist offices will also provide information on important events, festivals, performances and concerts.

SPECTATOR SPORT
Soccer (*calcio*) is the national passion and there are stadiums in all the major towns. If you'd rather watch a game than visit a Roman ruin, check newspapers for details of who's playing where.

THINGS TO BUY
Italy is synonymous with elegant, fashionable and high-quality clothing. The problem is that most of the clothes are very expensive. However, if you can manage to be in the country during the summer sales in July and August and the winter sales in December and January, you can pick up incredible bargains.

Italy is renowned for the quality of its leather goods, so plan to stock up on bags, wallets, purses, belts and gloves. At markets such as Porta Portese in Rome and the San Lorenzo leather market in Florence you can find some remarkable bargains – but check carefully for quality.

Other items of interest are Venetian glass, and the great diversity of ceramics produced throughout Italy, notably on the Amalfi Coast, at Deruta and Orvieto in Umbria, and in Sicily. The beautiful Florentine paper goods also make great gifts and are reasonably priced.

Getting There & Away

AIR
Although paying full fare to travel by plane in Europe is expensive, there are various discount options, including cut-price fares for students and people aged under 25 or 26 (depending on the airline). There are also stand-by fares which are usually around 60% of the full fare. Several airlines, including Alitalia, Qantas and

Air France, offer cut-rate fares on legs of international flights between European cities. These are usually the cheapest fares available, but the catch is that they are usually during the night or very early in the morning, and the days on which you can fly are severely restricted. Some examples of cheap one-way fares at the time of writing were: Rome-Paris L167,000 (L278,000 return); Rome-London L177,000 (L295,000 return); Rome-Amsterdam L250,000 (L340,000 return).

Another option is to travel on charter flights. There are several companies throughout Europe which operate these, and fares are usually cheaper than for normal scheduled flights. Italy Sky Shuttle (☎ 0181-748 1333), part of the Air Travel Group, 227 Shepherd's Bush Rd, London W6 7AS, specialises in charter flights, but also offers scheduled flights.

Look in the classified pages of the London Sunday newspapers for information on other cheap flights. Campus Travel (☎ 0171-730 3402), 52 Grosvenor Gardens, SW1W OAG, and STA Travel (☎ 0171-939 3232), 74 Old Brompton Rd, London SW7, both offer reasonably cheap fares. Within Italy, information on discount fares is available from CTS and Sestante CIT offices (see the earlier Useful Organisations section).

LAND

If you are travelling by bus, train or car to Italy, it will be necessary to cross various borders, so remember to check whether you require visas for those countries before leaving home.

Bus

Eurolines is the main international carrier in Europe, with representatives in Italy and throughout the continent. Its head office (☎ 0171-730 0202), is at 52 Grosvenor Gardens, Victoria, London SW1, and it has representatives in Italy and throughout Europe. The main bus company operating this service in Italy is Lazzi: in Florence (☎ 055-21 51 55), Piazza Adua; and Rome (☎ 06-884 08 40), Via Tagliamento 27b. Buses leave from Rome, Florence, Milan, Turin, Venice and Naples, as well as numerous other Italian towns, for major cities throughout Europe including London, Paris, Barcelona, Amsterdam, Vienna, Prague, Athens and Istanbul. A guide to the cost of one-way tickets is Rome-Paris L162,000;

Rome-London L217,000; and Rome-Barcelona L180,000.

Train

Eurocity (EC) trains run from major destinations throughout Europe direct to major Italian cities. On overnight hauls you can book a *cuccetta* (known outside Italy as a *couchette* or sleeping berth).

Travellers aged under 26 can take advantage of Billet International de Jeunesse tickets (BIJ, also known in Italy as BIGE), which can cut fares by up to 50%. They are sold at Transalpino offices at most train stations and at CTS and Sestante CIT offices in Italy, Europe and overseas. Examples of one-way fares include: Rome-Amsterdam L315,100 and Rome-London L280,700.

Examples of normal one-way 2nd-class fares are Rome-London L285,000; and Rome-Amsterdam L325,400. Throughout Europe and in Italy it is worth paying extra for a couchette on night trains. A couchette from Rome to Paris is an extra L24,500.

You can book tickets at train stations or at CTS, Sestante CIT and most other travel agency offices. Eurocity trains, like the internal intercity trains, carry a supplement (see Costs & Reservations in the Getting Around section).

Car & Motorcycle

Travelling with your own vehicle certainly gives you more flexibility. The drawbacks in Italy are that cars can be inconvenient in larger cities where you'll have to deal with heavy traffic, parking problems and the risk of car theft in some cities. Driving in Italy is expensive once you add up the cost of petrol and toll charges on the autostrade. Foreign tourists driving cars with non-Italian numberplates are entitled to a free breakdown service, including emergency tow-truck service. The service is provided by the Italian Automobile Club (ACI; see Car & Motorcycle in the Getting Around section).

You will need a valid driver's licence from your own country, or an International Driving Permit, as well as proof of ownership (if you are driving your own car) and a Green Card, an internationally recognised proof of insurance, which can be obtained from your insurer.

The main points of entry into Italy are the

ITALY

Mont Blanc tunnel from France at Chamonix, which connects to the A5 for Turin and Milan; the Grand St Bernard tunnel from Switzerland, which also connects to the A5; and the Brenner Pass from Austria, which connects with the A22 to Bologna. Italy has an excellent autostrada system; the main north-south link is the Autostrada del Sole from Milan to Reggio di Calabria (A1 from Milan to Rome, A2 from Rome to Naples and A3 to Reggio di Calabria).

Hitching

Your best bet is to enquire at hostels throughout Europe, where you can often arrange a lift. Otherwise, follow the same advice as for within Italy and stand, with a sign stating your destination, near the entrance to an autostrada (it is illegal to hitch on the autostrade).

SEA

Ferries connect Italy to Greece, Tunisia, Turkey and Malta. There are also services to Corsica (from Livorno) and Albania (from Trieste, Bari and Ancona). See Getting There & Away under Brindisi (ferries to/from Greece), Ancona (to/from Greece, Albania and Turkey), Venice (to/from Croatia), and Sicily (to/from Malta and Tunisia).

The company Adriatica runs the Albania service, with ferries leaving Trieste and Ancona twice a week for Durrës and three times a week from Bari. You can pick up an Adriatica brochure at many travel agencies. In Bari, contact the agency Agestea (☎ 080-523 58 25) at the Stazione Marittima. In Trieste, contact the agency Agemar (☎ 040-36 32 22), Piazza Duca degli Abruzzi 1a.

LEAVING ITALY

There is a departure tax on international flights, which is built into the cost of your ticket.

Getting Around

AIR

Travelling by plane is expensive within Italy and it makes much better sense to use the efficient and considerably cheaper rail and bus services. The domestic airlines are Alitalia and Meridiana. The main airports are in Rome,

Pisa, Milan, Naples, Catania and Cagliari, but there are other, smaller airports throughout Italy. Domestic flights can be booked directly with the airlines or through Sestante CIT, CTS and other travel agencies.

Alitalia offers a range of discounts for students, young people and families (40%), and weekend travel (50%). Another option is Apex fares, limited to certain flights and requiring a minimum two-night stay.

BUS

Bus travel within Italy is provided by numerous companies, and services vary from local routes linking small villages to major intercity connections. It is usually necessary to make reservations only for long trips, such as Rome to Palermo or Brindisi. Otherwise, just arrive early enough to claim a seat.

Buses can be a cheaper and faster way to get around if your destination is not on major rail lines, for instance from Umbria to Rome or Florence, and in the interior areas of Sicily and Sardinia. Some examples of prices for bus travel are Rome-Palermo L70,000; Rome-Siena L22,000; and Rome-Pompeii L25,000.

You can usually get bus timetables from local tourist offices and, if not, staff will be able to point you in the direction of the main bus companies. See Rome's Getting There & Away section for more details.

TRAIN

Travelling by train in Italy is simple, relatively cheap and generally efficient. The Ferrovie dello Stato (FS) is the partially privatised state train system and there are several private railway services throughout the country.

There are several types of trains: *regionale*, which usually stops at all stations and can be very slow; *interregionale*, which runs between the regions; *diretto*, which indicates that you do not need to change trains to reach the final destination; an *espresso*, which stops only at major stations; and an intercity (IC), or Eurocity (EC), which services only the major cities. There is also the new ETR 450, a fast train service between major cities, known as the *pendolino*, which has both 1st and 2nd class.

Costs & Reservations

To travel on the intercity, Eurocity and pendolino trains, you have to pay a *supplemento*, an additional charge determined by the distance you are travelling. For instance, on the intercity train between Florence and Bologna (about 100 km) you will pay a L4900 supplemento. Always check whether the train you are about to catch is an intercity or Eurocity, and pay the supplement before you get on the train, otherwise you will pay extra. It's obligatory to book a seat on the pendolino, since it doesn't carry standing-room passengers. The difference in second-class fares for the pendolino and intercity trains is around L8000 from Rome to Florence, and you arrive half an hour earlier.

There are left-luggage facilities at all major train stations and at other train stations, except for the smallest, throughout Italy. They are usually open seven days a week, 24 hours a day, but if not, they close for only a few hours after midnight.

Discounts
It is not worth buying a Eurail or Inter-Rail pass if you are going to travel only in Italy. The FS offers its own discount passes for travel within the country. These include the Cartaverde for those aged 26 years and under. It costs L40,000, is valid for one year, and entitles you to a 20% discount on all train travel. You can buy a *biglietto chilometrico* (kilometric ticket), which is valid for two months and allows you to cover 3000 km, with a maximum of 20 trips. It costs L186,000 (2nd class) and you must pay the rapido supplement if you catch an intercity train. Its main attraction is that it can be used by up to five people, either singly or together. Some examples of normal, 2nd-class train fares are: Rome-Florence L24,400 (plus L11,800 supplement); Rome-Naples L17,200 (plus L9700 supplement). A 2nd-class fare on the pendolino from Rome to Florence (less than a 1¾-hour journey) is L45,800.

CAR & MOTORCYCLE
Trains and buses are fine for travelling through most of Italy but, if you want to get off the beaten track, renting a car or motorcycle is a good idea, particularly in Sicily and Sardinia where some of the most interesting and beautiful places are difficult to reach by public transport. The Istituto Geografico de Agostini publishes detailed road maps for all of Italy. Its book entitled *Atlante Stradale Italiano* has road

maps as well as town maps. You can also buy individual maps of the regions you plan to visit.

Automobile Club d'Italia (ACI) offers free roadside assistance to tourists driving cars with foreign numberplates (☎ 116). They will also tow your car for free to the nearest garage – you will be up for the cost of repairs.

Roads are generally good throughout the country and there is an excellent system of autostrade (freeways). The main north-south link is the Autostrada del Sole, which extends from Milan to Reggio di Calabria (called the A1 from Milan to Naples and the A3 from Naples to Reggio). The only problem with the autostrade is that they are toll roads. Connecting roads provide access to Italy's major cities from the autostrada system.

Road Rules
Italian traffic, particularly in the cities, can appear extremely chaotic, and people drive at high speed on the autostrade (never remain in the left-hand fast lane longer than is necessary to pass a car).

In Italy, as throughout Continental Europe, people drive on the right-hand side of the road and pass on the left. Unless otherwise indicated, you must give way to cars coming from the right. It is compulsory to wear seat belts if they are fitted to the car (front seat belts on all cars and back seat belts on cars produced after 26 April 1990). Most Italians ignore this requirement and generally wear seat belts only on the autostrade. If caught not wearing your seat belt, you will be required to pay a L50,000 on-the-spot fine.

You don't need a licence to ride a moped under 50 cc, but you should be aged 14 years or over, and a helmet is compulsory up to age 18; you can't carry passengers or ride on the autostrade. To ride a motorcycle or scooter up to 125 cc, you must be at least 16 years old and have a licence (a car licence will do). Helmets are compulsory. Over 125 cc, you need a motorcycle licence and, of course, a helmet.

The limit on blood-alcohol content is 0.08% and random breath tests have now been introduced.

In Rome and Naples you might have difficulty negotiating the extraordinarily chaotic traffic, but remain calm, keep your eyes on the car in front of you and you should be OK. Most roads are well signposted and once you arrive

ITALY

in a city or village, follow the *centro* signs to reach the centre of town. Be extremely careful where you park your car. In the major cities it will almost certainly be towed away and you will pay a heavy fine if you leave it near a sign reading 'Zona di Rimozione' (Removal Zone) and featuring a tow truck.

Some Italian cities, including Rome, Florence, Milan and Turin, have introduced restricted access to motorists (both private and rental cars) in their historical centres. The restrictions, however, do not apply to vehicles with foreign registrations, to allow tourists to reach their hotels. If you are stopped by a traffic police officer, you will need to name the hotel where you are staying and produce a pass (provided by the hotel) if required. Motorcyclists with large bikes may be stopped, and *motorini* (mopeds) and scooters (such as Vespas) are able to enter the zones without any problems.

Speed limits, unless otherwise indicated by local signs, are: on autostrade 130 km/h for cars of 1100 cc or more, 110 km/h for smaller cars and motorcycles under 350 cc; on all main, non-urban highways 100 km/h; on secondary non-urban highways 90km/h; in built-up areas 50 km/h.

Expenses

Petrol prices are high in Italy – around L1800 per litre. Autostrada tolls are also expensive: you will pay around L55,000 for the trip from Rome to Milan. Petrol is called *benzina*, unleaded petrol is *benzina senza piombo* and diesel is *gasolio*. If you are driving a car which uses liquid petroleum gas (LPG), you will need to buy a special guide to service stations which have *gasauto*, also known as GPL. By law these must be located in nonresidential areas and are usually in the country or on city outskirts. The guides are available at service stations selling GPL.

Rental

It is cheaper to organise a rental car before you leave your own country, for instance through some sort of fly/drive deal. Most major firms, including Hertz, Avis and Budget, will arrange this and you simply pick up the vehicle at a nominated point when in Italy. Foreign offices of Sestante CIT can also help to organise car or camper-van rental before you leave home.

You will need to be aged 21 years or over (23 years or over for some companies) to rent a car in Italy, and you will find the deal a lot easier to organise if you have a credit card. You'll find that most firms will accept your standard licence or an International Driving Permit.

At the time of writing, Hertz was offering a special weekend rate which compared well with rates offered by other firms. This was L190,000 for a small car from Friday 9 am to Monday 9 am. The cost for a week was L611,000. Other discounts are also offered to tourists. If you need a baby car seat, call one day ahead to ensure the company has one available. They cost an extra L50,000.

Rental motorcycles are usually mopeds and scooters such as Vespas (50 cc and 125 cc), but it is also possible to rent big touring motorcycles. The cost for a 50-cc Vespa is around L60,000 a day or L300,000 a week. An 800-cc BMW costs L120,000 a day and L800,000 a week. Note that most places require a sizable deposit, sometimes around L300,000, and that you could be responsible for reimbursing part of the value of the vehicle if it is stolen. Always check the fine print in the contract.

Rental agencies are listed under the major cities in this chapter. Most tourist offices have information about where to rent a car or motorcycle, or you can look in the *Yellow Pages* for each town.

Purchase

Car Basically, it is not possible for foreigners to buy a car in Italy, since the law requires that you must be a resident to own and register one. However, if you manage to find a way around this, the average cost of a cheap car is L1,500,000 to L2,500,000, ranging up to around L5,000,000 for a decent second-hand Fiat Uno. The best way to find a car is to look in the classified section of local newspapers in each town or city.

Motorcycle The same laws apply to owning and registering a motorcycle. The cost of a second-hand Vespa ranges from L500,000 to L1,000,000, and a motorino will cost from L200,000 to L1,000,000. Prices for more powerful bikes start at L1,500,000.

BICYCLE

Bikes are available for rent in most Italian towns – the cost ranges from L8000 to L15,000 a day and up to L50,000 a week (see the Getting Around section in each city). But if you are planning to do a lot of cycling, consider buying a bike in Italy; you can buy a decent second-hand bicycle for L200,000. See the Activities section earlier in this chapter for some suggestions on places to cycle. Bikes can travel in the baggage compartment of Italian trains (not on the pendolino, Eurocities or intercities).

HITCHING

It is illegal to hitchhike on Italy's autostrade, but quite acceptable to stand near the entrance to the toll booths. It is not often done in Italy, but Italians are friendly people and you will generally find a lift. Women travelling alone should be extremely cautious about hitchhiking, particularly in the south, Sicily and Sardinia. It is preferable to travel with a companion in these areas. In Rome, go to the Enjoy Rome office (☎ 06-445 1843) at Via Varese 39 for advice.

BOAT

Navi (large ferries) service the islands of Sicily and Sardinia, and *traghetti* (smaller ferries) and *aliscafi* (hydrofoils) service areas such as Elba, the Aeolian Islands, Capri and Ischia. The main embarkation points for Sicily and Sardinia are Genoa, Livorno, Civitavecchia and Naples. In Sicily the main points of arrival are Palermo and Messina, and in Sardinia they are Cagliari, Arbatax, Olbia and Porto Torres. Tirrenia Navigazione is the major company servicing the Mediterranean and it has offices throughout Italy. The FS also operates ferries to Sicily and Sardinia. Further information is provided in the Getting There & Away sections under both islands. Most long-distance services are overnight and all ferries carry vehicles (you can usually take a bicycle free of charge).

LOCAL TRANSPORT

All the major cities have good transport systems, including buses and, in Rome, Milan and Naples, underground railways. In Venice, however, your only options are to get around by boat or on foot. Efficient bus services also operate between neighbouring towns and villages. Tourist offices will provide information on urban public transport systems, including bus routes and maps of the underground railway systems.

Bus

Urban buses are usually frequent and reliable and operate on an honour system. You must buy a ticket beforehand and validate it in the machine on the bus. Tickets generally cost from L1500 to L1800, although most cities offer 24-hour tourist tickets for around L4000 to L6000.

The trend in the larger cities is towards integration of public transport services, which means the same ticket is used for buses, trams and the underground. Tickets are sold at authorised tobacconists, bars and newspaper stands and at ticket booths at bus terminals (for instance, outside Stazione Termini in Rome where most of the major buses stop).

Think twice before travelling without a ticket, as in most cities the army of inspectors has been increased along with fines. In Rome you will be fined L50,000 on the spot if caught without a validated ticket.

Underground

On the underground railways (called the *Metropolitana*) in Rome, Naples and Milan (where they are referred to as the MM), you must buy tickets and validate them before getting on the train.

Taxi

Try to avoid using taxis in Italy, as they are very expensive, and you can usually catch a bus instead. The shortest taxi ride in Rome will cost around L10,000, since the flag fall is L6400. Generally taxis will not stop if you hail them in the street. Instead head for the taxi ranks at train and bus stations or you can telephone for one (radio taxi phone numbers are listed throughout this chapter in the Getting Around sections of the major cities).

ORGANISED TOURS

It is less expensive and more enjoyable to do some research and see the sights independently, but if you are in a hurry or prefer guided tours, go to Sestante CIT or American Express offices. Both offer city and package tours (see under Organised Tours in the major cities for further information). Offices of CIT abroad (see Useful Organisations earlier) can provide information about and organise package tours to Italy.

Rome

'I now realise all the dreams of my youth', wrote Goethe on his arrival in Rome in the winter of 1786. Perhaps Rome today is more chaotic, but certainly no less romantic or fascinating. A phenomenal concentration of history, legend and monuments coexists with an equally phenomenal concentration of people busily going about everyday life. It is easy to pick the tourists because they are the only ones to turn their heads as the bus passes the Colosseum.

Rome had its origins in Etruscan, Latin and Sabine settlements on the Palatine, Esquiline, Quirinal and surrounding hills (archaeological evidence shows that the Palatine settlement was the earliest). It is, however, the legend of Romulus and Remus which has captured the popular imagination. They were the twin sons of Rhea Silvia and the Roman war god Mars, and were raised by a she-wolf after being abandoned on the banks of the Tiber (Tevere). The myth says Romulus killed his brother during a battle over who should govern, and then established the city on the Palatine (Palatino), one of the famous Seven Hills of Rome. Romulus, who established himself as the first king of Rome, disappeared one day, enveloped in a cloud which carried him back to the domain of the gods.

From the legend grew an empire which eventually controlled almost the entire world known to Europeans at the time, an achievement described by a historian of the day as being 'without parallel in human history'.

In Rome there is visible evidence of the two great empires of the Western world: the Roman Empire and the Christian Church. On the one hand there are the forum and the Colosseum, and on the other St Peter's and the Vatican. In between, in almost every piazza, lies history on so many levels that what you actually see is only the tip of the iceberg – a phenomenon exemplified by St Peter's Basilica, which

stands on the site of an earlier basilica built by the Emperor Constantine over the necropolis where St Peter was buried.

Realistically, at least a week is probably a reasonable amount of time to explore Rome, but whatever time you devote to the city, put on your walking shoes, buy a good map and plan your time carefully – the city will eventually seem less chaotic and overwhelming than it first appears.

Orientation

Rome is a vast city, but the historical centre is relatively small. Most of the major sights are within walking distance of the central train station, Stazione Termini. It is, for instance, possible to walk from the Colosseum, through the Forum and the Palatine, up to the Spanish Steps and across to the Vatican in one day, though this is hardly recommended even for the most dedicated tourist. One of the great pleasures of Rome is to allow time for wandering through the many beautiful *piazzas* (squares), stopping now and again for a caffè and *paste* (pastries). All the major monuments are to the west of the station area, but make sure you use a map. Although it can be enjoyable to get lost in Rome, it can also be very frustrating and time-consuming.

It can be difficult to plan an itinerary if your time is limited. Some museums and galleries are now open all day, while others close around 1.30 pm – it is a good idea to check. Some of the major monuments which open in the afternoon include the Colosseum, St Peter's Basilica and the Roman Forum (the latter in summer only). Remember that many museums are closed on Monday.

Most new arrivals in Rome will end up at Stazione Termini. It is the terminus for all international and national trains; the main city bus terminus is in Piazza dei Cinquecento, directly in front of the station. Many intercity buses arrive and depart from the Piazzale Tiburtina, in front of the Stazione Tiburtina, accessible from Termini on the Metropolitana Linea B. Get off at Tiburtina.

The main airport is Leonardo da Vinci, at Fiumicino (about half an hour by train or an hour by car from the centre). For more information, see To/From the Airport under the following Rome Getting Around section.

If you're arriving in Rome by car, invest in

ITALY

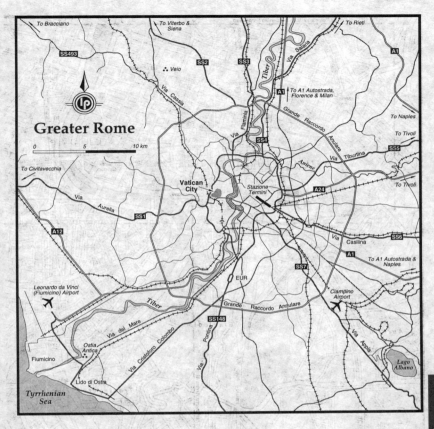

Greater Rome

0   5   10 km

To Bracciano
To Viterbo & Siena
To Rieti
SS493
SS2
SS3
Veio
A1
Via Salaria
Via Cassia
Tiber
Via Flaminia
To A1 Autostrada, Florence & Milan
A1
Grande Raccordo Anulare
To Naples
SS4
Aniene
To Tivoli
Via Tiburtina
SS5
To Civitavecchia
Vatican City
Stazione Termini
To Tivoli
A24
Via Aurelia
SS1
Via Casilina
SS6
A12
A1
To A1 Autostrada & Naples
SS7
EUR
Leonardo da Vinci (Fiumicino) Airport
Ciampino Airport
Tiber
Grande Raccordo Annulare
SS148
Via del Mare
Via Cristoforo Colombo
Via Pontina
Via Appia
Lago Albano
Ostia Antica
Fiumicino
Lido di Ostia
Tyrrhenian Sea

a good road map of the city beforehand so as to have an idea of the various routes into the city centre: easy access routes from the Grande Raccordo Anulare (the ring road encircling the city, which is connected to the Autostrada del Sole) include Via Salaria from the north, Via Aurelia from the north-west and Via Cristoforo Colombo from the south. Normal traffic is not permitted into the city centre, but tourists are allowed to drive to their hotels.

The majority of cheap hotels and pensioni are concentrated around Stazione Termini, but if you are prepared to go the extra distance, it is more expensive but definitely more enjoyable to stay closer to the centre. The area around the station, particularly to the south-west, is unpleasant, seedy and can be dangerous at night, especially for women, but it is the most popular area for budget travellers.

Invest L5000 in the street map and bus guide simply entitled *Roma*, with a red-and-blue cover, which is published by Editrice Lozzi in Rome; it is available at any newsstand in Stazione Termini. It lists all streets, with map references, as well as all bus routes.

Information
Tourist Offices There is a tourist information office (EPT) at Stazione Termini, open

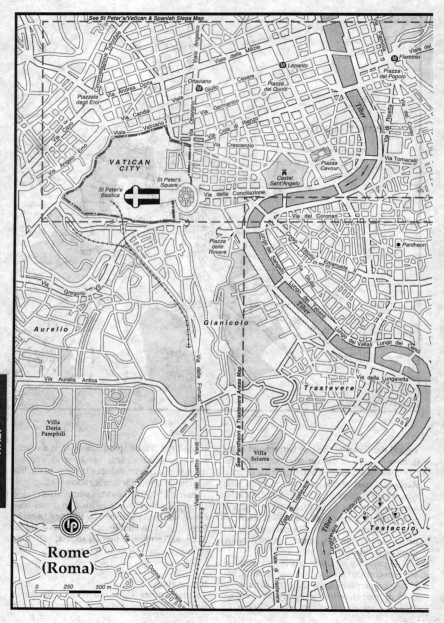

See St Peter's/Vatican & Spanish Steps Map

VATICAN CITY

St Peter's Basilica

St Peter's Square

Piazzale degli Eroi

Via Andrea Doria

Via Candia

Viale Vaticano

Via Angelo Emo

Via Ciro

Circonvallazione Trionfale

Viale Angelico

Viale delle Milizie

Ottaviano

Giulio

Cesare

Via Germanico

Via Ottaviano

Via Cola di Rienzo

Via Crescenzio

Lepanto

Piazza dei Quiriti

Flaminio

Viale del Flaminio

Piazza del Popolo

Tiber

Via di Ripetta

Via del Corso

Via Tomacelli

Castel Sant'Angelo

Piazza Cavour

Via della Conciliazione

Via dei Coronari

Pantheon

Corso Vittorio Emanuele II

Lungo dei Sangallo

Via Giulia

Lungo dei Tebaldi

Tiber

Lungo dei Vallati

Lungo dei Cenci

Via della Lungaretta

Trastevere

Piazza delle Rovere

Via Gregorio VII

Via

Aurelio

Via Aurelia Antica

Gianicolo

Via delle Fornaci

Villa Doria Pamphili

Via Vitellia

See Pantheon & Trastevere Areas Map

Viale dei Quattro Venti

Villa Sciarra

Viale di Trastevere

Viale di Trastevere

Testaccio

Tiber

Lungotevere Testaccio

Via di Donna Olimpia

Rome (Roma)

0   250   500 m

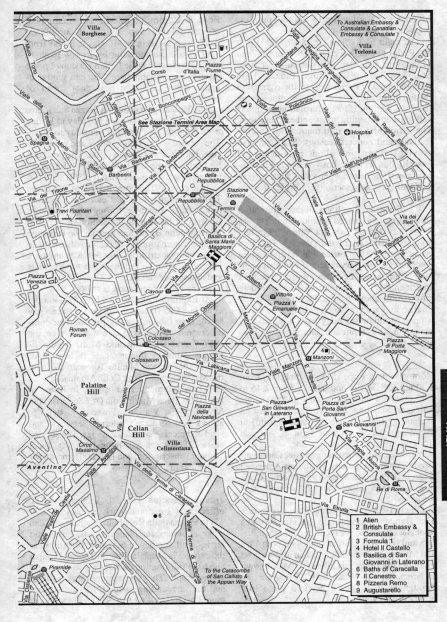

ITALY

1 Alien
2 British Embassy &
   Consulate
3 Formula 1
4 Hotel Il Castello
5 Basilica di San
   Giovanni in Laterano
6 Baths of Caracalla
7 Il Canestro
8 Pizzeria Remo
9 Augustarello

Monday to Saturday from 9 am to 7 pm. It is opposite platform No 4.

The main EPT office (☎ 48 89 92 53) is at Via Parigi 11 and is open from 8.15 am to 7 pm Monday to Saturday. Walk north-west from Stazione Termini, through Piazza della Repubblica. Via Parigi runs to the right from the top of the piazza, about a five-minute walk from the station. It has information on hotels and museum opening hours and entrance fees. The office also has information on summer festivals and concert seasons. Staff can also provide information about provincial and intercity bus services, but you need to be specific about where and when you want to go (see the Getting Around section for further information).

It's likely that you'll get all the information and assistance you need at Enjoy Rome (☎ 445 18 43; fax 445 07 34), Via Varese 39 (a few minutes north-east of the station). This is a privately run tourist office which offers a free hotel reservation service. Staff can also organise alternative accommodation such as apartments. They have extensive up-to-date information about Rome. The owners speak English and are very keen to help. The office is open Monday to Friday from 8.30 am to 1 pm and 3.30 to 6 pm and Saturday from 8.30 am to 1 pm.

Money Banks are open Monday to Friday from 8.30 am to 1.30 pm and usually from 2.45 to 3.45 pm. You will find a bank and exchange offices at Stazione Termini. There is also an exchange office (Banco di Santo Spirito) at Fiumicino airport, to your right as you exit from the customs area.

Numerous other exchange offices are scattered throughout the city, including American Express in Piazza di Spagna and Thomas Cook in Piazza della Repubblica and several other locations.

Otherwise, go to any bank in the city centre. The Banca Commerciale Italiana, Piazza Venezia, is reliable for receiving money transfers and will give cash advances on both Visa and MasterCard. Credit cards can also be used in automatic teller machines (ATMs), known as *bancomats*, to obtain cash 24 hours a day throughout Italy. You'll need to get a PIN number from your bank.

Post & Communications The main post office is at Piazza San Silvestro 19, just off Via del Tritone, and is open Monday to Friday from 8.30 am to 8 pm and Saturday from 8.30 am to noon. Fermo posta (the Italian version of poste restante) is available here. You can send telegrams from the office next door (open 24 hours).

The Vatican post office, in Piazza San Pietro (St Peter's Square), is open Monday to Friday from 8.30 am to 7 pm and Saturday to 6 pm. The service is supposedly faster and more reliable, but there's no fermo posta. The postcode for central Rome is 00100, although for fermo posta at the main post office it is 00186.

There is a Telecom office at Stazione Termini, from where you can make international calls direct or through an operator. Another office is near the station, in Via San Martino della Battaglia opposite the Pensione Lachea. International calls can easily be made with a phonecard from any public telephone. Phonecards can be purchased at tobacconists and newspaper stands.

Rome's telephone code is ☎ 06.

At Explorer Café (☎ 32 41 17 57), Via dei Gracchi 83/85 (near the Vatican), you can pay by the hour (about L12,000) to use their computers to have access to an e-mail service, the WWW and CD-Rom and Multi Media libraries. Another Internet café is Music All (☎ 784 29 33), Via Manlio Torquato 21 (near the Metro stop in Largo Colli Albani).

A new Internet centre opened in Rome in mid-1996. Itaca Multimedia (☎ 686 14 64; fax 689 60 96) at Via della Fosse di Castello 8, allows you to access Internet services, and send and receive e-mail messages. The service costs L7000 for a half-hour, L100,000 for a 10-hour subscription, and L30,000 a month for a personal mail box.

Travel Agencies There is a Sestante CIT office (Italy's national tourist agency; ☎ 4 79 41) in Piazza della Repubblica, where you can make bookings for planes, trains, buses and ferries, and another in Stazione Termini near the exit to Via Marsala. The staff speak English and have information on fares for students and young people. They also arrange tours of Rome and the surrounding areas. CTS (the student tourist centre; ☎ 4 67 91), Via Genova 16, off

Via Nazionale, offers much the same services and will also make hotel reservations, but focuses on discount and student travel. There is a branch office at Termini. The staff at both offices speak English. American Express (☎ 6 76 41 for travel information; ☎ 7 22 82 for 24-hour client service for lost or stolen cards; ☎ 167-87 20 00 for lost or stolen travellers' cheques), Piazza di Spagna 38, has a travel service similar to CIT and CTS, as well as a hotel reservation service, and can arrange tours of the city and surrounding areas.

Bookshops The Corner Bookshop, at Via del Moro 48 in Trastevere, is very well stocked with English-language books (including Lonely Planet guides). It is run by a helpful and friendly Australian woman named Claire Hammond. The Anglo-American Bookshop, Via della Vite 102, off Piazza di Spagna, also has an excellent selection of literature, travel guides and reference books. The Lion Bookshop, Via del Babuino 181, also has a good range, as does the Economy Book and Video Center, Via Torino 136, off Via Nazionale.

Laundry There is a coin laundrette, Onda Blu, at Via Principe Amadeo 70b, near the train station.

Medical Services Emergency medical treatment is available in the Pronto Soccorso (casualty sections) at public hospitals including: Policlinico Umberto I (☎ 446 23 41), Via del Policlinico 255, near Stazione Termini; Policlinico A Gemelli (☎ 3 01 51), Largo A Gemelli 8. The Rome American Hospital (☎ 2 56 71), Via E Longoni 69, is a private hospital and you should use its services only if you have health insurance and have consulted your insurance company. Rome's paediatric hospital is Bambino Gesù (☎ 68 59 23 51) on the Janiculum (Gianicolo) Hill at Piazza Sant'Onofrio.

For an ambulance call ☎ 5510, and for first aid call ☎ 118.

There is a pharmacy in Stazione Termini, open daily from 7 am to 11 pm (closed in August). For information (in Italian) on all-night pharmacies in Rome, ring ☎ 1921. Otherwise, closed pharmacies should post a list in their windows of others open nearby.

Emergency The questura (police headquarters; ☎ 4686) is at Via San Vitale 15. Its Foreigners' Bureau (Ufficio Stranieri; ☎ 46 86 29 87) is around the corner at Via Genova 2. It is open 24 hours a day and thefts can be reported here. For immediate police attendance call ☎ 112 or 113.

Dangers & Annoyances Thieves are very active in the areas in and around Stazione Termini, at major sights such as the Colosseum and Roman Forum, and in the city's most expensive shopping streets, such as Via Condotti. Pickpockets like to work on crowded buses, particularly No 64 from St Peter's to Termini and the No 27 from Termini to the Colosseum. For more comprehensive information on how to avoid being robbed see the Dangers and Annoyances section earlier in this chapter.

Things to See & Do
It would take years to explore every corner of Rome, months to begin to appreciate the incredible number of monuments and weeks for a thorough tour of the city. You can, however, cover most of the important monuments in five days, or three at a minimum.

Walking Tour A good, but rather long walk to help orient yourself in Rome is to start from Piazza della Repubblica and head north-west along Via Vittorio Emanuele Orlando, turning left into Via XX Settembre (which becomes Via del Quirinale) to reach the **Piazza del Quirinale**. Along the way you'll pass by two churches, Borromini's **San Carlo alle Quattro Fontane** at the intersection known as the Quattro Fontane, and Bernini's **Sant'Andrea al Quirinale**. Set on the Quirinal Hill, the Piazza del Quirinale affords an interesting view of Rome and St Peter's. Italy's president lives at the Palazzo del Quirinale. The palace and its gardens are opened to the public on the last Sunday of each month from 9 am to 1 pm. Admission is free. From Piazza del Quirinale walk back down Via del Quirinale and turn left into Via delle Quattro Fontane to get to **Piazza Barberini**. From here you can wander up **Via Veneto**, or take Via Sistina to the **Spanish Steps**.

From Piazza di Spagna wander down Via

ITALY

Condotti and turn left on to Via del Corso, crossing over Via del Tritone. Then take the second left (Via delle Muratte) to see the **Trevi Fountain**. Return to Via del Corso and cross into the **Piazza Colonna**. Things get a bit complicated here, but use a good map, follow the tourist signs and you won't get lost. Walk through the piazza into the **Piazza di Montecitorio**, and continue straight ahead along Via degli Uffici del Vicario, where you can buy a gelato at Giolitti. Then turn left at Via della Maddalena to get to the **Pantheon**.

Take Via Giustiniani from the north-western corner of Piazza della Rotonda to get to **Piazza Navona**. Leave the piazza from Via Cuccagna, cross Corso Vittorio Emanuele II and take Via Cancelleria to reach the **Campo de' Fiori**. From here go down Via Gallo into the **Piazza Farnese** and then walk directly ahead out of the piazza on Via dei Farnesi into **Via Giulia**.

If you still have the energy, you have two choices. Either continue along Via Giulia and cross the Ponte Vittorio Emanuele II to get to **St Peter's Basilica** and the **Vatican**, or cross the **Ponte Sisto** at the southern end of Via Giulia and wander through the streets of **Trastevere**.

Piazza del Campidoglio Designed by Michelangelo in 1538, the piazza is on the Capitolino (Capitoline Hill), the most important of Rome's seven hills. The hill was the seat of the ancient Roman government and is now the seat of Rome's municipal government. Michelangelo also designed the façades of the three palaces which border the piazza. A bronze equestrian statue of Emperor Marcus Aurelius once stood in the centre of the piazza. It was removed for restoration and is now on display in the ground floor portico of the Palazzo del Museo Capitolino. A copy will eventually be placed in the piazza. In the two palaces flanking the piazza are the **Musei Capitolini**, which are well worth visiting. They are open Tuesday to Saturday 9 am to 7 pm and Sunday until 1.30 pm. Admission is L10,000.

Walk to the right of the Palazzo del Senato to see a panorama of the Roman Forum. Walk to the left of the same building to reach the ancient Roman **Carcere Mamertino**, where prisoners were put through a hole in the floor to starve to death. St Peter was believed to have

been imprisoned there. The **Chiesa di Santa Maria d'Aracoeli** is between the Campidoglio and the Monumento Vittorio Emanuele II at the highest point of the Capitoline Hill. Built on the site where legend says the Tiburtine Sybil told Augustus of the coming birth of Christ, it features frescos by Pinturicchio in the first chapel of the south aisle.

Piazza Venezia This piazza is overshadowed by a monument dedicated to Vittorio Emanuele II, which is often referred to by Italians as the *macchina da scrivere* (typewriter) – because it resembles one.

Built to commemorate Italian unification, the piazza incorporates the **Altare della Patria** and the tomb of the unknown soldier, as well as the **Museo del Risorgimento**. Also in the piazza is the 15th-century **Palazzo Venezia**, which was Mussolini's official residence.

Roman Forum & Palatine Hill The commercial, political and religious centre of ancient Rome, the forum stands in a valley between the Capitoline and Palatine (Palatino) hills. Originally marshland, the area was drained during the early Republican era and became a centre for political rallies, public ceremonies and senate meetings. Its importance declined along with the empire after the 4th century, and the temples, monuments and buildings constructed by successive emperors, consuls and senators over a period of 900 years fell into ruin, eventually to be used as pasture land.

The area was systematically excavated in the 18th and 19th centuries, and excavations are continuing. You can enter the forum from Via dei Fori Imperiali, which leads from Piazza Venezia to the Colosseum. The forum and Palatine are open in summer from 9 am to 6 pm (3 pm in winter), and on Sunday from 9 am to 1 pm year-round. Admission is L12,000 and covers entrance to both the forum and the Palatine Hill.

As you enter the forum, to your left is the **Tempio di Antonino e Faustina**, erected by the Senate in 141 AD and transformed into a church in the 8th century. To your right are the remains of the **Basilica Aemilia**, built in 179 BC and demolished during the Renaissance, when it was plundered for its precious marble. The Via Sacra, which traverse the forum from north-west to south-east, runs in front of the basilica. Towards the Campidoglio is the **Curia**, once the meeting place of the Roman Senate and converted to a Christian church in the Middle Ages. The church was dismantled and the Curia restored in the 1930s. In front of the Curia is the **Lapis Niger**, a large piece of black marble which legend says covered the grave of Romulus. Under the Lapis Niger is the oldest known Latin inscription, dating to the 6th century BC.

The **Arco di Settimo Severo** was erected in 203 AD in honour of this emperor and his sons, and is considered one of Italy's major triumphal arches. A circular base stone beside the arch marks the *umbilicus urbis*, the symbolic centre of ancient Rome. To the south is the **Rostrum**, used in ancient times by public speakers and once decorated by the rams of captured ships.

South along the Via Sacra is the **Tempio di Saturno**, one of the most important temples in ancient Rome. Eight granite columns remain. The **Basilica Julia**, in front of the temple, was the seat of justice, and nearby is the Tempio di Giulio Cesare (Temple of Julius Caesar), which was erected by Augustus in 29 BC on the site where Caesar's body was burned and Mark Antony read his famous speech. Back towards the Palatine Hill is the **Tempio dei Castori**, built in 489 BC to mark the defeat of the Etruscan Tarquins and in honour of the Heavenly Twins, or Dioscuri. It is easily recognisable by its three remaining columns.

In the area south-east of the temple is the **Chiesa di Santa Maria Antiqua**, the oldest Christian church in the forum. It is closed to the public. Back on the Via Sacra is the **Case delle Vestali**, home of the virgins who tended the sacred flame in the adjoining **Tempio di Vesta**. If the flame went out, it was seen as a bad omen. The next major monument is the vast **Basilica di Costantino**. Its impressive design inspired Renaissance architects. The **Arco di Tito**, at the Colosseum end of the forum, was built in 81 AD in honour of the victories of the emperors Titus and Vespasian against Jerusalem.

From here climb the **Palatino**, where wealthy Romans built their homes and where legend says that Romulus founded the city. Archaeological evidence shows that the earliest settlements in the area were on the Palatine.

Like the forum, the buildings of the Palatine fell into ruin and in the Middle Ages the hill became the site of convents and churches. During the Renaissance, wealthy families established their gardens here. The Farnese gardens were built over the ruins of the Domus Tiberiana, which is now under excavation.

Worth a look are the impressive **Domus Augustana**, which was the private residence of the emperors, and the **Domus Flavia**, the residence of Domitian; the **Tempio della Magna Mater**, built in 204 BC to house a black stone connected with the Asiatic goddess, Cybele; and the **Casa di Livia**, thought to have been the house of the wife of Emperor Augustus, and decorated with frescos. Bring a picnic lunch.

Colosseum Originally known as the Flavian Amphitheatre, its construction was started by Emperor Vespasian in 72 AD in the grounds of Nero's Golden House, and completed by his son Titus. The massive structure could seat 80,000 and the bloody gladiator combat and wild beast shows, when thousands of wild animals were slashed to death, give some insight into Roman people of the day.

In the Middle Ages the Colosseum became a fortress and was later used as a quarry for travertine and marble for the Palazzo Venezia and other buildings. Restoration works have been underway since 1992. Opening hours are from 9 am to 7 pm in summer (3 pm in winter) and to 1 pm Wednesday, Sunday and public holidays. General entry is free, although there are plans to introduce an entry fee. It costs L8000 to go to the top levels.

Arch of Constantine On the west side of the Colosseum is the triumphal arch built to honour Constantine following his victory over his rival Maxentius at the battle of Milvian Bridge (near the present-day Zona Olimpica, north-west of the Villa Borghese) in 312 AD. Its decorative reliefs were taken from earlier structures. A major restoration was completed in 1987.

Circus Maximus There is not much to see here apart from the few ruins that remain of what was once a chariot racetrack big enough to hold more than 200,000 people.

Baths of Caracalla This huge complex, covering 10 hectares, could hold 1600 people and included shops, gardens, libraries and entertainment. Begun by Antonius Caracalla and inaugurated in 217 AD, the baths were used until the 6th century. From the 1930s to 1993 they were an atmospheric venue for opera performances in summer. These performances have now been banned to prevent further damage to the ruins. The baths are open in summer from 9 am to 6 pm and in winter until 3 pm. Entry is L8000.

Some Significant Churches Down Via Cavour from Stazione Termini is **Santa Maria Maggiore**, built in the 5th century. Its main baroque façade was added in the 18th century, preserving the 13th-century mosaics of the earlier façade. Its bell tower is Romanesque and the interior is baroque. There are 5th-century mosaics decorating the triumphal arch and nave. Follow Via Merulana to reach **San Giovanni in Laterano**, Rome's cathedral. The original church was built in the 4th century, the first Christian basilica in Rome. Largely destroyed over a long period of time, it was rebuilt in the 17th century. **San Pietro in Vincoli**, just off Via Cavour, is worth a visit because it houses Michelangelo's *Moses* and his unfinished statues of Leah and Rachel, as well as the chains worn by St Peter during his imprisonment before being crucified. **San Clemente**, in Via San Giovanni in Laterano, near the Colosseum, defines how history in Rome exists on many levels. The 12th-century church at street level was built over a 4th-century church which was, in turn, built over a 1st-century Roman house containing a temple dedicated to the pagan god of light, Mithras.

Santa Maria in Cosmedin, north-west of Circus Maximus, is regarded as one of the finest medieval churches in Rome. It has a seven-storey bell tower and its interior is heavily decorated with Cosmatesque inlaid marble, including the beautiful floor. The main attraction for the tourist hordes is, however, the **Bocca della Verità** (Mouth of Truth). Legend has it that if you put your right hand into the mouth, while telling a lie, it will snap shut. Located in Via Veneto, **Santa Maria della Concezione** is an austere 17th-century building; however, the Capuchin cemetery beneath the church (with access on the right of the church steps) features a bizarre display of monks' bones which were used to decorate the walls of a series of chapels.

Baths of Diocletian Started by Emperor Diocletian, these baths were completed in the 4th century. The complex of baths, libraries, concert halls and gardens covered about 13 hectares and could house up to 3000 people. After the aqueduct which fed the baths was destroyed by invaders in 536 AD, the complex fell into decay. Parts of the ruins are now incorporated into the church of Santa Maria degli Angeli and the Museo Nazionale Romano. The baths are open Tuesday to Saturday from 9 am to 2 pm and Sunday to 1 pm. Admission is L12,000.

Basilica di Santa Maria degli Angeli Designed by Michelangelo, this church incorporates what was the great central hall and tepidarium (lukewarm room) of the original baths. During the following centuries his work was drastically changed and little evidence of his design, apart from the great vaulted ceiling of the church, remains. An interesting feature of the church is a double meridian in the transept, one tracing the polar star and the other telling the precise time of the sun's zenith. The church is open from 7.30 am to 12.30 pm and from 4 to 6.30 pm. Through the sacristy is an entrance to a stairway leading to the upper terraces of the ruins. A plaque near the stairway records the traditional belief that the baths were built by thousands of Christian slaves.

Museo Nazionale Romano This museum houses an important collection of ancient art, including Greek and Roman sculpture. It also has a collection of frescos and mosaics from the Villa of Livia at Prima Porta. The museum is now largely located in the former Collegio Massimo, just across the road from the Baths of Diocletian, and is open from 9 am to 2 pm (1 pm on Sunday, closed Monday) and entry is L12,000.

Via Vittorio Veneto This was Rome's hot spot in the 1960s, where film stars could be spotted at the expensive outdoor cafés. These days you will find only tourists, and the atmosphere of Fellini's *Roma* is long dead.

Piazza di Spagna & Spanish Steps This piazza, church and famous staircase (Scalinata della Trinità dei Monti) have long provided a major gathering place for foreigners. Built with a legacy from the French in 1725, but named after the Spanish Embassy to the Holy See, the steps lead to the church of Trinità dei Monti, which was built by the French.

In the 18th century the most beautiful men and women of Italy gathered there, waiting to be chosen as artists' models. To the right as you face the steps is the house where Keats spent the last three months of his life, and where he died in 1821. In the piazza is the boat-shaped fountain of the **Barcaccia**, believed to be by Pietro Bernini, father of the famous Gian Lorenzo. One of Rome's most elegant shopping streets, **Via Condotti**, runs off the piazza towards Via del Corso.

Piazza del Popolo This vast piazza was laid out in the 16th century and redesigned in the early 19th century by Giuseppe Valadier. It is at the foot of the **Pincio Hill**, from where there is a panoramic view of the city.

Villa Borghese This beautiful park was once the estate of Cardinal Scipione Borghese. His 17th-century villa houses the **Museo e Galleria Borghese**, which has been undergoing renovations for more than a decade. It still houses a sculpture collection (entry L4000, open Tuesday to Saturday from 9 am to 1.30 pm and Sunday till 1 pm). Part of the gallery's collection of paintings is temporarily housed in the **Istituto San Michele a Ripa**, Via di San Michele a Ripa in Trastevere (open Tuesday to Saturday from 9 am to 7 pm, and Sunday 9 am to 1 pm). Entry is L4000. Just outside the park are the **Galleria Nazionale d'Arte Moderna**, Viale delle Belle Arti 131, and the important Etruscan museum, **Museo Nazionale di Villa Giulia**, along the same street in Piazzale di Villa Giulia. Both open Tuesday to Saturday from 9 am to 7 pm and Sunday to 1 pm. Entry at both is L8000.

Trevi Fountain The high-baroque Fontana di Trevi was designed by Nicola Salvi in 1732.

Its water was supplied by one of Rome's earliest aqueducts. Work to clean the fountain and its water supply was completed in 1991. The famous custom is to throw a coin into the fountain (over your shoulder while facing away) to ensure your return to Rome. If you throw a second coin you can make a wish.

Pantheon This is the best-preserved building of ancient Rome. The original temple was built in 27 BC by Marcus Agrippa, son-in-law of Emperor Augustus, and dedicated to the planetary gods. Although the temple was rebuilt by Emperor Hadrian around 120 AD, Agrippa's name remains inscribed over the entrance.

Over the centuries the temple was consistently plundered and damaged. The gilded bronze roof tiles were removed by an emperor of the eastern empire, and Pope Urban VIII had the bronze ceiling of the portico melted down to make the canopy over the main altar of St Peter's and 80 cannons for Castel Sant'Angelo. The Pantheon's extraordinary dome is considered the most important achievement of ancient Roman architecture. In 608 AD the temple was consecrated to the Virgin and all martyrs.

The Italian kings Vittorio Emanuele II and Umberto I and the painter Raphael are buried there. The Pantheon is in Piazza della Rotonda and is open Monday to Saturday from 9 am to 4 pm (9 am to 2 pm in winter) and 9 am to 1 pm Sunday and public holidays year-round. Admission is free.

Piazza Navona This is a vast and beautiful square, lined with baroque palaces. It was laid out on the ruins of Domitian's stadium and features three fountains, including Bernini's masterpiece, the **Fontana dei Fiumi** (Fountain of the Rivers), in the centre. Take time to relax on one of the stone benches and watch the artists who gather in the piazza to work.

Campo de' Fiori This is a lively piazza where a flower and vegetable market is held every morning except Sunday. Now lined with bars and trattorias, the piazza was a place of execution during the Inquisition.

The **Palazzo Farnese** (Farnese Palace), in the piazza of the same name, is just off Campo de' Fiori. A magnificent Renaissance building, it was started in 1514 by Antonio da Sangello,

ITALY

Via dell'Orso

V degli Uffici

Piazza Montecitorio

Piazza Colonna

Ponte Sant'Angelo

Ponte Vittorio Emanuele II

Via dei Coronari

2 ▼

1

Via Giustiniani

Piazza della Rotonda

12 ▼ 11

Via dei Coronari

14

13

Piazza Navona

Piazza della Rotonda

Via B. Vecchi

Corso Vittorio

Via del

▼16

17

18

Via del Governo Vecchio

15

Piazza S Eustachio

23

22

Corso Rinascimento

Piazza della Minerva

24

Lungo Giancolense

Lungo Sangallo

Lungo dei

Via del

Emanuele II

Pellegrino

19

20

21

Via di Monserrato

Via dei Cappellari

25 ▼

Corso Vittorio Emanuele II

Largo Argentina

Ponte Giuseppe Mazzini

Via d'Alberi

Via Mantellate

Via Giulia

Lungo dei Tebaldi

▼26 27

28

Campo de' Fiori

32

33

Via dei Giubbonari

Piazza Mattei

Piazza Campitelli

29

31

30

Piazza Farnese

42

Villa Orto Botanico

Tiber

Lungo della Farnesina

Via della Lungaretta

Via d. Pettinari

Via Arenula

Via Porta d'Ottavia

43

PLACES TO STAY
12 Albergo Abruzzi
21 Pensione Primavera
24 Pensione Mimosa
27 Albergo della Lunetta
28 Albergo del Sole
33 Albergo Pomezia

PLACES TO EAT
1   Gelateria Giolitti
2   Gelateria della
    Palme
4   Piccolo Arancio
11 Tazza d'Oro
13 Bevitoria Navona
14 Bar della Pace
15 Trattoria Pizzeria
    da Francesco
16 Osteria
17 Paladini
18 Pizzeria da
    Baffetto
19 Pizzeria
    Montecarlo
20 Cul de Sac 1
22 Caffé Sant'Eustachio
25 Pizza a Taglio
29 Hosteria Romanesca
32 Filetti di Baccalà
36 Gli Angeletti
38 Alle Carette
42 Sora Margherita
46 D'Augusto
48 Da Lucia
51 Bar San Callisto
52 Pizzeria da
    Vittorio
53 Pizzeria Ivo
55 McDonald's
56 Fonte della
    Salute
58 Frontoni

Ponte Sisto

Piazza Trilussa

Piazza de' Renzi

Lungo dei Vallati

Lungo dei Cenci

Ponte Garibaldi

Ponte Fabricio

Isola Tiberina

Ponte Cestio

Via G Garibaldi

Via della Lungara

Via della Scala

Via del Moro

46

47

48

49

50

Lungo R Sanzio

Lungo Anguillara

Ponte Palatino

Piazza Santa Maria

Piazza San Calisto

51

54

55

56

Ponte Palatino

Trastevere

Via Luciano Manara

52

53

Via San Francesco a Ripa

Via dei Genovesi

59

Lungo Ripa

Via Mameli

Piazza San Cosimato

57

58 ▼

Piazza Mastai

Via di Trastevere

Via Ardica

Via di S. Michele

Viale Glorioso

Via E Morosini

62

63

Tiber

Villa Sciarra

Ponte Sublicio

Ponte Sublicio

Via di Sabina

ITALY

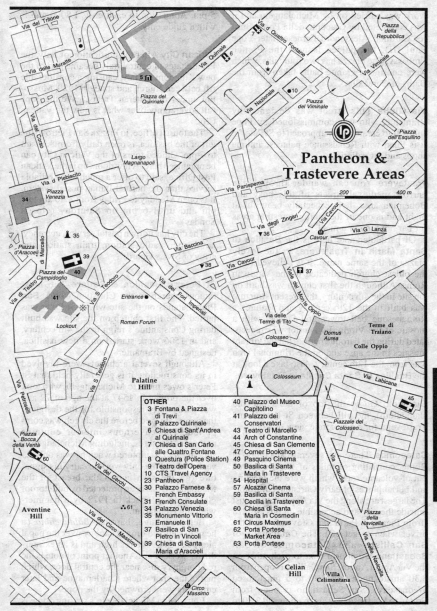

Pantheon & Trastevere Areas

0   200   400 m

OTHER

3 Fontana & Piazza di Trevi
5 Palazzo Quirinale
6 Chiesa di Sant'Andrea al Quirinale
7 Chiesa di San Carlo alle Quattro Fontane
8 Questura (Police Station)
9 Teatro dell'Opera
10 CTS Travel Agency
23 Pantheon
30 Palazzo Farnese & French Embassy
31 French Consulate
34 Palazzo Venezia
35 Monumento Vittorio Emanuele II
37 Basilica di San Pietro in Vincoli
39 Chiesa di Santa Maria d'Aracoeli
40 Palazzo del Museo Capitolino
41 Palazzo dei Conservatori
43 Teatro di Marcello
44 Arch of Constantine
45 Chiesa di San Clemente
47 Corner Bookshop
49 Pasquino Cinema
50 Basilica di Santa Maria in Trastevere
54 Hospital
57 Alcazar Cinema
59 Basilica di Santa Cecilia in Trastevere
60 Chiesa di Santa Maria in Cosmedin
61 Circus Maximus
62 Porta Portese Market Area
63 Porta Portese

ITALY

work was carried on by Michelangelo and it was completed by Giacomo della Porta. Built for Cardinal Alessandro Farnese (later Pope Paul III), the palace is now the French Embassy. The piazza has two fountains, which were enormous granite baths taken from the Baths of Caracalla.

Via Giulia This street was designed by Bramante, who was commissioned by Pope Julius II to create a new approach to St Peter's. It is lined with Renaissance palaces, antique shops and art galleries.

Trastevere You can wander through the narrow medieval streets of this busy and Bohemian area. It is especially beautiful at night and is one of the more interesting areas for bar-hopping or a meal.

Of particular note here is the **Basilica di Santa Maria in Trastevere**, in the lovely piazza of the same name. It is believed to be the oldest church dedicated to the Virgin in Rome. Although the first church was built on the site in the 4th century, the present structure was built in the 12th century and features a Romanesque bell tower and façade, with a mosaic of the Virgin. Its interior was redecorated during the baroque period, but the vibrant mosaics in the apse and on the triumphal arch date from the 12th century. Also take a look at the **Basilica di Santa Cecilia in Trastevere**.

Gianicolo Go to the top of the Gianicolo (Janiculum), the hill between St Peter's and Trastevere, for a panoramic view of Rome.

Catacombs There are several catacombs in Rome, consisting of miles of tunnels carved out of volcanic rock, which were the meeting and burial places of early Christians in Rome. The largest are along the Via Appia Antica, just outside the city and accessible on bus No 218 (from Piazza di Porta San Giovanni – ask the driver when to get off). The **Catacombs of San Callisto** and **Catacombs of San Sebastiano** are almost next to each other on the Via Appia Antica. San Callisto is open from 8.30 am to noon and 2.30 to 5 pm (closed Wednesday). San Sebastiano is open from Friday to Wednesday, 9 am to noon and 2.30 to

5 pm. Admission to each costs L8000 and is with a guide only.

Vatican City After the unification of Italy, the Papal States of central Italy became part of the new Kingdom of Italy, causing a considerable rift between church and state. In 1929, Mussolini, under the Lateran Treaty, gave the pope full sovereignty over what is now the Vatican City.

The tourist office, in Piazza San Pietro to the left of the basilica, is open daily from 8.30 am to 7 pm. Guided tours of the Vatican City can be organised here. A few doors up is the Vatican Post Office, said to offer a much more reliable service than the normal Italian postal system. It is open Monday to Friday from 8.30 am to 7 pm and until 6 pm on Saturday (closed Sunday).

The city has its own postal service, currency, newspaper, radio station, train station and army of Swiss Guards.

St Peter's Basilica & Square The most famous church in the Christian world, **San Pietro** stands on the site where St Peter was buried. The first church on the site was built during Constantine's reign in the 4th century, and in 1506 work started on a new basilica, designed by Bramante.

Although several architects were involved in its construction, it is generally held that St Peter's owes more to Michelangelo, who took over the project in 1547 at the age of 72 and was particularly responsible for the design of the dome. He died before the church was completed. The cavernous interior contains numerous treasures, including Michelangelo's superb *Pietà*, sculptured when he was only 25 years old and the only work to carry his signature (on the sash across the breast of the Madonna). It has been protected by bulletproof glass since an attack in 1972 by a hammer-wielding Hungarian.

Bernini's huge, baroque *Baldacchino* (a heavily sculpted bronze canopy over the papal altar) stands 29 metres high and is an extraordinary work of art. Another point of note is the red porphyry disc near the central door, which marks the spot where Charlemagne and later emperors were crowned by the pope.

Entrance to Michelangelo's soaring dome is

to the right as you climb the stairs to the atrium of the basilica. Make the entire climb on foot for L5000, or pay L6000 and take the elevator for part of the way (recommended).

The basilica is open daily from 7 am to 7 pm (6 pm in winter) and dress rules are stringently enforced – no shorts, miniskirts or sleeveless tops. Prams and strollers must be left in a designated area outside the basilica.

Bernini's **Piazza San Pietro** (St Peter's Square) is considered a masterpiece. Laid out in the 17th century as a place for Christians of the world to gather, the immense piazza is bound by two semicircular colonnades, each of which is made up of four rows of Doric columns. In the centre of the piazza is an obelisk that was brought to Rome by Caligula from Heliopolis (in ancient Egypt). When you stand on the dark paving stones between the obelisk and either of the fountains, the colonnades appear to have only one row of columns.

The pope usually gives a public audience at 10 or 11 am every Wednesday in the Papal Audience Hall. To attend, you must go to Prefettura della Casa Pontifica (☎ 69 88 30 17), through the bronze doors under the colonnade to the right as you face the basilica. The office is open from Monday to Saturday 9 am to 1 pm. Otherwise apply in writing to the Prefettura della Casa Pontifica, 00120 Città del Vaticano.

Vatican Museums From St Peter's follow the wall of the Vatican City (to the right as you face the basilica) to the museums, or catch the regular shuttle bus (L2000) from the piazza in front of the tourist office. The museums are open Monday to Saturday from 8.45 am to 1 pm. At Easter and during summer they are open to 4 pm. Admission is L15,000. The museums are closed on Sundays and public holidays, but open on the last Sunday of every month from 9 am to 1 pm (free admission, but queues are always very long). Guided visits to the Vatican gardens cost L18,000 and can be booked by calling ☎ 69 88 44 66.

The Vatican museums contain an incredible collection of art and treasures collected by the popes, and you will need several hours to see the most important areas and museums. The Sistine Chapel comes towards the end of a full visit, otherwise you can walk straight there and

then work your way back through the museums.

The **Museo Pio-Clementino**, containing Greek and Roman antiquities, is on the ground floor near the entrance. Through the Tapestry and Map galleries are the **Stanze di Rafaello**, once the private apartment of Pope Julius II, decorated with frescos by Raphael. Of particular interest is the magnificent **Stanza della Segnatura**, which features Raphael's masterpieces *The School of Athens* and *Disputation on the Sacrament*.

From Raphael's Rooms, go down the stairs to the sumptuous **Appartamento Borgia**, decorated with frescos by Pinturicchio, then go down another flight of stairs to the **Sistine Chapel**, the private papal chapel built in 1473 for Pope Sixtus IV. Michelangelo's wonderful frescos of the *Creation* on the barrel-vaulted ceiling and *Last Judgment* on the end wall have both been recently restored. It took him four years, at the height of the Renaissance, to paint the ceiling. Twenty-four years later he painted the extraordinary *Last Judgment*. The other walls of the chapel were painted by artists including Botticelli, Ghirlandaio, Pinturicchio and Signorelli.

Organised Tours

Walk Through the Centuries (☎ 323 17 33), Via Silla 10, offers walking tours of the city's main sights for L25,000 per person. Bus No 110 leaves from Piazzo dei Cinquecento, in front of Stazione Termini, for a three-hour tour of the city. The cost is L15,000. Vastours (☎ 481 43 09), Via Piemonte 34, operates half-day coach tours of Rome from L43,000 and full-day coach tours of the city from L110,000, as well as tours to Tivoli, the Castelli Romani and other Italian cities. American Express (☎ 676 41) in Piazza di Spagna, and the CIT office in Piazza della Repubblica also offer guided tours of the city.

Special Events

Although Romans desert their city in summer, particularly in August, when the weather is relentlessly hot and humid, cultural and musical events liven up the place. The Comune di Roma coordinates a diverse series of concerts, performances and events throughout summer under the general title Estate Romana (Roman Summer). The series usually features major international performers. Information is published in Rome's daily newspapers. A jazz festival is held in July and August in the Villa Celimontana, a park on top of the Celian Hill (access from Piazza della Navicella). The Festa de' Noantri is held in Trastevere in the last two weeks of July in honour of Our Lady of Mt Carmel. Street stalls line Viale di Trastevere, but head for the back streets for live music and street theatre. The Festa di San Giovanni is held on 23 and 24 June in the San Giovanni district of Rome and features much dancing and eating in the streets. Part of the ritual is to eat stewed snails and suckling pig.

At Christmas the focus is on the many churches of Rome, each setting up its own Nativity scene. Among the most renowned is the 13th-century crib at Santa Maria Maggiore. During Holy Week, at Easter, the focus is again religious and events include the famous procession of the cross between the Colosseum and the Palatine on Good Friday, and the Pope's blessing of the city and the world in St Peter's Square on Easter Sunday.

The Spanish Steps become a sea of pink azaleas during the Spring Festival in April.

Places to Stay

Camping About 15 minutes from the centre by public transport is *Village Camping Flaminio* (☎ 333 26 04), at Via Flaminia 821. It costs L13,000 per person and L12,400 for a site. Tents and bungalows are available for rent. From Stazione Termini catch bus No 910 to Piazza Mancini, then bus No 200 to the camping ground. At night, catch bus No 24N from Piazzale Flaminio (just north of Piazza del Popolo).

Hostel The HI *Ostello Foro Italico* (☎ 323 62 67), Viale delle Olimpiadi 61, costs L23,000 a night, breakfast and showers included. Take Metro Linea A to Ottaviano, then bus No 32 to Foro Italico. The head office of the Italian Youth Hostels Association (☎ 487 11 52) is at Via Cavour 44, 00184 Rome. It will provide information about all the hostels in Italy. You can also join HI here.

Hotels & Pensioni There is a vast number of cheap hotels and pensioni in Rome, concentrated mainly to the north-east and south-west

of Stazione Termini. The private tourist office, Enjoy Rome (see the earlier Tourist Offices section), will book you a room, but if you want to go it alone, either phone ahead or check your bags in and walk the streets to the left and right of the station. The area south-west is crowded, noisy and swarms with thieves and pickpockets who prey on newly arrived tourists. It can be unpleasant and dangerous, particularly for women at night, so it is important always to remain extremely alert. The area north-east is quieter and somewhat safer.

North-East of Stazione Termini To reach the pensioni in this area, head to the right as you leave the train platforms onto Via Castro Pretorio. *Pensione Giamaica* (☎ 49 01 21), Via Magenta 13, has OK singles/doubles for L40,000/65,000 and triples at L25,000 per person. Nearby at Via Magenta 39 is the excellent *Fawlty Towers* (☎ 445 03 74), which offers hostel-style accommodation at L25,000 per person, or L27,000 with private shower. Run by the people at Enjoy Rome, it offers lots of information about Rome and added bonuses are the sunny terrace and satellite TV.

Nearby in Via Palestro there are several reasonably priced pensioni. *Pensione Restivo* (☎ 446 21 72), Via Palestro 55, has reasonable singles/doubles for L60,000/100,000, including the cost of showers. A triple is L27,000 per person. There is a midnight curfew. In the same building, *Albergo Mari* (☎ 446 21 37) has singles/doubles for L45,000/70,000. A good choice is *Hotel Positano* (☎ 49 03 60), Via Palestro 49, which has very pleasant rooms for L80,000/100,000 with bathroom. *Pensione Katty* (☎ 444 12 16), Via Palestro 35, has basic singles/doubles for up to L55,000/70,000. Around the corner at Viale Castro Pretorio 25 is *Pensione Ester* (☎ 495 71 23) with comfortable doubles for L70,000 and L90,000 for a triple.

At Via San Martino della Battaglia 11, are three good pensioni in the same building. The *Pensione Lachea* (☎ 495 72 56) has large, newly renovated doubles/triples for L60,000/80,000. *Hotel Pensione Dolomiti* (☎ 49 10 58) has singles/doubles for L44,000/55,000; a triple is L25,000 per person. *Albergo Sandra* (☎ 445 26 12), Via Villafranca 10 (which runs between Via Vicenza and Via San Martino della

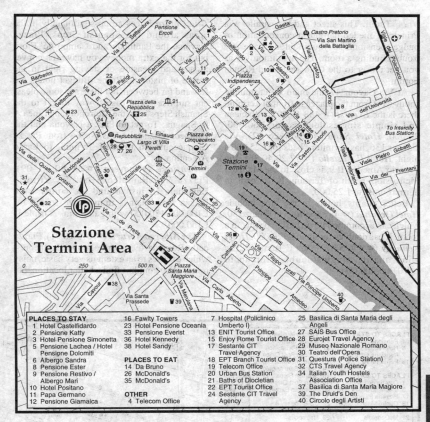

Stazione Termini Area

0   250   500 m

PLACES TO STAY
1 Hotel Castelfidardo
2 Pensione Katty
3 Hotel Pensione Simonetta
5 Pensione Lachea / Hotel
  Pensione Dolomiti
6 Albergo Sandra
8 Pensione Ester
9 Pensione Restivo /
  Albergo Mari
10 Hotel Positano
11 Papa Germano
12 Pensione Giamaica

16 Fawlty Towers
23 Hotel Pensione Oceania
33 Pensione Everist
36 Hotel Kennedy
38 Hotel Sandy

PLACES TO EAT
14 Da Bruno
26 McDonald's
35 McDonald's

OTHER
4 Telecom Office

7 Hospital (Policlinico
  Umberto I)
13 ENIT Tourist Office
15 Enjoy Rome Tourist Office
17 Sestante CIT
  Travel Agency
18 EPT Branch Tourist Office
19 Telecom Office
20 Urban Bus Station
21 Baths of Diocletian
22 EPT Tourist Office
24 Sestante CIT Travel
  Agency

25 Basilica di Santa Maria degli
  Angeli
27 SAIS Bus Office
28 Eurojet Travel Agency
29 Museo Nazionale Romano
30 Teatro dell'Opera
31 Questura (Police Station)
32 CTS Travel Agency
34 Italian Youth Hostels
  Association Office
37 Basilica di Santa Maria Maggiore
39 The Druid's Den
40 Circolo degli Artisti

Battaglia), is clean, with dark but pleasant rooms. Singles/doubles cost L50,000/70,000, including the cost of a shower. *Hotel Pensione Simonetta* (☎ 444 13 02), across from Piazza dell'Indipendenza at Via Palestro 34, has decent rooms for L70,000/85,000.

Papa Germano (☎ 48 69 19), at Via Calatafimi 14a, is one of the more popular budget places in the area. It has singles/doubles for L40,000/65,000, or L50,000/80,000 with private bathroom.

Hotel Castelfidardo (☎ 446 46 38), Via Castelfidardo 31, off Piazza Indipendenza, is one of Rome's better one-star pensioni. It has singles/doubles for L50,000/65,000 and triples

for L28,000 per person, or L38,000 per person with private bathroom. *Pensione Stella* (☎ 444 10 78), Via Castelfidardo 51, is a friendly establishment, with decent rooms for L40,000/ 60,000. Across Via XX Settembre, at Via Collina 48 (a 10-minute walk from the station) is *Pensione Ercoli* (☎ 474 54 54) with singles/ doubles for L43,000/60,000 and triples for L80,000.

West of Stazione Termini This area is decidedly seedier, but prices remain the same. As you exit to the left of the station, follow Via Gioberti to Via G Amendola, which becomes

Via F Turati. This street and the parallel Via Principe Amedeo harbour a concentration of budget pensioni, so you shouldn't have any trouble finding a room. The area improves as you get closer to the Colosseum and Roman Forum.

At Via Cavour 47, the main street running south-west from the piazza in front of Termini, there is the *Everest* (☎ 488 16 29), with clean and simple singles/doubles for L60,000/90,000. *Hotel Sandy* (☎ 445 26 12), Via Cavour 136, has dormitory beds for L25,000 a night. *Hotel Il Castello* (☎ 77 20 40 36), Via Vittorio Amedeo II 9, is close to the Manzoni Metro stop, south of Termini. It has beds in dorm rooms for L25,000.

Better quality hotels in the area include *Hotel Oceania* (☎ 482 46 96), Via Firenze 50, which can accommodate up to five people in a room. It has doubles for up to L170,000. *Hotel Kennedy* (☎ 446 53 73), Via F Turati 62, has good quality singles/doubles for up to L110,000/200,000.

City Centre Prices go up significantly in the areas around the Spanish Steps, Piazza Navona, the Pantheon and Campo de' Fiori, but for the extra money you have the convenience and pleasure of staying right in the centre of historical Rome. Budget hotels are few and far between, but there are some pleasant surprises. The easiest way to get to the Spanish Steps is on the Metropolitana Linea A to Spagna. To get to Piazza Navona and the Pantheon area, take Bus No 64 from Piazza Cinquecento, in front of Termini, to Largo Argentina.

Pensione Primavera (☎ 68 80 31 09), Piazza San Pantaleo 3 on Via Vittorio Emanuele II, just around the corner from Piazza Navona, has immaculate rooms for L100,000/130,000 with bathroom. A triple is L150,000.

The *Albergo Abruzzi* (☎ 679 20 21), Piazza della Rotonda 69, overlooks the Pantheon – which excuses to an extent its very basic, noisy rooms. You couldn't find a better location, but

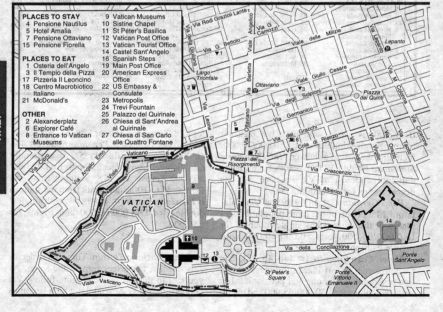

it is expensive at L83,000/110,000 for singles/ doubles. Triples are L150,000. Bookings are essential throughout the year at this popular hotel. *Pensione Mimosa* (☎ 68 80 17 53; fax 683 35 57), Via Santa Chiara 61 (off Piazza della Rotonda), has very pleasant singles/ doubles for L65,000/95,000. The owner imposes a strict no-smoking rule in the rooms.

The *Albergo del Sole* (☎ 654 08 73), Via del Biscione 76, off Campo de' Fiori, has expensive singles/doubles at L85,000/115,000 – but it's in a great location. Around the corner is *Albergo della Lunetta* (☎ 687 76 30; fax 689 20 28), Piazza del Paradiso 68, which charges L50,000/90,000 for singles/doubles, or L70,000/130,000 with private shower. Reservations are essential at both hotels.

The *Albergo Pomezia* (☎ & fax 686 13 71) at Via dei Chiavari 12 (which runs off Via dei Giubbonari from Campo de' Fiori) has doubles/triples for L100,000/130,000, breakfast included. Use of the communal shower is free.

Near the Spanish Steps is *Pensione Fiorella* (☎ 361 05 97), Via del Babuino 196; singles/ doubles cost L55,000/89,000, including breakfast.

Near St Peter's & the Vatican Bargains do not abound in this area, but it is comparatively quiet and still reasonably close to the main sights. Bookings are an absolute necessity because rooms are often filled with people attending conferences and so on at the Vatican. The simplest way to reach the area is on the Metropolitana Linea A to Ottaviano. Turn left into Via Ottaviano, and Via Germanico is a short walk away. Bus No 64 from Termini stops at St Peter's – walk away from the basilica along Via di Porta Angelica, which becomes Via Ottaviano after Piazza del Risorgimento, a five-minute walk.

The best bargain in the area is *Pensione Ottaviano* (☎ 39 73 72 53), Via Ottaviano 6, near Piazza Risorgimento. It has beds in dormitories for L25,000 per person. The owner

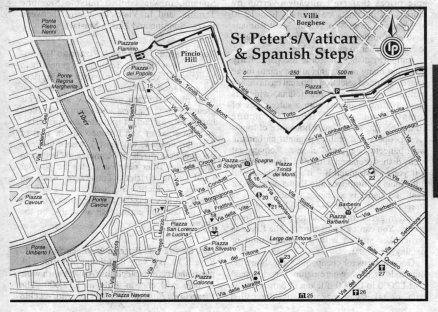

speaks good English. *Hotel Pensione Nautilus* (☎ 324 21 18), Via Germanico 198, offers basic doubles/triples for L90,000/L130,000 or L100,000/L140,000 with private bathroom (no singles). *Hotel Amalia* (☎ 39 72 33 56), Via Germanico 66 (near the corner of Via Ottaviano), has a beautiful courtyard entrance and clean, sunny rooms. Singles/doubles are L80,000/100,000 and include breakfast and use of the communal shower.

Rental Accommodation Apartments near the centre of Rome are expensive, so expect to pay around L2,000,000 a month. A good way to find a shared apartment is to buy *Wanted in Rome* or *Metropolitan*, two English-language fortnightly magazines which publish both classified advertisements and information about what's on in the city. Enjoy Rome (see Tourist Offices) can also help.

Places to Eat
Rome bursts at the seams with trattorias, pizzerias and restaurants – the trick is to locate an establishment that serves good food at reasonable prices that isn't already overrun by tourists. Eating times are generally from 12.30 to 3 pm and from 8 to 11 pm. Most Romans head out for dinner around 9 pm, so it's better to arrive earlier to claim a table.

Antipasto dishes in Rome are particularly good and many restaurants allow you to make your own mixed selection. Typical pasta dishes include: bucatini all'Amatriciana, which is large, hollow spaghetti with a salty sauce of tomato and *pancetta* (bacon); penne all'arrabbiata, which has a hot sauce of tomatoes, peppers and chilli; spaghetti carbonara, with pancetta, eggs and cheese. Romans eat many dishes prepared with offal. Try the paiata – if you can stomach it – it's pasta with veal intestines. Saltimbocca alla Romana (slices of veal and ham) is a classic meat dish, as is straccetti con la rucola, fine slices of beef tossed in garlic and oil and topped with fresh rocket. You can't go past carciofi alla Romana (artichokes stuffed with garlic and mint or parsley) in winter.

Good options for cheap, quick meals are the hundreds of bars, where panini (sandwiches) cost L2000 to L4000 if taken *al banco* (at the bar), or takeaway pizzerias, usually called *pizza a taglio*, where a slice of freshly cooked pizza, sold by weight, can cost as little as L2000. Bakeries are numerous and are another good choice for a cheap snack. Try a huge piece of pizza bianca, a flat bread resembling focaccia, costing from around L2000 a slice (sold by weight). Try *Paladini*, Via del Governo Vecchio 29, for sandwiches and *Pizza a Taglio*, Via Baullari, between Campo de' Fiori and Corso Vittorio Emanuele II, for takeaway pizza.

For groceries and supplies of cheese, prosciutto, salami and wine, shop at alimentari. For fresh fruit and vegetables there are numerous outdoor markets, notably the lively daily market in Campo de' Fiori. Other, cheaper food markets are held in Piazza Vittorio Emanuele, near the station, and in Via Andrea Doria, near Largo Trionfale, north of the Vatican. The huge wholesale food markets are in Via Ostiense, some distance from the centre, and are open to the public Monday to Saturday from 10 am to 1 or 2 pm.

But, if all you really want is a Big Mac, you'll find McDonald's outlets in Piazza della Repubblica (with outside tables), Piazza di Spagna, in Via Giolitti outside Stazione Termini, and in Viale Trastevere (between Piazza Sonnino and Piazza Mastai).

Restaurants, Trattorias & Pizzerias The restaurants near Stazione Termini are generally to be avoided if you want to pay reasonable prices for good food – although there are some great little places hidden away. The side streets around Piazza Navona and Campo de' Fiori harbour many budget trattorias and pizzerias, and the areas of San Lorenzo (to the east of Termini, near the university), where you can get the best pizza in Rome, and Testaccio (across the Tiber near Piramide) are popular local eating districts. Trastevere offers an excellent selection of rustic eating places hidden in tiny piazzas, and pizzerias where it doesn't cost the earth to sit at a table on the street.

City Centre The *Pizzeria Montecarlo*, Vicolo Savelli 12, is a very traditional pizzeria, with paper sheets for tablecloths. A pizza with wine or beer will cost as little as L15,000. The *Pizzeria da Baffetto*, Via del Governo Vecchio

11, on the corner of Via Sora, is a Roman institution. Expect to join a queue if you arrive after 9 pm and don't be surprised if you end up sharing a table. Funnily enough, for all this, the pizzas are nothing to write home about. Pizzas cost around L9000, a litre of wine costs L9000 and the coperto is only L1500. Further along the street at No 18 is a tiny, nameless *osteria* run by Antonio Bassetti, where you can eat an excellent, simple meal for around L20,000. There's no written menu, but don't be nervous – the owner/waiter will explain slowly (in Italian). Back along the street towards Piazza Navona, at Piazza Pasquino 73, is *Cul de Sac 1*, which has pleasant light meals at reasonable prices.

Trattoria Pizzeria da Francesco, Piazza del Fico 29, has good pasta dishes for around L12,000, as well as pizzas for L7000 to L14,000 and a good range of antipastos and vegetables. *Pizzeria Il Leoncino*, Via del Leoncino 28, going from Piazza Navona towards the Spanish Steps, has good pizzas at low prices. *Centro Macrobiotico Italiano*, Via della Vite 14, is a vegetarian restaurant. It charges an annual membership fee (which reduces as the year goes by), but tourists can usually eat there and pay only a small surcharge.

There are several small restaurants in the Campo de' Fiori. *Hostaria Romanesca* is tiny, so arrive early in winter. In summer there are numerous tables outside. A dish of pasta will cost around L10,000, a full meal around L25,000.

Along Via Giubbonari, off Campo de' Fiori, is *Filetti di Baccalà* in the tiny Largo dei Librari, which serves only deep-fried cod fillets for around L4000 and wine for L6000 a litre. Across Via Arenula, in the Jewish quarter, is *Sora Margherita*, Piazza delle Cinque Scole 30. It serves traditional Roman and Jewish food and a full meal will cost around L25,000.

Near the Trevi Fountain, in Vicolo Scanderbeg, you'll find *Piccolo Arancio*, which offers reasonable food at around L9000 for a first course and L9000 to L15,000 for a secondo. Most of the restaurants in this area are either high class and very expensive, or tourist traps.

West of the Tiber On the west bank of the Tiber, good-value restaurants are concentrated in Trastevere and the Testaccio district, past Piramide. Many of the establishments around St Peter's and the Vatican are geared for tourists and can be very expensive. There are, however, some good options. Try *Il Tempio della Pizza*, Viale Giulio Cesare 91, or *Osteria dell'Angelo*, Via G Bettolo 24, along Via Leone IV from the Vatican City, although this place can be difficult to get into.

In Trastevere's maze of tiny streets you will find any number of pizzerias and cheap trattorias. The area is beautiful at night and most establishments have outdoor tables. It is very popular, so arrive before 8.30 pm if you don't want to join a queue for a table.

Try *Frontoni*, on Viale di Trastevere, opposite Piazza Mastai, for fantastic panini made with pizza bianca. *D'Augusto*, Piazza dei Renzi, just around the corner from the Basilica Santa Maria in Trastevere (turn right as you face the church and walk to Via della Pelliccia), is one of the cheapest spots in town. The food might be average, but the atmosphere, especially in summer with tables outside in the piazza, is as traditionally Roman as you can get. A meal with wine will cost around L20,000. *Pizzeria Ivo*, Via di San Francesco a Ripa 158, has outdoor tables. It's popular with tourists, but the pizzas could be bigger for the price (from around L9000).

A much better pizza is to be had at *Pizzeria da Vittorio*, Via San Cosimato 14a. It is tiny and you have to wait if you arrive after 9 pm, but the atmosphere is great. A bruschetta, pizza and wine will cost around L15,000. *Da Lucia*, Vicolo del Mattinato 2, is more expensive at around L35,000 a full meal, but the food is good and the owners are delightful.

You won't find a cheaper, noisier, more chaotic pizzeria in Rome than *Pizzeria Remo*, Piazza Santa Maria Liberatrice 44, in Testaccio. *Il Canestro*, Via Maestro Giorgio, Testaccio, specialises in vegetarian food and is relatively expensive. *Augustarello*, Via G Branca 98, off the piazza, specialises in the very traditional Roman fare of offal dishes. The food is reasonable and a meal will cost around L20,000.

San Lorenzo District & between Termini & the Forum You will find typical local fare and good pizzas at prices students can afford at *Pizzeria l'Economica*, Via Tiburtina 44.

Another local favourite is *Formula 1*, Via degli Equi 13. Pizzas at both cost around L8000.

If you have no option but to eat near Stazione Termini, try to avoid the tourist traps offering overpriced full menus. *Trattoria da Bruno*, Via Varese 29, has great food at reasonable prices – around L8000 for pasta and up to L14,000 for a second course. They serve home-made gnocchi on Thursdays. A decent pizzeria is *Alle Carrette*, Vicolo delle Carrette 14, off Via Cavour near the Roman Forum. A pizza and wine will cost around L12,000. Just off Via Cavour in the tiny Via dell'Angeletto, is *Gli Angeletti*, an excellent little restaurant with prices at the higher end of the budget range. You'll pay around L12,000 for a pasta and around L15,000 for a second course.

Cafés & Bars Remember that prices skyrocket in bars as soon as you sit down, particularly near the Spanish Steps, in the Piazza della Rotonda and in Piazza Navona, where a cappuccino *a tavola* (at a table) can cost L5000 or more. The same cappuccino taken at the bar will cost around L1500 – but passing an hour or so watching the world go by over a cappuccino, beer or wine in any of the above locations can be hard to beat!

For the best coffee in Rome head for *Tazza d'Oro*, just off Piazza della Rotonda in Via degli Orfani, and *Caffè Sant'Eustachio*, Piazza Sant'Eustachio 82. Try the granita di caffè at either one. *Vineria* in Campo de' Fiori, also known as *Giorgio's*, has a wide selection of wine and beers. In summer it has tables outside, but prices are steep – better to stand at the bar. *Bar della Pace*, Via della Pace 3/7, is big with the young 'in' crowd, but 'cool' always has a price. *Bevitoria Navona*, Piazza Navona 72 has wine by the glass. *Bar San Callisto*, Piazza San Callisto, in Trastevere, has outside tables and you don't pay extra to sit down. The crowd is generally pretty scruffy. *The Druid's Den* is a popular Irish pub, which means you can get Guinness and Kilkenny on tap. It's at Via San Martino ai Monti 28, near Santa Maria Maggiore.

Gelati *Giolitti*, Via degli Uffici del Vicario 40, near the Pantheon and *Gelateria della Palma*, around the corner at Via della Maddalena 20, both have a huge selection of flavours. *Fonte della Salute*, Via Cardinale Marmaggi 2-6, in Trastevere, has arguably the best gelati in Rome.

Entertainment

Rome's primary entertainment guide is *Trovaroma*, a weekly supplement in the Thursday edition of the newspaper *La Repubblica*. Considered the bible for what is happening in the city, it provides a comprehensive listing, but in Italian only. The newspaper also publishes a daily listing of cinema, theatre and concerts.

Metropolitan is a fortnightly magazine for Rome's English-speaking community (L1500). It has good entertainment listings and is available at outlets including the Economy Book & Video Center, Via Torino 136 and newsstands in the city centre, including at Largo Argentina. Another excellent guide is *Roma C'è*, available at newspaper stands.

For information on Internet cafés see the earlier Rome, Post & Communications section.

Exhibitions & Concerts From November to May, opera is performed at the *Teatro dell'Opera*, Piazza Beniamino Gigli (☎ 481 70 03). A season of concerts is held in October and November at the *Accademia di Santa Cecilia*, Via della Conciliazione 4, and the *Accademia Filarmonica*, Via Flaminia 118. A series of concerts is held from July to the end of September at the *Teatro Marcello*, Via Teatro di Marcello 44, near Piazza Venezia. For information call ☎ 482 74 03.

Rock concerts are held throughout the year and are advertised on posters plastered all over the city. For information and bookings, contact the ORBIS agency (☎ 475 14 03) in Piazza Esquilino near Stazione Termini.

Nightclubs Nightclubs and discotheques are popular during winter. Among the more interesting and popular Roman live music clubs is *Radio Londra*, Via di Monte Testaccio 67, in the Testaccio area. Although entry is free, you might find it hard to get in here because the bouncers tend to pick and choose, but give it a try anyway. In the same street are the more sedate music clubs *Caruso Caffè* at No 36 and *Caffè Latino* at No 96, both generally offering jazz or blues. More jazz and blues can be heard at *Alexanderplatz*, Via Ostia 9, and *Big Mama*, Via San Francesco a Ripa 18, in Trastevere.

Metropolis, Via Rasella 5, near Piazza Barberini, is a rock club which often stages live concerts by young overseas bands. Membership costs L10,000. *Circolo degli Artisti*, Via Lamarmora 28, near Piazza Vittorio Emanuele, is a lively club, popular among Rome's 'cool' set.

Roman discos are outrageously expensive. Expect to pay up to L30,000 to get in (although women are often allowed in free of charge), which may or may not include one drink. Perennials include: *Alien*, Via Velletri 13; *Piper '90*, Via Tagliamento 9; and *Gilda-Swing*, Via Mario de' Fiori 97. The best gay disco is *L'Alibi*, Via di Monte Testaccio 44.

Cinema The cinema *Pasquino* (☎ 580 36 22), Vicolo del Piede 19, in Trastevere, screens films in English. It is just off Piazza Santa Maria in Trastevere. *Alcazar* (☎ 588 00 99), Via Merry del Val 14, Trastevere, shows an English-language film every Monday.

Things to Buy

The first things that come to mind when thinking of shopping in Rome are clothing and shoes. But it can be difficult to find bargains here, except during the sales.

It is probably advisable to stick to window-shopping in the expensive Ludovisi district, the area around Via Veneto. The major fashion shops are in Via Sistina and Via Gregoriana, heading towards the Spanish Steps. Via Condotti and the parallel streets heading from Piazza di Spagna to Via del Corso are lined with moderately expensive clothing and footwear boutiques, as well as shops selling accessories.

It is cheaper, but not as interesting, to shop along Via del Tritone and Via Nazionale. There are some interesting second-hand clothes shops along Via del Governo Vecchio.

If clothes don't appeal, wander through the streets around Via Margutta, Via Ripetta, Piazza del Popolo and Via Frattina to look at the art galleries, artists' studios and antiquarian shops. Antique shops line Via Coronari, between Piazza Navona and Lungotevere di Tor di Nona.

Everyone flocks to the famous Porta Portese market every Sunday morning. Hundreds of stalls selling anything you can imagine line the streets of the Porta Portese area parallel to Viale di Trastevere, near Trastevere. Here you can pick up a genuine 1960s evening dress for L1000, an antique mirror for L10,000 or a leather jacket for L40,000. Take time to rummage through the piles of clothing and bric-a-brac and you will find some incredible bargains. Catch bus No 280 from Largo Argentina and ask the bus driver where to get off (it's a 10-minute ride).

The market in Via Sannio, near Porta San Giovanni, sells new and second-hand clothes and shoes at bargain prices.

Getting There & Away

Air The main airline offices are in the area around Via Veneto and Via Barberini, north of the station. Qantas, British Airways, Alitalia, Air New Zealand, Lufthansa and Singapore Airlines are all in Via Bissolati. The main airport is Leonardo Da Vinci, at Fiumicino (see the Getting Around section).

Bus The main terminal for intercity buses is in Piazzale Tiburtina, in front of the Stazione Tiburtina. Catch the Metropolitana Linea B from Termini to Tiburtina. Buses connect with cities throughout Italy. Numerous companies, some of which are listed below, operate these services. For information about which companies operate services to which destinations, go to the EPT office, or Enjoy Rome (see Tourist Offices). At Eurojet, Piazza della Repubblica 54, you can buy tickets for and get information about several bus services. Otherwise, there are ticket offices for all of the companies inside the Tiburtina station. COTRAL buses, which service Lazio, depart from numerous points throughout the city, depending on their destinations. Again, the EPT or Enjoy Rome should be able to help.

Some useful bus lines are:

COTRAL – services throughout Lazio – via Ostiense 131 (☎ 722 24 70)
Lazzi – services to other European cities (Eurolines) and the Alps – via Tagliamento 27r (☎ 884 08 40)
Marozzi – services to Bari and Brindisi, as well as to Pompeii, Sorrento and the Amalfi Coast – information at Eurojet

SAIS & Segesta – services to Sicily – Piazza della Repubblica 42 (☎ 481 96 76)
SENA – service to Siena – information at Eurojet
SULGA – services to Perugia and Assisi – information at Eurojet

Train Almost all trains arrive at and depart from Stazione Termini. There are regular connections to all major cities in Italy and throughout Europe. An idea of trip time and cost for intercity trains from Rome (which require the rapido supplement) is as follows: Florence (two hours, L31,500); Milan (five hours, L57,700) and Naples (two hours, L23,000). For train timetable information phone ☎ 4775 (from 7 am to 10.40 pm), or go to the information office at the station (English is spoken). Timetables can be bought at most newsstands in and around Termini and are particularly useful if you are travelling mostly by train. Services at Termini include luggage storage beside tracks 1 and 22 (L5000 per piece for 12 hours), telephones and money exchange (see the Information section). Some trains depart from the stations in Trastevere and at Tiburtina.

Car & Motorcycle The main road connecting Rome to the north and south is the Autostrada del Sole A1, which extends from Milan to Reggio di Calabria. On the outskirts of the city it connects with the Grande Raccordo Anulare (GRA), the ring road encircling Rome. If you are entering or leaving Rome, use the Grande Raccordo and the major feeder roads which connect it to the city; it might be longer, but it is simpler and faster. From the Grande Raccordo there are 33 exits into Rome. If you're approaching from the north, take the Via Salaria, Via Nomentana or Via Flaminia exits. From the south, Via Appia Nuova, Via Cristoforo Colombo and Via del Mare (which connects Rome to the Lido di Ostia) all provide reasonable direct routes into the city. The A12 connects the city to Civitavecchia and to Fiumicino airport.

To rent a car, you will need to be at least 21 years old and have a valid driver's licence. It is cheaper to organise a car from your own country if you want one for a long period. If you have a small child, you can organise to have a baby car seat. It will cost around L46,000 extra for the entire rental period.

Car rental companies in Rome include: Avis (☎ toll-free 1678-6 30 63), Piazza Esquilino 1; Hertz (☎ toll-free 1678-2 20 99), Viale Leonardo da Vinci 421; Europcar (☎ 1678-6 80 88), Via Lombardia 7; and Maggiore (☎ toll-free 1678-6 70 67), Via Po 8. All have offices at Stazione Termini and at both airports. Happy Rent (☎ 481 81 85), Piazza Esquilino 8, rents cars, scooters and bicycles (with baby seats available), as well as videocameras. Another option for scooters and bicycles is I Bike Rome (☎ 322 52 40), Via Veneto 156.

Hitching It is illegal to hitchhike on the autostrade. To head north, wait for a lift on Via Salaria, near the autostrada exit. To go south to Naples, take the Metropolitana to Anagnina and wait in Via Tuscolana. Hitching is not recommended, particularly for women, either alone or in groups.

Boat Tirrenia and FS (state railway) ferries leave from Civitavecchia, near Rome, for various points in Sardinia (see the Sardinia's Getting There & Away section). Bookings can be made at Sestante CIT, or any travel agency displaying the Tirrenia or FS sign. You can also book directly with Tirrenia (☎ 474 20 41), Via Bissolati 41, Rome, or at the *Stazione Marittima* (ferry terminal) at the port in Civitavecchia. Bookings can be made at Stazione Termini for FS ferries.

Getting Around
To/From the Airport The main airport is Leonardo Da Vinci (☎ 65 95 1) at Fiumicino. Access to the city is via the airport-Stazione Termini direct train (follow the signs to the station from the airport arrivals hall), which costs L13,000. The train arrives at and leaves from platform No 22 at Termini and there is a ticket office on the platform. The trip takes 35 minutes. The first train leaves the airport for Termini at 7 am and the last at 10.50 pm. Another train makes stops along the way, including at Trastevere and Ostiense, and terminates at Stazione Tiburtina (L8000). A night bus runs from Stazione Tirburtina (accessible by bus No 42N from Piazza Cinquecento in front of Termini) to the airport. The airport is connected to Rome by an autostrada, accessible from the Grande Raccordo.

ITALY

Taxis are prohibitively expensive from the airport (see Taxi in the main Getting Around section of this chapter).

The other airport is Ciampino, which is used for most domestic and international charter. Blue COTRAL buses (running from 5.45 am to 10.30 pm) connect with the Metropolitana (Linea A at Anagnina), where you can catch the subway to Termini or the Vatican. But, if you arrive very late at night you could end up being forced to catch a taxi. A new metropolitan train line now under construction, which will be known as FM4, will connect the airport with Termini. The airport is connected to Rome by Via Appia Nuova.

Bus The city bus company is ATAC and most of the main buses terminate in Piazza Cinquecento in front of Stazione Termini. Details on which buses head where are available at the ATAC information booth in the centre of the piazza. Another central point for main bus routes in the centre is Largo Argentina, on Corso Vittorio Emanuele south of the Pantheon. Buses run from 6 am to midnight, with limited services throughout the night on some routes.

Travel on Rome's buses, subway and suburban railways has now been linked, and the same ticket is valid for all three. Tickets cost L1500 and are valid for 75 minutes. They must be purchased *before* you get on the bus and validated in the orange machine as you enter. The fine for travelling without a ticket is L50,000, to be paid on the spot, and there is no sympathy for 'dumb tourists'. Tickets can be purchased at any tobacconist, newsstand, or at the main bus terminals. Daily tickets cost L6000, weekly tickets cost L24,000 and monthly tickets are L50,000. ATAC was restructuring many routes in 1996. However, at the time of writing, useful bus numbers to remember were No 64 from Stazione Termini to St Peter's; No 27 from Termini to the Colosseum; No 218 from Piazza di Porta San Giovanni to the catacombs; and No 44 from Piazza Venezia to Trastevere.

Metropolitana The Metropolitana (Metro) has two lines, A and B. Both pass through Stazione Termini. Take Linea A for Piazza di Spagna, the Vatican (Ottaviano) and Villa Borghese (Flaminio), and Linea B for the Colosseum,

Circus Maximus and Piramide (for Testaccio and Stazione Ostiense). Tickets are the same as for city buses (see under Bus in this section). Trains run approximately every five minutes between 6 am and 11.30 pm.

Taxi Taxis are on radio call 24 hours a day in Rome. Cooperativa Radio Taxi Romana (☎ 3570) and La Capitale (☎ 4994) are two of the many operators. Major taxi ranks are at the airports and Stazione Termini and also at Largo Argentina in the historical centre. Remember that there are surcharges on Sunday and for luggage, night service, public holidays and travel to/from Fiumicino airport. The taxi flag fall is L6400 (for the first three km), then L1200 per km. There is a L3000 supplement from 10 pm to 7 am and L1000 from 7 am to 10 pm on Sunday and public holidays. There is a L15,000 supplement on travel to and from Fiumicino airport because it is outside the city limits. This means the fare will cost around L70,000.

Car & Motorcycle Negotiating Roman traffic by car is difficult enough, but be aware that you are taking your life in your hands if you ride a motorcycle in the city. The rule in Rome is to watch the vehicles in front and hope that the vehicles behind are watching you.

Most of the historic centre is closed to normal traffic, although tourists are permitted to drive to their hotels. *Vigili* (traffic police) control the entrances to the centre and will let you through once you mention the name of your hotel. Ask at the hotel for a parking permit for the centre, otherwise you might find a brace on your car wheel or, at worst, that the car has been towed away. If your car goes missing after being parked illegally, check with the traffic police (☎ 6 76 91). It will cost about L180,000 to get it back.

The major parking area close to the centre is at the Villa Borghese. Entrance is from Piazzale Brasile at the top of Via Veneto. There is a supervised car park at Stazione Termini. There are large car parks at Stazione Tiburtina and Piazza dei Partigiani at Stazione Ostiense (both accessible to the centre of Rome by the Metro). The EPT office has a list of cheap car parks on the outskirts of Rome; you can reach the centre by bus or Metro. (See the preceding

ITALY

Getting There & Away section for information about car, scooter and bike rental.)

In Rome, be wary when crossing at traffic lights because most motorcyclists don't stop at red lights. Neither motorcyclists nor motorists are keen to stop at pedestrian crossings, so be extremely careful. The accepted mode of crossing a road is to step into the traffic and walk at a steady pace. If in doubt, follow a Roman.

Around Rome

Rome demands so much of your time and concentration that most tourists forget that the city is part of the region of Lazio. There are some interesting places within easy day-trip distance of the city. In summer, avoid the polluted beaches close to the city and head south to Sabaudia or Sperlonga, or take the train from Ostiense to Lago di Bracciano.

OSTIA ANTICA

The Romans founded this port city at the mouth of the Tiber in the 4th century BC and it became a strategically important centre of defence and trade. It was populated by merchants, sailors and slaves, and the ruins of the city provide a fascinating contrast to a place such as Pompeii. It was abandoned after barbarian invasions and the appearance of malaria, but Pope Gregory IV re-established the city in the 9th century.

The Rome EPT office or Enjoy Rome can provide information about the ancient city.

Things to See & Do

Of particular note in the excavated city are the **Terme di Nettuno**; a **Roman theatre** built by Augustus; the **forum** and **temple**, dedicated to Jupiter, Juno and Minerva; and the **Piazzale delle Corporazioni**, where you can see the offices of Roman merchants, distinguished by mosaics depicting their trades. The site is open from 9 am to about an hour before sunset and entry is L8000.

Getting There & Away

To get to Ostia Antica take the Metropolitana Linea B to Magliana and then the Ostia Lido train (getting off at Ostia Antica).

TIVOLI

Set on a hill by the Anio River, Tivoli was a resort town of the ancient Romans and became popular as a summer playground for the rich during the Renaissance. It is famous today for the terraced gardens and fountains of the Villa d'Este and the ruins of the spectacular Villa Adriana, built by the Roman emperor Hadrian.

The local AAST tourist office (☎ 0774-31 12 49) is in Largo Garibaldi near the COTRAL bus stop.

Things to See & Do

Hadrian built his summer villa, **Villa Adriana**, in the 2nd century AD. Its construction was influenced by the architecture of the famous classical buildings of the day. It was successively plundered by barbarians and Romans for building materials and many of its original decorations were used to embellish the Villa d'Este. However, enough remains to give an idea of the incredible size and magnificence of the villa. You will need about four hours to wander through the vast ruins. Highlights include La Villa dell'Isola (the Villa of the Island), where Hadrian spent his pensive moments, the Imperial Palace and its Piazza d'Oro (Golden Square) and the floor mosaics of the Hospitalia. The villa is open from 9 am to about one hour before sunset, therefore to around 7 pm (last entry at 6 pm) in the warmer months and to around 5 pm in winter. Entry is L8000.

The Renaissance **Villa d'Este** was built in the 16th century for Cardinal Ippolito d'Este on the site of a Franciscan monastery. The villa's beautiful gardens are decorated with numerous fountains, which are its main attraction. Opening hours are the same as for Villa Adriana and entry is L8000. Villa d'Este is closed on Mondays.

Getting There & Away

Tivoli is about 40 km east of Rome and accessible by Cotral bus. Take Metro Linea B from Stazione Termini to Rebibbia; the bus leaves from outside the station every 15 minutes. The bus also stops near the Villa Adriana, about one km from Tivoli. Otherwise, catch local bus No 4 from Tivoli's Piazza Garibaldi to Villa Adriana.

ETRUSCAN SITES

Lazio has several important Etruscan archaeological sites, most within easy reach of Rome by car or public transport. These include Tarquinia (one of the most important cities of the Etruscan League), Cerveteri, Veio and Tuscania. The tombs and religious monuments discovered in the area have yielded the treasures which can now be seen in the large museums, including the Villa Giulia and the Vatican, although the small museums at Tarquinia and Cerveteri are worth visiting.

If you really want to lose yourself in a poetic journey, take along a copy of D H Lawrence's *Etruscan Places*.

Tarquinia

Believed to have been founded in the 12th century BC and to have been the home of the Tarquin kings who ruled Rome before the creation of the republic, Tarquinia was an important economic and political centre of the Etruscan League. The major attractions here are the painted tombs of its necropoli (burial grounds). The AAST tourist information office (☎ 0766-85 63 84) is at Piazza Cavour 1.

Things to See & Do The 15th-century Palazzo Vitelleschi houses the **Museo Nazionale de Tarquinia** and an excellent collection of Etruscan treasures, including frescos removed from the tombs. There are also numerous sarcophagi found in the tombs. The museum is open Tuesday to Sunday from 9 am to 7 pm (closed Monday). Admission costs L8000 and the same ticket admits you to the **necropolis**, a 15 to 20-minute walk away (same opening hours). Ask at the tourist office for directions. Only a small number of the thousands of tombs have been excavated and only a handful are open on any given day. You must wait until a group forms and a guide will then take you on a tour of four to six tombs. Beware of long waits in summer, when thousands of tourists visit the necropolis daily. The tombs are richly decorated with frescos, though many are seriously deteriorated. They are now maintained at constant temperatures to preserve the remaining decorations. This means that it is possible to see them only through glass partitions.

Take the time to wander through the streets of medieval Tarquinia and, if you have a car, ask for directions to the remains of Etruscan Tarquinia, on the crest of the Civita Hill nearby. There is little evidence of the ancient city, apart from a few limestone blocks that once formed part of the city walls. However, a large temple, the **Ara della Regina**, was discovered on the hill and has been excavated this century.

Places to Stay & Eat There is a camping ground by the sea, *Tusca Tirrenia* (☎ 8 82 94), Viale Neriedi. There are no budget options if you want to stay overnight and it can be difficult to find a room if you don't book well in advance. Try the *Hotel all'Olivo* (☎ 85 73 18), Via Togliatti 15, in the newer part of town, about a 10-minute walk downhill from the medieval centre. Rooms with private bath cost L60,000/90,000 for singles/doubles.

For a good, cheap meal, try *Cucina Casareccia*, at Via G Mazzini 5, off Piazza Cavour, or *Trattoria Arcadia* opposite at No 6.

Getting There & Away Buses leave approximately every hour for Tarquinia from Via Lepanto in Rome, near the Metropolitana Linea A Lepanto stop, arriving at Tarquinia a few steps away from the tourist office. You can also catch a train from Ostiense, but Tarquinia's station is at Tarquinia Lido (beach), approximately three km from the centre. You will then need to catch one of the regular local buses.

Cerveteri

Ancient Caere was founded by the Etruscans in the 8th century BC and enjoyed a period of great prosperity as a maritime centre from the 7th to 5th centuries BC. The main attractions here are the tombs known as *tumoli*, great mounds with carved stone bases. Treasures taken from the tombs can be seen in the Vatican Museums, the Villa Giulia Museum and the Louvre. The Pro Loco tourist office is at Piazza Risorgimento 19.

The main necropolis area, **Banditaccia**, is open daily from 9 am to 4 pm in winter and 9 am to 7 pm in summer and entry is L8000. You can wander freely once inside the area, though it is best to follow the recommended routes in order to see the best preserved tombs. Signs detailing the history of the main tombs are in Italian only. Banditaccia is accessible by local

ITALY

bus in summer only from the main piazza in Cerveteri, but it is also a pleasant three-km walk west from the town.

There is also a small **museum** in Cerveteri that contains an interesting display of pottery and sarcophagi. It is in the Palazzo Ruspoli and is open from 9 am to 2 pm (closed Monday). Entry is free.

Cerveteri is accessible from Rome by COTRAL bus from Via Lepanto, outside the Lepanto stop on Metropolitana Linea A.

Northern Italy

Italy's northern regions are its wealthiest and offer many and varied attractions to travellers. A tour of the north could take you from the beaches of the Italian Riviera in Liguria, to Milan for a shopping spree, into Emilia-Romagna to sample its remarkable *cucina* (cuisine), through countless medieval and Renaissance towns and villages, and into the Alps to ski or trek in the Dolomites, before taking a boat trip down the Grand Canal of timeless Venice.

GENOA

Travellers who think of Genoa (Genova) as simply a dirty port town and bypass the city for the coastal resorts don't know what they're missing. This once powerful maritime republic, birthplace of Christopher Columbus (1451-1506) and now capital of the region of Liguria, can still carry the title La Superba (the proud). It is a fascinating city that is full of contrasts. Here you can meet crusty old seafarers in the markets and trattorias of the port area, where some of the tiny streets are so narrow it is difficult for two people to stand together. But go round a corner and you will find young Genoese in the latest Benetton gear strolling through streets lined with grand, black-and-white marble palaces.

Orientation

Most trains stop at both of the main stations in Genoa: Stazione Principe and Stazione Brignole. The area around Brignole is closer to the city centre and offers more pleasant accommodation than does Principe, which is close to the port. Women travelling alone should avoid staying in the port area.

From Brignole walk straight ahead along Via Fiume to get to Via XX Settembre and the historical centre. It is easier to walk around Genoa than to use the local ATM bus service, but most useful buses stop outside both stations.

Information

Tourist Offices There are APT tourist offices at Stazione Principe and at the airport (both open from 8 am to 8 pm Monday to Saturday and 9 am to midday on Sunday) and at Via del Porto Antico (☎ 2 4871) in the Palazzina Santa Maria, open 8.30 am to 6.30 pm seven days a week.

Post & Communications The main post office is in Via Dante, just off Piazza de Ferrari. There is a Telecom office at Stazione Brignole, open from 8 am to 10 pm.

Genoa's postcode is 16100 and its telephone code is ☎ 010.

Medical Services The Ospedale San Martino (☎ 55 51) is in Via Benedetto XV. For an ambulance call ☎ 570 59 51.

Emergency Call ☎ 113 for the police.

Things to See & Do

Start by wandering around the port area, the oldest part of Genoa, to see the huge, 12th-century, black-and-white marble **Cattedrale di San Lorenzo** and the nearby **Palazzo Ducale**, in Piazza Matteotti. In the beautiful, tiny **Piazza San Matteo** are the palaces of the Doria family, one of the most important families of the city in the 14th and 15th centuries. Take a walk along **Via Garibaldi**, which is lined with palaces. Some are open to the public and contain art galleries, including the 16th-century **Palazzo Bianco** and the 17th-century **Palazzo Rosso**, where the Flemish painter Van Dyck lived. Both are open from 9 am to 7 pm Tuesday to Saturday and on Sunday from 9 am to 12.30 pm. Entry to each is L4000.

Take the kids to the **aquarium** (Europe's biggest and well worth a visit) to see the sharks, dolphins, penguins and myriad other marine life. Located on Ponte Spinola, it opens from

9.30 am to 7 pm Tuesday, Wednesday and Friday and 9.30 am to 8.30 pm Thursday, Saturday and Sunday.

Places to Stay

The HI *Ostello Genova* (☎ 242 24 57), is at Via Costanzi 120, at Righi, just outside Genoa. Bed and breakfast costs L22,000 and a meal is L15,000. Catch bus No 40 from Stazione Brignole. The *Casa della Giovane* (☎ 20 66 32), Piazza Santa Sabina 4, has cheap beds for women only.

Turn right as you leave Stazione Brignole and walk up Via de Amicis to Piazza Brignole. Turn right into Via Gropallo where there are some good hotels in a lovely old palazzo at No 4. *Pensione Mirella* (☎ 839 37 22) has singles/doubles for L37,000/65,000. A shower costs L2000 extra. The *Carola* (☎ 839 13 40) has very pleasant rooms for L45,000/75,000. *Albergo Rita* (☎ 87 02 07), a few doors up at No 8, has recently renovated singles/doubles for L30,000/65,000. *Albergo Vittoria* (☎ 58 15 17), Largo Archimede 1 (turn left as you leave Stazione Brignole), has large rooms for L35,000/45,000.

Places to Eat

Don't leave town without trying pesto genovese (pasta with a sauce of basil, garlic and pine nuts), torta pasqualina (made with artichokes, cheese and eggs), pansoti (ravioli), farinata (a torte made with chickpea flour) and, of course, focaccia. The best deal in town is at *Da Maria*, Vico Testa d'Oro 14, where a full meal is a set L12,000, including wine. Students and old seafarers dine here. *Trattoria Walter*, Vico Colalanza 2r, concentrates on Genoese specialities. Pasta dishes cost from L7000.

Entertainment

The Genoa Theatre Company performs at the *Politeama Genovese* (☎ 89 35 89) and the *Teatro della Corte* (☎ 570 24 72). Its main season is January to May. *Teatro della Tosse in Sant'Agostino* (☎ 29 57 20), Piazza R Negri, has a season of diverse shows from October to May.

Getting There & Away

Air The Cristoforo Colombo international airport at Sestri Ponente, six km west of the city, has regular domestic and international connections. An airport bus service, the Volabus (☎ 59 94 14), leaves from Piazza Verdi, just outside Stazione Brignole and also stops at Stazione Principe.

Bus Buses leave from Piazza della Vittoria for Rome, Florence, Milan and Perugia. Eurolines buses leave from the same piazza for Barcelona, Madrid and Paris. You can make bookings at Geotravels (☎ 58 71 81) in the piazza.

Train Genoa is connected by train to Turin, Milan, Pisa and Rome. For train information call ☎ 28 40 81.

Boat The city's busy port is a major embarkation point for ferries to Sicily, Sardinia and Corsica. Major companies are: Corsica Ferries (for Corsica), Piazza Dante 1 (☎ 59 33 01); Moby Lines (for Corsica), Ponte Asserato (☎ 25 27 55); and Tirrenia (for Sicily and Sardinia), at the Stazione Marittima, Ponte Colombo (☎ 275 80 41). For more information, see the Getting There & Away sections under Sicily and Sardinia, and under Corsica in the France chapter.

RIVIERA DI LEVANTE

This coastal area of the region of Liguria from Genoa to La Spezia, on the border with Tuscany, has a spectacular beauty to rival that of the Amalfi Coast. It also has several resorts which, despite attracting thousands of summer tourists, manage to remain unspoiled. The region's climate means that both spring and autumn can bring suitable beach weather.

The telephone code is ☎ 0185.

There are tourist offices in most of the towns, including at Santa Margherita (☎ 78 74 85), Via XXV Aprile, between the station and the sea, and at Camogli (☎ 77 10 66), Via XX Settembre 33, just as you leave the station. They will advise on accommodation.

Things to See & Do

Santa Margherita Ligure, a pretty resort town noted for its orange blossoms, is a good base from which to explore the area.

From Santa Margherita, the resorts of **Portofino**, a haunt of the rich and famous, and **Camogli**, a fishing village turned major resort

ITALY

town (but which still manages to look like a fishing village), are a short bus ride away. The fascinating fishing village of **San Fruttuoso** and its medieval Benedictine monastery are also close by.

Easily accessible by train are the beautiful **Cinque Terre**, literally meaning Five Lands. These five coastal towns (Monterosso, Vernazza, Corniglia, Manarola and Riomaggiore) are linked by walking tracks along the coast. Make a point of walking from Monterosso to Riomaggiore (about five hours).

Places to Stay & Eat
There are some excellent options in Santa Margherita. The *Albergo Nuovo Riviera* (☎ 28 74 03), in an old villa at Via Belvedere 10, has singles/doubles for L45,000/60,000 or doubles with private shower for L70,000. It also offers half and full board, which is compulsory in the high season. Full board is L70,000 per person. The friendly owners impose a strict no-smoking rule in the hotel's public areas. *Albergo Annabella* (☎ 28 65 31), Via Costasecca 10, has large, bright rooms for L45,000/65,000. Triples are L90,000.

In Camogli try the *Albergo la Camogliese* (☎ 77 14 02), Via Garibaldi 55, on the seafront. Some rooms have balconies and views and prices are graded accordingly. The cheapest rooms cost L60,000/90,000 a single/double. Full board in the high season is L90,000.

In Santa Margherita, *Trattoria San Siso*, at Corso Matteotti 137 (about 10 minutes from the seafront), has great food at low prices, with a full meal costing around L20,000. Try the panzotti, which are small ravioli in a walnut sauce.

Getting There & Away
The entire coast is served by train and all points are accessible from Genoa. From Santa Margherita, Camogli and the Cinque Terre are both accessible by train. Buses leave from Santa Margherita's Piazza Martiri della Libertà for Portofino. You can walk to San Fruttuoso from either Portofino or Camogli.

Boats leave from near the bus stop in Santa Margherita for Portofino (L9000 return), San Fruttuoso (L23,000 return) and the Cinque Terre (L35,000 return).

TURIN
Turin (Torino) is the capital of the Piedmont region. The House of Savoy, which ruled this region for hundreds of years (and Italy until 1945), built for itself a gracious baroque city. Its grandeur is often compared to that of Paris. Italy's industrial expansion began here with companies like Fiat and Olivetti.

Orientation & Information
The Porta Nuova train station is the point of arrival for most travellers. To reach the city centre walk straight ahead over the main east-west route, Corso Vittorio Emanuele II, through the grand Piazza Carlo Felice and along Via Roma until you come to Piazza San Carlo. The APT tourist office (☎ 011-53 51 81) is at Via Roma 226. There is a smaller office at the main train station and both are open Monday to Saturday from 9 am to 7.30 pm.

Things to See & Do
In Piazza San Carlo, known as Turin's drawing room, are the baroque churches of **San Carlo** and **Santa Cristina**, the latter designed by Filippo Juvarra. **Piazza Castello**, the centre of historical Turin, features the sumptuous **Palazzo Madama**, once the residence of Victor Amadeo I's widow Marie Cristina, and the **Museo Civico di Arte Antica**. Nearby is the **Palazzo Reale** (Royal Palace), an austere 17th-century building. Its gardens were designed in 1697 by Louis le Nôtre, whose other works include the gardens at Versailles.

The **Cattedrale di San Giovanni**, west of the Palazzo Reale, off Via XX Settembre, houses the **Shroud of Turin**, the linen cloth which some believed was used to wrap the crucified Christ. Scientists have been able to categorically establish that the shroud is simply not that old – instead it dates back to somewhere around the 12th century. The actual shroud is in the **Cappella della Santa Sindone** (Chapel of the Holy Shroud), topped by Guarini's honeycomb-like, black marble dome, while a copy adorns the walls of a nearby chapel.

Places to Stay & Eat
Cheap rooms can be hard to find. Call the APT in advance for a suggestion, although the staff won't make a reservation.

Campeggio Villa Rey (☎ 819 01 17), Strada Val San Martino Superiore 27, is open from March to October. The *Ostello Torino* (☎ 660 29 39), Via Alby 1, on the corner of Via Gatti, is in the hills east of the Po River and can be reached by bus No 52 from the Porta Nuova station. Bed and breakfast is L18,000 and a meal is L14,000.

The *Canelli* (☎ 54 60 78), Via San Dalmazzo 5b, off Via Garibaldi, has singles/doubles for L25,000/35,000. The *Albergo Magenta* (☎ 54 26 49), Corso Vittorio Emanuele II 67, has singles/doubles for L45,000/60,000.

One of the better self-service restaurants is *La Grangia*, Via Garibaldi 21, where you can eat a full meal for around L14,000. At *Pizzeria alla Baita dei 7 Nani*, Via A Doria 5, you can have a pizza and a beer for around L10,000. For excellent gelati, head for *Caffé Fiorio*, Via Po 8, and try the gianduia.

Getting There & Away
Turin is serviced by Caselle international airport (☎ 567 63 61), with flights to European and national destinations. The SADEM bus company (☎ 30 16 16) runs a service to the airport every 30 minutes from the bus station at Corso Inghilterra 3. Intercity buses also terminate here. Buses serve the Aostan valley, most of the towns and ski resorts in Piedmont and major Italian cities. Regular trains connect with Milan, Aosta, Venice, Genoa and Rome.

Getting Around
The city is well serviced by a network of buses and trams. A map of public transport routes is available from the APT.

AROUND TURIN
The main attractions of the Piedmont region are the Alps, including the **Parco Nazionale del Gran Paradiso** and the beautiful natural reserve around **Monte Rosa** in the far north. Walkers can tackle sections of the Grande Traversata delle Alpi, a 200-km track through the Alps, running from the Ligurian border to Lago Maggiore on the border with Lombardy. Information is available at Turin's APT office. Wine-lovers can visit the vineyards around **Asti**, a pleasant town in the Monferrato hills, which gives its name to Italy's best known sparkling wine, Asti Spumante.

MILAN
The economic and fashion capital of Italy, Milan (Milano) has long been an elegant and cultural city. Its origins are believed to be Celtic, but it was conquered by the Romans in 222 BC, and later became an important trading and transport centre. From the 13th century the city flourished under the rule of two powerful families: the Visconti and later the Sforza.

Orientation
From Milan's central train station (Stazione Centrale), it is simple to reach the centre of town and other major points on the efficient Milan underground (known as the MM, or Metropolitana). The MM3 will take you from the station to the Duomo and the centre of town. The city of Milan is huge, but most sights are in the centre. Use the Duomo and the Castello Sforzesco, at the other end of Via Dante, as your points of reference. The main shopping areas and sights are around and between the two.

Note that Milan closes down almost completely in August, when most of the city's inhabitants take their annual holidays. You will find few restaurants and shops open at this time.

Information
Tourist Offices The main branch of the APT (☎ 80 96 62) is at Via Marconi 1, in Piazza del Duomo, where you can pick up the useful *Milan is Milano*, one of the most comprehensive city guides in Italy. It is open Monday to Saturday from 8 am to 7 pm and Sunday and public holidays from 9 am to 12.30 pm and 1.30 to 5 pm. There is a branch office (open the same hours) at the Stazione Centrale.

Milan City Council operates an information office in Galleria V Emanuele II, just off Piazza del Duomo, Monday to Saturday from 8 am to 8 pm.

Foreign Consulates You will find the consulates of the following countries in Milan: Australia (☎ 77 70 41), Via Borgogna 2; Canada (☎ 675 81), Via Vittorio Pisani 19; France (☎ 655 91 41), Via Mangili 1; the UK (☎ 72 30 01), Via San Paolo 7; and the USA (☎ 29 03 51), Via P Amadeo 2/10.

ITALY

PLACES TO STAY
5 Hotel Italia
6 Albergo Salerno
7 Hotel Verona
8 Hotel Due Giardini
10 Hotel Nettuno
12 Hotels Kennedy &
    San Tomaso
14 Hotel Tris
22 Albergo Commercio
32 Hotel Nuovo
41 Hotel Speronari

PLACES TO EAT
13 Ciao
18 Bar Assodi Cuori
26 Ciao
30 Luini
31 Ristorante Di Gennaro
33 Ciao
34 Trattoria da Bruno
38 Peck Delicatessan
42 Pizzeria Dogana
43 Ciao
47 Popeye
49 Berlin Caffè

OTHER
1 Stazione Centrale, Tourist
   Information Office &
   Telecom Telephones
2 Piazza Duca d'Aosta

3 Stazione Centrale
   Metro Station
4 Piazza Caiazzo &
   Caiazzo Metro Station
9 Piazza Lima
11 Piazza della Repubblica
15 Piazza G Oberdan
16 Porta Venezia
   Metro Station
17 Piazza Cavour
19 Questura (Police Station)
20 Piazza San Marco
21 Palazzo Brera
23 Castello Sforzesco
24 Piazzale Cadorna
25 Cairoli Metro Station &
   Largo Cairoli
27 Piazza della Scala
28 La Scala Opera House
29 Piazza San Babila & San
   Babila Metro Station
35 Duomo
36 Galleria Vittorio Emanuele
   II & Telecom Telephones
37 Piazza del Duomo &
   Duomo Metro Station
39 Piazza Cordusio
40 Post Office
44 APT Tourist Office
45 Piazza Diaz
46 Underground Parking
48 Hospital

Milan
(Milano)

ITALY

0   250   500 m

Money Banks in Milan are open Monday to Friday from 8.30 am to 1.30 pm and from 3 to 4 pm. Exchange offices open at weekends include Banca Ponti, Piazza del Duomo 19, from 8.30 am to 1 pm Saturday. There are also exchange offices open seven days a week at the Stazione Centrale. The American Express office (☎ 72 00 36 94) is at Via Brera 3 and opens Monday to Thursday from 9 am to 5.30 pm and Friday to 5 pm.

Post & Communications The main post office is at Via Cordusio 4, off Via Dante, near Piazza del Duomo. Fermo Posta is here, open Monday to Friday from 8.15 am to 7.40 pm and Saturday to 3.30 pm. There are also post offices at the station and at Linate airport.

There are Telecom telephone offices at the central station (open daily from 8 am to 9.30 pm – telephone directories are here for all of Italy, Europe and the Mediterranean) and in Galleria V Emanuele II, open daily from 8 am to 9.30 pm.

Telecom has been changing telephone numbers in Milan for some years. If you have problems call ☎ 12 (they speak Italian only).

Milan's postcode is 20100 and its telephone code is ☎ 02.

Bookshops The American Bookstore, Via Campiero 16, has a good selection of English-language books.

Medical Services For an ambulance call ☎ 77 33 and for emergency first-aid call the Italian Red Cross on ☎ 38 83. If you need a hospital, the Ospedale Maggiore Policlinico (☎ 551 35 18) is at Via Francesco Sforza 35, close to the centre. There is an all-night pharmacy in the Stazione Centrale (☎ 669 09 35).

Emergency In an emergency call the police on ☎ 113 or ☎ 112. The *questura centrale* (police headquarters) office for foreigners is at Via Montebello (☎ 62 26 34 00). They speak English. For lost property call the Milan City Council (☎ 551 61 41).

Dangers & Annoyances Milan's main shopping areas are popular haunts for local groups of thieves. They are as numerous here as in Rome and also lightning fast. They use the same technique of waving cardboard or newspaper in your face to distract your attention while they head for your pockets or purse. Be particularly careful in the piazza in front of the Stazione Centrale – it is a major haunt of thieves who prey on tourists.

Things to See & Do
Start with the extraordinary **Duomo**, commissioned by Gian Galeazzo Visconti in 1386. The first glimpse of this spiky, tumultuous structure, with its marble façade shaped into pinnacles, statues and pillars, is certainly memorable.

Walk through the graceful **Galleria Vittorio Emanuele II** to **La Scala**, Milan's famous opera house. The theatre's **museum** is open Monday to Saturday from 9 am to midday and 2 to 6 pm, and on Sunday from 9.30 am to 12.30 pm and 2.30 to 6 pm. Admission is L5000.

At the end of Via Dante is the huge **Castello Sforzesco**, which was originally a Visconti fortress but was entirely rebuilt by Francesco Sforza in the 15th century. Its museums contain an interesting collection of sculpture, including Michelangelo's *Pietà Rondanini*. It is open Tuesday to Sunday from 9.30 am to 5.30 pm. Admission is free.

Nearby in Via Brera is the 17th-century **Palazzo di Brera**, which houses the **Pinacoteca di Brera**. This gallery's vast collection of paintings includes Mantegna's masterpiece, the *Dead Christ*. The gallery is open Tuesday to Saturday from 9 am to 5.30 pm and Sunday from 9 am to 12.30 pm. Admission is L8000.

An absolute must is Leonardo da Vinci's *Last Supper*, in the Cenacolo Vinciano, next to the **Chiesa di Santa Maria delle Grazie**, noted for Bramante's tribune. The *Last Supper* was restored in 1995, but centuries of damage from floods, bombing and decay have left their mark. The building is open Tuesday to Saturday from 8 am to 1.45 pm. Admission is L12,000.

Special Events
St Ambrose's Day (7 December) is one of Milan's major festivals, and features a traditional street fair near the Basilica di Sant'Ambrogio, off Via Carducci.

Places to Stay
Hostels The HI *Ostello Piero Rotta* (☎ 39 26

ITALY

70 95), Viale Salmoiraghi 2, is north-west of
the city centre. Bed and breakfast is L23,000.
Take the MM1 to the QT8 stop. The place is
closed from 9 am to 5 pm and lights out is 12.30
am. *Protezione della Giovane* (☎ 29 00 01 64),
Corso Garibaldi 123, is run by nuns for women
aged 16 to 25 years. Beds cost from L26,000 a
night.

Hotels Milan's hotels are among the most
expensive and heavily booked in Italy, so it's
strongly recommended that you book in
advance. There are numerous budget hotels
around Stazione Centrale, but quality varies.
The tourist office will make bookings, which
hotels will hold for one hour.

Stazione Centrale & Corso Buenos Aires
The *Nettuno* (☎ 29 40 44 81), Via Tadino 27
(turn right off Via D Scarlatti, which is to the
left as you leave the station), is a 10-minute
walk away. It has basic singles/doubles for
L44,000/64,000. A triple with bathroom is
L120,000.

In Via Vitruvio, to the left off Piazza Duca
d'Aosta as you leave the station, there are two
budget options. The *Albergo Salerno* (☎ 204
68 70) at No 18 has very clean singles/doubles
for L40,000/60,000 – an extra L20,000 with
bathroom. The *Italia* (☎ 669 38 26) at No 44
has less attractive rooms for L45,000/65,000.
The *Due Giardini* (☎ 29 52 10 93), Via
Lodovico Settala 46, has very comfortable
singles/doubles for L60,000/80,000 and triples
for L108,000, as well as a communal garden.
The *Verona* (☎ 66 98 30 91), at Via Carlo
Tenca 12, near Piazza della Repubblica, has
rooms for L50,000/80,000 with TV and telephone.

At Viale Tunisia 6, just off Corso Buenos
Aires, there are several hotels. The *Hotel
Kennedy* (☎ 29 40 09 34) has reasonable
singles/doubles for L60,000/80,000. A double
with private bathroom is L120,000 and triples
with bathroom are L40,000 per person. Bookings are accepted. The *Hotel San Tomaso*
(☎ 29 51 47 47) has small, clean singles/
doubles for L50,000/80,000 and triples for
L35,000 per person.

Closer to the centre, off Piazza G Oberdan,
is the quaint *Hotel Tris* (☎ 29 40 06 74), at Via

Sirtori 26. It has appealing doubles/triples with
private shower for L80,000/105,000.

The Centre The *Albergo Commercio* (☎ 86
46 38 80), Via Mercato 1, has very basic
singles/doubles with shower for L50,000/
60,000. From Piazza Cordusio walk down Via
Broletto, which becomes Via Mercato. The
entrance to the hotel is around the corner in Via
delle Erbe.

Very close to Piazza del Duomo is the *Hotel
Speronari* (☎ 86 46 11 25), Via Speronari 4,
which is eccentrically decorated but comfortable. Singles/doubles are L60,000/80,000. The
Hotel Nuovo (☎ 86 46 05 42) at Piazza Becca-
ria 6, is in a great location just off Corso
Vittorio Emanuele II and the Duomo. Singles/
doubles cost L50,000/65,000.

Places to Eat
Italians say that the cucina of Lombardy
(Lombardia) is designed for people who don't
have time to waste because they are always in
a hurry to get to work. In Milan, traditional
restaurants are being replaced by fast-food
outlets and sandwich bars as the favoured
eating places. Try the bar snacks laid in many
bars around 5 pm.

Restaurants Avoid the area around the station
and head for Corso Buenos Aires and the
centre.

Around Stazione Centrale Ciao, Corso
Buenos Aires 7, is part of a chain (there are
others in Corso Europa, Piazza del Duomo and
at Via Dante 5), but the food is first-rate and
relatively cheap. Pasta dishes cost around
L5000 and excellent salads go for around
L3000. *Ristorante Primavera d'Oriente*, Via
Palestrina 13, offers a standard Chinese meal
from L16,000.

City Centre The first time the Milanese tasted
pizza it was cooked at *Ristorante Di Gennaro*,
Via S Radegonda 3, though today there is not
much to set this place above others in the city.
The *Trattoria da Bruno*, Via Cavallotti 15, off
Corso Europa, has a set-price lunch for
L17,000. *Pizzeria Dogana*, on the corner of
Via Capellari and Via Dogana, also near the
Duomo, has outside tables. Pasta and pizza

each cost around L9000 and there's a good selection of contorni.

Popeye, Via San Tecla 8, near the Duomo, is reputed to have the best pizza in Milan. A pizza costs around L7000 to L10,000 and a full meal will come to around L25,000 or more.

Cafés & Sandwich Bars One of Milan's oldest fast-food outlets is **Luini**, Via S Radegonda 16, just off Piazza del Duomo. A popular haunt of teenagers and students, it sells panzerotti, similar to calzone (a savoury turnover made with pizza dough) but stuffed with tomatoes, garlic and mozzarella. They cost L3000.

Berlin Caffè, Via G Mora 9 (to the left off Corso Porta Ticinese, near Largo Carròbbio), has a small menu at night (L12,000 for one dish). Otherwise it is a pleasant place for coffee or wine.

A good sandwich bar is **Bar Assodi Cuori**, Piazza Cavour (where you can sit down for no extra charge). Not far from Stazione Centrale is **Pattini & Marinoni**, at Corso Buenos Aires 53, which sells bread, and also pizza by the slice.

For gourmet takeaway head for **Peck**. Its rosticceria is at Via Cesare Cantù 11, where you can buy cooked meats and vegetables. Another outlet is at Via Spadari 9 (near the Duomo).

Entertainment

Music, theatre and cinema dominate Milan's entertainment calendar. The opera season at **La Scala** opens on 7 December. For tickets go to the box office (☎ 55 18 13 77), but don't expect a good seat unless you book well in advance. There is also a summer season, which features operas, concerts and ballet.

In March/April and October/November organ concerts are performed at the Church of San Maurizio in the Monastero Maggiore, at Corso Magenta 15, the continuation of Via Meravigli. In April/May there is a jazz festival, Città di Milano, and in summer the city stages Milano d'Estate, a series of concerts, theatre and dance performances.

The main season for theatre and concerts starts in October. Full details of all events are available from the tourist office in Piazza del Duomo. For details on cinema read the listings

section in the daily newspaper *Corriere della Sera*.

Things to Buy

Every item of clothing you ever wanted to buy, but could never afford, is in Milan. The main streets for clothing, footwear and accessories are behind the Duomo around Corso Vittorio Emanuele II. You can window-shop for high-class fashions in Via Borgospesso and Via della Spiga.

The areas around Via Torino, Corso Buenos Aires and Corso XXII Marzo are less expensive. Markets are held in the areas around the canals (south-west of the centre), notably on Viale Papiniano on Tuesday and Saturday morning. A flea market is held in Viale Gabriele d'Annunzio each Saturday.

Getting There & Away

Air International flights use Malpensa airport, about 50 km north-west of Milan. Domestic and European flights use Linate airport, about seven km east.

Bus Bus stations are scattered throughout the city, although some major companies use Piazza Castello as a terminal. Check with the APT for assistance.

Train Regular trains go to Venice, Florence (and Bologna), Genoa, Turin and Rome, as well as major cities throughout Europe. For train timetable information go to the busy office in the station (they speak English), open 7 am to 11 pm or call ☎ 67 50 01.

Car & Motorcycle Milan is the major junction of Italy's motorways, including the Autostrada del Sole (A1) to Rome, the Milano-Torino (A5) and the Serenissima (A4) for Verona and Venice, and the A8 and A9 north to the lakes and the Swiss border.

All these roads meet with the Milan ring road, known as the Tangenziale Est and Tangenziale Ovest (the east and west bypasses). From here follow the signs which lead into the centre. The A4 in particular is an extremely busy road, where there are numerous accidents that can hold up traffic for hours. In winter all roads in the area become extremely hazardous because of rain, snow and fog.

ITALY

Getting Around

To/From the Airports STAM airport shuttle buses leave from Piazza Luigi di Savoia, on the east side of Stazione Centrale, for Malpensa airport (from 5.15 am to 10.15 pm, tickets L18,000) and for Linate airport (from 5.40 am to 9 pm, tickets L6000) every half-hour.

Bus & Metro Milan's public transport system is extremely efficient. The underground (MM) has three lines. The red MM1 provides the easiest access to the city centre. It is necessary to take the green MM2 from Stazione Centrale to Loreto metro station to connect with the MM1. The yellow MM3 also passes through Stazione Centrale and has a station in Piazza del Duomo. It's the easiest way to get around, but buses and trams are also useful. Tickets for the MM are L1500, valid for one underground ride and/or 75 minutes on buses and trams.

You can buy tickets in the MM stations, as well as at authorised tobacconists and newspaper stands.

Taxi Taxis won't stop if you hail them in the street – head for the taxi ranks, all of which have telephones. A few of the radio taxi companies serving the city are Radiotaxidata (☎ 53 53), Esperia (☎ 83 88) and Autoradiotaxi (☎ 85 85).

Car & Motorcycle Normal traffic is banned in the city centre from Monday to Friday 7.30 am to 6 pm, although tourists travelling to their hotels are allowed to enter. The city is dotted with expensive car parks (look for the blue sign with a white P). A cheaper alternative is to use one of the supervised car parks at the last stop on each MM line. Hertz, Avis, Maggiore and Europcar all have offices at Stazione Centrale.

MANTUA

Legend, perpetuated by Virgil and Dante, claims that Mantua (Mantova) was founded by the soothsayer Manto, daughter of Tiresias. Virgil was, in fact, born in a nearby village in 70 AD. From the 14th to the 18th century the city was ruled by the Gonzaga family, who embellished the town with their palaces and employed artists such as Andrea Mantegna and Pisanello to decorate them with their paintings

and frescos. You can easily see the city on a day trip from Milan, Verona or Bologna.

Information

The tourist office, Piazza Andrea Mantegna, is a 10-minute walk from the station along Corso Vittorio Emanuele, which becomes Corso Umberto 1. It is open from Monday to Saturday 9 am to noon and 3 to 6 pm.

Mantua's telephone code is ☎ 0376.

Things to See & Do

Start with the **Piazza Sordello**, which is surrounded by impressive buildings including the **cattedrale**, a strange building that combines a Romanesque tower, baroque façade and Renaissance interior. The piazza is dominated by the **Palazzo Ducale**, a huge complex of buildings, and seat of the Gonzaga family. There is much to see in the palace, in particular the Gonzaga **apartments** and art collection, and the famous **Camera degli Sposi** (Bridal Chamber), decorated with frescos by Andrea Mantegna in the 15th century. In the **Sala del Pisanello** (Pisanello's Room) are frescos by the Veronese painter (discovered in 1969 under two layers of plaster), depicting the cycle of chivalry and courtly love, which were. The palace is open Monday to Saturday from 9 am to 1 pm, 2.30 to 4.30 pm, and Sunday 9 am to 1 pm. Admission is L10,000.

Don't miss the **Palazzo Te**, the lavishly decorated summer palace of the Gonzaga. It is open Tuesday to Sunday from 9 am to 6 pm. Admission is L10,000. Take bus No 5 from the centre to the palace.

Places to Stay & Eat

The HI *Ostello per la Gioventù* (☎ 37 24 65) is just out of town at Lunetta San Giorgio. Take bus No 2M from the station. Bed and breakfast is L15,000. There is a *camping ground* next to the hostel which charges L4000 per person and L3500 for a tent space. Both are open from April to October.

At the *Albergo Roma Vecchia* (☎ 32 21 00), Via Corridoni 20, doubles cost L42,000. It is closed during August and part of December.

Self Service Nuvolari, Piazza Viterbi 11, is a self-service place with good food and cheap prices. *Caà Ramponi*, Piazza Broletto 7, offers pasta and pizza at reasonable prices. You could also buy fresh produce from the market in nearby Piazza Broletto and have a picnic in Piazza Virgiliana.

Getting There & Away
Mantua is accessible by train and bus from Verona (about 40 minutes), and by train from Milan and Bologna with a change at Modena.

VERONA
Forever associated with Romeo and Juliet, Verona has much more to offer than the relics of a tragic love story. Known as *la piccola Roma* (little Rome) for its importance as a Roman city, its golden era was during the 13th and 14th centuries, under the rule of the della Scala (also referred to as Scaliger) family. This was a period noted for the savage family feuding on which Shakespeare based his play.

Old Verona is small, but there is much to see and it is a popular base for exploring surrounding towns.

Orientation & Information
It's easy to find your way around Verona. Buses leave for the centre from outside the train station; otherwise walk to the right, past the bus station, cross the river and walk along Corso Porta Nuova to Piazza Brà. From there take Via Mazzini and turn left at Via Cappello to reach Piazza delle Erbe.

The main tourist office is at Via Leoncino 61 (☎ 59 28 28), on the corner of Piazza Brà facing the Roman Arena (open 8 am to 7 pm). There are branches at the train station (open 8 am to 6 pm) and at Piazza delle Erbe 42 (open only in summer from 8 am to 7 pm).

The main post office is at Piazza Viviani. The Ospedale Civile Maggiore (☎ 807 11 11) is at Piazza A Stefani.

Verona's telephone code is ☎ 045.

Things to See & Do
The pink-marble Roman amphitheatre, known as the **Arena**, in Piazza Brà, was built in the 1st century and is now Verona's opera house. Walk along Via Mazzini to Via Cappello and **Juliet's House** (Casa di Giulietta), its entrance smothered with lovers' graffiti. Further along the street to the right is **Porta Leoni**, one of the gates to the old Roman Verona; **Porta Borsari**, the other gate to the city, is north of the Arena at Corso Porta Borsari.

In the other direction is **Piazza delle Erbe**,

the former site of the Roman forum. Lined with the characteristic pink-marble palaces of Verona, the piazza today remains the lively centre of the city, but the permanent market stalls in its centre detract from its beauty. In the piazza is the **Fountain of Madonna Verona**. Just off the square is the elegant **Piazza dei Signori**, flanked by the Renaissance **Loggia del Consiglio**; the della Scala (Scaliger) residence now known as the **Governor's Palace** and partly decorated by Giotto; and the medieval town hall. Take a look at the **Duomo**, on Via Duomo, for its Romanesque main doors and Titian's *Assumption*.

Places to Stay & Eat
The HI *Ostello Villa Francescatti* (☎ 59 03 60), Salita Fontana del Ferro 15, should be your first choice. Bed and breakfast is L17,000 a night (including sheets) and a meal is L12,000. An HI or student card is necessary. Next door is a *camping ground*. To reserve a space, speak to the hostel management. Catch bus No 2 from the station to Piazza Isolo and then follow the signs.

The *Casa della Giovane* (☎ 59 68 80), Via Pigna 7, just off Via Garibaldi, is for women only and costs L25,000 or L30,000 a night for a bed in a small dormitory. Catch bus No 2 and ask the driver where to get off.

Albergo Castello (☎ 800 44 03), Corso Cavour 43, has singles/doubles for L30,000/48,000. *Albergo Ciopeta* (☎ 800 68 43), Vicolo Teatro Filarmonico 2, near Piazza Brà, has doubles for up to L100,000.

Known for its fresh produce, its crisp soave (a dry white wine) and its boiled meat, Verona offers delicious food at reasonable prices. In Piazza Brà, with a view of the Arena, is *Brek*, a good bet for cheap meals, with pasta dishes starting from around L6000. The *Pizzeria Liston*, Via dietro Liston 19, has good pizzas for around L8000. A full meal will cost around L24,000.

Entertainment
Throughout the year the city hosts musical and cultural events. These culminate in the season of opera and drama that runs from July to September at the *Arena* (tickets from around L40,000). There is a lyric-symphonic season in winter at the 18th-century *Teatro Filarmonico* (☎ 800 28 80), Via dei Mutilati 4, just off

ITALY

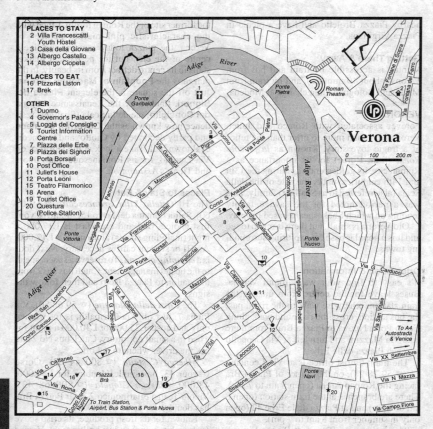

PLACES TO STAY
2 Villa Francescatti
   Youth Hostel
3 Casa della Giovane
13 Albergo Castello
14 Albergo Ciopeta

PLACES TO EAT
16 Pizzeria Liston
17 Brek

OTHER
1 Duomo
4 Governor's Palace
5 Loggia del Consiglio
6 Tourist Information
   Centre
7 Piazza delle Erbe
8 Piazza dei Signori
9 Porta Borsari
10 Post Office
11 Juliet's House
12 Porta Leoni
15 Teatro Filarmonico
18 Arena
19 Tourist Office
20 Questura
   (Police Station)

Piazza Brà, and Shakespeare is performed in the Roman Theatre in summer. Information and tickets for these events are available at the Ente Lirico Arena di Verona (☎ 800 51 51), Piazza Brà 28.

Getting There & Away
The Verona-Villafranca airport (☎ 51 30 39) is just outside the town and accessible by bus and train.

The main APT bus terminal is in the piazza in front of the station, an area known as Porta Nuova. Buses leave for surrounding areas, including Mantua, Ferrara and Brescia.

Verona is on the Brenner Pass railway line to Austria and Germany. It is directly linked by train to Milan, Venice, Florence and Rome.

The city is at the intersection of the Serenissima A4 (Milan-Venice) and the Brennero A22 autostrade.

Getting Around
There is an APT bus to the airport, which leaves from Porta Nuova and from Piazza Cittadella, off Corso Porta Nuova near Piazza Brà. Bus Nos 2 and 8 connect the station with Piazza Brà and No 32 with Piazza delle Erbe. A ticket costs L14000 and is valid for one hour. Otherwise it's a 15-minute walk along Corso Porta Nuova.

If you arrive by car, you should have no trouble reaching the centre. Simply follow the *centro* signs. There are also signs marking the directions to most hotels. There's a free car park in Via Città di Nimes (near the train station).

PADUA

Although famous as the city of St Anthony and for its university, which is one of the oldest in Europe, Padua (Padova) is often merely seen as a convenient and cheap place to stay while visiting Venice. The city, however, offers a rich collection of art treasures and its many piazzas and arcaded streets are a pleasure to explore.

Orientation & Information

From the train station it's a 10-minute walk to reach the centre of town, or you can take bus No 10 along Corso del Popolo, which becomes Corso Garibaldi, to the historical centre.

There is a tourist office at the station, open Monday to Saturday from 9.30 am to 5.30 pm and Sunday from 9 am to noon. There you can pick up a map, a list of hotels and other useful information.

The post office is at Corso Garibaldi 33 and there's a telephone office nearby at No 7, open 9 am to midday and 4 to 6 pm.

Padua's postcode is 35100 and its telephone code is ☎ 049.

Things to See & Do

Thousands of pilgrims arrive in Padua every year to visit the **Basilica del Santo** in the hope that St Anthony, patron saint of Padua and of lost things, will help them find whatever it is they are looking for. The saint's tomb is in the church along with important art works, including 14th-century frescos and bronze sculptures by Donatello which adorn the high altar. A bronze equestrian statue, known as the *Gattamelata* (Honeyed Cat), also by Donatello, is outside the basilica.

The **Cappella degli Scrovegni** is in the Giardini dell'Arena, off Piazza Eremitani. The interior walls of the chapel were completely covered in frescos by Giotto in the 14th century. Depicting the life of Christ and ending with the *Last Judgment*, the 38 panels are considered one of the greatest works of figurative art of all time. The chapel is open daily from 9 am to 7 pm. The **Palazzo della**

Ragione (Law Courts) is remarkable for its sloping roof and loggias; inside is the enormous, entirely frescoed **salon**, containing a huge wooden horse built for a joust in 1466.

A special L15,000 ticket (L10,000 for students) allows entry to the city's main monuments and you can buy it at any of the main sights. Since entry to the Scrovegni Chapel alone is L10,000, it's worth the price.

Places to Stay & Eat

Padua has no shortage of budget hotels, but they fill up quickly in summer. The non-HI *Ostello della Città di Padova* (☎ 875 22 19) is at Via A Aleardi 30. Bed and breakfast is L19,000. Take bus No 3, 8 or 12 from the station to Prato della Valle (a piazza about five minutes away) and then ask for directions. The *Verdi* (☎ 875 57 44), Via Dondi dell'Orologio 7, has basic and clean singles/doubles for L39,000/52,000 and is located in the university district off Via Verdi. The *Pavia* (☎ 66 15 58) at Via dei Papafava 11 has slightly dingy singles/doubles for L35,000/45,000. Follow Corso del Popolo until it becomes Via Roma and then turn right into Via Marsala.

Daily markets are held in the piazzas around the Palazzo Ragione, with fresh produce sold in Piazza delle Erbe and Piazza della Frutta, and bread, cheese and salami sold in the shops

Trattoria Voglia Di, Via Umberto, just before Prato della Valle, serves an excellent meal for around L20,000. It also has a bar where you can get a sandwich. A cheap but not very atmospheric place to eat a meal is the self-service restaurant, *Brek*, in Piazza Cavour, under the porticoes.

Getting There & Away

Padua is directly linked by train to Milan, Venice and Bologna and is easily accessible from most other major cities. Regular buses serve Venice, Milan, Trieste and surrounding towns. The terminal is in Piazzale Boschetti, off Via Trieste, near the station. There is a large public car park in Prato della Valle, a massive piazza near the Basilica del Santo.

VENICE

Perhaps no other city in the world has inspired the superlatives heaped upon Venice (Venezia) by great writers and travellers through the centuries. It was, and remains, a

ITALY

phenomenon – La Serenissima, the Most Serene Republic.

The secret to seeing and discovering the romance and beauty of Venice is to *walk*. Parts of Dorsoduro and Castello are devoid of tourists even in the high season (July to September). You could become lost for hours in the narrow winding streets between the Accademia and the station, where the signs pointing to San Marco and the Rialto never seem to make any sense – but what a way to pass the time!

After the fall of the Western Roman Empire, as waves of barbarians poured across the Alps, the people of the Veneto cities fled to the islands of the coastal lagoon. The waters that today threaten its existence once protected the city. Following years of Byzantine rule, Venice evolved into a republic ruled by a succession of doges (chief magistrates of the republic), a period of independence which lasted 1000 years. It was the point where East met West, and the city eventually grew in power to dominate the entire Mediterranean, the Adriatic and the trade routes to the Levant. It was from here that Marco Polo set out on his voyage to China.

Today, most of Venice is under restoration and this, together with the annual winter floods (caused by high tides) and soaring property values, make it increasingly unattractive as a place of residence. Most of the 'locals' in fact live in industrial Mestre, which is linked to the city by the four-km-long bridge across the lagoon. A project to install massive floodgates at the main entrances to the lagoon has been approved by the Italian government, but work has been delayed by the country's seemingly endless political turmoil. The floodgates would be designed to protect the city from disaster-level floods. This and other projects to 'save' Venice are supported by local and international bodies.

Orientation

Venice is built on 117 small islands and has some 150 canals and more than 400 bridges. Only three bridges cross the Grand Canal (Canale Grande): the Rialto, the Accademia

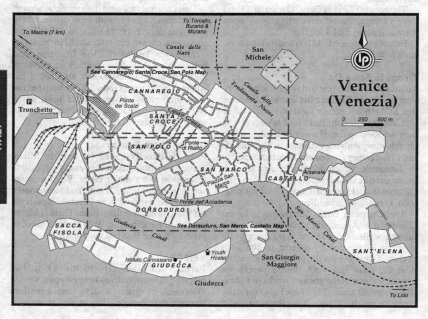

and the Scalzi at the train station. The city is divided into six *sestieri* (sections): Cannaregio, Castello, San Marco, Dorsoduro, San Polo and Santa Croce. The streets are called *calle*, *ruga* or *salizzada*; little side streets can be called *caletta* or *ramo*; a street beside a canal is a *fondamenta*; a canal is a *rio*; and a quay is a *riva*. The only square in Venice called a *piazza* is San Marco – all the others are called a *campo*. On maps, you will find the following abbreviations: Cpo for Campo, Sal for Salizzada, cl for Calle, Mto for Monumento and Fond for Fondamenta.

If all that isn't confusing enough, Venice also has its own style of street numbering. Instead of a system based on individual streets, there is instead a long series of numbers for each sestiere. There are no cars in the city and all public transport is via the canals, on *vaporetti*. To cross the Grand Canal between the bridges, use a *traghetto* (basically a public gondola) – a cheaper mode of transport than the tourist gondolas. Signs will direct you to the various traghetto points. The other mode of transportation is *a piedi* (on foot). To walk from the *ferrovia* (train station) to San Marco along the main thoroughfare, Lista di Spagna (whose name changes several times), will take a good half-hour – follow the signs to San Marco. From San Marco the routes to other main areas, such as the Rialto, the Accademia and the ferrovia, are well signposted but can be confusing, particularly in the Dorsoduro and San Polo areas.

The free map provided by the tourist office (see the following section) provides only a vague guide to the complicated network of streets. Pick up a cheap de Agostini map, simply titled *Venezia*, which lists all street names with map references.

Information

Tourist Offices There is an information office of the APT at the train station, open Monday to Saturday from 8 am to 7.30 pm. The main office (☎ 529 87 30) is in the Palazzetto Selva in the ex Giardini Reale. From Piazza San Marco, walk to the waterfront and turn right – the office is about 100 metres ahead. The staff will give you a map and list of hotels and will help you find a room.

Young people can buy a Rolling Venice card (L5000), which offers significant discounts on food, accommodation and entry to museums and galleries. It is available at the Assessorato all Gioventù, Corte Contarina 1529, just west of Piazza San Marco.

Foreign Consulates There is a British Consulate (☎ 522 72 07) at Palazzo Querini near the Accademia, Dorsoduro 1051. The French Consulate (☎ 522 23 92) is on the Fondamenta Zattere at Dorsoduro 1397.

Money Banks are always the most reliable places to change money and they offer the best rates. Most of the main banks have branches in the area around the Rialto and San Marco. After hours, the American Express office, Salizzada San Moisè (exit from the western end of Piazza San Marco onto Calle Seconda dell'Ascensione) will exchange money without charging commission. Normal opening hours are weekdays from 9 am to 5.30 pm and Saturday to 12.30 pm. For card-holders the office also has an ATM. Thomas Cook, in Piazza San Marco, is open Monday to Saturday from 9 am to 6 pm and Sunday from 9 am to 2 pm. There is also a bank at the train station, or you can change money at the train ticket office from 7 am to 8.30 pm daily.

Post & Communications The main post office is at Salizzada del Fontego dei Tedeschi, just near the Ponte di Rialto (Rialto Bridge) on the main thoroughfare to the station. You can buy stamps at window Nos 11 and 12 in the central courtyard. There is a branch post office just off the western end of Piazza San Marco.

A staffed Telecom office next to the main office is open Monday to Friday from 8 am to 12.30 pm and 4 to 7 pm.

Venice's postcode is 30100 and the telephone code is ☎ 041.

Bookshops There is a good selection of English-language guidebooks and general books on Venice at Studium, on the corner of Calle de la Canonica, on the way from San Marco to Castello. San Giorgio, Calle Larga XXII Marzo 2087, west of San Marco, has a good range of English-language books.

Medical Services If you need a hospital, the Ospedale Civili Riuniti di Venezia (☎ 520 56

22) is in Campo SS (Santissimi) Giovanni e Paolo. For an ambulance phone ☎ 523 00 00. Current information on all-night pharmacies is listed in *Un Ospite di Venezia*, available at the tourist offices.

Emergency For police emergencies call ☎ 113. The questura (☎ 520 32 22) is at Fondamenta di San Lorenzo in Castello.

Things to See & Do

Before you visit Venice's main monuments, churches and museums, catch the No 1 vaporetto along the Grand Canal and then go for a long walk around Venice. Start at **San Marco** and head for the **Accademia Bridge** to reach the narrow, tranquil streets and squares of **Dorsoduro** and **San Polo**. In these sestieri you will be able to appreciate just how beautiful and seductive Venice can be. Remember that most museums are closed on Monday.

Piazza & Basilica di San Marco One of the most famous squares in the world, San Marco was described by Napoleon as the finest drawing room in Europe. Enclosed by the basilica, the old Law Courts and the Libreria Vecchia (which houses the Archaeological Museum and the Marciana Library), the piazza hosts flocks of pigeons and tourists, both competing for space in the high season. Stand and wait for the famous bronze *mori* (Moors) to strike the bell of the Law Courts' 15th-century **clock tower**.

The **basilica**, with its elaborately decorated façade, was constructed to house the body of St Mark, which had been stolen from its burial place in Egypt by two Venetian merchants. The saint has been reburied several times in the basilica (at least twice the burial place was forgotten) and his body now lies under the high altar. The present basilica was built in the Byzantine style in the 11th century and richly decorated with magnificent mosaics and other embellishments over the next five centuries. The famous bronze horses which stood above the entrance have been replaced by replicas. The horses were part of Venice's booty from the famous Sack of Constantinople in 1204. The originals are now in the basilica's museum (entry is L3000).

Don't miss the stunning **Pala d'Oro**

(L3000), a gold altarpiece decorated with silver, enamel and precious stones. It is behind the basilica's altar.

In the piazza is the basilica's 99-metre-high freestanding **bell tower**. It was built in the 10th century, but suddenly collapsed on 14 July 1902 and was later rebuilt. It was closed to the public in 1996, but it normally costs L2000 to climb to the top.

Palazzo Ducale The official residence of the doges and the seat of the republic's government, this palace also housed many government officials and the prisons. The original palace was built in the 9th century, and later expanded and remodelled. Visit the **Sala del Maggior Consiglio** to see the paintings by Tintoretto and Veronese. The palace is open daily from 9 am to 7 pm. Admission is L10,000. The **Bridge of Sighs** (Ponte dei Sospiri) connects the palace to the old prisons. This bridge now evokes romantic images, probably because of its association with Casanova, a native of Venice who was incarcerated in the prisons. It was, however, the thoroughfare for prisoners being led to the dungeons.

Galleria dell'Accademia The Academy of Fine Arts contains an important collection of Venetian art, including works by Tintoretto, Titian and Veronese. It is open Wednesday to Monday from 9 am to 2 pm and Tuesday from 9 am to 7 pm, and admission is L12,000. For a change of pace visit the nearby **Collezione Peggy Guggenheim**, once the home of the American heiress. It contains her collection of modern art, including works by Jackson Pollock, Max Ernst, Salvador Dali and Marc Chagall, and is set in a sculpture garden where Miss Guggenheim and her many pet dogs are buried. It is open Wednesday to Sunday from 11 am to 6 pm (closed Tuesday). Admission is L10,000.

Churches On Giudecca Island, the **Chiesa del Redentore** (Church of the Redeemer) was built in the 16th century by the architect Palladio and is the scene of the annual Festa del Redentore (see the Special Events section). The **Chiesa di Santa Maria della Salute** was built at the entrance to the Grand Canal and dedicated to the Madonna after a plague in the

17th century. It contains works by Tintoretto and Titian. Be sure to visit the great Gothic churches **SS Giovanni e Paolo** and the **Frari**.

The Lido Easily accessible by vaporetto No 1, 2 or 82, this thin strip of land, east of the centre, separates Venice from the Adriatic. Once *the* most fashionable beach resort, it is still very popular and it is almost impossible to find a space on its long beach in summer.

Islands The island of **Murano** is the home of Venetian glass. Visit the Glassworks Museum to see the evolution of the famous glassware. **Burano**, despite the constant influx of tourists, is still a relatively sleepy fishing village, renowned for the lace-making of its women residents. Visit the tiny **Torcello** to see the Byzantine mosaics in its cathedral, notably the stunning mosaic of the Madonna in the apse. Excursion boats leave for the three islands from San Marco (L20,000 per hour). If you want to go it alone, vaporetto No 12 goes to all three and costs L4000 one way. It leaves from Fondamenta Nova.

Gondolas These might represent the quintessential romantic Venice, but at around L80,000 for a 50-minute ride they are very expensive. It is possible to squeeze up to five people into one gondola and still pay the same price. Prices are set for gondolas, so check with the tourist office if you have problems.

Organised Tours
Shop around the various travel agencies for the best deals, or try Ital-Travel (☎ 522 91 11), San Marco 72B, under the colonnade at Piazza San Marco's western end. It organises tours of the city on foot or by boat.

Special Events
The major event of the year is the famous Carnevale, held during the 10 days before Ash Wednesday, when Venetians don spectacular masks and costumes for what is literally a 10-day street party.

The Venice Biennale, a major exhibition of international visual arts, is held every odd-numbered year (for the time being), and the Venice International Film Festival is held every September at the Palazzo del Cinema, on the Lido.

The most important celebration on the Venetian calendar is the Festa del Redentore (Festival of the Redeemer), on the third weekend in July, which features a spectacular fireworks display. The regatta storica, a gondola race on the Grand Canal, is held on the first Sunday in September.

Places to Stay
Simply put, Venice is expensive. The average cost of singles/doubles without bath is now L40,000/60,000. The hostel and several religious institutions provide some respite for budget travellers. Hotel proprietors are inclined to inflate the bill by demanding extra for a compulsory breakfast, and, almost without exception, they increase their prices in the high season (usually July to October). It is advisable to make a booking before you arrive. As Venice does not have a traditional street numbering system, the best idea is to ring your hotel when you arrive and ask for specific directions. If you're travelling by car, you can save on car park costs by staying in Mestre.

Camping There are numerous camping grounds, many with bungalows, at Litorale del Cavallino, the coast along the Adriatic Sea, north-east of the city. The tourist office has a full list, but you could try the *Marina di Venezia* (☎ 96 61 46), Via Montello 6, at Punta Sabbioni, which is open from May to September.

Hostels The HI *Ostello Venezia* (☎ 523 82 11) is on the island of Giudecca, at Fondamenta delle Zitelle 86. It is open to members only, though you can buy a card there. Bed and breakfast is L23,000 and full meals are available for L14,000. Take vaporetto No 82 from the station (L4000 one way) and get off at Zitelle. The hostel is closed from 9 am to 2 pm and curfew is at 11.30 pm. *Istituto Canossiano* (☎ 522 21 57), nearby at Fondamenta del Piccolo 428, has dorm beds for women only at L18,000 per night. Take vaporetto No 82 and get of at Sant'Eufemia. The *Ostello Santa Fosca* (☎ 71 57 75), Cannaregio 2372, is about halfway between the station and San Marco. Walk along the Lista di Spagna for about 15 minutes and you will see signs directing you to the hostel. A bed in a dorm costs L23,000. It opens only in June, July and August. *Foresteria Valdese* (☎ 528 67 97), Castello 5150, has dorm beds for L25,000 a night. It also has beds in private rooms for L32,000 per night and two independent apartments at around L100,000 per day – great for families. Take Calle Lunga from Campo Santa Maria Formosa.

Hotels Most of the cheaper hotels are in Cannaregio; places around San Marco and in the Castello, Dorsoduro, San Polo and Santa Croce areas are more expensive.

Cannaregio This is the easiest area to find a bed because of the sheer number of pensioni, locande and alloggi. The *Locanda Antica Casa Carettoni* (☎ 71 62 31) at Lista di Spagna 130, has singles/doubles for L35,000/60,000. Just off the Lista di Spagna, at Calle della Misericordia 358, is *Hotel Santa Lucia* (☎ 71 51 80), in a newer building which has singles/doubles for up to L65,000/100,000. It also has small apartments for up to five people.

Hotel Villa Rosa (☎ 71 65 69), Calle della Misericordia 389, has singles/doubles for L60,000/90,000 and triples for L120,000, all with breakfast included. *Albergo Adua* (☎ 71 61 84) is at Lista di Spagna 233a, about 50 metres past Casa Carettoni on the right. It has slightly shabby but clean singles/doubles for L38,000/53,000 and triples for L80,000.

The *Hotel Rossi* (☎ 71 51 64) is also near the station in the tiny Calle de le Procuratie, off Lista di Spagna, and has singles/doubles for L60,000/90,000. Triples/quads with bathroom cost L120,000/180,000. At *Al Gobbo* (☎ 71 50 01), in Campo San Geremia, sparkling clean doubles are L90,000. In the same piazza at No 283 is the pleasant *Casa Gerotto*, with singles/doubles for L40,000/60,000 and triples for L75,000. Four-bed dorms cost L22,000 per person. In the same building is *Alloggi Calderan* (☎ 71 55 62), with singles/doubles for L40,000/60,000. *Alloggi Biasin* (☎ 72 06 42), Fondamenta di Cannaregio 1252, is just off the Lista di Spagna across the Ponte delle Guglie. Singles/doubles are L30,000/70,000

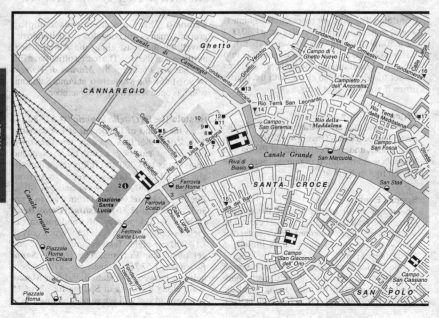

and rooms for three and four are around L30,000 a person. Rooms can be very small.

The **Hotel Minerva & Nettuno** (☎ 71 59 68), Lista di Spagna 230, has decent singles/doubles for L59,000/85,000.

San Marco Although this is the most touristy area of Venice, it has some surprisingly good-quality (relatively) budget pensioni. **Al Gambero** (☎ 522 43 84; fax 520 04 31), Calle dei Fabbri 4587, near Campo San Zulian, has small but pleasant singles/doubles for L61,000/100,000 and triples for L138,000, breakfast included. **Hotel Noemi** (☎ 523 81 44), at Calle dei Fabbri 909, is only a few steps from the piazza and has basic singles/doubles for L55,000/75,000. A triple is L94,000. Check the bed for comfort before accepting a room.

One of the nicest places in this area is **Locanda Casa Petrarca** (☎ & fax 520 04 30), San Marco 4386, which has singles/doubles for L60,000/90,000. Extra beds in a room are an additional 35%. Doubles with bath are L128,000. The friendly owner speaks English.

To get there, find Campo San Luca, go along Calle dei Fusari, then take the second street on the left and turn right into Calle Schiavone.

Castello This area is to the east of Piazza San Marco, and although close to the piazza, is less touristy. The easiest way to get there is to catch the No 1 vaporetto to Castello.

The **Locanda Piave** (☎ 528 51 74), is just off Campo Santa Maria Formosa at Ruga Giuffa 4838/40. Singles/doubles are L65,000/98,000, including breakfast. **Locanda Silva** (☎ 522 76 43), Fondamenta del Rimedio 4423, off Campo SM Formosa towards San Marco, has basic rooms for L50,000/85,000.

Dorsoduro, San Polo & Santa Croce The **Albergo Guerrato** (☎ 522 71 31) is just near the Rialto Bridge at Calle drio la Scimia 240a, to the right off Ruga de Speziale. Singles/doubles cost L95,000/125,000, but it's worth the extra expense. **Hotel Al Gallo** (☎ 523 67 61), Calle Amai 197, off Fondamenta Tolentini, has excellent doubles/triples for L80,000/130,000.

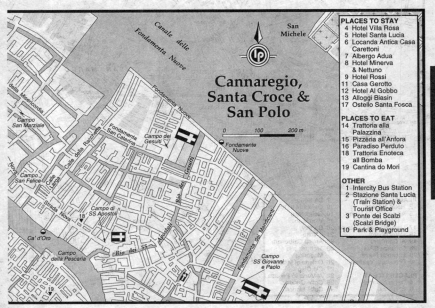

Cannaregio, Santa Croce & San Polo

PLACES TO STAY
4 Hotel Villa Rosa
5 Hotel Santa Lucia
6 Locanda Antica Casa Carettoni
7 Albergo Adua
8 Hotel Minerva & Nettuno
9 Hotel Rossi
11 Casa Gerotto
12 Hotel Al Gobbo
13 Alloggi Biasin
17 Ostello Santa Fosca

PLACES TO EAT
14 Trattoria alla Palazzina
15 Pizzeria all'Anfora
16 Paradiso Perduto
18 Trattoria Enoteca all Bomba
19 Cantina do Mori

OTHER
1 Intercity Bus Station
2 Stazione Santa Lucia (Train Station) & Tourist Office
3 Ponte dei Scalzi (Scalzi Bridge)
10 Park & Playground

ITALY

The **Casa Peron** (☎ 71 00 21), Salizzada San Pantalon 84, has clean rooms with shower for L50,000/85,000, including breakfast. The same owners run **Casa Diana** next door, which has singles/doubles for young people for L35,000/65,000. To get there from the station, cross the bridge (Ponte Scalzi) and follow the signs to San Marco and the Rialto till you reach Rio delle Muneghette, then cross the wooden bridge.

Lido The **Pensione La Pergola** (☎ 526 07 84), Via Cipro 15, has pleasant singles/doubles for L53,000/80,000, including breakfast. It's open all year and has a shady terrace. To get there

turn left off the Gran Viale Santa Maria Elisabetta into Via Zara, then turn right into Via Cipro.

Mestre Only 15 minutes away on bus No 7, Mestre is an economical alternative to staying in Venice. There are a number of good hotels as well as plenty of cafés and places to eat around the pleasant main square. If you're travelling by car, the savings on car-parking charges are considerable. **Albergo Roberta** (☎ 92 93 55), Via Sernaglia 21, has good-sized, clean rooms for L50,000/70,000. **Albergo Giovannina** (☎ 92 63 96), Via Dante 113, has decent singles/doubles for L40,000/85,000.

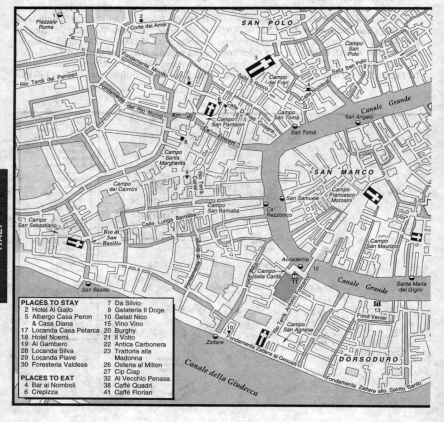

PLACES TO STAY
2 Hotel Al Gallo
5 Albergo Casa Peron & Casa Diana
17 Locanda Casa Petarca
18 Hotel Noemi
19 Al Gambero
28 Locanda Silva
29 Locanda Piave
30 Foresteria Valdese

PLACES TO EAT
4 Bar ai Nomboli
6 Crepizza
7 Da Silvio
9 Gelateria Il Doge
10 Gelati Nico
15 Vino Vino
20 Burghy
21 Il Volto
22 Antica Carbonera
23 Trattoria alla Madonna
26 Osteria al Milion
27 Cip Ciap
32 Al Vecchio Penasa
38 Caffè Quadri
41 Caffè Florian

Places to Eat

Eating in Venice can be an expensive pastime unless you choose very carefully. Many restaurants, particularly around San Marco, are tourist traps, where prices are high and the quality is poor.

Many bars serve a wide range of Venetian panini, with every imaginable filling. Tramezzini (three-pointed sandwiches) and huge bread rolls cost from L3000 to L5000 if you eat them while standing at the bar. Head for one of the many bacari or osterie, for wine by the glass and interesting snacks. The staples of the Veneto region's cucina are rice and beans. Try the risi e bisi (risotto with peas) and don't miss a risotto or pasta dish with radicchio trevisano (red chicory). The rich mascarpone dessert, tiramisù, is a favourite here.

Self-Catering For fruit and vegetables, as well as delicatessans, head for the market in the streets on the San Polo side of the Rialto Bridge. There is a *Standa* supermarket on Strada Nova and a *Mega 1* supermarket in Campo Santa Margherita.

Cannaregio The *Trattoria alla Palazzina*, Canregio 1509, is just over the first bridge after Campo San Geremia. It has a garden at the rear and serves good pizzas for L6000 to L13,000.

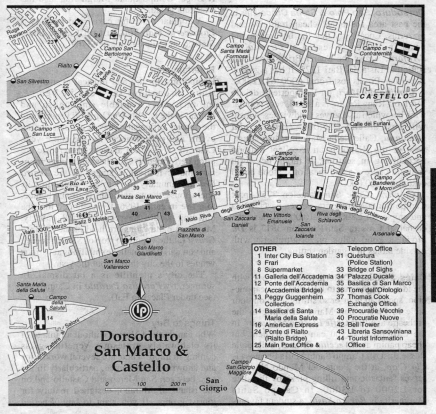

Dorsoduro, San Marco & Castello

OTHER
1 Inter City Bus Station
3 Frari
8 Supermarket
11 Galleria dell'Accademia
12 Ponte dell'Accademia (Accademia Bridge)
13 Peggy Guggenheim Collection
14 Basilica di Santa Maria della Salute
16 American Express
24 Ponte di Rialto (Rialto Bridge)
25 Main Post Office &
31 Questura (Police Station)
33 Bridge of Sighs
34 Palazzo Ducale
35 Basilica di San Marco
36 Torre dell'Orologio
37 Thomas Cook Exchange Office
39 Procuratie Vecchie
40 Procuratie Nuove
42 Bell Tower
43 Libreria Sansoviniana
44 Tourist Information Office

A full meal will cost around L25,000. *Trattoria Enoteca all Bomba*, Calle de l'Oca, parallel to Strada Nova near Campo SS Apostoli, has a tourist menu for L20,000. *Paradiso Perduto*, Fondamenta della Misericordia, is a restaurant/bar with live music and outside tables in summer.

Around San Marco & Castello *Vino Vino*, San Marco 2007, is a popular bar/osteria at Ponte Veste near Teatro La Fenice. The menu changes daily. A pasta or risotto costs L8000, a main dish around L13,000. Wine is sold by the glass. There's a *Burghy* outlet in Campo San Luca. At *Antica Carbonera*, in Calle Bembo, pasta around L8000.

Dorsoduro, San Polo & Santa Croce This is the best area for small, cheap trattorias and pizzerias. Locals say that the best pizza and pasta in Venice is served at *Pizzeria al-l'Anfora*, across the Scalzi Bridge from the station at Lista dei Bari 1223. It has a garden at the rear. Pizzas cost from L6000 to L12,000.

Cantina do Mori, on Sottoportego dei do Mori, off Ruga Rialto, is a small, very popular wine bar which also serves sandwiches. A meal will cost around L25,000. *Trattoria alla Madonna*, Calle della Madonna, two streets west of the Rialto, is an excellent trattoria specialising in seafood. It might be worth splurging here – a full meal of seafood could cost up to L60,000.

Crepizza, Calle San Pantalon 3757, past Campo Santa Margherita, serves pasta, pizza and crêpes for L8000 to L10,000. Around the corner at Crosera San Pantalon 3817 is *Da Silvio*, a good value pizzeria/trattoria with outside tables in a garden setting.

Cafés, Snacks & Osterie If you can cope with the idea of paying up to L10,000 for a cappuccino, spend an hour or so sitting at an outdoor table in Piazza San Marco, listening to the orchestra at either *Caffè Florian* or *Quadri*. In the Castello area you can get excellent but cheap panini at *Al Vecchio Penasa*, Calle delle Rasse. Just off Campo Santa Maria Formosa is *Cip Ciap*, at the Ponte del Mondo Novo. It serves fantastic and filling pizza by the slice for L2000 to L3000. In Campo Santa Margherita is *Bar La Sosta*, a student favour-ite. Panini cost from L1500 to L4000 and you can sit outside at no extra charge. *Bar ai Nomboli*, between Campo San Polo and the Frari on the corner of Calle dei Nomboli and Rio Terrà di Nomboli, has a great selection of gourmet sandwiches and tramezzini.

If you're looking for a good osteria, try *Il Volto*, Calle Cavalli, in the San Marco area, or *Osteria Al Milion*, Corta Prima del Milion, behind the Chiesa di San Giovanni Crisostomo.

Gelati & Pastries The best ice cream in Venice is said to be at *Gelati Nico*, Fondamenta Zattere 922. The locals take their evening stroll along the fondamenta while eating their gelati. *Il Doge*, Campo Santa Margherita, also has excellent gelati.

A popular place for cakes and pastries is *Pasticceria Marchini*, just off Campo Santo Stefano, at Calle del Spezier 2769.

Entertainment

Exhibitions, theatre and musical events continue throughout the year in Venice. Information is available (in English and Italian) in the weekly *Un Ospite di Venezia* and the tourist office also has brochures listing events and performances for the entire year. Concerts of classical and chamber music are often performed in churches and a contemporary music festival is staged at the *Teatro Goldoni* annually in October. Venice lost its opera house, the magnificent Teatro La Fenice, to a fire in early 1996. It was hoped that the building would be reconstructed quickly. Major art exhibitions are held at the *Palazzo Grassi* (at the vaporetto stop of San Samuele), and you will find smaller exhibitions at various venues in the city throughout the year.

The city's nightlife is a bit dismal. In summer, try *Paradiso Perduto* in Cannaregio (see under Places to Eat).

Things to Buy

Who can think of Venice without an image of its elaborately grotesque Venetian glass coming to mind? There are several workshops and showrooms in Venice, particularly in the area between San Marco and Castello and on the island of Murano, designed mainly for tourist groups. If you want to buy Venetian glass, shop around carefully because quality and prices vary dramatically.

The famous Carnevale masks make a beautiful, though expensive, souvenir of Venice. A small workshop and showroom in a small street off Campo SS Filippo and Giacomo, towards Piazza San Marco, is worth a look. Venice is also famous for its *carta marmorizzata* (marbled paper), sold at many outlets throughout the city.

The main shopping area for clothing, shoes, accessories and jewellery is in the narrow streets between San Marco and the Rialto, particularly the Merceria and the area around Campo San Luca. It is best to avoid shopping in the Piazza San Marco itself or at the Rialto bridge – prices are high for the tourists.

Getting There & Away

Air Marco Polo airport (☎ 260 92 60) is just east of Mestre and services domestic and European flights. It is accessible by regular *motoscafo* (motorboat) from San Marco and the Lido (L15,000). There are also ATVO buses from Piazzale Roma (L5000). A water taxi from San Marco will cost around L87,000.

Bus ACTV buses leave from Piazzale Roma for surrounding areas, including Mestre and Chioggia, a fishing port at the southernmost point of the lagoon. Buses also go to Padua and Treviso. Tickets and information are available at the office in the piazza.

Train The Stazione Santa Lucia, known in Venice as the *ferrovia*, is directly linked by train to Padua, Verona, Trieste, Milan and Bologna and thus is easily accessible from Florence and Rome. You can also leave from Venice for major points in Germany, Austria and the former Yugoslavia. The Venice Simplon Orient Express runs between Venice and London, via Verona, Zürich and Paris twice weekly. Ask at any travel agent.

Boat Kompas Italia (☎ 528 65 45), San Marco 1497, operates some ferry and hydrofoil services to Croatia. Kompas also operates day trips to towns on the Istrian peninsula.

Getting Around

As there are no cars in Venice, vaporetti are the city's mode of public transport.

Once you cross the bridge from Mestre, cars must be left at the car park on the island of Tronchetto or at Piazzale Roma (cars are allowed on the Lido – take car ferry No 17 from Tronchetto). The car parks are not cheap at around L22,000 a day. A cheaper alternative is to leave the car at Fusina, near Mestre, and catch the No 16 vaporetto to Zattere and then the No 82 either to Piazza San Marco or the train station. Ask for information at the tourist information office just before the bridge to Venice.

From Tronchetto or Piazzale Roma, vaporetto No 1 zigzags its way along the Grand Canal to San Marco and then to the Lido. There are faster and more expensive vaporetti if you are in a hurry. The No 12 vaporetto leaves from the Fondamenta Nuove for the islands of Murano, Burano and Torcello. A full timetable is available at the tourist office. Tickets cost L3000 for the No 1 and L4000 one way for all the other, faster vaporetti. A 24-hour ticket costs L15,000, a three-day ticket costs L30,000 and one week costs L55,000.

Water taxis are exorbitant, with a set charge of L27,000 for a maximum of seven minutes, then L500 every 15 seconds. It's an extra L8000 if you phone for a taxi, and various other surcharges add up to make a gondola ride seem cheap.

FERRARA

Ferrara was the seat of the Este dukes from the 13th century to the end of the 16th century. The city retains much of the austere splendour of its heyday – its streets are lined with graceful palaces and in its centre is the Castello Estense, surrounded by a moat.

Information

The tourist information office (☎ 20 93 70), Corso della Giovecca 21, opens Monday to Saturday from 9 am to 1 pm and from 2.30 to 5.30 pm. There's another office at Via Kennedy 2, open from April to October.

The Ferrara telephone code is ☎ 0532.

Things to See & Do

The historical centre is small, encompassing the medieval Ferrara to the south of the

ITALY

Castello Estense, and the area to the north, built under the rule of Duke Ercole I during the Renaissance. The castello now houses government offices, but certain areas are open to the public. Visit the **medieval prisons**, where in 1425 Duke Nicolò d'Este had his young second wife, Parisina Malatesta, and his son Ugo beheaded after discovering they were lovers, thereby inspiring the poet Robert Browning to write *My Last Duchess*.

The beautiful Romanesque-Gothic **Duomo** has an unusual pink-and-white marble triple façade and houses some important works of art in its museum. The 14th-century **Palazzo Schifanoia**, at Via Scandiana 23, one of the Este palaces, houses the Civic Museum and features interesting frescos. It is open daily from 9 am to 7 pm; entry is L6000.

Places to Stay & Eat

Ferrara is a cheap alternative to Bologna, and it can even be used as a base for Padua and Venice. The *Tre Stelle* (☎ 20 97 48), Via Vegri 15, has very basic singles/doubles for L30,000/40,000. *Pensione Artisti* (☎ 76 10 38), Via Vittoria 66, has singles/doubles for L26,000/46,000. Better rooms are available at *Albergo Nazionale* (☎ 20 96 04), Corso Porta Reno 32, for L55,000/90,000 with private bathroom.

A popular budget restaurant is *Trattoria da Giacomino*, Via Garibaldi 135, where a full meal will cost around L24,000. *Royal Pizzeria*, Via Vignatagliata 11, has pizzas for around L9000.

Getting There & Away

Ferrara is on the Bologna-Venice train line, with regular trains to both cities. It is 40 minutes from Bologna and 1½ hours from Venice. Regular trains also run directly to Ravenna. Buses run from the train station to Modena (also in the Emilia-Romagna region).

BOLOGNA

Elegant, intellectual and wealthy, Bologna stands out among the many beautiful cities of Italy. The regional capital of Emilia-Romagna, Bologna is famous for its porticoes (arcaded streets), its harmonious architecture, its university (which is one of the oldest in Europe) and, above all, its gastronomic tradition. The Bolognese have given the world tortellini, lasagne, mortadella and the ubiquitous spaghetti bolognese (known in Italy as *ragù*), hence one of the city's nicknames, Bologna la Grassa (Bologna the Fat).

Information

There is an Informazioni e Assistenza Turistica (IAT) office (☎ 23 96 60) in Piazza Maggiore, inside the Centro d'Informazione Comunale. It is open Monday to Saturday from 9 am to 7 pm and Sunday from 9 am to 1 pm. There are branch offices at the train station and the airport. Pick up a map and the useful booklet *A Guest in Bologna*, published monthly in English.

The main post office is in Piazza Minghetti. Telecom telephone offices are at Piazza VIII Agosto 24, and the train station. In a medical emergency call ☎ 118, or Ospedale Maggiore on ☎ 634 81 11. For the police call ☎ 113 or 112.

Bologna's telephone code is ☎ 051.

Things to See

The **Piazza Maggiore**, the adjoining **Piazza del Nettuno** and **Fontana di Nettuno** (Neptune's Fountain), sculpted in bronze by a French artist who became known as Giambologna, and the **Piazza Porta Ravegnana**, with its leaning towers to rival that of Pisa, form the beautiful centre of Bologna.

In Piazza Maggiore is the **Basilica di San Petronio**, dedicated to the city's patron saint. The red-and-white marble of its unfinished façade displays the colours of Bologna. It contains important works of art and it was here that Charles V was crowned emperor by the pope in 1530. The **Palazzo Comunale** (town hall) is a huge building, combining several architectural styles in remarkable harmony. It features a bronze statue of Pope Gregory XIII (a native of Bologna who created the Gregorian calendar), an impressive winding staircase and Bologna's collection of art treasures.

The **Chiesa di Santo Stefano** is in fact a group of four churches in the Romanesque style. In a small courtyard is a basin which legend says was used by Pontius Pilate to wash his hands after condemning Christ to death. In fact, it is an 8th century Lombard artefact.

Places to Stay & Eat

Budget hotels in Bologna are virtually nonexistent and it is almost impossible to find a single room. The city's busy trade-fair calen-

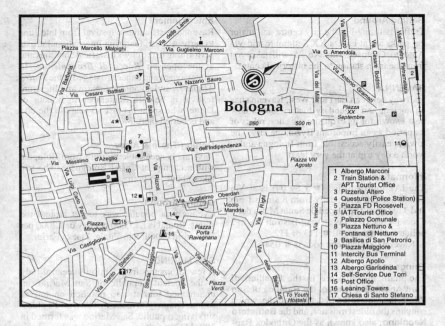

Bologna

1 Albergo Marconi
2 Train Station &
  APT Tourist Office
3 Pizzeria Altero
4 Questura (Police Station)
5 Piazza FD Roosevelt
6 IAT Tourist Office
7 Palazzo Comunale
8 Piazza Nettuno &
  Fontana di Nettuno
9 Basilica di San Petronio
10 Piazza Maggiore
11 Intercity Bus Terminal
12 Albergo Apollo
13 Albergo Garisenda
14 Self-Service Due Torri
15 Post Office
16 Leaning Towers
17 Chiesa di Santo Stefano

dar means that hotels are often heavily booked, so always book in advance. The best options are the two HI hostels: *Ostello San Sisto* (☎ 51 92 02), Via Viadagola 14, charges L18,000 with breakfast and *Ostello Due Torri* (☎ 50 18 10), in the same street at No 5, charges L20,000. Take bus No 93 or 20/b from Via Irnerio, off Via Independenza near the station, and ask the bus driver where to get off, then follow the signs to the hostel.

Albergo Garisenda (☎ 22 43 69), Galleria del Leone 1, is under the two towers and has decent singles/doubles for L65,000/85,000. The *Apollo* (☎ 22 39 55), Via Drapperie 5, off Via Rizzoli, has singles/doubles for L49,000/81,000 and triples with bathroom for L140,000. The *Albergo Marconi* (☎ 26 28 32), at Via G Marconi 22, has pleasant singles/doubles/triples for L45,000/70,000/96,000.

Fortunately, it is cheaper to eat in Bologna, particularly in the university district north of Via Rizzoli. *Pizzeria Bella Napoli*, Via San Felice 40, serves good pizzas at reasonable prices. *Trattoria da Boni*, Via Saragozza 88, is

another good option. *Pizzeria Altero*, Via Ugo Bassi 10, has good, cheap pizzas. Try the self-service *Due Torri*, Via dei Giudei 4, under the towers. It opens only for lunch and the food is good value. You can buy panini in most cafés and eat them standing at the bar.

Shop at the *Mercato Ugo Bassi*, Via Ugo Bassi 27, a covered market offering all the local fare. There is also a market in the streets south-east of Piazza Maggiore.

Getting There & Away

Bologna is a major transport junction for northern Italy and trains from virtually all major cities stop here. The only hitch is that many are intercity trains, which means you have to pay the rapido supplement.

Buses to major cities depart from the terminal in Piazza XX Settembre, around the corner from the train station in Piazza delle Medaglie d'Oro.

The city is linked to Milan, Florence and Rome by the A1 (Autostrada del Sole). The A13 heads directly for Venice and Padua, and the A14 goes to Rimini and Ravenna.

ITALY

Getting Around

Traffic is limited in the city centre and major car parks are at Piazza XX Settembre and Via Antonio Gramsci. Bus No 25 will take you from the train station to the historical centre.

RAVENNA

Halfway between East and West, Ravenna has an ancient and legendary history, but is now best known for its exquisite mosaics, relics of its period as an important Byzantine city. The town is easily accessible from Bologna and is worth a day trip at the very least.

Information

The IAT tourist office (☎ 3 54 04) is at Via Salara 8 and is open daily from 8 am to 1 pm and 3 to 6 pm. The Ospedale Santa Maria delle Croci (☎ 40 91 11) is at Via Missiroli 10. In a police emergency call ☎ 113 or 112.

Ravenna's telephone code is ☎ 0544.

Things to See

The main mosaics are in the **Basilica di Sant'Apollinare Nuovo**, the **Basilica di San Vitale**, the **Mausoleo di Galla Placidia**, which contains the oldest mosaics, and the **Battistero Neoniano**, also known as the Orthodox Baptistry. These are all in the town centre and an admission ticket to the four, as well as to the **Museo Arcivescovile**, costs L9000 – a bargain given that a ticket to only one monument costs L5000. The **Basilica di Sant'Apollinare Nuovo in Classe** is five km from Ravenna and accessible by bus No 4 from the station.

Places to Stay & Eat

The HI *Ostello Dante* (☎ 42 04 05) is at Via Aurelio Nicolodi 12. Take bus No 1 from Viale Pallavacini, to the left of the station. Bed and breakfast is L22,000 and family rooms are available. *Al Giaciglio* (☎ 3 94 03), at Via R Brancaleone 42, has singles/doubles for L35,000/50,000 and triples for L80,000. To find it, go straight ahead from the station along Viale Farini and turn right into Via Brancaleone from Piazza Mameli. The only other budget hotel, the Ravenna, at Via Maroncelli 12, was closed for renovation at the time of writing.

For a quick meal, try *Free Flow Bizantino*, Piazza Andrea Costa, next to the city's fresh-produce market.

Entertainment

Ravenna hosts a music festival from late June to early August, featuring international artists performing in the city's historical churches and at the open-air *Rocca di Brancaleone*. In winter, opera and dance are staged at the *Teatro Alighieri*, and an annual theatre and literature festival is held in September in honour of Dante, who spent his last 10 years in the city and is buried there.

Getting There & Away

Ravenna is accessible by train from Bologna, with a change at Castel Bolognese. The trip takes about 1½ hours.

Getting Around

Cycling is a popular way to get around the sights. Rental is L15,000 per day or L2000 per hour from COOP San Vitale, Piazza Farini.

SAN MARINO

A few kilometres from Rimini in central Italy is the ancient Republic of San Marino, an unashamed tourist trap perched on top of Monte Titano (600 metres). The world's oldest surviving republic, San Marino was formed in 300 AD by a stonemason said to have been escaping religious persecution. The tiny state (only 61 sq km) strikes its own coins, has its own postage stamps and its own army. Wander along the city walls and drop in at the two fortresses. The main attraction of a visit is the splendid view of the mountains and the coast. The Ufficio di Stato per il Turismo (☎ 0549-88 29 98), is in the Palazzo del Turismo, Contrada Omagnano 20.

The town is accessible from Rimini by ATR bus. There is no train to San Marino.

The Dolomites

This spectacular limestone mountain range in the Alps stretches across Trentino-Alto Adige into the Veneto. It is the Italians' favoured area for skiing and there are excellent hiking trails.

Information

Information can be obtained at the APT del Trentino (Azienda per la Promozione Turistica del Trentino) in Trent (☎ 0461-90 00 00) at Corso III Novembre 134; in Rome (☎ 06-679 42 16) at Via Poli 47; or Milan (☎ 02-87 43 87) at Piazza Diaz 5. The provincial tourist office for Alto Adige (☎ 0472-99 38 08) is at Piazza Parocchia 11, Bolzano. The APT delle Dolomiti Bellunesii (☎ 0473-94 00 83) can provide information on trekking along the Sentiero della Pace (Path of Peace), which traces the Italian/German frontline of WWI.

Skiing

There are numerous excellent ski resorts, including the expensive and fashionable Cortina d'Ampezzo and the less pretentious, more family-oriented resorts, such as those in the Val Gardena in Trentino-Alto Adige. All have helpful tourist offices with loads of information on facilities, accommodation and transport (some are listed in this section).

The high season is generally from Christmas to early January and from early February to April, when prices go up considerably, but actual dates vary throughout the Alps. A good way to save money is to buy a *settimana bianca* (literally, 'white week' – a package-deal ski holiday) through Sestante CIT, CTS or other travel agencies throughout Italy. This covers accommodation, food and ski passes for seven days.

If you want to go it alone, but plan to do a lot of skiing, invest in a ski pass. Most resort areas offer their own passes for unlimited use of lifts at several resorts for a nominated period. The cost in the 1996/97 high season for a seven-day pass was around L245,000. However, the best value is the Superski Dolomiti pass, which allows access to 450 lifts and more than 1100 km of ski runs. In the 1996/97 high season, a superski pass for seven days cost L296,000. Ring Superski Dolomiti (☎ 0471-79 53 98) for information. The average cost of ski and boot hire in the Alps is from L17,000 to L25,000 a day for downhill and around L15,000 for cross-country.

Trekking

Without doubt, the Dolomites provide the most breathtaking opportunities for walking in the Italian Alps – from a half-day stroll with the kids, to walks/treks for as many days as you like, and demanding treks which combine walking with mountaineering skills. The

walking season is roughly from July to late September. Alpine refuges usually close around September 20.

Buy a map of the hiking trails, which also shows the locations of Alpine refuges. The best maps are the Tabacco 1:25,000, which can be bought in newsagents and bookshops in the area where you plan to hike. They are also often available in major bookshops in larger cities. Lonely Planet's *Italy* guide has more detailed information about walking in the Dolomites, including suggested treks. A useful guide is *Walking in the Dolomites* by Gillian Price.

Hiking trails are generally very well marked with numbers on red-and-white painted bands (which you will find on trees and rocks along the trails), or by numbers inside different coloured triangles for the Alte Vie (the four High Routes through the Dolomites – ask for details at the tourist offices listed in this section). There are numerous organisations offering guided treks, climbs etc, as well as courses. One is the *Scuola Alpina Dolomiten* (☎ 0471-70 53 43; fax 0471-70 73 890), Via Vogelweider, Castelrotto, which has a summer programme including week-long treks, expeditions on horseback and mountain bike, and courses in rockclimbing. It also has a winter programme of ski expeditions and courses. Phone or fax for a programme.

Recommended areas to walk in the Dolomites include:

Brenta Group (Dolomiti di Brenta)
    accessible from either Molveno to the east or Madonna di Campiglio to the west
Sella Group
    accessible from either the Val Gardena to the west, or the Val Badia to the east
Pale di San Martino
    accessible from San Martino di Castrozza
Cortina area
    which straddles Trentino and Veneto and features the magnificent Parco Naturale di Fanes-Sennes-Braies, and, to the south, Mt Pelmo and Mt Civetta
Sesto Dolomites
    north of Cortina towards Austria.

Warning Remember that even in summer the weather is extremely changeable in the Alps and, though it might be sweltering when you set off, you should be prepared for very cold and wet weather on even the shortest of walks. Essentials include a pair of good-quality, worn-in walking boots, an anorak or pile/wind jacket, a lightweight backpack and water.

Getting There & Away

Trentino-Alto Adige has an excellent public transport network – the two main bus companies for the region are SAD in Alto Adige and Atesina in Trentino. The main towns and many of the ski resorts are also accessible from major cities throughout Italy, including Rome, Florence, Bologna, Milan and Genoa, by a network of long-distance buses operated by companies including Lazzi, SITA, Sena and STAT. Information about the services is available from tourist offices and *autostazioni* (bus stations) throughout Trentino-Alto Adige, or from the following offices: Lazzi Express (☎ 06-884 08 40), Via Tagliamento 27B, Rome, and in Florence at Piazza Adua 1 (055-21 51 55); SITA (☎ 055-21 47 21), Autostazione, Via Santa Caterina di Siena 17, Florence.

Getting Around

If you are planning to hike in the Alps during the warmer months, you will find that hitch-hiking is no problem, especially near the resort towns. The areas around the major resorts are well serviced by local buses, and tourist offices will be able to provide information on local bus services. During winter, most resorts have 'ski bus' shuttle services from the towns to the main ski facilities.

CORTINA D'AMPEZZO

The most famous, fashionable and expensive Italian ski resort, Cortina is also one of its best equipped and certainly the most picturesque. If you are on a tight budget, the prices for accommodation and food will be prohibitive, even in the low season. However, camping grounds and Alpine refuges (open only during summer) provide more reasonably priced alternatives.

Situated in the Ampezzo bowl, Cortina is surrounded by the stunning Dolomites, including the Cristallo and Marmarole groups and the Tofane. Facilities for both downhill and cross-country skiing are first class. The area is also very popular for trekking and climbing, with well-marked trails and numerous refuges. A memorable three-day walk starts at Passo Falzarego and incorporates sections of Alta Via No 1. It takes you through the beautiful Val di

Fanes and ends at Passo Cimabanche. Buy a good 1:25,000 map and plan your route.

Information

The main tourist information office (APT: ☎ 32 31) is at Piazzetta San Francesco 8, in the town centre. It has information on accommodation, ski passes and hiking trails. There is a small information office at Piazza Roma 1.

La Cortina's telephone code is 0436.

Places to Stay

The *International Camping Olympia* (☎ 50 57) is about five km north of Cortina at Fiames and is open all year. A local bus will take you there from Cortina. If you are trekking in the area, refuges are open from July to late September and charge roughly L20,000 per person. There are not many options for cheap accommodation in Cortina. You could try the *Albergo Cavallino* (☎ 26 14) or the *La Ginestrina* (☎ 86 02 55), both of which charge L70,000 or more per person, including breakfast, in the high season.

CANAZEI

Set in the Fassa Dolomites, the resort of Canazei has more than 100 km of trails and is linked to slopes in the Val Gardena and Val Badia by a network of runs known as the **Sella Ronda**, which enable skiers to make a day-long skiing tour of the valleys surrounding the Sella Group. Canazei also offers cross-country skiing and summer skiing on the Marmolada glacier. (At 3342 metres, the Marmolada peak is the highest in the Dolomites.) The Marmolada *camping ground* (☎ 0462-6 16 60) is open all year, or you have a choice of hotels, furnished rooms and apartments. Contact the AAST tourist office (☎ 6 11 13) for full details. The resort is accessible by Atesina bus from Trent and SAD bus from Bolzano and the Val Gardena.

VAL GARDENA

This is one of the most popular skiing areas in the Alps, due to its reasonable prices and excellent facilities for downhill, cross-country and alpine skiing. There are excellent walking trails in the Sella group and the Alpi Siusi. The Vallunga, behind Selva, is great for family walks and cross-country skiing.

The valley's main towns are Ortisei, Santa

Cristina and Selva, all offering lots of accommodation and easy access to runs. The tourist offices at Santa Cristina (☎ 0471-79 30 46) and Selva (☎ 79 51 22) have extensive information on accommodation and facilities. Staff speak English and will send details on request.

The Val Gardena is accessible from Bolzano by SAD bus. It is connected to major Italian cities by coach services (Lazzi, SITA and STAT).

MADONNA DI CAMPIGLIO

One of the five major ski resorts in Italy and situated in the Brenta Dolomites, Madonna di Campiglio is one of the more beautiful and well-equipped places to ski, but also one of the more expensive. The Brenta group offers challenging trails for mountaineers and cross-country skiers, while the nearby, beautiful Val di Genova is perfect for family walks. The resort is accessible by Atesina bus from Trent, and from Rome, Florence and Bologna by Lazzi or SITA coach. More information is available from the helpful APT office (☎ 0465-4 20 00).

SAN MARTINO DI CASTROZZA

Located in a sheltered position beneath the Pale di San Martino, this resort is popular among Italians and offers good facilities and ski runs, as well as cross-country skiing and a toboggan run. The APT office (☎ 0439-76 88 67) will provide a full list of accommodation, or try the *Suisse* (☎ 6 80 87), Via Dolomiti 1. Its singles/doubles cost L50,000/85,000. Buses travel regularly from Trent and, during the high season, from Milan, Venice, Padua and Bologna.

Central Italy

The landscape in central Italy is a patchwork of textures bathed in a beautiful soft light – golden pink in Tuscany, and a greenish gold in Umbria and the Marches. The people remain close to the land, but in each of the regions there is also a strong artistic and cultural tradition – even the smallest medieval hill town can harbour extraordinary works of art.

FLORENCE

Cradle of the Renaissance, home of Dante, Machiavelli, Michelangelo and the Medici, Florence (Firenze) is overwhelming in its wealth of art, culture and history, and is one of the most enticing cities in Italy.

Florence was founded as a colony of the Etruscan city of Fiesole in about 200 BC and later became the strategic Roman garrison settlement of Florentia. In the Middle Ages the city developed a flourishing economy based on banking and commerce, which sparked a period of building and growth previously unequalled in Italy. It was a major focal point for the Guelph and Ghibelline struggle of the 13th century, which saw Dante banished from the city. But Florence truly flourished in the 15th century under the Medici, reaching the height of its cultural, artistic and political development as it gave birth to the Renaissance.

The Grand Duchy of the Medici was succeeded in the 18th century by the House of Lorraine (related to the Austrian Hapsburgs). As a result of the Risorgimento, the Kingdom of Italy was formally proclaimed in March 1861, and Florence was the capital of the new kingdom from 1865 to 1871. During WWII, parts of the city, including all of the bridges except the Ponte Vecchio, were destroyed by bombing, and in 1966 a devastating flood destroyed or severely damaged many important works of art. A worldwide effort helped Florence in its massive restoration works.

In 1993, a bomb seriously damaged one of the principal corridors of the Uffizi Gallery. Several important works of art were lost in the attack, which was executed by the Mafia.

Orientation

Whether you arrive by train, bus or car, the central train station, Santa Maria Novella, is a good reference point. Budget hotels and pensioni are concentrated around Via Nazionale, to the east of the station, and Piazza Santa Maria Novella, to the south. The main thoroughfare to the centre is Via de' Panzani and then Via de' Cerretani, about a 10-minute walk. You'll know you've arrived when you first glimpse the Duomo.

Once at Piazza del Duomo you will find Florence easy to negotiate, with most of the major sights within easy walking distance.

ITALY

Florence (Firenze)

ITALY

OTHER
- 1 Tourist Medical Service
- 2 Questura (Police Station)
- 3 Museo di San Marco
- 4 Galleria dell'Accademia
- 10 Lazzi Bus Station & Ticket Office
- 11 ATAF Local Bus Station
- 12 Telecom Telephones
- 13 ATAF Ticket & Information Booth
- 16 Covered Market
- 19 APT Tourist Information Office
- 20 Feltrinelli Bookshop
- 21 Basilica di San Lorenzo
- 22 Cappelle Medicee
- 26 Comune di Firenze Tourist Information Office
- 27 SITA Bus Station
- 32 Chiesa di Santa Maria Novella
- 36 Onda Blu Laundry
- 37 Paperback Exchange Bookshop
- 38 Ponte alla Carraia
- 40 Ponte Santa Trinità
- 42 Cabiria
- 44 Palazzo Pitti
- 45 Forte di Belvedere
- 47 Ponte alle Grazie

PLACES TO STAY
- 5 Pensione Mary
- 6 Pensione Ausonia & Rimini & Pensione Kursaal
- 7 Locanda Daniel & Soggiorno Nazionale
- 8 Ostello Archi Rossi
- 9 Albergo Azzi & Albergo Anna
- 23 Pensione Accademia
- 24 Soggiorno Burchi
- 25 Pensione Bellavista & Pensione Le Cascine
- 28 La Romagnola & La Gigliola
- 29 Pensione Montreal
- 30 Pensione Margareth
- 31 La Scala
- 33 La Mia Casa
- 34 Pensione Ottaviani & Albergo Visconti
- 35 Pensione Toscana & Pensione Sole
- 41 Ostello Santa Monaca

PLACES TO EAT
- 14 Caffé degli Innocenti
- 15 Bondi
- 17 Café Za Za
- 18 Mario's
- 39 Angelino
- 43 Trattoria Casalinga
- 46 I Tarocchi

See Duomo to Ponte Vecchio Map

0   200   400 m

Think carefully, though, about how you spend your time. Most important museums close by 2 pm (with the exception of the Uffizi Gallery) and virtually all are closed on Monday. You will need to start your day early, but be careful not to overload your itinerary. Florence is a living art museum and you won't waste your time by just wandering the streets. Take the city ATAF buses for longer distances such as to Piazzale Michelangelo or the nearby suburb of Fiesole, both of which offer panoramic views of the city (see the Getting Around section that follows).

Information
Tourist Offices The city council (Comune di Firenze) operates a tourist information office (☎ 21 22 45) just outside the main train station in the covered area where local buses stop. During high season it opens from Monday to Saturday 8 am to 7.30 pm. The main APT office (☎ 29 08 32) is just north of the Duomo at Via Cavour 1r and opens Monday to Saturday 8.15 am to 7.15 pm and Sunday from 8.15 am to 1.45 pm. At both offices you can pick up a map of the city, a list of hotels and other useful information. The Consorzio ITA (☎ 28 28 93), inside the station on the main concourse, can check availability of hotel rooms and book you a night for a small fee.

A good map of the city, on sale at newsstands, is the one with the white, red and black cover (*Firenze: Pianta della Città*), which costs L8000.

Foreign Consulates The US Consulate (☎ 239 82 76) is at Lungarno Vespucci 38, and the UK Consulate (☎ 21 25 94) is at Lungarno Corsini 2. The French Consulate (☎ 230 25 56) is at Piazza Ognissanti 2.

Money The main banks are concentrated around Piazza della Repubblica. You can use the service at the information office in the station, but it has bad exchange rates.

Post & Communications The main post office is in Via Pellicceria, off Piazza della Repubblica, open weekdays from 8.15 am to 7 pm and Saturday to midday. Poste restante mail can be addressed to 50100 Firenze. There is a Telecom office at Via Cavour 21, open

daily from 8 am to 9.45 pm, and another at Stazione Santa Maria Novella, open Monday to Saturday from 8 am to 9.45 pm.

Florence's telephone code is ☎ 055.

Bookshops The Paperback Exchange, Via Fiesolana 31r (closed Sunday), has a vast selection of new and second-hand books. Internazionale Seeber, Via de' Tornabuoni 70r, and Feltrinelli, opposite the APT in Via Cavour, also have good selections of English-language books.

Laundry Onda Blu, Via degli Alfani 24bR, east of the Duomo, is self service and charges around L6000 for a 6.5 kilo load.

Medical Services The main public hospital is Ospedale Careggi (☎ 427 71 11), Viale Morgagni 85, north of the city centre. Tourist Medical Service (☎ 47 54 11), Via Lorenzo il Magnifico 59, is open 24 hours a day and the doctors speak English, French and German. An organisation of volunteer interpreters (English, French and German) called the Associazione Volontari Ospedalieri (☎ 234 45 67 or ☎ 40 31 26) will translate free of charge once you've found a doctor. Hospitals have a list of volunteers. All-night pharmacies include the Farmacia Comunale (☎ 28 94 35), inside the station, and Molteni (☎ 28 94 90), in the city centre at Via Calzaiuoli 7r.

Emergency For police emergency call ☎ 113. The questura (☎ 4 97 71) is at Via Zara 2. There is an office for foreigners where you can report thefts etc. Lost property (☎ 36 79 43) and towed-away cars can be collected from Via Circondaria 19 (south-west of the centre).

Dangers & Annoyances Crowds, heavy traffic and summer heat can combine to make Florence unpleasant. Air pollution can be a problem for small children, people with respiratory problems and the elderly, so check with your hotel or the tourist office. Pickpockets are active in crowds and on buses, and beware of the groups of dishevelled women and children carrying newspapers and cardboard. A few will distract you while the others rifle your bag and pockets.

ITALY

Things to See & Do

Duomo This beautiful cathedral, with its pink, white and green marble façade and Brunelleschi's famous dome dominating the Florence skyline, is one of Italy's most famous monuments. At first sight, no matter how many times you have visited the city, the Duomo will take your breath away. Named the Cattedrale di Santa Maria del Fiore, it was begun in 1296 by the Sienese architect Arnolfo di Cambio but took almost 150 years to complete. It is the fourth-largest cathedral in the world.

The Renaissance architect Brunelleschi won a public competition to design the enormous dome, the first of its kind since antiquity. Although now severely cracked and under restoration, it remains a remarkable achievement of design. The dome is decorated with frescos by Vasari and Zuccari and stained-glass windows by Donatello, Andrea del Castagno, Paolo Uccello and Lorenzo Ghiberti. Climb to the top of the dome for an unparalleled view of Florence (open from 9.30 am to 5.20 pm, entry L8000). The Duomo's marble façade was built in the 19th century to replace the original unfinished façade, which was pulled down in the 16th century.

Giotto designed and began building the **bell tower** next to the cathedral in 1334, but died before it was completed. This unusual and graceful structure is 82 metres high and you can climb its stairs from 9 am to 4.20 pm daily (L8000).

The Romanesque-style **baptistry**, believed to have been built between the 5th and 11th centuries on the site of a Roman temple, is the oldest building in Florence. Dante was baptised here. It is famous for its gilded bronze doors, particularly the celebrated east doors facing the duomo, the *Gates of Paradise*, by Lorenzo Ghiberti. The south door, by Andrea Pisano, dates from 1336 and is the oldest. The north door is also by Ghiberti, who won a public competition in 1401 to design it, but the *Gates of Paradise* remain his masterpiece. Most of the doors are copies – the original panels are being removed for restoration and are placed in the Museo dell'Opera del Duomo as work is completed. The baptistry is open Monday to Saturday from 1.30 to 6 pm and on Sunday from 9 am to 1.30 pm. An entry fee of around L3000 was to be introduced in 1996.

Uffizi Gallery The Palazzo degli Uffizi, built by Vasari in the 16th century, houses the most important art collection in Italy. The vast collection of paintings dating from the 13th to 18th centuries represents the great legacy of the Medici family.

You will need more than one visit to appreciate fully the extraordinary number of important works in the Uffizi, which include paintings by Giotto and Cimabue from the 14th century; 15th-century masterpieces including Botticelli's *Birth of Venus* and *Allegory of Spring*; and works by Filippo Lippi, Fra Angelico and Paolo Uccello. *The Annunciation* by Leonardo da Vinci is also here. There are 16th-century works by Raphael, Michelangelo's *Holy Family* and famous works by Titian, Andrea del Sarto, Tintoretto, Rembrandt, Caravaggio, Tiepolo, Rubens, Van Dyck and Goya. Most of the gallery's second corridor was damaged in the 1993 bomb attack. Restoration work on the art works and rooms was expected to be completed by the end of 1996. The gallery is open weekdays from 9 am to 7 pm and Sunday from 9 am to 2 pm (closed Monday). Entry is L12,000.

Piazza della Signoria & Palazzo Vecchio Built by Arnolfo di Cambio between 1299 and 1314, the Palazzo Vecchio is the traditional seat of the Florentine government. In the 16th century it became the ducal palace of the Medici before they moved to the Pitti Palace. Visit the beautiful Michelozzi courtyard just inside the entrance and the lavishly decorated apartments upstairs. It is open weekdays from 9 am to 7 pm and Sunday to 1 pm (closed Thursday). Admission is L10,000. The palace's turrets, battlements and 94-metre-high bell tower form an imposing and memorable backdrop to Piazza della Signoria, scene of many important political events in the history of Florence, including the execution of the religious and political reformer Savonarola. A bronze plaque marks the spot where he was burned at the stake in 1498. The **Loggia della Signoria**, at a right angle to the Palazzo Vecchio, contains important sculptures, including Cellini's *Perseus*.

Ponte Vecchio This famous 14th-century bridge, lined with gold and silversmiths' shops,

Duomo to Ponte Vecchio

0   100   200 m

1 Baptistry
2 Bell Tower
3 Duomo
4 Osteria Il Caminetto
5 Albergo Firenze
6 Pensione Maria
  Luisa de Medici
7 Brunori
8 Gelateria Perché No?
9 Internazionale Seeber
10 Post Office
11 Palazzo del Bargello &
   Museo Nazionale
12 Gelateria Vivoli
13 Palazzo Vecchio
14 Loggia della Signoria
15 Uffizi Gallery
16 Aily Home
17 Trattoria da Benvenuto
18 Angle's Pub
19 Fiaschetteria

was the only one to survive Nazi bombing in WWII. Originally, the shops housed butchers. A corridor along the 1st floor was built by the Medici to link the Pitti Palace and the Uffizi Gallery.

Palazzo Pitti The immense and imposing Palazzo Pitti, housing several museums, was originally designed by Brunelleschi. The **Galleria Palatina** (open Tuesday to Saturday from 9 am to 7 pm, Sunday 9 am to 2 pm; entry L12,000) has 16th and 17th-century works by Raphael, Filippo Lippi, Tintoretto, Veronese and Rubens, hung in lavishly decorated rooms. The royal apartments of the Medici, and later of the Savoy, show the splendour in which these rulers lived.

The other museums are the **Museo degli Argenti**, the **Galleria del Costume** and the **Galleria d'Arte Moderna**. They open Tuesday to Sunday 9 am to 2 pm. After the Pitti Palace, visit the beautiful Renaissance **Giardino di Boboli** (entry L4000).

Palazzo Bargello & Museo Nazionale del Bargello A medieval palace, also known as the Palazzo del Podestà, the Bargello was the seat of the local ruler and, later, of the chief of police. People were tortured at the site of the well in the centre of the courtyard.

The palace now houses Florence's rich collection of sculpture, notably works by Michelangelo, many by Benvenuto Cellini, and Donatello's stunning bronze *David*, the first sculpture since antiquity to depict a fully naked man (open Tuesday to Sunday 9 am to 2 pm; entry is L8000).

Galleria dell'Accademia Michelangelo's *David* is in this gallery (the one in Piazza della Signoria is a good copy), as are four of his unfinished *slaves* (or *prisoners*). The gallery upstairs houses many important works of the Florentine primitives. The gallery, at Via Ricasoli 60, is open Tuesday to Saturday from 9 am to 7 pm and Sunday to 2 pm. Entry is L12,000.

Basilica di San Lorenzo & Capelle Medicee The basilica, rebuilt by Brunelleschi in the early 15th century for the Medici, contains his **Sagrestia Vecchia** (Old Sacristy), which was decorated by Donatello. It's also worth visiting the **Biblioteca Laurenziana**, a huge library designed by Michelangelo to house the Medici collection of some 10,000 manuscripts.

Around the corner, in Piazza Madonna degli Aldobrandini, are the Medici Chapels. The **Cappella dei Principi**, sumptuously decorated with precious marble and semiprecious stones, was the principal burial place of the Medici grand dukes. The graceful and simple **Sagrestia Nuova** was designed by Michelangelo, but he left Florence for Rome before its completion. It contains his beautiful sculptures *Night & Day*, *Dawn & Dusk* and the *Madonna with Child*, which adorn the Medici tombs. The chapels are open Tuesday to Sunday from 9 am to 2 pm. Admission is L10,000.

Other Attractions The Dominican church of **Santa Maria Novella** was built during the 13th and 14th centuries, and its white-and-green marble façade was designed by Alberti in the 15th century. The church is decorated with frescos by Ghirlandaio (who was assisted by a very young Michelangelo) and Masaccio. The **Cappella di Filippo Strozzi** contains frescos by Filippo Lippi, and the beautiful **cloisters** feature frescos by Uccello and his students.

The **Convento di San Marco** (Monastery of St Mark) is a museum of the work of Fra Angelico, who covered its walls and many of the monks' cells with frescos and lived here from 1438 to 1455. Also worth seeing are the peaceful cloisters and the cell of the monk Savonarola. It also contains works by Fra Bartolomeo and Ghirlandaio. The monastery is open Tuesday to Sunday from 9 am to 2 pm and entry is L8000.

Head up to **Piazzale Michelangelo** for a magnificent view of Florence. To reach the piazzale, cross the Ponte Vecchio, turn left and walk along the river, then turn right at Piazza Giuseppe Roggi, or take bus No 13 from the station.

Cycling
I Bike Italy (☎ 234 23 71) offers reasonably priced full and half-day guided mountain-bike rides in the countryside around Florence, as well as longer tours in Tuscany and Umbria.

Courses
Florence has more than 30 schools offering courses in Italian language and culture. Numerous other schools offer courses in art, including painting, drawing and sculpture, as well as art history. While Florence might be the most attractive city in which to study Italian language or art, it is also one of the more expensive. Perugia, Siena and Urbino offer good-quality courses at much lower prices. The cost of language courses in Florence ranges from about L450,000 to L900,000, depending on the school and the length of the course (one month is usually the minimum duration). Here are the addresses of some of the language courses available in Florence:

Centro Linguistico Italiano Dante Alighieri
    Via dei Bardi 12, 50125, Florence (☎ 234 29 86)
Istituto Europeo
    Piazzale delle Pallottole 1, 50122 Florence
    (☎ 238 10 71)
Istituto di Lingua e Cultura Italiana per Stranieri Michelangelo
    Via Ghibellina 88, 50122 Florence (☎ 24 09 75)

Art courses range from one-month summer workshops (costing from L500,000 to more than L1,000,000) to longer-term professional diploma courses. These can be expensive, some of them costing more than L6,500,000 a year. Schools will organise accommodation for students, upon request, either in private apartments or with Italian families.

Brochures detailing courses and prices are available at Italian cultural institutes throughout the world. You can write in English to request information and enrolment forms – letters should be addressed to the *segretaria*. Some art schools include:

Istituto d'Arte di Firenze Lorenzo de' Medici
Via Faenza 43, 50122 Florence (☎ 28 71 43)
Istituto per l'Arte e il Restauro
Palazzo Spinelli, Borgo Santa Croce 10, 50122 Florence (☎ 234 58 98)

Special Events

The major festivals include the Festa del Patrono (the Feast of St John the Baptist) on June 24; the Scoppio del Carro (Explosion of the Cart), held in front of the Duomo on Easter Sunday (see Facts for the Visitor at the start of this chapter); and the lively Calcio Storico (Historical Football), featuring football matches played in 16th-century costume, which is held in June.

Places to Stay

There are more than 150 budget hotels in Florence, so even in peak season when the city is packed with tourists, you should be able to find a room. However, it is always advisable to make a booking, and you should arrive by late morning to claim your room.

Always ask the full price of a room before putting your bags down. Hotels and pensioni in Florence are notorious for bill-padding, particularly in summer. Many require an extra L5000 for a compulsory breakfast and will charge L3000 and more for a shower. Prices listed here are for high season and, unless otherwise specified, are for rooms without private bathroom.

Camping The *Italiani e Stranieri* camping ground (☎ 681 19 77), Viale Michelangelo 80, is near Piazzale Michelangelo. Take bus No 13 from the train station. *Villa Camerata* (☎ 60 03 15), Viale Augusto Righi 2/4, is next to the HI hostel (see the next section), north-east of the centre (take bus 17B from the station, 30 minutes). There is another camping ground at Fiesole, *Campeggio Panoramico* (☎ 59 90 69)

at Via Peramonda 1, which also has bungalows. Take bus No 7 to Fiesole from the station.

Hostels The HI *Ostello Villa Camerata* (☎ 60 14 51), Viale Augusto Righi 2/4, charges L23,000 for B&B, dinner is L14,000 and there is also a bar. Take bus No 17B, which leaves from the right of the station as you leave the platforms. The trip takes 30 minutes. Daytime closing is 9 am to 2 pm. It is open to HI members only and reservations can be made by mail (essential in summer).

The private *Ostello Archi Rossi* (☎ 29 08 04), Via Faenza 94r, is another good option for a bed in a dorm room. *Ostello Santa Monaca* (☎ 26 83 38), Via Santa Monaca 6, is also private. It is a 15 to 20-minute walk from the station. Go through Piazza Santa Maria Novella, along Via de' Fossi, across the Ponte alla Carraia and directly ahead along Via de' Serragli. Via Santa Monaca is on the right. A bed costs L20,000 and meals are available.

Hotels – around the station The *Pensione Bellavista* (☎ 28 45 28), Largo Alinari 15 (at the start of Via Nazionale), is small, but a knockout bargain if you manage to book one of the two double rooms with balconies and a view of the Duomo and Palazzo Vecchio. Singles/doubles cost L55,000/70,000, but they will hit you for L3500 to use the bath. In the same building is the *Pensione Le Cascine* (☎ 21 10 66), a two-star hotel with beautifully furnished rooms, some with balconies. Singles/doubles are L65,000/95,000, including use of the communal bathroom. Prices double for rooms with private bathrooms.

Albergo Azzi (☎ 21 38 06), Via Faenza 56, has a helpful management and singles/doubles cost L45,000/70,000, breakfast included. The same management runs the *Albergo Anna* upstairs.

Across Via Nazionale at Via Faenza 7, is *Pensione Accademia* (☎ 29 34 51). It has pleasant rooms and incorporates an 18th-century palace, replete with magnificent stained-glass doors and carved wooden ceilings; singles cost L90,000 and a double with bathroom is L130,000, breakfast and TV included. *Soggiorno Burchi* (☎ 41 44 54), Via Faenza 20, has triples for L75,000 and there is free use of the kitchen.

The *Locanda Daniel* (☎ 21 12 93), Via Nazionale 22, has doubles for L60,000 and beds in a large room for L25,000 per person. One of the rooms has a panoramic view of the Duomo. The owner will not take bookings, so arrive very early. In the same building is *Soggiorno Nazionale* (☎ 238 22 03). Singles/ doubles are L55,000/84,000 and triples are L114,000. Breakfast is included.

At No 24 is the *Pensione Ausonia & Rimini* (☎ 49 65 47), run by a young couple who go out of their way to help travellers. Singles/ doubles are L65,000/84,000 and a triple is L108,000. The price includes breakfast and use of the communal bathroom. The same couple also operates the more expensive *Pensione Kursaal* downstairs.

Pensione Mary (☎ 49 63 10), Piazza della Indipendenza 5, has singles/doubles for L60,000/85,000.

Hotels – around Piazza Santa Maria Novella

In the piazza at No 25, *La Mia Casa* (☎ 21 30 61) is a rambling place filled with backpackers. Singles/doubles are L35,000/50,000 and triples/quads are L65,000/80,000.

Via della Scala, which runs north-west off the piazza, is lined with pensioni. *La Romagnola* (☎ 21 15 97) at No 40 has large, clean rooms for L39,000/64,000. A triple room is L90,000. The same family runs *La Gigliola* (☎ 28 79 81) upstairs. *La Scala* (☎ 21 26 29) at No 21 is small and has doubles/triples for L80,000/110,000. The *Pensione Margareth* (☎ 21 01 38) at No 25 is pleasantly furnished and has singles/doubles for L45,000/60,000. A triple is L90,000. Use of the communal shower is L2500. *Pensione Montreal* (☎ 238 23 31) at No 43 has singles for L40,000 and doubles/ triples with bathroom for L80,000/120,000.

The *Sole* (☎ 239 60 94), Via del Sole 8, charges L45,000/65,000 for singles/doubles. A double with bathroom costs L85,000. Triples/ quads cost L78,000/92,000. The curfew is 1 am. Ask for a quiet room. In the same building is the *Pensione Toscana* (☎ 21 31 56), with singles/doubles for L70,000/ 110,000. The *Ottaviani* (☎ 239 62 23), at Piazza Ottaviani 1, just off Piazza Santa Maria Novella, has singles/doubles for L50,000/ 70,000, breakfast included. In the same build- ing is the *Visconti* (☎ 21 38 77), with a pleasant

terrace garden where you can have breakfast. Singles/doubles are L55,000/84,000, and a triple is L115,000. Breakfast is included.

Hotels – from the Duomo to the Arno
This area is a 15-minute walk from the station and is right in the heart of old Florence.

One of the best deals is the small *Aily Home* (☎ 329 65 05), overlooking the Ponte Vecchio at Piazza Santo Stefano 1. It has double rooms (three of which overlook the bridge) for L60,000 a night. *Albergo Firenze* (☎ 21 42 03; fax 21 23 70), Piazza dei Donati 4, just south of the Duomo, has singles/doubles for L55,000/82,000 including breakfast. The *Brunori* (☎ 28 96 48), Via del Proconsolo 5, has doubles for L66,000, or with private bathroom for L84,000. The *Maria Luisa de' Medici* (☎ 28 00 48), Via del Corso 1, is in a 17th-century palace. It has no singles, but its large rooms for up to five people cater for families. All prices include breakfast. A double is L93,000, a triple L129,000 and a quad L168,000.

Fiesole In the hills overlooking Florence is *Bencistà* (☎ 055-5 91 63), Via Benedetto da Maiano 4, about one km from Fiesole. It is an old villa and from its terrace there is a magnificent view of Florence. A double is L140,000, or L170,000 with bathroom, and half-pension is L105,000 per person. It might break the budget, but for one or two days it is well worth it.

Rental If you want an apartment in Florence, save your pennies and start searching well before you arrive. A one-room apartment with kitchenette, in the centre, will cost from L600,000 to L1,000,000 a month. Florence & Abroad (☎ 48 70 04), Via Zanobi 58, handles rental accommodation.

Places to Eat
Simplicity and quality best describe the food of Tuscany. Start your meal with fettunta (known elsewhere in Italy as bruschetta), a thick slice of toasted bread, rubbed with garlic and soaked with the rich, green Tuscan olive oil. Try the ribollita, a very filling soup of vegetables and white beans, reboiled with chunks of bread and garnished with olive oil. Another traditional dish is the deliciously simple fagiolini alla Fiorentina (green beans

and olive oil). Florence is renowned for its excellent bistecca Fiorentina (beefsteak Florentine) – thick, juicy and big enough for two people.

Eating at a good trattoria can be surprisingly economical, but many tourists fall into the trap of eating at the self-service restaurants which line the streets of the main shopping district between the Duomo and the Arno. Be adventurous and seek out the little eating places in the district of Oltrarno (the other side of the Arno from the centre) and near the Mercato Centrale (the covered market) in San Lorenzo. The market, open from Monday to Saturday 7 am to 2 pm (also Saturday from 4 to 8 pm), offers fresh produce, cheeses and meat at reasonable prices.

City Centre The *Trattoria da Benvenuto*, Via Mosca 16r, on the corner of Via dei Neri, is an excellent trattoria. A full meal will cost around L25,000 and a quick meal of pasta, bread and wine will cost around L12,000. *Angie's Pub*, Via dei Neri 35r, offers a vast array of sandwiches and focaccia (you can design your own) for L4500 to L6500, as well as hamburgers, served Italian-style with mozzarella and spinach, and hot dogs with cheese and mushrooms. There is a good range of beers and no extra charge if you sit down. At *Fiaschetteria*, Via dei Neri 17r, try the excellent ribollita for around L10,000. *Osteria Il Caminetto*, Via dello Studio 34, just south of Piazza del Duomo, has a small vine-covered terrace. A pasta dish costs around L9000, and a full meal around L30,000.

Around San Lorenzo Ask anyone in Florence where they go for lunch and they will answer *Mario's*. This small bar and trattoria at Via Rosina 2r, near the Mercato Centrale, is open only at lunchtime. It serves pasta dishes for around L4000 to L6000, and a secondo for L5000 to L9000. A few doors down, at Piazza del Mercato Centrale 20, is *Cafè Za Za*, another favourite with the locals. Prices are around the same as at Mario's. *Bondi*, Via dell'Ariento 85, specialises in focaccia and pizza from L2500.

In the Oltrarno A bustling place popular with the locals is *Trattoria Casalinga*, Via dei

Michelozzi 9r. The food is great and a filling meal of pasta, meat or contorni, and wine will cost you around L15,000 to L20,000. *I Tarocchi*, Via de' Renai 12-14r, serves excellent pizza, ranging from L6000 to L10,000, as well as dishes typical of the region, including a good range of pasta from L7000 to L8000, and plenty of salads and vegetable dishes from L5000 to L8000. The coperto is only L2000. *Angelino*, Via Santo Spirito 36, is an excellent trattoria where a full meal will cost around L35,000.

Cafés & Snack Bars Near the Mercato Centrale, Via Nazionale 57, *Caffè degli Innocenti* has a good selection of pre-prepared panini and cakes for around L2500 to L3500. The streets between the Duomo and the Arno harbour many pizzerias where you can buy pizza by the slice to take away for around L2000 to L4000, depending on the weight.

Gelati Among the best outlets for gelati are *Gelateria Vivoli*, Via dell'Isola delle Stinche, near Via Torta, and *Perché No?*, Via dei Tavolini 19r, off Via Calzaiuoli.

Entertainment

Several publications list the theatrical and musical events and festivals held in the city and surrounding areas. They include the bimonthly *Florence Today* and the monthly *Firenze Information* and *Firenze Avvenimenti*, all available at the tourist offices. *Firenze Spettacolo* is the city's definitive entertainment guide, available every 15 days for L2500 at newsstands.

Concerts, opera and dance are performed year-round at the *Teatro Comunale*, Corso Italia 16, with the main seasons running from September to December and from January to April. Contact the theatre's box office (☎ 277 92 36).

The *Astro Cinema* in Piazza San Simone, near Santa Croce, runs films in English every night except Monday. Nightclubs include *La Dolce Vita*, Piazza del Carmine, south of the Arno. *Cabiria*, in Piazza Santo Spirito, is a bar which is very popular among young people, especially in summer.

A more sedate pastime is the nightly passeggiata (stroll) in Piazzale Michelangelo, overlooking the city (take bus No 13 from the station or the Duomo).

Things to Buy

The main shopping area is between the Duomo and the Arno, with boutiques concentrated along Via Roma, Via dei Calzaiuoli and Via Por Santa Maria, leading to the goldsmiths lining the Ponte Vecchio. Window-shop along Via de' Tornabuoni, where the top designers, including Gucci, Yves Saint Laurent and Pucci, sell their wares.

The open-air market (open Monday to Saturday), located in the streets of San Lorenzo near the Mercato Centrale, offers leather goods, clothing and jewellery at low prices, but quality can vary greatly. Check the item carefully before you buy. You can bargain, but not if you want to use a credit card. The flea market at Piazza dei Ciompi, off Borgo Allegri near the Church of Santa Croce (Monday to Saturday), is not as extensive but there are great bargains. It opens roughly the same hours as retail shops and all day on the last Sunday of the month.

Florence is famous for its beautifully patterned paper, which is stocked in the many *cartolerie* (stationer's shops) throughout the city and at the markets.

Getting There & Away

Air The nearest international airport is Galileo Galilei at Pisa, just under an hour away from Florence. It has regular connections to major European and Italian cities. Amerigo Vespucci airport, a few km north-west of the city centre at Via del Termine, serves mainly domestic flights.

Bus The SITA bus terminal (☎ 21 47 21), Via Santa Caterina da Siena, is just to the west of the train station. Buses leave for Siena, the Colle Val d'Elsa, Poggibonsi (where there are connecting buses to San Gimignano and Volterra) and Arezzo. Full details on other bus services are available at the APT.

Train Florence is on the main Rome-Milan line and most of the trains are the fast intercities, for which you have to pay a rapido supplement. Regular trains also go to/from Venice (three hours) and Trieste. For train information ring ☎ 28 87 85.

Car & Motorcycle Florence is connected by the Autostrada del Sole (A1) to Bologna and Milan in the north and Rome and Naples to the south. The motorway to the sea, Autostrada del Mare (A11), joins Florence to Prato, Lucca, Pisa and the Mediterranean coast, and a superstrada (dual carriageway) joins the city to Siena. Exits from the autostrade into Florence are well signed, and either one of the exits marked 'Firenze nord' or 'Firenze sud' will take you to the centre of town. There are tourist information offices on the A1 both to the north and south of the city.

Getting Around

To/From the Airports Regular trains leave from platform number 5 at Florence's Santa Maria Novella station for Pisa airport daily from 5.55 am to 8 pm. Check your bags in at the air terminal (☎ 21 60 73) near platform 5. ATAF bus No 62 leaves regularly from the train station for Amerigo Vespucci airport.

Bus ATAF buses service the city centre and Fiesole. The terminal for the most useful buses is in a small piazza to the left as you go out of the station onto Via Valfonda. Bus No 7 leaves from here for Fiesole and also stops at the Duomo. Tickets must be bought before you get on the bus and are sold at most tobacconists or from automatic vending machines at major bus stops (L1400 for one hour, L1900 for two hours, L5000 for 24 hours).

Car & Motorcycle If you're spending the day in Florence, park the car at the Fortezza da Basso. It costs L1500 an hour. More expensive car parks are in Piazza del Mercato Centrale.

To rent a car, try Hertz (☎ 28 22 60), Via M Finiguerra 17r, or Avis (☎ 21 36 29), Borgognissanti 128r. For motorcycles and bicycles try Alinari (☎ 28 05 00), Via Guelfa 85r.

Taxi You can find taxis outside the station, or call ☎ 4798 or ☎ 4390 to book one.

PISA

Once a maritime power to rival Genoa and Venice, Pisa now seems content to have one remaining claim to fame: its leaning tower. On the banks of the Arno River near the Ligurian Sea, Pisa was once a busy port, the site of an important university and the home of Galileo Galilei (1564-1642). Devastated by the Genoese in the 13th century, its history eventually merged with that of Florence. Today Pisa is a pleasant town, but there is not a lot to see after you have explored the main square, the Campo dei Miracoli, and taken a walk around the old centre.

Information

There are APT tourist information offices at the train station, the airport and at Piazza Arcivescovado, next to the Campo dei Miracoli. In summer the station and Campo offices open daily from 8 am to 8 pm but the station office is closed on Sunday. Take bus No 1 from the station, which is across the river from the old town, to Piazza del Duomo.

Pisa's postcode is 56100 and the telephone code is ☎ 050.

Things to See & Do

The Pisans can justly claim that their **Campo dei Miracoli** (Field of Miracles) is one of the most beautiful squares in the world. Set in its sprawling lawns are the **cathedral**, the **baptistry** and the **leaning tower**. On any day the piazza is teeming with people – students studying, tourists wandering and Pisan workers eating their lunch.

The Romanesque cathedral, begun in 1064, has a beautiful façade of columns in four tiers and its huge interior is lined with 68 columns. The bronze doors of the transept, facing the leaning tower, are by Bonanno Pisano. The 16th-century bronze doors of the main entrance are by Giambologna and were made to replace the original doors which were destroyed in a fire. The marble baptistry, which was started in 1153 and took almost two centuries to complete, contains a beautiful pulpit by Nicola Pisano.

The famous leaning bell tower was in trouble from the start. Its architect, Bonanno Pisano, managed to complete three tiers before the tower started to lean. The problem is generally believed to have been caused by shifting soil, and the tower has continued to lean by an average one mm a year. Galileo climbed its 294 steps to experiment with gravity. Today it is no longer possible to follow in his footsteps. The tower has been closed for some years while the Italians have been trying to work out how to

stop its inexorable lean towards the ground. Finally, in early 1994, they found a solution – 600 tons of lead ingots which anchor the north foundation. The lean was stopped and the tower even began to straighten. However, in September 1995 the tower moved 2.5 mm in one night. While no-one has any intention of turning the leaning tower into a straight tower, many still believe that it will fall down eventually.

After seeing the Campo dei Miracoli, take a walk down Via Santa Maria, along the Arno and into the Borgo Stretto to explore the old city.

Places to Stay & Eat

Pisa has a reasonable number of budget hotels for a small town, but many double as residences for students during the school year, so it can be difficult to find a cheap room. The non-HI *Ostello per la Gioventù* (☎ 89 06 22), is at Via Pietrasantina 15 and is used by students. A bed is L20,000. The place is closed from 9 am to 6 pm. Take bus No 3 from the station. The *Albergo E Gronchi* (☎ 56 18 23), Piazza Arcivescovado 1, just near the Campo dei Miracoli, has modern singles/doubles for L32,000/50,000 and triples/quads for L68,000/84,000. *Albergo Giardino* (☎ 56 21 01), Piazza Manin 1, just west of Campo dei Miracoli, has singles/doubles for L40,000/60,000. The *Hotel di Stefano* (☎ 55 35 59), Via Sant'Apollonia 35, offers good-quality singles/doubles for L40,000/55,000.

Near the station is the *Albergo Milano* (☎ 23 162), Via Mascagni 14, with pleasant rooms and a friendly owner. Singles/doubles cost L45,000/60,000 and triples cost L80,000.

Being a university town, Pisa hosts a good range of cheap eating places. Head for the area around Borgo Stretto and the university. *Numeroundici*, Via Domenica Cavalca 11, has cheap snacks, as well as a full menu. *Pizzeria da Matteo*, Via Santa Maria 20, is another good choice. There is an open-air food market in Piazza delle Vettovaglie, off Borgo Stretto. Pick up supplies there and head for the Campo dei Miracoli for a picnic lunch.

Getting There & Away

The airport, with domestic and international (European) flights, is only a few minutes away by train, or by bus No 7 from the station. Lazzi (☎ 462 88) buses operate to Florence, Prato and Lucca. APT (☎ 233 84) runs buses to

ITALY

Volterra and Livorno. The city is linked by direct train to Florence, Rome and Genoa. Local trains head for Lucca and Livorno.

SIENA

Italy's best preserved medieval town, Siena is built on three hills and is still surrounded by its historic ramparts. Its medieval centre is bristling with majestic Gothic buildings in various shades of the colour known as burnt sienna. According to legend, Siena was founded by the sons of Remus (one of the founders of Rome). In the Middle Ages the city became a free republic, but its success and power led to serious rivalry with Florence. In a famous incident in the 13th century, the Florentines hurled dead donkeys and excrement into Siena, hoping to start a plague.

Painters of the Sienese School produced important works of art and the city was home to St Catherine and St Benedict. Siena is divided into 17 *contrade* (districts) and each year 10 are chosen to compete in the Palio, an extraordinary horse race and pageant held in the shell-shaped Piazza del Campo on 2 July and 16 August.

Orientation

Siena is well geared for tourism. Signs direct you through the modern town to the medieval city, and within the walls there are easy-to-follow signs to all the major sights.

From the train station catch bus No 2, 3 or 10 to Piazza Matteotti and walk into the centre along Via dei Termini (it takes about five minutes to reach the Campo). From the bus terminal in Piazza San Domenico, it's a five-minute walk along Via della Sapienza and then left into Via delle Terme to the Campo. No cars, apart from those of residents, are allowed in the medieval centre.

Information

Tourist Office The APT office (☎ 28 05 51) is at Piazza del Campo 56 and during summer is open Monday to Saturday from 8.30 am to 7.30 pm. For the rest of the year it opens Monday to Friday from 9 am to 1 pm and 3.30 to 6.30 pm.

Post & Communications The main post office is at Piazza Matteotti 1. The Telecom office is at Via dei Termini 40.

Siena's telephone code is ☎ 0577.

Medical Services For an ambulance, call ☎ 28 00 28. The public hospital (☎ 29 08 07) is in Viale Bracci, just north of Siena at Le Scotte.

Emergency For a police emergency call ☎ 113. The questura is at Via del Castoro 23 (near the Duomo) and its Foreigners' Office is in Piazza Jacopo della Quercia.

Things to See & Do

The **Piazza del Campo**, known simply as the Campo, is a magnificent shell-shaped, slanting piazza, its paving divided into nine sectors. At the lowest point of the piazza is the imposing **Palazzo Pubblico** (also known as Palazzo Comunale or town hall), considered one of the most graceful Gothic buildings in Italy. Inside the town hall are numerous important Sienese works of art, including Simone Martini's *Maestà* and Ambrogio Lorenzetti's frescos, *Allegories of Good & Bad Government*. There is also a chapel with frescos by Taddeo di Bartolo. As with all museums and monuments in Siena, the opening hours for the palace vary depending on the time of year. In summer it opens Monday to Saturday from 9.30 am to 7.30 pm and Sunday from 9.30 am to 1.45 pm. Entry is L6000, or L3000 for students.

The spectacular **Duomo** is one of the most beautiful in Italy. Its black-and-white striped marble façade has a Romanesque lower section, with carvings by Giovanni Pisano. Its upper section is 14th-century Gothic and there are 19th-century mosaics at the top. The interior features an inlaid marble floor, with various works depicting biblical stories. The beautiful **pulpit** was carved in marble and porphyry by Nicola Pisano, the father of Giovanni Pisano. Other important art works include a bronze statue of St John the Baptist by Donatello and statues of St Jerome and Mary Magdalene by Bernini.

Through a door from the north aisle is the **Libreria Piccolomini**, which Pope Pius III (pope during 1503) built to house the magnificent, illustrated books of his uncle, the former pope Pius II. It features frescos by Pinturicchio and a Roman statue of the Three Graces. Entry is L2000.

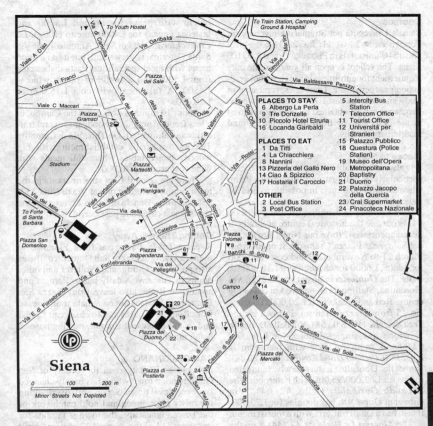

Siena

PLACES TO STAY
6 Albergo La Perla
9 Tre Donzelle
10 Piccolo Hotel Etruria
16 Locanda Garibaldi

PLACES TO EAT
1 Da Titti
4 La Chiacchiera
8 Nannini
13 Pizzeria del Gallo Nero
17 Hostaria il Caroccio

OTHER
2 Local Bus Station
3 Post Office

5 Intercity Bus
   Station
7 Telecom Office
11 Tourist Office
12 Universitá per
   Stranieri
15 Palazzo Pubblico
18 Questura (Police
   Station)
19 Museo dell'Opera
   Metropolitana
20 Baptistry
21 Duomo
22 Palazzo Jacopo
   della Quercia
23 Crai Supermarket
24 Pinacoteca Nazionale

0   100   200 m

Minor Streets Not Depicted

ITALY

The **Museo dell'Opera Metropolitana** (Duomo Museum) is in Piazza del Duomo. It houses many important works of art that formerly adorned the cathedral, including the famous *Maestà* by Duccio di Buoninsegna, formerly used as a screen for the cathedral's High Altar; and works by artists including Ambrogio Lorenzetti, Simone Martini and Taddeo di Bartolo. The collection also features tapestries and manuscripts. From mid-March to the end of September the museum is open daily from 9 am to 7.30 pm. In October it closes at 6 pm and during the rest of the year at 1.30 pm. Entry is L5000.

The **baptistry**, which is behind the cathe-dral, has a Gothic façade and is decorated with 15th-century frescos, a font by Jacopo della Quercia, and sculptures by artists such as Donatello and Ghiberti. Entry is L3000.

The 15th-century **Palazzo Buonsignori** houses the **Pinacoteca Nazionale** (National Picture Gallery), with innumerable masterpieces by Sienese artists, including the *Madonna dei Francescani* by Duccio di Buoninsegna, *Madonna col Bambino* by Simone Martini and a series of Madonnas by Ambrogio Lorenzetti. The gallery is open Tuesday to Saturday from 9 am to 7 pm and Sunday to 1 pm. Admission is L8000.

Courses

Siena's Università per Stranieri (University for Foreigners; ☎ 24 01 11; fax 28 31 63; e-mail unistra4@unisi.it) is in Piazzetta Grassi 2, 53100 Siena. The school is open all year and the only requirement for enrolment is a high school graduation/pass certificate. There are several areas of study and courses cost L725,000 for 10 weeks. Brochures can be obtained by making a request to the Secretary, or from the Italian Cultural Institute in your city.

Places to Stay

It is always advisable to book a hotel in Siena, particularly in August and during the Palio, when accommodation is impossible to find for miles around the city.

The *Colleverde* camping ground (☎ 28 00 44) is outside the historical centre at Strada di Scacciapensieri 47 (take bus No 8 from Piazza del Sale, near Piazza Gramsci). It opens from March 21 to November 10 and costs L13,000 for adults, L6500 for children and L18,000 for a site. The *Guidoriccio* hostel (☎ 52 212), Via Fiorentina, Stellino, is about two km out of the centre. Bed and breakfast is L20,000. Take bus No 15 from Piazza Gramsci. In town try the *Tre Donzelle* (☎ 28 03 58), Via delle Donzelle 5, which has singles/doubles for L38,000/62,000. A room for four with bathroom is L132,000. *Piccolo Hotel Etruria* (☎ 28 80 88), Via delle Donzelle 1, has newly renovated rooms for L62,000/95,000 with bathroom. The *Locanda Garibaldi* (☎ 28 42 04), Via Giovanni Dupré 18, has doubles for L70,000. It also has a small trattoria with a tourist menu.

The *Albergo La Perla* (☎ 47 144) is on the 2nd floor at Via delle Terme 25, a short walk from the Campo. Small but clean singles/doubles with shower are L60,000/90,000.

Agriturismo is well organised around Siena. The tourist office has a list of establishments, or contact Agriturismo in Rome (see Accommodation in the Facts for the Visitor section earlier in this chapter).

Places to Eat

Pizzeria del Gallo Nero, Via del Porrione 67, near the Campo, has good pizzas for around L8000 and there are no cover or service charges. In the Piazza del Campo is the cheap self-service *Ciao & Spizzico*. Off the Campo, at Via Casato di Sotto 32, is *Hostaria Il Car-roccio* with pasta for around L8000 and bistecca (steak) for L4000 an etto (100g). *La Chiacchiera*, Costa di Sant' Antonio 4, off Via Santa Caterina, is very small, but it has a good menu with local specialities. Pasta dishes cost from L5000 and a bottle of house wine is L4500. A full meal will cost L15,000 to L20,000.

About 10 minutes walk from the Campo, in a less frenetic neighbourhood, are several trattorias and alimentari. *Da Titti*, Via di Camollia 193, is a no-frills establishment with big wooden bench tables where full meals with wine cost around L20,000.

There are several *Crai* supermarkets in the town centre, including one at Via di Città 152-156. *Nannini*, Banchi di Sopra 22, is one of the city's finest cafés and pasticcerie.

Getting There & Away

Regular Tra-In buses run from Florence to Siena, arriving at Piazza San Domenico. Buses also go to San Gimignano, Volterra and other points in Tuscany. A daily bus to Perugia and another to Rome also leave from Piazza San Domenico. Siena is not on a main train line, so from Rome it is necessary to change at Chiusi and from Florence at Empoli, making buses a better alternative.

SAN GIMIGNANO

Few places in Italy rival the beauty of San Gimignano, a town which has barely changed since medieval times. Set on a hill overlooking the misty pink, green and gold patchwork of the Tuscan landscape, the town is famous for its towers (14 of the original 72 remain), built as a demonstration of power by its prominent families in the Middle Ages.

The town is packed with tourists at weekends, so try to visit during the week. The Pro Loco tourist information office (☎ 94 00 08) is in Piazza del Duomo in the town centre.

San Gimignano's telephone code is ☎ 0577.

Things to See

Climb San Gimignano's tallest tower, **Torre Grossa** (also known as the town hall tower), off Piazza del Duomo, for a memorable view of the Tuscan hills. The tower is reached from within the **Palazzo del Popolo**, which houses the **Museo Civico**, with paintings by Filippo Lippi and Pinturicchio. Also in the piazza is the

Duomo, with a Romanesque interior, frescos by Ghirlandaio in the **Cappella di Santa Fina** and a *Last Judgment* by Taddeo di Bartolo.

The **Piazza della Cisterna**, with a 13th-century well, is the most impressive piazza in San Gimignano. It is paved with bricks in a herringbone pattern and lined with towers and palaces.

Places to Stay & Eat

San Gimignano offers few options for budget travellers. The nearest camping ground is *Il Boschetto di Piemma* (☎ 94 03 52), about three km from San Gimignano at Santa Lucia. It costs L6000 a night for adults and L4000 for children, plus L8000 for a site. It is open from April until mid-October and there is a bus service to the site. The non-HI hostel (☎ 94 19 91) at Via delle Fonti opens from March 1 to October 31 and charges L21,000 for B&B. *Foresteria Convento di Sant'Agostino* (☎ 94 03 83), Piazza Sant'Agostino, has rooms for L25,000/35,000. Some rooms are very shabby, but the prices are hard to beat.

Hotels in town are expensive, but there are numerous rooms for rent in private homes. Agriturismo is well organised in this area. For information on both, contact the tourist office or the APT in Siena.

Pizzeria Pizzoteca, Via dei Fossi, outside the walls to the left of Porta San Matteo, has good pizzas, but forget about the pasta. *Trattoria Chiribiri*, Piazzetta della Madonna, off Via San Giovanni, has pasta at reasonable prices. Nearby is *Pizza a Taglio*, with pizza by the slice. There is a fresh produce market held on Thursday morning in Piazza del Duomo and there are several alimentari in Via San Matteo.

Getting There & Away

Regular buses connect San Gimignano with Florence and Siena, but for both you need to change at Poggibonsi. Buses arrive at Porta San Giovanni and timetables are posted outside the Pro Loco. Enter through the Porta and continue straight ahead to reach the Piazza del Duomo.

PERUGIA

One of Italy's best preserved medieval hill towns, Perugia, the capital of the Umbria Region, has a lively and bloody past. The city is noted for the internal feuding of its families, the Baglioni and the Oddi, and the violent wars

against its neighbours during the Middle Ages. Perugia also has a strong artistic and cultural tradition. It was the home of the painter Perugino, and Raphael, his student, also worked here. Its University for Foreigners, established in 1925, offers courses in Italian language and attracts thousands of students from all over the world. A full calendar of musical and cultural events, including the noted Umbria Jazz in July, makes the city even more appealing.

Orientation & Information

The centre of all activity in Perugia is the Corso Vannucci. The APT tourist information office (☎ 572 33 27) is in Piazza IV Novembre, opposite the cathedral at one end of the Corso, and is open Monday to Saturday from 8.30 am to 1.30 pm and 4 to 7.30 pm and Sunday from 9 am to 1 pm. The main post office is in Piazza Matteotti. For all events and useful information, get a copy of the monthly *Perugia What, Where, When* (L1000 at newsstands).

Perugia's telephone code is ☎ 075.

Things to See & Do

The **Palazzo dei Priori**, on Corso Vannucci, is a rambling 13th-century palace housing the impressively frescoed **Sala dei Notari** and the **Galleria Nazionale dell'Umbria**, with works by Pinturicchio, Perugino and Fra Angelico. Opposite the palazzo is the **duomo**, with an unfinished façade in the characteristic Perugian red-and-white marble. Inside are frescos, decorations and furniture by well-known artists from the 15th to 18th centuries.

Between the two buildings, in Piazza IV Novembre, is the 13th-century **Fontana Maggiore**, designed by Fra Bevignate in 1278 and carved by Nicola and Giovanni Pisano. The bas-relief panels represent scenes of the history and trades of Perugia, the sciences and the seasons. At the other end of Corso Vannucci is the **Rocca Paolina** (Paolina Fortress), the ruins of a massive 16th-century fortress built upon the foundations of the palaces and homes of the powerful families of the day, notably the Baglioni. The homes were destroyed and the materials used to build the fortress, under the orders of Pope Paul III, as a means of suppressing the Baglioni. Destroyed by the Perugians after the declaration of the Kingdom of Italy in 1860, it remains a symbol of their defiance against oppression.

ITALY

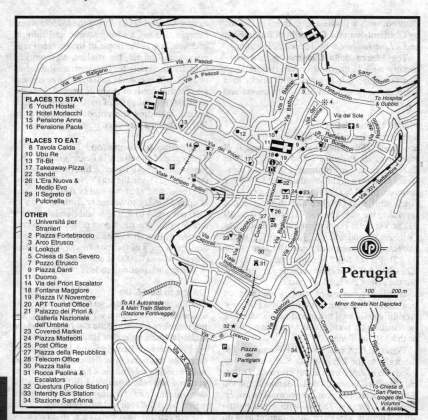

PLACES TO STAY
6 Youth Hostel
12 Hotel Morlacchi
15 Pensione Anna
16 Pensione Paola

PLACES TO EAT
8 Tavola Calda
10 Ubu Re
13 Tit-Bit
17 Takeaway Pizza
22 Sandri
26 L'Era Nuova &
    Medio Evo
29 Il Segreto di
    Pulcinella

OTHER
1 Universitá per
   Stranieri
2 Piazza Fortebraccio
3 Arco Etrusco
4 Lookout
5 Chiesa di San Severo
7 Pozzo Etrusco
9 Piazza Danti
11 Duomo
14 Via dei Priori Escalator
18 Fontana Maggiore
19 Piazza IV Novembre
20 APT Tourist Office
21 Palazzo dei Priori &
    Galleria Nazionale
    dell'Umbria
23 Covered Market
24 Piazza Matteotti
25 Post Office
27 Piazza della Repubblica
28 Telecom Office
30 Piazza Italia
31 Rocca Paolina &
    Escalators
32 Questura (Police Station)
33 Intercity Bus Station
34 Stazione Sant'Anna

Perugia

0   100   200 m

Minor Streets Not Depicted

In the **Chiesa di San Severo**, Piazza San Severo, is Raphael's magnificent fresco *Trinity with Saints*, one of the last works by the painter in Perugia and completed by Perugino after Raphael's death in 1520.

Etruscan remains in Perugia include the **Arco Etrusco** (Etruscan Arch), near the university, and the **Pozzo Etrusco** (Etruscan Well), off Piazza Piccinino, near the cathedral.

Courses

Perugia's University for Foreigners offers three and six-month courses in Italian language and culture for L720,000 for three months. The six-month courses are for advanced students.

Special one-month courses (L320,000) and intensive courses (L450,000 per month) are also offered. The quality of the courses is generally good, but there can be up to 70 students in a beginner's class during the summer months. You may need to apply for a study visa in your own country, and to obtain this you must have confirmation of enrolment in a course (see Visas & Embassies in the Facts for the Visitor section of this chapter). Since obtaining the necessary documentation from the university takes time, ensure that you send your enrolment form at least three to four months before your intended departure date.

The university will organise accommodation

on request. A room in an apartment (shared with other students), in a private room or with an Italian family will cost around L400,000 a month. Course details can be obtained from Italian cultural institutes in your country, or you can write to the secretary at the Università per Stranieri, Palazzo Gallenga, Piazza Fortebraccio 4, 06122 Perugia (☎ 574 62 11; fax 574 62 13).

Places to Stay
Perugia has a good selection of reasonably priced hotels, but if you arrive unannounced during Umbria Jazz in July, or during August, expect problems. The non-HI *Centro Internazionale per la Gioventù* (☎ 572 28 80), Via Bontempi 13, charges L14,000 a night. Sheets (for the entire stay) are an extra L1000. Its TV room has a frescoed ceiling and its terrace has one of the best views in Perugia (this floor was closed for renovation in 1996). Daylight closing is 9.30 am to 4 pm.

Pensione Anna (☎ 573 63 04), Via dei Priori 48, off Corso Vannucci, has singles/doubles for L36,000/55,000. The *Pensione Paola* (☎ 572 38 16), Via della Canapina 5, is five minutes from the centre, down the escalator from Via dei Priori. It has pleasant singles/doubles for L38,000/58,000. Just off Corso Vannucci, at Via Bonazzi 25, is the *Piccolo Hotel* (☎ 572 29 87), with small doubles for L60,000 (no singles). Showers cost an extra L3000.

The *Hotel Morlacchi* (☎ 572 03 19), Via Tiberi 2, north-west of Piazza IV Novembre, has singles/doubles for L45,000/70,000, or a triple with bathroom for L120,000.

The weekly *Cerco e Trovo* (L2500 at newsstands) lists rental accommodation.

Places to Eat
Being a student town, Perugia offers many budget eating options. Good places for pizza are *L'Era Nuova*, just behind the bar *Medio Evo* on Corso Vannucci, and *Tit-Bit*, Via dei Priori 105. Another option is the popular *Il Segreto di Pulcinella*, Via Larga 8. A pizza will cost from L5000 to L10,000 at each restaurant. There is a takeaway pizza place at Via dei Priori 3.

For a cheap meal try the *Tavola Calda* in Piazza Danti. For an excellent meal and lots of vegetables, try *Ubu Re*, Via Baldeschi 17. It's on the expensive side.

Sandri, in Corso Vannucci near the Palazzo dei Priori, is a great meeting place for a quiet coffee and cake, where you don't pay extra to sit down.

Getting There & Away
Perugia is not on the main Rome-Florence railway line. There are some direct trains from both cities, but most require a change, either at Foligno (from Rome) or Terontola (from Florence). Local trains (for towns such as Terni) leave from St Anna Station. Intercity buses leave from Piazza Partigiani, at the end of the Rocca Paolina escalators, for Rome (and Fiumicino airport), Florence, Siena and cities throughout Umbria including Assisi, Gubbio and nearby Lake Trasimeno. Full timetables for all trains and buses are available at the tourist office.

Getting Around
The main train station is a few km downhill from the historical centre. Catch any bus heading for Piazza Matteotti or Piazza Italia to get to this centre. Tickets cost L1000 and must be bought before you get on the bus.

If you arrive in Perugia by car, be prepared to be confused. Roads leading to the centre wind around a hill topped by the historical centre, and the normal driving time from the base of the hill to the centre is around 10 to 15 minutes. Signs to the centre are clearly marked 'centro' and by following these signs you should arrive at Piazza Italia, where you can leave the car and walk along Corso Vannucci to the tourist office.

Most of the centre is closed to normal traffic, but tourists are allowed to drive to their hotels. It is probably wiser not to do this, as driving in central Perugia is a nightmare because of the extremely narrow streets, most of which are one way. To accommodate other traffic, escalators from the historical centre take you to large car parks downhill. The Rocca Paolina escalator leads to Piazza Partigiani, where there is a supervised car park (L10,000 for one day, then L7500 per day), the intercity bus terminal, and escalators to Piazza Italia nearby. The Via dei Priori escalator leads to two major car parks.

ASSISI

Despite the millions of tourists and pilgrims it attracts every year, Assisi, home of St Francis, manages to remain a beautiful and tranquil refuge (as long as you keep away from the main tourist drags). From Roman times its inhabitants have been aware of the visual impact of the city, perched halfway up Mt Subasio. From the valley its pink-and-white marble buildings literally shimmer in the sunlight.

The APT tourist office (☎ 81 25 34), Piazza del Comune 12, has all the information you need on hotels, sights and events in Assisi.

The local telephone code is ☎ 075.

Things to See

Most people visit Assisi to see its religious monuments. **St Francis' Basilica** is composed of two churches, one built on top of the other. The lower church contains the crypt where St Francis is buried. The upper church was decorated by the great painters of the 13th and 14th centuries, including Giotto and Cimabue. Dress rules are applied rigidly – absolutely no shorts, miniskirts or low-cut dresses/tops are allowed.

The 13th-century **Basilica di Santa Chiara** has an impressive façade. Inside are interesting 14th-century frescos and the remains of St Clare, friend of St Francis and founder of the Order of Poor Clares. The **Cattedrale di San Rufino** is interesting for its impressive Romanesque façade. Its austere interior was altered in the 16th century, but retains the baptismal font where St Francis and St Clare were baptised. The **Piazza del Comune**, in the town centre, was the site of the Roman **Foro Romano**, parts of which have been excavated; access is from Via Portico (entry L3000). The piazza also contains the **Tempio di Minerva**. It is now a church, but retains its impressive pillared façade.

Assisi's 'crown' is the **Rocca Maggiore**, a remarkably well-preserved medieval castle. In the valley below Assisi is the **Basilica di Santa Maria degli Angeli**, a huge church built around the first Franciscan monastery, and the **Cappella del Transito**, where St Francis died in 1226.

Places to Stay & Eat

Assisi is well geared for tourists and there are numerous budget hotels and *affittacamere*

(rooms for rent). Peak periods, when you will need to book well in advance, are Easter, August and September, and the Feast of St Francis on 3 and 4 October. The tourist office has a full list of affittacamere and religious institutions.

The HI *Ostello della Pace* (☎ 81 67 67), Via Valecchi, is small and open all year. Bed and breakfast is L25,000. There is a non-HI *hostel* (L22,000 for B&B) and camping ground (☎ 81 36 36) just out of the town at Fontemaggio. From Piazza Matteotti, at the far end of town from St Francis' Basilica, walk uphill for about two km along Via Eremo delle Carceri till you reach the hostel. *Albergo La Rocca* (☎ 81 22 84), Via Porta Perlici 27, has singles/doubles for L31,000/48,000 and doubles with bath for L69,000. The *Albergo Italia* (☎ 81 26 25), Piazza del Comune, has singles/doubles for L35,000/47,000.

For a snack of pizza by the slice, head for *Pizza Vincenzo*, just off Piazza del Comune at Via San Rufina 1a. In the same complex as the camping ground at Fontemaggio is *La Stalla*, where you can eat a filling meal under an arbour for less than L20,000. In town try *Il Pozzo Romano*, Via Santa Agnese 10, off Piazza Santa Chiara. The pizzas cost around L7000. The restaurant at the *Albergo La Rocca* has home-made pasta for L5000 to L9000 and a three-course tourist menu for L19,000.

Getting There & Away

Buses connect Assisi with Perugia, Foligno and other local towns, leaving from Piazza Santa Chiara. Buses for Rome and Florence leave from Piazza San Pietro. Assisi's train station is in the valley, in the suburb of Santa Maria degli Angeli. It is on the same line as Perugia and there is a shuttle bus service between the town and the station.

SOUTH OF PERUGIA

Umbria is a mountainous region characterised by its many medieval hill towns. After Perugia and Assisi, visit **Orvieto**, **Spello** and **Spoleto** to appreciate the Romanesque and Gothic architecture, particularly Orvieto's cathedral, considered one of the most beautiful in Italy. Try to time your visit to take in the Festival of Two Worlds at Spoleto in late June and early July. These hill towns are accessible by bus or train from Perugia, and the tourist office there has information and timetables.

ANCONA
The main reason to visit Ancona is to catch a ferry to Croatia, Greece or Turkey. This industrial, unattractive port town in the region of the Marches does, however, have an interesting, though small and semi-abandoned, historical centre.

Orientation & Information
The easiest way to get from the train station to the port is by bus No 1. There are tourist information offices at the train station and the *stazione marittima* (seasonal). The main APT office (☎ 3 49 38) is out of the way at Via Thaon de Revel 4.

The main post office is at Piazza XXIV Maggio, open Monday to Saturday from 8.15 am to 7 pm. The Telecom office is opposite the train station.

The telephone code for Ancona is ☎ 071.

Things to See
Walk uphill to the old town and the **Piazzale del Duomo** for a view of the port and the Adriatic. The town's Romanesque **cathedral** was built on the site of a Roman temple and has Byzantine and Gothic features. The church of **San Francesco delle Scale** has a beautiful Venetian-Gothic doorway, and towards the port are the 15th-century **Loggia dei Mercanti** (Merchants' Loggia) and the Romanesque church of **Santa Maria della Piazza**, which has a remarkable, heavily adorned façade.

Places to Stay & Eat
Many people bunk down at the ferry terminal, although the city has many cheap hotels. *Albergo Fiore* (☎ 4 33 90), Piazza Rosselli 24, has singles/doubles for L40,000/65,000 and is just across from the train station. The *Pensione Centrale* (☎ 5 43 88), Via Marsala 10 (near Corso Stamira), has doubles for L50,000.

Trattoria da Dina, Vicolo ad Alto 17 in the old town, has full meals for around L10,000. *Osteria del Pozzo*, Via Bonda 2, just off Piazza del Plebiscito, has good, reasonably priced food. For atmosphere and good fare head for *Osteria Teatro Strabacco*, Via Oberdan 2, near Corso Stamira. The *Mercato Pubblico*, off

Corso Mazzini, has fresh fruit and vegetables and alimentari.

Getting There & Away
Bus Buses link Ancona with towns throughout the Marches region and also with major cities including Rome and Milan. Ancona is on the Bologna-Lecce train line and thus easily accessible from major towns throughout Italy. It is also directly linked to Rome via Foligno.

Car & Motorcycle Ancona is on the A14, which links Bologna and Bari. Tourists can park free at the port.

Boat All ferry operators have booths at the Stazione Marittima, off Piazza Kennedy. Here you can pick up timetables and price lists and make bookings. Remember that timetables are always subject to change and that prices fluctuate dramatically with the season. Most lines offer discounts on return fares. Prices listed are for one way, deck class in the 1996 high season.

Companies include the following: Minoan Lines (☎ 5 67 89) operates ferries to Igoumenitsa, Corfu, Kefallonia and Patras (Greece) for L123,000. Adriatica (☎ 207 43 34) ferries go to Durres in Albania (L155,000) and Split in Croatia (L70,000). Jadrolinija (☎ 20 28 05) goes to Patras (Greece) for L138,000. Marlines (☎ 20 25 66) goes to Patras (L110,000) and Kusadasi in Turkey (L270,000). Full information is available at the port.

URBINO
This town in the Marches can be difficult to reach, but it is worth the effort to see the birthplace of Raphael and Bramante, which has changed little since the Middle Ages and remains a centre of art, culture and learning.

The APT tourist information office (☎ 24 41) is at Piazza Duca Federico 35.

The telephone code for Urbino is ☎ 0722.

Things to See & Do
Urbino's main sight is the huge **Palazzo Ducale**, designed by Laurana and completed in 1482. The best view is from Corso Garibaldi to the west, from where you can appreciate the size of the building and see its towers and loggias. Enter the palace from Piazza Duca

ITALY

Federico and visit the **Galleria Nazionale delle Marches**, featuring works by Raphael, Paolo Uccello and Verrocchio. The palace is open daily from 9 am to 2 pm and entry is L8000. Also visit the **Casa di Rafaello**, Via Raffaello 57, where the artist Raphael was born, and the **Oratorio di San Giovanni Battista**, with 15th-century frescos by the Salimbeni brothers.

Courses

Urbino's Università degli Studi offers an intensive course in Italian language and culture for foreigners in August. The one-month courses cost around L500,000.

Brochures and enrolment forms can be obtained from Italian cultural institutes in your country or by writing to the Secretary, Università degli Studi di Urbino, Via Saffi 2, 61029 Urbino (☎ 30 52 50). You can arrange accommodation through the university by writing to Ufficio Alloggi dell'ERSU, Via Saffi 46, 61029 Urbino (☎ 29 34). The cost of accommodation is around L350,000 per month.

Places to Stay & Eat

Urbino is a major university town and most cheap beds are taken by students during the school year. The tourist office has a full list of affittacamere. The *Pensione Fosca* (☎ 32 96 22), Via Raffaello 67, has doubles/triples for L55,000/68,000. *Albergo Italia* (☎ 27 01), Corso Garibaldi 32, is next to the Palazzo Ducale and has singles/doubles from L42,000/55,000.

There are numerous bars around Piazza della Repubblica in the town centre and near the Palazzo Ducale which sell good panini. Try *Il Cortigiano* in Piazza del Rinascimento or *Pizzeria Galli*, Via Vittorio Veneto 19, for takeaway pizza by the slice. *Ristorante Da Franco*, just off Piazza del Rinascimento, next to the university, has a self-service section where you can eat a full meal for around L20,000.

Getting There & Away

There is no train service to Urbino, but it is connected by SAPUM and Bucci buses on weekdays to cities including Ancona, Pesaro and Arezzo. There is a bus link to the train station at the town of Fossato di Vico, on the Rome-Ancona line. There are also buses to Rome twice a day. All buses arrive at Borgo Mercatale, down Via Mazzini from Piazza della Repubblica. The tourist office has time-tables for all bus services.

Southern Italy

The land of the *mezzogiorno* (midday sun) will surprise even the most world-weary traveller. Rich in history and cultural traditions, the southern regions are poorer than those of the north, and certainly the wheels of bureaucracy grind increasingly more slowly as you travel closer to the tip of the boot. The attractions here are simpler and more stark, the people more vibrant and excitable, and myths and legends are inseparable from official history. Campania and Basilicata cry out to be explored and absolutely nothing can prepare you for Naples. Less well known among foreigners, Calabria has beautiful beaches and the striking scenery of the Sila Massif to offer visitors.

NAPLES

Crazy and confusing, but also seductive and fascinating, Naples (Napoli), capital of the Campania region, has an energy that is palpable. Beautifully positioned on the Bay of Naples and overshadowed by Mt Vesuvius, it is one of the most densely populated cities in Europe. You will leave Naples with a head full of its classic images – laundry strung across narrow streets, three people and a dog on one Vespa, cars speeding along alleys no wider than a driveway, and the same streets teeming with locals shopping at outdoor markets and drinking wine or caffè with friends.

Naples has its own secret society of criminals, the *Camorra*, which traditionally concentrated its activities on the import and sale of contraband cigarettes, but has now diversified into drugs, construction, finance and tourist developments.

Orientation

Both the Stazione Centrale (central train station) and the main bus terminal are in the vast Piazza Garibaldi. Naples is divided into *quartieri* (quarters). The main thoroughfare into the historical centre, Spaccanapoli, is

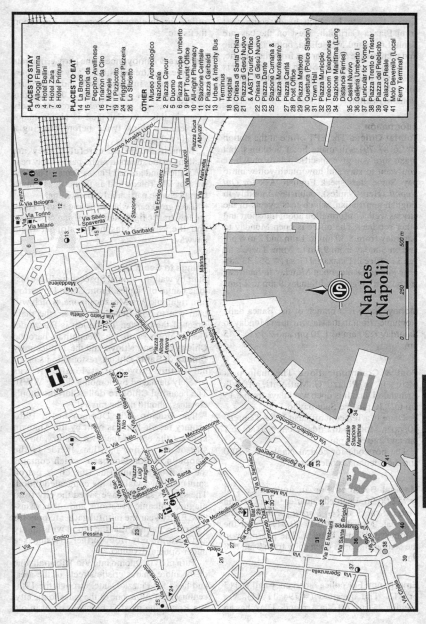

PLACES TO STAY
3 Alloggi Fiamma
4 Hotel Bellini
7 Hotel Zara
8 Hotel Primus

PLACES TO EAT
14 La Brace
15 Trattoria da
    Peppino Avellinese
16 Trianon da Ciro
17 Michele
19 Il Pizzicotto
24 Friggitoria Pizzeria
26 Lo Sfizietto

OTHER
1 Museo Archeologico
   Nazionale
2 Piazza Cavour
5 Duomo
6 Piazza Principe Umberto
9 EPT Tourist Office
10 All-night Pharmacy
11 Stazione Centrale
12 Piazza Garibaldi
13 Urban & Intercity Bus
    Terminus
18 Hospital
20 Chiesa di Santa Chiara
21 Piazza di Gesù Nuovo
    & AAST Tourist Office
22 Chiesa di Gesù Nuovo
23 Piazza Dante
25 Stazione Cumana &
    Stazione Montesanto
27 Piazza Carità
28 Post Office
29 Piazza Matteotti
30 Questura (Police Station)
31 Town Hall
32 Piazza Municipio
33 Telecom Telephones
34 Stazione Marittima (Long
    Distance Ferries)
35 Castel Nuovo
36 Galleria Umberto I
37 Funicular for Vomero
38 Piazza Trento e Trieste
39 Piazza del Plebiscito
40 Palazzo Reale
41 Molo Beverello (Local
    Ferry Terminal)

Naples
(Napoli)

ITALY

Corso Umberto I, which heads south-west from Piazza Garibaldi. West on the bay are Santa Lucia and Mergellina, both fashionable and picturesque and a far cry from the chaotic, noisy historical centre. South of Mergellina is Posillipo, where the ultra-wealthy live, and in the hills overlooking the bay is the residential Vomero district.

Information

Tourist Offices The EPT office at the station (☎ 26 87 79) will make hotel bookings, but make sure you give specific details on where you want to stay and how much you want to pay. Some staff speak English. Ask for *Qui Napoli* (Here Naples), published monthly in English and Italian, which lists events in the city, as well as information about transport and other services. The office is open Monday to Saturday from 8.30 am to 1 pm and 2 to 8 pm and on Sunday from 9 am to 2 pm. There's an AAST office in Piazza del Gesù (☎ 552 33 28), near Piazza Dante, open Monday to Saturday from 9 am to 6 pm and Sunday 9 am to 2 pm.

Money There is a branch of the Banca della Comunicazioni in the station, open Monday to Saturday 8.20 am to 1.20 pm and 2.45 to 3.45 pm.

Post & Communications The main post office is in Piazza G Matteotti, off Via Armando Diaz. It is open weekdays from 8.15 am to 7.30 pm and Saturday to 1 pm.

There is a Telecom office at Via A Depretis 40, open Monday to Friday from 9.30 am to 1 pm and 2 to 5.30 pm.

The postcode for central Naples is 80100 and the telephone code is ☎ 081.

Medical Services For an ambulance call ☎ 752 06 96. Each city quarter has a Guardia Medica, check in *Qui Napoli* for details. The Ospedale Monaldi (☎ 545 50 51) is near the Duomo, in Vico L Bianchi. The pharmacy in the central station is open daily from 8 am to 8 pm.

Emergency For police emergency call ☎ 113 or 112. The questura (☎ 794 11 11), Via Medina 75, just off Via Armando Diaz, has an office for foreigners where you can report thefts etc.

Dangers & Annoyances The petty crime rate in Naples is extremely high. Carry your money and documents in a money belt and never carry a bag or purse if you can help it. Pickpockets and thieves on motorcycles are extremely adept in this city. Car theft is also a major problem, so think twice before bringing a vehicle to the city.

Women should be careful if they are walking in the streets at night, particularly near the station and around Piazza Dante. The area west of Via Toledo and as far north as Piazza Capità can be particularly threatening.

Take great care when crossing roads. There are few traffic lights and pedestrian crossings, and the Neapolitans never stop at them anyway.

Things to See & Do

Start by walking around Spaccanapoli, the historic centre of Naples. From Corso Umberto I turn right into Via Mezzocannone, which will take you to Via Benedetto Croce, the main street of the quarter. To the left is Piazza del Gesù Nuovo, with the Neapolitan baroque **Chiesa di Gesù Nuovo** and the 14th-century **Chiesa di Santa Chiara**, restored to its original Gothic-Provençal style after it was severely damaged by bombing during WWII. The beautiful **Chiostro delle Clarisse** (nun's cloisters) should not be missed.

The **Duomo** (Via Duomo) has a 19th-century façade but was built by the Angevin kings at the end of the 13th century, on the site of an earlier basilica. Inside is the **Cappella di San Gennaro**, which contains the head of St Januarius (the city's patron saint) and two vials of his congealed blood. The saint is said to have saved the city from plague, volcanic eruptions and other disasters. Every year the faithful gather to pray for a miracle, namely that the blood will liquefy and save the city from further disaster (see under Special Events).

Turn off Via Duomo into **Via Tribunali**, one of the more characteristic streets of the area, and head for Piazza Dante, through the 17th-century **Port'Alba**, one of the gates to the city. Via Roma, the most fashionable street in old

Naples, heads to the left (becoming Via
Toledo) and ends at Piazza Trento e Trieste and
the **Piazza del Plebiscito**.

In the piazza is the **Palazzo Reale**, the
former official residence of the Bourbon and
Savoy kings, now a museum. It is open
Monday to Saturday from 9 am to 2 pm and to
1 pm Sunday and public holidays. Admission
is L6000. Just off the piazza is the **Teatro San
Carlo**, one of the most famous opera houses in
the world thanks to its perfect acoustics and
beautiful interior.

The 13th-century **Castel Nuovo** overlooks
Naples' ferry port. The early Renaissance **triumphal arch** commemorates the entry of
Alfonso I of Aragon into Naples in 1443. It is
possible to enter the courtyard of the castle, but
the building itself is not open to the public.
South-west along the waterfront, at Porto
Santa Lucia, is the **Castel dell'Ovo**, originally
a Norman castle, which is surrounded by a tiny
fishing village, the **Borgo Marinaro**.

The **Museo Archeologico Nazionale** is in
Piazza Museo, north of Piazza Dante. It contains one of the most important collections of
Graeco-Roman artefacts in the world, mainly
the rich collection of the Farnese family, and
the art treasures that were discovered at
Pompeii and Herculaneum. It is open Monday
to Saturday from 9 am to 2 pm and Sunday to
1 pm. Admission is L12,000.

From May to October, Naples' main
museums are open until 7 pm.

To escape the noise and general chaos of
historical Naples, catch the Funicolare Centrale in Via Toledo (funicular) to the suburb of
Vomero and visit the **Certosa di San Martino**,
a 14th-century Carthusian monastery, rebuilt
in the 17th century in Neapolitan baroque style.
It houses the **Museo Nazionale di San
Martino**. The monastery's church is well worth
a visit, as are its terraced gardens, which afford
spectacular views of Naples and the bay. The
monastery is open Tuesday to Sunday from 9
am to 2 pm. Entry is L8000.

Special Events
Religious festivals are lively occasions in
Naples, especially the celebration of St
Januarius, the patron saint of the city, held three
times a year: on the first Sunday in May, 19
September and 16 December in the Duomo.

Places to Stay
Hostel The HI *Ostello Mergellina Napoli*
(☎ 761 23 46), Salita della Grotta 23 in
Mergellina, is modern, safe and the best budget
option in the city. Bed and breakfast is
L20,000, or L22,000 per person for a family
room. Dinner is L14,000 and there is a bar. It
is open all year and imposes a maximum three-
night stay in summer. Take bus No 152 from
the station, or the Metropolitana to Mergellina,
and signs will direct you to the hostel from the
waterfront.

Hotels Most of the cheap hotels are near the
station and Piazza Garibaldi in a rather
unsavoury area, and some of the cheaper hotels
double as brothels. It is best to ask the tourist
office at the station to recommend or book a
room.

Station Area The following hotels are safe and
offer a reasonable standard of accommodation.
The *Hotel Zara* (☎ 28 71 25), Via Firenze 81,
is clean with singles/doubles for L28,000/
50,000. Doubles with private bath are L60,000.
Via Firenze is off Corso Novara, to the right as
you leave the train station. *Albergo Ginevra*
(☎ 28 32 10), Via Genova 116, the second
street to the right off Corso Novara, is another
reliable and well-kept place with newly renovated singles/doubles for L36,000/60,000 and
triples for L80,000. The *Casanova Hotel*
(☎ 26 82 87), Corso Garibaldi 333, is quiet and
safe. Singles/doubles are L28,000/51,000.
Triples with shower are L78,000. *Hotel
Primus* (☎ 554 73 54), Via Torino 26, has good
standard, renovated rooms with bathroom for
L50,000/90,000.

Piazza Dante Area The *Alloggi Fiamma*
(☎ 45 91 87), Via Francesco del Giudice has
basic singles/doubles with bathroom for
L40,000/ 70,000. Another option is *Hotel
Bellini* (☎ 45 69 96), Via San Paolo 44, with
singles/doubles for L35,000/65,000.

Out of the Centre Just off Piazza Amedeo in
Mergellina, at Via Martucci 72, is *Pensione
Ruggiero* (☎ 761 24 60). It has clean, bright
singles/doubles with bathroom for L90,000/
120,000. In Santa Lucia *Pensione Astoria*
(☎ 764 99 03), Via Santa Lucia 90, is a great

bargain, with well-kept singles/doubles for L30,000/50,000. In the same building is *Albergo Teresita* (☎ 764 0105) with singles/doubles for L40,000/55,000. At Vomero, just near the funicular station, is *Pensione Margherita* (☎ 556 70 44), Via D Cimarosa 29. This hotel is more up-market and charges L46,000/82,000 for singles/doubles. Ask for a room with a bay view. Have a L50 coin on hand for the lift.

Places to Eat
Naples is the home of pasta and pizza. In fact, once you have eaten a good Neapolitan pizza, topped with fresh tomatoes, oregano, basil and garlic, no other pizza will taste the same. Try a calzone, a filled version of a pizza, or mozzarella in carozza, which is mozzarella deep-fried in bread, sold at tiny street stalls. Also sold at street stalls is the misto di frittura (deep-fried vegetables). Don't leave town without trying the sfogliatelle (light, flaky pastry filled with ricotta).

City Centre According to the locals the best pizza in Naples is served at *Trianon da Ciro*, Via Pietro Colletta 46, near Via Tribunali. There's a wide selection, costing from L5500 to L12,000. Across the street is *Michele*, another good pizzeria. Nearer the station is *Trattoria Avellinese*, Via Silvio Spaventa 31-35, just off Piazza Garibaldi, which specialises in cheap seafood. Just down the street at No 14 is *La Brace*, a no-nonsense cheap place to eat. *Il Pizzicotto*, Via Mezzocannone 129, has good pizzas and full meals cost around L15,000.

Mergellina & Vomero Neapolitans head for the area around Piazza Sannazzaro, south-west of the centre, for a good meal. It is also handy to the youth hostel. *Pizzeria da Pasqualino*, Piazza Sannazzaro 79, has outdoor tables and serves good pizzas and seafood. A meal will cost around L20,000 with wine. *Mario Daniele*, Via A Scarlatti 104, is a bar with a restaurant upstairs. *Cibo Cibo*, Via Cimarosa 150, is another good budget spot.

Food Stalls On the corner of Vico Basilico Puoti and Via Pignasecca is *Lo Sfizietto*. *Friggitoria Pizzeria* is at Piazza Montesanto. Both offer lots of cheap goodies.

Entertainment
The monthly *Qui Napoli* and the local newspapers are the only real guides to what's on. In July there is a series of free concerts called *Luglio Musicale a Capodimonte* outside the Capodimonte Palace. The *Teatro San Carlo* has year-round performances of opera, ballet and concerts. Tickets start at L20,000. Call ☎ 797 21 11 for bookings and information.

Things to Buy
The area around Naples is famous for its ceramic products and many small shops in the city and surrounding areas sell hand-painted ceramics at reasonable prices. Young people shop along Via Roma and Via Toledo. More exclusive shops are found in Santa Lucia, along Via Chiaia to Piazza dei Martiri and down towards the waterfront. Naples is renowned for the work of its goldsmiths and for its *presepi* (nativity scenes). Most artisans are in Spaccanapoli. The narrow streets of Naples are full of markets, notably in the area off Via Mancinio (off Piazza Garibaldi), near Piazza Carità (which separates Via Roma and Via Toledo) and around Piazza Montesanto.

Getting There & Away
Air The Capodichino airport (☎ 789 62 68), Viale Umberto Maddalena, is about five km north-east of the city centre. There are connections to most Italian and several European cities.

Bus Buses leave from Piazza Garibaldi, just outside the train station, for destinations including Salerno, Benevento, Caserta (every 20 minutes) and Bari, Lecce and Brindisi in Apulia.

Train Naples is a major rail transport centre for the south, and regular trains for most major Italian cities arrive and depart from the Stazione Centrale in Piazza Garibaldi. There are up to 30 trains a day for Rome.

Car & Motorcycle Driving in Naples is not recommended. The traffic is chaotic and car and motorcycle theft is rife. The city is easily accessible from Rome on the A1. The Naples-Pompeii-Salerno road connects with the coastal road to Sorrento and the Amalfi Coast.

ITALY

Boat Traghetti and *aliscafi* (hydrofoils) leave for Capri, Sorrento, Ischia and Procida from the Molo Beverello, in front of the Castel Nuovo. Some hydrofoils leave for the bay islands from Mergellina and ferries for Ischia and Procida also leave from Pozzuoli. All operators have offices at the various ports from which they leave. Tickets for the hydrofoils cost around double those for ferries, but the trip takes half the time.

Ferries to Palermo and Cagliari (Tirrenia ☎ 720 11 11) and to the Aeolian Islands (Siremar ☎ 761 36 88) leave from the Stazione Marittima on Molo Angioino, next to Molo Beverello (see the Getting There & Away sections under Sicily and Sardinia). SNAV (☎ 761 23 48) runs regular hydrofoils to the islands.

Getting Around

You can make your way around Naples by bus, tram, Metropolitana (underground) and funicular. City buses leave from Piazza Garibaldi in front of the central station bound for the centre of Naples, as well as Mergellina. Tickets, called *GiraNapoli*, cost L1200 for 90 minutes and are valid for buses, trams, the Metropolitana and funicular services. Day tickets cost L4000. Useful buses include: 14 to the airport; CD and CS to Piazza Dante; C4 Mergellina to the city centre; 127R from Piazza Garibaldi to Piazza Cavour and the archaeological museum. Tram No 1 leaves from east of Stazione Centrale for the city centre. To get to Molo Beverello and the Stazione Marittima, take Bus No R2, 152 or M1 from Stazione Centrale.

The Metropolitana station is downstairs at central station. Trains head west to Mergellina, stopping at Piazza Amedeo and the funicular to Vomero, and Piazza Cavour, then head on to the Campi Flegrei and Pozzuoli. Another line, now under construction, will eventually connect Piazza Garibaldi and Piazza Medaglie d'Oro, with stops including the Duomo and the Museo Archeologico Nazionale.

The main funicular connecting the city centre with Vomero is the Funicolare Centrale, in Piazza Duca d'Aosta, next to Galleria Umberto I, on Via Toledo.

The Ferrovia Circumvesuviana operates trains for Pompeii, Herculaneum and Sorrento. The station is about 400 metres south-west of Stazione Centrale, in Corso Garibaldi (take the underpass from Stazione Centrale). The Ferrovia Cumana and the Circumflegrei, based at Stazione Cumana in Piazza Montesanto, operate services to Pozzuoli and Cumae every 20 minutes.

AROUND NAPLES

From Naples it is only a short distance to **Campi Flegrei** (Phlegraean Fields) of volcanic lakes and mudbaths, which inspired both Homer and Virgil in their writings. Today part of suburban Naples, the area is dirty and over-developed, but still worth a day trip. The Greek colony of **Cumae** is certainly worth visiting, particularly to see the Cave of the Cumaean Sybil, home of one of the ancient world's greatest oracles. Also in the area is **Lake Avernus**, the mythical entrance to the underworld.

Reached by CPTC bus from Naples' Piazza Garibaldi or by train from the Stazione Centrale is the **Palazzo Reale** at Caserta, usually called the Reggia di Caserta. Built by the Bourbon king Charles III, this massive 1200-room palace is set in gardens modelled on Versailles.

Pompeii & Herculaneum

Buried under a layer of lapilli (burning fragments of pumice stone) during the devastating eruption of Mt Vesuvius in 79 AD, **Pompeii** provides a fascinating insight into how the ancient Romans lived. It was a resort town for wealthy Romans, and among the vast ruins are impressive temples, a forum, one of the largest known Roman amphitheatres, and streets lined with shops and luxurious houses. Many of the site's mosaics and frescos have been moved to Naples Museo Archeologico Nazionale. The exception is the Villa dei Misteri, where the frescos remain *in situ*.

Most of the houses and shops are locked, but there are numerous official attendants who are supposed to open them on request. Single women should avoid attendants who are a bit too willing to take you to the more secluded sights.

There are tourist offices (AAST) at Via Sacra 1 (☎ 850 72 55) in the new town, and just outside the excavations at Piazza Porta Marina Inferiore 12 (☎ 861 09 13). *How to Visit Pompeii* (talk them down to L8000), is a comprehensive guide to the ancient city. The ruins

ITALY

are open from 9 am to one hour before sunset and entry is L12,000.

Catch the Circumvesuviana train from Naples and get off at the Pompeii-Villa dei Misteri stop; the Porta Marina entrance is close by.

Herculaneum (Ercolano) is closer to Naples and is also a good point from which to visit Mt Vesuvius. Legend says the city was founded by Hercules. First Greek, then Roman, it was also destroyed by the 79 AD eruption, buried under mud and lava. Most inhabitants of Herculaneum had enough warning and managed to escape. The ruins here are smaller and the buildings, particularly the private houses, are remarkably well preserved. Here you can see better examples of the frescos, mosaics and furniture that used to decorate Roman houses.

Herculaneum is also accessible on the Circumvesuviana train from Naples. The ruins are open daily from 9 am to one hour before sunset. Entry is L12,000.

Catch the SITA bus from the piazza in front of the Ercolano train station to Mt Vesuvius (L4000 return). The first bus leaves the station at 8.15 am and the last returns at 5.45 pm. You'll then need to walk about 1.5 km to the summit, where you must pay L3000 to be accompanied by a guide to the crater.

SORRENTO

This major resort town is in a particularly beautiful area, but is heavily overcrowded in summer with package tourists and traffic. However, it is handy to the Amalfi Coast and Capri.

Orientation & Information

The centre of town is Piazza Tasso, a short walk from the train station along Corso Italia. The AAST tourist office (☎ 807 40 33), Via Luigi de Maio 35, is inside the Circolo dei Forestieri complex. The office is open from Monday to Saturday from 8.30 am to 2 pm and 4 to 7 pm. The postcode is 80067.

The post office is at Corso Italia 210 and the Telecom telephone office is at Piazza Tasso 37. For medical assistance contact the Ospedale Civile (☎ 533 11 11). For the police call ☎ 113. Sorrento's telephone code is ☎ 081.

Places to Stay

There are several camping grounds, including *Nube d'Argento* (☎ 878 13 44), Via Capo 21, which costs L13,000 per person and up to L19,000 for a tent site.

The HI Ostello Surriento was closed at the time of writing.

Albergo City (☎ 877 22 10), Corso Italia 221, has singles/doubles with bathroom for 60,000/85,000. *Pensione Linda* (☎ 878 29 16), Via degli Aranci 125, has singles/doubles for L40,000/70,000.

Places to Eat

You can get a cheap meal at *Self Service Angelina Lauro*, Piazza Angelino Lauro. *Giardinello*, Via dell'Accademia 7, has pizzas for around L7000 and pasta from L5000. In Via San Cesareo, off Piazza Tasso, there are several alimentari where you can buy food for picnics.

Getting There & Away

Sorrento is easily accessible from Naples on the Circumvesuviana train line. SITA buses leave from outside the train station for the Amalfi Coast. Hydrofoils and ferries leave from the port, along Via de Maio and down the steps from the tourist office, for Capri and Ischia.

In summer, traffic is heavy along the coastal roads to Sorrento.

CAPRI

This beautiful island, an hour by ferry from Naples, retains the mythical appeal which attracted Roman emperors, including Augustus and Tiberius, who built 12 villas here. The town of Capri is packed with tourists in summer, but is more peaceful in the low season. A short bus ride will take you to Anacapri, the town uphill from Capri – a good alternative if rooms are full in Capri. The island is famous for its grottoes, but is also a good place for walking. There are tourist offices at Marina Grande (☎ 081-837 06 34), where all the ferries arrive, in Piazza Umberto I (☎ 837 06 86), in the centre of town, and at Piazza Vittoria 4 in Anacapri (☎ 837 15 24).

Things to See & Do

There are expensive boat tours of the grottoes, including the famous **Grotta Azzurra** (Blue Grotto). Boats leave from the Marina Grande and a round trip will cost about L23,000 (which includes the cost of a motorboat to the grotto, rowing boat into the grotto and entrance fee). It is cheaper to catch a bus from Anacapri (although the rowboat and entrance fee still total around L15,000). It is possible to swim into the grotto before 9 am and after 5 pm, but do so only in company and when the sea is very calm. You can walk to most of the interesting points on the island (pick up a walking guide from the tourist office). Sights include the **Giardini d'Augusto**, in the town of Capri, and **Villa Jovis**, the ruins of one of Tiberius' villas, along the Via Longano and Via Tiberio. The latter is a one-hour walk uphill from Capri. Also visit the **Villa San Michele** at Anacapri.

Places to Stay & Eat
The *Stella Maris* (☎ 837 04 52), Via Roma 27, just off Piazza Umberto I, is right in the noisy heart of town. Singles/doubles are L60,000/90,000 and triples/quads are an additional 30%. Prices go down significantly in the off season. Bookings must be made well in advance for summer. *Villa Louisa* (☎ 837 01 28), Via D Birago 1, has rooms with great views for L80,000 a double.

In Anacapri, the *Loreley* (☎ 837 14 40), Via G Orlandi 16, near the town centre, is one of the better deals. Singles/doubles with bathroom are L50,000/90,000. The *Caesar Augustus* (☎ 837 14 21), Via G Orlandi 4, is a beautiful hotel which becomes a knockout bargain in the off season and when they have empty rooms. Prices can go as low as L40,000 per person, so it is worth checking out. Another option on the island is affittacamere. The tourist office has a full list.

In Capri, try *La Cisterna*, Via M Serafina 5, for a pizza. In Anacapri try the *Trattoria il Solitario*, in a garden setting at Via G Orlandi 54. Another good place is *Il Saraceno*, Via Trieste e Trento 18, where a full meal could cost up to L30,000. Try their lemon liqueur.

Getting There & Away
See the Getting There & Away section under Naples.

Getting Around
From Marina Grande, the funicular directly in front of the port takes you to the town of Capri (L1500), which is at the top of a steep hill some

three km from the port up a winding road. Small local buses connect the port with Capri, Anacapri and other points around the island (L1500 for one trip).

AMALFI COAST
The Amalfi coast swarms with rich tourists in summer and prices are correspondingly high. However, it remains a place of rare and spectacular beauty and if you can manage to get there in spring or autumn, you will be surprised by the reasonably priced accommodation and peaceful atmosphere.

There are tourist information offices in the individual towns, including at Positano (☎ 87 50 67), Via Saracino 2, and Amalfi (☎ 87 11 07), on the waterfront at Marina Grande.

The telephone code for the area is ☎ 089.

Positano
This is the most beautiful town on the coast, but for exactly this reason it has also become the most fashionable. It is, however, still possible to stay here cheaply.

Villa Nettuno (☎ 87 54 01), Via Pasitea 208, has doubles for L90,000 in the high season, all with private bath, though prices vary according to the length of stay. Half of the rooms are new and have small balconies overlooking the sea. The older rooms are cheaper and open onto a large terrace. Book well in advance for summer.

Villa Maria Luisa (☎ 87 50 23), at Via Fornillo 40, has double rooms with terraces for L35,000 per person in the low season and L50,000 per person, breakfast included, in July. Half-pension (L85,000 per person) is obligatory during August. The *Villa delle Palme* (☎ 87 51 62), around the corner in Via Pasitea, is run by the same management and charges slightly higher prices. Next door is the pizzeria *Il Saraceno d'Oro*, Via Pasitea 254.

Around Positano
The hills behind Positano offer some great walks if you tire of lazing on the beach. The tourist office at Positano has a brochure listing four routes, ranging in length from two to four hours. Visit **Nocelle**, a tiny, isolated village above Positano, accessible by walking track from the end of the road from Positano. Have lunch at *Trattoria Santa Croce* (☎ 87 53 19), which has a terrace with panoramic views. It is

open for both lunch and dinner in summer, but at other times of the year it is best to telephone and check in advance. From Nocelle, a walking track leads directly up into the hills overlooking the Amalfi Coast. Nocelle is accessible by local bus from Positano, via Montepertuso; buses run roughly every half-hour in summer from 7.50 am to midnight.

On the way from Positano to Amalfi is the town of **Praiano**, which is not as scenic but has more budget options, including the only camping ground on the Amalfi Coast. *La Tranquillità* (☎ 87 40 84), has a pensione, bungalows and a small camping ground. It costs L14,000 per head to camp there if you have your own tent. For a double room or bungalow it is L80,000 (with breakfast) and in summer there is compulsory half-pension at L60,000 a head including room, private bathroom, breakfast and dinner. The SITA bus stops outside the pensione. The entire establishment closes down in winter, reopening at Easter. The *Pensione Aquila* (☎ 87 40 65) at Via degli Ulivi 15, charges L60,000 a double with breakfast, L70,000 with dinner and L90,000 in August. Signs from the coastal road make it easy to find.

Amalfi

One of the four powerful maritime republics of medieval Italy, Amalfi today is a major tourist resort. Despite this, it manages to retain a tranquil atmosphere. It has an impressive **Duomo**, and nearby is the **Grotta dello Smeraldo**, which rivals Capri's Blue Grotto.

In the hills behind Amalfi is **Ravello**, accessible by bus and worth a visit if only to see the magnificent 11th-century **Villa Rufolo**, once the home of popes and, later, of the German composer Wagner. The **Villa Cimbrone**, built this century, is set in beautiful gardens, which end at a terrace offering a spectacular view of the Gulf of Salerno. There are numerous walking paths in the hills between Amalfi and Ravello. Pick up the book *Walks from Amalfi – The Guide to a Web of Ancient Italian Pathways* (L10,000) in Amalfi.

Places to Stay & Eat The HI *Ostello Beato Solitudo* (☎ 081-802 50 48) is at Piazza G Avitabile, in Agerola, just west of Amalfi. It charges L13,000 for bed only. For a room in Amalfi, try the *Albergo Proto* (☎ 87 10 03), Salita dei Curiali 4, which has singles/doubles from L50,000/80,000, breakfast included. The *Hotel Lidomare* (☎ 87 13 32) is at Via Piccolomini 9 (follow the signs from Piazza del Duomo and go left up a flight of stairs). A double costs more than L100,000 in high season, but rates are affordable at other times of the year.

Cheaper accommodation can be found at Atrani, just around the corner from Amalfi towards Salerno. *A Scalinetta* (☎ 87 14 92), just off Piazza Umberto, has beds in dorms for two, four and six people from L25,000 per person, breakfast included.

In Amalfi, *Trattoria Pizzeria al Teatro*, Via Mara Francesca Panza 19 (follow the signs to the left from Via Pietro Capuana, the main shopping street of Piazza del Duomo), offers good food in very pleasant surroundings. A pizza costs between L5000 and L10,000, pasta costs up to L7000 and fish up to L15,000. *Trattoria da Maria*, Via Genova 14, is good value with main courses around L10,000. *A Scalinetta* also has a trattoria.

Getting There & Away

Bus The coast is accessible by regular SITA buses, which run between Salerno (a 40-minute train trip from Naples) and Sorrento (accessible from Naples on the Circumvesuviana train line). Buses stop in Amalfi at Piazza Flavio Gioia, from where you can catch a bus to Ravello.

Car & Motorcycle The coastal road is narrow and in summer it is clogged with traffic, so be prepared for long delays. At other times of the year you should have no problems. Hire a motorcycle in Sorrento or Salerno.

Boat Hydrofoils and ferries also service the coast, leaving from Salerno and stopping at Amalfi and Positano. From Positano you can catch a boat to Capri.

PAESTUM

The evocative image of three Greek temples standing in fields of poppies is not easily forgotten and makes the trek to this archaeological site well worth the effort. The three temples, just south of Salerno, are among the world's best preserved monuments of the ancient Greek world. There is a tourist office (☎ 0828-81 10 16) and a museum at the site. The ruins are open Tuesday to Sunday from 9 am to one hour before sunset and entry is L10,000.

Paestum is accessible from Salerno by ATACS bus or by train.

MATERA
This ancient city in the region of Basilicata evokes powerful images of a peasant culture which existed until just over 30 years ago. Its famous *sassi* – the stone houses built in the two ravines which slice through the city – were home to more than half of Matera's population (about 20,000 people) until the 1950s, when the local government built a new residential area just out of Matera and relocated the entire population.

Information
The tourist office (☎ 33 19 83), Via Viti de Marco 9, off Via Roma (which runs off Piazza V Veneto) can organise a professional tour guide (about L25,000 for an hour).

Matera's telephone code is ☎ 0835.

Things to See
The two sassi wards, known as **Barisano** and **Caveoso**, had no electricity, running water or sewerage system until well into this century. The oldest sassi are at the top of the ravines, and the dwellings which appear to be the oldest were established in this century. As space ran out in the 1920s, the population started moving into hand-hewn or natural caves, an extraordinary example of civilisation in reverse.

The sassi zones are accessible from Piazza Vittorio Veneto and Piazza del Duomo, in the centre of Matera. Be sure to see the rock churches, **Santa Maria d'Idris** and **Santa Lucia alla Malve**, both with amazingly well-preserved Byzantine frescos. The 13th-century Apulian-Romanesque **cathedral**, overlooking Sasso Barisano, is also worth a visit. In Sasso Caveoso you will be approached by young children wanting to act as tour guides. They might be small, but they know their sassi, so pay them a few thousand lire and take up the offer, even if you can't speak Italian. Some sassi are now being restored and young people have begun to move back into the area.

Recent excavations in Piazza Vittorio Veneto have revealed the ruins of parts of Byzantine Matera, including a castle and a rock church decorated with frescos. Access is restricted, so enquire at the tourist office.

Places to Stay & Eat
There are not a lot of options for budget accommodation here and it is best to book in advance. Try the *Albergo Roma* (☎ 33 39 12), Via Roma 62. Singles/doubles are L38,000/55,000. The local fare is simple and the focus is on vegetables. *Da Aulo*, Via Anza di Lucana, is economical and serves typical dishes of Basilicata. There is a fruit and vegetable market near Piazza V Veneto, between Via Lucana and Via A Persio.

Getting There & Away
SITA buses connect Matera with Potenza, Taranto and Metaponto. The town is on the private Ferrovie Apulo-Lucane train line, which connects with Bari, Altamura and Potenza. There is also a twice-daily Marozzi bus from Rome to Matera (see the Rome Getting There & Away section). Buses arrive in Piazza Matteotti, a short walk down Via Roma to the town centre.

APULIA
For the dedicated traveller, the Apulia (Puglia) region offers many rich experiences. There are the many beautiful Romanesque churches, notably the cathedrals at Trani, Bari, Bitonto and Ruvo di Puglia. Or visit the beaches and forest of the Gargano Peninsula, stopping off at the famous sanctuary of St Michael the Archangel at Monte Sant'Angelo, and making a side trip to the unspoiled Tremiti Islands. Also visit Alberobello to see its *trulli*, which are whitewashed, conical-shaped buildings, both ancient and modern.

Lecce
Baroque can be grotesque, but never in Lecce. The style here is so refined and particular to the city that the Italians call it *barocco leccese* (Lecce baroque). Lecce's numerous bars and restaurants are a pleasant surprise in such a small city.

There is an EPT office (☎ 30 44 43) in Piazza Sant'Oronzo, the town's main piazza. Take bus No 4 from the station to the town centre.

Lecce's telephone code is ☎ 0832.

ITALY

Things to See & Do The most famous example of Lecce baroque is the **Basilica di Santa Croce**. Artists worked for 150 years to decorate the building, creating an extraordinarily ornate façade. In the **Piazza del Duomo** are the 12th-century **cathedral** (which was completely restored in the baroque style by the architect Giuseppe Zimbalo of Lecce), and its 70-metre-high **bell tower**; the **Palazzo del Vescovo** (Bishop's Palace); and the **Seminario**, with its elegant façade and baroque well in the courtyard. In Piazza Sant'Oronzo are the remains of a **Roman amphitheatre**.

Places to Stay & Eat Cheap accommodation is not abundant in Lecce, but camping facilities abound in the province of Salento. Near Lecce is *Torre Rinalda* (☎ 65 21 61), near the sea at Torre Rinalda. You can get there by STP bus from the terminal in Via Adua. In town try *Hotel Cappello* (☎ 30 88 81) at Via Montegrappa 4, near the station. Singles/doubles are L40,000/60,000 with bathroom.

Eating in this city is both inexpensive and a pleasure. A good snack bar is *Guido e Figlio*, Via Trinchese 10. *Pizzeria Dolomiti*, Viale A Costa 5, has eat-in and takeaway pizzas.

Getting There & Away STP buses connect Lecce with towns throughout the Salentine Peninsula, leaving from Via Adua. Lecce is directly linked by train to Brindisi, Bari, Rome, Naples and Bologna. The Ferrovie del Sud Est runs trains to surrounding areas, including Otranto, Gallipoli and Taranto and major points in Apulia.

Otranto

Without a car it is difficult to tour the picturesque Adriatic coast of Salento, which extends to the tip of Italy's heel, at Capo Santa Maria di Leuca. However, Otranto is easy to reach by bus and on the Ferrovie del Sud Est train line.

The tourist office (☎ 80 14 36) is at Via Pantaleone Presbitero.

Otranto's telephone code is ☎ 0836.

Things to See This port town of whitewashed buildings is overrun by tourists in summer, but it is worth a visit if only to see the incredible **mosaic** that covers the floor of the Romanesque **cathedral**. The recently restored 12th-century mosaic, depicting the tree of life, is a masterpiece unrivalled in southern Italy and is stunning in its simplicity.

The tiny Byzantine **Chiesa di San Pietro** contains some well-preserved Byzantine paintings.

Places to Stay Unfortunately, the town is not geared for budget tourism and has no one-star hotels. *Il Gabbiano* (☎ 80 12 51), Via Porto Craulo 5, has singles/doubles with bath for L35,000/80,000.

Getting There & Away A Marozzi bus runs daily from Rome to Brindisi, Lecce and Otranto (see Rome's Getting There & Away section). Ferries leave from here for Corfu and Igoumenitsa (Greece). For information and reservations for both ferries and the Marozzi bus, go to Ellade Viaggi (☎ 80 15 78) at the port.

Brindisi

Most travellers associate Brindisi with waiting. As the major embarkation point for ferries from Italy to Greece, the city swarms with travellers in transit. There is not much to do here, other than wait, so most backpackers gather at the train station or at the port in the Stazione Marittima. The two are connected by Corso Umberto I, which becomes Corso Garibaldi, and they are a 10-minute walk from each other; otherwise, you can take bus No 6, 9 or 12.

The EPT tourist information office (☎ 56 21 26) is at Lungomare Regina Margherita 12. Another information office is inside the Stazione Marittima.

Brindisi's telephone code is ☎ 0831.

Dangers & Annoyances Thieves are very active in the area between the station and port. Carry valuables in a money belt, don't walk alone through the town at night and never leave luggage or valuables unattended in your car. It is inadvisable to sleep in any of the piazzas between the station and port (a homeless man was bashed to death by a group of youths in the piazza in front of the station a few years ago). If you arrive in Brindisi with a car during summer, allow extra time for the eternal traffic jam around the port.

ITALY

Things to See & Do From ancient Roman times Brindisi has been Italy's gateway to the east. It was from here that the Crusaders set off for the Holy Land. Tradition has it that Virgil died in a Roman house near the columns marking the end of the **Appian Way** on his return from Greece. In Piazza del Duomo is the 14th-century **Palazzo Balsamo**, with a beautiful *loggetta* (a building open on one or more sides). The town's main monument is the **Chiesa di Santa Maria del Casale**, about four km from the centre. Built by Prince Philip of Taranto around 1300, it is a Romanesque church with Gothic and Byzantine touches.

Places to Stay & Eat The non-HI *Ostello per la Gioventù* (☎ 41 31 23) is about two km out of town at Via N Brandi 4, in Casale. B&B costs L17,000. Take bus No 3 or 4 from Via Cristoforo Colombo near the train station. *Hotel Venezia* (☎ 52 75 11), Via Pisanelli 4, has singles/doubles for L25,000/ 40,000. Turn left off Corso Umberto I onto Via S Lorenzo da Brindisi to get there.

There are numerous takeaway outlets along the main route between the train and boat stations, but if you want a meal, head for the side streets. The *Osteria Spaghetti House*, Via Mazzini 57, near the station, has good-value meals for around L20,000. There is a fruit and vegetable market in Via Battisti, off Corso Umberto I, open from 7 am to 1 pm daily except Sunday.

Getting There & Away Marozzi runs several buses a day to/from Rome (Stazione Tiburtina), leaving from Viale Regina Margherita in Brindisi (see the Rome Getting There & Away for information section). Appia Travel (☎ 52 16 84), Viale Regina Margherita 8-9, sells tickets (L52,000 or L58,000). Brindisi is directly connected by train to the major cities of northern Italy, as well as Rome, Ancona and Naples.

Boat Ferries leave Brindisi for Greek destinations including Corfu, Igoumenitsa, Patras and Cefalonia. The major companies operating ferries from Brindisi are: Adriatica (☎ 52 38 25), Corso Garibaldi 85-87 (open from 9 am to 1 pm, 4 to 7 pm) and on the 1st floor of the Stazione Marittima, where you must go to

check in; Hellenic Mediterranean Lines (☎ 52 85 31), Corso Garibaldi 8; and Med Link Lines (☎ 52 76 67), Corso Garibaldi 49.

Adriatica and Hellenic are the most expensive, but also the most reliable. They are the only lines which can officially accept Eurail and Inter-Rail passes, which means you pay only L5000 for deck class, L34,000 for a poltrona and L66,000 for a second-class cabin bed. If you want to use your Eurail or Inter-Rail pass, it is important to reserve some weeks in advance in summer. Even with a booking in summer, you must still go to the Adriatic or Hellenic embarkation office in the Stazione Marittima to have your ticket checked.

Discounts are available for travellers under 26 years of age and holders of some Italian rail passes. Note that fares increase by 40% in July and August. Ferry services are also increased during this period. Average prices in the 1996 high season for deck class were: Adriatica and Hellenic to Corfu, Igoumenitsa, Cefalonia or Patras – L90,000 (L76,000 for the return); Med Link to the same destinations – L75,000.

Prices go up by an average L15,000 for a poltrona, and for the cheapest cabin accommodation prices jump by L30,000 to L40,000. Bicycles can be taken aboard free, but the average fare for a motorcycle is L50,000 in the high season. Fares for cars are around L100,000 in the high season.

The port tax is L10,000, payable when you buy your ticket. It is essential to check in at least two hours prior to departure.

CALABRIA

Much of Calabria is still to be discovered by travellers, even though the region's beaches have become popular destinations. Tourist development has begun along the region's Ionian and Tyrrhenian coastlines, but in most areas it is minimal compared with Italy's more touristy regions. This is an area with many small villages in picturesque settings where the pace of life is slow and things have remained largely unchanged over the years. Market days are still an important local feature and this is when you will find most activity in the villages and towns.

Although the fierce feuding of the 'Ndrangheta, Calabria's version of the Sicilian Mafia, continues to cause havoc and atrocious

ITALY

deaths among Calabrians, tourists travelling in the region should not be concerned.

The Italian government's Southern Italy Development Fund, established in 1950 to invest money in the southern regions and in Sicily and Sardinia (for irrigation, road construction and industrial development), has basically succeeded in dragging the region into the 20th century, but many Calabrians, particularly those in more remote areas, still live in extreme poverty. Few locals speak English and you are more likely to be well received if you at least make an attempt to speak Italian.

Catanzaro & Cosenza
The old town of **Catanzaro**, the region's capital, is strikingly set, high on a hill top overlooking the Ionian Sea. Calabria's **riviera**, along the Ionian coast, is overdeveloped and pockmarked with heavy industry, but remains popular among Germans and Italians. **Tropea**, to the north of the region on the Tyrrhenian Sea, was an isolated paradise only a decade ago. Today it too has been affected by tourist development, but is certainly worth a visit, along with nearby **Pizzo** and **Scalea**, further north. For accommodation at Tropea try the *Vulcano* (☎ 0963-6 15 98), Via Campo Superiore. There are camping grounds at Scalea, including the *Camping La Pantera Rossa* (☎ 0985-2 15 46), Corso Mediterraneo.

If adventure appeals, Calabria's **Sila Massif** is the place to visit. This beautiful wilderness area remains on the verge of massive development and incorporates a major national park. The Sila is divided into three areas: the **La Greca**, **La Grande** and **La Piccola**. The best point from which to start exploring the Sila Massif is **Cosenza**, accessible by train from Paola, which is on the Rome-Reggio di Calabria railway line on the coast. From Cosenza catch a bus or train to **Camigliatello Silano**. (Cosenza has two train stations – the national FS Stazione Nuova, and the Ferrovie della Calabria serving the Sila Massif area. You can get from one to the other on local bus No 5.)

The Cosenza tourist office (☎ 0984-2 78 21) is at Corso Mazzini 92. For a room try the *Albergo Bruno* (☎ 0984-7 38 89), Corso Mazzini 27. Rooms are L30,000/ 50,000.

At Camigliatello Silano you can obtain trekking and tourist information from the Pro Loco (☎ 0984-57 80 91), Via Roma 5. Opening

hours are irregular. For accommodation try the *Miramonti* (☎ 0984-57 90 67), Via Forgitelle.

Reggio di Calabria
The port city of Reggio di Calabria on the Strait of Messina is the capital of the province of Reggio di Calabria and was, until 1971, the capital of the region of Calabria. Founded in approximately 720 BC by Greek colonists, this city was destroyed by an earthquake in 1908, which also razed Messina, and was totally rebuilt. There is a tourist information booth at the station (☎ 2 71 20) and the main office (☎ 89 20 12) is at Corso Garibaldi 329, where you can pick up a map and a list of hotels.

Reggio's telephone code is ☎ 0965.

Things to See The **lungomare** (promenade along the port) overlooks Sicily and, in certain atmospheric conditions, such as at dawn, it is possible to see the fabled **mirage of Morgana**, the reflection of Messina in the sea. Reggio's only really impressive sight is the **Museo Nazionale** (National Museum), which houses a remarkable collection documenting Greek civilisation in Calabria. Of particular interest are the **Bronzi di Riace** (Bronze Warriors of Riace), two Greek statues found off the coast of Riace in the Ionian Sea in 1972.

Places to Stay & Eat Try *Albergo Noel* (☎ 89 09 65), Via Genoese Zerbi 13, north of the Stazione Lido, which has singles/doubles for L55,000/65,000.

There are numerous alimentari along Corso Garibaldi, where you can buy cheese, bread and wine. *Ristorante La Pignata*, Via D Tripepi 122, off Corso Garibaldi, has reasonably priced food.

Getting There & Away Reggio is directly connected by regular trains to Naples and Rome, and also to Metaponto, Taranto and Bari (Apulia). Its two stations are the Lido, at the port, and Centrale, in the town centre at Piazza Garibaldi.

Up to 20 hyrofoils run by SNAV (☎ 2 95 68) leave the port just north of Stazione Lido every day for Messina, some of them proceeding on to the Isole Eolie (Aeolian Islands). The FS runs several hydrofoils a day from the port to Messina.

It is easier, particularly if you arrive from the north by train, to depart from Villa San Giovanni, 15 minutes north of Reggio by train. Car ferries cross from here to Messina around the clock. All ferry companies have offices in Reggio or at the ferry terminal in Villa San Giovanni. If you arrive at Villa San Giovanni by train, you will most likely have already paid for the ferry passage across the strait. You can stay on your train (which is usually taken aboard the ferry), but the trip is short and it is more pleasant to sit on the boat deck.

Sicily

Think of Sicily (Sicilia) and two things immediately come to mind – beaches and the Mafia. While its beaches are beautiful and the Mafia still manages to assert a powerful influence on the Sicilian economy and way of life, Sicily is remarkably diverse.

The largest island in the Mediterranean, its strategic location made it a prize for successive waves of invaders and colonisers, so that it is now a place of Greek temples, Norman churches and castles, Arab and Byzantine domes and splendid baroque churches and palaces. Its landscape ranges from the fertile coast to the mountains of the north and the vast, dry plateau of its centre.

Sicily has a population of about five million. Long neglected by the Italian government after unification, it became a semiautonomous region in 1948, remaining under the control of the central Italian government, but with greater powers to legislate on regional matters. Although industry has developed on the island, its economy is still largely based on agriculture and its people remain strongly connected to the land.

Sicily's temperate climate means mild weather in winter, while summers are relentlessly hot and the beaches swarm with holidaying Italians and other Europeans. The best times to visit are in spring and autumn, when it is hot enough for the beach, but not too hot for sightseeing.

Sicilian food is hotter, spicier and sweeter than in other parts of Italy. The focus is on seafood, notably swordfish, and fresh produce.

Some say that fruit and vegetables taste better in Sicily. Their *dolci* (cakes and sweets) can be works of art but are very sweet. Try the cassata, both a ricotta cake (traditionally available only in winter) and a rich ice cream, and the *cannoli*, tubes of pastry filled with cream, ricotta or chocolate. Don't miss trying the *dolci di mandorle* (rich almond cakes and pastries) and the *granita*, a drink of crushed ice flavoured with lemon, strawberry or coffee, to name a few flavours.

As mentioned, the Mafia remains a powerful force in Sicily. Since the arrest of the Sicilian 'godfather', Salvatore 'Toto' Riina, in 1993, *Mafia pentiti* (grasses) have continued to blow the whistle on fellow felons, businesspeople and politicians, right up to former Prime Minister, Giulio Andreotti, who is on trial both in Palermo and Perugia. The Italian author Luigi Barzini wrote in his novel *The Italians*: 'The phenomenon has deep roots in history, in the character of the Sicilians, in local habits. Its origins disappear down the dim vistas of the centuries.' There is no need to fear you will be caught in the crossfire of a gang war while in Sicily. The 'men of honour' are little interested in the affairs of tourists.

Getting There & Away

Air There are flights from all major cities in Italy to Palermo and Catania. The two airports are also serviced by flights from major European cities. The easiest way to obtain information is from any Sestante CIT or Alitalia offices throughout Italy.

Bus & Train Direct bus services from Rome to Sicily are operated by two companies – SAIS and Segesta. In Rome the buses leave from Stazione Tiburtina. The SAIS bus runs to Agrigento, Catania and Syracuse, with connections to Palermo; it leaves daily from Rome at 8 pm. The Segesta bus runs directly to Palermo, leaving Rome at 7.45 am on Tuesday, Thursday and Saturday. One-way tickets for both cost L68,000.

One of the cheapest ways to reach Sicily is to catch a train to Messina. The cost of the ticket covers the ferry crossing from Villa San Giovanni (Calabria) to Messina. Direct trains run from Milan, Florence, Rome, Naples and Reggio di Calabria. (See the Getting There &

Away section under Reggio di Calabria for more details.)

Boat Sicily is accessible by ferry from Genoa, Livorno, Naples, Reggio di Calabria and Cagliari, and also from Malta and Tunisia. The main company servicing the Mediterranean is Tirrenia. Prices are determined by the season and jump considerably in the summer period (Tirrenia's high season varies according to your destination, but is usually from July to September). Timetables change completely each year and it is best to pick up the annual booklet listing all routes and prices at any Tirrenia office, or at a travel agency which takes ferry bookings. Be sure to book well in advance during summer, particularly if you have a car.

High-season prices in 1996 for a poltrona were: Genoa-Palermo – L109,700 (22 hours); Naples-Palermo – L69,000 (10½ hours); Palermo-Cagliari – L60,000 (14 hours); and Trapani-Tunisia–L92,000 (eight hours). A bed in a shared 2nd-class cabin costs an additional L10,000 to L20,000. Cars cost upwards of L100,000. Other main lines servicing the island are Grandi Traghetti for Livorno-Palermo and Gozo Channel for Sicily-Malta. For information on ferries going from the mainland directly to Lipari, see the Getting There & Away section under Aeolian Islands.

Getting Around
Bus is the best mode of public transport in Sicily. Numerous companies run services between Syracuse, Catania and Palermo as well as to Agrigento and towns in the interior. See the Getting Around section under each town for more details. The coastal train service between Messina and Palermo and Messina down to Syracuse is efficient and reliable.

Probably the best way to enjoy Sicily is by car. It is possible to hitchhike in Sicily, but don't expect a ride in a hurry. Women should not hitchhike alone under any circumstances.

PALERMO
An Arab emirate and later the seat of a Norman kingdom, Palermo was once regarded as the grandest and most beautiful city in Europe. Today it is in a remarkable state of decay – through neglect and heavy bombing during

WWII – yet enough evidence remains of its golden days to make Palermo one of the most fascinating cities in Italy.

Orientation
Palermo is a large but easily manageable city. The main streets of the historical centre are Via Roma and Via Maqueda, which extend from the central station to Piazza Castelnuovo, a vast square in the modern part of town.

Information
Tourist Offices The main APT tourist office (☎ 58 38 47) is at Piazza Castelnuovo 35. It opens Monday to Friday from 8 am to 8 pm and Saturday 8 am to 2 pm. The branch offices at the Stazione Centrale and at the port were closed indefinitely at the time of writing. There is a branch office at the airport.

Money There is an exchange office at the Stazione Centrale, open daily from 8 am to 8 pm.

Post & Communications The main post office is at Via Roma 322 and the main Telecom telephone office is opposite the station in Piazza G Cesare, open daily from 8.30 am to 9.30 pm.

The postcode for Palermo is 90100 and the telephone code is ☎ 091.

Medical Services For an ambulance call ☎ 30 66 44. There is a public hospital (☎ 666 11 11) at Via Carmelo Lazzaro. There is an all-night pharmacy, Lo Cascio, near the train station at Via Roma 1.

Emergency Call the police on ☎ 113. The police office for foreigners (☎ 21 01 11) is in Piazza della Vittoria, open 24 hours a day.

Dangers & Annoyances Petty crime is rife in Palermo and highly deft pickpockets and motorcycle bandits prey on tourists. Avoid wearing jewellery or carrying a bag and keep all your valuables in a money belt. It is unsafe for women to walk through the streets of the historical centre at night, even in Via Roma or Via Maqueda. At night, travellers should avoid the area north-east of the station, between Via Roma and the port.

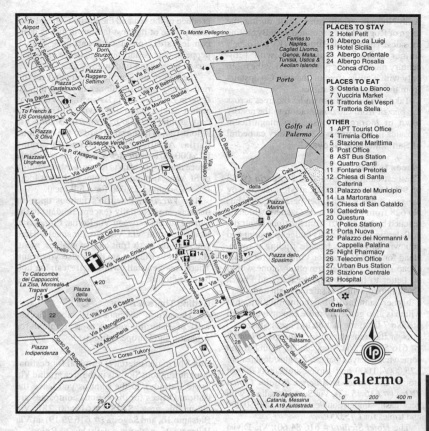

PLACES TO STAY
2 Hotel Petit
10 Albergo da Luigi
18 Hotel Sicilia
23 Albergo Orientale
24 Albergo Rosalia
    Conca d'Oro

PLACES TO EAT
3 Osteria Lo Bianco
7 Vucciria Market
16 Trattoria dei Vespri
17 Trattoria Stella

OTHER
1 APT Tourist Office
4 Tirrenia Office
5 Stazione Marittima
6 Post Office
8 AST Bus Station
9 Quattro Canti
11 Fontana Pretoria
12 Chiesa di Santa
    Caterina
13 Palazzo del Municipio
14 La Martorana
15 Chiesa di San Cataldo
19 Cattedrale
20 Questura
    (Police Station)
21 Porta Nuova
22 Palazzo dei Normanni &
    Cappella Palatina
25 Night Pharmacy
26 Telecom Office
27 Urban Bus Station
28 Stazione Centrale
29 Hospital

Palermo

0   200   400 m

ITALY

Things to See

The intersection of Via Vittorio Emanuele and Via Maqueda marks the **Quattro Canti** (four corners of Palermo). The four 17th-century Spanish baroque façades are each decorated with a statue. Nearby is **Piazza Pretoria**, with a beautiful fountain (**Fontana Pretoria**), created by Florentine sculptors in the 16th century. Locals used to call it the Fountain of Shame because of its nude figures. Also in the piazza are the baroque **Chiesa di Santa Caterina** and the **Palazzo del Municipio** (town hall). Just off the piazza is Piazza Bellini and Palermo's most famous church, **La Martorana**, with a beautiful Arab-Norman bell

tower and its interior decorated with Byzantine mosaics. Next to it is the Norman **Chiesa di San Cataldo**, which also mixes Arab and Norman styles and is easily recognisable by its red domes.

The huge Norman **cattedrale** is along Via Vittorio Emanuele, on the corner of Via Bonello. Although modified many times over the centuries, it remains an impressive example of Norman architecture. Opposite Piazza della Vittoria and the gardens is the **Palazzo Reale**, also known as the Palazzo dei Normanni, now the seat of the government. Enter from Piazza Indipendenza to see the **Cappella Palatina**, a magnificent example of

Arab-Norman architecture, built during the reign of Roger II and decorated with Byzantine mosaics. The **Sala di Ruggero** (King Roger's former bedroom), is decorated with 12th-century mosaics. It is possible to visit the room only with a guide (free of charge). Go upstairs from the Cappella Palatina.

Take bus No 8/9 from under the trees across the piazza from the train station to the nearby town of **Monreale** to see the magnificent mosaics in the famous 12th-century cathedral of **Santa Maria la Nuova**.

Places to Stay

The best camping ground is *Trinacria* (☎ 53 05 90), Via Barcarello 25, at Sferracavallo by the sea. It costs L7500 per person. Catch bus No 628 from Piazzale A de Gasperi, which is reached by bus No 101 from Stazione Centrale.

Palermo has numerous budget pensioni and you will have little trouble finding a room. Head for Via Maqueda or Via Roma for basic, cheap rooms. Women travelling alone would do better to head for the area around Piazza Castelnuovo, which is safer at night and offers a higher standard of accommodation, but which is also generally more expensive. Catch bus No 7 from the station to Piazza Sturzo.

Near the train station try *Albergo Orientale* (☎ 616 57 25), Via Maqueda 26, in an old and somewhat decayed palace. Singles/doubles are L25,000/40,000 and triples are L60,000. Just around the corner is *Albergo Rosalia Conca d'Oro* (☎ 616 45 43), Via Santa Rosalia 7, with very basic singles/doubles for L35,000/50,000 and triples for L75,000.

The *Hotel Sicilia* (☎ 616 84 60), Via Divisi 99, on the corner of Via Maqueda, has rooms of a higher standard. Singles/doubles are L35,000/50,000, or L45,000/65,000 with private shower. *Albergo da Luigi* (☎ 58 50 85), Via Vittorio Emanuele 284, next to the Quattro Canti, has singles/doubles from L25,000/50,000, or L40,000/60,000 with bathroom. Ask for a room with a view of the fountain.

Near Piazza Castelnuovo is the *Hotel Petit* (☎ 32 36 16), Via Principe di Belmonte 84, with clean and comfortable singles/doubles for L50,000/65,000 with private shower. A single without shower is L35,000.

Places to Eat

Palermo's cucina takes advantage of the fresh produce of the sea and the fertile Conca d'Oro Valley. One of its most famous dishes is pasta con le sarde (pasta with sardines, fennel, peppers, capers and pine nuts). Swordfish is served here sliced into huge steaks.

The Palermitani are late eaters and restaurants rarely open for dinner before 8 pm. At *Osteria Lo Bianco*, Via E Amari, off Via Roma at the Castelnuovo end of town, a full meal will cost around L20,000. *Trattoria Stella*, Via Alloro 104, is in the courtyard of the old Hotel Patria. A full meal will come to around L25,000. *Trattoria dei Vespri*, Piazza Santa Croce dei Vespri, off Via Roma, past the church of St Anna, has outdoor tables and great food. It costs around L25,000 for a full meal.

The *Vucciria*, Palermo's famous open-air markets, are held daily (except Sunday) in the narrow streets between Via Roma, Piazza San Domenico and Via Vittorio Emanuele. Here you can buy fresh fruit and vegetables, meat, cheese and virtually anything else you want. There are even stalls which sell steaming hot, boiled octopus.

Getting There & Away

Air The airport at Punta Raisi, about 30 km west of Palermo, serves as a terminal for domestic and European flights.

Bus The main (intercity) terminal for destinations throughout Sicily is in the area around Via Paolo Balsamo, to the right as you leave the station. Offices for the various companies are all in this area. SAIS (☎ 616 60 28), Via Balsamo 16, and Segesta (☎ 616 79 19), at Via Balsamo 26, both run a daily bus to Rome.

Train Regular trains leave from the Stazione Centrale for Milazzo, Messina, Catania and Syracuse, as well as for nearby towns such as Cefalù. Direct trains go to Reggio di Calabria, Naples and Rome (L92,600 one way).

Boat Boats leave from the port (Molo Vittorio Veneto) for Sardinia and the mainland (see the Getting There & Away section under Sicily). The Tirrenia office (☎ 33 33 00) is at the port.

Getting Around

Taxis to the airport cost upwards of L60,000. The cheaper option is to catch one of the regular blue buses which leave every 40 minutes from outside the station from 5.25 am to 9.45 pm (L5000). Palermo's buses are efficient and most stop outside the train station. Useful numbers to remember are the No 7 along Via Roma from the train station to near Piazza Castelnuovo and the No 39 from the station to the port. You must buy tickets before you get on the bus; they cost L1500 for one hour.

AEOLIAN ISLANDS

Also known as the Lipari Islands, the seven islands of this archipelago just north of Milazzo are volcanic in origin. They range from the well-developed tourist resort of Lipari and the understated jet-set haunt of Panarea, to the rugged Vulcano, the spectacular scenery of Stromboli (and its fiercely active volcano), the fertile vineyards of Salina, and the solitude of Alicudi and Filicudi, which remain relatively undeveloped. The islands have been inhabited since the Neolithic era, when migrants sought the valuable volcanic glass, obsidian. The Isole Eolie (Aeolian Islands) are so named because the ancient Greeks believed they were the home of Aeolus, the god of wind. Homer wrote of the islands in the *Odyssey*.

Information

The main AAST tourist information office (☎ 988 00 95) for the islands is on Lipari at Corso Vittorio Emanuele 202. Offices open on Stromboli, Vulcano and Salina during summer.

The telephone code for the islands is ☎ 090.

Things to See & Do

On **Lipari** visit the **castello**, with its archaeological park and museum. You can also go on excellent walks on the island. Catch a local bus from the town of Lipari to the hill-top village of **Quattrocchi** for a great view of Vulcano. Boat trips will take you around the island – contact the tourist office for information.

Vulcano, a strange, desolate place, with the smell of sulphur always in the air, is a short boat trip from Lipari's port. The main volcano (**Vulcano Fossa**) is still active, though the last recorded period of eruption was from 1888 to 1890. Though you can do the one-hour hike to the crater, be extremely careful of sudden bursts of sulphurous gas and landslides.

Stromboli is the most spectacular of the islands. Its volcano is the most active in Europe – climb Stromboli at night to see the **Sciara del Fuoco** (Trail of Fire), lava streaming down the side of the volcano, and the volcanic explosions from the crater. Many people make the trip (four to five hours) without a guide during the day, but at night you should go with a guided group. The Club Alpino Italiano (☎ 98 62 63), off Piazza San Vincenzo, in San Vincenzo, organises guided tours which depart at around 4 pm and return at 11.30 pm. It is best to contact them in advance to make a booking, since they only depart if groups are large enough. Remember to take warm clothes, wear heavy shoes and carry a torch and plenty of water. The return trip from Lipari to Stromboli is L25,400 by ferry and L45,000 by hydrofoil.

Places to Stay & Eat

Lipari provides the best options for a comfortable stay. It has numerous budget hotels, affittacamere and apartments, and the other islands are easily accessible by regular hydrofoils. When you arrive on Lipari you are likely to be approached by someone offering accommodation. This is worth checking because the offers are usually genuine.

The island's camping ground, *Baia Unci* (☎ 981 19 09), is at Canneto, about two km out of the Lipari township. It costs L15,000 a night per person, plus L25,000 for a site. The HI *hostel* (☎ 981 15 40), Via Castello 17, is inside the walls of the castle. A bed costs L12,000 a night, plus L2000 for a hot shower, or L2500 for breakfast. A meal costs L15,000. *Cassarà Vittorio* (☎ 981 15 23), Vico Sparviero 15, costs L35,000 per person, or L40,000 with private bathroom. There are two terraces with views, and use of the kitchen is L5000. The owner can be found (unless he finds you first) at Via Garibaldi 78, on the way from the port to the centre.

You can eat surprisingly cheaply on Lipari. For a pizza try *Il Galeone*, Corso V Emanuele 222. For an excellent meal eat at *Trattoria d'Oro*, Corso Umberto I. There is a L20,000 tourist menu.

Panarea is a beautiful haunt of the jet set. If you want seclusion, head for Filicudi or Alicudi. However, the hotels aren't exactly cheap. The *Ericusa* (☎ 988 99 02) on Alicudi costs L90,000 a double and the *Locanda la Canna* (☎ 988 99 56) on Filicudi charges

ITALY

L80,000 a double. On Stromboli try the *Locanda Stella* (☎ 98 60 20), Via Fabio Filzo 14, and on Vulcano, if you can cope with the sulphurous fumes, try *Pensione Agostino* (☎ 985 23 42), Via Favaloro 1 (close to the mud bath), which has doubles with bathroom for L85,000. Camping facilities are available on Salina and Vulcano. Most accommodation in summer is booked out well in advance on the smaller islands, particularly on Stromboli, and most hotels close during winter.

Getting There & Away

Ferries and hydrofoils leave for the islands from Milazzo (which is easy to reach by train from Palermo and Messina) and all ticket offices are along Via Rizzo at the port. SNAV runs hydrofoils (L18,100 one way). Siremar runs hydrofoils, as well as ferries for half the price. They both have offices at the port. SNAV runs hydrofoils from Palermo twice a day in summer and three times a week in the off season. If arriving at Milazzo by train, you will need to catch a bus to the port. If arriving by bus, simply make the five-minute walk back along Via Crispi to the port area.

You can travel directly to the islands from the mainland. Siremar runs regular ferries from Naples and SNAV runs hydrofoils from Naples (see the Naples Getting There & Away section), Messina and Reggio di Calabria. Note that the sea around the islands can be very rough.

Getting Around

Regular hydrofoil and ferry services operate between the islands. Both Siremar and Aliscafi SNAV have offices at the port on Lipari, where you can get full timetable information.

TAORMINA

Spectacularly located on a hill overlooking the sea and Mt Etna, Taormina was long ago discovered by the European jet set, which has made it one of the more expensive and touristy towns in Sicily. But its magnificent setting, its Greek Theatre and the nearby beaches remain as seductive now as they were for the likes of Goethe and D H Lawrence. The AAST tourist office (☎ 2 32 43) in Palazzo Corvaja, just off the main street, Corso Umberto, near Largo Santa Caterina, has extensive information on the town.

Taormina's telephone code is ☎ 0942.

Things to See

The **Greek Theatre** (entry L2000) was built in the 3rd century BC and later greatly expanded and remodelled by the Romans. Concerts and theatre are staged there in summer and it affords a wonderful view of Mt Etna. From the beautiful **villa comunale** (public gardens) there is a panoramic view of the sea. Along Corso Umberto is the **Duomo**, with a Gothic façade. The local beach is **Isola Bella**, a short bus ride from Via Pirandello. Trips to Mt Etna can be organised through CST (☎ 2 33 01), Corso Umberto 101.

Places to Stay & Eat

You can camp near the beach at *Campeggio San Leo* (☎ 2 46 58), Via Nazionale, at Capotaormina. The cost is L7500 per person per night, and L8000 for a tent site.

There are numerous affittacamere in Taormina and the tourist office has a full list. *Il Leone* (☎ 2 38 78), Via Bagnoli Croce 127, near the public gardens, has singles/doubles for L26,000/46,000, or L26,000 per person with private bathroom. *Pensione Ingeniere* (☎ 62 54 80), Via Timeo 8, charges L30,000 per person. At *Pensione Svizzera* (☎ 2 37 90), Via Pirandello 26, on the way from the bus stop to the town centre, very pleasant singles/doubles are L60,000/100,000, with private bathroom. Breakfast is included.

Eating is expensive here. For a light meal head for *Shelter Pub*, Via Fratelli Bandieri 10, off Corso Umberto, for sandwiches and salads from L4000 to L8000. *Ritrovo Trocadero*, Via Pirandello 1, has pizza and pasta at reasonable prices. At *Ristorante La Piazzetta*, Via Paladini 5, you can sit outside and an excellent full meal will cost around L30,000.

Getting There & Away

Bus is the easiest way to get to Taormina. SAIS buses leave from Messina and Catania. Taormina is on the main train line between Messina and Catania, but the station is on the coast and regular buses will take you to Via Pirandello, near the centre; bus services are heavily reduced on Sunday.

MT ETNA

Dominating the landscape in eastern Sicily between Taormina and Catania, Mt Etna (3350 metres) is Europe's largest live volcano and one of the world's most active. Eruptions occur frequently, both from the four live craters at the summit and on the volcano's slopes, which are littered with crevices and old craters. Its most recent eruption was in 1992, when a stream of lava threatened the town of Zafferana Etnea. The unpredictability of the volcano's activity means that people are no longer allowed to climb to the craters at the summit. Only a rope marks the point where it becomes unsafe to proceed, but it would be extremely foolish to ignore the warning signs and go further. To reach this point, you can either hike from the start of the cable car (a long, hard climb of about five hours return), or catch the cable car to 2500 metres (L25,000 return) and then one of the 4WD minibuses to 2920 metres (L27,000 return). Many people catch the minibuses uphill and then walk back to the cable car.

If you want to stay on the volcano, there is *Rifugio Sapienza* (☎ 095-91 10 62) near the cable car.

Mt Etna is best approached from Catania by AST bus (☎ 095-53 17 56), which leaves from Via L Sturzo in front of Catania's train station at 8.15 am and goes via Nicolosi to the cable car on Mt Etna. The bus returns to Catania at 4 pm. Another option is to circle Mt Etna on the private Circumetnea train line, which starts at Catania at Stazione Borgo, Via Caronda 352, accessible by bus No 29 or 36 from Catania's main train station. From Taormina, you can catch a train to Randazzo, where you can pick up the Circumetnea.

SYRACUSE

Once a powerful Greek city to rival Athens, Syracuse (Siracusa) is one of the highlights of a visit to Sicily. Founded in 743 BC by colonists from Corinth, it became a dominant sea power in the Mediterranean, prompting Athens to attack the city in 413 BC. In one of the great maritime battles in history, the Athenian fleet was destroyed. Syracuse was conquered by the Romans in 212 BC and, with the rest of Sicily, fell to a succession of invasions through the centuries. Syracuse was the birthplace of the Greek mathematician and physicist Archimedes, and Plato attended the court of the tyrant Dionysius, who ruled from 405 to 367 BC.

The main sights of Syracuse are in two areas: on the island of Ortygia and at the archaeological park two km across town. There are two tourist information offices. The AAT (☎ 46 42 55) is at Via Maestranza 33 on Ortygia. It opens Monday to Saturday from 8.30 am to 1.45 pm and 4.30 to 7.30 pm (closed afternoons in winter). The APT (☎ 677 10), Via San Sebastiano 43 (branch office at the archaeological zone), opens Monday to Saturday from 8 am to 7 pm and Sunday from 8 am to 1 pm.

The town's telephone code is ☎ 0931.

Things to See

The island of Ortygia is the spiritual and physical heart of the city. Its buildings are predominantly medieval, with some baroque palaces and churches. The 7th-century **Duomo** was built on top of the **Temple of Athena**, incorporating most of the original columns in its three-aisled structure. The **Piazza Duomo** is lined with baroque palaces. Walk down Via Picherali to the waterfront and the **Fonte Aretusa** (Fountain of Arethusa), a natural freshwater spring. According to Greek legend, the nymph Arethusa, pursued by the river god Alpheus, was turned into a fountain by the goddess Diana. Undeterred, Alpheus turned himself into the river which feeds the spring.

To get to the **Parco Archeologico**, catch bus No 1 from Riva della Posta on Ortygia. The main attraction here is the 5th-century BC **Greek theatre**, its seating area carved out of solid rock. Nearby is the **Orecchio di Dionisio**, an artificial grotto in the shape of an ear which the tyrant of Syracuse, Dionysius, used as a prison. Its extraordinary acoustics led the painter Caravaggio, during a visit in the 17th century, to give the grotto its current name. Caravaggio mused that the tyrant must have taken advantage of the acoustics to overhear the whispered conversations of his prisoners. The 2nd-century **Roman Amphitheatre** is impressively well preserved. The park is open daily from 9 am to one hour before sunset. Admission is L2000.

The **Museo Archeologico Paolo Orsi**, about 500 metres east of the archaeological zone, off Viale Teocrito, contains the best organised and most interesting archaeological collection in Sicily. The museum is open Tuesday to Saturday from 9 am to 1 pm and Wednesday also from 3.30 to 6.30 pm. Entry is L2000.

ITALY

Special Events

Since 1914 Syracuse has hosted a festival of Greek classical drama in May and June of every even-numbered year. Performances are given at the Greek Theatre. Tickets are available at the APT, at the theatre ticket booth. For information call ☎ 6 53 73.

Places to Stay

Camping facilities are at *Agriturista Rinaura* (☎ 72 12 24), about four km out of the city near the sea. Catch bus No 21, 22 or 24 from Corso Umberto. It costs L6000 per person and L8500 for a site. The non-HI *Ostello della Gioventù* (☎ 71 11 18), Viale Epipoli 45, is eight km west of Syracuse. Catch bus No 11 or 25 from Piazza Marconi. Beds are L20,000. If you can afford it, stay at the *Gran Bretagna* (☎ 6 87 65), on Ortygia at Via Savoia 21, just off Largo XXV Luglio. It has very pleasant rooms for L46,000/76,000. *Hotel Centrale* (☎ 605 28), close to the train station at Corso Umberto 141, has singles/doubles for L25,000/40,000 and triples for L55,000.

Places to Eat

Spaghetteria do Schoggiu, Via Scina 11, serves all types of pasta from L6500 a plate. *Pizzeria La Dolce Vita*, Via Roma 112, has outside tables in a small courtyard.

There is an open-air, fresh produce market in the streets behind the Temple of Apollo, open daily (except Sunday) until 1 pm. You will find several alimentari and supermarkets along Corso Gelone.

Getting There & Away

SAIS buses leave from Riva della Posta on Ortygia, for Catania, Palermo, Enna and surrounding small towns. The SAIS service for Rome also leaves from the piazza, connecting with the Rome bus at Catania. AST buses also service Palermo from Piazza della Posta. Syracuse is easy to reach by train from Messina and Catania. Boat services from Syracuse to Malta are in a state of flux. Check with the tourist offices (see the Malta chapter's Getting There & Away section).

AGRIGENTO

Founded in approximately 582 BC as the Greek Akragas, it is today a pleasant medieval town, but the Greek temples in the valley below are the real reason to visit. The Italian novelist and dramatist Luigi Pirandello (1867-1936) was born here, as was the Greek philosopher and scientist Empedocles (circa 490-430 BC). The AAST tourist office (☎ 204 54), Via Cesare Battisti 15, opens Monday to Friday from 8.30 am to 1.45 pm and 4 to 7 pm, and in the morning only on Saturday.

Agrigento's telephone code is ☎ 0922.

Things to See & Do

Agrigento's **Valley of the Temples** is one of the major Greek archaeological sights in the world. Its five main Doric temples were constructed in the 5th century BC and are in various states of ruin because of earthquakes and vandalism by early Christians. The only temple to survive relatively intact is the **Tempio della Concordia**, which was transformed into a Christian church. The **Tempio di Giunone**, a five-minute walk uphill to the east, has an impressive sacrificial altar. The **Tempio di Ercole** is the oldest of the structures. Across the main road which divides the valley is the massive **Tempio di Giove**, one of the most imposing buildings of ancient Greece. Although now completely in ruins, it used to cover an area measuring 112 metres by 56 metres, with columns 18 metres high. **Telamoni**, colossal statues of men, were also used in the structure. The remains of one of them are in the **Museo Archeologico**, just north of the temples on Via dei Templi (a copy lies at the archaeological site). Close by is the **Tempio di Castore e Polluce**, which was partly reconstructed in the 19th century. The temples are lit up at night until 11.30 pm and are open until 9 pm. To get to the temples from the town, catch bus No 1, 2 or 3 from the train station.

Places to Stay & Eat

The *Bella Napoli* (☎ 2 04 35), Piazza Lena 6, off Via Bic Bac at the end of Via Atenea, has clean and comfortable singles/doubles for L30,000/55,000, or L40,000/75,000 with private bathroom. For a decent, cheap meal try the *Trattoria la Concordia*, Via Porcello 6.

Getting There & Away

Intercity buses leave from Piazza Rosselli, just off Piazza Vittorio Emanuele, for Palermo, Catania and surrounding small towns.

Sardinia

The second-largest island in the Mediterranean, Sardinia (Sardegna) was colonised and invaded by the Greeks, Phoenicians and Romans, followed by the Pisans, Genoese and finally the Spaniards. But it is often said that the Sardinians, known on the island as *Sardi*, were never really conquered – they simply retreated into the hills.

The Romans were prompted to call the island's eastern mountains *Barbagia* because of their views on the lifestyle of the locals. This area is still known as the Barbagia. Even today the Sardinians are a strangely insular people. In the island's interior, some women still wear the traditional costume and shepherds still live in almost complete isolation, building enclosures of stone or wood for their sheep and goats as the ancients did. If you venture into the interior, you will find the people incredibly gracious and hospitable, but easily offended if they sense any lack of respect.

The first inhabitants of the island were the Nuraghic people, thought to have arrived here around 2000 BC. Little is known about them, but the island is dotted with thousands of *nuraghi*, their conical-shaped stone houses and fortresses.

Sardinia became a semiautonomous region in 1948, and the Italian government's Sardinian Rebirth Plan of 1962 made some impact on the development of tourism, industry and agriculture.

The island's cuisine is as varied as its history. Along the coast most dishes feature seafood and there are many variations of *zuppa di pesce* (fish soup). Inland you will find *porcheddu* (roast suckling pig), kid goat with olives, and even lamb's trotters in garlic sauce. The Sardi eat *pecorino* (sheep's milk cheese) and you will rarely find *parmigiano* (Parmesan cheese) here. The preferred bread throughout the island is the paper-thin *carta musica* (literally, music paper), also called *pane carasau*, often sprinkled with oil and salt.

The landscape of the island ranges from the 'savage, dark-bushed, sky-exposed land' described by D H Lawrence, to the incredibly beautiful gorges and valleys near Dorgali, the rugged isolation of the Gennargentu mountain range and the unspoiled coastline between Bosa and Alghero. Although hunters have been traditionally active in Sardinia, some wildlife remains, notably the albino donkeys on the island of Asinara, colonies of griffon vultures on the west coast, and miniature horses in the inland area of Giara di Gesturi, in the southwest. The famous colony of Mediterranean monk seals at the Grotta del Bue Marino, near the beach of Cala Gonone, has not been sighted for some years.

Try to avoid the island in August, when the weather is very hot and the beaches are overcrowded. Warm weather generally continues from May to September.

Getting There & Away

Air Airports at Cagliari, Olbia and Alghero link Sardinia with major Italian and European cities. For information contact Alitalia or the Sestante CIT or CTS offices in all major towns.

Boat The island is accessible by ferry from Genoa, Livorno, Civitavecchia, Naples, Palermo, Trapani, Bonifacio (Corsica) and Tunis. The departure points in Sardinia are Olbia, Golfo Aranci and Porto Torres in the north, Arbatax on the east coast and Cagliari in the south.

The main company is Tirrenia, though the national railway, Ferrovie dello Stato, runs a slightly cheaper service between Olbia and Civitavecchia. Moby Lines (which also runs Navarma Lines and Sardegna Lines) and Sardinia Ferries (also known as Elba and Corsica Ferries) both operate services from the mainland to Sardinia, as well as to Corsica and Elba. They depart from Livorno, Civitavecchia and arrive at either Olbia or Golfo Aranci. Most travel agencies in Italy have brochures on the various companies' services.

Timetables change every year and prices fluctuate according to the season.

Prices for a poltrona on Tirrenia ferries in the 1996 high season were as follows: Genoa-Cagliari – L94,000 (19 hours); Genoa-Porto Torres or Olbia – L60,000 (12½ hours); Civitavecchia-Cagliari – L70,000 (13½ hours); Civitavecchia-Olbia – L33,900 (seven hours); Naples-Cagliari – L65,000 (15 hours); and Palermo-Cagliari – L60,000 (12½ hours). The cost of taking a small car ranged from

ITALY

L138,000 to L241,000, and up to L50,000 for a motorcycle.

Getting Around

Bus The two main bus companies are ARST, which operates extensive services throughout the island, and PANI, which links the main towns.

Train The main FS train lines link Cagliari with Oristano, Sassari and Olbia. The private railways that link smaller towns throughout the island can be very slow. However, the *trenino* (little train), which runs from Cagliari to Arbatax through the Barbagia, is a relaxing way to see part of the interior (See the Getting There & Away section under Cagliari).

Car & Motorcycle The only way to explore Sardinia properly is by road. Rental agencies are listed under Cagliari and some other towns around the island.

Hitching You might find hitchhiking laborious once you get away from the main towns because of the light traffic. Women should not hitchhike in Sardinia under any circumstances.

CAGLIARI

This is a surprisingly attractive city which offers an interesting medieval section, a beautiful beach – Poetto – and a population of pink flamingos.

Orientation

If you arrive by bus, train or boat you will find yourself at the port area of Cagliari. The main street along the harbour is Via Roma, and the old city stretches up the hill behind it to the castle. Most of the budget hotels and restaurants are in the area near the port.

Information

Tourist Offices The AAST information booth (☎ 66 92 55) at Piazza Matteotti 1, is open daily from 8 am to 8 pm in the high season, and from 8 am to 2 pm in other months. There are also information offices at the airport and in the Stazione Marittima.

The ESIT (Ente Sardo Industrie Turistiche) office (☎ 6 02 31), Via Goffredo Mameli 97, is open daily from 8 am to 8 pm in high season.

Here you can pick up information on all of Sardinia.

Post & Communications The main post office is in Piazza del Carmine, up Via La Maddalena from Via Roma. The Telecom telephone office is at Via G M Angioj, north of Piazza Matteotti.

The postcode for Cagliari is 09100 and the telephone code is ☎ 070.

Medical Services For an ambulance ring ☎ 27 23 45, and for medical attention go to the Ospedale Civile (☎ 601 82 67), Via Ospedale.

Emergency Contact the police on ☎ 113, or go to the questura (☎ 4 44 44), Via Amat 9.

Things to See

The **Museo Archeologico Nazionale**, Piazza Arsenale, in the Citadella dei Musei, has a fascinating collection of Nuragic bronzes. It is open Monday to Saturday from 9 am to 2 pm, Sunday from 9 am to 1 pm and in the afternoon from 3.30 to 6.30 pm on Wednesday, Friday and Saturday. Entry is L4000.

It is enjoyable enough to wander through the medieval quarter. The Pisan-Romanesque **Duomo** was built in the 13th century, but later remodelled. It has an interesting Romanesque pulpit.

From the **Bastione di San Remy**, which is in the centre of town in Piazza Costituzione and once formed part of the fortifications of the old city, there is a good view of Cagliari and the sea.

The Pisan **Torre di San Pancrazio**, in Piazza Indipendenza, is also worth a look. The **Roman amphitheatre**, on Viale Buon Cammino, is considered the most important Roman monument in Sardinia. During summer, opera is performed here.

Spend a day on the **Spiaggia di Poetto** (east of the centre) and wander across to the salt lakes to see the flamingos.

Special Events

The Festival of Sant'Efisio, a colourful festival mixing the secular and the religious, is held annually for four days from 1 May.

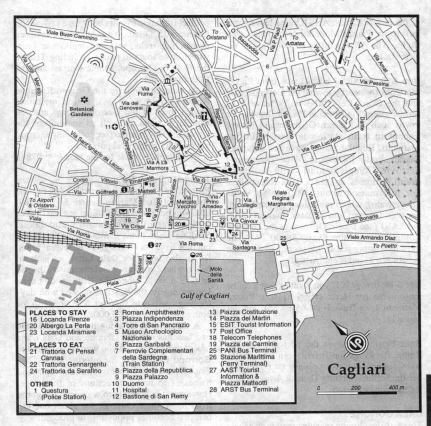

PLACES TO STAY
16 Locanda Firenze
20 Albergo La Perla
23 Locanda Miramare

PLACES TO EAT
21 Trattoria Ci Pensa Cannas
22 Trattoria Gennargentu
24 Trattoria da Serafino

OTHER
1 Questura (Police Station)

2 Roman Amphitheatre
3 Piazza Indipendenza
4 Torre di San Pancrazio
5 Museo Archeologico Nazionale
6 Piazza Garibaldi
7 Ferrovie Complementari della Sardegna (Train Station)
8 Piazza della Repubblica
9 Piazza Palazzo
10 Duomo
11 Hospital
12 Bastione di San Remy

13 Piazza Costituzione
14 Piazza dei Martiri
15 ESIT Tourist Information
17 Post Office
18 Telecom Telephones
19 Piazza del Carmine
25 PANI Bus Terminal
26 Stazione Marittima (Ferry Terminal)
27 AAST Tourist Information & Piazza Matteotti
28 ARST Bus Terminal

Cagliari

0   200   400 m

Places to Stay & Eat

There are numerous budget pensioni near the station. Try the **Locanda Firenze** (☎ 65 36 78), Corso Vittorio Emanuele 50, which has comfortable singles/doubles for L35,000/45,000. The **Locanda Miramare** (☎ 66 40 21), Via Roma 59, has singles/doubles for L55,000/60,000. Nearby is **Albergo La Perla** (☎ 66 94 46), Via Sardegna 18, with singles/doubles for L42,000/54,000.

Several reasonably priced trattorias can be found in the area behind Via Roma, particularly around Via Sardegna and Via Cavour. **Trattoria da Serafino**, Via Lepanto 6, on the corner of Via Sardegna, has excellent food at reasonable prices. **Trattoria Gennargentu**, Via Sardegna 60, has good pasta and seafood and a full meal costs around L20,000. **Trattoria Ci Pensa Cannas**, down the street at No 37, is another good choice, with meals for around L20,000. In Via Sardegna there are also grocery shops and bakeries.

Entertainment

During summer, opera is performed in the Roman amphitheatre.

Getting There & Away

Air Cagliari's airport (☎ 24 00 47) is north-west

ITALY

of the city at Elmas. ARST buses leave regularly from Piazza Matteotti to coincide with flights. The Alitalia office (☎ 60 10) is at Via Caprera 14.

Bus & Train ARST buses leave from Piazza Matteotti for nearby towns, the Costa del Sud and the Costa Rei. PANI buses leave from further along Via Roma at Piazza Darsena for towns such as Sassari, Oristano and Nuoro. The main train station is also in Piazza Matteotti. Regular trains leave for Oristano, Sassari, Porto Torres and Olbia. The private Ferrovie Complementari della Sardegna (train) station is in Piazza della Repubblica. For information about the Trenino Verde (green train), which runs along a scenic route between Cagliari and Arbatax, contact ESIT, the AAST (see Tourist Offices), or the Ferrovie Complementari directly (☎ 58 00 76). The most interesting and scenic section of the route is between Mandas and Arbatax.

Car & Motorcycle If you want to rent a car or motorcycle try Hertz (☎ 66 81 05), Piazza Matteotti 1, or Ruvioli (☎ 65 89 55), Via dei Mille 11.

Boat Ferries arrive at the port just off Via Roma. Bookings for Tirrenia can be made at Via Campidano 1, c/o Agenave (☎ 66 60 65). See the Sardinia Getting There & Away section for more information.

CALA GONONE
This fast-developing seaside resort is an excellent base from which to explore the coves along the coastline, as well as the Nuraghic sites and rugged terrain inland.

Major points are accessible by bus and boat, but you will need a car to explore.

Information
Tourist information is available at the boat ticket office at the port. There is a Pro Loco tourist office at nearby Dorgali (☎ 9 62 43) at Via Lamarmora 106, where you can pick up maps, a list of hotels and information to help you while visiting the area. The EPT office (☎ 3 00 83) in Nuoro, Piazza Italia 19, also has information on the area.

For information on trekking in the Barbagia,

contact Barbagia Insolita on ☎ 28 81 67, at Via Carducci 25, Oliena. You can choose between demanding treks, relaxing walks, or four-wheel drive tours to places including Tiscali, the Gola di Gorropu, Monte Corrasi and the Codula di Luna.

At Cala Gonone, try the Gruppo Ricerche Ambientali (☎ 9 34 24), which organises guided treks of the Gorropu Gorge and the Codula di Luna, as well as sections of the Grotta del Bue Marino (see following section) not open to the general public.

The telephone code for the area is ☎ 0784.

Things to See & Do
From Cala Gonone's port catch a boat to the **Grotta del Bue Marino**, where a guide will take you on a one-km walk to see vast caves with stalagmites, stalactites and lakes. Sardinia's last colony of monk seals lived here, but they have not been sighted in several years. Boats also leave for **Cala Luna**, an isolated beach where you can spend the day by the sea or take a walk along the **Codula di Luna**. Unfortunately, the beach is packed with day-tripping tourists in summer. The boat trip for both together costs L25,000.

A **walking track** along the coast links the two beaches of Cala Gonone and Cala Luna (about three hours). If you want to explore the **Gorropu Gorge**, ask for information at Cala Gonone, since it is necessary to use ropes and harnesses to traverse sections of the gorge. However, it is possible to walk into the gorge from its northern entrance for about one km before it becomes impossible to proceed.

Places to Stay
At Cala Gonone there is a *camping ground* (☎ 9 31 65) at Via Collodi. It is expensive in summer at up to L20,000 per person. Free camping is strictly forbidden throughout the area.

Hotels include the *Gabbiano* (☎ 9 31 30) at the port, with singles/doubles for L40,000/ 60,000.

Su Gologone (28 75 12), is a few km east of Oliena, near the entrance to the Lanaittu valley. It is on the expensive side at around L115,000 a double with bathroom, but it is in a lovely setting and organises guided tours and treks, as well as horse-riding expeditions. Its restaurant is renowned throughout the island.

Getting There & Away

Catch a PANI bus to Nuoro from Cagliari, Sassari or Oristano and then take an ARST bus to Dorgali and Cala Gonone. There is also a bus from Olbia's port to Dorgali, from where you can catch a bus (only every three hours) to Cala Gonone. If you are travelling by car, you will need a detailed road map of the area. One of the best is published by the Istituto Geografico de Agostini. The tourist office has maps which detail the locations of the main sights.

ALGHERO

One of the most popular tourist resorts in Sardinia, Alghero is on the island's west coast in the area known as the Coral Riviera.

The town is a good base from which to explore the magnificent coastline which links it to Bosa in the south and the famous Grotte di Nettuno (Neptune's Caves) on the Capocaccia, a cape just near Alghero, to the north.

Orientation & Information

The train station is in Via Don Minzoni, some distance from the centre, and is connected by a regular bus service to the centre of town.

The main tourist information office, AAST (☎ 97 90 54), is at Piazza Porta Terra 9, near the port and just across the gardens from the bus terminal. The old city and most hotels and restaurants are in the area west of the tourist office.

The main post office is at Via XX Settembre 108. There is a bank of public telephones on Via Vittorio Emanuele at the opposite end of the gardens from the tourist office.

The postcode for Alghero is 07041 and the telephone code is ☎ 079.

In an emergency ring the police on ☎ 113; for medical attention ring ☎ 93 05 33, or go to the Ospedale Civile (☎ 99 62 33), Via Don Minzoni.

Things to See & Do

It's worth wandering through the narrow streets of the old city and around the port. The most interesting church is the **Chiesa di San Francesco**, Via Carlo Alberto. The city's **cathedral** has been ruined by constant remodelling, but its bell tower remains a fine example of Gothic-Catalan architecture.

Near Alghero are the **Grotte di Nettuno**, accessible by hourly boats from the port (L15,000), or by the SFS bus from Via Catalogna. For some services you will need to change at Porto Conte (L2000 one way).

If you have your own means of transport, don't miss the beautiful **Capocaccia** and the **Nuraghe di Palmavera**, about 10 km out of Alghero on the road to Porto Conte.

The coastline between **Alghero** and **Bosa** is stunning. Rugged cliffs fall down to isolated beaches, and near Bosa is one of the last habitats of the griffon vulture. It is quite an experience if you are lucky enough to spot one of these huge birds. The only way to see the coast is by car or motorcycle, or by hitchhiking. If you want to rent a bicycle or motorcycle to explore the coast, try Cicloexpress (☎ 97 65 92), Via Lamarmora 39.

Places to Stay

It is virtually impossible to find a room in August unless you book months in advance. At other times of the year you should have little trouble.

Camping facilities include *Calik* (☎ 93 01 11) in Fertilia, about seven km out of town, at L15,000 per person.

The HI *Ostello dei Giuliani* (☎ 93 03 53) is at Via Zara 1, Fertilia. Take the hourly bus AF from Via Catalogna to Fertilia. Bed and breakfast costs L14,000, a shower is L1000 and a meal costs L14,000. The hostel is open all year.

In the old town is the *Hotel San Francesco* (☎ 97 92 58), Via Ambrogio Machin 2, with singles/doubles for L50,000/85,000. *Pensione Normandie* (☎ 97 53 02), Via Enrico Mattei 6, is out of the centre. To get there follow Via Cagliari, which becomes Viale Giovanni XXIII. It has slightly shabby but large singles/doubles for L35,000/65,000.

Places to Eat

A pleasant place to eat is *Trattoria il Vecchio Mulino*, Via Don Deroma 3. A full meal will cost around L25,000. A cheaper option is the *pizzeria* just off Via Roma at Vicolo Adami 17. Takeaway pizza by the slice costs about L2500. *Paninoteca al Duomo*, next to the cathedral in Piazza Civica, has good sandwiches.

ITALY

Entertainment

In summer Alghero stages the Estate Musicale Algherese (Alghero's Summer Music Festival) in the cloisters of the church of San Francesco, Via Carlo Alberto.

A festival, complete with fireworks display, is held annually on 15 August for the Feast of the Assumption.

Getting There & Away

Alghero is accessible from Sassari by train. The main bus station is in Via Catalogna, next to the public park. ARST buses leave for Sassari and Porto Torres; SFS buses also service Sassari and there is a special service to Olbia to coincide with ferry departures. Buses also run between Alghero and Bosa.

Liechtenstein

Blink and you might miss Liechtenstein; the country measures just 25 km from north to south, and an average of six km from west to east. In some ways you could be forgiven for mistaking it for a part of Switzerland. The Swiss franc is the legal currency, all travel documents valid for Switzerland are also valid for Liechtenstein, and the only border regulations are on the Austrian side. Switzerland also represents Liechtenstein abroad, subject to consultation.

But a closer look reveals that Liechtenstein is quite distinct from its neighbour. The ties with Switzerland began only in 1923 with the signing of a customs and monetary union. Before that, it had a similar agreement with Austria-Hungary. Although Liechtenstein shares the Swiss telephone and postal system, it issues its own postage stamps.

Unlike Switzerland, Liechtenstein joined the United Nations (1990) and, in 1995, the European Economic Area (EEA). Despite going separate ways over the EEA issue, the open border between Liechtenstein and Switzerland will remain intact. Liechtenstein has no plans to follow other EEA states which are seeking full EU membership.

Liechtenstein is a very prosperous country. In 1996 it suffered from an unusually high level of unemployment: 1.1% – 227 people!

Facts about the Country

Liechtenstein was created by the merger of the domain of Schellenberg and the county of Vaduz in 1712 by the powerful Liechtenstein family. It was a principality under the Holy Roman Empire from 1719 to 1806 and, after a spell in the German Confederation, it achieved full sovereign independence in 1866. The modern constitution was drawn up in 1921. Even today, the prince retains the power to dissolve parliament and must approve every act before it becomes law. Prince Franz Josef II was the first ruler to live in the castle above the capital city of Vaduz. He died in 1989 after a reign of 51 years, and was succeeded by his son, Prince Hans-Adam II.

Liechtenstein has no military service – its minuscule army (80 men!) was disbanded in 1868. It is a country known for its wines, postage stamps, and its status as a tax haven.

Despite its small size, Liechtenstein has two political regions (upper and lower) and three distinct geographical areas: the Rhine valley in the west, the edge of the Tirolean Alps in the south-east, and the northern lowlands. The current population is 30,600, with a third of that total made up of foreign residents.

Sightseeing highlights are few. Many tourists come to Liechtenstein only for the stamps – a stamp in the passport and stamps on a postcard for the folks back home. But it's worth lingering to appreciate the prince's art collection, and to enjoy the scenery.

See the Switzerland chapter for details on entry regulations, currency etc. The same emergency numbers apply as in Switzerland: dial ☎ 133 for the police, ☎ 144 for an ambulance, or ☎ 122 in the event of a fire.

The telephone code for all of Liechtenstein is ☎ 075.

Getting There & Away

Liechtenstein has no airport (the nearest is in Zürich), and only a few trains stop within its borders (at Schaan). Getting there by postbus is easiest. There are usually three buses an hour from the Swiss border towns of Buchs (Sfr2) and Sargans (Sfr3) which stop in Vaduz. Buses run hourly from the Austrian border town of Feldkirch, but you must change at Schaan to reach Vaduz (the Sfr3 ticket is valid for both buses).

By road, route 16 from Switzerland passes through Liechtenstein via Schaan and terminates at Feldkirch. The N13 follows the Rhine along the Swiss/Liechtenstein border; minor roads cross into Liechtenstein at each motorway exit.

Getting Around

Postbus travel within Liechtenstein is cheap and reliable; all fares cost Sfr2 or Sfr3. The only drawback is that some services finish early; the last of the hourly buses from Vaduz to Malbun, for example, leaves at 4.20 pm (6.20 pm in summer). Get a timetable from the Vaduz tourist office.

Vaduz

Although the capital of Liechtenstein, Vaduz is little more than a village, with a population of 5070.

Orientation & Information
Two adjoining streets, Städtle and Äulestrasse, enclose the town centre. Everything of importance is within this small area, including the bus station.

The Vaduz tourist office (☎ 232 14 43; fax 392 16 18), Städtle 37, has a free room-finding service and information on the whole country. It is open Monday to Friday from 8 am to noon and 1.30 to 5.30 pm. Depending on demand, the office is also open from June to August for limited hours on weekends. Staff members are kept busy putting surprisingly dull souvenir entry stamps in visitors' passports (Sfr2). Pick up the excellent *Tourist Guide*, which tells you everything you might want to know about the country.

The main post office (FL-9490), Äulestrasse 38, is open Monday to Friday from 8 am to 6 pm, and on Saturday from 8 to 11 am. Postal rates are the same as in Switzerland. The post office has an adjoining philatelic section which is open similar hours.

The hospital, Krankenhaus Vaduz (☎ 235 44 11), is at Heiligkreuz 25.

Bikes can be rented from Melliger AG (☎ 232 16 06), Kirchstrasse 10, for Sfr20 per day; they can be picked up the evening before rental begins.

Things to See & Do
Although the **castle** is not open to the public, it is worth climbing the hill for a closer look.

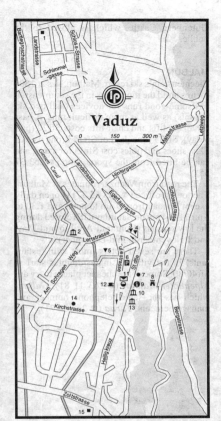

There's a good view of Vaduz and the mountains, and a network of marked walking trails along the ridge.

The **State Art Collection** at Städtle 37 has good temporary exhibitions; it is open daily, and entry costs Sfr5 (students Sfr3). The **Postage Stamp Museum**, next to the tourist office, contains 300 frames of national stamps issued since 1912 (free; open daily). A **Ski Museum** awaits at Bangarten 10 (Sfr5; open weekday afternoons). The **National Museum**, Städtle 43, will be closed until the end of the century. Look out for processions and fireworks on 15 August, Liechtenstein's national holiday.

Places to Stay

The SYHA *hostel* (☎ 232 50 22), Untere Rütigasse 6, is open from March to November. Beds cost Sfr26.30 including breakfast. From 10 am to 5 pm reception is closed and the doors are locked. The hostel is a 30-minute walk from Buchs and a 10-minute walk from Schaan. Take the road to Vaduz and turn right at Marianumstrasse.

Check the tourist office hotel list for private rooms or cheaper accommodation outside Vaduz. *Hotel Falknis* (☎ 322 63 77), Landstrasse, is a 15-minute walk (or take the postbus) from the centre of Vaduz, towards Schaan. Reasonable singles/doubles are Sfr50/100, with a shower on each floor. *Gasthof Au* (☎ 232 11 17), Austrasse 2, is the only other budget option in Vaduz. Singles/doubles with private shower are Sfr80/120, or Sfr60/95 without; triples are Sfr145. Eating is pleasant and fairly inexpensive in its garden restaurant.

Places to Eat

Restaurants are pricey in Vaduz, so look out for lunchtime specials. *Hotel Engel*, Städtle 13, has good meals from Sfr17, with vegetarian choices. At No 5, *City-Snack* provides cheap but basic fodder. On Äulestrasse, try *Café Amann* (closed Sunday), or stock up in the *Denner* supermarket. By Denner is *Azzurro*, a stand-up place with big pizzas from Sfr7.50.

AROUND VADUZ

The lowlands (Unterland) of Northern Liechtenstein are dotted with small communities. There's little to do except enjoy the quiet pace of life and view the village churches. Pottery-making is demonstrated on weekdays at Schaedler Keramik (☎ 373 14 14) in **Nendeln** (admission free). The Rofenberg in **Eschen-Nendeln** was formerly a place of public execution and is now the site of the Holy Cross Chapel. **Schellenberg** has a Russian monument, commemorating the night in 1945 when a band of 500 heavily armed Russian soldiers crossed the border. They had been fighting for the German army, but they came to defect, not attack.

Triesenberg, on a terrace above Vaduz, commands an excellent view over the Rhine valley and has a pretty onion-domed church. There's also a museum devoted to the Walser community, which journeyed from Valais (Switzerland) to settle here in the 13th century (admission Sfr2; students Sfr1). The Walser dialect is still spoken here.

Balzers, in the extreme south of the country, is dominated by the soaring sides of Gutenberg Castle, which is closed to the public.

MALBUN

Liechtenstein's ski resort, Malbun, lies at 1600 metres amid the mountains in the south-east. It has some good runs for novices (and two ski schools) as well as more difficult runs. A pass for all ski lifts and chair lifts costs Sfr22 (half a day), Sfr33 (one day) or Sfr143 (one week). Skis, shoes and poles cost Sfr43 for a day, and can be hired from the sports shop (☎ 263 37 55).

The road from Vaduz terminates at Malbun. The tourist office (☎ 263 65 77) is open daily except Sunday from 9 am to noon and 1.30 to 5 pm (1 to 4 pm on Saturday). It's closed during the low seasons (from mid-April to mid-May, and 1 November to mid-December).

There are seven hotels (most with restaurants) in the village; singles/doubles start at Sfr40/80. Some of the cheaper places to try are *Alpenhotel Malbun* (☎ 263 11 81), *Galina*, which has the same telephone number and management, and *Turna* (☎ 263 34 21).

Luxembourg

The Grand Duchy of Luxembourg (Luxemburg, Letzeburg) has long been a transit land. For centuries, ownership passed from one European superpower to another; and for decades, travellers wrote it off as merely an expensive stepping stone to other destinations.

While it's true that this tiny country is more a tax shelter for financial institutions than a budget haven for travellers, many people miss the best by rushing through. Its countryside is beautiful, dotted with feudal castles, deep river valleys and quaint wine-making towns, while the capital, Luxembourg City, is often described as the most dramatically situated in Europe.

Facts about the Country

HISTORY

Luxembourg's history reads a little like the fairy tale its name evokes. More than 1000 years ago, in 963, a count called Sigefroi (or Siegfried, count of Ardennes) built a castle high on a promontory, laying the foundation stone of the present-day capital and the beginning of a dynasty which spawned rulers throughout Europe.

By the end of the Middle Ages, the strategically placed, fortified city was much sought after – the Burgundians, Spanish, French, Austrians and Prussians all waging bloody battles to conquer and secure it. Besieged, devastated and rebuilt more than 20 times in 400 years, it became the strongest fortress in Europe after Gibraltar, hence its nickname, 'Gibraltar of the north'.

Listed as a French 'forestry department' during Napoleon's reign, it was included in the newly formed United Kingdom of the Netherlands, along with Belgium, in 1814. It was cut in half 16 years later when Belgium severed itself from the Netherlands and Luxembourg was split between them. This division sparked the Grand Duchy's desire for independence,

and in 1839 the Dutch portion became present-day Luxembourg. Later, after the country declared itself neutral, the long-contested fort was blown up.

Luxembourg entered the 20th century riding on the wealth of its iron-ore deposits. When this industry slumped in the mid-1970s, the Grand Duchy survived by introducing favourable banking and taxation laws, which made it a world centre of international finance.

GEOGRAPHY

On maps of Europe, Luxembourg usually gets allocated a 'Lux' tag – and even that abbreviation is often too big to fit the space it occupies on the map between Belgium, Germany and France. At only 82 km long and 57 km wide, riddled with rivers, its 2600 sq km are divided between the forested Ardennes highlands to the north, and farming and mining country to the south.

GOVERNMENT & POLITICS

One of Europe's smallest sovereign states,

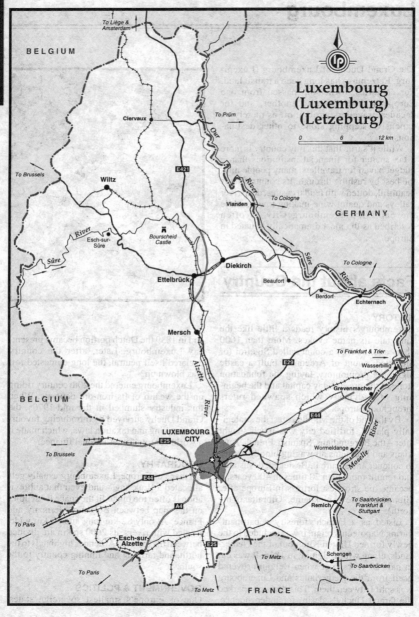

Luxembourg
(Luxemburg)
(Letzeburg)

BELGIUM

To Liège & Amsterdam

Clervaux

To Prüm

To Brussels

Wiltz

To Brussels

River

Sûre

Esch-sur-Sûre

Bourscheid Castle

Vianden

To Cologne

GERMANY

Diekirch

Ettelbrück

Beaufort

Berdorf

Echternach

To Cologne

Mersch

To Frankfurt & Trier

Wasserbillig

Alzette River

Grevenmacher

BELGIUM

LUXEMBOURG CITY

Wormeldange

Moselle River

To Brussels

To Paris

Remich

To Saarbrücken, Frankfurt & Stuttgart

Esch-sur-Alzette

To Metz

Schengen

To Saarbrücken

To Paris

To Metz

FRANCE

0   6   12 km

Luxembourg is a constitutional monarchy headed by Grand Duke Jean, who came to the throne after his mother's abdication in 1964. The main political parties are the Christian-Social, Democratic and Workers-Socialist.

POPULATION & PEOPLE

A motto seen carved in stone walls sums up the people's character: *Mir wëlle bleiwe wat mir sin* – We want to remain what we are. Despite a history of foreign domination, Luxembourg's 400,000 inhabitants steadfastly adhere to an independent character.

ARTS

Few Luxembourgers are internationally known in the arts, which is probably why Edward Steichen, one of the pioneers of American photography, is held in such high regard in his native land. The expressionist painter Joseph Kutter introduced modern art to Luxembourg. Roger Manderscheid is a respected, contemporary author who often writes in Letzeburgesch, the national language.

RELIGION

Christianity was established early, and today Catholicism reigns supreme. More than 95% of the population are Roman Catholic, with the church dominating many facets of life, including politics, the media and education.

LANGUAGE

There are three official languages in Luxembourg: French, German and Letzeburgesch. The latter is most closely related to German and was proclaimed as the national tongue in 1985. Luxembourgers speak Letzeburgesch to each other on the streets and in their homes; a couple of words often overheard are *moien* (good morning/hello) and *äddi* (goodbye). Like French speakers, Luxembourgers say *merci* for 'thank you'. In the business world, the judiciary or the press, French or German are automatically used. For a rundown on these two languages, see the Language Guide at the back of this book. English is widely spoken in the capital, but less so around the countryside.

Facts for the Visitor

PLANNING

Climate & When to Go

Luxembourg has a temperate climate with warm summers and cold winters – especially cold in the Ardennes, which often get snow. The sunniest months are May to August, although April and September can be sunny as well. Precipitation is spread pretty evenly over the year. Luxembourg in spring can be a riot of wild flowers and blossoms.

SUGGESTED ITINERARIES

Depending on the length of your stay, you might want to see and do the following things (though if you're relying on public transport, you might need a few more days to cover these areas):

Two days
    Spend one day in Luxembourg City and another day touring the Moselle Valley.
One week
    Spend two days in Luxembourg City, three days in the centre and north (Vianden, Clervaux, Wiltz, Ettelbrück and Diekirch) and two days exploring the Little Switzerland region (Echternach and Beaufort) and the Moselle Valley.

HIGHLIGHTS

Luxembourg's highlights include strolling along the capital's Chemin de la Corniche at sunset; spending a lazy morning tasting local Moselle Valley wines; hiking almost anywhere in the north; and taking in the expansive view from Bourscheid Castle.

TOURIST OFFICES

The Office National du Tourisme headquarters (☎ 400808; fax 404748), PO Box 1001, L-1010, Luxembourg City, is not open to the public, but will send you information.

Tourist Offices Abroad

UK
    122-124 Regent St, London W1R 5FE
    (☎ 0171-434 2800)
USA
    17 Beekman Place, New York, NY 10022
    (☎ 212-935 8888)

VISAS & EMBASSIES

Most nationals from Western Europe and

Scandinavia, and travellers from Australia, Canada, Israel, Japan, New Zealand, the USA and 29 other countries, need only a valid passport for a stay of up to three months. Everyone else needs a visa before entering the country.

Luxembourg Embassies Abroad

In countries where there is no representative, contact the Belgian or Dutch diplomatic missions. Luxembourg embassies and consulates include:

Australia
  Landmark Building, Level 5, 345 George St, Sydney, NSW 2000 (☎ 02-9320 0255)
Canada
  3877 Ave Draper, Montréal, Que H4A 2N9 (☎ 04-489 6052)
UK
  27 Wilton Crescent, London SW1X 8SD (☎ 0171-235 6961)
USA
  2200 Massachusetts Ave, NW Washington, DC 20008 (☎ 202-265 4171)

Foreign Embassies in Luxembourg

The nearest Australian, Canadian and New Zealand embassies are in Belgium (see the Belgium Facts for the Visitor section). The following embassies are all in Luxembourg City:

Belgium
  4 Rue des Girondins, L-1626 (☎ 442746)
France
  9 Blvd Prince Henri, L-1724 (☎ 475 5881)
Germany
  20-22 Ave Emile Reuter, L-2420 (☎ 453 4451)
Japan
  17 Rue Beaumont, L-1219 (☎ 464151)
Netherlands
  5 Rue C M Spoo, L-2546 (☎ 227570)
UK
  14 Blvd Roosevelt, L-2450 (☎ 229864)
USA
  22 Blvd Emmanuel Servais, L-2535 (☎ 460123)

CUSTOMS

Petrol, alcohol and tobacco products are cheap in Luxembourg and people from neighbouring countries often come here to stock up. Travellers from EU countries may import 800 cigarettes or 200 cigars or 1000g of tobacco; 10l of spirits or 20l of aperitifs; 90l of wine and 110l of beer. Visitors from non-EU countries can bring in one-quarter of the above tobacco products and just one litre of spirits or two litres of either aperitifs or wine.

MONEY

The unit of currency is the Luxembourg franc – written as 'f' or 'flux' – which is issued in f1, f5, f20 and f50 coins, and f100, f1000 and f5000 notes. It's equal to the Belgian franc (for exchange rates, see the Belgium Facts for the Visitor section), but while Belgian currency is commonly used in Luxembourg, the reverse does not apply. Banks are best for changing money, and all major credit cards are commonly accepted. Prices are on a par with Belgium – except petrol, which is much cheaper. Tipping is not obligatory and bargaining is downright impossible.

Consumer Taxes

Value-added tax (abbreviated in French as TVA) is calculated at 15%, except for hotel, restaurant and camping ground prices, which enjoy only a 3% levy. The procedure for claiming the tax back is tedious (a lot of paperwork and a good six-month wait) unless you buy from shops displaying the 'Tax Free for Tourists' signs, and you'll still only get 10% returned. The tourist office has a booklet explaining all the details.

POST & COMMUNICATIONS

Post offices (except in Luxembourg City) are open similar weekday hours to shops. It costs f16 to send a letter (under 20g) within Europe and f25 outside. Expect mail to Australia, Canada, New Zealand and the USA to take at least a week. To the UK and within Europe, it'll take two or three days. There's a f16 fee (sometimes waived) for poste restante.

Local telephone calls cost f5 for about four minutes. International phone calls can be made from some post offices, telephone centres or public phones using f250 or f550 phonecards. To telephone outside of Luxembourg, the international access code is ☎ 00. There are no telephone area codes in Luxembourg. Faxes can be sent from telephone centres and cost f20/37/55 per minute to the UK/USA/Australia. It costs f80 to receive a fax.

To make international telephone calls to Luxembourg, the country code from *most* countries is ☎ 352 (from Austria, for example, it's ☎ 432).

NEWSPAPERS & MAGAZINES

The only English-language newspaper is the weekly *Luxembourg News*, which gives a brief rundown of local news and has entertainment listings. Foreign newspapers, and magazines such as *Time* and *Newsweek*, are readily available.

PHOTOGRAPHY & VIDEO

Processing and developing charges are moderate – about f20 per print plus f100 for developing in a one-hour shop. A 36-exposure Kodak 64 slide film costs f495 including developing. A normal/Hi8 8mm video cassette (90 minutes) costs f255/550.

TIME

Noon in Luxembourg is 3 am in San Francisco, 6 am in New York and Toronto, 11 am in London, 9 pm in Sydney and 11 pm in Auckland. The 24-hour clock is commonly used. Daylight-saving time comes into effect at 2 am on the last Sunday in March, when clocks are moved an hour forward; they're moved an hour back at 2 am on the last Sunday in October.

ELECTRICITY

The current used is 220V, 50 Hz, and the socket used is the two-pin variety.

WEIGHTS & MEASURES

The metric system is used. Like other Continental Europeans, Luxembourgers indicate decimals with commas and thousands with points.

LAUNDRY

While not profuse, you can generally find a self-service *laverie* in larger towns. A five-kg wash costs about f290; dryers are f30 for 10 minutes.

TOILETS

Public toilets in Luxembourg are not profuse. Those that have an attendant warrant a f10 charge; those that don't are usually ill-kept and best avoided.

HEALTH

Hotels and tourist offices can usually assist in finding an English-speaking doctor. In the case of a medical emergency or if you need a phar-macy outside normal working hours call ☎ 112.

WOMEN TRAVELLERS

Women should face few problems travelling around Luxembourg. However, in the event of attack, contact the women's crisis organisation Waisse Rank (☎ 402040) at 84 Rue Adolphe Fischer in Luxembourg City.

GAY & LESBIAN TRAVELLERS

Luxembourg has no national homosexual or lesbian organisations, and attitudes to homosexuality are still quite conservative. Only in the capital, Luxembourg City, will you find the odd gay bar. The age of consent is 16.

DISABLED TRAVELLERS

Disabled travellers will find little joy in getting around in Luxembourg – lifts are not commonplace, ramps are few, and pavements are uneven. For information it's best to contact Info-Handicap (☎ 366466), 20 Rue de Contern, L-5955 Itzig.

SENIOR TRAVELLERS

Only Luxembourg citizens are entitled to discounts for seniors on local transport, and there are no discounts for the elderly at museums.

DANGERS & ANNOYANCES

Luxembourg is a safe country to travel around. In the event of an emergency, call ☎ 113 for the police or ☎ 112 for medical assistance.

BUSINESS HOURS

Trading hours are weekdays 9 am to 5.30 pm (except Monday when some shops open about noon), and a half or full day on Saturday. Many shops close for lunch between noon and 2 pm. Banks have shorter hours: weekdays from 9 am to 4.30 pm and, in the capital, on Saturday mornings – country branches close for lunch.

PUBLIC HOLIDAYS & SPECIAL EVENTS

Public holidays include New Year's Day, Easter Monday, May Day (1 May), Ascension Day, Whit Monday, National Day (23 June), Assumption Day (15 August), All Saints' Day (1 November) and Christmas Day.

For a small country, Luxembourg is big on festivals. Pick up the tourist office's *Calendar* of Events brochure for local listings. The biggest national events are carnival, held six weeks before Easter, and Bonfire Day (Bürgsonndeg), one week later.

ACTIVITIES

With a dense network of marked walking paths, the Grand Duchy is a hiker's haven. National routes are indicated by yellow signposts. Tracks marked by white triangles connect the 13 Hostelling International hostels. The hostel association headquarters (see the following Accommodation section) is the best place for buying detailed national and regional hiking maps, though local tourist offices also stock walking maps of their area.

WORK

Seasonal grape picking is available in the Moselle Valley for about six weeks from mid-September. Wages vary: the average is about f1000 a day including accommodation and meals. No permit is needed, but the work is popular with locals, so if possible organise your job in advance directly with a farmer or through a vineyard.

ACCOMMODATION

Unless you're camping, there are few cheap alternatives. Singles/doubles in no-star hotels start at f1000/1400 for a basic room with breakfast. In country areas, B&Bs are often cosier options and cost about f1200 for two people.

Hostels are a good bet because they're often scenically located near castles or overlooking valleys. However, they close sporadically during winter. The nightly dorm rate, including breakfast, varies from f345 to f415 for members under 26 years of age, and f425 to f500 for older members. Nonmembers must pay an extra f110 a night. For more details contact Hostelling International (HI) (☎ 225588), 18 Place d'Armes, L-2013 Luxembourg City.

Camping grounds are profuse, though mainly in the central and northern regions. Rates for one adult per night range from f45 in the rare 'Category 3' grounds to between f100 and f180 in the more plentiful 'Category 1'. In general, children are charged half the adult rate, and a tent site is equivalent to an adult rate.

The national tourist office has free hotel and camping brochures, and farm-holiday, apartment and cottage lists (local offices have B&B lists). The national office will reserve accommodation free of charge. In summer, it's wise to book ahead for all accommodation.

FOOD & DRINK

Luxembourg's cuisine is similar to that in Belgium's Wallonia region – plenty of pork, freshwater fish and game meat – but with a German influence in local specialities like liver dumplings with sauerkraut. Eating out will rapidly burn up your budget because even a plat du jour (plate of the day) in the cheapest café will cost f260, and strict vegetarians will find little joy. On a brighter note, beer, both local (Mousel) and Belgian, is plentiful, and the Moselle Valley white wines are highly drinkable.

ENTERTAINMENT

Nightlife outside Luxembourg City is very tame. In summer, terrace cafés take over town squares and are the place for people-watching, especially during local festivals. Cinemas generally screen films in their original language with French, and sometimes German, subtitles.

Getting There & Away

AIR

The international airport, Findel, is six km east of the capital, and is serviced by frequent buses (see the Luxembourg City Getting Around section). The national carrier, Luxair, flies to a number of European destinations, including Amsterdam, Athens and London. It has offices at Findel and in the city centre at Place de la Gare (☎ 481820). Icelandair (☎ 4027 2727), at 59 Rue Glesener, has regular flights to the USA. Departure tax is included in ticket prices.

LAND

Train

Eurail, Inter-Rail, Europass and Flexipass are valid; so is the 'Benelux Tourrail' pass (see the Belgium Getting Around section), which costs f6320/4220 for a 1st/2nd-class ticket for people above 26 years and f3160 (2nd class only) for those under 26. The Benelux Tourrail pass is also valid for travelling on Luxembourg Railways' buses. There are hourly trains to Brussels (f782 for a one-way, 2nd-class ticket, 2¾ hours) and to Amsterdam via Brussels (f1950, 5½ hours) or less frequently but cheaper via Liège (f1750, six hours). To Liège itself the fare is f750. Other destinations include Paris (f1468, four hours, four trains per day) and Trier in Germany (f280, 40 minutes, 11 per day). The station office (☎ 492424) in Luxembourg City is open 24 hours for international and national enquiries.

Car & Motorcycle

The A4 is the major route to Brussels and Paris; the A31 via Dudelange leads to Metz in France. The main route to Germany is the A48 via Trier.

RIVER

It's possible to take the MV *Princesse Marie-Astrid* from Grevenmacher along the Moselle as far as Bernkastel in Germany. This tourist boat has summer-only services: once weekly to Bernkastel (f600 one way, 6½ hours) and three times a week to Trier (f260, two hours). For more details, see the Moselle Valley section.

Getting Around

BUS & TRAIN

Unlike its Benelux partners, Luxembourg does not have an extensive rail system, so getting around, once you leave the main north-south rail line, can take time. The bus network is thorough and the fare system for both train and bus is simple: f40 for a 'short' (about 10 km or less) trip, or f160 for a 2nd-class unlimited day ticket, which is also good for travelling on inner-city buses. It's valid from the time of purchase until 8 am the next day. For information on national (CFL) buses and trains call ☎ 492424.

In most train stations, you'll find either a luggage room (f60 per article for 24 hours) or luggage lockers, which come in an array of sizes and prices – f60, f80 or f100 for 48 hours.

If you arrive somewhere by bus, you can expect to have to lug your stuff with you.

CAR & MOTORCYCLE

Luxembourgers drive on the right-hand side, wearing seat belts is compulsory, and drink-driving penalties are high. The speed limit is 30 km/h in dense residential areas, 50 km/h in towns, 90 km/h outside towns and 120 km/h on motorways. The maximum permissible blood-alcohol concentration is 0.08%. The price of fuel is among the cheapest in Western Europe: a litre of super costs f29.40, lead-free f26.40, and diesel f21.60. For all other motoring information, contact the Automobile Club de Luxembourg (☎ 450045) 54 Route de Longwy, L-8007 Bertrange.

Car rental is expensive at f2585/12207 per day/week (including insurance, VAT and unlimited km) for a small Citroën.

BICYCLE

Cycling is more of a popular pastime than the way of life it is elsewhere in Benelux. Bikes can be hired for about f400 per day – local tourist offices have rental details and cycling maps. It costs f40 to take your bike on a train.

HITCHING

Getting a ride is rarely a problem, but away from the capital city, traffic can be light. It's illegal to hitch on motorways.

BOAT

For details of passenger boat services along the Moselle, see the Moselle Valley section.

LOCAL TRANSPORT

Luxembourg City has a good local bus network. Elsewhere there is little public transport besides taxis. Taxis cost f32 per km plus a 10% night surcharge; 25% extra on Sundays.

ORGANISED TOURS

Day trips by bus from Luxembourg City take in either the Moselle Valley and Echternach, or Vianden and the Little Switzerland region. They only run from June to September; for details ask the tourist office for the *Sightseeing Luxembourg* brochure.

Luxembourg City

Strikingly situated high on a promontory overlooking the Pétrusse and Alzette valleys, the Grand Duchy's 1000-year-old capital is a composed blend of old and new. One of Europe's financial leaders, it's a wealthy city with an uncommonly tranquil air and unusually clean streets.

Orientation

The city centre has three sections. The main one is the old-town hub, north of the valleys and based around two large pedestrian squares, Place d'Armes and Place Guillaume. The modern commercial centre is across the Pétrusse Valley to the south, connected by two bridges, Pont Adolphe and Pont Passerelle. This area ends around the train station, a 20-minute walk from Place d'Armes. The train station quarter is being spruced up, but some of the backstreets are still seedy. The Grund, or lower town, is a picturesque, cobblestoned quarter, built well below the fortifications, and home these days to some brisk nightlife. Across the Alzette Valley rise the modern towers of the European Centre (Centre Européen).

Information

Tourist Offices
The city tourist office (☎ 222809) is on Place d'Armes. It's open Monday to Saturday from 9 am to 6 pm (in summer until 7 pm and also open on Sunday). It hands out free city maps, a comprehensive walking tour pamphlet and the handy *Luxembourg Weekly* events guide.

There are two national offices. The airport bureau (☎ 400808) is open weekdays 10 am to 2.30 pm and then from 4 to 7 pm, Saturday from 10 am to 1.45 pm and Sunday from 10 am to 2.30 pm and 3.30 to 6.30 pm. More centrally located, the train station office (☎ 481199), next to the Luxair office on Place de la Gare, is open from 1 July to mid-September daily from 9 am to 7 pm, and from mid-September to 30 June from 9 am to noon and 2 to 6.30 pm (closed Sundays from 1 November to 31 March). It provides city and national information and reserves rooms.

Money
The Banque de Luxembourg, opposite the station, has average rates. American Express (☎ 471 7541) is at 34 Ave de la Porte Neuve, is north of the old-town hub. Outside banking hours, exchange offices with poorer rates are open daily at the train station from 8.30 am to 9 pm, and at the airport from 7 am to 8.30 pm (Sunday from 9 am).

Post & Communications
The main post office is at 25 Rue Aldringen, open Monday to Saturday from 7 am to 7 pm. The post office branch at 38 Place de la Gare, near the train station, is open weekdays from 8 am to 7 pm and Saturday until noon. Phone calls and faxes can be made from the new telephone office, open the same hours, round the corner on Rue d'Épernay.

Travel Agencies
Sotours (☎ 461514), 15 Place du Théâtre, specialises in student and youth fares. Nouvelles Frontières (☎ 46 4140), in the arcade between Rue des Bains and Blvd Royal, has occasional discount airfares.

Bookshops
The best place for (expensive) English-language books is Magasin Anglais (☎ 224925), 19 Allée Scheffer, a 15-minute walk north-west of Place d'Armes.

Laundry
The Quick Wash on Place de Strasbourg is open weekdays from 8.30 am to 7 pm and Saturday until 6 pm.

Medical Services
In the case of a medical emergency or if you need a pharmacy outside normal working hours call ☎ 112.

Things to See & Do

Luxembourg is easily covered on foot. The city seems made for leisurely wandering, with lookouts and serene parks dotting the southern rim of the old town, where you'll find most of the sights.

Walking Tour From Place d'Armes, head south down Rue Chimay to the coach-infested **Place de la Constitution**, where you have excellent views over the green Pétrusse Valley and the spectacular bridges that span it. East along Blvd Roosevelt, the gardens which cover the 17th-century **Citadelle du St Esprit** offer superb panoramas up both valleys and over the Grund.

Follow the natural curve north to the **Chemin de la Corniche** – a pedestrian promenade hailed as 'Europe's most beautiful balcony' – which winds up to the **Bock**, the cliff on which Count Sigefroi built his mighty fort. The castle and much of the fortifications were blown up between 1867 and 1883. There's little left – the main attractions are the view and the nearby entrance to the Casemates, a 21-km network of underground passages spared from destruction because of their delicate position in relation to the town. The **Grund** lies in the valley directly below, accessible from the other side of the Bock or by a free lift dug in the cliff near the citadel at Place du St Esprit.

From the Bock, continue north up Blvd Victor Thorn, past the row of Spanish turrets overlooking the HI hostel, to the 1000-year-old **Three Turrets**. From here, it's just a short walk back to the centre via Rue du Marché-aux-Herbes, where you'll find the **Grand Ducal Palace**, built in the 16th and 18th centuries and extensively restored in recent years (open to visitors from mid-July to 31 August only), and **Place Guillaume**, with its formal government edifices.

Casemates The Casemates are a honeycomb of damp, rock rooms carved out under the Bock. Long ago, they used to house bakeries, slaughterhouses and thousands of soldiers; during WWI and WWII they were used as a bomb shelter for 35,000 people. They are open everey day from March to October from 10 am to 5 pm; entry costs f70/40 for adults/children.

Museums Just north of the Grand Ducal Palace, the **Musée National** on Place Marché-aux-Poissons is a blend of Roman and medieval relics, fortification models and art from the 13th century up to the present day. It's open Tuesday to Friday from 10 am to 4.45 pm, Saturday from 2 to 5.45 pm, and Sunday from 10 to 11.45 am and 2 to 5.45 pm. The new **Museum of the History of Luxembourg City** on Rue du St is open Tuesday to Saturday from 10 am to 6 pm. Admission to both museums is free.

Market On Wednesday and Saturday mornings, there's a food market on Place Guillaume. On the second and fourth Saturday morning of each month, it's bric-a-brac time on Place d'Armes.

Organised Tours

The *Pétrusse Express* is a toy train that runs from Place de la Constitution down to the Grund. It operates daily from Easter to October and costs f230/160 for adults/children. Alternatively, Sales-Lentz/Segatos (☎ 461617) at 49 Blvd Royal, operates two-hour city bus trips for f400/250 for adults/children.

Special Events

Two festivals are worth catching: Octave, a Catholic festival held from late April to early May, which climaxes with a street parade headed by the royal family; and Schueberfouer, a fortnight-long fun fair in late August, during which decorated sheep take to the streets.

Places to Stay

The cheap hotels are clustered north of the station, though most backpackers end up in the scenically situated hostel.

Camping There are two 'category 1' camp sites south of the city. *1 Kockelscheuer* (☎ 471815), 22 Route de Bettembourg in Kockelscheuer, is about four km away (take bus No 2 from the train station). It's open from Easter to 31 October. *Bon Accueil* (☎ 367069), on Route de Thionville, Alzingen, is about five km south of the city (the bus to Alzingen from the train station stops nearby). It's open from 1 April to 30 September.

Hostels The *hostel* (☎ 226889) at 2 Rue du Fort Olizy is excellently located in a valley below the old city. Bus No 9 from the airport or train station (last one at 11 pm) stops at the top of the embankment, otherwise it's a 25-minute walk from the station. The hostel is open all year, and charges f550/1100 for members under 26 and f650/1300 for members over 26. Dorms start at f415 for members aged under 26, and f500 for older members. Non-members pay an extra f110 a night.

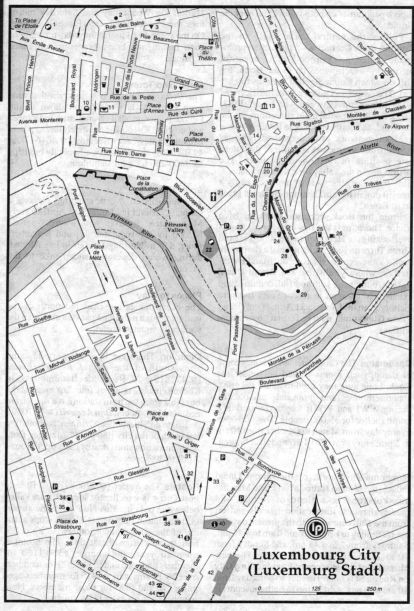

Luxembourg City
(Luxemburg Stadt)

0   125   250 m

PLACES TO STAY

6	Youth Hostel
18	Hôtel Schintgen
30	Hôtel le Parisien
31	Auberge le Papillon
38	Hôtel Bristol
39	Carlton Hôtel

PLACES TO EAT

3	Chez Mami
9	Monopol Cafeteria
17	Brasserie Chimay
19	Bacchus
23	Mesa Verde
32	Monopol Cafeteria
37	As Arcadas

OTHER

1	French Embassy
2	Nouvelles Frontiéres
4	Sotour Travel
5	Three Turrets
7	Interview
8	Um Piquet
10	Bus Station
11	Main Post Office
12	City Tourist Office
13	Musée National
14	Grand Ducal Palace
15	Casemates
16	Bock
20	History of Luxembourg City Museum
21	Cathedral
22	British Embassy
24	Café des Artistes
25	Scott's Pub
26	Café Häffchen
27	Vélo en Ville
28	Grund Lift
29	Citadelle du St Esprit
33	Supermarket
34	Iceland Air
35	Supermarket
36	Laundry
40	National Tourist Office
41	Banque de Luxembourg
42	Train Station
43	Telephone Office
44	Station Post Office

Hotels There are a couple of OK options on Rue de Strasbourg near the train station. The cheapest is the huge and old *Carlton Hôtel* (☎ 484802) at No 9 which has clean rooms for f750/1400/1800. *Hôtel Bristol* (☎ 485829) at No 11 has spotless rooms from f1800/2000, and parking for f300 – but ask to see the rooms first because some are no bigger than walk-in wardrobes.

Hôtel le Parisien (☎ 492397), 46 Rue Sainte Zithe, is in a slightly quieter area, and has decent rooms starting at f1200/1700. Similarly priced and just as good is *Brasserie/Auberge le Papillon* (☎ 494490) at 9 Rue Origer.

The only reasonable alternative in the old centre is the *Hôtel Schintgen* (☎ 222844), at 6 Rue Notre Dame, where rooms start at f2000/3000.

Places to Eat

Near the train station, the Portuguese-run *As Arcadas* (☎ 491264), 29 Rue Joseph Junck, serves an excellent, lunchtime-only, two-course meal for f270.

Up in the old town is *Chez Mami*, 15 Rue des Bains, a Portuguese family-run café with port straight from the home country and decent steaks for f350. More centrally, *Brasserie Chimay* on Rue Chimay has a plat du jour for f350, and steaks from f400. The *Monopol* store on Rue Génistre has a 5th-floor cafeteria which has great views and a lunchtime f225 plat du jour; there's another *Monopol* cafeteria on Ave de la Liberté.

One of the city's trendiest Italian restaurants is *Bacchus* (☎ 471397), at 32 Rue du Marché-aux-Herbes. Pizzas start at f270; bookings are advisable. In the Grund, *Scott's Pub* overlooks the river and serves snacks (see the following Entertainment section). The only vegetarian option, and it's not a cheap one, is *Mesa Verde* (☎ 464126), 11 Rue du St Esprit (closed Sunday and Monday).

Otherwise, there's a supermarket at Place de Strasbourg, and another in the basement of the Centre Commercial.

Entertainment

Even on weekends, nightlife is modest, but a few well-patronised watering holes are not hard to find. The Grund area is one of the most popular spots, and when the cliffs are lit up in summer, it's a pleasant stroll down to the taverns which huddle here. The *Café des Artistes* at 22 Montée du Grund has live piano music and spontaneous singing until 2 am. Just across the bridge on Bisserweg is *Scott's Pub*, a raucous, weekend live blues and rock venue; it's calmer on weekdays. Over the road, the tranquil courtyard of *Café Häffchen* – one of the city's oldest meeting spots – has been attracting drinkers since the early 1800s.

In the old centre, *Interview* (19 Rue Aldringen) and the nearby *Um Piquet* (30 Rue de la Poste) are popular, trendy bar/cafés. There are biker bars, North African haunts and a few nightclubs around the station and along Rue Joseph Junck. The city's small gay scene revolves around *Chez Mike* just before Place de l'Étoile on Ave Émile Reuter.

Getting There & Away

For information on airlines and international trains, see the Getting There & Away section at the beginning of this chapter. For national destinations, see the Getting There & Away section in each place. Turn left as you leave the train station to find CFL buses heading to towns within Luxembourg.

Getting Around

To/From the Airport Bus No 9 (three services hourly) connects Findel airport with the hostel and station; it costs f40 (and f40 extra for luggage). There's also a more expensive (f120) but quicker Luxair bus which leaves from outside the Luxair office at the station. For a taxi to Findel, reckon on about f650.

Bus Turn right as you leave the train station to find city buses. In the old town, the main bus terminal is Centre Hamilius, opposite the post office on Ave Monterey. Free bus route maps are handed out at the tourist office.

Car While street parking and car parks are readily available, it's better to leave the car behind and stroll around the sights in the old-town hub, most of which is a pedestrian zone.

Most of the large car-rental companies have offices at the airport. Head offices are as follows:

Autolux
  33 Blvd Prince Henri, L-1724 (☎ 221181)
Avis
  2 Place de la Gare, L-1616 (☎ 489595)
Budget
  Luxembourg Airport, L-1110 (☎ 437575)
Hertz
  20 Rue de Cessange, L-1320 (☎ 485485)
Rent a Car
  191 Route de Longwy, L-1941 (☎ 440861)

Bicycle The HI hostel can organise rental bikes or try *Vélo en Ville* (☎ 4796 2383) at 8 Bisserweg which charges f250 per half-day, f400 a day or f2000 a week (20% off for those aged under 26).

Around Luxembourg

MOSELLE VALLEY

Less than half an hour's drive east of the capital, the Luxembourg section of the Moselle Valley is one of Europe's smallest and most charming wine regions. More than a dozen towns line the **Route du Vin** (Wine Road), which follows the Moselle from Wasserbillig, through the region's capital at Grevenmacher, the picturesque, hillside village of Wormeldange and the popular, waterfront playground of Remich, to the small, southern border town of Schengen.

You'll find only two tourist offices along the way. The largest is in Grevenmacher (☎ 758275) at 10 Route du Vin, open weekdays from 10 am to noon and 2 to 5 pm; the other is at Remich (☎ 698488), in the bus station on the Esplanade, open only in July and August from 10.30 am to 12.30 pm and 2.30 to 6.30 pm.

Things to See & Do

Wine tasting is the obvious attraction and there are about six *caves* (cellars) en route where you can sample the fruity, white vintages. The smaller caves are often the most atmospheric: on Sunday mornings they turn into lively meetings spots for the villages' older folk. Try the **Cellars of Poll-Fabaire** at Wormeldange, open daily from 1 May to 31 August; or in Grevenmacher, the larger **Caves Bernard-Massard**, which are open daily from April to 31 October. In Remich, **St Martin** is open the same months as Massard. All three places run tours (f70 to f90) which end with a 'free' drink.

From April to September, it's possible to travel the 'wine river' on board the MS *Princesse Marie-Astrid*, which plies the Moselle, calling in at the major towns between Bernkastel in Germany and Schengen in Luxembourg. As an example of the prices,

Wasserbillig to Wormeldange costs f190/290 for a one-way/return ticket.

Special Events
The wine festivals start in August and climax with November's 'New Wine' festival in Wormeldange; each village celebrates nearly all stages of the wine-making process.

Places to Stay
Camping grounds are few and far between in this region. Next to the butterfly garden in Grevenmacher, there's *Camping de la Route du Vin* (☎ 75234), open from April to September. In Remich, *Camp Europe* (☎ 698018) is 100m from the bus station on the main Esplanade. It's open from Easter to mid-September.

Even the tiniest village has at least one hotel-cum-restaurant, but the only *hostel* is in Grevenmacher (☎ 75222), at 15 Gruewereck, on the hill behind the town. It's open from mid-March to 31 December.

If it's a hotel you're after, the *Mosellan* (☎ 75157), 35 Rue de Trèves, near the bus station in Grevenmacher, has rooms from f800/1500. In Wormeldange, *Relais du Postillon* (☎ 768485), 113 Rue Principale, has rooms from f1500/1900. Remich has several riverfront choices, the cheapest being *Beau Séjour* (☎ 698126), 30 Quai de la Moselle, which has rooms from f1100/1900.

Getting There & Away
The region is difficult to explore by train because the line to Germany only goes through the northern tip of the area at Wasserbillig. Otherwise, there are twice-daily buses from Luxembourg City to Grevenmacher, with frequent connections to the smaller towns further south. Alternatively, there's the boat (see the previous Things to See & Do section).

CENTRAL LUXEMBOURG
While there's not much to keep you in central Luxembourg, the area can make a good exploration base. The most conveniently situated town is **Ettelbrück**, the nation's central road and rail junction; while nearby **Diekirch** is home to the region's main wartime museum.

The tourist office in Ettelbrück (☎ 82068) is at the train station. It's open weekdays from 8.30 am to noon and 1.30 to 4.45 pm (in July and August, it's also open on weekends). The

tourist office in Diekirch (☎ 803023) is at 1 Esplanade, a 10-minute walk from the station. It's open weekdays from 9 am to noon and 2 to 5 pm (from 1 July to 15 August, it's open from 9 am to 6 pm, and weekends from 10 am to noon and 2 to 4 pm).

Things to See & Do
The **National Military Museum** in Diekirch details the 1944 Battle of the Bulge and the liberation of Luxembourg by US troops. From Easter to 31 October, it's open every day from 10 am to noon and 2 to 6 pm.

If you have a car, it's well worth taking the winding drive north-west of Diekirch to the 1000-year-old **Bourscheid Castle**, which is situated on a plateau overlooking farmland and the Sûre River. The castle is open daily from April to October, and on weekends from November to March.

Places to Stay
Kalkesdelt (☎ 82185) on Chemin du Camping, in Ettelbrück is 2.5 km from the station. In Diekirch, *Camping de la Sûre* (☎ 809425) is on Route de Gilsdorf. Both are open from 1 April to 30 September. The Ettelbrück *hostel* (☎ 82269) is at Rue G D Joséphine-Charlotte, a 20-minute walk from the station. It's closed at various times during the year – ring before you arrive. B&Bs are the next best bet, or there's *Auberge Herckmans* (☎ 817428) at 3 Place de la Résistance which has rooms from f850/1350. In Diekirch, the cheapest hotel in town is *Hôtel Ernzbach* (☎ 803636), 4 Ave de la Gare, with rooms from f1000/1200.

Getting There & Away
Hourly trains from Luxembourg City to Ettelbrück take 30 minutes; to Diekirch, it takes 40 minutes.

LITTLE SWITZERLAND
Centred around the old, Christian town of Echternach, in a pocket of woodland north-east of the capital, is the Little Switzerland (Petite Suisse) region where outdoor enthusiasts go on retreat – though rarely a solitary one. Hiking, cycling and rock climbing make it one of Luxembourg's prime tourist areas.

There's an information office in Echternach (☎ 72230) at Porte St Willibrord, open weekdays from 9 am to noon and 2 to 5 pm (also on weekends in July and August). There are smaller offices in the two other main towns in the region: at Berdorf (☎ 79643), in the town hall, which is open weekdays from 9 am to noon and 2 to 6 pm; and in Beaufort (☎ 86081), at 9 Rue de l'Église, open weekdays from 8 am to noon (from 15 July to 31 August daily from 8 am to noon and 1 to 5 pm).

Things to See & Do

If you're in Echternach on Whit Sunday, look out for the handkerchief pageant in honour of St Willibrord, a missionary who died in the town centuries ago. If not, you can visit the **basilica** where St Willibrord's remains lie in a white, marble sarcophagus. Behind the Basilica, there's a Benedictine **abbey**.

You can also head west to the walking paths which wind through rocky chasms and waterfalls to **Berdorf**, situated on the tableland six km away, and on to the crumbling castle of **Beaufort**, open daily from 1 April to 25 October from 9 am to 6 pm.

Places to Stay

Camping grounds are abundant throughout this region, the loveliest ones of course being away from the towns. But if you're stuck, *Camp Officiel* (☎ 72272) is about 200m from the bus station in Echternach.

There are two *hostels* – one in Echternach (☎ 72158), 9 Rue André Duchscher, and the other at Beaufort (☎ 86075), 6 Rue de l'Auberge. Both close irregularly throughout the year, so ring ahead.

Hotels are plentiful in Echternach: try *Aigle Noir* (☎ 72383) at 4 Rue de la Gare, or *Hôtel de l'Abbaye* (☎ 729184) at 2 Rue des Merciers. Both have rooms from f1000/1450. In Berdorf, *Auberge Lenert* (☎ 79811), at 35 Rue d'Echternach, prices start from f900/1400. In Beaufort, the *Auberge Écu de Beaufort* (☎ 86118), at 11 Rue de l'Église, has rooms from f800/1400.

Getting There & Away

There are only buses from the capital city to Echternach, and they take 40 minutes. From Echternach, buses connect to other towns.

THE NORTH

Known as the Luxembourg Ardennes, the Grand Duchy's northern region is its most

spectacular. Winding valleys with fast-flowing rivers cut deep through green plateaus crowned by castles. Of the three main towns, Clervaux, in the far north, is the most accessible; while Vianden, in the east, is arguably Luxembourg's most touristic town. To the west, the town of Wiltz holds no special appeal, though the tiny nearby hamlet of Esch-sur-Sûre attracts a staggering number of tourists simply because of its location.

Clervaux's tourist office (☎ 920072) is ensconced in its castle, and is open weekdays from Easter to 30 June from 2 to 5 pm, from 1 July to 30 September from 9.45 to 11.45 am and 2 to 6 pm, and in October 9.45 to 11.45 am and 1 to 5 pm. Outside these hours, the town hall, also in the castle, has local information. The slick Vianden office (☎ 84257), 37 Rue de la Gare, is open daily from 1 April to 30 October from 9.30 am to noon and 2 to 6 pm. Outside these months, it's closed on Wednesday. The tourist office in Wiltz (☎ 957444) is also in the castle. Its opening hours are irregular but, basically, it is open in summer daily from 10 am to 6 pm and in winter on Tuesday from 2 to 5 pm.

Clervaux

This town has two main sights: its feudal **castle**, in the town centre, and the turreted Benedictine **abbey**, high in the forest above. The castle houses several exhibits, including Edward Steichen's famous photography collection, *Family of Man*. It's open Tuesday to Sunday from 10 am to 6 pm (closed January and February).

Vianden

Though little more than a village, Vianden's attractions are considerable. Besides its 9th-century charm, the town's most noted feature is its impeccably restored, but now somewhat sterile, **chateau**. It's open daily from 10 am to 4 pm (to 6 pm in summer). The chateau's striking position can be photographed from the **chair lift** which climbs the nearby hill daily from Easter to mid-October.

Vianden's other ace is the former home – now museum-cum-tourist office – of the French author Victor Hugo, who lived here in exile in the 1860s.

Wiltz

Built on the side of a small plateau, Wiltz is more spacious, but less picturesque, than Clervaux or Vianden. It's divided in two: the Ville Haute (High Town), where most of the sights are located, is situated on a crest, while the Ville Basse and the train station are down below. The rather sterile **chateau** sits on the edge of the Ville Haute and is home to an exhibition on the 1944 Battle of the Bulge (also known as the Ardennes Offensive). It's open daily from 1 June to mid-September from 10 am to noon and 1 to 5 pm.

Esch-sur-Sûre

The tiny village of Esch-sur-Sûre draws most people to the area south of Wiltz (off the main road to Ettelbrück). It's built on a rocky peninsula skirted by the Sûre River, and lorded over by steep cliffs and a ruined castle. The village lures hordes of tourists, evident by the disproportionate number of hotels here.

Places to Stay

Clervaux In Clervaux, the closest camping ground is *Reuler* (☎ 920160), about 1.5 km from the train station. There's no hostel; the nearest is six km away in Troisvierges (☎ 98018), at 24 Rue de la Gare (closed February and November).

The *Hôtel du Parc* (☎ 91068) at 2 Rue du Parc is the best-value hotel in this overpriced town. It occupies a beautiful, old chateau and has rooms from f1500/2300.

Vianden There are several camping grounds in Vianden. The closest to the centre is *Op dem Deich* (☎ 84375), on the river to the south. It's open from Easter to 31 September. Vianden's *hostel* (☎ 84177) is at 3 Montée du Château, in the shadow of the chateau. It's closed from 1 December to 28 February.

There are heaps of hotels, but most are pricey and many are open from Easter to October only. The most expensive of them line the Grand Rue. For something cheaper, try *Hôtel Berg en Dal* (☎ 84127) at 3 Rue de la Gare or *Hôtel Cheng Bao* (☎ 84348) at 13 Rue Victor Hugo. Both have rooms from f800/1300.

Wiltz *Camping Kaul* (☎ 950079) on Rue Simon Jos, about 800m from the train station, is open from 1 May to 1 October. The clean *hostel* (☎ 958039), at 6 Rue de la Montagne, is a one km climb from the train station, behind the Ville Haute. In the Ville Basse, *Auberge du Pont* (☎ 958103), at 11 Rue du Pont, has rooms for f950/1500.

Getting There & Away

There are trains every two hours to Clervaux (one hour) from Luxembourg City. To reach Vianden, take the Luxembourg City-Ettelbrück train and then take a connecting bus. To get to Wiltz (1½ hours), take the Luxembourg City-Clervaux train and change trains in Kautenbach.

The Netherlands

A small country with a big reputation for liberalism, the Netherlands (Nederland, or Holland as it's commonly, but incorrectly, known) swims in a sea of familiar images. A land of bikes and dykes, of blazing flower fields, and mills but few hills – these are all quintessential Netherlands, and largely true outside the major cities and the once-radical, still exuberant, capital of Amsterdam.

While Amsterdam tops most travellers' itineraries, there is plenty to entice you away from the 'anything goes' capital. The countryside's endlessly flat landscape, broken only by slender church steeples in scenes which inspired the nation's early artists, is a cyclist's nirvana. And while you may be pressed to find wide-open, untouched spaces and solitude, you'll discover a hard-fought-for land, with proud people and farmers who, yes, still wear traditional clogs.

Facts about the Country

HISTORY

The Netherlands' early history is linked with Belgium and Luxembourg: the three were known as the 'Low Countries' until the 16th century when the present-day Netherlands' boundaries were roughly drawn. Originally the land was inhabited by tribal groups: the Germanic Batavi drained the sea lagoons while the Frisii lived on mounds in the remote north.

In the late 16th century, the region's northern provinces united to fight the Spanish (see the Belgium History section). The most powerful of these provinces was Holland with its main city of Amsterdam, and to the outside world, Holland became synonymous with the independent country that was to emerge in this corner of Europe (a bit like saying England when you mean Britain).

Led by Prince William of Orange, nicknamed William the Silent for his refusal to enter into religious arguments, the Revolt of the Netherlands lasted 80 years, ending in 1648 with a treaty that recognised the 'United Provinces' as an independent republic. As part of the deal, the Scheldt River was closed to all non-Dutch ships. This destroyed the trade of the largest port in that time, Antwerp, but ensured the prosperity of its rival, Amsterdam.

Amsterdam stormed onto the European scene in what was the province of Holland's most glorified period: the Golden Age from about 1580 to about 1740, after which the British began dominating the world seas. The era's wealth was generated by the Dutch East India Company, which sent ships to the Far East in search of spices and other exotic goods, while colonising the Cape of Good Hope and Indonesia and establishing trading posts throughout Asia. Later the West Indies Company sailed to West Africa and the Americas, creating colonies in Surinam, the Antilles and New Amsterdam (today's New York).

Meanwhile Amsterdam's bourgeoisie indulged in fine, gabled canal houses and paintings of themselves and the remains of last night's dinner.

The Netherlands
(Nederland)

0   25   50 km

To Kristiansand

NORTH
SEA

To Newcastle

To Hull/Harwich

To Sheeness

This in turn stimulated the arts and brought renown to painters such as Rembrandt.

But it didn't last. In 1795 the French invaded and Napoleon appointed his younger brother Louis as king. When the largely unpopular French occupation came to an end, the United Kingdom of the Netherlands – incorporating Belgium and Luxembourg – was born. The first king, King William I of Orange, was crowned in 1814, and the House of Orange rules to this day. In 1830 the Belgians rebelled and became independent; Luxembourg did the same soon after.

While the Netherlands stayed neutral in WWI, it was unable to do so in WWII. The Germans invaded on 10 May 1940, obliterating much of Rotterdam in a bombing blitz four days later. Although a sound Dutch resistance movement formed, only a small minority of the country's Jews survived the war.

In 1949, despite military attempts to hold on to Indonesia, the colony won independence. Surinam followed much later with a peaceful handover of sovereignty in 1975. The Antilles are still a colony, with a large degree of self-rule.

In 1953 one of the country's worst disasters hit when a high spring tide coupled with a severe storm breached the dykes in Zeeland, drowning 1835 people. To ensure the tragedy would never be repeated, the Delta Plan was conceived (see the Delta Region section later in this chapter).

The 1960s social consciousness found fertile ground in the Netherlands, especially in Amsterdam which became the radical heart of Europe. The riotous squatter's movement stopped the demolition of much cheap inner-city housing, the lack of which is a continuing problem.

In 1995, the largest mandatory evacuation in the Netherlands since the Zeeland disaster was carried out after heavy rain in France and Belgium caused the Meuse and Waal rivers to flood. Some 240,000 people were relocated from Gelderland, the region based around Nijmegen, due to fears that dykes along the two rivers would burst.

GEOGRAPHY & ECOLOGY

Bordered by the North Sea, Belgium and Germany, the Netherlands is largely artificial, its lands reclaimed from the sea over many centuries and the drained polders protected by dykes. More than half of the country lies below sea level. Only in the south-east Limburg province will you find hills.

The south-west province of Zeeland is the combined delta area of the Scheldt, Meuse (Maas in Dutch), Lek and Waal rivers; the Lek and Waal are branches of the Rhine, carrying most of its water to the sea – the mighty Rhine itself peters out in a pathetic little stream (the Oude Rijn, or Old Rhine) at the coast near Katwijk.

On the whole, the Dutch public takes environmental issues such as pollution very seriously, and sound legislation has been set up to help preserve and protect the environment.

GOVERNMENT & POLITICS

Against the European trend, the Netherlands developed from a republic to a constitutional monarchy, headed today by Queen Beatrix who took over from her mother, Juliana, in 1980. Coalition governments pursue policies of compromise. The three main parties are the socialist PvdA, the Catholic-Protestant CDA, and the conservative Liberal VVD. However, at the last general election in 1994, considerable gains were made by two other parties – the centre-left D66 and the General Old People's Union.

The country consists of 12 provinces, one of which, Flevoland, only came into existence in 1967 after it had been claimed from the sea. The province of Holland was split into North Holland (capital: Haarlem) and South Holland (capital: The Hague) during the Napoleonic era. The Catholic half of the population lives mainly in the south-eastern provinces of North Brabant and Limburg. The province of Zeeland gave New Zealand its name (Australia used to be known as New Holland).

As with Belgians and Luxembourgers, the Dutch view European Union as a fact of life, and further integration is taken much for granted.

ECONOMY

Despite its small size, the Netherlands is currently ninth in the world's GDP rankings. It is a leader in service industries such as banking as well as electronics (Philips) and multimedia (Polygram) and also has a highly developed

NETHERLANDS

horticultural industry – bulbs and cut flowers. Agriculture plays an important role, particularly dairy farming and glasshouse fruits and vegetables Rotterdam harbour, which has the largest tonnage in the world, is vital to the economy as are the country's large supplies of natural gas in the north-east.

POPULATION & PEOPLE

Western Europe's most densely populated country, there are 15.4 million people, and a lot of Frisian cows, in its 34,000 sq km. This concentration is intensified in the Randstad – the western hoop of cities including Amsterdam, The Hague and Rotterdam – which is one of the most densely populated conurbations on earth.

ARTS

Over the centuries the Netherlands has spawned a realm of famous painters. The earliest artist of note was Hieronymus Bosch whose 15th-century religious works are charged with fear, distorted creatures and agonised people. Rembrandt, with his use of light and shadow, created shimmering religious scenes and led the historic artists of the Golden Age. Meanwhile, Frans Hals and Jan Vermeer were the masters in portraiture and common life scenes, two revolutionary themes which became popular due to the decline in the influence of the traditional patron, the church.

Of more recent note was Vincent van Gogh (1853-90), whose earlier works, including the dour *Potato Eaters*, were painted in his homeland though he spent much of the remainder of his career in Belgium and later France where he was greatly influenced by the impressionists. A little later, Piet Mondriaan was introducing his cubic De Stijl movement, while this century has seen the perplexing designs of Maurits Escher.

The Netherlands shines internationally in other artistic fields, including jazz (The Hague hosts the world's largest jazz festival each summer) and dance. The latter is highlighted by the respected Nationaal Ballet company and the Nederlands Danstheater with its innovative modern dance.

Though relatively little Dutch literature has been translated into English you can find some classic tales such as *Max Havelaar* by Eduard D Dekker, better known as Multatuli, and Simon Vestdijk's *The Garden Where the Brass Band Played*. Noted contemporary authors include Harry Mulisch *(The Assault)* and Cees Nooteboom *(A Song of Truth and Semblance* and *In the Dutch Mountains)*.

The Diary of Anne Frank, an autobiography written by a Jewish teenager, movingly describes life in hiding in Nazi-occupied Amsterdam.

CULTURE

The Dutch are well known for their tolerance which perhaps has stemmed largely from *verzuiling* (pillarisation), the custom of dividing society into compartments or pillars which, although separate from each other, support society as a whole. In this way any group which demands a place in society can have it and the balance is kept by an overall attitude of 'agreeing to disagree'.

RELIGION

The number of former churches that these days house art galleries is the most obvious sign of today's attitude to religion – and art. The Dutch Reformed Church, to which half the population belonged 100 years ago, attracts 20% today though it's still the official church of the royal family. Catholicism remains strong in the south-east, in theory if not in practice.

LANGUAGE

Most English speakers use the term 'Dutch' to describe the language spoken in the Netherlands, and 'Flemish' for that spoken in the northern half of Belgium and a tiny northwestern corner of France. Both are in fact the same language, the correct term for which is Netherlandic, or *Nederlands*, a West Germanic language spoken by about 25 million people worldwide.

The people of the northern Fryslân (Friesland) province speak their own language. Although Frisian is actually the nearest relative of the English language, you won't be able to make much sense of it when you hear it spoken.

The differences between Dutch and Flemish *(Vlaams)*, in their spoken as well as written forms, are similar to those between UK and North American English.

Like many other languages, Netherlandic gives its nouns genders. There are three genders: masculine, feminine (both with *de* for 'the') and neuter (with *het*). Where English uses 'a' or 'an', Netherlandic uses *een* (pronounced *ern*), regardless of gender.

Netherlandic also has a formal and an informal version of the English 'you'. The formal version is *U* (written with a capital letter and pronounced *ü*), the informal version is *je* (pronounced *yer*). As a general rule, people who are older than you should still be addressed with *U*.

See the Language Guide at the back of the book for pronunciation guidelines and useful words and phrases.

Facts for the Visitor

PLANNING
Climate & When to Go
The Netherlands has a temperate maritime climate with cool winters and mild summers. Spring is the ideal time to visit as there's less chance of rain and the bulbs are in bloom – April for daffodils, tulips in May. The wettest months are July and August, though precipitation is spread pretty evenly over the year. The sunniest months are May to August, and the warmest are June to September. Because it's such a flat country, wind has free reign – something you'll soon notice if you take to cycling.

Books & Maps
For a humorous look at Dutch ways, pick up the *The UnDutchables* by the non-Dutch Colin White & Laurie Boucke. The two best road maps of the Netherlands are those produced by Michelin (scale: 1:400,000) and the ANWB (scale: 1:300,000). The ANWB also puts out provincial maps detailing cycling paths and picturesque road routes (scale: 1:100,000).

SUGGESTED ITINERARIES
Depending on the length of your stay, you might want to see and do the following things:

Two days
    Visit Amsterdam.
One week
    Spend two days in Amsterdam, one day each in Haarlem (make sure you visit the Keukenhof gardens), Leiden, The Hague and the Hoge Veluwe national park, and the remaining day visiting Rotter-

dam, the Kinderdijk windmills and the Delta Expo (see the Delta Region section).
Two weeks
    Spend three days in Amsterdam, two days each in Haarlem (Keukenhof), The Hague and Schiermonnikoog, one day each in Leiden, Delft, Rotterdam (Kinderdijk), the Delta Region (Delta Expo and Middelburg) and the Hoge Veluwe national park, and if you have any time left over you can throw in Maastricht or Den Bosch.
One month
    This should give you enough time to have a look around the whole country.

HIGHLIGHTS
After Amsterdam, the Keukenhof gardens (see the Around Haarlem section) are a must, especially for flower aficionados, while anyone into a bit of dirt should investigate *wadlopen* – mud-flat-walking (see The North section). Museum and cycling buffs will be in their glory throughout – a visit to the Kröller-Müller Museum (see the Hoge Veluwe section) can superbly combine the two.

TOURIST OFFICES
Local Tourist Offices
The ubiquitous VVV – the national tourist organisation – sells brochures on everything and maps for everywhere. Its offices are generally open Monday to Friday from 9 am to 5 pm, Saturday from 10 am to noon, and will book accommodation for a fee of f4 a person. In larger cities, and during the summer months of July and August, opening hours are extended. Many VVV offices have telephone numbers prefixed by 06 (these numbers cost 50 to 75 cents a minute) and answered by recorded messages in Dutch – wait for the message to end to be answered personally.

The Netherlands Board of Tourism (NBT) head office (☎ 070-370 57 05) is at Vlietweg 15, Postbus 458, 2260 MG Leidschendam. This office, as well as some of the NBT offices abroad, take postal and telephone enquiries only.

Tourist Offices Abroad
NBT has offices overseas, including the following:

Belgium
    Louizalaan 89, Postbus 136, 1050 Brussels (☎ 02-534 04 10)

NETHERLANDS

Canada
    25 Adelaide St East, suite 710, Toronto, Ont M5C
    1Y2 (☎ 416-363 1577)
Germany
    Friesenplatz 1, Postfach 270580, 50511 Cologne
    (☎ 0221-257 0383)
Japan
    NK Shinwa Building, 5F 5-1, Koijmachi, Chiyoda-
    ku, Tokyo 102 (☎ 03-3222 1112)
UK
    PO Box 523, London, SW1E 6NT (☎ 0171-828
    7900)
USA
    355 Lexington Ave (21st floor), New York, NY 10017
    (☎ 212-370 7367)
    Suite 103, 9841 Airport Blvd (10th floor), Los
    Angeles, CA 90045 (☎ 310-348 9339)
    225 N Michigan Ave, suite 326, Chicago, IL 60601
    (☎ 312-819 1500)

VISAS & EMBASSIES

Travellers from Australia, Canada, Israel,
Japan, New Zealand, Norway, the USA and
many other countries need only a valid passport – no visa – for a stay of up to three months.
EU nationals and most other Europeans can
enter for three months with just their national
identity card or a passport expired for not more
than five years. After three months, extensions
can be applied for through the Vreem-
delingendienst (Foreigners' Service)
department of the police. Nationals of most
other countries need to get a Netherlands visa
before entry.

Dutch Embassies Abroad
Australia
    120 Empire Circuit, Yarralumla, Canberra, ACT 2600
    (☎ 06-273 3111)
Canada
    Suite 2020, 350 Albert St, Ottawa, Ont K1R 1A4
    (☎ 613-237 5030)
New Zealand
    10th floor, Investment House, Ballance &
    Featherston St, Wellington (☎ 04-473 8652)
UK
    38 Hyde Park Gate, London SW7 5DP (☎ 0171-584
    5040)
USA
    4200 Linnean Ave, NW Washington, DC 20008
    (☎ 202-244 5300)

Foreign Embassies in the Netherlands
Embassies (in The Hague) and consulates (in
Amsterdam) of other countries in the Nether-
lands include:

Australia
    Carnegielaan 4, 2517 KH The Hague (☎ 070-310 82
    00)
Belgium
    Lange Vijverberg 12, 2513 AC The Hague (☎ 070-
    364 49 10)
Canada
    Sophialaan 7, 2514 JP The Hague (☎ 070-311 16 00)
France
    Embassy: Smidsplein 1, 2514 BT The Hague
    (☎ 070-364 14 31)
    Consulate: Vijzelgracht 2, 1017 HR Amsterdam
    (☎ 020-624 83 46). Visas are issued at the side office
    on 1e Weteringdwarsstraat between 9 am and noon.
Germany
    Embassy: Groot Hertoginnelaan 18, 2517 EG The
    Hague (☎ 070-342 06 00)
    Consulate: De Lairessestraat 172, 1075 HM Amster-
    dam (☎ 020-673 62 45)
Japan
    Tobias Asserlaan 2, 2517 KC The Hague (☎ 070-346
    95 44)
New Zealand
    Carnegielaan 10, 2517 KH The Hague (☎ 070-346
    93 24)
UK
    Embassy: Lange Voorhout 10, 2514 ED The Hague
    (☎ 070-364 58 00)
    Consulate: Koningslaan 44, 1075 EJ Amsterdam
    (☎ 020-676 43 43)
USA
    Embassy: Lange Voorhout 102, 2514 EJ The Hague
    (☎ 070-310 92 09)
    Consulate: Museumplein 19, 1071 DJ Amsterdam
    (☎ 020-575 53 09)

CUSTOMS

Visitors from non-EU countries can import
goods and gifts valued up to f380 as well as
200 cigarettes (or 50 cigars or 250g of
tobacco), one litre of liquor more than 22% by
volume or two litres less than 22% by volume
or two litres of sparkling wine, two litres of
non-sparkling wine, 50g of perfume spirits and
0.25 litre of eau de toilette. Tobacco and
alcohol may only be brought in by people aged
17 and over.

MONEY

Overall, banks have the best exchange rates
and charge f5 commission for travellers'
cheques and f3 for cash. De Grenswissel-
kantoren (The Border Exchange Offices,
GWK), the national exchange organisation,
has similar rates and fees. You'll find GWK
branches at all major border posts and train
stations, open Monday to Saturday from 8 am
to 8 pm, Sunday 10 am to 4 pm. The branches

at Amsterdam's Centraal Station and Schiphol airport operate 24 hours. With a student card there's no commission for exchanging cash. In larger cities there are exchange services (mainly for cash) at the post office, as well as many private exchange bureaus that close late but generally demand exorbitant fees or offer lousy rates. All major credit cards are accepted.

Currency

The currency is the guilder, divided into 100 cents and symbolised as 'Dfl' or 'f' (originally 'florin'). There are 5c, 10c, 25c, f1, f2.50 and f5 coins, and f10, f25, f50, f100, f250 and f1000 notes.

Exchange Rates

Australia	A$1	=	f1.31
Belgium	Bf1	=	f0.05
Canada	C$1	=	f1.21
France	1FF	=	f0.33
Germany	DM1	=	f1.13
Japan	¥100	=	f1.54
New Zealand	NZ$1	=	f1.16
United Kingdom	UK£1	=	f2.59
United States	US$1	=	f1.66

Costs

Living in hostels and eating in cheap restaurants, you'll be looking at spending roughly f50 a day. Travelling costs relatively little due to the country's size. Tipping is not compulsory, but 'rounding up' the bill is always appreciated in taxis, restaurants and pubs with table or pavement service. Forget about bargaining here, though the Dutch themselves sometimes manage to get away with it at flea markets.

Avid museum goers should consider the yearly Museumcard, which gives free entry into 400 museums and art galleries. It costs f45 for adults (f15 for those aged under 18) and is issued at museums or tourist information (VVV) offices. Unless stated otherwise, all the museums and art galleries mentioned in this chapter are free with the Museumcard.

Consumer Taxes

The value-added tax (BTW in Dutch) is calculated at 17.5% for most goods except consumer items like food, for which you pay 6%. Travellers from non-EU countries can have it refunded on goods over f300 providing they're bought from one shop on one day and are exported within three months.

To claim the tax back, ask the shop owner to provide an export certificate when you make the purchase. When you leave for a non-EU country, get the form endorsed by the Dutch customs, who will send the certificate to the supplier, who in turn refunds you the tax by cheque or money order. If you want the tax before you leave the country, it's best to buy through shops displaying the 'Tax Free For Tourists' sign (but because of red tape, you'll lose about 5% of the refund). In this case the shopkeeper will give you a stamped cheque which can be cashed at the border.

Buying with a credit card is the best system as you won't pay any tax providing you get customs to stamp the receipt the shop owner gave you and that you send the receipt back to the shop.

POST & COMMUNICATIONS

In general, post offices are open Monday to Friday from 8.30 am to 5 pm, Saturday to noon. Letters cost f1 for up to 20g within Europe, f1.60 outside, and will take about a week to the USA and Canada, six to 10 days to Australia and New Zealand, and two to three days to the UK.

Local telephone calls cost 25 cents for roughly five minutes, except when you use cardphones inside public centres (such as post offices, some train stations and tourist offices) which charge 54 cents for the first five minutes. To determine the type of phone, watch the digital message displayed when you pick up the receiver. If it reads 'eerste tik – f0.54' you'll know it's an expensive one. Telephone numbers prefixed with '☎ 06' are also more expensive (between 50 and 75 cents a minute) to call. In local telephone books, similar surnames are listed alphabetically by address, not by initials.

Telephones take f0.25, f1, f2.50 and f5 coins, or f5, f10 and f25 phonecards and, in some cases, credit cards. International calls can be made from public phones, post offices or telephone kiosks. Depending on the country you are calling, it may be cheaper to buy a PTT Telecom Country Card rather than an ordinary phonecard as the former gives a 15% to 20% discount on calls to certain countries. Country Cards are available for the USA (f25), Canada

NETHERLANDS

(f25), and Australia, New Zealand and South Africa (all f50). Note, these cards look like a normal phonecard and can be used at public phones but they must not be inserted into a cardphone – ask at any post office for details on how they work.

International faxes can also be sent from public fax machines at post offices in some large cities but they are very expensive – f25 for the first page to countries outside Europe and f22.50 within, plus f5/2.50 respectively for each additional page. Telegraph services are more expensive still.

For making international telephone calls to the Netherlands, the country code is ☎ 31. To telephone abroad, the international access code is ☎ 00.

MEDIA
There's no English-language newspaper, but international papers and magazines are easy to find and London's BBC radio World Service can be tuned to on 648 kHz medium wave.

PHOTOGRAPHY & VIDEO
A Kodak 64 (36-exposure) slide film costs about f22. Film developing is f5.50 plus f1 per print. Films for video cameras cost around f7.50/24 for 30/90 minutes. In red-light districts, 'No photo' stickers often adorn windows and should be taken seriously.

TIME
The Netherlands is in the Central European Time zone. Noon is 11 am in London, 6 am in New York, 3 am in San Francisco, 6 am in Toronto, 9 pm in Sydney, and 11 pm in Auckland. The 24-hour clock is commonly used. Daylight-saving time comes into effect at 2 am on the last Sunday in March, when clocks are moved an hour forward, and ends at 2 am on the last Saturday in October, when they're moved an hour back again.

ELECTRICITY
The electric current is 220V, 50 Hz and plugs are of the two-round-pin variety.

WEIGHTS & MEASURES
The metric system is used. In shops, 100g is referred to as an *ons* and 500g is a *pond*. EU directives have prohibited the use of *ons* in pricing and labelling, but the term is so ingrained it will take a while to disappear. Like other Continental Europeans, the Dutch indicate decimals with commas and thousands with points.

LAUNDRY
If you can push past all the piles of clothes in a typical Dutch *wassalon*, you're lucky – at least you're in the front door. Generally, self-service laundrettes are no more than a few machines put aside for do-it-yourselfers in staffed laundries. In large cities, you'll also find the traditional unattended laundrette. A five-kg wash costs an average of f10 including drying.

TOILETS
Public toilets are not abundant which is why most people tend to duck into a café or pub. Occasionally you'll see streetside toilet cubicles – put a coin in the slot and the door will open.

HEALTH
The Netherlands has reciprocal health arrangements with other EU countries and Australia. For minor health concerns pop into a local *apotheek* (pharmacy); for more serious problems you'll find English-speaking staff at almost any *ziekenhuis* (hospital). In an emergency, the national telephone number for police, ambulance and fire brigade is ☎ 06 11.

WOMEN TRAVELLERS
The women's movement has a strong foothold and women travellers will find *vrouwen* (women's) cafés, bookshops and help centres in many cities. Het Vrouwenhuis (Women's House ☎ 020-625 20 66) at Nieuwe Herengracht 95, 1011 RX Amsterdam, is well known.

Unwanted attention from men is not a big problem in the Netherlands, however, in the event of rape or attack, Opvang Sexueel Geweld (☎ 020-612 75 76) is an Amsterdam-based help line, open weekdays from 10.30 am to 11.30 pm and on weekends from 3.30 to 11.30 pm.

GAY & LESBIAN TRAVELLERS
The Netherlands has long had the reputation of being the most liberal country in Europe where attitudes to homosexuality are concerned. The age of consent is 16, and discrimination on the

basis of homosexual orientation is illegal. Most provincial capitals have at least one gay and lesbian bar or café, as well as a branch of COC, a gay and lesbian information service. COC's headquarters (☎ 020-623 11 92) is at Rozenstraat 14, 1016 NX Amsterdam; here too is a coffee shop open Monday to Friday from 9 am to 5 pm. Another useful organisation may be the Gay & Lesbian Switchboard (☎ 020-623 65 65), an information and help line based in Amsterdam and staffed daily from 10 am to 10 pm. *Gay News Amsterdam* is a free, monthly, English/Dutch publication.

DISABLED TRAVELLERS

Travellers with a mobility problem will find the Netherlands well equipped to meet specialised needs. A large number of government buildings, museums, hotels and restaurants have lifts and/or ramps. Many trains and some taxis have wheelchair access, and most train stations have a toilet for the handicapped.

For the visually impaired, train timetables are published in braille and bank notes have raised symbols on the corners for identification.

For more information contact Mobility International Nederland (☎ 024-399 71 38) Postbus 165, 6560 AD Groesbeek.

SENIOR TRAVELLERS

Senior travellers should encounter few problems when travelling around the Netherlands. Many buildings have lifts or ramps, and public transport is quite accessible.

The 60+ Seniorenkaart provides 30% discount on trains for one year but, at f99, it's not worth it for most foreign visitors. Generally museums do not offer discounts to seniors though there's nothing to stop you trying.

DANGERS & ANNOYANCES

The number of tales of travellers in Amsterdam having their wallets swiped could fill a book. Pickpockets often use distraction as their key tool, so keep your hands on your valuables especially at Centraal Station in Amsterdam, the post office, telephone centres and tourist strongholds. Cyclists too should be warned: the stolen bicycle racket is rife. Locals use two chains to lock up their bikes, and even that's no guarantee.

Despite popular belief to the contrary, drugs are illegal. Possession of more than 30g of marijuana or hash can, strictly speaking, get you a f5000 fine and/or land you in jail – hard drugs can definitely land you in jail. Small amounts of 'soft' drugs for personal use are generally, though not officially, tolerated, but could complicate matters if you're already in trouble with the police over something else.

In the event of an emergency, the national telephone number for police, ambulance and fire brigade is ☎ 06 11.

BUSINESS HOURS

The working week starts leisurely at around lunchtime on Monday. For the rest of the week, most shops open at 8.30 or 9 am and close at 5.30 or 6 pm, except Thursday or Friday when many close at 9 pm, and on Saturday, at 4 pm. In Amsterdam and tourist centres, you will find many shops open on Sunday too. Banks are generally open Monday to Friday from 9 am to 4 or 5 pm. Many museums are closed on Mondays.

PUBLIC HOLIDAYS & SPECIAL EVENTS

Public holidays are: New Year's Day, Good Friday (but most shops stay open), Easter Monday, Queen's Birthday (30 April), Ascension Day, Whit Monday, Christmas Day, Boxing Day.

The Holland Festival brings many of the top names in music, opera, dance and theatre to Amsterdam for performances throughout June. Another big event in Amsterdam is Koninginnedag (Queen's Day), the 30 April national holiday held on the former Queen Juliana's birthday. On this day the whole central city becomes a huge street market/party where people sell whatever they've dug out of their attics.

Religious celebrations like carnival are confined to the Catholic south.

ACTIVITIES

Along with cycling, windsurfing, sailing and boating are some of the most popular Dutch pastimes, especially in the waterlogged provinces of Fryslân and Zeeland.

WORK

Australian, New Zealand and US citizens are legally allowed to work in the Netherlands.

However, there is a mound of red tape to get through before you can do so, and the bottom line is that you must be filling a job that no Dutch or EU national has the skill to do. In other words, there are few legal openings for non-EU nationals. Illegal jobs, known as working 'in the black', are also pretty rare. Even work in the bulb fields around Leiden (June to October) has dried up for non-EU nationals. Some travellers' hotels in Amsterdam employ touts to drum up guests by pouncing on newly arrived backpackers – the pay isn't much but you may get free lodging.

ACCOMMODATION

Rarely cheap and often full, budget accommodation in peak times is best booked ahead. This applies to summer and public holidays, but also if you're going to be in the Randstad during the Keukenhof season.

The cheapest alternative is the 37 official hostels run by the Nederlandse Jeugdherberg Centrale (NJHC; ☎ 020-551 31 55), Prof Tulpstraat 2, 1018 HA Amsterdam. The NJHC has three categories of hostels, with nightly rates in a dorm varying from f21 to f25 for members (f5 more if you're a non-member) including breakfast. Some hostels have double rooms ranging from f25 to f30 per person. In some cities there's a f2.50 summer surcharge. In large cities you'll find similarly priced unofficial hostels and cheaper 'sleep-ins'.

Camping grounds are copious but prices vary – on average f6.50/7/4 per adult/tent/car. The NBT has a selective list of sites or there's the ANWB's annual camping guide (f27.95 for non-members), both available from the VVV or bookshops.

Hotels start at f55/75 single/double for basic rooms that are rarely flash, with continental breakfast included. Prices sometimes rise during the high season (roughly 15 March to 15 November); prices quoted throughout this chapter are for the high season. B&Bs are a good alternative and start at f30 per person a night. Local VVVs have lists or you can book through Bed & Breakfast Holland (☎ 020-615 75 27; fax 020-669 15 73) at Theophile de Bockstraat 3, 1058 TV Amsterdam. If you go through the latter, you must book a minimum of two nights and there's a f10 administration fee.

You can book hotel accommodation ahead (no deposit required) either in writing or by telephone or fax to the Netherlands Reservation Centre (☎ 070-320 25 00; fax 070-320 26 11) Postbus 404, 2260 AK Leidschendam. You must supply all the relevant details and allow time for them to confirm the booking with you (in writing or by fax).

FOOD

While gastronomical delights are not a Dutch forte, you won't go hungry. What the cuisine lacks in taste sensation, it makes up for in quantity. And thanks to the sizeable Indonesian, Chinese, Surinamese, Turkish and Italian communities there are plenty of spicy alternatives. Vegetarians will find that many eetcafés have at least one meat-free dish.

Snacks

On the savoury side, the national fast-food habit is *frites* – chips or French fries. *Kroketten*, or croquettes (crumbed fried concoctions), are sold hot from vending machines; *broodjes* (open sandwiches) are everywhere; and mussels, raw herrings and deep-fried fish are popular coastal snacks.

As for sweets, *appelgebak* (apple pie) ranks up there with frites, while *poffertjes* (fried doughy balls sprinkled with icing sugar) are sure-fire tourist food, as are *pannekoeken* (pancakes) and *stroopwafels* (hot wafers glued together with syrup).

Main Dishes

Dinner traditionally comprises thick soups and meat, fish or chicken dishes fortified with potatoes. Most restaurants have a *dagschotel* (dish of the day) for about f18, while *eetcafés* ('eating pubs') serve meals or cheap snacks. Otherwise, the Indonesian *rijsttafel* ('rice table') of boiled rice with oodles of side dishes is pricey but worth a try, as are Zeeland mussels, best during months with an 'r' in their name (or so local tradition has it).

Self-Catering

The national Albert Heijn chain has saturated the country with supermarkets. The Vroom & Dreesmann (V & D) department stores occasionally have basement supermarkets.

DRINKS

Beer is the staple, served cool and topped by a two-finger-thick head of froth – a sight which can horrify Anglo-Saxon drinkers. According to the Heineken tour guide, it's not to 'rip off English uninitiates' but to 'capture the flavour bubbles which would otherwise fly away'! Apparently it's reason enough for bar staff to coolly respond to requests of 'no head please'. Many Belgian beers – such as Duvel and Westmalle Triple – have become immensely popular in the Netherlands, and are reasonably priced.

Dutch gin *(genever)* is made from juniper berries; a common combination, known as a *kopstoot* ('head butt'), is a glass of genever with a beer chaser – two or three of those is all most people can handle. There are plenty of indigenous liqueurs, including *advocaat* (a kind of eggnog) and the herb-based *Beerenburg*.

ENTERTAINMENT

You'll rarely have to search for nightlife. In summer, parks come alive with festivals while city squares reverberate with the sounds of street musicians. Bars and cafés abound, from pavement terraces filled with sun-seekers to old brown cafés thick with conversation and smoke. Movies screen in their original language with Dutch subtitles.

THINGS TO BUY

Diamonds and flowers are the specialities, the latter cheap and plentiful all year. For flower bulbs it's easiest to buy through one of the specialist mail-order companies. They'll handle all the red tape including the 'health certificate' many countries require for importing bulbs. As for diamonds, if you've got the budget to buy them, you probably don't need advice.

Getting There & Away

AIR

The Netherlands has just one main international airport, Schiphol, about 10 km south-west of Amsterdam. One of Western Europe's major international hubs, it services flights from airlines worldwide as well as the national carrier, KLM Royal Dutch Airlines. Most foreign airlines have offices in Amster-

dam (see the Amsterdam Getting There & Away section).

The airport is connected by frequent train services to the nearby Randstad cities including Amsterdam (f6, 20 minutes), The Hague (f12.25, 40 minutes) and Rotterdam (f18, 45 minutes). For flight information, ring ☎ 06-35 03 40 50; for other general Schiphol information, ☎ 020-601 91 11.

LAND
Bus

Eurolines and Hoverspeed Citysprint are the two international bus companies servicing the Netherlands. Tickets can be bought in most travel agencies as well as at Netherlands Railways (NS) Reisburos (Travel Bureaus) at large train stations. Both offer reduced fares for those aged under 26.

Eurolines has regular buses to a crop of Western, Eastern, Mediterranean and central European destinations as well as Scandinavia and North Africa. Hoverspeed Citysprint buses run only between London, Belgium and the Netherlands. Depending on the service, there are stops in Breda, Rotterdam, The Hague and Utrecht as well as Antwerp and Brussels in Belgium. Some Eurolines buses and all Citysprint buses cross the Channel from Calais in France. Travellers using either service should check whether they'll require a French visa.

For more detailed information on both companies, see the Amsterdam (or other relevant city) Getting There & Away section.

Train

Eurail, Inter-Rail, Europass and Flexipass tickets are valid for use on NS, which operates regular and efficient services to all its neighbouring countries from Amsterdam, the country's international hub. For all international train information and reservations, you'll find 'International' offices in all large train stations or you can call ☎ 06-92 96. In peak periods, it's wise to reserve seats in advance.

There are two main lines south from Amsterdam. One passes through The Hague and Rotterdam and on to Antwerp (f46, 2¼ hours, hourly trains) and Brussels (f56, three hours, hourly trains) and then on to either Paris (f123 plus a f8 EuroCity supplement, six hours, 10 a day) or Luxembourg City (f102, six

NETHERLANDS

hours). The other line goes via Utrecht and Maastricht to Luxembourg City (f98, six hours) and on to France and Switzerland. The line south-east runs via Utrecht and Arnhem to Cologne (f69 plus an f8 EuroCity supplement, 2½ hours, every two hours) and further into Germany. The line east goes to Berlin, with a branch north to Hamburg. All these fares are one way in 2nd class; people aged under 26 get a 25% discount.

The new high-speed train, *Thalys*, runs four times per day between Amsterdam and Antwerp (f55, two hours), Brussels (f63, 2½ hours) and Paris (f132, 4¾ hours). Those aged under 26 get a 45% discount and seniors with a Rail Europe Senior (RES) card are entitled to 30% off.

The UK To London, there are two train-ferry routes. The basic one-way fare for either from Amsterdam is f158 – reservations are strongly recommended. One service goes via Hook of Holland (Hoek van Holland) on the coast near Rotterdam to Harwich in England and on to London's Liverpool St Station. The daytime run takes 10½ hours and the overnight service takes 13 hours. There's an obligatory f16 reservation fee for the overnight run.

The other service goes via Ostend in Belgium to Ramsgate and on to Victoria Station. There are three services per day but journey lengths vary greatly depending on whether a jetfoil or ferry is used to cross the Channel. Using the jetfoil, the total trip takes nine hours but you must pay a f16 to f25 jetfoil supplement (it varies according to season). The daytime ferry takes 11 hours; the overnight ferry 12 to 13 hours.

Alternatively, you can get a train from Amsterdam to Brussels and connect there with Eurostar trains which operate through the Channel Tunnel. From Amsterdam, the one-way trip to London's Waterloo Station takes about five hours and costs f215, or f145 for Apex fares (these must be reserved 14 days in advance). Those under 25 years pay f110. There are six to seven services per day (five on Sundays).

Car & Motorcycle

The main entry points from Belgium are the E22 (Antwerp-Breda) and the E25 (Liège-

Maastricht). From Germany there are many border crossings, but the main links are the E40 (Cologne-Maastricht), the E35 (Düsseldorf-Arnhem), and the A1 (Hanover -Amsterdam). For details about car ferries from England, see the following section.

SEA

Four companies operate car/passenger ferries between the Netherlands and England, and one company has a ferry to Norway. For information on train-ferry services, see the previous Train section. Most travel agents have information on the following services.

Stena Sealink Line sails from Hook of Holland to Harwich and has day (6½ hours) and night (nine hours) boats. Fares for a car with driver range from f236 to f420 depending on the season. There are also special deals whereby you can take a car and a maximum of six people for f310/610 in the low/high season. An adult one-way passenger ticket costs f90/120 in the low/high season; cabins cost extra and start at f30 a person.

North Sea Ferries operates an overnight boat (13½ hours) between Europoort (near Rotterdam) and Hull. Basic rates for cars start at f175/200 in the low/high season and adult tickets are f106/135.

Flushing (Vlissingen) and Sheerness are linked by Eurolink Ferries with day (eight hours) and night (9½ hours) services. Fares for a car and up to five people are f190/250 for the day/night boat in the low season; high-season fares are f275/356. The ordinary passenger fare is f78.

Scandinavian Seaways sails from IJmuiden (near Amsterdam) to Newcastle twice a week from April to October. The journey takes 16 hours. Rates for cars are f90/150 in the low/high season; passenger fares start at f95/140. Cabins begin at f100/145 per person.

The same company also sails three times a week from IJmuiden to Kristiansand (Norway) from May to August. Fares for the 20-hour voyage start at f130/200 for a car in the low/high season. Passengers must be paid for separately, and seasonal rates start at f190/230, or f210/250 in a cabin. Future Line Travel (see the Amsterdam Travel Agencies section) has information and discount tickets for NJHC members.

RIVER

Several companies offer riverboat cruises from either Rotterdam or Arnhem along the Scheldt to Belgium (six days) or via the Rhine and Moselle rivers to Germany and Luxembourg (eight to 14 days). Most travel agents have brochures.

LEAVING THE NETHERLANDS

There is an f8 departure tax for airline passengers leaving from the Netherlands; however, most travellers will find that this tax is incorporated in the price of their airline ticket.

Getting Around

The Netherlands' public transport system is excellent. For all national train/bus/tram information, there's one central telephone number: ☎ 06-92 92.

BUS

Buses are used for regional transport rather than for long distances, which are better travelled by train. They provide a vital service, especially in parts of the north and east, where trains are less frequent or non-existent. The national *strippenkaart* (see the following Local Transport section) is used on many regional buses.

TRAIN

NS trains are fast and efficient, with at least one InterCity train every 15 minutes between major cities, and half-hourly trains on branch lines. Most train stations have small and large luggage lockers which cost f4/6 respectively for 24 hours.

Costs

Fares are calculated per km – on average, 100 km will cost f26/44 single/return. If you're returning on the same day, it's cheaper to buy a *dagretour* (day return) rather than two single tickets.

There's a mélange of discount fares but you'd have to live on the trains to make most of them worthwhile. A 'One-Day Ticket' gives unlimited 2nd/1st-class travel (after 9 am) and costs f66/99. With this ticket you can also buy

a 'Public Transport Link Ticket' for f7.50 which gives unlimited use of city buses, trams and metros. The 'Meermans Kaart', or Group Ticket, gives two to six people (f98 to f168) unlimited travel all day on weekends but only after 9 am on weekdays (except in July and August when there is no weekday restriction). The 'Euro Domino Holland' pass entitles adults to three/five/10 days' travel within one month for f90/140/250. Those under 26 years pay f65/99/175. For a supplement of f17/28/45, you can travel free on all public transport. From June to August there's an alternative 'Summer Tour' pass which gives three days' travel in 10 for one/two people for f79/114. Also in summer (and at various holiday periods throughout the year), those under 19 years can get a 'Tour Time' pass which gives four days' travel in 10 in both the Netherlands and Belgium for f65. For an extra f15, you can ride on all public transport in the Netherlands.

For the full list, get the *Exploring Holland by Train* brochure, which also details discount 'Rail Idee' or day excursion tickets.

CAR & MOTORCYCLE

Foreign drivers need a Green Card as proof of insurance. Road rules are basically stick to the right and give way to the right (except at major crossroads and roads with right of way). Speed limits are 50 km/h in towns, 80 km/h outside and 120 km/h on motorways. Fuel prices per litre are f2.04 for super, f1.96 to f2 for lead-free ('Euro loodvrij', also called Super 95 and Super Plus 98) and f1.36 for diesel. The maximum permissible blood-alcohol concentration is 0.05%. For other motoring information, contact the Royal Dutch Touring Association (ANWB) at either Wassenaarseweg 220, 2596 EC The Hague (☎ 070-314 14 20), or Museumplein 5, 1071 DJ Amsterdam (☎ 020-673 08 44).

BICYCLE

With 10,000 km of cycling paths, a *fiets* (bicycle) is *the* way to go. The ANWB publishes cycling maps for each province. Major roads have separate bike lanes, and, except for motorways, there's virtually nowhere bicycles can't go. That said, in places such as the Delta region and along the coast you'll often need muscles to combat the North Sea headwinds.

NETHERLANDS

To take a bicycle on a train (not allowed in peak hours) costs f10 for up to 80 km, or f15 for greater distances.

While about 85% of the population own bikes and there are more bikes than people, they're also abundantly available for hire. In most cases you'll need to show your passport, and leave an imprint of your credit card or a deposit (from f50 to f200). Private operators charge f10 to f12.50 per day, and f50 per week. Train-station hire shops (called Rijwiel shops), uniformly charge f6/24 a day/week if you have a valid train ticket. Without a ticket, the rate is f8/32. You must return the bike to the same station.

Alternatively, it can work out much cheaper to buy a 'second-hand' bike from a street market for upwards of f25, bearing in mind it's probably part of the stolen bike racket.

HITCHING
Hitching is usually effortless, but illegal on motorways. Be wary of the usual dangers and aware of the risks you take.

BOAT
Ferries connect the mainland with the five Frisian Islands (see The North section for details) and are also used as road connections in Zeeland, two of the principal links being Flushing (Vlissingen in Dutch) to Breskens and Kruiningen to Perkpolder.

LOCAL TRANSPORT
Bus & Tram
Buses and/or trams operate in most cities, and Amsterdam and Rotterdam also have metros.

Fares operate nationally. You buy a *strippenkaart* (strip card) which is valid throughout the country, and stamp off a number of strips depending on how many zones you cross. The ticket is then valid on all buses, trams, metros and city trains for an hour, or longer depending on the number of strips you've stamped. Around central Amsterdam for example, you'll use two strips – one for the journey plus one for the zone. A zone further will cost three strips, and so on. When riding on trams it is an honesty system – it's up to you to stamp your card (fare dodgers will face a f64 on-the-spot fines). The buses are more conventional, with drivers stamping the strips as you get on. Bus and tram drivers sell two-strip

cards for f3, three-strip cards for f4.50 and eight-strip cards for f12. More economical are 15-strip cards for f11 or 45-strip ones for f32.25 which you must purchase in advance at train or bus stations, post offices, some VVV offices or tobacconists.

Taxi
Usually booked by phone (officially you're not supposed to wave them down on the street), taxis also hover outside train stations and hotels and cost roughly f20 for five km. There are also *treintaxis* (train taxis) which charge a flat rate of f6 a person to anywhere within a certain radius (it varies from city to city) of the train station. You can buy your treintaxi voucher at the train station. They do not operate in Amsterdam, The Hague or Rotterdam.

ORGANISED TOURS
It's possible to whip through villages, windmills, cheese factories and historic towns in neighbouring Belgium all in a day trip from Amsterdam (see the Around Amsterdam section for more details). Local tourist offices can advise on bus, canal, bike or walking tours available in their own town or city.

Amsterdam (003 20)

For many travellers, Amsterdam is a city of preconceived ideas. Personal freedom, liberal drug laws, the gay centre of Europe – these are images synonymous with the Dutch capital since the heady 1960s and 1970s when it led as Europe's most radical city. While the exuberance dimmed somewhat during the 1980s, it was not extinguished. Tolerance still holds pride of place although it's being increasingly tested with a chronic housing shortage, growing numbers of homeless and signs of racial tension.

More obvious, however, are the rich historical and lively contemporary airs that meld here, as you'll feel when exploring the myriad art galleries and museums, relaxing in the canalside cafés or enjoying the open-air entertainment that beats through the heart of summer.

Orientation

By capital-city standards, Amsterdam (population 725,000) is small. Its major sights, accommodation and nightlife are scattered around a web of concentric canals (*grachten*) known as the canal belt, which gives the city an initially confusing, yet ultimately orderly and unique feel.

The centre, easily and enjoyably covered on foot, has two main parts: the old, medieval core and the 'newer', 17th-century canal-lined quarters which surround it. Corked to the north by Centraal Station (CS), the old city centre is encased by the Kloveniersburgwal and Singel canals. After Singel come Herengracht, Keizersgracht and Prinsengracht, the newer canals dug to cope with Amsterdam's Golden Age expansion. The city's central point is Dam Square, five minutes walk straight down Damrak from Centraal Station. Main streets bisect the canal belt like spokes in a wheel.

Information

Tourist Offices The VVV has four offices around town. The two busiest are at CS: one is inside the main hall, open Monday to Saturday from 8 am to 7.30 pm and Sunday from 8 am to 4 pm, and the other is outside at Stationsplein 10, open daily from 9 am to 5 pm. A third tourist office at Leidseplein operates every day from 9 am to 7 pm (until 6 pm on Sunday), and the Stadionplein tourist office (good for motorists entering the city from the west or south) is open daily from 9 am to 5 pm. During peak summer months, some of these opening hours may be extended slightly. There's also an office in the plaza at Schiphol airport, open daily from 7 am to 10 pm. For telephone information on weekdays, you can call ☎ 06-34 03 40 66 (75 cents a minute) from 9 am to 5 pm.

The VVVs sell a f29.90 Amsterdam Pass which gives free entry to several museums and discounts on a range of things from canal boats to restaurants.

Money There are 24-hour GWK offices at CS and Schiphol airport; otherwise, there's a throng of midnight-trading change bureaus along Damrak and Leidsestraat which charge horrendous commissions. Check Change Express at Damrak 86 (☎ 020-624 66 82) or Leidseplein 1 (☎ 622 14 25): its rates are often comparable to banks and commissions surprisingly low.

American Express is at Damrak 66, and is open weekdays from 9 am to 5 pm and on Saturday 9 am to noon; to report lost or stolen cards, call ☎ 020-642 44 88, or for travellers' cheques, ☎ 06-022 01 00. Thomas Cook has offices at Damrak 1-5 (☎ 020-620 32 36), open daily until 8 pm; and at Leidseplein 31a (☎ 020-626 70 00), until about 5.30 pm (4 pm on Sunday).

Post & Communications The main post office is at Singel 250, and is open weekdays from 9 am to 6 pm and Saturday from 9 am to 3 pm. International phone calls can be made daily between 8 am and 2 am nearby at Telecenter, Raadhuisstraat 48-50.

Amsterdam's telephone code is ☎ 020.

Travel Agencies Amsterdam is a major European centre for cheap fares to anywhere in the world. A few of the better known budget agencies are:

Amber Reisbureau (☎ 685 11 55) Da Costastraat 77; cheap flights to outside Europe and often no queues
Budget Air (☎ 627 12 51) Rokin 34
Budget Bus (☎ 627 51 51) Rokin 10; for Eurolines tickets
Future Line Travel (☎ 622 28 59) Prof Tulpstraat 2; reduced ferry fares to Norway for youth hostel members
ILC Reizen (☎ 620 51 21 for flights, ☎ 622 43 42 for other queries) NZ Voorburgwal 256; plane and bus tickets and paid car lifts to other European capitals
Malibu Travel (☎ 626 66 11) Damrak 30; long-time, cheap flight specialists
NBBS Reizen (☎ 624 09 89) Rokin 38 or (☎ 638 17 36) Leidsestraat 53; nationwide 'student' travel agency

Bookshops English-language books are plentiful but horribly expensive. Try the following:

Allert de Lange (☎ 624 67 44) Damrak 62; long established with good travel section
American Book Centre (☎ 625 55 37) Kalverstraat 185; good travel-guide section, cheaper than competitors, extra 10% off for students
De Slegte (☎ 622 59 33) Kalverstraat 48-52; Amsterdam's specialist in remaindered novels and coffee-table books
Pied à terre (☎ 627 44 55) Singel 393; huge range of travel literature, maps, hiking and trekking information
The Book Exchange (☎ 626 62 66) Kloveniersburgwal 58; rabbit warren of second-hand books

NETHERLANDS

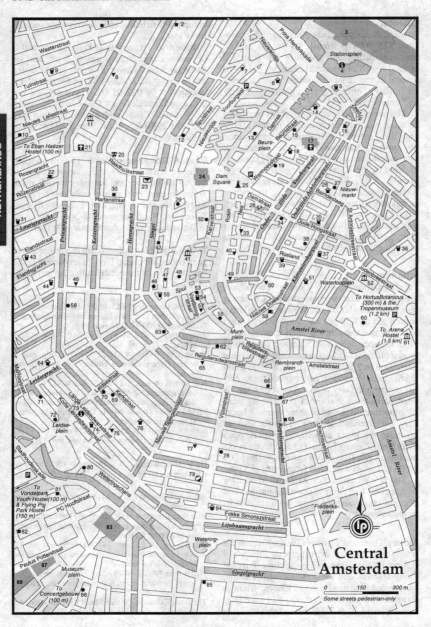

Central
Amsterdam

Some streets pedestrian-only

0   150   300 m

NETHERLANDS

PLACES TO STAY
2   Keizersgracht Hotel
6   Flying Pig Downtown
    Hostel
10 Hotel van Onna
14 Kabul Hostel
15 Hotel Beursstraat
16 The Crown
18 Nelly's Inn Hostel
26 The Shelter
30 Hotel Belga
42 Hotel Estheréa
51 Stadsdoelen Youth
    Hostel
64 International Budget
    Hotel
66 The Veteran
68 Seven Bridges
76 Hans Brinker Hostel
81 Hotel Wynnobel
82 Hotel P C Hooft
84 Euphemia Budget Hotel

PLACES TO EAT
7   De Keuken van 1870
8   Pancake Bakery
33 Café Frascati
40 Sisters
45 Miramare
47 Haesje Claes
49 La Margarita
50 Atrium
57 Vlaams Frites Huis
65 Rose's Cantina

75 Piccolino
77 Hollandse Glorie

OTHER
1   Laundry
3   Centraal Station (CS)
4   Tourist Office
5   In den Olofspoort
9   Café de Tuin
11 Anne Frank's House
12 Moped Rental Service
13 Allert de Lange
    Bookshop
17 Westerkerk
19 Condomerie
20 Telephone Centre
21 Oude Kerk
22 COC Café
23 Main Post Office
24 Royal Palace
25 National Monument
27 Supermarket
28 Damstraat Rent-a-Bike
29 Vrolijk Bookshop
31 Pie
32 De Slegte Bookshop
34 Laundry
35 Goa
36 Bimhuis
37 De Engelbewaarder
38 The Book Exchange
39 Rusland
41 Historical Museum &
    Schuttersgallerij

43 Saarein
44 La Tertulia
46 Pied à terre Bookshop
48 Begijnhof
52 Rembrandt's House
53 W H Smith Bookshop
54 Café de Schutter
55 Hoppe
56 Public Library & Café
58 American Book Centre
59 Café de Jaren
60 City Hall /
    Muziektheater
61 Jewish Historical
    Museum
62 Flower Market
63 Supermarket
67 Bridge of 15 Bridges
69 Laundry
70 Big Bananas Night
    Shop
71 Milky Way
72 Stadsschouwburg
73 Tourist Office
74 Café Alto
78 Supermarket
79 French Consulate
80 Paradiso
83 Rijksmuseum
85 Heineken Brewery
86 ANWB
87 Van Gogh Museum
88 Stedelijk Museum

Vrolijk (☎ 623 51 42) Paleisstraat 135; lesbian and gay
  bookshop
W H Smith (☎ 638 38 21) Kalverstraat 152; strong on
  guides, maps and novels (translated Dutch literature
  on 1st floor)

Laundry The Clean Brothers have a laundrette
near Leidseplein at Kerkstraat 56, open daily
from 7 am to 9 pm, and another at Westerstraat
26. In the red-light district, service washes can
be done at Happy Inn, Warmoesstraat 30, open
Monday to Saturday from 9 am to 6 pm, or
there's a bigger laundrette at Damstraat 12.

Medical & Emergency Services For medical
emergencies, phone the 24-hour Tourist
Medical Service (☎ 624 57 93) or the Dental
Service (☎ 06-821 22 30). The closest hospitals to the centre are VU Ziekenhuis (☎ 548 91
11), de Boelelaan 1117, or Onze Lieve Vrouwe
Gasthuis (☎ 599 91 11), 1e Oosterparkstraat
170. For police, ambulance and fire brigade,

the national number is ☎ 06 11. The main
police station (☎ 559 91 11) is at Elandsgracht
117.

Things to See & Do
With 141 art galleries and 42 museums,
Amsterdam is justly famed for its cultural pro-
liferation.

Walking Tour The best place to start is **Dam
Square** (the 'Dam'), where the Amstel River
was dammed in the 13th century, giving the
city its name. Today it's the crossroads for the
crowds surging along the pedestrianised
Kalverstraat and Nieuwendijk shopping
streets, and the pivotal point to interesting
outer quarters. Here too is the **National Monument**, a 22-metre-high obelisk dedicated to
those who died in WWII.

  Heading west from Dam Square along
Raadhuisstraat, you'll cross the main canals to

the towered **Westerkerk** whose 17th-century carillon chimes a concert every Tuesday between noon and 1 pm. In the church's shadow stands a statue of **Anne Frank**, the young Jewish diarist who hid for years with her family in a nearby house only to be tragically discovered near the end of WWII. Across Prinsengracht from here spreads the **Jordaan**, an area built up in the 17th century to house the city's lower class. Revived in the 1960s as a student ghetto, today its many renovated gabled houses sit atop canal-front cafés in Amsterdam's trendiest quarter.

South from the Dam along NZ Voorburgwal, the quaint **Spui** square acts as a façade to hide one of the inner city's most tranquil spots, the **Begijnhof**. Such *hofjes*, or groupings of almshouses, were built throughout the Low Countries in the Middle Ages to house Catholic women, the elderly and poor. From the Begijnhof you can walk though the **Schuttersgalerij** (Civic Guard Gallery), a glass-covered passageway adorned with 15 enormous paintings, to Amsterdam's **Historical Museum** at Kalverstraat 92.

Continuing south, Leidsestraat ends where the city's nightlife takes off at **Leidseplein**. From there it's just a few minutes walk southeast past **Vondelpark** – a summer-long entertainment venue – to the ever-inundated Museumplein where you'll find the Rijksmuseum, Van Gogh Museum and Stedelijk Museum (see the following section). Follow Singelgracht two blocks east to the **Heineken Brewery**.

Back across the canals, the **Muntplein** tower denotes the colourful **Bloemenmarkt**. Close by is **Rembrandtplein**, one of the nightlife hubs, and the **'Bridge of 15 Bridges'**, so called because from here you can see 15 bridges (they're best viewed at night when lit up). Further north, the sleaze of the **red-light district** extends along the parallel OZ Voorburgwal and OZ Achterburgwal canals, past **Oude Kerk**, the city's oldest church, to **Zeedijk**, once the heroin nerve centre and *the* street not to go. It has been face-lifted in recent years but plenty of drugs are still going down in the alleys leading to the stark **Nieuwmarkt**.

South-east of here is the city's Jewish quarter or **Jodenhoek** and the **Jewish Historical Museum**. The nearby **Rembrandthuis** and **Waterlooplein market** attract hordes.

Further east, the **Hortus Botanicus** (Botanical Garden) is home to the world's oldest potplant.

Museums & Galleries If you intend visiting more than a few museums, it can be worth buying the Museumcard (see Money in the Facts for the Visitor section earlier in this chapter). The **Rijksmuseum** on Stadhouderskade 42 is the Netherlands' largest art collection, concentrating on Dutch artists from the 15th to 19th centuries and housing Rembrandt's famous *Night Watch*. Opening hours are 10am to 5 pm daily, and entry costs f12.50/5 for adults/children.

The **Van Gogh Museum** at Paulus Potterstraat 7 boasts the largest collection of his works in the world – 200 paintings plus 600 or so drawings. It's open daily from 10 am to 5 pm; admission costs f12.50/5 for adults/children. Next door, the **Stedelijk Museum** has contemporary Dutch art and is open daily from 11 am to 5 pm; admission is f8/4 for adults/children.

Excerpts from **Anne Frank's** diary movingly describe the Jewish teenager's last years in the house at Prinsengracht 263. It's open Monday to Saturday from 9 am to 5 pm and Sunday from 10 am (from June to August daily until 7 pm) and costs f8/4.50 for adults/children; Museumcards are not accepted.

For a wider picture, the **Jewish Historical Museum** at Jonas Daniël Meijerplein 2 details Jewish society and the Holocaust. It's open daily from 11 am to 5 pm, and costs f7/3.50 for adults/children; take tram No 9 from the CS or the metro to Waterlooplein.

The **Verzetsmuseum** (Resistance Museum) at Lekstraat 63 gives another angle, telling the story of Dutch resistance. Open Tuesday to Friday from 10 am to 5 pm, weekends 1 to 5 pm, it costs f4.50/2 for adults/children; take tram No 4 or 25.

The **Rembrandthuis** at Jodenbreestraat 4-6 displays sketches by the master in his former home. It's open Monday to Saturday 10 am to 5 pm, Sunday from 1 to 5 pm, and costs f7.50/5 for adults/children. Take the metro to Waterlooplein.

The excellent **Scheepvaart Museum** (Dutch Maritime Museum), Kattenburgerplein 1, is lorded over by the superbly restored, 18th-century, United East India Company rig,

Amsterdam. Open Tuesday to Saturday from 10 am to 5 pm (and, from June to September also on Monday), Sunday from noon, admission costs f12.50/8 for adults/children. It's about 15 minutes walk east of CS, or take bus No 22.

The **Tropenmuseum** (Museum of the Tropics) at Linnaeusstraat 2 realistically depicts African, Asian and Latin American lifestyles. It's open weekdays 10 am to 5 pm, weekends from noon to 5 pm, and costs f10/5 for adults/children; take tram No 9 or bus No 22 from CS.

Royal Palace Occasionally used by the royal family who opt more for their residences in The Hague, the Dam Square palace is open in June and August daily from 12.30 to 5 pm. The rest of the year it's open on Tuesday, Wednesday and Thursday from 1 to 4 pm.

Heineken Brewery Beer production stopped in 1988 but the 125-year-old brewery at Stadhouderskade 78 still coerces beer buffs to its weekday tours at 9.30 and 11 am, and 1 and 2.30 pm (from mid-September to 1 June morning tours only). In July and August, there are extra tours on Saturday at noon and 2 pm. Tickets (f2) go on sale at 9 am but come early, as even first thing Monday there are plenty of takers.

Markets There's a profusion of street markets. Most are open daily except Sunday, from 9 or 10 am to 5 pm. The biggest flea market is **Waterlooplein**, good for cheap bikes and locks. The **Bloemenmarkt** on Singel is a floating flower market, established in 1862 and popular with tourists and pickpockets.

Organised Tours
Yellow Bike (☎ 620 69 40) at Nieuwezijds Kolk 29 (just off NZ Voorburgwal) organises bicycle tours that take in the waterland reserve to the north in a 6½-hour tour for f42.50; bring your own lunch. City tours can be done by bike (f29, three hours) or walking (f15, 1¾ hour).

Places to Stay
Amsterdam is popular all year but in peak times it's overrun – bookings are essential.

Camping Backpackers are generally directed to the two 'youth camps'. The closest is *Vliegenbos* (☎ 636 88 55) at Meeuwenlaan 138, across the harbour from CS, open from April to September, charging f9.25 for one person with a tent plus f3.25/4.25 for a motorbike/car. Take either bus No 32 or 36 from CS. The other, *Zeeburg* (☎ 694 44 30), at Zuiderzeeweg 29, is open March to December. It charges f6.50 a person, plus f3.50/3.50/6 for a tent/motorbike/car. Bus No 37 from Amstel Station stops at the door, or you can take bus No 22 from CS.

Hostels & Youth Hotels Most of the private hostels and youth hotels don't take advance bookings, so turn up early.

Old City Centre Accurately advertised as the 'cheapest B&B in town', *The Shelter* (☎ 625 32 30) at Barndesteeg 21 is a Christian hostel in the red-light district just over 10 minutes walk from CS. It has huge, single-sex dorms and midnight curfews, but at f18 there are few complaints. Follow the signs from CS or get the metro to Nieuwmarkt.

Five minutes walk south is *Stadsdoelen* (☎ 624 68 32), Kloveniersburgwal 97, one of the city's two official NJHC hostels. It's on one of the city's oldest canals, charges f24.50 and has a 2 am curfew; the closest metro is Nieuwmarkt. In the heart of the red-light district is the lively *Kabul* (☎ 623 71 58) at Warmoesstraat 38. Singles/doubles/triples go for f72/92/137 and dorms cost f32. Down the road at Warmoesstraat 115 is *Nelly's Inn* (☎ 638 01 25). It has good security, lockers and no curfews; a bed in a dorm (from eight to 24 beds) costs f35, and there's a popular bar.

One of the newest places in town is the *Flying Pig Downtown* (☎ 420 6822) at Nieuwendijk 100. It has small singles/doubles for f100/170 and an assortment of dorms from f23.50 per person. It features a café popular with travellers.

Beyond Old City Centre The main NJHC hostel, *Vondelpark* (☎ 683 17 44), is at Zandpad 5, open all year, popular with teenage school groups, and charges f26.50 for members. Get tram No 1, 2 or 5 to Leidseplein from where it's a five-minute walk. Immediately opposite is the *Flying Pig Par!*

(☎ 421 05 83), Vossiusstraat 46, which is slightly cheaper than its counterpart in the old city centre (see previous section).

Ideally sited in a colourful, old canal house near Leidseplein, the *International Budget Hotel* (☎ 624 27 84) at Leidsegracht 76 is a great choice. It's run by two friendly New Zealanders, there's no curfew and there's 24-hour security. Depending on the season, a bed in a four-person room costs f25-35, singles go for between f65-80, and doubles are from f80-110; breakfast is f3-5 extra. From CS, take tram No 1, 2 or 5 to Prinsengracht. If it's full, they also run the larger *Euphemia Budget Hotel* (☎ 622 90 45) at Fokke Simonszstraat 1 – f35/100 for a dorm/double; take tram No 16, 24 or 25 from CS and get off at Prinsengracht. Closer to Leidseplein is the huge, modern *Hans Brinker* (☎ 622 06 87) at Kerkstraat 136. It's popular with well-off visiting students and has singles/doubles/dorms from f77/120/42 a person.

A Christian hostel similar to The Shelter, but in a more urbane area than its red-light counterpart, is *Eban Haëzer* (☎ 624 47 17) at Bloemstraat 179; you'll find the same prices, rules and big dorms – get tram No 13 or 17 to Marnixstraat. For even bigger dorms, try the *Arena* (☎ 694 74 44) at 's-Gravesandestraat 51. A 1960s survivor (and previously known as the *Sleep-In*), it's the haunt of dope and Doors fans and regularly has live bands. There's no curfew and there's parking. A bunk in a dorm costs f25.50; double rooms start at f100. Breakfast is f7 extra. Take the metro to Weesperplein then follow the signs for 10 minutes, or jump on tram No 6.

Near the Jordaan, the *Keizersgracht Hotel* (☎ 625 13 64) at Keizersgracht 15-17 has tight security, a big bar and 3 am curfew; singles/doubles cost f70/105 and triples/quads f120/150 without breakfast (f8 extra).

Hotels The following rates, unless stated otherwise, include breakfast. Many hotels lower their prices in winter.

Old City Centre The *Hotel Beursstraat* (☎ 626 37 01), at Beursstraat 7, is ordinary but secure and clean, and there's public parking nearby. Doubles cost f75 without breakfast. About three blocks east on one of the main red-light canals is *The Crown* (☎ 626 96 64) at OZ Voorburgwal

21. There's plenty of dope, a lively bar, and singles/doubles start at f70/100. Those with guilders to burn should consider *Hotel Estheréa* (☎ 624 51 46) at Singel 303. It occupies a charming 17th-century canal house and has elegant rooms for f265/365.

Beyond Old City Centre A sage choice on a quiet canal is *Seven Bridges* (☎ 623 13 29) at Reguliersgracht 31. A spiral staircase leads up to lofty singles/doubles/triples which start at f100/130/180. It's already been discovered so book well ahead. Note the interesting eagle gable on the house across the canal. Two blocks away, *The Veteran* (☎ 620 26 73) on the canal at Herengracht 561 is another good option. Cheery and welcoming, double/triple rooms start at f130/160.

Near the museum stronghold, the *Hotel P C Hooft* (☎ 662 71 07) at P C Hooftstraat 63 is a reasonable option in a district free of dog turds. Singles/doubles start at f65/95. Also here is *Hotel Wynnobel* (☎ 662 22 98), Vossiusstraat 9, which has 11 modest rooms for f70/110.

In the Jordaan, *Hotel Belga* (☎ 624 90 80) at Hartenstraat 8 is a charming blend of the old and new. Singles/doubles start at f80/125 – rooms 4, 8 and 9 are the best. For something brand-new head to the friendly *Hotel van Onna* (☎ 626 58 01) at Bloemgracht 104. Rooms in the old/new sections go for f55/65 per person.

Places to Eat

Restaurants abound: try the neon-lit streets off Leidseplein for a veritable diner's market, the Jordaan for discreet eetcafés or the city centre for fast-food factories, student cafeterias and vegetarian hideaways.

Restaurants Amsterdam's restaurants beckon with variety and a casual approach.

Old City Centre The *De Keuken van 1870* (☎ 624 89 65) on Spuistraat 4 is an unpretentious Dutch diner that began last century as a soup kitchen. Open until 8 pm, it offers hearty soups for f3 and main courses, all served with potatoes, from f9. For classier Dutch, try *Haesje Claes* (☎ 624 99 98) on NZ Voorburgwal 320 near Spui. This refined restaurant has traditional fare like salted herrings for f7, seafood and other main courses from f17 to f31.

Nearby, the city's favourite friture, *Vlaams Frites Huis* at Voetboogstraat 33, is a must for chip fans. In a seemingly age-old tradition, young and old queue for a f3 paper cone of 'Amsterdam's best' sauce-smothered frites which they then stand and eat in an air of camaraderie in the alley. Even if you don't like frites, it's a great sight.

A couple of serene options are tucked away in the Nes – the easily missed lane off Dam Square's south-east corner. *Café Frascati* (☎ 624 13 24) at Nes 59 is modernly spacious with mains from f20, while further along, *Sisters* (☎ 626 39 70) at No 102 is a slightly cheaper vegetarian haunt with generous servings and an amiable atmosphere.

A block south, *La Margarita* (☎ 624 05 29) at Langebrugsteeg 6 serves huge Mexican nachos for f14.50. Follow Langebrugsteeg east to the university's student cafeteria, *Atrium*, at OZ Achterburgwal 237, for f6.50 meals weekdays only, from noon to 2 pm and 5 to 7 pm.

Beyond Old City Centre Indonesian, Greek and Italian cuisine compete fiercely with steak houses and Dutch fare in the streets off Leidseplein. Here you'll find *Piccolino* (☎ 623 14 95) at Lange Leidsedwarsstraat 63 which has big pizzas from f8.50.

The *Hollandse Glorie* (☎ 624 47 64) at Kerkstraat 222 is laced and intimate, with Dutch mains from f23. *Rose's Cantina* (☎ 625 97 97) at Reguliersdwarsstraat 38 is a big Mexican restaurant with even bigger pitchers of sangria.

In the Jordaan, the amiable *Miramare* (☎ 625 88 95) at Runstraat 6 has tasty pizzas from f10, while the *Pancake Bakery* (☎ 625 13 33), in the basement of an old warehouse at Prinsengracht 191, serves platter-sized pancakes from f7 to f15.

Cafés & Eetcafés Amsterdam has a plethora of cafés where you can have a coffee, beer or a snack, and an increasing number of pubs that also serve meals.

The huge *Café de Jaren* at Nieuwe Doelenstraat 20 near Muntplein has a popular sun deck and English newspapers. Just up the canal at Kloveniersburgwal 59, *De Engel-*

bewaarder is a pleasant, one-time literary café, or for the contemporary real thing, try the *coffee shop* at the Openbare Bibliotheek (Public Library) at Prinsengracht 587, where there are English magazines and papers (closed Sundays). Opposite the Tropenmuseum, the terraced *East of Eden* café with its huge tusker mural is a fitting finale to an afternoon in the museum.

Self-Catering The *Big Bananas* on Leidsestraat is open until late each night. *Albert Heijn* supermarkets are located at Vijzelstraat 119, on Nieuwmarkt, and on the corner of Singel and Leidsestraat.

Entertainment
While the infamous youth clubs, 'smoking' coffee shops and red-light district live on, the radical air is largely gone. These days you'll see groups of elderly tourists herded en masse past the windowed women while the younger set head for the music cafés, designer bars and nightclubs dotted throughout the city.

Classical music, theatre and ballet are high on the priorities, as are African and world music. Pick up the fortnightly, f3.50 'What's On' guide from the VVV or from the Amsterdam Uit Buro (AUB) ticket shop on the corner of Leidseplein and Marnixstraat.

Gay nightlife is centred on Reguliersdwarsstraat and Kerkstraat and the streets off Rembrandtplein. The COC (see the Gay & Lesbian Travellers section earlier in this chapter) has a list of homosexual and lesbian clubs and bars.

Pubs Pubs, bars, brown cafés, cafés – call them what you like, but places to drink abound. For the intimate atmosphere of the old brown café, try *Hoppe* at Spui 18 – it's been enticing drinkers behind its thick curtain for more then 300 years (the entrance is to the right of the pub-with-terrace of the same name). Bigger and more modern but with the same smoke-stained brown walls is *Café de Schutter* on Voetboogstraat. In the Jordaan, *Café de Tuin* at 2e Tuinstraat 13 has an impressive view of the Westerkerk tower, especially when it's backed by an azure evening sky. At the top end of the red-light district, *In den Olofspoort* at Nieuwebrugsteeg 13 is a typical genever-tasting house.

There's a throng of gay bars and cafés, although not nearly as many options for lesbians. *Saarein* at Elandsstraat 119 is the most popular women's bar, open until about 1 am (closed Monday). *COC Café* at Rozenstraat 14 is a daytime gay and lesbian café.

Live Music The Dutch favour live jazz, and Amsterdam's no exception. There are plenty of venues. *Café Alto* (☎ 626 32 49) at Korte Leidsedwarsstraat 15 has nightly sessions from 9.30 pm. A larger venue is the *Bimhuis* (☎ 623 13 61) at Oude Schans 73.

The legendary *Melkweg* (Milky Way) (☎ 624 17 77), behind Leidseplein on Lijnbaansgracht 234a, moves from late until early with live rock, reggae and African rhythm. The equally hallowed *Paradiso* (☎ 626 45 21) at Weteringschans 6 these days has everything from Turkish theatre to heavy rock or classical. The *Arena* (see the previous Places to Stay section) features live rock from 10 pm every night in summer (twice a week for the rest of the year). *Soeterijn* (☎ 568 85 00), downstairs at the Tropenmuseum, is a leading venue for music, film and theatre, often in English, from developing countries.

'Smoking' Coffee Shops Although the once omnipresent hemp leaf stickers have largely come unstuck, you'll have little difficulty pinpointing the coffee shops whose trade is marijuana, hash and spacecakes rather than tea, coffee and cookies. The most famous and expensive is *The Bulldog*, with five branches around town, the chief one being at Leidseplein 13-17. *Goa* at Kloveniersburgwal 42 sells slices of spacecake; more discreet is *Rusland* at Rusland 16. *La Tertulia* on the corner of Prinsengracht and Oude Looiersstraat is big with backpackers while in the Jordaan, the canalside *Pie* on Lauriergracht is the pick of the crop.

Nightclubs For discoing, there's *Mazzo* at Rozengracht 114 in the Jordaan. *IT* at Amstelstraat 24 is the largest gay nightclub. Two mixed nightclubs are *Havana* at Reguliersdwarsstraat 17 and *Roxy* at Singel 465.

Cinema Cafés and the like have posters stuck to their windows listing what's screening at the mainstream cinemas. For foreign and art films,

try *Desmet* (☎ 627 34 34) on Plantage Middenlaan 4a.

Theatre & Dance The city's premier performing arts venues are the *Stadsschouwburg* (☎ 624 23 11) at Leidseplein 26 and the *Muziektheater* (☎ 625 54 55) at Amstel 3.

Things to Buy
Amsterdam is a shopper's city, and there are exclusive outlets everywhere. Here's a random selection of some interesting shops:

Condomerie
Warmoesstraat 141 – well situated for its trade (☎ 627 41 74)
De Klompenboer
NZ Voorburgwal 20 – clog specialist (☎ 623 06 32)
De Witte Tandenwinkel
Runstraat 5 – toothbrush trader (☎ 623 34 43)
Musiques du Monde
Singel 281 – world music (☎ 624 13 54)
The Headshop
On the corner of Nieuwe Hoogstraat and Kloveniersburgwal – all kinds of drug devices (☎ 624 90 61)

Getting There & Away
Air Schiphol airport is one of Western Europe's major international hubs, and Amsterdam has long been known for its cheap bucket-shop tickets (see Travel Agents in the Amsterdam Information section). Airline offices in Amsterdam include:

KLM
Gabriël Metsustraat 2-6, on the corner of Museumplein (☎ 474 77 47 for 24-hour reservations and information)
Malaysia Airlines
Weteringschans 24a (☎ 626 24 20)
Qantas
Stadhouderskade 6 (☎ 683 80 81)

Bus Eurolines (☎ 694 17 91) operates from Amstel Station, connected to CS by metro. Tickets can be bought from Budget Bus (☎ 627 51 51) on Rokin 10. It has services to many European and Scandinavian destinations, including three or four buses a day to London – a one-way ticket for those aged over/under 26 years costs f100/90. The trip to London takes between 10 and 12 hours, depending on the route and whether it's a daytime or overnight service. Many of the buses cross the Channel at Calais in France (check whether you need a French visa) while others cross from Ostend in Belgium. Buses go either via Utrecht and Breda, and Antwerp and Bruges in Belgium or, less frequently, via The Hague and Rotterdam.

Other Eurolines services include Antwerp (f35, 3½ hours), Brussels (f35, five hours), Cologne (f50, 4½ hours), Copenhagen (f125, 13 hours) and Paris (f85, 8½ hours).

Hoverspeed Citysprint (☎ 664 66 26) buses to London leave from Van Tuyll van Serooskerkenweg 125 – to get there take tram No 24 from CS. Arrivals from London are dropped more centrally at Leidseplein. A one-way ticket for those aged over/under 26 years costs f90/80. Hoverspeed buses usually go via Utrecht and Breda (or, in summer only, also via The Hague and Rotterdam), and cross the Channel with the SeaCat or Hovercraft from Calais in France (check whether you need a French visa), ending at London's Victoria Station. The departure times and frequency of Citysprint services vary depending on the season but, all year, there is at least one daily daytime bus (10 hours) and, in summer, there is usually also an overnight service (10¾ hours).

Most travel agents have details on these services.

Train There's an international information and reservations office (☎ 620 22 66) at CS, open daily from 6.30 am to 10 pm. For national information call ☎ 06-92 92, or ask at the ticket windows. In peak times you'll have to queue for luggage lockers here.

For fares and journey times to other destinations in the Netherlands, check the Getting There & Away sections in those places. For prices and times of trains to neighbouring countries, as well as information on the train/ferry services to London, see Train in the Getting There & Away section at the beginning of this chapter.

Car & Motorcycle Local companies have the cheapest car rental – about f60 per day, plus km fees. Try the following in Amsterdam:

Avis
  Nassaukade 380, 1054 AD Amsterdam
  (☎ 683 60 61)

Diks Autohuur
  Van Ostadestraat 278, 1073 TW Amsterdam
  (☎ 662 33 66)
Europcar
  Overtoom 51, 1054 HB Amsterdam (☎ 683 21 23)
Kaspers en Lotte
  Van Ostadestraat 232, 1073 TT Amsterdam
  (☎ 662 66 14)

For motorbikes, Gilex Motoren (☎ 623 45 50) at Marnixstraat 186 rents machines for f120 per day.

Hitching For Groningen and northern Germany, take the metro to Amstel Station and get onto Gooiseweg; for Utrecht, Belgium and central/southern Germany, take tram No 25 to Nieuwe Utrechtseweg; for Schiphol, Leiden and The Hague, get tram No 6, 16 or 24 to Stadionplein and head out on Amstel-veenseweg; for Haarlem and Alkmaar, get tram No 12 or bus No 15 to Haarlemmerweg.

Ferry For details on train-ferry services to the UK and ferries to Norway, see the Getting There & Away section at the beginning of this chapter.

Getting Around
To/From the Airport There are trains every 15 minutes to Amsterdam CS (20 minutes), costing f6 one way. Taxis cost about f60.

Bus, Tram & Metro CS is the hub of Amsterdam's comprehensive network of public transport. It is operated by the Gemeente-vervoerbedrijf (GVB), which has an information office next to the VVV on Stationsplein, open weekdays 7 am to 9 pm and weekends from 8 am. It has free transport maps of the central city area.

Buses, trams and metros use strip cards (see Getting Around: Local transport in the section before Amsterdam), or you can buy one to nine-day unlimited tickets for between f12 and f42.25 from the GVB (one to four-day tickets are sold from VVV offices also).

All services run from about 5 or 6 am until midnight when the more limited night buses take over. For all information, call the national public transport number (☎ 06-92 92).

Taxi & Watertaxi Both are expensive, but watertaxis, with their minimum half-hour rental fee of f60, prohibitively so. For watertaxi information and bookings call ☎ 622 21 81; for road taxis, ☎ 677 77 77.

Car & Motorcycle A 17th-century city enmeshed by waterways is hardly the place for motorised transport. Anti-car feelings are strong and the city council has done much to restrict access and parking. The *Amsterdam by Car* leaflet, free from the VVV, pinpoints parking areas and direly warns of penalties – usually a fine of f121 and a wheel clamp – for nonconformists.

Parking spaces within the central canal zone have a system where you buy a ticket from a central 'parking pole' (f4 per hour). The cheapest parking garage is under the modern City Hall/Muziektheater (the 'Stopera') on Waterlooplein. It may work out cheaper to buy a f24/60 one/three-day parking card, sold from many hotels.

Motorcycles can usually be parked on pavements so long as they don't obstruct pedestrians, but security is a big problem with any parked vehicle, irrespective of the time of day. For any queries, contact the Parking Department (☎ 555 98 00) at Prins Hendrikkade 108.

Moped The Moped Rental Service has two offices – one (☎ 422 02 66) at Spuistraat 98 and the other (☎ 420 19 00) at Marnixstraat 208. The rental rate is f12 for the first hour plus f10/7.50 for the 2nd/3rd hours, or f35/60 for six hours/one day. No driving licence is required to rent a moped.

Bicycle Tram tracks and the other 550,000 bikes are the only real obstacle to cycling; local cyclists can get very impatient when pedestrians block cycle paths. It's advisable to book rental bikes ahead in summer. Try the following places:

Damstraat Rent-a-Bike, Pieter Jacobszdwarsstraat 11 (just off Damstraat) (☎ 625 50 29) – f10/50 per day/week

Rijwiel Shop, Stationsplein 33 (☎ 624 83 91) – f8/32 per day/week, f200 deposit or credit card imprint, returned by 10 pm

Canal Boat, Bus & Bike A horde of operators sell canal cruises (f12 an hour), leaving from in front of CS, along Damrak and Rokin and near the Rijksmuseum. The Canal Bus (☎ 623 98 86) stops at the tourist enclaves between CS and the Rijksmuseum and has one/two-day tickets for f19.50/27.50. The Museumboot (☎ 622 21 81) offers a f22 day ticket (f15 if you buy it after 1 pm) good for unlimited travel. In summer, canal 'bikes' can be hired from kiosks at CS and Leidseplein, with two/four-seaters costing f25/41 per hour.

AROUND AMSTERDAM

Nearby sights are easily reached by public transport or guided tours. Tours can be booked through the VVV, and include trips to Aalsmeer, Alkmaar, The Hague, Delft and the Afsluitdijk.

The world's biggest flower auction is held daily (except weekends) at **Aalsmeer**, south of Amsterdam, in a complex the size of 100 football fields; take bus No 172 from CS. Bidding starts early, so arrive between 7.30 and 9 am. Admission costs f4.50 for anyone aged over 12 (free for those under).

The **Molen van Sloten** is the only working windmill in the vicinity of Amsterdam. It's 30 minutes on bus No 144 from Leidseplein and is open daily from 10 am to 4 pm. Admission costs f5 for adults.

To get to the once typical, but unfortunately now tourist-filled, fishing village of **Volendam**, take bus No 110 from CS (35 minutes). To the similar village and former island of **Marken**, now connected to the mainland by a dyke, get bus No 111 (45 minutes) or go to Volendam and take the ferry (summer only, f6/8 single/return).

The **Alkmaar cheese market**, which is staged at 10 am every Friday in summer in the town's main market square, attracts droves. Arrive early if you want to get more than a fleeting glimpse of the famous round cheeses being whisked away. There are two trains per hour from CS (30 minutes) and it's a 10-minute walk at the other end.

The Randstad

The Netherlands' most densely populated region, the Randstad (literally, 'Urban

Agglomeration') spreads in a circle from Amsterdam, incorporating The Hague, Rotterdam and Utrecht, and smaller towns like Haarlem, Leiden and Delft. A compact area, its many sights are highlighted by the bulb fields, which explode in intoxicating colours between March and May. They're best viewed between Haarlem and Leiden; even from the window of a train, they're a spectacular sight.

HAARLEM
Less than 15 minutes by train from Amsterdam, Haarlem is close to the spectacular colours of the Keukenhof and the wealthy seaside resort of Zandvoort. It's a small but vibrant town, home to the country's oldest museum as well as one dedicated to the city's favourite son, Frans Hals.

Orientation & Information
The impressive train station (built in 1908) and neighbouring bus depot are 10 minutes walk, straight up Kruisweg, from the Grote Markt, Haarlem's central square. Zandvoort is 10 minutes down the railway line.

Haarlem's telephone code is (☎ 023).

Tourist Offices The Haarlem VVV (☎ 06-32 02 40 43), at Stationsplein 1 to the right outside the train station, is open Monday to Saturday from 9 am to 5.30 pm (from 1 October to 30 March on Saturday from 10 am to 4 pm).

The Zandvoort office (☎ 571 79 47) is at Schoolplein 1.

Things to See & Do
Haarlem's main attractions are its museums, which can be covered in a day if you're not planning on visiting the nearby Keukenhof and Zandvoort as well.

Museums The **Frans Hals Museum** at Groot Heiligland 62 features many of the 17th-century artist's portraits. It's open Monday to Saturday 11 am to 5 pm, Sunday from 1 pm, and costs f6.50/3 for adults/children.

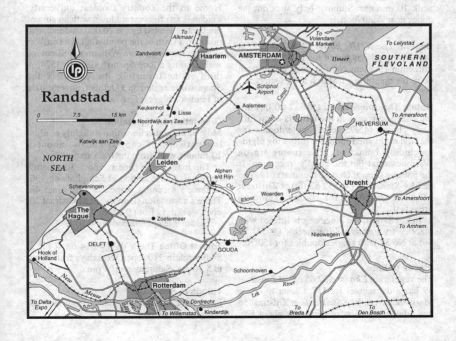

Close to the town centre, the **Teyler Museum** at Spaarne 16 is the country's oldest, housing a curious collection including drawings by Michelangelo and Raphael. It's open Tuesday to Saturday from 10 am to 5 pm, Sunday from noon, and costs f7.50/3.50 for adults/children.

St Bavo Church Also known as the Grote Kerk, the St Bavokerk on the Grote Markt is home to the Müller organ which a young Mozart played, and which you can hear in summer on Tuesday at 8.15 pm and Thursday at 3 pm. The church itself is open to visitors Monday to Saturday from 10 am to 4 pm; entry is f2.50/1.50.

Places to Stay
There are a few reasonably priced hotels in Haarlem, or else try the pensions at Zandvoort.

Camping The *De Liede* (☎ 533 23 60) at Liewegje 17 is open all year – take bus No 2 (direction Zuiderpolder) to Zoete Inval and walk 10 minutes. Summer-only sites dot the dunes near Zandvoort.

Hostels The *NJHC hostel* (☎ 537 37 93) at Jan Gijzenpad 3 is out of town, but bus No 2 (direction Haarlem Noord) stops at the front door. It's open from 1 March to 31 October.

Hotels The *Joops Hotel* (☎ 532 20 08) has the cheapest rooms in town but is often full. They charge f45/75 for a single/double for the first night and f30/60 for following nights (excluding breakfast). The rooms are on Warmoesstraat but the hotel's 'reception' is the antique shop at Oude Groenmarkt 12. The nearby *Stadscafé* (☎ 532 52 02) at Zijlstraat 56 charges f50/75 for rooms excluding breakfast.

In Zandvoort, the Hogeweg is littered with places – try *Pension Zilvermeeuw* (☎ 571 72 86) at No 32 with singles/doubles for f50/70.

Places to Eat
The vegetarian *Eko* (☎ 532 65 68) at Zijlstraat 39 has a dagschotel for f17. Closer to Grote Markt the tavern-like *Stadscafé* at Zijlstraat 56 has a huge selection of meals for about f26.

Self-caterers will find a *Deka Markt* supermarket at Gedempte Oude Gracht 58.

Getting There & Away
InterCity trains run every 15 minutes to/from Amsterdam CS (f6, 15 minutes) and Leiden (f8.75, 30 minutes).

AROUND HAARLEM
Near the town of Lisse between Haarlem and Leiden, the world's largest garden, the **Keukenhof**, attracts a staggering 800,000 people for a mere eight weeks every year. Its beauty is something of an enigma, combining nature's talents with artificial precision to create a garden where millions of tulips and daffodils bloom every year, perfectly in place and exactly on time. It's open from late March to May but dates vary slightly, so check with the VVV or the Keukenhof (☎ 0252-46 55 55). Take bus No 50 or 51 from Haarlem station. The Keukenhof costs f16/8 for adults/children.

LEIDEN
Home to the country's oldest university, Leiden is an effervescent town with an aura of intellect generated by the 20,000 students who make up a sixth of the population. The university was a present from William the Silent for withstanding a long Spanish siege in 1574. A third of the townsfolk starved before the Spaniards retreated on 3 October, now the date of Leiden's biggest festival.

Orientation & Information
Most of the sights lie within a slightly confusing network of central canals, about a 10-minute walk from the train station.

The main post office is about 300 metres north-east of the station at Schipholweg 130, or there's a central branch at Breestraat 46. There's a wassalon (laundry) at Morsstraat 50, open weekdays from 9 am to 9 pm.

Leiden's telephone code is ☎ 071.

Tourist Office The VVV (☎ 514 68 46) is at Stationsplein 210, open weekdays from 9 am to 5.30 pm, Saturday until 4 pm.

Things to See & Do
In summer, canal cruises leave from near the bridge at Beestenmarkt.

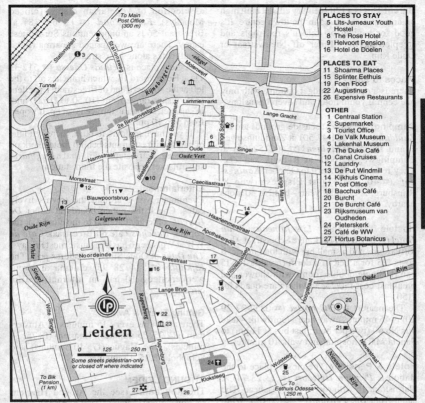

PLACES TO STAY
5 Lits-Jumeaux Youth Hostel
8 The Rose Hotel
9 Helvoort Pension
16 Hotel de Doelen

PLACES TO EAT
11 Shoarma Places
15 Splinter Eethuis
19 Foen Food
22 Augustinus
26 Expensive Restaurants

OTHER
1 Centraal Station
2 Supermarket
3 Tourist Office
4 De Valk Museum
6 Lakenhal Museum
7 The Duke Café
10 Canal Cruises
12 Laundry
13 De Put Windmill
14 Kijkhuis Cinema
17 Post Office
18 Bacchus Café
20 Burcht
21 De Burcht Café
23 Rijksmuseum van Oudheden
24 Pieterskerk
25 Café de WW
27 Hortus Botanicus

Leiden

0   125   250 m

Some streets pedestrian-only or closed off where indicated

NETHERLANDS

Museums Located at Rapenburg 28, the **Rijksmuseum van Oudheden** (National Museum of Antiquities) tops Leiden's list of 11 museums. Its striking entrance hall contains the Temple of Taffeh, a gift from Egypt for the Netherlands' help in saving ancient monuments from inundation when the Aswan High Dam was built. It's open Tuesday to Saturday from 10 am to 5 pm, Sunday from noon, and costs f5/4 for adults/children.

The 17th-century **Lakenhal** (Cloth Hall) at Oude Singel 28 houses an assortment of works by old masters, period rooms and temporary exhibitions. It's open weekdays from 10 am to 5 pm and weekends from noon, and costs f5/2.50 for adults/children.

De Valk (Falcon), Leiden's landmark windmill, is a museum that will blow away notions that windmills were a Dutch invention. It's at Binnenvestgracht 1, open Tuesday to Saturday from 10 am to 5 pm, Sunday from 1 pm, and costs f5/3 for adults/children.

Hortus Botanicus Europe's oldest botanical garden, dating back 400 years, is at Rapenburg 73. It's open daily from 9 am to 5 pm (on Sundays from 10 am), but closed Saturdays in winter. Admission costs f5/2.50 for adults/children.

Burcht This is a 12th-century citadel built high on an artificial mound in the town centre. It's good for a view of Leiden's red roofs and steepled skyline. Enter off Nieuwstraat or Oude Rijn.

Places to Stay

There is a dearth of budget options, with only one central youth hotel and several pensions.

Camping The closest seaside grounds are *De Zuidduinen* (☎ 401 47 50) at Zuidduinseweg 1 and *De Noordduinen* (☎ 402 52 95) at Campingweg 1, both at Katwijk aan Zee. They're open from April to October. *Koningshof* (☎ 402 60 51) at Elsgeesterweg 8, Rijnsburg, is open all year – bus No 40 stops nearby.

Hostels The friendly *Lits-Jumeaux Youth Hotel* (☎ 512 84 57) at Lange Scheistraat 9 has lofty rooms and a small bar with loud music. It costs f25 for a bed in a dorm (breakfast is f5 extra). Single/double rooms with shower and breakfast cost f50/75, and there are quads for f150.

The nearest *NJHC hostel* (☎ 0252-37 29 20) is 45 minutes away near Noordwijk – take bus No 60 (two per hour; last bus at 11 pm) to Sancta Maria hospital and walk 10 minutes.

Hotels & Pensions The closest place to the station is *Pension Helvoort* (☎ 13 23 74) at Narmstraat 1b with rooms for f40 a head. The canal-front *Bik Pension* (☎ 12 26 02), Witte Singel 92 south of the town centre, is similarly priced – take bus No 43. *The Rose Hotel* (☎ 514 66 30) at Beestenmarkt 14 is a lovely little place (six rooms only) with a great location. The rooms all have private shower cubicles, and cost f75/100. Alternatively, on the canal near the Rijksmuseum is the stately *Hotel de Doelen* (☎ 512 05 27) at Rapenburg 2; all rooms have a shower and toilet, and start at f110/165.

Places to Eat

The best value in town is *Augustinus*, a mensa (student cafeteria) on Rapenburg 24 with meals from f6, open weekdays from 5 to 9 pm.

The *Splinter Eethuis* (☎ 514 95 19) at Noordeinde 30 has a dagschotel for f13.50 and a selection of vegetarian dishes (closed Mondays). *Foen Food* (☎ 12 61 78) at Breestraat 56 is an unpretentious Surinamese eatery. There are well-priced shoarma (pitta-bread) cafés along Morsstraat.

A great place is *Eethuis Odessa* (☎ 512 33 11) at Hogewoerd 18, which branches off to the left at the southern end of Breestraat. Excellent pasta dishes range from f10.50 to f16.50 and, in summer, a floating terrace is set up. It's open from 5 to 10 pm.

If you have guilders to burn, there is a lane of candle-lit restaurants behind Pieterskerk on Kloksteeg. Self-caterers will find a *Dagmarkt* supermarket opposite the train station.

Entertainment

Evenings revolve around the town's lively cafés. Check the notice boards at either *De Burcht*, a literary bar next to the citadel or the popular *Bacchus* café on Breestraat. *Café de WW* at Wolsteeg 6 has live music most Fridays; *The Duke* at Oude Singel 2 features jazz. The *Kijkhuis* (☎ 514 28 95) cinema at Vrouwenkerksteeg 10 has an alternative film circuit.

Getting There & Away

There are trains every 15 minutes to Amsterdam (f12.25, 35 minutes), Haarlem (f8.75, 30 minutes), The Hague (f7, 10 minutes) and Schiphol (f8.75, 17 minutes).

AROUND LEIDEN

The **Keukenhof** (see the Around Haarlem section earlier) is about 10 km north of Leiden. It can be reached by NZH bus No 54 (20 minutes, two per hour), which runs directly there (during the flower season only) and leaves from the train station.

THE HAGUE

Officially known as 's-Gravenhage ('the Count's Domain') because a count built a castle here in the 13th century, The Hague – Den Haag in Dutch – is the country's seat of government and residence of the royal family, though the capital city is Amsterdam. It has a refined air, created by the many stately mansions and palatial embassies that line its green boulevards.

It's known for its prestigious art galleries, a huge jazz festival held annually near the seaside suburb of Scheveningen, and the mini-iature town of Madurodam. There is a poorer side to all the finery, though, and the area south of the centre is far removed from its urbane neighbours to the north.

Orientation & Information

Trains stop at Station HS (Hollands Spoor), 20 minutes walk south of the city, or CS (Centraal Station), five minutes from the centre – head straight up Herengracht.

Tourist Offices The main VVV (☎ 06-34 03 50 51) is at Koningin Julianaplein 30 next to CS; the other is in Scheveningen, at Gevers Deynootweg 1134 near the Kurhaus. Both are open from Monday to Saturday from 9 am to 5.30 pm. In July and August, they're also open on Sunday from 10 am to 5 pm.

Money Besides the GWK office in CS, there's an American Express (☎ 070-370 11 00) at Venestraat 20.

Post & Communications The main post office is on Kerkplein next to the Grote Kerk.
The Hague's telephone code is ☎ 070.

Laundry There's a wassalon to the east behind CS at Theresiastraat 250.

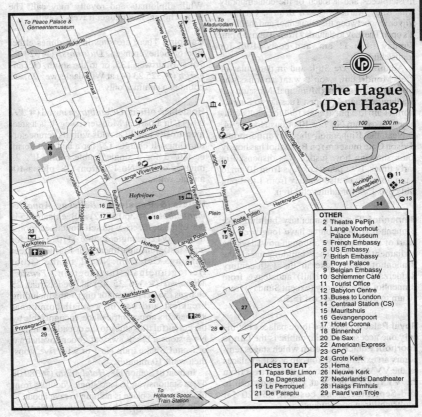

The Hague (Den Haag)

0   100   200 m

OTHER
2 Theatre PePijn
4 Lange Voorhout Palace Museum
5 French Embassy
6 US Embassy
7 British Embassy
8 Royal Palace
9 Belgian Embassy
10 Schlemmer Café
11 Tourist Office
12 Babylon Centre
13 Buses to London
14 Centraal Station (CS)
15 Mauritshuis
16 Gevangenpoort
17 Hotel Corona
18 Binnenhof
20 De Sax
22 American Express
23 GPO
24 Grote Kerk
25 Hema
26 Nieuwe Kerk
27 Nederlands Danstheater
28 Haags Filmhuis
29 Paard van Troje

PLACES TO EAT
1 Tapas Bar Limon
3 De Dageraad
19 Le Perroquet
21 De Paraplu

NETHERLANDS

Medical & Emergency Services For general medical information call ☎ 345 53 00; for an after-hours doctor, ☎ 346 96 69; for an emergency dentist, ☎ 397 44 91; and for general police enquiries ☎ 310 49 11.

Things to See & Do
The Hague has a good selection of galleries and historical edifices. Scheveningen has the beach, dominated by the highbrow Kurhaus Hotel.

Museums & Galleries The showpiece is the **Mauritshuis**, an exquisite 17th-century mansion housing a superb collection of Dutch and Flemish masterpieces and a touch of the contemporary with Andy Warhol's *Queen Beatrix*. On Korte Vijverberg between the Binnenhof and the Plein, it's open Tuesday to Saturday from 10 am to 5 pm, Sunday from 11 am, and costs f10/5 for adults/children.

Admirers of De Stijl, and in particular of Piet Mondriaan, won't want to miss the **Gemeentemuseum** (Municipal Museum) at Stadhouderslaan 41. Open Tuesday to Sunday from 11 am to 5 pm, it costs f8/4 for adults/children – take tram No 7 or 10 or bus No 4 or 14.

Near the Binnenhof, the **Gevangenpoort** (Prison Gate museum) on Buitenhof has hourly tours showing how justice was dispensed in early times. It's open weekdays from 10 am to 4 pm, in summer also Sunday from 1 to 4 pm, and costs f5/3 for adults/children.

Binnenhof The parliamentary buildings, or Binnenhof (Inner Court), have long been the heart of Dutch politics although nowadays the parliament meets in a new building outside the Binnenhof. Tours take in the 13th-century Ridderzaal (Knight's Hall) and leave from Binnenhof 8a, every day (except Sunday) from 10 am to 3.45 pm and cost f5.50.

Royal Palace There are three palaces but the only one accessible to the public is the **Lange Voorhout Palace Museum** which stages temporary art exhibitions. You can pass the palaces on the VVV's 'Royal Tour' which leaves from the VVV office at CS at 1 pm (mid-April to mid-September) and costs f27.50/20 for adults/children and students.

Peace Palace Home of the International Court of Justice, the Peace Palace on Carnegieplein can be visited by guided tours (only) which cost f5/3 for adults/children and must be booked – enquire at the palace or the VVV. To get there, take tram No 7 or bus No 4 from CS.

Madurodam Everything that's quintessential Netherlands is in this tiny 'town' that's big with tourists. Newly renovated, it's open daily from 9 am to 10 pm (until 5 pm from October to March), and costs f19.50/14 for adults/children. Take tram Nos 1 and 9 or bus No 22 from the CS.

Places to Stay
While diplomats and royalty may call The Hague home, few budget travellers will.

Camping There are sites in the dunes either side of Scheveningen. *Duinhorst* (☎ 324 22 70) at Buurtweg 135, or to the south, *Ockenburgh* (☎ 325 23 64) at Wijndaelerweg 25, are both open summer only.

Hostel The official *Ockenburgh* hostel (☎ 397 00 11), in a park at Monsterseweg 4, is a steel monstrosity totally at odds with its serene surroundings. It charges f27 for a bed in a dorm, or f40/73 for a single/double room. It's 25 minutes on bus No 122 from CS, plus a 10-minute walk.

Hotels & Pensions *Bellevue Appartementenhotel* (☎ 360 55 52) at Beeklaan 415 is one of the best bets, with self-contained rooms from f60/120 single/double (f10 extra for breakfast), plus apartments for four and street parking. Get tram No 11 to the Groot Hertoginnelaan intersection. *Pension Minnema* (☎ 346 35 42) at Dedelstraat 25 charges f55 per person for big rooms including breakfast and use of a small communal kitchen. It's an eccentric place, recognisable by the colourful tiles stuck to the outside wall. Bus No 5 stops a block away at Groenhovenstraat or from CS take tram No 1 or 9 for five stops, then walk 10 minutes.

In front of Station HS, *Hotel Aristo* (☎ 389 08 47) at Stationsweg 164 has singles/doubles from f48/80 but this place is nothing to rave about.

In Scheveningen, the best option is *Pension*

AAlberts (☎ 354 97 90) at Harstenhoekweg 189, a few minutes walk from the beach. Immaculate rooms with private toilet and shower cost f55 per person. The *El Cid Pension* (☎ 354 66 67), 200 metres before the Kurhaus at Badhuisweg 51, has musty rooms for f45 or f50 per person. Tram No 1 or 9 will get you close to either of these places. For the desperate, there's *Schuur* (☎ 355 65 83) at Badhuiskade 2, which charges f44/82 – take tram No 7 to the stop 'Badhuiskade'.

Still in Scheveningen but more up-market is the *Hotel Duinzicht* (☎ 350 69 99) at Alkmaarsestraat 6. It has singles/doubles with shower for f85/117, and parking.

For a diplomat-style splurge there's *Hotel Corona* (☎ 363 79 30) at Buitenhof 39, with charming rooms from f265/335.

Places to Eat

Fortunately you get a more versatile outlook on eating than sleeping. The cobbled streets off Denneweg, north of the Lange Voorhout royal palace, are one of the livelier areas with canalside cafés, intimate restaurants, theatres and bars. Here you find *De Dageraad* (☎ 364 56 66) at Hooikade 4, a rustic vegetarian place with main dishes for about f20; it's open daily until 9 pm. *Tapas Bar Limon* (☎ 356 14 65) at Denneweg 59a is also good.

Le Perroquet (☎ 363 97 86) on Lange Poten serves huge satay specials for f14.50. It's also good for the ubiquitous 'koffie met appelgebak' (coffee with apple pie). *Schlemmer Café* (☎ 360 90 90) at Lange Houtstraat 17 is tastefully decorated and frequented by similarly dressed people; a lunchtime dagschotel costs f18.50. In Bagijnestraat, an alley off Lange Poten, you'll find a gourmet's UN as well as the music café *De Paraplu* (☎ 364 71 34). It boasts a dagschotel for f18.50 and 23 types of beer.

The *Hema* on Grote Marktstraat in the city centre and the *Albert Heijn* on Harstenhoekplein in Scheveningen both sell basic supplies for self-caterers.

Entertainment

Although it's more a city for fine dining than raging, there are a few lively cafés, and in the second week of July the North Sea Jazz Festival considerably invigorates the music scene. If you're into ballet, be sure to catch a perfor-

mance by the renowned *Nederlands Danstheater* in its theatre off the Spui (casual dress will do; no performances in July and August).

On a daily level, there's the happening little bar *De Sax* on Korte Houtstraat 14a just off the Plein, or *Theatre PePijn* (☎ 346 03 54) on Nieuwe Schoolstraat 21, with a solid live jazz line-up. Just up the street at No 2 is *Stairs*, a gay bar/disco. At Spui 191 there's the *Haags Filmhuis* (☎ 365 60 30), which screens foreign and art movies.

The *Paard van Troje* (☎ 360 18 38), Prinsegracht 12, is The Hague's answer to Amsterdam's Melkweg and Paradiso 'cultural activity centres', with bands often performing on Thursday, Friday and Saturday, and occasional theatre performances – otherwise, there's film or disco. Admission costs f7.50 to f30 depending on what's happening. It's usually closed Monday and Tuesday.

Getting There & Away

Bus Eurolines and Hoverspeed buses stop at Anna van Bueren Straat to the east behind CS. Tickets for both can be bought at Broere Reizen (☎ 382 40 51) travel agent inside the Babylon Centre next to the VVV. London services all originate in Amsterdam, arriving in The Hague about 50 minutes later. For more details, see the Amsterdam Getting There & Away section.

Train Trains to Amsterdam (f16, 45 minutes), Delft (f3.75, five minutes), Leiden (f7, 10 minutes) and Rotterdam (f7, 15 minutes) depart from Station HS, though the line that takes in Schiphol airport (f12.25, 40 minutes) via Leiden on its way to Amsterdam South leaves from CS. Trains to Utrecht (f16, 45 minutes) leave from CS. For all national rail, bus and tram enquiries call ☎ 06-92 92.

Tram Just nine km away, Delft can be reached by tram No 1 (30 minutes), which departs from next to CS.

Getting Around

Public transport maps are sold (f1) from the tourist office at CS. Buses and some trams leave from above CS, while other trams take off from the side. Tram No 7 goes to Scheveningen via the Peace Palace, while tram

Nos 1 and 9 follow Nieuwe Parklaan past Madurodam to the coast. Tram Nos 8, 9 and 12 link CS and HS.

DELFT
Had the potters who lived in Delft long ago not been such accomplished copiers, today's townsfolk would probably live in relative peace. But the distinctive blue-and-white pottery which the 17th-century artisans duplicated from Chinese porcelain became famous worldwide as delftware. If you're here in summer you'll probably wish you weren't; in winter its old-world charm and narrow, canal-lined streets make a pleasant day trip from nearby Rotterdam or The Hague. Delft is home to the country's largest technical university, which helps explain the high proportion of young males.

Orientation & Information
The train and neighbouring bus station are a 10-minute stroll south of the central Markt. The post office is on Hippolytusbuurt. There's a laundry at Koornmarkt 68.

Delft's telephone code is ☎ 015.

Tourist Office The VVV (☎ 212 61 00) at Markt 85 is open weekdays from 9 am to 6 pm, Saturday until 5 pm, and in summer Sunday from 10 am to 3 pm.

Things to See & Do
Buying pottery tops most visitors' priorities. There are three factories where you can watch working artists while being set straight on identifying genuine from fake. Alternatively, a smattering of museums and churches attract passers-by, and canal boats cruise around in summer, leaving from **Koornmarkt**.

Delftware The most central and modest outfit is **Atelier de Candelaer** at Kerkstraat 14, a small operation going since 1975. The other two factories sit poles apart outside the centre. **De Delftse Pauw** at Delftweg 133 is the smaller, employing 35 painters who work mainly from their homes; take tram No 1 to Pasgeld, walk up Broekmolenweg to the canal and turn left. It has daily tours but you won't see the painters on weekends. **De Porceleyne Fles**, south at Rotterdamseweg 196, is the only

original factory, operating since the 1650s. It's slick and pricey; bus No 63 from the train station stops nearby, or it's a 25-minute walk from the town centre.

Churches The 14th-century **Nieuwe Kerk** houses the crypt of the Dutch royal family as well as the mausoleum of William the Silent. Open daily except Sunday, it costs f2.50/1 for adults/children. The Gothic **Oude Kerk**, with 140 years' seniority and a two-metre tilt in its tower, is at Heilige Geestkerkhof. A combination ticket costs f4/1.50 for adults/children.

Prinsenhof Across from Oude Kerk at St Agathaplein 1, the Prinsenhof is where William the Silent held court until assassinated here in 1584. It now has historical and contemporary art, is open Tuesday to Saturday from 10 am to 5 pm, Sunday from 1 pm, and costs f5/2.75 for adults/children.

Places to Stay
There's a camping ground, *Delftse Hout* (☎ 213 00 40), at Korftlaan 5 to the north-east of town; it's open all year. Get bus No 64 from the station.

Unless you want to part with plenty of guilders for rooms often resembling wardrobes, the best bets are the pensions near the station, however in summer they are heavily booked. *Van Leeuwen Pension* (☎ 212 37 16) at Achterom 143 is welcoming, with plenty of rooms for f35 per person. *De Vos Pension* (☎ 212 32 58) at Breestraat 5 has doubles (no singles) for f65. Alternatively, on the Markt, *Hotel Dalmacya* (☎ 212 37 14) at No 39 has large singles/doubles for f62/74 or there's *Les Compagnons Hotel* (☎ 214 01 02) at No 61 with rooms for f100/135. You'll get old-world charm and some space at *Hotel Leeuwenbrug* (☎ 214 77 41), Koornmarkt 16. Rooms start at f131/158.

Places to Eat
De Ruif Café (☎ 214 22 06) at Kerkstraat 23 has a floating terrace and serves generous meals – the dagschotel (f13.50) and vegetarian dishes (f17.50) are particularly good value. *Uit de Kunst* (☎ 212 13 19) at Oude Delft 140 has a delightful conservatory and a relaxing ambience.

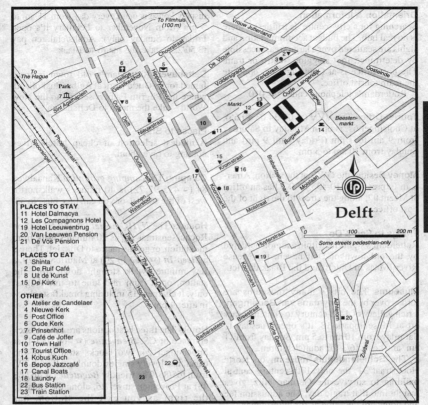

PLACES TO STAY
11 Hotel Dalmacya
12 Les Compagnons Hotel
19 Hotel Leeuwenbrug
20 Van Leeuwen Pension
21 De Vos Pension

PLACES TO EAT
1 Shinta
2 De Ruif Café
8 Uit de Kunst
15 De Kurk

OTHER
3 Atelier de Candelaer
4 Nieuwe Kerk
5 Post Office
6 Oude Kerk
7 Prinsenhof
9 Café de Joffer
10 Town Hall
13 Tourist Office
14 Kobus Kuch
16 Bepop Jazzcafé
17 Canal Boats
18 Laundry
22 Bus Station
23 Train Station

Delft

Some streets pedestrian-only

The newly renovated *Shinta* (☎ 213 09 46) at Voldersgracht 31 is a little Indonesian eatery with rijsttafel for f35 (closed Wednesday). Otherwise, there's great, reasonably priced, local cuisine at *De Kurk* (☎ 214 14 74) at Kromstraat 20.

Entertainment

Delft is no raving metropolis. The *Bepop Jazzcafé* on Kromstraat is the liveliest spot. The *Filmhuis* (☎ 214 02 26), at Doelenplein 5 to the north of the centre, has an alternative film circuit. The local crowds at *Café de Joffer* inevitably spill out onto Nieuwstraat, or for a slightly quieter haunt, try *Kobus Kuch* on Beestenmarkt 1.

Getting There & Away

It's 10 minutes by train to Rotterdam, less to The Hague. Tram No 1 leaves every 15 minutes from in front of the train station for The Hague (30 minutes).

ROTTERDAM

Rotterdam's catastrophic bombardment on 14 May 1940 left it crippled then and, sadly, somewhat soulless today. Its centre is modern, with mirrored skyscrapers and some extraordinarily innovative buildings. The city prides itself on this experimental architecture as well as having the world's largest port.

Orientation & Information

Searching for a city 'centre' is fruitless – there is no real hub. The budget accommodation and sights are scattered over a large area, accessible by determined foot-slogging, metro or tram. The post office is at Coolsingel 42, opposite the main tourist office.

Rotterdam's telephone code is ☎ 010.

Tourist Office The VVV (☎ 06-34 03 40 65), at Coolsingel 67, is open Monday to Saturday from 9 am to 7 pm (Friday until 9 pm) and Sunday from 10 am to 5 pm.

Money Besides the GWK at the station, American Express (☎ 010-433 03 00) has an office at Meent 92, along the street to the right of the post office.

Things to See & Do

Rotterdam's sights lie within a region bordered by the old town of Delfshaven, the Meuse River (Maas in Dutch) and the Blaak district.

Museums The city's many museums are lorded over by the **Boymans van Beuningen**, a rich gallery of 14th-century to contemporary art at Museumpark 18. It's open Tuesday to Saturday from 10 am to 5 pm, Sunday from 11 am, and costs f6/3 for adults/children.

The **Schielandshuis** museum on Korte Hoogstraat 31, the only 17th-century central building to survive the German blitz, gives insight into that tragic day. The admission fee and hours are the same as for the Boymans.

Cruises Spido (☎ 413 54 00) runs daily, 75-minute harbour cruises which cost f13/6.50 for adults/children, and day trips from f35 to the harbour heart at Europoort, or through the northern part of the Delta works (f42.50), taking in Kinderdijk (see Around Rotterdam) and Willemstad (see the Delta Region section) but not the Delta Expo on the Eastern Scheldt.

Euromast This 185-metre-high tower pricks the skyline at Parkhaven 20; admission is f14.50/9 for adults/children. Take tram No 6 or 9, or the metro to Dijkzigt.

Kijk-Kubus With Escher-like design, the 'cube houses' offer a new angle to modern living. The display house is open every day from 11 am to 5 pm (from November to February it's open Friday to Sunday only). Adults/children pay f3.50/2.50; take the metro to Blaak.

Delfshaven Rotterdam's old town is most famed for its **Oude Kerk** at Aelbrechtskolk 20, where the Pilgrim Fathers set sail to the New World – take the metro to Delfshaven.

Places to Stay

A modest selection of cheap hotels gives nothing to rave about.

Camping The *camping ground* at Kanaalweg 84 (☎ 415 97 72) is 40 minutes walk northwest of the station, or you can take bus No 33.

Hostels The *NJHC hostel* (☎ 436 57 63) on Rochussenstraat 107 is 20 minutes walk from the station, or get the metro to Dijkzigt. There's a *Sleep-In* (☎ 412 14 20) at Mauritsweg 29, a few minutes walk straight down from the station, open from mid-June to mid-August only. It charges f15 including breakfast; check in after 4 pm.

Hotels The three best options are out the back entrance of CS. *Bienvenue* (☎ 466 93 94) at Spoorsingel 24, two blocks straight up the canal, has lovely singles/doubles, all with TV, from f65/85. The friendly *Bagatelle* (☎ 467 63 48) at Provenierssingel 26, along the canal to the right as you exit the station, has singles/doubles for f39/68 without breakfast. The *Hotel Holland* (☎ 465 31 00), just across the canal at No 7, has small rooms with narrow metal beds for f52.50/62.50.

Otherwise, *Orion* (☎ 476 38 01) at Zwaerdecroonstraat 40, just round the corner from the Jazzcafé Dizzy, has OK rooms for f40/70 (not including breakfast).

Maritime romantics might enjoy a night at the *Hotel New York* (☎ 439 05 00) at Koninginnenhoofd 1. This palatial building, the former headquarters of the Holland-America shipping line, sits on a spit of land in the heart of Rotterdam's old harbour. Tower rooms with magnificent views start at f160.

Places to Eat

Near the hostel, *Jazzcafé Dizzy* (☎ 477 30 14)

at 's-Gravendijkwal 127 buzzes with live jazz and has snacks or pricey meals. The *Wester Paviljoen* (☎ 436 26 45), on the corner of Mathenesserlaan and Nieuwe Binnenweg, is a rustic café popular with all types. Basic meals cost between f9 and f15. *Loos* (☎ 411 77 23) at Westplein is a trendier version of the same, with an exquisite restaurant and cheaper 'pub' fare.

In Delfshaven, *Het Eethuisje* at Mathenesserdijk 436a is a humble café with f9.75 meals, weekdays from 4 to 9 pm. At Mauritsweg 28 near the Sleep-In, *De Eend* (☎ 412 98 07) has unpretentious meals from f11.95, but is open weekdays only from 4.30 to 8 pm.

Self-caterers will find an *Albert Heijn* supermarket at Nieuwe Binneweg 288.

Entertainment
Rotterdam is home to one of the country's biggest music venues, the *Ahoy'* (☎ 410 42 04) – check the VVV's entertainment guide for listings. On a local level, try the *Jazzcafé Dizzy* (see Places to Eat).

Two great places for a drink are *Zochers'*, a restored 1830s merchant house at Baden Powellaan 12 in Park de Heuvel, and the *Hotel New York* (see Places to Stay), accessible by one of the hotel's quaint private water taxis from Veerhaven.

Getting There & Away
Bus Eurolines and Hoverspeed buses stop at Conradstraat (to the right as you leave the train station) where Eurolines also has an office (☎ 412 44 44). Hoverspeed tickets are available from NBBS Reizen (☎ 414 98 22) at Meent 126 near the main VVV. Services to London leave from Amsterdam (for details, see Bus in the Amsterdam Getting There & Away section) and generally arrive in Rotterdam 1¼ hours later.

Train There are trains every 15 minutes to Amsterdam (f21.75, one hour), Delft (f4.75, 10 minutes), The Hague (f7, 15 minutes) and Utrecht (f14, 40 minutes). Half-hourly services run to Middelburg (f31, 1½ hours) and Hook of Holland (f8, 30 minutes).

Ferry For information on the ferries from Hook of Holland and Europoort to England, see the main Getting There & Away section at the beginning of this chapter. North Sea Ferries has a bus (f10) which leaves daily at 4 pm from CS to connect with the awaiting ferry at Europoort.

Getting Around
Trams leave from in front of the train station; the metro from underneath. Both run until about 1 am; on Fridays and Saturdays, night buses then take over. Free maps are available from the public transport kiosk in front of the station.

AROUND ROTTERDAM
The **Delta Expo** (see Middelburg Things to See in the Delta Region section) can be reached from CS by taking the metro to Zuidplein, then the NZH bus No 133 to Burgh-Haamstede and then bus No 104.

The **Kinderdijk**, the Netherlands' picture-postcard string of 19 working windmills, sits between Rotterdam and Dordrecht near Alblasserdam. On Saturday afternoons in July and August (and on the first Saturday of the month during the rest of the year) the mills' sails are set in motion. One windmill is open daily from April to September – get the metro to Zuidplein, then bus No 154.

UTRECHT
Lorded over by the Dom, the country's tallest church tower, Utrecht is an antique frame surrounding an increasingly modern interior. Its 14th-century sunken canals, once-bustling wharfs and cellars now brim with chic shops, restaurants and cafés. Also home to the country's largest university, its student population adds spice to a once largely church-oriented community.

Orientation & Information
A compact city, the most appealing quarter lies between Oudegracht and Nieuwegracht and the streets around the Dom. Unfortunately, none of the past character is evident when arriving at the train station, which lies behind Hoog Catharijne, the Netherlands' largest indoor shopping centre and a modern-day monstrosity.

Utrecht's telephone code is ☎ 030.

Tourist Office The VVV (☎ 06-34 03 40 85) is five minutes from the station at Vredenburg

NETHERLANDS

90, open weekdays from 9 am to 6 pm and Saturday until 4 pm.

Things to See & Do

The 102-metre-high Dom tower and some unusual museums can elevate your visit. Canal cruises leave from Oudegracht.

Dom Tower The 465 steps lead up to excellent views. In winter the tower is open only on weekends from noon to 5 pm; from 1 April to 31 October, it opens weekdays from 10 am to 5 pm and weekends from noon to 5 pm. Entry costs f4/2 for adults/children.

Museums There are 14 museums, but many are little more than bizarre hideaways for particular paraphernalia – a laundry museum is one example.

The **Grocery Museum** on Hoogt 6 is worth 10 minutes. The one-roomed museum sits above a sweet shop filled with the popular Dutch *drop* (a sweet or salted liquorice). It's open from Tuesday to Saturday from 12.30 to 4.30 pm, and entry is free.

The **Van Speelklok tot Pierement** ('From Musical Clock to Street Organ') museum has a colourful collection including 18th-century instruments demonstrated with gusto during hourly tours. It's at Buurkerkhof 10, open Tuesday to Saturday from 10 am to 5 pm, Sunday from 1 pm, and costs f7.50/5/4 for adults/students/children.

For religious and medieval art buffs, **Het Catharijneconvent** museum winds through a 15th-century convent at Nieuwegracht 63 and has the country's largest collection of medieval Dutch art. Open Tuesday to Friday from 10 am to 5 pm, weekends from 11 am, it costs f5/3.50 for adults/students and children.

Places to Stay

Camping De Berekuil (☎ 271 38 70) at Ariënslaan 5 is easily reached by bus No 57 from the station and is open all year.

You can join the destitutes at the *Snurk-huis* (Sleep-Inn) (☎ 231 53 26) at Jansveld 51, 10 minutes walk from the station – head straight up Vredenburg to the post office, take Voorstraat to the left and it's two streets on your right; it costs f8 with breakfast, and you can only book in between 9 pm and 1 am. Alterna-

tively, the *Youth Hostel* (☎ 656 12 77) at Rhijnauwenselaan 14 in Bunnik is eight km east, 20 minutes on bus No 40 or 41.

As for hotels, the *Domstad* (☎ 231 01 31) at Parkstraat 5, 20 minutes walk from the station (or bus No 3), has singles/doubles with communal bathrooms for f60/75. The *Park Hotel* (☎ 251 67 12) at Tolsteegsingel 34 has homy rooms with private shower and toilet for f57/95 single/double, and parking; it's on a tree-lined canal about 25 minutes walk from the station, or take bus No 2.

Places to Eat

The Oudegracht is lined with outdoor restaurants and cafés, though many of them are expensive. For pasta, join the crowds at *Toque Toque* (☎ 231 87 87) on the corner of Oudegracht and Vinkenburgstraat. *De Werfkring* (☎ 231 17 52) at wharf No 123 on Oudegracht is a reasonable vegetarian haunt (closed Sunday). *De Baas* on Lijnmarkt is a cheap, popular eatery run by a collective; tips go to selected aid organisations. Near the Sleep-Inn in Voorstraat, there are pizza and shoarma (pitta-bread) places. *Eettafel Veritas* is a student mensa at Kromme Nieuwe Gracht 54, open weeknights from 5 to 7.30 pm.

For self-caterers, there's a *V & D* supermarket in Hoog Catharijne, or an *Albert Heijn* on Voorstraat 38 near the Sleep-Inn.

Getting There & Away

Bus Eurolines and Hoverspeed buses stop at Jaarbeursplein out the back of the train station; tickets can be bought from Wasteels (☎ 293 08 70) at Jaarbeurstraverse 6 (on the covered walkway which joins Hoog Catharijne to Jaarbeursplein). For information on both services, see the Amsterdam Getting There & Away section.

Train As Utrecht is the national rail hub, there are frequent trains to Amsterdam (f10.75, 30 minutes), Arnhem (f16, 40 minutes), Den Bosch (f12.25, 30 minutes), Maastricht (f39, two hours), Rotterdam (f14, 40 minutes) and The Hague (f16, 45 minutes).

Getting Around

Buses leave from underneath Hoog Catharijne, and in summer, canal bikes can be hired on Oudegracht.

Arnhem & the Hoge Veluwe

About an hour's drive east of Amsterdam, the Hoge Veluwe is the Netherlands' largest national park and home of the prestigious Kröller-Müller museum. Literally meaning 'High' Veluwe, it's little more than a bump on the flat lands around it, but here it is possible to touch on a sense of isolation and wilderness found nowhere else on the Dutch mainland.

To the south, the town of Arnhem was the site of fierce fighting between the Germans and British and Polish airborne troops during the failed Operation Market Garden in WWII. Today it's a peaceful town, the closest base to the nearby war museum and the park.

Orientation & Information

The VVV (☎ 06-32 02 40 75) is at Stationsplein, to the left out of Arnhem's station, open Monday from 11 am to 5.30 pm, Tuesday to Friday from 9 am to 5.30 pm, and Saturday from 10 to 4 pm. Buses leave from the right as you exit the station. The town's pedestrianised centre, based around the well-hidden Korenmarkt, is five minutes walk away – head down Utrechtsestraat, cross over Willemsplein and cut through Korenstraat.

Arnhem's telephone code is ☎ 026.

Things to See & Do

In Arnhem itself, the main attraction is the **Museum of Fine Art** at Utrechtseweg 87 which occupies a neoclassical building overlooking the Rhine. It's a 10-minute walk from the station.

Outside the town, Oosterbeek's wartime **Airborne Museum** at Utrechtseweg 232 is open weekdays from 11 am to 5 pm and Sundays from noon – get bus No 1. The **Open-Air Museum** at Schelmseweg 89 has a collection of rural buildings including windmills, workshops and farmhouses. It's open April to October only – take bus No 3.

Hoge Veluwe Stretching for nearly 5500 hectares, the Hoge Veluwe is a strange mix of forests and woods, shifting sands and heathery moors. It's home to red deer, wild boar, moufflon (a Mediterranean goat), and the Kröller-Müller Museum, with its vast collection of Van Goghs.

The Hoge Veluwe is most inviting from mid-August to mid-September when ablaze with heather, or during the red deer's rutting season in September and October. It's best seen on foot or bicycle – 400 of the latter are available free of charge from the visitors' centre inside the park.

There are three entrances, but if you're using public transport the easiest route is with a special bus (No 12) which leaves from the VVV in Arnhem and goes to the visitors' centre. It runs at least three times daily from early April to 31 October and costs f7.35/4.15 return for adults/children.

Alternatively, you could catch the hourly bus No 107 from Arnhem bus station to Otterlo. From there, you can either follow the signs to the entrance one km away and then walk the remaining four km to the visitors' centre or wait for the hourly bus No 110 to Hoenderloo which will drop you at the visitors' centre.

The park is open daily from 8 or 9 am to sunset and costs f8/4/8 for adults/children/cars. The yearly Museumcard is not valid.

Kröller-Müller Museum Near the Hoge Veluwe visitors' centre, the museum's 278 Van Goghs are only a start. There are works by Picasso and Mondriaan, and out the back is Europe's largest sculpture garden. Once in the park, the museum is free. It's open Tuesday to Sunday from 10 am to 5 pm.

Places to Stay & Eat

There are camping grounds on the outside perimeter of the Hoge Veluwe, but closer to Arnhem try **Camping Arnhem** (☎ 443 16 00) at Kemperbergerweg 771 – it's 20 minutes on bus No 2 and a one-km walk from the bus station (next to the train station) in Arnhem.

The **Alteveer Youth Hostel** (☎ 442 01 14) at Diepenbrocklaan 27 is 10 minutes on bus No 3.

As for hotels, **Pension Parkzicht** (☎ 442 06 98) at Apeldoornsestraat 16 is 10 minutes downhill from the station and charges f47.50 a person. One block away and similarly priced is the musty **Hotel Rembrandt** (☎ 442 01 53) at Paterstraat 1.

Mozaik (☎ 351 55 65) on Ruiterstraat 46

near the main post office is a popular Turkish restaurant. It also has vegetarian meals from f14. Cheaper is the mainly takeaway fare at **Picolino Pizza House** (☎ 443 81 23) three blocks away on Hoogstraat 4. Terrace cafés rim the Korenmarkt – *Wampie* is the oldest and arguably the most popular.

Getting There & Away

Trains to Amsterdam (f25.25, 65 minutes) and Rotterdam (f28.75, 75 minutes) go via Utrecht (f16, 40 minutes), while the line south passes Den Bosch (f16, 45 minutes) and continues to Maastricht (f33.75, two hours).

The Delta Region

The Netherlands' aptly named province of Zeeland ('Sea Land') makes up most of the Delta region. Spreading out over the south-west corner of the country, it was until recent decades a solitary place, where isolated islands

were battered by howling winds and white-capped seas, and where little medieval towns, nestled somewhere in a protected groove, were seemingly lost in time.

But after the 1953 flood (see the History section at the beginning of this chapter) came the decision to defend Zeeland from the sea – and thus bring it into the present day. One by one the islands were connected by causeways and bridges, and the Delta Project (see the Around Middelburg section that follows) became a reality.

These days there's still a sense of a wild land, interspersed with quaint towns like Middelburg and Zierikzee, the port of Flushing (Vlissingen in Dutch), and further north-east, the fortified village of Willemstad.

Without a car, the region can be difficult to explore, although local buses do connect towns and villages.

MIDDELBURG

The long-time capital of Zeeland and the province's largest town, Middelburg is close to

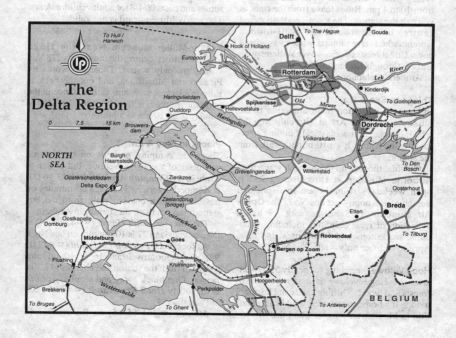

the Delta Expo and is the best base for exploring this windswept region.

Information

The VVV (☎ 0118-61 68 51) is at Markt 65a, open Monday to Saturday from 9.30 am to 5 pm (until 3 pm on Saturday from 1 November to 1 February) and Sunday from noon to 4 pm (March to October only).

Middelburg's telephone code is ☎ 0118.

Things to See

Dating back to the mid-1400s, the Gothic **Town Hall** was destroyed (like much of the central district) during the 1940 German blitz which flattened Rotterdam. Convincingly restored, it's open for guided visits only between 1 March and 1 November. A few streets away is **Lange Jan**, the town's other distinctive tower, which rises from the former 12th-century **Abdij** (Abbey) complex, later converted to Protestant churches. The tower can be climbed from mid-April to 31 October. For insight into the province's history, visit the **Zeeuws Museum** (Zeeland Museum) inside the Abbey.

Places to Stay & Eat

Between early April and mid-October, campers can try *Camping Middelburg* (☎ 62 53 95) at Koninginnelaan 55.

The nearest NJHC hostel, *Westhove* (☎ 58 12 54), is in a medieval castle about 15 km west between the villages of Domburg and Oostkapelle. It's open from mid-March to mid-October – from Middelburg station, take ZWN bus No 54.

In town near the Abbey, *Pension Bij de Abdij* (☎ 61 30 32) at Bogaardstraat 14 has single/double rooms from f40/80. Closer to the station, *Pension Huize Orliëns* (☎ 63 81 00) at Nieuwstraat 23 is similarly priced.

Restaurants and tearooms line the Markt, and more are along Vlasmarkt opposite the tourist office. *De Geere* (☎ 61 30 83) at Langeviele 51 is a popular café, as is the trendy *Café Bommel* on Markt 85.

Getting There & Away

Train For all national information call ☎ 06-92 92. Major destinations north-east include Amsterdam (f44.50, 2½ hours) and Rotterdam (f31, 1½ hours).

AROUND MIDDELBURG

The disastrous 1953 flood was the impetus for the Delta Project in which the south-west river deltas were blocked using a network of dams, dykes and a remarkable 3.2-km storm surge barrier. Lowered only in rough conditions, this barrier was built following environmental opposition to plans to dam the Eastern Scheldt (Oosterschelde). It can be dropped during abnormally high tides but generally remains open to allow normal tidal movements and the survival of the region's shellfish.

Finished in 1986, the project is exhibited at the **Delta Expo** (☎ 0111-65 27 02) which sits steadfastly on top of the barrier. Open daily from 10 am to 5.30 pm (closed Monday and Tuesday from 1 November to 31 March), it costs f16.50/11.50 for adults/children in summer, and f12.50/7.50 in winter. To get there from Middelburg, take the ZWN bus No 104 (30 minutes, buses every half-hour). If you are driving or you want to try your hand hitching, head onto the N57 in the direction of 'Burgh-Haamstede'.

WILLEMSTAD

Sitting on the edge of the Delta region but officially part of Brabant province, Willemstad is a picturesque medieval village with a big place in Dutch hearts and on their day-tripping calender. Built in the mid-16th century, the village was given to the nation's saviour, William the Silent, as compensation for his expenses in leading the Revolt of the Netherlands.

The VVV (☎ 0168-47 35 55) is at Voorstraat 2a in the centre of the village.

Overnighters will find only two hotel choices: *Willemstad Hotel* (☎ 0168-47 37 00) at Voorstraat 42 charges f100/120 for a single/double (breakfast f15 extra), or there's the slick, harbour-front *Het Wapen van Willemstad* (☎ 0168-47 35 50) at Benedenkade 12 with rooms from f110/150 including breakfast. There are also two B&Bs – ask at the VVV.

Without a car, it's up to your thumb, the BBA bus (one every hour) from Roosendaal or Breda, or ZWN buses from Rotterdam. It takes 1½ hours to get to Rotterdam by bus – you must change at Oud Beyerland.

The North

The Netherlands' northern region is made up of several provinces, including Fryslân and Groningen. Capped by the Frisian Islands, the region's shores are washed by the shallow Waddenzee which is home to a small number of seals and the unique Dutch sport of wadlopen (see the Groningen section).

Even to the Dutch, the lakeland province of Fryslân is a bit 'different' from the rest of the Netherlands. For here the people have their own flag, anthem and language, Frysk (Frisian) which, since 1980, has been a mandatory subject for primary school students in the province. In 1996, the province's name was officially changed from Friesland to Fryslân (as it is spelt in Frysk).

AFSLUITDIJK

The 30-km long Afsluitdijk or 'Barrier Dyke' connects the provinces of North Holland and Fryslân and transformed the old Zuiderzee into the IJsselmeer lake. Driving along the dyke's A7 motorway, you'll pass the **Stevinsluizen**, sluices named after the 17th-century engineer, Henri Stevin, who first mooted the idea of reclaiming the Zuiderzee.

Tours to Fryslân from Amsterdam usually take in the Afsluitdijk. Otherwise, without your own wheels, you can cross it on the hourly bus No 350 from Alkmaar to Leeuwarden, but not by train.

LEEUWARDEN

As the economic and cultural capital of Fryslân, Leeuwarden radiates an air of proud independence. The city developed from three *terp* (artificial dwelling mound) settlements which merged in the 15th century, though it's better remembered as the birth place of Mata Hari, the dancer executed by the French in 1917 on suspicion of spying for the Germans.

The VVV (☎ 06-32 02 40 60) at Stationsplein 1 has provincial information including boating details and booklets describing the Frisian language and 'national' symbols. More can be gained from the **Frisian Museum** at Turfmarkt 11 as well as the **Frisian Literary Museum**, Grote Markt 28, in Mata Hari's former house.

The cheapest hotel in town is *De Pauw* (☎ 058-212 36 51) at Stationsweg 10 near the train station. *Havana* (☎ 058-216 09 81) at Uniabuurt 4 is a good eetcafé.

From Amsterdam there are twice-hourly trains to Leeuwarden (f44.50, 1¾ hours) or you can take bus No 350 from Alkmaar across the Afsluitdijk.

GRONINGEN

This lively provincial capital has been an important trading centre since the 13th century, its prosperity increasing with the building in 1614 of the country's second oldest university and, later, the discovery of natural gas. The VVV (☎ 06-32 02 30 50) is at Gedempt Kattendiep 6, between the train station and the city centre.

The city's newest and most colourful attraction is the **Groninger Museum** at Museumeiland 1, opposite the train and bus stations. It's open Tuesday to Sunday from 10 am to 5 pm.

Groningen is the best place to arrange **wadlopen**, a serious pastime – strenuous and at times dangerous – involving km-long, low-tide walks in mud that can come up to your thighs. To get into the thick of it, contact Henk Schildhuis (☎ 0596-57 28 86) at Badweg 42, Loppersum, north-east of Groningen, who specialises in groups of less than 15 people, or Dijkstra Wad Walking Tours (☎ 0595-52 83 45) at Pieterburen to the north.

For overnighters, there's the clean *Simplon* (☎ 050-313 52 21) at Boterdiep 73. This youth centre (take bus No 1 from the train station) has cheap beers, a small cinema, live music and beds in large dorms for f19 per person. More centrally, *Hotel Friesland* (☎ 050-312 13 07) at Kleine Pelsterstraat 4 has doubles for f77.

Twice-hourly trains depart from Amsterdam to Groningen (f47.25, 2¼ hours) and from Groningen to Leeuwarden (f14, 50 minutes).

FRISIAN ISLANDS

Known as the Frisian or Wadden Islands, the country's five northern isles stretch in an arc from Texel to Schiermonnikoog. They are important bird-breeding grounds as well as being an escape for stressed southerners wanting to touch roots with nature. Ferries connect the islands to the mainland, and there are (mainly summer) hostels on all except

Vlieland. Bikes are a good way to get around and can be hired.

Texel

The largest and most populated island, Texel's 24 km of beach can seem overrun all summer but even more so in June when the world's largest catamaran race is staged here. The biggest village is Den Burg where you'll find the VVV (☎ 31 47 41) on Groeneplaats 9.

For information on the island's ecology, visit **Ecomare** at Ruyslaan 92. Set up in the 1950s to protect the tourist-inundated environment, it's also a hospital for sick seals from the pollution-embattled Waddenzee population.

The telephone code for Texel is ☎ 0222.

Places to Stay For isolated camping, head to *Loodsmansduin* (☎ 31 92 03) at Rommelpot 19 near Den Hoorn. *De Krim* camping (☎ 31 66 66) at Roogeslootweg 6 in Cocksdorp is open all year.

There are two NJHC hostels on opposite sides of Den Burg. The pleasant *Panorama* (☎ 31 54 41) is at Schansweg 7 – bus No 29; *De Eyercoogh* at Pontweg 106 is 10 minutes walk from town, or get bus No 28 from the ferry.

The *Hotel De Merel* (☎ 31 31 32) at Warmoesstraat 22 has rooms for f55 per person; *'t Koogerend* (☎ 31 33 01) at Kogerstraat 94 charges f81/112.

Getting There & Away Trains from Amsterdam to Den Helder (1½ hours) are met by a bus that whips you to the awaiting, hourly car ferry. The trip takes 20 minutes, and costs f11.25/5.75 return for adults/children; cars/bicycles are charged f50/6.50.

Vlieland & Terschelling

Both connected by ferry to the mainland town of Harlingen, Vlieland is one of the two car-free isles, while Terschelling is the group's longest. A popular family island, Vlieland has one village: Oost-Vlieland; its western sister drowned in the 1700s. The VVV (☎ 45 11 11) is on Havenweg 10.

Thirty-km-long Terschelling is known as a good-time isle but it also has some stunning scenery and is great for biking. Its main village is West-Terschelling, where the VVV (☎ 44 30

00) is at Willem Barentszkade 19 opposite the ferry terminal.

The telephone code for Vlieland and Terschelling is ☎ 0562.

Places to Stay On Vlieland there's *De Stortemelk* camping ground (☎ 45 12 25) at Kampweg 1, while the 'cheapest' hotel is *De Herbergh van Flielant* (☎ 45 14 00) at Dorpsstraat 105 with doubles for f130.

On Terschelling, *Dellewal* camping ground (☎ 44 26 02) is next to the *NJHC hostel* (☎ -44 31 15) on Burg van Heusdenweg 39. On the same road, *Dellewal Hotel* (☎ 44 23 05) at No 42 charges f55 per person. In the town centre, *Hotel NAP* (☎ 44 32 10) at Torenstraat 50 has stunning rooms from f115/150 a single/double.

Getting There & Away Twice-hourly trains run from Leeuwarden to Harlingen (f8, 25 minutes) where three boats a day (in summer) make the 1¾-hour voyage to Vlieland; two do so in winter. A return costs f39.40/19.70/16.70 for adults/children/bicycles. The trip to Terschelling takes the same time and costs the same – cars can be taken but that's expensive. There's also a faster ferry – twice a day to Terschelling and once daily to Vlieland – which costs f7.50 extra each way and takes 45 minutes.

Ameland

Ameland has no real notable features except its quaint villages and the number of tourists who explode onto the scene in summer. There are four villages; the main one, Nes, is home to the VVV (☎ 0519-54 20 20) at Rixt van Doniaweg 2.

The telephone code for Ameland is ☎ 0519.

Places to Stay At Nes, there's *Camping Duinoord* (☎ 54 20 70) at Jan van Eijckweg 4. The *NJHC hostel* (☎ 55 41 33) is at Oranjeweg 59 near the lighthouse at Hollum – get bus No 130 from Nes. The *Hotel de Jong* (☎ 54 20 16) across from the VVV in Nes has singles/doubles from f57/120. In the quieter village of Ballum, the *Hotel Nobel* (☎ 55 41 57) at Kosterweg 16 has rooms for f70/140.

Getting There & Away From Leeuwarden, take bus No 66 to the port at Holwerd; from Groningen it's bus No 34. On weekdays there are six boats a day, weekends four. Returns cost f18.80/9.90/8.90 for adults/children/bikes, and cars start at f99 (in winter, all prices are slightly cheaper). The journey takes 45 minutes.

Schiermonnikoog

With one of the nation's most tongue-tying names, Schiermonnikoog is the smallest island, off limits to cars. In the only village, about three km from the ferry terminus, you'll find the VVV (☎ 53 12 33) at Reeweg 5.

The telephone code for Schiermonnikoog is ☎ 0519.

Places to Stay Any bus will drop you at the *NJHC hostel* (☎ 53 12 57) at Knuppeldam 2. Alternatively, there's *Seedune* camping (☎ 53 13 98) at Seeduneweg 1, or *Hotel Zonneweelde* (☎ 53 11 33) at Langestreek 94 with singles/doubles for f75/150.

Getting There & Away There are four ferries on weekdays (fewer on weekends) from the village of Lauwersoog, between Leeuwarden and Groningen. To get there from Leeuwarden, take bus No 50; from Groningen, bus No 63. The voyage takes 45 minutes each way and return tickets cost f18.30/9.90/8.40 for adults/children/bikes (in winter, fares are a few guilders cheaper).

The South-East

Sprinkled with woods, heather and the odd incline, the Netherlands' south-eastern corner is a world apart from everything up north. Best described in art terms, it's the Burgundian Netherlands of Hieronymus Bosch and Pieter Paul Rubens (the latter from neighbouring Antwerp), rather than the Netherlands which inspired northerners like Frans Hals and Rembrandt. Made up of the North Brabant and Limburg provinces, its two main towns, Den Bosch and Maastricht, are intimate and energetic, and easily able to win you to the ways of the south.

DEN BOSCH

Capital of the province of North Brabant, Den Bosch (officially known as 's-Hertogenbosch,

'The Count's Forest') has several rich museums and many decorative gables. As for the name, it's the townsfolk of long ago you can thank for shortening it from the official version to the more pronounceable Den Bosch.

Orientation & Information

The town's pedestrianised centre is based around the Markt, a 10-minute walk east of the train station. To get there, head straight up Stationsweg and along Visstraat; at the end, turn right into Hogesteenweg which leads down to the Markt, on the way passing the town's oldest building, now home to the VVV (☎ 06-91 12 23 34) at Markt 77. It's open weekdays from 9 am to 5.30 pm, Saturday to 4 pm.

The telephone code for Den Bosch is ☎ 073.

Things to See

The **Noordbrabants Museum**, housed in the former governor's residence at Verwersstraat 41, features exhibits about Brabant life and art from earlier times. It's open Tuesday to Friday from 10 am to 5 pm, weekends from noon.

The other main attraction is **St Jan's Cathedral**, one of the most ornate churches in the Netherlands. It's a few minutes walk from the Markt at the end of Kerkstraat, the main shopping thoroughfare.

Places to Stay & Eat

Regional camping grounds are profuse. One of the closest is *De Wildhorst* (☎ 0413-29 14 66) at Meerstraat 30 in Heeswijk-Dinther about 12 km to the south-east. It's open all year; take bus No 158 to the church at Heeswijk and then it's two km.

As for hotels, the *Terminus* (☎ 613 06 66) at Stationsplein 19 next to the station has decent singles/doubles from f45/85 (closed Sunday). One block east of the Markt, *Hotel All In* (☎ 613 40 57) at Gasselstraat 1 has rooms for f45/75, but it's rougher around the edges and breakfast is f10 extra. Note the gold elephant gable across the street.

There's no shortage of atmospheric cafés and restaurants – try Korte Putstraat or Molenstraat. At No 4 on the latter is *Van Puffelen* (☎ 689 04 14), a spacious eetcafé (closed Monday) with good-value local cuisine.

Getting There & Away

Den Bosch's new train station should be finished by the end of 1997. Trains run regularly to Amsterdam (f21.75, one hour) via Utrecht (f12.25, 30 minutes), and to Arnhem (f16, 45 minutes) and Maastricht (f31, 1½ hours).

MAASTRICHT

The Netherlands' oldest city, Maastricht sits at the bottom end of the thin finger of land which juts down between Belgium and Germany – and which is influenced by them both. Capital of the largely Catholic Limburg province, its history stretches back to 50 BC when the Romans set up camp on the bank of the River Meuse.

Today spanning both banks, this lively city with its small student population has a reputation even in its own country as being something a little 'foreign'. For here you can pay for a beer in Belgian francs or German marks; you can sample the distinct tastes of neighbouring cuisines; and, before Lent, party with the rest of the revellers in the Netherlands' largest carnival festival.

Orientation & Information

The west bank of the Meuse is the city's main hub. Here you'll find the old, now largely pedestrianised, centre with its trendy Stokstraat quarter. On the east bank there's the Wyck, an area of 17th-century houses and intimate cafés and bars. To the south of the Wyck a new commercial area, Céramique, is being developed on a site long occupied by the pottery industry.

The main post office is at Grote Staat 5. There's a laundry just up from the Markt at Boschstraat 82, open weekdays from 8.30 am to 5 pm.

Maastricht's telephone code is ☎ 043.

Tourist Office The VVV (☎ 325 21 21) is housed in Het Dinghuis ('The Thing House') on the corner of Kleine Staat and Jodenstraat. It's open Monday to Saturday from 9 am to 5

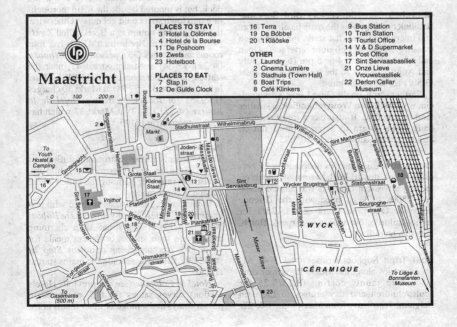

Maastricht

PLACES TO STAY
3 Hotel la Colombe
4 Hotel de la Bourse
11 De Poshoorn
18 Zwets
23 Hotelboot

PLACES TO EAT
7 Stap In
12 De Guide Clock

16 Terra
19 De Böbbel
20 't Kläöske

OTHER
1 Laundry
2 Cinema Lumière
5 Stadhuis (Town Hall)
6 Boat Trips
8 Café Klinkers

9 Bus Station
10 Train Station
13 Tourist Office
14 V & D Supermarket
15 Post Office
17 Sint Servaasbasiliek
21 Onze Lieve
   Vrouwebasiliek
22 Derlon Cellar
   Museum

0   100   200 m

or 6 pm. From May to October, it's also open on Sundays from 11 am to 3 pm.

Money The GWK office at the train station is open daily from 8 am to 9 pm.

Things to See & Do
The VVV has a brochure on a walk around the fortification walls which still partly surround the city.

Museums The premier museum, **Bonnefanten**, occupies a new purpose-built complex at Ave Céramique 250 in Céramique. The museum features art and architecture from the Limburg area, and is open Tuesday to Sunday from 11 am to 5 pm. Admission costs f10/7.50 for adults/children. Take bus No 5 or 8 from the Markt.

For a glimpse of life in Maastricht in Roman times, there's the **Derlon Cellar Museum** in the basement of the Derlon Hotel at Plankstraat 21. Opening hours are limited: Sunday from noon to 4 pm only; admission is free.

Churches The 10th-century **Sint Servaasbasiliek** on Vrijthof is the main basilica – large and internally somewhat stark, but with a rich treasure house of religious artefacts. Open daily from 10 am to 4 or 5 pm (6 pm in July and August), entry to the treasure trove costs f3.50/1 for adults/children.

Further south, on the Onze Lieve Vrouweplein, is **Onze Lieve Vrouwebasiliek**, a smaller Gothic structure. It also has a treasury, open daily from 11 am to 5 pm (from 1 pm on Sunday); admission costs f5.50/3.25.

Casemates Eight metres deep and lit by kerosine lamps, this 10-km labyrinth of tunnels on the city's western outskirts was started in the late 1500s to keep pace with the defence network. One-hour tours cost f5.25/3 for adults/children, but unless you speak Dutch, they can be dull.

Boat Trips Stiphout Cruises (☎ 325 41 51) operates trips along the Meuse River including 50-minute jaunts costing f8.75/5.25 for adults/children and day cruises to Liège in Belgium. Trips leave from Maaspromenade 27.

Places to Stay
There's a small range of averagely priced hotels, but book ahead around carnival and in summer.

Camping The closest camp site is the five-star *De Dousberg* (☎ 343 21 71) at Dousbergweg 102, one km from the hostel (to get there, see the following Hostels section). It's open from 1 March to 31 October, and there's an on-site restaurant serving reasonably-priced meals.

Hostels Part of a sporting complex, the *NJHC hostel* (☎ 346 67 77) is at Dousbergweg 4, about six km from the train station. Bus No 8 (two per hour, last bus 5.30 pm) runs to the front door (providing you tell the driver your destination). At night time, Call-Bus No 17 will get you there. It charges f28 for a bed in a dorm, or f66 for a double room – check in after 3 pm.

Hotels Just downstream from the centre is the *Hotelboot* (☎ 321 90 23) at Maasboulevard 95. It has singles/doubles from f55/75 and a sun deck, but is moored beside the main thoroughfare into town so it could get noisy. Otherwise, the best central option is a B&B called *Zwets* (☎ 321 64 82) at Bredestraat 41. It has four rooms and charges f35 a person. *De Poshoorn* (☎ 321 73 34) at Stationsstraat 47, near the station, has decent rooms from f110/135. *Hotel la Colombe* (☎ 321 57 74) at Markt 30 charges f135/155 for rooms, or there's *Hotel de la Bourse* (☎ 321 81 12) at Markt 37 which has double rooms from f105.

Places to Eat
Thanks mainly to the gastronomic influences of its Belgian and German neighbours, Maastricht ranks high among the Dutch where cuisine is concerned.

In the centre, Platielstraat is lined with restaurants and cafés. Nearby, there's *De Bóbbel* (☎ 321 74 13) at Wolfstraat 32, a charming brown café with snacks or decent meals for about f10. Another cheap option is *Stap In* (☎ 321 97 10) at Kesselkade 61; mains start at f12.50.

Hotel la Colombe (see the previous Hotels section) serves satays for f16, or there are pricier satays and a range of other meals at *De*

Gulde Clock (☎ 325 27 09), Wycker Brugstraat 54.

If you're dying to splurge on local cuisine, *'t Klääöske* (☎ 321 81 18) at Plankstraat 20 has sumptuous mains starting from f25. The tranquil *Terra* (☎ 325 54 13) at Brusselsestraat 47 is a vegetarian restaurant with a dagschotel for f17.50 (closed Monday).

For self-caterers, there's a *V & D* supermarket on Kleine Staat.

Entertainment

If the weather's good, Vrijthof and Onze Lieve Vrouweplein are taken over by people-watching terrace cafés. Alternatively, you can cross the river to Rechtstraat where there are several cosy cafés including *Klinkers* at No 12 and *Take One* at No 28. *Cinema Lumière* (☎ 321 40 80) at Bogaardenstraat 40 screens non-mainstream films.

Getting There & Away

Within the Netherlands, major train lines include those to Amsterdam (f47.25, 2½ hours) and Den Bosch (f31, 1½ hours). Major international connections include those to Liège in Belgium (f8.60, 30 minutes, one train per hour), Cologne in Germany (f34.80, 1½ hours, every two hours), and Luxembourg City (f48.60, three hours, every two hours). For national information call ☎ 06-92 92; for international information call ☎ 325 62 70.

Getting Around

City Bus (☎ 329 25 74) buses run the local routes as do Call-Buses (☎ 329 25 66), minibuses which must be booked by telephone an hour in advance and which usually run in the evening when there's less demand. There are also VOM-taxis (☎ 362 22 22), share taxis which operate from 8.30 am to 11.30 pm and are cheaper than normal taxis. The main bus station is next to the train station. Bikes can be hired at the Rijwiel shop to the left out of the train station.

Portugal

Spirited yet unassuming, Portugal has a dusty patina of faded grandeur; the quiet remains of a far-flung colonialist realm. Even as it flows towards the economic mainstream of the European Union (EU), it still seems to gaze over its shoulder and out to sea.

For visitors, this far side of Europe offers more than beaches and port wine. Beyond the crowded Algarve, one finds wide appeal: a simple but hearty cuisine based on seafood and lingering conversation, an enticing architectural blend that wanders from the Moorish to Manueline to surrealist styles, and a changing landscape that occasionally lapses into impressionism. Like the *emigrantes*, economically inspired Portuguese vagabonds who eventually find their way back to their roots, *estrangeiros*, or foreigners, who have had a taste of the real Portugal can only be expected to return.

Facts about the Country

HISTORY

The early history of Portugal goes back to the Celts who settled the Iberian Peninsula around 700 BC. A subsequent pattern of invasion and reinvasion was established by the Phoenicians, Greeks, Romans and Visigoths in succession.

In the 8th century, the Moors crossed the Strait of Gibraltar and commenced a long occupation which introduced their culture, architecture and agricultural techniques to Portugal. Resistance to the Moors culminated in their ejection during the 12th century.

In the 15th century, Portugal entered a phase of conquest and discovery under the rule of Henry the Navigator. Famous explorers such as Vasco da Gama, Ferdinand Magellan and Bartolomeu Diaz set off to discover new trade routes and assisted in creating a huge empire that, at its peak, extended to India, the Far East, Brazil and Africa.

This period of immense power and wealth faded towards the end of the 16th century when Spain occupied Portugal. Although the Portuguese regained their country within a few decades, the momentum of the empire steadily declined over the following centuries.

At the close of the 18th century, Napoleon sent several expeditions to invade Portugal but he was eventually trounced by the troops of the Anglo-Portuguese alliance.

During the 19th century, Portugal's economy fell apart. There was a general muddle of civil war and political mayhem which culminated in the abolition of the monarchy in 1910 and the founding of a democratic republic.

The democratic phase was brief, lasting until a military coup in 1926 set the stage for a long period of dictatorship under Antonio de Oliveira Salazar, who clung tenaciously to power until 1968 when he died after falling off a chair! General dissatisfaction with the repressive regime and a pointless and ruinous colonial war in Africa led to the Revolution of the Carnations, a peaceful military coup on 25 April 1974.

During the 1970s and early 1980s, Portugal

Portugal

0   50   100 km

went through some painful adjustments: the political scene was marked by extreme swings between right and left, and the economy suffered from strikes over government versus private ownership. The granting of independence to Portugal's African colonies in 1974-75 resulted in a flood of nearly a million refugees into the country. Entry into the EU in 1986 secured a measure of stability, buttressed by the acceptance of Portugal as a full member of the European Monetary System in 1992.

Although EU membership has given a tremendous boost to Portugal's development and modernisation, the 1990s have been troubled by recession, rising unemployment, and continuing backwardness in the agricultural and educational sectors. In the 1995 elections, the electorate showed its dissatisfaction with the scandal-tainted Social Democrat Party by switching back to socialism after 10 years of conservatism.

The next big dates on the country's calendar are the Lisbon Expo in 1998 which is expected to attract eight million visitors (and coincide with the opening of the new 12 km Vasco da Gama bridge across the Tejo), and the difficult goal of European monetary union in 1999.

GEOGRAPHY & ECOLOGY

Portugal is one of Europe's smaller countries – approximately twice the size of Switzerland. From north to south it's 560 km and from east to west, 220 km.

The northern and central regions are densely populated, particularly near the coast. The inland region is characterised by lush vegetation and mountains; the highest range is the Serra da Estrela, peaking at Torre (1993 metres). The south is less populated and, apart from the mountainous backdrop of the Algarve, much flatter and drier.

Portugal has one international-standard national park (70,290-hectare Peneda-Gerês), 10 *parques naturals* (natural parks) (of which the biggest and best known is 101,060-hectare Serra da Estrela), eight nature reserves and three other protected areas. The government's Instituto da Conservação da Natureza (ICN) manages all of them; its information office (☎ 01-352 3317) at Rua Ferreira Lapa 29-A, Lisbon, provides maps and information, though each park has its own information centre as well.

GOVERNMENT & POLITICS

Portugal has a Western-style democracy based on the Assembleia da República, a single-chamber parliament with 230 members and an elected president. The two main parties are the ruling Socialist Party (Partido Socialista or PS) and the opposition right-of-centre Social Democratic Party (Partido Social Democrata or PSD). There are several other parties, including the United Democratic Coalition (CDU), which links the Communist Party with the Greens (Partido Ecologista Os Verdes or PEV). The Greens are occasionally referred to as 'watermelons' – green on the outside and red on the inside!

The general election of October 1995 saw the ousting of the PSD after 10 years of rule and the return to power of the Socialist Party. The 46-year-old prime minister, António Guterres, has reassured many by expressing a strong commitment to budgetary discipline and to European monetary unification but it remains to be seen whether he can fulfil his promise to improve health care and education.

ECONOMY

After severe economic problems and rampant inflation in the 1980s, Portugal has tamed the inflation rate to around 4%. The tight grip of state ownership has been relaxed and privatisation continues to accelerate, even under the new socialist government. Agriculture plays a decreasing role in the economy as services (such as real estate, banking and tourism) and industry take over. In addition, Portugal looks set to benefit from its low labour costs, young population (nearly a quarter of the population is under 15 years old), and traditional trading links with South America and Africa. EU membership has led to dramatic changes: the EU provides vital funding (a stunning US$12.8 million a day for the rest of the century) which has already helped to improve the country's infrastructure. However, competition from within the single European market, and a massive budget deficit, are beginning to sour the EU honeymoon.

POPULATION & PEOPLE

Portugal's population of 10.6 million does not include an estimated three million Portuguese living abroad as migrant workers.

PORTUGAL

ARTS

Music

The best-known form of Portuguese music is the melancholy, nostalgic *fado*, songs popularly considered to have originated with the yearnings of 16th-century sailors. Much of what is offered in tourist shows in Lisbon is overpriced and far from authentic. Amália Rodrigues is *the* star of Portuguese fado; her recordings can be bought in most record shops in Portugal.

Literature

During the 16th century, Gil Vicente, who excelled at farces and religious dramas, set the stage for Portugal's dramatic tradition. Later in the same century, Luís de Camões wrote *Os Lusíadas*, an epic poem celebrating the age of discovery and exploration. He is now considered the national poet of Portugal. The romantic dramatist Almeida Garrett was one of Portugal's leading literary figures during the 19th century, while Fernando Pessoa is arguably the finest Portuguese poet and dramatist to emerge this century and one of the few contemporary Portuguese writers to be widely read abroad.

For a look at Portuguese literature in translation, try Camões' *The Lusiads* and works by Eça de Queiroz *(The Maias)*, Fernando Pessoa *(Selected Poems)*, Fernando Namora *(Mountain Doctor)* and Mario Braga. For a recent Portuguese 'whodunit' – close to the political bone – pick up *The Ballad of Dog's Beach* (Dent, 1986) by José Cardoso Pires.

Architecture

Of special interest is the development during the 16th century of Manueline architecture, named after King Manuel I (1495-1521). The style represents the zest for discovery during that era and is characterised by the use of boisterous twists and spirals as columns, and nautical themes for decoration.

Crafts

The most striking Portuguese craft is the making of decorative tiles known as *azulejos*, a technique learnt in the 15th century from the Moors. Today, superb examples of this craft are to be seen all over Portugal. Lisbon has its own azulejos museum.

CULTURE

Despite growing prosperity and influences from abroad, the Portuguese are keeping a firm grip on their culture. Traditional folk dancing is still the pride of villages throughout the land, and local festivals are celebrated with gusto. Soccer is one modern element now ingrained in male Portuguese life – watching matches on TV ensures the continuation of the traditional long lunch break.

The Portuguese are famous for their friendliness, but they're also fairly conservative: you'll endear yourself to them more quickly if you avoid looking too outlandish and if you greet and thank them in Portuguese. Skimpy beachwear is tolerated at beach resorts, but shorts (and hats) are considered very offensive inside churches.

RELIGION

The Portuguese population is 99% Roman Catholic. The Protestant community numbers less than 120,000 and there are approximately 5000 Jews.

LANGUAGE

Like French, Italian, Spanish and Romanian, Portuguese is a Romance language, closely derived from Latin. It is spoken by more than 10 million people in Portugal, 130 million in Brazil, and is also the official language of five African nations. In large cities such as Porto and Lisbon, it's easy to find Portuguese who speak English, but in remoter areas few locals speak foreign languages, unless they are returned emigrants. See the Language Guide at the back of the book for pronunciation guidelines and useful words and phrases.

Facts for the Visitor

PLANNING

Climate & When to Go

Portugal's climate is temperate; it's only searingly hot in midsummer in the Algarve and Alentejo. The tourist season in the Algarve lasts from late February to November. Peak season extends from June to September; prices for accommodation and museums outside peak season can be discounted by as much as 50%. Prices in this chapter are for peak season.

During winter, the north receives plenty of rain, and temperatures can be chilly. Snowfall is common in the mountains, particularly the Serra da Estrela, which has basic ski facilities. Tourist season in the north extends from approximately May to September.

You can take advantage of fewer crowds, seasonal discounts and spectacular foliage in spring (late March and April) and late summer (September and early October).

Books & Maps
They Went to Portugal and *They Went to Portugal Too* by Rose Macaulay follow the experiences of a wide variety of visitors from medieval times to the 19th century. For a general overview of Portugal and its place in the modern world try *The Portuguese: The Land and Its People* by Marion Kaplan.

The Michelin map of Portugal is accurate and extremely useful even if you are not using a car. The maps produced by the Automóvel Club de Portugal (ACP) provide slightly more up-to-date, but less detailed, coverage.

Walkers should pack the *Landscapes of Portugal* series (Sunflower Books, UK) by Brian & Aileen Anderson, with both car tours and walks in various regions, including the Algarve, Sintra/Estoril and the Costa Verde. More detailed is *Walking in Portugal* by Bethan Davies & Ben Cole.

Military and civilian topographic maps of Portugal are sold at the Porto Editora bookshop (☎ 02-200 7669), Rua da Fabrica 90, Porto. ICN (☎ 01-352 3317), Rua Ferreira Lapa 29-A, Lisbon, the state agency that administers national/natural parks, has a few maps. Better information is available at information offices in or near the parks, though little of it is in the kind of detail needed by trekkers.

SUGGESTED ITINERARIES
Depending on the length of your stay you might want to see the following places:

Two days
    Visit Lisbon.
One week
    Three days in Lisbon, two in Sintra, one in Óbidos and Nazaré.
Two weeks
    As above, plus the Algarve, including two days each in Tavira, Lagos and Sagres.

One month
    As above, plus three days each in Porto, Évora, Serra da Estrela Natural Park, Peneda-Gerês National Park, and two days in Castelo de Vide and Marvão.
Two months
    All of the above, but spending twice as long in each place.

HIGHLIGHTS
For scenery, you can't beat the wild mountain landscapes of the Serra da Estrela and Peneda-Gerês National Park. Architecture buffs should make a beeline for the monasteries at Belém and Batalha, and the palaces of Pena (in Sintra) and Buçaco. Combining the best of both worlds are Portugal's old walled towns such as Évora and Marvão, which are architectural gems surrounded by stunning scenery. Not to be missed in Lisbon is the Gulbenkian, a giant of a museum.

TOURIST OFFICES
Local Tourist Offices
Known as *postos de turismo* or *turismos*, local tourist offices are found throughout Portugal and will provide brochures and varying degrees of assistance.

Tourist Offices Abroad
Countries with Portuguese tourist offices operating under the administrative umbrella of ICEP (Investimentos, Comércio e Turismo de Portugal) include:

Canada
    Portuguese Trade & Tourism Office, 60 Bloor Street West, suite 1005, Toronto, Ont M4W 3B8 (☎ 416-921 7376)
Spain
    Oficina de Turismo de Portugal, Gran Via 27, 1st floor, 28013 Madrid (☎ 91-522 9354)
UK
    Portuguese Trade & Tourism Office, 22-25a Sackville St, London W1X 1DE (☎ 0171-494 1441)
USA
    Portuguese Trade & Tourism Office, 590 Fifth Ave, 4th floor, New York, NY 10036-4704 (☎ 212-354 4403)

There are ICEP offices in many other countries, including Austria, Belgium, France, Germany, Holland, Italy and Switzerland.

VISAS & EMBASSIES
Nationals of all EU countries, as well as those from Australia, Canada, Ireland, Israel, New

PORTUGAL

Zealand and the USA, can stay up to three months in any half-year without a visa. Some others, including nationals of South Africa and Singapore, need a visa and must produce evidence of financial responsibility, eg a fixed sum of money plus an additional amount per day of their stay (the amounts vary depending on nationality), unless they are the spouse or child of EU citizens.

Portugal is one of the signatories of the Schengen Convention on the abolition of mutual border controls (the others are Austria, Belgium, France, Germany, Greece, Italy, Luxembourg, Netherlands and Spain). You can apply for visas for more than one of these states on the same form, though a visa for one does not automatically grant you entry to the others.

Visa Extensions & Re-entry Visas

Outside Portugal, information is supplied by Portuguese consulates. Inside Portugal, contact the Foreigners' Registration Service (Serviço de Estrangeiros e Fronteiras), Avenida António Augusto de Aguiar 20, Lisbon (☎ 01-346 6141 or 01-352 3112), open 9 am to 3 pm on weekdays.

Portuguese Embassies Abroad

Australia
    23 Culgoa Circuit, O'Malley, ACT 2606 (☎ 06-290 1733)
Canada
    645 Island Park Drive, Ottawa, Ont K1Y 0B8 (☎ 613-729 0883)
Ireland
    Knock Sinna House, Knock Sinna, Fox Rock, Dublin 18 (☎ 01-289 4416)
Spain
    Calle del Pinar 1, Madrid 6 (☎ 91-261 7808)
UK
    62 Brompton Road, London SW3 1BJ (☎ 0171-581 3598; premium-rate recorded message ☎ 0891-600202; fax 0171-581 3085)
USA
    2125 Kalorama Rd NW, Washington, DC, 20008 (☎ 202-328 8610)

Foreign Embassies in Portugal

Foreign embassies in Lisbon include:

Canada
    Edifício MCB, Avenida da Liberdade 144 (☎ 01-347 4892)
France
    Calçada Marquês de Abrantes (☎ 01-395 6056)
Germany
    Campo do Mártires da Pátria 38 (☎ 01-352 3961)

Ireland
    Rua da Imprensa à Estrela 1 (☎ 01-396 1569)
Spain
    Rua do Salitre 1 (☎ 01-347 2381)
UK
    Rua de São Domingos à Lapa 37 (☎ 01-396 1191)
USA
    Avenida das Forças Armadas (☎ 01-726 6600)

There are no embassies for Australia or New Zealand in Portugal, but both countries have honorary consuls in Lisbon. Australian citizens can call ☎ 01-353 0750 on weekdays between 1 and 2 pm (the nearest Australian embassy is in Paris); New Zealand citizens should call ☎ 01-357 4134 during business hours (the nearest New Zealand embassy is in Rome).

CUSTOMS

There is no limit on the importation of currency. But if you leave with more than 100,000$00 in escudos or 500,000$00 in foreign currency you will have to prove that you brought in at least this much. The duty-free allowance for travellers from non-EU countries is 200 cigarettes (or 250g of tobacco or 50 cigars or 100 cigarillos); one litre of alcoholic beverage over 22% alcohol by volume or two litres of wine or beer. EU travellers can arrive loaded up with 800 cigarettes, plus 10 litres of spirits, 20 litres of apéritifs or sparkling wine, or a mind-boggling 90 litres of still wine or 110 litres of beer! Everyone can bring in enough coffee, tea etc for personal use.

MONEY

Portuguese banks can change most foreign currencies and travellers' cheques but charge a nasty commission of at least 2000$00, plus 140$00 government tax. Eurocheques often have a 500$00 commission charge. The best deals for travellers' cheques are at private exchange bureaus in Lisbon, Porto and popular tourist resorts: these often charge no commission, but their exchange rates are fairly low.

Better value (and more convenient) are the 24-hour Multibanco credit-card machines found at nearly all banks. There's a handling fee of about 1.5% included in the transaction and exchange rates are reasonable. Automatic exchange machines are found only in a few major cities.

Major credit cards are widely accepted – especially Visa and MasterCard.

Currency

The unit of Portuguese currency is the escudo, further divided into 100 centavos. Prices are usually written with a $ sign between escudos and centavos; eg 25 escudos 50 centavos is written 25$50.

There are 200$00, 100$00, 50$00, 20$00, 10$00, 5$00, 2$50 and 1$00 coins. Notes currently in circulation are 10,000$00, 5000$00, 2000$00, 1000$00 and 500$00. The Portuguese frequently refer to 1000$00 as a *conto*.

Exchange Rates

Australia	A$1	=	119$25
Canada	C$1	=	110$90
France	1FF	=	30$35
Germany	DM1	=	102$85
Japan	¥100	=	140$70
New Zealand	NZ$1	=	106$15
Spain	100 ptas	=	120$90
United Kingdom	UK£1	=	237$00
United States	US$1	=	152$15

Costs

Although costs are beginning to rise noticeably, Portugal is still one of the cheapest places to travel in Europe. On a rock-bottom budget – using hostels or camping grounds, and mostly self-catering – you can squeeze by with about US$25 a day. With bottom-end accommodation and the occasional inexpensive restaurant meal, daily costs will hover around US$30. Travelling with a companion and timing your trip to take advantage of off-season discounts (see the Climate & When to Go section), you can eat and sleep in style for around US$70 per day for two. Outside major tourist areas, prices dip appreciably.

Tipping & Bargaining

A reasonable restaurant tip is 5% to 10%. For just a snack at a *cervejaria*, *pastelaria* (see the Food section that follows) or café, a bit of loose change is sufficient. Taxi drivers appreciate 5% to 10% of the fare, and petrol station attendants 30$00 to 60$00.

Good-humoured bargaining is acceptable in markets but you'll find the Portuguese tough opponents! Off season, you can sometimes bargain down the price of accommodation.

Consumer Taxes

A 17% sales tax, called IVA, is levied on hotel and other accommodation, restaurant meals, car rental and some other bills.

If they are resident outside the EU, foreign tourists can claim an IVA refund on goods from shops which are members of Europe Tax-Free Shopping Portugal. The minimum purchase eligible for a refund at the time of research was 11,700$00 in any one shop. The shop assistant fills in a cheque for the amount of the refund (minus an administration fee). When you leave Portugal present the goods, the cheque and your passport at the tax-refund counter at customs for a cash, postal-note or credit-card refund. This service is presently available at the airports in Lisbon, Porto and Faro, and at Lisbon harbour (customs section). If you are leaving overland, contact customs at the last EU border point. Further details are available from Europe Tax-Free Shopping Portugal (☎ 01-840 8813) in the international departures concourse of Lisbon airport.

POST & COMMUNICATIONS
Post

Postal Rates Postcards and letters up to 20g cost 140$00 to destinations outside Europe, 98$00 to non-EU European destinations and 78$00 to EU destinations. For delivery to the USA or Australia, allow eight to 10 days; delivery times for destinations within Europe average four to six days.

Sending Mail If you're sending a parcel, 'economy air' (or surface airlift – SAL) costs about a third less than air mail, but usually arrives a week or so later. Printed matter is cheapest (and simplest) to send in batches of under two kg. Postal regulations for large parcels can tie both you and the counter clerk in knots. The post office at Praça dos Restauradores in Lisbon and the main post office in Porto are open into the evening and on weekends.

Receiving Mail Most major towns have a post office with *posta restante* service, but it can take time to find out exactly which post office feels responsible. A charge of 60$00 is levied for each item of mail received, at least in Lisbon and Porto.

Addresses Addresses in Portugal are written with the street name first, followed by the

PORTUGAL

building address and often a floor number with a ° symbol, eg 15-3°. An alphabetical tag on the address eg 2-A indicates an adjoining entrance or building. The tag R/C *(rés do chão)* means ground floor.

Telephone

The largest coin accepted by standard pay phones is 50$00, making these phones impractical for international calls. Local calls start at 20$00. Much more useful for both domestic and international calls are the increasingly common 'Credifones', which accept plastic cards available from newsagents, tobacconists and telephone offices. Credifone cards are currently in 875$00 or 2100$00 denominations. A separate TLP (Telefones de Lisboa e Porto) phonecard system is used in Lisbon and Porto as well.

Calls can be made from public telephones as well as booths in Portugal Telecom offices and post offices. International calls average 300$00 per minute to Europe; 450$00 per minute off-peak to Australia and the USA (600$00 per minute at peak times). Charges from private phones are about a third less than those from public phones. Calls from a hotel room are almost double the standard rate. It's generally cheapest to phone between 8 pm and 8 am and on weekends.

To call Portugal from abroad, dial the international access code, ☎ 351 (the country code for Portugal), the area code and the number. Important area codes include ☎ 01 (Lisbon) and ☎ 02 (Porto). From Portugal, the international access code is ☎ 00.

Fax

Post offices now operate a domestic and international fax service known as CORFAX, costing 1350$00 for the first page to Europe, North America or Australia.

E-mail

Telepac, Portugal's biggest Internet provider, has a public user's centre in Lisbon called Quiosque Internet (☎ 01-314 2527; e-mail email@telepac.pt), where you can plug into the net or send e-mail (but not receive it) for 125$00 per quarter-hour. It's open weekdays from 9 am to 5 pm in the Forum Picoas building beside Picoas metro station.

NEWSPAPERS & MAGAZINES

Major Portuguese-language newspapers include *Diário de Notícias*; the dailies *Público* and *Jornal de Notícias*; and the gossip tabloid *Correio da Manhã*, which may lack finesse but licks all the others for circulation. Weeklies include *O Independente* and *Expresso*. For entertainment listings, check the local dailies or the municipality's calendar of events (usually available at tourist offices).

English-language newspapers published in Portugal include *Portugal Post*, an English-language weekly which aims to serve all of Portugal; *The News*, 'Portugal's National English-Language Paper', which has various regional editions featuring relevant local news and classified pages; and the similar *APN* (Anglo-Portuguese News).

English-language newspapers and magazines from abroad are widely available in most major cities and tourist resorts.

RADIO & TV

Portuguese radio is represented by the state-owned stations *Antenna Um* and *Antenna Dois*, by *Rádio Renascença* and by a clutch of recently established local stations. *Rádio Difusão Portuguesa* transmits daily programmes to visitors in English and other languages. Portuguese TV has expanded from two state-run channels (RTP-1 or Canal 1, and RTP-2 or TV2) to include two private channels (SIC and TVI). Soaps (known as *telenovelas*) take up the lion's share of broadcasting time.

BBC World Service broadcasts can be picked up on 15.070 MHz shortwave.

PHOTOGRAPHY & VIDEO

It's best to take film and camera equipment with you, especially if you hanker after Kodachrome, which is generally not available or very expensive. Other brands of E6 slide film, as well as print film and video cassettes, are widely available for reasonable prices at franchised photo shops in larger towns. Print film processing is as fast and inexpensive as anywhere in Europe.

TIME

Portugal is GMT/UTC in winter and GMT/UTC plus one hour in summer. Clocks are set forward by an hour on the last Sunday in March and back on the last Sunday in October.

ELECTRICITY
Electricity is 220V, 50 Hz. Plugs are normally of the two-round-pin variety.

WEIGHTS & MEASURES
Portugal uses the metric system; decimals are indicated with commas and thousands with points.

LAUNDRY
You'll find *lavandarias* providing laundry services at reasonable cost all over the place, though it make take a day or two. Genuine self-service is rare – though in Lisbon and Porto some can do your wash in a few hours, as cheaply as doing it yourself. Expect to pay around 1500$00 for a 10-kg load.

TOILETS
When available (which isn't often), public toilets in towns are of the sit-down variety, generally clean, and usually free. Most people, however, go to the nearest café for a drink or pastry and take advantage of the facilities there.

HEALTH
There is little to worry about in Portugal. Avoid swimming on beaches which are not marked as safe – Atlantic currents are notoriously dangerous. Take the usual precautions against sunburn and sunstroke. If you are an EU national, make sure you get an E111 or similar form a few weeks before your departure; this entitles you to free emergency medical treatment in Portugal. Considering the relatively small investment required, travel insurance is advisable as a backup.

For minor health problems you can pop into a local chemist (just ask directions to a *farmácia*). For more serious problems, ask your embassy or the local tourist office to refer you to the nearest hospital with an English-speaking doctor. The number to dial in any emergency is ☎ 112.

WOMEN TRAVELLERS
Women travelling around Portugal on their own or in small groups may be accorded attention by males who have the curious habit of

hissing. The attention is wearisome, but generally unfocused and best ignored.

DISABLED TRAVELLERS
The Secretariado Nacional de Rehabilitação (☎ 01-793 6517; fax 01-796 5182), Avenida Conde de Valbom 63, Lisbon, publishes the Portuguese-language *Guia de Turismo* with sections on barrier-free accommodation, transport, shops, restaurants and sights in Portugal. It's only available at their offices.

A private agency called Turintegra, also called APTTO (Associação Portuguesa de Turismo Para Todos; ☎ & fax 01-859 5332), Praça Dr Fernando Amado, Lote 566-E, 1900 Lisbon, keeps a keener eye on developments and arranges holidays for disabled travellers. The public transport agencies of Lisbon, Coimbra and Porto offer dial-a-ride services at costs comparable to those of taxis.

DANGERS & ANNOYANCES
Crime against foreigners in Portugal usually involves pickpocketing, theft from cars or pilfering from camping grounds (though armed robberies are also on the increase), mostly in heavily touristed areas such as the Algarve, specific parts of Lisbon and a few other major cities. With the usual precautions (use a money belt or something similar and don't leave valuables in cars or tents) there is little cause for worry. For peace of mind take out travel insurance.

The national emergency number is ☎ 112, for police, fire and other emergencies anywhere in Portugal. For more routine police matters and direct access to the fire brigade there are also telephone numbers for each town or district.

BUSINESS HOURS
Most banks are open weekdays from 8.30 am to 3 pm. Most museums and other tourist attractions are open weekdays from 10 am to 5 pm but are often closed at lunchtime and all day Monday. Shopping hours generally extend from 9 am to 7 pm on weekdays, and from 9 am to 1 pm on Saturday. Lunch is given serious and lingering attention between noon and 3 pm.

PUBLIC HOLIDAYS & SPECIAL EVENTS
Public holidays in Portugal include New Year's Day, Carnival & Shrove Tuesday

(February/March), Good Friday, Anniversary of the Revolution (25 April), May Day, Corpus Christi (May), National Day (Camões Day; 10 June), Feast of the Assumption (15 August), Republic Day (5 October), All Saints' Day (1 November), Independence Day (1 December), Feast of the Immaculate Conception (8 December) and Christmas Day.

The most interesting cultural events in Portugal include:

Holy Week Festival
This is celebrated at Braga during Easter week and features a series of colourful processions of which the most famous is the Ecce Homo procession, featuring hundreds of barefoot penitents carrying torches.
Festas das Cruzes (Festival of the Crosses)
Held in Barcelos in May, this festival is noted for its processions, performances of folk music and dance, and exhibitions of regional handicrafts.
Feira Nacional da Agricultura (National Agricultural Fair)
In June, Santarém holds a grand country fair with bullfighting, folk singing and dancing.
Festa do Santo António (Festival of Saint Anthony)
This street festival is held in Lisbon (mainly in the Alfama district) on June 13.
Festas de São João (St John's Festival)
From 16 to 24 June, Porto parties – the night of the 23rd sees virtually all the townsfolk out on the streets amicably bashing each other over the head with leeks or plastic hammers.
Festas da Nossa Senhora da Agonia (Agonia Fair & Festival)
This is held in Viana do Castelo on the first Sunday after 15 August and is famed for its folk arts, parades, fireworks, and handicrafts fair.
Feira de São Martinho (National Horse Festival)
Equine enthusiasts will want to gallop off to Golegã between 3 and 11 November to see all manner of horses, riding contests and bullfights.

ACTIVITIES
Hiking & Pony Trekking
Despite some magnificent rambling country, walking ranks low among Portuguese passions: there are no national walking clubs or official cross-country trails, though some parks are establishing trails (see Serra da Estrela in the Central Portugal section and Peneda-Gerês in the North section). See Information under Lisbon, Évora and Serra da Estrela in the Central Portugal section, and Peneda-Gerês in the North section, for some local outfits specialising in walking and pony treks.

Water Sports
Water sports popular in Portugal include white-water rafting, water-skiing, surfing, windsurfing and motorised and unmotorised boating. For local specialists in these sports see Information under Lagos and Sagres in the Algarve section and Peneda-Gerês in the North section.

Canyoning & Hydrospeed
Canyoning is a relatively new adventure sport which involves tackling every possible outdoor challenge offered by a canyon: swimming, trekking, abseiling and rock climbing. Hydrospeed is a version of white-water boating, without the boat. A few agencies offer these high-adrenalin activities, including Trilhos (see Information under Porto).

Multi-Activity & Adventure Programmes
Movijovem, the country's central booking office for Hostelling International (see Lisbon), organises adventure holidays in Portugal for 16 to 26-year-olds, which include rafting, caving and horse riding. TurAventur (see Évora) offers walking, biking and jeep trips across the plains of the Alentejo. Montes d'Aventura and Trote-Gerês (see Peneda-Gerês) can organise trekking, horse riding, canoeing, cycling and combination trips in the Peneda-Gerês National Park.

For the full range of available sports, ask the National Tourist Office for its brochure.

ACCOMMODATION
Most local tourist offices have lists of accommodation to suit a wide range of budgets and they can help you locate and book it. Although the government uses one to five stars to grade some types of accommodation, the criteria seem erratic. For a room with a double bed, ask for a *quarto de casal*; for twin beds, ask for a *duplo*; and for a single room, ask for a *quarto individual*.

Camping
Camping is widespread and popular in Portugal, and easily the cheapest option. The *Roteiro Campista* (1500$00), published annually in March and sold in most large bookshops, is an excellent multilingual guide with details of camping grounds in Portugal and regulations for camping outside these sites. Depending on

the facilities and the season, prices per night run at about 500$00 to 600$00 for an adult (or child over 10 years old), plus 400$00 to 500$00 for a car and the same again for a small tent. Considerably lower prices apply in less touristed regions and in the low season.

Hostels

Portugal has a network of 20 youth hostels, called *pousadas de juventude*, part of the Hostelling International (HI) system. Low rates are offset by restrictions including a midnight curfew and exclusion from the hostel for part of the day at most (but not all) of them. Prices are higher for popular hostels, particularly Lisbon's, but for most others a dorm bed costs 1200$00 to 1400$00 in the low season and 1450$00 to 1600$00 in the high season. Some hostels also offer private doubles from 2200$00 to 3700$00 per room per night. Breakfast is included in the price; lunch or dinner costs 950$00 more.

Demand is high, so advance reservations (for which you are charged 1000$00) are essential. If you don't already have a card from your national hostel association, you can get an HI membership by paying an extra 400$00 each (and having a 'guest card' stamped) at the first six hostels you stay at. For more information, contact Movijovem (☎ 01-355 9081; fax 01-352 8621), Avenida Duque d'Ávila 137, 1000 Lisbon – Portugal's central HI reservations office, where you can book hostels anywhere in Portugal or abroad.

Cheap Rooms

Another cheap option is a *quarto particular* (private room), or *quarto*, usually just a room in a private house. Home-owners may approach you in the street or at the bus or train station; otherwise watch for 'quartos' signs. Tourist offices sometimes have relevant lists. The rooms are usually clean, cheap (around 3500$00 a double) and free from the restrictions of hostels, and the owners can be interesting characters. A more commercial variant is a *dormida* or rooming house, where doubles cost about 4000$00 in the high season. You may be able to bargain for less in the low season.

Guesthouses

The most common types of guesthouses, the Portuguese equivalent of B&Bs, are the *residencial* and the *pensão* (plural *pensões*). Both are graded from one to three stars, and the top-rated establishments are often cheaper and better-run than some hotels clinging to their last star(s). During the high season, rates for a double in the cheapest pensão start at around 4500$00; expect to pay slightly more for a residencial, where breakfast is normally included in the price. There are often cheaper rooms with communal bathrooms. During the low season, rates drop by at least a third.

Hotels

Hotels are graded from one to five stars. For a double in high season you'll pay between 15,000$00 and 30,000$00 at the top end and around 9000$00 to 12,000$00 at the low end. In the same category, but more like up-market inns, are the *estalagem* and *albergaria*. In the low season, prices drop spectacularly, with a double in a spiffy four-star hotel for as little as 8000$00. Breakfast is usually included.

Other Accommodation

There is a wide selection of other opulent accommodation. *Pousadas* are government-run former castles, monasteries or palaces, often in spectacular locations. Details are available from tourist offices.

Private counterparts of pousadas are mostly operated under a scheme called Turismo de Habitação ('Turihab') and smaller schemes called Turismo Rural and Agroturismo, which allow you to stay in anything from a farmhouse to a mansion as the guest of the owner. Some also have self-catering cottages. A hefty book, *Turismo no Espaço Rural*, describing most of the available places, is available for about 2800$00 from Turismo de Habitação, Praça da República 4990, Ponte de Lima (☎ 058-741 672; fax 058-741444), from the Lisbon tourist office or from Portuguese national tourist offices abroad.

Prices usually include breakfast and are graded by quality and season. For a double in high season you will pay a minimum of 14,500$00 in a pousada, and 11,500$00 in a manor house belonging to the Turihab scheme. In low season, prices drop by as much as 50% and you can literally stay in a palace for the price of an average B&B elsewhere in Europe.

PORTUGAL

FOOD

Eating and drinking get serious attention in Portugal, where hearty portions and excellent value for money are the norm. Portugal has solidly ignored the fast-food era in favour of leisurely dining and devotion to wholesome ingredients.

The line between snacks and full-scale meals is blurred. Bars and cafés often sell snacks or even offer a small menu. For full-scale meals try a *casa do pasto* (a simple and cheap eatery, most popular at lunchtimes), a *restaurante*, a *cervejaria* (a type of bar and restaurant), or a *marisqueira* (a restaurant with an emphasis on seafood). The *prato do dia* (dish of the day) is often an excellent deal at around 700$00. In more touristed regions, restaurants may advertise an *ementa turística* (tourist menu). In contrast to the prato do dia, these are not real bargains.

The titbits offered at the start of a meal, known as the *couvert*, often include bread rolls, cheese and butter; you will be charged additionally for this. A full portion, ample for two decent appetites, is a *dose*; or you can ask for a *meia dose* (half-portion) usually about a third cheaper. Lunchtime moves at a leisurely pace from noon to 3 pm; evening meals are taken between 7 and 10.30 pm.

Snacks

Typical snacks include *sandes* (sandwiches), *prego em pão* (a slab of meat with egg sandwiched in a roll), *pastéis de bacalhau* (cod fish cakes), and *tosta mista* (a toasted cheese and ham sandwich). Prices start at around 250$00. Soups are also cheap and filling.

Main Dishes

Seafood in Portugal offers exceptional value, especially fish dishes such as *linguado grelhado* (grilled sole), *bife de atúm* (tuna steak), and the omnipresent *bacalhau* (cod) cooked in dozens of different ways. Meat is hit-and-miss, but worth sampling are *presunto* (ham); lamb, usually roasted, and known as *borrego* by the gourmets of Alentejo; and *cabrito* (kid). Prices for main dishes start at around 900$00.

Desserts & Cheeses

In most cafés and *pastelarias* (pastry shops), you can gorge yourself on some of the sweetest desserts *(sobremesas)* and cakes *(bolos)* imaginable. Cheeses from Serra da Estrela, Serpa and the Azores are also worth sampling but relatively expensive at about 2300$00 a kg.

Self-Catering

The lively local markets offer excellent fresh seafood, vegetables and fruit. Go early to get the best choice.

DRINKS

Nonalcoholic Drinks

Surprisingly, fresh fruit juices are a rarity. Mineral water *(água mineral)* is excellent, either carbonated *(com gás)* or still *(sem gás)*.

Coffee is a hallowed institution with its own convoluted nomenclature. A small black espresso is usually called a *bica*. For coffee with lots of milk, ask for a *galão*. In the north, half coffee and half milk is a *meia de leite*; elsewhere, it's a *café com leite*. Tea *(chá)* comes with lemon *(com limão)* or with milk *(com leite)*.

Alcohol

Local brands of beer *(cerveja)* include Sagres, Super Bock and Tuborg (produced under licence). To order draught beer, ask for a *fino* or an Imperial.

Portuguese wine *(vinho)* offers excellent value in all its varieties: mature red *(tinto)*, white *(branco)* and semi-sparkling young *(vinho verde)*, which is usually white but occasionally red. Restaurants often have *vinho da casa* (house wine) for as little as 250$00 for a 350-ml bottle or jug, though for less than 800$00 you can buy a bottle to please the most discerning taste buds.

Port, synonymous with Portugal, is produced in the Douro Valley near Porto and drunk in three forms: ruby, tawny and white. Dry white port with sardines makes a memorable feast. Local brandy *(aguardente)* is also worth a try. For some rough stuff that tries hard to destroy your throat, ask for a *bagaço* (grape marc). Most bartenders in Portugal have the pleasant habit of serving large measures: a single brandy often contains the equivalent of a triple in the UK or the USA.

ENTERTAINMENT

Cinemas are inexpensive – around 700$00 a ticket – and prices are often reduced once a week in a bid to lure audiences from their home videos. Foreign films are normally shown in the original language with Portuguese subtitles.

For dance, music (rock, jazz and classical) and other cultural events, ask at the tourist offices or pick up a copy of the local newspaper for listings.

Discos abound in Lisbon, Porto and the Algarve (where the town of Albufeira has a reputation as Portugal's hot spot).

Perhaps the most original forms of entertainment are the local festivals (see the earlier Public Holidays & Special Events section).

SPECTATOR SPORT

Football (soccer) dominates the sporting scene – literally everything stops for a big match. The season lasts from August to May and almost every village and town finds enough players for a team. The three main teams are Benfica and Sporting in Lisbon, and FC Porto in Porto. Ask at the tourist office about forthcoming matches.

Bullfighting is still popular in Portugal, despite pressure from international animal-rights activists. If you want to see a *tourada*, the season runs from late April to October. The rules for the Portuguese version of bullfighting prohibit a public kill, though the hapless beast must often be dispatched in private afterwards. In Lisbon, bullfights are held at the Campo Pequeno on Thursday. Ribatejo is the region where most bulls are bred; major fights are staged in Vila Franca de Xira and Santarém.

THINGS TO BUY

Leather goods, especially shoes and bags, are good value, as are textiles such as lace and embroidered linen. Handicrafts range from inexpensive pottery and basketwork to substantial purchases like rugs from Arraiolos, filigree gold or silver jewellery, and sets of azulejos made to order.

Getting There & Away

AIR

British Airways and TAP (Air Portugal) have direct flights between London and Lisbon.

They also provide direct services to Porto and Faro. Fare categories are extremely complicated and seem to change every six months.

A discounted London-Lisbon return fare is about £130 in low season, or about £200 to £240 in high season. It's sometimes possible to get deals as low as £100 for charter or package return flights between London and Faro. For a general idea of prices from England, call TAP (☎ 0171-828 0262) or British Airways (☎ 0181-897 4000) direct. Both BA and TAP offer discounted youth and student fares. You could also try the travel agencies Abreu (☎ 0171-229 9905) or Latitude 40 (☎ 0171-229 3164), or ask the Portuguese National Tourist Office for its *Tour Operators' Guide: Portugal*. Campus Travel (☎ 0171-730 3402) is one of the UK's best youth-fare agencies.

For prices *to* England, try the youth travel agencies Tagus Travel (☎ 01-352 5509) and Jumbo Expresso (☎ 01-793 9264); other options are Top Tours (☎ 01-315 5885), TAP (☎ 01-841 6990) and British Airways (☎ 01-346 4353), all in Lisbon.

Since France, and Paris in particular, has a huge population of Portuguese immigrants, there are also frequent flights at reasonable prices between the two countries. For details, from France call Air France (☎ 01 44 08 24 24) or TAP (☎ 01 44 86 89 89). Both offer discounted prices to those under 26.

Madeira and the Azores are served by direct flights from Lisbon. There are also direct flights to Madeira from London, and to the Azores from New York and Montreal. The standard fare for a return flight with TAP from Lisbon is about UK£145 to Madeira or UK£210 to the Azores. Package deals offered by UK travel agencies may offer even better value.

LAND

Bus

Spain Intercentro, Portugal's main Eurolines agent, operates bus services three times a week between Lisbon and Madrid (11 hours) for 6860$00. Eurolines also has services between other Portuguese towns and Spain; for information and reservations, call ☎ 91-530 7600 (Madrid) or ☎ 01-357 7715 (Lisbon).

Internorte (☎ 02-600 4223 in Porto) runs coaches to/from northern Portuguese cities, including a service between Porto and Madrid

(5230$00) four times a week. In the Algarve, Intersul has express services between Lagos and Seville about four times weekly, via Vila Real de Santo António.

England & France Intercentro/Eurolines has regular services between central Portugal (Lisbon and other cities) and France, with a bus change in Paris for London, five times a week. Allow about 40 hours for the trip from London (Victoria coach station) to Lisbon; a standard ticket costs UK£112 one way. For more information call Eurolines in England on %y0990-143219 or in Portugal on %y01-357 7715.

Internorte (Porto ☎ 02-600 4223) has similar services to/from northern Portugal (Porto and other cities), with a change in Paris, as well as a once-weekly direct Porto-London coach. A one-way Porto-London ticket is about UK£95.

The private line IASA (☎ 01-793 6451 in Lisbon, ☎ 02-208 4338 in Porto) runs coaches five times a week between Lisbon and Paris (via Coimbra and other towns) and between Porto and Paris (via Braga and other towns). Both journeys take about 27 hours and cost about UK£65 one way.

Train
Spain The main rail route is Madrid-Lisbon via Valência de Alcântara; the journey (with an express departure daily) takes about 10 hours. Other popular routes include Vigo-Porto (expresses three times a day) and, in southern Spain, Seville-Ayamonte, across the river from the Portuguese town of Vila Real de Santo António in the Algarve. Also, the daily Lisbon-Paris train (see the following section) goes via Salamanca, Valladolid, Burgos, Vitória and San Sebastian.

England & France In general, it's only worth taking the train if you can take advantage of special under-26 rail passes such as Inter-Rail (see the Getting Around chapter at the beginning of this book for details).

Services from London to Lisbon and other destinations in Portugal run via Paris, where you change trains. There are two standard routes. The *Sud Express* runs from Paris via Irún (where you must change trains again) and across Spain to Pampilhosa in Portugal (con-

nections for Porto) before continuing to Lisbon. The other route runs from Paris to Madrid, where you can catch the *Lisboa Express* via Entroncamento (connections for Porto) to Lisbon. Allow at least 30 hours for the trip from London to Lisbon. A one-way, 2nd class, under-26 ticket is UK£94.

Car & Motorcycle The quickest routes from the UK are by ferry via northern Spain – from Plymouth to Santander with Brittany Ferries (☎ 0990-360360) or from Portsmouth to Bilbao with P&O Ferries (☎ 0990-980111). Alternatively, take the ferry or Channel Tunnel to France, motor down the coast via Bordeaux, through Spain via Burgos and Salamanca to Portugal. One option to reduce driving time on this route is to use Motorail for all or part of the trip from Paris to Lisbon; for information in England call French Railways (☎ 0171-803 3030).

All border posts are open around the clock.

LEAVING PORTUGAL
There is an airport departure tax of about 2000$00 for international departures and about 800$00 for domestic departures (the exact amount depends on your destination), but this is invariably included in the price of the ticket.

Getting Around

AIR
Flights inside Portugal are extremely expensive and hardly worth considering for the short distances involved – unless you have an under-26 card. Portugália operates daily flights between Lisbon, Porto and Faro (14,280$00 – about UK£65 – for the 50-minute Lisbon-Faro flight), with a handsome 50% discount for youth-card holders. For further information, phone Portugália in Lisbon (☎ 01-840 8999).

TAP also has some domestic connections, including Lisbon-Porto, and daily Lisbon-Faro flights that connect with all international TAP arrivals and departures at Lisbon.

BUS
The now defunct, state-run Rodoviária Nacional (RN) has spawned a host of private regional

companies which together operate a dense network of bus services of two types: *expressos* which provide comfortable, fast and direct connections between major cities and towns, and *carreiras* which stop at every crossroad. Local weekend services, especially up north, can thin out to almost nothing, especially when school is out in summer. In the boondocks, timetables are a rare commodity: stock up on information at tourist offices or bus stations in major towns.

An express coach from Lisbon to Faro takes just under five hours and costs about 2000$00 (2500$00 for the luxury four-hour EVA express); Lisbon-Porto takes 3½ hours and costs about 1800$00.

TRAIN

Caminhos de Ferro Portugueses (CP), the state railway company, operates three main types of service: *rápido* or *intercidade* (marked IC on timetables); *interregional* (marked IR); and *regional* (marked R). Tickets for the first two types cost at least double the price of a regional service, and reservations are either mandatory or highly recommended. A special intercidade service called Alfa, with fewer stops than usual, operates between selected northern cities (eg Lisbon and Porto). Frequent train travellers may want to buy a copy of the *Guia Horário Oficial* (360$00), which lists all domestic and international timetables, from the ticket windows at all the major stations in Lisbon.

If you can match your itinerary and pace to a regional service, travel by rail is cheaper, if slower, than by bus. Children from four to 12 years old and adults over 65 travel at half-price. Holders of youth cards get 30% off regional and interregional services only. There are also family discounts. Tourist tickets (*bilhetes turísticos*) are available for seven (17,500$00), 14 (28,300$00) or 21 (40,000$00) days, but are only worthwhile if you plan to spend a great deal of time moving around. The same discounts apply as for regular tickets. With intercidade and Alfa services everyone – even rail-pass holders – must pay an additional booking charge.

CAR & MOTORCYCLE

ACP (Automóvel Club de Portugal) is Portugal's representative for various foreign car and touring clubs. It provides medical, legal and car breakdown assistance for its members, but anyone can get road information and maps from its head office (☎ 01-356 3931; fax 01-357 4732) at Rua Rosa Araújo 24, Lisbon.

Road Rules

There are indeed rules, but the two guiding principles for Portuguese drivers seem to be: find the fastest route between two points; and defy the law of mortality in doing so. Although city driving (and parking) is hectic, minor roads in the countryside have surprisingly little traffic. Recent EU subsidies have ensured that the road system has been upgraded and there are now several long stretches of motorway – some of which are toll roads.

Petrol is pricey – 156$00 and up for a litre of 95-octane unleaded fuel. Unleaded petrol (*sem chumbo*) is readily available in most parts of the country. Speed limits in Portugal are 60 km/h in cities and public centres, unless otherwise indicated; 90 km/h on normal roads; and 120 km/h on motorways. Driving is on the right, and front passengers are required by law to wear seat belts.

Car Rental

There are dozens of local car-rental firms in Portugal, but the best deals are often arranged from abroad, either as part of a package with the flight, or through an international car-rental firm. From the UK, for example, for a small car expect to pay about UK£130 for seven days in the high season or UK£65 in low season; in Portugal, figure on around UK£160 in the high season or UK£130 in the low season (including tax, insurance and unlimited mileage). You must be at least 23 years old and have held your licence for over a year.

BICYCLE

The Portuguese are still bemused by the idea of cycling for pleasure, though the rental of mountain bikes (nicknamed BTT, for *bicyclete tudo terrano*) is catching on in some touristed areas (for anywhere from 1500$00 to 3500$00 a day). Elsewhere, bike shops and rental outfits are rare; if you're bringing your own machine, pack plenty of spares.

You can take your bike on any regional or interregional train for 1200$00.

PORTUGAL

HITCHING

Thumbing a ride takes considerable time because drivers in remote regions tend to be going short distances. You get to meet some interesting characters, but you may only advance from one field to the next! You'll make more progress on major roads.

LOCAL TRANSPORT

Bus

Except in big cities like Lisbon there is little reason to take a municipal bus. Most areas have regional bus services of some kind, but timetables can be scarce and/or bewildering, with many new private companies operating similar routes – and services can simply disappear on summer weekends, especially in the north.

Metro

Lisbon's underground system, the metro, is handy for the city centre, and by the time of Expo '98 it will extend much further. See the Lisbon section for more details.

Taxi

Taxis offer good value over short distances – especially for two or more people – and are usually plentiful in towns. Flag fall is 250$00; a fare of 500$00 is often enough for a zip across town. Once a taxi leaves the town or city limits, you may pay a higher fare, and possibly the cost of a return trip – whether you take it or not.

Other Transport

Enthusiasts for stately progress should not miss the trams of Lisbon and Porto, an endangered species. Also worth trying are the funiculars and elevators (both called *elevadores*) in Lisbon, Bom Jesus (Braga), Nazaré and elsewhere.

Commuter ferries run back and forth across the Rio Tejo all day between Lisbon and Cacilhas (and other points).

ORGANISED TOURS

Gray Lines (☎ 01-352 2594; fax 01-353 3291), Avenida Praia da Vitória 12-B, Lisbon, organises three to seven-day bus tours to selected regions throughout Portugal, normally through local travel agents or upper-end tourist hotels. The AVIC coach company (☎ 058-829705), Avenida Combatentes 206, Viana do Castelo, entices travellers on short tours of the lovely Douro and Lima valleys. Miltours (☎ 089-890 4600), Verissimo de Almeida 20, Faro, gives you a choice of day trips not only in the Algarve but all over Portugal; they also have offices in Lisbon (Rua Conde de Redondo 21, ☎ 01-352 4166) and Porto (Rua J Simão Bolivar 209, ☎ 02-941 4671).

Several unusual tours of Portugal are organised by UK travel agencies, eg art and music tours by Martin Randall Travel (☎ 0181-742 3355; fax 0181-742 1066) and wine tours in Alentejo and the Douro by Arblaster & Clarke Wine Tours (☎ 01730-893344). Further listings are available from the Portuguese National Tourist Office.

Two UK travel agencies that specialise in hiking holidays are Explore Worldwide (☎ 01252-319448) and Ramblers Holidays (☎ 01707-331133). Refer to Activities under Facts for the Visitor for information on adventure-travel specialists within Portugal.

Lisbon

Although it bustles with the crowds, noise and traffic of a capital city, Lisbon's low skyline and breezy position beside the Rio Tejo (River Tagus) lend it a small and manageable feel. Its unpretentious atmosphere and pleasant blend of architectural styles conspire with diverse attractions – and a few unique quirks – to make it a favourite with a wide range of visitors. Furthermore, Lisbon (Lisboa to the Portuguese) is one of Europe's most economical destinations. Lovers of Art Deco shouldn't wait: façades are fast disappearing in a frenzy of redevelopment.

Orientation

Apart from the puff required to negotiate the hills, orientation is straightforward. Activity centres on the lower part of the city, the Baixa district, focused on Praça Dom Pedro IV, which nearly everyone calls 'the Rossio'. Just north of the Rossio is Praça dos Restauradores, at the bottom of Avenida da Liberdade. West of the Rossio it's a steep climb to the Bairro Alto district where one section, the Chiado, is under renovation after a huge fire in 1988. East of the Rossio, it's another climb to the Castelo de São Jorge and the adjacent Alfama district, a maze of tiny streets. Several km to the west is Belém with its cluster of attractions.

Information

Tourist Offices The main tourist office (☎ 346 6307) in Palácio Foz, Praça dos Restauradores, near Rossio metro station, offers brochures and can help with accommodation. Ask here about museum opening times, which delight in being fickle. The office is open from 9 am to 8 pm every day. There is also a tourist office at the airport (☎ 849 4323), open daily from 6 am to 2 am.

Money There are useful banks with 24-hour exchange machines (for foreign cash) at the airport; at Santa Apolónia train station; opposite Rossio station (at Rua 1 de Dezembro 118-A); and at Rua Augusta 24 near Praça do Comércio. A better deal is the private exchange bureau, Cota Câmbios, at Rua do Áurea 283, open from 9 am to 8 pm weekdays (to 6 pm Saturday). Banco Borges e Irmão (☎ 342 1068) at Avenida da Liberdade 9-A is open from 8.30 am to 7.30 pm on weekdays and on alternate Saturdays.

Post & Communications The central post office is on Praça do Comércio. Mail addressed to Posta Restante, Central Correios, Terreira do Paço, 1100 Lisboa, will go to counter 13 or 14 here. A fee of 60$00 is charged for each letter collected. A telephone office at Rossio 68 is open daily from 8 am to 11 pm. A more convenient post and telephone office (☎ 347 1122), on Praça dos Restauradores opposite the tourist office, is open weekdays from 8 am to 11 pm and weekends and holidays from 9 am to 6 pm.

The telephone code for Lisbon is ☎ 01.

Travel Agencies Top Tours (☎ 315 5885; fax 315 5873), Avenida Duque de Loulé 108, is Lisbon's American Express representative. It offers commission-free currency exchange, help with lost cards or travellers' cheques, and outbound ticketing, and will forward and hold mail and faxes. It's closed at weekends. Good youth travel agencies are Tagus Travel (☎ 352 5509 for air bookings, ☎ 352 5986 for youth cards and other services) at Rua Camilo Castelo Branco 20, and Jumbo Expresso

(☎ 793 9264), Avenida da República 97, near Entre Campos metro station.

Two agencies specialising in adventure travel are Rotas do Vento (☎ 364 9852; fax 364 9843) at Rua dos Lusíadas 5, which organises weekend guided walks to remote corners of Portugal; and Turnatur (☎ 207 6886; fax 207 7675), Rua Almirante Reis 60 in Barreiro, just across the Tejo, which organises nature walks, jeep safaris, canoeing and canyoning expeditions.

Bookshops The central Diário de Notícias at Rossio 11 has a modest range of guides and maps. The city's biggest bookseller is Livraria Bertrand, with at least half a dozen shops, the biggest at Rua Garrett 7. If you're into classy bookshops, seek out Livraria Buchholz at Rua Duque de Palmela 4 (by Rotunda metro station), with its extensive collection. For second-hand books, there are two or three shops along Calçada do Carmo, which climbs up behind Rossio station.

Cultural Centres The USA's Abraham Lincoln Center (☎ 357 0102), at Avenida Duque de Loulé 22-B, is open weekdays from 2 to 5.30 pm. The library has a massive stock of American books and magazines. The British Council (☎ 347 6141), at Rua de São Marçal 174, also has a good library. It's open Tuesday through Friday from noon to 6 pm. At Avenida Luis Bivar 91 is the Institut Franco-Portugais de Lisbonne (☎ 311 1400).

Maps Along with their microscopic city map the tourist office sometimes has a good 1:15,000 *Lisboa* map free of charge. The detailed, oblique-perspective *Lisbon City Map – Vista Aérea Geral*, available from kiosks and bookshops, is great for spotting landmarks.

Laundry Lavandaria Sous'ana (☎ 888 0820) on the 1st floor of the Centro Comércial da Mouraria on Largo Martim Moniz (metro: Socorro) is self-service, but they'll do your wash in a few hours for the same price; they're open 9.30 am to 8.30 pm except Sunday. The Texas Lavandaria at Rua da Alegria 7, with dry-cleaning, washing and ironing, is open weekdays.

PORTUGAL

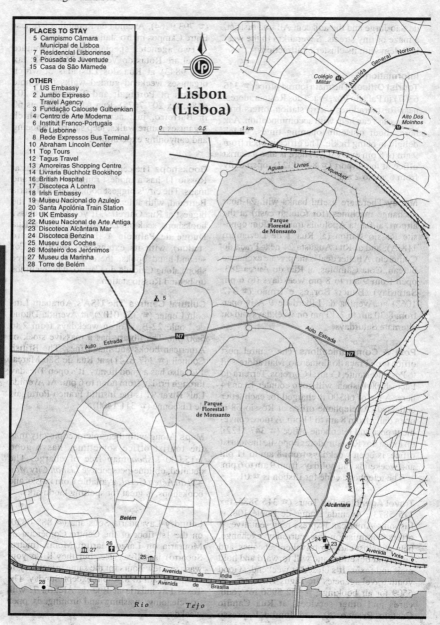

PLACES TO STAY
5 Campismo Câmara
   Municipal de Lisboa
7 Residencial Lisbonense
9 Pousada de Juventude
15 Casa de São Mamede

OTHER
1 US Embassy
2 Jumbo Expresso
   Travel Agency
3 Fundação Calouste Gulbenkian
4 Centro de Arte Moderna
6 Institut Franco-Portugais
   de Lisbonne
8 Rede Expressos Bus Terminal
10 Abraham Lincoln Center
11 Top Tours
12 Tagus Travel
13 Amoreiras Shopping Centre
14 Livraria Buchholz Bookshop
16 British Hospital
17 Discoteca A Lontra
18 Irish Embassy
19 Museu Nacional do Azulejo
20 Santa Apolónia Train Station
21 UK Embassy
22 Museu Nacional de Arte Antiga
23 Discoteca Alcântara Mar
24 Discoteca Benzina
25 Museu dos Coches
26 Mosteiro dos Jerónimos
27 Museu da Marinha
28 Torre de Belém

Lisbon
(Lisboa)

0   0.5   1 km

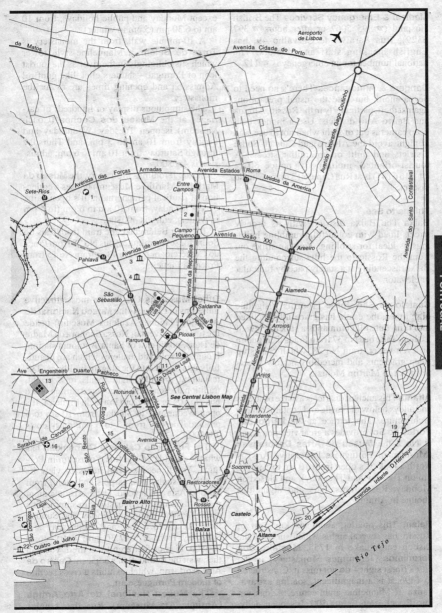

Aeroporto
de Lisboa

Avenida Cidade do Porto

de Matos

Avenida das Forças Armadas

Avenida Estados Unidos da America

Avenida Almirante Gago Coutinho

Avenida do Santo Contestável

Sete-Rios

1

Entre Campos

Avenida de Berna

2

Pahlavā

3

Campo Pequeno

Avenida João XXI

Areeiro

4

São Sebastião

6
Marquès de
Luis Braz

Avenida da República

Alameda

Saldanha

7

Casa
Museo

8

Reis

Parque

9

Picoas

Arroios

10

Avenida Engenheiro Duarte Pacheco

11

Duque de Loulé

12

Anjos

13

Rotunda

14

See Central Lisbon Map

Avenida de Liberdade

Avenida

Intendente

Saraiva

15

Avenida

Almirante

Rua Escola Politécnica

de Carvalho

16

Socorro

19

Rua de São Bento

17

18

Restauradores

Bairro Alto

Rossio

Castelo

Baixa

Avenida Infante D Henrique

21

São Domingos

Lapa

20

22

Quatro de Julho

Alfama

Rio Tejo

PORTUGAL

PORTUGAL

Medical & Emergency Services The British Hospital (☎ 395 5067 or after hours ☎ 397 6329), Rua Saraiva de Carvalho 49, has English-speaking staff and doctors. The national number for an emergency is ☎ 112.

Dangers & Annoyances There's no need to be paranoid, but take the usual precautions against theft, particularly in the Rossio, Alfama and Bairro Alto districts. Use a money belt, keep cameras out of sight when not in use, and at night avoid the Alfama and Cais do Sodré districts and unlit or unfamiliar streets. A tourist-oriented, multilingual police office (☎ 346 6141) is at Rua Capelo 13 in the Chiado district.

Things to See

Baixa The Baixa district, with its orderly streets lined with colourful, crumbling buildings, is ideal for strolling. You can strike out from the Rossio to the hills surrounding the Baixa, ascending at a stately pace by funicular or elevator.

Castelo de São Jorge From its Visigothic high times, the castle has gracefully declined into ruin, but still commands a superb view of Lisbon. Take bus No 37 from Praça da Figueira or, even better, tram No 28, which clanks up steep gradients and incredibly narrow streets from Largo Martim Moniz.

Alfama This ancient district is a maze of streets and alleys below the castle and contains superb architecture. The terrace at the **Largo das Portas do Sol** provides a great viewpoint, and at No 2 the **Museu de Artes Decorativas** (Museum of Portuguese Decorative Arts) is worth a look. It's open from 10 am to 5 pm (8 pm on Tuesday and Thursday), and closed on Monday. Restaurants, bars and nightclubs abound in Alfama.

Belém This quarter, about six km west of Rossio, has several sights which survived the Lisbon earthquake in 1755. **Mosteiro dos Jerónimos** (Jerónimos Monastery) is the city's finest sight – do not miss it. Constructed in 1496, it is a magnificent, soaring extravaganza of Manueline architecture. Admission into the cloisters is 400$00. It's open daily,

except Monday and public holidays, from 10 am to 6.30 pm (5 pm in winter).

A 10-minute walk from the monastery is **Torre de Belém**, a Manueline-style tower which sits obligingly in the river as *the* tourist icon of Portugal – shutters click like gunfire! Admission and opening times are as for the monastery.

The sumptuous display of hundreds of carriages at the **Museu dos Coches** (Coach Museum) is open Tuesday, Wednesday and Sunday from 10 am to 3 pm, and Thursday through Saturday from 10 am to 6 pm; admission is 450$00.

Beside Jerónimos Monastery, the **Museu da Marinha** (Maritime Museum) houses a collection of nautical paraphernalia. It's open daily, except Monday, from 10 am to 6 pm (to 5 pm in winter); entry is 300$00.

To reach Belém take the train from Cais do Sodré for seven minutes; bus No 28 from Praça do Comércio; or bus No 43 or tram No 15 from Praça da Figueira.

Other Museums One of the most attractive museums in Lisbon is the **Museu Nacional do Azulejo** (National Azulejos Museum) inside the former convent of Nossa Senhora da Madre de Deus, north-east of Santa Apolónia station. It contains splendid azulejos which are beautifully integrated into the elegant buildings. The restaurant provides light meals in a bright, traditional kitchen or in a covered garden. Take bus No 104 or 105 from Praça da Figueira. It's open Wednesday to Sunday from 10 am to 6 pm and Tuesday from 2 to 6 pm; entry costs 350$00.

The **Fundação Calouste Gulbenkian** has what is considered the finest museum in Portugal. You'll need several hours to view its paintings, sculptures, carpets and more, from Europe, Asia and beyond. The most convenient metro station is São Sebastião. In summer it's open Tuesday, Thursday, Friday and Sunday from 10 am to 5 pm, and Wednesday and Saturday from 2 to 7.30 pm; entry costs 500$00. If your feet aren't too tired, you can then visit the Foundation's adjacent **Centro de Arte Moderna**, which exhibits a cross section of modern Portuguese art.

The **Museu Nacional de Arte Antiga** (Antique Art Museum), Rua das Janelas

Verdes, houses the national collection of works by Portuguese painters. Opening times are Wednesday to Sunday from 10 am to 6 pm and Tuesday from 2 to 6 pm. Admission costs 500$00. Take bus No 40 or 60 from Praça da Figueira.

Mercado da Ribeira This municipal market (also called Mercado Municipal 24 de Julho) is Lisbon's biggest market, diagonally opposite Cais do Sodré station. Get there early in the day to see vegetables, fruit, seafood and more, sold by feisty vendors.

Places to Stay
Camping The *Campismo Câmara Municipal de Lisboa* (☎ 760 2061/2063) in Parque Florestal de Monsanto is about six km northwest of Rossio. Take bus No 14 or 43 from Praãa da Figueira.

Hostels Close to the centre is the *pousada de juventude* (☎ 353 2696) on Rua Andrade Corvo 46 (off Ave Fontes Pereira de Melo). It's open 24 hours a day. The closest metro station is Picoas, or take bus No 46 from Santa Apolónia station or Rossio and get off at Marquês de Pombal. It's very popular, so reservations are essential.

The *Pousada de Juventude de Catalazete* (☎ 443 0638) is at Estrada Marginal (next to Inatel) in Oeiras. This is a very pleasant beachside hostel, 12 km west of central Lisbon. Take the train from Cais do Sodré station to Oeiras, a trip of 20 to 25 minutes. The hostel is open 24 hours a day. Reservations are essential.

Hotels & Guesthouses The tourist office in Restauradores will make enquiries but not reservations for accommodation in Lisbon. During the high season advance bookings are imperative for accommodation near the centre.

Baixa & Chiado If you don't mind climbing four flights of stairs, the central *Pensão Galicia* (☎ 342 8430) at Rua do Crucifixo 50 and *Pensão Moderna* (☎ 346 0818) at Rua dos Correeiros 205 are good value, with doubles for 4500$00.

Pensão Estrela do Chiado (☎ 342 6110) at Rua Garrett 29, involves similar exercise and has doubles from 4000$00. Close to Rossio

station, *Residencial Estrela do Mondego* (☎ 346 7109) at Calçada do Carmo 25, has bigger rooms for the same price. Also up behind Rossio station at Calçada do Duque 53, *Pensão Duque* (☎ 346 3444) has plain, clean doubles with shared bathroom for about 3500$00.

Restauradores & Rato At Rua Jardim do Regedor 24, *Residencial Campos* (☎ 346 2864) is a friendly place surrounded by restaurants. Doubles start at 4000$00. At Rua da Glória 21, the *Pensão Monumental* (☎ 346 9807) has functional doubles from 6000$00, but street noise can be annoying. *Hotel Suiço-Atlântico* (☎ 346 1713), Rua da Glória 3, has well-maintained rooms and is close to the tourist office. Doubles start at around 9500$00.

Casa de São Mamede (☎ 396 3166), Rua Escola Politécnica 159, is a stylish hotel in an elegant old house with doubles from 10,000$00. With similar rates is the well-run *Hotel Jorge V* (☎ 356 2525), just off Avenida da Liberdade at Rua Mouzinho da Silveira 3.

Bairro Alto At Rua do Teixeira 37, close to the Elevador da Glória, the pleasant *Pensão Globo* (☎ 346 2279) has doubles without shower for as little as 3500$00. Nearby, the popular *Pensão Londres* (☎ 346 2203) at Rua Dom Pedro V 53 has several floors of spacious rooms, the upper ones with great city views. Doubles start at 5300$00.

Saldanha The bright and pleasant *Residencial Lisbonense* (☎ 354 4628), at Rua Pinheiro Chagas 1, has doubles from 7000$00.

Castelo de São Jorge Below the castle at Costa do Castelo 74, *Pensão Ninho das Aguias* (☎ 886 7008) offers amazing views after a steep climb. Reservations are essential. Doubles start at around 6500$00.

Places to Eat
Most of the city's good restaurants and cafés are in the Baixa and Bairro Alto districts. Eateries in the streets off Praça dos Restauradores tend to be poorer value or lower quality.

Baixa One of several similar bargain restaurants along Rua dos Coreeiros is *Lagosta*

PORTUGAL

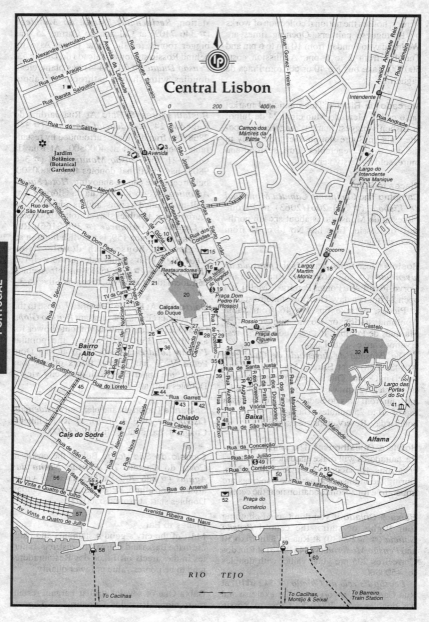

Central Lisbon

0   200   400 m

Rua Alexandre Herculano
Rua Rosa Araújo
Rua Barata Salgueiro
Avenida da Liberdade
Rua Rodrigues Sampaio
Rua — Gomez — Freire

1

Rua — do — Salitre

Jardím
Botânico
(Botanical
Gardens)

2 Avenida

3

Campo dos
Mártires da
Pátria

4

Largo do
Intendente
Pina Manique

Intendente

Avenida Almirante Reis

Rua Palmeira

Rua Andrade

Rua da Palma

Rua da Escola Politécnica

da Alegria

5

Ruo de
São Marçal

6

Rua Dom Pedro V

13

Avenida da Liberdade

Avenida da Liberdade

Rua das Portas de Santo Antão

8

Rua dos Condes

9
10
11
12

15

14

Restauradores

16 17

Rua do Jardim do Regedor

21

20

Praça Dom
Pedro IV
(Rossio)

19

Socorro

Largo
Martim
Moniz

18

Rua de São Pedro de Alcântara
TV da Carra

23

24

Calçada
do Duque

25

Rossio

26

27

28 29

Calçada Carmo

Praça da
Figueira

30

do Castelo

31

32

Bairro
Alto

37

36

34

33

35

39

Rua de Santa Justa

R dos Correeiros
R da Prata
Rua Augusta
Rua Áurea

Costa

Largo das
Portas
do Sol

41

Calçada do Combro

Rua do Loreto

38

45

Rua Garrett
44

43 42

Chiado

Rua Capelo

46

47

Rua Nova do Trindade

Rua do Alecrim

Cais do Sodré

Rua de São Paulo

Rua das Remedeiros

56

55 54
53

57

Av Vinte e Quatro de Julho

Av Vinte e Quatro de Julho

Avenida Ribeira das Naus

Rua das Franqueiras

Rua dos Douradores
Rua da Vitória
Rua de São Nicolau

Baixa

Rua da Conceição

Rua da Madalena

Rua de São Mamede

Rua de São Julião

Rua do Comércio
49

50

51

Rua dos Bacalhoeiros

Rua da Alfândega

Alfama

52

Praça do
Comércio

Rua do Arsenal

58

59

60

RIO   TEJO

To Cacilhas

To Cacilhas,
Montijo & Seixal

To Barreiro
Train Station

PORTUGAL

Vermelha (☎ 342 4832), a typically casual casa de pasto at No 155. *Restaurante Pinóquio* (☎ 346 5106), Praça dos Restauradores 79, is more expensive, though the seafood is good. *Restaurante O Sol* (☎ 347 1944), Calçada do Duque 23, is an inexpensive vegetarian option with set meals for under 1000$00.

For a coffee or a meal, *Nicola*, at Rossio 24, is the celebrated grande dame of Lisbon's turn-of-the-century cafés. It is closed on Sunday. *Martinho da Arcada* café (☎ 887 9259), Praça do Comércio 3, was once a haunt of the literary set, including Fernando Pessoa, but renovation has cost it some of that lustre. It closes at 9 pm; both the café and the adjacent, overpriced restaurant are closed on Sunday.

Bairro Alto The cavernous *Cervejaria da Trindade* (☎ 342 3506), Rua Nova da Trindade 20-C, is a converted convent decorated with azulejos. Main dishes start at around 1200$00. It stays open until 1 am.

Restaurante O Brunhal (☎ 347 8634), Rua

da Glória 27, close to the tourist office, is an unpretentious place with simple cheap food.

Restaurante Porto de Abrigo (☎ 346 0873) is at Rua dos Remolares 18, close to Cais do Sodré station. The seafood dishes are recommended: figure on 800$00 to 1700$00 a dish; it's closed on Sunday. One of several cheapies in the same area, the *Pastelaria & Snack Bar Brasilia* (☎ 346 6902) at Praça Duque da Terceira 10, has good-value daily specials.

Restaurante O Tacão Pequeno (☎ 347 2848) at Travessa da Carra 3-A, is a cosy dive with some unusual décor. Nearby, the bright, plain *Cafetaria Brasil* at Rua de São Pedro de Alcântara 51 has pratos do dia (dishes of the day) from 600$00.

A Brasileira (☎ 346 9547), Rua Garrett 120, is another venerable café with strong literary traditions.

Entertainment
For current listings, pick up a copy of the free monthly *Agenda Cultural* from the tourist office, or *Público* from a newsstand.

Music In its authentic form, fado is fascinating. However, the sad truth in Lisbon is that many casas de fado (which are also restaurants) produce pale tourist imitations, often at prices which may make you feel like groaning as much as the fado singer. Even the simplest places now have a minimum charge of 1800$00 to 3000$00. In the Bairro Alto you could try *Adega Machado* (☎ 342 8713), Rua do Norte 91, or the simpler *Adega do Ribatejo* (☎ 346 8343), at Rua Diário de Notícias 23. The tourist office can suggest others.

Hot Clube de Portugal (☎ 346 7369), Praça da Alegria 39, is at the centre of a thriving Lisbon jazz scene. You can listen to live music there three or four nights a week. It's open from 10 pm to 2 am, closed on Sunday and Monday.

Homesick Dubliners craving a draft Guinness should head down to *Ó Gilíns Irish Pub* (☎ 342 1899) at Rua dos Remolares 8-10, by Cais do Sodré station. It's open daily from 11 am to 2 am and has live Irish music most Saturday nights and jazz with brunch on Sunday.

Discos boom and bust at lightning speed. Try *Benzina* (☎ 363 3959), Travessa de Teixeira Júnior 6 in the Alcântara district, or *Alcântara Mar* (☎ 363 6432), just down the road at Rua da Cozinha Económica 11, both raving from midnight until 6 or 7 am.

The African music scene (predominantly Cape Verdean) bops in numerous bars in the area around Rua de São Bento; one of the best known is *Discoteca A Lontra* at No 155.

Cinemas There are plenty of cinemas around the city. The Amoreiras shopping centre has a multiscreen cinema (☎ 383 1275) showing almost a dozen different films every night. Tickets are 700$00 (500$00 on Monday).

Spectator Sport The local football teams are Benfica and Sporting. The tourist office can advise on match dates and tickets. If you must see one, bullfights are staged at Campo Pequeno between April and October.

Things to Buy
For azulejos, try Fabrica Sant'Ana at Rua do Alecrim 95, or Cerâmica Viúva Lamego (☎ 885 2402), Largo do Intendente Pina Manique 25 (metro: Intendente). The Museu Nacional do Azulejo also has a small shop. On Tuesday and Saturday mornings, visit the Feira da Ladra, a kind of flea market in the Alfama district. Or just wander the backstreets of Baixa and Bairro Alto.

Getting There & Away
For information on international and domestic connections, see the Getting There & Away and Getting Around sections at the beginning of this chapter.

Air Lisbon's airport is 20 minutes from the centre (but 45 minutes or more in rush hour). For arrival and departure information phone ☎ 840 4500.

Bus What's left of the state-run RN service (notably Rede Expressos), plus international coaches and a few private companies such as EVA (from the Algarve), uses the main bus terminal (☎ 354 5439) at Avenida Casal Ribeiro 18, not far from Picoas and Saldanha metro stations. The private Renex company (☎ 887 4871 or 888 2829), including Resende, Caima and Frota Azul services, operates from Rua dos Bacalhoeiros, a few blocks east of Praça do Comércio.

Train Santa Apolónia station (☎ 888 4025 for train information) is the terminus for trains from north and central Portugal, and for all international services. Cais do Sodré station is used by trains heading to Cascais and Estoril. Rossio station is centrally placed and serves Sintra and Estremadura. Barreiro station lies across the river and is the terminus for services from the south of Portugal and the Algarve; connecting ferries leave frequently from the pier at Terréiro do Paço, by Praça do Comércio.

Ferry Ferries of the Transtejo line run back and forth across the Rio Tejo from Praça do Comércio to Cacilhas (90$00) every 10 minutes all day, and to Montijo (270$00) and Seixal (200$00) every hour or so. There is also a car ferry to Cacilhas from Cais do Sodré

Getting Around
To/From the Airport Bus No 91, called the Aero-Bus, is a special service running about every 20 minutes from 7 am to 9 pm and taking

20 to 45 minutes (depending on traffic) between the airport and the city centre, including a stop right outside the tourist office. It costs 430$00/1000$00 and includes a ticket useable for one/three days on all buses, trams and funiculars. Local bus Nos 8, 44, 45 and 83 also run near the tourist office but are a nightmare in rush hour if you have baggage. A taxi will cost about 1500$00, plus an extra 300$00 if your luggage needs to go in the boot.

Bus & Tram Individual bus and tram tickets cost 150$00 or half that if purchased beforehand. Prepaid tickets are sold at kiosks with the Carris logo, most conveniently at Praça da Figueira and the Santa Justa elevator. If you plan to spend a few days in Lisbon, tourist passes valid for all trams and buses and the metro are available for four days (1550$00) or one week (2190$00).

Buses and trams run from about 5 or 6 am to 1 am, with some night services. You can get a transport map (*Planta dos Transportes Públicas da Carris*) from the tourist office and sometimes from Carris kiosks, but thanks to the city's building frenzy, route changes are so frequent the map is not always reliable.

Wheelchair users can all Carris on ☎ 363 2044 for information on their dial-a-ride service. The clattering, antediluvian trams (*eléctricos*) are an endearing component of Lisbon. Don't leave without riding tram No 28 to the old quarter from Rua da Conceiçao.

Metro The metro isn't extensive (though plenty of expansion is underway), but it's useful for short hops across the centre of town. Individual tickets cost 70$00 or it's 500$00 for a *caderneta* of 10 tickets. A day ticket costs 200$00. The metro operates from 6.30 am to 1 am. Pickpockets can be a nuisance.

Taxi Compared with the rest of Europe, Lisbon's taxis are fast, cheap and plentiful. Either flag taxis down on the street or go to a rank. Some of the taxis that haunt the airport are a bit unscrupulous, so watch your map.

Car Car-rental companies in Lisbon include Avis (☎ 356 1176), Europcar (☎ 353 5115), Kenning (☎ 354 9182) and Solcar (☎ 356 0500).

Around Lisbon

SINTRA
If you make only one side trip from Lisbon, Sintra should receive top priority. Long favoured by Portuguese royalty and English nobility (Lord Byron was dotty about it), the thick forests and unusual architecture of Sintra provide a complete change from urban Lisbon. The very efficient tourist office (☎ 923 1157), on the ground floor of the Sintra Regional Museum on Praça da República (near the Palácio Nacional), has a good map and photos of accommodation options. During weekends and the annual music festival held in July expect droves of visitors. In high season it's wise to book ahead for more up-market accommodation.

The telephone code for Sintra is ☎ 01.

Things to See
The **Palácio Nacional de Sintra**, recently repainted a shocking bright white, dominates the town with its twin kitchen chimneys. From Moorish origins, the palace has been developed into a synthesis of Manueline and Gothic architecture. Highlights include the **Magpie Room** and the **Swan Room**. It's open daily, except Wednesday, from 10 am to 1 pm and 2 to 5 pm; entry is 400$00. Ticket sales finish 30 minutes before closing time.

A steep three-km climb from the centre leads to the **Palácio da Pena**, built in 1839 in exuberant Romantic style. The grounds are ideal for botanical forays. It's open daily, except Monday, from 10 am to 1 pm and from 2 to 5 pm; entry is 400$00. The nearby ruins of **Castelo dos Mouros**, which provide a magnificent view over the town and surroundings, are open daily from 10 am to 6 pm (5 pm in winter).

Rambling and romantic, the **Monserrate Gardens** are a four-km walk from the town, past the brazenly luxurious **Palácio de Seteais** hotel. The gardens are open from 10 am to 6 pm (5 pm in winter) and entry is 200$00.

More beguiling is the **Convento dos Capuchos**, a tiny 16th-century hermitage in the forest nine km from Sintra, with cells hewn from rock and lined with cork. Walkers can

PORTUGAL

approach it from Monserrate, though the path isn't always clear; guidance is provided in the *Landscapes of Portugal* walkers' guidebook for this area (see Books & Maps earlier in this chapter).

Places to Stay

The nearest decent camping ground is *Camping Praia Grande* (☎ 929 0581), on the coast 11 km from Sintra and linked by a frequent bus service.

The *pousada de juventude* (☎ 924 1210) is at Santa Eufémia, four km from the town centre. Along with dormitory beds, it has doubles for 3300$00. Advance reservations are essential.

Casa de Hospedes Adelaide (☎ 923 0873), Rua Guilherme Gomes Fernandes 11, a 10-minute walk from the station, has comfortable doubles without bath from around 3500$00. Closer to the station, at Largo Afonso d'Albuquerque 25, *Pensão Nova Sintra* (☎ 923 0220) is a cosy old house with doubles at 5000$00 (without private bath) and a pleasant outdoor patio. Across the railway, at Rua João de Deus 70, *Piela's* (☎ 924 1691) has immaculate doubles at 6500$00. For 24,000$00 you can have an exquisite double in the *Quinta da Capela* (☎ 929 0170), an 18th-century manor house in a wooded valley below Monserrate Gardens.

Places to Eat

Tulhas (☎ 923 2378), close to the tourist office at Rua Gil Vicente 4-6, is an excellent restaurant; it's closed on Wednesday. The simple *A Tasca do Manel* (☎ 923 0215) by the town hall at Largo Dr Vergilio Horta 5, serves all the usual favourite fare for around 800$00 a dish, while the nearby *Topico Bar & Restaurant* (☎ 923 4825) at Rua Dr Alfredo Costa 8, has live music on Wednesday, Friday and Saturday. For something special, try *Orixás* (☎ 924 1672), an expensive Brazilian restaurant-cum-art gallery at Avenida Adriano Júlio Coelho 7. *Fonte da Pipa* (☎ 923 4437), Rua Fonte da Pipa 11-13, is a cosy bar with snacks and inexpensive drinks.

Getting There & Away

The bus and train stations are together in the north of the town on Avenida Dr Miguel Bombarda, two km from the Palácio Nacional. Trains from Lisbon's Rossio station take about 50 minutes (180$00). Buses run from Sintra to Estoril, Cascais and Mafra.

Getting Around

Taxis are a convenient though expensive way to get around: a three-hour sightseeing trip is 6000$00 plus 20% at weekends and holidays (the tourist office has a full list of prices). Horse-drawn carriages are a romantic alternative: figure on 6000$00 to Monserrate and back. Horse riding is available at Centro Hipico Penha Longa Country Club (☎ 924 9033) for around 3500$00 an hour.

ESTORIL

Estoril is a beach resort with Europe's biggest casino and a genteel ambience favoured by the rich and famous. The tourist office (☎ 466 3813) is on Arcadas do Parque. Attractions are limited to the casino, and strolls in the public gardens. Estoril's telephone code is ☎ 01.

Accommodation and restaurants are both better value in Cascais, just a couple of km further west along the coastline, but if you feel like lingering to gamble your escudos away, the pick of the pensões is *Pensão Smart* on Rua José Viana 3 (☎ 468 2164). Doubles with breakfast start at 6500$00. Cheaper digs are at nearby *Casa de Hóspedes Paula Castro* (☎ 01-468 0699), Rua da Escola 4, which has basic doubles from 5000$00. From Cais do Sodré station in Lisbon it's a half-hour trundle by train to Estoril (180$00).

CASCAIS

Cascais is similar to Estoril, but has become the 'in' beach resort. Cascais tourist office (☎ 486 8204), Rua Visconde de Luz 14, has accommodation lists and bus timetables.

The telephone code for Cascais is ☎ 01.

Things to See & Do

Two km west of the town centre is the **Boca do Inferno** (literally, 'mouth of hell'), where the sea roars into the coast. **Cabo da Roca**, the westernmost point of Europe, is a spectacular and often very windy spot 16 km from Cascais and Sintra (served by buses from both towns) – pop into the tiny windswept post office for a commemorative certificate. Those who like their beaches long and wild will appreciate **Guincho**, three km from Cascais, the venue for the 1991 World Surfing Championships.

Bicycles and motorcycles can be rented from Gesrent at Centro Commercial Cisne (☎ 486 4566), Avenida Marginal Bloco 3 (near the post office).

Places to Stay
Camping Orbitur do Guincho (☎ 487 1014), seven km from Cascais near Guincho beach, is useful if you have your own transport.

Getting There & Away
From Cais do Sodré station in Lisbon it's a 25-minute train trip (180$00) to Cascais.

QUELUZ
The 17th-century **Palácio Nacional de Queluz**, with later additions inspired by Versailles, has sumptuous rooms and fine gardens. The throne room and the gargantuan kitchen (now a restaurant) are highlights. It's open Wednesday to Monday from 10 am to 1 pm and 2 to 5 pm; entry is 400$00.

Frequent trains from Rossio station make the 20-minute trip (150$00) to Queluz.

MAFRA
The only attraction here is the colossal **Palácio Nacional de Mafra**, which tops the league for size on the Iberian Peninsula. Its size (an estimated 4500 doors!) and austerity make the tour rather depressing. It's open from 10 am to 1 pm and from 2 to 5 pm, except Tuesday and public holidays; admission is 300$00 (free on Sunday mornings).

Buses from Lisbon take 1½ hours (530$00), or from Sintra it's a 45-minute bus ride (370$00).

The Algarve

Loud, boisterous and full of foreigners, the Algarve is about as far from quintessential Portugal as one can get. While sun and sand are the major drawcards, there are some other attractions. West of Lagos are wild and all-but-deserted beaches. The coast east of Faro is dotted with enticing, colourful fishing villages. And for those who've filled up on seascapes, there are the forested slopes of Monchique, the

fortified village of Silves and the past glory of Estói Palace tucked away in the mountains.

Orientation
The southernmost slice of Portugal, the Algarve divides neatly into five regions: the Costa Vicentina facing west into the teeth of Atlantic gales, the windward coast (Sotavento) from Sagres to Lagos, the central coast from Lagos to Faro, the leeward coast (Barlavento) from Faro to Vila Real de Santo António, and the interior.

The largest town, and district capital, is Faro. The easternmost town, Vila Real de Santo António, is a border crossing to Ayamonte, Spain – linked to it by a car ferry and a highway bridge across the mouth of Rio Guadiana. The beach, golf, disco and nightclub scenes are focused on the central Algarve, particularly Albufeira and Portimão. West of Lagos, the shore grows increasingly steep and rocky.

Information
Leaflets describing every Algarve community from tiny Alcoutim to booming Albufeira are available from the district tourist office in Faro. A host of English-language newspapers like the *Algarve News*, *APN* and *Algarve Resident*, which are aimed primarily at expatriates, provide entertainment listings and information on attractions and coming events. Walkers should pick up *Algarve: Guide to Walks* (250$00) from the Faro tourist office.

Dangers & Annoyances Take extra precautions against theft on the Algarve. Paranoia is unwarranted, but don't leave anything of value in your vehicle or unattended on the beach.

Swimmers should beware of dangerous currents, especially on the west coast. Beaches are marked by coloured flags: red means the beach is closed to bathing, yellow means swimming is prohibited but wading is fine, green means anything goes.

Things to Buy
Few souvenirs are actually made in the Algarve, but Moorish-influenced ceramics and local woollens (cardigans and fishing pullovers) are good value. You may want to try Algarviana, a local amaretto (bitter almond liqueur), or the salubrious bottled waters of Monchique, on sale everywhere.

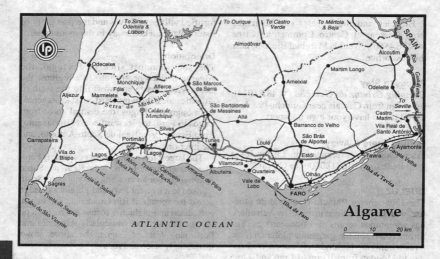

Getting There & Away

The major airport at Faro serves both domestic and international flights. For details see the introductory Getting There & Away section of this chapter.

Several companies, including Rede Expressos and EVA, operate regular and express services to all the major towns on the Algarve. It's about 5½ hours from Lisbon to Faro. Services also run between Lagos and Seville (Spain) via major Algarve towns (5½ hours).

From Barreiro in Lisbon there are several trains daily to Lagos and Faro (four to five hours, half an hour less by intercidade train).

For motorists arriving from Ayamonte in Spain, a bridge completed in 1991 four km north of Vila Real de Santo António now bypasses the old ferry connection. The most direct route from Lisbon to Faro takes about five hours.

Getting Around

There's an efficient network of bus services between the major towns of the Algarve. Via Infante, the superhighway planned to run the length of the coast to Spain, is only partially completed. Bicycles, scooters and motorcycles can be rented all over; see individual town listings.

FARO

The capital of the Algarve, Faro is also the main transport hub and a thriving commercial centre, but is otherwise of little interest. The tourism office (☎ 803604), Rua da Misericórdia, can provide a wide range of tourist literature.

The telephone code for Faro is ☎ 089.

Things to See & Do

The waterfront around Praça de Dom Francisco Gomes has pleasant gardens and cafés. Faro's beach, **Praia de Faro**, is six km southwest of the city on Ilha de Faro. Take bus No 16 from in front of the tourist office; another option between May and September is a ferry from Arco da Porta Nova, close to Faro's port.

At Estói, 12 km north of Faro, the wonderful crumbling wreck of **Estói Palace** is a surreal garden of statues, balustrades and azulejos – highly recommended. The bus from Faro to São Brás de Alportel goes via Estói.

Places to Stay & Eat

There are some camping facilities at Faro beach. Conveniently close to the port and the train station is the *Residencial Avenida* (☎ 823347) at Avenida da República 150, where a double costs 7000$00/5000$00 with/

without bath. Singles/doubles at the nearby *Residencial Madalena* (☎ 805806), Rua Conselheiro Bivar 109, are about 5000$00/7000$00. Slightly cheaper is the good *Residencial Alameda* (☎ 801962), Rua José de Matos 31.

The *Restaurante Mariqueira Ramirez*, Rua Filipe Alistão 19, serves excellent seafood. A *Garrafeira do Vilaça* (☎ 802150) at Rua São Pedro 33 is popular with students; next door at No 31 is the pricier *Restaurante Queda d'Água*. Worth lingering at is *Café Aliança*, a turn-of-the-century gem on Rua Dom Francisco Gomes.

Getting There & Away
The airport is six km from the city centre. Bus No 18 runs there until around 8 pm. A taxi into town costs about 1100$00.

The bus station is in the centre, close to the harbour. There are at least 10 express buses to Lisbon (1900$00) daily, including four non-stops, and frequent buses to other coastal towns.

The train station is just a few minutes on foot west of the bus station. Around six trains go to Lisbon daily (1800$00), and a similar number go to Albufeira and Portimão.

TAVIRA
Tavira is one of the Algarve's oldest and most beautiful towns. Graceful bridges cross Rio Gilão which divides the town. The excellent tourist office (☎ 22511) is at Rua da Galeria 9. Bicycles and motorcycles can be rented from Loris rent, Rua Damiao Augusto de Brito, 4 (☎ 325203, mobile ☎ 0931-274766).

The telephone code for Tavira is ☎ 081.

Things to See & Do
In the old part of town is the **Igreja da Misericórdia**, with a striking Renaissance doorway. From there, it's a short climb to the **castle** dominating the town.

Two km from Tavira is **Ilha da Tavira**, an attractive island beach connected to the mainland by ferry. Walk two km beside the river to reach the ferry terminal at Quatro Águas or take the bus from the bus station.

For a look at the way the Algarve used to be, take a bus to **Cacela Velha**, an unspoilt hamlet eight km from Tavira. Another worthwhile day trip is to the church and colourful quay at

Olhão, 22 km west of Tavira. Drop in for a delicious and fresh seafood lunch at *Papy's*, opposite the park.

Places to Stay & Eat
There's a *camping ground* on Ilha da Tavira, but the ferry stops running at 11 pm (usually 1 am from July to September). *Pensão Residencial Lagoas* (☎ 22252), at Rua Almirante Cândido dos Reis 24, has singles/doubles from 2500$00/4000$00 without bath. *Princesa do Gilão* (☎ 325171), Rua Borda d'Água de Aguiar 10, beside the river, charges 5000$00/6000$00 a single/double, but street-side rooms can be noisy. In the heart of town, *Pensão Residencial Castelo* (☎ 23942) at Rua da Liberdade 4, has rooms for 5000$00/5500$00 with bath.

Restaurante O Pátio (☎ 23008) at Rua António Cabreira 30 serves excellent Algarve specialties such as cataplana (shellfish cooked in a sealed wok).

Getting There & Away
Running between Faro and Tavora there are 15 trains a day (taking between 40 and 60 minutes) as well as seven buses a day (four at weekends), taking an hour.

LAGOS
Lagos is a major tourist resort with some of the finest beaches on the Algarve. The breathtakingly unhelpful tourist office (☎ 763031) is on Largo Marquês de Pombal in the centre of town.

The telephone code for Lagos is ☎ 082.

Things to See & Do
In the old part of town, the **municipal museum** houses an odd assortment of ecclesiastical treasures, handicrafts and preserved animal fetuses. The adjacent **Chapel of Santo António** contains some extraordinarily intricate baroque woodwork.

The beach scene includes **Meia Praia**, a vast strip of sand to the east; and to the west **Praia da Luz** and the more secluded **Praia do Pinhão**.

Espadarte do Sul (☎ 761820) operates **boat trips** from Docapesca harbour, including snorkelling and game fishing. Bom Dia (☎ 764670) has classier outings on a traditional schooner. Local fishermen trawl for customers along the seaside promenade and offer motorboat jaunts to the nearby grottoes.

Landlubbers can go **horse riding** at Tiffany's equestrian centre (☎ 69395), about 10 km west on the N125 road; they'll even come and get you in Lagos.

Places to Stay & Eat

Two nearby camping grounds are *Trindade* (☎ 763893), 200 metres south of the town walls, and *Imulagos* (☎ 760031), with a shuttle bus from the waterfront road. The *pousada de juventude* (☎ 761970) is at Rua Lançarote de Freitas 50. *Residencial Marazul* (☎ 769749), Rua 25 de Abril 13, has smart singles/doubles from 6500$00/8000$00. Private rooms are plentiful and usually cost around 5000$00 a double.

For standard food with fado accompaniment, try *Restaurante A Muralha* (☎ 763659), Rua da Atalaia 15. *O Cantinho Algarvio* (☎ 761289), at Rua Afonso d'Almeida 17, offers good Algarve specialities. The *Barroca Jazz Bar & Restaurant* (☎ 767162), at the south end of Rua da Barroca, is open from 7 pm to 2 am, with live jazz most nights in summer.

Getting There & Away

Both bus and train services depart up to six times daily to Lisbon.

Getting Around

You can rent bicycles and mopeds from Safari Moto (☎ 764314) at Rua Lucinda Santos 4 (near the main bus terminal), or from Motoride (☎ 761720) at Rua José Afonso 23. Figure on about 1300$00 a day for a mountain bike or 2000$00 for a moped.

MONCHIQUE

This quiet highland town in the forested Serra de Monchique offers an alternative to the discos and lazy beach life on the coast.

The telephone code for Monchique is ☎ 082.

Things to See & Do

In Monchique itself, the **Igreja Matriz** has an amazing Manueline portal – about the closest you'll get to seeing stone tied in knots! Follow the brown signs which lead pedestrians up above the bus station round the old town's narrow streets.

Six km south is the drowsy hot-spring community of **Caldas de Monchique**. Have a soak in the spa or try the bottled water.

The best excursion from Monchique is to drive or hike eight km through thick forest to the 'rooftop' of the Algarve at **Fóia**. If you can ignore the forests of radio masts, the views are terrific.

Places to Stay & Eat

The *Residencial Miradouro* (☎ 92163), Rua dos Combatentes do Ultramar, has singles/doubles for 3500$00/4500$00. *Restaurante A Charrete* (☎ 92142), Rua Samora Gil, is friendly and unpretentious. Winning rave reviews from travellers (who have scribbled recommendations on the walls) is the cosy *Restaurante Central*, Rua da Igreja 5. *Barlefante* (☎ 92774), at Travessa da Guerreira, is a popular bar which stays open until 1 am.

Getting There & Away

Over a dozen daily buses run between Lagos and Portimão, where eight services daily run to Monchique.

SILVES

Silves was once the Moorish capital of the Algarve and rivalled Lisbon in its influence. Times are quieter now, but the town's huge castle is a reminder of past grandeur and well worth a visit.

The switched-on tourist office (☎ 442255), Rua 25 de Abril, can also help with accommodation.

The telephone code for Silves is ☎ 082.

Places to Stay & Eat

The *Residencial Sousa* (☎ 442502), Rua Samoura Barros 17, has singles/doubles for 3500$00/4000$00. The eye-catching *Residencial Ponte Romana* (☎ 443275) beside the old bridge has rooms for around 5000$00/6000$00.

Restaurante Rui (☎ 442682), Rua C Vitarinho 23, is the best (and most expensive) fish restaurant in town; it serves a memorable arroz de marisco (shellfish rice). For cheaper meals, head for the riverfront restaurants opposite the bus stop.

Getting There & Away
Silves train station is two km from town; buses meet Faro trains seven times daily (five times daily at weekends). Another bus service connects Silves with Portimão via Lagoa.

SAGRES
Sagres is a small fishing port perched on dramatic, windswept cliffs at the south-western extremity of Portugal.

The telephone code for Sagres is ☎ 082.

Things to See & Do
In the **fort**, on a wide windy promontory, Henry the Navigator established his school of navigation and primed the explorers who later founded the Portuguese empire.

There are several beaches close to Sagres. A particularly pleasant one is at the fishing village of **Salema**, 17 km east.

No visit to Sagres would be complete without a trip to precipitous **Cabo de São Vicente** (Cape St Vincent), six km from Sagres. A solitary lighthouse stands on this barren cape which proclaims itself the south-westernmost point of Europe.

Places to Stay & Eat
The well-maintained *Camping Sagres* (☎ 64351) is two km from town, off the Lisbon road. Scooters are available for hire here. Some locals in Sagres rent out rooms for around 3500$00 a double. Cheap, filling meals can be had at the *Restaurante A Sagres* (☎ 64171) at the roundabout as you enter the village, and the *Café Atlântico* (☎ 64236) on the main street near the turn-off to the elegant *Pousada do Infante* (☎ 64222).

Getting There & Away
There are about a dozen buses daily between Sagres and Lagos, fewer on Sundays and holidays; at least three connect Sagres to Faro.

Central Portugal

Central Portugal, good for weeks of desultory rambling, deserves more attention than it receives. From the beaches of the Costa de Prata to the lofty Serra da Estrela and the sprawling Alentejo plains dotted with curious megaliths, it is a landscape of extremes.

Some of Portugal's finest wines come from the Dão region, while further south, the hills and plains are studded with the country's equally famous cork oaks. To literally top it off, the centre is graced with scores of fortresses and walled cities where you can wander along ancient cobbled streets, breathe clean air, and contemplate the awe-inspiring expanses below.

ÉVORA
One of the architectural gems of Portugal, the walled town of Évora is the capital of Alentejo province – a vast district with surprisingly varied landscapes of olive groves, vineyards and wheat fields, and in spring brilliant wild flowers. Évora's charm lies in the narrow one-way streets (mind those wing mirrors!) of the remarkably well preserved inner town.

Orientation & Information
The focal point of Évora is Praça do Giraldo. From here you can wander through backstreets until you meet the city walls. Poor maps with some walking routes are available from the tourist office (☎ 22671), Praça do Giraldo 73, while the good *Planta de Évora* map, and a few books in English, can be found at Nazareth bookshop, Praça do Giraldo 46.

Outside the tourist office there's an automatic exchange machine which accepts a wide range of currencies. The post office is on Rua de Olivença. The hospital (☎ 22132) is on Rua do Valasco.

The telephone code for Évora is ☎ 066.

Things to See
On Largo do Marquês de Marialva is the **Sé**, Évora's cathedral. It has cloisters and a museum of ecclesiastical treasures, both closed Monday. Admission is 300$00.

Next door, the **Museu de Évora**, features Roman and Manueline sculptures, and also paintings by 16th-century Portuguese artists. Admission is 250$00. Opposite the museum is the Roman-era **Temple of Diana**, subject of Évora's top-selling postcard.

The **Igreja de São Francisco**, a few blocks south of Praça do Giraldo, includes the ghoulish Capela dos Ossos (Chapel of Bones),

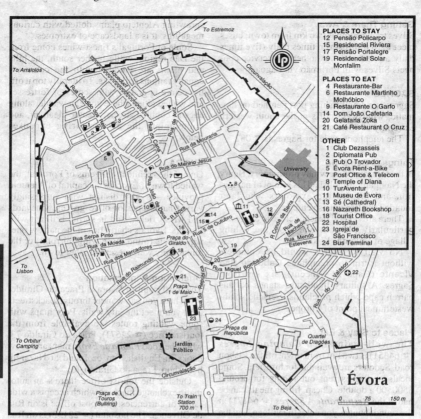

PORTUGAL

PLACES TO STAY
12 Pensão Policarpo
15 Residencial Riviera
17 Pensão Portalegre
19 Residencial Solar
   Monfalim

PLACES TO EAT
4 Restaurante-Bar
6 Restaurante Martinho
   Molhóbico
9 Restaurante O Garfo
14 Dom João Cafetaria
20 Gelataria Zoka
21 Café Restaurant O Cruz

OTHER
1 Club Dezasseis
2 Diplomata Pub
3 Pub O Trovador
5 Évora Rent-a-Bike
7 Post Office & Telecom
8 Temple of Diana
10 TurAventur
11 Museu de Évora
16 Sé (Cathedral)
16 Nazareth Bookshop
18 Tourist Office
22 Hospital
23 Igreja de
   São Francisco
24 Bus Terminal

Évora

0   75   150 m

constructed with the bones and skulls of several thousand people.

Places to Stay

Accommodation gets very tight in Évora, which is popular with Spanish tourists. The tourist office can help, but in summer you should definitely book ahead.

Camping *Orbitur* (☎ 25190) is about two km south of the town; take a bus towards Alcáçovas or a taxi.

Guesthouses The *Residencial Solar Monfalim* (☎ 22031), Largo da Misericórdia 1, is a

mini-palace with fading singles/doubles from 10,000$00/12,000$00. Doubles at the *Pensão Policarpo* (☎ 22424), Rua da Freiria de Baixo 16, another historical charmer, are 8500$00/6500$00 with/without bath. In the backstreets at Travessa do Barão 18 is the run-down *Pensão Portalegre* (☎ 22326), with quiet rooms at 2000$00/3000$00. The *Residencial Riviera* (☎ 23304), Rua 5 de Outubro 49, is like a quality hotel and is good value with doubles for 9000$00.

Places to Eat

Restaurante O Garfo (☎ 29256), Rua de Santa Catarina 13, provides healthy servings of feijoada ha alentejana (lamb and bean stew) and other lamb dishes at reasonable prices in traditional surroundings. *Restaurante Martinho* (☎ 23057), Largo Luis de Camões 24-25, is one of many places specialising in borrego (lamb) dishes. The friendly *Café Restaurant O Cruz* (☎ 744779), at Praça 1 de Maio 20, dishes out good bacalhau and tasty carne com ameijoas (meat with clams). Another good-value place is the *Restaurante-Bar Molhóbico* (☎ 744343) at Rua de Aviz 91, offering meat dishes and half a dozen versions of bacalhau until 1.30 am. The town's most popular ice-cream parlour is *Gelataria Zoka* at Largo de São Vicente 14 (west end of Rua Miguel Bombarda).

Entertainment

Among popular student hang-outs are a cluster of bars north-west of the centre – *Club Dezasseis* (☎ 26559) at Rua do Escrivão da Cámara 16; the *Diplomata Pub* (☎ 25675), with frequent live music, at Rua do Apóstolo 4; and the *Pub O Trovador* (☎ 27370) at Rua da Mostardeira 4. Another student focal point that stays open late is *Dom João Cafetaria* (☎ 20493), Rua Vasco da Gama 10.

The Feira de São João is Évora's big bash, held from approximately 22 June to 2 July and renowned as one of Alentejo's biggest country fairs.

Getting There & Away

Bus There are at least five buses a day to Lisbon (3¾ hours) and to Estremoz, and at least three to Faro; all buses depart from the terminal (☎ 22121) on Rua da República.

Train There are several express trains to Lisbon (three hours) daily, plus slower services. There are also trains to the Algarve (tedious and indirect), Coimbra (changes required) and regional chug-a-lug services to Beja.

Getting Around

Évora Rent-a-Bike (☎ 761453), on Praça Joaquim António de Aguiar, has mountain bikes for about 1500$00 a day. TurAventur (☎ & fax 743134) at Rua João de Deus 21, can organise everything from walking and biking tours to drive-yourself jeep safaris.

MONSARAZ

Monsaraz, a magical walled town perched high above the plain, is well worth the effort spent getting there for its eerie medieval atmosphere, clear light and magnificent views. It's small and easily covered on foot in a couple of hours. Of architectural interest are the **Misericórdia** hospital and the **Museu de Arte Sacra**, probably a former tribunal which houses a rare 15th-century fresco of the allegory of justice. Clamber onto the castle's parapets for the best views.

Places to Stay & Eat

The tourist office (☎ 066-55136) on the main square can help with accommodation, including private rooms, Turihab places, and a couple of posh establishments just outside town. There are three fairly expensive restaurants and a tiny grocery store near the main gate. Eat before 8 pm, as the town goes to bed early.

Getting There & Away

With infrequent direct buses from Évora (only one or two a day), it's best to stay overnight in Monsaraz. There are also a few buses daily from Reguengos de Monsaraz (17 km west), which has more regular connections with Évora and several places to stay overnight.

ESTREMOZ

The Estremoz region is dominated by huge mounds of marble extracted from its quarries. The town's architectural appeal lies in its elegant, gently deteriorating buildings, which are liberally embellished with marble, of course.

Information

The welcoming tourist office (☎ 332071/2/3), in a kiosk on the south-western corner of the main square (known as the Rossio), has maps and accommodation lists.

The telephone code for Estremoz is ☎ 068.

Things to See & Do

The upper section of Estremoz is crowned by the **Torre de Menagem**. At the foot of the castle is a former palace, converted into a pousada. The focus of the lower section is the Rossio, and two interesting sights nearby are the **Igreja de São Francisco** and the **Misericórdia** hospital.

PORTUGAL

There's a small food and pottery **market** every Saturday in the Rossio. The clothes and shoes section is on the eastern outskirts of town. One of Portugal's most charming museums is the **Museu Rural** at Rossio 62 and full of handmade miniatures. It's open daily, except Monday, from 10 am to 1 pm and 3 to 5.30 pm; entry is 100$00.

Vila Viçosa, 17 km from Estremoz, is an easy bus trip. The major attraction is the **Palácio Ducal** – the ancestral home of the dukes of Bragança – with its horde of carpets, furniture and artworks. It's open daily, except Monday and public holidays, from 9.30 am to 1 pm and 2 to 6 pm (last tour at 5 pm). Admission (with a mandatory guided tour, usually in Portuguese only) costs 1000$00 which includes the fee for the armoury museum. The coach museum costs another 250$00.

Places to Stay & Eat
Spacious singles/doubles at the *Pensão-Restaurante Mateus* (☎ 22226), Rua Almeida 41, are good value at 2500$00/4500$00. Prices include breakfast in the restaurant which is also good for other meals.

Getting There & Away
About 12 buses daily (including three expressos) run from Estremoz to Évora, and six buses run to Portalegre daily, with less frequent connections to and from Lisbon.

CASTELO DE VIDE & MARVÃO
From Portalegre (near the Spanish border, north-east of Lisbon) it's a short hop to **Castelo de Vide**, noted for its mineral water and picturesque houses clustered around a castle. Highlights are the **Judiaria** (Old Jewish Quarter) in the well-preserved network of medieval backstreets, and the view from the castle.

Try to spend at least one night in **Marvão**, a magnificent medieval walled village tucked into a mountaintop 12 km from Castelo de Vide. The grand views from its castle encompass large chunks of Spain and Portugal.

Information
The tourist offices at Castelo de Vide (☎ 91361), Rua de Bartolomeu Álvares da Santa 81, and at Marvão (☎ 93104), Rua Dr Matos Magalhães, can both help with accom-

modation, including private rooms and Turihab places.

The telephone code for Marvão and Castelo de Vide is ☎ 045.

Getting There & Away
In summer, from Portalegre there are four or five buses daily to Castelo de Vide five times daily and one or two to Marvão. Two buses run daily from Lisbon to Castelo de Vide and Marvão. There are three direct connections daily between Castelo de Vide and Marvão. Outside the summer season you may find no buses at all on weekends and holidays.

NAZARÉ
The peaceful 17th-century fishing village of Nazaré was 'discovered' by tourism in the 1970s and dubbed Portugal's most picturesque fishing village. Today, the old fishing skills and distinctive local dress have gone overboard and in the high season the place is a tourist circus. But the beauty of the coastline and the superb seafood make it a worthwhile place to visit.

The tourist office (☎ 561194) is at the funicular end of Avenida da República. The telephone code for Nazaré is ☎ 062.

Things to See & Do
The lower part of Nazaré's beachfront has retained a core of narrow streets which now cater to the tourist trade. The upper section, O Sítio, on the cliffs overlooking the beach, is reached by a vintage funicular railway. The cliff-top view along the coast is superb.

The beaches attract huge summer crowds and pollution is an increasing problem. Beware of dangerous currents. The tourist office will tell you which beaches are safe for swimming.

Places to Stay & Eat
Many locals rent private rooms: you will probably be pounced on when you arrive at the bus station. Singles/doubles start around 3000$00/4500$00. *Camping Golfinho* (☎ 553680) is an inexpensive camping ground off the main Estrada Nacional 242 just north of town; two other sites, including an Orbitur one, are 2.5 km from Nazaré. There are dozens of pensões, but prices jump in high season.

One compelling reason to visit is the superb and abundant seafood, though the seafront restaurants are expensive. For cheaper fare in simple surroundings, try *Casa Marques* (☎ 551680) at Rua Gil Vicente 37, run by a troika of Nazarean women. The friendly *A Tasquinha* (☎ 551945) at Rua Adrião Batalha 54 does a superb carne de porco à Alentejana for under 1000$00. Another attractively priced place is *Casa O Pescador* (☎ 553326) at Rua António Carvalho Laranjo 18-A. The caldeirada (fish stew) is a tasty bargain at 900$00.

Getting There & Away
The nearest train station, six km away at Valado, is connected to Nazaré by frequent buses. There are numerous bus connections to Lisbon, Alcobaça, Óbidos and Coimbra.

ALCOBAÇA
Alcobaça's attraction is the immense **Mosteiro de Santa Maria de Alcobaça**, founded in 1178. The original Gothic style has undergone Manueline, Renaissance and baroque additions. Of interest are the tombs of Pedro I and Inês de Castro, the cloisters, the kings' room and the kitchens. It's open from 9 am to 7 pm (5 pm in winter); entry is 400$00.

The tourist office (☎ 062-42377) is opposite the monastery.

Getting There & Away
Alcobaça is an easy day trip from Nazaré. There are frequent buses to Nazaré, Batalha and Leiria. The closest train station is five km north-west at Valado dos Frades, from where there are buses to Alcobaça.

BATALHA
Batalha's single highlight is its monastery, the **Mosteiro de Santa Maria de Vitória**, a colossal Gothic masterpiece constructed between 1388 and 1533. Earthquakes and vandalism by French troops have taken their toll, but a full restoration was completed in 1965. Highlights include the Founder's Chapel (with the tomb of Henry the Navigator), the Royal Cloisters, Chapter House and the Unfinished Chapels. It's open from 9 am to 6 pm daily; entry is 400$00.

The tourist office (☎ 044-96180) is in a nearby shopping complex on Largo Paulo VI. The telephone code for Batalha is ☎ 044.

Getting There & Away
There are frequent bus connections to Alcobaça, Nazaré, Tomar and Leiria, and at least three direct buses to Lisbon daily.

ÓBIDOS
The impressive walled town of Óbidos has preserved its medieval streets and alleys almost too perfectly. It's easily seen in a day. The friendly tourist office (☎ 959231), Rua Direita, has information on Óbidos and the region.

The telephone code for Óbidos is ☎ 062.

Things to See
Climb onto the town walls and do a circuit for the views and your bearings. Then wander through the back alleys before popping into **Igreja de Santa Maria**, featuring fine azulejos, and the adjacent **museu municipal**.

Places to Stay & Eat
Accommodation in Óbidos isn't cheap but it's plentiful, with both residencials and a number of private rooms for around 4500$00 a double. Look for the signs around town. You might fancy dishing out for the romantic *Casa do Poço* (☎ 959358) in Travessa da Mouraria; its four double rooms around a courtyard are 11,500$00 each. A cheaper alternative is the *Residencial Martim de Freitas* (☎ 959185), just outside the walls on the Estrada Nacional 8, with doubles from 6000$00.

Restaurants are not cheap either. The supermarket inside the town gate would suit self-caterers. *Restaurante Alcaide* (☎ 959220) at Rua Direita has excellent main dishes from 1200$00 and you can eat on the terrace in warm weather. It's closed on Monday and during November.

Getting There & Away
There are excellent bus connections to Lisbon, Porto, Coimbra, Tomar and the surrounding region. From the train station, outside the walls at the foot of the hill, there are five services daily to Lisbon (most with a change at Cacém).

COIMBRA
Coimbra is famed for its university, dating back to the 13th century, and its traditional role as a centre of culture and art, complemented in recent times by industrial development.

PORTUGAL

The regional tourist office (☎ 23886) on Largo da Portagem has a good city map and information on cultural events. There are friendlier and more efficient municipal tourist offices (☎ 32591 or 33202) in Praça Dom Dinis by the university, and down below in Praça da República.

Coimbra's annual highlight is the Queima das Fitas (literally, 'burning of ribbons') when students celebrate the end of the academic year by burning their faculty ribbons. This boisterous week of fado and revelry begins the first Thursday in May.

The telephone code for Coimbra is ☎ 039.

Things to See
In lower Coimbra, the most interesting sight is **Mosteiro de Santa Cruz** with its ornate pulpit, medieval tombs and intricate sacristy.

In the upper town, the main attractions are the **old university** with its baroque library and Manueline chapel, and the **Machado de Castro Museum**, with a fine collection of sculpture and painting. The back alleys of the university quarter are filled with student hangouts and an exuberant atmosphere.

At **Conímbriga**, 16 km south of Coimbra, are the excavated remains of a Roman city (open from 9 am to 1 pm and 2 to 8 pm; to 6 pm in winter), including impressive mosaic floors, baths and fountains. The site museum (open from 10 am to 1 pm and 2 to 6 pm) has a variety of Roman artefacts and a good restaurant. Both are open daily except Monday. Entry costs 350$00. Buses run frequently to Condeixa, a km from the site, or you can take a direct bus (245$00) at 9.05 or 9.35 am (9.35 am only at weekends) from the AVIC terminal at Rua João de Ruão 18; it returns at 1 and 6 pm (6 pm only at weekends).

Activities
O Pioneiro do Mondego (☎ 478385) rents out kayaks at 2500$00 a day for paddling down the Rio Mondego (a free minibus whisks you upriver to Penacova at 10 am).

Horse riders can trot around Choupal Park by contacting the Coimbra Riding Centre (☎ 37695), Mata do Choupal.

Places to Stay & Eat
The *pousada de juventude* (☎ 22955), Rua Henriques Seco 12-14, is Coimbra's youth hostel; take bus No 5 from Largo de Portagem or No 5 from Coimbra A. *Residencial Antunes* (☎ 23048), Rua Castro Matoso 8, near the university, has singles/doubles from 3200$00/4800$00 (without bath) and deluxe doubles at 10,000$00. Overlooking the central Praça do Comércio, the quiet *Pensão Rivoli* (☎ 25550) has rooms for 2500$00/4500$00. One of the cheapest places in the town centre is the spartan *Hospedaria Simões* (☎ 34638), Rua Fernandes Tomás 69, where singles/doubles cost around 2000$00/3000$00.

There are numerous cheap eateries around the Praça do Comércio. *Diligência Bar* (☎ 27667), Rua Nova 30, is also a popular venue for amateur and professional fadistas. The vaulted *Café Santa Cruz*, in the Praça 8 de Maio, is an addictive place for coffee breaks. In a seedy backstreet at Beco do Forno 12, *Zé Manel* (☎ 23790) is a wacky little dive with crazy décor and huge servings. Go before 8 pm to beat the queues. The cosy *Restaurante Ticino* (☎ 35989), near the hostel at Rua Bernardo de Albuquerque 120, serves good Italian dishes from around 1200$00.

Getting There & Away
At least a dozen buses and an equal number of trains run daily to Lisbon and Porto and there are frequent express buses to Évora and Faro. Coimbra has three train stations: Coimbra Parque for Lousã; Coimbra A for Figueira da Foz; and the main Coimbra B for all other services (including international). Coimbra A and B are linked by a regular shuttle train service.

Getting Around
Mountain bikes can be rented from O Pioneiro do Mondego (☎ 478385) from 1 to 3 pm and 8 to 10 pm.

Car-rental agencies include Avis (☎ 34786), Hertz (☎ 37491) and Salitur (☎ 20594).

LUSO & BUÇACO FOREST
Walkers will appreciate the Buçaco Forest, which was chosen by monks as a retreat in the 6th century and has escaped serious harm since then. It's a few km from the spa resort of Luso, where the tourist office (☎ 939133) on Avenida Emídio Navarro has a general map of the forest and more detailed leaflets describing

trails past wayside shrines and more than 700 species of trees and shrubs.

The telephone code for Luso is ☎ 031.

Places to Stay & Eat

The Luso tourist office has accommodation lists. *Pensão Central* (☎ 939254), Avenida Emídio Navarro, has bright singles/doubles from 2700$00/4500$00 and a good summer-time restaurant with patio seating.

For a touch of class, try the *Palace Hotel* (☎ 930101; fax 930509), a former royal hunting lodge in the forest and as zany and beautiful an expression of Manueline style as any in Portugal. Figure on spending at least 2500$00 per dish or 5000$00 for the res-taurant's set menu. If you want to stay in this positively elegant five-star establishment, you'll pay around 25,000$00/30,000$00.

Getting There & Away

Five buses a day go to Luso and Buçaco from Coimbra and Viseu (only two on weekends). There are three trains daily from Coimbra to Luso.

SERRA DA ESTRELA

Serra da Estrela, Portugal's highest mountain range, stretches between Guarda and Castelo Branco. With steep valleys, forests and streams, it offers superb scope for hiking and is a designated parque natural. The highest peak, Torre (1993 metres), is snow-covered for much of the year.

Orientation & Information

The best sources of information are at the tourist offices in Covilhã (☎ 075-322170), Manteigas (☎ 075-981129) and Guarda (☎ 071-222251), and the park office in Manteigas (☎ 075-982382). Covilhã is an uninteresting industrial hub, but a good base for excursions; another is the hostel at Penhas da Saúde. The regional tourist administration publishes the walking guide *À Descoberta da Estrela*, with maps and narratives. It is avail-able from the Covilhã, Manteigas and Seia tourist offices, and park offices in Gouveia, Seia and Manteigas, for 840$00 (English edition). A more detailed map for 1050$00 is also available.

Serious hikers might want to contact the Club Nacional de Montanhismo (☎ 075-

323364; fax 075-313514) in Covilhã, which organises weekend walking, camping, skiing and other expeditions.

Places to Stay

The *pousada de juventude* (☎ 075-25375) at Penhas da Saúde, high in the mountains nine km from Covilhã, has full facilities for meals (theirs or do-it-yourself) and accommodation. There are buses from Covilhã on weekends in July and August only, and hitching is fairly safe and easy; the only other options are your feet or bike, or a taxi.

Getting There & Away

There are several buses a day from Coimbra to Seia, Covilhã and Guarda, as well as some from Porto and Lisbon to Covilhã and Guarda. Twice-daily intercidade trains link Coimbra to Guarda, and twice-daily interregional trains stop at Gouveia as well. Covilhã and Guarda are on the Lisbon-Paris line, with several fast trains a day and connections from Porto.

Getting Around

There are twice-daily buses (and some week-end express services) linking Guarda and Covilhã, but nothing across the park.

The North

Most visitors are surprised by Portugal's north-ern tier. With considerable tracts of forest, rich viticultural country, the peaks of Peneda-Gerês National Park, and a strand of undeveloped beaches, it is Portugal's new tourism horizon. The urban scene focuses on Porto with its magnificent vantage point on the Rio Douro. Within easy reach of Porto are a trio of stately historical cities: Braga, Portugal's religious centre; beautifully situated Viana do Castelo; and Guimarães, which proudly declares itself the country's birthplace.

PORTO

Porto is Portugal's second-largest city. Despite its reputation as a grimy industrial hub, it has considerable charm beyond the imbibing of port wine.

Orientation

The city is divided by the Rio Douro, which is spanned by four bridges. On the north bank is central Porto; on the south bank is Vila Nova de Gaia with its port-wine lodges.

The focus of central Porto is Avenida dos Aliados. Major shopping areas are eastward around Rua de Santa Catarina, and westward around Rua dos Clérigos. Praça da Liberdade marks the southern end of Avenida dos Aliados, close to São Bento station and its cavernous booking hall covered with superb azulejos. The picturesque Ribeira district lies below Ponte de Dom Luís I, several streets south of São Bento.

Information

Tourist Offices The municipal tourist office (☎ 312740) is at Rua Clube dos Fenianos 25, close to the town hall. It's open weekdays from 9 am to 5.30 pm (to 4 pm on Saturday). Between July and September it's open on weekdays until 7 pm and on Sunday from 10 am to 1 pm. A smaller national tourist office (☎ 317514) is found at Praça Dom João I, 43. It's open weekdays from 9 am to 7 pm and on weekends from 9 am to 3.30 pm.

Foreign Consulates There is no longer a US Consulate here. The UK Consulate (☎ 618 4789; fax 610 0438), Avenida da Boavista 3072, is open weekdays from 9.30 am to 12.30 pm and 3 to 5 pm.

Money Several banks line Avenida dos Aliados, with a currency exchange machine at No 138. Better deals are at Portocambios, Rua Rodrigues Sampaio 193, and at InterContinental, Rua de Ramalho Ortigão 8.

Post & Communications The main post office (the place to collect poste-restante mail) is on Praça General Humberto Delgado, opposite the main tourist office; it's open weekdays from 8 am to 9 pm and weekends from 9 am to 6 pm. The main telephone office is at Praça da Liberdade 62; it's open weekdays from 8 am to midnight and on Sundays and holidays from 10 am to 1 pm and 2 pm to midnight. The telephone office in the main post office is open weekdays from 9 am to 6 pm.

The telephone code for Porto is ☎ 02.

Travel Agencies Top Tours (☎ 208 2785; fax 325367), Rua Alferes Malheiro 96, is the American Express representative. Youth travel specialist Jumbo Express Viagens (☎ 208 1561), Rua de Ceuta 47, can arrange youth and student travel, including car-rental discounts.

Laundry The Pinguim Lavandaria (☎ 609 5032), in the basement of the Brasilia shopping centre, Praça Mouzinho de Albuquerque, Boavista, has laundry, dry-cleaning and self-service facilities. It's open from 10 am to 10.30 pm Monday to Saturday.

Medical Services The Santo António Hospital (☎ 200 5241 day; 200 7354 night) has some English-speaking staff.

Things to See & Do

The **Torre dos Clérigos** on Rua dos Clérigos is the highest tower in Portugal. Its 200-plus steps lead to the best panorama of the city. It's open daily, except Wednesday, from 10.30 am to noon and from 2.30 to 5 pm, for 100$00.

The formidable **Sé**, the cathedral dominating central Porto, is worth a visit for its mixture of architectural styles and ornate interior. It's open daily from 9 am to 12.30 pm and 2.30 to 6 pm. Admission to the cloisters and chapter house (closed Sunday) is 200$00.

The **Soares dos Reis National Museum**, on Rua Dom Manuel II, has finally reopened after renovation and is open daily except Monday, from 10 am to 12.30 pm and 2 to 5.30 pm. It displays masterpieces of Portuguese painting and sculpture from the 19th and 20th centuries. Admission is 350$00 (140$00 for students with youth cards) and is free on Sunday morning.

In Vila Nova de Gaia you can tour the cellars of some of the **port-wine lodges** and sample the goods. Large lodges include Porto Sandeman (☎ 370 2293), Largo Miguel Bombarda 3, and Ferreira (☎ 370 0010), Rua Carvalhosa 19.

In Porto the **Solar do Vinho do Porto** (☎ 694749) is at Rua de Entre Quintas 220. Select from a huge port list and sip it on a terrace offering excellent views across the city. It's open until 11.45 pm on weekdays and until 10.45 pm on Saturday (closed on Sunday and public holidays).

Bolhão is a fascinating market north-east of

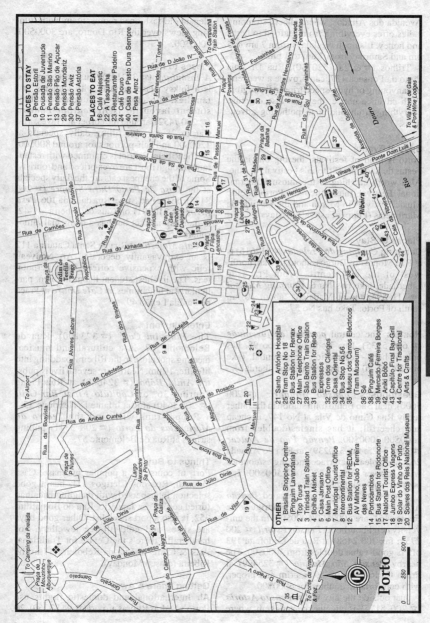

Avenida dos Aliados, where cheery strapping ladies offer everything from seafood to herbs and honey. It's open weekdays from 7 am to 5 pm and Saturday from 7 am to 1 pm.

Trilhos (☎ & fax 520740), Rua Dr Luis Pinto da Fonseca 137, can provide a weekend of canyoning or hydrospeed trips in the region. With advance notice, they can also organise everything from biking to potholing adventures.

Special Events

Porto is fond of festivals: the big one is the Festas de São João (St John's Festival) in June. Also worth catching is the unusual International Festival Intercéltico do Porto (Celtic Music Festival) in March and the Festival de Marionetas (Puppet Festival) in May.

Places to Stay

Camping *Camping da Prelada* (☎ 812616) is at Rua Monte dos Burgos, about five km northwest of the city centre. From Praça da Liberdade, take bus No 6. *Camping Marisol* (☎ 711 5942) is at Madalena, about 10 km south of Porto. Take bus No 57.

Hostels The central *pousada de juventude* (☎ 606 5535), Rua Rodrigues Lobo 98, has only 50 beds – reservations are essential. Take bus No 52, 20 or 3 from Praça da Liberdade.

Guesthouses *Pensão Mondariz* (☎ 200 5600), near São Bento train station in the rather seedy Rua Cimo de Vila at No 147, is cheap and cheerful; it has singles/doubles from 1500$00/3000$00. *Pensão Pão de Açucar* (☎ 200 2425; fax 310239), at Rua do Almada 262, has a pleasant terrace and singles/doubles with shower from 5500$00/7500$00. It's popular, so bookings are essential.

Rooms at the recently renovated *Pensão Aviz* (☎ 320722) at Avenida Rodrigues de Freitas 451, are 5000$00/6000$00. In the university neighbourhood, *Pensão Estoril* (☎ 200 2751; fax 208 2468) at Rua de Cedofeita 193 offers good-value doubles from 4000$00. The nearby *Pensão São Marino* (☎ 325499) at Praça Carlos Alberto 59 is prim and proper, with comfortable doubles for 6000$00.

Just outside the city walls, *Pensão Astória* (☎ 200 8175) is an unexpected gem where elegant old-fashioned rooms, many with stunning views over the Rio Douro, are 3000$00/5000$00.

Places to Eat

A Tasquinha (☎ 322145), Rua do Carmo 23, is a folksy place popular with students and families. It's closed on Sunday. Another student favourite is *Restaurant Padeiro* (☎ 200 7452), around the corner at Travessa do Carmo 28-A, with filling daily specials at 1200$00 and half-portions for around 800$00.

The Ribeira district is crammed with restaurants, though most are over-priced and touristy. Some of the cheapest eats are the daily specials at the *Casa de Pasto Dura Sempre* (☎ 200 8488), on the backstreet Rua da Lada 106. *Pesa Arroz* (☎ 310291) on Cais da Ribeira, 41-42, is more up-market but has a congenial atmosphere.

Café Majestic at Rua de Santa Catarina 112 is an extravagantly decorated Art Nouveau relic with expensive coffees and afternoon teas. The liveliest student haunt in town, particularly at lunchtimes, is *Café Douro* at Praça de Parada Leitão 49.

Entertainment

The *Pinguim Café* (☎ 323100), Rua de Belomonte 67, is a cultural and musical meeting spot close to the Ribeira, paddling into life after 10 pm. Nearby are several lively pubs: try *Aniki Bóbó* (☎ 324669) at Rua Fonte Taurina 36, or *Capitúlo Final Bar-Grill* (☎ 208 3640) at Rua Infante D'Henrique 35.

Puppet-fans will find the *Teatro de Marionetas do Porto* (☎ 208 3341) pulling strings at Rua de Belomonte 57.

Things to Buy

Port, of course, is a popular purchase. Casa Oriental, Rua dos Clérigos 111, has a good selection interspersed with dangling bacalhau (dried cod). Casa Januário, Rua do Bonjardim 352, is also a port specialist. Other good buys are shoes and gold-filigree jewellery. For handicrafts, there's the Centre for Traditional Arts & Crafts at Rua da Reboleira 37 in the Ribeira (closed Monday).

Getting There & Away

Air International and domestic flights use Porto's Pedras Rubras airport (☎ 941 3260), 20 km north-west of the city centre. Domestic connections include daily Portugália flights to/from Lisbon and Faro, and some TAP flights to/from Lisbon. Both TAP and British Airways link Porto with London.

Bus There are several places where you can catch long-distance buses. Renex (☎ 208 2398) at Rua Carmelitas 32 is the best choice for Lisbon and the Algarve, and also runs to Braga; the ticket office is open 24 hours a day. From Praça Filipa de Lencastre, REDM (☎ 200 3152) goes mainly to Braga; AV Minho (☎ 200 6121) to Viana do Castelo; and João Terreira das Neves (☎ 200 0881) to Guimarães. From a terminal at Rua Alexandre Herculano 370, Rede Expressos (☎ 200 6954) buses go all over Portugal. Rodonorte (☎ 200 5637) departs from Rua Ateneu Comércial do Porto 19 and goes mainly to Bragança and Vila Real.

Train Porto, a rail hub for northern Portugal, has three major stations. Most international connections, and all intercidade links throughout Portugal, start at Campanhã (☎ 564141), the main and largest station. Inter-regional and regional connections depart from either the very central São Bento station or from Campanhã (bus No 35 runs frequently between these two stations). Trindade station is for Póvoa de Varzim and Guimarães only.

Car & Motorcycle Driving in the city centre is a real pain, thanks to gridlocked traffic, one-way streets and scarce parking.

Getting Around

To/From the Airport Take bus No 56 from Jardim da Cordoaria or a taxi (2400$00 plus a possible baggage charge of 300$00). During peak times allow an hour from the city centre.

Bus An extensive bus system operates from Jardim da Cordoaria (also called Jardim de João Chagas) and Praça Dom João I. Individual tickets cost 160$00 or you can buy a caderneta (book of 20 tickets) for 1400$00, or a one-day (350$00), four-day (1700$00) or one-week (2200$00) Passe Turístico (Tourist Pass), from kiosks near the bus stops or opposite São Bento station.

Tram Porto's trams used to be one of the delights of the city but only one is left: the No 18, trundling from Carmo out to Foz and back to Boa Vista every quarter-hour all day (except Sunday when a No 18 bus does the route). Sentimental fans can stop en route at the **Museu dos Carros Eléctricos** (Tram Museum), Cais do Bicalho (look for the STCP building), which has dozens of restored old cars in a cavernous tram warehouse. It's open Tuesday to Saturday from 9 am to noon and 2 to 5 pm; entry is 100$00.

Taxi Taxis are good value. For a zip across town, figure on about 500$00. An additional charge is made if you cross the Ponte Dom Luís to Vila Nova de Gaia or leave the city limits.

Car Porto's car-rental agencies include Hertz (☎ 312387), Europcar (☎ 318398), Turiscar (☎ 600 8401), and AA Castanheira (☎ 606 5256).

ALONG THE DOURO

The Douro Valley is one of Portugal's scenic highlights, with some 200 km of bold, expansive panoramas from Porto to the Spanish border. In the upper reaches, port-wine vineyards wrap round every crew-cut hillside, interrupted only by the occasional bright-white port company manor house.

The river, tamed by eight dams and locks since the late 1980s, is now navigable all the way, making boat tours an ideal option. Vistadouro (☎ 938 7949) organises one or two-day cruises throughout the year. Highly recommended, too, is the train trip from Porto to Peso da Régua (about a dozen trains daily, 2½ hours). The last 50 km cling dramatically to the river bank. The further you go, the better it gets: four trains continue daily along the valley to Pocinho (4½ hours).

Bike and car travellers have an enticing choice of river-hugging roads along the south and north banks – but both are wriggly and crowded with Porto escapees at weekends. Grayline (☎ 316597), Rua Guedes de Azevedo, Edificio Silo-Auto, operates a day-long Douro Valley coach tour which includes some nearby attractions.

The detailed colour map *Rio Douro*

PORTUGAL

(1000$00), available from Porto bookshops, is a handy source of information.

VIANA DO CASTELO

This port, attractively set at the mouth of the Rio Lima, is renowned for its historic old town and its promotion of folk traditions.

The helpful tourist office (☎ 822620) on Praça da Erva has information on festivals and other tourist literature about the region. The telephone code for Viana do Castelo is ☎ 058.

During August, the town hosts the Festas de Nossa Senhora da Agonia. See the Facts for the Visitor section at the start of this chapter for more details.

Things to See & Do

The focal point of the town is the splendid Praça da República with its delicate fountain and elegant buildings, including the **Ingreja de Misericórdia**.

At the top of the steep Santa Luzia hill, four km above town, is **Ingreja de Santa Luzia**, with a grand panorama across the coast from its dome lookout. A funicular railway climbs the hill from 9 am to 7 pm (hourly in the morning, every 30 minutes in the afternoon) from behind the train station.

Places to Stay & Eat

The tourist office has extensive accommodation listings, and can book Turihab places from 6000$00 for a double. *Pensão Guerreiro* (☎ 822099), Rua Grande 14 (1st floor), has clean singles/doubles for 2000$00/4000$00 (without bath). The *Residencial Magalhães* (☎ 823293), Rua Manuel Espregueira 24, has comfortable doubles from 5000$00.

The family-run *Restaurante Minho* (☎ 823261), Rua Gago Coutinho 103-5, serves wholesome, inexpensive dishes until midnight. Folksy *Os Três Potes* (☎ 829928), Rua Beco dos Fornos 9, has seafood dishes from around 1300$00, and dancers skipping between the tables on Saturday nights in summer! For other seafood specials try *Neiva-Mar Marisqueira* (☎ 820669), Largo Infante D. Henrique 1 (at the corner of Largo de Santa Catarina), opposite the fish market.

Getting There & Away

During the week, over a dozen buses daily go to Porto including four express services (1½

hours). Ten buses daily go to Braga (one hour). Train services run north to Spain and south to Porto.

BRAGA

Crammed with churches, Braga is considered Portugal's religious capital. During Easter week, huge crowds attend its Holy Week Festival.

The tourist office (☎ 22550), Avenida da Liberdade 1, can help with accommodation and maps. The telephone code for Braga is ☎ 053.

Things to See & Do

At Bom Jesus do Monte, a pilgrimage site on a hill seven km from the city, is an extraordinary stairway called **Escadaria do Bom Jesus**, with sculpted representations of the five senses, and a superb view. Buses run from Braga to the site, where you can either climb the steps or ride a funicular railway to the top.

In the centre of Braga is the **Sé**, a bewildering cathedral complex. Admission to its rambling treasury museum and several tomb chapels is 300$00.

It's an easy day trip to **Guimarães**, considered the cradle of Portugal, of interest for its medieval town centre and the palace of the dukes of Bragança.

Places to Stay

The *pousada de juventude* (☎ 616163), Rua de Santa Margarida 6, is a friendly hostel near the city centre. The *Grande Residência Avenida* (☎ 22955), Avenida da Liberdade 738, is good value with doubles from around 4500$00. Cheap but not very cheerful is the *Casa Santa Zita* (☎ 618331), a hostel for pilgrims (and others) at Rua São João 20, with singles/doubles for 2750$00/5500$00. Rooms with stunning views at the *Hotel Sul-Americano* (☎ 481237) at Bom Jesus start at 5500$00/7500$00; it's very popular, so reserve a place.

Places to Eat

Café Brasileira (☎ 22104) is a turn-of-the-century special at the corner of Rua de São Marcos and Rua do Souto, just off Praça da República; order a coffee and watch the world pass by. At *Retiro da Primavera* (☎ 72482), Rua Gabriel Pereira Castro 100, the prato do dia is probably the best-value meal in town. More congenial is the rustic, family-run *Casa*

Grulha (☎ 22883) at Rua dos Biscainhos 95, with an excellent cabrito assado (roast kid, a local specialty). Two good-value places (pratos for under 1000$00) on Praça Velha are *Taberna Rexío da Praça* at No 17 (closed on Sunday) and the casa de pasto *Pregão* at No 18.

Getting There & Away
The completion of an expressway from Porto has put Braga within easy day-trip reach. Train services connect Braga north to Viana do Castelo and Spain and south to Porto and Coimbra. There are excellent bus services to Porto and Lisbon, and local bus lines to Guimarães and Bom Jesus.

PENEDA-GERÊS NATIONAL PARK
This fine wilderness park along the Spanish border has spectacular scenery and a wide variety of fauna and flora. The Portuguese day-trippers and holiday-makers tend to stick to the main camping areas, leaving the rest of the park to hikers.

The main centre for the park is **Caldas do Gerês** (also called just Gerês), a sleepy, hot-spring village.

Orientation & Information
You can obtain information from the tourist office (☎ 391133) in the colonnade at the upper end of Caldas do Gerês. The Peneda-Gerês National Park has a small information office nearby (☎ 391181), others at Arcos de Valdevez and Montalegre just outside the park, and a head office (☎ 600 3480) in Braga at Avenida António Macedo, Quinta das Parretas. All sell a useful park map (530$00), with some roads and tracks (but not trails), and a booklet (105$00) on the park's features; most other information is in Portuguese.

The telephone code for Braga and Caldas do Gerês is ☎ 053.

Activities
Hiking The lack of decent trail maps can be a problem on a long trip, though most tracks are pleasant enough for short walks. From Caldas do Gerês, avoid the popular **Miradouro do Gerês** route at weekends when it's packed with car-trippers. A good option which offers the possibility of a swim is an old Roman road from Albergaria (10 km up-valley from Caldas by taxi or hitching), past the **Vilarinho**

das Furnas reservoir to **Campo do Gerês**. Further afield, the walks to Ermida and Cabril are excellent and both have simple accommodation and cafés.

An official long-distance trail is slowly being established, with eight itineraries spanning the park, mostly following traditional routes. Five have been completed so far, and descriptive map-brochures (300$00, in Portuguese) are available for two of these; contact a park office for details.

Montes d'Aventura (mobile ☎ 0936-673739, or Porto ☎ 02-208 8175), with a base at the pousada de juventude in Campo do Gerês, and Trote-Gerês (☎ 053-659860) near Cabril, organise guided walks for under 1800$00 per person per day.

Horse Riding The national park operates horse-riding facilities (☎ 391181) from beside their Vidoeiro camping ground, near Caldas do Gerês, for around 1300$00 an hour. Two other equine outfits are Equi Campo (☎ 357022) at Campo do Gerês, and Trote-Gerês (☎ 659860) near Cabril.

Canoeing & Other Water Sports Rio Caldo, eight km south of Caldas do Gerês, is the base for water sports on the Caniçada reservoir. The English-run outfit Água Montanha Lazer (☎ 391740) rents out kayaks for 600$00 to 1000$00 per hour, four-person canoes for 1500$00, plus small outboard boats. For paddling the Salamonde reservoir, Trote-Gerês (☎ 659860) rents canoes at 1000$00 an hour from their camping ground at Cabril. There's a swimming pool in Caldas do Gerês' Parque das Termas; park admission is 130$00 and pool admission is 700$00 on weekdays or 1100$00 on weekends.

Organised Tours
For an organised spin through the major sights in the park, Agência no Gerês (☎ 391112), next to the Universal Hotel in Caldas do Gerês, operates two to five-hour trips for 1000$00 to 1250$00 per person.

Places to Stay
The *Pousada de Juventude de Vilarinho das Furnas* (☎ 351339) and the very good *Cerdeira Camping Ground*, both at Campo

do Gerês, make good bases for hikes. One km north of Caldas do Gerês at Vidoeiro is a good park-run camping ground (☎ 391289). Other camping grounds are at Lamas de Mouro, Entre-Ambos-os-Rios and Cabril.

Caldas do Gerês has plenty of pensões, though these are often block-booked by spa patients in summer. Try *Pensão da Ponte* (☎ 391121) beside the gushing river, with doubles from 6000$00, or *Pensão Príncipe* (same owners, same rates) just up the hill. At the top of the hill, with the best views, is *Pensão Adelaide* (☎ 391188), with doubles from 5000$00/4000$00 with/without bath. For more rural accommodation, Trote-Gerês (☎ 659860) operates the cheerful, comfortable *Pousadinho* cottage in Paradela, with doubles from 4200$00.

Places to Eat
Most pensões at Caldas do Gerês provide hearty meals, usually available to non-guests,

too. Pensão Adelaide has a popular restaurant, or you can try the *Baltasar Pensão Restaurant* (☎ 391131), next to the park office, with huge servings from 900$00 a dish. There are several small stores in the main street for picnic provisions.

Getting There & Away
From Braga at least 10 buses a day run to Caldas do Gerês and at least two a day to Campo do Gerês (plus more on weekdays). Coming from Lisbon or Porto, change at Braga.

Getting Around
Unless you have your own transport, you must rely on infrequent bus connections to a limited number of places in or near the park, or walk.

Mountain bikes are available from Trote-Gerês (☎ 659860) at its Cabril camping ground, and from Pensão Carvalho Araújo (☎ 391185) in Caldas do Gerês.

Spain

Spaniards approach life with such exuberance that most visitors have to stop and stare. In almost every town in the country, the nightlife will outlast the foreigners. Then just when they think they are coming to terms with the pace, they are surrounded by the beating drums of a fiesta, with day and night turning into a blur of dancing, laughing, eating and drinking. Spain also holds its own in cultural terms with exciting museums like the Prado in Madrid, Cuenca's abstract art museum, the wacky Dalí museum in Figueres, and the Picasso and Miró museums in Barcelona.

Then, of course, you have the weather and the highly varied landscape. From April to October the sun shines with uncanny predictability on the Mediterranean coast and the Balearic Islands. Elsewhere you can enjoy good summer weather in the more secluded coves of Galicia, in the Pyrenees or the mountains of Andalucía, or on the surf beaches of western Andalucía or the País Vasco (Basque Country).

A wealth of history awaits the visitor to Spain: fascinating prehistoric displays at the archaeological museums in Teruel and Madrid; and from Roman times the aqueduct in Segovia, the seaside amphitheatre in Tarragona and the buried streets of Roman Barcelona made accessible via an underground walkway. After Roman times, the Moorish era left perhaps the most powerful cultural and artistic legacy – focused on Granada's Alhambra, Córdoba's mosque and Seville's *alcázar* – but Christian Spain also constructed hundreds of impressive castles, cathedrals, monasteries, palaces and mansions, which still stand throughout the length and breadth of the country.

Facts about the Country

HISTORY
Ancient History
Located at the crossroads between Europe and Africa, the Iberian Peninsula has always been a target for invading peoples and civilisations. From around 8000 to 3000 BC, people from North Africa known as the Iberians crossed the Strait of Gibraltar and settled the peninsula. Around 1000 BC Celtic tribes entered northern Spain, while Phoenician merchants were establishing trading settlements along the Mediterranean coast. They were followed by Greeks and Carthaginians who arrived around 600 to 500 BC.

The Romans arrived in the 3rd century BC, but took two centuries to subdue the peninsula. Christianity came to Spain during the 1st century AD, but was initially opposed by the Romans, leading to persecution and martyrdoms. In 409 AD Roman Hispania was invaded by Germanic tribes and by 419 the Christian Visigoths, another Germanic people, had established a kingdom which lasted until 711, when the Moors – Muslim Berbers and Arabs from North Africa – crossed the Strait of Gibraltar and defeated Roderic, the last Visigoth king.

SPAIN

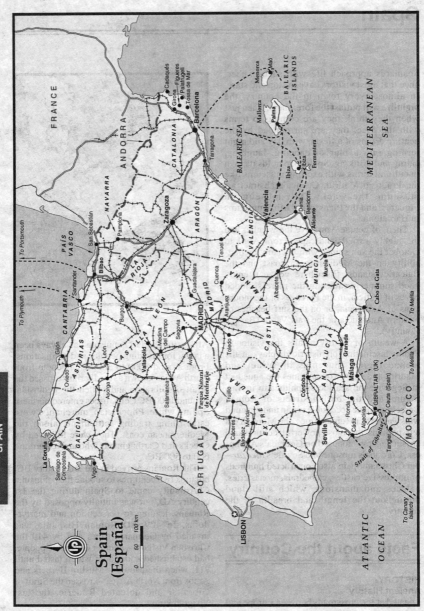

Spain
(España)

Moorish Spain & the Reconquista

By 714, the Muslim armies had occupied the entire peninsula, apart from some northern mountain regions. Moorish dominion was to last almost 800 years in parts of Spain. In the Moorish-held areas – known as al-Andalus – arts and sciences prospered, new crops and agricultural techniques were introduced, and palaces, mosques, schools, gardens and public baths were built.

In 722 a small army under the Visigothic leader Pelayo inflicted the first defeat on the Moors at Covadonga in northern Spain. This marked the beginning of the Reconquista, the very gradual and unsteady reconquest of Spain by the Christians. By the beginning of the 11th century the frontier between Christian and Muslim Spain stretched across the peninsula from Barcelona to the Atlantic.

In 1085 Toledo was taken by Alfonso VI, king of León and Castile, prompting the Moors to request military help from northern Africa which arrived in the form of the Almoravids, who recaptured much territory and ruled it until the 1140s. The Almoravids were followed by the Almohads, another north African people, who ruled until 1212. By the mid-13th century, the Christians had taken most of the peninsula except for the state of Granada.

In the process the kingdoms of Castile and Aragón emerged as Christian Spain's two main powers, and in 1469 they were united by the marriage of Isabel, princess of Castile, and Fernando, heir to the throne of Aragón. Known as the Catholic Monarchs, they united all of Spain and laid the foundations for the Spanish golden age. They also revived the notorious Inquisition, which expelled and executed thousands of Jews and other non-Christians. In 1492 the last Moorish ruler of Granada surrendered to them, marking the completion of the Reconquista.

The Golden Age

Also in 1492, while searching for an alternative passage to India, Columbus stumbled on the Bahamas and claimed the Americas for Spain. This sparked a period of exploration and exploitation which was to yield Spain enormous wealth while destroying the ancient American empires. For three centuries, gold and silver from the New World were used to finance the expansion of the Spanish empire.

In 1516 Fernando was succeeded by his grandson Carlos, of the Habsburg dynasty. Carlos was elected Holy Roman Emperor in 1519, and ruled over an empire that included Austria, southern Germany, the Netherlands, Spain and the American colonies. But he and his successors were to lead Spain into a series of expensive wars and, despite the influx of American gold and silver, the empire was soon bankrupt. In 1588 the mighty Spanish Armada was annihilated by Sir Francis Drake's English fleet. The Thirty Years' War (1618-48) saw Spain in conflict with the Netherlands, France and England. By the reign of the last Habsburg monarch, Carlos II (1655-1700), the Spanish empire was in debt and decline.

The 18th & 19th Centuries

Carlos II died without an heir. At the end of the subsequent War of the Spanish Succession (1702-13), Felipe V, grandson of French king Louis XIV, became the first of the Bourbon dynasty. The Bourbons unified Spain, overseeing a period of stability, enlightened reforms and economic growth, but this recovery was ended by events after the French Revolution of 1789.

When Louis XVI was guillotined in 1793, Spain initially declared war on the new French republic, but then turned to alliance with France and war against Britain, in which the Battle of Trafalgar (1805) ended Spanish sea power. In 1807-08 Napoleon's troops entered Spain, supposedly en route to invade Portugal, but Napoleon convinced Carlos IV, the Spanish king, to abdicate, and installed his own brother Joseph Bonaparte as king of Spain. The Spanish people united against the French and fought a five-year war of independence. In 1815 Napoleon was defeated by Wellington and a Bourbon, Fernando VII, was restored to the Spanish throne.

Fernando's reign was a disastrous advertisement for monarchy: the Inquisition was re-established, liberals and constitutionalists were persecuted, free speech was repressed, Spain entered a severe recession and the American colonies won their independence. After his death in 1833 came the First Carlist War (1834-39), fought between conservative forces led by Don Carlos, Fernando's brother, and liberals who supported the claim of Fernando's daughter Isabel (later Isabel II) to the throne.

SPAIN

In 1868 the monarchy was overthrown during the Septembrina Revolution and Isabel II was forced to flee the country. The First Republic was declared in 1873, but within 18 months the army had restored the monarchy, with Isabel's son Alfonso XII on the throne. Despite political turmoil, Spain's economy prospered in the second half of the 19th century, fuelled by industrialisation.

The disastrous Spanish-American War of 1898 marked the end of the Spanish empire. Spain was defeated by the USA in a series of naval battles, resulting in the loss of its last overseas possessions – Cuba won its independence and Puerto Rico, Guam and the Philippines passed to the USA.

The 20th Century

The early 20th century was characterised by military disasters in Morocco and growing political and social instability as radical forces struggled to overthrow the established order. In 1923, with Spain on the brink of civil war, Miguel Primo de Rivera made himself military dictator, and ruled until 1930. In 1931 Alfonso XIII fled the country, and the Second Republic was declared.

Like its predecessor, the Second Republic also fell victim to internal conflict. The 1936 elections told of a country split in two, with the Republican government (an uneasy alliance of leftist parties known as the Popular Front) and its supporters on one side, and the right-wing Nationalists (an alliance of the army, Church and the fascist-style Falange Party) on the other.

Nationalist plotters in the army rose against the government in July 1936. During the subsequent Spanish Civil War (1936-39), the Nationalists, led by General Francisco Franco, received almost unlimited military and financial support from Nazi Germany and fascist Italy, while the elected Republican government received support only from Russia and, to a lesser degree, from the International Brigades made up of foreign leftists.

By 1939 Franco had won and an estimated 350,000 Spaniards had died. After the war, thousands of Republicans were executed, jailed or forced into exile. Franco's 35-year dictatorship began with Spain isolated internationally and crippled by recession. It wasn't until the 1950s and 1960s, when the rise in

tourism and a treaty with the USA combined to provide much needed funds, that the country began to recover. By the 1970s Spain had the fastest-growing economy in Europe.

Franco died in 1975, having named Juan Carlos, grandson of Alfonso XIII, his successor. King Juan Carlos is widely credited with having overseen Spain's transition from dictatorship to democracy. The first elections were held in 1977, a new constitution was drafted in 1978, and a failed military coup in 1981 was seen as a futile attempt to turn back the clock. Spain joined the EU in 1986, and celebrated its return to the world stage in style in 1992, with Expo '92 in Seville and the Olympic Games in Barcelona.

GEOGRAPHY & ECOLOGY

Spain is probably Europe's most geographically diverse country, with landscapes ranging from the near-deserts of Almería to the green, Wales-like countryside and deep coastal inlets of Galicia, and from the sunbaked plains of Castilla-La Mancha to the rugged mountains of the Pyrenees.

The country covers around 80% of the Iberian Peninsula and spreads over nearly 505,000 sq km, more than half of which is high tableland – the *meseta*. This is supported and divided by several mountain chains. The main ones are the Pyrenees along the border with France; the Cordillera Cantábrica backing the north coast; the Sistema Ibérico from the central north towards the middle Mediterranean coast; the Cordillera Central from north of Madrid towards the Portuguese border; and three east-west chains across Andalucía, one of which includes the highest range of all, the Sierra Nevada.

The major rivers are the Ebro, Duero, Tajo (Tagus), Guadiana and Guadalquivir, each draining a different basin between the mountains and all flowing into the Atlantic Ocean, except for the Ebro which reaches the Mediterranean Sea.

Flora & Fauna

The brown bear, wolf, lynx and wild boar all survive in Spain, though only the boar exists in healthy numbers. Spain's high mountains harbour the goat-like chamois and Spanish ibex (the latter rare) and big birds of prey such as eagles, vultures and the lammergeier. The marshy Ebro delta and Guadalquivir estuary are very important for waterbirds, the spectacular greater flamingo among them. Many of Spain's 5500 seed-bearing plants occur nowhere else in Europe because of the barrier of the Pyrenees. Spring wildflowers are spectacular in many country and hill areas.

The conservation picture has improved by leaps and bounds in the past 20 years and Spain now has 25,000 sq km of protected areas, including 10 national parks. But overgrazing, reservoir creation, tourism, housing developments, agricultural and industrial effluent, fires and hunting all still threaten plant and animal life.

GOVERNMENT & POLITICS
Spain is a constitutional monarchy. The 1978 constitution restored parliamentary government and grouped the country's 50 provinces into 17 autonomous communities, each with its own regional government. From 1982 to 1996 Spain was governed by the centre-left PSOE party led by Felipe González. In the 1996 election the PSOE, weakened by a series of scandals and long-term economic problems, was finally unseated by the right-of-centre Partido Popular, led by José María Aznar.

ECONOMY
Spain has experienced an amazing economic turnabout in the 20th century, raising its living standards from the lowest in Western Europe to a level comparable with the rest of the continent. But its booming economy came back to earth with a thud in the early 1990s, and has since recovered only slowly. The unemployment rate is by far the highest in Western Europe, at over 20%. Service industries employ over six million people and produce close to 60% of the country's GDP. The arrival of over 50 million tourists every year brings work to around 10% of the entire labour force. Industry accounts for about one-third of both workforce and GDP, but agriculture accounts for only 4% of GDP compared to 23% in 1960, although it employs one in 10 workers.

POPULATION & PEOPLE
Spain has a population of 39 million, descended from all the many peoples who have settled here over the millennia, among them Iberians, Celts, Romans, Jews, Visigoths and Moors. The biggest cities are Madrid (three million), Barcelona (1.7 million), Valencia (750,000) and Seville (715,000). Each region proudly preserves its own unique culture, and some – Catalonia and the País Vasco in particular – display a fiercely independent spirit.

ARTS
Cinema
Early Spanish cinema was hamstrung by a lack of funds and technology, and perhaps the greatest of all Spanish directors, Luis Buñuel, made his silent surrealist classics *Un Chien Andalou* (1928) and *L'Age d'Or* (1930) in France. Buñuel, however, returned to Spain to make *Tierra sin Pan* (Land without Bread, 1932), a film about rural poverty in the Las Hurdes area of Extremadura.

Under Franco there was strict censorship, but satirical and uneasy films like Juan Antonio Bardem's *Muerte de un Ciclista* (Death of a Cyclist, 1955) and Luis Berlanga's *Bienvenido Mr Marshall* (Welcome Mr Marshall, 1953) still managed to appear. Carlos Saura, with films like *Ana y los Lobos* (Anna & the Wolves, 1973), and Victor Erice, with *El Espiritu de la Colmena* (Spirit of the Beehive, 1973) and *El Sur* (The South, 1983), looked at the problems of young people scarred by the Spanish Civil War and its aftermath.

After Franco, Pedro Almodóvar broke away from this serious cinema dwelling on the past with his humorous films set amid the social and artistic revolution of the late 1970s and 80s – notably *Mujeres al Borde de un Ataque de Nervios* (Women on the Verge of a Nervous Breakdown, 1988). Almodóvar has brought Spanish films for the first time to a non-arthouse public outside Spain, and has made international stars of two of his actors, Antonio Banderas and Carmen Maura.

Painting
The golden age of Spanish art (1550-1650) was strongly influenced by Italy but the great Spanish artists developed their talents in unique ways. The giants were the Toledo-based El Greco (originally from Crete), and Diego Velázquez, perhaps Spain's most revered painter. Both excelled with insightful portraits, among other things. Francisco Zurbarán and Bartolomé Esteban Murillo were also prominent. The genius of the 18th and

SPAIN

19th centuries was Francisco Goya, whose versatility ranged from unflattering royal portraits and anguished war scenes to bullfight etchings.

Catalonia was the powerhouse of early 20th-century Spanish art, engendering the hugely prolific Pablo Picasso, the colourful symbolist Joan Miró, and Salvador Dalí, who was obsessed with the unconscious and weird. Works by these and other major Spanish artists can be found in galleries throughout the country.

Architecture

The earliest architectural relics are the prehistoric monuments on Menorca. Reminders of Roman times include the ruins of Mérida and Tarragona, and Segovia's amazing aqueduct. The Moors created some uniquely beautiful Islamic buildings such as Granada's Alhambra, Córdoba's mosque and Seville's alcázar (fortress) – the latter an example of Mudéjar architecture, the name given to Moorish work done in Christian-held territory.

The first main Christian architectural movement was Romanesque, in the north in the 11th and 12th centuries, which has left countless lovely country churches and several cathedrals, notably that of Santiago de Compostela. Later came the many great Gothic cathedrals (Toledo, Barcelona, León, Salamanca and Seville) of the 13th to 16th centuries, as well as Renaissance styles, such as the plateresque work so prominent in Salamanca and the austere work of Juan de Herrera, responsible for El Escorial. Spain then followed the usual path to baroque (17th and 18th centuries) and neoclassicism (19th century) before Catalonia produced its startling modernist movement around the turn of the 20th century, of which Antoni Gaudí's La Sagrada Família church is the most stunning example. More-recent architecture is only likely to excite specialists.

Literature

One of the earliest works of Spanish literature is the *Cantar de mío Cid*, an anonymous epic poem describing the life of El Cid, an 11th-century Christian knight. Miguel de Cervantes' novel *Don Quixote de la Mancha* is the masterpiece of the literary flowering of the 16th and 17th centuries, and one of the world's great works of fiction. The playwrights Lope de Vega and Pedro Calderón de la Barca were also leading lights of the age.

The next highpoint, in the early 20th century, grew out of the crisis of the Spanish-American War which spawned the intellectual 'Generation of '98'. Philosophical essayist Miguel de Unamuno was prominent, but the towering figure was poet and playwright Federico García Lorca, whose tragedies *Blood Wedding* and *Yerma* won international acclaim before he was murdered in the civil war for his Republican sympathies. Camilo José Cela, author of the civil war aftermath novel *The Family of Pascal Duarte*, won the 1989 Nobel Prize for literature. Juan Goytisolo is probably the major contemporary writer; his most approachable work is his autobiography *Forbidden Territory*. There has been a proliferation of women – particularly feminist – writers in the last 25 years, in which prominent figures include Adelaide Morales, Ana María Matute and Montserrat Roig.

CULTURE

Most Spaniards are economical with etiquette but this does not signify unfriendliness. They're gregarious people, on the whole very tolerant and easy-going towards foreigners. It's not easy to give offence. Disrespectful behaviour – including excessively casual dress – in churches won't go down well though.

Siesta

Contrary to popular belief, most Spaniards do not sleep in the afternoon. The siesta is generally devoted to a long leisurely lunch and lingering conversation. Then again, if you've stayed out until 5 am...

Flamenco

Getting to see real, deeply emotional, flamenco can be hard, as it tends to happen semi-spontaneously in little bars. Andalucía is its traditional home. You'll find plenty of clubs there and elsewhere offering flamenco shows: these are generally aimed at tourists and are expensive, but some are good. Your best chance of catching the real thing is probably at one of the flamenco festivals in the south, usually held in summer.

RELIGION

Only about 20% of Spaniards are regular churchgoers, but Catholicism is deeply ingrained in the culture. As the writer

Unamuno said, 'Here in Spain we are all Catholics, even the atheists'. Many Spaniards have a deep-seated scepticism of the Church: during the civil war, churches were burnt and clerics shot because they represented repression, corruption and the old order.

LANGUAGE

Spanish, or Castilian *(castellano)* as it is often and more precisely called, is spoken by just about all Spaniards, but there are also three widely spoken regional languages: Catalan (another Romance language, closely related to Spanish and French) is spoken by about two-thirds of people in Catalonia and the Balearic Islands and half the people in the Valencia region; Galician (another Romance language which sounds like a cross between Spanish and Portuguese) is spoken by many in the northwest; and Basque (of obscure, non-Latin origin) is spoken by a minority in the País Vasco and Navarra.

English isn't as widely spoken as many travellers seem to expect. In the main cities and tourist areas it's much easier to find people who speak at least some English, though generally you'll be better received if you at least try to communicate in Spanish.

See the Language Guide at the back of the book for pronunciation guidelines and useful words and phrases.

Facts for the Visitor

PLANNING

Climate & When to Go

For most purposes the ideal months to visit Spain are May, June and September (plus April and October in the south). At these times you can rely on good weather, yet avoid the sometimes extreme heat – and main crush of Spanish and foreign tourists – of July and August, when temperatures may climb to 45°C in parts of Andalucía and when Madrid is unbearably hot and almost deserted.

The summer overflows with festivals, including Sanfermines, with the running of the bulls in Pamplona, and Semana Grande all along the north coast (dates vary from place to

place), but there are excellent festivals during the rest of the year too.

In winter the rains never seem to stop in the north, except when they turn to snow. Madrid regularly freezes in December, January and February. At these times Andalucía is the place to be, with temperatures reaching the mid-teens in most places and good skiing in the Sierra Nevada.

Books & Maps

The New Spaniards by John Hooper is a fascinating account of modern Spanish society and culture. For a readable and thorough, but not over-long, survey of Spanish history, *The Story of Spain* by Mark Williams is hard to beat.

Classic accounts of life and travel in Spain include Gerald Brenan's *South from Granada* (1920s), Laurie Lee's *As I Walked Out One Midsummer Morning* (1930s), George Orwell's *Homage to Catalonia* (the civil war), and *Iberia* by James Michener (1960s). Among the best of more recent books are *Homage to Barcelona* by Colm Tóibín, *Spanish Journeys* by Adam Hopkins and *Cities of Spain* by David Gilmour.

Of foreign literature set in Spain, Ernest Hemingway's civil war novel *For Whom the Bell Tolls* is a must.

If you're planning in-depth travels in Spain, get hold of Lonely Planet's *Spain – travel survival kit*.

Some of the best maps for travellers are published by Michelin, which produces a 1:1 million *Spain Portugal* map and six 1:400,000 regional maps. The country map doesn't show railways, but the regional maps do.

Online Services

An Internet search under 'Spain, Travel' will reveal dozens of sites including the national tourist office's useful *Discover Spain* (www.spaintour.com).

What to Bring

You can buy anything you need in Spain, but some articles, such as sun-screen lotion, are more expensive than elsewhere. Books in English tend to be expensive and are hard to find outside main cities.

A pair of strong shoes and a towel are essential. A money belt or shoulder wallet can be useful in big cities. Bring sunglasses if glare

SPAIN

gets to you. If you want to blend in, don't just pack T-shirts, shorts and runners – Spaniards are quite dressy and many tourists just look like casual slobs to them.

SUGGESTED ITINERARIES

If you want to whiz around as many places as possible in limited time, the following itineraries might suit you:

Two days
  Fly to Madrid, Barcelona or Seville, or nip into Barcelona or San Sebastián overland from France.

One week
  Spend two days each in Barcelona, Madrid and Seville, allowing one day for travel.

Two weeks
  As above, plus San Sebastián, Toledo, Salamanca and/or Cuenca, Córdoba and/or Granada, and maybe Cáceres and/or Trujillo.

One month
  As above, plus some of the following: side trips from the cities mentioned above; an exploration of the north, including Santiago de Compostela and the Picos de Europa; visits to Teruel, Mallorca, Formentera, Segovia, Ávila, or some smaller towns and more remote regions such as North-East Extremadura or Cabo de Gata.

HIGHLIGHTS
Beaches

Yes, it's still possible to have a beach to yourself in Spain. In summer it may be a little tricky, but spots where things are bound to be quiet are such gems as the beaches of Cabo Favàritx in Menorca, and some of the secluded coves on Cabo de Gata in Andalucía. There are also good, relatively uncrowded beaches on the Costa de la Luz, between Tarifa and Cádiz. On the Galician coast, between Noia and Pontevedra, are literally hundreds of beaches where even in mid-August you won't feel claustrophobic.

Museums & Galleries

Spain is home to some of the finest art galleries in the world. The Prado in Madrid has very few rivals, and there are outstanding art museums in Bilbao, Seville, Barcelona, Valencia and Córdoba. There are also fascinating smaller galleries, such as the Dalí museum in Figueres and the abstract art museum in Cuenca. Tarragona and Teruel have excellent archaeological museums.

Buildings

Try not to miss Andalucía's Moorish gems – the Alhambra in Granada, the alcázar in Seville and the mezquita in Córdoba – or Barcelona's extraordinary La Sagrada Família church. The fairy-tale alcázar in Segovia has to be seen to be believed. For even more exciting views, and loads of medieval ghosts, try to reach the ruined castle in Morella, Valencia province.

Scenery

There's outstanding mountain scenery – often coupled with highly picturesque villages – in the Pyrenees and Picos de Europa in the north and in parts of Andalucía such as the Alpujarras. On the coasts, the rugged inlets of Galicia and stark, hilly Cabo de Gata in Andalucía stand out.

TOURIST OFFICES

Most towns (and many villages) of any interest have a tourist office (*oficina de turismo*). These will supply you with a map and brochures with basic information on local sights, attractions, accommodation, history etc. Some can also provide info on other places too. Their staff are generally helpful and often speak some English.

Tourist Offices Abroad

Spain has tourist information centres in 20 countries including:

Canada
  102 Bloor St West, 14th floor, Toronto, Ontario M5S 1M8 (☎ 416-961 3131)

France
  43ter Ave Pierre 1er de Serbie, 75381 Paris (☎ 01 47 20 90 54)

Portugal
  Avenida Fontes Pereira de Melo 51, 4th floor, 1000 Lisbon (☎ 01-354 1992; fax 354 0332)

UK
  57-58 St James's St, London SW1A 1LD (☎ 0171-499 0901)

USA
  665 Fifth Ave, New York, NY 10022 (☎ 212-759 8822)

USEFUL ORGANISATIONS

The travel agency TIVE, with offices in major cities throughout Spain, specialises in discounted tickets and travel arrangements for students and young people. Its head office (☎ 91-347 7700) is at Calle José Ortega y Gasset 71, 28006 Madrid.

VISAS & EMBASSIES

Citizens of EU countries can enter Spain with their national identity card or passport. UK citizens must have a full passport – a British visitor passport won't do. Non-EU nationals must take their passport.

EU, Norway and Iceland citizens require no visa. Nationals of Canada, Israel, Japan, New Zealand, Switzerland and the USA need no visa for stays of up to 90 days but must have a passport valid for the whole visit.

Australians and South Africans are among nationalities who do need a visa for Spain. It's best to obtain the visa in your country of residence to avoid possible bureaucratic problems. Both 30-day single-entry and 90-day triple-entry visas are available, though if you apply in a country where you're not resident the 90-day option may not be available. Triple-entry visas will save you a lot of time and trouble if you plan to leave Spain – say to Gibraltar or Morocco – then re-enter it.

The Schengen 'System'

Spain is one of the seven Schengen countries – the others are Belgium, France, Germany, Luxembourg, the Netherlands and Portugal – which have theoretically done away with passport control on travel between them. (In fact some checks have still been known to occur at airports and on some Lisbon-Madrid trains.) But confusingly, the seven countries have not standardised their lists of nationalities that require visas. So Australians, for example, need a visa to visit France or Spain, but not for Portugal. Despite the removal of most passport controls between Schengen countries, it's still illegal for Australians to enter Spain without a visa, and can lead to deportation.

One good thing about the Schengen system is that a visa for one Schengen country is valid for other Schengen countries too – so, for instance, a French visa is good for Spain too, and vice-versa. Compare validity periods, prices and the number of permitted entries before you apply, as these can differ between countries.

Stays of Longer than 90 Days

EU, Norway and Iceland nationals planning to stay in Spain more than 90 days are supposed to apply during their first month in the country for a residence card. This is a lengthy, compli-cated procedure: if you intend to subject yourself to it, consult a Spanish consulate before you go to Spain, as you'll need to take certain documents with you.

Other nationalities are not normally allowed more than one 90-day stay in any six-month period. Visa carriers may be able to get short visa extensions at their local Comisaría de Policía (National Police station), but don't count on it. Otherwise, for stays of longer than 90 days you're supposed to get a residence card. This is a nightmarish process, starting with a residence visa issued by a Spanish consulate in your country of residence: start the process light-years in advance.

Spanish Embassies Abroad

Spanish embassies include:

Australia
  15 Arkana St, Yarralumla, Canberra 2600, ACT (☎ 06-273 3555); consulates in Sydney and Melbourne
Canada
  350 Sparks St, suite 802, Ottawa K1R 7S8 (☎ 613-237 2193); consulates in Toronto and Montreal
France
  22 Ave Marceau, 75381 Paris (☎ 01 44 43 18 00); consulates in Marseille, Bayonne, Hendaye, Pau etc
New Zealand
  represented in Australia
Portugal
  Rua do Salitre 1, 1296 Lisbon (☎ 01-347 2381); consulates in Porto and Valença do Minho
UK
  39 Chesham Place, London SW1X 8SB (☎ 0171-235 5555); consulates in Edinburgh and Manchester
USA
  2375 Pennsylvania Ave NW, Washington, DC, 20037 (☎ 202-452 0100); consulates in New York, Los Angeles, San Francisco, Chicago Miami and other cities

Foreign Embassies in Spain

Some 70 countries have embassies in Madrid, including:

Australia
  Paseo de la Castellana 143 (☎ 579 04 28)
Canada
  Calle de Nuñez de Balboa 35 (☎ 431 43 00)
France
  Calle de Salustiano Olozoga 9 (☎ 435 55 60)
Germany
  Calle de Fortuny 8 (☎ 319 91 00)
Ireland
  Calle de Claudio Coello 73 (☎ 576 35 00)

SPAIN

Japan
    Calle de Joaquín Costa 29 (☎ 562 55 46)
Morocco
    Calle de Serrano 179 (☎ 562 42 84)
New Zealand
    Plaza Lealtad 2 (☎ 523 0226)
Portugal
    Calle del Pinar 1 (☎ 561 78 00)
UK
    Calle de Fernando el Santo 16 (☎ 319 02 00)
USA
    Calle de Serrano 75 (☎ 577 40 00)

CUSTOMS

EU internal borders are customs-free. From outside the EU, you are allowed to bring in one litre of spirits, 50 grams of perfume and 200 cigarettes duty-free.

MONEY
Currency

Spain's unit of currency is the peseta (pta). The legal denominations are coins of one, five (known as a *duro*), 10, 25, 50, 100, 200 and 500 ptas. There are notes of 1000, 2000, 5000 and 10,000 ptas. In the past, several different forms of coin have circulated for each value, but from February 1997 only one type of coin for each value will be legal tender. Take care not to confuse the 500-pta coin with the 100-pta coin.

Exchange Rates

Banks – mostly open Monday to Friday from 8.30 am to 2 pm, Saturday from 8.30 am to 1 pm – generally give better exchange rates than currency-exchange offices, and travellers' cheques attract a slightly better rate than cash. ATMs accepting a wide variety of cards are common.

Australia	A$1	=	99 ptas
Canada	C$1	=	92 ptas
France	1FF	=	25 ptas
Germany	DM1	=	85 ptas
Japan	¥100	=	116 ptas
Portugal	100$00	=	83 ptas
New Zealand	NZ$1	=	88 ptas
United Kingdom	UK£1	=	196 ptas
USA	US$1	=	126 ptas

Costs

Spain is one of Western Europe's more affordable countries. If you are particularly frugal, it's possible to scrape by on US$20 to US$25 a day; this would involve staying in the cheapest possible accommodation, avoiding eating in restaurants or going to museums or bars, and not moving around too much. Places like Madrid, Barcelona, Seville and San Sebastián will place a greater strain on your money belt.

A more reasonable budget would be US$35 to US$40 a day. This would allow you 1500 to 2000 ptas for accommodation; 300 ptas for breakfast (coffee and a pastry); 800 to 1000 ptas for a set lunch; 250 ptas for public transport (two metro or bus rides); 500 ptas for a major museum; and 600 ptas for a light dinner, with a bit over for a drink or two and intercity travel.

Tipping & Bargaining

In restaurants, menu prices include a service charge, and tipping is a matter of personal choice – most people leave some small change and 5% is plenty. It's common to leave small change in bars and cafés. The only places in Spain where you are likely to bargain are markets and, occasionally, cheap hotels – particularly if you're staying for a few days.

Consumer Taxes & Refunds

In Spain, VAT (value-added tax) is known as IVA *(impuesto sobre el valor añadido)*. On accommodation and restaurant prices, there's a flat rate of 7% IVA which is usually – but not always – included in quoted prices. To check, ask if the price is 'con IVA' (with VAT) or 'sin IVA' (without VAT).

On retail goods, alcohol, electrical appliances etc, IVA is 16%. Visitors are entitled to a refund of IVA on any item costing more than 15,000 ptas that they are taking out of the EU. Ask the shop for a Europe Tax-Free Shopping Cheque when you buy, then present the goods and cheque to customs when you leave within three months. Customs stamps the cheque and you then cash it at a booth with the Tax-Free logo and Cash Refund sign. There are booths at all main Spanish airports, the border crossings at Algeciras, Gibraltar and Andorra, and similar refund points throughout the EU.

POST & COMMUNICATIONS
Post

Main post offices in towns are usually open Monday to Friday from about 8.30 am to 8.30 pm, and Saturday from about 9 am to 1.30 pm. Stamps are also sold at *estancos* (tobacconist shops with the 'Tabacos' sign in yellow letters on a maroon background). A standard air-mail letter or card costs 60 ptas to Europe, 87 ptas to the USA or Canada, and 108 ptas to Australia or New Zealand. Mail to/from Europe normally takes up to a week, and to North America, Australia or New Zealand around 10 days – but there may be some unaccountable long delays.

Poste-restante mail can be addressed to you at either poste restante or *lista de correos*, the Spanish name for it, in the city in question. It's a fairly reliable system, although you must be prepared for mail to arrive late. American Express card or travellers' cheque holders can use the free client mail service (see the Facts for the Visitor chapter at the beginning of this book).

Common abbreviations used in Spanish addresses are 1°, 2°, 3° etc, which mean 1st, 2nd, 3rd floor, and s/n *(sin número)*, which means the building has no number.

Telephone & Fax

When calling Spain from other countries, omit the initial 9 of the Spanish area code. Public pay phones are blue, common and easy to use. They accept coins, phonecards *(tarjetas telefónicas)* and, in some cases, credit cards. Phonecards come in 1000 and 2000-pta denominations and are available at main post offices and estancos. A three-minute call from a pay phone costs 15 ptas within a local area, 72 ptas to other places in the same province, or 184 ptas to other provinces. Calls are around 15% cheaper between 10 pm and 8 am and all day Sunday and holidays.

International reverse-charge (collect) calls are simple to make: from a pay phone or private phone dial ☎ 900 99 00 followed by ☎ 61 for Australia, ☎ 44 for the UK, ☎ 64 for New Zealand, ☎ 15 for Canada, and for the USA ☎ 11 (AT&T) or ☎ 14 (MCI).

Most main post offices have a fax service, but you'll often find cheaper rates at shops or offices with 'Fax Público' signs.

NEWSPAPERS & MAGAZINES

The major daily newspapers in Spain are the solid liberal *El País*, the conservative *ABC*, and *El Mundo*, which specialises in breaking political scandals. For a laugh, have a look at *¡Hola!*, a weekly magazine devoted to the lives and loves of the rich and famous. There's also a welter of regional dailies, some of the best being in Barcelona, the País Vasco and Andalucía.

International press such as the *International Herald Tribune*, *Time* and *Newsweek*, and daily papers from Western European countries reach major cities and tourist areas on the day of publication; elsewhere they're harder to find and are a day or two late.

RADIO & TV

There are hundreds of radio stations, mainly on the FM band – you'll hear a substantial proportion of British and American music. The national pop/rock station, Radio 3, has admirably varied programming.

Spaniards are Europe's greatest TV-watchers after the British, but do a lot of their watching in bars and cafés which makes it more of a social activity. Most TVs receive six channels – two state-run (TVE1 and TVE2), three privately run (Antena 3, Tele 5 and Canal+, and one regional channel. Apart from news, TV seems to consist mostly of game and talk shows, sport, soap operas, sitcoms, and English-language films dubbed into Spanish.

PHOTOGRAPHY & VIDEO

Main brands of film are widely available and processing is fast and generally efficient. A roll of print film (36 exposures, 100 ASA) costs around 650 ptas and can be processed for around 1700 ptas – though there are often better deals if you have two or three rolls developed together. The equivalent in slide film is around 850 ptas plus the same for processing. Nearly all pre-recorded videos in Spain use the PAL image-registration system common to Western Europe and Australia. These won't work on many video players in France, North America and Japan.

TIME

Spain is one hour ahead of GMT/UTC during winter, and two hours ahead from the last Sunday in March to the last Sunday in September.

ELECTRICITY

Electric current in Spain is 220V, 50 Hz, but some places are still on 125 or 110V. In fact, the voltage sometimes differs in the same building. Plugs have two round pins.

WEIGHTS & MEASURES

The metric system is used. Like other Continental Europeans, the Spanish indicate decimals with commas and thousands with points.

LAUNDRY

Self-service laundrettes are rare. Laundries (*lavanderías*) are common but not particularly cheap. They will usually wash, dry and fold a load for 1000 to 1200 ptas.

HEALTH

Apart from the dangers of contracting STDs, the main thing you have to be wary of is the sun – in both cases, use protection. Tap water is safe to drink throughout most of the country – if in doubt ask *¿Es potable el agua?* – although taste-wise it varies from great to blah. Bottled water is available everywhere, generally for 40 to 75 ptas for a 1.5-litre bottle.

Health care is available for free to EU citizens on provision of an E111 form (available free in your home country – contact your health service before you come to Spain to find out how to get it), but others will have to pay cash, so travel insurance is a must. In a health emergency, the local tourist office or police (☎ 091 or ☎ 092) can advise on where to go. *Farmacias* (chemists) can treat many ailments. Emergency dental treatment is available at most public hospitals.

WOMEN TRAVELLERS

The best way for women travellers to approach Spain is simply to be ready to ignore stares, cat calls and unnecessary comments. However, Spain has one of the lowest incidences of reported rape in the developed world, and even physical harassment is much less frequent than you might expect. The Asociación de Asistencia a Mujeres Violadas in Madrid (☎ 91-574 01 10, Monday to Friday from 10 am to 2 pm and 4 to 7 pm; recorded message in Spanish at other times) offers advice and help to rape victims, and can provide details of similar centres in other cities, though only limited English is spoken.

GAY & LESBIAN TRAVELLERS

Attitudes are pretty tolerant, especially in the cities. Madrid, Barcelona, Sitges, Ibiza and Cádiz all have active gay and lesbian scenes. Gay and lesbian travellers wanting information can call Gai-Inform in Madrid (☎ 91-523 00 70) daily from 5 to 9 pm.

DISABLED TRAVELLERS

Spanish tourist offices in other countries can provide a basic information sheet with some useful addresses, and give info on accessible accommodation in specific places. Mobility International (☎ 02-410 6274; fax 02-410 6297), Rue de Manchester 25, Brussels B1070, Belgium, has researched facilities for disabled tourists in Spain. INSERSO (☎ 91-347 88 88), Calle Ginzo de Limea 58, 28029 Madrid, is the government department for the disabled, with branches in all of Spain's 50 provinces.

You'll find some wheelchair-accessible accommodation in main centres, but it may not be in the budget category – although 25 Spanish youth hostels are classed as suitable for wheelchair users.

DANGERS & ANNOYANCES

It's a good idea to take your car radio and any other valuables with you any time you leave your car. In fact it's best to leave nothing at all – certainly nothing visible – in a parked car. In youth hostels, don't leave belongings unattended – there is a high incidence of theft. Beware of pickpockets in cities and tourist resorts (Barcelona and Seville have bad reputations). There is also a relatively high incidence of mugging in such places, so keep your wits about you. Emergency numbers for the police throughout Spain are ☎ 091 (national police) and ☎ 092 (local police).

Drugs

In 1992 Spain's liberal drug laws were severely tightened. No matter what anyone tells you, it is not legal to smoke dope in public bars. There is a reasonable degree of tolerance when it comes to people having a smoke in their own home, but not in hotel rooms or guesthouses.

BUSINESS HOURS

Generally, people work Monday to Friday from 9 am to 2 pm and then again from 4.30 or 5 pm for another three hours. Shops and travel agencies are usually open these hours on Saturday too, though some may skip the evening session. Museums all have their own unique opening hours: major ones tend to open for something like normal business hours (with or without the afternoon break), but often have their weekly closing day on Monday, not Sunday.

PUBLIC HOLIDAYS

Spain has something like 15 official holidays a year – some observed nationwide, some very local – but you'll often find banks, post offices and shops winding down early before holidays or opening up late after them. When a holiday falls close to a weekend, Spaniards like to make a *puente* (bridge) – meaning they take the intervening day off too. The following holidays are observed just about everywhere: 1 January (New Year's Day), 6 January (Epiphany or Three Kings' Day, when children receive presents), Good Friday, 1 May (Labour Day), 15 August (Feast of the Assumption), 12 October (National Day), 1 November (All Saints' Day), 6 December (Constitution Day), 8 December (Feast of the Immaculate Conception) and 25 December (Christmas). The two main periods when Spaniards go on holiday are Semana Santa (the week leading up to Easter Sunday) and the month of August. At these times accommodation in resorts can be scarce and transport heavily booked, but other cities are often half-empty.

SPECIAL EVENTS

Spaniards indulge their love of colour, noise, crowds and partying at innumerable local fiestas and *ferias* (fairs): even small villages will have at least one, probably several, during the year. Many fiestas are religion-based but still highly festive. Local tourist offices can always supply detailed info.

Among festivals to look out for are La Tamborada in San Sebastián on 20 January, when the whole town dresses up and goes berserk; *carnaval*, a time of fancy-dress parades and merrymaking celebrated around the country about seven weeks before Easter (wildest in Cádiz and Sitges); Valencia's week-long mid-March party, Las Fallas, with all-night dancing and drinking, first-class fireworks, and processions; Semana Santa with its parades of holy images and huge crowds, notably in Seville; Seville's Feria de Abril, a week-long party in late April, a kind of counterbalance to the religious peak of Semana Santa; Sanfermines, with the running of the bulls, in Pamplona in July; Semana Grande, another week of heavy drinking and hangovers, all along the north coast during the first half of August; and Barcelona's week-long party, the Festes de la Mercè, around 24 September.

ACTIVITIES

Surfing & Windsurfing

The País Vasco has some good surf spots – San Sebastián, Zarauz and the legendary left at Mundaca, among others. Tarifa, Spain's southernmost point, is windsurfer's heaven, with constant strong breezes and long, empty beaches too.

Skiing

Skiing in Spain is cheap and the facilities and conditions are surprisingly good. The season runs from around December to May. The most accessible resorts are in the Sierra Nevada (very close to Granada), the Pyrenees (north of Barcelona) and in the ranges north of Madrid. The tourist offices in these cities have information on the various ski fields, and affordable day trips can be booked through travel agents.

Cycling

Bike touring isn't as common as in other parts of Europe because of deterrents like the often-mountainous terrain, crowded roads and summer heat. It's a more viable option on the Balearic Islands than on much of the mainland, though it's popular in autumn and spring in the south. Mountain biking is increasingly popular and areas like Andalucía and Catalonia have km upon km of good tracks for this. Finding bikes to rent is a hit-and-miss affair so if you're set on the idea it's best to bring your own.

Trekking & Walking

Spain is a trekker's paradise, so much so that Lonely Planet has published a guide to some of the best treks in the country, *Trekking in Spain*. See also the Mallorca and Picos de Europa sections of this chapter.

Walking country roads and paths, between settlements, can also be highly enjoyable and

SPAIN

a great way to meet the locals. Two organisations publish detailed maps of Spain.

The Instituto Geográfico Nacional (IGN) covers the country in over 4000 1:25,000 sheets, mostly fairly up-to-date. The IGN and the Army Cartographic Service (SCE) both publish 1:50,000 series – the SCE's tend to be more up to date, but the IGN's are more traveller/hiker oriented. Also very useful for hiking and exploring small areas are the *Guía Cartográfica* and *Guía Excursionista y Turística* booklets published in Spanish by Editorial Alpina. Covering most of the mountainous parts of the country (except the south), these include detailed maps at scales ranging from 1:25,000 to 1:50,000, and are well worth their price (around 500 ptas). You may well find IGE, SCE and Alpina publications in local bookshops but it's more reliable to get them in advance from specialist map or travel shops like La Tienda Verde in Madrid, and Altaïr and Quera in Barcelona, or you can obtain them from some overseas specialists. IGN (☎ 91-554 14 50), Calle General Ibañez de Íbero 3, 28003 Madrid, can supply you with a free catalogue.

If you fancy a really long walk, there's the Camino de Santiago. This route, which has been followed by Christian pilgrims for centuries, can be commenced at various places in France. It then crosses the Pyrenees and runs via Pamplona, Logroño and León all the way to the cathedral in Santiago de Compostela. There are numerous guidebooks explaining the route, and the best map is published by IGN.

COURSES

The best place to take a language course in Spain is generally at a university. Those with the best reputations include Salamanca, Santiago de Compostela and Santander. It can also be fun to combine study with a stay in one of Spain's most exciting cities such as Barcelona, Madrid or Seville. There are also dozens of private language colleges throughout the country; the Instituto Cervantes (☎ 0171-935 1518), at 22-23 Manchester Square, London W1M 5AP, can send you lists of these and of universities that run courses. Some Spanish embassies and consulates also have info.

Other courses available in Spain include art, cookery and photography. Spanish tourist offices can help with information.

WORK

EU, Norway and Iceland nationals are allowed to work in Spain without a visa, but if they plan to stay more than three months, they are supposed to apply within the first month for a residence card (see Visas & Embassies earlier in this chapter). Virtually everyone else is supposed to obtain, from a Spanish consulate in their country of residence, a work permit and, if they plan to stay more than 90 days, a residence visa. These procedures are even more difficult (see Visas & Embassies). That said, quite a few people do manage to work in Spain one way or another – though with Spain's unemployment rate running at over 20%, don't rely on it. Teaching English is an obvious option – a TEFL certificate will be a big help. Another possibility is summer work in a bar or restaurant in a tourist resort. Quite a lot of these are run by foreigners.

ACCOMMODATION

Camping

Spain has more than 800 camping grounds. Facilities and settings vary enormously, and grounds are officially rated from 1st class to 3rd class. You can expect to pay around 450 ptas per person, 450 ptas per car and 450 ptas per tent. Tourist offices can direct you to the nearest camping ground. Many sites are open all year, though quite a few close from around October to Easter. With certain exceptions (such as many beaches and environmentally protected areas), it is legal to camp outside camping grounds. You'll need permission to camp on private land.

Hostels

Spain's youth hostels (*albergues juveniles*) are often the cheapest place to stay for lone travellers, but two people can usually get a double room elsewhere for a similar price. With some notable exceptions, hostels are only moderate value. Many have curfews and/or are closed during the day, or lack cooking facilities (though if so they usually have a cafeteria). They can, too, be lacking in privacy, and are often heavily booked by school groups. Most are members of the country's Hostelling International (HI) organisation, Red Española de Albergues Juveniles (REAJ), whose head office (☎ 91-347 77 00) is at Calle José Ortega y Gasset 71, 28006 Madrid. Prices often depend on the season or whether you're under 26: typically you pay 900 to 1500 ptas. Some hostels require HI membership, others don't but may charge more if you're not a member. You can buy HI cards for 1800 ptas at virtually all hostels.

Other Accommodation

Officially, all establishments are either *hoteles* (from one to five stars), *hostales* (one to three stars) or *pensiones*. In practice, there are all sorts of overlapping categories, especially at the budget end of the market. In broad terms, the cheapest are usually *fondas* and *casas de huéspedes*, followed by pensiones. All these normally have shared bathrooms, and singles/doubles for 1000/2000 to 1500/3000 ptas. Some hostales and *hostal-residencias* come in the same price range, but others have rooms with private bathroom costing anywhere up to 6000 ptas or so. Hoteles are usually beyond the budgets of shoestringers. The luxurious state-run *paradores*, often converted historic buildings, are prohibitively expensive.

Room rates in this chapter are high-season prices, which in most resorts and other heavily touristed places means July and August, Semana Santa and sometimes Christmas-New Year. At other times prices in many places go down by 5% to 25%.

FOOD

It's a good idea to reset your stomach's clock in Spain, unless you want to eat alone or only with other tourists. Most Spaniards start the day with a light breakfast (*desayuno*), perhaps coffee with a *tostada* (toasted roll) or *pastel* (pastry). *Churros con chocolate* (long, deep-fried doughnuts with thick hot chocolate) are a delicious start to the day and unique to Spain. Lunch (*almuerzo* or *comida*) is usually the main meal of the day, eaten between about 1.30 and 4 pm. The evening meal (*cena*) is usually lighter and may be eaten as late as 10 or 11 pm. It's common (and a great idea!) to go to a bar or café for a snack around 11 am and again around 7 or 8 pm.

Spain has a huge variety of local cuisines. Seafood as well as meat is prominent almost everywhere. One of the most characteristic dishes, from the Valencia region, is paella – rice, seafood, the odd vegetable and often chicken or meat, all simmered up together,

with a yellow colour traditionally produced by saffron. Another dish, of Andalucian origin, is gazpacho, a soup made from tomatoes, breadcrumbs, cucumber and/or green peppers, eaten cold. *Tortillas* (omelettes) are an inexpensive standby and come in many varieties. *Jamón serrano* (cured ham) is a treat for meat-eaters but can be expensive.

Cafés & Bars

If you want to follow Spanish habits, you'll be spending plenty of time in cafés and bars. In almost all of them you'll find *tapas* available. These saucer-sized mini-snacks are part of the Spanish way of life and come in infinite varieties from calamari rings to potato salad to spinach with chickpeas to a small serving of tripe. A typical tapa costs 100 to 200 ptas, but check before you order because some are a lot dearer. A *ración* is a meal-sized serving of these snacks; a *media ración* is a half-ración.

The other popular snacks are *bocadillos*, long filled white bread rolls. Spaniards eat so many bocadillos that there are cafés that sell nothing else. Try not to leave Spain without sampling a *bocadillo de tortilla de patata* or *de jamón serrano*, a roll filled with potato omelette or cured ham.

You can often save 10% to 20% by ordering and eating food at the bar rather than at a table.

Restaurants

Throughout Spain, you'll find plenty of restaurants serving good, simple food at affordable prices, often featuring regional specialities. Many restaurants offer a *menú del día* – the budget traveller's best friend. For between 500 and 1200 ptas, you typically get a starter, a main course, dessert, bread and wine – often with a choice of two or three dishes for each course. The *plato combinado* is a near relative of the menú. It literally translates as 'combined plate' – maybe a steak and egg with chips and salad, or fried squid with potato salad. You'll pay more for your meals if you order à la carte, but the food will be better.

Vegetarian Food

Finding vegetarian fare can be a headache. It's not uncommon for 'meatless' food to be flavoured with meat stock. But in larger cities and important student centres there's a growing awareness of vegetarianism, so that if

SPAIN

there isn't a vegetarian restaurant, there are often vegetarian items on menus. A good vegetarian snack at almost any place with bocadillos or sandwiches is a *bocadillo* (or *sandwich*) *vegetal*, which has a filling of salad and, often, fried egg (*sin huevo* means without egg).

Self-Catering

Every town of any substance has a *mercado* (food market). These are fun and great value. Even big eaters should be able to put together a filling meal of bread, chorizo (spiced sausage), cheese, fruit and a drink for 400 ptas or less. If you shop carefully you can eat three healthy meals a day for as little as 600 ptas.

DRINKS

Coffee in Spain is strong. Addicts should specify how they want their fix: *café con leche* is about 50% coffee, 50% hot milk; *café solo* is a short black; *café cortado* is a short black with a little milk.

The most common way to order a beer (*cerveza*) is to ask for a *caña* (pronounced 'can-ya'), which is a small draught beer. *Corto* and, in the País Vasco, *zurrito*, are other names for this. A larger beer (about 300 ml) is often called a *tubo*, or in Catalonia a *jarra*. All these words apply to draught beer (*cerveza de barril*) – if you just ask for a cerveza you're likely to get bottled beer, which is more expensive.

Wine (*vino*) comes white (*blanco*), red (*tinto*) or rosé (*rosado*). *Tinto de verano*, a kind of wine shandy, is good in summer. There are also many regional grape specialities such as *jerez* (sherry) in Jerez de la Frontera and *cava* (like champagne) in Catalonia. *Sangría*, a sweet punch made of red wine, fruit and spirits, is refreshing and very popular with tourists.

The cheapest drink of all is, of course, water. To specify tap water (which is safe to drink almost everywhere), just ask for *agua de grifo*.

ENTERTAINMENT

Spain has some of the best nightlife in Europe – wild and *very* late nights, especially on Friday and Saturday, are an integral part of the Spain experience. Many young Spaniards don't even think about going out till midnight or so. Bars, which come in all shapes, sizes and themes, are the main attractions until around 2 or 3 am. Some play great music which will get

you hopping before – if you can afford it – you move on to a disco till 5 or 6 am. Discos are generally expensive, but not to be missed if you can manage to splurge. Spain's contributions to modern dance music are *bakalao* and *makina*, kinds of frenzied (150 to 180 bpm) techno.

The live-music scene is less exciting. Spanish rock and pop tends to be imitative, though the bigger cities usually offer a reasonable choice of bands. See the earlier Culture section for info on flamenco.

Cinemas abound and are good value, though foreign films are usually dubbed into Spanish.

SPECTATOR SPORT

The national sport is *fútbol* (soccer). The best teams to see – for their crowd support as well as their play – are usually Real Madrid and Barcelona, though the atmosphere can be electric anywhere. The season runs from September to May.

Bullfighting is enjoying a resurgence despite continued pressure from international animal-rights activists. It's a complex activity that's regarded as much as an art form as a sport by aficionados. If you decide to see a *corrida de toros*, the season runs from March to October. Madrid, Seville and Pamplona are among the best places to see one.

THINGS TO BUY

Many of Spain's best handicrafts are fragile or bulky – inconvenient unless you're going straight home. Pottery comes in a great range of attractive regional varieties. Some lovely rugs and blankets are made in places like the Alpujarras and Níjar in Andalucía. There's some pleasing woodwork available too, such as Granada's marquetry boxes and chess sets. Leather jackets, bags and belts are quite good value in many places.

Getting There & Away

AIR

Spain has many international airports including Madrid, Barcelona, Bilbao, Santiago de Compostela, Seville, Málaga, Almería, Alicante, Valencia, Palma de Mallorca, Ibiza and Maó (Menorca). In general, the cheapest destinations are Málaga, the Balearic Islands, Barcelona and Madrid.

Australia

In general, the best thing to do is to fly to London, Paris, Frankfurt or Rome, and then make your way overland. Alternatively, some flight deals to these centres include a couple of short-haul flights within Europe, and Madrid or Barcelona are usually acceptable destinations for these. Some round-the-world (RTW) fares include stops in Spain. STA Travel should be able to help you out with a good price. Generally speaking, a return fare to Europe for under A$1700 is too good to pass up.

North America

Return fares to Madrid from Miami, New York, Atlanta or Chicago range from US$620 to US$680 on Iberia or Delta. On the west coast, agencies such as Pelican Travel in Concord, California, can put together return fares from around US$770.

London

Scheduled flights to Spain are generally expensive, but with the huge range of charter, discount and low-season fares, it's often cheaper to fly than to take a bus or train. Check the travel sections of *TNT* or *Time Out* magazines or the weekend newspapers. The following are examples of short-notice low-season return fares from London:

Destination	Fare	Agent	Phone
Barcelona	£109	Charter Flight Centre	☎ 0171-630 5757
Ibiza	£95	Flight Dealers	☎ 0171-630 9494
Madrid	£89	Comet Travel	☎ 0171-636 6060
Málaga	£79	Alpha Flights	☎ 0181-579 3508

From Spain

For northern Europe, check the ads in local English-language papers in tourist centres like the Costa del Sol, the Costa Blanca and the Balearic Islands. You may pick up a one-way fare to London for around 12,000 ptas. The youth and student travel agency TIVE, and the general travel agency Halcón Viajes, both with branches in most main cities, have some good fares: generally you're looking at around 13,000 to 15,500 ptas one way to London, Paris

or Amsterdam, and at least 30,000 ptas to the USA.

LAND
Bus

There are regular bus services to Spain from all major centres in Europe, including Lisbon, London and Paris. In London, Eurolines (☎ 0171-730 8235) has services at least twice a week to Barcelona (24 hours), Madrid (27 hours) and Málaga (34 hours). One-way fares are £70 to £90. Tickets are sold by major travel agencies, and people under 26 and senior citizens qualify for a 10% discount. In Spain, services to the major European cities are operated by Eurolines affiliates such as Linebús and Julià Via. There are also bus services to Morocco from some Spanish cities.

Train

Reaching Spain by train is more expensive than bus unless you have a rail pass, though fares for those under 26 come close to the bus price. Normal one-way fares from London to Madrid (via Paris) are around £115. For more details, contact British Rail International in London (☎ 0171-834 2345) or a travel agent. See the introductory Getting Around chapter for more on rail passes and train travel through Europe.

Car & Motorcycle

If you're driving or riding to Spain from England, you'll have to choose between going through France (check visa requirements) or taking a direct ferry from England to Spain (see the following section). The cheapest way is one of the shorter ferries from England to France, then a quick drive down through France.

SEA
Britain

There are two direct ferry services. Brittany Ferries (in England ☎ 0990-360360) runs Plymouth-Santander ferries twice weekly from about mid-March to mid-November (24 hours), and a Portsmouth-Santander service (30 hours), usually once a week, in other months. P&O European Ferries (in England ☎ 0990-980980) runs Portsmouth-Bilbao ferries twice weekly almost all year (35 hours). Prices on all services are similar: one-way passenger fares range from about £45 in winter to £75 in summer (cabins extra); a car and driver costs from £145 to £260, or you can take a vehicle and several passengers for £223 to £411.

Morocco

Ferry services between Spain and Morocco include Algeciras-Tangier, Algeciras-Ceuta, Gibraltar-Tangier, Málaga-Melilla and Almería-Melilla. Those to/from Algeciras are the fastest, cheapest and most frequent, with up to nine daily Ceuta sailings (1½ hours) and four Tangier sailings (2½ hours). One-way passenger/car/motorcycle fares are 1800/8250/1875 ptas (Ceuta) and 2960/9300/2650 ptas (Tangier). You can buy tickets at Algeciras harbour, but it's more convenient to go to one of the many agencies on the waterfront. The price doesn't vary from shop to shop, so just look for the place with the shortest queue. A word of advice – don't buy Moroccan currency until you reach Morocco, as you will get ripped off in Algeciras.

LEAVING SPAIN

There is no departure tax in Spain.

Getting Around

AIR

Spain now has four main domestic airlines – Iberia, Aviaco, Air Europa and Spanair – and competition produces some fares which can make flying worthwhile if you're in a hurry, especially for longer trips or return trips. Málaga or Seville to Barcelona with Air Europa, for example, is 13,900 ptas (20,900 ptas return), against 7000 to 9000 ptas each way by bus or train. You can fly from Barcelona to the Balearic Islands with Spanair for 7950 ptas, or there and back with Aviaco for 12,500 ptas, not very much more than the ferry fare.

Among travel agencies, TIVE and Halcón Viajes (see Air under Getting There & Away earlier) are always worth checking for fares. There are some useful deals if you're under 26 (or, in some cases, over 63).

BUS

Spain's bus network is operated by dozens of independent companies and is more extensive than its train system, serving remote towns and villages as well as the major routes. The choice between bus and train depends on the particular trip you're taking: for the best value, compare fares, journey times and frequencies each time you move. Buses to/from Madrid are often cheaper than cross-country routes: for instance Seville to Madrid costs 2680 ptas while the shorter Seville-Granada trip is 2710 ptas.

Many towns and cities have one main bus station where most buses arrive and depart, and these usually have an information desk giving info on all services. Tourist offices can also help with info but don't sell tickets.

TRAIN

The Spanish train system has improved beyond imagination in the last 15 years. Trains are mostly modern and comfortable, and late arrivals are now the exception rather than the rule. The main headache is deciding which compartment on which train gives you best value for money.

RENFE, the national railway company, runs numerous types of train, and travel times can vary a lot on the same route. So can fares, which may depend not just on the type of train but also the day of the week and time of day. Among long-distance (largo recorrido) trains the best, quickest and most expensive type is normally a Talgo. Next quickest is usually an Intercity, then a Diurno or Rápido and finally an Estrella. Some trains have both 1st and 2nd class, some have only one or the other. There's also a category of overnight train called Tren Hotel, usually 1st class only and quite quick. Best of all is the AVE high-speed service that links Madrid and Seville in just 2½ hours.

Regionales are RENFE trains that travel shorter distances, usually with a lot of stops and cheaper fares. Cercanías are suburban trains run by various local authorities, not RENFE.

There's also a bewildering range of accommodation types, especially on overnight trains. RENFE publishes a fare guide, but it's 500 pages long and to understand it fully you'd need a PhD in cryptography! For any one route, there are up to 24 different fares per class (fares quoted in this chapter are typical 2nd-class seat fares). Fortunately ticket clerks understand the problem and are usually happy to go through a few options with you. The cheapest sleeper option is usually a *litera*, a bunk in a six-berth 2nd-class compartment.

You can buy tickets and make reservations at stations, RENFE offices in many city centres, and travel agencies which display the RENFE logo. For long-distance trains a reservation is always needed and costs 500 ptas or more per ticket.

Train Passes
Rail passes are valid for all RENFE trains, but Inter-Rail users have to pay supplements on Talgo and Intercity services, and full fare on the high-speed AVE service between Madrid and Seville. All pass-holders, like everyone else, have to make reservations for long-distance trains and pay the reservation fee of 500 ptas or more.

RENFE's Tarjeta Turistica is a rail pass valid for four to 10-days travel in a two-month period: in 2nd class, four days costs 22,646 ptas, while 10 days is 48,374 ptas.

CAR & MOTORCYCLE
If you're driving or riding around Spain, consider investing 1900 ptas in the *Mapa Oficial de Carreteras*, which is published annually by the Ministry of Public Works, Transport & Environment. It's a handy atlas with detailed road maps as well as maps of all the main towns and cities.

Spain's roads vary enormously but are generally quite good. Fastest are the *autopistas*, multilane freeways between major cities. On some, mainly in the north, you have to pay hefty tolls (from the French border to Barcelona, for example, it's around 1750 ptas). Minor routes can often be slow going but are usually more scenic. Petrol is relatively expensive at around 110 ptas for a litre of unleaded.

The head office of the Spanish automobile club Real Automovil Club de España (RACE) is at Calle José Abascal 10, 28003 Madrid (☎ 91-447 32 00). For RACE's 24-hour, nationwide, on-road emergency service, call ☎ 91-593 3333.

Road Rules
A general disrespect for road rules has given Spain the dubious honour of having one of the highest road-death tolls in the developed world. Speed limits are 120 km/h on autopistas, 90 or 100 km/h on other country roads and 50 km/h in built-up areas. The maximum allowable blood-alcohol level is 0.08%. Seat belts must be worn, and motorcyclists must always wear a helmet.

Trying to find a parking spot can be a nightmare in larger towns and cities. Spanish drivers just park anywhere to save themselves the hassle of a half-hour search, but *grúas* (tow trucks) will tow your car away if given the chance. The cost of bailing out a car hovers around the 6000 ptas mark.

Rental
Rates vary widely from place to place. The best deals tend to be in major tourist areas, including at their airports. At Málaga airport you can rent a small car for under 20,000 ptas a week. More generally, you're looking at something like 2500 ptas for a day plus 25 ptas a km (taxes and insurance included), or around 40,000 ptas a week with unlimited km. Local companies often have better rates than the big firms.

BICYCLE
See the Activities section earlier.

HITCHING
It's still possible to thumb your way around parts of Spain, but large doses of patience and common sense are necessary. Women should avoid hitching alone. Hitching is illegal on autopistas and difficult on major highways. Your chances are better on minor roads, although the going can still be painfully slow.

BOAT
For information on ferries to, from and between the Balearic Islands, see that section of this chapter.

LOCAL TRANSPORT
In many Spanish towns you will not need to use public transport, as transport terminals and accommodation are centralised and within walking distance of most tourist attractions.

Most towns in Spain have an effective local bus system. In larger cities, these can be complicated, but tourist offices can advise on which buses you need. Barcelona and Madrid both have efficient underground systems which are cheaper, faster and easier to use than the bus systems.

Taxis are still pretty cheap. If you split a cross-town fare between three or four people, it can be a decidedly good deal. Rates vary slightly from city to city: in Barcelona, they cost 270 ptas, plus 92 to 107 ptas per km; in Madrid they're a bit cheaper. There are supplements for luggage and airport trips.

Madrid

Whatever apprehensions you may have about Madrid when you first arrive, Spain's capital is sure to grow on you. Madrid may lack the glamour or beauty of Barcelona and the historical richness of so many Spanish cities (it was insignificant until Felipe II made it his capital in 1561), but it more than makes up for this with a remarkable collection of museums and galleries, some lovely parks and gardens and a really wild nightlife.

Orientation

The area of most interest to visitors lies between Parque del Buen Retiro in the east and Campo del Moro in the west. These two parks are more or less connected by Calle de Alcalá and Calle Mayor, which meet in the middle at Puerta del Sol. Calle Mayor passes the main square, Plaza Mayor, on its way from Puerta del Sol to the Palacio Real in front of Campo del Moro.

The main north-south thoroughfare is Paseo de la Castellana, which runs (changing names to Paseo de Recoletos and finally Paseo del Prado) all the way from Chamartín train station in the north to Madrid's other big station, Atocha.

Information

Tourist Offices Madrid's main tourist office (☎ 541 23 25) is in the Torre de Madrid on Plaza de España. It's open weekdays from 9 am to 7 pm (to 1 pm on Saturday). There are other tourist offices at Calle Duque de Medinaceli 2 (☎ 429 49 51), open the same hours, and at Plaza Mayor 3 (☎ 366 54 77), open weekdays from 10 am to 8 pm (to 2 pm on Saturday). The offices in Chamartín train station and Barajas

airport are open weekdays from 8 am to 8 pm and Saturday from 9 am to 1 pm.

Money Large banks like the Caja de Madrid usually have the best rates, but check commissions first. Banking hours are weekdays from 9 am to 2 pm (Saturday to 1 pm). El Corte Inglés department stores (see Things to Buy earlier) and American Express (see Post & Communications following) also have reasonable exchange rates. If you're desperate there are plenty of *bureaux de change* around Puerta del Sol and Plaza Mayor, which offer appalling rates but are open until midnight. One exception on both counts is Cambios Uno, Calle de Alcalá 20 – open daily from 9 am to 9 pm (Sunday till 3 pm).

Post & Communications The main post office is in the gigantic Palacio de Comunicaciones on Plaza de la Cibeles. Poste restante (lista de correos) is at window 17 and is open weekdays from 8 am to 9.30 pm and on Saturday from 8.30 am to 2 pm. American Express (☎ 322 54 24) is not too far away for those using its client mail service, at Plaza de las Cortes 2. It's open weekdays from 9 am to 5.30 pm and Saturday from 9 am to noon.

There are plenty of public phones on the streets. The Telefónica *locutorios* (phone centres) at Gran Vía 30 and Paseo de Recoletos 41 (near Plaza Colón) have phone books for the whole country and cabins where you can make calls in relative peace. Both are open daily from 9.30 am to 11.30 pm. Madrid's telephone code is ☎ 91.

Travel Agencies For cheap travel tickets try Viajes Zeppelin (☎ 547 79 03), Plaza Santo Domingo 2; or TIVE, the student and youth travel organisation, at Calle Fernando el Católico 88 (☎ 543 02 08) or in the Instituto de la Juventud at Calle José Ortega y Gasset 71 (☎ 347 77 00), both open Monday to Friday from 9 am to 1 pm.

Bookshops Librería Turner, Calle de Génova 3, has an excellent selection of English-language books – literature, fiction and guidebooks – as well as French and German books. Booksellers, at Calle José Abascal 48, is another good English bookshop. Librería de Mujeres, Calle San Cristóbal 17, is a women's bookshop and a well-known feminist meeting place.

La Tienda Verde, Calle Maudes 38 (metro: Cuatro Caminos), has about the best selection of walking guides and maps for many parts of Spain, including many IGN and SCE 1:25,000, 1:50,000 and 1:100,000 maps.

Laundry Laundrettes include Lavandería España on Calle Infante, Lavomatique on Calle de Cervantes, and Lavandería Alba at Calle del Barco 26.

Medical & Emergency Services The most central police station is beside the ticket office in Puerta del Sol metro station. You can call the police on ☎ 091. For medical emergencies, there's a clinic and 24-hour first-aid station at the Centro de Salud (☎ 521 00 25), Calle Navas de Tolosa 10. You can also ring ☎ 061 in a medical emergency. For an ambulance ring the Cruz Roja (Red Cross) on ☎ 522 22 22. For English-speaking medical services, try the Anglo-American Medical Unit (☎ 435 18 23) at Calle Conde de Aranda 1 (metro: Retiro).

Things to See

Madrid will make a lot more sense if you spend some time just walking around before you start getting into the city's cultural delights. The following walking tour could take anywhere from a few hours to a few days – it's up to you. You'll find more detail on the major sights in following sections.

Walking Tour The most fitting place to start getting to know Madrid is **Puerta del Sol**. Sol, as it's known to locals, is not much more than a huge traffic-junction-cum-bus-stop, but it's as central as you can get – on the south side, a small plaque in the footpath marks **Km 0**, from which distances along Spain's highways are measured. The statue of a bear climbing a tree on the north side of Sol is one of Madrid's favourite meeting places.

Walk up Calle de Preciados and take the second street on the left, which will bring you to Plaza de las Descalzas. Note the **doorway** to the Caja de Ahorros in the Caja de Madrid building – it was built for King Felipe V in 1733. It faces the 16th-century **Convento de las Descalzas Reales**. Moving along, head south down Calle San Martín to the **Iglesia de San Ginés**. This is one of Madrid's oldest churches – there is evidence that it has been here in one form or another since the 14th century. It houses some fine paintings, including El Greco's *Cleansing of the Temple*, but is only open for services. Behind the church is the wonderful **Chocolatería de San Ginés**, which specialises in chocolate con churros; it's generally open from 7 to 10 pm and 1 to 7 am.

Continue down to and across Calle Mayor and into Madrid's most famous square. On a sunny day the cafés on the early 17th-century **Plaza Mayor** do a roaring trade, with some 500 tables on the square – definitely a place to be seen, as the prices indicate. In the middle is a **statue of Felipe III**, who was responsible for the building of the square. The colourful murals on the **Real Casa de la Panadería**, on the north side, were painted in the early 1990s.

From Plaza Mayor, head west along Calle Mayor to the historic **Plaza de la Villa**, with Madrid's 17th-century ayuntamiento (city hall). Also here are the 16th-century **Casa de Cisneros** and the Gothic-Mudéjar **Torre de los Lujanes**, one of the city's oldest buildings, dating from the Middle Ages.

Take the street down the left side of Casa de Cisneros, cross the road at the end, go down the stairs and follow cobbled Calle del Cordón out on to Calle Segovia. Almost directly in front of you is the Mudéjar tower of the **Iglesia de San Pedro**. Turn right when you come to Plaza de la Cruz Verde. A little way up the hill behind you is the domed **Iglesia de San Andrés** – the decoration inside the dome is rather unusual and worth a peek.

Walk up Calle de la Villa past the military church on to Calle Mayor, and turn left, passing the **Capitanía General**, the national military headquarters. Calle Mayor brings you out on to Calle Bailén.

As you walk northward, you will pass Madrid's cathedral, the **Iglesia de la Almudena**, a stark and cavernous building which was finally completed in mid-1992, after more than 110 years under construction. A little further along is the **Palacio Real**, opposite which is the lovely **Plaza de Oriente**, with its collection of statues, fountains and mazes. On the far side of the plaza is Madrid's **Teatro Real**.

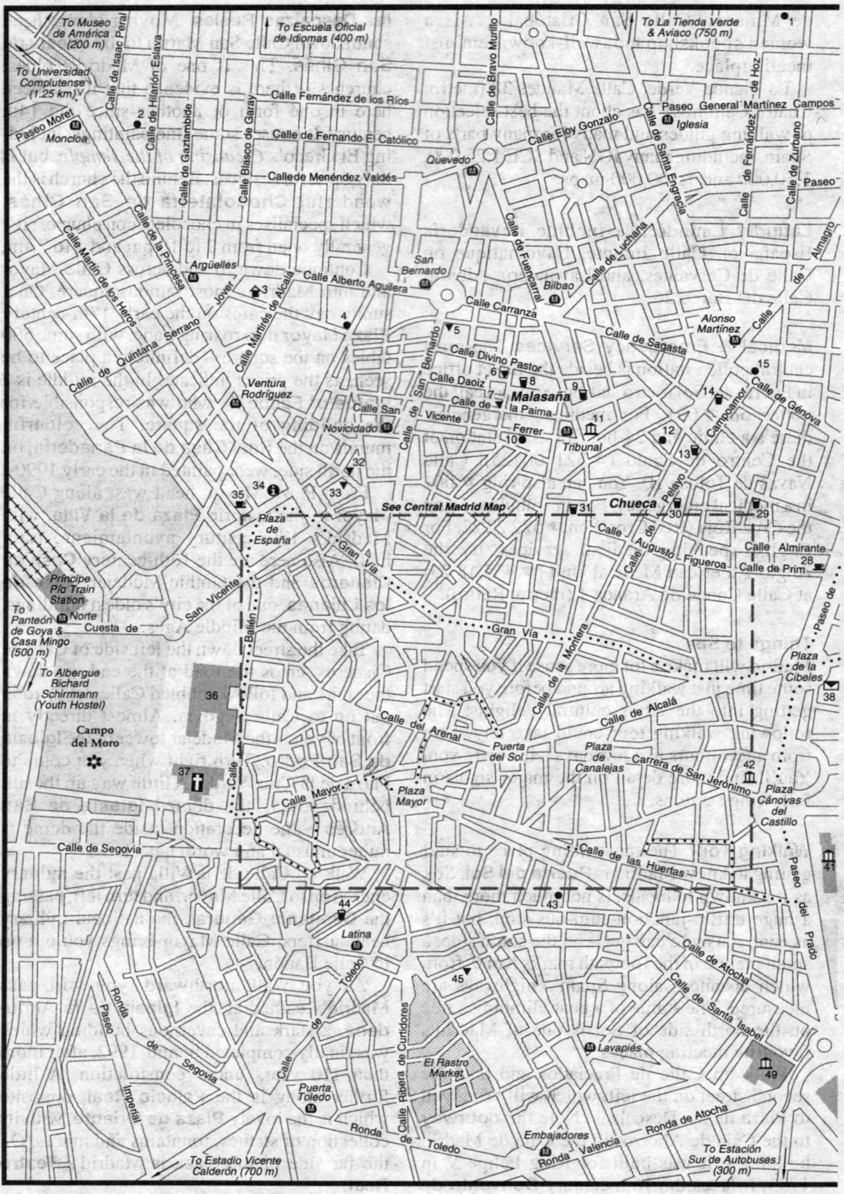
To Museo de América (200 m)
To Escuela Oficial de Idiomas (400 m)
To La Tienda Verde & Aviaco (750 m)
To Universidad Complutense (1.25 km)
Calle de Isaac Peral
Calle de Hilarión Eslava
Calle de Bravo Murillo
Calle Fernández de los Ríos
Calle de Fernando El Católico
Calle de Menéndez Valdés
Calle de Gaztambide
Calle Blasco de Garay
Paseo Moret
Moncloa
Quevedo
Calle Eloy Gonzalo
Calle de Santa Engracia
Calle de Fernández de Hoz
Calle de Zurbano
Paseo General Martínez Campos
Iglesia
Paseo
Calle Martín de los Heros
Calle de la Princesa
Argüelles
Calle Mártires de Alcalá
Calle Alberto Aguilera
San Bernardo
Calle de Fuencarral
Calle de Luchana
Bilbao
Calle de Almagro
Jover
Calle de Quintana
Serrano
Calle Carranza
Calle de Sagasta
Alonso Martínez
Calle de San Bernardo
Calle Divino Pastor
Calle Daoiz
Calle de la Palma
Malasaña
Calle San Vicente
Ventura Rodríguez
Novicidado
Ferrer
Tribunal
Calle de Génova
Campoamor
Calle de Pelayo
See Central Madrid Map
Chueca
Plaza de España
Gran Vía
Calle Augusto Figueroa
Calle Almirante
Calle de Prim
Paseo de
Príncipe Pío Train Station
Norte
To Panteón de Goya & Casa Mingo (500 m)
Cuesta de San Vicente
To Albergue Richard Schirrmann (Youth Hostel)
Calle Bailén
Calle de la Montera
Plaza de la Cibeles
Campo del Moro
Calle del Arenal
Calle de Alcalá
Puerta del Sol
Plaza de Canalejas
Carrera de San Jerónimo
Plaza Cánovas del Castillo
Calle Mayor
Plaza Mayor
Calle de Segovia
Calle de las Huertas
Paseo del Prado
Latina
Calle de Atocha
Calle de Toledo
Calle de Santa Isabel
Ronda de Segovia
Paseo Imperial
Calle Ribera de Curtidores
Lavapiés
El Rastro Market
Puerta Toledo
Ronda de Toledo
Ronda de Atocha
Embajadores
Ronda Valencia
To Estadio Vicente Calderón (700 m)
To Estación Sur de Autobuses (300 m)
1
2
3
4
5
6
7
8
9
10
11
12
13
14
15
28
29
30
31
32
33
34
35
36
37
38
41
42
43
44
45
49

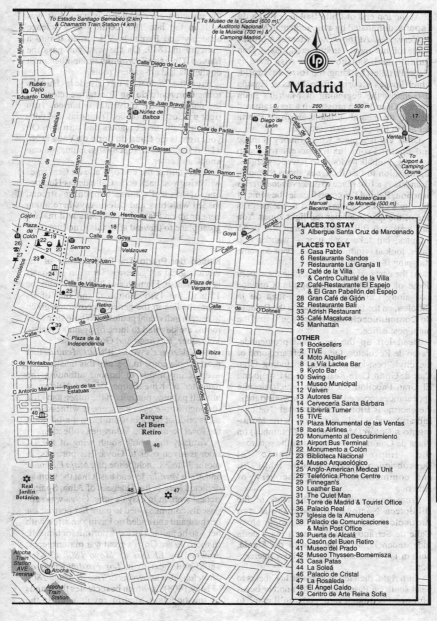

Madrid

0   250   500 m

To Estadio Santiago Bernabéu (2 km)
& Chamartín Train Station (4 km)

To Museo de la Ciudad (600 m),
Auditorio Nacional
de la Música (700 m) &
Camping Madrid

To Museo Casa
de Moneda (500 m)

To
Airport &
Camping
Osuna

Calle Miguel Angel

Rubén
Darío
Eduardo Dato

Calle Diego de León

Calle Velázquez

Calle de Juan Bravo

Calle Príncipe de Vergara

Calle Núñez de
Balboa

Calle de Padilla

Diego de
León

Calle de Francisco Silvela

Ventas

Calle José Ortega y Gasset

Calle Conde de Peñalver

Calle de Alcántara

Calle Don Ramon

de la Cruz

Paseo de la Castellana

Calle de Serrano

Calle Lagasca

16

Manuel
Becerra

Calle de Hermosilla

Calle

Alcalá

Colón

Plaza
de
Colón

18

Calle de Goya

Goya

26
22 19
21 20
27
23
24

Serrano

Calle Jorge Juan

Velázquez

Calle Núñez

Calle de Villanueva

Calle

25

Plaza de
Vergara

Retiro

Calle

de

O'Donnell

de

Alcalá

Recoletos

39

Plaza de la
Independencia

Ibiza

C de Montalban

Avenida Menéndez Pelayo

C Antonio Maura

Paseo de las
Estatuas

40

Parque
del Buen
Retiro

46

Calle de Alfonso XII

Real
Jardín
Botánico

48 47

Atocha
Train
Station
AVE
Terminal

Atocha

Atocha
Train
Station

17

PLACES TO STAY
3   Albergue Santa Cruz de Marcenado

PLACES TO EAT
5   Casa Pablo
6   Restaurante Sandos
7   Restaurante La Granja II
19 Café de la Villa
    & Centro Cultural de la Villa
27 Café-Restaurante El Espejo
    & El Gran Pabellón del Espejo
28 Gran Café de Gijón
32 Restaurante Bali
33 Adrish Restaurant
35 Café Macaluca
45 Manhattan

OTHER
1   Booksellers
2   TIVE
4   Moto Alquiler
8   La Vía Lactea Bar
9   Kyoto Bar
10 Swing
11 Museo Municipal
12 Valven
13 Autores Bar
14 Cervecería Santa Bárbara
15 Librería Turner
16 TIVE
17 Plaza Monumental de las Ventas
18 Iberia Airlines
20 Monumento al Descubrimiento
21 Airport Bus Terminal
22 Monumento a Colón
23 Biblioteca Nacional
24 Museo Arqueológico
25 Anglo-American Medical Unit
26 Telefónica Phone Centre
29 Finnegan's
30 Leather Bar
31 The Quiet Man
34 Torre de Madrid & Tourist Office
36 Palacio Real
37 Iglesia de la Almudena
38 Palacio de Comunicaciones
    & Main Post Office
39 Puerta de Alcalá
40 Casón del Buen Retiro
41 Museo del Prado
42 Museo Thyssen-Bornemisza
43 Casa Patas
44 La Soleá
46 Palacio de Cristal
47 La Rosaleda
48 El Ángel Caído
49 Centro de Arte Reina Sofia

SPAIN

At the top end of Calle Bailén is **Plaza de España**, dominated by a monument to Miguel de Cervantes. At the writer's feet is a bronze statue of his most famous creations – Don Quixote and Sancho Panza. Also here is Madrid's tallest building, the **Torre de Madrid**, which houses a tourist office. Plaza de España also marks the beginning of Madrid's main street – Gran Vía, a crosstown artery rammed through the neighbourhoods north of Puerta del Sol in the early 20th century.

Gran Vía is a place where money is made and spent. From luxury hotels to cheap hostales, pinball parlours to jewellery shops, high fashion to fast food, sex shops to banks, Gran Vía is a fine place to observe *madrileños* in action. Behind the grand façades lie some of the city's tackier scenes – just to the north is one of the city's sleazier red-light zones. You can walk the full length of Gran Vía in 15 minutes, but take your time – wander into cafés, look at window displays, even do some shopping if you can afford to.

At the east end of Gran Vía, note the superb dome of the **Edificio Metrópolis**. Continue east along Calle de Alcalá to **Plaza de la Cibeles**, on the far side of which is the **Palacio de Communicaciones**, where you'll find the main post office.

Head left up the tree-lined promenade, Paseo de Recoletos. On your left are some of the city's best-known cafés, including Gran Café de Gijón, Café-Restaurante El Espejo and El Gran Pabellón del Espejo which, despite appearances, opened in 1990! On your right is the enormous **Biblioteca Nacional** (National Library), and a little further on is the **Monumento a Colón** (Monument to Columbus) on Plaza de Colón. At the far end of the square is the impressive **Monumento al Descubrimiento**, sculpted in the mid-1970s and commemorating the 'discovery' of America.

From here walk round the back of the Biblioteca Nacional to where the **Museo Arqueológico** is housed. Walk south along Calle de Serrano until you reach Plaza de la Independencia, with the **Puerta de Alcalá**, built in 1778, in the middle of a busy intersection.

Turn right, then left at Plaza de la Cibeles to head south on Paseo del Prado, another beautiful tree-lined boulevard, and you'll come to the museum after which it is named. It was built in the late 18th century as a science academy and Fernando VII turned it into a museum in 1819. On the way you pass the **Museo Thyssen-Bornemisza**, another must on the Madrid art-gallery route.

From the Prado walk up Calle de las Huertas to the **Convento de las Trinitarias** (closed to the public), where Cervantes is buried. Turn right up Costanilla de las Trinitarias and continue to Calle de Cervantes and turn left. On your right is the **Casa de Lope de Vega** at No 11 – if the 'abierto' (open) sign is up, you can knock and enter.

A left turn at the end of Calle de Cervantes will bring you back on to Calle de las Huertas, one of Madrid's more happening streets, loaded with bars and cafés. Anywhere along here or up on Plaza de Santa Ana will make a great place to unwind after this gruelling tour!

Museo del Prado The Prado is one of the world's great art galleries. Its main emphasis is on Spanish, Flemish and Italian art from the 15th to the 19th centuries, and one of its strengths lies in the generous coverage given to certain individual geniuses. Whole strings of rooms are devoted to three of Spain's greats – Velázquez, El Greco and Goya.

Of Velázquez's works, it's *Las Meninas* that most people come to see, and this masterpiece – depicting maids of honour attending the daughter of King Felipe IV, and Velázquez himself painting portraits of the queen and king (through whose eyes the scene is witnessed) – takes pride of place in room 12 on the 1st floor, the focal point of the Velázquez collection.

Virtually the whole south wing of the 1st floor is given over to Goya. His portraits, in rooms 34 to 38, include the pair *Maja Desnuda* and *Maja Vestida*: legend has it that the woman depicted here is the Duchess of Alba, Spain's richest woman in Goya's time. Goya was supposedly commissioned to paint her portrait for her husband and ended up having an affair with her – so he painted an extra portrait for himself. In room 39 are Goya's great war masterpieces, crowned by *El Dos de Mayo 1808* (2 May 1808) and, next to it, *Los Fusilamientos de Moncloa*, also known as *El Tres de Mayo 1808* (3 May 1808), in which he recreates the pathos of the hopeless Madrid revolt against the

Central Madrid

0   125   250 m

PLACES TO STAY
1   Hostal El Pinar
2   Hostal Besaya
6   Hostal Médieval
9   Hostal América
10 Hotel Laris
12 Hostal Flores
16 Hotel Regente
23 Pensión Luz
27 Hostal Eureka
35 Hostal Leonesa
36 Hostal Rifer
37 Hostal Riesco
40 Hostal Santa Cruz
43 Hostal Tineo & Hostal Gibert
46 Hostal La Rosa
51 Pensión Poza
52 Hostal Lucense & Hostal Prado
57 Hostal Mondragón & Hostal León
66 Hostal Vetusta

73 Hostal La Macarena
74 Hostal Los Gallegos
78 Hostal Castro & Hostal San Antonio
80 Hostal Casanova
83 Hostal López
85 Hostal Matute

PLACES TO EAT
11 Bar Restaurante Cuchifrito
15 Restaurante Integral Artemisa
19 Taberna del Alabardero
20 Restaurante La Paella Real
22 Café del Real
33 Chocolatería de San Ginés
38 Restaurante Pontejos
41 Museo de Jamón
44 La Casa del Abuelo
47 Las Bravas
48 La Trucha
53 La Trucha
56 Mesón La Caserola
58 Restaurante Integral Artemisa
64 Café Principal
67 Restaurante Madrid 1600
75 Restaurante Sobrino de Botín
79 Restaurante Pasadero
82 Restaurante La Biotika
84 Restaurante La Sanabresa

OTHER
3   Bali Hai Disco
4   Morocco Disco
5   Lavandería Alba (Laundrette)
7   Cruising Bar
8   Rimmel Bar
13 Telefónica Phone Centre

14 Cock Bar
17 Centro de Salud
18 Viajes Zeppelin
21 Teatro Real
24 Convento de las Descalzas Reales
25 El Corte Inglés Department Store
26 Police Station
28 Edificio Metropolis
29 RENFE Train Booking Office
30 Police Station
31 Teatro de la Zarzuela
32 Cambios Uno
34 Iglesia de San Ginés
42 La Cartuja Disco
49 Torero Disco
54 Suristán
57 Teatro de la Comedia
54 Viva Madrid
55 La Venencia Bar
59 Carbones Bar
60 American Express
61 Tourist Office
62 Casa de Lope de Vega
63 Lavomatique (Laundrette)
65 La Moderna Bar
68 Mercado de San Miguel
69 Capitanía General
70 Ayuntamiento (City Hall)
71 Casa de Cisneros
72 Torre de los Lujanes
76 Tourist Office
77 Lavandería España (Laundrette)
81 Convento de las Trinitarias
86 Iglesia de San Pedro
87 Iglesia de San Andrés

SPAIN

French. There's more Goya in rooms 66 and 67 on the ground floor.

Other well-represented artists include El Greco, the Flemish masters Hieronymus Bosch and Peter Paul Rubens, and the Italians Tintoretto, Titian and Raphael.

The Prado is open Tuesday to Saturday from 9 am to 7 pm, and on Sundays and holidays from 9 am to 2 pm. Entry is 400 ptas (200 ptas if you have a student card) and includes the Casón del Buen Retiro, a subsidiary a short walk east which contains the collection's 19th-century works. It's free for all on weekends from 2.30 to 7 pm, as well as on some national holidays. A 'Paseo del Arte' ticket for 1050 ptas gives a year's access to the Prado, Centro de Arte Reina Sofia and Museo Thyssen-Bornemisza.

Centro de Arte Reina Sofia

At Calle de Santa Isabel 52, opposite Atocha station, the Reina Sofia museum houses a superb collection of predominantly Spanish art. The exhibition focuses on the period 1900 to 1940, and includes, in room 7, Picasso's famous *Guernica*, his protest at the German bombing of the Basque town of Guernica during the Spanish Civil War in 1937. The day of the bombing, 26 April, had been a typical market day in the town of 5000 people. Because of the market there were another 5000 people selling their wares or doing their weekly shopping. The bombs started to drop at 4 pm. By the time they stopped, three hours later, the town and thousands of the people in it had been annihilated.

Guernica was painted in Paris. Picasso insisted that it stay outside Spain until Franco and his cronies were gone and democracy had been restored. It was secretly brought to Spain in 1981, and moved here from the Casón del Buen Retiro in 1992. It's displayed with a collection of preliminary sketches and paintings which Picasso put together in May 1937.

The museum also contains further work by Picasso, while room 9 is devoted to Salvador Dalí's surrealist work and room 13 contains a collection of Joan Miró's late works, characterised by their remarkable simplicity.

Reina Sofia is open every day, except Tuesday, from 10 am to 9 pm (Sunday to 2.30 pm). Entry is 400 ptas (200 ptas for students with ID); free on Saturday afternoon and Sunday.

Museo Thyssen-Bornemisza

Purchased by Spain in 1993 for something over US$300 million (a snip), this extraordinary collection of 800 paintings was formerly the private collection of the Dutch steel magnate Heinrich von Thyssen. Starting with medieval religious art, it moves on through Titian, El Greco and Rubens to Cézanne, Monet and Van Gogh, then from Miró, Picasso and Gris to Pollock, Dalí and Lichtenstein, thereby offering one of the best and most comprehensive art-history lessons you'll ever have. The museum is at Paseo del Prado 8, almost opposite the Prado, and opens Tuesday to Saturday from 10 am to 7 pm, and Sunday from 9 am to 2 pm. Entry is 600 ptas (350 ptas for students with ID); free from 2.30 pm on Saturday and Sunday.

Palacio Real

Madrid's 18th-century Royal Palace is a lesson in what can happen if you give your interior decorators a free hand. You'll see some of the most elaborately decorated walls and ceilings imaginable, including the sublime Throne Room (and other rooms of more dubious merit). This over-the-top palace hasn't been used as a royal residence for some time and today is only used for official receptions and, of course, tourism.

The first series of rooms you strike after buying your ticket is the Farmacia Real (Royal Pharmacy), an unending array of medicine jars and stills for mixing royal concoctions. The Armería Real (Royal Armoury) is a shiny collection of mostly 16th and 17th-century weapons and royal suits of armour. Elsewhere are a good selection of Goyas, 215 absurdly ornate clocks from the Royal Clock Collection, and five Stradivarius violins, still used for concerts and balls. Most of the tapestries in the palace were made in the Royal Tapestry Factory. All the chandeliers are original and no two are the same.

The palace is open daily from 9 am to 6 pm (Sunday to 3 pm) and costs 850 ptas (students 350 ptas); free on Wednesday. A 50-minute guided tour is included in the price, but you may have to wait a while for your language to come up. The nearest metro station is Opera.

Convento de las Descalzas Reales

The Convent of the Barefoot Royals, on Plaza Descalzas, was founded in 1559 by Juana of

Austria, daughter of the Spanish king Carlos I, and became one of Spain's richest religious houses thanks to gifts from noblewomen. Much of the wealth came in the form of art: on the obligatory guided tour you'll be confronted by a number of tapestries based on works by Rubens, and a wonderful painting entitled *The Voyage of the 11,000 Virgins*. Juana of Austria is buried here. Opening hours are Tuesday to Saturday from 10.30 am to 12.30 pm and (except Friday) from 4 to 5.30 pm. On Sunday it's open from 11 am to 1.30 pm. Entry is 650 ptas (students 250 ptas); free on Wednesday.

Panteón de Goya Also called the Ermita de San Antonio de la Florida, this little church contains not only Goya's tomb, directly in front of the altar, but also one of his greatest works – the entire ceiling and dome, beautifully painted with religious scenes (and recently restored). The scenes on the dome depict the miracle of St Anthony. The panteón is the first of two small churches 700 metres north-west along Paseo de la Florida from Norte metro station. It's open Tuesday to Friday from 10 am to 2 pm and 4 to 8 pm, and weekends from 10 am to 2 pm. Entry is 300 ptas (free on Wednesday and Sunday).

Museo Arqueológico This museum on Calle de Serrano traces the history of the peninsula from the earliest prehistoric cave paintings to the Iberian, Roman, Carthaginian, Greek, Visigothic, Moorish and Christian eras. Exhibits include mosaics, pottery, fossilised bones and a reconstructed prehistoric burial site. It's open Tuesday to Saturday from 9.30 am to 8.30 pm, and Sunday from 9 am to 2 pm. Entry is 400 ptas (students 200 ptas); free from 2 pm on Saturday and on Sunday.

Other Museums Madrid almost has more museums than the Costa del Sol has high-rise apartments. If you can digest any more, they include: the **Museo Municipal**, with assorted art including some Goyas, and some beautiful old maps, scale models, silver, porcelain and period furniture; the **Museo Casa de la Moneda**, which follows the history of coinage in great detail and contains a mind-boggling collection of coins and paper money; the **Museo de América** with stuff brought from

the Americas from the 16th to 20th centuries; and even the **Museo de la Ciudad**, perfectly described by one traveller as 'a must for infrastructure buffs!', which rather drily traces the growth of Madrid. Check the tourist office's *Enjoy Madrid* brochure for more details.

Real Jardín Botánico The perfect answer to an overdose of art and history could be this beautiful botanic garden next door to the Prado. It's open daily from 10 am to 7 pm and entry costs 200 ptas (students 100 ptas).

Parque del Buen Retiro This is another great place to escape hustle and bustle. On a warm spring day walk between the flowerbeds and hedges or just sprawl out on one of the lawns.

Stroll along **Paseo de las Estatuas**, a path lined with statues originally from the Palacio Real. It ends at a lake overlooked by a **statue of Alfonso XII**. There are rowing boats for rent at the northern end when the weather is good.

Perhaps the most important, and certainly the most controversial, of the park's other monuments is *El Ángel Caído* (The Fallen Angel). First-prize winner at an international exhibition in Paris in 1878, this is said to be the first statue in the world dedicated to the devil.

You should also visit some of the park's gardens, such as the exquisite **La Rosaleda** (rose garden), and the **Chinese Garden** on a tiny island near the Fallen Angel. The all-glass **Palacio de Cristal** in the middle of the park occasionally stages modern-art exhibitions.

Campo del Moro This serene and stately garden is directly behind the Palacio Real, and the palace is visible through the trees from just about all points. This is one of the few places in the city where the roar of the traffic is reduced to a whisper and it's quite a haven for local birdlife. A couple of fountains and statues, a thatch-roofed pagoda and a carriage museum provide artificial diversions, but nature is the real attraction here.

El Rastro If you get up early on a Sunday morning you'll find the city almost deserted, until you get to El Rastro. The Rastro is one of the biggest flea markets you're ever likely to see, and if you're prepared to hunt around, you can find almost anything. The market spreads along and between Calle Ribera de Curtidores and Calle Embajadores (metro: Latina). It's said to be the place to go if you want to buy your car stereo back – watch your pockets and bags.

Language Courses
Madrid's Universidad Complutense offers a range of language and culture courses throughout the year, ranging from beginners to advanced. Contact the Secretaría de los Cursos para Extranjeros (☎ 394 53 25; fax 394 52 98), Facultad de Filosofía y Letras (Edificio A), Universidad Complutense, Ciudad Universitaria, 28040 Madrid. Another option is the rather overworked Escuela Oficial de Idiomas (☎ 533 58 05), Calle de Jesús Maestro s/n, which has Spanish-language courses at most levels from beginners up. There are many private language schools too.

Organised Tours
Madrid Vision tourist buses trace a circular route around the city, stopping at major sights, including the Prado and near Plaza Mayor, with taped commentaries in four languages including English. You can board at any of 13 clearly marked stops. One full round trip is 1500 ptas; a 2200-pta ticket gives you two full days. Either way, the metro is a quicker and cheaper way of getting around. The buses run five times daily except Sunday and holidays (when they go three times), and Monday when they don't run at all.

Special Events
Madrid's major fiesta celebrates its patron saint, San Isidro Labrador, throughout the third week of May. There are free music performances around the city and one of the country's top bullfight seasons at the Plaza Monumental de las Ventas. The Malasaña district, already busy enough (see Entertainment later), has its biggest party on 2 May, and the Fiesta de San Juan is held in the Parque del Buen Retiro for the seven days leading up to 24 June. The few locals who haven't left town in August will be celebrating the consecutive festivals of La Paloma, San Cayetano and San Lorenzo. The last week of September is Chamartín's Fiesta de Otoño (Autumn Festival) – about the only time you would go to Chamartín other than to catch a train.

Places to Stay
Finding a place to stay in Madrid is never really a problem.

Camping There are only two camping grounds relatively close to the city, but both are open all year, charging 525 ptas per person, 525 ptas per tent and 525 ptas per car. *Camping Osuna* (☎ 741 05 10), on Avenida de Logroño near the airport, is the better of the two (though smaller, with room for just 360): take the metro to Canillejas at the end of line 5, from where it's about 500 metres. *Camping Madrid* (☎ 302 28 35) is at Km 11 on the N-I road to Burgos. Take the Alcobendas bus from the stop outside Plaza de Castilla metro station to Los Dominicos, from where it's a 15-minute walk.

Hostels Madrid has two HI hostels within striking distance of the centre. Both are cheap (B&B at 900 ptas for those under 26, 1200 ptas for others), but they're also institutional, inconveniently located and almost always full with school groups. *Albergue Santa Cruz de Marcenado* (☎ 547 45 32), at Calle Santa Cruz de Marcenado 28, is a five-minute walk from Argüelles metro station, and has a 1.30 am curfew. *Albergue Richard Schirrmann* (☎ 463 56 99) is in Casa de Campo, a huge public park five km west of the centre. The hostel is a 15-minute walk from El Lago metro, but the park area is not safe to walk in at night. On the plus side, the hostel is open 24 hours a day and there's parking space.

Hostales & Pensiones These tend to cluster in three or four parts of the city and the price-to-quality ratio is fairly standard. In summer the city is drained of people, thanks to the horrific heat, so if you are mad enough to be here then, you may well be able to make a hot deal on the price. At other times it's only worth trying to bargain if you intend to stay a while.

Around Plaza de Santa Ana Santa Ana is well on the way to becoming one of Madrid's 'in' places. Close to Sol and within walking distance of the Prado and Atocha train station, it's also in one of Madrid's nightlife areas and has plenty of good budget restaurants.

North of the plaza, there's a choice of at least five hostales at Carrera de San Jerónimo 32.

Hostal Mondragón (☎ 429 68 16) (4th floor) is pretty good value at 1800/2700 ptas for biggish singles/doubles. *Hostal León* (☎ 429 67 78) in the same building is not bad and has heating in winter. It charges 2000/3500 ptas.

There are a number of very popular places on Calle Núñez de Arce. *Hostal Lucense* (☎ 522 48 88) at No 15 and *Pensión Poza* (☎ 232 20 65) at No 9 are owned by the same people (who used to live in Australia). Small, sometimes windowless, rooms start at 1000/2000 ptas, but there are better ones for 1500/2200 ptas. A hot shower is 200 ptas extra. In the same building as the Lucense, *Hostal Prado* (☎ 521 30 73) offers reasonable rooms from 1500/2800 ptas.

Hostal La Rosa (☎ 532 58 05), further up at Plaza de Santa Ana 15 (3rd floor), is good value with spacious rooms for 1800/3000 ptas.

Hostal Vetusta (☎ 429 64 04), Calle de las Huertas 3, has small but cute rooms with private shower for 2000/3500 ptas – try for one overlooking the street. On a quiet part of this street at No 54 (1st floor), *Hostal López* (☎ 429 43 49) is a good option. Rooms start at 2400/3800 ptas, or 3600/4800 ptas with private bath. The impressive *Hostal Matute* (☎ 429 55 85), Plaza de Matute 11, has spacious rooms for 2500/4300 ptas, or 3500/5500 ptas with private bath.

Hostal Casanova (☎ 429 56 91), Calle de Lope de Vega 8, has simple rooms at 1800/2600 ptas. Up around the corner at Calle de León 13, the attractive *Hostal Castro* (☎ 429 51 47) has good, clean rooms at 2000/3500 ptas with private bath. *Hostal San Antonio* (☎ 429 51 37), the next floor up, also has some nice rooms at similar prices.

Around Puerta del Sol You can't get more central than Plaza Puerta del Sol. Generally you'll pay for this privilege, but there are still some good deals in the surrounding streets.

Hostal Eureka (☎ 531 94 60), Calle de la Montera 7 (3rd floor), has bright, simple singles/doubles for 1500/2500 ptas. The pick of this area's bunch is *Hostal Riesco* (☎ 522 26 92) at Calle de Correo 2 (3rd floor), with comfortable rooms looking right on to the plaza. They cost 3200/4300 ptas with shower, or 3600/5000 ptas with full bathroom. *Hostal Rifer* (☎ 532 31 97) at Calle Mayor 5 (4th floor) is not quite as good but still reasonable at 4000/5000 ptas.

Hostal Gibert (☎ 522 42 14), Calle Victoria 6 (2nd floor), has rooms for 2000/3500 ptas, or doubles with private bath for 4000 ptas. In the same building on the 1st floor, *Hostal Tineo* (☎ 521 49 43) is perfectly adequate with singles/doubles at 2000/3500 ptas.

Around Plaza Mayor Plaza Mayor, Madrid's true heart, is not a major accommodation area, but there are a few good options scattered among all the open-air cafés, tapas bars, ancient restaurants and souvenir shops.

Hostal Los Gallegos (☎ 366 58 84) at Calle de Toledo 4 has singles/doubles for 1400/3000 ptas and one of the best positions in the city. *Hostal Santa Cruz* (☎ 522 24 41) at Plaza de Santa Cruz 6 (2nd floor) is equally well positioned and has much better rooms for 2400/3600 ptas, or 2800/4400 ptas with bath. The more up-market *Hostal La Macarena* (☎ 365 92 21), Calle Cava San Miguel 8, is also perfectly located. All rooms have private bath and they cost 3500/5500 ptas.

Further north, *Hostal Leonesa* (☎ 559 43 60), Calle Costanilla de Santiago 2 (2nd floor), has bright rooms for 1800/2800 ptas. *Pensión Luz* (☎ 542 07 59), Calle de las Fuentes 10 (3rd floor), is a bargain at 2000/3500 ptas.

Around Gran Vía The hostales on and around Gran Vía tend to be a little more expensive. All the same, it's another popular area.

Hostal El Pinar (☎ 547 32 82), Calle Isabel la Católica 19, has singles/doubles at 2500/3800 ptas. The stylish *Hostal Besaya* (☎ 541 32 06), Calle San Bernardo 13, has good rooms from 3600/4800 ptas.

Hostal Flores (☎ 522 81 52) at Gran Vía 30 (entrance at Calle G Jiménez Quesada 2, 8th floor) offers good views and rooms for 2300/3500 ptas, or 3500/4500 ptas with private bath.

Hotel Laris (☎ 521 46 80), Calle del Barco 3, is a good mid-range hotel with rooms for 5000/7900 ptas, all with air-con and colour TV. Garage space is available (2000 ptas). *Hotel Regente* (☎ 521 29 41), Calle Mesoneros Romanos 9, has similar standards and prices.

There are loads of places on Calle Valverde. *Hostal América* (☎ 522 26 14) at No 9 (4th floor) is excellent value, with rooms at 1700/

SPAIN

3500 ptas. Calle de Fuencarral also has plenty of options. At No 45, *Hostal Medieval* (☎ 522 25 49) has spacious and bright rooms from 3000/4200 ptas.

Rental Many of the hostales mentioned above will do a deal on long stays. This may include a considerable price reduction, meals and laundry. It is simply a matter of asking. For longer stays, check the rental pages of *Segundamano* magazine or notice boards at universities, the Escuela Oficial de Idiomas and cultural institutes like the British Council or Alliance Française.

Places to Eat

Around Santa Ana If you are staying around Santa Ana, you needn't look far for good-value eats. *Restaurante La Sanabresa*, Calle Amor de Dios 12, has some of the brightest lights and best value food in the city – main meals start at about 500 ptas and desserts at 150 ptas. At No 3 in the same street, *Restaurante La Biotika* is an earthy and aromatic vegetarian restaurant, with a menú for 950 ptas and salads and mains from 700 ptas. *Restaurante Pasadero*, Calle Lope de Vega 9, is a popular local place with a solid set lunch for 975 ptas. *Restaurante Integral Artemisa* at Calle Ventura de la Vega 4 is an excellent vegetarian restaurant with a tasty set menú for 1200 ptas. They have another branch at Calle Tres Cruces 4 off Gran Vía. *Mesón La Caserola*, Calle de Echegaray 3, is an unassuming and popular place for seafood. Ask for a fritura, a mixed platter of deep-fried seafood.

The *Museo de Jamón*, Carrera de San Jerónimo 6, is one of several branches of this Madrid institution. Huge clumps of every conceivable type of ham dangle all over the place. Check prices as some are very expensive. There are cheap bocadillos and platos combinados too.

Excellent tapas joints in the Santa Ana area include *La Casa del Abuelo*, Calle Victoria 14, a classic old wine bar with superb grilled or garlic king prawns; *Las Bravas*, on Calle Álvarez Gato, with the best patatas bravas (spicy potatoes) you'll ever eat; and *La Trucha*, with two branches just off Plaza de Santa Ana on Calle Núñez de Arce and Calle Manuel Fernández y González.

Around Plaza Mayor You know you're getting close to Plaza Mayor when you see signs in English saying 'Typical Spanish Restaurant' and 'Hemingway Never Ate Here'. Nevertheless, when the sun's shining (or rising) there's not a finer or more popular place to be than at one of the outdoor cafés in the plaza.

Calle Cava San Miguel and Calle de Cuchilleros are packed with mesones that aren't bad for a little tapas hopping. Among them is *Restaurante Madrid 1600* at Cava San Miguel 7. A cut above the rest is *Restaurante Sobrino de Botín*, Calle de Cuchilleros 17, one of Europe's oldest restaurants (established in 1725), where the set menú costs about 3200 ptas – it's popular with those who can afford it.

The popular *Restaurante Pontejos*, Calle San Cristóbal 11, is a reliable place where you can often get a good paella. A full meal with wine will be about 2500 ptas.

Other Areas Just about anywhere you go in central Madrid, you can find cheap restaurants with good food.

Manhattan, half a km south of Plaza Mayor at Calle Encomienda 5, is a busy, no-frills establishment that fills up quickly for its 800-pta lunch menú. *Bar Restaurante Cuchifrito* at Calle Valverde 9 is a plain, simple eating house with a set menú for 900 ptas. *Casa Mingo* at Paseo de la Florida 2, near the Panteón de Goya, is a great old place for chicken and cider. A full roast bird, salad and bottle of cider – enough for two – comes to less than 2000 ptas.

If you're after paella at all costs, head for *Restaurante La Paella Real*, Calle de Arrieta 2 near Plaza de Oriente, which does a whole range of rice-based dishes from 1500 ptas. For a really first-class meal in a cosy atmosphere try *Taberna del Alabardero*, nearby at Calle Felipe V 6. Expect little change from 5000 ptas per person. If this is a bit steep, consider a couple of the mouthwatering tapas at the bar.

In the Malasaña area around Plaza Dos de Mayo, *Restaurante La Granja II* on Calle San Andrés has a vegetarian menú for 900 ptas. *Restaurante Sandos*, Plaza Dos de Mayo 8, can do you a cheap outdoor pizza and beer. A couple of blocks away, *Casa Pablo*, also known as La Glorieta, Calle de Manuela

Malasaña 37, is a rather polished place with good, modestly priced food – the 950-pta menú is excellent value.

The Plaza de España area is a good hunting ground for non-Spanish food, though you're looking at 2000 to 2500 ptas for a meal in the better places. *Restaurante Bali*, Calle San Bernardino 6, has authentic Indonesian fare. The *Adrish*, virtually across the street at No 1, is about Madrid's best Indian restaurant.

Cafés Madrid has so many fine places for a coffee and a light bite that you'll certainly find your own favourites. Ours include: *Café Principal*, Calle del Príncipe 33, an old-fashioned place near Plaza de Santa Ana; the historic, very elegant *Café-Restaurante El Espejo*, Paseo de Recoletos 31 (you could also sit at the turn-of-the-century-style *El Gran Pabellón del Espejo* outside); the equally graceful *Gran Café de Gijón* just down the road; the more down-to-earth *Café de la Villa* in the cultural centre of the same name on Plaza Colón, a cheery den for arty types and office workers; *Café del Real*, Plaza Isabel II, an atmospheric place with a touch of faded elegance, good for breakfast and busy at night too; and *Café Macaluca*, at Calle Juan Álvarez Mendizabal 4, just off Plaza de España, with fabulous crêpes and cheesecake.

Self-Catering The *Mercado de San Miguel*, just west of Plaza Mayor, is a good place to stock up on food for a cheap lunch.

Entertainment

A copy of the weekly *Guía del Ocio* (125 ptas at newsstands) will give you a good rundown of what's on in Madrid. Its comprehensive listings include music gigs, art exhibitions, cinema, TV and theatre. It's very handy even if you can't read Spanish.

Bars The epicentres of Madrid's nightlife are the Santa Ana-Calle de las Huertas area, and the Malasaña-Chueca zone north of Gran Vía. The latter has a decidedly lowlife element.

Any of the bars on Plaza de Santa Ana makes a pleasant stop, especially when you can sit outside in the warmer months. *La Moderna* attracts a mixed and buzzy crowd. Though it gets very crowded at weekends, you should look into *Viva Madrid*, Calle Manuel Fernández y González 7; its tiles and heavy wooden ceilings make a distinctive setting for the earlier stage of your evening. On the same street, *Carbones* is a busy place open till about 4 am with good mainstream music on the jukebox. *La Venencia*, Calle Echegaray 7, is an ill-lit, woody place that looks as if it hasn't been cleaned in years – perfect for sampling one of its six varieties of sherry.

In Malasaña, *Cervecería Santa Bárbara* at Plaza Santa Bárbara 8 is a classic Madrid drinking house and a good place to kick off a night out. Irish pubs are very popular in Madrid: two good ones are *The Quiet Man*, Calle Valverde 44, and *Finnegan's*, Plaza de las Salesas 9. *La Vía Lactea*, Calle Velarde 18, is a bright place with thumping mainstream music, a young crowd and a good drinking atmosphere. *Kyoto* bar on Calle Barceló is another popular hang-out. Calle de Pelayo Campoamor is lined with an assortment of bars, graduating from noisy rock bars at the north end to gay bars at the south end, where you've reached the Chueca area, the heart of Madrid's gay nightlife. *Autores*, No 6, can usually be relied on to be busy when other bars are thinning out in the wee hours. *Leather* at No 42 is just one of the many gay bars. *Rimmel*, Calle Luis de Góngora 4, and *Cruising*, Calle Pérez Galdós 5, are other popular gay haunts.

The quaintly named *Cock Bar*, Calle de la Reina 16, once served as a discreet salon for high-class prostitution. The ladies in question have gone but this popular bar retains plenty of atmosphere.

Live Music & Discos Latin rhythms have quite a hold in Madrid. A good place to indulge is *Vaiven*, Travesía de San Mateo 1 in Malasaña. Thursday is the big night, with the band La Única working magic. Entry is free and a beer is about 600 ptas. *Suristán*, Calle de la Cruz 7, near Plaza Santa Ana, pulls in a wide variety of bands, from Cuban to African, usually starting at 11.30 pm, sometimes with a cover charge up to 1000 ptas. *Swing*, Calle San Vicente Ferrer 23 in Malasaña, always has something on, including Caribbean music and, on Friday, pop and soul. Entry hovers around 1000 ptas. *Morocco*, at Calle Marqués de

SPAIN

Leganés 7 in Malasaña, is still a popular stop on the Madrid disco circuit, though some say it's past its prime. It gets going about 1 am. From 5 am a lively, noisy crowd makes for *Bali Hai*, nearby in Calle de la Flor Alta, where you can lose weight to the sound of bakalao.

Near Plaza de Santa Ana, Calle de la Cruz has a couple of good dance spaces: try to pick up fliers for them before you go – they may save you queueing. *Torero*, No 26, has Spanish music upstairs and international fare downstairs. *La Cartuja*, No 10, is also pretty popular and is open till 6 am.

La Soleá, Calle de la Cava Baja 27, is regarded by some as the last real flamenco bar in Madrid. *Casa Patas*, Calle Cañizares 10, hosts recognised masters of flamenco song, guitar and dance. Bigger flamenco names also play some of Madrid's theatres – check listings.

Concerts, Theatre & Opera There's plenty happening, except in summer. The city's grandest stage, the *Teatro Real*, is still undergoing an overhaul. The beautiful old *Teatro de la Comedia*, Calle del Príncipe 14, home to the Compañía Nacional de Teatro Clásico, often stages gems of classic Spanish and European theatre. The *Teatro de la Zarzuela*, Calle Jovellanos 4, fills the gap left by the Teatro Real as Madrid's top opera venue. The *Centro Cultural de la Villa*, under the waterfall at Plaza de Colón, stages everything from classical concerts to comic theatre, opera and even classy flamenco. Also important for classical music is the *Auditorio Nacional de Música*, Avenida Príncipe de Vergara 146 (metro: Cruz del Rayo), which often hosts the Orquesta Nacional de España.

Cinema Cinemas are very reasonably priced, with tickets around 700 ptas. Films in their original language (with Spanish subtitles) are usually marked VO (versión original) in listings. A good part of town for these is on and around Calle Martín de los Heros and Calle de la Princesa, near Plaza de España. The *Renoir*, *Alphaville*, *Lumière* and *Princesa* complexes here all screen VO movies.

Spectator Sport
Spending an afternoon or evening at a football (soccer) match provides quite an insight into Spanish culture. Tickets can be bought on the day of the match, starting from around 1000 ptas, although big games may be sold out. Real Madrid's home is the huge Estadio Santiago Bernabéu (metro: Lima). Atlético Madrid play at Estadio Vicente Calderón (metro: Pirámides).

Madrid is one of the best places in Spain to see a bullfight. These take place most Sundays between March and October – more often during the festival of San Isidro Labrador in May, and in summer. Madrid has Spain's largest bullring, Plaza Monumental de las Ventas (metro: Ventas), and a second bullring by metro Vista Alegre. Tickets are best bought in advance, from agencies or at the rings, and cost from about 2000 ptas.

Things to Buy
For general shopping needs, start at either the markets or the large department stores. The most famous market is El Rastro (see the section in Things to See, earlier). The largest department store chain is El Corte Inglés, with a central branch just north of Sol on Calle de Preciados.

The city's premier shopping street is Calle Serrano, a block east of Paseo de la Castellana. Calle del Almirante off Paseo de Recoletos has a wide range of engaging, less-mainstream shops. For guitars and other musical instruments, hunt around the area near the Palacio Real. For leather try the shops on Calle del Príncipe and Gran Vía, or Calle Fuencarral for shoes. For designer clothing, try the Chueca area.

Getting There & Away
Air Scheduled and charter flights from all over the world arrive at Madrid's Barajas airport, 13 km north-east of the city. With nowhere in Spain more than 12 hours away by bus or train, domestic flights are generally not very good value unless you're in a burning hurry. Nor is Madrid the budget international flight capital of Europe. That said, you *can* find bargains to popular destinations such as London, Paris and New York, and for domestic flights it's worth hunting around the airlines and a few travel agents. Some of the more interesting domestic fares from Madrid at the time of writing included:

Destination	Airline	Fare (one way/return)
Barcelona	Air Europa	6900/13,800 ptas
		(youth fare)
Canary Islands	Spanair	18,100/28,900 ptas
Palma de		
Mallorca	Spanair	9900/13,800 ptas
Málaga	Air Europa	9900/14,900 ptas
Santiago de		
Compostela	Spanair	9900/13,800 ptas

For more on fares and agents, see Travel Agencies under Information earlier in this Madrid section, and this chapter's introductory Getting There & Away and Getting Around sections.

Airline offices in Madrid include:

Air Europa
    Barajas airport (☎ 542 73 38, information ☎ 902-30 06 00)
American Airlines
    Calle de Pedro Teixeira 8 (☎ 597 20 68)
Aviaco
    Calle Maudes 51 (☎ 554 36 00)
British Airways
    Calle Serrano 60 (☎ 431 75 75)
Delta Airlines
    Calle de Goya 8 (☎ 577 06 50)
Iberia
    Calle de Goya 29 (☎ 587 87 87 or 587 81 09)
Spanair
    Barajas airport (☎ 393 67 35, information and reservations ☎ 902-13 14 15)

Bus There are eight bus stations dotted around Madrid. Tourist offices can tell you which you need for your destination. Most buses to the south, and some to other places (including a number of international services), use the Estación Sur de Autobuses (☎ 468 42 00 for information) at Calle de las Canarias 17 (metro: Palos de la Frontera). The choice between bus and train depends largely on where you're going – more detail on services to/from Madrid is given in other city sections in this chapter.

Train Atocha station, south of the centre, is used by most trains to/from southern Spain and many destinations around Madrid. Some trains from the north also terminate here, passing through Chamartín, the other main station (in the north of the city), on the way. Chamartín (metro: Chamartín) is smaller and generally serves destinations north of Madrid, though this rule is not cast-iron: some trains to the south use Chamartín and don't pass through

Atocha. A third station, Príncipe Pío (metro: Norte), is used by some trains to/from Galicia, Extremadura and Salamanca.

The main RENFE booking office (☎ 328 90 20) is at Calle Alcalá 44 and is open Monday to Friday from 9.30 am to 8 pm.

For information on fares, see the Getting There & Away section under the city you are going to.

Car & Motorcycle Madrid is surrounded by two ring-road systems, the older M-30 and the now almost completed M-40, considerably further out. Roads in and out of the city can get pretty clogged at peak hours (around 8 to 10 am, 2 pm, 4 to 5 pm and 8 to 9 pm), and on Sunday night.

Car-rental companies in Madrid include Atesa/Eurodollar (☎ 571 19 31), Avis (☎ 547 20 48), Budget (☎ 402 14 80), Europcar (☎ 541 88 92) and Hertz (☎ 900-10 01 11). All these have offices at the airport, in the city centre, and often at the main train stations. Recently there's been a spate of robberies on hire-cars leaving the airport, which makes it wiser to pick up your car elsewhere.

You can rent motorbikes from Moto Alquiler (☎ 542 06 57), Calle Conde Duque 13, but it's pricey, starting at 4000 ptas plus 16% tax a day for a 49-cc Vespino, with a 40,000-pta deposit. Something like a Yamaha 250 will cost you 10,000 ptas a day plus tax, with a 75,000-pta deposit.

Hitching & Car Pooling If you intend to hitch out of Madrid, you need to get well out of town first – choose a town along your route and start from there. For Andalucía, your chances of long rides improve dramatically south of Aranjuez.

A good alternative to hitching, and cheaper than buses and trains, is to prearrange a ride to your destination. You can do this through Auto Compartido (☎ 522 77 72), Calle de Santa Lucía 15. There's an annual membership fee of 1160 ptas, and then you pay a further 5 ptas per km.

Getting Around
To/From the Airport An airport bus service runs to/from an underground terminal in Plaza de Colón every 12 to 15 minutes. The trip takes

SPAIN

30 minutes in average traffic and costs 360 ptas. An alternative is to take bus No 1 (180 ptas) between the airport (where it uses the same stop as the airport bus) and Canillejas metro station. A taxi between the airport and city centre should cost around 2400 ptas.

Bus In general, the underground (metro) is faster and easier than city buses for getting around central Madrid. Bus route maps are available from tourist offices. A single ride costs 130 ptas. Night owls may find the 20 night bus lines, running from midnight to 6 am, useful. They run from Puerta del Sol and Plaza de la Cibeles.

Metro Madrid has a very efficient, safe and simple underground system. Trains run from 6.30 am to 1.30 am. Single rides cost 130 ptas and a ticket for 10 rides is 645 ptas.

Taxi Madrid's taxis are inexpensive by European standards. They're handy late at night, though in peak hours it's quicker to walk. From Chamartín station to Plaza de Colón costs about 1000 ptas.

Car & Motorcycle There's little point subjecting yourself to Madrid's traffic just to move from one part of the city to another, especially at peak hours. Most on-street parking space in central Madrid is designated for people with special permits, but almost everybody ignores this – also ignoring the 12,000 parking tickets slapped on vehicles every day. But you risk being towed if you park in a marked no-parking or loading zone, or if you double-park. There are plenty of car parks across the city, but they cost about 200 ptas an hour.

Around Madrid

EL ESCORIAL
The extraordinary 16th-century monastery-palace complex of San Lorenzo de El Escorial lies about one hour north-west of Madrid, just outside the town of the same name.

El Escorial was built by Felipe II, king of Spain, Naples, Sicily, Milan, the Netherlands and large parts of the Americas, to commemo-rate his victory over the French in the battle of San Quintín (1557) and as a mausoleum for his father Carlos I, the first of Spain's Habsburg monarchs. Felipe began searching for a site in 1558, deciding on El Escorial in 1562. The last stone was placed in 1584, and the next 11 years were spent on decoration and other finishing touches. El Escorial's austere style, reflecting not only Felipe's wishes but also the watchful eye of architect Juan de Herrera, is loved by some, hated by others. Either way, it's a quint-essential monument of Spain's golden age.

Almost all visitors to El Escorial make it a day trip from Madrid. It's open daily from 10 am to 6 pm (to 5 pm from October to March), and you should allow at least 2½ hours for a visit.

Information
You can get information on El Escorial from tourist offices in Madrid, or from the tourist office (☎ 91-890 15 54) close to the monastery at Calle Floridablanca 10. It's open weekdays from 10 am to 2 pm and 3 to 4.45 pm and on Saturday from 10 am to 1.45 pm.

You will have to pay for all but the most basic of the printed information at the monastery; guidebooks are on sale in the souvenir shop, starting from 700 ptas.

Things to See
Above the monastery's main gateway, on its west side, stands a **statue of San Lorenzo**, holding a symbolic gridiron, the instrument of his martyrdom (he was roasted alive on one). Inside, across the Patio de los Reyes, stands the restrained **basílica**, a cavernous church with a beautiful white-marble Crucifixion by Benvenuto Cellini, sculpted in 1576. At either side of the altar stand bronze statues of Carlos I and his family (to the left), and Felipe II with three of his four wives and his eldest son (on the right).

From the basílica, follow signs to the ticket office (*taquilla*), where you must pay 850 ptas (students 350 ptas) to see the other open parts of El Escorial. The price includes an optional guided tour of the *panteones* and one or two other sections.

The route you have to follow leads first to the **Museo de Arquitectura**, detailing in Spanish how El Escorial was built, and the **Museo de Pintura**, with 16th and 17th-century Spanish, Italian and Flemish fine art. You then head upstairs to the richly decorated **Palacio de Felipe II**, in one room of which the monarch died in 1598; his bed was positioned so that he could watch proceedings at the basilica's high altar. Next you descend to the **Panteón de los Reyes**, where almost all Spain's monarchs since Carlos I, and their spouses, lie in gilded marble coffins. Three empty sarcophagi await future arrivals. Backtracking a little, you find yourself in the **Panteón de los Infantes**, a larger series of chambers and tunnels housing the tombs of princes, princesses and other lesser royalty.

Finally, the **Salas Capitulares** in the southeast of the monastery house a minor treasure trove of El Grecos, Titians, Tintorettos and other old masters.

When you emerge, it's worth heading back to the entrance, where you can gain access to the **biblioteca** (library), once one of Europe's finest and still a haven for some 40,000 books. You can't handle them, but many historic and valuable volumes are on display.

Getting There & Away

Herranz bus line runs up to 30 buses a day to El Escorial from Calle de la Princesa, near Moncloa metro station in Madrid. The bus (700 ptas return) takes around one hour and drops you off near the monastery. There are also frequent trains (costing about the same as the bus) from Madrid's Atocha station, and local buses will take you the two km from the train station up to the monastery. Some trains continue to Ávila from El Escorial.

Castilla y León

The one-time centre of the mighty Christian kingdom of Castile, Castilla y León is one of Spain's most historic regions. From Segovia's Roman aqueduct to the walled city of Ávila, and from León's magnificent cathedral to the beautifully preserved old centre of Salamanca, it is crowded with reminders of its prominent role in Spain's past.

SEGOVIA

Segovia is justly famous for its magnificent

Roman aqueduct, but also has a splendid ridgetop old city which is worthy of more than a fleeting visit from Madrid. Originally a Celtic settlement, Segovia was conquered by the Romans around 80 BC. The Visigoths and Moors also left their mark before the city finally ended up in Castilian hands in the 11th century.

There are two tourist offices, one on Plaza Mayor (☎ 46 03 34) and another on Plaza del Azoguejo down beside the aqueduct.

The telephone code for Segovia is ☎ 921.

Things to See

You can't help but see the **aqueduct**, stretching away from the east end of the old city – it's over 800 metres long with 163 arches. The dates are a little hazy, but it was probably built in the 1st century AD.

At the heart of the old city is the 16th-century Gothic **catedral** on the very pretty Plaza Mayor. The first thing that catches your attention inside is its brightness. With a very high ceiling and no transepts, its sheer volume is quite overwhelming.

Perched on a craggy clifftop at the west end of the old city, Segovia's **alcázar**, with its turrets, towers and spires, is a fairy-tale 15th-century castle. It was virtually destroyed by fire in 1862, but has since been completely rebuilt and converted into a museum (open daily; entry 350 ptas).

Places to Stay

Two km along the road to La Granja is *Camping Acueducto* (☎ 42 50 00), open April to September.

Fonda Aragón (☎ 46 09 14) and *Fonda Cubo* (☎ 46 09 17), both at Plaza Mayor 4, are shabby but among the cheapest in town: 1200/2500 ptas for singles/doubles at the Aragón, a bit less at the Cubo. If you have no luck with these, *Hostal Juan Bravo* (☎ 43 55 21), Calle de Juan Bravo 12, will often have a room. Adequate rooms with private bath cost 4000/4200 ptas. There are a couple of dingy doubles without bath for 3300 ptas. More pleasant is *Hostal Plaza* (☎ 46 03 03), Calle Cronista Lecea 11, where rooms start at 3000/4000 ptas without private bath.

Further from the centre, but about the best deal in town, is the spick and span *Hostal Don Jaime* (☎ 44 47 87), near the aqueduct at Calle de Ochoa Ondategui 8. Rooms with TV cost 3000/5000 ptas.

If you can't find anywhere to stay in Segovia, it may be worth continuing to La Granja (see Around Segovia), which has a few cheap pensiones and considerably better nightlife.

Places to Eat

Bar Yiyo's, Calle de Doctor Sánchez 3, has hamburgers and the like and also one of the cheapest set lunches you're likely to find in Segovia – 875 ptas. At **Restaurante La Codorniz**, Calle Aniceto Marinas 3, you can expect to pay about 1500 ptas for a good main meal. Segovia's speciality is cochinillo asado (roast suckling pig); a set meal featuring this is 2100 ptas at one local favourite, **Mesón José María** at Calle del Cronista Lecea 11.

Getting There & Away

There are up to 16 buses a day to Madrid, and daily buses to Ávila and Salamanca. The bus station is 500 metres south of the aqueduct, just off Paseo Ezequiel González. There are also up to nine trains daily to Madrid (Chamartín or Atocha stations) but they are pretty slow. Trains also run north to Valladolid.

Getting Around

Bus No 3 runs between Plaza Mayor and the train station, passing the bus station on the way.

AROUND SEGOVIA

In the mountain village of San Ildefonso de la Granja, 11 km south-east, you can visit the royal palace and glorious gardens of **La Granja**, a Spanish version of Versailles built by Felipe V in 1720. Up to 10 buses daily run from Segovia to San Ildefonso.

About 50 km north-west of Segovia, the **Castillo de Coca** is also well worth a visit. One of the best known castles in Spain, this beautiful all-brick building dates from the 15th century. It is now a forestry school, but guided tours (☎ 911-58 63 59 or ☎ 911-58 66 47) are conducted by the students. Coca is on the Segovia-León railway, and up to three buses a day run from Segovia.

ÁVILA

Ávila deservedly lays claims to being one of the world's best preserved, and most impress-ive, walled cities. The 11th and 12th-century walls surrounding the old town are 2.5 km long, up to 12 metres high and three metres thick, with 90 turrets. The city has nine gates, the most beautiful of which are those of San Vicente and the alcázar.

Ávila also is also distinguished by being the highest city in Spain (1127 metres); the birth-place of St Teresa of Ávila, the 16th-century mystical writer and reformer of the Carmelite order; and – less to be boasted about – the place where Tomás de Torquemada orchestrated the most brutal phase of the Spanish Inquisition, sending off 2000 people to be burnt at the stake in the late 15th century.

Ávila's tourist office (☎ 21 13 87) is at Plaza de la Catedral 4.

The telephone code for Ávila is ☎ 920.

Things to See & Do

Of the numerous convents, museums and mon-uments you can visit here, the most outstanding is the **catedral** (open daily), built into the eastern end of the walls. Construction started in the 12th century in Romanesque style, although other sections, such as the Gothic towers, date from the 14th and 15th centuries. Later renovations were carried out in the baroque style, and the façade is adorned with an intricate Renaissance frieze. Art works in the small museum include a portrait by El Greco.

A short distance outside the eastern walls is the 16th-century **Palacio de los Deanes**, on Plaza de Nalvillos, which houses Ávila's inter-esting provincial museum – mainly ethnological and archaeological exhibits (200 ptas). A couple of minutes walk further east, on Calle Duque de Alba, **Convento de San José** was the first convent founded by St Teresa. Its museum is full of memorabilia (open daily).

Los Cuatros Postes, a lookout point around 2.5 km from the city gates on the Salamanca road, has the best view of the city and its perfectly preserved walls.

If you are in the region in October, don't miss the Festival of Santa Teresa (8 to 15 October). Semana Santa in Ávila is also recom-mended.

Places to Stay & Eat

Hostal Las Cancelas (☎ 21 22 49), just south of the cathedral at Calle de la Cruz Vieja 6, has simple singles/doubles from 2500/3500 ptas. *Hotel Jardín* (☎ 21 10 74), Calle de San Segundo 38, is a fairly scruffy place with rooms starting at 2500/3500 ptas. Better is the *Hostal Mesón El Rastro* (☎ 21 12 18), Plaza del Rastro 1, which is full of character and has a good restaurant. Rooms start at 3200/4000 ptas.

Restaurante Los Leales, Plaza de Italia 4, has a solid menú for 900 ptas. For a cheap, decent pizza, try *Telepizza* on the corner of Avenida de Portugal and Calle de San Segundo.

Getting There & Away

There are up to 17 trains a day between Ávila and Madrid. The two-hour trip costs 755 ptas. Trains to Salamanca cost the same. Buses also connect Ávila with Madrid, Segovia and Salamanca.

The bus and train stations are around 700 metres and 1.5 km east of the old town respectively. Bus No 1 links the train station with the old town.

SALAMANCA

Salamanca on a warm, sunny day is a great place to be. The cafés in the beautiful Plaza Mayor fill the square with tables and chairs, and the street artists and musicians come out of their winter hiding places. This is one of Spain's most inspiring cities, both in terms of history and modern life.

Information

The municipal tourist office (☎ 21 83 42) on Plaza Mayor, open daily, concentrates on information about the city. For more information, including details of language courses at Salamanca University, which is one of the best places in Spain to study Spanish, go to the oficina de turismo (☎ 26 85 71) in the Casa de las Conchas, open Monday to Friday from 10 am to 2 pm and 5 to 8 pm, and Saturday from 10 am to 2 pm.

The post office is at Gran Vía 25. There's no shortage of banks around the centre.

The telephone code for Salamanca is ☎ 923.

Things to See

As in many Spanish cities, one of the joys of Salamanca is to simply wander around the streets. Salamanca's beautiful **Plaza Mayor**

was designed in 1733 by the Spanish architect José Churriguera and built almost entirely in golden sandstone. The most outstanding building on the square, the **ayuntamiento** (town hall), was not completed until 1755.

The 15th-century **Casa de las Conchas** on the corner of Rua Mayor and Calle de la Compañía is a symbol of Salamanca. The original owner was a knight of St James *(caballero de Santiago)* and had the façades decorated with carved sandstone shells, the emblem of his order. The entrance to the **university**, on Calle Libreros, is another wonder. The best place to admire its intricacy from, the **Patio de las Escuelas**, is open from 9.30 am to 1.30 pm and 4 to 6.30 pm.

Next, brace yourself for the **Catedral Nueva** (New Cathedral) on Rua Mayor. This incredible Gothic structure, completed in 1733, took 220 years to build. As you try to take in the detailed relief around the entrance, you may wonder how they did it so fast. From inside the cathedral, you can enter the adjacent **Catedral Vieja** (Old Cathedral) for 300 ptas. A Romanesque construction begun in the early 11th century, this was consecrated in 1160, and has a particularly beautiful dome which helps to create a surprisingly spacious interior. Both cathedrals are open daily from 10 am to 1.30 pm and 4 to 7.30 pm.

At the southern end of Gran Vía is the magnificent **Convento de San Esteban**, where Columbus is said to have once stayed. Across the road, the smaller **Convento de las Dueñas** has a lovely courtyard with views of the cathedrals' domes and spires. Both convents are open daily.

Places to Stay

Salamanca is a very popular place to spend a few days, and accommodation can be hard to find. Persevere as it's worth the effort.

It is hard to beat a room in one of the little places right on Plaza Mayor. *Pensión Los Angeles* (☎ 21 81 66), No 10, has rather basic singles/doubles with washbasin for 1500/2500 ptas. Not far south of the plaza, *Hostal La Perla Salamantina* (☎ 21 76 56) at Calle de Sánchez Barbero 7 has rooms with bath for 2000/4000 ptas. *Hostal Tormes* (☎ 21 96 83) at Rua Mayor 20 has a range of rooms up to 2400/3300 ptas. The simple but decent *Pensión Estefanía* (☎ 21 73 72), Calle Jesús

SPAIN

Salamanca

0   100   200 m

PLACES TO STAY
3 Hotel Las Torres
6 Hostal Orly
9 Pensión Los Angeles
17 Hostal La Perla
   Salamantina
18 Hostal Tormes
23 Pensión Estefanía
32 Pensión Feli

PLACES TO EAT
7 Restaurante El Clavel
8 Restaurante Llamas
12 Music-Arte Cafe
16 El Patio Chico
22 Restaurante El Bardo
24 Restaurante El Trigal
25 Café El Ave Turuta

OTHER
1 Bus Stop for Train
   Station
2 Post Office
4 O'Neill's Irish Pub
5 Ayuntamiento
10 Municipal Tourist Office
11 Mercado Central
13 Bus Stop for Bus Station
14 Koalas
15 Café El Corrillo
19 Café Luxor
20 Taberna La Rayuela
21 Casa de las Conchas &
   Tourist Office
26 Patio de las Escuelas
27 University
28 Catedral Nueva
29 Convento de las Dueñas
30 Convento de San Esteban
31 Catedral Vieja

3-5, has one single at 1750 ptas and doubles from 3000 ptas.

Further south, *Pensión Feli* (☎ 21 60 10), Calle de los Libreros 58, has a handy location near the university and cheerful rooms for 2000/2800 ptas.

If you're looking for a little extra comfort, *Hostal Orly* (☎ 21 61 25), at Calle del Pozo Amarillo 5-7, offers good, modern rooms with TV, phone and heating for 4280/5350 ptas. *Hotel Las Torres*, (☎ 21 21 00), Calle de Concejo 4, has comfortable rooms with all mod cons for 9630/12,840 ptas.

Places to Eat

The best place to look for cheap eats (for those on a really low budget) is the excellent *mercado central* (food market), right by Plaza Mayor. *Restaurante Llamas*, nearby at Calle del Clavel 9, has a tasty menú for 950 ptas. There are also dozens of eateries around Plaza Mayor. *Music-Arte Cafe*, Plaza del Corrillo 20, has tasty filled baguettes and croissants for 375 ptas and good pastries. *El Patio Chico* on Calle de Melendez is a lively place to sit around and drink beers; filling tapas are around 400 ptas a throw.

Restaurante El Bardo, inside the Casa de las Conchas, has a good menú at 900 ptas (vegetarian or carnivorous). Another vegetarian place with similar prices is *Restaurante El Trigal* at Calle Libreros 20. Along the street at No 24, there's a respectable 800-pta menú at *Café El Ave Turuta*.

For a splurge, try the *Restaurante El Clavel*, at Calle del Clavel 6. You're looking at about 4000 ptas for a full meal.

Entertainment

When the university is in session, the nightlife in Salamanca is bound to please. Most of the places to be seen are on or around Gran Vía. Make sure you see the amazing décor at *Cafe Luxor*, a little way east up Calle de San Justo from Gran Vía. *Koalas* at Gran Vía 63 is, of course, a must for homesick Aussies, and as the day grows old, this place can really start to move. A popular, pleasantly low-lit place for earlier in the evening is *Taberna La Rayuela*, Rua Mayor 19. *O'Neill's Irish Pub*, Calle de Zamora 14, is one of the Irish-style pubs increasingly in vogue in Spain, and it's always busy. *Café El Corrillo* on Calle de Meléndez

is a great place to have a beer while catching some live jazz.

Getting There & Away

Bus Salamanca's bus station (☎ 23 67 17) is at Avenida Filiberto Villalobos 85, about a km north-west of Plaza Mayor. AutoRes has up to 16 express buses daily to Madrid, taking 2½ hours for 2210 ptas, plus stopping buses for 1770 ptas.

Among many other destinations served by regular buses are Santiago de Compostela, Cáceres, Ávila, Segovia, León and Valladolid.

Train The station is on Paseo de la Estación, 1.3 km north-east of the centre. At least five trains leave daily for Madrid (three hours, 1560 ptas) via Ávila (1¾ hours, 805 ptas). There are also direct trains daily to León, Valladolid and Barcelona. You can reach Santiago de Compostela via Medina del Campo, and Santander via Valladolid. A train for Lisbon leaves at 4.55 am.

Getting Around

From the train station, take bus No 1, which heads to the city centre along Calle Azafranal. Going the other way, it can be picked up on Gran Vía near the post office. From the bus station, bus No 4 runs round the old town perimeter to Gran Vía. Heading back, pick it up outside Plaza Mayor.

LEÓN

León is far too often left off travellers' itineraries. For those who get here, a fresh and pleasant city awaits. It's a city of long, wide boulevards, open squares and excellent nightlife, with one of Spain's greatest cathedrals. León was at its mightiest in the 10th to 13th centuries, as capital of the expanding Christian kingdom of the same name.

The tourist office (☎ 23 70 82), opposite the cathedral at Plaza de la Regla 3, is open Monday to Saturday from 10 am to 2 pm and 5 to 8 pm, and on Sunday from 11 am to 2 pm and 4.30 to 8.30 pm.

León's telephone code is ☎ 987.

Things to See

León's **catedral**, built primarily in the 13th century, is a wonder of Gothic architecture. Its

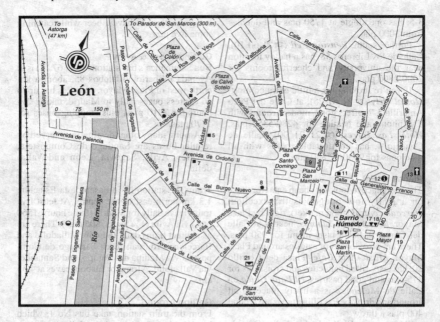

León

most outstanding feature is its breathtaking stained-glass windows. Of course, you'll have to go inside to appreciate their beauty. Opening hours are 9.30 am to 1 pm and 4 to 6.30 pm (closed Sunday afternoon). At the northern end of Calle del Cid is a great monument from the earlier Romanesque age: the **Real Basílica de San Isidoro** containing the **Panteón Real**, burial place of Leonese royalty with some wonderful 12th-century ceiling frescos. The panteón can be visited only by guided tour (300 ptas).

Plaza Mayor in the old town, a short distance south of the cathedral, is a little run down, but this is part of its romance. It is also the heart of León's buzzing nightlife. Also of interest is the **Casa de Botines** on Plaza San Marcelo, designed by the Catalan genius Antoni Gaudí, although it's rather conservative by his standards.

Places to Stay

There's plenty of budget accommodation, mostly on or near Avenida de Ordoño II,

Avenida de Roma and Plaza Mayor in the old town. **Pensión Berta** (☎ 25 70 39), Plaza Mayor 8, has basic singles/doubles for 1500/2200 ptas. The position is unbeatable.

Fonda Roma (☎ 22 46 63), Avenida de Roma 4, is in an attractive old building, with dirt-cheap rooms at 900/1500 ptas. More expensive is the **Hostal Central** (☎ 25 18 06), Avenida de Ordoño II 27, with reasonable rooms for 1800/2700 ptas. **Hostal Bayón** (☎ 23 14 46), Calle del Alcázar de Toledo 6, is run by a friendly woman who keeps clean rooms costing 2650/3500 ptas. **Hostal Orejas** (☎ 25 29 09), Calle de Villafranca 8, is a pretty good deal: rooms with bath and TV are 3200/5150 ptas.

Hotel Paris (☎ 23 86 00; fax 27 15 72), Calle de Generalísimo Franco 20, is a wonderful old hotel with moderate prices, at 4150/6250 ptas. If you're really an oil sheikh masquerading as a backpacker, you'll probably stay at the magnificent 15th-century **Parador de San Marcos** (☎ 23 73 00), Plaza de San Marcos 7. Doubles fit for royalty start from 17,500 ptas.

```
PLACES TO STAY
 3  Fonda Roma
 5  Hostal Bayón
 6  Hostal Orejas
 7  Hostal Central
11  Hotel Paris
19  Pensión Berta

PLACES TO EAT
10  Restaurante Bodega Regia
16  Restaurante El Tizón
17  Restaurante El Palomo
18  Restaurante & Sidrería Vivaldi
20  Restaurante Honoré

OTHER
 1  Train Station
 2  Pub La Morgue
 4  Real Basílica de San Isidoro & Panteón
    Real
 8  La Fundación
 9  Casa de Botines
12  Tourist Office
13  Catedral
14  Mercado
15  Bus Station
21  Post Office
```

Places to Eat

There are lots of good places within a short walk of the cathedral or Plaza Mayor. *Restaurante Honoré*, Calle de los Serradores 4, has a good menú for 750 ptas. *Restaurante El Palomo*, on tiny Calle de la Escalerilla, is a quality establishment with a lunch menú for 1300 ptas. Next door is the popular *Restaurante & Sidrería Vivaldi*, where you can wash down your meal with a cider from Asturias.

Restaurante El Tizón, Plaza San Martín 1, is good for wine and meat dishes, and offers an abundant menú for 1600 ptas. There are a few decent pizzerias and bars on the same square. For a really good meal in a cosy atmosphere, you can't go past the award-winning *Restaurante Bodega Regia* at Calle General Mola 5. They have a menú for 1700 ptas, and you can eat really well à la carte from 2500 ptas or so.

Entertainment

León's nocturnal activity flows thickest in the aptly named Barrio Húmedo (Wet Quarter), the crowded tangle of lanes leading south off Calle del Generalísimo Franco. Plaza San Martín is a particularly pleasant spot for drinks. Calle de Cervantes and Calle de Fernando Regueral north of Calle del Generalísimo Franco, are also lined with bars to suit most tastes.

As the night grows older, the action slides west towards the river. Friday nights are the best for dancing till dawn at *Pub La Morgue*, a noisy place for the young bakalao scene on Avenida de Roma. A more mixed crowd and music can be had until 6 am at *La Fundación*, just off Calle del Burgo Nuevo. There are more places on and around Avenida de Lancia.

Getting There & Away

Bus The bus station is on Paseo del Ingeniero Saenz de Miera, on the west bank of the Río Bernesga. Empresa Fernández has as many as eight buses to Madrid a day. The trip takes $3\frac{1}{2}$ to $4\frac{1}{2}$ hours and costs 2600 to 4000 ptas. Other destinations include Bilbao, Zamora, Salamanca and Valladolid.

Train The train station too is across the river, on Avenida de Astorga. Up to 10 trains a day leave for Madrid. A regional train (the slowest) costs 2550 ptas. Plenty of trains head north to Oviedo and Gijón and south to Valladolid. There are three trains daily to Barcelona and up to five to La Coruña and other destinations in Galicia.

AROUND LEÓN

A more extravagant example of Gaudí's work is in the town of **Astorga**, 47 km south-west of Léon. His Palacio Episcopal (1889) is also home to the moderate Museo de los Caminos, with Roman artefacts and religious art. Next door, the cathedral is a hotchpotch of 15th to 18th-century styles. Both are open in summer from 10 am to 2 pm and 4 to 8 pm, and in winter from noon to 2 pm and 3.30 to 6.30 pm (250 ptas each or 400 ptas for both). Several buses a day go from León.

Castilla-La Mancha

Best known as the home of Don Quixote, Castilla-La Mancha conjures up images of endless empty plains and sweeping windmills.

This Spanish heartland is also home to two exceptionally scenic and fascinating cities, Toledo and Cuenca.

TOLEDO

Toledo is one of Spain's most magnificent historic cities. The narrow, winding streets of the old city, perched on a small hill above the Río Tajo, are crammed with fascinating museums, monuments, churches and castles. As the main city of Muslim central Spain, Toledo was the peninsula's leading centre of learning and the arts in the 11th century. Taken by the Christians in 1085, it soon became the headquarters of the Spanish Church and was one of the most important of Spain's numerous early capitals. Until 1492, Christians, Jews and Muslims coexisted peaceably here, for which Toledo still bears the label 'Ciudad de las Tres Culturas' (City of the Three Cultures). Its unique architectural combinations, with Arabic influences everywhere, are a strong reminder of Spain's mixed heritage. El Greco lived here from 1577 to 1614 and many of his works can still be seen in the city.

Toledo is quite expensive and packed with tourists and souvenir shops. Try to stay here at least overnight, since you can enjoy the street and café life after the tour buses have headed north in the evening.

Information

The main tourist office (☎ 22 08 43) is on Carretera de Madrid, just outside the Puerta Nueva de Bisagra gate at the northern entrance to the old city. There's also an information booth on Plaza de Zocodover, the main square of the old city. Both are open daily.

The telephone code for Toledo is ☎ 925.

Things to See

Most of Toledo's attractions open from about 10 am to 1.30 pm and about 4 to 6 pm (7 pm in summer). Many, including the alcázar, Sinagoga del Tránsito and Casa y Museo de El Greco – but not the cathedral – are closed Sunday afternoon and/or all day Monday.

The **catedral**, in the heart of the old city, is awesome. You could easily spend hours in here, admiring the glorious stone architecture, stained-glass windows, tombs of kings in the Capilla Mayor, and art by the likes of El Greco, Velázquez and Goya. Entry to the cathedral is free, but you have to buy a ticket (500 ptas) to enter four areas – the Coro, Sacristía, Capilla de la Torre and Sala Capitular – which contain some of the finest art and artisanry.

The **alcázar**, Toledo's number-one landmark, just south of Plaza de Zocodover, was fought over repeatedly from the Middle Ages to the civil war, when it was besieged by Republican troops. Today it's a military museum, created by the Nationalist victors of the civil war, with most of the displays – which are fascinating – relating to the 1936 siege. Entry is 125 ptas.

The **Museo de Santa Cruz** on Calle de Cervantes contains a large and sometimes surprising collection of furniture, fading tapestries, military and religious paraphernalia, and paintings. Upstairs is an impressive collection of El Grecos including the masterpiece *La Asunción* (Assumption of the Virgin). Note also *La Sagrada Familia*: during cleaning of the painting in the 1980s, San José appeared in the background to the surprise and delight of all concerned. Entry is 200 ptas (free on Saturday afternoon and Sunday).

In the south-west of the old city, the queues outside an unremarkable church, the **Iglesia de Santo Tomé** on Plaza del Conde, indicate there must be something special inside. That something is El Greco's masterpiece *El Entierro del Conde de Orgaz*. The painting depicts the burial of the Count of Orgaz in 1322 by San Esteban (St Stephen) and San Agustín (St Augustine), observed by a heavenly entourage, including Christ, the Virgin, John the Baptist and Noah. Entry is 150 ptas.

The so-called **Casa y Museo de El Greco** on Calle de Samuel Leví, in Toledo's former Jewish quarter, contains the artist's famous *Vista y Plano de Toledo*, plus about 20 of his minor works and other 17th-century Spanish artworks. The house was apparently not really El Greco's; it was simply decorated in the style of his era. Entry is 400 ptas (200 ptas for students).

Nearby, the **Sinagoga del Tránsito** on Calle de los Reyes Católicos is one of two synagogues left in Toledo. Built in 1355 and handed over to the Catholic church in 1492, when most of Spain's Jews were expelled from the country, it houses the interesting Museo Sefardí, examining Jewish culture in Spain before 1492. Entry is 400 ptas (free on Saturday afternoon and Sunday).

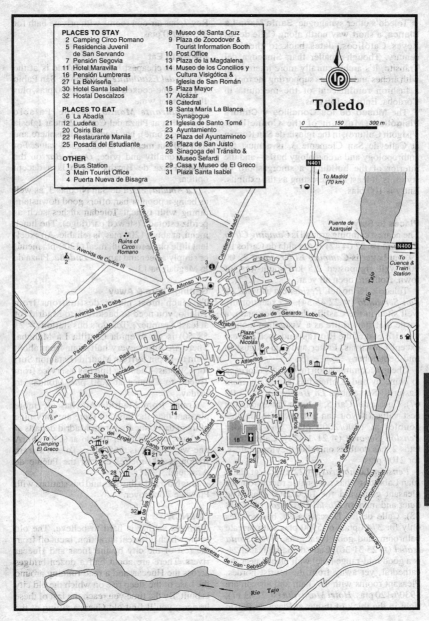

PLACES TO STAY
2 Camping Circo Romano
5 Residencia Juvenil
   de San Servando
7 Pensión Segovia
11 Hotel Maravilla
16 Pensión Lumbreras
27 La Belviseña
30 Hotel Santa Isabel
32 Hostal Descalzos

PLACES TO EAT
6 La Abadía
12 Ludeña
20 Osiris Bar
22 Restaurante Manila
25 Posada del Estudiante

OTHER
1 Bus Station
3 Main Tourist Office
4 Puerta Nueva de Bisagra

8 Museo de Santa Cruz
9 Plaza de Zocodover &
   Tourist Information Booth
10 Post Office
13 Plaza de la Magdalena
14 Museo de los Concilios y
   Cultura Visigótica e
   Iglesia de San Román
15 Plaza Mayor
17 Alcázar
18 Catedral
19 Santa María La Blanca
   Synagogue
21 Iglesia de Santo Tomé
23 Ayuntamiento
24 Plaza del Ayuntamineto
26 Plaza de San Justo
28 Sinagoga del Tránsito &
   Museo Sefardi
29 Casa y Museo de El Greco
31 Plaza Santa Isabel

Toledo

0   150   300 m

Toledo's other synagogue, **Santa María La Blanca**, a short way north along Calle de los Reyes Católicos, dates back to the 12th century. Though smaller than Sinagoga del Tránsito, it's architecturally more interesting, with arches and columns supporting the roof in a fashion reminiscent of the mezquita in Córdoba. Entry is 150 ptas.

The **Museo de los Concilios y Cultura Visigótica** (Museum of the Councils & Visigoth Culture), in the Iglesia de San Román at Calle de San Clemente 3, is a must for anthropology and archaeology buffs – and the interior of the building, a smorgasbord of styles, is at least as interesting as the exhibits. Entry is 100 ptas.

Places to Stay

The nearest camping ground is *Camping Circo Romano* (☎ 22 04 42) at Avenida de Carlos III 19, but better is *Camping El Greco* (☎ 22 00 90), well signposted 2.5 km south-west of town. Both are open all year.

Toledo's HI hostel, *Residencia Juvenil de San Servando* (☎ 22 45 54), is exceptionally well sited in the Castillo de San Servando, a castle that started life as a Visigothic monastery. It's east of the Río Tajo and open all year except Christmas, Easter and mid-August to mid-September.

Cheap accommodation in the city is not easy to come by and is often full, especially from Easter to September. *La Belviseña* (☎ 22 00 67), Cuesta del Can 5, is basic but among the best value (if you can get in), with singles/doubles at 1000/2000 ptas. The friendly *Pensión Segovia* (☎ 21 11 24), Calle Recoletos 2, has doubles only, but they're spotless, for 2100 ptas.

Pensión Lumbreras (☎ 22 15 71) at Calle Juan Labrador 9 has reasonable rooms round a pleasant courtyard for 1600/2500 ptas. The quiet and modern *Hostal Descalzos* (☎ 22 28 88), Calle de los Descalzos 30, has doubles only for 3745 ptas, or 5900 ptas with private bathroom, and good breakfasts. *Hotel Santa Isabel* (☎ 25 31 36), Calle de Santa Isabel 24, is a good mid-range hotel well placed near the cathedral, yet away from the tourist hordes. Pleasant rooms with TV, bath and air-con are 3930/6120 ptas. *Hotel Maravilla* (☎ 22 83 17), right in the thick of things at Plaza de Barrio

Rey 7, has air-con rooms with private bath for 3750/6000 ptas.

Places to Eat

About the cheapest lunch in Toledo is at the *Posada del Estudiante*, Callejón de San Pablo 2. The home-cooked menú costs 600 ptas, plus 100 ptas for wine.

Restaurante Manila, in the Palacio Fuensalida at Plaza del Conde 2 (near Iglesia de Santo Tomé), has loads of atmosphere and its 1100-pta menú is usually good value. For similar quality and price, *Osiris Bar* on the shady Plaza de Barrio Nuevo is a decent option.

La Abadía, Plaza de San Nicolás 3, as well as being a popular bar, offers good downstairs dining with typical Toledan dishes such as perdiz estofada (stewed partridge). The lunch menú, at about 1200 ptas, is reliable. An excellent little place for a full meal (1200-pta menú) or simply a beer and tapas is *Ludeña*, Plaza de la Magdalena 13.

Getting There & Away

To reach most major destinations from Toledo, you need to backtrack to Madrid (or at least Aranjuez). Toledo's bus station (☎ 21 58 50) is on Avenida Castilla La Mancha. There are buses every half-hour from about 6 am to 10 pm to/from Madrid (Estación Sur) for 550 ptas. The Aisa line has a service from Toledo to Cuenca at 5.30 pm, Monday to Friday.

Trains from Madrid (Atocha) are more pleasant than the bus, but there are only nine of them daily (the first from Madrid departs at 7.20 am, the last from Toledo at 9.30 pm). A one-way ticket is 565 ptas. Toledo's train station is 400 metres east of the Puente de Azarquiel.

Bus No 5 links the train and bus stations with Plaza de Zocodover.

CUENCA

Cuenca's setting is hard to believe. The old town, which is its real attraction, is cut off from the rest of the city by the Júcar and Huécar rivers. There are about half a dozen bridges across the Huécar, and a road running around the base of the steep rise on which the old city is built. By the time you reach the last of these bridges, you'll find old Cuenca sitting at the top of a deep gorge, with its most famous monuments teetering on the edge – a photographer's delight.

Don't follow the signs to the tourist office in the new town – there's a more useful one (☎ 23 21 19) up in the old town at Calle de San Pedro 6, just up the hill from Plaza Mayor.

The telephone code for Cuenca is ☎ 969.

Things to See & Do
Cuenca's **Casas Colgadas** (Hanging Houses) originally built in the 15th century, are precariously positioned on a clifftop, their balconies literally hanging over the gorge. A footbridge across the gorge provides access to spectacular views of these buildings (and the rest of the old town) from the other side. Inside the Casas Colgadas is the **Museo de Arte Abstracto Español**. This exciting collection is based around works by Spain's 'abstract generation', a group of artists who were particularly active in the 1950s. Opening hours are Tuesday to Friday from 11 am to 2 pm and 4 to 6 pm, Saturday from 11 am to 2 pm and 4 to 8 pm, and Sunday from 11 am to 2 pm. Entry is 300 ptas.

Nearby, on Calle del Obispo Valero, is the very different **Museo Diocesano**, with beautiful textiles, tapestries and religious art and artefacts dating as far back as the 13th century. Entry is 200 ptas; it's open Tuesday to Saturday from 11 am to 2 pm and 4 to 6 pm, Sunday from 11 am to 2 pm.

On Plaza Mayor you'll find Cuenca's strange **catedral**. The lines of the unfinished façade are Norman-Gothic and reminiscent of French cathedrals, and the stained-glass windows look like they'd be more at home in the abstract art museum.

As you wander the old town's beautiful streets, check the **Torre de Mangana**, the remains of a Moorish fortress in a square west of Calle de Alfonso VIII, overlooking the plain below.

Places to Stay & Eat
Pensión Real (☎ 22 99 77), in virtually the last house in the highest part of the old town at Calle Larga 99, is a typical family-run place with singles/doubles for 1700/4000 ptas. *Posada Huécar* (☎ 21 42 01), at Paseo del Huécar 3 at the foot of the old town, is quiet and comfortable with rooms from

2000/3800 to 3000/5000 ptas. *Posada de San José* (☎ 21 13 00), behind the tourist office at Ronda de Julián Romero 4, is a lovely 16th-century residence with doubles costing up to 4920 ptas, or up to 9500 ptas with private bathroom. Most of the restaurants and cafés around Plaza Mayor are better for a drink and people-watching than for good-value eating, but *Mesón Mangana* just down from the plaza has tasty tapas and a menú for 1500 ptas.

Down in the new town, there are several places on Calle Ramón y Cajal, which runs from near the train station towards the old town, including two no-frills pensiones at No 53: *Pensión Adela* (☎ 22 25 33) charging 1250 ptas per person plus 200 ptas for a shower, and *Pensión Marín* (☎ 22 19 78) upstairs, which is marginally better value at 1300/2400 ptas for singles/doubles. At No 49, *Hostal Cortés* (☎ 22 04 00) is more comfortable but characterless. Rooms with bath and TV are 3430/5350 ptas. *El Mesón*, Calle de Colón 56, is an atmospheric place to eat, with a good-value 1300-pta menú. It opens for lunch, and Friday and Saturday evenings only.

Getting There & Away
There are up to nine buses a day to Madrid (2½ hours, 1260 ptas), and daily buses to Barcelona, Teruel and Valencia. There are five trains a day direct to Madrid (Atocha), taking 2½ hours and costing 1215 ptas one way. There are also three trains a day to Valencia.

Bus No 1 or 2 from near the bus and train stations will take you up to Plaza Mayor in the old town.

AROUND CUENCA
A 35-km drive north of Cuenca is the bizarre **Ciudad Encantada** (Enchanted City). This 'city', open daily from 9.30 am to sunset (200 ptas), is a series of fantastically shaped rocks, many now given names that refer somewhat imaginatively to their shapes, such as Crocodile & Elephant Fighting, Mushrooms and Roller Coaster. If you have a car, it is worth the trip. The scenery on the way is great and the Ciudad Encantada itself makes a wonderful playground – a must if you are with kids. Take food and drink, as the café is expensive.

SPAIN

Catalonia

Catalonia (Catalunya in Catalan, Cataluña in Spanish) is one of the most fiercely independent regions in Spain and also the wealthiest. The Catalans speak a distinct language, Catalan, and many don't consider themselves Spanish. Catalonia's golden age was the 12th to 14th centuries, when it was the leading light in the medieval kingdom of Aragón, and Barcelona was capital of a big Mediterranean seafaring empire. The region has much to offer: Barcelona apart, there's the Costa Brava to its north, Tarragona with its fine Roman remains, Sitges with Spain's most forthright gay community and a vibrant carnaval, and Figueres with the bizarre Dalí museum. Away from the towns and cities, the Pyrenees offer good walking in many areas, especially the Parc Nacional d'Aigües Tortes i Sant Maurici, and skiing in winter.

BARCELONA

If you only visit one city in Spain, it probably should be Barcelona. After hosting the Olympic Games in 1992, it has finally taken its place on the list of the world's great cities. Catalonia's modernist architecture of the late 19th and early 20th centuries – a unique melting pot of Art Nouveau, Gothic, Moorish and other styles – climaxes here in the inspiring creations of Antoni Gaudí, among them La Sagrada Família church and Parc Güell. Barcelona also has world-class museums including two devoted to Picasso and Miró, a fine old quarter (the Barri Gòtic) and nightlife as good as anywhere in the country.

Orientation

Plaça de Catalunya is Barcelona's main square, and a good place to get your bearings when you arrive. The main tourist office is nearby at Gran via de les Corts Catalanes 658. Most travellers base themselves in Barcelona's old city (Ciutat Vella), the area bordered by the harbour Port Vell (south), Plaça de Catalunya (north), Ronda de Sant Pau (west) and Parc de la Ciutadella (east).

La Rambla, the city's best known boulevard, runs through the heart of the old city from Plaça de Catalunya down to the harbour. On the east side of La Rambla is the Gothic quarter (Barri Gòtic), and on the west the somewhat seedy Barri Xinès. North of the old city is the gracious suburb l'Eixample, where you'll find the most outstanding examples of Barcelona's modernist architecture.

Information

Tourist Offices Barcelona's main tourist office, the Catalunya Oficina de Turisme (☎ 301 74 43) at Gran Via de les Corts Catalanes 658, is open on weekdays from 9 am to 7 pm (Saturday to 2 pm). It can get very busy in summer but has a great deal of useful information and reasonable maps. There is another helpful office (☎ 412 91 71) at Estació Sants, the main train station, open on weekdays (and every day in summer) from 8 am to 8 pm, and on weekends from 8 am to 2 pm.

Money Banks usually have the best rates for both cash and travellers' cheques. Banking hours are usually weekdays from 8 am to 2 pm. The American Express office at Passeig de Gràcia 101 is open weekdays from 9.30 am to 6 pm and Saturday from 10 am to noon. You can also change money at El Corte Inglés department store on Plaça de Catalunya, open from 10.30 am to 9.30 pm except Sunday. Both these places have reasonable rates. For after-hours emergencies, there are currency exchanges along La Rambla.

Post & Communications The main post office is on Plaça d'Antoni López. For most services including poste restante (lista de correos), it's open weekdays from 8 am to 9 pm, and Saturday from 9 am to 2 pm.

Barcelona's telephone code is ☎ 93.

Travel Agencies Viva (☎ 483 83 78) at Carrer de Rocafort 116-122 (metro: Rocafort) offers youth and student fares. It's open weekdays from 10 am to 8 pm, and Saturday from 10 am to 1.30 pm, but expect long queues.

Bookshops In the Barri Gòtic, Quera at Carrer de Petritxol 2 specialises in maps and guides; Próleg at Carrer de la Dagueria 13 is a good women's bookshop.

In l'Eixample, Altaïr, Carrer de Balmes 71, is a superb travel bookshop; Librería Francesa at Passeig de Gràcia 91, Come In at Carrer de Provença 203 and BCN at Carrer d'Aragó 277 are good for novels and books on Spain, and dictionaries.

Laundry Lavandería Tigre at Carrer Rauric 20 in the Barri Gòtic will wash and dry five kg in a couple of hours for 1075 ptas. Doing it yourself saves 100 ptas.

Emergency There's a handy Guàrdia Urbana police station (☎ 301 90 60), with English spoken, at La Rambla 43 opposite Plaça Reial. The emergency police numbers are ☎ 091 or ☎ 092. For an ambulance or emergency medical help call ☎ 061.

Dangers & Annoyances Watch your pockets, bags and cameras on the train to/from the airport, on La Rambla, in the Barri Gòtic south of Plaça Reial and in the Barri Xinès – especially at night. These last two areas, once very seedy, have been somewhat cleaned up in recent years but there are still some pickpockets, bag-snatchers and intimidating beggars about.

Things to See

☆**La Rambla** The best way to introduce yourself to Barcelona is by a leisurely stroll from Plaça de Catalunya down **La Rambla**, the magnificent boulevard of a thousand faces. This long pedestrian strip, shaded by leafy trees, is an ever-changing blur of activity, lined with newsstands, bird and flower stalls, and cafés. It's populated by artists, buskers, human statues, shoe-shine merchants, beggars, and a constant stream of people promenading and just enjoying the sights.

About halfway down La Rambla is the wonderful **Mercat de la Boqueria**, which is worth going to just for the sights and sounds, but is also a good place to stock up on fresh fruit, vegetables, nuts, bread, pastries – everything you'll need for a park picnic. Just off La Rambla, further south, **Plaça Reial** was, until a few years ago, a seedy square of ill repute, but it's now quite pleasant, with numerous cafés, bars and a couple of music clubs. Just off the other side of La Rambla at Carrer Nou de la Rambla 3-5 is Gaudí's moody **Palau Güell**,

open daily, except Sunday, from 10 to 2 pm and 4 to 8 pm (300 ptas; students 150 ptas).

Down at the end of La Rambla stands the **Monument a Colom**, a statue of Columbus atop a tall pedestal. A small lift will take you to the top of the monument (225 ptas). Just west is the **Museu Marítim**, in the beautiful 14th-century Royal Shipyards, with an impressive array of boats, models, maps and more. If you like boats and the sea, you won't be disappointed – open daily, except Monday, from 10 am to 7 pm (800 ptas).

Barri Gòtic Barcelona's serene Gothic **catedral** is open daily from 8 am to 1.30 pm and 5 to 7.30 pm – be sure to visit the lovely cloister. Each Sunday at noon, crowds gather in front of the cathedral to dance the Catalan national dance, the *sardana*. Just east of the cathedral is the fascinating **Museu d'Història de la Ciutat** (City History Museum) composed of several buildings around **Plaça del Rei**, the palace courtyard of the medieval monarchs of Aragón. From the royal chapel, climb the multi-tiered Mirador del Rei Martí for good views. The museum also includes a remarkable subterranean walk through excavated portions of Roman and Visigothic Barcelona. It's all open Monday to Saturday from 10 am to 2 pm and 4 to 8 pm, and Sunday from 10 am to 2 pm. Entry is 500 ptas (250 ptas for students under 26 and pensioners).

A few minutes walk west of the cathedral, **Plaça de Sant Josep Oriol** is something of a hang-out for bohemian musicians and buskers. The plaza is surrounded by cafés and towards the end of the week becomes an outdoor art and craft market.

Waterfront For a look at the new face of Barcelona, take a stroll along the waterfront areas, once drab and seedy, but now attractively redeveloped with marinas, pedestrian promenades and more. From the bottom of La Rambla you can cross the Rambla de Mar footbridge to the **Moll d'Espanya**, a former wharf in the middle of the old harbour, Port Vell, where you'll find **L'Aquàrium**, one of Europe's best aquariums, open daily from 10 am to 9 pm, but not cheap at 1300 ptas. North-east of Port Vell, on the far side of the drab La Barceloneta area, begin the city **beaches**. Along the beachfront, after 1.25

SPAIN

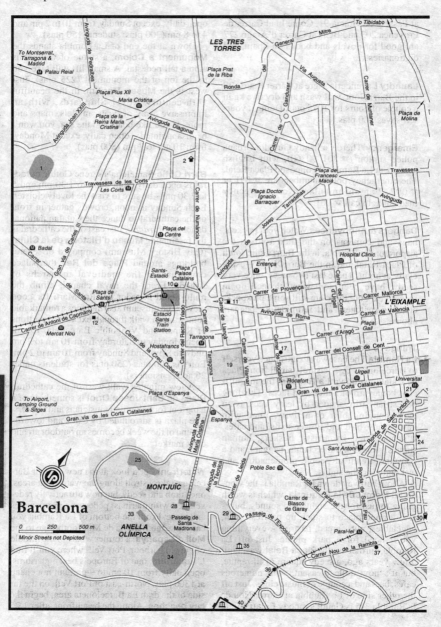

To Tibidabo

To Montserrat, Tarragona & Madrid

Palau Reial

LES TRES TORRES

Mitre

General

Via Augusta

Carrer del Muntaner

Plaça de Molina

Plaça Prat de la Riba

Ronda

Carrer de Ganduxer

Plaça Pius XII

Maria Cristina

Plaça de la Reina Maria Cristina

Avinguda Diagonal

1

Travessera de les Corts

Les Corts

2

Plaça de Francesc Macià

Travessera

Plaça Doctor Ignacio Barraquer

Avinguda

Tarradellas

Plaça del Centre

Avinguda de Josep

Hospital Clínic

Entença

L'EIXAMPLE

Sants-Estació

Plaça Països Catalans

10

Carrer de Provença

Carrer del Comte d'Urgell

Carrer Mallorca

Carrer de València

Badal

Gran via de Carles III

de Sants

Plaça de Sants

11

Avinguda de Roma

Plaça Gail

Carrer de Antoni de Capmany

12

Mercat Nou

Estació Sants Train Station

Carrer del Rector Triadó

Carrer de Llançà

Carrer d'Aragó

Carrer del Consell de Cent

Tarragona

17

Hostafrancs

Carrer de la Creu Coberta

Carrer de Vilamarí

Carrer de Rocafort

Rocafort

Urgell

Universitat

21

To Airport, Camping Ground & Sites

Plaça d'Espanya

19

Gran via de les Corts Catalanes

Gran via de les Corts Catalanes

Avinguda Reina Maria Cristina

Espanya

Sant Antoni

Ronda de Sant Antoni

24

25

MONTJUÏC

Avinguda del la Tècnica

Carrer de Lleida

Poble Sec

Avinguda del Paral·lel

Ronda de Sant Pau

30

33

28

Passeig de Santa Madrona

29

Passeig de l'Exposició

Carrer de Blasco de Garay

ANELLA OLÍMPICA

34

35

Paral·lel

37

Barcelona

0   250   500 m

Minor Streets not Depicted

36

40

Carrer Nou de la Rambla

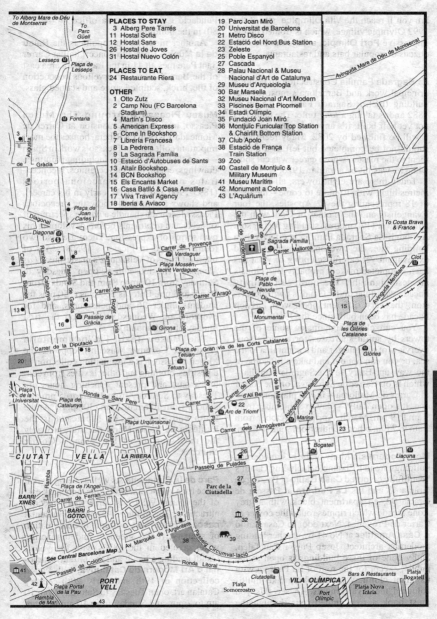

PLACES TO STAY
3 Alberg Pere Tarrés
11 Hostal Sofia
12 Hostal Sans
26 Hostal de Joves
31 Hostal Nuevo Colón

PLACES TO EAT
24 Restaurante Riera

OTHER
1 Otto Zutz
2 Camp Nou (FC Barcelona Stadium)
4 Martin's Disco
5 American Express
6 Come In Bookshop
7 Librería Francesa
8 La Pedrera
9 La Sagrada Família
10 Estació d'Autobuses de Sants
13 Altair Bookshop
14 BCN Bookshop
15 Els Encants Market
16 Casa Batlló & Casa Amatller
17 Viva Travel Agency
18 Iberia & Aviaco

19 Parc Joan Miró
20 Universitat de Barcelona
21 Metro Disco
22 Estació del Nord Bus Station
23 Zeleste
25 Poble Espanyol
27 Cascada
28 Palau Nacional & Museu Nacional d'Art de Catalunya
29 Museu d'Arqueologia
30 Bar Marsella
32 Museu Nacional d'Art Modern
33 Piscines Bernat Picornell
34 Estadi Olímpic
35 Fundació Joan Miró
36 Montjuïc Funicular Top Station & Chairlift Bottom Station
37 Club Apolo
38 Estació de França
39 Zoo
40 Castell de Montjuïc & Military Museum
41 Museu Marítim
42 Monument a Colom
43 L'Aquàrium

SPAIN

km you'll reach the **Vila Olímpica**, site of the 1992 Olympic village, which is fronted by the impressive **Port Olímpic**, a large marina with dozens of popular bars and restaurants.

La Sagrada Família Construction on Gaudí's principal work and Barcelona's most famous building (metro: Sagrada Família) began in 1882 and is taking a *long* time. The church is not yet half built: it's anyone's guess whether it will be finished by 2082. Many feel that it should not be completed but left as a monument to the master, whose career was cut short when he was hit by a tram in 1926.

Today there are eight towers, all over 100 metres high, with 10 more to come – the total of 18 representing the 12 Apostles, the four Evangelists and the mother of God, with the tallest tower (170 metres) standing for her son. Although La Sagrada Família is effectively a building site, the awesome dimensions and extravagant yet careful sculpting of what has been completed make it probably Barcelona's greatest highlight. The north-east Nativity Façade was done under Gaudí's own supervision, the very different north-west Passion Façade has been built since the 1950s.

You can climb high inside some of the towers by spiral staircases for a vertiginous overview of the interior and a panorama to the sea, or you can opt out and take a lift some of the way up. Entry to La Sagrada Família – which is on Carrer de Sardenya, on the corner of Carrer de Mallorca – is 750 ptas for everyone. It's open daily – May to September from 9 am to 9 pm, March, April and October from 9 am to 7 pm, other months from 9 am to 6 pm.

More Modernism Many of the best modernist buildings are in l'Eixample, including Gaudí's beautifully coloured **Casa Batlló** at Passeig de Gràcia 43 and his **La Pedrera** at Passeig de Gràcia 92, an apartment block with a grey stone façade which ripples round the corner of Carrer de Provença. Next door to Casa Batlló is **Casa Amatller** at No 41 by another leading modernist architect, Josep Puig i Cadafalch. Sadly none of these buildings is open to the public, except for the roof of La Pedrera with its giant chimney pots looking like multicoloured medieval knights. To see this you must book a free guided tour through the

Fundació Caixa Catalunya office (☎ 484 59 80) in the building.

Another modernist highpoint is the **Palau de la Música Catalana** concert hall at Carrer Sant Pere mes alt 11 in the La Ribera area east of the Barri Gòtic – a marvellous concoction of tile, brick, sculpted stone and stained glass.

Museu Picasso & Around The Museu Picasso, in a medieval mansion at Carrer de Montcada 15-19 in La Ribera, houses the most important collection of Picasso's work in Spain – more than 3000 pieces, including paintings, drawings, engravings and ceramics. It concentrates on Picasso's Barcelona periods (1895-1900 and 1901-04, early in his career), and shows fascinatingly how the precocious Picasso learned to handle a whole spectrum of subjects and treatments before developing his own forms of expression. There are also two rooms devoted to Picasso's 1950s series of interpretations of Velázquez's masterpiece *Las Meninas*. The museum is open Tuesday to Saturday from 10 am to 8 pm and Sunday from 10 am to 3 pm. Entry is 500 ptas (250 ptas for students under 26 and pensioners, and for everyone on Wednesday; free on the first Sunday of each month).

The **Museu Tèxtil i d'Indumentària** (Textile & Costume Museum), opposite the Museu Picasso, has a fascinating collection of tapestries, clothing and other textiles from centuries past and present. Opening hours are Tuesday to Saturday from 10 am to 5 pm and Sunday from 10 am to 2 pm (300 ptas). At the south end of Carrer de Montcada is the **Església de Santa Maria del Mar**, probably the most perfect of Barcelona's Gothic churches.

Parc de la Ciutadella As well as being a great place for a picnic or a stroll, this large park east of the Ciutat Vella has some more specific attractions. Top of the list are the monumental **cascada** (waterfall), a dramatic combination of statuary, rocks, greenery and thundering water created in the 1870s with the young Gaudí lending a hand; and the **Museu Nacional d'Art Modern de Catalunya**, with a good collection of 19th and early 20th-century Catalan art, open Tuesday to Saturday from 10 am to 7 pm, and Sunday from 10 am to 2 pm

(200 ptas). At the southern end of the park is Barcelona's **zoo**, open daily from 10 am to 5 pm (950 ptas) and famed for its albino gorilla.

Parc Güell This park, in the north of the city, is where Gaudí turned his hand to landscape gardening. It's a strange, enchanting place where Gaudí's passion for natural forms really took flight – to the point where the artificial almost seems more natural than the natural.

The main, lower gate, flanked by buildings which have the appearance of Hansel and Gretel's gingerbread house, sets the mood of the entire park, with its winding paths and carefully tended flower beds, skewed tunnels with rough stone columns resembling tree roots, and the famous dragon of broken glass and tiles. The house in which Gaudí lived most of his last 20 years has been converted into a museum, open Sunday to Friday from 10 am to 2 pm and 4 to 6 pm (250 ptas). The simplest way to Parc Güell is to take the metro to Lesseps then walk 10 to 15 minutes: follow the signs north-east along Travessera de Dalt then left up Carrer de Larrard. The park is open daily from 10 am – May to August to 9 pm, April and September to 8 pm, March and October to 7 pm, other months to 6 pm (free).

Montjuïc This hill overlooking the city centre from the south-west is home to some of Barcelona's best museums and attractions, some fine parks, and the main 1992 Olympics sites – well worth some of your time.

On the north side of the hill, the impressive **Palau Nacional** houses the **Museu Nacional d'Art de Catalunya**, with a wonderful collection of Romanesque frescos, woodcarvings and sculpture from medieval Catalonia. Opening hours are Tuesday to Saturday from 10 am to 7 pm, and Sundays and holidays from 10 am to 2.30 pm. Entry is 500 ptas.

Nearby is the **Poble Espanyol** (Spanish Village), by day a tour group's paradise with its craft workshops, souvenir shops and creditable copies of famous Spanish architecture; after dark it becomes a nightlife jungle, with bars and restaurants galore. It's open from 9 am daily (Monday to 8 pm; Tuesday to Thursday to 2 am; Friday and Saturday to 4 am; Sunday to midnight). Entry is 950 ptas (450 ptas with

a student card) but free after 9 pm except Friday and Saturday.

Downhill east of the Palau Nacional, the **Museu d'Arqueologia** (Archaeological Museum) has a good collection from Catalonia and the Balearic Islands. Opening hours are Tuesday to Saturday from 9.30 am to 1.30 pm and from 3.30 to 7 pm, and Sunday from 9.30 am to 2 pm. Entry is 200 ptas (free on Sunday).

Above the Palau Nacional is the **Anella Olímpica** (Olympic Ring), where you can swim in the Olympic pool, the **Piscines Bernat Picornell**, open daily from 7.30 am to 9 pm (2.30 pm on Sunday) for 1000 ptas, and wander into the main **Estadi Olímpic** (open daily from 10 am to 6 pm; admission free).

The **Fundació Joan Miró**, a short distance downhill east of the Estadi Olímpic, is one of the best modern art museums in Spain. Aside from many works by Miró, there are both permanent and changing exhibitions of other modern art. It's open Tuesday to Saturday from 11 am to 7 pm (Thursday to 9.30 pm), Sundays and holidays from 10.30 am to 2.30 pm. Entry is 600 ptas (300 ptas for students).

At the top of Montjuïc is the **Castell de Montjuïc**, with a military museum and great views.

To get to Montjuïc you can either walk or take a bus from Plaça d'Espanya (metro: Espanya). Bus No 61 from here links most of the main sights and ends at the foot of a chairlift (375 ptas) up to the castle. A funicular railway (185 ptas) from Paral-lel metro station also runs to the chairlift. From November to mid-June, the chairlift and funicular run only on weekends and holidays.

Tibidabo At 542 metres, this is the highest hill in the wooded range that forms the backdrop to Barcelona – a good place for a change of scene, some fresh air and, if the air's clear, 70-km views. At the top are the **Temple del Sagrat Cor**, a church topped by a giant Christ statue, and the **Parc d'Atraccions** funfair. A short distance along the ridge is the 288-metre **Torre de Collserola** telecommunications tower, with a hair-raising external glass lift – open daily from 11 am to 2.30 pm and 4 to 6 pm (500 ptas).

The fun way to Tibidabo is to take a suburban train from Plaça de Catalunya to Avinguda

SPAIN

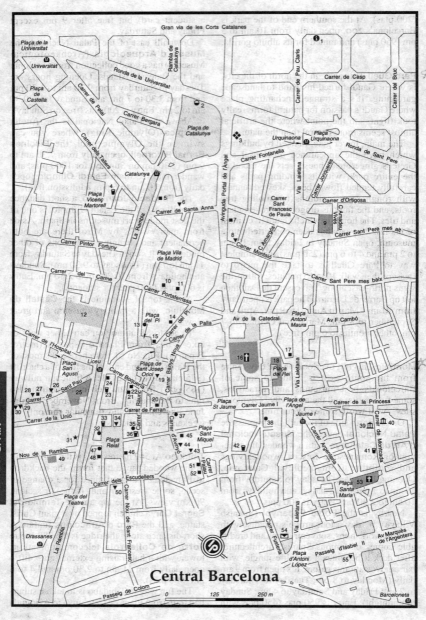

Central Barcelona

0   125   250 m

PLACES TO STAY					
5	Hotel Continental	19	Mesón Jesús	18	Museu d'Història de la
7	Hostal Lausanne	26	Bar-Restaurante		Ciutat
10	Pensión-Hostal Fina		Romescu	23	Cafè de l'Òpera
11	Hostal-Residencia	28	Restaurante Els Tres	25	Gran Teatre del Liceu
	Rembrandt		Bots	31	Guàrdia Urbana
14	Hostal Galerias Maldà	29	Restaurante Pollo Rico		(Police Station)
15	Hotel Jardi	30	Kashmir Restaurant	32	Barcelona Pipa Club
17	Hostal Layetana		Tandoori	33	Glaciar Bar
20	Pensión Fernando	34	Les Quinze Nits	35	Lavandería Tigre
21	Pensión Bienestar	43	Bar Restaurant	36	Bar Malpaso
22	Pensión Europa		Cervantes	37	CIAJ (Youth
24	Hotel Internacional	44	El Gallo Kiriko		Information Centre)
27	Hotel Peninsular	50	La Fonda Escudellers	38	Próleg Bookshop
45	Hostal Levante	55	Restaurante Set Portes	39	Museu Textil i
46	Hotel Roma Reial				d'Indumentària
48	Youth Hostel Kabul	**OTHER**		40	Museu Picasso
51	Casa Huéspedes	1	Main Tourist Office	41	El Xampanyet Bar
	Mari-Luz	2	Catalunya Train Station	42	Bar L'Ascensor
52	Alberg Palau	3	El Corte Inglés	47	Jamboree & Sala
			Department Store		Tarantos
PLACES TO EAT		4	L'Ovella Negra	49	Palau Güell
6	Self-Naturista	9	Palau de la Música	53	Església de Santa
8	Els Quatre Gats		Catalana		Maria del Mar
12	Mercat de la Boqueria	13	Quera Bookshop	54	Main Post Office
		16	Catedral		

de Tibidabo (10 minutes), then hop on the *tramvia blau* tram (175 ptas) across the road, which will take you up to the foot of the Tibidabo funicular railway. The funicular climbs to the church at top of the hill for 300 ptas. All these run every 10 or 15 minutes from at least 9 am to 9.30 pm.

Els Encants Market This good second-hand market by Plaça de les Glòries Catalanes, runs on Monday, Wednesday, Friday and Saturday between 8 am and 6 pm (8 pm in summer).

Courses
The Universitat de Barcelona runs good-value one-month Spanish courses (80 hours tuition, 40,000 ptas) about four times a year. Contact its Instituto de Estudios Hispánicos (☎ 318 42 66 ext 2084; fax 302 59 47) at Gran via de les Corts Catalanes 585. The main tourist office and the CIAJ youth information centre at Carrer de Ferran 32 in the Barri Gòtic have further information on courses. There are also notice boards with ads for classes at the above-mentioned university building and at Come In bookshop, Carrer de Provença 203. Also advertised at Come In are some jobs for English teachers.

Organised Tours
Bus No 100 (Bus Turístic), which starts at Plaça de Catalunya, is a special tourist bus that operates from mid-June to late October. It leaves every 20 minutes and does a city circuit linking virtually all the major sights. You can get on or off anywhere along the route. Tickets cost 1200 ptas for one day or 1700 ptas for two consecutive days, and include discounts to many attractions. This beats the other tours hands down on price.

Special Events
Barcelona's biggest festival is the Festes de la Mercè, several days of merrymaking around 24 September including *castellers* (human-castle builders), dances of giants and *correfocs* – a parade of firework-spitting dragons and devils. There are many others – tourist offices can clue you in.

Places to Stay
Camping *Camping Cala Gogo* (☎ 379 46 00), nine km south-west, is the closest camping ground to Barcelona and can be reached by bus No 65 from Plaça d'Espanya. Two to three km further out in Viladecans, on Carretera C-246, *El Toro Bravo* (☎ 637 34 62) and *La Ballena Alegre* (☎ 658 05 04) are much more pleasant,

SPAIN

and there are several more camping grounds within a few more km on Carretera C-246. To get to any of these, take bus No L95 from the corner of Ronda de la Universitat and Rambla de Catalunya.

Hostels A handful of places in Barcelona provide dormitory accommodation. For two people they're not great value, but they're certainly good places to meet other travellers. All require you to rent sheets, at 150 to 350 ptas for your stay, if you don't have them (or a sleeping bag). Ring before you go as the hostels can get booked up.

Youth Hostel Kabul (☎ 318 51 90), at Plaça Reial 17, is a rough-and-ready place but it has no curfew and is OK if you're looking for somewhere with a noisy party atmosphere; it has 150 places and charges 1300 ptas a night (no card needed). Security is slack but there are safes available for your valuables. Bookings are not taken.

Alberg Palau (☎ 412 50 80) at Carrer Palau 6 has just 40 places and is more pleasant. It charges 1200 ptas a night including breakfast and has a kitchen. It's open from 7 am to midnight. No card is needed.

Hostal de Joves (☎ 300 31 04), near metro Arc de Triomf at Passeig de Pujades 29, is quite clean and modern, with 68 beds and a kitchen, and charges 1300 ptas including breakfast; there's a 1 or 2 am curfew. A hostel card is only needed during the six peak summer weeks.

Alberg Mare de Déu de Montserrat (☎ 210 51 51) is the biggest and most comfortable hostel, but is four km north of the centre at Passeig Mare de Déu del Coll 41-51. It has 180 beds and charges 1500 ptas if you're under 26 or have an ISIC or IYTC card, 2075 ptas otherwise (breakfast included). A hostel card is needed. It's closed during the day and you can't get in after 3 am. It's a 10-minute walk from Vallcarca metro or a 20-minute ride from Plaça de Catalunya on bus No 28.

Alberg Pere Tarrés, (☎ 410 23 09) at Carrer de Numància 149 (about five minutes walk from Les Corts metro), has 90 beds at 1300 ptas for those under 26, 1550 ptas for others, plus 250 ptas for non-HI members (rates include breakfast). It has a kitchen, but is closed during the day and you can't get in after 2 am.

Pensiones & Hostales Most of the cheaper options are scattered through the old city, on either side of La Rambla. Generally, the areas closer to the port and on the west side of La Rambla are seedier and cheaper, and as you move north towards Plaça de Catalunya standards (and prices) rise.

Hostal Galerias Maldà (☎ 317 30 02), upstairs in an arcade off Carrer del Pi 5, is about as cheap as you'll find. It's a rambling family-run establishment with basic but clean doubles at 2000 ptas and a couple of singles for 1000 ptas. The ever-popular *Casa Huéspedes Mari-Luz* (☎ 317 34 63), Carrer Palau 4, has doubles and dorms for 1300 ptas a person. The same people own the clean if somewhat spartan *Pensión Fernando* (☎ 301 79 93), Carrer de la Volta del Remei 4, with around 100 rooms, mostly doubles, for 1500 ptas a person. The nearby *Pensión Bienestar* (☎ 318 72 83), Carrer Quintana 3, has 30 clean, ordinary singles/doubles from 1500/2600 ptas. At Carrer Boqueria 18, *Pensión Europa* (☎ 318 76 20) has above-average security and 40 plain, reasonable-sized rooms for 1600/3200 ptas, or 2100/3400 ptas with shower.

Hostal Levante (☎ 317 95 65), Baixada de Sant Miquel 2, is a good family-run place with singles/doubles for 2500/4000 ptas and doubles with bath for 5000 ptas. Up near Plaça de Catalunya is the excellent *Hostal Lausanne* (☎ 302 11 39), Avinguda Portal de l'Àngel 24 (1st floor), with good security and rooms from 2000/3200 ptas. Quiet Carrer Portaferrissa has a couple of good hostales: *Hostal-Residencia Rembrandt* (☎ 318 10 11) at No 23, and *Pensión-Hostal Fina* (☎ 317 97 87) at No 11. Both charge around 2500/3600 ptas for comfortable singles/doubles. *Hostal Layetana* (☎ 319 20 12) at Plaça de Berenguer Gran 2 is very well kept, with good-sized rooms at 2350/3650 ptas.

Opposite Estació de França, the impressive *Hostal Nuevo Colón* (☎ 319 50 77), Avinguda Marquès de l'Argentera 19, has rooms from 2000/3200 ptas.

Accommodation near Estació Sants is inconvenient for the centre, but if you arrive late at night, *Hostal Sofia* (☎ 419 50 40), at Avinguda de Roma 1-3, has very good rooms from 3500/4500 ptas. The modern *Hostal Sans* (☎ 331 37 00) at Carrer de Antoni de Capmany 82 charges 2100/3100 ptas, or 3100/4700 ptas with bath.

Hotels Higher up the scale, but good value, is the *Hotel Roma Reial* (☎ 302 03 66) at Plaça Reial 11. Modern singles/doubles with bath cost 3500/5800 ptas. The once-grand *Hotel Peninsular* (☎ 302 31 38), Carrer de Sant Pau 34, has singles/doubles from 3245/4815 ptas, although the rooms don't quite live up to the impressive foyer and central atrium.

Hotel Jardi (☎ 301 59 00), Plaça de Sant Josep Oriol 1, is well located, clean and plain, with rooms from 6500 to 8000 ptas single or double. On La Rambla itself, *Hotel Continental* (☎ 301 25 70) at No 138 and *Hotel Internacional* (☎ 302 25 66) at No 78-80 are among the best value. The Continental has pleasant, well-decorated rooms from 7450/9250 ptas including a good breakfast; the Internacional charges 6300/8100 ptas.

Places to Eat

For quick food, the *Bocatta* and *Pans & Company* chains, with numerous branches around the city, do good hot and cold baguettes with a range of fillings for 300 to 400 ptas.

The greatest concentration of cheaper restaurants is within walking distance of La Rambla. There are a few good-value ones on Carrer de Sant Pau, west off La Rambla. *Kashmir Restaurant Tandoori* at No 39 does tasty curries and biryanis from around 750 ptas. *Restaurante Pollo Rico*, No 31, has a somewhat seedy downstairs bar where you can have a quarter chicken or an omelette, with chips, bread and wine, for 300 to 400 ptas; the restaurant upstairs is more salubrious and only slightly more expensive. *Restaurante Els Tres Bots*, No 42, is grungy but cheap, with a menú for 750 ptas. Just off Carrer de Sant Pau on Carrer de l'Arc de Sant Agustí, tiny *Bar Restaurante Romescu* has good, home-style food at great prices, with most main courses around 400 or 500 ptas.

One of Barcelona's best value meals is the 695-pta, four-course menú (available evenings too) at the *Restaurante Riera*, Carrer de Joaquín Costa 30. Servings are generous and there's plenty to choose from (closed Friday night and Saturday).

There are lots more places in the Barri Gòtic. *Self-Naturista*, a self-service vegetarian restaurant at Carrer de Santa Anna 13, does a good lunch menú for 810 ptas. *Mesón Jesús*, Carrer dels Cecs de la Boqueria 4, and *Bar-Restaurant*

Cervantes, Carrer de Cervantes 7, do good lunch menús for 900 to 1000 ptas. *El Gallo Kiriko* at Carrer d'Avinyó 19 is a friendly Pakistani restaurant busy with travellers. Tandoori chicken and salad, or couscous with beef or vegetables, is just 450 ptas.

For something a bit more up-market, *Les Quinze Nits* at Plaça Reial 6 and *La Fonda Escudellers* on Carrer dels Escudellers are two stylish bistro-like restaurants, under the same management, with a big range of good Catalan and Spanish dishes at reasonable prices – which can mean long queues in summer and at weekends. Three courses with wine and coffee will be about 2000 ptas. Carrer dels Escudellers also has a couple of good night-time takeaway falafel joints – 200 to 300 ptas a serve. Or there's *Restaurante Set Portes* (☎ 319 30 33) at Passeig d'Isabel II 14, which dates from 1836 and specialises in paella (1200 to 2000 ptas). It's advisable to book. Another famous institution is *Els Quatre Gats*, Picasso's former hang-out at Carrer Montsió 3.

The *Mercat de la Boqueria* on La Rambla has a great selection of food.

Entertainment

Barcelona's entertainment bible is the weekly *Guía del Ocio* (125 ptas at newsstands). Its excellent listings (in Spanish) include films, theatre, music and art exhibitions.

Bars Barcelona's huge variety of bars are mostly at their busiest from about 11 pm to 1 am, especially on Friday and Saturday.

Cafè de l'Òpera at La Rambla 74, opposite the Liceu opera house, is the liveliest place on La Rambla. It gets packed with all and sundry at night. *Glaciar* on Plaça Reial gets very busy with a young crowd of foreigners and locals. Tiny *Bar Malpaso* at Carrer Rauric 20, just off Plaça Reial, packs in a young, casual crowd and plays great Latin and African music. Not far away, *Bar L'Ascensor*, Carrer de Bellafila 3, is a cosy little place with more good music and a young crowd.

El Xampanyet at Carrer de Montcada 22 near the Museu Picasso is another small place, specialising in cava (Catalan champagne, around 500 ptas a bottle), with good tapas too.

West of La Rambla, *L'Ovella Negra*, Carrer de les Sitges 5, is a noisy, barn-like tavern with

SPAIN

a young crowd. **Bar Marsella**, Carrer de Sant Pau 65, specialises in absinthe (absenta in Catalan), a potent but mellow beverage with supposed narcotic qualities (500 ptas a shot).

Another great bar area is the Port Olímpic, with many bright and lively spots with open-air tables out front; some have good music inside too.

Live Music & Discos Many music places have dance space and some discos have bands on around midnight or so, to pull in some custom before the real action starts about 3 am. If you go for the band, you can normally stay for the disco at no extra cost and avoid bouncers' whims about what you're wearing etc. Women – and maybe male companions – may get in free at some discos if the bouncers like their looks. Count on 300 to 800 ptas for a beer in any of these places.

On Plaça Reial, **Barcelona Pipa Club**, No 3, has jazz Thursday to Saturday around midnight (ring the bell to get in); **Jamboree**, No 17, has jazz nightly and a lively disco later, from about 1.30 am; **Sala Tarantos**, next door, has classy flamenco some nights. **Club Apolo**, Carrer Nou de la Rambla 113, has live world music several nights a week, followed by live salsa or a varied disco.

Otto Zutz, Carrer de Lincoln 15, is, as its blurb says, 'where the beautiful people go…2000 ptas. Worth it'. The crowd's cool and the atmosphere's great – just don't wear running shoes and if in doubt, do wear black.

Zeleste, Carrer dels Almogàvers 122, Poble Nou, is a cavernous warehouse-type club, regularly hosting visiting bands. **Mirablau** at the foot of the Tibidabo funicular is a bar with great views and a small disco floor; it's open till 4.30 am and entry is free.

The two top gay discos are **Metro**, Carrer de Sepúlveda 185, and **Martin's** at Passeig de Gràcia 130. Metro attracts some lesbians and heteros as well as gay men; Martin's is for gay men only.

Opera & Classical Music The Gran Teatre del Liceu opera house on La Rambla, gutted by fire in 1994, is due to reopen in 1998. Until then, opera and orchestral music are shared among other theatres, the lovely Palau de la Música

Catalana at Carrer de Sant Pere mes alt 11 being the chief venue.

Cinema For films in their original language (with Spanish subtitles), check listings for those marked VO (versión original). A ticket is usually 600 to 700 ptas but many cinemas reduce prices on Monday.

Getting There & Away

Air Barcelona's airport, 14 km south-west of the city centre at El Prat de Llobregat, caters to international as well as domestic flights. For any flight it's well worth comparing the range of available fares, at any travel agent. One-way fares to Madrid range from 6900 ptas (Air Europa's youth fare) to 14,950 ptas on some Iberia flights. Other Air Europa fares include Seville or Santiago de Compostela for 13,900 ptas one way or 20,900 ptas return. Spanair flies to Palma de Mallorca from 9900 ptas return. One-way flights to London start from around 17,000 ptas, and to New York from 35,000 ptas (a bit less for students and those under 26).

Iberia and Aviaco (☎ 412 56 67) are at Passeig de Gràcia 30; Spanair (☎ 478 66 91) and Air Europa (☎ 412 77 33) are at the airport.

Bus The terminal for virtually all domestic and international buses is the Estació del Nord at Carrer d'Alí Bei 80 (metro: Arc de Triomf). Its information desk (☎ 265 65 08) is open daily from 7 am to 9 pm. A few international buses go from Estació d'Autobuses de Sants beside Estació Sants train station.

Several buses a day go to most main Spanish cities. Madrid is seven or eight hours away (2690 to 3450 ptas), San Sebastián 6½ hours (2375 ptas), Valencia 4½ hours (2650 ptas), Granada 13 to 15 hours (7540 ptas). Buses run several times a week to London (14,450 ptas), Paris (11,125 ptas) and other European cities.

Train Virtually all trains travelling to/from destinations within Spain stop at Estació Sants (metro: Sants-Estació); most international trains use Estació de França (metro: Barceloneta).

For some international destinations you have to change trains at Montpellier or the French border. A 2nd-class seat to Paris is

11,795 to 13,420 ptas, a sleeping berth 15,500 to 39,500 ptas.

Daily trains run to most major cities in Spain. To Madrid there are seven trains a day (6½ to 9½ hours, 4800 ptas); to San Sebastián two (eight to 10 hours, 4500 ptas); to Valencia 10 (four to 4½ hours, 3000 ptas), to Seville four (11 to 13½ hours, 6600 to 9200 ptas).

Tickets and information are available at the stations or from the RENFE office in Passeig de Gràcia metro/train station on Passeig de Gràcia, open daily from 7 am to 9 pm.

Car & Motorcycle Tolls on the A-7 autopista add up to over 1700 ptas from the French border to Barcelona, and over 6000 ptas from Barcelona to Alicante. The N-II from the French border and N-340 southbound are slower but toll-free. The fastest route to Madrid is via Zaragoza on the A-2 (1890 ptas), which heads west off the A-7 south of Barcelona, then the toll-free N-II from Zaragoza.

Getting Around

To/From the Airport Trains link the airport to Estació Sants and Catalunya station on Plaça de Catalunya every half-hour. They take 15 to 20 minutes and a ticket is 300 ptas (335 ptas at weekends). The A1 Aerobús does the 40-minute run between Plaça de Catalunya and the airport every 15 minutes, or every half-hour at weekends. The fare is 435 ptas. A taxi from the airport to Plaça de Catalunya is around 2000 ptas.

Bus, Metro & Train Barcelona's metro system spreads its tentacles around the city in such a way that most places of interest are within 10 minutes walk of a station. Buses and suburban trains are only needed for a few destinations – but note the Bus Turístic under Organised Tours earlier in this section.

A single metro, bus or suburban train ride costs 130 ptas, but a T-1 ticket, valid for 10 rides, costs only 700 ptas, while a T-DIA ticket (500 ptas) gives unlimited city travel in one day.

Car & Motorcycle While traffic flows smoothly thanks to an extensive one-way system, navigating can be extremely frustrating. Parking a car is also difficult and, if you

choose a parking garage, quite expensive. It's better to ditch your car and rely on public transport.

Taxi Barcelona's black-and-yellow taxis are plentiful, reasonably priced and especially handy for late-night transport. From Plaça de Catalunya, it costs around 600 ptas to Estació Sants.

MONESTIR DE MONTSERRAT

Unless you are on a pilgrimage, the prime attraction of Montserrat, 50 km north-west of Barcelona, is its setting. The Benedictine Monastery of Montserrat sits high on the side of an amazing 1236-metre mountain of truly weird rocky peaks, and is best reached by cable car. The monastery was founded in the 11th century to commemorate an apparition of the Virgin Mary on this site. Pilgrims still come from all over Christendom to pay homage to its Black Virgin (La Moreneta), a 12th-century wooden sculpture of Mary, regarded as Catalonia's patroness.

Information

Montserrat's information centre (☎ 835 02 51, ext 586), to the left along the road from the top cable-car station, is open daily from 9 am to 6 pm. It has a good free leaflet/map on the mountain and monastery, and an official guidebook for 475 ptas.

Montserrat's telephone code is ☎ 93.

Things to See & Do

If you are making a day trip to Montserrat, come early. Apart from the monastery, exploring the mountain is a treat.

The two-part **Museu de Montserrat**, on the plaza in front of the monastery's basilica (church), has an excellent collection ranging from an Egyptian mummy to art by El Greco, Monet and Picasso. It's open daily from 10.30 am to 2 pm and 3 to 6 pm (400 ptas, students 200 ptas).

Daily from 8 to 10.30 am, and noon to 6.30 pm, you can file past the image of the Black Virgin, high above the main altar of the 16th-century **basilica**, the only part of the monastery proper open to the public. The famous Montserrat Boys' Choir sings in the basilica every day at 1 and 7 pm, except in July.

SPAIN

The church fills up quickly, so try to arrive early.

You can explore the mountain above the monastery on a web of paths leading to small chapels and some of the peaks. The Funicular de Sant Joan (475/775 ptas one way/return) will lift you up the first 250 metres from the monastery.

Places to Stay & Eat

There are several accommodation options (all ☎ 835 02 51) at the monastery. A small camping ground 300 metres along the road past the lower Sant Joan funicular station is open from Semana Santa to October. The cheapest rooms are in the *Cel-les de Montserrat*, blocks of simple apartments, with showers, for up to 10 people. Two people pay 2360 ptas, or 2555 to 3155 ptas with kitchen. The *Hotel El Monestir*, open from Semana Santa to October, has singles/doubles from 2200/3800 ptas. *Hotel Abat Cisneros* charges from 4700/7900 ptas, but little more than half that in the off season.

The *Snack Bar* near the top cable-car station has platos combinados from 875 ptas and bocadillos from 325 ptas. *Cafeteria Self-Service* along the road has great views but is dearer – 1650 ptas for a three-course menú. *Hotel Abat Cisneros* has a menú for 2900 ptas.

Getting There & Away

Trains run from Plaça d'Espanya in Barcelona to Aeri de Montserrat daily, every two hours from 7.10 am to 9.10 pm – a 1½-hour ride. Return tickets for 1560 ptas include the exciting cable car up to the monastery from Aeri de Montserrat.

There's also a daily bus to the monastery from Estació d'Autobuses de Sants in Barcelona at 9 am (plus 8 am in July and August), for a return fare of 1090 ptas (1240 ptas at weekends).

COSTA BRAVA

The Costa Brava ranks with Spain's Costa Blanca and Costa del Sol among Europe's most popular holiday spots. It stands alone, however, in its spectacular scenery and proximity to northern Europe, both of which have sent prices skyrocketing in the most appealing places.

The main jumping-off points for the Costa Brava are the inland towns Girona (Gerona in Castilian) and Figueres (Figueras). Both places are on the A-7 autopista and the toll-free N-II highway which connect Barcelona with France. Along the coast the most appealing resorts are, from north to south, Cadaqués, L'Escala (La Escala), Tamariu, Llafranc and Calella de Palafrugell and Tossa de Mar.

Tourist offices along the coast are very helpful, with information on accommodation, transport and other things; they include Girona (☎ 22 65 75), Figueres (☎ 50 31 55), Palafrugell (☎ 30 02 28), and Cadaqués (☎ 25 83 15).

The telephone code for the Costa Brava is ☎ 972.

Coastal Resorts

The Costa Brava (Rugged Coast) is all about picturesque inlets and coves. Some longer beaches at places like L'Estartit and Empúries are worth visiting out of season, but there has been a tendency to build tall buildings wherever engineers think it can be done. Fortunately, in many places it just can't.

Cadaqués, about one hour's drive east of Figueres at the end of an agonising series of hairpin bends, is perhaps the most picturesque of all Spanish resorts, and haunted by the memory of the artist Salvador Dalí, who lived here. It's very short on beaches, so people tend to spend a lot of time sitting at waterfront cafés or wandering along the beautiful rocky coast. About 10 km north-east of Cadaqués is **Cap de Creus**, a rocky peninsula with a single restaurant at the top of a craggy cliff. This is paradise for anyone who likes to scramble around rocks risking life and limb with every step.

Further down the coast, past L'Escala and L'Estartit, you eventually come to Palafrugell, itself a few km inland with little to offer, but near three beach towns that have to be seen to be believed. The most northerly of these, and also the smallest, least crowded and most exclusive, is **Tamariu**. **Llafranc** is the biggest and busiest, and has the longest beach. **Calella de Palafrugell**, with its picture-postcard setting, is never overcrowded and always relaxed. If you're driving down this coast, it's worth making the effort to stop at some of these towns, particularly out of season.

Other Attractions

When you have had enough beach for a while, make sure you put the **Teatre-Museu Dalí**, on Plaça Gala i Salvador Dalí in Figueres, at the top of your list. This 19th-century theatre was converted by Dalí himself and houses a huge and fascinating collection of his strange creations. From July to September it's open from 9 am to 7.15 pm daily; in other months it's open from 10.30 am to 5.15 pm daily, except Mondays and 1 January and 25 December. Entry is 1000 ptas (students 700 ptas). Expect huge crowds and long queues in summer.

Historical interest is provided by **Girona**, with a lovely medieval quarter centred on a Gothic cathedral, and the ruins of the Greek and Roman town of **Empúries**, two km from L'Escala.

For a spectacular stretch of coastline, take a drive north from Tossa de Mar to San Feliu de Guíxols. There are 360 curves in this 20-km stretch of road, which, with brief stops to take in the scenery, can take a good two hours.

Among the most exciting attractions on the Costa Brava are the **Illes Medes**, off the coast from the package resort of L'Estartit. These seven islets and their surrounding coral reefs, with a total land area of only 21.5 hectares, have been declared a natural park to protect their extraordinarily diverse flora and fauna. Almost 1500 different life forms have been identified on and around the islands. A two-hour snorkelling or glass-bottom boat trip from L'Estartit costs around 1400 ptas; diving is easily arranged too.

Places to Stay

Most visitors to the Costa Brava rent apartments. If you are interested in renting an apartment for a week or so, contact local tourist offices in advance for information.

Figueres Figueres' HI hostel, the *Alberg Tramuntana* (☎ 50 12 13), is two blocks from the tourist office at Carrer Anicet Pagès 2. It charges 1500 ptas if you're under 26 or have an ISIC or IYTC card, 2075 ptas otherwise (breakfast included). Alternatively, *Hotel España* (☎ 50 08 69), a block east of the Dalí museum at Carrer de La Jonquera 26, has decent singles/doubles for 2000/4000 ptas. Don't sleep in Figueres' Parc Municipal – people have been attacked here at night.

Girona Girona's modern HI hostel, *Alberg Residencia Cerverí* (☎ 21 81 21), is perfectly situated in the middle of the old town at Carrer dels Ciutadans 9. The price is the same as at Figueres, if you can get a place – from October to June it's usually full with students. Otherwise, head down the road to *Pensión Viladomat* (☎ 20 31 76) at Carrer dels Ciutadans 5, which has comfortable singles/doubles for 1800/3600 ptas.

Cadaqués *Camping Cadaqués* (☎ 25 81 26) is at the top of the town as you head towards Cabo de Creus. It charges 500 ptas a car, 650 ptas a tent and 525 ptas a person. At these prices, a single person is probably better off staying in town near the waterfront. *Hostal Marina* (☎ 25 81 99) at Carrer Riera 3 has singles/doubles from 2140/4280 ptas.

Near Palafrugell There are camping grounds at all three of Palafrugell's satellites. In Calella de Palafrugell try *Camping Moby Dick* (☎ 61 43 07); in Llafranc, *Kim's Camping* (☎ 30 11 56); and in Tamariu, *Camping Tamariu* (62 04 22).

Hotel and pensión rooms are relatively thin on the ground here, as many people come on package deals and stay in apartments. In Calella de Palafrugell, the friendly *Hostería del Plancton* (☎ 61 50 81) is one of the best deals on the Costa Brava, with rooms from 1500/3000 to 1800/3600 ptas, but it's only open from June to September. *Residencia Montaña* (☎ 30 04 04) at Carrer Cesárea 2 in Llafranc is well positioned near the beach and has singles/doubles for 2570/4815 ptas, or 2835/5450 ptas with shower, including breakfast. In Tamariu, the *Hotel Sol d'Or* (☎ 62 01 72), five minutes walk from the beach at Carrer Riera 18, has doubles with bathroom for 5620 ptas.

Getting There & Away

A few buses daily run from Barcelona to Tossa del Mar, L'Estartit and Cadaqués, but for the small resorts near Palafrugell you need to get to Girona first. Girona and Figueres are both on the railway connecting Barcelona to France. The dozen or so trains daily from Barcelona to Port Bou at the border all stop in Girona, and most in Figueres. The fare from Barcelona to Girona is 845 ptas, to Figueres 1195 ptas.

Getting Around

There are two or three buses a day from Figueres to Cadaqués and three or four to L'Escala. Figueres bus station (☎ 67 42 98) is across the road from the train station.

Several buses daily run to Palafrugell from Girona (where the bus station is behind the train station), and there are buses from Palafrugell to Calella de Palafrugell, Llafranc and Tamariu. Most other coastal towns (south of Cadaqués) can be reached by bus from Girona.

TARRAGONA

Tarragona makes a perfect contrast to the city life of Barcelona. Founded in 218 BC, it was for a long time the capital of much of Roman Spain, and Roman structures figure among its most important attractions. Other periods of history are also well represented, including the medieval cathedral and 17th-century British additions to the old city walls. The city's archaeological museum is one of the most interesting in Spain. Today, Tarragona is a modern city with a large student population and a lively beach scene – and Spain's answer to EuroDisney, Port Aventura, is just a few km south.

Orientation & Information

Tarragona's main street is Rambla Nova, which runs approximately north-west from a clifftop overlooking the Mediterranean. A couple of blocks to the east, parallel to Rambla Nova, is Rambla Vella, which marks the beginning of the old town. To the south-west, on the coast, is the train station.

Tarragona's main tourist office (☎ 24 50 64) is at Carrer Major 39. There is also a regional tourist office at Carrer Fortuny 4.

The telephone code for Tarragona is ☎ 977.

Things to See & Do

The **Museu d'Història de Tarragona** comprises four separate Roman sites. A single 400-pta ticket (free for students and pensioners) from any of them is good for all. The sites are open daily except Monday: from July to September, hours are 10 am to 8 pm; hours vary in other months. A good site to start with is the **Museu de la Romanitat** on Plaça del Rei,

which includes part of the vaults of the Roman circus, where chariot races were held. Nearby, close to the beach, is the very well preserved Roman **amphitheatre**, where gladiators battled each other, or wild animals, to the death. On Carrer Lleida, a few blocks west of Rambla Nova, are substantial remains of a **Roman forum**. The **Passeig Arqueològic** is a peaceful walkway along a stretch of the old city walls, which are a combination of Roman, Iberian and 17th-century British efforts.

Tarragona's **Museu Arqueològic**, on Plaça del Rei, gives further insight into the city's rich history. The carefully presented exhibits include frescos, mosaics, sculpture and pottery dating back to the 2nd century BC. The museum is open daily except Monday (100 ptas, free on Tuesday). Also worth seeing is the **Museu d'Art Modern** at Carrer Santa Anna 8.

The **catedral** sits grandly at the highest point of Tarragona, overlooking the old town. Some parts of the building date back to the 12th century AD. It's open for tourist visits Monday to Friday from 10 am to 2 pm (300 ptas). Entrance is through the beautiful cloister with the excellent Museu Diocesà.

If you're here in summer, Platja del Miracle is the main city beach. It is reasonably clean but can get terribly crowded. Several other beaches dot the coast north of town, but in summer you will never be alone.

Port Aventura

Port Aventura (☎ 902-20 22 20), which opened in 1995 near Salou, 10 km south-west of Tarragona, is Spain's newest, biggest and best funfair. It's divided into five theme areas – China, a Mediterranean fishing village, the Wild West, Polynesia and ancient Mexico. It has a hectic street life that includes wild-west shoot-outs and Polynesian dance troupes, theatres with Chinese acrobats, and of course hair-raising rides like the Dragon Khan, claimed to be Europe's biggest roller coaster. If you have 3900 ptas to spare, it makes a really fun day out with never a dull moment. Port Aventura is open daily, from Semana Santa to October, from 10 am to 8 pm. At peak periods it may stay open till midnight, with special night tickets, valid from 7 pm to midnight, costing 2300 ptas. Trains run to Port Aventura's own station several times a day from Tarragona and Barcelona.

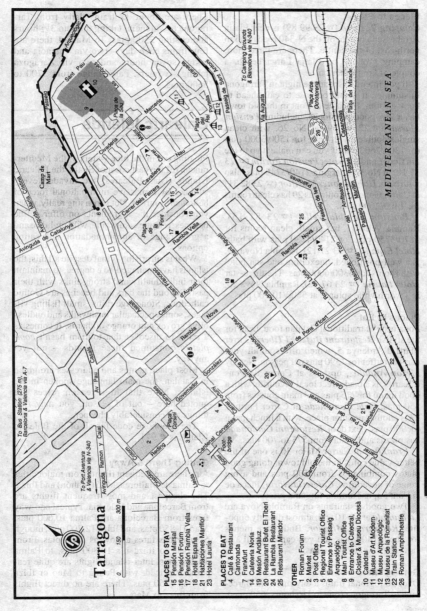

Tarragona

```
0    150    300 m
```

To Bus Station (275 m),
Barcelona & Valencia via A-7

To Port Aventura
& Valencia via N-340

To Camping Grounds
& Barcelona via N-340

MEDITERRANEAN SEA

SPAIN

PLACES TO STAY
15 Pensión Marsal
16 Pensión Forum
17 Pensión Rambla Vella
18 Hotel España
21 Habitaciones Mariflor
23 Hotel Lauria

PLACES TO EAT
4 Café & Restaurant
  Cantonada
7 Frankfurt
14 Cafetería Noria
19 Mesón Andaluz
20 Restaurant Bufet El Tiberi
24 La Rambla Restaurant
25 Restaurant Mirador

OTHER
1 Roman Forum
2 Market
3 Post Office
5 Regional Tourist Office
6 Entrance to Passeig
  Arqueològic
8 Main Tourist Office
9 Entrance to Catedral,
  Cloister & Museu Diocesà
10 Catedral
11 Museu d'Art Modern
12 Museu Arqueològic
13 Museu de la Romanitat
22 Train Station
26 Roman Amphitheatre

Places to Stay

Camping Tàrraco (☎ 23 99 89) is near Platja Arrabassada beach, off the N-340 road two km north-east of the centre. There are three more camping grounds on Platja Larga beach, a couple of km further on.

If you intend to spend the night in Tarragona in summer, it would be wise to call ahead to book a room. Plaça de la Font in the old town has a few good pensiones, including *Pensión Marsal* (☎ 22 40 69) at No 26, with clean singles/doubles with bath for 1500/3000 ptas (or 1300/2600 ptas if you can make it up to the 5th floor), and the better *Pensión Forum* (☎ 23 17 18) at No 37, charging 2140/3745 ptas, also with bath. *Habitaciones Mariflor* (☎ 23 82 31) at Carrer General Contreras 29 has clean rooms for 1400/2600 ptas.

Pensión Rambla Vella (☎ 23 81 15), Rambla Vella 31, has small, clean rooms for 1870/3750 ptas, or 2140/4280 ptas with bath. *Hotel España* (☎ 23 27 12), Rambla Nova 49, is a well-positioned, unexciting one-star hotel with rooms for 3300/6000 ptas. The three-star *Hotel Lauría* (☎ 23 67 12), Rambla Nova 20, is a worthwhile splurge at 5800/10,700 ptas.

Places to Eat

For a taste of traditional Catalan food, head for the stylish *Restaurant Bufet El Tiberi*, Carrer Martí d'Ardenya 5, which offers an all-you-can-eat buffet for 1390 ptas per person. Nearby *Mesón Andaluz*, upstairs at Carrer de Pons d'Icart 3, is a backstreet local favourite, with a good menú for 775 ptas and main courses from 350 ptas. *Café Cantonada* at Carrer Fortuny 23 is another popular place, with a lunch menú for 900 ptas; next door, *Restaurant Cantonada* has pizzas and pasta from 575 to 700 ptas.

Frankfurt at Carrer Major 30 is one of the better-value cafés in the old town, doing good platos combinados from 500 ptas and a big range of bocadillos. *Cafeteria Noria*, Plaça de la Font 53, has similar fare and prices.

Two good restaurants on Rambla Nova are *La Rambla* at No 10 and, almost directly opposite, *Restaurant Mirador*. Both have menús for about 1400 ptas and you can eat well à la carte for 2500 to 3000 ptas.

Getting There & Away

Over 20 regional trains a day run from Barcelona to Tarragona (one to 1½ hours, 650 ptas).

There are about 12 trains daily from Tarragona to Valencia, taking three to 3½ hours and costing 2500 ptas. To Madrid, there are four trains each day – two via Valencia and taking seven hours and two via Zaragoza taking six hours. Fares range from 3700 to 5600 ptas.

Balearic Islands

Floating out in the blue waters of the Mediterranean off the east coast of Spain, the Balearic Islands (Islas Baleares) are invaded every summer by a massive multinational force of hedonistic tourists. Not surprising really, when you consider the ingredients on offer – fine beaches, relentless sunshine, wild nightlife and a great range of accommodation and eating options.

What is surprising is that despite all this, the islands have managed, to a degree, to maintain their individuality and strong links with their past. Beyond the bars and beaches are Gothic cathedrals, Stone Age ruins, small fishing villages, some spectacular bushwalks and endless olive groves and orange orchards. It comes as a relief to discover that tourism hasn't *completely* consumed these islands – not yet anyway.

Most place names and addresses are given in Catalan, the main language spoken in the islands. Note that high-season prices are quoted here – out of season, you may find things are considerably cheaper.

The telephone code for all of the Balearic Islands is ☎ 971.

Getting There & Away

Air There are frequent flights from major cities to Palma de Mallorca, Maó (Mahón) and Ibiza. The cheapest and most frequent flights are from Barcelona and Valencia. Typical one-way fares from Barcelona are Palma 10,600 ptas, Maó 11,850 ptas, and Ibiza 12,700 ptas, though Spanair has fares as low as 7950 ptas. From Valencia to Ibiza it's 10,800 ptas, to Palma 12,100 ptas. Inter-island flights are quite reasonably priced, with Palma to Maó or Ibiza costing 6650 ptas. There are no direct flights from Ibiza to Maó.

Return fares are double the one-way fare, unless you can manage to meet the not-too-stringent advance-booking conditions for deals like Aviaco's *tarifa azul* (around 12,000 ptas return from Barcelona to Ibiza or Maó) or Spanair's *super reducida* Barcelona-Palma return fare of 9900 ptas.

Boat Trasmediterránea, with offices in (and services between) Barcelona (☎ 93-443 25 32), Valencia (☎ 96-367 65 12), Palma, Maó and Ibiza, is the major ferry company serving the islands.

It has a 'four seasons' timetable – the warmer it is, the more frequent the sailings. In summer, scheduled ferries are: Barcelona-Palma, nine a week; Barcelona-Ibiza, five a week; Barcelona-Maó, Valencia-Palma and Valencia-Ibiza, all six a week; and Valencia-Maó, one a week. There are also inter-island services, although it's not much more expensive to fly.

During summer, one-way fares from the mainland to any of the islands are 6300 ptas for a *butaca turista* (seat), except for Valencia-Ibiza which costs 5040 ptas. Alternatively, you can take a berth in a cabin, which ranges from around 10,500 ptas (four-share) to 15,750 ptas (twin-share) per person. To take a small car from the mainland costs around 18,000 ptas; a motorcycle is around 4500 ptas. Off-season fares are considerably lower.

Another company, Flebasa (☎ 96-578 40 11), has services from Denia on the mainland (between Valencia and Alicante) to both Ibiza and Formentera. See the Formentera section later for details on ferries there from Ibiza.

MALLORCA

Mallorca is the largest of the Balearic Islands. Most of the five million annual visitors to the island are here for the three *s* words: sun, sand and sea. There are, however, other reasons for coming to Mallorca. Palma, the main population centre, is in itself worth visiting, and the island offers a number of noncoastal attractions.

Orientation & Information

The capital, Palma de Mallorca, is on the southern side of the island, in a bay famous for its brilliant sunsets. The Serra de Tramuntana

mountain range, which runs parallel with the north-west coastline, is trekkers' heaven. Mallorca's best beaches are along the north-east and east coasts – so are most of the big tourist resorts.

All of the major resorts have at least one tourist office. Palma has four – on Plaça d'Espanya (☎ 71 15 27), at Carrer Sant Domingo 11 (☎ 72 40 90), on Plaça Major and at the airport. Palma's post office is on Carrer de la Constitució.

Things to See & Do

Palma is a pleasant town and worth spending a day or so exploring. The enormous **catedral** on Plaça Almoina is the first landmark you will see as you approach the island by ferry. It houses an excellent museum, and some of the cathedral's interior features were designed by Antoni Gaudí; entry costs 400 ptas.

In front of the cathedral is the **Palau de l'Almudaina**, the one-time residence of the Mallorcan monarchs. Inside is a collection of tapestries and artworks, although it's not really worth the 450 ptas entry. Instead, visit the rich and varied **Museu de Mallorca** (300 ptas).

Also near the cathedral are the interesting **Museu Diocesà** and the delicate **Banys Àrabs** (Arab baths), the only remaining monument to the Moorish domination of the island. Also worth visiting is the collection of the **Fundació Joan Miró**, housed in the artist's Palma studios at Carrer Joan de Saridakis 29, two km west of the centre.

Mallorca's north-west coast is a world away from the concrete jungles on the other side of the island. Dominated by the Serra de Tramuntana mountains, it's a beautiful region of olive groves, pine forests and small villages with stone buildings; it also has a rugged and rocky coastline. There are a couple of highlights for drivers: the hair-raising road down to the small port of **Sa Calobra** and the amazing trip along the peninsula leading to the island's northern tip, **Cap Formentor**.

If you don't have your own wheels, take the **Palma to Sóller train** (see Getting Around later). It's one of the most popular and spectacular excursions on the island. Sóller is also the best place to base yourself for trekking – the easy three-hour return walk from here to the beautiful village of Deià is a fine introduction to trekking on Mallorca. The tourist office's

SPAIN

Palma de Mallorca

0   150   300 m   Parc de la Mar

Some streets pedestrian-only

PLACES TO STAY
7   Hotel Born
9   Pensión Costa Brava
11   Hostal Pons
13   Hostal Apuntadores
14   Hostal Ritzi

PLACES TO EAT
12   Vecchio Giovanni & Abaco
17   Casa Julio
20   Rincón del Artista
21   Restaurante Sa Impremta
23   Mario's Cafe

OTHER
1   Train Stations (to Sóller & Inca)
2   Bus Station & Airport Bus
3   Tourist Office
4   Hospital
5   Santa Magadalena Church
6   Mercat de l'Olivar (Market)
8   Teatro Principal
10   Tourist Office
15   Post Office
16   Main Tourist Office
18   Ayuntamiento (Town Hall)
19   Santa Eulalia Church
22   Basílica de Sant Francesc
24   Palau de l'Almudaina
25   Catedral
26   Museu Diocesá
27   Museu de Mallorca
28   Banys Árabs (Arab Baths)

SPAIN

Hiking Excursions brochure covers 20 of the island's better walks, or for more detailed information see Lonely Planet's *Trekking in Spain*.

Most of Mallorca's best beaches have been consumed by tourist developments, although there are exceptions. There are long stretches of sandy, undeveloped beach south of **Port d'Alcúdia** on the north-east coast. The lovely **Cala Mondragó** on the south-east coast is backed by a solitary hostal, and a little further south the attractive port town of **Cala Figuera** has escaped many of the ravages of mass tourism. There are also some good quiet beaches near the popular German resort of **Colonia San Jordi**, particularly Ses Arenes and Es Trenc, both a few km back up the coast towards Palma.

Places to Stay
Palma The *Pensión Costa Brava* (☎ 71 17 29), Carrer Martí Feliu 16, is a back-street cheapie with reasonable rooms from 1300/2300 ptas. The cluttered 19th-century charm of *Hostal Pons* (☎ 72 26 58), Carrer del Vi 8, overcomes its limitations (spongy beds, only one bathroom); it charges 2000 ptas per person. At Carrer Apuntadores 8, *Hostal Apuntadores* (☎ 71 34 91) has smartly renovated singles/doubles at 2000/3530 ptas and doubles with bathroom at 4100 ptas. Next door, *Hostal Ritzi* (☎ 71 46 10) has good security and comfortable rooms at 2300/3300 ptas, or doubles with shower/bath for 3800/4500 ptas.

The superb *Hotel Born* (☎ 71 29 42), in a restored 18th-century palace at Carrer de Sant Jaume 3, has B&B from 6000/8500 ptas.

Other Areas If you've got time (and sense), have a quick look around Palma and then head for the hills. In Deià, the charming *Pensión Villa Verde* (☎ 63 90 37) charges 2300 ptas per person for B&B, while *Hostal Miramar* (☎ 63 90 84), overlooking the town, has B&B at 3600/6000 ptas (during summer, it's half-board only, from 5100/9000 ptas). Beside the train station in Sóller, the popular *Hotel El Guía* (☎ 63 02 27) has rooms for 4815/6420 ptas, or nearby (go past El Guía and turn right) the cosy *Casa de Huéspedes Margarita Thás Vives* (☎ 63 42 14) has doubles/triples/quads at 2800/3600/5000 ptas.

If you want to stay on the south-east coast, the large *Hostal Playa Mondragó* (☎ 65 77 52) at Cala Mondragó has B&B for 3900/5800 ptas. At Cala Figuera, *Hostal Ca'n Jordi* (☎ 64 50 35) has rooms from 2500/4200 ptas.

If you're camping, *Camping Club Picafort* (☎ 53 78 63) on the north coast (nine km south of Port d'Alcúdia) has excellent facilities and good beaches opposite. There are also several youth hostels and a couple of quirky old monasteries around the island where you can sleep cheap – ask at the tourist offices for full details.

Places to Eat
For Palma's best range of eateries, wander through the maze of streets between Plaça de la Reina and the port. Carrer Apuntadors is lined with restaurants and should have something to suit everyone – seafood, Chinese, Italian – even a few Spanish restaurants! Around the corner at Carrer Sant Joan 1 is the deservedly popular *Vecchio Giovanni*, which has a good menú for 950 ptas. Right next door is the amazing *Abaco*, the bar of your wildest dreams (with the drinks bill of your darkest nightmares). At *Mario's Cafe*, on Carrer de la Mar, you can have pizza or pasta from 700 ptas.

There are a couple of good places over near Plaça de Santa Eulalia, both with menús for 800 ptas: the excellent *Casa Julio*, Calle Previsio 4, specialises in local rice dishes (open for lunch only, Monday to Saturday) and, nearby at Carrer d'En Morey 4, *Restaurante Sa Impremta* is a friendly little bar-eatery.

Getting Around
Bus No 17 runs every half-hour between the airport and Plaça Espanya in central Palma (265 to 295 ptas). Alternatively, a taxi will cost around 1800 ptas.

Most parts of the island are accessible by bus from Palma. Buses generally depart from or near the bus station at Plaça Espanya – the tourist office's *Public Tourist Bus Routes* brochure lists all the gory details. Mallorca's two train lines also start from Plaça Espanya. One goes to the inland town of Inca (250 ptas one way) and the other goes to Sóller (420 ptas one way).

The best way to get around the island is by car – it's worth renting one just for the drive along the north-west coast. There are about 30 rental agencies in Palma. If you want to

SPAIN

compare prices many of them have harbour-side offices along Passeig Marítim. Rates vary substantially, depending on the season and hire period. If you're looking for a cheapish deal, places worth trying include Casa Mascaro (☎ 73 61 03), Iber-Auto (☎ 28 54 48) and Entercar (☎ 74 30 51).

IBIZA

Ibiza (Eivissa in Catalan) is the most extreme of the Balearic islands, both in terms of its landscape and the people it attracts. Hippies, gays, fashion victims, nudists, party animals – this is truly one of the world's most bizarre melting pots. The island receives over a million visitors each year. Apart from the weather and the desire to be 'seen', the main drawcards are the notorious nightlife and the many pictur-esque beaches.

Orientation & Information

The capital, Ibiza (Eivissa) city, is on the south-eastern side of the island. This is where most travellers arrive (the airport is to the south, and most ferries operate from the port here) and it's also the best base. The next-largest towns are Santa Eulária des Riu on the east coast and Sant Antoni de Portmany on the west coast. Other big resorts are scattered around the island.

In Ibiza city, the tourist office (☎ 30 19 00) is at Passeig Vara de Rey 13. There is a Telefónica phone centre on Avinguda Santa Eulària by the port, while the post office is at Carrer Madrid 23. You'll find a good laun-drette, Lavandería Master Clean, at Carrer Felipe II 12.

Things to See & Do

Shopping seems to be a major pastime in Ibiza city – the port area of **Sa Penya** is crammed with funky and trashy clothes boutiques and hippy market stalls. From here you can wander up into the **D'Alt Vila**, the old walled town, with its up-market restaurants, galleries and the **Museu d'Art Contemporani**. There are fine views from the walls and from the **catedral** at the top, and the **Museu Arqueològic** nearby is worth a visit.

The heavily developed **Platja de ses Figueretes** beach is a 20-minute walk south of Sa Penya – you'd be better off taking the half-hour bus ride (105 ptas) south to the beaches at **Ses Salines**.

If you're prepared to explore, there are still numerous unspoiled and relatively undevel-oped beaches around the island. On the north-east coast, **Cala de Boix** is the only black-sand beach in the islands, while further north are the lovely beaches of **S'Aigua Blanca**. On the north coast near Portinatx, **Cala Xarraca** is in a picturesque, semi-protected bay, and near Port de Sant Miquel is the attractive **Cala Benirras**. On the south-west coast, **Cala d'Hort** has a spectacular setting overlooking two rugged rock-islets, Es Verda and Es Verdranell.

Places to Stay

Ibiza City There are quite a few hostales in the streets around the port, although in mid-summer cheap beds are as scarce as hen's teeth. The friendly *Hostal Sol y Brisa* (☎ 31 08 18), Avinguda Bartolomé Vincent Ramón 15, has excellent singles/doubles at 1800/3400 ptas. Nearby at Carrer Vincente Cuervo 14, *Hostal Ripoll* (☎ 31 42 75) has similar prices, as well as good studio apartments (2000 to 9000 ptas a night).

On the waterfront, *Hostal-Restaurante La Marina* (☎ 31 01 72), Andenes del Puerto 4, has good doubles with sea views at 3200 ptas and sleepless singles with disco views at 1700 ptas. *Casa de Huéspedes Navarro* (☎ 31 08 25), Carrer de la Cruz 20 (3rd floor), also has some rooms with harbour views (and a sunny rooftop) for 1600/3200 ptas.

If you're after rooms with bath, *Hostal-Residencia Parque* (☎ 30 13 58) at Carrer Vincente Cuervo 3 has rooms for 3100/6200 ptas. Perfectly located at Passeig Vara del Rey 2, *Hotel Montesol* (☎ 31 01 61) has rooms with TV and phone for around 4900/7900 ptas.

Other Areas One of the best of Ibiza's half-dozen camping grounds is *Camping Cala Nova* (☎ 33 17 74), 500 metres north of the resort town of Cala Nova and close to a good beach.

If you want to get away from the resort developments the following places are all worth checking out. Near the Ses Salines beach (and bus stop), *Casa de Huéspedes Escandell* (☎ 39 65 83) is a simple six-room guesthouse with doubles from 3500 ptas; next door *Hostal Mar y Sal* (☎ 39 65 84) has doubles at 4600 ptas. On the south-west coast at Cala d'Hort, *Restaurante y Habitaciones Del Carmen* (☎ 14 26 61) has good rooms upstairs with bath and sea views from 4225/6500 ptas. Near the S'Aigua Blanca beaches, *Pensión Sa Plana* (☎ 33 5073) has a pool, rooms with bath from 4000/4500 ptas and a menú for 1000 ptas.

Places to Eat

Bland, overpriced eateries abound in the port area, but there are a few exceptions worth searching out. The no-frills *Comidas Bar San Juan*, Carrer Montgri 8, is outstanding value with main courses from 400 to 750 ptas. At Carrer de la Cruz 19, *Ca'n Costa* is another family-run eating house with a menú for 900 ptas. *Chi Chi's*, Carrer del Mar 16, isn't particularly cheap but its Tex-Mex tucker is particularly good. Pizzas and pastas are around 800 ptas at the *Pizzería Da Franco Er Romano* (below Hostal Sol y Brisa) – it also has a menú for 1250 ptas.

Entertainment

Ibiza's nightlife is renowned. The gay scene is wild and the dress code expensive. Dozens of bars keep Ibiza city's port area jumping until the early hours, and after they wind down you can continue on to one of the island's world-famous discos – if you can afford the 3000 to 5000 ptas entry, that is. The big-names are *Pacha*, on the north side of Ibiza city's port; *Privilege* and *Amnesia*, both six km out on the road to Sant Antoni; and *Kiss* and *Space*, both south of Ibiza city in Platja d'En Bossa.

Getting Around

Buses run between the airport and Ibiza city hourly (100 ptas); otherwise, a taxi costs around 1500 ptas. Buses to other parts of the island leave from the series of bus stops along Avenida Isidoro Macabich – pick up a copy of the handy bus timetable from the tourist office.

If you are intent on getting to some of the more secluded beaches you will need to rent wheels. Agencies in Ibiza city include Ribas (☎ 30 18 11), at Calle Vincente Cuervo 3, and Valentin (☎ 31 08 22), at Avinguda Bartolomé Vincent Ramón 19. Both have cars (4000 to 6000 ptas a day), scooters (2500 to 4000 ptas a day) and bicycles (700 to 1000 ptas a day).

FORMENTERA

A short boat ride south of Ibiza, Formentera is the smallest and least developed of the four main Balearic Islands. This idyllic island has fine beaches and some excellent short walking and cycling trails to explore. It's a popular day trip destination from Ibiza and can get pretty crowded in midsummer, but most of the time it is still possible to find yourself a strip of sand out of sight of tourist colonies and out of earshot of other tourists.

Orientation & Information

Formentera is about 20 km from east to west. Ferries arrive at La Savina on the north-west coast; the tourist office (☎ 32 20 57) is behind the rental agencies you'll see when you disembark. Three km south is the island's capital, Sant Francesc Xavier, where you'll find most of the banks. From here, the main road runs along the middle of the island before climbing to the highest point (192 metres). At the eastern end of the island is the Sa Mola lighthouse. Three km east of La Savina, Es Pujols is the main tourist resort (and the only place with any nightlife to speak of).

Things to See & Do

Some of the island's best and most popular beaches are the beautiful white strips of sand along the narrow promontory which stretches north towards Ibiza. A two-km walking trail leads from the La Savina-Es Pujols road to the far end of the promontory, from where you can wade across a narrow strait to **S'Espalmador**, a tiny islet with beautiful, quiet beaches. Along Formentera's south coast, **Platja de Migjorn** is made up of numerous coves and beaches – tracks lead down to these off the main road. On the west coast is the lovely **Cala Saona** beach.

The tourist office's *Green Tours* brochure outlines 19 excellent walking and cycling trails that take you through some of the island's most scenic areas.

Places to Stay

Camping is not allowed on Formentera. Sadly, the coastal accommodation places mainly cater to German and British package-tour agencies and are overpriced and/or booked out in summer. In Es Pujols you could try *Hostal Tahiti* (☎ 32 81 22), with B&B at 5200/8600 ptas. If you prefer peace and quiet you would

SPAIN

be better off in Es Caló – *Fonda Rafalet* (☎ 32 70 16) has good rooms on the waterfront for 3000/5500 ptas, or across the road the tiny and simple *Casa de Huéspedes Miramar* (☎ 32 70 60) charges 2000/3000 ptas.

Perhaps the best budget bet is to base yourself in one of the small inland towns and bike it to the beaches. In Sant Ferran (1.6 km south of Es Pujols), the popular *Hostal Pepe* (☎ 32 80 33) has B&B with bath at 3110/4975 ptas. In Sant Francesc Xavier, *Restaurant Casa Rafal* (☎ 32 22 05) charges 2000/3500 ptas (3000/5000 ptas with bath). La Savina isn't the most thrilling place, but *Hostal La Savina* (☎ 32 22 79) has excellent rooms from 2750/4250 ptas.

Getting There & Away
There are 20 to 25 ferries daily between Ibiza city and Formentera. The trip takes about 25 minutes by jet ferry (3600 ptas return), or about an hour by car ferry (1500 to 2200 ptas return; 5000 ptas for a small car). Prices vary from company to company, so check around.

Getting Around
A string of rental agencies line the harbour in La Savina. Bikes are the best way to get around, and daily rates range from 500 ptas to 1000 ptas for a mountain bike. If you're in a tearing hurry (or lazy), there are also scooters (1500 to 4000 ptas) and cars (4000 to 7000 ptas). A regular bus service connects all the main towns.

MENORCA
Menorca is perhaps the least overrun and most low-key of the Balearic Islands. In 1993, the island was declared a Biosphere Reserve by UNESCO, with the aim of preserving its important environmental areas such as the Albufera d'es Grau wetlands and its unique collection of archaeological relics and monuments.

Orientation & Information
The capital, Maó (Mahón in Spanish), is at the eastern end of the island. Its busy port is the arrival point for most ferries, and Menorca's airport is seven km south-west. The main road runs down the middle of the island to Ciutadella, Menorca's second-largest town,

with secondary roads leading north and south to the major coastal resorts and beaches.

The main tourist office is in Maó (☎ 36 37 90) at Plaça de S'Esplanada 40. During summer there are offices at the airport and in Ciutadella on Plaça des Born. Maó's post office is on Carrer del Bon Aire.

Things to See & Do
Maó and Ciutadella are both harbour towns, and from either place you'll have to commute to the beaches. Maó absorbs most of the tourist traffic – while you're here you can take a boat cruise around its impressive harbour and sample the local gin at the **Xoriguer distillery**. Ciutadella, with its smaller harbour and historic buildings, has a more distinctively Spanish feel about it.

In the centre of the island, the 357-metre-high **Monte Toro** has great views of the whole island, and on a clear day you can see as far as Mallorca.

With your own transport and a bit of footwork you'll be able to discover some of Menorca's off-the-beaten-track beaches. North of Maó, a drive across a lunar landscape leads to the lighthouse at **Cap de Favàritx**. If you park just before the gate to the lighthouse and climb up the rocks behind you, you'll see a couple of the eight beaches that are just waiting for scramblers like yourself to grace their sands.

On the north coast, the picturesque town of **Fornells** is on a large bay that is popular with windsurfers. Further west at the beach of Binimella, you can continue (on foot) to the unspoilt Cala Pregonda.

North of Ciutadella is **La Vall**, another stretch of untouched beach backed by a private nature park (600 ptas entry per car). On the south coast, there are two good beaches either side of the resort of Santa Galdana – Cala Mitjana to the east, and Macarella to the west.

Menorca's beaches aren't its only attractions. The interior of the island is liberally sprinkled with reminders of its rich and ancient heritage. Pick up a copy of the tourist office's excellent *Archaeological Guide to Minorca*.

Places to Stay
The only *camping ground* is near the beach of Cala Galdana, 10 km south of Ferreries. It is only open in summer.

Maó and Ciutadella both have a handful of good budget options. In Maó at Carrer de la Infanta 19, *Hostal Orsi* (☎ 36 47 51) is owned by a young English couple who are a mine of information about the island. With singles/doubles/triples at 2200/3800/5400 ptas, it is highly recommended. *Hostal La Isla* (☎ 36 64 92), Carrer de Santa Catalina 4, has excellent rooms with bath at 2000/4000 ptas.

In Ciutadella at Carrer de Sant Isidre 33, *Hostal Oasis* (☎ 38 21 97) is set around a spacious courtyard and has its own Italian restaurant; rooms with bath are 2500/4300 ptas. *Hotel Geminis* (☎ 38 58 96), Carrer Josepa Rossinyol 4, is a friendly and stylish two-star with excellent rooms for 3500/6500 ptas.

In Fornells, *Hostal La Palma* (☎ 37 66 34), Plaça S'Algaret 3, has singles/doubles from 3000/5750 ptas.

Places to Eat

In Maó, the *American Bar* in Plaça Reial has a limited but tasty menú for 950 ptas. *La Dolce Vita*, an Italian bistro at Carrer de Sant Roc 25, has great home-made bread, pasta, fresh salads, pizza, and a menú for 1000 ptas. Maó's waterfront road, Andén de Levante, is lined with restaurants with outdoor terraces. The excellent *Roma*, at No 295, has pizzas and pastas from 700 ptas and a menú for 1100 ptas.

Ciutadella's port is also lined with restaurants, and you won't have any trouble finding somewhere to eat. After dinner, check out *Sa Clau*, a hip little jazz and blues bar set in the old city walls.

Getting Around

From the airport, a taxi into Maó costs around 1200 ptas – there are no buses.

TMSA (☎ 36 03 61) runs six buses a day between Maó and Ciutadella, with connections to the major resorts on the south coast. In summer there are also daily bus services to most of the coastal towns from both Maó and Ciutadella.

If you're planning to hire a car, rates vary seasonally (from around 3500 to 7000 ptas a day) – during summer, minimum hire periods apply. Places worth trying include Ibercars (☎ 36 42 08), GB International (☎ 36 24 32) and Autos Confort (☎ 36 94 70). In Maó, Hostal Orsi rents mountain bikes (800 ptas a day). Motos Rayda (☎ 35 47 86) also rents

bikes as well as a range of scooters (1500 to 2500 ptas a day).

Valencia & Murcia

Though perhaps best known for the package resorts of the Costa Blanca, this region also includes Spain's lively third city, Valencia, and a fairy-tale castle at Morella.

VALENCIA

Valencia comes as a pleasant surprise to many. Home to paella and, they claim, the Holy Grail, it is also blessed with great weather and Las Fallas (in March), one of the wildest parties in the country.

Orientation

Plaza del Ayuntamiento marks the centre of Valencia. Most points of interest lie to the north of the train station and are generally within easy walking distance. The Río Turia cuts the central region of the city from the northern and eastern suburbs. This once mighty river is now almost dry, and has been turned into a city-length park, the Jardines del Turia.

Many Valencian streets now have signs in Catalan as well as the Spanish used in this section. You'll often find Catalan and Spanish signs at opposite ends – or sides – of the street.

Information

Valencia's main tourist office (☎ 351 04 17) on Plaza del Ayuntamiento is open weekdays from 8.30 am to 2.15 pm and from 4.15 to 6.15 pm, and Saturday from 9.15 am to 12.45 pm. There's a regional tourist office (☎ 352 85 73) at the train station, open weekdays from 9 am to 6.30 pm.

The post office is on Plaza del Ayuntamiento, and there's a telephone centre at the train station. Valencia's telephone code is ☎ 96.

A good selection of English-language novels is available at the English Book Centre at Calle Pascual y Genis 16. There is a laundrette, Lavandería El Mercat, at Plaza del Mercado 12.

SPAIN

Things to See & Do

Valencia's **Museo de Bellas Artes**, north across the river on Calle San Pio V, ranks among the very best museums in the country. It contains a beautiful collection including works by El Greco, Goya, Velázquez and a number of Valencian impressionists. It opens Tuesday to Saturday between 9 am and 2 pm and 4 and 6 pm, and Sunday from 9 am to 2 pm; entry is free. Another museum with works by El Greco is the **Real Colegio del Patriarca** on Plaza del Patriarca (open daily 11 am to 1.30 pm; entry 100 ptas). The **Instituto Valenciano Arte Moderno (IVAM)**, north-west of the centre at Calle Guillem de Castro 118, houses an impressive collection of 20th-century Spanish art (open Tuesday to Sunday from 11 am to 6 pm; entry 350 ptas).

Valencia's **catedral** is also worth a visit. Climb to the top of the tower for a great view of the sprawling city. The cathedral's museum also claims to be home to the Holy Grail (Santo Cáliz), and contains works by Goya.

The baroque **Palacio de Marqués de dos Aguas**, on Calle Poeta Querol, is fronted by an extravagantly sculpted façade and houses the **Museo Nacional de Cerámica**. It was closed for renovations at the time of writing but should be open by the time you read this.

Valencia has OK city beaches east of the centre, but a better bet is to take a bus 10 km south to the **Playas del Saler**.

Special Events

Valencia's Las Fallas de San José is one of Spain's most unique festivals, an exuberant and anarchic blend of fireworks, music, festive bonfires *(fallas)* and all-night partying. If you're in Spain between 12 and 19 March, don't miss it.

Places to Stay

The nearest camping ground, *Camping del Saler* (☎ 183 00 23), is on the coast 10 km south of Valencia. There is an HI hostel, *Albergue La Paz* (☎ 369 01 52), three km east of the centre at Avenida del Puerto 69 (open July to mid-September).

Central Valencia's accommodation zones are distinctively different. A few dodgy hostales cluster around the train station but there are better options north of the mercado central, which puts you close to Valencia's best nightlife (and, unfortunately, the red-light district). *Hospedería del Pilar* (☎ 391 66 00), Plaza del Mercado 19, has clean and bright singles/doubles at 1300/2400 ptas (1900/3400 ptas with bath). At Calle de la Carda 11, the old *Hostal El Rincón* (☎ 391 79 98) has similar prices. *Hostal El Cid* (☎ 392 23 23), Calle Cerrajeros 13, charges 1400/2700 ptas, or 3000/3700 ptas for doubles with shower/bath.

The areas around and east of Plaza del Ayuntamiento are more up-market. At Calle Salva 12, *Pensión Paris* (☎ 352 67 66) has spotless singles/doubles/triples at 2000/3000/4500 ptas (doubles with shower 3600 ptas). The stylish *Hostal Comedias* (☎ 394 1692), Calle de las Comedias 19, has excellent rooms with bath at 2500/5000 ptas. *Hostal Moratín* (☎ 352 12 20), Calle Moratín 15, has spacious rooms for 2200/3750 ptas, while nearby at Calle Barcelonina 1, *Hotel Londres* (☎ 351 22 44) has well-worn but cosy rooms with TV, phone and bath for 4400/7600 ptas (3750/6500 ptas on weekends).

Places to Eat

The *mercado central* is on Plaza del Mercado. Across the road, *Café del Mercat* has tasty tapas, a lunchtime menú for 1200 ptas and a dinner menú for 1800 ptas. At Calle En Llop 2, *Bar Cafetería Olimpya* has an excellent menú for 950 ptas; they also do pretty good salads, breakfasts and tapas.

Restaurante El Generalife, just off Plaza de la Virgen at Calle Caballeros 5, has a menú for around 1000 ptas that often includes a Valencian paella. *Café de las Horas*, Conde de Almodóvar 1, is a wonderful salon-style tearoom serving up sandwiches, salads and cakes – very soothing. Across the road from here is the popular subterranean *Las Cuevas* restaurant. For a splurge, you can't go wrong at *Restaurante Nuevo Don Ramón*, Plaza Rodrigo Botet 4, with a weekday lunch menú for 1100 ptas and main courses in the 1000 to 2200 ptas range.

Entertainment

Valencia's 'what's on' guides, *Que y Donde* and *Turia*, are both available from newsstands. On Plaza Ayuntamiento, *Filmoteca* (☎ 351 23 36) screens classic and art-house films in their original language (200 ptas entry!).

Finnigan's, an Irish pub on Plaza de la

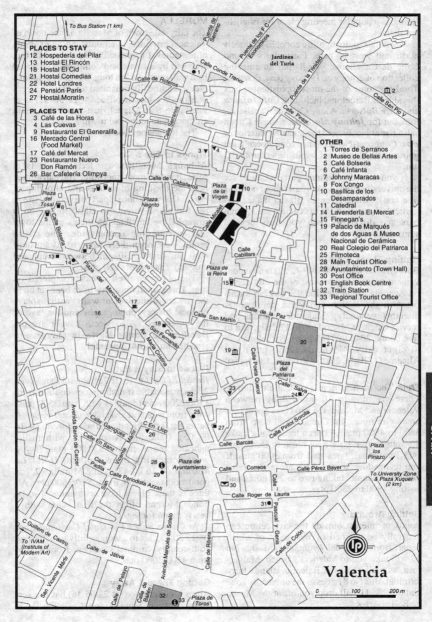

To Bus Station (1 km)

PLACES TO STAY
12 Hospedería del Pilar
13 Hostal El Rincón
18 Hostal El Cid
21 Hostal Comedias
22 Hotel Londres
24 Pensión Paris
27 Hostal Moratín

PLACES TO EAT
3 Café de las Horas
4 Las Cuevas
9 Restaurante El Generalife
16 Mercado Central
(Food Market)
17 Café del Mercat
23 Restaurante Nuevo
Don Ramón
26 Bar Cafetería Olimpya

Jardines
del Turia

Calle Conde Trenor
Calle de Roteros
Calle Serranos
Puente de Serranos
Puente de los F C.
Económicos
Puente de la Trinidad
Calle Pintor
Calle San Pío V

Plaza
del
Tosal
Calle Bolsería
Calle de Caballeros
Plaza
Negrito
Plaza de
la Virgen
Calle Micalet
Calle Cabillars
Plaza de
la Reina

OTHER
1 Torres de Serranos
2 Museo de Bellas Artes
5 Café Bolsería
6 Café Infanta
7 Johnny Maracas
8 Fox Congo
10 Basílica de los
Desamparados
11 Catedral
14 Lavandería El Mercat
15 Finnegan's
19 Palacio de Marqués
de dos Aguas & Museo
Nacional de Cerámica
20 Real Colegio del Patriarca
25 Filmoteca
28 Main Tourist Office
29 Ayuntamiento (Town Hall)
30 Post Office
31 English Book Centre
32 Train Station
33 Regional Tourist Office

Plaza del
Mercado
Calle San Martín
Calle de la Paz
Calle
San Fernando
Av. María Cristina
Calle Poeta Querol
Plaza
del
Patriarca
Calle Salvá
Calle Garrigues
Calle En Sanz
C En Llop
Calle
Pedía
Calle Periodista Azzati
San Vicente Mártir
Calle Pintor Sorolla
Calle Barcas
Plaza
los
Pinazo
Avenida Barón de Cárcer
Plaza del
Ayuntamiento
Calle
Correos
Calle Pérez Bayer
Calle Roger de Lauria
To University Zone
& Plaza Xuquer
(2 km)
C Guillem de Castro
To IVAM
(Institute of
Modern Art)
Calle de Játiva
Avenida Marqués de Sotelo
Calle de Ribera
Pascual y Genís
Calle de Colón
San Vicente Mártir
Calle de Pelayo
Calle de Bailén
Calle de
Bailén
Plaza de
Toros

SPAIN

Valencia

0   100   200 m

Reina, is a popular meeting place for English-speakers.

Valencia's main nightlife zone, El Carme, is north and west of here. Particularly around Calle de Caballeros, you'll find an amazing collection of grungy and groovy bars. Plaza del Tosal has some of the most sophisticated bars this side of Barcelona, including *Café Infanta* and *Cafe Bolseria*. Along Calle de Caballeros, look out for *Johnny Maracas*, a suave Cuban salsa bar at No 39, and the amazing interior of *Fox Congo* at No 35. This zone doesn't get going until 11 pm, and winds down around 3 am.

If you want to continue partying, head for the university zone two km east (about 600 ptas in a taxi). Along Avenida Blasco Ibáñez and particularly around Plaza Xuquer are enough bars and discos to keep you busy beyond sunrise.

Getting There & Away

Bus The bus station (☎ 349 72 22) is an inconvenient two km north-west of the city centre on Avenida Menéndez Pidal – bus No 8 runs between the station and Plaza del Ayuntamiento (eventually). Major destinations and services include Madrid (10 to 12 daily, four to five hours, 2845 to 3145 ptas), Barcelona (six to eight daily, 4½ hours, 2650 ptas) and Alicante (12 daily, 2¼ to 4½ hours, 1890 ptas).

Train The train station is on Calle de Játiva. There are nine to 10 trains daily between Valencia and Madrid; the trip takes about four hours (six hours via Cuenca) and costs from 3800 to 4800 ptas. A dozen trains daily make the four to five-hour haul north to Barcelona (via Tarragona); fares start from 3000 ptas. If you're heading south, there are eight trains daily to Alicante, taking two to 2½ hours and costing 1800 to 2300 ptas.

Getting Around

Points of interest outside the city centre can generally be reached by bus, most of which depart from Plaza del Ayuntamiento. Bus No 19 will take you to Valencia's beach, Malvarrosa, as well as to the Balearic Islands ferry terminal. Bus No 81 goes to the university zone and bus No 11 will drop you off at the Museo de Bellas Artes.

MORELLA

The fairy-tale town of Morella, in the north of Valencia province, is an outstanding example of a medieval fortress. Perched on a hill top, crowned by a castle and completely enclosed by a wall over two km long, it is one of Spain's oldest continually inhabited towns.

Morella's tourist office (☎ 17 30 32) is at Puerta de San Miguel, just inside the main entrance gate to the old town.

The telephone code is ☎ 964.

Things to See & Do

Although Morella's wonderful castle is in ruins, it is still most imposing. You can almost hear the clashing of swords and clip-clop of horses that were once a part of everyday life in the fortress. A strenuous climb to the top is rewarded by breathtaking views of the town and surrounding countryside. The castle grounds are open daily from 10.30 am until 6.30 pm (until 7.30 pm between May and August). Entry costs 200 ptas.

The old town itself is easily explored on foot. Three small museums have been set up in the towers of the ancient walls, with displays on local history, photography and the 'age of the dinosaurs'. Also worth a visit are the **Basílica de Santa María la Mayor** and attached **Museo Arciprestal**.

Places to Stay & Eat

Hostal El Cid (☎ 16 01 25), Puerta San Mateo 2, has reasonable if drab singles/doubles from 1300/2200 ptas (doubles with bath 3500 ptas) – the front rooms at least have decent views. A better bet is the friendly *Fonda Moreno* (☎ 16 01 05), Calle San Nicolás 12, with rustic, unheated rooms from 950/1800 ptas. If you want something more modern, *Hotel La Muralla* (☎ 16 02 43), Calle Muralla 12, has good rooms with bath from 2800/3500 ptas. All three of these places have restaurants of sorts; Fonda Moreno offers the best value with a hearty menú for 900 ptas.

At Cuesta Suñer 1 is *Hotel Cardenal Ram* (☎ 17 30 85), set in a wonderfully transformed 16th-century cardinal's palace. Rooms start from 4300/7000 ptas.

Getting There & Away

Autos Mediterraneo (☎ 22 05 36) has bus services between Morella and Castellón de la

Plana (daily, 1015 ptas) and Vinaròs (Monday to Saturday, 710 ptas), both on the coast north of Valencia, as well as to Alcañiz in Aragón (Monday, Wednesday and Thursday; 2000 ptas).

If you are driving to Morella in winter, check the weather forecast first, as the town is sometimes snowed in for days.

THE COSTA BLANCA

Alicante and the surrounding coastal area, the Costa Blanca, is one of Europe's most heavily touristed regions. Who hasn't heard of nightmares such as Benidorm and Torrevieja? If you want to find a secluded beach in midsummer, you should keep well away from here. If, however, you are looking for a lively social life, good beaches and a suntan...

The telephone code for the Costa Blanca is ☎ 96.

Alicante

Alicante is a surprisingly refreshing town with wide boulevards, long white sandy beaches and a number of other attractions.

The main tourist office (☎ 520 00 00) is at Explanada de España 2; there's another tourist office at the bus station on Calle Portugal.

Things to See & Do The most obvious of Alicante's attractions is the **Castillo de Santa Bárbara**, a 16th-century fortress overlooking the city. There is a lift shaft deep inside the mountain which will take you right to the castle (200 ptas return) – the lift entrance is opposite Playa del Postiguet. The castle opens daily from 10 am to 8 pm (9 am to 7 pm from October to March); entry is free.

The **Colección de Arte de Siglo XX** on Plaza Santa María houses an excellent collection of modern art including a handful of works by Dalí, Miró and Picasso. It opens daily from 10.30 am to 1.30 pm and 6 to 9 pm (but from October to April from 10 am to 1 pm and 5 to 8 pm) except on Monday, Sunday afternoon and public holidays. Entry is free.

Kontiki (☎ 521 63 96) runs boat trips most days to the popular **Isla de Tabarca** south of Alicante. The island has quiet beaches and good snorkelling, plus a small hotel. Return fares are 1500 ptas.

Playa del Postiguet is Alicante's city beach, but you are better off heading north to the cleaner and less-crowded beaches of San Juan or Campello.

Places to Stay At Calle Monges 2, the outstanding *Pensión Les Monges* (☎ 521 50 46) is more like a boutique hotel than a pensión. Its eight rooms range from 1800/3400 ptas to 2600/4200 ptas with bath – book ahead. At Calle Villavieja 8, *Pensión La Milagrosa* (☎ 521 69 18) has clean and bright rooms and a small guest kitchen; it charges 1200 to 1500 ptas per person. At Calle Mayor 5, *Hostal Mayor* (☎ 520 13 83) has singles/doubles/triples with bath for 2200/4000/5700 ptas. Opposite the bus station at Calle Portugal 26, *Hostal Portugal* (☎ 592 92 44) charges 2000/3000 ptas, or 3000/3800 ptas with bath.

The three-star *Hotel Palas* (☎ 520 93 09), Plaza Puerta del Mar, is a rambling, semigrand hotel with a weird collection of art works, furniture and mirrors. Rooms with mod cons (and a few odd ones) cost 5240/8425 ptas.

Places to Eat The *Restaurante Ciudad Imperial*, Calle de Gravina 8, has tasty Chinese tucker, a budget menú at 500 ptas and banquet menús from 695 to 950 ptas. At Calle Maldonado 25, *Restaurante El Canario* is a no-frills local eatery with a hearty menú for 850 ptas. *Cafetería Capri*, Calle San Ildefonso 6, has 22 different platos combinados costing from 600 to 1400 ptas and a menú for 925 ptas. *Restaurante El Refugio*, at Calle Rafael Altamira 19, has menús from 1200 to 2400 ptas.

You can try local seafood specialties at the stylish *Boutique del Mar* at Calle San Fernando 16, where main courses range from 750 to 1500 ptas and the menú costs 1500 ptas.

Restaurante Mixto Vegetariano on Plaza Santa María is a basic little place doing reasonable vegetarian or carnivorous menús for 850 ptas

Entertainment Alicante's El Barrio nightlife zone clusters around the cathedral – look out for the heavenly (and very weird) *Celestial Copas*, *La Naya*, *Potato-Bar Cafe*, and *Jamboree Bar*. Down on Explanada de España, the very cool *Cool* has live salsa, jazz and blues bands.

SPAIN

PLACES TO STAY
10 Hostal Mayor
11 Hostal Portugal
16 Pensión Les Monges
25 Pensión
La Milagrosa
28 Hotel Palas

PLACES TO EAT
4 Cafetería Capri
15 Boutique del Mar
16 Restaurante El Refugio
21 Restaurante El Canario
24 Restaurante
Mixto Vegetariano
30 Restaurante
Ciudad Imperial

OTHER
1 Estación de Madrid
(Train Station)
2 Museo Arqueológico
Provincial
3 Mercado Central

5 Astoria Minicines
6 Celestial Copas
7 Concatedral de San Nicolás
8 La Naya & Potato-Bar Cafe
9 Jamboree Bar
12 Bus Station, Telephone Centre
& Municipal Tourist Office
13 Post Office
14 Cool
17 Plaza Ayuntamiento
18 Ayuntamiento (Town Hall)
& Tourist Office
19 Plaza Santísima
22 Colección de
Arte de Siglo XX
23 Iglesia de Santa María
26 Train Ticket Office
27 Main Tourist Office
29 Téléphone Centre
31 Entrance to lift shaft to
Castillo de Santa Bárbara
32 Buses to San Juan
33 Boats to Isla de Tabarca

Alicante

Getting There & Away Alicante is the gateway to the Costa Blanca; the airport is 12 km west of the town centre.

There are daily services from the bus station (☎ 513 07 00) on Calle Portugal to Almería (2500 ptas), Granada (3090 ptas), Valencia (1890 ptas), Barcelona (4300 ptas), Madrid (2950 ptas) and the towns along the Costa Blanca.

The train station (☎ 521 02 02) is on Avenida Salamanca. Services include Madrid (10 daily, 3500 to 4500 ptas), Valencia (eight daily, 1800 to 2300 ptas) and Barcelona (three daily, 3500 to 5000 ptas).

Jávea

Jávea (Xàbia), 10 km south-east of the port of Denia, is worth a visit early in the season, when the weather has started to improve but the masses haven't arrived yet. This laid-back place is in three parts: the old town (three km inland), the port and the beach zone of El Arenal, which is lined with pleasant bar-restaurants that stay open late during summer. If you have wheels, you might try to get to **Cabo La Nao**, known for its spectacular views, or **Granadella**, with its small, uncrowded beach – both are a few km to the south of Jávea.

Camping El Naranjal (☎ 579 29 89) is about 10 minutes walk from El Arenal. The port area is very pleasant and has some reasonably priced pensiones: *Fonda del Mar* (☎ 579 01 17) at Calle Cristo del Mar 12 has singles/doubles for 2000/4000 ptas, and a good restaurant with a menú for 1300 ptas. At Avenida de la Marina Española 8, *Hostal La Marina* (☎ 579 31 39) is run by an amiable Scottish family and has good rooms from 2000/3000 to 4500/5500 ptas with bath and sea views. In their restaurant you can try Valencian paella, or maybe the haggis?

Calpe

One of the Costa's more pleasant seaside towns, Calpe (22 km north-east of Benidorm) is dominated by the Gibraltaresque **Peñon de Ilfach**, a towering monolith that juts out into the sea. The climb to the 332-metre-high summit is especially popular – while you're up there you can choose which of Calpe's two long sandy beaches to grace with your presence later in the day.

There are a couple of good places to bed down. *Pensión Centrica* (☎ 583 55 28) on Plaza de Ilfach has cosy, pretty rooms for 1600 ptas per person, while a stone's throw from the beachfront, *Hostal Crespo* (☎ 583 39 31) at Calle La Pinta 1 has doubles (some with sea views) ranging from 2500 to 4000 ptas.

Altea

Altea's beaches may be a blend of pebbles, rocks and sand, but it beats Benidorm hands down when it comes to character (which, admittedly, isn't saying much). With what's left of the old town perched on a hill top overlooking the sea, Altea (11 km north-east of Benidorm) is a good place to spend a few days relaxing away from the nearby hustle and bustle. The tourist office (☎ 584 41 14) is at Calle San Pedro 9.

Hotel San Miguel (☎ 584 04 00), on the waterfront at Calle La Mar 65, has pleasant rooms with bath for 3500/6000 ptas (plus IVA). The seafood restaurant downstairs has a good menú for 1650 ptas.

Benidorm

Infamous Benidorm supposedly represents all that is bad about tourism in Spain. If you're thinking about coming out of sheer curiosity – can it really be that bad? – allow us to save you the trip. It's worse – much, much worse than you could possibly imagine. Five km of white sandy beaches backed by a relentless jungle of concrete high-rise; streets overwhelmed with tourists toting tacky souvenirs and plastic beach toys; slabs of pasty-white flesh committing outrageous sins in the name of summer fashion...

Benidorm's tourist office (☎ 585 32 24) is near the waterfront in the old town at Calle Martínez Alejos 16. Almost everyone here is on some kind of package deal, but if you need to stay there are a few hostales in the old town. *Hostal Calpi* (☎ 585 78 48), Costera del Barco 6, has rooms with bath for 2000 to 3000 ptas per person. *Hostal La Santa Faz* (☎ 585 40 63), Calle Santa Faz 18, has dim rooms with bath for 3250/6000 ptas.

Santa Pola

Apart from being yet another beachfront concrete jungle, Santa Pola (20 km south of Alcante) is the jumping-off point for the Isla

SPAIN

de Tabarca. The town's tourist office (☎ 669 22 76) is on Plaza de la Diputación.

Beaches in and around Santa Pola worth visiting include Gran Playa and Playa Lisa. Also try the beaches in Santa Pola del Este. In the centre of town on Plaza de la Glorieta, a well-preserved, 16th-century **fortress** stands besieged by 20th-century high-rise architecture. Inside there's a small **aquarium** and **archaeological museum** (100 ptas).

Camping Bahía (☎ 541 10 12) is about 15 minutes walk from the town centre at Calle Partida Rural de Valverde Bajo 9. The friendly *Hostal Chez Michel* (☎ 541 18 42), Calle Felipe 11, has refurbished rooms with bath at 2625/4000 ptas.

Torrevieja
A heavily developed but not completely unpleasant coastal resort, Torrevieja has good beaches and a lively nightlife, but be warned that you will probably not get to know many, if any, Spaniards here. The tourist office (☎ 571 59 36) is centrally located on Plaza Capdepont.

The best budget bet is *Hostal Fernández* (☎ 571 00 09), well located at Calle Ramón Gallud 16; rooms with bath are 3000/5000 ptas. Near the bus station at Calle Zoa 53, *Hotel Cano* (☎ 670 09 58) has modern rooms with bath at 3500/5000 ptas. At Avenida Dr Gregorio Marañon 22, *Hostal Reina* (☎ 670 19 04) has cheap rooms with marshmallow beds for 1800/3000 ptas.

MURCIA
The Murcian coast beyond Cartagena has some of the least developed beaches on the Mediterranean coast, and towns in the interior, such as Lorca, have a flavour unique to this part of the country.

The best known and most touristed beaches in the area are in the so-called Mar Menor, just south of the Valencia-Murcia border. You are better off passing them by and heading on to **Mazarrón** to the west of Cartagena, or even further south-west to the golden beaches at **Águilas**. Both Mazarrón and Águilas have camping grounds and it is possible to swim there (without dying of hypothermia) as early as the beginning of March.

Andalucía

The stronghold of the Moors for nearly eight centuries and the pride of the Christians for many more thereafter, Andalucía is perhaps Spain's most exotic and colourful region. The home of flamenco, bullfighting and some of the country's most brilliant fiestas, it's peppered with reminders of the Moorish past – from treasured monuments like the Alhambra in Granada and the mezquita in Córdoba to the white villages clinging to its hillsides. The regional capital, Seville, is one of Spain's most exciting cities.

Away from the main cities and resorts, Andalucía is surprisingly untouristed and makes for some great exploring. Its scenery ranges from semideserts to lush river valleys, from gorge-ridden mountains to the longest coastline of any Spanish region. The coast stretches from the quiet beaches of Cabo de Gata, past the mayhem of the Costa del Sol, to come within 14 km of Africa at the windsurfing centre Tarifa, before opening up to the Atlantic Ocean on the Costa de la Luz, where long beaches sweep by Cádiz and the famous wetlands of Doñana National Park to the Portuguese border.

SEVILLE
Seville (Sevilla) is one of the most exciting cities in Spain, with an atmosphere both relaxed and festive, a rich history, some great monuments, beautiful parks and gardens, and a large, lively student population. Located on the Río Guadalquivir, which is navigable to the Atlantic Ocean, Seville was once the leading Muslim city in Spain. It reached its height later, in the 16th and 17th centuries, when it held a monopoly on Spanish trade with the Americas. Expo '92, in 1992, once again plunged Seville into the international limelight.

Seville is an expensive place, so it's worth planning your visit carefully. In high summer, the city is stiflingly hot and not a fun place to be. It's best during its unforgettable spring festivals, though rooms then (if you can get one) are expensive.

Information
The main tourist office at Avenida de la Constitución 21 (☎ 422 14 04) is open week-

days from 9 am to 7 pm and Saturday from 10 am to 2 pm. It's often extremely busy, so you might try the other offices – at Paseo de las Delicias 9 (☎ 423 44 65), open Monday to Friday from 8.30 am to 6.30 pm, and on Calle Arjona (☎ 421 36 30), open weekdays from 9 am to 8.45 pm, and weekend mornings. There's also a tourist office (☎ 444 91 28) at the airport.

Seville's telephone code is ☎ 95.

Librería Beta, at Avenida de la Constitución 9 and 27, has guidebooks and novels in English. Tintorería Roma at Calle Castelar 4 will wash, dry and fold a load of washing for 1000 ptas.

Things to See & Do

Cathedral & Giralda Seville's immense cathedral – the biggest in the world, says the *Guinness Book of Records* – was built on the site of Moorish Seville's main mosque between 1401 and 1506. The structure is primarily Gothic, though most of the internal decoration is in later styles. The adjoining tower, La Giralda, was the mosque's minaret and dates from the 12th century. The climb up La Giralda affords great views and is quite easy as there's a ramp (not stairs) all the way up inside. One highlight of the cathedral's lavish interior is Christopher Columbus' supposed tomb inside the south door (no-one's 100% sure that his remains didn't get mislaid somewhere in the Caribbean). The four crowned sepulchre-bearers represent the four kingdoms of Spain at the time of Columbus' sailing. Entry to the cathedral and Giralda is 600 ptas (students and pensioners 200 ptas). Opening hours for both are Monday to Saturday from 11 am to 5 pm, and Sunday from 2 to 4 pm. The Giralda alone is open on Sunday from 10.30 am to 1.30 pm.

Alcázar Seville's alcázar, a residence of Muslim and Christian royalty for many centuries, was founded in the 10th century as a Moorish fortress. It has been adapted by Seville's rulers in almost every century since, which makes it a mish-mash of styles, but adds to its fascination. The highlights are the **Palacio de Don Pedro**, exquisitely decorated by Moorish artisans for the Castilian king Pedro the Cruel in the 1360s, and the large, immaculately tended **gardens** – the perfect

place to ease your body and brain after some intensive sightseeing. The alcázar is open Tuesday to Saturday from 10.30 am to 5 pm, and Sundays and holidays from 10 am to 1 pm. Entry is 600 ptas (students free).

Walks & Parks If you're not staying in the **Barrio de Santa Cruz**, the old Jewish quarter immediately east of the cathedral and alcázar, make sure you take a stroll among its quaint streets and lovely plant-bedecked plazas. Another enjoyable walk is along the **riverbank**, where the 13th-century Torre del Oro contains a small, crowded maritime museum.

South of the centre, large **Parque de María Luisa** is a very pleasant place to get lost in, with its maze of paths, tall trees, flowers, fountains and shaded lawns.

Museums The **Archivo de Indias**, beside the cathedral, houses over 40 million documents dating from 1492 through to the decolonisation of the Americas. Most can only be consulted with special permission, but there are rotating displays of fascinating maps and documents. Entry is free, and it's open Monday to Friday from 10 am to 1 pm.

The **Museo de Bellas Artes**, on Calle Alfonso XII, has an outstanding, beautifully housed collection of Spanish art, focusing on Seville artists like Murillo and Zurbarán. It's open Tuesday to Sunday from 9 am to 3 pm (250 ptas, free for EU citizens).

Expo '92 Site The Expo '92 site is west of the Guadalquivir across the Puente del Cachorro. A **Parque de Atracciones** (adventure park) is due to reopen here in 1997. Two other areas are open to visitors. One is **Puerta de Triana**, with exhibits on sea exploration in the Pabellón de la Navegación (400 ptas). The other is the **Conjunto Monumental de La Cartuja**, a 15th-century monastery where Columbus used to stay, later converted into a china factory (300 ptas). Both sites are closed Monday. You can wander round the rest of the Expo grounds and admire the pavilions, but it's rather lifeless.

Special Events

The first of Seville's two great festivals is Semana Santa, the week leading up to Easter Sunday. Throughout the week long processions

SPAIN

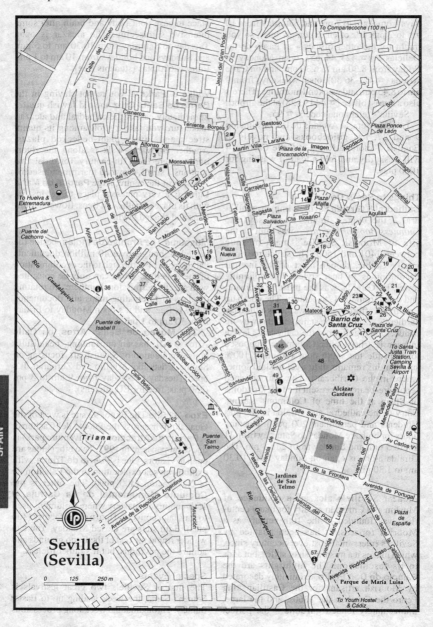

To Compartecoche (100 m)

Calle del Tornео

Jesús del Gran Poder

Cisneros

Teniente Borges

J Gestoso

2

Martín Villa   Laraña

Plaza Ponce
de León

Calle Alfonso XII

3

Monsalves

6

8

9

Imagen

Apodaca

Plaza de la
Encarnación

Sol

Santiago

Imperial

Pedro del Toro

San Eloy

Velázquez

10

Plaza de la
Encarnación

5

To Huelva &
Extremadura

Murillo

O'Donnell

Cerrajería

Cuna

11

12

13

14

Plaza
Alfalfa

17

Aguilas

Marqués de Paradas

Canalejas

San Pablo

Moratín

Méndez

Núñez

Tetuán

Sierpes

Sagasta

Plaza
Salvador

Cta Rosario

Alvarez

17

18

Levíes

19

20

Argote de Molina

Puente
del Cachorro

Arjona

Reyes Católicos

Almansa

Pastor y Landero

Santas Patronas

15

16

Zaragoza

Calle Castelar

33

Plaza
Nueva

32

Quintero

Hernando Colón

21

22

23

24

25

26

27

Santa María La Blanca

Río

Guadalquivir

37

Adriano

38

34

42

43

G Vinuesa

Avenida de la Constitución

31

30

Mateos

29

28

Gago

Barrio de
Santa Cruz

46

47

Plaza de
Santa Cruz

36

Trenal

Calle de

40

41

Díaz

Antonia

Dos

de

Mayo

39

Puente de
Isabel II

Paseo de Cristóbal Colón

Fernando

44

45

Santo Tomás

48

To Santa
Justa Train
Station,
Camping
Sevilla &
Airport

Santander

49

50

Alcázar
Gardens

Calle Betis

51

Almirante Lobo

Calle San Fernando

56

52

53

54

Puente
San Telmo

Av Sanjurjo

Avenida de Roma

Avenida del Cid

Av Carlos V

Triana

Paseo de las Delicias

55

Palos de la Frontera

Avenida de Portugal

Avenida de la República Argentina

Asunción

Jardines de
San Telmo

Avenida del Perú

Avenida María Luisa

Río

Guadalquivir

Avenida de Isabel la Católica

Plaza
de
España

57

Avenida Rodríguez Caso

Parque de María Luisa

Avenida Menéndez Pelayo

Seville
(Sevilla)

0   125   250 m

To Youth Hostel
& Cádiz

PLACES TO STAY		25	Restaurant El Cordobés	36	Tourist Office
2	Hostal Pino	28	Pizzeria San Marco	38	Arena
6	Hostal Alfonso XII	29	Bodega Santa Cruz	39	Plaza de Toros de la
7	Hostal Lis II	33	Bodega Paco Góngora		Maestranza (Bull-
10	Hostal Lis	37	Mercado del Arenal		ring)
17	Hostal Sierpes	46	El Rincón de Pepe	40	Habana
18	Hostal Sánchez	54	Pizzeria San Marco	41	A3
	Sabariego			42	Bar Populus
20	Huéspedes La	**OTHER**		44	Main Post Office
	Montoreña	1	Expo 92 Site	45	Archivo de Indias
21	Hostal Bienvenido	4	Museo de Bellas Artes	47	Los Gallos
23	Pensión Fabiola	5	Plaza de Armas Bus	48	Alcázar
24	Pensión San Pancracio		Station	49	Main Tourist Office
26	Pensión Cruces El	11	El Mundo	50	Librería Beta
	Patio	12	Sopa de Ganso	51	Torre del Oro & Museo
27	Hostal Toledo	13	Bare Nostrum		Marítimo
35	Hotel La Rábida	14	Lamentable	52	Alambique, Mui d'Aqui
43	Hotel Simón	15	Bestiario		& Big Ben
		16	American Express	53	SVQ
PLACES TO EAT		19	La Carbonería	55	University
3	Bodegón Alfonso XII	30	La Giralda	56	Prado de San
8	Patio San Eloy	31	Catedral		Sebastián Bus
9	Pizzeria San Marco	32	Librería Beta		Station
22	Cervecería Alta-Mira &	34	Tintorería Roma	57	Tourist Office
	Bar Casa Fernando		(Laundry)		

of religious brotherhoods *(cofradías)*, dressed in strange penitents' garb with tall pointed hoods, accompany sacred images through the city, watched by huge crowds. The Feria de Abril, a week in late April, is a kind of release after this solemnity: the festivities involve six days of music, dancing, horse riding and traditional dress on a site in the Los Remedios area west of the river, plus daily bullfights and a general city-wide party.

Places to Stay

The summer prices given here can come down substantially from October to March, but during Semana Santa and the Feria de Abril they can rise by anything up to 200%.

Seville's 200-place HI hostel *Albergue Juvenil Sevilla* (☎ 461 31 50) was closed for renovation but may be open by the time you get there. It's at Calle Isaac Peral 2, about 10 minutes by bus No 34 from opposite the main tourist office.

Barrio de Santa Cruz has a few fairly good-value places to stay. *Hostal Bienvenido* (☎ 441 36 55) at Calle Archeros 14 has singles for 1500 or 1700 ptas, and doubles for 3000 ptas. *Huéspedes La Montoreña* (☎ 441 24 07), Calle San Clemente 12, has clean, simple singles/doubles at 1500/3000 ptas. *Pensión*

San Pancracio (☎ 441 31 04), at Plaza de las Cruces 9, has small singles for 1800 ptas and bigger doubles for 3200 ptas, or 4000 ptas with bath. *Pensión Cruces El Patio* (☎ 422 96 33), Plaza de las Cruces 10, has a few dorm beds at 1200 ptas, singles at 2500 ptas, and doubles at 4000 and 5000 ptas. The friendly *Hostal Toledo* (☎ 421 53 35), Calle Santa Teresa 15, has good singles/doubles with bath for 2500/5000 ptas. *Pensión Fabiola* (☎ 421 83 46) at Calle Fabiola 16 has simple, well-kept rooms from 3000/5500 ptas.

The area north of Plaza Nueva, only 10 minutes walk from all the hustle and bustle, has some good value too. *Hostal Pino* (☎ 421 28 10), Calle Tarifa 6, is one of the cheapest, at 1600/2600 ptas, or 2000/3200 ptas with shower. *Hostal Lis II* (☎ 456 02 28), in a beautiful house at Calle Olavide 5, charges 1700 ptas for singles and 3500 ptas for doubles with toilet. The same family owns *Hostal Lis* (☎ 421 30 88) at Calle Escarpín 10, where singles/doubles with shower are 2000/3500 ptas. The friendly *Hostal Alfonso XII* (☎ 421 15 98) at Calle Monsalves 25 has singles for 2000 ptas and doubles with bath for 4000 ptas.

On Corral del Rey, east of Plaza Nueva, *Hostal Sánchez Sabariego* (☎ 421 44 70) at No 23 has singles for 2000 ptas and doubles

SPAIN

with bath for 4000 ptas. Almost opposite, at No 22, *Hostal Sierpes* (☎ 422 49 48) is a good larger place with a garage space. Singles with bath are 4300 ptas, doubles are 4300 to 6700 ptas. They'll pay your taxi fare from the train or bus stations.

Hotel Simón (☎ 422 66 60), at Calle García de Vinuesa 19, in a typical 18th-century Seville house, has very pleasant singles/doubles with bath from 5350/7500 ptas. The impressive *Hotel La Rábida* (☎ 422 09 60), Calle Castelar 24, has rooms with bath at 5600/8825 ptas, and a restaurant.

Places to Eat

In central Seville, Barrio de Santa Cruz is the best area for decent-value eating. The excellent, very popular *Pizzeria San Marco*, in a stylishly refurbished building at Calle Mesón del Moro 6, has pizzas and pasta dishes for 700 to 800 ptas (there are two more branches at Calle de la Cuna 6 and Calle Betis 68). Calle Santa María La Blanca has several good places: at *Cervecería Alta-Mira*, No 6, a media-ración of tortilla Alta-Mira (made with potatoes and vegetables) is almost a full meal for 600 ptas; *Bar Casa Fernando* round the corner has a decent 800-pta lunch menú; *Restaurant El Cordobés* at No 20 is good for breakfasts such as eggs, bacon, bread and coffee for 350 ptas. *Bodega Santa Cruz* on Calle Mateos Gago is a popular bar with a big choice of good-sized tapas for 150 ptas. Near the alcázar, *El Rincón de Pepe* at Calle Gloria 6 has folksy décor and a menú of gazpacho or salad, paella and dessert for 1050 ptas.

West of Avenida de la Constitución, *Bodega Paco Góngora* at Calle Padre Marchena 1 has a huge range of good seafood at decent prices – media-raciones of fish a la plancha (grilled) are mostly 600 ptas. Further north, *Patio San Eloy* at Calle San Eloy 9 is a bright, busy place with lots of good tapas for 115 to 175 ptas. *Bodegón Alfonso XII* at Calle Alfonso XII 33 has deals like a breakfast of bacon, eggs and coffee for 350 ptas.

Mercado del Arenal, on Calle Pastor y Landero, is the only food market in the central area.

Entertainment

Seville's nightlife is among the liveliest in Spain. On fine nights throngs of people block the streets outside popular bars, while teenagers and students just bring their own bottles to mass gathering spots such as the Mercado del Arenal. Seville also has some great music bars, often with dance space. As everywhere in Spain, the real action is on Friday and Saturday nights.

Drinking & Dancing Until about midnight, Plaza Salvador is a popular spot for an open-air drink, with a student crowd and couple of little bars selling carry-out drinks. The east bank of the Guadalquivir is busy into the early hours – in summer it's dotted with temporary bars.

There are some hugely popular bars just north of the cathedral, but the crowds from about midnight around Calle de Adriano, west of Avenida de la Constitución, have to be seen to be believed. Busy music bars on Adriano itself include *A3*, *Habana*, *Bar Populus* and *Arena*. Nearby on Calle García de Vinuesa and Calle Dos de Mayo are some quieter bodegas (traditional wine bars), some with good tapas, that attract a more mature crowd.

Calle Pérez Galdós off Plaza Alfalfa has three lively music bars – *Lamentable*, *Bare Nostrum* and *Sopa de Ganso* which serves vegetarian tapas. It's fairly busy by midnight. Across the river, *Alambique*, *Mui d'Aqui* and *Big Ben*, side by side on Calle Betis two blocks north of the Puente de San Telmo, all play good music and attract an interesting mix of students and travellers.

For serious disco action, try the bakalao frenzy at *Bestiario* on Calle Zaragoza, or the funkier *SQV* at Calle Betis 67. SQV opens until around dawn from Thursday to Saturday and entry is free – though before about 2 am the crowd is *very* young.

Flamenco Seville is Spain's flamenco capital but even here it can be hard to find authentic flamenco unless you're present for the Feria de Abril, or the Bienal de Arte Flamenco festival, held in September and/or October in even-numbered years. Bars which put on fairly regular flamenco, of erratic quality, include *La Carbonería*, Calle Levies 18, and *El Mundo*, Calle Siete Revueltas 5 (usually Tuesday at midnight). There are also several tourist-oriented venues with regular shows, and some of these, though hardly spontaneous, are good.

The best is *Los Gallos* on Plaza Santa Cruz, with two shows nightly; entry is 3000 ptas.

Spectator Sport
Seville's bullfights are among the best in the country. The season runs from Easter to October, with fights most Sundays about 6 pm, and almost every day during the Feria de Abril and the week or two before it. The bullring is on Paseo de Cristóbal Colón. Tickets start around 2000 ptas.

Getting There & Away
Air Seville airport (☎ 451 06 77) has quite a range of domestic and international flights. Air Europa flies to Barcelona for 13,900 ptas (from 20,900 ptas return).

Bus Buses to Extremadura, Madrid, Portugal and Andalucía west of Seville leave from the Plaza de Armas bus station (☎ 490 80 40). Buses to other parts of Andalucía use the Prado de San Sebastián bus station (☎ 441 71 11).

Daily services include around 10 buses each to Córdoba (two hours, 1200 ptas), Granada (three hours, 2710 ptas), Málaga (three hours, 2245 ptas) and Madrid (six hours, 2680 ptas). To Lisbon there are three direct buses a week (eight hours, 4350 ptas), and daily buses with a transfer at the border (nine hours, 2540 ptas). For the Algarve you need to change buses at Huelva, or Ayamonte on the border.

Train Seville's Santa Justa train station (☎ 454 02 02) is about 1.5 km north-east of the city centre on Avenida Kansas City.

To/from Madrid, there are up to a dozen super-fast AVE trains each day, covering the 471 km in just 2½ hours and costing from 7600 to 9200 ptas in the cheapest class (turista); a couple of Talgos taking 3½ hours for 6700 to 7300 ptas in 2nd class; and the evening Tren Hotel, taking 3¾ hours for 5100 ptas in a seat. Inter-Rail cards are not valid on AVEs; Eurail pass-holders pay 1400 ptas.

Other daily trains include about 20 to Córdoba (43 minutes to 1¾ hours, 875 to 2500 ptas); four to Barcelona (11 to 14 hours, from 6600 ptas); and three each to Granada (4½ hours, 1950 ptas) and Málaga (three hours, 1790 ptas). For Lisbon (16 hours, 6500 ptas),

there's one train a day with a change in Cáceres.

Car Pooling Compartecoche (☎ 490 78 52) at Calle González Cuadrado 49 is an intercity car-pooling service. Its service is free to drivers, while passengers pay an agreed transfer rate. Ring them for details.

Getting Around
The airport is about seven km from the centre, off the N-IV Córdoba road. Airport buses (750 ptas) run up to 12 times daily – tourist offices have details.

Bus Nos C1 and C2, across the road from the front of Santa Justa train station, follow a circular route via Avenida de Carlos V, close to Prado de San Sebastián bus station and the city centre, and Plaza de Armas bus station. Bus No C4, south on Calle de Arjona from Plaza de Armas bus station, goes straight to the centre.

GRANADA
From the 13th to 15th centuries, Granada was capital of the last Moorish kingdom in Spain, and the finest city on the peninsula. Today it's home to the greatest Moorish legacy in the country, and one of the most magnificent buildings on the continent – the Alhambra. South-east of the city, the Sierra Nevada mountain range (Spain's highest), and the Alpujarras valleys, with their picturesque, mysterious villages, are well worth exploring if you have time to spare.

Information
Granada's main tourist office (☎ 22 66 88), on Plaza de Mariana Pineda, opens on weekdays from 9.30 or 10.30 am to 1.30 or 2 pm (depending on the season) and from 4.30 to 6.30 or 7 pm, and on Saturday from 10 am to 1 pm. There's another office on Calle Mariana Pineda, open Monday to Friday from 9 am to 7 pm and Saturday from 10 am to 2 pm.

Granada's telephone code is ☎ 958.

Lavandería Duquesa, Calle de la Duquesa 26, will wash and dry a load of clothes for 900 ptas.

Things to See
La Alhambra One of the greatest accomplishments of Islamic art and architecture, the Alhambra is simply breathtaking. Much has

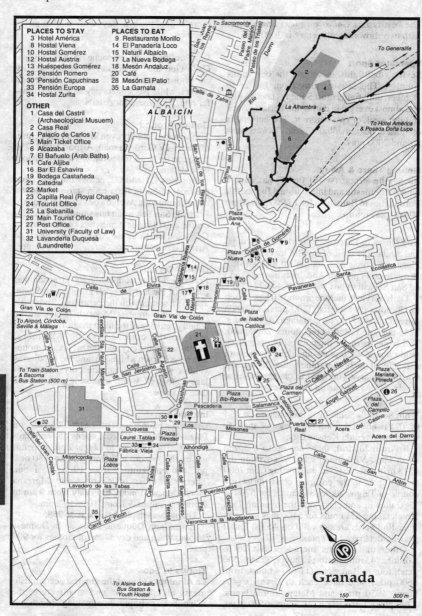

PLACES TO STAY
3   Hotel América
8   Hostal Viena
10 Hostal Gomérez
12 Hostal Austria
13 Huéspedes Gomérez
29 Pensión Romero
30 Pensión Capuchinas
33 Pensión Europa
34 Hostal Zurita

PLACES TO EAT
9   Restaurante Morillo
14 El Panadería Loco
15 Naturii Albaicín
17 La Nueva Bodega
18 Mesón Andaluz
20 Café
28 Mesón El Patio
35 La Garnata

OTHER
1   Casa del Castril
    (Archaeological Musuem)
2   Casa Real
4   Palacio de Carlos V
5   Main Ticket Office
6   Alcazaba
7   El Bañuelo (Arab Baths)
11 Cafe Aljibe
16 Bar El Eshavira
19 Bodega Castañeda
21 Catedral
22 Market
23 Capilla Real (Royal Chapel)
24 Tourist Office
25 La Sabanilla
26 Main Tourist Office
27 Post Office
31 University (Faculty of Law)
32 Lavandería Duquesa
    (Laundrette)

SPAIN

Granada

ALBAICÍN

La Alhambra

To Sacromonte

To Generalife

To Hotel América
& Posada Doña Lupe

To Airport, Córdoba,
Seville & Málaga

To Train Station
& Bacoma
Bus Station (500 m)

To Alsina Graells
Bus Station &
Youth Hostel

0   150   300 m

been written about its fortress, palace, patios and gardens, but nothing can really prepare you for what you will see.

The **Alcazaba** is the Alhambra's fortress, dating from the 11th to the 13th centuries. The views of the city from the tops of the towers are great. The **Casa Real** (Royal Palace), built for Granada's rulers in its 14th and 15th-century heyday, is the centrepiece of the Alhambra. The intricacy of the stonework, epitomised by the Patio de los Leones (Patio of the Lions) and Sala de las Dos Hermanas (Hall of the Two Sisters), is stunning. Finally, there is the **Generalife**, the summer palace of the sultans, set in soul-soothing gardens. This is a great spot to relax and contemplate the rest of the Alhambra from afar.

Cuesta de Gomérez leads up to the Alhambra from Plaza Nueva in the city. The complex opens at 9 am, closing at 7.45 pm in summer (5.45 pm on Sunday) and at 6 pm in winter. There are also night-time sessions. Admission is 675 ptas, but free on Sunday. You'll enjoy your visit much more if you can avoid the bus-tour crowds – go first thing in the morning or during siesta. On weekends and holidays and in high summer you'll have to queue a while for your ticket.

Other Attractions Simply wandering around the narrow streets of the **Albaicín** Moorish district, across the river from the Alhambra (not too late at night), or the area around **Plaza Bib-Rambla** is a real pleasure. On your way, stop by the **Casa del Castril** (archaeological museum) and **El Bañuelo** (Arab baths), both on Carrera del Darro in the Albaicín, and the **Capilla Real** (Royal Chapel) on Gran Vía de Colón in which Fernando and Isabel, the Christian conquerors of Granada in 1492, are buried along with their daughter and son-in-law. Next door to the chapel is Granada's **catedral**, which dates in part from the early 16th century. The Gypsy caves of **Sacromonte**, in the north of the city, are another popular attraction.

Places to Stay
Granada's youth hostel, *Albergue Juvenil Granada* (☎ 27 26 38), is near the bus station at Camino de Ronda 171. It charges 1100 ptas per person if you're under 26, 1400 ptas if you're older. An alternative budget option is

the *Posada Doña Lupe* (☎ 22 14 73), on Avenida del Generalife, just above the Alhambra car park, which has plentiful singles/doubles from 1000/1950 ptas including a light breakfast.

Most of Granada's budget accommodation clusters in two areas – on the east side of Plaza Nueva (well placed for the Albaicín and Alhambra) and around Plaza Trinidad. In the first area, *Hostal Gomérez* (☎ 22 44 37), Cuesta de Gomérez 10, is cheap and cheerful with rooms for 1400/2300 ptas. *Huéspedes Gomérez* (☎ 22 63 98), Cuesta de Gomérez 2, is also friendly and even cheaper at 1200/2000 ptas. *Hostal Viena* (☎ 22 18 59), in Calle Hospital de Santa Ana 2 (off Cuesta de Gomérez), has rooms from 1500/3000 ptas and doubles with bath for 3500 ptas. The same owners run *Hostal Austria* (☎ 22 70 75), Cuesta de Gomérez 4, where rooms with bath cost from 2500/3500 ptas.

Hotel América (☎ 22 74 71) is not a budget hotel, but it simply must be mentioned because of its magical position. Yes, you too can have a room within the walls of the Alhambra, if you can afford 6500/11,000 ptas.

Around Plaza de la Trinidad there's plenty of choice. *Pensión Romero* (☎ 26 60 79), Calle Sílleria 1, on the corner of Calle Mesones, has rooms from 1400/2600 ptas. The small *Pensión Capuchinas* (☎ 26 53 94), Calle Capuchinas 2 (2nd floor), has rooms from 1500/2500 ptas, but the proprietors can be picky about who they let in. *Pensión Europa* (☎ 27 87 44), Calle Fábrica Vieja 16, is run by a family and has rooms from 2000/3900 ptas; meals are available. *Hostal Zurita* (☎ 27 50 20), Plaza de la Trinidad 7, is friendly and good value with rooms from 1875/3750 ptas and off-street parking for 1000 ptas a day.

Places to Eat
There are some great deals on food in Granada, and bar flies will be delighted to hear that you often don't pay for tapas in Granada's bars. *La Nueva Bodega* in Calle Cetti Meriém has a menú for 850 ptas, and around the corner on Calle de Elvira, *Mesón Andaluz* has various menús from 950 ptas. There are a few cheapies on Cuesta de Gomérez, heading up to the Alhambra: *Restaurante Morillo* (summer

SPAIN

only) at No 20 has 18 menús from 750 to 1400 ptas.

Don't miss the tasty Arabic food at the *Café* on Plaza Nueva – you can eat in or take away. The teterías (Arabic-style tea houses) on Calderería Nueva, a picturesque pedestrian street west of Plaza Nueva, are atmospheric but expensive. *Naturii Albaicín*, Calderería Nueva 10, is a good vegetarian restaurant. A few doors up the street is an excellent wholemeal bakery, *El Panadería Loco*.

Mesón El Patio, Calle Mesones 50, has an outdoor courtyard, cheap bocadillos, reasonably priced main dishes and excellent bread. For late-night snacks, but also open during the day, *La Garnata*, a modern cafetería at Carril del Picón 22, is a great place for churros and chocolate and has delicious, affordable sandwiches including a very nice BLT.

Entertainment

The highest concentration of nightspots is on and around Calle Pedro Antonio de Alarcón: to get there, walk south on Calle Tablas from Plaza Trinidad. After 11 pm, you can't miss it. Another interesting street is Carrera del Darro and its continuation, known as Paseo de los Tristes, which leads from Plaza Nueva up into the Albaicín.

Bars in the streets west of Plaza Nueva get very lively on weekend nights. *Bodega Castañeda*, on Calle Almireceros, is one of the most famous bars in Granada and an institution among locals and tourists alike.

Granada's oldest bar, *La Sabanilla*, in Calle Tundidores, is showing its age but is worth a visit. Don't miss *Bar El Eshavira*, a basement jazz and flamenco club down a dark alley at Placeta de la Cuna. For great late-night music try *Cafe Aljibe*, above Plaza de Cuchilleros.

In the evening many travellers go to Sacromonte to see flamenco, but it's extremely touristy and a bit of a rip-off.

Getting There & Away

Most buses to other parts of Andalucía and further afield leave from the Alsina Graells bus station (☎ 25 13 58) on Camino de Ronda, 1.5 km south-west of the centre. Long-distance buses (to Madrid, Barcelona etc) are also run by Bacoma, on Avenida Andaluces opposite the train station, 1.5 km south-west of the centre.

Of the two trains daily to Madrid, one takes 9½ hours (3300 ptas), the other takes six hours (4000 ptas). To Seville, there are three trains a day (four hours, from 1950 ptas). For Málaga and Córdoba, you have to change trains in Bobadilla. There's one train daily to Valencia and Barcelona (6300 ptas).

CÓRDOBA

In Roman times Córdoba was the capital of Hispania Ulterior province and then, after a reorganisation, of Baetica province. With the building of the mezquita (mosque) in the 8th century it became the most important Moorish city in Spain and the most splendid city in Europe, a position it held for 200 or so years until the Córdoban Caliphate broke up after the death of its great ruler Al-Mansur in 1002. Thereafter Córdoba was overshadowed by Seville and in the 13th century both cities fell to the Christians in the Reconquista. The legacy of these great civilisations makes Córdoba one of the most interesting and important historical centres in Spain.

Orientation

Córdoba centres on and around the mezquita, which lies near the banks of the Río Guadalquivir. The mezquita is surrounded by the Judería (old Jewish quarter) to its west and the old Muslim quarter to its east, which make up the old town. The commercial centre of modern Córdoba is Plaza de las Tendillas, a few hundred metres north of the mezquita. Further north-west is the train station, on Avenida de América.

Information

There are two tourist offices: the municipal tourist office (☎ 47 20 00 ext 209) on Plaza de Judá Leví, and the provincial tourist office (☎ 47 12 35) on Calle Torrijos, near the entrance to the mezquita. The main post office is on Calle de José Cruz Conde. There are plenty of telephones on Plaza de las Tendillas.

Córdoba's telephone code is ☎ 957.

Things to See & Do

After Granada and Seville, Córdoba seems almost provincial. It is quite a laid-back town and a pleasant place to spend a couple of days just relaxing. Its most important attraction is the **mezquita**. Built by the Emir of Córdoba,

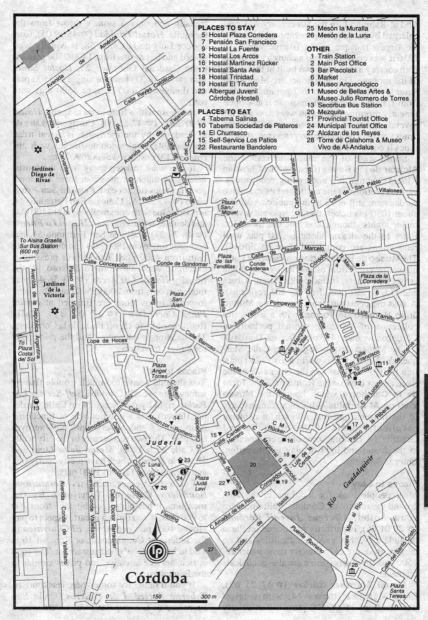

PLACES TO STAY
5 Hostal Plaza Corredera
7 Pensión San Francisco
9 Hostal La Fuente
12 Hostal Los Arcos
16 Hostal Martínez Rücker
17 Hostal Santa Ana
18 Hostal Trinidad
19 Hostal El Triunfo
23 Albergue Juvenil
 Córdoba (Hostel)

PLACES TO EAT
4 Taberna Salinas
10 Taberna Sociedad de Plateros
14 El Churrasco
15 Self-Service Los Patios
22 Restaurante Bandolero

25 Mesón la Muralla
26 Mesón de la Luna

OTHER
1 Train Station
2 Main Post Office
3 Bar Piscolabi
6 Market
8 Museo Arqueológico
11 Museo de Bellas Artes &
 Museo Julio Romero de Torres
13 Secorbus Bus Station
20 Mezquita
21 Provincial Tourist Office
24 Municipal Tourist Office
27 Alcázar de los Reyes
28 Torre de Calahorra & Museo
 Vivo de Al-Andalus

Córdoba

0   150   300 m

SPAIN

Abd al-Rahman I, in the 8th century AD, and enlarged by subsequent generations, it became the largest mosque in the Islamic world. In 1236 it was converted into a church and in the 16th century a cathedral was built in the centre of the mosque. Opening hours are Monday to Saturday from 10.30 am to 7 pm and Sunday from 1.30 to 7.30 pm. The mosque is also open for early morning masses on weekdays and for several masses on Sunday mornings. At these times you may be allowed to enter free; at other times it costs 750 ptas.

South-west of the mezquita stands the **Alcázar de los Reyes** (Castle of the Christian Kings). Though it's undergoing renovations, various sections of the castle and its extensive gardens are still open to the public. Ask here about 1050-pta tickets that incorporate several major sights, though alas not the mezquita. Entry to the alcázar alone is 300 ptas until renovations are completed (free on Friday). The **Museo de Bellas Artes** on Plaza del Potro houses a collection of works by Córdoban artists and others, including Zurbarán, Ribera and Goya (250 ptas, free for EU residents). Across the courtyard from here is the **Museo Julio Romero de Torres**, with a wonderful collection of his dark, sensual portraits of Córdoban women (425 ptas, free on Tuesday).

The **Museo Arqueólogico** on Calle Marqués del Villar is also worth a visit (250 ptas, free for EU citizens). On the other side of the river, across the **Puente Romano**, is the **Torre de la Calahorra** which houses the **Museo Vivo de Al-Andalus**. Although some aspects of the museum are rather kitsch, it contains excellent models of the mezquita and Granada's Alhambra; some of the commentary in the sound-and-light display is interesting. Entry is 400 ptas.

Places to Stay

Most people look for lodgings in the area around the mezquita. Córdoba's ultra-modern youth hostel, *Albergue Juvenil Córdoba* (☎ 29 01 66), is perfectly positioned on Plaza de Judá Leví, has excellent facilities and no curfew. Beds are 1175 ptas for those under 26, 1500 ptas for others – there are also good deals on meals.

Hostal Martínez Rücker (☎ 47 25 62), Calle Mártinez Rücker 14, with singles/doubles from 1500/3500 ptas, is particularly

friendly and only a stone's throw from the mezquita. *Hostal Trinidad* (☎ 48 79 05), Corregidor Luis de la Cerda 58, is equally well placed and has rooms from 1400/2700 ptas. At Calle Cardenal González 25, *Hostal Santa Ana* (☎ 48 58 37) has one single at 1500 ptas and doubles at 3000 ptas, or 4500 ptas with bath.

For those with a little extra to spend, *Hostal El Triunfo* (☎ 47 55 00), Corrigedor Luis de la Cerda 79 by the mezquita, is a real treat. Comfortable singles/doubles/triples with air-con and TV cost 3500/5800/6900 ptas.

If you want to keep away from the tourist masses as much as possible, there are some good hostales further east. *Pensión San Francisco* (☎ 47 27 16), Calle de San Fernando 24, is good value with one small single at 1500 ptas and doubles from 3500 ptas. *Hostal La Fuente* (☎ 48 78 27), Calle de San Fernando 51, has compact singles at 1800 ptas and doubles with bath from 4500 ptas. The shower pressure is excellent! At Calle Romero Barroso 14, the friendly *Hostal Los Arcos* (☎ 48 56 43) has modern rooms from 2000/3500 ptas. Or, check to see if renovations are finished at *Hostal Plaza Corredera* (☎ 47 05 81), Calle Rodriguez Marín 15, off Plaza de la Corredera. The location is interesting and the price right for budget travellers.

Places to Eat

You shouldn't have too much trouble finding somewhere to eat in Córdoba. *Self-Service Los Patios*, right by the mezquita on Calle Cardenal Herrero, has a good choice of functional main courses and desserts with nothing over 600 ptas. The two restaurants in the city walls on Calle de la Luna, *Mesón de la Luna* and *Mesón la Muralla*, both have pretty courtyards and menús from 1200 to 1900 ptas.

For a first-class meal try *Restaurante Bandolero*, Calle de Torrijos 6 by the mezquita. It has platos combinados from 700 to 900 ptas; if you order à la carte expect to pay around 4000 ptas per person. *El Churrasco* in the Judería at Calle Almanzor Romero 16 is said to be Córdoba's best restaurant. The food is rich, service attentive and prices similar to the Bandolero.

If you'd rather try somewhere less touristy, *Taberna Sociedad de Plateros*, Calle San Francisco 6, is a popular local tavern with a good range of tapas and raciones to choose from. Likewise *Taberna Salinas* at Calle Tundidores 3 offers good, cheap, local fare.

There is an excellent market in Plaza de la Corredera, another part of town beyond the tourist precinct. The market opens from Monday to Saturday and gets going at around 9.30 am – Saturday is the busiest day. There are lots of good bakeries with pastries, cakes and bocadillos in both the old and new parts of town; try Calle Concepción off the south end of the Avenida del Gran Capitán pedestrian mall.

Entertainment

As you might expect, Córdoba has pretty good nightlife. Most of the action is in the new town, in the area around Plaza de las Tendillas. In particular, try Plaza San Miguel and Calle del Caño. The pubs and bars around Plaza Costa del Sol in Ciudad Jardín, a km or so west of Plaza Tendillas, are also popular. If you're getting peckish in the early hours, head for *Bar Piscolabi* or one of its neighbours in Calle Conde de Cárdenas, for some of the cheapest bocadillos in Spain to go with your drink.

Getting There & Away

Buses to cities around Andalucía leave from the Alsina Graells Sur bus station (☎ 23 64 74) at Avenida Medina Azahara 29-31. Long-distance buses to Barcelona and other cities on the Mediterranean coast, operated by Bacoma (☎ 45 65 14), also leave from this bus station. Buses to Madrid are run by Secorbus (☎ 46 80 40), Camino de los Sastres, on the corner of Avenida República Argentina some 600 metres north-west of the mezquita and behind the big Hotel Melia.

There are plenty of trains daily from Córdoba to Seville. Options range from AVEs (45 minutes, from 2100 ptas) to stopping trains (1¾ hours, 875 ptas). From Córdoba to Madrid, AVEs take 1¾ to two hours (from 5500 ptas) and the night train takes 6½ hours (3400 ptas). There are around eight trains to Bobadilla daily (875 to 1400 ptas). Most of them continue to Málaga (1300 to 2400 ptas). For Granada, you usually need to change trains at Bobadilla but connections are good (3¾ to 5½ hours, from 1700 ptas).

COSTA DE ALMERÍA

The Costa de Almería in south-east Andalucía, running from the Golfo de Almería round Cabo de Gata to the border of Murcia, is perhaps the last section of Spain's Mediterranean coast where you can have a beach completely to yourself. In high summer forget it, but this is Spain's hottest region, so even in late March it can be warm enough to take in some rays and try out your new swimsuit.

Orientation & Information

The most useful tourist offices are in Almería (☎ 27 43 55), San José (☎ 38 02 99) and Mojácar (☎ 47 51 62). Change money before going to Cabo de Gata as there are no banks there.

The telephone code for the region is ☎ 950.

Things to See & Do

The **Alcazaba**, an enormous 10th-century Moorish fortress, is the highlight of Almería city. In its heyday the city it dominated was more important than Granada. In the desert 25 km inland on the N-340 is **Mini-Hollywood** (☎ 36 52 36), where *A Fistful of Dollars* and other classic Westerns were shot. It's fun to drop in: the Western town set is preserved and shoot-outs are staged daily (entry 925 ptas). From Almería you can get there on a Tabernas bus.

The best thing about the region is the wonderful 50-km coastline and semidesert scenery of **Cabo de Gata**. All along the coast from Cabo de Gata village to Agua Amarga, some of the most beautiful and empty beaches on the Mediterranean alternate with precipitous cliffs and scattered villages. At Las Salinas, three km south of Cabo de Gata village, is a famous **flamingo colony**. The main village is laid-back **San José**, from where you can walk or drive to some of the best beaches such as **Playa Genoveses** and **Playa Monsul**. Some other beaches can only be reached on foot or by boat.

Mojácar, 30 km north of Agua Amarga, is a white town of Moorish origin, perched on a hill two km from the coast. Although a long resort strip, Mojácar Playa, has grown up below, Mojácar is still a very pretty place and it's not hard to spend some time here, especially if you fancy a livelier beach scene than Cabo de Gata offers.

SPAIN

Places to Stay & Eat

A good cheapie in Almería is *Hostal Universal* (☎ 23 55 57), in the centre at Puerta de Purchena 3, with singles/doubles for 1500/ 3000 ptas. *Restaurante Alfareros*, nearby at Calle Marcos 6, has a good three-course lunch and dinner menú for 900 ptas.

In high summer it's a good idea to ring ahead about accommodation on Cabo de Gata, as some places fill up. There are four camping grounds: *Camping Los Escullos* (☎ 38 98 11) and *Camping Las Negras* (☎ 52 52 37) are open year-round. San José's *albergue juvenil* (youth hostel; ☎ 38 03 53), on Calle Montemar, opens from late June to late September, plus holidays, and charges 1250 ptas. In San José village centre, *Fonda Costa Rica* has doubles with bath for 5000 ptas. *Hostal Bahía* (☎ 38 03 06) nearby on Calle Correo has lovely singles/doubles for 5000/7500 ptas. *Restaurante El Emigrante* across the road does good fish and meat dishes for 900 or 1000 ptas, and big salads and tortillas for 300 to 400 ptas. There's accommodation in other villages too.

In Mojácar, the cheaper places are mostly up in the town. *Pensión Casa Justa* (☎ 47 83 72), Calle Morote 7, is good value with rooms at 1500/3000 ptas, or 4000 ptas for doubles with bath. *Hostal La Esquinica* (☎ 47 50 09), nearby at Calle Cano 1, charges 1750/3500 ptas. *Pensión La Luna* (☎ 47 80 32), Calle Estación Nueva 15, is more comfortable with doubles at 5000 ptas and good meals available. *Restaurante El Viento del Desierto* on Plaza Frontón by the church is good value with main courses such as chicken kebabs or rabbit in mustard for 550 to 700 ptas. The only true budget place to stay down at the beach is *El Cantal* camping ground (☎ 47 82 04). *Antonella*, 1.5 km south, is popular for its pizzas and pasta for 600 to 1200 ptas.

Getting There & Away

Almería has an international and domestic airport and is accessible by bus and train from Madrid, Barcelona, Granada and Seville, and by bus from Málaga and Murcia. Buses run from Almería to Cabo de Gata village and (except on Sunday) to San José. Mojácar can be reached by bus from Almería, Murcia, Granada and Madrid.

MÁLAGA & THE COSTA DEL SOL

The Costa del Sol, a string of tightly packed high-rise resorts running south-west from Málaga towards Gibraltar, is geared for – and incredibly popular with – package-deal tourists from Britain and Germany and the time-share crowd. The main resorts are Torremolinos (which has acquired such a bad reputation that it has been dubbed 'Terrible Torre'), Fuengirola and Marbella. From Marbella onwards, you can see the Rif Mountains in Morocco on a clear day.

The telephone code for Málaga and the coast is ☎ 95.

Things to See & Do

The Costa del Sol pulls in the crowds because of its weather, beaches, warm Mediterranean water and cheap package deals. The resorts were once charming Spanish fishing villages, but that aspect has all but disappeared in most cases. If you're more interested in Spain than in foreign package tourists, **Málaga** itself is a better place to stop over. It has a bustling street life, a 16th-century cathedral and a Moorish palace/fortress, the Alcazaba, from which the walls of the Moorish castle, the Gibralfaro, climb to the top of the hill dominating the city.

Torremolinos and **Fuengirola** are a concrete continuum designed to squeeze as many paying customers as possible into the smallest possible area. You'll be surprised if you hear someone speak Spanish. **Marbella** is more inviting: its old town has managed to retain some of its original character and has a well-preserved 15th-century castle. **Puerto Banús**, four km west, is the only town on the Costa del Sol which could be called attractive. Consequently it's also exorbitant. Its harbour is often a port of call for yachts that moor in Monte Carlo at other times of the year. A lot of the money here is rumoured to be on the crooked side, but nobody asks any questions.

Probably the only reason to stay long on the Costa del Sol is to work. If you go about it the right way, you may get work on one of the yachts in Puerto Banús. Some young travellers make good money in Marbella, Fuengirola and Torremolinos, touting for time-share salespeople.

Places to Stay

In Málaga the friendly *Pensión Córdoba* (☎ 221 44 69), Calle Bolsa 9, has singles/

doubles at 1600/2800 ptas. The basic but clean *Hospedajes La Perla* (☎ 221 84 30), Calle Luis de Velázquez 5 (3rd floor), charges 1300/2600 ptas. Both are near the central Plaza de la Constitución.

Rooms down the coast are expensive in July, August and maybe September but prices usually come down sharply at other times from the levels given here. In Terrible Torre, *Hostal Prudencio* (☎ 238 14 52), Calle Carmen 43, at 2800/5600 ptas, is a stone's throw from the beach. *Hostal Guillot* (☎ 238 01 44), Calle Río Mundo 4, is nowhere near as pleasant, but has cheaper doubles at 3500 ptas.

At Fuengirola, the British-run *Pensión Coca* (☎ 247 41 89), Calle de la Cruz 3, has decent rooms at 2800/4800 ptas. *Pensión Andalucía* (☎ 246 33 30), Calle Troncón 59, has doubles only at 3300 ptas (4500 ptas in August). Both are just a short walk from the beach.

Marbella has an excellent modern HI *hostel* (☎ 277 14 91) at Calle Trapiche 2; rooms have just two or three beds and half have private bath. It's 1175 ptas for those under 26, and 1500 ptas for others. The British-run *Hostal del Pilar* (☎ 282 99 36), in the old town at Calle Mesoncillo 4, is popular with backpackers and charges 2000 ptas a person.

Places to Eat

Near the cathedral in Málaga, *Bar Restaurante Tormes*, Calle San Agustín 13 (closed Monday), and the slightly fancier *El Jardín* on Calle Cister both have good menús for 1100 ptas. For local flavour, sample fish dishes at outdoor tables at the reasonably priced marisquerías on Calle Comisario. In Torremolinos and Fuengirola, it's just a matter of going for a walk along the beachfront – you'll find plenty of places with menús for well under 1000 ptas.

In Marbella, *Bar El Gallo* at Calle Lobatos 44 in the old town does great-value burgers and fish and meat dishes for 325 to 475 ptas. *Restaurante Sol de Oro* on the seafront in front of the tourist office has a good menú for 925 ptas including wine.

Getting There & Away

Málaga is the main landing and launching pad for the Costa del Sol and its airport has a good range of domestic as well as international flights. Málaga is linked by train and bus to all major Spanish centres, including Madrid, Barcelona, Seville, Granada and Algeciras. Málaga's bus and train stations are round the corner from each other, one km west of the centre.

Getting Around

Trains run every half-hour from Málaga airport to the city centre and west to Torremolinos and Fuengirola. There are even more frequent buses from Málaga to Torremolinos, Fuengirola and Marbella.

RONDA

One of the prettiest and most historic towns in Andalucía, Ronda is a world apart from the nearby Costa del Sol. Straddling the savagely deep and steep El Tajo gorge, the town stands at the heart of some lovely hill country dotted with white villages and ripe for exploring.

The main tourist office (☎ 287 12 72) is at Plaza de España 1.

Ronda's telephone code is ☎ 95.

Things to See & Do

Ronda is a pleasure to wander around, but during the day you'll have to contend with bus loads of day-trippers up from the coast.

The **Plaza de Toros** (1785) is considered the home of bullfighting and is something of a mecca for aficionados; inside is the small but fascinating **Museo Taurino**. Entry to both is 225 ptas.

To cross the gorge to the originally Moorish old town, you have a choice of three bridges. The 18th-century **Puente Nuevo** (New Bridge) is an amazing feat of engineering and the views from here are great. The old town itself is littered with ancient churches, monuments and palaces. The **Palacio de Mondragón** houses a rather inconsequential museum, but is almost worth the 200 ptas entry (students 100 ptas) for the views alone. You can walk down into the gorge from nearby Plaza María Auxiliadora. Also of interest are **Santa María la Mayor**, a medieval church whose tower was once the minaret of a mosque, and the **Baños Arabes** (Arab Baths), also dating from the 13th century.

Places to Stay & Eat

Camping El Sur (☎ 287 59 39) is in a pleasant

SPAIN

setting two km south-west of town and has a swimming pool and restaurant.

Fonda La Española (☎ 287 10 52), in the street behind the main tourist office at Calle José Aparicio 3, has clean, basic singles/doubles from 1200/2400 ptas. The friendly *Pensión La Purisima* (☎ 287 10 50), Calle Sevilla 10, is also good value with rooms for 1500/3000 ptas.

There are several good places to eat on and just off Plaza del Socorro, a block west of the bullring. *El Molino* here has pizzas, pasta and platos combinados from 500 to 700 ptas, and tables outside. A few metres up Calle Lorenzo Borrego, *Pizzeria Michelangelo* is also good value; *Cervecería Patatín-Patatán* next door has great tapas.

Getting There & Away

There are several buses daily to Seville (2½ hours, 1235 ptas) and Málaga (two to three hours, 875 to 1100 ptas, some via the Costa del Sol), and one (except Sunday) to La Línea (Gibraltar) for 990 ptas. The bus station is on Plaza Concepción Garcia Redondo.

Daily trains go to Seville (three hours, 1650 ptas), Málaga (two to 2½ hours, 1080 ptas), Granada and Córdoba, mostly with a change at Bobadilla, and there are direct trains to Algeciras. The station is on Avenida de Andalucía.

Gibraltar

The British colony of Gibraltar occupies a huge lump of limestone, five km long and one km wide, at the mouth of the Mediterranean Sea. It's a curious and interesting port of call if you're in the region. Gibraltar has certainly had a rocky history; it was the bridgehead for the Moorish invasion of Spain in 711 AD and Castile didn't finally wrest it from the Moors until 1462. Then in 1704 an Anglo-Dutch fleet captured Gibraltar after a one-week siege. Spain gave up military attempts to regain it from Britain after the failure of the 3½-year Great Siege in 1779-83, but during the Franco period Gibraltar was an extremely sore point between Britain and Spain, and the border was closed for years.

Today Gibraltar is self-governing and depends on Britain only for defence. An overwhelming majority of Gibraltarians – many of whom are of Genoese or Jewish ancestry – want to remain with Britain.

Information

EU, US, Canada, Australia, New Zealand, Israel, South Africa and Singapore passport-holders are among those who do *not* need visas for Gibraltar, but anyone who needs a visa for Spain should have at least a double-entry Spanish visa if they intend to return to Spain from Gibraltar.

Gibraltar has helpful tourist offices at: the border; the Piazza, Main St (☎ 74982); and the Gibraltar Museum, 18-20 Bomb House Lane (☎ 74805). All are open Monday to Friday from 10 am to 6 pm, the last two are also open on Saturday from 10 am to 2 pm.

The currency is the Gibraltar pound or pound sterling. You can use pesetas but conversion rates aren't in your favour. Exchange rates for buying pesetas are, however, a bit better than in Spain. Change any unspent Gibraltar pounds before you leave.

To phone Gibraltar from Spain, the telephone code is ☎ 9567; from the UK dial ☎ 00, then ☎ 350 (the code for Gibraltar) and the local number.

Things to See & Do

Downtown Gibraltar is nothing very special – you could almost be in Bradford or Bletchley – but the **Gibraltar Museum**, 18-20 Bomb House Lane, has an interesting historical, architectural and military collection and includes a Moorish bathhouse. It's open the same hours as the tourist office. Entry is £2. Many graves in the **Trafalgar Cemetery** are of those who died at Gibraltar from wounds received in the Battle of Trafalgar (1805).

The large **Upper Rock Nature Reserve**, covering most of the upper rock, has spectacular views and several interesting spots to visit. It's open daily from 9.30 am to sunset. Entry, at £5 a person and £1.50 a vehicle, includes all the following sites, which are open to 6.15 pm. Cable-car tickets (see Getting Around later) include entry to the reserve, the Apes' Den and St Michael's Cave.

The rock's most famous inhabitants are its colony of **Barbary macaques**, the only wild

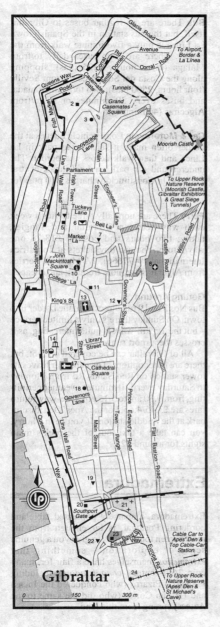

primates (apart from *Homo sapiens*) in Europe. Some of these hang around the **Apes' Den** near the middle cable-car station, others can often be seen at the top station or Great Siege Tunnels.

From the top cable-car station, there are views as far as Morocco in decent weather. **St Michael's Cave**, 20 minutes downhill walk south from here, is a big natural grotto renowned for its stalagmites and stalactites. Apart from attracting tourists in droves, it's used for concerts, plays and even fashion shows. The **Great Siege Tunnels**, 30 minutes walk north (downhill) from the top cable-car station, are a series of galleries in the rock hewn out by the British during the Great Siege to provide new gun emplacements. Worth a stop on the way down to the town from here are the **Gibraltar: a city under siege** exhibition and a **Moorish castle**.

Places to Stay

The *Emile Youth Hostel* (☎ 51106) at Montagu Bastion, Line Wall Rd, is a step up from Gibraltar's other budget options. It has 44 places in two to eight-person rooms for £10 including continental breakfast. The *Toc H Hostel* (☎ 73431), a ramshackle old place tucked into the city walls at the south end of Line Wall Road, has beds at £5 a night and cold showers. *Miss Seruya Guest House* (☎ 73220), 92/1A Irish Town (1st floor), has four very small and basic rooms and one shower. Singles/doubles cost from £8/12 to £16/18.

The *Queen's Hotel* (☎ 74000) at 1 Boyd St is in a different league, with a restaurant, bar, games room and singles/doubles at £16/24, or £20/36 with private bath or shower. Reduced rates of £14/20 and £16/24 are offered to students and young travellers. The *Cannon Hotel* (☎ 51711) at 9 Cannon Lane also has decent rooms, each sharing a bathroom with one other room, for £25 single or double.

There are some economical options in the Spanish border town La Línea. *Pensión La Perla* (☎ 95-76 95 13), Calle Clavel 10, has spacious pink-trimmed singles/doubles for 1700/3000 ptas.

Places to Eat
Most of the many pubs in town do pub meals with all sorts of British goodies on the menu. One of the best is *The Clipper* at 78B Irish Town, where a generous serve of fish and chips and a pint of beer will set you back £6. *Three Roses Bar* at 60 Governor's St does a huge all-day British breakfast for £2.80. At the popular *Piccadilly Gardens* pub on Rosia Rd you can sit in the garden and have a three-course lunch for £6. *Maxi Manger* on Main St is a good fast-food spot with burgers (including vegetarian) for £1.60 and calamari for £2.25.

If you fancy a restaurant meal, there's great Indian food at the *Viceroy of India*, 9-11 Horse Barrack Court, which has a three-course lunch special for £6.50. À la carte there are vegetarian dishes for £2 to £3 and main courses from £6 to £10. *The Piazza*, 156 Main St, does decent pizzas for £5 to £6, and fish and meat main courses from £5.50 to £8. *Minister's Restaurant*, 310 Main St, does good servings of fish and seafood for £3.50 to £4, or fish, meat or pasta with chips or salad from £5.

Getting There & Away
Air GB Airways (☎ 79300) flies daily to London for £99 one way. It also has flights to Morocco.

Bus There are no regular buses to Gibraltar itself, but the bus station in the Spanish town La Línea is only a five-minute walk from the border. There are four buses daily to/from Málaga (three hours, 1225 ptas), stopping along the Costa del Sol; three to/from Seville (four hours, 2500 ptas); two to/from Granada; and buses every 30 minutes or so to/from Algeciras (40 minutes).

Car & Motorcycle Long vehicle queues at the border often make it sensible to park in La Línea and then walk across the border. The underground car park on La Línea's central Plaza de la Constitución charges 810 ptas for 24 hours.

Ferry There are normally three ferries a week each way between Gibraltar and Tangier, taking two hours and costing £18/28 one way/return. You can buy tickets at Tourafrica International (☎ 77666), 2A Main St. Ferries from Algeciras are more frequent and cheaper.

Getting Around
Bus Nos 3 and 9 run direct from the border into town. On Sunday there's only a limited service – but the 1.5 km-walk is quite interesting, as it crosses the airport runway.

All of Gibraltar can be covered on foot, but there are other options. The cable car leaves its lower station on Red Sands Rd from Monday to Saturday every 10 minutes, weather permitting, from 9.30 am to 5.15 pm. One-way/return fares are £3.45/4.65. For the Apes' Den, disembark at the middle station. If you're in a hurry, you can take a taxi tour of the rock's main sights for around £25.

Extremadura

Extremadura, a sparsely populated tableland bordering Portugal, is far enough from the most beaten tourist trails to give you a genuine sense of exploration – something that *extremeños* themselves have a flair for: many epic 16th-century *conquistadores* including Francisco Pizarro (who conquered the Incas) and Hernán Cortés (who did the same to the Aztecs) sprang from this land.

Trujillo and Cáceres are the two not-to-be-missed old towns here, while a spot of hiking, or just relaxing, in the valleys of north-east Extremadura makes the perfect change from urban life. Elsewhere, Mérida has Spain's biggest collection of Roman ruins, and the Parque Natural de Monfragüe, famous for its birds of prey, is a great stop for drivers north of Trujillo. If you can, avoid June, July and August, when Extremadura is *very* hot.

The telephone code for all places in this section is ☎ 927.

TRUJILLO

With just 9000 people, Trujillo can't be much bigger now than in 1529, when its most famous son Francisco Pizarro set off with his three brothers and a few local buddies for an expedition that culminated in the bloody conquest of the Inca empire three years later. Trujillo is blessed with a broad and fine Plaza Mayor, from which rises its remarkably preserved old town, packed with aged buildings exuding history. If you approach from the Plasencia direction you might imagine that you've driven through a time warp into the 16th century. The tourist office (☎ 32 26 77) is on Plaza Mayor.

Things to See

A **statue of Pizarro**, done by an American, Charles Rumsey, in the 1920s, dominates the Plaza Mayor. On the plaza's south side, the **Palacio de la Conquista** (closed to visitors) sports the carved images of Francisco Pizarro and the Inca princess Inés Yupanqui. Their daughter Francisca lived in this house with her husband Hernando, the only Pizarro brother to return alive to Spain. Two noble mansions which you can visit are the 16th-century **Palacio de los Duques de San Carlos**, also on the Plaza Mayor, and the **Palacio de Orellana-Pizarro**, through the alley in the plaza's south-west corner.

Up the hill, the **Iglesia de Santa María la Mayor** is an interesting hotchpotch of 13th to 16th-century styles, with some fine paintings by Fernando Gallego of the Flemish school. Higher up, the **Casa-Museo de Pizarro** has informative displays (in Spanish) on the lives and adventures of the Pizarro family. At the top of the hill, Trujillo's **castillo** is an impressive though empty structure, primarily of Moorish origin.

Places to Stay & Eat

Cheap accommodation is in rather short supply. *Camas Boni* (☎ 32 16 04), about 100 metres east of Plaza Mayor at Calle Domingo Ramos 7, is good value with singles/doubles from 1500/3000 ptas and doubles with bath for 4000 ptas. *Casa Roque* (☎ 32 23 13), further along the street at No 30, is a second option, at 1500/3500 ptas. On Plaza Mayor at No 27, *Hostal Nuria* (☎ 32 09 07) has nice rooms with bath for 3000/5000 ptas. *Hostal La Cadena* (☎ 32 14 63) at No 8 is also good, with rooms for 4000/5000 ptas.

The menú at *Restaurante La Troya* on Plaza Mayor costs 1900 ptas, but if you're a meat-eater it will save you from eating much else for the next couple of days. Portions are gigantic and they also give you a large omelette and a salad for starters, and an extra main course later on! If you're not quite that hungry there are great tapas here too. Elsewhere on Plaza Mayor *Cafetería Nuria* has platos combinados for 750 to 900 ptas. *Café-Bar El Escudo* up the hill on Plaza Santiago is also moderately priced.

Getting There & Away

The bus station (☎ 32 12 02) is 500 metres south of Plaza Mayor, on Carretera de Badajoz. At least 12 buses daily run to Madrid (2000 ptas, 2½ to four hours), and seven or more run to Cáceres and Mérida. There's daily service to Salamanca, but only three buses a week to Parque Natural de Monfragüe and Plasencia.

CÁCERES

Cáceres is larger than Trujillo and has an even bigger old town, created in the 15th and 16th centuries and so perfectly preserved that it can seem lifeless at times – but if things seem a bit quiet, the student-led nightlife around Plaza Mayor, on the north-west side of the old town, more than makes up for that on weekends. The tourist office (☎ 24 63 47) is on Plaza Mayor.

Things to See

The old town is still surrounded by walls and towers raised by the Almohads in the 12th century. Entering it from Plaza Mayor, you'll see ahead the fine 15th-century **Iglesia de Santa María**, Cáceres' cathedral. Any time from February to September, Santa María's tower will be topped by the ungainly nests of

SPAIN

the large storks which make their homes on every worthwhile vertical protuberance in the old city.

Many of the old city's churches and imposing medieval mansions can only be admired from outside, but you *can* enter the good **Museo de Cáceres** on Plaza Veletas, housed in a 16th-century mansion built over a 12th-century Moorish cistern *(aljibe)* which is the museum's prize exhibit. It's open daily, except Monday, from 9 am to 2.30 pm (200 ptas). Also worth a look is the **Casa-Museo Árabe Yussuf Al-Borch** at Cuesta del Marqués 4, a private house decked out with oriental and Islamic trappings to capture the feel of Moorish times. The **Arco del Cristo** at the bottom of this street is a Roman gate.

Places to Stay
The best area to stay is around Plaza Mayor, though it gets noisy at weekends. *Pensión Márquez* (☎ 24 49 60), just off the low end of the plaza at Calle Gabriel y Galán 2, is a friendly family-run place with clean singles/doubles at 1250/2500 ptas. *Hostal Castilla* (☎ 24 44 04), one block west at Calle Ríos Verdes 3, has adequate rooms for 2000/4000 ptas. *Hotel Iberia* (☎ 24 82 00), off the top end of the plaza at Calle Pintores 2, is a step up with characterful singles/doubles for 4000/5000 ptas including private bath, TV and air-con or heating.

Places to Eat
If you're hungry, Cáceres has another *Restaurante La Troya* on the same lines as the one in Trujillo, at Calle Juan XXIII 1, a 1.5-km walk south from Plaza Mayor.

On Plaza Mayor at No 9, the popular *Cafetería El Puchero* has a huge range of options from good bocadillos (around 300 ptas) and all sorts of raciones to sizeable platos combinados (675 to 900 ptas) and à la carte fare. *Cafetería El Pato*, a block down the arcade, has an upstairs restaurant with a good menú for 1285 ptas.

Cafetería Lux at Calle Pintores 32, off the high end of Plaza Mayor, does basic platos combinados from 375 to 650 ptas.

Getting There & Away
The bus and train stations are both a little over two km south-west of Plaza Mayor, more or less opposite each other. Bus No L-1 from the stop beside the petrol station by the big roundabout outside the train station will take you into town.

There are at least seven buses daily to Madrid (3½ to 4¼ hours, 2385 ptas) via Trujillo, and a handful each day to Mérida, Seville, Salamanca and points beyond.

Five trains a day go to Madrid (3½ to five hours, from 2200 ptas). If you're heading for Portugal, the daily train to Lisbon (six hours, from 4400 ptas) leaves in the middle of the night (3 am). One train a day, except Sunday, goes to Seville, and three a day go to Mérida and Plasencia.

NORTH-EAST EXTREMADURA
From Plasencia, the green, almost Eden-like valleys of La Vera, Valle del Jerte and Valle del Ambroz stretch north-east into the Sierra de Gredos and its western extensions. Watered by rushing mountain streams called *gargantas*, and dotted with medieval villages, these valleys offer some excellent walking routes and attract just enough visitors to provide a good network of places to stay.

Information
The Editorial Alpina booklet *Valle del Jerte, Valle del Ambroz, La Vera* (600 ptas) includes a 1:50,000 map of the area showing walking routes. Try to get it from a map or book shop before you come: if not, the tourist office in Cabezuela del Valle may have copies.

There are tourist offices at Plasencia (☎ 42 21 59), Jaraiz de la Vera (☎ 46 00 24), Jarandilla de la Vera (☎ 56 04 60) and Cabezuela del Valle (☎ 47 21 22). Most sizeable villages have banks.

Things to See & Do
La Vera About halfway up the valley, **Cuacos de Yuste** has its share of narrow village streets with half-timbered houses leaning at odd angles, their overhanging upper storeys supported by timber or stone pillars. Two km north-west up a side road is the **Monasterio de Yuste**, to which in 1555 Carlos I, once the world's most powerful man, retreated for his dying years. The simple royal chambers and the monastery church are open Monday to Saturday from 9.30 am to 12.30 pm and 3.30 to 6 pm and on Sundays and holidays from 9.30

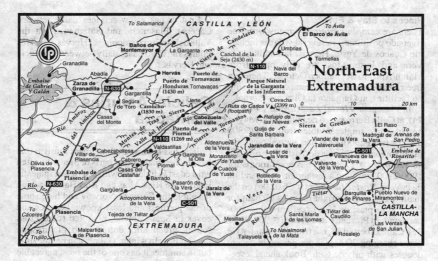

North-East Extremadura

to 11.30 am, 1 to 1.30 pm and 3.30 to 6 pm.) Entry is 100 ptas.

The road continues past the monastery to **Garganta la Olla**, another typically picturesque village, from where you can head over the 1269-metre **Puerto del Piornal** pass into the Valle del Jerte.

Jarandilla de la Vera is a bigger village, with a 15th-century fortress-church on the main square (below the main road), and a parador occupying a castle-palace where Carlos I stayed while Yuste was being readied for him. The tourist office beside the church has a basic leaflet suggesting some good walks from Jarandilla. Of the longer hikes, the Ruta de Carlos V (see Valle del Jerte) is the most enticing. If you want to do it in reverse, ask for directions at Camping Jaranda.

Valle del Jerte This valley grows half of Spain's cherries and turns into a sea of white at blossom time in April. **Piornal**, high on the south flank, is a good base for walks along the Sierra de Tormantos. In the bottom of the valley, **Cabezuela del Valle** has a particularly medieval main street. A 35-km road crosses from just north of here over the 1430-metre Puerto de Honduras pass to Hervás in the Valle del Ambroz. For hikers, the PR-10 trail climbs roughly parallel, to the south. From **Jerte** you can walk into the beautiful **Parque Natural de la Garganta de los Infiernos**.

Tornavacas, near the head of the valley, is the starting point of the **Ruta de Carlos V**, a 28-km marked trail following the route by which Carlos I (who was also Carlos V of the Holy Roman Empire) was carried over the mountains to Jarandilla on the way to Yuste. It can be walked in one long day – just as Carlos' bearers did it back then.

Valle del Ambroz Towards the head of the valley **Hervás**, a pleasant small town, has the best surviving 15th-century Barrio Judío (Jewish quarter) in Extremadura, where many Jews took refuge in hope of avoiding the Inquisition. About 22 km west by paved roads across the valley, **Granadilla** is a picturesque old fortified village that was abandoned after the Embalse de Gabriel y Galán reservoir almost surrounded it in the 1960s. Now it's restored as an educational centre and you can visit, free, from 10 am to 1 pm and 5 to 7 pm daily, except Saturday morning, Sunday afternoon and from 15 December to 30 January.

SPAIN

Places to Stay & Eat

There are *camping grounds* – many with fine riverside positions – in several villages including Cuacos de Yuste, Hervás, Jarandilla de la Vera and Jerte. Most are only open from March/April to September/October. There are free *zonas de acampada*, camping areas with no facilities, at Garganta la Olla and Piornal.

In Plasencia, *Hostal La Muralla* (☎ 41 38 74), at Calle Berrozana 6 near the Plaza Mayor, has adequate singles/doubles from 1500/2800 ptas, or from 2900/3000 ptas with shower. On the main road in Cuacos de Yuste, *Pensión Sol de Vettonia* (☎ 17 22 41) has good rooms for 1900/2700 ptas, and a restaurant. In Jarandilla de la Vera, *Hostal Jaranda* (☎ 56 02 06) on the main road has big, bright rooms with bath for 2675/5350 ptas, and an excellent-value 800-pta menú. In Piornal, *Casa Verde* (☎ 908-92 19 72), Calle Libertad 38, is a friendly hostel-style place charging 2000 ptas per person in decent doubles with private bath. Book ahead, especially in spring. *Pensión Los Piornos* (☎ 47 60 55) on Plaza de las Eras, has plain singles/doubles for 2000/2500 ptas.

In Cabezuela del Valle, the good *Hotel Aljama* (☎ 47 22 91), Calle Federico Bajo s/n, has nice modern rooms for 2500/4500 ptas. There are numerous places to eat and drink on nearby Calle El Hondón. *Hostal Puerto de Tornavacas* (☎ 47 01 01), a couple of km up the N-110 from Tornavacas, is a country inn-style place with rooms 2500/4600 ptas.

The only rooms in Hervás are at the dull *Hostal Sinagoga* (☎ 48 11 91), outside the town centre at Avenida de la Provincia 2, for 2500/5000 ptas with bath and TV.

Getting There & Away

Your own wheels are a big help but if you do use the buses, you can at least walk over the mountains without worrying about how to get back to your vehicle! The following bus services run Monday to Friday, with a much reduced service on weekends. Mirat (☎ 42 36 43) runs three or four Plasencia-Madrid buses daily along La Vera, and one from Cáceres to La Vera. Doaldi (☎ 17 03 59) and La Sepulvedana (☎ 91-530 48 00) also run Madrid-La Vera services.

León Álvarez runs four daily buses from Plasencia up the Valle del Jerte to Tornavacas, and one to Piornal.

Enatcar has a few services daily between Cáceres, Plasencia and Salamanca via the Valle del Ambroz, stopping at Hervás. Los Tres Pilares runs two buses daily between Plasencia and Hervás.

Galicia, Asturias & Cantabria

Galicia has been spared the mass tourism that has reached many other parts of Spain. Its often wild coast is indented with a series of majestic inlets – the Rías Altas and Rías Bajas – which resemble the fjords of Norway and hide some of the prettiest and least known beaches and coves in Spain. Inland, potholed roads cross rolling green hills dotted with picturesque farmhouses. In winter, Galicia can be freezing, but in summer it has one of the most agreeable climates in Europe – though you must expect a little rain.

Highlights of the Asturias and Cantabria regions, east of Galicia, are the wonderful cave paintings at Altamira and the Picos de Europa mountains.

SANTIAGO DE COMPOSTELA

This beautiful small city is the end of the Camino de Santiago, a collective name for several major medieval pilgrim routes from as far away as France, still followed by plenty of faithful today. Thanks to its university, Santiago is a lively city almost any time, but is at its most festive around 25 July, the Feast of Santiago (St James). Its tourist office (☎ 58 40 81) at Rúa do Vilar 43 is open from 10 am to 2 pm and 4 to 7 pm daily.

The city's telephone code is ☎ 981.

Things to See & Do

The goal of the Camino de Santiago is the **catedral** on magnificent **Praza do Obradoiro**. Under the main altar lies the supposed tomb of Santiago Apóstol (St James the Apostle). It's believed the saint's remains were buried here in the 1st century AD and rediscovered in 813, after which he grew into the patron saint of the Christian Reconquista, and his tomb attracted streams of pilgrims from all over western Europe. The cathedral is a superb

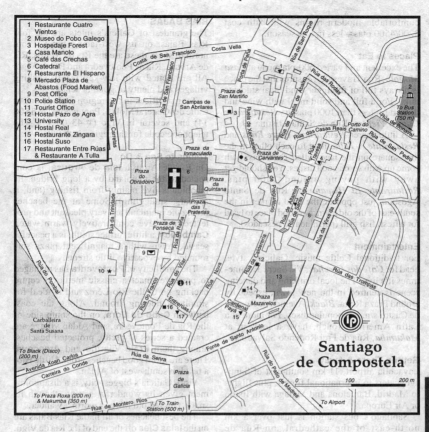

1 Restaurante Cuatro
   Vientos
2 Museo do Pobo Galego
3 Hospedaje Forest
4 Casa Manolo
5 Café das Crechas
6 Catedral
7 Restaurante El Hispano
8 Mercado Plaza de
   Abastos (Food Market)
9 Post Office
10 Police Station
11 Tourist Office
12 Hostal Pazo de Agra
13 University
14 Hostal Real
15 Restaurante Zingara
16 Hostal Suso
17 Restaurante Entre Rúas
   & Restaurante A Tulla

Santiago
de Compostela

Romanesque creation of the 11th to 13th centuries, with later decorative flourishes, and its masterpiece is the Pórtico de la Gloria inside the west façade.

Santiago's compact old town is a work of art, and a walk around the cathedral will take you through some of its most inviting squares. It's also good to stroll in the beautifully landscaped **Carballeira de Santa Susana** park south-west of the cathedral. Just north-east of the old city, off Porta do Camino, an impressive old convent houses the **Museo do Pobo Galego**, covering Galician life from fishing through music and crafts to traditional costume (open Monday to Saturday, free).

Places to Stay

Santiago is jammed with cheap pensiones, but many are full with students. A quiet and cheap central option with decent rooms is **Hospedaje Forest** (☎ 57 08 11), Callejón de Don Abril Ares 7, where singles/doubles start at 1300/2400 ptas. **Hostal Real** (☎ 56 66 56), Rúa da Caldererthe 49, has good-sized rooms for 2000/3000 ptas. The attractive **Hostal Pazo de Agra** (☎ 58 90 45), Rúa da Caldererthe 37, is a spotlessly kept old house with rooms for 2000/3000 ptas, or 3000/4500 ptas with private bath. Enquire at Restaurante Zingara, Rúa de Cardenal Payá. The popular little **Hostal Suso** (☎ 58 66 11), Rúa do Vilar 65, has amiable hosts;

SPAIN

comfortable modern rooms with bath cost 3200/4500 ptas – less in low season.

Places to Eat

The excellent and varied 600-pta menú at *Casa Manolo*, Rúa Travesa 27, ensures that the place is always full of foreigners and local students alike. For a full and solid meal with wine and dessert for less than 1000 ptas, try *Restaurante Cuatro Vientos*, Rúa de Santa Cristina 19.

A little dearer, *Restaurante Entre Rúas* and *Restaurante A Tulla*, next to each other in the tiny square on the lane called Entrerúas, both come up with some good dishes. You should get away with paying around 1500 ptas. *Restaurante El Hispano* on Rúa de Santo Agostiño, just opposite the food market in the south-east of the old town, is a good place to head for a fresh fish grill (parrillada de pescados).

Entertainment

For traditional Celtic music, Galician style, head for *Café das Crechas*, Via Sacra 3. Sometimes it's live. The local drinking and dancing scene is centred in the new town, especially around Praza Roxa. *Black*, Avenida de Rosalía de Castro s/n, is a popular disco. For more of a Latin American touch, have a look in at *Makumba*, Rúa de Frei Rodendo Salvado 16.

Getting There & Away

Lavacolla airport, 11 km south-east of Santiago, caters to international flights, plus flights to Madrid, Barcelona and Málaga with Iberia or Air Europa.

Santiago's bus station is just over a km north-east of the cathedral, on Rúa de Rodriguez Viguri. City bus No 10 runs to Praza de Galicia, on the south edge of the old town. Buses leave hourly to Vigo (900 ptas), via Pontevedra, and north to La Coruña (775 ptas), and there are regular buses to Salamanca, Madrid, Barcelona and Cáceres. Buses to Porto take five hours and cost 1800 ptas; there are two a week in winter, six a week in summer.

The train station is 600 metres south of the old town at the end of Rúa do Horreo. Bus Nos 6 and 9 from near the station go to Praza de Galicia. Up to four trains a day run to Madrid (eight to 11 hours, from 5000 ptas), and frequent trains head to La Coruña (1½ hours, 450 ptas), Pontevedra (one hour, 450 ptas) and Vigo.

RÍAS BAJAS

The grandest of Galicia's inlets are the four Rías Bajas, on its west-facing coast. From north to south these are the Ría de Muros, Ría de Arousa, Ría de Pontevedra and Ría de Vigo. All are dotted with low-key resorts, fishing villages and plenty of good beaches.

Tourist offices in the region include one at Calle del General Mola 3, Pontevedra (☎ 85 08 14) and several in Vigo (☎ 43 05 77). The telephone code for the region is ☎ 986.

Things to See & Do

On Ría de Arousa, **Isla de Arousa**, is connected to the mainland by a long bridge. Its inhabitants live mainly from fishing (and, it appears, smuggling). Some of the beaches facing the mainland are very pleasant and protected and have comparatively warm water. **Cambados**, a little further south, is a peaceful seaside town with a magnificent plaza surrounded by evocative little streets.

The small city of **Pontevedra** has managed to preserve intact a classic medieval centre backing on to the Río Lérez and is ideal for simply wandering around. Along the coast between **Cabo de Udra**, on the south side of the Ría de Pontevedra, and Aldán village are cradled a series of pretty, protected beaches, among them **Praia Vilariño** and **Areacova**. There are more good beaches around little **Hío**, a few km south-west of Aldán.

Vigo, Galicia's biggest city, is a disappointment given its wonderful setting, though its small, tangled old town is worth a wander.

The best beaches of all in the Rías Bajas are on the **Islas Cíes** off the end of the Ría de Vigo. Of the three islands, one is off limits for conservation reasons. The other two, Isla del Faro and Isla de Monte Agudo, are linked by a white sandy crescent – together forming a nine-km breakwater in the Atlantic. You can only visit the islands from mid-June to the end of September, and numbers are strictly limited. A return boat ticket from Vigo costs 1700 ptas: the frequency of services depends largely on the weather.

Places to Stay & Eat

A couple of *camping grounds* open in summer on Isla de Arousa. In Cambados, *Hostal Pazos Feijoo* (☎ 54 28 10), Calle de Curros Enriquez 1, near the waterfront in the newer part of town, has singles/doubles for 2500/4000 ptas. The *Café-Bar* on Rúa Caracol does reasonable seafood meals for about 1000 ptas.

In the old town in Pontevedra, *Hospedaje Penelas* (☎ 85 57 05) at Rúa Alta 17 has small but decent rooms for 2000/3000 ptas, and *Casa Alicia* (☎ 85 70 79), Avenida Santa María 5, has homely doubles for 2500 to 3000 ptas. You can eat cheaply on Calle de San Nicolás at *Casa Fidel O' Pulpeiro* at No 7, *Bar Barrantes* at No 6, or *O' Noso Bar* at No 5.

Hostal Stop (☎ 32 94 75) in Hío has rooms for as little as 1000/2000 ptas in winter, but more like 3000/5000 ptas in summer.

In Vigo, *Hostal Madrid* (☎ 22 55 23), Rúa de Alfonso XIII 63, near the train station, has doubles for 1800 ptas, or 2500 ptas with shower. Not too far away, *Hostal Krishna* (☎ 22 81 61), Rúa de Urzaiz 57, has modern singles/doubles for 2000/3000 ptas. Old Vigo is laced with tapas bars and eateries of all descriptions. *Patio Gallego* at Rúa dos Cesteiros 7, off Praza da Constitución, has a decent set lunch for 1000 ptas.

Camping is the only option if you want to stay on the Islas Cíes: you must book the camp site (520 ptas per person and per tent) at the office in the estación marítima in Vigo – places are limited. You can then organise a round-trip boat ticket for the days you require.

Getting There & Away
Pontevedra and Vigo are the area's transport hubs, with a reasonable network of local buses fanning out from them. Both are well served by buses and trains from Santiago de Compostela and La Coruña, and Vigo has services from more distant places like Madrid and Barcelona, as well as Aviaco flights from those cities. Three trains a day run from Vigo to Porto in Portugal (3½ hours).

LA CORUÑA
La Coruña (A Coruña in Galician), Galicia's capital, is an attractive port city with decent beaches and a wonderful seafront promenade, the Paseo Marítimo. The older part of town, the **Ciudad Vieja**, is huddled on the headland east of the port, while the most famous attraction, the **Torre de Hércules** lighthouse, originally built by the Romans (open daily from 10 am to 7 pm), caps the headland's northern end. The north side of the isthmus joining the headland

to the mainland is lined with sandy **beaches**, more of which stretch along the 30-km sweep of coast west of the city.

La Coruña's telephone code is ☎ 981.

Places to Stay & Eat
Calle de Riego de Agua, a block back from the waterfront Avenida de la Marina on the southern side of the isthmus, is a good spot to look for lodgings. *Hospedaje María Pita* (☎ 22 11 87) at No 38 (3rd floor), is good value with basic singles/doubles for 1200/1800 ptas. *Hostal Roma* (☎ 22 80 75), nearby at Rúa Nueva 3, offers basic doubles for 2100 ptas.

Calle de la Franja, the street behind Hospedaje María Pita, has several good places to eat. *Casa Jesusa* at No 8 offers a tasty seafood set lunch for 1000 ptas. You may have to queue for *O' Calexo* at No 34, but there's a good reason: the great fish grill (parrillada de pescado) for 2500 ptas for two.

Getting There & Away
There are daily trains and buses to Santiago de Compostela, Vigo, Santander, León, Madrid and Barcelona.

RÍAS ALTAS
North-east of La Coruña stretches the alternately pretty and awesome coast called the Rías Altas. This has some of the most dramatic scenery in Spain, and beaches that in good weather are every bit as inviting as those on the better known Rías Bajas. Spots to head for include the medieval towns **Betanzos, Pontedeume** and **Viveiro** (all with budget accommodation), the tremendous cliffs of **Cabo Ortegal** and the **beaches** between it and Viveiro. Buses from La Coruña and Santiago de Compostela will get you into the area – after that you'll need local buses and the occasional walk or lift.

PICOS DE EUROPA
This small mountainous region straddling Asturias, Cantabria and Castilla y León is some of the finest walking country in Spain. Spectacular scenery, combined with unique flora and fauna, ensures a continual flow of visitors from all over Europe and beyond.

The Picos are 25 km from the coast, and only around 40 km long and 40 km wide. They are comprised of three limestone massifs. In the south-east is the Andara Massif, with a summit of 2441 metres, and in the west is the Cornión Massif, with a summit of 2596 metres. In the centre is the best known and largest, the Uriello Massif, soaring to 2648 metres.

Books & Maps

Serious trekkers would be well advised to buy a copy of Lonely Planet's *Trekking in Spain*. If you want to buy detailed topographical maps of the area before coming to Spain, Edward Stanford, 12-14 Long Acre, London WC2E 9LP, can send you a list of those available. Try getting hold of the *Mapa Excursionista del Macizo Central de los Picos de Europa* by Miguel Andrade (1:25,000) and *Mapa del Macizo del Cornión* by José Ramón Lueje (1:25,000).

Things to See & Do

Serious trekkers should allow plenty of time for the Picos. If you're not quite that adventurous, perhaps the least strenuous way to get a feel for the area is to drive up to **Lago La Ercina** from Covadonga in the west of the Picos or to **Sotres** in the east. From either of these places you can set out on well-marked walking trails into the heart of the mountains.

Places to Stay & Eat

In a remote, beautiful setting off the road to Lago La Ercina, *Refugio de Enol* (☎ 98-584 85 76) is a simple stone building with bunk beds at 500 ptas (BYO sleeping bag) and good meals. In Sotres, *Pensión Los Picos* (☎ 98-594 50 24), also called Pensión Cipriano, is both the place to stay and the place to eat. Bunk beds cost 900 ptas, doubles range from 3000 to 4000 ptas and there is a menú for 1000 ptas. *Hostal Remoña* (☎ 942-73 66 05) in Espinama has singles/doubles from 2500/3500 ptas and a good menú for 950 ptas. The main access towns – Cangas de Onís, Arenas de Cabrales and Potes – all have a wide range of hostales.

Getting There & Away

The Picos are encircled by a ring road, from which three main routes lead into the heart of the mountains: from Cangas de Onís to Covadonga and Lago La Ercina; from Arenas de Cabrales to Sotres; and from Potes to Fuente Dé.

There are bus services from Santander, León, Oviedo and Gijón to the three main access towns, plus regular buses from Potes to Fuente Dé, and from Cangas de Onís to Covadonga and (in summer only) Lago La Ercina.

SANTANDER

Santander, capital of Cantabria, is a modern, cosmopolitan city with wide waterfront boulevards, leafy parks and crowded beaches. Semana Grande in August is a pretty wild party, but you won't find any accommodation here, or anywhere else on the north coast at that time, without booking well in advance.

The main tourist office (☎ 31 07 08) is in the estación marítima (ferry terminal); there's also a municipal tourist office (☎ 21 61 20) in the harbour-front Jardines de Pereda.

The telephone code for Santander is ☎ 942.

Things to See & Do

Santander's main attractions are the nightlife (see Entertainment later) and El Sardinero beach. As you come round to El Sardinero on bus No 1 or 2, you may notice an uncanny resemblance to Bondi Beach in Australia, with surfers out in force by mid-March, despite the cold. The streets back from the sea near El Sardinero are lined with beautiful houses. This is some of Spain's most expensive real estate.

Places to Stay

Camping Bellavista (☎ 27 48 43), on Cabo Mayor, is less than one km north of El Sardinero beach. From the centre, take bus No 9 (marked 'Cueto'), which stops 200 metres from the site – ask the driver where to get off.

Rooms are expensive in high summer, but the rates given here come down substantially from October to May. *Fonda Perla de Cuba* (☎ 21 00 41), Calle Hernán Cortés 8 (1st floor), is one of the better deals in town, with singles/doubles at 2000/4000 ptas. *Pensión La Corza* (☎ 21 29 50), down the same street at No 25 (3rd floor), has pleasant doubles for 5500 ptas. *Pensión Picos de Europa* (☎ 22 53 74), very near the bus station at Calle Calderón de la Barca 5 (3rd floor), is a cosy house with singles for around 2500 ptas and doubles with private shower for 4500 ptas.

If you have just arrived on the ferry from England, you might be looking for a little more luxury. *Hotel México* (☎ 21 24 50) at Calle

Calderón de la Barca 3 is a good bet. Featuring a collection of impressive paintings by the owners' son, it has singles/doubles with all mod cons for 5550/10,165 ptas.

Places to Eat

A good area for cheap eats is around Plaza Cañadio, three blocks back from the municipal tourist office. On the plaza itself the stylish *Restaurante Cañadio* serves first-class seafood and local specialities, with a lunch menú for 1550 ptas.

Just off the plaza, Calle Daoiz y Velarde has lots of options including *Mesón el Portón* at No 29 with a simple 850-pta lunch menú, and the *Bierhaus* at No 27 serving Spanish and German food. Also on this street are Tex-Mex and Chinese places and the old *Bodega Cigalaña* wine bar with good seafood.

Entertainment

Nightlife in Santander is centred around Calle Santa Lucía and is particularly good between Calle Santa Lucía and the waterfront. In summer, there is also quite a good scene in El Sardinero along the main drag.

Getting There & Away

Santander is one of the major entry points to Spain, thanks to its ferry link with Plymouth in England (see Getting There & Away at the start of this chapter).

The ferry terminal and train and bus stations are all in the centre of Santander, within 200 metres of each other. There are hourly buses to Bilbao (two hours, 875 ptas), five a day to San Sebastián (three hours, 1800 ptas), and two a day to La Coruña (10 hours, 5000 ptas) and Santiago de Compostela (11 hours, 5200 ptas).

Trains to Bilbao (one to three daily, 2½ hours, 855 ptas) and Oviedo are run by FEVE, a private line which does not accept rail passes. Trains to Madrid (via Ávila) and Galicia are run by RENFE, so rail passes are valid. To Madrid there are three trains daily (5½ to nine hours, from 3550 ptas). Trains to La Coruña and Santiago de Compostela follow a roundabout route taking 13 hours or more, with changes at Palencia or Medina del Campo, and cost from 7100 ptas.

SANTILLANA DEL MAR

The beautiful village of Santillana del Mar, 30 km west of Santander, has a wonderful feeling of timelessness. Cobbled streets lined with well-preserved old houses give it a character all its own. When it rains, water pours off the overhanging roofs in a torrent, somehow adding to the unusual charm of the town.

The telephone code for Santillana is ☎ 942.

Things to See & Do

Santillana's fame lies as much in the **Cueva de Altamira**, two km west, as in the town itself. The 14,000-year-old animal paintings in the Altamira cave reduce many people to tears, and all those lucky enough to gain entry are deeply moved by what they see. A maximum of 20 people a day are allowed into the cave and if you want to be one of them, you must ask permission at least a year in advance, listing three or four preferred dates, by writing to: Centro de Investigación Altamira, 39330 Santillana del Mar, Cantabria, Spain. If you're one of the lucky ones, admission is 400 ptas. Some people turn up on the day in the hope that someone has cancelled and they can get lucky. There's a small museum, open to all, at the cave; its hours are Tuesday to Sunday from 9.30 am to 2.30 pm.

Places to Stay & Eat

The good *Camping Santillana* (☎ 81 82 50), about 500 metres west of town on the main highway, charges around 500 ptas per person, 500 ptas per tent and 500 ptas per car.

In the old town, the best place to stay is *Posada Octavio* (☎ 81 81 99) at Plaza Las Arenas 4, run by the friendly González family. In summer, singles cost 3000 to 3500 ptas and doubles are 4500 to 5000 ptas. Most of the other places in the old town are considerably dearer, but there are plenty of options along the highway to the east, among them *Hostal Montañes* (☎ 81 8177) at Calle Le Dorat 8, with singles/doubles at 3500/5000 ptas in summer. Restaurants here tend to be expensive. A couple of exceptions are *Casa Cossío*, Plaza Abad Francisco Navarro 12, which does good seafood and has a menú for 950 ptas, and *Restaurant Altamira*, at Calle del Cartón 1, with a reliable lunch menú for 1100 ptas.

Getting There & Away

There are four buses a day (six in summer) between Santander and Santillana del Mar.

País Vasco, Navarra & Aragón

The Basque people have lived for thousands of years in Spain's País Vasco (Basque Country, or Euskadi in the Basque language) and the adjoining Pays Basque across the border in France. They have their own ancient language (Euskara), a distinct physical appearance, a rich culture and a proud history. Along with this strong sense of identity has come, among a significant minority of Basques in Spain, a desire for independence. The Basque nationalist movement was born in the 19th century. During the Franco years the Basque people were brutally repressed and Euskadi ta Askatasuna (ETA), a radical separatist movement, began its terrorist activities. With Spain's changeover to democracy in the late 1970s, the País Vasco was granted a large degree of autonomy, but ETA has continued to pursue full independence with terrorist tactics.

While ETA terrorism is still a deterrent to tourism, the País Vasco remains one of the most beautiful regions of Spain. Although the Bilbao area is heavily industrialised, the region has a spectacular coastline, a green and mountainous interior and the elegance of San Sebastián. Another great reason to visit is to sample the delights of Basque cuisine, considered the best in Spain.

South-east of the País Vasco, the Navarra and Aragón regions reach down from the Pyrenees into drier, more southern lands. Navarra has a high Basque population and its capital is Pamplona, home of the Sanfermines festival with its world-famous running of the bulls. The Aragonese Pyrenees offer the best range of opportunities for walking and skiing on the Spanish side of this mountain range. Head for the Parque Nacional de Ordesa for the best walking (the park entrance is at Torla) but note – especially in the peak Spanish holiday period, mid-July to mid-August – that a maximum 1500 visitors are allowed into the park at any time. Weatherwise the best months up there are late June to mid-September. Aragón has half a dozen decent ski resorts – the regional tourist office in Zaragoza has plenty of information about them.

SAN SEBASTIÁN

San Sebastián (Donostia in Basque) is stunning. Famed as a ritzy resort for wealthy Spaniards who want to get away from the hordes in the south, it has also been a stronghold of Basque nationalist feeling since well before Franco. The surprisingly relaxed town, of 180,000 people, curves round the beautiful Bahía de la Concha. Those who live here consider themselves the luckiest people in Spain, and after spending a few days on the beaches in preparation for the wild evenings, you may well begin to understand why.

Information

The very helpful municipal tourist office (☎ 48 11 66) is on the corner of Paseo de la República Argentina and Calle Reina Regente. From June to September it's open daily from 8 am to 8 pm (Sunday from 10 am to 1 pm); otherwise it's open weekdays from 9 am to 2 pm and 3.30 to 7 pm, and Saturday from 9 am to 2 pm. There's also a Basque regional tourist office (☎ 42 62 82) at Paseo de los Fueros 1.

The main post office is on Calle Urdaneta, behind the cathedral. The telephone code for San Sebastián is ☎ 943.

Lavomatique, in the Parte Vieja (old town) at Calle de Iñigo 14, is a rarity in Spain – a good self-service laundrette.

Things to See

The **Playa de la Concha** and **Playa de Ondarreta** make up one of the most beautiful city beaches in Spain. You can get out to **Isla de Santa Clara**, in the middle of the bay, by boat from the port – but it's more exciting to swim. In summer, rafts are anchored about halfway from Ondarreta to the island to serve as rest stops.

If you intend to spend your evenings as the locals do, you won't be up to much more than sitting on the beach during the day. However, there is some worthwhile sightseeing to be done in and around San Sebastián.

The **Museo de San Telmo**, in a 16th-century monastery on Plaza de Zuloaga, has a bit of everything – ancient tombstones, agriculture and carpentry displays, a good art collection – and the squeakiest floors in Spain. It's open Tuesday to Saturday from 10.30 am to 1.30 pm and 4 to 7.30 pm and is free.

Overlooking Bahía de la Concha from the

SPAIN

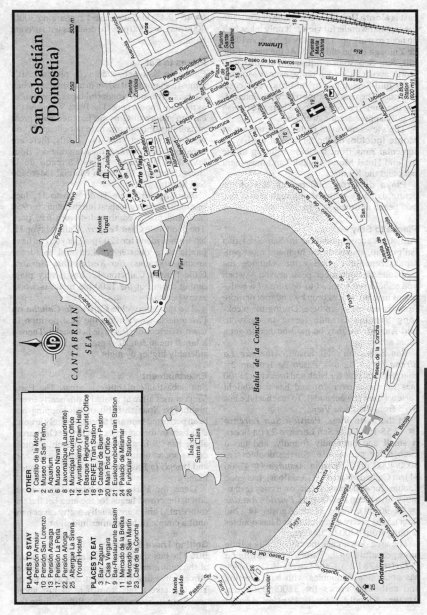

San Sebastián (Donostia)

CANTABRIAN SEA

Bahía de la Concha

Isla de Santa Clara

Monte Urgull

Monte Igueldo

Ondarreta

Gros

Urumea

Río

Puente Santa Catalina

Puente María Cristina

Puente Zurriola

Parte Vieja

Paseo Nuevo

Paseo República Argentina

Paseo de los Fueros

Plaza de España

To Bus Station (600 m)

PLACES TO STAY
4 Pensión Amaiur
10 Pensión San Lorenzo
13 Pensión Arsuaga
17 Pensión La Peña
22 Pensión Ahorga
25 Albergue La Sirena (Youth Hostel)

PLACES TO EAT
3 Bar Zaguan
7 Casa Vergara
9 Bar-Restaurante Basarri
11 Mercado de la Brexa
16 Mercado San Martín
23 Café de la Concha

OTHER
1 Castillo de la Mota
2 Museo de San Telmo
5 Aquarium
6 Museo Naval
8 Lavomatique (Laundrette)
12 Municipal Tourist Office
14 Ayuntamiento (Town Hall)
15 Basque Regional Tourist Office
18 RENFE Train Station
19 Catedral de Buen Pastor
20 Main Post Office
21 Euskotrenbideak Train Station
24 Palacio de Miramar
26 Funicular Station

east is **Monte Urgull**, with a statue of Christ on the top and wonderful views. It only takes half an hour to walk up: a stairway starts from Plaza de Zuloaga in the old town. At the base of the hill, San Sebastián's **aquarium** is also well worth a visit. It's open daily, except Monday from mid-September to mid-May and costs 450 ptas. The nearby **Museo Naval** is interesting too, and free, but you need to read Spanish to fully appreciate the displays.

The views are even better from the top of **Monte Igueldo**, on the far side of the bay. A funicular runs from the base right up to the top-end Hotel Monte Igueldo, an amusement park and the Ku disco.

Playa de Gros, 500 metres east of the centre, is badly polluted although it is a fine surf beach at times.

Places to Stay

Although accommodation in San Sebastián isn't cheap, standards are high and most pensiones represent good value. Outside the mid-June to September peak season – when you should book ahead to be sure of a bed – prices in many places drop by a quarter or more from the levels given here. During the week-long Semana Grande fiesta in early to mid-August you may be hard-pushed to get a room at all.

San Sebastián's HI hostel, *Albergue La Sirena* (☎ 31 02 68), Paseo de Igueldo 25, charges 1500 ptas for bunk and breakfast (1700 ptas for those over 26) and has a midnight curfew (2 am at weekends). To reach it take bus No 5 from the Parte Vieja.

In the Parte Vieja, *Pensión San Lorenzo* (☎ 42 55 16), Calle San Lorenzo 2 (1st floor), is small and eminently friendly, and has a kitchen for guests' use. Singles/doubles are 3000/4000 ptas. *Pensión Arsuaga* (☎ 42 06 81), at Calle de Narrika 3 (3rd floor), has good doubles for 4000 ptas, and its own cosy restaurant with a menú for 900 ptas. *Pensión Amaiur* (☎ 42 96 54), Calle 31 de Agosto 44 (2nd floor), is as pretty as a picture and has doubles ranging from 4300 to 5500 ptas.

The area down near the cathedral is a little more peaceful than the Parte Vieja. *Pensión La Perla* (☎ 42 81 23), Calle Loyola 10 (1st floor), has great singles/doubles with bath, heating and cathedral views for 3200/5350 ptas. Another friendly place is *Pensión Añorga*

(☎ 46 79 45) at Calle Easo 12, charging 3000/4000 ptas, or 5000 ptas for doubles with private bath.

Places to Eat

Eating in San Sebastián is a pleasure. It's almost a shame to sit down in a restaurant when the bars have such wonderful tapas, or pinchos, as they are known here. The Parte Vieja and the eastern suburb of Gros are jammed with great restaurants, though most are not cheap. If you want to construct your own meals, there are excellent *food markets* on Alameda del Boulevard in the Parte Vieja (Mercado de la Bretxa), and on Calle San Marcial (Mercado San Martín).

Bar Zaguan, Calle 31 de Agosto 31, does one of the town's cheapest lunch menús for 950 ptas, and platos combinados from 650 ptas. The good little *Casa Vergara*, Calle Mayor 21, has a lunch menú for 1200 ptas, or you can have paella or a quarter-chicken and salad for around 800 ptas. *Bar-Restaurante Basarri*, Calle Fermín Calbetón 17, has a very plain dining room but the 1200-pta menú is worth every peseta.

The incredibly chic *Café de la Concha* on Paseo de la Concha has the best position in town, overlooking Playa de la Concha. There's a lunch menú for 1050 ptas – prices are considerably higher by night.

Entertainment

San Sebastián's nightlife is great. The Parte Vieja comes alive at around 8 pm nearly every night. The Spanish habit of bar-hopping has been perfected here and there are surely around 200 bars in the compact old town. One street alone has 28 in a 300-metre stretch! Typical drinks are a zurrito (a very small, cheap beer) and txacolí (a Basque wine, not to everyone's liking).

Once the Parte Vieja begins to quieten down, the crowd heads for the area behind the cathedral. Things are usually pretty quiet here until a couple of hours after midnight.

Getting There & Away

Bus The bus station is 20 minutes walk south of the centre on Plaza de Pio XII, with ticket offices spreading along the streets to its north. You can take a bus from here to just about anywhere in Spain. Buses to Bilbao along the autopista go every half-hour, take a little over an hour and cost 1030 ptas. You can also go via Zarauz and the coast which takes about three hours. The bus to Pamplona takes over two hours and costs 750 ptas.

Train The RENFE train station is across the river on Paseo de Francia, on a line linking Paris with Madrid. There are six trains a day to Madrid (six to 8½ hours, from 4600 ptas), and two to Barcelona (nine to 10½ hours, from 4600 ptas) via Pamplona and Zaragoza. To Paris (six to eight hours, from 10,500 ptas), there's one direct train a day and several others with a change at Hendaye. Other destinations include Salamanca, La Coruña and Algeciras.

Trains to Bilbao, and some to Hendaye, are run by a private company, Euskotrenbideak, from a separate station on Calle de Easo.

COSTA VASCA
Spain's often ruggedly beautiful Costa Vasca (Basque Coast) is one of its least touristed coastal regions. A combination of cool weather, rough seas and terrorism tends to put some people off.

Things to See & Do
Between the French border and San Sebastián, **Fuenterrabia** (Hondarribia) is a picturesque fishing town with good beaches nearby, while **Pasajes de San Juan** (Pasaia Donibane) has a pretty old section and some good-value fish restaurants.

West of San Sebastián, the coast extends to Bilbao, passing through some of the finest **surfing** territory in Europe. Keep your wet suit handy though, as the water here can be pretty chilly. **Zarauz** (Zarautz), about 15 km west of San Sebastián, stages a round of the World Surfing Championship each September, when all the big names turn up for one of Europe's greatest surfing spectacles. Slightly west, the picturesque village of **Guetaria** (Getaria) has a small beach, but the main attraction is just in wandering around the narrow streets and the fishing harbour.

Mundaca (Mundaka), 12 km north of Guernica (Gernika), is a surfing town. For much of the year, surfers and beach bums hang around waiting for the almost legendary 'left-hander' to break. When it does, it's one of the longest and best lefts you'll ever see! If you're interested in renting a surfboard or stocking up on Aussie surf gear, ask the locals to direct you to Craig's shop (Craig is an Australian who came here to surf some years ago and never managed to leave).

In Bilbao, the showpiece (when it opens in 1997) will be the **Museo Guggenheim de Arte Contemporáneo**, in a new waterfront building that looks for all the world like a huge scrap-metal yard seen through the eyes of someone on a strong dose of LSD. Inside will be art by Picasso, Dalí, Miró, Matisse, Pollock and other 20th-century greats. On a more old-fashioned note, the excellent **Museo de Bellas Artes** in Parque de Doña Casilda de Iturriza has works by El Greco, Velázquez and Goya, and an important collection of Basque art.

Places to Stay & Eat
San Sebastián and Bilbao are the most obvious bases for excursions along the Basque coast. In Bilbao you might try *Hostal Jofra* (☎ 94-421 29 49), at Calle Elcano 34, which has singles/doubles from 1700/3000 ptas.

In the smaller towns the easiest and cheapest option is generally camping. *Camping Talai-Mendi* (☎ 943-83 00 42) in Zarauz is 500 metres from the beach and signposted from the highway on the east side of town; it's open from July to mid-September only. Guetaria is well known for its excellent seafood and has a couple of harbourside restaurants where you can watch the fishing boats unload.

In Mundaca, *Camping Portuondo* (☎ 94-687 63 68) is on the riverfront about one km south of town, on the road to Guernica. For food, you will be pretty much limited to sandwiches or do-it-yourself fare, as anything else is prohibitively expensive. There is an excellent *food market* in nearby Bermeo (west of Mundaca).

Getting Around
The coastal road is best explored by car. If you don't have your own transport, there are buses from San Sebastián to Zarauz and Guetaria, and from Bilbao to Guernica. From Guernica you can take a bus to Bermeo which will drop you in Mundaca. Hitching can be painfully slow.

PAMPLONA

The madcap festivities of Sanfermines in Pamplona (Iruñea in Basque) run from 6 to 14 July and are characterised by nonstop partying, out-of-control drunkenness and, of course, the bulls being set free in the streets of the old town. Every year there are injuries, and occasionally deaths, as the frenzied crowd runs through the streets in front of, behind and around the bulls. Inevitably, someone always gets a little too close, with predictably gory consequences.

The safest place to watch the running (*encierro*) is on TV. If this is too tame for you, see if you can sweet-talk your way on to a balcony in one of the streets where the bulls run. You might have to pay, but it is well worth the cost if you can afford it. The other places to watch from are Plaza Santo Domingo where the action begins, or near the entrance to the bullring. The bulls are let out at 8 am, but if you want to get a good vantage point you will have to be there around 6 am.

If you visit at any other time of year, you'll find a very pleasant and modern city, with lovely parks and gardens, a compact and partly walled old town, and a large proportion of students among the population of 185,000. The tourist office (☎ 22 07 41) is just south of the old town at Calle Duque de Ahumada 3.

Pamplona's telephone code is ☎ 948.

Places to Stay & Eat

The nearest camping ground is *Camping Ezcaba* (☎ 33 03 15), seven km north of the city. To get there, take an Arre or Oricain bus from Calle Teovaldos near the bullring. The camping ground fills up a couple of days before Sanfermines.

If you want to stay in a pensión or hostal during Sanfermines, you'll need to book well in advance (and pay a substantial premium). During the festival, beds are also available in private houses (casas particulares) – check with the tourist office or haggle with the locals at the bus and train stations. Otherwise, you'll have to do what everyone else does and sleep in one of the parks, plazas or shopping malls. You can leave your bags for 200 ptas in the consigna at the bus station. Alternatively, you could make day trips here from San Sebastián or other towns.

Fonda La Montañesa (☎ 22 43 80), Calle San Gregorio 2, has clean and basic singles/doubles for 1300/2600 ptas. *Pensión Casa García* (☎ 22 38 93), along the street at No 12, is a little better at 1400/2700 ptas.

The best way to eat cheaply in Pamplona is to fill up on tapas. There are some good places on Calle San Lorenzo; *Lanzale* at No 31 and *El Erburo* at No 19 have menús for 1000 and 1200 ptas respectively.

Getting There & Away

The bus station is on Avenida de Yanguas y Miranda, a five-minute walk south of the old town. There are up to 12 buses a day to San Sebastián (2½ hours, 700 ptas) and daily services to Madrid, Zaragoza and Bilbao.

The train station is about two km north-west of the old town. There are daily trains to San Sebastián (2½ hours, 1200 ptas), Zaragoza and Barcelona.

ZARAGOZA

Zaragoza, capital of Aragón and home to half its 1.2 million people, is often said to be the most Spanish city of all. Once an important Roman city, under the name Caesaraugusta, and later a Muslim centre for four centuries, it is today relatively untouched by tourism. The old town is full of lively bars and restaurants, and Aragonese cooking is good.

Information

The city tourist office (☎ 20 12 00) is in a surreal-looking glass cube on Plaza del Pilar. From Monday to Saturday, it's open from 9.30 am to 1.30 pm and from 4.30 to 7.30 pm; on Sunday it's open from 10 am to 2 pm. There's also a regional tourist office (☎ 39 35 37) in the Torreón de la Zuda, a Mudéjar tower on Plaza Cesar Augusto.

The post office is at Paseo de la Independencia 33. The telephone code for Zaragoza is ☎ 976.

Things to See

Zaragoza's focus is the vast 500-metre-long main square, **Plaza de Nuestra Señora del Pilar**. Dominating the north side is the **Basílica de Nuestra Señora del Pilar**, a 17th-century church of epic proportions. People flock to kiss a piece of marble pillar – believed to have been left by the Virgin Mary when she appeared to Santiago (St James) in a vision here in AD 40

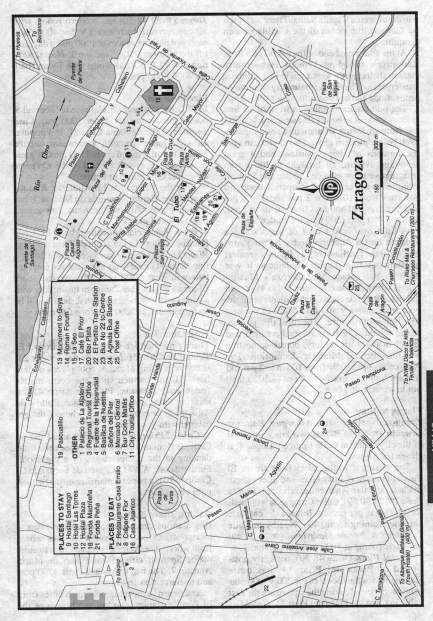

PLACES TO STAY
9   Hostal Santiago
10 Hotel Las Torres
12 Hostal Plaza
18 Fonda Madrileña
21 Fonda Peña

PLACES TO EAT
2   Restaurante Casa Emilio
8   Crêperie Flor
16 Casa Juanico

19 Pascualillo

OTHER
1   Palacio de La Aljafería
3   Regional Tourist Office
4   Fuente de la Hispanidad
5   Basílica de Nuestra,
      Señora del Pilar
6   Mercado Central
7   Bar Corto Maltés
11 City Tourist Office

13 Monument to Goya
14 Roman Forum
15 La Seo
17 Café El Prior
20 Bar Plata
23 El Portillo Train Station
23 Bus No 22 to Centre
24 Agreda Bus Station
25 Post Office

Río Ebro

Puente de Piedra

Puente de Santiago

Plaza del Pilar

Plaza César Augusto

Plaza San Felipe

Plaza Santa Cruz

El Tubo

Plaza de España

Plaza de la Independencia

Plaza del Carmen

Plaza de San Miguel

Plaza de Aragón

Plaza de Toros

Zaragoza

To Huesca

To Barcelona

To Madrid

To Risko Mar & Churrasco Restaurante (300 m)

To KVM Disco (2 km), Teruel & Valencia

To Albergue Baltasar Gracián (Youth Hostel)

SPAIN

300 m

150

– in the church's Capilla Santa. There's a fresco by Goya in the dome of the Capilla de San Joaquín.

At the south-east end of the plaza is **La Seo**, Zaragoza's brooding 12th to 16th-century cathedral. Its north-west façade is a Mudéjar masterpiece. The inside is undergoing major renovations and has been closed for some time.

The odd trapezoid thing in front of La Seo is the outside of a remarkable structure housing the **Roman forum** of ancient Caesaraugusta. Well below modern ground level you can visit the remains of shops, porticos and a great sewerage system, all brought to life by an imaginative show of slides, music and Spanish commentary. The forum is open Tuesday to Saturday from 10 am to 2 pm and 5 to 8 pm and Sundays and holidays from 10 am to 2 pm. Entry is 400 ptas (200 ptas for students).

A little over a km west of the plaza, the **Palacio de La Aljafería**, today housing Aragón's *cortes* (parliament), is Spain's greatest Muslim building outside Andalucía. It was built as the palace of Zaragoza's Muslim rulers, who held the city from 714 to 1118, and the inner Patio de Santa Isabel displays all the geometric mastery and fine detail of the best Muslim architecture. The upstairs palace, added by the Christian rulers Fernando and Isabel in the 15th century, boasts some fine Muslim-inspired Mudéjar decoration. The Aljafería is open daily from 10 am to 2 pm and (except Sunday) from 4 to 8 pm (4.30 to 6.30 pm in winter). It's free.

Places to Stay
Zaragoza's HI hostel, *Albergue Baltásar Gracián* (☎ 55 13 87), is two km south-west of the city centre at Calle Franco y López 4. It closes for August.

The cheapest rooms elsewhere are in El Tubo, the maze of busy lanes and alleys south of Plaza del Pilar. An excellent choice is *Fonda Peña* (☎ 29 90 89), Calle Cinegio 3, with beds for 1100 ptas per person. It has a decent little comedor (dining room) too. Nearby at Calle Estébanes 4, *Fonda Madrileña* (☎ 29 81 49) has basic rooms at 1000 ptas per person. *Hostal Plaza* (☎ 29 48 30), perfectly positioned at Plaza del Pilar 14, has quite reasonable singles/doubles for 2000/3000 ptas – the rooms overlooking the square are the best value in town. At Plaza del Pilar 11, *Hotel Las Torres* (☎ 39 42 50) has modern rooms with air-con, private bath and TV for 4000/6500 ptas, and parking spaces at 1000 ptas a day. Just off the plaza at Calle Santiago 3, *Hostal Santiago* (☎ 39 45 50) has rooms with TV and bath for 3000/4000 ptas.

Places to Eat
In El Tubo, *Pascualillo*, Calle de la Libertad 5, does a good menú for under 1000 ptas. *Casa Juanico*, Calle de Santa Cruz 21, is a popular old-style tapas bar with a comedor out the back. The solid menú costs 1100 ptas. A great dessert of crêpes can be had in the *Crêperie Flor*, just off Plaza San Felipe.

Near the Palacio de La Aljafería, *Restaurante Casa Emilio*, Avenida de Madrid 5, is a simple place with wholesome, low-priced home-cooked meals.

For a higher class of eating, head for Calle Francisco Vitoria, a km south of Plaza del Pilar. *Risko Mar*, Calle de Francisco Vitoria 16, is a fine fish restaurant – an excellent set meal for two will cost 5000 ptas. Across the road, *Churrasco* is another Zaragoza institution, with a wide variety of meat and fish dishes. You'll be up for as much as 3000 ptas for a full meal.

Entertainment
There's no shortage of bars in and around El Tubo. *Bar Corto Maltés*, Calle del Temple 23, is one of a string of rather cool places on this lane. All the barmen sport the corto maltés (sideburns). *Chastón*, Plaza de Ariño 4, is a relaxing little jazz club. *Bar Plata*, Calle 4 de Agosto, is a bar cantante, where you get cabaret with your drinks.

Café El Prior, near Plaza de Santa Cruz on Calle de Contamina, is a good place for a little dancing in the earlier stages of a night out. Further south, *KWM* at Paseo de Fernando El Católico 70 is a popular mainstream disco open until about 5 am.

Getting There & Away
Bus stations are scattered all over town – tourist offices can tell you what goes where from where. The Agreda company runs to most major Spanish cities from Paseo de María Agustín 7. The trip to Madrid costs 1750 ptas and to Barcelona 1640 ptas.

Trains run to most main Spanish cities from El Portillo station, one km south-west of the centre on Calle José Anselmo Clave, linked by bus No 22 to Plaza de España in the centre. Up to 14 trains daily run to both Madrid (three to 4½ hours, from 2600 ptas) and Barcelona (3½ to 4½ hours, from 3000 ptas). Some Barcelona trains go via Tarragona. There are two trains a day to Valencia (six hours, from 2200 ptas) via Teruel, and two to San Sebastián (four or 5½ hours, from 2400 ptas), with a stop in Pamplona.

TERUEL
Aragón's hilly deep south is culturally closer to Castilla-La Mancha or the backlands of Valencia than to some other regions of Aragón itself. A good stop on the way to the coast from Zaragoza, or from Cuenca in Castilla-La Mancha, is the town of Teruel, which has a flavour all its own thanks to four centuries of Muslim domination in the middle ages and some famous Mudéjar architecture dating from after its capture by the Christians in 1171.

The tourist office (☎ 60 22 79) is at Calle Tomás Nogués 1.

Teruel's telephone code is ☎ 978.

Things to See
Teruel has four magnificent Mudéjar towers, on the cathedral of **Santa María** (12th and 13th centuries) and the churches of **San Salvador** (13th century), **San Martín** and **San Pedro** (both 14th century). These, and the ceiling inside Santa María, are among Spain's best Mudéjar architecture. Note the complicated brickwork and colourful tiles on the towers, so typical of the style. A further example of Mudéjar work is **La Escalinata**, the flight of stairs leading down to the train station from Paseo del Óvalo, on the edge of the old town.

The **Museo Provincial de Teruel** on Plaza Padre Polanco is well worth a visit, mainly for its fascinating, well-presented archaeological collection going back to the days of *Homo erectus*. Entry is free; hours are Tuesday to Friday from 10 am to 2 pm and 4 to 7 pm, and weekends from 10 am to 2 pm.

Places to Stay & Eat
Fonda El Tozal (☎ 60 10 22) at Calle Rincón 5 is great value. It's an amazing rickety old house run by a wonderful, friendly family, and most of the rooms have cast-iron beds, enamelled chamber pots and exposed ceiling beams. Singles/doubles cost 1300/2500 ptas. In winter, you might prefer *Hostal Aragón* (☎ 60 13 87), Calle Santa María 4, which is also charming but has mod cons such as heating. Rooms are 1620/2750 ptas, or 2775/4450 ptas with private bath. Both these places are just a couple of minutes walk from the main square, Plaza Carlos Caste.

Teruel is famed for its jamón. If you can't fit a whole leg of ham in your backpack, at least sample a tostada con jamón, with tomato and olive oil. At *Bar Gregori*, Paseo del Óvalo 6, you can choose from a tasty range of tapas, or raciones from 400 to 900 ptas. *Bar El Torreón* at Ronda de Ambeles 28, in one of the turrets of what were the city walls, offers a filling lunch menú for 800 ptas.

Getting There & Away
The bus station (☎ 60 20 04) is on Ronda de Ambeles. There are daily buses to Barcelona (six hours, 3000 ptas), Cuenca (2¾ hours, 1050 ptas), Valencia (2½ hours, 1050 ptas) and Madrid (4½ hours, 2215 ptas).

By rail, Teruel is about midway between Valencia and Zaragoza, with three trains a day to both places, taking just under three hours and costing around 1100 ptas.

To get to the old town, walk out of the train station, take a deep breath, and start climbing the stairway in front of you.

SPAIN

Switzerland

Switzerland (Schweiz, Suisse, Svizzera, Svizzra) offers its fair share of clichés – irresistible chocolates, kitsch cuckoo clocks, yodelling Heidis, humourless bankers – but plenty of surprises, too. The visitor will find a flavour of Germany, France and Italy, but always seasoned with a unique Swissness.

Goethe described Switzerland as a combination of 'the colossal and the well-ordered', a succinct reference to the indomitable and majestic Alpine terrain set against the tidy, efficient, watch-precision towns and cities. The combination of these elements provides a peerless attraction. Unfortunately, high costs may prompt you to rush through the whole landscape faster than you would like.

Facts about the Country

HISTORY

The first inhabitants of the region were a Celtic tribe, the Helvetii. The Romans appeared on the scene in 107 BC by way of the Great St Bernard Pass, but owing to the difficulty of the terrain their attempted conquest of the area was never decisive. They were gradually driven back by the Germanic Alemanni tribe which settled in the region in the 5th century. Burgundians and Franks also settled the area, and Christianity was gradually introduced.

The territory was united under the Holy Roman Empire in 1032 but central control was never very tight, allowing neighbouring nobles to contest each other for local influence. That was all changed by the Germanic Habsburg family, which became the most powerful dynasty in central Europe. Habsburg expansion was spearheaded by Rudolph I, who gradually brought the squabbling nobles to heel.

The Swiss Confederation

Upon Rudolph's death in 1291, local leaders saw a chance to gain independence. The forest communities of Uri, Schwyz and Nidwalden formed an alliance on 1 August 1291. Their pact of mutual assistance is seen as the origin of the Swiss Confederation, and their struggles against the Habsburgs is idealised in the familiar legend of William Tell. Duke Leopold responded by dispatching a powerful Austrian army in 1315 which was routed by the Swiss at Morgarten. The effective action of the union soon prompted other communities to join. Lucerne (1332) was followed by Zürich (1351), Glarus and Zug (1352), and Bern (1353). Further defeats of the Habsburgs followed at Sempach (1386) and Näfels (1388).

Encouraged by these successes, the Swiss gradually acquired a taste for territorial expansion. Further land was seized from the Habsburgs. They took on Charles the Bold, the Duke of Burgundy, and defeated him at Grandson and Morat. Fribourg, Solothurn, Basel, Schaffhausen and Appenzell joined the Confederation, and the Swiss gained independence from Holy Roman Emperor Maximilian I after their victory at Dornach in 1499. Finally the Swiss over-reached themselves. They took on a superior force of French and Venetians at

Switzerland
(Schweiz)
(Suisse)
(Svizzera)
(Svizra)

Marignano in 1515 and lost. The defeat prompted them to withdraw from the international scene. Realising they could no longer compete against larger powers with better equipment, they renounced expansionist policies and declared their neutrality. Even so, Swiss mercenaries continued to serve in other armies for centuries to come, and earned an unrivalled reputation for skill and courage.

The Reformation in the 16th century caused upheaval throughout Europe. The Protestant teachings of Luther, Zwingli and Calvin spread quickly, although the inaugural cantons remained Catholic. This caused internal unrest that dragged on for centuries, but the Swiss did at least manage to avoid international disputes. At the end of the Thirty Years' War in 1648 they were recognised in the Treaty of Westphalia as a neutral state. Switzerland was free to prosper as a financial and intellectual centre.

The French Republic invaded Switzerland in 1798 and established the Helvetic Republic. The Swiss vehemently resisted such centralised control, causing Napoleon to restore the former confederation of cantons in 1803. Yet France retained overall jurisdiction. Further cantons also joined the Confederation: Aargau, St Gallen, Graubünden, Ticino, Thurgau and Vaud. Napoleon was finally sent packing following his defeat by the British and Prussians at Waterloo. The ensuing Congress of Vienna guaranteed Switzerland's independence and permanent neutrality, as well as adding the cantons of Valais, Geneva and Neuchâtel.

The Modern State

Throughout the gradual move towards one nation, each canton remained fiercely independent, even to the extent of controlling its own coinage and postal services. They lost these powers in 1848 when a new federal constitution was agreed upon (revised in 1874), which is largely still in place today. Bern was established as the capital and the Federal Assembly was set up to take care of national issues. The cantons retained legislative (Grand Council) and executive (States Council) powers to deal with local matters.

Having achieved political stability, Switzerland was able to concentrate on economic and social matters. Relatively poor in mineral resources, it developed industries predomi-

nantly dependent on highly skilled labour. A network of railways and roads was built, opening up previously inaccessible regions of the Alps and helping the development of tourism. The international Red Cross was founded in Geneva in 1863 by Henri Dunant, and compulsory free education was introduced.

The Swiss have carefully guarded their neutrality in the 20th century. Their only involvement in WWI lay in the organising of Red Cross units. Switzerland joined the League of Nations after peace was won, under the proviso that its involvement would be purely financial and economic rather than entailing any possible military sanctions. Despite some accidental bombing, WWII also left Switzerland largely unscathed, and its territory proved to be a safe haven for escaping Allied prisoners.

While the rest of Europe underwent the painful process of rebuilding from the ravages of war, Switzerland was able to expand from an already powerful commercial, financial and industrial base. Zürich developed as an international banking and insurance centre. Many international bodies, such as the World Health Organisation (WHO), based their headquarters in Geneva. Agreements between workers and employers were struck, under which industrial weapons such as strikes and lockouts were renounced. Social reforms were also introduced, such as old-age pensions in 1948.

Afraid that its neutrality would be compromised, Switzerland declined to become a member of the United Nations (though it currently has 'observer' status, ie it gives money but doesn't have a vote) or the North Atlantic Treaty Organisation (NATO). It did, however, join the European Free Trade Association (EFTA). In the face of other EFTA nations applying for European Union (EU, then known as the European Community) membership, Switzerland finally made its own application in 1992. As a prelude to full EU membership Switzerland was to join the EEA (European Economic Area), yet the government's strategy lay in ruins after citizens rejected the EEA in a referendum in December 1992. Switzerland's EU application has consequently been put on ice; in the meantime the government has been laying the groundwork for closer integration with the EU, in the hope that the people will eventually come round.

Defence

Despite its long-standing neutrality, Switzerland maintains a 400,000-strong civilian army. Every able-bodied male undergoes national service at age 20 and stays in the reserves for 22 years, all the while keeping his rifle and full kit at home. In addition, a whole infrastructure is in place to repel any invasion, including the planned destruction of key roads and bridges. All new buildings must have a substantial airraid capacity, and underground car parks can be instantly converted to bunkers. Fully equipped emergency hospitals, unused yet maintained, await underneath ordinary hospitals. It's a sobering thought, as you explore the countryside, to realise that those apparently undisturbed mountains and lakes hide a network of military installations and storage depots. Potential invaders would be well advised not to mess with the Swiss.

GEOGRAPHY & ECOLOGY

Mountains make up 70% of Switzerland's 41,285 sq km. The land is 45% meadow and pasture, 24% forest and 6% arable. Farming of cultivated land is intensive and cows graze on the upper slopes in the summer as soon as the retreating snow line permits.

The Alps occupy the central and southern regions of the country. The Dufour summit (4634 metres) of Monte Rosa is the highest point, although the Matterhorn (4478 metres) is more well known. A series of high passes in the south provide overland access into Italy. Glaciers account for an area of 2000 sq km, most notably the Aletsch Glacier which at 169 sq km is the largest valley glacier in Europe.

The St Gotthard Massif in the centre of Switzerland is the source of many lakes and rivers, such as the Rhine and the Rhône. The Jura Mountains straddle the northern border with France. These mountains peak at around 1700 metres and are less steep and less severely eroded than the Alps.

Between the two mountain systems is the Mittelland, also known as the Swiss Plateau, a region of hills crisscrossed by rivers, ravines and winding valleys. This area has spawned the most populous cities and is also where much of the agricultural activity takes place.

Switzerland has long been an environmentally aware nation. Citizens diligently recycle household waste and cities encourage the use of public rather than private transport. The policy in the mountains is to contain rather than expand existing resorts.

GOVERNMENT & POLITICS

The modern Swiss Confederation is made up of 23 cantons; three are subdivided, bringing the total to 26. Each has its own constitution and legislative body for dealing with local issues. The Jura achieved full cantonal status as late as 1979.

National legislative power is in the hands of the Federal Assembly which consists of two chambers. The lower chamber, the National Council, has 200 members, elected by proportional representation. The upper chamber, the States Council, is composed of 46 members, two per full canton. The Federal Assembly elects seven members to form the Federal Council, which holds executive power. All elections are for a four-year term except the posts of president and vice-president of the Confederation, which are rotated annually. The vice-president always succeeds the president, meaning the governing body is not dominated by any one individual.

Under the 1874 constitution, Swiss citizens enjoy direct democracy: 50,000 signatories are needed to force a full referendum on proposed laws, and 100,000 to initiate legislation. Citizens regularly vote in referenda on national, local and communal issues. Yet surprisingly, women only won the right to vote in federal elections in 1971, and it was 1991 before women gained a cantonal vote in Appenzell. Appenzell is one of the few cantons which still votes by a show of hands in an open-air parliament called the *Landsgemeinde*.

ECONOMY

Switzerland has a mixed economy with the emphasis on private ownership. The only industries nationalised outright are telecommunications, post and the federal railway. Other than municipal enterprises, everything else is in private hands and operates according to capitalist principles, with the occasional subsidy thrown in. A good proportion of the wealth generated is returned to the community via social welfare programmes. The system is efficient (though price-fixing cartels are a problem); even so, Switzerland is not immune from world recession.

Unemployment, previously virtually unknown, has crept to over 4%. Inflation is expected to keep below 2% in 1997.

In the absence of other raw materials, hydroelectric power has become the main source of energy. Chemicals, machine tools and watches and clocks are the most important exports. Silks and embroidery, also important, are produced to a high quality. Swiss banks are a magnet for foreign funds attracted by political and monetary stability. Tourism, although recently dented by the strong Swiss franc, is still the country's third-biggest industry and the well-established infrastructure makes life easy for visitors (it's especially easy to spend too much money!). Swiss breakthroughs in science and industry include vitamins, DDT, gas turbines and milk chocolate. They also, for their sins, developed the modern formula for life insurance.

POPULATION & PEOPLE

With a population of seven million, Switzerland averages 169 inhabitants per sq km. The Alpine districts are sparsely populated, meaning that the Mittelland is densely settled, especially round the shores of the larger lakes. Zürich is the largest city with 363,000 inhabitants, next comes Geneva (190,000), Basel (172,000) and Bern (133,000). Most of the people are of Germanic origin as reflected in the breakdown of the four national languages spoken (see the Language section). One-fifth of people living in the country are residents but not Swiss citizens; the foreign influx started after WWII, particularly from southern Europe.

ARTS

Switzerland does not have a very strong tradition in the arts, even though many foreign writers and artists have visited and settled, attracted by the beauty and tranquillity of the mountains and lakes. Among them were Voltaire, Byron and Shelley. Paul Klee is the best-known native painter. He created abstract works which used colour, line and form to evoke a variety of sensations. The 18th-century writings of Rousseau in Geneva played an important part in the development of democracy. Carl Jung, with his research in Zürich, was instrumental in developing modern psychoanalysis.

Arthur Honegger is the only Swiss composer of note. Despite that, music is strongly emphasised with a full symphony orchestra in every main city. Gothic and Renaissance architecture are evident in urban areas, especially Bern. Rural Swiss houses vary according to region, but are generally characterised by ridged roofs with wide, overhanging eaves, and balconies and verandahs which are usually enlivened by colourful floral displays (especially geraniums).

CULTURE

In general the Swiss are a law-abiding nation; even minor transgressions such as littering can cause offence. Always shake hands when being introduced to a Swiss, and again when leaving. Formal titles should also be used (*Herr* for men and *Frau* for women). It is also customary to greet shopkeepers when entering their shops. Public displays of affection are OK, but are more common in French and Italian Switzerland than in the slightly more formal German-speaking parts.

In a few mountain regions such as Valais, people still wear traditional rural costumes, but dressing up is usually reserved for festivals. Every spring hardy herders climb to Alpine pastures with their cattle and live in summer huts while tending their herds. They gradually descend back to village level as the grassland is grazed. Both the departure and the return is a cause for celebrations and processions. Yodelling and playing the alp horn are also part of the Alpine tradition, as is Swiss wrestling.

RELIGION

Protestantism and Roman Catholicism are equally widespread, though the concentration varies between cantons. Strong Protestant areas are Bern, Vaud and Zürich, whereas Valais, Ticino and Uri are mostly Catholic. Some churches are supported entirely by donations from the public, others receive state subsidies.

LANGUAGE

Located in the corner of Europe where the German, French and Italian language areas meet, the linguistic melting pot which is Switzerland has three official federal languages: German (spoken by 64% of the population),

Language Areas

- Romansch
- German
- French
- Italian

Facts for the Visitor

PLANNING
Climate & When to Go

Ticino in the south has a hot, Mediterranean climate, and Valais in the south-west is noted for being dry. Elsewhere the temperature is typically 20°C to 25°C in summer and 2°C to 6°C in winter, with spring and autumn hovering around the 7°C to 14°C mark. Summer tends to bring a lot of sunshine, but also the most rain. You will need to be prepared for a range of temperatures dependent on altitude.

Look out for the *Föhn*, a hot, dry wind that sweeps down into the valleys and can be oppressively uncomfortable. It can strike at any time of year. Daily weather reports covering 25 resorts are displayed in major train stations. Switzerland is visited throughout the year – December to April for winter sports, and May to October for general tourism and hiking. Alpine resorts all but close down in May and November.

Books & Maps

For more detail, refer to Lonely Planet's *Switzerland* guide and *Walking in Switzerland*. Switzerland Tourism sells various useful publications. *Living and Working in Switzerland* by David Hampshire is an excellent practical guide for those doing what the title suggests. *Why Switzerland?* by Jonathan Steinberg looks at the country's history and culture, and enthusiastically argues that Switzerland is *not* a boring country. *The Xenophobe's Guide to the Swiss* by Paul Bilton is an informative and sometimes amusing small volume. Fiction about Switzerland is surprisingly scarce, but Anita Brookner won the Booker Prize in 1984 for *Hotel du Lac*, a novel set around Lake Geneva.

Michelin covers the whole country with four maps. The *Landeskarte der Schweiz* (Topographical Survey of Switzerland) series is larger in scale and especially useful for hiking. Kümmerly & Frey maps are also good for hikers. All these maps are sold throughout Switzerland. Swiss banks, especially UBS and SBC, are a good source of free maps.

English-language books are widely available in Switzerland, though for foreign titles

French (19%) and Italian (8%). A fourth language, Rhaeto-Romanic, or Romansch, is spoken by under 1% of the population, mainly in the canton of Graubünden. Derived from Latin, it's a linguistic relic which, along with Friulian and Ladin across the border in Italy, has survived in the isolation of mountain valleys. Romansch was recognised as a national language by referendum in 1938 and was given federal protection in 1996.

Though German-speaking Swiss have no trouble with standard High German, they use Swiss German, or *Schwyzertütsch*, in private conversation and in most nonofficial situations. Swiss German covers a wide variety of melodic dialects that can differ quite markedly from High German. Visitors will probably note the frequent use of the suffix *-li* to indicate the diminutive, or as a term of endearment.

You will have few problems being understood in English in the German-speaking parts of Switzerland. However, it is simple courtesy to greet people with the Swiss-German *Grüezi* (Hello) and to enquire *sprechen sie Englisch?* (do you speak English?) before launching into English. In French Switzerland you shouldn't have too many problems either, though the locals' grasp of English is likely to be less complete than that of German speakers. Italian Switzerland is where you will have the greatest difficulty. Most locals speak some French and/or German in addition to Italian. English has a lower priority, but you'll still find that the majority of hotels and restaurants have at least one English-speaking staff member. See the Language Guide at the back of the book for German, French and Italian pronunciation guidelines and useful words and phrases.

you always pay more in francs than the cover price. Check second-hand bookshops in the cities.

What to Bring
Take a sturdy pair of boots if you intend to walk in the mountains, and warm clothing for those cold nights at high altitude. Hostel membership is invaluable, and it's cheaper to join before you get to Switzerland.

SUGGESTED ITINERARIES
Depending on the length of your stay, you might want to see and do the following things:

Two days
Visit the sights in Geneva and take a trip on the lake. Don't miss Château de Chillon in Montreux.
One week
Visit Geneva and Montreux. En route to Zürich, spend a couple of days exploring Interlaken and the Jungfrau Region.
Two weeks
As above, but spend longer in the mountains. Detour to Bern, Basel and Lucerne.
One month
As above, but after Zürich, explore St Gallen and eastern Switzerland before looping down to take in Graubünden, Ticino and Valais.
Two months
As above, but take your time. Visit Neuchâtel and the Jura Mountains from Bern.

HIGHLIGHTS
Endless beautiful vistas greet you in this country. The views from Schilthorn or its neighbour, Jungfrau, are unforgettable. Zermatt combines inspiring views of the Matterhorn and quality skiing. Be sure to take a boat trip: Lake Lugano reveals the sunny side of Switzerland's Italian canton, and Lake Thun offers snowcapped scenery and several castles. Excursions are also excellent on lakes Lucerne and Geneva.

The Château de Chillon near Montreux is justifiably the most famous castle in Switzerland. Picturesque town centres include Bern, Lucerne, St Gallen and Stein am Rhein. Zürich, Basel and Geneva are bursting with fine museums and art galleries. Lausanne features a unique collection of bizarre 'outsider' art.

TOURIST OFFICES
Switzerland Tourism abroad and local tourist offices (Verkehrsbüro) in Switzerland are extremely helpful and have plenty of literature to give out, including maps (nearly always free). Somebody invariably speaks English. Local offices can be found everywhere tourists are likely to go, and will often book hotel rooms and organise excursions.

If staying in resorts, ask the local tourist office if there's a Visitor's Card, as these are good for discounts.

Anglo-Phone (☎ 157 5014) is an English-language information service; it costs Sfr2.13 a minute throughout Switzerland.

Tourist Offices Abroad
Canada
    Switzerland Tourism, 926 The East Mall, Etobicoke, Toronto, Ontario M9B 6K1 (☎ 416-695 20 90; fax 695 27 74)
UK
    Switzerland Tourism, Swiss Centre, Swiss Court, London W1V 8EE (☎ 0171-734 1921; fax 437 4577)
USA
    Switzerland Tourism, Swiss Center, 608 Fifth Ave, New York, NY 10020 (☎ 212-757 59 44; fax 262 61 16)

Switzerland Tourism also has offices in Los Angeles, Chicago, Paris, Milan, Munich and Vienna. It has no office in Australia – contact the embassy in Canberra (see the following section).

VISAS & EMBASSIES
Visas are not required for passport holders of the UK, the USA, Canada, Australia or New Zealand. A maximum three-month stay applies although passports are rarely stamped. The few Third World and Arab nationals who require visas should have a passport valid for at least six months after their intended stay.

Swiss Embassies Abroad
Australia
    7 Melbourne Ave, Forrest, Canberra, ACT 2603 (☎ 06-273 3977; fax 273 34 28)
Canada
    5 Marlborough Ave, Ottawa, Ontario K1N 8E6 (☎ 613-235 1837; fax 563 1394)
New Zealand
    22 Panama St, Wellington (☎ 04-472 1593; fax 499 6302)
UK
    16-18 Montague Place, London W1H 2BQ (☎ 0171-723 0701; fax 724 7001)
USA
    2900 Cathedral Ave NW, Washington, DC 20008-3499 (☎ 202-745 7900; fax 387 2564)

Foreign Embassies in Switzerland

All embassies are in Bern, including:

Australia
  Alpenstrasse 29 (☎ 351 01 43)
Canada
  Kirchenfeldstrasse 88 (☎ 352 63 81)
France
  Schosshaldenstrasse 46 (☎ 351 24 24)
Germany
  Willadingweg 83 (☎ 359 41 11)
UK
  Thunstrasse 50 (☎ 352 50 21)
USA
  Jubiläumsstrasse 93 (☎ 357 70 11)

Check the Bern tourist office or phone book for other embassies. New Zealand has no embassy; its consulate and mission is in Geneva (see the city section). Consulates can be found in many other towns, particularly Geneva and Zürich.

CUSTOMS

Visitors arriving from Europe may import 200 cigarettes, 50 cigars or 250 grams of pipe tobacco. Visitors arriving from non-European countries may import twice as much. The allowance for alcoholic beverages is the same for everyone: one litre above 15% and two litres below 15%. Tobacco and alcohol may only be brought in by people aged 17 or over.

MONEY

Currency

Swiss francs are divided into 100 centimes (usually called *Rappen* in German-speaking Switzerland). There are notes for 10, 20, 50, 100, 500 and 1000 francs, and coins for five, 10, 20 and 50 centimes, as well as for one, two and five francs.

All major travellers' cheques and credit cards are equally acceptable. Virtually all train stations have money-exchange facilities which are open daily, and many offer Visa card cash advances. Commission is not charged for changing cash or cheques (except in some airport terminals) but shop around for the best exchange rates. Hotels usually have the worst rates. Getting electronic funds sent to a Swiss bank is straightforward, but there may be charges made by the receiving bank (sometimes depending upon the currencies involved). There should be no charge at Union

Bank of Switzerland (UBS) branches if the money is accepted in Swiss francs. There are no charges at the Swiss end for American Express' Moneygram transfer system.

There are no restrictions on the amount of currency that can be brought in or taken out of Switzerland.

Exchange Rates

Australia	A$1	=	Sfr0.95
Canada	C$1	=	Sfr0.88
France	1FF	=	Sfr0.24
Germany	DM1	=	Sfr0.82
Japan	¥100	=	Sfr1.12
New Zealand	NZ$1	=	Sfr0.84
United Kingdom	UK£1	=	Sfr1.88
United States	US$1	=	Sfr1.21

Costs

Prices are higher in Switzerland than anywhere else in Europe. Some travellers can scrimp by on little more than Sfr40 a day after buying a rail pass. This is survival level – camping or hostelling, self-catering when possible and allowing nothing for nonessentials. If you want to stay in pensions and have the odd beer, count on spending twice as much. Taking cable cars is a major expense; if you're fit enough, walk instead.

Tipping & Bargaining

Tipping is rarely necessary as hotels, restaurants and bars are required by law to include a 15% service charge on bills (though locals often 'round-up'). Even taxis normally have a charge included. Prices are fixed, but people have successfully haggled for lower hotel rates in the low season.

Consumer Taxes

On 1 January 1995, VAT (MWST) on goods and services replaced the old 'turnover' tax which applied only to goods. The rate is 6.5%, though it was later reduced to 3% for hotel bills. Nonresidents can claim the tax back on purchases over Sfr500. Ask for the documentation when making the purchase.

If you're driving to Switzerland, see the Getting There & Away section for important information about paying the motorway tax.

POST & COMMUNICATIONS

Postcards and letters to Europe cost Sfr1.10/0.90 *priority/economy*; to elsewhere they cost Sfr1.80/1.10. The term 'poste restante' is widely understood although you might prefer to use the German term, *postlagernde briefe*. Mail can be sent to any town with a post office and is held for 30 days, but you need to show your passport in order to collect it. American Express also holds mail for one month for people who use its cheques or cards.

Post office opening times vary but typically are Monday to Friday from 8 am to noon and 2 to 6.30 pm, and Saturday from 8 am to 11 am. The larger post offices offer services outside normal hours (every day to late evening), but some transactions are subject to a Sfr1 to Sfr2 surcharge.

Nearly all post offices have telephones. Hotels can charge as much as they like for telephone calls, and they usually charge plenty, even for direct-dial. Even in payphones the minimum charge is a massive Sfr0.60. Calls within Switzerland are 60% cheaper on weekdays between 5 pm and 7 pm and between 9 pm and 8 am, and throughout the weekend. International calls to Europe are cheaper from 9 pm to 8 am on weekdays, and throughout the weekend. You can dial to just about anywhere worldwide. Phonecards *(taxcard)* are available for Sfr10 and Sfr20. To send a fax self-service at post offices costs Sfr2 plus the telephone call time.

The country code for Switzerland is ☎ 41. Drop the initial zero on the area code when dialling in from overseas.

NEWSPAPERS & MAGAZINES
English-language newspapers and magazines are widely available and cost around Sfr3 to Sfr6.

RADIO & TV
The BBC World Service broadcasts on medium wave (1296 and 648 kHz), and American Forces Network is on the FM band (101.8 mHz). Swiss Radio International (3985, 6165 or 9535 kHz) broadcasts in English at 6 and 8 am and later on at 1 pm. Multi-channel, multi-language cable TV is widespread, including in nearly all hotels.

PHOTOGRAPHY & VIDEO
Allow plenty of film for those mountain views. Film is around Sfr6.50 for Kodak Gold and Sfr16.50 for Kodachrome (36 exposures). The Inter Discount chain has the lowest prices. Switzerland uses the PAL video system.

TIME
Swiss time is GMT/UTC plus one hour. Daylight saving comes into effect at midnight on the last Saturday in March, when the clocks are moved forward one hour; they go back again on the last Saturday in September.

ELECTRICITY
The electric current is 220V, 50Hz. The standard Continental plug, with two round pins, can be used in the Swiss three-pin socket, but not if, as is common, the socket is recessed to receive the Swiss six-sided plug. International adapters don't fit these – it's best to buy and fit a Swiss plug on arrival.

WEIGHTS & MEASURES
The metric system is used. Note that cheese and other foods may be priced per 100 grams rather than per kg (a futile attempt to cushion the shock of the high prices?). Like other Continental Europeans, the Swiss indicate decimals with commas and thousands with points.

LAUNDRY
There is no shortage of coin-operated or service laundrettes in cities. Expect to pay around Sfr10 to wash and dry a five-kg load. Many hostels also have washing machines, and prices are usually slightly cheaper.

TOILETS
Public toilets are invariably spick-and-span. Urinals are free but there's often a pay slot for cubicles.

HEALTH
No inoculations are required for entry to healthy Switzerland. All medical treatment must be paid for, whether in cantonal or university hospitals or private clinics. Charges are high, so medical insurance is strongly advised. Remember that the air is thinner at high altitude. Take things easy above 3000 metres, and if you start feeling light-headed, come down to a lower altitude.

WOMEN TRAVELLERS
Women travellers should experience few prob-

lems with sexual harassment in Switzerland. However, Ticino males suffer from the same machismo leanings as their Italian counterparts, so advice given in the Italy chapter applies to some extent there too.

GAY & LESBIAN TRAVELLERS

Attitudes to homosexuality are reasonably tolerant. The *Cruiser* magazine (☎ 01-261 82 00), Postfach 599, CH-8025, Zürich, has extensive listings of gay and lesbian organisations, bars and events in Switzerland (Sfr4). The age of consent is 16.

DISABLED TRAVELLERS

Switzerland Tourism can provide useful information. Many hotels have disabled access, and 150 train stations have a mobile lift for train-boarding. The Swiss Invalid Association (☎ 062-212 12 62), or Schweizerischer Invalidenverband, is at Froburgstrasse 4, CH-4600 Olten.

DANGERS & ANNOYANCES

Crime rates may be low but don't neglect security. There are a lot of young drug addicts in Switzerland who may cause problems when they congregate in groups in cities. Emergency telephone numbers are police ☎ 117, fire brigade ☎ 118, ambulance (most areas) ☎ 144. Take special care in the mountains: helicopter rescue (☎ 383 11 11) is extremely expensive (make sure your travel insurance covers Alpine sports).

BUSINESS HOURS

Most shops are open from 8 am to 6.30 pm, Monday to Friday, with a 90-minute or two-hour break for lunch at noon. Some are closed on Monday morning and Wednesday afternoon, and some towns have late opening on Thursday. Banks are open Monday to Friday from 8.30 am to 4.30 pm with some local variations.

PUBLIC HOLIDAYS & SPECIAL EVENTS

National holidays are 1 January, Good Friday, Easter Monday, Ascension Day, Whit Monday, 1 August (National Day), and 25 and 26 December. Some cantons observe 2 January, 1 May (Labour Day), Corpus Christi and All Saints' Day. Numerous events take place at a local level throughout the year, so it's worth checking with the local tourist office. Most dates vary from year to year. This is just a brief selection:

January
    Costumed sleigh rides, Engadine
February
    Carnival in Basel, Lucerne and elsewhere
March
    Engadine Skiing Marathon, Graubünden
April
    Start of summer-long *Combats de Reines* (cow fighting; yes, the cows fight each other!), lower Valais
    Landsgemeinde meetings in Appenzell, Hundwil (or Trogen), Sarnen and Stans (last Sunday of the month)
May
    May Day, especially St Gallen and Vaud
June
    Geneva Rose Week
July
    Montreux Jazz Festival
August
    National Day, Swiss wrestling in Emmental
    Geneva Festival
September
    Knabenschiessen shooting contest, Zürich
October
    Vintage festivals in wine-growing regions such as Morges, Neuchâtel and Lugano
November
    Open-air markets including the Onion Market in Bern
December
    St Nicholas Day (6 December)
    Escalade Festival in Geneva

ACTIVITIES

Water Sports

Water-skiing, sailing and windsurfing are possible on most lakes. Courses are usually available, especially in Graubünden and central Switzerland. There are over 350 lake beaches. Anglers should contact the local tourist office for a fishing permit valid for lakes and rivers. The Rotsee near Lucerne is a favourite place for rowing regattas. Rafting is possible on many Alpine rivers including the Rhine and the Rhône. Canoeing is mainly centred on the Muota in Schwyz canton and on the Doubs in the Jura.

Skiing

There are dozens of ski resorts throughout the Alps, the pre-Alps and the Jura, incorporating some 200 ski schools. Those resorts favoured by the package-holiday companies do not necessarily have better skiing facilities, but they do tend to have more diversions off the slopes, in terms of sightseeing and nightlife.

Equipment can always be hired at resorts; for one day you'll pay about Sfr43/20 for downhill/cross-country gear. You can buy new equipment at reasonable prices, or try asking to buy ex-rental stock – affluent Swiss spurn such equipment so you might pick up real bargains.

Ski passes (around Sfr50 for one day; multi-day passes are cheaper per day) allow unlimited use of mountain transport. Beginners could save money by buying ski coupons instead (where available) if they only want to try a couple of experimental runs.

Hiking & Mountaineering
There are 50,000 km of designated footpaths with regular refreshment stops en route. Bright yellow signs marking the trail make it difficult to get lost; each gives an average walking time to the next destination. Zermatt is a favourite destination for mountaineers, but you should never climb on your own, or without proper equipment. For information contact the Swiss Alpine Club (☎ 031-351 36 11), or Schweizer Alpenclub (SAC), Helvetiaplatz 4, CH-3005 Bern.

Walking
Walking is popular, and an exhilarating activity in rural areas. Switzerland Tourism shows the way with its *Switzerland Step by Step* booklets detailing 100 walks to mountain lakes, over mountain passes, and from town to town. Lonely Planet's *Walking in Switzerland* contains track notes for walking in the Swiss countryside.

WORK
Officially, only foreigners with special skills can work legally but people still manage to find work in ski resorts – anything from snow clearing to washing dishes. Hotel work has the advantage of including meals and accommodation. In theory, jobs and work permits should be sorted out before arrival, but if you find a job once there, the employer may well have unallocated work permits. The seasonal 'A' permit *(Permis A, Saisonbewilligung)* is valid for up to nine months, and the elusive and much sought-after 'B' permit *(Permis B, Aufenthaltsbewilligung)* is renewable and

valid for a year. Expect·regulations for EU citizens to ease over the next few years. Many resort jobs are advertised in the Swiss weekly newspaper, *Hotel + Touristik Revue*. Casual wages are higher than in most other European countries.

ACCOMMODATION
Camping
There are about 450 camping grounds, which are classified from one to five stars depending upon amenities and convenience of location. Charges per night are around Sfr6 per person plus Sfr3 to Sfr8 for a tent, and from Sfr3 for a car. Many sites offer a slight discount if you have a Camping Carnet. Free camping is not actively encouraged and you should be discreet. The Swiss Camping & Caravanning Federation (☎ 041-210 48 22) – Schweizerischer Camping und Caravanning-Verband (SCCV) – is at Habsburgerstrasse 35, CH-6004 Lucerne.

Hostels
There are 73 official Swiss Youth Hostels *(jugendherberge, auberge de jeunesse, alloggio per giovani)* spread throughout the country, which are automatically affiliated to the international network. Most Swiss hostels include breakfast in the price; most also add an extra Sfr2.50 for the first night's stay (exceptions are the hostels in Bern, Bruson, Geneva, Lugano and Vaduz). It is the full *first night's charge* that is quoted in this chapter. Sheets are nearly always included, and some places have double or family rooms available (with single or bunk beds). Around half of the Swiss hostels have kitchen facilities. Membership cards must be shown at hostels. Nonmembers pay a Sfr5 'guest fee' to stay in Swiss hostels; six of these add up to a full international membership card. However, you're better off paying a one-off fee of Sfr25 for international membership, or becoming a member in your country of residence should be even cheaper.

Hostels do get full, and telephone reservations are not accepted. Write, or use the excellent telefax service. Under this system, Swiss hostels will reserve ahead to the next hostel for you but you must give specific dates. The cost is Sfr1 plus a Sfr9 refundable deposit, and you must claim your bed by 7 pm. A map, giving full details of all hostels on the reverse, including fax numbers, is available free from hostels and some tourist offices. The Swiss Youth Hostel Association (SYHA), or Schweizerischer Jugendherbergen (☎ 01-360 14 14), is at Schaffhauserstrasse 14, CH-8042, Zürich.

Hotels

Swiss accommodation is geared towards value for money rather than low cost, so even bottom-of-the-range rooms are fairly comfortable. High-season prices can be 10% (towns) to 40% (Alpine resorts) higher than in the low season, but exactly when the high season occurs varies from region to region. Hotels are star rated. Prices start at around Sfr40/70 for a basic single/double. Count on at least Sfr10 more for a room with a private shower. Rates generally include breakfast, which tends to be a buffet in mid-range and above hotels. Note that some train stations have hotel information boards with a free telephone. The Swiss Hotel Association (☎ 031-370 41 11), or Schweizer Hotelier-Verein (SHV), is at Monbijoustrasse 130, CH-3001 Bern.

Other Accommodation

'Hotel Garni' means a B&B establishment without a restaurant. Private houses in rural areas sometimes offer inexpensive rooms; look out for signs saying *Zimmer frei* (room(s) vacant). Some farms also take paying guests. Self-catering accommodation is available in holiday chalets, apartments or bungalows. Local tourist offices have full lists of everything on offer in the area. The Swiss Alpine Club maintains around 150 mountain huts at higher altitudes. Some hotels in mountain resorts have a cheap dormitory annexe (*Massenlager* or *dortoir*).

FOOD

The Swiss emphasis on quality extends to meals. Basic restaurants provide simple but well-cooked food although prices are generally high. Many budget travellers rely on picnic provisions from supermarkets, but even here prices can be a shock with cheese costing over Sfr20 a kg!

The main supermarket chains (closed Sunday, except at some train stations) are Migros and Coop. Larger branches have good quality self-service restaurants, which typi-

cally open to around 6.30 pm on weekdays and to 4 pm on Saturday. These, along with EPA department store restaurants, are usually the cheapest places for hot food, with dishes starting at around Sfr7. Likewise at university restaurants (*mensas*); when mentioned in this chapter they are open to everyone, but note that serving times are limited (typically weekdays from 11.30 am to 1.30 pm and 5.30 to 7.30 pm, and perhaps for Saturday lunch). They're sometimes open during university holidays. Buffet-style restaurant chains, like Manora and Inova, offer good food at low prices. The food is freshly cooked in front of you, and you can sometimes select the ingredients yourself.

In restaurants the best value is a fixed-menu dish of the day (*Tagesteller*, *plat du jour*, or *piatto del giorno*). Fast-food joints are proliferating. Some wine bars (*Weinstübli*) and beer taverns (*Bierstübli*) serve meals. Main meals are eaten at noon. Cheaper restaurants (except pizzerias) tend to be fairly rigid about when they serve. Go to a hotel or more up-market restaurant for more flexible, later eating. Vegetarian restaurants can be hard to come by, though many places offer non-meat choices. Restaurants tend to have a closing day (often Monday).

Swiss food borrows characteristics from its larger neighbours. Breakfast is of the Continental variety. *Müsli* (muesli) was invented in Switzerland at the end of the 19th century but few people seem to eat it in its country of origin. Soups are popular and often very filling. Cheeses form an important part of the Swiss diet. Emmental and Gruyère are combined with white wine to create *fondue*, which is served up in a vast pot and eaten with bread cubes. *Raclette* is another cheese dish, served with potatoes. *Rösti* (fried, shredded potatoes) is German Switzerland's national dish. A wide variety of *Wurst* (sausage) is available. Veal is highly rated throughout Switzerland; in Zürich it is thinly sliced and served in a cream sauce (*Geschnetzeltes Kalbsfleisch*). *Bündnerfleisch* is dried beef, smoked and thinly sliced. Swiss chocolate, excellent by itself, is often used in desserts and cakes.

DRINKS

Mineral water is readily available but tap water is fine to drink. Note that milk from Alpine cows contains a high level of fat.

Alcohol licensing laws in Switzerland aren't too restrictive – you're more likely to be restricted by the high prices. Fortunately, beer and wine prices in supermarkets aren't too bad. In bars, lager beer comes in 0.58 or 0.3-litre bottles or on draught *(vom Fass)* with measures ranging from 0.2 to 0.5 litre.

Wine is considered an important part of the meal even though it is rather expensive. Local wines are generally good but you may not have heard of them before, as output cannot even meet domestic demand so they are rarely exported. The main growing regions are the Italian and French-speaking parts of the country, particularly in Valais and by Lake Neuchâtel and Lake Geneva. Both red and white wines are produced, and each region has its own speciality (eg Merlot in Ticino). There is also a choice of locally produced fruit brandies, often served with or in coffee.

ENTERTAINMENT

Cinemas usually show films in their original language. Check posters for the upper-case letter: for instance, E/d/f indicates English with German and French subtitles. In French Switzerland you might see 'VO' instead, which signifies 'original version'. Nightlife is not all it could be in the cities, and is generally expensive. Geneva is the best place for late nightclubs *(boîtes)*, although Zürich is also lively. Several cheaper, alternative-style venues are mentioned in this chapter. In ski resorts the 'après ski' atmosphere can keep things lively until late. Listening to music is popular. Classical, folk, jazz and rock concerts are performed in all major cities.

THINGS TO BUY

Watches and chocolates are on many people's shopping lists. Swiss army knives range from simple blades (Sfr10) to mini-toolboxes (Sfr100 or more). A grotesquely tacky cuckoo clock with a girl bouncing on a spring will set you back at least Sfr25, a musical box anything upwards of Sfr35. Should you want a cowbell to warn people of your arrival, one with a decorative band will cost from Sfr8 to a fortune depending on the size. If you're after textiles and embroidery look around St Gallen, and for woodcarvings go to Brienz.

Getting There & Away

AIR

The main entry points for flights are Zürich and Geneva. Each has several nonstop flights a day to major transport hubs such as London, Paris and Frankfurt. Both airports are linked directly to the Swiss rail network. The airport serving Basel is on the French side of the border at Mulhouse. Bern has a small airport with some international flights (eg direct to/from London's Stansted airport by Air Engiadina). Swissair luggage check-in facilities are at major Swiss train stations.

LAND
Bus
The international bus service to Switzerland is minimal. Buses go to both Zürich (one or three per week, via Basel) and Geneva (three per week) from London's Victoria coach station. Either way, the journey takes 20 hours and costs UK£99 (£89 for those under 26). Geneva also has bus connections to Chamonix and Barcelona (see Geneva for details). Eurolines' representative in Zürich is Marti Travel (☎ 01-221 04 72), Usteristrasse 10.

Train
Located at the heart of Europe, it is not surprising that Switzerland has excellent and frequent train connections to the rest of the continent. Zürich is the busiest international terminus. It has two direct day trains to Vienna (nine hours) and one night train. There are several trains a day to both Geneva and Lausanne from Paris, and journey time is three to four hours by super-fast TGV. Paris to Bern takes 4½ hours by TGV. Most connections from Germany pass though Zürich or Basel. Nearly all connections from Italy pass through Milan before branching off to Zürich, Lucerne, Bern or Lausanne. Reservations on international trains are subject to a surcharge of Sfr5 to Sfr22, depending on the day and/or service.

Car & Motorcycle
Roads into Switzerland are good despite the difficulty of the terrain, but special care is needed when negotiating mountain passes. Some, such as the N5 route from Morez (in

France) to Geneva are not recommended if you have not had previous experience. Upon entering Switzerland you will need to decide whether you wish to use the motorways. There is a one-off charge of Sfr40 if you do. Organise this money beforehand, since you might not always be able to change money at the border. Better still, buy it in advance from Switzerland Tourism or a motoring organisation. The sticker (called a *vignette*) you receive is valid for a year and must be displayed on the windscreen. A separate fee must be paid for trailers and caravans (motorcyclists must pay, too), Some Alpine tunnels incur additional tolls.

BOAT

Basel can be reached by Rhine steamer from Amsterdam or other towns en route. The total journey time is more than four days. Switzerland can also be reached by steamer from several lakes: from Germany via Lake Constance (Bodensee in German); from Italy via Lake Maggiore; and from France via Lake Geneva (Lac Lémon).

LEAVING SWITZERLAND

Swiss airport taxes of around Sfr15 are always included in the ticket price – there is no other departure tax to pay.

Getting Around

PASSES & DISCOUNTS

Swiss public transport is a fully integrated and comprehensive system incorporating trains, buses, boats and funiculars – some say it's the most efficient network in the world. Various special tickets are available to the tourist to make the system even more attractive.

The best deal for people planning to travel extensively is the Swiss Pass, entitling the holder to unlimited travel on Swiss Federal Railways, boats, most Alpine postbuses and also on trams and buses in 35 towns. Reductions of 25% apply on funiculars and mountain railways. Passes are valid for four days (Sfr210), eight days (Sfr264), 15 days (Sfr306) and one month (Sfr420) – prices are for 2nd-class tickets.

The Swiss Card allows a free return journey from your arrival point to any destination in Switzerland, 50% off rail, boat and bus excursions, and reductions on mountain railways. The cost is Sfr140 (2nd class) or Sfr170 (1st class) and it is valid for a month. The Half-Fare Card is a similar deal minus the free return trip. The cost is Sfr90 for one month or Sfr150 for one year.

The Swiss Flexi Pass allows free, unlimited trips for three days out of 15. The cost is Sfr210 for 2nd class. All these cards are best purchased before arrival in Switzerland from Switzerland Tourism or a travel agent, as they can be bought at only a few major transport centres once you're there.

The Family Card gives free travel for children aged under 16 accompanied by at least one parent; accompanied unmarried children from 16 to under 25 pay 50%. Most vendors of the various Swiss travel passes will supply this free to pass purchasers; if not, the Family Card can be bought from major Swiss railway station for Sfr20.

Regional passes, valid for a specific tourist region, provide free travel on certain days and half-price travel on other days within a seven or 15-day period.

All the larger lakes are serviced by steamers, for which rail passes are usually valid (including Eurail; Inter-Rail often gets 50% off). A Swiss Navigation Boat Pass costs Sfr35 and entitles the bearer to 50% off fares of the main operators. It is valid year-round, but few boats sail in winter.

AIR

Internal flights are not of great interest to the visitor, owing to the excellent ground transport. Crossair, a subsidiary of Swissair, is the local carrier, and links major towns and cities several times daily.

BUS

Yellow postbuses are a supplement to the rail network, following postal routes and linking towns to the more inaccessible regions in the mountains. In all, routes cover some 8000 km of terrain. They are extremely regular, and departures tie in with train arrivals. Postbus stations are next to train stations.

TRAIN

The Swiss rail network covers 5000 km and is

a combination of state-run and private lines. Trains are clean, reliable, frequent and as fast as the terrain will allow. Prices are high, though the travel passes mentioned above will cut costs. All fares quoted are for 2nd class; 1st-class fares are about 65% higher. In general, Eurail passes are not valid for private lines and Inter-Rail gets 50% off. All major stations are connected to each other by hourly departures, but services stop from around midnight to 6 am.

Train stations invariably offer luggage storage, either at a counter (usually Sfr5 per piece) or in 24-hour lockers (Sfr2 to Sfr5). They also have excellent information counters which give out free timetable booklets and advice on connections. Single/return train tickets over 80/160 km are valid for two days/one month; you can break the journey but tell the conductor of your intentions. Train schedules are revised yearly, so double-check details before travelling.

CAR & MOTORCYCLE
Be prepared for winding roads, high passes and long tunnels. Normal speed limits are 50 km/h in towns, 120 km/h on motorways, 100 km/h on semi-motorways (roadside rectangular pictograms show a white car on a green background) and 80 km/h on other roads. Don't forget you need a vignette to use motorways and semi-motorways (see the Getting There & Away section). Mountain roads are good but stay in low gear whenever possible and remember that ascending traffic has right of way over descending traffic, and postbuses always have right of way. Snow chains are recommended in winter. Use dipped lights in *all* road tunnels. Some minor Alpine passes are closed from November to May – check with tourist offices or motoring organisations. The Swiss Automobile Club (☎ 031-311 77 22), or Automobil-Club der Schweiz (ACS), is at Wasserwerkgasse 39, CH-3000 Bern 13.

Ring ☎ 140 for the national 24-hour breakdown service. Switzerland is tough on drink-driving, so don't risk it; the BAC limit is 0.08%, and if caught exceeding this limit, you face a large fine or imprisonment.

Rental
One-way drop-offs are usually free of charge within Switzerland, though collision damage

waiver costs extra. Weekend rates (noon Friday to 9 am Monday) for Budget and Europcar are Sfr190; this is cheaper than Hertz and Avis, though all charge from about Sfr185 for the normal daily unlimited rate. Look to local operators for the lowest prices (the local tourist office will have details). Overall, pre-booked rates are lower than in France, Italy and Austria, and higher than in Germany.

BICYCLE
Despite the hilly countryside, cycling is popular in Switzerland. Cycles can be hired from most train stations and returned to any station with a rental office, though there is a Sfr6 surcharge if you don't return it to the same station (declare your intentions at the outset). The cost is Sfr22 per day or Sfr88 per week. Bikes can be transported on normal trains but not on InterCity (IC) or EuroCity (EC) trains. Switzerland Tourism issues three free, useful booklets on cycling holidays, concentrating on the Pre-Alps, the Midlands, and from the Rhine to Ticino.

Swiss railway stations sell a new Bike Pass, combining transportation and bicycle rental.

HITCHING
Although illegal on motorways, hitching is allowed on other roads and can be fairly easy. At other times it can be quite slow. Indigenous Swiss are not all that sympathetic towards hitchers, and you'll find that most of your lifts will come from foreigners. A sign is helpful. Make sure you stand in a place where vehicles can stop. To try to get a ride on a truck, ask around the customs post at border towns.

LOCAL TRANSPORT
City Transport
All local city transport is linked together on the same ticketing system and you need to buy tickets before boarding. One-day passes are usually available and are much better value than paying per trip. There are regular checks for fare dodgers; those caught without a ticket pay an on-the-spot fine of Sfr40 to Sfr60.

Taxis are always metered and tend to wait around train stations. Beware – they are expensive!

Mountain Transport
There are five main modes of transport used in steep Alpine regions. A funicular (*funiculaire*

or *Standseilbahn)* is a pair of counterbalancing cars drawn by cables. A cable car *(téléphérique* or *Luftseilbahn)* is dramatically suspended from a cable high over a valley. A gondola *(télécabine* or *Gondelbahn)* is a smaller version of a cable car except that the gondola is hitched onto a continuously running cable once the passengers are inside. A cable chair *(télésiège* or *Sesselbahn)* is likewise hitched onto a cable but is unenclosed. A ski lift *(téléski* or *Schlepplift)* is a T-bar hanging from a cable, which the skiers hold onto while their feet slide along the snow.

In practice, the terms 'gondola' and 'cable car' are more or less interchangeable, and T-bars are gradually being phased out.

ORGANISED TOURS

Tours are booked through local tourist offices. The country is so compact that excursions to the major national attractions are offered from most towns. A trip up to Jungfraujoch, for example, is available from Zürich, Geneva, Bern, Lucerne or Interlaken. Most tours represent reasonable value.

Bern (Berne)

Founded in 1191 by Berchtold V, Bern (Berne in French) is Switzerland's capital and fourth-largest city (population 133,000). The story goes that the city was named for the bear (*bärn* in local dialect) that was Berchtold's first kill when hunting in the area. Even today the bear remains the heraldic mascot of the city. Despite playing host to the nation's politicians, Bern retains a relaxed, small-town charm. A picturesque old town contains six km of covered arcades and 11 historic fountains, as well as the descendants of the city's first casualty who perform tricks for tourists. The world's largest Paul Klee collection is housed in the Museum of Fine Arts.

Orientation

The compact centre of the old town is contained within a sharp U-bend of the Aare River. The main train station is within easy reach of all the main sights and has bicycle rental (daily

from 6.10 am to 11.45 pm), Swissair check-in, and expensive showers.

Information

Tourist Office The Offizielles Verkehrsbüro Bern (☎ 311 66 11) is in the train station and is open daily from 9 am to 8.30 pm. From 1 October to 31 May it shuts two hours earlier and Sunday hours are reduced to 10 am to 5 pm. Services include hotel reservations (Sfr3 commission, so use the free hotel phone outside) and excursions.

The tourist office's free booklet, *Bern aktuell*, contains much practical and recreational information in three languages. Some shops are shut on Monday morning, and many stay open till 9 pm on Thursday.

Money The SBB exchange office is in the lower level of the train station, open daily from 6.15 am to 8.45 pm (9.45 pm in summer).

Post & Communications The main post office (Schanzenpost 3001) is on Schanzenstrasse; it is open Monday to Friday from 7.30 am to 6.30 pm and on Saturday from 7.30 to 11 am.

The telephone code for Bern is ☎ 031.

Travel Agencies Kehrli & Oeler Reisebüro (☎ 311 00 22), Bubenbergplatz 9, is the American Express travel service representative. The budget and student travel agency SSR (☎ 302 03 12) has two offices: Falkenplatz 9 and Rathausgasse 64. Both are open Monday to Friday only.

Bookshops Stauffacher, Neuengasse 25, has many English-language books. Check Rathausgasse or Kramgasse for second-hand bookshops.

Medical & Emergency Services The university hospital (☎ 632 21 11) is on Fribourgstrasse. Important phone numbers are: police ☎ 117; fire brigade ☎ 118; ambulance ☎ 144.

Things to See

Walking Tour The city map from the tourist office details a picturesque walk through the old town. The core of the walk is Marktgasse and Kramgasse with their covered arcades and colourful fountains. Dividing the two streets is the **Zeitglockenturm**, a clock tower on which revolving figures herald the chiming hour. Congregate a few minutes before the hour on the east side to see them twirl. Originally a city gate, the clock was installed in 1530. The **Einstein House**, Kramgasse 49, is where the physicist developed his special theory of relativity (Sfr2). There's not much to see, but it's relatively interesting.

The unmistakably Gothic, 15th-century **cathedral** (*Münster*), is noted for its stained-glass windows and elaborate main portal. Just over the River Aare are the **bear pits** (*Bärengraben*). Bears have been at this site since 1857, although records show that as far back as 1441 the city council bought acorns to feed the ancestors of these overgrown pets. Up the hill is the **Rose Garden**, which has 200 varieties of roses and an excellent view of the city.

Parliament Well worth a visit are the Bundeshäuser, home of the Swiss Federal Assembly. There are free daily tours when the parliament is not in session (watch from the public gallery when it is). Arrive early and reserve a place for later in the day. A multilingual guide takes you through the impressive chambers, and highlights the development of the Swiss constitution.

Museums There is no shortage of museums. The **Museum of Fine Arts** (Kunstmuseum), Hodlerstrasse 8-12, holds the Klee collection and an interesting mix of Italian masters, Swiss and modern art. It is open Tuesday from 10 am to 9 pm, and Wednesday to Sunday from 10 am to 5 pm; entry costs Sfr6 (students Sfr4).

Many museums are grouped together on the south side of the Kirchenfeldbrücke – buy the day pass for Sfr7 (Sfr4 students and seniors) if you want to visit more than one. The best is the **Bern Historical Museum** (Bernisches Historisches Museum), Helvetiaplatz, open Tuesday to Sunday from 10 am to 5 pm (admission Sfr5, students Sfr3, free on Saturday). Highlights include the original sculptures from the Münster doorway depicting the Last Judgement, Niklaus Manuel's macabre *Dance of Death* panels, and the ridiculous codpiece on the William Tell statue upstairs.

Also worthwhile is the **Natural History Museum** (Naturhistorisches Museum) on Bernastrasse, with animals depicted in realistic dioramas. It is open Monday from 2 to 5 pm, Tuesday to Saturday from 9 am to 5 pm, and Sunday from 10 am to 5 pm (Sfr3, Sfr1.50 for students, free on Sunday).

Markets An open-air vegetable, fruit and flower market is at Bundesplatz on Tuesday and Saturday. On the fourth Monday in November, Bern hosts its famous onion market.

Organised Tours
The two-hour city tour by coach (Sfr22) has informative commentary; the on-foot version costs Sfr12. Get details from the tourist office.

Places to Stay
Camping To get to *Camping Kappelenbrücke* (☎ 901 10 07), take postbus No 3 or 4 from the train station to Eymatt. It's open year-round and reception is shut from 1 to 4 pm. Cost is Sfr6 per person and Sfr6 for a car and tent. Near the river but south of town is *Camping Eichholz* (☎ 961 26 02), Strandweg 49. Take tram No 9 from the train station to Wabern. The site is open from 1 May to 30 September, and charges are Sfr5.50 per person, from Sfr4 for a tent, and Sfr2 for parking. Cheap two-bed rooms are also available.

Hostel The SYHA *hostel* (☎ 311 63 16), Weihergasse 4, is in a good location below Parliament (signposted). It is usually full in summer, when a three-day maximum stay applies. Reception shuts down from 9.30 am to 3 pm (summer) or 5 pm (winter), but bags can be left in the common room during the day. Dorm beds are Sfr17, breakfast is Sfr6 and lunch and dinner are Sfr11 each. There are lockers, a midnight curfew, and washing machines (Sfr4 to wash and from Sfr1 to dry).

Hotels There's a limited choice of budget rooms in Bern. *Bahnhof-Süd* (☎ 992 51 11), Bümplizstrasse 189, to the west of town beyond the autobahn, has singles/doubles with hall showers from Sfr50/80 without breakfast. To get there, take bus No 13 from the city centre. Take bus No 20 from Bahnhofplatz for *Marthahaus Garni* (☎ 332 41 35), Wyttenbachstrasse 22A. It's a friendly place with

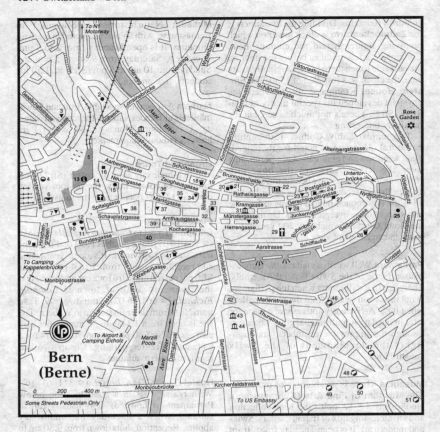

Bern (Berne)

To N1 Motorway

Rose Garden

Aargauerstalden

Some Streets Pedestrian Only

0   200   400 m

To Camping Kappelenbrücke

To Airport & Camping Eicholz

Marzili Pools

To US Embassy

comfortable rooms and two TV lounges. Singles/doubles are Sfr60/95 and triples/quads are Sfr120/140. Add around Sfr25 per room if you want private shower/toilet and TV. Convenient for the train station is *National* (☎ 381 19 88), Hirschengraben 24. It has good-for-the-price singles/doubles from Sfr60/100, or Sfr85/120 with private shower and toilet.

In the old town, in an 18th-century building is *Hospiz zur Heimat* (☎ 311 04 36), Gerechtigkeitsgasse 50, with singles/doubles for Sfr64/96, and triples/quads for Sfr126/168. Rooms with shower/toilet are around Sfr30 extra. *Goldener Schlüssel* (☎ 311 02 16),

Rathausgasse 72, charges a little more, but has TV and radio in all rooms. Rooms are clean and reasonably spacious in both places.

Goldener Adler (☎ 311 17 25), at Gerechtigkeitsgasse 7, has similar rooms (with TV) for Sfr105/140 with private shower or Sfr75/130 without. Another good choice for mid-price accommodation is *Hotel Krebs* (☎ 311 49 42), Genfergasse 8, near the train station. Singles with shower, toilet, TV and breakfast buffet are expensive at Sfr128, but the corresponding doubles are a much better deal at Sfr158; the family room for four costs Sfr245.

PLACES TO STAY					
1	Marthahaus Garni	37	Mazot	26	Wasserwerk
9	National	38	Della Casa	29	Cathedral
16	Hotel Krebs			31	Einstein House
20	Goldener Schlüssel	**OTHER**		32	Theaterplatz
24	Hospiz zur Heimat	2	Reithalle	33	Zeitglockenturm
27	Goldener Adler	4	Bus Station	39	Bundesplatz
41	SYHA Hostel	5	Train Station	40	Parliament
		6	Post Office	42	Helvetiaplatz
PLACES TO EAT		8	Bubenbergplatz	43	Bern Historical Museum
3	Mensa	10	Kehrli & Oeler	44	Natural History
7	Café Bubenberg Vegi		Reijebüro		Museum
11	Manora	12	Public Transport Office	45	Dampfzentrale
23	Klötzlikeller	13	Tourist Office	46	South African Embassy
28	Ratskeller	14	Bahnhofplatz	47	Australian Embassy
30	Menuetto	15	Stauffacher Bookshop	48	British Embassy
34	Restaurant Brasserie	17	Museum of Fine Arts	49	Irish Embassy
	Anker	18	Kornhauskeller	50	Canadian Embassy
35	EPA	19	Kornhausplatz	51	Italian Embassy
36	Migros & GD	21	SSR Travel Agency		
	Restaurant	22	Rathaus		
		25	Bear Pits		

Places to Eat

The *EPA* department store, between Markt-gasse and Zeughausgasse, has meals from Sfr7 in its self-service restaurant. *Migros* supermarket at Marktgasse 46 has a cheap self-service restaurant on the 1st floor. On the same floor is *G D Restaurant* with regional dishes from Sfr10; both are open normal shop hours, with late opening to 9 pm on Thursday, though Migros is closed on Monday until 2 pm. Also good value is the university *mensa*, Gesellschaftsstrasse 2, on the 1st floor. Meals cost around Sfr8 to Sfr12, with reductions for students. It is open Monday to Friday 11.30 am to 1.45 pm and (Monday to Thursday) from 5.45 to 7.30 pm. The café downstairs keeps longer hours for drinks and snacks.

Manora, Bubenbergplatz 5a, is a busy buffet-style restaurant with tasty dishes for Sfr9 to Sfr16. The pile-it-on-yourself salad is Sfr4.20 to Sfr9.40 per plate. Nearby is *Café Bubenberg Vegi*, 1st floor, Bubenbergplatz 8, which has terrace seating and good vegetarian food for Sfr15 to Sfr20. It is open Monday to Saturday from 7.30 am to 10.30 pm. Slightly more expensive but also recommended for vegetarian food is *Menuetto* (☎ 311 14 48), Münstergasse 47, open daily except Sunday from 11 am to 10 pm.

Several pleasant restaurants with outside seating line Bärenplatz, though there's little to choose between them. Go to *Mazot* at No 5 to try Swiss specialities such as Rösti (Sfr12.50) and fondue (Sfr19). *Restaurant Brasserie Anker* at Zeughausgasse 1 has standard Swiss food for a similar price. Its front section is popular with beer drinkers (Sfr3.80 for half a litre).

The dingy exterior of *Della Casa* (☎ 311 21 42), Schauplatzgasse 16, hides a good-quality restaurant within. The local speciality, Bernerplatte (a selection of meats with sauerkraut and beans) costs Sfr39, but perhaps you can find it on the excellent three-course daily menu for Sfr19.50 (different menu lunch and dinner; not available in the plusher upstairs section). It's open Monday to Friday from 8.30 to 11.30 pm (menu to 9 pm) and Saturday from 8.30 am to 3 pm.

For good-quality fish and meat dishes (Sfr17.50 to Sfr45) in a calm setting, try *Ratskeller*, Gerechtigkeitsgasse 81 (open daily). *Klötzlikeller* (☎ 311 74 56) is an atmospheric wine cellar at Gerechtigkeitsgasse 62, with live music every second Wednesday in winter. Menus (ranging from cheapish to mid-price) change every two months in which food and wine from different regions are featured. It is open Tuesday to Saturday from 4 pm till after midnight.

Entertainment

On Monday, cinemas cost Sfr10 instead of the usual Sfr15. Open-air swimming pools, such as those at Marzili, are free (open May to September). A favoured activity in the summer is to walk upriver then float in the swift current of the Aare back to Marzili.

There are various late-night clubs in the centre but entry and drink prices are high. Young people with fewer francs go to places like **Wasserwerk**, Wasserwerkgasse 5. There's a bar with pool tables (open 8 pm), a disco (Sfr5 to Sfr15; from 10 pm) and live music (Sfr10 to Sfr35). **Dampfzentrale** (☎ 311 63 37), Marzilistrasse 47, is a venue for jazz and other music, plus art exhibitions. The **Reithalle** (☎ 302 63 17), Schützenmattstrasse, is a centre for alternative arts, offering reasonable admission prices for dance, theatre, cinema, and live music, as well as a bar, restaurant and women's centre. The place looks a bit seedy, and there have been safety problems in the past. Nowadays, however, it is said to be safe and almost respectable.

Kornhauskeller (☎ 311 11 33), at Kornhausplatz 17, is a traditional beer hall with live piano music nightly, and a summer folklore show on Monday (free entry). Food can get pricey, though there is Rösti from Sfr10. It is open Monday to Saturday from 11.30 am to around midnight. On Sunday it has a jazz matinee from 11 am to 1 pm (Sfr15).

Getting There & Away
Air There are daily flights to/from London, Paris, Lugano, Munich, Brussels and other European destinations from the small airport.

Bus Postbuses depart from the west side of the train station.

Train There are at least hourly connections to most Swiss towns, including Geneva (Sfr48, takes 1¾ hours), Basel (Sfr34, 70 minutes), Interlaken (Sfr24, 50 minutes) and Zürich (Sfr42, 1½ hours).

Car & Motorcycle There are three motorways which intersect at the northern part of the city. The N1 is the route from Neuchâtel in the west and Basel and Zürich in the north-east. The N6 connects Bern with Thun and the Interlaken region in the south-east. The N12 is the route from Geneva and Lausanne in the south-west.

Getting Around
To/From the Airport Belp airport is nine km south-east of the city centre. A small white bus links the airport to the train station (Sfr14). It takes 20 minutes and is coordinated with flight arrivals and departures.

Bus Getting around on foot is easy enough if you're staying in the city centre. Bus and tram tickets cost Sfr1.50 (under seven stops) or Sfr2.40. A day pass for the city and regional network is Sfr7.50. Buy single-journey tickets at stops and daily cards from the tourist office or the public transport office at Bubenbergplatz 5.

Taxi Many taxis wait by the station. The cost is Sfr6.50 plus Sfr2.70 (Sfr3 on Sunday and at night) per km.

AROUND BERN
There are some excellent excursions close to Bern. **Fribourg**, 30 minutes away by train (Sfr10.40), offers an old town-centre, fine views and a well-presented Art & History Museum. Further south is **Gruyères**, about an hour away from either Fribourg or Montreux. It has a 13th-century castle on the hill, and next to the train station is a dairy (☎ 026-921 14 10) offering daily free cheese-making tours. About 30 km west of Bern is **Murten**, a historic walled town overlooking a lake (hourly trains from Fribourg and Bern).

Neuchâtel

Neuchâtel (population 34,000) is inside the French-speaking region of Switzerland, on the north-west shore of the lake that shares its name. This relaxing town offers easy access to the mountain areas of the Jura, where there's good cross-country skiing and hiking.

Orientation & Information
The tourist office (☎ 725 42 42), Rue de la Place d'Armes 7, is open Monday to Friday from 9 am to noon and 1.30 to 5.30 pm, and Saturday from 9 am to noon (open daily in summer). Pick up a copy of its walking tour of the town centre. The train station (Gare CFF)

changes money daily and rents bikes. A post office is opposite (Poste, 2002 Neuchâtel 2). The central pedestrian zone is less than one km away down the hill along Ave de la Gare. Place Pury is the hub of local buses (Sfr1.60 to Sfr2.60 per trip, or Sfr6 for a day pass) and is close to the tourist office.

Neuchâtel's telephone code is ☎ 032.

Things to See

The centrepiece of the old town is the **castle** and the adjoining **Collegiate Church**. The castle dates from the 12th century and now houses cantonal offices. The church contains a striking cenotaph of 15 statues dating from 1372. Nearby, the **Prison Tower** (entry Sfr0.50) offers a good view of the area and has interesting models showing the town as it was in the 15th and 18th centuries.

One of the town's several museums, the **Museum of Art and History** (Musée d'Art et d'Histoire), 2 quai Léopold Robert, is especially noted for three 18th-century clockwork figures. Unfortunately they are only activated on the first Sunday of each month. Entry is Sfr7, or Sfr4 for students; the museum is shut on Monday and free on Thursday. The tourist office has information on nearby walking trails and boat trips on the lake.

Places to Stay & Eat

The SYHA *hostel* (☎ 731 31 90), Rue du Suchiez 35, is over two km from the town centre; take bus No 1 to Vauseyon then follow the signs. It is a small, pleasant, family-run place with good evening meals and a laundry service. Beds are Sfr22 and it closes from mid-December to mid-February. La Chaux-de-Fonds also has a SYHA *hostel* (☎ 968 43 15), Rue de Doubs 34, which is closed in November and December.

Hôtel du Poisson (☎ 753 30 31), Ave Bachelin 7, Marin (take bus No 1 from Place Pury), has singles/doubles for Sfr41/76 with private shower. In Neuchâtel, the ageing *Hôtel Terminus* (☎ 725 20 21), opposite the train station, has the cheapest rooms: Sfr90/120 with shower or Sfr50/90 without. *Marché* (☎ 724 58 00) is ideally central at Place des Halles 4. Singles/doubles for Sfr70/100 vary in size, use hall shower and have a TV. An extra bed in the room costs Sfr35.

Cheap self-service restaurants are at *Coop*,

Rue de la Treille 4; *EPA*, opposite the tourist office; and at *Cité Universitaire*, Ave de Clos-Brochet (open weekdays and for Saturday lunch). *Crêperie* is at Rue de l'Hôpital 7. If you don't like thin pancakes you'll think this place is a load of crêpe, because that's all it serves – but they're very tasty with many sweet or savoury fillings.

Café du Cerf, Rue de l'Ancien 4, has good Asian food (from Sfr17 to Sfr30), and lots of different beers for evening drinkers. You can eat upstairs, too, in the more formal part. A unique feature of Neuchâtel is its *restaurants de nuit*, open from around 9 pm to 6 am. They provide an excellent opportunity for revellers to drink all night. *Garbo Café*, Rue des Chavannes 7, is one such place.

Getting There & Away

There are hourly fast trains to Geneva (70 minutes, Sfr41), Bern (35 minutes, Sfr16.60) and many other destinations. Postbuses leave from outside the station.

AROUND NEUCHÂTEL

Six km to the east of town at Marin (take bus No 1 from Place Pury) is **Papiliorama**, with over 1000 butterflies of all sizes and hues, and **Nocturama**, with Latin American night creatures. They're in the Marin Centre and open daily (Sfr11).

Twenty km north-west of Neuchâtel and accessible by train in 30 minutes, is **La Chaux-de-Fonds**. This watch-making town is worth visiting for its Horology Museum (Sfr8, students Sfr4; closed Monday) at Rue des Musées 29.

The Jura canton is known for **horse riding**; contact the tourist office in Saignelégier (☎ 951 26 26). Costs are relatively low in this part of Switzerland.

Geneva

Geneva (Genève, Genf, Ginevra) is Switzerland's third-largest city (population 175,630), comfortably encamped on the shore of Lake Geneva (Lac Léman). Geneva belongs not so much to French-speaking Switzerland as to the whole world. It is truly an international city, a destination where belligerents

Geneva
(Genève)

0   250   500 m

Minor Streets not Depicted

PLACES TO STAY		48	Cave Valaisanne et		27	Permanence Médico
4	Centre Masaryk		Chalet Suisse			Chirurgicale
5	SYHA Hostel	53	Café Universal		28	Place des 22 Cantons
9	Hôtel de la Cloche				32	l'Usine
20	Hotel Lido	**OTHER**			33	Librairie Prior
31	Armée du Salut Hostel	1	Red Cross & Red			(Bookshop)
49	Hôtel Beau-site		Crescent Museum		34	Tourist Office
51	Hôtel Aïda	2	Palais des Nations		36	CGN Ticket Booth
54	Centre Universitaire	3	Place des Nations		37	Jardin Anglais
	Zofingien	6	Horizon Motos		40	Artou (Bookshop)
55	Hôtel le Prince		(Motorbike Rental)		41	Cathedral St Pierre
		8	Sixt-Alsa (car rental)		43	Maison Tavel
PLACES TO EAT		12	Bureau de Change		44	Alhambar
7	Migros	13	Tourist Office		45	Rousseau's Birthplace
10	Auberge de Savièse	14	Ilot 13		46	Reformation Monument
11	Le Blason	17	Notre-Dame		47	Flanagan's Irish Bar
15	Kong Restaurant	18	CAR (Information		50	Centre Sportif des
16	La Trattoria		Centre)			Vernets
26	Miyako	19	Place de Cornavin		52	SSR (Travel Agency)
29	Restaurant Manora	21	Post Café		56	Museum of Art &
30	Auberge de Coutance	22	Post Office			History
35	Café du Centre	23	Place des Alpes		57	Museum of Natural
38	l'Amiral	24	International Bus			History
39	Dent de Lion		Terminal			
42	EPA	25	American Express			

worldwide come to settle their differences by negotiation. One in three residents are non-Swiss and many world organisations are based here, not least the United Nations (European headquarters).

After gaining respite from the Duke of Savoy in 1530, Geneva was ripe for the teachings of John Calvin two years later; it soon became known as the Protestant Rome, during which time fun became frowned upon. Thankfully this legacy barely lingers and today Geneva offers a varied nightlife. In 1798 the French annexed the city and held it for 16 years before it was admitted to the Swiss Confederation as a canton in 1815.

Orientation
The Rhône River runs through the city, dividing it into *rive droite* (north of the Rhône) and *rive gauche* (the south). Conveniently in the centre of town on the north side is the main train station, Gare de Cornavin. To the south of the river lies the old part of town, where many important buildings are located. In the summer, Geneva's most visible landmark is the Jet d'Eau, a giant fountain on the southern shore.

Information
Tourist Offices The busy tourist office (☎ 738 52 00) is in the train station, and is open

Monday to Saturday from 9 am to 6 pm. From mid-June to 31 August it's open daily from 8 am to 8 pm (6 pm weekends). Hotel reservations cost Sfr5. There's another tourist office (☎ 311 98 27) in the old town at Place du Molard.

The Centre d'Accueil et de Renseignements (CAR) (☎ 731 46 47) has tourist and accommodation information, and a car-sharing agency. It is based in a yellow bus at the station end of Rue du Mont-Blanc and is open mid-June to 31 August, daily from 8 am to 11 pm.

Foreign Consulates These include:

Australia
    56-58 Rue de Moillebeau (☎ 918 29 00)
Canada
    1 Pré de la Bichette (☎ 919 92 00)
France
    11 Rue J Imbert Galloix (☎ 311 34 41)
Italy
    14 Rue Charles Galland (☎ 346 47 44)
New Zealand
    28A Chemin du Petit-Saconnex (☎ 734 95 30)
UK
    37-39 Rue de Vermont (☎ 734 12 04)
USA
    1-3 Ave de la Paix (☎ 738 76 13)

Money The exchange office in Gare de Cornavin is open every day from 6.45 am to

9.30 pm. The best rates seen while researching this edition were in the Bureau de Change at 32 Rue de Zürich, open weekdays and Saturday morning. Don't exchange banknotes at the airport (Sfr5 commission, though this doesn't apply to travellers' cheques) – cash them commission-free at the adjoining train station.

Post & Communications The main post office is at 18 Rue du Mont-Blanc, 1211 Genève 1. It is open Monday to Friday from 7.30 am to 6 pm, and Saturday from 7.30 to 11 am.

Geneva's telephone code is ☎ 022.

Travel Agencies American Express (☎ 731 76 00) is at 7 Rue du Mont-Blanc, near many other travel agents and airline offices. The budget and student travel agency SSR (☎ 329 97 34) is at 3 Rue Vignier (closed Saturday).

Bookshops Librairie des Amateurs, 15 Grand-Rue, and Librairie Prior, 6 Rue de la Cité, both have second-hand English-language books from Sfr3. Artou (☎ 818 02 40), 8 Rue de Rive, is good for travel books.

Medical Services Ring ☎ 111 (premium rate) for medical information. The Cantonal Hospital (☎ 382 33 11) is at 24 Rue Micheli du Crest. Permanence Médico Chirurgicale (☎ 731 21 20), 21 Rue de Chantepoulet, is a private clinic, open 24 hours a day. Emergency dental treatment (☎ 733 98 00) is at 60 Ave Wendt.

Things to See

Walking Tour The centre of the city is so compact that it is easy to see many of the main sights on foot. Start a scenic walk through the old town at the **Île Rousseau**, noted for a statue in honour of the celebrated free thinker.

Turn right along the south side of the Rhône until you reach the 13th-century **Tour d'Île**, once part of the medieval city fortifications. Walk south down the narrow, cobbled Rue de la Cité until it becomes Grand-Rue. Here at No 40 is Rousseau's birthplace. A short detour off Grand-Rue is the partially Romanesque, partially Gothic **Cathedral St Pierre**. John Calvin preached here from 1536 to 1564. There is a good view from the tower, which is open daily to 5.30 pm (entry Sfr2.50). The cathedral is on

a significant but unspectacular archaeological site (entry Sfr5, students Sfr3, closed Monday). Grand-Rue terminates at **Place du Bourg-de-Four**, the site of a medieval marketplace which now has a fountain and touristy shops.

Take Rue de la Fontaine to reach the lakeside. Anti-clockwise round the shore is the **Jet d'Eau**. Calling this a fountain is something of an understatement. The water shoots up with incredible force (200 km/h, 1360 horsepower) to create a 140-metre-high plume. At any one time, seven tonnes of water is in the air, and much of it, depending on the whims of the wind, falls on spectators who venture out on the pier. It's not activated in winter.

Parks & Gardens On the lakefront near the old town, the **Jardin Anglais** features a large clock composed of flowers. Colourful flower gardens and the occasional statue line the promenade on the north shore of the lake, and lead to two relaxing parks. One of these, the **Jardin Botanique**, features exotic plants, llamas and an aviary. Entry is free and it is open every day from 7 am to 7.30 pm. South of Grand-Rue is **Promenade des Bastions**. This park contains a massive monument to the Reformation: the giant figures of Bèze, Calvin, Farel and Knox are flanked by smaller statues of other important figures, and depictions in relief of events instrumental in the spread of the movement.

Museums Geneva is not a bad place to get stuck on a rainy day as there are plenty of museums, many of which are free. The most important is the **Museum of Art and History** (Musée d'Art et d'Histoire), 2 Rue Charles Galland, with a vast and varied collection including paintings, sculpture, weapons and archaeology. The nearby **Museum of Natural History** (Musée d'Histoire Naturelle), Route de Malagnou, has dioramas, minerals and anthropological displays. In the old town, **Maison Tavel**, 6 Rue du Puits Saint Pierre, is notable for a detailed relief map of Geneva in 1850, covering 35 sq metres. All these museums are free and open Tuesday to Sunday from 10 am to 5 pm.

By the UN is the **International Red Cross & Red Crescent Museum**, a vivid multimedia illustration of the history of those two humanitarian organisations. It's open Wednesday to

Monday from 10 am to 5 pm (entry Sfr8, or Sfr4 for students and senior citizens).

United Nations The European arm of the UN is housed in the Palais des Nations, former home of its deceased parent, the League of Nations, and is the focal point for a resident population of 3000 international civil servants. The hour-long tour of the interior is pricey and only moderately interesting (Sfr8.50; students Sfr6.50). There is no charge to walk around the gardens where there's a towering grey monument coated with heat-resistant titanium, donated by the former USSR to commemorate the conquest of space.

The gardens are open Monday to Friday from November to March and daily from April to October. Guided tours are from 10 am to noon and 2 to 4 pm, and 9 am to noon and 2 to 6 pm in July and August. You need to show your passport to gain admittance.

Excursions In France, **Mont Salève** yields an excellent view of the city and Lake Geneva. Take bus No 8 to Veyrier and walk across the border. The cable car up costs Sfr15 return (students Sfr9.20) and runs daily in summer, infrequently in winter. **CERN**, near Meyrin, is a research laboratory into particle physics, and has an interesting free exhibition (with English text) open Monday to Saturday from 10 am to 5 pm. Three-hour guided tours of the site and particle accelerator are on Saturday only (free; reserve ahead on ☎ 767 84 84). Take bus No 15 from the station. You pass into France on the tour; as it's not an official crossing you won't need a visa, but take your passport.

Activities

Centre Sportif des Vernets (☎ 343 88 50), 4 Rue Hans Wilsdorf, has swimming (Sfr4.50; students Sfr1.50) and ice skating (same price) and is open daily except Monday from 9 am. At weekends in the summer Lake Geneva is alive with the bobbing white sails of sailing boats. Swim in the lake at Genève Plage (Sfr5, including entry to a large pool with waterslide) on the south shore and Jetée des Pâquis (Sfr1) on the north shore.

Special Events

The Geneva Festival, held in the second weekend of August, is a time of fun, fireworks and parades. L'Escalade on 11 December celebrates the foiling of an invasion by the Duke of Savoy in 1602.

Places to Stay

Camping The most central camping ground, *Sylvabelle* (☎ 347 06 03), 10 Chemin de Conches, is reached by bus No 8 from Gare de Cornavin or Rond-Point de Rive. Four-person bungalows are available and camping is Sfr6 per person, Sfr5 per tent and Sfr3 per car (closed in winter).

Seven km north-east of the city centre on the southern lakeshore is *Camping Pointe à la Bise* (☎ 752 12 96), Vesenaz; it costs Sfr6 per person, plus from Sfr7 for tents. Take bus E from Rive. Further (at the terminus of bus E) and cheaper is *Camping D'Hermance* (☎ 751 14 83), Chemin des Glerrets. Both sites are open from around April to October and prices include car parking.

Hostels A good selection of dormitory accommodation is listed in the *Young People Info* leaflet issued by the tourist office, including some that take women only.

North of the Rhône The SYHA *hostel* (☎ 732 62 60), 28-30 Rue Rothschild, is big, modern and busy, with helpful and knowledgeable staff. Dorms are Sfr23 and there are a few family rooms and doubles (Sfr60 with shower). Three-course dinners are Sfr11.50, and there's a TV room, laundry and kitchen facilities. The hostel is closed from 10 am to 5 pm (to 4 pm in summer) and there is a flexible midnight curfew.

Centre Masaryk (☎ 733 07 72), 11 Ave de la Paix, has dorms for Sfr25 with an 11 pm curfew. Singles/doubles/triples cost Sfr38/ 64/ 90 and you can get a key for late access. Take bus No 5 or 8 from Gare de Cornavin.

The *Armée du Salut Hostel* (☎ 344 91 21), Chemin Galiffe 4, will take travellers. At just Sfr10 per person in very simple double rooms it's a bargain, but expect insalubrious co-habites. The hostel is closed from 9 am to 6 pm in winter, 8 am to 7 pm in summer; there's a two nights maximum stay for foreigners.

South of the Rhône The *Cité Universitaire* (☎ 346 23 55), at 46 Ave Miremont, has 500 beds, but dorms (Sfr15) are only available in July and August. Take bus No 3 from Cornavin to the terminus at Champel, south of the city centre. Singles/doubles cost Sfr40/55, or Sfr34/50 for students. A double studio with kitchen, toilet and shower costs Sfr61. Prices exclude breakfast (from Sfr5). Reception is open from 8 am to noon (9 to 11 am on Sunday) and 2 pm (6 pm on weekends) to 10 pm.

Centre Universitaire Zofingien (☎ 329 11 40), 6 Rue des Voisins, has well-equipped rooms which are excellent value even if they are slightly cramped. Singles/doubles/triples with toilet, shower and sink are Sfr48/72/90.

Hotels In addition to the affordable choices mentioned below, there are many high-class, high-cost hotels catering to visitors on limitless budgets or generous expense accounts.

North of the Rhône At 6 Rue de la Cloche, the *Hôtel de la Cloche* (☎ 732 94 81), is small, old-fashioned, friendly, and liable to be full unless you call ahead. Big singles/doubles using hall shower are Sfr50/75; doubles with private shower cubicle are Sfr85. Breakfast costs Sfr5.

Hôtel Lido (☎ 731 55 30), 8 Rue de Chantepoulet, has a better ambience, decent-sized rooms, and genial staff. Singles/doubles with private shower, toilet, TV and radio start at Sfr75/120, and there are a couple of rooms for Sfr65/110 using hall shower.

There's not much to choose between the tourist-class hotels clustered round the train station. *Bernina* (☎ 731 49 50), *Astoria* (☎ 732 10 25) and *Excelsior* (☎ 732 09 45) all have comfortable singles/doubles with shower or bath and toilet for around Sfr110/150. *Hôtel Suisse* (☎ 732 66 30), 10 Place de Cornavin, is the pick of them, with a nice swirling staircase and better appointed rooms, but it's also more expensive, starting at Sfr135/180.

South of the Rhône Try the *Hôtel Aïda* (☎ 320 12 66), 6 Ave Henri-Dunant, which has renovated singles/doubles (using hall shower) for Sfr55/75. Rooms with shower/toilet cost Sfr75/100 and also have a TV. *Hôtel Beau-Site* (☎ 328 10 08), 3 Place du Cirque, has good-sized, old-fashioned rooms with high ceiling and creaky wood floors. Singles/doubles/

triples are Sfr59/80/96 (hall shower), Sfr64/85/110 (private shower cubicle) or Sfr75/102/120 (private bathroom). *Hôtel le Prince* (☎ 329 85 44/5), 16 Rue des Voisins, has comfortable if smallish rooms with shower/toilet, TV and telephone. Singles/doubles are Sfr80/102, or Sfr60/80 using hall shower.

Places to Eat

Eating is generally cheaper around Gare de Cornavin, or south of the old town in the vicinity of the university. Fondue and raclette are widely available. Also popular is locally caught perch, but it costs well over Sfr20 unless you can find it as a plat du jour. There is a small *fruit & vegetable market* open daily on Rue de Coutance. *Migros* supermarket on Rue des Pâquis has a cheap self-service restaurant. *Aperto*, a supermarket in the train station, is open daily from 6 am to 9 pm. See the following Entertainment section for more places to eat.

North of the Rhône The buffet-style *Restaurant Manora*, 4 Rue de Cornavin, has tasty daily dishes from Sfr10 and extensive salad and dessert bars. It is open daily from 7 am to 9.30 pm (9 am to 9 pm on Sunday). Opposite, *Auberge de Coutance* (☎ 732 79 19) is recommended for exquisite specialities from Sfr26, including duck delicacies. It's an atmospheric below-ground restaurant at 25 Rue de Coutance (closed Saturday evening and Sunday).

La Trattoria, 1 Rue de la Servette, near the station, has excellent Italian food from Sfr14 (closed Sunday). Along the road at No 31 is *Kong Restaurant*, providing tasty Chinese dishes for Sfr20. Visit at lunchtime, when every weekday there are meals for Sfr12 including rice and starter, and (Tuesday, Wednesday and Thursday only) Sfr17.50 secures an all-you-can-eat buffet.

Le Blason, 23 Rue des Pâquis, looks like a typical bar/restaurant by day, with meals from Sfr14, but it also courts late night clubbers by opening daily from 4 am to 2 am (4 am to midnight on weekends). *Auberge de Savièse*, nearby at No 20 has lunchtime plats du jour from Sfr13, and Swiss specialities such as fondue from Sfr18.90 (closed Saturday lunchtime and Sunday).

Take advantage of the international flavour of Geneva to vary your diet. Explore the streets north of Rue des Alpes for cheapish Mexican and Asian food. *Miyako* (☎ 738 01 20), 11 Rue de Chantrepoulet, is expensive but the quality is excellent. This Japanese restaurant has three-course business lunches from Sfr29, and a full evening meal will cost around Sfr50 or more (closed Sunday).

South of the Rhône For the cheapest eating in the old town, make for the restaurant in the *EPA* department store on Rue de la Croix d'Or. Meals are Sfr8 to Sfr14. *Le Zofage*, downstairs in the Centre Universitaire Zofingien (see Places to Stay), has a plat du jour for Sfr11.50 (Sfr10 for students) and is open every day from 7 am to midnight.

Café du Centre, 5 Place du Molard, has outside seating in a pleasant square near the old town. Office staff relax here after work over a coffee or a beer. The lunchtime plat du jour costs Sfr15 on weekdays (open every day from 7 am to 2 am). *Dent de Lion*, 14 Rue des Eaux-Vives, is a small vegetarian place, open Monday to Friday from 9 am to 3 pm and 6 to 10 pm. Three-course lunches are Sfr15.

More up-market is the large and popular *Cave Valaisanne et Chalet Suisse* (☎ 328 12 36), 23 Blvd Georges Favon. It's an excellent place to try many varieties of fondue (starting at Sfr19.80); the scent of bubbling cheese inside could give a mouse palpitations at 20 paces. It's open from 8 am to 1 am daily.

Café Universal, 26 Blvd du Pont d'Arve, is atmospheric, French and smoky, with theatrical patrons (closed Sunday and Monday in summer). Plats du jour are from Sfr15 and dinners are mostly above Sfr20. Another good place for those with slightly larger budgets is *l'Amiral* (☎ 735 18 08), 24 Quai Gustave-Ador, near the Jet d'Eau. The 'menu du touriste' is fillet of perch with salad and dessert for Sfr32 (open daily).

Entertainment

Geneva has a good selection of nightclubs but unless you have money to burn, steer clear. These, along with dance, music and theatre events, are listed in *Geneva Agenda*, free from the tourist office.

Alternative arts flourish in the city. *L'Usine* (☎ 781 34 90), 4 Place des Volontaires, is a converted old factory (hence the name), now a centre for cinema, cabaret, theatre, concerts and homeless art objects (closed Monday). It has a bar and a good restaurant with inexpensive food (closed Saturday to Monday). Also explore *Ilot 13*, 12 Rue de Montbrillant, a collection of squats offering art shows, organic food, drinks, music and theatre.

A good British/Irish bar is *Post Café*, 7 Rue de Berne, with draught cider and Guinness, and British sports on Sky TV. A similar, larger place in the old town is *Flanagan's Irish Bar*, Rue du Cheval-Blanc. *Alhambar* (☎ 312 30 11), 1st floor, 10 Rue de la Rôtisserie, has food, drinks and live music (closed Monday). *Au Chat Noir* (☎ 343 49 98), 13 Rue Vautier, is a jazz club with interesting murals and live music.

Getting There & Away

Air Geneva airport is an important transport hub and has frequent connections to every major European city. Enquire at Swissair (☎ 799 59 99) about youth fares (aged under 25) and one-off offers; the office is by the station on Rue de Lausanne, open Monday to Friday from 8.30 am to 6 pm.

Bus International buses depart from Place Dorcière (☎ 732 02 30), off Rue des Alpes. There are three buses a week to London (Sfr150) and Barcelona (Sfr90), and several buses a day to Chamonix (Sfr47, Sfr81 return).

Train There are more or less hourly connections to most Swiss towns; Zürich takes three hours (Sfr74), as does Interlaken Ost (Sfr60), both via Bern. There are regular international trains to Paris (Sfr78 by TGV, reservations essential), Hamburg (Sfr261), Milan (Sfr71) and Barcelona (Sfr99). Gare des Eaux-Vives is the station for Annecy and Chamonix. To get there from Gare de Cornavin, take bus No 8 or 1 to Rond-Point de Rive and then tram No 12.

Car & Motorcycle An autoroute bypass skirts Geneva, with major routes intersecting southwest of the city: the N1 from Lausanne joins with the E62 to Lyon (130 km) and the E25 heading south-east towards Chamonix. Toll-free main roads follow the course of these motorways.

Sixt-Alsa (☎ 732 90 90), 1 Place de la Navigation, has the best daily car rental rates (from Sfr115 per day, unlimited km) and offers one-way drop-offs to Zürich airport. Its weekend deals (Sfr205) are for 72 hours. Horizon Motos (☎ 731 23 39), 51 Rue de Lausanne, has motorcycles (weekend rates from Sfr117, unlimited mileage).

Boat Compagnie Générale de Navigation (CGN) (☎ 311 25 21) by the Jardin Anglais operates a steamer service to all towns and major villages bordering Lake Geneva, including those in France. Most boats only operate between May and September, such as those to Lausanne (3½ hours, Sfr27) and Montreux (4½ hours, Sfr34). Both Eurail and Swiss passes are valid on CGN boats, or there are CGN boat day passes for Sfr47. CGN also has circular excursions and dancing cruises.

Getting Around
To/From the Airport Getting from Cointrin airport is easy with 200 trains a day into Gare de Cornavin (six minutes, Sfr4.80). Bus No 10 (Sfr2.20) does the same five-km trip. A taxi would cost around Sfr30.

Bus A combination of buses, trolleybuses and trams makes getting around just as easy. There are ticket dispensers at bus stops. A ticket valid for one hour costs Sfr2.20; a book of six such tickets costs Sfr12, while a book of 12 costs Sfr22. One, two or three-day passes for the whole canton cost Sfr8.50, Sfr15 or Sfr19, though most people will only need a city day pass (Sfr5, or Sfr27 for six passes). Passes and multi-tickets are available from the tourist office bus section, from Transports Publics Genevois at the lower level of Gare de Cornavin (by the yellow escalators), or at Rond-Point de Rive.

Taxi The cost for most taxis is Sfr6.30 plus Sfr2.70 per km, though some operators have higher prices.

Bicycle The bike rental office at Gare de Cornavin is open daily from 7 am to 6.45 pm (7.45 pm at weekends). It has a leaflet showing cycle routes in and around the city.

Boat In addition to CGN (see the previous Getting There & Away section) smaller companies operate excursions on the lake between April and October but no passes are valid. Ticket offices and departures are along Quai du Mont-Blanc and by the Jardin Anglais. Trips range from half an hour (Sfr10, several departures a day) to two hours (Sfr25), with commentary in English.

Lake Geneva Region

LAUSANNE
Capital of the canton of Vaud, this hilly city is Switzerland's fifth largest (population 128,000). Don't miss l'Art Brut, one of Europe's most unusual art collections.

Orientation & Information
In the train station is a tourist office, open daily (closed mornings in winter); bicycle rental (summer only) and money-changing facilities. The main post office (Poste Principale 1001), is by the station. The cathedral, shopping streets and Place St François (the main hub for local transport) are up the hill to the north.

The main tourist office (☎ 617 14 27), 2 Ave de Rhodanie, is by the picturesque harbour of Ouchy. It's open Monday through to Saturday from 8 am to 7 pm, and Sunday from 9 am to noon and 1 to 6 pm. From 1 October to 31 March it's open to 6 pm on weekdays and weekend hours are Saturday only from 8 am to noon and 1 to 5 pm. Commission is charged for hotel reservations.

Lausanne's telephone code is ☎ 021.

Things to See & Do
The fine Gothic **cathedral** was built in the 12th and 13th centuries and has an impressive main portal and attractive stained-glass windows. The church and tower are open daily, though the famous rose window is undergoing renovations until 1999.

The **Musée de l'Art Brut**, 11 Ave de Bergières, should not be missed. It's a fascinating amalgam of art created by untrained

Lausanne

0   200   400 m

Some Minor Streets not Depicted

PLACES TO STAY
22 Hôtel d'Angleterre

PLACES TO EAT
6   Migros
8   Café de l'Everche
10 Manora
13 Au Couscous

OTHER
1   Palais de Beaulieu
2   Musée de l'Art Brut
3   Castle St Marie
4   Palais de Rumine
    & Museum of Fine Arts
5   Place de la Riponne
7   Cathedral
9   Place de la Palud
11 Place St François
12 St François Church
14 Post Office
15 Main Train Station
16 Main Post Office
17 Musée de l'Elysée
18 CGN Head Office
19 Tourist Office
20 Regional Tourist Office
21 Ouchy Metro
23 Musée Olympique
24 CGN Boat Departure Point

To Neuchâtel (75 km)
& N1 Motorway

Avenue de Bergières

Avenue de France

Avenue de Beaulieu

Avenue Vinet

To Morges

Avenue d'Echallens

Avenue de Morges

Rue de Genève

To Ada - Logements

Avenue de Tivoli

Rue des Terreaux

Rue Neuve

Rue St Laurent

Rue de Genève

Pont Chauderon

Avenue Jules Gonin

Rue du Grand-Chêne

La Grand Pont

Rue Centrale

Rue de Bourg

Rue du Tunnel

Rue Dr César - Roux

Rue St - Martin

Rue Curtat

Place Bessières

To Place
de l'Ours,
Murten &
Bern

Avenue Marc-Dufour

Avenue Louis - Ruchonnet

Rue du Petit-Chêne

Avenue du Théâtre

Mon-Repos

Place
de la Gare

Avenue de la Gare

Avenue Mont d'Or

To SYHA Hostel
& Jeunotel

Ave. Fraisse

Boulevard

de Grancy

Avenue

Dapples

Botanical
Gardens

Avenue de la Harpe

Avenue de Cour

Avenue d'Ouchy

Avenue de l'Elysée

Avenue de Rhodanie

Chemin de Bellerive

To
Camping
de Vidy &
Geneva (62 km)

Avenue d'Ouchy

Port d'Ouchy

Quai d'Ouchy

To
Montreux
(31 km)

Lake Geneva

SWITZERLAND

artists – the mentally-unhinged, eccentrics and incarcerated criminals. Some of the images created are startling, others merely strange. Biographies and explanations are in English and the collection is open Tuesday to Sunday from 11 am to 1 pm and 2 to 6 pm. Entry costs Sfr6, or Sfr4 for students.

Lausanne is the headquarters of the International Olympic Committee, so it is perhaps inevitable that there's a museum devoted to the Games. The lavish **Olympic Museum** (Musée Olympique), 1 Quai d'Ouchy, is open daily except Monday (Sfr14, students Sfr9), and tells the Olympic story using videos, archive film, interactive computers and memorabilia.

The large **Palais de Rumine** contains several museums. The most important is the Museum of Fine Arts (Musée Cantonal des Beaux-Arts), which exhibits many works by Swiss artists, and holds temporary exhibitions (entry fee varies). The other museums in the building are free and cover natural history and other sciences (closed Monday).

The lake provides plenty of sporting opportunities. Vidy Sailing School (☎ 617 90 00) offers courses on windsurfing, water-skiing and sailing, and equipment rental for these activities. For less athletic entertainment, try a tour of the nearby wine-growers' cellars, centring on Lavaux and Chablais to the east and La Côte to the west. Get details from the tourist office.

Places to Stay

Year-round lakeside camping is possible at *Camping de Vidy* (☎ 624 20 31), just to the west of the Vidy sports complex. The SYHA *hostel* (☎ 616 57 82), 1 Chemin du Muguet, Ouchy, can be reached from the train station by bus No 1 or a 20-minute walk. Dorms cost Sfr24 per night and dinners are Sfr11.50. Reception is closed from 9 am to 5 pm and curfew is at 11.30 pm.

Newly opened in 1993, *Jeunotel* (☎ 626 02 22), 36 Chemin du Bois de Vaud, offers no-frills accommodation in dorms (Sfr21), singles/doubles (Sfr64/74 with shower or Sfr54/58 without), and triples/quads (Sfr69/92 without). The self-service restaurant serves cheap meals; if you want breakfast add Sfr7. *Villa Cherokee* (☎ 647 57 20), 4 Chemin de Charmilles, is family-run and has singles/doubles from Sfr35/60 excluding breakfast.

To get there, take bus No 2 and get off at Presbytère.

The best mid-range deal is the *Hôtel d'Angleterre* (☎ 616 41 45) on the Quai d'Ouchy. It's a stately old building and has large, comfortable rooms with TV and views of the lake. Singles/doubles start at Sfr100/140 with shower or Sfr65/110 without. It's closed between Christmas and 31 January. Byron wrote the *Prisoner of Chillon* here in 1816.

Places to Eat

There is a *Migros* restaurant at Rue Neuve, but you're better off heading for the buffet-style *Manora*, 17 Place St François, open daily to 10.30 pm. There's a good choice of vegetables, salad and fruit, and main dishes are around Sfr10. *Café de l'Everche*, 4 Rue Louis Curtat, by the cathedral, has a lunch and evening two-course menu for Sfr14.50 and a pleasant garden at the back. It is open daily from 7 am to midnight.

Restaurant *Au Couscous* (☎ 312 20 17), 2 Rue Enning, on the 1st floor, has a wide menu including Tunisian, vegetarian and macrobiotic food. Meals start at Sfr12 and it's open daily to 1 am.

Getting There & Away

There are three trains an hour to/from Geneva (Sfr19.40; takes 40 to 50 minutes), and one or two an hour to Bern. Trains to Interlaken Ost cost Sfr50 either via Bern or the scenic route via Montreux. For boat services, see the Geneva section.

MONTREUX

Centrepiece of the so-called Swiss Riviera, Montreux offers marvellous lakeside walks and access to the ever-popular Château de Chillon.

Orientation & Information

The train station and main post office are on Ave des Alpes, which down to the south leads to Place de la Paix and the main streets of Grand-Rue and Ave du Casino. The tourist office (☎ 962 84 84) is a few minutes away in the Pavillon on the lakeshore; it is open Monday to Friday from 9 am to noon and 1.30 to 6 pm, and on Saturday from 9 am to noon. Hours are extended in the summer, when the place is open daily.

The telephone code for Montreux is ☎ 021.

Things to See

Montreux is known for the **Château de Chillon** (pronounced 'Sheeyoh'), which receives more visitors than any other historical building in Switzerland. Occupying a stunning position right on Lake Geneva, the fortress caught the public imagination when Lord Byron wrote about the fate of Bonivard, a follower of the Reformation, who was chained to the fifth pillar in the dungeons for four years in the 16th century. Byron etched his own name on the third pillar.

The castle, still in excellent condition, dates from the 11th century and has been much modified and enlarged since then. Allow at least two hours to view the tower, courtyards, dungeons and numerous rooms containing weapons, utensils, frescos and furniture. Entry costs Sfr6.50 for adults, Sfr5.50 for students and Sfr3 for children, and the castle opens daily at 10 am (9 am from April to September). The closing time varies throughout the year: it is 4.45 pm from November to February; 5.30 pm in March and October; 6.30 pm in April, May, June and September; and 7 pm in July and August. The castle is a pleasant 45-minute walk along the lakefront from Montreux (15 minutes from the hostel), or it's also accessible by train or bus No 1 (Sfr1.70).

Nearby **Vevey**, to the west, has several interesting museums and is easily reached by bus No 1.

Montreux's other claim to fame is the **Jazz Festival** in early July. The programme is announced in May and tickets are available shortly afterwards from the Montreux tourist office or from the ticket corner in branches of the Swiss Bank Corporation throughout Switzerland.

Places to Stay

The SYHA *hostel* (☎ 963 49 34) is at 8 Passage de l'Auberge, Territet, a 30-minute walk along the lake clockwise from the tourist office (or take the train or bus No 1). It's open year-round, near the waterfront and under the railway line. It has renovated facilities throughout; dorms are Sfr27 and doubles (bunk beds) are Sfr74.

Villa Germaine (☎ 963 15 28), 3 Ave de Collonges, Territet, is the same price year-round. Singles/doubles are Sfr65/100 with shower or Sfr50/85 without. *Pension Wilhelm*

(☎ 963 14 31), 13 Rue de Marché, charges Sfr60/90 for singles/doubles (some with own shower) in an old-fashioned, family-run hotel. *Hostellerie du Lac* (☎ 963 32 71), 12 Rue du Quai, has rooms with high ceilings, big balconies and views of the lake. Doubles start at Sfr70 with hall shower or Sfr110 with private facilities, and all rooms have TV and radio. Subtract Sfr10/20 for single occupancy (closed mid-December to late February).

Places to Eat

Migros supermarket on Ave du Casino has a self-service restaurant, with late opening (to 7.45 pm) on Thursday and Friday. *Restaurant City*, 37 Ave des Alpes, is also self-service with meals for under Sfr12. The main advantage of this place is the sunny terrace overlooking the lake (open daily).

Tea-Room Les Arcades, Rue Industrielle, offers fantastic value for a weekday lunch (to 2 pm): soup, main course, dessert and a drink is only Sfr13. *Brasserie des Alpes*, 23 Ave des Alpes, serves good French and Italian fare from Sfr14 and is open daily. On the lake along Rue de Quay, check out *Palais Hoggar*, decked out in fake inlays, looking like a low-budget version of the Taj Mahal. It has Asian food for around Sfr25 to Sfr35.

Getting There & Away

Hourly trains run to/from Geneva and take 70 minutes (Sfr27). From Lausanne, there are three trains an hour (Sfr8.40) which take around 25 minutes. Slow local trains continue eastwards from Montreux to stop at Territet for the hostel, and Chillon for the castle. Interlaken can be reached via a scenic rail route, with changeovers at Zweisimmen and Spiez (rail passes valid, though there is a Sfr6 supplement for 'Panorama Express' trains only). The track winds its way up the hill for an excellent view over Lake Geneva. For boat services, see Getting There & Away in the Geneva section.

VAUD ALPS

If you're in this region in late January, don't miss the International Hot Air Balloon Week, a visually spectacular event in **Château d'Oex**, on the Montreux-Interlaken rail line. Contact its tourist office (☎ 026-924 77 88).

To get off the beaten track, consider staying in quiet, untouristed **Gryon** (1130 metres). It is scenically situated, close to the Villars ski area and 30 minutes by train from Bex (which is on the Lausanne-Sion rail route). There are several cheap places to stay – ask the tourist office (☎ 024-498 14 22). *Swiss Alp Retreat* (☎ 024-498 33 21), based in the Chalet Martin, has traveller-oriented Swiss/Australian owners who rent ski gear (only Sfr15) and bikes (Sfr10), and organise excursions. Dorms cost Sfr15 in summer (Sfr18 in winter) and doubles or family rooms are Sfr20 (Sfr25) per person, plus Sfr1 or Sfr2 for sheets. There's a kitchen (no breakfast) and check-in is from 9 am to 9 pm. Telephone ahead.

Valais

The dramatic Alpine scenery of Valais (Wallis in German) once made it one of the most inaccessible regions of Switzerland. Nowadays the mountains and valleys have been opened up by an efficient network of roads, railways and cable cars. It is an area of great natural beauty and, naturally enough, each impressive panorama has spawned its own resort. Skiing (47 listed centres) in the winter and hiking in the summer are primary pursuits, but angling, swimming, mountaineering, even tennis, are widely enjoyed.

Valais is also known for its Combats de Reines (Kuhkämpfe in German) – cow fights organised in villages to determine which beast is most suited to lead the herd up to the summer pastures. They usually take place on selected Sundays through the summer from April, accompanied by much celebration and consumption of Valaisan wine. The combatants rarely get hurt. There is a grand final in Aproz on Ascension Day, and the last meeting of the season is at the Martigny Fair in October.

SION

Sion, the capital of the Lower Valais, merits a perusal en route from Montreux to Zermatt. Its historical pre-eminence (the Bishops of Sion formerly held the powers of temporal princes) is hinted at by the two ancient fortifications that dominate the town: Tourbillon Castle and on the neighbouring hill, the Valère church. Both provide a fine view of the Rhône valley.

The regional museums of Valais are here too; get details from the Sion tourist office (☎ 027-322 85 86), Place de la Planta. The regional tourist office (☎ 027-322 31 61), 6 Rue Pré-Fleuri, can help you plan excursions to other attractions in the Valais.

If you want to stop over, there's a SYHA *hostel* (☎ 027-323 74 70), Rue de l'Industrie 2, behind the station (exit left and turn left under the tracks). All trains on the Lausanne-Brig express route stop at Sion.

ZERMATT

Skiing, hiking and mountaineering are the main attractions in this resort, all overseen by the Matterhorn, the most famous peak in the Alps.

Orientation & Information

The massive Matterhorn (4478 metres) stands sentinel at the head of the valley. Zermatt is car-free except for electric taxis, and there are few street names.

The tourist office (☎ 967 01 81), beside the train station, is open Monday to Friday from 8.30 am to noon and 2 to 6 pm, and Saturday from 8.30 am to noon. During the summer and winter high season it is also open Saturday afternoon and Sunday. Next door is a travel agent which changes money. The mountain guides office *(Bergführerbüro)* (☎ 967 34 56) on the main street near the post office is another good information source. Some hotels and restaurants close between seasons.

Zermatt's telephone code is ☎ 027.

Activities

Zermatt has many demanding slopes to test the experienced skier; beginners have fewer possibilities. February to April is peak time, but in early summer the snow is still good and the lifts are less busy. There are excellent views of mountain panoramas, including Mt Rosa and the Matterhorn, from the network of cable cars and gondolas.

The cog-wheel railway to Gornergrat (3100 metres) is a particular highlight. The Klein Matterhorn is topped by the highest cable station in Europe, at 3820 metres, and provides access to summer skiing slopes. It is possible to ski into Italy from here along the Ventina route to Cervinia but don't forget to take your passport. There are footpaths to and from many of the cable-car terminals. A day pass for all ski lifts, excluding Cervinia, costs Sfr60. Ski shops open daily for rental – for one day, hire prices for skis and stocks are Sfr38 and boots are Sfr19.

A walk in the cemetery is a sobering experience for would-be mountaineers, as numerous monuments tell of deaths on Mt Rosa and the Matterhorn. Also wander around the traditional Valais wooden barns in the Hinter Dorf area, just north of the church.

Places to Stay & Eat
Camping Spiss (☎ 967 39 21), to the left of the train station, is open from June to September.

The SYHA *hostel* (☎ 967 23 20) has an excellent view of the Matterhorn. Turn left at the church, cross the river and take the second right. Dorm beds at half-board cost Sfr38, plus Sfr6 in high season. Laundry loads cost Sfr8. The doors stay open during the day, but curfew is at 11.30 pm. The hostel is shut during May, and from late November to mid-December.

Opposite the train station and popular with mountaineers is *Hotel Bahnhof* (☎ 967 24 06), with dorms for Sfr26 or Sfr28 and singles/doubles for Sfr46/76, all without breakfast. There's a kitchen, a few showers and no curfew or daytime closing. *Hotel Gabelhorn* (☎ 967 22 35), in the Hinter Dorf area of the village, is small and friendly, costing from Sfr45 per person.

Most other places are significantly cheaper in the low season – make use of the hotel board with free phone in both the tourist office and train station. *Hotel Garni Malva* (☎ 967 30 33), overlooking the east side of the river, costs from Sfr55 per person; doubles with private shower are from Sfr132.

North Wall Bar, near the hostel, is one of the cheapest and best bars in the village, and is popular with resort workers. It has ski videos, music, good pizzas from Sfr10 and beer at Sfr4.50 for half a litre. The bar is closed during the off season, otherwise it's open daily from 6.30 pm to midnight. Down the hill, the more expensive *Papperla Pub* is also popular.

Beyond the church on the main street, *Restaurant Weisshorn* and the *Café du Pont* next door are both good places for food. Also recommended is *Walliserkanne*, by the post office, which has pizzas, fondue, fish dishes and Valais specialities from Sfr14 to Sfr24.

Getting There & Away
Hourly trains depart from Brig, calling at Visp en route. The steep and scenic journey takes 80 minutes and costs Sfr34 one way, or Sfr58 return. It is a private railway; Eurail passes are not valid, Inter-Rail earns 50% off and the Swiss Pass gets free travel. See the St Moritz section for information on the Glacier Express. The only way out is back, but if you're going to Saas Fee you can divert there from Stalden-Saas.

As Zermatt is car-free, you need to park cars at Täsch (Sfr3 to Sfr10 per day) and take the train from there (Sfr6.60). Parking is free in Visp if you take the Zermatt train (for details, ☎ 923 13 33).

SAAS FEE
In the valley adjoining Zermatt, Saas Fee may not have the Matterhorn, but there are plenty of other towering peaks to keep you occupied.

Orientation & Information
The village centre and ski lifts are to the left of the bus station, which contains a post office. The high season is from mid-December to mid-April. The tourist office (☎ 957 14 57), opposite the bus station, is open from Monday to Friday from 8.30 am to noon and 2 to 6.30 pm, Saturday from 8 am to 7 pm, and Sunday from 3 to 6 pm. During the low season, weekend opening is reduced depending on demand.

Saas Fee's telephone code is ☎ 027.

Activities
Saas Fee is surrounded by an impressive panorama of 4000-metre peaks and rivals Zermatt as a summer skiing centre. There is also ski mountaineering along the famous Haute Route to Chamonix. The highest metro in the world operates all year to Mittelallalin at 3500 metres, where there's an ice pavilion explaining interesting facts about glaciers.

A general lift pass costs Sfr51 for one day. Ski rental prices are as for Zermatt. The tourist office has a map of summer walking trails. Even in winter, 30 km of marked footpaths remain open.

Places to Stay & Eat
The *Albana* has beds in shared rooms with shower from Sfr30, including a great breakfast.

It's advisable to book in advance in winter, and it's closed in the off-season. Reception is in the adjoining *Hotel Mascotte* (☎ 957 27 24), which has singles/doubles for Sfr55/110 with private toilet and shower. In the south of the village, convenient for the ski lifts, is *Garni Feehof* (☎ 957 33 44), with good-value singles/doubles for Sfr53/106 with shower or Sfr46/92 without.

Eat pizza at *Boccalino* near the ski lifts. In the extreme north of the village, *Restaurant Alp Hitta* (☎ 957 10 50) has a rustic atmosphere, complete with background Alpine music. Raclette is Sfr6, fondue is Sfr20, and other Walliser meals start at Sfr14. It's closed in the off-season, though the restaurant manages two to four-person apartments, each with a small kitchen, which are available all year. The price of Sfr39 per person includes breakfast. *La Ferme*, near the tourist office, is good for mid-range food.

Getting There & Away
Saas Fee cannot be reached by train. Hourly buses depart from Brig via Visp, take one hour and cost Sfr17.40.

Like Zermatt, Saas Fee is car-free. Park at the entrance to the village, where daily charges are Sfr13 (get Sfr4 off with the Guest Card, supplied by your hotel in Saas Fee).

OTHER RESORTS
The best known resort in west Valais is **Verbier**, with 400 km of ski runs. Ski passes cost Sfr59 for one day or Sfr355 for a week. Across the valley (reached by bus) is **Bruson**, an unspoiled village with traditional homes. It has a very cheap SYHA *hostel* (☎ 776 23 56), closed in November. Lesser-known resorts can have perfectly adequate skiing yet be much cheaper. Ski passes in **Leukerbad**, for example, west of Brig, are Sfr38 (students Sfr32) for one day or Sfr200 (students Sfr158) for a week. Leukerbad is also a health spa with the added attraction of hot springs.

Ticino

Situated south of the Alps and enjoying a Mediterranean climate, Ticino (Tessin in German) gives more than just a taste of Italy. Indeed, it belonged to Italy until the Swiss Confederation seized it in 1512. The people are darker skinned than their compatriots, and the cuisine, architecture and vegetation reflect that found further south. Italian is the official language of the canton. Many people also speak French and German but you will find English less widely spoken than in the rest of Switzerland. The region offers mountain hikes and dramatic gorges in the north, water sports and relaxed, leisurely towns in the south. A 10-day fishing permit for Ticino's lakes and rivers costs Sfr50 at tourist offices. Free open-air music festivals include Bellinzona's Piazza Blues (late June), and Lugano's Estival Jazz (early July) and Worldmusic Festival (end of August). There are others – check with local tourist offices.

The telephone code for the whole canton is ☎ 091.

LOCARNO
Locarno (Population 15,000) lies at the northern end of Lake Maggiore. It's Switzerland's lowest town, at 205 metres above sea level.

Orientation & Information
The centre of town is the Piazza Grande where the main post office can be found. The tourist office (☎ 751 03 33) is nearby at Largo Zorzi, within the casino complex. It has brochures on many parts of Switzerland. It's open Monday to Friday from 8 am to 7 pm, and Saturday and Sunday from 9 am to noon and 1 to 5 pm. From around November to March, opening hours are reduced to Monday to Friday from 8 am to noon, and 2 to 6 pm.

A five-minute walk away is the train station, where money exchange counters are open daily from 6 am to 8.40 pm, and bikes can be rented daily from 8 am and returned up to 7 pm or later.

Things to See & Do
The principal attraction is the **Madonna del Sasso**, up on the hill with a good view of the lake and the town. The sanctuary was built after the Virgin Mary appeared in a vision in 1480. It contains some 15th-century paintings, a small museum and several distinctive statue groups. There is a funicular from the town centre, but the 20-minute walk up is not demanding (take Via al Sasso off Via

Cappuccini) and you pass some shrines on the way.

In the town, as well as exploring the Italianate piazzas and arcades, there are a couple of churches worth a look, including the 17th-century **Chiesa Nuova** on Via Cittadella, with an ornate ceiling complete with frolicking angels.

Locarno has more hours of sunshine than anywhere else in Switzerland, just right for strolls round the lake. **Giardini Jean Arp** is a small lakeside park off Lungolago Motta, where sculptures by the surrealist artist are scattered among the palm trees and tulips.

Places to Stay

Delta Camping (☎ 751 60 81) is very expensive. It'll cost Sfr38 for two people, or Sfr54 from 1 June to 31 August.

A new SYHA *hostel* is to open in spring 1997; enquire at the tourist office.

Pensione Città Vecchia (☎ 751 45 54), Via Toretta 13, off Piazza Grande (head up the hill by the sign for 'Innovazione'), is a private hostel without curfew or daytime closing. Beds in different-sized dorms are Sfr22, plus Sfr4.50 each if you require sheets or breakfast. Both are provided in singles/doubles at Sfr33 per person, and it is open from 1 March to November. *Osteria Reginetta* (☎ 752 35 53), not far away at Via della Motta 8, has singles/doubles/triples for Sfr39 per person, or Sfr45 including breakfast.

Convenient for the station is *Garni Montaldi* (☎ 743 02 22), Piazza Stazione. Renovated singles/doubles with shower and cable TV are Sfr60/120, or Sfr52/104 without. You can get some great deals out of season (closed January). Reception is also here for *Stazione*, an older building to the rear where singles/doubles are Sfr40/80, also with shower. Stazione closes from 1 November to 31 March.

Hotel Ristorante Zurigo (☎ 743 16 17), Via Verbano 9, offers comfortable accommodation overlooking the lake. Gold-coloured metal bedsteads, tastefully arranged pictures and patterned tiled floors give the rooms some style. Prices start at Sfr87/124 for a single/double in winter, rising to Sfr147/184 in summer. All rooms have cable TV and private shower/toilet.

Places to Eat

The *Coop* supermarket on Piazza Grande has a deli counter. *Inova*, Via Stazione 1, by the train station, has good self-service dishes from Sfr9, help-yourself salad plates from Sfr4.20 to Sfr10.50, and beer for only Sfr2.60 a glass. It is open daily to 10 pm. *Trattoria Campagna Ristorante*, Via Castelrotto, west of St Antonio church, has a piatto del giorno (dish of the day) for Sfr14, and pizza and pasta from Sfr11. It is closed on Sunday evening.

Try fish specialities (Sfr30 to Sfr45) in the upstairs section at *Ristorante Cittadella*, Via Cittadella 18. Downstairs, there are pizzas from Sfr11.50 (closed Monday). The restaurant at Hotel Ristorante Zurigo serves good, mid-range food.

Getting There & Away

The St Gotthard pass provides the road link (N2) to central Switzerland. There are trains every two hours from Brig, passing through Italy en route. The cost is Sfr48 and it takes around three hours. You change trains at Domodossola across the border, so bring your passport.

One-day travel passes for boats on Lake Maggiore cost Sfr10 to Sfr19 depending upon the area they're valid for on the lake. For more information, contact Navigazione Lago Maggiore on ☎ 751 18 65. There is a regular boat and hydrofoil service from Italy.

BELLINZONA

The capital of Ticino is a city of castles. It is set in a valley of lush mountains, and stands at the southern side of two important Alpine passes, San Bernardino and St Gotthard.

Orientation & Information

The train station has money-exchange (open daily from 6 am to 9 pm), bike rental and a supermarket (open daily to 9 pm). Postbuses depart one block in front on Via C Molo. The tourist office (☎ 825 21 31), Via Camminata 2, Palazzo Civico, is open Monday to Friday from 8 am to noon and 1.30 to 6.30 pm, and Saturday from 9 am to noon. To get there, turn left out of the station and walk for 10 minutes, passing the main post office (Posta 1, 6500) on the way.

The telephone code for Bellinzona is ☎ 091.

Things to See

The three medieval castles which dominate the town are testimony to Bellinzona's historical importance, based on its key location at the crossroads of major Alpine routes. All the castles are well preserved, free to enter, and offer fine views of the town and surrounding mountains.

Castel Grande, dating from around the 6th century, is the largest and most central; **Castello di Montebello** is slightly above the town. Both are open daily. Quite a trek up the hill is the smaller **Castello di Sasso Corbaro**, open from 1 April to 31 October from 9 am to noon and 2 to 5 pm (closed Monday). No buses go up there but it's easy to beg a lift back down again from the car park. Each castle has a small museum covering history and archaeology (Sfr4, students Sfr2, closed Monday); if you want to see them all, buy a combined ticket for Sfr8 (students Sfr4).

The **Santa Maria delle Grazie** church in the town features an impressive 15th-century fresco of the Crucifixion, similar to that in Lugano.

Places to Stay

The *camping ground* (☎ 829 11 18), Bosco di Molinazzo, costs Sfr6.20 per person, Sfr5.20 per tent and Sfr16 for a camper van. The few budget hotels in town fill quickly. Two places to try near the station are *Metropoli* (☎ 825 11 79), Via Ludovico il Moro, with singles/doubles from Sfr50/90, and *San Giovanni* (☎ 825 19 19), Via San Giovanni 7, with singles/doubles for Sfr50/95, with access to a hall shower. *Croce Federale* (☎ 825 16 67), at Viale Stazione 12, has singles/doubles/triples for Sfr95/130/160. All rooms have shower, toilet and TV.

Places to Eat

Cheap self-service restaurants are at *Coop*, on Via H Guisan, the nearby *Migros*, and *Inova*, in the Innovazione department store on Viale Stazione. *Birreria Corona*, opposite the tourist office at Via Camminata 5, provides a range of meals, including pizzas from Sfr9.50. All these places are closed on Sunday. *Speranza*, Piazza Collegiata 1, only has limited lunches, but go there on Friday and Saturday nights for free blues concerts.

Pedemonte (☎ 825 33 33), Via Pedemonte 12, by the station on the east side of the tracks,

is a great place for mid-price food. Personal service is paramount – there's not even a written menu; instead, the staff explain the dishes to you. It is closed Monday.

Getting There & Away

Bellinzona is on the train route connecting Locarno (Sfr6.60, 25 minutes) and Lugano (Sfr10.40, 30 minutes). It is also on the Zürich-Milan route. Postbuses head north-east to Chur (Sfr5 supplement applies even with travel passes). You need to reserve your postbus seat the day before on ☎ 825 77 55. There is a good cycling track along the Ticino River to Lake Maggiore and Locarno.

LUGANO

Switzerland's southernmost tourist town offers an excellent combination of lazy days, watery pursuits and hillside hikes.

Orientation & Information

The old town lies down the hill to the east of the train station, which offers money-exchange, bike rental and an Aperto super-market, all open daily. About 10-minutes walk away, the tourist office (☎ 921 46 64) over-looks Lake Lugano, on Riva G Albertolli. Opening hours are Monday to Friday 9 am to at least 6 pm, reducing in winter to 9 am to noon and from 2 to 5 pm. On Saturday between April and October it is open from 9 am to 5 pm.

The main post office (Posta 1, 6900) is in the centre of the old town at Via della Posta 7. The Italian Consulate (☎ 922 05 13) is at Via Monte Ceneri 16.

Lugano's telephone code is ☎ 091.

Things to See & Do

Winding alleyways, pedestrian-only piazzas and colourful parks make Lugano an ideal town for walking around. The **Santa Maria degli Angioli** church, Piazza Luini, has a vivid fresco of the Crucifixion by Bernardino Luini dating from 1529.

The **Thyssen-Bornemisza Gallery**, Villa Favorita, Castagnola, is a famous private art collection. It covers every modern style from abstract to photorealism, though the Old Masters were removed to Spain in 1992. Admission is expensive at Sfr10 for adults or Sfr7 for students, and it's open April to Novem-ber, Friday to Sunday from 10 am to 5 pm. The

Cantonal Art Museum, Via Canova 10, also has a worthwhile modern selection. Entry costs Sfr7 (students Sfr5), though exhibitions are extra. It's open Wednesday through Sunday from 10 am to 5 pm and Tuesday 2 to 5 pm.

The **Lido**, east of the Cassarate River, offers a swimming pool and sandy beaches for Sfr6 a day, and it's open daily from 1 May to mid-September. A boat tour of **Lake Lugano** is a very enjoyable excursion. There are boat and bus departures approximately every 90 minutes to nearby Melide, where **Swissminiatur** displays 1:25 scale models of national attractions (Sfr10.50, children Sfr6; closed in winter, otherwise open daily). Picturesque villages, reachable by boat, are Gandria (visit the customs museum across the shore) and Morcote.

The tourist office has hiking information, and even conducts free guided walks of the town on Tuesday in the summer (book the day before). There are excellent hikes and views from **Monte San Salvatore** and **Monte Brè**. The funicular from Paradiso up Monte San Salvatore operates from mid-March to mid-November only and costs Sfr11 to go up or Sfr17 return. To get up Monte Brè, you can take the year-round funicular from Cassarate which costs Sfr12 to go up or Sfr18 return.

Places to Stay

The relaxed SYHA *hostel* (☎ 966 27 28), Via Cantonale 13, is a hard 20-minute walk uphill from the train station (signposted), or take bus No 5 to Crocifisso (Sfr1.70). Beds are Sfr15, plus (if required) Sfr2 for sheets and Sfr6 for breakfast. It also has private rooms from Sfr20 per person. Reception is closed noon to 3 pm and curfew is at 10 pm. The hostel has private grounds and a swimming pool and closes from 31 October to late March.

Close to the train station is *Hotel Montarina* (☎ 966 72 72), Via Montarina 1, with beds in large dorms for Sfr20 (excluding sheets), singles/doubles from Sfr40/80 and triples/quads for Sfr111/148, all without breakfast. It's convenient but not as friendly as the hostel, and has a garden. Reception is open from 9 am to 9 pm and there's no curfew. It closes from 31 October to about two weeks before Easter.

Hotel Restaurant Pestalozzi (☎ 921 46 46), Piazza Indipendenza 9, has good singles/doubles/triples for Sfr88/138/190 with own

shower/toilet or Sfr54/96/125 without. *Zurigo* (☎ 923 43 43), along the road at Corso Pestalozzi 13, also has rooms with various facilities, all starting at Sfr60/100. It has plenty of off-street parking spaces.

Around the bay in Paradiso is *Victoria au Lac* (☎ 994 20 31), Via General Guisan 3, which sometimes has space when places in town are full (take bus No 1). It's old-fashioned and atmospheric; singles/doubles are Sfr65/110, or Sfr95/138 with shower. Parking is no problem, and it's open from 1 April to 31 October.

Places to Eat

There is a large *Migros* supermarket on Via Pretorio opposite Via Emilio Bossi. Its restaurant is open to 8 pm daily except Sunday. The *EPA* department store on Piazzetta San Carlo also has a cheap restaurant. Similarly priced is *Ristorante Inova*, up the stairs on the north side of Piazza Cioccaro, with excellent buffet-style food (open daily to 10 pm). Also good and cheap for Italian and vegetarian food is *Pestalozzi* (see Places to Stay), open daily from 6 am to 10 pm.

As you might expect, pizza and pasta abound. On the south side of Piazza Cioccaro is the large *Sayonara*. It has the usual selection, as well as local dishes (open daily). *La Tinèra*, Via dei Gorini, off Piazza della Riforma, is also good for Ticinese food, and has meals for Sfr11 to Sfr25. At lunch you may have to queue to be seated. It's closed on Sunday.

Getting There & Away

Lugano is on the same road and rail route as Bellinzona. To St Moritz, two postbuses run (daily in summer; only Friday, Saturday and Sunday in winter). It costs Sfr54 (plus a Sfr5 supplement, not covered by Swiss travel passes) and takes four hours. You need to reserve your seat the day before at the bus station, the train information office, or by phoning ☎ 807 95 20. Buses leave from the bus station on Via Serafino Balestra, though the St Moritz bus also calls at the train station. A seven-day regional holiday pass costs Sfr92 and is valid for all regional public transport including funiculars and boats on Lake Lugano.

Graubünden

Once upon a time, tourists in Switzerland were a summer phenomenon. Then in 1864, Johannes Badrutt, the owner of the Engadiner Kulm Hotel in St Moritz, offered four English summer guests free accommodation if they returned for the winter. He told them they were missing the best time of the year. Although dubious, the English were unable to refuse a free offer. They returned, enjoyed themselves, and winter tourism was born.

Today Graubünden (Grisons, Grigioni, Grishun) has some of the most developed and best known winter sports centres in the world, including Arosa, Davos, Klosters, Flims, and, of course, St Moritz. Away from the international resorts, Graubünden is a relatively unspoiled region of rural villages, Alpine lakes and hilltop castles. The people speak German, Italian or Romansch.

The Graubünden tourist office (☎ 081-302 61 00; fax 302 14 14), north of Chur in the Heidiland motorway service station on the N13 autobahn, is open 365 days a year.

CHUR

Chur (population 32,900) is the canton's capital and largest town, yet it has a very compact centre. It has been continuously inhabited since 3000 BC.

Orientation & Information

Money exchange is possible in the train station daily from 7 am to 8 pm. A five-minute walk straight ahead down Bahnhofstrasse is Postplatz. To the right is a post office (7002) and to the left is the tourist office (☎ 252 18 18), Grabenstrasse 5, open Monday to Friday from 8 am to noon and 1.30 to 6 pm, and Saturday from 9 am to noon. Pick up a free copy of the walking tour of the centre of town. The regional tourist office, Alexanderstrasse 24, has information on the whole canton (open weekdays 8 am to noon and 1.30 to 5.30 pm).

Chur's telephone code is ☎ 081.

Things to See

Chur has an attractive old town with 16th-century buildings, fountains and alleyways. Augusto Giacometti designed three of the windows in the 1491 **Church of St Martin**. In the impressive **cathedral**, built from 1150, take note of the crypt, the high altar and the carved heads on the choir stalls. The **Kunstmuseum** on Postplatz is closed Monday and contains modern art, including a generous gathering of stuff by the three Giacomettis: Alberto, Augusto and Giovanni. Note also the sci-fi work by local artist, HR Giger, who created the monsters in the *Alien* films. Entry costs Sfr5 (students Sfr3). If you like sci-fi themes, visit Giger's creatively decorated bar at Comercialstrasse 23.

For swimming and other sports, look to the **Obere Au Sportzentrum** (☎ 254 42 88) northwest of town (take bus No 2).

Places to Stay

Camp Au (☎ 284 22 83), by the sports centre, costs Sfr6.10 per person and from Sfr5.50 for a tent. The old SYHA *hostel* has been closed down, but a new one should open up in 1997. Check with the tourist office.

The central *Franziskaner* (☎ 252 12 61), Kupfergasse 18, has adequate singles/doubles from Sfr50/90. A better deal is *Rosenhügel* (☎ 252 23 88), up the hill at Malixerstrasse 32. Prices start at Sfr45/90, and it's a five-minute walk south of the old town. Greater comfort and arty décor can be found at *Hotel Drei Könige* (☎ 252 17 25), Reichsgasse 18. Singles/doubles are Sfr92/136 with shower or Sfr70/110 without. There's parking nearby and it also stages occasional concerts.

Places to Eat

Cheap self-service restaurants are at *Coop* on Bahnhofstrasse and at *Migros* on Gürtelstrasse, both with late opening till 9 pm on Friday. For pizzas, there are two restaurants side by side on Grabenstrasse.

Speise Restaurant Zollhaus, at Malixerstrasse 1, has two parts (open daily). Bierschwemme is the downstairs bar and serves hot meals from only Sfr8.70. The daily special with soup is Sfr10.80 (available from 11 am to 1 pm and 6 to 8 pm). Upstairs is the calmer and more cultured Bündnerstube, where meals are mostly above Sfr20.

For well-prepared food in wooden, rustic surroundings, go to *Hotel Stern*, opposite Drei Könige on Reichsgasse. Main evening dishes are around Sfr18 to Sfr40. Lunchtime eating is cheaper, with three menus (one vegetarian) from Sfr16 including soup.

Entertainment

At night the hectic, crowded *John Bull* pub on Grabenstrasse attracts young drinkers, and there are lots of loud music bars in the streets behind.

Getting There & Away

Postbuses leave from the depot above the train station, including the express service to Bellinzona (reserve ahead on ☎ 252 38 23). There are rail connections to Davos, Klosters and Arosa, and fast trains to Sargans (the station for Liechtenstein, only 25 minutes away) and Zürich (85 minutes, Sfr37). Chur can be visited on the Glacier Express route (see the following St Moritz section).

ST MORITZ

This resort needs little introduction. Playground of today's international jet-setters, the curative properties of its waters have been known for 3000 years.

Orientation & Information

St Moritz exudes health and wealth. The train station near the lake rents bikes and changes money from 6.50 am to 8.10 pm daily. Just up the hill is the post office (7500) and five minutes further on is the tourist office or *Kurverein* (☎ 837 33 33) at Via Maistra 12. It's open Monday to Friday from 9 am to noon and 2 to 6 pm, on Saturday morning, and also on Saturday afternoon during the high season. To the south-west, two km around the lake from the main town, St Moritz Dorf, lies St Moritz Bad; buses run between the two. Not much stays open during November, May and early June.

The telephone code for St Moritz is ☎ 081.

Activities

In the St Moritz region there are 350 km of downhill runs, although the choice for beginners is limited. A one-day ski pass costs Sfr54, and ski and boot rental is about Sfr43 for one day. There are also 160 km of cross-country trails (equipment rental Sfr20) and 120 km of marked hiking paths.

Numerous other sporting activities are on offer: golf (including on the frozen lake in winter), tennis, squash, fishing, horse riding, sailing, windsurfing and river rafting, to mention just a few. The tourist office has a list of the inevitable high prices. If you can't afford to partake in the activities, at least people-watching is fun and free. Buying a health treatment in the spa is another way to spend money, or you could pop into the **Engadine Museum** or the **Segantini Museum**.

Places to Stay

The *Olympiaschanze* camping ground (☎ 833 40 90) is one km south-west of St Moritz Bad and is open from 1 June to late September.

The modern SYHA *Stille Hostel* (☎ 833 39 69), Via Surpunt 60, St Moritz Bad, is a 30-minute walk round the lake from the tourist office. Half-pension per person prices are Sfr41.50 in four-bed dorms and Sfr54 in double rooms. Laundry costs Sfr4 per load. Reception is closed from 9 am to 4 pm (but the doors stay open), curfew is at midnight and the hostel is open year-round. If it's full, try the *Sporthotel Stille* (☎ 833 69 48) next door. Per person prices start at Sfr50 in summer or Sfr80 (for half-board) in winter.

Hotel prices fluctuate according to the season, reaching a peak from around mid-December to mid-February, and these are the prices quoted below. The summer high season, July and August, isn't quite as expensive. In some places in winter you must take half-board. *Bellaval* (☎ 833 32 45), right by the train station on the south side, has singles/doubles from Sfr62/120 using hall shower. St Moritz Bad has the cheaper options, such as *Hotel Bernina* (☎ 833 60 22), Via dal Bagn. However, this hotel is only good value in the summer (closed May) when rooms start at Sfr75/145 with private shower or Sfr55/107 without.

Most of the hotels in the centre of St Moritz Dorf sport four or five stars. The best three-star choices are close together on Via Veglia near the tourist office: *Hotel Eden Garni* (☎ 833 61 61) at Sfr100/90 and *Hotel Languard Garni* (☎ 833 31 37) at Sfr100/200.

Places to Eat

The cheapest restaurants are between Dorf and Bad. A *Coop* supermarket is on Via dal Bagn. Next door there's *Bellevue*, a self-service restaurant with meals from Sfr10 (open supermarket hours). Beside it is *Al Tavolo*, offering food for a range of prices (open daily). The popular *Hotel Sonne*, Via Sela 11, close to the hostel, serves pasta, salads and tasty pizzas (after 5 pm) from Sfr12. It is open daily from 7 am to midnight.

In Dorf, look for lunch specials or go to *Hotel Steinbock*, down from the post office, where meals start at Sfr16. Try an expensive taste of the highlife at the top of the Corviglia funicular by sampling the truffles, caviar and desserts at *La Marmite* (☎ 833 63 55). Queue or reserve ahead in season.

Getting There & Away
To Lugano, two postbuses run (daily in summer; only on Friday, Saturday and Sunday in winter). You must reserve a seat the day before on ☎ 833 30 72, and the route incurs a Sfr5 supplement. A train-and-bus combination will get you to Landeck in Austria.

At least nine daily trains travel south to Tirano in Italy with connections to Milan. The famous Glacier Express connects St Moritz to Zermatt via the 2033-metre Oberalp Pass, taking 7½ hours to cover 290 scenic km and crossing 291 bridges (Sfr125). Novelty drink glasses in the dining car have sloping bases to compensate for the hills – but you must remember to keep turning them around! Beware of the Sfr9 reservation fee that's payable only on some trains on both routes.

AROUND ST MORITZ
The Engadine Valley, running north-east and south-west of St Moritz, offers a combination of plush resorts and unspoilt villages. In the latter category are **Guarda** and **Zuoz**, where you can see homes displaying traditional *sgraffito* designs (patterns scratched on wall plaster) that are characteristic of the Engadine. The annual cross-country ski marathon between Maloja and Zuoz takes place on the second Sunday in March. The route crosses ice-covered lakes and passes by St Moritz lake. Trains and buses run regularly along the Engadine Valley.

Flora and fauna abound in the 169 sq km of the **Swiss National Park** (open June to October). The park information centre (☎ 081-856 13 78), Zernez, has details of hiking routes and the best places to see particular animals. Trains to Zernez from St Moritz cost Sfr15.80.

Other Ski Resorts
In the **Davos/Klosters** region there are 320 km of ski runs, mostly medium to difficult, including one of the hardest runs in the world, the Gotschnawang. **Arosa** is another top-notch resort, easily reached by a scenic train ride from Chur. Most other ski resorts in Graubünden have predominantly easy to medium runs. Ski passes average Sfr50 for one day (cheaper by the week).

Zürich

Zürich (population 363,000) started life as a Roman customs post until it graduated to the status of a free city under the Holy Roman Empire in 1218. Today, Switzerland's most populous city offers an ambience of affluence and plenty of cultural diversions. Banks and art galleries will greet you at every turn, in a strange marriage of finance and aesthetics.

The city's reputation as a cultural and intellectual centre began after it joined the Swiss Confederation in 1351. Zwingli helped things along with his teachings during the Reformation. In the 19th century, Zürich's international status as an industrial and business centre was given impetus by the energetic administrator and railway magnate, Alfred Escher. WWI saw the influx of luminaries such as Lenin, Trotsky and James Joyce; also Tristan Tzara and Hans Arp, key figures in the founding of Dadaism in 1916 at the Cabaret Voltaire.

Orientation
Zürich is at the northern end of Lake Zürich (Zürichsee), with the city centre split by the Limmat River. Like many Swiss cities, it is compact and conveniently laid out. The main train station (Hauptbahnhof) is on the west or left bank of the river, close to the old centre.

Information
Tourist Offices The main tourist office (☎ 211 40 00), Bahnhofplatz 15, arranges car rentals and excursions. From April to October it is open Monday to Friday from 8.30 am to 9.30 pm, and Saturday and Sunday from 8.30 am to 8.30 pm; from November to March it closes two hours earlier each day. Staff charge for

PLACES TO STAY
1 Justinusheim
2 Hotel Poly
15 Scheuble
16 Martahaus
20 Splendid
21 City Backpacker
22 Rothus
42 OASE Evangelisches Haus
43 Foyer Hottingen
47 St Georges

PLACES TO EAT
8 Mr Wong
10 Clipper Restaurant
11 Migros City
14 Mensa Polyterrace
17 Rheinfelder Bierhalle
19 Café Zähringer
23 Stadtküche
28 Manora
29 Hiltl Vegi
30 Bernerhof
31 EPA
35 Mère Catherine
36 Bodega Española
40 Café Schlauch
44 EPA

OTHER
3 Mitfahrzentrale
4 SSR (Travel Agency)
5 Limmat Boat Terminus
6 Swiss National Museum
7 Tourist Information
9 Post Office
12 Coop (Supermarket)
14 Cantonal Hospital
18 Pestalozzi Library
24 Police Station
25 Billettzentrale Ticket Agency
26 Ståheli English Bookshop
27 Globetrotter Travel Agency
32 Café Münz
33 St Peter's Church
34 Grossmünster Cathedral
37 Oliver Twist
38 Travel Bookshop
39 Casa Bar
41 Kunsthaus (Art Gallery)
45 Fraumünster Church
46 American Express
48 Lake Steamers Landing Stage
49 Arboretum

Zürich

0   200   400 m

Minor Streets not Depicted

maps – get one free from one of the larger city banks instead. There is an airport tourist office in Terminal B (☎ 816 40 81), open daily from 10 am to 7 pm.

The headquarters of Switzerland Tourism (☎ 288 11 11; fax 288 12 05) is located at Bellariastrasse 38, and has information on the whole of Switzerland. It's open Monday to Friday from 8 to 11.45 am and 1 to 5 pm.

Zurich's telephone code is ☎ 01.

Foreign Consulates These include:

Austria
    Minervastrasse 116 (☎ 383 72 00)
Germany
    Kirchgasse 48 (☎ 265 65 65)
South Africa
    Basteiplatz 7 (☎ 221 11 88)
UK
    Dufourstrasse 56 (☎ 261 15 20)
USA
    Zollikerstrasse 141 (☎ 422 25 66)

Money There's no shortage of choice when exchanging money in this banking city. Banks are open Monday to Friday 8.15 am to 4.30 pm (6 pm Thursday). The exchange office by platform 16 in the Hauptbahnhof is open daily from 6.30 am to 10.45 pm. In the airport, exchange money in terminal A to avoid paying commission on cash.

Post & Communications The main post office is Sihlpost (☎ 296 21 11), Kasernenstrasse 95-97, 8021. It is open Monday to Friday from 7.30 am to 6.30 pm, and Saturday from 7.30 to 11 am. Like many other large Swiss post offices, it also has a counter open daily till late but some transactions incur a Sfr1 surcharge outside normal hours. Another post office is at the Hauptbahnhof.

Travel Agencies American Express (☎ 211 83 70), Bahnhofstrasse 20, is open Monday to Friday from 8.30 am to 5.30 pm and Saturday from 9 am to noon. SSR is a specialist in student, youth and budget fares. Branches are at Leonhardstrasse 10 (open Monday to Friday) and Bäckerstrasse 40 (open Monday afternoon to Saturday morning), or call ☎ 297 11 11 for telephone sales. Globetrotter (☎ 211 77 80), Rennweg 35, also has worldwide budget fares, and a travel noticeboard and magazine.

Bookshops & Libraries Stäheli English Bookshop (☎ 201 33 02), Bahnhofstrasse 70, has fiction, nonfiction and travel. English and French-language books are at Librairie Poyot, Bahnhofstrasse 9. The Travel Book Shop (☎ 252 38 83), Rindermarkt 20, has a huge selection of English-language travel books and can order anything you want. It also runs the map shop next door. Read English-language newspapers in the Pestalozzi Library, Zähringerstrasse 17 (open to 8 pm weekdays, 5 pm Saturday).

Medical & Emergency Services For medical and dental help, ring ☎ 261 61 00. The Cantonal University Hospital (☎ 255 11 11), Ramistrasse 100, has a casualty department. There is a 24-hour chemist at Bellevue Apotheke (☎ 252 56 00), Theaterstrasse 14. The police (☎ 216 71 11) are at Bahnhofquai 3.

Dangers & Annoyances Crime and drug-addiction have grown apace in Zürich in recent years. Crime still isn't high by international standards, but keep alert.

Things to See & Do
Walking Tour The pedestrian streets of the old town on either side of the Limmat contain most of the major sights. Features to notice are winding alleyways, 16th and 17th-century houses and guildhalls, courtyards and fountains. Zürich has 1030 fountains and the locals insist the water is drinkable in them all. Don't be surprised if a waiter heads for the nearest fountain if you ask for tap water in a restaurant!

The elegant **Bahnhofstrasse** was built on the site of the city walls which were torn down 150 years ago. Underfoot are bank vaults crammed full of gold and silver. Zürich is one of the world's premier precious metals markets but the vaults (for some reason) aren't open to the public.

The 13th-century tower of **St Peter's Church**, St Peterhofstatt, has the largest clock face in Europe (8.7 metres in diameter). The **Fraumünster Church** nearby is noted for the distinctive stained-glass windows in the choir created by Marc Chagall, which were completed when he was 83. Augusto Giacometti also did a window here, as well as in the **Grossmünster Cathedral** across the river where Zwingli preached in the 16th century. The figure glowering from the south tower of the Grossmünster is Charlemagne.

Museums The most important of many is the **Museum of Fine Arts** (Kunsthaus), Heimplatz 1. The large permanent collection ranges from 15th-century religious art to the various schools of modern art. Swiss artists Füssli and Hodler are well represented, as are the sculptures of Alberto Giacometti. It is open Tuesday to Thursday from 10 am to 9 pm, and Friday to Sunday from 10 am to 5 pm. Entry costs Sfr5 (students and seniors Sfr3) except on Sunday when it's free. Temporary exhibitions always cost extra. Look out also for the numerous private galleries round the city.

The **Swiss National Museum** (Schweizerisches Landesmuseum), Museumstrasse 2, has a definitive section on church art, plus weapons, coins, costumes and utensils all housed in a pseudo-castle built in 1898. Opening hours are Tuesday to Sunday from 10 am to 5 pm and entry is free.

The **Lindt & Sprüngli chocolate factory**, Seestrasse 204 (take bus No 165 from Bürkliplatz to Schooren), offers a museum, film, and generous chocolate gift – all free! It's open Monday to Thursday; phone ahead on ☎ 716 22 33.

Zoo The large zoo has 2500 animals from all around the world; it's open daily from 8 am to 6 pm (5 pm November to February). Entry costs Sfr12 (students Sfr6) and you can get there by tram No 5 or 6. The zoo backs on to Zürichberg, a large wood ideal for walks away from the noise of the city.

Other Attractions Informative if expensive guided walks around the old town, organised by the tourist office in summer, last around two hours and cost Sfr18. Walks around the Zürichsee (Lake Zürich) are pleasant. The concrete walkways give way to trees and lawns in the Arboretum on the west bank. Look out for the flower clock face at nearby Bürkliplatz. On the east bank, the Zurichhorn park has sculptures and a so-so Chinese Garden (Sfr7).

Special Events
On the third Monday in April Zürich holds its

spring festival, Sechseläuten. Guild members parade the streets in historical costume and tour the guildhalls, playing music. A fireworks-filled 'snowman' (the Böögg), is ignited at 6 pm. Another local holiday is Knabenschiessen, on the second weekend of September, a shooting competition for 12 to 16-year-old youths.

Fasnacht brings lively musicians and a large, costumed procession. The carnival commences with typical Swiss precision at 11.11 am on 11 November, though the biggest parades are in February. A huge fairground takes over central Zürich during the **Züri Fäscht**, every third year (1997 etc) in early July. The International June Festival concentrates on music and the arts, and the International Jazz Festival takes place at the end of October.

Places to Stay – bottom end
Accommodation can be a problem, particularly from August to October. Cheaper hotels fill early. Book ahead if you can, or use the information board and free phone in the train station. The tourist office can sometimes get lower rates (Sfr5 booking fee). Private rooms are virtually nonexistent.

Camping *Camping Seebucht* (☎ 482 16 12) is on the west shore of the lake, four km from the city centre, at Seestrasse 559. It is well signposted and can be reached by bus No 161 or 165 from Bürkliplatz. It has good facilities including a shop and café, but it is only open from 1 May to 30 September. Prices are Sfr5.50 per person (10% discount with Camping Carnet), Sfr8 for a tent or Sfr10 for a camper van.

Hostels Some of the places mentioned are not strictly hostels, but they appear here because they offer dorm beds as well as comfortable private rooms.

The SYHA *hostel* (☎ 482 35 44) is at Mutschellenstrasse 114, Wollishofen, and has 24-hour service. Take tram No 6 or 7 to Morgental, or the S-Bahn to Wollishofen. Four or six-bed dorms (with lockers) are Sfr29. There's a restaurant, laundry facilities (Sfr8 to wash and dry) and TV room.

More convenient is *City Backpacker* (☎ 251 90 15), Schweizerhofgasse 5, otherwise known as Hotel Biber. Small dorms are

Sfr30, with reductions for multiple nights; singles/doubles are Sfr65/85 and triples/quads are Sfr115/140. Prices are without breakfast but there are kitchens, and showers are in the hall. Reception is closed from 11 am to 3 pm. Also ideally central is *Martahaus* (☎ 251 45 50), at Zähringerstrasse 36. Singles/doubles/triples cost Sfr66/98/117, and Sfr32 gets you a place in a six-bed dorm which is separated into individual cubicles by partitions and curtains. There is a comfortable lounge and breakfast room, and a shower on each floor. Book ahead (telephone reservations OK), particularly for single rooms.

Foyer Hottingen (☎ 261 93 15), Hottingerstrasse 31, is run by nuns. Women, couples (married, ideally) and families are welcome, but the sisters of the cloth are wary of carousing young men, so single males are only accepted in an emergency. Singles/ doubles are Sfr55/90 and triples/quads are Sfr105/120. Dorms (with lockers) for women only are Sfr25 or Sfr30. Showers cost Sfr1.50 and there's a midnight curfew. Telephone reservations are accepted.

OASE Evangelisches Haus (☎ 267 35 35), Freiestrasse 38, is a student residence with kitchen facilities, available to tourists from July to October. Singles/doubles are Sfr80/130 with shower or Sfr65/110 without. Dorms with canvas beds are Sfr35. At weekends there's no breakfast and prices reduce by Sfr5 per person. Check-in by noon or from 5 to 7 pm.

Justinusheim (☎ 361 38 06), at Freuden-bergstrasse 146, is another student home. Beds are available during student holidays (particularly in the summer), with only a few vacancies in term time. Singles/doubles are Sfr60/90 with shower or Sfr50/80 without. Triples (hall shower) are Sfr120. It's just a few paces away from the woods of Zürichberg, and has a terrace with good views of Zürich and the lake. Take tram No 10 from the Hauptbahnhof to Rigiplatz and then the frequent Seilbahn to the top (city network tickets are valid).

The *Salvation Army* (Heilsarmee; ☎ 298 90 00), Molkenstrasse 6, will reluctantly take travellers (Sfr32 per person in four-bed rooms) though it's really for disadvantaged locals.

Hotels In the old town, *Hotel Splendid* (☎ 252 58 50), Rosengasse 5, offers a choice of old or new rooms. Either type is good value, with

singles/doubles/triples for Sfr58/96/127 (hall showers). The optional breakfast is Sfr10 and there's live piano music nightly in the bar downstairs.

Dufour (☎ 422 36 55), Seefeldstrasse 188, has acceptable singles/doubles for Sfr65/75, again using hall showers, and without break-fast. Reception in the bar downstairs is open daily from 9 am to midnight. Get there by tram No 2 or 4.

Hotel Poly (☎ 362 94 40), at Univer-sitätsstrasse 63, has fresh singles/doubles for Sfr55/80 using hall showers. Rooms from Sfr75/110 are bigger and have TV and private shower.

Hotel St Georges (☎ 241 11 44), at Weber-strasse 11, on the west bank of the Sihl River, is quiet and comfortable and has a lift; singles/doubles are Sfr69/98, using hall showers.

Places to Stay – middle

In the city centre, *Hotel Limmathof* (☎ 261 42 20), Limmatquai 142, has modern fittings but is in a noisy location. Singles/doubles with bath or shower and toilet are Sfr100/125, and triples are Sfr180. The nearby *Alexander Guesthouse* (☎ 251 82 03), Niederdorfstrasse 40, costs from Sfr95/140 for a similar standard.

Goldenes Schwert (☎ 252 59 40), Markt-gasse 14, has rooms for Sfr150/190 with private bath/toilet. The staff thoughtfully (and significantly) lay out ear plugs in each room. Reception is opposite in the *Hotel Rothus*, where rooms using hall shower are Sfr75/115. The three-star *Hotel Scheuble* (☎ 251 87 95), also in the old town at Mühlegasse 17, has rooms from Sfr110/140 (Sfr95/135 in winter).

Places to Eat – bottom

Zürich has hundreds of restaurants serving all types of local and international cuisine. The Zürich speciality, Geschnetzeltes Kalbsfleisch (thinly sliced veal in a cream sauce), generally costs above Sfr20. Fast-food stands offer Brat-wurst and bread from around Sfr4.50. There is a large *Coop* opposite the Hauptbahnhof.

Self-Service The large and busy *Mensa Poly-terrace*, Leonhardstrasse 34, is next to the Seilbahn (funicular) top station. It has good meals for Sfr10.50 (Sfr8.10 for ISIC holders) including vegetarian options. It's open Monday to Friday from 11.15 am to 1.30 pm and 5.30 to 7 pm, and every second Saturday from 11.30 am to 1 pm. From mid-July to around mid-October it's open for lunch only. There is a café upstairs which is also popular. Just along the road, there is another *mensa* in the university building, Rämistrasse 71, open Monday to Friday from 7.30 am to 8 pm, and on alternate Saturdays to the Polyterrace.

Food is just as cheap in *Stadtküche*, Schipfe 16, one of several state-subsidised kitchens (weekday lunches only). The *EPA* department stores at Sihlporte and Stadelhoferstrasse have a cheap restaurant, or you could try *Silberkugel*, below ground by the station, or *Migros Restaurant* in the Migros City shopping centre. The Manor department store on Bahnhofstrasse has a good *Manora* buffet-style restaurant. Like the EPA restaurants, it has late opening on Thursday. *Mr Wong*, opposite the train station, serves big portions of Asian food from Sfr11.

Other Restaurants *Clipper Restaurant*, Lagerstrasse 1, is basic and busy with good-value if simple food. Seating opens on to the pavement making it nice and cool in the summer. Most main dishes cost as little as Sfr9 to Sfr13. The cheap beer (Sfr4 for half a litre) attracts many local drinkers. It is open daily from 10 am to 11.30 pm.

Bernerhof, Zeughausstrasse 1, has satisfying, filling food in an unpretentious environment. Several daily menus from Sfr11.80 (including soup) are available midday and evening. It's open daily from 8 am (weekdays), 10 am (Sunday) or 3 pm (Saturday) until midnight (kitchen till 9 pm). In the evening, locals come to drink and play board and card games.

Rheinfelder Bierhalle, Niederdorfstrasse 76, has all-day menus, including soup starting from Sfr12.80, and the beer's cheap, too (Sfr4.10 for half a litre). Opening hours are from 9 am to midnight daily.

Café Zähringer on Spitalgasse serves up mostly organic food (from Sfr15) to alternative types, and it's a good place to linger for a game of chess, or for live music most Wednesdays (closed during the day and on Monday). *Café Schlauch*, Münstergasse 20, is another possibility for vegetarians (closed Monday and Tuesday).

Places to Eat – middle
Vegetarians will have a field day in the meat-free environment of *Hiltl Vegi* (☎ 221 38 71), Sihlstrasse 28, on two floors. Varied lunches cost from Sfr16 and the salad buffet is both extensive and expensive. Every evening at 6 pm there's an Indian buffet which costs Sfr4 per 100 grams, or it's Sfr36 for all you can eat.

Mère Catherine (☎ 262 22 50), Nägelhof 3, is a popular French restaurant in a small courtyard. The food is tasty but not cheap unless you choose the lunchtime menus from Sfr14.50 (not available Sunday). Quality Spanish fare (Sfr18 to Sfr45) can be had at *Bodega Española* (☎ 251 23 10), on the 1st floor at Münstergasse 15. It has a good selection of Spanish wines from Sfr33.50 a bottle.

Splurge on French food amid the mirrors and gleaming metal of *Brasserie Lipp Restaurant* (☎ 211 11 55), Uraniastrasse 9 (opposite Billettzentrale on the map). Its elegant clientele are attracted by a wide choice of sumptuous dishes in the Sfr20 to Sfr40 range (open daily). *Restaurant JOSEF* (☎ 271 65 95), Gasometerstrasse 24, greets mainly youngish diners. There are interesting and varied daily specials (Sfr24 to Sfr34), often with an Italian emphasis. It's closed Saturday and Sunday lunchtime.

Entertainment
Pick up from the tourist office the free events magazines, *Züritip* and *Zürich next*. Tickets for most events can be obtained from Billettzentrale (☎ 221 22 83), Werdmühleplatz, off Bahnhofstrasse; it's open Monday to Friday from 10 am to 6.30 pm and Saturday to 2 pm. This government agency has minimal commission charges, and closes in July and August when activity in the arts dies down. Cinema prices are reduced to Sfr11 every Monday from their normal price of around Sfr15. Films are usually in the original language.

Zürich has numerous cafés where you can linger over a coffee. Try the entertaining *Cafeteria zur Münz*, Münzplatz 3, where Jean Tinguely mobiles hang from the ceiling. It is open Monday to Friday from 6.30 am to 7 pm (9 pm on Thursday), and Saturday from 8 am to 5 pm.

Many late-night pubs, clubs and discos are in Niederdorfstrasse and adjoining streets in the old town. This area is also a red-light district. The *Casa Bar*, Münstergasse 30, is a busy pub with live jazz from 8 pm. English-speakers gravitate towards *Oliver Twist*, an Irish pub on Rindermarkt. The *Comedy Club* performs plays in English – check venues in the events magazines.

Rote Fabrik (☎ 481 98 11 for music, ☎ 482 42 12 for theatre), Seestrasse 395, is a centre for the arts (take Bus No 161 or 165 from Bürkliplatz). It has concerts most nights ranging from rock and jazz to avant-garde (Sfr15 to Sfr25), original-language films (Sfr10), theatre and dance (all closed Monday).

Getting There & Away

Air Kloten airport, the major gateway, is 10 km north of the city centre and has several daily flights to/from all major destinations. Swissair and Austrian Airlines share an office in the Hauptbahnhof (open weekdays and Saturday morning). For Swissair reservations around the clock, call ☎ 258 34 34.

Train The busy Hauptbahnhof has direct trains to Stuttgart (Sfr63), Munich (Sfr90), Innsbruck (Sfr66) and Milan (Sfr68) as well as to many other international destinations. There are also hourly departures to most Swiss towns including Lucerne (50 minutes, Sfr19.40), Bern (70 minutes, Sfr42) and Basel (65 minutes, Sfr30).

Car & Motorcycle The N3 approaches Zürich from the south along the shore of Lake Zürich. The N1 is the fastest route from Bern and Basel and the main entry point from the west. The N1 also services routes to the north and east of Zürich.

Hitching Zürich's Mitfahrzentrale (☎ 632 56 17) is at Leonhardstrasse 15. This agency links drivers and hitchers, but only for international journeys. There is a commission of Sfr10 to Sfr20. It's open Monday to Friday from noon to 1 pm.

Getting Around

To/From the Airport Taxis cost around Sfr40, so take the train for Sfr5.40 (five an hour, takes 10 minutes) – it's much cheaper to buy the ticket *before* boarding.

Public Transport There is a comprehensive and unified bus, tram and S-Bahn service in the city, which includes boats on the Limmat River. All tickets must be bought in advance from dispensers at stops. The variety of tickets and zones available can be confusing. Short trips of five stops or less are Sfr2.10. For the city of Zürich, a one-hour pass costs Sfr3.60 and a 24-hour pass is Sfr7.20. Getting to the airport involves travel in an extra zone (Sfr10.80 for a 24-hour pass). A 24-hour pass valid for unlimited travel within the whole canton of Zürich costs Sfr28.40, including extended tours of the lake.

Lake steamers leave from Bürkliplatz, departing every 30 to 60 minutes from early April to late October (Swiss Pass and Eurail valid, Inter-Rail 50% discount). For boat information, phone ☎ 482 10 33.

Other Transport Taxis in Zürich are expensive, even by Swiss standards, at Sfr6 plus Sfr3.20 per km. There's bicycle rental in the Hauptbahnhof, but use of city bikes is free from early May to late October at Werdemühleplatz and a couple of other less central points. The depots open weekdays from 7 am – take your passport. The tourist office has a list of car-parking garages near the central pedestrian zone. A Sfr10 pass from a police station allows all-day street parking in a blue zone.

Central Switzerland

This is the region which many visitors think of as the 'true' Switzerland. Not only is it rich in typical Swiss features – mountains, lakes, tinkling cowbells, Alpine villages and ski resorts – but it is also where Switzerland began as a nation 700 years ago. The original pact of 1291, signed by the communities of Uri, Schwyz and Nidwalden, can be viewed today in the Bundesbriefarchiv hall in Schwyz town centre.

LUCERNE

Ideally situated in the historic and scenic heart of Switzerland, Lucerne (Luzern in German) is an excellent base for a variety of excursions, yet it also has a great deal of charm in its own right, particularly the medieval town centre.

Orientation & Information

The town centre is on the north bank of the River Reuss. The train station is nearby on the south bank; extensive station facilities below ground level include bike rental (from 7 am to 7.45 pm) and money exchange.

Exit left for the tourist office (☎ 410 71 71), Frankenstrasse 1, which is open Monday to Friday from 8.30 am to 6 pm and Saturday from 9 am to 5 pm. From 1 November to 31 March it closes at 1 pm on Saturday and for two hours at noon on weekdays.

In front of the train station is the boat landing stage, and close by is the main post office (Hauptpost, Luzern 1, 6000). Across the river is American Express (☎ 410 00 77), Schweizerhofquai 4, open weekdays and Saturday morning.

Lucerne's telephone code is ☎ 041.

Things to See

The picturesque old centre offers 15th-century buildings with painted façades, and the towers of the city walls. Some of these towers can be climbed for extensive views. Be sure to walk along the two covered bridges, **Kapellbrücke**, with its water tower that appears in just about

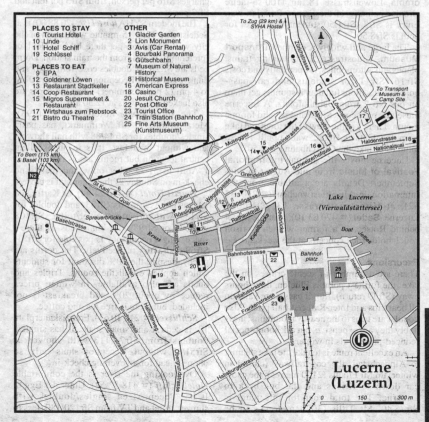

PLACES TO STAY
6 Tourist Hotel
10 Linde
11 Hotel Schiff
19 Schlüssel

PLACES TO EAT
9 EPA
12 Goldener Löwen
13 Restaurant Stadtkeller
14 Coop Restaurant
15 Migros Supermarket & Restaurant
17 Wirtshaus zum Rebstock
21 Bistro du Theatre

OTHER
1 Glacier Garden
2 Lion Monument
3 Avis (Car Rental)
4 Bourbaki Panorama
5 Gütschbahn
7 Museum of Natural History
8 Historical Museum
16 American Express
18 Casino
20 Jesuit Church
22 Post Office
23 Tourist Office
24 Train Station (Bahnhof)
25 Fine Arts Museum (Kunstmuseum)

To Zug (29 km) & SYHA Hostel

To Transport Museum & Camp Site

To Bern (115 km) & Basel (103 km)

Lake Lucerne (Vierwaldstättersee)

Boat Jetties

Lucerne (Luzern)

0   150   300 m

every photograph of Lucerne, and **Spreuer-brücke**. Both contain a series of pictorial panels under the roof. Kapellbrücke dates from 1333, and was rebuilt in 1993 after suffering fire damage.

The poignant **Lion Monument**, carved out of natural rock in 1820, is dedicated to the Swiss soldiers who died in the French Revolution. Next to it is the fascinating **Gletschergarten** (Glacier Garden), Denkmalstrasse 4, where giant glacial potholes prove that 20 million years ago Lucerne was a subtropical palm beach. The potholes can be perused daily (except Monday in winter), and admission costs Sfr7 (students Sfr5). Also worth a look is the nearby **Bourbaki Panorama**, Löwenstrasse 18, an 1100-sq-metre circular painting of the Franco-Prussian war. Entry is Sfr3 (Sfr1.50 students). A ticket for both is Sfr8.50.

The large and widely acclaimed **Transport Museum**, Lidostrasse 5, containing trains, planes and automobiles, is open daily and costs Sfr16 (Sfr11 for students and rail passholders). It's more fun than it sounds; get there on bus No 2 from Bahnhofplatz. A Lucerne museums pass costs Sfr25 and is valid for one month. There's a fine **view** of the town and lake from the Gütsch Hotel; walk uphill for 20 minutes or take the Gütschbahn (Sfr2.50).

Lucerne hosts the annual **International Festival of Music** from mid-August to mid-September. Details are available from the Internationale Musikfestwochen (☎ 210 35 62), at Hirschmattstrasse 13, CH-6002 Lucerne. **Sedel** (☎ 420 63 10), near the hostel behind Rotsee, is a former women's prison which holds rock concerts at the weekend.

Excursions

There are a number of scenic cruises on the lake; the furthest point is Flüelen, three hours away (Sfr39 return). Eurail passes are valid on all boat trips and Inter-Rail gets half price. Also popular are trips to the nearby mountains; inevitably they are expensive, but ask about special reduced-price deals in winter.

An excellent route is to take the lake steamer to Alpnachstad, the cog railway (closed in winter) up Mt Pilatus (2100 metres), the cable car down to Kriens and the bus back to Lucerne. The total cost for this jaunt is Sfr75.40. Mt Titlis (3020 metres) can be reached by train from Engelberg (Sfr14.20 each way) and then by a series of cable cars (Sfr73 return), but the tourist office's all-in guided bus tour (Sfr85 from Lucerne) is cheaper. A combination steamer, cog railway and cable-car excursion up Mt Rigi (1800 metres) costs Sfr78. There are reductions on all these prices with rail passes.

Places to Stay

A Visitor's Card is available, valid for useful discounts.

Camp Lido (☎ 370 21 46), Lidostrasse 8, is on the north shore of the lake and east of the town. It is open from March to October and charges Sfr6 per person, from Sfr5 per tent and Sfr3 per car.

The modern SYHA *hostel* (☎ 420 88 00) is at Sedelstrasse 12, a 15-minute walk north of the city walls. You can get there by bus No 1 or (preferably) No 18 from the train station. Dorm beds are Sfr28.50, doubles cost from Sfr67 and dinners are Sfr11. Reception is shut from 10 am to 4 pm (2 pm in summer) when the doors are also locked. Curfew is at 12.30 am.

The small *Linde* hotel (☎ 410 31 93), Metzgerrainle 3, off Weinmarkt, has basic singles/doubles for Sfr44/88 with hall showers and without breakfast. It is in an excellent central location but rooms are available from 1 April to 31 October only, and there's no check-in on Sunday as the restaurant is closed.

Tourist Hotel (☎ 410 24 74), St Karli Quai 12, has large dorms for Sfr33, and doubles for Sfr134 with private shower/toilet, Sfr108 without, or Sfr98 with bunk beds. If there's space, single occupancy is possible for Sfr81, Sfr69 and Sfr64 respectively. The dorms are pricey, despite the 10% discount for students which applies on all the rooms. Triples and quads are also available. In winter, prices reduce by around 20% and breakfast is not included, but there is free tea and coffee.

Schlüssel (☎ 210 10 61), Franziskanerplatz 12, is central and small-scale. It has singles/doubles from Sfr74/113 with shower or Sfr51/86 without. Reception shuts early, so phone ahead for an evening check-in.

Overlooking the river is the comfortable *Hotel Schiff* (☎ 418 52 52), Unter der Egg 8. It has decent-sized singles/doubles with shower, toilet and TV from Sfr120/180 (less in winter), and some rooms using hall shower for Sfr70/115.

Places to Eat

Tagesmenus (daily menus) in town are in the range of Sfr13 to Sfr15. Look out for the local speciality, Kügelipastetli, a vol-au-vent stuffed with meat and mushrooms and served with a rich sauce.

Coop and *Migros* have restaurants close together on Hertensteinstrasse. *EPA* department store, Mühlenplatz, has an excellent self-service restaurant with unbeatable prices for Switzerland: meals from Sfr8, soup from Sfr1.50, salad buffet at Sfr1.80 per 100 grams, and tea or coffee for Sfr1.80. They're all open till 9 pm on Thursday. *Bistro du Theatre*, Theaterstrasse 5, is popular amongst mainly young people for fairly inexpensive eating and drinking.

Goldener Löwen, Eisengasse 1, has a typical local ambience, despite the tourist signs outside. Swiss specialities start at around Sfr15 in this small place. *Restaurant Stadtkeller* (☎ 410 47 33), Sternenplatz 3, has two folklore shows a day to allow you to yodel with your mouth full. Dishes cost from Sfr20 at lunch and Sfr30 in the evening, plus it's Sfr10 for the show (there's a bar – you don't have to eat). Reservations are usually necessary for meals. From November to mid-March, the show is replaced by live music (evening only).

Wirtshaus zum Rebstock (☎ 410 35 81), St Leodegar Strasse 3, has meals from Sfr13 to Sfr35. There are several eating areas providing variety in style and cuisine, including the linked *Hofgarten* vegetarian restaurant beyond the garden. *Hotel-Restaurant Schiff* (see Places to Stay), has lunch specials with soup from Sfr15, but it's also a good place to shed some francs and gain some pounds on quality evening dining. Cuisine from different nationalities is featured on a regular basis in winter.

Getting There & Away

Hourly trains connect Lucerne to Interlaken (Sfr23), Bern (Sfr31), Zürich (Sfr19.40), Lugano (Sfr55) and Geneva (Sfr65, via Olten or Langnau). The N2/E9 motorway connecting Basel and Lugano passes by Lucerne, and the N14 provides the road link to Zürich.

INTERLAKEN

Interlaken (population 15,000), flanked by Lake Thun and Lake Brienz and within striking distance of the mighty peaks of the Jungfrau, Mönch and Eiger, is an ideal starting point for exploring the surrounding delights. It is the centre of the Bernese Oberland, where the scenic wonders of Switzerland come into their own. People often end up staying longer than they planned.

Orientation & Information

Most of Interlaken is coupled between its two train stations. Each station offers bike rental and daily money exchange facilities, and behind each is a boat landing for boat services on the lakes. The main shopping street, Höheweg, runs between the two stations. You can walk from one to the other in under 20 minutes.

The tourist office (☎ 822 21 21), Höheweg 37, is nearer to Interlaken West and it's open Monday to Friday from 8 am to noon and 2 to 6 pm, and Saturday from 8 am to noon. During July and August, hours are extended. Staff will book rooms (no commission), or you can use the hotel board and free phone outside and at both railway stations. The main post office (3800, Postplatz) is near the Interlaken West station.

Interlaken's telephone code is ☎ 033.

Things to See & Do

Numerous hiking trails dot the area surrounding Interlaken, all with signposts giving average walking times. The funicular up to **Harder Kulm** (Sfr20 return) yields an excellent panorama and further prepared paths. There are worthwhile boat trips to several towns and villages around the lakes. European rail passes are valid on all boats. On **Lake Thun**, both the towns of Spiez (Sfr11.60 each way by steamer, Sfr6.60 by train) and Thun (Sfr15.60 by steamer, Sfr14 by train) have a castle. Other resorts offer water sports. A short, Sfr6 boat ride from Interlaken are the **St Beatus Höhlen** (St Beatus Caves), with some impressive stalagmite formations and a small museum. Combined entry is Sfr12, or Sfr11 for students. The department store dummies in a 'realistic reconstruction of a prehistoric settlement' are a laugh. Photography is prohibited in the caves as it holds up the guided tour

– not that that stops anybody. The caves can also be reached from Interlaken by bus or a 90-minute walk, and are open from Palm Sunday to October, daily from 9.30 am to 5 pm.

Lake Brienz has a more rugged shoreline than its neighbour, and fewer resorts. Brienz itself (Sfr12.40 by steamer, or Sfr6 by train) is the centre of the Swiss woodcarving industry and is close to the **Freilichtmuseum Ballenberg**, a huge open-air park displaying typical Swiss crafts and houses. The park is open daily from mid-April to the end of October, and admission costs Sfr12 (students Sfr10).

Places to Stay

The Guest Card gets useful discounts. Private rooms are good value: *Walter* (☎ 822 76 88), Oelestrasse 35, has four doubles (hall shower) for Sfr20 per person; the huge breakfast is Sfr7.

There are five camping grounds close together north-west of Interlaken West. *Alpenblick* (☎ 822 77 57), on Seestrasse by the Lombach River, costs Sfr5.80 per person, from Sfr9 per tent and Sfr4 for a car. Just along the road by the lake is *Manor Farm* (☎ 822 22 64), which is more expensive but has more facilities. Both are open all year.

The SYHA *hostel* (☎ 822 43 53), Aareweg 21, am See, Bönigen, is a 20-minute walk round the lake from Interlaken Ost, or take bus No 1. It has an excellent lakeside location, with swimming facilities and a kitchen. Beds in large dorms are Sfr17, breakfast is Sfr7 and dinner is Sfr11. The reception shuts between 9 am and 4 pm but the communal areas stay open. There is a 1 am curfew, and the hostel is closed from mid-December to mid-March.

Balmer's Herberge (☎ 822 19 61), at Hauptstrasse 23, is a 15-minute walk (signposted) from either station. Excellent communal facilities include a reading room, games room, music room, store, cellar bar and nightly videos. Balmer's organises excursions, rents bikes and gets discounts on adventure activity packages. There's a great atmosphere and it's a refreshing change of style from SYHA hostels, even if it's sometimes noisy and too much like an American summer camp. Beds are Sfr17 in dorms, Sfr27 in doubles and Sfr22 in triples and quads. Showers are Sfr1, optional sheet rental is Sfr4, and evening meals are Sfr5 to Sfr10. Sign for a bed during the day

(facilities are open) and check in at 5 pm. If it's full, get a mattress on the floor for Sfr11.

The Alp Lodge (☎ 822 47 48), an annexe of the Bellevue Hotel on Marktgasse, has creatively-decorated rooms for one to six people at Sfr39 per person with shower/toilet or Sfr29 without (no singles in summer). There's 24-hour access, with check-in from 3 pm. By Interlaken West train station is *Touriste Garni* (☎ 822 28 31), with a few parking spaces. Good-value singles/doubles are Sfr55/110 with shower or Sfr48/90 without.

Hotel Splendid (☎ 822 76 12), Höheweg 33, offers three-star comfort with well-presented singles/doubles for Sfr110/182 with private shower/toilet or Sfr80/117 without. Rooms have tea and coffee-making facilities. *Hotel Europe* (☎ 822 71 41), near Interlaken Ost station at Höheweg 94, offers renovated rooms with all facilities for Sfr150/220. There's ample free parking.

Places to Eat

Get cheap meals at the self-service restaurants of the supermarkets, *Migros*, opposite Interlaken West (late opening on Thursday), and *Coop*, Bahnhofstrasse, overlooking the river (late opening on Thursday and open on Sunday). A good, inexpensive place for Italian food is *Pizzeria Mercato*, Postgasse, off Höheweg, open daily to 11.30 pm.

Anker Restaurant, Marktgasse 57, is good and inexpensive for Swiss food. There is a games area at the back, and weekly live music in winter (closed Thursday). The *Hotel Europe* (see Places to Stay) has tasty two-course meals for Sfr13 (Sfr18 on Sunday), and a three-course vegetarian menu for Sfr17; other dishes cost Sfr15 to Sfr25.

The *Vegetaris* section of the Hotel Weisses Kreuz, Höheweg (opposite Buddy's Pub), is the place for vegetarians to head, with meals from Sfr13. For traditional food (for about Sfr30) in a typical chalet, go to *Gasthof Hirschen*, on the corner of Hauptstrasse and Parkstrasse (closed Wednesday lunch and Tuesday). The 1st floor restaurant in *Hotel Metropole*, by the tourist office, is expensive, but has affordable lunches. The hotel also has the *Panoramic Bar/Café* on the 15th floor – it's worth going up for a drink or snack to admire the view and to walk round the balcony.

Entertainment

Evening entertainment in Interlaken encompasses the casino with its folklore show, and several discos around town. Good places for a drink are *Mr Pickwick*, Postgasse 3, where there's a free disco or live music on weekends, and *Buddy's Pub*, Höheweg 33.

Getting There & Away

Trains to Lucerne depart hourly from Interlaken Ost. Trains to Brig and to Montreux (via Bern or Zweisimmen) depart from Interlaken West or Ost. Main roads head east to Lucerne and west to Bern, but the only way south for vehicles, without a big detour around the mountains, is to take the car-carrying train from Kandersteg, south of Spiez.

JUNGFRAU REGION

The views keep getting better the further south you go from Interlaken, and it's an ideal region for hiking and skiing. Train stations here offer poor rates for money-exchange.

The telephone code for the whole area is ☎ 033.

Grindelwald

Only 40 minutes by train from Interlaken Ost (Sfr9 each way) is Grindelwald, a busy resort under the north face of the Eiger. In the First region there are 90 km of hiking trails above 1200 metres. Of these, 48 km stay open year-round. In winter, the First is also the main skiing area, with a variety of runs stretching from Oberjoch at 2486 metres, right down to the village at 1050 metres. The cable car from Grindelwald-Grund to Männlichen, where there are more good views and hikes, is the longest in Europe (Sfr27 up, Sfr43 return). Grindelwald can be reached by road.

The tourist office (☎ 854 12 12) is in the centre at the Sportzentrum, 200 metres up from the train station. It's open daily in summer, but closed Sunday the rest of the year.

Places to Stay & Eat Grindelwald has several *camping grounds*, and a SYHA *hostel* (☎ 853 10 09), which is at Terrassenweg, a 20-minute climb from the train station. Dorm beds are Sfr29.50 and doubles cost from Sfr69. Reception is shut from 9 am to 3 pm (5 pm on Sunday) and the hostel closes down in the off-season. Close to the hostel is the *Naturfreundehaus*

(☎ 853 13 33), which has dorms from Sfr32 (closed in the off-season). Other dorms are listed in the tourist office leaflet.

In the centre of the village, just off the main street (signposted), is *Lehmann's Herberge* (☎ 853 31 41), with good-value rooms for one to six people costing Sfr40 or Sfr45 per person (plus Sfr5 for single-night stays). At the same turning on the main street is *Hotel Tschuggen* (☎ 853 17 81), with attractive singles/doubles for Sfr77/120 with private shower/toilet or Sfr57/100 without. Next door is *Ristorante Mercado*, one of the cheapest places to eat in this pricey village; small pizzas start at Sfr11, and there's a terrace. Nearby, *Restaurant Rendez-vous* has decent meals from Sfr13, or try *Hotel Derby* by the train station. There's a *Coop* supermarket opposite the tourist office.

A good mid-range choice for both food and accommodation is *Fiescherblick* (☎ 853 44 53), on the eastern side of the village.

Lauterbrunnen Valley

This valley is the other fork branching out from Interlaken into the mountains. The first village reached by car or rail is **Lauterbrunnen**, known mainly for the cascading Staubbach Falls just outside the village, and the even more impressive Trümmelbach Falls, which are somewhat further out (Sfr10 entry, open April to November). Find out more from the tourist office (☎ 855 19 55) on the main street.

Above the village (via funicular) is Grütschalp, where you switch to the train to **Mürren** (Sfr8.40), a skiing and hiking resort. The ride yields tremendous unfolding views across the valley to the Jungfrau, Mönch and Eiger peaks. Mürren's efficient tourist office (☎ 856 86 86) is in the sports centre. A 40-minute walk down the hill from Mürren is tiny **Gimmelwald**, relatively undisturbed by tourism.

Gimmelwald and Mürren can also be reached from the valley floor by the Stechelberg cable car, which runs all the way up to **Schilthorn** at 2971 metres. From the top there's a fantastic 360° panorama, and film shows will remind you that James Bond performed his stunts here in *On Her Majesty's Secret Service*. The return cable fare is a wallet-withering Sfr83, but ask about low season or first/last ascent of the day discounts.

SWITZERLAND

Places to Stay & Eat Gimmelwald and especially Lauterbrunnen are bargains for accommodation, but Mürren is more touristy and therefore more expensive. Another suitable base is Wengen, perched on the eastern side of the valley. It has several hotels with dormitories: enquire at the local tourist office (☎ 855 14 14).

Lauterbrunnen Both *Camping Schützenbach* (☎ 855 12 68) and *Camping Jungfrau* (☎ 856 20 10) have cheap dorms and bungalows in addition to camping. *Matratzenlager Stocki* (☎ 855 17 54) has a sociable atmosphere, kitchen facilities, and dorms beds for Sfr12 without breakfast. *Chalet im Rohr* (☎ 855 21 82) has singles/doubles for around Sfr24 per person. There's a kitchen but no breakfast.

Eating on the cheap is less easy. Stock up in the *Coop*, or try one of the hotel restaurants. *Hotel Horner* has pizza and pasta from Sfr11.

Gimmelwald The *Mountain Hostel* (☎ 855 17 04), close to the cable-car station and with a great view, was renovated in 1996. Dorms without breakfast cost Sfr18. It has kitchen facilities, daytime check-in and no curfew. *Restaurant-Pension Gimmelwald* (☎ 855 17 30), next door, with simple accommodation and hot meals from Sfr11. It adjoins a shop that's open just a few mornings a week. Five minutes up the hill is *Mittaghorn* (☎ 855 16 58), sometimes known as Walter's. Singles/doubles are Sfr55/60, triples/quads are Sfr85/105, and dormitory beds in the loft are Sfr25. Beds are available from May to mid-November only, as it's pre-booked in winter. Beer in the small café costs Sfr4 for an 0.58-litre bottle, but the tasty meals are only for guests who must pre-order.

Mürren The only budget places are two pensions about a 30-minute walk up the hill, *Suppenalp* (☎ 855 17 26) and *Sonnenberg* (☎ 855 11 27). Each charges Sfr37 in dorms and around Sfr100 for double rooms.

Hotel Edelweiss (☎ 855 13 12), with singles/doubles for Sfr95/180, is one of the cheaper village hotels. It has reasonable food from Sfr12, and good views from the south-facing terrace.

The small *Staegerstübli*, next to the *Coop* supermarket, is another affordable place for food (open daily).

Jungfraujoch

The trip to Jungfraujoch by railway (the highest in Europe) is excellent. Unfortunately, the price is as steep as the track and is hardly worth it unless you have very good weather – call ☎ 855 10 22 for forecasts, or check the live pictures on cable TV. From Interlaken Ost, trains go via Grindelwald or Lauterbrunnen to Kleine Scheidegg. From here, the line is less than 10 km long but took 16 years to build. Opened in 1912, the track powers through both the Eiger and the Mönch with majestic views from two windows blasted in the mountainside, before terminating at 3454 metres at Jungfraujoch.

On the summit, there is free entry to the **ice palace** (a maze cut in a glacier). From the terrace of the Sphinx Research Institute (a weather station) the panorama of peaks and valleys is unforgettable, including the Aletsch Glacier to the south, and mountains as distant as the Jura and the Black Forest. Take warm clothing and sunglasses (for glacier walking). There's a self-service restaurant in the complex.

From Interlaken Ost, return journey time is 2½ hours each way and the fare is Sfr158 (Eurail Sfr116, Inter-Rail Sfr76.60, Swiss Pass Sfr105). Allow at least three hours at the site. There's a cheaper (or more accurately, less exorbitant) 'good morning ticket' of Sfr120 (Eurail Sfr101, Inter-Rail Sfr76.60, Swiss Pass Sfr90) if you take the first train (6.35 am from Interlaken) and leave the summit by noon. From 1 November to 30 April the reduction is valid for the 6.35 and 7.38 am trains, and the noon restriction doesn't apply. It is not possible to walk up beyond Kleine Scheidegg.

Other Destinations

Marvellous views and hikes compete for attention from various other vantage points in the Jungfrau region, such as **Schynige Platte**, **Männlichen** and **Kleine Scheidegg**.

Skiing is a major activity in the winter months, with a good variety of intermediate runs plus the demanding run down from the Schilthorn. Resort ski passes cost Sfr50 or Sfr52 for a day, or Sfr100 for a minimum of two days in the whole Jungfrau region.

Northern Switzerland

This part of the country is important for industry and commerce, yet it is by no means lacking in tourist attractions. Take time to explore Lake Constance, the Rhine and the picturesque town centres of the region.

BASEL

Basel (Bâle in French) joined the Swiss Confederation in 1501. Although an industrial city of 190,000 people, it retains an attractive old town and offers many interesting museums. The famous Renaissance humanist, Erasmus of Rotterdam, was associated with the city and his tomb rests in the cathedral.

Orientation & Information

Basel's strategic position on the Rhine at the dual border with France and Germany has been instrumental in its development as a commercial and cultural centre. On the north bank of the Rhine is Kleinbasel (Little Basel), surrounded by German territory. The pedestrian-only old town and most of the sights are on the south bank in Grossbasel (Greater Basel).

The main tourist office (☎ 261 50 50) is by the Mittlere bridge at Schifflände 5, open Monday to Friday from 8.30 am to 6 pm, and Saturday from 10 am to 4 pm. Under two km south is the main SBB Bahnhof which has bike rental, money exchange (6 am to 9 pm daily), a grocery store (7 am to 11.30 pm daily) and another tourist office (☎ 271 36 84), open Monday to Friday from 8.30 am to 6 pm and Saturday from 8.30 am to 12.30 pm. Its opening hours are extended between April and September to 7 pm weekdays, 1.30 to 6 pm Saturday, and (between June and September) Sunday from 10 am to 2 pm.

The main post office (4001 Basel 1, Freie Strasse) is in the centre, though the office by the train station has a daily emergency counter (surcharge payable).

Basel's telephone code is ☎ 061.

Things to See & Do

The tourist office has free guides to walks through the old town, taking in cobbled streets, colourful fountains and 16th-century buildings. The restored **Rathaus** (town hall) is very impressive and has a frescoed courtyard. The 12th-century **Münster** (cathedral) is another highlight with its Gothic spires and Romanesque St Gallus doorway.

Of the many museums (a three-day pass costs Sfr23), the most important is the **Kunstmuseum**, St Albangraben 16, with a good selection of religious, Swiss and modern art. It is open Tuesday to Sunday from 10 am to 5 pm, and costs Sfr7 (students Sfr5) except on the first Sunday of the month when it's free. It has an excellent collection of Picassos. The artist was so gratified when the people of Basel paid a large sum for two of his paintings that he donated a further four from his own collection.

Basel's **zoo** is one of the best in Switzerland (open daily; Sfr10, students Sfr8). Be sure to take a look at the **fountain** on Theaterplatz. It's a typical display by the Swiss sculptor Jean Tinguely, with madcap machinery playing water games with hoses – art with a juvenile heart.

Basel is also a carnival town. At the end of January, *Vogel Gryff* is when winter is chased away. On the Monday after Ash Wednesday, three days of festivities begin. Known as *Fasnacht*, it's a spectacle of parades, masks, music and costumes, all starting at 4 am!

Places to Stay

Hotels are expensive and liable to be full during numerous trade fairs and conventions. Be sure to book ahead. Unusually, July and August aren't too bad in Basel. The tourist office in the SBB Bahnhof reserves rooms for Sfr10 commission, compared to Sfr5 in the main tourist office. Check the tourist office hotel list for cheaper, out-of-town accommodation.

Six km south of the train station is *Camp Waldhort* (☎ 711 64 29) at Heideweg 16, Reinach.

The SYHA *hostel* (☎ 272 05 72) is fairly near the centre of town at St Alban Kirchrain 10. Dorm beds are Sfr26.80 and double rooms are Sfr37.80 per person. Reception is shut from 11 am to 2 pm, when the doors are also locked. Curfew is at midnight.

In the old town, *Stadthof* (☎ 261 87 11), Gerbergasse 84, has standard singles/doubles for Sfr80/160, without breakfast and using hall showers. Near the pedestrian zone is

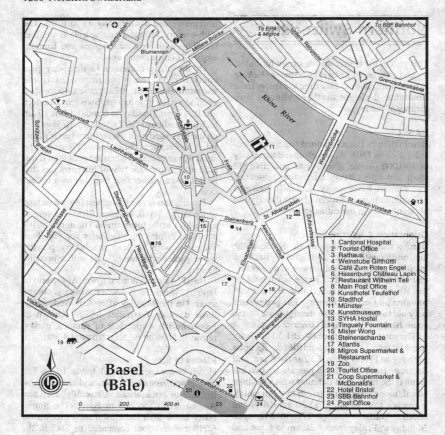

1 Cantonal Hospital
2 Tourist Office
3 Rathaus
4 Weinstube Gifthüttli
5 Café Zum Roten Engel
6 Hasenburg Château Lapin
7 Restaurant Wilhelm Tell
8 Main Post Office
9 Kunsthotel Teufelhof
10 Stadthof
11 Münster
12 Kunstmuseum
13 SYHA Hostel
14 Tinguely Fountain
15 Mister Wong
16 Steinenschanze
17 Atlantis
18 Migros Supermarket & Restaurant
19 Zoo
20 Tourist Office
21 Coop Supermarket & McDonald's
22 Hotel Bristol
23 SBB Bahnhof
24 Post Office

Basel (Bâle)

Steinenschanze (☎ 272 53 53), Steinengraben 69, which has singles/doubles with private shower/toilet for Sfr100/140. The price for students is reduced to Sfr50 per person for the first three nights. By the station, the two-star *Hotel Bristol* (☎ 271 38 22) has a variety of rooms ranging from small 'B-Zimmer' singles for Sfr75 to doubles with their own bathroom for Sfr170.

If you can afford to splash out on accommodation, there is a unique possibility in the *Kunsthotel Teufelhof* (☎ 261 10 10), Leonhardsgraben 47. Each of the rooms was assigned to a different artist to create environmental art. All rooms will stay intact for about

two years before being reassigned to a new artist. The shock of waking up in a piece of art is quite something. The rooms have shower and toilet, and prices start at Sfr215/280 for a single/double, or Sfr145/260 in the new Galeriehotel annexe. Some rooms are more elaborately kitted out than others, but all are a welcome respite from standard hotel fixtures. It also has a quality restaurant.

Places to Eat

The *EPA* department store, Untere Rebgasse, Kleinbasel, has a cheap self-service restaurant, open till 8 pm on Thursday. *Migros* supermarket restaurants are opposite EPA and on

Sternengasse. *Mister Wong*, Steinenvorstadt 1a, also self-service, offers a reasonable choice of Asian dishes from Sfr10. It has a salad bar and is open daily to at least 10.30 pm. *Restaurant Wilhelm Tell*, Spalenvorstadt 38, by the Spalentor city gate, is very small, simple and busy, but it's still worth paying a visit for tasty Swiss dishes from Sfr14.50. It's open daily, with Röstis available evening only.

For Basel specialities in a typical ambience, try *Weinstube Gifthüttli* (☎ 261 16 56), Schneidergasse 11. Meals start at Sfr14.50 – check the menus written in bizarre local dialect (closed Sunday). Opposite is the slightly more down-to-earth *Hasenburg Château Lapin*. Vegetarians should check the environmentally-sound *Café Zum Roten Engel* in the adjoining courtyard (outside tables). It serves organic vegetarian food for around Sfr12.50 to Sfr15, as well as milky coffee, breakfast and many types of tea.

Entertainment
For evening entertainment, try *Atlantis* (☎ 272 20 38), Klosterberg 13. It has live music nightly (mainly rock, jazz and R&B); there's usually a cover charge (Sfr5 to Sfr35).

Getting There & Away
Basel is a major European rail hub. For most international trains you pass the border controls in the station, so allow extra time. All trains to France go from SBB Bahnhof. There are four to five trains a day to Paris (Sfr68) and connections to Brussels and Strasbourg. Trains to Germany stop at BBF Bahnhof on the north bank; local trains to the Black Forest stop only at BBF, though fast EC services stop at SBB too. Main destinations along this route are Frankfurt (Sfr79, plus around Sfr11 German rail supplement), Cologne, Hamburg and Amsterdam. Services within Switzerland go from SBB: there are two fast trains an hour to both Geneva (Sfr67; via Bern or Biel/Bienne) and Zürich (Sfr30). By motorway, the E25/E60 heads down from Strasbourg and passes by Mulhouse airport, and the E35/A5 hugs the German side of the Rhine.

Getting Around
The yellow bus outside the Swissair office at SBB station goes to/from Mulhouse airport (Sfr2.60). City buses and trams run every six

to 10 minutes. Tickets cost Sfr1.80 for up to and including four stops, or Sfr2.60 for the whole central zone. Multi-journey cards are available, but you're better off with a day pass for Sfr7.40.

AROUND BASEL
See the Germany chapter for information on the **Black Forest**; it's an easy excursion from Basel. To the south lies **Solothurn**, well worth looking at on the way to/from Bern. It has an Italianate cathedral, a baroque Jesuit church, historic fountains and a good fine art museum (housing Hodler's classic painting of William Tell).

SCHAFFHAUSEN
The capital of the canton that bears its name, this communications and arms centre was accidentally bombed by the USA in 1944. Thankfully its medieval town centre remains intact. The Rhine Falls is three km down river.

Orientation & Information
Schaffhausen is in a bulge of Swiss territory surrounded by Germany on the north bank of the Rhine. The train station is adjacent to the old town, where you'll find the tourist office (☎ 625 51 41) at Fronwagturm. It is open weekdays and (in summer) to noon Saturday. Postbuses depart from the rear of the station and local buses from the front. The main post office is also opposite the station.

The telephone code for Schaffhausen is ☎ 052.

Things to See
The attractive old town is bursting with oriel windows, painted façades and ornamental fountains. The best streets are Vordergasse, which has the 16th-century **Haus zum Ritter** with its painted historical scenes, and Vorstadt; they intersect at Fronwagplatz. Get an overview of the town from the **Munot** fortress up on the hill (open daily, free). The **Allerheiligen Museum**, by the cathedral in Klosterplatz, houses a collection ranging from ancient bones to modern art (free, closed Monday).

The **Rhine Falls** (Rheinfall) can be reached by a 40-minute stroll westward along the river, or by bus No 1 or 9 to Neuhausen. The largest waterfall in Europe drops 23 metres and makes a tremendous racket as 600 cubic metres of water crashes down every second. The 45 km of the Rhine from Schaffhausen to Constance is one of the river's most beautiful stretches, passing by meadows, castles and ancient villages, not the least being picturesque **Stein am Rhein**, 20 km to the east, with a central square (Rathausplatz) that's one of the most photogenic in Switzerland.

Places to Stay

The SYHA *hostel* (☎ 625 88 00) is a 15-minute walk west of the train station (or take bus No 3 to Breite), at Randenstrasse 65 (closed November to late February). Dorms cost Sfr21.50, and the reception is closed from 9 am to 5.30 pm. The cheapest deal in the town centre is *Steinbock* (☎ 625 42 60), Webergasse 47, with singles/doubles for Sfr48/75 with hall showers. There's no breakfast, but the rooms are clean and reasonably sized. *Park Villa* (☎ 625 27 37), Parkstrasse 18, is atmospheric and often luxurious. It costs from Sfr105/159 for rooms with shower/toilet, or Sfr70/100 without.

Places to Eat

Eat for under Sfr12 at either the *Migros* supermarket and restaurant at Vorstadt 39, the *EPA* department store restaurant at Vordergasse 69, or at *Manora* in the Manor department store by the tourist office. The best Italian food (from Sfr13) is at *Pizzeria Romana*, Unterstadt 18 (closed Wednesday).

For a taste treat, go to *Rheinhotel Fischerzunft* (☎ 625 32 81), Rheinquai 8. It's one of Switzerland's top restaurants; main dishes are around Sfr50 and combine Asian and European styles.

Getting There & Away

Hourly trains run to Zürich (Sfr15). Constance and Basel can be reached by either Swiss or (cheaper) German trains. Steamers travel to Constance several times a day in summer, and the trip takes four hours; they depart from Freier Platz (call ☎ 625 42 82 for information). Schaffhausen has good roads radiating out in all directions.

ST GALLEN

In 612, an itinerant Irish monk called Gallus fell into a briar. Relying on a peculiar form of Irish logic, the venerable Gallus interpreted this clumsy act as a sign from God and decided

to stay put and build a hermitage. From this inauspicious beginning the town of St Gallen evolved and developed into an important medieval cultural centre.

Orientation & Information

The main post office (Bahnhofplatz, 9001) is opposite the train station. Two minutes away is the tourist office (☎ 227 37 37), Bahnhofplatz 1a, open Monday to Friday from 9 am to noon and 1 to 6 pm, and on Saturday from 9 am to noon. It has a free hotel booking service for personal and telephone callers, and a useful *Tourist Information* booklet. A few minutes to the east is the pedestrian-only old town.

The telephone code for St Gallen is ☎ 071.

Things to See

St Gallen has an interesting old-city centre. Several buildings have distinctive oriel windows: the best are on Gallusplatz, Spisergasse and Kugelgasse. The twin-tower **cathedral** cannot and should not be missed. Completed in 1766, it's immensely impressive and impressively immense. The ceiling frescos were by Josef Wannenmacher; look out also for the pulpit, arches, statue groups and woodcarvings around the confessionals.

Adjoining the church is the **Stiftsbibliothek** (Abbey Library), containing some beautifully etched manuscripts from the Middle Ages and a splendidly opulent rococo interior. There's even an Egyptian mummy, dating from 700 BC and as well preserved as the average grandparent. Entry is Sfr5, students Sfr3, and it's closed for three weeks in November, and on Sunday from 1 December to 30 April.

The **Grabenhalle**, Blumenberg Platz, is a major venue for concerts and other arts events.

Places to Stay

The SYHA *hostel* (☎ 245 47 77) is a signposted, 15-minute walk east of the old town at Jüchstrasse 25 (follow hostel signs with the adult and child – the other hostel signs are for drivers). Alternatively, take the Trogenerbahn from outside the station to 'Schülerhaus'. Beds are Sfr23 in a dorm or Sfr32 in a double room. Reception is closed from 9 am to 5 pm but there's usually day-time access to communal areas. Get a key to avoid the curfew. The hostel closes from mid-

December to early March, though it's sometimes open in January.

Weisses Kreuz (☎ 223 28 43) on Engelgasse is the best value hotel. It has varying singles/doubles for Sfr40/75 using hall showers, or from Sfr55/80 with private shower. The reception is in the bar downstairs. *Touring Garni* (☎ 222 58 01) is virtually opposite. Singles/doubles for Sfr54/95 have private shower; those for Sfr44/75 have a sink but no access to a shower. *Elite Garni* (☎ 222 12 36), Metzgergasse 9-11, is a small step up in price and quality.

Places to Eat

Eating can be pretty good in St Gallen. At the lower end, look out for various fast-food stalls selling St Gallen sausage and bread for around Sfr4. The university *Hochschule Mensa*, east of the rail tracks at Dufourstrasse, offers cheap weekday lunches.

On St Leonhardstrasse is *Migros* supermarket and restaurant. Equally economical is the *EPA* department-store restaurant at Bohl, in the centre. Both have late closing on Thursday to 9 pm. Next door to EPA is *Stein*, which, if building renovations don't alter the food, has tasty but cheap fare. Close by are two places straddling Marktplatz and Neugasse, *Hörni* and *Marktplatz*. Both are similar, offering food at a range of prices. Hörni has a wide selection of beers, but you can only get the cheaper draught stuff on the ground floor.

A good mid-range place is *Wirtschaft Zur Alten Post* (☎ 222 66 01), Gallusstrasse 4. The food is typically Swiss, with meat and fish dishes mostly above Sfr30, though there are cheaper lunch menus. Small and cosy, this restaurant fills quickly so reserve ahead. It's closed on Sunday and Monday.

Getting There & Away

St Gallen is a short train ride from Lake Constance (Bodensee), upon which boats sail to Bregenz in Austria, and to Constance and Lindau in Germany (not in winter). There are also regular trains to Bregenz (Sfr12), Constance (Sfr15.80), Chur (Sfr32) and Zürich (Sfr26).

APPENZELL

If you ever hear a joke in Switzerland, the inhabitants of Appenzell are likely to be its target. They are known for their parochialism and are considered (a little unfairly) to be several stages lower on the evolutionary ladder than the rest of humanity. Women were finally allowed to vote in local affairs in 1991, and then only after the supreme court ruled their exclusion by the men unconstitutional.

Appenzell has an old-fashioned air and attracts plenty of tourists. The village is a delight to wander around, with traditional old houses, painted façades and lush surrounding countryside. The streets are bedecked with flags and flowers on the last Sunday in April when the locals vote on cantonal issues by a show of hands in the open-air parliament (Landsgemeinde). Everyone wears traditional dress for the occasion and many of the men carry swords or daggers as proof of citizenship.

Getting There & Away

There are hourly connections from St Gallen by a narrow-gauge train (Swiss Pass and Eurail valid; Inter-Rail gets half-price) which meanders along, mostly following the course of the road (45 minutes). There are two routes so you can make it a circular trip.

Appendix I – Climate Charts

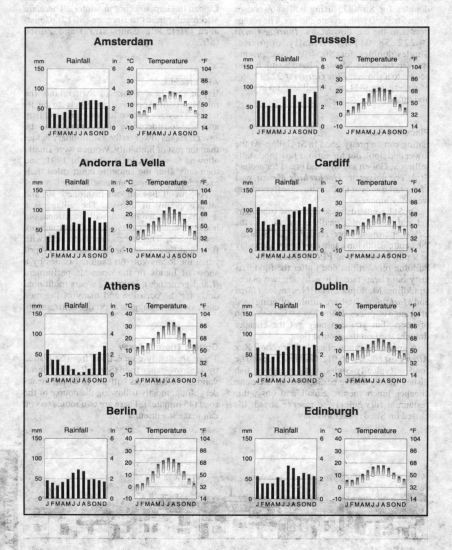

Amsterdam

Brussels

Andorra La Vella

Cardiff

Athens

Dublin

Berlin

Edinburgh

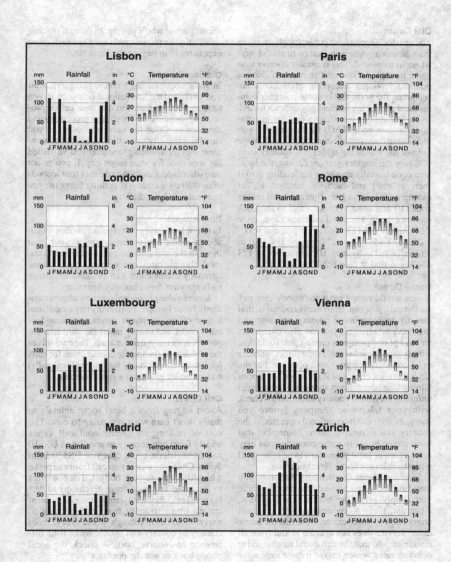

Appendix II – Telephones

Dial Direct

You can dial directly from public telephone boxes from almost anywhere in Europe to almost anywhere in the world. This is usually cheaper than going through the operator. In much of Europe, public telephones accepting phonecards are becoming the norm and in some countries coin-operated phones are increasingly difficult to find.

To call abroad you simply dial the international access code (IAC) for the country you are calling from (most commonly 00 in Europe but see the following table), the country code (CC) for the country you are calling, the local area code (usually dropping the leading zero if there is one) and then the number. If, for example, you are in Italy (international access code 00) and want to make a call to the USA (country code 1), San Francisco (area code 212), number ☎ 123 4567, then you dial ☎ 00-1-212-123 4567. To call from the UK (00) to Australia (61), Sydney (02), number ☎ 123 4567, you dial ☎ 00-61-2-1234 5678.

Home Direct

If you would rather have somebody else pay for the call, you can, from many countries, dial directly to your home country operator and then reverse charges; you can also charge the call to a phone company credit card. To do this, simply dial the relevant 'home direct' number to be connected to your own operator. For the USA there's a choice of AT&T, MCI or Sprint Global One home direct services. Home direct numbers vary from country to country – check with your telephone company before you leave, or with the international operator in the country you're ringing from. Remember that from phone boxes in some countries you may need a coin or local phonecard to be connected with the relevant home direct operator.

In some places (particularly airports), you may find dedicated home direct phones where you simply press the button labelled USA, Australia, Hong Kong or whatever for direct connection to the operator. Note that the home direct service does not operate to and from all countries, and that the call could be charged at operator rates, which makes it quite expensive

for the person who's paying. In general placing a call on your phone credit card is much more expensive than paying the local tariff.

Dialling Tones

In some countries (eg France, Hungary), after you've dialled the international access code, you have to wait for a second dial tone before proceeding with the code for your target country and the number. Often the same applies when you ring from one city to another within these countries: wait for a dialling tone after you've dialled the area code for your target city. If you're not sure what to do, simply wait three or four seconds after dialling a code – if nothing happens, you can probably keep dialling.

Phonecards

In major locations you may find phones which accept credit cards: simply swipe your card through the slot and the call is charged to the card, though rates can be very high. Phone company credit cards can be used to charge calls via your home country operator.

Stored-value phonecards are now almost standard all over Europe. You usually buy a card from a post office, telephone centre, newsstand or retail outlet and simply insert the card into the phone each time you make a call. The card solves the problem of finding the correct coins for calls (or lots of correct coins for international calls) and generally gives you a small discount.

Call Costs

Avoid ringing from a hotel room unless you really don't care what it's going to cost. The cost of making an international call varies widely from one country to another. A US$10 call from Britain could cost you US$30 from Spain. Choosing where you call from can make a big difference to your budget. The countries in the table are rated from * (cheap) to *** (expensive). Reduced rates are available at certain times (usually from mid-evening to early morning), though these vary from country to country and should make little difference to relative costs – check the local phone book or ask the operator.

Telephone Codes

	CC	cost (see text)	IAC	IO
Albania	355			
Andorra	376	***	00	821111
Austria	43	**	00	09
Belgium	32	***	00	1224 (private phone) 1223 (public phone)
Belarus	375		8(w)10	
Bulgaria	359	**	00	
Croatia	385	***	99	901
Cyprus	357	***	00	
Cyprus (Turkish)	905		00	
Czech Republic	42	***	00	0131
Denmark	45	**	00	141
Estonia	372	***	8(w)00	007
Finland	358	*	990	020222
France	33	**	00(w)	12
Germany	49	**	00	00118
Gibraltar	350	***	00	100
Greece	30	*	00	161
Hungary	36	*	00(w)	09
Iceland	354		90	09
Ireland	353	*	00	114
Italy	39	***	00	15
Latvia	371	***	00	115
Liechtenstein	41 75	***	00	114
Lithuania	370	***	8(w)10 8(w)	194/195
Luxembourg	352	**	00	0010
Macedonia	389		99	
Malta	356	**	00	194
Morocco	212	***	00(w)	12
Netherlands	31	***	00	060410
Norway	47	*	095	181
Poland	48	**	0(w)0	901
Portugal	351	**	00	099
Romania			40	071
Russia	7		8(w)10	
Slovakia	42	**	00	0131
Slovenia	386	**	00	901
Spain	34	***	07(w)	91389
Sweden	46	**	009(w)	0018
Switzerland	41	***	00	114
Tunisia	216	***	00	
Turkey	90	**	00	115
UK	44	*	00	155
Yugoslavia	381	**	99	901

CC – Country Code (to call *into* that country)
IAC – International Access Code (to call abroad *from* that country)
IO – International Operator (to make enquiries)
(w) – wait for dialling tone
Other country codes include: Australia 61, Canada 1, Hong Kong 852, India 91, Indonesia 62, Israel 972, Japan 81, Macau 853, Malaysia 60, New Zealand 64, Singapore 65, South Africa 27, Thailand 66, USA 1

Appendix III – European Organisations

	Council of Europe	EU	EFTA	NATO	Nordic Council	OECD	WEU
Albania	✓	–	–	–	–	–	–
Andorra	✓	–	–	–	–	–	–
Austria	✓	✓	–	–	–	✓	–
Belgium	✓	✓	–	✓	–	✓	✓
Bulgaria	✓	–	–	–	–	–	–
Croatia	•	–	–	–	–	–	–
Cyprus	✓	–	–	–	–	–	–
Czech Republic	✓	–	–	–	–	✓	–
Denmark	✓	✓	–	✓	✓	✓	–
Estonia	✓	–	–	–	–	–	–
Finland	✓	✓	–	–	✓	✓	–
France	✓	✓	–	✓	–	✓	–
Germany	✓	✓	–	✓	–	✓	✓
Greece	✓	✓	–	✓	–	✓	✓
Hungary	✓	–	–	–	–	✓	–
Iceland	✓	–	✓	✓	✓	✓	–
Ireland	✓	✓	–	–	–	✓	–
Italy	✓	✓	–	✓	–	✓	✓
Latvia	✓	–	–	–	–	–	–
Lithuania	✓	–	–	–	–	–	–
Luxembourg	✓	✓	–	✓	–	✓	✓
Macedonia	✓	–	–	–	–	–	–
Malta	✓	–	–	–	–	–	–
Netherlands	✓	✓	–	✓	–	✓	✓
Norway	✓	–	✓	✓	✓	✓	–
Poland	✓	–	–	–	–	–	–
Portugal	✓	✓	–	✓	–	✓	✓
Romania	✓	–	–	–	–	–	–
Slovakia	✓	–	–	–	–	–	–
Slovenia	✓	–	–	–	–	–	–
Spain	✓	✓	–	✓	–	✓	✓
Sweden	✓	✓	–	–	✓	✓	–
Switerland	✓	–	✓	–	–	✓	–
Turkey	✓	–	–	✓	–	✓	–
UK	✓	✓	–	✓	–	✓	✓
Yugoslavia	–	–	–	–	–	✓	–

✓ – full memeber
• – special guest status

Council of Europe

Established in 1949, the Council of Europe is the oldest of Europe's political institutions. It aims to promote European unity, protect human rights, and assist in the cultural, social and economic development of its member states, but its powers are purely advisory. Founding states were Belgium, Denmark, France, Ireland, Italy, Luxembourg, the Netherlands, Norway, Sweden and the UK. Its headquarters are in Strasbourg.

European Union (EU)

Founded by the Treaty of Rome in 1957, the European Economic Community, or Common Market as it used to be known, broadened its scope far beyond economic measures as it developed into the European Community and finally the European Union. Its original aims were to develop and expand the economies of its member states by abolishing customs tariffs, coordinating transportation systems and general economic policies, establishing a common economic policy towards nonmember states, and promoting the free movement of labour and capital within its borders. Further measures included the abolishment of border controls and the linking of currency exchange rates. Since the Maastricht treaty of December 1991, the EU is committed to establishing a common foreign and security policy, close cooperation in home affairs and the judiciary, and a single European currency to be called the euro.

The EEC's founding states were Belgium, France, West Germany, Italy, Luxembourg and the Netherlands – the Treaty of Rome was an extension of the European Coal and Steel Community (ECSC) founded by these six states in 1952. Denmark, Ireland and the UK joined in 1973, Greece in 1981, Spain and Portugal in 1986 and Austria, Finland and Sweden in 1995. The main EU organisations are the European Parliament (elected by direct universal suffrage, with growing powers), the European Commission (the daily 'government'), the Council of Ministers (ministers of member states who make the important decisions) and the Court of Justice. The European Parliament meets in Strasbourg; Luxembourg is home to the Court of Justice. Other EU organisations are based in Brussels.

European Free Trade Association (EFTA)
Established in 1960 as a response to the creation of the European Economic Community, EFTA aims to eliminate trade tariffs on industrial products between member states, though each member retains the right to its own commercial policy towards nonmembers. Most members cooperate with the EU through the European Economic Area agreement. Denmark and the UK left EFTA to join the EU in 1973 and others have since followed suit, leaving EFTA's future in doubt. Its headquarters are in Geneva.

North Atlantic Treaty Organisation (NATO)
The document creating this defence alliance was signed in 1949 by the USA, Canada and 10 European countries to safeguard their common political, social and economic systems against external threats (read: against the powerful

Soviet military presence in Europe after WW II). An attack against any member state would be considered an attack against them all. Greece and Turkey joined in 1952, West Germany in 1955, and Spain in 1982; France withdrew from NATO's integrated military command in 1966 and Greece did likewise in 1974, though both remain members. NATO's Soviet counterpart, the Warsaw Pact founded in 1955, collapsed with the democratic revolutions of 1989 and the subsequent disintegration of the Soviet Union; most of its former members are now NATO associates in the 'Partnership for Peace' programme. NATO's headquarters are in Brussels.

Nordic Council
Established in Copenhagen in 1953, the Nordic Council aims to promote economic, social and cultural cooperation among its member states (Denmark, Finland, Iceland, Norway and Sweden). Since 1971, the Council has acted as an advisory body to the Nordic Council of Ministers, a meeting of ministers from the member states responsible for the subject under discussion. Decisions taken by the Council of Ministers are usually binding, though member states retain full sovereignty. Environmental, tariff, labour and immigration policies are often coordinated.

Organisation for Economic Cooperation and Development (OECD)
The OECD was set up in 1961 to supersede the Organisation for European Economic Cooperation, which allocated US aid under the Marshall Plan and coordinated the reconstruction of postwar Europe. Sometimes seen as the club of the world's rich countries, the OECD aims to encourage economic growth and world trade. Its member states include most of Europe, as well as Australia, Canada, Japan, Mexico, New Zealand and the USA. Its headquarters are in Paris.

Western European Union (WEU)
Set up in 1955, the WEU was designed to coordinate the military defences between member states, to promote economic, social and cultural cooperation, and to encourage European integration. Social and cultural tasks were transferred to the Council of Europe in 1960, and these days the WEU is sometimes touted as a future, more 'European', alternative to NATO. Its headquarters are in Brussels.

Appendix IV – Alternative Place Names

The following abbreviations are used:

(B) Basque
(C) Catalan
(D) Dutch/Flemish
(E) English
(F) French
(Fl) Flemish/Dutch
(G) German
(Gr) Greek
(Ir) Irish
(I) Italian
(L) Luxembourgian
(I) Italian
(P) Portuguese
(Rh) Romansch
(S) Spanish

AUSTRIA
Österreich

Carinthia (E) – Kärnten (G)
Danube (E) – Donau (G)
East Tirol (E) – Osttirol (G)
Lake Constance (E) – Bodensee (G)
Lower Austria (E) – Niederösterreich (G)
Upper Austria (E) – Oberösterreich (G)
Styria (E) – Steiermark (G)
Tirol (E, G) – Tyrol (G)
Vienna (E) – Wien (G)
Vienna Woods (E) – Wienerwald (G)

BELGIUM
België (Fl), Belgique (F)

Antwerp (E) – Antwerpen (Fl), Anvers (F)
Bruges (E, F) – Brugge (Fl)
Brussels (E) – Brussel (Fl), Bruxelles (F)
Ghent (E) – Gent (Fl), Gand (F)
Liège (E, F) – Luik (Fl), Lüttich (G)
Louvain (E, F) – Leuven (Fl)
Mechlin (E) – Mechelen (Fl), Malines (F)
Meuse (River) (E, F) – Maas (Fl)
Mons (E, F) – Bergen (Fl)
Namur (E, F) – Namen (Fl)
Ostend (E) – Oostende (Fl), Ostende (F)
Scheldt (River) (E) – Schelde (Fl), Escaut (F)
Tournai (E, F) – Doornik (Fl)
Ypres (E, F) – Ieper (Fl)

FRANCE

Bayonne (F, E) – Baiona (B)
Basque Country (E) – Euskadi (B), Pays Basque (F)
Burgundy (E) – Bourgogne (F)

Brittany (E) – Bretagne (F)
Corsica (E) – Corse (F)
French Riviera (E) – Côte d'Azur (F)
Dunkirk (E) – Dunkerque (F)
Channel Islands (E) – Îles Anglo-Normandes (F)
English Channel (E) – La Manche (F)
Lake Geneva (E) – Lac Léman (F)
Lyons (E) – Lyon (F)
Marseilles (E) – Marseille (F)
Normandy (E) – Normandie (F)
Rheims (E) – Reims (F)
Rhine (River) (E) – Rhin (F), Rhein (G)
Saint Jean de Luz (F) – Donibane Lohizune (B)
Saint Jean Pied de Port (F) – Donibane Garazi (B)
Sark (Channel Islands) (E) – Sercq (F)

GERMANY
Deutschland

Aachen (E, G) – Aix-la-Chapelle (F)
Baltic Sea (E) – Ostsee (G)
Bavaria (E) – Bayern (G)
Bavarian Alps (E) – Bayerische Alpen (G)
Bavarian Forest (E) – Bayerischer Wald (G)
Black Forest (E) – Schwarzwald (G)
Cologne (E) – Köln (G)
Constance (E) – Konstanz (G)
Danube (E) – Donau (G)
East Friesland (E) – Ostfriesland (G)
Federal Republic of Germany (E) –
  Bundesrepublik Deutschland (abbrev BRD) (G)
Franconia (E) – Franken (G)
Hamelin (E) – Hameln (G)
Hanover (E) – Hannover (G)
Harz Mountains (E) – Harzgebirge (G)
Hesse (E) – Hessen (G)
Lake Constance (E) – Bodensee (G)
Lower Saxony (E) – Niedersachsen (G)
Lüneburg Heath (E) – Lüneburger Heide (G)
Mecklenburg-Pomerania (E) –
  Mecklenburg-Vorpommern (G)
Munich (E) – München (G)
North Friesland (E) – Nordfriesland (G)
North Rhine-Westphalia (E) –
  Nordrhein-Westfalen (G)
Nuremberg (E) – Nürnberg (G)
Pomerania (E) – Pommern (G)
Prussia (E) – Preussen (G)
Rhine (E) – Rhein (G)
Rhineland-Palatinate (E) – Rheinland-Pfalz (G)
Romantic Road (E) – Romantische Strasse (G)
Saarbrücken (E, G) – Sarrebruck (F)
Saxon Switzerland (E) –
  Sachsische Schweiz (G)
Saxony (E) – Sachsen (G)
Swabia (E) – Schwaben (G)

Thuringia (E) – Thüringen (G)
Thuringian Forest (E) – Thüringer Wald (G)

GREECE
Hellas (or Ellaν)

Athens (E) – Athina (Gr)
Corfu (E) – Kerkyra (Gr)
Crete (E) – Kriti (Gr)
Patras (E) – Patra (Gr)
Rhodes (E) – Rodos (Gr)
Salonica (E) – Thessaloniki (Gr)
Samothrace (E) – Samothraki (Gr)
Santorini (E, I) – Thira (Gr)

IRELAND
Eire

Aran Islands (E) – Oileáin Árainn (Ir)
Athlone (E) – Baile Átha Luain (Ir)
Bantry (E) – Beanntraí (Ir)
Belfast (E) – Béal Feirste (Ir)
Cork (E) – Corcaigh (Ir)
Derry/Londonderry (E) – Doire (Ir)
Dingle (E) – An Daingean (Ir)
Donegal (E) – Dún na nGall (Ir)
Dublin (E) – Baile Átha Cliath (Ir)
Galway (E) – Gaillimh (Ir)
Kilkenny (E) – Cill Chainnigh (Ir)
Killarney (E) – Cill Áirne (Ir)
Kilronan (E) – Cill Ronáin (Ir)
Limerick (E) – Luimneach (Ir)
Roscommon (E) – Ros Comáin (Ir)
Rossaveal (E) – Ros an Mhil (Ir)
Shannon (E) – Sionann (Ir)
Tipperary (E) – Tiobraid Árann (Ir)
Waterford (E) – Port Láirge (Ir)
Wexford (E) – Loch Garman (Ir)

ITALY
Italia

Aeolian Islands (E) – Isole Eolie (I)
Apulia (E) – Puglia (I)
Florence (E) – Firenze (I)
Genoa (E) – Genova (I)
Herculaneum (E) – Ercolano (I)
Lombardy (E) – Lombardia (I)
Mantua (E) – Mantova (I)
Milan (E) – Milano (I)
Naples (E) – Napoli (I)
Padua (E) – Padova (I)
Rome (E) – Roma (I)
Sicily (E) – Sicilia (I)
Sardinia (E) – Sardegna (I)

Syracuse (E) – Siracusa (I)
Tiber (River) (E) – Tevere (I)
Venice (E) – Venezia (I)

LUXEMBOURG
Letzeburg (L), Luxembourg (F), Luxemburg (G)

THE NETHERLANDS
Nederland

Den Bosch (E, D) – 's-Hertogenbosch (D)
Flushing (E) – Vlissingen (D)
Hook of Holland (E) – Hoek van Holland (D)
Meuse (River) (E, F) – Maas (D)
Rhine (River) (E) – Rijn (D)
The Hague (E) – Den Haag (or 's-Gravenhage) (D)

PORTUGAL
Cape St Vincent (E) – Cabo de São Vicente (P)
Lisbon (E) – Lisboa (P)
Oporto (E) – Porto (P)

SPAIN
España
Andalusia (E) – Andalucía (S)
Balearic Islands (E) – Islas Baleares (S)
Basque Country (E) – Euskadi (B), País Vasco (S)
Catalonia (E) – Catalunya (C), Cataluña (S)
Cordova (E) – Córdoba (S)
Corunna (E) – La Coruña (S)
Majorca (E) – Mallorca (S)
Minorca (E) – Menorca (S)
Navarre (E) – Navarra (S)
San Sebastián (E, S) – Donostia (B)
Saragossa (E) – Zaragoza (S)
Seville (E) – Sevilla (S)

SWITZERLAND
Schweiz (G), Suisse (F), Svizzera (I), Svizra (Rh)

Basel (E, G) – Basle (E), Bâle (F), Basilea (I)
Bern (E, G) – Berne (E, F), Berna (I)
Fribourg (E, F) – Freiburg (G), Friburgo (I)
Geneva (E) – Genève (F), Genf (G), Ginevra (I)
Graubünden (E, G) – Grisons (F), Grigioni (I), Grishun (Rh)
Lake Constance (E) – Bodensee (G)
Lake Geneva (E) – Lac Léman (F)
Lake Maggiore (E) – Lago Maggiore (I)
Lucerne (E, F) – Luzern (G), Lucerna (I)
Neuchâtel (E, F) – Neuenburg (G)
Ticino (E, I) – Tessin (G, F)
Valais (E, F) – Wallis (G)
Zürich (G) – Zurich (F), Zurigo (I)

Appendix V – International Country Abbreviations

The following is a list of official country abbreviations that you may encounter on motor vehicles in Europe. Other abbreviations are likely to be unofficial ones, often referring to a particular region, province or even city. A vehicle entering a foreign country must carry a sticker identifying its country of registration, though this rule is not always enforced.

A	–	Austria	GE	–	Georgia
AL	–	Albania	GR	–	Greece
AND	–	Andorra	H	–	Hungary
AUS	–	Australia	HKJ	–	Jordan
B	–	Belgium	HR	–	Croatia
BG	–	Bulgaria	I	–	Italy
BIH	–	Bosnia-Herzegovina	IL	–	Israel
BY	–	Belarus	IRL	–	Ireland
CC	–	Consular Corps	IS	–	Iceland
CD	–	Diplomatic Corps	L	–	Luxembourg
CDN	–	Canada	LAR	–	Libya
CH	–	Switzerland	LT	–	Lithuania
CY	–	Cyprus	LV	–	Latvia
CZ	–	Czech Republic	M	–	Malta
D	–	Germany	MA	–	Morocco
DK	–	Denmark	MC	–	Monaco
DZ	–	Algeria	MD	–	Moldavia
E	–	Spain	MK	–	Macedonia
EST	–	Estonia	N	–	Norway
ET	–	Egypt	NL	–	Netherlands
F	–	France	NZ	–	New Zealand
FIN	–	Finland	P	–	Portugal
FL	–	Liechtenstein	PL	–	Poland
FR	–	Faroe Islands	RL	–	Lebanon
GB	–	Great Britain	RO	–	Romania
GBA	–	Alderney	RSM	–	San Marino
GBG	–	Guernsey	RUS	–	Russia
GBJ	–	Jersey	S	–	Sweden
GBM	–	Isle of Man	SK	–	Slovakia
GBZ	–	Gibraltar	SLO	–	Slovenia
			SYR	–	Syria
			TN	–	Tunisia
			TR	–	Turkey
			UA	–	Ukraine
			USA	–	United States of America
			V	–	Vatican City
			WAN	–	Nigeria
			YU	–	Yugoslavia
			ZA	–	South Africa

Language Guide

This Language Guide contains pronunciation guidelines and basic vocabulary to help you get around Western Europe. For background information about each language see the individual country chapters. For more extensive coverage of the languages included here, see Lonely Planet's *Western Europe phrasebook* and *Mediterranean Europe phrasebook*.

DUTCH

Pronunciation

Vowels Single vowels are pretty straightforward, with long and short sounds for each:

a	short, as the 'u' in 'cut'
aa	long, like the 'a' in 'father'
au, ou	both pronounced somewhere between the 'ow' in 'how' and the 'ow' in 'glow'
e	short, like the 'e' in 'bet', or the 'er' in 'fern'
e, ee	long, like the 'ay' in 'day'
ei, ij	like the 'ey' in 'they'
eu	as the British queen would pronounce the 'o' in 'over' if she were exaggerating
i	short, like the 'i' in 'in'
i, ie	like the 'ee' in 'meet', but clipped
o	short, as in 'pot'
oe	like the 'oo' in 'zoo'
o, oo	long, like the 'o' in 'note'
u	short, similar to the 'u' in 'urn'
u, uu	long, like the 'u' in the German *über*
ui	no equivalent sound in English; in French, the 'eui' in *fauteuil* is close (if you leave out the slide towards the 'l')

Consonants These, too, are pretty straightforward, except for the 'ch' and 'g' which make (northern) Netherlandic sound so harsh:

ch & g	in the north, a hard 'kh' sound as in the Scottish *loch*; in the south, a softer, lisping sound
j	as the 'y' in 'yes'; also as the 'j' or 'zh' sound in 'jam' or 'pleasure'
r	in the south, a trilled sound; in the north it varies, often guttural
s	as the 's' in 'sample'; sometimes as the 'zh' sound in 'pleasure'
w	at the beginning of a word, a clipped sound almost like a 'v'; at the end of a word as the English 'w'

Basics

Hello	*Dag/hallo*
Goodbye	*Dag*
Yes/No	*Ja/Nee*
Please	*Alstublieft/alsjeblieft*
Thank you	*Dank U/je (wel)*
You're welcome	*Geen dank*
Excuse me	*Pardon*
Sorry	*Sorry*

Do you speak English?
Spreekt U/spreek je Engels?
How much is it?
Hoeveel kost het?
What is your name?
Hoe heet U/je?
My name is ...
Ik heet ...

Getting Around

What time does the ... leave/arrive?
Hoe laat vertrekt/arriveert...?

next	*volgende*
the boat	*de boot*
the bus/tram	*de bus/tram*
the train	*de trein*

I would like to hire a car/bicycle.
Ik wil graag een auto/fiets huren.
I would like a one-way ticket/a return ticket.
Ik wil graag een enkele reis/een retour.

1st/2nd class	*eerste/tweede klas*
left luggage locker	*bagagekluis*
bus/tram stop	*bushalte/tramhalte*
train station/ferry terminal	*treinstation/ veerhaven*

Where is the ...?	*Waar is de ...?*
far/near	*ver/dichtbij*
Go straight ahead.	*Ga rechtdoor.*
Turn left/right.	*Ga linksaf/rechtsaf.*

Around Town

a bank	*een bank*
the...embassy	*de...ambassade*
my hotel	*mijn hotel*
the post office	*het postkantoor*
the market	*de markt*
the pharmacy	*de drogist*
the newsagency/ stationer's	*de krantenwinkel kantoorboek- handel*
telephone centre	*de telefooncentrale*
tourist information office	*de VVV/het toeristenbureau*

What time does it open/close?
Hoe laat opent/sluit het

Accommodation

hotel	*hotel*
guesthouse	*pension*
youth hostel	*jeugdherberg*
camping ground	*camping*

Do you have any rooms available?
Heeft U kamers vrij?

a single/double room	*een eenpersoons/ tweepersoons- kamer*
one nights/two nights	*één nacht/twee nachten*

How much is it per night/per person?
Hoeveel is het per nacht/per persoon?
Does it include breakfast?
Zit er ontbijt bij inbegrepen?

Time, Days & Numbers
What time is it?
Hoe laat is het?

today	*vandaag*
tomorrow	*morgen*
in the morning/ afternoon	*'s-morgens/ 's-middags*

Monday	*maandag*
Tuesday	*dinsdag*
Wednesday	*woensdag*
Thursday	*donderdag*
Friday	*vrijdag*
Saturday	*zaterdag*
Sunday	*zondag*

0	*nul*
1	*één*
2	*twee*
3	*drie*
4	*vier*
5	*vijf*
6	*zes*
7	*zeven*
8	*acht*
9	*negen*
10	*tien*
100	*honderd*
1000	*duizend*
one million	*één miljoen*

Emergencies

Help!	*Help!*
Call a doctor!	*Haal een dokter!*
Call the police!	*Haal de politie!*
Go away!	*Ga weg!*
I'm lost.	*Ik ben de weg kwijt.*

FRENCH

Pronunciation
French has a number of sounds which are diffi-cult for Anglophones to produce. These include:

- The distinction between the 'u' sound (as in *tu*) and 'oo' sound (as in *tout*). For both

sounds, the lips are rounded and projected forward, but for the 'u' the tongue is towards the front of the mouth, its tip against the lower front teeth, whereas for the 'oo' the tongue is towards the back of the mouth, its tip behind the gums of the lower front teeth.

- The nasal vowels. During the production of nasal vowels the breath escapes partly through the nose and partly through the mouth. There are no nasal vowels in English; in French there are three, as in *bon vin blanc*, 'good white wine'. These sounds occur where a syllable ends in a single 'n' or 'm'; the 'n' or 'm' is silent but indicates the nasalisation of the preceding vowel.
- The 'r'. The standard 'r' of Parisian French is produced by moving the bulk of the tongue backwards to constrict the air flow in the pharynx while the tip of the tongue rests behind the lower front teeth. It is similar to the noise made by some people before spitting, but with much less friction.

Basics

Hello	*Bonjour*
Goodbye	*Au revoir*
Yes/No	*Oui/Non*
Please	*S'il vous plaît*
Thank you	*Merci*
That's fine, you're welcome	*Je vous en prie*
Excuse me (attention)	*Excusez-moi*
Sorry (excuse me, forgive me)	*Pardon*

Do you speak English?
  Parlez-vous anglais?
How much is it?
  C'est combien?

```
Signs
ENTRANCE                ENTRÉE
EXIT                    SORTIE
FULL, NO VACANCIES      COMPLET
INFORMATION             RENSEIGNEMENTS

OPEN/CLOSED             OUVERT/FERMÉ
PROHIBITED              INTERDIT
POLICE STATION          (COMMISSARIAT
                        DE) POLICE
ROOMS AVAILABLE         CHAMBRES
                        LIBRES
TOILETS (MEN'S/         TOILETTES, WC
WOMEN'S)                (HOMMES/
                        FEMMES)
```

What is your name?
  Comment vous appelez-vous?
My name is ...
  Je m'appelle ...

Getting Around
What time does the next ... leave/arrive?
  À quelle heure part/arrive le prochain ...?

boat	*bateau*
bus (city)	*bus*
bus (intercity)	*car*
tram	*tramway*
train	*train*

I would like to hire a car/bicycle.
  Je voudrais louer une voiture/un vélo.
I would like a one-way ticket.
  Je voudrais un billet aller simple.
I would like a return ticket
  Je voudrais un billet aller retour.

1st/2nd class	*première/ deuxième classe*
left luggage (office)	*consigne*
timetable	*horaire*
bus/tram stop	*arrêt d'autobus/ de tramway*
train station/ferry terminal	*gare/gare maritime*

Where is ...?	*Où est ...?*
far/near	*loin/proche*
Go straight ahead.	*Continuez tout droit.*
Turn left/right.	*Tournez à gauche/à droite.*

Around Town

a bank	*une banque*
the...embassy	*l'ambassade de...*
my hotel	*mon hôtel*
the post office	*le bureau de poste*
the market	*le marché*
the chemist/ pharmacy	*la pharmacie*
the newsagency/ stationer's	*l'agence de presse/la papeterie*
a public telephone	*une cabine téléphonique*
the tourist information office	*l'office de tourisme/le syndicat d'initiative*

What time does it open/close?
  Quelle est l'heure de l'ouverture?

Accommodation

the hotel	*l'hôtel*
the youth hostel	*l'auberge de jeunesse*
the camping ground	*le camping*

Do you have any rooms available?
Est-ce que vous avez des chambres libres?

for one/two people	*pour une personne/ deux personnes*

How much is it per night/per person?
Quel est le prix par nuit/par personne?

Is breakfast included?
Est-ce que le petit déjeuner est compris?

Time, Days & Numbers

What time is it?
Quelle heure est-il?

today	*aujourd'hui*
tomorrow	*demain*
yesterday	*hier*
morning/afternoon	*matin/après-midi*
Monday	*lundi*
Tuesday	*mardi*
Wednesday	*mercredi*
Thursday	*jeudi*
Friday	*vendredi*
Saturday	*samedi*
Sunday	*dimanche*

0	*zéro*
1	*un*
2	*deux*
3	*trois*
4	*quatre*
5	*cinq*
6	*six*
7	*sept*
8	*huit*
9	*neuf*
10	*dix*
100	*cent*
1000	*mille*
one million	*un million*

Emergencies

Help!	*Au secours!*
Call a doctor!	*Appelez un médecin!*
Call the police!	*Appelez la police!*
Leave me alone!	*Fichez-moi la paix!*
I'm lost.	*Je me suis égaré/ égarée.*

GERMAN

Pronunciation

Unlike English or French, German has no real silent letters: you pronounce the **k** at the start of the word *Knie* (knee), the **p** at the start of *Psychologie* (psychology), and the **e** at the end of *ich habe* (I have).

Vowels As in English, vowels can be pronounced long, like the 'o' in 'pope', or short, like the 'o' in 'pop'. As a rule, German vowels are long before one consonant and short before two consonants: the **o** is long in the word *Dom* (cathedral), but short in the word *doch* (after all).

a	short, like the 'u' in 'cut', or long, as in 'father'
au	as in 'vow'
ä	short, as in 'act', or long, as in 'hair'
äu	as in 'boy'
e	short, as in 'bet', or long, as in 'day'
ei	like the 'ai' in 'aisle'
eu	as in 'boy'
i	short, as in 'in', or long, as in 'see'
ie	as in 'see'
o	short, as in 'pot', or long, as in 'note'
ö	like the 'er' in 'fern'
u	like the 'u' in 'pull'
ü	similar to the 'u' in 'pull' but with stretched lips

Consonants Most German consonants sound similar to their English counterparts. One important difference is that **b**, **d** and **g** sound like 'p', 't' and 'k', respectively, at the end of a word.

b	normally like the English 'b', but as 'p' at end of a word
ch	like the 'ch' in Scottish *loch*
d	normally like the English 'd', but like 't' at end of a word

g	normally like the English 'g', but as 'k' at the end of a word, or 'ch' in the Scottish *loch* at the end of a word when after 'i'
j	like the 'y' in 'yet'
qu	like 'k' plus 'v'
r	can be trilled or guttural, depending on the region
s	normally like the 's' in 'sun', but like the 'z' in 'zoo' when followed by a vowel
sch	like the 'sh' in 'ship'
sp, st	the **s** sounds like the 'sh' in 'ship'when at the start of a word
ß	like the 's' in 'sun' (written as '**ss**' in this book)
tion	the **t** sounds like the 'ts' in 'hits'
v	as the 'f' in 'fan'
w	as the 'v' in 'van'
z	as the 'ts' in 'hits'

Basics

Good day	*Guten Tag*
Hello (in southern Germany)	*Grüss Gott*
Goodbye	*Auf Wiedersehen*
Bye bye	*Tschüss*
Yes/No	*Ja/Nein*
Please	*Bitte*
Thank you	*Danke*
That's fine/You're welcome	*Bitte sehr*
Sorry (excuse me, forgive me)	*Entschuldigung*

Do you speak English?
Sprechen Sie Englisch?
How much is it ?
Wieviel kostet es?
What is your name?
Wie heissen Sie?
My name is ...
Ich heisse ...

Signs

ENTRANCE	*EINGANG*
EXIT	*AUSGANG*
FULL, NO VACANCIES	*VOLL, BESETZT*
INFORMATION	*AUSKUNFT*
OPEN/CLOSED	*OFFEN/ GESCHLOSSEN*
POLICE STATION	*POLIZEIWACHE*
ROOMSAVAILABLE	*ZIMMER FREI*
TOILETS (MEN'S/ WOMEN'S)	*TOILETTEN (WC) (HERREN/ DAMEN)*

Getting Around

What time does ... leave?
Wann fährt ...ab?
What time does ... arrive?
Wann kommt ...an?
What time is the next boat?
Wann fährt das nächste Boot?

the boat	*das Boot*
the bus (city)	*der Bus*
the bus (intercity)	*der (überland) Bus*
the tram	*die Strassenbahn*
the train	*der Zug*

I would like to hire a car/bicycle.
Ich möchte ein Auto/einen Fahrrad mieten.
I would like a one-way ticket/return ticket.
Ich möchte eine Einzelkarte/Rückfahrkarte.

1st/2nd class	*erste/zweite Klasse*
left luggage	*Gepäckaufbewahrr raum*
timetable	*Fahrplan*
bus stop/tram stop	*Bushaltestelle/ Strassenbahn- haltestelle*
train station/ferry terminal	*Bahnhof (Bf)/ Fährhafen*

Where is the ...?	*Wo ist die ...?*
far/near	*weit/nahe*
Go straight ahead.	*Gehen Sie geradeaus.*
Turn left/right.	*Biegen Sie links ab/ rechts ab.*

Around Town

a bank	*eine Bank*
the...embassy	*die...Botschaft*
my hotel	*mein Hotel*
the post office	*das Postamt*
the market	*der Markt*
the pharmacy	*die Apotheke*
the newsagency/ stationers	*der Zeitungshändler/ Schreibwaren- geschäft*
the telephone centre	*die Telefonzentrale*
the tourist office	*das Verkehrsamt*

What time does it open/close?
Um wieviel Uhr macht es auf/zu?

Accommodation

hotel	*Hotel*
guesthouse	*Pension, Gästehaus*
youth hostel	*Jugendherberge*
camping ground	*Campingplatz*

Do you have any rooms available?
Haben Sie noch freie Zimmer?
a single room/ *ein Einzelzimmer/*
double room *Doppelzimmer*
for one/two nights *eine Nacht/zwei*
Nächte
How much is it per night/per person?
Wieviel kostet es pro Nacht/pro Person?
Is breakfast included?
Ist Frühstück inbegriffen?

Time, Days & Numbers

What time is it?	*Wie spät ist es?*
today	*heute*
tomorrow	*morgen*
yesterday	*gestern*
in the morning/	*morgens/nachmittags*
afternoon	

Monday	*Montag*
Tuesday	*Dienstag*
Wednesday	*Mittwoch*
Thursday	*Donnerstag*
Friday	*Freitag*
Saturday	*Samstag, Sonnabend*

Sunday	*Sonntag*
0	*null*
1	*eins*
2	*zwei (zwo* on phone or public announcements)
3	*drei*
4	*vier*
5	*fünf*
6	*sechs*
7	*sieben*
8	*acht*
9	*neun*
10	*zehn*
100	*hundert*
1000	*tausend*
one million	*eine Million*

Emergencies

Help!	*Hilfe!*
Call a doctor!	*Holen Sie einen Arzt!*
Call the police!	*Rufen Sie die Polizei!*
I'm lost.	*Ich habe mich verirrt.*

GREEK

Pronunciation

Greek letters are shown by the closest English sound.

A α	**a**	like the 'a' in 'father'
B β	**v**	like the 'v' in 'vine'
Γ γ	**gh, y**	like a rough 'g', or like 'y' in 'yes'
Δ δ	**dh**	like the 'th' in 'there'
E ε	**e**	like the 'e' in 'egg'
Z ζ	**z**	like the 'z' in 'zoo'
H η	**i**	like the 'ee' in 'feet'
Θ θ	**th**	like the 'th' in 'throw'
I ι	**i**	like the 'ee' in 'feet'
K κ	**k**	like the 'k' in 'kite'
Λ λ	**l**	like the 'l' in 'leg'
M μ	**m**	like the 'm' in 'man'
N ν	**n**	like the 'n' in 'net'
Ξ ξ	**x**	like the 'ks' in 'looks'
O o	**o**	like the 'o' in 'hot'
Π π	**p**	like the 'p' in 'pup'
P ρ	**r**	slightly trilled 'r'
Σ σ	**s**	like the 's' in 'sand' (ς at the end of a word)
T τ	**t**	like the 't' in 'tap'
Y υ	**i**	like the 'ee' in 'feet'
Φ φ	**f**	like the 'f' in 'find'
X χ	**kh, h**	like the 'ch' in 'loch', or like a rough 'h'
Ψ ψ	**ps**	like the 'ps' in 'lapse'
Ω ω	**o**	like the 'o' in 'hot'

ει, οι	like the 'ee' in 'feet'
αι	like the 'e' in 'bet'
ου	like the 'oo' in 'mood'
μπ	like the 'b' in 'beer', or 'mb' as in 'amber', or 'mp' as in 'ample'
ντ	like the 'd' in 'dot', or as the 'nt' in 'sent', or as the 'nd' in 'bend'
γκ, γγ	like the 'g' in 'god', or as the 'ng' in 'angle'
γξ	like the 'ks' in 'minks'
τζ	like the 'ds' in 'hands'

Some pairs of vowels are pronounced separately if the first has an acute accent ( ), or the second has a dieresis (..).

All Greek words of two or more syllables have an acute accent which indicates where the stress falls. In the following list the stressed syllable is indicated by bold type. The suffix of some Greek words depends on the gender of the speaker eg, *asthmatikos* (m) and *asthmatikya* (f), or *epileptikos* (m) and *epileptikya* (f).

Basics

Hello	*ya*su (inf)/*ya*sas (formal, plural)
Goodbye	*andio*
Yes/No	*one/okhi*
Please	*sas parakalo*
Thank you	*sas efkharisto*
That's fine. You're welcome.	*ine endaksi parakalo*
Excuse me/Sorry	*signomi*

Do you speak English?
  milate anglika
How much is it?
  poso kani
What is your name?
  pos sas lene/pos legeste
My name is ...
  me lene ...

Signs

ENTRANCE	ΕΙΣΟΔΟΣ
EXIT	ΕΞΟΔΟΣ
INFORMATION	ΠΛΗΡΟΦΟΡΙΕΣ
OPEN/CLOSED	ΑΝΟΙΚΤΟ/ΚΛΕΙΣΤΟ
POLICE STATION	ΑΣΤΥΝΟΜΙΚΟΣ ΣΤΑΘΜΟΣ
PROHIBITED	ΑΠΑΓΟΡΕΥΕΤΑΙ
TOILETS (MEN'S/WOMEN'S)	ΤΟΥΑΛΕΤΕΣ (ΑΝΔΡΩΝ/ΓΥΝΑΙΚΩΝ)

Getting Around

What time does the next...leave/arrive?
  ti ora fevyi/ apohorito...
  the boat *to plio*
  the bus (city) *to leoforio (ya tin boli)*
  the bus (intercity) *to leoforio (ya ta proastia)*
  the tram *to tram*
  the train *to treno*

I would like a one-way ticket/a return ticket.
  tha ithela isitirio horis epistrofi/isitirio met epistrois.
  1st/2nd class *proti/dhefteri thesi*
  left luggage *horos aspokevon*
  timetable *dhromologhio*
  bus stop *i stasi tu leoforiu*
  Go straight ahead. *pighenete efthia*
  Turn left/right. *stripste aristera/ dheksya.*

Around Town

a bank	*mia trapeza*
the...embassy	*i...presvia*
the hotel	*to ksenodho khio*
the post office	*to takhidhromio*
the market	*i aghora*
the pharmacy	*farmakio*
the newsagency	*efimeridhon*
the telephone centre	*to tilefoniko kentro*
the tourist information office	*to ghrafio turistikon pliroforion*

What time does it open/close?
  ti ora aniyi/klini

Accommodation

hotel	ΞΕΝΟΔΟΧΕΙΟ
rooms (domatia)	ΔΩΜΑΤΙΑ
youth hostel	ΠΑΝΔΟΧΕΙΟ ΝΕΩΝ
camping ground	ΚΑΤΑΣΚΗΝΩΣΗ

I'd like... *thelo*
  a single room/ double room *ena dhomatio ya ena atomo/dhio atoma*
How much is it per night/per person?
  poso kostizi ya ena vradhi ya ena atomo

Time, Days & Numbers

What time is it?
  ti ora ine
today *simera*
tomorrow *avrio*
yesterday *hthes*
in the morning/ afternoon *to proi/to apoyevma*

Monday	*dheftera*	7	*epta*
Tuesday	*triti*	8	*okhto*
Wednesday	*tetarti*	9	*enea*
Thursday	*pempti*	10	*dheka*
Friday	*paraskevi*	100	*ekato*
Saturday	*savato*	1000	*khilya*
Sunday	*kiryaki*	one million	*ena ekatomirio*

0	*midhen*
1	*ena*
2	*dhio*
3	*tria*
4	*tesera*
5	*pende*
6	*eksi*

Emergencies

Help!	*voithia*
Call a doctor!	*fona kste ena yatro*
Call the police!	*tilefoniste stin astinomia*
Go away!	*fighe!/dhromo*
I'm lost.	*eho hathi*

ITALIAN

Pronunciation

Italian is not difficult to pronounce once you learn a few easy rules. Although some of the more clipped vowels and stress on double letters, require careful practice for English speakers, it is easy enough to make yourself understood.

Vowels Vowels are generally more clipped than in English.

a	like the second 'a' in 'camera'
e	like the 'ay' in 'day', but without the 'i' sound
i	as in 'see'
o	as in 'dot'
u	as in 'too'

Consonants The pronunciation of many Italian consonants is similar to that of English. The following sounds depend on certain rules:

c	like 'k' before **a**, **o** and **u**; or like the 'ch' in 'choose' before **e** and **i**
ch	a hard 'k' sound
g	a hard 'g' as in 'get' before **a**, **o**
gh	a hard 'g' as in 'get'
gli	like the 'lli' in 'million'
gn	like the 'ny' in 'canyon'
h	always silent
r	a rolled 'rrr' sound
sc	like the 'sh' in 'sheep' before **e** and **i**; or a hard sound as in 'school' before **h**, **a**, **o** and **u**

z	like the 'ts' in 'lights' or as the 'ds' in 'beds'

Note that when 'ci', 'gi' and 'sci' are followed by **a**, **o** or **u**, unless the accent falls on the 'i', it's not pronounced. Thus the name 'Giovanni' is pronounced 'joh-VAHN-nee', with no 'i' sound after the 'G'.

Stress Double consonants are pronounced as a longer, often more forceful sound than a single consonant.

Stress often falls on the next to last syllable, as in 'spaghetti'. When a word has an accent, the stress is on that syllable, as in *città* (city).

Basics

Hello	*Buongiorno/Ciaŏ*
Goodbye	*Arrivederci/Ciao*
Yes/No	*Si/No*
Please	*Per favore/Per piacere*
Thank you	*Grazie*
That's fine/You're welcome	*Prego*
Excuse me	*Mi scusi*
Sorry (Excuse me, forgive me)	*Mi scusi/Mi perdoni*

Do you speak English?	*Parla (Parli) inglese?*
How much is it?	*Quanto costa?*

What is your name?
Come si chiama?
My name is ...?
Mi chiamo...

Signs

ENTRANCE	INGRESSO/ENTRATA
EXIT	USCITA
FULL/NO VACANCIES	COMPLETO
INFORMATION	INFORMAZIONE
OPEN/CLOSED	APERTO/CHIUSO
PROHIBITED	PROIBITO/VIETATO
POLICE	POLIZIA/ CARABI-NIERI
POLICE STATION	QUESTURA
ROOMS AVAILABLE	CAMERE LIBERE
TOILETS (MEN'S/WOMEN'S)	GABINETTI/BAGNI (UOMINI/DONN)

Getting Around

What time does the next... leave/arrive?
A che ora parte/ arriva il prossimo/la prossima...?

boat	la barca
ferry	il traghetto
bus	l'autobus
tram	il tram
train	il treno

I'd like to hire a car/bicycle.
Vorrei noleggiare una macchina/ bicicletta.
I'd like a one-way/return ticket.
Vorrei un biglietto di solo andata/di andata e ritorno

1st/2nd class	prima/seconda classe
left luggage	deposito bagagli
timetable	orario
bus stop	fermata dell'autobus
train station	stazione
ferry terminal	stazione marittima

Where is ...?	Dov'è ...?
far/near	lontano/vicino
Go straight ahead.	Si va sempre diritto.
Turn left/ right.	Gira a sinistra/ destra.

Around Town

a bank	un banco
the ... embassy	l'ambasciata di ...
my hotel	il mio albergo
the post office	la posta
the market	il mercato
the chemist/ pharmacy	la farmacia
the newsagency/ stationer's	l'edicola/il cartolaio
the telephone centre	il centro telefonico
the tourist information office	l'ufficio del turismo

What time does it open/close?
A che ora (si) apre/chiude?

Accommodation

hotel	albergo
guesthouse	pensione
youth hostel	ostello per la gioventù
camping ground	campeggio

Do you have any rooms available?
Ha delle camere libere?/C'è una camera libera?

a single room	una camera singola
a double room	una camera matrimoniale/ doppia
for one/two nights	per una notte/ due notti

How much is it per night/per person?
Quanto costa per la notte/ciascuno?
Is breakfast included?
È compresa la colazione?

Time, Days & Numbers

What time is it?
Che ora è?/Che ore sono?

today	oggi
tomorrow	domani
yesterday	ieri
morning/afternoon	mattina/pomeriggio

Monday	lunedì
Tuesday	martedì
Wednesday	mercoledì
Thursday	giovedì
Friday	venerdì
Saturday	sabato
Sunday	domenica

0	zero		100	cento
1	uno		1000	mille
2	due		one million	un milione
3	tre			
4	quattro			

Emergencies

5 cinque	Help!	Aiuto!

5	cinque	
6	sei	
7	sette	
8	otto	
9	nove	
10	dieci	

Emergencies

Help!	Aiuto!
Call a doctor!	Chiama un dottore/ un medico!
Call the police!	Chiama la polizia!
Go away!	Vai via! (informal)
I'm lost.	Mi sono perso/persa.

PORTUGUESE

Pronunciation

Pronunciation of Portuguese is difficult; like English, vowels and consonants have more than one possible sound depending on position and stress. Moreover, there are nasal vowels and diphthongs in Portuguese with no equivalent in English.

Vowels Single vowels should present relatively few problems:

a	short, like the 'u' sound in 'cut', or long like the 'ur' sound in 'hurt'
e	short, as in 'bet', or longer as in French été and English 'laird'
é	short, as in 'bet'
ê	long, like the 'a' sound in 'gate'
e	silent final 'e', like the final 'e' in English 'these'; also silent in unstressed syllables
i	as in 'see', or short as in 'ring'
o	short, as in 'pot'; long as in 'note'; or like 'oo' as in 'good'
ô	long, as in 'note'
u	'oo', as in 'good'

Nasal Vowels Nasalisation is represented by an 'n' or an 'm' after the vowel, or by a tilde, (~) over it. The nasal 'i' exists in English as the 'ing' in 'sing'. For other vowels, try to pronounce a long 'a', 'ah', or 'e', 'eh', holding your nose, as if you had a cold.

Diphthongs Double vowels are relatively straightforward:

au	as in 'now'
ai	as in 'pie'

ei	as in 'day'
eu	pronounced together
oi	similar to 'boy'

Nasal Diphthongs Try the same technique as for nasal vowels. To say não, pronounce 'now' through your nose.

ão	nasal 'now' (owng)
ãe	nasal 'day' (eing)
õe	nasal 'boy' (oing)
ui	similar to the 'uing' in 'ensuing'

Consonants The following consonants are specific to Portuguese:

c	hard, as in 'cat' before a, o or u
c	soft as in 'see' before e or i
ç	as in 'see'
g	hard, as in 'garden' before a, o or u
g	soft, as in 'treasure' before e or i
gu	hard, as in 'get' before e or i
h	never pronounced at the beginning of a word
nh	like the 'ni' sound in 'onion'
lh	like the 'll' sound in 'million'
j	as in 'treasure'
m	in final position is not pronounced, it simply nasalises the previous vowel: um (oong), bom (bõ)
qu	like the 'k' in 'key' before e or i
qu	like the 'q' in 'quad' before a or o
r	at the beginning of a word, or rr in the middle of a word, is a harsh, guttural sound similar to the French rue, Scottish loch, or German Bach. In some areas of Portugal this r is not guttural, but strongly rolled.

r	in the middle or at the end of a word is a rolled sound stronger than the English 'r'
s	like the 's' in 'see' (at the beginning of a word)
ss	like the 's' in 'see' (in the middle of a word)
s	like the 'z' in 'zeal' (between vowels)
s	like the 'sh' in 'ship' (before another consonant, or at the end of a word)
x	like the 'sh' in 'ship'; the 'z' in 'zeal'; or the 'ks' sound in 'taxi'

Word stress is important in Portuguese, as it can change the meaning of the word. Many Portuguese words have a written accent and the stress must fall on that syllable when you pronounce the word.

Basics

Hello/Goodbye	*Olá/adeus*
Yes/No	*Sim/não*
Please	*Se faz favor*
Thank you	*Obrigado/a*
That's fine/You're welcome	*De nada*
Excuse me	*Desculpe/com licença*
Sorry (excuse me, forgive me)	*Desculpe*

Do you speak English?
  Fala Inglês?
How much is it?
  Quanto custa?
What is your name?
  Como se chama?
My name is...
  Chamo-me...

Signs

ENTRANCE	*ENTRADA*
EXIT	*SAÍDA*
FREE ADMISSION	*ENTRADA GRÁTIS*
INFORMATION	*INFORMAÇÕES*
OPEN/CLOSED	*ABERTO/ENCERRADO (OR FECHADO)*
PROHIBITED	*PROIBIDO*
POLICE STATION	*ESQUADRA DA POLÍCIA*
ROOMS AVAILABLE	*QUARTOS LIVRES*
TOILETS	*WC*

Getting Around

What time does the next ... leave/arrive?
  A que horas parte/chega o próximo ...?

boat	*o barco*
bus (city)	*o autocarro*
bus (intercity)	*a camioneta*
tram	*o eléctrico*
train	*o combóio*

I'd like to hire a car/bicycle.
  Queria alugar um carro/uma bicicleta.
I'd like a one-way ticket.
  Queria um bilhete simples/de ida
I'd like a return ticket.
  Queria um bilhete de ida e volta

1st/2nd class	*primeira/segunda classe*
timetable	*horário*
bus stop	*paragem de autocarro*
train station	*estação ferroviária*

Where is ... ?	*Onde é ... ?*
far/near	*longe/perto*
Go straight ahead.	*Siga sempre a direito/sempre em frente.*
Turn left/right.	*Vire à esquerda/ direita...*

Around Town

a bank	*dum banco*
the...embassy	*da embaixada de ...*
my hotel	*do meu hotel*
the post office	*dos correios*
the market	*do mercado/da praça*
chemist/pharmacy	*da farmácia*
newsagency/ stationer's	*papelaria/tabacaria*
the telephone centre	*da central de telefones*
the tourist information office	*do turismo/do serviço de informações para turistas*

What time does it open/close?
  A que horas abre/fecha?

Accommodation

hotel	*hotel*
guesthouse	*pensão*
youth hostel	*albergue de juventude*

| camping ground | *parque de campismo* |

Do you have any rooms available?
Tem quartos livres?

a single room	*um quarto individual*
a double room	*um quarto duplo/de casal*
for one/two nights	*para uma/duas noites*

How much is it per night/per person?
Quanto é por noite/por pessoa?
Is breakfast included?
O pequeno almoço está incluído?

Time, Days & Numbers
What time is it?
Que horas são?

today	*hoje*
tomorrow	*amanhã*
yesterday	*ontem*
morning/afternoon	*manhã/ tarde*

Monday	*segunda-feira*
Tuesday	*terça-feira*
Wednesday	*quarta-feira*
Thursday	*quinta-feira*
Friday	*sexta-feira*
Saturday	*sábado*
Sunday	*domingo*

0	*zero*
1	*um/uma*
2	*dois/duas*
3	*três*
4	*quatro*
5	*cinco*
6	*seis*
7	*sete*
8	*oito*
9	*nove*
10	*dez*
100	*cem*
1000	*mil*
one million	*um milhão (de)*

Emergencies
Help!	*Socorro!*
Call a doctor!	*Chame um médico!*
Call the police!	*Chame a polícia!*
Go away!	*Deixe-me em paz!*
I'm lost.	*Estou perdido/a.*

SPANISH

Pronunciation
Pronunciation of Spanish is not difficult, given that many Spanish sounds are similar to their English counterparts, and there is a clear and consistent relationship between pronunciation and spelling. If you stick to the following rules you should have very few problems in being understood.

Vowels Unlike English, each of the vowels in Spanish has a uniform pronunciation which does not vary. For example, the Spanish 'a' has one pronunciation rather than the numerous pronunciations we find in English, such as the 'a' in 'cake', 'art' and 'all'. Many Spanish words have a written accent. The acute accent (as in *días*) generally indicates a stressed syllable and it doesn't change the sound of the vowel. Vowels are pronounced clearly even if they are in unstressed positions or at the end of a word.

a	like the 'u' in 'nut', or a shorter sound than the 'a' in 'art'
e	like the 'e' in 'met'
i	somewhere between the 'i' sound in 'marine' and the 'i' in 'flip'
o	similar to the 'o' in 'hot'
u	as the 'oo' in 'hoof'

Consonants Some Spanish consonants are the same as their English counterparts. The pronunciation of other consonants varies according to which vowel follows and also according to which part of Spain you happen to be in. The Spanish alphabet also contains three consonants that are not found within the English alphabet: 'ch', 'll' and 'ñ'.

b	soft; also (less commonly) like the 'b' in 'book' when initial, or preceded by a nasal
c	a hard 'c' as in 'cat' when followed by a, o, u or a consonant; like the 'th' in 'thin' before e or i
ch	like the 'ch' in choose

d	like the 'd' in 'dog' when initial; elsewhere as the 'th' in 'then'
g	like the 'g' in 'gate' when initial and before **a**, **o** and **u**; elsewhere much softer. Before **e** or **i** it's a harsh, breathy sound, similar to the 'h' in 'hit'
h	silent
j	a harsh, guttural sound similar to the 'ch' in Scottish 'loch'
ll	like the 'll' in 'million'; some people pronounce it rather like the 'y' in 'yellow'
ñ	a nasal sound like the 'ni' in 'onion'
q	like the 'k' in 'kick'; 'q' is always followed by a silent **u** and is combined only with the vowels **e** (as in *que*) and **i** as in *qui*
r	a rolled 'r' sound; longer and stronger when initial or doubled
s	like the 's' in 'send'
v	the same sound as **b**
x	like the 'ks' sound in 'taxi', when between two vowels; like the 's' in 'say' when it precedes a consonant
z	like the 'th' in 'thin'

Semiconsonant Spanish also has the semi-consonant 'y'. This is pronounced like the Spanish 'i' when it's at the end of a word or when it stands alone as a conjunction. As a consonant, its sound is somewhere between the 'y' in 'yonder' and the 'g' in 'beige', depending on the region.

Basics

Hello/Goodbye	*¡Hola!/¡Adiós!*
Yes/No	*Sí/No*
Please	*Por favor*
Thank you	*Gracias*
That's fine/ You're welcome	*De nada*
Excuse me	*Permiso*
Sorry (excuse me, forgive me)	*Lo siento/Discúlpeme*

Do you speak English?
: *¿Habla inglés?*

How much is it?
: *¿Cuánto cuesta?/¿Cuánto vale?*

What is your name?
: *¿Cómo se llama?*

My name is...
: *Me llamo ...*

Signs	
ENTRANCE	*ENTRADA*
EXIT	*SALIDA*
FULL, NO VACANCIES	*OCUPADO, COMPLETO*
INFORMATION	*INFORMACIÓN*
OPEN/CLOSED	*ABIERTO/ CERRADO*
PROHIBITED	*PROHIBIDO*
POLICE STATION	*ESTACIÓN DE POLICÍA*
ROOMS AVAILABLE	*HABITACIONES LIBRES*
TOILETS (MEN/WOMEN)	*SERVICIOS/ ASEOS (HOMBRES/ MUJERES*

Getting Around

What time does the next ...leave/arrive?
: *¿A qué hora sale/llega el próximo ...?*

the boat	*el barco*
the bus (city)	*el autobús, el bus*
the bus (intercity)	*el autocar*
the train	*el tren*
the tram	*el tranvía*

I'd like to hire a car/bicycle.
: *Quisiera alquilar un coche/una bicicleta.*

I'd like a one-way ticket.
: *Quisiera un billete sencillo*

I'd like a return ticket.
: *Quisiera un billete de ida y vuelta*

1st class/2nd class	*primera/segunda clase*
left luggage	*consigna*
timetable	*horario*
bus stop	*parada de autobus*
train station	*estación (de ferrocarril)*

Where is ... ?	*¿Dónde está ... ?*
far/near	*lejos/cerca*
Go straight ahead.	*Siga/Vaya todo derecho.*
Turn left.	*Doble a la izquierda.*
Turn right.	*Doble a la derecha.*

Around Town

a bank	*un banco*
the...embassy	*la embajada...*
my hotel	*mi hotel*
the post office	*los correos*

the market	*el mercado*
the chemist/pharmacy	*la farmacia*
the newsagency/ stationer's	*papelería*
the telephone centre	*la central telefónica*
the tourist office	*la oficina de turismo*

What time does it open/close?
  ¿A qué hora abren/cierran?

Accommodation
hotel	*hotel*
guesthouse	*pensión/casa de huespedes*
youth hostel	*albergue juvenil*
camping ground	*terreno de camping*

Do you have any rooms available?
  ¿Tiene habitaciones libres?
a single room	*una habitación individual*
a double room	*una habitación doble*
for/one two nights	*para una/dos noches*
How much is it per night/per person?
  ¿Cuánto cuesta por noche/por persona?
Is breakfast included?
  ¿Incluye el desayuno?

Time, Days & Numbers
What time is it?
  ¿Qué hora es?/¿Qué horas son?
| today | *hoy* |
| tomorrow | *mañana* |

| yesterday | *ayer* |
| morning/ afternoon | *mañana/tarde* |

Monday	*lunes*
Tuesday	*martes*
Wednesday	*miércoles*
Thursday	*jueves*
Friday	*viernes*
Saturday	*sábado*
Sunday	*domingo*

0	*cero*
1	*uno, una*
2	*dos*
3	*tres*
4	*cuatro*
5	*cinco*
6	*seis*
7	*siete*
8	*ocho*
9	*nueve*
10	*diez*
100	*cien/ciento*
1000	*mil*
one million	*un millón*

Emergencies
Help!	*¡Socorro!\¡Auxilio!*
Call a doctor!	*¡Llame a un doctor!*
Call the police!	*¡Llame a la policía!*
Go away!	*¡Váyase!*
I'm lost.	*Estoy perdido/ perdida.*

Index

1308 Index

TEXT

to Milano   8:45

                            Verona 10:23
               10:03
                           11:46

11:16 → 13:32
12:16 → 14:15

             München
13:30
                  20:30

12:37 Wien   20:32
                    22:35

LONELY PLANET PHRASEBOOKS

LONELY PLANET PHRASEBOOKS

Building bridges,
Breaking barriers,
Beyond babble-on

Listen for the gems

Speak your own words

Ask your own
questions

Master of
your
own
image

- handy pocket-sized books
- easy to understand Pronunciation chapter
- clear and comprehensive Grammar chapter
- romanisation alongside script to allow ease of pronunciation
- script throughout so users can point to phrases
- extensive vocabulary sections, words and phrases for every situations
- full of cultural information and tips for the traveller

'...vital for a real DIY spirit and attitude in language learning' – Backpacker

'the phrasebooks have good cultural backgrounders and offer solid advice for challenging situations in remote locations' – San Francisco Examiner

'...they are unbeatable for their coverage of the world's more obscure languages' – The Geographical Magazine

---

Arabic (Egyptian)
Arabic (Moroccan)
Australia
  Australian English, Aboriginal and Torres Strait languages
Baltic States
  Estonian, Latvian, Lithuanian
Bengali
Burmese
Brazilian
Cantonese
Central Europe
  Czech, French, German, Hungarian, Italian and Slovak
Eastern Europe
  Bulgarian, Czech, Hungarian, Polish, Romanian and Slovak
Egyptian Arabic
Ethiopian (Amharic)
Fijian
French
German
Greek

Hindi/Urdu
Indonesian
Italian
Japanese
Korean
Lao
Latin American Spanish
Malay
Mandarin
Mediterranean Europe
  Albanian, Croatian, Greek, Italian, Macedonian, Maltese, Serbian, Slovene
Mongolian
Moroccan Arabic
Nepali
Papua New Guinea
Pilipino (Tagalog)
Quechua
Russian
Scandinavian Europe
  Danish, Finnish, Icelandic, Norwegian and Swedish

South-East Asia
  Burmese, Indonesian, Khmer, Lao, Malay, Tagalog (Pilipino), Thai and Vietnamese
Spanish
Sri Lanka
Swahili
Thai
Thai Hill Tribes
Tibetan
Turkish
Ukrainian
USA
  US English, Vernacular Talk, Native American languages and Hawaiian
Vietnamese
Western Europe
  Basque, Catalan, Dutch, French, German, Irish, Italian, Portuguese, Scottish Gaelic, Spanish (Castilian) and Welsh

---

LONELY PLANET JOURNEYS

JOURNEYS is a unique collection of travel writing – published by the company that understands travel better than anyone else. It is a series for anyone who has ever experienced – or dreamed of – the magical moment when they encountered a strange culture or saw a place for the first time. They are tales to read while you're planning a trip, while you're on the road or while you're in an armchair, in front of a fire.

JOURNEYS books catch the spirit of a place, illuminate a culture, recount a crazy adventure, or introduce a fascinating way of life. They always entertain, and always enrich the experience of travel.

THE GATES OF DAMASCUS
Lieve Joris
Translated by Sam Garrett

This best-selling book is a beautifully drawn portrait of day-to-day life in modern Syria. Through her intimate contact with local people, Lieve Joris draws us into the fascinating world that lies behind the gates of Damascus. Hala's husband is a political prisoner, jailed for his opposition to the Assad regime; through the author's friendship with Hala we see how Syrian politics impacts on the lives of ordinary people.

Lieve Joris, who was born in Belgium, is one of Europe's leading travel writers. In addition to an award-winning book on Hungary, she has published widely acclaimed accounts of her journeys to the Middle East and Africa. *The Gates of Damascus* is her fifth book.

'Expands the boundaries of travel writing' – Times Literary Supplement

---

KINGDOM OF THE FILM STARS
Journey into Jordan
Annie Caulfield

Kingdom of the Film Stars is a travel book and a love story. With honesty and humour, Annie Caulfield writes of travelling in Jordan and falling in love with a Bedouin. Her book offers fascinating insights into the country – from the traditional tent life of nomadic tribes to the first woman MP's battle with fundamentalist colleagues. *Kingdom of the Film Stars* unpicks some of the tight-woven Western myths about the Arab world, presenting cultural and political issues within the intimate framework of a compelling love story.

Annie Caulfield, who was born in Ireland and currently lives in London, is an award-winning playwright and journalist. She has travelled widely in the Middle East.

'Annie Caulfield is a remarkable traveller. Her story is fresh, courageous, moving, witty and sexy!' – Dawn French

LONELY PLANET TRAVEL ATLASES

Lonely Planet has long been famous for the number and quality of its guidebook maps. Now we've gone one step further and in conjunction with Steinhart Katzir Publishers produced a handy companion series: Lonely Planet travel atlases – maps of a country produced in book form.

Unlike other maps, which look good but lead travellers astray, our travel atlases have been researched on the road by Lonely Planet's experienced team of writers. All details are carefully checked to ensure the atlas corresponds with the equivalent Lonely Planet guidebook.

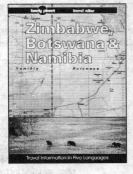

The handy atlas format means no holes, wrinkles, torn sections or constant folding and unfolding. These atlases can survive long periods on the road, unlike cumbersome fold-out maps. The comprehensive index ensures easy reference.

- full-colour throughout
- maps researched and checked by Lonely Planet authors
- place names correspond with Lonely Planet guidebooks
  – no confusing spelling differences
- legend and travelling information in English, French, German, Japanese and Spanish
- size: 230 x 160 mm

Available now:
Chile & Easter Island • Egypt • India & Bangladesh • Israel & the Palestinian Territories •Jordan, Syria & Lebanon • Kenya • Laos • Portugal • South Africa, Lesotho & Swaziland • Thailand • Turkey • Vietnam • Zimbabwe, Botswana & Namibia

---

LONELY PLANET TV SERIES & VIDEOS

Lonely Planet travel guides have been brought to life on television screens around the world. Like our guides, the programmes are based on the joy of independent travel, and look honestly at some of the most exciting, picturesque and frustrating places in the world. Each show is presented by one of three travellers from Australia, England or the USA and combines an innovative mixture of video, Super-8 film, atmospheric soundscapes and original music.

Videos of each episode – containing additional footage not shown on television – are available from good book and video shops, but the availability of individual videos varies with regional screening schedules.

Video destinations include: Alaska • American Rockies • Australia – The South-East • Baja California & the Copper Canyon • Brazil • Central Asia • Chile & Easter Island • Corsica, Sicily & Sardinia – The Mediterranean Islands • East Africa (Tanzania & Zanzibar) • Ecuador & the Galapagos Islands • Greenland & Iceland • Indonesia • Israel & the Sinai Desert • Jamaica • Japan • La Ruta Maya • Morocco • New York • North India • Pacific Islands (Fiji, Solomon Islands & Vanuatu) • South India • South West China • Turkey • Vietnam • West Africa • Zimbabwe, Botswana & Namibia

The Lonely Planet TV series is produced by:
Pilot Productions
The Old Studio
18 Middle Row
London W10 5AT UK

For video availability and ordering information contact your nearest Lonely Planet office.

Music from the TV series is available on CD & cassette.

PLANET TALK

Lonely Planet's FREE quarterly newsletter

We love hearing from you and think you'd like to hear from us.

*When...*is the right time to see reindeer in Finland?
*Where...*can you hear the best palm-wine music in Ghana?
*How...*do you get from Asunción to Areguá by steam train?
*What...*is the best way to see India?

For the answer to these and many other questions read PLANET TALK.

Every issue is packed with up-to-date travel news and advice including:

* a letter from Lonely Planet co-founders Tony and Maureen Wheeler
* go behind the scenes on the road with a Lonely Planet author
* feature article on an important and topical travel issue
* a selection of recent letters from travellers
* details on forthcoming Lonely Planet promotions
* complete list of Lonely Planet products

To join our mailing list contact any Lonely Planet office.

Also available: Lonely Planet T-shirts. 100% heavyweight cotton.

LONELY PLANET ONLINE

Get the latest travel information before you leave or while you're on the road

Whether you've just begun planning your next trip, or you're chasing down specific info on currency regulations or visa requirements, check out Lonely Planet Online for up-to-the minute travel information.

As well as travel profiles of your favourite destinations (including maps and photos), you'll find current reports from our researchers and other travellers, updates on health and visas, travel advisories, and discussion of the ecological and political issues you need to be aware of as you travel.

There's also an online travellers' forum where you can share your experience of life on the road, meet travel companions and ask other travellers for their recommendations and advice. We also have plenty of links to other online sites useful to independent travellers.

And of course we have a complete and up-to-date list of all Lonely Planet travel products including guides, phrasebooks, atlases, Journeys and videos and a simple online ordering facility if you can't find the book you want elsewhere.

www.lonelyplanet.com
or
AOL keyword: lp

LONELY PLANET PRODUCTS

Lonely Planet is known worldwide for publishing practical, reliable and no-nonsense travel information in our guides and on our web site. The Lonely Planet list covers just about every accessible part of the world. Currently there are eight series: *travel guides*, *shoestring guides*, *walking guides*, *city guides*, *phrasebooks*, *audio packs*, *travel atlases* and *Journeys* – a unique collection of travel writing.

EUROPE

Amsterdam • Austria • Baltic States phrasebook • Britain • Central Europe on a shoestring • Central Europe phrasebook • Czech & Slovak Republics • Denmark • Dublin • Eastern Europe on a shoestring • Eastern Europe phrasebook • Estonia, Latvia & Lithuania • Finland • France • French phrasebook • German phrasebook • Greece • Greek phrasebook • Hungary • Iceland, Greenland & the Faroe Islands • Ireland • Italian phrasebook • Italy • Mediterranean Europe on a shoestring • Mediterranean Europe phrasebook • Paris • Poland • Portugal • Portugal travel atlas • Prague • Russia, Ukraine & Belarus • Russian phrasebook • Scandinavian & Baltic Europe on a shoestring • Scandinavian Europe phrasebook • Slovenia • Spain • Spanish phrasebook • St Petersburg • Switzerland • Trekking in Greece • Trekking in Spain • Ukrainian phrasebook • Vienna • Walking in Britain • Walking in Switzerland • Western Europe on a shoestring • Western Europe phrasebook

Travel Literature: The Olive Grove: Travels in Greece

NORTH AMERICA

Alaska • Backpacking in Alaska • Baja California • California & Nevada • Canada • Florida • Hawaii • Honolulu • Los Angeles • Mexico • Miami • New England • New Orleans • New York City • New York, New Jersey & Pennsylvania • Pacific Northwest USA • Rocky Mountain States • San Francisco • Southwest USA • USA phrasebook • Washington, DC & the Capital Region

CENTRAL AMERICA & THE CARIBBEAN

Bermuda • Central America on a shoestring • Costa Rica • Cuba • Eastern Caribbean • Guatemala, Belize & Yucatán: La Ruta Maya • Jamaica

SOUTH AMERICA

Argentina, Uruguay & Paraguay • Bolivia • Brazil • Brazilian phrasebook • Buenos Aires • Chile & Easter Island • Chile & Easter Island travel atlas • Colombia • Ecuador & the Galápagos Islands • Latin American Spanish phrasebook • Peru • Quechua phrasebook • Rio de Janeiro • South America on a shoestring • Trekking in the Patagonian Andes • Venezuela

Travel Literature: Full Circle: A South American Journey

ANTARCTICA

Antarctica

ISLANDS OF THE INDIAN OCEAN

Madagascar & Comoros • Maldives • Mauritius, Réunion & Seychelles

AFRICA

Africa - the South • Africa on a shoestring • Arabic (Moroccan) phrasebook • Cape Town • Central Africa • East Africa • Egypt • Egypt travel atlas • Ethiopian (Amharic) phrasebook • Kenya • Kenya travel atlas • Malawi, Mozambique & Zambia • Morocco • North Africa • South Africa, Lesotho & Swaziland • South Africa, Lesotho & Swaziland travel atlas • Swahili phrasebook • Trekking in East Africa • West Africa • Zimbabwe, Botswana & Namibia • Zimbabwe, Botswana & Namibia travel atlas

Travel Literature: The Rainbird: A Central African Journey • Songs to an African Sunset: A Zimbabwean Story